The Gun Digest® Book of EXPLODED GUN DRAWINGS

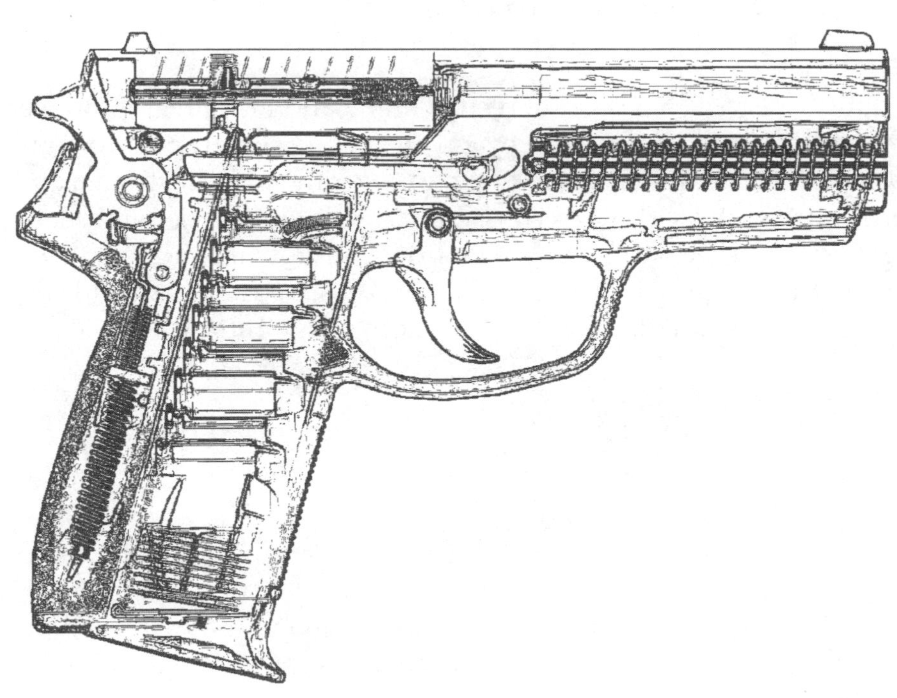

Harold A. Murtz

Published by

700 East State Street • Iola, WI 54990-0001
715-445-2214 • 888-457-2873

Our toll-free number to place an order or obtain
a free catalog is (800) 258-0929.

Library of Congress Catalog Number: 2004115355

ISBN: 0-89689-141-0

Designed by Kara Grundman
Edited by Dan Shideler

Printed in the United States of America

Visit us on-line at
e-GunParts.com
GUN PARTS
NUMRICH
Established 1950
CORPORATION
For more than 50 years Numrich Gun Parts Corporation has been helping keep America's firearms in perfect working order by supplying our customers with quality gun parts at a reasonable price.
You've made us the WORLD'S LARGEST supplier of current, obsolete, and military gun parts, gunsmith supplies, military surplus, and shooting accessories.
With over 650 million parts, it's very likely we have the parts you need to repair, modify or accessorize your firearm.
Catalog #27
The only catalog of its kind, featuring fine products from...
• Colt • Winchester • Remington
• Mossberg and more...
• More than 1,200 pages
• 180,000+ individual items
• Over 500 schematics
• Firearm parts lists
• Store brand name to original manufacturer cross reference.
FIREARMS PARTS CATALOG #27
The Reference Guide for Antique, Obsolete, Military and Current Parts and Accessories
TABLE OF CONTENTS...
Parts By Manufacturer page 13
Surplus Items page 1089
Gunsmithing Supplies page 1133
Safety Accessories page 1159
Firearm And Shooting Accessories page 1186
Cross-Reference By Firearms Manufacturer page 1194
TOLL-FREE ORDER LINE: 866.686.7424 | Web: e-GunParts.com
Call our friendly service representatives, toll free at 866-NUMRICH (866-686-7424), or visit our web site at:
e-GunParts.com
Catalog #27
ITEM#SC-27 $14.95
U.S. Orders: (Bulk Mail) Shipping charges included.
Foreign Orders: Air Mail – 30 day delivery or surface – 90 day delivery. Shipping charges additional.
226 Williams Lane, P.O. Box 299 • West Hurley, New York 12491 • Toll-Free Fax: 877- GUNPART

THE LARGEST SOURCE FOR CURRENT, OBSOLETE, MILITARY & COMMERCIAL FIREARMS PARTS AND ACCESSORIES

ANSCHUTZ .22LR MATCH GRADE BARREL BLANK

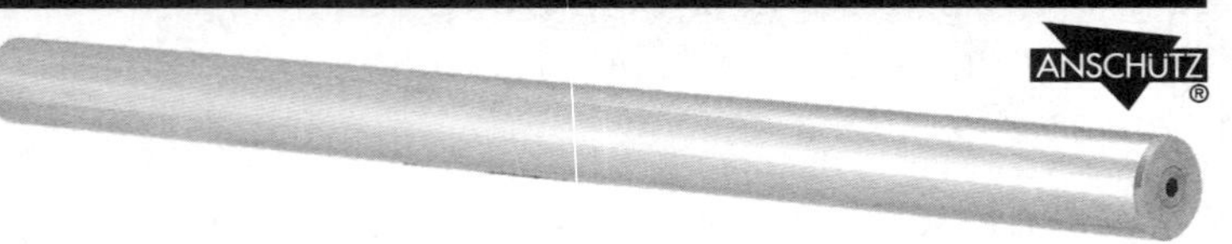

Air-gauged using premium German tool steel with 6% carbon steel.Measures 1 1/4" OD x 19 5/8" long, in the white. Features 8-groove rifling and a 1/16 rate of twist. Note: Circular marking around one end of the bore represents the chamber end. Weight, 6.6 lbs.

ITEM#SC884540 $89.95

MAUSER 98 RIFLE 3 ROUND DETACHABLE MAGAZINES

Quickly convert your top loading Mauser 98 rifle into a detachable magazine model without alteration. Simply remove the military style floorplate and replace it with a brand new, quality crafted, blued-steel magazine. They were originally manufactured by the Gibbs Rifle Co. for Mauser 98 Sporter Rifles. Available in long or short action.

Long Action - Fits .25-06/.270/.30-06/8mm
Cartridges. . . . . **ITEM#SC808870 $26.50**
Short Action - Fits .22-250/.243/.308
Cartridges. . . . . **ITEM#SC808880 $26.50**

BOLT HANDLE FORGING BLOCKS

For use with Mauser 93, 94, 95, 96 & 98 rifle bolts. Machined from quality tool steel. Note: Can be modified to function with Springfield 1903/1903A3 bolts.

ITEM#SC928490 $34.95

Shipping and handling costs for parts orders additional. Call for details.

MAUSER 98 SINGLE & DOUBLE SET TRIGGER SPORTER ACTIONS

Fully-forged large ring actions for use with standard calibers including 7 x 57 through .30-06. Features include a complete bolt assembly with commercial bolt sleeve, an adjustable trigger assembly with side safety, a push-button, hinged trigger guard assembly and a blued finish. Bolt can be opened in the cocked and safe position. Manufactured in Yugoslavia by Zastava. Choose from either a single trigger (3 1/2 lbs. to 6 lbs.) or a double set trigger (1 1/2 lbs. to 4 1/2 lbs.) configuration. Note: Magazine well measures 3 3/8" in length and bolt face measures .470" in diameter. FFL Require

Single Trigger Action -
Regular Price $292.95 . . . . **ITEM#SC851010 $199.00**
Double Set Trigger Action -
Regular Price $499.95 . . . . **ITEM#SC851020 $299.00**

WINCHESTER 1894 .30 W.C.F. HALF OCTAGON BARREL KIT

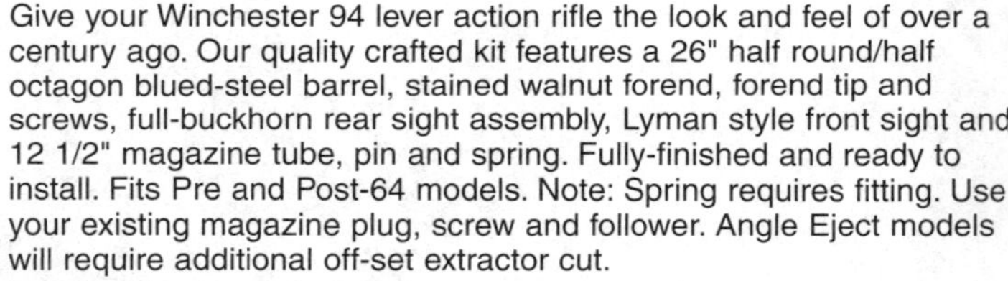

Give your Winchester 94 lever action rifle the look and feel of over a century ago. Our quality crafted kit features a 26" half round/half octagon blued-steel barrel, stained walnut forend, forend tip and screws, full-buckhorn rear sight assembly, Lyman style front sight and 12 1/2" magazine tube, pin and spring. Fully-finished and ready to install. Fits Pre and Post-64 models. Note: Spring requires fitting. Use your existing magazine plug, screw and follower. Angle Eject models will require additional off-set extractor cut.

ITEM#SC715730 $279.95

COLT G / K / Q FRAME .22 CALIBER CONVERTIBLE CYLINDERS

Blued-steel, 6 shot, caliber stamped. CNC machined and hardened to th original Colt factory specifications. Fits Colt Buntline Scout, Frontier Sco Frontier Scout '62, New Frontier and Peacemaker revolvers. Purchase the cylinders individually or in a set.

.22 LR Cylinder
ITEM#SC189810 $85.00
.22 Magnum Cylinder
ITEM#SC881510 $85.00
Cylinder Set
ITEM#SC885950 $149.95

Visit us on-line at
e-GunParts.com

TOLL-FREE: 866-NUMRICH (866-686-7424)
TOLL-FREE FAX (877-GUNPART)
226 Williams Lane, P.O. Box 299 • West Hurley, New York 12491

ACKNOWLEDGMENTS

We wish to give special thanks to the following individuals, companies and associations for their contributions to EXPLODED HANDGUN DRAWINGS.

Mr. Jack First of Jack First Distributors; Ms. Nancy Padua of Blacksmith Corporation; Mr. Jerry Krasne and Tony Schmidt of Triple K Manufacturing Company; The Gun Parts Corporation; the National Rifle Association; Mr. Dennis Riordan; Mr. Thomas E. Wessel; the late Mr. James M. Triggs; and the myriad manufacturers and importers of U.S.- and foreign-made handguns.

CONTENTS

EXPLODED LONG GUN DRAWINGS

EXPLODED HAND GUN DRAWINGS

CX22/CXC22 Auto

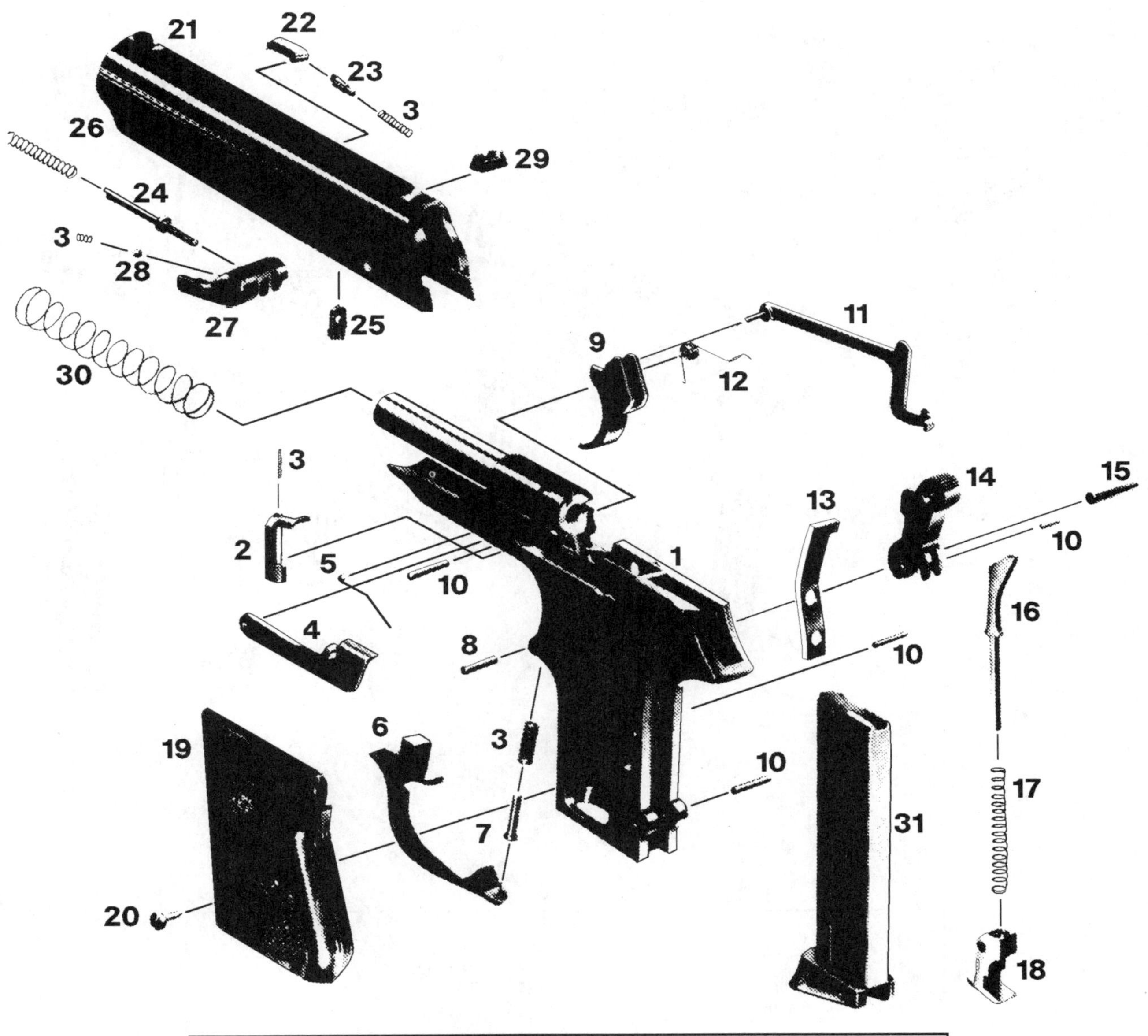

1	Frame	17	Mainspring
2	Firing Pin Stop	18	Magazine Catch
3	Spring	19	Grip Plates
4	Breech Block Catch Link	20	Grip Plate Screw and Bushing
5	Leaf Spring	21	Slide
6	Trigger Guard	22	Extractor
7	Trigger Guard Spring Pin	23	Extractor Pin
8	Trigger Guard Pin	24	Firing Pin
9	Trigger	25	Firing Pin Plug
10	Pin	26	Firing Pin Spring
11	Trigger Bar	27	Safety-Lever
12	Trigger Bar Spring	28	Steel Ball
13	Sear	29	Rear Sight
14	Hammer	30	Recoil Spring
15	Hammer Pin	31	Magazine
16	Mainspring Guide Rod		

EP380 Auto

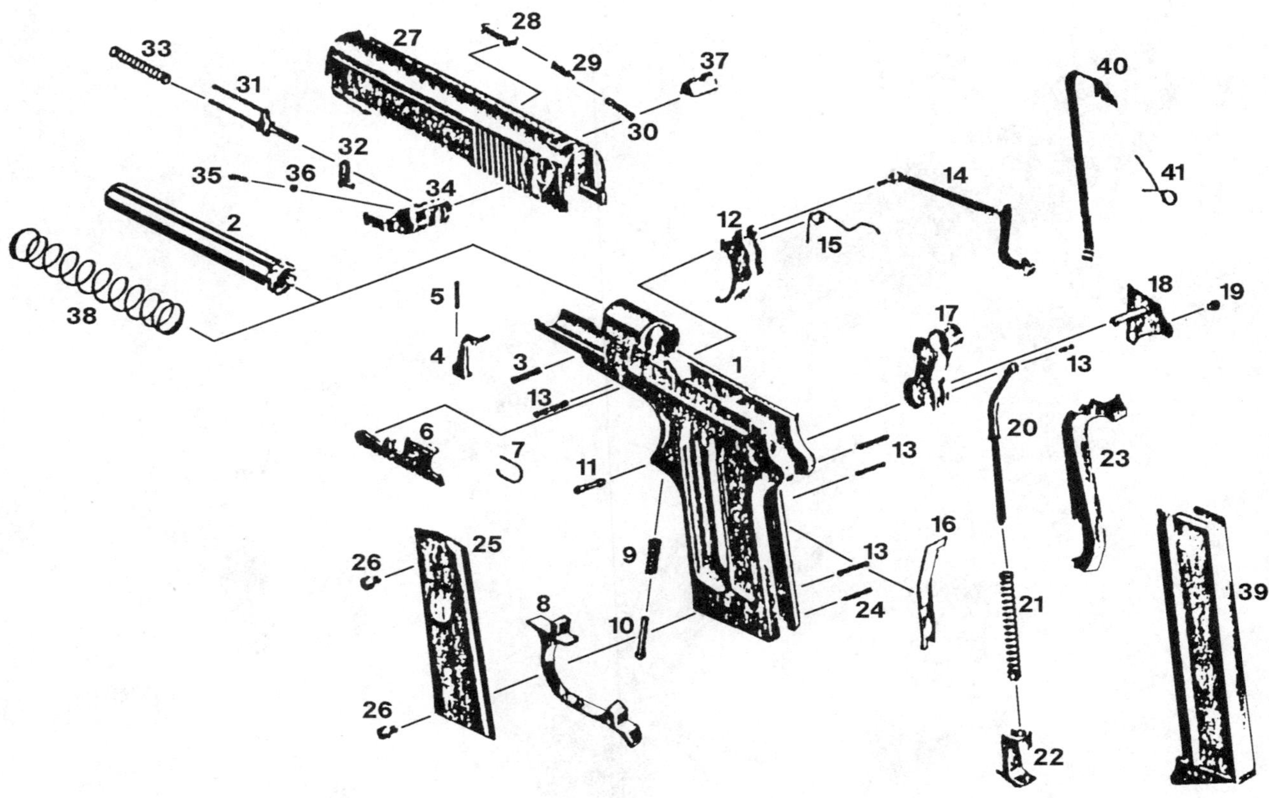

1	Frame	22	Magazine Catch
2	Barrel	23	Backstrap
3	Conical Pin	24	Pin
4	Firing Pin Stop	25	Grip Plates
5	Spring	26	Grip Plate Screws
6	Breech Block Catch Link	27	Slide
7	Breech Block Catch Link Spring	28	Extractor
8	Trigger Guard	29	Extractor Pin
9	Trigger Guard Spring	30	Extractor Spring
10	Trigger Guard Spring Pin	31	Firing Pin
11	Trigger Guard Pin	32	Firing Pin Plug
12	Trigger	33	Firing Pin Spring
13	Cylindrical Pin	34	Safety-Lever
14	Trigger Bar	35	Safety-Lever Spring
15	Trigger Bar Spring	36	Steel Ball
16	Sear	37	Rear Sight
17	Hammer	38	Recoil Spring
18	Sideplate	39	Magazine
19	Screw	40	Magazine Safety-Lever
20	Mainspring Guide Rod	41	Magazine Safety-Lever Spring
21	Mainspring		

P98 Auto

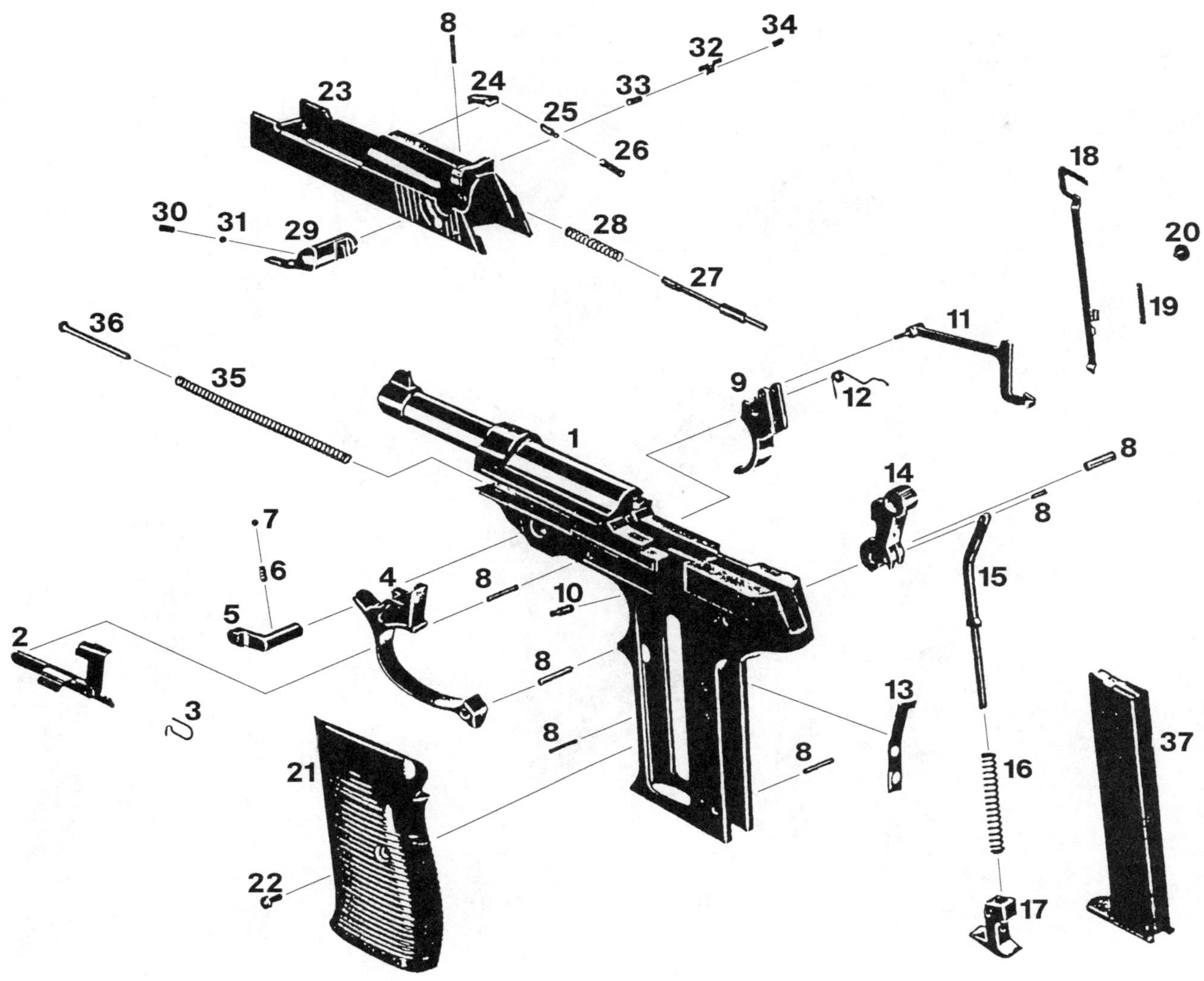

1	Frame	20	Countersunk Screw
2	Breech Block Catch Link	21	Grip Plates
3	Breech Block Catch Link Spring	22	Grip Plate Screw
4	Trigger Guard	23	Slide
5	Locking Lever for Trigger Guard	24	Extractor
6	Spring	25	Extractor Pin
7	Steel Ball	26	Extractor Spring
8	Cylindrical Pin	27	Firing Pin
9	Trigger	28	Firing Pin Spring
10	Set Screw	29	Safety-Lever
11	Trigger Bar	30	Safety-Lever Spring
12	Trigger Bar Spring	31	Steel Ball
13	Sear	32	Rear Sight Blade
14	Hammer	33	Spring
15	Mainspring Guide Rod	34	Rear Sight Windage Screw
16	Mainspring	35	Recoil Spring
17	Magazine Catch	36	Spring Bar
18	Magazine Safety-Lever	37	Magazine
19	Spring		

PK22 Auto

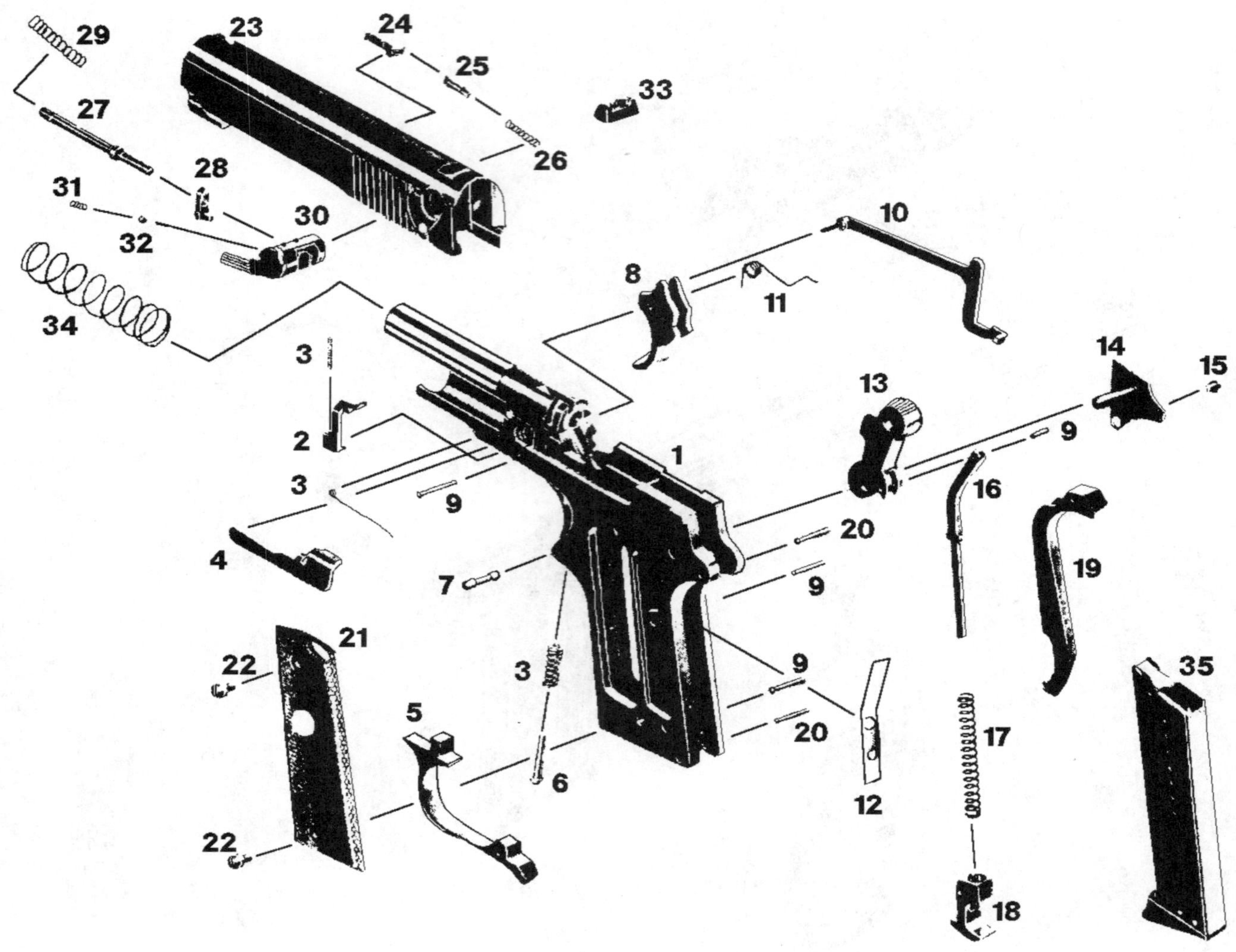

1	Frame	19	Backstrap
2	Firing Pin Stop	20	Pin
3	Spring	21	Grip Plates
4	Breech Block Catch Link	22	Grip Plate Screw
5	Trigger Guard	23	Slide
6	Trigger Guard Spring Pin	24	Extractor
7	Trigger Guard Pin	25	Extractor Pin
8	Trigger	26	Extractor Spring
9	Cylindrical Pin	27	Firing Pin
10	Trigger Bar	28	Firing Pin Plug
11	Trigger Bar Spring	29	Firing Pin Spring
12	Sear	30	Safety-Lever
13	Hammer	31	Safety-Lever Spring
14	Sideplate	32	Steel Ball
15	Screw	33	Rear Sight
16	Mainspring Guide Rod	34	Recoil Spring
17	Mainspring	35	Magazine
18	Magazine Catch		

PX22 Auto

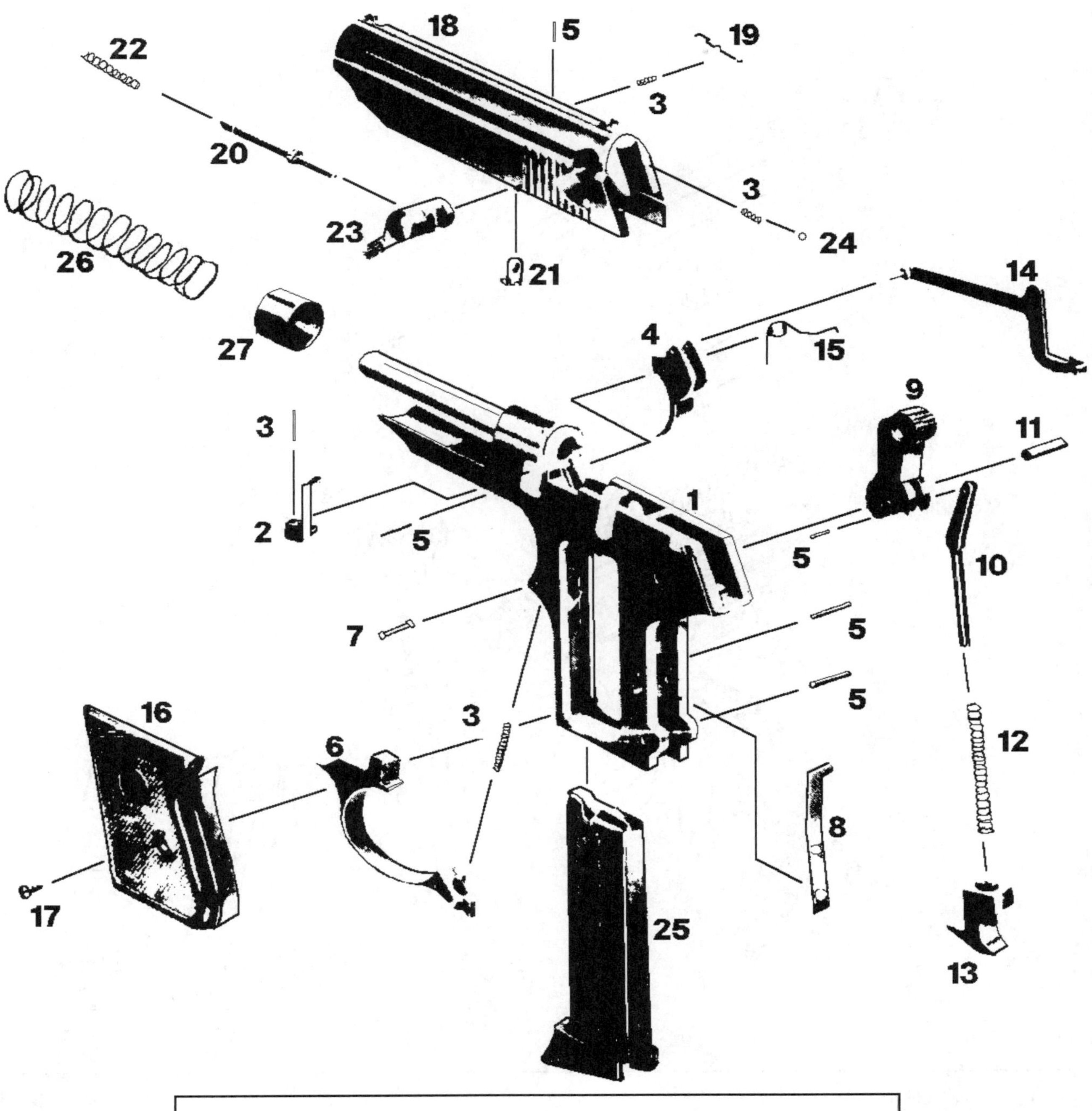

1	Frame	15	Trigger Bar Spring
2	Firing Pin Stop	16	Grip Plates
3	Spring	17	Grip Plate Screw
4	Trigger	18	Slide
5	Cylindrical Pin	19	Extractor
6	Trigger Guard	20	Firing Pin
7	Trigger Guard Pin	21	Firing Pin Plug
8	Sear	22	Firing Pin Spring
9	Hammer	23	Safety-Lever
10	Mainspring Guide Rod	24	Steel Ball
11	Hammer Pin	25	Magazine
12	Mainspring	26	Recoil Spring
13	Magazine Catch	27	Sear Spring Plunger
14	Trigger Bar		

ZC380 Auto

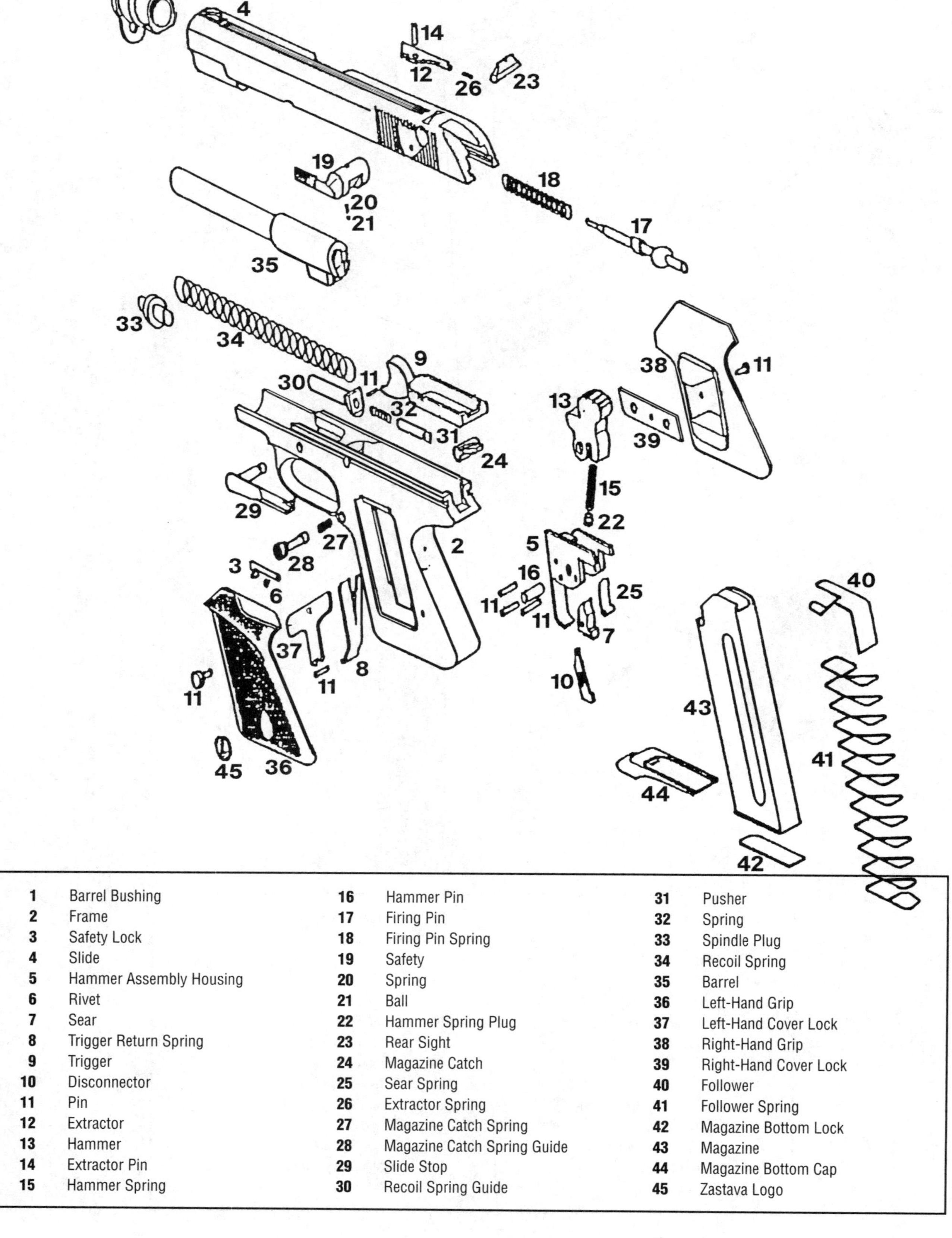

1	Barrel Bushing	**16**	Hammer Pin	**31**	Pusher
2	Frame	**17**	Firing Pin	**32**	Spring
3	Safety Lock	**18**	Firing Pin Spring	**33**	Spindle Plug
4	Slide	**19**	Safety	**34**	Recoil Spring
5	Hammer Assembly Housing	**20**	Spring	**35**	Barrel
6	Rivet	**21**	Ball	**36**	Left-Hand Grip
7	Sear	**22**	Hammer Spring Plug	**37**	Left-Hand Cover Lock
8	Trigger Return Spring	**23**	Rear Sight	**38**	Right-Hand Grip
9	Trigger	**24**	Magazine Catch	**39**	Right-Hand Cover Lock
10	Disconnector	**25**	Sear Spring	**40**	Follower
11	Pin	**26**	Extractor Spring	**41**	Follower Spring
12	Extractor	**27**	Magazine Catch Spring	**42**	Magazine Bottom Lock
13	Hammer	**28**	Magazine Catch Spring Guide	**43**	Magazine
14	Extractor Pin	**29**	Slide Stop	**44**	Magazine Bottom Cap
15	Hammer Spring	**30**	Recoil Spring Guide	**45**	Zastava Logo

380 Backup Auto

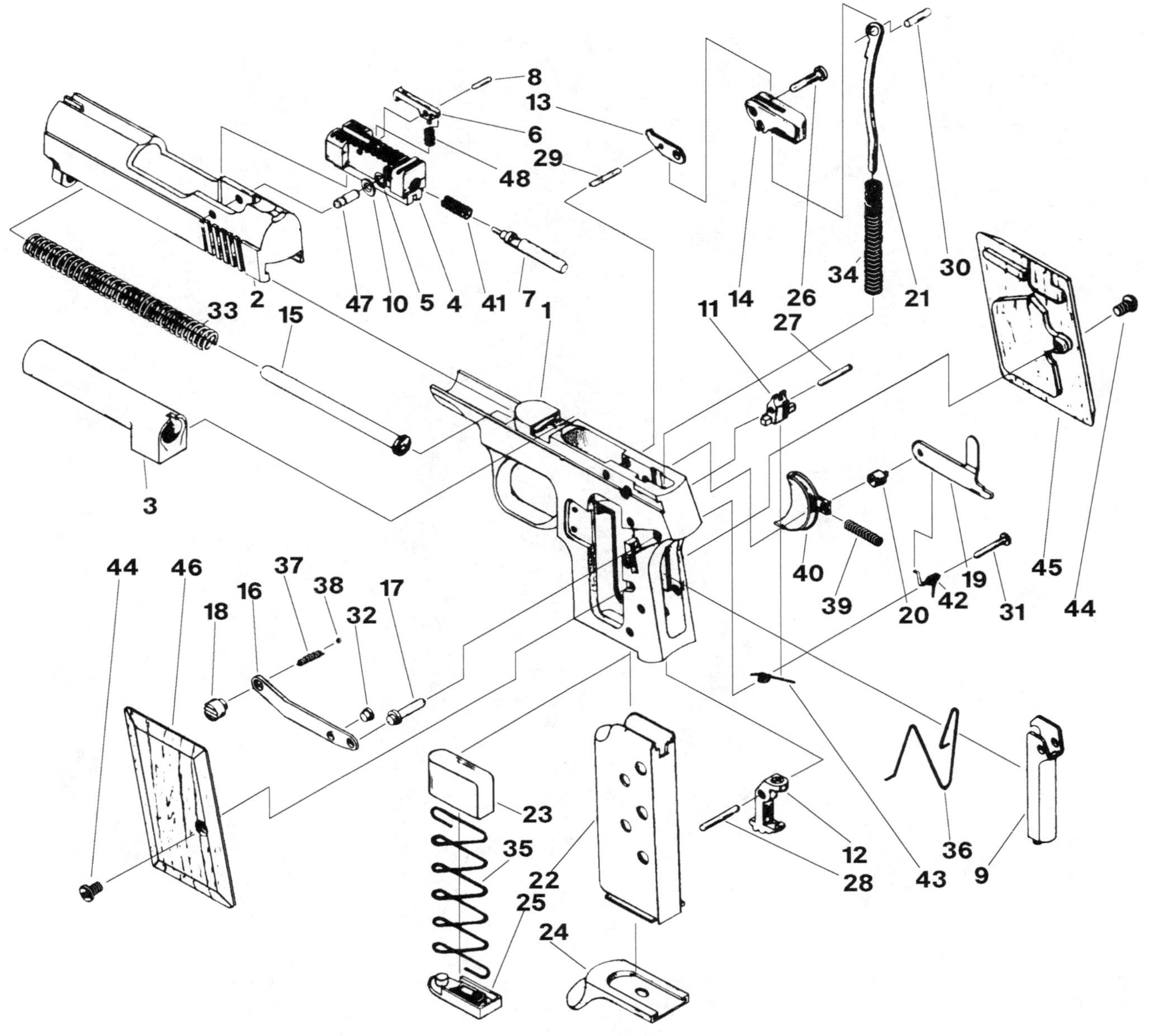

1	Frame	**17**	Safety Pin	**33**	Recoil Spring
2	Slide	**18**	Safety Knob	**34**	Hammer Spring
3	Barrel	**19**	Disconnector	**35**	Magazine Spring
4	Bolt	**20**	Disconnector Pin	**36**	Arch Housing Spring
5	Snap Ring	**21**	Strut	**37**	Safety Spring
6	Extractor	**22**	Magazine Body	**38**	Safety Spring Ball
7	Firing Pin	**23**	Magazine Follower	**39**	Trigger Spring
8	Extractor Pin	**24**	Magazine Floorplate Extension	**40**	Trigger
9	Arch Housing	**25**	Magazine Floorplate	**41**	Firing Pin Spring
10	Washer	**26**	Hammer Pin	**42**	Disconnector Spring
11	Sear	**27**	Sear Pin	**43**	Sear Spring
12	Magazine Latch	**28**	Magazine Latch Pin	**44**	Grip Screw
13	Ejector	**29**	Ejector Pin	**45**	Grip (Right)
14	Hammer	**30**	Hammer Strut Pin	**46**	Grip (Left)
15	Recoil Rod	**31**	Sear Disconnector Spring Pin	**47**	Bolt Retaining Pin
16	Safety	**32**	Safety Stop Pin	**48**	Extractor Spring

45 Hardball, Combat and Longslide Autos

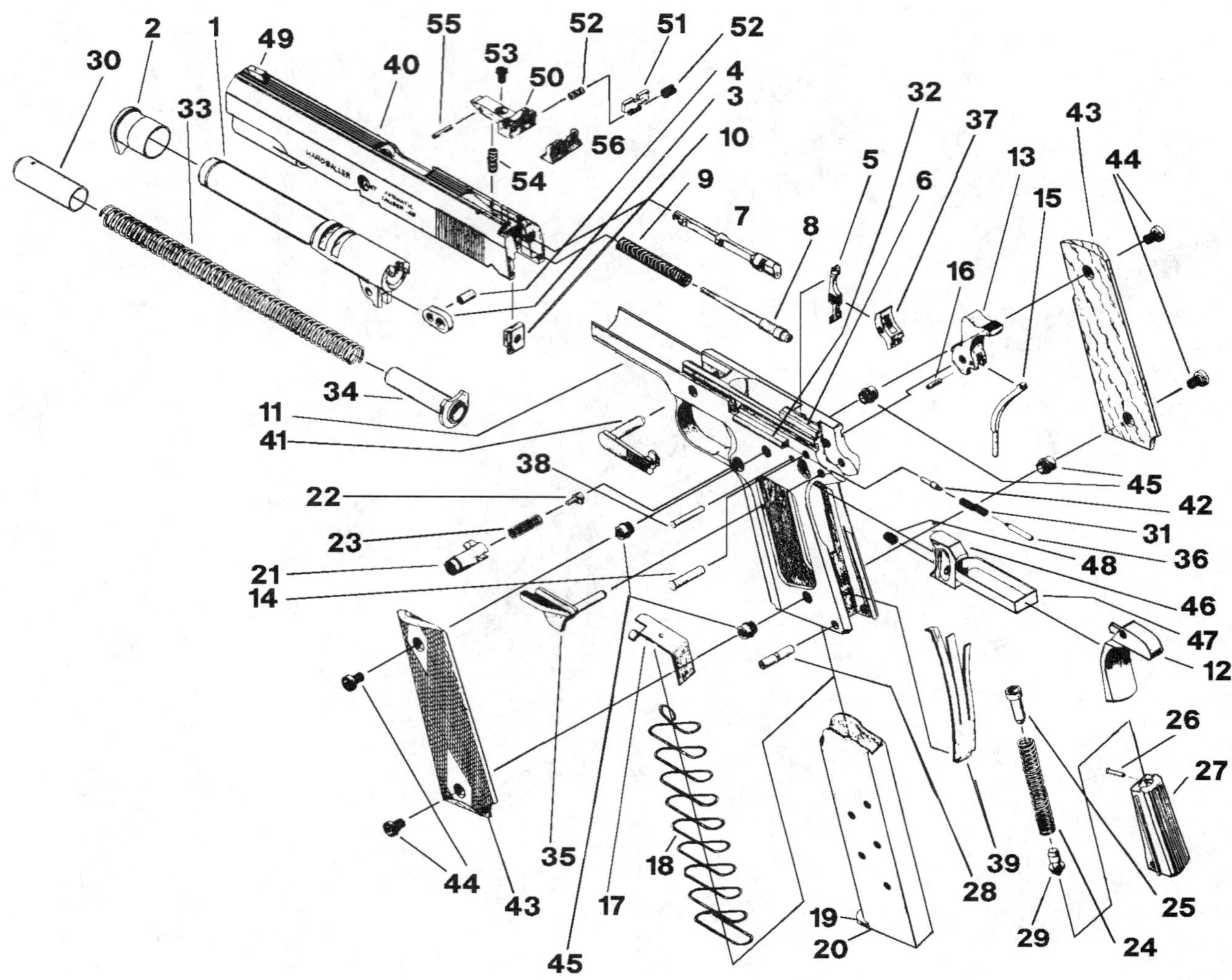

1	Barrel	21	Magazine Catch Assembly	41	Slide Stop
2	Barrel Bushing	22	Magazine Catch Retainer	42	Slide Stop Plunger
3	Barrel Link	23	Magazine Catch Spring	43	Grips (Black Neoprene)
4	Barrel Link Pin	24	Mainspring	44	Stock Screws
5	Disconnector	25	Mainspring Cap	45	Stock Screw Bushings
6	Ejector	26	Mainspring Cap Pin	46	Trigger
7	Extractor	27	Mainspring Housing	47	Trigger Bar
8	Firing Pin	28	Mainspring Housing Pin	48	Trigger Stop Adjustment Screw
9	Firing Pin Spring	29	Mainspring Housing Pin Retainer	49	Front Sight
10	Firing Pin Stop	30	Recoil Spring Plug	50	Rear Sight Base
11	Frame	31	Plunger Spring	51	Rear Sight Blade
12	Grip Safety	32	Plunger Tube	52	Rear Sight Windage Screws
13	Hammer	33	Recoil Spring	53	Rear Sight Elevation Screw
14	Hammer Pin	34	Recoil Spring Guide	54	Rear Sight Elevation Screw Spring
15	Hammer Strut	35	Safety Lock	55	Rear Sight Base Pin
16	Hammer Strut Pin	36	Safety Lock Plunger	56	Rear Sight, Fixed
17	Magazine Follower	37	Sear	**Parts Not Shown**	
18	Magazine Spring	38	Sear Pin		Ejector Pin
19	Magazine Floorplate	39	Sear Spring		
20	Magazine Body	40	Slide		

Lightning Auto

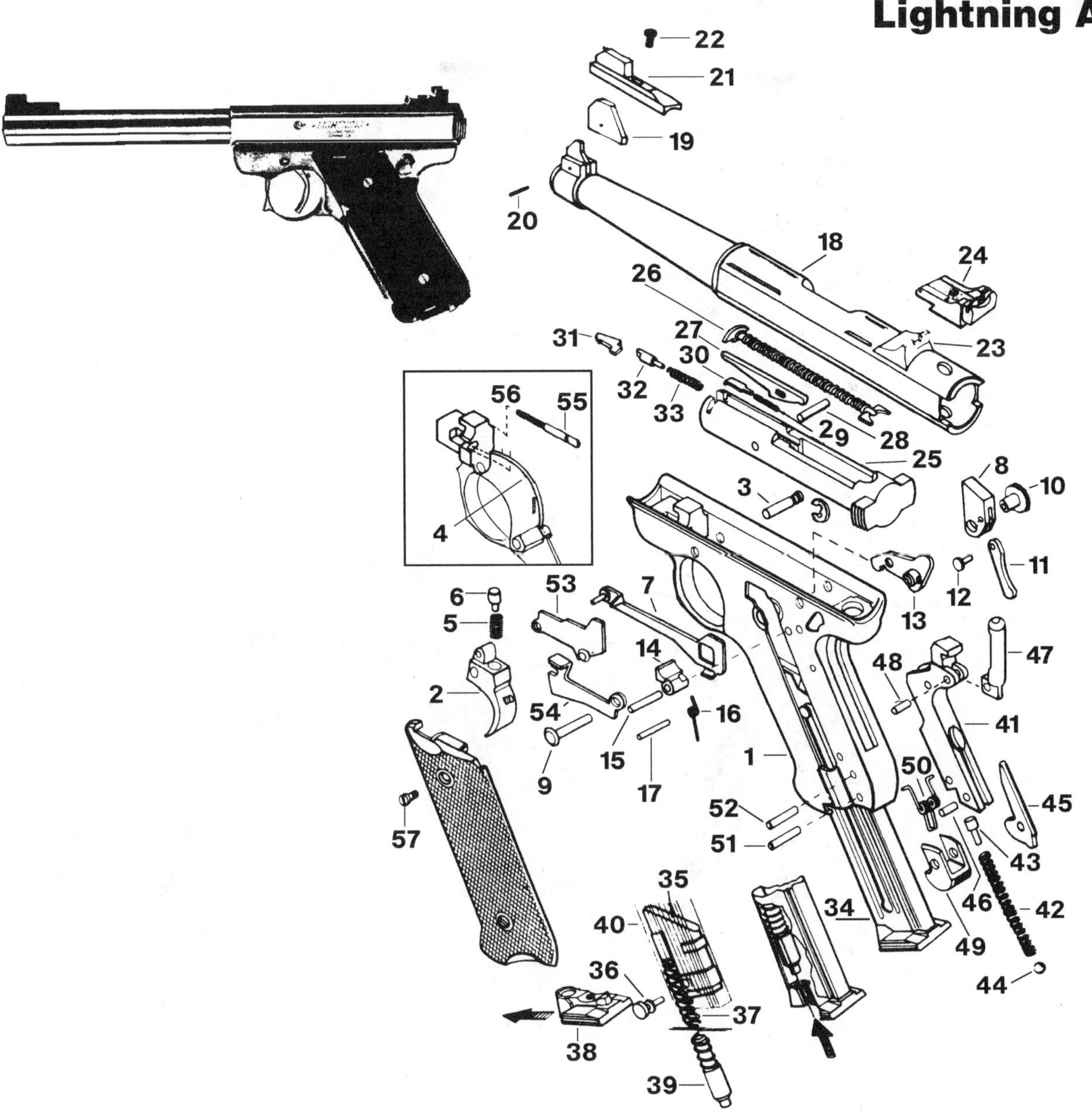

1	Grip Frame	20	Front Sight Pin	39	Magazine Floorplate Retainer
2	Trigger with Adjustment Screw	21	Front Sight (Ramp Style)	40	Magazine Body
3	Trigger Pin	22	Ramp Sight Screw	41	Mainspring Housing
4	Trigger Pin Retainer	23	Rear Sight (Standard Model)	42	Mainspring
5	Trigger Spring	24	Rear Sight (Adjustable)	43	Mainspring Plunger
6	Trigger Spring Plunger	25	Bolt	44	Detent Ball
7	Disconnector	26	Recoil Spring Assembly	45	Housing Latch
8	Hammer	27	Firing Pin	46	Housing Latch Pin
9	Hammer Pin	28	Firing Pin Stop	47	Bolt Stop Pin
10	Hammer Bushing	29	Firing Pin Spring	48	Bolt Stop Pin Pivot
11	Hammer Strut	30	Firing Pin Spring Support	49	Magazine Latch
12	Hammer Strut Pin	31	Extractor	50	Magazine Latch Spring
13	Safety (Complete)	32	Extractor Plunger	51	Magazine Latch Pin
14	Sear	33	Extractor Spring	52	Magazine Latch Stop Pin
15	Sear Pin	34	Magazine (Complete)	53	Bolt Stop Assembly
16	Sear Spring	35	Magazine Follower	54	Bolt Stop Thumb-Piece
17	Sear Spring Stop Pin	36	Magazine Follower Button	55	Bolt Stop Plunger
18	Barrel/Receiver Assembly	37	Magazine Spring	56	Bolt Stop Plunger Spring
19	Front Sight Blade	38	Magazine Floorplate	57	Grip Screws

Skipper Auto

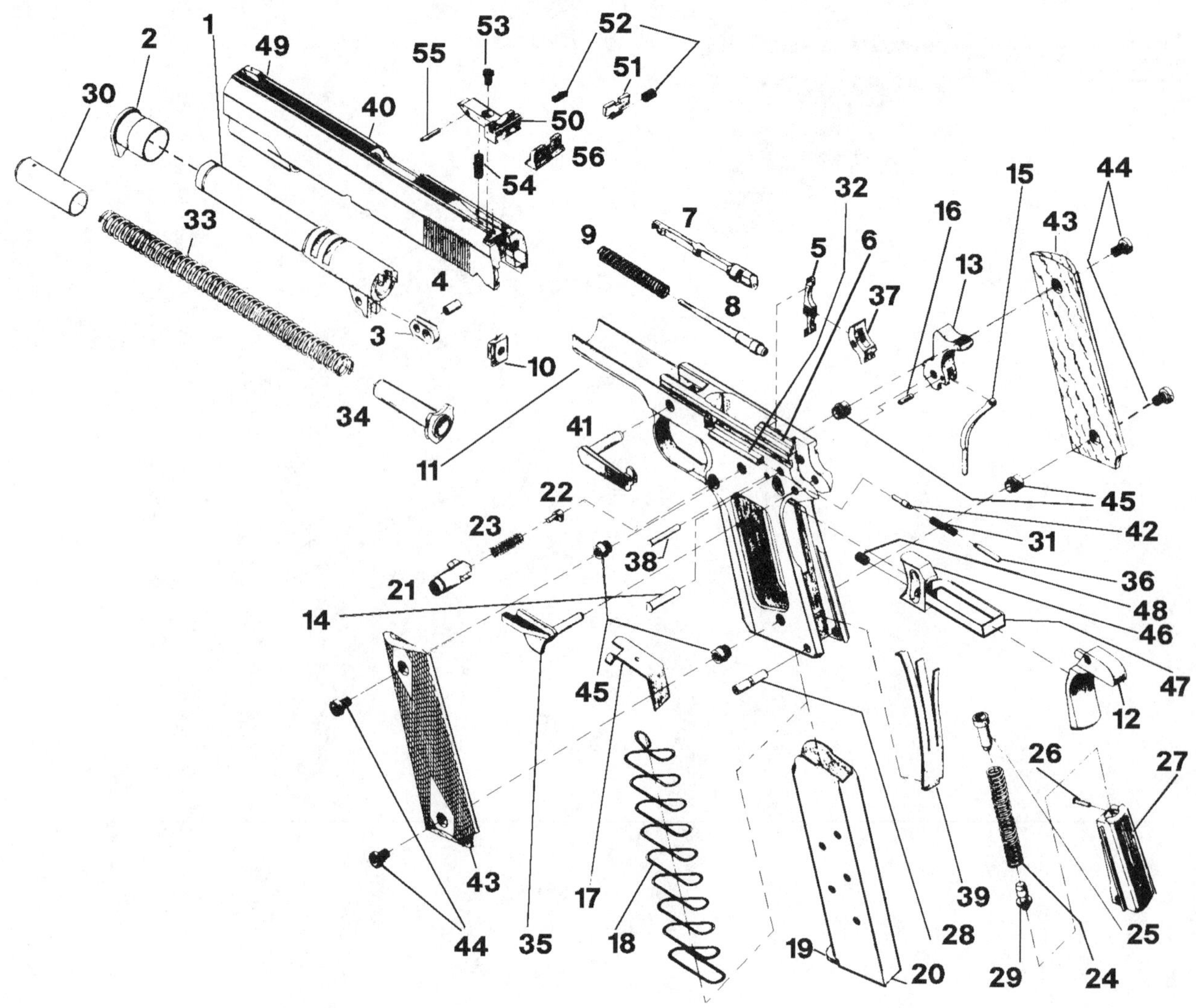

1	Barrel	**21**	Magazine Catch Assembly	**40**	Slide
2	Barrel Bushing	**22**	Magazine Catch Retainer	**41**	Slide Stop
3	Barrel Link	**23**	Magazine Catch Spring	**42**	Slide Stop Plunger
4	Barrel Link Pin	**24**	Mainspring	**43**	Grips
5	Disconnector	**25**	Mainspring Cap	**44**	Stock Screws
6	Ejector	**26**	Mainspring Cap Pin	**45**	Stock Screw Bushings
7	Extractor	**27**	Mainspring Housing	**46**	Trigger
8	Firing Pin	**28**	Mainspring Housing Pin	**47**	Trigger Bar
9	Firing Pin Spring	**29**	Mainspring Housing Pin Retainer	**48**	Trigger Stop Adjustment Screw
10	Firing Pin Stop	**30**	Recoil Spring Plug	**49**	Front Sight
11	Frame	**31**	Plunger Spring	**50**	Rear Sight Base
12	Grip Safety	**32**	Plunger Tube	**51**	Rear Sight Blade
13	Hammer	**33**	Recoil Spring	**52**	Rear Sight Windage Screw
14	Hammer Pin	**34**	Recoil Spring Guide	**53**	Rear Sight Elevation Screw
15	Hammer Strut	**35**	Safety Lock	**54**	Rear Sight Elevation Screw Spring
16	Hammer Strut Pin	**36**	Safety Lock Plunger	**55**	Rear Sight Base Pin
17	Magazine Follower	**37**	Sear	**56**	Rear Sight, Fixed
18	Magazine Spring	**38**	Sear Pin	**Parts Not Shown**	
19	Magazine Floorplate	**39**	Sear Spring		Ejector Pin
20	Magazine Body				

Exemplar Bolt Action

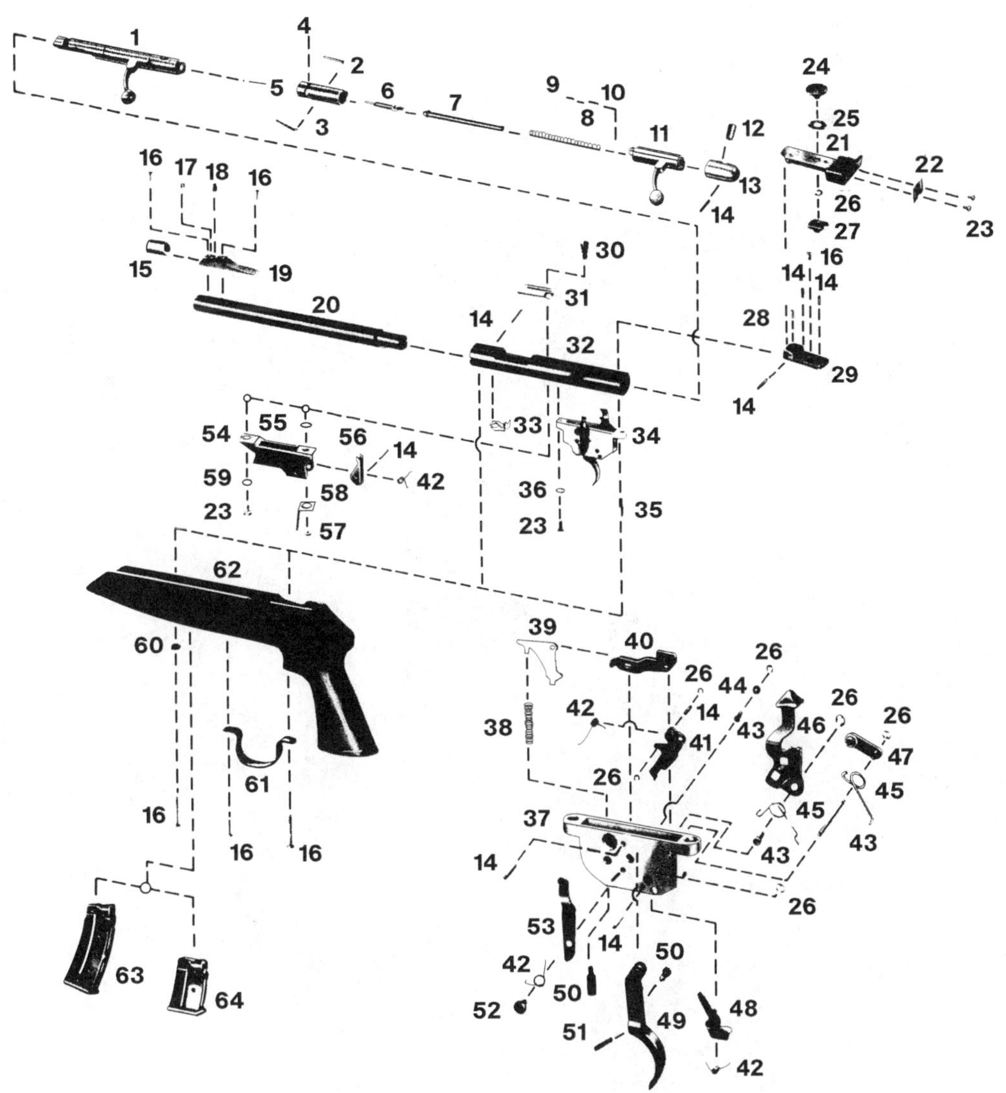

1	Bolt Assembly	23	Pan Head Screw	45	Spring
2	Extractor	24	Elevation Screw	46	Safety-Lever
3	Cartridge Retainer	25	Click Spring	47	Catch Lever
4	Spring Clamp	26	Retaining Collar	48	Release Latch
5	Bolt Head	27	Screw Socket	49	Trigger
6	Firing Pin	28	Compression Spring	50	Adjusting Screw
7	Striker Pin	29	Rear Sight Base	51	Set-Screw
8	Striker Spring	30	Ejector	52	Shoulder Screw
9	Catch Bolt	31	Bolt Guide	53	Bolt Release Lever
10	Catch Bolt Spring	32	Receiver	54	Magazine Guide
11	Bolt with Handle	33	Cartridge Guide	55	Distance Ring
12	Guide Bolt	34	Two-Stage Trigger Assembly	56	Magazine Retainer
13	Cocking Piece	35	Hexagon Threaded Bolt	57	Nut
14	Cylindrical Pin	36	Toothed Lock Washer	58	Guide Tongue
15	Front Sight Hood	37	Trigger Housing	59	Spring Washer
16	Countersunk Head Screw	38	Trigger Spring	60	Sleeve
17	Safety Plug	39	Cam Lever	61	Trigger Guard
18	Front Sight	40	Release Plunger	62	Stock with Partial Fittings
19	Front Sight Base	41	Catch Link	63	10-Shot Magazine
20	Barrel	42	Torsional Spring	64	5-Shot Magazine
21	Rear Sight Flap	43	Pivot		
22	Rear Sight Blade	44	Washer		

Trifire Auto

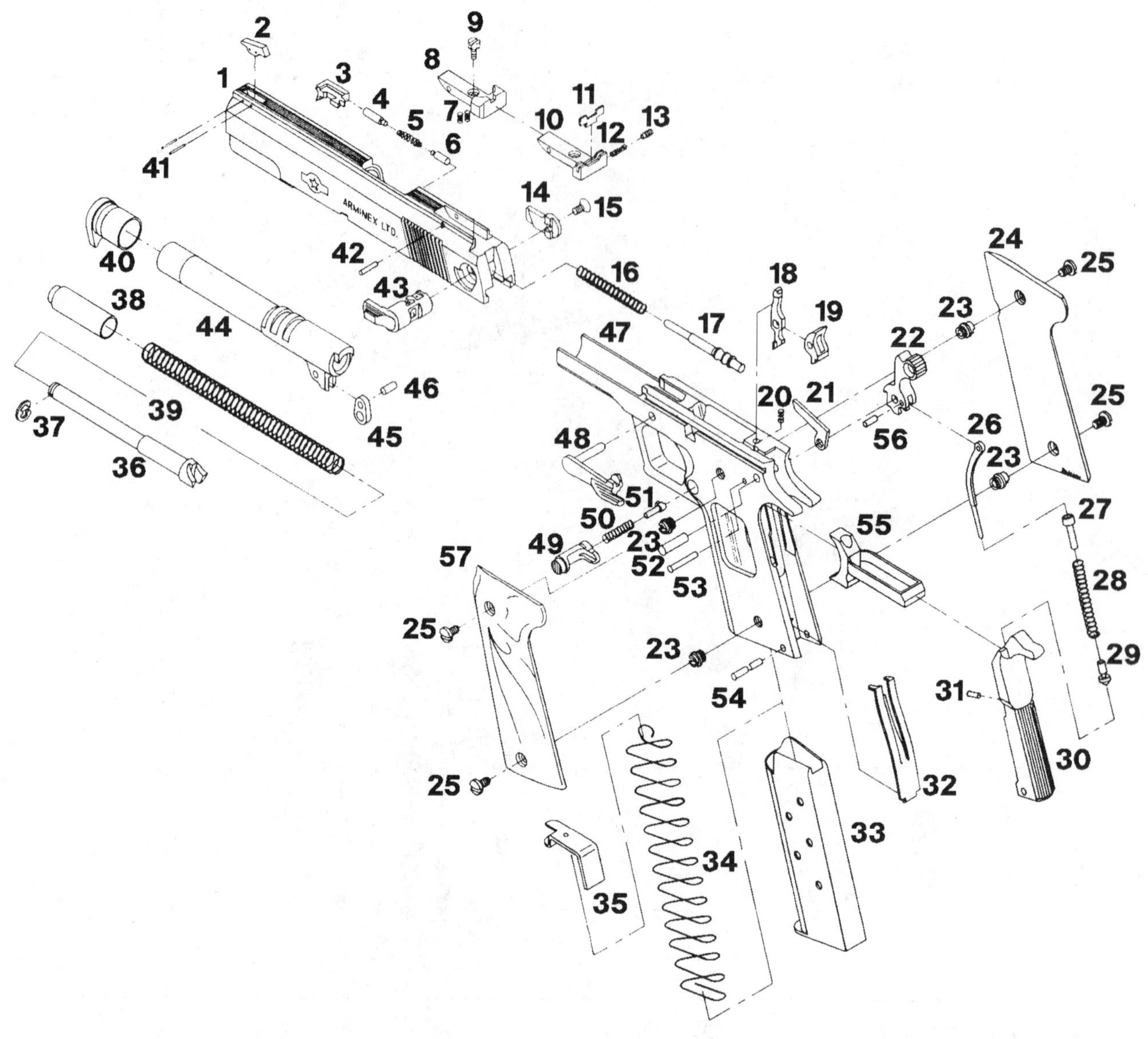

1	Slide	20	Ejector Spring	38	Recoil Spring Plug
2	Front Sight	21	Ejector	39	Recoil Spring
3	Extractor	22	Hammer	40	Barrel Bushing
4	Extractor Plunger	23	Grip Screw Bushings	41	Front Sight Pin
5	Extractor Spring	24	Grips	42	Rear Sight Pin
6	Safety Plunger	25	Grip Screws	43	Firing Pin Lock, Left
7	Rear Sight Elevation Spring	26	Hammer Strut	44	Barrel
8	Rear Sight, Fixed	27	Mainspring Cap	45	Barrel Link
9	Rear Sight Elevation Screw	28	Mainspring	46	Barrel Pin
10	Rear Sight, Adjustable	29	Mainspring Housing Pin Retainer	47	Frame
11	Rear Sight Blade	30	Backstrap	48	Slide Stop
12	Rear Sight Windage Spring	31	Mainspring Cap Pin	49	Magazine Catch
13	Rear Sight Windage Screw	32	Sear Spring	50	Magazine Spring
14	Firing Pin Lock, Right	33	Magazine	51	Magazine Catch Guide
15	Firing Pin Lock Screw	34	Magazine Spring	52	Hammer Pin
16	Firing Pin Spring	35	Magazine Follower	53	Sear Pin
17	Firing Pin	36	Recoil Spring Guide Rod	54	Mainspring Housing Pin
18	Disconnector	37	Recoil Spring Clip	55	Trigger
19	Sear			56	Hammer Strut Pin

Cadix Revolver

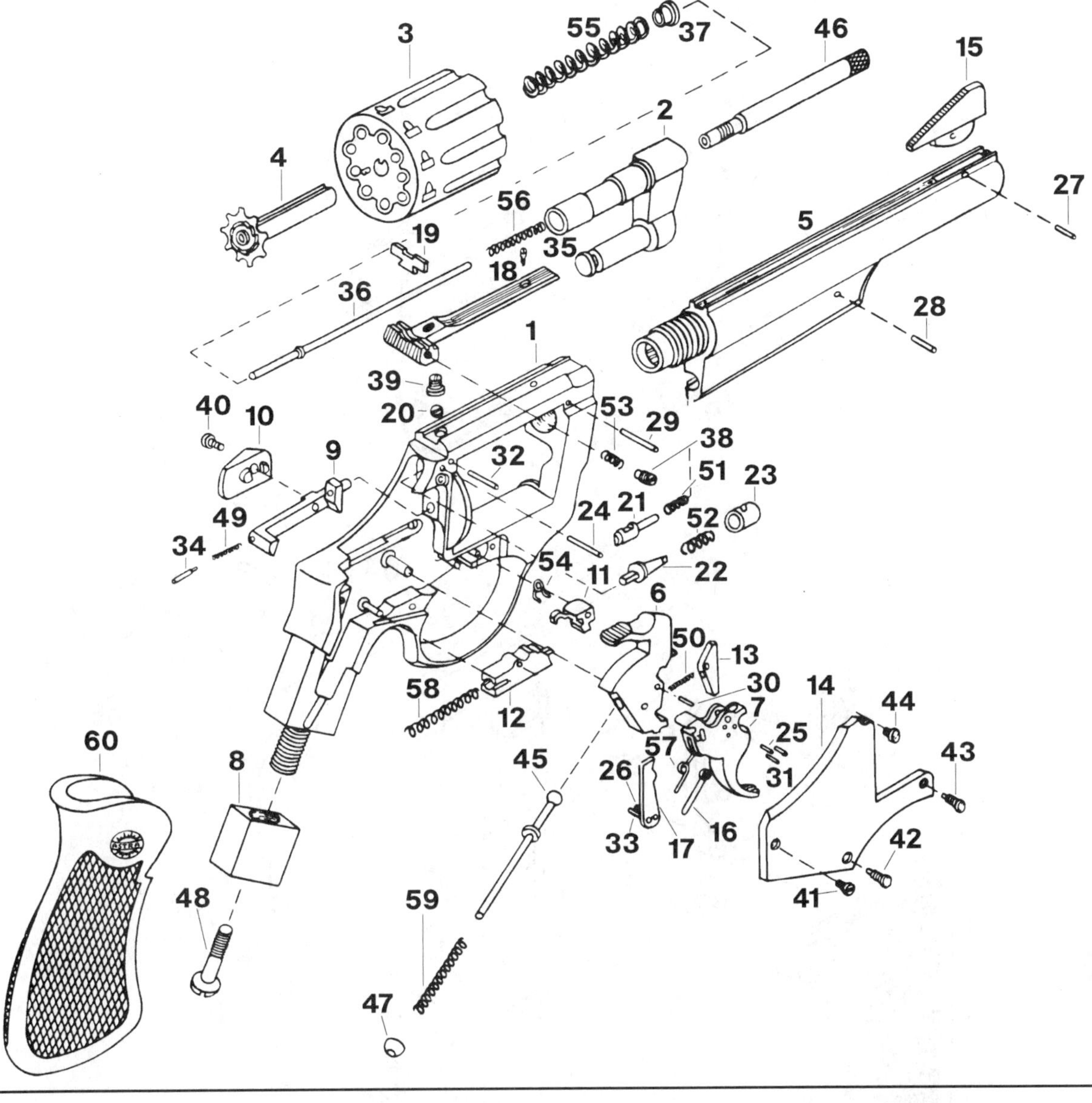

1	Frame	**21**	Locking Bolt	**41**	Flat Head Sideplate Screw
2	Crane	**22**	Firing Pin	**42**	Rear Sideplate Screw
3	Cylinder	**23**	Firing Pin Bushing	**43**	Front Sideplate Screw
4	Extractor	**24**	Firing Pin Retaining Pin	**44**	Top Sideplate Screw
5	Barrel	**25**	Lever Spring Pin	**45**	Hammer Strut
6	Hammer	**26**	Lever Spring Collar Pin	**46**	Extractor Rod
7	Trigger	**27**	Front Sight Pin (Not for 2")	**47**	Mainspring Cap
8	Grip Adjusting Block (Not for 2")	**28**	Locking Bolt Pin	**48**	Grip Adjusting Screw (Not for 2")
9	Bolt	**29**	Barrel Pin	**49**	Bolt Spring
10	Thumb-Piece	**30**	Sear Pin	**50**	Sear Spring
11	Cylinder Stop	**31**	Hand Torsion Spring Pin	**51**	Locking Bolt Spring
12	Rebound Slide	**32**	Firing Pin Bushing Retaining Pin	**52**	Firing Pin Spring
13	Sear	**33**	Cylinder Lever Pin	**53**	Sight Slide Spring (Not for 2")
14	Slide Plate	**34**	Bolt Plunger	**54**	Cylinder Stop Spring
15	Front Sight (Not for 2")	**35**	Sight Leaf Screw (Not for 2")	**55**	Extractor Spring
16	Trigger Lever	**36**	Center Pin	**56**	Center Pin Spring
17	Hand	**37**	Extractor Rod Collar	**57**	Hand Torsion Spring
18	Rear Sight Leaf (Not for 2")	**38**	Windage Screw (Not for 2")	**58**	Rebound Slide Spring
19	Sight Slide (Not for 2")	**39**	Elevation Screw (Not for 2")	**59**	Mainspring
20	Elevating Stud (Not for 2")	**40**	Thumb-Piece Screw	**60**	Grip

Camper Auto

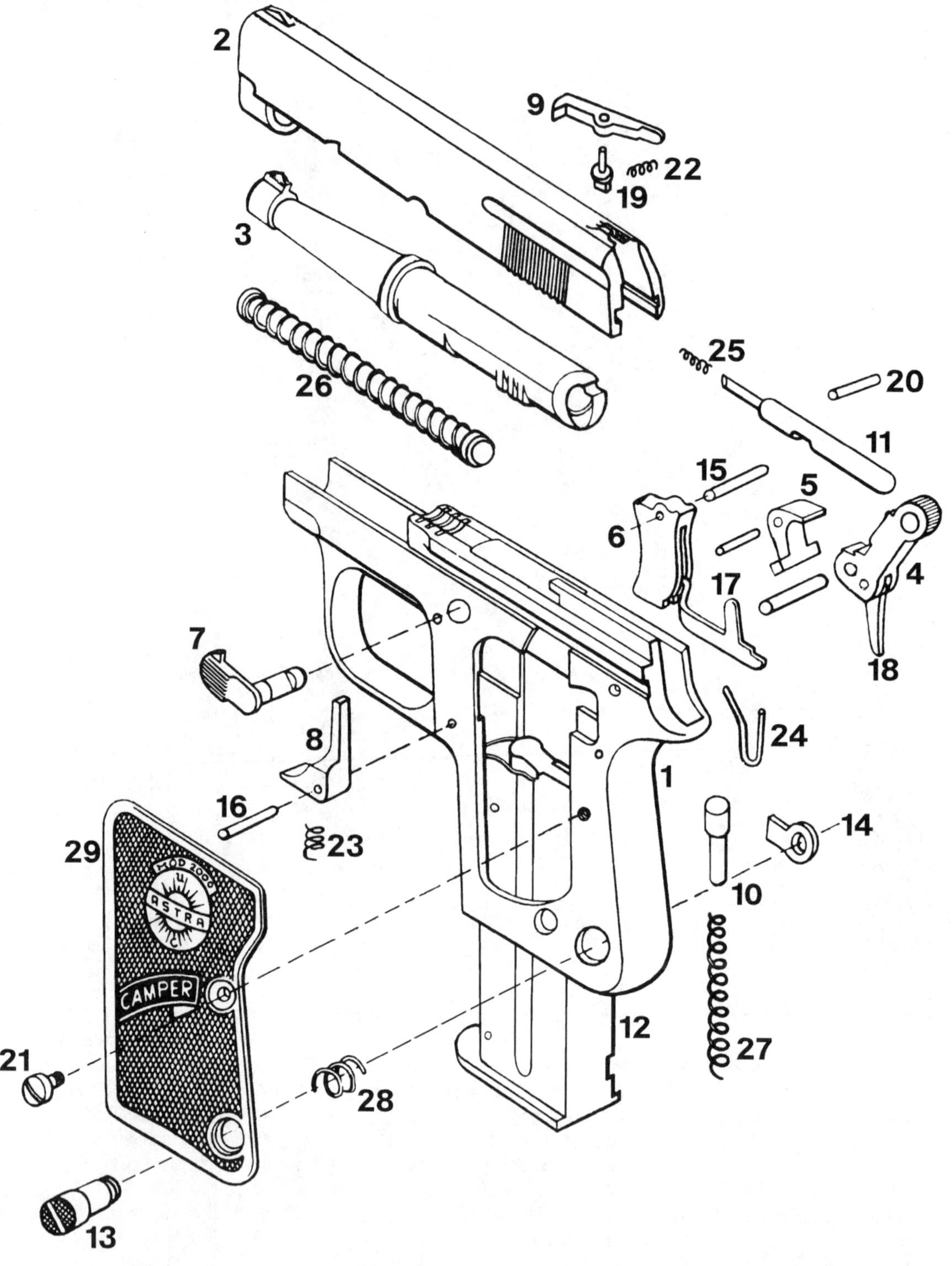

1	Frame	11	Firing Pin	21	Grip Screw
2	Slide	12	Magazine	22	Extractor Spring
3	Barrel	13	Magazine Catch Button	23	Magazine Safety Spring
4	Hammer with Strut and Pin	14	Magazine Catch	24	Sear Spring
5	Sear	15	Trigger Pin	25	Firing Pin Spring
6	Trigger with Disconnector	16	Magazine Safety Pin	26	Recoil Spring Assembly
7	Thumb Safety	17	Sear Pin	27	Hammer Spring
8	Magazine Safety	18	Hammer Pin	28	Magazine Catch Spring
9	Extractor	19	Extractor Pin	29	Grips
10	Hammer Spring Guide	20	Firing Pin Retaining Pin		

Constable Auto

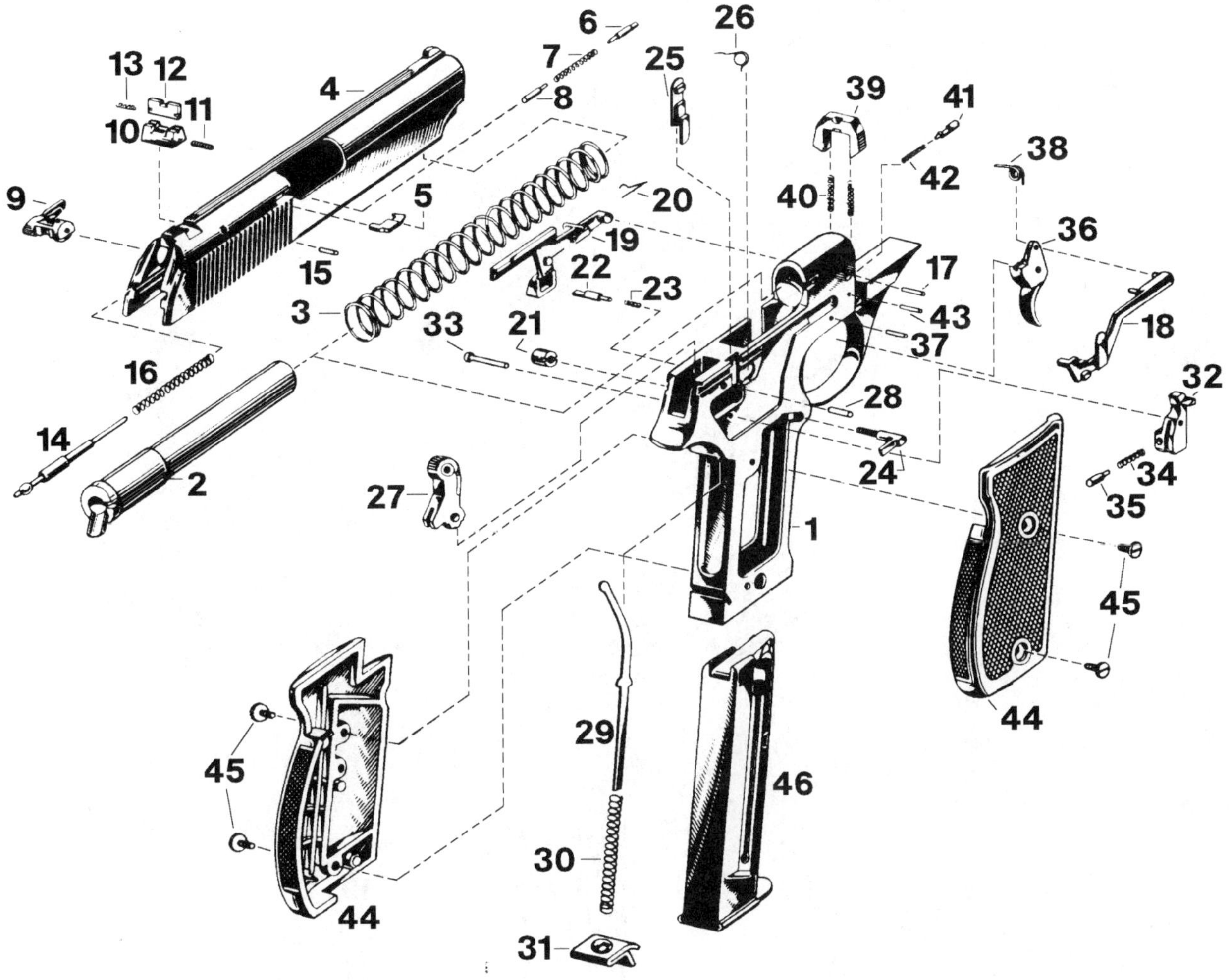

1	Frame	24	Magazine Catch
2	Barrel	25	Disconnector
3	Recoil Spring	26	Disconnector Spring
4	Slide	27	Hammer
5	Extractor	28	Hammer Pin
6	Extractor Pin	29	Mainspring Guide
7	Extractor Spring	30	Mainspring
8	Safety Detent	31	Mainspring Retainer
9	Thumb Safety	32	Sear
10	Rear Sight Base, Adjustable	33	Sear Pin
11	Rear Sight Windage Screw	34	Sear Spring
12	Rear Sight Leaf	35	Sear Plunger
13	Rear Sight Windage Spring	36	Trigger
14	Firing Pin	37	Trigger Pin
15	Firing Pin Retainer	38	Trigger Spring
16	Firing Pin Spring	39	Disassembly Latch
17	Barrel Retainer Pin	40	Disassembly Latch Spring
18	Trigger Bar	41	Disassembly Latch Plunger
19	Ejector Slide Stop	42	Disassembly Latch Plunger Spring
20	Ejector Slide Stop Spring	43	Disassembly Latch Pin
21	Magazine Button	44	Grip
22	Magazine Catch Plunger	45	Grip Screw
23	Magazine Catch Spring	46	Magazine

Cub Auto

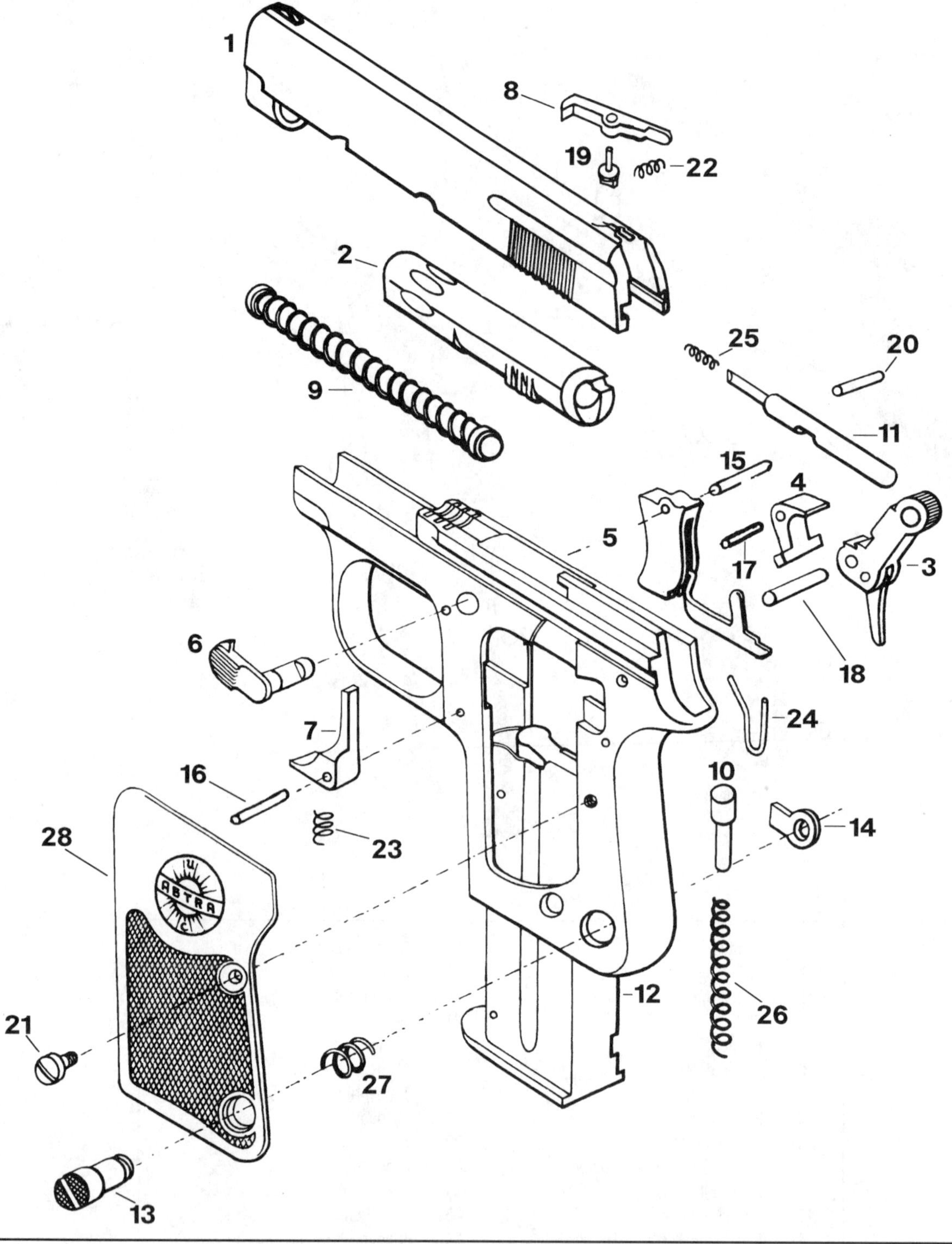

1	Slide	**11**	Firing Pin	**21**	Grip Screw
2	Barrel	**12**	Magazine	**22**	Extractor Spring
3	Hammer with Strut and Pin	**13**	Magazine Catch Button	**23**	Magazine Safety Spring
4	Sear	**14**	Magazine Catch	**24**	Sear Spring
5	Trigger with Disconnector	**15**	Trigger Pin	**25**	Firing Pin Spring
6	Thumb Safety	**16**	Magazine Safety Pin	**26**	Hammer Spring
7	Magazine Safety	**17**	Sear Pin	**27**	Magazine Catch Spring
8	Extractor	**18**	Hammer Pin	**28**	Grips
9	Recoil Spring Assembly	**19**	Extractor Pin		
10	Hammer Spring Guide	**20**	Firing Pin Retaining Pin		

Falcon Auto

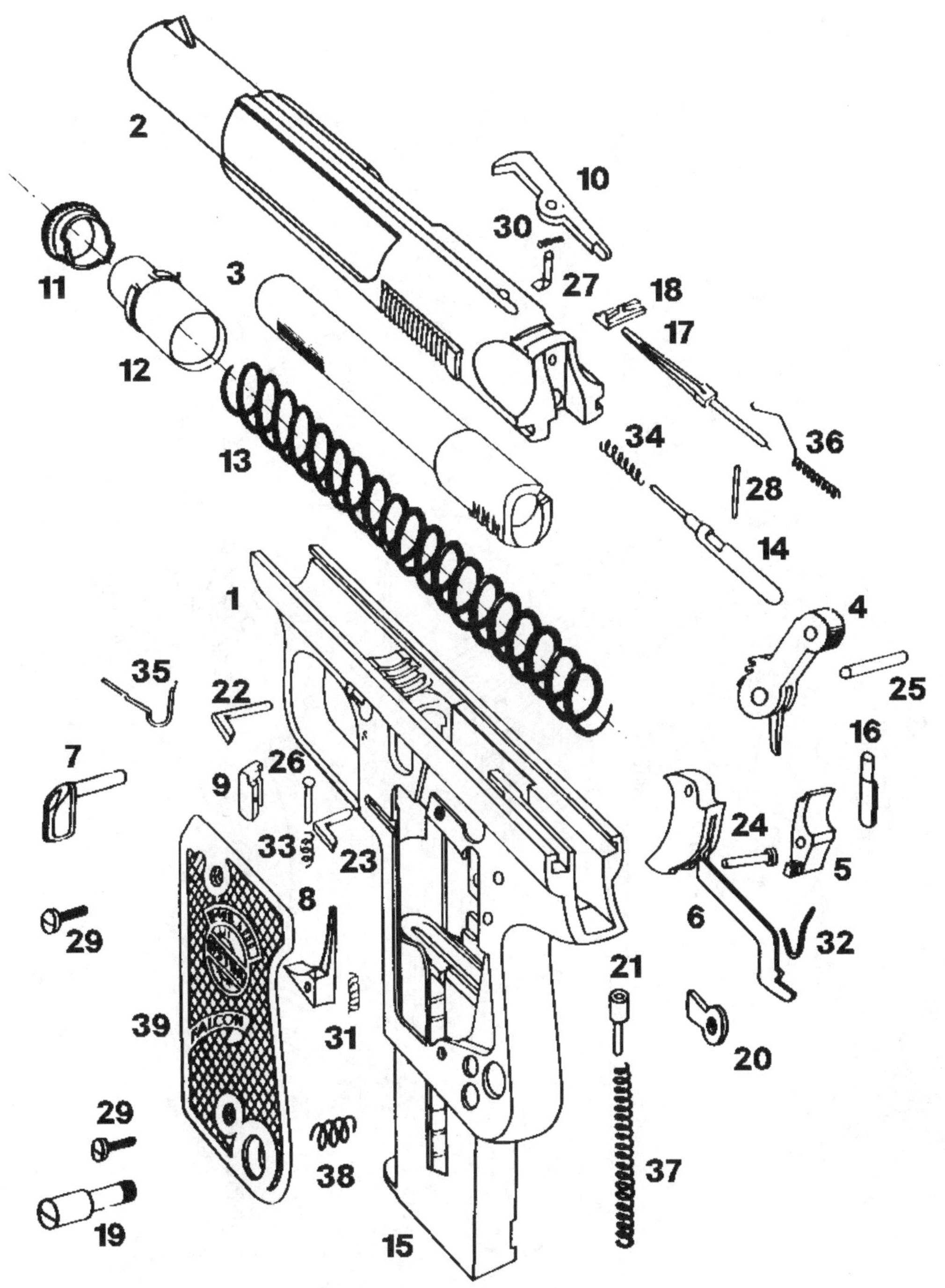

1	Frame	**14**	Firing Pin	**27**	Extractor Retaining Pin
2	Slide	**15**	Magazine	**28**	Loaded Chamber Retaining Pin
3	Barrel	**16**	Firing Pin Retainer	**29**	Grip Screws (4)
4	Hammer with Strut	**17**	Loaded Chamber Indicator	**30**	Extractor Spring
5	Sear	**18**	Rear Sight	**31**	Magazine Safety Spring
6	Trigger with Bar	**19**	Magazine Catch Button	**32**	Sear Spring
7	Safety-Lever	**20**	Magazine Catch	**33**	Safety Plunger Spring
8	Magazine Safety	**21**	Hammer Spring Plunger	**34**	Firing Pin Spring
9	Slide Latch	**22**	Trigger Pin	**35**	Slide Latch Spring
10	Extractor	**23**	Magazine Safety Pin	**36**	Loaded Chamber Indicator Spring
11	Barrel Bushing Lock	**24**	Sear Pin	**37**	Hammer Spring
12	Barrel Bushing	**25**	Hammer Pin	**38**	Magazine Catch Spring
13	Recoil Spring	**26**	Safety Plunger	**39**	Grip Panel

Firecat Auto

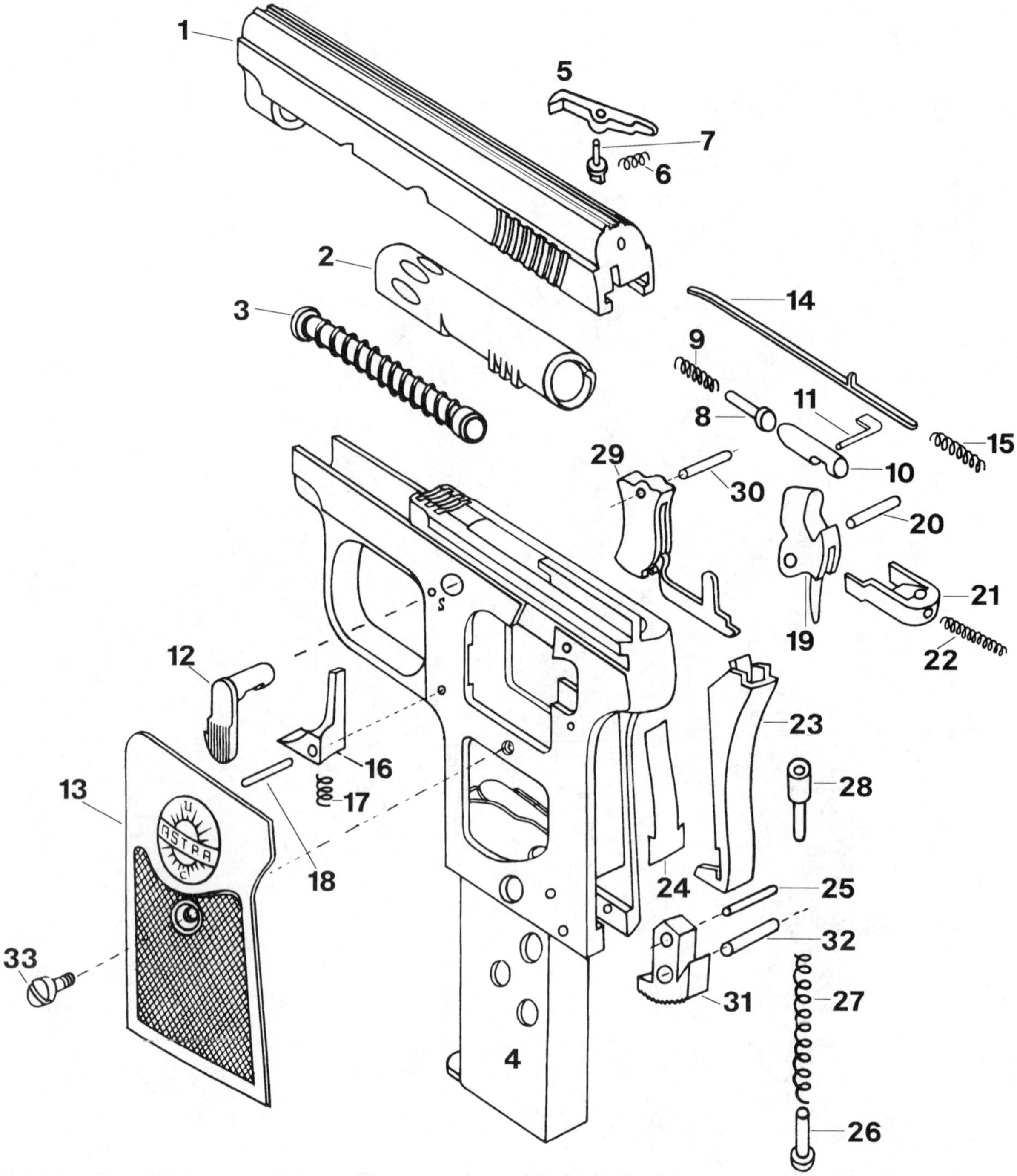

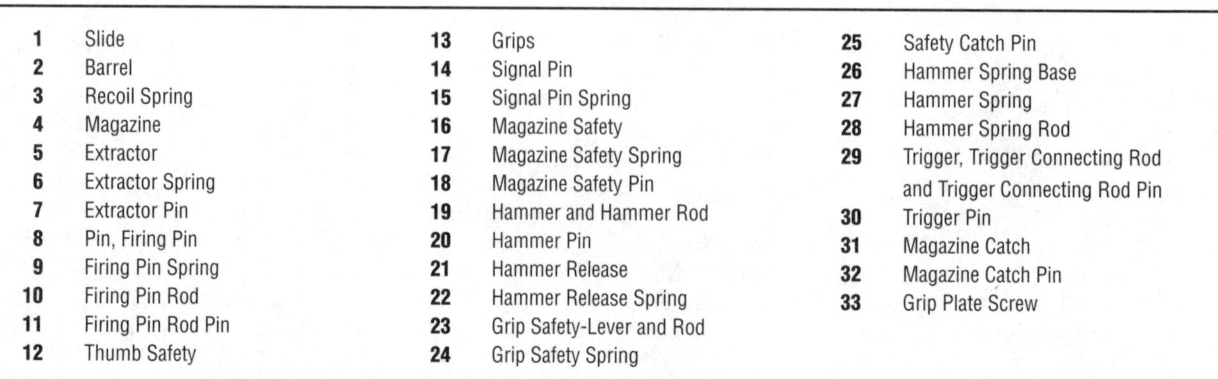

1	Slide	13	Grips	25	Safety Catch Pin
2	Barrel	14	Signal Pin	26	Hammer Spring Base
3	Recoil Spring	15	Signal Pin Spring	27	Hammer Spring
4	Magazine	16	Magazine Safety	28	Hammer Spring Rod
5	Extractor	17	Magazine Safety Spring	29	Trigger, Trigger Connecting Rod and Trigger Connecting Rod Pin
6	Extractor Spring	18	Magazine Safety Pin	30	Trigger Pin
7	Extractor Pin	19	Hammer and Hammer Rod	31	Magazine Catch
8	Pin, Firing Pin	20	Hammer Pin	32	Magazine Catch Pin
9	Firing Pin Spring	21	Hammer Release	33	Grip Plate Screw
10	Firing Pin Rod	22	Hammer Release Spring		
11	Firing Pin Rod Pin	23	Grip Safety-Lever and Rod		
12	Thumb Safety	24	Grip Safety Spring		

Model 357 AST Revolver

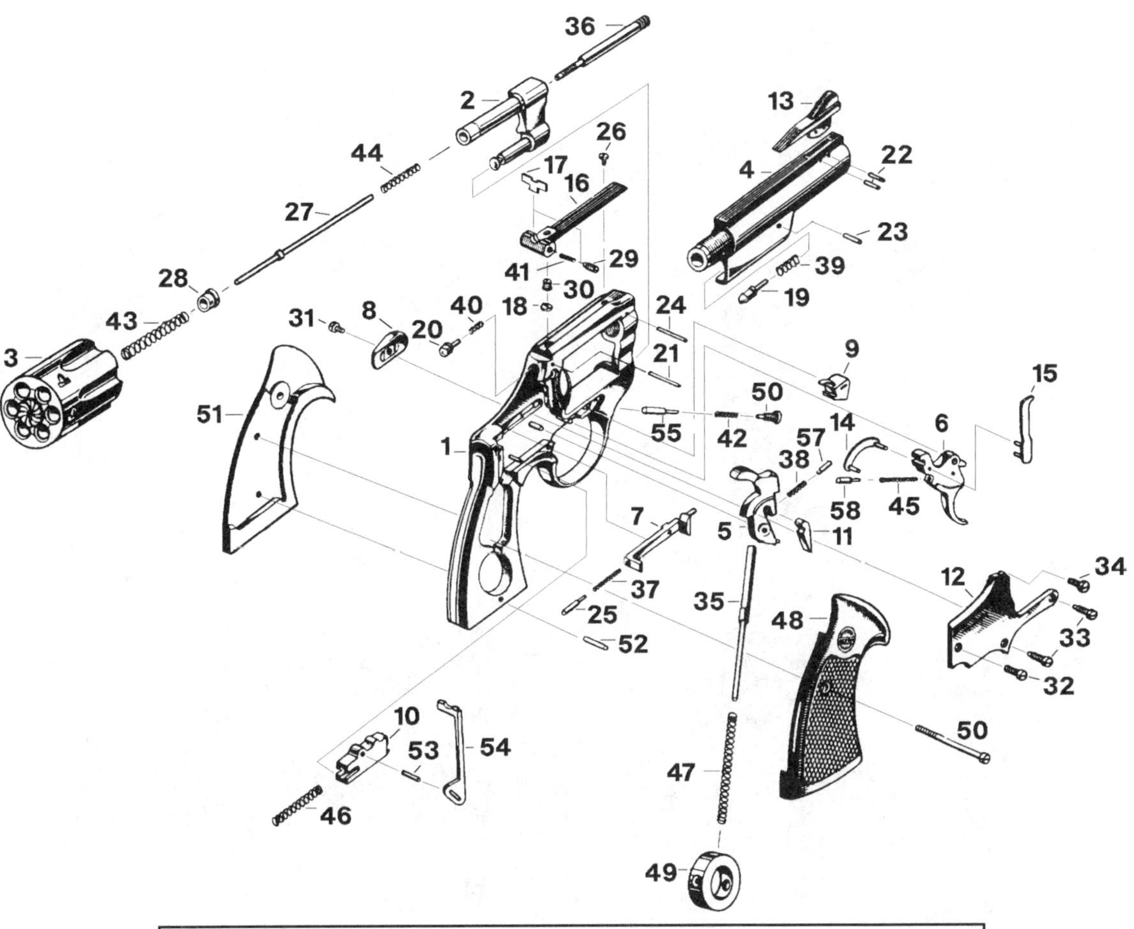

1	Frame	**30**	Elevator Screw
2	Crane	**31**	Thumb-Piece Screw
3	Cylinder with Extractor and Pins	**32**	Flat Head Sideplate Screw
4	Barrel	**33**	Front Lower Sideplate Screw
5	Hammer	**34**	Top Sideplate Screw
6	Trigger	**35**	Hammer Strut
7	Bolt	**36**	Extractor Rod
8	Thumb-Piece	**37**	Bolt Spring
9	Cylinder Stop	**38**	Sear Spring
10	Rebound Slide	**39**	Locking Bolt Spring
11	Sear	**40**	Firing Pin Spring
12	Slideplate	**41**	Sight Slide Spring
13	Front Sight	**42**	Cylinder Stop Spring
14	Trigger Lever	**43**	Extractor Spring
15	Hand	**44**	Center Pin Spring
16	Rear Sight Leaf	**45**	Hand Torsion Spring
17	Sight Slide	**46**	Rebound Slide Spring
18	Screw Plate of Rear Sight Leaf Elevator	**47**	Hammer Spring
19	Locking Bolt	**48**	Right Grip
20	Firing Pin	**49**	Regulation Ring
21	Firing Pin Retaining Pin	**50**	Holder Grip Screw
22	Front Sight Pins	**51**	Left Grip
23	Locking Bolt Pin	**52**	Holder Grip Pin
24	Barrel Pin	**53**	Safety Pin
25	Bolt Plunger	**54**	Safety
26	Sight Leaf Screw	**55**	Cylinder Stop Plunger
27	Central Pin	**56**	Cylinder Stop Screw
28	Extractor Rod Collar	**57**	Sear Plunger
29	Windage Screw	**58**	Hand Plunger

Model 400 Auto

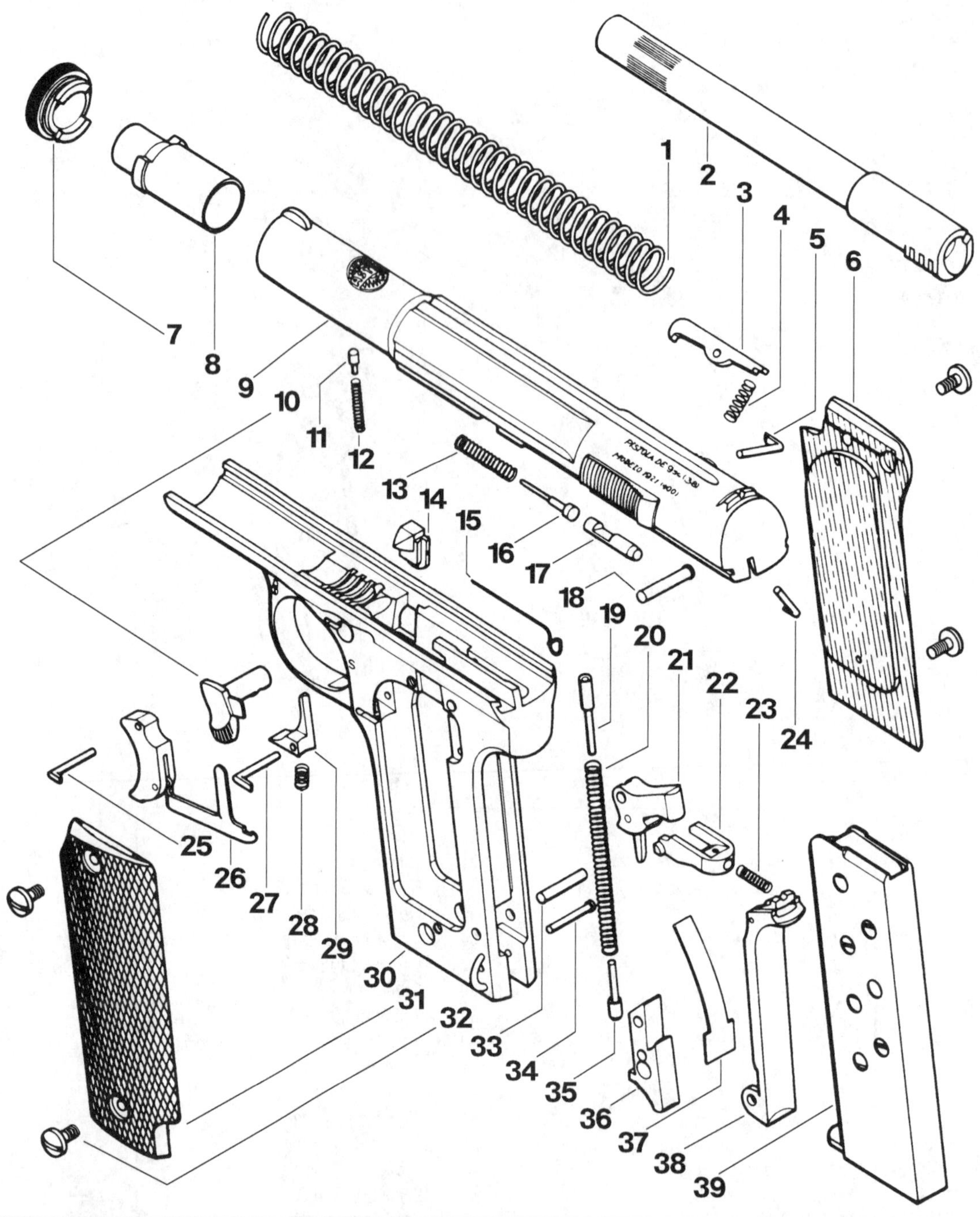

1	Recoil Spring	**14**	Slide Stop	**27**	Magazine Safety Pin
2	Barrel	**15**	Slide Stop Spring	**28**	Magazine Safety Spring
3	Extractor	**16**	Firing Pin	**29**	Magazine Safety
4	Extractor Spring	**17**	Firing Pin Extension	**30**	Frame
5	Firing Pin Retainer Pin	**18**	Hammer Pin	**31**	Left Grip
6	Right Grip	**19**	Hammer Plunger	**32**	Grip Screws (4)
7	Barrel Bushing Lock	**20**	Hammer Spring	**33**	Grip Safety Pin
8	Barrel Bushing	**21**	Hammer and Strut	**34**	Magazine Catch Stop
9	Slide	**22**	Sear	**35**	Magazine Catch Plunger
10	Safety Catch	**23**	Sear Spring	**36**	Magazine Catch
11	Safety Detent	**24**	Extractor Pin	**37**	Grip Safety Spring
12	Safety Spring	**25**	Trigger Pin	**38**	Grip Safety
13	Firing Pin Spring	**26**	Trigger and Trigger Bar	**39**	Magazine

Model A-60 DA Auto

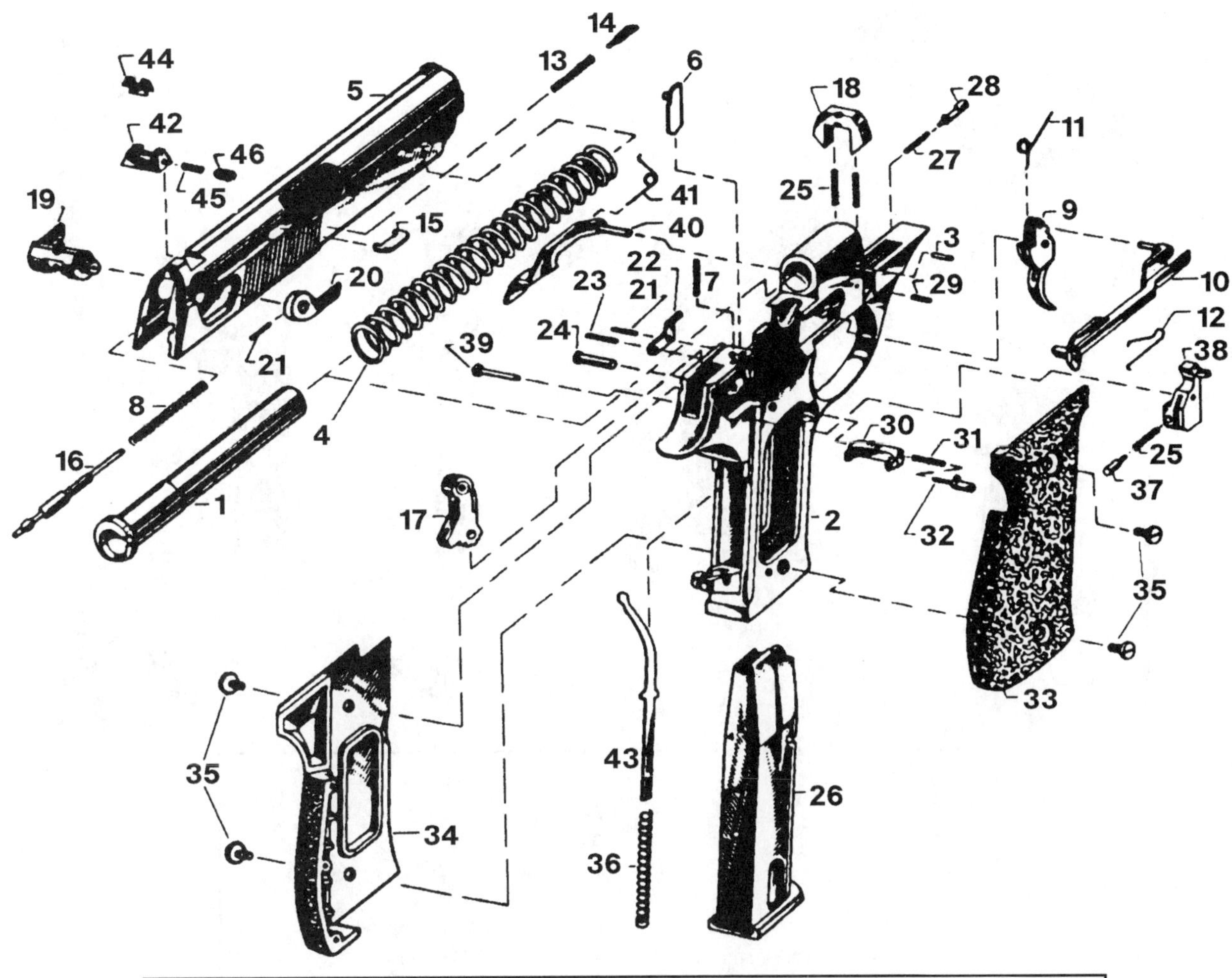

1	Barrel	**24**	Hammer Pin
2	Frame	**25**	Sear Spring and Takedown Yoke Spring
3	Barrel Pin	**26**	Magazine Complete
4	Recoil Spring	**27**	Takedown Plunger Spring
5	Slide	**28**	Takedown Plunger
6	Disconnector	**29**	Takedown Plunger Pin
7	Disconnector Spring	**30**	Magazine Catch
8	Firing Pin Spring	**31**	Magazine Catch Spring
9	Trigger	**32**	Magazine Catch Retainer
10	Sear Bar	**33**	Right Grip
11	Trigger Spring	**34**	Left Grip
12	Sear Bar Spring	**35**	Grip Screws
13	Extractor Spring	**36**	Mainspring
14	Extractor Retainer	**37**	Sear Plunger
15	Extractor	**38**	Sear
16	Firing Pin	**39**	Sear Pin
17	Hammer	**40**	Slide Retainer
18	Takedown Yoke	**41**	Slide Retainer Spring
19	Thumb Safety	**42**	Rear Sight
20	Right Thumb Safety	**43**	Hammer Strut
21	Thumb Safety Pin and Front Ejector Pin	**44**	Sight Slide
22	Ejector	**45**	Sight Slide Spring
23	Ejector Rear Pin	**46**	Windage Screw

Model A-80 DA Auto

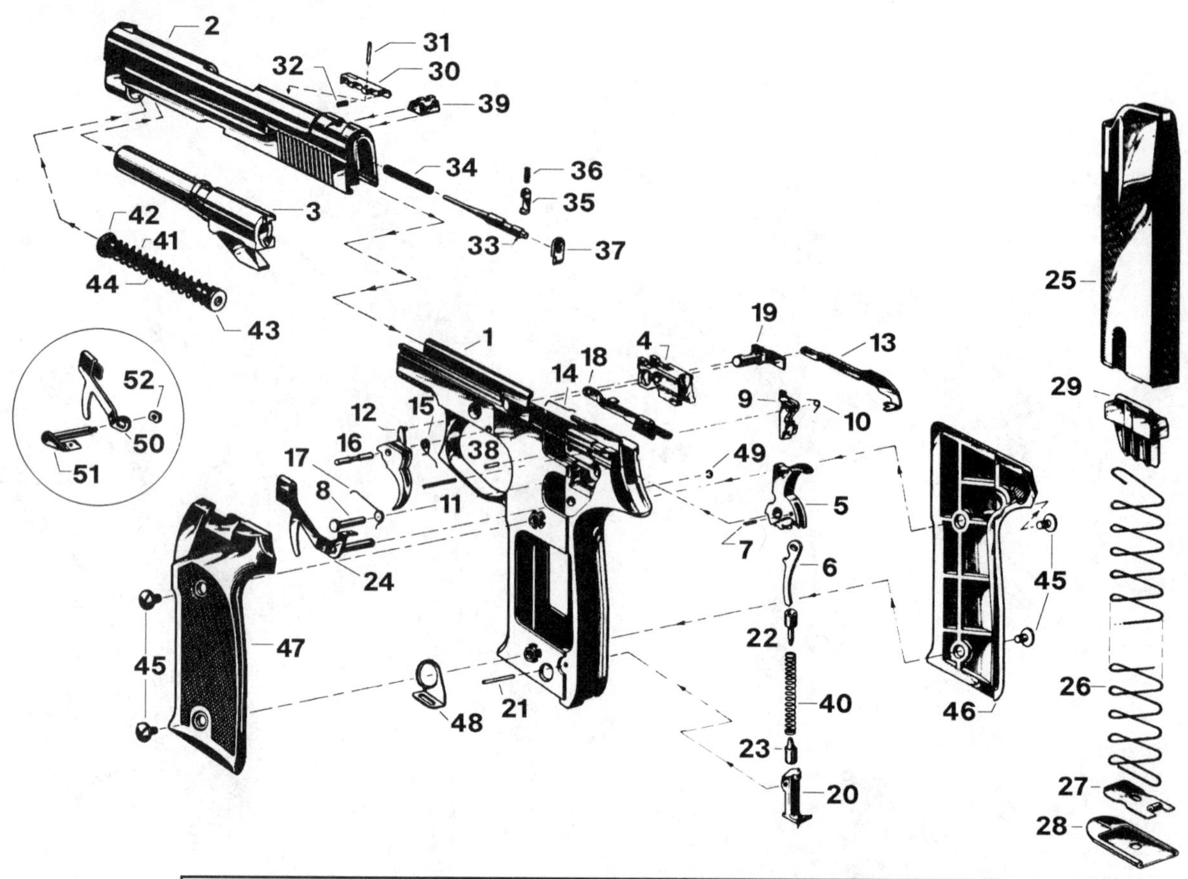

1	Frame	**31**	Extractor Pin
2	Slide	**32**	Extractor Spring
3	Barrel	**33**	Firing Pin
4	Barrel Stop	**34**	Firing Pin Spring
5	Hammer	**35**	Firing Pin Block
6	Hammer Strut	**36**	Firing Pin Block Spring
7	Hammer Strut Pin	**37**	Firing Pin Stop Plate
8	Hammer Pin	**38**	Sear Spring Stop Pin
9	Sear	**39**	Rear Sight
10	Sear Spring	**40**	Hammer Spring
11	Sear Pin	**41**	Recoil Spring
12	Trigger	**42**	Recoil Spring Washer
13	Sear Bar	**43**	Guide Nut
14	Sear Bar Spring	**44**	Recoil Spring Guide
15	Trigger Spring	**45**	Grip Screw
16	Trigger Pin	**46**	Right Grip
17	Slide Retainer and Hammer-Lowering Lever Spring	**47**	Left Grip
18	Slide Retainer	**48**	Lanyard Loop
19	Takedown Latch	**49**	Lever Snap Ring
20	Magazine Catch	**50**	Hammer-Lowering Lever (Left-Handed)
21	Magazine Catch Pin	**51**	Hammer-Lowering Lever Arm (Left-Handed)
22	Hammer Spring Upper Guide	**52**	Hammer-Lowering Lever Nut (Left-Handed)
23	Hammer Spring Lower Guide		
24	Hammer-Lowering Lever	**Parts Not Shown**	
25	Magazine		Lanyard Loop (Left-Handed)
26	Magazine Spring		Right Grip (Left-Handed)
27	Magazine Plate		Left Grip (Left-Handed)
28	Magazine Floorplate		
29	Follower		
30	Extractor-Loaded Chamber Indicator		

Model A-90 DA Auto

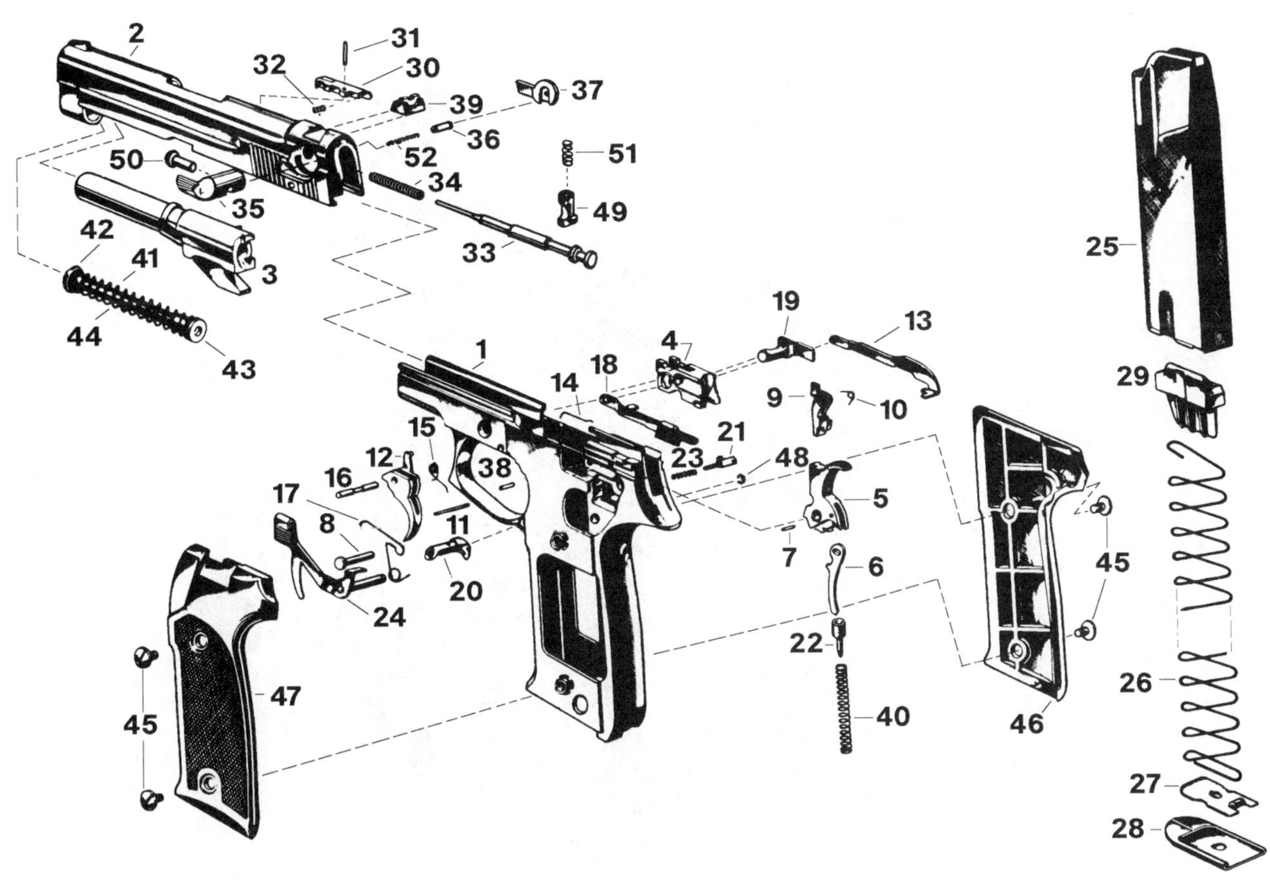

1	Frame	**27**	Magazine Plate
2	Slide	**28**	Magazine Floorplate
3	Barrel	**29**	Follower
4	Barrel Stop	**30**	Extractor-Loaded Chamber Indicator
5	Hammer	**31**	Extractor Pin
6	Hammer Strut	**32**	Extractor Spring
7	Hammer Strut Pin	**33**	Firing Pin
8	Hammer Pin	**34**	Firing Pin Spring
9	Sear	**35**	Manual Safety
10	Sear Spring	**36**	Manual Safety Bolt
11	Sear Pin	**37**	Manual Safety Retainer Arm
12	Trigger	**38**	Sear Spring Stop Pin
13	Sear Bar	**39**	Rear Sight
14	Sear Bar Spring	**40**	Hammer Spring
15	Trigger Spring	**41**	Recoil Spring
16	Trigger Pin	**42**	Recoil Spring Washer
17	Slide Retainer and Hammer Lowering Lever Spring	**43**	Guide Nut
18	Slide Retainer	**44**	Recoil Spring Guide
19	Takedown Latch	**45**	Grip Screws
20	Magazine Catch	**46**	Right Grip
21	Magazine Catch Retainer	**47**	Left Grip
22	Hammer Spring Upper Guide	**48**	Lever Snap Ring
23	Magazine Catch Spring	**49**	Firing Pin Block
24	Hammer Lowering Lever	**50**	Back Firing Pin
25	Magazine	**51**	Firing Pin Block Spring
26	Magazine Spring	**52**	Manual Safety Bolt Spring

Model 41, 44 and 45 Revolver

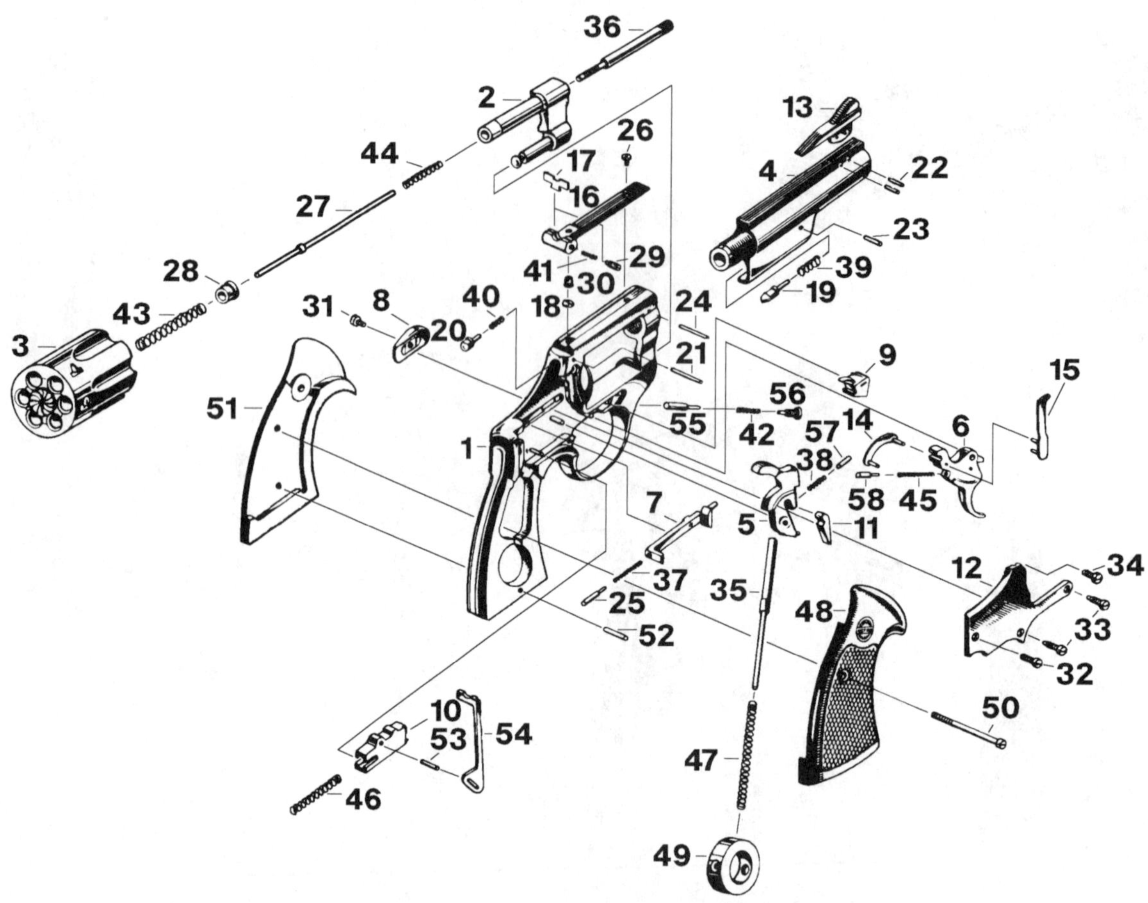

1	Frame
2	Crane
3	Cylinder with Extractor and Pins
4	Barrel
5	Hammer
6	Trigger
7	Bolt
8	Thumb-Piece
9	Cylinder Stop
10	Rebound Slide
11	Sear
12	Slide Plate
13	Front Sight
14	Trigger Lever
15	Hand
16	Rear Sight Leaf
17	Sight Slide
18	Screw Plate of Rear Sight Leaf Elevator
19	Locking Bolt
20	Firing Pin
21	Firing Pin Retaining Pin
22	Front Sight Pin
23	Locking Bolt Pin
24	Barrel Pin
25	Bolt Plunger
26	Sight Leaf Screw
27	Central Pin
28	Extractor Rod Collar
29	Windage Screw
30	Elevator Screw
31	Thumb-Piece Screw
32	Flat Head Sideplate Screw
33	Front Lower Sideplate Screw
34	Top Sideplate Screw
35	Hammer Strut
36	Extractor Rod
37	Bolt Spring
38	Sear Spring
39	Locking Bolt Spring
40	Firing Pin Spring
41	Sight Slide Spring
42	Cylinder Stop Spring
43	Extractor Spring
44	Center Pin Spring
45	Hand Torsion Spring
46	Rebound Slide Spring
47	Hammer Spring
48	Right Grip
49	Regulation Ring
50	Holder Grip Screw
51	Left Grip
52	Holder Grip Pin
53	Safety Pin
54	Safety
55	Cylinder Stop Plunger
56	Cylinder Stop Screw
57	Sear Plunger
58	Hand Plunger

Model 180 Auto

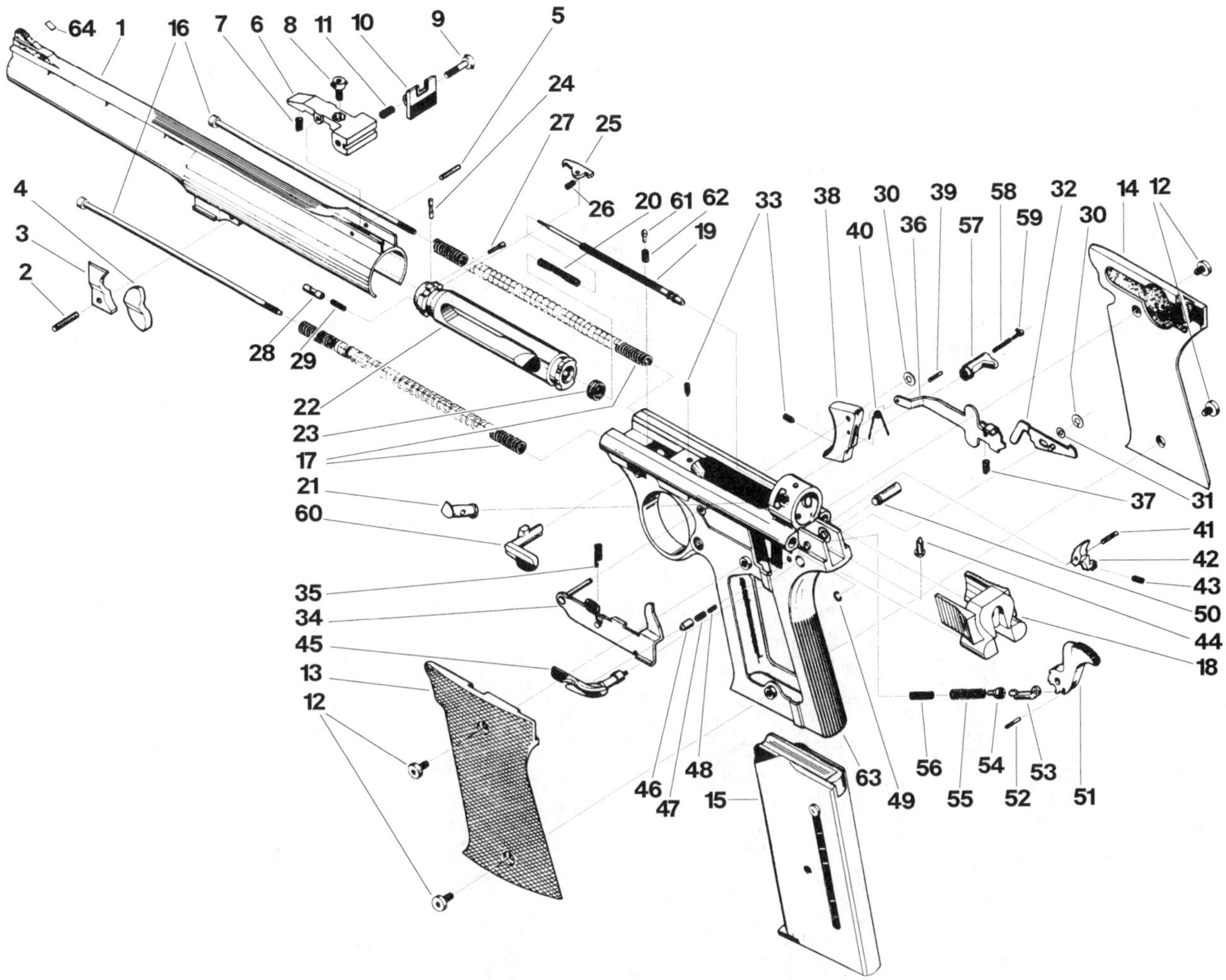

1	Barrel and Extension Assembly
2	Accelerator Block Pin
3	Accelerator Block
4	Accelerator
5	Rear Sight Pin
6	Rear Sight Platform
7	Rear Sight Elevation Spring
8	Elevation Adjustment Screw Assembly
9	Windage Adjustment Screw Assembly
10	Rear Sight Blade
11	Rear Sight Windage Spring
12	Grip Screw
13	Left Grip
14	Right Grip
15	Magazine Assembly
16	Recoil Rod
17	Recoil Spring
18	Cocking Piece
19	Firing Pin
20	Firing Pin Spring
21	Bolt Rotation Pin
22	Bolt
23	Bolt Rotation Spring
24	Extractor Retaining Pin
25	Extractor
26	Extractor Spring
27	Ejector Retaining Pin
28	Ejector
29	Ejector Spring
30	Retaining Ring
31	Safety Plate Spacer
32	Safety Plate
33	Trigger Adjustment Screw
34	Hold Open Assembly
35	Hold Open Spring
36	Trigger Bar
37	Trigger Bar Spring
38	Trigger
39	Trigger Bar Pin
40	Trigger Spring
41	Sear Pin
42	Sear
43	Sear Spring
44	Bolt Safety Tappet
45	Safety-Lever
46	Safety-Lever Detent Plunger
47	Safety-Lever Detent Spring (Outer)
48	Safety-Lever Detent Spring (Inner)
49	Hammer Pin Retaining Ring
50	Hammer Pin
51	Hammer
52	Hammer Strut Pin
53	Hammer Strut
54	Hammer Strut Guide
55	Hammer Spring (Outer)
56	Hammer Spring (Inner)
57	Magazine Latch
58	Magazine Latch Spring
59	Magazine Latch Retainer
60	Barrel Latch
61	Barrel Latch Detent Plunger
62	Barrel Latch Detent Spring
63	Frame
64	Sight Insert Material

Model 1911-A1 Auto

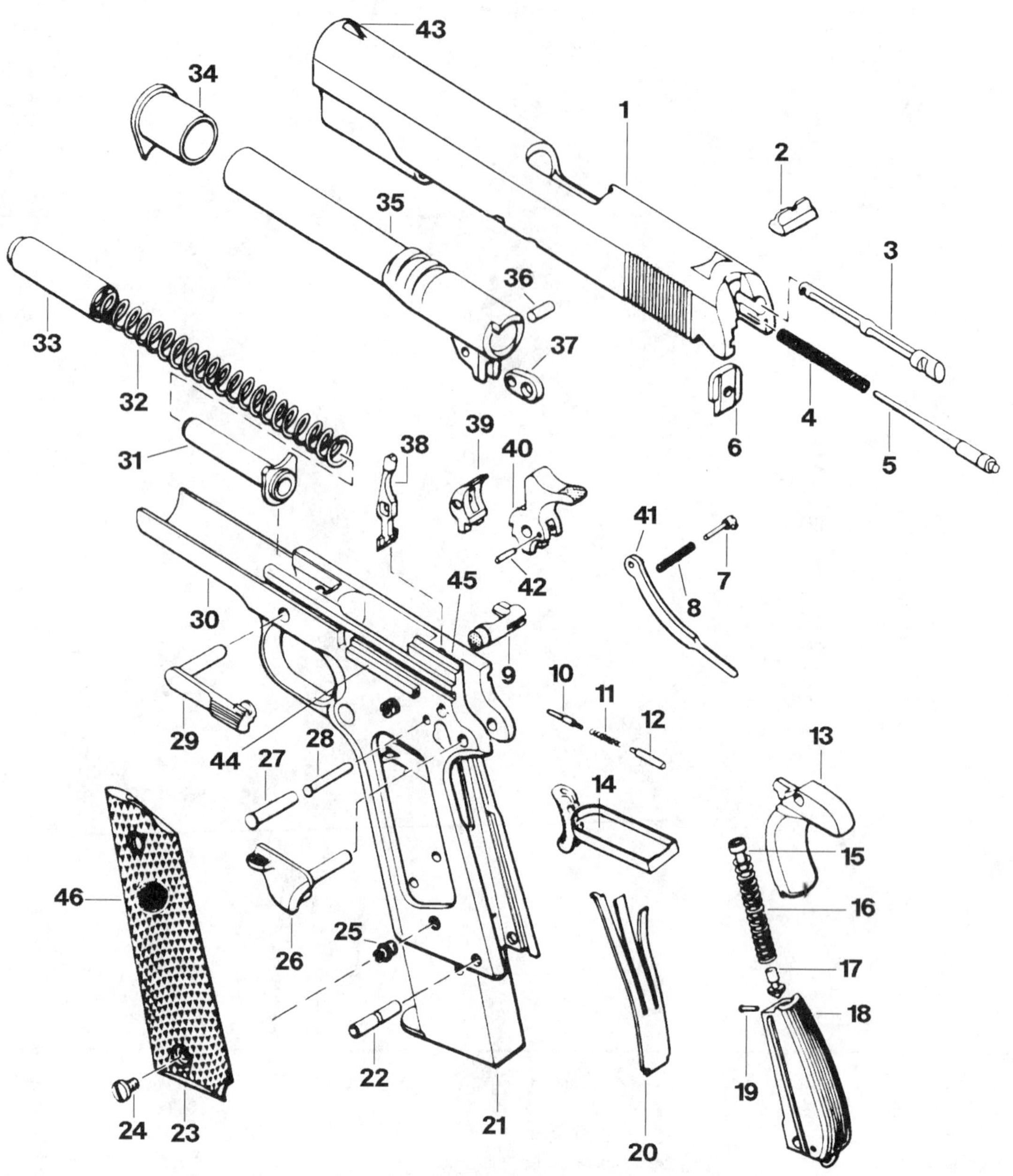

1	Slide	17	Mainspring Housing Pin Retainer	33	Plug
2	Rear Sight	18	Mainspring Housing	34	Barrel Bushing
3	Extractor	19	Mainspring Cap Pin	35	Barrel
4	Firing Pin Spring	20	Sear Spring	36	Barrel Link Pin
5	Firing Pin	21	Magazine	37	Barrel Link
6	Firing Pin Stop Plate	22	Mainspring Housing Pin	38	Disconnector
7	Magazine Catch Lock	23	Hand Grip with Medallion	39	Sear
8	Magazine Catch Spring	24	Grip Screw	40	Hammer
9	Magazine Catch	25	Stock Screw Bushing	41	Hammer Strut
10	Slide Stop Plunger	26	Safety Catch	42	Hammer Strut Pin
11	Plunger Spring	27	Hammer Pin	43	Front Sight
12	Safety Catch Plunger	28	Sear and Disconnector Pin	44	Plunger Tube
13	Grip Safety	29	Slide Stop	45	Ejector
14	Trigger	30	Frame (Receiver)	46	Medallion
15	Mainspring Cap	31	Recoil Spring Guide	**Parts Not Shown**	
16	Mainspring	32	Recoil Spring		Ejector Pin

Model 1915-1919 Auto

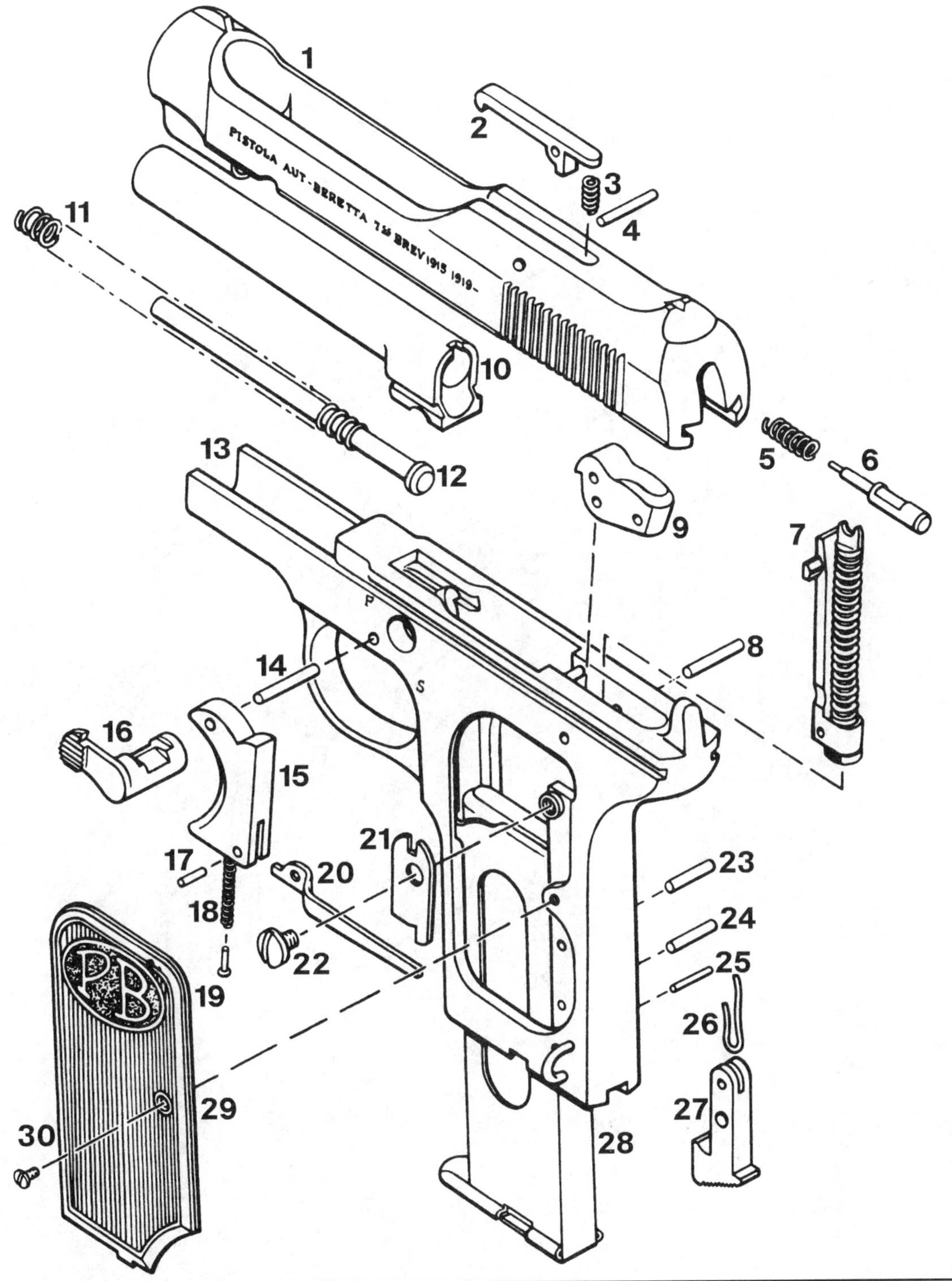

1	Slide	11	Recoil Spring	21	Sear Lever
2	Extractor	12	Recoil Spring Guide	22	Sear Lever Screw
3	Extractor Spring	13	Frame	23	Sear Pin
4	Extractor Pin	14	Trigger Pivot Pin	24	Magazine Catch Pin
5	Firing Pin Spring	15	Trigger	25	Magazine Catch Limit Pin
6	Firing Pin	16	Safety-Lever	26	Magazine Catch Spring
7	Sear/Hammer Spring Assembly	17	Trigger Bar Pin	27	Magazine Catch
8	Hammer Pivot	18	Trigger Bar Spring	28	Magazine Assembly
9	Hammer	19	Trigger Bar Spring Plunger	29	Grip Panel (2)
10	Barrel	20	Trigger Bar	30	Grip Screw (2)

Model 1934 Auto

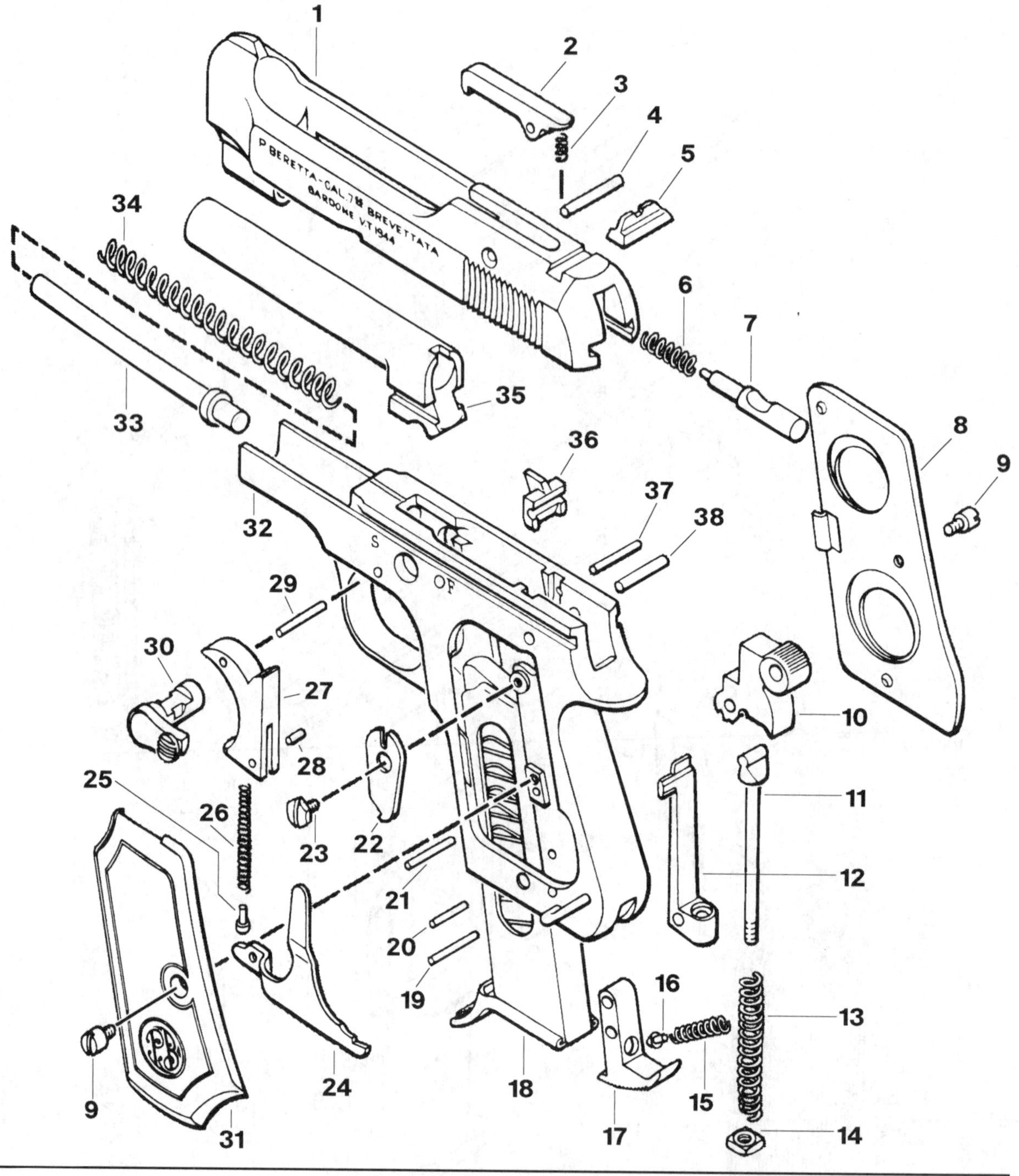

1	Slide	14	Hammer Strut Nut	27	Trigger
2	Extractor	15	Magazine Catch Spring	28	Trigger Bar Pin
3	Extractor Spring	16	Spring Follower	29	Trigger Pin
4	Extractor Pin	17	Magazine Catch	30	Safety Catch
5	Rear Sight	18	Magazine Assembly	31	Left-Hand Grip
6	Firing Pin Spring	19	Magazine Catch Pin	32	Receiver
7	Firing Pin	20	Magazine Catch Hinge Pin	33	Recoil Spring Guide
8	Right-Hand Grip	21	Sear Lever Pin	34	Recoil Spring
9	Grip Screws (2)	22	Sear Plate	35	Barrel
10	Hammer	23	Sear Plate Screw	36	Ejector
11	Hammer Strut	24	Trigger Bar	37	Ejector Pin
12	Sear Lever	25	Trigger Spring Plunger	38	Hammer Pin
13	Hammer Spring	26	Trigger Spring		

Model 20 Auto

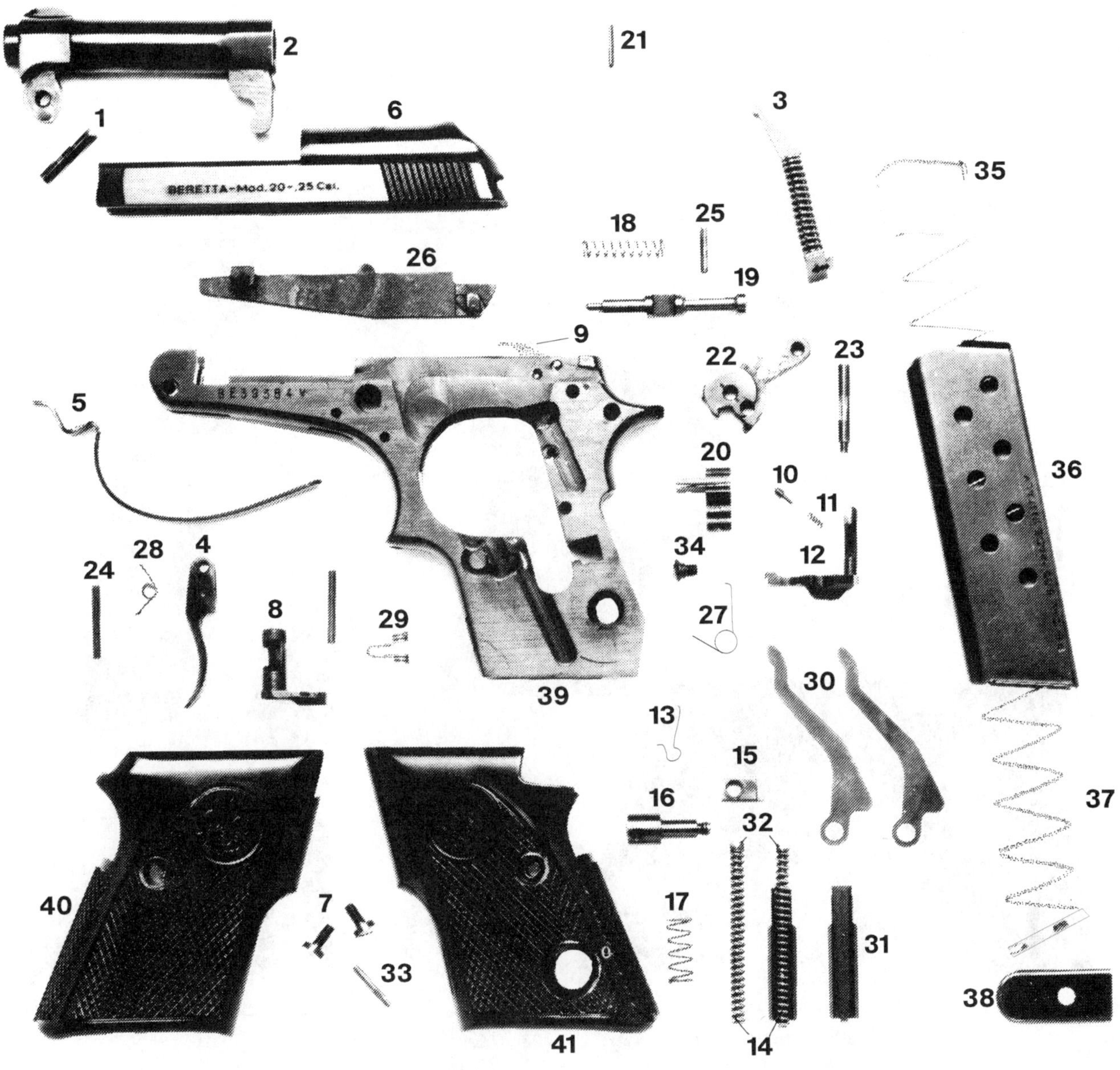

1	Barrel Front Mount Pin
2	Barrel Assembly
3	Hammer Spring Guide Assembly
4	Trigger
5	Trigger Guard
6	Slide
7	Grip Screws
8	Ejector
9	Ejector Pin
10	Safety Plunger
11	Safety Spring
12	Safety
13	Sear Spring
14	Recoil Spring
15	Magazine Release
16	Magazine Release Button
17	Magazine Release Button Spring
18	Firing Pin Spring
19	Firing Pin
20	Sear
21	Sear Pin
22	Hammer
23	Hammer Pin
24	Trigger Pin
25	Firing Pin Retaining Pin
26	Trigger Bar
27	Trigger Bar Spring
28	Trigger Spring
29	Barrel Lever Spring
30	Recoil Spring Lever
31	Recoil Spring Cover
32	Recoil Spring Plunger
33	Grip Junction Roll Pin
34	Trigger Bar Spring Screw
35	Magazine Follower
36	Magazine Body
37	Magazine Spring
38	Magazine Floorplate
39	Frame
40	Right Grip Panel
41	Left Grip Panel
Parts Not Shown	
	Barrel Release

Model 21A Auto

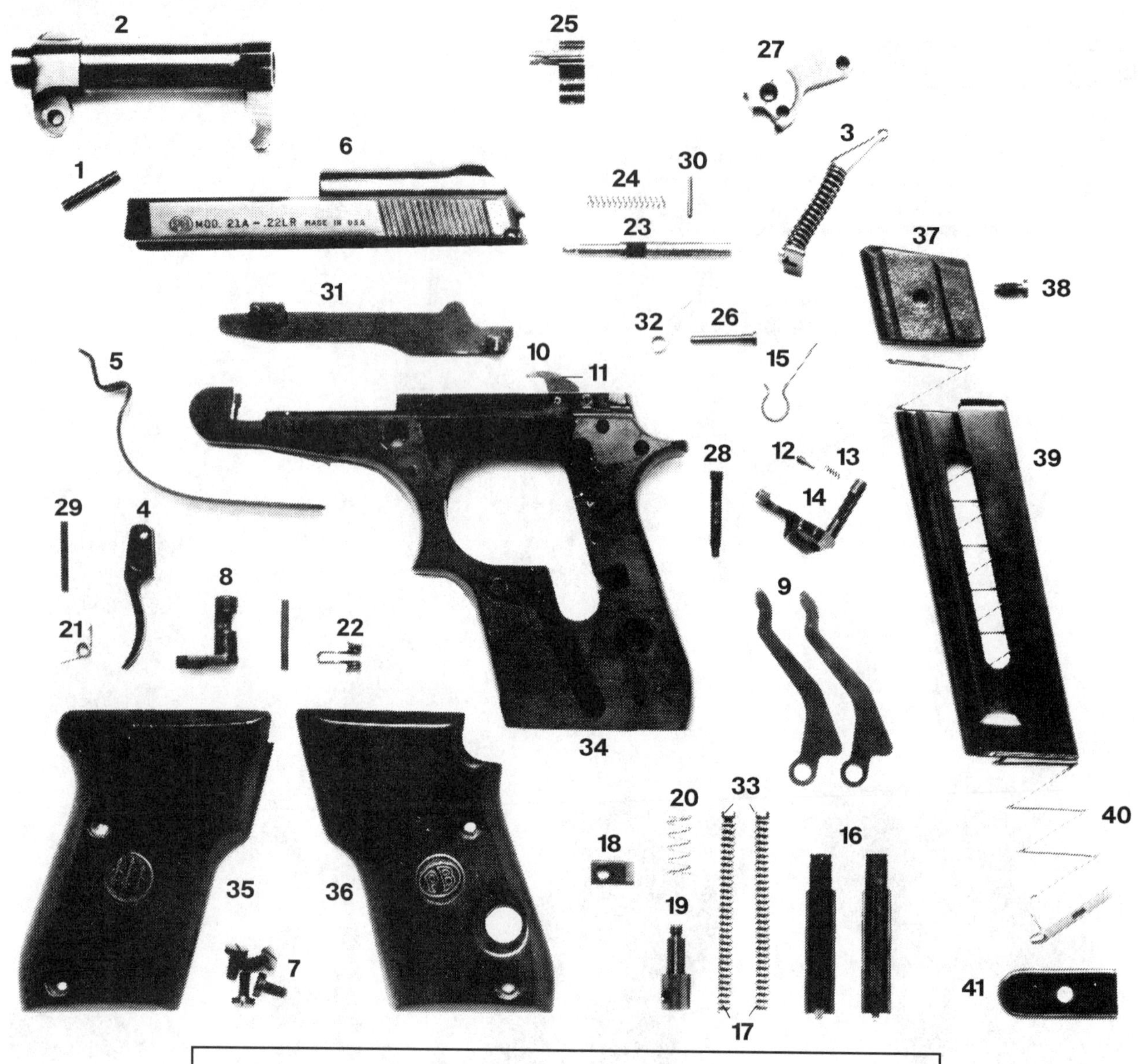

1	Barrel Front Mount Pin	22	Barrel Release Spring
2	Barrel Assembly	23	Firing Pin
3	Hammer Spring Guide Assembly	24	Firing Pin Spring
4	Trigger	25	Sear
5	Trigger Guard	26	Sear Pin
6	Slide	27	Hammer
7	Grip Screws	28	Hammer Pin
8	Barrel Release	29	Trigger Pin
9	Recoil Bar	30	Firing Pin Retaining Pin
10	Ejector	31	Trigger Bar
11	Ejector Pin	32	Trigger Bar Spring
12	Safety Plunger	33	Recoil Spring Plunger
13	Safety Spring	34	Frame
14	Safety	35	Right Grip Panel
15	Sear Spring	36	Left Grip Panel
16	Recoil Spring Cover	37	Magazine Follower
17	Recoil Spring	38	Magazine Follower Screw
18	Magazine Release	39	Magazine Body
19	Magazine Release Button	40	Magazine Spring
20	Magazine Release Spring	41	Magazine Floorplate
21	Trigger Spring		

Model 70 Auto

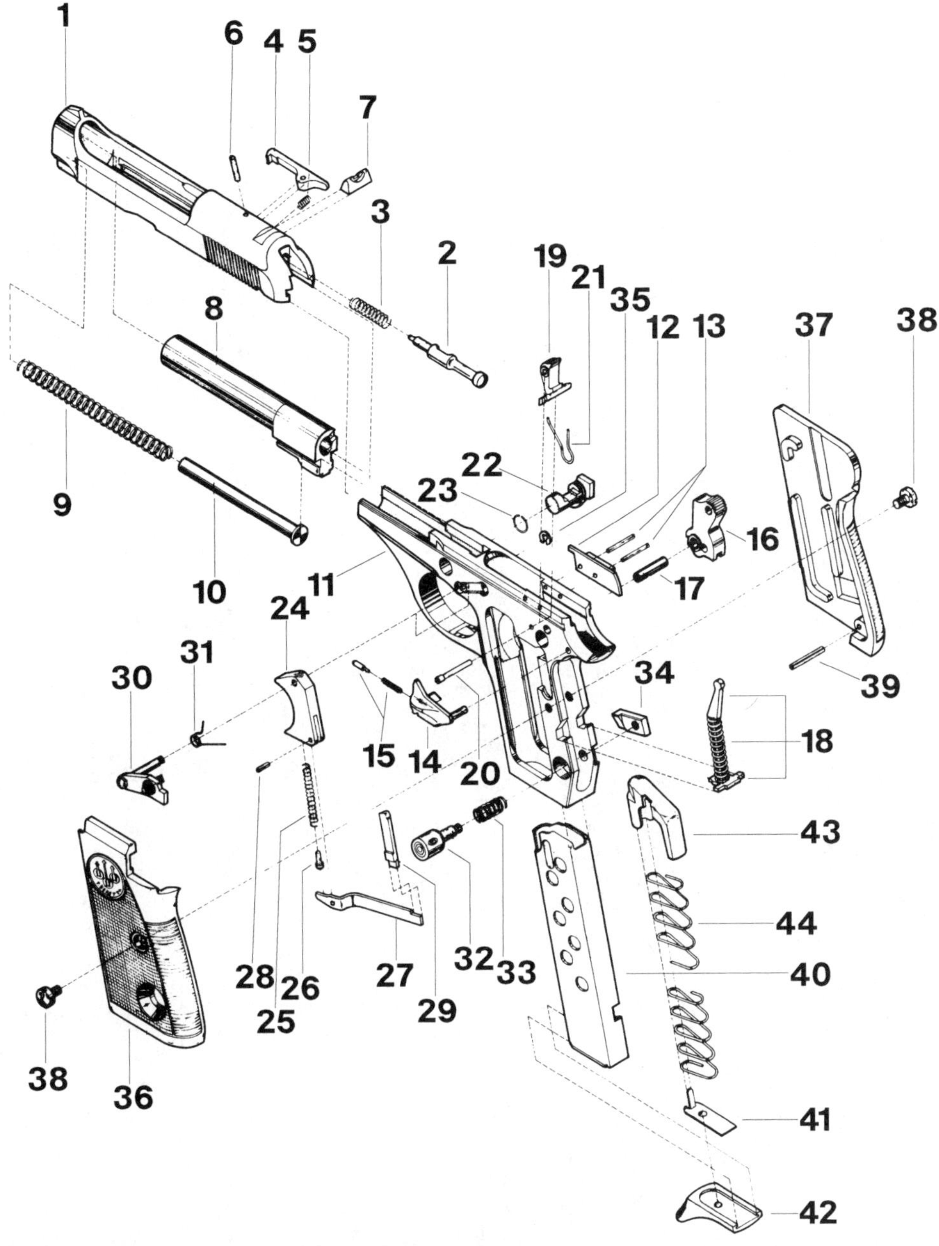

1	Slide	**17**	Hammer Pin	**32**	Magazine Release Push Button
2	Firing Pin	**18**	Hammer Spring/Strut/ Nut Assembly	**33**	Magazine Release Spring
3	Firing Pin Spring	**19**	Sear	**34**	Magazine Release Catch
4	Extractor	**20**	Sear Pin	**35**	Trigger Pin E Clip
5	Extractor Spring	**21**	Sear Spring	**36**	Left Grip Panel
6	Extractor Pin	**22**	Slide Lock with Circlip	**37**	Right Grip Panel
7	Rear Sight	**23**	Slide Lock Circlip	**38**	Grip Screws (2)
8	Barrel	**24**	Trigger	**39**	Grip Junction Rod
9	Recoil Spring	**25**	Trigger Bar Spring	**40**	Magazine Body
10	Recoil Spring Guide	**26**	Trigger Bar Spring Plungers (2)	**41**	Magazine Spring Plate
11	Frame	**27**	Trigger Bar	**42**	Magazine Floorplate Extension
12	Ejector	**28**	Trigger Bar Pin	**43**	Follower
13	Ejector Pins (2)	**29**	Disconnector	**44**	Magazine Spring
14	Safety-Lever	**30**	Slide Catch		**Parts Not Shown**
15	Safety-Lever Spring and Plunger	**31**	Slide Catch Spring		Trigger Pin
16	Hammer				Slide Catch Spring Screw

Model 76 Auto

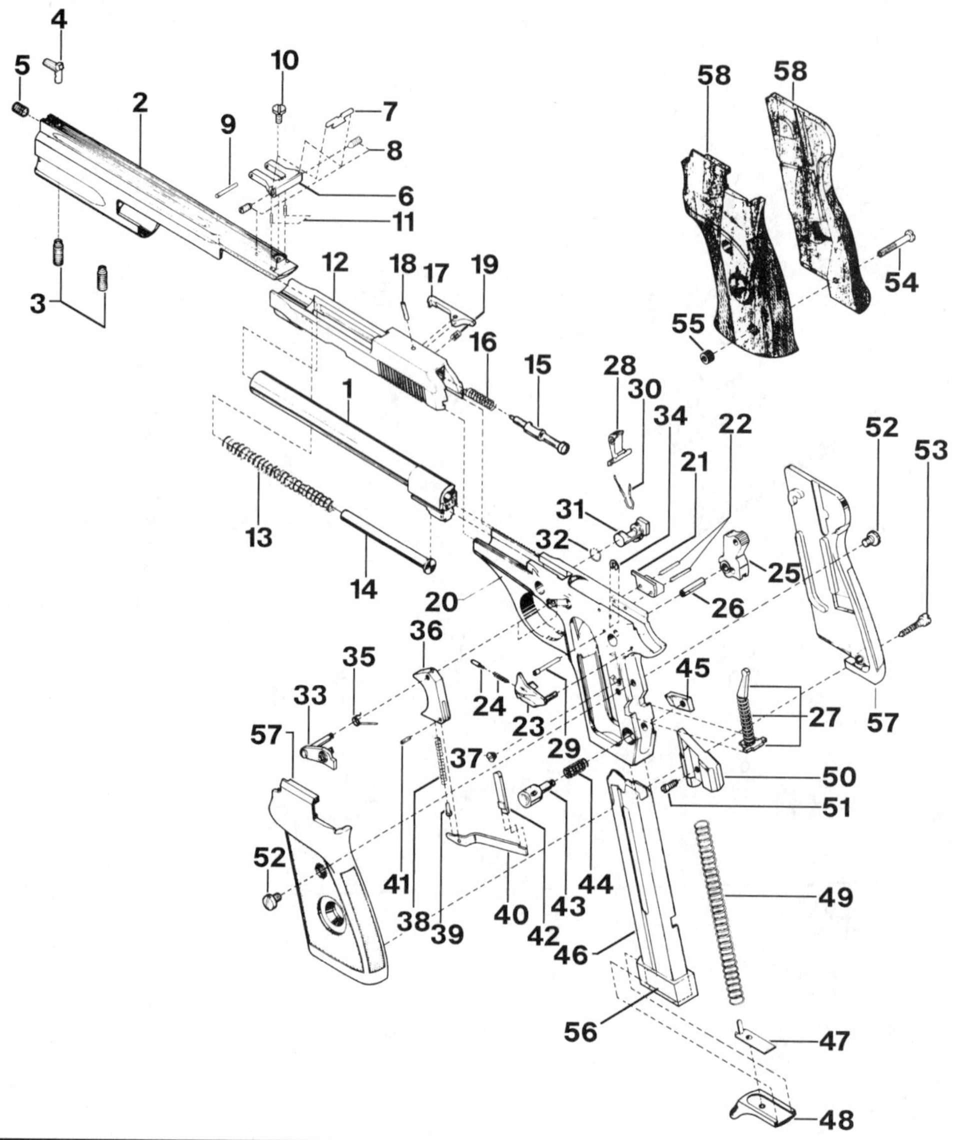

1 Barrel
2 Barrel Weight
3 Barrel Weight Lock Screws
4 Interchangeable Front Sight
5 Front Sight Screw
6 Rear Sight Base
7 Rear Sight Blade
8 Rear Sight Windage Screws
9 Rear Sight Assembly Pin
10 Rear Sight Assembly Elevating Screw
11 Rear Sight Assembly Springs (2)
12 Slide
13 Recoil Spring
14 Recoil Spring Guide
15 Firing Pin
16 Firing Pin Spring
17 Extractor
18 Extractor Pin
19 Extractor Spring
20 Frame
21 Ejector
22 Ejector Pins (2)
23 Safety-Lever
24 Safety Spring and Plunger Assembly
25 Hammer
26 Hammer Pin
27 Hammer Spring Assembly
28 Sear
29 Sear Pin
30 Sear Spring
31 Disassembly Catch
32 Disassembly Catch Circlip
33 Slide Catch
34 Slide Catch E Spring
35 Slide Catch Spring
36 Trigger
37 Trigger Spring
38 Trigger Bar Spring
39 Trigger Bar Spring Plunger
40 Trigger Bar
41 Trigger Bar Pin
42 Disconnector
43 Magazine Release Push Button
44 Magazine Release Spring
45 Magazine Release Catch
46 Magazine Box
47 Magazine Floorplate
48 Magazine Floorplate Extension
49 Magazine Spring
50 Follower
51 Follower Retaining Screw
52 Grip Screws (2)
53 Grip Junction Screw, Plastic Grip
54 Grip Junction Screw, Wood Grip
55 Grip Junction Screw Bushing
56 Magazine Spacer
57 Plastic Grip
58 Wood Grip

Parts Not Shown

Barrel Weight Pin
Slide Catch Screw

Model 81 and 84 Auto

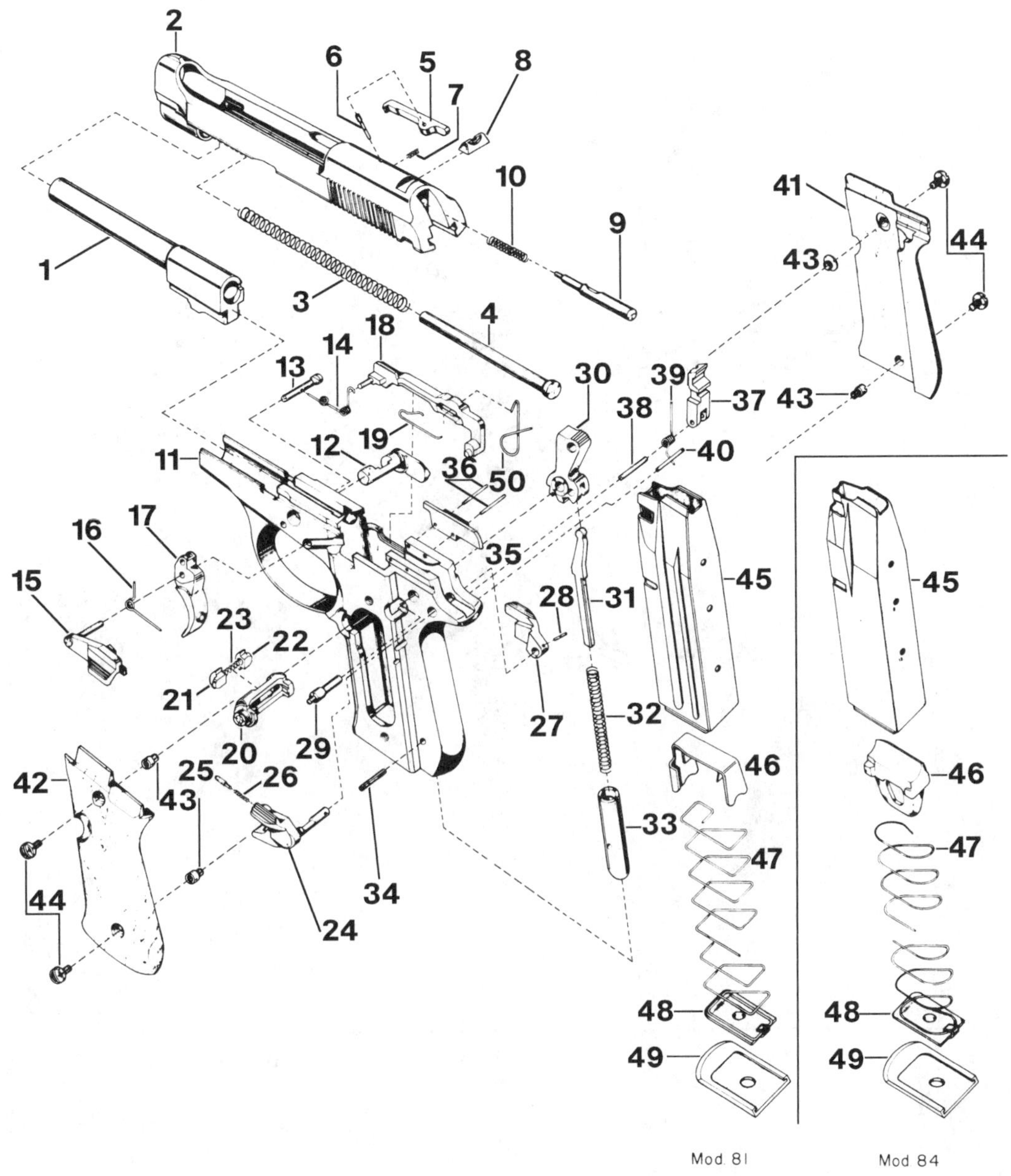

1	Barrel	**19**	Trigger Bar Spring	**34**	Hammer Strut Guide Pin
2	Slide	**20**	Magazine Release Button	**35**	Ejector
3	Recoil Spring	**21**	Magazine Release Button Spring Bushing	**36**	Ejector Pin (2)
4	Recoil Spring Guide	**22**	Magazine Release Button Spring Bushing	**37**	Sear
5	Extractor	**23**	Magazine Release Button Spring	**38**	Sear Pin
6	Extractor Pin	**24**	Left Safety	**39**	Sear Spring
7	Extractor Spring	**25**	Safety Spring Pin	**40**	Sear Spring Pin
8	Rear Sight	**26**	Safety Spring	**41**	Right Grip Panel
9	Firing Pin	**27**	Right Safety Wing	**42**	Left Grip Panel
10	Firing Pin Spring	**28**	Safety Pin	**43**	Grip Bushing
11	Frame	**29**	Hammer Pin	**44**	Grip Screw (4)
12	Disassembly Latch	**30**	Hammer	**45**	Magazine Body
13	Disassembly Latch Release Button	**31**	Hammer Spring Strut	**46**	Magazine Follower
14	Trigger Spring	**32**	Hammer Spring	**47**	Magazine Spring
15	Slide Catch	**33**	Hammer Strut Guide	**48**	Magazine Plate
16	Slide Catch Spring			**49**	Magazine Floorplate
17	Trigger			**50**	Magazine Safety Spring
18	Trigger Bar				

Model 85B and 85BB Auto

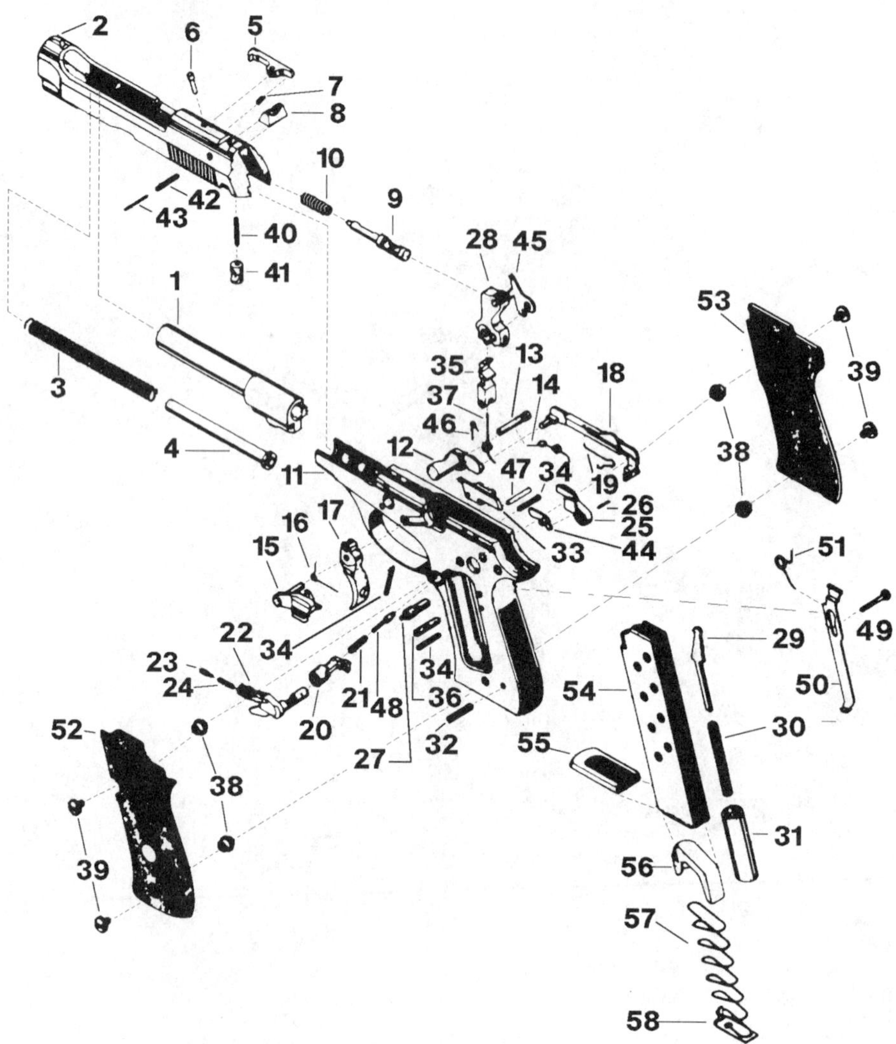

1	Barrel	**24**	Safety Spring	**47**	Ejector Front Pin
2	Slide	**25**	Right Safety	**48**	Magazine Catch Spring Guide Plunger
3	Recoil Spring	**26**	Safety Pin	**49**	Sear Spring and Magazine Safety Pin
4	Recoil Spring Guide	**27**	Hammer Pin	**50**	Magazine Safety
5	Extractor	**28**	Hammer	**51**	Magazine Safety Spring
6	Extractor Pin	**29**	Hammer Spring Guide	**52**	Left Grip Panel
7	Extractor Spring	**30**	Hammer Spring	**53**	Right Grip Panel
8	Rear Sight	**31**	Hammer Spring Cap	**54**	Magazine Body
9	Firing Pin	**32**	Hammer Spring Cap Pin	**55**	Magazine Floorplate
10	Firing Pin Spring	**33**	Ejector	**56**	Magazine Follower
11	Frame	**34**	Spring Pin	**57**	Magazine Spring
12	Disassembly Latch	**35**	Sear	**58**	Magazine Spring Plate
13	Disassembly Latch Release Button	**36**	Sear Pin		**Parts Not Shown**
14	Trigger Spring	**37**	Sear Spring		Magazine Release Button Spring Bushing, Long
15	Slide Catch	**38**	Grip Bushing		Magazine Release Button Spring Bushing, Short
16	Slide Catch Spring	**39**	Grip Screws		Magazine Safety Spring Retaining Bushing
17	Trigger	**40**	Firing Pin Catch Spring		Safety Magazine Spring
18	Trigger Bar	**41**	Firing Pin Catch		Magazine Follower Screw
19	Trigger Bar Spring	**42**	Firing Pin Retaining Pin (Outer Pin)		
20	Magazine Release Button	**43**	Firing Pin Retaining Pin (Inner Pin)		
21	Magazine Release Button Spring	**44**	Trigger Release Lever		
22	Left Safety	**45**	Firing Pin Catch Lever		
23	Safety Spring Plunger	**46**	Firing Pin Catch Lever Spring		

Model 87 Auto

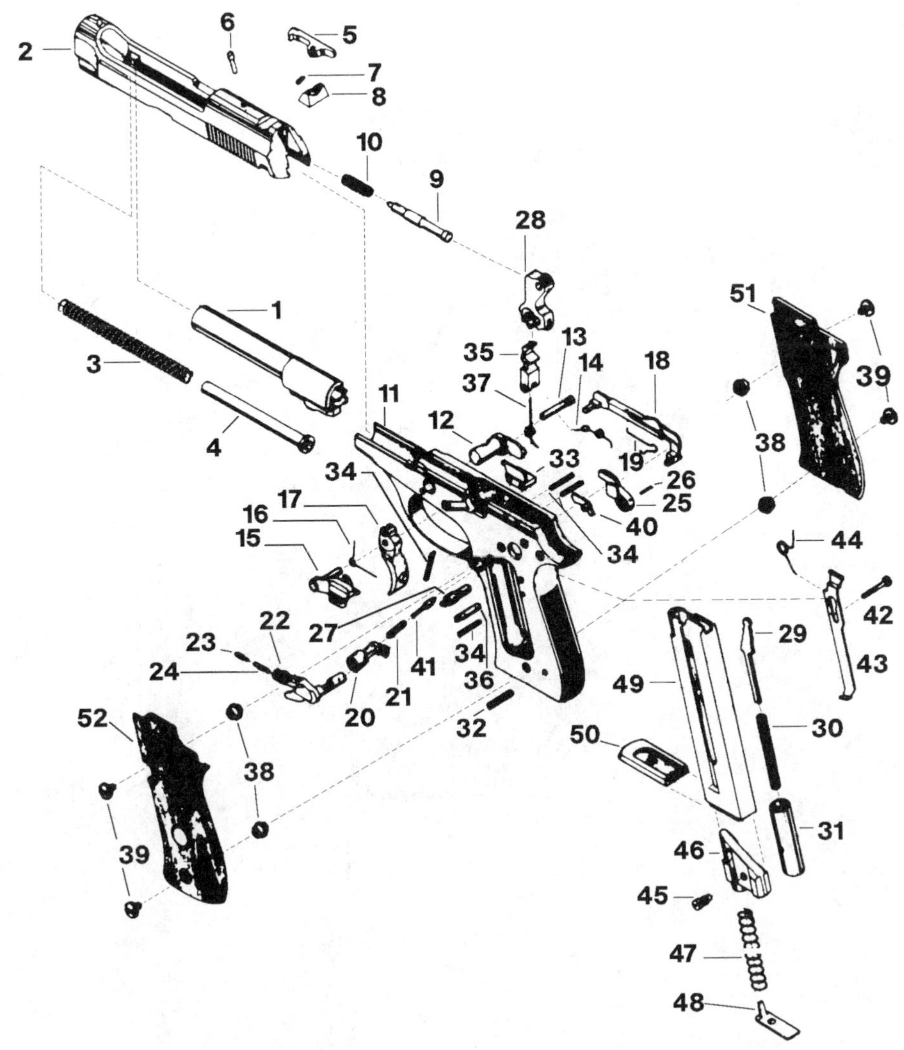

1	Barrel	**25**	Right Safety	**48**	Magazine Spring Plate
2	Slide	**26**	Safety Pin	**49**	Magazine Body
3	Recoil Spring	**27**	Hammer Pin	**50**	Magazine Floorplate
4	Recoil Spring Guide	**28**	Hammer	**51**	Right Grip Panel
5	Extractor	**29**	Hammer Spring Guide	**52**	Left Grip Panel
6	Extractor Pin	**30**	Hammer Spring	**Parts Not Shown**	
7	Extractor Spring	**31**	Hammer Spring Cap		Magazine Release Button
8	Rear Sight	**32**	Hammer Spring Cap Pin		Spring Bushing, Long
9	Firing Pin	**33**	Ejector		Magazine Release Button
10	Firing Pin Spring	**34**	Spring Pin		Spring Bushing, Short
11	Frame	**35**	Sear		Magazine Safety, Spring
12	Disassembling Latch	**36**	Sear Pin		Retaining Bushing
13	Disassembling Latch Release Button	**37**	Sear Spring		Safety Magazine Spring
14	Trigger Spring	**38**	Grip Bush		Firing Pin Catch Spring
15	Slide Catch	**39**	Grip Screws		Firing Pin Catch
16	Slide Catch Spring	**40**	Trigger Release Lever		Firing Pin Retaining Pin (Outer Pin)
17	Trigger	**41**	Magazine Catch Spring Guide Plunger		Firing Pin Retaining Pin (Inner Pin)
18	Trigger Bar	**42**	Sear Spring and Magazine Safety Pin		Firing Pin Catch Lever
19	Trigger Bar Spring	**43**	Magazine Safety		Firing Pin Catch Lever Spring
20	Magazine Release Button	**44**	Magazine Safety Spring		Ejector Front Pin
21	Magazine Release Button Spring	**45**	Magazine Follower Screw		
22	Left Safety	**46**	Magazine Follower		
23	Safety Spring Plunger	**47**	Magazine Spring		
24	Safety Spring				

Model 90 Auto

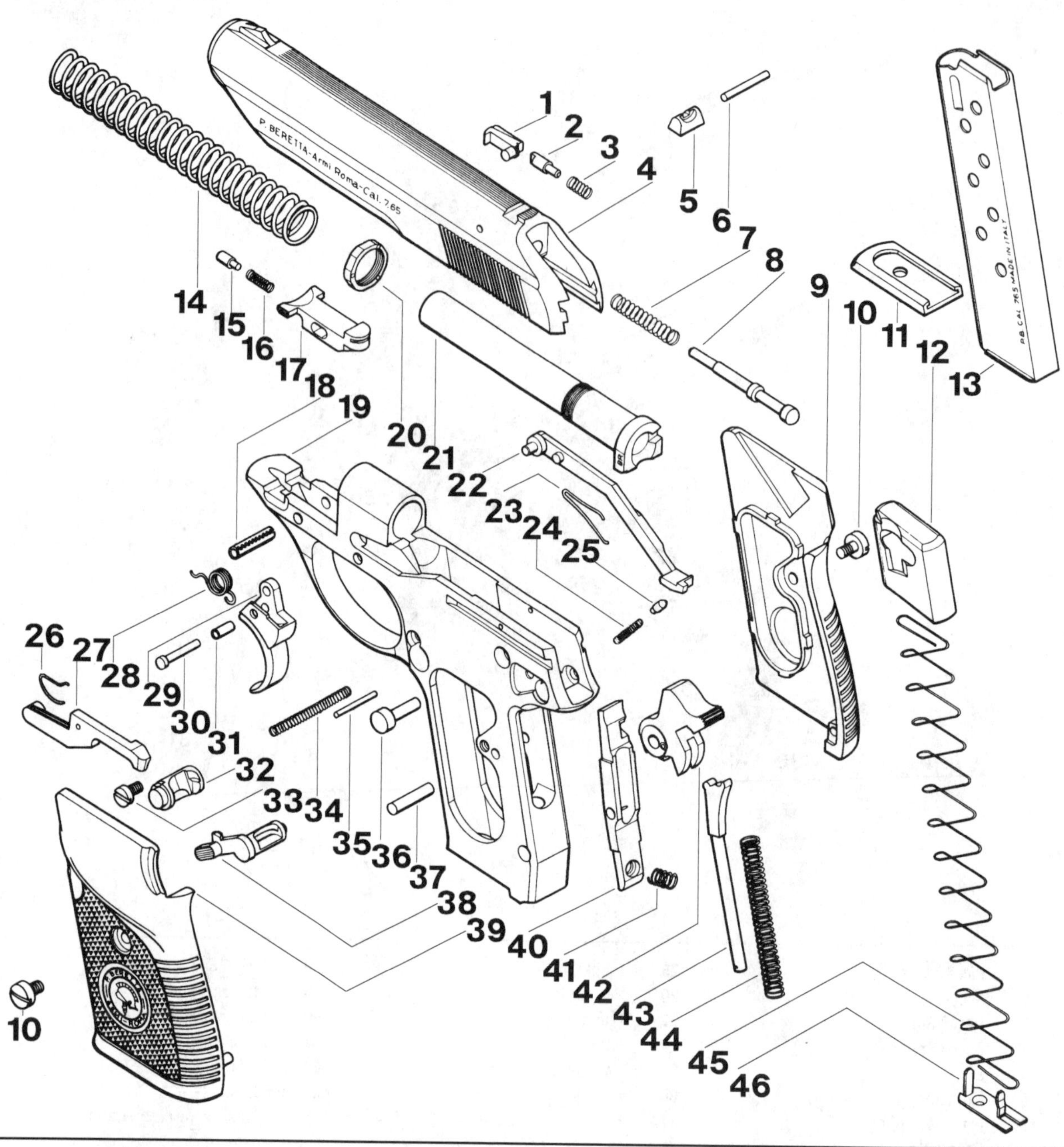

1	Extractor
2	Extractor Plunger
3	Extractor Spring
4	Slide
5	Rear Sight
6	Firing Pin Retainer
7	Firing Pin Spring
8	Firing Pin
9	Right Grip
10	Grip Screw
11	Magazine Floorplate
12	Magazine Follower
13	Magazine Body
14	Recoil Spring
15	Slide Catch Plunger
16	Slide Catch Spring
17	Slide Catch
18	Slide Catch Pin
19	Frame
20	Barrel Nut
21	Barrel
22	Trigger Bar
23	Trigger Bar Spring
24	Safety Spring
25	Safety Plunger
26	Ejector Spring
27	Ejector/Empty Magazine Indicator
28	Trigger Spring
29	Trigger
30	Trigger Pin
31	Trigger Pin Sleeve
32	Magazine Catch
33	Magazine Catch Screw
34	Magazine Catch Spring
35	Hammer Stop Pin
36	Hammer Pin
37	Sear Pin
38	Safety
39	Left Grip
40	Sear
41	Sear Spring
42	Hammer
43	Hammer Strut
44	Hammer Spring
45	Magazine Spring
46	Magazine Bottom Plate

Model 92 Auto

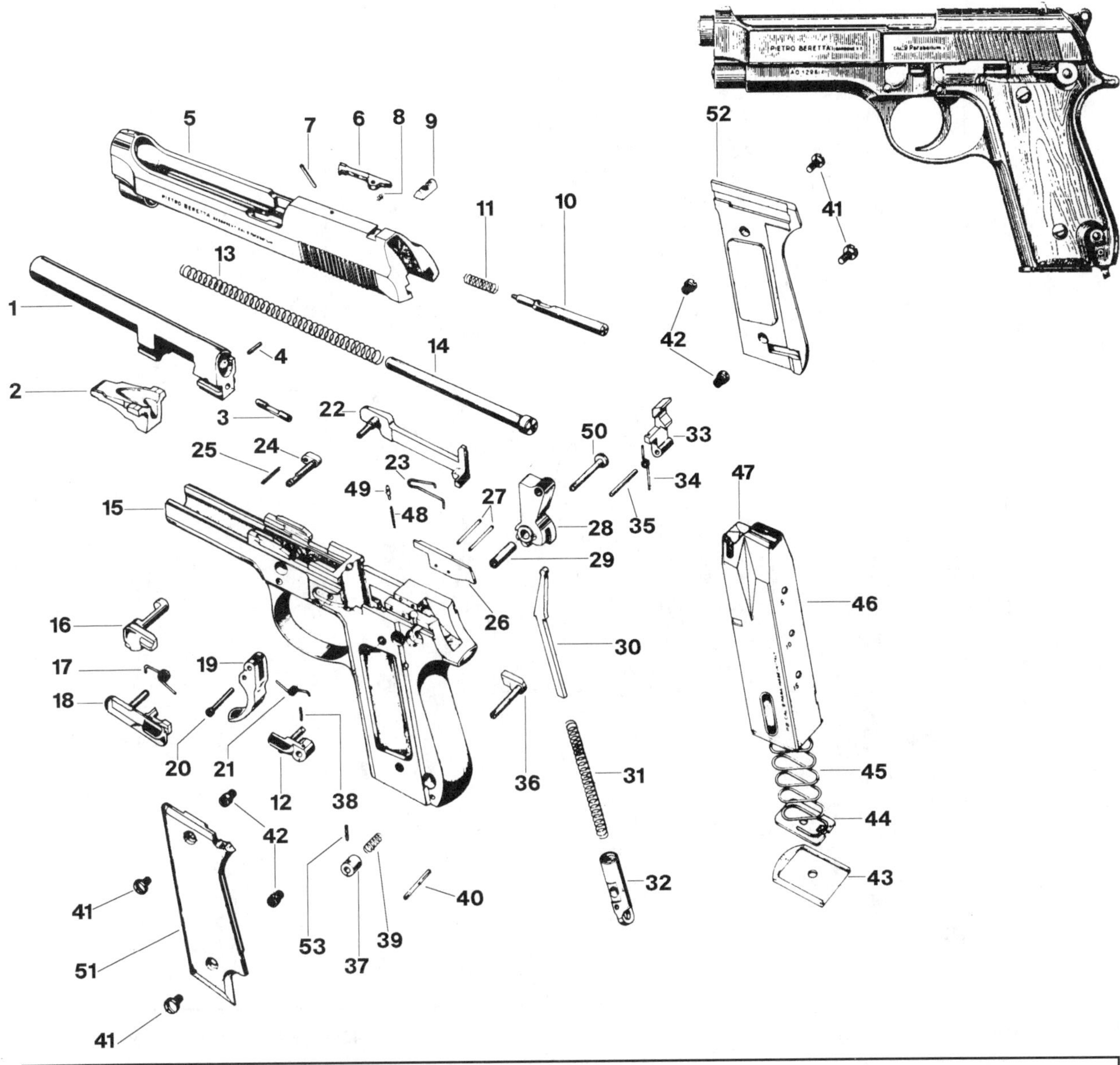

1	Barrel	20	Trigger Pin	38	Safety Pin
2	Locking Block	21	Trigger Spring	39	Magazine Release Button Spring
3	Locking Block Plunger	22	Trigger Bar	40	Hammer Spring Cap Pin
4	Spring Pin/Locking Block	23	Trigger Bar Spring	41	Grip Screws
5	Slide	24	Disassembly Latch Release Button	42	Grip Bush
6	Extractor	25	Disassembly Latch Release Button Spring	43	Magazine Floorplate
7	Extractor Pin	26	Ejector	44	Magazine Spring Plate
8	Extractor Spring	27	Ejector Pins	45	Magazine Spring
9	Rear Sight	28	Hammer	46	Magazine Body
10	Firing Pin	29	Hammer Pin	47	Magazine Follower
11	Firing Pin Spring	30	Hammer Spring Guide	48	Safety Plunger Spring
12	Safety	31	Hammer Spring	49	Safety Plunger
13	Recoil Spring	32	Hammer Spring Cap	50	Safety Pin
14	Recoil Spring Guide	33	Sear	51	Left Grip Panel
15	Frame	34	Sear Spring	52	Right Grip Panel
16	Disassembly Latch	35	Sear Pin	53	Magazine Release Button Spring Pin
17	Slide Catch Spring	36	Magazine Release Button		
18	Slide Catch	37	Magazine Release Button Bushing		
19	Trigger				

Model 92F and 92F Compact Auto

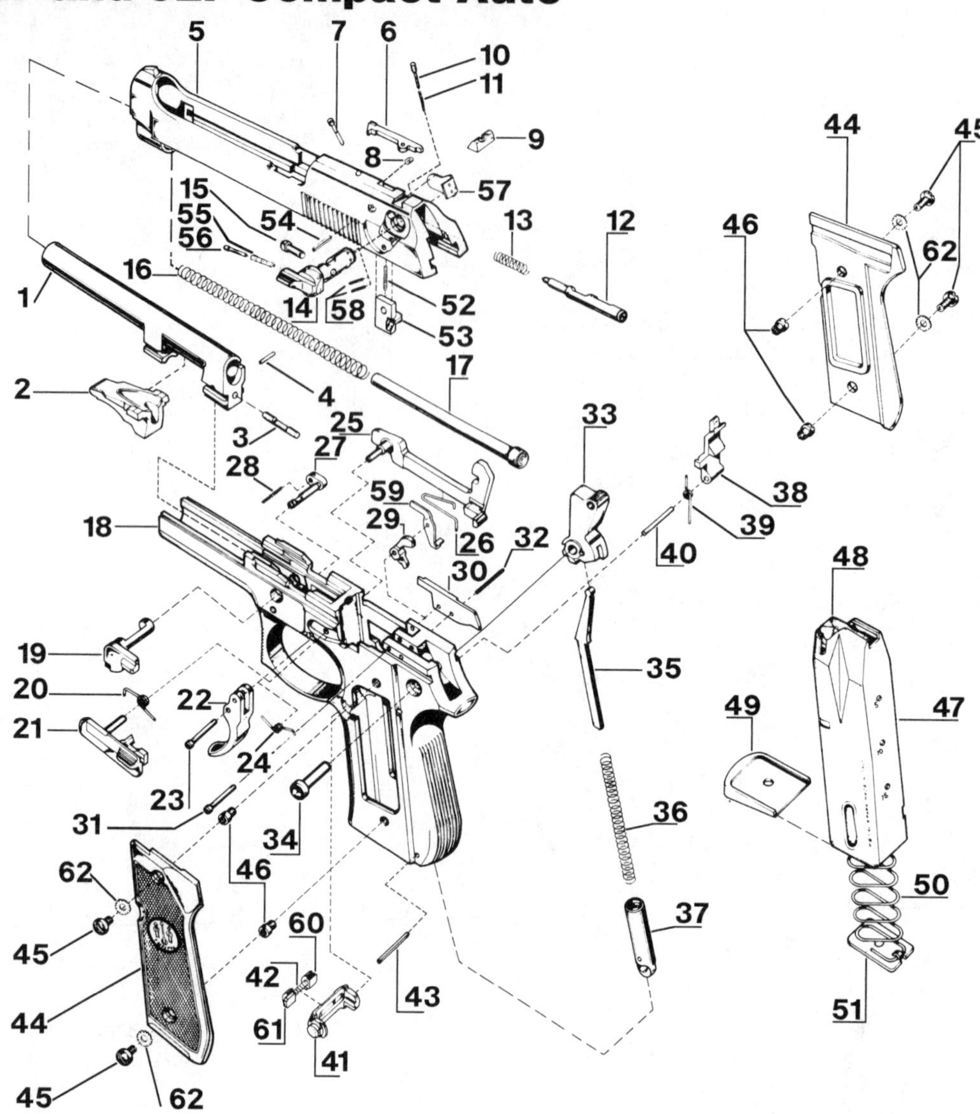

No.	Part	No.	Part	No.	Part
1	Barrel (Factory fitting required)	22	Trigger	42	Magazine Release Button Spring
2	Locking Block	23	Trigger Pin	43	Hammer Spring Cap Spring Pin
3	Locking Block Plunger	24	Trigger Spring	44	Grips
4	Locking Block Plunger—Retaining Pin	25	Trigger Bar	45	Grip Screws
5	Slide	26	Trigger Bar Spring	46	Grip Bush
6	Extractor	27	Disassembling Latch Release Button	47	Magazine Box
7	Extractor Pin	28	Disassembling Latch Release Button Spring	48	Magazine Follower
8	Extractor Spring	29	Hammer Release Lever	49	Magazine Bottom
9	Rear Sight	30	Ejector	50	Magazine Spring
10	Trigger Bar Release Plunger	31	Hammer Release Lever Pin	51	Magazine Lockplate
11	Trigger Bar Release Plunger Spring	32	Ejector Spring Pin	52	Firing Pin Catch Spring
12	Firing Pin	33	Hammer	53	Firing Pin Catch
13	Firing Pin Spring	34	Hammer Pin	54	Firing Pin Catch Retaining Spring Pin
14	Safety	35	Hammer Spring Guide	55	Safety Plunger Spring
15	Firing Pin Plunger	36	Hammer Spring	56	Safety Plunger
16	Recoil Spring	37	Hammer Spring Cap	57	Right Safety-Lever
17	Recoil Spring Guide	38	Sear	58	Right Safety-Lever Spring Pin
18	Frame	39	Sear Spring	59	Firing Pin Catch Lever
19	Disassembling Latch	40	Sear Pin	60	Magazine Catch Spring Bush (Short)
20	Slide Catch Spring	41	Magazine Release Button	61	Magazine Catch Spring (Long)
21	Slide Catch			62	Spring Washers

Model 92S Auto

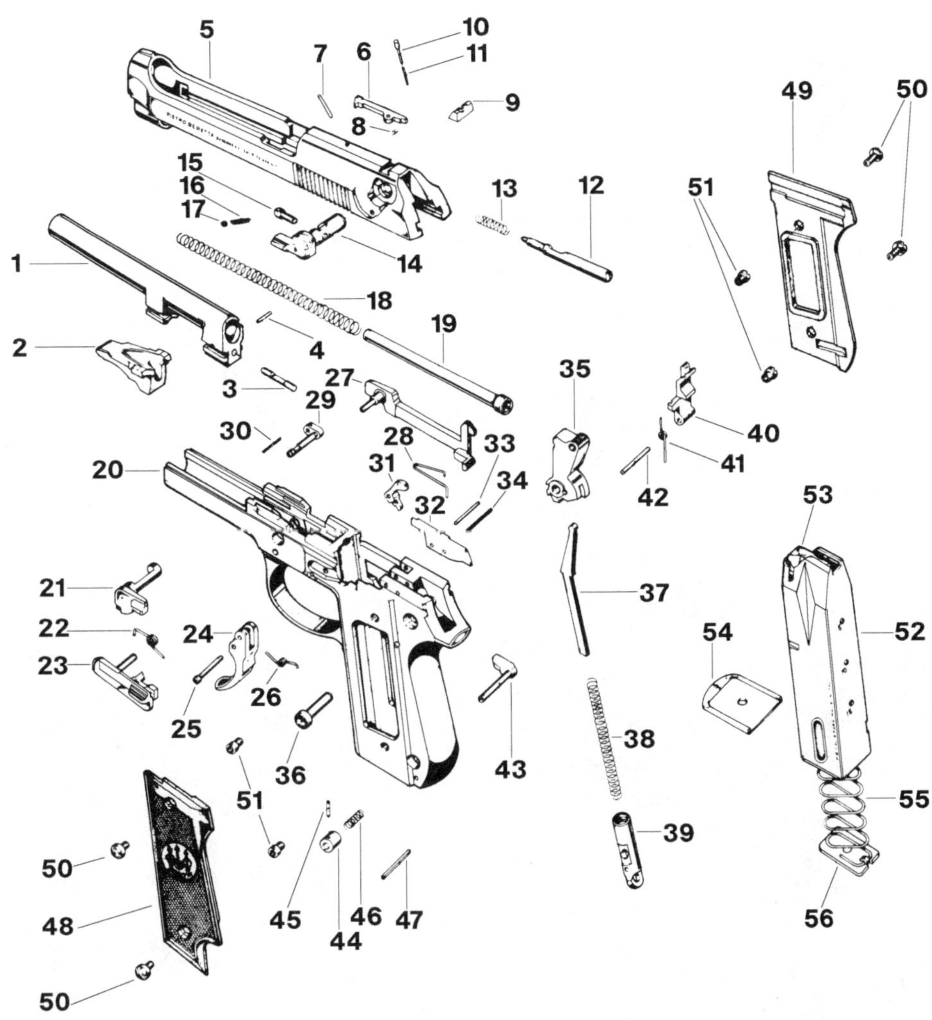

1	Barrel	**26**	Trigger Spring	**50**	Grip Screws
2	Locking Block	**27**	Trigger Bar	**51**	Grip Screw Bushings
3	Locking Block Plunger	**28**	Trigger Bar Spring	**52**	Magazine Body
4	Locking Block Spring Pin	**29**	Disassembly Latch Release Button	**53**	Magazine Follower
5	Slide	**30**	Disassembly Latch Release Button Spring	**54**	Magazine Floorplate
6	Extractor	**31**	Hammer Release Lever	**55**	Magazine Spring
7	Extractor Pin	**32**	Ejector	**56**	Magazine Spring Plate
8	Extractor Spring	**33**	Hammer Release Lever Pin	**Parts Not Shown**	
9	Rear Sight	**34**	Ejector Pin		Firing Pin Catch Spring
10	Trigger Bar Release Plunger	**35**	Hammer		Firing Pin Catch
11	Release Plunger Spring	**36**	Hammer Pin		Spring Pin
12	Firing Pin	**37**	Hammer Spring Guide		Safety Plunger Spring
13	Firing Pin Spring	**38**	Hammer Spring		Safety Plunger
14	Safety	**39**	Hammer Spring Cap		Right Safety-Lever
15	Firing Pin Plunger	**40**	Sear		Safety Lever Pin
16	Safety Ball Spring	**41**	Sear Spring		Firing Pin Catch Lever
17	Safety Ball	**42**	Sear Pin		Magazine Release Button
18	Recoil Spring	**43**	Magazine Release Button		Spring Bush (Short)
19	Recoil Spring Guide	**44**	Magazine Release Button Bushing		Magazine Release Button
20	Frame	**45**	Safety Pin		Spring Bush (Long)
21	Disassembling Latch	**46**	Magazine Release Button Spring		Magazine Release Button
22	Slide Catch Spring	**47**	Hammer Spring Cap Pin		Spring Bush Plunger
23	Slide Catch	**48**	Left Grip Panel		
24	Trigger	**49**	Right Grip Panel		
25	Trigger Pin				

Model 92SB, 92SB Compact and 98 Auto

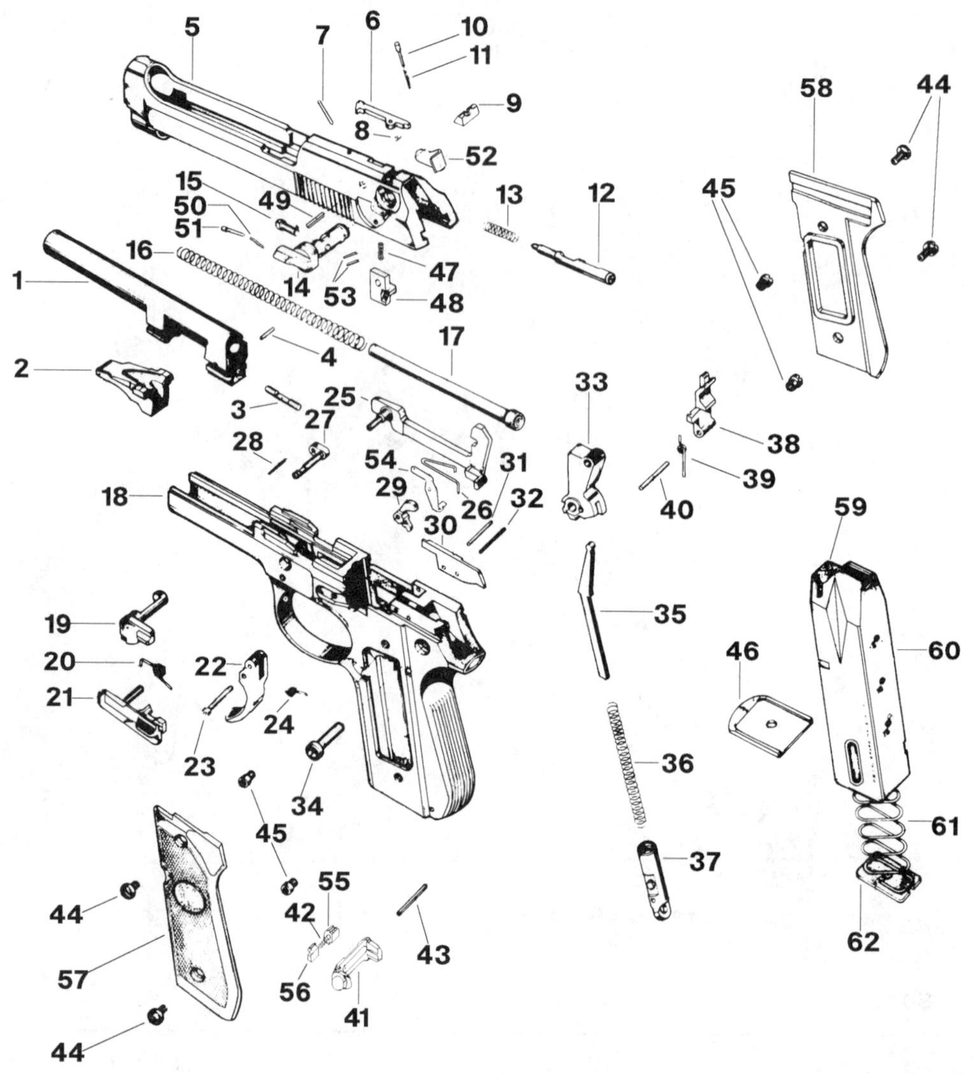

1	Barrel	23	Trigger Pin	43	Hammer Spring Cap Pin
2	Locking Block	24	Trigger Spring	44	Grip Screws
3	Locking Block Plunger	25	Trigger Bar	45	Grip Screw Bushings
4	Locking Block Spring Pin	26	Trigger Bar Spring	46	Magazine Floorplate
5	Slide	27	Disassembly Latch Release Button	47	Firing Pin Catch Spring
6	Extractor	28	Disassembly Latch Release Button Spring	48	Firing Pin Catch
7	Extractor Pin	29	Hammer Release Lever	49	Spring Pin
8	Extractor Spring	30	Ejector	50	Safety Plunger Spring
9	Rear Sight	31	Hammer Release Lever Pin	51	Safety Plunger
10	Trigger Bar Release Plunger	32	Ejector Pin	52	Right Safety-Lever
11	Trigger Bar Release Plunger Spring	33	Hammer	53	Safety-Lever Pins
12	Firing Pin	34	Hamer Pin	54	Firing Pin Catch lever
13	Firing Pin Spring	35	Hammer Spring Guide	55	Magazine Release Button Spring Bush (Short)
14	Safety	36	Hammer Spring	56	Magazine Release Button Spring Bush (Long)
15	Firing Pin plunger	37	Hammer Spring Cap	57	Left Grip Panel
16	Recoil Spring	38	Sear	58	Right Grip Panel
17	Recoil Spring Guide	39	Sear Spring	59	Magazine Follower
18	Frame	40	Sear Pin	60	Magazine Body
19	Disassembly Latch	41	Magazine Release Button	61	Magazine Spring
20	Slide Catch Spring	42	Magazine Release Button Spring	62	Magazine Spring Plate
21	Slide Catch				
22	Trigger				

Model 950 B and 950 BS Auto

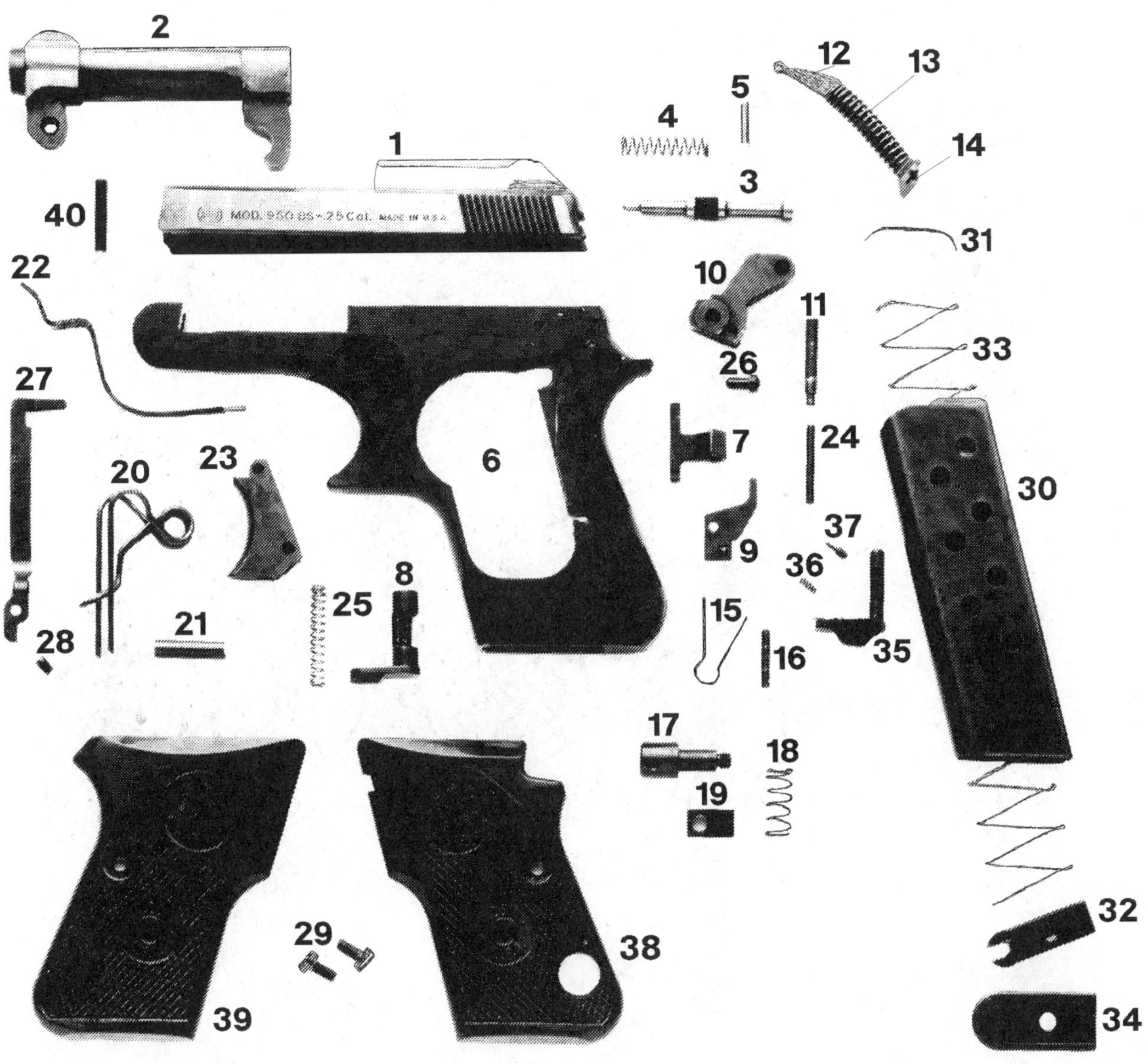

1	Slide	**16**	Sear Pin	**31**	Follower
2	Barrel	**17**	Magazine Release Button	**32**	Magazine Spring Plate
3	Firing Pin	**18**	Magazine Catch Spring	**33**	Magazine Spring
4	Firing Pin Spring	**19**	Magazine Catch	**34**	Magazine Floorplate
5	Firing Pin Retaining Pin	**20**	Recoil Spring	**35**	Safety
6	Frame	**21**	Recoil Spring Pin	**36**	Safety Spring
7	Ejector	**22**	Trigger Guard	**37**	Safety Spring Plunger
8	Barrel Lever	**23**	Trigger	**38**	Left Grip Panel
9	Ejector Pin	**24**	Trigger Pin	**39**	Right Grip Panel
10	Hammer	**25**	Trigger Bar Spring	**40**	Barrel Mounting Pin
11	Hammer/Safety Stop Pin (950 BS)	**26**	Trigger Bar Spring Plunger	**Parts Not Shown**	
12	Hammer Strut	**27**	Trigger Bar		Sear
13	Hammer Spring	**28**	Trigger Bar Pin		Magazine Follower Retaining Screw
14	Hammer Spring Retainer	**29**	Grip Screws		Barrel Lever Stop Screw
15	Sear Spring	**30**	Magazine Body		

Model 1908 Auto

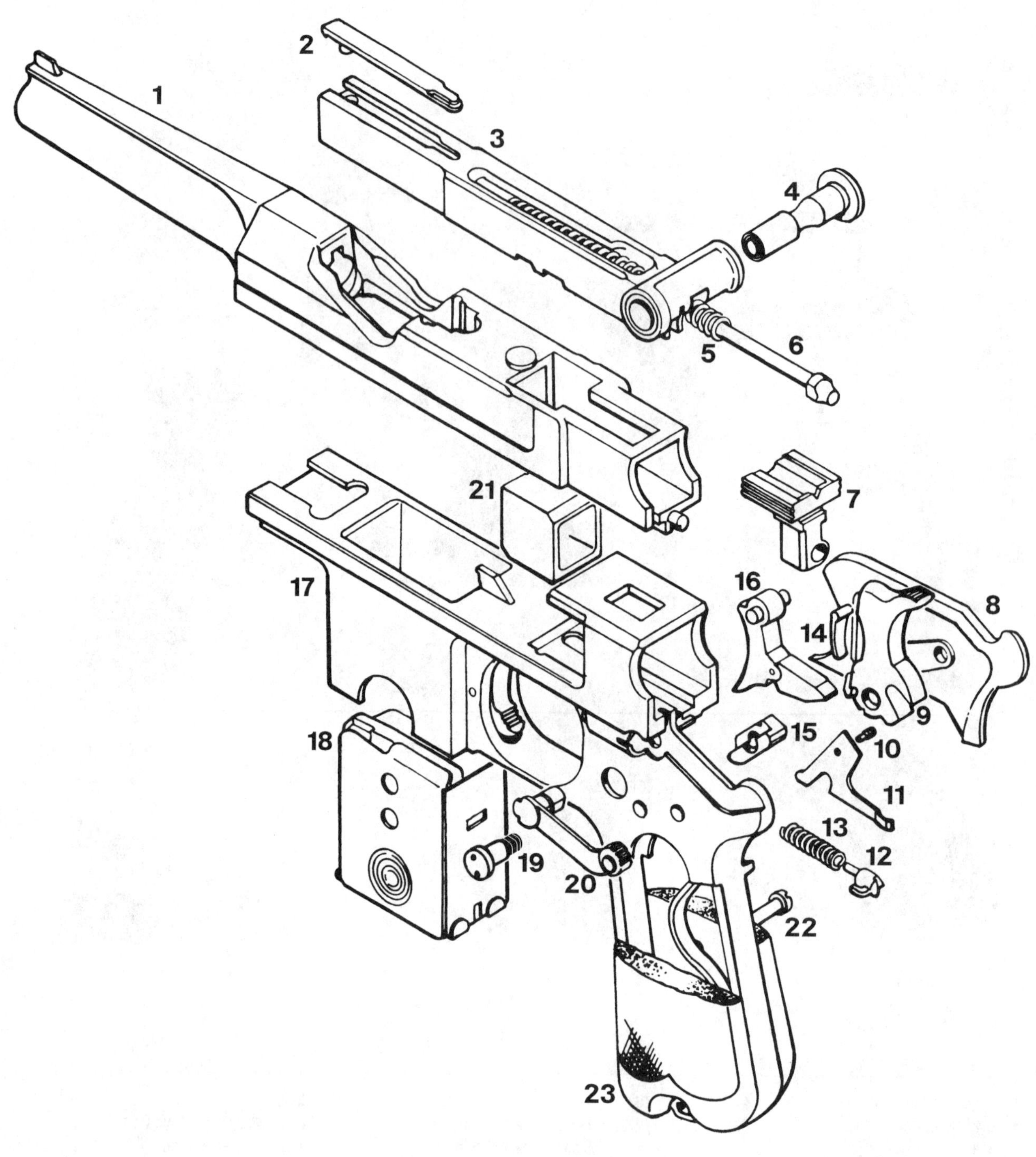

1	Barrel and Extension	9	Hammer	17	Frame
2	Extractor	10	Disconnector Screw	18	Magazine Assembly
3	Bolt	11	Disconnector	19	Sideplate Retainer
4	Bolt Knob Insert	12	Safety Plunger	20	Safety-Lever
5	Firing Pin Spring	13	Safety Spring	21	Locking Block
6	Firing Pin	14	Sear Spring	22	Grip Screw
7	Rear Sight/Bolt Retainer	15	Sear	23	Grip Panel
8	Sideplate	16	Trigger Assembly		

Special Auto

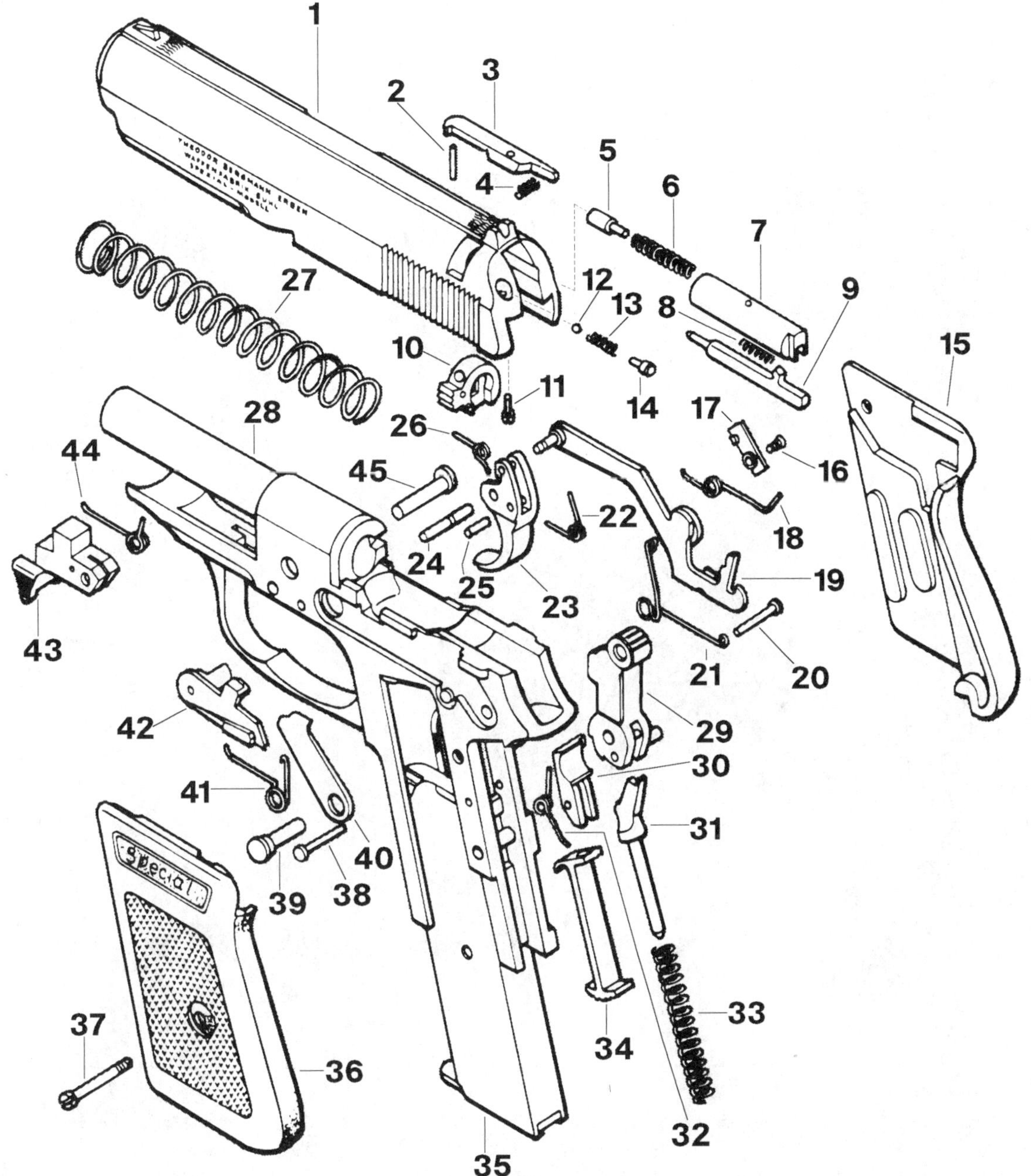

1	Slide	16	Retainer Plate Screw	31	Hammer Strut
2	Extractor Pin	17	Spring Retainer Plate	32	Sear Spring
3	Extractor	18	Trigger Bar Guide Spring	33	Hammer Spring
4	Extractor Spring	19	Trigger Bar	34	Magazine Catch
5	Housing Plunger	20	Spring Retainer Pin	35	Magazine
6	Plunger Spring	21	Trigger Bar Spring	36	Left Grip
7	Firing Pin Housing	22	Pin Retainer Spring	37	Grip Screw
8	Firing Pin Spring	23	Trigger	38	Sear Stop Pin
9	Firing Pin	24	Trigger Pin	39	Hammer Pin
10	Safety Catch	25	Retainer Spring Pin	40	Ejector
11	Detent Retainer Screw	26	Trigger Spring	41	Hold-Open Spring
12	Detent Ball	27	Recoil Spring	42	Hold-Open Catch
13	Detent Spring	28	Frame and Barrel Assembly	43	Takedown Latch
14	Spring Guide	29	Hammer	44	Takedown Latch Spring
15	Right Grip	30	Sear	45	Takedown Latch Pin

BERNARDELLI

Model 60 Auto

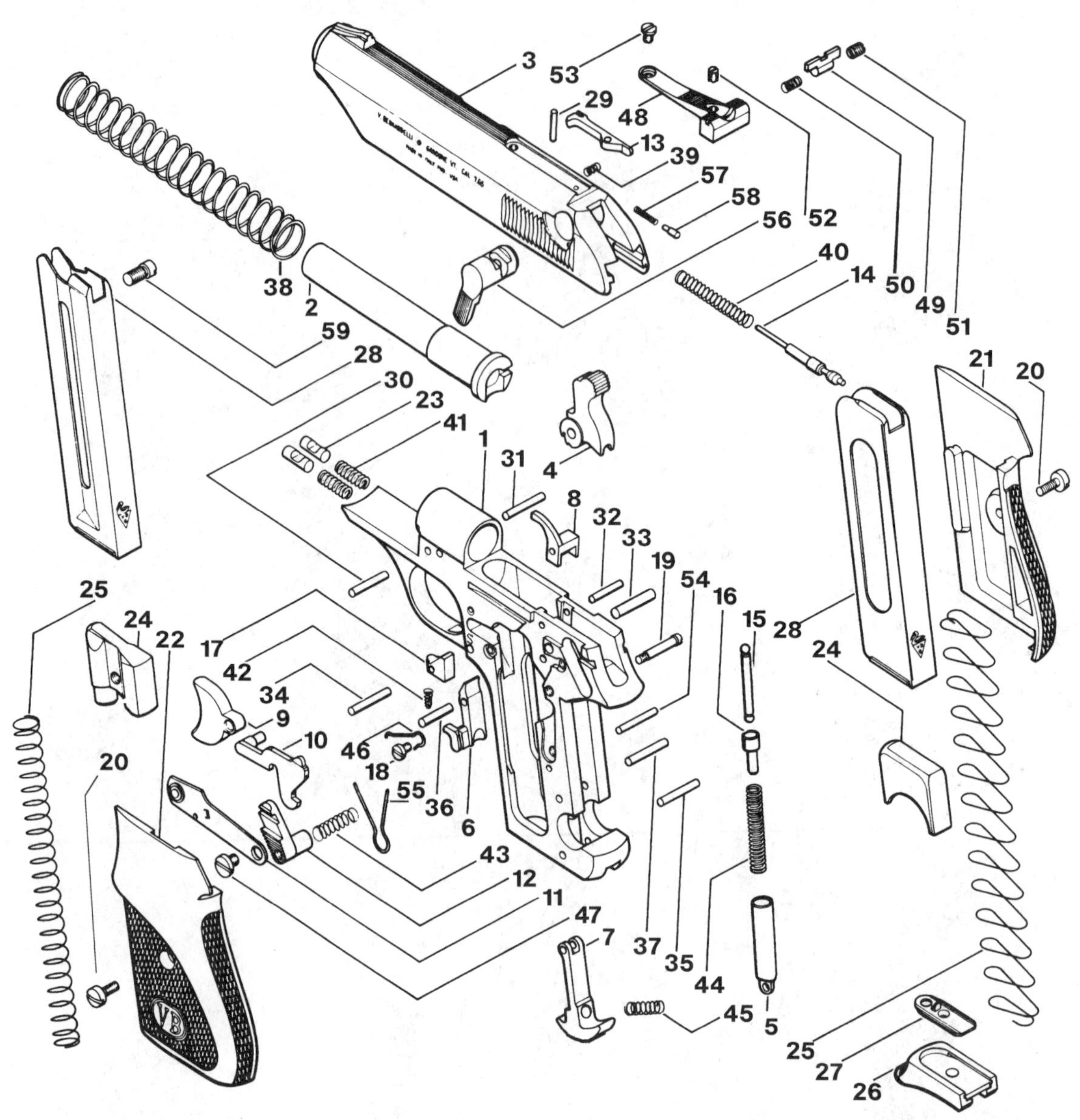

1	Receiver	**21**	Right Grip	**41**	Buffer Spring
2	Barrel	**22**	Left Grip	**42**	Magazine Safety Spring
3	Slide	**23**	Slide Buffer	**43**	Takedown Button Spring
4	Hammer	**24**	Magazine Platform	**44**	Mainspring
5	Mainspring Holder	**25**	Magazine Spring	**45**	Magazine Catch Spring
6	Sear	**26**	Finger Extension	**46**	Trigger Bar Spring
7	Magazine Catch	**27**	Magazine Bottom Plate	**47**	Safety Screw
8	Ejector	**28**	Magazine Shell	**48**	Rear Sight Leaf
9	Trigger	**29**	Extractor Pin	**49**	Sight Blade
10	Trigger Bar	**30**	Buffer Pin	**50**	Windage Spring
11	Safety	**31**	Barrel Pin	**51**	Windage Screw
12	Takedown Button	**32**	Ejector Pin	**52**	Elevation Screw
13	Extractor-Indicator Pin	**33**	Hammer Pin	**53**	Leaf Sight Screw
14	Firing Pin	**34**	Magazine Safety Pin	**54**	Mainspring Holder Stop Pin
15	Mainspring Strut	**35**	Magazine Catch Pin	**55**	Sear Spring
16	Mainspring Guide	**36**	Sear Pin	**56**	Safety Lock
17	Magazine Safety	**37**	Mainspring Holder and Grip Pin	**57**	Safety Lock Spring
18	Trigger Bar Spring Screw	**38**	Recoil Spring	**58**	Safety Lock Spring Detent
19	Takedown Button Screw	**39**	Extractor Spring	**59**	Magazine Follower Stud
20	Grip Screw	**40**	Firing Pin Spring		

Model 80 Auto

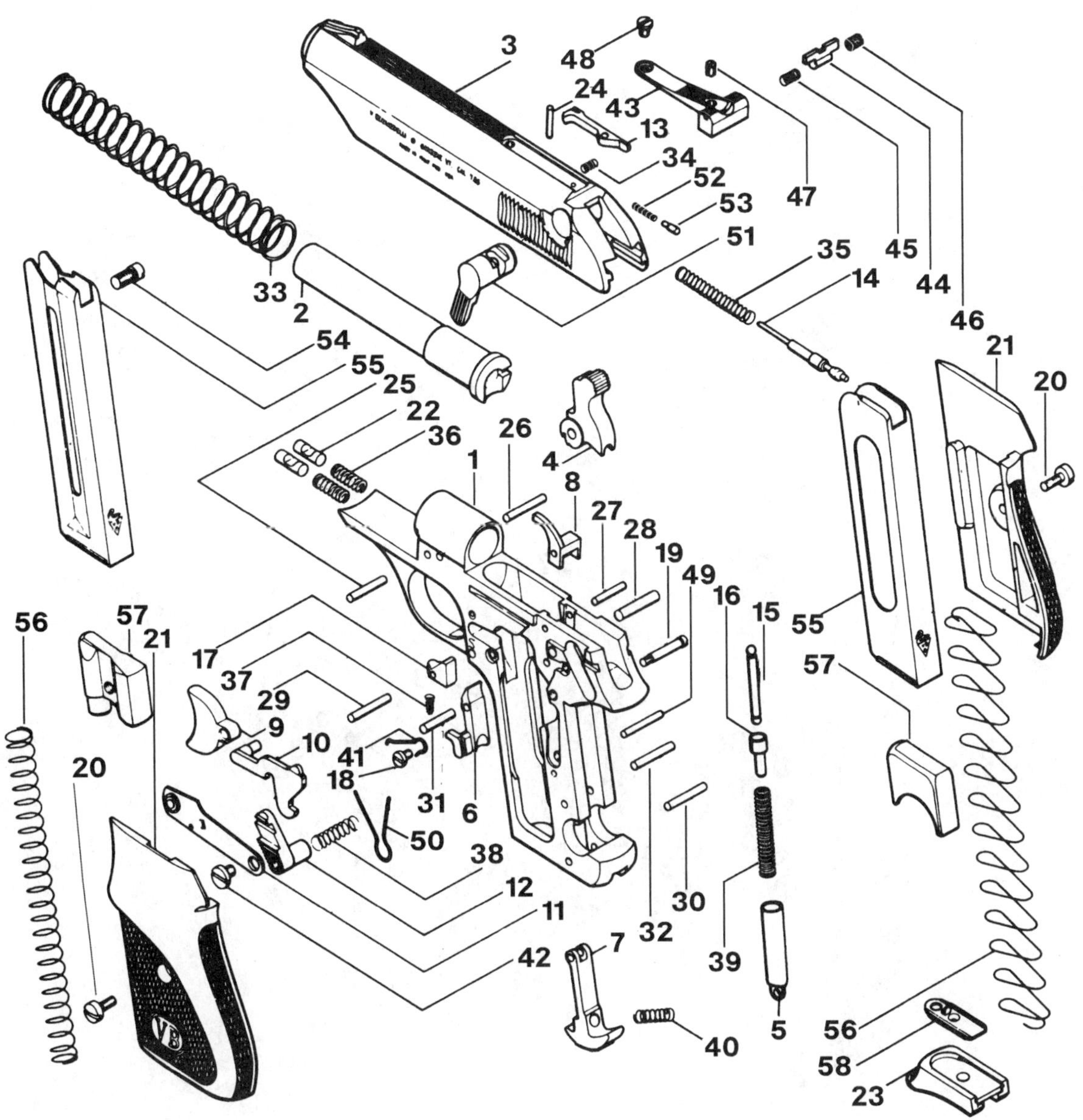

1	Frame	21	Grips	41	Magazine Catch Spring
2	Barrel	22	Slide Buffers	42	Trigger Bar Spring
3	Slide	23	Magazine Finger Rest	43	Safety-Lever Screw
4	Hammer	24	Extractor Pin	44	Front Sight Ramp
5	Mainspring Guide	25	Firing Pin Stop Pin	45	Front Sight Spring
6	Sear	26	Buffer Pin	46	Front Sight Screw Ring
7	Magazine Catch	27	Barrel Pin	47	Rear Sight Base
8	Ejector	28	Ejector Pin	48	Rear Sight Leaf
9	Trigger	29	Hammer Pin	49	Windage Spring
10	Trigger Bar	30	Magazine Safety Pin	50	Windage Screw
11	Safety-Lever	31	Magazine Catch Stop Pin	51	Elevation Screw
12	Takedown Button	32	Sear Pin	52	Rear Sight Screw
13	Extractor	33	Magazine Catch Pin	53	Mainspring Guide Stop Pin
14	Firing Pin	34	Recoil Spring	54	Sear Spring
15	Mainspring Strut	35	Extractor Spring	55	Magazine Follower
16	Mainspring Plunger	36	Firing Spring	56	Magazine Spring
17	Magazine Safety	37	Buffer Springs	57	Magazine Body
18	Trigger Bar Spring Screw	38	Magazine Safety Spring	58	Magazine Follower Stud
19	Takedown Button Screw	39	Takedown Button Spring	59	Magazine Spring Plate
20	Grip Screws	40	Mainspring		

Model 90 Auto

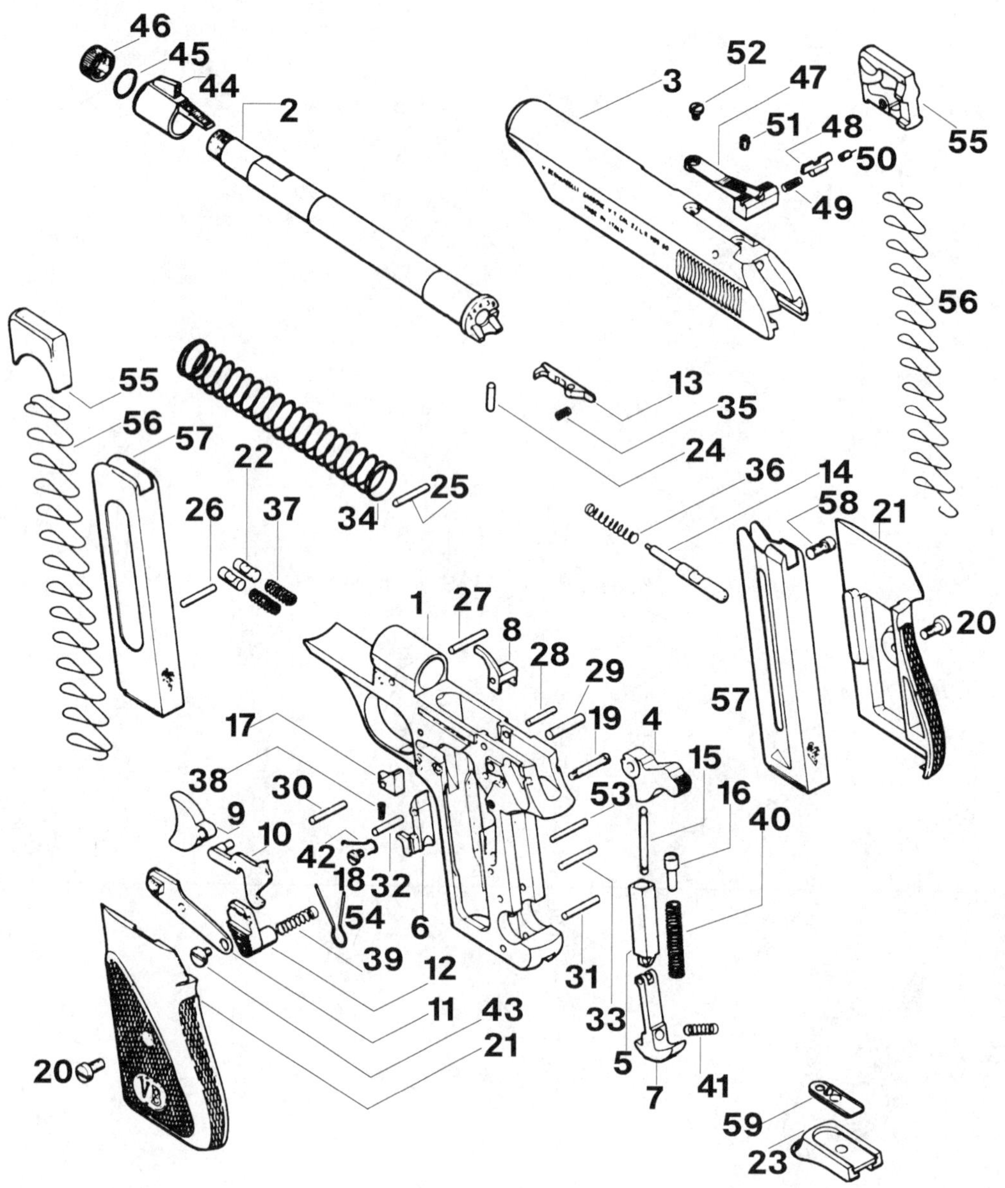

1	Frame	**21**	Grips	**41**	Magazine Catch Spring
2	Barrel	**22**	Slide Buffers	**42**	Trigger Bar Spring
3	Slide	**23**	Magazine Finger Rest	**43**	Safety-Lever Screw
4	Hammer	**24**	Extractor Pin	**44**	Front Sight Ramp
5	Mainspring Guide	**25**	Firing Pin Stop Pin	**45**	Front Sight Spring
6	Sear	**26**	Buffer Pin	**46**	Front Sight Screw Ring
7	Magazine Catch	**27**	Barrel Pin	**47**	Rear Sight Base
8	Ejector	**28**	Ejector Pin	**48**	Rear Sight Leaf
9	Trigger	**29**	Hammer Pin	**49**	Windage Spring
10	Trigger Bar	**30**	Magazine Safety Pin	**50**	Windage Screw
11	Safety-Lever	**31**	Magazine Catch Stop Pin	**51**	Elevation Screw
12	Takedown Button	**32**	Sear Pin	**52**	Rear Sight Screw
13	Extractor	**33**	Magazine Catch Pin	**53**	Mainspring Guide Stop Pin
14	Firing Pin	**34**	Recoil Spring	**54**	Sear Spring
15	Mainspring Strut	**35**	Extractor Spring	**55**	Magazine Follower
16	Mainspring Plunger	**36**	Firing Spring	**56**	Magazine Spring
17	Magazine Safety	**37**	Buffer Springs	**57**	Magazine Body
18	Trigger Bar Spring Screw	**38**	Magazine Safety Spring	**58**	Magazine Follower Stud
19	Takedown Button Screw	**39**	Takedown Button Spring	**59**	Magazine Spring Plate
20	Grip Screws	**40**	Mainspring		

Model PO-18 Auto

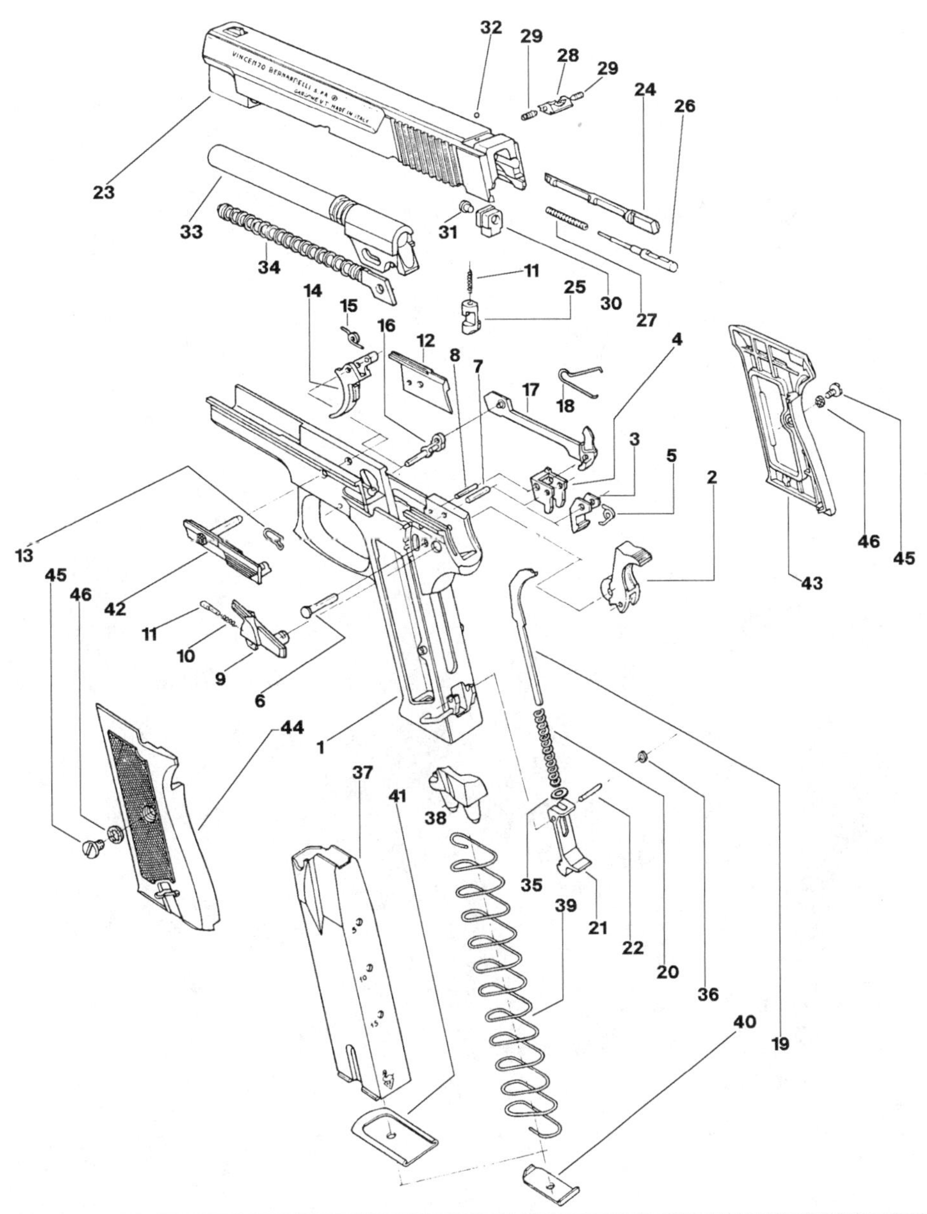

1	Frame	**19**	Hammer Spring Strut	**35**	Hammer Spring Washer
2	Hammer	**20**	Hammer Spring	**36**	Hammer Spring Base Pin Spacer
3	Sear	**21**	Hammer Spring Base/ Magazine Catch	**37**	Magazine Body
4	Sear Lever	**22**	Hammer Spring Base/ Magazine Catch Pin	**38**	Magazine Follower
5	Sear Spring	**23**	Slide	**39**	Magazine Spring
6	Hammer Pin	**24**	Extractor	**40**	Magazine Spring Plate
7	Sear Pin	**25**	Firing Pin Block	**41**	Magazine Floorplate
8	Sear Spring Detent Pin	**26**	Firing Pin	**42**	Slide Latch
9	Safety	**27**	Firing Pin Spring	**43**	Right Grip Panel
10	Safety Catch Plunger Spring	**28**	Rear Sight Blade	**44**	Left Grip Panel
11	Safety Catch Plunger	**29**	Rear Sight Windage Screws	**45**	Grip Screws
12	Ejector	**30**	Firing Pin Retainer	**46**	Grip Screw Bushings
13	Slide Stop Spring	**31**	Firing Pin Piston		
14	Trigger	**32**	Rear Sight Positioning Ball		
15	Trigger Return Spring	**33**	Barrel		
16	Trigger Pivot	**34**	Recoil Spring and Guide		
17	Trigger Bar				
18	Trigger Bar Spring				

NOTE: Gun shown is very early production. Later Production guns have a one-piece firing pin retained by a cross pin and other differences.

Model VB60 Auto

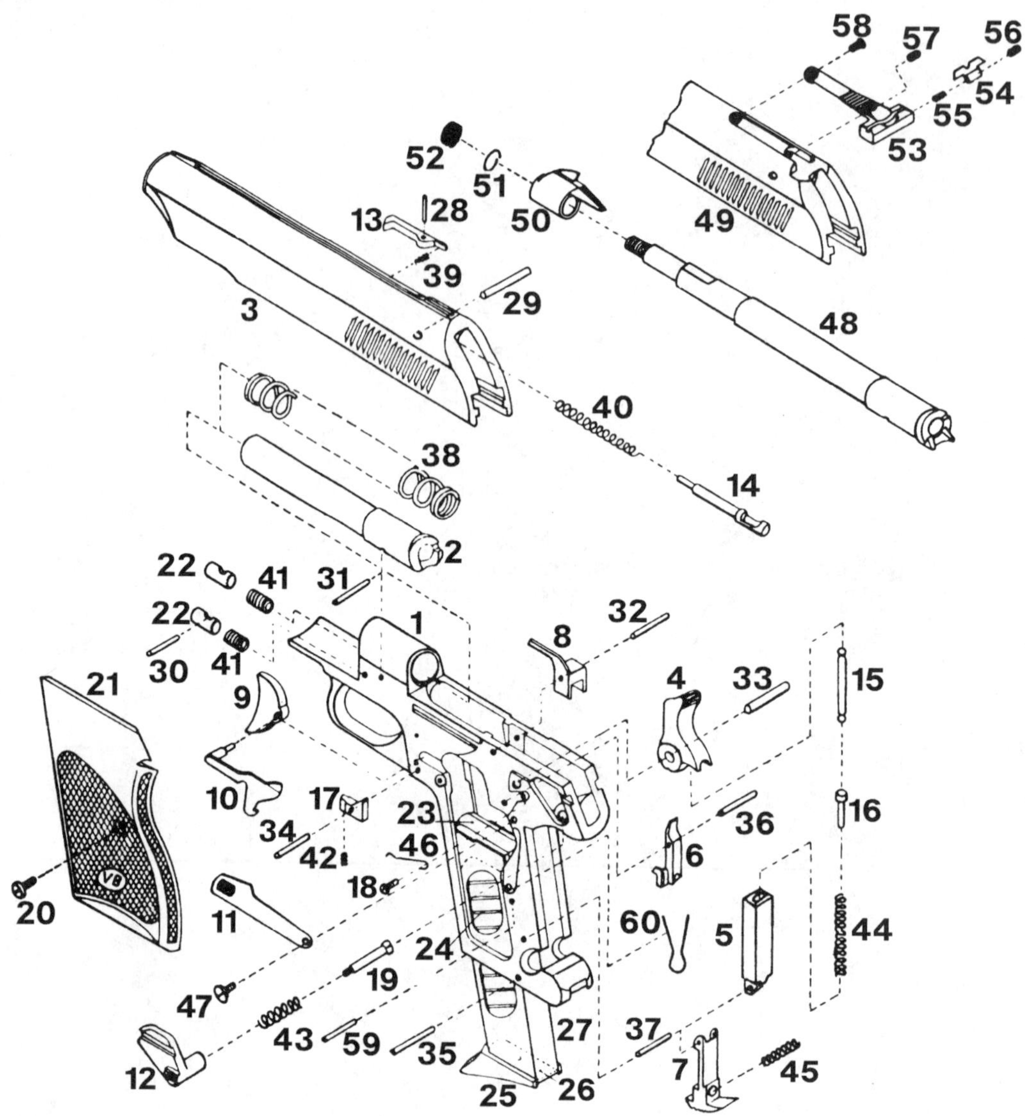

1	Receiver	22	Slide Buffer	43	Takedown Button Spring
2	Barrel	23	Magazine Platform	44	Mainspring
3	Slide	24	Magazine Spring	45	Magazine Catch Spring
4	Hammer	25	Finger Extension	46	Trigger Bar Spring
5	Mainspring Holder	26	Magazine Bottom Plate	47	Thumb Safety Screw
6	Sear	27	Magazine Shell	48	Barrel (Prolonged)
7	Magazine Catch	28	Extractor Pin	49	Slide for Rear Sight
8	Ejector	29	Firing Pin Pin	50	Front Sight Ramp
9	Trigger	30	Buffer Pin	51	Front Sight Spring
10	Trigger Bar	31	Barrel Pin	52	Front Sight Screwed Ring
11	Thumb Safety	32	Ejector Pin	53	Rear Sight Leaf
12	Takedown Button	33	Hammer Pin	54	Sight Blade
13	Extractor	34	Magazine Safety Pin	55	Windage Spring
14	Firing Pin	35	Magazine Catch Pin	56	Windage Screw
15	Mainspring Strut	36	Sear Pin	57	Elevation Screw
16	Mainspring Guide	37	Mainspring Holder Pin	58	Leaf Sight Screw
17	Magazine Safety	38	Recoil Spring	59	Mainspring Holder Pin
18	Trigger Bar Spring Screw	39	Extractor Spring	60	Sear Spring
19	Takedown Button Screw	40	Firing Pin Spring	**Parts Not Shown**	
20	Grip Screw	41	Buffer Spring		Magazine Follower Screw
21	Grips	42	Magazine Safety Spring		Magazine Assembly

Model 644 Auto

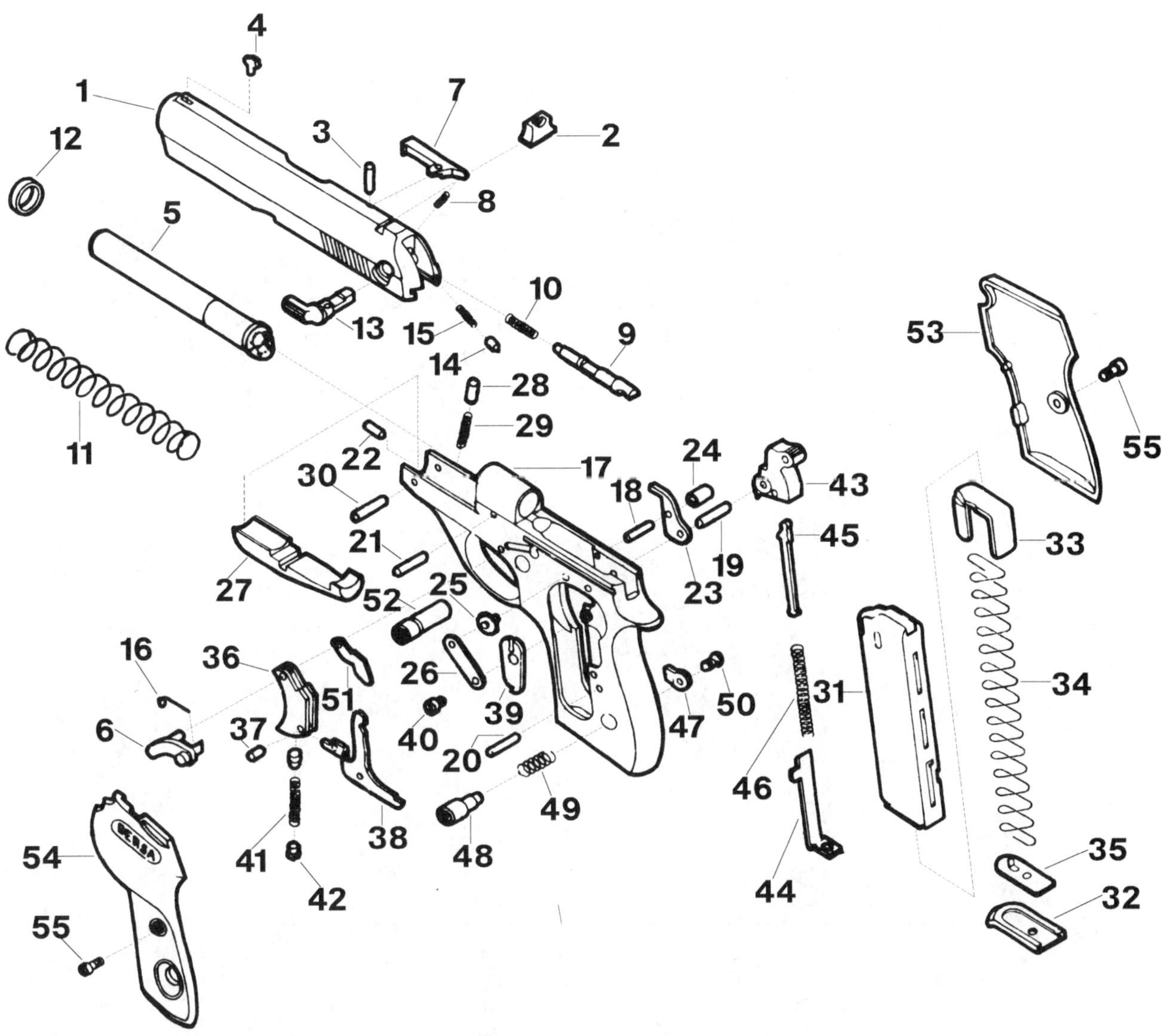

1	Slide	**20**	Sear Bar Pin	**39**	Sear Activator
2	Rear Sight	**21**	Barrel Retainer Pin	**40**	Sear Activator Screw
3	Extractor Pin	**22**	Disassembly Latch Limit Pin	**41**	Trigger Spring
4	Front Sight	**23**	Ejector	**42**	Trigger Spring Guide
5	Barrel	**24**	Ejector Bushing	**43**	Hammer
6	Slide Stop	**25**	Magazine Safety	**44**	Sear Bar
7	Extractor	**26**	Magazine Safety Spring	**45**	Hammer Spring Guide
8	Extractor Spring	**27**	Takedown Latch	**46**	Hammer Spring
9	Firing Pin	**28**	Takedown Latch Spring Plug	**47**	Magazine Latch
10	Firing Pin Spring	**29**	Takedown Latch Spring	**48**	Magazine Release Button
11	Recoil Spring	**30**	Takedown Latch Pin	**49**	Magazine Latch Spring
12	Barrel Bushing	**31**	Magazine Body	**50**	Magazine Latch Screw
13	Firing Pin Safety	**32**	Magazine Floorplate	**51**	Trigger Safety Bar
14	Firing Pin Safety Stop	**33**	Magazine Follower	**52**	Trigger Safety Button
15	Firing Pin Safety Spring	**34**	Magazine Spring	**53**	Right Grip Panel
16	Slide Stop Spring	**35**	Magazine Floorplate Latch	**54**	Left Grip Panel
17	Frame	**36**	Trigger	**55**	Grip Screws
18	Ejector Pin	**37**	Disconnector Pin		
19	Hammer Pin	**38**	Disconnector		

Model 83-73 Auto

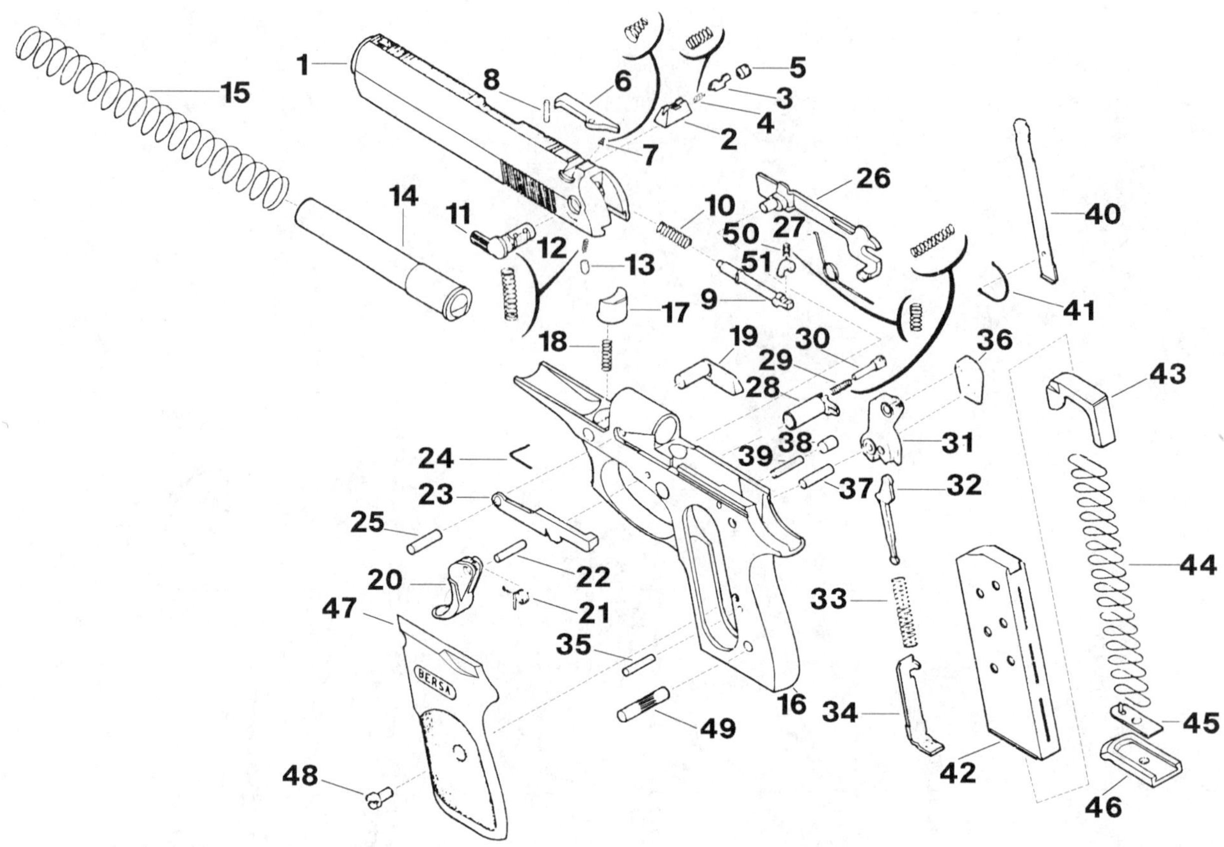

1	Slide	**27**	Disconnector Spring
2	Rear Sight	**28**	Magazine Catch
3	Rear Sight Blade	**29**	Magazine Catch Spring
4	Rear Sight Spring	**30**	Magazine Catch Pin
5	Rear Sight Screw	**31**	Hammer
6	Extractor	**32**	Hammer Spring Guide
7	Extractor Spring	**33**	Hammer Spring
8	Extractor Pin	**34**	Cocking Piece
9	Firing Pin	**35**	Cocking Piece Pin
10	Firing Pin Spring	**36**	Hammer Release
11	Safety	**37**	Hammer Pin
12	Safety Spring	**38**	Hammer Release Bush
13	Safety Stop	**39**	Hammer Release Pin
14	Barrel	**40**	Magazine Safety
15	Recoil Spring	**41**	Magazine Safety Spring
16	Frame	**42**	Magazine
17	Slide Stop	**43**	Feeder Platform
18	Slide Stop Spring	**44**	Magazine Spring
19	Disassembly Bar	**45**	Magazine Bottom Holder
20	Trigger	**46**	Magazine Bottom
21	Trigger Spring	**47**	Grip
22	Trigger Pin	**48**	Grip Screw
23	Slide Catch	**49**	Grip Pin
24	Slide Catch Spring	**50**	Firing Pin Stop Spring
25	Slide Catch Pin	**51**	Firing Pin Stop
26	Disconnector		

Model 223 Auto

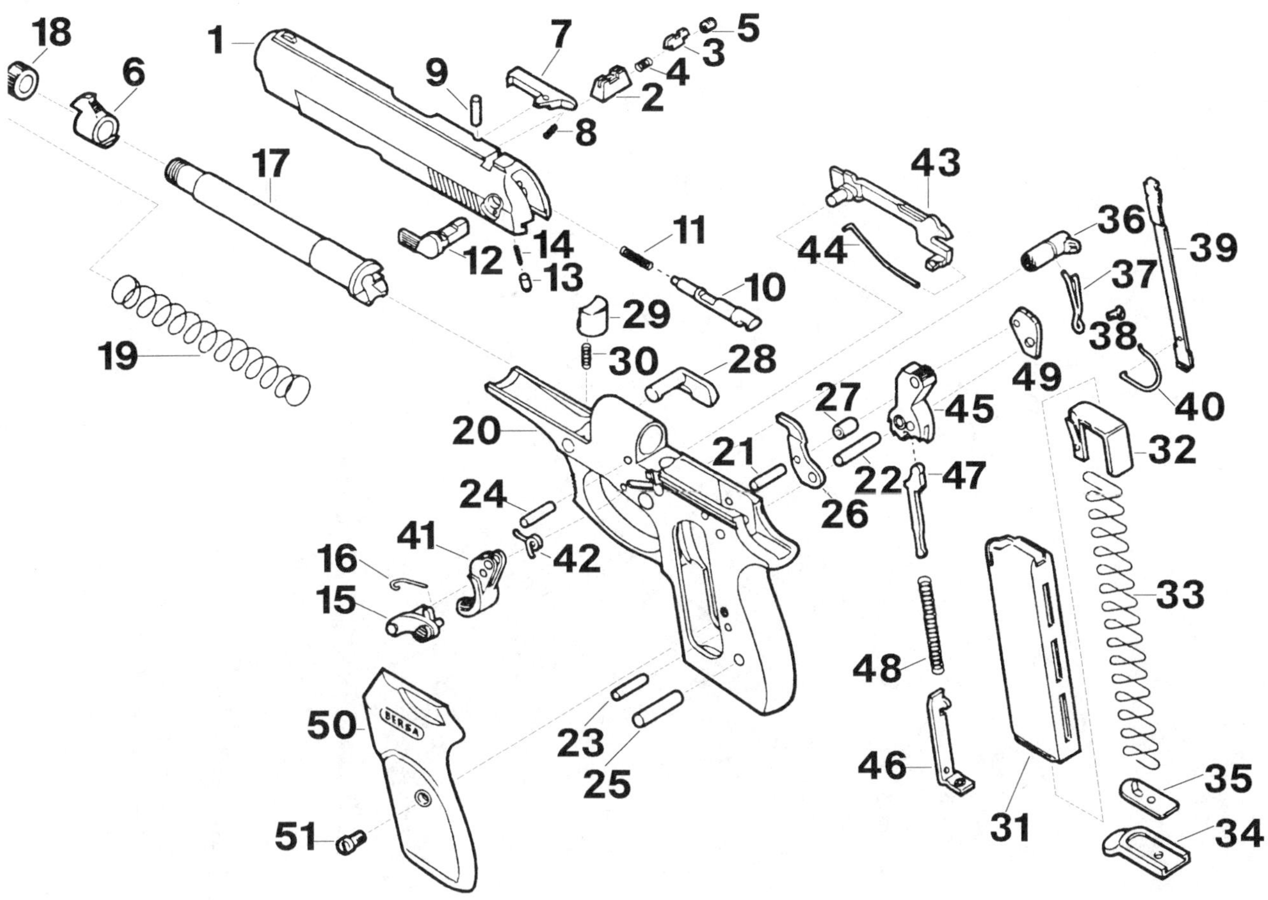

1	Slide	27	Ejector Bush
2	Rear Sight	28	Disassembly Piece
3	Rear Sight Blade	29	Slide Stop
4	Rear Sight Spring	30	Slide Stop Spring
5	Rear Sight Screw	31	Magazine
6	Front Sight	32	Feeder Platform
7	Extractor	33	Magazine Spring
8	Extractor Spring	34	Magazine Bottom
9	Extractor Pin	35	Magazine Bottom Holder
10	Firing Pin	36	Magazine Catch
11	Firing Pin Spring	37	Magazine Catch Spring
12	Safety	38	Magazine Catch Screw
13	Safety Stop	39	Magazine Safety
14	Safety Spring	40	Magazine Safety Spring
15	Catch Slide	41	Trigger
16	Catch Slide Spring	42	Trigger Spring
17	Barrel	43	Disconnector
18	Front Sight Nut	44	Disconnector Spring
19	Recoil Spring	45	Hammer
20	Frame	46	Cocking Piece
21	Ejector Pin	47	Hammer Spring Guide
22	Hammer Pin	48	Hammer Spring
23	Cocking Piece Pin	49	Hammer Release
24	Barrel Pin	50	Grip Plate
25	Grip Pin	51	Grip Plate Screw
26	Ejector		

Model 224, 225 and 226 Auto

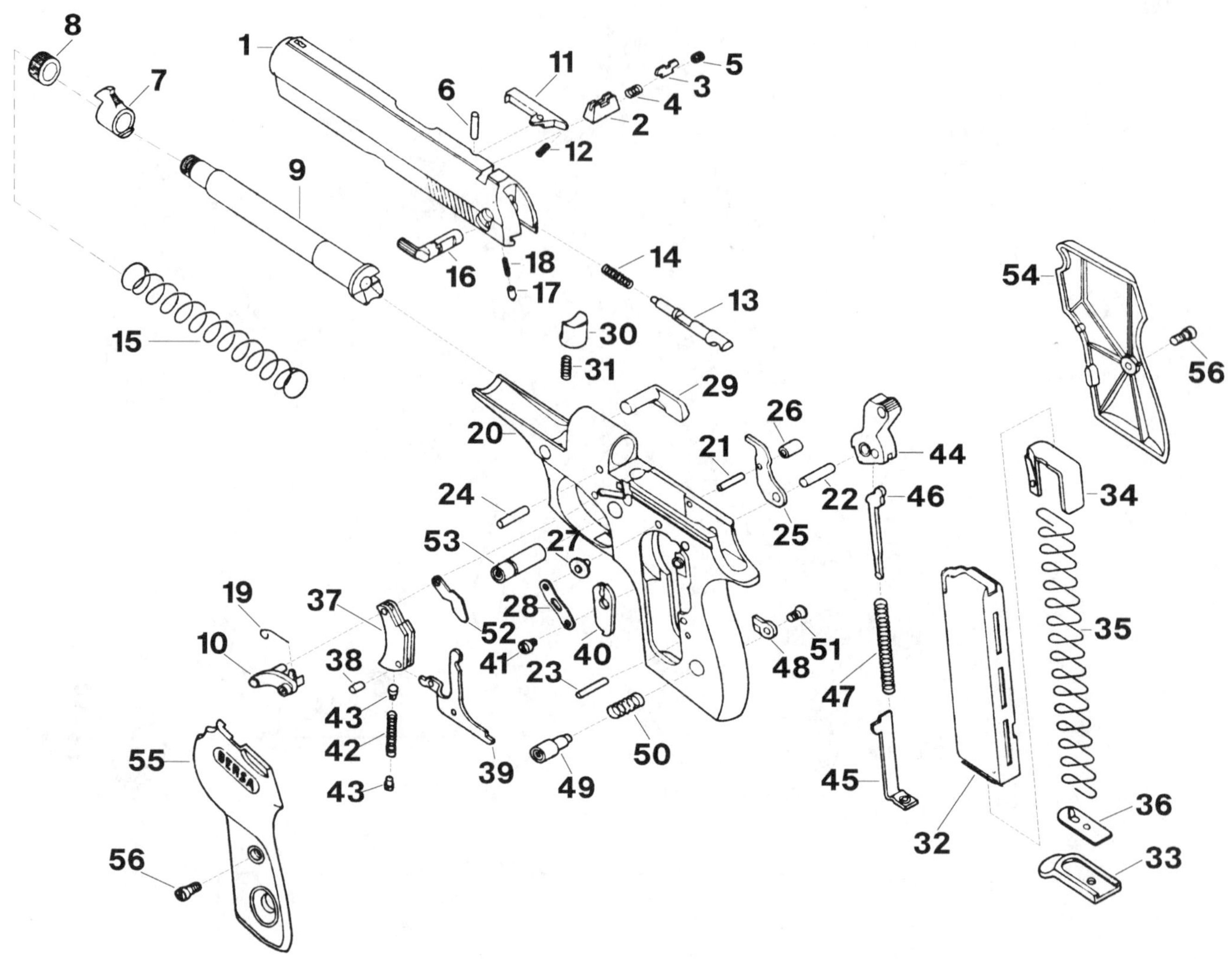

1	Slide	**20**	Frame	**39**	Disconnector
2	Rear Sight Body	**21**	Ejector Pin	**40**	Release Piece
3	Rear Sight Blade	**22**	Hammer Pin	**41**	Release Piece Screw
4	Rear Sight Spring	**23**	Cocking Piece Pin	**42**	Trigger Spring
5	Rear Sight Screw	**24**	Barrel Pin	**43**	Trigger Spring Pin
6	Extractor Pin	**25**	Ejector	**44**	Hammer
7	Front Sight	**26**	Ejector Bush	**45**	Cocking Piece
8	Front Sight Nut	**27**	Magazine Safety	**46**	Hammer Spring Guide
9	Barrel	**28**	Magazine Safety Spring	**47**	Hammer Spring
10	Catch Slide	**29**	Disassembly Piece	**48**	Magazine Catch
11	Extractor	**30**	Slide Top	**49**	Magazine Button
12	Extractor Spring	**31**	Slide Top Spring	**50**	Magazine Catch Spring
13	Firing Pin	**32**	Magazine Body	**51**	Magazine Catch Screw
14	Firing Pin Spring	**33**	Magazine Bottom	**52**	Trigger Safety
15	Recoil Spring	**34**	Feeder Platform	**53**	Safety Button
16	Firing Pin Safety	**35**	Magazine Spring	**54**	Grip Plate Right
17	Firing Pin Safety Top	**36**	Magazine Bottom Holder	**55**	Grip Plate Left
18	Firing Pin Safety Spring	**37**	Trigger	**56**	Grip Screws
19	Catch Slide Spring	**38**	Disconnector Pin		

Autoloading Pistol

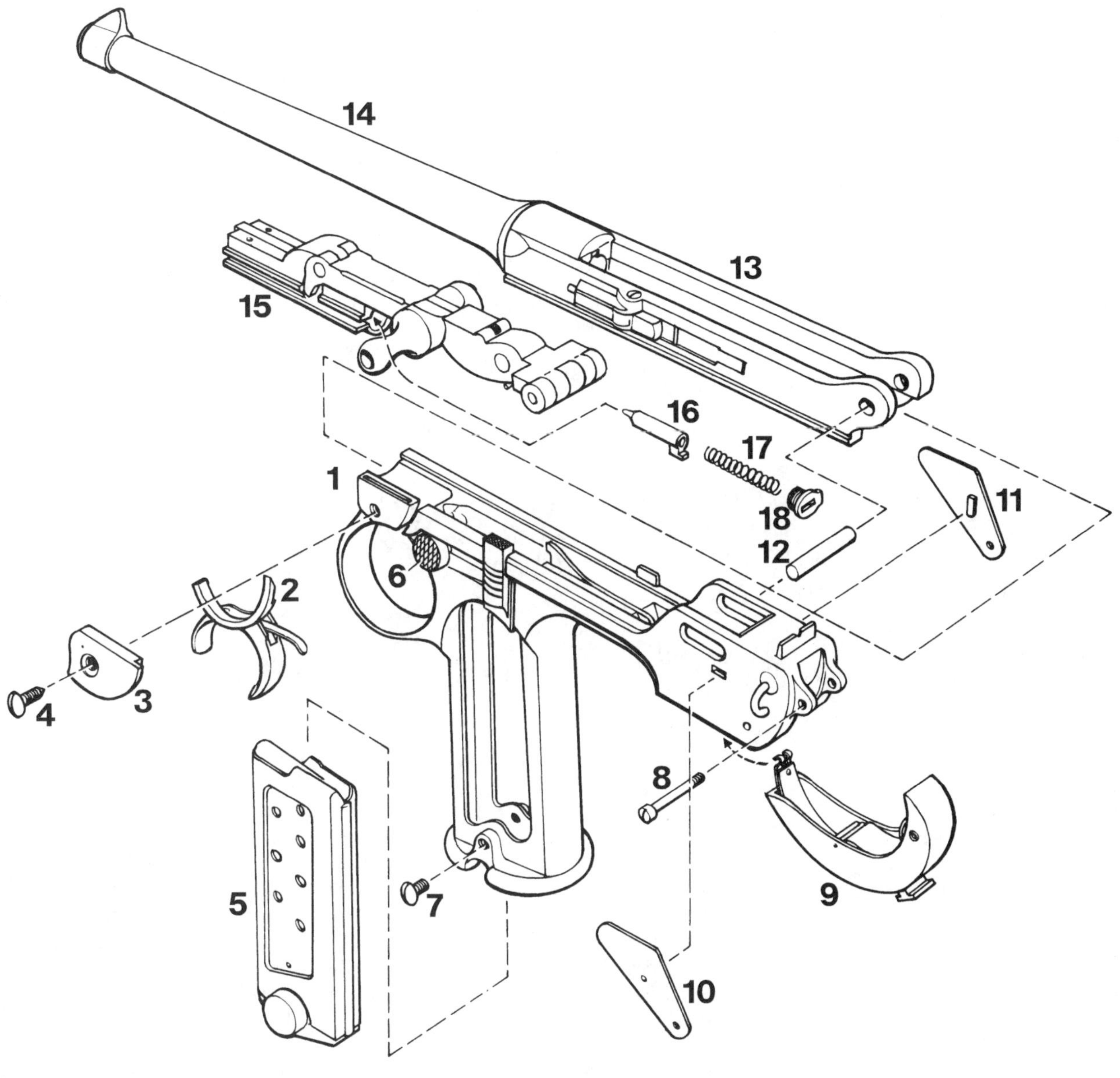

1	Frame	11	Cover Plate (Right)
2	Trigger	12	Connecting Pin
3	Trigger Cover	13	Receiver
4	Trigger Cover Screw	14	Barrel
5	Magazine Assembly	15	Breechblock and Toggle Links
6	Magazine Catch Button	16	Firing Pin
7	Grip Screw	17	Firing Pin Spring
8	Recoil Spring Housing Screw	18	Firing Pin Screw
9	Recoil Spring Housing with Recoil Spring	**Parts Not Shown**	
10	Cover Plate (Left)		Grips

Combat Auto

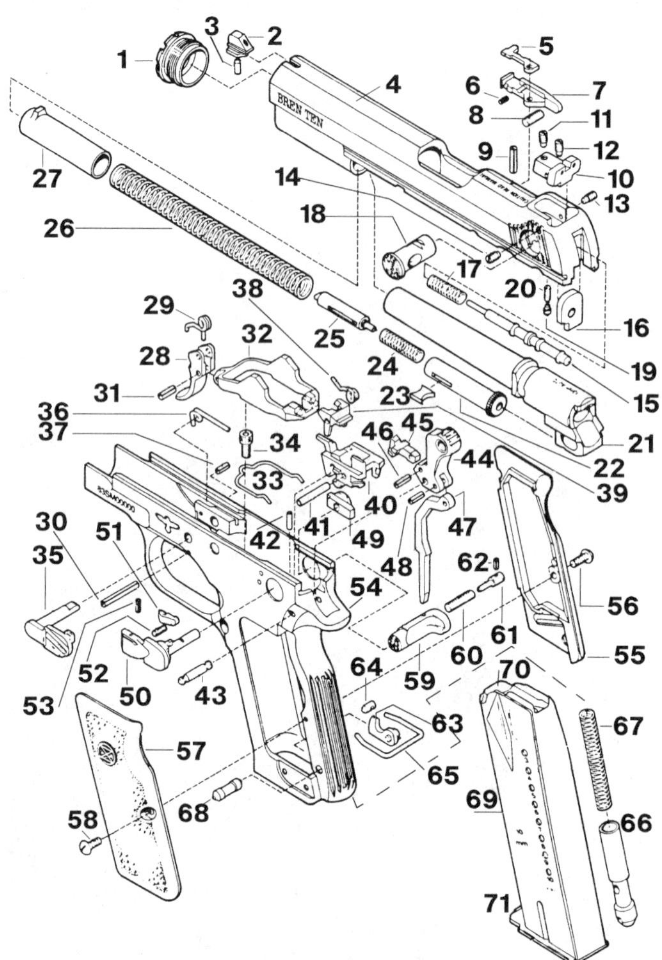

1	Barrel Bushing
2	Front Sight
3	Front Sight Plug
4	Slide
5	Loaded Chamber Indicator
6	Loaded Chamber Indicator Spring
7	Extractor
8	Extractor Spring
9	Extractor Pin
10	Rear Sight
11	Forward Rear Sight Elevation Adjustment Screw
12	Rearward Rear Sight Elevation Adjustment Screw
13	Right Rear Sight Windage Adjustment Screw
14	Left Rear Sight Windage Adjustment Screw
15	Firing Pin
16	Firing Pin Retainer
17	Firing Pin Spring
18	Firing Pin Block
19	Firing Pin Block Detent
20	Firing Pin Block Detent Spring
21	Barrel
22	Recoil Spring Guide
23	Screwdriver Lock Key
24	Recoil Buffer Spring
25	Screwdriver/Recoil Buffer
26	Recoil Spring
27	Recoil Spring Tube/Barrel Bushing Lock
28	Trigger
29	Trigger Return Spring
30	Trigger Pivot Pin
31	Trigger Bar Pivot Pin
32	Trigger Bar
33	Trigger Bar Spring
34	Trigger Bar Spring Screw
35	Slide Stop
36	Slide Stop Spring
37	Slide Stop Spring Pin
38	Sear Spring
39	Sear
40	Sear Housing
41	Sear Pin
42	Hammer Pin Retainer
43	Hammer Pin
44	Hammer
45	Double Action Hook
46	Hook Pin
47	Hammer Strut
48	Strut Pin
49	Thumb Safety Bushing
50	Thumb Safety-Lever
51	Thumb Safety-Lever Detent
52	Thumb Safety-Lever Detent Spring
53	Thumb Safety-Lever Detent Pin
54	Receiver (Frame)
55	Right Stock
56	Right Stock Screw
57	Left Stock
58	Left Stock Screw
59	Magazine Release
60	Magazine Release Spring
61	Magazine Release Lock
62	Magazine Release Lock Pin
63	Magazine Catch Selector Cam
64	Magazine Catch Selector Keeper
65	Magazine Catch Selector Keeper Spring
66	Lanyard Loop/Mainspring Retainer
67	Mainspring
68	Lanyard Loop/Mainspring Retainer Pin
69	Magazine Body
70	Magazine Follower
71	Magazine Floorplate

Parts Not Shown

Magazine Floorplate Retainer

Magazine Spring

Pocket Auto

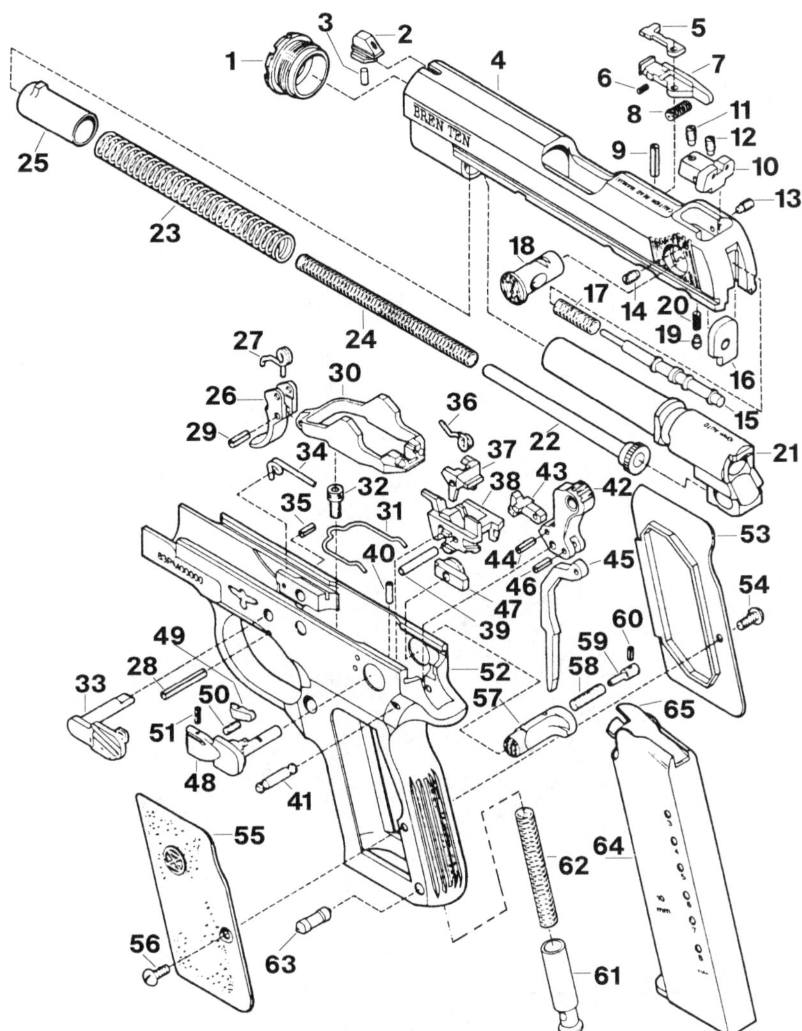

1	Barrel Bushing	21	Barrel	44	Hook Pin
2	Front Sight	22	Recoil Spring Guide	45	Hammer Strut
3	Front Sight Plug	23	Recoil Spring, Outer	46	Strut Pin
4	Slide	24	Recoil Spring, Inner	47	Thumb Safety Bushing
5	Loaded Chamber Indicator	25	Recoil Spring Tube/Barrel Bushing Lock	48	Thumb Safety-Lever
6	Loaded Chamber Indicator Spring	26	Trigger	49	Thumb Safety-Lever Detent
7	Extractor	27	Trigger Return Spring	50	Thumb Safety-Lever Detent Spring
8	Extractor Spring	28	Trigger Pivot Pin	51	Thumb Safety-Lever Detent Pin
9	Extractor Pin	29	Trigger Bar Pivot Pin	52	Receiver (Frame)
10	Rear Sight	30	Trigger Bar	53	Right Stock
11	Forward Rear Sight Elevation Adjustment Screw	31	Trigger Bar Spring	54	Right Stock Screw
12	Rearward Rear Sight Elevation Adjustment Screw	32	Trigger Bar Spring Screw	55	Left Stock
13	Right Rear Sight Windage Adjustment Screw	33	Slide Stop	56	Left Stock Screw
14	Left Rear Sight Windage Adjustment Screw	34	Slide Stop Spring	57	Magazine Release
15	Firing Pin	35	Slide Stop Spring Pin	58	Magazine Release Spring
16	Firing Pin Retainer	36	Sear Spring	59	Magazine Release Lock
17	Firing Pin Spring	37	Sear	60	Magazine Release Lock Pin
18	Firing Pin Block	38	Sear Housing	61	Mainspring Retainer
19	Firing Pin Block Detent	39	Sear Pin	62	Mainspring
20	Firing Pin Block Detent Spring	40	Hammer Pin Retainer	63	Mainspring Retainer Pin
		41	Hammer Pin	64	Magazine Body
		42	Hammer	65	Magazine Follower
		43	Double Action Hook	**Parts Not Shown**	
					Magazine Spring

Special Forces Model Auto

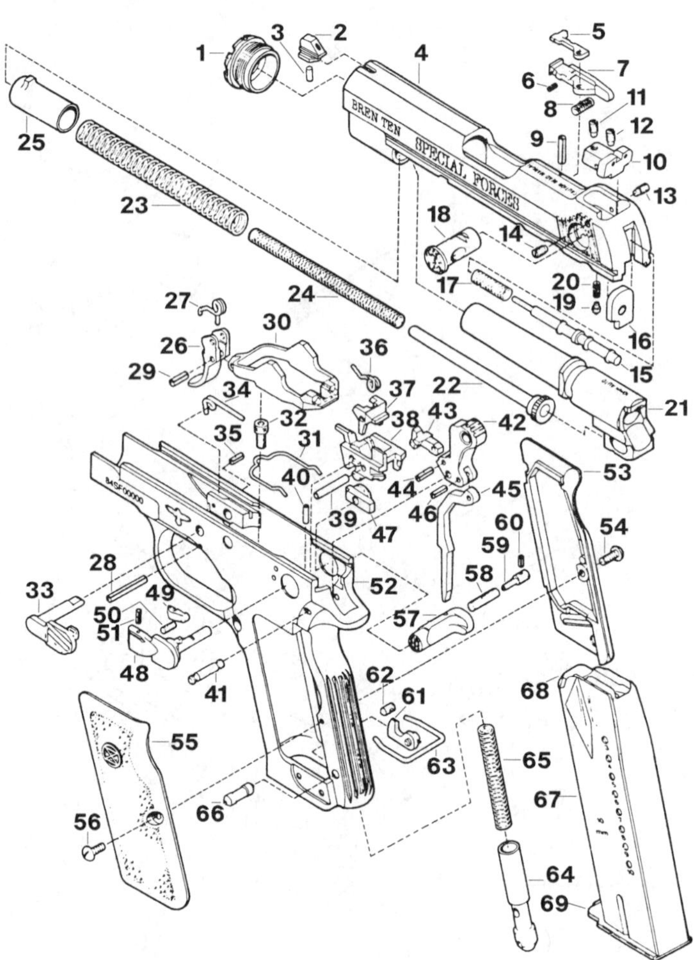

1	Barrel Bushing
2	Front Sight
3	Front Sight Plug
4	Slide
5	Loaded Chamber Indicator
6	Loaded Chamber Indicator Spring
7	Extractor
8	Extractor Spring
9	Extractor Pin
10	Rear Sight
11	Forward Rear Sight Elevation Adjustment Screw
12	Rearward Rear Sight Elevation Adjustment Screw
13	Right Rear Sight Windage Adjustment Screw
14	Left Rear Sight Windage Adjustment Screw
15	Firing Pin
16	Firing Pin Retainer
17	Firing Pin Spring
18	Firing Pin Block
19	Firing Pin Block Detent
20	Firing Pin Block Detent Spring
21	Barrel
22	Recoil Spring Guide
23	Recoil Spring, Outer
24	Recoil Spring, Inner
25	Recoil Spring Tube/Barrel Bushing Lock
26	Trigger
27	Trigger Return Spring
28	Trigger Pivot Pin
29	Trigger Bar Pivot Pin
30	Trigger Bar
31	Trigger Bar Spring
32	Trigger Bar Spring Screw
33	Slide Stop
34	Slide Stop Spring
35	Slide Stop Spring Pin
36	Sear Spring
37	Sear
38	Sear Housing
39	Sear Pin
40	Hammer Pin Retainer
41	Hammer Pin
42	Hammer
43	Double Action Hook
44	Hook Pin
45	Hammer Strut
46	Strut Pin
47	Thumb Safety Bushing
48	Thumb Safety-Lever
49	Thumb Safety-Lever Detent
50	Thumb Safety-Lever Detent Spring
51	Thumb Safety-Lever Detent Pin
52	Receiver (Frame)
53	Right Stock
54	Right Stock Screw
55	Left Stock
56	Left Stock Screw
57	Magazine Release
58	Magazine Release Spring
59	Magazine Release Lock
60	Magazine Release Lock Pin
61	Magazine Catch Selector Cam
62	Magazine Catch Selector Keeper
63	Magazine Catch Selector Keeper Spring
64	Lanyard Loop/Mainspring Retainer
65	Mainspring
66	Lanyard Loop/Mainspring Retainer Pin
67	Magazine Body
68	Magazine Follower
69	Magazine Floorplate

Parts Not Shown

Magazine Floorplate Retainer

Magazine Spring

Model CZ-75 Auto

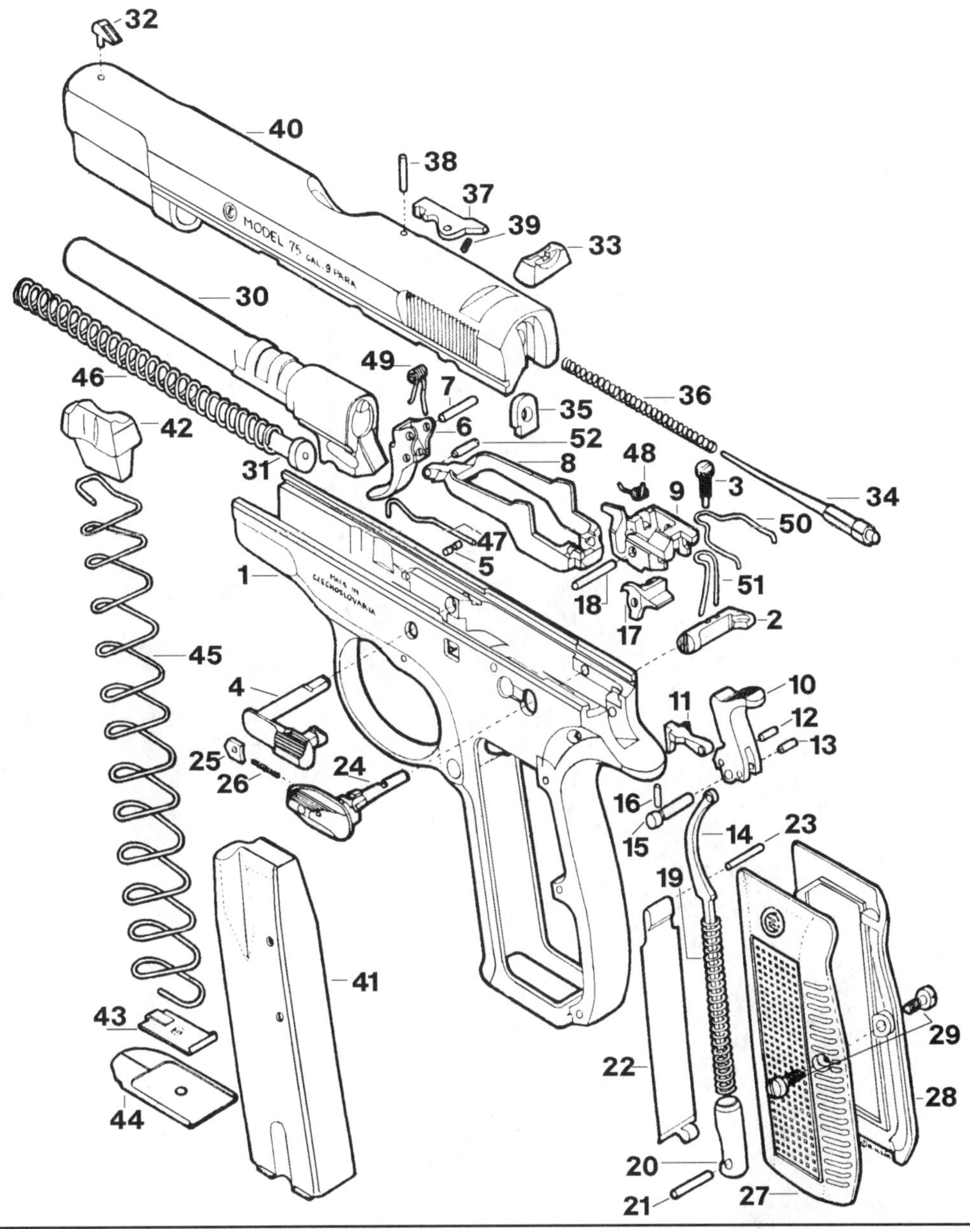

1	Frame	**18**	Sear Pin	**36**	Firing Pin Spring
2	Magazine Catch	**19**	Hammer Spring	**37**	Extractor
3	Trigger Bar Spring Screw	**20**	Hammer Spring Base	**38**	Extractor Pivot Pin
4	Slide Stop	**21**	Hammer Spring Base Pin	**39**	Extractor Spring
5	Slide Stop Pin Spring Pin	**22**	Magazine Security Spring Plate	**40**	Slide
6	Trigger	**23**	Magazine Security Spring Plate Pin	**41**	Magazine Body
7	Trigger Pin	**24**	Safety-Lever	**42**	Magazine Follower
8	Trigger Bar	**25**	Safety-Lever Detent Plate	**43**	Magazine Spring Plate
9	Sear Assembly Housing with Ejector	**26**	Safety-Lever Detent Plate Spring	**44**	Magazine Floorplate
		27	Left Grip	**45**	Magazine Spring
10	Hammer	**28**	Right Grip	**46**	Recoil Spring
11	Interruptor	**29**	Grip Screw	**47**	Slide Stop Pin Spring
12	Interruptor Pin	**30**	Barrel	**48**	Hammer Stop Spring
13	Hammer Strut Pin	**31**	Recoil Spring Guide	**49**	Trigger Spring
14	Hammer Strut	**32**	Front Sight	**50**	Trigger Bar Spring
15	Hammer Pin	**33**	Rear Sight	**51**	Magazine Catch Spring
16	Hammer Pin Retaining Pin	**34**	Firing Pin	**52**	Trigger Bar Pin
17	Sear	**35**	Firing Pin Retainer		

25 Auto

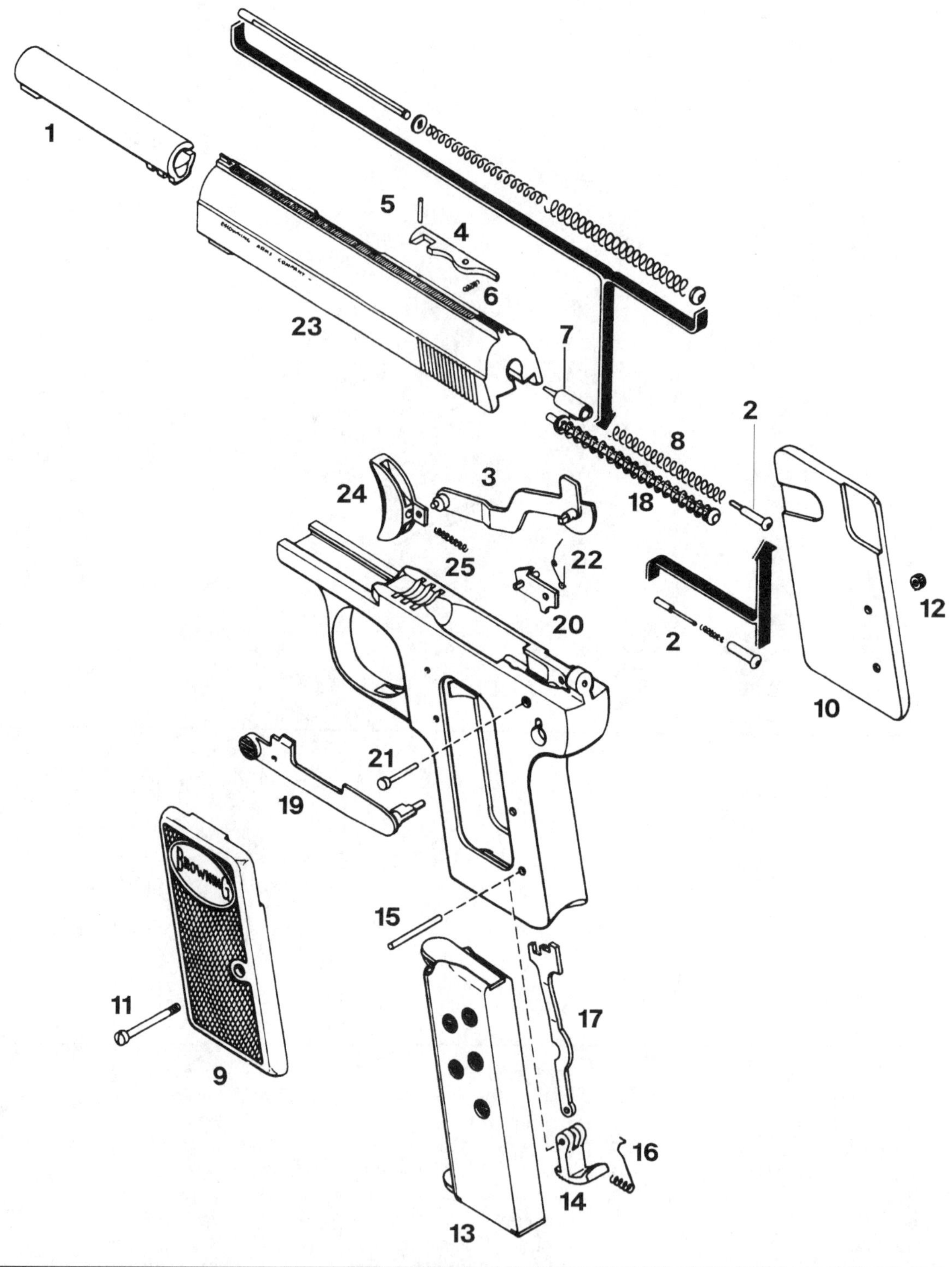

1	Barrel	**10**	Grip Plate, Right	**19**	Safety
2	Cocking Indicator Assembly	**11**	Grip Plate Screw	**20**	Sear
3	Connector	**12**	Grip Plate Escutcheon	**21**	Sear Pin
4	Extractor	**13**	Magazine	**22**	Sear Spring
5	Extractor Pin	**14**	Magazine Latch	**23**	Slide
6	Extractor Spring	**15**	Magazine Latch Pin	**24**	Trigger
7	Firing Pin	**16**	Magazine Latch Spring	**25**	Trigger Spring
8	Firing Pin Spring	**17**	Magazine Safety		
9	Grip Plate, Left	**18**	Recoil Spring Assembly		

380 and 32 Auto (Pre-1969)

Note: Can be used for FN/Browning Model 1910

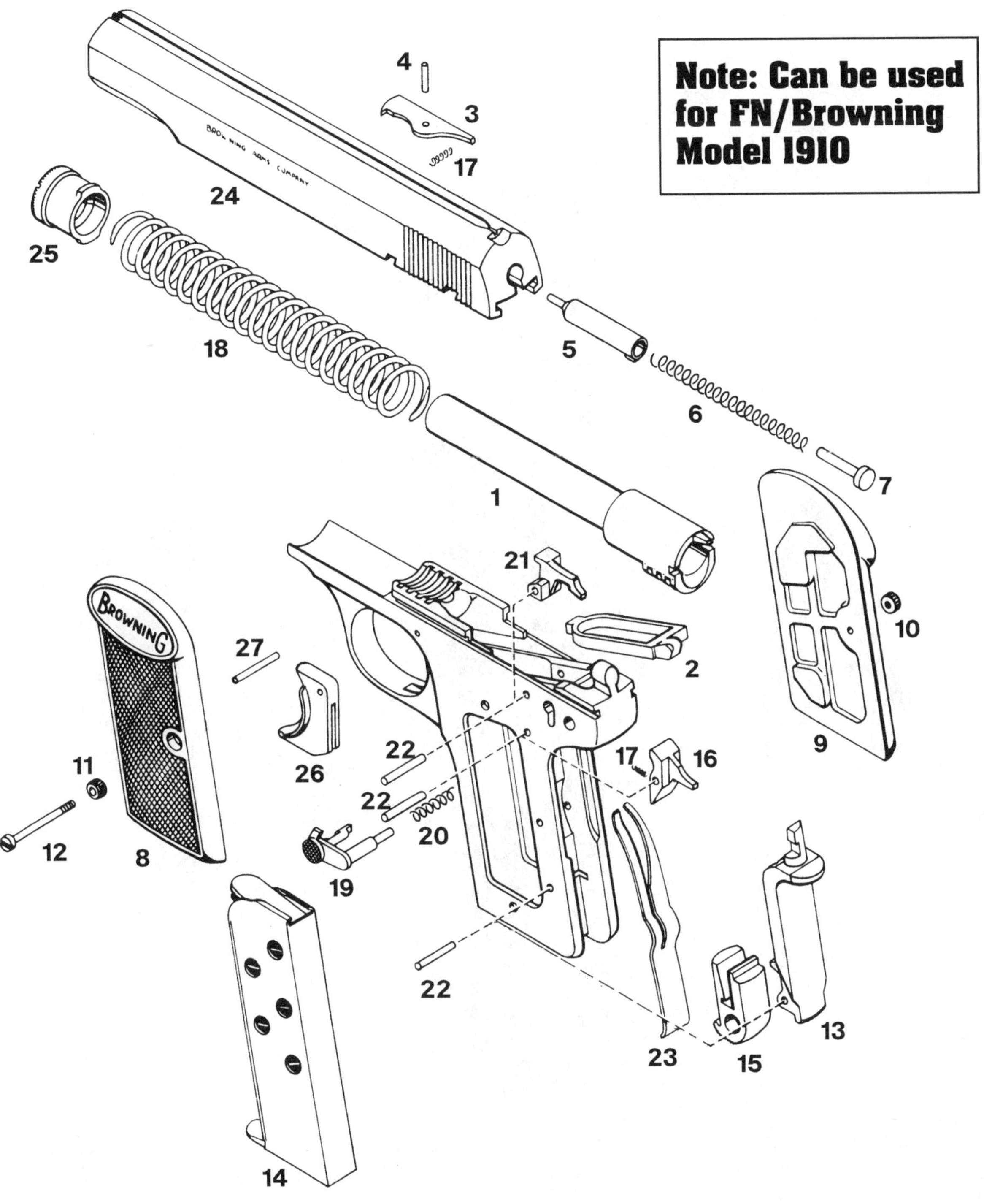

1	Barrel	**11**	Grip Plate Escutcheon, Unthreaded	**20**	Safety Spring
2	Connector	**12**	Grip Plate Screw	**21**	Sear
3	Extractor	**13**	Grip Safety	**22**	Sear Pin, Magazine Safety Pin and Grip Safety Pin
4	Extractor Pin	**14**	Magazine Complete	**23**	Sear Spring
5	Firing Pin	**15**	Magazine Latch	**24**	Slide
6	Firing Pin Spring	**16**	Magazine Safety	**25**	Slide Ring
7	Firing Pin Spring Guide	**17**	Magazine Safety and Extractor Spring	**26**	Trigger
8	Grip Plate, Left	**18**	Recoil Spring	**27**	Trigger Pin
9	Grip Plate, Right	**19**	Safety		
10	Grip Plate Escutcheon, Threaded				

380 Auto (1969-1974)

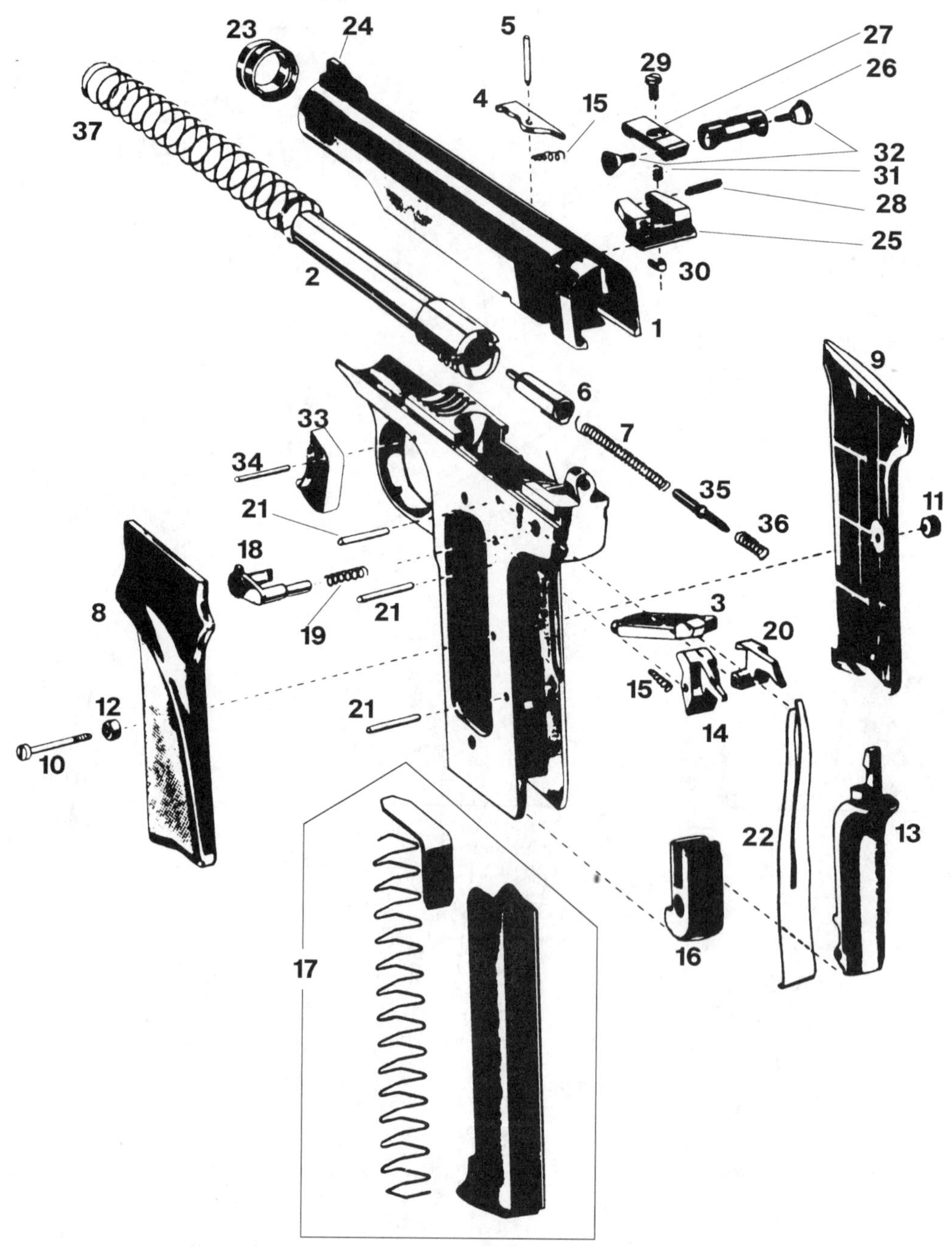

1	Slide	**14**	Magazine Safety	**25**	Sight Base, Rear
2	Barrel	**15**	Magazine Safety and Extractor Spring	**26**	Sight Aperture, Rear
3	Connector			**27**	Sight Aperture Housing, Rear
4	Extractor	**16**	Magazine Latch	**28**	Sight Aperture Housing Pin, Rear
5	Extractor Pin	**17**	Magazine Assembly	**29**	Sight Elevation Screw, Rear
6	Firing Pin	**18**	Safety	**30**	Sight Elevation Screw Spring, Rear
7	Firing Pin Spring	**19**	Safety Spring	**31**	Sight Elevation Spring, Rear
8	Grip Plate, Left	**20**	Sear	**32**	Sight Windage Screw, Rear
9	Grip Plate, Right	**21**	Sear Pin, Magazine Safety Pin and Grip Safety Pin	**33**	Trigger
10	Grip Plate Screw			**34**	Trigger Pin
11	Grip Escutcheon, Threaded	**22**	Sear Spring	**35**	Cocking Indicator
12	Grip Escutcheon, Unthreaded	**23**	Slide Ring	**36**	Cocking Indicator Spring
13	Grip Safety	**24**	Sight with Ramp, Front	**37**	Recoil Spring

BDA DA Auto (1969 - 1974)

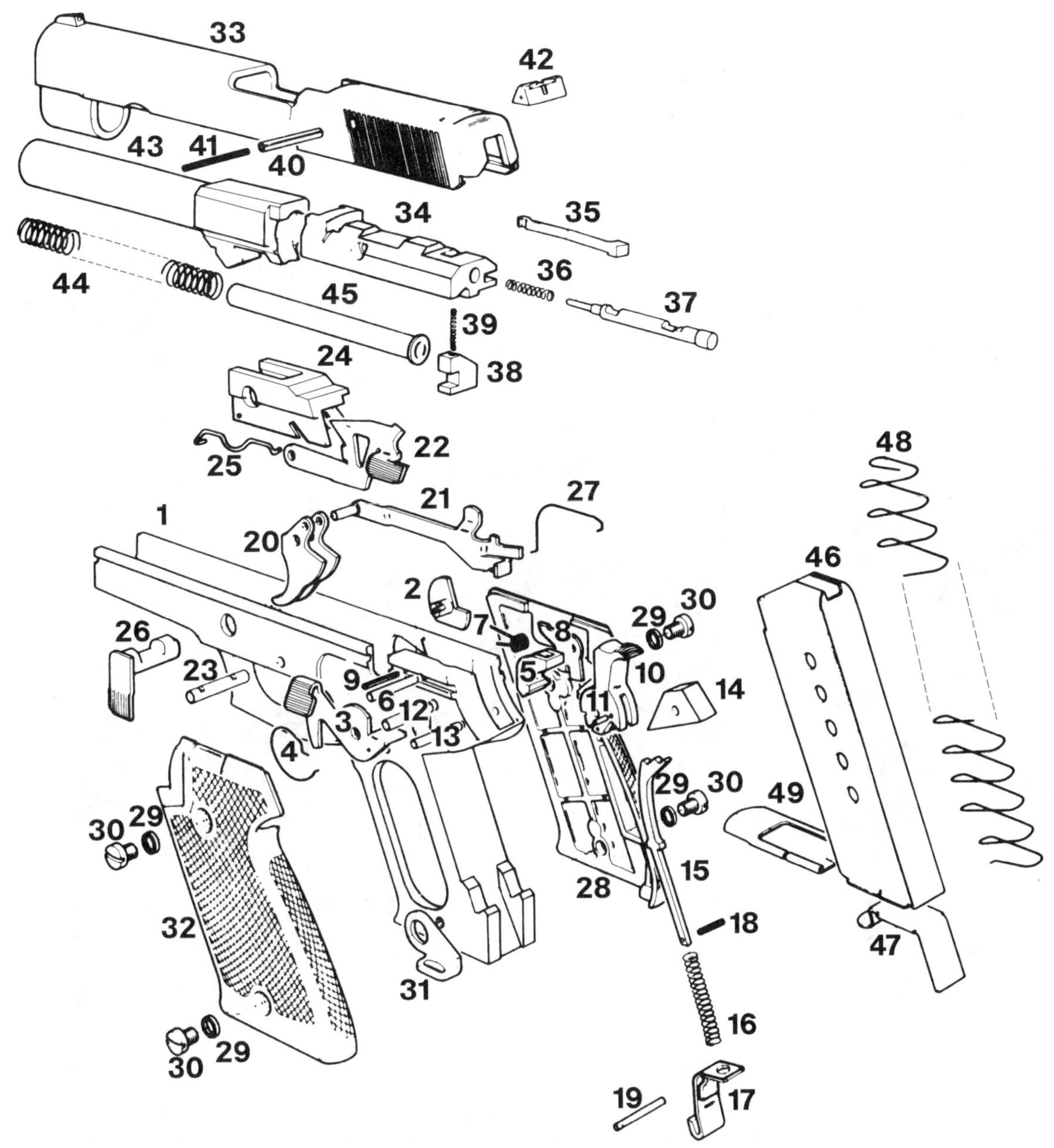

1	Frame	**18**	Hammer Spring Pin	**35**	Extractor
2	Decocking Lever Seat	**19**	Magazine Catch Pin	**36**	Firing Pin Spring
3	Decocking Lever	**20**	Trigger	**37**	Firing Pin
4	Decocking Lever Spring	**21**	Trigger Rod	**38**	Safety Slide
5	Sear	**22**	Slide Release	**39**	Safety Slide Spring
6	Sear Pin	**23**	Trigger Pin	**40**	Firing Pin Retaining Pin, Outer
7	Sear Torsion Spring	**24**	Locking Insert	**41**	Firing Pin Retaining Pin, Inner
8	Safety-Lever	**25**	Slide Release	**42**	Sight, Rear
9	Sear Torsion Spring Pin	**26**	Disassembly Lever	**43**	Barrel
10	Hammer	**27**	Trigger Spring	**44**	Recoil Spring
11	Hammer Pin	**28**	Grip Plate, Right	**45**	Recoil Spring Guide
12	Hammer Axle	**29**	Grip Plate Washer	**46**	Magazine
13	Hammer Stop Pin	**30**	Grip Plate Screw	**47**	Magazine Follower
14	Hammer Stop	**31**	Strap Ring	**48**	Magazine Spring
15	Mainspring Guide	**32**	Grip Plate, Left	**49**	Magazine Base Plate
16	Mainspring	**33**	Slide		
17	Magazine Catch	**34**	Rear Insert		

BDA 380 Auto

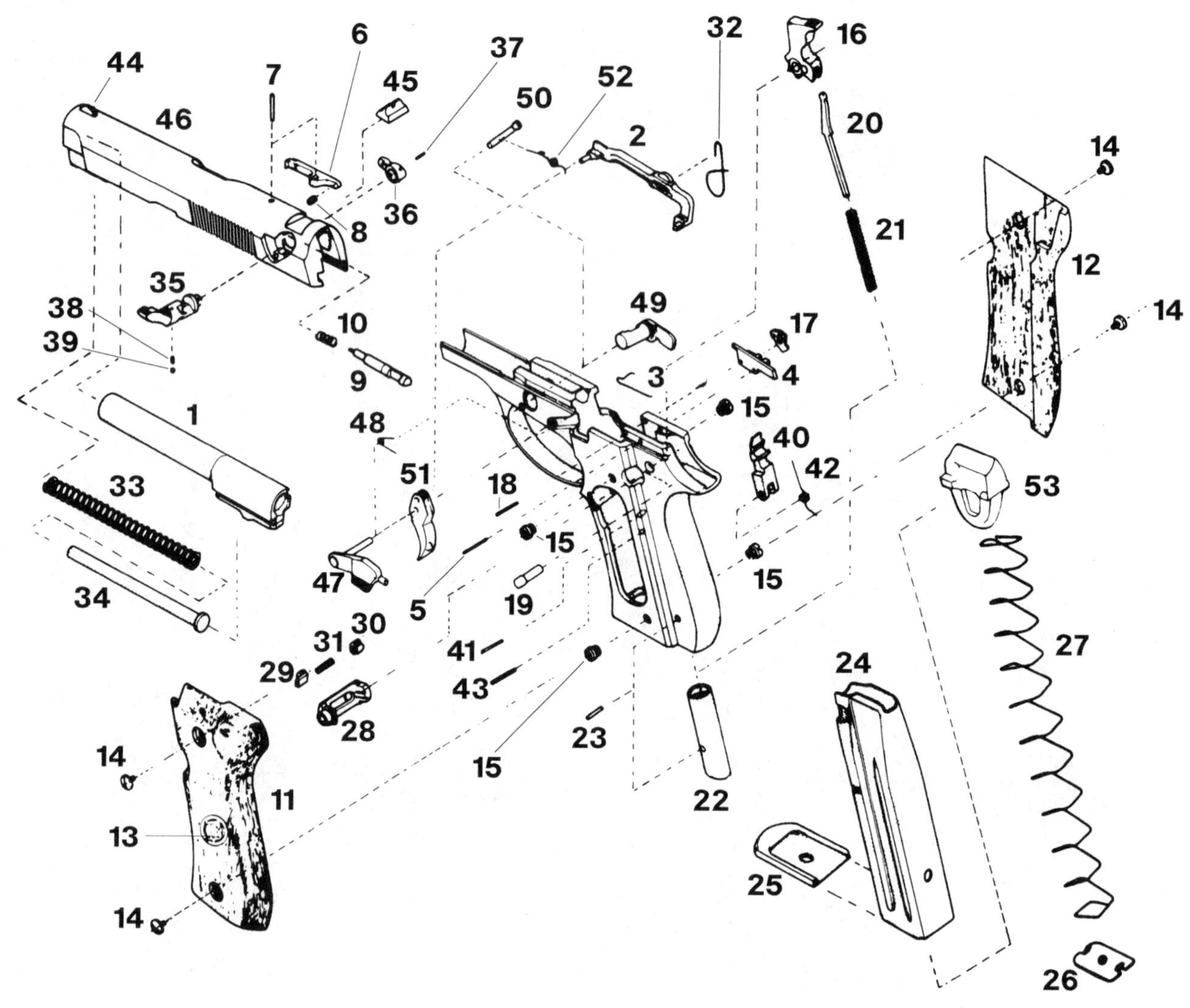

1	Barrel	19	Hammer Pin	37	Safety and Decocking Lever Pin
2	Disconnector	20	Hammer Strut	38	Safety Spring
3	Disconnector Spring	21	Mainspring	39	Safety Spring Ball
4	Ejector	22	Mainspring Guide	40	Sear
5	Ejector Pin	23	Mainspring Pin	41	Sear Pin
6	Extractor	24	Magazine Body	42	Sear Spring
7	Extractor Pin	25	Magazine Floorplate	43	Sear Spring Pin
8	Extractor Spring	26	Magazine Floorplate Retainer	44	Front Sight Blade
9	Firing Pin	27	Magazine Spring	45	Rear Sight
10	Firing Pin Spring	28	Magazine Latch	46	Slide
11	Grip Plate, Left	29	Magazine Latch Retainer, Left	47	Slide Stop
12	Grip Plate, Right	30	Magazine Latch Retainer, Right	48	Slide Stop Spring
13	Grip Plate Medallion	31	Magazine Latch Retainer Spring	49	Takedown Lever
14	Grip Plate Screws	32	Magazine Safety Spring	50	Takedown Lever Stop
15	Grip Plate Bushings	33	Recoil Spring	51	Trigger
16	Hammer	34	Recoil Spring Guide	52	Trigger Spring
17	Hammer Disconnector	35	Safety and Decocking Lever, Left	53	Magazine Follower
18	Hammer Disconnector Pin	36	Safety and Decocking Lever, Right		

BDA 380 (1978-Present)

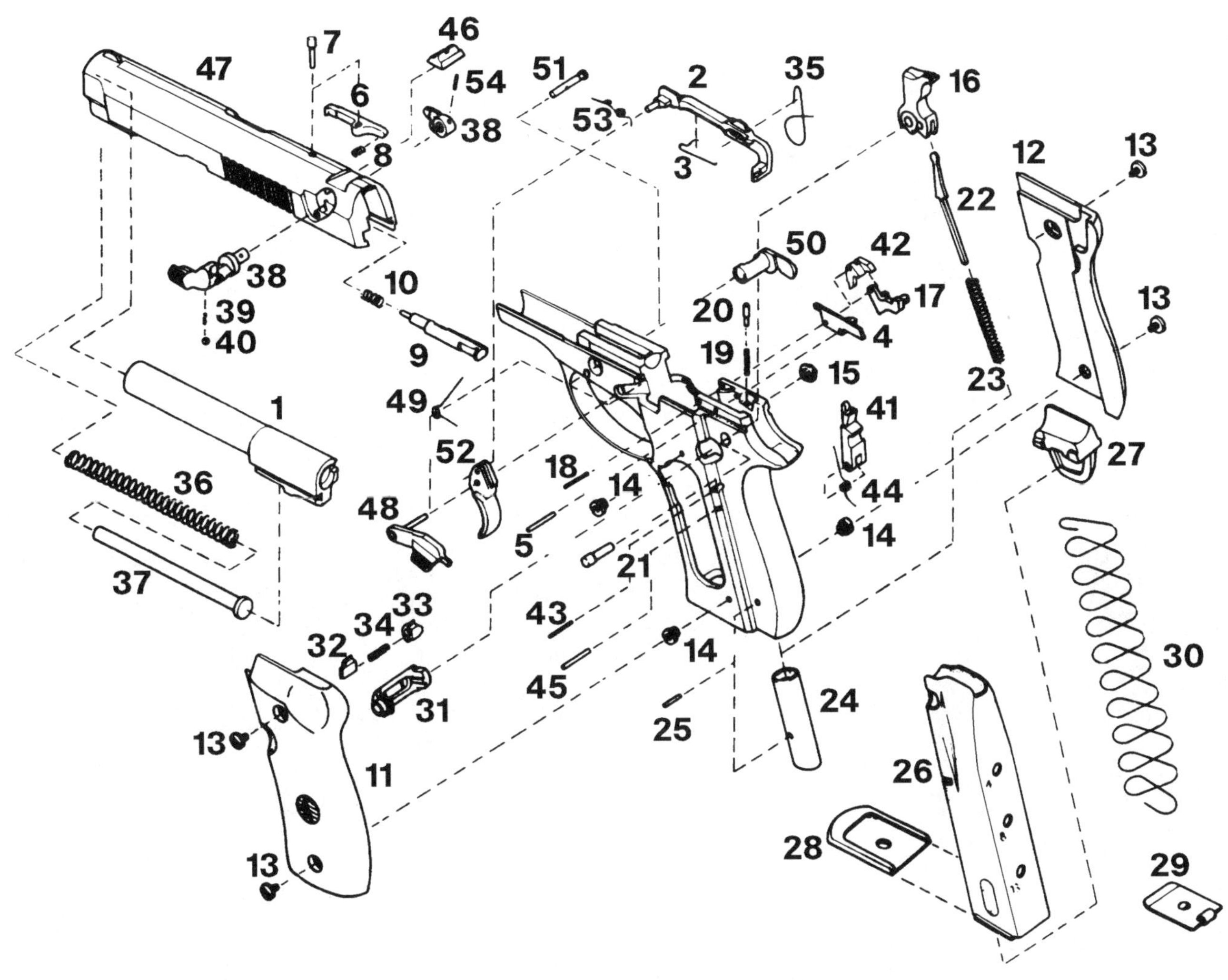

1	Barrel	**20**	Hammer Disconnector Spring Plunger	**39**	Safety Spring
2	Disconnector	**21**	Hammer Pin	**40**	Safety Spring Ball
3	Disconnector Spring	**22**	Hammer Strut	**41**	Sear
4	Ejector	**23**	Mainspring	**42**	Sear Disconnector
5	Ejector Pin	**24**	Mainspring Guide	**43**	Sear Pin
6	Extractor	**25**	Mainspring Pin	**44**	Sear Spring
7	Extractor Pin	**26**	Magazine Body	**45**	Sear Spring Pin
8	Extractor Spring	**27**	Magazine Follower	**46**	Sight, Rear
9	Firing Pin	**28**	Magazine Floorplate	**47**	Slide
10	Firing Pin Spring	**29**	Magazine Floorplate Retainer	**48**	Slide Stop
11	Grip Plate, Left	**30**	Magazine Spring	**49**	Slide Stop Spring
12	Grip Plate, Right	**31**	Magazine Latch	**50**	Takedown Lever
13	Grip Plate Screw	**32**	Magazine Latch Retainer, Left	**51**	Takedown Lever Stop
14	Grip Plate Bushing	**33**	Magazine Latch Retainer, Right	**52**	Trigger
15	Grip Plate Bushing and Spring Retainer	**34**	Magazine Latch Retainer Spring	**53**	Trigger Spring
16	Hammer	**35**	Magazine Safety Spring	**54**	Safety Assembly Pin
17	Hammer Disconnector	**36**	Recoil Spring	**Parts Not Shown**	
18	Hammer Disconnector Pin	**37**	Recoil Spring Guide		Grip Plate Medallion
19	Hammer Disconnector Spring	**38**	Safety Assembly		

Buckmark Auto

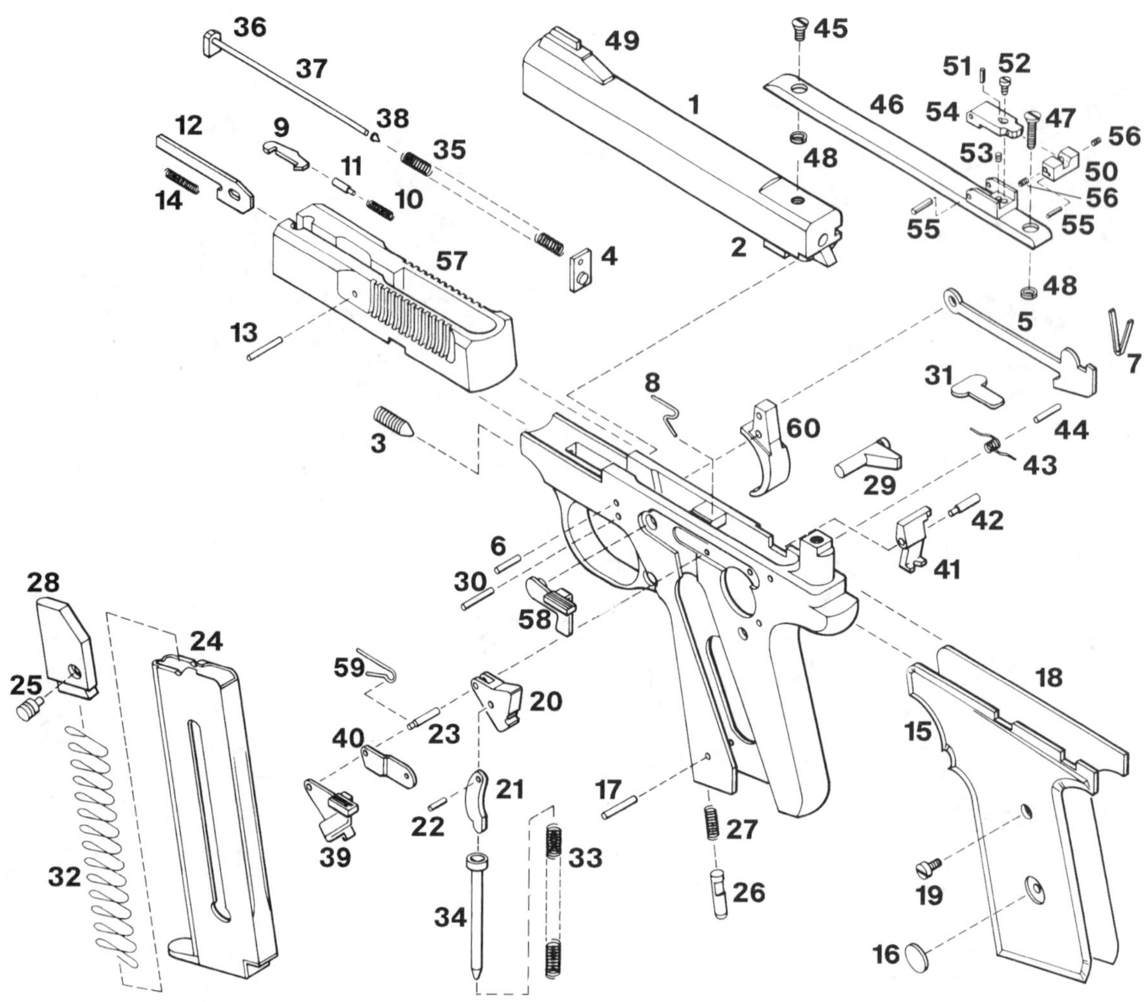

- **1** Barrel Assembly
- **2** Barrel Block
- **3** Barrel Mounting Screw
- **4** Buffer
- **5** Disconnector
- **6** Disconnector Pin
- **7** Disconnector Spring
- **8** Ejector
- **9** Extractor
- **10** Extractor Spring
- **11** Extractor Spring Plunger
- **12** Firing Pin
- **13** Firing Pin Retainer
- **14** Firing Pin Spring
- **15** Grip, Left
- **16** Grip Medallion
- **17** Grip Pin
- **18** Grip, Right
- **19** Grip Screw
- **20** Hammer
- **21** Hammer Link
- **22** Hammer Link Pin
- **23** Hammer Pin
- **24** Magazine Body
- **25** Magazine Button
- **26** Magazine Ejector
- **27** Magazine Ejector Spring
- **28** Magazine Follower
- **29** Magazine Latch
- **30** Magazine Latch Pin and Trigger Pin
- **31** Magazine Latch Spring
- **32** Magazine Spring
- **33** Mainspring
- **34** Mainspring Plunger
- **35** Recoil Spring
- **36** Recoil Spring Guide
- **37** Recoil Spring Guide Rod
- **38** Recoil Spring Guide Rod Retaining Ring
- **39** Safety Assembly with Thumb-Piece
- **40** Safety Click Plate
- **41** Sear
- **42** Sear Pin
- **43** Sear Spring
- **44** Sear Spring Pin
- **45** Sight Base Screw, Front
- **46** Sight Base, Rear
- **47** Sight Base Screw, Rear
- **48** Sight Base Screw-Lock Washer
- **49** Sight, Front
- **50** Rear Sight Blade
- **51** Rear Sight Detent Pin
- **52** Rear Sight Elevation Screw
- **53** Rear Sight Elevation Spring
- **54** Rear Sight Leaf
- **55** Rear Sight Leaf/Friction Pin
- **56** Rear Sight Windage Screw
- **57** Slide
- **58** Stop Open Latch Assembly with Thumb-Piece
- **59** Stop Open Latch Spring
- **60** Trigger

Parts Not Shown

- Recoil Spring Guide Assembly
- Sight Blade
- Sight Blade Screw
- Sight Elevation Screw
- Sight Rear Assembly Complete
- Sight Front Pin
- Sight Front Screw
- Sight Leaf
- Sight Rivet

Buckmark Silhouette Auto

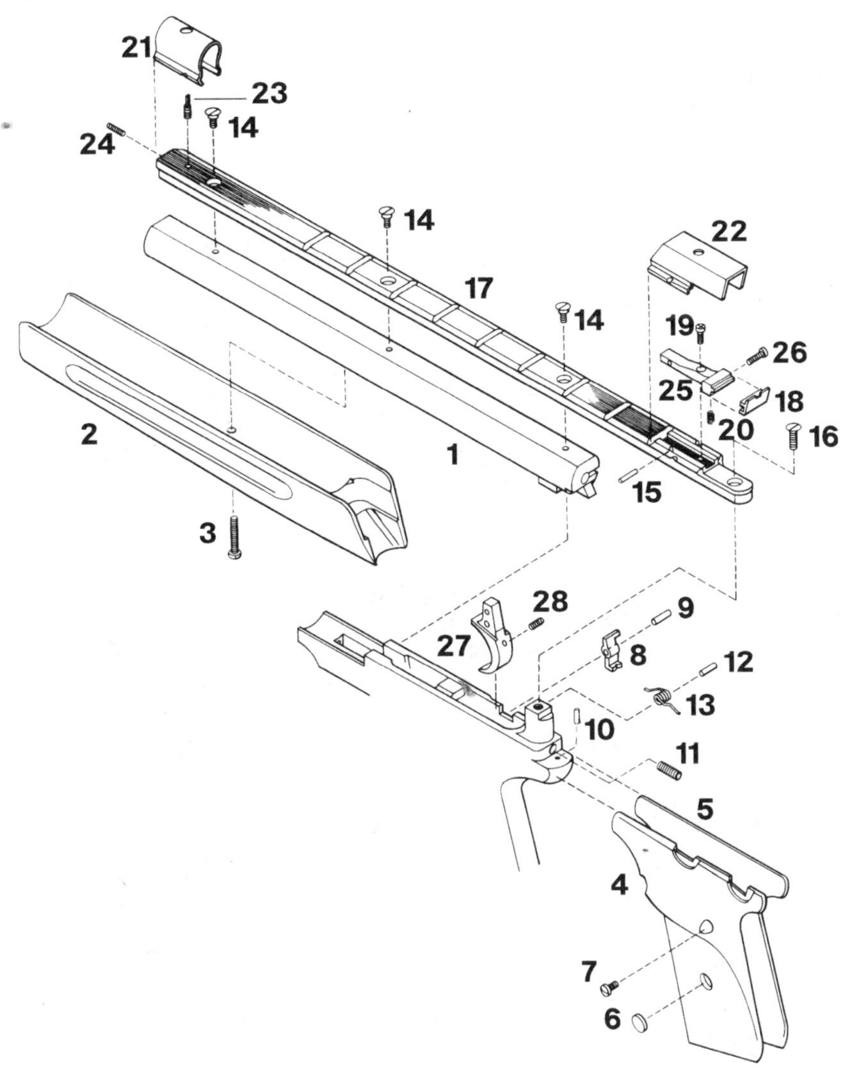

1	Barrel
2	Forearm
3	Forearm Screw
4	Grip, Left
5	Grip, Right
6	Grip Medallion
7	Grip Screw
8	Sear
9	Sear Pin
10	Sear Screw Stop Pin
11	Sear Spring Adjusting Screw
12	Sear Spring Pin
13	Sear Spring
14	Sight Base Screw Front
15	Sight Base Retaining Pin
16	Sight Base Screw Rear
17	Sight Base
18	Sight Blade
19	Sight Elevation Screw
20	Sight Elevation Spring
21	Sight Hood, Front
22	Sight Hood, Rear
23	Sight Post Front
24	Sight Post Lock Screw
25	Sight Windage Screw Retainer
26	Sight Windage Screw
27	Trigger Adjustable
28	Trigger Limit Screw

Parts Not Shown
(See Challenger I and II)

Barrel Block
Barrel Mounting Screw
Disconnector Assembly
Ejector
Extractor
Extractor Spring
Extractor Spring Plunger
Firing Pin
Firing Pin Retaining Pin
Hammer
Hammer Link
Hammer Link Pin
Hammer Pin
Magazine Body
Magazine Button
Magazine Ejector
Magazine Ejector Spring
Magazine Follower
Magazine Latch
Magazine Latch Pin and Trigger Pin
Magazine Latch Spring
Mainspring
Mainspring Plunger
Recoil Spring
Recoil Spring Guide
Recoil Spring Guide Rod
Safety Assembly with Thumb-Piece
Safety Click Plate
Stop Open Latch
Stop Open Latch Spring

Buckmark Varmint Auto

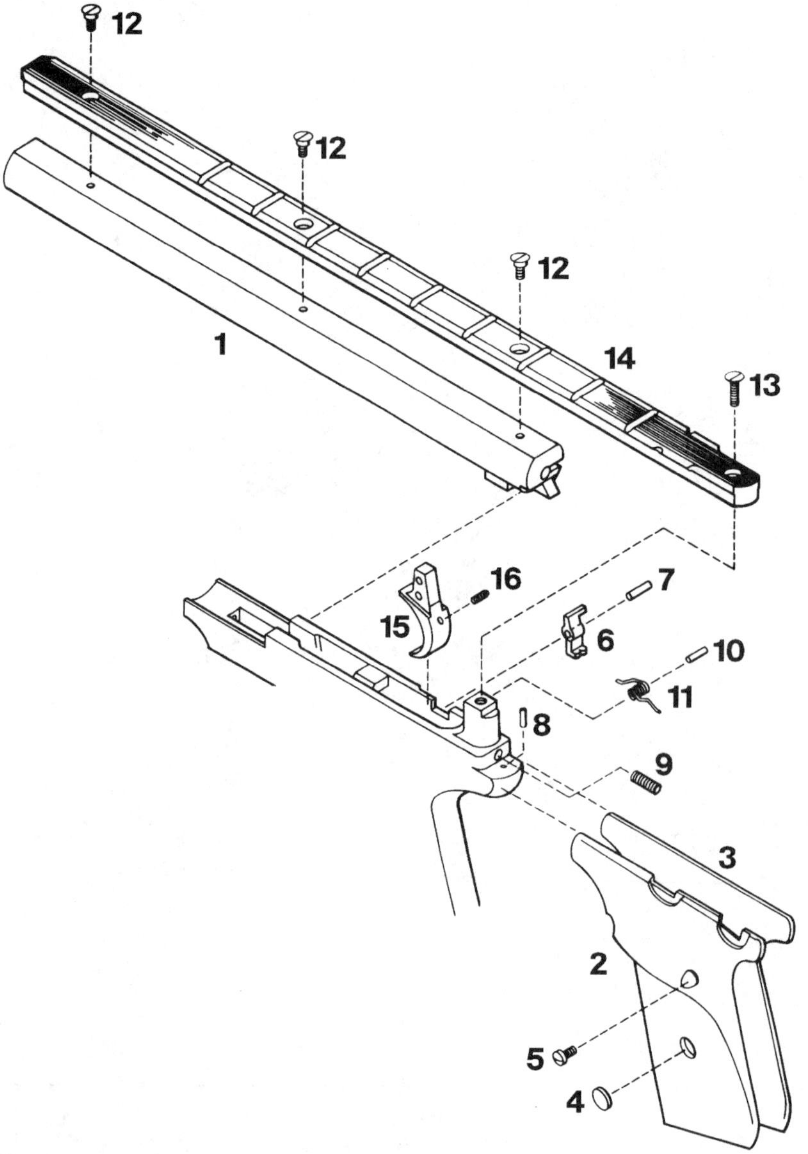

1	Barrel Assembly
2	Grip, Left
3	Grip, Right
4	Grip Medallion
5	Grip Screw
6	Sear
7	Sear Pin
8	Sear Screw Stop Pin
9	Sear Spring Adjusting Screw
10	Sear Spring Pin
11	Sear Spring
12	Sight Base Screw, Front
13	Sight Base Screw, Rear
14	Sight Base
15	Trigger, Adjustable
16	Trigger Limit Screw

Parts Not Shown
(See Challenger II and III)

Barrel Block
Barrel Mounting Screw
Disconnector Assembly
Disconnector Spring
Ejector
Extractor
Extractor Spring
Extractor Spring Plunger
Firing Pin
Firing Pin Retaining Pin
Forearm
Forearm Screw
Hammer
Hammer Link
Hammer Link Pin
Hammer Pin
Magazine Body
Magazine Button
Magazine Ejector
Magazine Ejector Spring
Magazine Follower
Magazine Latch
Magazine Latch Spring
Magazine Spring
Mainspring
Mainspring Plunger
Recoil Spring
Recoil Spring Guide
Recoil Spring Guide Rod
Safety Assembly with Thumb-Piece
Safety Click Plate
Stop Open Latch
Stop Open Latch Spring

Challenger II Auto

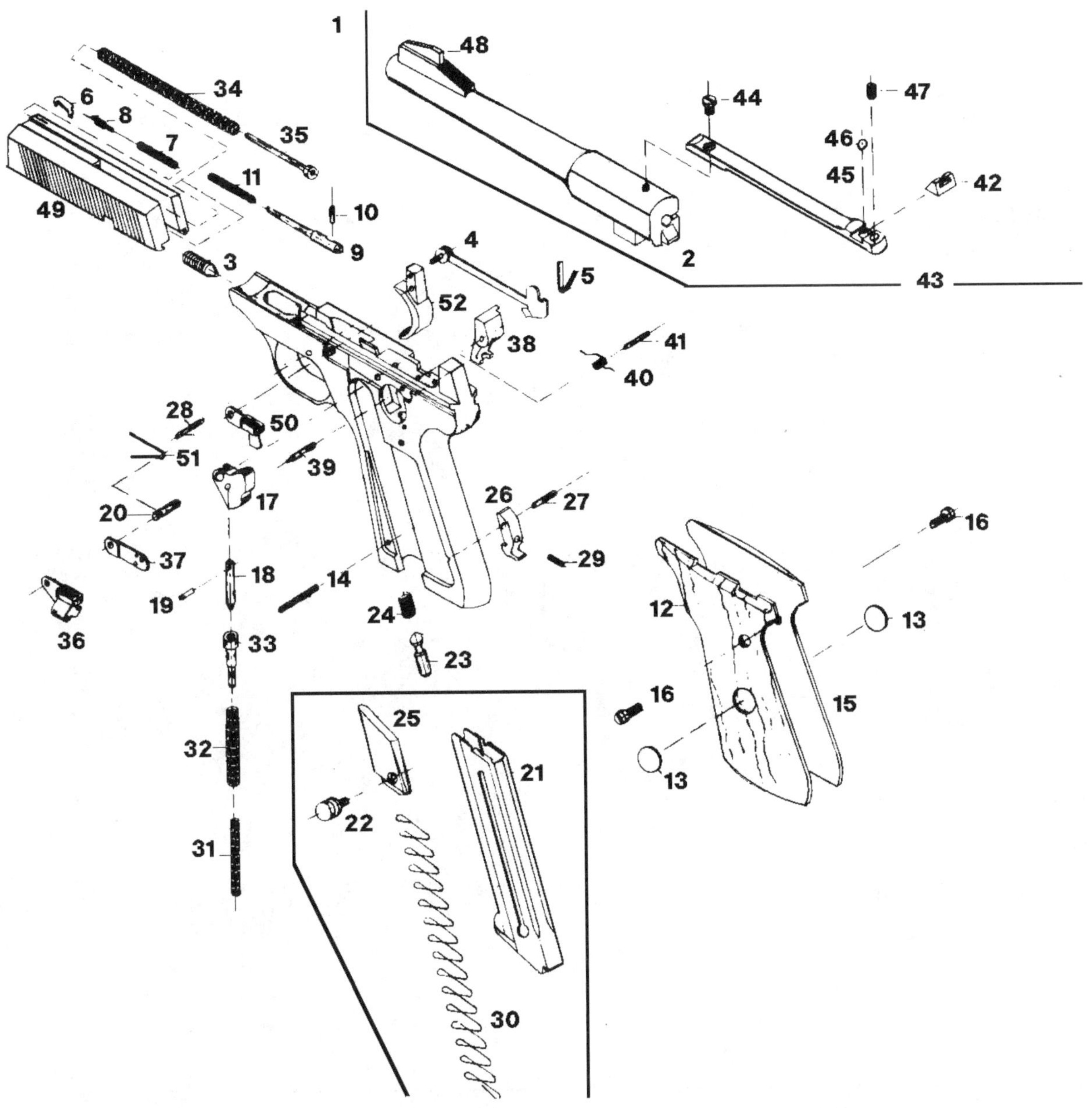

1	Barrel Assembly	**19**	Hammer Link Pin	**37**	Safety Click Plate
2	Barrel Block	**20**	Hammer Pin	**38**	Sear
3	Barrel Mounting Screw	**21**	Magazine Body	**39**	Sear Pin
4	Disconnector Assembly	**22**	Magazine Button	**40**	Sear Spring
5	Disconnector Spring	**23**	Magazine Ejector	**41**	Sear Spring Pin
6	Extractor	**24**	Magazine Ejector Spring	**42**	Sight Aperture, Rear
7	Extractor Spring	**25**	Magazine Follower	**43**	Sight Assembly, Rear
8	Extractor Spring Plunger	**26**	Magazine Latch	**44**	Sight Base Mounting Screw
9	Firing Pin	**27**	Magazine Latch Pin	**45**	Sight Base Rear
10	Firing Pin Retaining Pin	**28**	Trigger Pin	**46**	Sight Base Rear Spring
11	Firing Pin Spring	**29**	Magazine Latch Spring	**47**	Sight Elevation Screw, Rear
12	Grip, Left	**30**	Magazine Spring	**48**	Sight, Front
13	Grip Medallion	**31**	Mainspring, Inner	**49**	Slide
14	Grip Pin	**32**	Mainspring, Outer	**50**	Stop Open Latch Assembly with Thumb-Piece
15	Grip, Right	**33**	Mainspring Plunger	**51**	Stop Open Latch Spring
16	Grip Screw	**34**	Recoil Spring	**52**	Trigger
17	Hammer	**35**	Recoil Spring Guide		
18	Hammer Link	**36**	Safety Assembly with Thumb-Piece		

Challenger III Auto

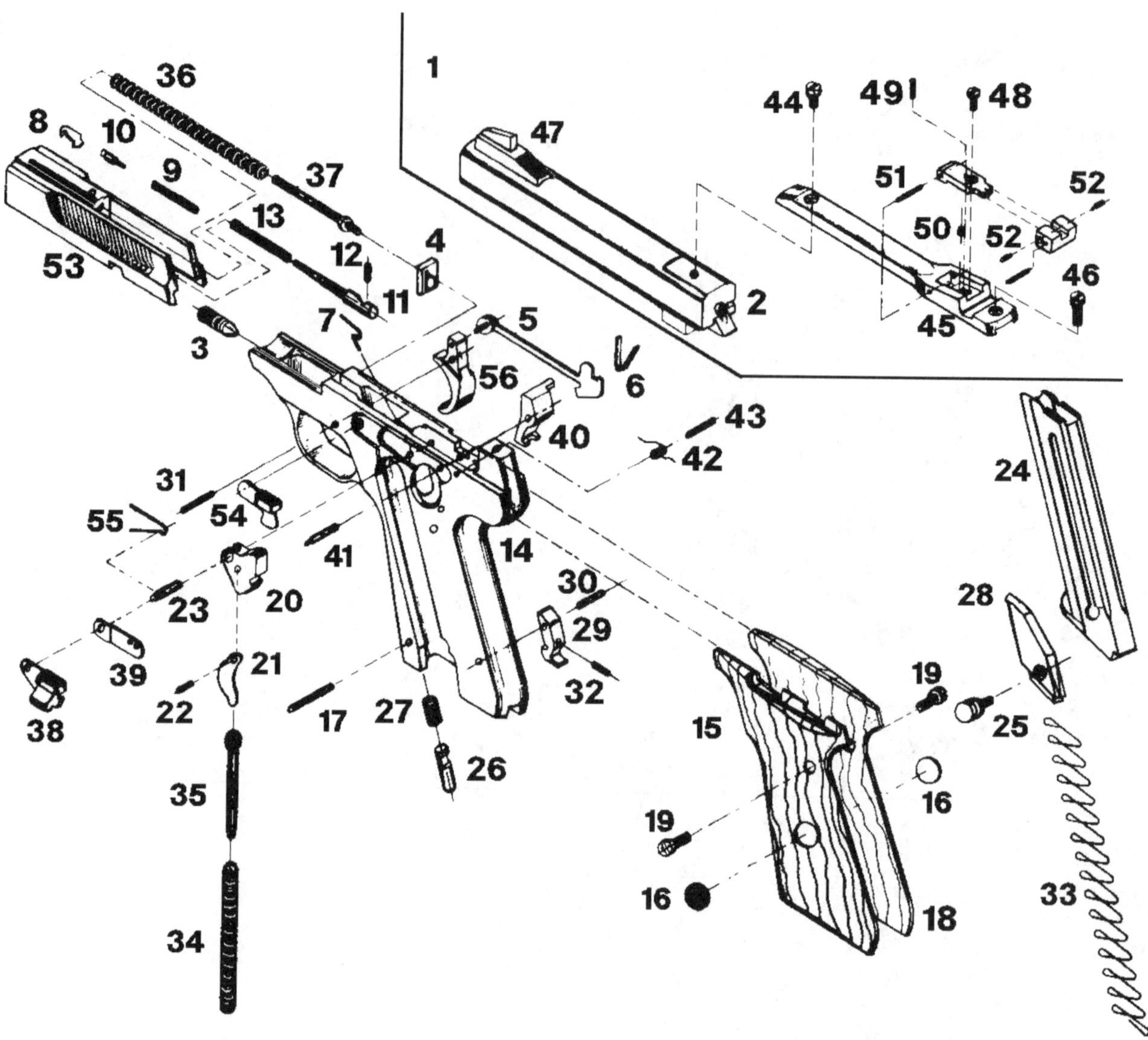

1	Barrel Assembly	20	Hammer	39	Safety Click Plate
2	Barrel Block	21	Hammer Link	40	Sear
3	Barrel Mounting Screw	22	Hammer Link Pin	41	Sear Pin
4	Buffer	23	Hammer Pin	42	Sear Spring
5	Disconnector Assembly	24	Magazine Body	43	Sear Spring Pin
6	Disconnector Spring	25	Magazine Button	44	Sight Base Rear, Front Screw
7	Ejector	26	Magazine Ejector	45	Sight Base Rear
8	Extractor	27	Magazine Ejector Spring	46	Sight Base Rear, Rear Screw
9	Extractor Spring	28	Magazine Follower	47	Sight, Front
10	Extractor Spring Plunger	29	Magazine Latch	48	Rear Sight Elevation Screw
11	Firing Pin	30	Magazine Latch Pin	49	Rear Sight Elevation Spring
12	Firing Pin Retaining Pin	31	Trigger Pin	50	Rear Sight Leaf/Friction Pin
13	Firing Pin Spring	32	Magazine Latch Spring	51	Rear Sight Pin
14	Frame	33	Magazine Spring	52	Rear Sight Windage Screw
15	Grip, Left	34	Mainspring	53	Slide
16	Grip Medallion	35	Mainspring Plunger	54	Stop Open Latch Assembly with Thumb-Piece
17	Grip Pin	36	Recoil Spring	55	Stop Open Latch Spring
18	Grip, Right	37	Recoil Spring Guide	56	Trigger
19	Grip Screw	38	Safety Assembly with Thumb-Piece		

9mm Hi-Power Auto

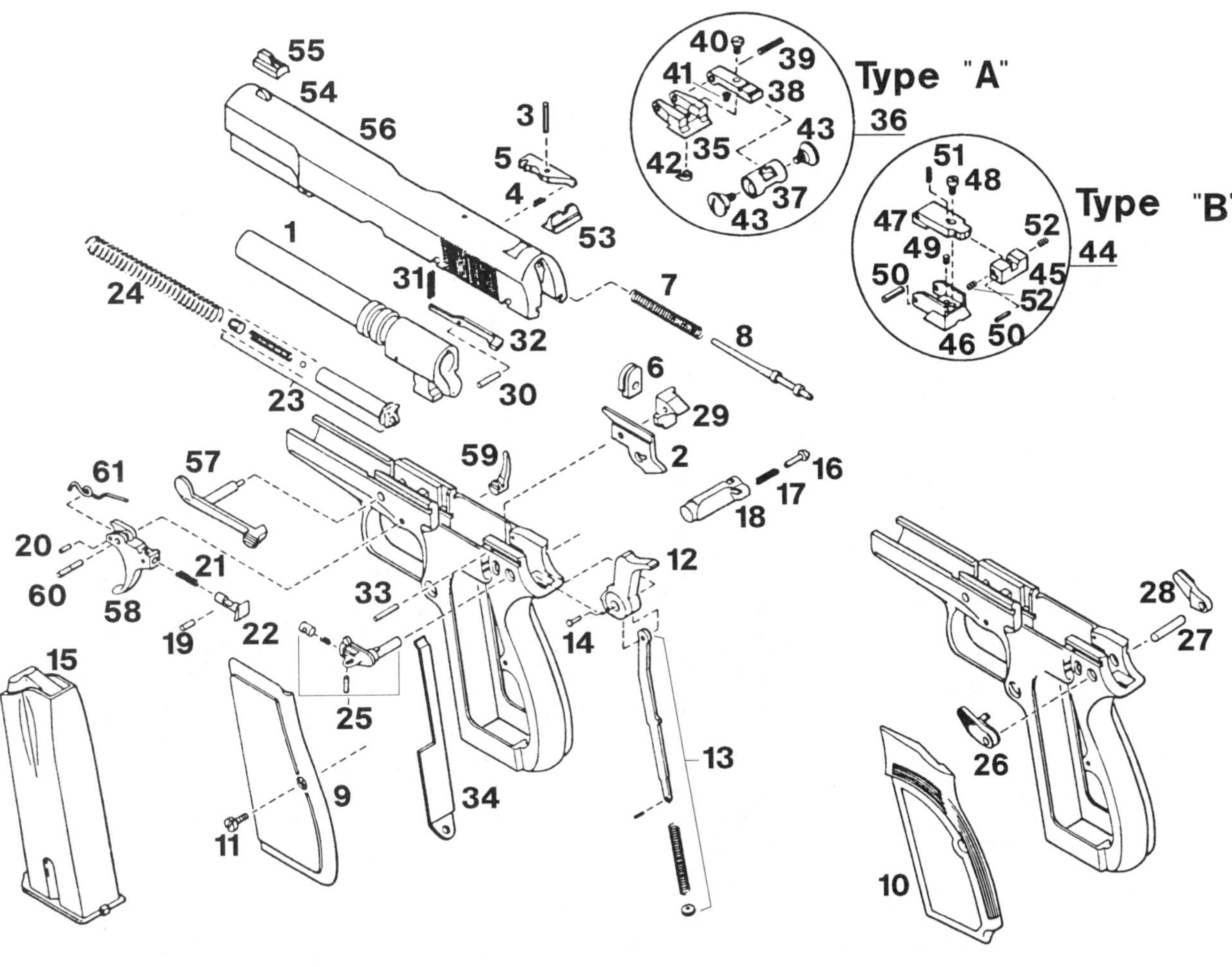

1	Barrel	23	Recoil Spring Guide Assembly with Slide Stop Retaining Ball, Spring and Cap	42	Sight Elevation Spring, Adjustable
2	Ejector	24	Recoil Spring	43	Sight Windage Screw Rear, Adjustable
3	Extractor Pin	25	Safety Assembly, Complete	44	Rear Sight, Complete
4	Extractor Spring	26	Safety-Lever, Left	45	Rear Sight Blade
5	Extractor	27	Safety-Lever Pin	46	Rear Sight Complete, Adjustable
6	Firing Pin Retaining Plate	28	Safety-Lever, Right	47	Rear Sight Leaf
7	Firing Pin Spring	29	Sear	48	Rear Sight Elevation Screw
8	Firing Pin	30	Sear Lever Pin	49	Rear Sight Elevation Spring
9	Grip, Left Black Plastic	31	Sear Lever Spring	50	Rear Sight Leaf/Friction Pin
10	Grip, Left Moulded Contour	32	Sear Lever	51	Rear Sight Detent Pin
11	Grip Screw	33	Sear Pin	52	Rear Sight Windage Screw
12	Hammer	34	Sear Spring with Button	53	Sight, Rear
13	Hammer Strut Assembly with Mainspring, Mainspring Support Pin and Nut	35	Rear Sight Base, Adjustable	54	Sight, Front
14	Hammer Strut Pin	36	Rear Sight Complete, Adjustable	55	Sight, Adjustable Front
15	Magazine	37	Sight Aperture Rear, Adjustable	56	Slide with Fixed Front Sight
16	Magazine Latch Spring Guide	38	Sight Aperture Housing Rear, Adjustable	57	Slide Stop
17	Magazine Latch Spring	39	Sight Aperture Housing Pin Rear, Adjustable	58	Trigger
18	Magazine Latch	40	Sight Elevation Screw Rear, Adjustable	59	Trigger Lever
19	Trigger Spring Pin	41	Sight Elevation Screw Spring Rear, Adjustable	60	Trigger Pin
20	Magazine Safety Pin			61	Trigger Spring
21	Magazine Safety Spring				
22	Magazine Safety				

Parts Not Shown

Grip, Right Black Plastic

Grip, Left Moulded Contour

Model 1900 Auto

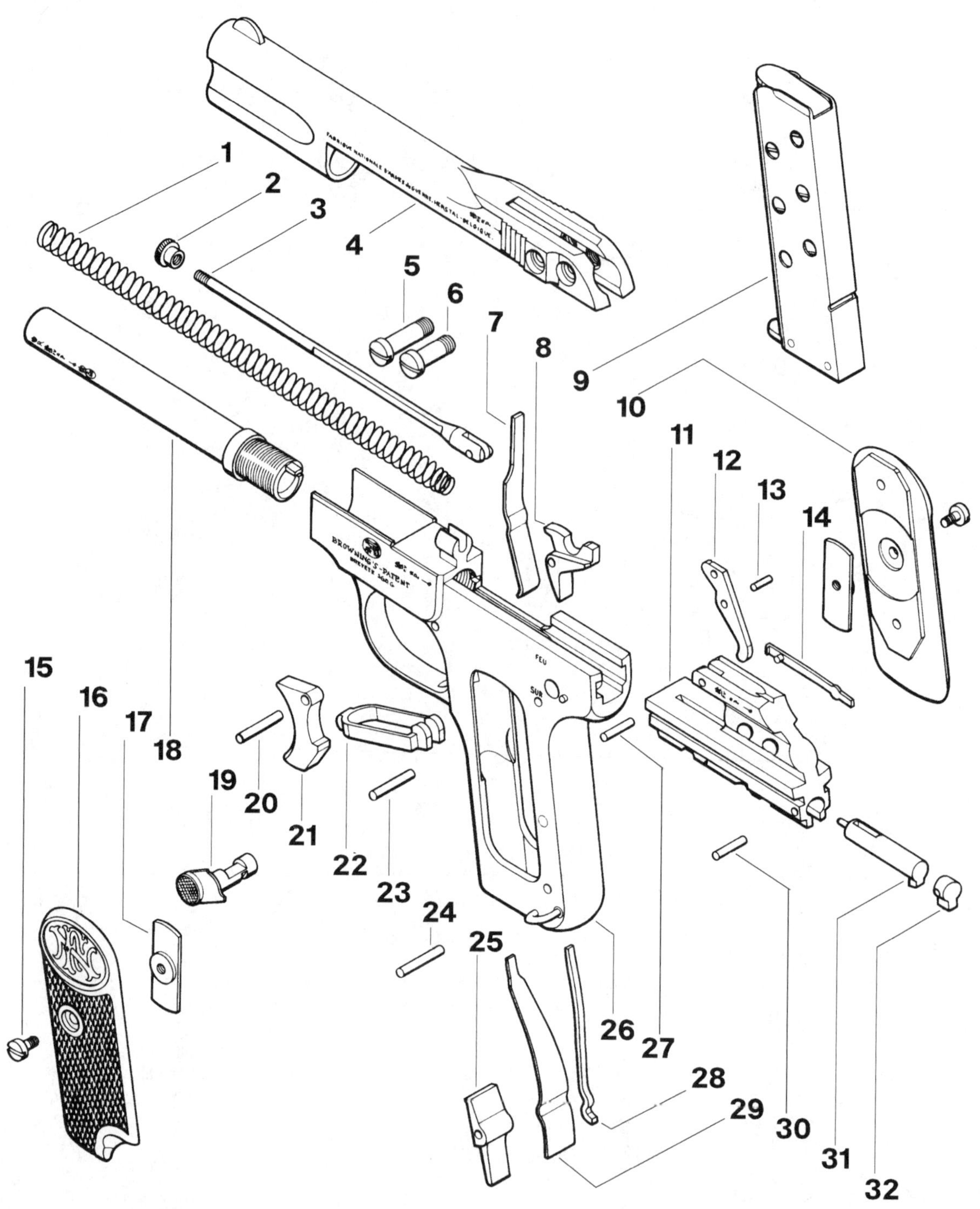

1	Recoil Spring
2	Recoil Spring Guide Nut
3	Recoil Spring Guide
4	Slide
5	Breechblock Screw (Long)
6	Breechblock Screw (Short)
7	Sear Spring
8	Sear
9	Magazine
10	Right Grip
11	Breechblock
12	Cocking Lever
13	Recoil Spring Guide Pin
14	Extractor
15	Grip Screw
16	Left Grip
17	Grip Retainer
18	Barrel
19	Safety
20	Trigger Pin
21	Trigger
22	Trigger Bar
23	Sear Pin
24	Magazine Catch Pin
25	Magazine Catch
26	Frame
27	Cocking Lever Pin
28	Safety Spring
29	Trigger Bar Spring
30	Breechblock Plug Pin
31	Firing Pin
32	Breechblock Plug

Model 1910 Auto

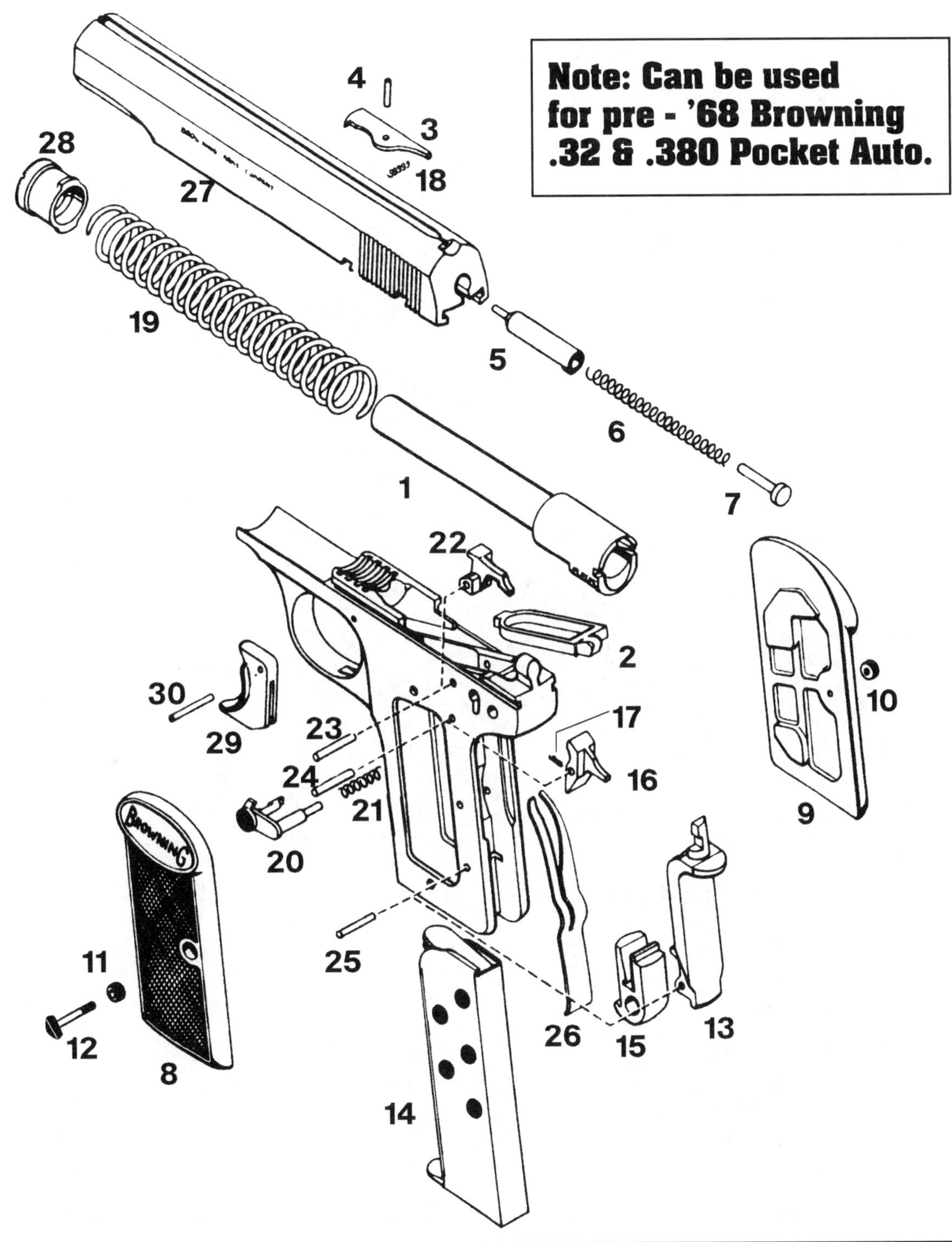

1	Barrel	**11**	Grip Escutcheon, Unthreaded	**21**	Safety Spring
2	Connector	**12**	Grip Plate Screw	**22**	Sear
3	Extractor	**13**	Grip Safety	**23**	Sear Pin
4	Extractor Pin	**14**	Magazine, Complete	**24**	Magazine Safety Pin
5	Firing Pin	**15**	Magazine Latch	**25**	Grip Safety Pin
6	Firing Pin Spring	**16**	Magazine Safety	**26**	Sear Spring
7	Firing Pin Spring Guide	**17**	Magazine Safety Spring	**27**	Slide
8	Grip Plate, Left	**18**	Extractor Spring	**28**	Slide Ring
9	Grip Plate, Right	**19**	Recoil Spring	**29**	Trigger
10	Grip Escutcheon, Threaded	**20**	Safety	**30**	Trigger Pin

Model 1922 Auto

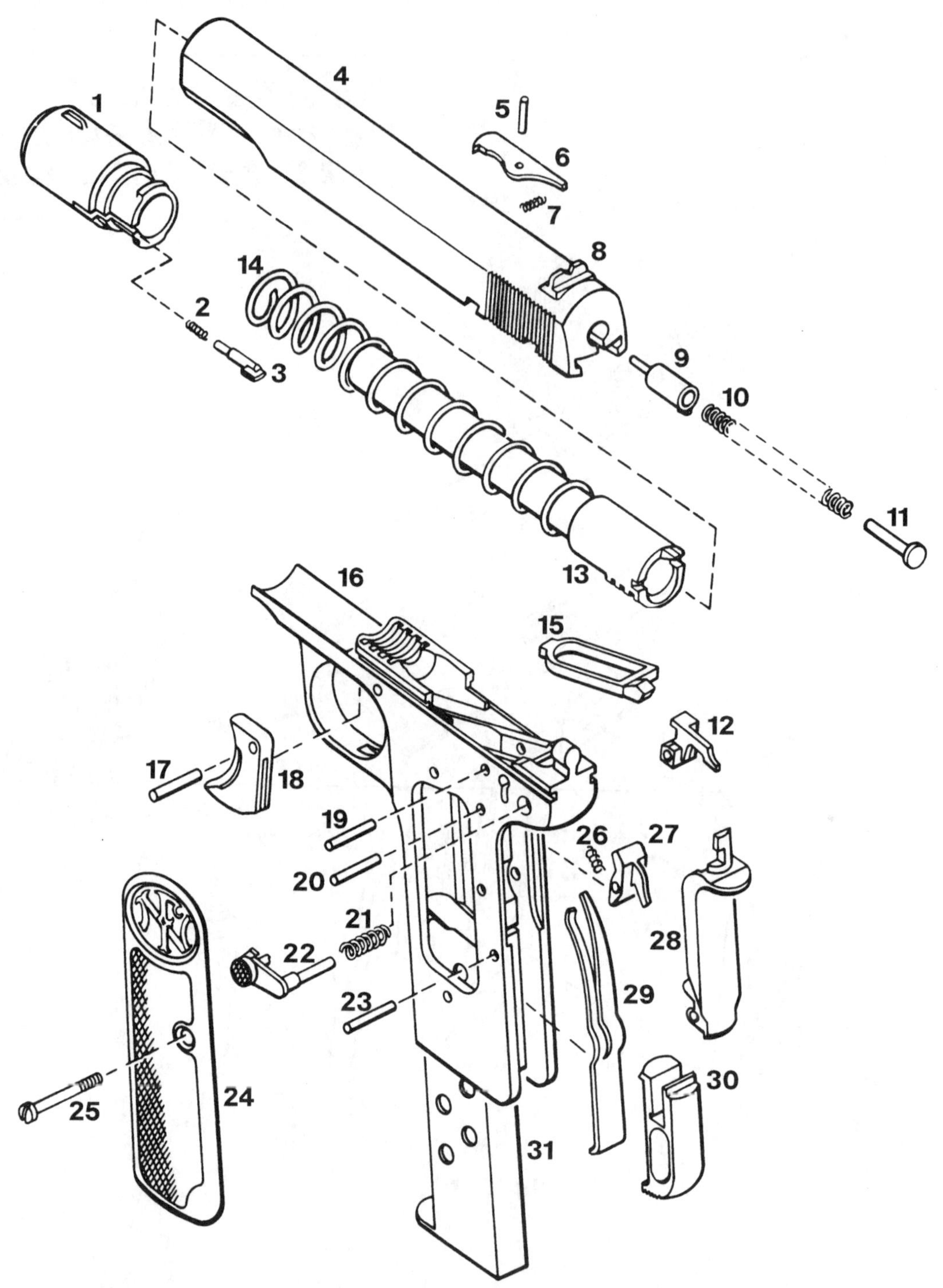

1	Slide Extension	**12**	Sear	**23**	Grip Safety Hinge Pin
2	Slide Extension Spring	**13**	Barrel	**24**	Left Grip Panel
3	Slide Extension Catch	**14**	Recoil Spring	**25**	Grip Screw
4	Slide	**15**	Trigger Bar	**26**	Magazine Safety Spring
5	Extractor Pin	**16**	Frame	**27**	Magazine Safety
6	Extractor	**17**	Trigger Pin	**28**	Grip Safety
7	Extractor Spring	**18**	Trigger	**29**	Mainspring
8	Rear Sight	**19**	Sear Pin	**30**	Magazine Catch
9	Firing Pin	**20**	Magazine Safety Pin	**31**	Magazine
10	Firing Pin Spring	**21**	Safety Catch Spring		
11	Spring Follower	**22**	Safety Catch		

Model 1935 Hi-Power Auto

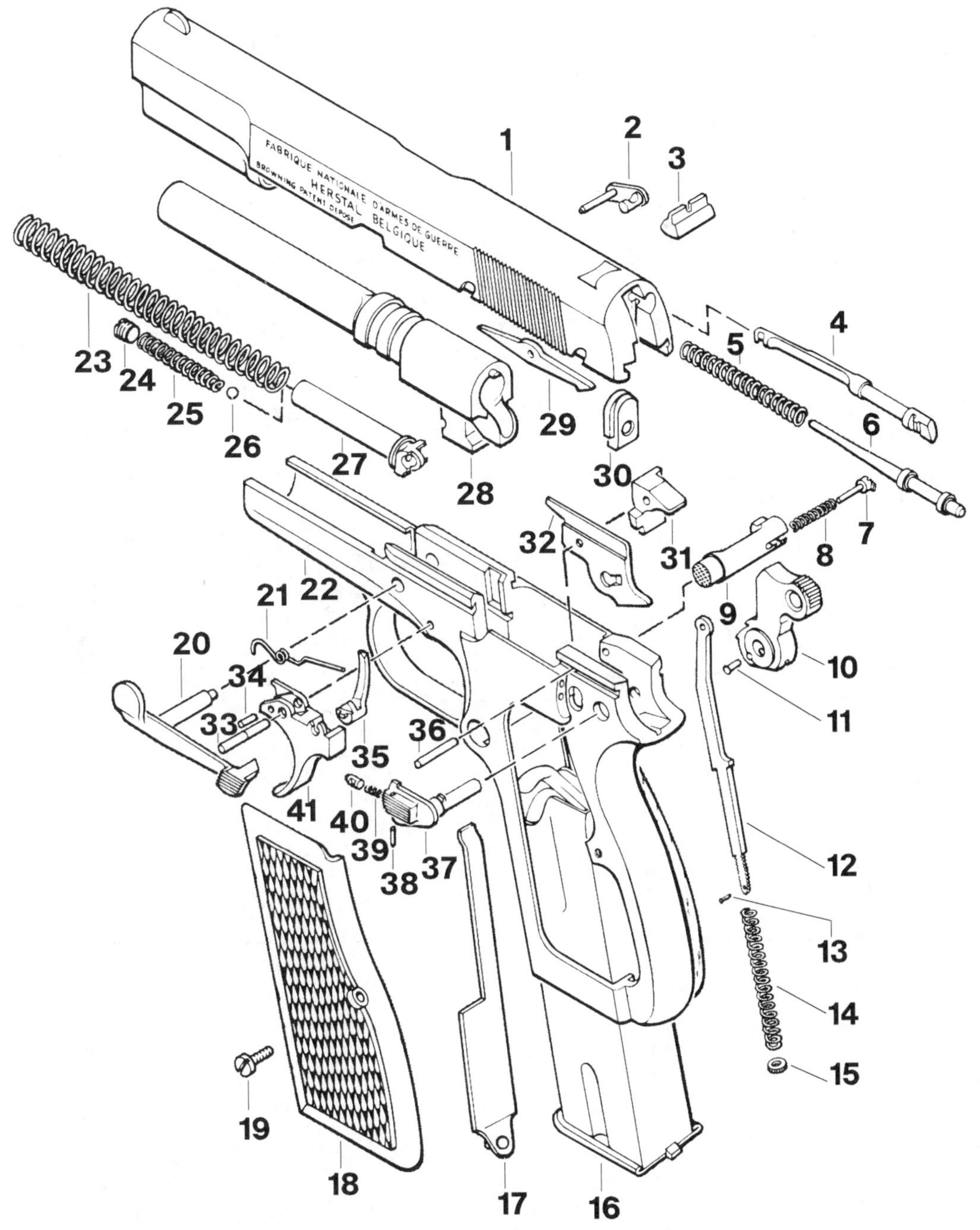

1	Slide	15	Hammer Spring Support	29	Sear Lever
2	Sear Lever Retainer	16	Magazine	30	Firing Pin Retainer Plate
3	Rear Sight	17	Sear Spring	31	Sear
4	Extractor	18	Left-Hand Grip	32	Ejector
5	Firing Pin Spring	19	Grip Screw	33	Trigger Pin
6	Firing Pin	20	Slide Stop	34	Trigger Spring Pin
7	Magazine Catch Spring Guide	21	Trigger Spring	35	Trigger Lever
8	Magazine Catch Spring	22	Frame (Receiver)	36	Sear Pin
9	Magazine Catch	23	Recoil Spring	37	Safety Catch
10	Hammer	24	Spring Retainer	38	Stud Retainer Pin
11	Hammer Pin	25	Detent Ball Spring	39	Stud Spring
12	Hammer Strut	26	Detent Ball	40	Stud
13	Hammer Strut Pin	27	Recoil Spring Guide	41	Trigger
14	Hammer Spring	28	Barrel		

Nomad, Challenger and Medalist Auto

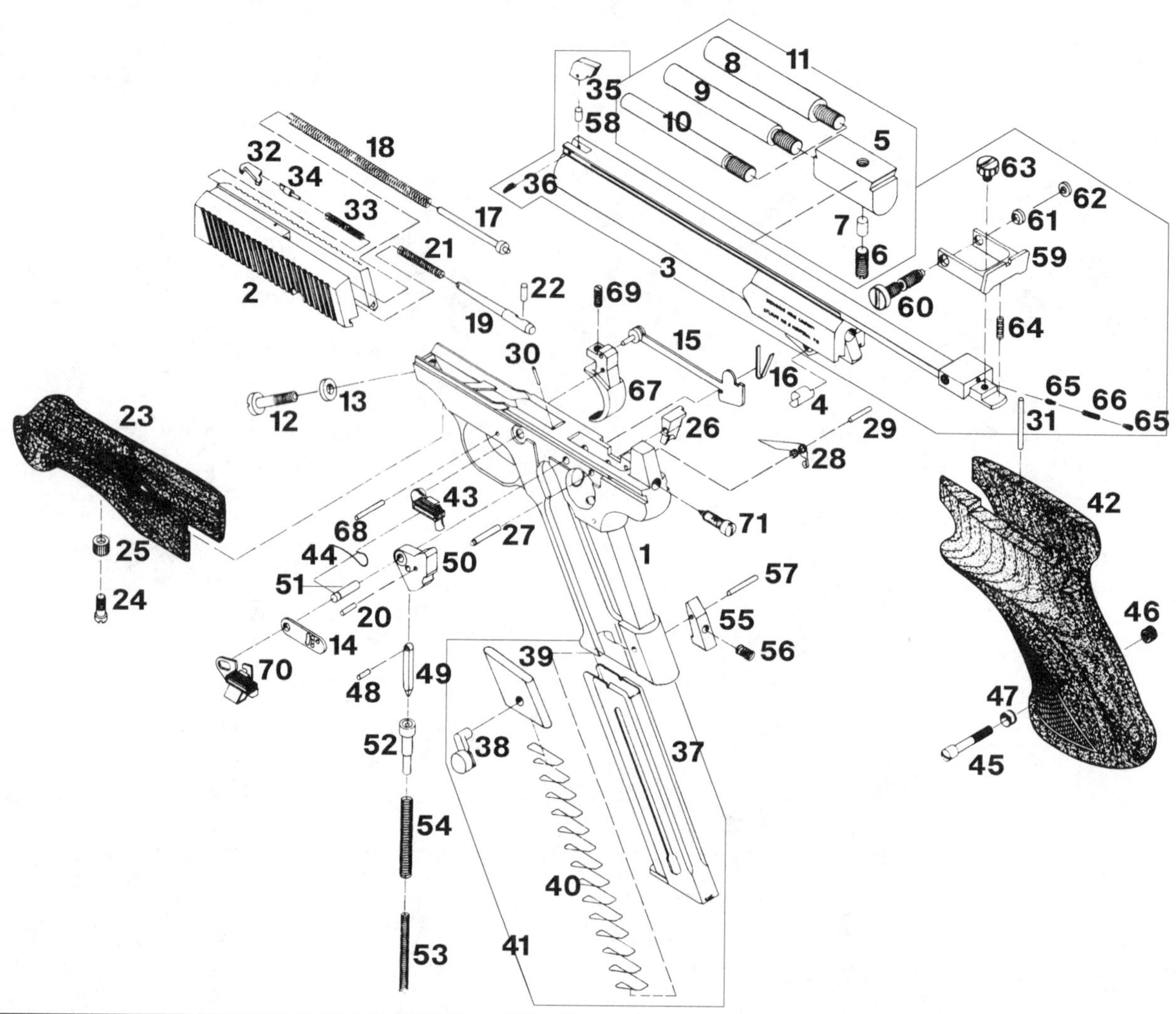

1	Frame
2	Slide
3	Barrel with Ventilated Rib
4	Barrel Guide Pin
5	Counterweight Support
6	Counterweight Support Screw
7	Counterweight Support Bushing
8	Counterweight 2.52 oz.
9	Counterweight 1.79 oz.
10	Counterweight .94 oz.
11	Counterweight Support and Weights
12	Barrel Mounting Screw
13	Barrel Mounting Screw Washer
14	Click Plate
15	Disconnector
16	Disconnector Spring
17	Recoil Spring Guide
18	Recoil Spring
19	Firing Pin
20	Fire Pin For Dry Firing
21	Firing Pin Spring
22	Firing Pin Retaining Pin
23	Forend
24	Forend Screw
25	Forend Screw Escutcheon
26	Sear
27	Sear Pin
28	Sear Spring
29	Sear Spring Pin
30	Ejector
31	Ejector Deflection Pin
32	Extractor
33	Extractor Spring
34	Extractor Plunger
35	Sight Blade, Front
36	Sight Blade Retaining Pin, Front
37	Magazine
38	Magazine Button
39	Magazine Follower
40	Magazine Spring
41	Magazine Complete
42	Grip, Right-Hand
43	Stop Open Latch
44	Stop Open Latch Spring
45	Grip Screw
46	Grip Escutcheon, Threaded
47	Grip Escutcheon, Unthreaded
48	Hammer Link Pin
49	Hammer Link
50	Hammer
51	Hammer Pin
52	Mainspring Plunger
53	Mainspring, Inner
54	Mainspring, Outer
55	Magazine Latch
56	Magazine Latch Spring
57	Magazine Latch Pin
58	Ventilated Rib Retaining Pin
59	Sight Aperture, Rear
60	Sight Windage Screw, Rear
61	Sight Windage Bushing, Rear
62	Sight Windage Washer, Rear
63	Sight Elevation Screw, Rear
64	Sight Elevation Spring
65	Sight Adjusting Screw Follower, Windage or Elevation
66	Sight Adjusting Screw Follower Spring, Windage and Elevation
67	Trigger
68	Trigger Pin
69	Trigger Backlash Adjustment Screw
70	Safety
71	Trigger Pull Adjustment Screw

Swedish Model 1907

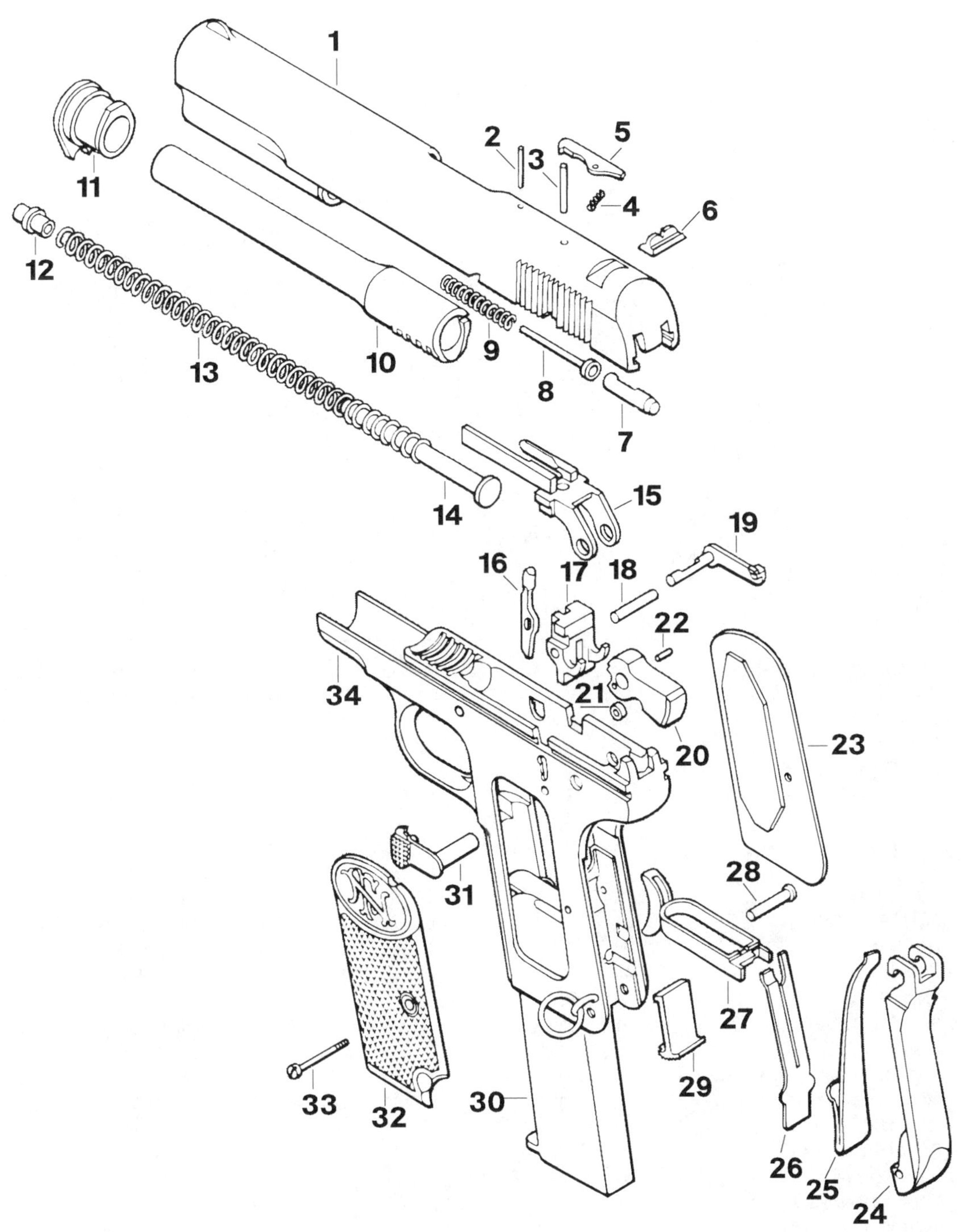

1	Slide	13	Recoil Spring	25	Hammer Spring
2	Extractor Pin	14	Recoil Spring Guide	26	Sear Spring
3	Firing Pin Retainer Pin	15	Ejector and Cartridge Guide	27	Trigger
4	Extractor Spring	16	Disconnector	28	Grip Safety Pin
5	Extractor	17	Sear	29	Magazine Catch
6	Rear Sight	18	Sear Pin	30	Magazine
7	Firing Pin Extension	19	Slide Stop	31	Safety
8	Firing Pin	20	Hammer	32	Left Grip
9	Firing Pin Spring	21	Hammer Roll	33	Grip Screw
10	Barrel	22	Roll Axis Pin	34	Receiver
11	Barrel Bushing	23	Right Grip		
12	Bushing Stop	24	Grip Safety		

Model 100 Auto

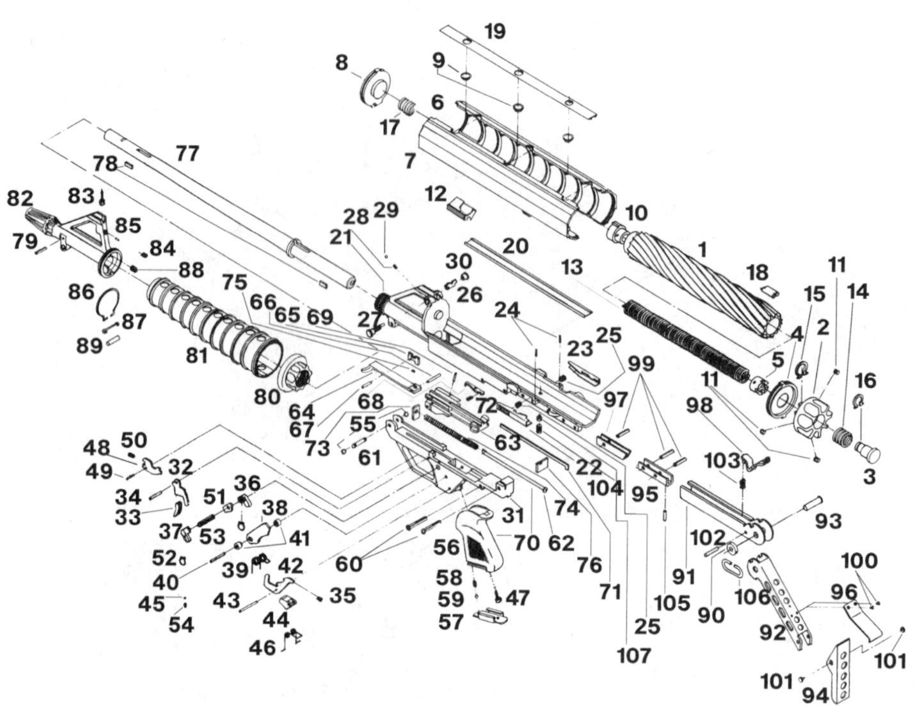

1	Fluted Cartridge Carrier
2	Rear End Cap
3	Spring Release Button
4	Clutch Plate
5	Drive Spring Retainer
6	Magazine Outer Shell, Right
7	Magazine Outer Shell, Left
8	Front End Cap
9	Magazine Lens
10	Splined Driver
11	Clutch Roller Bearing
12	Feed Lips
13	Drive Spring
14	Clutch Spring
15	Snap Ring, Large
16	Snap Ring, Small
17	Magazine Compression Spring
18	Magazine Follower
19	Ribbon Clamp, Upper
20	Ribbon Clamp, Lower
21	Upper Receiver
22	Magazine Catch, Left
23	Magazine Catch, Right
24	Magazine Catch Pins
25	Magazine Catch Spring
26	Rear Sight Blade
27	Rear Sight Screw
28	Rear Sight Spring
29	Rear Sight Ball
30	Rear Sight Bushing
31	Lower Receiver
32	Trigger
33	Trigger Pad
34	Trigger Pin
35	Trigger Spring
36	Safety-Lever, Right
37	Safety-Lever, Left
38	Hammer
39	Hammer Spring
40	Hammer Pin
41	Hammer Bushing
42	Sear
43	Sear Pivot Pin
44	Disconnector
45	Safety Ball
46	Disconnector Spring
47	Pistol Grip Mounting Screw
48	Bolt Catch
49	Bolt Catch Pin
50	Bolt Catch Spring
51	Safety
52	Safety C-Ring
53	Safety Shaft
54	Safety Spring
55	C-Rings
56	Pistol Grip
57	Pistol Grip Cover
58	Pistol Grip Cover Spring
59	Pistol Grip Cover Ball
60	Takedown Pins
61	Hinge Pin
62	Return Spring Washer
63	Bolt
64	Bolt Handle
65	Firing Pin
66	Bolt Handle Pin
67	Firing Pin Stop Pin
68	Extractor
69	Extractor Pin
70	Return Spring Rod
71	Ejector
72	Extractor Spring
73	Return Spring Retainer
74	Return Spring Bolt
75	Firing Pin Spring
76	Buffer
77	Barrel
78	Barrel Key
79	Barrel Cross Pin
80	Barrel Nut
81	Barrel Shroud
82	Front Sight
83	Front Sight Post
84	Front Sight Post Spring
85	Front Sight Post Pin
86	Sling Ring
87	Sling Ring Clasp
88	Barrel Shroud Spring
89	Sling Sleeve
90	Pivot Pin Washer
91	Sliding Arm
92	Pivoting Arm
93	Pivot Pin
94	Buttplate
95	Sliding Arm Lock
96	Leaf Spring
97	Sliding Arm Track
98	Buttstock Release Lever
99	Sliding Arm Lock and Track Pins
100	Leaf Spring Rivets
101	Knurled Hinge Pins
102	Release Lever Roll Pin
103	Release Lever Spring
104	Sliding Arm Lock Spring
105	Stop Dowell
106	Stock Ring
107	Magazine Ejector Button

Bulldog 44 Special Revolver

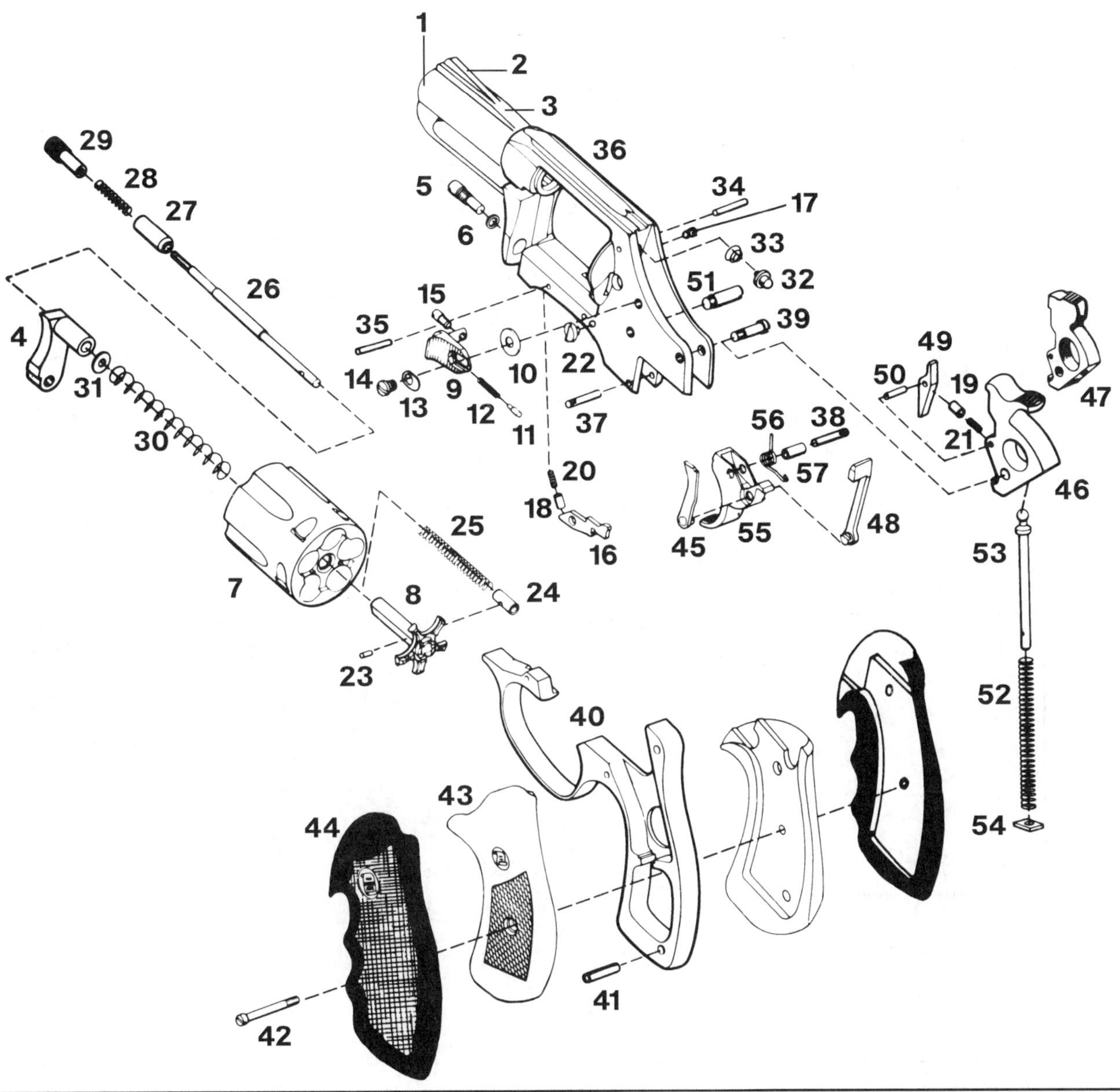

1	Barrel	20	Cylinder Plunger Spring	39	Frame Assembly Screw
2	Front Sight	21	Hammer Plunger Spring	40	Grip Frame and Trigger Guard
3	Shroud	22	Cylinder Stud	41	Grip Locating Pin
4	Crane	23	Ejector Rod Assembly Pin	42	Grip Screw
5	Crane Screw	24	Ejector Rod Bushing	43	Grips, Bulldog Style
6	Crane Screw Washer	25	Ejector Rod Lock Spring	44	Grips, Neoprene
7	Cylinder	26	Ejector Rod	45	Hand
8	Ejector	27	Ejector Rod Collar	46	Hammer
9	Cylinder Latch	28	Ejector Rod Collar Spring	47	Hammer Spurless
10	Cylinder Latch Washer	29	Ejector Rod Head	48	Hammer Block
11	Cylinder Latch Plunger	30	Ejector Rod Return Spring	49	Hammer Pawl
12	Cylinder Latch Plunger Spring	31	Ejector Rod Washer	50	Hammer Pawl Pin
13	Cylinder Latch Cover Plate	32	Firing Pin	51	Hammer Screw
14	Cylinder Latch Retaining Screw	33	Firing Pin Spring	52	Mainspring
15	Cylinder Latch Release Screw	34	Firing Pin Retaining Pin	53	Mainspring Guide Rod
16	Cylinder Stop	35	Cylinder Retaining Pin	54	Mainspring Seat
17	Cylinder Stop Bushing	36	Frame Assembly	55	Trigger
18	Cylinder Plunger	37	Frame Assembly Pin	56	Trigger Spring
19	Hammer Plunger	38	Trigger Pin	57	Trigger Spring Bushing

Bulldog Tracker Revolver

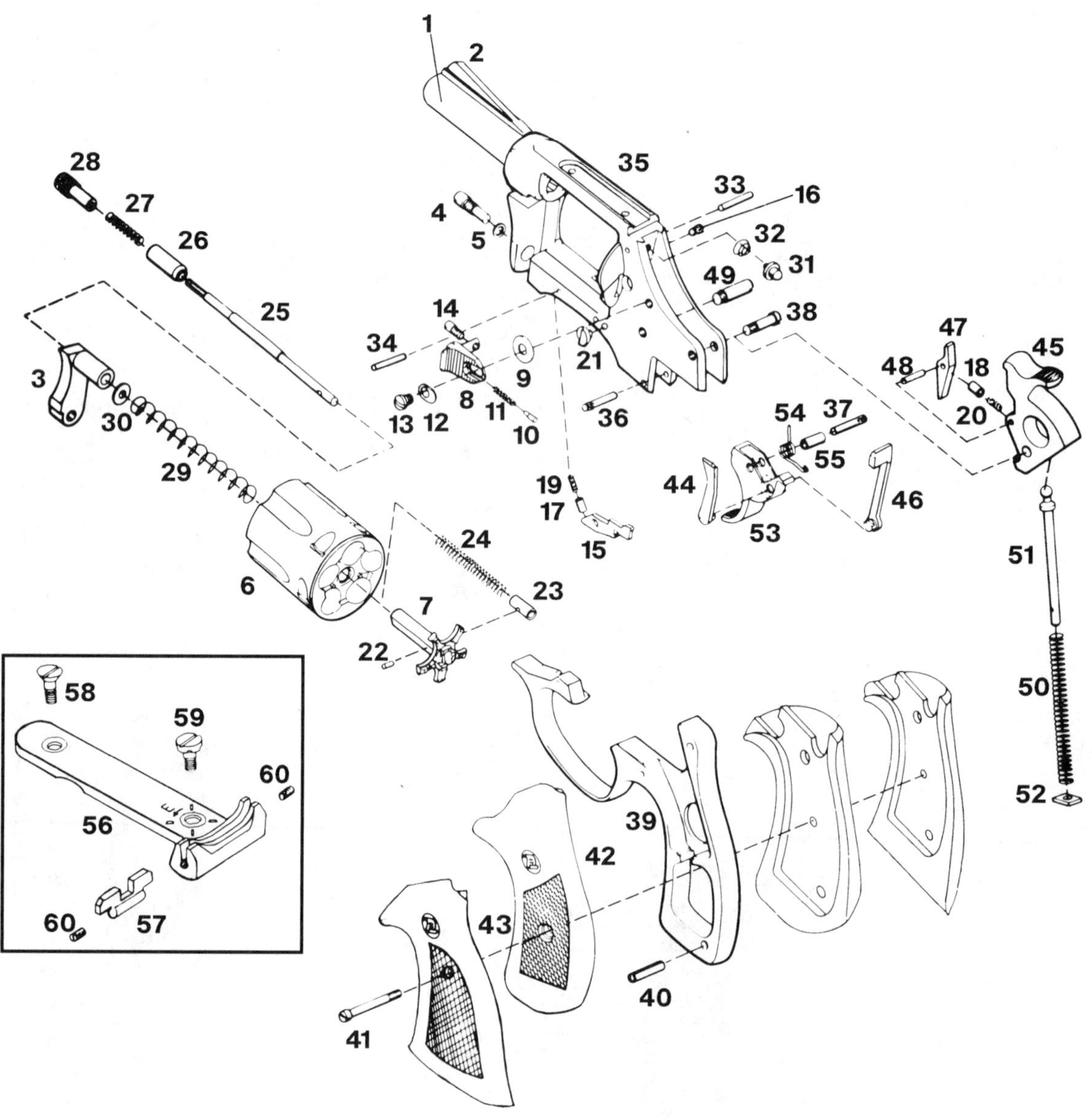

1	Barrel	**21**	Cylinder Stud	**41**	Grip Screw
2	Front Sight	**22**	Ejector Rod Assembly Pin	**42**	Grips, Bulldog Style
3	Crane	**23**	Ejector Rod Bushing	**43**	Grips, Square Butt
4	Crane Screw	**24**	Ejector Rod Lock Spring	**44**	Hand
5	Crane Screw Washer	**25**	Ejector Rod	**45**	Hammer
6	Cylinder	**26**	Ejector Rod Collar	**46**	Hammer Block
7	Ejector	**27**	Ejector Rod Collar Spring	**47**	Hammer Pawl
8	Cylinder Latch	**28**	Ejector Rod Head	**48**	Hammer Pawl Pin
9	Cylinder Latch Washer	**29**	Ejector Rod Return Spring	**49**	Hammer Screw
10	Cylinder Latch Plunger	**30**	Ejector Rod Washer	**50**	Mainspring
11	Cylinder Latch Plunger Spring	**31**	Firing Pin	**51**	Mainspring Guide Rod
12	Cylinder Latch Cover Plate	**32**	Firing Pin Spring	**52**	Mainspring Seat
13	Cylinder Latch Retaining Screw	**33**	Firing Pin Retaining Pin	**53**	Trigger
14	Cylinder Latch Release Screw	**34**	Cylinder Retaining Pin	**54**	Trigger Spring
15	Cylinder Stop	**35**	Frame Assembly	**55**	Trigger Spring Bushing
16	Cylinder Stop Bushing	**36**	Frame Assembly Pin	**56**	Rear Sight Body
17	Cylinder Plunger	**37**	Trigger Pin	**57**	Rear Sight Blade
18	Hammer Plunger	**38**	Frame Assembly Screw	**58**	Rear Sight Retaining Screw
19	Cylinder Plunger Spring	**39**	Grip Frame and Trigger Guard	**59**	Rear Sight Elevation Screw
20	Hammer Plunger Spring	**40**	Grip Locating Pin	**60**	Rear Sight Windage Screws

Off-Duty Revolver

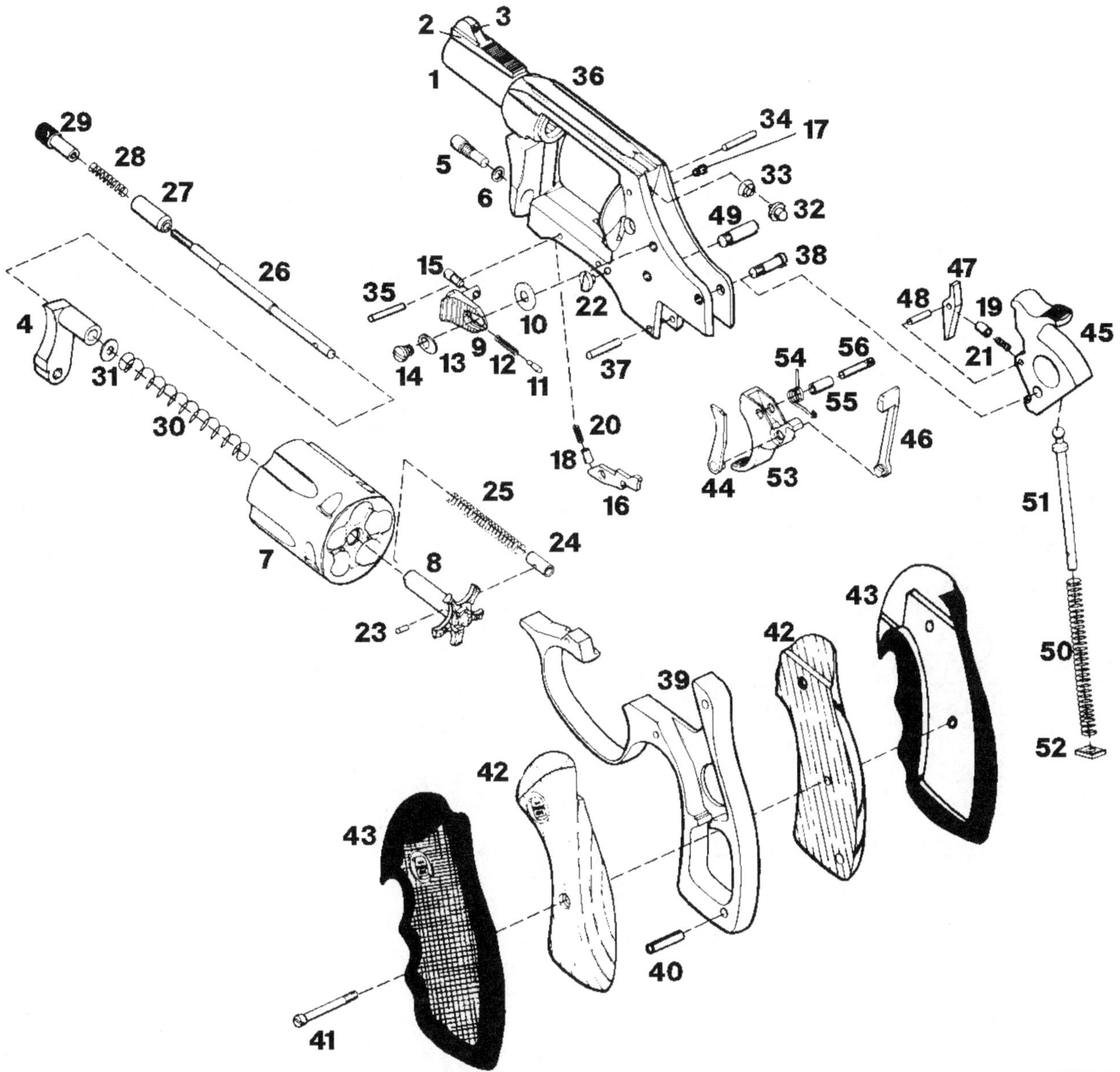

1	Barrel Assembly	20	Cylinder Plunger Spring	39	Grip Frame and Trigger Guard
2	Front Sight	21	Hammer Plunger Spring	40	Grip Locating Pin
3	Sight Insert	22	Cylinder Stop Stud	41	Grip Screw
4	Crane	23	Ejector Rod Assembly Pin	42	Grips, Plain Panel
5	Crane Screw	24	Ejector Rod Bushing	43	Grips, Neoprene
6	Crane Screw Washer	25	Ejector Rod Lock Spring	44	Hand
7	Cylinder	26	Ejector Rod	45	Hammer
8	Ejector	27	Ejector Rod Collar	46	Hammer Block
9	Cylinder Latch	28	Ejector Rod Collar Spring	47	Hammer Pawl
10	Cylinder Latch Washer	29	Ejector Rod Head	48	Hammer Pawl Pin
11	Cylinder Latch Plunger	30	Ejector Rod Return Spring	49	Hammer Screw
12	Cylinder Latch Plunger Spring	31	Ejector Rod Washer	50	Mainspring
13	Cylinder Latch Cover Plate	32	Firing Pin	51	Mainspring Guide Rod
14	Cylinder Latch Retaining Screw	33	Firing Pin Spring	52	Mainspring Seat
15	Cylinder Latch Release Screw	34	Firing Pin Retaining Pin	53	Trigger
16	Cylinder Stop	35	Cylinder Retaining Pin	54	Trigger Spring
17	Cylinder Stop Bushing	36	Frame Assembly	55	Trigger Spring Bushing
18	Cylinder Plunger	37	Frame Assembly Pin	56	Trigger Pin
19	Hammer Plunger	38	Frame Assembly Screw		

Pathfinder Revolver

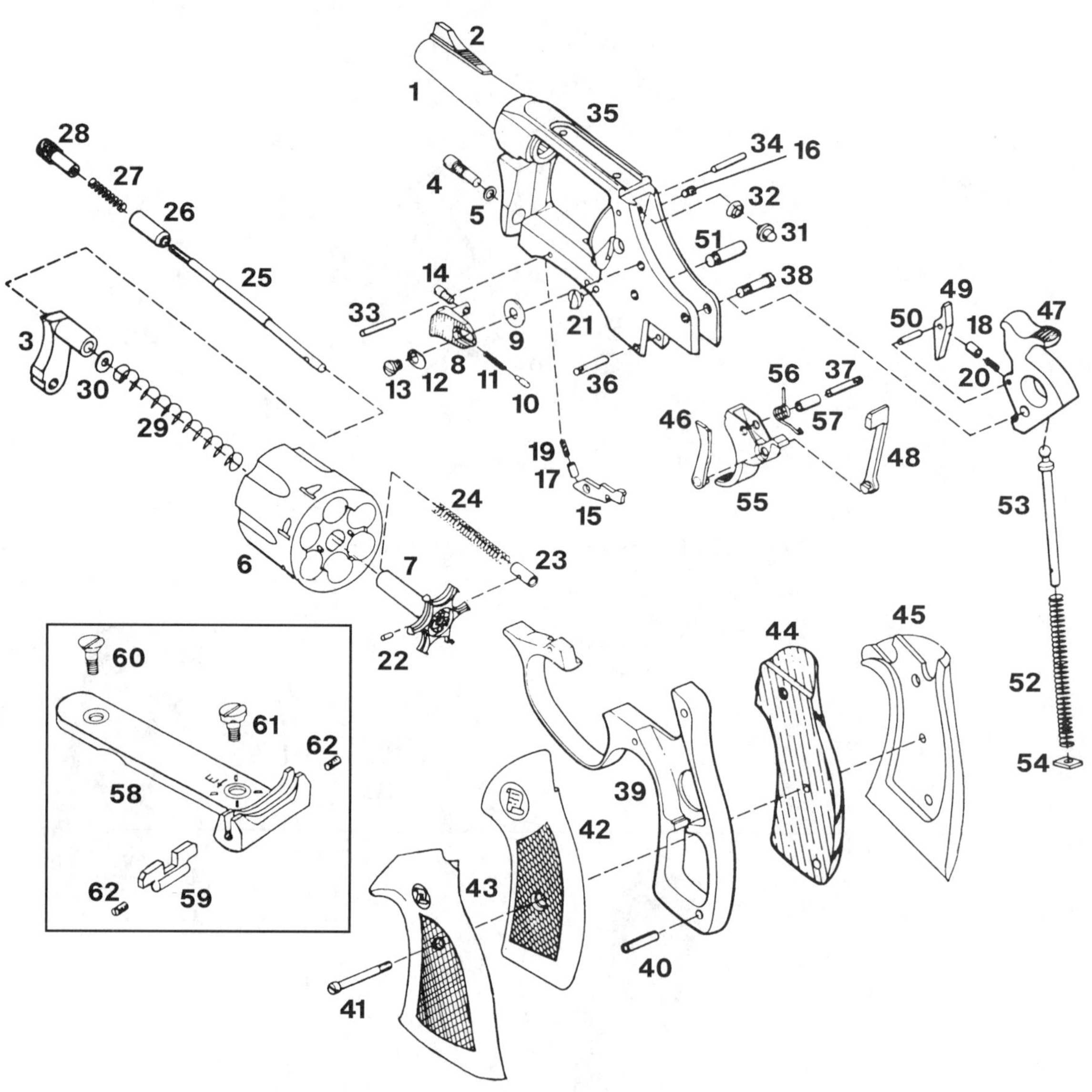

1	Barrel
2	Front Sight
3	Crane
4	Crane Screw
5	Crane Screw Washer
6	Cylinder
7	Ejector
8	Cylinder Latch
9	Cylinder Latch Washer
10	Cylinder Latch Plunger
11	Cylinder Latch Plunger Spring
12	Cylinder Latch Cover Plate
13	Cylinder Latch Retaining Screw
14	Cylinder Latch Release Screw
15	Cylinder Stop
16	Cylinder Stop Bushing
17	Cylinder Plunger
18	Hammer Plunger
19	Cylinder Plunger Spring
20	Hammer Plunger Spring
21	Cylinder Stud
22	Ejector Rod Assembly Pin
23	Ejector Rod Bushing
24	Ejector Rod Lock Spring
25	Ejector Rod
26	Ejector Rod Collar
27	Ejector Rod Collar Spring
28	Ejector Rod Head
29	Ejector Rod Return Spring
30	Ejector Rod Washer
31	Firing Pin
32	Firing Pin Spring
33	Cylinder Retaining Pin
34	Firing Pin Retaining Pin
35	Frame
36	Frame Assembly Pin
37	Trigger Pin
38	Frame Assembly Screw
39	Grip Frame/Trigger Guard
40	Grip Locating Pin
41	Grip Screw
42	Left Grip, Round Butt
43	Left Grip, Square Butt
44	Right Grip, Round Butt
45	Right Grip, Square Butt
46	Hand
47	Hammer
48	Hammer Block
49	Hammer Pawl
50	Hammer Pawl Pin
51	Hammer Screw
52	Hammer Spring
53	Hammer Spring Strut
54	Hammer Spring Seat
55	Trigger
56	Trigger Spring
57	Trigger Spring Bushing
58	Rear Sight Base
59	Rear Sight Blade
60	Rear Sight Retaining Screw
61	Rear Sight Elevation Screw
62	Rear Sight Windage Screws

Police Bulldog and Police Undercover Revolver

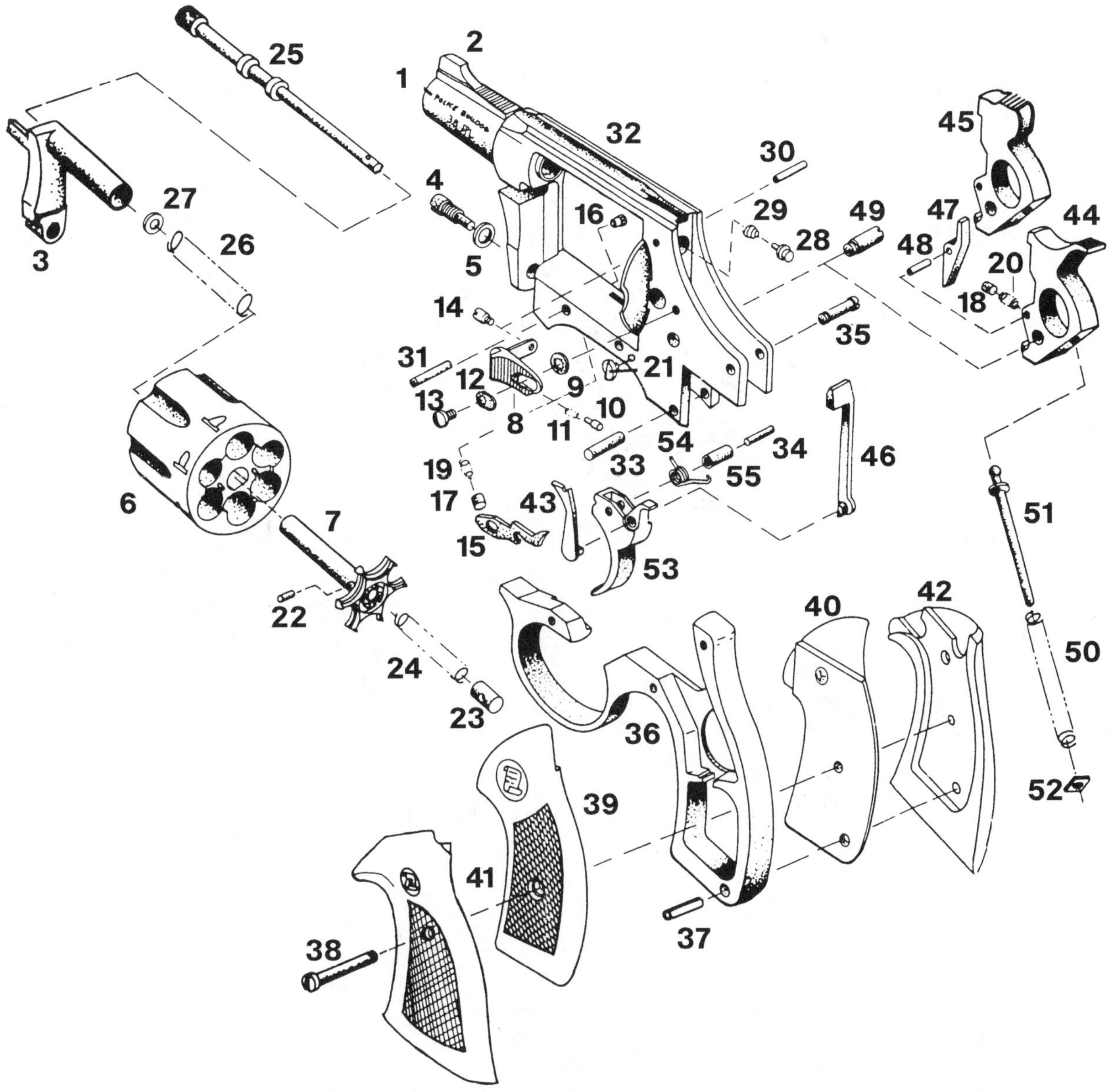

1	Barrel	**20**	Hammer Plunger Spring	**39**	Left Grip, Round Butt
2	Front Sight	**21**	Cylinder Stop Stud	**40**	Right Grip, Round Butt
3	Crane	**22**	Ejector Rod Assembly Pin	**41**	Left Grip, Square Butt
4	Crane Screw	**23**	Ejector Rod Bushing	**42**	Right Grip, Square Butt
5	Crane Screw Washer	**24**	Ejector Rod Lock Spring	**43**	Cylinder Hand
6	Cylinder	**25**	Ejector Rod	**44**	Hammer, Regular
7	Ejector	**26**	Ejector Rod Return Spring	**45**	Hammer, Spurless
8	Cylinder Latch	**27**	Ejector Rod Washer	**46**	Hammer Block
9	Cylinder Latch Washer	**28**	Firing Pin	**47**	Hammer Pawl
10	Cylinder Latch Plunger	**29**	Firing Pin Spring	**48**	Hammer Pawl Pin
11	Cylinder Latch Plunger Spring	**30**	Firing Pin Retaining Pin	**49**	Hammer Screw
12	Cylinder Latch Cover Plate	**31**	Cylinder Retaining Pin	**50**	Hammer Spring
13	Cylinder Latch Retaining Screw	**32**	Frame	**51**	Hammer Spring Strut
14	Cylinder Latch Release Screw	**33**	Frame Assembly Pin	**52**	Hammer Spring Seat
15	Cylinder Stop	**34**	Trigger Pin	**53**	Trigger
16	Cylinder Stop Bushing	**35**	Frame Assembly Screw	**54**	Trigger Spring
17	Cylinder Plunger	**36**	Grip Frame/Trigger Guard	**55**	Trigger Spring Bushing
18	Hammer Plunger	**37**	Grip Locating Pin		
19	Cylinder Plunger Spring	**38**	Grip Screw		

Target Bulldog Revolver

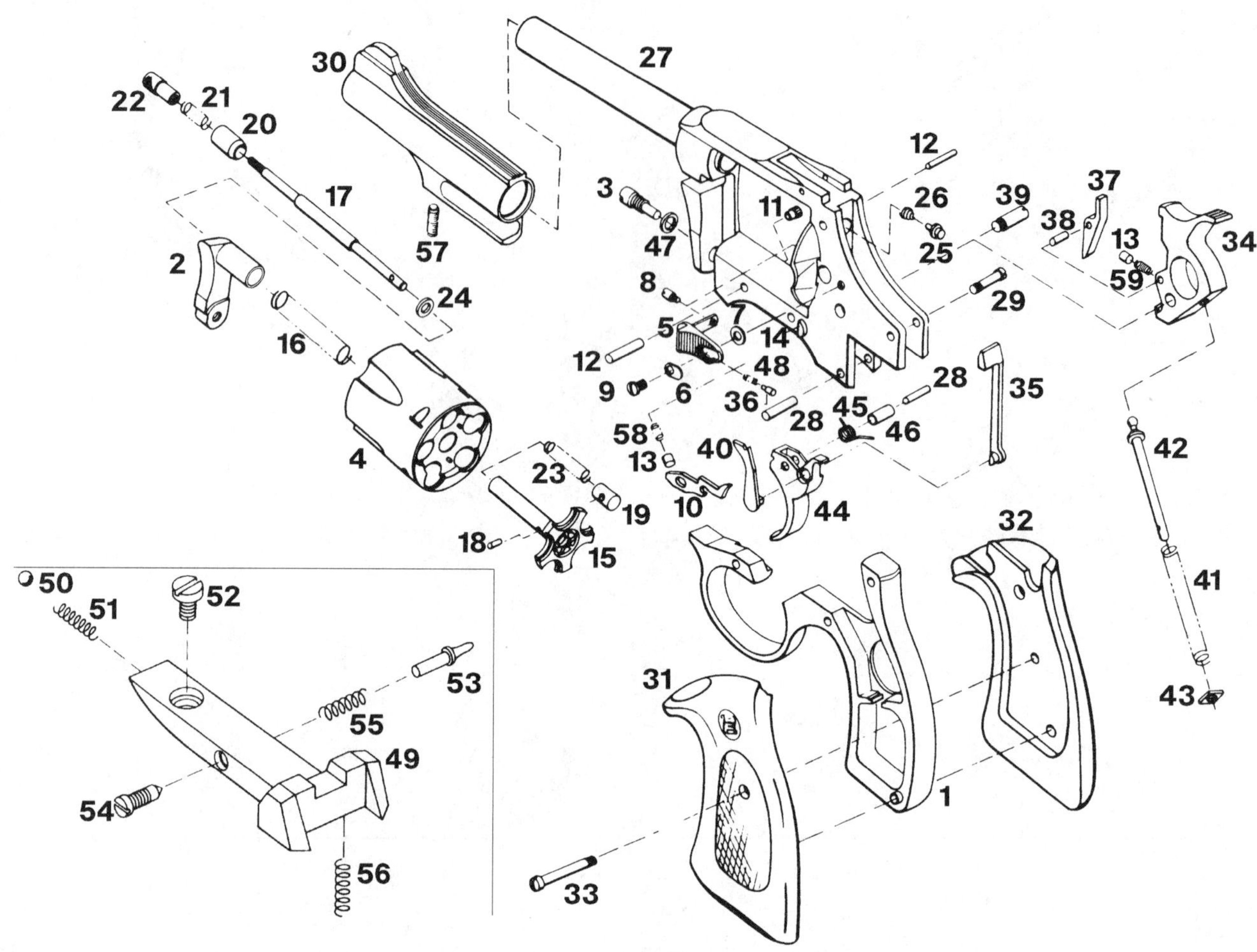

1	Grip Frame	**21**	Ejector Rod Collar Spring	**43**	Mainspring Seat
2	Crane	**22**	Ejector Rod Head	**44**	Trigger
3	Crane Screw	**23**	Ejector Rod Lock Spring	**45**	Trigger Spring
4	Cylinder	**24**	Ejector Rod Washer	**46**	Trigger Spring Bushing
5	Cylinder Latch	**25**	Firing Pin	**47**	Crane Screw Washer
6	Cylinder Latch Cover Plate	**26**	Firing Pin Spring	**48**	Cylinder Latch Spring
7	Cylinder Latch Washer	**27**	Frame and Barrel	**49**	Rear Sight Base
8	Cylinder Latch Release Screw	**28**	Frame Assembly and Trigger Pins	**50**	Sight Detent Ball
9	Cylinder Latch Retaining Screw	**29**	Frame Assembly Screw	**51**	Sight Detent Spring
10	Cylinder Stop	**30**	Barrel Shroud	**52**	Sight Elevation Screw
11	Cylinder Stop Bushing	**31**	Left Grip	**53**	Sight Windage Plunger
12	Cylinder Stop and Firing Pin Retaining Pins	**32**	Right Grip	**54**	Sight Windage Screw
		33	Grip Screw	**55**	Sight Windage Spring
13	Cylinder Stop and Hammer Pawl Plungers	**34**	Hammer	**56**	Sight Elevation Spring
		35	Hammer Block Assembly	**57**	Barrel Shroud Screw
14	Ejection Stud	**36**	Cylinder Latch Plunger	**58**	Cylinder Stop Plunger Spring
15	Ejector	**37**	Hammer Pawl	**59**	Hammer Pawl Plunger Spring
16	Ejector Return Spring	**38**	Hammer Pawl Pin	**Parts Not Shown**	
17	Ejector Rod	**39**	Hammer Screw		Grip Escutcheon
18	Ejector Rod Assembly Pin	**40**	Hand Assembly		Grip Escutcheon Nut
19	Ejector Rod Bushing	**41**	Mainspring		Grip Locating Pin
20	Ejector Rod Collar	**42**	Mainspring Strut		

Undercover Revolver

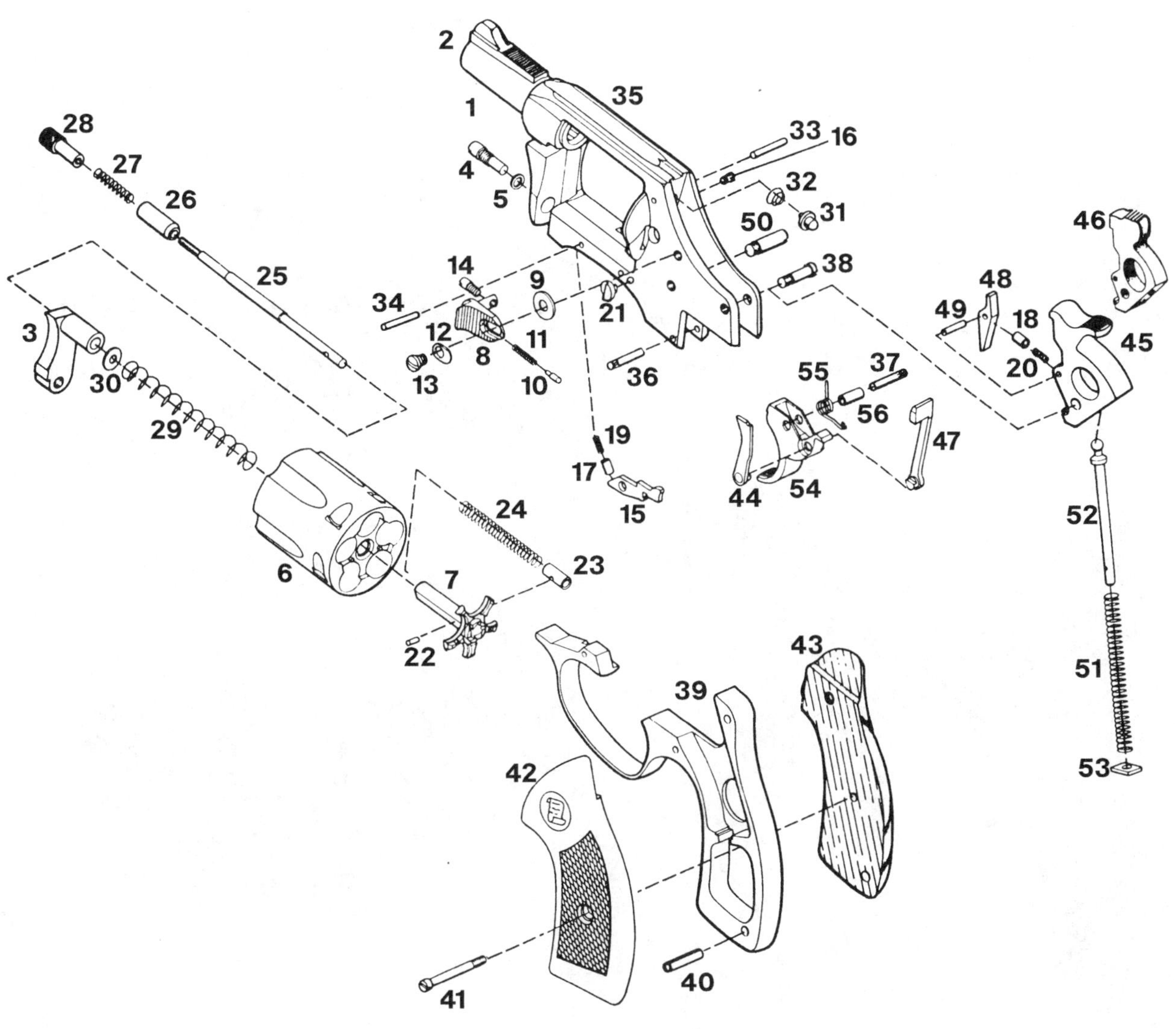

1	Barrel	20	Hammer Plunger Spring	39	Grip Frame/Trigger Guard
2	Front Sight	21	Cylinder Stop Stud	40	Grip Locating Pin
3	Crane	22	Ejector Rod Assembly Pin	41	Grip Screw
4	Crane Screw	23	Ejector Rod Bushing	42	Left Grip
5	Crane Screw Washer	24	Ejector Rod Lock Spring	43	Right Grip
6	Cylinder	25	Ejector Rod	44	Hand
7	Ejector	26	Ejector Rod Collar	45	Hammer, Regular
8	Cylinder Latch	27	Ejector Rod Collar Spring	46	Hammer, Spurless
9	Cylinder Latch Washer	28	Ejector Rod Head	47	Hammer Block
10	Cylinder Latch Plunger	29	Ejector Rod Return Spring	48	Hammer Pawl
11	Cylinder Latch Plunger Spring	30	Ejector Rod Washer	49	Hammer Pawl Pin
12	Cylinder Latch Cover Plate	31	Firing Pin	50	Hammer Screw
13	Cylinder Latch Retaining Screw	32	Firing Pin Spring	51	Hammer Spring
14	Cylinder Latch Release Screw	33	Firing Pin Retaining Pin	52	Hammer Spring Strut
15	Cylinder Stop	34	Cylinder Retaining Pin	53	Hammer Spring Seat
16	Cylinder Stop Bushing	35	Frame	54	Trigger
17	Cylinder Plunger	36	Frame Assembly Pin	55	Trigger Spring
18	Hammer Plunger	37	Trigger Pin	56	Trigger Spring Bushing
19	Cylinder Plunger Spring	38	Frame Assembly Screw		

Flintlock Revolver

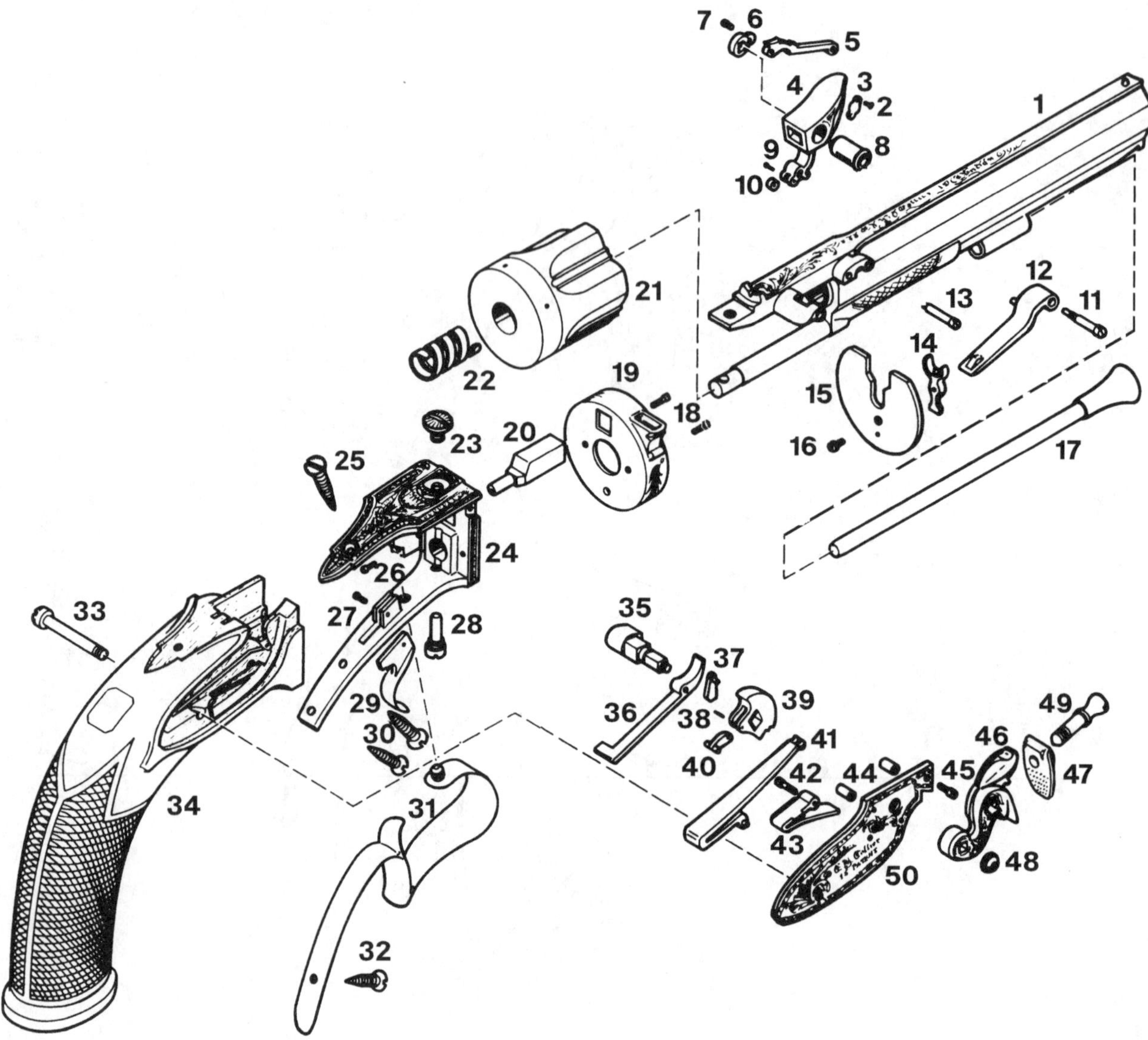

Key					
1	Barrel	17	Ramrod	34	Stock
2	Priming Reservoir Cover Screw	18	Pan Housing Screws	35	Hammer Pivot
3	Priming Reservoir Cover	19	Pan Housing	36	Sear
4	Frizzen	20	Pan Housing Index Block	37	Fly
5	Priming Drum Lever	21	Cylinder	38	Stirrup Pin
6	Priming Drum Retainer Lock	22	Cylinder Spring	39	Tumbler
7	Priming Drum Retainer Lock Screw	23	Upper Barrel Mounting Screw	40	Stirrup
8	Priming Drum	24	Frame	41	Mainspirng
9	Frizzen Spring Roller Screw	25	Tang Screw	42	Sear Spring Screw
10	Frizzen Spring Roller	26	Pan Housing Index Block Screw	43	Sear Spring
11	Frizzen Spring Screw	27	Trigger Pivot Screw	44	Lockplate Bushings
12	Frizzen Spring	28	Lower Barrel Mounting Screw	45	Lockplate Screw
13	Frizzen Pivot	29	Trigger	46	Hammer
14	Cylinder Plate Yoke	30	Tang Screws	47	Top Jaw
15	Cylinder Plate	31	Trigger Guard	48	Hammer Cap Nut
16	Cylinder Plate Screw	32	Trigger Guard Screw	49	Jaw Screw
		33	Lockplate Screw	50	Lockplate

1849 Revolver

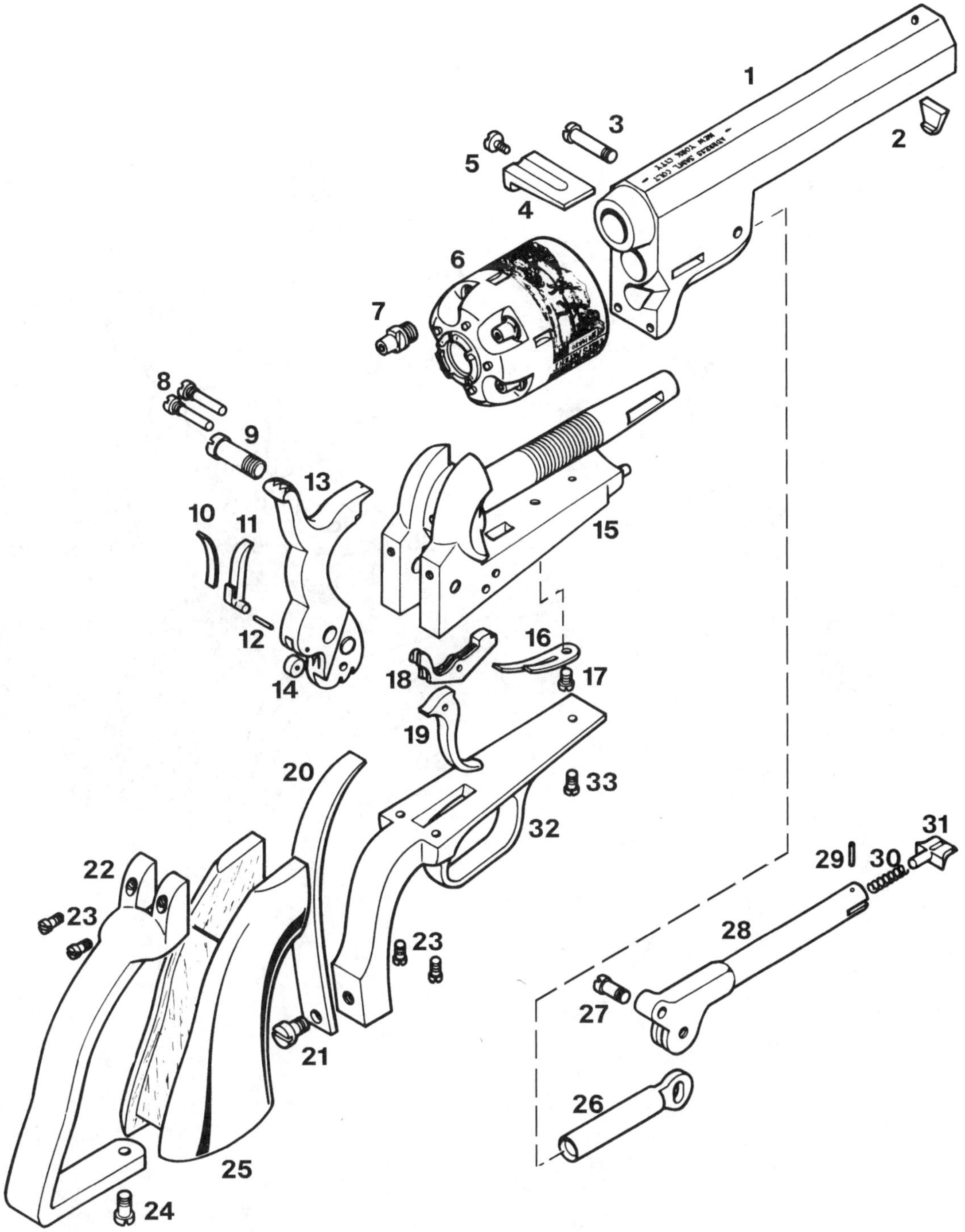

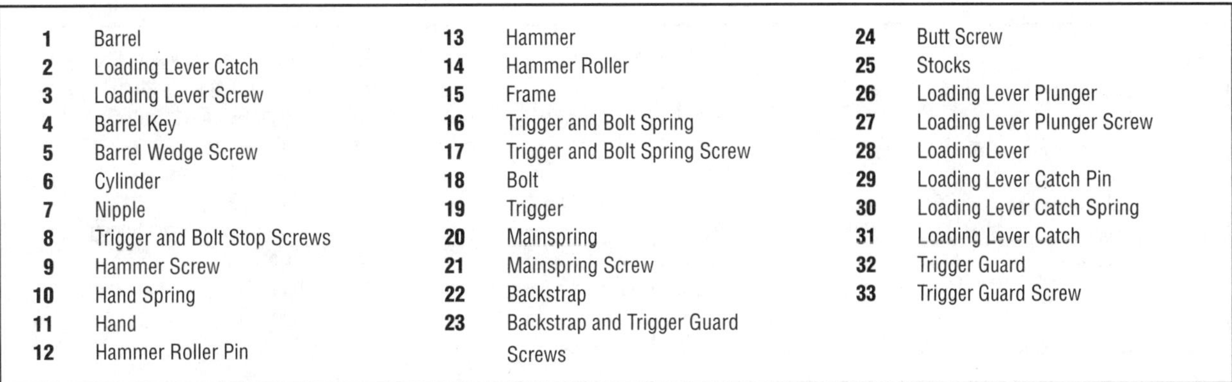

1	Barrel	13	Hammer	24	Butt Screw
2	Loading Lever Catch	14	Hammer Roller	25	Stocks
3	Loading Lever Screw	15	Frame	26	Loading Lever Plunger
4	Barrel Key	16	Trigger and Bolt Spring	27	Loading Lever Plunger Screw
5	Barrel Wedge Screw	17	Trigger and Bolt Spring Screw	28	Loading Lever
6	Cylinder	18	Bolt	29	Loading Lever Catch Pin
7	Nipple	19	Trigger	30	Loading Lever Catch Spring
8	Trigger and Bolt Stop Screws	20	Mainspring	31	Loading Lever Catch
9	Hammer Screw	21	Mainspring Screw	32	Trigger Guard
10	Hand Spring	22	Backstrap	33	Trigger Guard Screw
11	Hand	23	Backstrap and Trigger Guard Screws		
12	Hammer Roller Pin				

1851 Navy and 1862 Pocket Navy Revolver

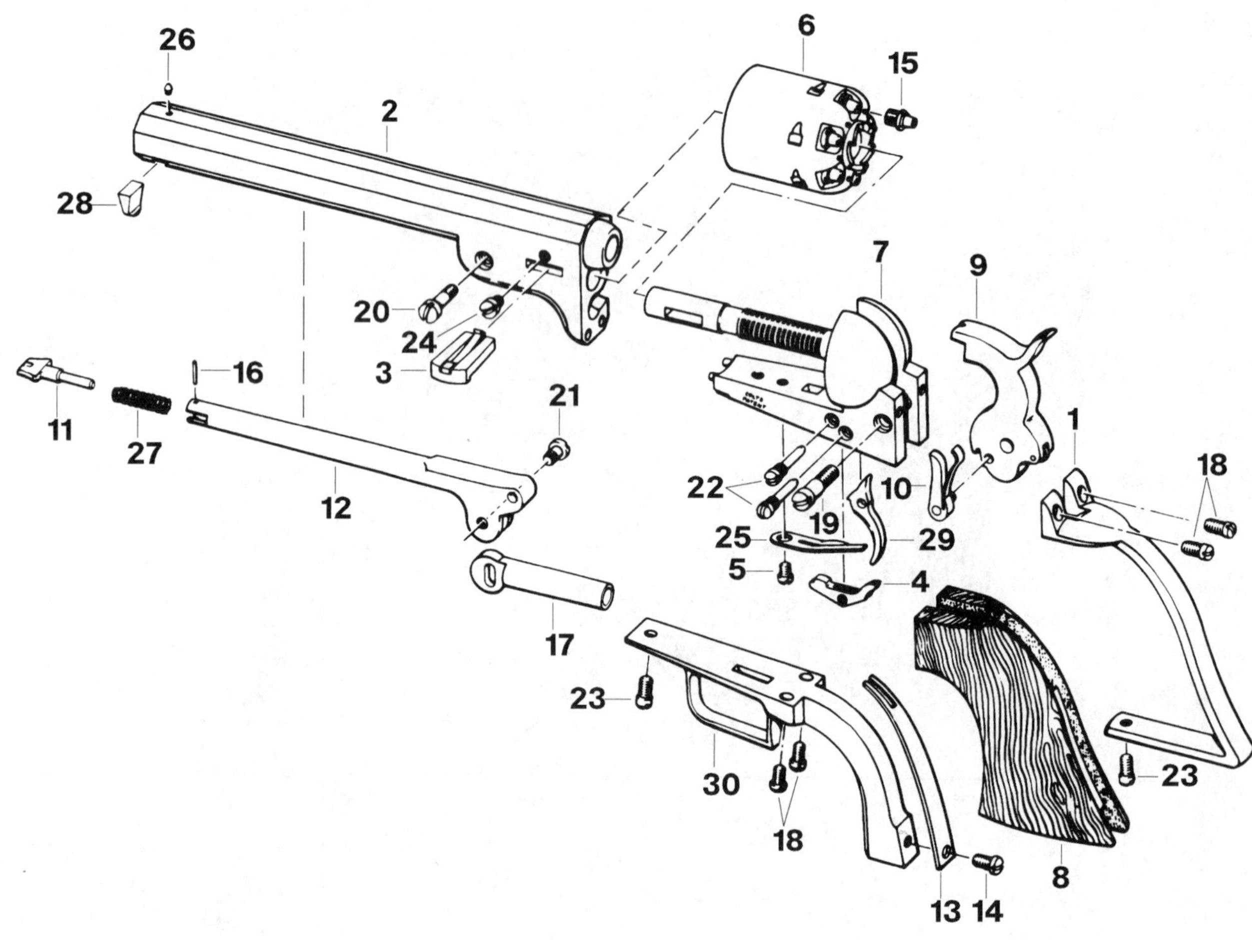

Key

1	Backstrap	**11**	Loading Lever Latch	**21**	Loading Lever Plunger Screw
2	Barrel	**12**	Loading Lever	**22**	Bolt and Trigger Screws
3	Barrel Wedge	**13**	Mainspring	**23**	Trigger Guard and Butt Screws
4	Bolt	**14**	Mainspring Screw	**24**	Wedge Screw
5	Bolt Spring Screw	**15**	Nipple	**25**	Sear and Bolt Spring
6	Cylinder	**16**	Loading Lever Latch Retaining Pin	**26**	Front Sight
7	Frame	**17**	Loading Lever Plunger	**27**	Loading Lever Latch Spring
8	Stocks	**18**	Backstrap and Guard Screws	**28**	Barrel Stud
9	Hammer	**19**	Hammer Screw	**29**	Trigger
10	Hand and Spring Assembly	**20**	Loading Lever Screw	**30**	Trigger Guard

1855 Sidehammer Revolver

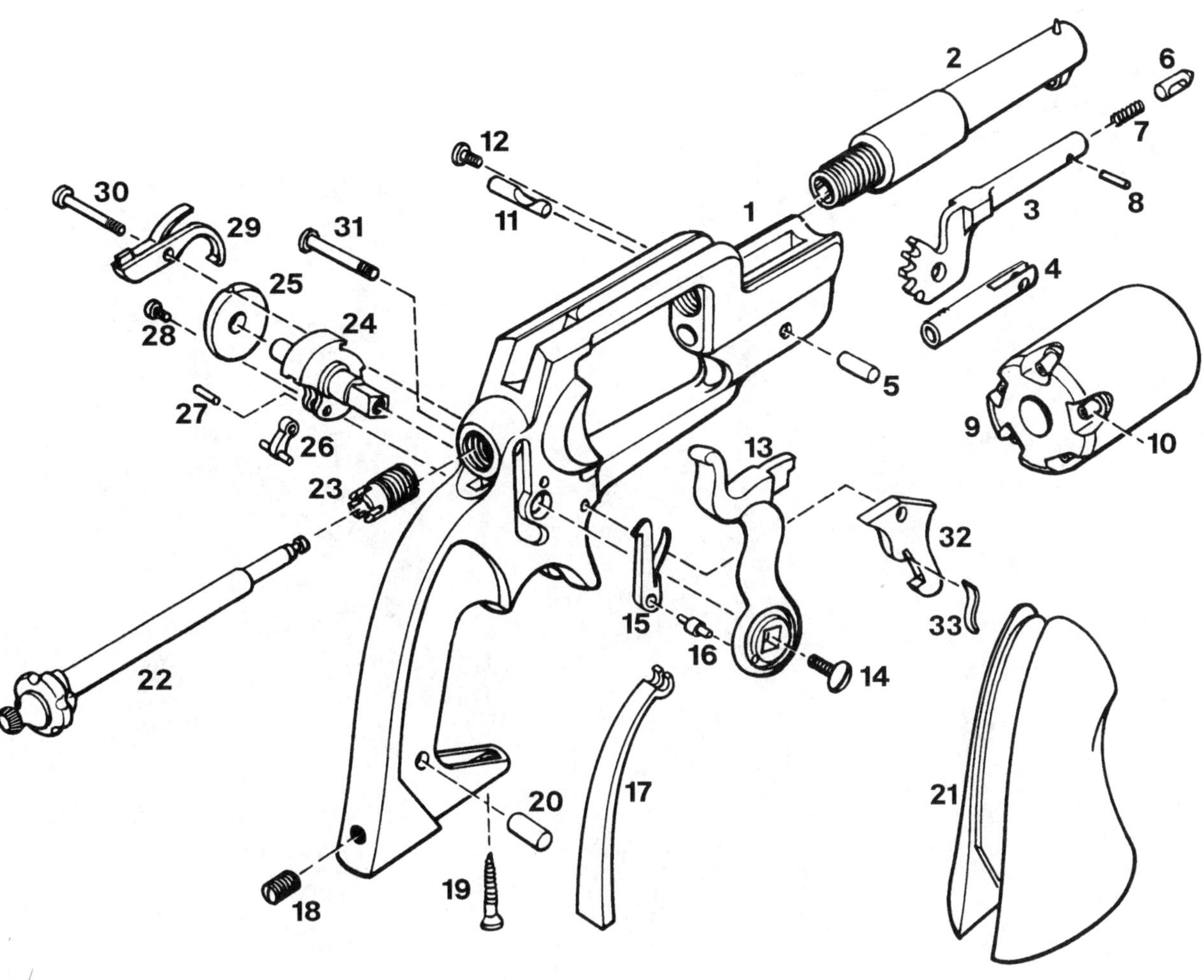

1	Frame	17	Mainspring
2	Barrel	18	Mainspring Tension Screw
3	Loading Lever	19	Grip Screw
4	Loading Lever Plunger	20	Mainspring Pin
5	Loading Lever Plunger Pin	21	Stocks
6	Loading Lever Latch	22	Cylinder Arbor
7	Loading Lever Latch Spring	23	Cylinder Arbor Sleeve
8	Loading Lever Latch Pin	24	Sear
9	Cylinder	25	Sideplate
10	Nipple	26	Stirrup
11	Cylinder Arbor Retaining Pin	27	Stirrup Pin
12	Cylinder Arbor Retaining Pin Screw	28	Sideplate Screw
13	Hammer	29	Cylinder Stop and Spring
14	Hammer Screw	30	Cylinder Stop Screw
15	Hand and Hand Spring	31	Trigger Screw
16	Hand Pin	32	Trigger
		33	Trigger Spring

1860 Army, 1861 Navy and 1862 Police Revolver

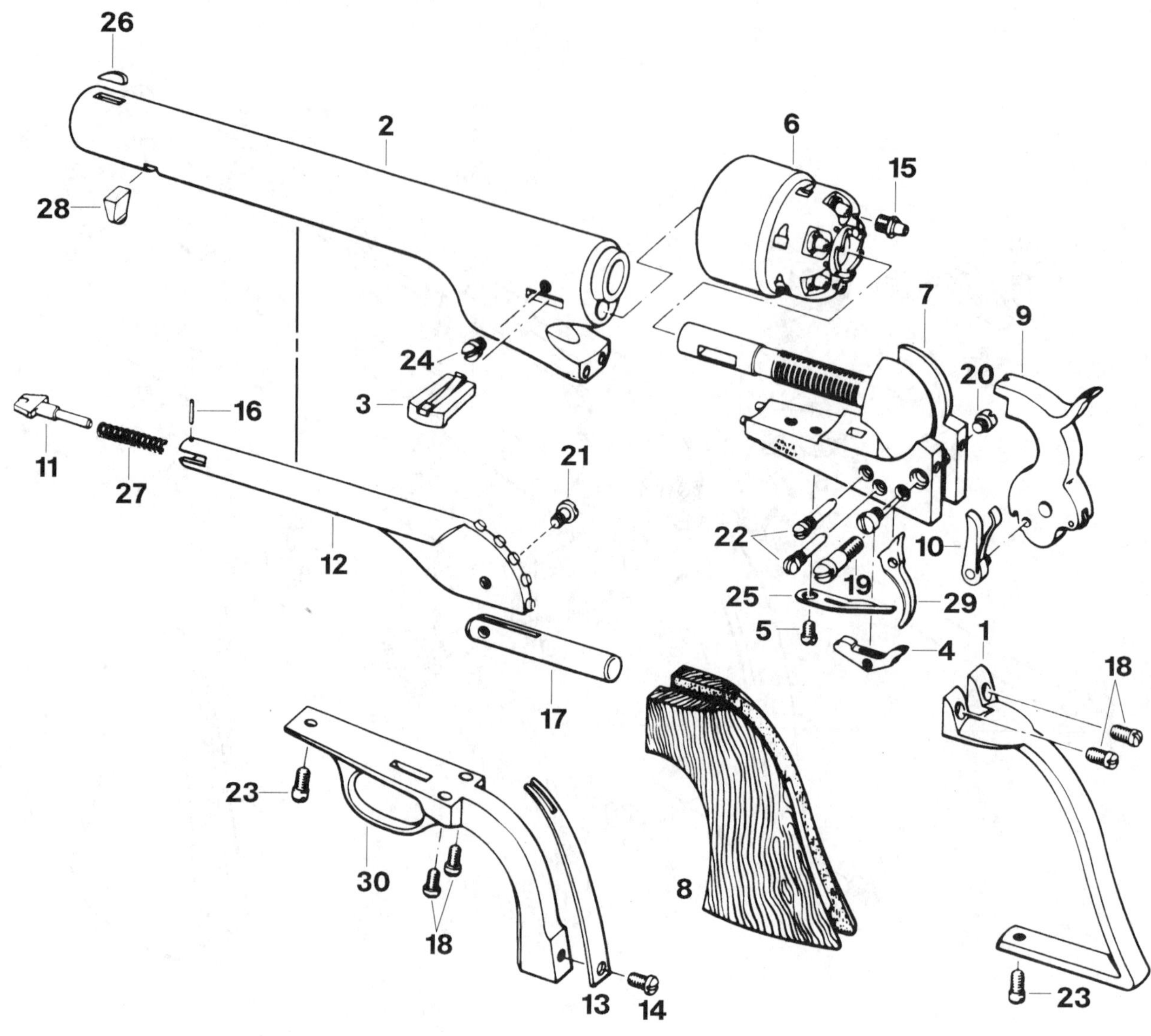

1	Backstrap	16	Loading Lever Latch Retaining Pin
2	Barrel	17	Loading Lever Plunger
3	Barrel Wedge	18	Backstrap and Guard Screws
4	Bolt	19	Hammer Screw
5	Bolt Spring Screw	20	Guide Screw
6	Cylinder	21	Loading Lever Plunger Screw
7	Frame	22	Bolt and Trigger Screws
8	Stocks	23	Trigger Guard and Butt Screw
9	Hammer	24	Wedge Screw
10	Hand and Spring Assembly	25	Sear and Bolt Spring
11	Loading Lever Latch	26	Front Sight
12	Loading Lever	27	Loading Lever Latch Spring
13	Mainspring	28	Barrel Stud
14	Mainspring Screw	29	Trigger
15	Nipple	30	Trigger Guard

22-Caliber Conversion Unit

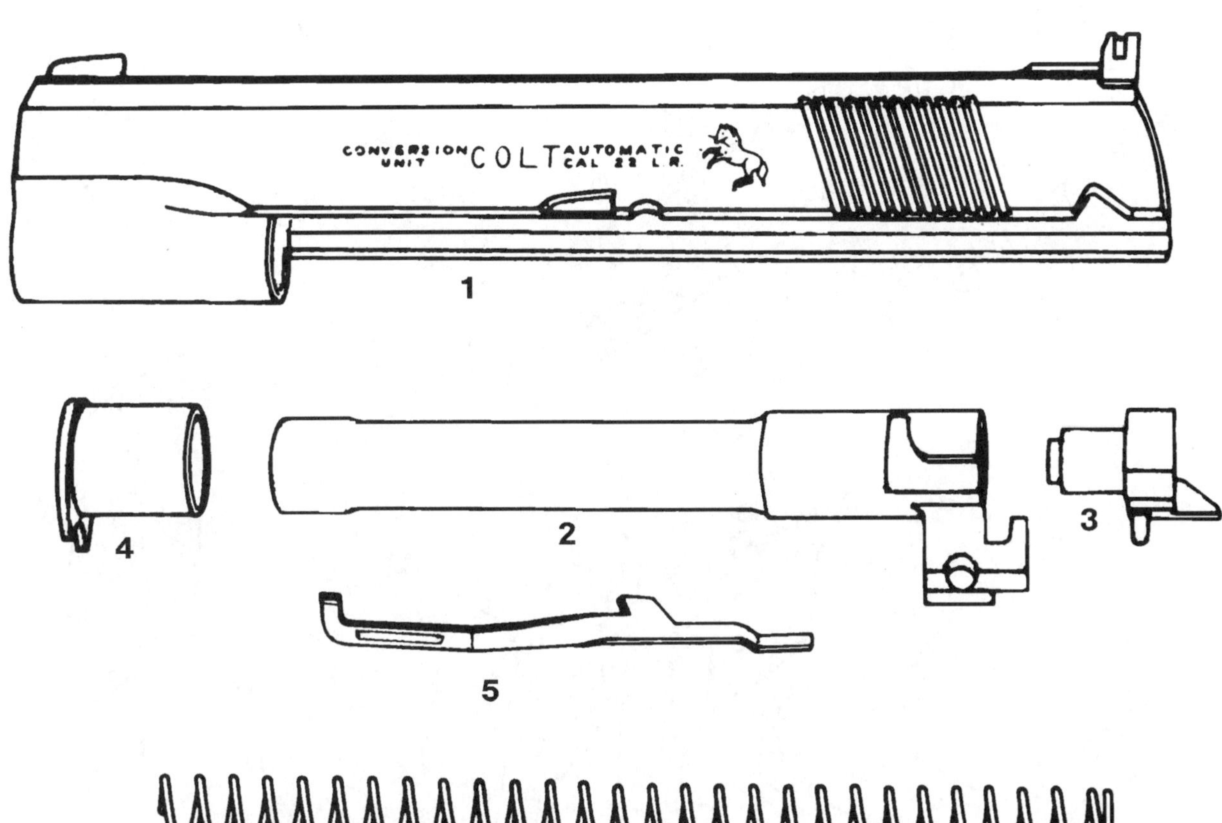

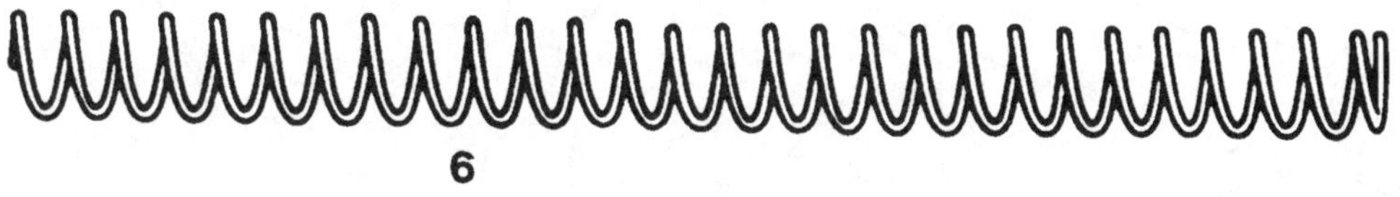

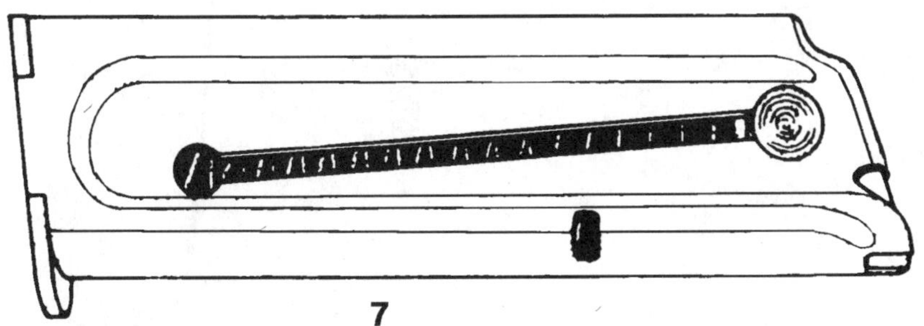

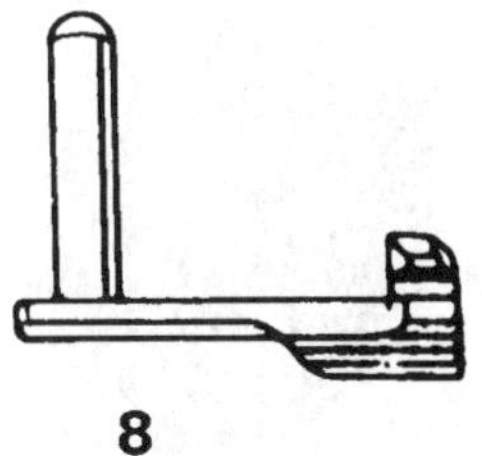

1	Slide (with Sights)	**5**	Ejector
2	Barrel	**6**	Recoil Spring
3	Floating Chamber	**7**	Magazine
4	Barrel Bushing	**8**	Slide Stop

22 Short and 25 ACP Pocket Auto

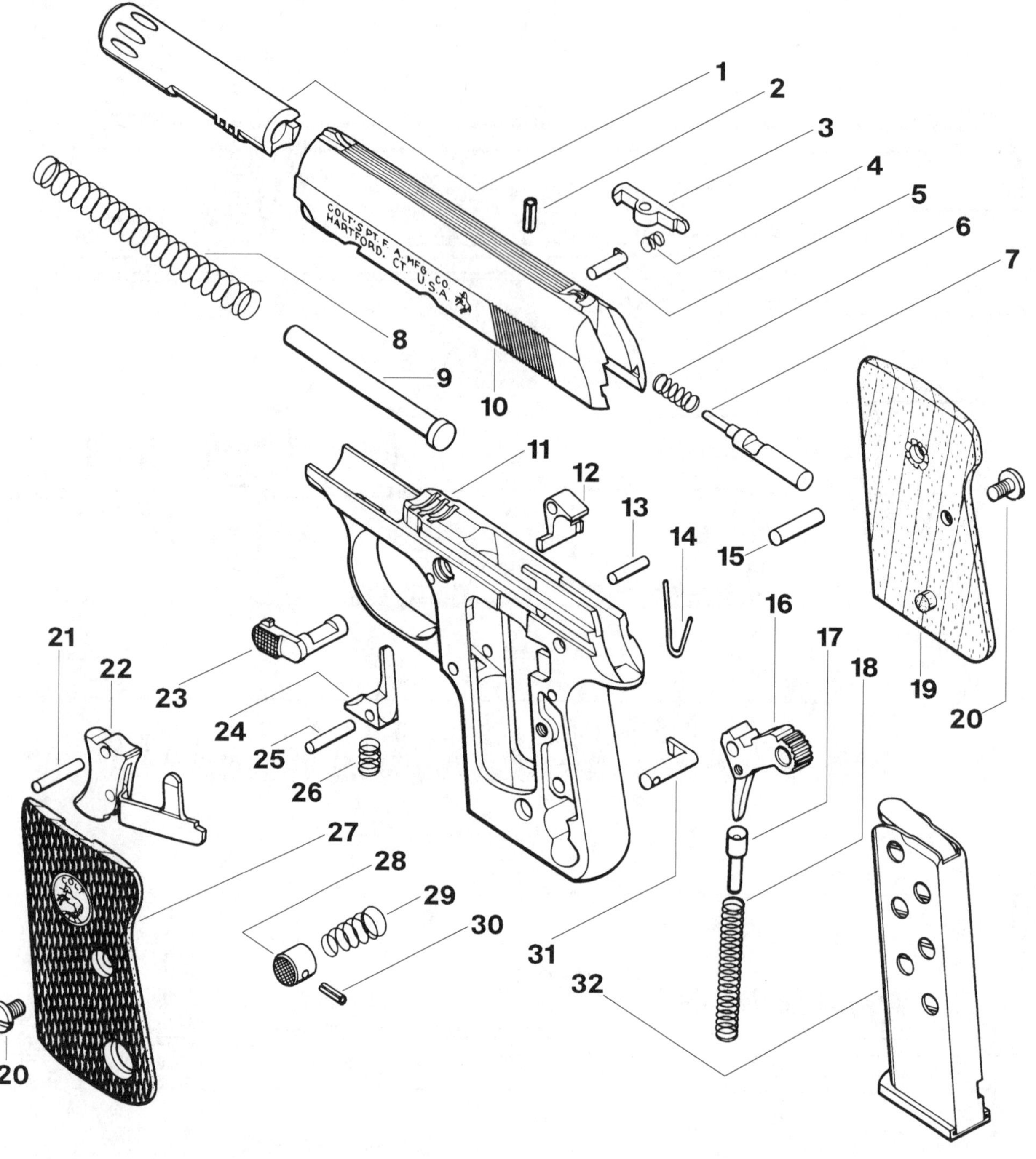

1	Barrel
2	Extractor Pivot Pin
3	Extractor
4	Extractor Spring
5	Firing Pin Retaining Pin
6	Firing Pin Spring
7	Firing Pin
8	Recoil Spring
9	Recoil Spring Plunger
10	Slide
11	Frame
12	Sear
13	Sear Pin
14	Sear Spring
15	Hammer Pin
16	Hammer
17	Hammer Spring Guide
18	Hammer Spring
19	Right Grip
20	Grip Screw
21	Trigger Pin
22	Trigger with Disconnector
23	Thumb Safety
24	Magazine Safety
25	Magazine Safety Pin
26	Magazine Safety Spring
27	Left Grip
28	Magazine Catch Button
29	Magazine Catch Spring
30	Magazine Catch Button Pin
31	Magazine Catch
32	Magazine

1908 Model M Pocket Auto 32 ACP and 380 ACP

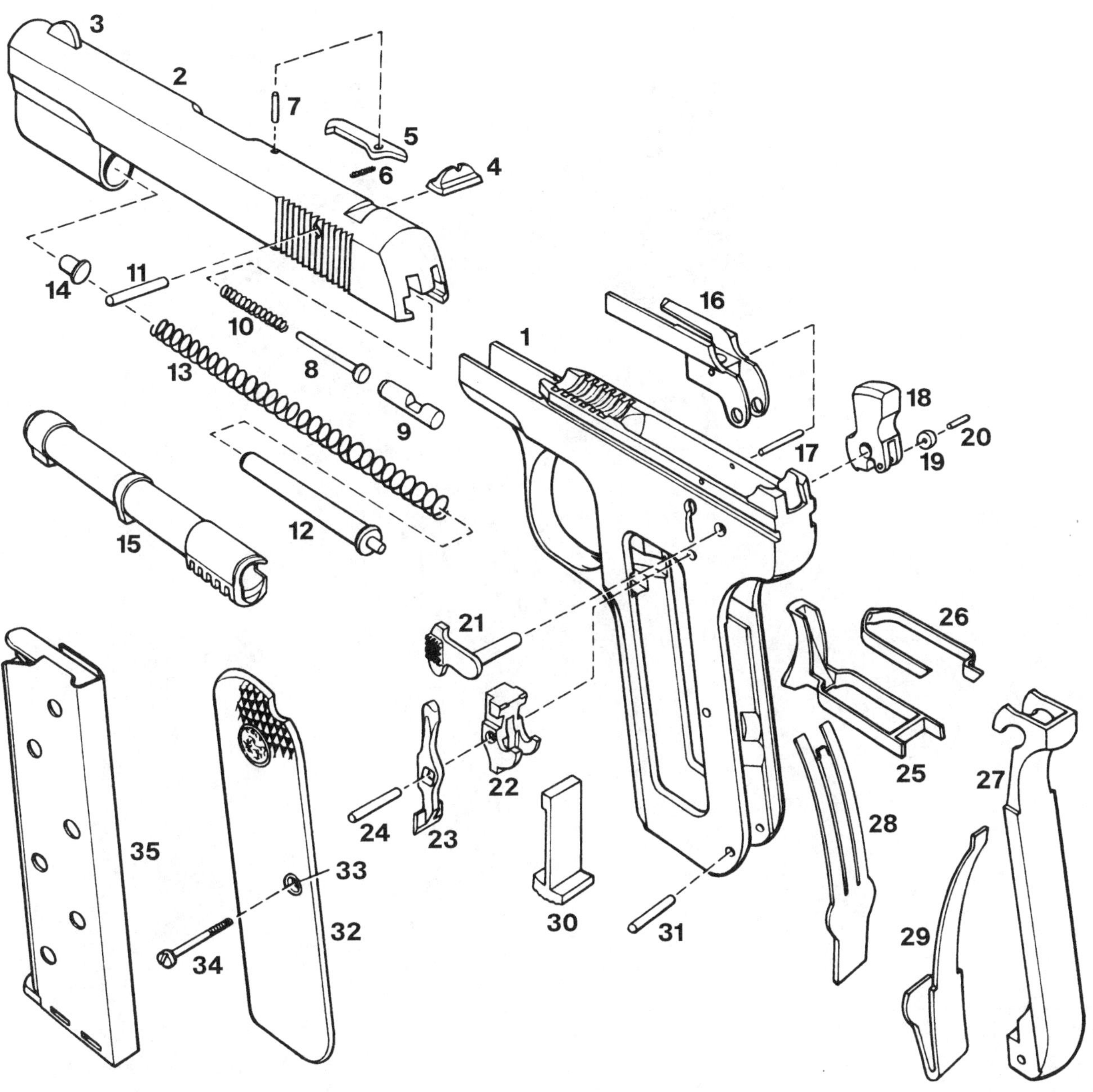

1	Frame	13	Recoil Spring	25	Trigger
2	Slide	14	Recoil Spring Plug	26	Depressor
3	Front Sight	15	Barrel	27	Grip Safety
4	Rear Sight	16	Ejector	28	Sear Spring
5	Extractor	17	Ejector Pin	29	Mainspring
6	Extractor Spring	18	Hammer	30	Magazine Catch
7	Extractor Pivot Pin	19	Hammer Roller Bushing	31	Grip Safety Pin
8	Firing Pin	20	Hammer Roller Pin	32	Grip
9	Firing Pin Impeller	21	Slide Lock	33	Grip Escutcheon
10	Firing Pin Spring	22	Sear	34	Grip Screw
11	Firing Pin Lock Pin	23	Disconnector	35	Magazine with Spring and Follower
12	Recoil Spring Guide	24	Sear Pin		

Anaconda Revolver

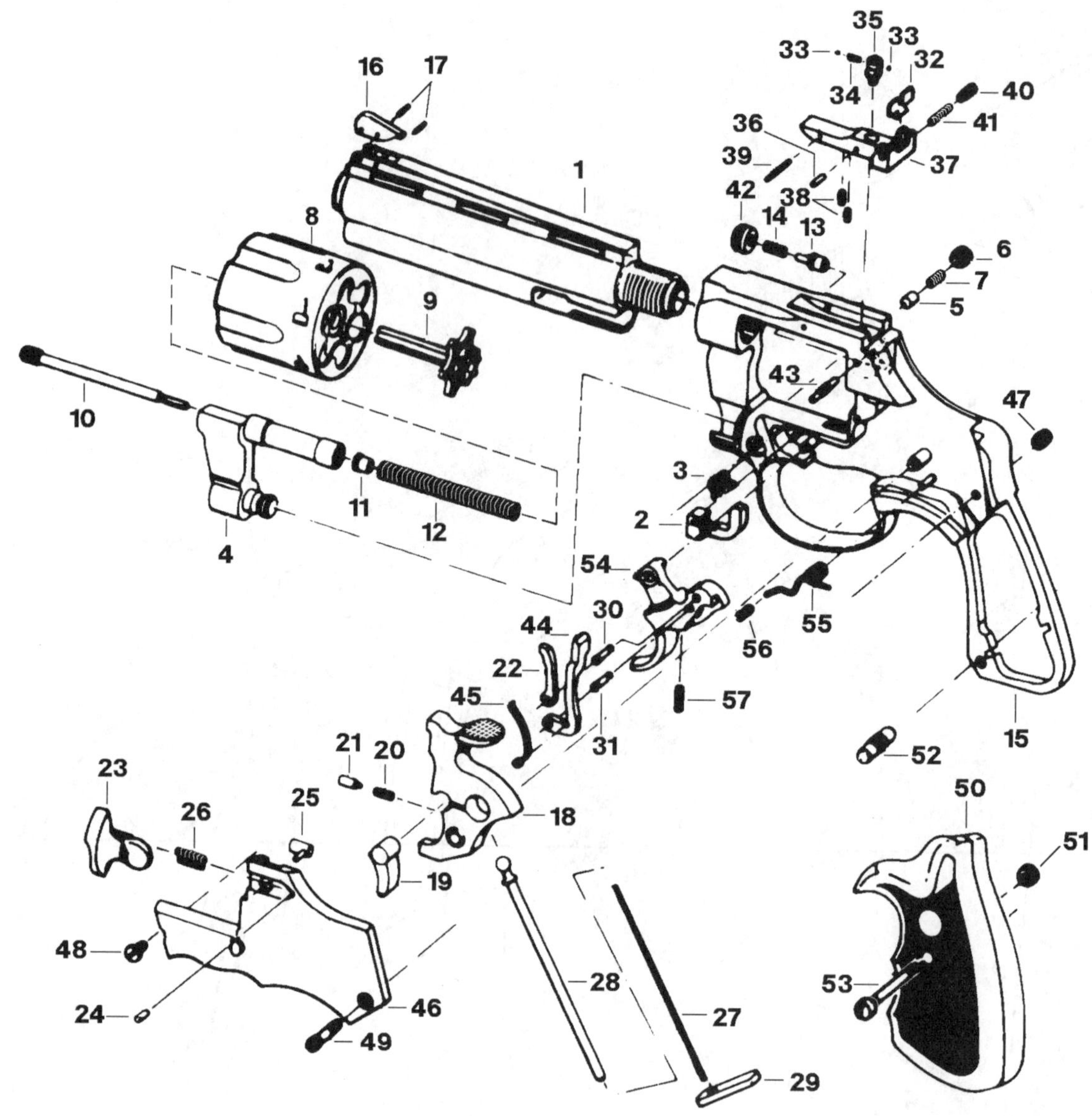

No.	Part	No.	Part	No.	Part
1	Barrel	20	Hammer Strut Spring	39	Rear Sight Leaf Pin
2	Bolt	21	Hammer Strut Spring Guide	40	Rear Sight Windage Screw
3	Bolt Spring	22	Hand	41	Rear Sight Windage Spring
4	Crane	23	Latch	42	Recoil Plate
5	Crane Lock Detent	24	Latch Insert	43	Recoil Plate Pin
6	Crane Lock Screw	25	Latch Pin Assembly	44	Safety Connector
7	Crane Lock Spring	26	Latch Spring	45	Safety Connector and Hand Spring
8	Cylinder	27	Hammer Spring	46	Sideplate
9	Ejector Ratchet and Stem	28	Hammer Spring Guide	47	Sideplate Nut
10	Ejector Rod	29	Hammer Spring Seat	48	Sideplate Screw
11	Ejector Rod Bushing	30	Hand Pivot Pin	49	Sideplate and Stock Screw
12	Ejector Spring	31	Safety-Lever Pivot Pin	50	Stock
13	Firing Pin	32	Rear Sight Blade	51	Stock Screw Nut
14	Firing Pin Spring	33	Rear Sight Detent Balls	52	Stock Pin
15	Frame	34	Rear Sight Detent Spring	53	Stock Screw
16	Front Sight Blade	35	Rear Sight Elevation Screw	54	Trigger Assembly
17	Front Sight Blade Pin	36	Rear Sight Elevation Screw Pin	55	Trigger Return Spring
18	Hammer	37	Rear Sight Base	56	Trigger Return Spring Guide
19	Hammer Strut	38	Rear Sight Base Elevation Springs	57	Trigger Screw

Buntline Special Revolver

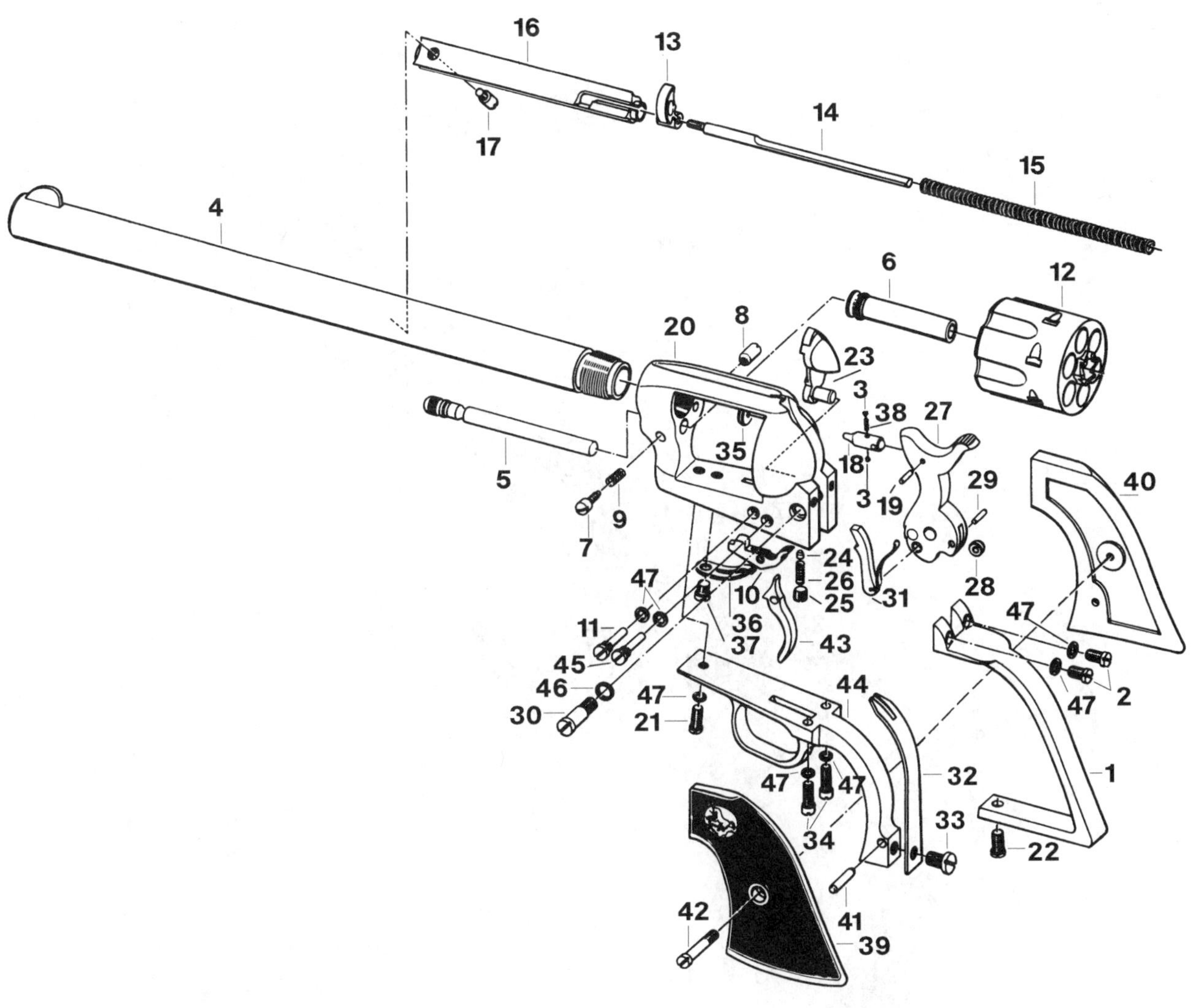

1	Backstrap	**17**	Ejector Rod Tube Screw	**33**	Mainspring Screw
2	Backstrap Screws	**18**	Firing Pin	**34**	Rear Guard Screws
3	Firing Pin Ball	**19**	Firing Pin Rivet	**35**	Recoil Plate
4	Barrel	**20**	Frame	**36**	Sear and Bolt Spring
5	Cylinder Base Pin	**21**	Front Guard Screw	**37**	Sear and Bolt Spring Screw
6	Cylinder Base Pin Bushing	**22**	Front Backstrap Screw	**38**	Firing Pin Detent Spring
7	Cylinder Base Pin Screw	**23**	Loading Gate	**39**	Stock, Left
8	Cylinder Base Pin Screw Nut	**24**	Loading Gate Catch	**40**	Stock, Right
9	Cylinder Base Pin Spring	**25**	Loading Gate Catch Screw	**41**	Stock Pin
10	Bolt	**26**	Loading Gate Spring	**42**	Stock Screw
11	Bolt Screw	**27**	Hammer	**43**	Trigger
12	Cylinder	**28**	Hammer Roller Bushing	**44**	Trigger Guard
13	Ejector Head	**29**	Hammer Roller Pin	**45**	Trigger Screw
14	Ejector Rod	**30**	Hammer Screw	**46**	Hammer Screw Washer
15	Ejector Rod Spring	**31**	Hand and Hand Spring	**47**	Washer
16	Ejector Rod Tube	**32**	Mainspring		

Cobra Revolver (Old Model)

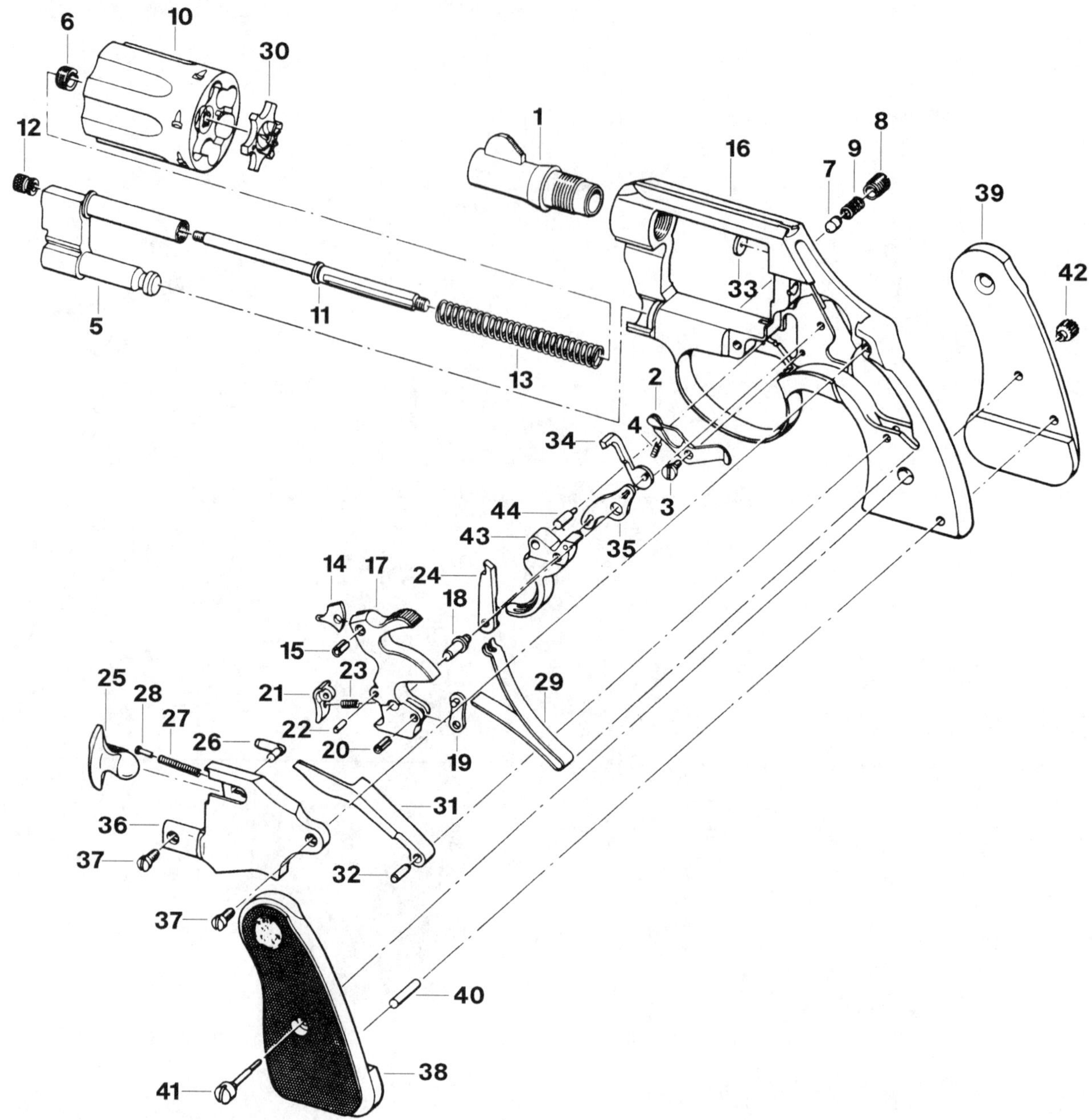

1	Barrel	**16**	Frame	**31**	Rebound Lever
2	Bolt	**17**	Hammer	**32**	Rebound Lever Pin
3	Shoulder Screw	**18**	Hammer Pivot Pin	**33**	Recoil Plate
4	Bolt Spring	**19**	Hammer Stirrup	**34**	Safety
5	Crane	**20**	Hammer Stirrup Pin	**35**	Safety-Lever
6	Crane Bushing	**21**	Hammer Strut	**36**	Sideplate
7	Crane Lock Detent	**22**	Hammer Strut Pin	**37**	Sideplate Screws
8	Spring Retaining Screw	**23**	Hammer Strut Spring	**38**	Left Grip
9	Crane Lock Spring	**24**	Hand	**39**	Right Grip
10	Cylinder	**25**	Cylinder Latch	**40**	Grip Alignment Pin
11	Ejector Rod	**26**	Cylinder Latch Pin	**41**	Grip Screw
12	Ejector Rod Head	**27**	Cylinder Latch Spring	**42**	Grip Screw Nut
13	Ejector Spring	**28**	Cylinder Latch Spring Guide	**43**	Trigger
14	Firing Pin	**29**	Mainspring	**44**	Trigger Shoulder Pin
15	Firing Pin Roll Pin	**30**	Ejector Ratchet		

Combat Commander, 10mm Delta Elite, Lightweight Commander MK.IV, Officers ACP MK.IV Series 80 and Gold Cup National Match MK.IV Series 80 Auto

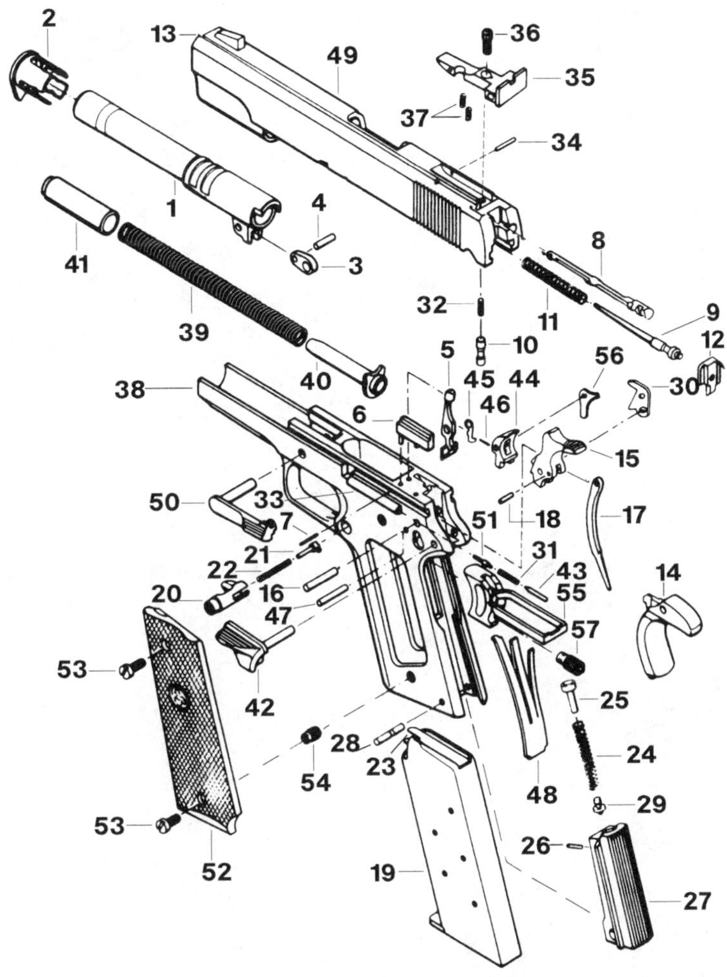

1	Barrel
2	Barrel Bushing
3	Barrel Link
4	Barrel Link Pin
5	Disconnector
6	Ejector
7	Ejector Pin
8	Extractor
9	Firing Pin
10	Firing Pin Plunger
11	Firing Pin Spring
12	Firing Pin Stop
13	Front Sight
14	Grip Safety
15	Hammer
16	Hammer Pin
17	Hammer Strut
18	Hammer Strut Pin
19	Magazine Assembly
20	Magazine Catch
21	Magazine Catch Lock
22	Magazine Catch Spring
23	Magazine Follower
24	Mainspring
25	Mainspring Cap
26	Mainspring Cap Pin
27	Mainspring Housing (Flat)
28	Mainspring Housing Pin
29	Mainspring Housing Pin Retainer
30	Plunger Lever
31	Plunger Spring
32	Firing Pin Plunger Spring
33	Plunger Tube
34	Rear Sight Leaf Pin
35	Rear Sight Leaf
36	Rear Sight Elevation Screw
37	Rear Sight Elevation Springs
38	Receiver
39	Recoil Spring
40	Recoil Spring Guide
41	Recoil Spring Plug
42	Safety Lock
43	Safety Lock Plunger
44	Sear
45	Depressor
46	Depressor Spring
47	Sear Pin
48	Sear Spring
49	Slide
50	Slide Stop
51	Slide Stop Plunger
52	Stock
53	Stock Screws
54	Stock Screw Bushing
55	Trigger Assembly
56	Trigger Bar Lever
57	Trigger Stop

Parts Not Shown

- Firing Pin Block Plunger
- Firing Pin Block Plunger Spring
- Magazine Spring
- Rear Sight Blade
- Rear Sight Detent Ball
- Rear Sight Elevating Screw Pin
- Rear Sight Windage Screw
- Rear Sight Windage Spring
- Sear Depressor Spring (Gold Cup only)
- Sear Depressor (Gold Cup only)

Commando, Diamondback and Viper Revolver

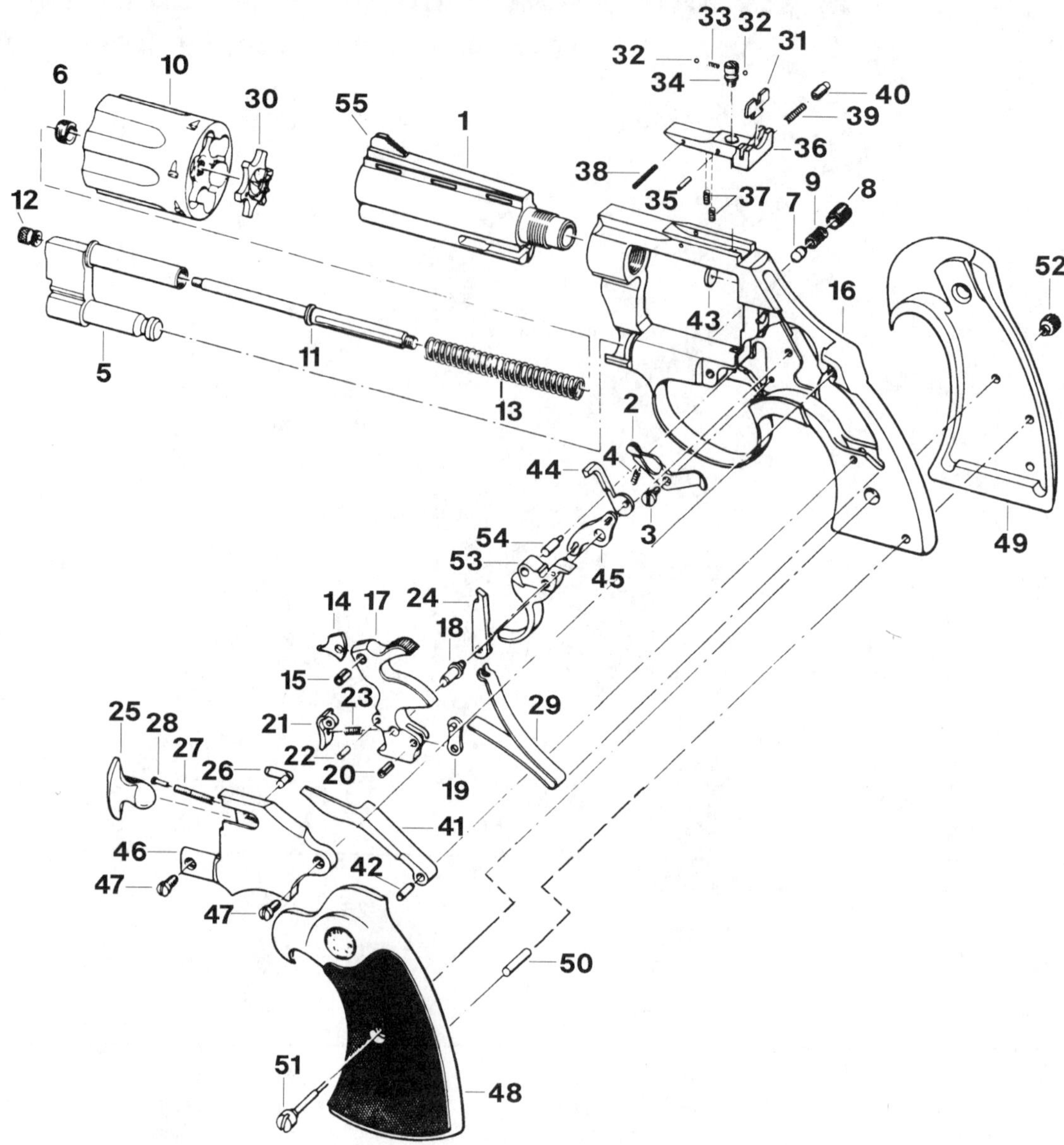

1	Barrel	**21**	Hammer Strut	**40**	Rear Sight Windage Screw
2	Bolt	**22**	Hammer Strut Pin	**41**	Rebound Lever
3	Bolt Screw	**23**	Hammer Strut Spring	**42**	Rebound Lever Pin
4	Bolt Spring	**24**	Hand	**43**	Recoil Plate
5	Crane	**25**	Latch	**44**	Safety
6	Crane Bushing	**26**	Latch Pin	**45**	Safety-Lever
7	Crane Lock Detent	**27**	Latch Spring	**46**	Sideplate
8	Crane Lock Screw	**28**	Latch Spring Guide	**47**	Sideplate Screw
9	Crane Lock Spring	**29**	Mainspring	**48**	Stock, Left
10	Cylinder	**30**	Ratchet	**49**	Stock, Right
11	Ejector Rod	**31**	Rear Sight Blade	**50**	Stock Pin
12	Ejector Rod Head	**32**	Rear Sight Detent Balls	**51**	Stock Screw
13	Ejector Spring	**33**	Rear Sight Detent Spring	**52**	Stock Screw Nut
14	Firing Pin	**34**	Rear Sight Elevation Screw	**53**	Trigger
15	Firing Pin Rivet	**35**	Rear Sight Elevation Screw Pin	**54**	Trigger Pin
16	Frame	**36**	Rear Sight Leaf	**55**	Front Sight
17	Hammer	**37**	Rear Sight Leaf Elevation Springs	**Parts Not Shown**	
18	Hammer Pin	**38**	Rear Sight Leaf Pin		Ejector Bushing
19	Hammer Stirrup	**39**	Rear Sight Windage Spring		
20	Hammer Stirrup Pin				

Derringer #3

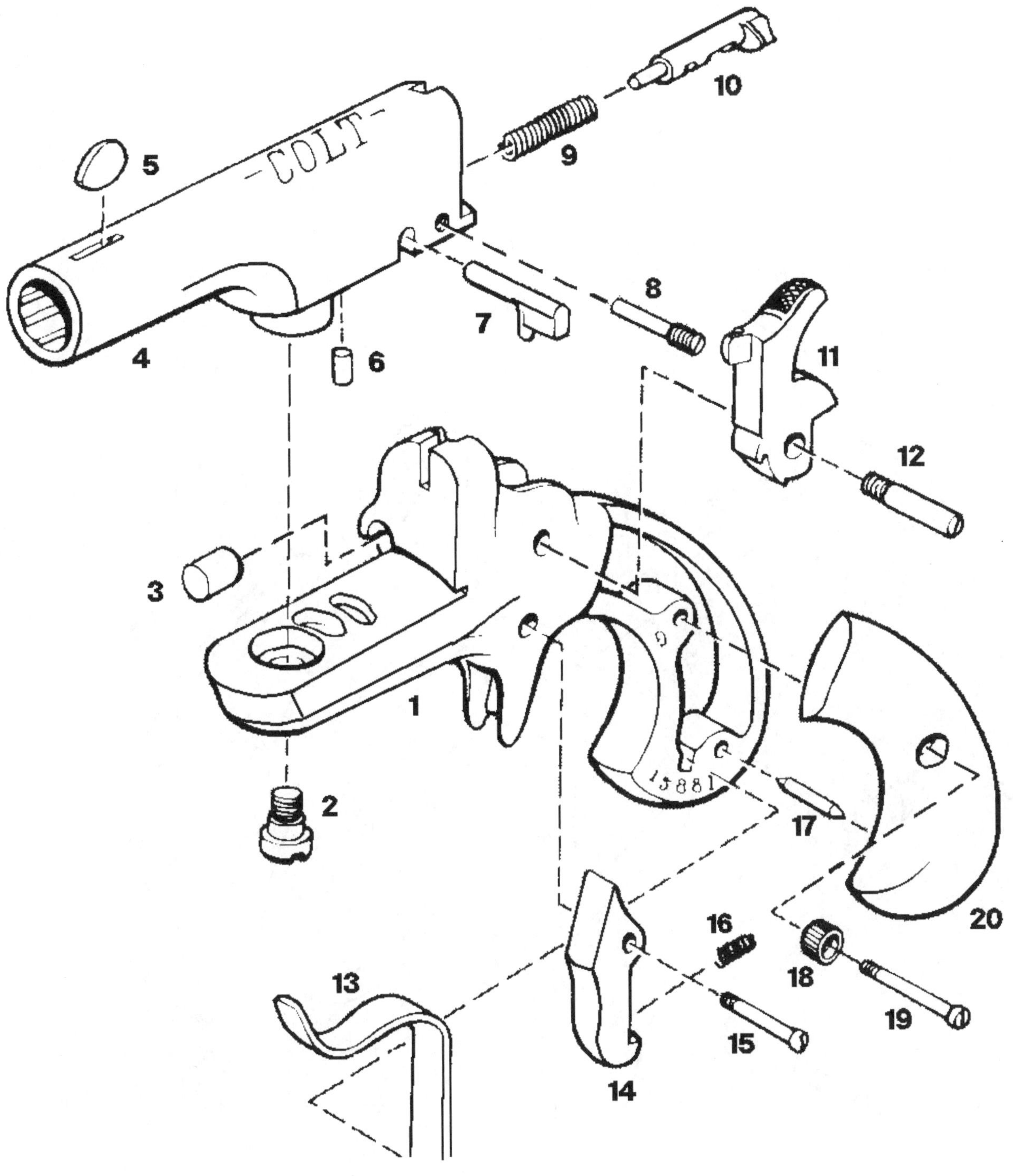

1	Frame	**8**	Barrel Latch and Ejector Screw	**15**	Trigger Screw
2	Barrel Screw	**9**	Barrel Latch and Ejector Spring	**16**	Trigger Spring (Flat or Coil Type)
3	Barrel Latch Bushing	**10**	Barrel Latch and Ejector	**17**	Grip Pin
4	Barrel	**11**	Hammer	**18**	Escutcheon
5	Front Sight	**12**	Hammer Screw	**19**	Grip Screw
6	Barrel Stop Pin	**13**	Mainspring	**20**	Grip
7	Barrel Latch Release Pin	**14**	Trigger		

Derringer #4

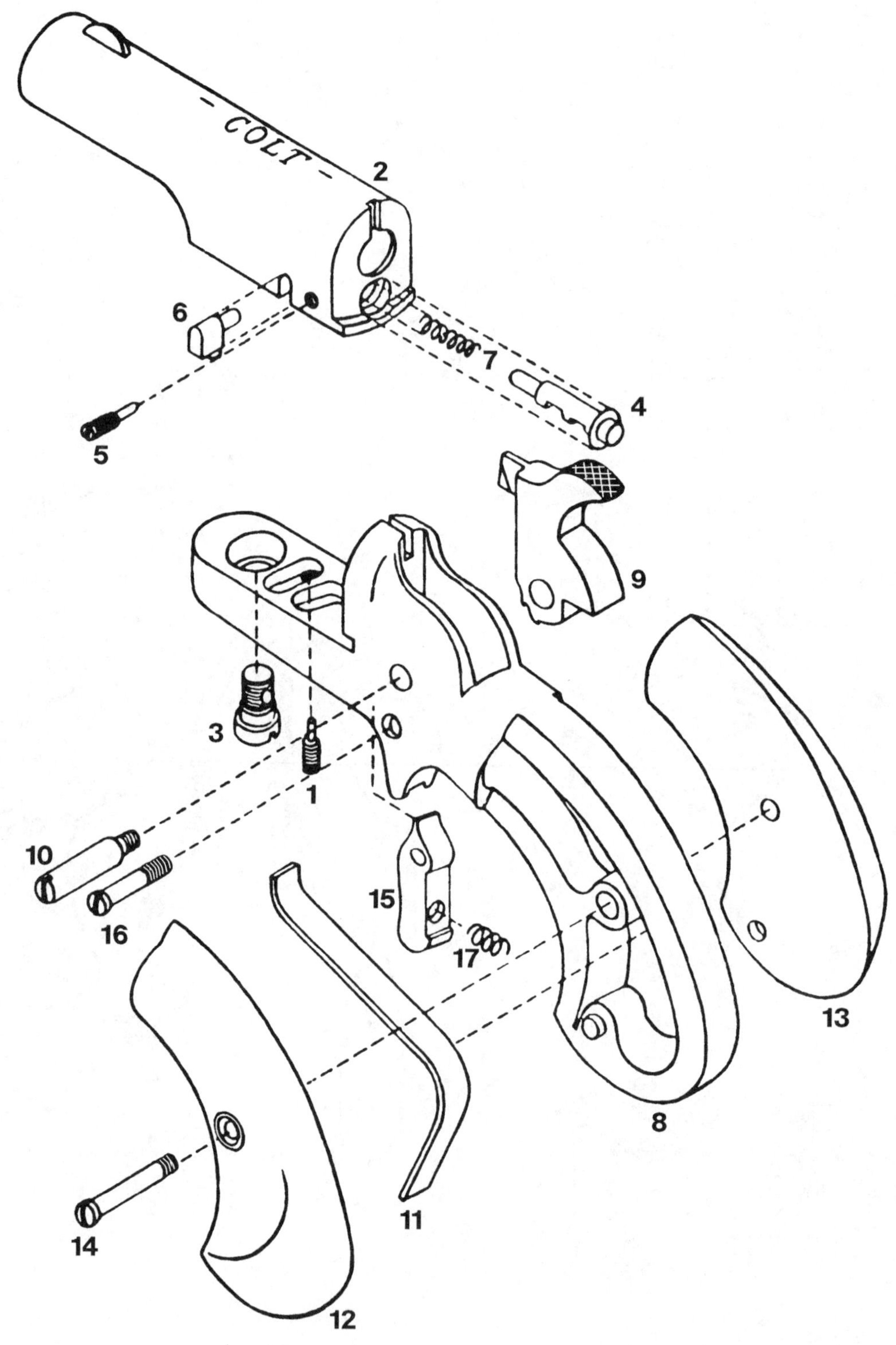

1	Assembly Screw	7	Ejector Spring	13	Stock, Left
2	Barrel	8	Frame	14	Stock Screw
3	Barrel Pivot Screw	9	Hammer	15	Trigger
4	Ejector	10	Hammer Screw	16	Trigger Screw
5	Ejector Retaining Screw	11	Mainspring	17	Trigger Spring
6	Ejector Sear	12	Stock, Right		

Detective Special and Agent (Old Model) Revolver

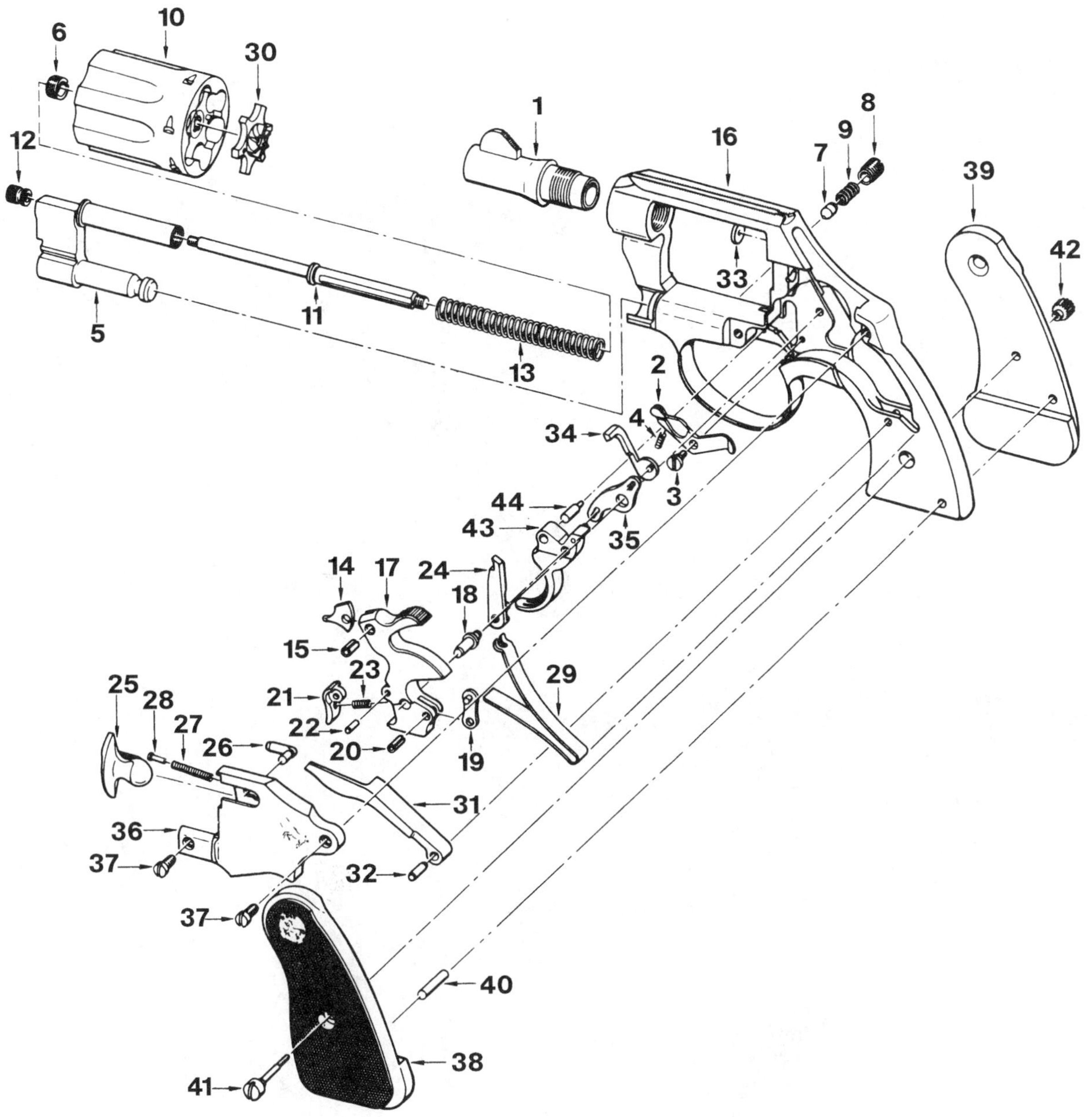

1	Barrel	**16**	Frame	**31**	Rebound Lever
2	Bolt	**17**	Hammer	**32**	Rebound Lever Pin
3	Bolt Screw	**18**	Hammer Pin	**33**	Recoil Cup
4	Bolt Spring	**19**	Hammer Stirrup	**34**	Safety
5	Crane	**20**	Hammer Stirrup Pin	**35**	Safety-Lever
6	Crane Bushing	**21**	Hammer Strut	**36**	Sideplate
7	Crane Detent	**22**	Hammer Strut Pin	**37**	Sideplate Screws
8	Spring Retaining Screw	**23**	Hammer Strut Spring	**38**	Stock, Left
9	Crane Lock Spring	**24**	Hand	**39**	Stock, Right
10	Cylinder	**25**	Latch	**40**	Stock Pin
11	Ejector Rod	**26**	Latch Pin	**41**	Stock Screw
12	Ejector Rod Head	**27**	Helical-Compression Spring	**42**	Stock Screw Nut
13	Ejector Spring	**28**	Latch Spring Guide	**43**	Trigger
14	Firing Pin	**29**	Mainspring	**44**	Headless Shoulder Pin
15	Roll Pin	**30**	Ejector Ratchet		

Detective Special, Agent and Cobra (New Model) Revolver

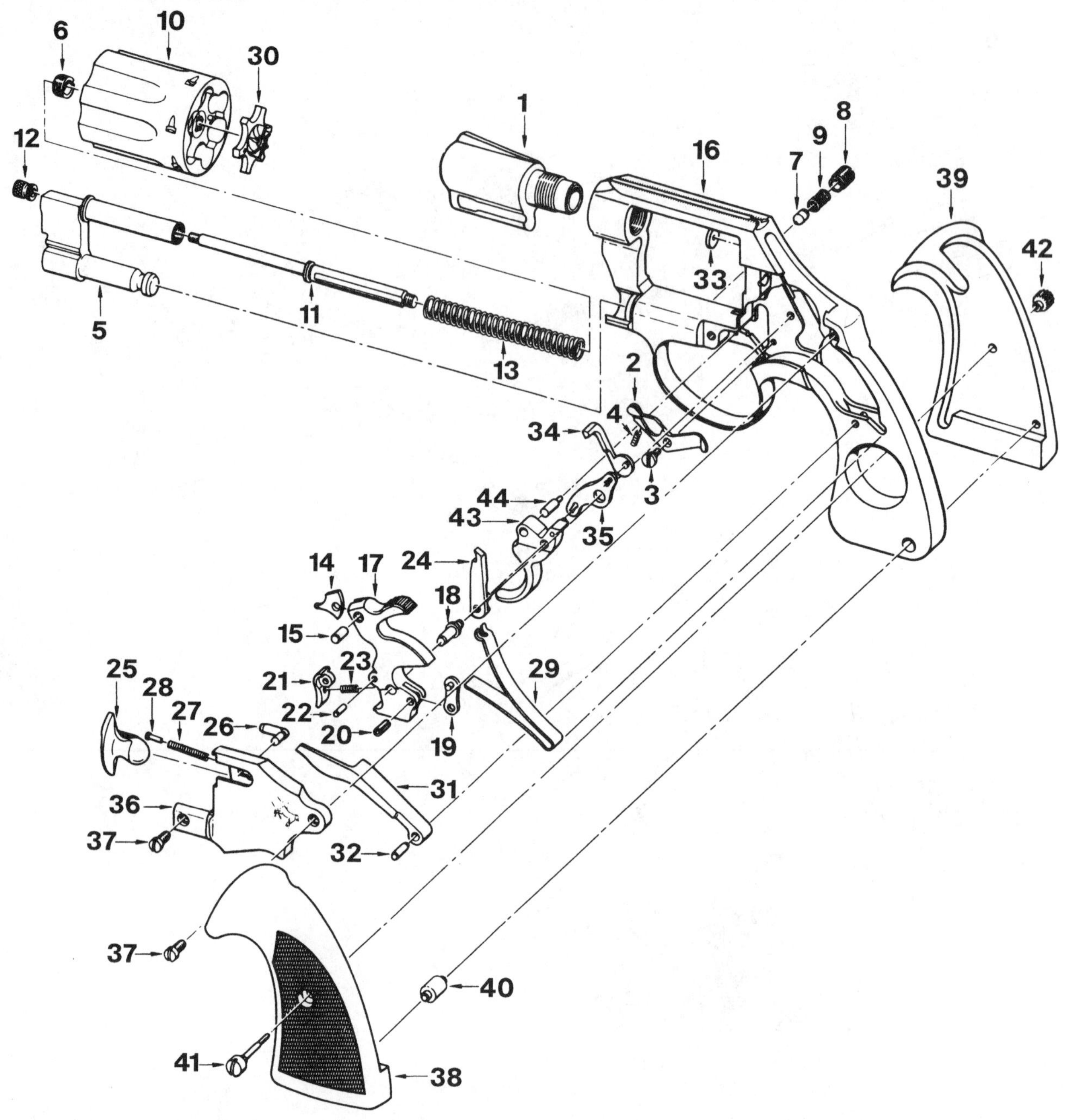

No.	Part	No.	Part	No.	Part
1	Barrel Assembly	16	Frame Assembly	31	Rebound Lever
2	Bolt	17	Hammer Assembly	32	Rebound Lever Pin
3	Bolt Screw	18	Hammer Pin	33	Recoil Plate
4	Bolt Spring	19	Hammer Stirrup	34	Safety Assembly
5	Crane	20	Hammer Stirrup Pin	35	Safety-Lever
6	Crane Bushing	21	Hammer Strut	36	Sideplate
7	Crane Detent	22	Hammer Strut Pin	37	Sideplate Screws
8	Spring Retaining Screw	23	Hammer Strut Spring	38	Stock, Left
9	Crane Lock Spring	24	Hand Detent Assembly	39	Stock, Right
10	Cylinder	25	Latch	40	Stock Pin
11	Ejector Rod	26	Latch Pin	41	Stock Screw
12	Ejector Rod Head	27	Latch Spring	42	Stock Screw Nut
13	Ejector Spring	28	Latch Spring Guide	43	Trigger
14	Firing Pin	29	Mainspring	44	Trigger Pin
15	Firing Pin Rivet	30	Ejector Ratchet		

Double Eagle Auto

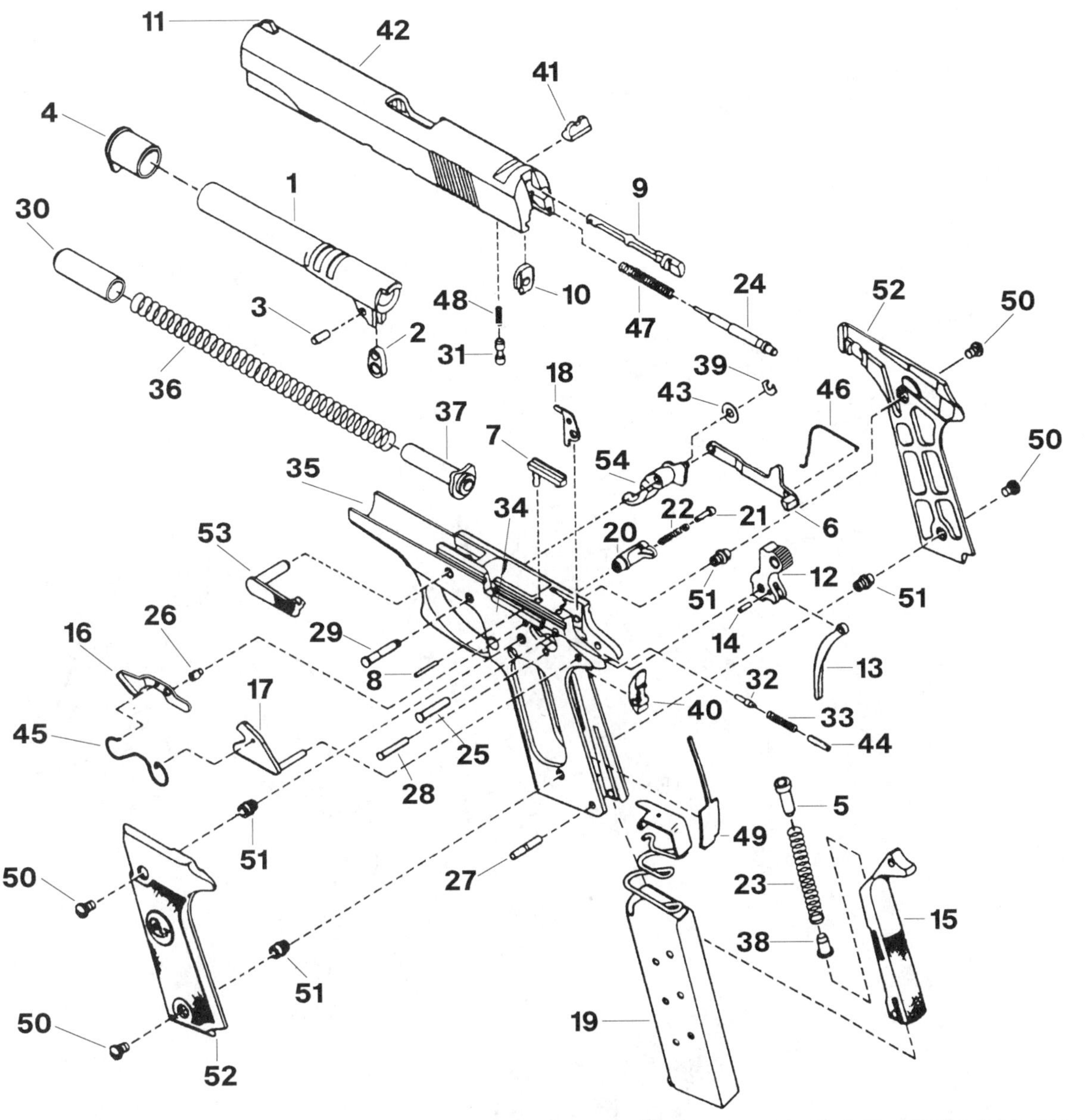

1	Barrel	19	Magazine Assembly	37	Recoil Spring Guide
2	Barrel Link	20	Magazine Catch	38	Pin Retainer
3	Barrel Link Pin	21	Magazine Catch Lock	39	Trigger Retaining Ring
4	Barrel Bushing	22	Magazine Catch/Gate Spring	40	Sear
5	Mainspring Cap	23	Mainspring	41	Rear Sight
6	Drawbar	24	Firing Pin	42	Slide
7	Ejector	25	Hammer Pin	43	Spacer Washer
8	Ejector Pin	26	Decocking Lever Pin	44	Spiral Pin
9	Extractor	27	Mainspring Housing Pin	45	Decocking Spring
10	Firing Pin Stop	28	Sear Pin	46	Drawbar Spring
11	Front Sight	29	Trigger Pin	47	Firing Pin Spring
12	Hammer	30	Recoil Spring Plug	48	Firing Pin Plunger Spring
13	Hammer Strut	31	Firing Pin Plunger	49	Sear Spring
14	Hammer Strut Pin	32	Slide Stop Plunger	50	Stock Screws
15	Mainspring Housing	33	Plunger Spring	51	Stock Screw Bushings
16	Forward Decocking Lever	34	Plunger Tube	52	Stocks
17	Rear Decocking Lever	35	Receiver	53	Slide Stop
18	Plunger Lever	36	Recoil Spring	54	Trigger

Frontier Scout and Buntline Scout Revolver

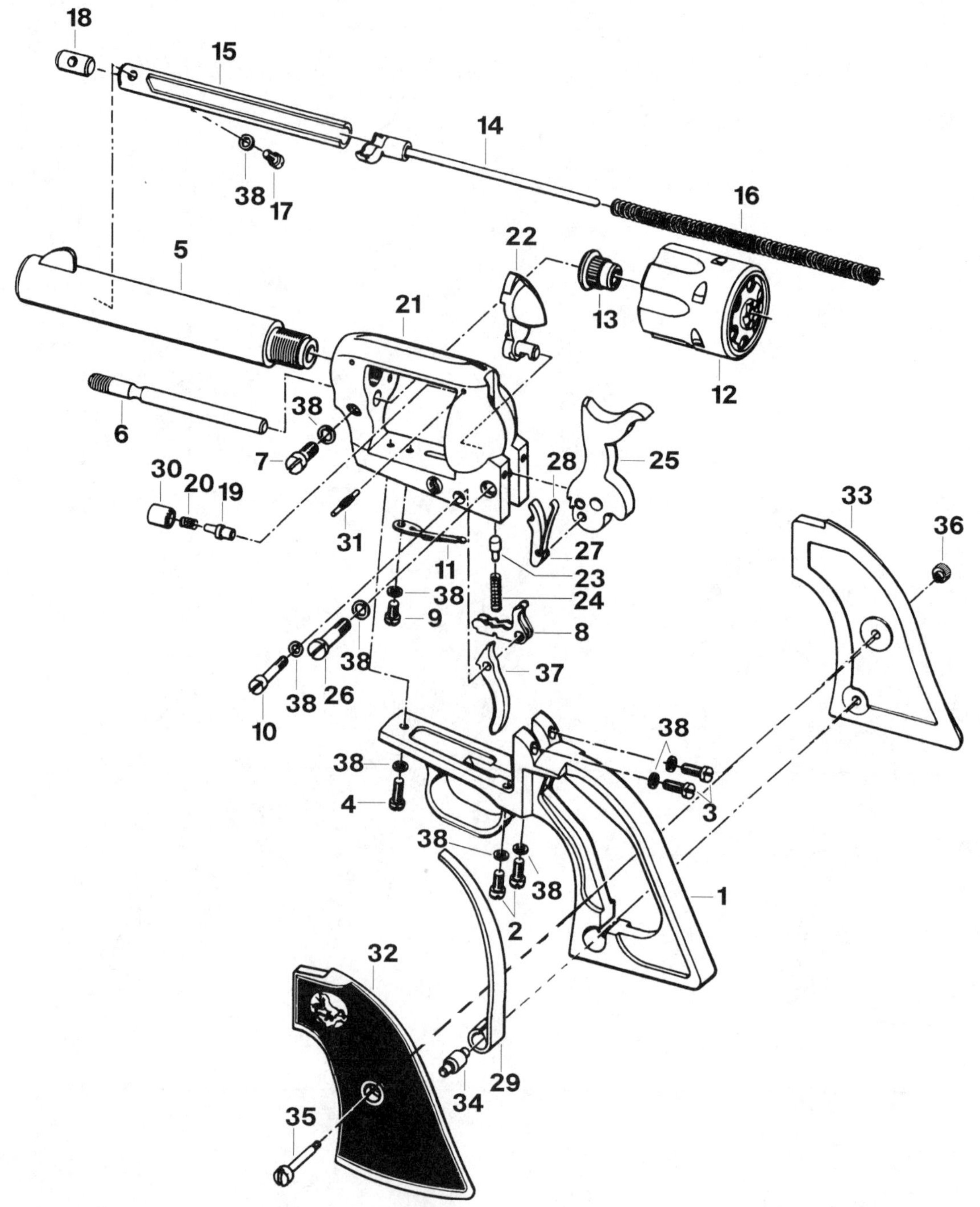

1	Backstrap	**14**	Ejector Rod	**27**	Hand and Post Assembly
2	Backstrap Screws, Bottom	**15**	Ejector Rod Tube	**28**	Hand Spring
3	Backstrap Screws, Top	**16**	Ejector Spring	**29**	Mainspring
4	Backstrap Screw, Front	**17**	Ejector Tube Screw	**30**	Recoil Cup
5	Barrel	**18**	Ejector Tube Plug	**31**	Recoil Cup Pin
6	Base Pin	**19**	Firing Pin	**32**	Stock, Left
7	Base Pin Screw	**20**	Firing Pin Spring	**33**	Stock, Right
8	Bolt	**21**	Frame	**34**	Stock Pin
9	Bolt Spring Screw	**22**	Gate	**35**	Stock Screw
10	Bolt and Trigger Screw	**23**	Gate Detent	**36**	Stock Screw Nut
11	Bolt and Trigger Spring	**24**	Gate Spring	**37**	Trigger
12	Cylinder	**25**	Hammer	**38**	Washer
13	Cylinder Bushing	**26**	Hammer Screw		

Gold Cup New Model Auto

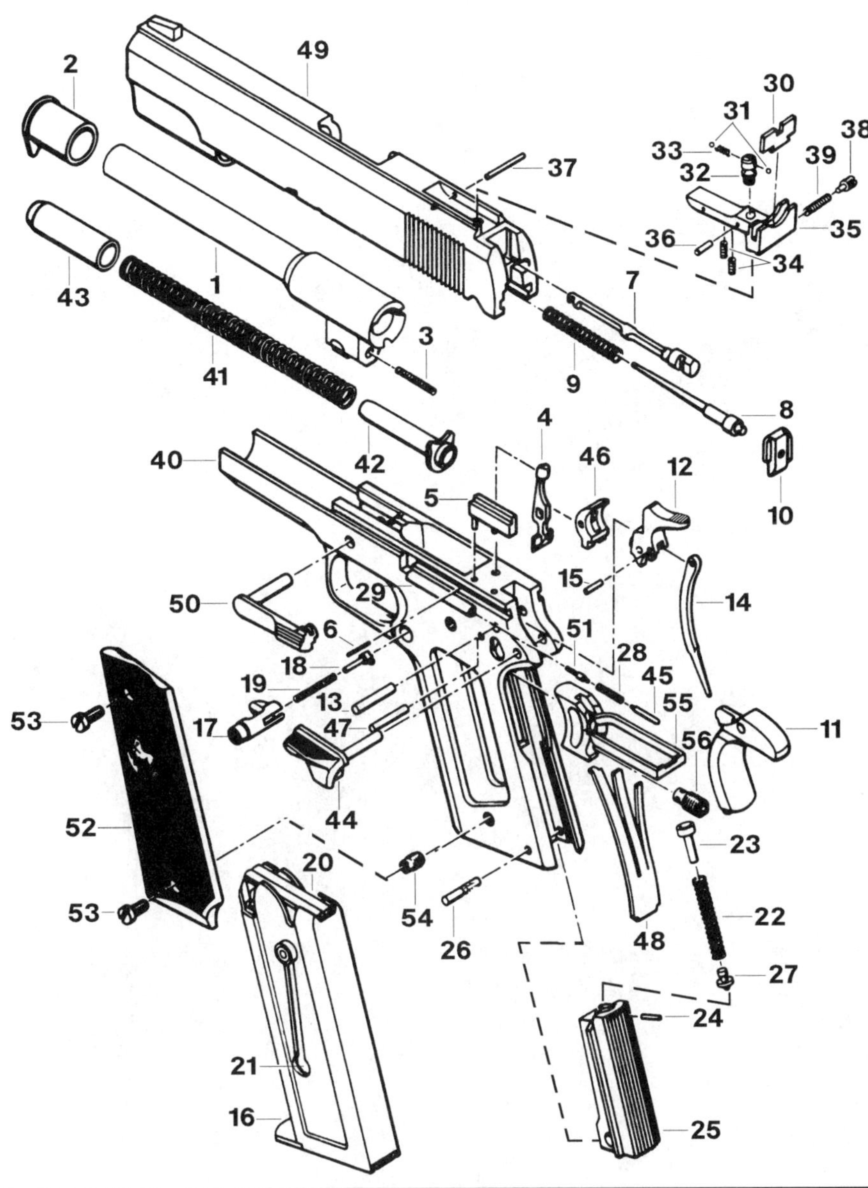

No.	Part	No.	Part	No.	Part
1	Barrel	20	Magazine Follower Assembly	38	Rear Sight Windage Screw
2	Barrel Bushing	21	Magazine Spring Assembly	39	Rear Sight Windage Spring
3	Barrel Return Spring	22	Mainspring	40	Receiver
4	Disconnector	23	Mainspring Cap	41	Recoil Spring
5	Ejector	24	Mainspring Cap Pin	42	Recoil Spring Guide
6	Ejector Pin	25	Mainspring Housing	43	Recoil Spring Plug
7	Extractor	26	Mainspring Housing Pin	44	Safety Lock
8	Firing Pin	27	Mainspring Housing Pin Retainer	45	Safety Lock Plunger
9	Firing Pin Spring	28	Plunger Spring	46	Sear
10	Firing Pin Stop	29	Plunger Tube	47	Sear Pin
11	Grip Safety	30	Rear Sight Blade	48	Sear Spring
12	Hammer	31	Rear Sight Detent Balls	49	Slide Assembly
13	Hammer Pin	32	Rear Sight Elevation Screw	50	Slide Stop
14	Hammer Strut	33	Rear Sight Detent Spring	51	Slide Stop Plunger
15	Hammer Strut Pin	34	Rear Sight Elevation Springs	52	Stock Assembly
16	Magazine Assembly	35	Rear Sight Leaf	53	Stock Screws
17	Magazine Catch	36	Rear Sight Elevation Screw Pin	54	Stock Screw Bushing
18	Magazine Catch Lock	37	Rear Sight Leaf Pin	55	Trigger Assembly
19	Magazine Catch Spring			56	Trigger Stop

Government Model 380 and 380 Mustang Auto

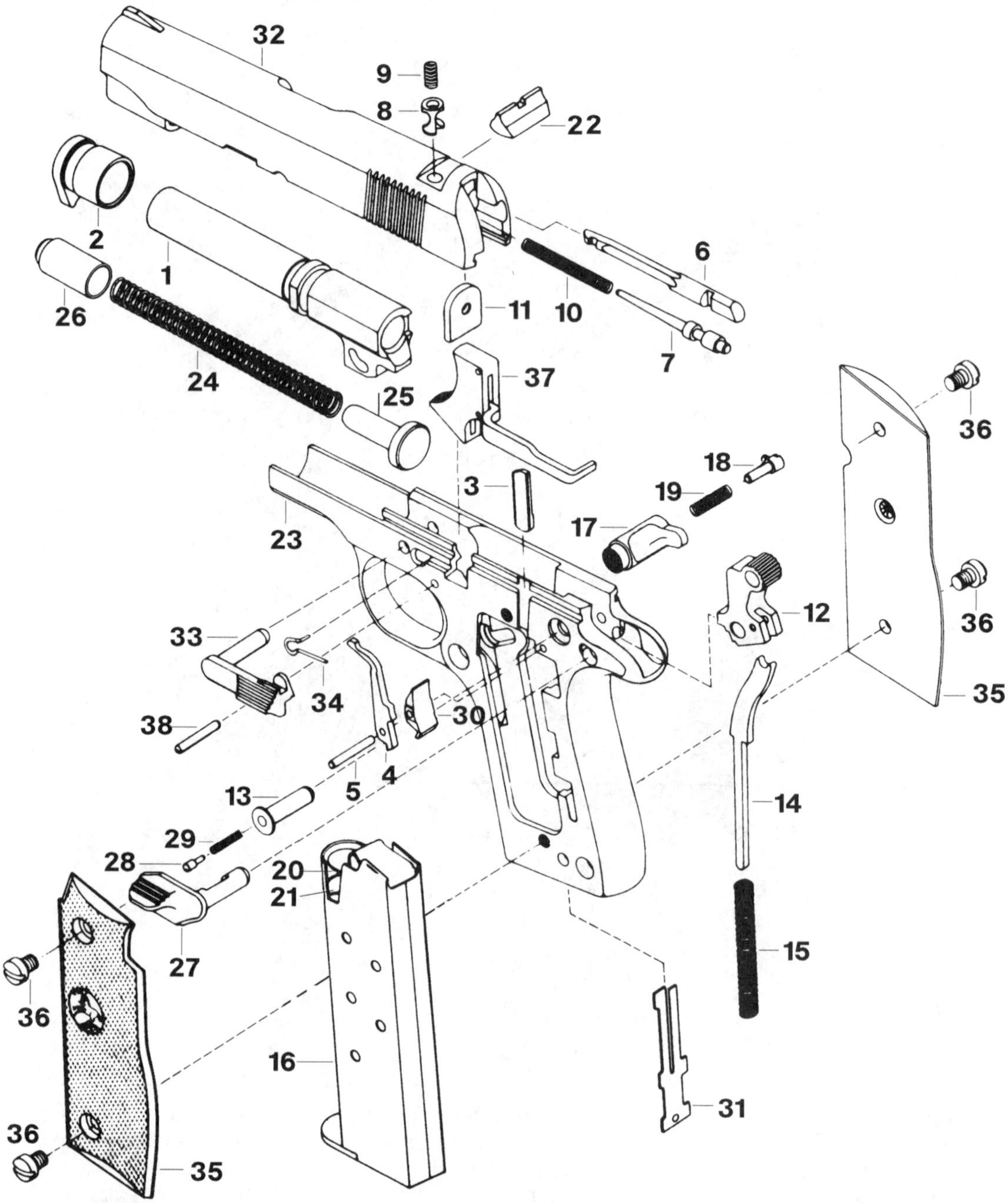

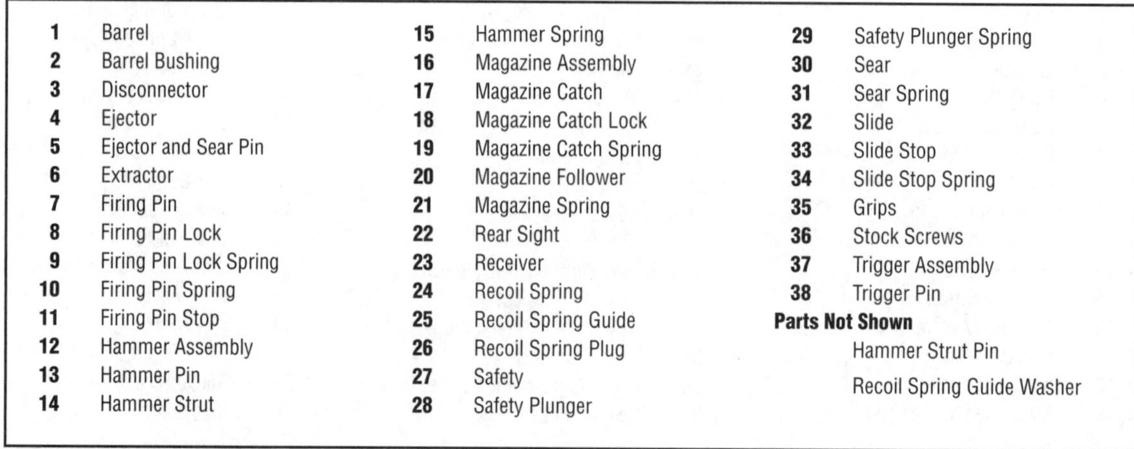

No.	Part	No.	Part	No.	Part
1	Barrel	15	Hammer Spring	29	Safety Plunger Spring
2	Barrel Bushing	16	Magazine Assembly	30	Sear
3	Disconnector	17	Magazine Catch	31	Sear Spring
4	Ejector	18	Magazine Catch Lock	32	Slide
5	Ejector and Sear Pin	19	Magazine Catch Spring	33	Slide Stop
6	Extractor	20	Magazine Follower	34	Slide Stop Spring
7	Firing Pin	21	Magazine Spring	35	Grips
8	Firing Pin Lock	22	Rear Sight	36	Stock Screws
9	Firing Pin Lock Spring	23	Receiver	37	Trigger Assembly
10	Firing Pin Spring	24	Recoil Spring	38	Trigger Pin
11	Firing Pin Stop	25	Recoil Spring Guide	**Parts Not Shown**	
12	Hammer Assembly	26	Recoil Spring Plug		Hammer Strut Pin
13	Hammer Pin	27	Safety		Recoil Spring Guide Washer
14	Hammer Strut	28	Safety Plunger		

King Cobra Revolver

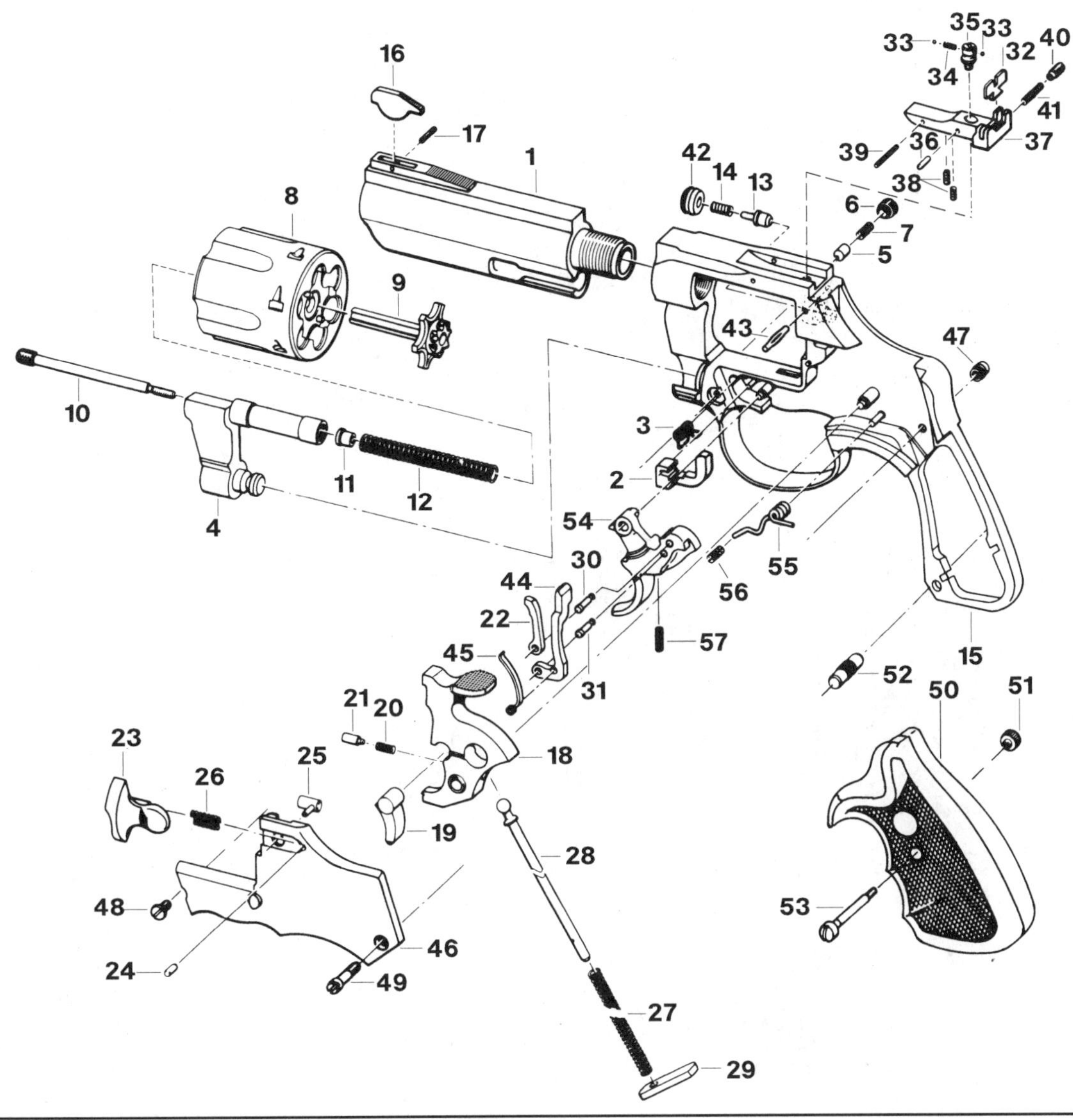

1	Barrel	**22**	Hand	**43**	Recoil Plate Pin
2	Bolt	**23**	Latch	**44**	Safety Connector
3	Bolt Spring	**24**	Latch Insert	**45**	Safety Connector and Hand Spring
4	Crane Assembly	**25**	Latch Pin Assembly	**46**	Sideplate
5	Crane Lock Detent	**26**	Latch Spring	**47**	Sideplate Nut
6	Crane Lock Screw	**27**	Mainspring	**48**	Sideplate Screw
7	Crane Lock Spring	**28**	Mainspring Guide	**49**	Sideplate and Stock Screw
8	Cylinder	**29**	Mainspring Seat	**50**	Stock Assembly
9	Ejector Ratchet and Stem	**30**	Hand Pivot Pin	**51**	Stock Nut
10	Ejector Rod	**31**	Safety-Lever Pivot Pin	**52**	Stock Pin
11	Ejector Rod Bushing	**32**	Rear Sight Blade	**53**	Stock Screw
12	Ejector Spring	**33**	Rear Sight Detent Balls	**54**	Trigger Assembly
13	Firing Pin	**34**	Rear Sight Detent Spring	**55**	Trigger Return Spring
14	Firing Pin Spring	**35**	Rear Sight Elevation Screw	**56**	Return Spring Guide
15	Frame Detent Assembly	**36**	Rear Sight Elevation Screw Pin	**57**	Trigger Screw
16	Front Sight Blade	**37**	Rear Sight Leaf	**Parts Not Shown**	
17	Front Sight Blade Pin	**38**	Rear Sight Leaf Elevation Springs		Bolt Pivot Pin
18	Hammer	**39**	Rear Sight Leaf Pin		Hammer Pivot Pin
19	Hammer Strut	**40**	Rear Sight Windage Screw		Pivot Pin Spring
20	Hammer Strut Spring	**41**	Rear Sight Windage Spring		Trigger Pivot Pin
21	Hammer Strut Spring Guide	**42**	Recoil Plate		

Lawman Mk. III, Metro Police Mk. III, Official Police Mk. III, Trooper Mk. III and Peacekeeper Revolver

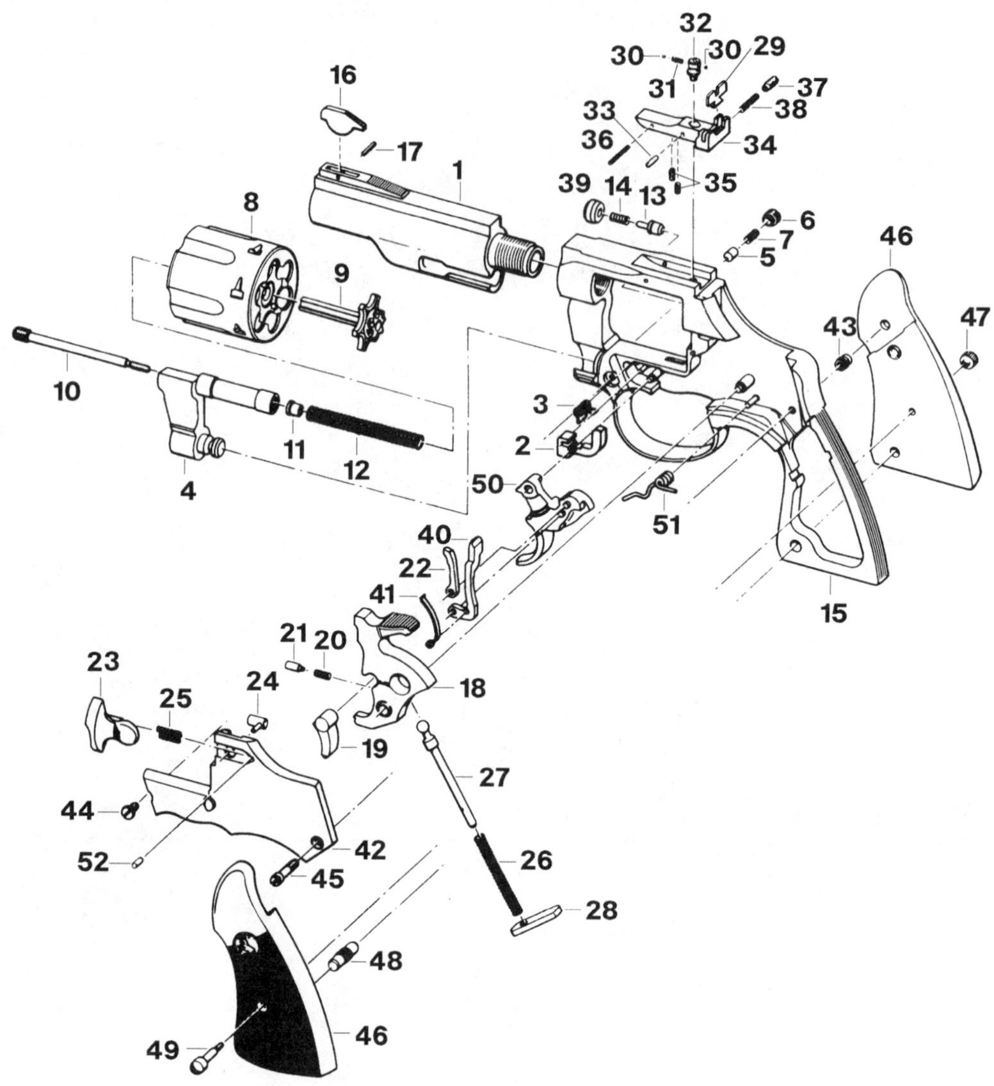

1	Barrel	**22**	Hand	**43**	Sideplate Nut
2	Bolt	**23**	Latch	**44**	Sideplate Screw
3	Bolt Spring	**24**	Latch Pin Assembly	**45**	Sideplate and Stock Screw
4	Crane Assembly	**25**	Latch Spring	**46**	Grips
5	Crane Lock Detent	**26**	Mainspring	**47**	Stock Nut
6	Crane Lock Screw	**27**	Mainspring Guide	**48**	Stock Pin
7	Crane Lock Spring	**28**	Mainspring Seat	**49**	Stock Screw
8	Cylinder	**29**	Rear Sight Blade	**50**	Trigger Assembly
9	Ejector Ratchet and Stem	**30**	Rear Sight Detent Balls	**51**	Trigger Return Spring
10	Ejector Rod	**31**	Rear Sight Detent Spring	**52**	Latch Insert
11	Ejector Rod Bushing	**32**	Rear Sight Elevation Screw	**Parts Not Shown**	
12	Ejector Spring	**33**	Rear Sight Elevation Screw Pin		Bolt Pivot Pin
13	Firing Pin	**34**	Rear Sight Leaf		Hammer Pivot Pin
14	Firing Pin Spring	**35**	Rear Sight Leaf Elevation Springs		Pivot Pin
15	Frame	**36**	Rear Sight Leaf Pin		Pivot Pin Spring
16	Front Sight Blade	**37**	Rear Sight Windage Screw		Recoil Plate Pin
17	Front Sight Blade Pin	**38**	Rear Sight Windage Spring		Trigger Pivot Pin
18	Hammer	**39**	Recoil Plate		Trigger Screw
19	Hammer Strut	**40**	Safety Connector		
20	Hammer Strut Spring	**41**	Safety Connector and Hand Spring		
21	Hammer Strut Spring Guide	**42**	Sideplate		

Lightning Revolver

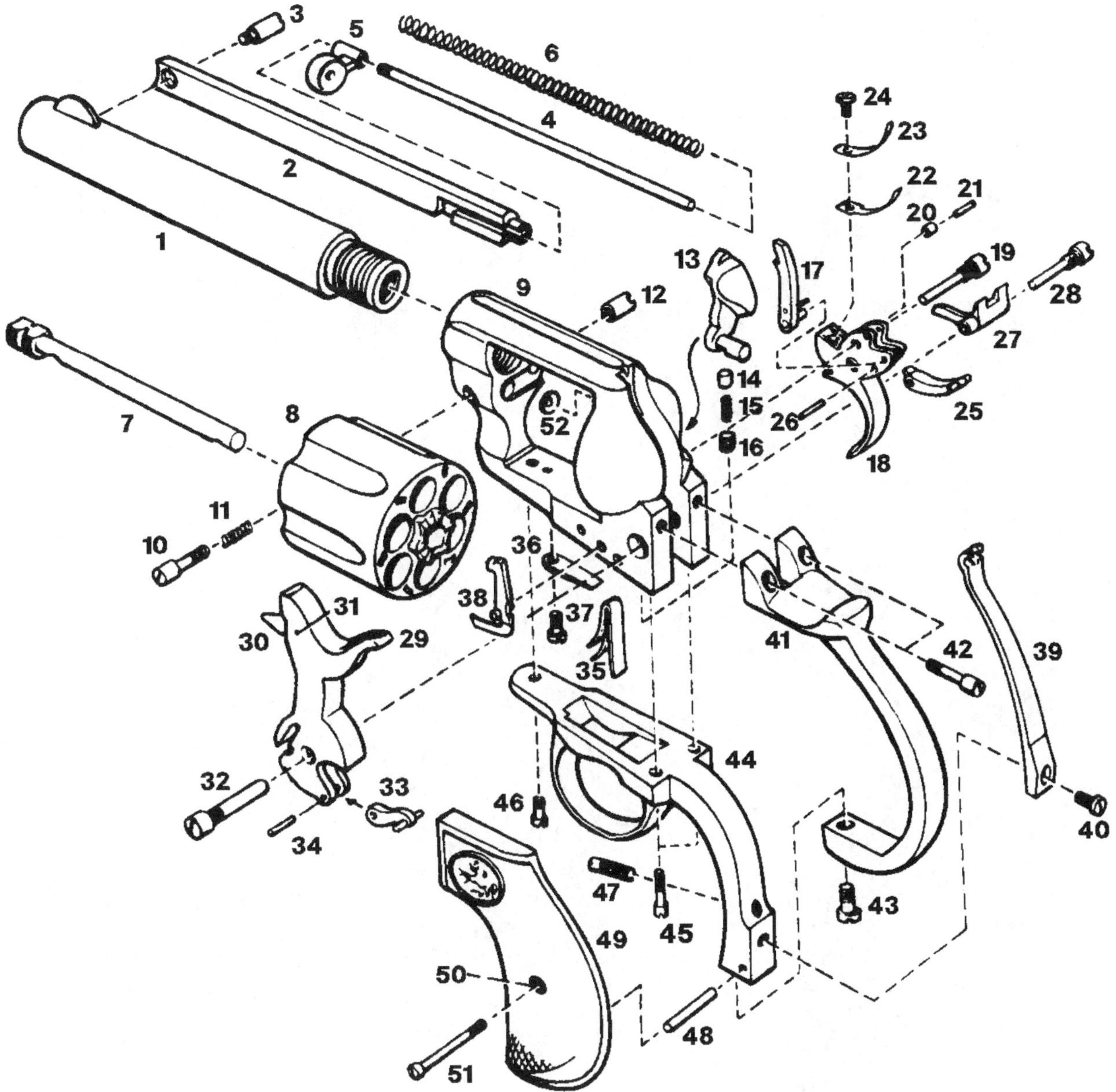

1	Barrel	19	Trigger Screw	37	Trigger Spring Screw
2	Ejector Housing	20	Trigger Roll	38	Cylinder Stop
3	Ejector Housing Screw	21	Trigger Roll Pin	39	Mainspring
4	Ejector Rod	22	Trigger Strut Spring	40	Mainspring Screw
5	Ejector Rod Head	23	Hand Spring	41	Backstrap
6	Ejector Spring	24	Hand and Strut Spring Screw	42	Backstrap Screws
7	Cylinder Pin	25	Trigger Strut	43	Butt Screw
8	Cylinder	26	Trigger Strut Pin	44	Trigger Guard
9	Frame	27	Sear	45	Rear Trigger Guard Screws
10	Cylinder Pin Lock Screw	28	Sear Screw	46	Front Trigger Guard Screw
11	Cylinder Pin Lock Screw Spring	29	Hammer	47	Mainspring Tension Screw
12	Cylinder Pin Lock Nut	30	Firing Pin	48	Grip Pin
13	Loading Gate	31	Firing Pin Rivet	49	Grip, Rubber
14	Loading Gate Catch	32	Hammer Screw	50	Escutcheon
15	Loading Gate Catch Spring	33	Stirrup	51	Grip Screw
16	Loading Gate Catch Screw	34	Stirrup Pin	52	Recoil Plate
17	Hand	35	Hand and Cylinder Stop Tension Spring		
18	Trigger	36	Trigger Spring		

Model 1911-1911A1 Auto

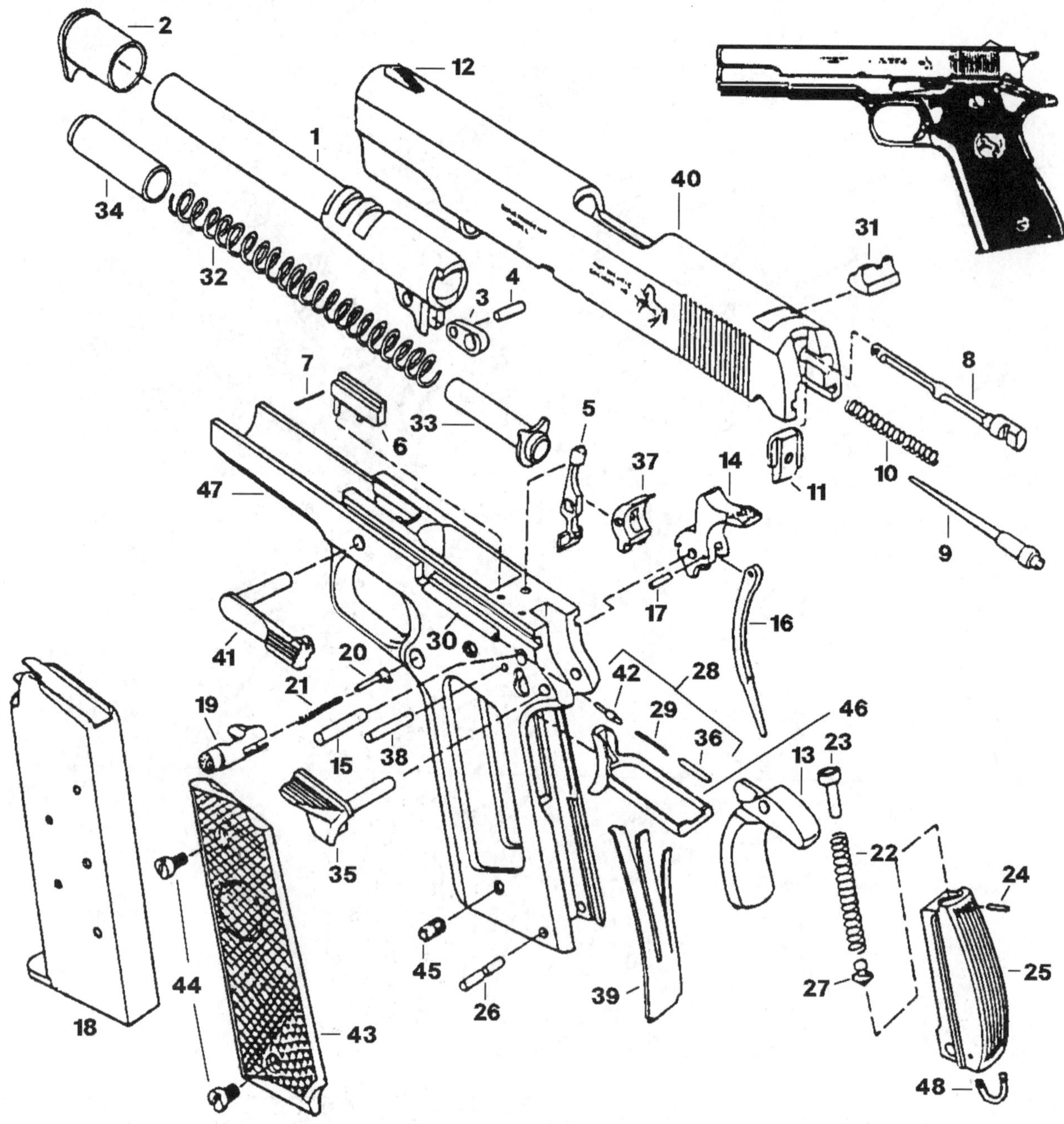

1	Barrel	**17**	Hammer Strut Pin	**33**	Recoil Spring Guide
2	Barrel Bushing	**18**	Magazine Assembly	**34**	Recoil Spring Plug
3	Barrel Link	**19**	Magazine Catch	**35**	Safety Lock
4	Barrel Link Pin	**20**	Magazine Catch Lock	**36**	Safety Lock Plunger
5	Disconnector	**21**	Magazine Catch Spring	**37**	Sear
6	Ejector	**22**	Mainspring	**38**	Sear/Disconnector Pin
7	Ejector Pin	**23**	Mainspring Cap	**39**	Sear Spring
8	Extractor	**24**	Mainspring Cap Pin	**40**	Slide
9	Firing Pin	**25**	Mainspring Housing	**41**	Slide Stop
10	Firing Pin Spring	**26**	Mainspring Housing Pin	**42**	Slide Stop Plunger
11	Firing Pin Stop	**27**	Mainspring Housing Pin Retainer	**43**	Stock Assembly
12	Front Sight	**28**	Plunger Spring Assembly	**44**	Stock Screws
13	Grip Safety	**29**	Plunger Spring	**45**	Stock Screw Bushing
14	Hammer	**30**	Plunger Tube	**46**	Trigger
15	Hammer Pin	**31**	Rear Sight	**47**	Frame
16	Hammer Strut	**32**	Recoil Spring	**48**	Lanyard Loop

New Army and New Navy Revolver

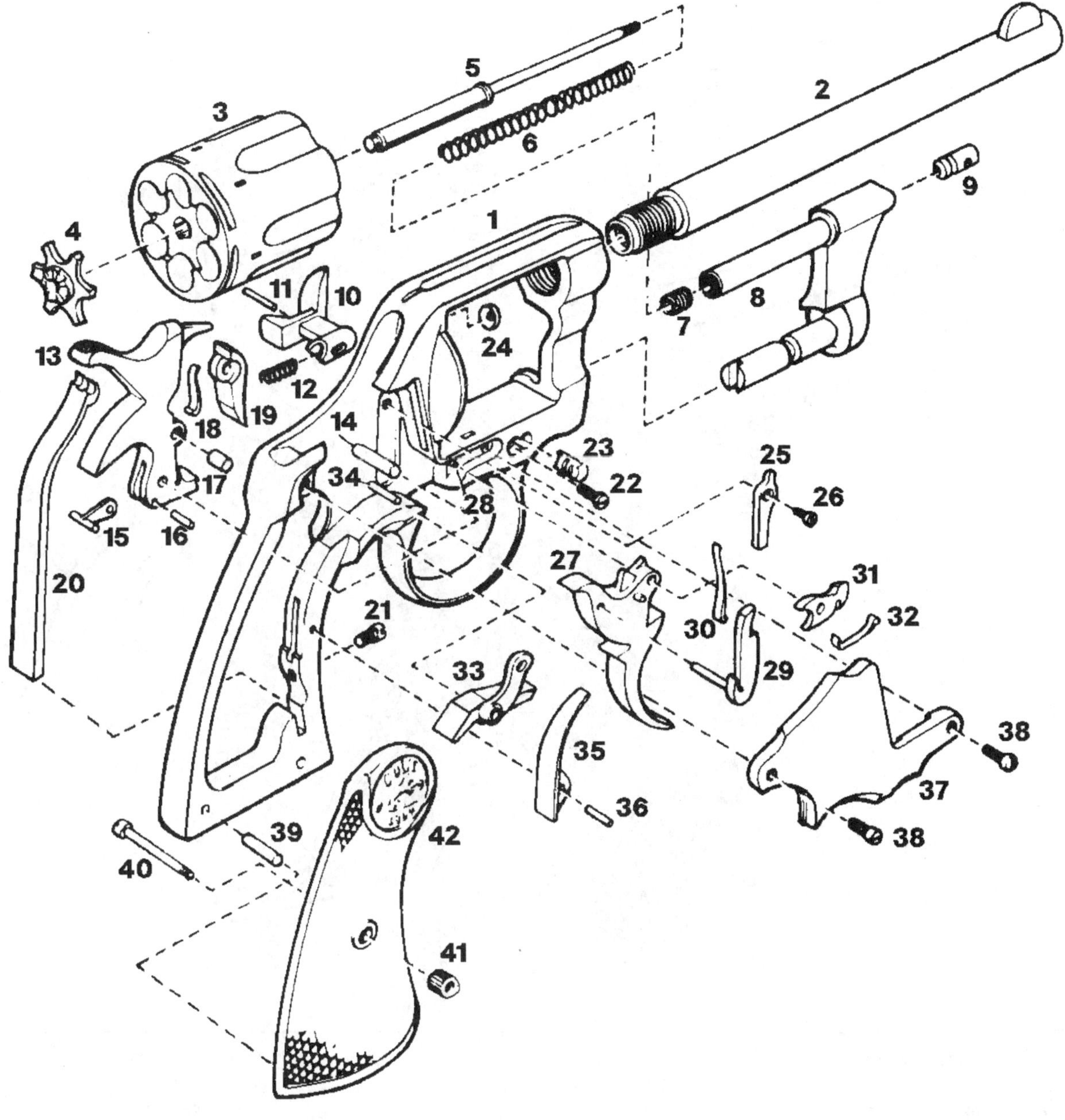

1	Frame	**15**	Hammer Stirrup	**29**	Cylinder Hand
2	Barrel	**16**	Hammer Stirrup Pin	**30**	Cylinder Hand Spring
3	Cylinder	**17**	Hammer Strut Spring Roller	**31**	Cylinder Stop
4	Ejector Ratchet	**18**	Hammer Strut Spring	**32**	Cylinder Stop Spring
5	Ejector Rod	**19**	Hammer Strut	**33**	Rebound Lever
6	Ejector Rod Spring	**20**	Mainspring	**34**	Rebound Lever Pin
7	Crane Bushing	**21**	Mainspring Tension Screw	**35**	Rebound Lever Spring
8	Crane	**22**	Crane Lock Screw	**36**	Rebound Lever Spring Pin
9	Ejector Rod Head	**23**	Crane Lock	**37**	Sideplate
10	Cylinder Latch	**24**	Firing Pin Bushing	**38**	Sideplate Screws
11	Cylinder Latch Retaining Pin	**25**	Locking Lever	**39**	Grip Locator Pin
12	Cylinder Latch Spring	**26**	Locking Lever Screw	**40**	Grip Screw
13	Hammer	**27**	Trigger	**41**	Grip Screw Bushing
14	Hammer Pin	**28**	Trigger Axis Pin	**42**	Grip

New Frontier 22 Revolver

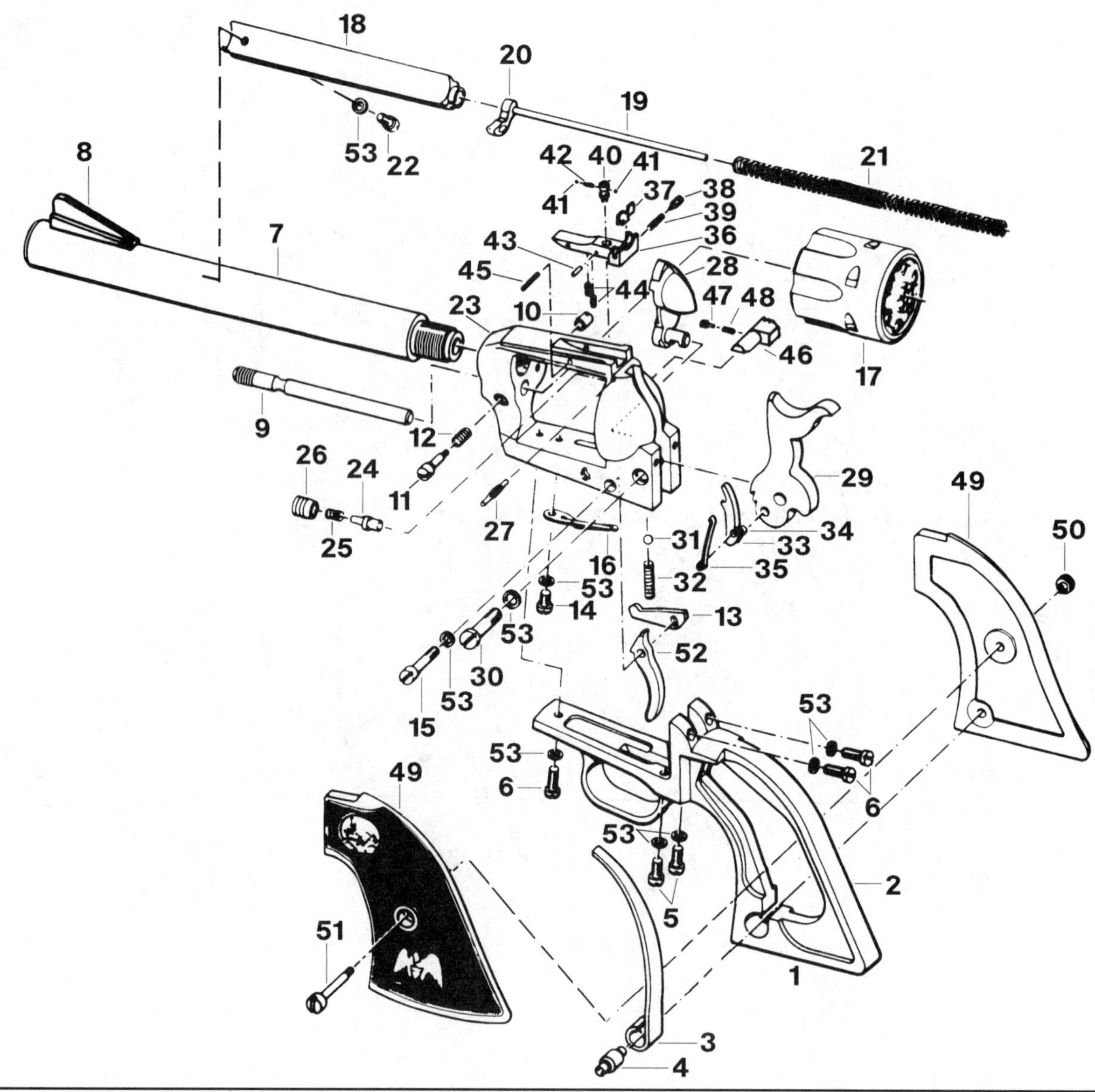

1	Backstrap Assembly	**21**	Ejector Spring	**41**	Elevation Detent Balls
2	Backstrap	**22**	Ejector Tube Screw	**42**	Elevation Detent Spring
3	Mainspring	**23**	Frame	**43**	Elevation Screw Pin
4	Stock Pin	**24**	Firing Pin	**44**	Elevation Springs
5	Grip Frame Screws, Bottom	**25**	Firing Pin Spring	**45**	Rear Sight Retention Pin
6	Grip Frame Screws, Front and Top	**26**	Recoil Plate	**46**	Safety Bolt
7	Barrel	**27**	Recoil Plate Pin	**47**	Safety Detent
8	Front Sight	**28**	Gate	**48**	Safety Detent Spring
9	Base Pin	**29**	Hammer	**49**	Stock Assembly
10	Base Pin Lock Nut	**30**	Hammer Screw	**50**	Stock Nut
11	Base Pin Lock Screw	**31**	Gate Detent	**51**	Stock Screw
12	Base Pin Lock Spring	**32**	Gate Detent Spring	**52**	Trigger
13	Bolt	**33**	Hand	**53**	Washers
14	Bolt Spring Screw	**34**	Hand Post	**Parts Not Shown**	
15	Bolt and Trigger Screw	**35**	Hand Spring		Base Pin Screw
16	Bolt and Trigger Spring	**36**	Rear Sight Leaf		Cylinder Bushing
17	Cylinder	**37**	Rear Sight Blade		Ejector Tube Plug
18	Ejector Tube	**38**	Windage Screw		Ejector Tube
19	Ejector Rod	**39**	Windage Detent Spring		
20	Ejector Rod Head	**40**	Elevation Screw		

New Frontier SAA Revolver

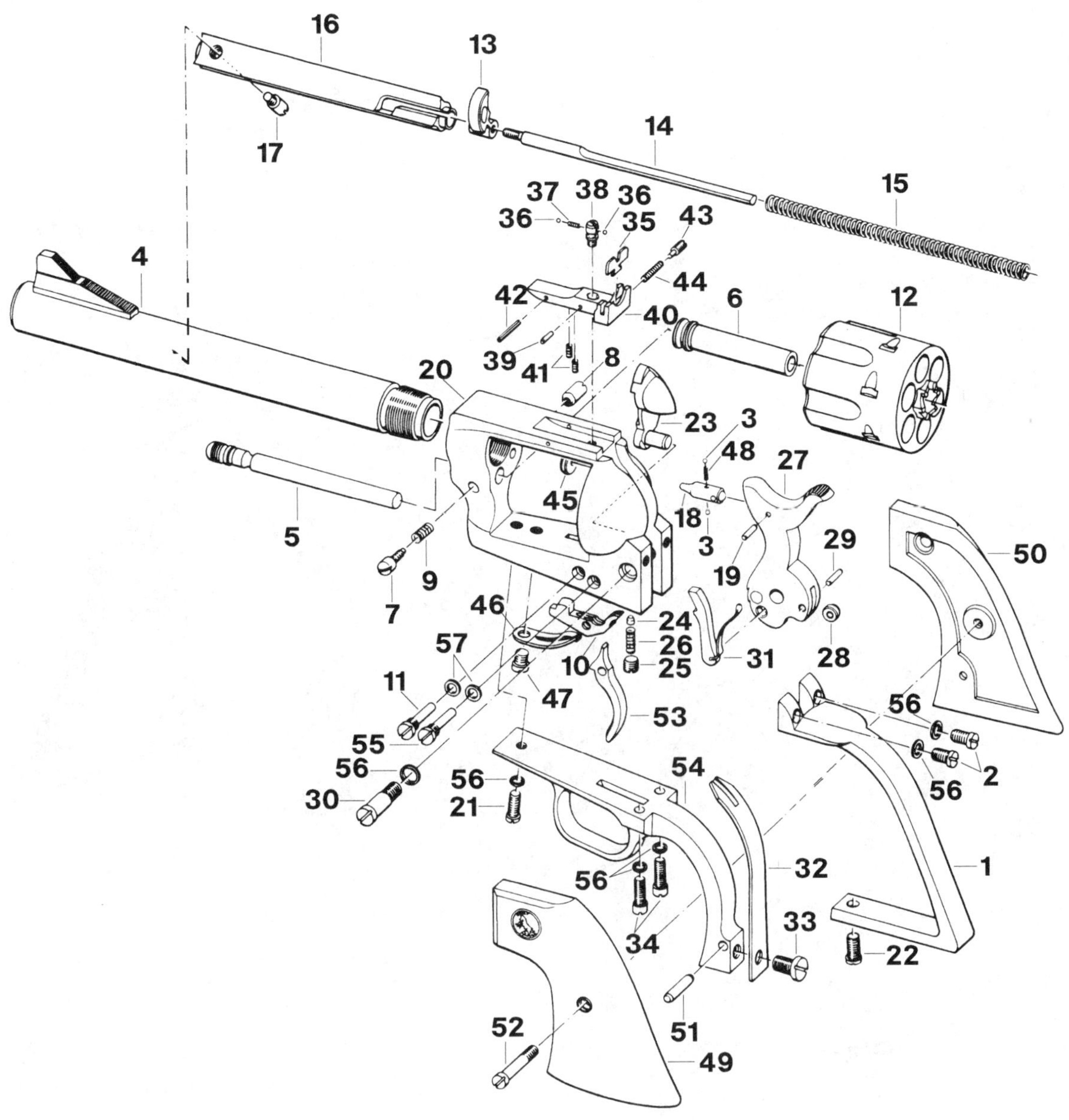

No.	Part	No.	Part	No.	Part
1	Backstrap	20	Frame	39	Rear Sight Elevation Screw Pin
2	Backstrap Screws	21	Front Guard Screw	40	Rear Sight Leaf
3	Balls	22	Frontstrap Screw	41	Rear Sight Leaf Elevation Springs
4	Barrel	23	Gate	42	Rear Sight Leaf Pin
5	Base Pin	24	Gate Catch	43	Rear Sight Windage Screw
6	Base Pin Bushing	25	Gate Catch Screw	44	Rear Sight Windage Spring
7	Base Pin Screw	26	Gate Spring	45	Recoil Plate
8	Base Pin Screw Nut	27	Hammer Assembly	46	Sear and Bolt Spring
9	Base Pin Spring	28	Hammer Roll	47	Sear and Bolt Spring Screw
10	Bolt	29	Hammer Roll Pin	48	Spring
11	Bolt Screw	30	Hammer Screw	49	Left Grip
12	Cylinder	31	Hand	50	Right Grip
13	Ejector Head	32	Mainspring	51	Stock Pin
14	Ejector Rod	33	Mainspring Screw	52	Stock Screw
15	Ejector Spring	34	Rear Guard Screws	53	Trigger
16	Ejector Tube	35	Rear Sight Blade	54	Trigger Guard
17	Ejector Tube Screw	36	Rear Sight Detent Balls	55	Trigger Screw
18	Firing Pin	37	Rear Sight Detent Spring	56	Washers
19	Firing Pin Rivet	38	Rear Sight Elevation Screw		

Officer's Model Match Revolver

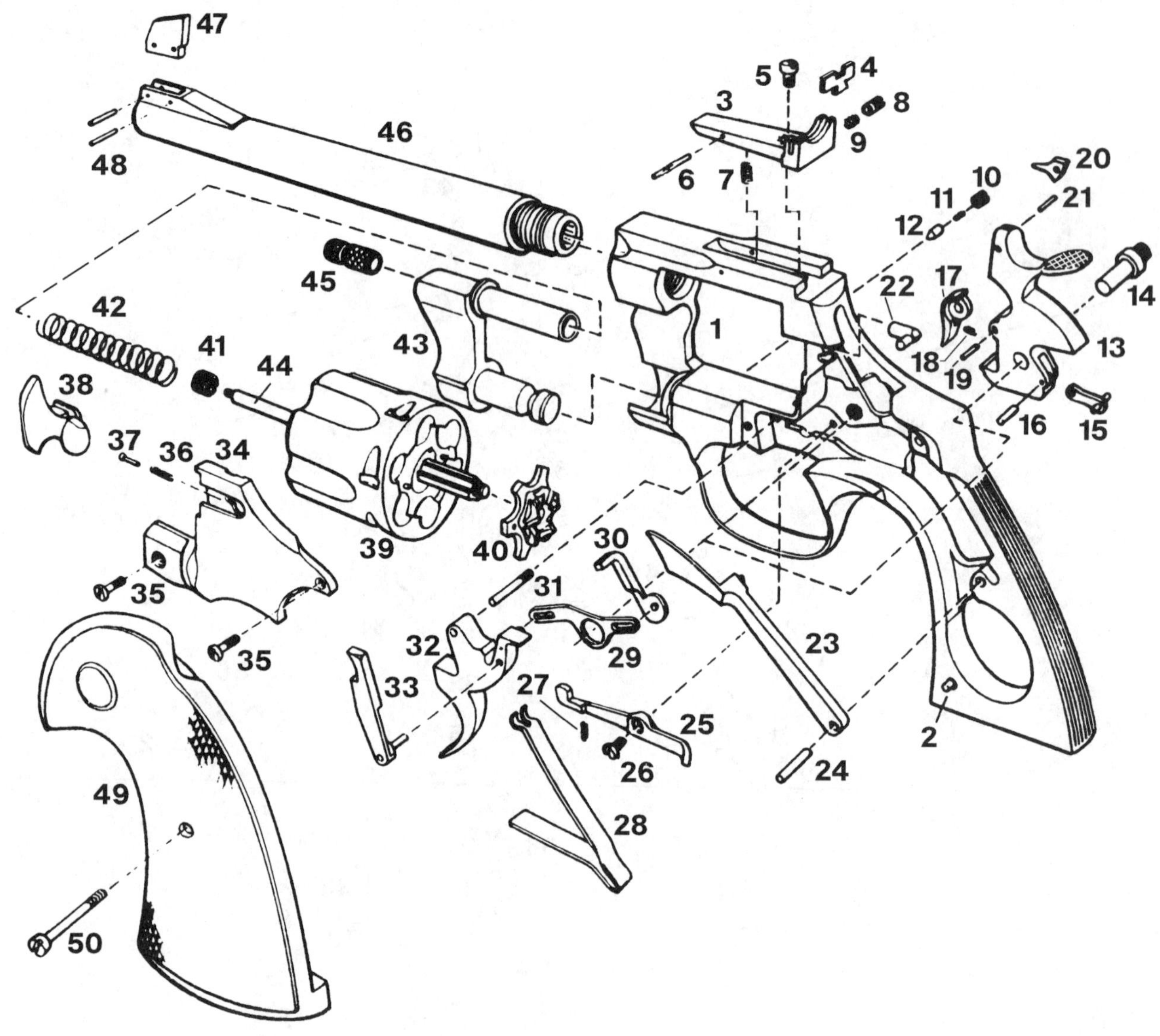

1	Frame	18	Strut Spring	35	Sideplate Screws
2	Stock Pin	19	Strut Pin	36	Latch Spring
3	Rear Sight Leaf	20	Firing Pin	37	Latch Spring Guide
4	Rear Sight Blade	21	Firing Pin Rivet	38	Latch
5	Rear Sight Elevation Screw	22	Latch Pin	39	Cylinder
6	Rear Sight Elevation Pin	23	Rebound Lever	40	Ratchet
7	Rear Sight Elevation Spring	24	Rebound Lever Pin	41	Crane Bushing
8	Rear Sight Windage Screw	25	Bolt	42	Ejector Spring
9	Rear Sight Windage Spring	26	Bolt Screw	43	Crane
10	Crane Lock Screw	27	Bolt Spring	44	Ejector Rod
11	Crane Lock Spring	28	Mainspring	45	Ejector Rod Head
12	Crane Lock Detent	29	Safety-Lever	46	Barrel
13	Hammer	30	Safety	47	Front Sight Blade
14	Hammer Pin	31	Trigger Pin	48	Front Sight Pins
15	Hammer Stirrup	32	Trigger	49	Stock
16	Hammer Stirrup Pin	33	Hand	50	Stock Screw
17	Strut	34	Sideplate		

Official Police Revolver

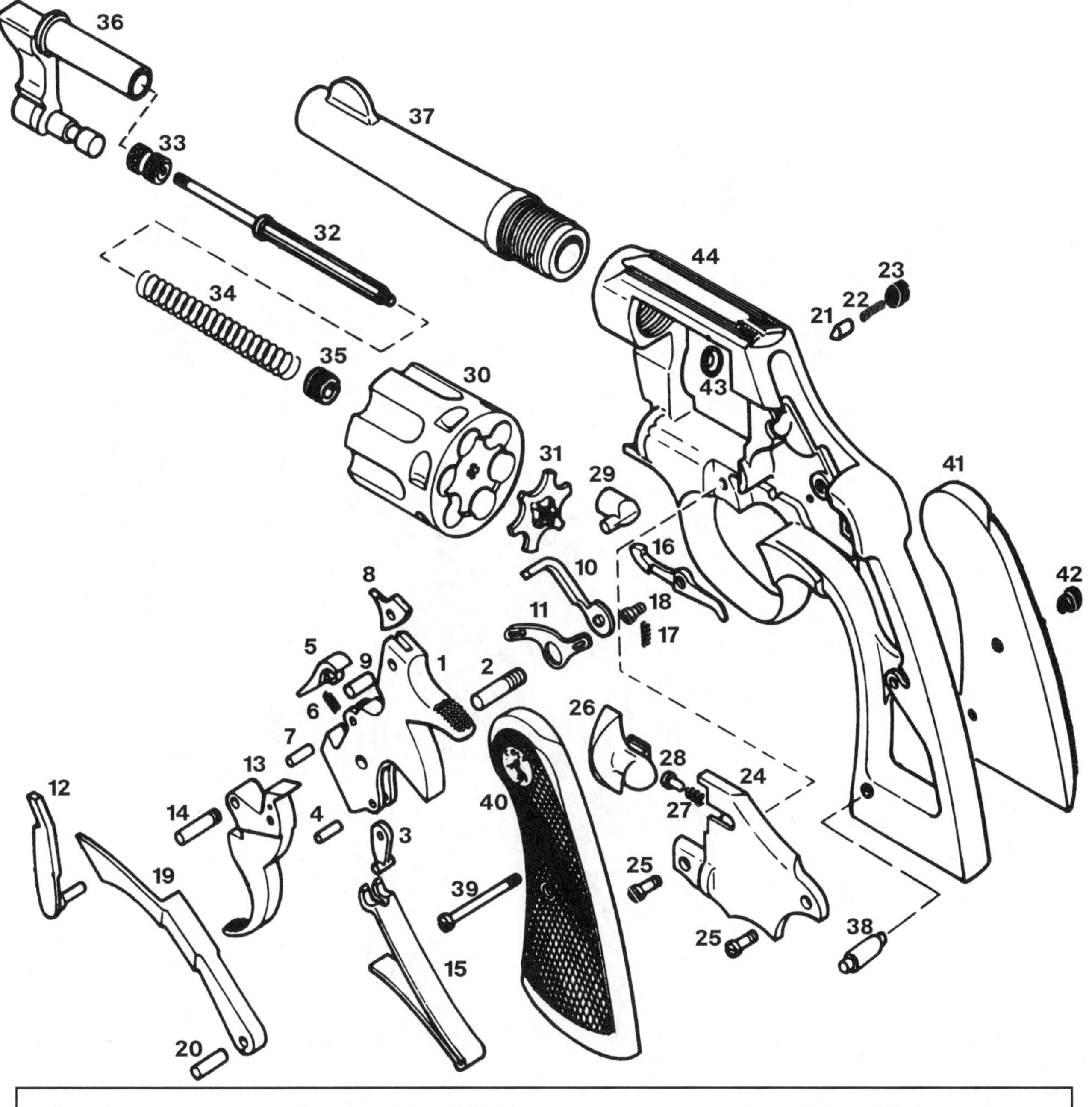

1	Hammer	**17**	Bolt Spring	**33**	Ejector Rod Head
2	Hammer Pin	**18**	Bolt Screw	**34**	Ejector Spring
3	Hammer Stirrup	**19**	Rebound Lever	**35**	Crane Bushing
4	Hammer Stirrup Pin	**20**	Rebound Lever Pin	**36**	Crane
5	Strut	**21**	Crane Lock Detent	**37**	Barrel
6	Strut Spring	**22**	Crane Lock Spring	**38**	Stock Pin
7	Strut Pin	**23**	Crane Lock Screw	**39**	Stock Screw
8	Firing Pin	**24**	Sideplate	**40**	Stock, Left
9	Firing Pin Rivet	**25**	Sideplate Screws	**41**	Stock, Right
10	Safety	**26**	Latch	**42**	Stock Screw Nut
11	Safety-Lever	**27**	Latch Spring	**43**	Recoil Plate
12	Hand	**28**	Latch Spring Guide	**44**	Frame
13	Trigger	**29**	Latch Pin	**Parts Not Shown**	
14	Trigger Pin	**30**	Cylinder		Cylinder Bushing
15	Mainspring	**31**	Ratchet		Cylinder Bushing Pin
16	Bolt	**32**	Ejector Rod		

Paterson Revolver

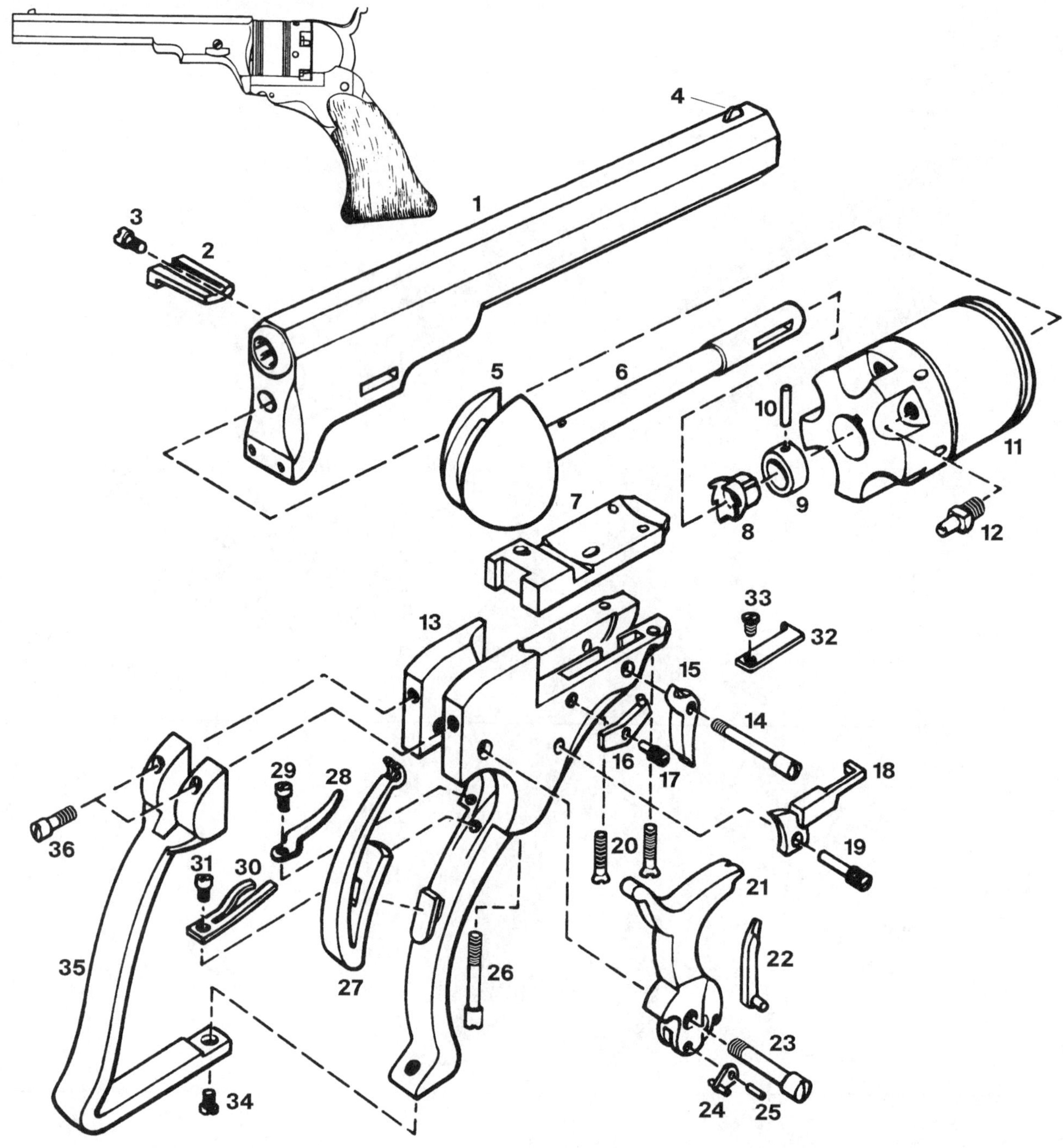

1	Barrel	**14**	Trigger Screw	**27**	Mainspring
2	Wedge	**15**	Trigger	**28**	Hand Spring
3	Wedge Screw	**16**	Bolt	**29**	Hand Spring Screw
4	Front Sight	**17**	Bolt Screw	**30**	Trigger and Bolt Spring
5	Recoil Shield	**18**	Trigger Actuating Bar	**31**	Trigger and Bolt Spring Screw
6	Cylinder Arbor	**19**	Trigger Actuating Bar Screw	**32**	Upper Trigger Spring
7	Frame Plate	**20**	Frame Plate Screws	**33**	Upper Trigger Spring Screw
8	Ratchet	**21**	Hammer	**34**	Butt Screw
9	Retaining Collar	**22**	Hand	**35**	Backstrap
10	Retaining Collar Pin	**23**	Hammer Screw	**36**	Backstrap Screws
11	Cylinder	**24**	Stirrup	**Parts Not Shown**	
12	Nipple	**25**	Stirrup Pin		Grip
13	Frame	**26**	Recoil Shield Screw		

Peacemaker, Peacemaker Buntline, New Frontier and New Frontier Buntline Revolver

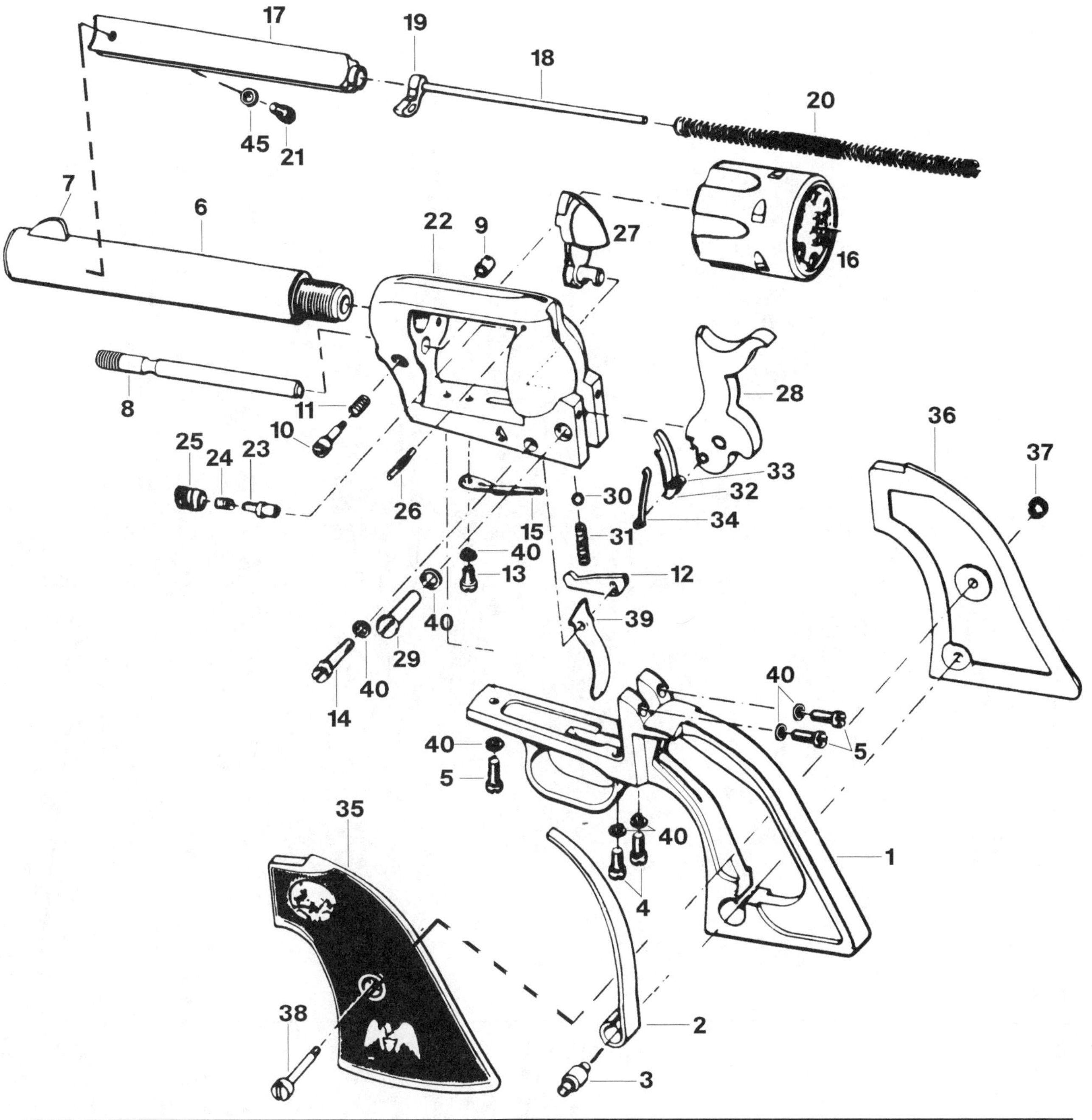

1	Backstrap	**15**	Bolt and Trigger Spring	**29**	Hammer Screw
2	Mainspring	**16**	Cylinder	**30**	Gate Detent
3	Stock Pin	**17**	Ejector Tube	**31**	Gate Detent Spring
4	Backstrap Screws, Bottom	**18**	Ejector Rod	**32**	Hand
5	Backstrap Screws, Front and Top	**19**	Ejector Rod Head	**33**	Hand Post
6	Barrel	**20**	Ejector Spring	**34**	Hand Spring
7	Front Sight	**21**	Ejector Tube Screw	**35**	Stock, Left
8	Base Pin	**22**	Frame	**36**	Stock, Right
9	Base Pin Lock Nut	**23**	Firing Pin	**37**	Stock Nut
10	Base Pin Lock Screw	**24**	Firing Pin Spring	**38**	Stock Screw
11	Base Pin Lock Spring	**25**	Recoil Plate	**39**	Trigger
12	Bolt	**26**	Recoil Plate Pin	**40**	Washers
13	Bolt Spring Screw	**27**	Gate		
14	Bolt and Trigger Screw	**28**	Hammer		

Pocket Auto

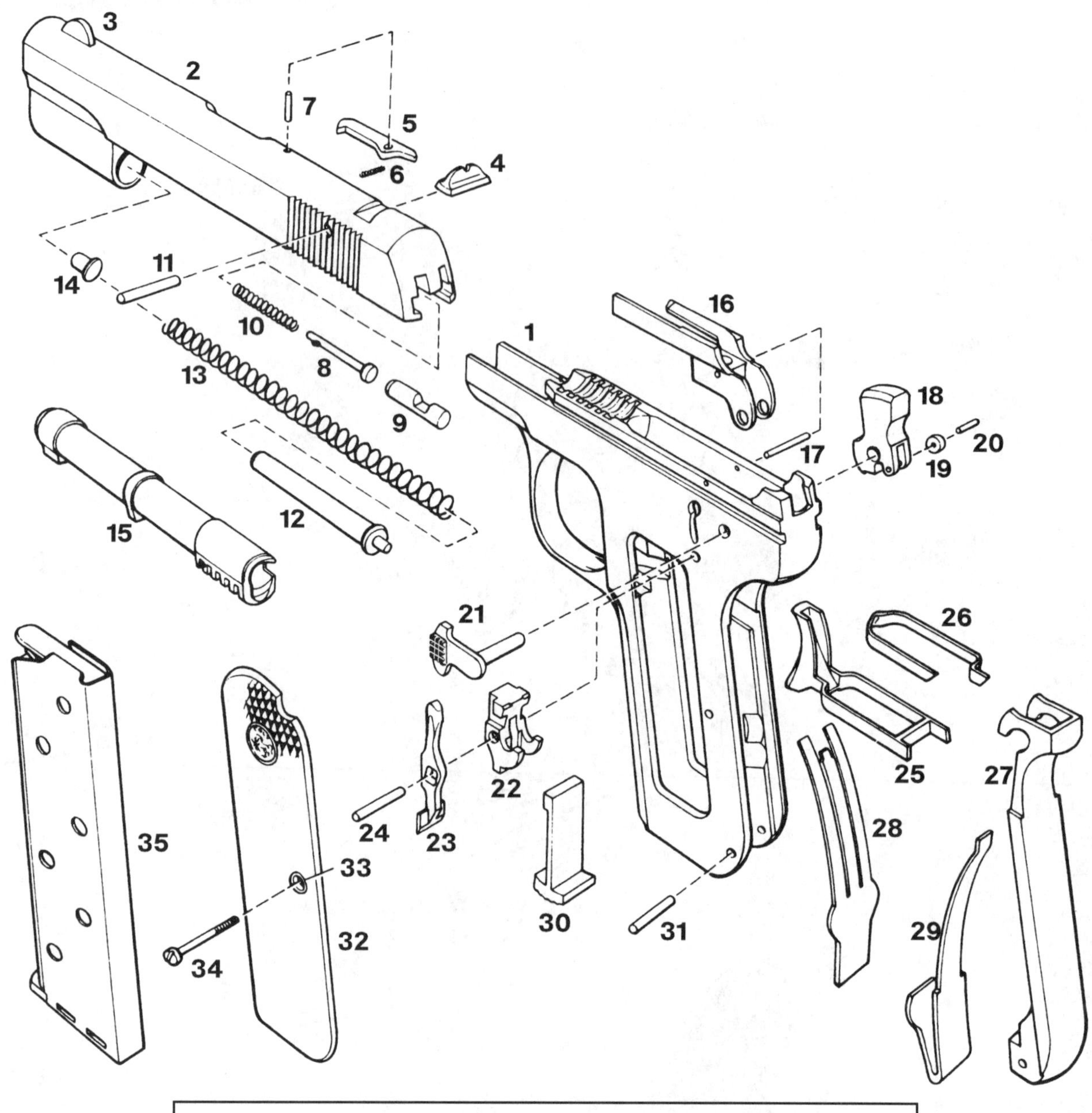

1	Frame	**19**	Hammer Roll
2	Slide	**20**	Hammer Roll Pin
3	Front Sight	**21**	Slide Lock Safety
4	Rear Sight	**22**	Sear
5	Extractor	**23**	Disconnector
6	Extractor Spring	**24**	Sear Pin
7	Extractor Pin	**25**	Trigger
8	Front Firing Pin	**26**	Depressor
9	Rear Firing Pin	**27**	Grip Safety
10	Firing Pin Spring	**28**	Sear Spring
11	Firing Pin Lock	**29**	Mainspring
12	Recoil Spring Guide	**30**	Magazine Catch
13	Recoil Spring	**31**	Grip Safety Pin
14	Plug	**32**	Grip
15	Barrel	**33**	Escutcheon
16	Ejector	**34**	Grip Screw
17	Ejector Pin	**35**	Magazine
18	Hammer		

Police Positive Special Revolver

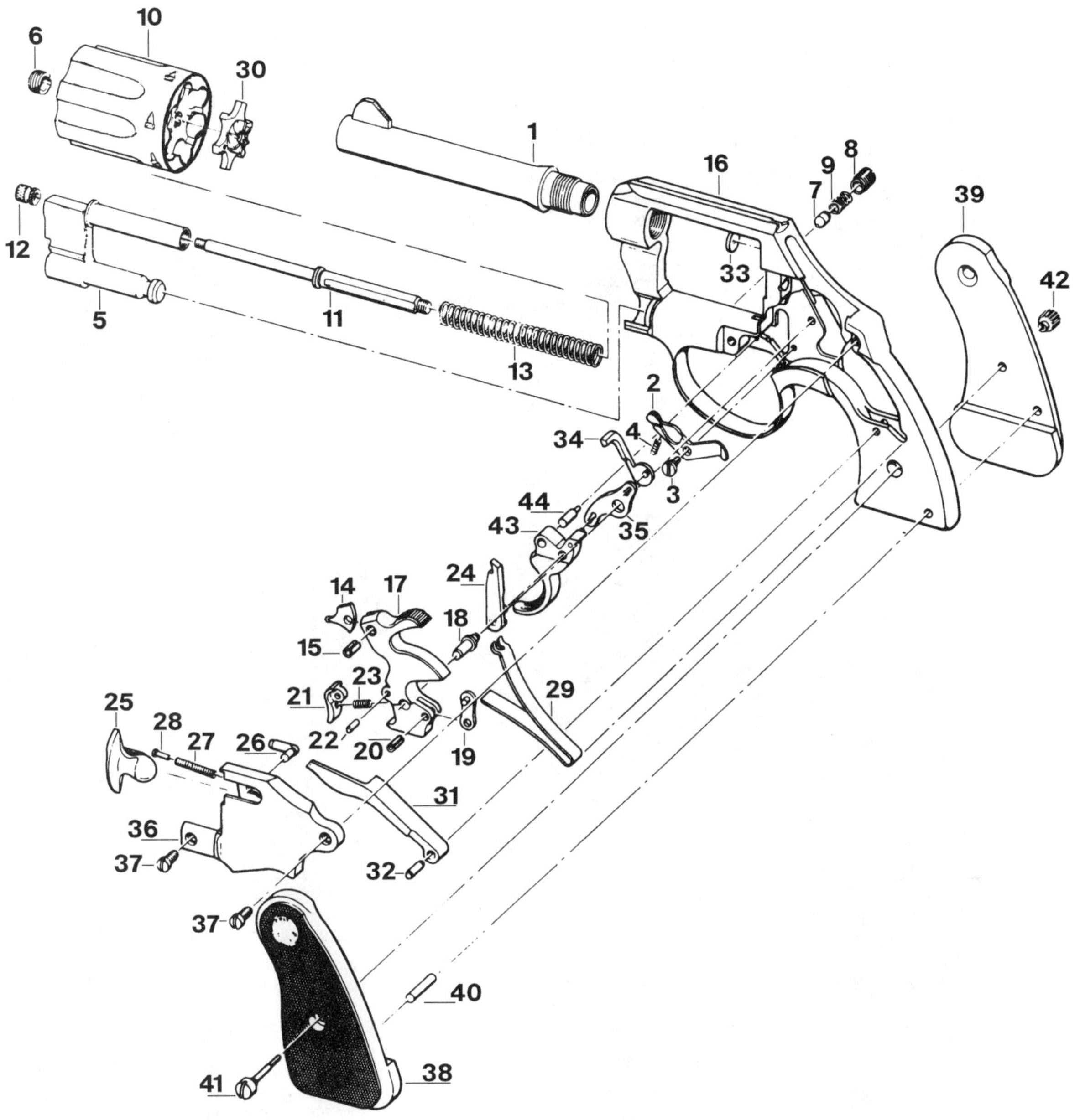

1	Barrel	16	Frame	31	Rebound Lever
2	Bolt	17	Hammer Assembly	32	Rebound Lever Pin
3	Bolt Screw	18	Hammer Pin	33	Recoil Plate
4	Bolt Spring	19	Hammer Stirrup Detent Assembly	34	Safety Assembly
5	Crane	20	Stirrup Pin (Roll Pin)	35	Safety-Lever
6	Crane Bushing	21	Hammer Strut	36	Sideplate
7	Crane Lock Detent	22	Hammer Strut Pin	37	Sideplate Screws
8	Spring Retaining Screw	23	Hammer Strut Spring	38	Stock, Left
9	Crane Lock Spring	24	Hand	39	Stock, Right
10	Cylinder	25	Latch	40	Stock Pin
11	Ejector Rod	26	Latch Pin	41	Stock Screw
12	Ejector Rod Head	27	Helical-Compression Spring	42	Stock Screw Nut
13	Ejector Spring	28	Latch Spring Guide	43	Trigger
14	Firing Pin	29	Mainspring	44	Headless Shoulder Pin
15	Roll Pin	30	Ejector Ratchet		

Police Python, Python and Trooper (Old Model) Revolver

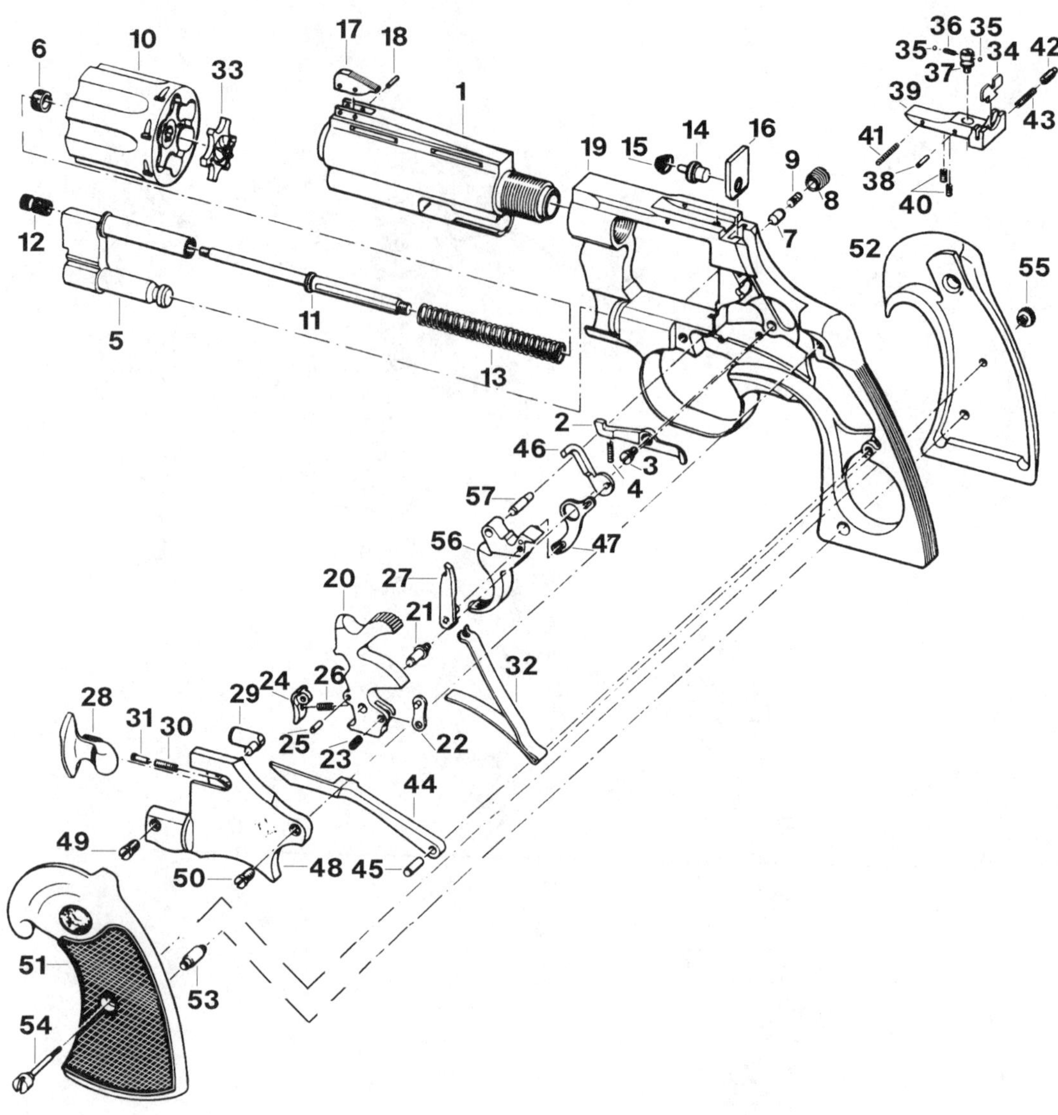

1	Barrel	**22**	Hammer Stirrup	**43**	Rear Sight Windage Spring
2	Bolt	**23**	Roll Pin	**44**	Rebound Lever
3	Bolt Screw	**24**	Hammer Strut	**45**	Rebound Lever Pin
4	Bolt Spring	**25**	Hammer Strut Pin	**46**	Safety
5	Crane	**26**	Hammer Strut Spring	**47**	Safety-Lever
6	Crane Bushing	**27**	Hand	**48**	Sideplate
7	Crane Lock Detent	**28**	Latch	**49**	Sideplate Screw, Front
8	Crane Lock Screw	**29**	Latch Pin	**50**	Sideplate Screw, Target
9	Crane Lock Spring	**30**	Latch Spring	**51**	Left Grip
10	Cylinder Detent Assembly	**31**	Latch Spring Guide	**52**	Right Grip
11	Ejector Rod	**32**	Mainspring	**53**	Stock Pin
12	Ejector Rod Head	**33**	Ratchet	**54**	Stock Screw, Target
13	Ejector Spring	**34**	Rear Sight Blade	**55**	Stock Screw Nut
14	Firing Pin	**35**	Rear Sight Detent Balls	**56**	Trigger
15	Firing Pin Spring	**36**	Rear Sight Detent Spring	**57**	Trigger Pin
16	Firing Pin Stop	**37**	Rear Sight Elevation Screw	**Parts Not Shown**	
17	Front Sight Blade	**38**	Rear Sight Elevation Screw Pin		Ejector Bushing
18	Front Sight Pin	**39**	Rear Sight Leaf		Firing Pin Rivet
19	Frame	**40**	Rear Sight Leaf Elevation Springs		Latch Insert
20	Hammer Assembly	**41**	Rear Sight Leaf Pin		Recoil Plate
21	Hammer Pin	**42**	Rear Sight Windage Screw		

Single Action Army Revolver

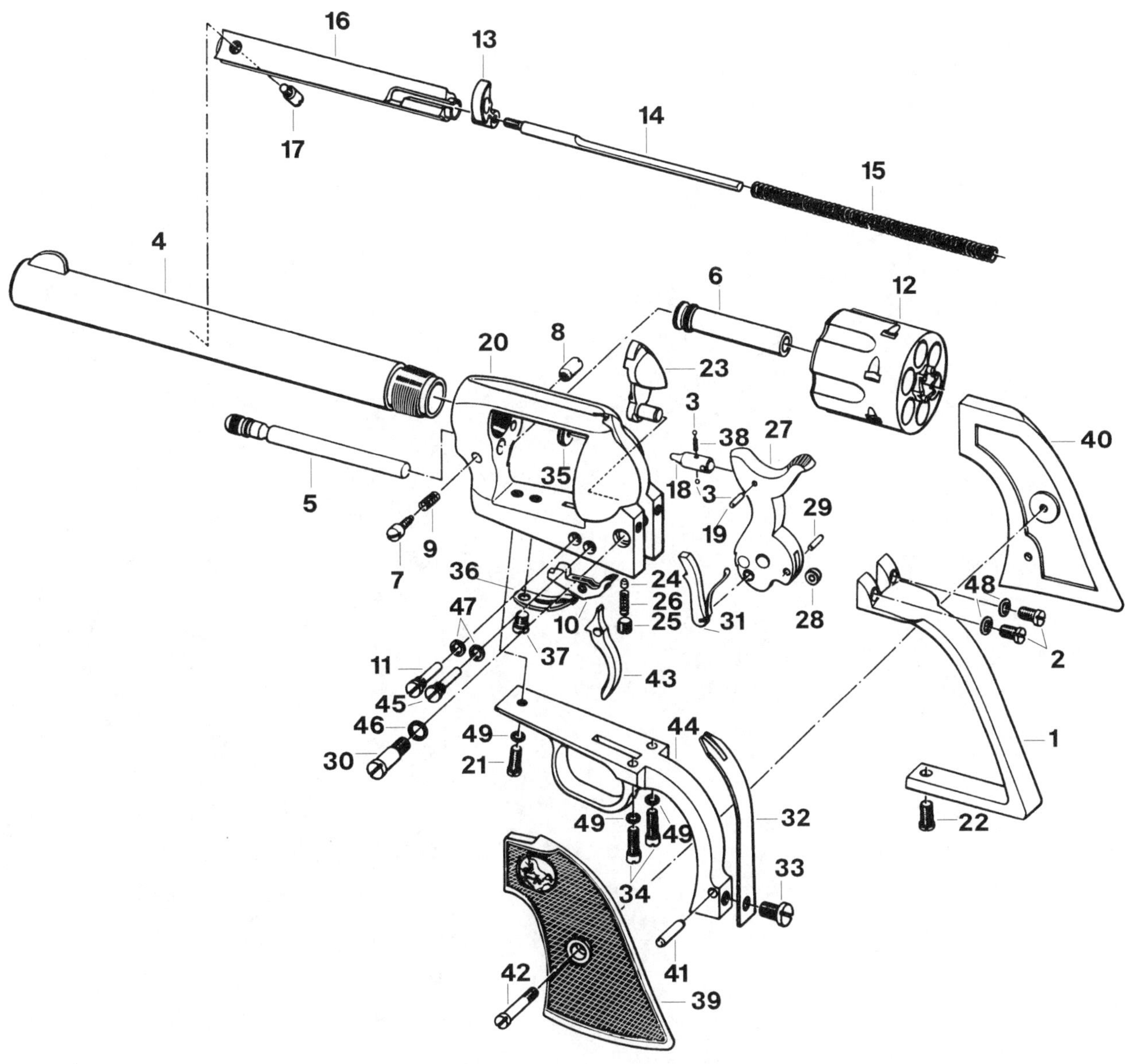

1	Backstrap	**18**	Firing Pin	**35**	Recoil Plate
2	Backstrap Screws	**19**	Firing Pin Rivet	**36**	Sear and Bolt Spring
3	Balls	**20**	Frame	**37**	Sear and Bolt Spring Screw
4	Barrel	**21**	Front Guard Screw	**38**	Spring
5	Base Pin	**22**	Front Strap Screw	**39**	Stock, Left
6	Base Pin Bushing	**23**	Gate	**40**	Stock, Right
7	Base Pin Screw	**24**	Gate Catch	**41**	Stock Pin
8	Base Pin Screw Nut	**25**	Gate Catch Screw	**42**	Stock Screw
9	Base Pin Spring	**26**	Gate Spring	**43**	Trigger
10	Bolt	**27**	Hammer	**44**	Trigger Guard
11	Bolt Screw	**28**	Hammer Roll	**45**	Trigger Screw
12	Cylinder	**29**	Hammer Roll Pin	**46**	Hammer Screw Washer
13	Ejector Head	**30**	Hammer Screw	**47**	Bolt Screw Washers
14	Ejector Rod	**31**	Hand Assembly	**48**	Backstrap Screw Washers
15	Ejector Spring	**32**	Mainspring	**49**	Rear Guard Screw Washers
16	Ejector Tube	**33**	Mainspring Screw		
17	Ejector Tube Screw	**34**	Rear Guard Screws		

Walker and 1st, 2nd and 3rd Dragoon Revolver

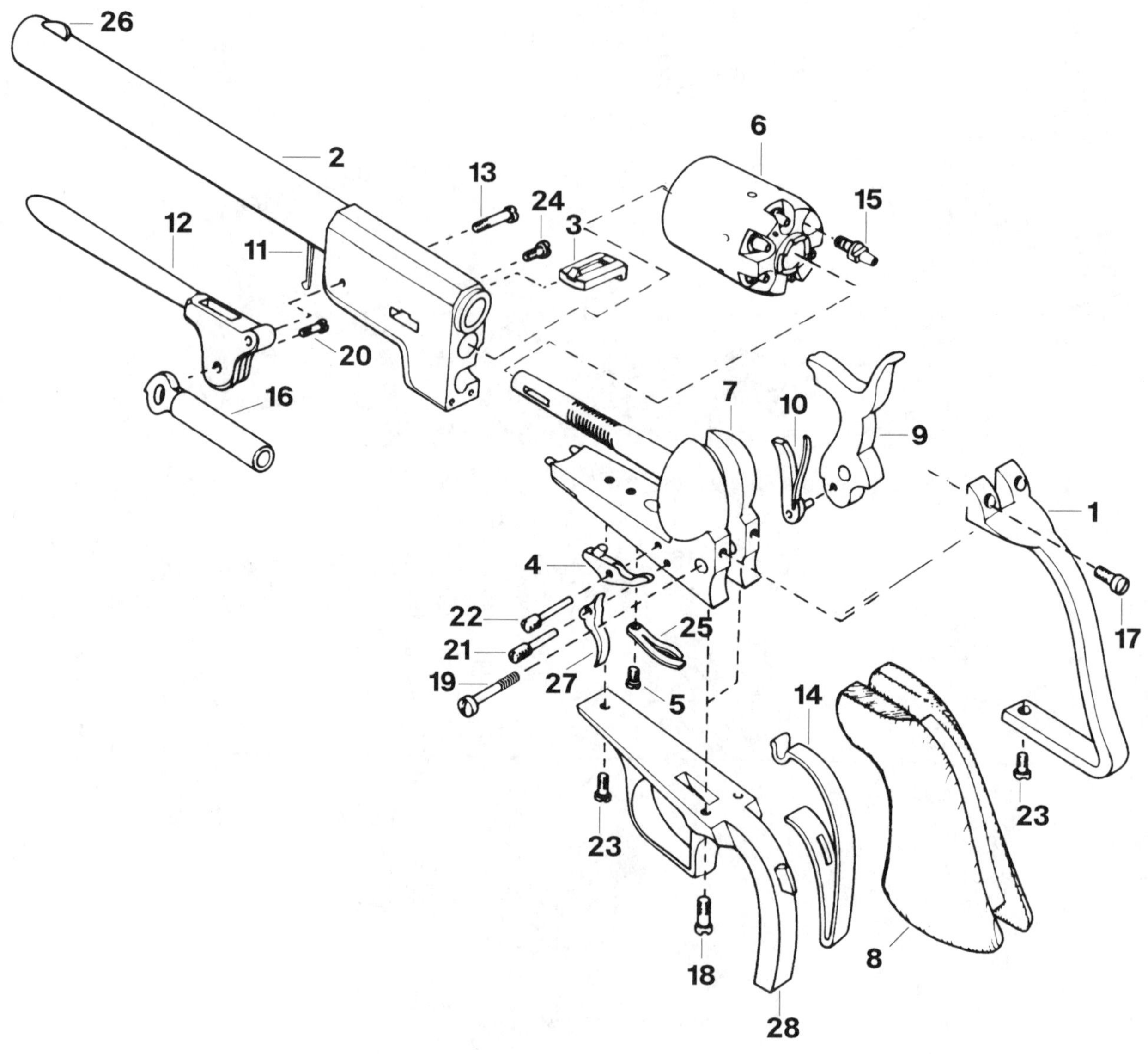

1	Backstrap	17	Backstrap Screw
2	Barrel	18	Guard Screw
3	Barrel Wedge Assembly	19	Hammer Screw
4	Bolt	20	Plunger Screw
5	Bolt Spring Screw	21	Trigger Screw
6	Cylinder Assembly	22	Trigger Bolt Screw
7	Frame Assembly	23	Trigger Guard and Butt Screw
8	Grip	24	Wedge Screw
9	Hammer	25	Sear and Bolt Spring
10	Hand and Spring Assembly	26	Front Sight
11	Loading Lever Latch	27	Trigger
12	Loading Lever	28	Trigger Guard
13	Loading Lever Screw	**Parts Not Shown**	
14	Mainspring		Base Pin
15	Nipple		Hand Assembly
16	Loading Plunger		Latch Spring

Woodsman Match Target, Target, Sport, Huntsman and Targetsman

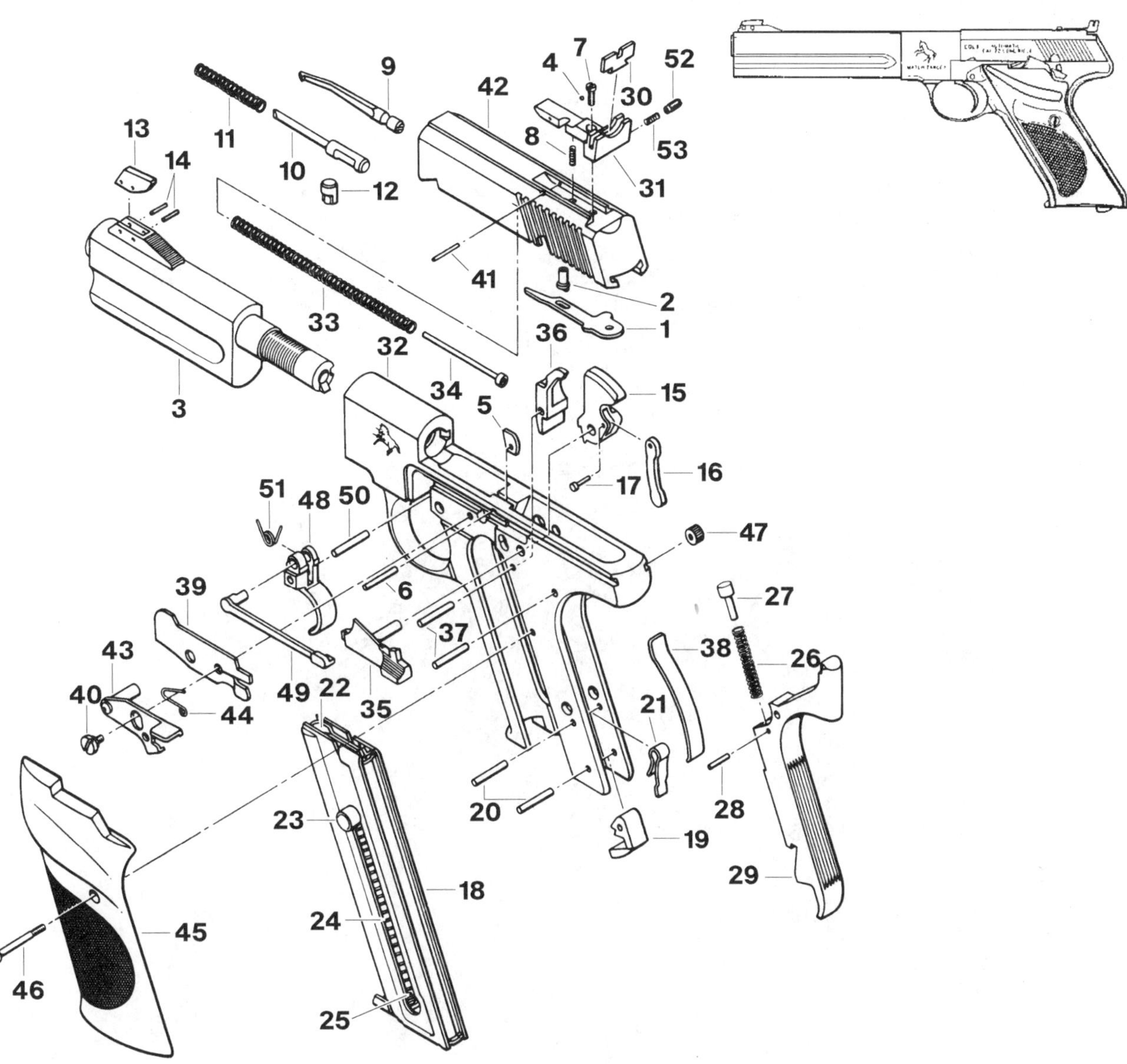

No.	Part
1	Assembly Lock
2	Assembly Lock Plunger
3	Barrel Detent Assembly
4	Rear Sight Detent Ball
5	Ejector
6	Ejector Pin
7	Rear Sight Elevation Screw
8	Rear Sight Elevation Spring
9	Extractor
10	Firing Pin
11	Firing Pin Spring
12	Firing Pin Stop
13	Front Sight Blade
14	Front Sight Blade Pins
15	Hammer
16	Hammer Strut
17	Hammer Strut Pin
18	Magazine Assembly
19	Magazine Catch
20	Magazine Catch Pin and Magazine Housing Lock Pin
21	Magazine Catch Spring
22	Magazine Follower
23	Magazine Follower Stud
24	Magazine Spring
25	Magazine Spring Guide
26	Mainspring
27	Mainspring Cap
28	Mainspring Cap Pin
29	Mainspring Housing
30	Rear Sight Blade
31	Rear Sight Leaf Assembly
32	Receiver
33	Recoil Spring
34	Recoil Spring Guide
35	Safety Lock Detent Assembly
36	Sear
37	Sear Pin and Mainspring Retainer Pin
38	Sear Spring
39	Sideplate
40	Sideplate Screw
41	Rear Sight Leaf Pin
42	Slide Detent Assembly
43	Slide Stop Detent Assembly
44	Slide Stop Spring
45	Stock Assembly
46	Stock Screw
47	Stock Screw Nut
48	Trigger
49	Trigger Bar
50	Trigger Pin
51	Trigger Spring
52	Rear Sight Windage Screw
53	Rear Sight Windage Spring

Parts Not Shown

Rear Sight Detent Ball

Rear Sight Detent Spring

Model A 357 Magnum Auto

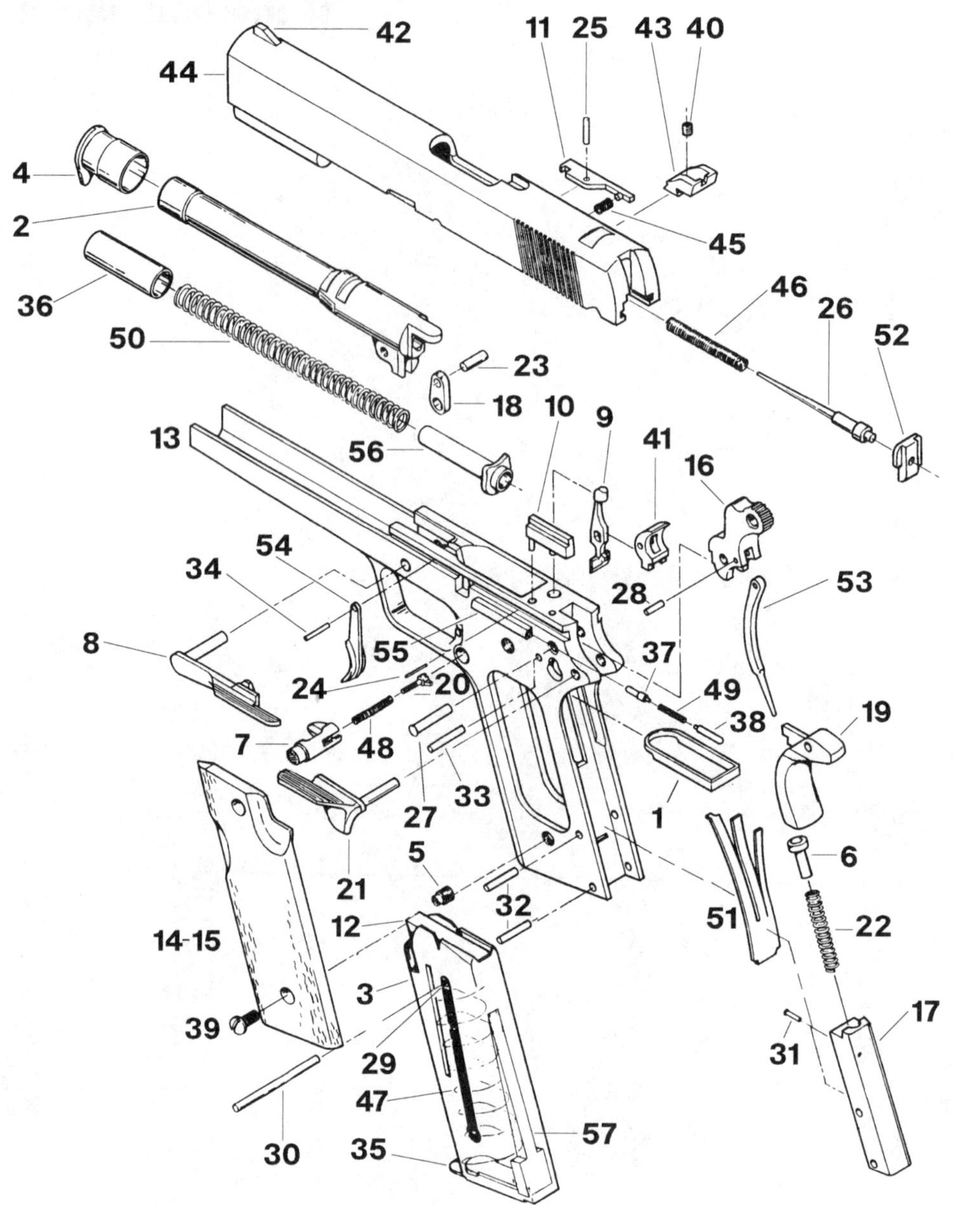

1	Trigger Bar	**20**	Magazine Catch Lock	**39**	Grip Screw
2	Barrel	**21**	Thumb Lock	**40**	Rear Sight Screw
3	Magazine Body	**22**	Mainspring	**41**	Sear
4	Barrel Bushing	**23**	Barrel Link Pin	**42**	Front Sight
5	Grip Screw Bushing	**24**	Ejector Pin	**43**	Rear Sight
6	Mainspring Cap	**25**	Extractor Pin	**44**	Slide
7	Magazine Catch	**26**	Firing Pin	**45**	Extractor Spring
8	Slide Catch	**27**	Hammer Pin	**46**	Firing Pin Spring
9	Disconnector	**28**	Hammer Strut Pin	**47**	Magazine Spring
10	Ejector	**29**	Magazine Follower Pin	**48**	Magazine Catch Spring
11	Extractor	**30**	Magazine Loading Pin	**49**	Plunger Tube Spring
12	Magazine Follower	**31**	Mainspring Cap Pin	**50**	Recoil Spring
13	Frame	**32**	Mainspring Housing Pins	**51**	Sear Spring
14	Grip, Left	**33**	Sear Pin	**52**	Firing Pin Stop
15	Grip, Right	**34**	Trigger Pin	**53**	Hammer Strut
16	Hammer	**35**	Magazine Floorplate	**54**	Trigger
17	Mainspring Housing	**36**	Recoil Plug	**55**	Plunger Tube
18	Barrel Link	**37**	Slide Stop Plunger	**56**	Recoil Spring Plunger Tube
19	Grip Lock	**38**	Thumb Lock Plunger	**57**	Magazine Wedge

4-Shot Derringer

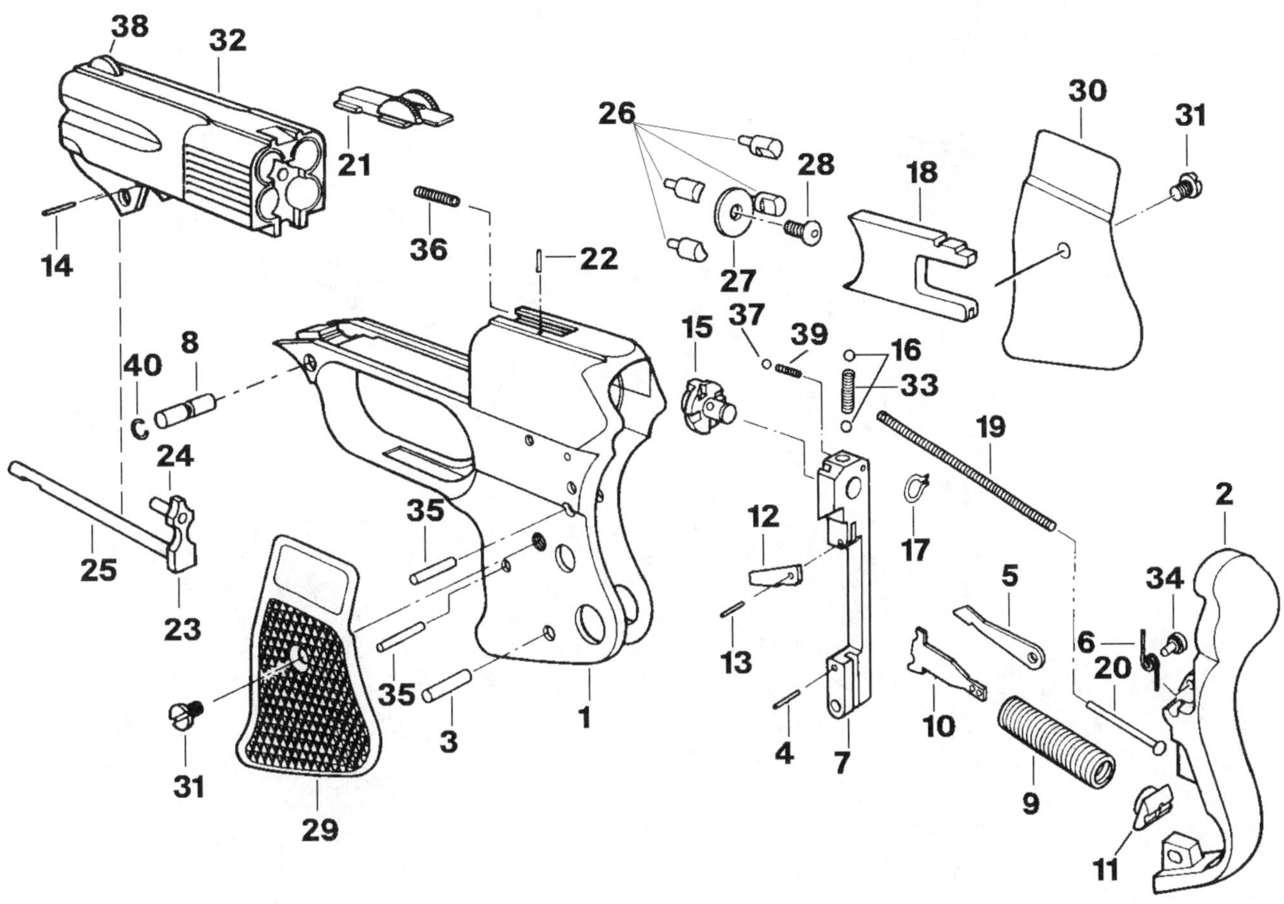

1	Frame	**23**	Extractor
2	Backstrap	**24**	Extractor Guide
3	Mounting Pin	**25**	Extractor Push Rod
4	Hammer Strut Bearing Pin	**26**	Firing Pins
5	Hand	**27**	Firing Pin Retaining Washer
6	Hand Spring	**28**	Firing Pin Retaining Washer Screw
7	Hammer	**29**	Left Grip
8	Barrel Pin	**30**	Right Grip
9	Hammer Spring	**31**	Grip Screws
10	Strut	**32**	Barrel
11	Bearing	**33**	Ratchet Plunger Spring
12	Sear	**34**	Hand Pivot Pin
13	Sear Pin	**35**	Hammer Pivot and Mounting Pin
14	Extractor Stop Pin	**36**	Latch Spring
15	Ratchet	**37**	Ratchet Retainer Ball
16	Ratchet Plungers	**38**	Front Sight
17	Ratchet Retaining Ring	**39**	Ratchet Ball Spring
18	Trigger	**40**	Pivot Pin Retaining Ring
19	Trigger Spring	**Parts Not Shown**	
20	Trigger Spring Guide Rod		Hand Spring Retainer
21	Latch		Barrel Pivot Retaining Pin
22	Latch Stop Pin		

CZ Model 50 Auto

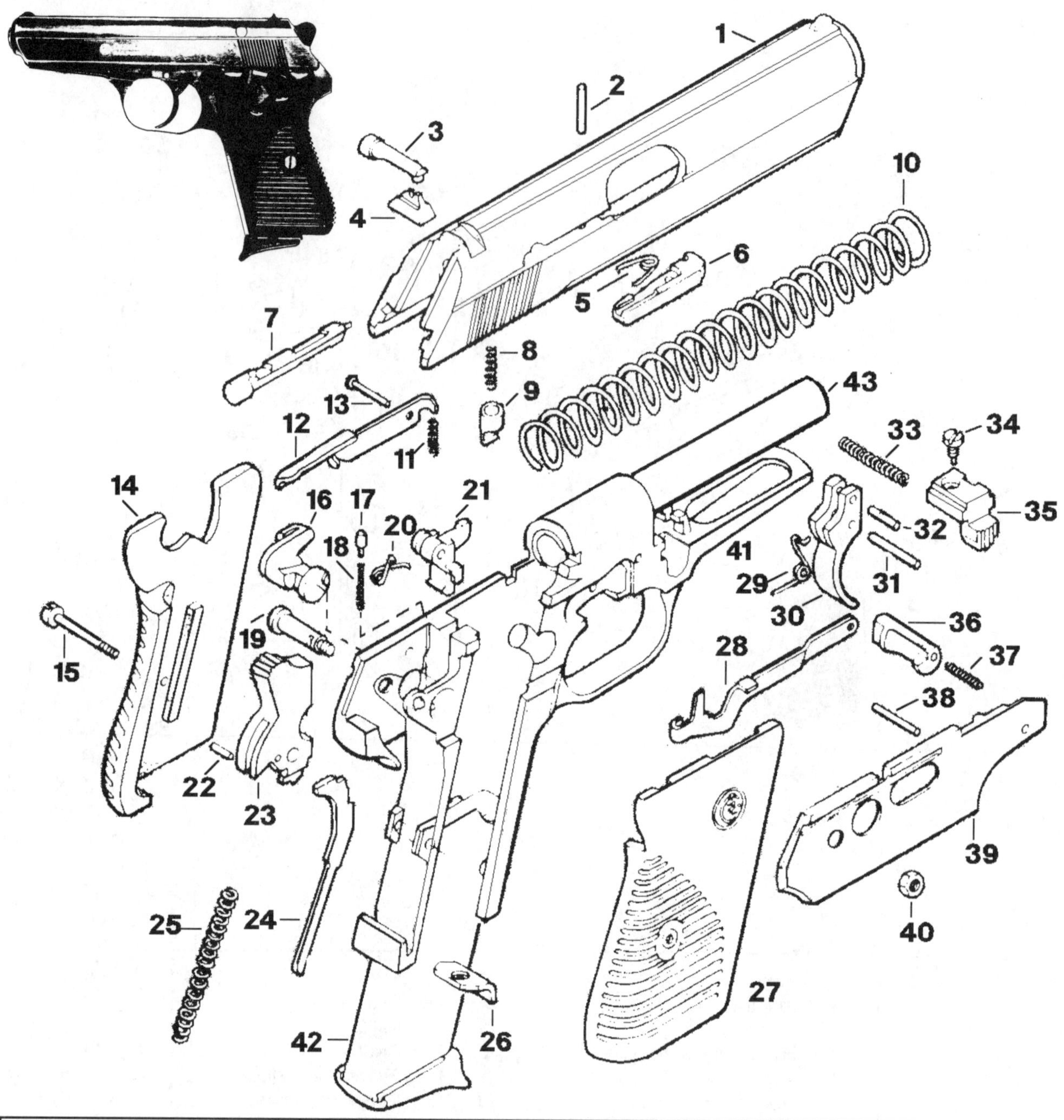

1	Slide	16	Safety	31	Trigger Pin
2	Extractor Pin	17	Safety Plunger	32	Trigger Bar Pin
3	Cartridge Indicator	18	Safety Spring	33	Takedown Catch Spring
4	Rear Sight	19	Hammer Bolt	34	Takedown Catch Screw
5	Extractor Spring	20	Sear Spring	35	Takedown Catch
6	Extractor	21	Sear	36	Magazine Catch
7	Firing Pin	22	Hammer Strut Pin	37	Magazine Catch Spring
8	Firing Pin Lock Spring	23	Hammer	38	Sear Pin
9	Firing Pin Lock	24	Hammer Strut	39	Sideplate
10	Recoil Spring	25	Hammer Spring	40	Hammer Bolt Nut
11	Hold-Open Latch Spring	26	Spring Retainer	41	Receiver
12	Hold-Open Latch and Ejector	27	Right Grip	42	Magazine
13	Hold-Open Hinge Pin	28	Trigger Bar	43	Barrel
14	Left Grip	29	Trigger Spring		
15	Grip Screw	30	Trigger		

CZ Model 1927 Auto

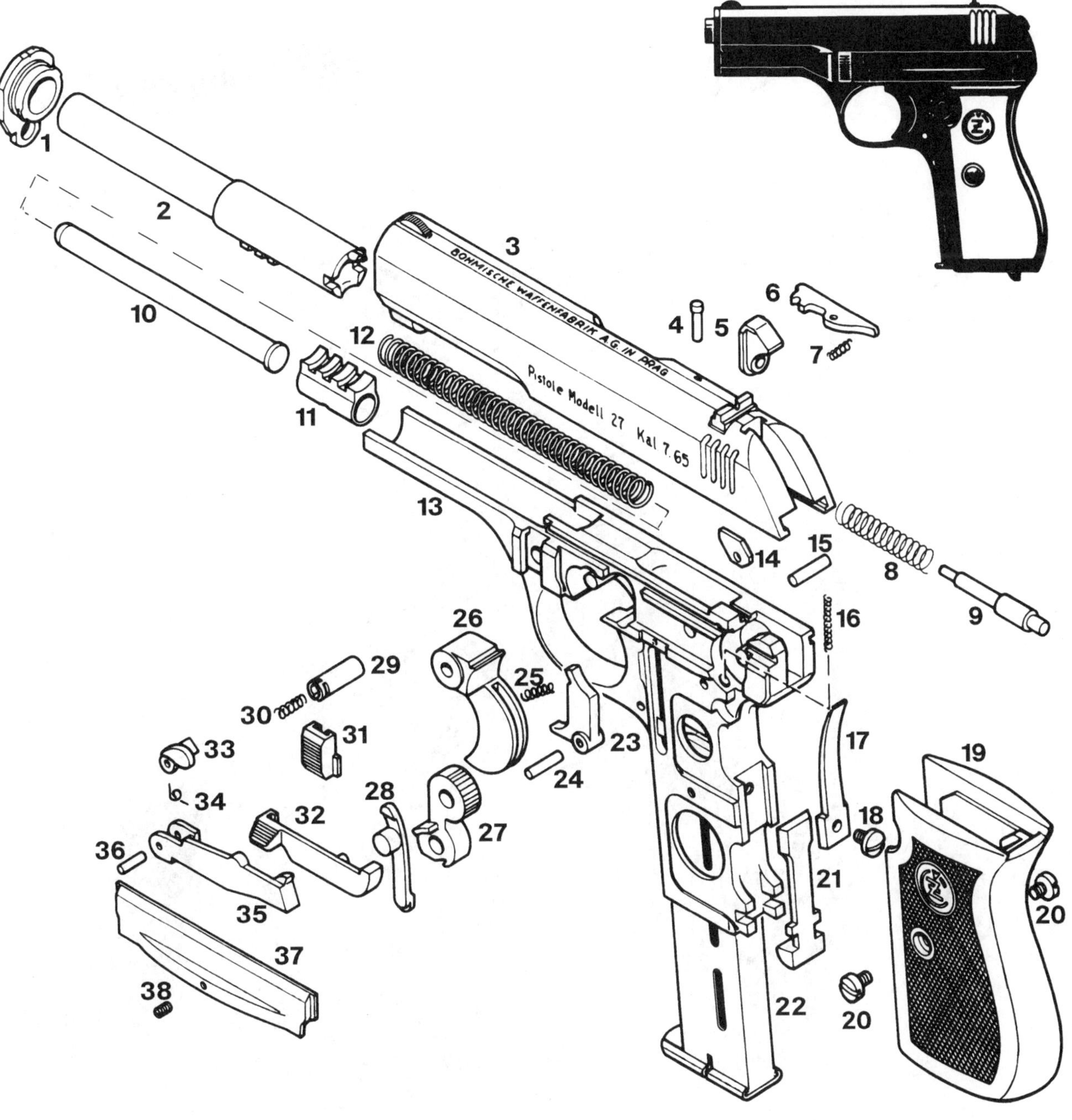

1	Barrel Bushing	**14**	Ejector	**27**	Hammer
2	Barrel	**15**	Ejector Pin	**28**	Safety Release
3	Slide	**16**	Safety and Trigger Bar Spring	**29**	Takedown Cross Pin
4	Extractor Pin	**17**	Hammer Spring	**30**	Takedown Catch Spring
5	Firing Pin Retainer	**18**	Hammer Spring Retaining Screw	**31**	Takedown Catch
6	Extractor	**19**	Grip	**32**	Safety Catch
7	Extractor Spring	**20**	Grip Screws	**33**	Disconnector
8	Firing Pin Spring	**21**	Magazine Catch	**34**	Disconnector Spring
9	Firing Pin	**22**	Magazine	**35**	Trigger Bar
10	Recoil Spring Guide	**23**	Magazine Disconnector	**36**	Trigger Bar Hinge Pin
11	Barrel Retainer	**24**	Disconnector Hinge Pin	**37**	Sideplate
12	Recoil Spring	**25**	Trigger Spring	**38**	Sideplate Screw
13	Frame	**26**	Trigger		

CZ Model 1938 Auto

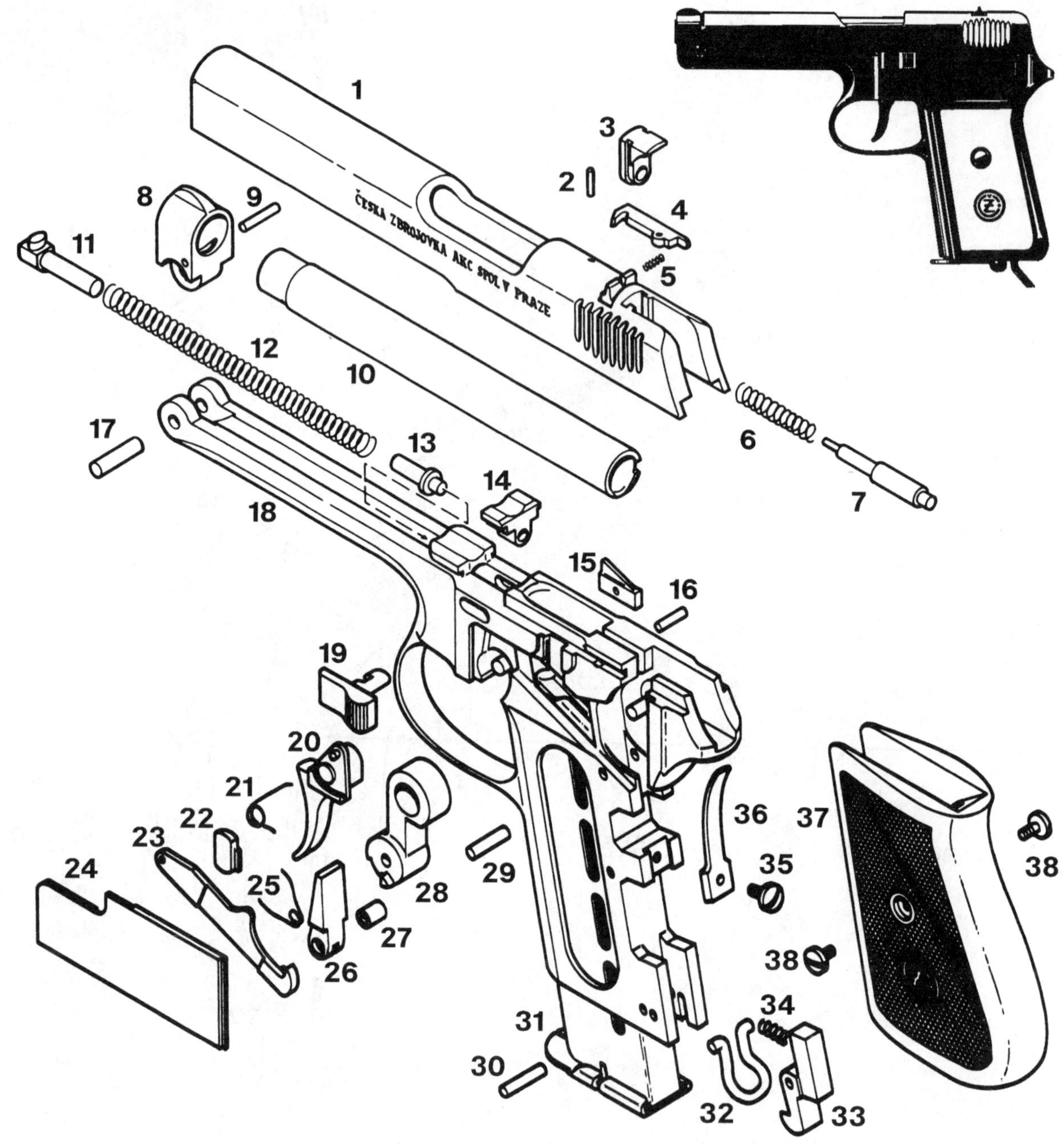

No.	Part	No.	Part	No.	Part
1	Slide	14	Slide Locking Block	27	Sear Pivot Sleeve
2	Extractor Pin	15	Ejector	28	Hammer
3	Firing Pin Retainer	16	Ejector Pin	29	Sear Pin
4	Extractor	17	Hinge Pin	30	Magazine Catch Pin
5	Extractor Spring	18	Frame	31	Magazine
6	Firing Pin Spring	19	Takedown Latch	32	Lanyard Loop
7	Firing Pin	20	Trigger	33	Magazine Catch
8	Barrel Mount	21	Trigger Spring	34	Magazine Catch Spring
9	Barrel Bushing Pin	22	Disconnector	35	Hammer Spring Screw
10	Barrel	23	Trigger Bar	36	Hammer Spring
11	Recoil Spring Guide	24	Sideplate	37	Grip
12	Recoil Spring	25	Sear Spring	38	Grip Screw
13	Takedown Latch Plunger	26	Sear		

CZ Model 1945 Auto

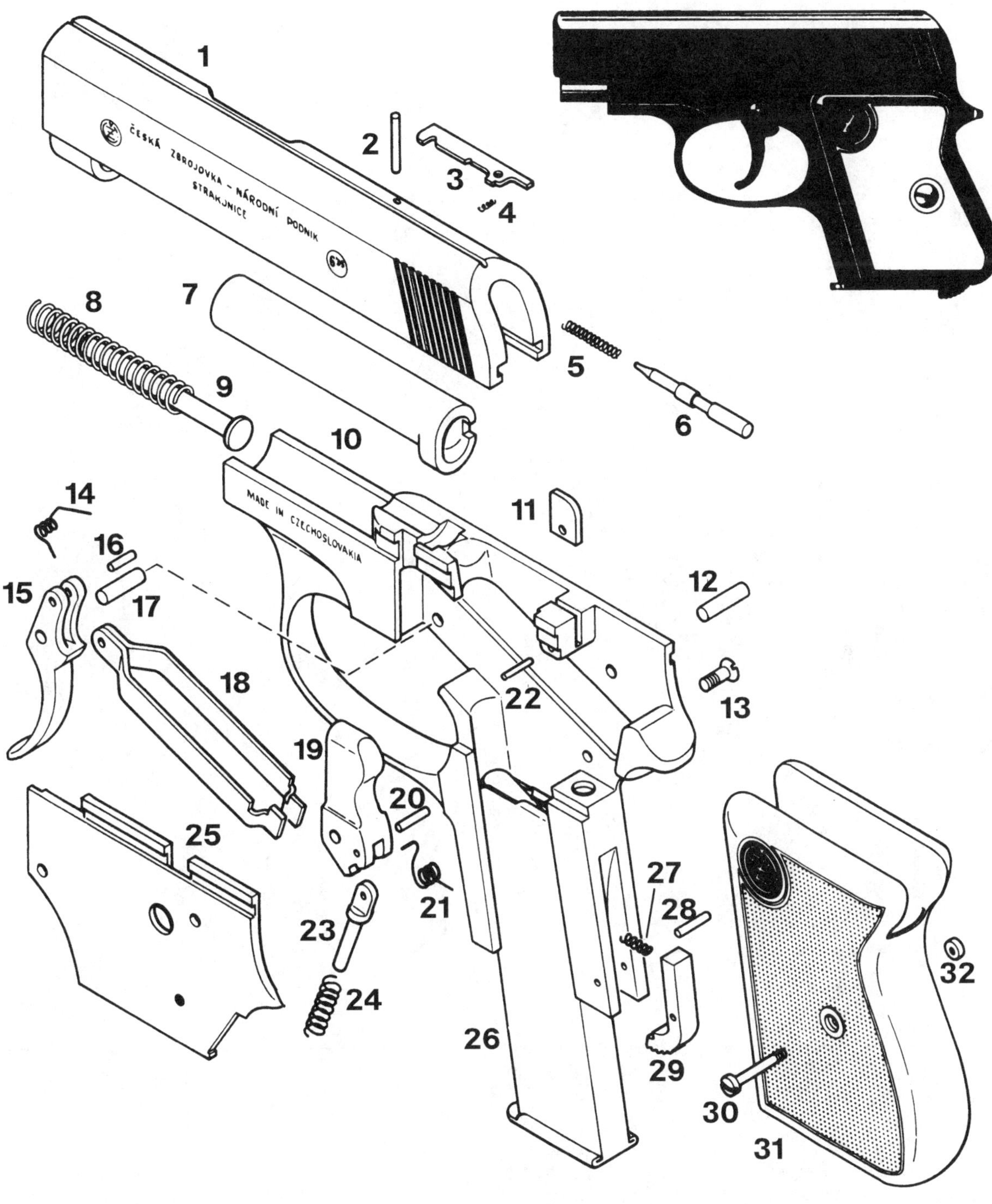

1	Slide	12	Hammer Pin	23	Hammer Strut
2	Extractor Pin	13	Sideplate Screw	24	Hammer Spring
3	Extractor	14	Trigger Spring	25	Sideplate
4	Extractor Spring	15	Trigger	26	Magazine
5	Firing Pin Spring	16	Trigger Bar Pin	27	Magazine Catch Spring
6	Firing Pin	17	Trigger Hinge Pin	28	Magazine Catch Pin
7	Barrel	18	Trigger Bar	29	Magazine Catch
8	Recoil Spring	19	Hammer	30	Grip Screw
9	Recoil Spring Guide	20	Hammer Strut Pin	31	Grip
10	Frame	21	Trigger Bar Return Spring	32	Grip Screw Nut
11	Ejector	22	Ejector Pin		

Model 12 Revolver

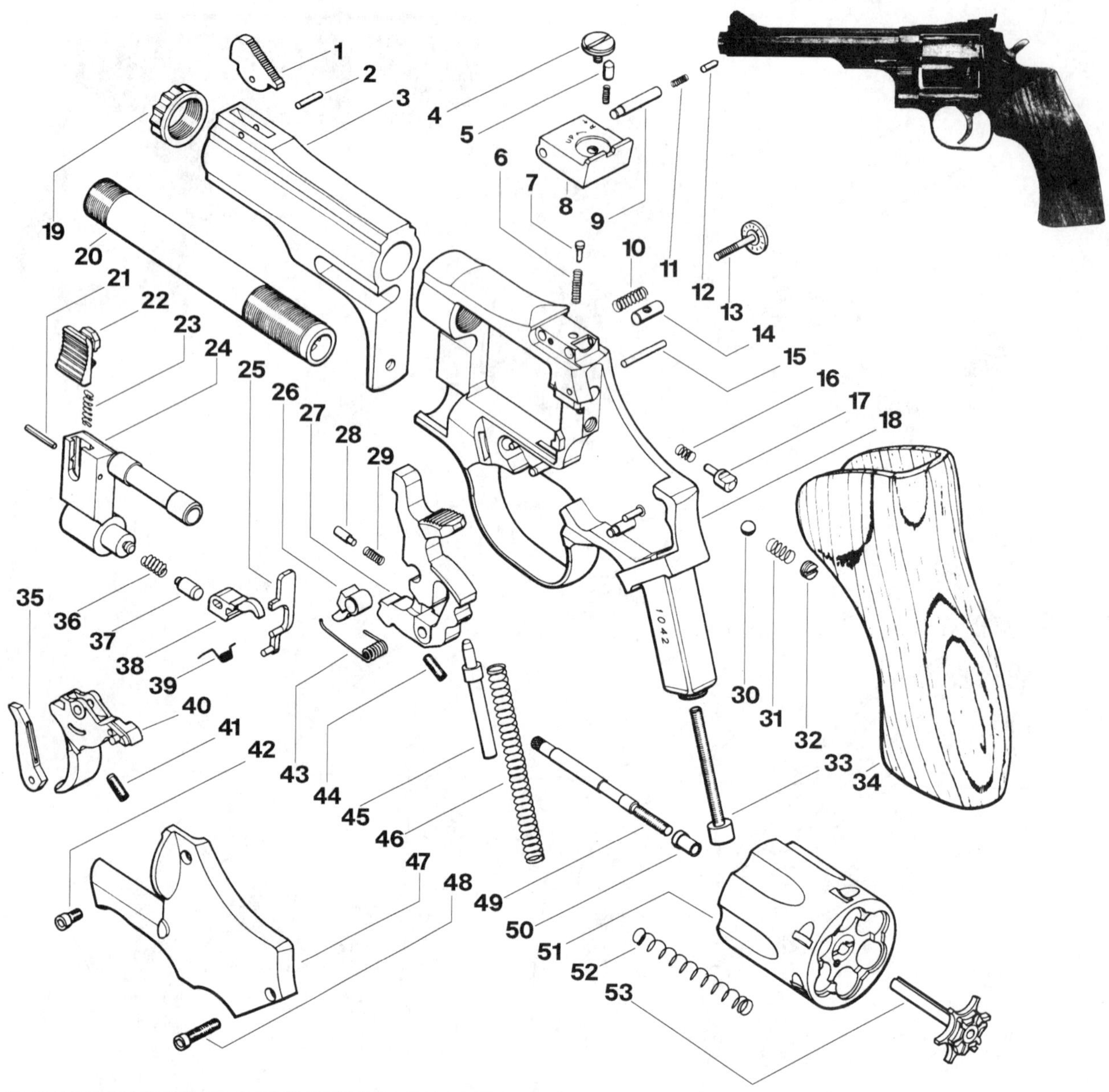

1	Front Sight	**19**	Barrel Nut	**37**	Bolt Plunger
2	Front Sight Pin	**20**	Barrel	**38**	Bolt
3	Shroud	**21**	Latch Retaining Pin	**39**	Hand Spring
4	Elevation Screw	**22**	Latch	**40**	Trigger
5	Elevation Click Plunger	**23**	Latch Spring	**41**	Trigger Stop Screw
6	Elevation Tension Spring	**24**	Crane	**42**	Sideplate Screw, Short
7	Elevation Tension Plunger	**25**	Firing Pin Connector	**43**	Trigger Return Spring
8	Rear Sight Body	**26**	Strut	**44**	Hammer Pin
9	Hinge Pin	**27**	Hammer	**45**	Mainspring Guide
10	Windage Tension Spring	**28**	Strut Plunger	**46**	Mainspring
11	Plunger Spring	**29**	Strut Spring	**47**	Sideplate
12	Windage Click Plunger	**30**	Cylinder Aligning Ball	**48**	Sideplate Screw, Long
13	Windage Screw	**31**	Aligning Ball Spring	**49**	Ejector Rod
14	Elevation Nut	**32**	Aligning Ball Screw	**50**	Ejector Rod Bushing
15	Firing Pin Retaining Pin	**33**	Grip Screw	**51**	Cylinder
16	Firing Pin Spring	**34**	Grip	**52**	Ejector Spring
17	Firing Pin	**35**	Hand	**53**	Extractor
18	Frame	**36**	Bolt Spring		

Model 8-2S, 14-2S, 708 and 714 Revolver

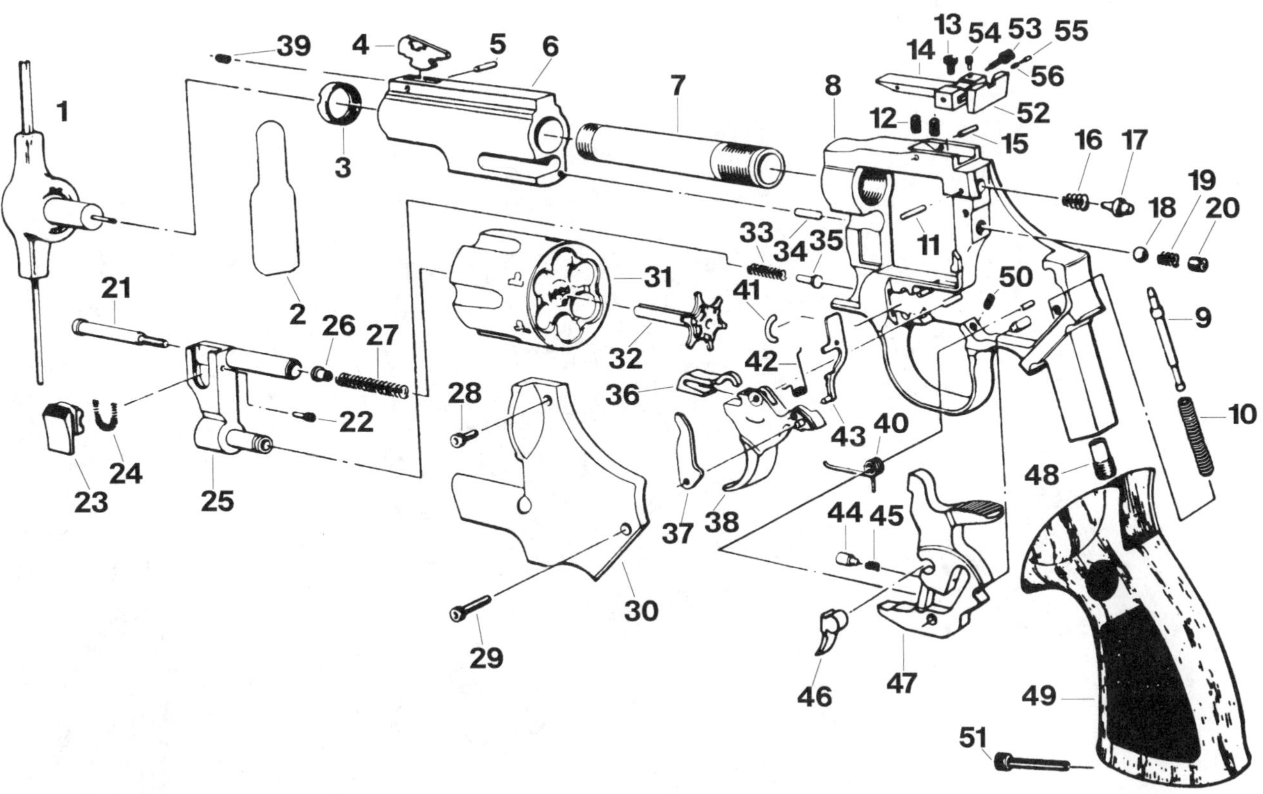

No.	Part	No.	Part
1	Wrench	29	Long Sideplate Screw
2	Gauge, Barrel and Cylinder Clearance	30	Sideplate
3	Barrel Nut	31	Cylinder
4	Front Sight	32	Extractor
5	Front Sight Pin	33	Bolt Spring
6	Shroud	34	Shroud Locating Pin
7	Barrel	35	Bolt Plunger
8	Frame	36	Bolt
9	Mainspring Guide	37	Hand
10	Mainspring	38	Trigger
11	Firing Pin Retaining Pin	39	Front Sight Retaining Screw
12	Rear Sight Elevation Tension Springs	40	Trigger Return Spring
13	Rear Sight Elevation Screw	41	Crane Lock
14	Rear Sight Body	42	Hand Spring
15	Rear Sight Retaining Pin	43	Connector
16	Firing Pin Spring	44	Strut Plunger
17	Firing Pin	45	Strut Spring
18	Cylinder Aligning Ball	46	Strut
19	Cylinder Aligning Ball Spring	47	Hammer
20	Aligning Ball Screw	48	Mainspring Seat
21	Ejector Rod	49	Grip
22	Latch Retaining Screw	50	Trigger Stop Screw
23	Latch	51	Grip Screw
24	Latch Spring	52	Rear Sight Blade
25	Crane	53	Windage Screw Retainer
26	Ejector Rod Bushing	54	Windage Screw
27	Ejector Spring	55	Windage Plunger Spring
28	Short Sideplate Screw	56	Windage Plunger

Model 8-2, 9-2, 14-2 and 15-2 Revolver

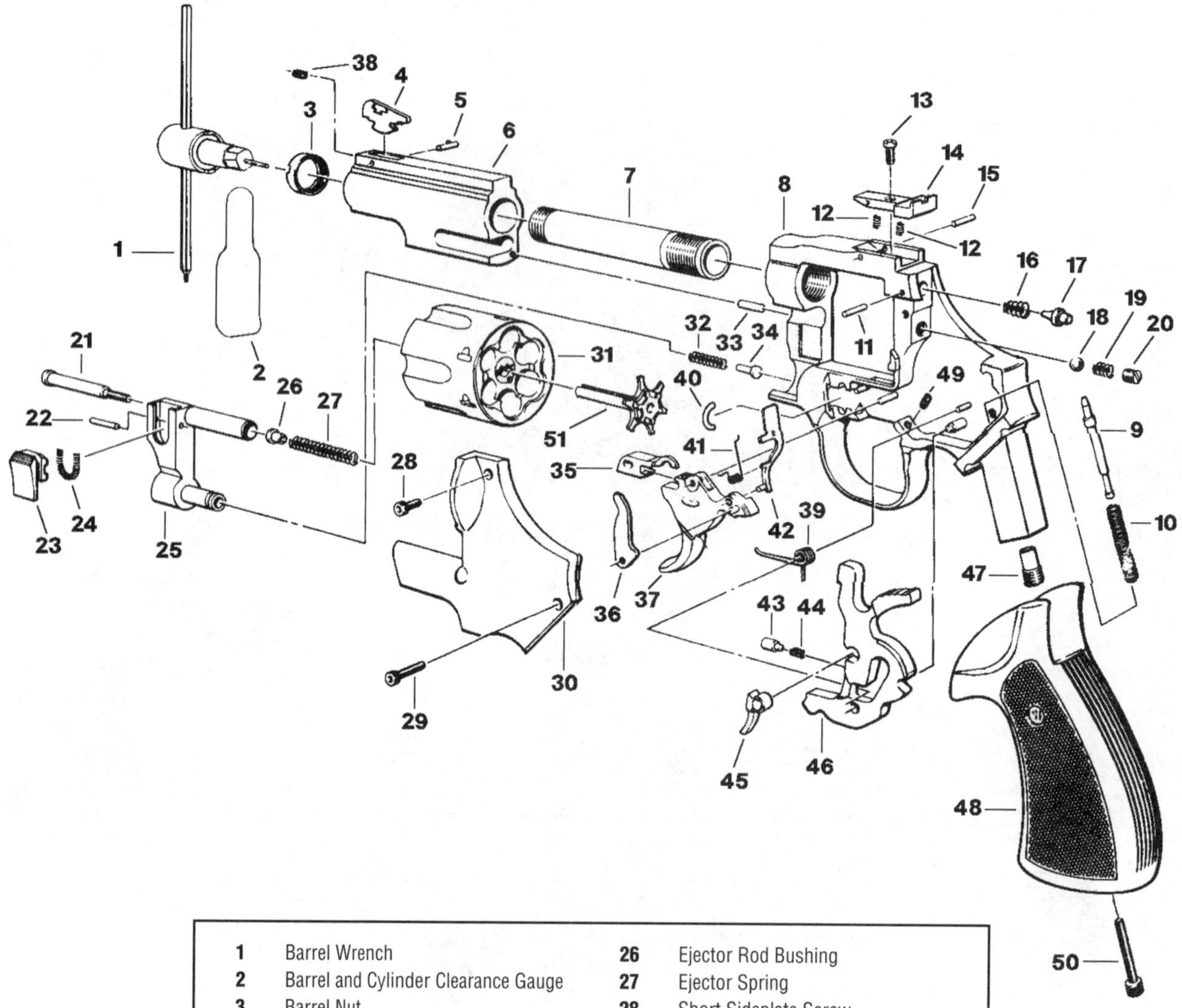

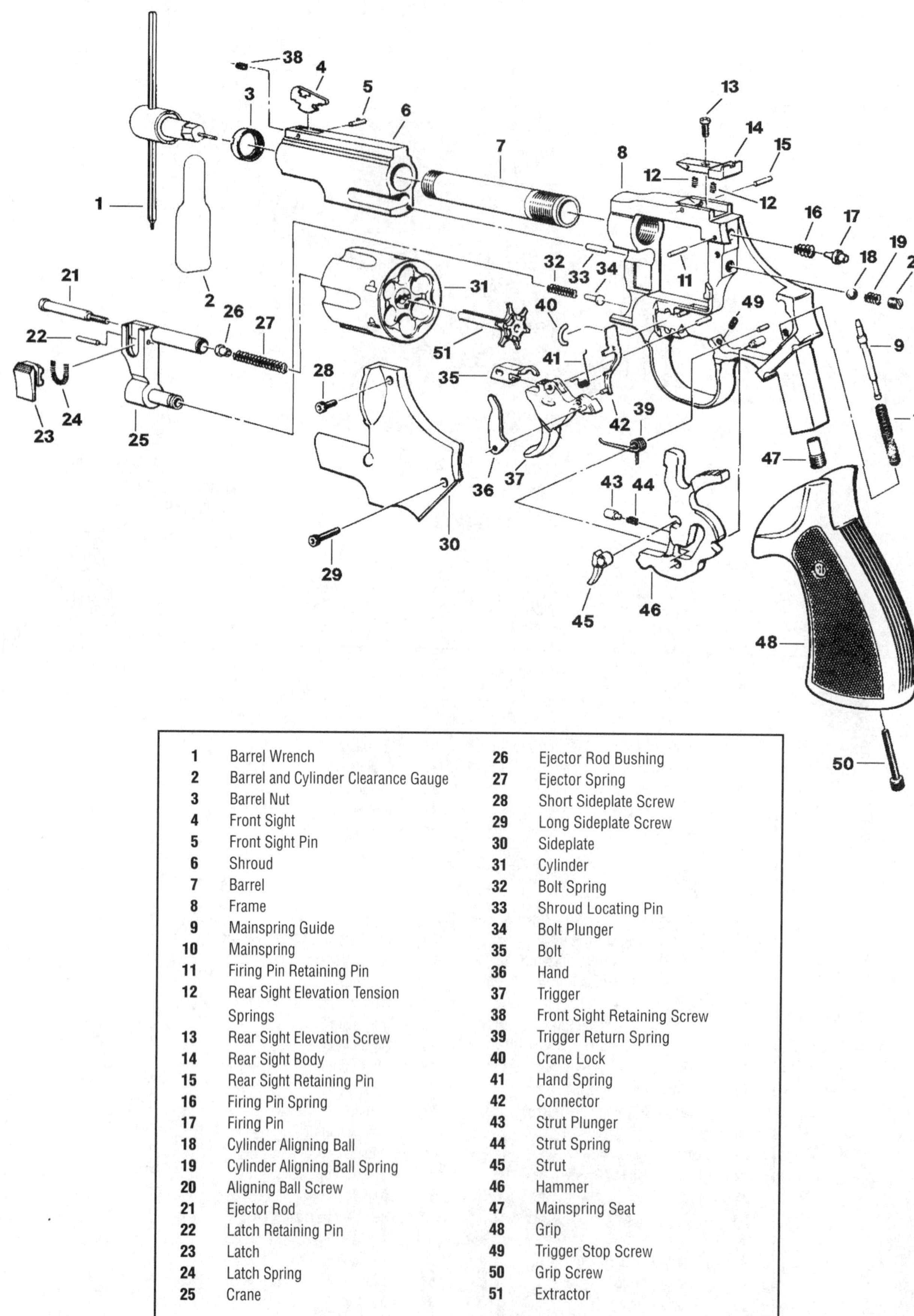

1	Barrel Wrench	26	Ejector Rod Bushing
2	Barrel and Cylinder Clearance Gauge	27	Ejector Spring
3	Barrel Nut	28	Short Sideplate Screw
4	Front Sight	29	Long Sideplate Screw
5	Front Sight Pin	30	Sideplate
6	Shroud	31	Cylinder
7	Barrel	32	Bolt Spring
8	Frame	33	Shroud Locating Pin
9	Mainspring Guide	34	Bolt Plunger
10	Mainspring	35	Bolt
11	Firing Pin Retaining Pin	36	Hand
12	Rear Sight Elevation Tension Springs	37	Trigger
13	Rear Sight Elevation Screw	38	Front Sight Retaining Screw
14	Rear Sight Body	39	Trigger Return Spring
15	Rear Sight Retaining Pin	40	Crane Lock
16	Firing Pin Spring	41	Hand Spring
17	Firing Pin	42	Connector
18	Cylinder Aligning Ball	43	Strut Plunger
19	Cylinder Aligning Ball Spring	44	Strut Spring
20	Aligning Ball Screw	45	Strut
21	Ejector Rod	46	Hammer
22	Latch Retaining Pin	47	Mainspring Seat
23	Latch	48	Grip
24	Latch Spring	49	Trigger Stop Screw
25	Crane	50	Grip Screw
		51	Extractor

Model 375, 40, 41, 44, 45, 740, 741 and 744 Revolver

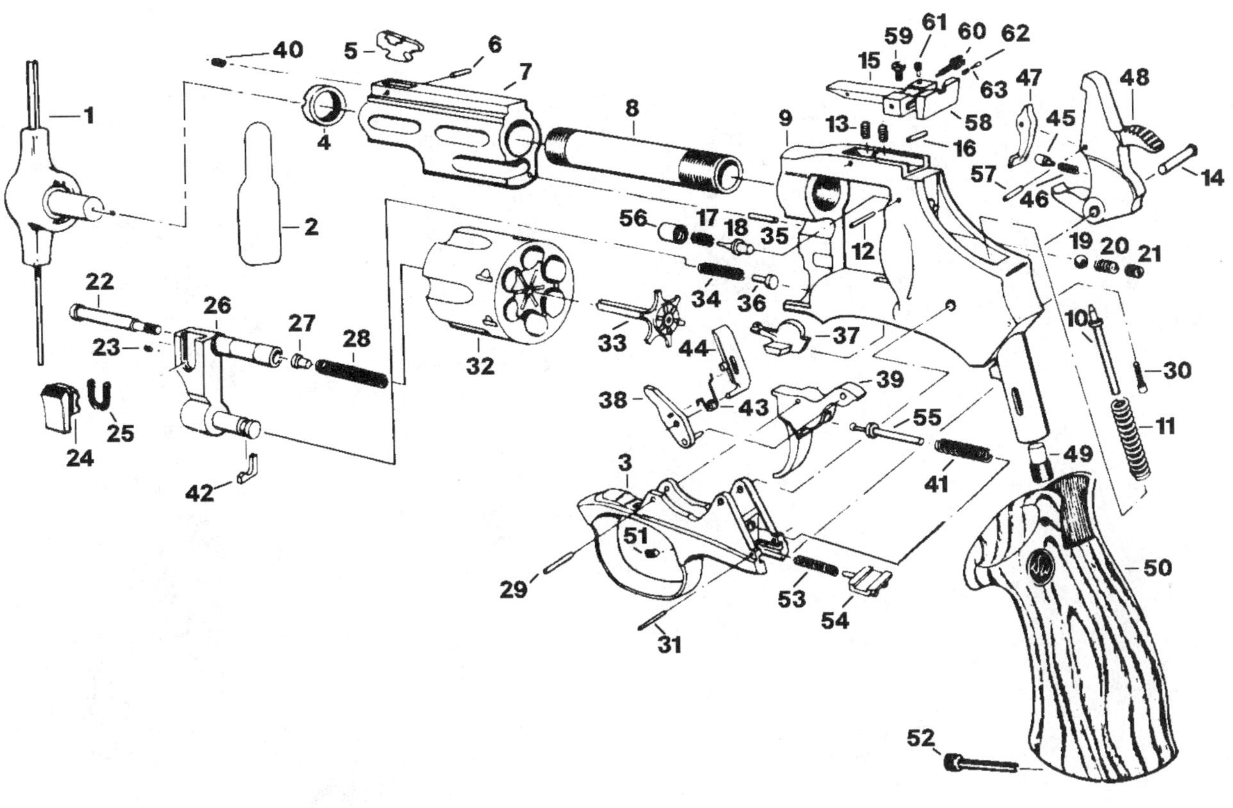

1	Wrench		21	Aligning Ball Screw		42	Crane Lock
2	Barrel and Cylinder Clearance Gauge		22	Ejector Rod		43	Hand Spring
3	Trigger Guard		23	Latch Retaining Screw		44	Connector
4	Barrel Nut		24	Latch		45	Strut Plunger
5	Front Sight		25	Latch Spring		46	Strut Spring
6	Front Sight Pin		26	Crane		47	Strut
7	Shroud		27	Ejector Rod Bushing		48	Hammer
8	Barrel		28	Ejector Spring		49	Mainspring Seat
9	Frame		29	Trigger Pivot Pin		50	Grip
10	Mainspring Guide		30	Mainspring Retaining Screw		51	Trigger Stop Screw
11	Mainspring		31	Trigger Assembly Latch Retaining Pin		52	Grip Screw
12	Firing Pin Retaining Pin		32	Cylinder		53	Trigger Assembly Latch Spring
13	Rear Sight ElevationTension Springs		33	Extractor		54	Trigger Assembly Latch
14	Hammer Pivot Pin		34	Bolt Plunger Spring		55	Trigger Return Spring Guide
15	Rear Sight Body		35	Shroud Locating Pin		56	Firing Pin Bushing
16	Rear Sight Retaining Pin		36	Bolt Plunger		57	Strut Pivot Pin
17	Firing Pin Spring		37	Bolt		58	Rear Sight Blade
18	Firing Pin		38	Hand		59	Elevation Screw
19	Cylinder Aligning Ball		39	Trigger		60	Windage Screw
20	Cylinder Aligning Ball Spring		40	Sight Retaining Screw		61	Windage Screw Retainer
			41	Trigger Return Spring		62	Windage Plunger
						63	Windage Plunger Spring

Model 44 Revolver

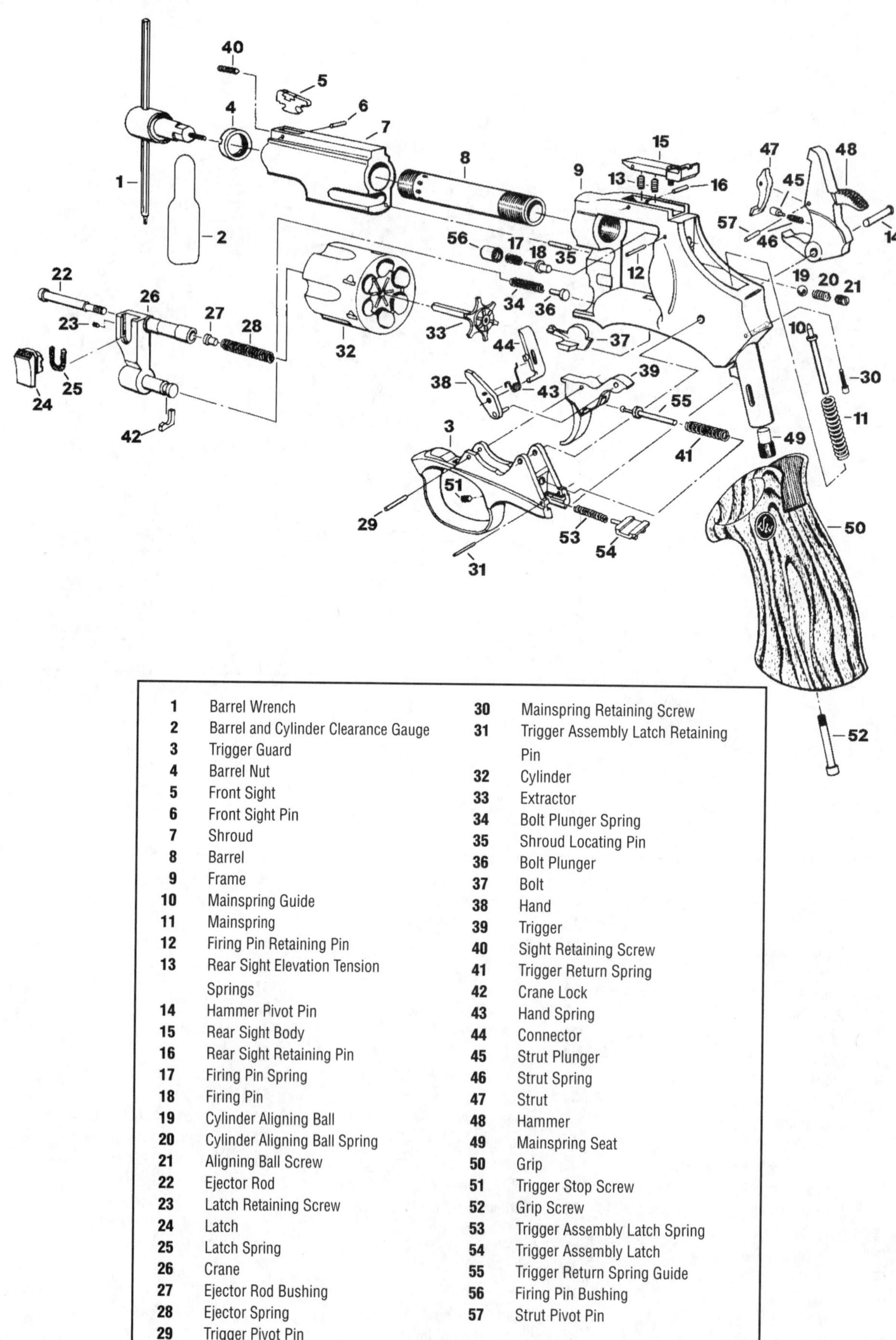

1	Barrel Wrench	30	Mainspring Retaining Screw
2	Barrel and Cylinder Clearance Gauge	31	Trigger Assembly Latch Retaining Pin
3	Trigger Guard	32	Cylinder
4	Barrel Nut	33	Extractor
5	Front Sight	34	Bolt Plunger Spring
6	Front Sight Pin	35	Shroud Locating Pin
7	Shroud	36	Bolt Plunger
8	Barrel	37	Bolt
9	Frame	38	Hand
10	Mainspring Guide	39	Trigger
11	Mainspring	40	Sight Retaining Screw
12	Firing Pin Retaining Pin	41	Trigger Return Spring
13	Rear Sight Elevation Tension Springs	42	Crane Lock
14	Hammer Pivot Pin	43	Hand Spring
15	Rear Sight Body	44	Connector
16	Rear Sight Retaining Pin	45	Strut Plunger
17	Firing Pin Spring	46	Strut Spring
18	Firing Pin	47	Strut
19	Cylinder Aligning Ball	48	Hammer
20	Cylinder Aligning Ball Spring	49	Mainspring Seat
21	Aligning Ball Screw	50	Grip
22	Ejector Rod	51	Trigger Stop Screw
23	Latch Retaining Screw	52	Grip Screw
24	Latch	53	Trigger Assembly Latch Spring
25	Latch Spring	54	Trigger Assembly Latch
26	Crane	55	Trigger Return Spring Guide
27	Ejector Rod Bushing	56	Firing Pin Bushing
28	Ejector Spring	57	Strut Pivot Pin
29	Trigger Pivot Pin		

Derringer

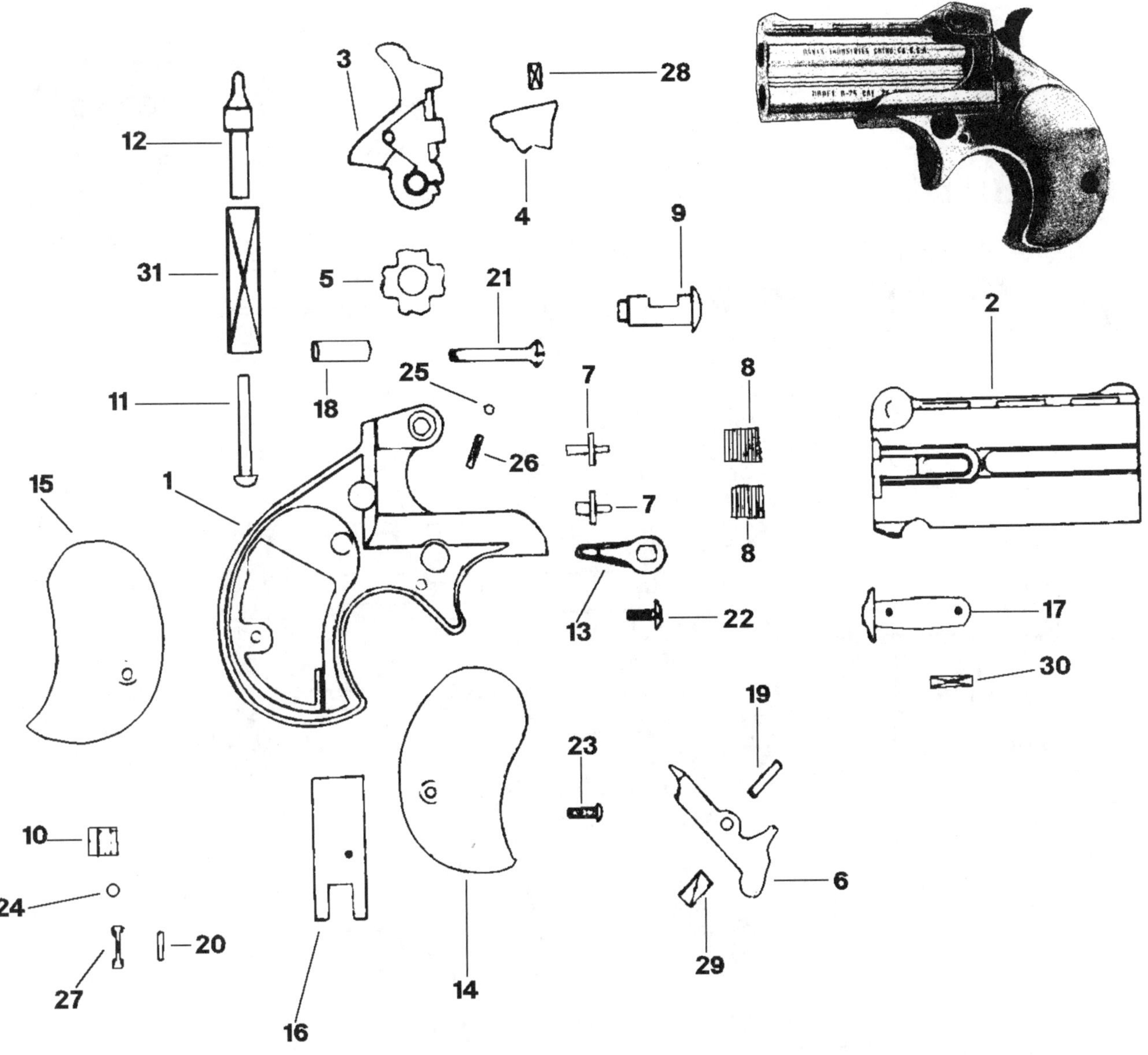

1	Frame	17	Extractor
2	Barrel	18	Hammer Pivot Pin
3	Hammer	19	Trigger Pin
4	Selector	20	Safety Pin
5	Cam	21	Hinge Screw
6	Trigger	22	Lock Screw
7	Firing Pins	23	Grip Screw
8	Bushings	24	Safety Ball
9	Lock	25	Lock Ball
10	Safety	26	Lock Spring
11	Screw	27	Safety Spring
12	Guide Pin	28	Selector Spring
13	Locking Lever	29	Trigger Spring
14	Right Grip	30	Extractor Spring
15	Left Grip	31	Mainspring
16	Cam Spring		

P-32 and P-380 Auto

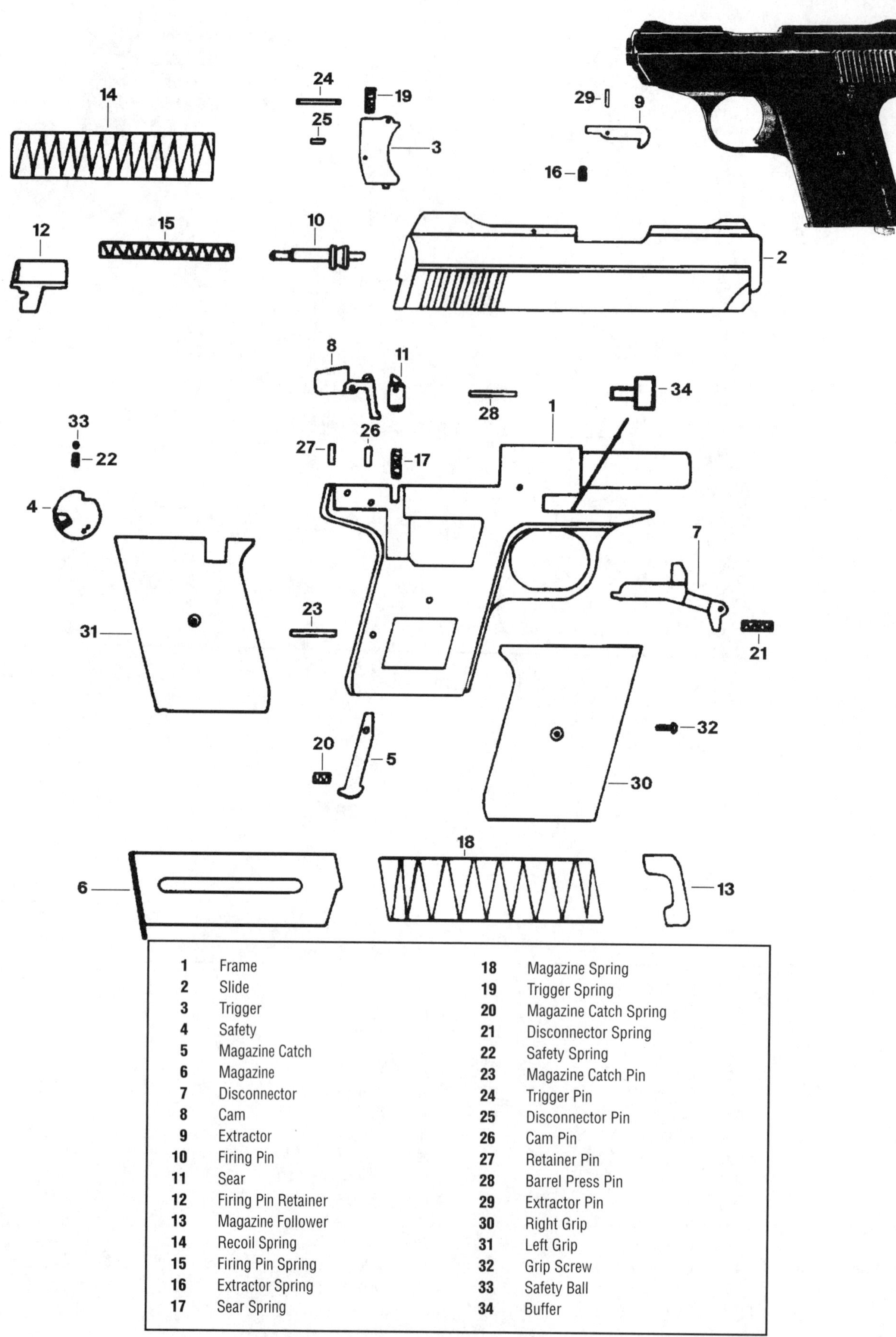

No.	Part	No.	Part
1	Frame	**18**	Magazine Spring
2	Slide	**19**	Trigger Spring
3	Trigger	**20**	Magazine Catch Spring
4	Safety	**21**	Disconnector Spring
5	Magazine Catch	**22**	Safety Spring
6	Magazine	**23**	Magazine Catch Pin
7	Disconnector	**24**	Trigger Pin
8	Cam	**25**	Disconnector Pin
9	Extractor	**26**	Cam Pin
10	Firing Pin	**27**	Retainer Pin
11	Sear	**28**	Barrel Press Pin
12	Firing Pin Retainer	**29**	Extractor Pin
13	Magazine Follower	**30**	Right Grip
14	Recoil Spring	**31**	Left Grip
15	Firing Pin Spring	**32**	Grip Screw
16	Extractor Spring	**33**	Safety Ball
17	Sear Spring	**34**	Buffer

357/41/44 Magnum Auto

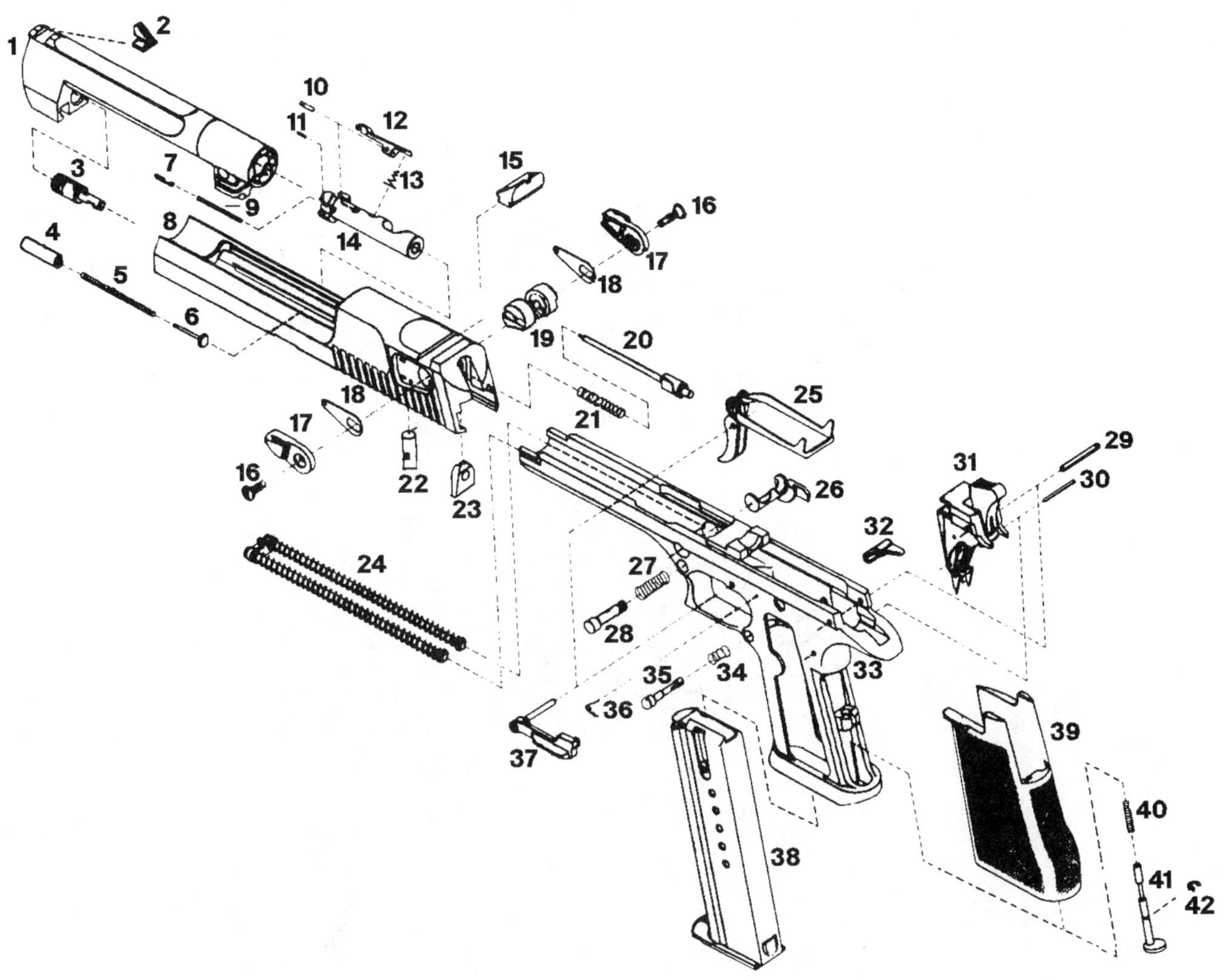

1	Barrel	**22**	Bolt Guide Pin
2	Front Sight	**23**	Firing Pin Stop
3	Gas Piston	**24**	Recoil Spring Assembly
4	Bolt Stabilizer Pin	**25**	Trigger Assembly
5	Bolt Stabilizer Spring	**26**	Barrel Lock
6	Guide Pin	**27**	Barrel Lock Spring
7	Ejector	**28**	Barrel Lock Pin
8	Slide	**29**	Hammer Pin
9	Ejector Spring	**30**	Sear Pin
10	Extractor Pin	**31**	Hammer Mechanism Assembly
11	Ejector Pin	**32**	Magazine Catch
12	Extractor	**33**	Frame
13	Extractor Spring	**34**	Magazine Catch Spring
14	Bolt	**35**	Magazine Catch Pin
15	Rear Sight	**36**	Slide Catch Spring
16	Safety Screws	**37**	Slide Catch
17	Safety-Lever	**38**	Magazine Assembly
18	Safety Springs	**39**	Grip
19	Safety Drum	**40**	Grip Pin Spring
20	Firing Pin	**41**	Grip Pin
21	Firing Pin Spring	**42**	Retaining Ring

Combat Master Auto

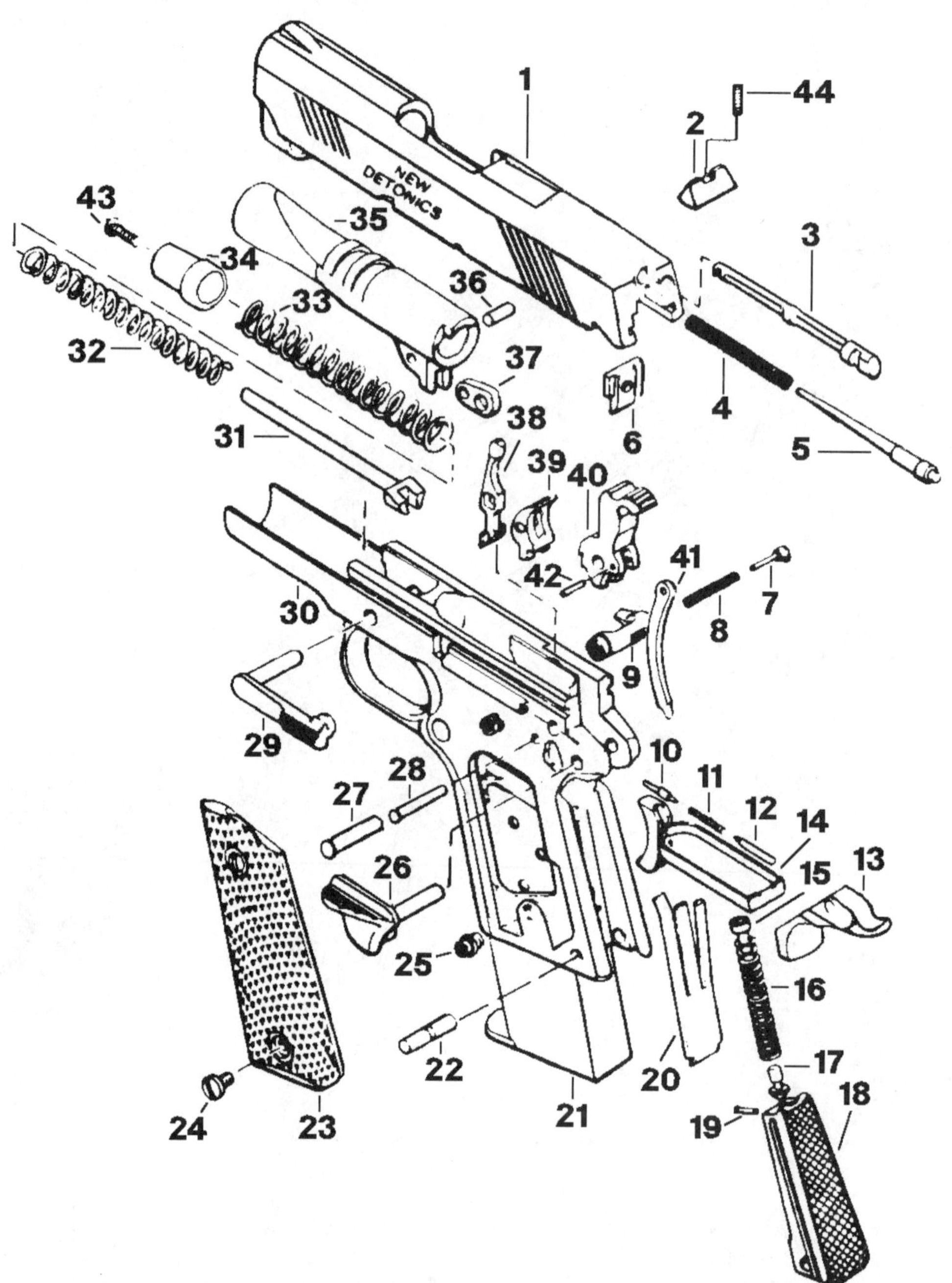

1	Slide	**16**	Mainspring	**30**	Frame
2	Rear Sight	**17**	Mainspring Housing Pin Retainer	**31**	Recoil Spring Guide
3	Extractor	**18**	Mainspring Housing	**32**	Inner Recoil Spring
4	Firing Pin Spring	**19**	Mainspring Cap Pin	**33**	Outer Recoil Spring
5	Firing Pin	**20**	Sear Spring	**34**	Recoil Spring Cap
6	Firing Pin Stop	**21**	Magazine Assembly	**35**	Barrel
7	Magazine Catch Lock	**22**	Mainspring Housing Pin	**36**	Barrel Link Pin
8	Magazine Catch Spring	**23**	Left Grip	**37**	Barrel Link
9	Magazine Catch	**24**	Stock Screw	**38**	Disconnector
10	Slide Stop Plunger	**25**	Stock Screw Bushing	**39**	Sear
11	Slide Stop Plunger Spring	**26**	Safety-Lever	**40**	Hammer
12	Safety Lock Plunger	**27**	Hammer Pin	**41**	Hammer Strut
13	Beavertail Grip Extension	**28**	Sear Pin	**42**	Hammer Strut Pin
14	Trigger	**29**	Slide Stop	**43**	Recoil Spring Guide Screw
15	Mainspring Guide			**44**	Rear Sight Retention Screw

Model 1907 Auto

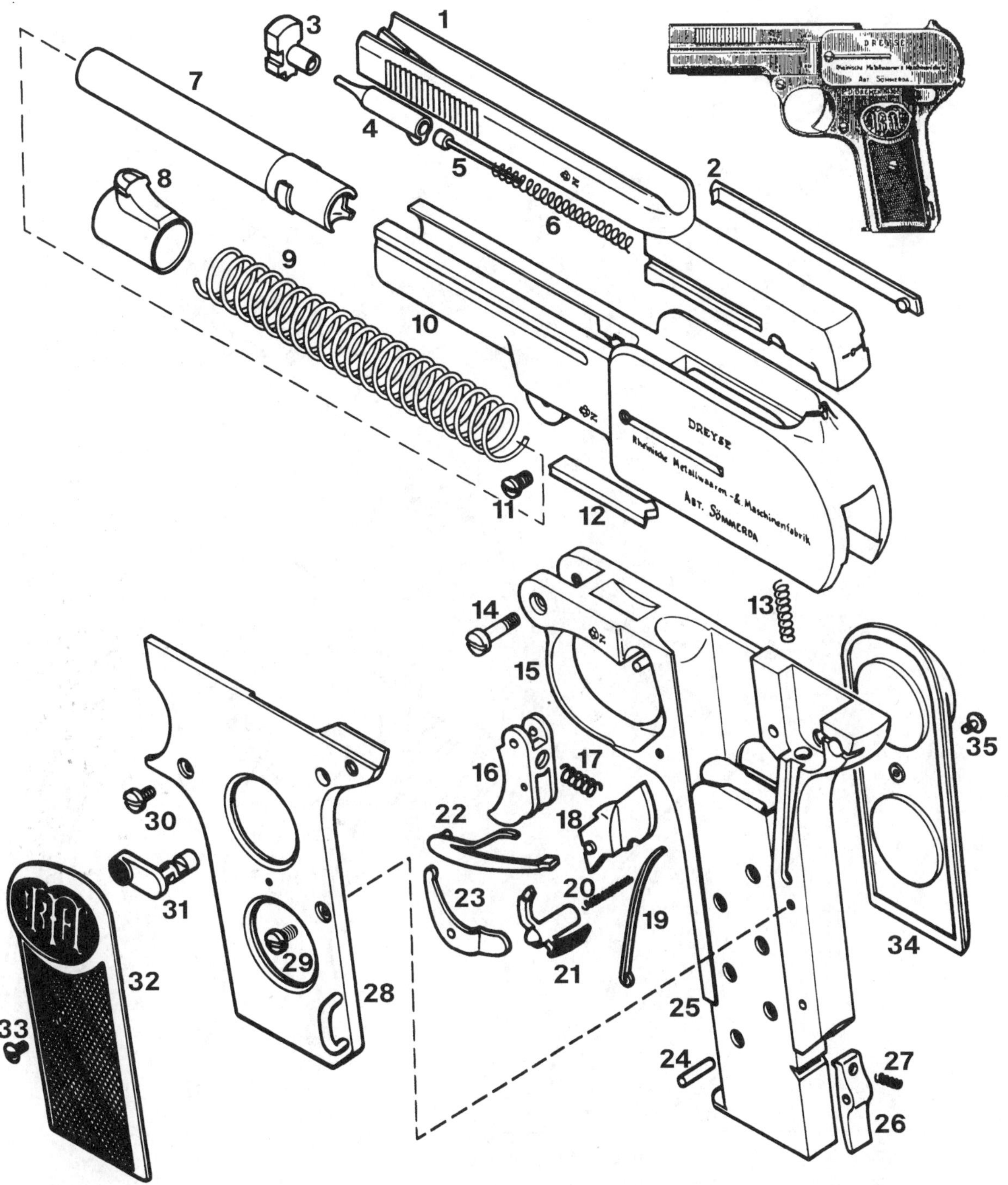

1	Slide	**13**	Sear Spring	**25**	Magazine
2	Extractor	**14**	Hinge Screw	**26**	Magazine Catch
3	Bolt Head	**15**	Grip Frame	**27**	Magazine Catch Spring
4	Firing Pin	**16**	Trigger	**28**	Sideplate
5	Cocking Indicator	**17**	Trigger Spring	**29**	Sideplate Screw
6	Firing Pin Spring	**18**	Sear	**30**	Front Sideplate Screw
7	Barrel	**19**	Safety Catch Spring	**31**	Safety Catch
8	Barrel Spring Follower	**20**	Frame Latch Spring	**32**	Left Grip Panel
9	Recoil Spring	**21**	Frame Latch	**33**	Left Grip Screw
10	Upper Frame	**22**	Trigger Bar	**34**	Right Grip Panel
11	Ejector Screw	**23**	Disconnector	**35**	Right Grip Screw
12	Ejector	**24**	Magazine Catch Pin		

Dakota Model 1873 Revolver

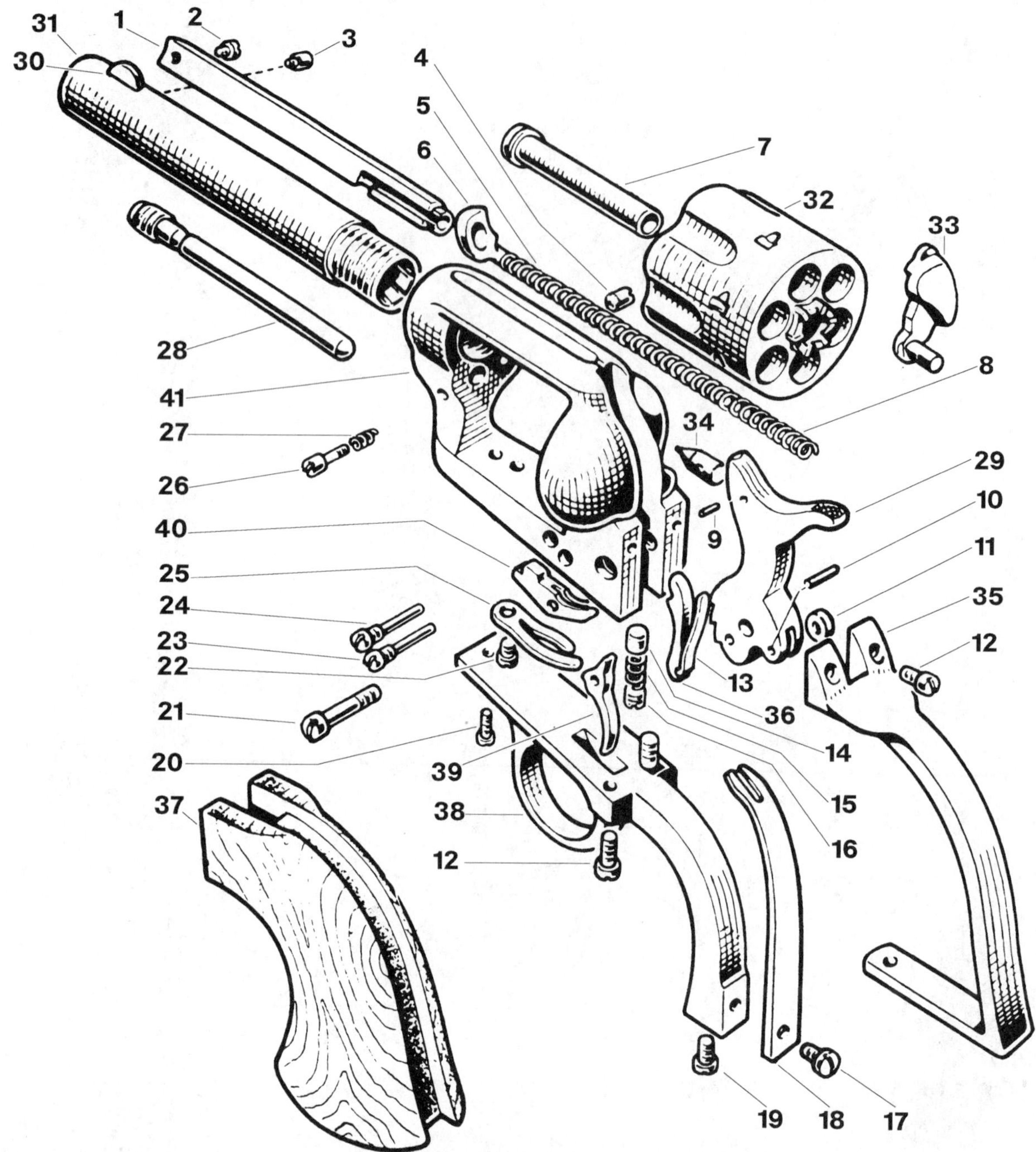

1	Ejector Tube	15	Loading Gate Spring	29	Hammer
2	Ejector Tube Screw	16	Loading Gate Catch Screw	30	Front Sight
3	Ejector Tube Screw Bushing	17	Mainspring Screw	31	Barrel
4	Ejector Pin Nut	18	Mainspring	32	Cylinder
5	Ejector Rod	19	Front Backstrap Screw	33	Loading Gate
6	Ejector Rod Head	20	Front Trigger Guard Screw	34	Firing Pin
7	Base Pin Bushing	21	Hammer Screw	35	Backstrap
8	Ejector Spring	22	Bolt Spring Screw	36	Hand
9	Firing Pin Lock Pin	23	Trigger Screw	37	Stock
10	Mainspring Roller Pin	24	Bolt Screw	38	Trigger Guard
11	Mainspring Roller	25	Sear and Bolt Spring	39	Trigger
12	Backstrap Screw	26	Cylinder Base Pin Screw	40	Bolt
13	Hand Spring	27	Cylinder Base Pin Spring	41	Frame
14	Loading Gate Catch	28	Cylinder Base Pin		

Remington 1875 Army Revolver

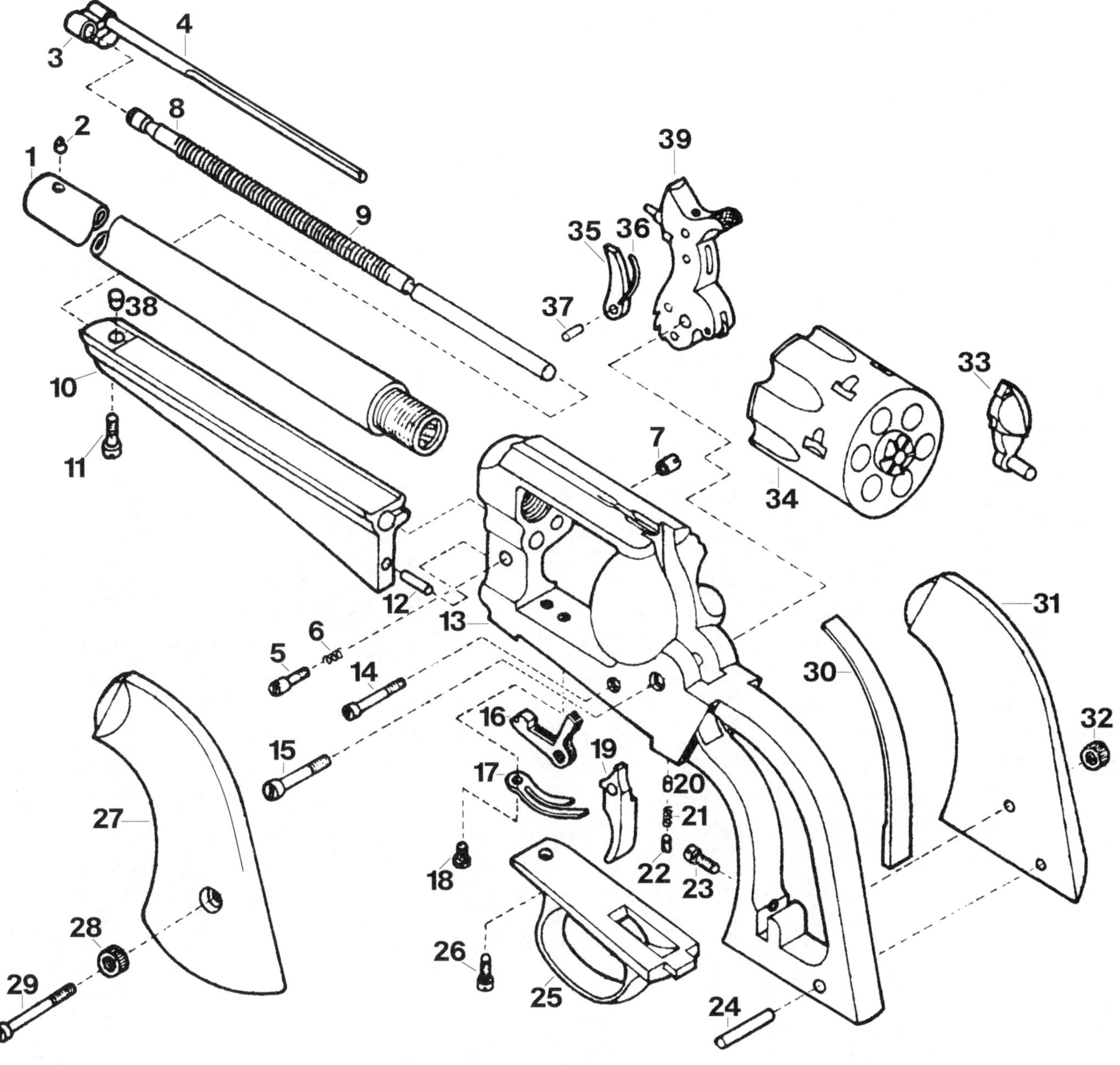

1	Barrel	14	Trigger and Bolt Screw	27	Left Grip
2	Front Sight	15	Hammer Screw	28	Left Grip Escutcheon
3	Ejector Rod Head	16	Cylinder Locking Bolt	29	Grip Screw
4	Ejector Rod	17	Trigger and Bolt Spring	30	Mainspring
5	Cylinder Lock Screw	18	Trigger and Bolt Spring Screw	31	Right Grip
6	Cylinder Lock Spring	19	Trigger	32	Right Grip Escutcheon
7	Cylinder Lock Nut	20	Gate Plunger	33	Loading Gate
8	Cylinder Pin	21	Gate Plunger Spring	34	Cylinder
9	Ejector Spring	22	Gate Plunger Screw	35	Hand
10	Ejector Housing	23	Mainspring Screw	36	Hand Spring
11	Ejector Housing Screw	24	Pin	37	Hand Axis Pin
12	Ejector Housing Pin	25	Trigger Guard	38	Ejector Housing Stud
13	Frame	26	Trigger Guard Screw	39	Hammer Assembly

No. 2 Mk. I Revolve

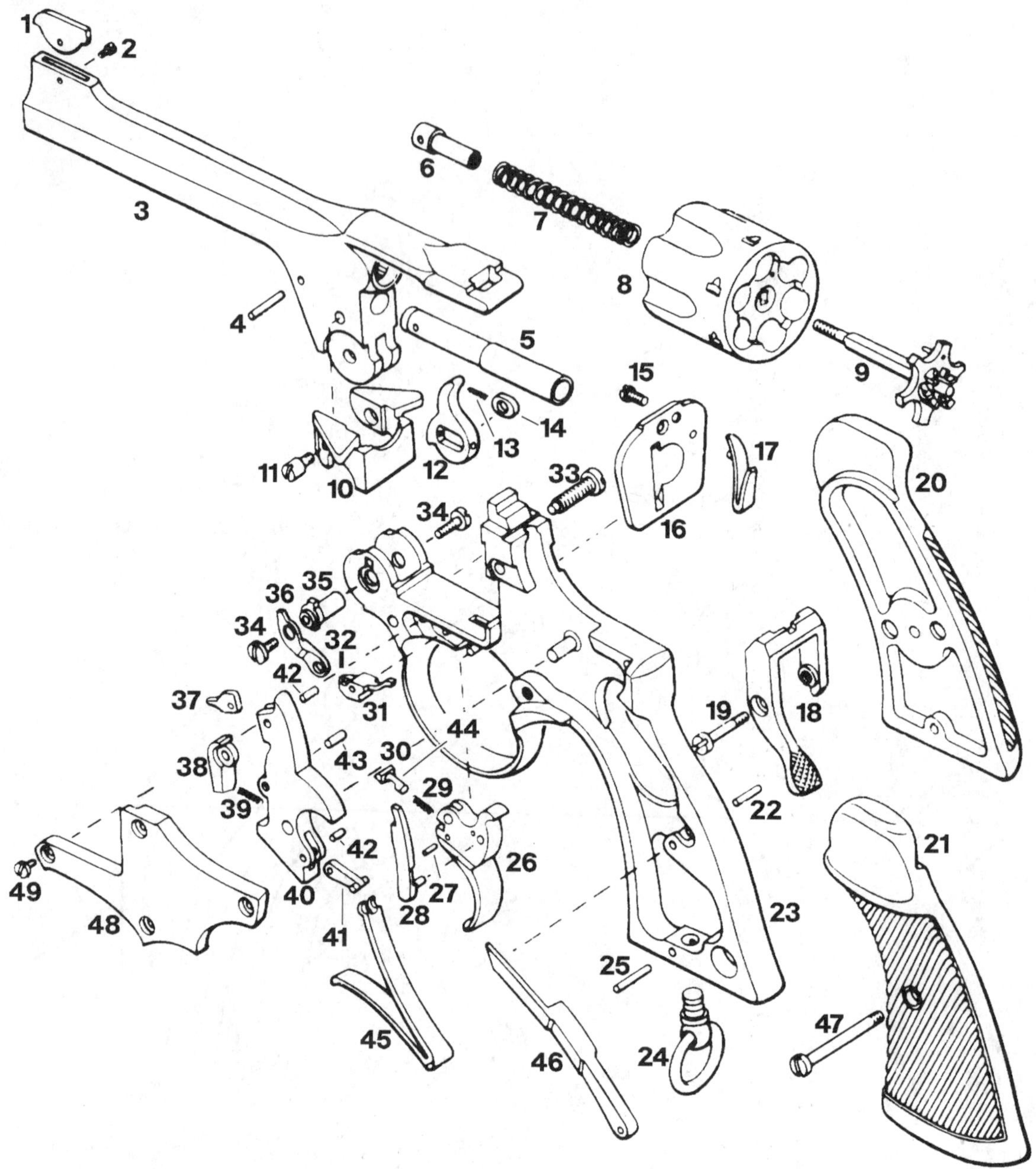

1	Front Sight Blade	18	Barrel Latch	35	Hinge Pin
2	Front Sight Screw	19	Barrel Latch Screw	36	Cam Lever
3	Barrel	20	Right Grip	37	Hammer Nose
4	Cylinder Arbor Retaining Pin	21	Left Grip	38	Hammer Catch
5	Cylinder Arbor	22	Mainspring Lever Pin	39	Hammer Catch Spring
6	Extractor Nut	23	Frame	40	Hammer
7	Extractor Spring	24	Lanyard Ring	41	Hammer Swivel
8	Cylinder	25	Grip Pin	42	Hammer Swivel Pin
9	Extractor	26	Trigger	43	Hammer Catch Retaining Pin
10	Cylinder Retaining Cam	27	Stop Operating Catch Pin	44	Nose Retaining Pin
11	Cylinder Cam Screw	28	Hand	45	Mainspring
12	Extractor Lever	29	Stop Operating Catch Spring	46	Mainspring Lever
13	Extractor Lever Spring	30	Stop Operating Catch	47	Grip Screw
14	Extractor Lever Roller	31	Cylinder Stop	48	Sideplate
15	Recoil Plate Screw	32	Cylinder Stop Spring	49	Sideplate Screw
16	Recoil Plate	33	Cam Lever Screw		
17	Barrel Latch Spring	34	Hinge Pin Screws		

22 Auto

Courtesy of Dennis Riordan

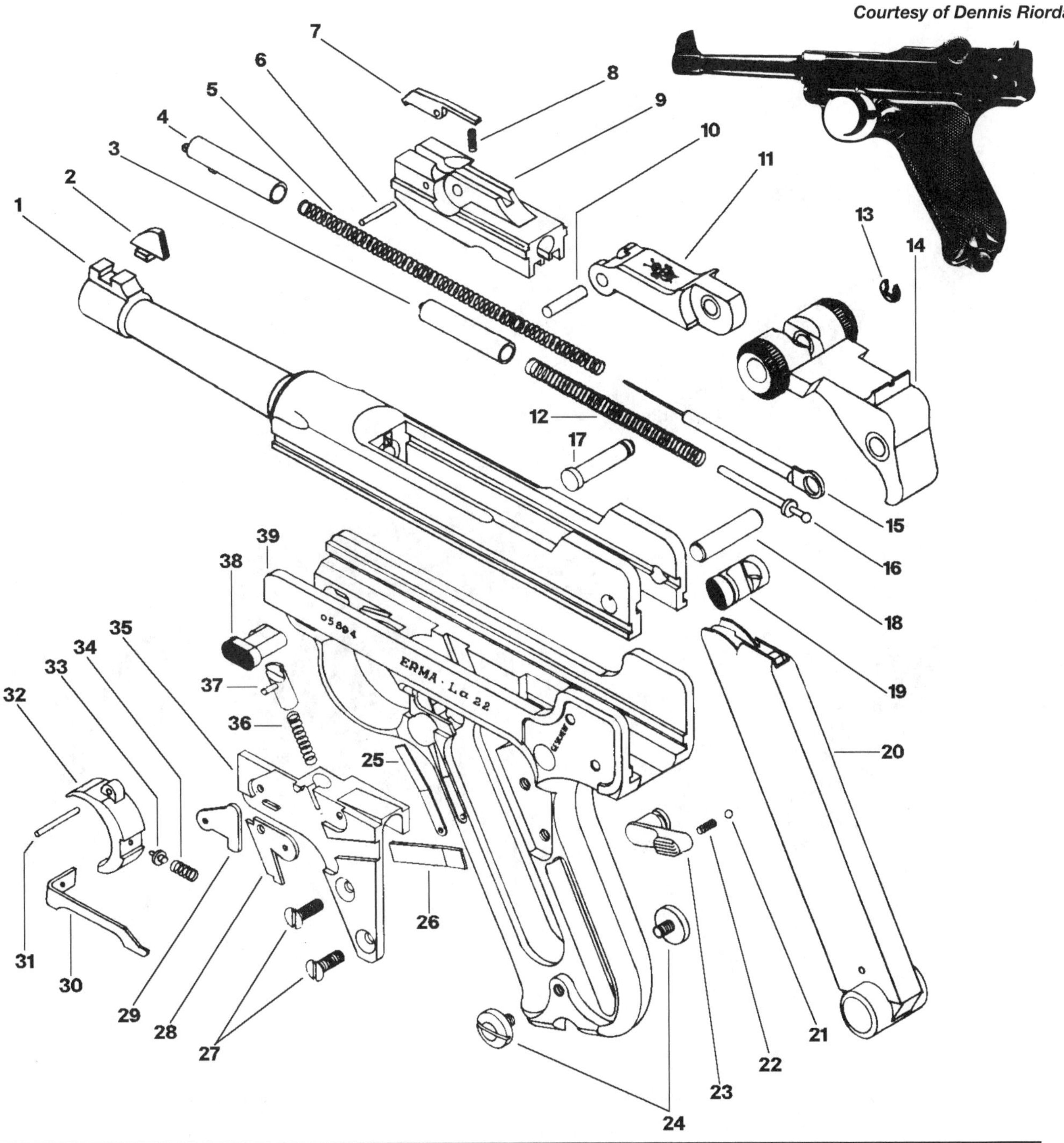

1	Barrel and Receiver	15	Firing Pin Spring Guide and Ejector	29	Disconnector
2	Front Sight	16	Recoil Spring Guide	30	Trigger Bar
3	Recoil Spring Sleeve	17	Toggle Axle Pin	31	Trigger Pin
4	Firing Pin	18	Receiver Axle Pin	32	Trigger
5	Firing Pin Spring	19	Magazine Catch	33	Trigger Plunger
6	Extractor Pin	20	Magazine Assembly	34	Trigger Spring
7	Extractor	21	Safety Ball	35	Sear Housing
8	Extractor Spring	22	Safety Spring	36	Sear Spring
9	Breechblock	23	Safety-Lever	37	Sear
10	Breechblock Pin	24	Grip Screws	38	Locking Bolt
11	Front Toggle Link	25	Magazine Catch Spring	39	Frame
12	Recoil Spring	26	Safety Bar	**Parts Not Shown**	
13	Toggle Axle Lockwasher	27	Sear Housing Screws		Grips
14	Rear Toggle Link	28	Sear Lever		

KGP68A Auto

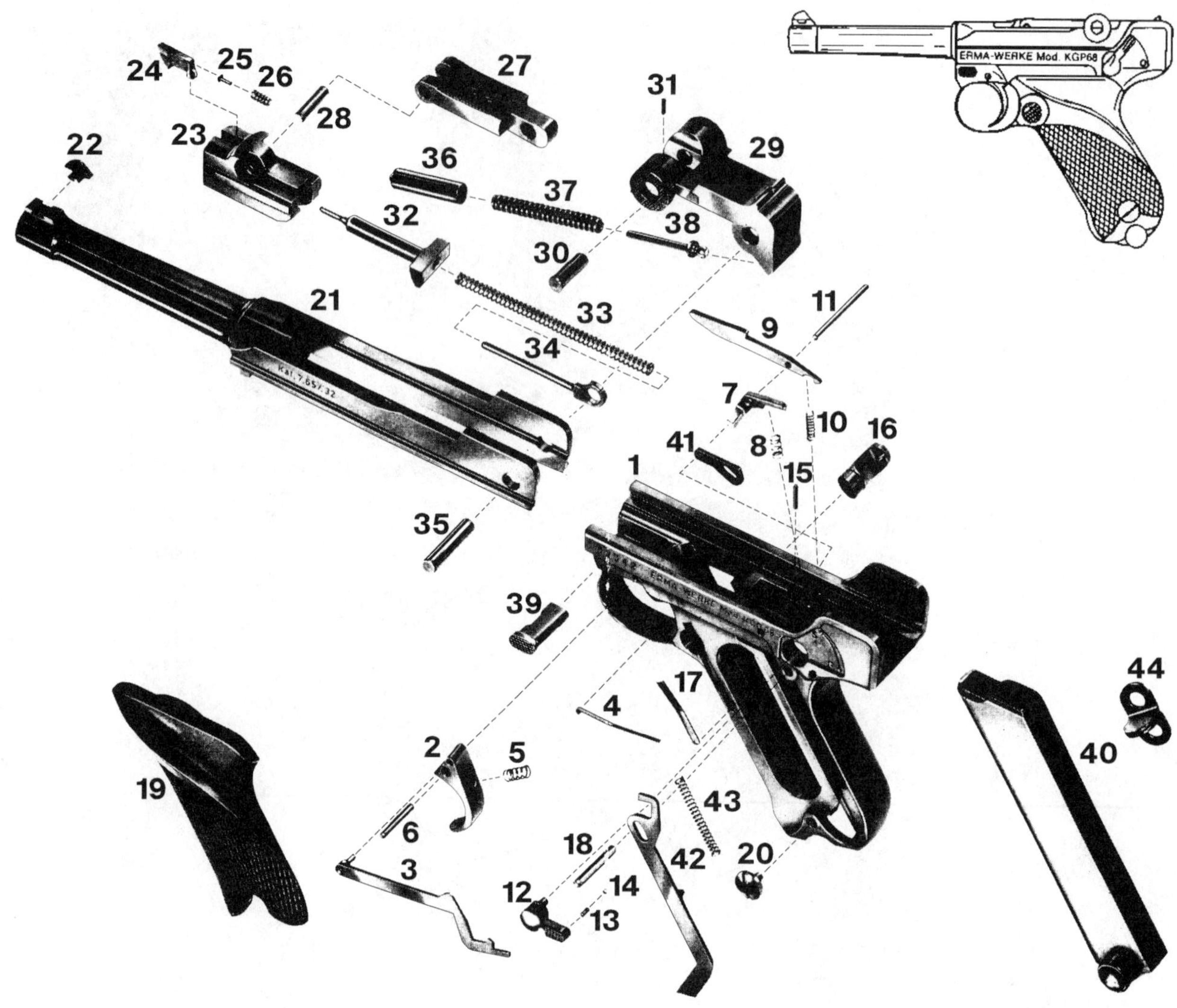

1	Frame	**17**	Magazine Catch Spring	**33**	Firing Pin Spring
2	Trigger	**18**	Grip Pin	**34**	Firing Pin Spring Bolt
3	Trigger Bar	**19**	Left Grip	**35**	Rear Toggle Axis Pin
4	Trigger Bar Spring	**20**	Grip Screw	**36**	Recoil Spring Tube
5	Trigger Spring	**21**	Barrel and Receiver	**37**	Recoil Spring
6	Trigger Pin	**22**	Front Sight	**38**	Recoil Spring Guide
7	Sear	**23**	Breechblock	**39**	Locking Bolt
8	Sear Spring	**24**	Extractor	**40**	Magazine Assembly
9	Breechblock Catch Link	**25**	Extractor Plunger	**41**	Safety Plate
10	Breechblock Catch Link Spring	**26**	Extractor Spring	**42**	Magazine Safety-Lever
11	Cylindrical Pin	**27**	Front Toggle Link	**43**	Safety Spring
12	Safety Catch	**28**	Front Link Connecting Pin	**44**	Magazine Follower Depressor
13	Safety Catch Spring	**29**	Rear Toggle Link	**Parts Not Shown**	
14	Safety Catch Ball Detent	**30**	Toggle Link Connecting Pin		Right Grip
15	Safety Catch Pin	**31**	Toggle Link Pin Retaining Pin		
16	Magazine Catch	**32**	Firing Pin		

KGP69 Auto

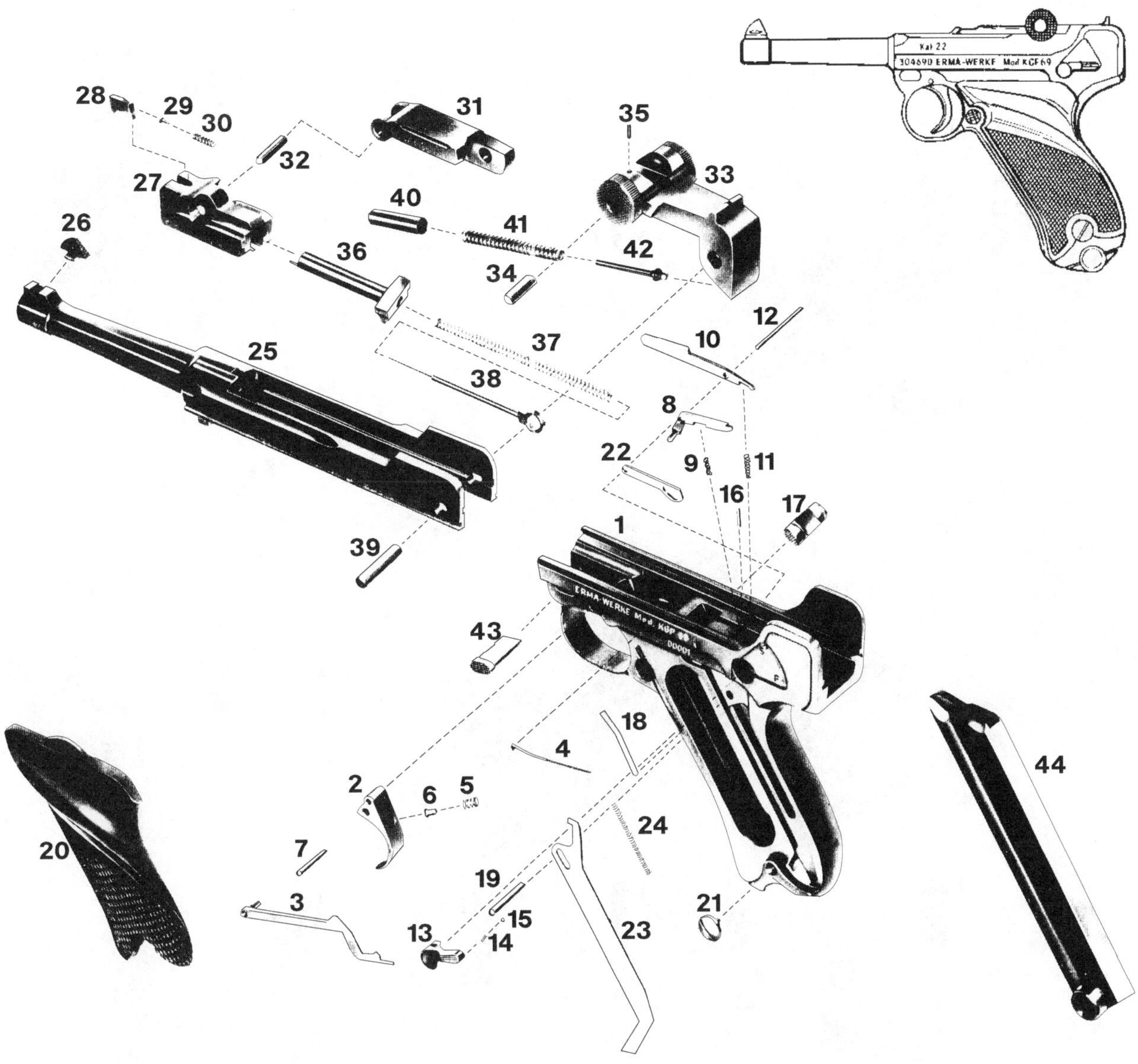

1	Frame
2	Trigger
3	Trigger Bar
4	Trigger Bar Spring
5	Trigger Spring
6	Trigger Spring Plunger
7	Trigger Pin
8	Sear
9	Sear Spring
10	Breechblock Catch Link
11	Breechblock Catch Link Spring
12	Breechblock Catch Link Pin
13	Safety-Lever
14	Safety-Lever Spring
15	Safety-Lever Ball Detent
16	Cylindrical Pin
17	Magazine Catch
18	Magazine Catch Spring
19	Magazine Safety-Lever Pin
20	Left Grip
21	Grip Screw
22	Safety Plate
23	Magazine Safety-Lever
24	Safety Spring
25	Barrel and Receiver
26	Front Sight
27	Breechblock
28	Extractor
29	Extractor Spring Plunger
30	Extractor Spring
31	Front Toggle Link
32	Front Toggle Link Pin
33	Rear Toggle Link
34	Toggle Link Connecting Pin
35	Toggle Link Pin Retaining Pin
36	Firing Pin
37	Firing Pin Spring
38	Ejector
39	Rear Toggle Axis Pin
40	Recoil Spring Tube
41	Recoil Spring
42	Recoil Spring Guide
43	Locking Bolt
44	Magazine Assembly

Parts Not Shown

Right Grip

RX22 Auto

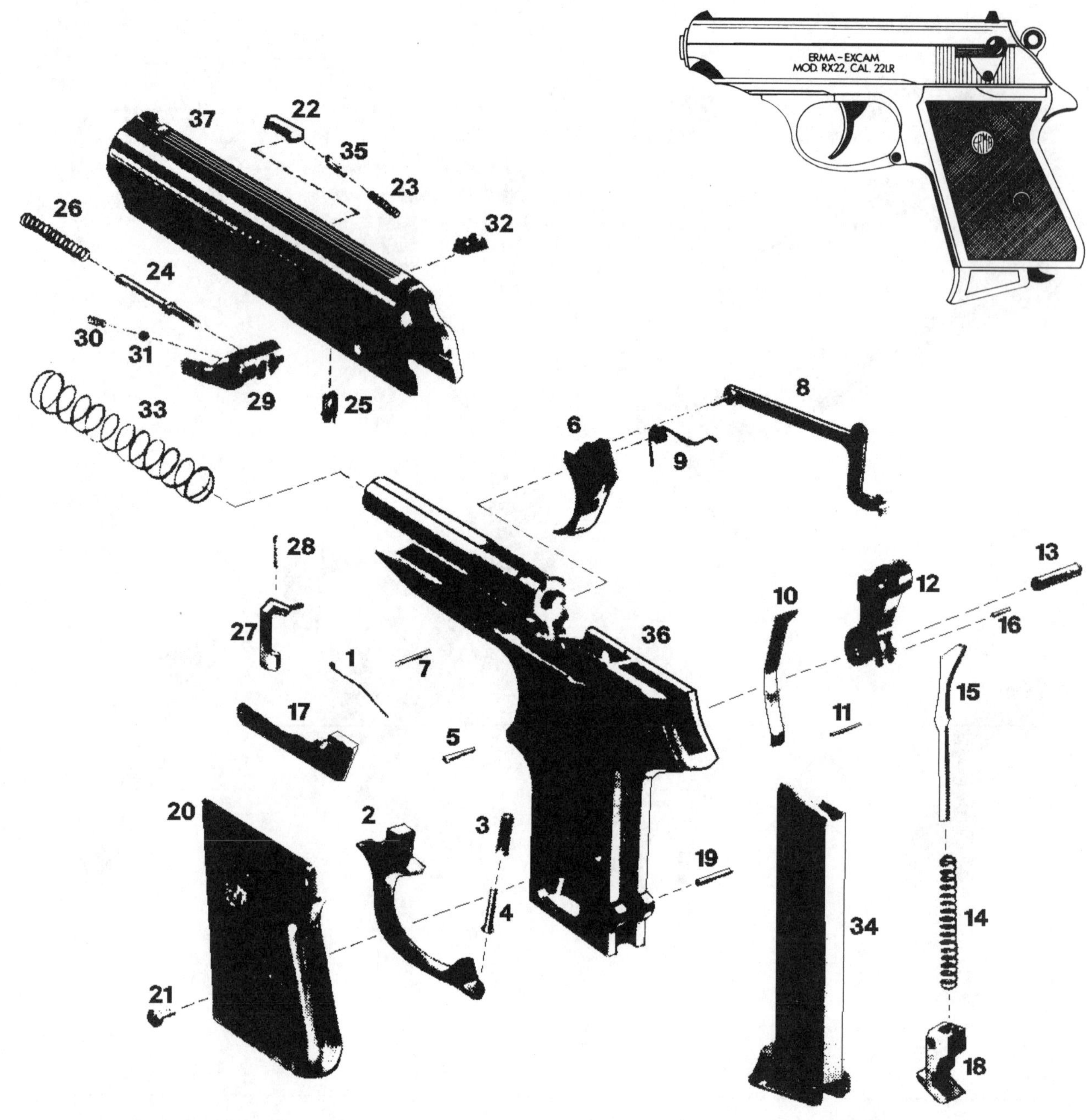

1	Leaf Spring
2	Trigger Guard
3	Lock Spring
4	Spring Pin
5	Guard Pin
6	Trigger
7	Trigger Pin
8	Trigger Bar
9	Trigger Bar Spring
10	Sear
11	Sear Pin
12	Hammer
13	Hammer Pin
14	Mainspring
15	Mainspring Guide
16	Mainspring Guide Pin
17	Catch Link
18	Magazine Catch
19	Magazine Catch Pin
20	Left Grip
21	Grip Screw
22	Extractor
23	Extractor Spring
24	Firing Pin
25	Firing Pin Retainer
26	Firing Pin Spring
27	Safety Link
28	Safety Spring
29	Thumb Safety
30	Thumb Spring
31	Thumb Safety Detent Ball
32	Rear Sight
33	Recoil Spring
34	Magazine Assembly
35	Extractor Pin
36	Frame Assembly
37	Slide

C-96 Auto

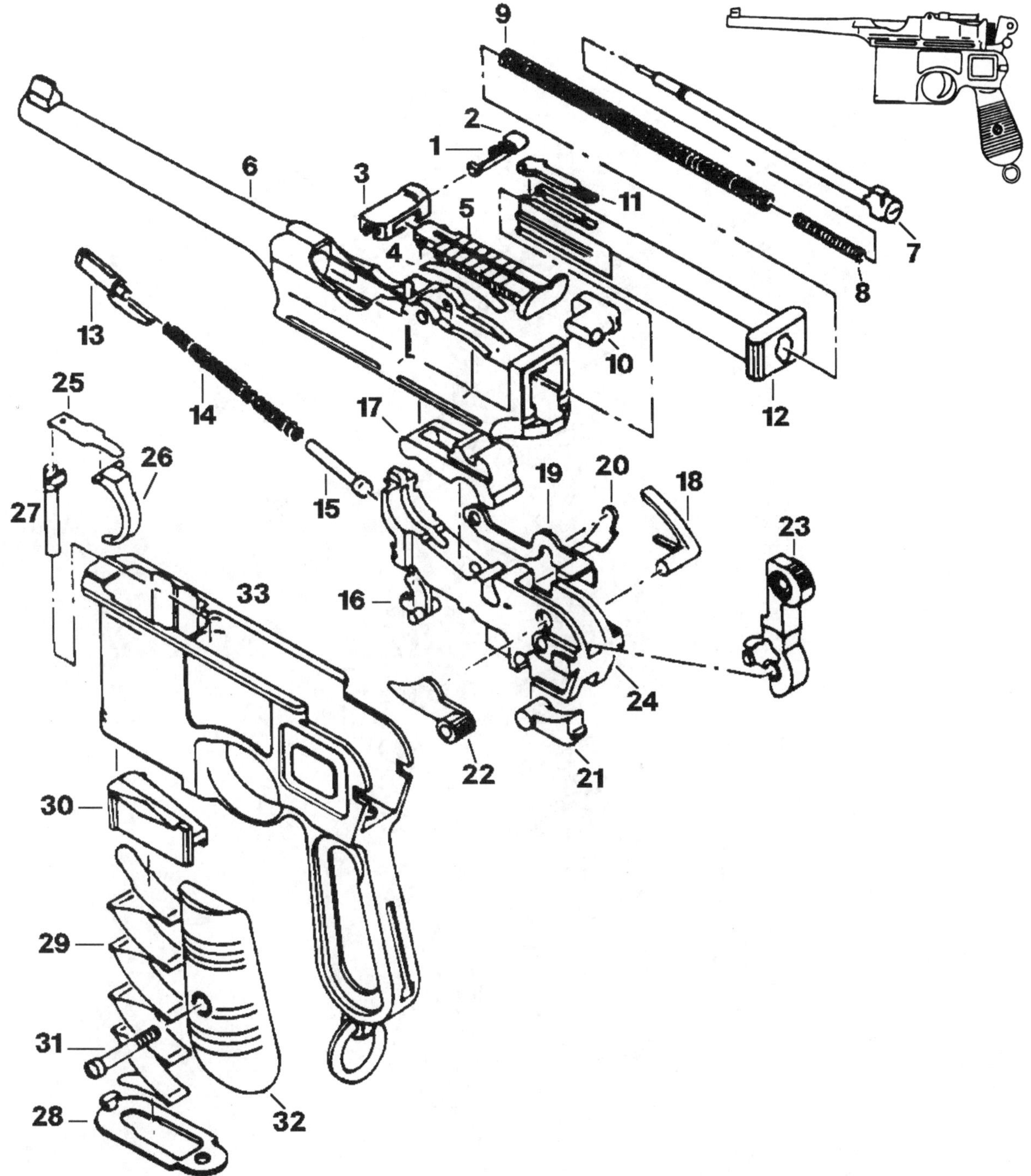

1	Rear Sight Slide Lock Spring	**13**	Rocker Plunger	**25**	Trigger Spring
2	Rear Sight Slide Lock	**14**	Mainspring	**26**	Trigger
3	Rear Sight Slide	**15**	Mainspring Plunger	**27**	Magazine Plunger
4	Rear Sight Spring	**16**	Rocker Coupling	**28**	Floorplate
5	Rear Sight	**17**	Bolt Locking Block	**29**	Magazine Spring
6	Receiver	**18**	Sear Spring and Hammer Pivot	**30**	Magazine Follower
7	Firing Pin	**19**	Sear Arm	**31**	Grip Screw
8	Firing Pin Spring	**20**	Sear	**32**	Left Grip
9	Recoil Spring	**21**	Lock Frame Stop	**33**	Frame
10	Bolt Stop	**22**	Safety-Lever	**Parts Not Shown**	
11	Extractor	**23**	Hammer		Right Grip
12	Bolt	**24**	Lock Mechanism Frame		

Model 714 Auto

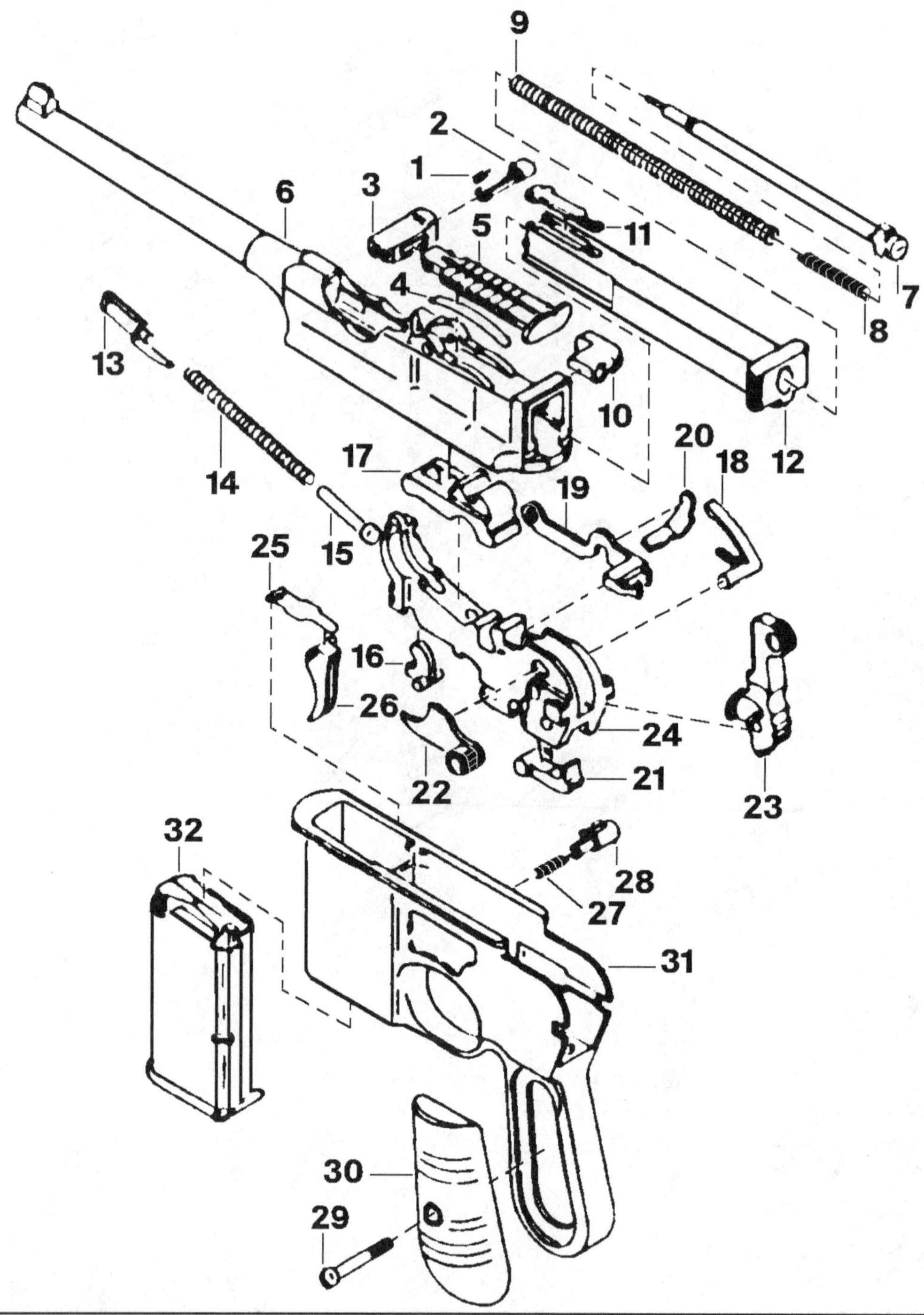

1	Rear Sight Slide Lock Spring	13	Rocker Plunger	25	Trigger Spring
2	Rear Sight Slide Lock	14	Mainspring	26	Trigger
3	Rear Sight Slide	15	Mainspring Plunger	27	Magazine Release Spring
4	Rear Sight Spring	16	Rocker Coupling	28	Magazine Release
5	Rear Sight	17	Bolt Locking Block	29	Grip Screw
6	Receiver	18	Sear Spring and Hammer Pivot	30	Left Grip
7	Firing Pin	19	Sear Arm	31	Frame
8	Firing Pin Spring	20	Sear	32	Magazine
9	Recoil Spring	21	Lock Frame Stop	**Parts Not Shown**	
10	Bolt Stop	22	Safety		Right Grip
11	Extractor	23	Hammer		
12	Bolt	24	Lock Mechanism Frame		

Casull Revolver

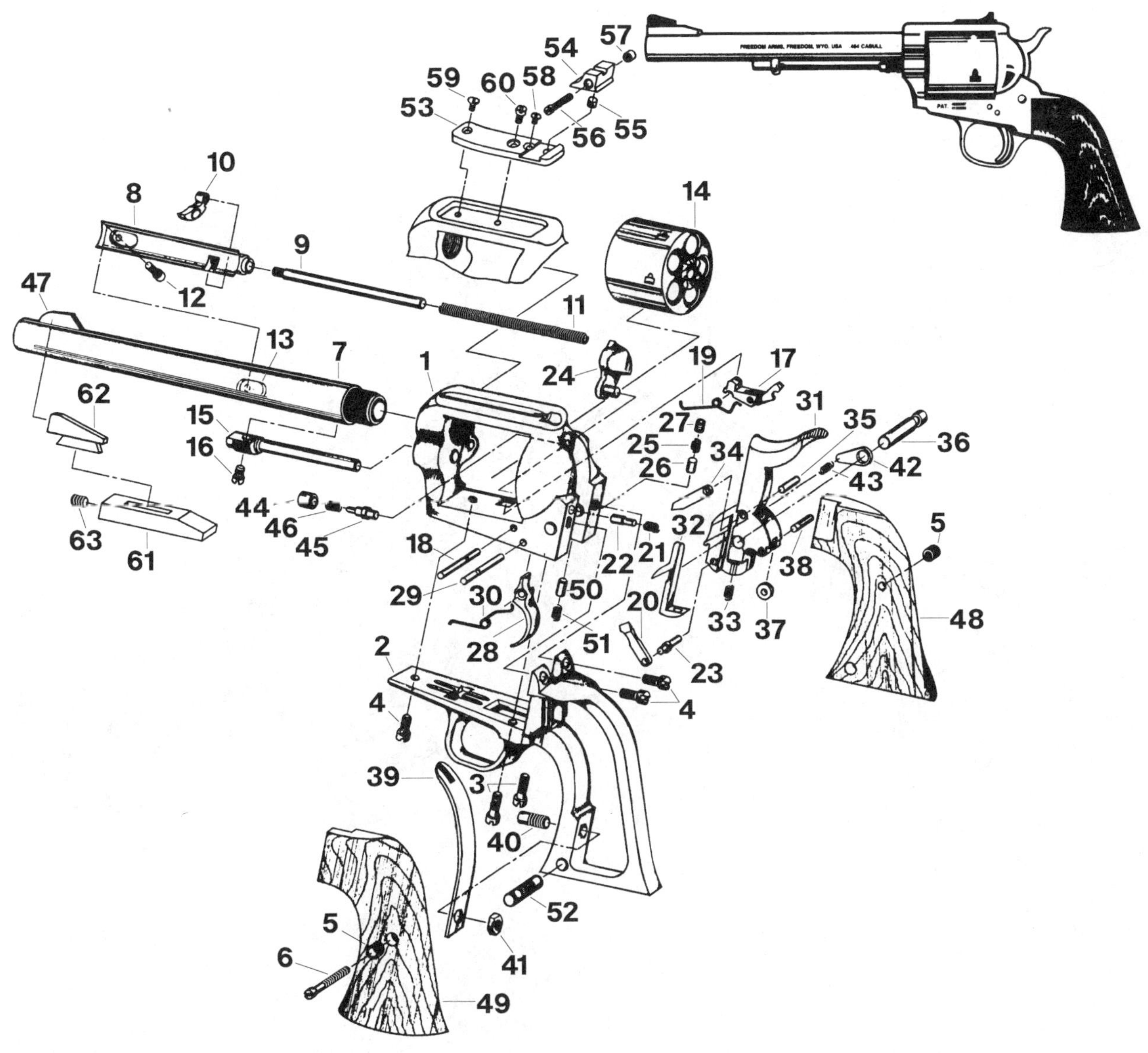

1	Cylinder Frame	22	Cylinder Hand Plunger	43	Trippet Spring
2	Grip Frame	23	Cylinder Hand Pin	44	Recoil Bushing
3	Frame Screws, Bottom	24	Loading Gate	45	Firing Pin
4	Frame Screws, Back and Bottom	25	Loading Gate Spring	46	Firing Pin Spring
5	Grip Escutcheons	26	Loading Gate Plunger	47	Front Sight
6	Grip Screw	27	Loading Gate Screw	48	Right Grip
7	Barrel	28	Trigger	49	Left Grip
8	Ejector Tube	29	Trigger Axis Pin	50	Hammer Axis Pin Retaining Pin
9	Ejector Rod	30	Trigger Spring	51	Hammer Axis Pin Retaining Spring
10	Ejector Rod Head	31	Hammer	52	Grip Locating Pin
11	Ejector Spring	32	Hammer Safety Bar	53	Spring Sight Base
12	Ejector Screw	33	Hammer Safety Bar Spring	54	Sight Leaf
13	Ejector Tube Recoil Lug	34	Hammer Safety Bar Actuator	55	Sight Adjustment Lug
14	Cylinder	35	Hammer Safety Bar Actuator Pin	56	Windage Screw
15	Cylinder Axis Pin	36	Hammer Axis Pin	57	Windage Screw Nut
16	Cylinder Axis Pin Screw	37	Hammer Roller	58	Sight Lock Screw
17	Cylinder Lock	38	Hammer Roller Pin	59	Sight Hold-Down Screw
18	Cylinder Lock Axis Pin	39	Mainspring	60	Sight Elevation Screw
19	Cylinder Lock Spring	40	Mainspring Anchor Bolt	61	Front Sight Ramp
20	Cylinder Hand	41	Mainspring Anchor Screw Nut	62	Front Sight Blade
21	Cylinder Hand Spring	42	Trippet	63	Front Sight Blade Set Screw

Mini Revolver

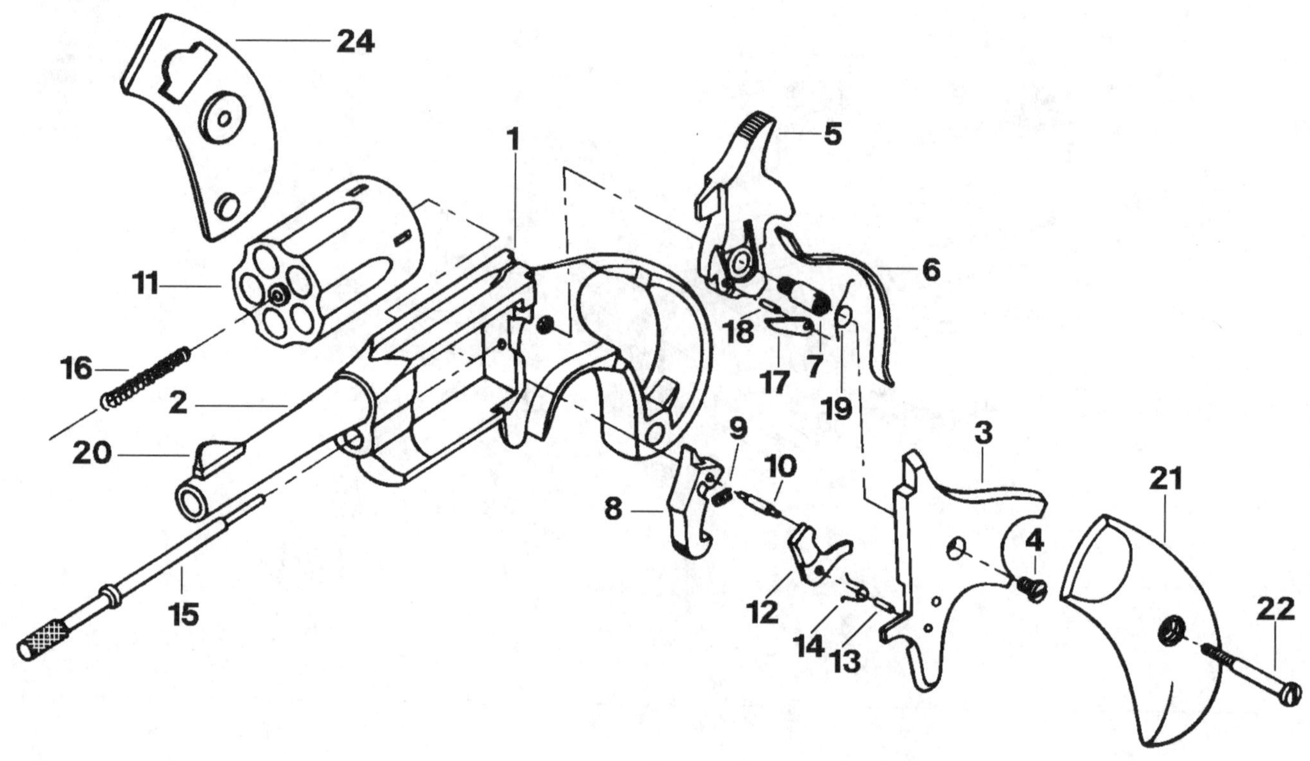

1	Receiver	12	Cylinder Lock
2	Barrel	13	Cylinder Lock Axis Pin
3	Sideplate Cover	14	Cylinder Lock Spring
4	Sideplate Cover Screw	15	Cylinder Pin
5	Hammer	16	Cylinder Pin Spring
6	Mainspring	17	Hand
7	Hammer Axis Pin	18	Hand Pin
8	Trigger	19	Hand Pin Spring
9	Trigger Spring	20	Front Sight
10	Trigger Axis Pin	21	Grip
11	Cylinder	22	Grip Screw

Model 1892 Ordnance Revolver

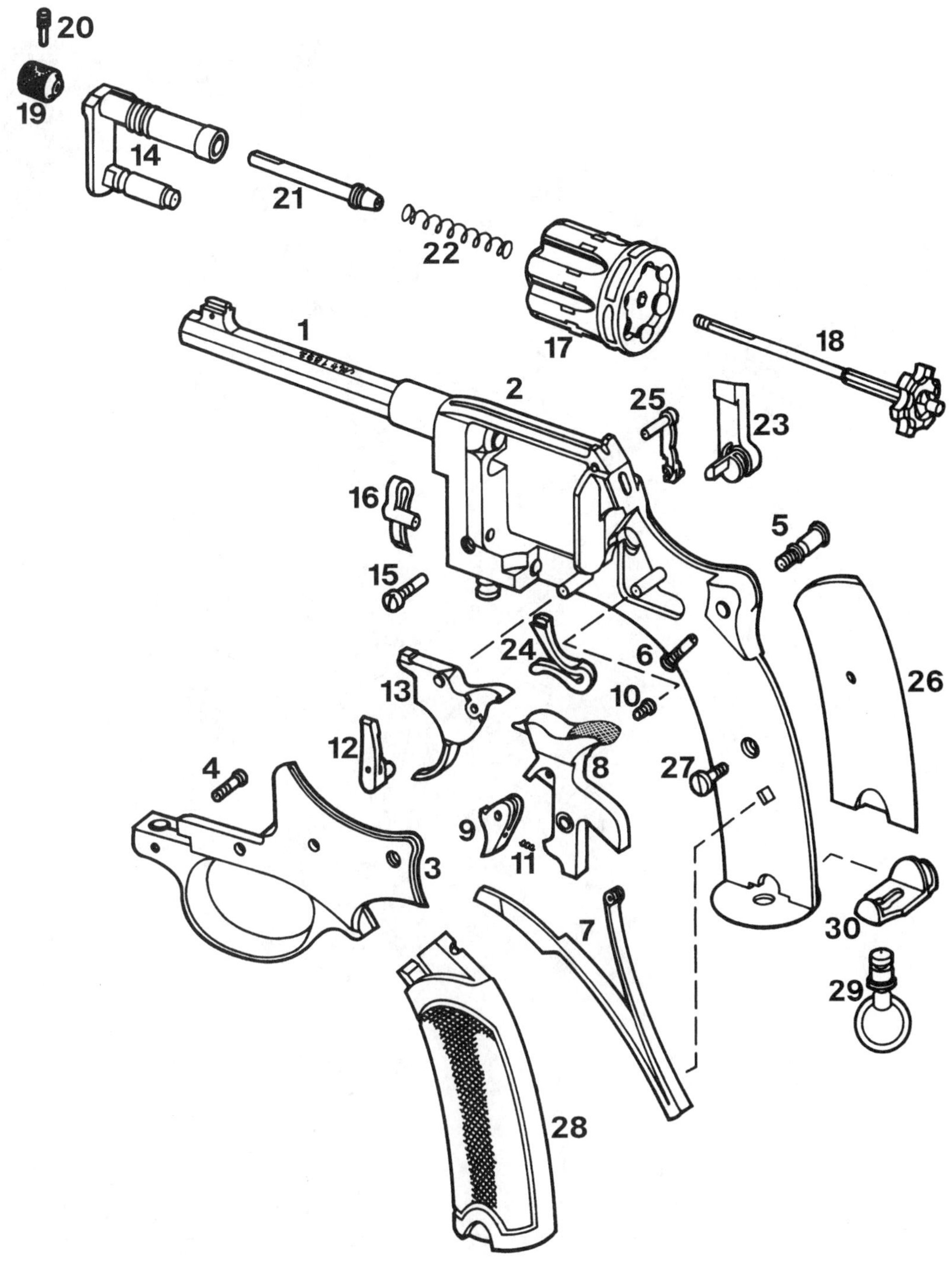

1	Barrel	11	Strut Spring	21	Extractor Bearing
2	Frame	12	Pawl	22	Extractor Spring
3	Sideplate	13	Trigger	23	Cylinder Gate
4	Sideplate Screw	14	Crane	24	Cylinder Gate Spring
5	Disassembly Screw	15	Crane Screw	25	Cylinder Catch
6	Disassembly Set-Screw	16	Crane Spring	26	Right Grip
7	Mainspring	17	Cylinder	27	Right Grip Screw
8	Hammer	18	Extractor	28	Left Grip
9	Strut	19	Extractor Knob	29	Lanyard Ring
10	Strut Screw	20	Extractor Knob Screw	30	Lanyard Ring Plate

Model 1935A Auto

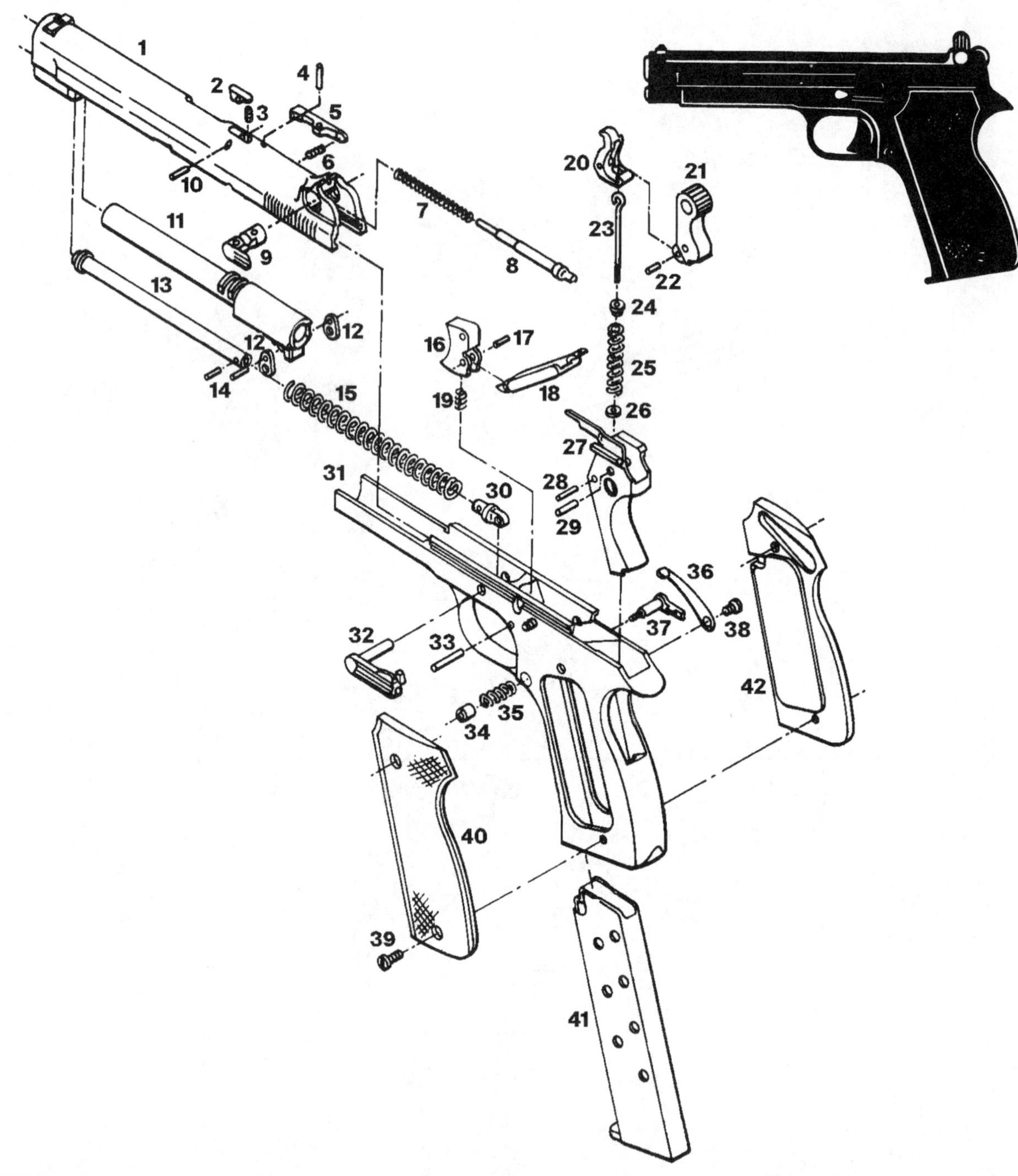

1	Slide	15	Recoil Spring	30	Recoil Spring Guide Tip
2	Cartridge Indicator	16	Trigger	31	Frame
3	Indicator Spring	17	Trigger Bar Pin	32	Slide Stop
4	Extractor Pin	18	Trigger Bar Disconnector	33	Trigger Pin
5	Extractor	19	Trigger Bar Spring	34	Magazine Catch Nut
6	Extractor Spring	20	Sear	35	Magazine Catch Spring
7	Firing Pin Spring	21	Hammer	36	Magazine Safety
8	Firing Pin	22	Hammer Strut Pin	37	Magazine Catch
9	Safety	23	Hammer Strut	38	Magazine Safety Screw
10	Cartridge Indicator Pin	24	Sear Pressure Plate	39	Grip Screw
11	Barrel	25	Hammer Spring	40	Left Grip
12	Barrel Link	26	Hammer Strut Nut	41	Magazine
13	Recoil Spring Guide	27	Ejector/Sear Housing	42	Right Grip
14	Recoil Spring Guide and Barrel Link Pins	28	Sear Pin		
		29	Hammer Pin		

Stop Auto

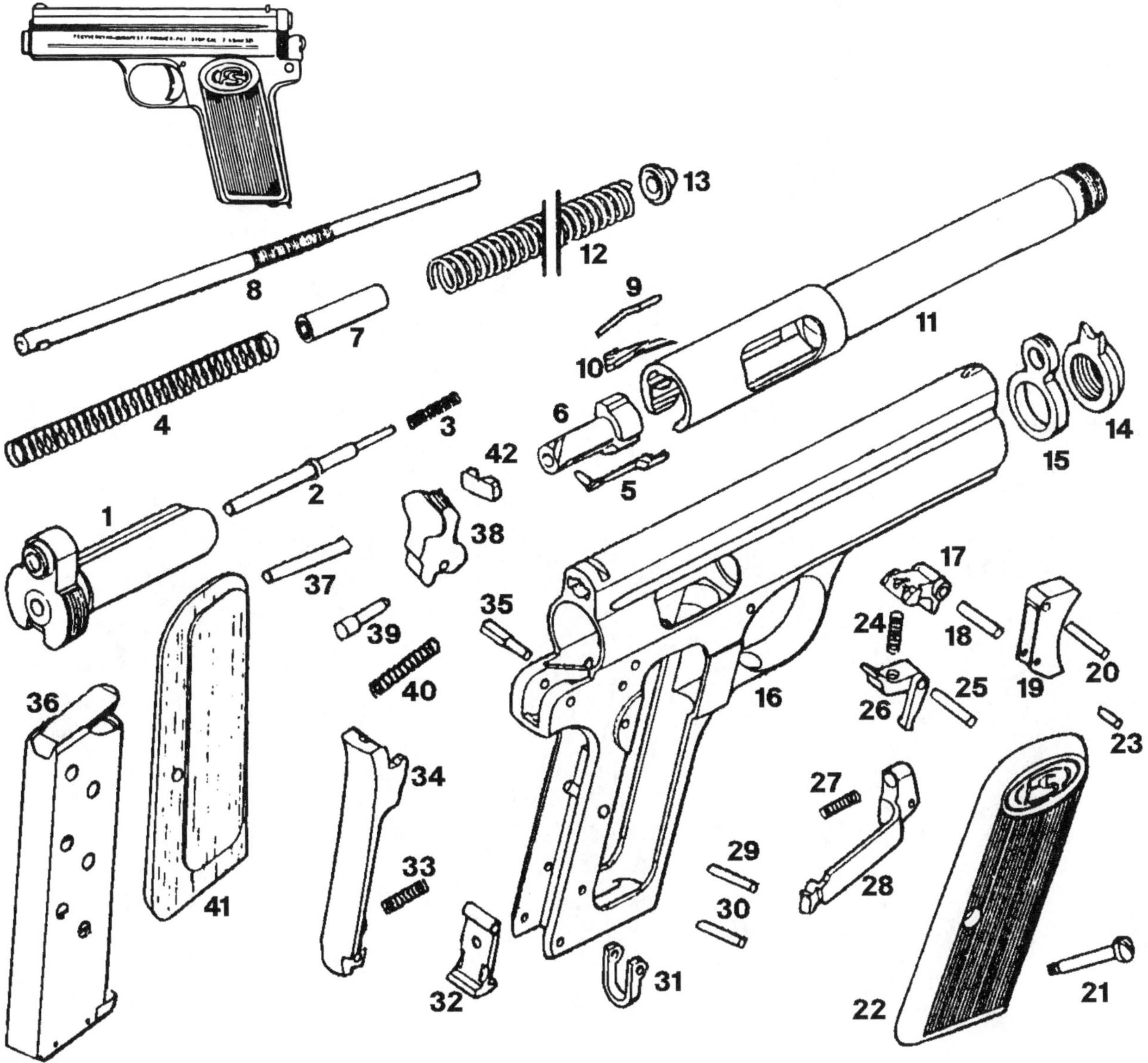

1	Bolt Body	16	Frame	31	Lanyard Loop
2	Firing Pin	17	Bolt Catch	32	Magazine Catch
3	Firing Pin Spring	18	Bolt Catch Pin	33	Grip Safety Spring
4	Bolt Return Spring	19	Trigger	34	Grip Safety
5	Extractor	20	Trigger Pin	35	Disconnector Pin
6	Bolt Head	21	Grip Screw	36	Magazine
7	Recoil Spring Guide Sleeve	22	Right Grip	37	Hammer Pin
8	Recoil Spring Guide Assembly	23	Trigger Bar Pin	38	Hammer
9	Ejector Spring	24	Sear Spring	39	Hammer Plunger
10	Ejector	25	Sear Pin	40	Hammer Spring
11	Barrel and Extension	26	Sear	41	Left Grip
12	Recoil Spring	27	Trigger Spring	42	Rear Sight
13	Barrel Nut Retainer	28	Trigger Bar		
14	Barrel Nut	29	Magazine Catch Pin		
15	Barrel Guide	30	Grip Safety Pin		

Model 1910 Auto

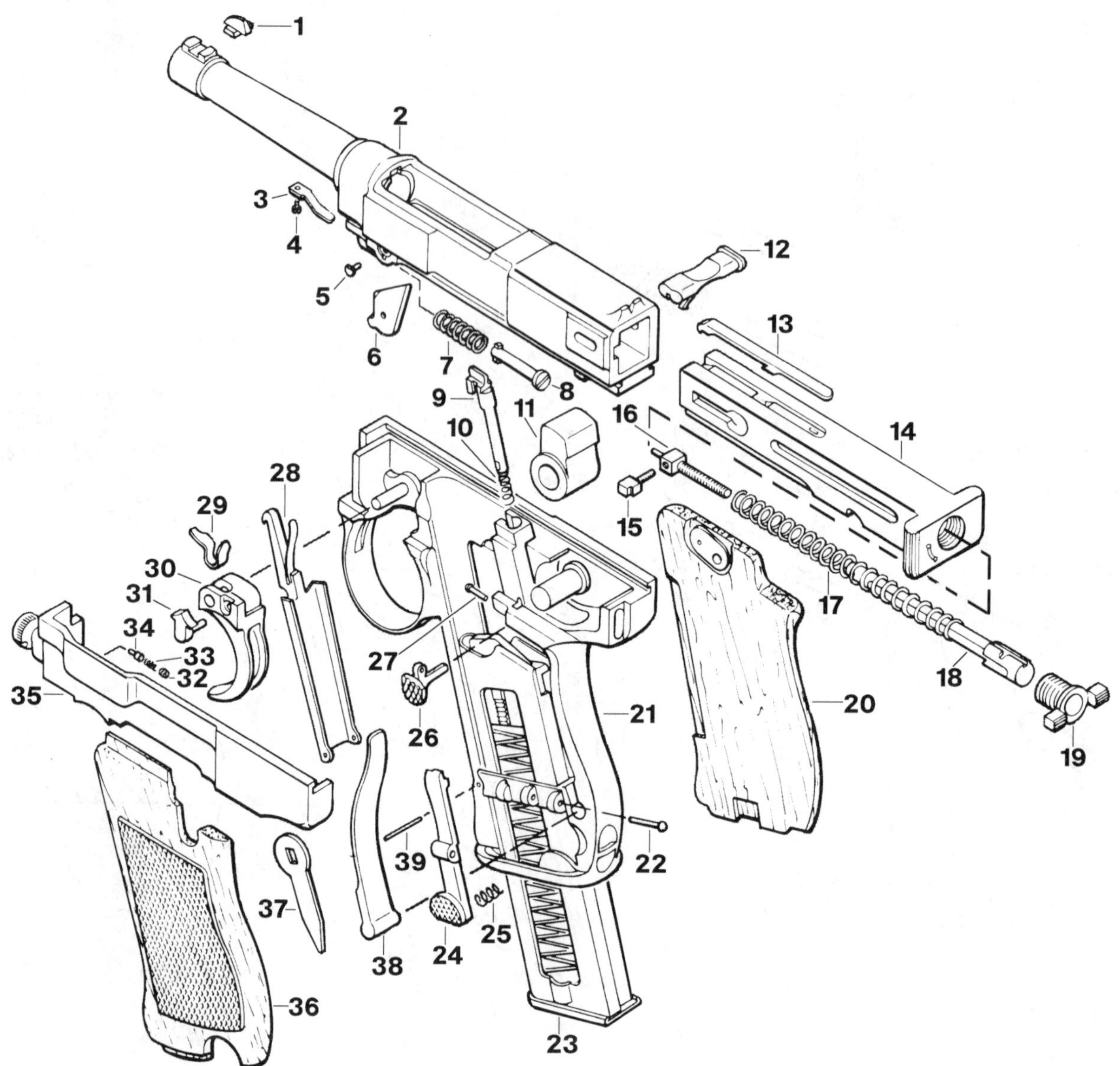

1	Front Sight	**15**	Firing Pin Guide	**29**	Trigger Spring
2	Barrel and Receiver	**16**	Firing Pin Head	**30**	Trigger
3	Sear Spring	**17**	Firing Pin Spring	**31**	Disconnector
4	Screw	**18**	Firing Pin Body	**32**	Set-Screw
5	Sear Pin	**19**	Safety Catch	**33**	Spring
6	Sear	**20**	Right Grip	**34**	Plunger
7	Barrel Return Spring	**21**	Frame	**35**	Sideplate Assembly
8	Barrel Spring Guide	**22**	Magazine Catch Pin	**36**	Left Grip
9	Ejector and Hold-Open Catch	**23**	Magazine	**37**	Disassembly Tool
10	Hold-Open Spring	**24**	Magazine Catch	**38**	Recoil Spring
11	Locking Block	**25**	Magazine Catch Spring	**39**	Grip Safety Pin
12	Cross Key	**26**	Hold-Open Catch	**Parts Not Shown**	
13	Extractor	**27**	Hold-Open Catch Pin		Takedown Screw
14	Bolt	**28**	Grip Safety		

Model 17 Auto

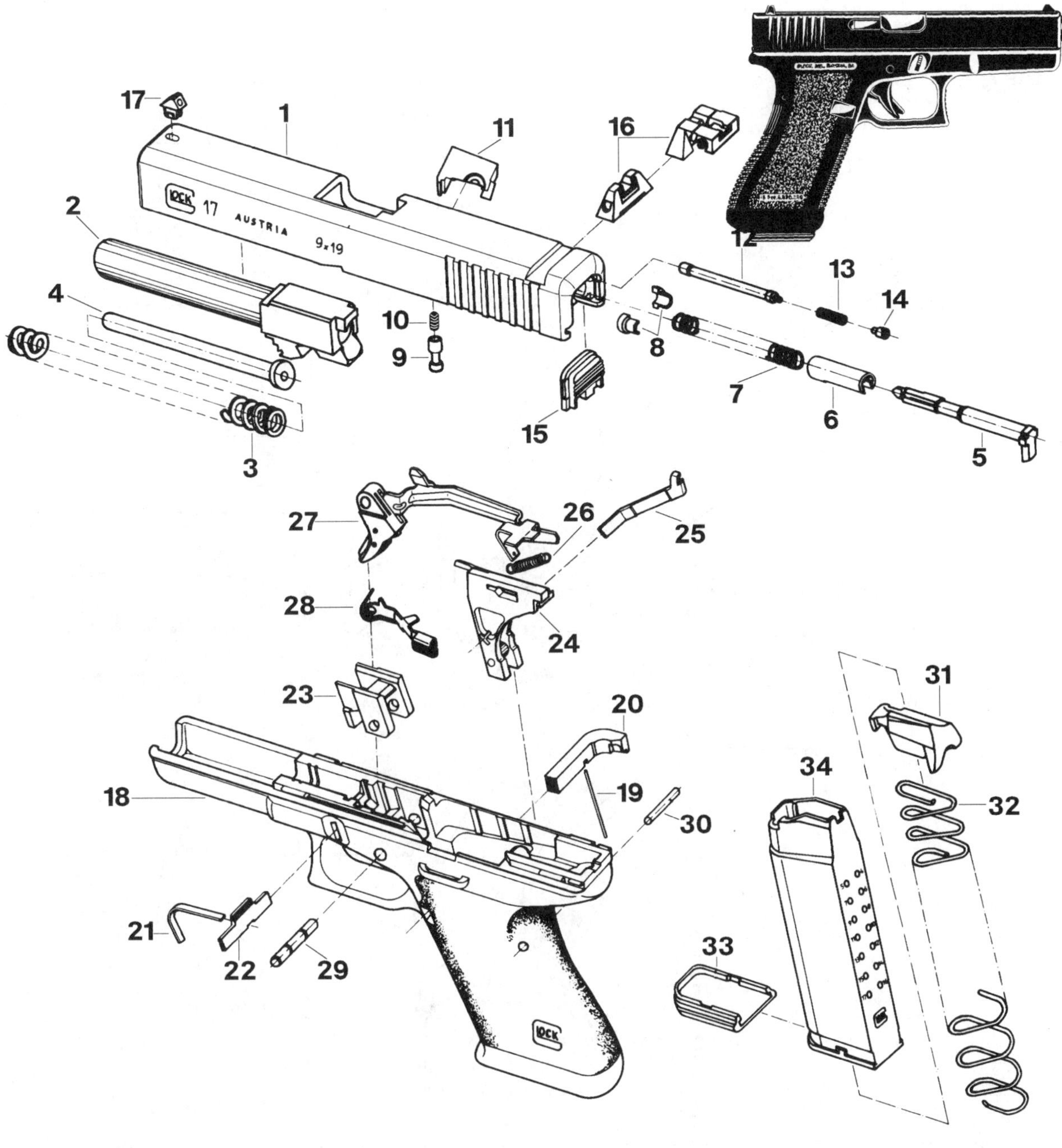

1	Slide	**13**	Extractor Depressor Plunger Spring	**24**	Trigger Mechanism Housing with Ejector
2	Barrel	**14**	Spring-Loaded Bearing	**25**	Connector
3	Recoil Spring	**15**	Slide Cover Plate	**26**	Trigger Spring
4	Recoil Spring Tube	**16**	Rear Sight Assembly	**27**	Trigger with Trigger Bar
5	Firing Pin	**17**	Front Sight	**28**	Slide Stop Lever
6	Spacer Sleeve	**18**	Receiver	**29**	Trigger Pin
7	Firing Pin Spring	**19**	Magazine Catch Spring	**30**	Trigger Mechanism Housing Pin
8	Spring Cups	**20**	Magazine Catch	**31**	Follower
9	Firing Pin Safety	**21**	Slide Lock Spring	**32**	Magazine Spring
10	Firing Pin Safety Spring	**22**	Slide Lock	**33**	Magazine Floorplate
11	Extractor	**23**	Locking Block	**34**	Magazine Tube
12	Extractor Depressor Plunger				

Single-Action Revolver

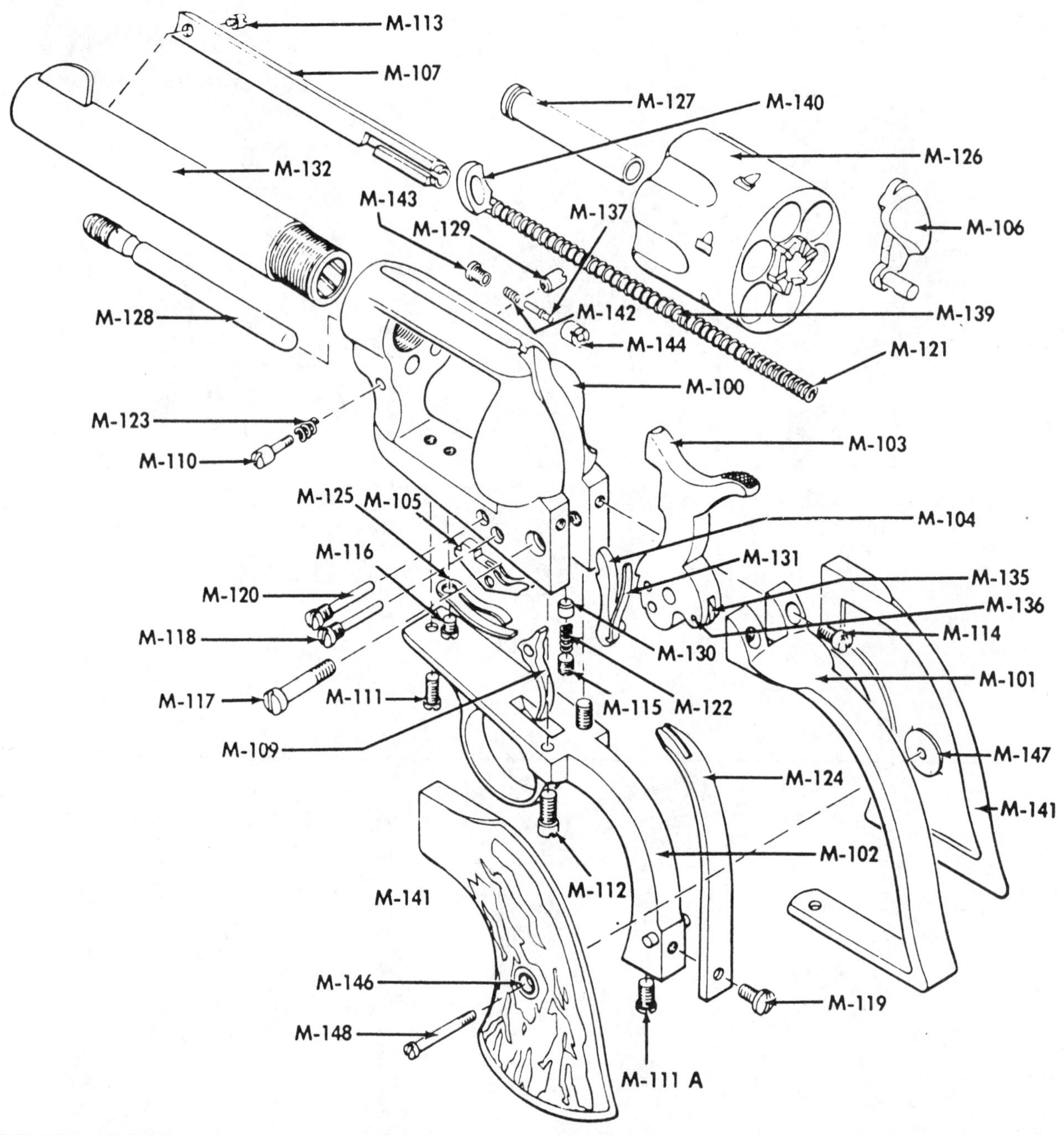

100	Frame	**115**	Gate Catch Screw	**130**	Gate Catch
101	Backstrap	**116**	Sear and Bolt Spring Screw	**131**	Hand Spring
102	Triggerguard	**117**	Hammer Screw	**132**	Barrel
103	Hammer	**118**	Trigger Screw	**135**	Main Spring Roller
104	Hand Assembly	**119**	Mainspring Screw	**136**	Main Spring Roller Pin
105	Bolt	**120**	Bolt Screw	**137**	Firing Pin
106	Gate	**121**	Ejector Screw	**139**	Ejector Rod
107	Ejector Tube	**122**	Gate Spring	**140**	Ejector Rod Head
108	Ejector Rod Assembly	**123**	Base Pin Catch Spring	**141**	Grips
109	Trigger	**124**	Main Spring	**142**	Firing Pin Spring
110	Base Pin Catch Screw	**125**	Sear and Bolt Spring	**143**	Flash PLate
111	Front Triggerguard Scew	**126**	Cylinder	**144**	Firing Pin Cap
112	Rear Triggergard Screw	**127**	Base Spring Bushing	**145**	Firing Pin Assembly
113	Ejector Tube Screw	**128**	Base Pin	**146-48**	Grip Inserts
114	Upper Backstrap Screw	**129**	Base Pin Catch Nut		

Derringer

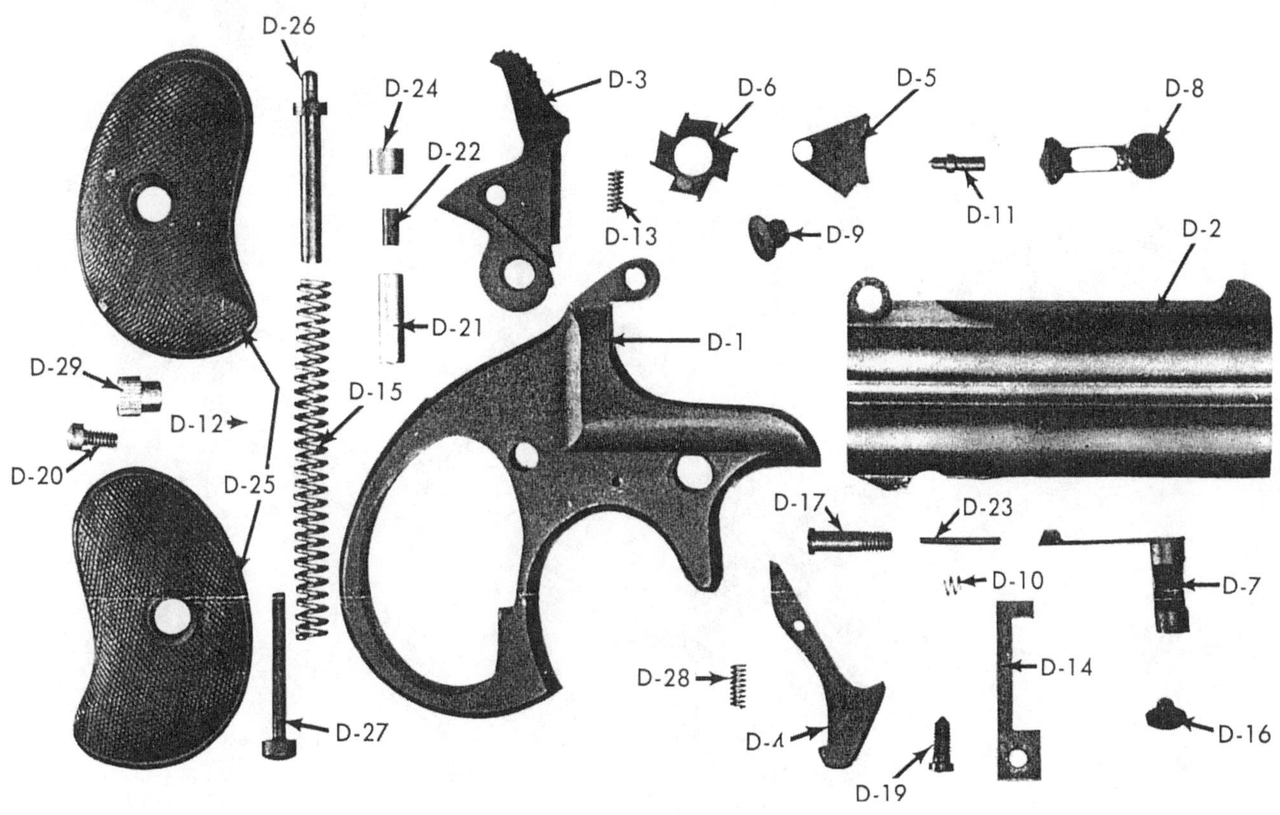

D-1	Frame	**D-16**	Barrel Lock Screw
D-2	Barrel	**D-17**	Barrel Hinge Screw
D-3	Hammer	**D-18**	Ejector Screw
D-4	Trigger	**D-19**	Selector Star Spring Scew
D-5	Selector	**D-20**	Grip Screws
D-6	Selector Star	**D-21**	Hammer Pin
D-7	Barrel Lock	**D-22**	Selector Pin
D-8	Ejector	**D-23**	Trigger Pin
D-9	Flashplates	**D-24**	Selector Star Bushing
D-10	Firing Pin Spring	**D-25**	Grips
D-11	Firing Pin	**D-26**	Main Spring Guide
D-12	Grip Yoke	**D-27**	Main Spring Guide Pin
D-13	Selector Spring	**D-28**	Trigger Spring
D-14	Selector Star Spring	**D-29**	Grip Inserts
D-15	Main Spring		

P-10 Auto

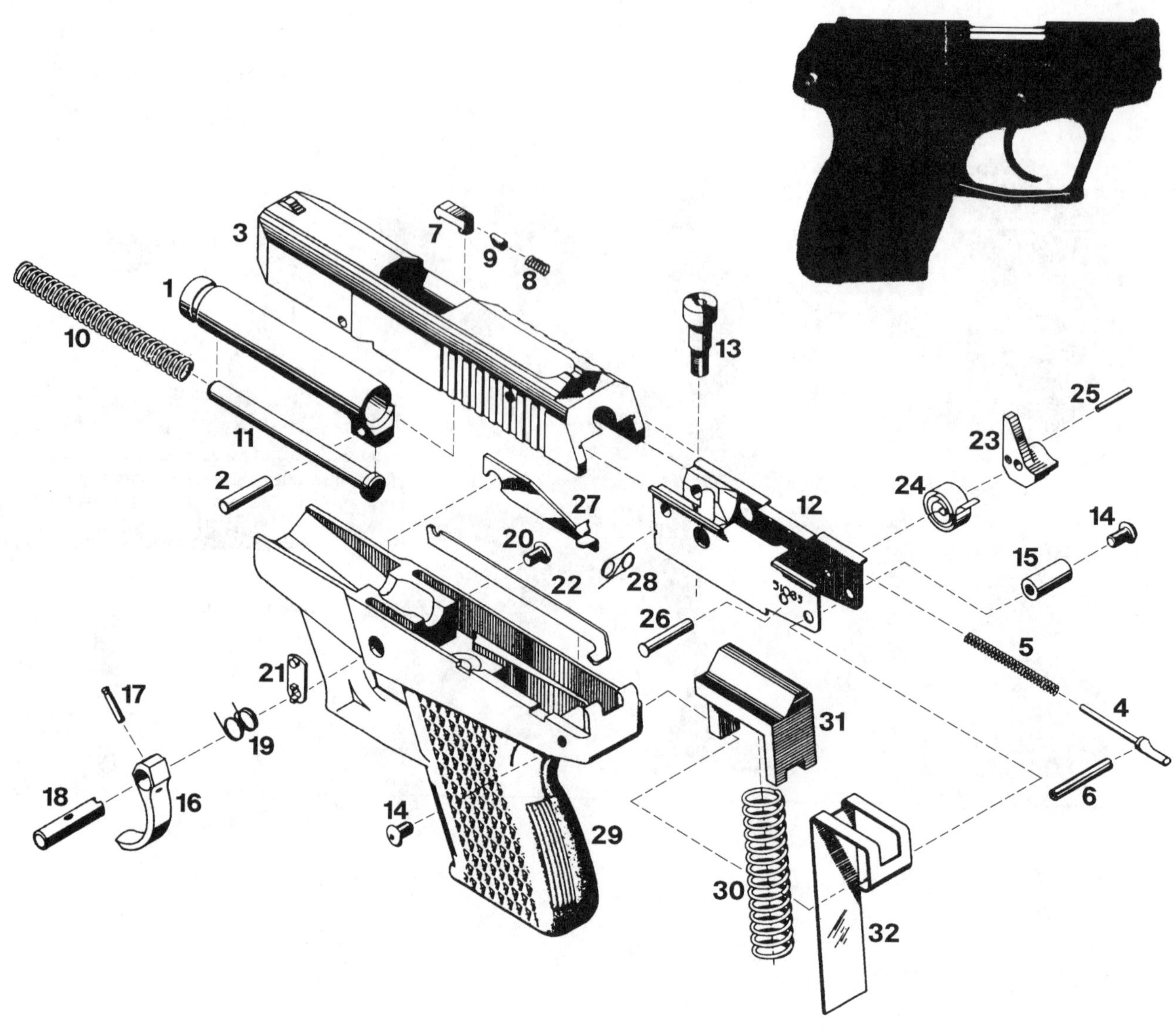

1	Barrel	**12**	Frame	**23**	Hammer
2	Barrel Pin	**13**	Frame Screw, Middle	**24**	Hammer Spring
3	Slide	**14**	Frame Screw, Rear	**25**	Hammer Pin
4	Firing Pin	**15**	Frame Bar	**26**	Hammer Axis
5	Firing Pin Spring	**16**	Trigger	**27**	Slide Stop
6	Firing Pin Pin	**17**	Trigger Pin	**28**	Slide Stop Spring
7	Extractor	**18**	Trigger Axis	**29**	Grip
8	Extractor Spring	**19**	Trigger Spring	**30**	Magazine Spring
9	Extractor Plunger	**20**	Trigger Screw	**31**	Magazine Follower
10	Recoil Spring	**21**	Trigger Lever	**32**	Magazine Plate
11	Recoil Spring Guide	**22**	Trigger Bar		

Model 1 Auto

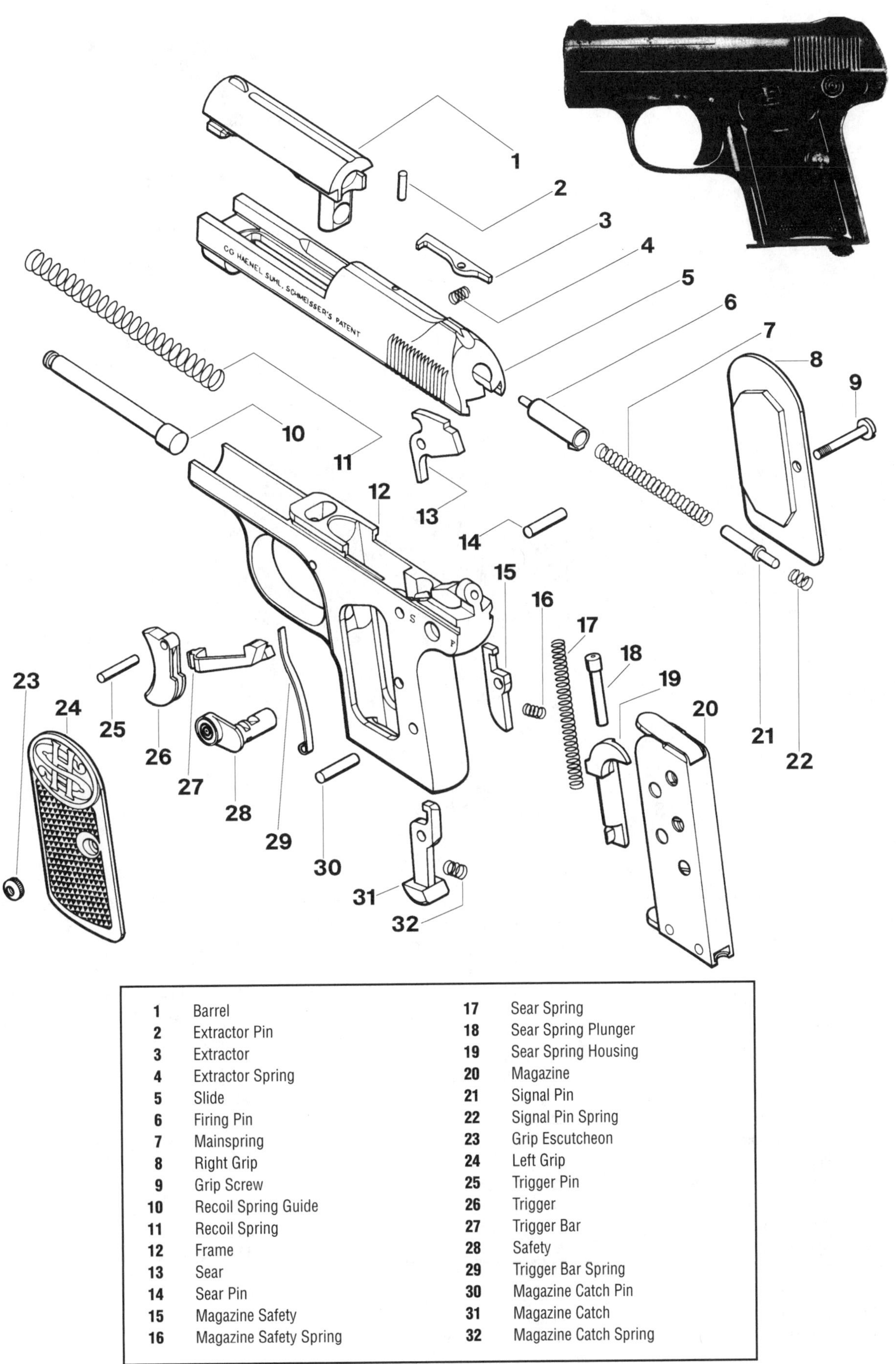

1	Barrel	17	Sear Spring
2	Extractor Pin	18	Sear Spring Plunger
3	Extractor	19	Sear Spring Housing
4	Extractor Spring	20	Magazine
5	Slide	21	Signal Pin
6	Firing Pin	22	Signal Pin Spring
7	Mainspring	23	Grip Escutcheon
8	Right Grip	24	Left Grip
9	Grip Screw	25	Trigger Pin
10	Recoil Spring Guide	26	Trigger
11	Recoil Spring	27	Trigger Bar
12	Frame	28	Safety
13	Sear	29	Trigger Bar Spring
14	Sear Pin	30	Magazine Catch Pin
15	Magazine Safety	31	Magazine Catch
16	Magazine Safety Spring	32	Magazine Catch Spring

Model 103 Single Shot

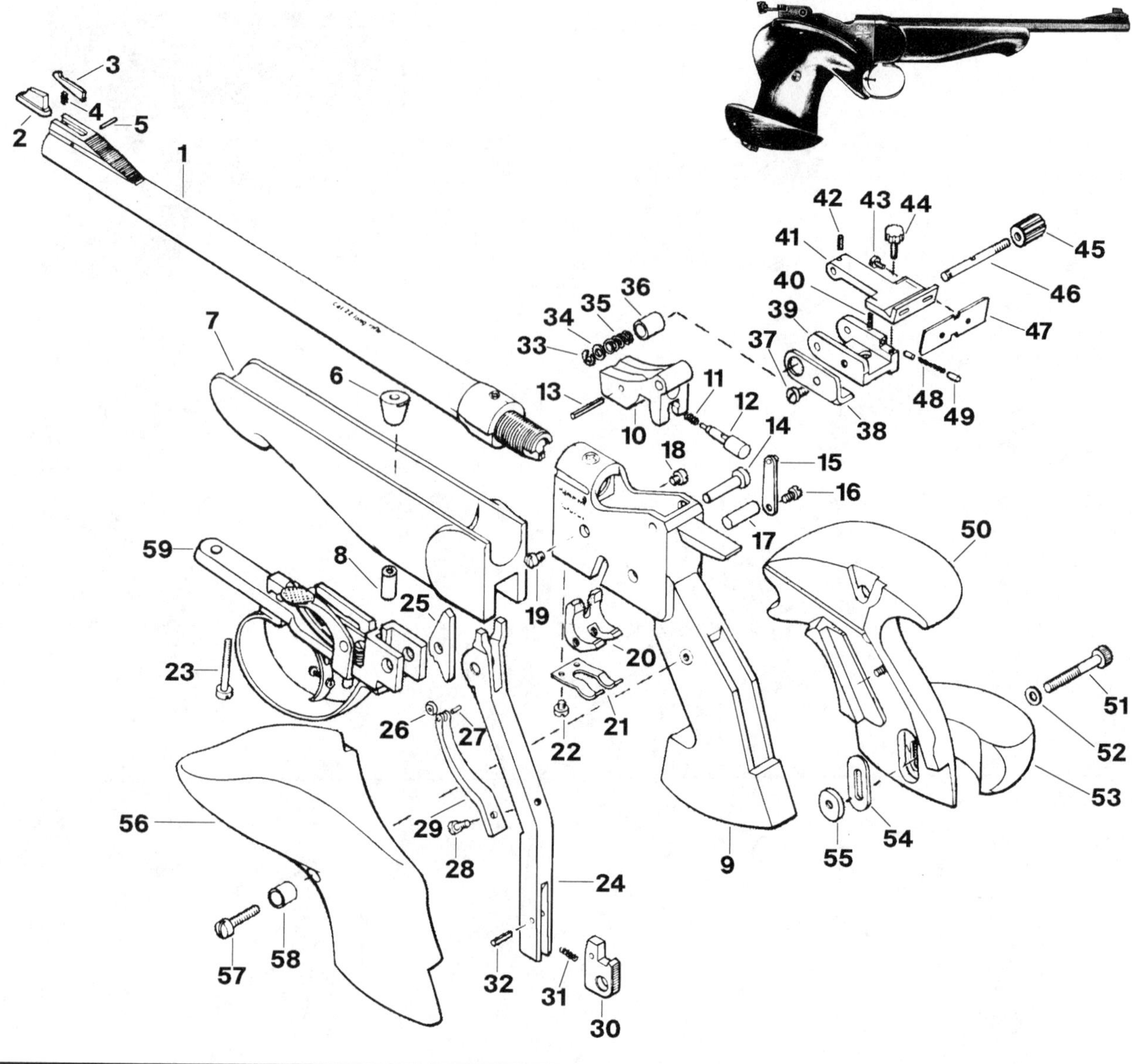

1	Barrel	21	Extractor Spring	41	Sight Leaf
2	Front Sight Blade	22	Extractor Spring Screw	42	Retainer Pin
3	Front Sight Latch	23	Front Guard Screw	43	Sight Blade Screw
4	Sight Latch Spring	24	Lever	44	Sight Elevating Screw
5	Latch Hinge Pin	25	Hammer	45	Windage Screw
6	Barrel Lug	26	Spring Roller	46	Sight Leaf Hinge
7	Forestock	27	Roller Pin	47	Sight Blade
8	Bushing	28	Mainspring Retaining Screw	48	Detent Spring
9	Frame	29	Mainspring	49	Detent
10	Breechblock	30	Lever Latch	50	Right Grip
11	Firing Pin Spring	31	Latch Spring	51	Heel Support Screw
12	Firing Pin	32	Latch Pin	52	Washer
13	Firing Pin Retaining Pin	33	C-Washer	53	Heel Support
14	Breechblock Hinge Pin	34	Washer	54	Elongated Washer
15	Hinge Pin Retaining Spring	35	Spring	55	Nut
16	Spring Retaining Screw	36	Nut	56	Left Grip
17	Cross Pin	37	Sight Retainer Screw	57	Grip Screw
18	Right Extractor Screw	38	Retainer Plate	58	Bushing
19	Left Extractor Screw	39	Sight Base	59	Trigger Assembly
20	Extractor	40	Sight Leaf Spring		

Model 120 Single Shot

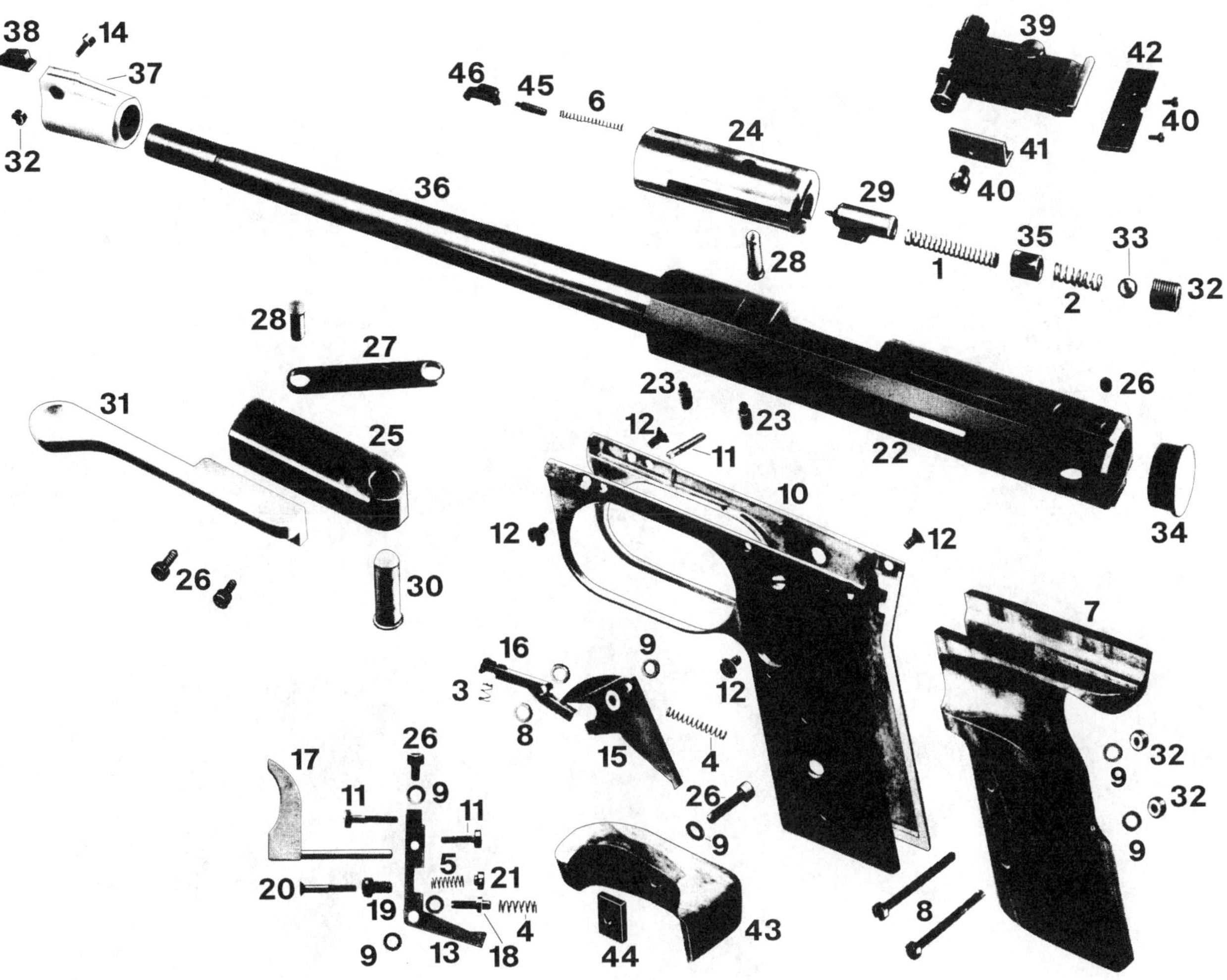

1	Mainspring	24	Breech
2	Locking Spring	25	Locking Piece
3	Sear Spring	26	Allen Screws
4	Springs	27	Connecting Piece
5	Let-Off Spring	28	Hinge Pin
6	Extractor Spring	29	Firing Pin
7	Grip	30	Support Pin
8	Grip Screws	31	Breech Lever
9	Washers	32	Nuts
10	Frame	33	Ball
11	Pins	34	End Cover
12	Counter-Sunk Screws	35	Mainspring Support
13	Trigger Bar	36	Barrel
14	Allen Set Screw	37	Front Sight Mounting
15	Striking Piece	38	Front Sight
16	Sear	39	Rear Sight
17	Trigger Latch	40	Screws
18	Adjustment Screw	41	Fixation Piece
19	Let-Off Screw	42	Rear Sight Blade
20	Let-Off Spring Screw	43	Hand Support
21	Hexagonal Nut	44	Nut Disc
22	Breech Housing	45	Extractor Bolt
23	Barrel Screws	46	Extractor

Model 150 Single Shot

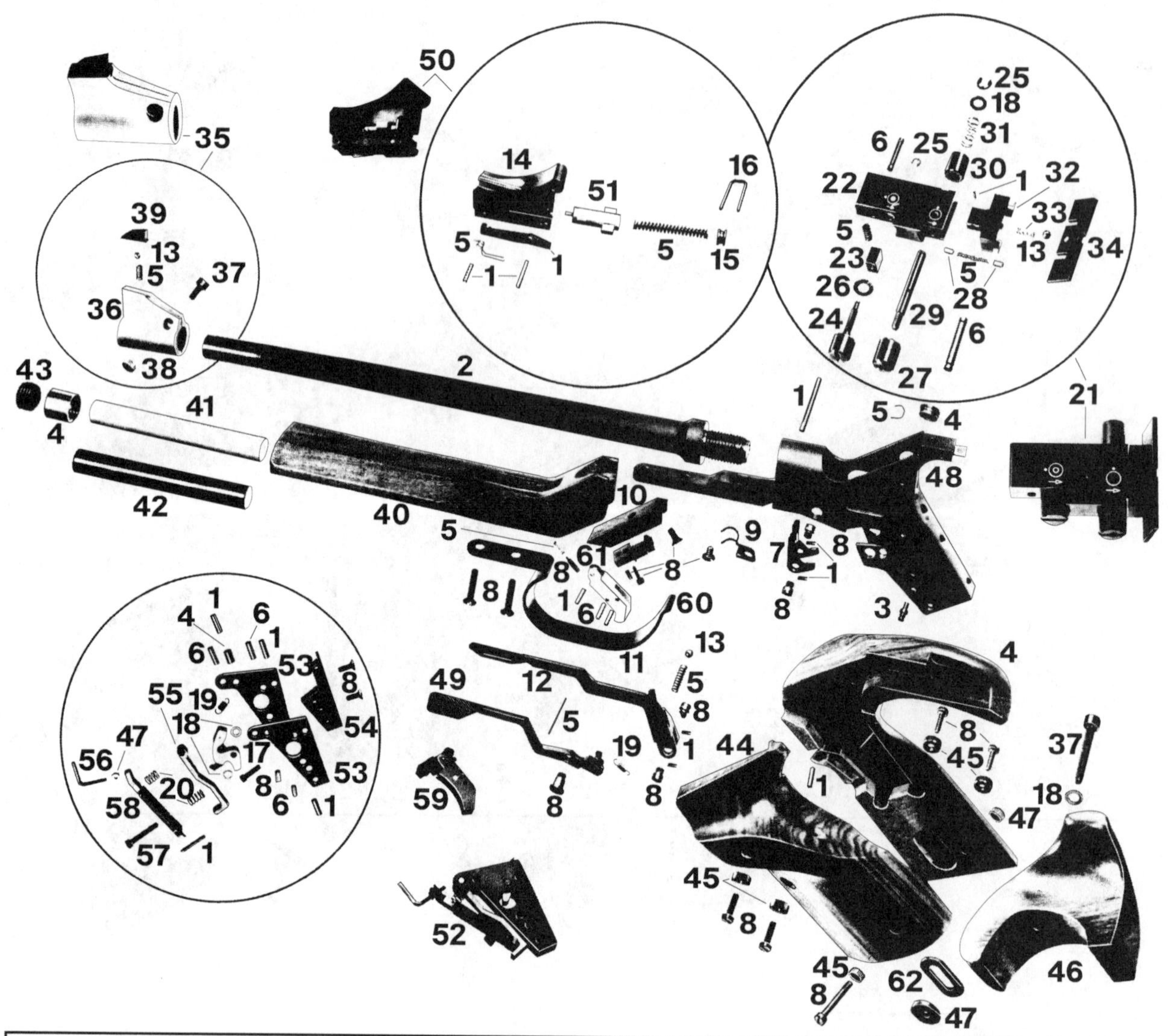

1	Pins	23	Elevation Piece	45	Screw Guides
2	Barrel	24	Micro-Screw	46	Hand Support
3	Spring Pin	25	Benzing Washers	47	Nuts
4	Annulus	26	Special Washer	48	Receiver
5	Springs	27	Micro-Nut	49	Trigger Cocking Lever
6	Bolts	28	Click Pins	50	Breech, Complete
7	Ejector	29	Windage Axle	51	Firing Pin
8	Screws	30	Spring Housing	52	Hair Trigger, Complete
9	Ejector Spring	31	Spring for Windage	53	Trigger Plates
10	Trigger Sear	32	Rear Sight Leaf	54	Trigger Base
11	Trigger Guard	33	Spring for Rear Sight Blade	55	Trigger Sear
12	Breech Lever	34	Rear Sight Blade	56	Short Lever
13	Balls	35	Front Sight Mounting, Complete	57	Trigger Spring Screw
14	Breech	36	Front Sight Mounting	58	Lever
15	Spring Ring	37	Allen Screws	59	Trigger Latch, Complete
16	Clamp	38	Female Screw	60	Trigger Latch
17	Hammer	39	Front Sight	61	Sliding Piece
18	Washers	40	Forend	62	Metal Insertion
19	Small Spring	41	Insertion	**Parts Not Shown**	
20	Trigger Springs	42	Extra Weight		Long Screw
21	Rear Sight, Complete	43	Forend Screw		Strong Trigger Spring
22	Rear Sight Base	44	Grips		Lever, Complete

Model 152 Single Shot

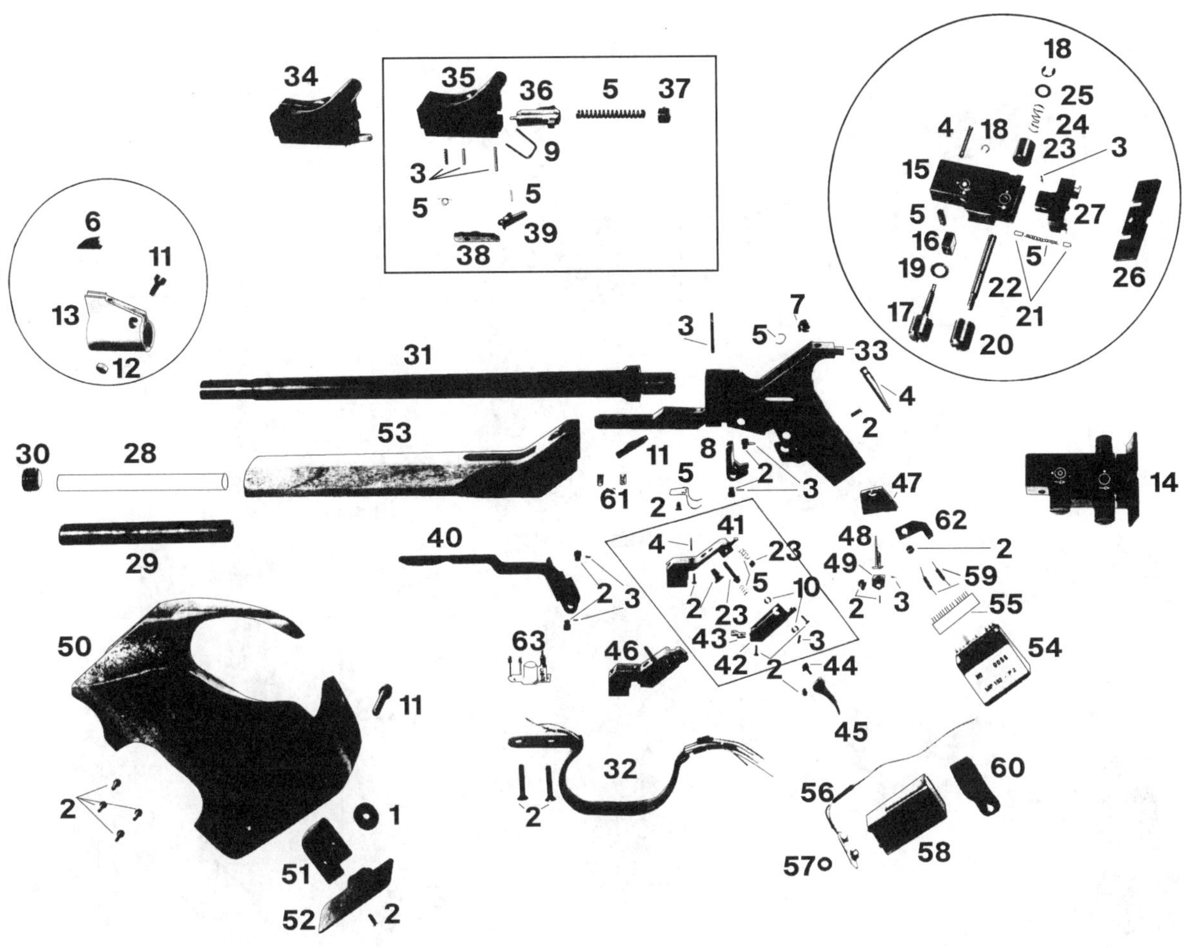

1	Nut	23	Spring Housing	45	Trigger Latch
2	Screws	24	Spring for Windage	46	Mechanical Part of Trigger, Complete
3	Pins	25	Washer	47	Support of Magnet
4	Bolts	26	Rear Sight Blade	48	Core
5	Springs	27	Rear Sight Leaf	49	Adjusting Angle
6	Front Sight	28	Insertion	50	Target Grip
7	Annulus	29	Extra Weight	51	Guard
8	Ejector	30	Forend Screw	52	Cover Plate
9	Clamp	31	Barrel	53	Forend
10	Ball Bearings	32	Trigger Guard, Complete	54	Electronic Print P 2
11	Allen Screws	33	Receiver	55	Plug Socket
12	Female Screw	34	Breech Complete	56	Press Button Contacts
13	Front Sight Mounting	35	Breech	57	O-Washer
14	Rear Sight Complete	36	Firing Pin	58	Battery
15	Rear Sight Base	37	Spring Washer	59	Black Strands
16	Elevation Piece	38	Catch Release	60	Battery Extractor Strap
17	Micro-Screw	39	Catch	61	Insulation Pipes
18	Benzing Washer	40	Breech Lever, Complete	62	Wire Stopper
19	Special Washer	41	Trigger Base	63	Switch and Indicator Print
20	Micro-Nut	42	Trigger Support		
21	Click-Pins	43	Switch Cell		
22	Windage Axle	44	Trigger Fixation		

Model 208/211 and 214/215 Auto

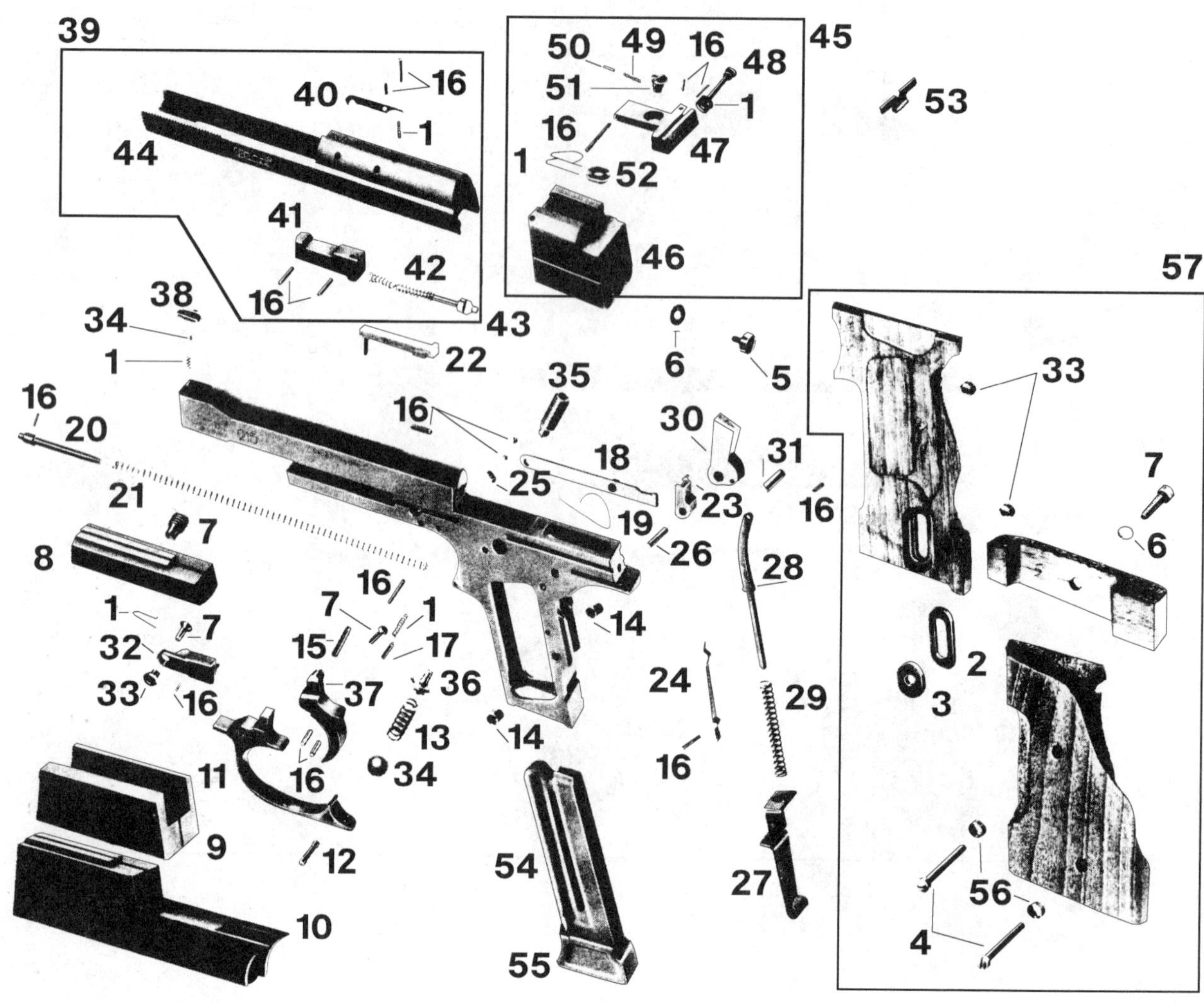

1	Springs	23	Sear	45	Rear Sight, Complete
2	Metal Insertion	24	Sear Spring	46	Rear Sight Support
3	Nut Disc	25	Sear Screw	47	Rear Sight Leaf
4	Grip Plate Screws	26	Sear Pin	48	Adjustable Windage Screw
5	Fixing Screw	27	Magazine Holder	49	Click Spring
6	Washers	28	Hammer Strut	50	Click Bolt
7	Screws	29	Mainspring	51	Adjustable Elevation Screw
8	Normal Weight	30	Hammer	52	Adjustable Elevation Nut
9	Heavy Weight	31	Hammer Bolt	53	Rear Sight Blade
10	Extra Heavy Weight	32	Blocking Piece	54	Magazine, Complete
11	Trigger Guard	33	Nuts	55	Magazine Extension
12	Trigger Guard Pin	34	Balls	56	Foundations
13	Trigger Guard Spring	35	Pressure Piece	57	Grips, Complete
14	Annulus	36	Safety	**Parts Not Shown**	
15	Trigger Pin	37	Trigger Latch, Complete		Short Trigger Latch, Complete
16	Pins	38	Front Sight		Magazine Feeder
17	Trigger Screw	39	Breech, Complete		Magazine Support
18	Trigger Bar	40	Extractor		Slide
19	Trigger Bar Spring	41	Firing Pin Support		Magazine Spring
20	Spring Pin	42	Firing Pin Spring		
21	Recuperator Spring	43	Firing Pin		
22	Ejector	44	Breech		

Model 232 Auto

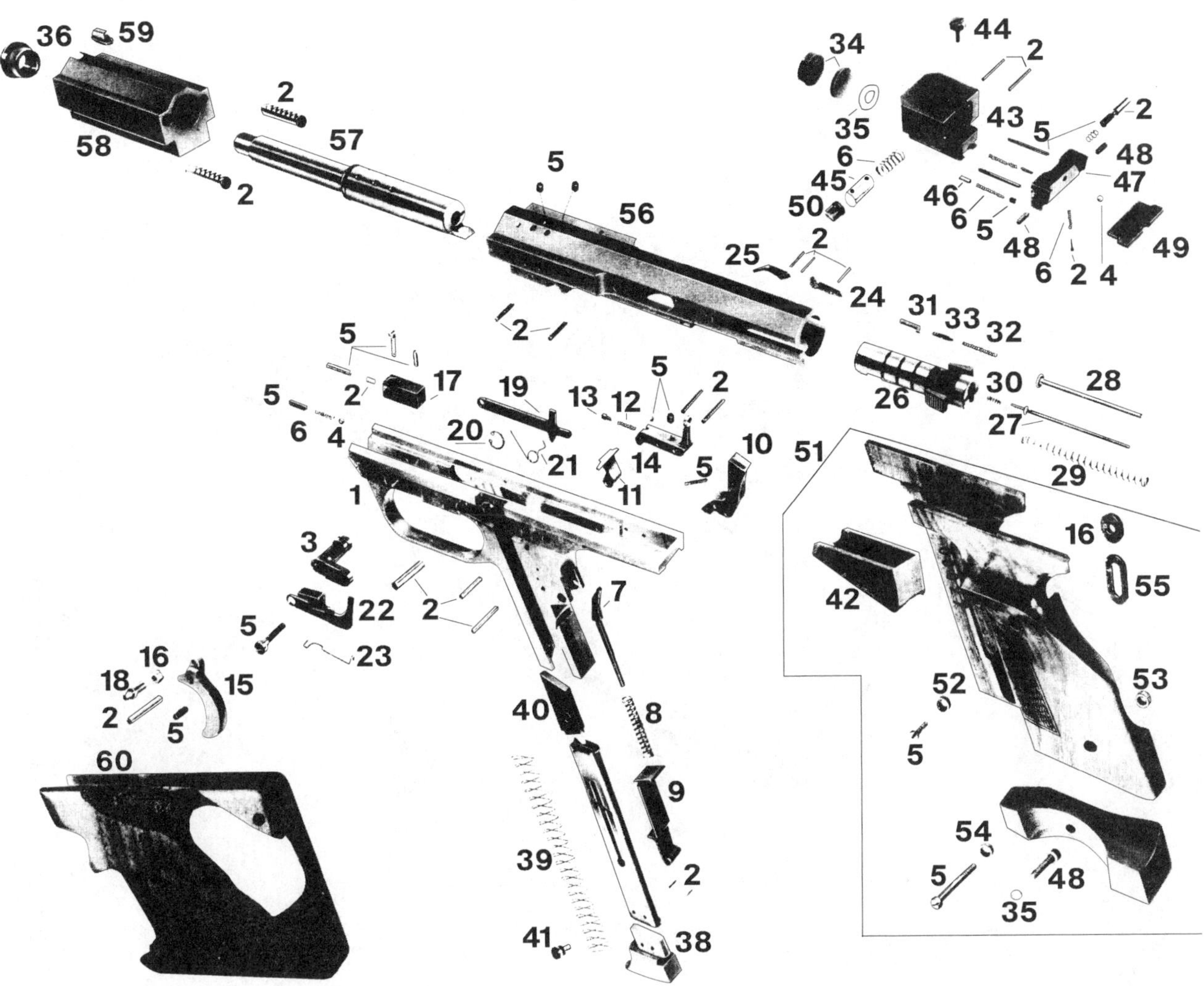

1	Frame	**21**	Trigger Bar Spring	**41**	Feeder Button
2	Pins	**22**	Breech Catch	**42**	Rubber Wedge
3	Locking Lever	**23**	Breech Catch Spring	**43**	Rear Sight
4	Balls	**24**	Disconnector	**44**	Elevation Screw
5	Screws	**25**	Ejector	**45**	Pivot Pin
6	Springs	**26**	Breech	**46**	Click Pin
7	Hammer Strut	**27**	Firing Pin	**47**	Rear Sight Support
8	Mainspring	**28**	Firing Pin Guide	**48**	Allen Screw
9	Magazine Catch	**29**	Recoil Spring	**49**	Rear Sight Blade
10	Hammer	**30**	Firing Pin Spring	**50**	Windage Screw
11	Trigger Sear	**31**	Extractor	**51**	Adjustable Grips
12	Sear Spring	**32**	Extractor Spring	**52**	Screw Guide
13	Sear Spring Screw	**33**	Extractor Spring Pin	**53**	Female Screw
14	Bearing	**34**	Buffer	**54**	Foundation
15	Trigger Latch	**35**	Washer	**55**	Metal Insertion
16	Nuts	**36**	Muzzle Nut	**56**	Receiver
17	Adjustment Piece	**37**	Magazine Body	**57**	Barrel
18	Trigger Screw	**38**	Magazine Extension	**58**	Barrel Sleeve
19	Trigger Bar	**39**	Magazine Spring	**59**	Front Sight
20	Positioning Washer	**40**	Feeder	**60**	Target Grip

Model 280 Auto

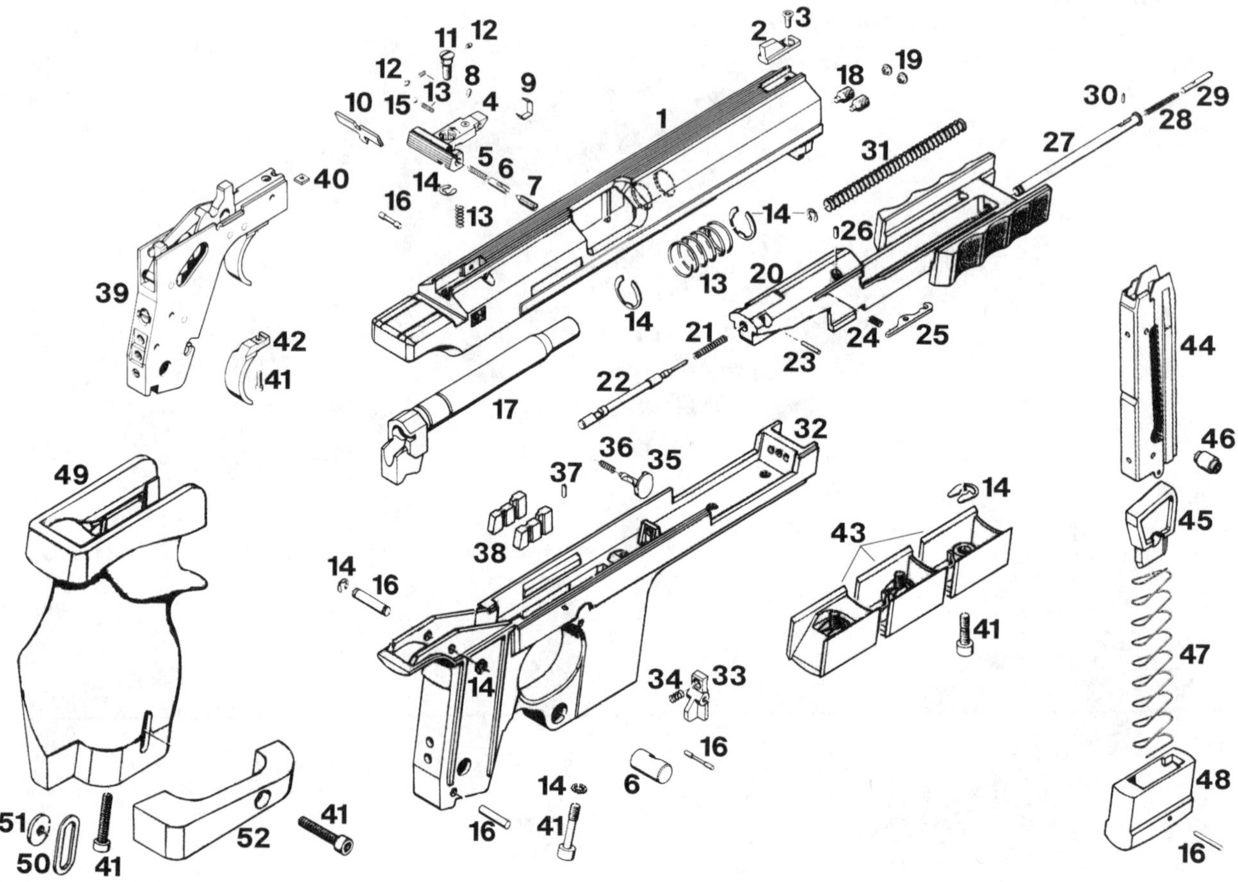

1	Receiver
2	Foresight
3	Countersunk Allen Screw
4	Rear Sight Mount
5	Pressure Stud Spring
6	Pressure Stud
7	Windage Adjustment Screw
8	Windage Click Pin
9	Leaf Spring
10	Rear Sight Blade
11	Elevation Adjustment Screw
12	Click Pin
13	Compression Springs
14	Circlips
15	Ball
16	Pins
17	Barrel, Complete
18	Screws
19	Plugs
20	Slide, Complete
21	Firing Pin Spring
22	Firing Pin
23	Conex Pin
24	Extractor Spring
25	Extractor
26	Expansion Pin
27	Recoil Spring Guide
28	Compression Stud Spring
29	Compression Stud
30	Expansion Pin
31	Recoil Spring
32	Frame
33	Magazine Catch
34	Compression Spring for Magazine Catch
35	Slide Catch, Complete
36	Slide Catch Spring
37	Grub Screw
38	Buffers
39	Trigger Action, Complete
40	Square Nut
41	Allen Screws
42	Trigger
43	Counterweights
44	Magazine Box, Complete
45	Magazine Follower
46	Loading Button
47	Magazine Spring
48	Magazine Extension
49	Adjustable Grip, Complete
50	Metal Insert
51	Nut
52	Palm Shelf

Parts Not Shown

Trigger Pin
Trigger Allen Screw
Trigger Circlip

Handy Gun

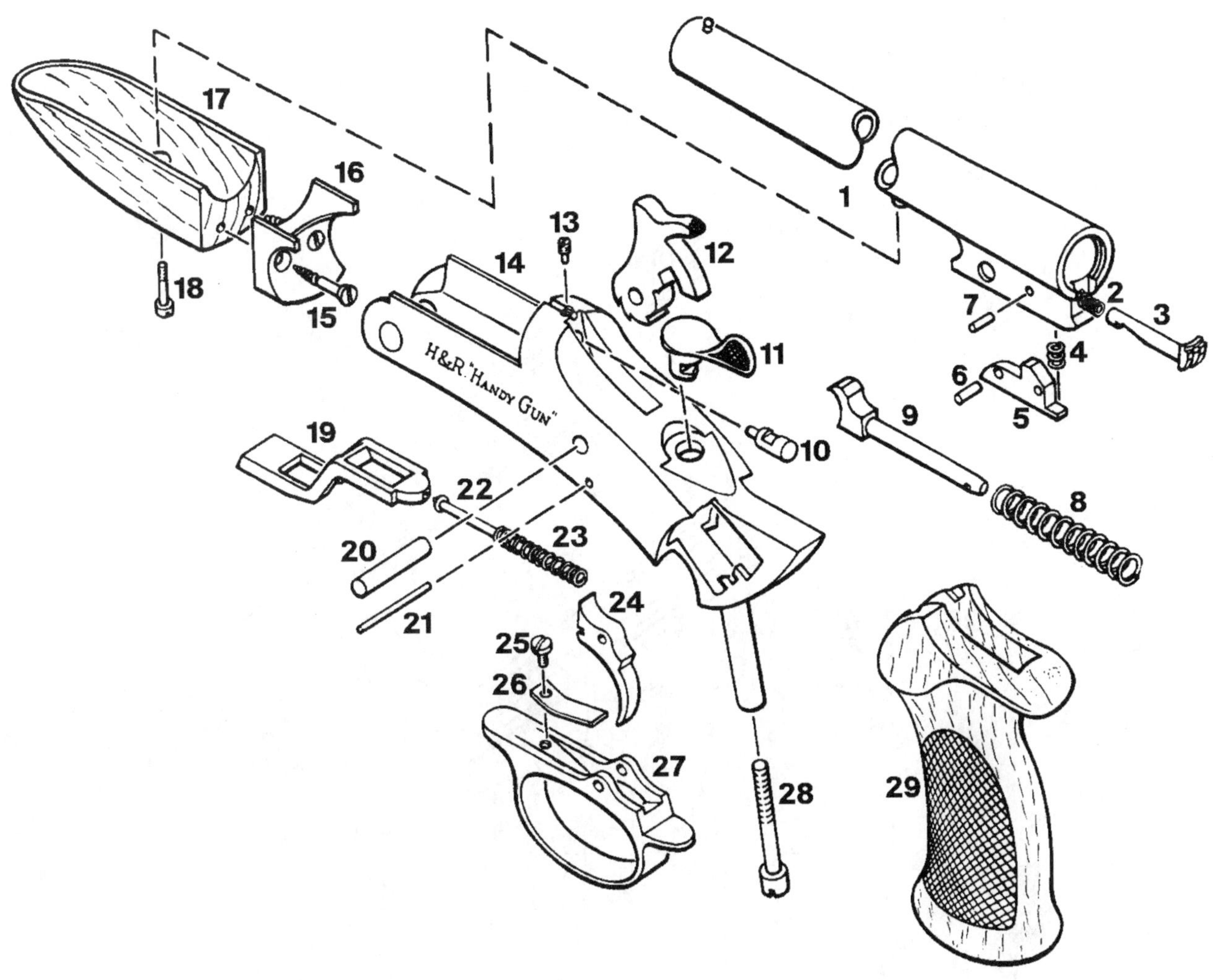

1	Barrel	**16**	Forend Iron
2	Ejector Spring	**17**	Forend
3	Ejector	**18**	Forend Screw
4	Ejector Sear Spring	**19**	Barrel Latch
5	Ejector Sear	**20**	Hammer Pin
6	Ejector Sear Trip Pin	**21**	Trigger Pin
7	Ejector Sear Pivot	**22**	Barrel Latch Plunger
8	Hammer Spring	**23**	Barrel Latch Spring
9	Hammer Strut	**24**	Trigger
10	Firing Pin	**25**	Trigger Spring Screw
11	Barrel Latch Lever	**26**	Trigger Spring
12	Hammer	**27**	Trigger Guard
13	Firing Pin Retaining Screw	**28**	Grip Screw
14	Frame	**29**	Grip
15	Forend Iron Screws		

32 Auto

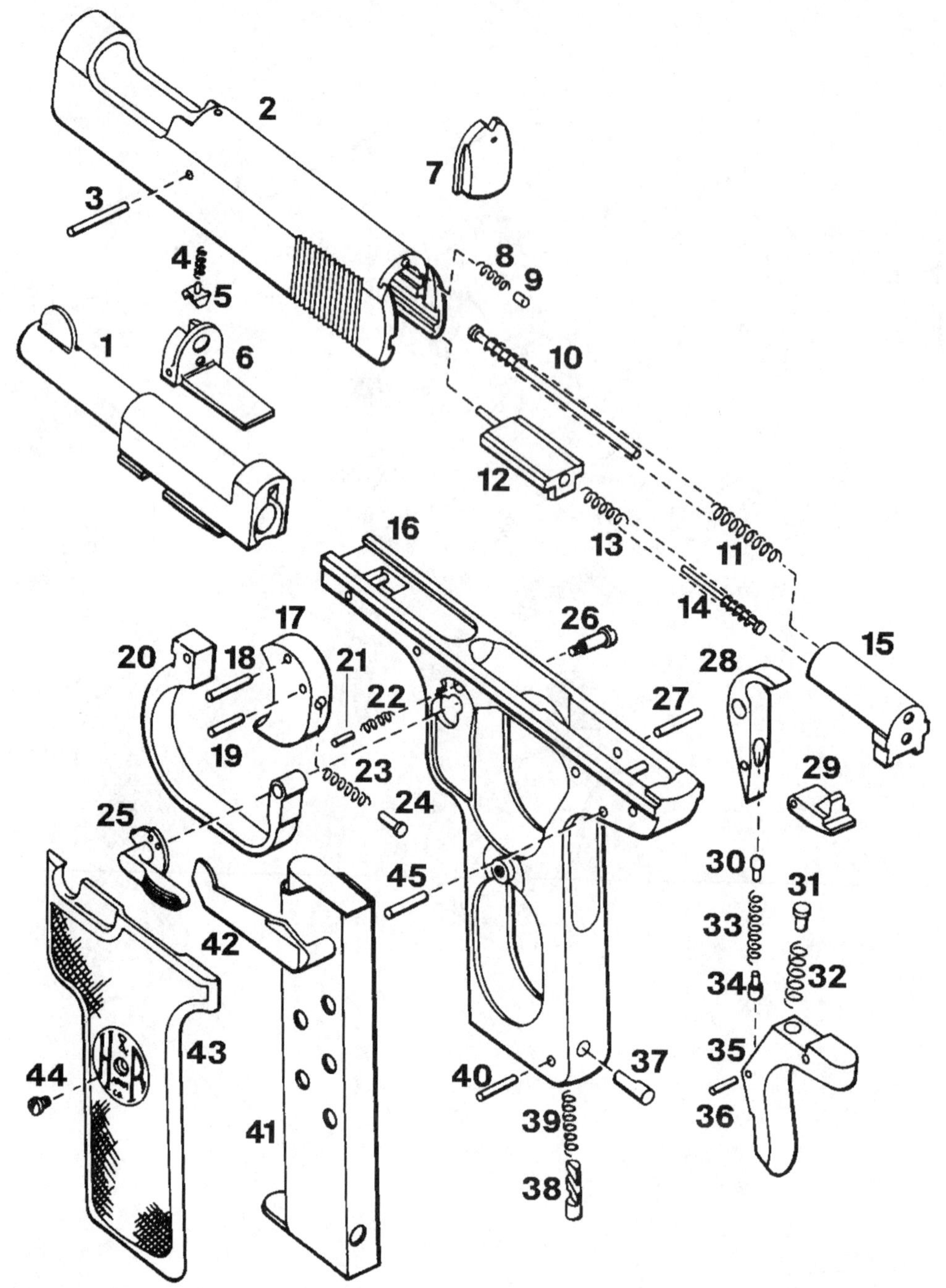

1	Barrel	16	Frame	31	Sear Spring Follower
2	Slide	17	Trigger	32	Sear Spring
3	Bolt Face Retainer Pin	18	Trigger Pin	33	Magazine Safety Spring
4	Extractor Spring	19	Trigger Stop Pin	34	Magazine Safety Spring Plunger
5	Extractor	20	Trigger Guard	35	Grip Safety
6	Bolt Face	21	Safety Catch Detent	36	Magazine Safety Pin
7	Slide End Plate	22	Safety Catch Detent Spring	37	Magazine Catch
8	End Plate Detent Spring	23	Trigger Spring	38	Magazine Release Button
9	End Plate Detent	24	Trigger Spring Plunger	39	Magazine Catch Spring
10	Recoil Spring Guide	25	Thumb Safety	40	Magazine Catch Pin
11	Recoil Spring	26	Trigger Guard Hinge Screw	41	Magazine Assembly
12	Firing Pin	27	Sear Pin	42	Trigger Bar
13	Firing Pin Spring	28	Magazine Safety	43	Grip
14	Firing Pin Spring Guide	29	Sear	44	Grip Screw
15	Slide Return Block	30	Trigger Bar Detent	45	Grip Safety Stop Pin

Model 603, 604, 903, 904, 905, 504, 826, 829 and 832 Revolver

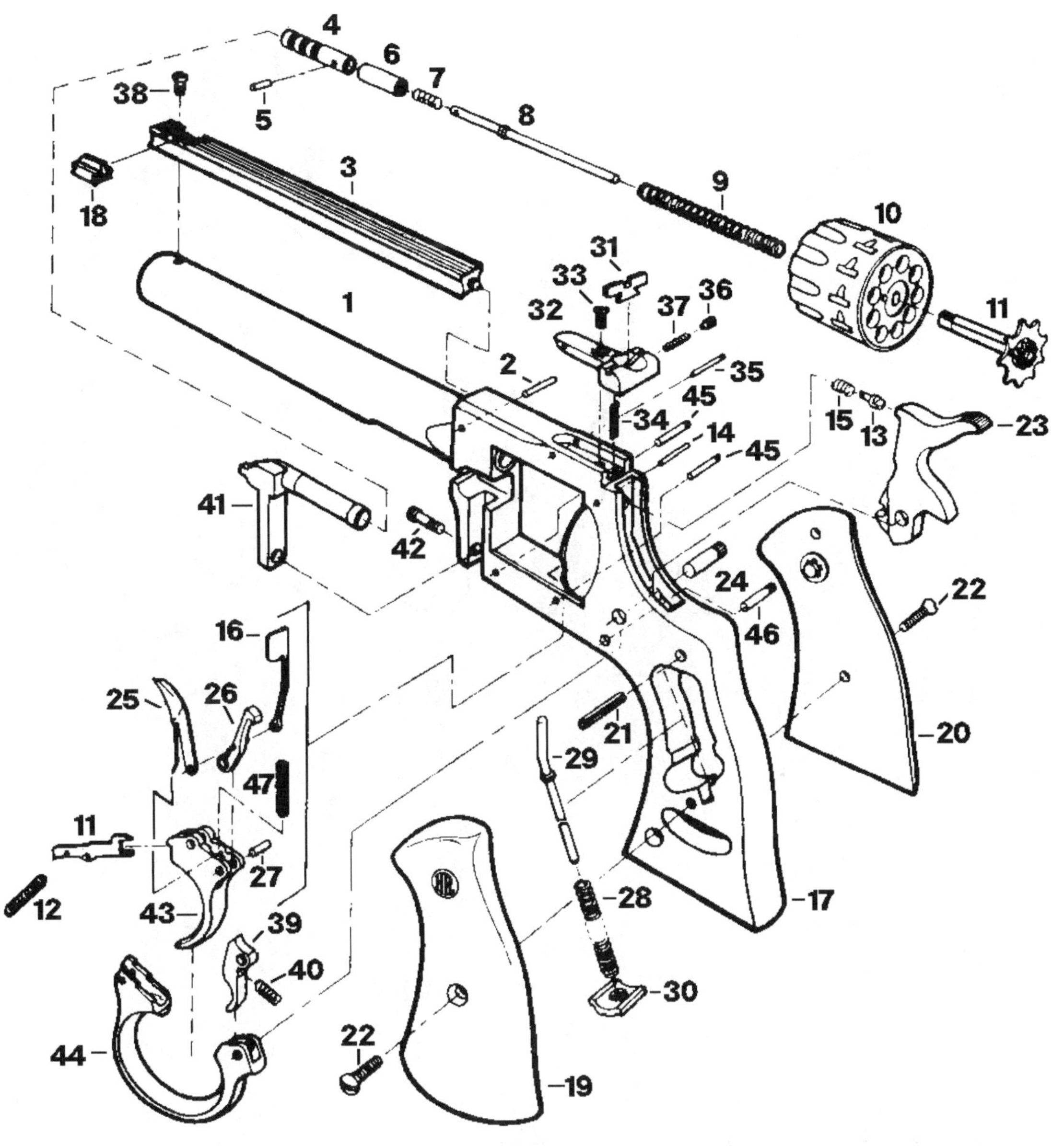

1	Barrel	17	Frame	33	Rear Sight Elevation Screw
2	Barrel Retaining Pin	18	Front Sight	34	Rear Sight Elevation Spring
3	Barrel Rib	19	Left Grip	35	Rear Sight Pivot Pin
4	Center Pin Head	20	Right Grip	36	Rear Sight Windage Screw
5	Center Pin Head Retaining Pin	21	Grip Pin	37	Rear Sight Windage Spring
6	Center Pin Spring Bushing	22	Grip Screws	38	Barrel Rib Screw
7	Center Pin Spring	23	Hammer	39	Sear
8	Center Pin	24	Hammer Pin	40	Sear Spring
9	Extractor Spring	25	Lever and Spring Assembly	41	Cylinder Crane
10	Cylinder	26	Lifter	42	Cylinder Crane Pivot Pin
11	Cylinder Stop	27	Lifter Pin	43	Trigger
12	Cylinder Stop Spring	28	Mainspring	44	Trigger Guard
13	Firing Pin	29	Mainspring Guide Rod	45	Front Trigger Guard and Trigger Pins
14	Firing Pin Retaining Pin	30	Mainspring Guide Seat		
15	Firing Pin Spring	31	Rear Sight Blade	46	Rear Trigger Guard and Sear Pin
16	Firing Pin Striker	32	Rear Sight Base	47	Trigger Spring

Model 732 and 733 Revolver

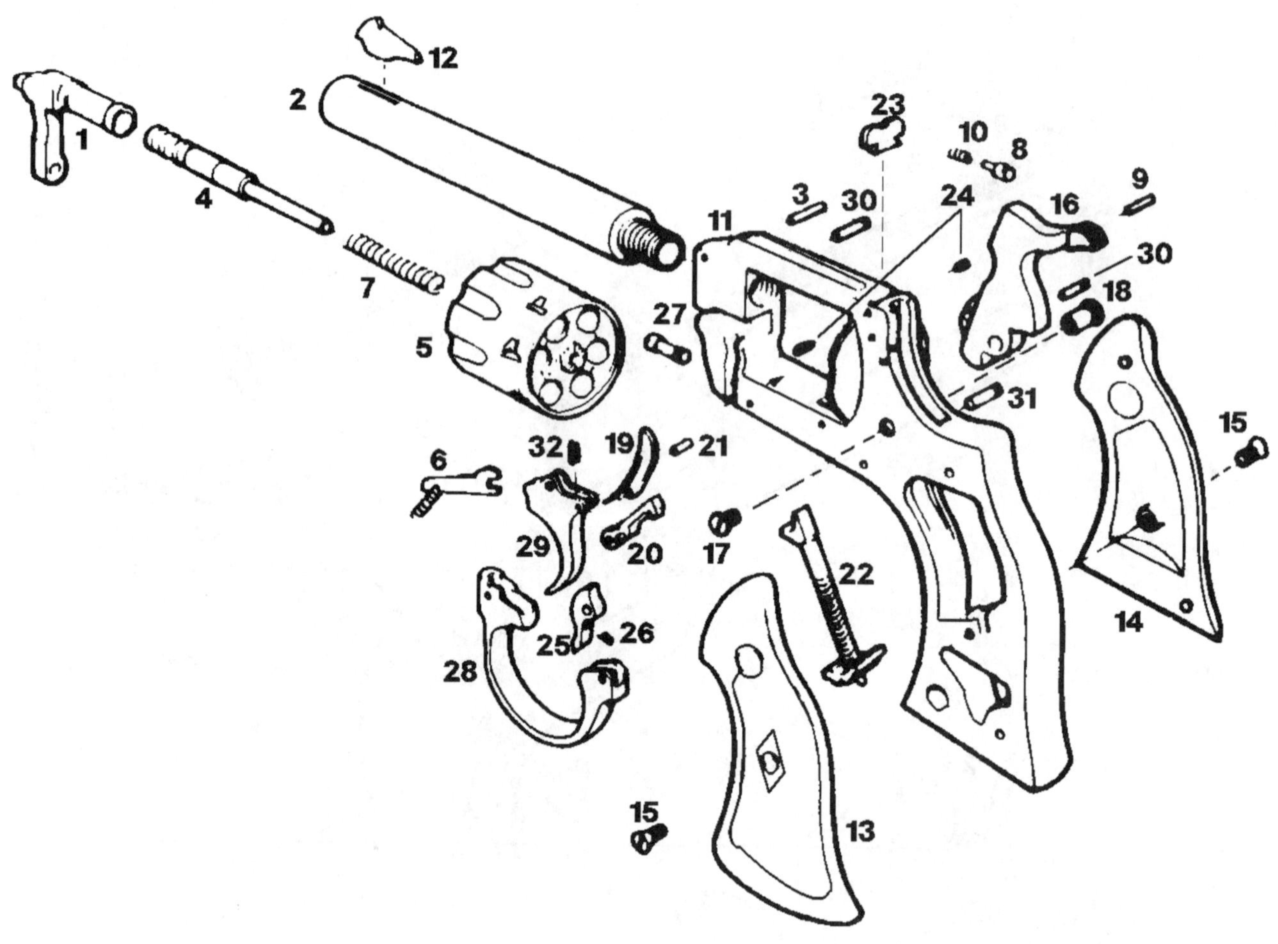

1	Cylinder Crane	18	Hammer Screw Stud
2	Barrel	19	Lever and Spring Assembly
3	Barrel Retaining Pin	20	Lifter
4	Center Pin Assembly	21	Lifter Pin
5	Cylinder and Extractor Assembly	22	Mainspring and Guide Assembly
6	Cylinder Stop and Spring	23	Rear Sight
7	Extractor Spring	24	Rear Sight Windage Screws
8	Firing Pin	25	Sear
9	Firing Pin Retaining Pin	26	Sear Spring
10	Firing Pin Spring	27	Crane Pivot Pin
11	Frame	28	Trigger Guard
12	Front Sight	29	Trigger
13	Grip, Left	30	Trigger Pin and Front Guard Pins
14	Grip, Right	31	Trigger Guard Rear Pin and Sear Pin
15	Grip Screws	32	Trigger Spring
16	Hammer		
17	Hammer Screw		

Model 922 and 933 Revolver

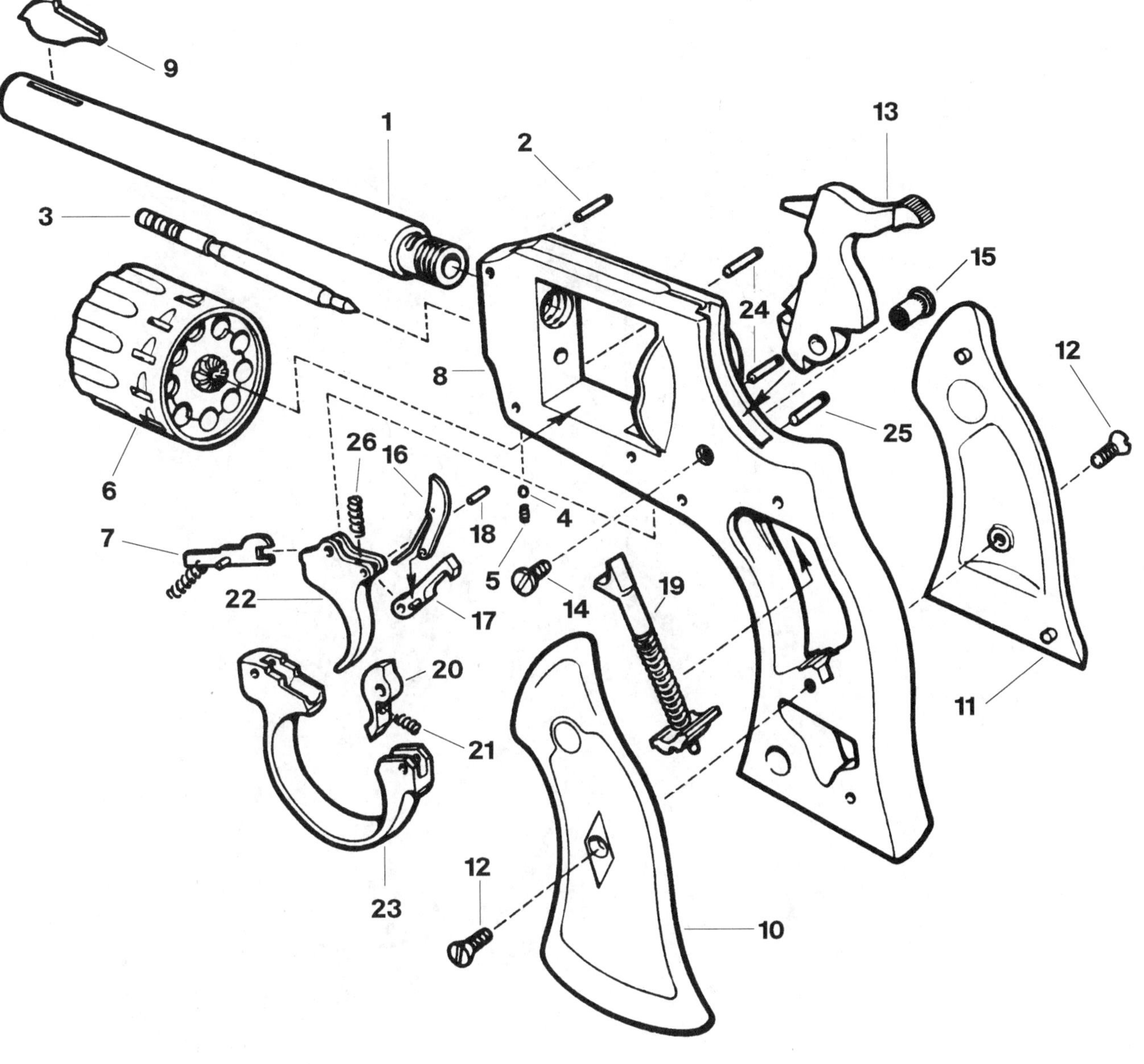

1	Barrel	**15**	Hammer Screw Stud
2	Barrel Retaining Pin	**16**	Lever and Spring Assembly
3	Center Pin	**17**	Lifter
4	Center Pin Ball Detent	**18**	Lifter Pin
5	Center Pin Ball Detent Spring	**19**	Mainspring and Guide Assembly
6	Cylinder and Extractor Assembly	**20**	Sear
7	Cylinder Stop and Spring	**21**	Sear Spring
8	Frame	**22**	Trigger
9	Front Sight	**23**	Trigger Guard
10	Left Grip	**24**	Trigger Pin and Guard Pin (Small)
11	Right Grip	**25**	Trigger Guard Rear Pin and Sear Pin (Large)
12	Grip Screws	**26**	Trigger Spring
13	Hammer		
14	Hammer Screw		

Model 925 Revolver

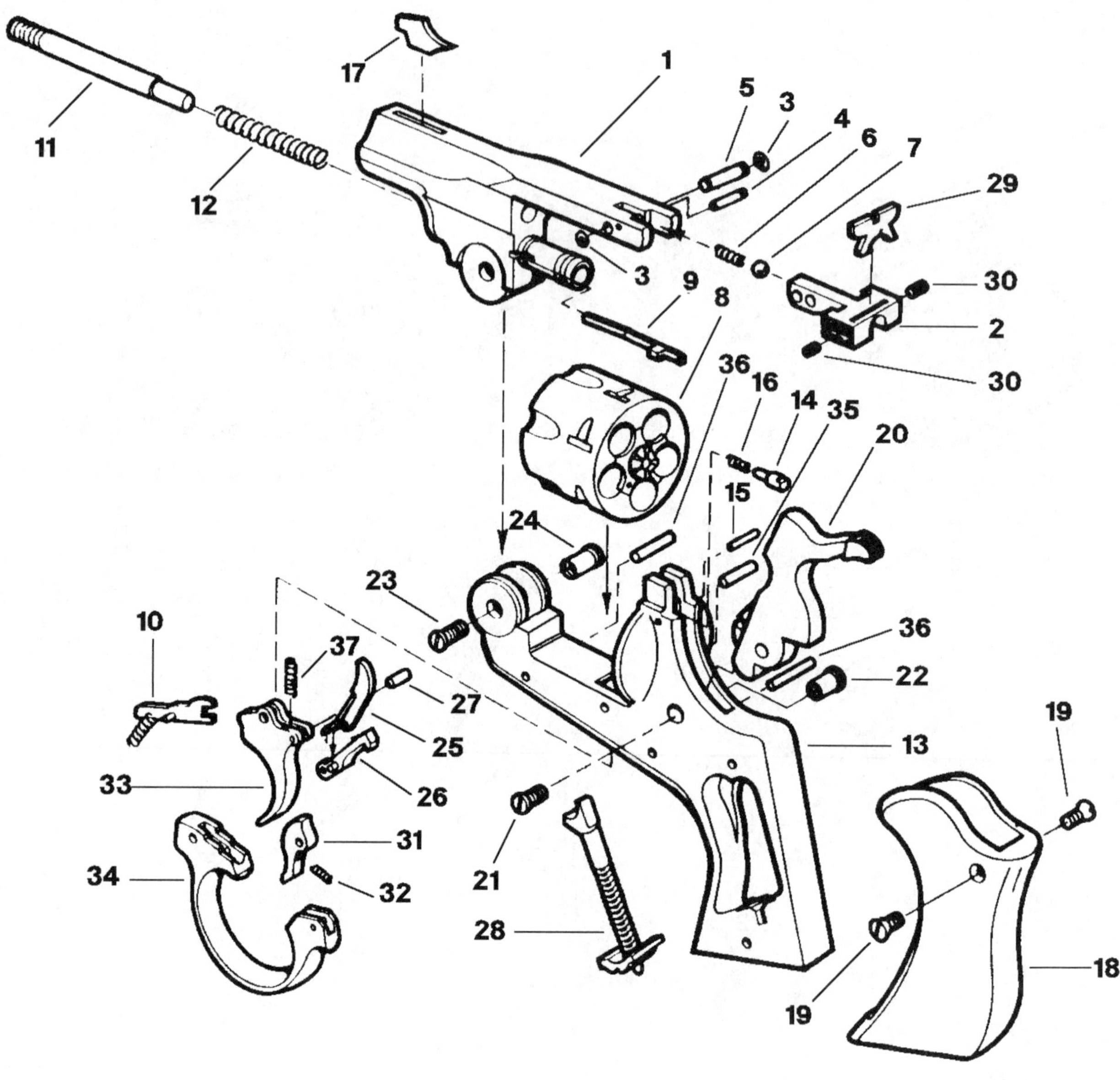

Key

1 Barrel
2 Barrel Catch
3 Barrel Catch Locking Spring
4 Barrel Catch Pin
5 Barrel Catch Pivot Pin
6 Barrel Catch Spring
7 Barrel Catch Spring Follower
8 Cylinder and Extractor Assembly
9 Cylinder Catch
10 Cylinder Stop Assembly
11 Ejector Rod
12 Ejector Spring
13 Frame
14 Firing Pin
15 Firing Pin Retaining Pin
16 Firing Pin Spring
17 Front Sight
18 Grip
19 Grip Screws
20 Hammer
21 Hammer Screw
22 Hammer Screw Stud
23 Hinge Screw
24 Hinge Screw Stud
25 Lever and Spring Assembly
26 Lifter
27 Lifter Pin
28 Mainspring and Guide Assembly
29 Rear Sight Blade
30 Rear Sight Windage Screws
31 Sear
32 Sear Spring
33 Trigger
34 Trigger Guard
35 Trigger Pin
36 Trigger Guard Rear Pin and Sear Pin (Large)
37 Trigger Spring

Parts Not Shown

Front Sight Screw
Front Sight Pin
Front Sight Spring

Model 929 Revolver

Courtesy James M. Triggs/NRA

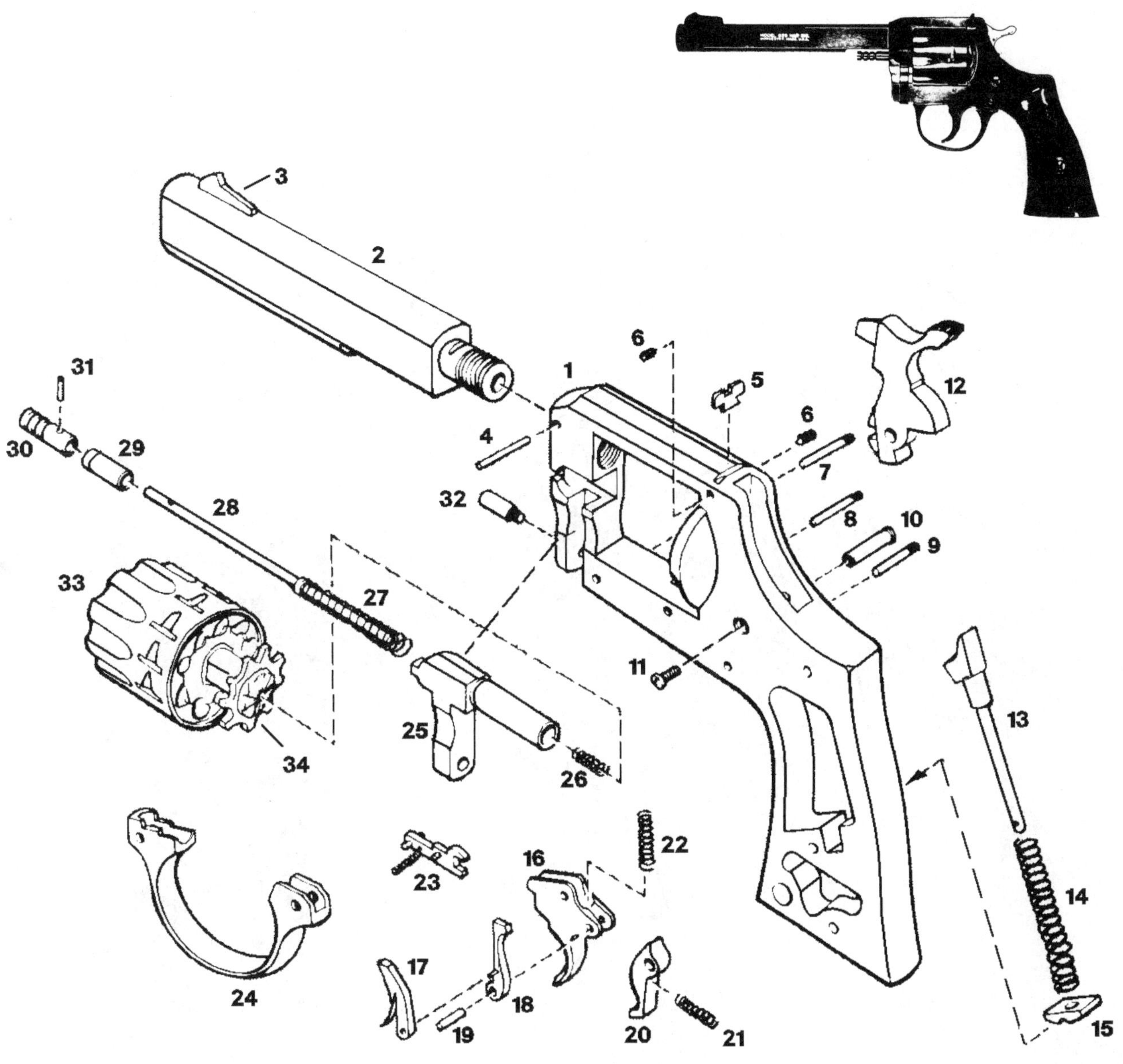

Key					
1	Frame	**13**	Mainspring Guide	**26**	Center Pin Spring
2	Barrel	**14**	Mainspring	**27**	Extractor Spring
3	Front Sight	**15**	Mainspring Seat	**28**	Center Pin
4	Barrel Retaining Pin	**16**	Trigger	**29**	Center Pin Guide
5	Rear Sight Leaf	**17**	Lever and Spring Assembly	**30**	Center Pin Head
6	Rear Sight Windage Screws	**18**	Lifter	**31**	Center Pin Head Pin
7	Front Trigger Guard Pin	**19**	Lifter Pin	**32**	Cylinder Crane Pivot Pin
8	Trigger Pin	**20**	Sear	**33**	Cylinder
9	Rear Trigger Guard and Sear Pin	**21**	Sear Spring	**34**	Extractor
10	Hammer Screw Stud	**22**	Trigger Spring		**Parts Not Shown**
11	Hammer Screw	**23**	Cylinder Stop Assembly		Right Grip
12	Hammer	**24**	Trigger Guard		Left Grip
		25	Swingout Arm Assembly		Grip Screws

Model 949, 950, 976, 649, 650, 660, 666, 676 and 686 Revolver

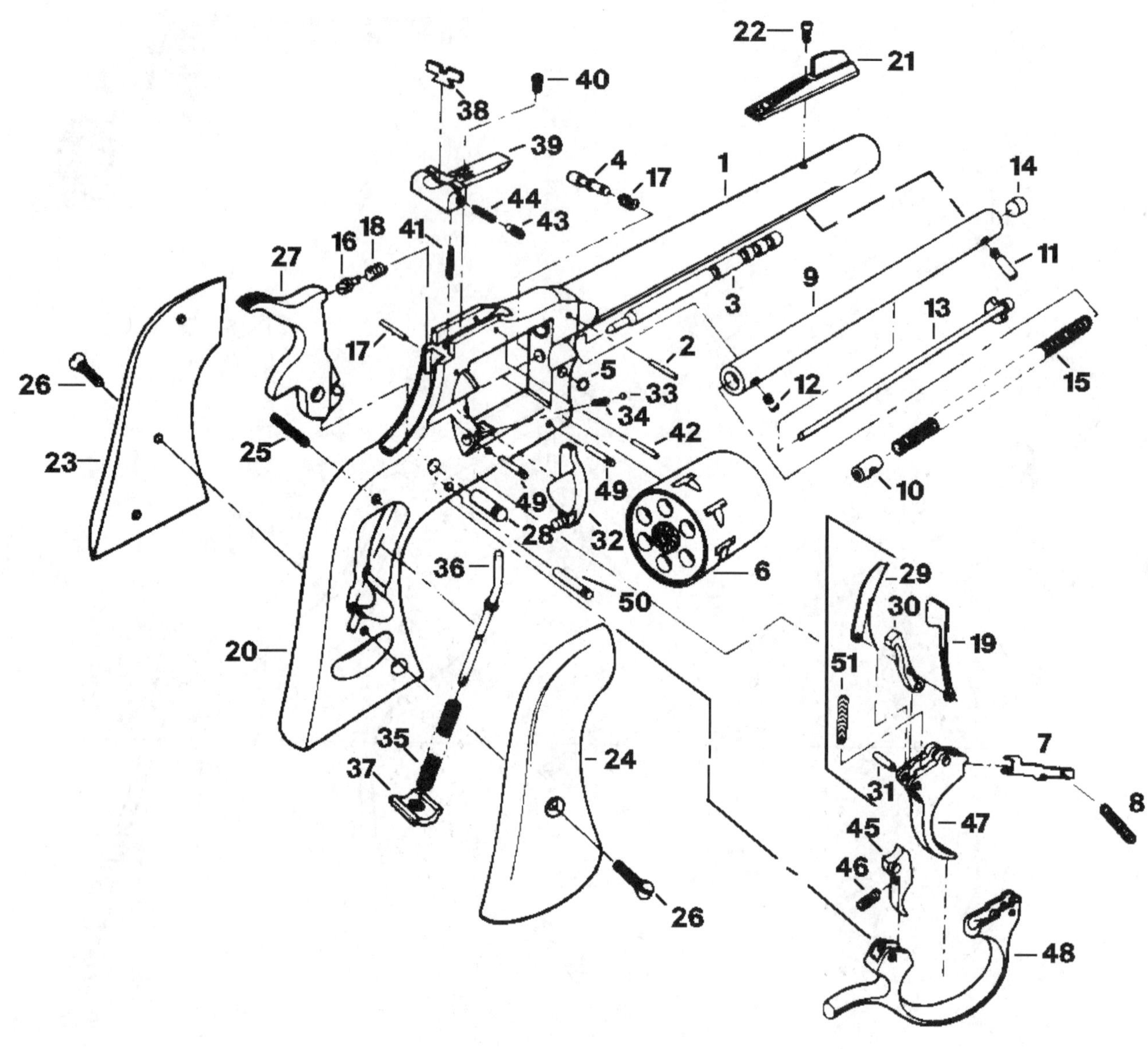

No.	Part	No.	Part	No.	Part
1	Barrel	18	Firing Pin and Center Pin Catch Spring	34	Loading Gate Ball Spring
2	Barrel Retaining Pin	19	Firing Pin Striker	35	Mainspring
3	Center Pin	20	Frame	36	Mainspring Guide Rod
4	Center Pin Catch	21	Front Sight	37	Mainspring Guide Seat
5	Center Pin Catch Retainer	22	Front Sight Screw	38	Rear Sight Blade
6	Cylinder	23	Left Grip	39	Rear Sight Base
7	Cylinder Stopt	24	Right Grip	40	Rear Sight Elevation Screw
8	Cylinder Stop Spring	25	Grip Pin	41	Rear Sight Elevation Spring
9	Ejector Housing	26	Grip Screws	42	Rear Sight Pivot Pin
10	Ejector Housing Bushing	27	Hammer	43	Rear Sight Windage Screw
11	Front Ejector Housing Screw	28	Hammer Pin	44	Rear Sight Windage Spring
12	Rear Ejector Housing Screw	29	Lever and Spring Assembly	45	Sear
13	Ejector Rod	30	Lifter	46	Sear Spring
14	Ejector Rod Stop	31	Lifter Pin	47	Trigger
15	Ejector Spring	32	Loading Gate	48	Trigger Guard
16	Firing Pin	33	Loading Gate Ball	49	Front Trigger Guard and Trigger Pin
17	Firing Pin Retaining Pin			50	Rear Trigger Guard and Sear Pin
				51	Trigger Spring

Model 999 Sportsman Revolver

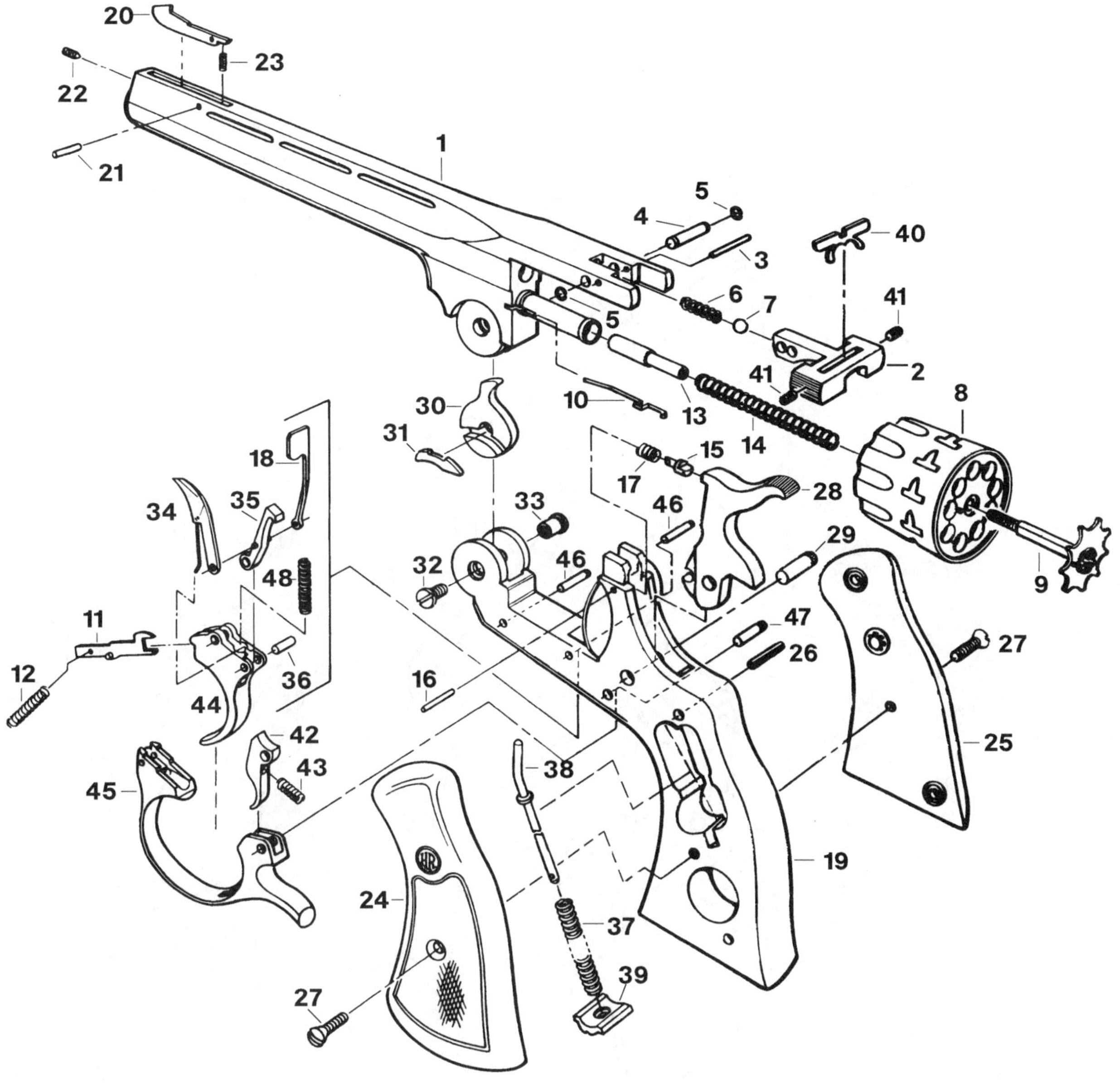

1	Barrel and Cylinder Arbor Assembly	**17**	Firing Pin Spring	**34**	Lever and Spring Assembly
2	Barrel Catch	**18**	Firing Pin Striker	**35**	Lifter
3	Barrel Catch Pin	**19**	Frame	**36**	Lifter Pin
4	Barrel Catch Pivot Pin	**20**	Front Sight	**37**	Mainspring
5	Barrel Catch Pivot Pin Retainers	**21**	Front Sight Pin	**38**	Mainspring Guide Rod
6	Barrel Catch Spring	**22**	Front Sight Adjusting Screw	**39**	Mainspring Guide Seat
7	Barrel Catch Spring Follower	**23**	Front Sight Spring	**40**	Rear Sight Blade
8	Cylinder	**24**	Left Grip	**41**	Rear Sight Windage Screws
9	Extractor	**25**	Right Grip	**42**	Sear
10	Cylinder Catch	**26**	Grip Pin	**43**	Sear Spring
11	Cylinder Stop	**27**	Grip Screws	**44**	Trigger
12	Cylinder Stop Spring	**28**	Hammer	**45**	Trigger Guard
13	Extractor Extension	**29**	Hammer Pin	**46**	Front Trigger Guard Pin and Trigger Pin
14	Extractor Spring	**30**	Hook	**47**	Rear Trigger Guard Pin and Sear Pin
15	Firing Pin	**31**	Hook Slide	**48**	Trigger Spring
16	Firing Pin Retaining Pin	**32**	Barrel Hinge Screw		
		33	Barrel Hinge Screw Stud		

Top Break 22 7-Shot Revolver

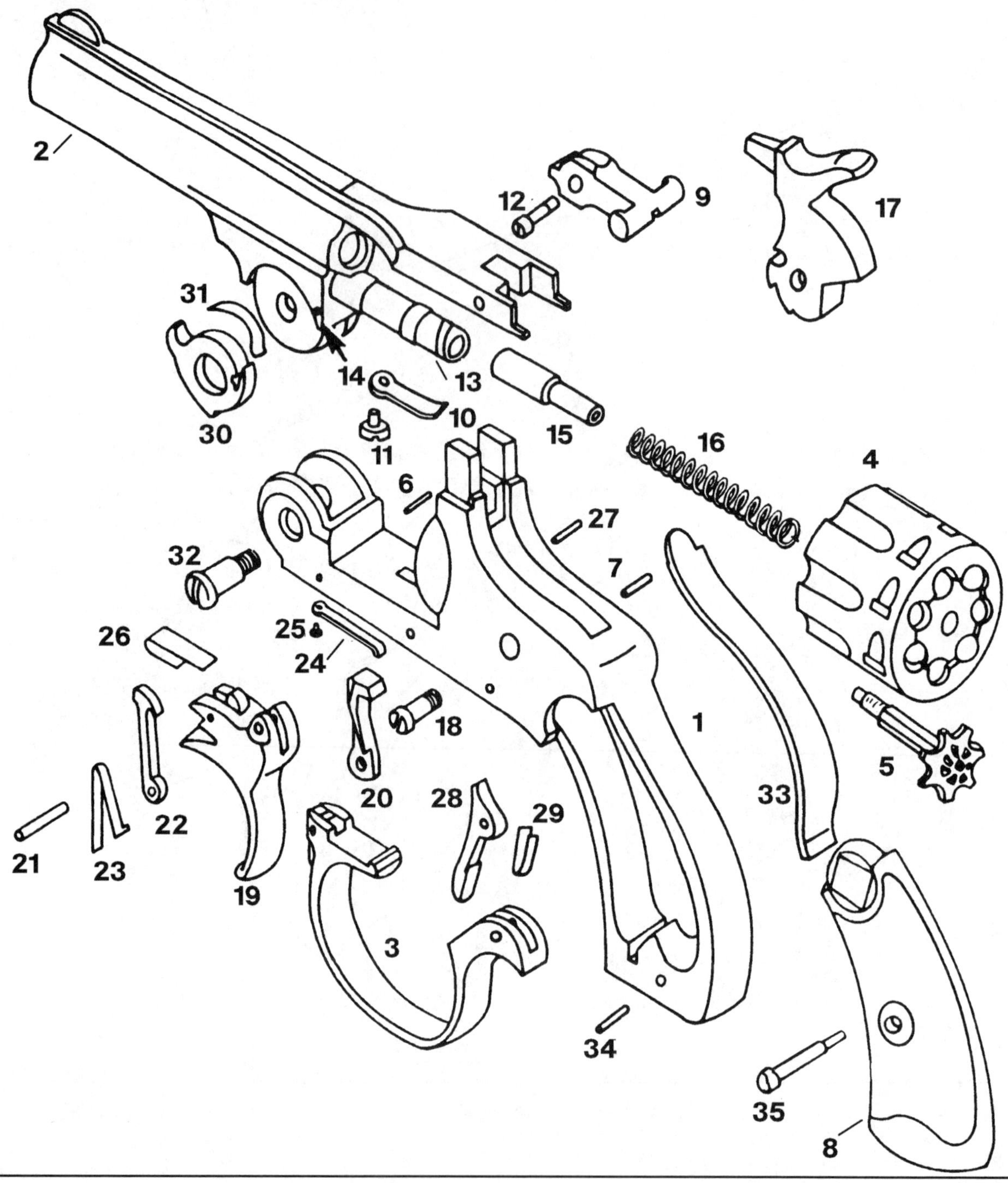

1	Frame	**14**	Cylinder Arbor Pin	**27**	Trigger Pin
2	Barrel	**15**	Extractor Extension	**28**	Sear
3	Trigger Guard	**16**	Extractor Spring	**29**	Sear Spring
4	Cylinder	**17**	Hammer	**30**	Extractor Hook
5	Extractor	**18**	Hammer Screw	**31**	Hook Spring
6	Front Guard Pin	**19**	Trigger	**32**	Barrel Hinge Screw
7	Guard/Sear Pin	**20**	Lifter	**33**	Mainspring
8	Left Grip	**21**	Lifter Pin	**34**	Grip Pin
9	Barrel Catch	**22**	Hand	**35**	Grip Screw
10	Barrel Catch Spring	**23**	Hand Spring	**Parts Not Shown**	
11	Barrel Catch Spring Screw	**24**	Cylinder Stop		Right Grip
12	Barrel Catch Pivot Screw	**25**	Cylinder Stop Screw		
13	Cylinder Arbor	**26**	Trigger Spring		

HK-4 Auto

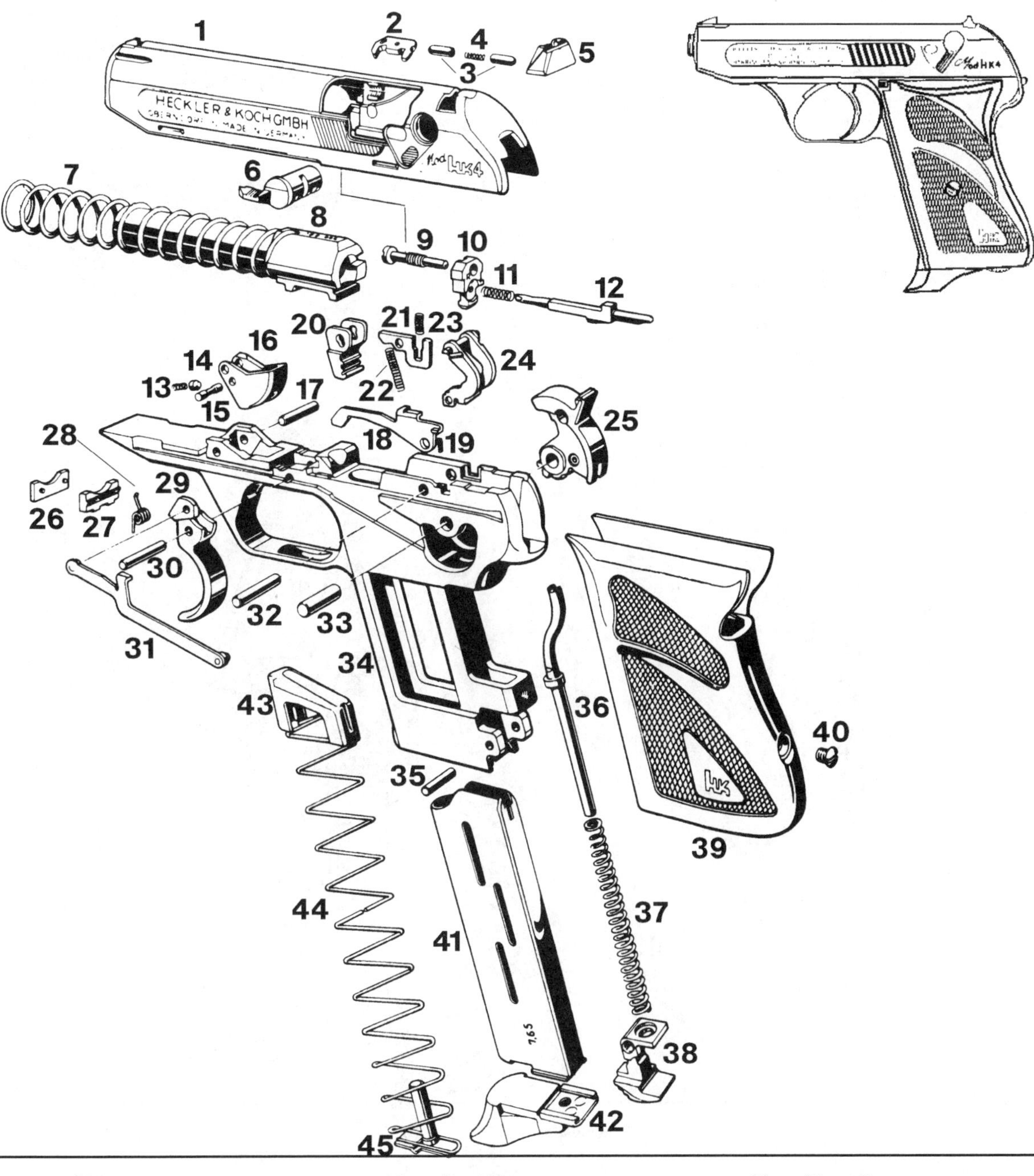

1	Slide	16	Barrel Clamp	31	Trigger Bar
2	Extractor	17	Cylindrical Pin	32	Cylindrical Pin
3	Set Bolts	18	Ejector	33	Hammer Pin
4	Compression Spring	19	Ejector Spring	34	Receiver
5	Rear Sight	20	Sear	35	Cylindrical Pin
6	Safety Pin	21	Spring Support	36	Spring Rod
7	Recoil Spring	22	Drag Spring	37	Mainspring
8	Barrel	23	Disconnector Spring	38	Magazine Catch
9	Cylinder-Head Screw	24	Disconnector	39	Grip
10	Face Plate	25	Hammer	40	Lens Head Countersunk Screw
11	Firing Pin Spring	26	Buffer Plate	41	Magazine Housing
12	Firing Pin	27	Buffer	42	Floorplate with Grip Extension
13	Plunger Spring	28	Elbow Spring	43	Follower
14	Plunger	29	Trigger	44	Follower Spring
15	Stop Pin	30	Cylindrical Pin	45	Locking Plate Assembly

P7 Auto

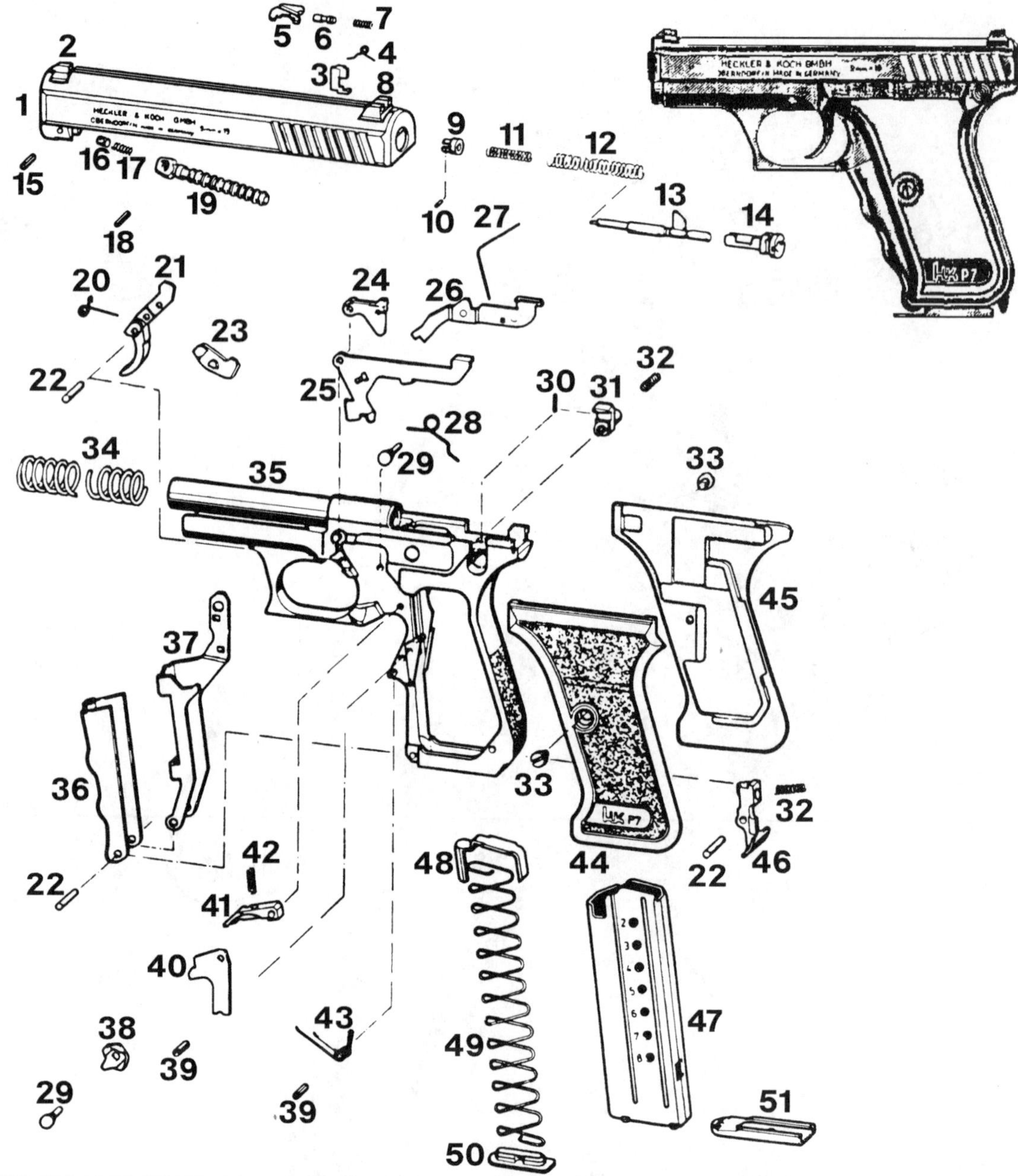

1	Slide
2	Front Sight
3	Drop Safety Catch
4	Elbow Spring
5	Extractor
6	Pressure Pin
7	Compression Spring
8	Rear Sight
9	Ring
10	Cylindrical Pin
11	Inner Firing Pin Spring
12	Outer Firing Pin Spring
13	Firing Pin
14	Bushing
15	Clamping Sleeve
16	Fixing Pin
17	Compression Spring
18	Clamping Pin
19	Piston
20	Elbow Spring
21	Trigger
22	Cylindrical Pins
23	Sear
24	Sear Control Lever
25	Catch Lever
26	Ejector Lever
27	Spring
28	Elbow Spring
29	Locking Pins
30	Clamping Sleeve
31	Slide Retaining Catch
32	Compression Spring
33	Grip Screws
34	Recoil Spring
35	Receiver with Barrel
36	Squeeze Cocker
37	Drag Lever
38	Rocker
39	Clamping Levers
40	Cocking Lever Stop
41	Cocking Latch
42	Compression Spring
43	Elbow Spring
44	Grip Shell, Left
45	Grip Shell, Right
46	Magazine Catch
47	Magazine Housing
48	Follower
49	Follower Spring
50	Locking Plate
51	Floorplate

P7M8 Auto

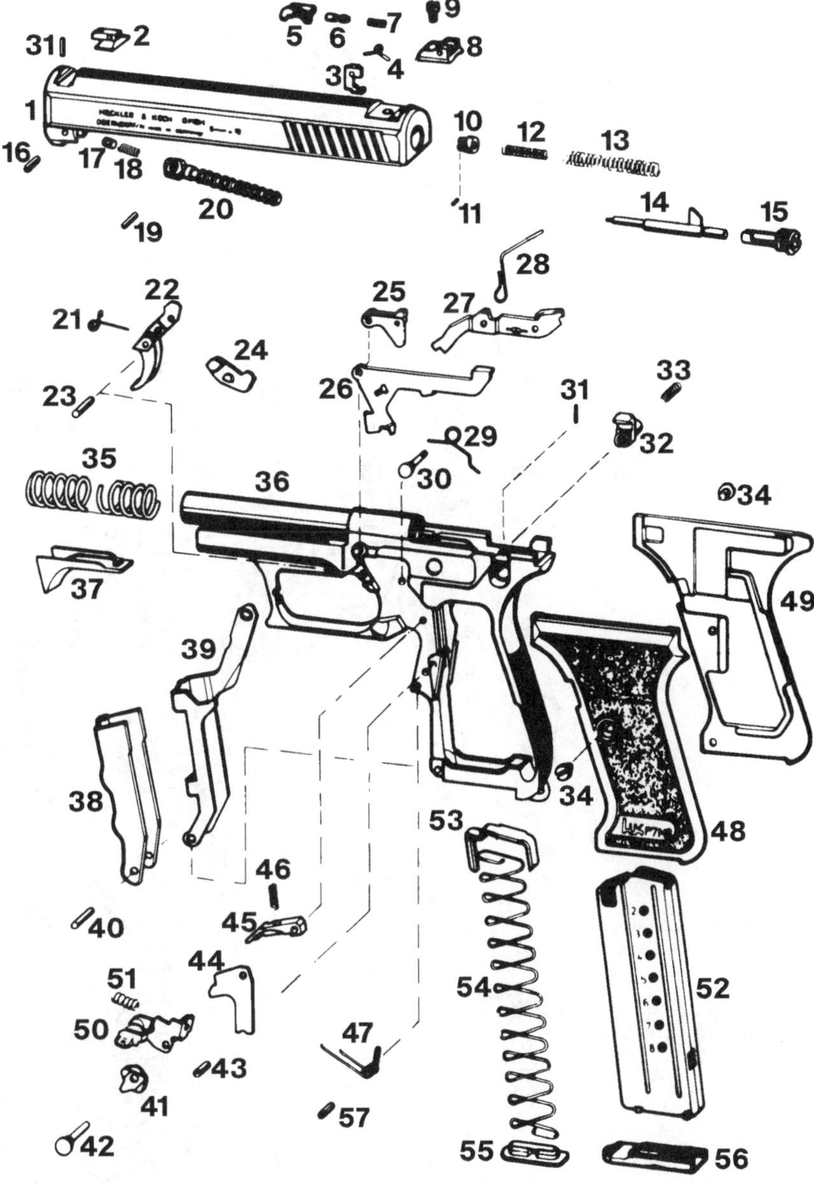

1	Slide	20	Piston	39	Drag Lever
2	Front Sight	21	Trigger Spring	40	Cocking Lever Axle
3	Drop Safety Catch	22	Trigger	41	Rocker
4	Drop Safety Catch Spring	23	Trigger Pin	42	Magazine Catch Axle
5	Extractor	24	Transmission Lever	43	Roll Pin
6	Extractor Plunger	25	Disconnector	44	Stop
7	Extractor Spring	26	Slide Stop	45	Cocking Latch
8	Rear Sight	27	Sear Lever	46	Cocking Latch Spring
9	Rear Sight Screw	28	Sear Spring	47	Cocking Lever Spring
10	Firing Pin Collar	29	Rocker Spring	48	Grip, Left
11	Firing Pin Collar Pin	30	Rocker Spring Axle	49	Grip, Right
12	Firing Pin Return Spring	31	Front Sight/Slide Retainer Pin	50	Magazine Catch
13	Firing Pin Spring	32	Slide Removal Button	51	Magazine Catch Spring
14	Firing Pin	33	Slide Removal Button Spring	52	Magazine Housing
15	Firing Pin Bushing	34	Grip Screws	53	Follower
16	Piston Roll Pin	35	Recoil Spring	54	Follower Spring
17	Piston Plunger	36	Receiver with Barrel	55	Magazine Lockplate
18	Piston Plunger Spring	37	Trigger Heat Shield	56	Magazine Floorplate
19	Plunger Retaining Roll Pin	38	Cocking Lever	57	Cocking Lever Spring Pin

HECKLER & KOCH

P7M13

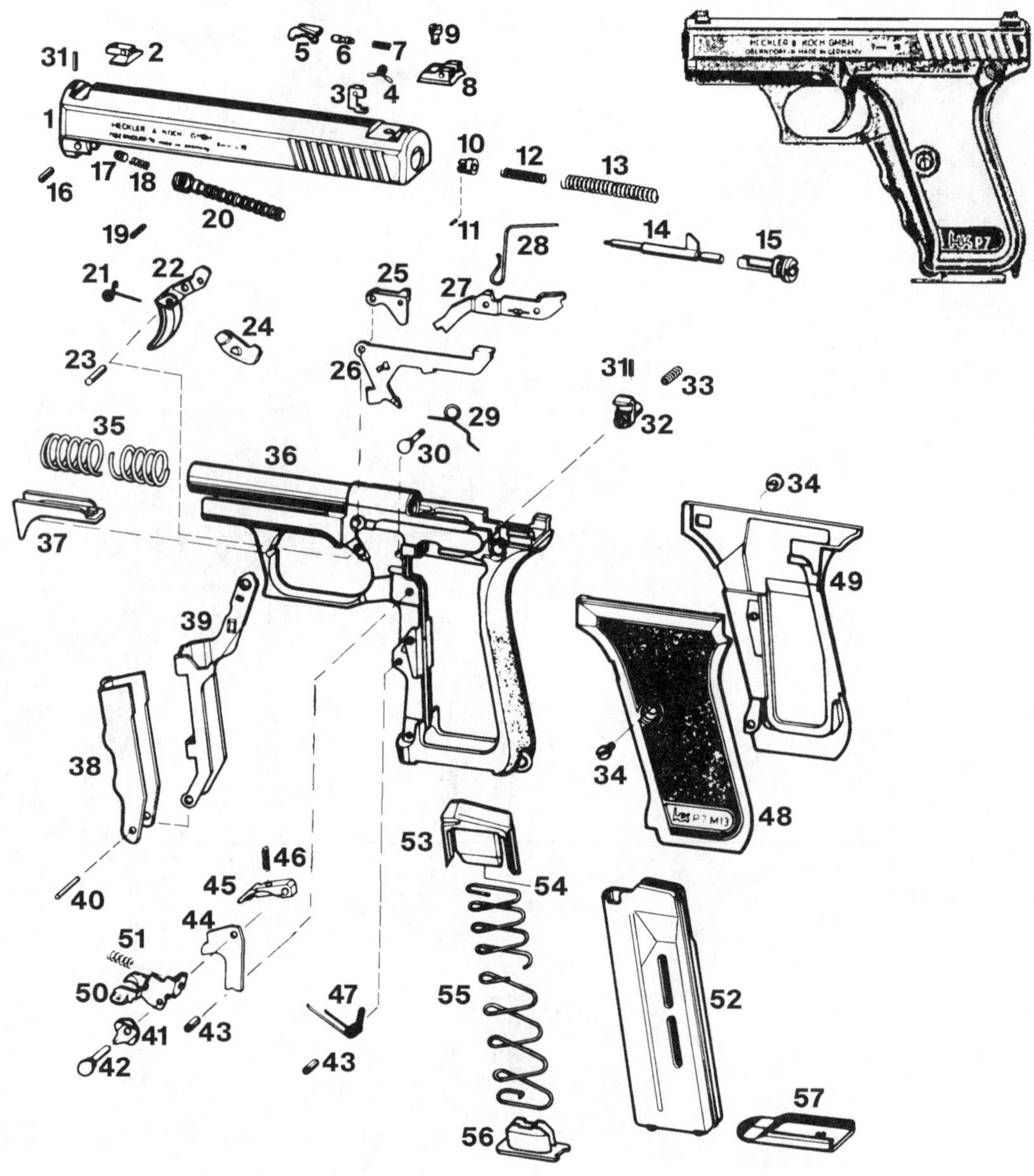

1	Slide	**20**	Piston	**39**	Drag Lever
2	Front Sight	**21**	Trigger Spring	**40**	Cocking Lever Axle
3	Drop Safety Catch	**22**	Trigger	**41**	Rocker
4	Drop Safety Catch Spring	**23**	Trigger Pin	**42**	Magazine Catch Axle
5	Extractor	**24**	Transmission Lever	**43**	Roll Pins
6	Extractor Plunger	**25**	Disconnector	**44**	Stop
7	Extractor Spring	**26**	Slide Stop	**45**	Cocking Latch
8	Rear Sight	**27**	Sear Lever	**46**	Cocking Latch Spring
9	Rear Sight Screw	**28**	Sear Spring	**47**	Cocking Lever Spring
10	Firing Pin Collar	**29**	Rocker Spring	**48**	Grip, Left
11	Firing Pin Collar Pin	**30**	Rocker Spring Axle	**49**	Grip, Right
12	Firing Pin Return Spring	**31**	Front Sight/Slide Retainer Pin	**50**	Magazine Catch
13	Firing Pin Spring	**32**	Slide Removal Button	**51**	Magazine Catch Spring
14	Firing Pin	**33**	Slide Removal Button Spring	**52**	Magazine Housing
15	Firing Pin Bushing	**34**	Grip Screws	**53**	Follower
16	Piston Roll Pin	**35**	Recoil Spring	**54**	Follower Insert
17	Piston Plunger	**36**	Receiver with Barrel	**55**	Follower Spring
18	Piston Plunger Spring	**37**	Trigger Heat Shield	**56**	Locking Plate
19	Plunger Retaining Roll Pin	**38**	Cocking Lever	**57**	Magazine Floorplate

P7 (PSP) Auto

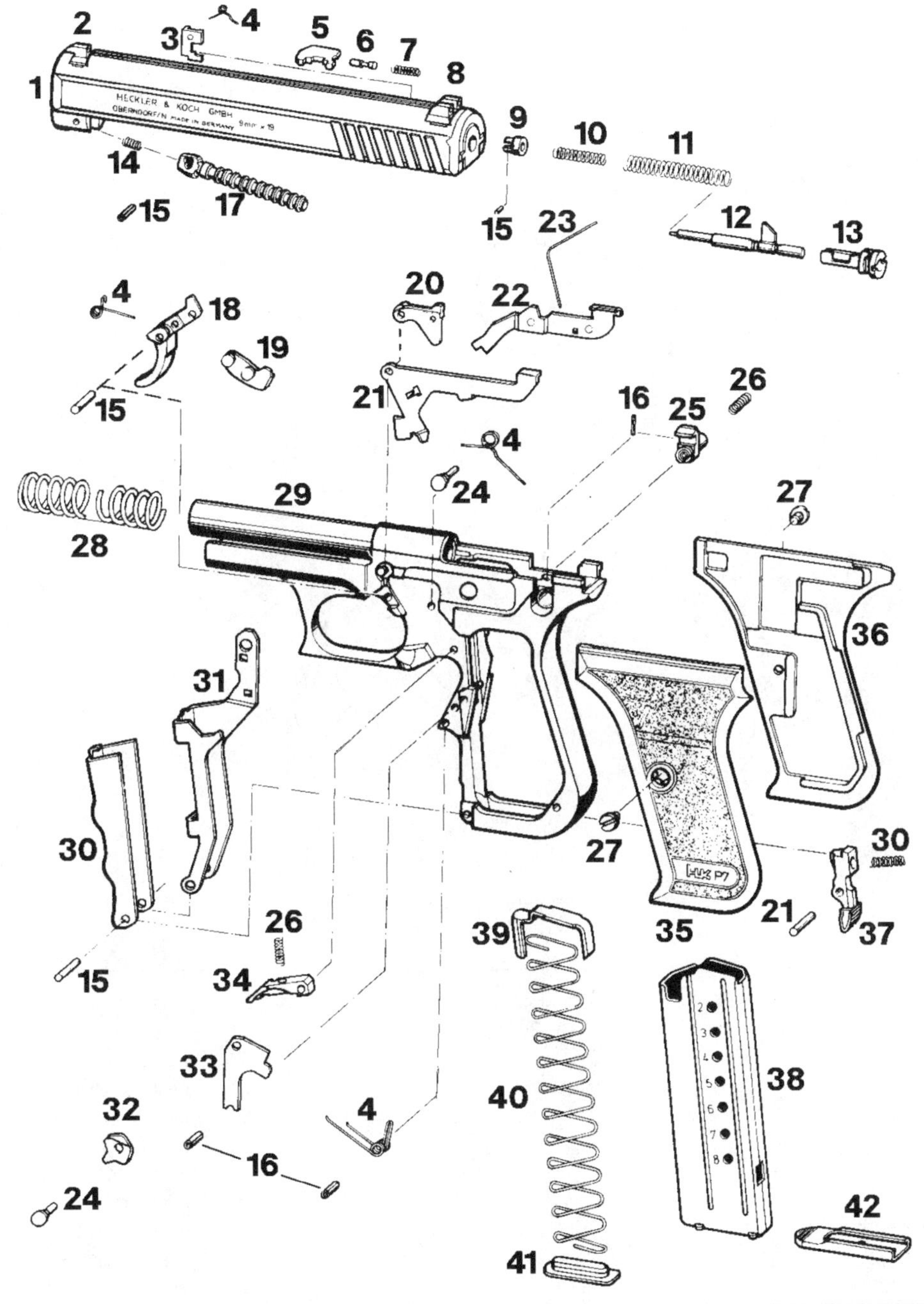

1	Slide	**15**	Cylindrical Pins	**29**	Grip with Barrel
2	Front Sight	**16**	Clamping Sleeves	**30**	Squeeze Cocker
3	Drop Safety Catch	**17**	Retarder Piston	**31**	Drag Lever
4	Elbow Spring	**18**	Trigger	**32**	Rocker
5	Extractor	**19**	Sear	**33**	Stop
6	Pressure Pin	**20**	Disconnector	**34**	Catch
7	Extractor Spring	**21**	Slide Catch Lever	**35**	Grip, Left
8	Rear Sight	**22**	Transmission Lever	**36**	Grip, Right
9	Spacer Ring	**23**	Spring	**37**	Magazine Catch
10	Return Spring	**24**	Bearing Pins	**38**	Magazine Housing
11	Firing Pin Spring	**25**	Stripping Button	**39**	Follower
12	Firing Pin	**26**	Compression Spring	**40**	Follower Spring
13	Cap	**27**	Grip Screws	**41**	Follower Spring Locking Plate
14	Piston Spring	**28**	Recoil Spring	**42**	Magazine Floorplate

P9S 9mm Auto

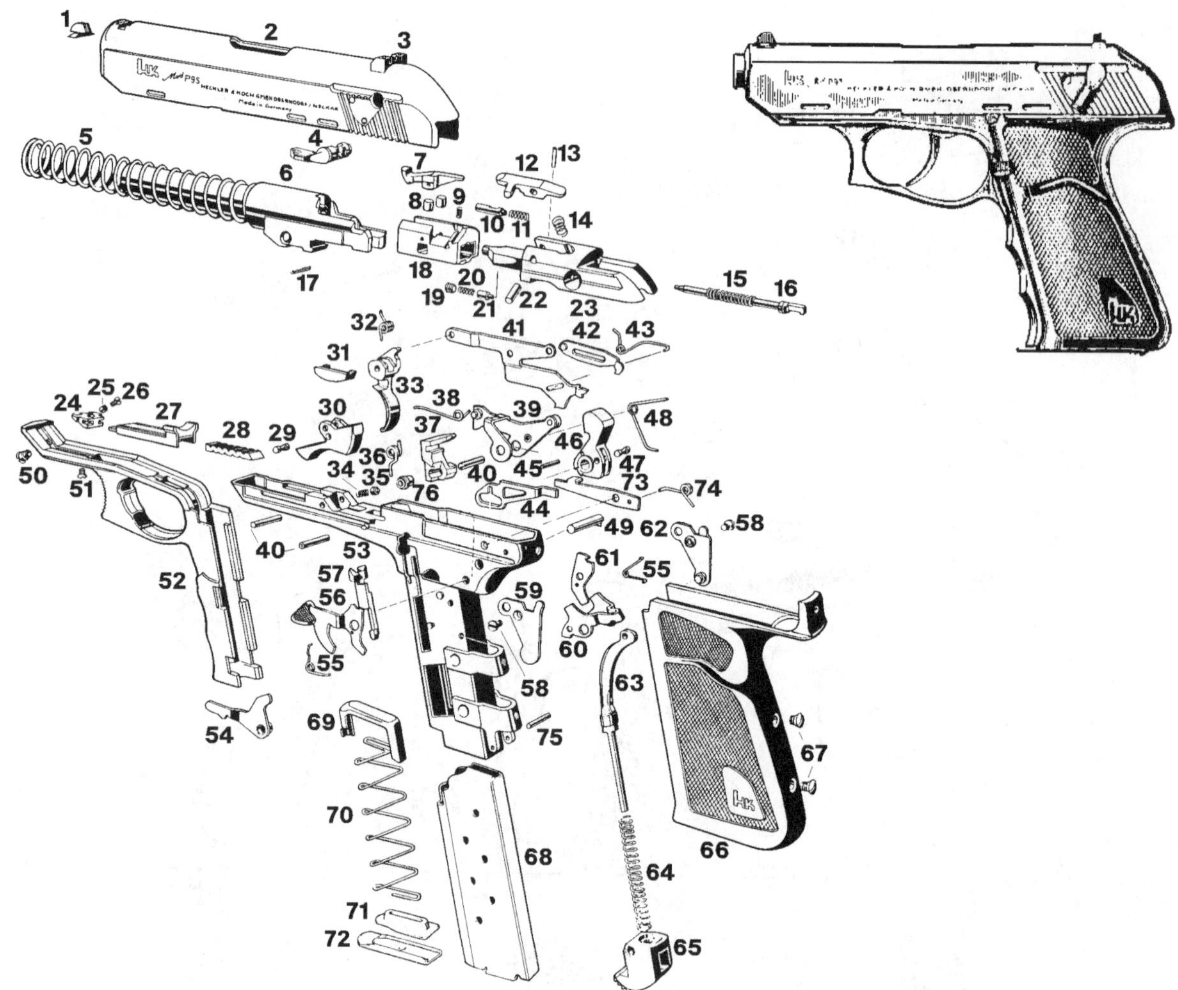

No.	Part
1	Front Sight
2	Slide
3	Rear Sight
4	Safety
5	Recoil Spring
6	Barrel
7	Extractor
8	Locking Rollers
9	Compression Spring
10	Pressure Pin
11	Compression Spring for Pressure Pin
12	Locking Catch
13	Clamping Sleeve
14	Compression Spring
15	Firing Pin Spring
16	Firing Pin
17	Spiral Pin
18	Bolt Head
19	Threaded Pin
20	Compression Spring
21	Catch Bolt
22	Cylindrical Pin
23	Bolt Head Carrier
24	Support
25	Sleeve
26	Raised Countersunk Head Screw
27	Buffer Housing
28	Plastic Buffer
29	Stop Pin
30	Barrel Catch
31	Insert Piece
32	Trigger Spring
33	Trigger
34	Compression Spring
35	Catch Bolt
36	Elbow Spring
37	Catch Lever
38	Catch Spring
39	Disconnector
40	Cylindrical Pins
41	Pull Bar
42	Trigger Lever
43	Pull Bar Spring
44	Indicator Pin
45	Spiral Pin
46	Hammer
47	Stop Pin
48	Disconnector Spring
49	Hammer Axle
50	Threaded Bushing
51	Raised Countersunk Head Screw
52	Trigger Guard
53	Receiver
54	Safety Catch
55	Elbow Spring
56	Cocking Lever
57	Catch
58	Countersunk Screw
59	Bearing Plate, Left
60	Angle Lever
61	Intermediate Lever
62	Bearing Plate, Right
63	Shank
64	Compression Spring
65	Magazine Catch
66	Combat Grip
67	Raised Head Countersunk Screws
68	Magazine Housing
69	Follower
70	Follower Spring
71	Follower Spring Support
72	Magazine Floorplate
73	Ejector
74	Ejector Spring
75	Magazine Catch Pin
76	Flanged Bush

SP89 Auto

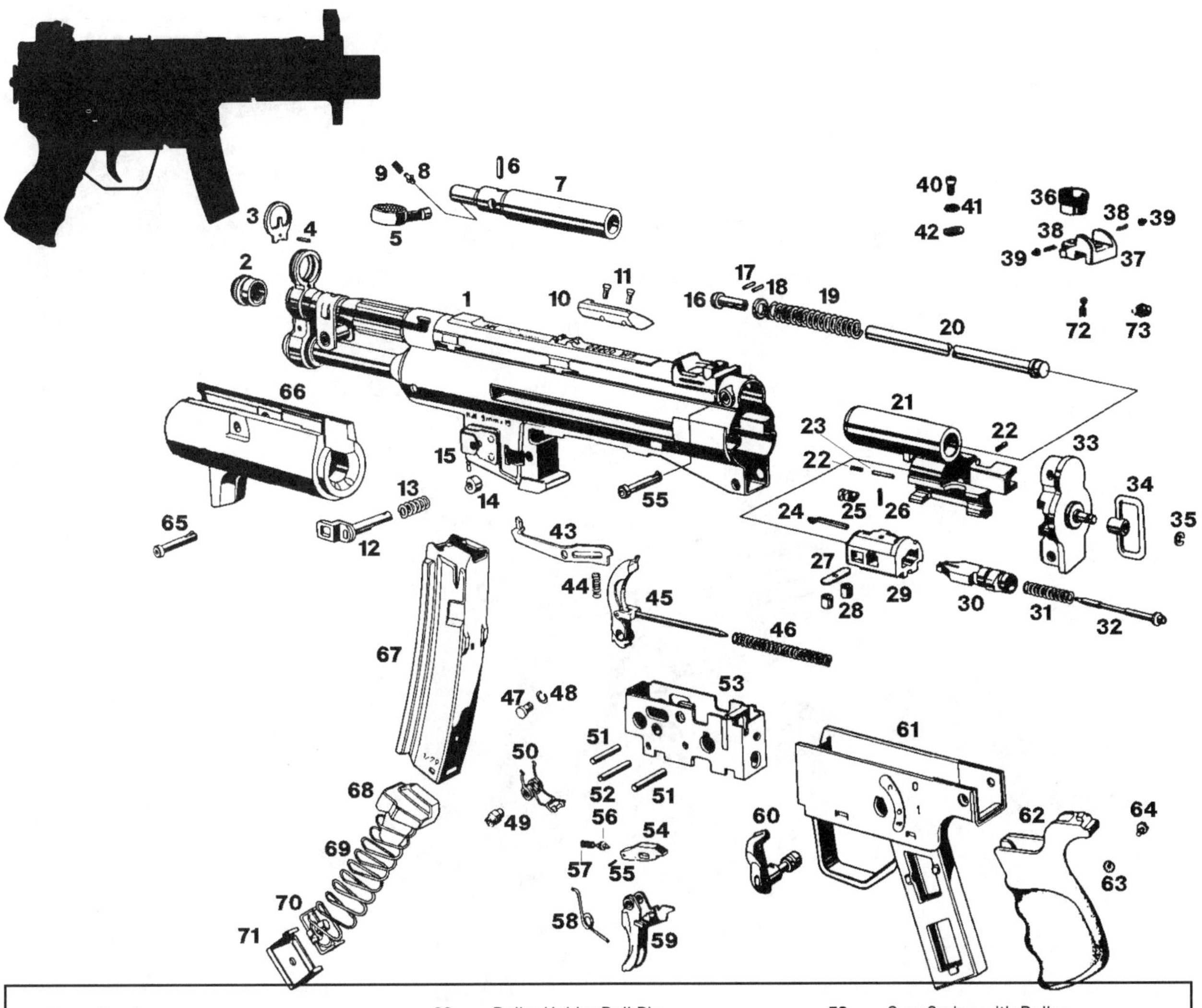

1	Receiver	26	Roller Holder Roll Pin	50	Sear Spring with Roller
2	Cocking Tube Cap	27	Roller Holder	51	Trigger and Sear Pins
3	Front Sight Element	28	Locking Rollers	52	Hammer Pin
4	Front Sight Element Pin	29	Bolt Head	53	Trigger Housing
5	Cocking Handle	30	Bolt Head Locking Piece	54	Sear
6	Cocking Handle Roll Pin	31	Firing Pin Spring	55	Sear Spring Pin
7	Cocking Handle Support	32	Firing Pin	56	Sear Spring Plunger
8	Plunger	33	Butt Cap Assembly	57	Sear Spring
9	Plunger Spring	34	Butt Cap Sling Ring	58	Trigger Spring
10	Cartridge Case Deflector	35	Butt Cap Sling Ring Retainer	59	Trigger
11	Case Deflector Rivets	36	Rear Sight Drum	60	Safety-Lever
12	Magazine Catch	37	Rear Sight Base	61	Grip Frame
13	Magazine Catch Spring	38	Windage Adjustment Springs	62	Grip
14	Magazine Catch Button	39	Windage Adjustment Screws	63	Grip Screw Lock Washer
15	Magazine Catch Roll Pin	40	Sight Base Mounting Screw	64	Grip Screw
16	Stop Pin	41	Sight Base Mounting Screw Spring Washer	65	Forend Pin
17	Stop Pin Rivets			66	Forend
18	Guide Ring	42	Sight Base Flat Washer	67	Magazine Body
19	Recoil Spring	43	Ejector	68	Magazine Follower
20	Recoil Spring Tube	44	Ejector Spring	69	Magazine Spring
21	Bolt Head Carrier	45	Hammer with Strut	70	Magazine Spring Locking Plate
22	Bolt Head Carrier Roll Pin	46	Hammer Spring	71	Magazine Floorplate
23	Locking Piece Stop Pin	47	Ejector Axle	72	Sight Base Ball Detent
24	Extractor Spring	48	Ejector Axle Spring	73	Sight Base Spring
25	Extractor	49	Spacer Sleeve		

VP70Z Auto

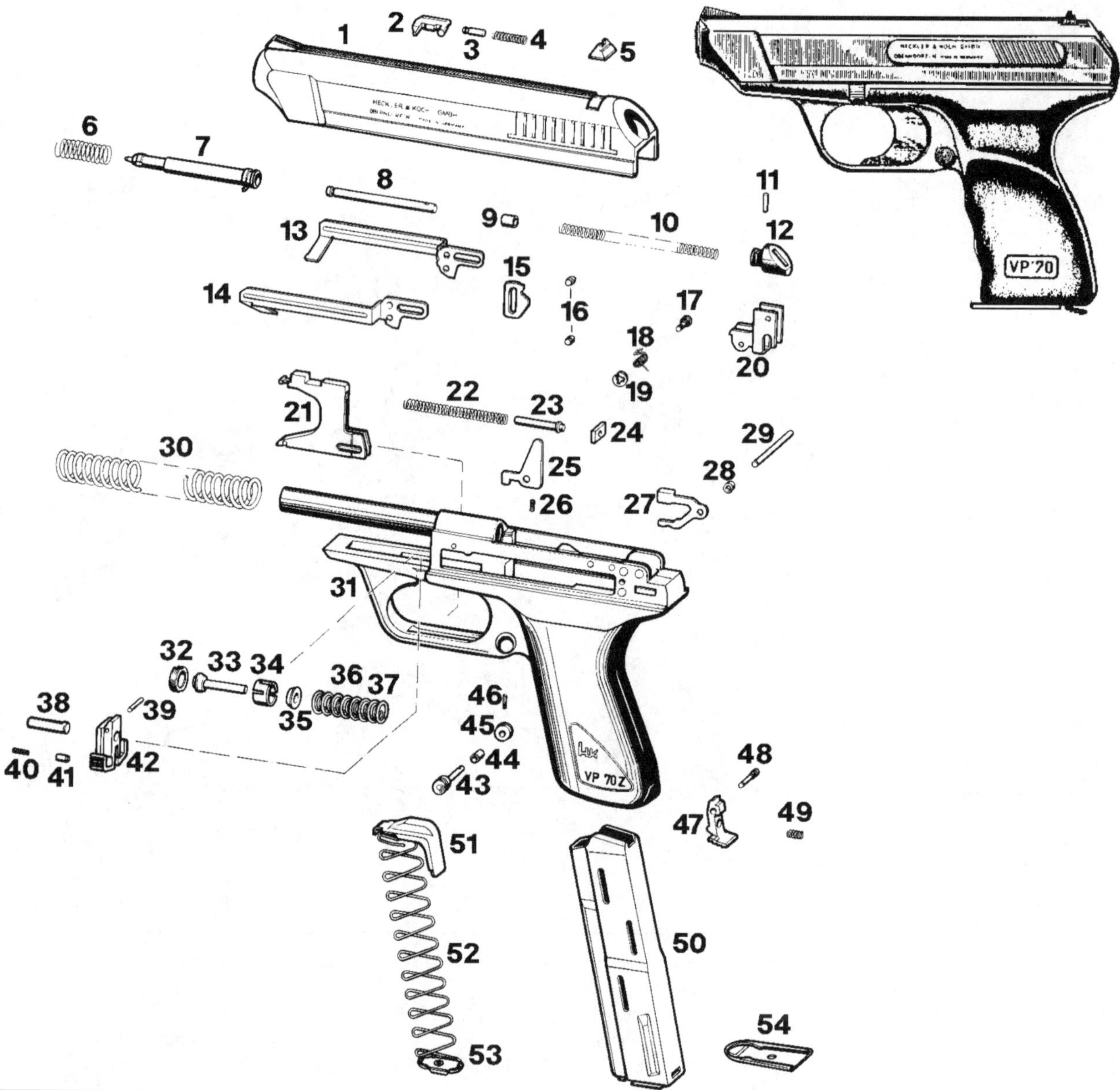

1	Slide
2	Extractor
3	Extractor Plunger
4	Extractor Spring
5	Rear Sight
6	Firing Pin Spring
7	Firing Pin
8	Firing Pin Spring Guide Rod
9	Firing Pin Spring Guide Rod Bushing
10	Firing Pin Spring
11	Slide Cap Retaining Pin
12	Slide Cap
13	Trigger Lever, Right
14	Trigger Lever, Left
15	Trigger Lever Driver
16	Trigger Lever Guide Bolts
17	Elbow Spring Axle
18	Elbow Spring
19	Elbow Spring Circlip
20	Trigger Lever Driver Control Lever
21	Trigger
22	Trigger Spring
23	Trigger Spring Plunger
24	Trigger Spring Support Plate
25	Drop Safety
26	Drop Safety Compression Spring
27	Catch Fork
28	Guide Roller
29	Guide Roller Pin
30	Recoil Spring
31	Receiver with Barrel
32	Buffer Spring Threaded Ring
33	Buffer Spring Guide Bolt
34	Buffer Spring Brake Ring
35	Buffer Spring Contact Piece
36	Inner Buffer Spring
37	Outer Buffer Spring
38	Buffer Bolt
39	Buffer Bolt Roll Pin
40	Compression Spring
41	Retaining Bushing
42	Retaining Catch
43	Safety Button
44	Safety Button Guide Bushing
45	Safety Button Locking Bushing
46	Safety Button Retaining Pin
47	Magazine Catch
48	Magazine Catch Screw
49	Magazine Catch Spring
50	Magazine Body
51	Magazine Follower
52	Magazine Spring
53	Magazine Spring Locking Plate
54	Magazine Floorplate

Derringer

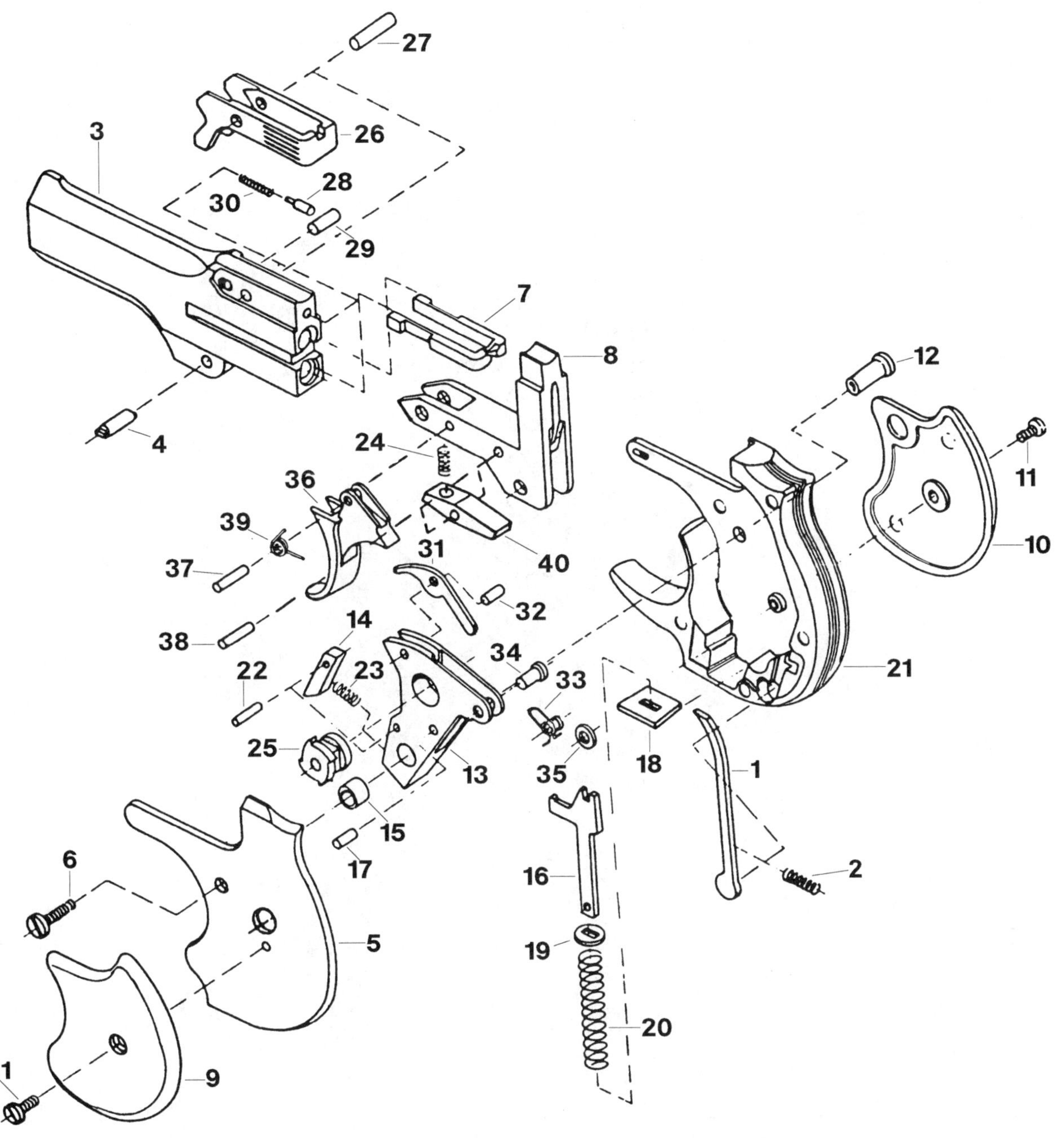

1	Actuator	15	Hammer Pivot Sleeve	29	Stirrup Roller
2	Actuator Spring	16	Hammer Strut	30	Stirrup Plunger Spring
3	Barrel	17	Hammer Strut Pin	31	Striker
4	Barrel Pivot Pin	18	Hammer Strut Plate	32	Striker Pivot Pin
5	Cover Plate	19	Hammer Strut Washer	33	Striker Spring
6	Cover Plate Screw	20	Hammer Spring	34	Striker Spring Retaining Pin
7	Extractor	21	Housing	35	Striker Spring Spacer Washer
8	L Frame	22	Hammer Pawl Pin	36	Trigger
9	Grip, Left	23	Hammer Pawl Spring	37	Trigger Pivot Pin
10	Grip, Right	24	Hammer Safety Block Spring	38	Hammer Safety Block Pin
11	Grip Screws	25	Ratchet	39	Trigger Spring
12	Hammer Pivot Screw	26	Stirrup	40	Hammer Safety Block
13	Hammer	27	Stirrup Pivot Pin		
14	Hammer Pawl	28	Stirrup Plunger		

Duramatic Auto

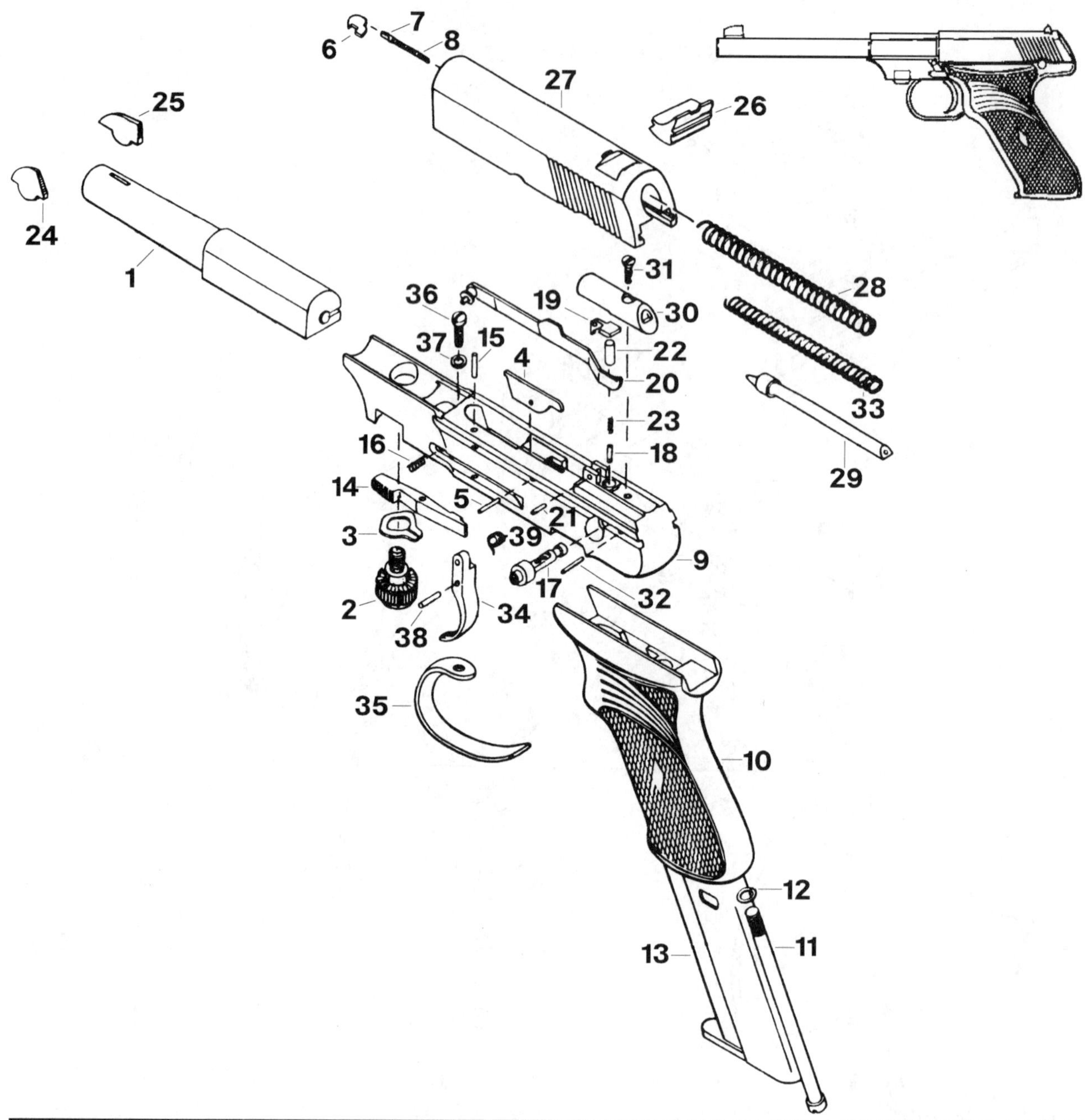

1 Barrel and Front Sight Assembly
2 Barrel Screw
3 Barrel Nut Lockwasher
4 Ejector
5 Ejector Pin
6 Extractor
7 Extractor Plunger
8 Extractor Spring
9 Frame
10 Grip
11 Grip Bolt
12 Grip Bolt Washer
13 Magazine Assembly
14 Magazine Catch
15 Magazine Catch Pin
16 Magazine Catch Spring
17 Safety
18 Safety Detent
19 Sear
20 Sear Bar and Trigger<R>Pull Pin Assembly
21 Sear Pin
22 Sear Plunger
23 Sear Spring
24 Front Sight, Short Barrel
25 Front Sight, Long Barrel
26 Rear Sight
27 Slide
28 Slide Spring
29 Striker
30 Striker Sleeve
31 Striker Sleeve Screw
32 Striker Sleeve Screw Locking Pin
33 Striker Spring
34 Trigger
35 Trigger Guard
36 Trigger Guard Screw
37 Trigger Guard Screw Lock Washer
38 Trigger Pin
39 Trigger Spring

Parts Not Shown

Magazine Button
Magazine Follower
Magazine Spring
Trigger Pull Pin

Mark I Sentinel Revolver

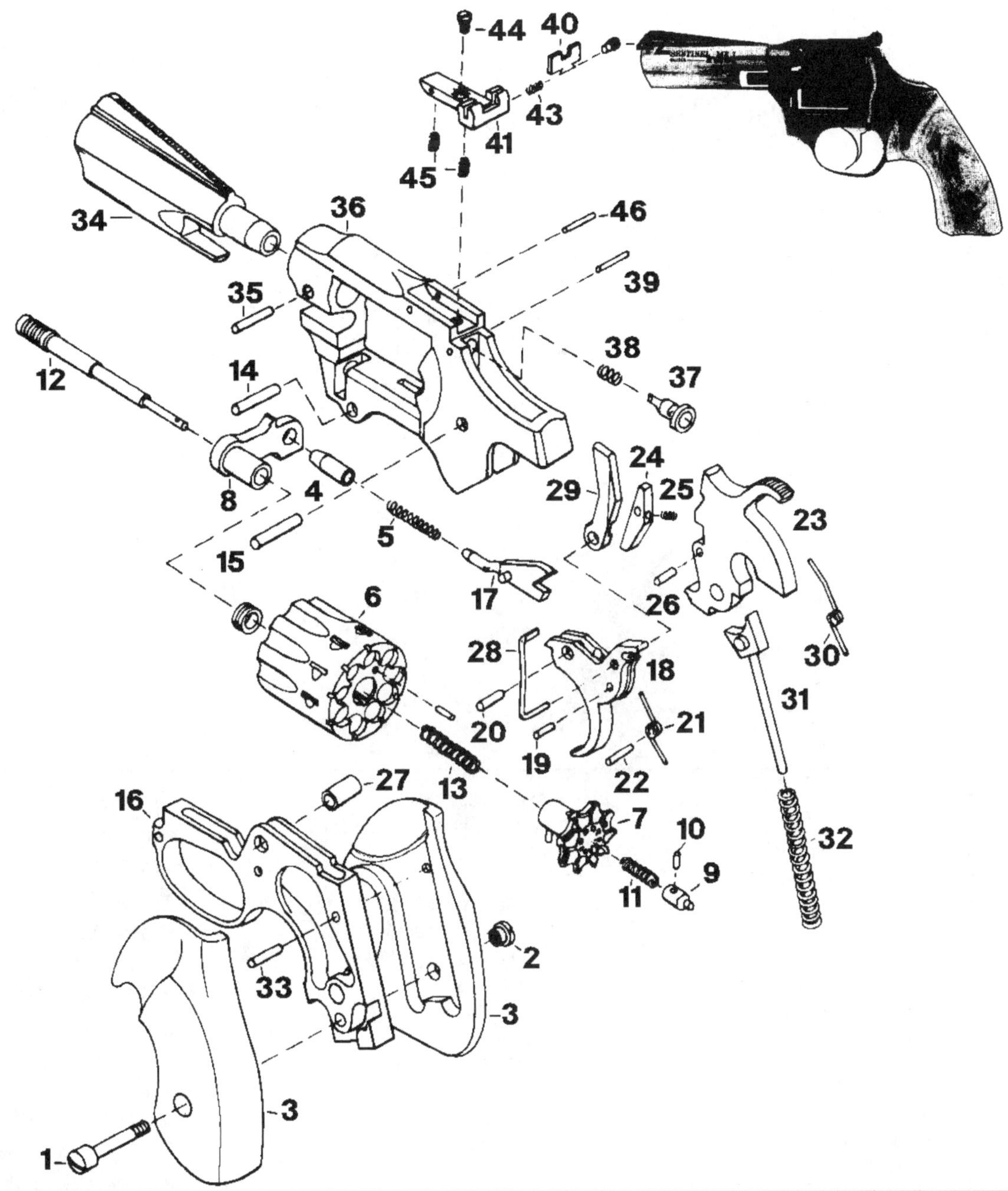

1	Grip Screw	**17**	Cylinder Stop Assembly	**33**	Grip Alignment Pin
2	Escutcheon Nut	**18**	Trigger	**34**	Barrel
3	Grips	**19**	Trigger Spring Contact Pin	**35**	Barrel Retention Pin
4	Link Pivot Pin	**20**	Trigger Pivot Pin	**36**	Frame
5	Cylinder Stop Spring	**21**	Trigger Spring	**37**	Firing Pin
6	Cylinder	**22**	Trigger Spring Returning Pin	**38**	Firing Pin Spring
7	Ejector	**23**	Hammer	**39**	Firing Pin Retention Pin
8	Crane Assembly	**24**	Hammer Pawl	**40**	Rear Sight Blade
9	Cylinder Lock Plunger	**25**	Hammer Pawl Spring	**41**	Rear Sight Base
10	Cylinder Lock Plunger Pin	**26**	Hammer Pawl Pin	**42**	Windage Screw
11	Cylinder Lock Plunger Spring	**27**	Hammer Sleeve	**43**	Windage Spring
12	Ejector Rod	**28**	Hammer Safety Stop	**44**	Elevation Screw
13	Ejector Rod Return Spring	**29**	Hand	**45**	Elevation Springs
14	Trigger Guard Assembly Pin	**30**	Hand Spring	**46**	Rear Sight Pin
15	Hammer Pivot Pin	**31**	Hammer Spring Guide Assembly		
16	Trigger Guard	**32**	Hammer Spring		

Military Model 107 Auto

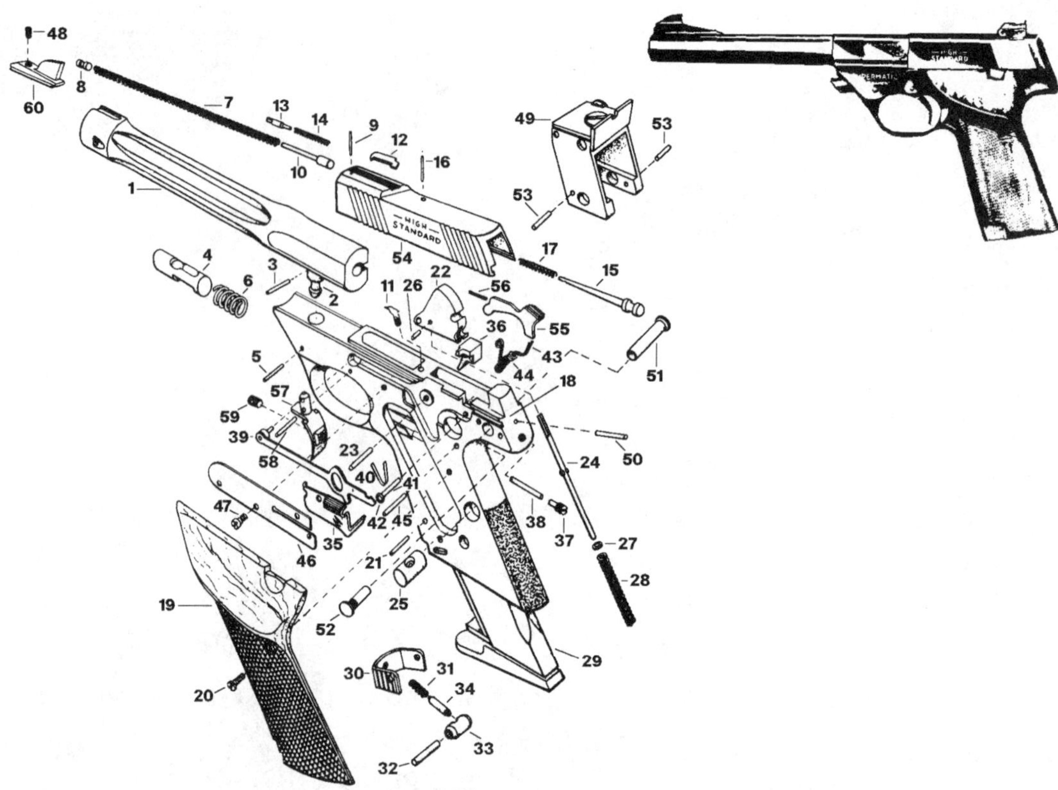

1 Barrel
2 Barrel Stud
3 Barrel Stud Retaining Pin
4 Barrel Takedown Plunger
5 Barrel Takedown Plunger Pin
6 Barrel Takedown Plunger Spring
7 Driving Spring
8 Driving Spring Plug
9 Driving Spring Plug Pin
10 Driving Spring Plunger
11 Ejector
12 Extractor
13 Extractor Plunger
14 Extractor Spring
15 Firing Pin
16 Firing Pin Retaining Pin
17 Firing Pin Spring
18 Frame
19 Grips
20 Grip Screw
21 Grip Alignment Pin
22 Hammer
23 Hammer Pin
24 Hammer Strut
25 Hammer Strut Anchor Pin
26 Hammer Strut Pin
27 Hammer Strut Washer
28 Hammer Spring
29 Magazine Assembly
30 Magazine Catch
31 Magazine Catch Spring
32 Magazine Catch Roller Pin
33 Magazine Catch Roller
34 Magazine Catch Spring Guide Pin
35 Safety
36 Sear
37 Sear Adjustment Screw
38 Sear Adjustment Screw Plunger
39 Sear Bar and Trigger Pull Pin Assembly
40 Sear Bar Spring
41 Sear Pin
42 Sear Pin Retaining Ring
43 Sear Spring
44 Sear Spring Leg Retainer
45 Sear Spring Pin
46 Sideplate
47 Sideplate Screw
48 Front Sight Screw
49 Rear Sight Adjustable Assembly
50 Rear Sight Base Frame Assembly Pins
51 Rear Sight Base Sleeve
52 Rear Sight Base Stud
53 Rear Sight Base Alignment Pins
54 Slide
55 Slide Lock Lever
56 Slide Lock Spring
57 Trigger
58 Trigger Pin
59 Trigger Stop Screw
60 Front Sight Assembly

Parts Not Shown

Barrel Weight
Barrel Filler Screws
Barrel Weight Lock Screws
Grip Screw Washer
Magazine Button
Magazine Follower
Magazine Spring
Rear Sight Base
Rear Sight Base Bracket
Rear Sight Cross Member
Rear Sight Elevation Adjustment Screw
Rear Sight Elevation Ball
Rear Sight Elevation Detent Plunger
Rear Sight Elevation Plunger
Rear Sight Elevation Spring
Rear Sight Leaf
Rear Sight Leaf Pivot Pin
Rear Sight Windage Screw
Rear Sight Retaining Pin
Rear Sight Windage Detent Plunger
Rear Sight Windage Detent Plunger Spring
Rear Sight Windage Spring
Slide Assembly
Weight
Weight Bracket

Model 100 and 101 Auto

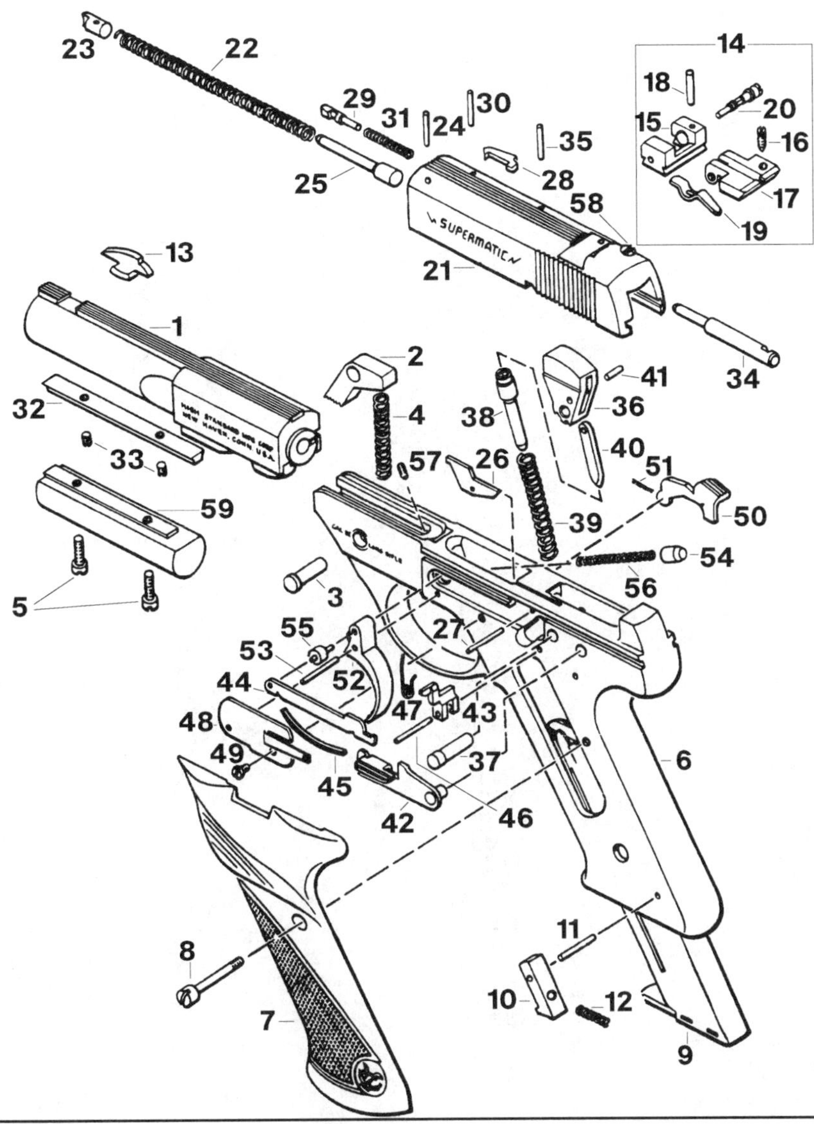

1	Barrel
2	Barrel Catch
3	Barrel Catch Pin
4	Barrel Catch Spring
5	Barrel Weight Screws
6	Frame
7	Grips
8	Grip Screw
9	Magazine
10	Magazine Catch
11	Magazine Catch Pin
12	Magazine Catch Spring
13	Front Sight
14	Rear Sight, Fixed
15	Rear Sight Base
16	Rear Sight Elevation Screw
17	Rear Sight Leaf
18	Rear Sight Retaining Pin
19	Rear Sight Spring
20	Rear Sight Windage Screw
21	Slide
22	Driving Spring
23	Driving Spring Plug
24	Driving Spring Plug Pin
25	Driving Spring Plunger
26	Ejector
27	Ejector Pin
28	Extractor
29	Extractor Plunger
30	Extractor Plunger Retaining Pin
31	Extractor Spring
32	Filler Plate
33	Filler Plate Screws
34	Firing Pin
35	Firing Pin Retaining Pin
36	Hammer
37	Hammer Pin
38	Hammer Plunger
39	Hammer Spring
40	Hammer Strut
41	Hammer Strut Pin
42	Safety-Lever
43	Sear
44	Sear Bar
45	Sear Bar Spring
46	Sear Pin
47	Sear Spring
48	Sideplate
49	Sideplate Screw
50	Slide Lock Lever
51	Slide Lock Spring
52	Trigger
53	Trigger Pin
54	Trigger Plunger
55	Trigger Pull Pin
56	Trigger Spring
57	Trigger Stop Screw
58	Wear Plug
59	Barrel Weight

Parts Not Shown

Grip Screw Nut
Grip Escutcheon
Magazine Button

Model 104 Super Citation Auto

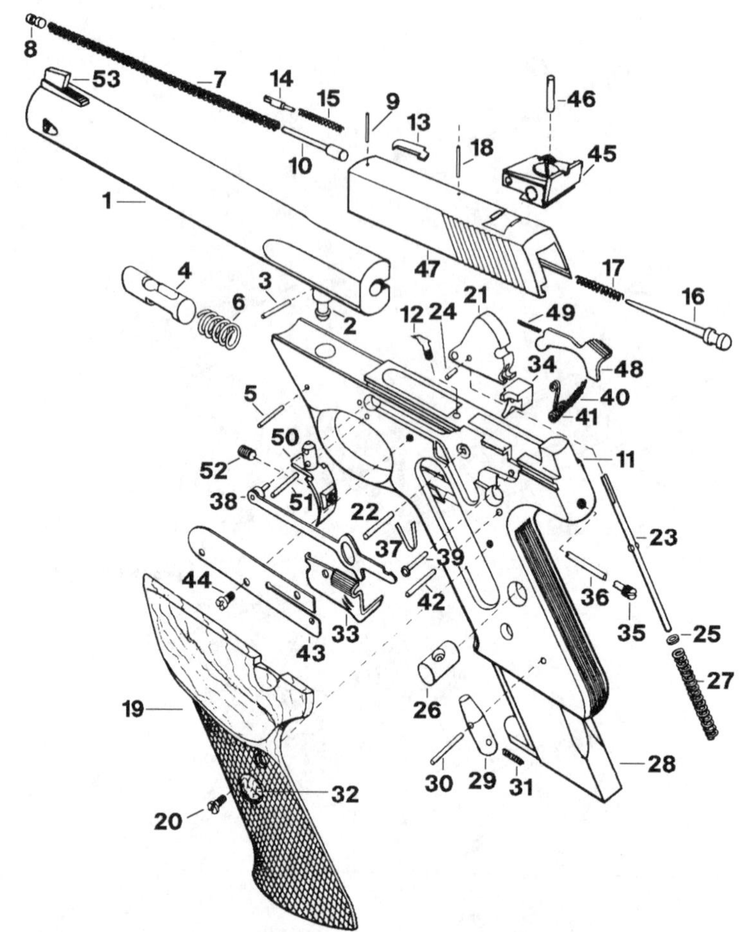

1	Barrel	**29**	Magazine Catch	Barrel Weight
2	Barrel Stud	**30**	Magazine Catch Pin	Barrel Weight Lock Screws
3	Barrel Stud Pin	**31**	Magazine Catch Spring	Grip Screw Washers
4	Barrel Takedown Plunger	**32**	Medallion	Magazine Button
5	Barrel Takedown Plunger Pin	**33**	Safety	Magazine Follower
6	Barrel Takedown Plunger Spring	**34**	Sear	Magazine Spring
7	Driving Spring	**35**	Sear Adjustment Screw	Front Sight Screw
8	Driving Spring Plug	**36**	Sear Adjustment Screw Plunger	Rear Sight Base
9	Driving Spring Plug Pin	**37**	Sear Bar Spring	Rear Sight Cross Member
10	Driving Spring Plunger	**38**	Sear Bar and Trigger Pull Pin Assembly	Rear Sight Elevation Screw
11	Frame	**39**	Sear Pin	Rear Sight Elevation Ball
12	Ejector	**40**	Sear Spring Leg Retainer	Rear Sight Elevation Detent Plunger
13	Extractor	**41**	Adjustable Sear Spring	Rear Sight Elevation Spring
14	Extractor Plunger	**42**	Sear Spring Pin	Rear Sight Leaf
15	Extractor Spring	**43**	Sideplate	Rear Sight Leaf Pivot Pin
16	Firing Pin	**44**	Sideplate Screw	Rear Sight Windage Screw
17	Firing Pin Spring	**45**	Adjustable Rear Sight	Rear Sight Windage Detent Plunger Spring
18	Firing Pin Retaining Pin	**46**	Rear Sight Retaining Pin	Rear Sight Windage Spring
19	Grips	**47**	Slide	Weight Bracket
20	Grip Screws	**48**	Slide Lock Lever	Weight
21	Hammer	**49**	Slide Lock Spring	Weight Screw
22	Hammer Pin	**50**	Trigger	
23	Hammer Strut	**51**	Trigger Pin	
24	Hammer Strut Pin	**52**	Trigger Stop Screw	
25	Hammer Strut Ring	**53**	Front Sight	
26	Hammer Strut Anchor Pin	**Parts Not Shown**		
27	Hammer Spring		Barrel Filler Screws	
28	Magazine Assembly			

Model HB Auto

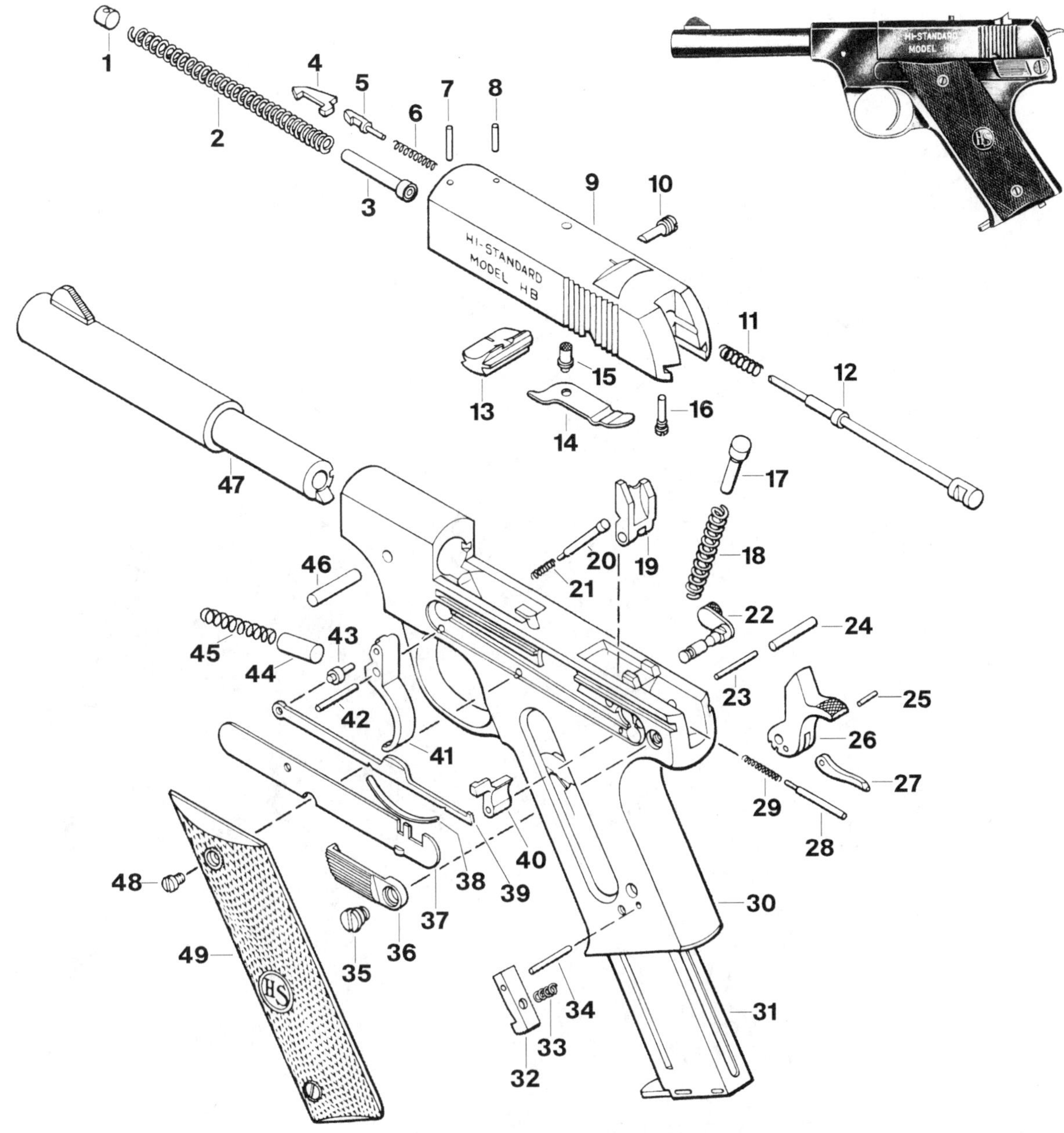

1	Recoil Spring Stop	18	Mainspring	35	Safety Catch Screw
2	Recoil Spring	19	Slide Stop	36	Safety Catch
3	Recoil Spring Guide	20	Slide Stop Plunger	37	Sideplate
4	Extractor	21	Slide Stop Spring	38	Trigger Bar Spring
5	Extractor Plunger	22	Takedown Latch	39	Trigger Bar
6	Extractor Spring	23	Sear Pin	40	Sear
7	Recoil Spring Stop Pin	24	Hammer Pin	41	Trigger
8	Extractor Pin	25	Hammer Strut Pin	42	Trigger Pin
9	Slide	26	Hammer	43	Pull Pin
10	Assembly Lock Screw	27	Hammer Strut	44	Trigger Spring Plunger
11	Firing Pin Spring	28	Sear Plunger	45	Trigger Spring
12	Firing Pin	29	Sear Spring	46	Barrel Pin
13	Rear Sight	30	Frame	47	Barrel
14	Assembly Lock Plunger	31	Magazine Assembly	48	Grip Screws
15	Assembly Lock	32	Magazine Catch	49	Grip, Left
16	Firing Pin Retaining Screw	33	Magazine Catch Spring		
17	Mainspring Guide	34	Magazine Catch Pin		

Model R-101 Revolver

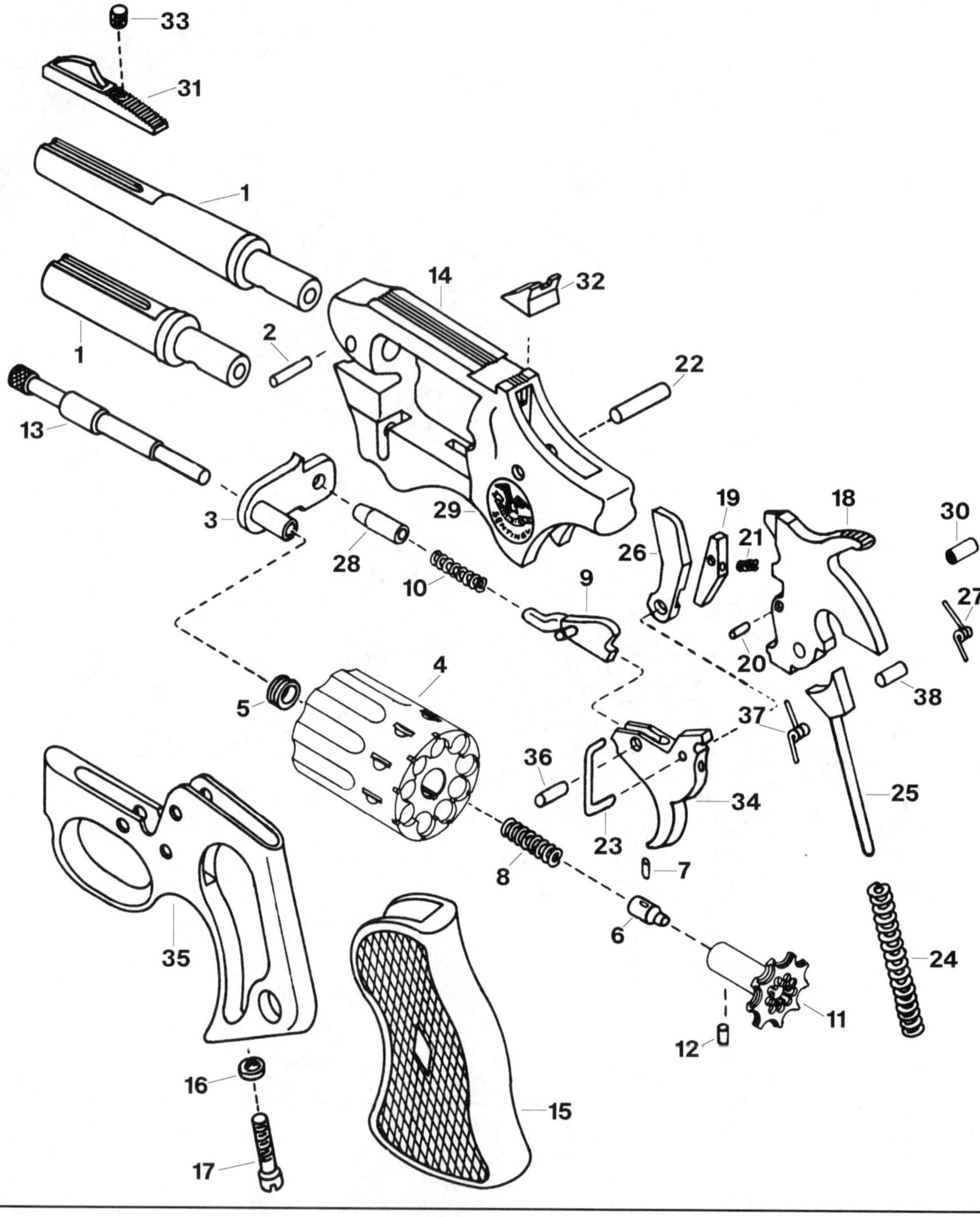

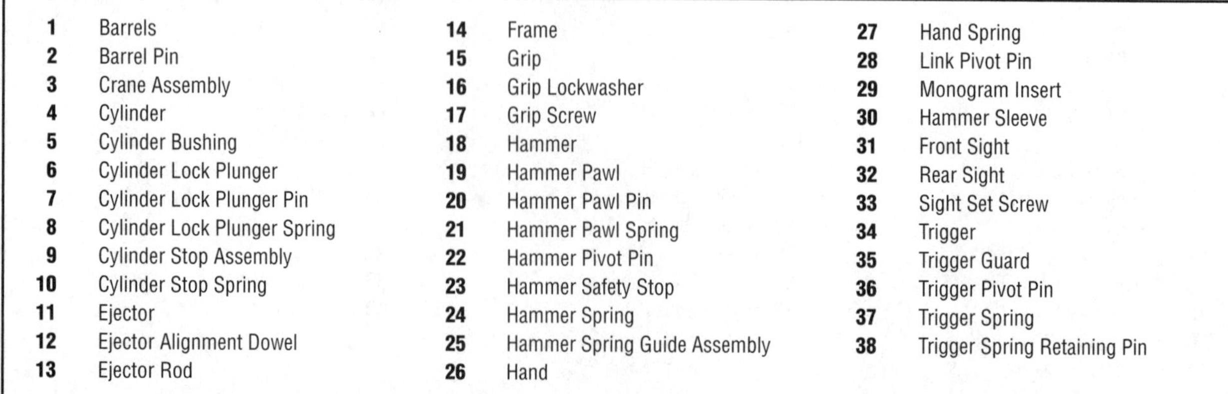

No.	Part	No.	Part	No.	Part
1	Barrels	**14**	Frame	**27**	Hand Spring
2	Barrel Pin	**15**	Grip	**28**	Link Pivot Pin
3	Crane Assembly	**16**	Grip Lockwasher	**29**	Monogram Insert
4	Cylinder	**17**	Grip Screw	**30**	Hammer Sleeve
5	Cylinder Bushing	**18**	Hammer	**31**	Front Sight
6	Cylinder Lock Plunger	**19**	Hammer Pawl	**32**	Rear Sight
7	Cylinder Lock Plunger Pin	**20**	Hammer Pawl Pin	**33**	Sight Set Screw
8	Cylinder Lock Plunger Spring	**21**	Hammer Pawl Spring	**34**	Trigger
9	Cylinder Stop Assembly	**22**	Hammer Pivot Pin	**35**	Trigger Guard
10	Cylinder Stop Spring	**23**	Hammer Safety Stop	**36**	Trigger Pivot Pin
11	Ejector	**24**	Hammer Spring	**37**	Trigger Spring
12	Ejector Alignment Dowel	**25**	Hammer Spring Guide Assembly	**38**	Trigger Spring Retaining Pin
13	Ejector Rod	**26**	Hand		

Model R-108 Revolver

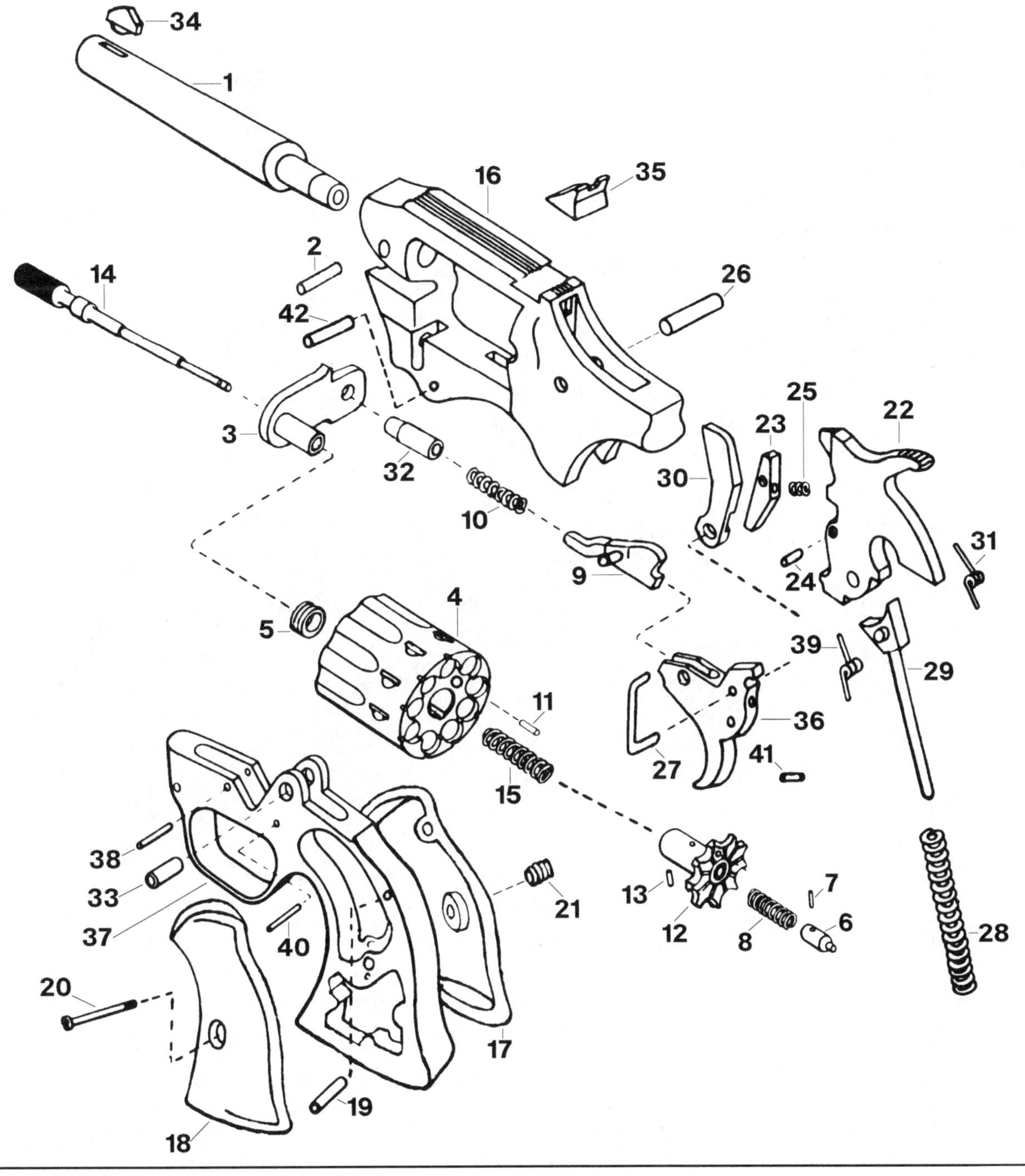

1	Barrel	15	Ejector Rod Return Spring	29	Hammer Spring Guide Assembly
2	Barrel Pin	16	Frame	30	Hand
3	Crane Assembly	17	Grip, Right	31	Hand Spring
4	Cylinder	18	Grip, Left	32	Link Pivot Pin
5	Cylinder Bushing	19	Grip Alignment Pin	33	Hammer Sleeve
6	Cylinder Lock Plunger	20	Grip Screw	34	Sight, Front
7	Cylinder Lock Plunger Pin	21	Grip Escutcheon Nut	35	Sight, Rear
8	Cylinder Lock Plunger Spring	22	Hammer	36	Trigger
9	Cylinder Stop Assembly	23	Hammer Pawl	37	Trigger Guard
10	Cylinder Stop Spring	24	Hammer Pawl Pin	38	Trigger Pivot Pin
11	Cylinder Ejector Alignment Pin	25	Hammer Pawl Spring	39	Trigger Spring
12	Ejector	26	Hammer Pivot Pin	40	Trigger Spring Retaining Pin
13	Ejector Alignment Dowel	27	Hammer Safety Stop	41	Trigger Spring Contact Pin
14	Ejector Rod	28	Hammer Spring	42	Trigger Guard Assembly Pin

Model W-102 and Model W-103 Revolver

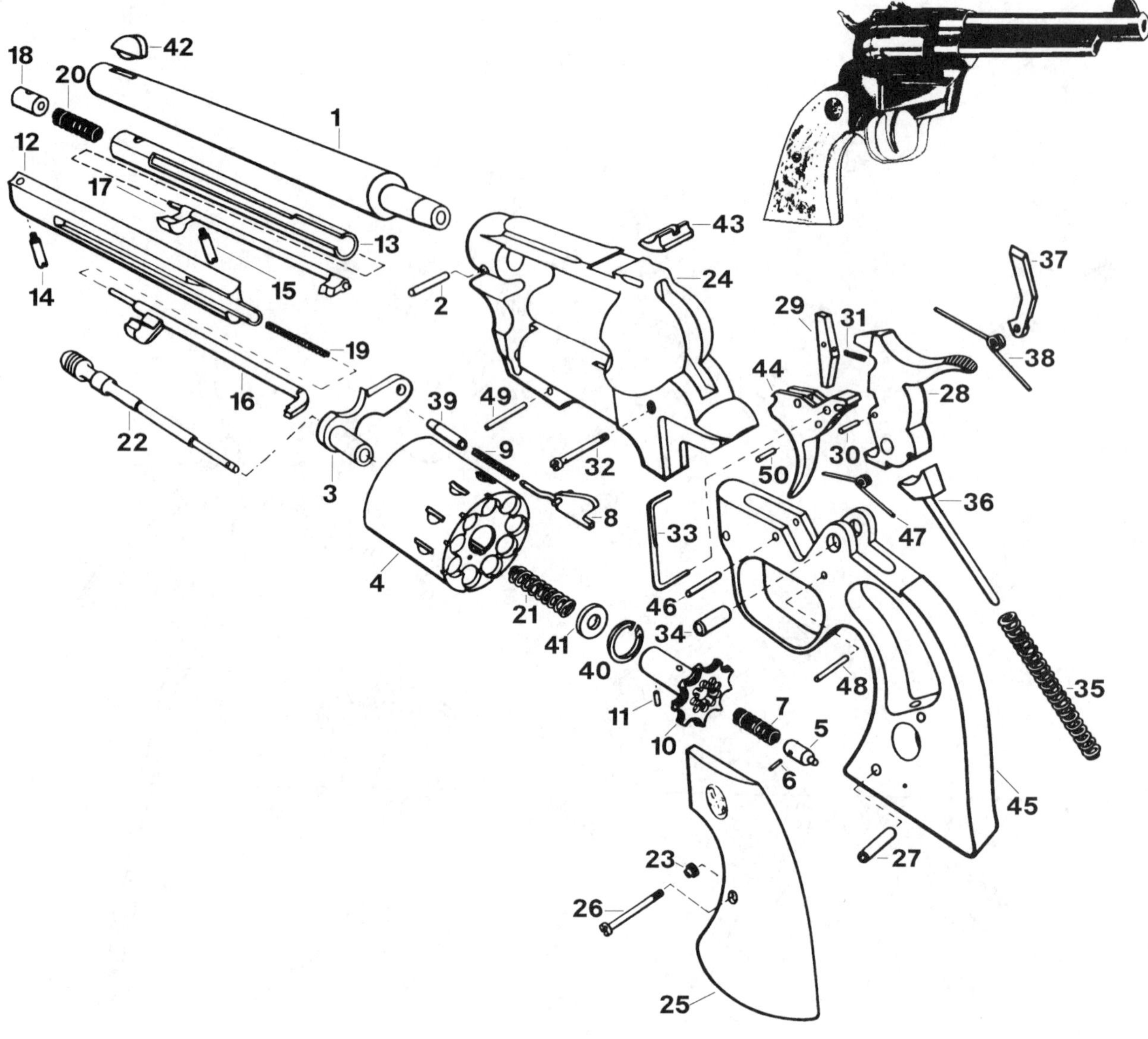

1	Barrel	**16**	Ejector Latch Rod Assembly (Model W-102)	**32**	Hammer Pivot Screw
2	Barrel Pin	**17**	Ejector Latch Rod Assembly (Model W-103)	**33**	Hammer Safety Stop
3	Crane Assembly	**18**	Ejector Latch Housing Plug	**34**	Hammer Sleeve
4	Cylinder	**19**	Ejector Latch Rod Spring (Model W-102)	**35**	Hammer Spring
5	Cylinder Lock Plunger	**20**	Ejector Latch Rod Spring (Model W-103)	**36**	Hammer Spring Guide Head Assembly
6	Cylinder Lock Plunger Pin	**21**	Ejector Rod Return Spring	**37**	Hand
7	Cylinder Lock Plunger Spring	**22**	Ejector Rod	**38**	Hand Spring
8	Cylinder Stop Assembly	**23**	Escutcheon Nut	**39**	Link Pivot Pin
9	Cylinder Stop Spring	**24**	Frame	**40**	Retaining Ring
10	Ejector	**25**	Grips	**41**	Return Spring Washer
11	Ejector Alignment Dowel	**26**	Grip Screw	**42**	Front Sight
12	Ejector Latch Housing (Model W-102)	**27**	Grip Alignment Pin	**43**	Rear Sight
13	Ejector Latch Housing (Model W-103)	**28**	Hammer	**44**	Trigger
14	Ejector Latch Housing Screw (Model W-102)	**29**	Hammer Pawl	**45**	Trigger Guard
15	Ejector Latch Housing Screw (Model W-103)	**30**	Hammer Pawl Pin	**46**	Trigger Pivot Pin
		31	Hammer Pawl Spring	**47**	Trigger Spring
				48	Trigger Spring Retaining Pin
				49	Trigger Guard Assembly Pin
				50	Trigger Spring Contact Pin

Model W-104 and Model W-105 Revolver

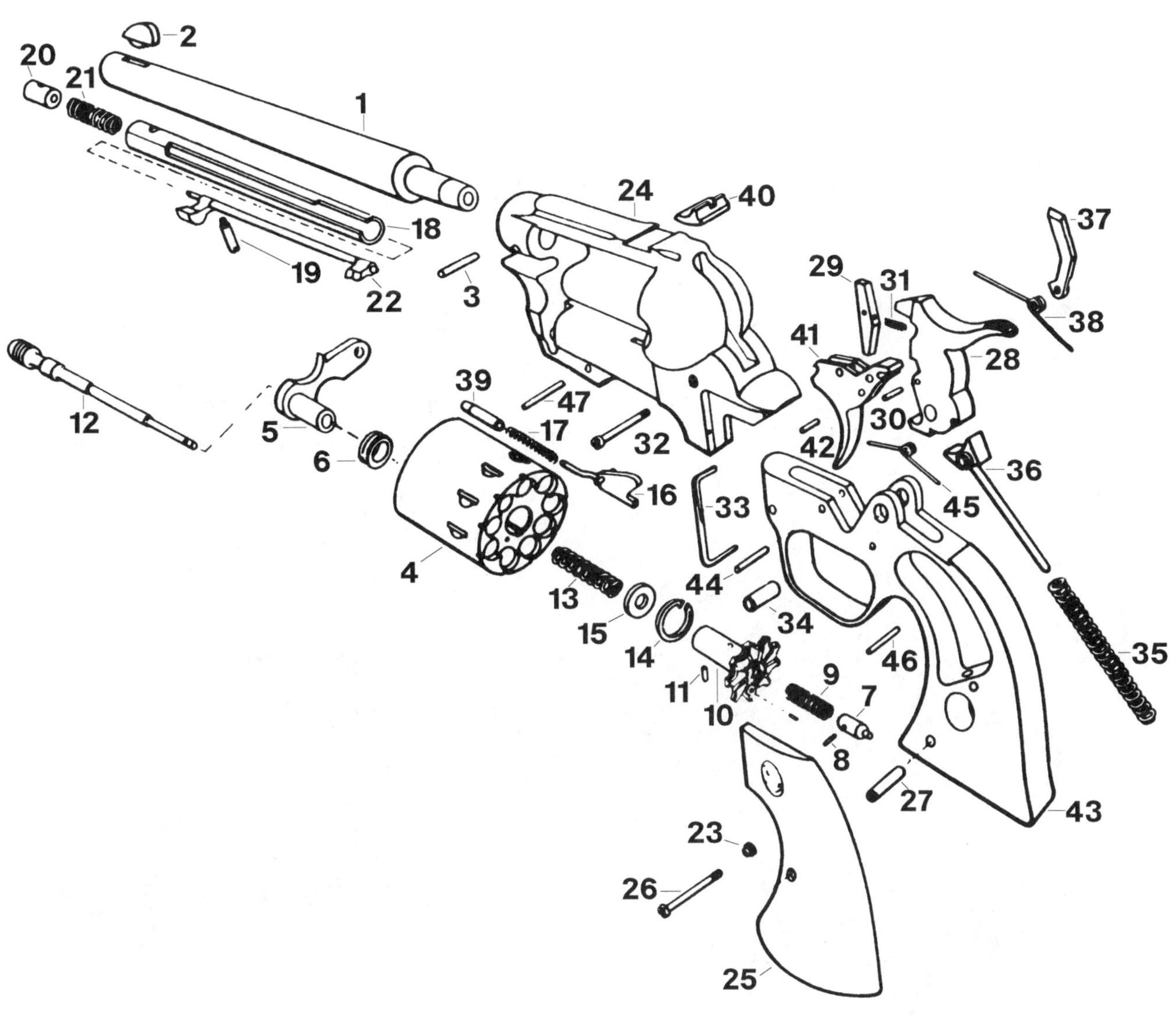

1	Barrel	17	Cylinder Stop Spring	33	Hammer Safety Stop
2	Front Sight	18	Ejector Latch Housing	34	Hammer Sleeve
3	Barrel Pin	19	Ejector Latch Housing Screw	35	Hammer Spring
4	Cylinder	20	Ejector Latch Housing Plug	36	Hammer Spring Guide Head Assembly
5	Crane Assembly	21	Ejector Latch Rod Spring	37	Hand
6	Cylinder Bushing	22	Ejector Latch Rod Assembly	38	Hand Spring
7	Cylinder Lock Plunger	23	Escutcheon Nut	39	Link Pivot Pin
8	Cylinder Lock Plunger Pin	24	Frame	40	Rear Sight
9	Cylinder Lock Plunger Spring	25	Grips	41	Trigger
10	Ejector	26	Grip Screw	42	Trigger Spring Contact Pin
11	Ejector Alignment Dowel	27	Grip Alignment Pin	43	Trigger Guard
12	Ejector Rod	28	Hammer	44	Trigger Pivot Pin
13	Ejector Rod Return Spring	29	Hammer Pawl	45	Trigger Spring
14	Retaining Ring	30	Hammer Pawl Pin	46	Trigger Spring Retaining Pin
15	Return Spring Washer	31	Hammer Pawl Spring	47	Trigger Guard Assembly Pin
16	Cylinder Stop Assembly	32	Hammer Pivot Screw		

Sentinel Deluxe Revolver

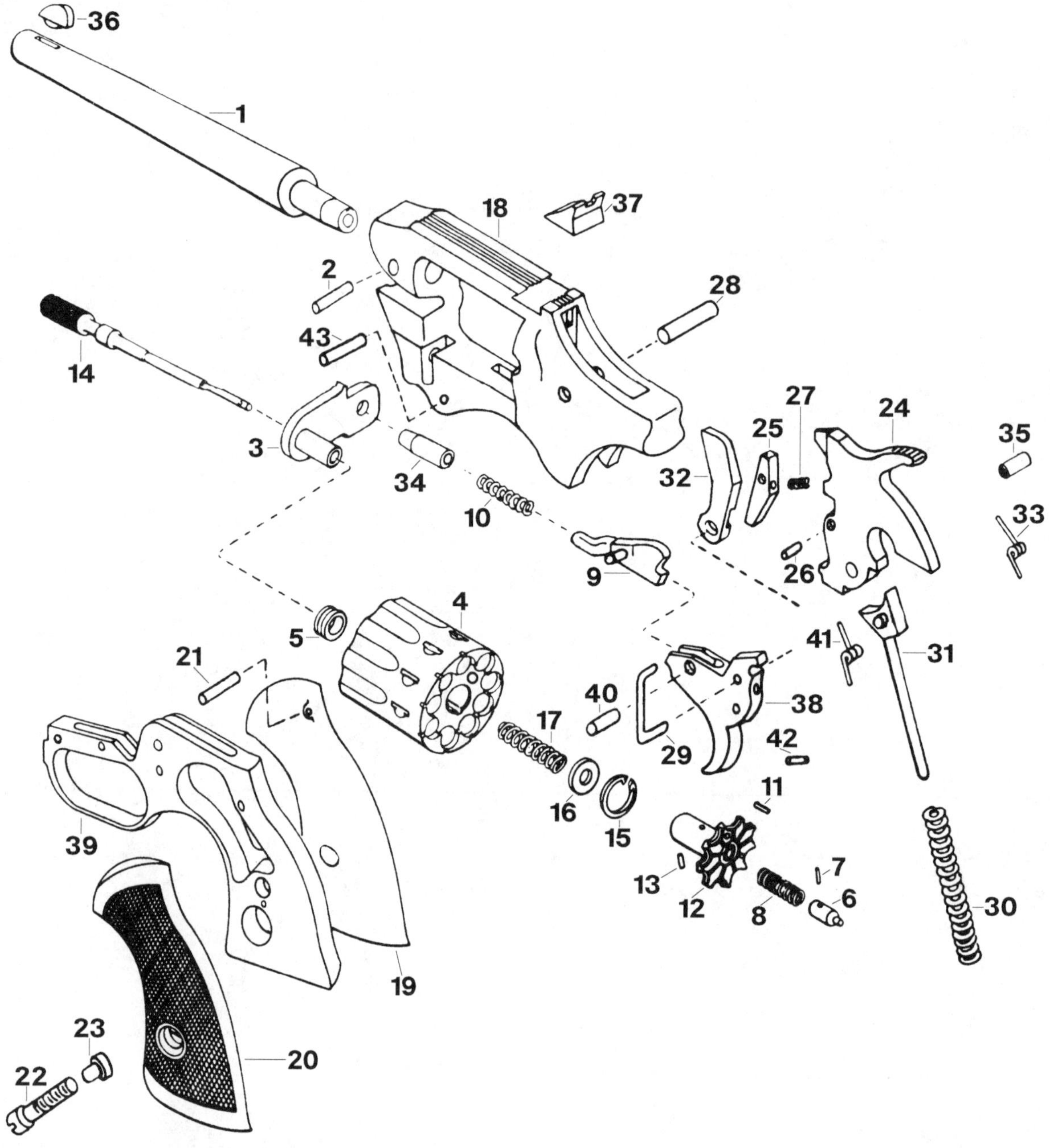

1	Barrel	**16**	Ejector Rod Return Spring Washer	**31**	Hammer Spring Guide Assembly
2	Barrel Pin	**17**	Ejector Rod Return Spring	**32**	Hand
3	Crane Assembly	**18**	Frame	**33**	Hand Spring
4	Cylinder	**19**	Grip, Right	**34**	Link Pivot Pin
5	Cylinder Bushing	**20**	Grip, Left	**35**	Hammer Sleeve
6	Cylinder Lock Plunger	**21**	Grip Alignment Pin	**36**	Front Sight
7	Cylinder Lock Plunger Pin	**22**	Grip Screw	**37**	Rear Sight
8	Cylinder Lock Plunger Spring	**23**	Grip Escutcheon Nut	**38**	Trigger
9	Cylinder Stop Assembly	**24**	Hammer	**39**	Trigger Guard
10	Cylinder Stop Spring	**25**	Hammer Pawl	**40**	Trigger Pivot Pin
11	Cylinder Ejector Alignment Pin	**26**	Hammer Pawl Pin	**41**	Trigger Spring
12	Ejector	**27**	Hammer Pawl Spring	**42**	Trigger Spring Contact Pin
13	Ejector Alignment Dowel	**28**	Hammer Pivot Pin	**43**	Trigger Guard Assembly Pin
14	Ejector Rod	**29**	Hammer Safety Stop	**Parts Not Shown**	
15	Ejector Rod Retaining Ring	**30**	Hammer Spring		Trigger Spring Retaining Pin

Sport King Auto

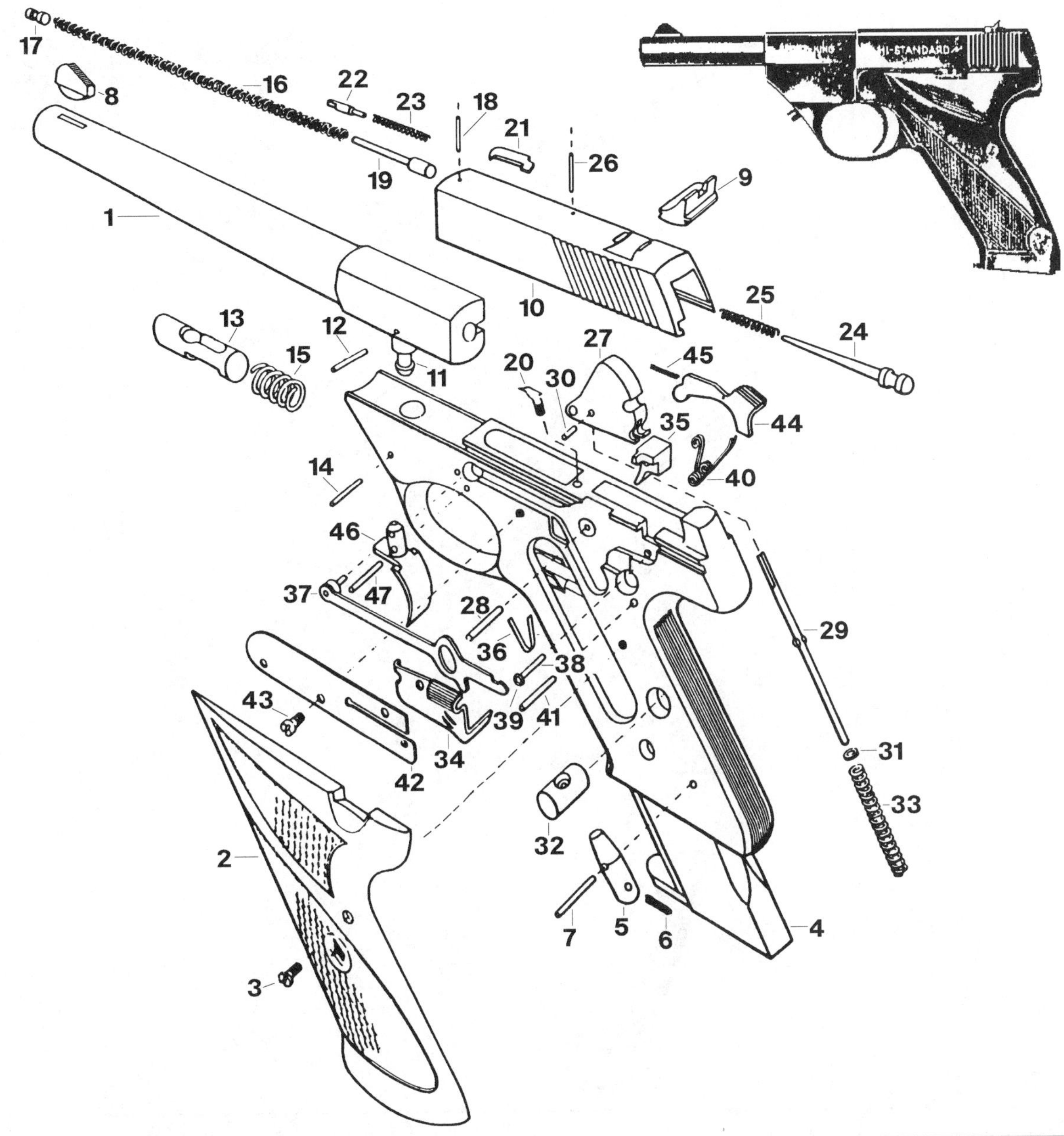

1	Barrel	**19**	Driving Spring Plunger	**37**	Sear Bar and Trigger Pull Pin Assembly
2	Grips	**20**	Ejector	**38**	Sear Pin
3	Grip Screw	**21**	Extractor	**39**	Sear Pin Retaining Ring
4	Magazine	**22**	Extractor Plunger	**40**	Sear Spring
5	Magazine Catch	**23**	Extractor Spring	**41**	Sear Spring Pin
6	Magazine Catch Spring	**24**	Firing Pin	**42**	Slideplate
7	Magazine Catch Pin	**25**	Firing Pin Spring	**43**	Slideplate Screw
8	Front Sight	**26**	Firing Pin Retaining Pin	**44**	Slide Lock Lever
9	Rear Sight	**27**	Hammer	**45**	Slide Lock Spring
10	Slide	**28**	Hammer Pin	**46**	Trigger
11	Barrel Stud	**29**	Hammer Strut	**47**	Trigger Pin
12	Barrel Stud Pin	**30**	Hammer Strut Pin	**Parts Not Shown**	
13	Barrel Takedown Plunger	**31**	Hammer Strut Ring		Magazine Button
14	Barrel Takedown Plunger Pin	**32**	Hammer Strut Anchor Pin		Magazine Follower
15	Barrel Takedown Plunger Spring	**33**	Hammer Spring		Magazine Spring
16	Driving Spring	**34**	Safety		Medallion
17	Driving Spring Plug	**35**	Sear		
18	Driving Spring Plug Pin	**36**	Sear Bar Spring		

Supermatic Auto

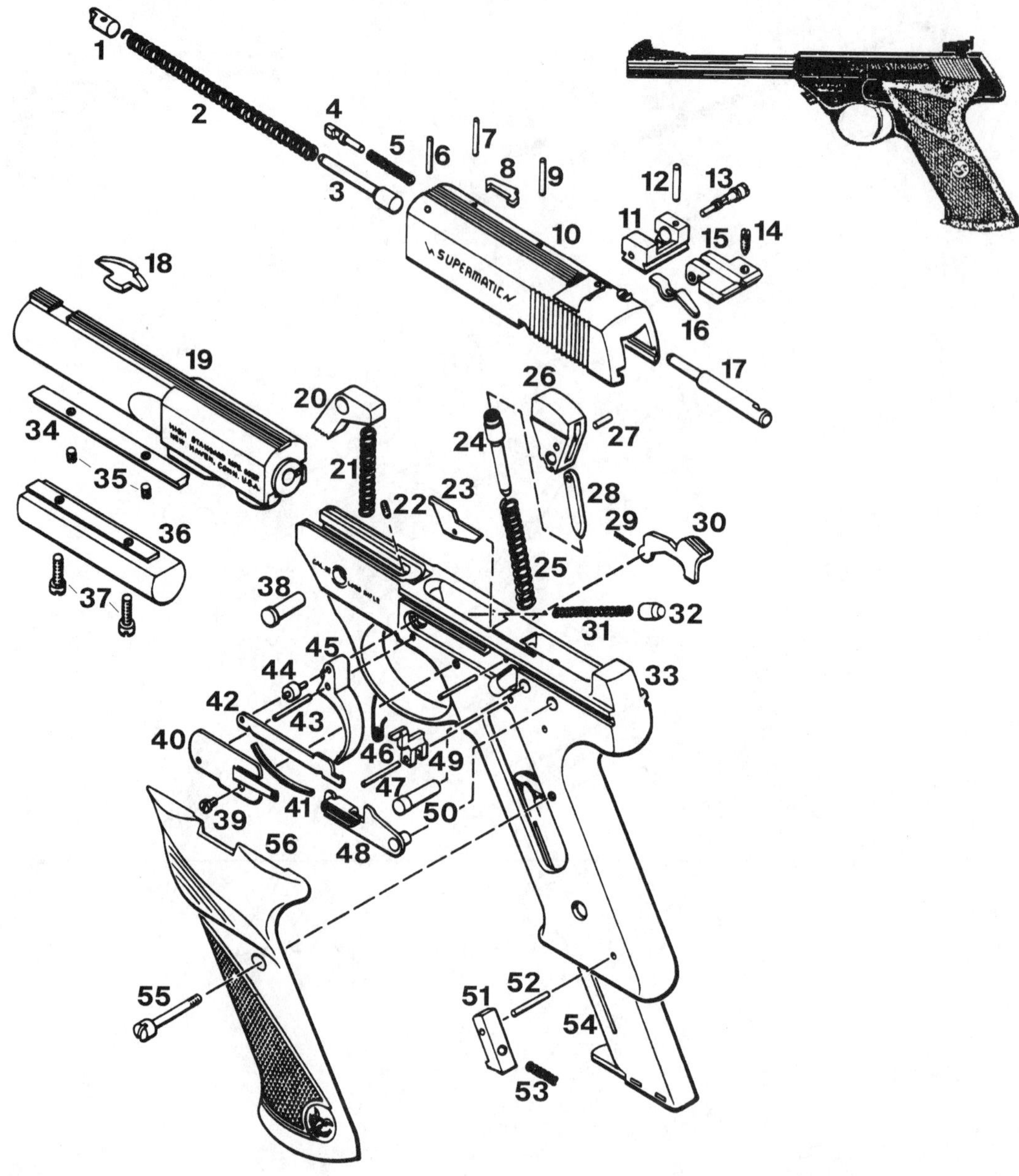

1	Driving Spring Plug	20	Takedown Plunger	39	Sideplate Screw
2	Driving Spring	21	Takedown Plunger Spring	40	Sideplate
3	Driving Spring Plunger	22	Trigger Stop Adjusting Screw	41	Trigger Bar Spring
4	Extractor Plunger	23	Ejector	42	Sear Bar
5	Extractor Spring	24	Hammer Spring Plunger	43	Trigger Pin
6	Driving Spring Plug Pin	25	Hammer Spring	44	Trigger Bar Stud
7	Extractor Limit Pin	26	Hammer	45	Trigger
8	Extractor	27	Hammer Strut Pin	46	Sear Spring
9	Firing Pin Retaining Pin	28	Hammer Strut	47	Sear Pin
10	Slide	29	Slide Stop Spring	48	Safety
11	Rear Sight Base	30	Slide Stop	49	Sear
12	Rear Sight Pin	31	Trigger Spring	50	Hammer Pivot
13	Windage Adjustment Screw	32	Trigger Spring Plunger	51	Magazine Catch
14	Elevation Adjustment Screw	33	Frame	52	Magazine Catch Pin
15	Rear Sight Blade	34	Weight Bracket	53	Magazine Catch Spring
16	Rear Sight Tension Spring	35	Bracket Screws	54	Magazine
17	Firing Pin	36	Barrel Weight	55	Grip Screw
18	Front Sight	37	Barrel Weight Screws	56	Grip Panel
19	Barrel	38	Takedown Plunger Pin		

Takedown Model Auto

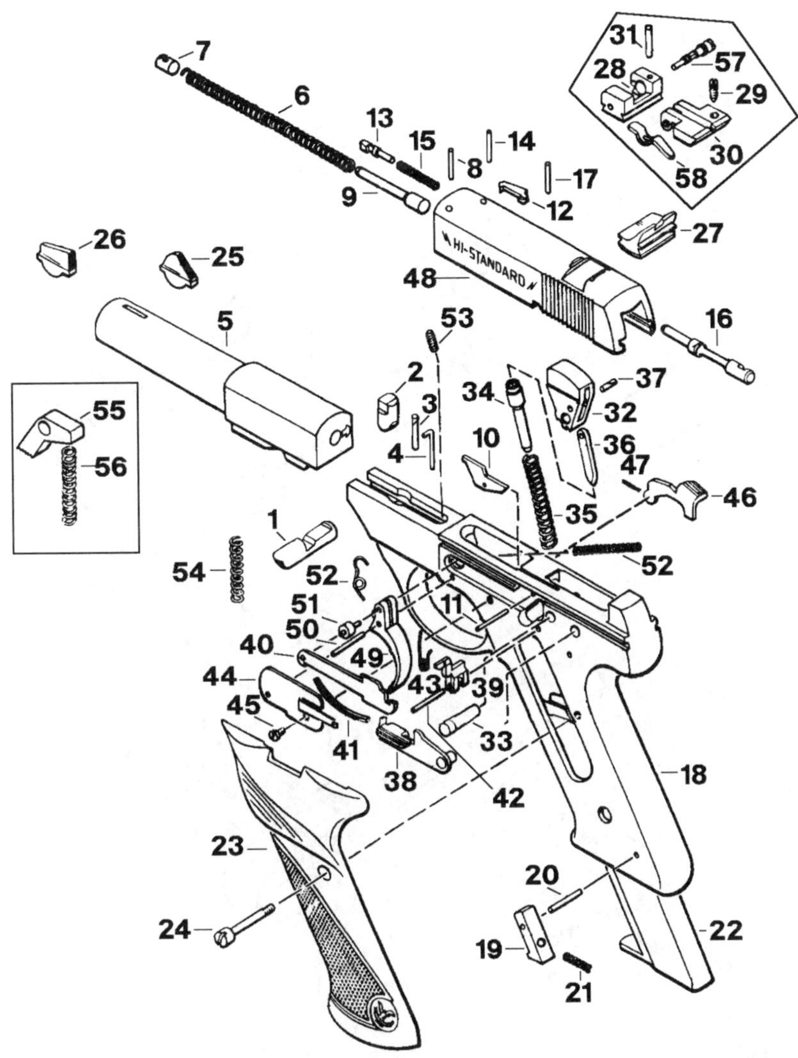

1	Barrel Plunger Cam	**25**	Front Sight (4 1/2" barrel)	**49**	Trigger
2	Barrel Lock	**26**	Front Sight (6 3/4" barrel)	**50**	Trigger Pin
3	Barrel Lock Pin	**27**	Rear Sight, Fixed	**51**	Trigger Pull Pin
4	Barrel Lock Retaining Pin	**28**	Rear Sight Base	**52**	Trigger Springs
5	Barrel	**29**	Rear Sight Elevation Screw	**53**	Trigger Stop Screw
6	Driving Spring	**30**	Rear Sight Leaf	**54**	Takedown Plunger Spring
7	Driving Spring Plug	**31**	Rear Sight Retaining Pin	**55**	Barrel Lock (Alternate Model)
8	Driving Spring Plug Pin	**32**	Hammer	**56**	Barrel Lock Spring (Alternate Model)
9	Driving Spring Plunger	**33**	Hammer Pin	**57**	Rear Sight Windage Screw
10	Ejector	**34**	Hammer Plunger	**58**	Rear Sight Elevation Spring
11	Ejector Pin	**35**	Hammer Spring		**Parts Not Shown**
12	Extractor	**36**	Hammer Strut		Magazine Button
13	Extractor Plunger	**37**	Hammer Strut Pin		Magazine Follower
14	Extractor Plunger Retaining Pin	**38**	Safety-Lever		Magazine Spring
15	Extractor Spring	**39**	Sear		Grip Screw Nut
16	Firing Pin	**40**	Sear Bar		Grip Escutcheon
17	Firing Pin Retaining Pin	**41**	Sear Bar Spring		Front Sight Set-Screw
18	Frame	**42**	Sear Pin		Firing Pin Sleeve
19	Magazine Catch	**43**	Sear Spring		Wear Plug
20	Magazine Catch Pin	**44**	Sideplate		
21	Magazinc Catch Spring	**45**	Sideplate Screw		
22	Magazine	**46**	Sidelock Lever		
23	Grip	**47**	Sidelock Spring		
24	Grip Screw	**48**	Slide		

Model P-37 Auto

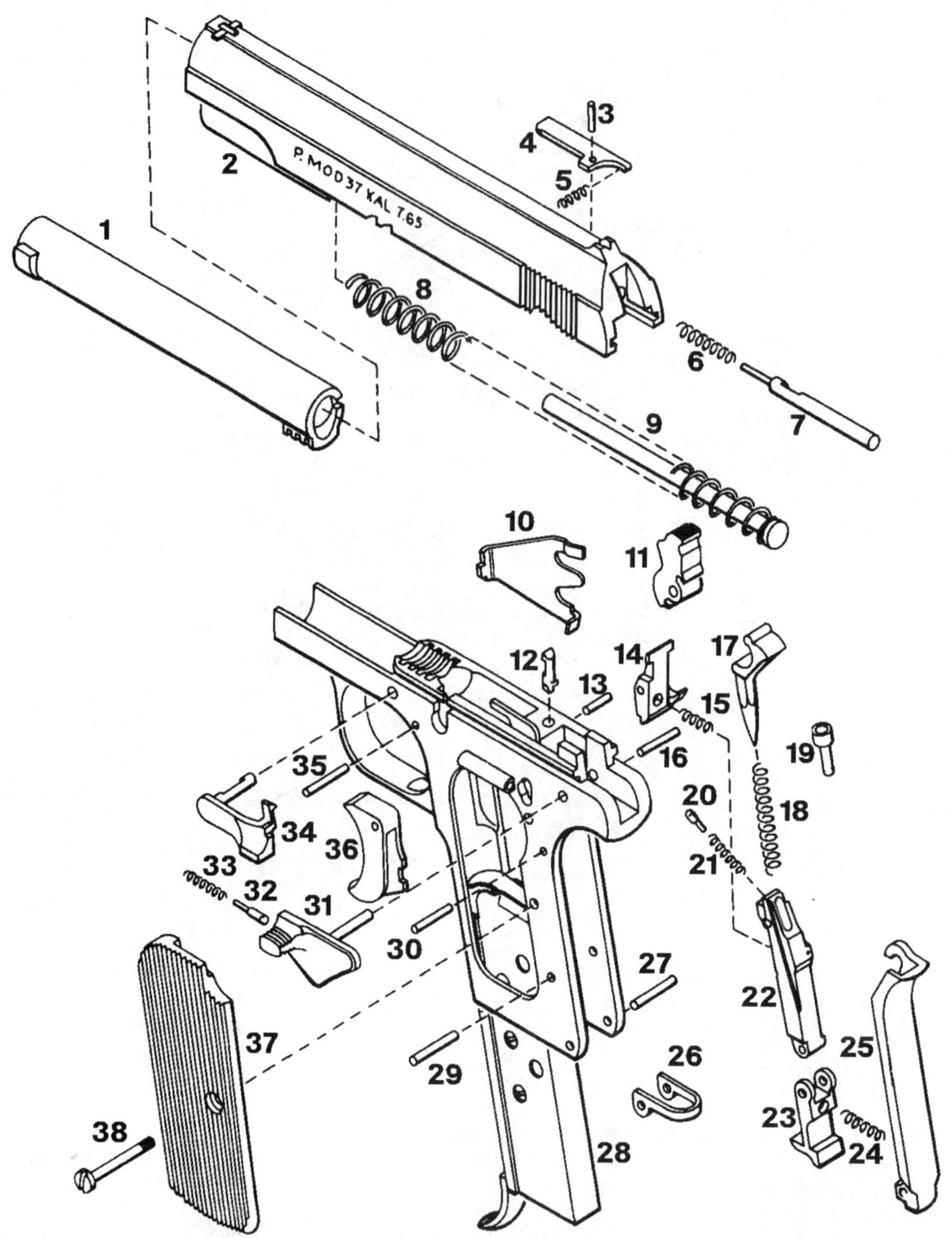

1	Barrel	14	Sear	27	Lanyard Loop Pin
2	Slide	15	Sear Spring	28	Magazine
3	Extractor Pin	16	Hammer Pin	29	Magazine Catch Pin
4	Extractor	17	Hammer Strut	30	Housing Retaining Pin
5	Extractor Spring	18	Hammer Spring	31	Thumb Safety
6	Firing Pin Spring	19	Hammer Spring Follower	32	Safety Detent
7	Firing Pin	20	Trigger Spring Follower	33	Safety Detent Spring
8	Recoil Spring	21	Trigger Spring	34	Slide Stop
9	Recoil Spring Guide	22	Hammer Spring Housing	35	Trigger Hinge Pin
10	Trigger Bar	23	Magazine Latch	36	Trigger
11	Hammer	24	Magazine Latch Spring	37	Grip Panel
12	Disconnector	25	Grip Safety	38	Grip Screw
13	Disconnector and Ejector Pin	26	Lanyard Loop		

Javelina Auto

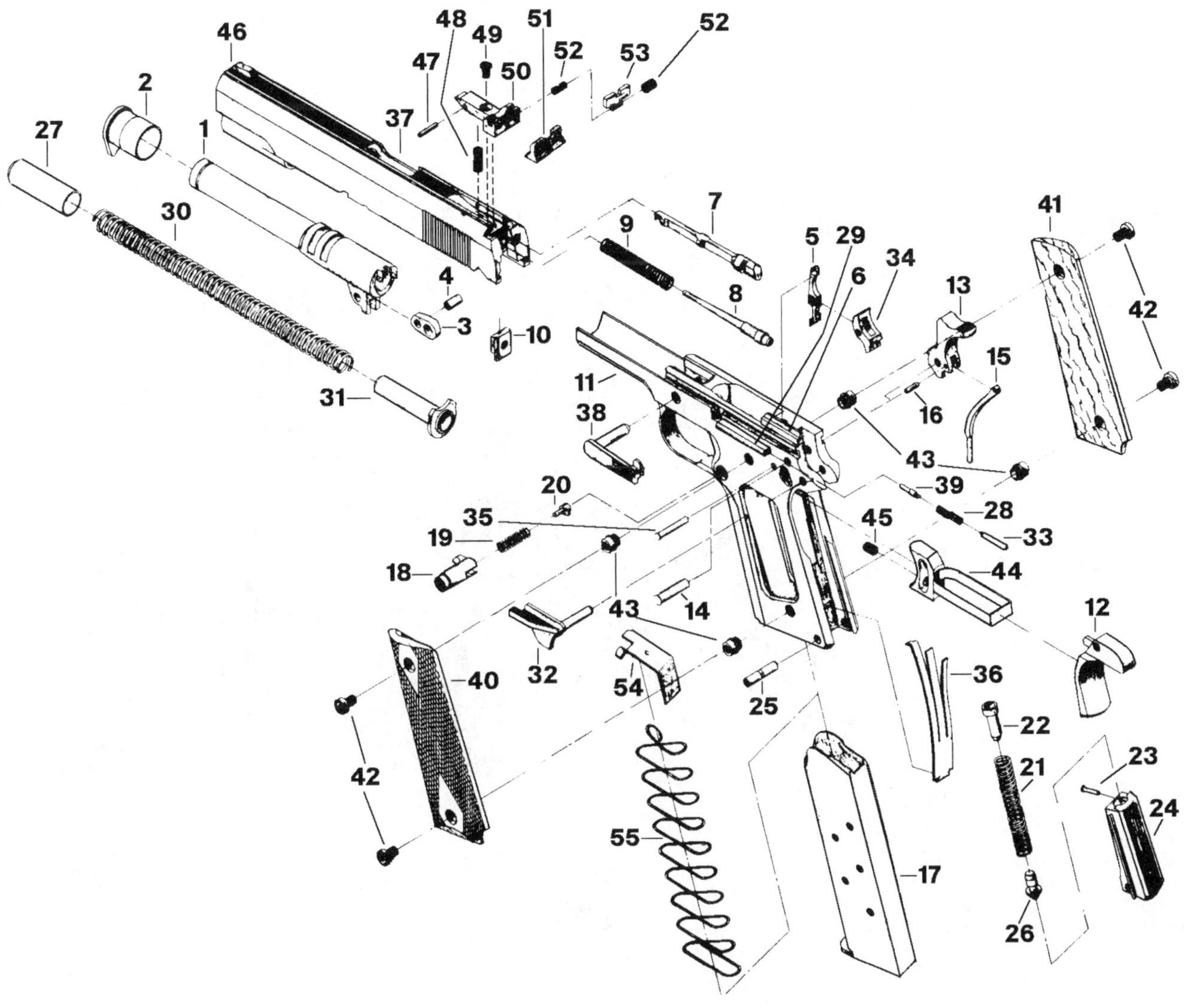

1	Barrel	**20**	Magazine Catch Retainer	**39**	Slide Stop Plunger
2	Barrel Bushing	**21**	Mainspring	**40**	Left Grip
3	Barrel Link	**22**	Mainspring Cap	**41**	Right Grip
4	Barrel Link Pin	**23**	Mainspring Cap Pin	**42**	Grip Screws
5	Disconnector	**24**	Mainspring Housing	**43**	Grip Screw Bushings
6	Ejector	**25**	Mainspring Housing Pin	**44**	Trigger Assembly
7	Extractor	**26**	Mainspring Housing Pin Retainer	**45**	Trigger Stop Screw
8	Firing Pin	**27**	Recoil Spring Plug	**46**	Front Sight
9	Firing Pin Spring	**28**	Slide Stop Plunger Spring	**47**	Rear Sight Pivot Pin
10	Firing Pin Stop	**29**	Slide Stop Plunger Tube	**48**	Rear Sight Spring
11	Frame	**30**	Recoil Spring	**49**	Rear Sight Elevation Screw
12	Grip Safety	**31**	Recoil Spring Guide	**50**	Rear Sight Base
13	Hammer	**32**	Thumb Safety	**51**	Fixed Rear Sight
14	Hammer Pin	**33**	Thumb Safety Lock Plunger	**52**	Rear Sight Windage Screws
15	Hammer Strut	**34**	Sear	**53**	Rear Sight Blade
16	Hammer Strut Pin	**35**	Sear Pin	**54**	Magazine Follower
17	Magazine Body	**36**	Sear Spring	**55**	Magazine Spring
18	Magazine Catch	**37**	Slide	**Parts Not Shown**	
19	Magazine Catch Spring	**38**	Slide Stop		Ejector Pin

Model R9 Auto

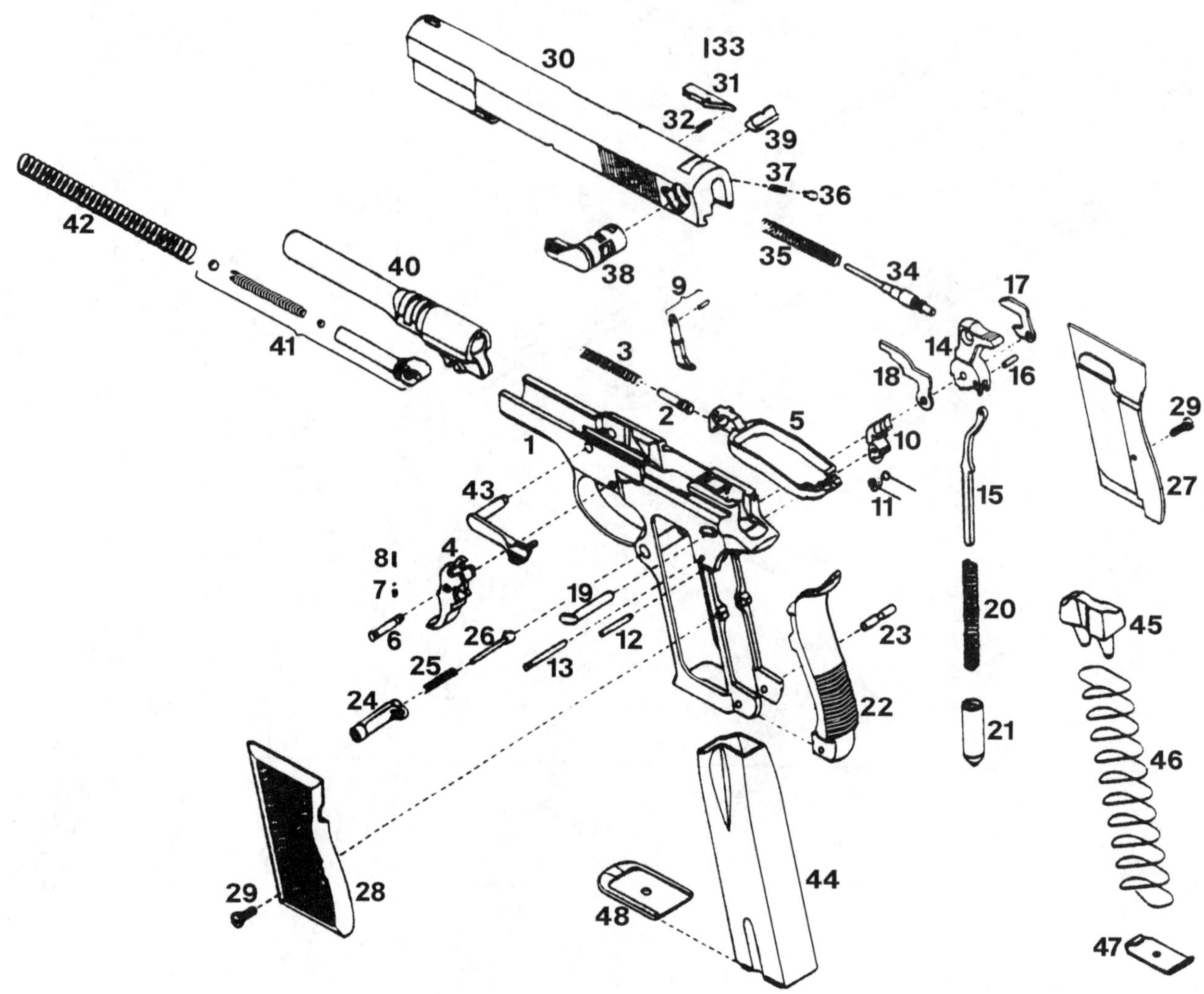

1	Frame	**17**	Sear Trip	**33**	Extractor Pin
2	Trigger Drawbar Plunger	**18**	Ejector	**34**	Firing Pin
3	Trigger Drawbar Plunger Spring	**19**	Hammer Axle Pin	**35**	Firing Pin Spring
4	Trigger	**20**	Hammer Spring	**36**	Safety Plunger
5	Trigger Drawbar	**21**	Hammer Spring Cap	**37**	Safety Plunger Spring
6	Trigger Pin	**22**	Rear Grip Insert	**38**	Safety
7	Trigger Pin Retainer	**23**	Rear Grip Insert Pin	**39**	Rear Sight
8	Trigger Pin Retainer Spring	**24**	Magazine Catch	**40**	Barrel
9	Disconnector	**25**	Magazine Catch Spring	**41**	Recoil Spring Guide
10	Sear	**26**	Magazine Retainer Catch	**42**	Recoil Spring
11	Sear Spring	**27**	Right Grip	**43**	Slide Stop
12	Sear Spring Retainer Pin	**28**	Left Grip	**44**	Magazine Body
13	Sear Pin	**29**	Grip Screws	**45**	Magazine Follower
14	Hammer	**30**	Slide	**46**	Magazine Spring
15	Hammer Strut	**31**	Extractor	**47**	Magazine Spring Plate
16	Hammer Strut Pin	**32**	Extractor Spring	**48**	Magazine Floorplate

Derringer

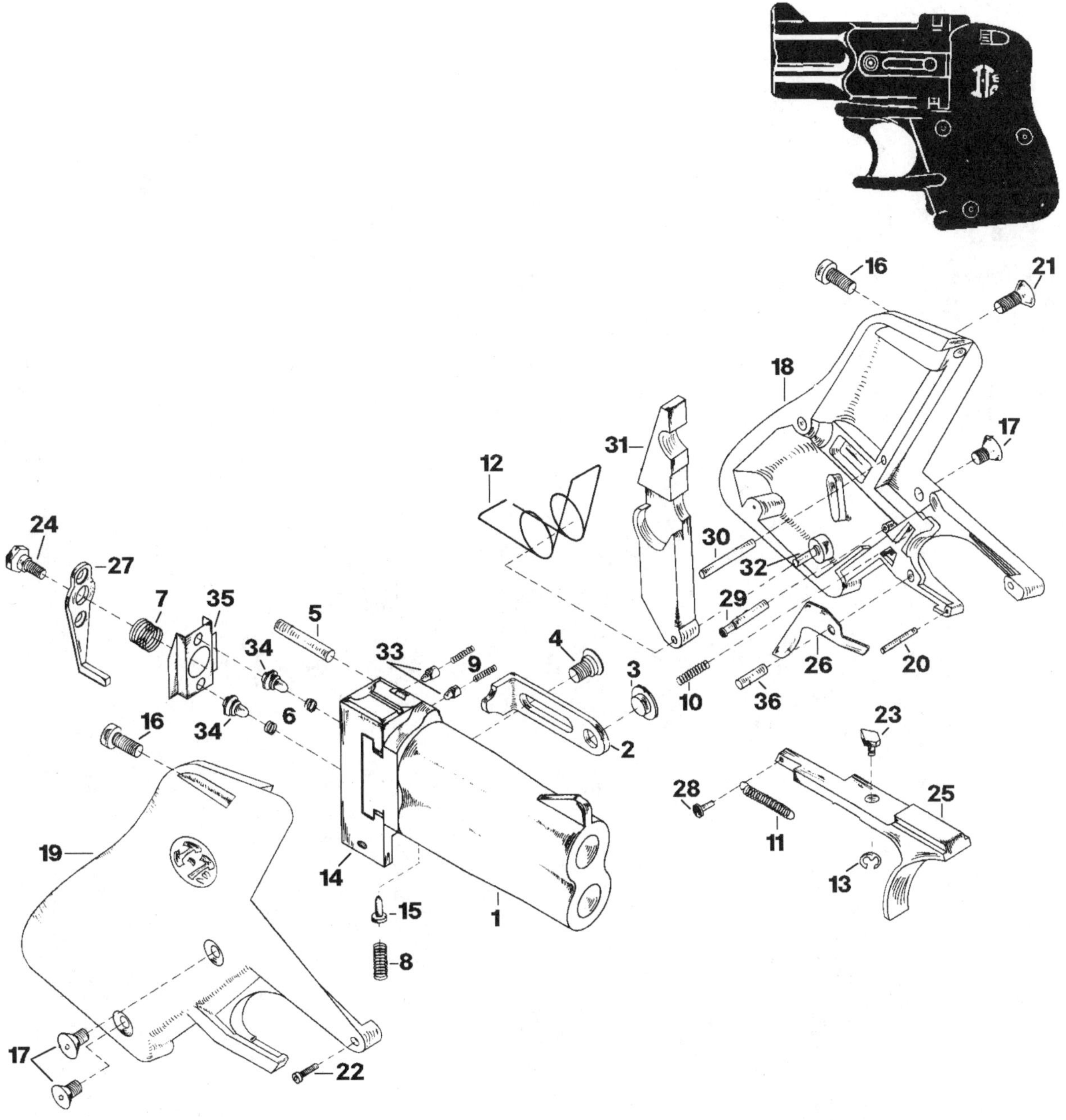

1	Barrel	**13**	Trigger Cam Spring	**25**	Trigger
2	Ejector	**14**	Frame	**26**	Safety
3	Ejector Knob	**15**	Barrel Lock	**27**	Selector
4	Ejector Screw	**16**	Upper Frame Screw	**28**	Upper Trigger Spring Pin
5	Barrel Axis	**17**	Frame and Hammer Axis Screws	**29**	Lower Trigger Spring Pin
6	Firing Pin Springs	**18**	Left Grip	**30**	Selector Pin
7	Selector Spring	**19**	Right Grip	**31**	Hammer
8	Barrel Lock Spring	**20**	Grip Pin	**32**	Hammer Axis
9	Poppett Springs	**21**	Large Grip Screw	**33**	Centering Poppetts
10	Safety Spring	**22**	Small Grip Screw	**34**	Firing Pins
11	Trigger Return Spring	**23**	Trigger Cam	**35**	Firing Pin Retainer
12	Hammer Spring	**24**	Selector Screw	**36**	Safety Axis

TEC-22 Auto

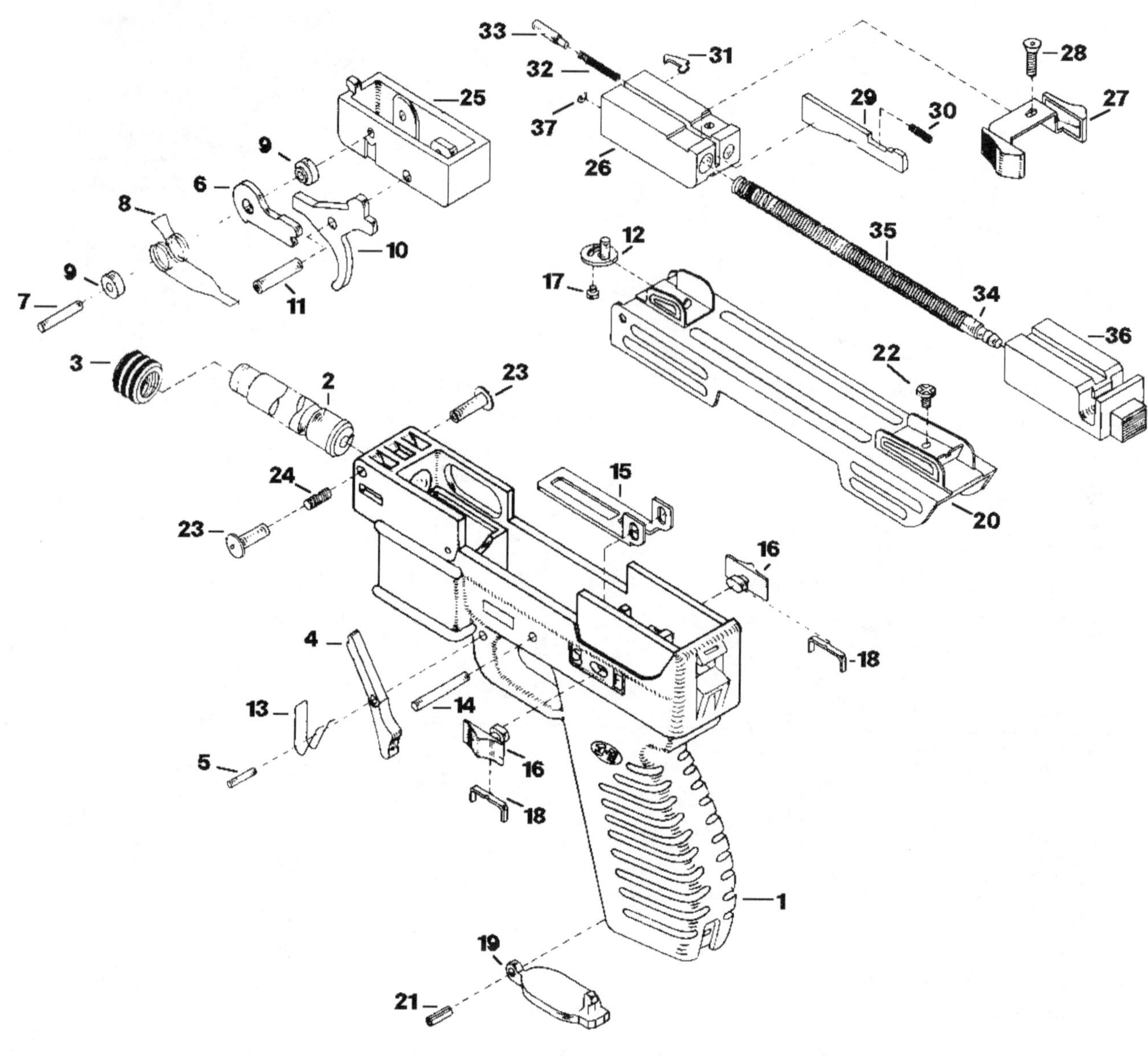

1	Frame	14	Insert Pin	27	Operating Handle
2	Barrel	15	Safety	28	Operating Handle Screw
3	Threaded Cover	16	Safety Buttons	29	Firing Pin
4	Magazine Catch Lever	17	Front Sight Screw	30	Firing Pin Spring
5	Magazine Catch Axis	18	Safety Springs	31	Extractor
6	Hammer	19	Butt	32	Extractor Spring
7	Hammer Axis	20	Cover	33	Extractor Pin
8	Mainspring	21	Butt Pin	34	Recoil Spring Guide
9	Hammer Bushing	22	Rear Sight Elevation Screw	35	Recoil Spring
10	Trigger	23	Cover Axes	36	Latch Button
11	Trigger Bushing	24	Cover Axis Screw	37	E-Ring
12	Front Sight	25	Insert		
13	Magazine Catch Spring	26	Bolt		

TEC-9 Auto

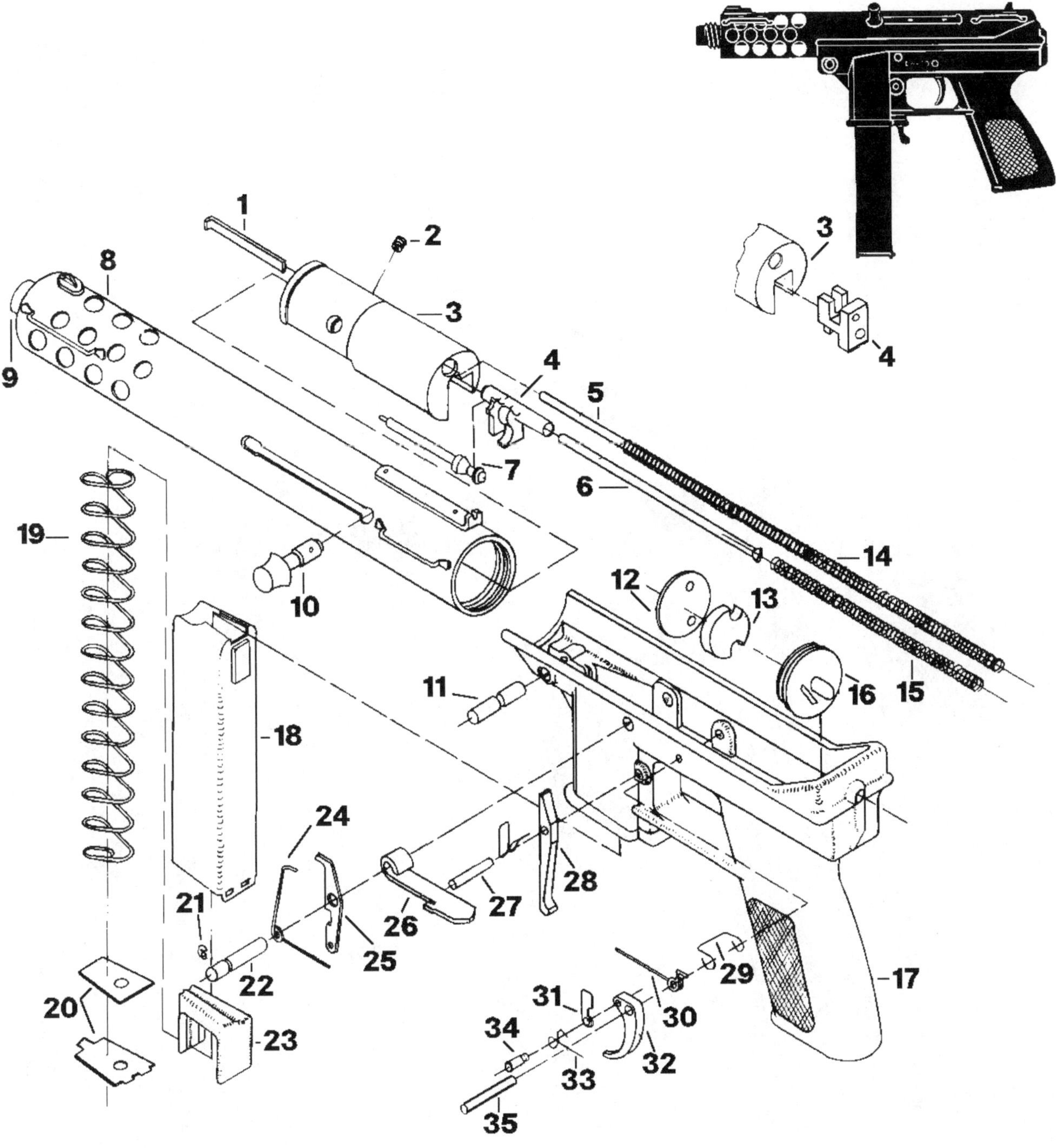

1	Extractor	13	Buffer	25	Ejector
2	Extractor Screw	14	Recoil Spring	26	Sear
3	Bolt	15	Striker Spring	27	Magazine Catch Axis
4	Striker	16	Rear Stabilizing Disk Cap	28	Magazine Catch
5	Recoil Spring Guide	17	Frame	29	Sear Retainer
6	Striker Guide	18	Magazine	30	Trigger Spring
7	Firing Pin	19	Magazine Spring	31	Disconnector
8	Upper Receiver	20	Magazine Bottom Plates	32	Trigger
9	Barrel	21	Large E-Ring	33	Disconnector Spring
10	Operating Handle	22	Sear Axis	34	Disconnector Axis
11	Assembly Pin	23	Follower	35	Trigger Axis
12	Buffer Plate	24	Sear Spring		

J-22 Auto

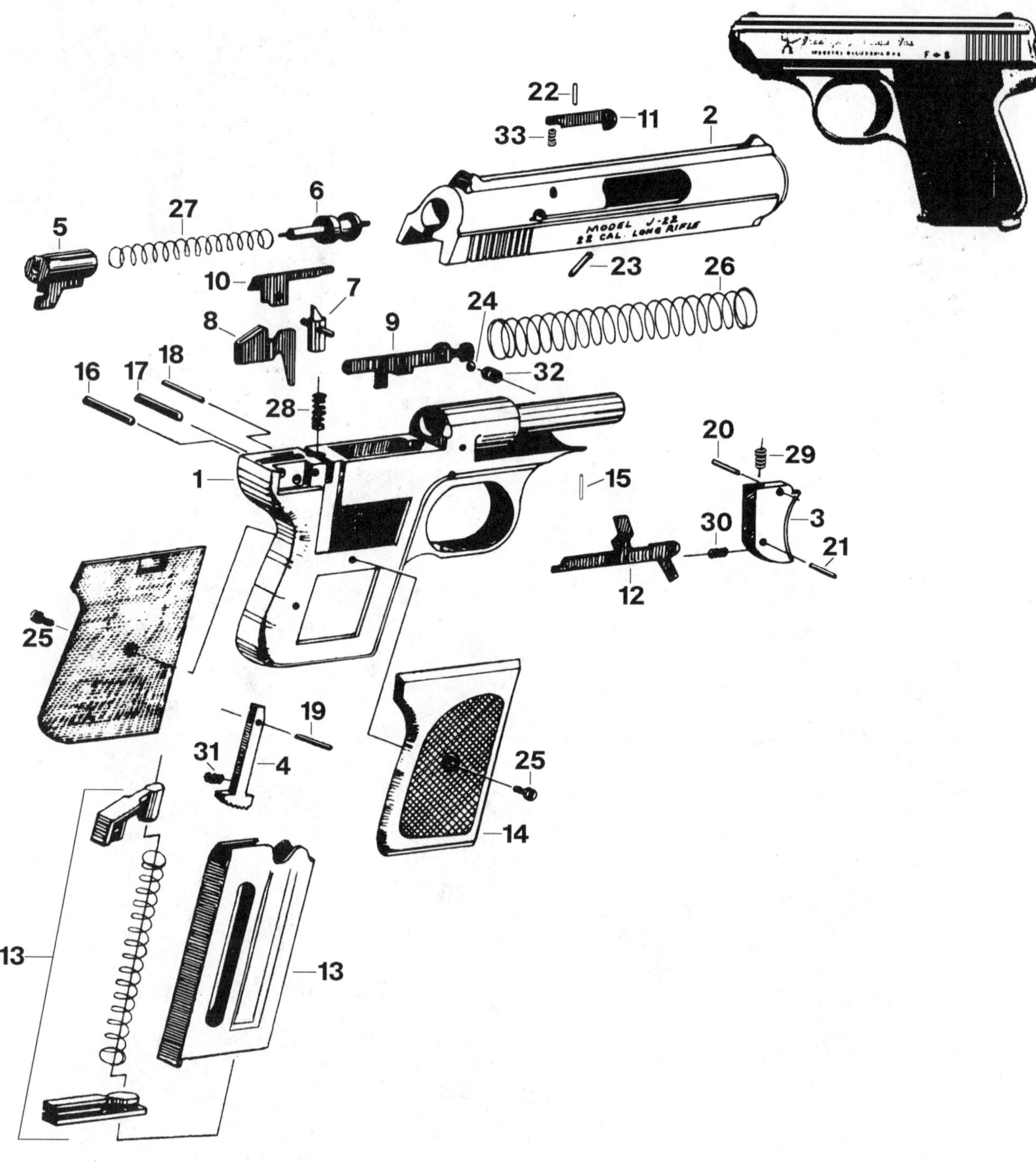

1	Frame	**12**	Trigger Bar Assembly	**23**	Wear Pin
2	Slide	**13**	Magazine Assembly	**24**	Safety Ball
3	Trigger	**14**	Grips	**25**	Grip Screws
4	Catch	**15**	Barrel Cross Pin	**26**	Recoil Spring
5	Takedown Button	**16**	Takedown Cross Pin	**27**	Firing Pin Spring
6	Firing Pin	**17**	Cam Pivot Pin	**28**	Sear Spring
7	Sear Assembly	**18**	Ejector Cross Pin	**29**	Trigger Retaining Spring
8	Cam	**19**	Catch Cross Pin	**30**	Trigger Bar Spring
9	Safety	**20**	Trigger Cross Pin	**31**	Catch Spring
10	Ejector	**21**	Trigger Bar Cross Pin	**32**	Safety Ball Spring
11	Extractor	**22**	Extractor Pin	**33**	Extractor Spring

Model 50 Revolver

Courtesy of James M. Triggs/NRA

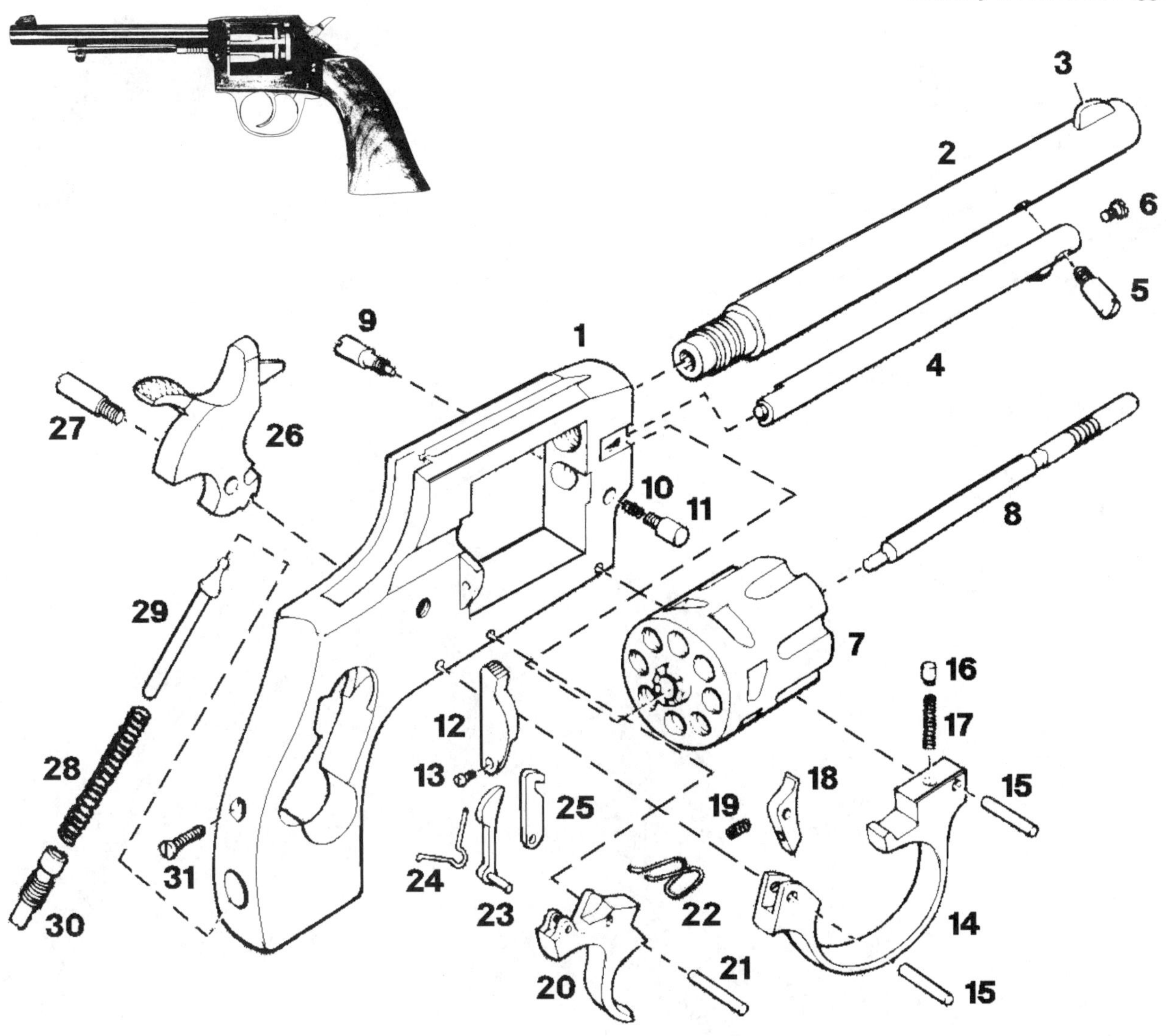

1	Frame	**12**	Loading Gate	**23**	Lever
2	Barrel	**13**	Loading Gate Screw	**24**	Lever Spring
3	Front Sight Blade	**14**	Trigger Guard	**25**	Lifter
4	Ejector Assembly	**15**	Trigger Guard Pins	**26**	Hammer
5	Ejector Tube Screw	**16**	Cylinder Friction Stud	**27**	Hammer Screw
6	Ejector Lock Screw	**17**	Cylinder Friction Stud Spring	**28**	Mainspring
7	Cylinder	**18**	Sear	**29**	Mainspring Plunger
8	Center Pin	**19**	Sear Spring	**30**	Mainspring Adjusting Screw
9	Center Pin Catch Nut	**20**	Trigger	**31**	Grip Screw
10	Center Pin Catch Spring	**21**	Trigger Pin	**Parts Not Shown**	
11	Center Pin Catch Screw	**22**	Trigger Spring		One-Piece Grip

Model 66 Revolver

Courtesy of James M. Triggs/NRA

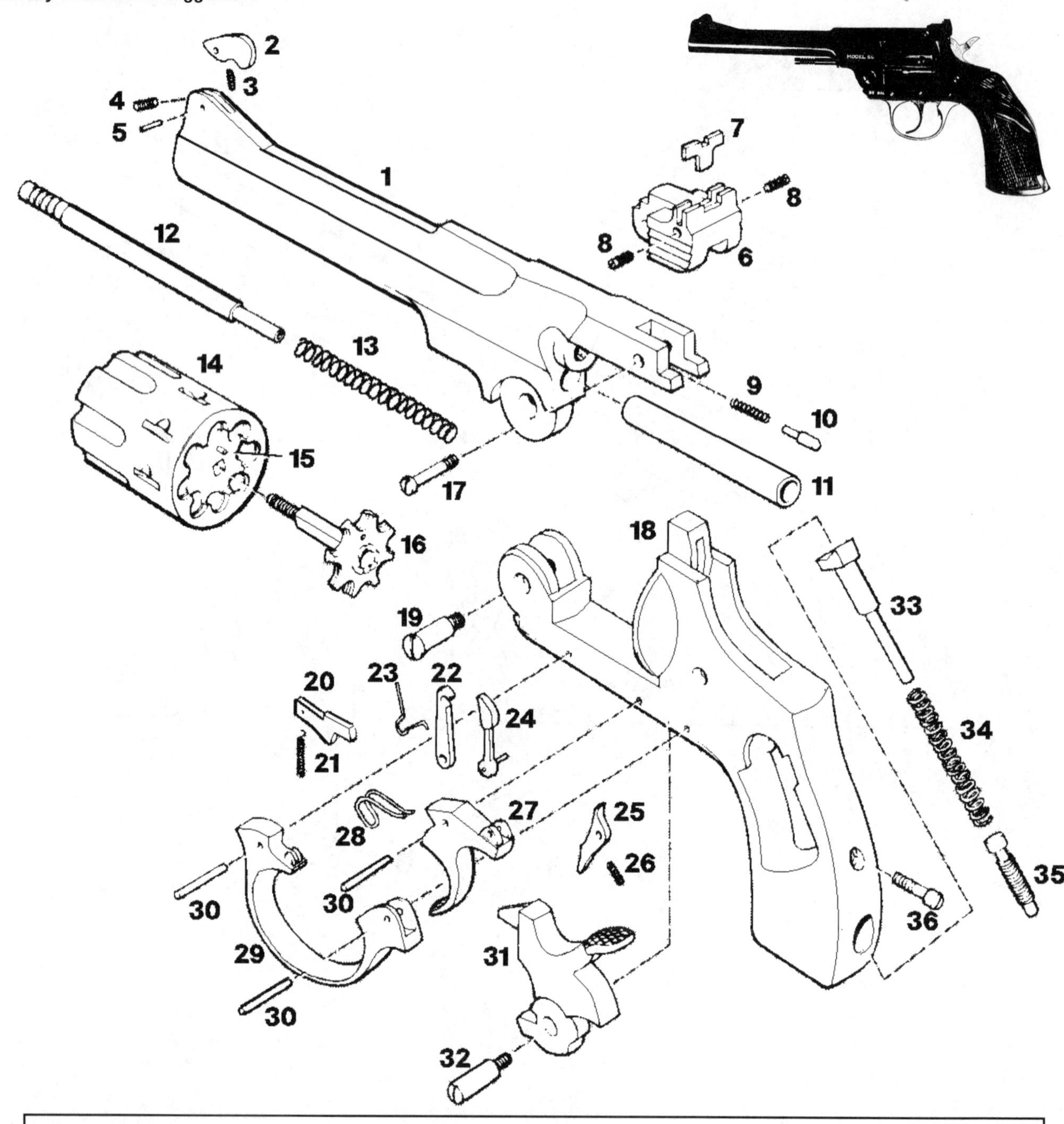

1	Barrel	**15**	Extractor Pin	**29**	Trigger Guard
2	Front Sight Blade	**16**	Extractor	**30**	Trigger and Guard Pins
3	Front Sight Spring	**17**	Barrel Catch Screw	**31**	Hammer
4	Front Sight Adjusting Screw	**18**	Frame	**32**	Hammer Screw
5	Front Sight Pin	**19**	Joint Screw	**33**	Mainspring Plunger
6	Barrel Catch	**20**	Cylinder Stop	**34**	Mainspring
7	Rear Sight Blade	**21**	Cylinder Stop Spring	**35**	Mainspring Adjusting Screw
8	Rear Sight Adjusting Screws	**22**	Lifter	**36**	Grip Screw
9	Barrel Catch Spring	**23**	Lever Spring	**Parts Not Shown**	
10	Barrel Catch Plunger	**24**	Lever and Pin		Grip (Large, One-Piece)
11	Quill	**25**	Sear		Grip (Small, Two-Piece)
12	Ejector Rod	**26**	Sear Spring		Tang Plug Screw
13	Extractor Spring	**27**	Trigger		
14	Cylinder	**28**	Trigger Spring		

Pony Auto

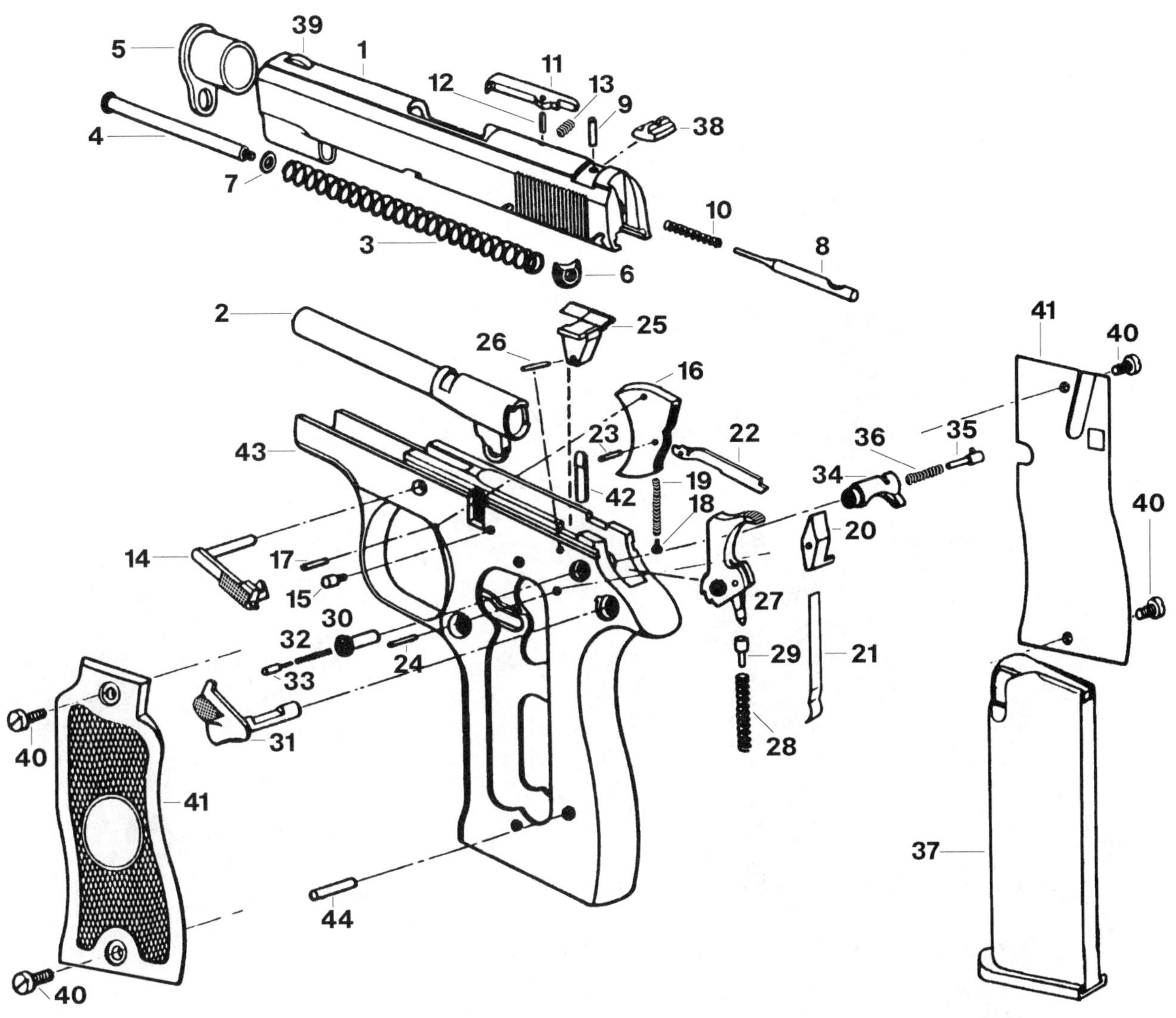

1	Slide	18	Trigger Plunger	35	Magazine Catch Lock
2	Barrel with Link and Pin	19	Trigger Plunger Spring	36	Magazine Catch Lock Spring
3	Recoil Spring	20	Sear	37	Magazine
4	Recoil Spring Guide	21	Sear Spring	38	Rear Sight
5	Barrel Bushing	22	Sear Bar	39	Front Sight
6	Recoil Spring Guide Head	23	Sear Bar Pin	40	Grip Screws
7	Recoil Spring Guide Washer	24	Sear Pin	41	Grips
8	Firing Pin	25	Ejector	42	Disconnector
9	Firing Pin Retaining Pin	26	Ejector Pin	43	Frame
10	Firing Pin Spring	27	Hammer with Strut and Pin	44	Grip Locator Pin
11	Extractor	28	Hammer Spring	**Parts Not Shown**	
12	Extractor Pin	29	Hammer Spring Plunger		Link
13	Extractor Spring	30	Hammer Pin		Link Pin
14	Slide Stop	31	Thumb Safety		Hammer Strut
15	Slide Stop Plunger Screw	32	Safety Spring		Hammer Strut Pin
16	Trigger	33	Safety Plunger		Recoil Spring Assembly
17	Trigger Pin	34	Magazine Catch		

Top-Break Revolver

Courtesy of Blacksmith Corporation

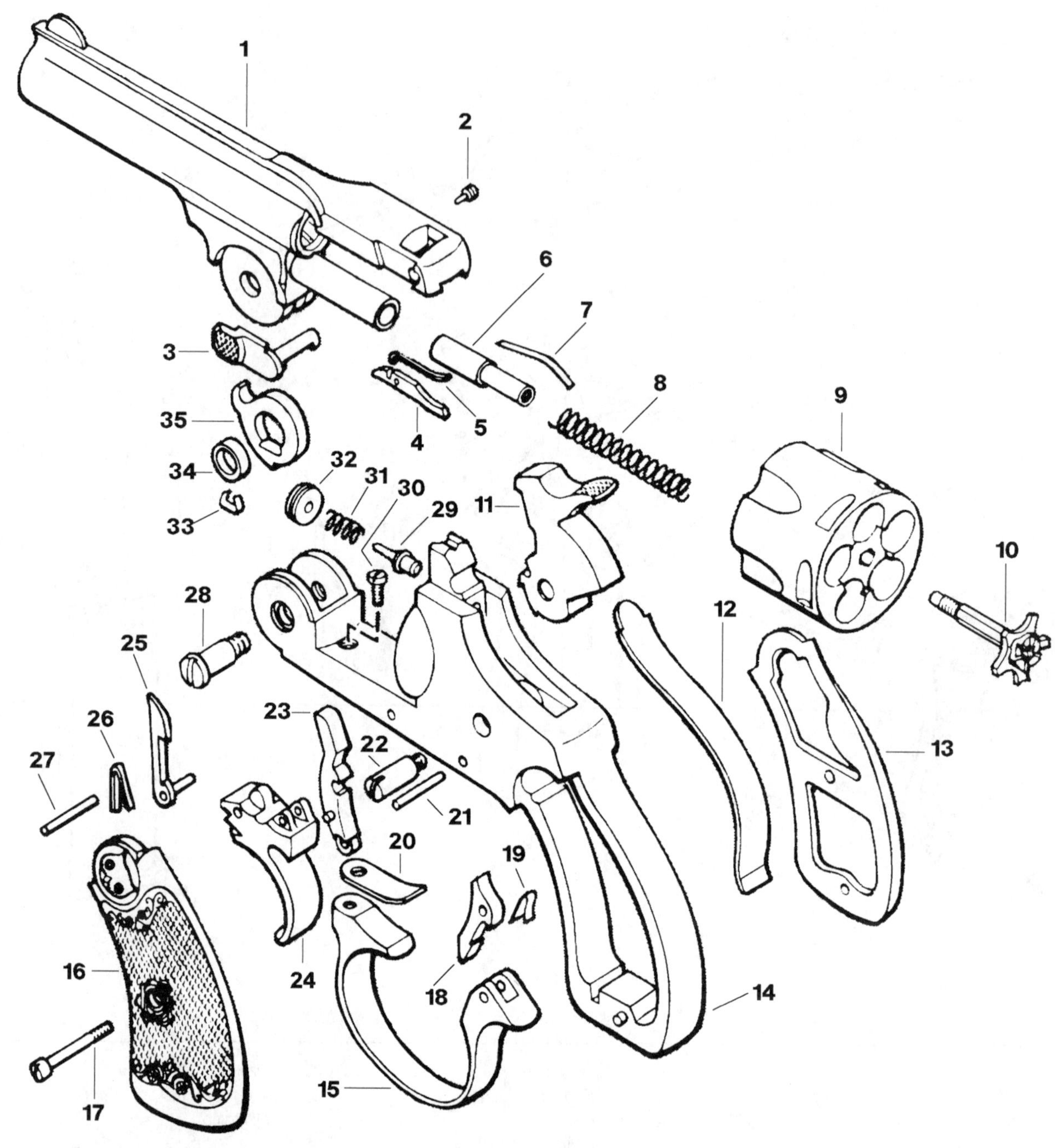

1	Barrel Assembly	**13**	Right Grip	**25**	Hand
2	Barrel Catch Screw	**14**	Frame	**26**	Hand Spring
3	Barrel Catch	**15**	Trigger Guard	**27**	Trigger Pin
4	Barrel Catch Spring Cover	**16**	Left Grip	**28**	Hinge Screw
5	Barrel Catch Spring	**17**	Grip Screw	**29**	Firing Pin
6	Extractor Stem	**18**	Sear	**30**	Trigger Guard Screw
7	Cylinder Friction Spring	**19**	Sear Spring	**31**	Firing Pin Spring
8	Extractor Spring	**20**	Trigger Spring	**32**	Firing Pin Bushing
9	Cylinder	**21**	Trigger Guard Pin	**33**	Extractor Spring
10	Extractor	**22**	Hammer Screw	**34**	Extractor Bushing
11	Hammer	**23**	Lifter	**35**	Extractor Cam
12	Hammer Spring	**24**	Trigger		

TP22 Auto

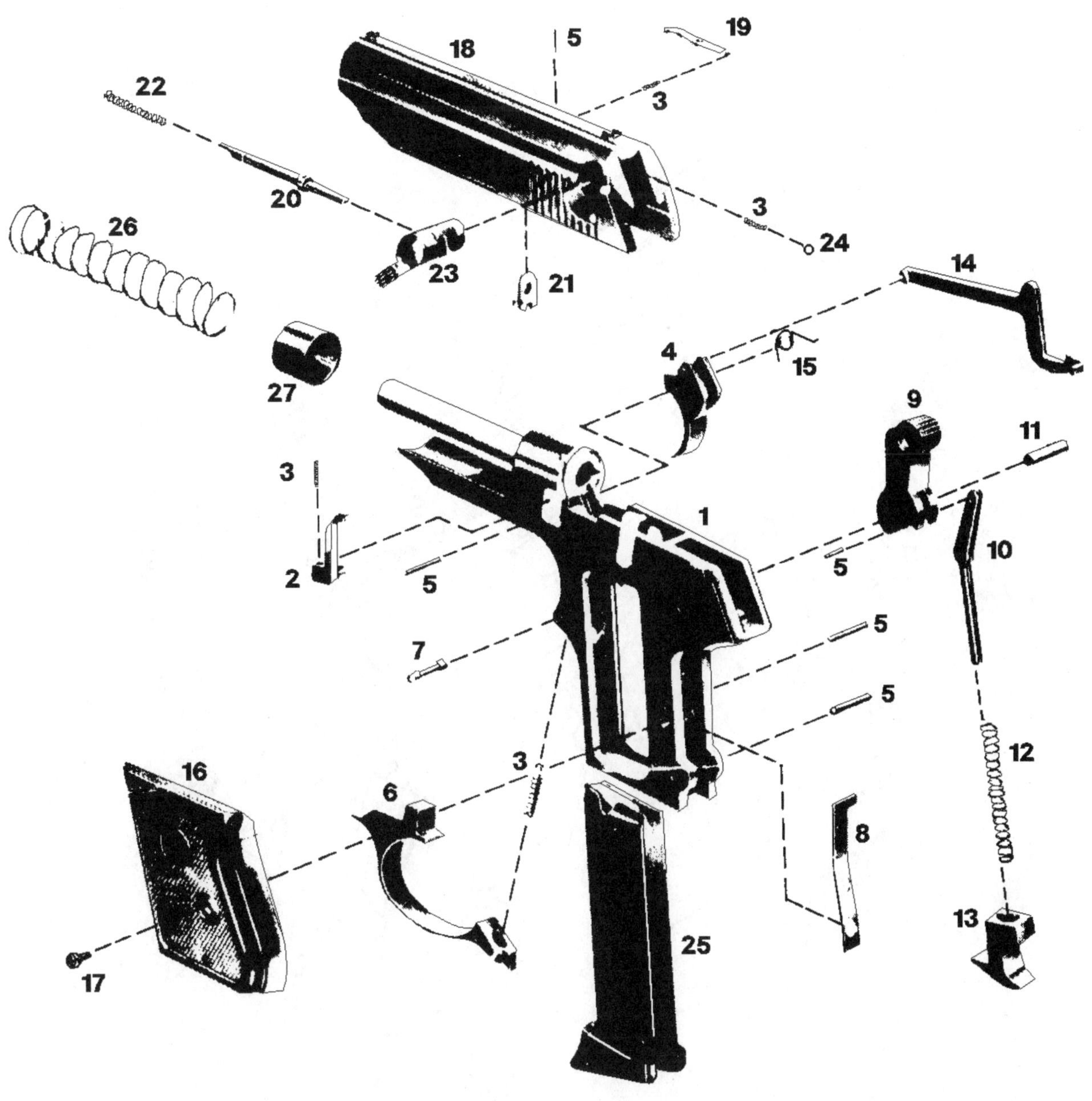

1	Frame	**10**	Mainspring Guide Rod	**19**	Extractor
2	Firing Pin Stop	**11**	Hammer Pin	**20**	Firing Pin
3	Springs	**12**	Mainspring	**21**	Firing Pin Plug
4	Trigger	**13**	Magazine Catch	**22**	Firing Pin Spring
5	Cylindrical Pins	**14**	Trigger Bar	**23**	Safety-Lever
6	Trigger Guard	**15**	Trigger Bar Spring	**24**	Steel Ball
7	Trigger Guard Pin	**16**	Grip Plates	**25**	Magazine Assembly
8	Sear	**17**	Grip Plate Screw	**26**	Recoil Spring
9	Hammer	**18**	Slide	**27**	Sear Spring Plunger

Baby Nambu Auto

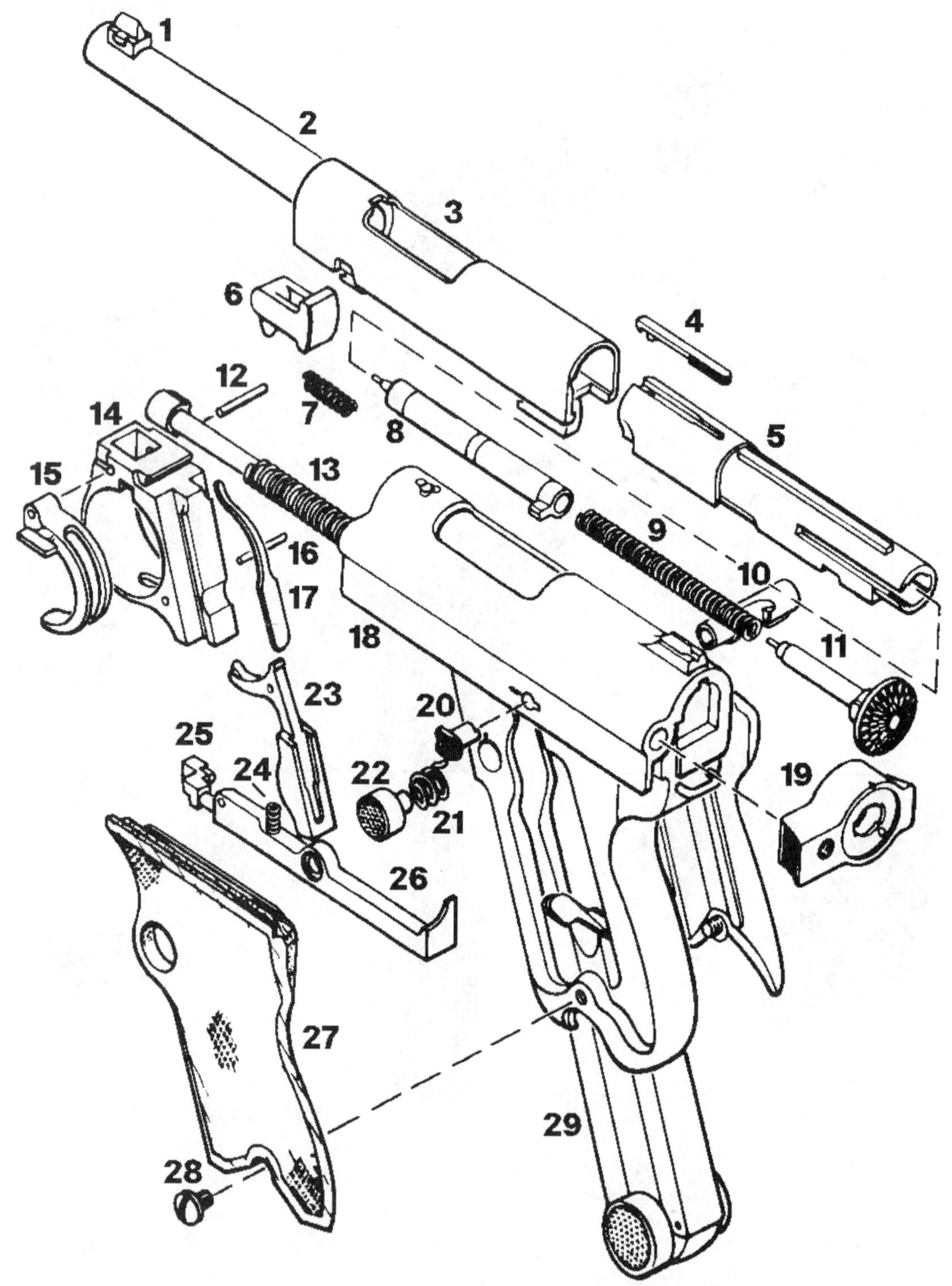

1	Front Sight	**11**	Firing Pin Retainer	**21**	Magazine Catch Spring
2	Barrel	**12**	Trigger Pin	**22**	Magazine Catch Button
3	Barrel Extension	**13**	Recoil Spring and Guide	**23**	Grip Safety
4	Extractor	**14**	Trigger Guard	**24**	Sear Spring
5	Bolt	**15**	Trigger	**25**	Disconnector
6	Locking Block	**16**	Grip Safety Pin	**26**	Sear
7	Locking Block Spring	**17**	Grip Safety Spring	**27**	Grip Panel
8	Firing Pin	**18**	Frame	**28**	Grip Screw
9	Firing Pin Spring	**19**	Cocking Knob	**29**	Magazine Assembly
10	Magazine Catch	**20**	Bolt Latch		

Nambu Type 14 Auto

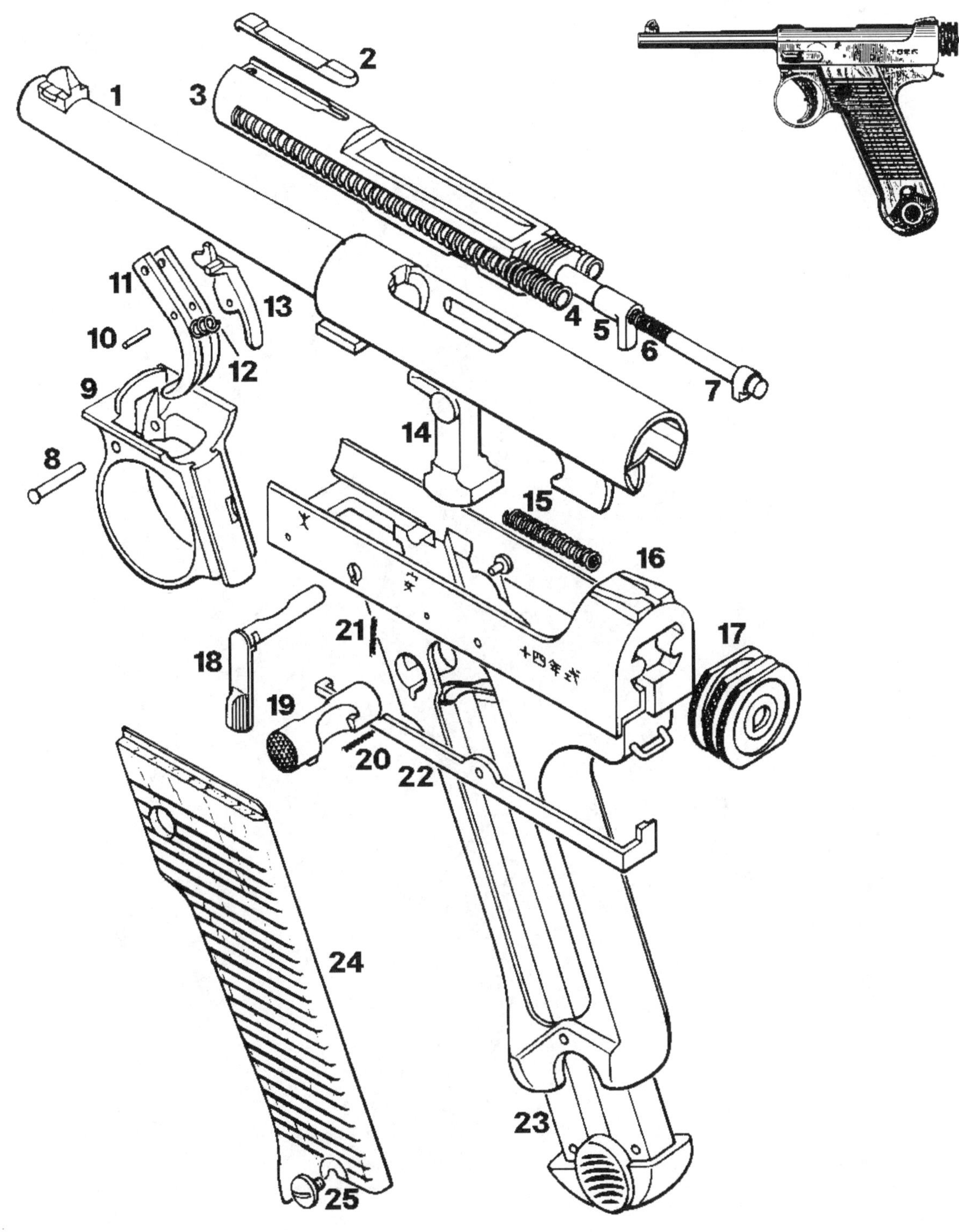

1	Barrel and Barrel Extension	**10**	Trigger Sear Pin	**19**	Magazine Catch
2	Extractor	**11**	Trigger	**20**	Magazine Catch Spring
3	Bolt	**12**	Sear Spring	**21**	Magazine Safety Spring with Plunger
4	Recoil Spring	**13**	Trigger Sear	**22**	Trigger Bar
5	Firing Pin	**14**	Locking Block	**23**	Magazine Assembly
6	Firing Pin Spring	**15**	Locking Block Spring	**24**	Grip Panel
7	Firing Pin Extension	**16**	Frame	**25**	Grip Screw
8	Trigger Hinge Pin	**17**	Cocking Piece		
9	Trigger Guard	**18**	Safety		

Type 26 Revolver

Courtesy of Blacksmith Corporation

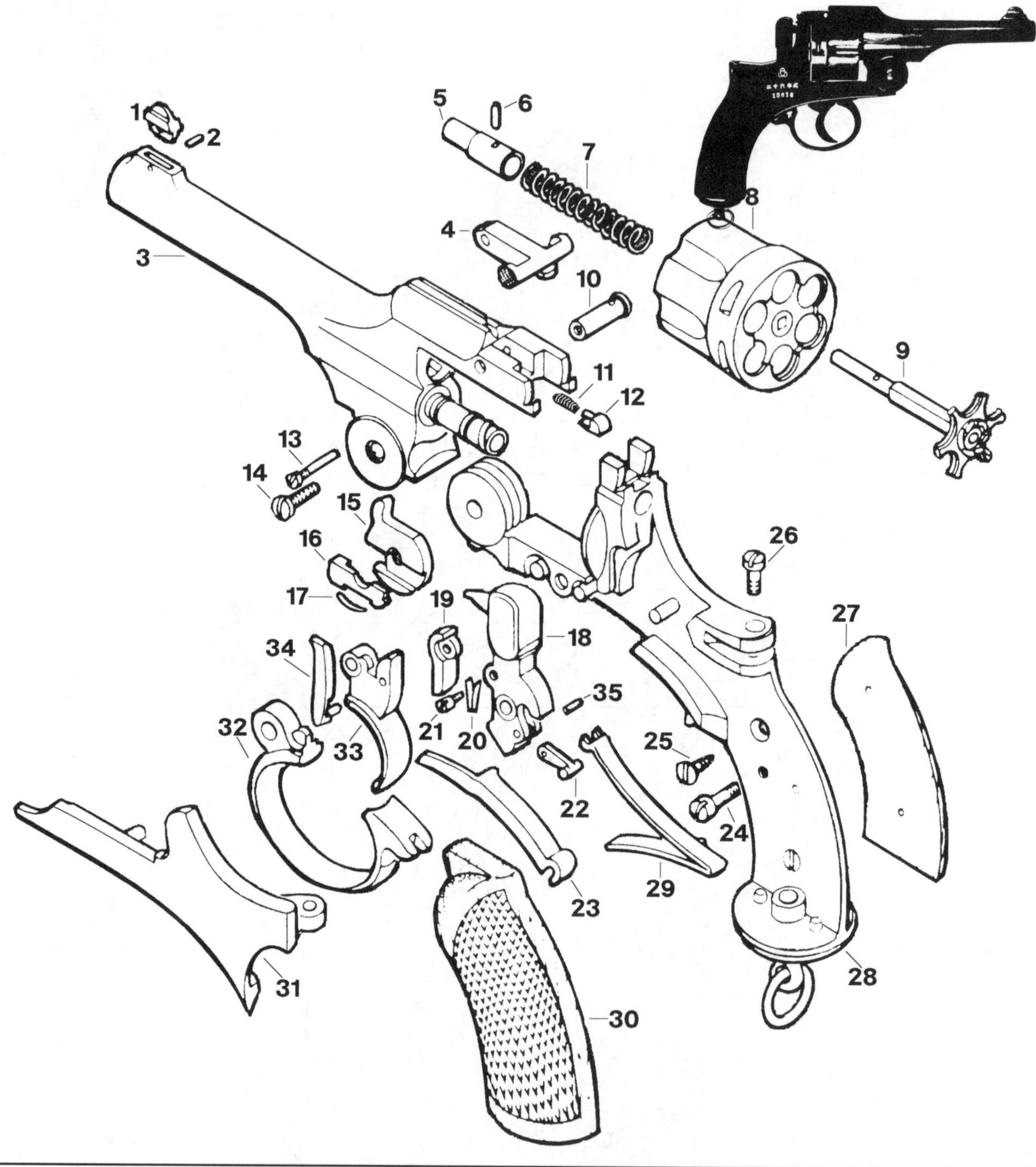

1	Front Sight	**13**	Latch Screw	**25**	Right Grip Screw
2	Front Sight Pin	**14**	Hinge Pin Screw	**26**	Sideplate Hinge Screw
3	Barrel	**15**	Extractor Cam	**27**	Right Grip
4	Latch	**16**	Extractor Release	**28**	Frame
5	Extractor Bearing	**17**	Release Tension Spring	**29**	Mainspring
6	Extractor Bearing Pin	**18**	Hammer	**30**	Left Grip
7	Extractor Spring	**19**	Strut	**31**	Sideplate
8	Cylinder	**20**	Strut Spring	**32**	Trigger Guard
9	Extractor	**21**	Strut Screw	**33**	Trigger
10	Barrel Hinge Pin	**22**	Hammer Stirrup	**34**	Hand
11	Latch Spring	**23**	Rebound Lever	**35**	Hammer Stirrup Pin
12	Latch Spring Plunger	**24**	Rebound Lever Screw		

Type 94 Auto

Courtesy of Blacksmith Corporation

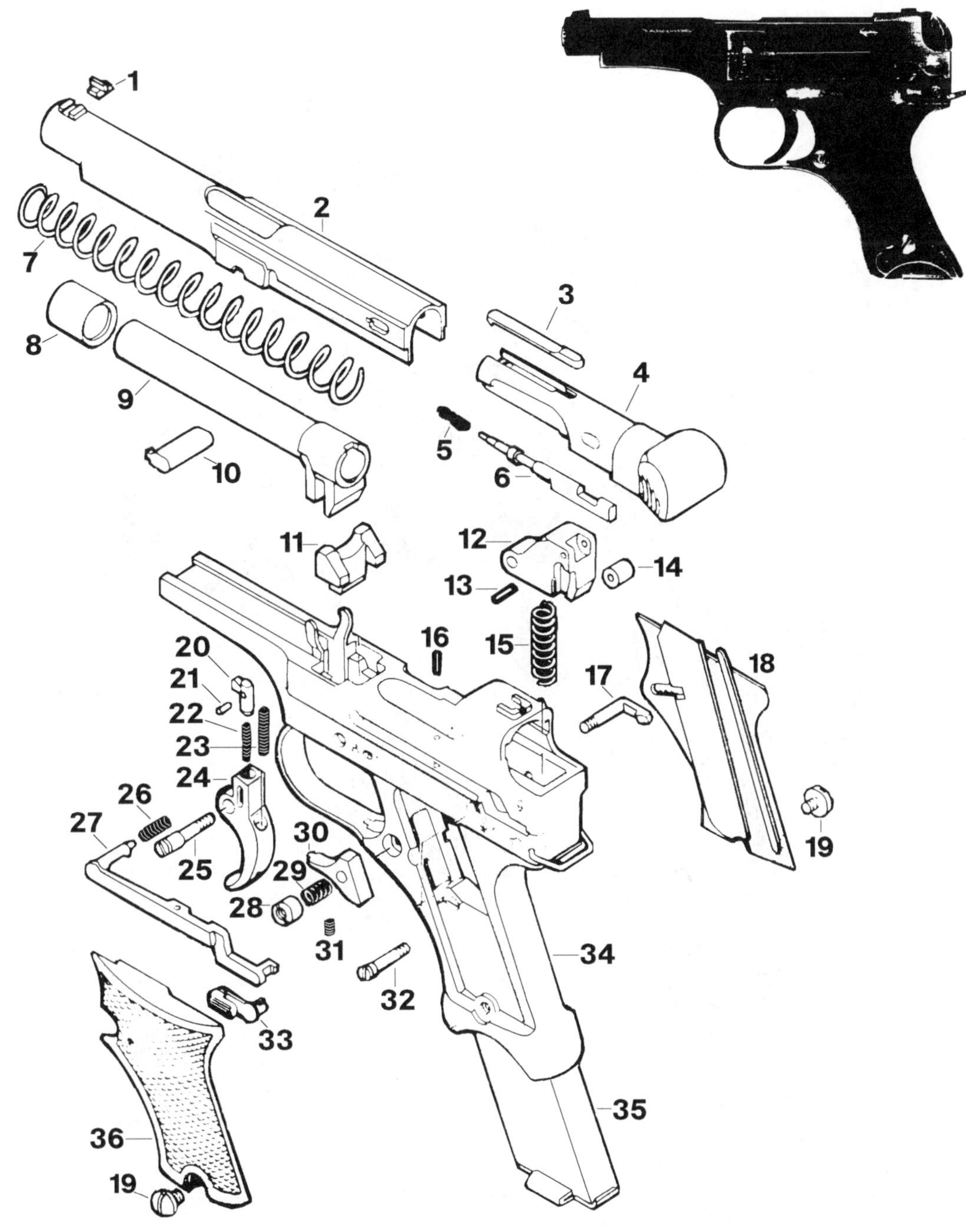

1	Front Sight	**13**	Hammer Roller Pin	**25**	Trigger Screw
2	Slide	**14**	Hammer Roller	**26**	Sear Spring
3	Extractor	**15**	Hammer Spring	**27**	Sear and Trigger Bar
4	Breechbolt	**16**	Sear Hinge Pin	**28**	Magazine Catch Nut
5	Firing Pin Spring	**17**	Magazine Catch	**29**	Magazine Catch Spring
6	Firing Pin	**18**	Right Grip	**30**	Magazine-Operated Safety
7	Recoil Spring	**19**	Grip Screw	**31**	Magazine Safety Spring
8	Recoil Spring Collar	**20**	Disconnector	**32**	Hammer Screw
9	Barrel	**21**	Disconnector Pin	**33**	Safety Catch
10	Cross Bolt	**22**	Disconnector Spring	**34**	Frame
11	Locking Block	**23**	Trigger Spring	**35**	Magazine Assembly
12	Hammer	**24**	Trigger	**36**	Left Grip

J-22 Auto

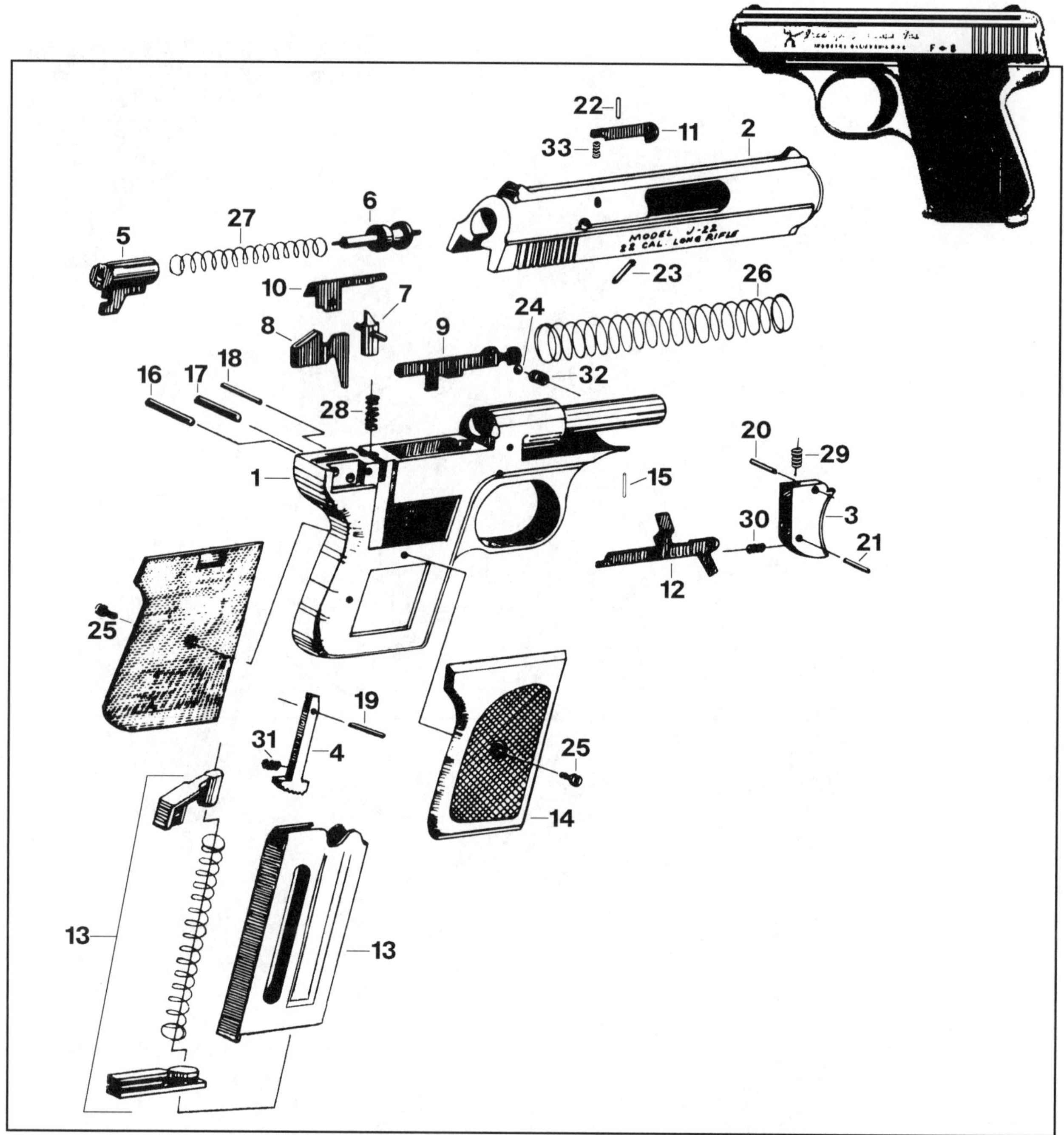

1 Frame
2 Slide
3 Trigger
4 Catch
5 Takedown Button
6 Firing Pin
7 Sear Assembly
8 Cam
9 Safety
10 Ejector
11 Extractor
12 Trigger Bar Assembly
13 Magazine Assembly
14 Grips
15 Barrel Cross Pin
16 Takedown Cross Pin
17 Cam Pivot Pin
18 Ejector Cross Pin
19 Catch Cross Pin
20 Trigger Cross Pin
21 Trigger Bar Cross Pin
22 Extractor Pin
23 Wear Pin
24 Safety Ball
25 Grip Screws
26 Recoil Spring
27 Firing Pin Spring
28 Sear Spring
29 Trigger Retaining Spring
30 Trigger Bar Spring
31 Catch Spring
32 Safety Ball Spring
33 Extractor Spring

941 Auto/IMI Baby Eagle

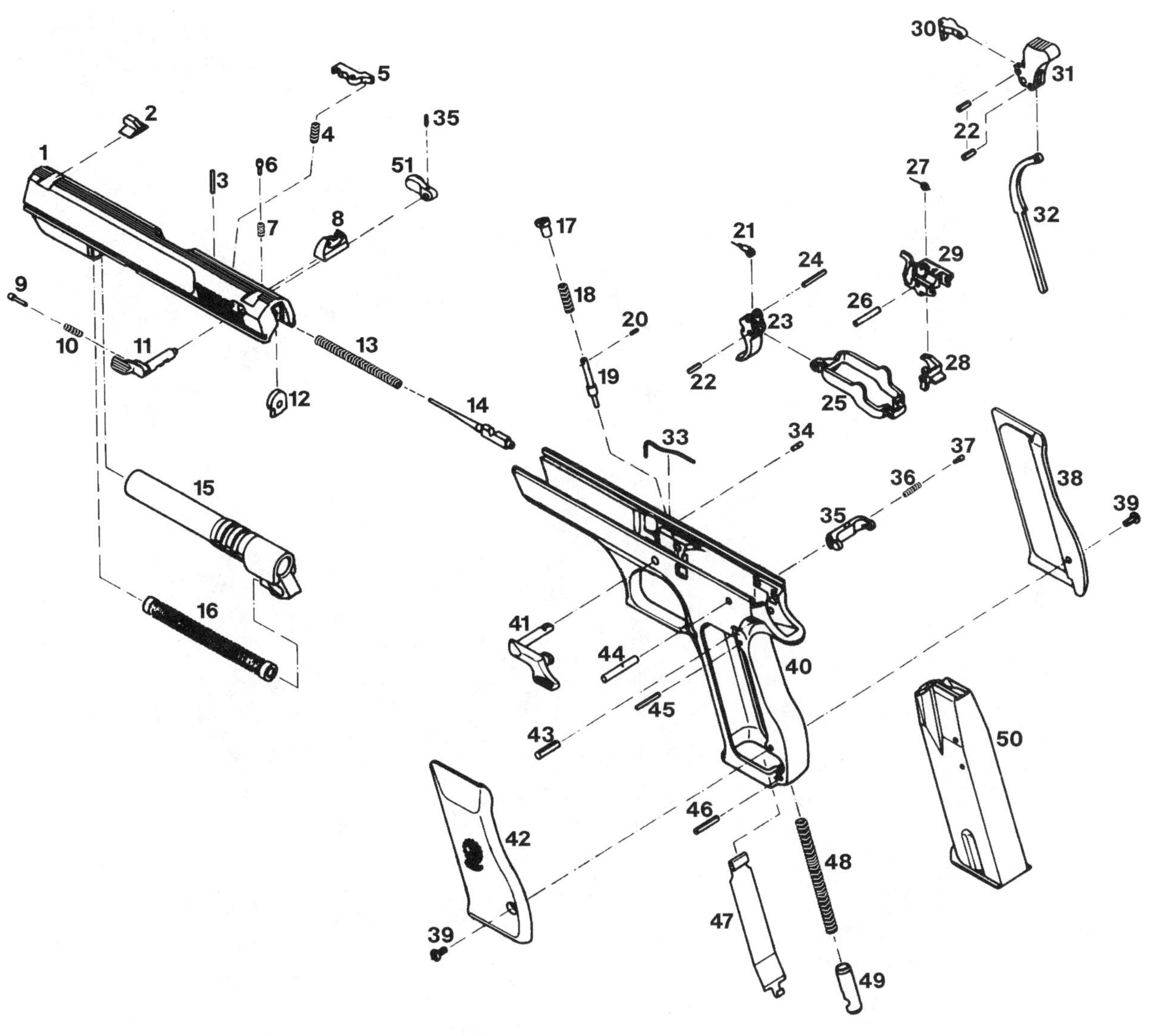

1	Slide	**18**	Plunger Spring	**35**	Magazine Catch
2	Front Sight	**19**	Plunger Pin	**36**	Magazine Catch Spring
3	Extractor Pin	**20**	Safety Pin	**37**	Magazine Catch Plunger
4	Extractor Spring	**21**	Trigger Spring	**38**	Right Grip
5	Extractor	**22**	Pins	**39**	Grip Screws
6	Firing Pin Safety	**23**	Trigger	**40**	Frame
7	Firing Pin Safety Spring	**24**	Trigger Pin	**41**	Slide Catch
8	Rear Sight	**25**	Trigger Bar	**42**	Left Grip
9	Safety Plunger	**26**	Sear Pin	**43**	Hammer Pin
10	Safety Spring	**27**	Sear Spring	**44**	Sear Housing Pin
11	Safety	**28**	Sear	**45**	Magazine Plate Pin
12	Firing Pin Plate	**29**	Sear Housing	**46**	Hammer Spring Cup Pin
13	Firing Pin Spring	**30**	Interruptor	**47**	Magazine Plate
14	Firing Pin	**31**	Hammer	**48**	Hammer Spring
15	Barrel	**32**	Hammer Rod	**49**	Hammer Spring Cup
16	Recoil Springs Assembly	**33**	Slide Catch Spring	**50**	Magazine Assembly
17	Trigger Plunger	**34**	Slide Catch Spring Pin		

Grizzly Win. Mag. Mark II Auto

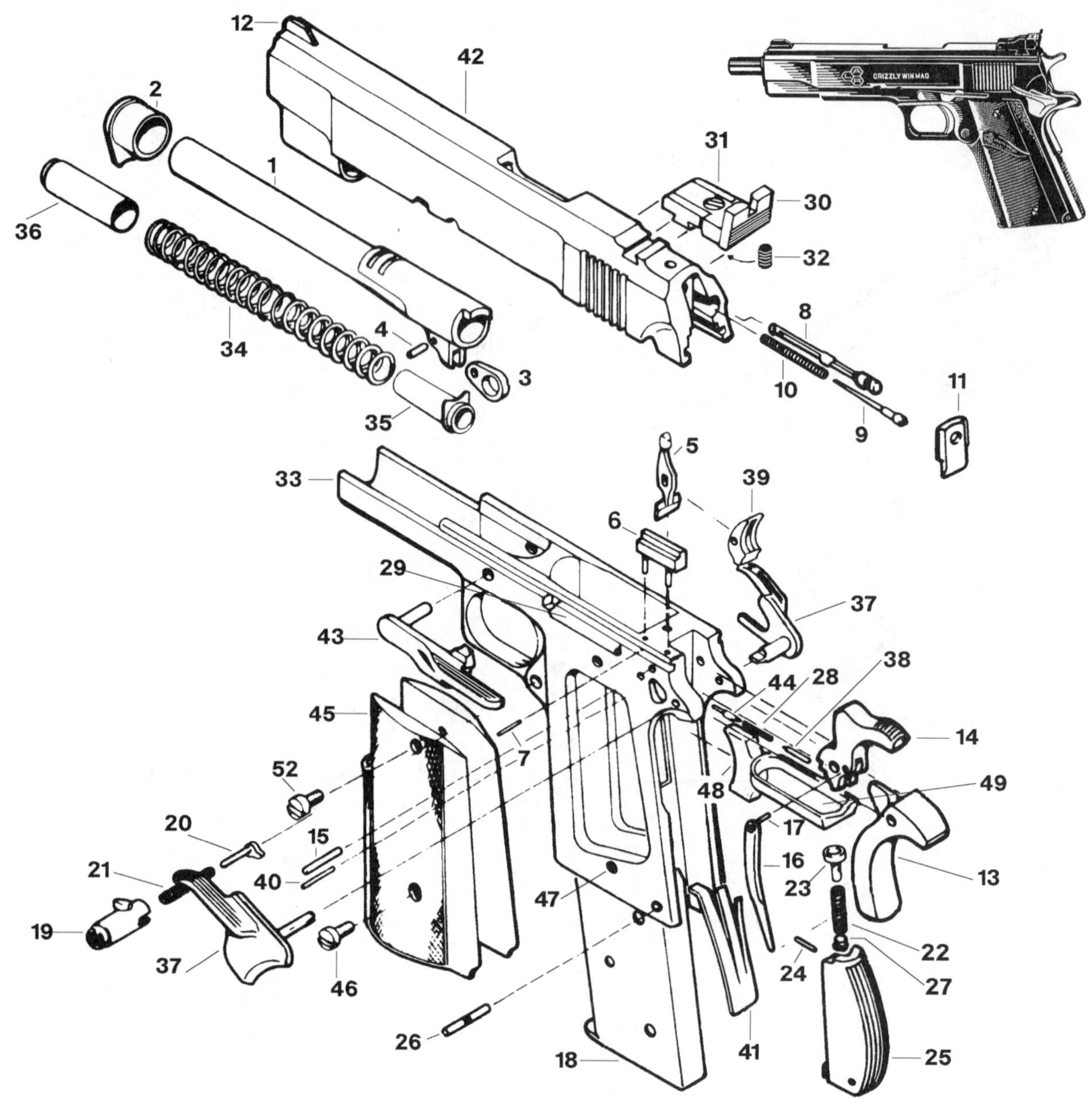

1	Barrel	**19**	Magazine Catch	**36**	Recoil Spring Plug
2	Barrel Bushing	**20**	Magazine Catch Lock	**37**	Safety Lock
3	Barrel Link	**21**	Magazine Catch Spring	**38**	Safety Lock Plunger
4	Barrel Link Pin	**22**	Mainspring	**39**	Sear
5	Disconnector	**23**	Mainspring Cap	**40**	Sear Pin
6	Ejector	**24**	Mainspring Cap Pin	**41**	Sear Spring
7	Ejector Pin	**25**	Mainspring Housing	**42**	Slide
8	Extractor	**26**	Mainspring Housing Pin	**43**	Slide Stop
9	Firing Pin	**27**	Mainspring Housing Pin Retainer	**44**	Slide Stop Plunger
10	Firing Pin Spring	**28**	Plunger Spring	**45**	Stock Assembly
11	Firing Pin Stop	**29**	Plunger Tube	**46**	Stock Screws
12	Front Sight	**30**	Rear Sight	**47**	Stock Screw Bushings
13	Grip Safety	**31**	Rear Sight Adjustment Screw	**48**	Trigger Assembly
14	Hammer	**32**	Rear Sight Spring	**49**	Trigger Bar
15	Hammer Pin	**33**	Receiver	**Parts Not Shown**	
16	Hammer Strut	**34**	Recoil Spring		Magazine Follower
17	Hammer Strut Pin	**35**	Recoil Spring Guide		Magazine Spring
18	Magazine Assembly				

9mm Browning Auto

Courtesy of Blacksmith Corporation

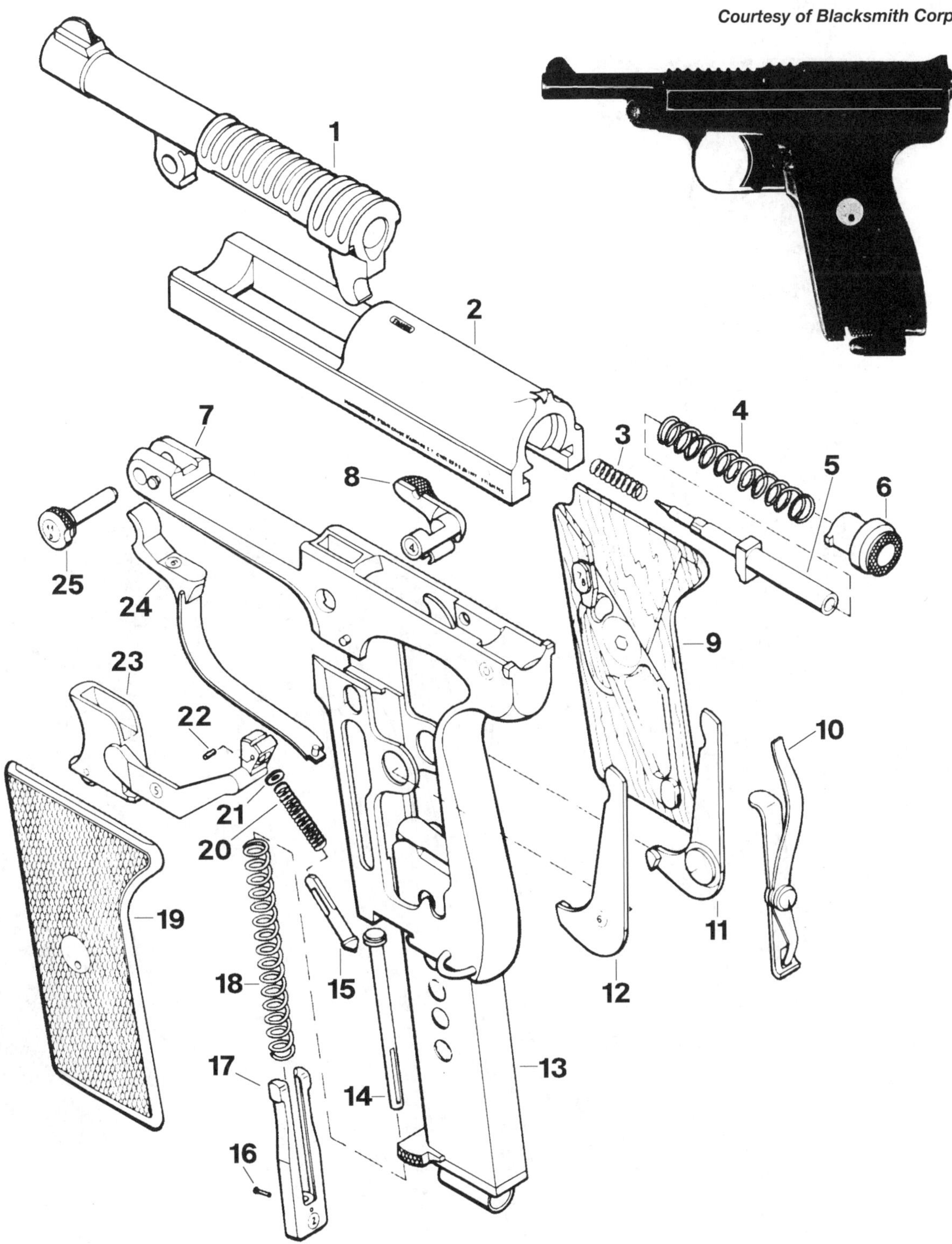

1	Barrel	10	Barrel Lever Spring	19	Left Grip
2	Slide	11	Right Recoil Lever	20	Trigger Spring
3	Firing Pin Rebound Spring	12	Left Recoil Lever	21	Trigger Spring Washer
4	Mainspring	13	Magazine Assembly	22	Trigger Strut Pin
5	Firing Pin	14	Recoil Spring Guide	23	Trigger
6	Slide Cap	15	Trigger Strut	24	Trigger Guard
7	Frame	16	Recoil Link Pin	25	Barrel Hinge Pin
8	Barrel Lever	17	Recoil Link		
9	Right Grip	18	Recoil Spring		

Pocket Model Auto

Courtesy of Dennis Riordan

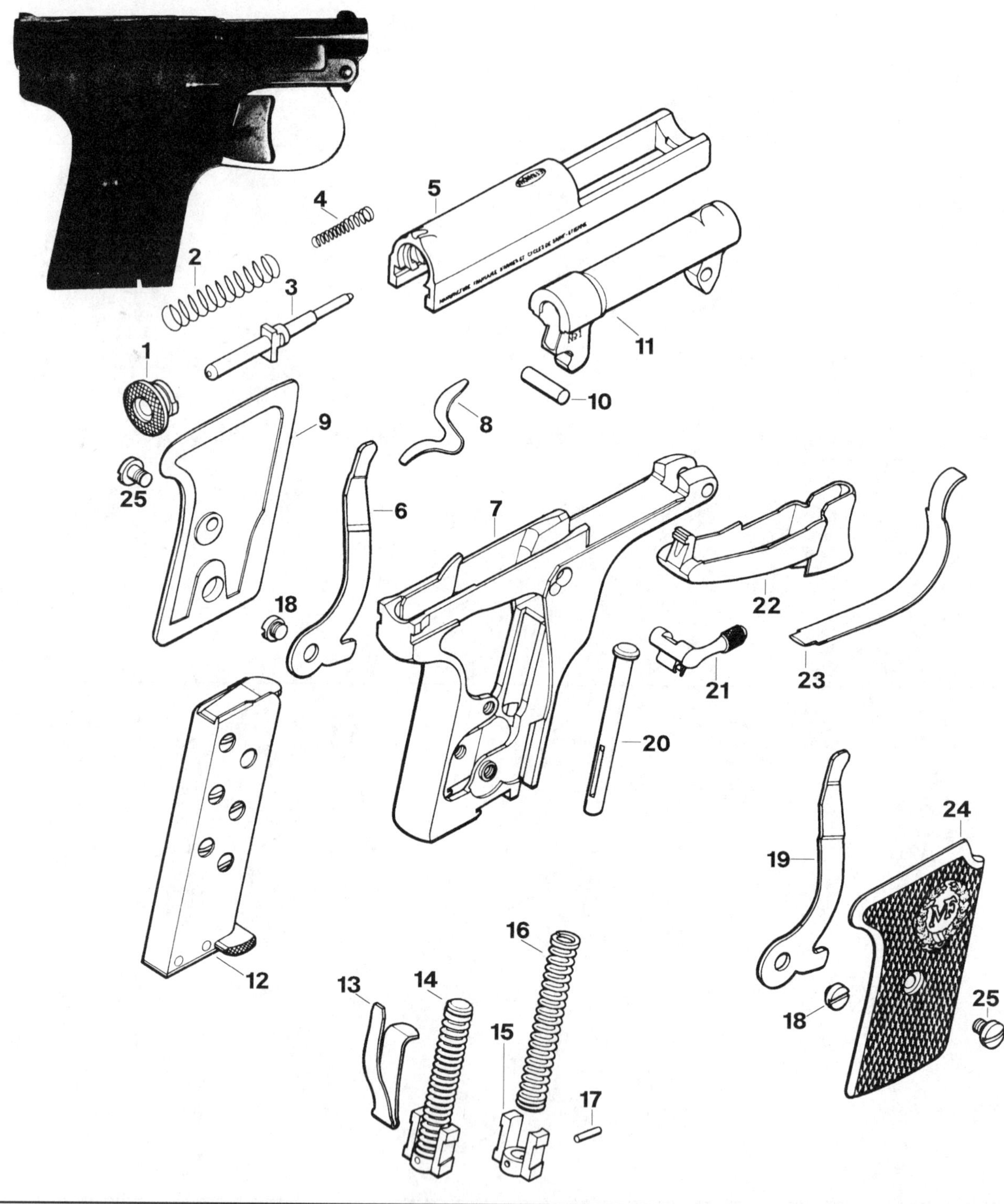

1	Slide Cap	**10**	Barrel Pin	**19**	Right Recoil Lever
2	Mainspring	**11**	Barrel	**20**	Recoil Spring Guide
3	Firing Pin	**12**	Magazine Assembly	**21**	Barrel Lever
4	Firing Pin Rebound Spring	**13**	Barrel Lever Spring	**22**	Trigger
5	Slide	**14**	Recoil Spring Assembly	**23**	Trigger Guard
6	Left Recoil Lever	**15**	Recoil Link	**24**	Right Grip
7	Frame	**16**	Recoil Spring	**25**	Grip Screws
8	Trigger Spring	**17**	Recoil Link Pin		
9	Left Grip	**18**	Recoil Lever Screws		

22 Auto

1	Frame	16	Mainspring Cap	31	Magazine Catch
2	Slide	17	Mainspring	32	Magazine Catch Spring
3	Barrel	18	Mainspring Housing Pin	33	Magazine Catch Lock
4	Hammer	19	Mainspring Cap Pin	34	Magazine Assembly
5	Hammer Pin	20	Barrel Bushing	35	Plunger Tube
6	Hammer Strut	21	Slide Stop	36	Slide Stop Plunger
7	Hammer Strut Pin	22	Recoil Spring Guide	37	Safety Lock Plunger
8	Sear	23	Plug	38	Plunger Spring
9	Sear Pin	24	Recoil Spring	39	Plunger Screws
10	Disconnector	25	Firing Pin	40	Grips
11	Trigger	26	Firing Pin Spring	41	Grips Screws
12	Grip Safety	27	Firing Pin Lock	42	Extractor
13	Safety Lock	28	Adjustable Sight	43	Extractor Spring
14	Sear Spring	29	Adjustable Sight Ball	44	Extractor Pin
15	Mainspring Housing	30	Adjustable Sight Screws		

32 Auto

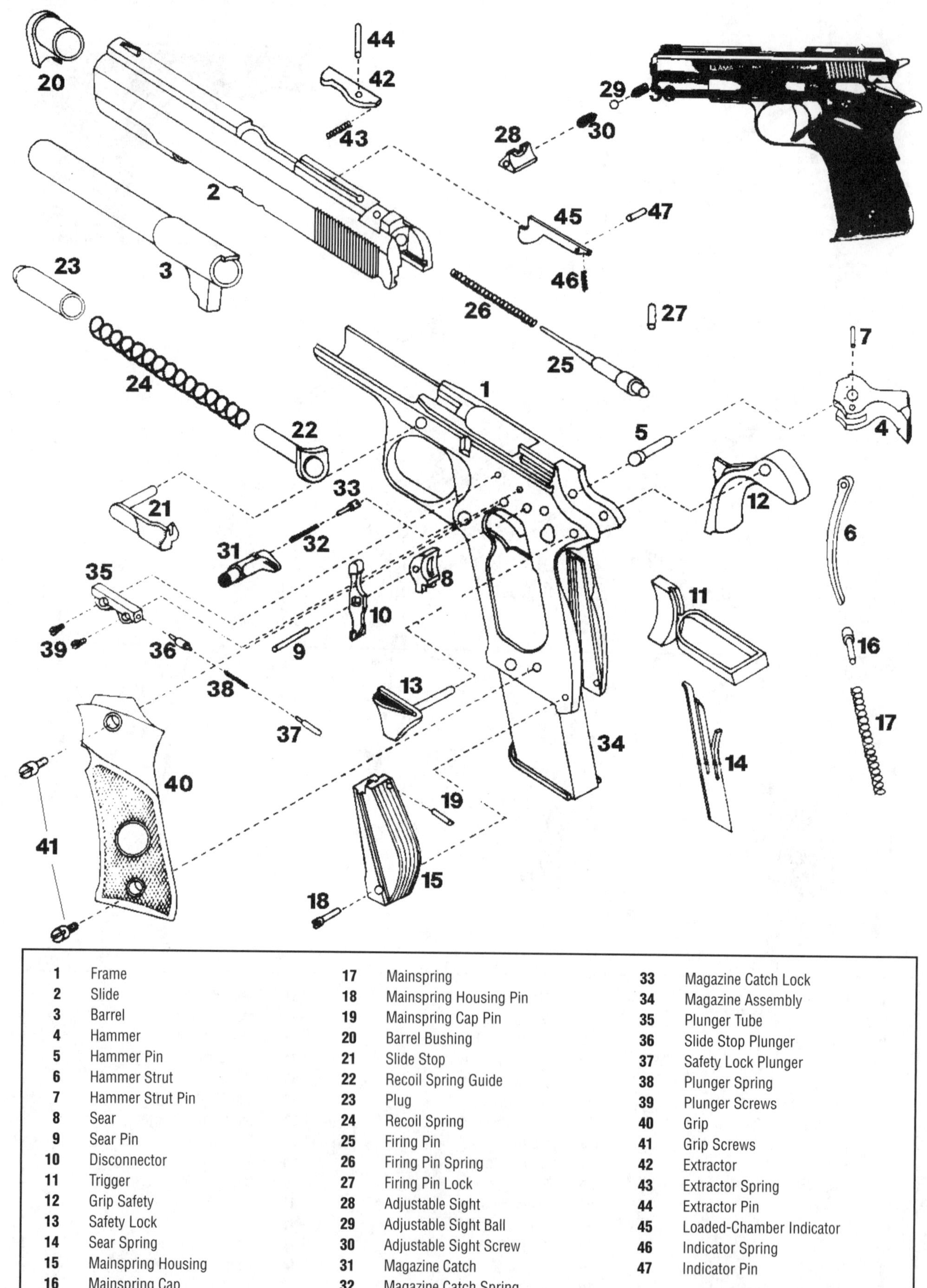

1	Frame	17	Mainspring	33	Magazine Catch Lock
2	Slide	18	Mainspring Housing Pin	34	Magazine Assembly
3	Barrel	19	Mainspring Cap Pin	35	Plunger Tube
4	Hammer	20	Barrel Bushing	36	Slide Stop Plunger
5	Hammer Pin	21	Slide Stop	37	Safety Lock Plunger
6	Hammer Strut	22	Recoil Spring Guide	38	Plunger Spring
7	Hammer Strut Pin	23	Plug	39	Plunger Screws
8	Sear	24	Recoil Spring	40	Grip
9	Sear Pin	25	Firing Pin	41	Grip Screws
10	Disconnector	26	Firing Pin Spring	42	Extractor
11	Trigger	27	Firing Pin Lock	43	Extractor Spring
12	Grip Safety	28	Adjustable Sight	44	Extractor Pin
13	Safety Lock	29	Adjustable Sight Ball	45	Loaded-Chamber Indicator
14	Sear Spring	30	Adjustable Sight Screw	46	Indicator Spring
15	Mainspring Housing	31	Magazine Catch	47	Indicator Pin
16	Mainspring Cap	32	Magazine Catch Spring		

357 Revolver

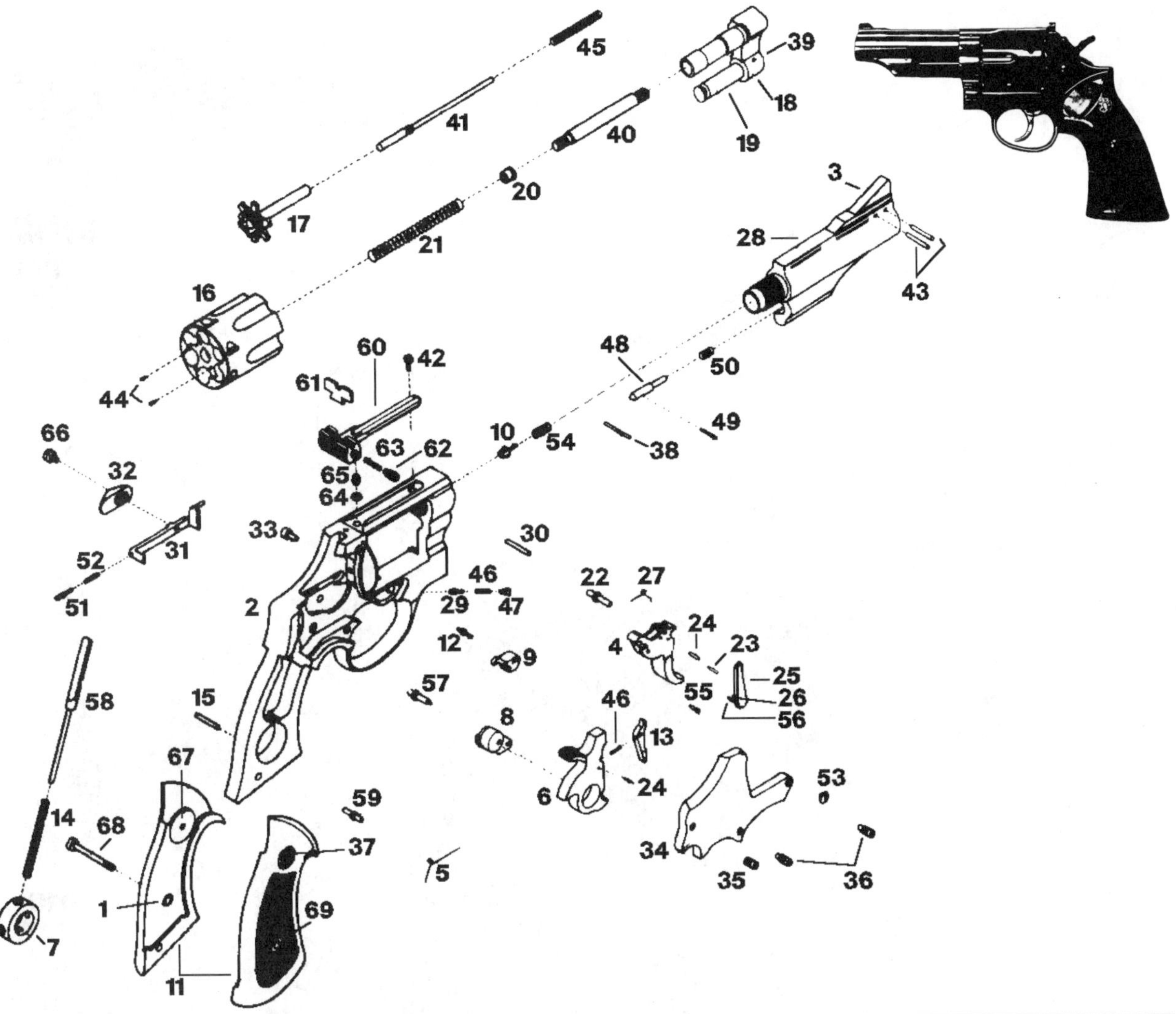

1	Washer	**25**	Hand	**48**	Locking Bolt
2	Frame	**26**	Hand Spring Stop	**49**	Locking Bolt Pin
3	Front Sight	**27**	Hand Spring	**50**	Locking Bolt Spring
4	Trigger	**28**	Barrel	**51**	Bolt Plunger
5	Trigger Spring	**29**	Cylinder Stop Plunger	**52**	Bolt Spring
6	Hammer	**30**	Barrel Pin	**53**	Upper Plate Screw
7	Pressure Regulator	**31**	Bolt	**54**	Firing Nose Spring
8	Hammer Cam	**32**	Thumb-Piece	**55**	Trigger Spring Plunger
9	Cylinder Stop	**33**	Frame Lug	**56**	Hand Axle
10	Firing Nose	**34**	Sideplate	**57**	Hammer Stud
11	Stocks	**35**	Plate Screw	**58**	Hammer Strut
12	Cylinder Stop Center	**36**	Yoke Screws	**59**	Trigger Spring Pin
13	Sear	**37**	Medallion	**60**	Rear Sight Leaf
14	Hammer Spring	**38**	Firing Nose Pin	**61**	Rear Sight
15	Stock Guide Pin	**39**	Yoke Pin	**62**	Rear Sight Windage Screw
16	Cylinder	**40**	Extractor Rod	**63**	Rear Sight Spring
17	Extractor	**41**	Center Pin	**64**	Nut Plate of Rear Sight Leaf Elevator
18	Yoke	**42**	Rear Sight Leaf Screw		
19	Yoke Center	**43**	Front Sight Pins	**65**	Rear Sight Elevating Nut
20	Extractor Collar	**44**	Extractor Guide Plungers	**66**	Thumb-Piece Screw
21	Extractor Spring	**45**	Extractor Spring	**67**	Rivet for Medallion
22	Trigger Stud	**46**	Cylinder Stop Plunger Spring and Sear Spring	**68**	Stock Screw
23	Hand Spring Pin			**69**	Nut
24	Sear Pin and Hand Spring Axle	**47**	Cylinder Stop Screw		

380 Auto

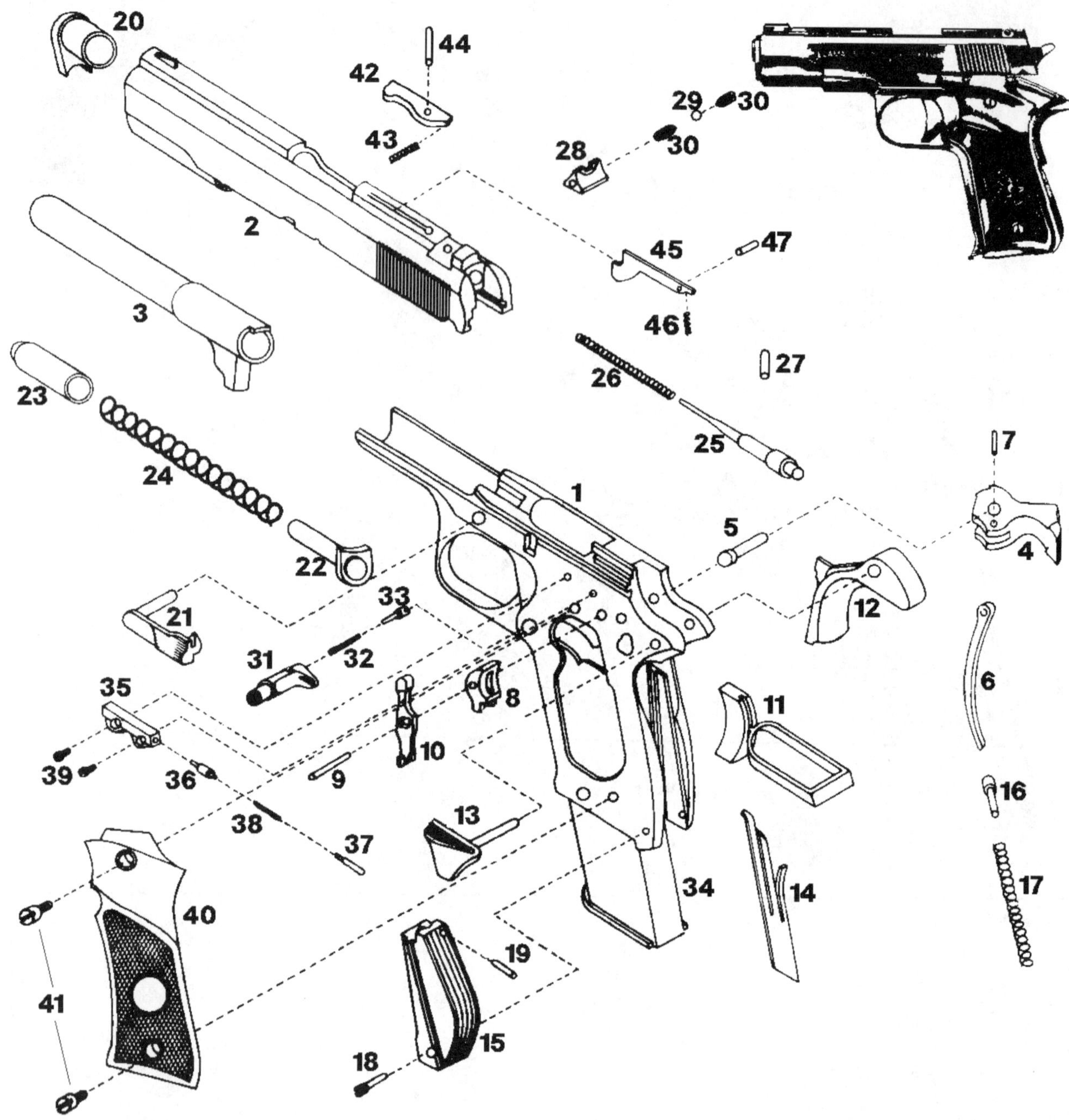

6	Hammer Strut	20	Barrel Bushing	34	Magazine
7	Hammer Strut Pin	21	Slide Stop	35	Plunger Tube
8	Sear	22	Recoil Spring Guide	36	Slide Stop Plunger
9	Sear Pin	23	Plug	37	Safety Lock Plunger
10	Disconnector	24	Recoil Spring	38	Plunger Spring
11	Trigger	25	Firing Pin	39	Plunger Screws
12	Grip Safety	26	Firing Pin Spring	40	Grip
13	Safety Lock	27	Firing Pin Lock	41	Grip Screws
14	Sear Spring	28	Adjustable Sight	42	Extractor
15	Mainspring Housing	29	Adjustable Sight Ball	43	Extractor Spring
16	Mainspring Cap	30	Adjustable Sight Screws	44	Extractor Pin
17	Mainspring	31	Magazine Catch	45	Loaded-Chamber Indicator
18	Mainspring Housing Pin	32	Magazine Catch Spring	46	Indicator Spring
19	Mainspring Cap Pin	33	Magazine Catch Lock	47	Indicator Pin

44 Magnum Revolver

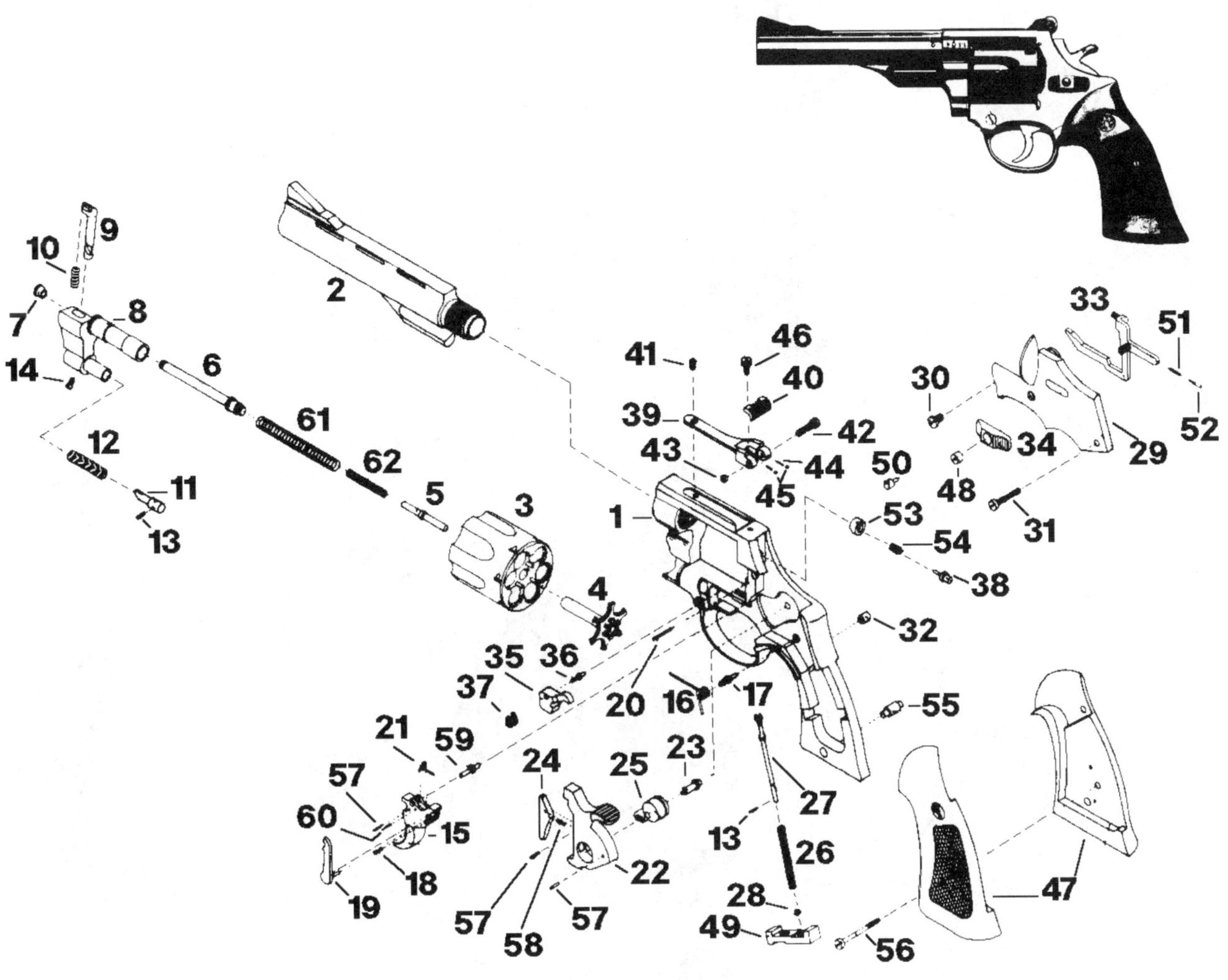

1	Frame	22	Hammer	43	Rear Sight Screw Nut
2	Barrel	23	Hammer Stud	44	Elevating Nut Springs
3	Cylinder	24	Sear	45	Elevating Nut Balls
4	Extractor	25	Hammer Cam	46	Rear Sight Elevating Nut
5	Center Pin	26	Hammer Spring	47	Stocks
6	Extractor Rod	27	Hammer Strut	48	Thumb-Piece Nut
7	Extractor Rod Collar	28	Hammer Spring Prop	49	Pressure Regulator
8	Yoke	29	Sideplate	50	Frame Lug
9	Yoke Bolt	30	Plate Screw	51	Bolt Plunger Spring
10	Bolt Spring	31	Grip Screw Guide	52	Bolt Plunger
11	Bolt Disconnector	32	Grip Screw Guide Nut	53	Pin Bush
12	Disconnector Spring	33	Bolt	54	Firing Nose Spring
13	Disconnector Spring Pins	34	Thumb-Piece	55	Stock Guide Pin
14	Yoke Screw	35	Cylinder Stop	56	Stock Screw
15	Trigger	36	Cylinder Stop Center	57	Sear Pin and Hammer Strut Pin
16	Trigger Spring	37	Cylinder Stop Spring	58	Sear Spring
17	Trigger Spring Pin	38	Firing Nose	59	Trigger Stud
18	Trigger Spring Plunger	39	Rear Sight Leaf	60	Hand Spring Pin
19	Hand	40	Rear Sight	61	Extractor Spring
20	Hand Stop	41	Rear Sight Leaf Screw	62	Center Pin Spring
21	Hand Spring	42	Rear Sight Windage Screw		

45 Auto

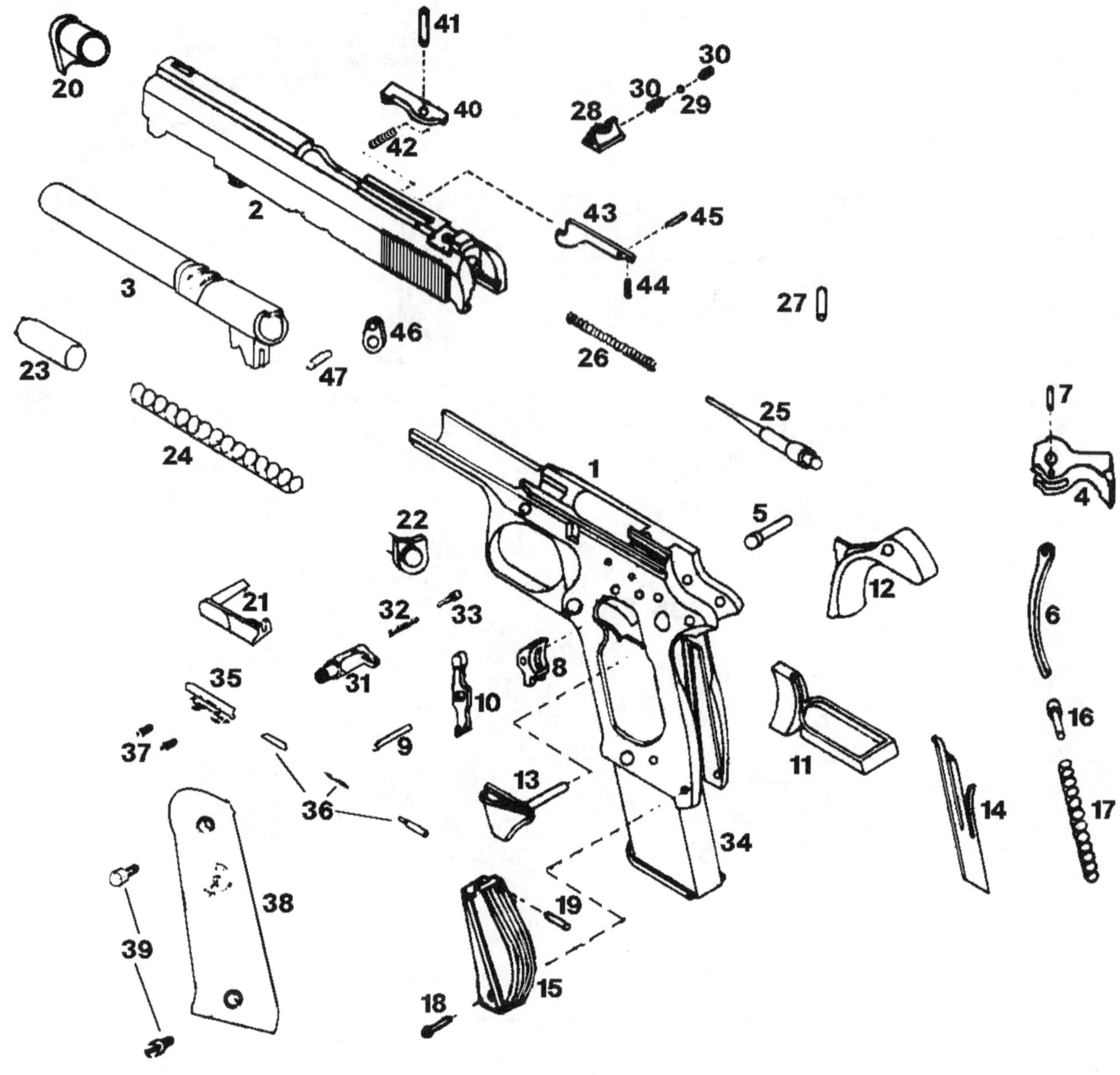

1	Frame	18	Mainspring Housing Pin	35	Plunger Tube
2	Slide	19	Mainspring Cap Pin	36	Plunger Complete
3	Barrel	20	Barrel Bushing	37	Plunger Screws
4	Hammer	21	Slide Stop	38	Grip
5	Hammer Pin	22	Recoil Spring Guide	39	Grip Screws
6	Hammer Strut	23	Plug	40	Extractor
7	Hammer Strut Pin	24	Recoil Spring	41	Extractor Pin
8	Sear	25	Firing Pin	42	Extractor Spring
9	Sear Pin	26	Firing Pin Spring	43	Loaded-Chamber Indicator
10	Disconnector	27	Firing Pin Lock	44	Indicator Spring
11	Trigger	28	Adjustable Rear Sight	45	Indicator Pin
12	Grip Safety	29	Adjustable Sight Ball	46	Barrel Link
13	Safety Lock	30	Adjustable Sight Screws	47	Barrel Link Pin
14	Sear Spring	31	Magazine Catch	**Parts Not Shown**	
15	Mainspring Housing	32	Magazine Catch Spring		Front Sight
16	Mainspring Cap	33	Magazine Catch Lock		
17	Mainspring	34	Magazine		

45 Omni Auto

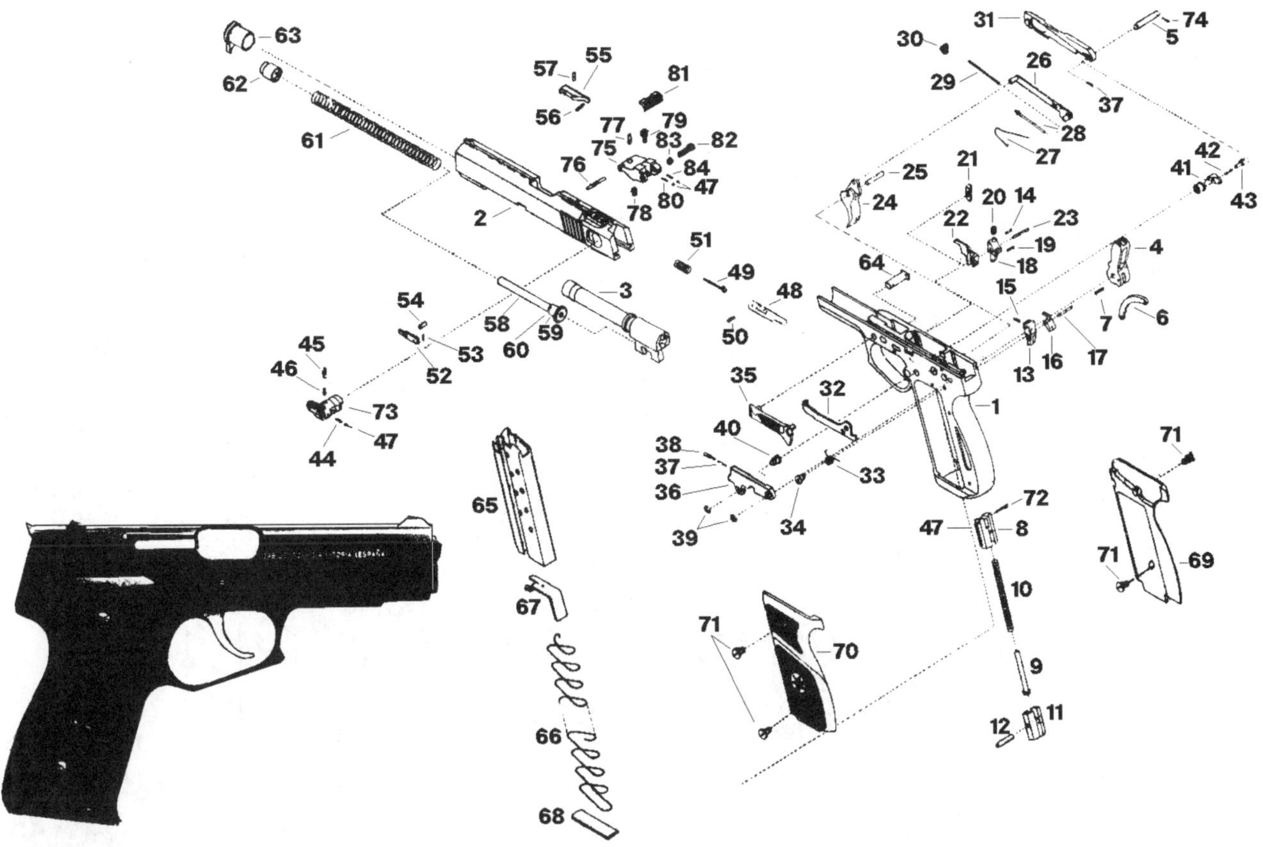

1	Frame	29	Double Action Trigger Bar Spring	57	Extractor Pin
2	Slide	30	Double Action Trigger Bar Spring Support	58	Recoil Spring Guide
3	Barrel	31	Bolt	59	Recoil Spring Guide Head
4	Hammer	32	Single Action Trigger Bar	60	Recoil Spring Guide Pin
5	Hammer Pin	33	Single Action Trigger Bar Spring	61	Recoil Spring
6	Stirrup	34	Single Action Trigger Bar Spring Pin	62	Recoil Spring Plug
7	Stirrup Pin	35	Slide Stop	63	Barrel Bushing
8	Hammer Spring Carriage	36	Plunger Tube	64	Barrel Pin
9	Hammer Spring Guide	37	Plunger Tube Spring/Bolt Spring	65	Magazine
10	Hammer Spring	38	Tube Spring Plunger	66	Magazine Spring
11	Hammer Spring Stop	39	Tube Fixing Washer	67	Magazine Follower
12	Hammer Spring Stop Pin	40	Tube Fixing Pin	68	Magazine Buttplate
13	Sear	41	Magazine Catch	69	Right Stock
14	Automatic Safety Lock Spring Pin	42	Magazine Catch Spring	70	Left Stock
15	Sear Spring	43	Catch Screw	71	Stock Screws
16	Automatic Safety Lock Disconnector	44	Manual Safety Lock Ball Spring	72	Hammer Spring Carriage Pin
17	Sear Pin	45	Safety Lock Plunger	73	Manual Safety Lock
18	Automatic Safety Lock	46	Safety Lock Plunger Spring	74	Hammer Pin Transverse Pin
19	Automatic Safety Lock Pin	47	Carriage Ball Bearings	75	Rear Sight Leaf
20	Automatic Safety Lock Spring	48	Rear Part of Firing Pin	76	Leaf Stud
21	Manual Safety Lock	49	Front Part of Firing Pin	77	Rear Sight Pin Fastening Pin/ Firing Nose Butt Pin
22	Ejector	50	Firing Pin Stud	78	Rear Sight Elevating Spring
23	Ejector Pin	51	Firing Pin Spring	79	Rear Sight Elevating Screw
24	Trigger	52	Firing Pin Safety Lock	80	Elevating Screw Spring
25	Trigger Pin	53	Firing Pin Safety Lock Spring	81	Rear Sight
26	Double Action Trigger Bar	54	Firing Pin Safety Lock Pin	82	Rear Sight Windage Screw
27	Double Action Trigger Bar Raising Spring	55	Extractor	83	Rear Sight Windage Spring
28	Double Action Trigger Bar Spring Guide	56	Extractor Spring	84	Rear Sight Windage Screw Spring

M-87 Auto

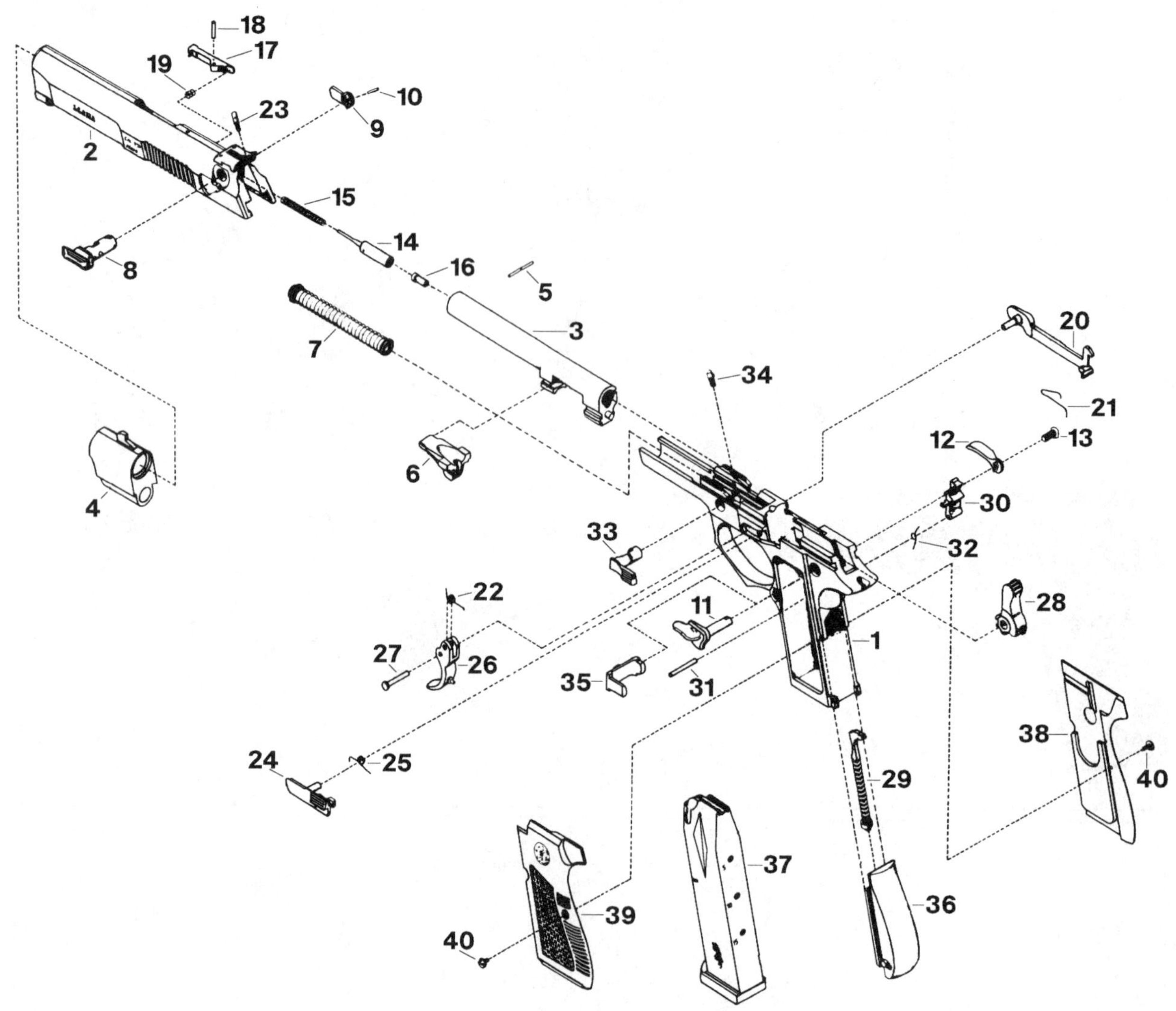

1	Frame	14	Firing Pin	28	Hammer
2	Slide	15	Firing Pin Spring	29	Hammer Spring
3	Barrel	16	Firing Pin Impeller	30	Sear
4	Muzzle Compensator	17	Extractor	31	Sear Pin
5	Muzzle Compensator Fastening Pin	18	Extractor Pin	32	Sear Spring
6	Locking Block	19	Extractor Spring	33	Disassembling Latch
7	Recoil Spring	20	Trigger Bar	34	Disassembling Latch Fixing Pin
8	Left Safety	21	Trigger Bar Spring	35	Magazine Catch
9	Right Safety	22	Trigger Spring	36	Hammer Spring Housing
10	Right Safety Pin	23	Trigger Bar Disconnector	37	Magazine Assembly
11	Safety Lock	24	Slide Stop	38	Right Grip
12	Right Grip Safety	25	Slide Stop Spring	39	Left Grip
13	Grip Fastening Screw	26	Trigger	40	Grip Screws
		27	Trigger Pin		

9mm DA M-82 Auto

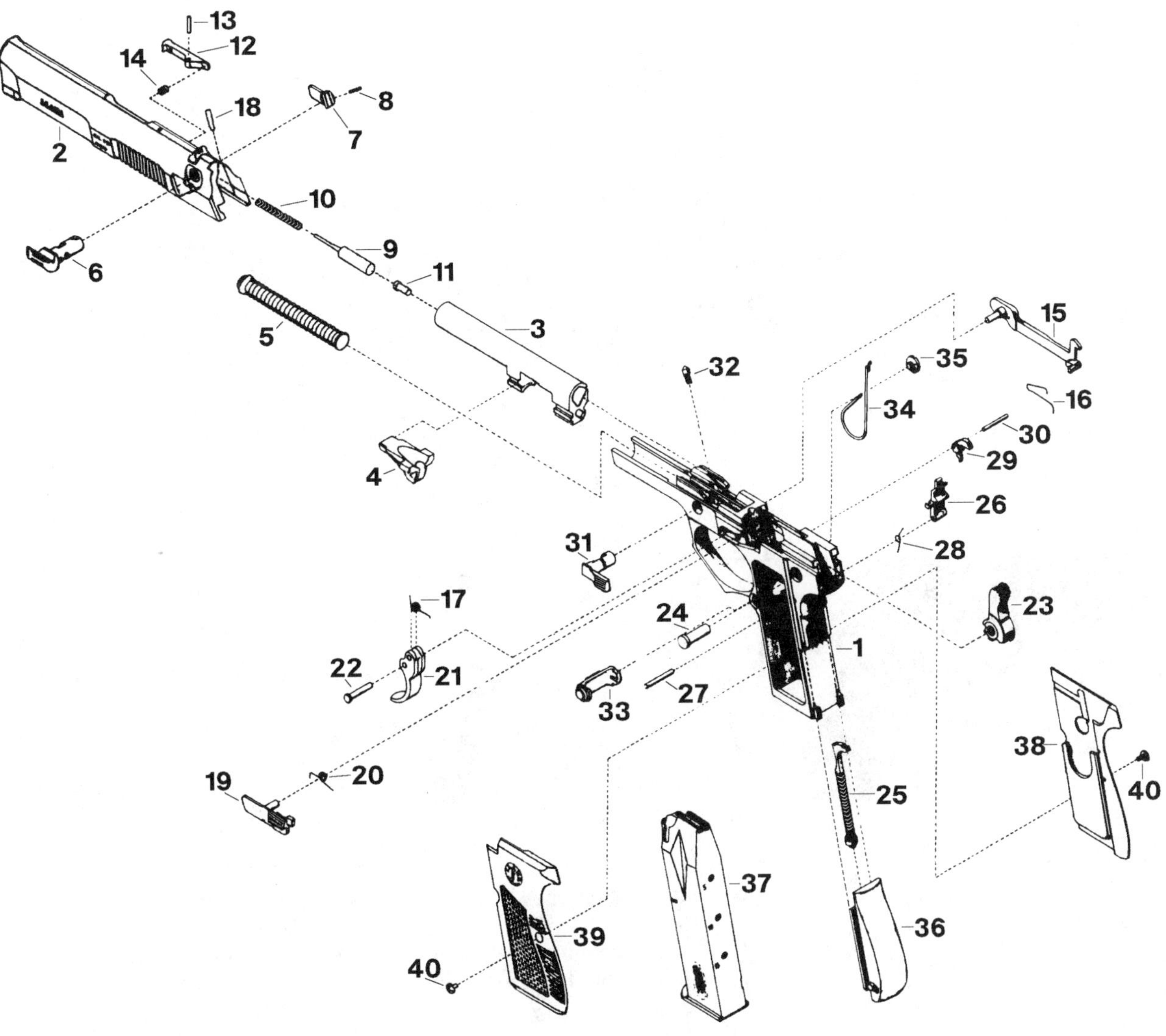

1	Frame	21	Trigger
2	Slide	22	Trigger Pin
3	Barrel	23	Hammer
4	Locking Block	24	Hammer Pin
5	Recoil Spring	25	Hammer Spring
6	Left Safety	26	Sear
7	Right Safety	27	Sear Pin
8	Right Safety Pin	28	Sear Spring
9	Firing Pin	29	Sear Disconnector
10	Firing Pin Spring	30	Sear Disconnector Pin
11	Firing Pin Impeller	31	Disassembling Latch
12	Extractor	32	Disassembling Latch Fixing Pin
13	Extractor Pin	33	Magazine Catch
14	Extractor Spring	34	Magazine Safety
15	Trigger Bar	35	Magazine Safety Screw
16	Trigger Bar Spring	36	Hammer Spring Housing
17	Trigger Spring	37	Magazine
18	Trigger Bar Disconnector	38	Right Grip
19	Slide Stop	39	Left Grip
20	Slide Stop Spring	40	Grip Screws

9mm Omni Auto

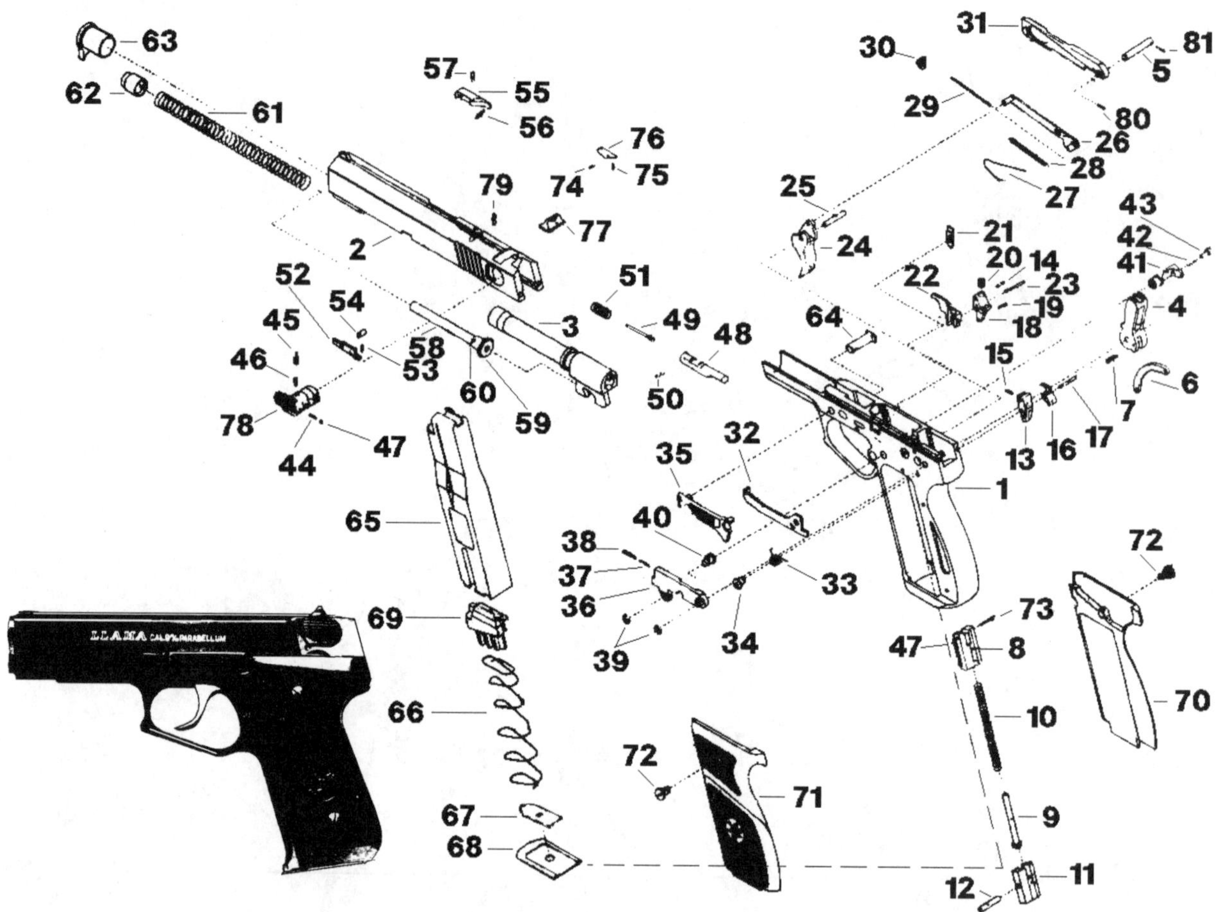

1	Frame
2	Slide
3	Barrel
4	Hammer
5	Hammer Pin
6	Stirrup
7	Stirrup Pin
8	Hammer Spring Carriage
9	Hammer Spring Guide
10	Hammer Spring
11	Hammer Spring Stop
12	Hammer Spring Stop Pin
13	Sear
14	Automatic Safety Lock Spring Pin
15	Sear Spring
16	Automatic Safety Lock Disconnector
17	Sear Pin
18	Automatic Safety Lock
19	Automatic Safety Lock Pin
20	Automatic Safety Lock Spring
21	Manual Safety Lock
22	Ejector
23	Ejector Pin
24	Trigger
25	Trigger Pin
26	Double Action Trigger Bar
27	DA Trigger Bar Raising Spring
28	Double Action Trigger Bar Spring Guide
29	Double Action Trigger Bar Spring
30	Double Action Trigger Bar Spring Support
31	Bolt
32	Single Action Trigger Bar
33	Sirgle Action Trigger Bar Spring
34	Single Action Trigger Bar Spring Pin
35	Slide Stop
36	Plunger Tube
37	Plunger Tube Spring
38	Tube Spring Plunger
39	Tube Fixing Washers
40	Tube Fixing Pin
41	Magazine Catch
42	Magazine Catch Spring
43	Catch Screw
44	Manual Safety Lock Ball Spring
45	Safety Lock Plunger
46	Safety Lock Plunger Spring
47	Carriage Ball Bearing
48	Rear Part of Firing Pin
49	Front Part of Firing Pin
50	Firing Pin Stud
51	Firing Pin Spring
52	Firing Pin Safety Lock
53	Firing Pin Safety Lock Spring
54	Firing Pin Safety Lock Pin
55	Extractor
56	Extractor Spring
57	Extractor Pin
58	Recoil Spring Guide
59	Recoil Spring Guide Head
60	Recoil Spring Guide Pin
61	Recoil Spring
62	Recoil Spring Plug
63	Barrel Bushing
64	Barrel Pin
65	Magazine
66	Magazine Spring
67	Magazine Buttplate Catch
68	Magazine Buttplate
69	Magazine Follower
70	Right Stock
71	Left Stock
72	Stock Screws
73	Hammer Spring Carriage Pin
74	Indicator Pin
75	Indicator Spring
76	Loaded-Chamber Indicator
77	Rear Sight
78	Manual Safety Lock
79	Firing Pin Stop Pin
80	Bolt Spring
81	Hammer Pin Transverse Pin

9mm Parabellum Auto

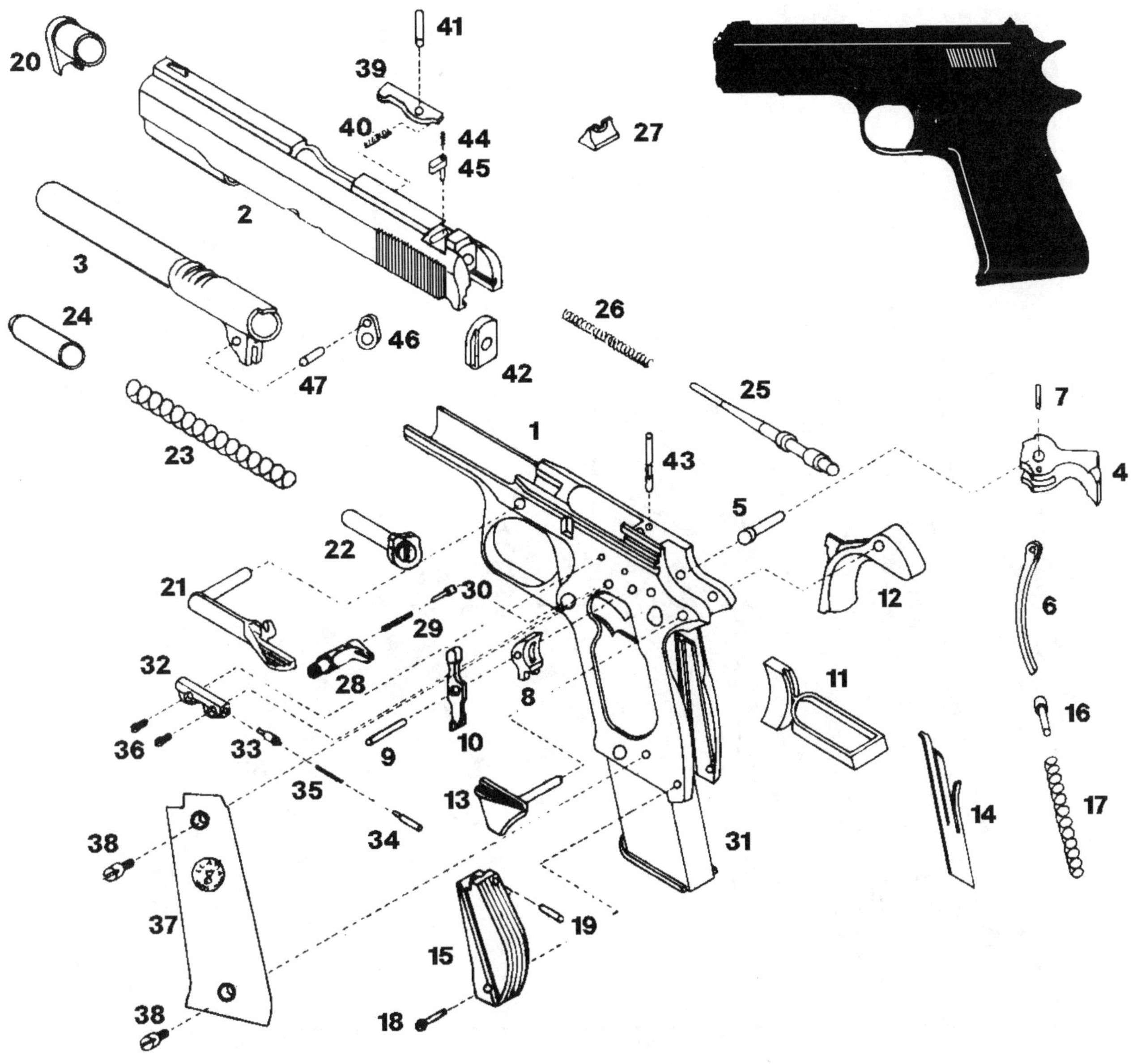

1	Frame	17	Mainspring	33	Slide Stop Plunger
2	Slide	18	Mainspring Housing Pin	34	Safety Lock Plunger
3	Barrel	19	Mainspring Cap Pin	35	Plunger Spring
4	Hammer	20	Barrel Bushing	36	Plunger Screws
5	Hammer Pin	21	Slide Stop	37	Grip
6	Hammer Strut	22	Recoil Spring Guide	38	Grip Screws
7	Hammer Strut Pin	23	Recoil Spring	39	Extractor
8	Sear	24	Plug	40	Extractor Spring
9	Sear Pin	25	Firing Pin	41	Extractor Pin
10	Disconnector	26	Firing Pin Spring	42	Firing Pin Retainer
11	Trigger	27	Rear Sight	43	Firing Pin Safety Disconnector
12	Grip Safety	28	Magazine Catch	44	Firing Pin Safety Spring
13	Safety Lock	29	Magazine Catch Spring	45	Firing Pin Safety
14	Sear Spring	30	Magazine Catch Lock	46	Catenary
15	Mainspring Housing	31	Magazine	47	Catenary Pin
16	Mainspring Cap	32	Plunger Tube		

Comanche III Revolver

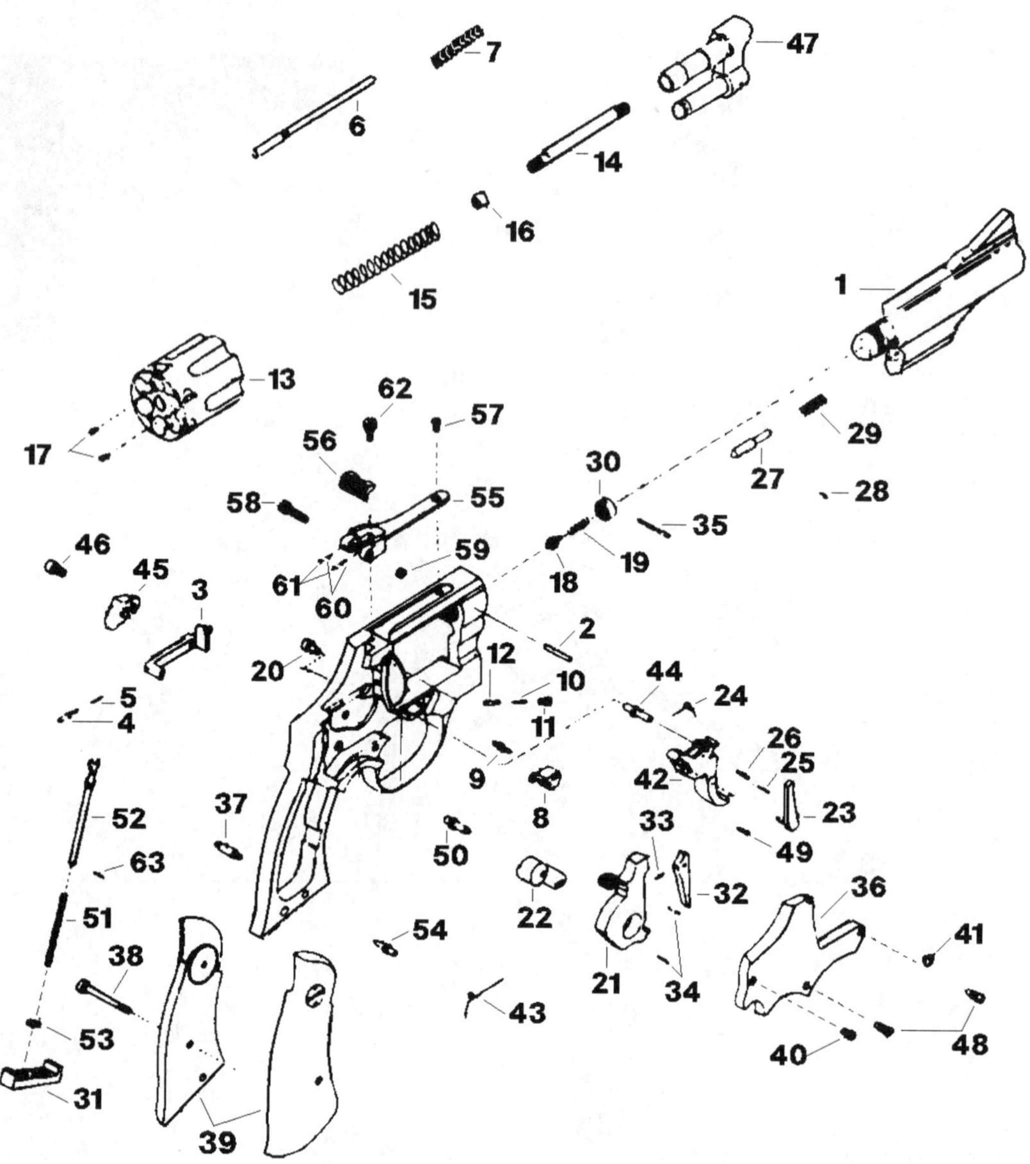

1	Barrel	**22**	Hammer Cam	**43**	Trigger Spring
2	Barrel Pin	**23**	Hand	**44**	Trigger Stud
3	Bolt	**24**	Hand Spring	**45**	Thumb-Piece
4	Bolt Plunger	**25**	Hand Spring Pin	**46**	Thumb-Piece Screw
5	Bolt Spring	**26**	Hammer Strut Pin	**47**	Yoke
6	Center Pin	**27**	Locking Bolt	**48**	Yoke Screws
7	Center Pin Spring	**28**	Locking Bolt Pin	**49**	Trigger Spring Plunger
8	Cylinder Stop	**29**	Locking Bolt Spring	**50**	Hammer Stud
9	Cylinder Stop Center	**30**	Pin Bushing	**51**	Hammer Spring
10	Cylinder Stop Plunger Spring	**31**	Pressure Regulator	**52**	Hammer Strut
11	Cylinder Stop Screw	**32**	Sear	**53**	Hammer Strut Prop
12	Cylinder Stop Plunger	**33**	Sear Spring	**54**	Trigger Spring Pin
13	Cylinder/Extractor	**34**	Sear Pin	**55**	Rear Sight Leaf
14	Extractor Rod	**35**	Steady Pins	**56**	Rear Sight
15	Extractor Spring	**36**	Sideplate	**57**	Rear Sight Leaf Screw
16	Extractor Collar	**37**	Stock Guide Pin	**58**	Rear Sight Windage Screw
17	Extractor Pins	**38**	Stock Screw	**59**	Rear Sight Screw Nut
18	Firing Nose	**39**	Stocks	**60**	Ball Springs
19	Firing Nose Spring	**40**	Plate Screw	**61**	Elevation Nut Balls
20	Frame Lug	**41**	Plate Screw, Upper	**62**	Rear Sight Elevation Nut
21	Hammer	**42**	Trigger	**63**	Disconnector Spring Pin

Large Frame IX-A Auto

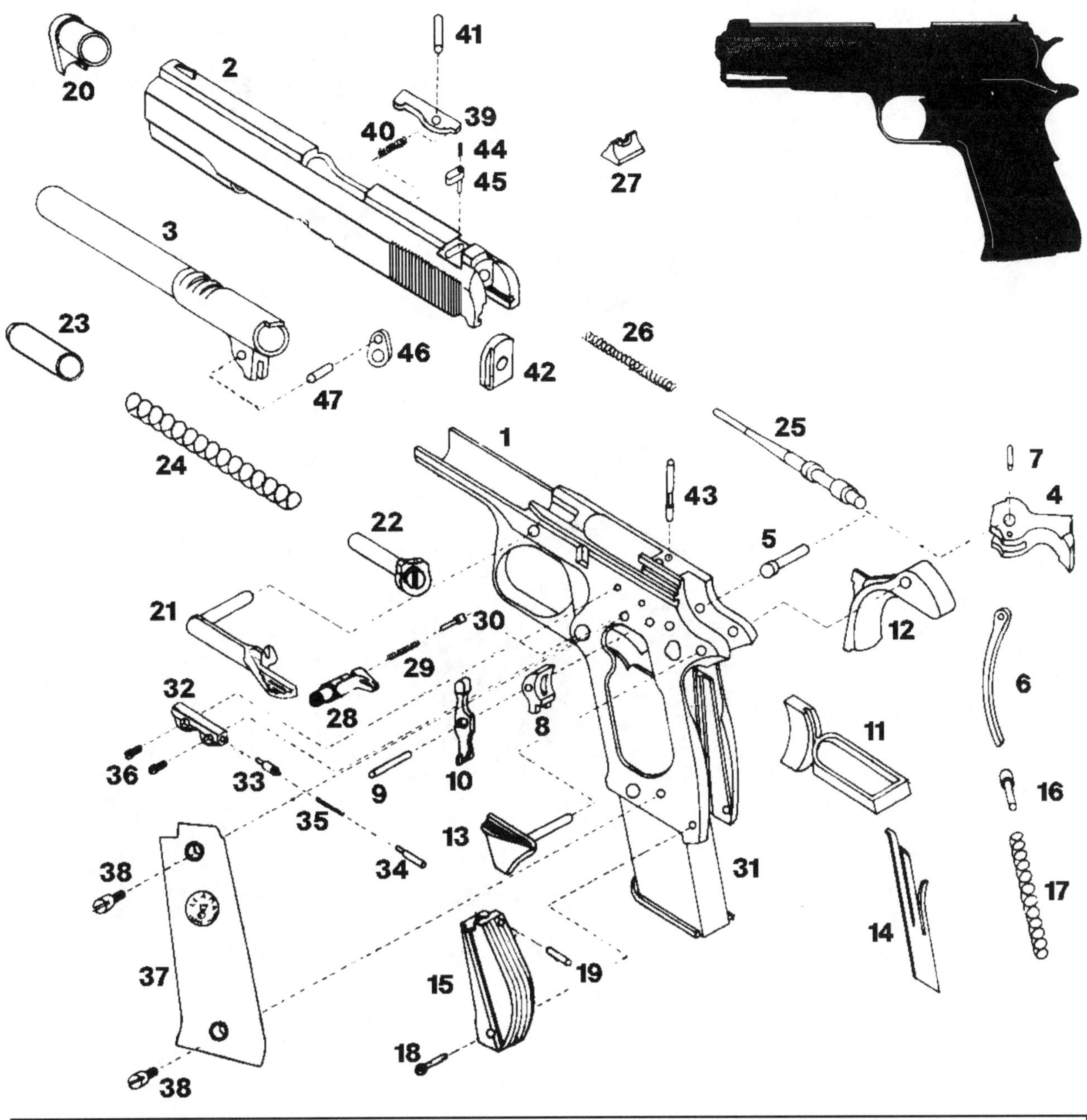

1	Frame	**17**	Mainspring	**33**	Slide Stop Plunger
2	Slide	**18**	Mainspring Housing Pin	**34**	Safety Lock Plunger
3	Barrel	**19**	Mainspring Cap Pin	**35**	Plunger Spring
4	Hammer	**20**	Barrel Bushing	**36**	Plunger Screws
5	Hammer Pin	**21**	Slide Stop	**37**	Grip
6	Hammer Strut	**22**	Recoil Spring Guide	**38**	Grip Screws
7	Hammer Strut Pin	**23**	Plug	**39**	Extractor
8	Sear	**24**	Recoil Spring	**40**	Extractor Spring
9	Sear Pin	**25**	Firing Pin	**41**	Extractor Pin
10	Disconnector	**26**	Firing Pin Spring	**42**	Firing Pin Retainer
11	Trigger	**27**	Rear Sight	**43**	Firing Pin Safety Disconnector
12	Grip Safety	**28**	Magazine Catch	**44**	Firing Pin Safety Spring
13	Safety Lock	**29**	Magazine Catch Spring	**45**	Firing Pin Safety
14	Sear Spring	**30**	Magazine Catch Lock	**46**	Catenary
15	Mainspring Housing	**31**	Magazine	**47**	Catenary Pin
16	Mainspring Cap	**32**	Plunger Tube		

Large Frame IX-B

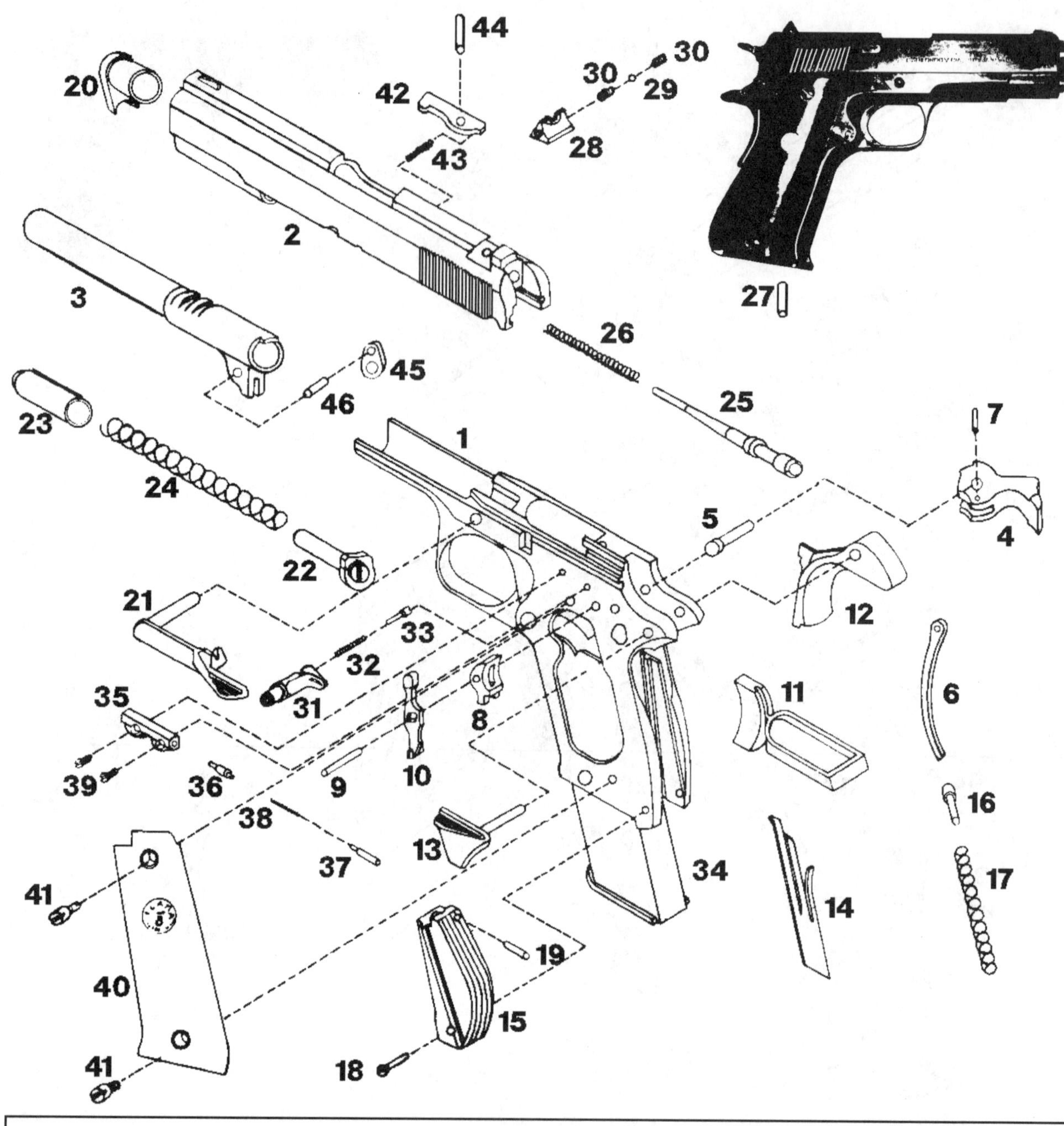

1	Frame	17	Mainspring	33	Magazine Catch Lock
2	Slide	18	Mainspring Housing Pin	34	Magazine
3	Barrel	19	Mainspring Cap Pin	35	Plunger Tube
4	Hammer	20	Barrel Bushing	36	Slide Stop Plunger
5	Hammer Pin	21	Slide Stop	37	Safety Lock Plunger
6	Hammer Strut	22	Recoil Spring Guide	38	Plunger Spring
7	Hammer Strut Pin	23	Plug	39	Plunger Screws
8	Sear	24	Recoil Spring	40	Grip
9	Sear Pin	25	Firing Pin	41	Grip Screws
10	Disconnector	26	Firing Pin Spring	42	Extractor
11	Trigger	27	Firing Pin Lock	43	Extractor Spring
12	Grip Safety	28	Adjustable Sight	44	Extractor Pin
13	Safety Lock	29	Adjustable Sight Ball	45	Catenary
14	Sear Spring	30	Adjustable Sight Screws	46	Catenary Pin
15	Mainspring Housing	31	Magazine Catch		
16	Mainspring Cap	32	Magazine Catch Spring		

Martial 38 and 22 Revolver

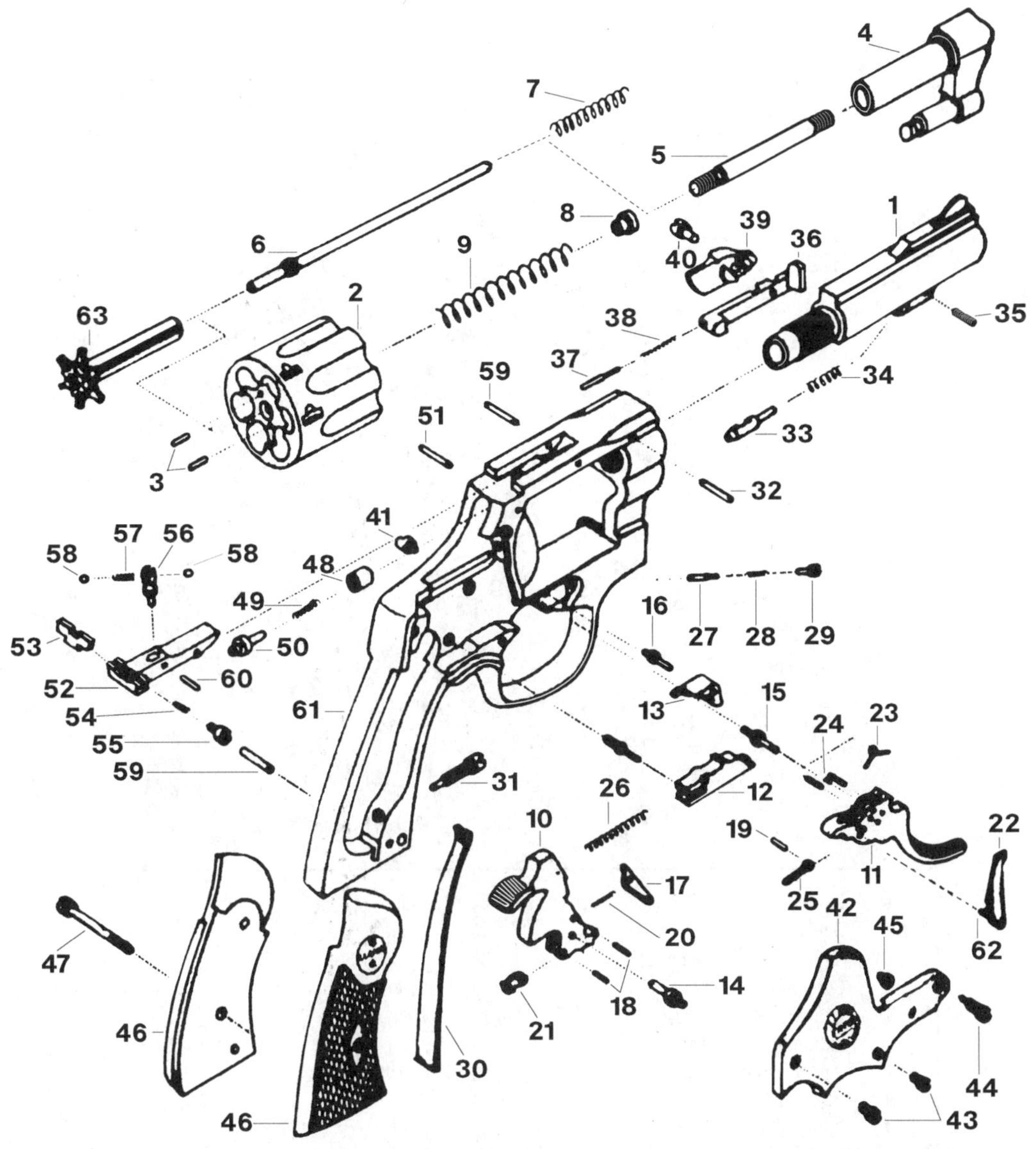

1	Barrel	22	Hand	43	Sideplate Screws
2	Cylinder	23	Hand Lever Spring	44	Yoke Screw
3	Extractor Pins	24	Hand Spring Pins	45	Sideplate Screw
4	Yoke	25	Trigger Lever	46	Grip Panels
5	Extractor Rod	26	Rebound Slide Spring	47	Grip Screw
6	Center Pin	27	Cylinder Stop Plunger	48	Pin Bushing
7	Center Pin Spring	28	Cylinder Stop Spring	49	Firing Pin Nose Spring
8	Extractor Collar	29	Cylinder Stop Screw	50	Firing Pin Nose
9	Extractor Spring	30	Mainspring	51	Steady Pin
10	Hammer	31	Strain Screw	52	Rear Sight Base
11	Trigger	32	Barrel Pin	53	Rear Sight Leaf
12	Rebound Slide	33	Lock Bolt	54	Rear Sight Spring
13	Cylinder Stop	34	Lock Bolt Spring	55	Rear Sight Windage Screw
14	Hammer Stud	35	Lock Bolt Pin	56	Rear Sight Elevation Nut
15	Trigger Stud	36	Bolt	57	Elevation Screw Spring
16	Cylinder Stop Center	37	Bolt Plunger	58	Elevation Screw Detents
17	Sear	38	Bolt Spring	59	Leaf Stud
18	Sear Pins	39	Thumb-Piece	60	Block Pin
19	Stirrup Pin	40	Thumb Screw	61	Frame
20	Sear Spring	41	Frame Lug	62	Hand Pin
21	Stirrup	42	Sideplate	63	Extractor

Super Comanche 44 Magnum Revolver

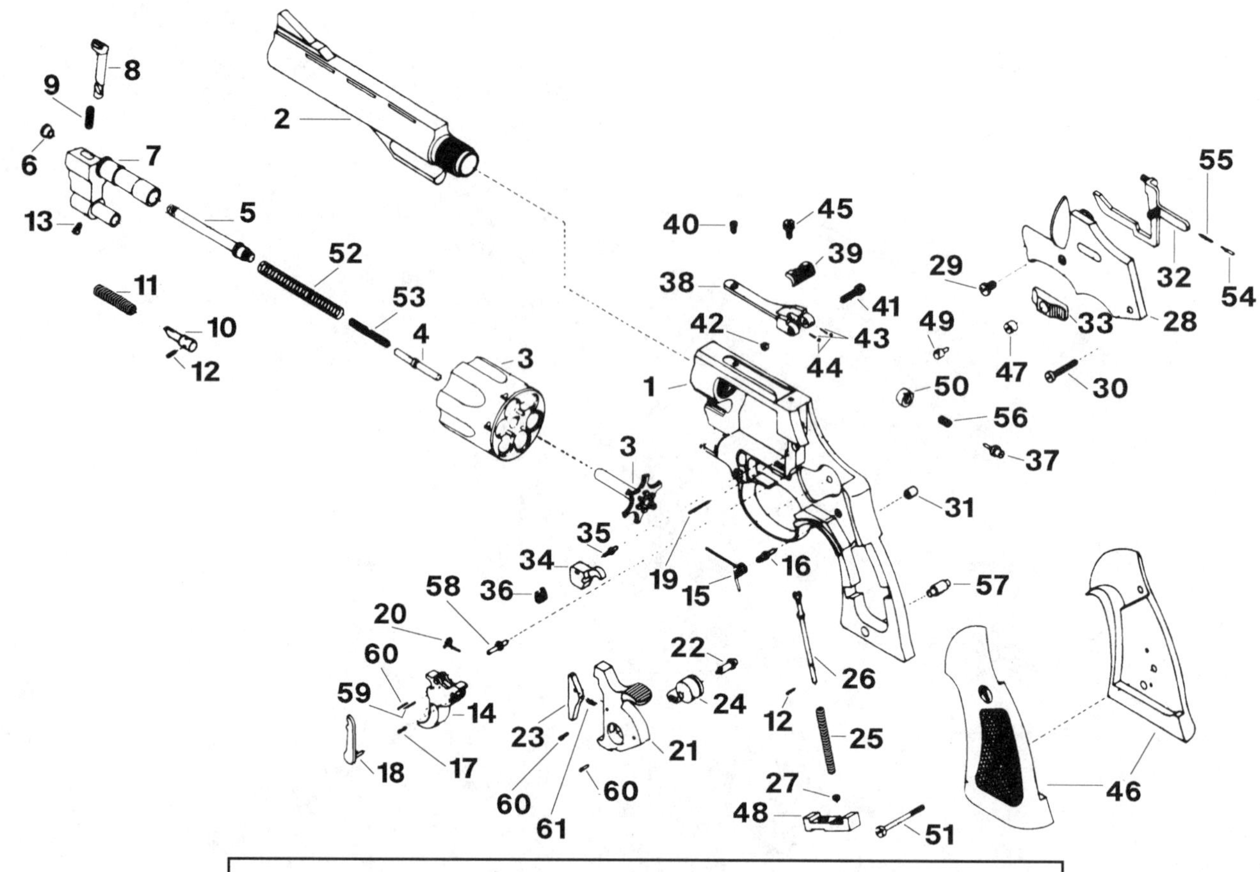

1	Frame	32	Bolt
2	Barrel	33	Thumb-Piece
3	Cylinder and Extractor	34	Cylinder Stop
4	Center Pin	35	Cylinder Stop Center
5	Extractor Rod	36	Cylinder Stop Spring
6	Extractor Rod Collar	37	Firing Nose
7	Yoke (Crane)	38	Rear Sight Leaf
8	Yoke Bolt	39	Rear Sight
9	Bolt Spring	40	Rear Sight Leaf Screw
10	Bolt Disconnector	41	Rear Sight Windage Screw
11	Disconnector Spring	42	Rear Sight Screw Nut
12	Disconnector Spring Pin	43	Elevating Nut Springs
13	Yoke Screw	44	Elevating Nut Balls
14	Trigger	45	Rear Sight Elevation Nut
15	Trigger Spring	46	Stocks
16	Trigger Spring Pin	47	Thumb-Piece Nut
17	Trigger Spring Plunger	48	Pressure Regulator
18	Hand	49	Frame Lug
19	Hand Stop	50	Pin Bushing
20	Hand Spring	51	Stock Screw
21	Hammer	52	Extractor Spring
22	Hammer Stud	53	Center Pin Spring
23	Sear	54	Bolt Plunger
24	Hammer Cam	55	Bolt Plunger Spring
25	Hammer Spring	56	Firing Nose Spring
26	Hammer Strut	57	Stock Guide Pin
27	Hammer Spring Prop	58	Trigger Stud
28	Sideplate	59	Hand Spring Pin
29	Plate Screw	60	Sear Pin and Hammer Strut Pin
30	Grip Screw Guide	61	Sear Spring
31	Grip Screw Guide Nut		

Conversion Unit

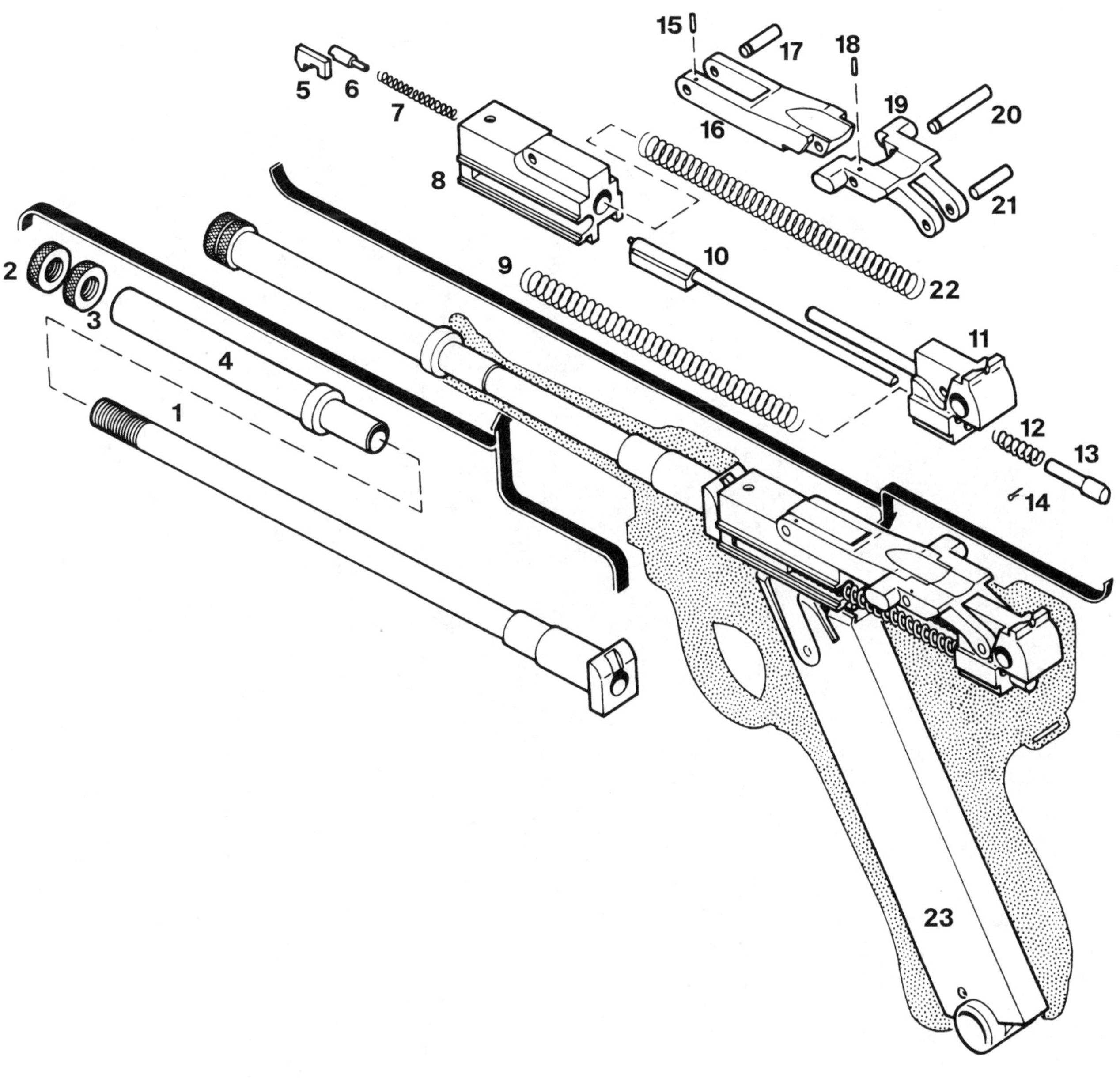

1	Barrel Liner	9	Firing Pin Spring	17	Front Toggle Pin
2	Front Barrel Lock Nut	10	Firing Pin	18	Center Pin Key
3	Rear Barrel Lock Nut	11	Rear Sight Block	19	Rear Toggle Link
4	Barrel Adaptor Sleeve	12	Buffer Spring	20	Center Toggle Pin
5	Extractor	13	Buffer	21	Rear Toggle Pin
6	Extractor Plunger	14	Retaining Clip	22	Recoil Spring
7	Extractor Spring	15	Front Toggle Pin Key	23	Magazine
8	Breechblock	16	Center Toggle Link		

Model 1900-02 Auto

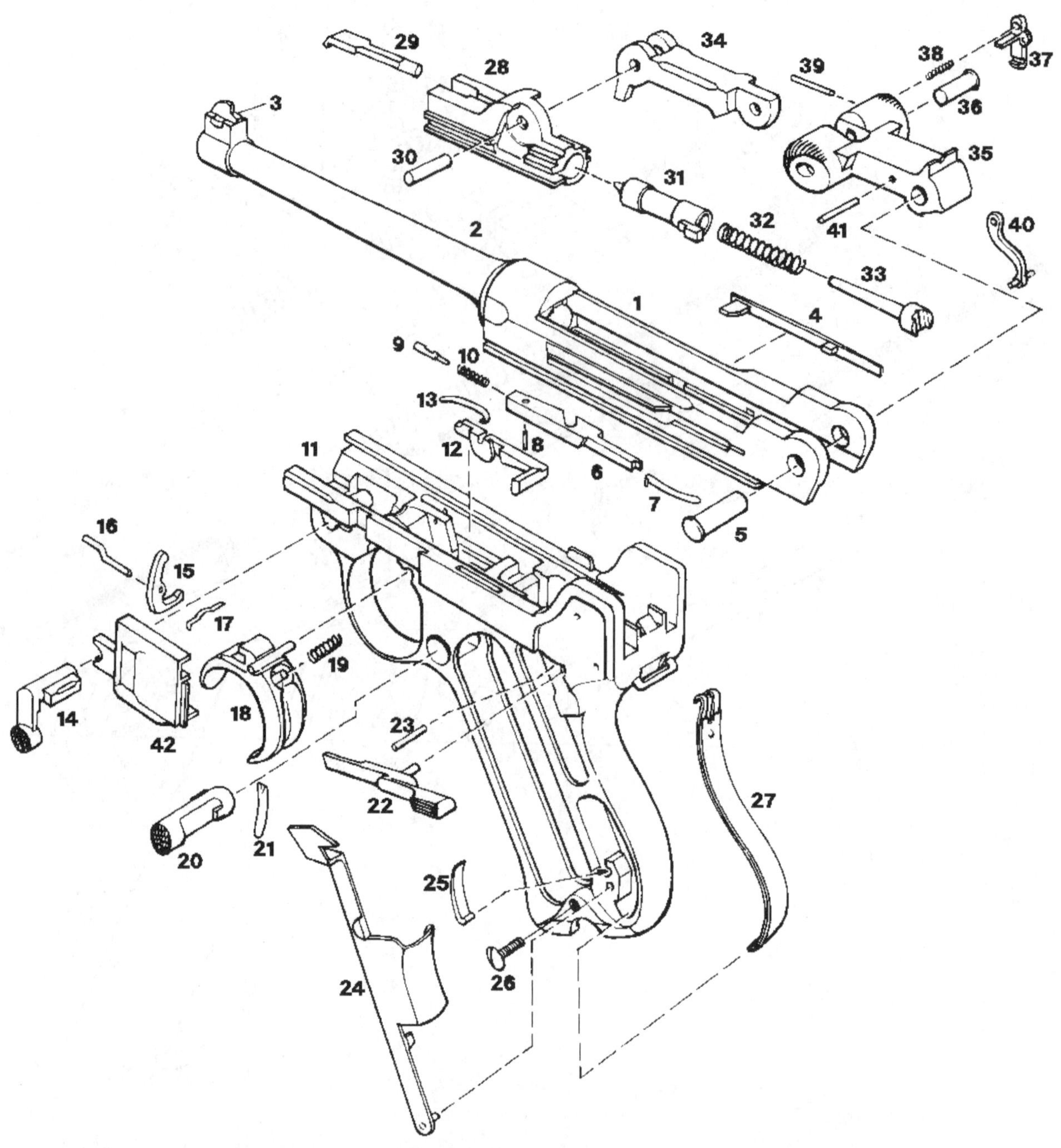

1	Receiver	**15**	Trigger Lever	**29**	Extractor
2	Barrel	**16**	Trigger Lever Pin	**30**	Breechblock Connecting Pin
3	Front Sight	**17**	Locking Bolt Spring	**31**	Firing Pin
4	Ejector	**18**	Trigger	**32**	Firing Pin Spring
5	Connecting Pin	**19**	Trigger Spring	**33**	Firing Pin Spring Retainer
6	Sear Bar	**20**	Magazine Catch	**34**	Forward Toggle Link
7	Sear Bar Spring	**21**	Magazine Catch Spring	**35**	Rear Toggle Link
8	Sear Bar Plunger Pin	**22**	Safety-Lever	**36**	Forward and Rear Toggle Link Pin
9	Sear Bar Plunger	**23**	Safety-Lever Pin	**37**	Toggle Lock
10	Sear Bar Plunger Spring	**24**	Grip Safety	**38**	Toggle Lock Spring
11	Frame	**25**	Grip Safety Spring	**39**	Toggle Lock Pin
12	Hold-Open Latch	**26**	Grip Screw	**40**	Coupling Link
13	Hold-Open Latch Spring	**27**	Recoil Spring	**41**	Coupling Link Pin
14	Locking Bolt	**28**	Breechblock	**42**	Trigger Plate

Model 1908 Auto

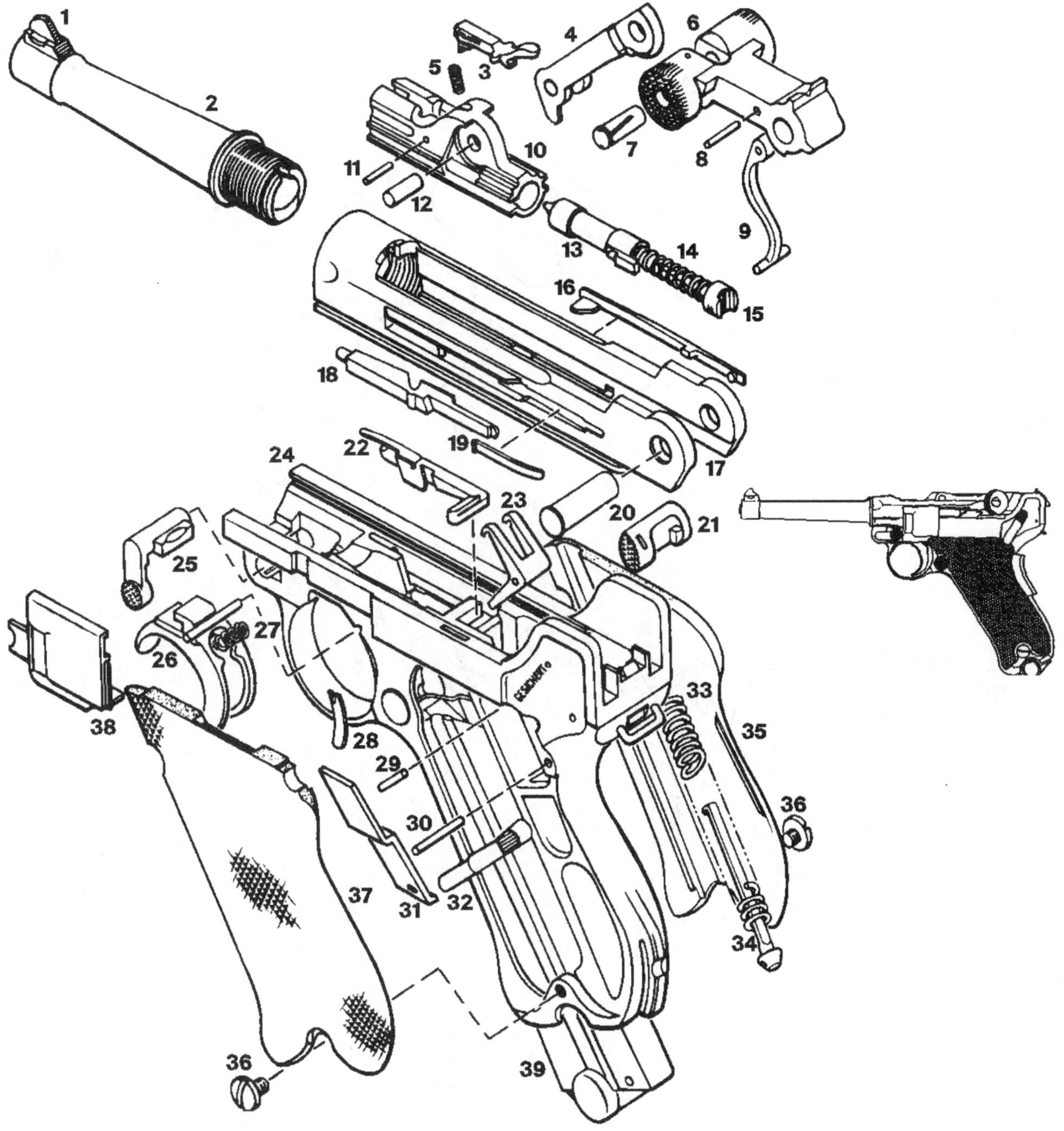

1	Front Sight	14	Firing Pin Spring	27	Trigger Spring
2	Barrel	15	Firing Pin Spring Retainer	28	Magazine Catch Spring
3	Extractor	16	Ejector	29	Safety-Lever Pin
4	Center Toggle Link	17	Barrel Extension (Receiver)	30	Recoil Lever Pin
5	Extractor Spring	18	Sear Bar	31	Safety Bar
6	Rear Toggle Link	19	Sear Bar Spring	32	Safety-Lever
7	Center Toggle Pin	20	Rear Toggle Pin	33	Mainspring
8	Coupling Link Pin	21	Magazine Catch	34	Mainspring Guide
9	Coupling Link	22	Hold-Open Latch with Spring	35	Right Grip Panel
10	Breechblock	23	Recoil Spring Lever	36	Grip Screws
11	Extractor Pin	24	Frame	37	Left Grip Panel
12	Breechblock Pin	25	Locking Bolt	38	Trigger Sideplate
13	Firing Pin	26	Trigger	39	Magazine

1851 Navy Revolver

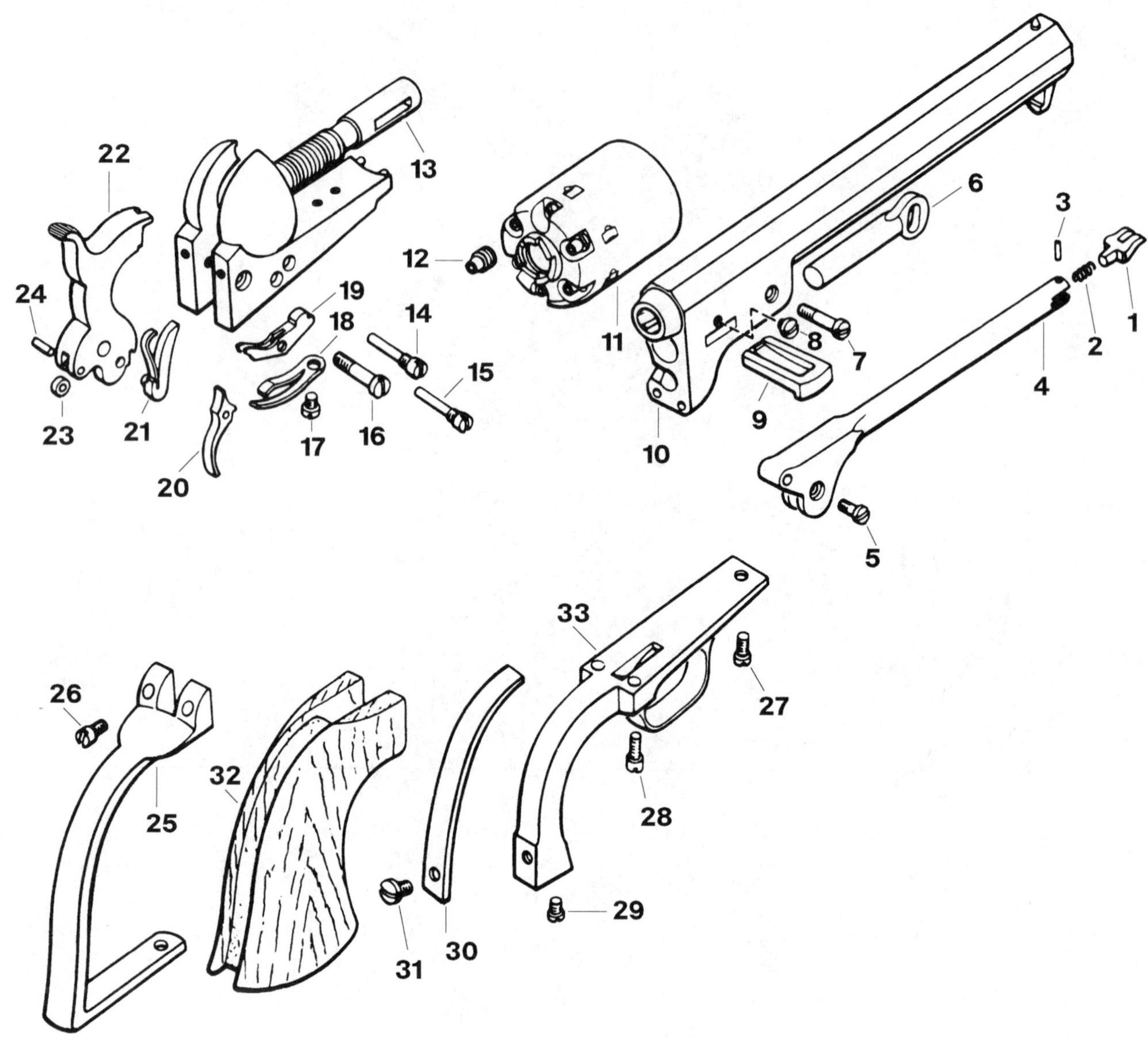

1	Loading Lever Latch	**12**	Nipple	**23**	Roller
2	Loading Lever Latch Spring	**13**	Base Pin	**24**	Roller Pin
3	Loading Lever Latch Pin	**14**	Bolt Screw	**25**	Backstrap
4	Loading Lever	**15**	Trigger Screw	**26**	Rear Backstrap Screws
5	Plunger Screw	**16**	Hammer Screw	**27**	Front Trigger Guard Screw
6	Plunger	**17**	Trigger and Bolt Spring Screw	**28**	Rear Trigger Guard Screws
7	Loading Lever Screw	**18**	Trigger and Bolt Spring	**29**	Lower Backstrap Screw
8	Wedge Screw	**19**	Bolt	**30**	Mainspring
9	Wedge	**20**	Trigger	**31**	Mainspring Screw
10	Barrel	**21**	Hand and Spring	**32**	Grip
11	Cylinder	**22**	Hammer	**33**	Trigger Guard

1860 Army Revolver

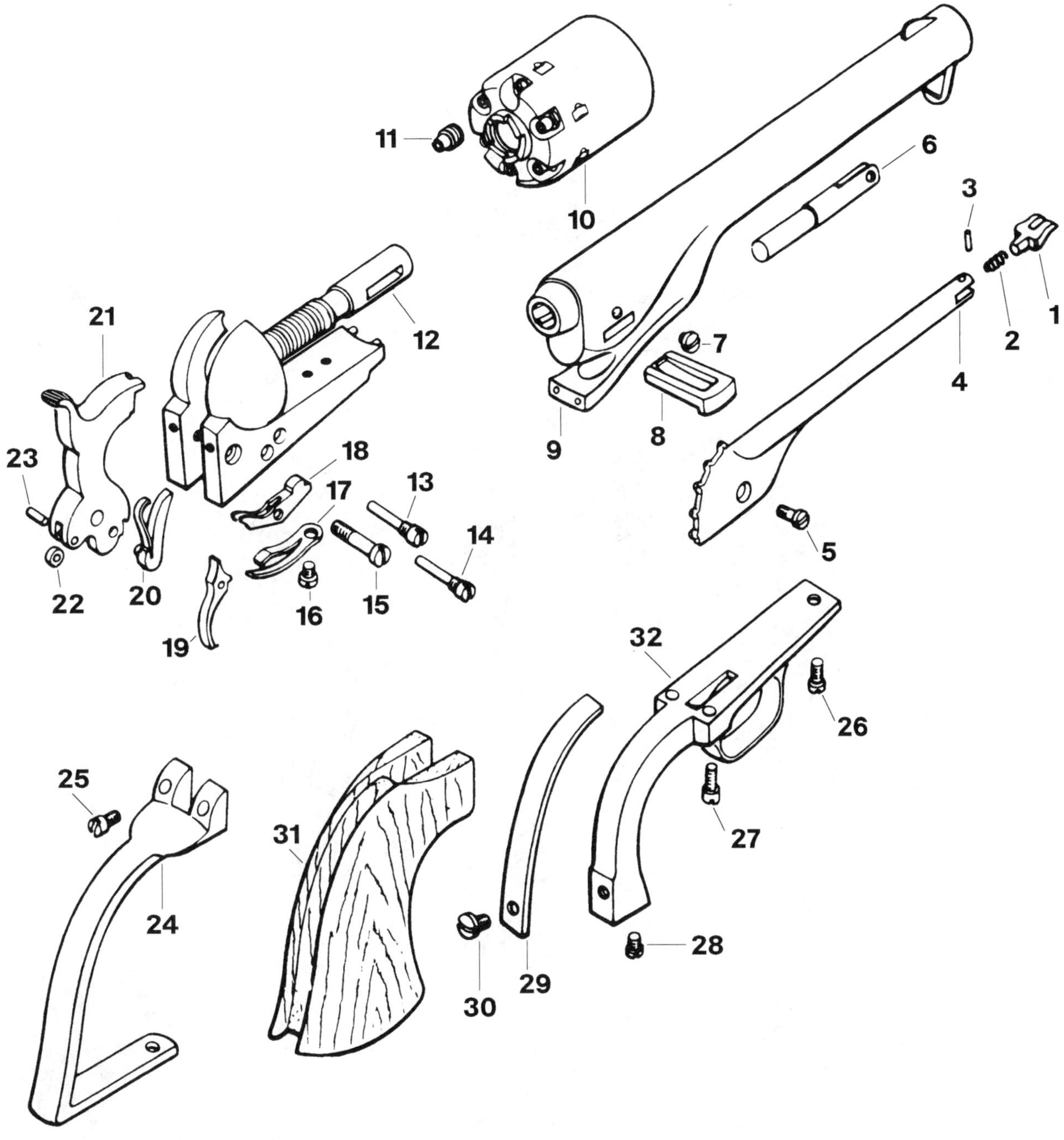

1	Loading Lever Latch	**12**	Base Pin	**23**	Roller Pin
2	Loading Lever Latch Spring	**13**	Bolt Screw	**24**	Backstrap
3	Loading Lever Latch Pin	**14**	Trigger Screw	**25**	Rear Backstrap Screws
4	Loading Lever	**15**	Hammer Screw	**26**	Front Trigger Guard Screw
5	Plunger Screw	**16**	Trigger and Bolt Spring Screw	**27**	Rear Trigger Guard Screws
6	Plunger	**17**	Trigger and Bolt Spring	**28**	Lower Backstrap Screw
7	Wedge Screw	**18**	Bolt	**29**	Mainspring
8	Wedge	**19**	Trigger	**30**	Mainspring Screw
9	Barrel	**20**	Hand and Spring	**31**	Grip
10	Cylinder	**21**	Hammer	**32**	Trigger Guard
11	Nipple	**22**	Roller		

Model A Auto

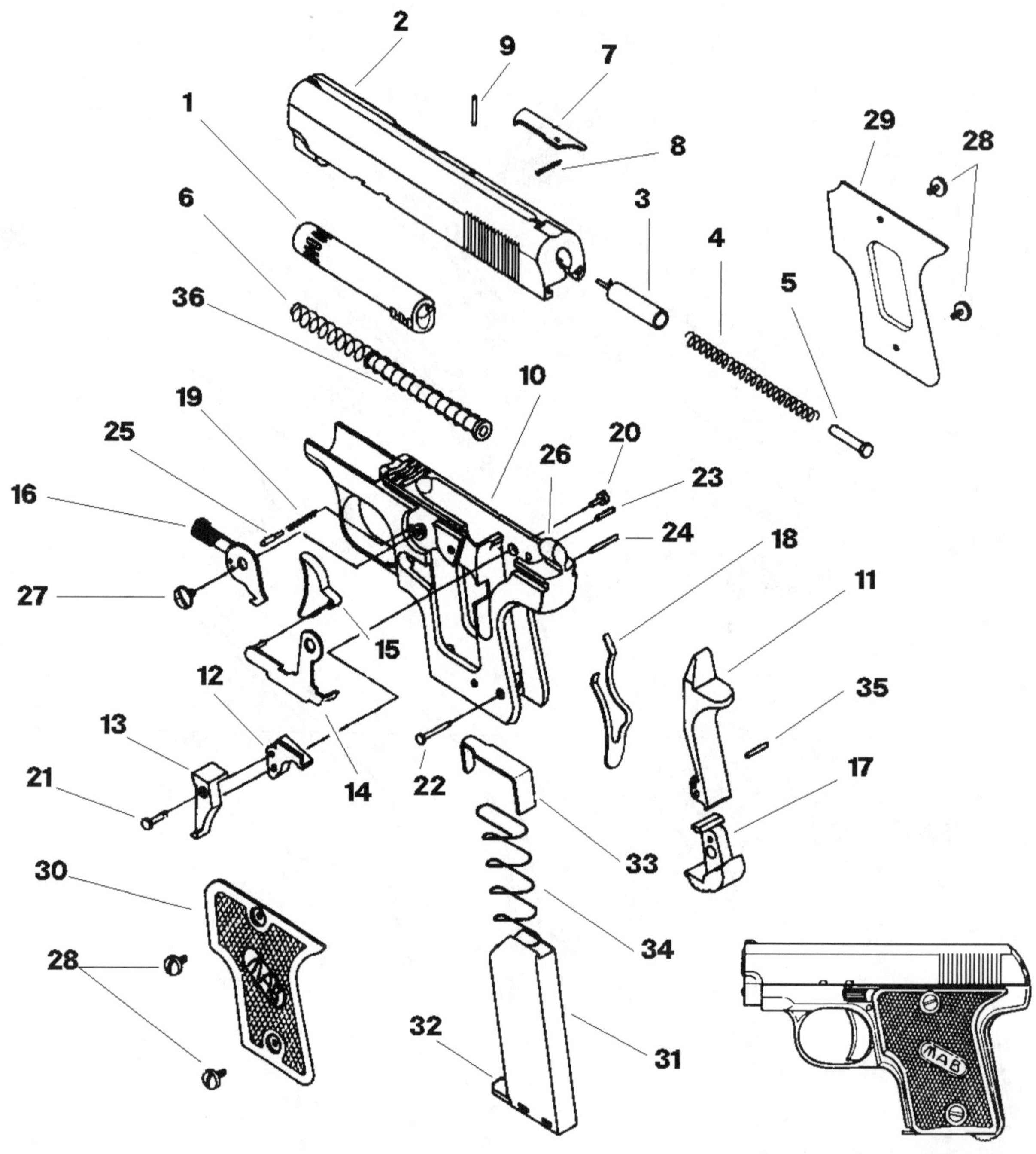

1	Barrel	13	Magazine Safety	25	Thumb Safety Plunger
2	Slide	14	Connector	26	Striker Spring Base
3	Firing Pin	15	Trigger	27	Thumb Safety Screw
4	Firing Pin Spring	16	Safety Catch	28	Grip Screws
5	Firing Pin Spring Guide	17	Magazine Catch	29	Grip, Right
6	Recoil Spring	18	Mainspring	30	Grip, Left
7	Extractor	19	Safety Catch Spring	31	Magazine Body
8	Extractor Spring	20	Sear Pin	32	Magazine Floorplate
9	Extractor Pin	21	Magazine Safety Pin	33	Magazine Follower
10	Frame	22	Grip Safety Axis Pin	34	Magazine Spring
11	Grip Safety	23	Grip Safety Stud	35	Magazine Catch Pin
12	Sear	24	Striker Spring Base Pin	36	Recoil Spring Guide

Model D Auto

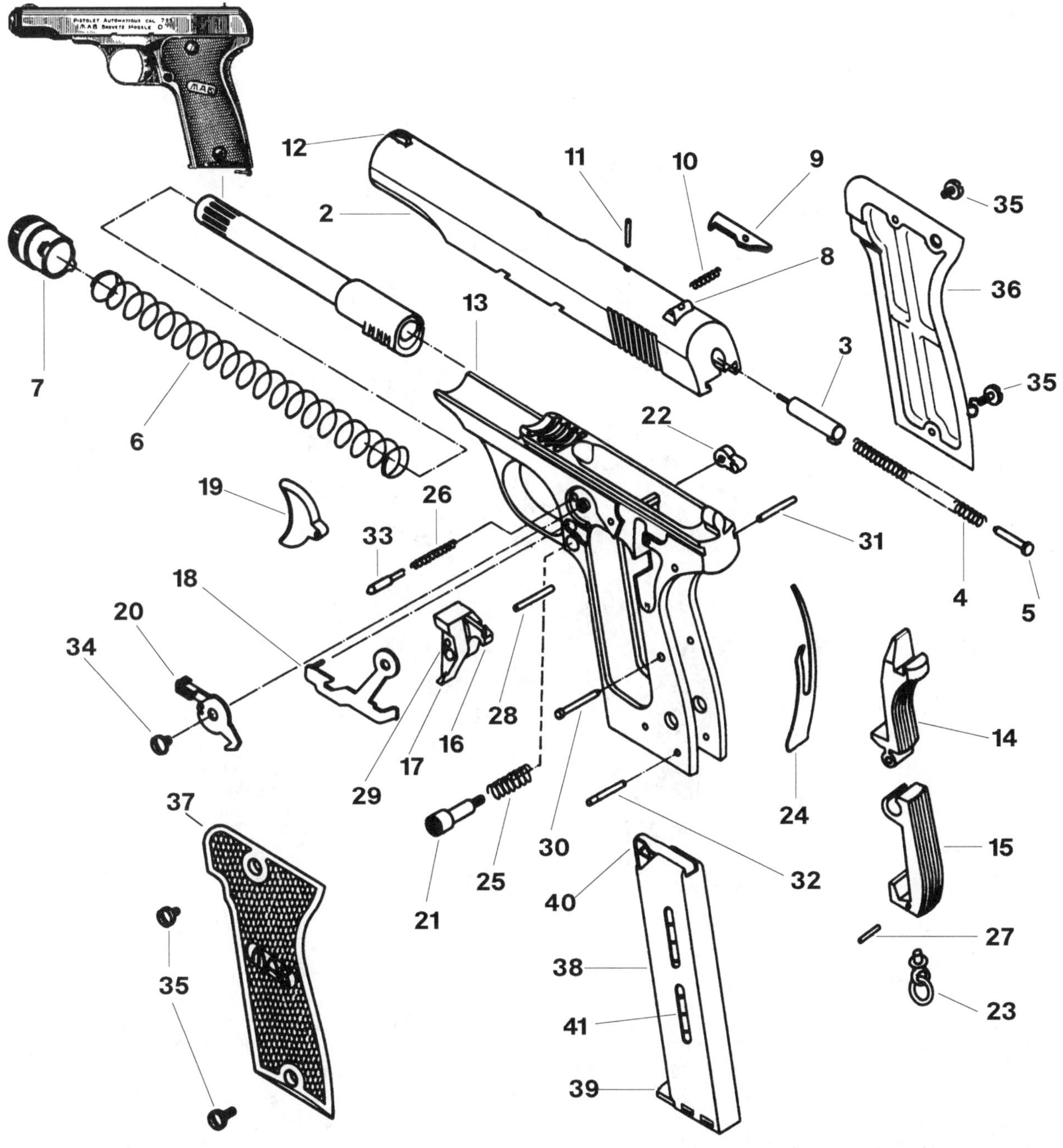

1	Barrel
2	Slide
3	Firing Pin
4	Firing Pin Spring
5	Firing Pin Spring Guide
6	Recoil Spring
7	Muzzle Bushing
8	Rear Sight
9	Extractor
10	Extractor Spring
11	Extractor Pin
12	Front Sight
13	Frame
14	Grip Safety
15	Lower Backstrap Insert
16	Sear
17	Magazine Safety
18	Connector
19	Trigger
20	Safety Catch
21	Magazine Release Button
22	Magazine Release Catch
23	Lanyard Loop
24	Mainspring
25	Magazine Catch Spring
26	Safety Spring
27	Lanyard Loop Pin
28	Sear Pin
29	Magazine Safety Pin
30	Takedown Pin
31	Grip Safety Stud
32	Grip Safety Axis Pin
33	Safety Plunger
34	Safety Screw
35	Grip Screws
36	Grip, Right
37	Grip, Left
38	Magazine Body
39	Magazine Floorplate
40	Magazine Follower
41	Magazine Spring

Model P8 Auto

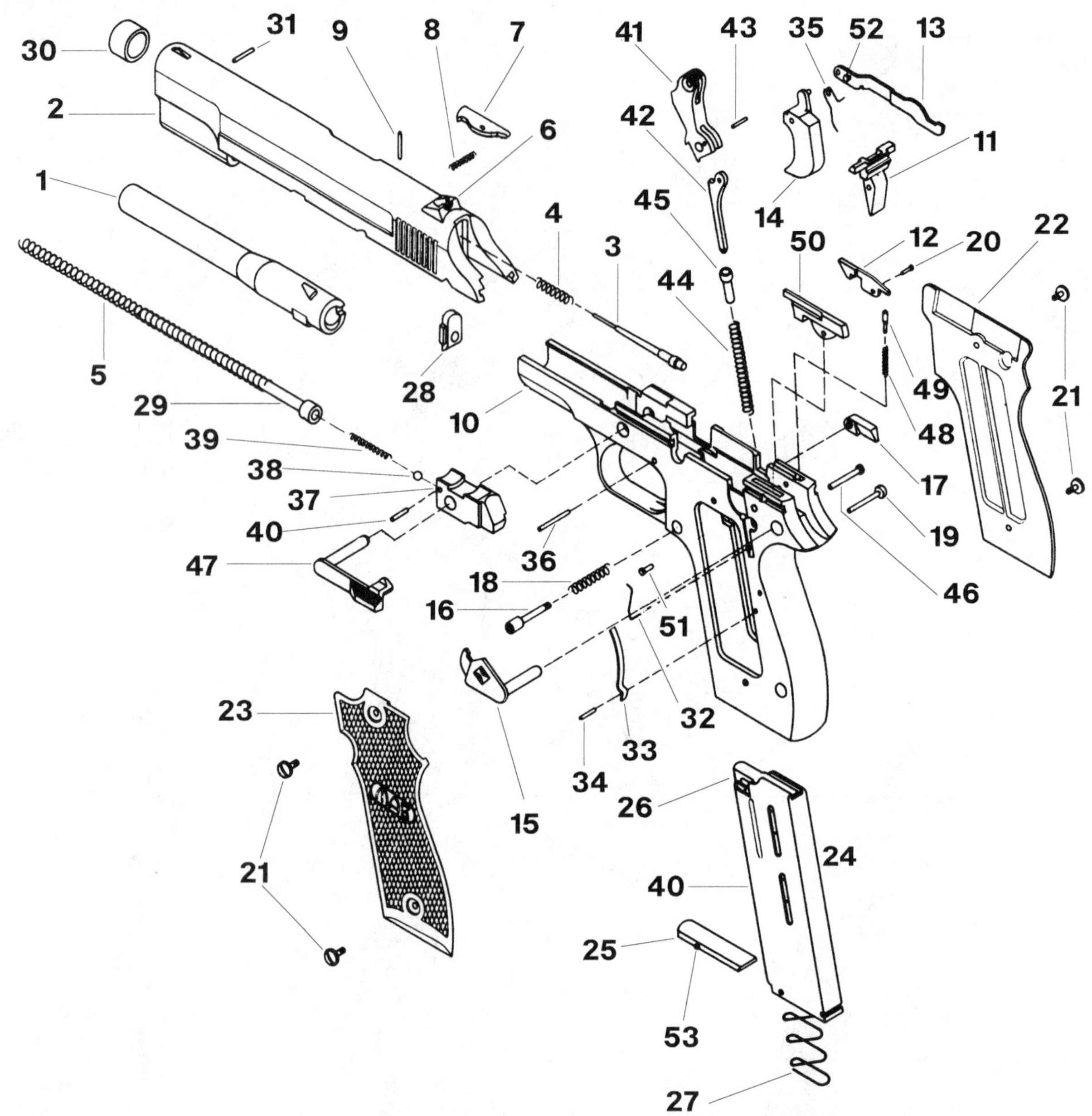

1	Barrel	19	Sear Pin	37	Barrel Block
2	Slide	20	Magazine Safety Pin	38	Slide Latch Spring Ball
3	Firing Pin	21	Grip Screws	39	Slide Latch Spring
4	Firing Pin Spring	22	Grip, Right	40	Recoil Spring Guide Pin
5	Recoil Spring	23	Grip, Left	41	Hammer
6	Rear Sight	24	Magazine Body	42	Hammer Strut
7	Extractor	25	Magazine Floorplate	43	Hammer Strut Pin
8	Extractor Spring	26	Magazine Follower	44	Hammer Spring
9	Extractor Pin	27	Magazine Spring	45	Hammer Spring Plunger
10	Frame	28	Firing Pin Retainer	46	Hammer Pivot
11	Sear	29	Recoil Spring Guide	47	Slide Lock Lever
12	Magazine Safety	30	Slide Ring	48	Magazine Safety Spring
13	Trigger Connector	31	Slide Ring Retainer Pin	49	Magazine Safety Spring Plunger
14	Trigger	32	Safety Catch Spring	50	Ejector
15	Safety-Lever	33	Sear Spring	51	Ejector Pin
16	Magazine Catch Button	34	Sear Spring Pin	52	Trigger Spring Stud
17	Magazine Catch	35	Trigger Spring	53	Magazine Floorplate Pin
18	Magazine Catch Spring	36	Trigger Pin		

Model P15 Auto

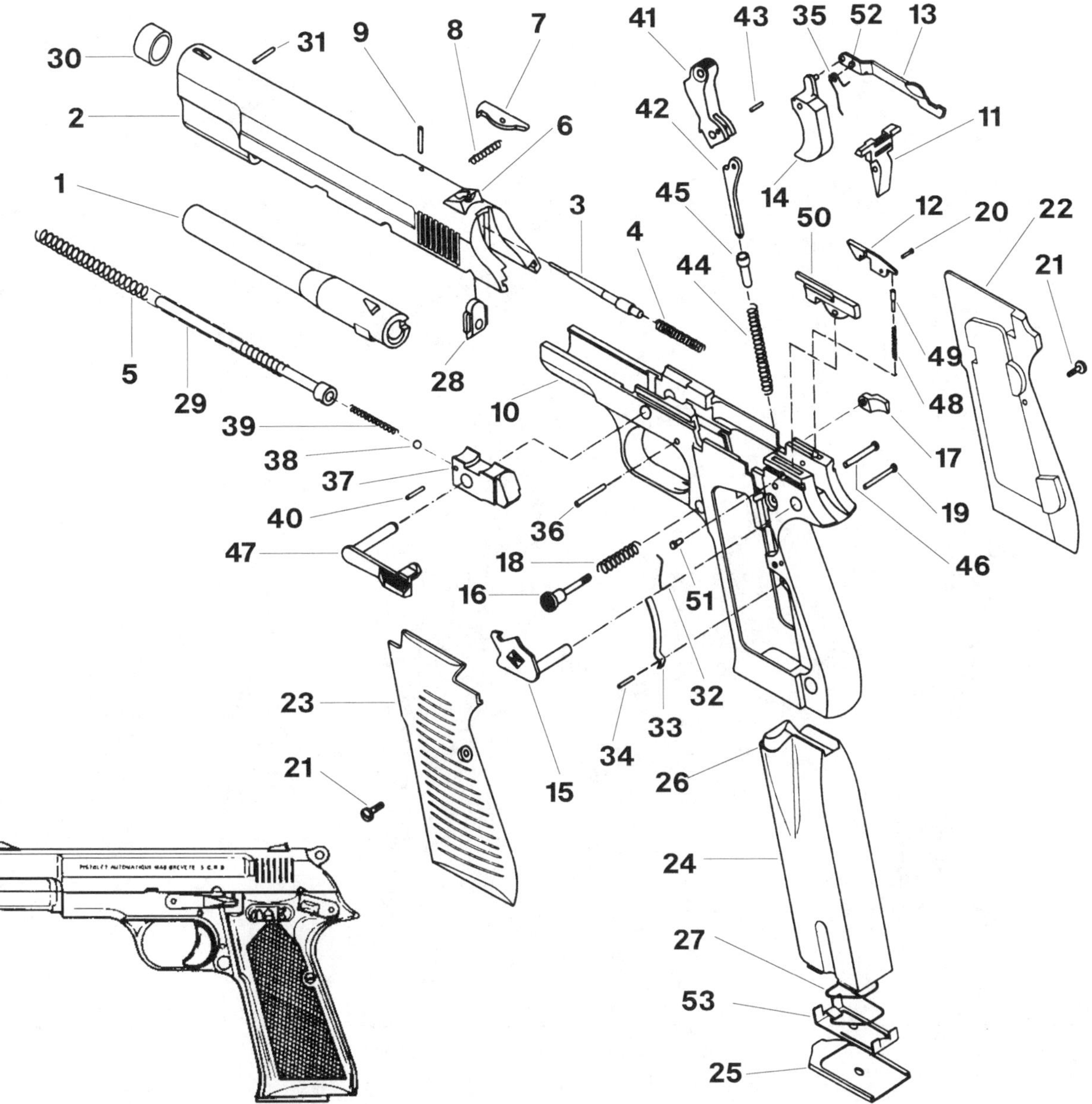

1	Barrel	19	Sear Pin	37	Barrel Block
2	Slide	20	Magazine Safety Pin	38	Slide Latch Spring Ball
3	Firing Pin	21	Grip Screws	39	Slide Latch Spring
4	Firing Pin Spring	22	Grip, Right	40	Recoil Spring Guide Pin
5	Recoil Spring	23	Grip, Left	41	Hammer
6	Rear Sight	24	Magazine Body	42	Hammer Strut
7	Extractor	25	Magazine Floorplate	43	Hammer Strut Pin
8	Extractor Spring	26	Magazine Follower	44	Hammer Spring
9	Extractor Pin	27	Magazine Spring	45	Hammer Spring Plunger
10	Frame	28	Firing Pin Retainer	46	Hammer Pivot
11	Sear	29	Recoil Spring Guide	47	Slide Lock Lever
12	Magazine Safety	30	Slide Ring	48	Magazine Safety Spring
13	Trigger Connector	31	Slide Ring Retainer	49	Magazine Safety Spring Plunger
14	Trigger	32	Safety Catch Spring	50	Ejector
15	Safety-Lever	33	Sear Spring	51	Ejector Pin
16	Magazine Catch Button	34	Sear Spring Pin	52	Trigger Connector Spring Stud
17	Magazine Catch Retainer	35	Trigger Spring	53	Magazine Floorplate Retainer
18	Magazine Catch Spring	36	Trigger Pin		

Model R22 Auto

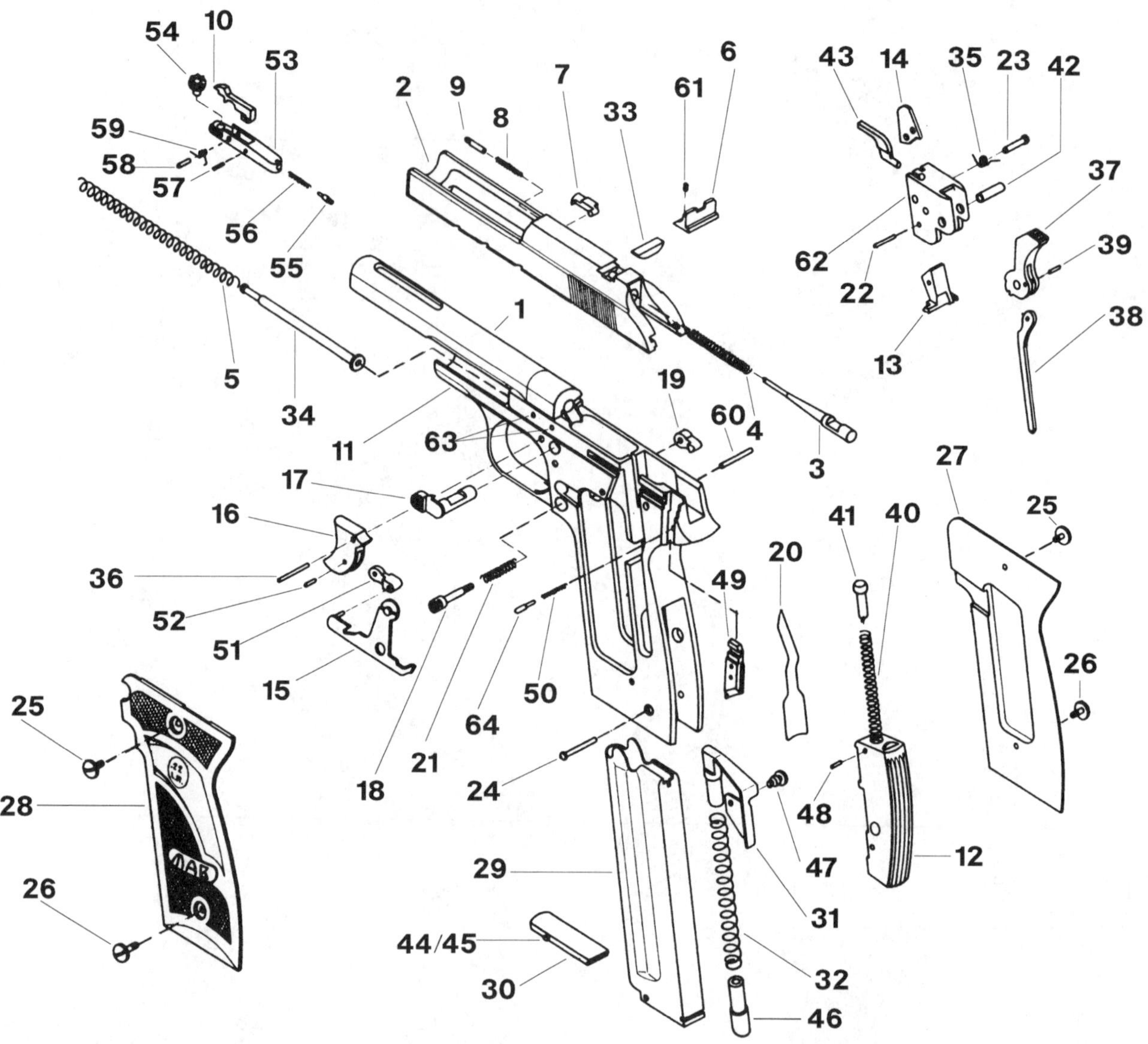

1 Barrel
2 Slide
3 Firing Pin
4 Firing Pin Spring
5 Recoil Spring
6 Rear Sight
7 Extractor
8 Extractor Spring
9 Extractor Spring Plunger
10 Front Sight
11 Frame
12 Hammer Spring Housing
13 Sear
14 Magazine Safety
15 Trigger Bar
16 Trigger
17 Thumb Safety
18 Magazine Button
19 Magazine Catch Retainer
20 Mainspring
21 Magazine Catch Spring
22 Sear Pivot Pin
23 Magazine Safety Pin
24 Hammer Spring Housing Pin
25 Grip Screws, Short
26 Grip Screws, Long
27 Grip, Right
28 Grip, Left
29 Magazine Body
30 Magazine Floorplate
31 Magazine Follower
32 Magazine Spring
33 Firing Pin Retainer
34 Recoil Spring Guide
35 Sear Spring
36 Trigger Pivot Pin
37 Hammer
38 Hammer Strut
39 Hammer Strut Pin
40 Hammer Spring
41 Hammer Spring Plunger
42 Hammer Pin
43 Ejector
44 Magazine Floorplate Plunger
45 Magazine Floorplate Plunger Spring
46 Magazine Spring Guide
47 Magazine Follower Stud
48 Hammer Spring Housing Pin
49 Slide Retainer
50 Slide Retainer Plunger Spring
51 Trigger Link
52 Trigger Link Pin
53 Front Sight Base
54 Front Sight Adjusting Screw
55 Front Sight Base Plunger
56 Front Sight Base Plunger Spring
57 Front Sight Pin
58 Front Sight Spring Pin
59 Front Sight Spring
60 Hammer Block Pin
61 Rear Sight Screw
62 Hammer Block
63 Barrel Pins
64 Slide Retainer Plunger

Winfield Auto

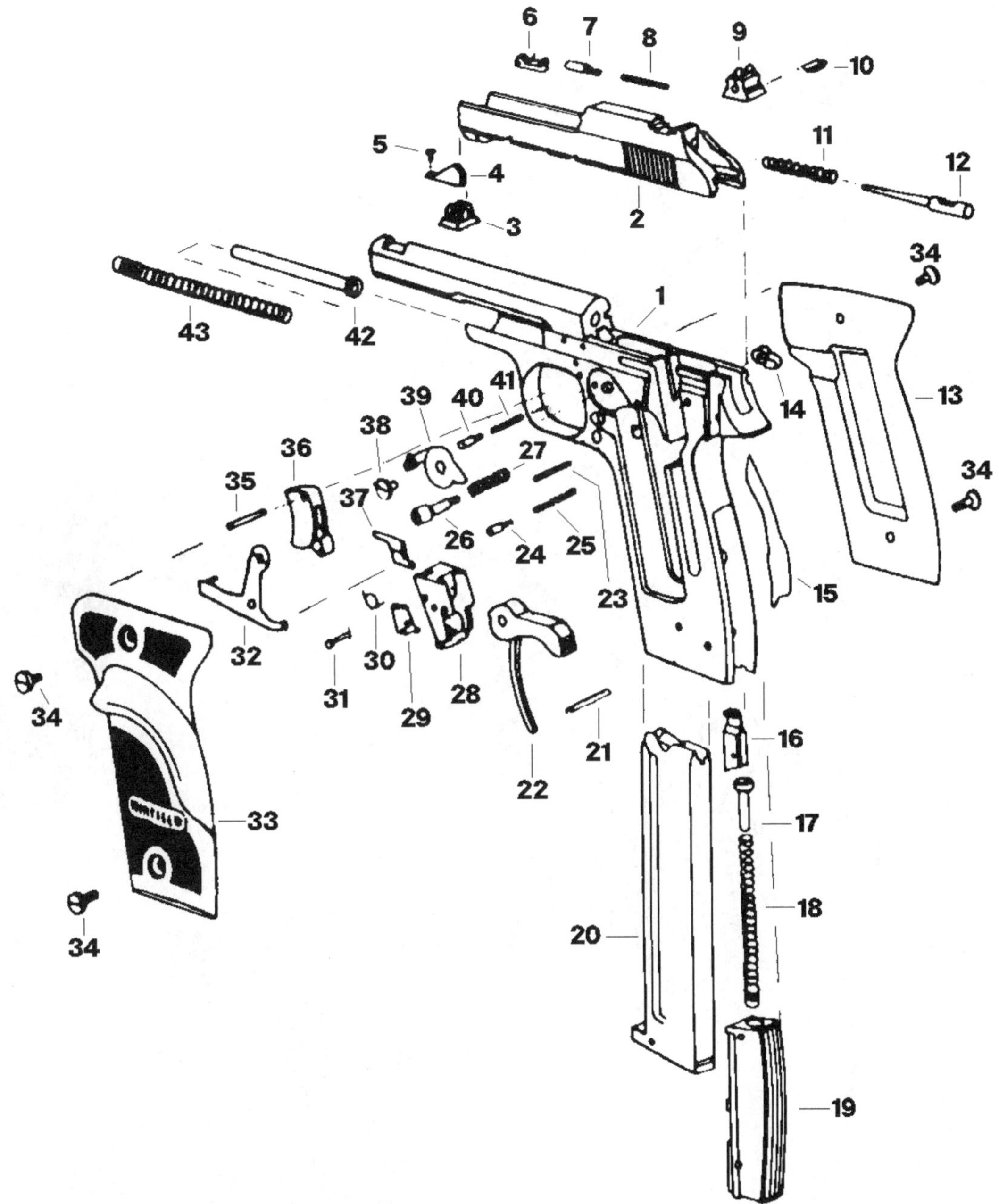

1	Frame
2	Slide
3	Front Sight Base
4	Front Sight Blade
5	Front Sight Blade Screw
6	Extractor
7	Extractor Spring Plunger
8	Extractor Spring
9	Rear Sight
10	Firing Pin Retainer
11	Firing Pin Spring
12	Firing Pin
13	Right Grip
14	Magazine Catch
15	Trigger/Sear Spring
16	Takedown Latch
17	Hammer Spring Plunger
18	Hammer Spring
19	Hammer Spring Housing
20	Magazine Assembly
21	Trigger/Sear Spring Pin
22	Hammer with Strut and Pin
23	Sear Housing Pin
24	Magazine Catch Lock Plunger
25	Magazine Catch Lock<R>Plunger Spring
26	Magazine Catch Button
27	Magazine Catch Spring
28	Hammer Block
29	Magazine Safety
30	Magazine Safety Spring
31	Magazine Safety Pin
32	Trigger Bar and Disconnector
33	Left Grip
34	Grip Screws
35	Trigger Axis Pin
36	Trigger
37	Ejector
38	Safety-Lever Screw
39	Safety-Lever
40	Safety Spring Plunger
41	Safety Spring
42	Recoil Spring Guide
43	Recoil Spring

Parts Not Shown

Sear

Sear Housing

9mm Auto

Courtesy of Blacksmith Corporation

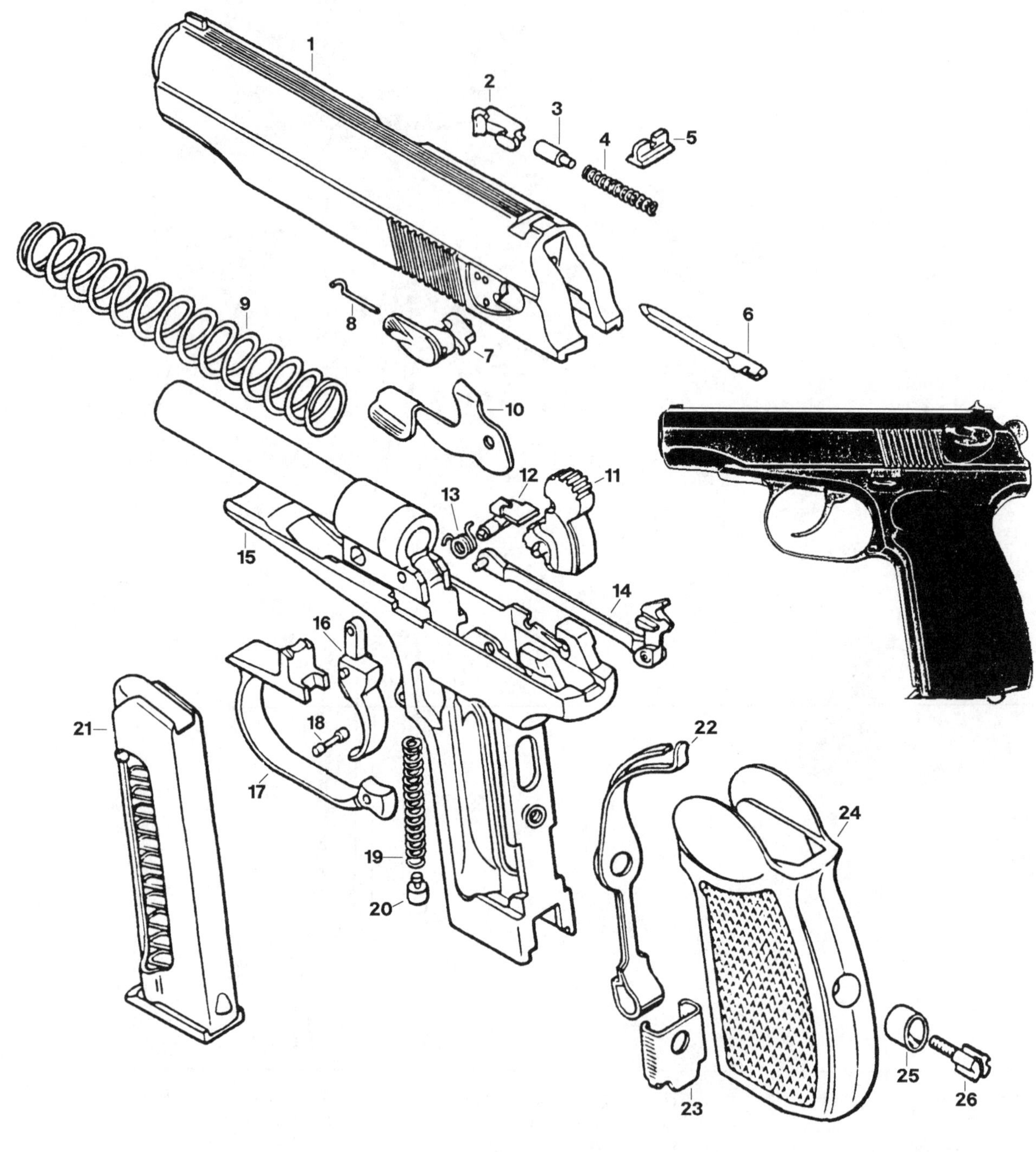

1	Slide	**10**	Ejector and Slide Stop	**19**	Trigger Guard Spring
2	Extractor	**11**	Hammer	**20**	Spring Plunger
3	Extractor Plunger	**12**	Sear	**21**	Magazine Assembly
4	Extractor Spring	**13**	Sear and Slide Stop Spring	**22**	Hammer and Trigger Spring
5	Rear Sight	**14**	Trigger Bar Assembly	**23**	Spring Retainer
6	Firing Pin	**15**	Frame and Barrel Assembly	**24**	Grip
7	Safety	**16**	Trigger	**25**	Grip Screw Detent Bushing
8	Safety Detent Spring	**17**	Trigger Guard	**26**	Grip Screw
9	Recoil Spring	**18**	Trigger Guard Pin		

Auto

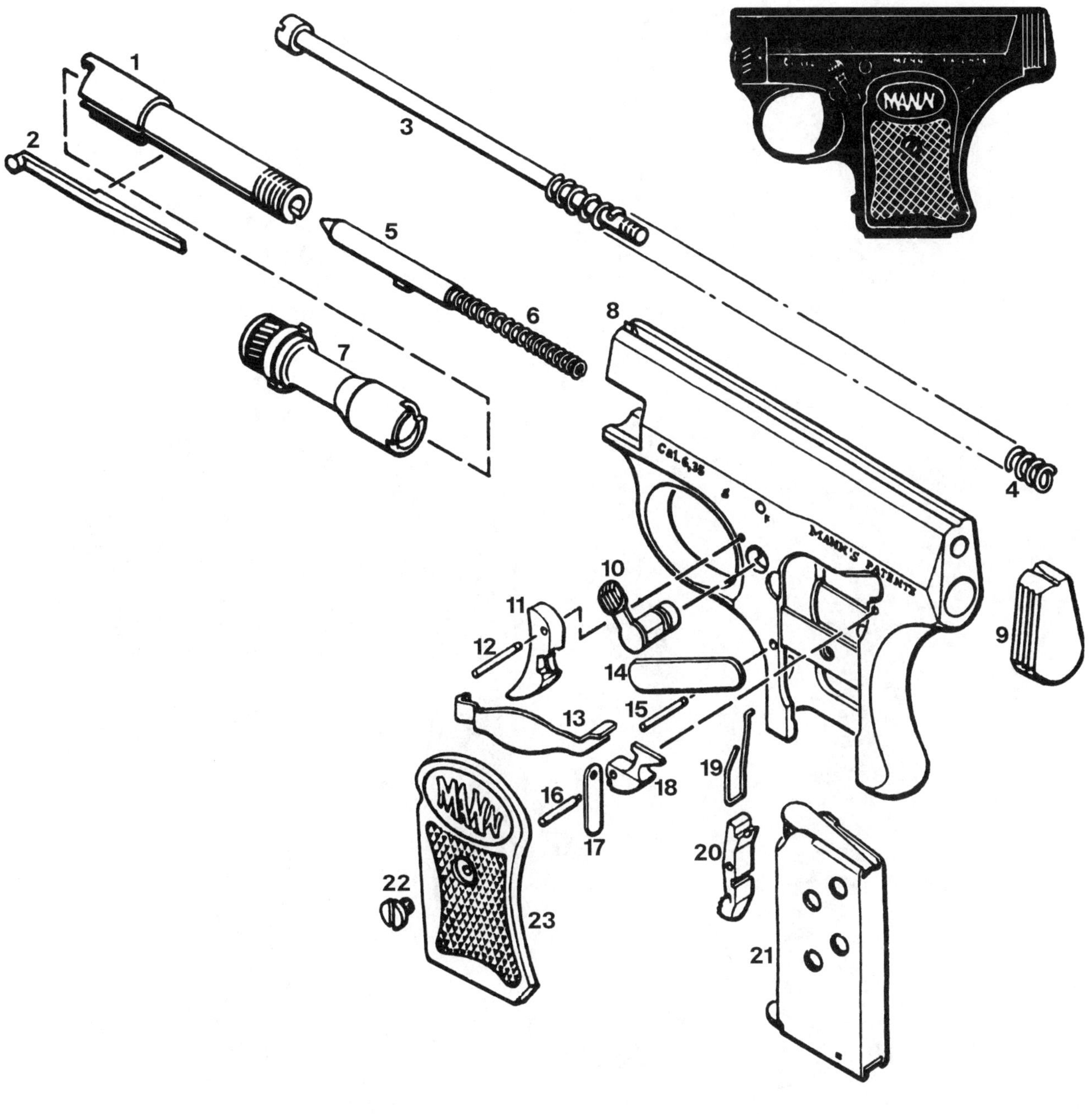

1	Breechblock	13	Trigger Bar
2	Ejector	14	Sideplate
3	Recoil Spring Guide	15	Magazine Catch Pivot
4	Recoil Spring	16	Sear Pin
5	Firing Pin	17	Sear Spring
6	Firing Pin Spring	18	Sear
7	Barrel	19	Magazine Catch Spring
8	Frame	20	Magazine Catch
9	Bolt Knob	21	Magazine Assembly
10	Safety-Lever	22	Grip Screws
11	Trigger	23	Grip Panels
12	Trigger Pin		

Model 1901 Auto

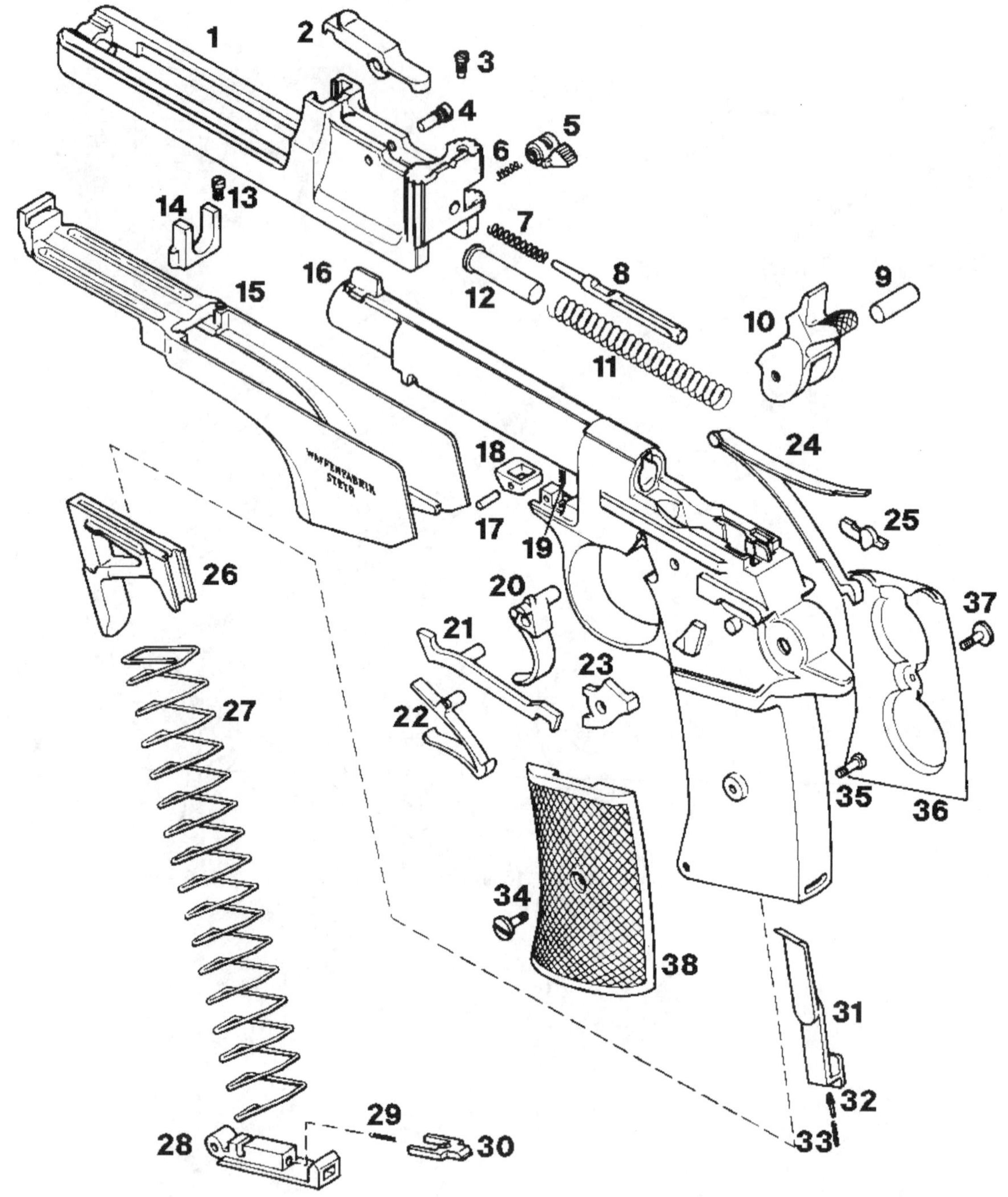

1	Slide	**14**	Yoke	**27**	Magazine Spring
2	Extractor	**15**	Frame Sleeve	**28**	Magazine Floorplate
3	Safety Catch Screw	**16**	Barrel and Frame	**29**	Floorplate Latch Spring
4	Extractor Pivot Screw	**17**	Takedown Latch Pin	**30**	Floorplate Latch
5	Safety	**18**	Takedown Latch	**31**	Magazine Unloading Latch
6	Safety Spring	**19**	Takedown Latch Spring	**32**	Magazine Unloading Latch Plunger
7	Firing Pin Spring	**20**	Trigger	**33**	Magazine Unloading Latch Spring
8	Firing Pin	**21**	Trigger Bar	**34**	Left Grip Screw
9	Hammer Axis Pin	**22**	Trigger/Sear Spring	**35**	Floorplate Pivot Screw
10	Hammer	**23**	Sear	**36**	Right Grip
11	Recoil Spring	**24**	Mainspring	**37**	Right Grip Screw
12	Recoil Spring Guide	**25**	Locking Block	**38**	Left Grip
13	Yoke Retaining Screw	**26**	Magazine Follower		

Model HSc Auto

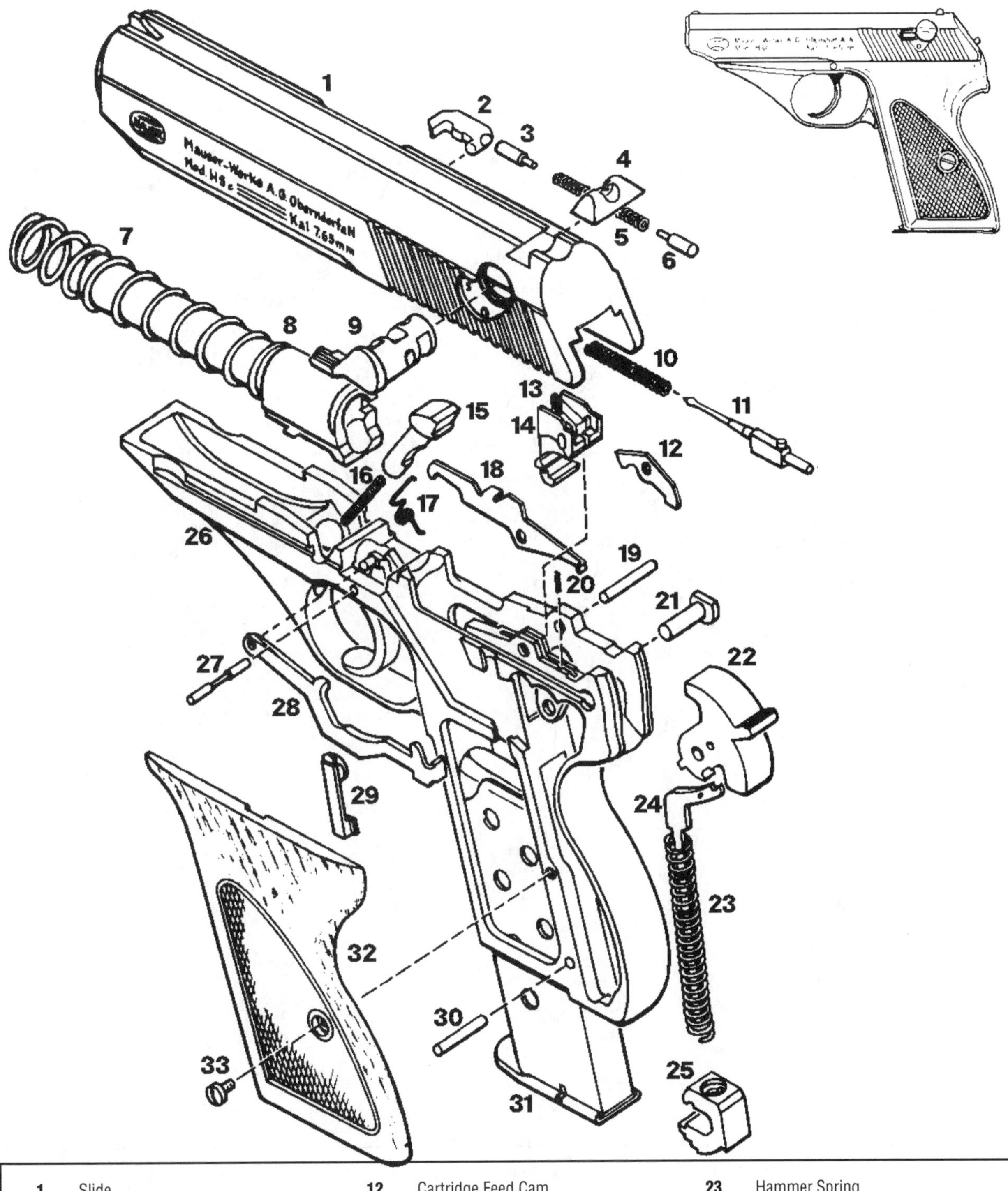

1	Slide	12	Cartridge Feed Cam	23	Hammer Spring
2	Extractor	13	Sear Spring	24	Hammer Strut
3	Extractor Plunger	14	Sear	25	Magazine Catch
4	Rear Sight	15	Takedown Latch	26	Frame
5	Extractor Spring	16	Takedown Latch Spring	27	Trigger Pin
6	Safety Detent Plunger	17	Trigger Spring	28	Trigger Bar
7	Recoil Spring	18	Magazine Safety	29	Disconnector
8	Barrel	19	Sear Hinge Pin	30	Magazine Catch Pin
9	Safety	20	Magazine Safety Spring	31	Magazine Assembly
10	Firing Pin Spring	21	Hammer Axis Pin	32	Grip Panels
11	Firing Pin	22	Hammer	33	Grip Screws

Model HSc (Post-1945) Auto

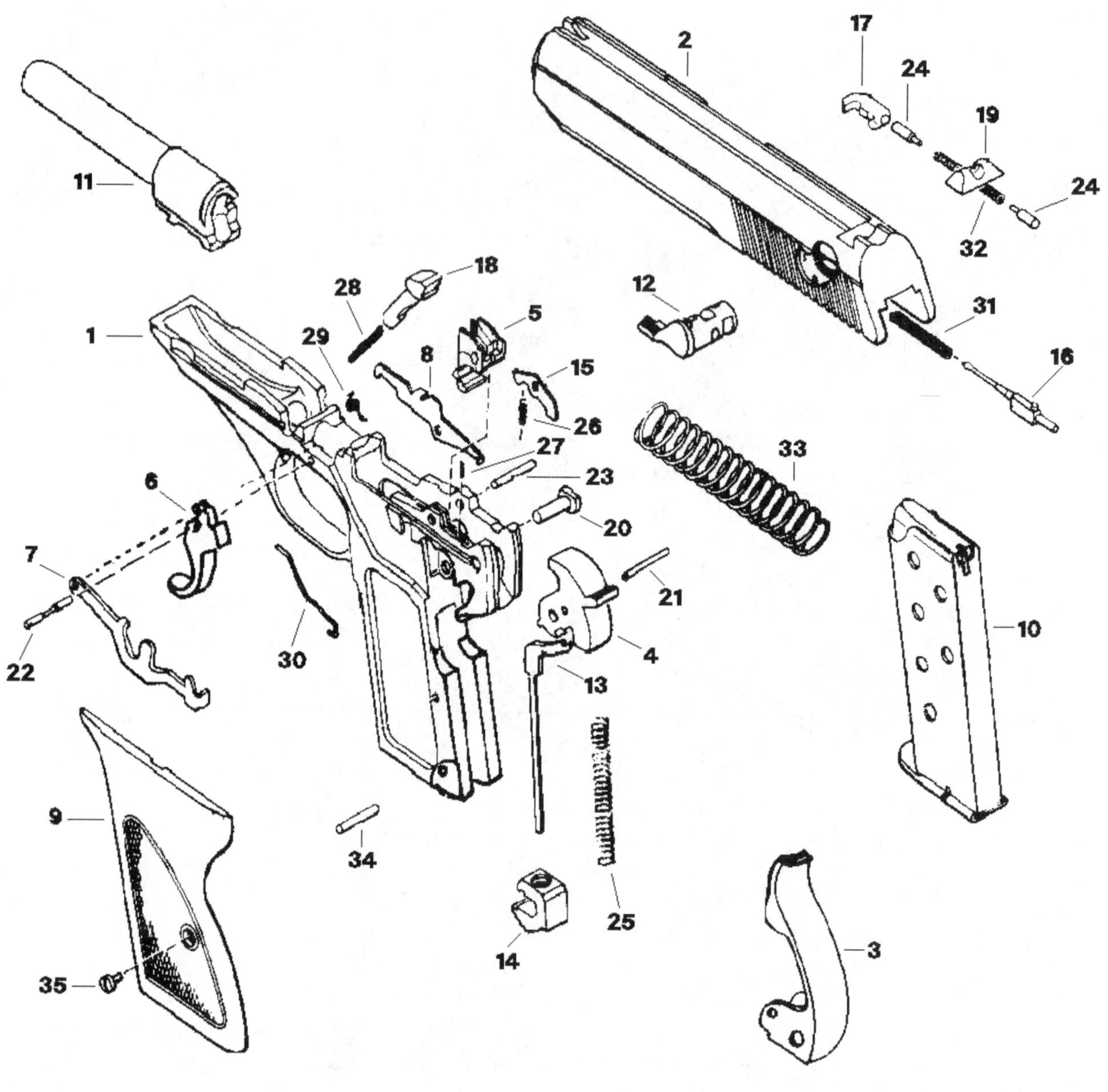

1	Frame	**13**	Hammer Strut	**25**	Mainspring
2	Slide	**14**	Magazine Release	**26**	Sear Spring
3	Backstrap	**15**	Magazine Safety	**27**	Ejector Spring
4	Hammer	**16**	Firing Pin	**28**	Takedown Latch Spring
5	Sear	**17**	Extractor	**29**	Trigger Spring
6	Trigger	**18**	Takedown Latch	**30**	Trigger Bar Spring
7	Trigger Bar	**19**	Rear Sight	**31**	Firing Pin Spring
8	Ejector	**20**	Hammer Axis Pin	**32**	Extractor Spring
9	Grips	**21**	Hammer Strut Pin	**33**	Recoil Spring
10	Magazine Assembly	**22**	Trigger Pin	**34**	Magazine Release Pin
11	Barrel	**23**	Sear Pin	**35**	Grip Screws
12	Safety	**24**	Extractor Pins		

Model 1896 "Broomhandle" (Early Type Cone Hammer) Auto

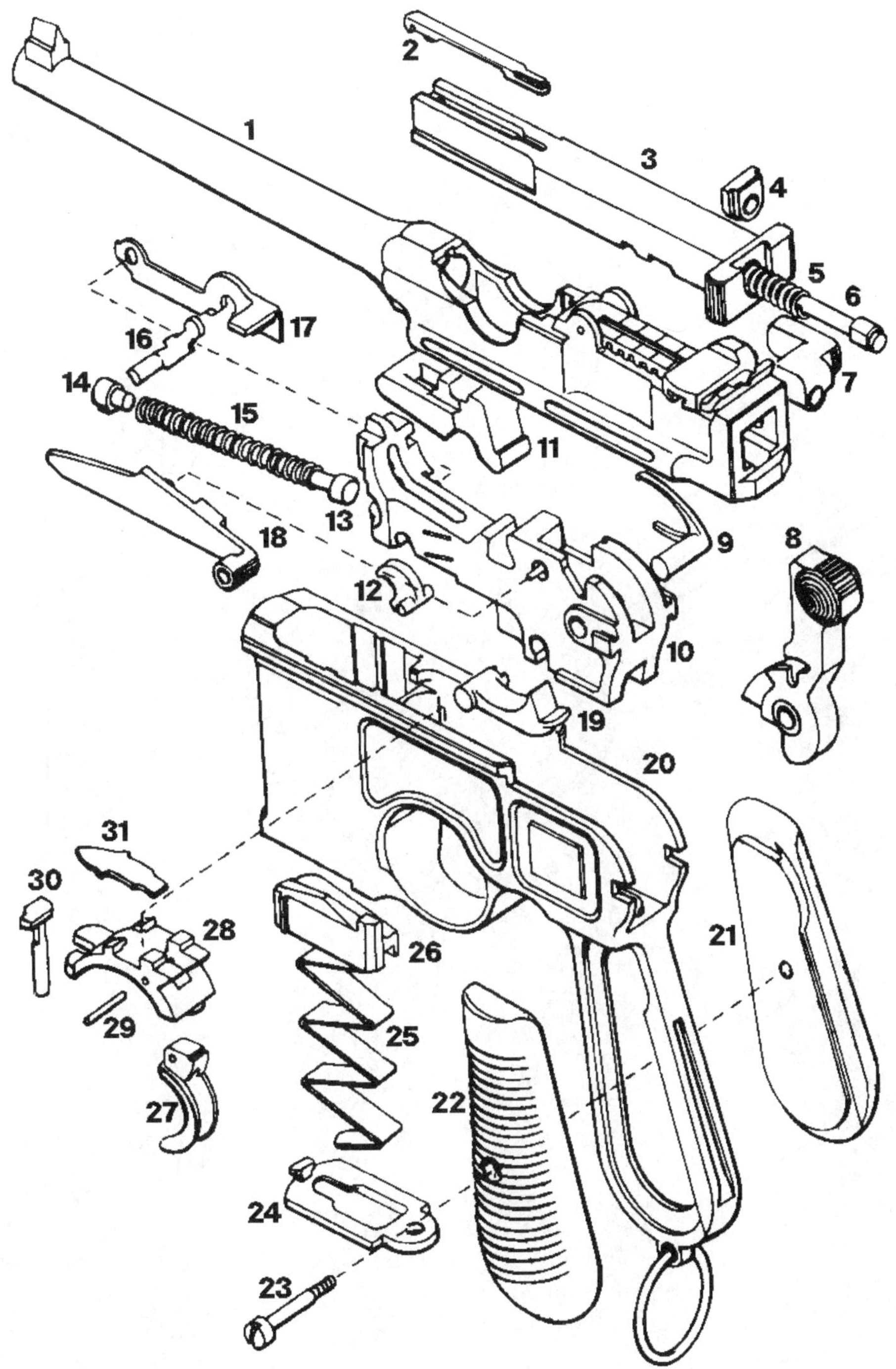

1	Barrel and Barrel Extension	12	Rocker Coupling	23	Grip Screw
2	Extractor	13	Mainspring Plunger	24	Magazine Floorplate
3	Bolt	14	Rocker Plunger	25	Magazine Spring
4	Firing Pin Retainer	15	Mainspring	26	Magazine Follower
5	Firing Pin Spring	16	Sear	27	Trigger
6	Firing Pin	17	Sear Arm	28	Trigger Housing
7	Bolt Stop	18	Safety	29	Trigger Pin
8	Hammer	19	Lock Frame Stop	30	Floorplate Plunger
9	Sear Spring and Hammer Pivot	20	Receiver	31	Trigger Spring
10	Lock Mechanism Frame	21	Right Grip Panel		
11	Bolt Locking Block	22	Left Grip Panel		

Model 1909-1910 Pocket Auto

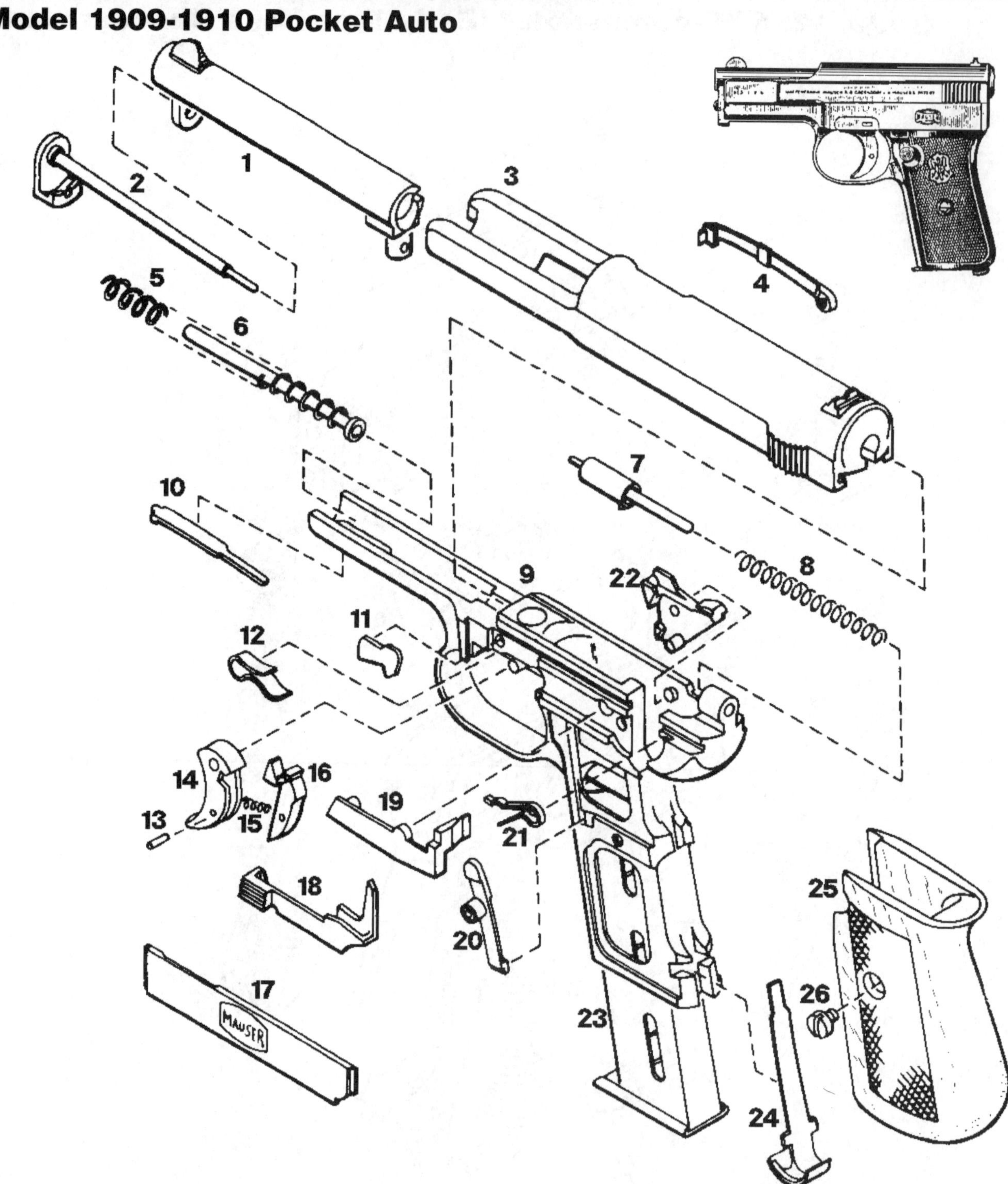

1	Barrel	10	Takedown Rod Catch	19	Trigger Bar
2	Takedown Rod	11	Disconnector	20	Safety Catch Release
3	Slide	12	Trigger Spring	21	Trigger Bar Spring
4	Extractor	13	Trigger Sear Pin	22	Ejector/Hold-Open Catch
5	Recoil Spring	14	Trigger	23	Magazine Assembly
6	Recoil Spring Guide	15	Trigger Sear Spring	24	Magazine Catch
7	Firing Pin	16	Trigger Sear	25	Grip
8	Firing Pin Spring	17	Sideplate	26	Grip Screws
9	Frame	18	Safety Catch		

Model 1910-1934 Pocket Auto

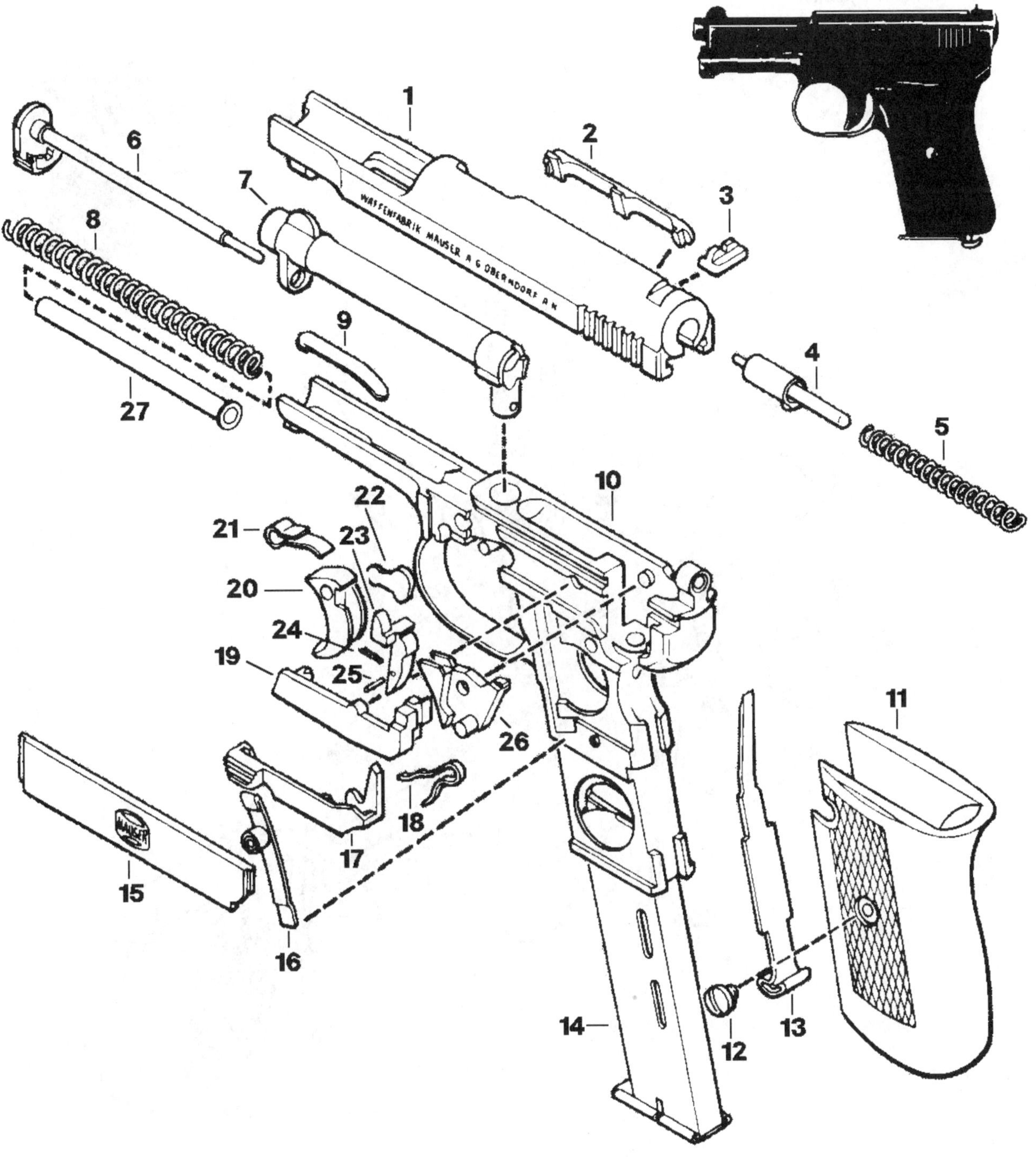

1	Slide	10	Frame	19	Trigger Bar
2	Extractor	11	Grip	20	Trigger
3	Rear Sight	12	Grip Screw	21	Trigger Spring
4	Firing Pin	13	Magazine Catch	22	Disconnector
5	Firing Pin Spring	14	Magazine Assembly	23	Trigger Sear
6	Takedown Rod	15	Sideplate	24	Trigger Sear Spring
7	Barrel	16	Safety Catch Release	25	Trigger Sear Pin
8	Recoil Spring	17	Safety Catch	26	Ejector and Hold-Open Catch
9	Takedown Rod Catch	18	Trigger Bar Spring	27	Recoil Spring Guide

W.T.P. Old Model Auto

Courtesy of Blacksmith Corporation

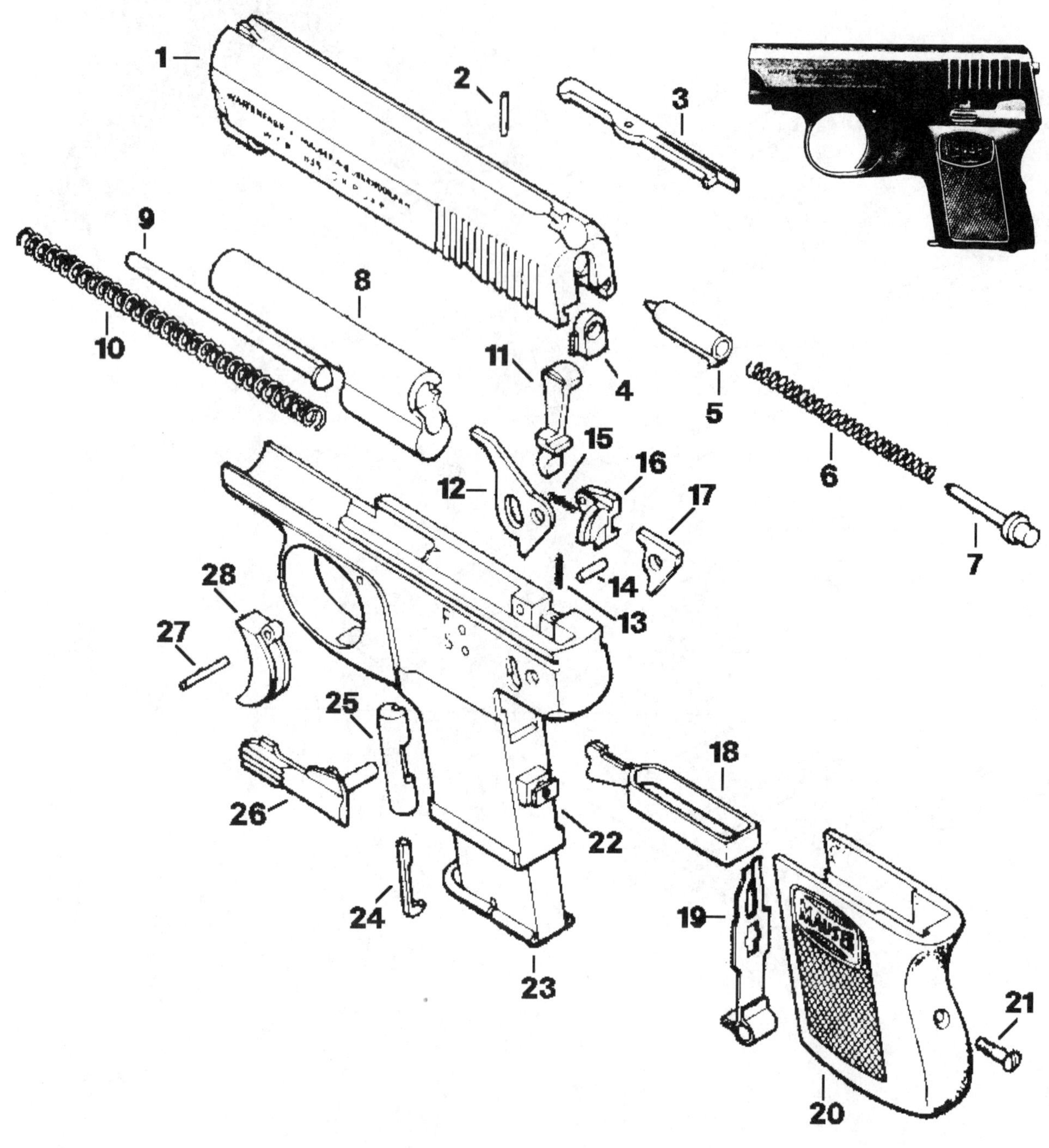

1	Slide	11	Disconnector	21	Grip Screw
2	Extractor Pin	12	Magazine Disconnector	22	Frame
3	Extractor	13	Disconnector Spring	23	Magazine Assembly
4	Firing Pin Retainer	14	Sear Pin	24	Takedown Catch Spring
5	Firing Pin	15	Sear Spring	25	Takedown Catch
6	Firing Pin Spring	16	Sear	26	Safety Catch
7	Firing Pin Spring Guide	17	Trigger Lever	27	Trigger Pin
8	Barrel	18	Trigger Bar	28	Trigger
9	Recoil Spring Guide Rod	19	Magazine Catch		
10	Recoil Spring	20	Grip		

22 Rimfire Revolver

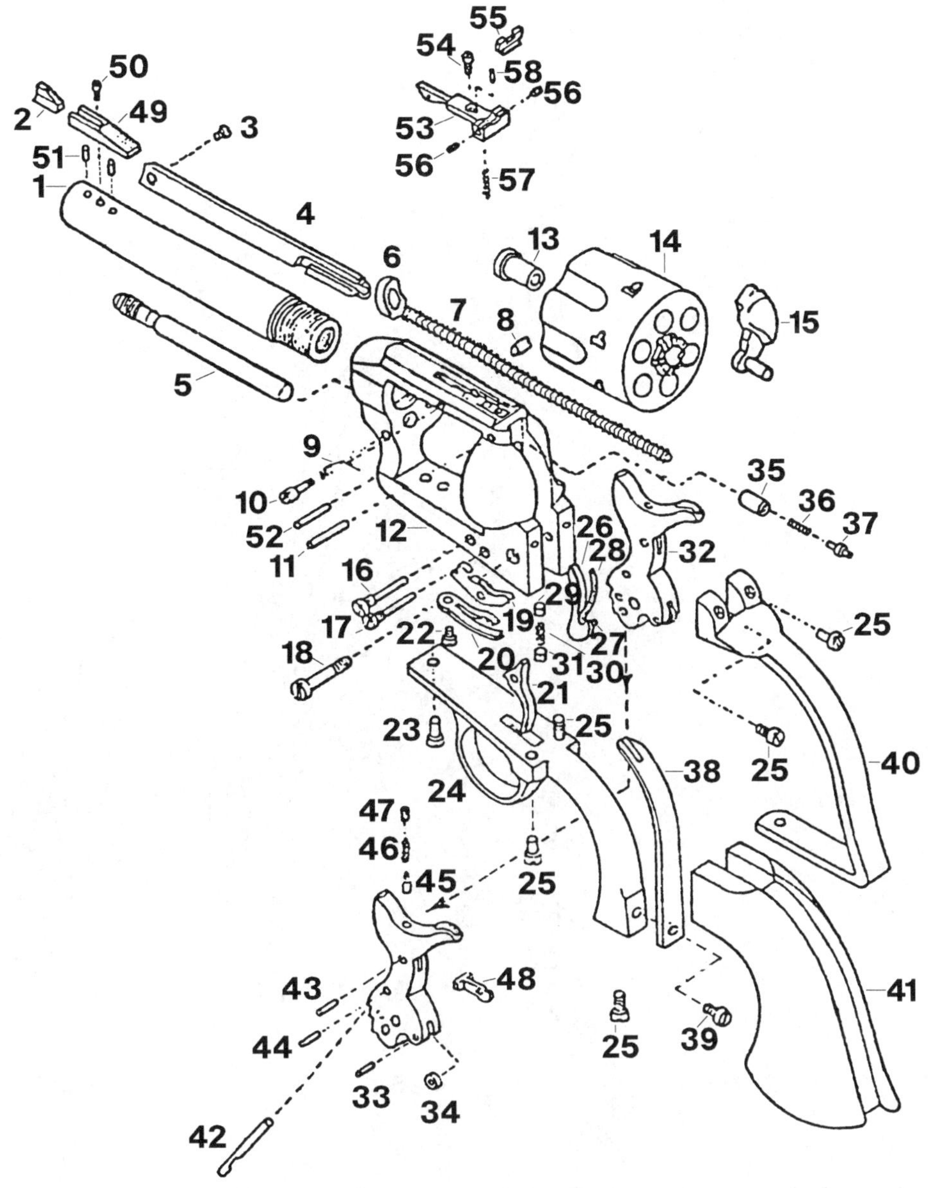

1	Barrel	21	Trigger	41	Grip
2	Front Sight	22	Sear and Bolt Spring Screw	42	Safety Block Rod
3	Ejector Rod Housing Screw	23	Front Guard Screw	43	Safety Block Pin
4	Ejector Rod Housing	24	Trigger Guard	44	Safety Block Rod Pin
5	Base Pin	25	Trigger Guard/Backstrap Screws	45	Safety Block Plunger
6	Ejector Rod with Head	26	Hand	46	Safety Block Plunger Spring
7	Ejector Rod Spring	27	Hand Pin	47	Safety Block Plunger Screw
8	Base Pin Screw Nut	28	Hand Spring	48	Safety Block
9	Base Pin Spring	29	Gate Catch Detent	49	Front Sight Base
10	Base Pin Screw	30	Gate Catch Spring	50	Front Sight Base Screw
11	Firing Pin Rivet Pin	31	Gate Catch Screw	51	Front Sight Pins
12	Frame	32	Hammer	52	Rear Sight Leaf Pin
13	Base Pin Bushing	33	Hammer Roll Pin	53	Rear Sight Base
14	Cylinder	34	Hammer Roll	54	Rear Sight Elevation Screw
15	Gate	35	Firing Pin Bearing (2)	55	Rear Sight Blade
16	Bolt Screw	36	Firing Pin Spring	56	Rear Sight Windage Screws
17	Trigger Screw	37	Firing Pin	57	Rear Sight Elevation Spring
18	Hammer Screw	38	Mainspring	58	Rear Sight Elevation Detent
19	Bolt	39	Mainspring Screw		
20	Sear and Bolt Spring	40	Backstrap		

SA Target/Silhouette Revolver

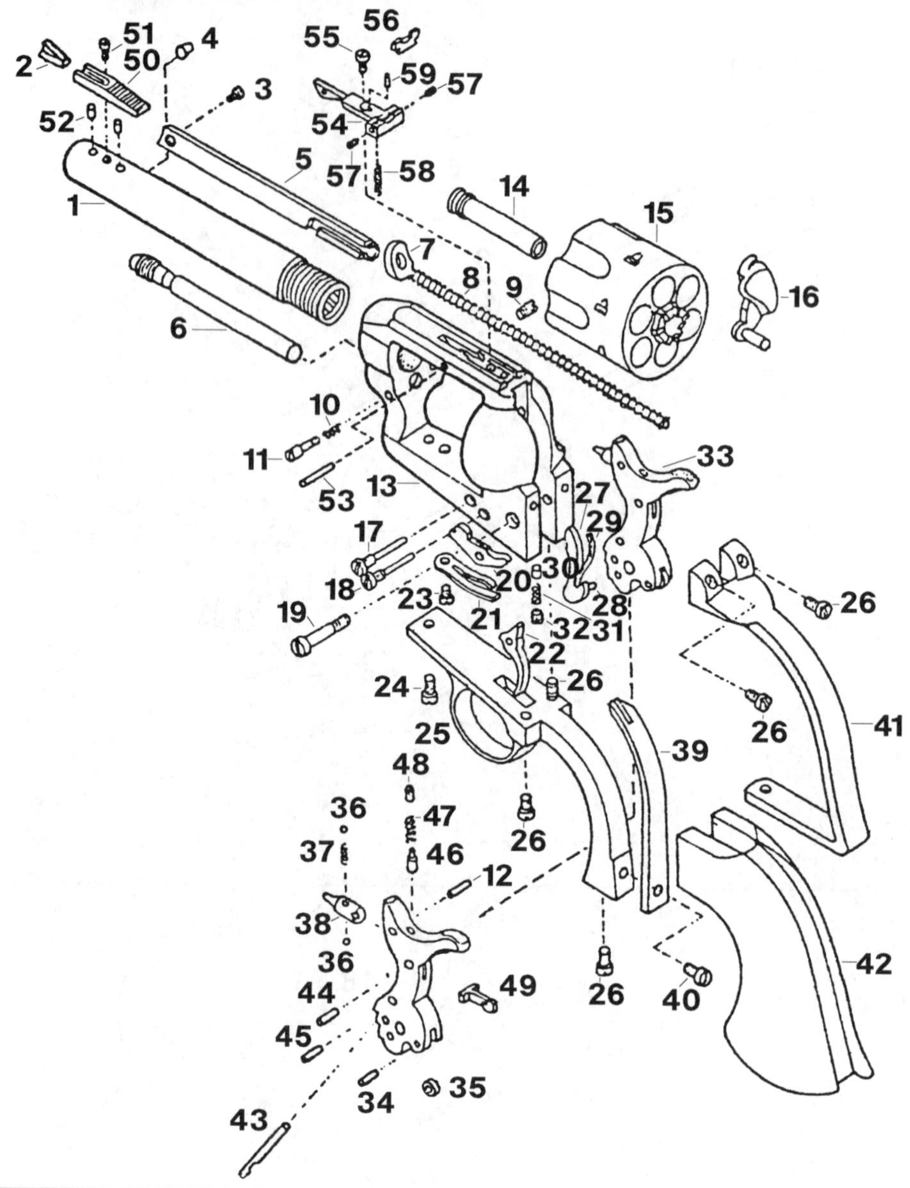

1	Barrel	21	Sear and Bolt Spring	41	Backstrap
2	Front Sight	22	Trigger	42	Grip
3	Ejector Rod Housing Screw	23	Sear and Bolt Spring Screw	43	Safety Block Rod
4	Ejector Rod Housing Lug	24	Front Guard Screw	44	Safety Block Pin
5	Ejector Rod Housing	25	Trigger Guard	45	Safety Block Rod Pin
6	Base Pin	26	Trigger Guard/Backstrap Screws	46	Safety Block Detent
7	Ejector Rod with Head	27	Hand	47	Safety Block Detent Spring
8	Ejector Rod Spring	28	Hand Assembly	48	Safety Block Detent Screw
9	Base Pin Screw Nut	29	Hand Spring	49	Safety Block
10	Base Pin Spring	30	Gate Catch Detent	50	Front Sight Base
11	Base Pin Screw	31	Gate Catch Spring	51	Front Sight Base Screw
12	Firing Pin Retaining Pin	32	Gate Catch Screw	52	Front Sight Base Pins
13	Frame	33	Hammer	53	Rear Sight Base Pin
14	Base Pin Bushing	34	Hammer Roll Pin	54	Rear Sight Base
15	Cylinder	35	Hammer Roll	55	Rear Sight Elevation Screw
16	Gate	36	Firing Pin Housing	56	Rear Sight Blade
17	Bolt Screw	37	Firing Pin Spring	57	Rear Sight Windage Screws
18	Trigger Screw	38	Firing Pin	58	Rear Sight Elevation Spring
19	Hammer Screw	39	Mainspring	59	Rear Sight Elevation Detent
20	Bolt	40	Mainspring Screw		

Single Action Revolver

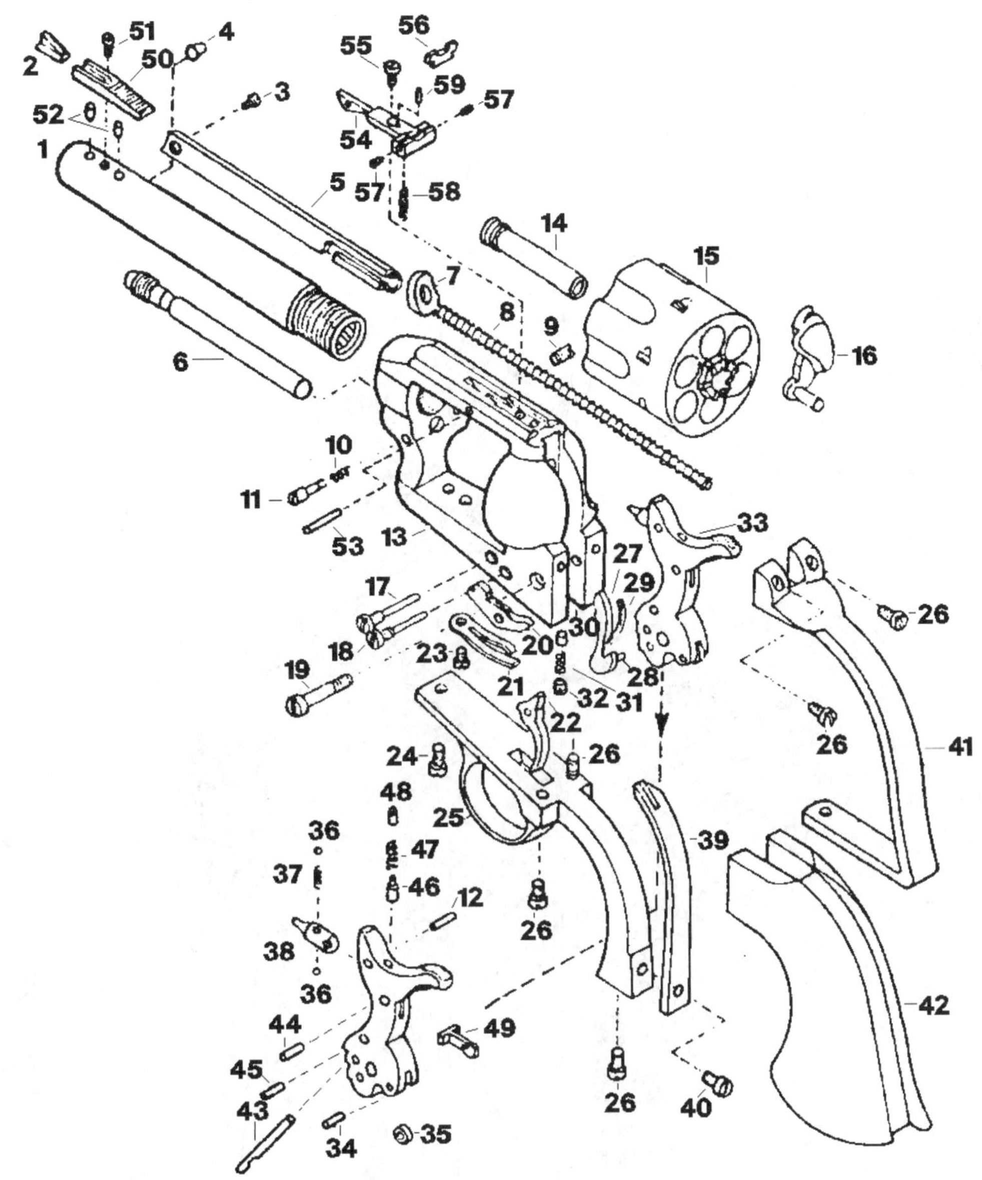

1	Barrel	21	Sear and Bolt Spring	41	Backstrap
2	Front Sight Blade	22	Trigger	42	Grip
3	Ejector Rod Housing Screw	23	Sear and Bolt Spring Screw	43	Safety Block Rod
4	Ejector Rod Housing Lug	24	Front Guard Screw	44	Safety Block Pin
5	Ejector Rod Housing	25	Trigger Guard	45	Safety Block Rod Pin
6	Base Pin	26	Trigger Guard/Backstrap Screws	46	Safety Block Plunger
7	Ejector Rod and Head	27	Hand	47	Safety Block Plunger Spring
8	Ejector Rod Spring	28	Hand Pin	48	Safety Block Plunger Screw
9	Base Pin Screw Nut	29	Hand Spring	49	Safety Block
10	Base Pin Spring	30	Gate Catch	50	Front Sight Base
11	Base Pin Screw	31	Gate Catch Spring	51	Front Sight Base Screw
12	Firing Pin Rivet	32	Gate Catch Screw	52	Front Sight Pins
13	Frame	33	Hammer	53	Rear Sight Leaf Pin
14	Base Pin Bushing	34	Hammer Roll Pin	54	Rear Sight Base
15	Cylinder	35	Hammer Roller	55	Rear Sight Elevation Screw
16	Gate	36	Firing Pin Bearings	56	Rear Sight Blade
17	Bolt Screw	37	Firing Pin Spring	57	Rear Sight Windage Screws
18	Trigger Screw	38	Firing Pin	58	Rear Sight Elevation Spring
19	Hammer Screw	39	Mainspring	59	Rear Sight Elevation Detent
20	Bolt	40	Mainspring Screw		

Turkish 380 Auto

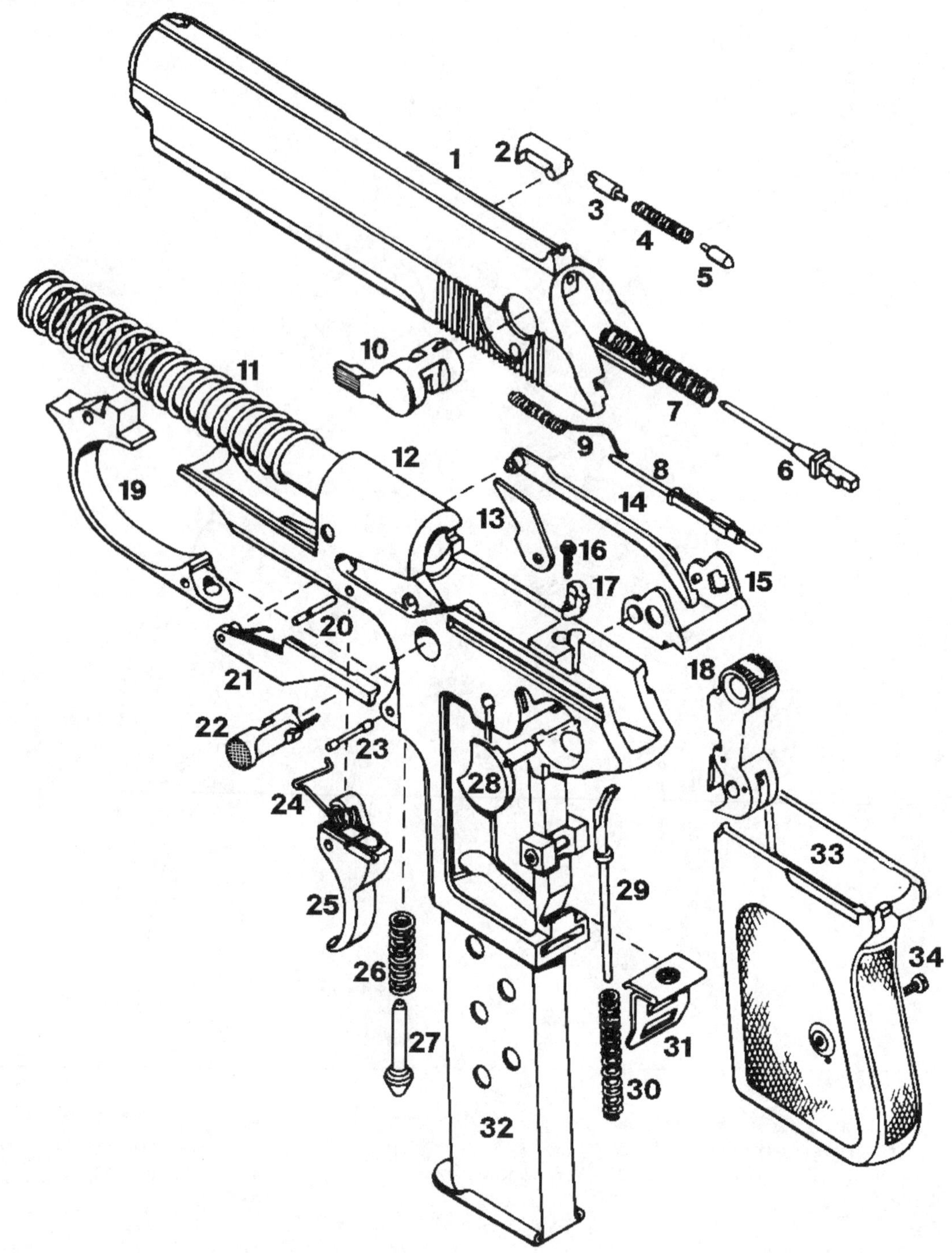

1	Slide	13	Hammer Release	24	Trigger Spring
2	Extractor	14	Trigger Bar	25	Trigger
3	Extractor Plunger	15	Cocking Piece	26	Trigger Guard Spring
4	Extractor Spring	16	Hammer Block Plunger and Spring	27	Trigger Guard Plunger
5	Safety Catch Plunger	17	Hammer Block	28	Hammer Pin
6	Firing Pin	18	Hammer	29	Hammer Strut
7	Firing Pin Spring	19	Trigger Guard	30	Hammer Spring
8	Cartridge Indicator	20	Trigger Pin	31	Lanyard Loop/Mainspring Retaining Bar
9	Indicator Spring	21	Ejector and Spring	32	Magazine Assembly
10	Safety Catch	22	Magazine Catch	33	Grip
11	Recoil Spring	23	Trigger Guard Pin	34	Grip Screw
12	Frame and Barrel				

Scoremaster/Servicemaster Auto

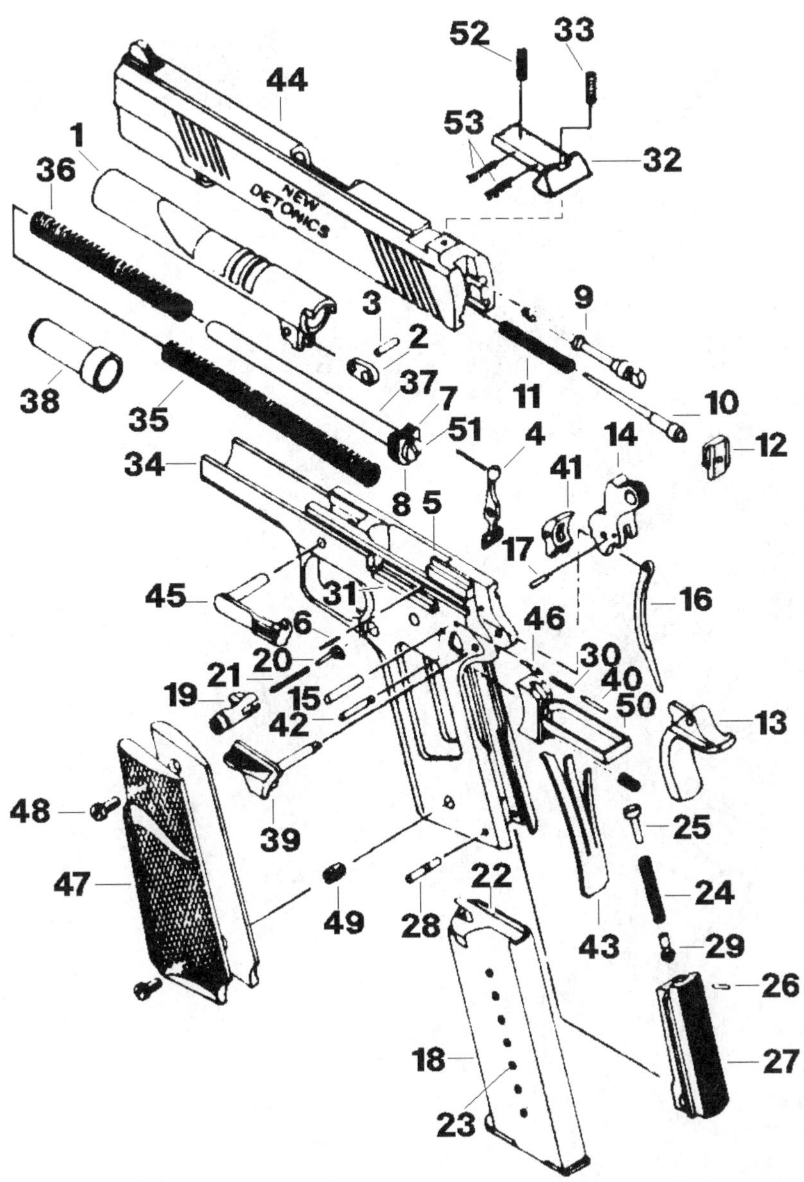

1	Barrel	19	Magazine Catch	36	Recoil Spring—Inner
2	Barrel Link	20	Magazine Catch Lock	37	Recoil Spring Guide
3	Barrel Link Pin	21	Magazine Catch Spring	38	Recoil Spring Cap
4	Disconnector	22	Magazine Follower	39	Safety Lock
5	Ejector	23	Magazine Spring	40	Safety Lock Plunger
6	Ejector Pin	24	Mainspring	41	Sear
7	Elastomer	25	Mainspring Cap	42	Sear Pin
8	Elastomer Retaining Plate	26	Mainspring Cap Spring	43	Sear Spring
9	Extractor	27	Mainspring Housing	44	Slide
10	Firing Pin	28	Mainspring Housing Pin	45	Slide Stop
11	Firing Pin Spring	29	Mainspring Housing Pin Retainer	46	Slide Stop Plunger
12	Firing Pin Stop			47	Stock
13	Grip Safety	30	Plunger Spring	48	Stock Screws
14	Hammer	31	Plunger Tube	49	Stock Screw Bushing
15	Hammer Pin	32	Rear Sight Windage Screw	50	Trigger Assembly
16	Hammer Strut	33	Rear Sight Elevation Screw	51	Recoil Spring Guide Screw
17	Hammer Strut Pin	34	Receiver	52	Rear Sight Retention Pin
18	Magazine Assembly	35	Recoil Spring—Outer	53	Rear Sight Springs

NORINCO

213 Auto

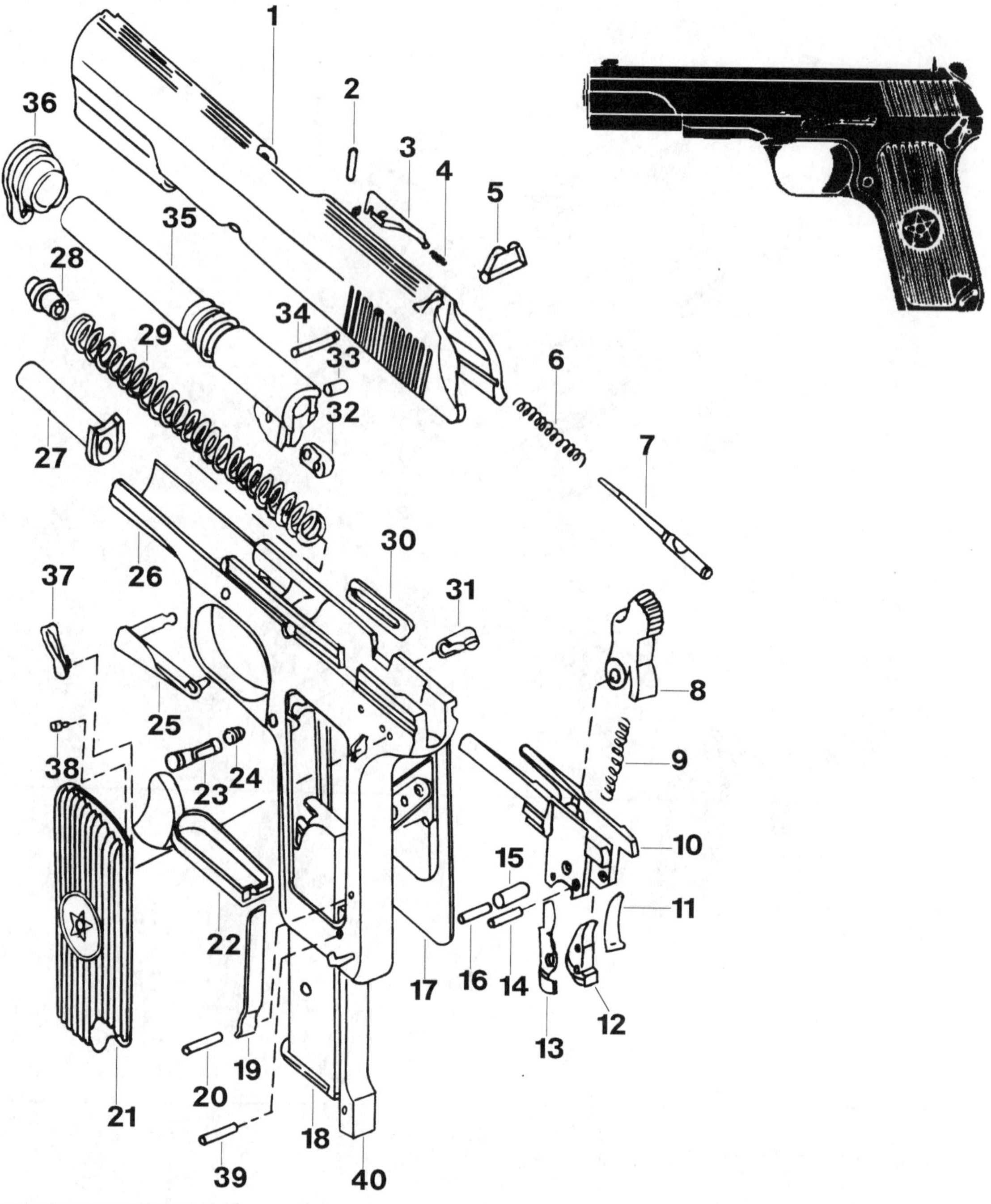

1	Slide	15	Hammer Pin	29	Recoil Spring
2	Extractor Pin	16	Sear Pin	30	Slide Stop Clip
3	Extractor	17	Right Grip	31	Magazine Catch Lock
4	Extractor Spring	18	Magazine Assembly	32	Barrel Link
5	Rear Sight	19	Trigger Spring	33	Barrel Link Pin
6	Firing Pin Spring	20	Trigger Spring Fixing Pin	34	Firing Pin Retainer Pin
7	Firing Pin	21	Left Grip	35	Barrel
8	Hammer	22	Trigger	36	Barrel Bushing
9	Hammer Spring	23	Magazine Catch	37	Safety Assembly
10	Hammer and Sear Housing	24	Magazine Catch Spring	38	Safety Fixing Screw
11	Sear Spring	25	Slide Stop	39	Insert Pin
12	Sear	26	Frame	40	Insert
13	Disconnector	27	Recoil Spring Guide		
14	Hammer Spring Stop	28	Recoil Spring Plug		

450 Magnum Revolver

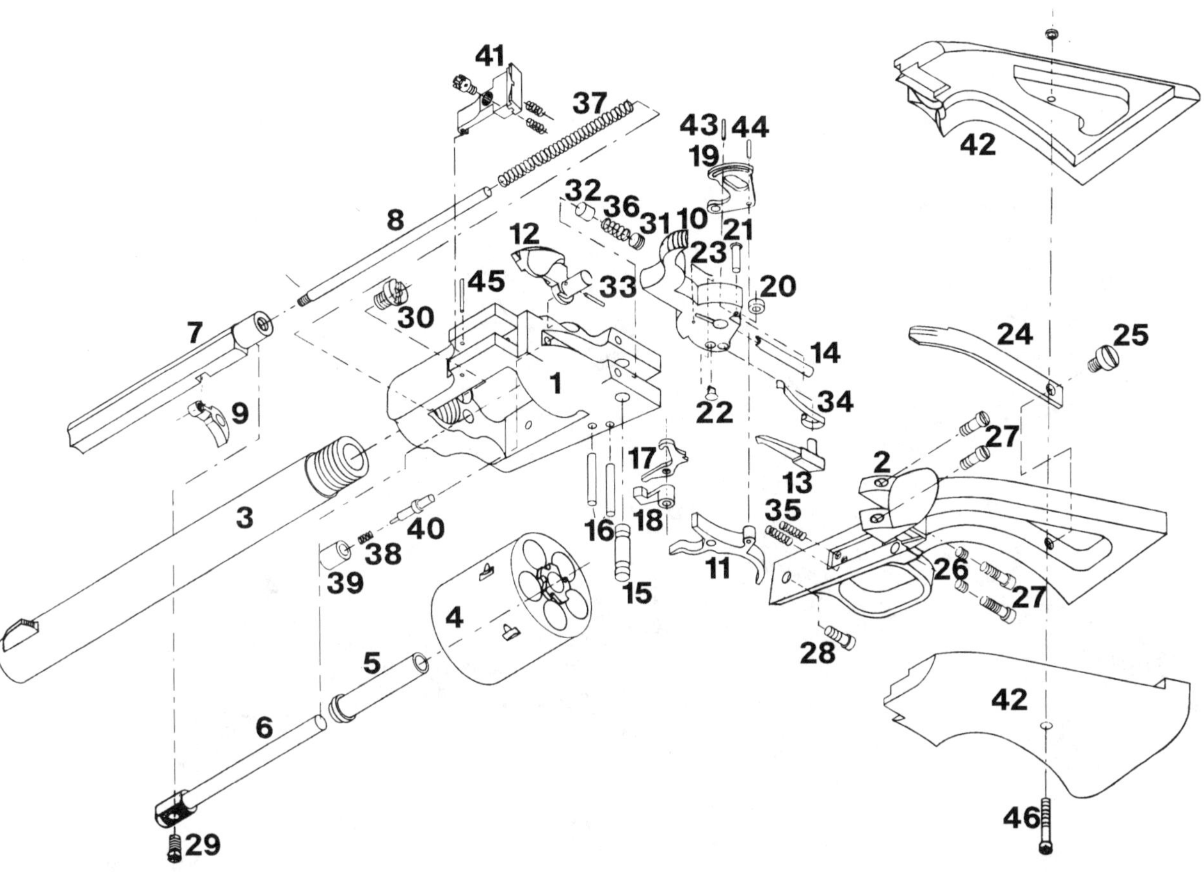

1	Cylinder Frame	**24**	Mainspring
2	Grip Frame	**25**	Mainspring Screw
3	Barrel	**26**	Hammer Pin Lock Screws
4	Cylinder	**27**	Frame Screws
5	Cylinder Bushing	**28**	Front Trigger Guard Screw
6	Cylinder Pin	**29**	Cylinder Pin Screw
7	Ejector Housing	**30**	Ejector Housing Screw
8	Ejector Rod	**31**	Gate Screw
9	Ejector Tab	**32**	Gate Piston
10	Hammer	**33**	Gate Pin
11	Trigger	**34**	Hand Spring
12	Gate	**35**	Trigger Bolt Springs
13	Hand	**36**	Gate Spring
14	Auxiliary Firing Pin	**37**	Ejector Spring
15	Hammer Pin	**38**	Firing Pin Spring
16	Hammer Pin and Trigger Pin	**39**	Recoil Plate
17	Latch Cam	**40**	Firing Pin
18	Latch	**41**	Rear Sight Assembly
19	Auxiliary Firing Pin Cam	**42**	Grips
20	Roller	**43**	Auxiliary Firing Pin Pin
21	Roller Pin	**44**	Cam Pin Tab
22	Button Latch	**45**	Rear Sight Assembly Pin
23	Button Latch Spring	**46**	Grip Screw

A-22S-5 Mini Revolver/also other NAA Mini Revolvers

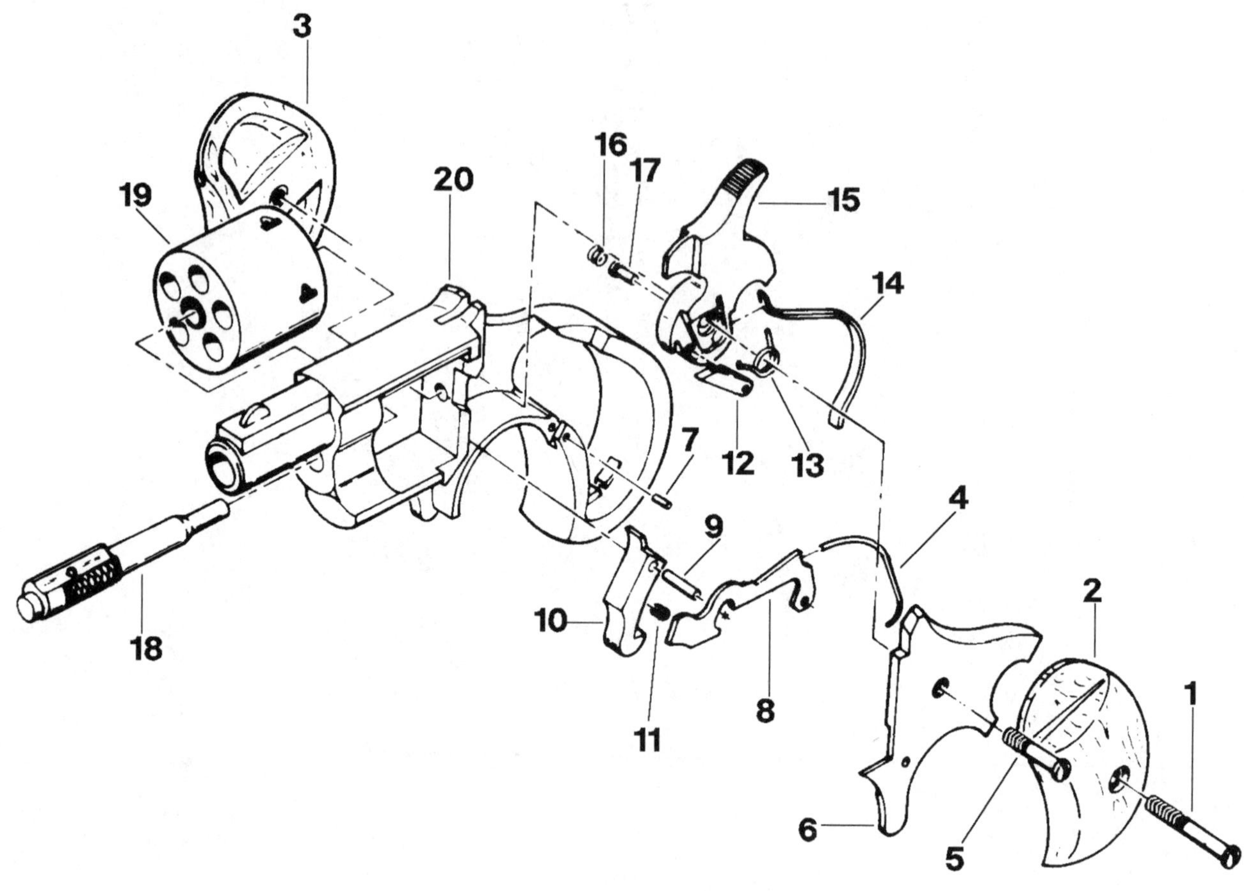

1	Grip Screw	11	Trigger Spring
2	Left Grip Panel	12	Cylinder Hand
3	Right Grip Panel	13	Hand Spring
4	Latch Spring	14	Mainspring
5	Hammer Screw	15	Hammer
6	Sideplate	16	Index Spring
7	Latch Pin	17	Index Pin
8	Cylinder Bolt	18	Cylinder Pin Assembly
9	Trigger Pin	19	Cylinder
10	Trigger	20	Frame

Pocket Auto

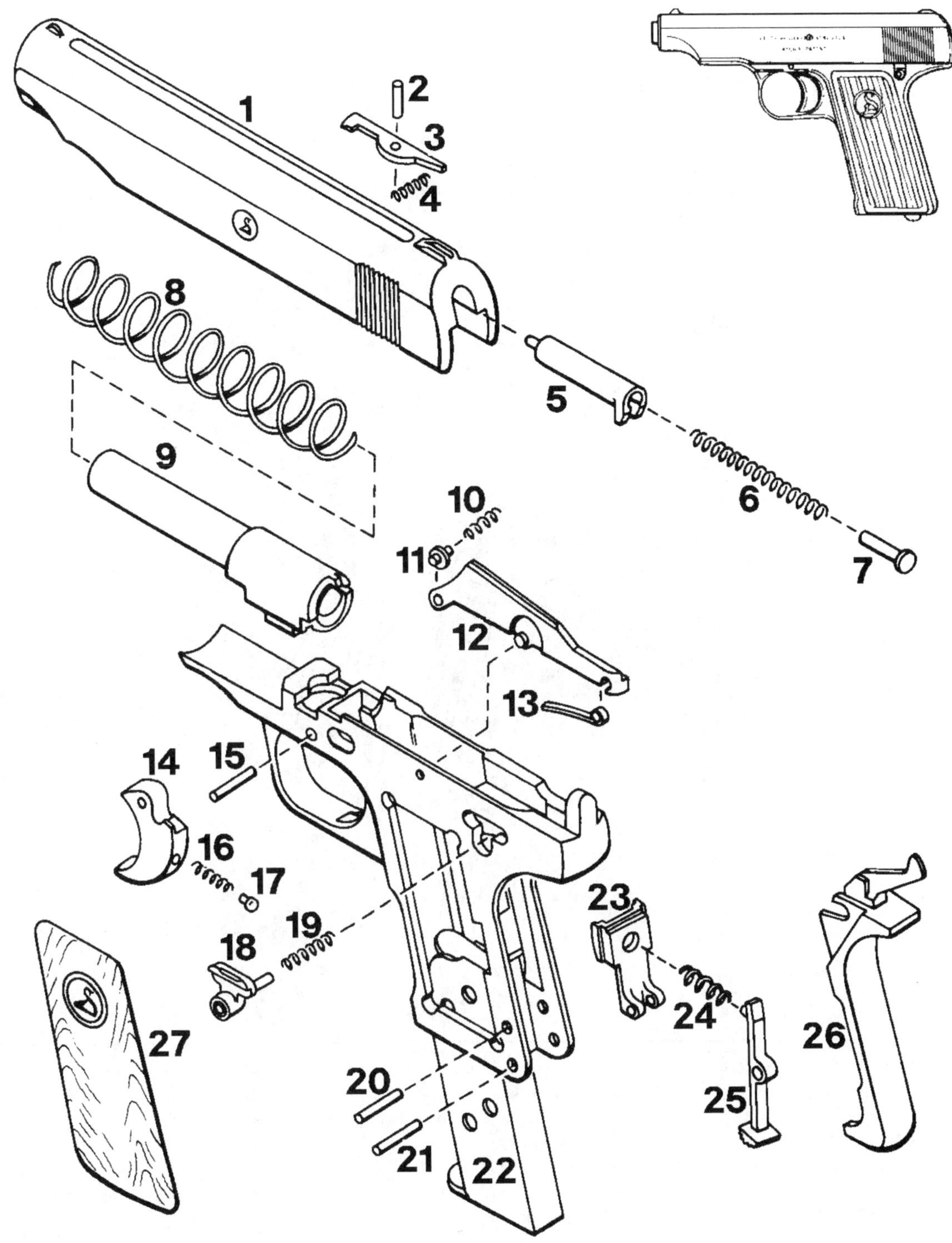

1	Slide	11	Disconnector	20	Magazine and Left Grip Latch Hinge Pin
2	Extractor Pin	12	Sear	21	Grip Safety Hinge Pin
3	Extractor	13	Sear Spring	22	Magazine
4	Extractor Spring	14	Trigger	23	Grip Latch
5	Firing Pin	15	Trigger Pin	24	Magazine Catch Spring
6	Firing Pin Spring	16	Trigger Spring	25	Magazine Catch
7	Firing Pin Spring Guide	17	Trigger Spring Plunger	26	Grip Safety
8	Recoil Spring	18	Takedown Catch	27	Grip Panel
9	Barrel	19	Takedown Catch Spring		
10	Disconnector Spring				

P14-45 Auto

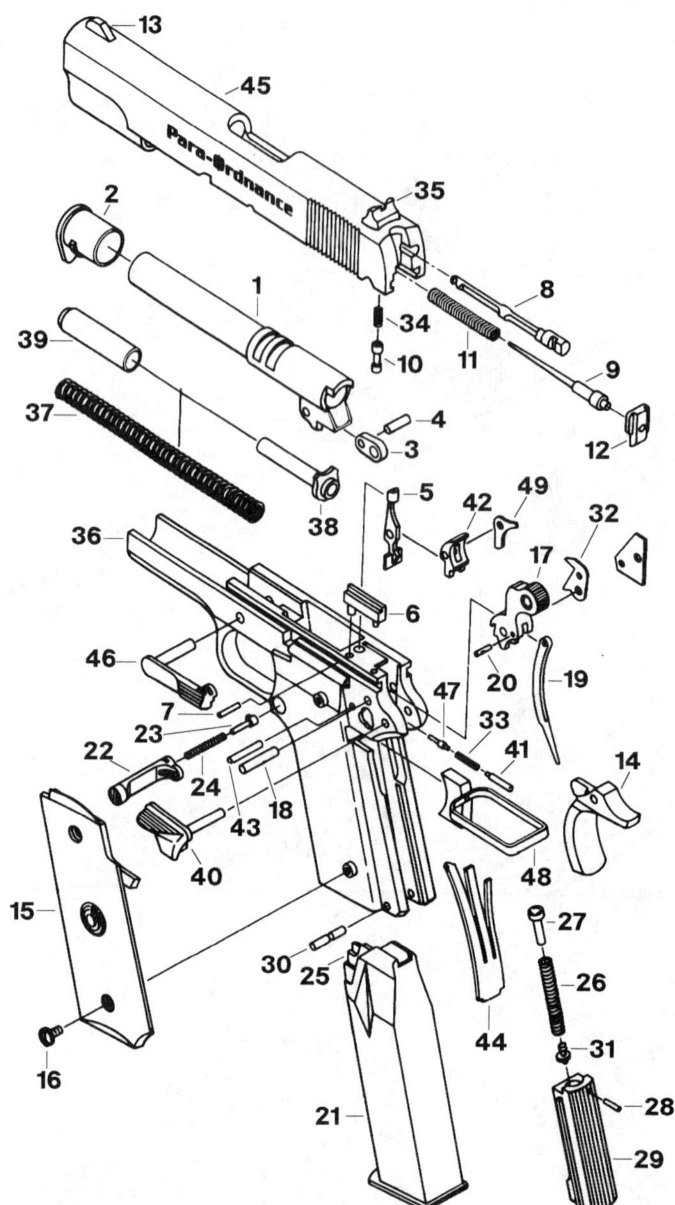

1	Barrel	**19**	Hammer Strut	**36**	Receiver
2	Barrel Bushing	**20**	Hammer Strut Pin	**37**	Recoil Spring
3	Barrel Link	**21**	Magazine Assembly	**38**	Recoil Spring Guide
4	Barrel Link Pin	**22**	Magazine Catch	**39**	Recoil Spring Plug
5	Disconnector	**23**	Magazine Catch Lock	**40**	Safety Lock
6	Ejector	**24**	Magazine Catch Spring	**41**	Safety Lock Plunger
7	Ejector Pin	**25**	Magazine Follower	**42**	Sear
8	Extractor	**26**	Mainspring	**43**	Sear Pin
9	Firing Pin	**27**	Mainspring Cap	**44**	Sear Spring
10	Firing Pin Plunger	**28**	Mainspring Cap Pin	**45**	Slide
11	Firing Pin Spring	**29**	Mainspring Housing (Flat)	**46**	Slide Stop
12	Firing Pin Stop	**30**	Mainspring Housing Pin	**47**	Slide Stop Plunger
13	Front Sight	**31**	Mainspring Housing Pin Retainer	**48**	Trigger Assembly
14	Grip Safety	**32**	Plunger Lever	**49**	Trigger Bar Lever
15	Grip	**33**	Plunger Spring	**Parts Not Shown**	
16	Grip Screw	**34**	Firing Pin Plunger Spring		Magazine Floorplate
17	Hammer	**35**	Rear Sight		Magazine Floorplate Retainer
18	Hammer Pin				Magazine Spring

Model 1935 (P-35) Auto

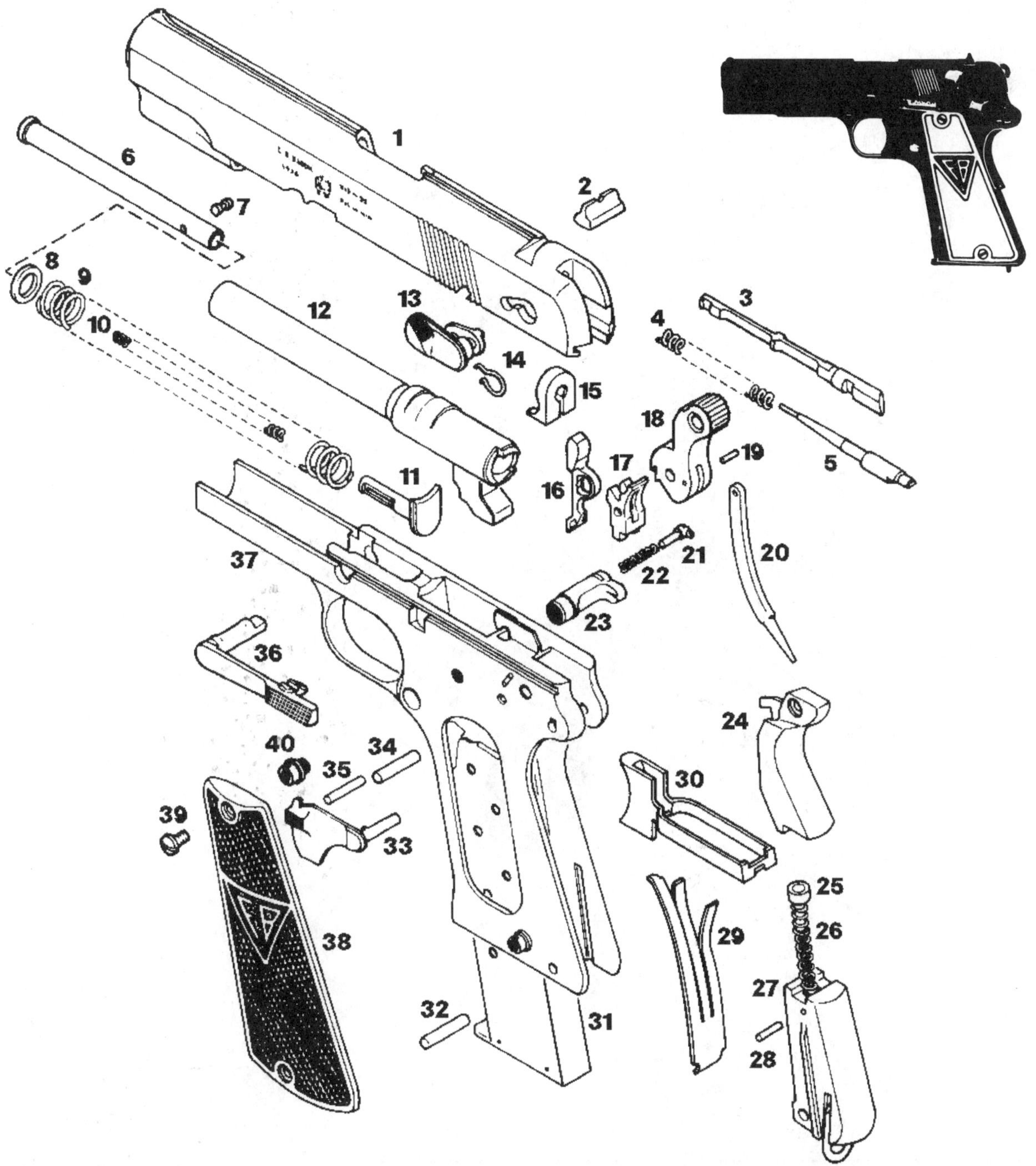

1	Slide	15	Firing Pin Retainer	29	Sear Spring
2	Rear Sight	16	Disconnector	30	Trigger
3	Extractor	17	Sear	31	Magazine
4	Firing Pin Spring	18	Hammer	32	Mainspring Housing Pin
5	Firing Pin	19	Hammer Strut Pin	33	Takedown Latch
6	Recoil Spring Guide	20	Hammer Strut	34	Hammer Pin
7	Spring Guide Retainer Pin	21	Magazine Catch Spring Guide	35	Sear and Disconnector Pin
8	Recoil Spring Stop	22	Magazine Catch Spring	36	Slide Stop/Hold-Open
9	Recoil Spring	23	Magazine Catch	37	Frame
10	Auxiliary Recoil Spring	24	Grip Safety	38	Grip Panel
11	Recoil Spring Guide Extension	25	Mainspring Cap	39	Grip Screw
12	Barrel	26	Mainspring	40	Grip Escutcheon
13	Hammer Drop Catch	27	Mainspring Housing		
14	Hammer Drop Catch Spring	28	Mainspring Retainer Pin		

Exactor Auto

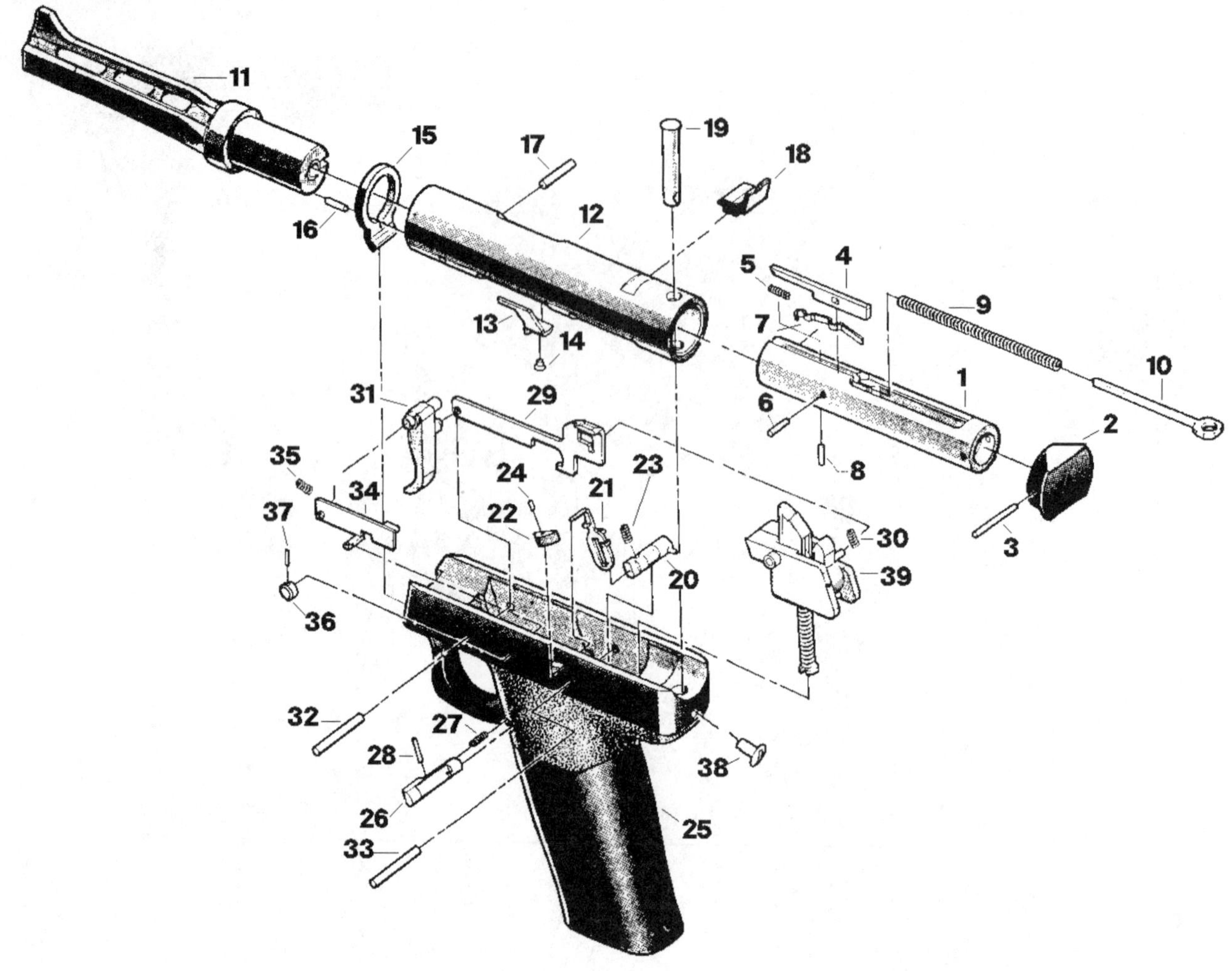

1	Bolt	**15**	Recoil Lug	**29**	Disconnector
2	Actuator Handle	**16**	Alignment Pin	**30**	Disconnector Spring
3	Actuator Pin	**17**	Shank Pin	**31**	Trigger Sub-Assembly
4	Firing Pin	**18**	Fixed Rear Sight	**32**	Trigger Retaining Pin
5	Firing Pin Spring	**19**	Bolt Stop Pin	**33**	Frame Retaining Pin
6	Firing Pin Pin	**20**	Hammer Block Sub-Assembly	**34**	Bolt Hold-Open
7	Extractor	**21**	Safety-Lever Sub-Assembly	**35**	Bolt Hold-Open Spring
8	Extractor Pin	**22**	Safety Knob	**36**	Bolt Hold-Open Knob
9	Recoil Spring	**23**	Safety Spring	**37**	Bolt Hold-Open Pin
10	Recoil Spring Guide	**24**	Safety Knob Pin	**38**	Takedown Screw
11	Barrel Sub-Assembly	**25**	Grip Body	**39**	Fire Control Sub-Assembly
12	Receiver	**26**	Magazine Latch	**Parts Not Shown**	
13	Ejector	**27**	Magazine Latch Spring		Adjustable Rear Sight
14	Ejector Screw	**28**	Magazine Latch Pin		Magazine

Model P-25 and MP-25 Auto

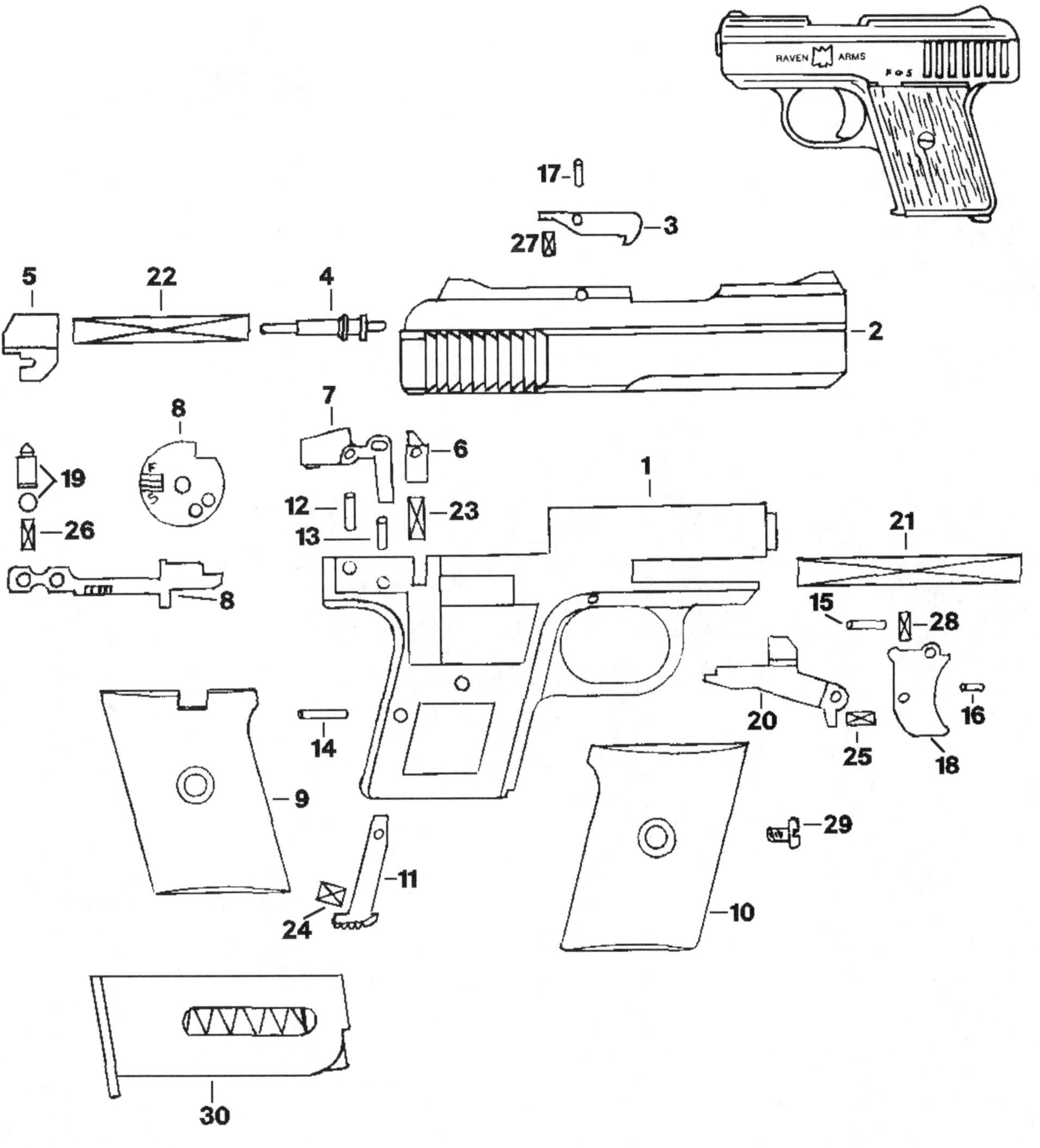

1	Frame	**11**	Magazine Catch	**21**	Recoil Spring
2	Slide	**12**	Retainer Pin	**22**	Striker Spring
3	Extractor	**13**	Cam Pin	**23**	Sear Spring
4	Firing Pin	**14**	Catch Pin	**24**	Catch Spring
5	Retainer	**15**	Pivot Pin	**25**	Trigger Spring
6	Sear Assembly	**16**	Trigger Pin	**26**	Plunger Spring
7	Cam	**17**	Extractor Pin	**27**	Extractor Spring
8	Safety Assembly	**18**	Trigger	**28**	Return Spring
9	Left Grip	**19**	Plunger and Ball	**29**	Grip Screw
10	Right Grip	**20**	Disconnector	**30**	Magazine Assembly

Double Derringer Auto

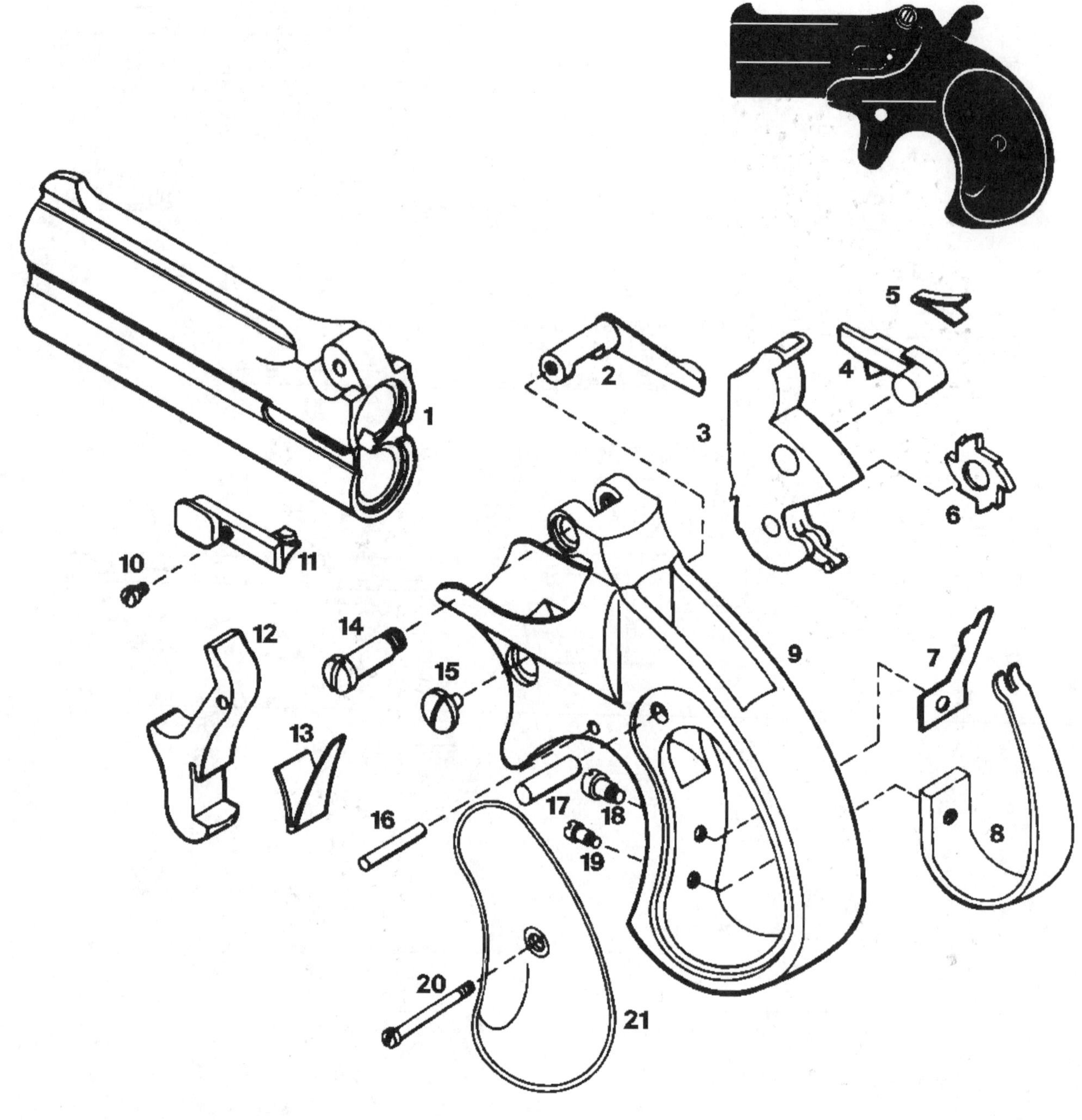

1	Barrels	12	Trigger
2	Barrel Lock	13	Trigger Spring
3	Hammer	14	Barrel Hinge Screw
4	Firing Pin	15	Barrel Lock Screw
5	Firing Pin Spring	16	Trigger Pin
6	Firing Pin Ratchet	17	Hammer Pin
7	Firing Pin Ratchet Spring	18	Firing Pin Ratchet Spring Screw
8	Mainspring	19	Mainspring Screw
9	Frame	20	Grip Screw
10	Ejector Screw	21	Grip Panel
11	Ejector		

Model 1890 Frontier Revolver

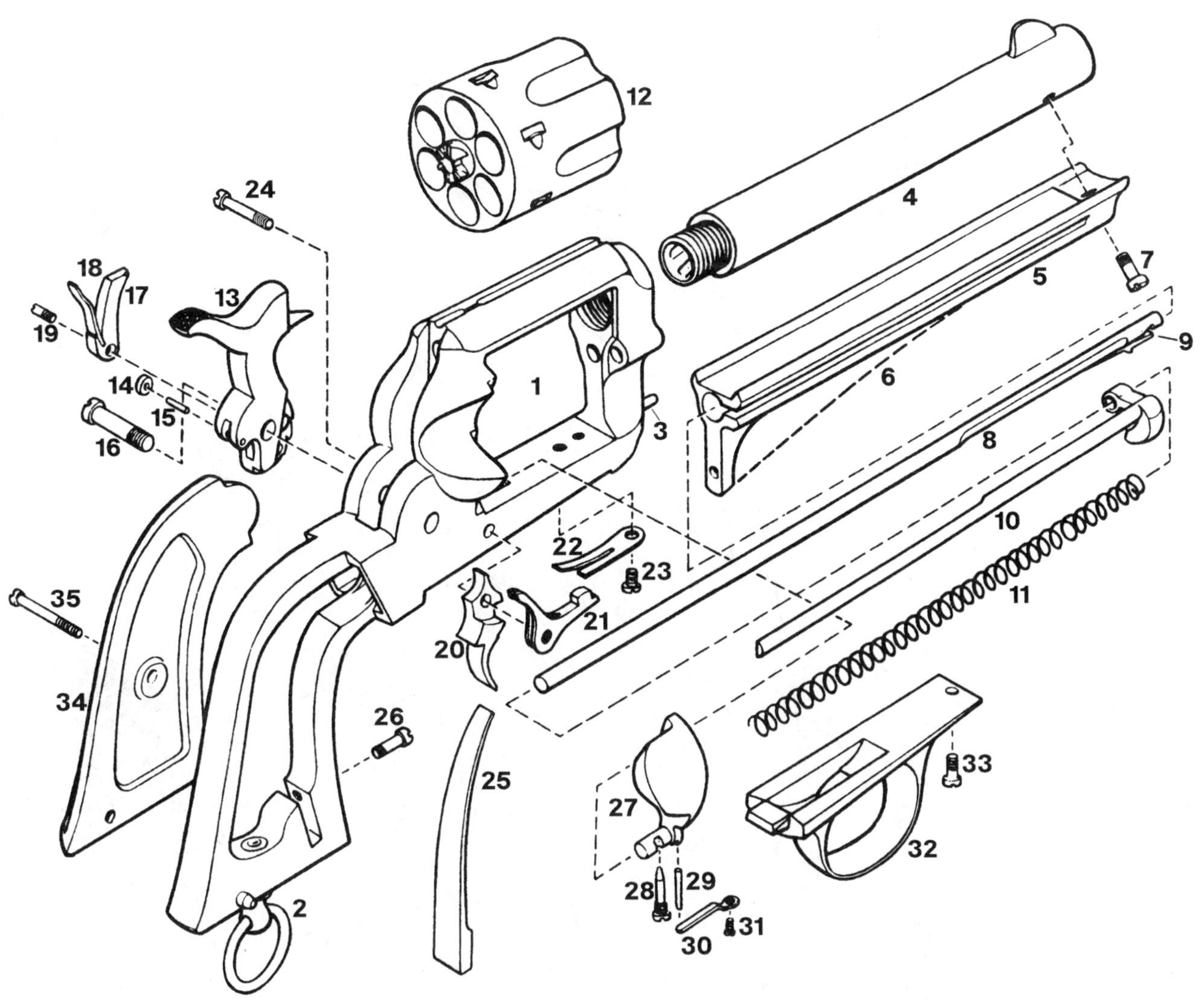

1	Frame	13	Hammer	25	Mainspring
2	Lanyard Swivel Ring Assembly	14	Hammer Roll	26	Strain Screw
3	Ejector Housing Stud	15	Hammer Roll Pin	27	Gate
4	Barrel	16	Hammer Screw	28	Gate Retaining Screw
5	Ejector Housing	17	Hand	29	Gate Plunger
6	Ejector Housing for Model 1875	18	Hand Spring	30	Gate Plunger Spring
7	Ejector Housing Screw	19	Hand Stud	31	Gate Plunger Spring Screw
8	Base Pin	20	Trigger	32	Trigger Guard
9	Base Pin Catch Spring	21	Bolt	33	Trigger Guard Screw
10	Ejector Rod	22	Trigger and Bolt Spring	34	Grip
11	Ejector Spring	23	Trigger and Bolt Spring Screw	35	Grip Screw
12	Cylinder	24	Trigger and Bolt Screw		

Model 51 Auto

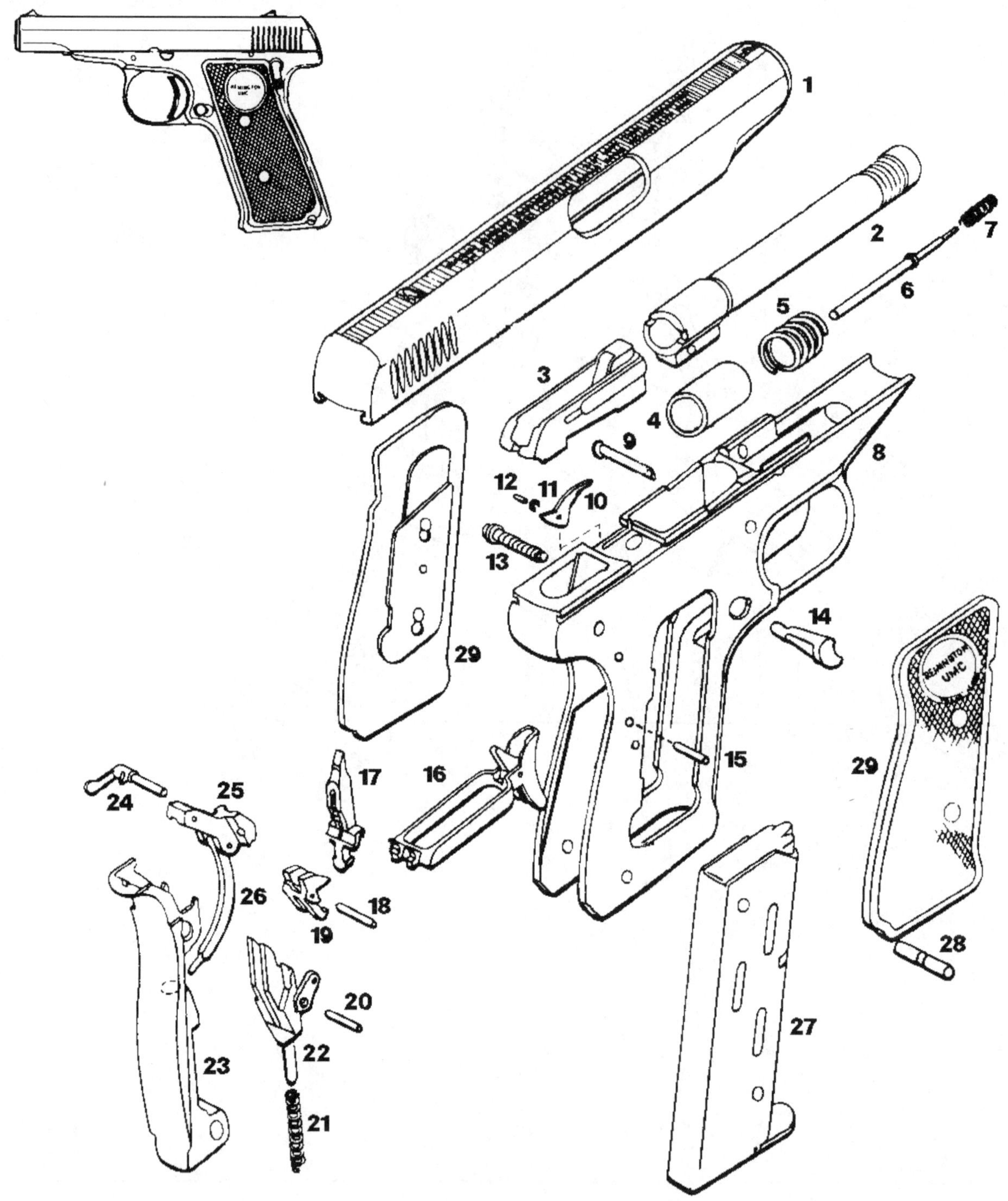

1	Slide	**11**	Ejector Spring	**20**	Sear Lock Lever Pin
2	Barrel	**12**	Ejector Pin	**21**	Mainspring
3	Breech Bolt	**13**	Magazine Lock Spring and Follower	**22**	Sear Lock
4	Recoil Spring Bushing	**14**	Magazine Lock	**23**	Grip Safety
5	Recoil Spring	**15**	Sear Lock Pin	**24**	Safety-Lever
6	Firing Pin	**16**	Trigger	**25**	Hammer
7	Firing Pin Spring	**17**	Disconnector	**26**	Mainspring Strut
8	Frame	**18**	Sear Pin	**27**	Magazine Assembly
9	Barrel Lock Pin	**19**	Sear	**28**	Grip Safety Pin
10	Ejector			**29**	Grip Panel

New Model Army 44 Revolver

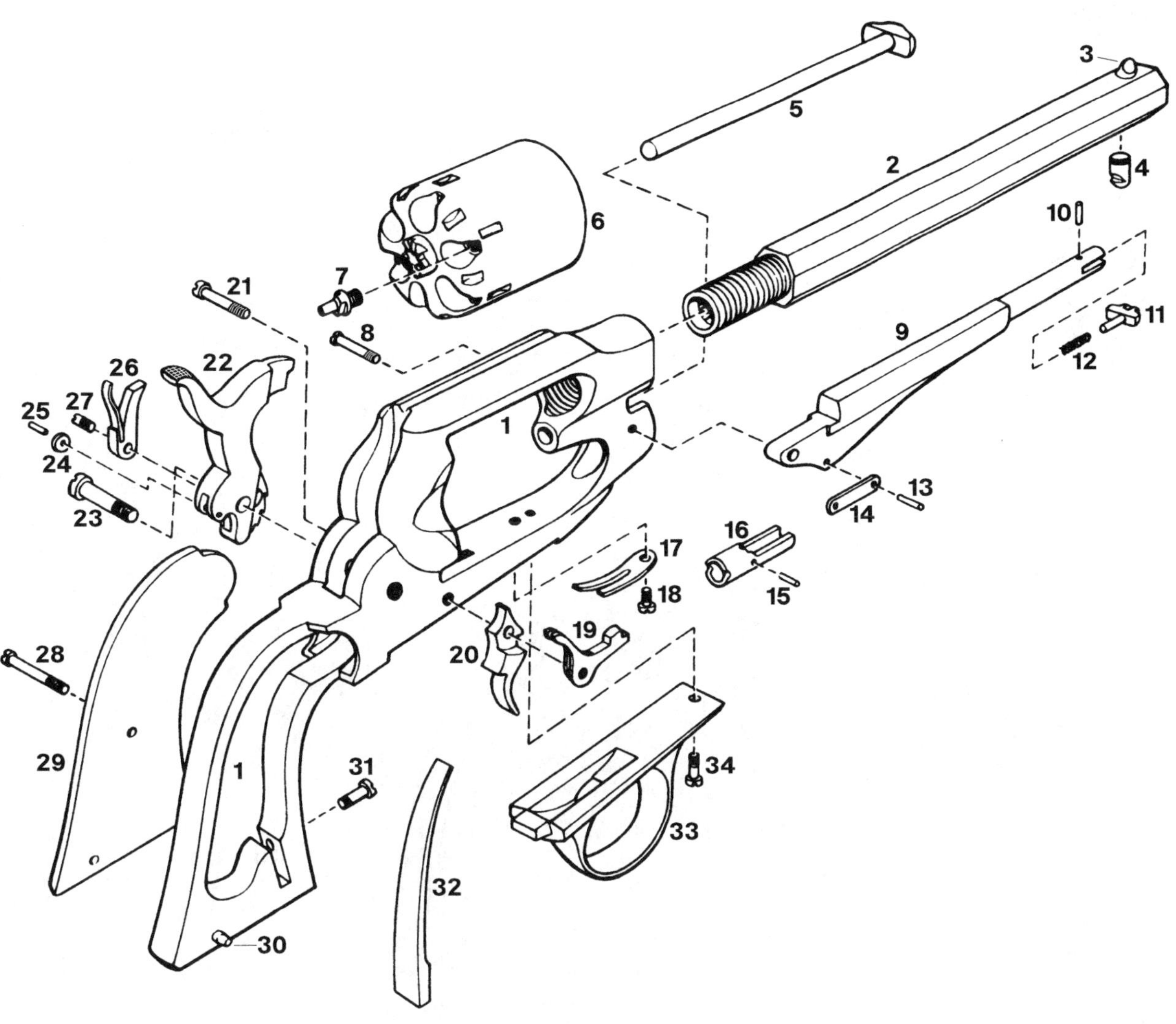

1	Frame	13	Front Plunger Link Pin	24	Hammer Roll
2	Barrel	14	Plunger Link	25	Hammer Roll Pin
3	Front Sight	15	Rear Plunger Link Pin	26	Hand and Hand Spring
4	Barrel Stud	16	Plunger	27	Hand Screw
5	Cylinder Pin	17	Trigger and Cylinder Stop Spring	28	Grip Screw
6	Cylinder	18	Trigger and Cylinder Stop Spring Screw	29	Grip
7	Nipple			30	Grip Pin
8	Loading Lever Screw	19	Cylinder Stop	31	Mainspring Set Screw
9	Loading Lever	20	Trigger	32	Mainspring
10	Latch Pin	21	Trigger and Cylinder Stop Screw	33	Trigger Guard
11	Latch	22	Hammer	34	Trigger Guard Screw
12	Latch Spring	23	Hammer Screw		

New Model Pocket Revolver

Courtesy of Blacksmith Corporation

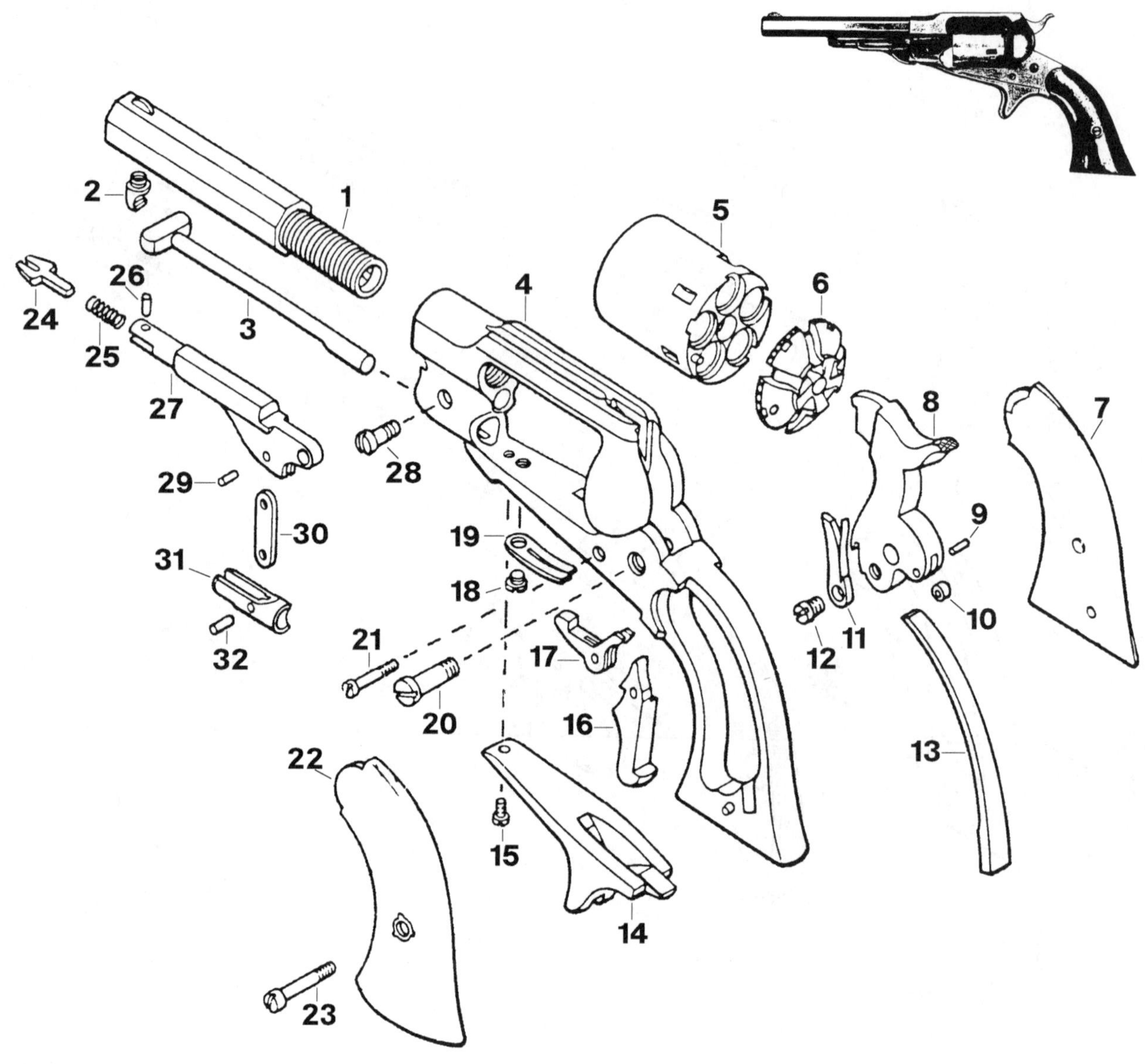

1	Barrel	**12**	Hand Retaining Screw	**23**	Grip Screw
2	Rammer Latch	**13**	Mainspring	**24**	Loading Lever Latch
3	Cylinder Pin	**14**	Trigger Guard	**25**	Latch Spring
4	Frame	**15**	Trigger Guard Screw	**26**	Latch Pin
5	Cylinder	**16**	Trigger	**27**	Loading Lever
6	Cylinder Backplate	**17**	Cylinder Stop	**28**	Lever Screw
7	Right Grip	**18**	Trigger Spring Screw	**29**	Lever Link Pin
8	Hammer	**19**	Trigger Spring	**30**	Link
9	Roller Pin	**20**	Hammer Screw	**31**	Rammer
10	Roller	**21**	Trigger Screw	**32**	Rammer Link Pin
11	Hand	**22**	Left Grip		

XP-100 Bolt Action

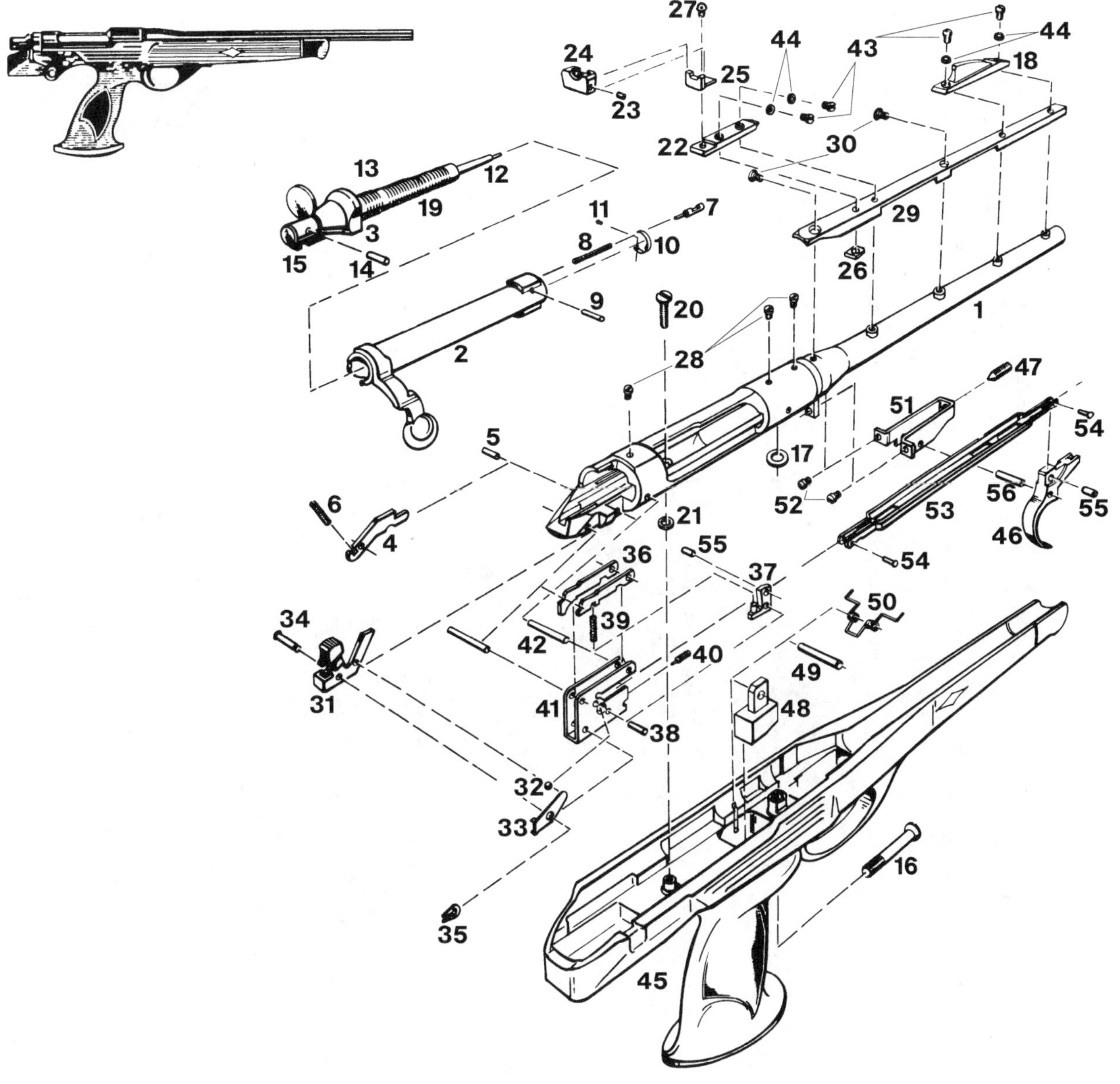

1	Barrel	**20**	Rear Receiver Screw	**39**	Sear Block Spring
2	Bolt Assembly	**21**	Rear Receiver Screw Washer	**40**	Sear Block Stop Screw
3	Bolt Plug	**22**	Rear Sight Base	**41**	Sear Housing
4	Bolt Stop	**23**	Rear Sight Elevation Screw	**42**	Sear Pins
5	Bolt Stop Pin	**24**	Rear Sight Eyepiece	**43**	Sight Screws
6	Bolt Stop Spring	**25**	Rear Sight Leaf	**44**	Sight Washers
7	Ejector	**26**	Rear Sight Nut	**45**	Stock Assembly
8	Ejector Spring	**27**	Rear Sight Windage Screw	**46**	Trigger
9	Ejector Pin	**28**	Receiver Plug Screws	**47**	Trigger Adjustment Screw
10	Extractor	**29**	Rib	**48**	Trigger Balance
11	Extractor Rivet	**30**	Rib Screws	**49**	Trigger Balance Pin
12	Firing Pin	**31**	Safety Assembly	**50**	Trigger Balance Spring
13	Firing Pin Assembly	**32**	Safety Detent Ball	**51**	Trigger Housing
14	Firing Pin Cross Pin	**33**	Safety Detent Spring	**52**	Trigger Housing Screws
15	Firing Pin Head	**34**	Safety Pivot Pin	**53**	Trigger Link
16	Forward Receiver Screw	**35**	Safety Snap Washer	**54**	Trigger Link Pins
17	Forward Receiver Screw Washer	**36**	Sear Safety Cam	**55**	Trigger Link Roller
18	Front Sight	**37**	Sear Block Assembly	**56**	Trigger Pin
19	Mainspring	**38**	Sear Block Pin		

22 and 25 Auto

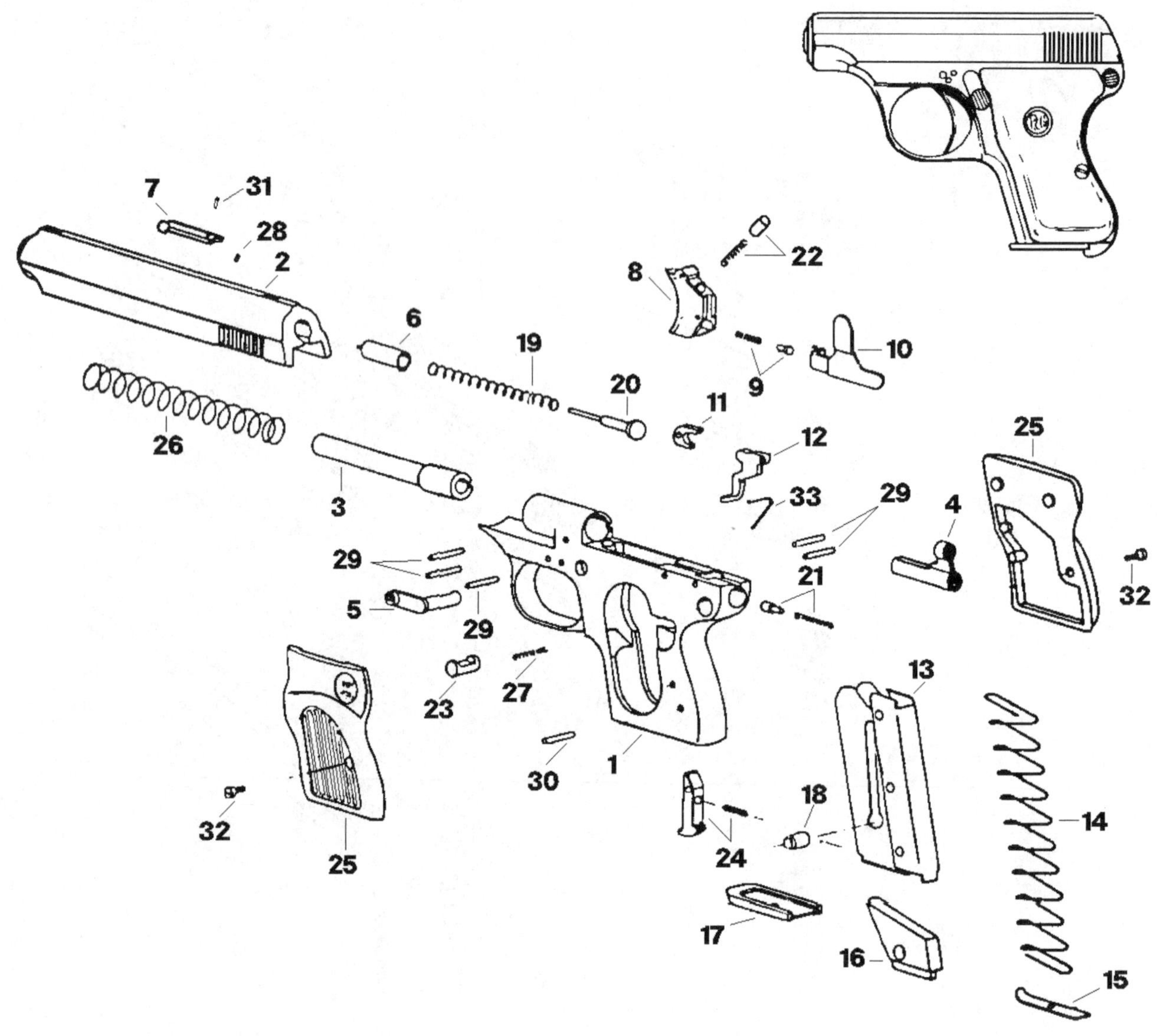

1	Receiver	18	Magazine Follower Thumb-Piece
2	Slide	19	Firing Pin Spring
3	Barrel	20	Firing Pin Follower
4	Hammer	21	Sear Cam Spring and Follower
5	Safety	22	Safety Spring and Follower
6	Firing Pin	23	Disconnector Button
7	Extractor	24	Magazine Retainer and Spring
8	Trigger	25	Grips
9	Trigger Bar Spring and Plunger	26	Barrel Spring
10	Trigger Bar	27	Disconnector Button Spring
11	Sear	28	Extractor Spring
12	Sear Cam	29	Dowel Pins
13	Magazine Body	30	Magazine Retainer Pin
14	Magazine Spring	31	Extractor Pin
15	Magazine Base Plate	32	Grip Screws
16	Magazine Follower	33	Sear Spring
17	Magazine Floorplate		

RG 63 Revolver

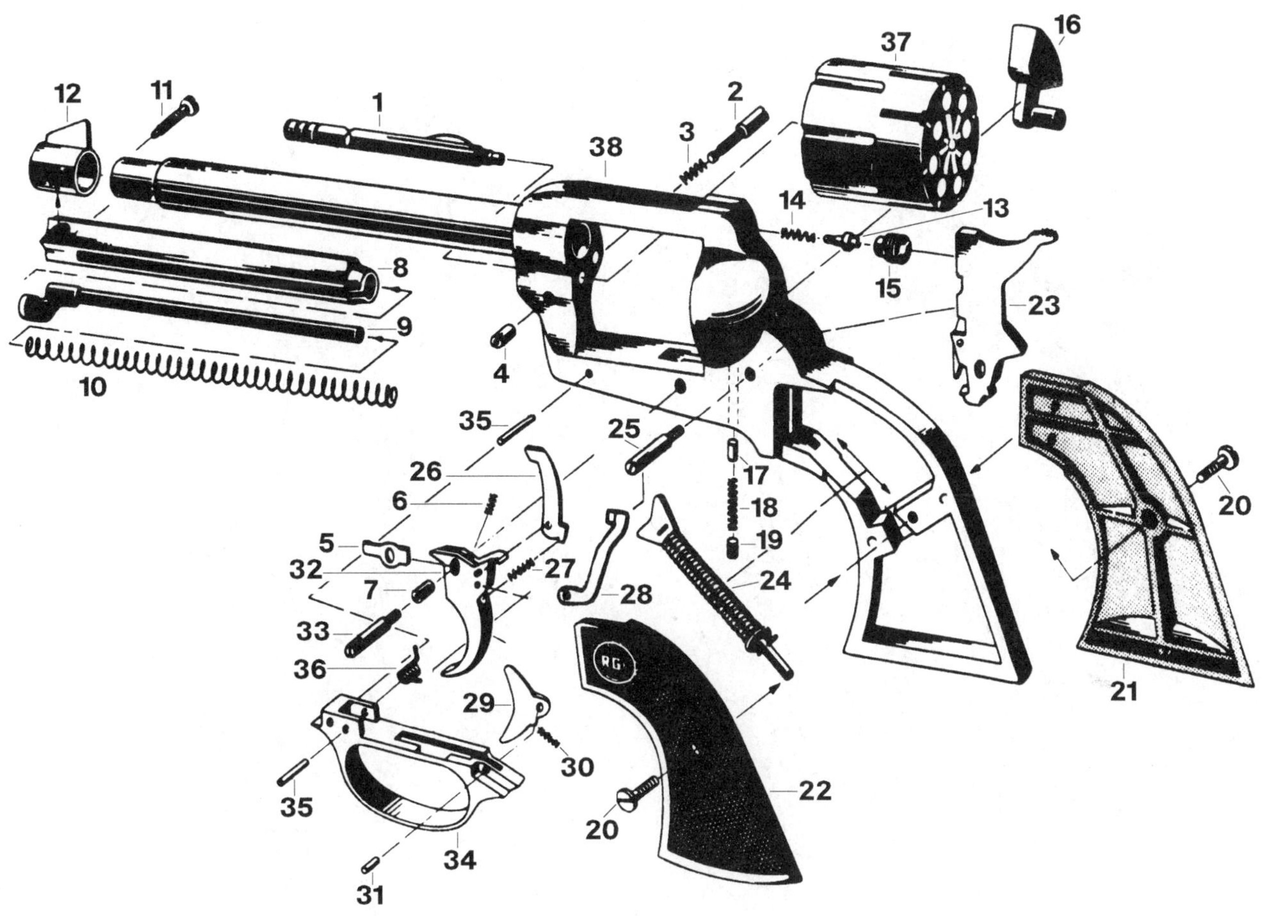

1	Cylinder Pin, Complete	**21**	Right Grip Plate
2	Attachment Pin	**22**	Left Grip Plate
3	Pressure Spring	**23**	Hammer, Complete
4	Slotted Nut	**24**	Mainspring Assembly
5	Cylinder Stop	**25**	Hammer Screw
6	Pressure Spring	**26**	Hand
7	Trigger Bushing	**27**	Hand Spring
8	Ejector Tube	**28**	Hammer Safety
9	Ejector Rod	**29**	Tension Latch
10	Pressure Spring	**30**	Tension Latch Spring
11	Lens Head Screw	**31**	Straight Pin
12	Front Sight	**32**	Trigger
13	Firing Pin	**33**	Trigger Screw
14	Firing Pin Spring	**34**	Trigger Guard
15	Firing Pin Sleeve	**35**	Straight Pin
16	Loading Gate	**36**	Trigger Spring
17	Straight Pin	**37**	Cylinder
18	Pressure Spring	**38**	Frame
19	Threaded Pin	**Parts Not Shown**	
20	Grip Plate Screws		Barrel Pin

ROSSI

22 Senator Revolver

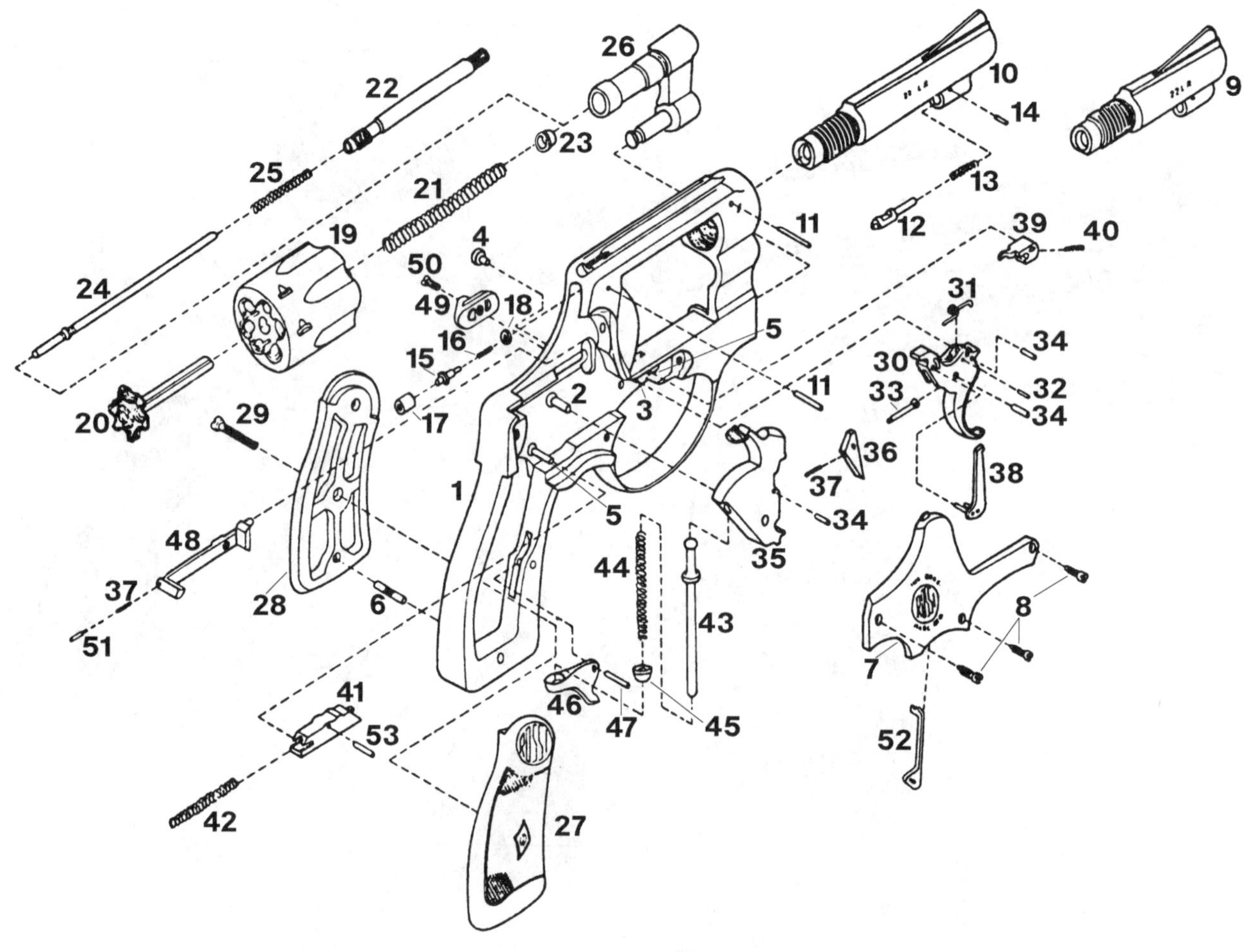

1	Frame with Bushing and Pins	28	Left Grip
2	Hammer Pin	29	Grip Screw
3	Trigger Pin	30	Trigger
4	Frame Lug	31	Hand Lever Spring
5	Cylinder Stop and Rebound Slide Pin	32	Hand Lever Spring Pin
6	Stock Pin	33	Trigger Lever
7	Sideplate	34	Trigger Lever Pins and Sear Spring Pin
8	Sideplate Screws	35	Target Hammer
9	Barrel, 2"	36	Sear
10	Barrel, 3"	37	Sear Spring and Bolt Plunger Spring
11	Barrel Pin and Firing Pin Retainer Pin	38	Hand
12	Locking Bolt	39	Cylinder Stop
13	Locking Bolt Spring	40	Cylinder Stop Spring
14	Locking Bolt Pin	41	Rebound Slide
15	Firing Pin	42	Rebound Slide Spring
16	Firing Pin Spring	43	Mainspring Rod
17	Firing Pin Bushing	44	Mainspring
18	Firing Pin Washer	45	Mainspring Swivel
19	Cylinder	46	Mainspring Stop
20	Extractor	47	Mainspring Stop Pin
21	Extractor Spring	48	Bolt
22	Extractor Rod	49	Thumb-Piece
23	Extractor Collar	50	Thumb-Piece Screw
24	Center Pin	51	Bolt Plunger
25	Center Pin Spring	52	Hammer Block
26	Yoke (Crane)	53	Hammer Block Pin
27	Right Grip		

Model 68, 69, 70 and 31 Revolver

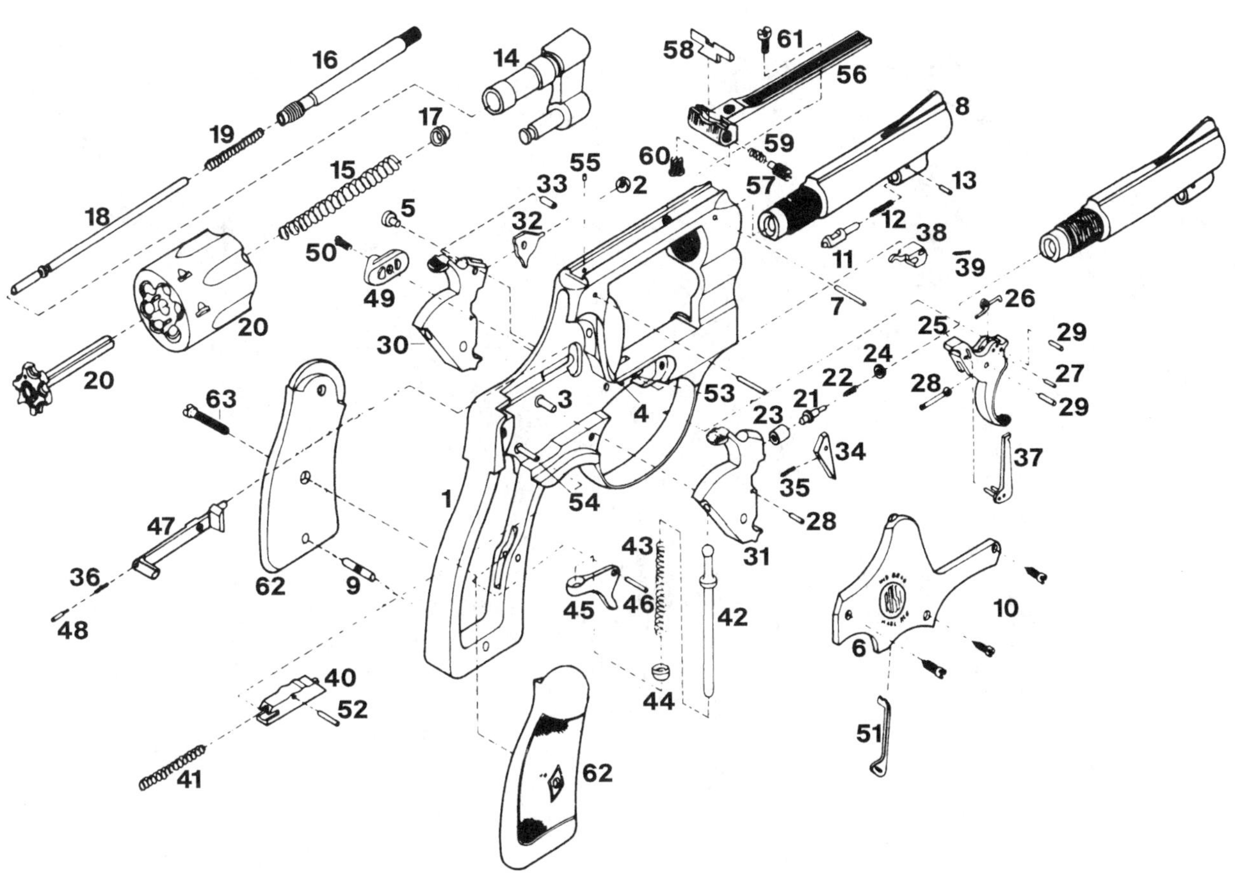

1	Frame	**22**	Firing Pin Spring	**43**	Mainspring
2	Hammer Nose Bushing	**23**	Firing Pin Bushing	**44**	Mainspring Swivel
3	Hammer Pin	**24**	Firing Pin Washer	**45**	Mainspring Stop
4	Trigger Pin	**25**	Trigger	**46**	Mainspring Stop Pin
5	Frame Lug	**26**	Hand Lever Spring	**47**	Bolt
6	Sideplate	**27**	Hand Lever Spring Pin	**48**	Bolt Plunger
7	Barrel Pin	**28**	Trigger Lever	**49**	Thumb-Piece
8	Barrel	**29**	Trigger Lever Pins	**50**	Thumb-Piece Screw
9	Stock Pin	**30**	Target Hammer	**51**	Hammer Block
10	Plate Screws	**31**	Standard Hammer	**52**	Hammer Block Pin
11	Locking Bolt	**32**	Hammer Nose	**53**	Cylinder Stop Pin
12	Locking Bolt Spring	**33**	Hammer Nose Rivet	**54**	Rebound Slide Pin
13	Locking Bolt Pin	**34**	Sear	**55**	Elevation Screw Pin
14	Yoke (Crane)	**35**	Sear Spring	**56**	Rear Sight Base
15	Extractor Spring	**36**	Bolt Spring	**57**	Rear Sight Windage Screw
16	Extractor Rod	**37**	Hand	**58**	Rear Sight Leaf
17	Extractor Collar	**38**	Cylinder Stop	**59**	Rear Sight Windage Spring
18	Center Pin	**39**	Cylinder Stop Spring	**60**	Rear Sight Elevation Screw
19	Center Pin Spring	**40**	Rebound Slide	**61**	Rear Sight Lock Screw
20	Cylinder with Extractor and Pins	**41**	Rebound Slide Spring	**62**	Grips
21	Firing Pin	**42**	Mainspring Rod	**63**	Grip Screw

Target Revolver

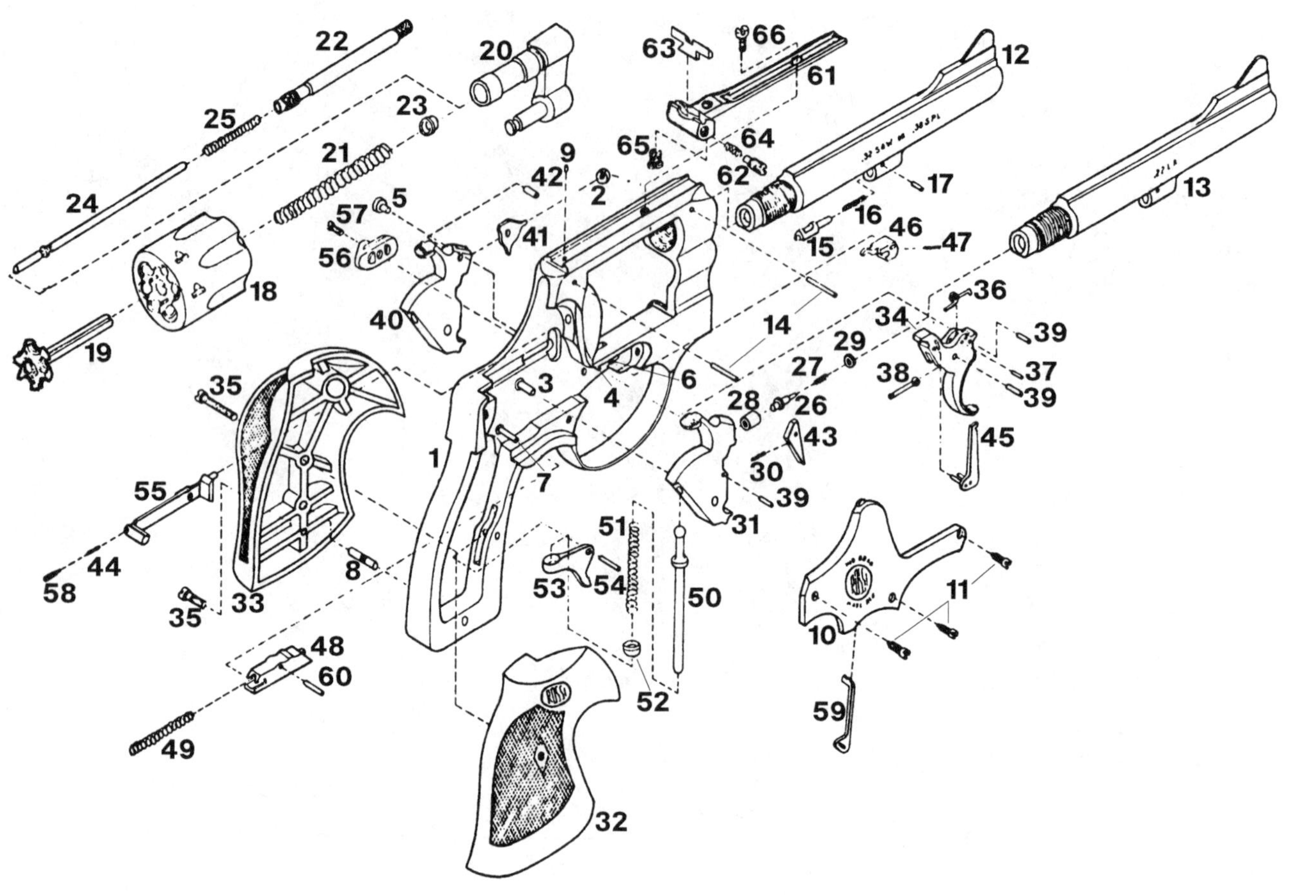

1	Frame with Bushing and Pins	23	Extractor Collar	45	Hand
2	Hammer Nose Bushing	24	Center Pin	46	Cylinder Stop
3	Hammer Pin	25	Center Pin Spring	47	Cylinder Stop Spring
4	Trigger Pin	26	Firing Pin	48	Rebound Slide
5	Frame Lug	27	Firing Pin Spring	49	Rebound Slide Spring
6	Cylinder Stop Pin	28	Firing Pin Bushing	50	Mainspring Rod
7	Rebound Slide Pin	29	Firing Pin Washer	51	Mainspring
8	Stock Pin	30	Sear Spring	52	Mainspring Swivel
9	Elevation Screw Pin	31	Target Hammer (Rimfire)	53	Mainspring Stop
10	Sideplate	32	Right Grip	54	Mainspring Stop Pin
11	Sideplate Screws	33	Left Grip	55	Bolt
12	Barrel 38	34	Trigger	56	Thumb-Piece
13	Barrel 22	35	Grip Screw	57	Thumb-Piece Screw
14	Barrel Pins	36	Hand Lever Spring	58	Bolt Plunger
15	Locking Bolt	37	Hand Lever Spring Pin	59	Hammer Block
16	Locking Bolt Spring	38	Trigger Lever	60	Hammer Block Pin
17	Locking Bolt Pin	39	Trigger Lever Pins	61	Rear Sight Base
18	Cylinder	40	Target Hammer (Centerfire)	62	Rear Sight Windage Screw
19	Extractor	41	Hammer Nose	63	Rear Sight Leaf
20	Yoke (Crane)	42	Hammer Nose Rivet	64	Rear Sight Spring
21	Extractor Spring	43	Sear	65	Rear Sight Elevation Screw
22	Extractor Rod	44	Bolt Plunger Spring	66	Rear Sight Lock Screw

44 Magnum Blackhawk Revolver

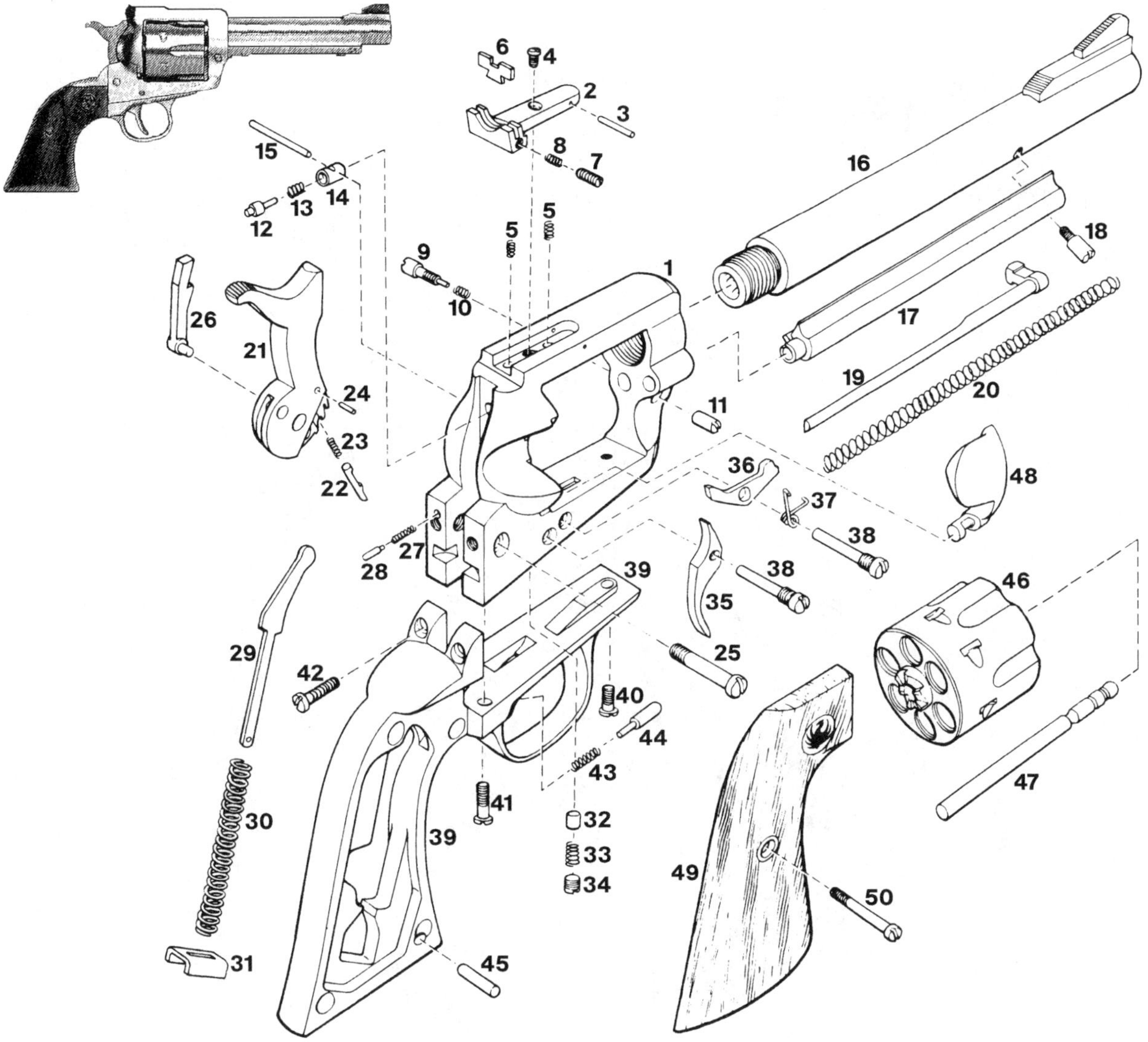

1	Cylinder Frame	18	Ejector Housing Screw	35	Trigger
2	Rear Sight	19	Ejector Rod Assembly	36	Cylinder Latch
3	Rear Sight Pivot Pin	20	Ejector Spring	37	Cylinder Latch Spring
4	Rear Sight Elevation Screw	21	Hammer	38	Trigger and Latch Pivot Screws
5	Rear Sight Elevation Springs	22	Hammer Plunger	39	Grip Frame
6	Rear Sight Leaf	23	Hammer Plunger Spring	40	Front Grip Frame Screw
7	Rear Sight Leaf Screw	24	Hammer Plunger Retaining Pin	41	Lower Grip Frame Screws
8	Rear Sight Leaf Spring	25	Hammer Pivot Screw	42	Rear Grip Frame Screws
9	Base Pin Latch	26	Pawl	43	Trigger Spring
10	Base Pin Latch Spring	27	Pawl Spring	44	Trigger Spring Plunger
11	Base Pin Latch Nut	28	Pawl Spring Plunger	45	Grip Pin
12	Firing Pin	29	Hammer Strut	46	Cylinder
13	Firing Pin Spring	30	Mainspring	47	Base Pin
14	Recoil Plate	31	Mainspring Seat	48	Gate
15	Recoil Plate Retaining Pin	32	Gate Detent Plunger	49	Grip Panels
16	Barrel	33	Gate Detent Plunger Spring	50	Grip Screw
17	Ejector Housing	34	Gate Detent Plunger Screw		

357 Maximum Blackhawk

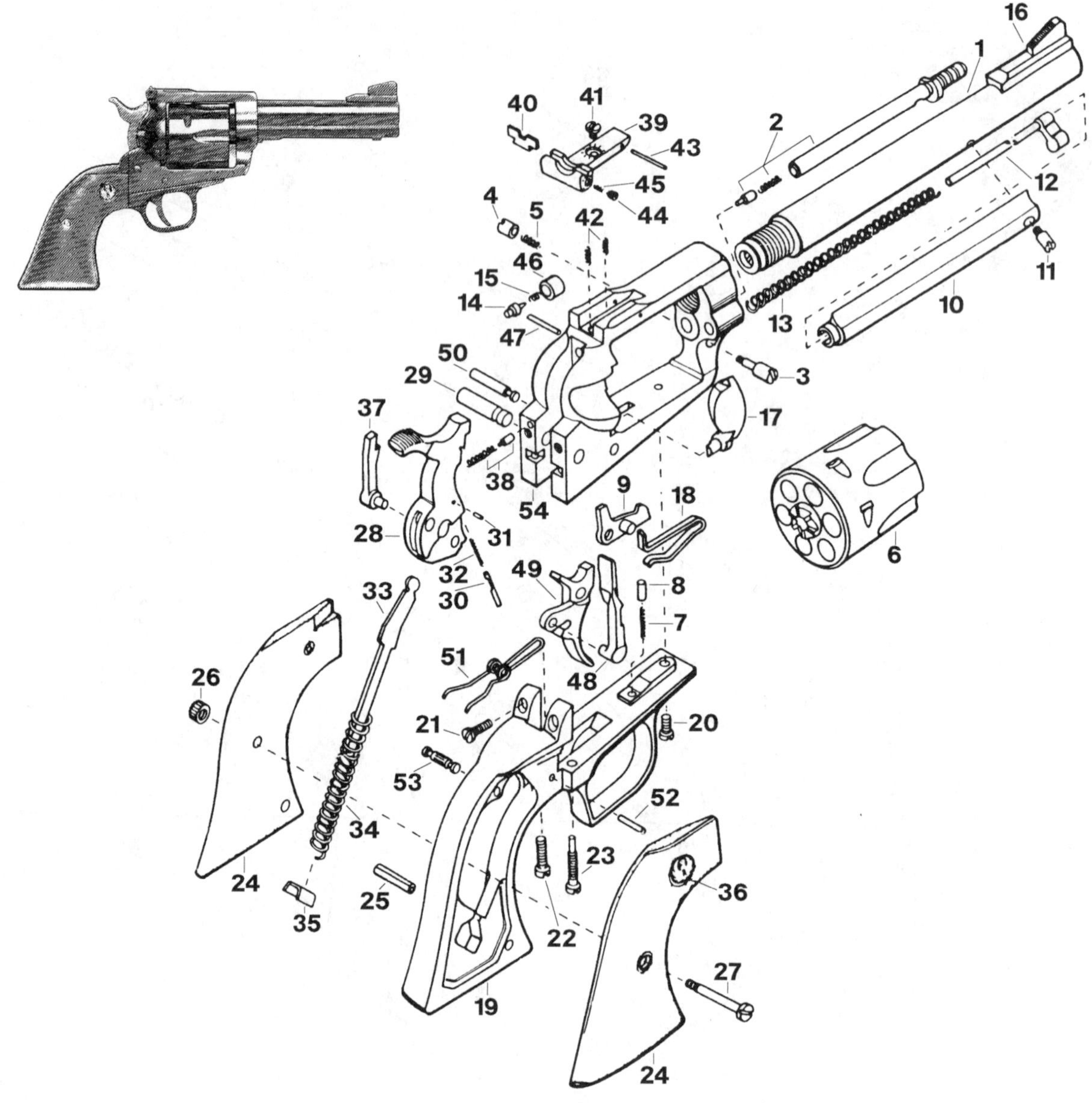

1	Barrel	**20**	Grip Frame Screw, Front	**39**	Rear Sight Assembly
2	Base Pin Assembly	**21**	Grip Frame Screw, Top	**40**	Rear Sight Blade
3	Base Pin Latch	**22**	Grip Frame Screw, Bottom	**41**	Rear Sight Elevation Screw
4	Base Pin Latch Nut	**23**	Grip Frame Screw and Pivot Lock	**42**	Rear Sight Elevation Springs
5	Base Pin Latch Spring	**24**	Grip Panels, Complete	**43**	Rear Sight Pivot Pin
6	Cylinder	**25**	Grip Panel Dowel	**44**	Rear Sight Windage Adjusting Screw
7	Cylinder Latch Spring	**26**	Grip Panel Ferrule, Left	**45**	Rear Sight Windage Spring
8	Cylinder Latch Spring Plunger	**27**	Grip Panel Screw	**46**	Recoil Plate
9	Cylinder Latch	**28**	Hammer Assembly	**47**	Recoil Plate Cross Pin
10	Ejector Housing	**29**	Hammer Pivot	**48**	Transfer Bar
11	Ejector Housing Screw	**30**	Hammer Plunger	**49**	Trigger
12	Ejector Rod	**31**	Hammer Plunger Pin	**50**	Trigger Pivot
13	Ejector Rod Spring	**32**	Hammer Plunger Spring	**51**	Trigger Spring
14	Firing Pin	**33**	Hammer Strut	**52**	Trigger Spring Pin
15	Firing Pin Rebound Spring	**34**	Mainspring	**53**	Trigger Spring Retaining Pin
16	Front Sight	**35**	Mainspring Seat	**54**	Frame
17	Gate	**36**	Medallion	**Parts Not Shown**	
18	Gate Detent Spring	**37**	Pawl		Grip Panel Ferrule, Right
19	Grip Frame	**38**	Pawl Spring and Plunger		Rear Sight Detent Ball

Bearcat 22 Revolver

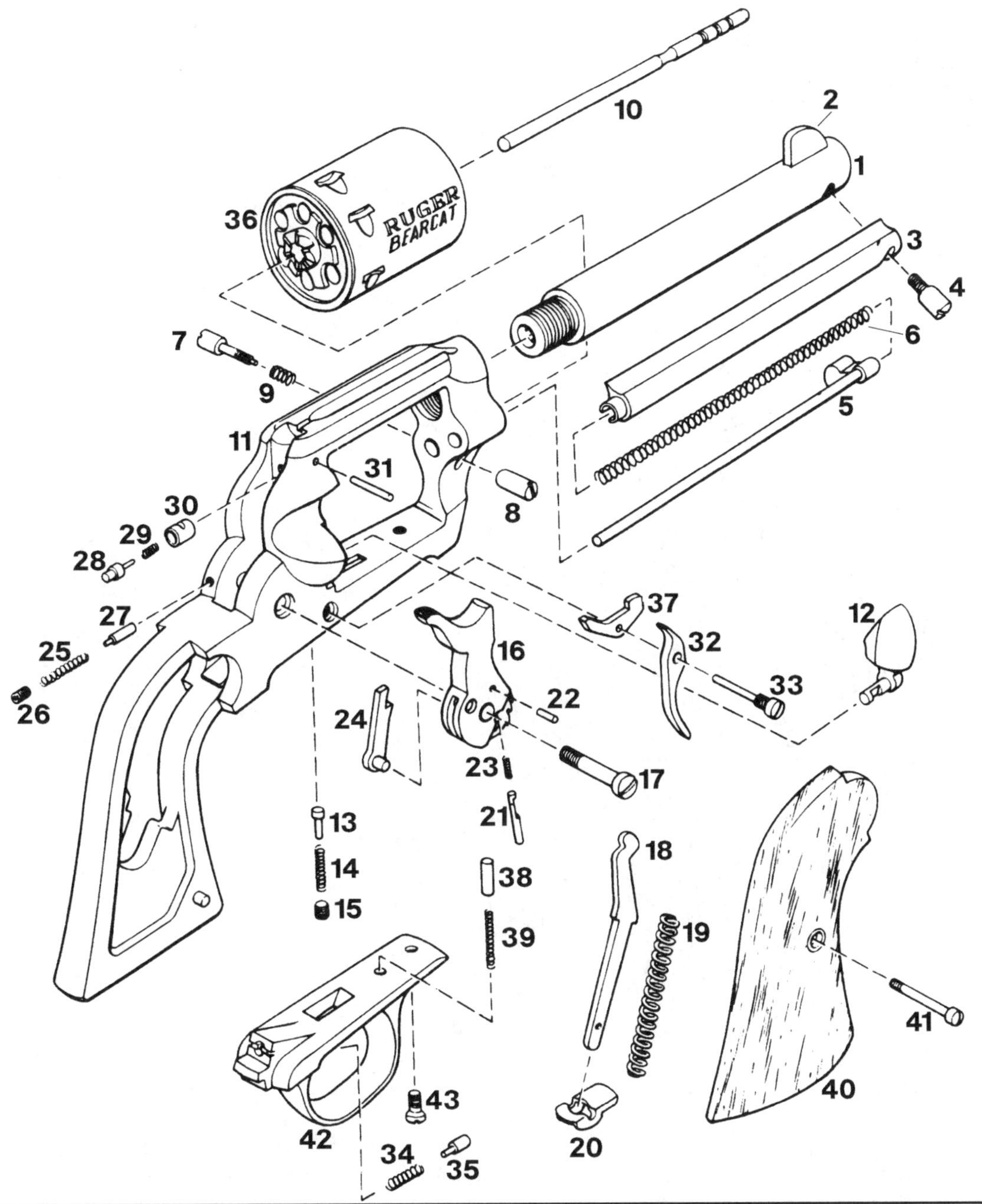

1	Barrel	16	Hammer	31	Recoil Plate Cross Pin
2	Front Sight	17	Hammer Pivot	32	Trigger
3	Ejector Housing	18	Hammer Strut	33	Trigger Pivot
4	Ejector Housing Screw	19	Hammer Spring	34	Trigger Spring
5	Ejector Rod Assembly	20	Hammer Spring Seat	35	Trigger Spring Plunger
6	Ejector Spring	21	Hammer Plunger	36	Cylinder
7	Base Pin Latch Body	22	Hammer Plunger Pin	37	Cylinder Latch
8	Base Pin Latch Nut	23	Hammer Plunger Spring	38	Cylinder Latch Plunger
9	Base Pin Latch Spring	24	Pawl	39	Cylinder Latch Spring
10	Base Pin	25	Pawl Spring	40	Grip Panel
11	Frame	26	Pawl Screw	41	Grip Panel Screw
12	Gate Assembly	27	Pawl Spring Plunger	42	Trigger Guard
13	Gate Detent Plunger	28	Firing Pin	43	Trigger Guard Screw
14	Gate Detent Spring	29	Firing Pin Rebound Spring		
15	Gate Retaining Screw	30	Recoil Plate		

Bisley Revolver

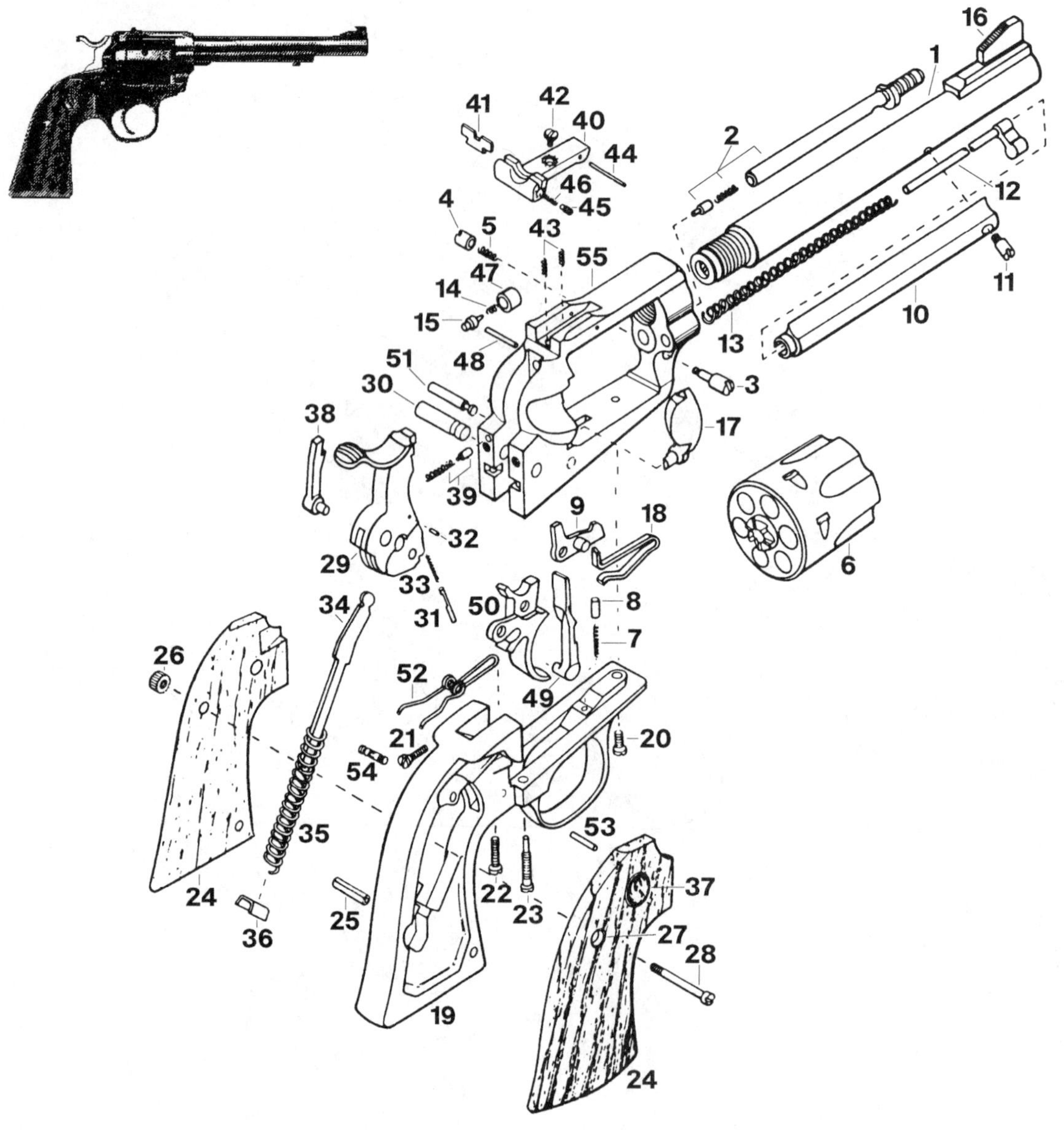

1	Barrel	**20**	Grip Frame Screw, Front	**39**	Pawl Spring and Plunger
2	Base Pin Assembly	**21**	Grip Frame Screw, Back	**40**	Rear Sight Assembly, Complete
3	Base Pin Latch	**22**	Grip Frame Screw, Bottom	**41**	Rear Sight Blade
4	Base Pin Latch Nut	**23**	Grip Frame Screw and Pivot Lock	**42**	Rear Sight Elevation Screw
5	Base Pin Latch Spring	**24**	Grip Panels	**43**	Rear Sight Elevation Springs
6	Cylinder	**25**	Grip Panel Dowel	**44**	Rear Sight Pivot Pin
7	Cylinder Latch Spring	**26**	Grip Panel Ferrule, Left	**45**	Rear Sight Windage Adjusting Screw
8	Cylinder Latch Spring Plunger	**27**	Grip Panel Ferrule, Right	**46**	Rear Sight Windage Spring
9	Cylinder Latch	**28**	Grip Panel Screw	**47**	Recoil Plate
10	Ejector Housing	**29**	Hammer Assembly	**48**	Recoil Plate Cross Pin
11	Ejector Housing Screw	**30**	Hammer Pivot	**49**	Transfer Bar
12	Ejector Rod Assembly	**31**	Hammer Plunger	**50**	Trigger
13	Ejector Rod Spring	**32**	Hammer Plunger Pin	**51**	Trigger Pivot
14	Firing Pin Rebound Spring	**33**	Hammer Plunger Spring	**52**	Trigger Spring
15	Firing Pin	**34**	Hammer Strut	**53**	Trigger Spring Pin
16	Front Sight	**35**	Mainspring	**54**	Trigger Spring Retaining Pin
17	Gate	**36**	Mainspring Seat	**55**	Frame
18	Gate Detent Spring	**37**	Medallion	**Parts Not Shown**	
19	Grip Frame	**38**	Pawl		Rear Sight Detent Ball

Bisley Rimfire Revolver

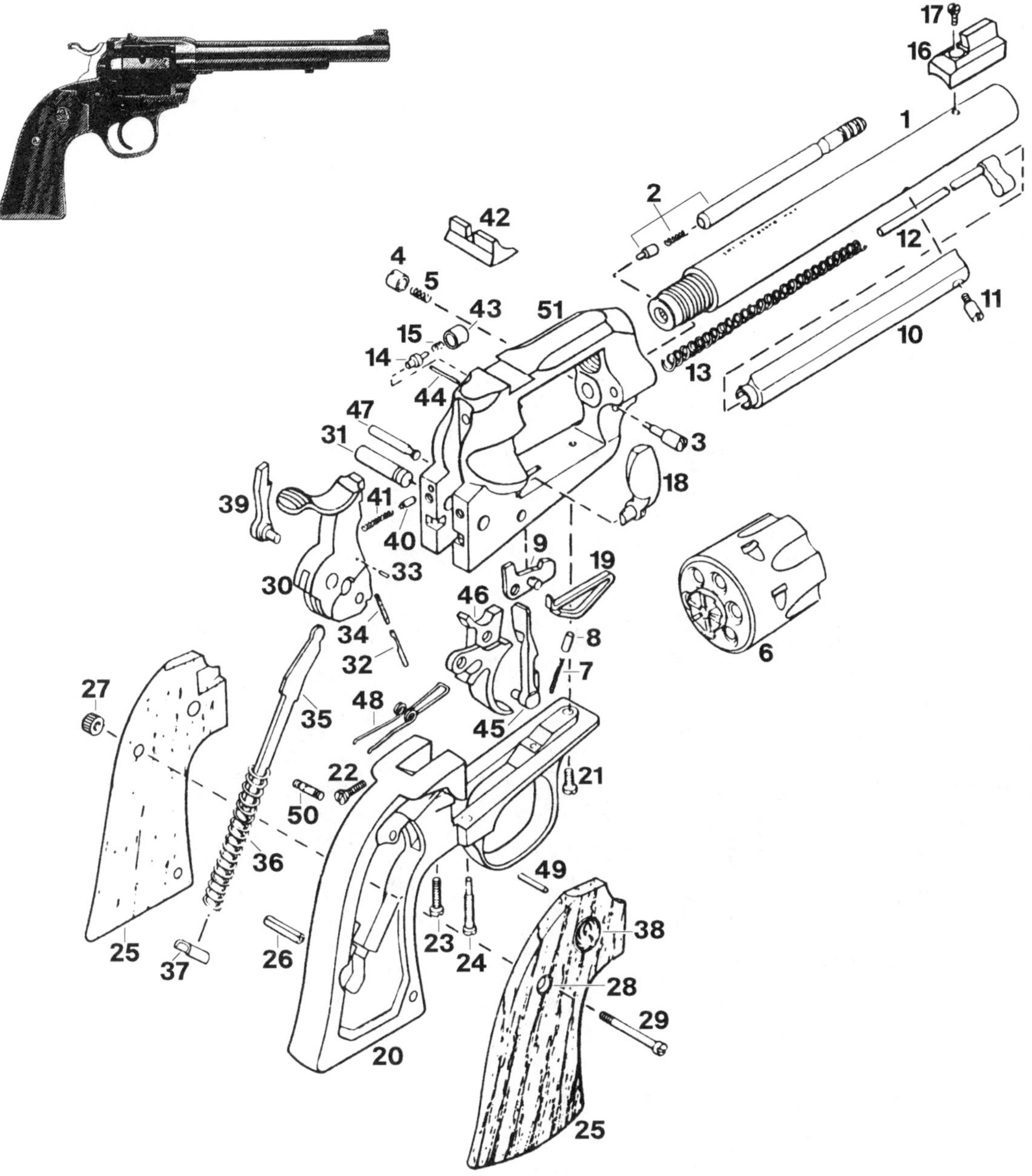

1	Barrel	18	Gate	35	Hammer Strut
2	Base Pin Assembly	19	Gate Detent Spring	36	Mainspring
3	Base Pin Latch	20	Grip Frame	37	Mainspring Seat
4	Base Pin Latch Nut	21	Grip Frame Screw, Front	38	Medallion
5	Base Pin Latch Spring	22	Grip Frame Screw, Back	39	Pawl
6	Cylinder	23	Grip Frame Screw, Bottom	40	Pawl Plunger
7	Cylinder Latch Spring	24	Grip Frame Screw and Pivot Lock	41	Pawl Plunger Spring
8	Cylinder Latch Spring Plunger	25	Grip Panels, Complete	42	Rear Sight
9	Cylinder Latch	26	Grip Panel Dowel	43	Recoil Plate
10	Ejector Housing	27	Grip Panel Ferrule, Left	44	Recoil Plate Cross Pin
11	Ejector Housing Screw	28	Grip Panel Ferrule, Right	45	Transfer Bar
12	Ejector Rod Assembly	29	Grip Panel Screw	46	Trigger
13	Ejector Rod Spring	30	Hammer Assembly	47	Trigger Pivot
14	Firing Pin	31	Hammer Pivot	48	Trigger Spring
15	Firing Pin Rebound Spring	32	Hammer Plunger	49	Trigger Spring Pin
16	Front Sight	33	Hammer Plunger Pin	50	Trigger Spring Retaining Pin
17	Front Sight Screw	34	Hammer Plunger Spring	51	Frame

Blackhawk and Super Blackhawk Revolver

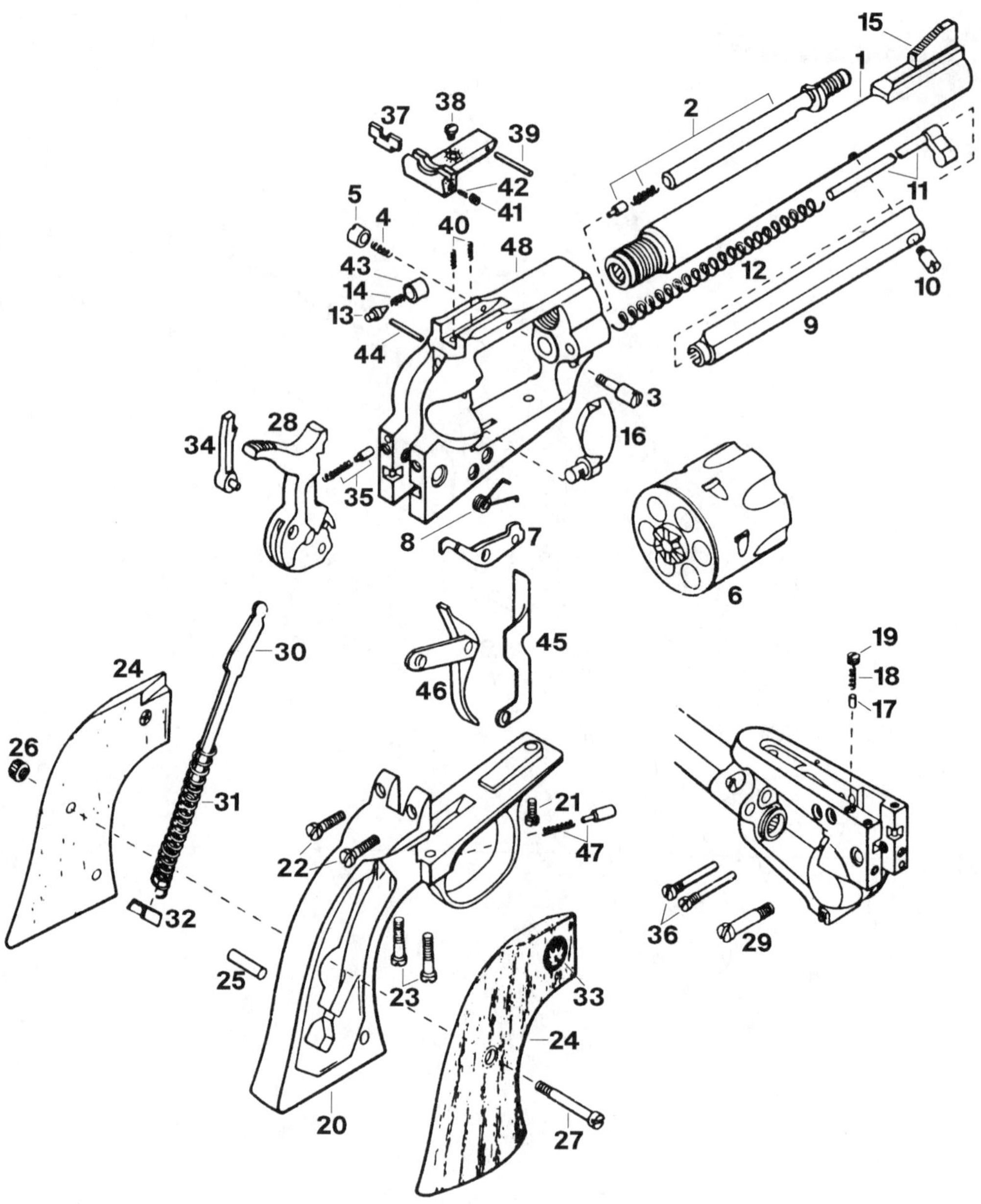

1	Barrel	**18**	Gate Detent Spring	**35**	Pawl Spring and Plunger
2	Base Pin Assembly	**19**	Gate Spring Screw	**36**	Pivot Screws
3	Base Pin Latch	**20**	Grip Frame	**37**	Rear Sight Blade
4	Base Pin Latch Spring	**21**	Grip Frame Screw, Front	**38**	Rear Sight Elevation Screw
5	Base Pin Nut	**22**	Grip Frame Screws, Back	**39**	Rear Sight Pivot Pin
6	Cylinder	**23**	Grip Frame Screws, Bottom	**40**	Rear Sight Springs
7	Cylinder Latch	**24**	Grip Panels	**41**	Rear Sight Windage Adjusting<R>Screw
8	Cylinder Latch Spring	**25**	Grip Panel Dowel	**42**	Rear Sight Windage Spring
9	Ejector Housing	**26**	Grip Panel Ferrule, Left	**43**	Recoil Plate
10	Ejector Housing Screw	**27**	Grip Panel Screw	**44**	Recoil Plate Cross Pin
11	Ejector Rod Assembly	**28**	Hammer	**45**	Transfer Bar
12	Ejector Spring	**29**	Hammer Pivot	**46**	Trigger
13	Firing Pin	**30**	Hammer Strut	**47**	Trigger Spring and Plunger
14	Firing Pin Rebound Spring	**31**	Mainspring	**48**	Frame
15	Front Sight	**32**	Mainspring Seat	**Parts Not Shown**	
16	Gate Assembly	**33**	Medallion		Grip Panel Ferrule, Right
17	Gate Detent Plunger	**34**	Pawl		

GP-100 Revolver

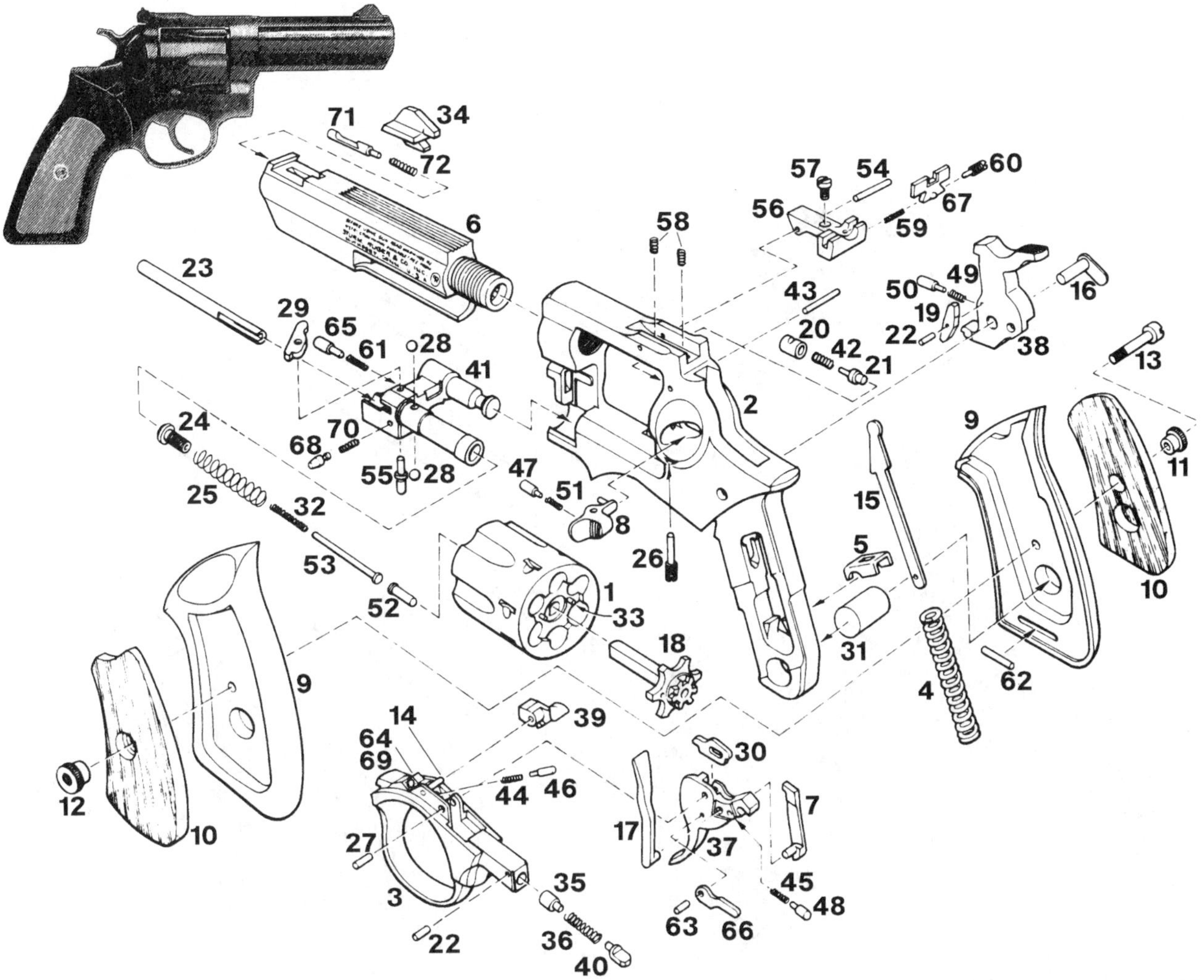

1	Cylinder
2	Frame
3	Trigger Guard
4	Mainspring
5	Mainspring Seat
6	Barrel
7	Pawl
8	Crane Latch
9	Grip Panels
10	Panel Inserts
11	Grip Ferrule, Right
12	Grip Ferrule, Left
13	Grip Panel Screw
14	Cylinder Latch Pivot
15	Hammer Strut
16	Hammer Pivot Assembly
17	Transfer Bar
18	Ejector
19	Hammer Dog
20	Recoil Plate
21	Firing Pin
22	Hammer Dog Pivot Pin and Trigger Guard Latch Pin
23	Ejector Rod
24	Ejector Retainer
25	Ejector Spring
26	Crane Latch Pivot
27	Trigger Pivot Pin
28	Cylinder Retaining Balls
29	Front Latch
30	Trigger Plunger
31	Grip Panel Locator
32	Center Pin Spring
33	Ejector Alignment Pins
34	Front Sight
35	Trigger Link Plunger
36	Trigger Guard Latch Spring
37	Trigger
38	Hammer
39	Cylinder Latch
40	Trigger Guard Latch
41	Crane and Crane Pivot Assembly
42	Firing Pin Rebound Spring
43	Recoil Plate Cross Pin
44	Cylinder Latch Spring
45	Pawl Plunger Spring
46	Cylinder Latch Plunger
47	Crane Latch Spring Plunger
48	Pawl Plunger
49	Hammer Dog Spring
50	Hammer Dog Spring Plunger
51	Crane Latch Spring
52	Center Pin Lock
53	Center Pin Rod
54	Rear Sight Cross Pin
55	Front Latch Pivot Pin
56	Rear Sight Base
57	Rear Sight Elevation Screw
58	Rear Sight Elevation Springs
59	Rear Sight Windage Spring
60	Rear Sight Windage Adjustment Screw
61	Front Latch Spring
62	Disassembly Pin
63	Trigger Link Pin
64	Crane Pivot Lock Plunger
65	Front Latch Spring Plunger
66	Trigger Link
67	Rear Sight Blade
68	Front Latch Pivot Lock
69	Crane Pivot Lock Spring
70	Front Latch Pivot Lock Spring
71	Front Sight Plunger
72	Front Sight Plunger Spring

Hawkeye

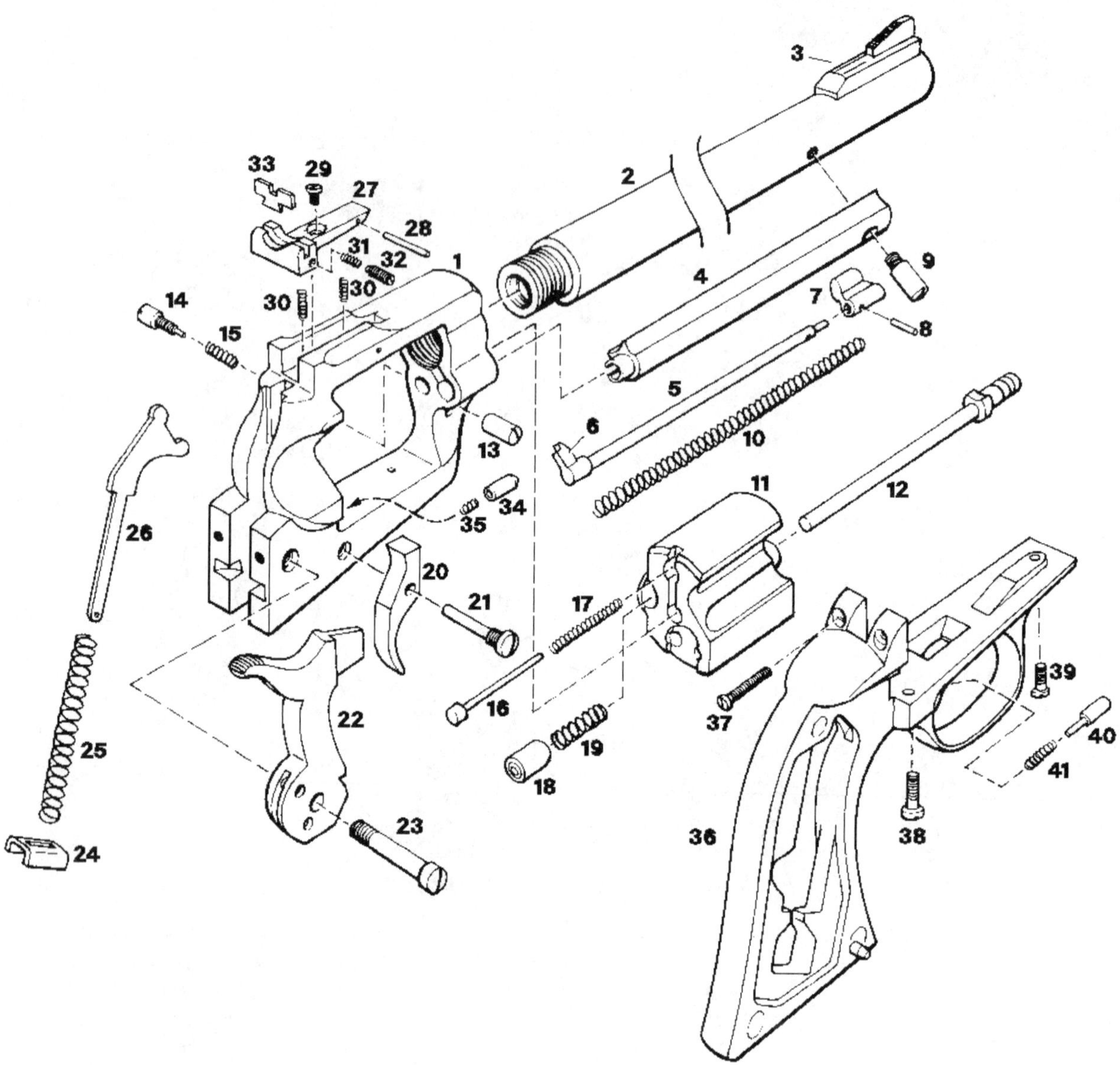

1	Frame	**15**	Base Pin Latch Spring	**29**	Elevating Screw
2	Barrel	**16**	Firing Pin	**30**	Elevating Springs
3	Front Sight	**17**	Firing Pin Spring	**31**	Windage Spring
4	Ejector Housing	**18**	Breechblock Lock Plunger	**32**	Windage Screw
5	Ejector Rod	**19**	Lock Plunger Spring	**33**	Rear Sight Leaf
6	Ejector	**20**	Trigger	**34**	Detent Plunger
7	Ejector Thumb-Piece	**21**	Trigger Screw	**35**	Detent Plunger Spring
8	Ejector Thumb-Piece Pin	**22**	Hammer	**36**	Grip Frame
9	Ejector Housing Screw	**23**	Hammer Screw	**37**	Rear Grip Frame Screws
10	Ejector Spring	**24**	Mainspring Seat	**38**	Lower Grip Frame Screws
11	Breechblock	**25**	Mainspring	**39**	Front Grip Frame Screw
12	Base Pin	**26**	Hammer Strut	**40**	Trigger Spring Plunger
13	Base Pin Latch Nut	**27**	Rear Sight Assembly	**41**	Trigger Spring
14	Base Pin Latch	**28**	Rear Sight Pivot Pin		

Mark II Standard and Target Auto

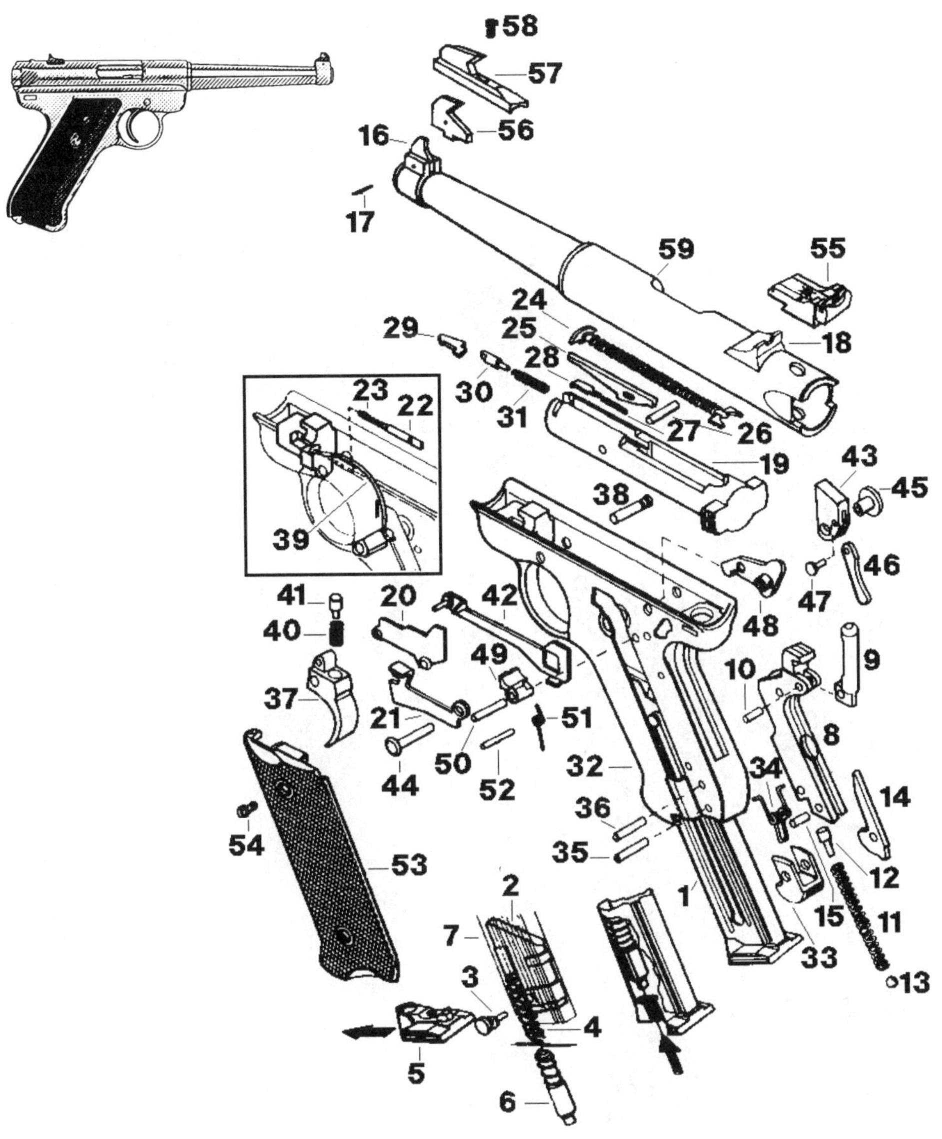

1	Magazine, Complete	**21**	Bolt Stop Thumb-Piece	**42**	Disconnector
2	Magazine Follower	**22**	Bolt Stop Plunger	**43**	Hammer
3	Magazine Follower Button	**23**	Bolt Stop Plunger Spring	**44**	Hammer Pivot
4	Magazine Spring	**24**	Recoil Spring Assembly	**45**	Hammer Bushing
5	Magazine Block (Bottom)	**25**	Firing Pin	**46**	Hammer Strut
6	Magazine Block Retaining Plunger	**26**	Firing Pin Stop	**47**	Hammer Strut Pin
		27	Rebound Spring	**48**	Safety
7	Magazine Body	**28**	Rebound Spring Support	**49**	Sear
8	Mainspring Housing	**29**	Extractor	**50**	Sear Pivot
9	Bolt Stop Pin	**30**	Extractor Plunger	**51**	Sear Spring
10	Bolt Stop Pivot Pin	**31**	Extractor Spring	**52**	Sear Spring Stop Pin
11	Mainspring	**32**	Grip Frame with Trigger Guard	**53**	Grip Panels
12	Mainspring Plunger	**33**	Magazine Latch	**54**	Grip Panel Screws
13	Detent Ball	**34**	Magazine Latch Spring	**55**	Adjustable Rear Sight, Target
14	Housing Latch	**35**	Magazine Latch Pin	**56**	Front Sight Blade, Target
15	Housing Latch Pivot	**36**	Magazine Latch Stop Pin	**57**	Ramp Front Sight, Target
16	Front Sight Blade	**37**	Trigger	**58**	Ramp Front Sight Screw, Target
17	Front Sight Pin	**38**	Trigger Pivot	**59**	Barrel
18	Rear Sight (Standard Model)	**39**	Trigger Pivot Retainer	**Parts Not Shown**	
19	Bolt	**40**	Trigger Spring		Medallion
20	Bolt Stop Assembly	**41**	Trigger Spring Plunger		Trigger with Overstop Travel

New Model Bisley Revolver

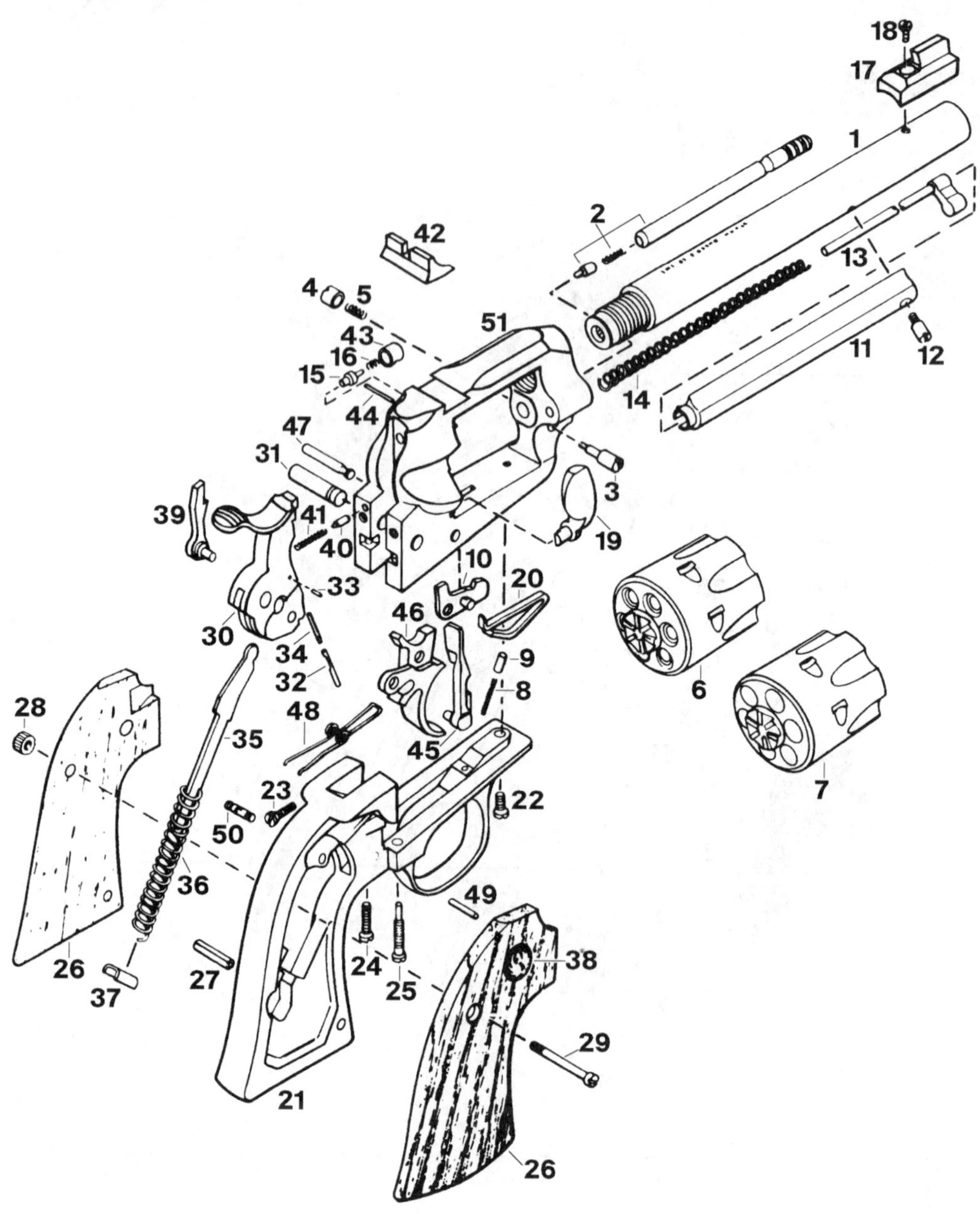

1	Barrel	18	Front Sight Screw	35	Hammer Strut
2	Base Pin Assembly	19	Gate	36	Mainspring
3	Base Pin Latch	20	Gate Detent Spring	37	Mainspring Seat
4	Base Pin Latch Nut	21	Grip Frame	38	Medallion
5	Base Pin Latch Spring	22	Grip Frame Screw, Front	39	Pawl
6	Cylinder (22 L.R.)	23	Grip Frame Screw, Back	40	Pawl Plunger
7	Cylinder (32 H&R Mag.)	24	Grip Frame Screw, Bottom	41	Pawl Plunger Spring
8	Cylinder Latch Spring	25	Grip Frame Screw and Pivot Lock	42	Rear Sight
9	Cylinder Latch Spring Plunger	26	Grip Panels, Complete	43	Recoil Plate
10	Cylinder Latch	27	Grip Panel Dowel	44	Recoil Plate Cross Pin
11	Ejector Housing	28	Grip Panel Ferrule, Left	45	Transfer Bar
12	Ejector Housing Screw	29	Grip Panel Screw	46	Trigger
13	Ejector Rod Assembly	30	Hammer Assembly	47	Trigger Pivot
14	Ejector Rod Spring	31	Hammer Pivot	48	Trigger Spring
15	Firing Pin	32	Hammer Plunger	49	Trigger Spring Pin
16	Firing Pin Rebound Spring	33	Hammer Plunger Pin	50	Trigger Spring Retaining Pin
17	Front Sight Ramp	34	Hammer Plunger Spring	51	Frame

New Model Blackhawk Revolver

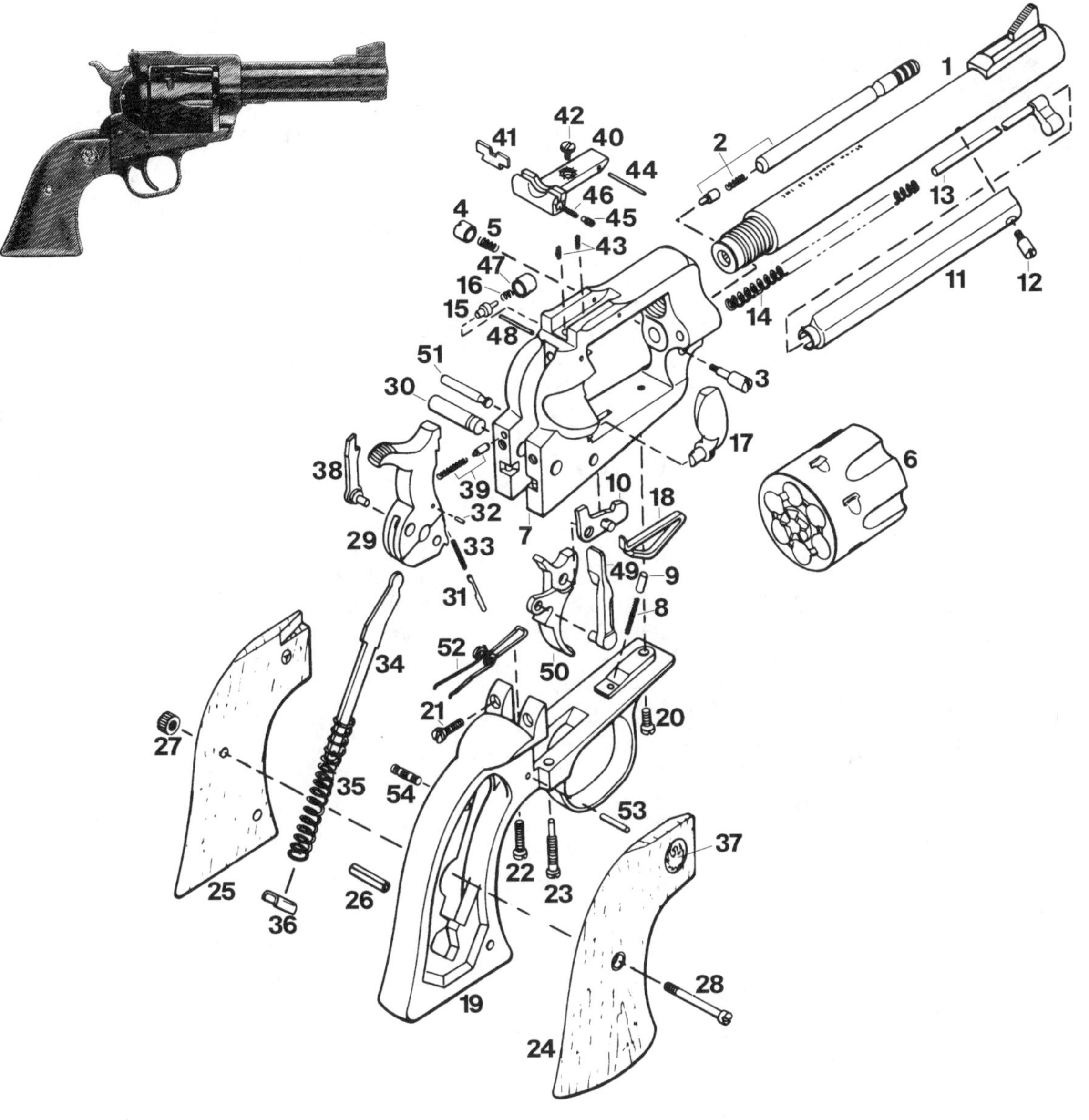

1	Barrel	**20**	Grip Frame Screw, Front	**39**	Pawl Spring and Plunger
2	Base Pin Assembly	**21**	Grip Frame Screw, Back	**40**	Rear Sight Assembly, Complete
3	Base Pin Latch	**22**	Grip Frame Screw, Bottom	**41**	Rear Sight Blade
4	Base Pin Latch Nut	**23**	Grip Frame Screw and Pivot Lock	**42**	Rear Sight Elevation Screw
5	Base Pin Latch Spring	**24**	Grip Panel, Right	**43**	Rear Sight Elevation Springs
6	Cylinder	**25**	Grip Panel, Left	**44**	Rear Sight Pivot Pin
7	Cylinder Frame	**26**	Grip Panel Dowel	**45**	Rear Sight Windage Adjustment Screw
8	Cylinder Latch Spring	**27**	Grip Panel Ferrule, Left	**46**	Rear Sight Windage Spring
9	Cylinder Latch Spring Plunger	**28**	Grip Panel Screw	**47**	Recoil Plate
10	Cylinder Latch	**29**	Hammer Assembly	**48**	Recoil Plate Cross Pin
11	Ejector Housing	**30**	Hammer Pivot	**49**	Transfer Bar
12	Ejector Housing Screw	**31**	Hammer Plunger	**50**	Trigger
13	Ejector Rod Assembly	**32**	Hammer Plunger Pin	**51**	Trigger Pivot
14	Ejector Rod Spring	**33**	Hammer Plunger Spring	**52**	Trigger Spring
15	Firing Pin	**34**	Hammer Strut	**53**	Trigger Spring Pin
16	Firing Pin Rebound Spring	**35**	Mainspring	**54**	Trigger Spring Retaining Pin
17	Gate	**36**	Mainspring Seat	**Parts Not Shown**	
18	Gate Detent Spring and Retainer	**37**	Medallion		Grip Panel Ferrule, Right
19	Grip Frame	**38**	Pawl		

New Model Single-Six SA Revolver

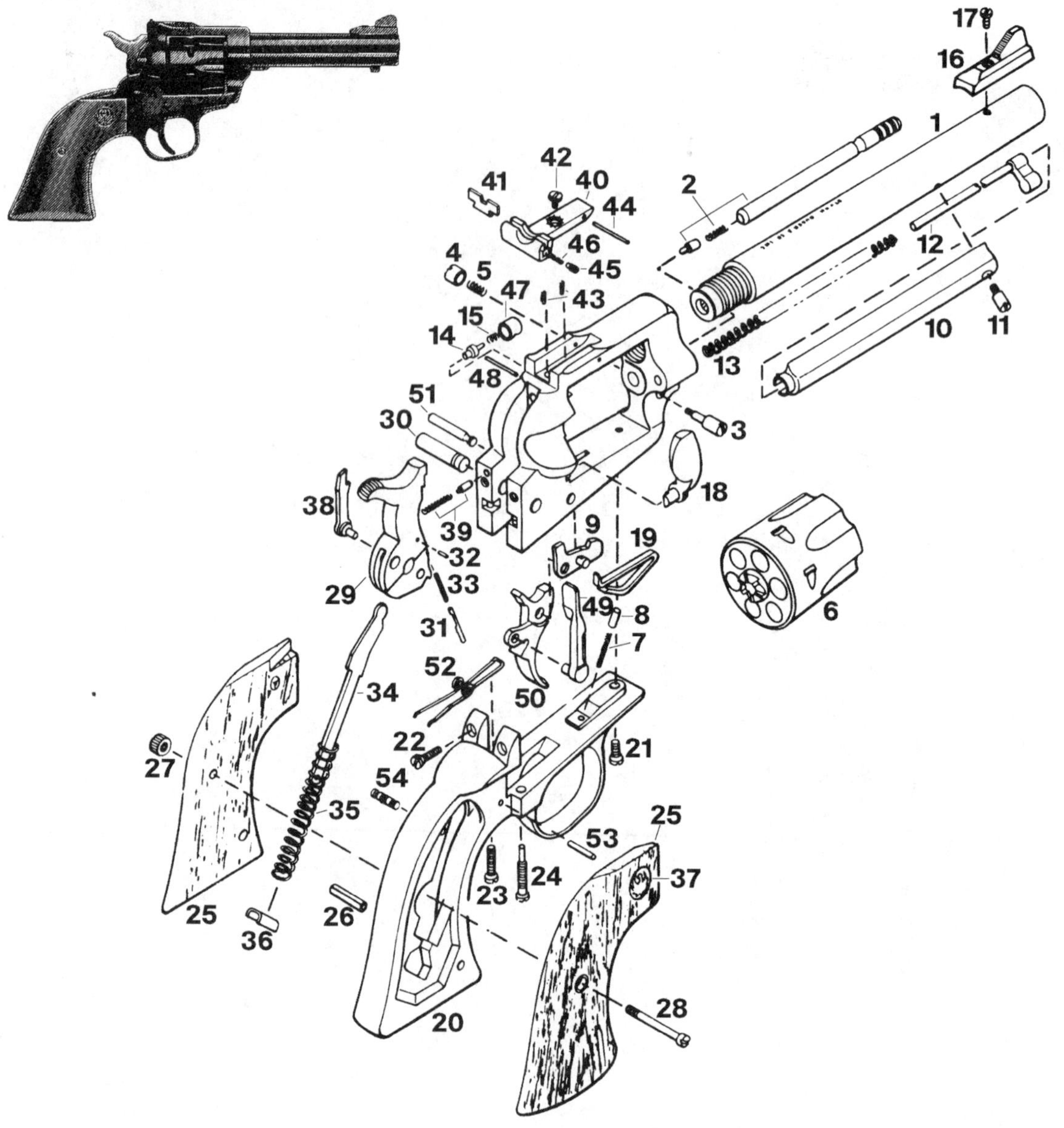

1	Barrel	20	Grip Frame	39	Pawl Spring and Plunger
2	Base Pin Assembly	21	Grip Frame Screw, Front	40	Rear Sight Assembly, Complete
3	Base Pin Latch	22	Grip Frame Screw, Back	41	Rear Sight Blade
4	Base Pin Latch Nut	23	Grip Frame Screw, Bottom	42	Rear Sight Elevation Screw
5	Base Pin Latch Spring	24	Grip Frame Screw and Pivot Lock	43	Rear Sight Elevation Springs
6	Cylinder	25	Grip Panels, Complete	44	Rear Sight Pivot Pin
7	Cylinder Latch Spring	26	Grip Panel Dowel	45	Rear Sight Windage Adjusting Screw
8	Cylinder Latch Spring Plunger	27	Grip Panel Ferrule, Left	46	Rear Sight Windage Spring
9	Cylinder Latch	28	Grip Panel Screw	47	Recoil Plate
10	Ejector Housing	29	Hammer Assembly	48	Recoil Plate Cross Pin
11	Ejector Housing Screw	30	Hammer Pivot	49	Transfer Bar
12	Ejector Rod Assembly	31	Hammer Plunger	50	Trigger
13	Ejector Rod Spring	32	Hammer Plunger Pin	51	Trigger Pivot
14	Firing Pin	33	Hammer Plunger Spring	52	Trigger Spring
15	Firing Pin Rebound Spring	34	Hammer Strut	53	Trigger Spring Pin
16	Front Sight	35	Mainspring	54	Trigger Spring Retaining Pin
17	Front Sight Screw	36	Mainspring Seat	**Parts Not Shown**	
18	Gate	37	Medallion		Grip Panel Ferrule, Right
19	Gate Detent Spring	38	Pawl		

New Model Super Blackhawk Hunter Model Revolver

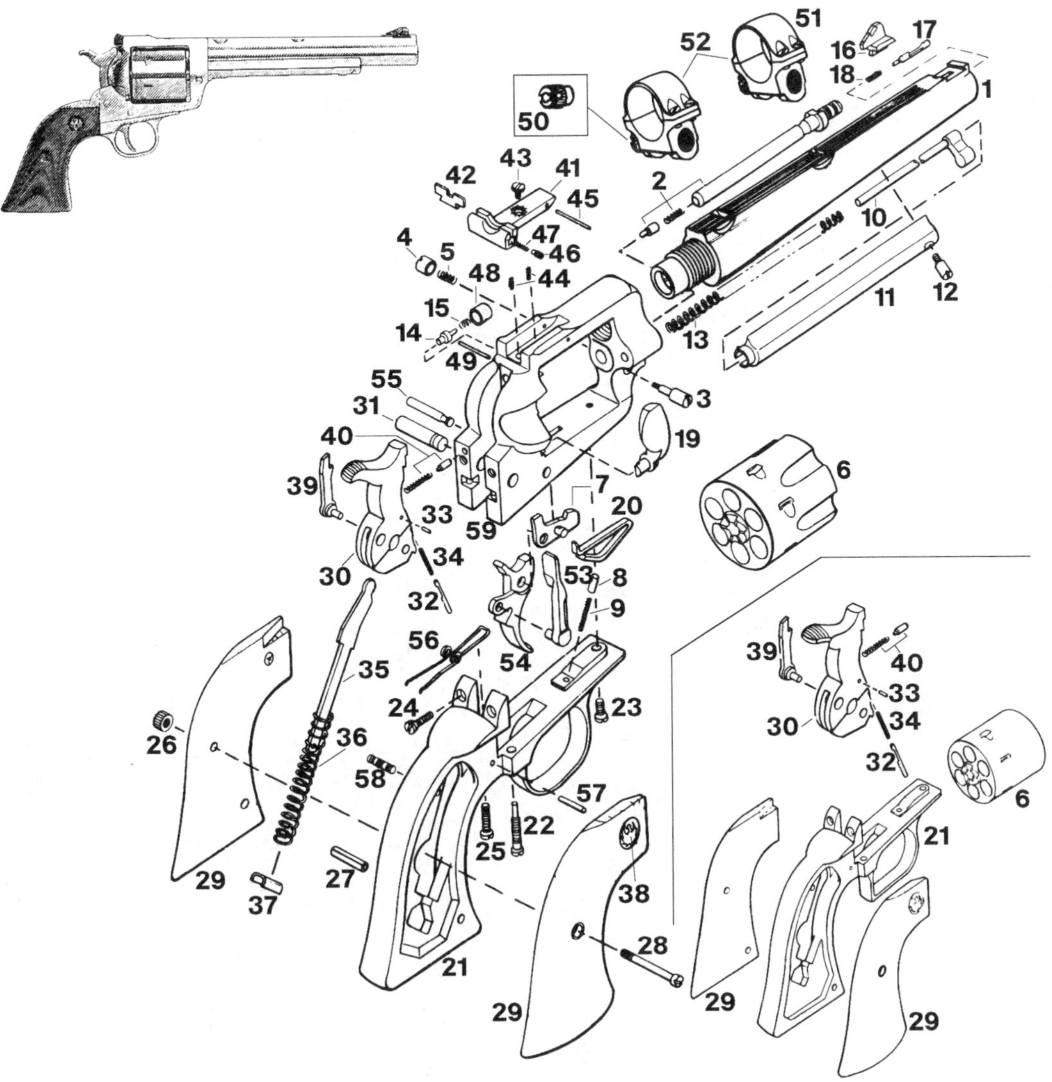

1	Barrel
2	Base Pin Assembly
3	Base Pin Latch
4	Base Pin Latch Nut
5	Base Pin Latch Spring
6	Cylinder
7	Cylinder Latch
8	Cylinder Latch Plunger
9	Cylinder Latch Spring
10	Ejector Rod Assembly
11	Ejector Housing
12	Ejector Housing Screw
13	Ejector Rod Spring
14	Firing Pin
15	Firing Pin Rebound Spring
16	Front Sight
17	Front Sight Plunger
18	Front Sight Spring
19	Gate
20	Gate Detent Spring
21	Grip Frame
22	Grip Frame Screw and Pivot Lock
23	Grip Frame Screw, Front
24	Grip Frame Screw, Back
25	Grip Frame Screw, Bottom
26	Grip Panel Ferrule, Left
27	Grip Panel Locating Pin
28	Grip Panel Screw
29	Grip Panels
30	Hammer Assembly
31	Hammer Pivot
32	Hammer Plunger
33	Hammer Plunger Cross Pin
34	Hammer Plunger Spring
35	Hammer Strut
36	Mainspring
37	Mainspring Seat
38	Medallion
39	Pawl
40	Pawl Spring and Plunger
41	Rear Sight
42	Rear Sight Blade
43	Rear Sight Elevation Screw
44	Rear Sight Elevation Springs
45	Rear Sight Pivot Pin
46	Rear Sight Windage Adjustment Screw
47	Rear Sight Windage Spring
48	Recoil Plate
49	Recoil Plate Cross Pin
50	Scope Base Nut
51	Scope Ring Screw
52	Scope Rings
53	Transfer Bar
54	Trigger
55	Trigger Pivot
56	Trigger Spring
57	Trigger Spring Pin
58	Trigger Spring Retaining Pin
59	Frame

Parts Not Shown

- Cylinder Latch Stud
- Grip Panel Ferrule, Right
- Rear Sight Detent Ball
- Scope Base Clamp

Old Army Blackpowder Revolver

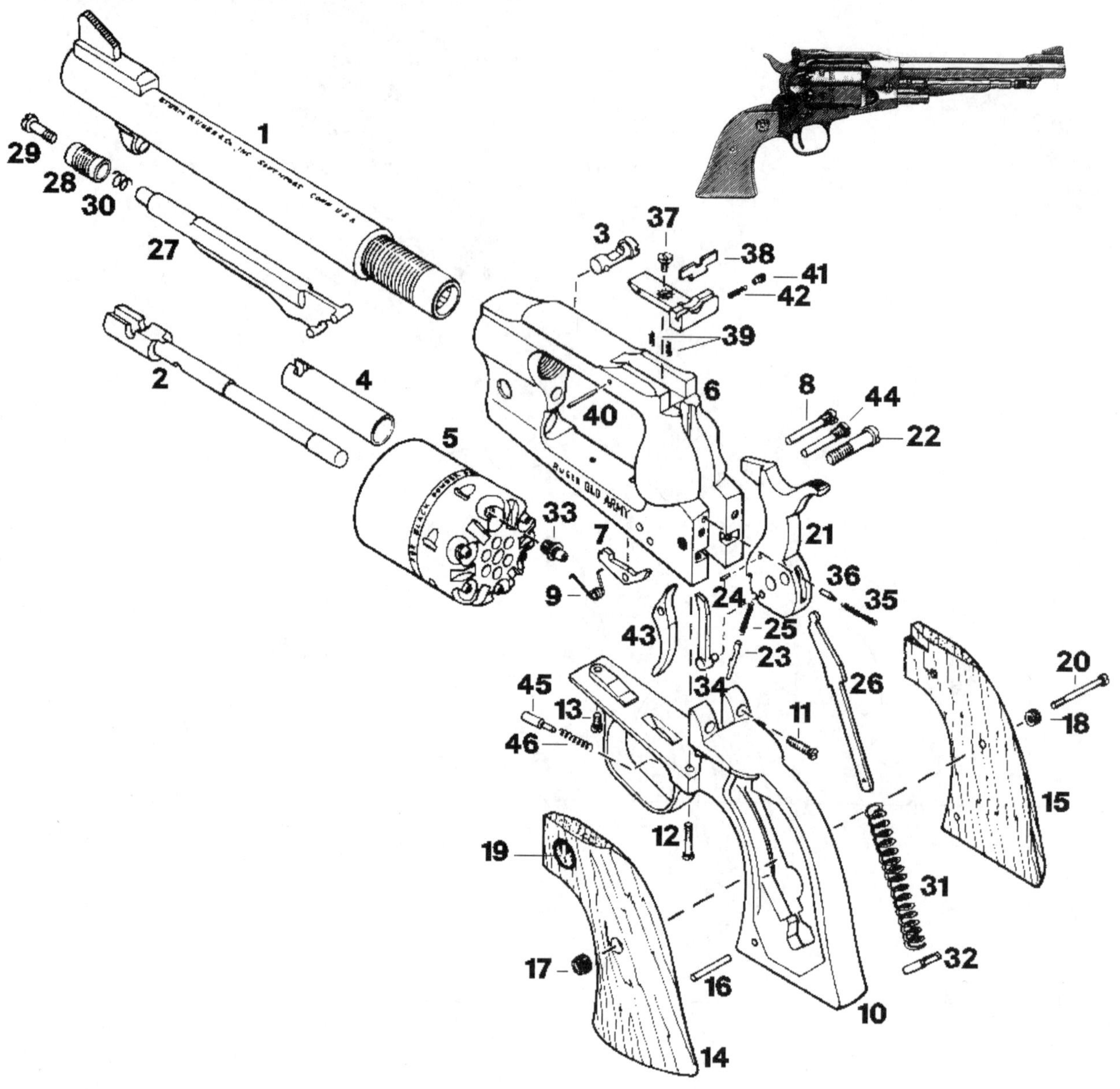

1	Barrel Assembly	**17**	Grip Panel Ferrule, Left	**33**	Nipple
2	Base Pin	**18**	Grip Panel Ferrule, Right	**34**	Pawl
3	Base Pin Retaining Pin Assembly	**19**	Grip Panel Medallion	**35**	Pawl Spring
4	Bullet Rammer	**20**	Grip Panel Screw	**36**	Pawl Spring Plunger
5	Cylinder	**21**	Hammer	**37**	Rear Sight Elevation Screw
6	Cylinder Frame	**22**	Hammer Pivot	**38**	Rear Sight Blade
7	Cylinder Latch	**23**	Hammer Plunger	**39**	Rear Sight Elevation Springs
8	Cylinder Latch Pivot	**24**	Hammer Plunger Pin	**40**	Rear Sight Pivot Pin
9	Cylinder Latch Spring	**25**	Hammer Plunger Spring	**41**	Rear Sight Windage Adjustment Screw
10	Grip Frame	**26**	Hammer Strut	**42**	Rear Sight Windage Spring
11	Grip Frame Screw, Back	**27**	Loading Lever	**43**	Trigger
12	Grip Frame Screw, Bottom	**28**	Loading Lever Catch	**44**	Trigger Pivot Screw
13	Grip Frame Screw, Front	**29**	Loading Lever Catch Screw	**45**	Trigger Plunger
14	Grip Panel, Left	**30**	Loading Lever Catch Spring	**46**	Trigger Spring
15	Grip Panel, Right	**31**	Mainspring		
16	Grip Panel Dowel	**32**	Mainspring Seat		

P85 Auto

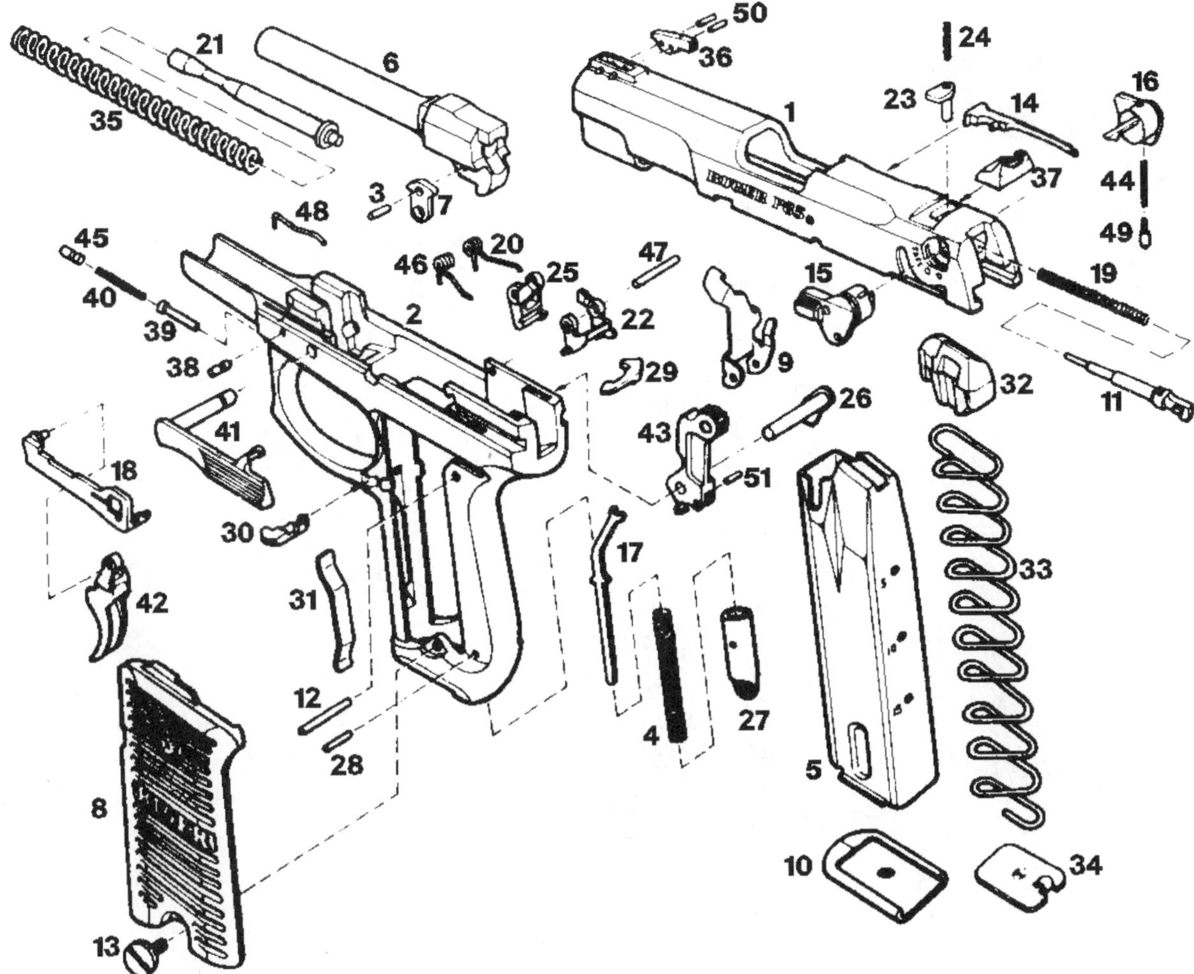

1	Slide	28	Hammer Spring Seat Pin
2	Frame	29	Magazine Latch, Right
3	Barrel Link Pin	30	Magazine Latch, Left
4	Hammer Spring	31	Magazine Latch Spring
5	Magazine Body	32	Magazine Follower
6	Barrel	33	Magazine Spring
7	Barrel Link	34	Magazine Spring Seat
8	Grip Panel, Left	35	Recoil Spring
9	Ejector	36	Sight, Front
10	Magazine Floorplate	37	Sight, Rear
11	Firing Pin	38	Slide Stop Spring Retainer
12	Ejector Pin	39	Trigger Bar Plunger
13	Grip Panel Screws	40	Trigger Bar Plunger Spring
14	Extractor	41	Slide Stop
15	Safety, Left	42	Trigger
16	Safety, Right	43	Hammer
17	Hammer Strut	44	Safety Detent Plunger Spring
18	Trigger Bar	45	Trigger Bar Spring Retainer
19	Firing Pin Spring	46	Sear Spring
20	Blocker Lever Spring	47	Sear Pivot Pin
21	Guide Rod	48	Slide Stop Spring
22	Blocker Lever	49	Safety Detent Plunger
23	Firing Pin Block	50	Front Sight Cross Pins
24	Firing Pin Block Spring	51	Hammer Strut Pin
25	Sear	**Parts Not Shown**	
26	Hammer Pivot Assembly		Grip Panel, Right
27	Hammer Spring Seat		

New Model Blackhawk Revolver

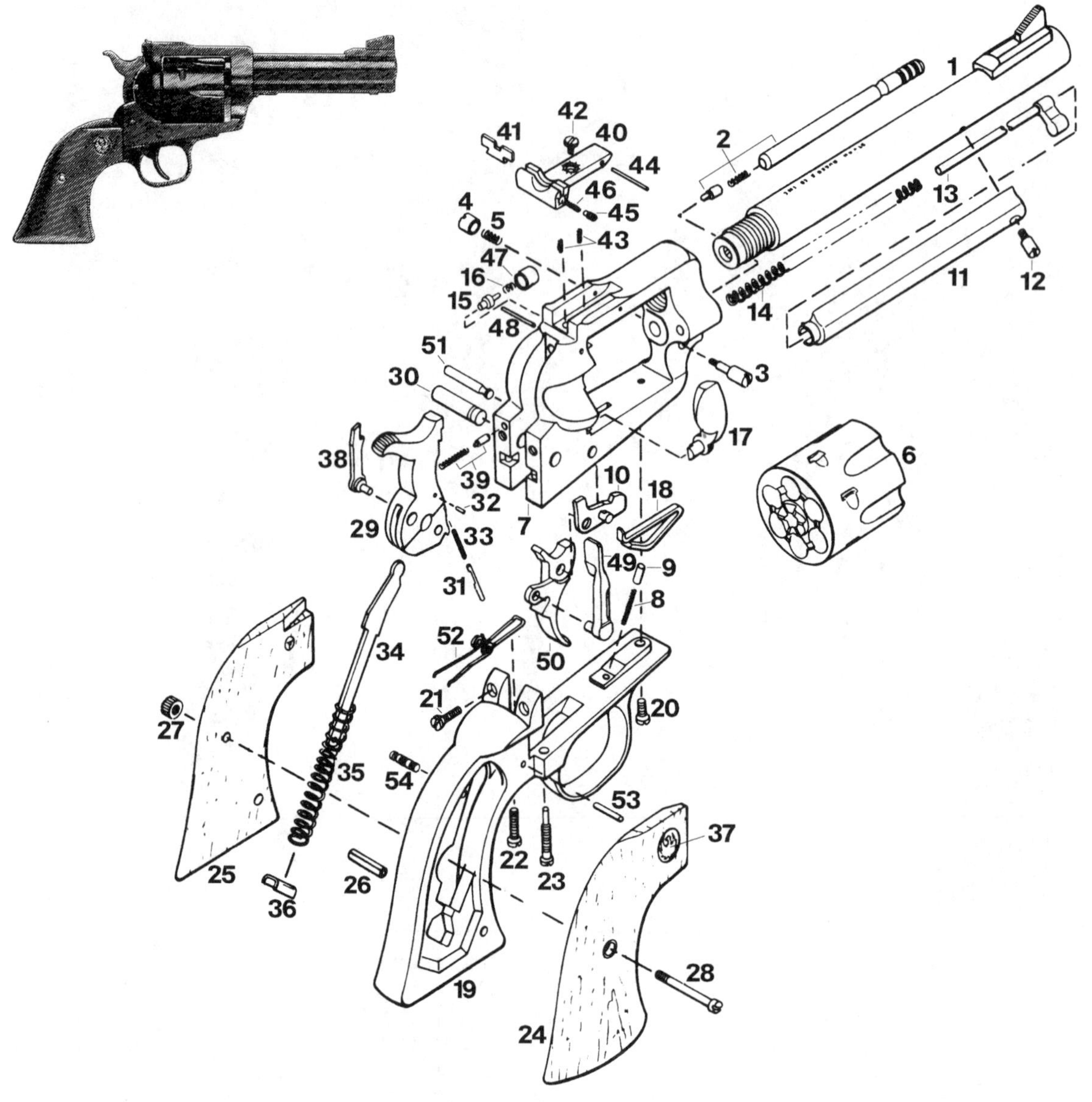

1	Barrel	**20**	Grip Frame Screw, Front	**39**	Pawl Spring and Plunger
2	Base Pin Assembly	**21**	Grip Frame Screw, Back	**40**	Rear Sight Assembly, Complete
3	Base Pin Latch	**22**	Grip Frame Screw, Bottom	**41**	Rear Sight Blade
4	Base Pin Latch Nut	**23**	Grip Frame Screw and Pivot Lock	**42**	Rear Sight Elevation Screw
5	Base Pin Latch Spring	**24**	Grip Panel, Right	**43**	Rear Sight Elevation Springs
6	Cylinder	**25**	Grip Panel, Left	**44**	Rear Sight Pivot Pin
7	Cylinder Frame	**26**	Grip Panel Dowel	**45**	Rear Sight Windage Adjustment Screw
8	Cylinder Latch Spring	**27**	Grip Panel Ferrule, Left	**46**	Rear Sight Windage Spring
9	Cylinder Latch Spring Plunger	**28**	Grip Panel Screw	**47**	Recoil Plate
10	Cylinder Latch	**29**	Hammer Assembly	**48**	Recoil Plate Cross Pin
11	Ejector Housing	**30**	Hammer Pivot	**49**	Transfer Bar
12	Ejector Housing Screw	**31**	Hammer Plunger	**50**	Trigger
13	Ejector Rod Assembly	**32**	Hammer Plunger Pin	**51**	Trigger Pivot
14	Ejector Rod Spring	**33**	Hammer Plunger Spring	**52**	Trigger Spring
15	Firing Pin	**34**	Hammer Strut	**53**	Trigger Spring Pin
16	Firing Pin Rebound Spring	**35**	Mainspring	**54**	Trigger Spring Retaining Pin
17	Gate	**36**	Mainspring Seat	**Parts Not Shown**	
18	Gate Detent Spring and Retainer	**37**	Medallion		Grip Panel Ferrule, Right
19	Grip Frame	**38**	Pawl		

New Model Single-Six SA Revolver

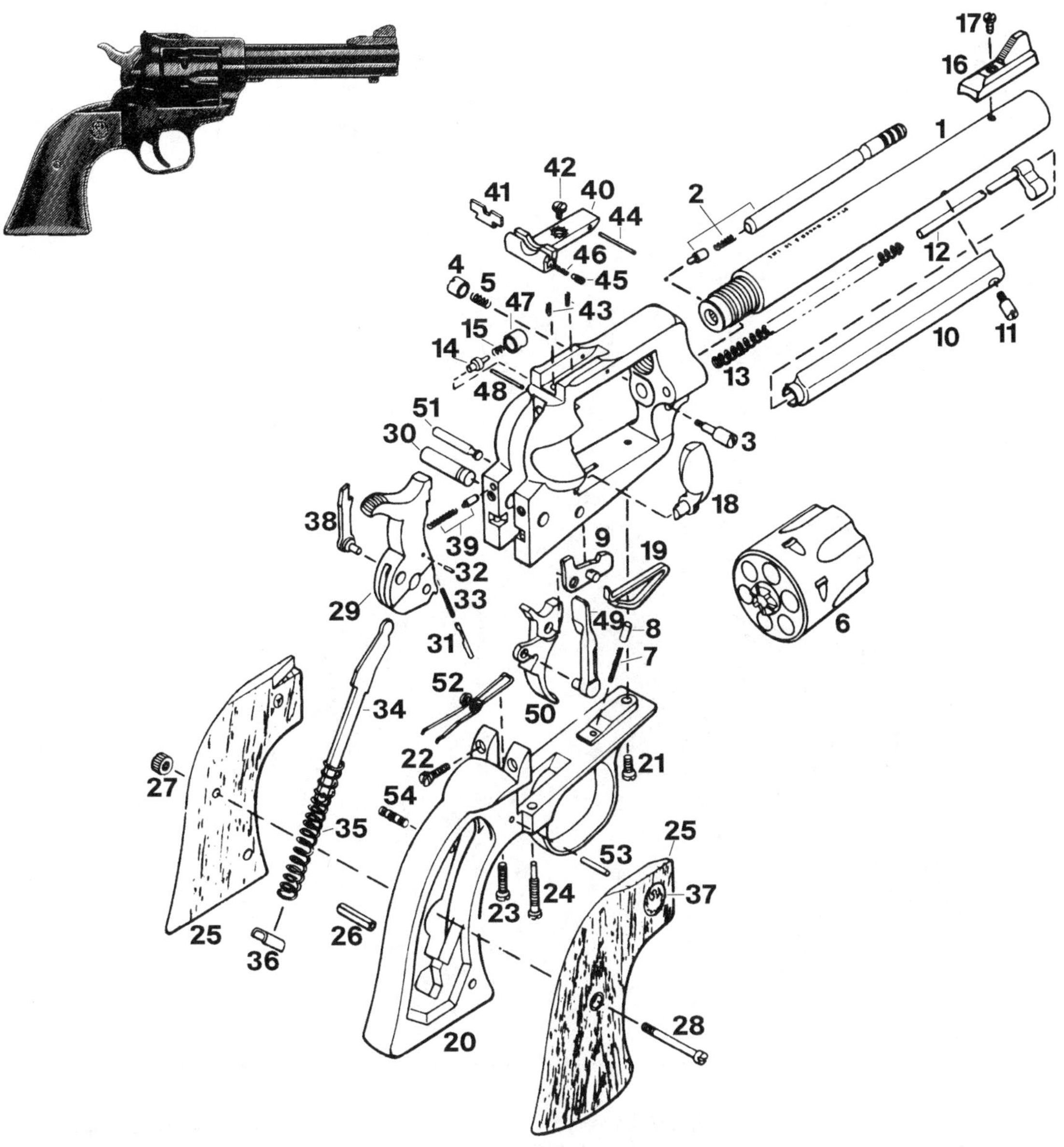

1	Barrel	20	Grip Frame	39	Pawl Spring and Plunger
2	Base Pin Assembly	21	Grip Frame Screw, Front	40	Rear Sight Assembly, Complete
3	Base Pin Latch	22	Grip Frame Screw, Back	41	Rear Sight Blade
4	Base Pin Latch Nut	23	Grip Frame Screw, Bottom	42	Rear Sight Elevation Screw
5	Base Pin Latch Spring	24	Grip Frame Screw and Pivot Lock	43	Rear Sight Elevation Springs
6	Cylinder	25	Grip Panels, Complete	44	Rear Sight Pivot Pin
7	Cylinder Latch Spring	26	Grip Panel Dowel	45	Rear Sight Windage Adjusting Screw
8	Cylinder Latch Spring Plunger	27	Grip Panel Ferrule, Left	46	Rear Sight Windage Spring
9	Cylinder Latch	28	Grip Panel Screw	47	Recoil Plate
10	Ejector Housing	29	Hammer Assembly	48	Recoil Plate Cross Pin
11	Ejector Housing Screw	30	Hammer Pivot	49	Transfer Bar
12	Ejector Rod Assembly	31	Hammer Plunger	50	Trigger
13	Ejector Rod Spring	32	Hammer Plunger Pin	51	Trigger Pivot
14	Firing Pin	33	Hammer Plunger Spring	52	Trigger Spring
15	Firing Pin Rebound Spring	34	Hammer Strut	53	Trigger Spring Pin
16	Front Sight	35	Mainspring	54	Trigger Spring Retaining Pin
17	Front Sight Screw	36	Mainspring Seat	**Parts Not Shown**	
18	Gate	37	Medallion		Grip Panel Ferrule, Right
19	Gate Detent Spring	38	Pawl		

New Model Super Blackhawk Hunter Model Revolver

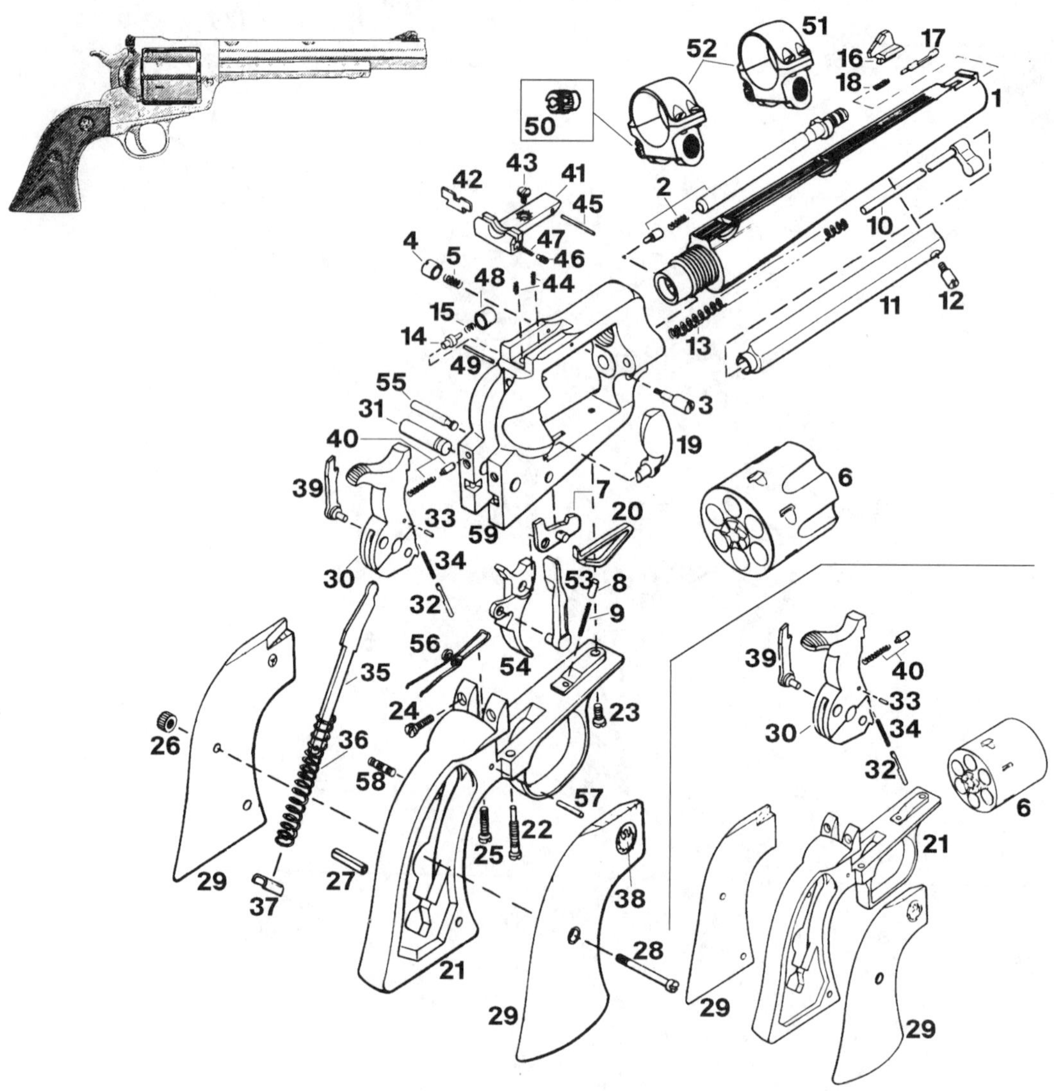

1	Barrel	23	Grip Frame Screw, Front	45	Rear Sight Pivot Pin
2	Base Pin Assembly	24	Grip Frame Screw, Back	46	Rear Sight Windage Adjustment Screw
3	Base Pin Latch	25	Grip Frame Screw, Bottom	47	Rear Sight Windage Spring
4	Base Pin Latch Nut	26	Grip Panel Ferrule, Left	48	Recoil Plate
5	Base Pin Latch Spring	27	Grip Panel Locating Pin	49	Recoil Plate Cross Pin
6	Cylinder	28	Grip Panel Screw	50	Scope Base Nut
7	Cylinder Latch	29	Grip Panels	51	Scope Ring Screw
8	Cylinder Latch Plunger	30	Hammer Assembly	52	Scope Rings
9	Cylinder Latch Spring	31	Hammer Pivot	53	Transfer Bar
10	Ejector Rod Assembly	32	Hammer Plunger	54	Trigger
11	Ejector Housing	33	Hammer Plunger Cross Pin	55	Trigger Pivot
12	Ejector Housing Screw	34	Hammer Plunger Spring	56	Trigger Spring
13	Ejector Rod Spring	35	Hammer Strut	57	Trigger Spring Pin
14	Firing Pin	36	Mainspring	58	Trigger Spring Retaining Pin
15	Firing Pin Rebound Spring	37	Mainspring Seat	59	Frame
16	Front Sight	38	Medallion	**Parts Not Shown**	
17	Front Sight Plunger	39	Pawl		Cylinder Latch Stud
18	Front Sight Spring	40	Pawl Spring and Plunger		Grip Panel Ferrule, Right
19	Gate	41	Rear Sight		Rear Sight Detent Ball
20	Gate Detent Spring	42	Rear Sight Blade		Scope Base Clamp
21	Grip Frame	43	Rear Sight Elevation Screw		
22	Grip Frame Screw and Pivot Lock	44	Rear Sight Elevation Springs		

P85 MKII Auto

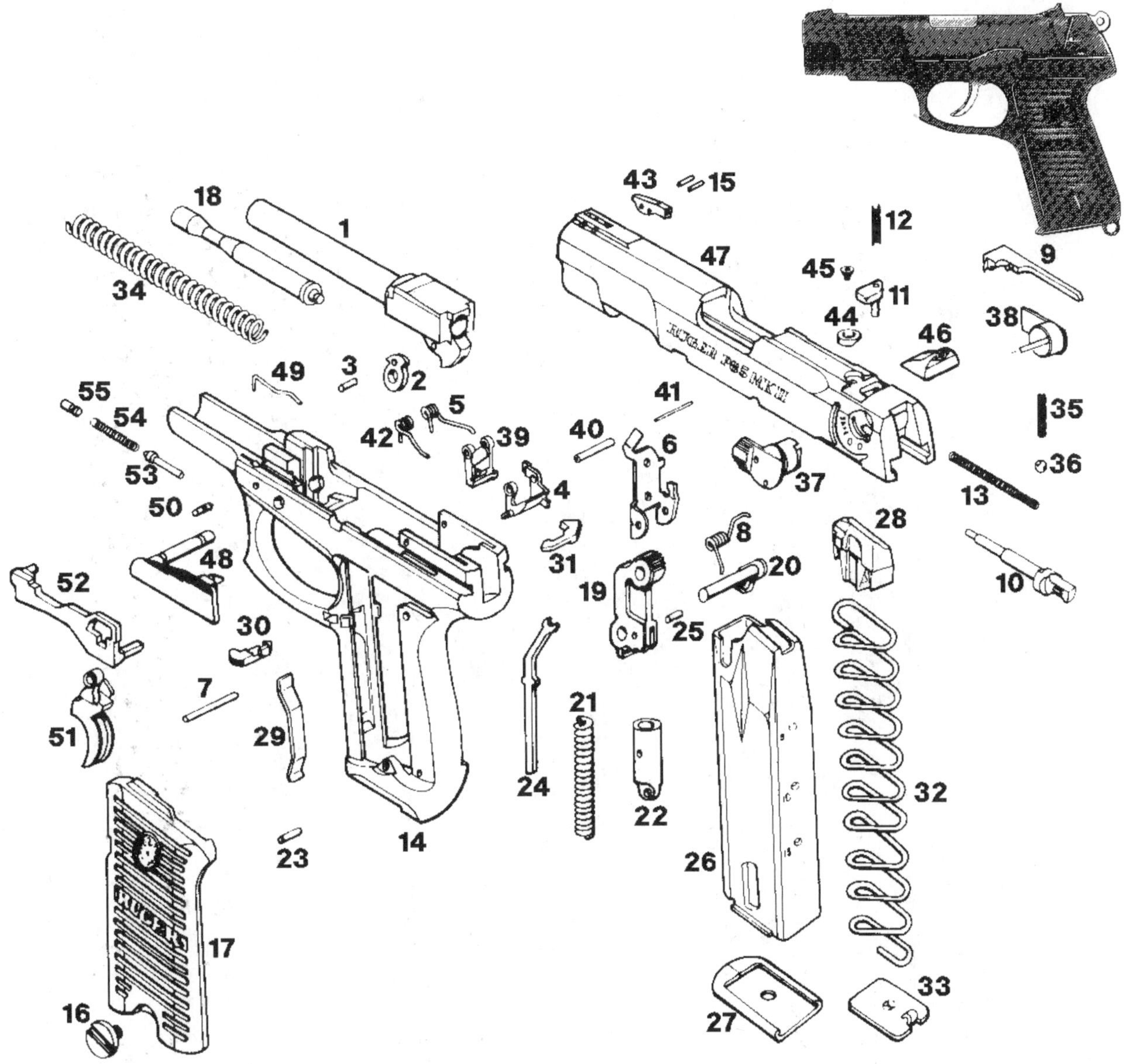

1	Barrel	21	Hammer Spring	41	Sear Pivot Pin
2	Barrel Link	22	Hammer Spring Seat	42	Sear Spring
3	Barrel Link Pin	23	Hammer Spring Seat Pin	43	Sight, Front
4	Blocker Lever	24	Hammer Strut	44	Sight Lock
5	Blocker Lever Spring	25	Hammer Strut Pin	45	Sight Lock Screw
6	Ejector	26	Magazine Body	46	Sight, Rear
7	Ejector Pin	27	Magazine Floorplate	47	Slide
8	Ejector Spring	28	Magazine Follower	48	Slide Stop
9	Extractor	29	Magazine Latch Spring	49	Slide Stop Spring
10	Firing Pin	30	Magazine Latch, Left	50	Slide Stop Spring Retainer
11	Firing Pin Block	31	Magazine Latch, Right	51	Trigger
12	Firing Pin Block Spring	32	Magazine Spring	52	Trigger Bar
13	Firing Pin Spring	33	Magazine Spring Seat	53	Trigger Bar Plunger
14	Frame	34	Recoil Spring	54	Trigger Bar Plunger Spring
15	Front Sight Cross Pins	35	Safety Detent Plunger Spring	55	Trigger Bar Spring Retainer
16	Grip Panel Screws	36	Safety Detent Ball	**Parts Not Shown**	
17	Grip Panel, Left	37	Safety, Left		Grip Panel, Right
18	Guide Rod Assembly	38	Safety, Right		Magazine Loader
19	Hammer	39	Sear		
20	Hammer Pivot Assembly	40	Sear Pivot Bearing		

P89DC Auto

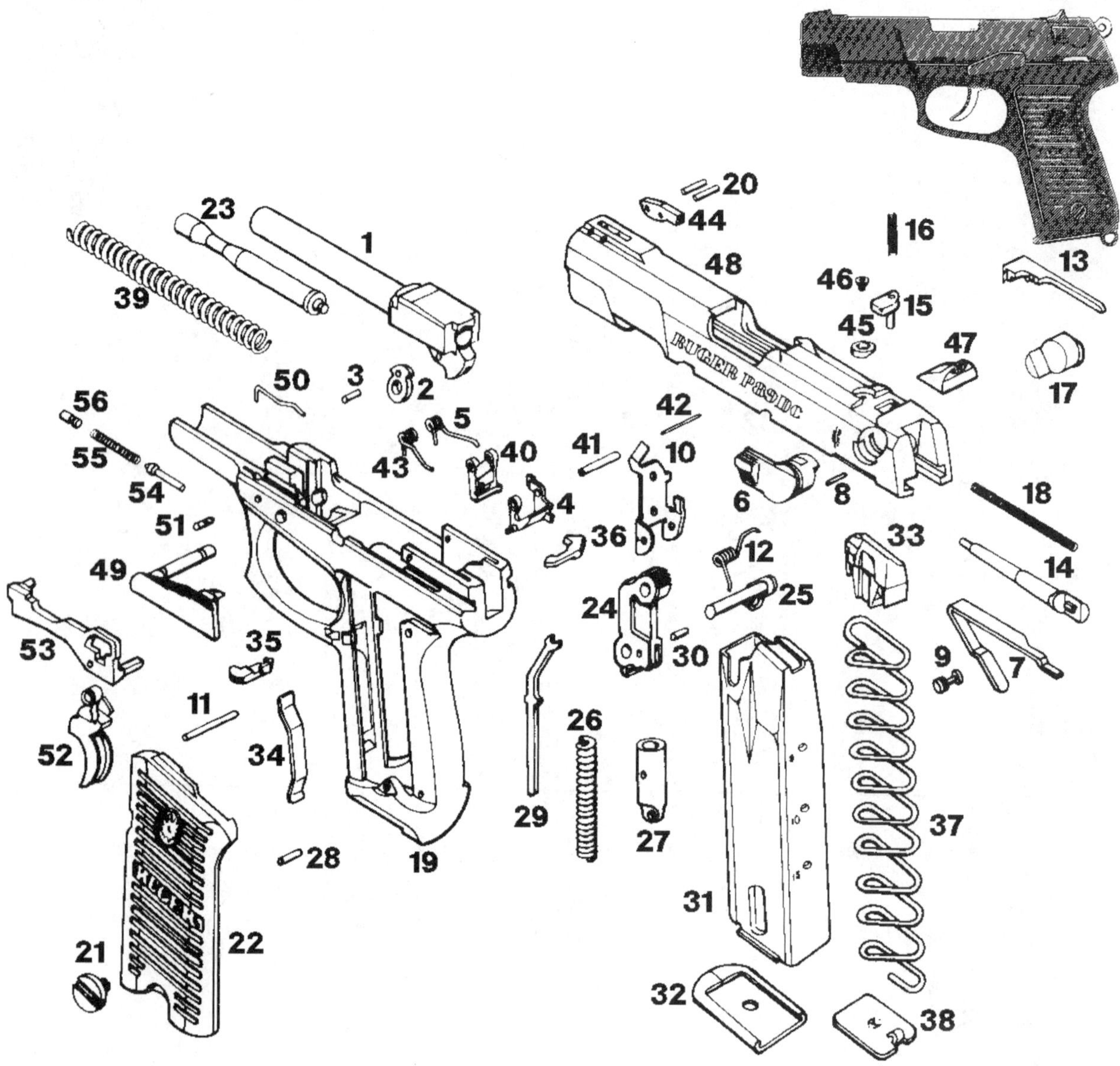

1	Barrel	21	Grip Panel Screws	41	Sear Pivot Bearing
2	Barrel Link	22	Grip Panel, Left	42	Sear Pivot Pin
3	Barrel Link Pin	23	Guide Rod Assembly	43	Sear Spring
4	Blocker Lever	24	Hammer	44	Sight, Front
5	Blocker Lever Spring	25	Hammer Pivot Assembly	45	Sight Lock
6	Decocker Lever	26	Hammer Spring	46	Sight Lock Screw
7	Decocker Lever Spring	27	Hammer Spring Seat	47	Sight, Rear
8	Decocker Lever Spring Pin	28	Hammer Spring Seat Pin	48	Slide
9	Decocker Lever Spring Retainer	29	Hammer Strut	49	Slide Stop
10	Ejector	30	Hammer Strut Pin	50	Slide Stop Spring
11	Ejector Pin	31	Magazine Body	51	Slide Stop Spring Retainer
12	Ejector Spring	32	Magazine Floorplate	52	Trigger
13	Extractor	33	Magazine Follower	53	Trigger Bar
14	Firing Pin	34	Magazine Latch Spring	54	Trigger Bar Plunger
15	Firing Pin Block	35	Magazine Latch, Left	55	Trigger Bar Plunger Spring
16	Firing Pin Block Spring	36	Magazine Latch, Right	56	Trigger Bar Spring Retainer
17	Firing Pin Stop	37	Magazine Spring	**Parts Not Shown**	
18	Firing Pin Spring	38	Magazine Spring Seat		Grip Panel, Right
19	Frame	39	Recoil Spring		
20	Front Sight Cross Pins	40	Sear		

P90DC Auto

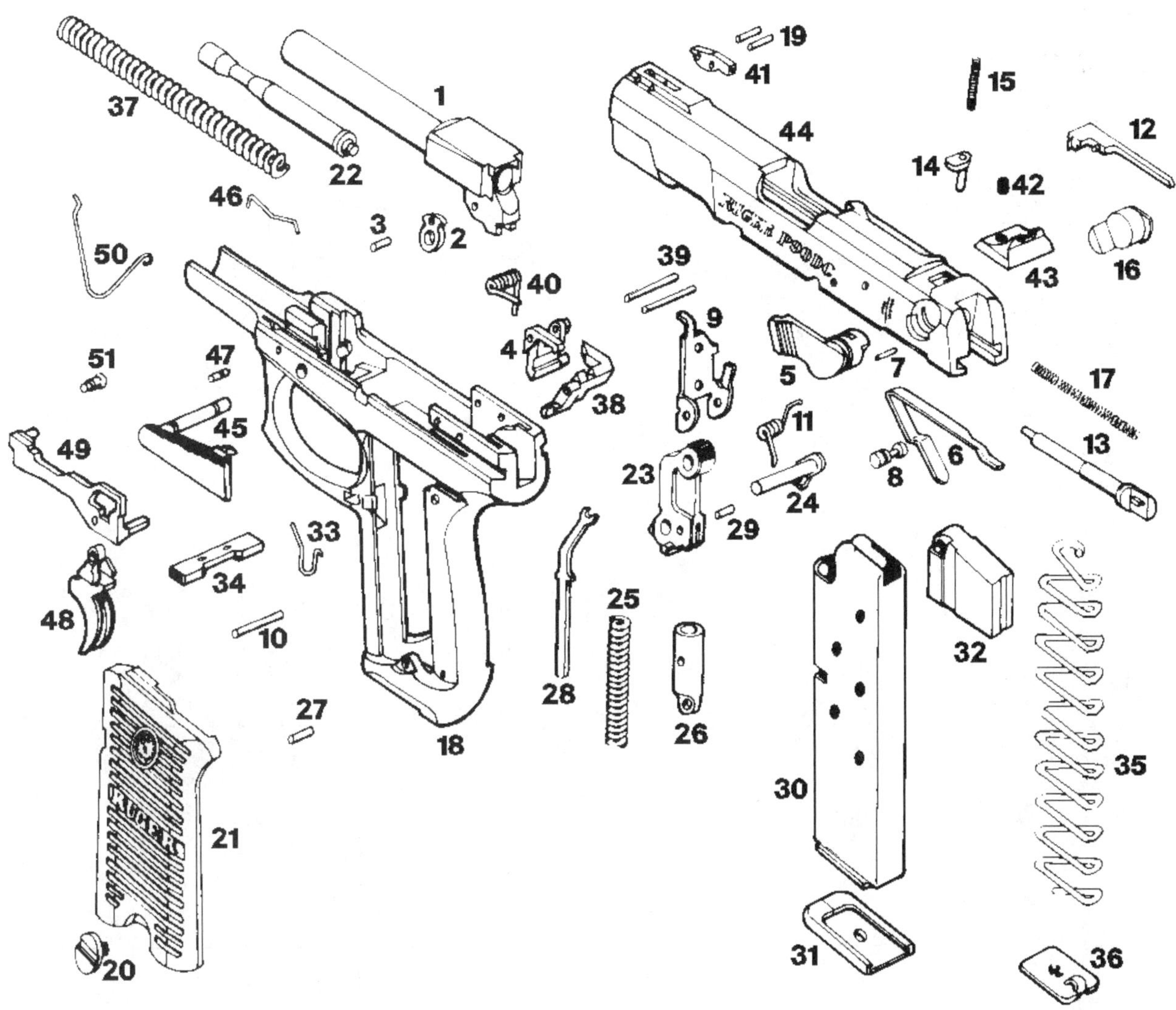

1	Barrel	**19**	Front Sight Cross Pins	**37**	Recoil Spring
2	Barrel Link	**20**	Grip Panel Screws	**38**	Sear
3	Barrel Link Pin	**21**	Grip Panel, Left	**39**	Sear Pivot Pins
4	Blocker Lever	**22**	Guide Rod Assembly	**40**	Sear Spring
5	Decocker Lever	**23**	Hammer	**41**	Sight, Front
6	Decocker Lever Spring	**24**	Hammer Pivot Assembly	**42**	Sight Lock Screw
7	Decocker Lever Spring Pin	**25**	Hammer Spring	**43**	Sight, Rear
8	Decocker Lever Spring Retainer	**26**	Hammer Spring Seat	**44**	Slide
9	Ejector	**27**	Hammer Spring Seat Pin	**45**	Slide Stop
10	Ejector Pin	**28**	Hammer Strut	**46**	Slide Stop Spring
11	Ejector Spring	**29**	Hammer Strut Pin	**47**	Slide Stop Spring Retainer
12	Extractor	**30**	Magazine Body	**48**	Trigger
13	Firing Pin	**31**	Magazine Floorplate	**49**	Trigger Bar
14	Firing Pin Block	**32**	Magazine Follower	**50**	Trigger Bar Spring
15	Firing Pin Block Spring	**33**	Magazine Latch Spring	**51**	Rivet
16	Firing Pin Stop	**34**	Magazine Latch	**Parts Not Shown**	
17	Firing Pin Spring	**35**	Magazine Spring		Grip Panel, Right
18	Frame	**36**	Magazine Spring Seat		

Redhawk Revolver

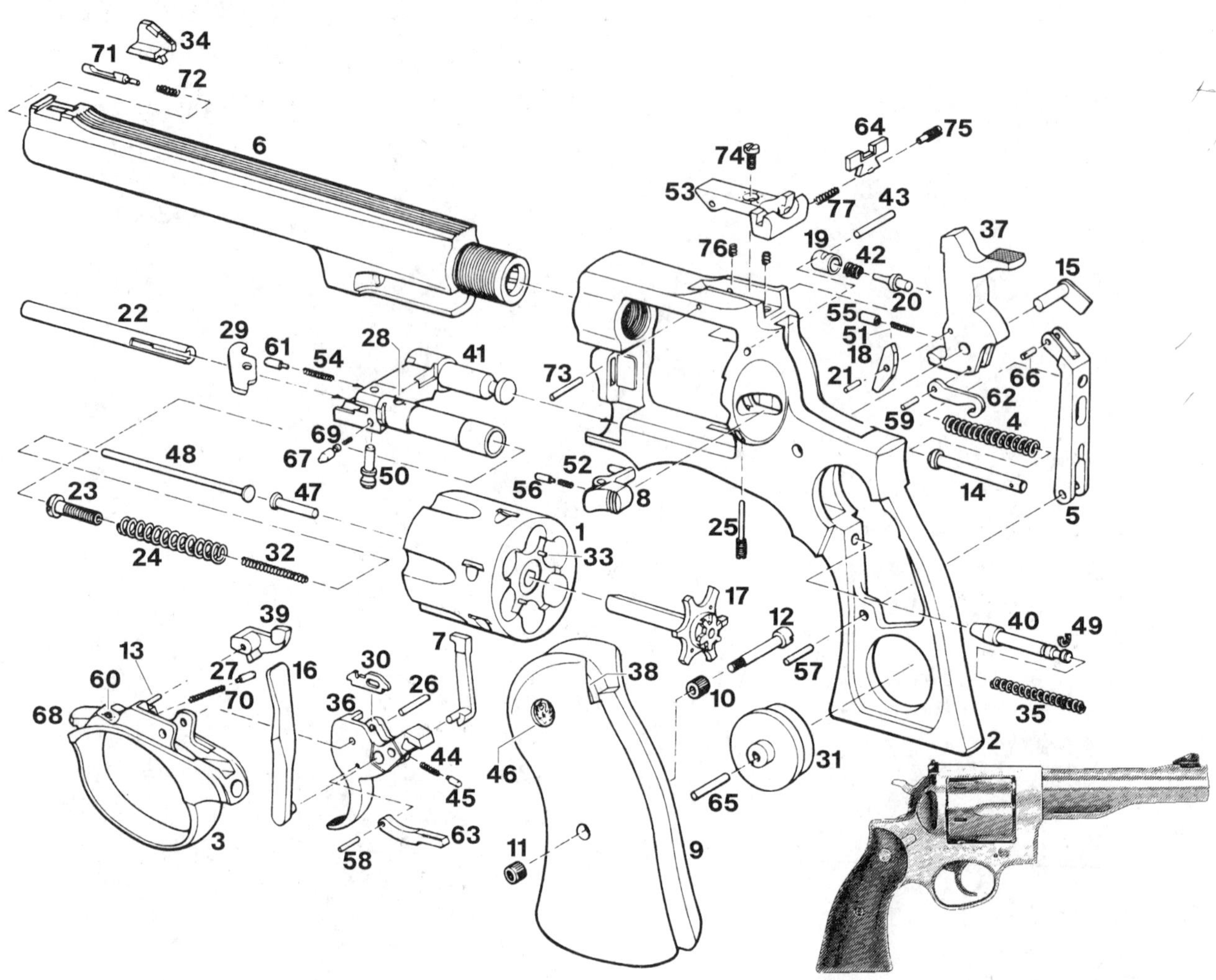

No.	Part	No.	Part	No.	Part
1	Cylinder	27	Cylinder Latch Plunger	52	Crane Latch Spring
2	Frame	28	Cylinder Retaining Balls	53	Rear Sight Base
3	Trigger Guard	29	Front Latch	54	Front Latch Spring
4	Mainspring	30	Trigger Plunger	55	Hammer Dog Spring Plunger
5	Mainspring Lever	31	Grip Panel Locator	56	Crane Latch Spring Plunger
6	Barrel	32	Center Pin Spring	57	Lever Pivot Pin
7	Pawl	33	Ejector Alignment Pins	58	Trigger Cross Pin
8	Crane Latch	34	Front Sight	59	Hammer Cross Pins
9	Grip Panels	35	Trigger Guard Latch Spring	60	Crane Pivot Lock Plunger
10	Grip Panel Ferrule, Right	36	Trigger	61	Front Latch Spring Plunger
11	Grip Panel Ferrule, Left	37	Hammer	62	Hammer Link
12	Grip Panel Screw	38	Grip Panel Boss	63	Trigger Link
13	Cylinder Latch Pivot	39	Cylinder Latch	64	Rear Sight Blade
14	Mainspring Strut	40	Trigger Guard Latch	65	Disassembly Pin
15	Hammer Pivot Assembly	41	Crane and Crane/Pivot Assembly	66	Mainspring Lever Cross Pin
16	Transfer Bar	42	Firing Pin Rebound Spring	67	Front Latch Pivot Lock
17	Ejector	43	Recoil Plate Cross Pin	68	Crane Pivot Spring
18	Hammer Dog	44	Pawl Plunger Spring	69	Front Latch Pivot Spring
19	Recoil Plate	45	Pawl Plunger	70	Cylinder Latch Spring
20	Firing Pin	46	Grip Medallions	71	Front Sight Plunger
21	Hammer Dog Pivot Pin	47	Center Pin Lock	72	Front Sight Plunger Spring
22	Ejector Rod	48	Center Pin Rod	73	Rear Sight Pivot Pin
23	Ejector Retainer	49	Trigger Guard Latch Retaining<R>Ring	74	Rear Sight Elevation Screw
24	Ejector Spring	50	Front Latch Pivot Pin	75	Rear Sight Windage Screw
25	Crane Latch Pivot	51	Hammer Dog Spring	76	Rear Sight Elevation Springs
26	Trigger Pivot Pin			77	Rear Sight Windage Spring

Security-Six, SP-6 and PS-6 Revolver

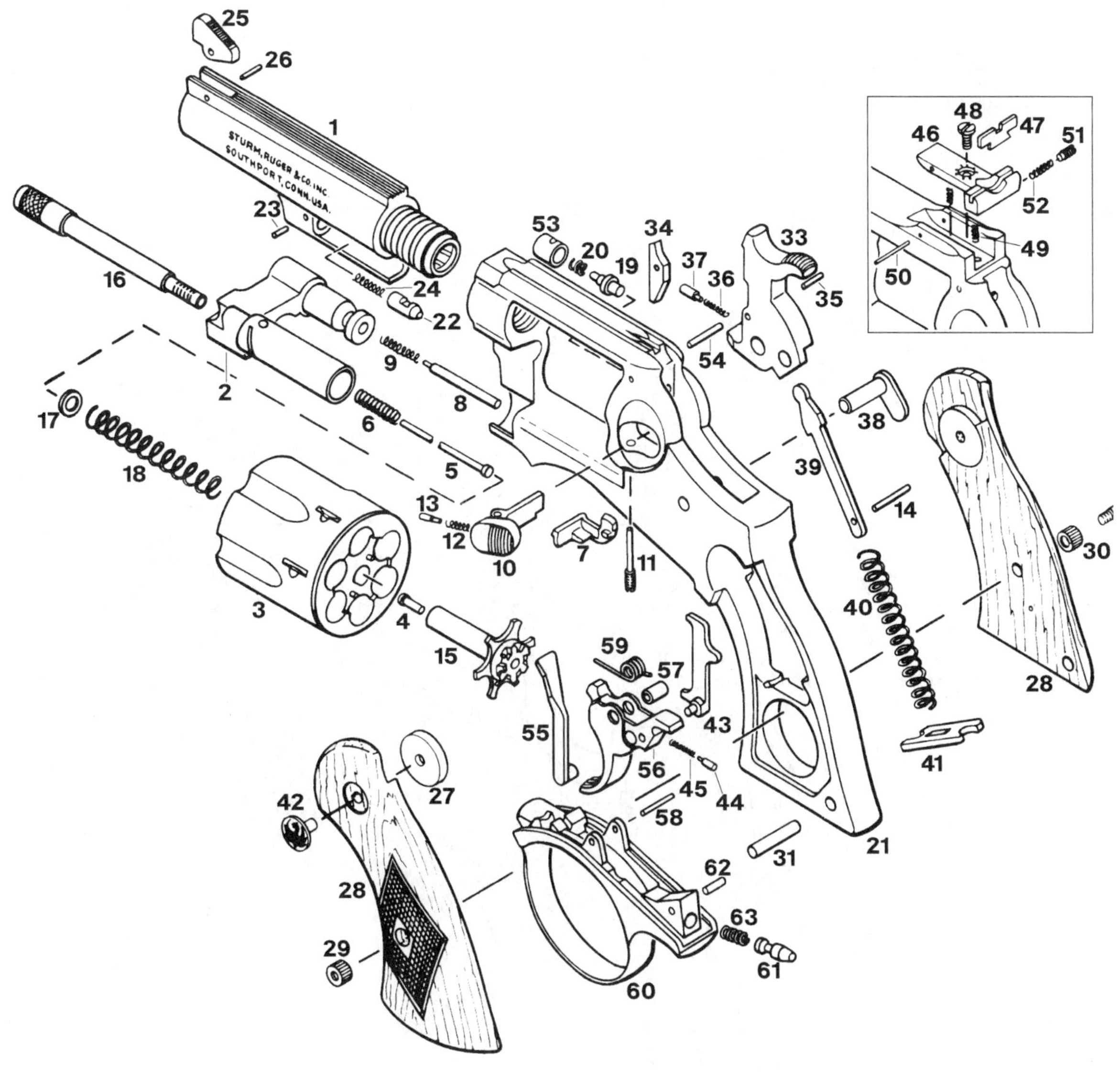

1	Barrel	22	Front Latch	43	Pawl
2	Crane/Crane Pivot Assembly	23	Front Latch Cross Pin	44	Pawl Plunger
3	Cylinder	24	Front Latch Spring	45	Pawl Spring
4	Cylinder Center Lock Pin	25	Front Sight Blade	46	Rear Sight
5	Cylinder Center Pin Rod	26	Front Sight Cross Pin	47	Rear Sight Blade
6	Cylinder Center Pin Spring	27	Grip Panel Boss	48	Rear Sight Elevation Screw
7	Cylinder Latch	28	Grip Panels	49	Rear Sight Elevation Springs
8	Cylinder Latch Plunger	29	Grip Panel Ferrule, Left	50	Rear Sight Pivot Pin
9	Cylinder Latch Spring	30	Grip Panel Ferrule, Right	51	Rear Sight Windage Screw
10	Cylinder Release Button	31	Grip Panel Dowel	52	Rear Sight Windage Spring
11	Cylinder Release Pivot	32	Grip Panel Screw	53	Recoil Plate
12	Cylinder Release Spring	33	Hammer	54	Recoil Plate Cross Pin
13	Cylinder Release Spring Plunger	34	Hammer Dog	55	Transfer Bar
14	Disassembly Pin	35	Hammer Dog Pivot Pin	56	Trigger
15	Ejector	36	Hammer Dog Spring	57	Trigger Bushing
16	Ejector Rod	37	Hammer Dog Spring Plunger	58	Trigger Pivot Pin
17	Ejector Rod Washer	38	Hammer Pivot Assembly	59	Trigger Spring
18	Ejector Spring	39	Hammer Strut	60	Trigger Guard
19	Firing Pin	40	Mainspring	61	Trigger Guard Plunger
20	Firing Pin Rebound Spring	41	Mainspring Seat	62	Trigger Guard Plunger Cross Pin
21	Frame	42	Grip Medallion	63	Trigger Guard Plunger Spring

Old Model Single-Six Revolver

Courtesy of Thomas E. Wessel/NRA

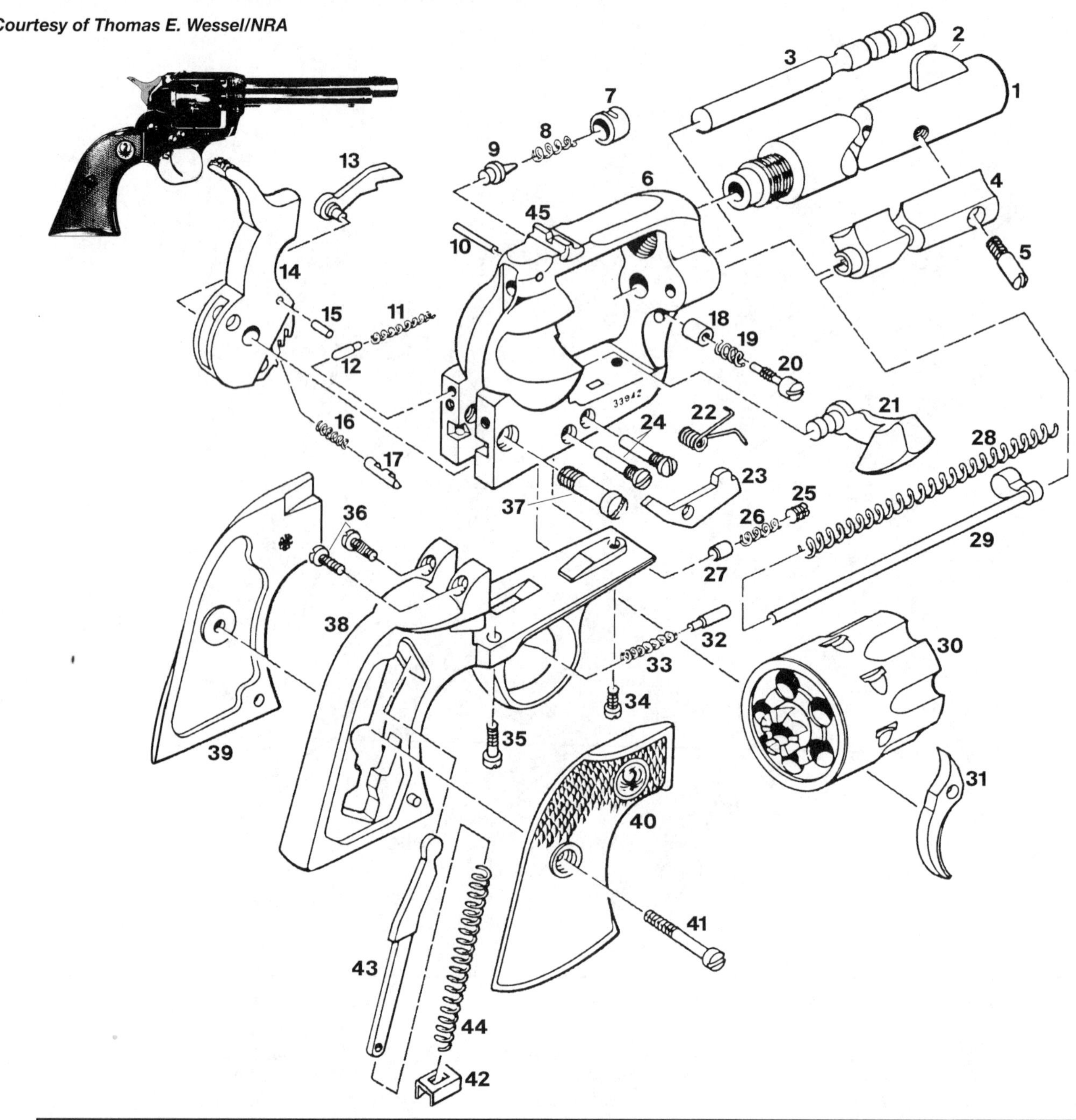

1	Barrel	16	Hammer Plunger Spring	31	Trigger
2	Front Sight	17	Hammer Plunger	32	Trigger Plunger
3	Base Pin	18	Base Pin Nut	33	Trigger Spring
4	Ejector Housing	19	Base Pin Nut Latch Spring	34	Grip Frame Screw, Front
5	Ejector Housing Screw	20	Base Pin Latch	35	Grip Frame Screw, Lower
6	Cylinder Frame	21	Gate Assembly (Contoured)	36	Grip Frame Screws, Rear
7	Recoil Plate	22	Cylinder Latch Spring	37	Hammer Pivot Screw
8	Rebound Spring	23	Cylinder Latch	38	Grip Frame
9	Firing Pin	24	Pivot Screws	39	Grip Panel, Left
10	Recoil Plate Pin	25	Gate Spring Screw	40	Grip Panel, Right
11	Pawl Spring	26	Gate Detent Spring	41	Grip Panel Screw
12	Pawl Plunger	27	Gate Detent Plunger	42	Mainspring Seat
13	Pawl	28	Ejector Spring	43	Hammer Strut
14	Hammer	29	Ejector Rod Assembly	44	Mainspring
15	Hammer Plunger Pin	30	Cylinder	45	Rear Sight

SP101 Revolver

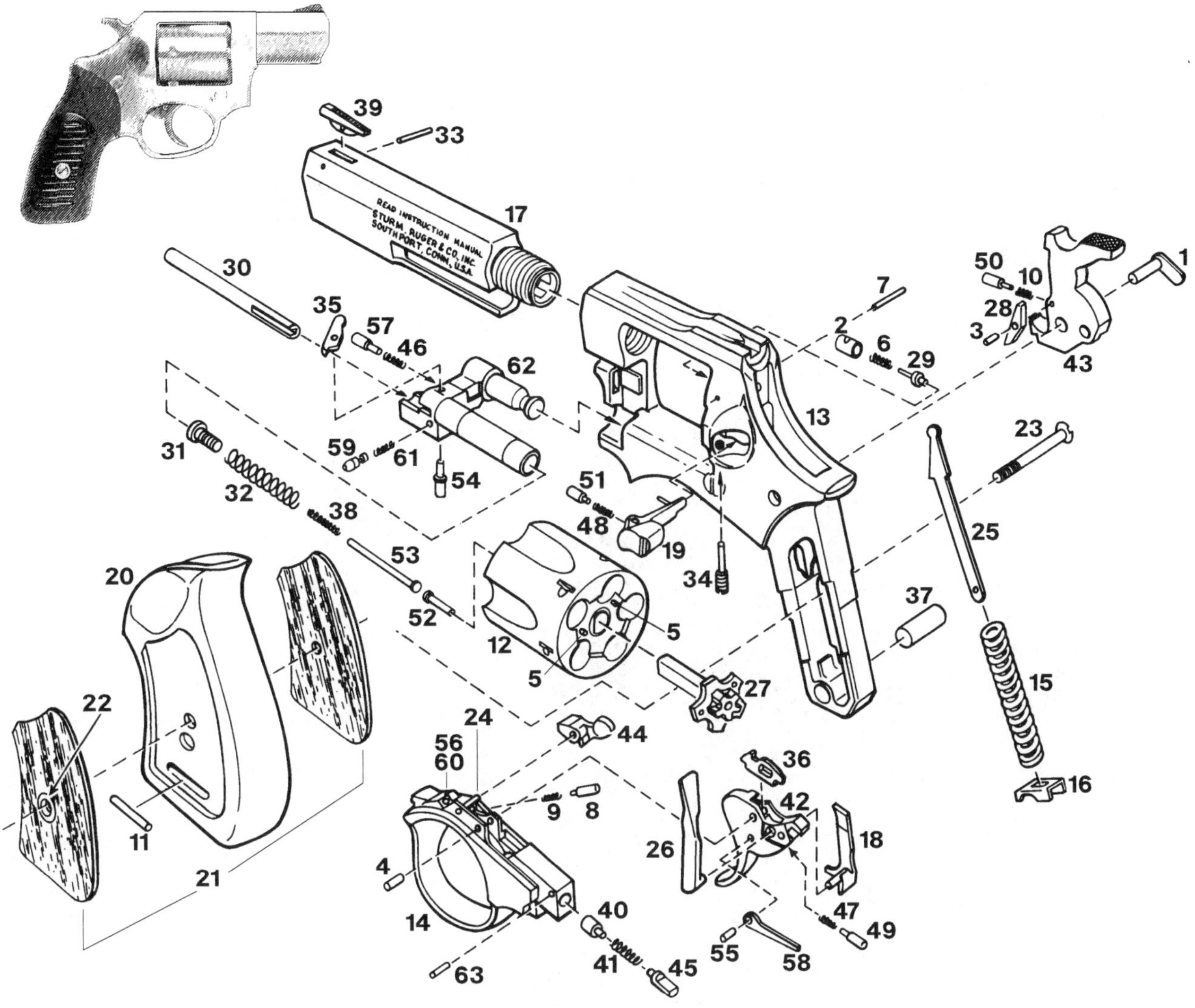

1	Hammer Pivot Assembly	**23**	Grip Panel Screw	**45**	Trigger Guard Latch
2	Recoil Plate	**24**	Cylinder Latch Pivot	**46**	Pawl Plunger Spring
3	Hammer Dog Pivot Pin	**25**	Hammer Strut	**47**	Front Latch Spring
4	Trigger Pivot Pin	**26**	Transfer Bar	**48**	Cylinder Latch Spring
5	Ejector Alignment Pins	**27**	Ejector	**49**	Pawl Plunger
6	Firing Pin Rebound Spring	**28**	Hammer Dog	**50**	Hammer Dog Spring Plunger
7	Recoil Plate Cross Pin	**29**	Firing Pin	**51**	Crane Latch Spring Plunger
8	Cylinder Latch Plunger	**30**	Ejector Rod	**52**	Center Pin Lock
9	Crane Latch Spring	**31**	Ejector Retainer	**53**	Center Pin Rod
10	Hammer Dog Spring	**32**	Ejector Spring	**54**	Front Latch Pivot Pin
11	Disassembly Pin	**33**	Front Sight Cross Pin	**55**	Trigger Link Pin
12	Cylinder	**34**	Crane Latch Pivot	**56**	Crane Pivot Lock Plunger
13	Frame	**35**	Front Latch	**57**	Front Latch Spring Plunger
14	Trigger Guard	**36**	Trigger Plunger	**58**	Trigger Link
15	Mainspring	**37**	Grip Panel Locator	**59**	Front Latch Pivot Lock
16	Mainspring Seat	**38**	Center Pin Spring	**60**	Crane Pivot Lock Spring
17	Barrel	**39**	Front Sight	**61**	Front Latch Pivot Lock Spring
18	Pawl	**40**	Trigger Link Plunger	**62**	Crane and Crane Pivot Assembly
19	Crane Latch	**41**	Trigger Guard Latch Spring	**63**	Trigger Guard Latch Pin
20	Pistol Grip	**42**	Trigger	**Parts Not Shown**	
21	Pistol Grip Insert	**43**	Hammer		Safety Disc
22	Ferrule	**44**	Cylinder Latch		

Stainless New Model Blackhawk and Super Blackhawk Revolver

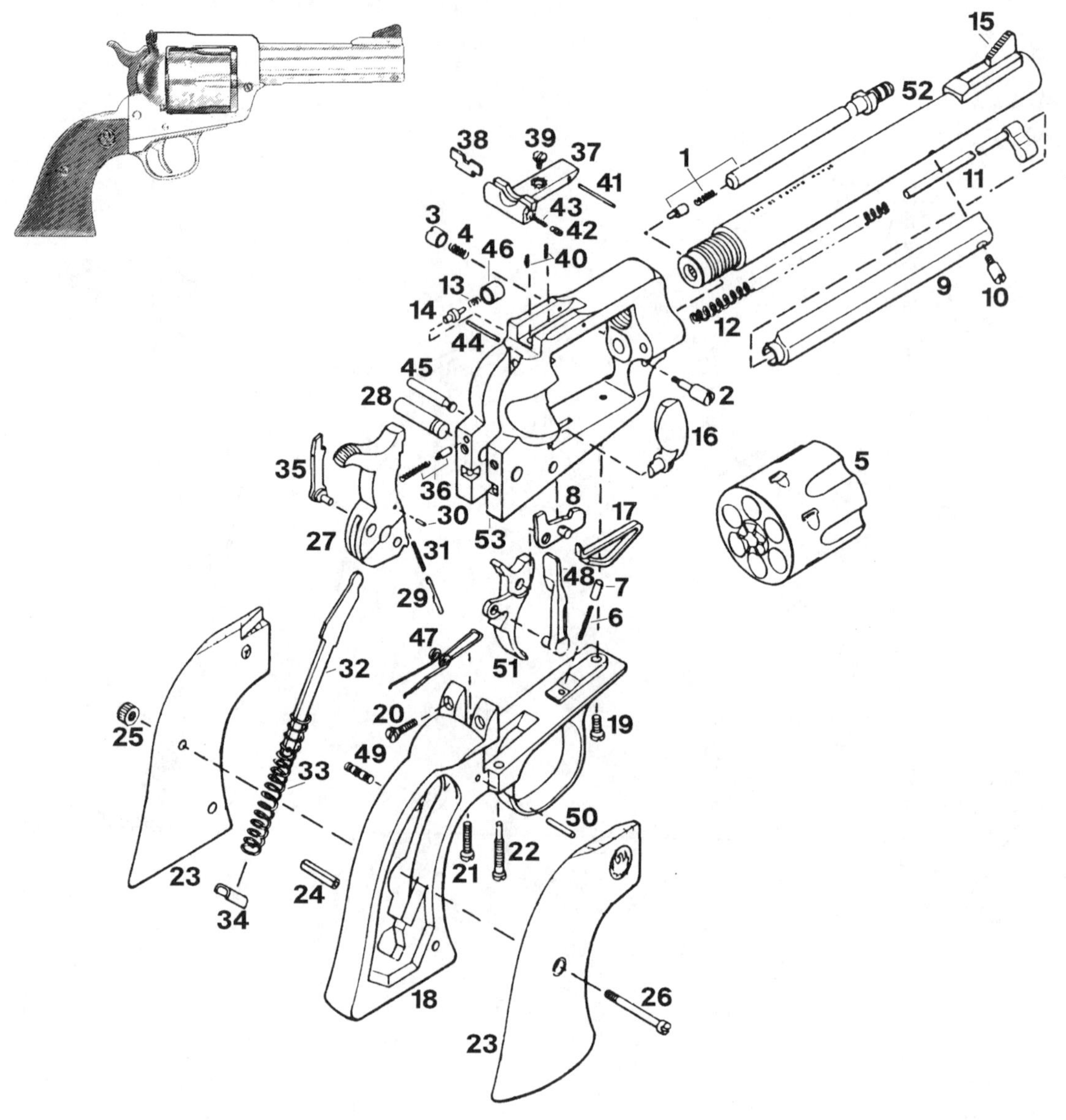

1	Base Pin Assembly	**21**	Grip Frame Screw, Bottom	**40**	Rear Sight Elevation Springs
2	Base Pin Latch	**22**	Grip Frame Screw and Pivot Lock	**41**	Rear Sight Pivot Pin
3	Base Pin Latch Nut	**23**	Grip Panels	**42**	Rear Sight Windage Adjusting Screw
4	Base Pin Latch Spring	**24**	Grip Panel Dowel	**43**	Rear Sight Windage Spring
5	Cylinder	**25**	Grip Panel Ferrule	**44**	Recoil Plate Cross Pin
6	Cylinder Latch Spring	**26**	Grip Panel Screw	**45**	Trigger Pivot
7	Cylinder Latch Spring Plunger	**27**	Hammer Assembly	**46**	Recoil Plate
8	Cylinder Latch	**28**	Hammer Pivot	**47**	Trigger Spring
9	Ejector Housing	**29**	Hammer Plunger	**48**	Transfer Bar
10	Ejector Housing Screw	**30**	Hammer Plunger Pin	**49**	Trigger Spring Retaining Pin
11	Ejector Rod Assembly	**31**	Hammer Plunger Spring	**50**	Trigger Spring Pin
12	Ejector Roll Spring	**32**	Hammer Strut	**51**	Trigger
13	Firing Pin Rebound Spring	**33**	Mainspring	**52**	Barrel
14	Firing Pin	**34**	Mainspring Seat	**53**	Frame
15	Front Sight	**35**	Pawl	**Parts Not Shown**	
16	Gate	**36**	Pawl Spring and Plunger		Front Sight Blade
17	Gate Detent Spring	**37**	Rear Sight Assembly, Complete		Front Sight Blade Cross Pin
18	Grip Frame	**38**	Rear Sight Blade		Rear Sight Detent Ball
19	Grip Frame Screw, Front	**39**	Rear Sight Elevation Screw		
20	Grip Frame Screw, Back				

Stainless New Model Single-Six Revolver

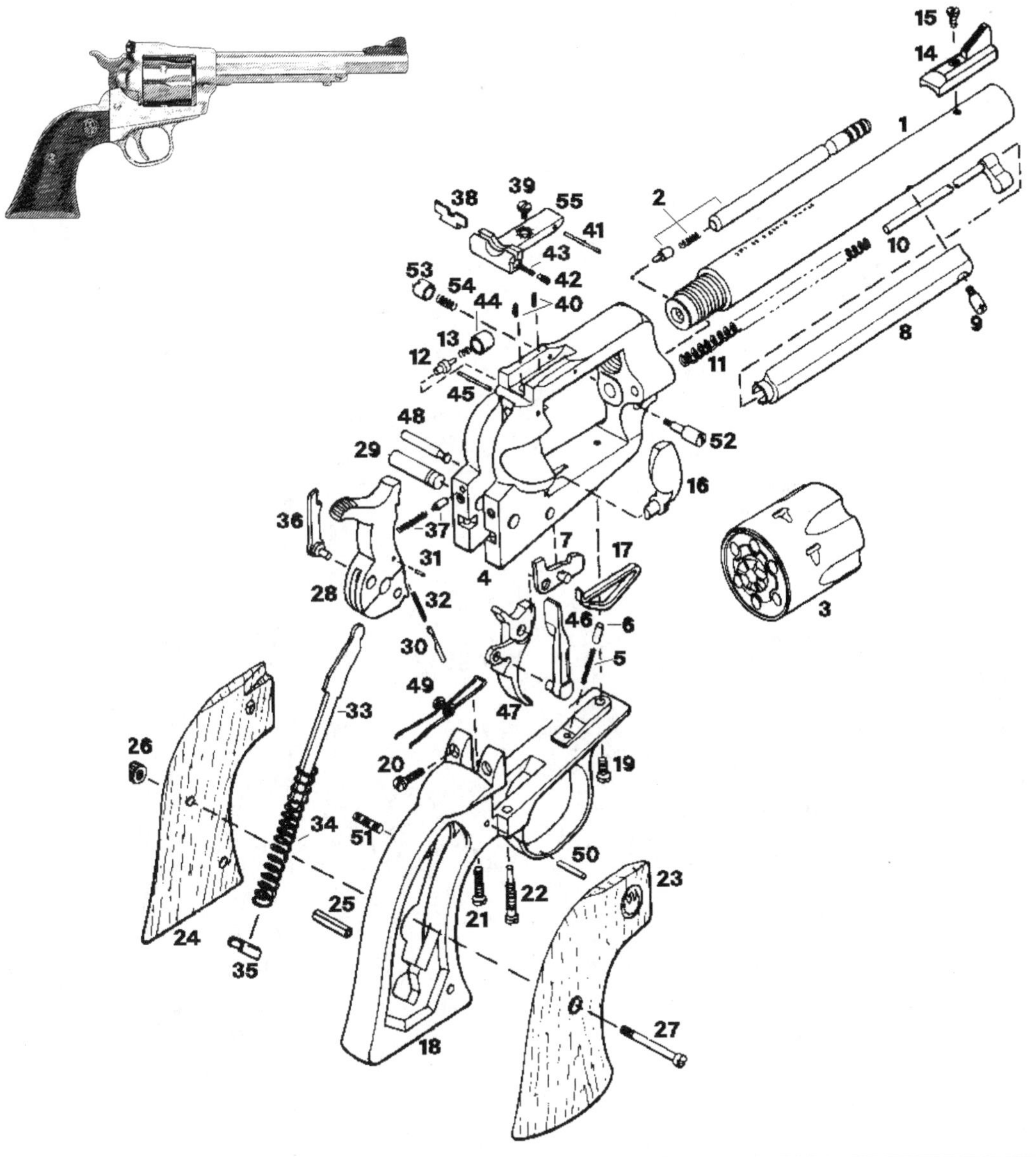

1	Barrel	**21**	Grip Frame Screw, Bottom	**40**	Rear Sight Elevation Springs
2	Base Pin Assembly	**22**	Grip Frame Screw and Pivot Lock	**41**	Rear Sight Pivot Pin
3	Cylinder	**23**	Grip Panel, Right	**42**	Rear Sight Windage Adjustment Screw
4	Cylinder Frame	**24**	Grip Panel, Left	**43**	Rear Sight Windage Spring
5	Cylinder Latch Spring	**25**	Grip Panel Dowel	**44**	Recoil Plate
6	Cylinder Latch Spring Plunger	**26**	Grip Panel Ferrule	**45**	Recoil Plate Cross Pin
7	Cylinder Latch	**27**	Grip Panel Screw	**46**	Transfer Bar
8	Ejector Housing	**28**	Hammer Assembly	**47**	Trigger
9	Ejector Housing Screw	**29**	Hammer Pivot	**48**	Trigger Pivot
10	Ejector Rod Assembly	**30**	Hammer Plunger	**49**	Trigger Spring
11	Ejector Rod Spring	**31**	Hammer Plunger Pin	**50**	Trigger Spring Pin
12	Firing Pin	**32**	Hammer Plunger Spring	**51**	Trigger Spring Retaining Pin
13	Firing Pin Rebound Spring	**33**	Hammer Strut	**52**	Base Pin Latch
14	Front Sight	**34**	Mainspring	**53**	Base Pin Latch Nut
15	Front Sight Screw	**35**	Mainspring Seat	**54**	Base Pin Latch Spring
16	Gate	**36**	Pawl	**55**	Rear Sight Base
17	Gate Detent Spring and Retainer	**37**	Pawl Spring and Plunger	**Parts Not Shown**	
18	Grip Frame	**38**	Rear Sight Blade		Medallion
19	Grip Frame Screw, Front	**39**	Rear Sight Elevation Screw		Rear Sight Detent Ball
20	Grip Frame Screw, Back				

Standard and Target Mark I Auto

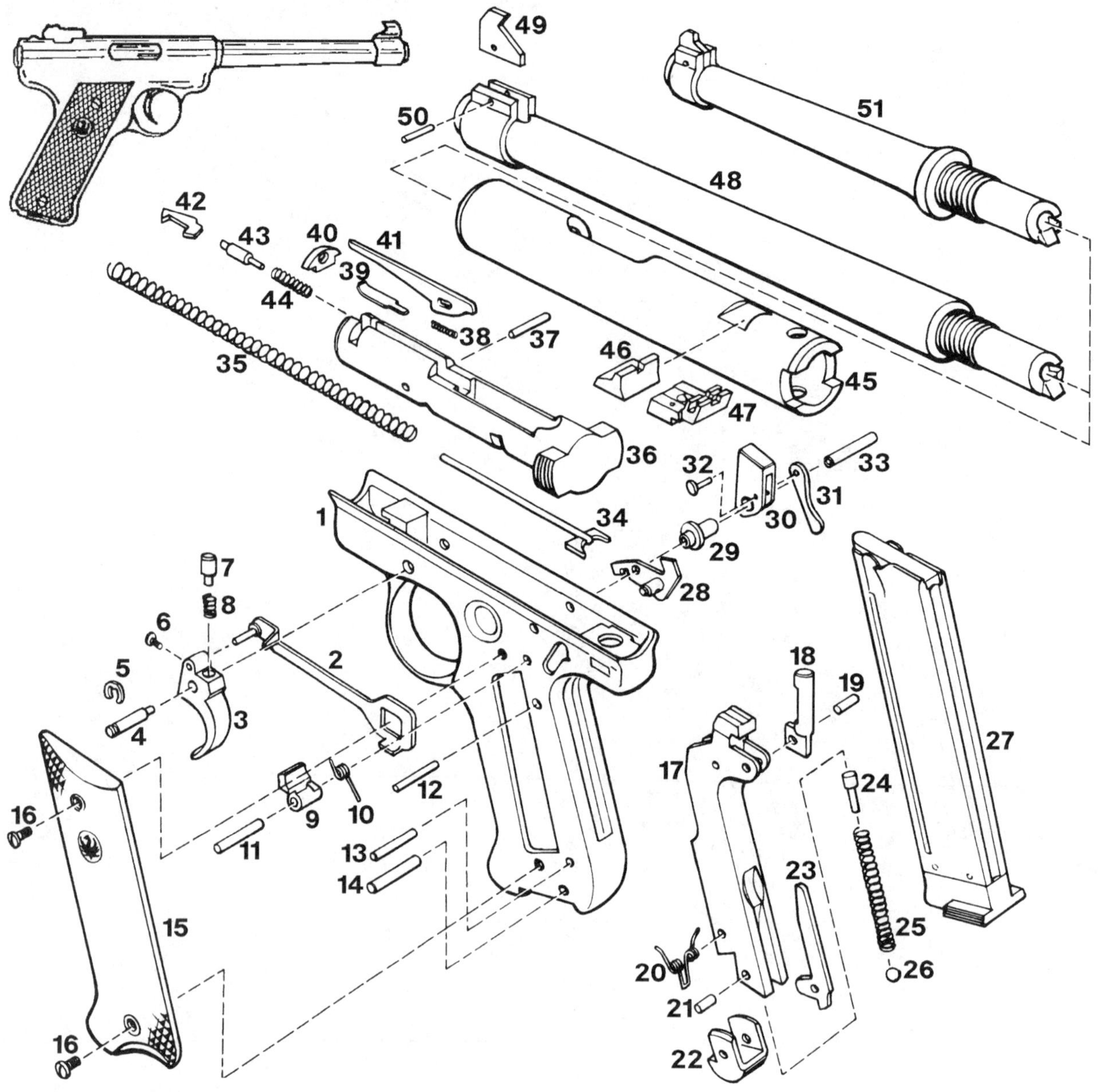

1	Frame	18	Bolt Stop	35	Recoil Spring
2	Disconnector	19	Bolt Stop Pivot Pin	36	Bolt
3	Trigger	20	Magazine Catch Spring	37	Firing Pin Stop
4	Trigger Pin	21	Housing Latch Pivot Pin	38	Rebound Spring
5	Trigger Pin Lock Washer	22	Magazine Catch	39	Rebound Spring Support
6	Trigger Stop Screw (Mk. I)	23	Housing Latch	40	Recoil Spring Support
7	Trigger Spring Plunger	24	Mainspring Plunger	41	Firing Pin
8	Trigger Spring	25	Mainspring	42	Extractor
9	Sear	26	Detent Ball	43	Extractor Plunger
10	Sear Spring	27	Magazine Assembly	44	Extractor Spring
11	Sear Pivot Pin	28	Safety Catch	45	Receiver
12	Sear Spring Stop Pin	29	Hammer Bushing	46	Rear Sight (Standard)
13	Magazine Catch Stop Pin	30	Hammer	47	Micro Rear Sight (Mk. I)
14	Magazine Catch Pivot Pin	31	Hammer Strut	48	Barrel (Mk. I)
15	Grip	32	Hammer Strut Pin	49	Front Sight Blade (Mk. I)
16	Grip Screws	33	Hammer Pivot Pin	50	Front Sight Pin (Mk. I)
17	Mainspring Housing	34	Recoil Spring Guide	51	Barrel Assembly (Standard)

Super Redhawk

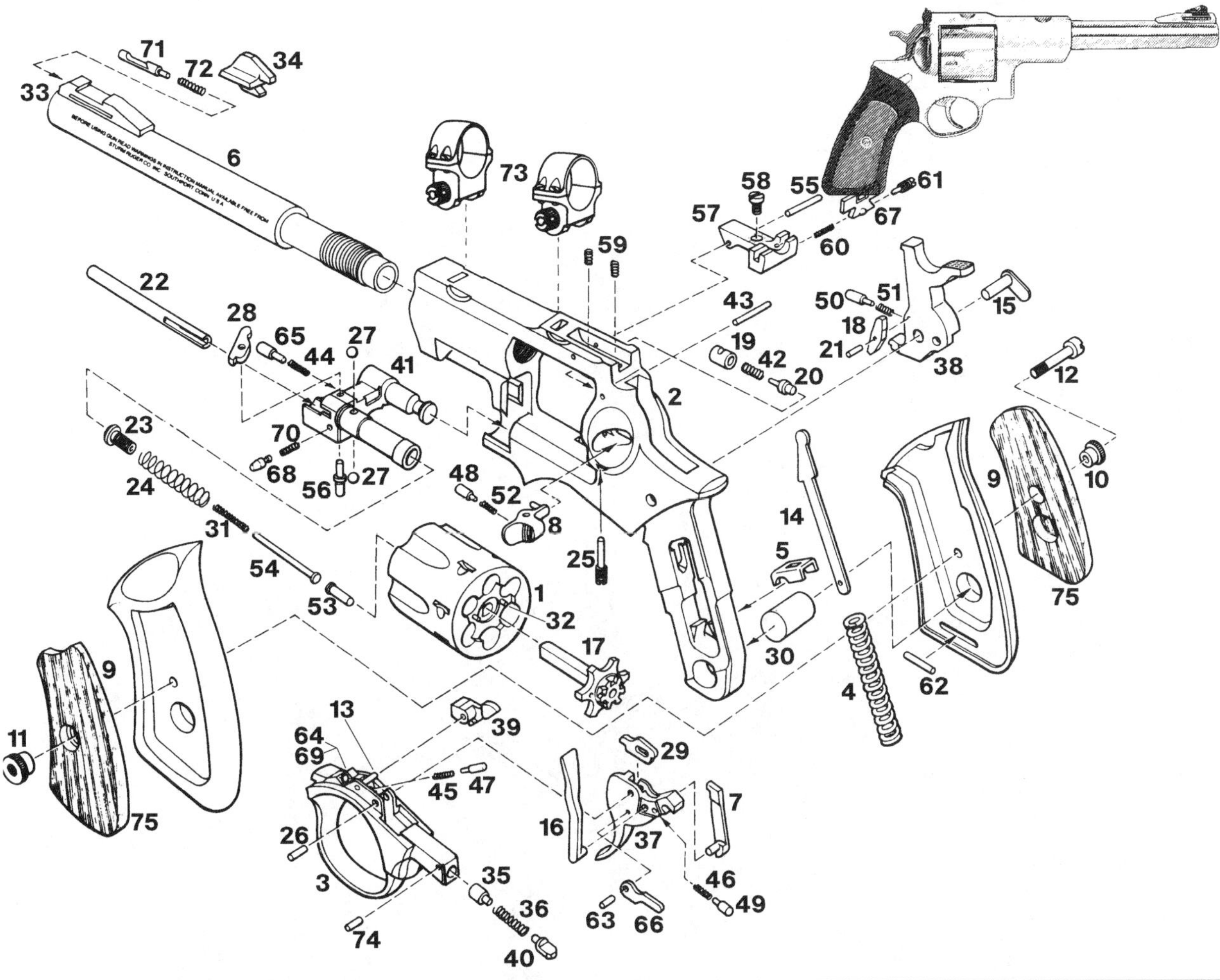

1	Cylinder	27	Cylinder Retaining Balls	53	Center Pin Lock
2	Frame	28	Front Latch	54	Center Pin Rod
3	Trigger Guard	29	Trigger Plunger	55	Rear Sight Cross Pin
4	Mainspring	30	Grip Panel Locator	56	Front Latch Pivot Pin
5	Mainspring Seat	31	Center Pin Spring	57	Rear Sight Base
6	Barrel	32	Ejector Alignment Pins	58	Rear Sight Elevation Screw
7	Pawl	33	Front Sight Base	59	Rear Sight Elevation Springs
8	Crane Latch	34	Front Sight	60	Rear Sight Windage Spring
9	Grip Panels/Panel Insert	35	Trigger Link Plunger	61	Rear Sight Windage Adjustment Screw
10	Grip Ferrule, Right	36	Trigger Guard Latch Spring	62	Disassembly Pin
11	Grip Ferrule, Left	37	Trigger	63	Trigger Link Pin
12	Grip Panel Screw	38	Hammer	64	Crane Pivot Lock Plunger
13	Cylinder Latch Pivot	39	Cylinder Latch	65	Front Latch Spring Plunger
14	Hammer Strut	40	Trigger Guard Latch	66	Trigger Link
15	Hammer Pivot Assembly	41	Crane and Crane Pivot Assembly	67	Rear Sight Blade
16	Transfer Bar	42	Firing Pin Rebound Spring	68	Front Latch Pivot Lock
17	Ejector	43	Recoil Plate Cross Pin	69	Crane Pivot Lock Spring
18	Hammer Dog	44	Cylinder Latch Spring	70	Front Latch Pivot Lock Spring
19	Recoil Plate	45	Front Latch Spring	71	Front Sight Plunger
20	Firing Pin	46	Pawl Plunger Spring	72	Front Sight Plunger Spring
21	Hammer Dog Pivot Pin	47	Cylinder Latch Plunger	73	Scope Rings
22	Ejector Rod	48	Crane Latch Plunger	74	Trigger Guard Latch Pin
23	Ejector Retainer	49	Pawl Plunger	75	Grips
24	Ejector Spring	50	Hammer Dog Plunger		
25	Crane Latch Pivot	51	Hammer Dog Spring		
26	Trigger Pivot Pin	52	Crane Latch Button Spring		

Tokarev Auto

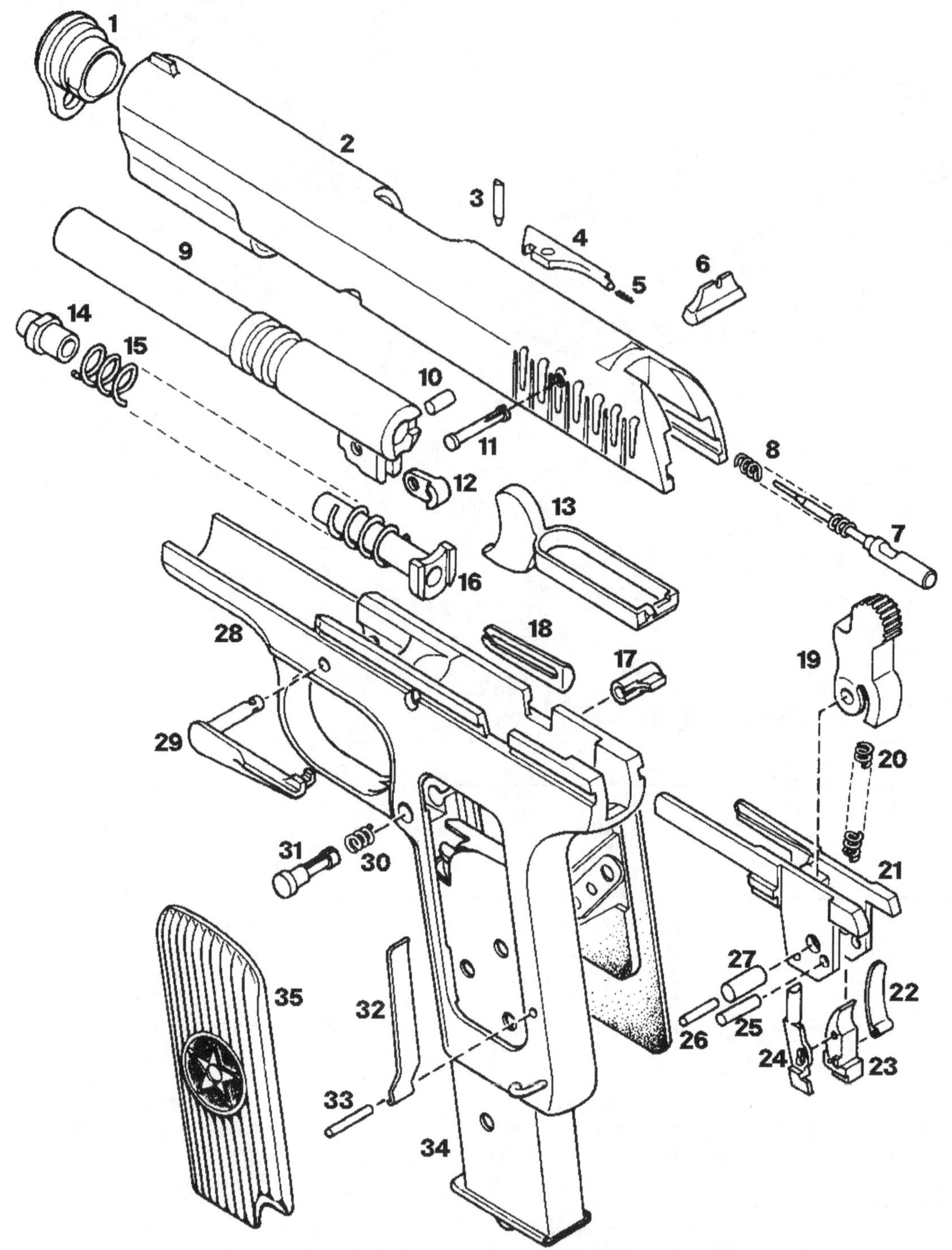

1	Barrel Bushing	13	Trigger	25	Spring Retainer Pin
2	Slide	14	Recoil Spring Retainer	26	Sear Pin
3	Extractor Pin	15	Recoil Spring	27	Hammer Pin
4	Extractor	16	Recoil Spring Guide	28	Frame
5	Extractor Spring	17	Magazine Catch	29	Slide Latch
6	Rear Sight	18	Slide Stop Retainer Clip	30	Magazine Catch Spring
7	Firing Pin	19	Hammer	31	Magazine Catch Spring Guide
8	Firing Pin Spring	20	Hammer Spring	32	Trigger Return Spring
9	Barrel	21	Hammer Mechanism Housing	33	Spring Retainer Pin
10	Barrel Link Pin	22	Sear Spring	34	Magazine Assembly
11	Firing Pin Retainer Pin	23	Sear	35	Grip Panel
12	Barrel Link	24	Disconnector		

Enforcer and Matchmaster Auto

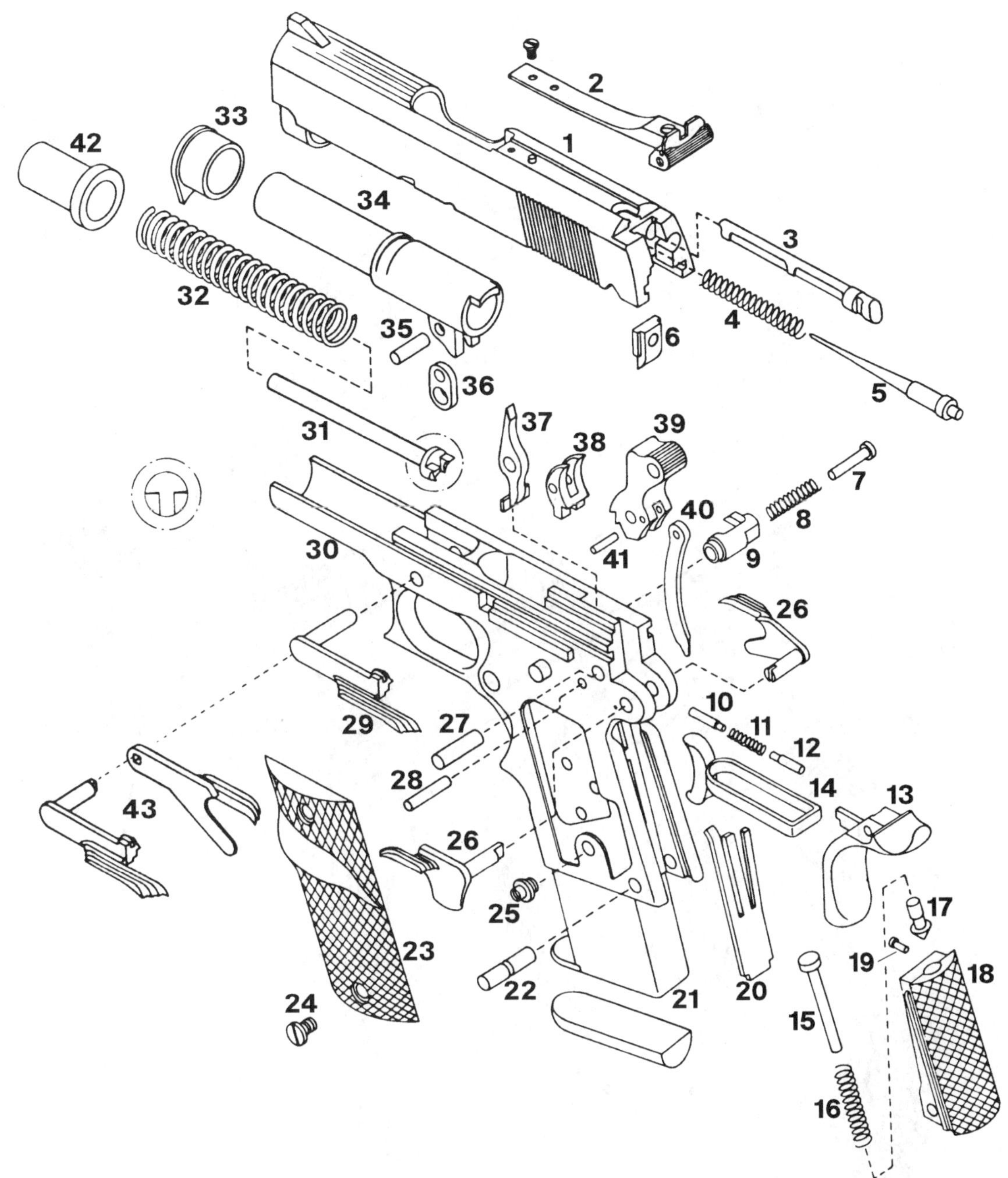

1	Slide	16	Mainspring	31	Recoil Spring Guide
2	Rear Sight and Screw	17	Mainspring Retainer	32	Recoil Spring
3	Extractor	18	Mainspring Housing	33	Barrel Bushing
4	Firing Pin Spring	19	Mainspring Cap Pin	34	Barrel
5	Firing Pin	20	Sear Spring	35	Barrel Link Pin
6	Firing Pin Stop	21	Magazine Assembly	36	Barrel Link
7	Magazine Catch Lock	22	Mainspring Housing Retention Pin	37	Disconnector
8	Magazine Catch Spring	23	Grips	38	Sear
9	Magazine Catch	24	Grip Screw	39	Hammer
10	Slide Stop Plunger	25	Grip Screw Escutcheon	40	Hammer Strut
11	Plunger Spring	26	Safety	41	Hammer Strut Pin
12	Safety Plunger	27	Hammer Pin	42	Recoil Spring Plug
13	Beaver Tail	28	Sear Pin	43	Ambidextrous Slide Stop
14	Trigger	29	Slide Stop		
15	Mainspring Cap	30	Frame		

Model 1913 Auto

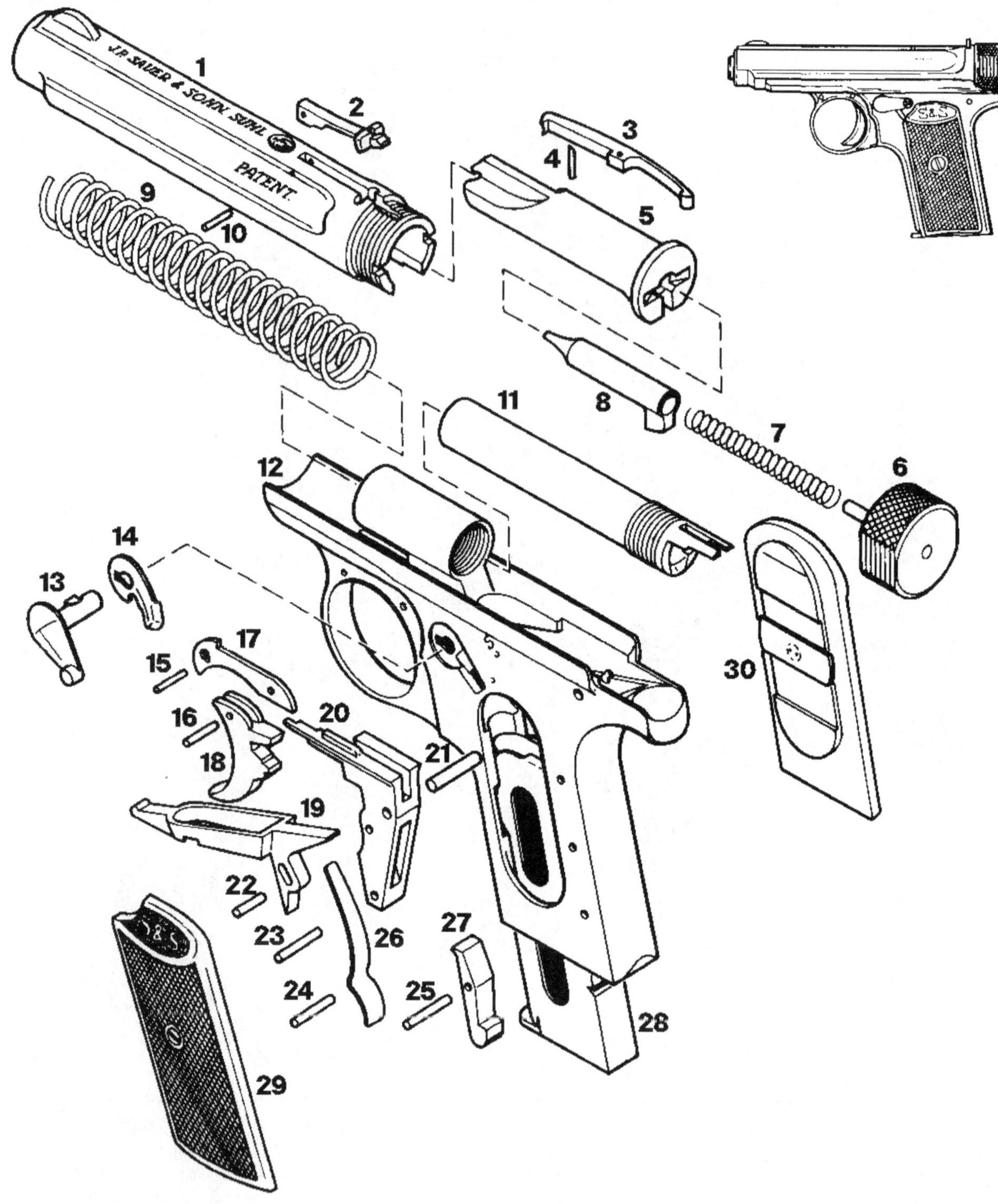

1	Slide	**11**	Barrel	**21**	Upper Sub-Frame Pin
2	Rear Sight and Latch	**12**	Frame	**22**	Trigger Bar Pin
3	Extractor	**13**	Safety Catch	**23**	Lower Sub-Frame Pin
4	Extractor Pin	**14**	Safety Catch Spring	**24**	Magazine Catch Spring Pin
5	Breechbolt	**15**	Slide Lock Pin	**25**	Magazine Catch Pin
6	Slide End Cap	**16**	Trigger Pin	**26**	Sear/Magazine Catch Spring
7	Firing Pin Spring	**17**	Slide Lock	**27**	Magazine Catch
8	Firing Pin	**18**	Trigger	**28**	Magazine Assembly
9	Recoil Spring	**19**	Trigger Bar and Sear	**29**	Grip Panel, Left
10	Rear Sight Pin	**20**	Mechanism Housing	**30**	Grip Panel, Right

Model 38H

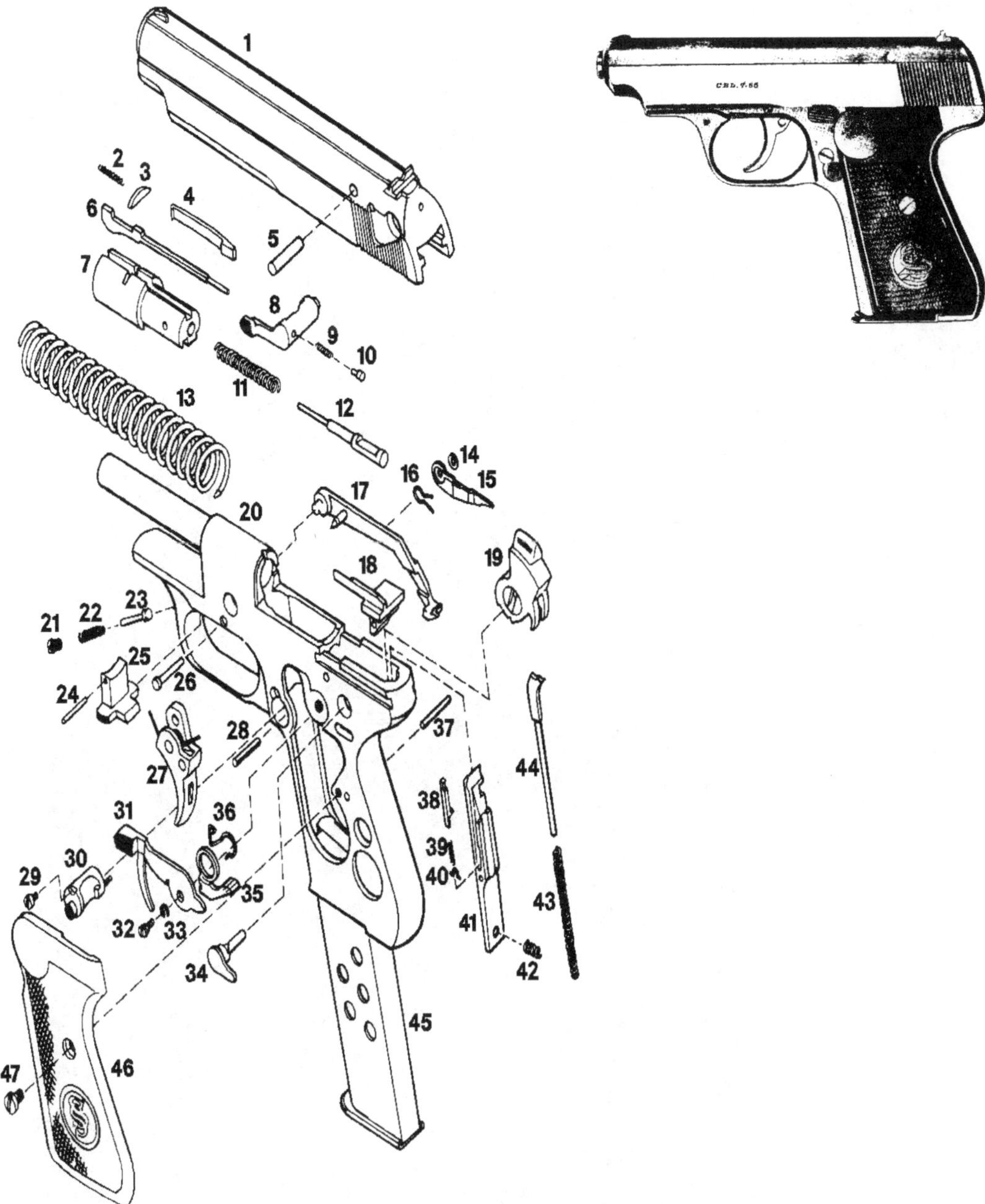

1	Slide	**17**	Trigger Bar	**33**	Cocking Lever Hinge Screw Retainer Clip
2	Cartridge Indicator Spring	**18**	Ejector	**34**	Hammer Extension
3	Cartridge Indicator Spring Retainer	**19**	Hammer	**35**	Hammer Lever
4	Extractor	**20**	Barrel and Frame Assembly	**36**	Cocking Lever Spring
5	Breechblock Retainer Pin	**21**	Takedown Detent Spring Retainer	**37**	Sear Hinge Pin
6	Cartridge Indicator	**22**	Takedown Detent Spring	**38**	Sear Disconnector
7	Breechblock	**23**	Takedown Detent	**39**	Disconnector Spring
8	Safety Catch	**24**	Takedown Latch Pin	**40**	Disconnector Spring Retainer
9	Safety Detent Spring	**25**	Takedown Latch	**41**	Sear
10	Safety Detent	**26**	Trigger Pin	**42**	Sear Spring
11	Firing Pin Spring	**27**	Trigger and Trigger Spring	**43**	Hammer Spring
12	Firing Pin	**28**	Ejector Pin	**44**	Hammer Strut
13	Recoil Spring	**29**	Magazine Catch Retaining Screw	**45**	Magazine Assembly
14	Magazine Safety Retainer	**30**	Magazine Catch and Spring	**46**	Grip Panel
15	Magazine Safety Bar	**31**	Cocking Lever	**47**	Grip Screws
16	Magazine Safety Spring	**32**	Cocking Lever Hinge Screw		

Model 1930 Auto

Courtesy of Blacksmith Corporation

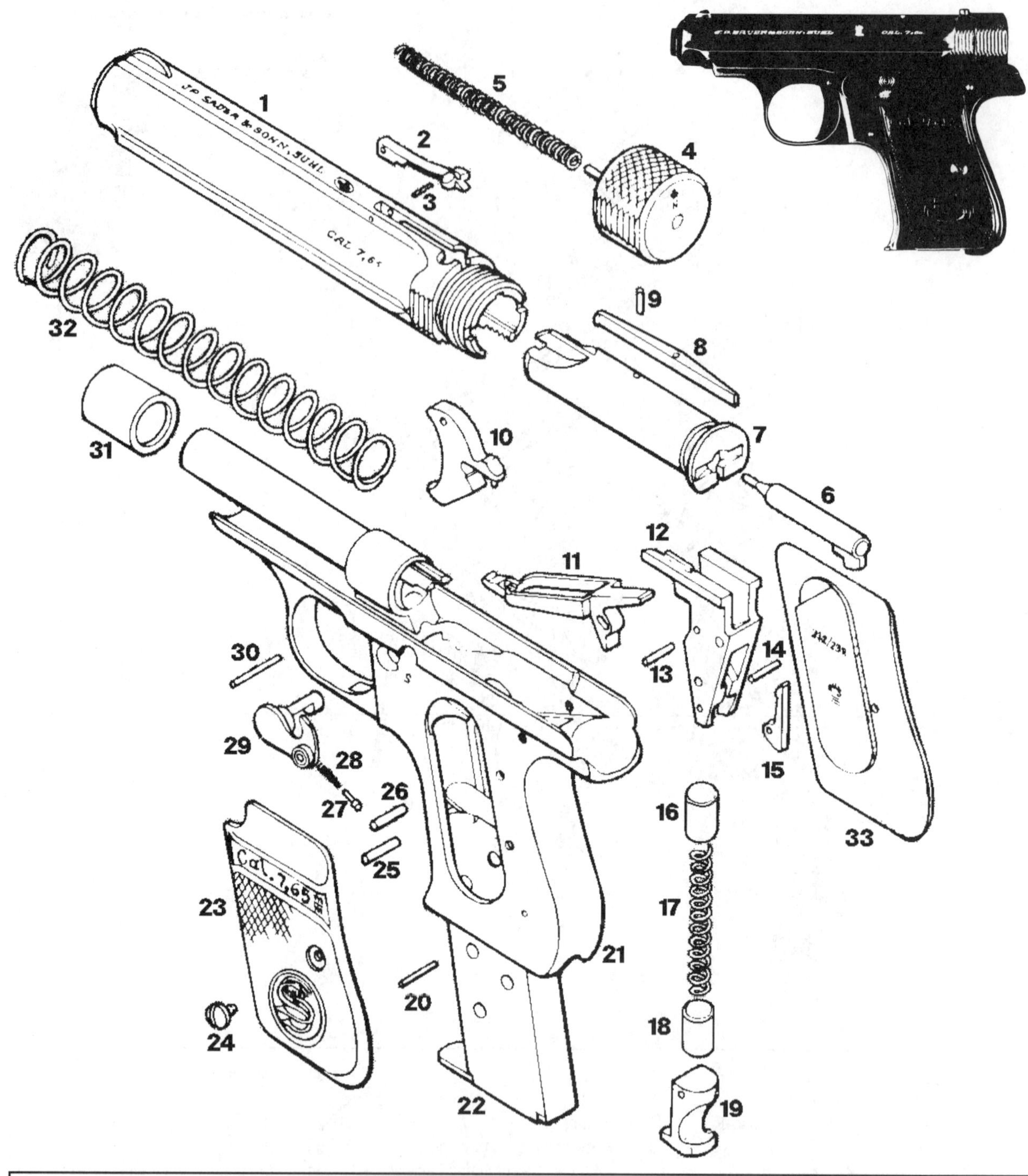

1	Slide	12	Mechanism Housing	23	Left Grip Panel
2	Rear Sight and Latch	13	Sear Pin	24	Grip Screws
3	Rear Sight and Latch Pin	14	Sear Cam Pin	25	Lower Mechanism Housing Pin
4	Slide Cap	15	Sear Cam	26	Upper Mechanism Housing Pin
5	Firing Pin Spring	16	Mainspring Follower	27	Safety Catch Detent Pin
6	Firing Pin	17	Mainspring	28	Safety Catch Detent Spring
7	Breechblock	18	Mainspring Cap	29	Safety Catch
8	Extractor	19	Magazine Catch	30	Trigger Pin
9	Extractor Pin	20	Magazine Catch Pin	31	Recoil Spring Guide
10	Trigger	21	Frame	32	Recoil Spring
11	Trigger Bar and Sear	22	Magazine Assembly	33	Right Grip Panel

Model 1910 Auto

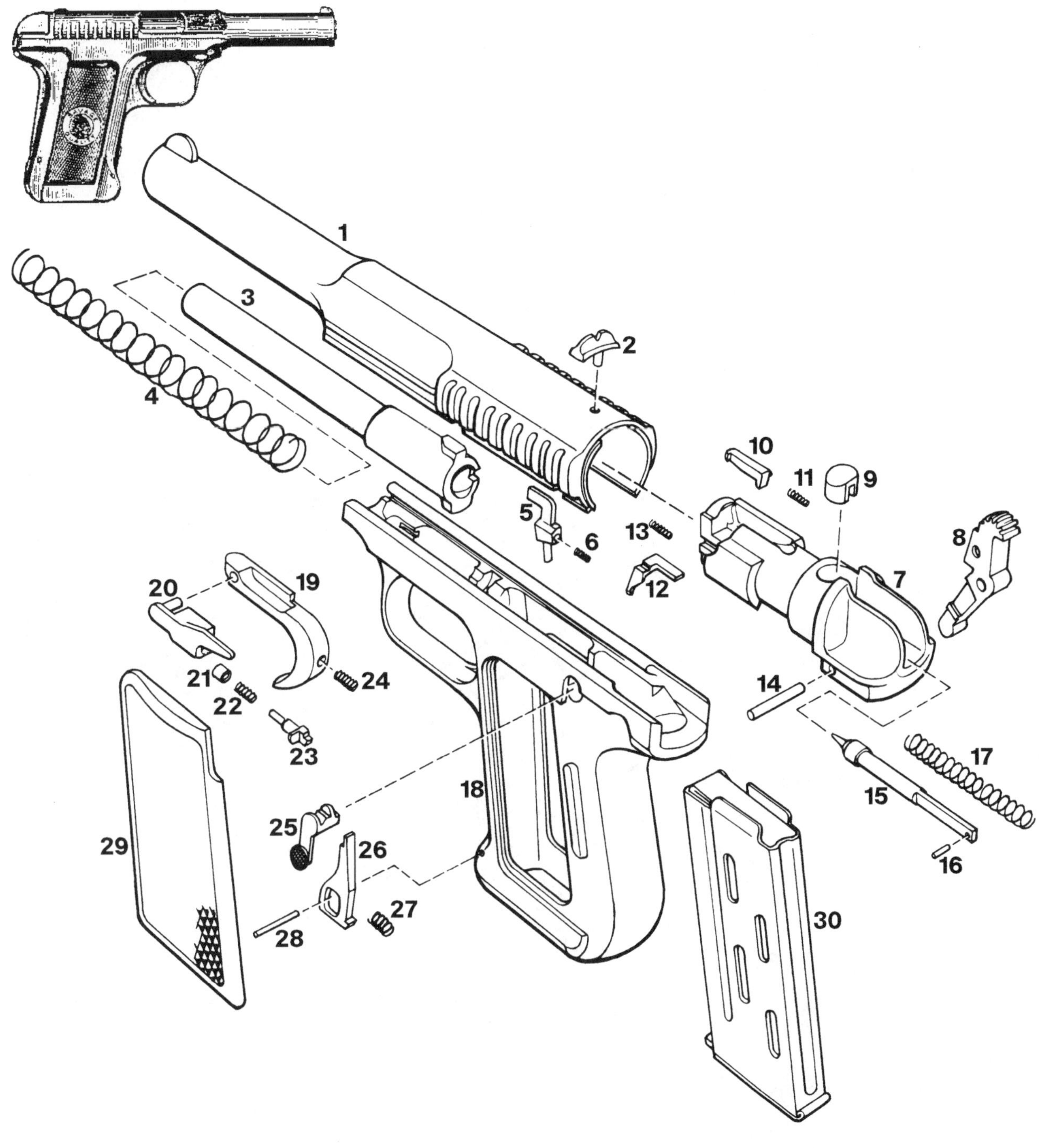

1	Slide	11	Extractor Spring	21	Sear Trip Lifter
2	Rear Sight	12	Sear	22	Sear Trip Spring
3	Barrel	13	Sear Spring	23	Sear Trip Catch
4	Recoil Spring	14	Cocking Lever Hinge Pin	24	Trigger Spring
5	Ejector	15	Firing Pin	25	Safety Catch
6	Safety Catch Spring	16	Firing Pin Hinge Pin	26	Magazine Catch
7	Breech Plug	17	Firing Pin Spring	27	Magazine Catch Spring
8	Cocking Lever Hammer	18	Frame	28	Magazine Catch Pin
9	Firing Pin Retainer	19	Trigger	29	Grip
10	Extractor	20	Sear Trip	30	Magazine Assembly

Model 1917 Auto

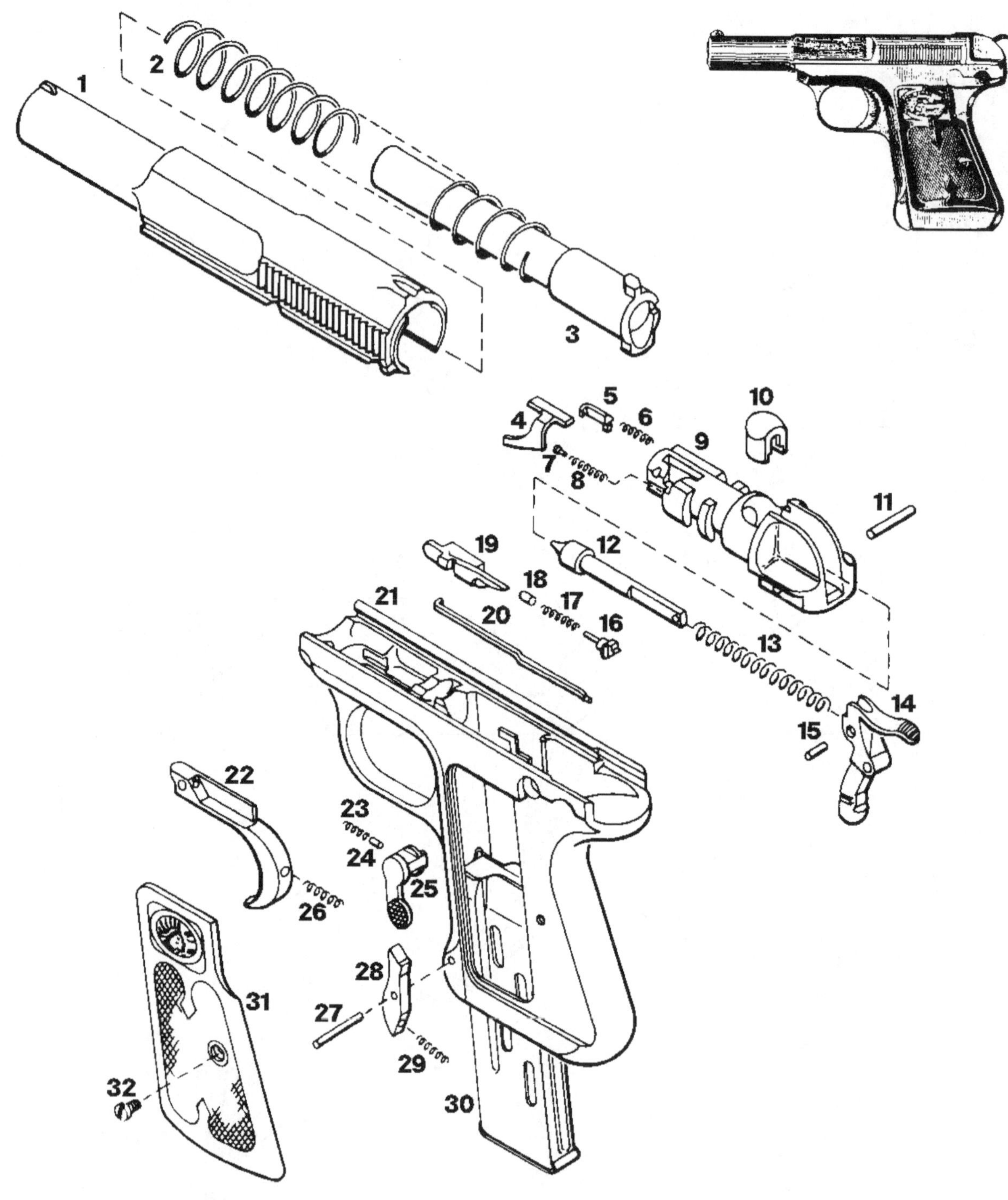

1	Slide	12	Firing Pin	23	Safety Catch Spring
2	Recoil Spring	13	Firing Pin Spring	24	Safety Catch Spring Plunger
3	Barrel	14	Cocking Lever	25	Safety Catch
4	Sear	15	Firing Pin Hinge Pin	26	Trigger Spring
5	Extractor	16	Sear Trip Catch	27	Magazine Catch Pin
6	Extractor Spring	17	Sear Trip Spring	28	Magazine Catch
7	Sear Spring Plunger	18	Sear Trip Lifter	29	Magazine Catch Spring
8	Sear Spring	19	Sear Trip	30	Magazine Assembly
9	Breech Plug	20	Trigger Bar	31	Grip Panel
10	Firing Pin Retainer	21	Frame	32	Grip Screws
11	Cocking Lever Hinge Pin	22	Trigger		

Auto

Courtesy of Blacksmith Corporation

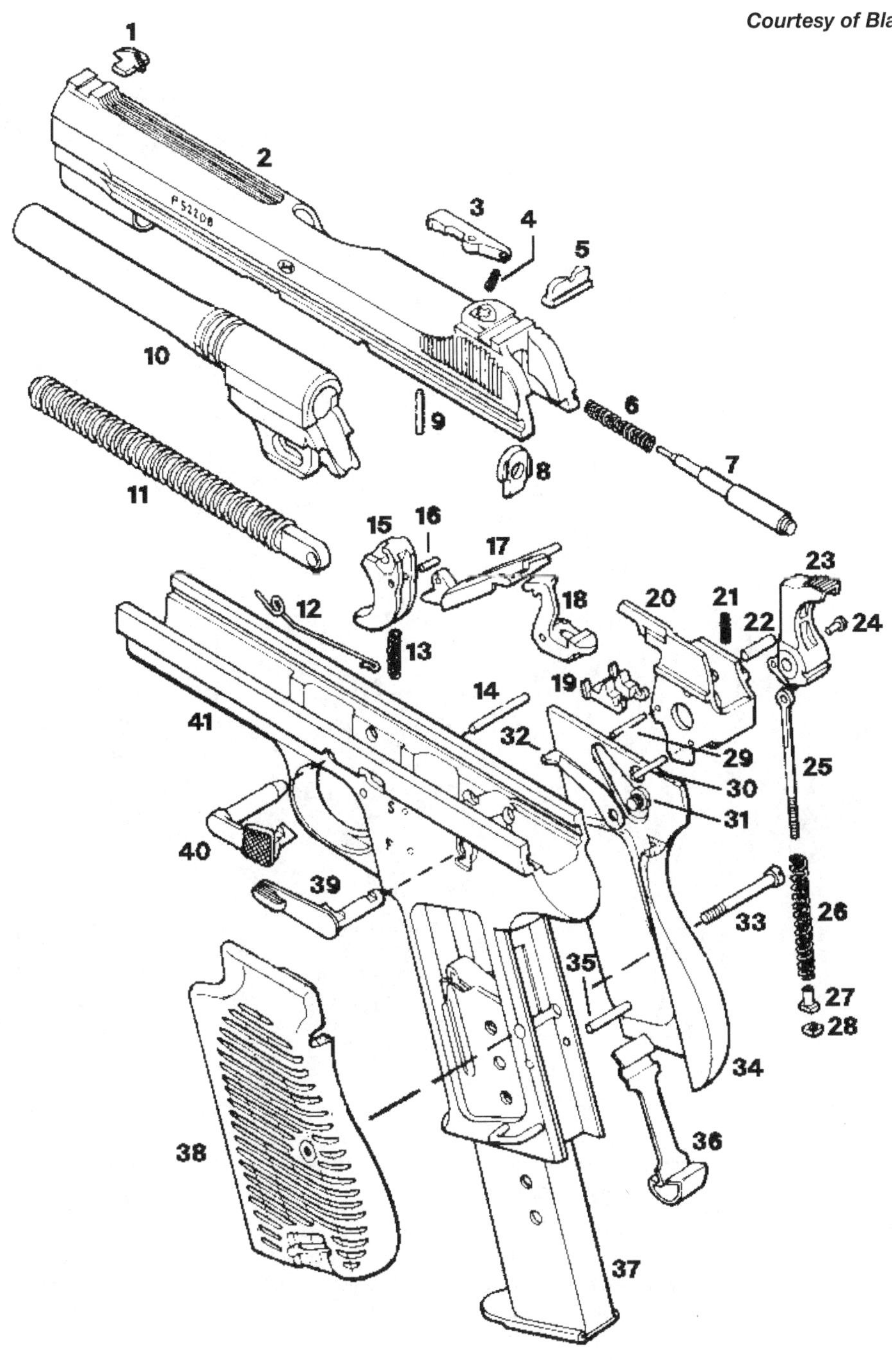

1	Front Sight	**15**	Trigger	**29**	Sear Hinge Pin
2	Slide	**16**	Trigger Bar Pin	**30**	Pressure Plate Stop Pin
3	Extractor	**17**	Trigger Bar	**31**	Magazine Disconnector Screw
4	Extractor Spring	**18**	Sear	**32**	Magazine Disconnector
5	Rear Sight	**19**	Sear Pressure Plate	**33**	Grip Screw
6	Firing Pin Spring	**20**	Sear and Hammer Housing	**34**	Right Grip Panel
7	Firing Pin	**21**	Sear Spring	**35**	Magazine Catch Pin
8	Firing Pin Retainer	**22**	Hammer Hinge Pin	**36**	Magazine Catch
9	Extractor Hinge Pin	**23**	Hammer	**37**	Magazine Assembly
10	Barrel	**24**	Hammer Strut Pin	**38**	Left Grip Panel
11	Recoil Spring Assembly	**25**	Hammer Strut	**39**	Safety Catch
12	Slide Stop Spring	**26**	Hammer Spring	**40**	Slide Stop
13	Trigger Spring	**27**	Hammer Spring Retainer Nut	**41**	Frame
14	Trigger Hinge Pin	**28**	Hammer Spring Retainer Lock Nut		

P220 Auto

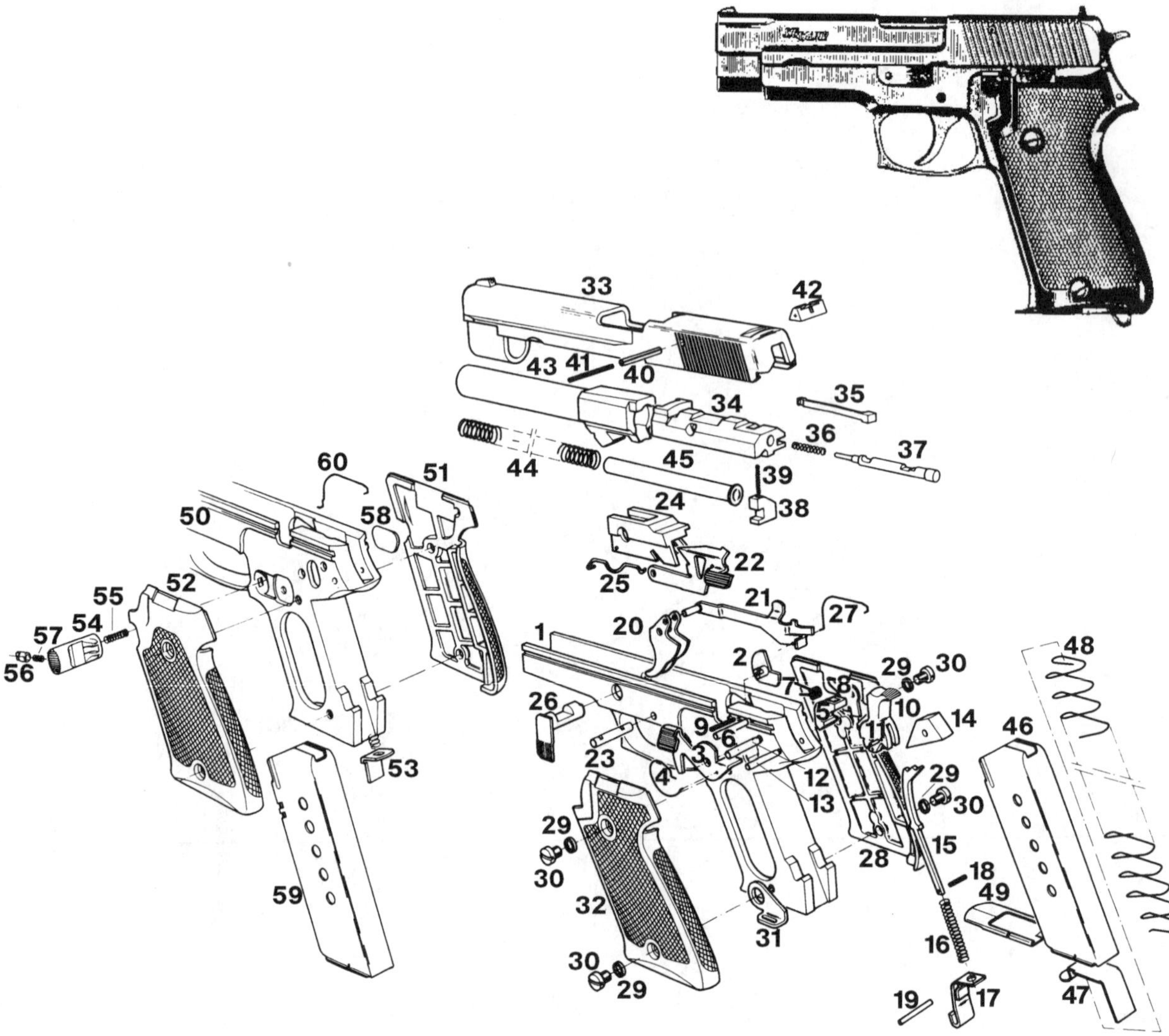

1	Frame
2	Decocking Lever Bearing
3	Decocking Lever
4	Decocking Lever Spring
5	Sear
6	Sear Shaft
7	Sear Spring
8	Safety-Lever
9	Spring Pin
10	Hammer
11	Hammer Strut Pin
12	Hammer Pivot Pin
13	Hammer Stop Pin
14	Hammer Stop
15	Hammer Strut
16	Mainspring
17	Magazine Catch
18	Mainspring Retaining Pin
19	Magazine Catch Pin
20	Trigger
21	Trigger Bar
22	Slide Catch Lever
23	Trigger Pivot
24	Locking Insert
25	Slide Catch Lever Spring
26	Takedown Lever
27	Trigger Bar Spring
28	Right Grip Panel
29	Grip Screw Washers
30	Grip Screws
31	Lanyard Loop
32	Left Grip Panel
33	Slide
34	Breechblock
35	Extractor
36	Firing Pin Spring
37	Firing Pin
38	Safety Lock
39	Safety Lock Spring
40	Outer Breechblock Retaining Pin
41	Inner Breechblock Retaining Pin Lock Pin
42	Rear Sight
43	Barrel
44	Recoil Spring
45	Recoil Spring Guide
46	Magazine Body
47	Magazine Follower
48	Magazine Spring
49	Magazine Floorplate
P220 American Parts Only	
50	Frame
51	Right Grip Panel
52	Left Grip Panel
53	Mainspring Seat
54	Magazine Catch
55	Magazine Catch Spring
56	Magazine Catch Stop
57	Magazine Catch Stop Spring
58	Support Plate
59	Magazine Body
60	Trigger Bar Spring

P225 Auto

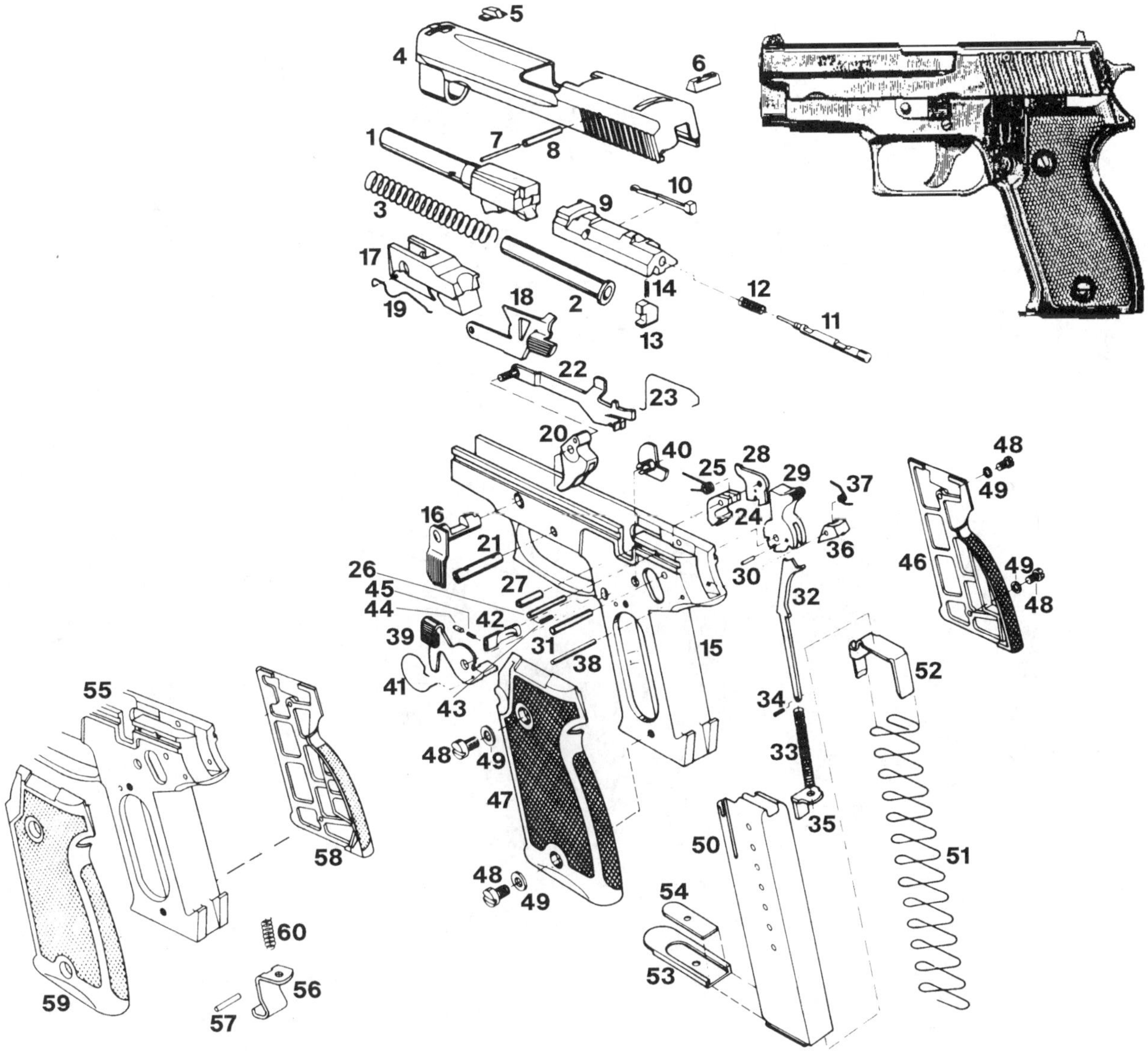

1 Barrel
2 Recoil Spring Guide
3 Recoil Spring
4 Slide
5 Front Sight
6 Rear Sight
7 Breechblock Retaining Pin Lock Pin
8 Breechblock Retaining Pin
9 Breechblock
10 Extractor
11 Firing Pin
12 Firing Pin Spring
13 Safety Lock
14 Safety Lock Spring
15 Frame
16 Takedown Lever
17 Locking Insert
18 Slide Catch Lever
19 Slide Catch Lever Spring
20 Trigger
21 Trigger Pivot
22 Trigger Bar
23 Trigger Bar Spring
24 Sear
25 Sear Spring
26 Sear Shaft
27 Sear Spring Pin
28 Safety-Lever
29 Hammer
30 Hammer Strut Pin
31 Hammer Pivot Pin
32 Hammer Strut
33 Mainspring
34 Mainspring Retaining Pin
35 Mainspring Seat
36 Hammer Stop
37 Reset Spring
38 Hammer Stop Pin
39 Decocking Lever
40 Decocking Lever Bearing
41 Decocking Lever Spring
42 Magazine Catch
43 Magazine Catch Spring
44 Magazine Catch Stop
45 Magazine Stop Spring
46 Right Grip Panel
47 Left Grip Panel
48 Grip Screws
49 Grip Screw Washers
50 Magazine Body
51 Magazine Spring
52 Magazine Follower
53 Magazine Floorplate
54 Magazine Spring Retainer

P225 with Bottom Magazine Catch Parts Only

55 Frame
56 Magazine Catch
57 Magazine Catch Pin
58 Right Grip Panel
59 Left Grip Panel
60 Magazine Catch Spring

P226 Auto

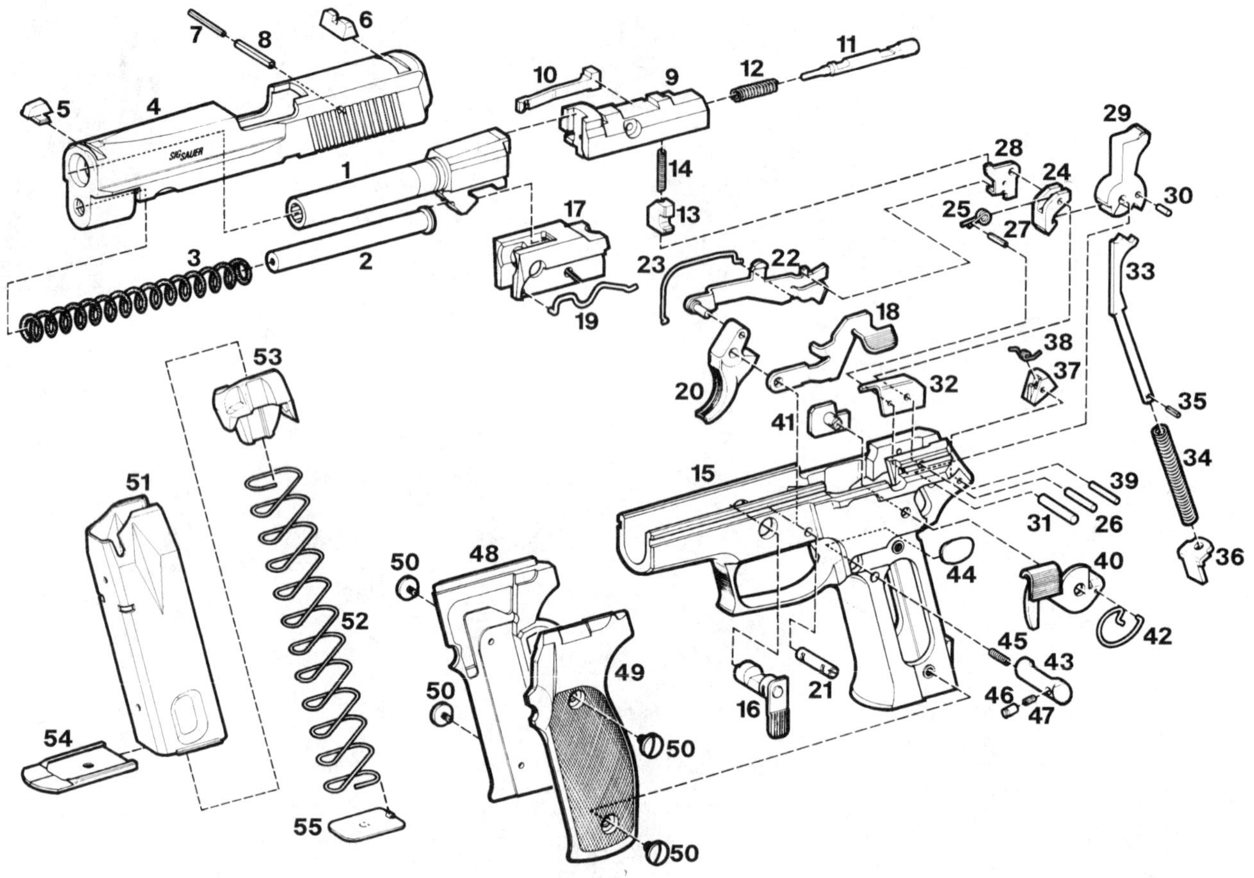

1	Barrel	**18**	Slide Catch Lever	**37**	Hammer Stop
2	Recoil Spring Guide	**19**	Slide Catch Lever Spring	**38**	Reset Spring
3	Recoil Spring	**20**	Trigger	**39**	Hammer Stop Pin
4	Slide	**21**	Trigger Pivot	**40**	Decocking Lever
5	Front Sight	**22**	Trigger Bar	**41**	Decocking Lever Bearing
6	Rear Sight	**23**	Trigger Bar Spring	**42**	Decocking Lever Spring
7	Breechblock Retaining Pin Lock Pin	**24**	Sear	**43**	Magazine Catch
8	Breechblock Retaining Pin	**25**	Sear Spring	**44**	Support Plate
9	Breechblock	**26**	Sear Shaft	**45**	Magazine Catch Spring
10	Extractor	**27**	Sear Spring Pin	**46**	Magazine Catch Stop
11	Firing Pin	**28**	Safety-Lever	**47**	Magazine Catch Stop Spring
12	Firing Pin Spring	**29**	Hammer	**48**	Right Grip Panel
13	Safety Lock	**30**	Hammer Strut Pin	**49**	Left Grip Panel
14	Safety Lock Spring	**31**	Hammer Pivot Pin	**50**	Grip Screws
15	Frame	**32**	Ejector	**51**	Magazine Body
16	Takedown Lever	**33**	Hammer Strut	**52**	Magazine Spring
17	Locking Insert	**34**	Mainspring	**53**	Magazine Follower
		35	Mainspring Retaining Pin	**54**	Magazine Floorplate
		36	Mainspring Seat	**55**	Magazine Spring Retainer

P228 Auto

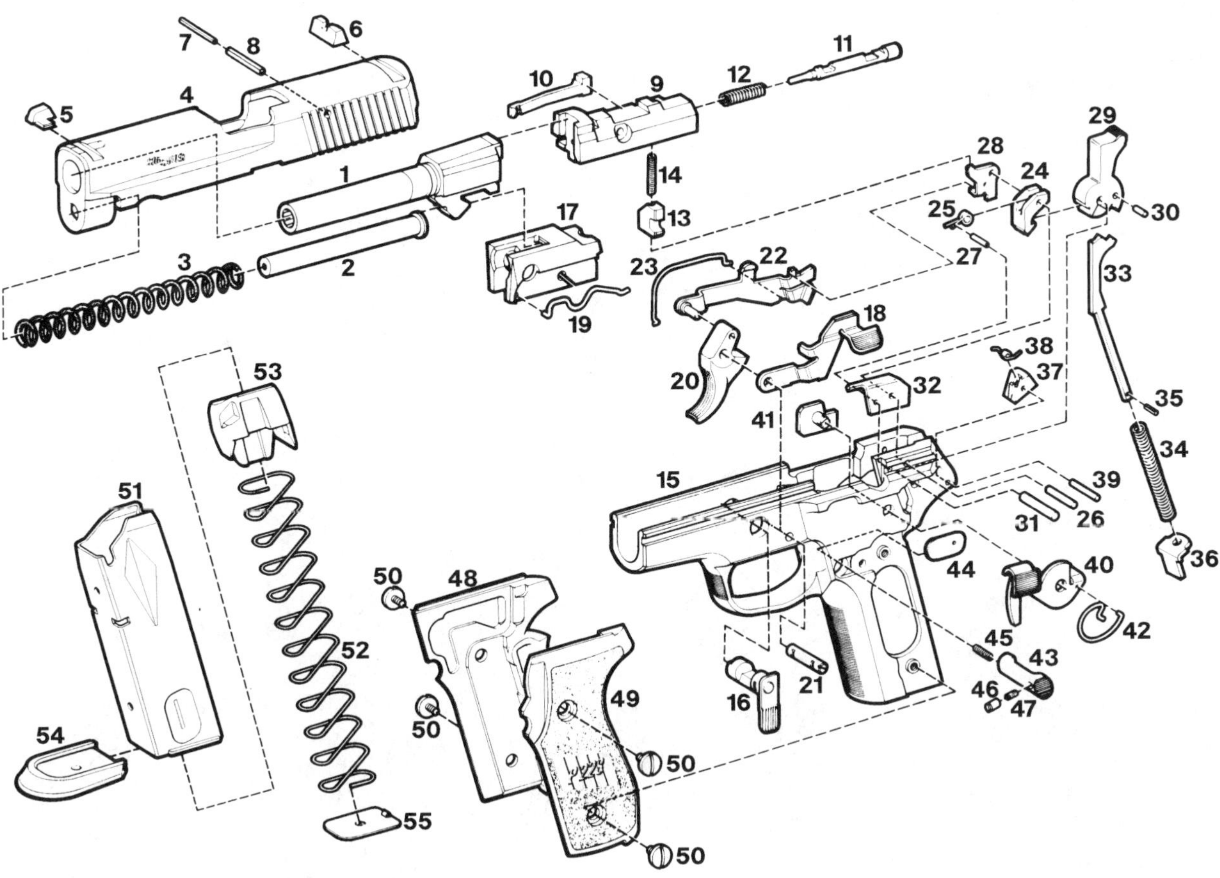

1	Barrel	**19**	Slide Catch Lever Spring	**38**	Reset Spring
2	Recoil Spring Guide	**20**	Trigger	**39**	Hammer Stop Pin
3	Recoil Spring	**21**	Trigger Pivot	**40**	Decocking Lever
4	Slide	**22**	Trigger Bar	**41**	Decocking Lever Bearing
5	Front Sight	**23**	Trigger Bar Spring	**42**	Decocking Lever Spring
6	Rear Sight	**24**	Sear	**43**	Magazine Catch
7	Breechblock Retaining Pin Lock Pin	**25**	Sear Spring	**44**	Support Plate
		26	Sear Shaft	**45**	Magazine Catch Spring
8	Breechblock Retaining Pin	**27**	Sear Spring Pin	**46**	Magazine Catch Stop
9	Breechblock	**28**	Safety-Lever	**47**	Magazine Catch Stop Spring
10	Extractor	**29**	Hammer	**48**	Right Grip Panel
11	Firing Pin	**30**	Hammer Strut Pin	**49**	Left Grip Panel
12	Firing Pin Spring	**31**	Hammer Pivot Pin	**50**	Grip Screws
13	Safety Lock	**32**	Ejector	**51**	Magazine Body
14	Safety Lock Spring	**33**	Hammer Strut	**52**	Magazine Spring
15	Frame	**34**	Mainspring	**53**	Magazine Follower
16	Takedown Lever	**35**	Mainspring Retaining Pin	**54**	Magazine Floorplate
17	Locking Insert	**36**	Mainspring Seat	**55**	Magazine Spring Retainer
18	Slide Catch Lever	**37**	Hammer Stop		

P230 Auto

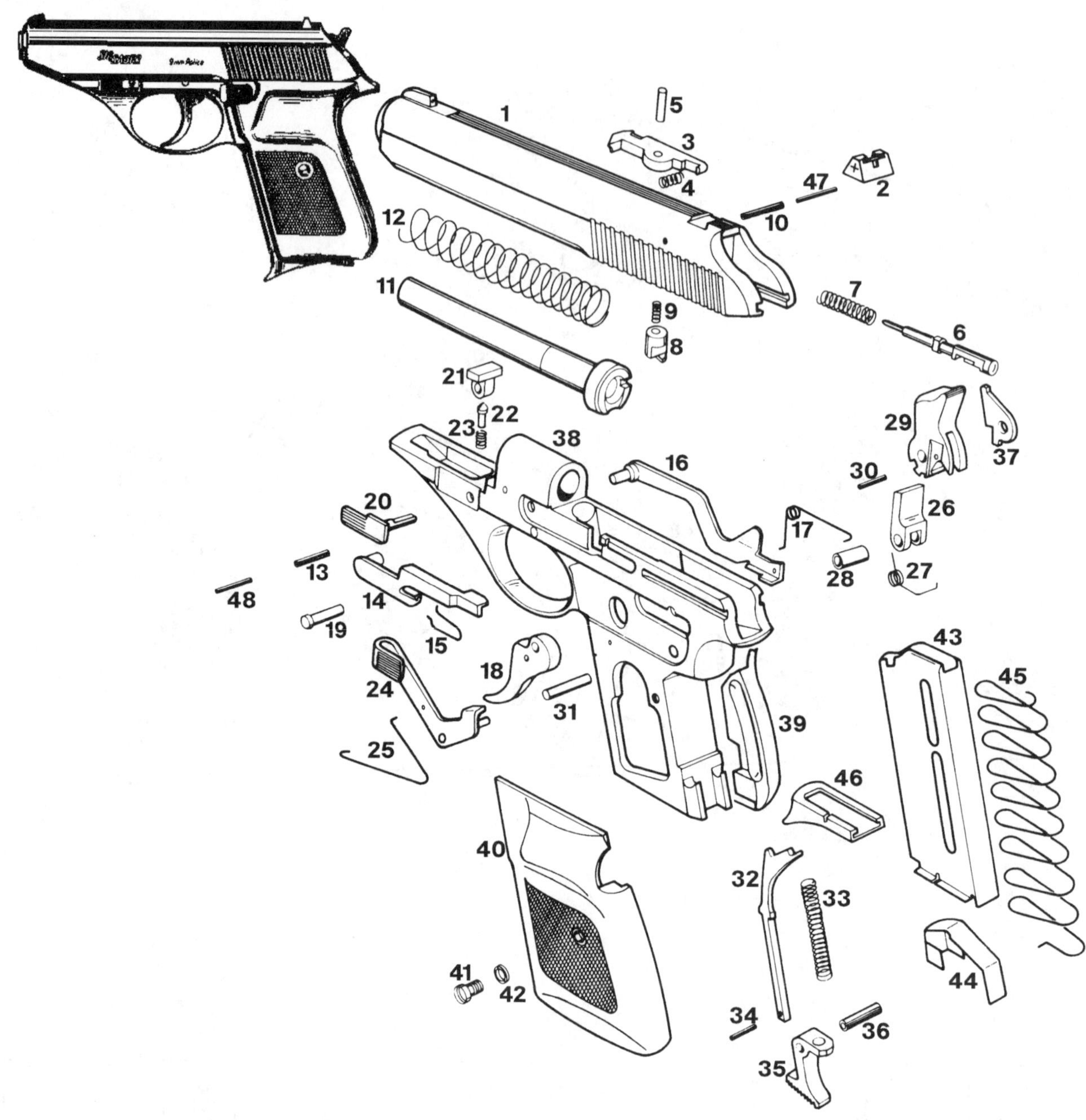

1	Slide	17	Trigger Bar Spring	33	Mainspring
2	Rear Sight	18	Trigger	34	Mainspring Retaining Pin
3	Extractor	19	Trigger Pivot	35	Magazine Catch
4	Extractor Spring	20	Takedown Latch Lever	36	Magazine Catch Pin
5	Extractor Pin	21	Takedown Latch	37	Safety-Lever
6	Firing Pin	22	Takedown Latch Plunger	38	Frame
7	Firing Pin Spring	23	Takedown Latch Spring	39	Right Grip Panel
8	Safety Lock	24	Decocking Lever	40	Left Grip Panel
9	Safety Lock Spring	25	Decocking Lever Spring	41	Grip Screws
10	Firing Pin Retaining Pin	26	Sear	42	Grip Screw Washers
11	Barrel	27	Sear Spring	43	Magazine Body
12	Recoil Spring	28	Sear Shaft	44	Magazine Follower
13	Barrel Retaining Pin	29	Hammer	45	Magazine Spring
14	Slide Catch Lever	30	Hammer Strut Pin	46	Magazine Floorplate
15	Slide Catch Spring	31	Hammer Pivot Pin	47	Firing Pin Retaining Pin Lock Pin
16	Trigger Bar	32	Hammer Strut	48	Barrel Retaining Pin Lock Pin

22 Model 1 (Second Issue) Revolver

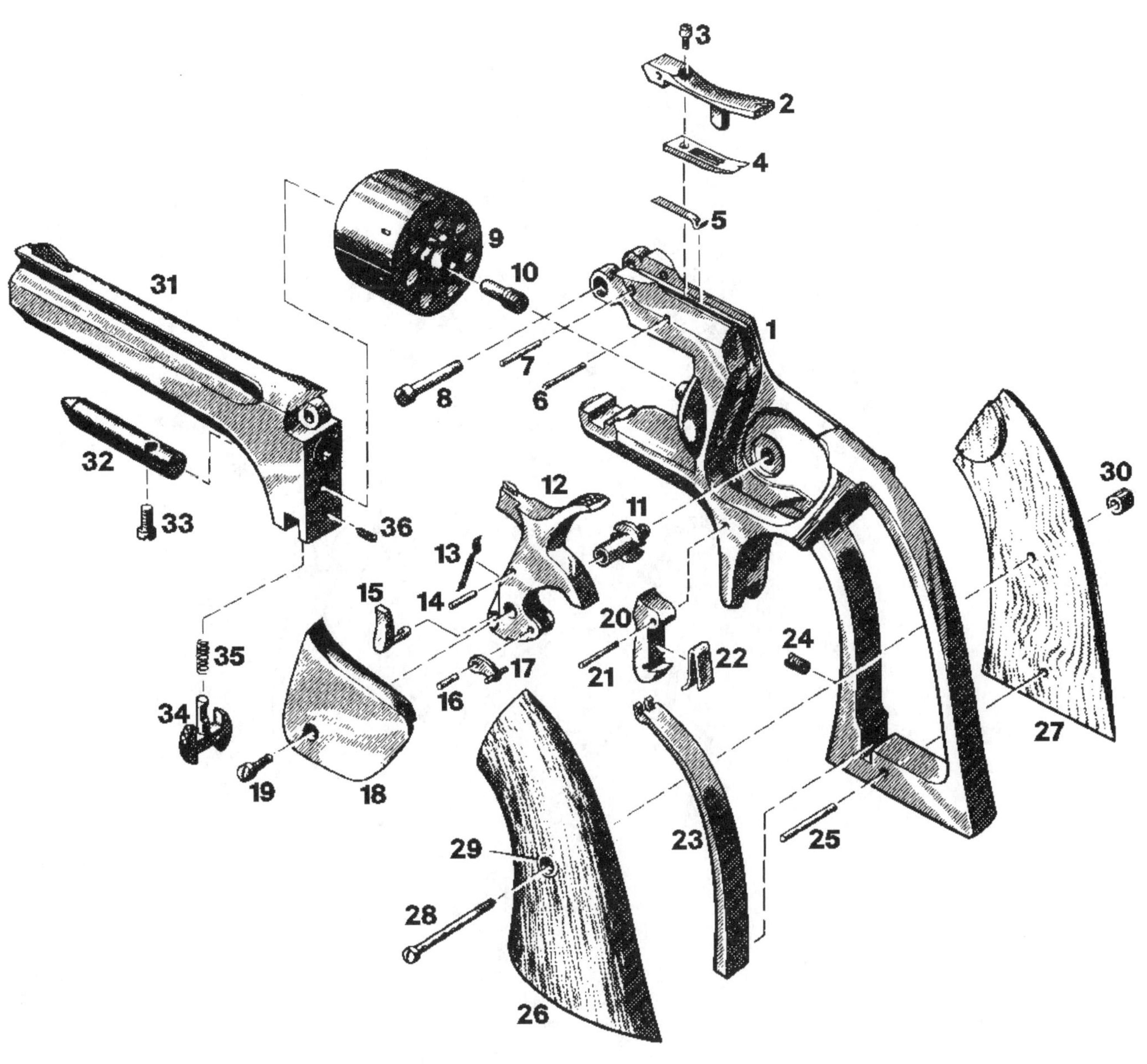

1	Frame	**13**	Hand Spring	**25**	Stock Locator Pin
2	Cylinder Stop	**14**	Hand Spring Pin	**26**	Left Grip
3	Cylinder Stop Screw	**15**	Hand	**27**	Right Grip
4	Cylinder Stop Striker	**16**	Stirrup Pin	**28**	Grip Screw
5	Cylinder Stop Spring	**17**	Stirrup	**29**	Grip Escutcheon
6	Cylinder Stop Spring Pin	**18**	Sideplate	**30**	Grip Escutcheon Nut
7	Cylinder Stop Pin	**19**	Sideplate Screw	**31**	Barrel
8	Barrel Pivot Screw	**20**	Trigger	**32**	Ejector Pin
9	Cylinder	**21**	Trigger Pin	**33**	Ejector Pin Screw
10	Cylinder Stud	**22**	Trigger Spring	**34**	Barrel Latch
11	Hammer Axis	**23**	Mainspring	**35**	Barrel Latch Spring
12	Hammer	**24**	Mainspring Strain Screw	**36**	Barrel Latch Screw

38 Safety Hammerless/ New Depature

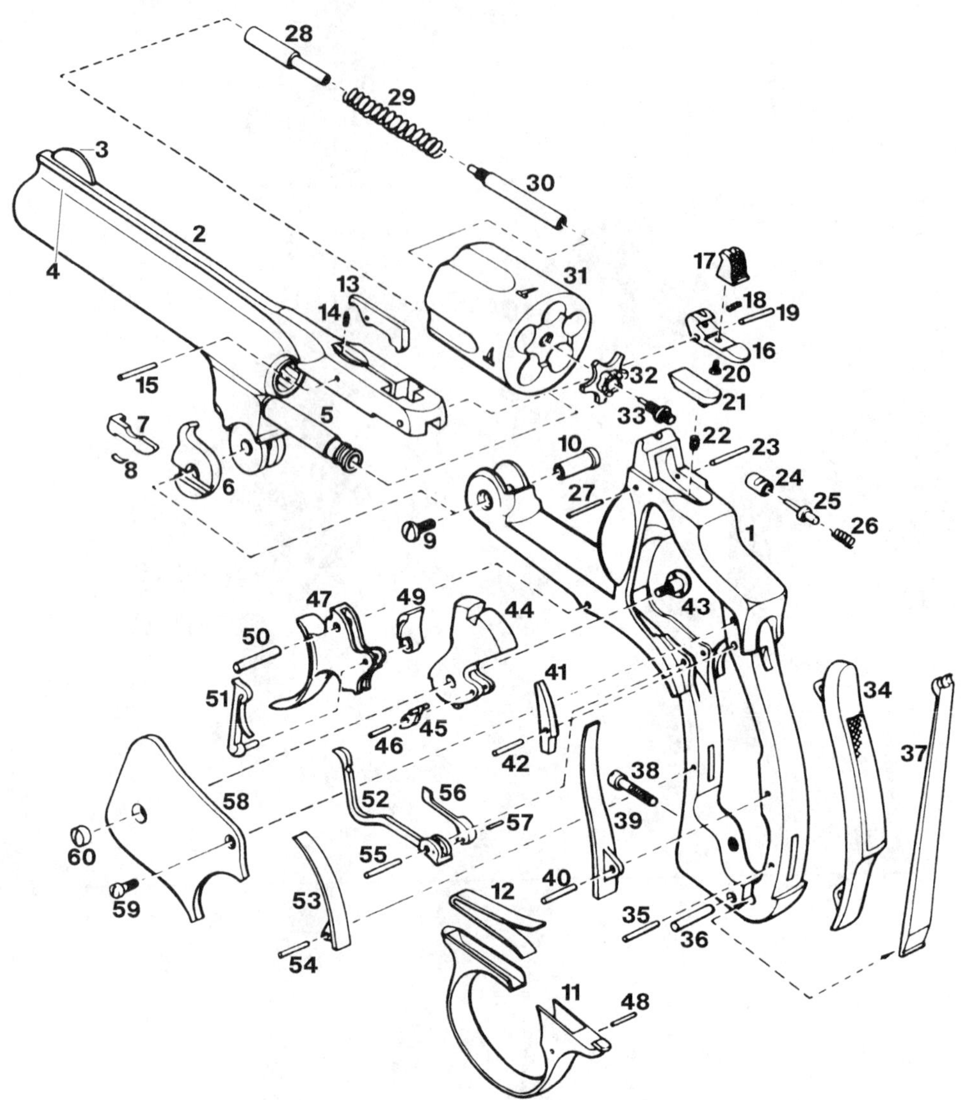

1	Frame	**23**	Barrel Catch Plate Pin	**45**	Stirrup
2	Barrel	**24**	Firing Pin Bushing	**46**	Stirrup Pin
3	Front Sight	**25**	Firing Pin	**47**	Trigger
4	Front Sight Pin	**26**	Firing Pin Spring	**48**	Trigger Stop Pin
5	Cylinder Base Pin	**27**	Firing Pin Bushing Retaining Pin	**49**	Sear
6	Extractor Cam	**28**	Extractor Post	**50**	Trigger Pin
7	Extractor Cam Latch	**29**	Extractor Spring	**51**	Hand and Spring
8	Extractor Cam Latch Spring	**30**	Extractor Rod	**52**	Cylinder Stop
9	Barrel Pivot Screw	**31**	Cylinder	**53**	Cylinder Stop Spring
10	Barrel Pivot	**32**	Extractor	**54**	Cylinder Stop Spring Pin
11	Trigger Guard	**33**	Extractor Stud	**55**	Cylinder Stop Pin
12	Trigger Spring	**34**	Safety-Lever	**56**	Split Spring
13	Cylinder Catch	**35**	Safety-Lever Pin	**57**	Split Spring Pin
14	Cylinder Catch Spring	**36**	Stock Pin	**58**	Sideplate
15	Cylinder Catch Pin	**37**	Mainspring	**59**	Slideplate Screw
16	Barrel Catch	**38**	Strain Screw	**60**	Hammer Stud Nut
17	Barrel Catch Thumb-Piece	**39**	Latch Spring	**Parts Not Shown**	
18	Barrel Catch Spring	**40**	Latch Spring Pin		Right Grip
19	Barrel Catch Pin	**41**	Latch		Left Grip
20	Barrel Catch Thumb-Piece Screw	**42**	Latch Pin		Grip Screw
21	Barrel Catch Plate	**43**	Hammer Stud		
22	Barrel Catch Plate Spring	**44**	Hammer		

44 American Revolver

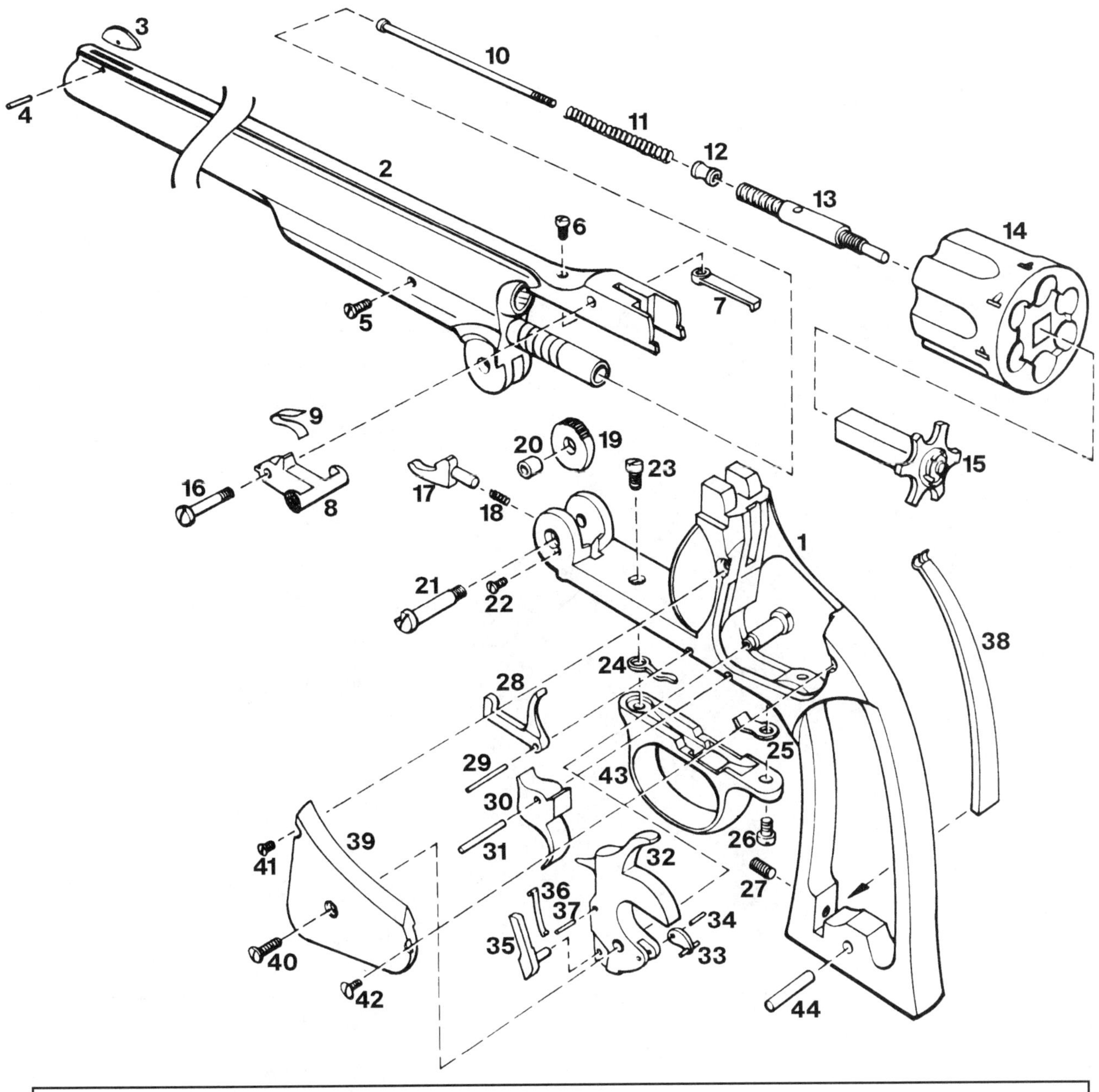

1	Frame	18	Ratchet Spring	35	Hand
2	Barrel	19	Ratchet	36	Hand Spring
3	Front Sight	20	Ratchet Bushing	37	Hand Spring Pin
4	Front Sight Pin	21	Barrel Pivot Screw	38	Mainspring
5	Cylinder Pin Screw	22	Barrel Pivot Locking Screw	39	Sideplate
6	Cylinder Catch Screw	23	Upper Trigger Guard Screw	40	Sideplate Hammer Pivot Screw
7	Cylinder Catch	24	Cylinder Stop Spring	41	Front Sideplate Screw
8	Barrel Release Catch	25	Trigger Spring	42	Rear Sideplate Screw
9	Barrel Release Spring	26	Lower Trigger Guard Screw	43	Trigger Guard
10	Extractor Lock Screw	27	Mainspring Set Screw	44	Grip Pin
11	Extractor Spring	28	Cylinder Stop	**Parts Not Shown**	
12	Extractor Spring Collar	29	Cylinder Stop Pin		Left Grip
13	Cylinder Lift Screw	30	Trigger		Right Grip
14	Cylinder	31	Trigger Pin		Grip Screw
15	Extractor	32	Hammer		
16	Barrel Catch Screw	33	Stirrup		
17	Ratchet Pawl	34	Stirrup Pin		

Model 10 Revolver

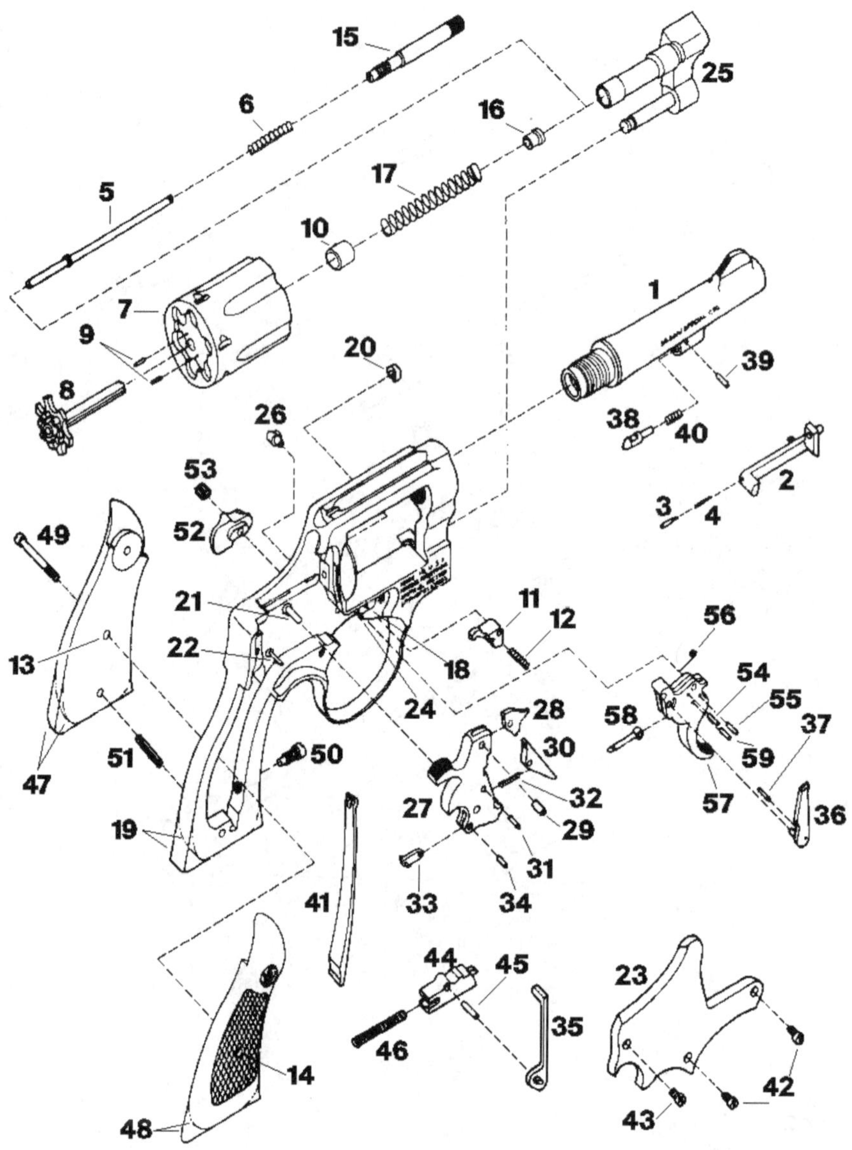

1	Barrel	21	Hammer Stud	41	Mainspring
2	Bolt	22	Rebound Slide Stud	42	Yoke Screws
3	Bolt Plunger	23	Sideplate	43	Sideplate Screw
4	Bolt Plunger Spring	24	Trigger Stud	44	Rebound Slide
5	Cylinder Center Pin	25	Yoke	45	Rebound Slide Pin
6	Cylinder Center Pin Spring	26	Frame Lug	46	Rebound Slide Spring
7	Cylinder	27	Hammer	47	Left Grip
8	Extractor	28	Hammer Nose	48	Right Grip
9	Extractor Pins	29	Hammer Nose Rivet	49	Grip Screw
10	Gas Ring	30	Sear	50	Mainspring Strain Screw
11	Cylinder Stop	31	Sear Pin	51	Grip Locator Pin
12	Cylinder Stop Spring	32	Sear Spring	52	Cylinder Latch Thumb-Piece
13	Grip Escutcheon	33	Stirrup	53	Cylinder Latch Thumb-Piece Nut
14	Grip Escutcheon Nut	34	Stirrup Pin	54	Hand Spring Pin
15	Extractor Rod	35	Hammer Block	55	Hand Spring Torsion Pin
16	Extractor Rod Collar	36	Hand	56	Hand Torsion Spring
17	Extractor Spring	37	Hand Pin	57	Trigger
18	Cylinder Stop Stud	38	Locking Bolt	58	Trigger Lever
19	Frame	39	Locking Bolt Pin	59	Trigger Lever Pin
20	Hammer Nose Bushing	40	Locking Bolt Spring		

Model 12 Revolver

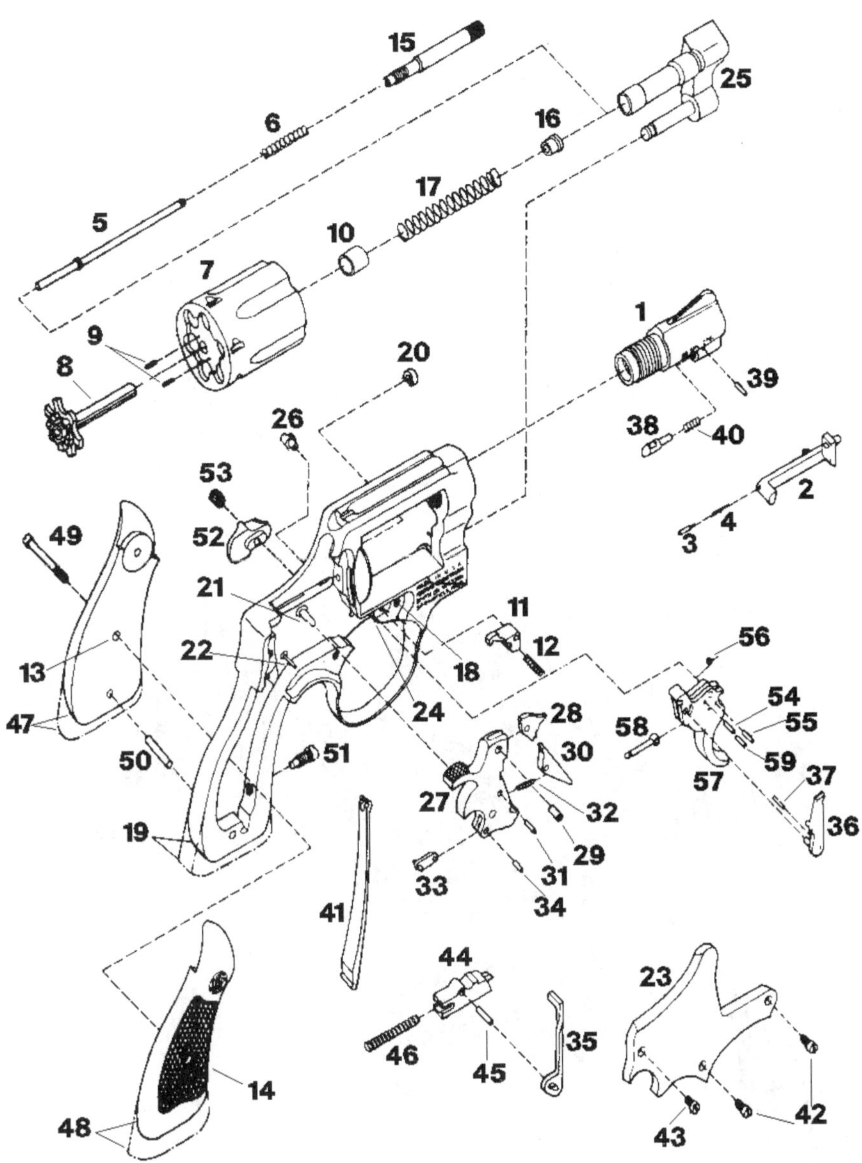

1	Barrel	21	Hammer Stud	41	Mainspring
2	Bolt	22	Rebound Slide Stud	42	Crowned Sideplate Screws
3	Bolt Plunger	23	Sideplate	43	Flat Sideplate Screw
4	Bolt Plunger Spring	24	Trigger Stud	44	Rebound Slide
5	Cylinder Center Pin	25	Yoke	45	Rebound Slide Pin
6	Cylinder Center Pin Spring	26	Frame Lug	46	Rebound Slide Spring
7	Cylinder	27	Hammer	47	Left Grip
8	Extractor	28	Hammer Nose	48	Right Grip
9	Extractor Pins	29	Hammer Nose Rivet	49	Grip Screw
10	Gas Ring	30	Sear	50	Grip Locator Pin
11	Cylinder Stop	31	Sear Pin	51	Mainspring Strain Screw
12	Cylinder Stop Spring	32	Sear Spring	52	Cylinder Latch Thumb-Piece
13	Grip Escutcheon	33	Stirrup	53	Cylinder Latch Thumb-Piece Nut
14	Grip Escutcheon Nut	34	Stirrup Pin	54	Hand Spring Pin
15	Extractor Rod	35	Hammer Block	55	Hand Spring Torsion Pin
16	Extractor Rod Collar	36	Hand	56	Hand Torsion Spring
17	Extractor Spring	37	Hand Pin	57	Trigger
18	Cylinder Stop Stud	38	Locking Bolt	58	Trigger Lever
19	Frame	39	Locking Bolt Pin	59	Trigger Lever Pin
20	Hammer Nose Bushing	40	Locking Bolt Spring		

SMITH & WESSON

Model 13 Revolver

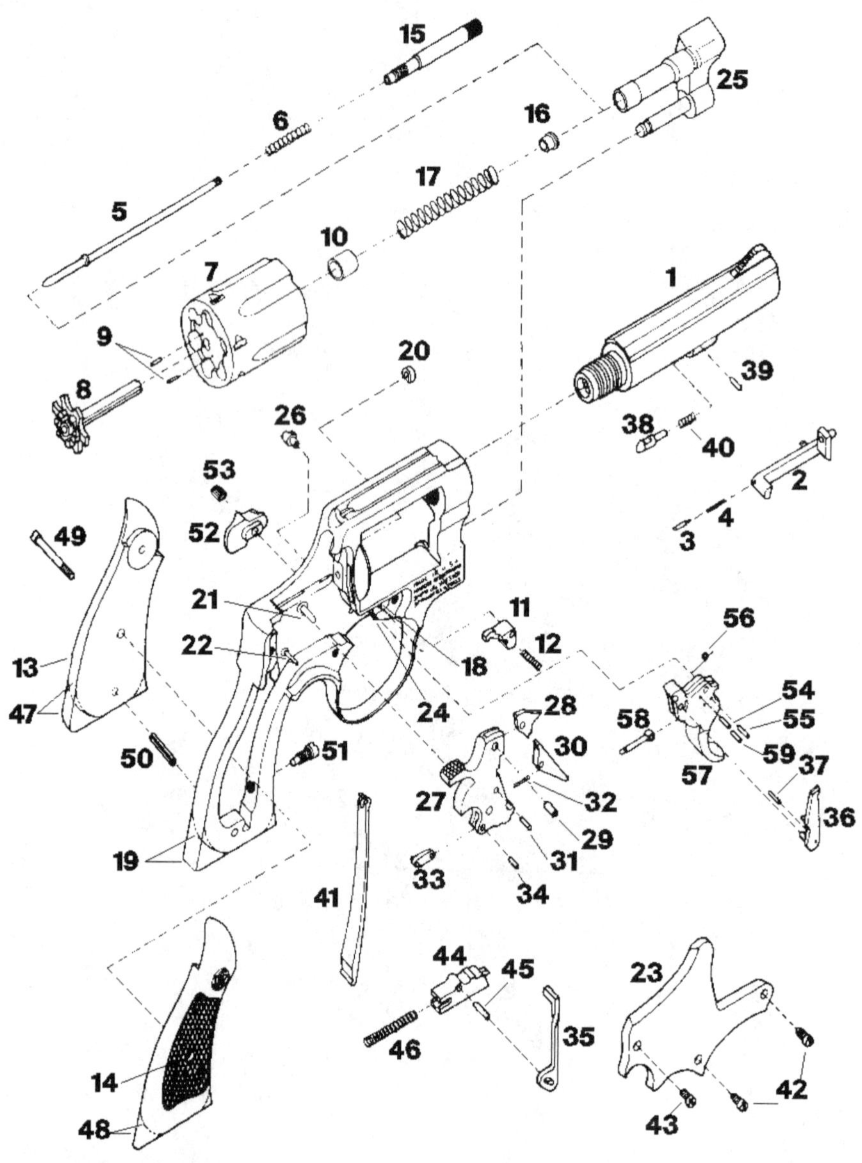

1	Barrel	21	Hammer Stud	41	Mainspring
2	Bolt	22	Rebound Slide Stud	42	Yoke Screws
3	Bolt Plunger	23	Sideplate	43	Sideplate Screw
4	Bolt Plunger Spring	24	Trigger Stud	44	Rebound Slide
5	Cylinder Center Pin	25	Yoke	45	Rebound Slide Pin
6	Cylinder Center Pin Spring	26	Frame Lug	46	Rebound Slide Spring
7	Cylinder	27	Hammer	47	Left Grip
8	Extractor	28	Hammer Nose	48	Right Grip
9	Extractor Pins	29	Hammer Nose Rivet	49	Grip Screw
10	Gas Ring	30	Sear	50	Grip Locator Pin
11	Cylinder Stop	31	Sear Pin	51	Mainspring Strain Screw
12	Cylinder Stop Spring	32	Sear Spring	52	Cylinder Latch Thumb-Piece
13	Grip Escutcheon	33	Stirrup	53	Cylinder Latch Thumb-Piece Nut
14	Grip Escutcheon Nut	34	Stirrup Pin	54	Hand Spring Pin
15	Extractor Rod	35	Hammer Block	55	Hand Spring Torsion Pin
16	Extractor Rod Collar	36	Hand	56	Hand Torsion Spring
17	Extractor Spring	37	Hand Pin	57	Trigger
18	Cylinder Stop Stud	38	Locking Bolt	58	Trigger Lever
19	Frame	39	Locking Bolt Pin	59	Trigger Lever Pin
20	Hammer Nose Bushing	40	Locking Bolt Spring		

Model 14 Revolver

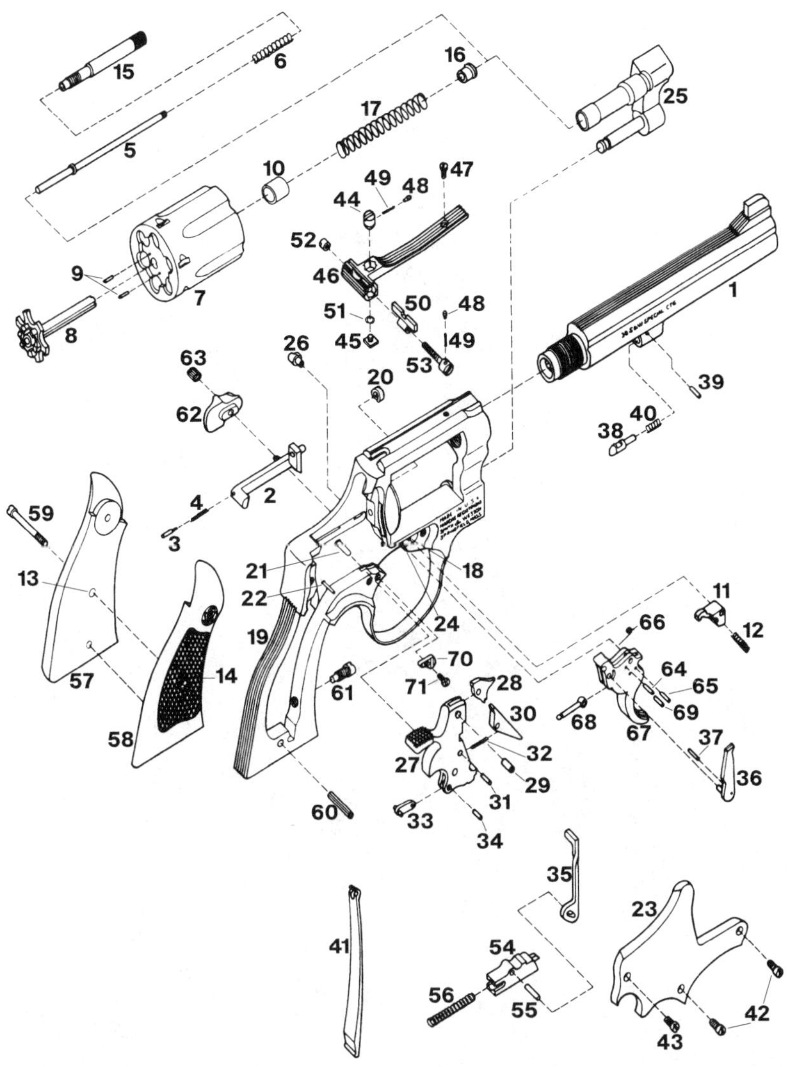

1	Barrel	**25**	Yoke	**49**	Rear Sight Plunger Spring
2	Bolt	**26**	Frame Lug	**50**	Rear Sight Slide
3	Bolt Plunger	**27**	Hammer	**51**	Rear Sight Spring Clip
4	Bolt Plunger Spring	**28**	Hammer Nose	**52**	Rear Sight Windage Nut
5	Cylinder Center Pin	**29**	Hammer Nose Rivet	**53**	Rear Sight Windage Screw
6	Cylinder Center Pin Spring	**30**	Sear	**54**	Rebound Slide
7	Cylinder	**31**	Sear Pin	**55**	Rebound Slide Pin
8	Extractor	**32**	Sear Spring	**56**	Rebound Slide Spring
9	Extractor Pins	**33**	Stirrup	**57**	Left Grip
10	Gas Ring	**34**	Stirrup Pin	**58**	Right Grip
11	Cylinder Stop	**35**	Hammer Block	**59**	Grip Screw
12	Cylinder Stop Spring	**36**	Hand	**60**	Grip Locator Pin
13	Grip Escutcheon	**37**	Hand Pin	**61**	Mainspring Strain Screw
14	Grip Escutcheon Nut	**38**	Locking Bolt	**62**	Cylinder Latch Thumb-Piece
15	Extractor Rod	**39**	Locking Bolt Pin	**63**	Cylinder Latch Thumb-Piece Nut
16	Extractor Rod Collar	**40**	Locking Bolt Spring	**64**	Hand Spring Pin
17	Extractor Spring	**41**	Mainspring	**65**	Hand Spring Torsion Pin
18	Cylinder Stop Stud	**42**	Yoke Screws	**66**	Hand Torsion Spring
19	Frame	**43**	Sideplate Screw	**67**	Trigger
20	Hammer Nose Bushing	**44**	Rear Sight Elevation Nut	**68**	Trigger Lever
21	Hammer Stud	**45**	Rear Sight Elevation Stud	**69**	Trigger Lever Pin
22	Rebound Slide Stud	**46**	Rear Sight Leaf	**70**	Trigger Stop
23	Sideplate	**47**	Rear Sight Leaf Screw	**71**	Trigger Stop Screw
24	Trigger Stud	**48**	Rear Sight Plunger		

Model 15 Revolver

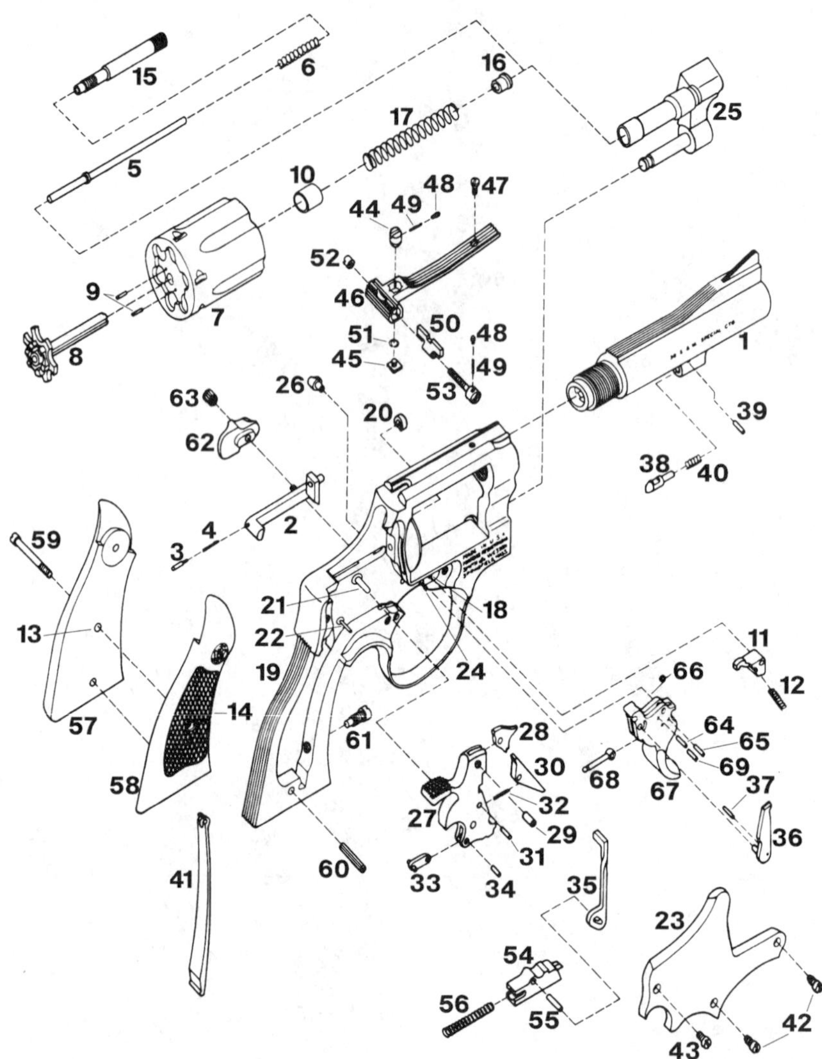

1	Barrel	**25**	Yoke	**49**	Rear Sight Plunger Spring
2	Bolt	**26**	Frame Lug	**50**	Rear Sight Slide
3	Bolt Plunger	**27**	Hammer	**51**	Rear Sight Spring Clip
4	Bolt Plunger Spring	**28**	Hammer Nose	**52**	Rear Sight Windage Nut
5	Cylinder Center Pin	**29**	Hammer Nose Rivet	**53**	Rear Sight Windage Screw
6	Cylinder Center Pin Spring	**30**	Sear	**54**	Rebound Slide
7	Cylinder	**31**	Sear Pin	**55**	Rebound Slide Pin
8	Extractor	**32**	Sear Spring	**56**	Rebound Slide Spring
9	Extractor Pins	**33**	Stirrup	**57**	Left Grip
10	Gas Ring	**34**	Stirrup Pin	**58**	Right Grip
11	Cylinder Stop	**35**	Hammer Block	**59**	Grip Screw
12	Cylinder Stop Spring	**36**	Hand	**60**	Grip Locator Pin
13	Grip Escutcheon	**37**	Hand Pin	**61**	Mainspring Strain Screw
14	Grip Escutcheon Nut	**38**	Locking Bolt	**62**	Cylinder Latch Thumb-Piece
15	Extractor Rod	**39**	Locking Bolt Pin	**63**	Cylinder Latch Thumb-Piece Nut
16	Extractor Rod Collar	**40**	Locking Bolt Spring	**64**	Hand Spring Pin
17	Extractor Spring	**41**	Mainspring	**65**	Hand Spring Torsion Pin
18	Cylinder Stop Stud	**42**	Yoke Screws	**66**	Hand Torsion Spring
19	Frame	**43**	Sideplate Screw	**67**	Trigger
20	Hammer Nose Bushing	**44**	Rear Sight Elevation Nut	**68**	Trigger Lever
21	Hammer Stud	**45**	Rear Sight Elevation Stud	**69**	Trigger Lever Pin
22	Rebound Slide Stud	**46**	Rear Sight Leaf	**70**	Trigger Stop
23	Sideplate	**47**	Rear Sight Leaf Screw		
24	Trigger Stud	**48**	Rear Sight Plunger		

Model 16 Revolver

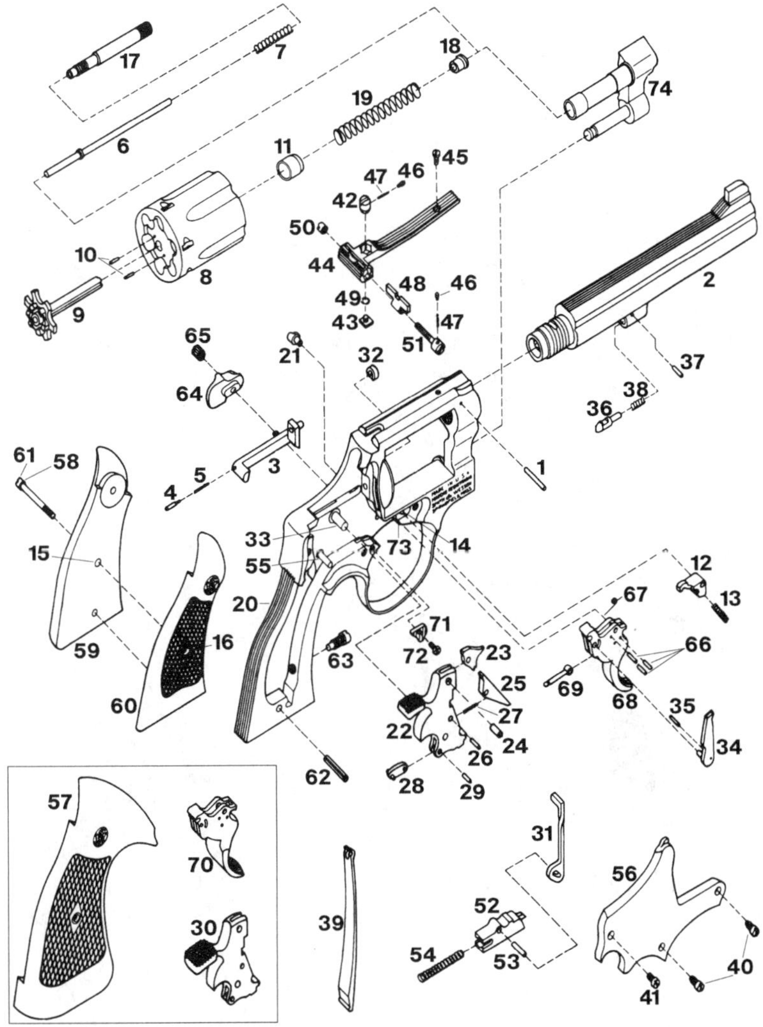

1	Barrel Pin	**26**	Sear Pin	**51**	Rear Sight Windage Screw
2	Barrel	**27**	Sear Spring	**52**	Rebound Slide
3	Bolt	**28**	Stirrup	**53**	Rebound Slide Pin
4	Bolt Plunger	**29**	Stirrup Pin	**54**	Rebound Slide Spring
5	Bolt Plunger Spring	**30**	Hammer, Target	**55**	Rebound Slide Stud
6	Cylinder Center Pin	**31**	Hammer Block	**56**	Sideplate
7	Cylinder Center Pin Spring	**32**	Hammer Nose Bushing	**57**	Stock Assembly, Target
8	Cylinder	**33**	Hammer Stud	**58**	Stock Screw, Target
9	Extractor Assembly	**34**	Hand	**59**	Left Grip
10	Extractor Pins	**35**	Hand Pin	**60**	Right Grip
11	Gas Ring	**36**	Locking Bolt	**61**	Grip Screw
12	Cylinder Stop	**37**	Locking Bolt Pin	**62**	Grip Locator Pin
13	Cylinder Stop Spring	**38**	Locking Bolt Spring	**63**	Mainspring Strain Screw
14	Cylinder Stop Stud	**39**	Mainspring	**64**	Cylinder Latch Thumb-Piece
15	Grip Escutcheon	**40**	Yoke Screws	**65**	Cylinder Latch Thumb-Piece Nut
16	Grip Escutcheon Nut	**41**	Sideplate Screw	**66**	Hand Spring Pins
17	Extractor Rod	**42**	Rear Sight Elevation Nut	**67**	Hand Torsion Spring
18	Extractor Rod Collar	**43**	Rear Sight Elevation Stud	**68**	Trigger
19	Extractor Spring	**44**	Rear Sight Leaf	**69**	Trigger Lever
20	Frame	**45**	Rear Sight Leaf Screw	**70**	Trigger, Target
21	Frame Lug	**46**	Rear Sight Plunger	**71**	Trigger Stop
22	Hammer	**47**	Rear Sight Plunger Springs	**72**	Trigger Stop Screw
23	Hammer Nose	**48**	Rear Sight Slide	**73**	Trigger Stud
24	Hammer Nose Rivet	**49**	Rear Sight Spring Clip	**74**	Yoke
25	Sear	**50**	Rear Sight Windage Nut		

Model 17 Revolver

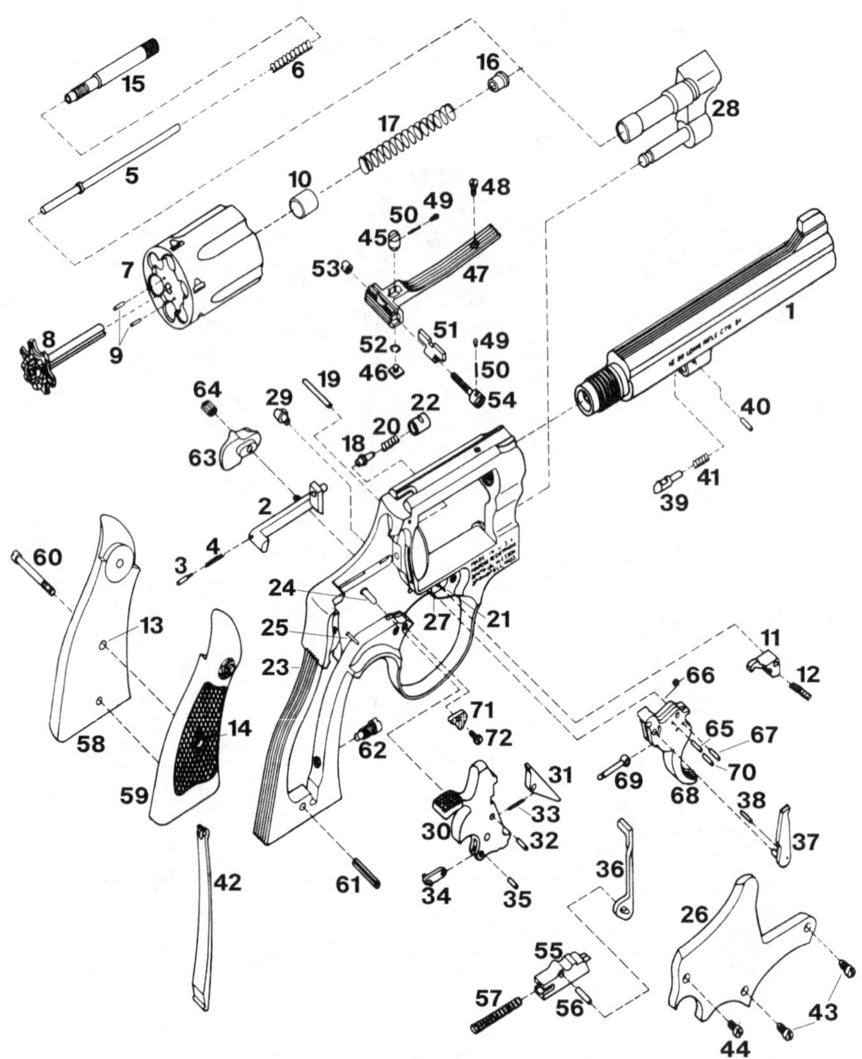

1	Barrel	25	Rebound Slide Stud	49	Rear Sight Plungers
2	Bolt	26	Sideplate	50	Rear Sight Plunger Springs
3	Bolt Plunger	27	Trigger Stud	51	Rear Sight Slide, Blue
4	Bolt Plunger Spring	28	Yoke	52	Rear Sight Spring Clip
5	Cylinder Center Pin	29	Frame Lug	53	Rear Sight Windage Nut
6	Cylinder Center Pin Spring	30	Hammer	54	Rear Sight Windage Screw
7	Cylinder	31	Sear	55	Rebound Slide
8	Extractor	32	Sear Pin	56	Rebound Slide Pin
9	Extractor Pins	33	Sear Spring	57	Rebound Slide Spring
10	Gas Ring	34	Stirrup	58	Left Grip
11	Cylinder Stop	35	Stirrup Pin	59	Right Grip
12	Cylinder Stop Spring	36	Hammer Block	60	Grip Screw
13	Grip Escutcheon	37	Hand	61	Grip Locator Pin
14	Grip Escutcheon Nut	38	Hand Pin	62	Mainspring Strain Screw
15	Extractor Rod	39	Locking Bolt	63	Cylinder Latch Thumb-Piece
16	Extractor Rod Collar	40	Locking Bolt Pin	64	Cylinder Latch Thumb-Piece Nut
17	Extractor Spring	41	Locking Bolt Spring	65	Hand Spring Pin
18	Firing Pin	42	Mainspring	66	Hand Torsion Spring
19	Firing Pin Bushing Pin	43	Yoke Screws	67	Hand Torsion Spring Pin
20	Firing Pin Spring	44	Sideplate Screw	68	Trigger
21	Cylinder Stop Stud	45	Rear Sight Elevation Nut	69	Trigger Lever
22	Firing Pin Bushing	46	Rear Sight Elevation Stud	70	Trigger Lever Pin
23	Frame	47	Rear Sight Leaf	71	Trigger Stop
24	Hammer Stud	48	Rear Sight Leaf Screw	72	Trigger Stop Screw

Model 18 Revolver

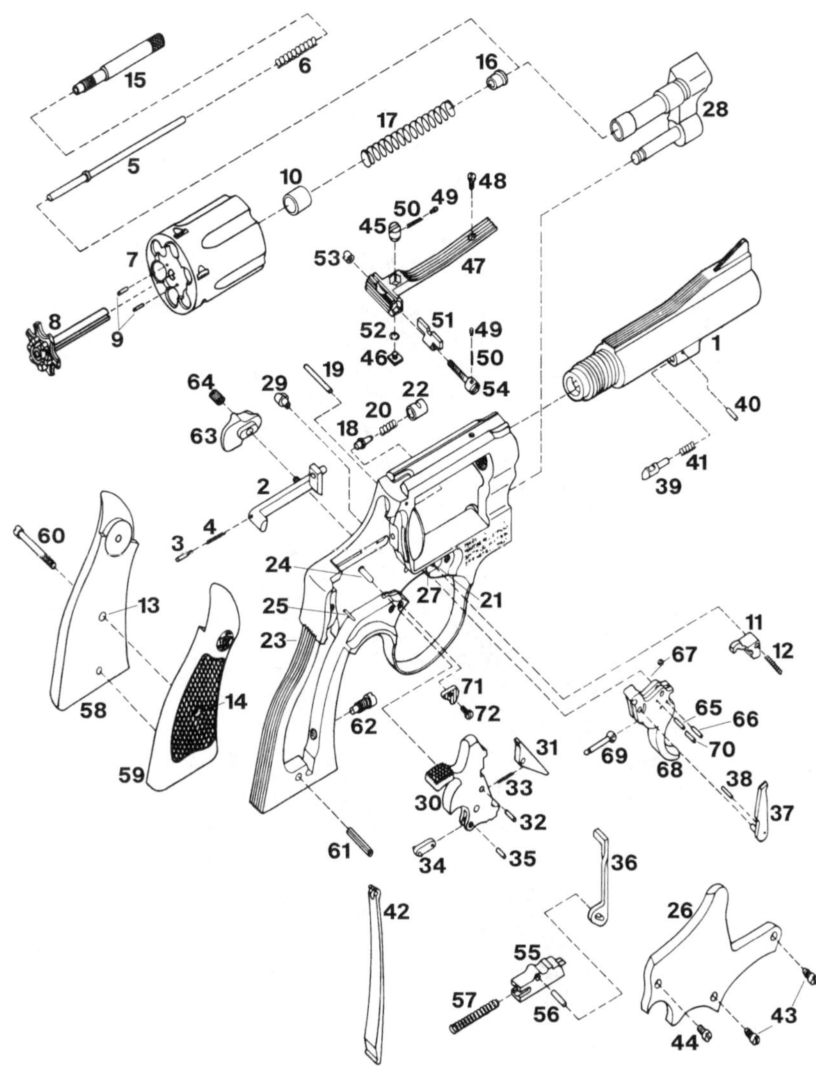

1	Barrel	**25**	Rebound Slide Stud	**49**	Rear Sight Plungers
2	Bolt	**26**	Sideplate	**50**	Rear Sight Plunger Springs
3	Bolt Plunger	**27**	Trigger Stud	**51**	Rear Sight Slide
4	Bolt Plunger Spring	**28**	Yoke	**52**	Rear Sight Spring Clip
5	Center Pin	**29**	Frame Lug	**53**	Rear Sight Windage Nut
6	Center Pin Spring	**30**	Hammer	**54**	Rear Sight Windage Screw
7	Cylinder	**31**	Sear	**55**	Rebound Slide
8	Extractor	**32**	Sear Pin	**56**	Rebound Slide Pin
9	Extractor Pins	**33**	Sear Spring	**57**	Rebound Slide Spring
10	Gas Ring	**34**	Stirrup	**58**	Stock, Left
11	Cylinder Stop	**35**	Stirrup Pin	**59**	Stock, Right
12	Cylinder Stop Spring	**36**	Hammer Block	**60**	Stock Screw
13	Escutcheon	**37**	Hand	**61**	Stock Pin
14	Escutcheon Nut	**38**	Hand Pin	**62**	Strain Screw
15	Extractor Rod	**39**	Locking Bolt	**63**	Thumb-Piece
16	Extractor Rod Collar	**40**	Locking Bolt Pin	**64**	Thumb-Piece Nut
17	Extractor Spring	**41**	Locking Bolt Spring	**65**	Hand Spring Pin
18	Firing Pin	**42**	Mainspring	**66**	Hand Spring Torsion Pin
19	Firing Pin Bushing Pin	**43**	York Screws, Crowned	**67**	Hand Torsion Spring
20	Firing Pin Spring	**44**	Plate Screw, Flat Head	**68**	Trigger
21	Cylinder Stop Stud	**45**	Rear Sight Elevation Nut	**69**	Trigger Lever
22	Firing Pin Bushing	**46**	Rear Sight Elevation Stud	**70**	Trigger Lever Pin
23	Frame	**47**	Rear Sight Leaf	**71**	Trigger Stop
24	Hammer Stud	**48**	Rear Sight Leaf Screw	**72**	Trigger Stop Screw

Model 19 Revolver

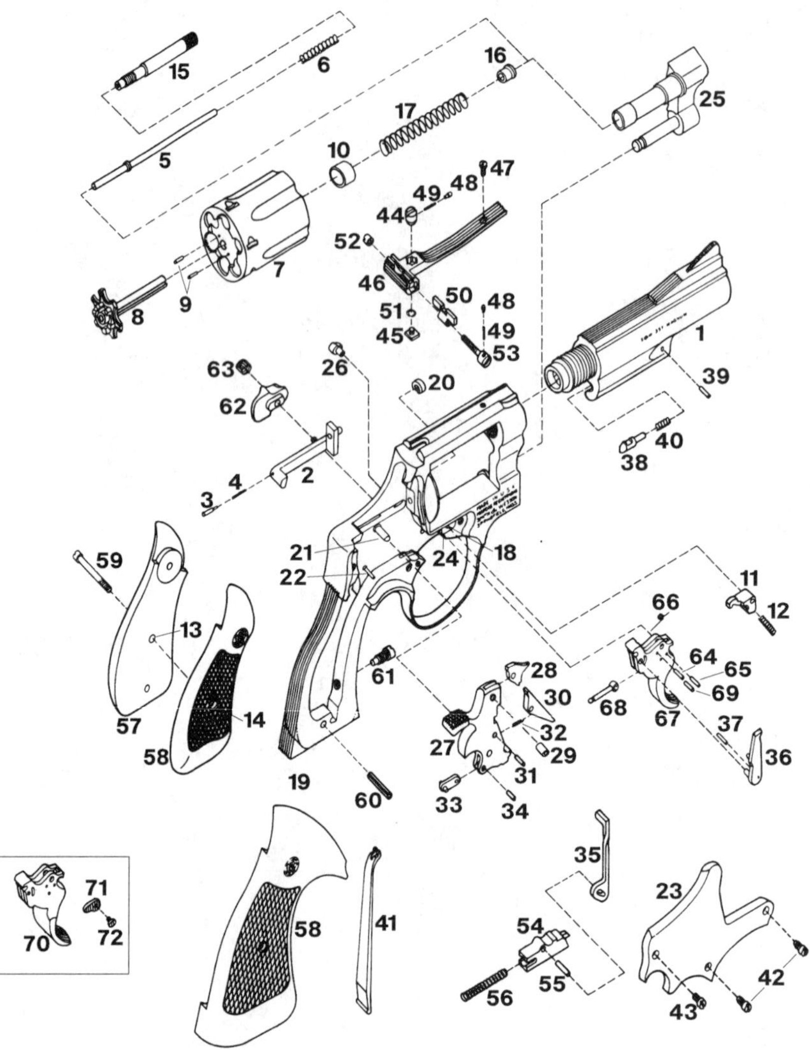

1	Barrel	**25**	Yoke	**49**	Rear Sight Plunger Spring
2	Bolt	**26**	Frame Lug	**50**	Rear Sight Slide
3	Bolt Plunger	**27**	Hammer	**51**	Rear Sight Spring Clip
4	Bolt Plunger Spring	**28**	Hammer Nose	**52**	Rear Sight Windage Nut
5	Center Pin	**29**	Hammer Nose Rivet	**53**	Rear Sight Windage Screw
6	Center Pin Spring	**30**	Sear	**54**	Rebound Slide
7	Cylinder	**31**	Sear Pin	**55**	Rebound Slide Pin
8	Extractor	**32**	Sear Spring	**56**	Rebound Slide Spring
9	Extractor Pins	**33**	Stirrup	**57**	Stock, Left
10	Gas Ring	**34**	Stirrup Pin	**58**	Stock, Right
11	Cylinder Stop	**35**	Hammer Block	**59**	Stock Screw
12	Cylinder Stop Spring	**36**	Hand	**60**	Stock Pin
13	Escutcheon	**37**	Hand Pin	**61**	Strain Screw
14	Escutcheon Nut	**38**	Locking Bolt	**62**	Thumb-Piece
15	Extractor Rod	**39**	Locking Bolt Pin	**63**	Thumb-Piece Nut
16	Extractor Rod Collar	**40**	Locking Bolt Spring	**64**	Hand Spring Pin
17	Extractor Spring	**41**	Mainspring	**65**	Hand Spring Torsion Pin
18	Cylinder Stop Stud	**42**	Yoke Screws, Crowned	**66**	Hand Torsion Spring
19	Frame	**43**	Plate Screw, Flat Head	**67**	Trigger
20	Hammer Nose Bushing	**44**	Rear Sight Elevation Nut	**68**	Trigger Lever
21	Hammer Stud	**45**	Rear Sight Elevation Stud	**69**	Trigger Lever Pin
22	Rebound Slide Stud	**46**	Rear Sight Leaf	**70**	Trigger, Target
23	Sideplate	**47**	Rear Sight Leaf Screw	**71**	Trigger Stop
24	Trigger Stud	**48**	Rear Sight Plunger	**72**	Trigger Stop Screw

Model 22/32 Kit Gun Revolver

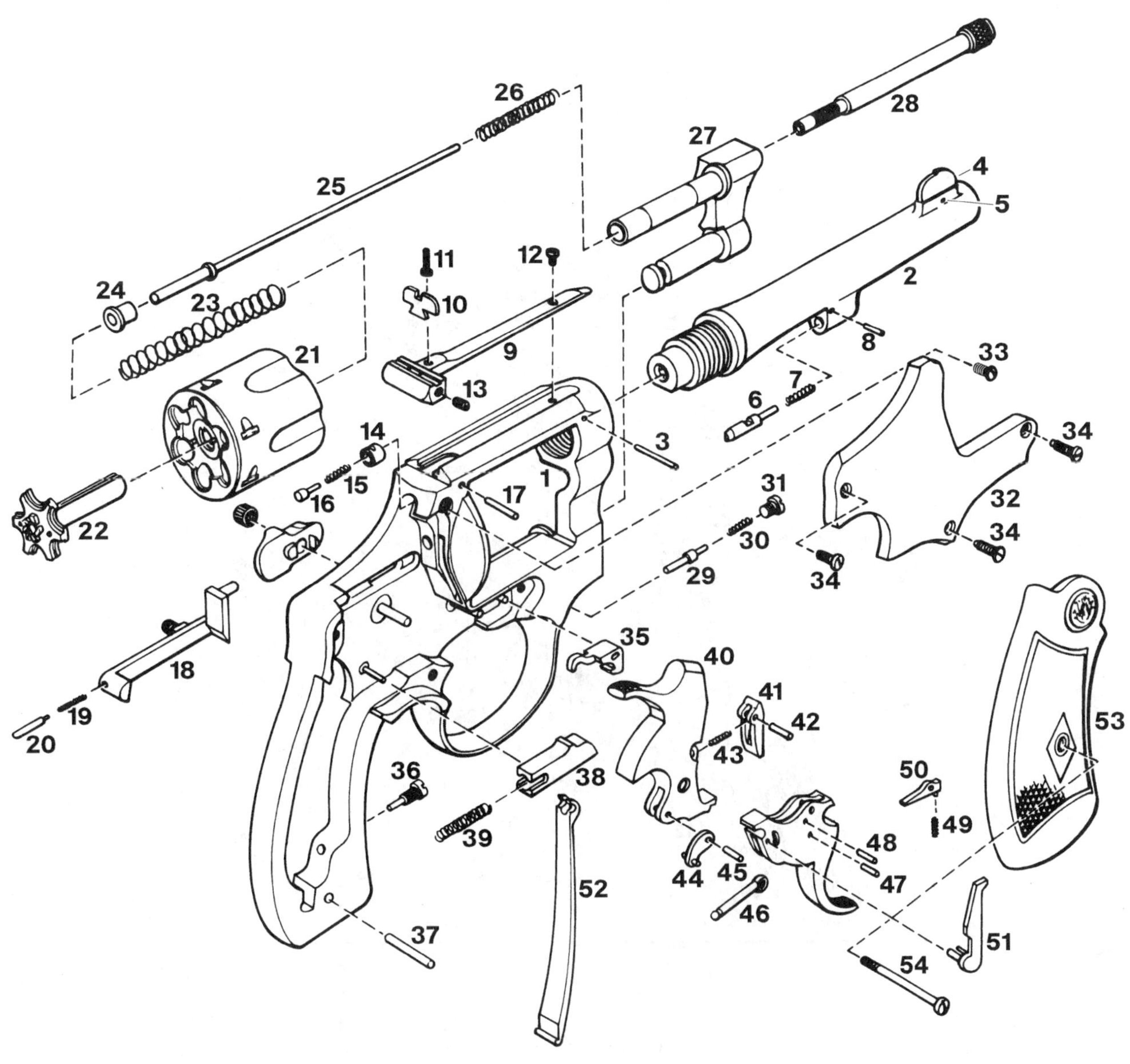

1	Frame	19	Bolt Plunger Spring	37	Stock Pin
2	Barrel	20	Bolt Plunger	38	Rebound Slide
3	Barrel Pin	21	Cylinder	39	Rebound Slide Spring
4	Front Sight Blade	22	Extractor	40	Hammer
5	Front Sight Pin	23	Extractor Spring	41	Sear
6	Locking Bolt	24	Extractor Rod Collar	42	Sear Pin
7	Locking Bolt Spring	25	Center Pin	43	Sear Spring
8	Locking Bolt Pin	26	Center Pin Spring	44	Stirrup
9	Rear Sight Leaf	27	Yoke	45	Stirrup Pin
10	Rear Sight Slide	28	Extractor Rod	46	Trigger Lever
11	Rear Sight Elevation Screw	29	Cylinder Stop Plunger	47	Trigger Lever Pin
12	Rear Sight Forward Screw	30	Cylinder Stop Plunger Spring	48	Hand Lever Pin
13	Rear Sight Windage Screws	31	Cylinder Stop Plunger Screw	49	Hand Lever Spring
14	Firing Pin Bushing	32	Sideplate	50	Hand Lever
15	Firing Pin Spring	33	Large Head Sideplate Screw	51	Hand
16	Firing Pin	34	Round Head Sideplate Screws	52	Mainspring
17	Firing Pin Bushing Pin	35	Cylinder Stop	53	Stocks
18	Bolt	36	Strain Screw	54	Stock Screw

Model 24 Revolver

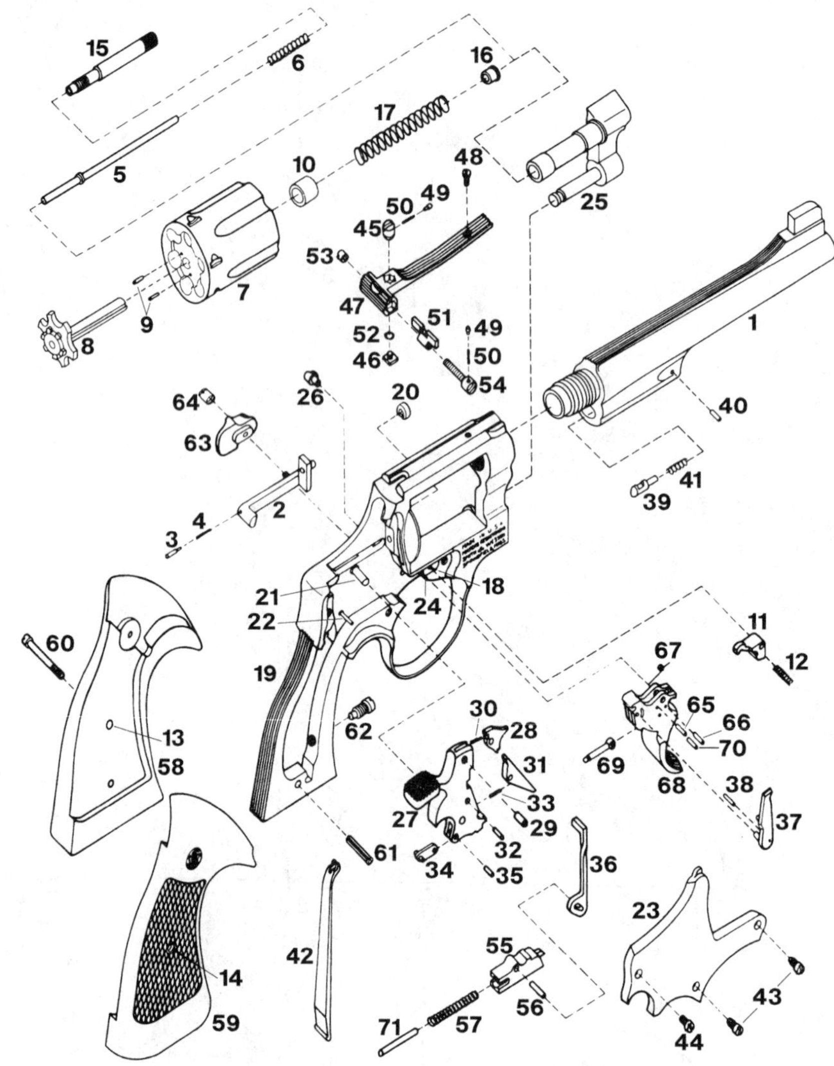

1	Barrel	**25**	Yoke	**49**	Rear Sight Plunger
2	Bolt	**26**	Frame Lug	**50**	Rear Sight Plunger Spring
3	Bolt Plunger	**27**	Hammer	**51**	Rear Sight Slide
4	Bolt Plunger Spring	**28**	Hammer Nose	**52**	Rear Sight Spring Clip
5	Center Pin	**29**	Hammer Nose Rivet	**53**	Rear Sight Windage Nut
6	Center Pin Spring	**30**	Hammer Nose Spring	**54**	Rear Sight Windage Screw
7	Cylinder	**31**	Sear	**55**	Rebound Slide
8	Extractor	**32**	Sear Pin	**56**	Rebound Slide Pin
9	Extractor Pins	**33**	Sear Spring	**57**	Rebound Slide Spring
10	Gas Ring	**34**	Stirrup	**58**	Stock, Left
11	Cylinder Stop	**35**	Stirrup Pin	**59**	Stock, Right
12	Cylinder Stop Spring	**36**	Hammer Block	**60**	Stock Screw
13	Escutcheon	**37**	Hand	**61**	Stock Pin
14	Escutcheon Nut	**38**	Hand Pin	**62**	Strain Screw
15	Extractor Rod	**39**	Locking Bolt	**63**	Thumb-Piece
16	Extractor Rod Collar	**40**	Locking Bolt Pin	**64**	Thumb-Piece Nut
17	Extractor Spring	**41**	Locking Bolt Spring	**65**	Hand Spring Pin
18	Cylinder Stop Stud	**42**	Mainspring	**66**	Hand Spring Torsion Pin
19	Frame	**43**	Plate Screws, Crowned	**67**	Hand Torsion Spring
20	Hammer Nose Bushing	**44**	Plate Screw, Flat Head	**68**	Trigger
21	Hammer Stud	**45**	Rear Sight Elevation Nut	**69**	Trigger Lever
22	Rebound Slide Stud	**46**	Rear Sight Elevation Stud	**70**	Trigger Lever Pin
23	Sideplate	**47**	Rear Sight Leaf	**71**	Trigger Stop Rod
24	Trigger Stud	**48**	Rear Sight Leaf Screw		

Model 25 Revolver

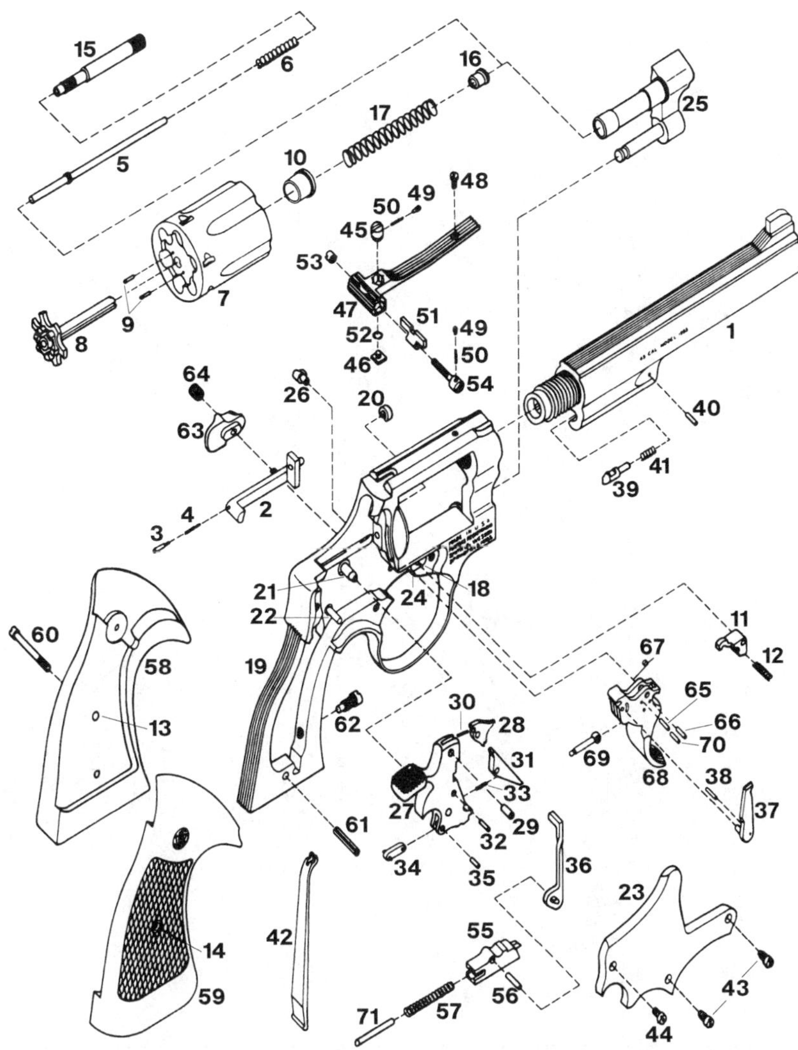

1	Barrel	**25**	Yoke	**49**	Rear Sight Plunger
2	Bolt	**26**	Frame Lug	**50**	Rear Sight Plunger Spring
3	Bolt Plunger	**27**	Hammer	**51**	Rear Sight Slide
4	Bolt Plunger Spring	**28**	Hammer Nose	**52**	Rear Sight Spring Clip
5	Center Pin	**29**	Hammer Nose Rivet	**53**	Rear Sight Windage Nut
6	Center Pin Spring	**30**	Hammer Nose Spring	**54**	Rear Sight Windage Screw
7	Cylinder	**31**	Sear	**55**	Rebound Slide
8	Extractor	**32**	Sear Pin	**56**	Rebound Slide Pin
9	Extractor Pins	**33**	Sear Spring	**57**	Rebound Slide Spring
10	Gas Ring	**34**	Stirrup	**58**	Stock, Left
11	Cylinder Stop	**35**	Stirrup Pin	**59**	Stock, Right
12	Cylinder Stop Spring	**36**	Hammer Block	**60**	Stock Screw
13	Escutcheon	**37**	Hand	**61**	Stock Pin
14	Escutcheon Nut	**38**	Hand Pin	**62**	Strain Screw
15	Extractor Rod	**39**	Locking Bolt	**63**	Thumb-Piece
16	Extractor Rod Collar	**40**	Locking Bolt Pin	**64**	Thumb-Piece Nut
17	Extractor Spring	**41**	Locking Bolt Spring	**65**	Hand Spring Pin
18	Cylinder Stop Stud	**42**	Mainspring	**66**	Hand Spring Torsion Pin
19	Frame	**43**	Plate Screws, Crowned	**67**	Hand Torsion Spring
20	Hammer Nose Bushing	**44**	Plate Screw, Flat Head	**68**	Trigger
21	Hammer Stud	**45**	Rear Sight Elevation Nut	**69**	Trigger Lever
22	Rebound Slide Stud	**46**	Rear Sight Elevation Stud	**70**	Trigger Lever Pin
23	Sideplate	**47**	Rear Sight Leaf	**71**	Trigger Stop Rod
24	Trigger Stud	**48**	Rear Sight Leaf Screw		

Model 27 Revolver

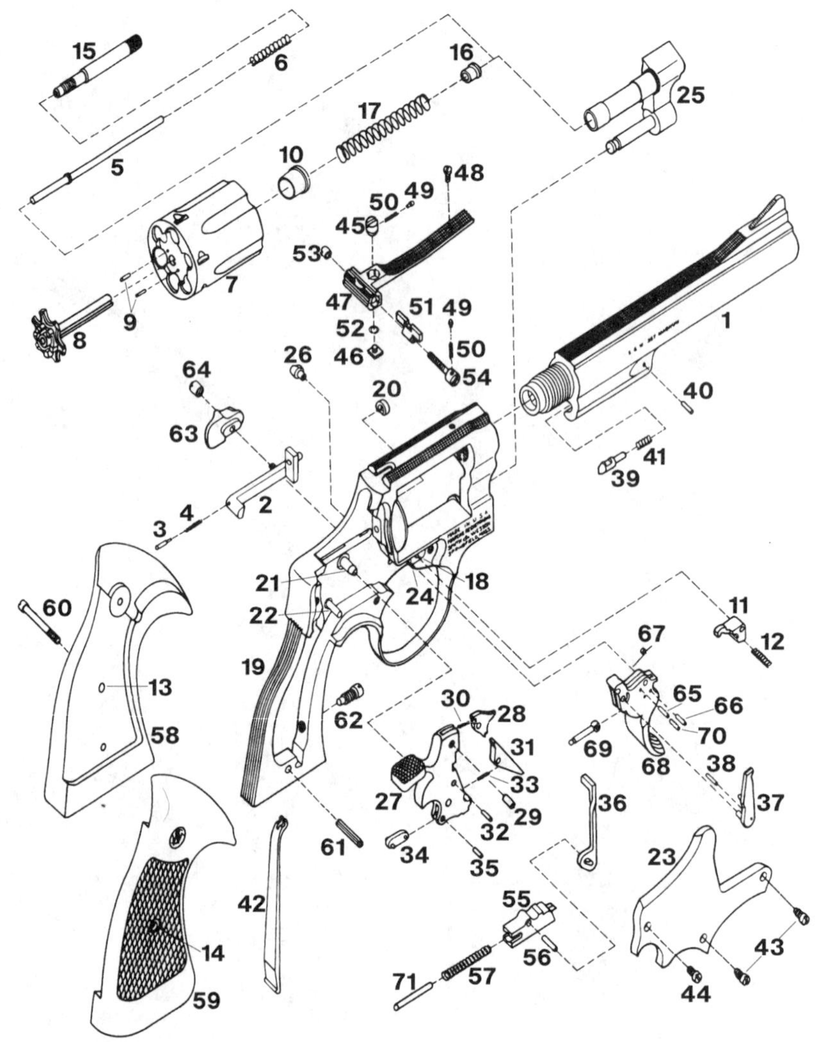

1	Barrel	26	Frame Lug	51	Rear Sight Slide
2	Bolt	27	Hammer	52	Rear Sight Spring Clip
3	Bolt Plunger	28	Hammer Nose	53	Rear Sight Windage Nut
4	Bolt Plunger Spring	29	Hammer Nose Rivet	54	Rear Sight Windage Screw
5	Center Pin	30	Hammer Nose Spring	55	Rebound Slide
6	Center Pin Spring	31	Sear	56	Rebound Slide Pin
7	Cylinder	32	Sear Pin	57	Rebound Slide Spring
8	Extractor	33	Sear Spring	58	Stock, Left
9	Extractor Pins	34	Stirrup	59	Stock, Right
10	Gas Ring	35	Stirrup Pin	60	Stock Screw
11	Cylinder Stop	36	Hammer Block	61	Stock Pin
12	Cylinder Stop Spring	37	Hand	62	Strain Screw
13	Escutcheon	38	Hand Pin	63	Thumb-Piece
14	Escutcheon Nut	39	Locking Bolt	64	Thumb-Piece Nut
15	Extractor Rod	40	Locking Bolt Pin	65	Hand Spring Pin
16	Extractor Rod Collar	41	Locking Bolt Spring	66	Hand Spring Torsion Pin
17	Extractor Spring	42	Mainspring	67	Hand Torsion Spring
18	Cylinder Stop Stud	43	Plate Screws, Crowned	68	Trigger
19	Frame	44	Plate Screw, Flat Head	69	Trigger Lever
20	Hammer Nose Bushing	45	Rear Sight Elevation Nut	70	Trigger Lever Pin
21	Hammer Stud	46	Rear Sight Elevation Stud	71	Trigger Stop Rod
22	Rebound Slide Stud	47	Rear Sight Leaf	**Parts Not Shown**	
23	Sideplate	48	Rear Sight Leaf Screw		Barrel Pin
24	Trigger Stud	49	Rear Sight Plunger		
25	Yoke	50	Rear Sight Plunger Spring		

Model 28 Revolver

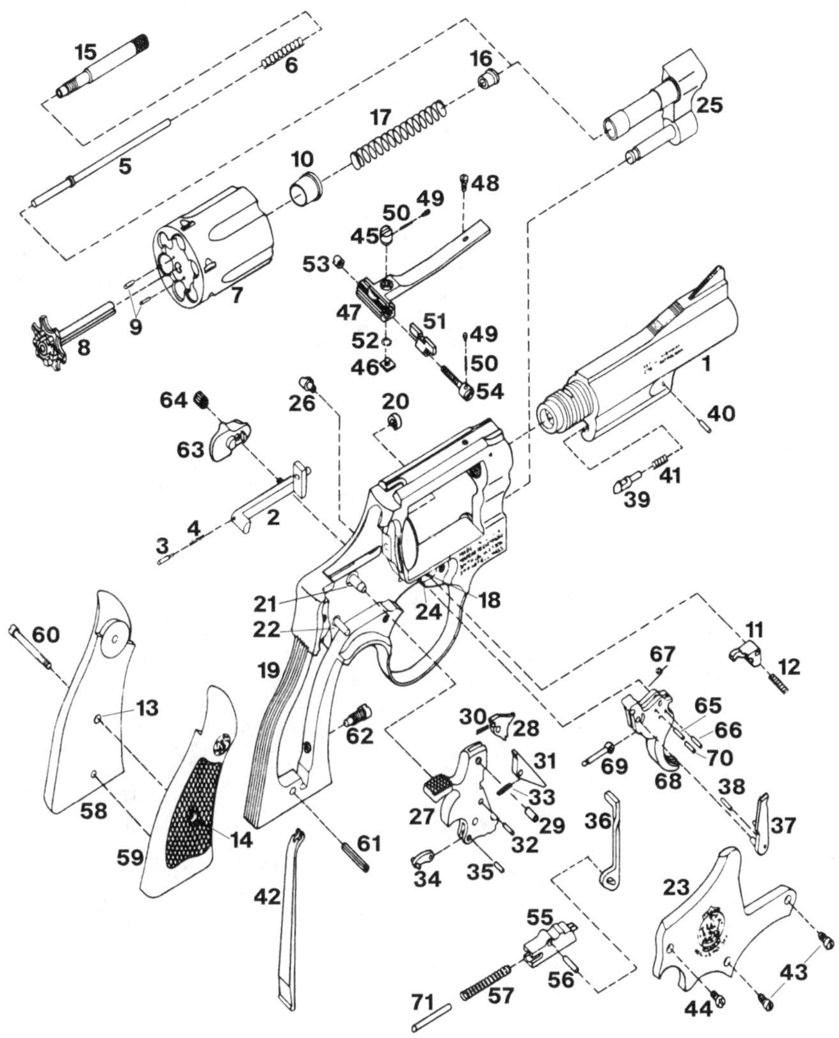

1 Barrel
2 Bolt
3 Bolt Plunger
4 Bolt Plunger Spring
5 Center Pin
6 Center Pin Spring
7 Cylinder
8 Extractor
9 Extractor Pins
10 Gas Ring
11 Cylinder Stop
12 Cylinder Stop Spring
13 Escutcheon
14 Escutcheon Nut
15 Extractor Rod
16 Extractor Rod Collar
17 Extractor Spring
18 Cylinder Stop Stud
19 Frame
20 Hammer Nose Bushing
21 Hammer Stud
22 Rebound Slide Stud
23 Sideplate
24 Trigger Stud
25 Yoke
26 Frame Lug
27 Hammer
28 Hammer Nose
29 Hammer Nose Rivet
30 Hammer Nose Spring
31 Sear
32 Sear Pin
33 Sear Spring
34 Stirrup
35 Stirrup Pin
36 Hammer Block
37 Hand
38 Hand Pin
39 Locking Bolt
40 Locking Bolt Pin
41 Locking Bolt Spring
42 Mainspring
43 Plate Screws, Crowned
44 Plate Screw, Flat Head
45 Rear Sight Elevation Nut
46 Rear Sight Elevation Stud
47 Rear Sight Leaf
48 Rear Sight Leaf Screw
49 Rear Sight Plungers
50 Rear Sight Plunger Springs
51 Rear Sight Slide
52 Rear Sight Spring Clip
53 Rear Sight Windage Nut
54 Rear Sight Windage Screw
55 Rebound Slide
56 Rebound Slide Pin
57 Rebound Slide Spring
58 Stock, Left
59 Stock, Right
60 Stock Screw
61 Stock Pin
62 Strain Screw
63 Thumb-Piece
64 Thumb-Piece Nut
65 Hand Spring Pin
66 Hand Spring Torsion Pin
67 Hand Torsion Spring
68 Trigger
69 Trigger Lever
70 Trigger Lever Pin
71 Trigger Stop Rod

Model 29 Revolver

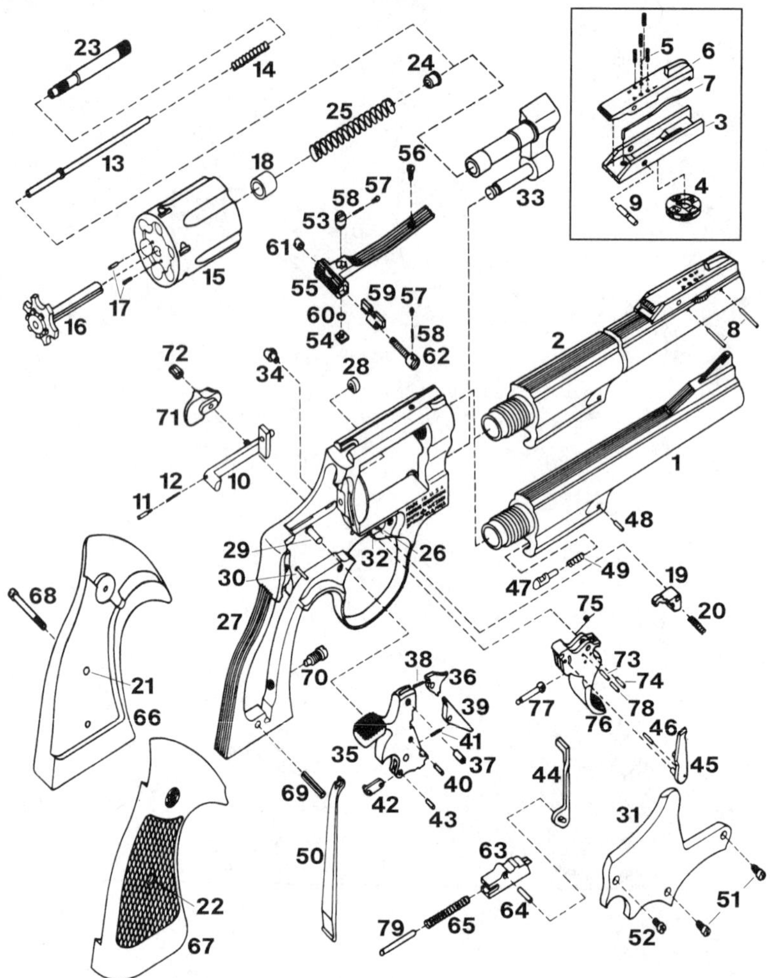

1	Barrel, Short	**28**	Hammer Nose Bushing	**55**	Rear Sight Leaf
2	Barrel, Long	**29**	Hammer Stud	**56**	Rear Sight Leaf Screw
3	Front Sight Base	**30**	Rebound Slide Stud	**57**	Rear Sight Plungers
4	Front Sight Cam	**31**	Sideplate	**58**	Rear Sight Plunger Springs
5	Front Sight Elevation Screws	**32**	Trigger Stud	**59**	Rear Sight Slide
6	Front Sight Leaf	**33**	Yoke	**60**	Rear Sight Spring Clip
7	Front Sight Leaf Spring	**34**	Frame Lug	**61**	Rear Sight Windage Nut
8	Front Sight Pins	**35**	Hammer	**62**	Rear Sight Windage Screw
9	Front Sight Pivot Pin	**36**	Hammer Nose	**63**	Rebound Slide
10	Bolt	**37**	Hammer Nose Rivet	**64**	Rebound Slide Pin
11	Bolt Plunger	**38**	Hammer Nose Spring	**65**	Rebound Slide Spring
12	Bolt Plunger Spring	**39**	Sear	**66**	Stock, Left
13	Center Pin	**40**	Sear Pin	**67**	Stock, Right
14	Center Pin Spring	**41**	Sear Spring	**68**	Stock Screw
15	Cylinder	**42**	Stirrup	**69**	Stock Pin
16	Extractor	**43**	Stirrup Pin	**70**	Strain Screw
17	Extractor Pins	**44**	Hammer Block	**71**	Thumb-Piece
18	Gas Ring	**45**	Hand	**72**	Thumb-Piece Nut
19	Cylinder Stop	**46**	Hand Pin	**73**	Hand Spring Pin
20	Cylinder Stop Spring	**47**	Locking Bolt	**74**	Hand Spring Torsion Pin
21	Escutcheon	**48**	Locking Bolt Pin	**75**	Hand Torsion Spring
22	Escutcheon Nut	**49**	Locking Bolt Spring	**76**	Trigger
23	Extractor Rod	**50**	Mainspring	**77**	Trigger Lever
24	Extractor Rod Collar	**51**	Plate Screws, Crowned	**78**	Trigger Lever Pin
25	Extractor Spring	**52**	Plate Screw, Flat Head	**79**	Trigger Stop Rod
26	Cylinder Stop Stud	**53**	Rear Sight Elevation Nut	**Parts Not Shown**	
27	Frame	**54**	Rear Sight Elevation Stud		Barrel Pin

Model 30 and 31 Revolver

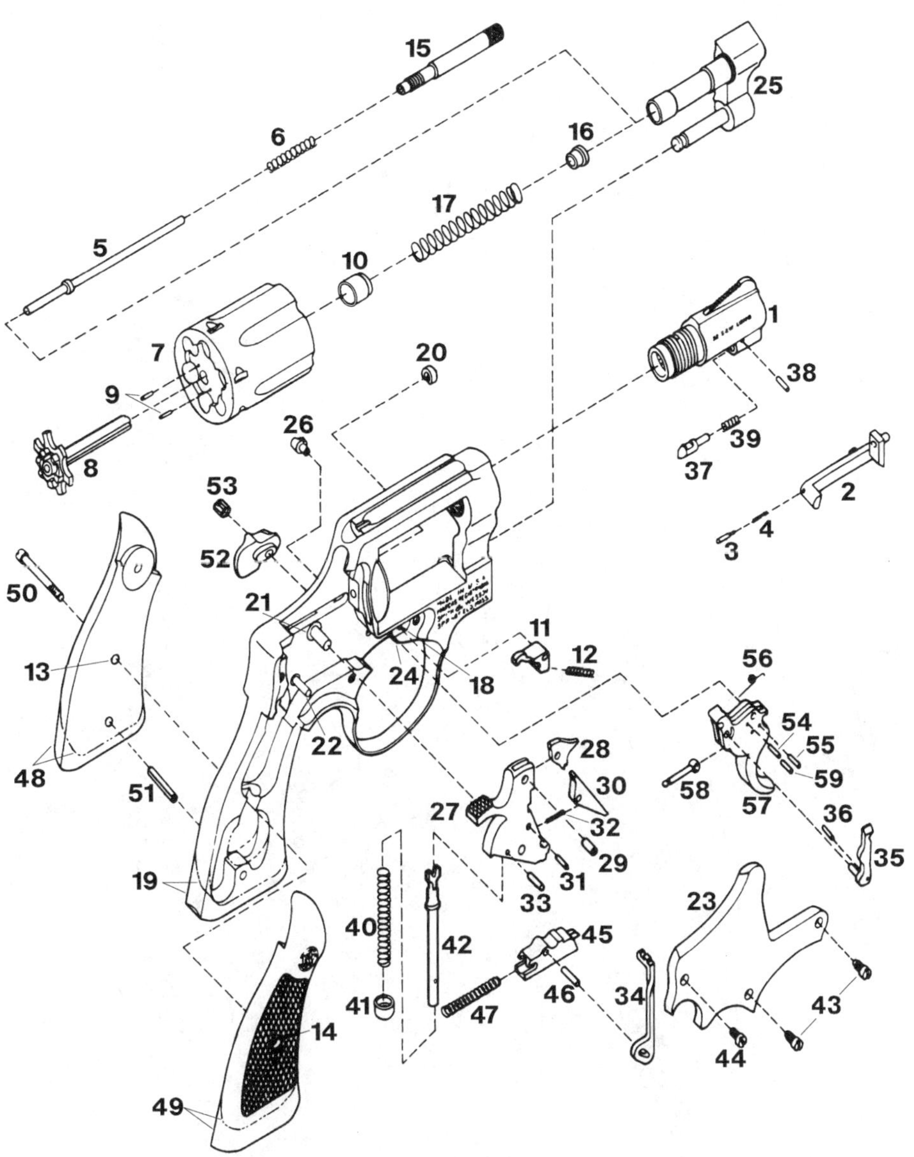

1	Barrel	**22**	Rebound Slide Stud	**43**	Plate Screws, Crowned
2	Bolt	**23**	Sideplate	**44**	Plate Screw, Flat Head
3	Bolt Plunger	**24**	Trigger Stud	**45**	Rebound Slide
4	Bolt Plunger Spring	**25**	Yoke	**46**	Rebound Slide Pin
5	Center Pin	**26**	Frame Lug	**47**	Rebound Slide Spring
6	Center Pin Spring	**27**	Hammer	**48**	Stock, Left
7	Cylinder	**28**	Hammer Nose	**49**	Stock, Right
8	Extractor	**29**	Hammer Nose Rivet	**50**	Stock Screw
9	Extractor Pins	**30**	Sear	**51**	Stock Pin
10	Gas Ring	**31**	Sear Pin	**52**	Thumb-Piece
11	Cylinder Stop	**32**	Sear Spring	**53**	Thumb-Piece Nut
12	Cylinder Stop Spring	**33**	Stirrup Pin	**54**	Hand Spring Pin
13	Escutcheon	**34**	Hammer Block	**55**	Hand Spring Torsion Pin
14	Escutcheon Nut	**35**	Hand	**56**	Hand Torsion Spring
15	Extractor Rod	**36**	Hand Pin	**57**	Trigger
16	Extractor Rod Collar	**37**	Locking Bolt	**58**	Trigger Lever
17	Extractor Spring	**38**	Locking Bolt Pin	**59**	Trigger Lever Pin
18	Cylinder Stop Stud	**39**	Locking Bolt Spring	**Parts Not Shown**	
19	Frame	**40**	Mainspring		Barrel Pin
20	Hammer Nose Bushing	**41**	Mainspring Rod Swivel		
21	Hammer Stud	**42**	Mainspring Stirrup		

Model 32 and 33 Revolver

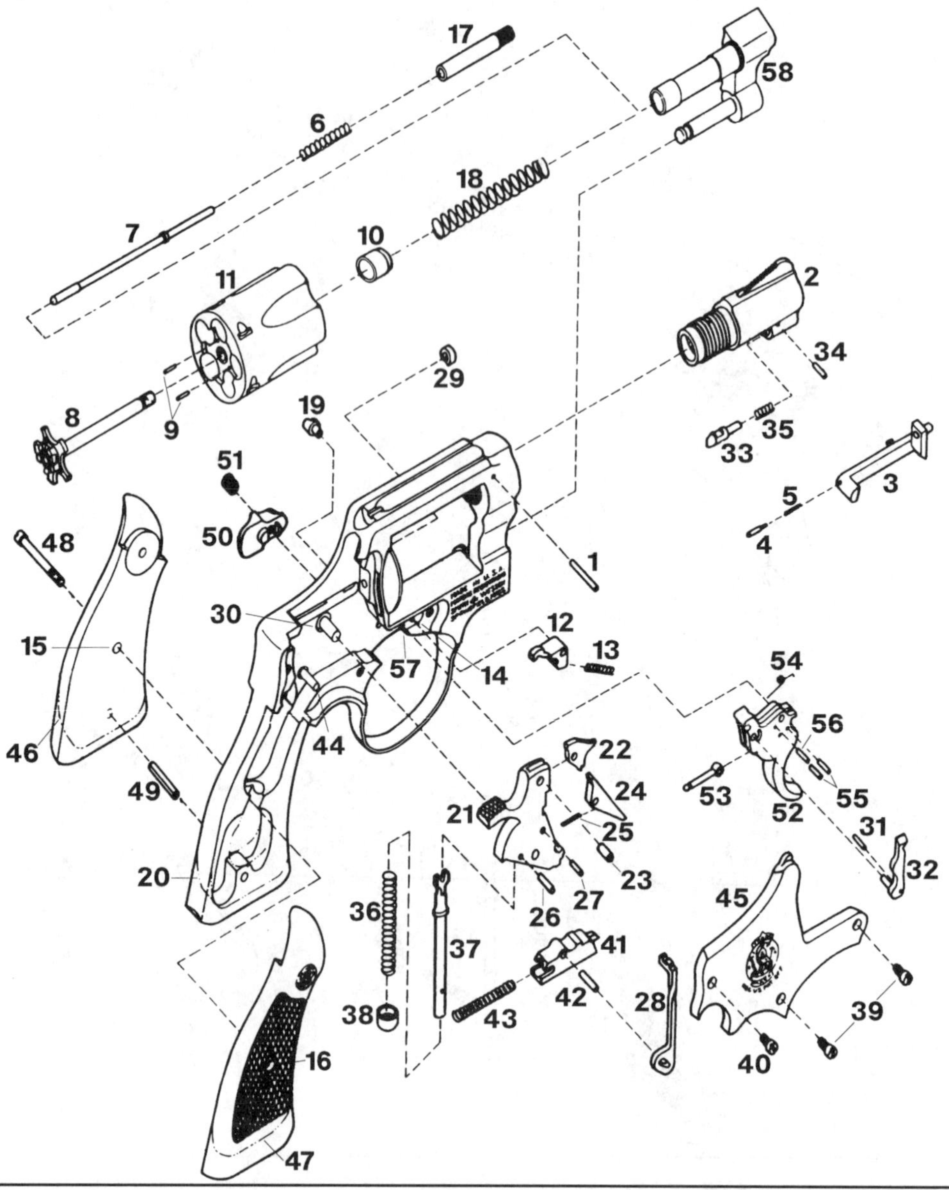

1	Barrel Pin	**21**	Hammer	**41**	Rebound Slide
2	Barrel	**22**	Hammer Nose	**42**	Rebound Slide Pin
3	Bolt	**23**	Hammer Nose Rivet	**43**	Rebound Slide Spring
4	Bolt Plunger	**24**	Sear	**44**	Rebound Slide Stud
5	Bolt Plunger Spring	**25**	Sear Spring	**45**	Sideplate
6	Center Pin Spring	**26**	Stirrup Pin	**46**	Stock, Left
7	Center Pin	**27**	Sear Pin	**47**	Stock, Right
8	Extractor Assembly	**28**	Hammer Block	**48**	Stock Screw
9	Extractor Pins	**29**	Hammer Nose Bushing	**49**	Stock Pin
10	Gas Ring	**30**	Hammer Stud	**50**	Thumb-Piece
11	Cylinder	**31**	Hand Pin	**51**	Thumb-Piece Nut
12	Cylinder Stop	**32**	Hand	**52**	Trigger
13	Cylinder Stop Spring	**33**	Locking Bolt	**53**	Trigger Lever
14	Cylinder Stop Stud	**34**	Locking Bolt Pin	**54**	Hand Torsion Spring
15	Escutcheon	**35**	Locking Bolt Spring	**55**	Trigger Lever Pins
16	Escutcheon Nut	**36**	Mainspring	**56**	Hand Spring Torsion Pin
17	Extractor Rod	**37**	Mainspring Stirrup	**57**	Trigger Stud
18	Extractor Spring	**38**	Mainspring Swivel	**58**	Yoke
19	Frame Lug	**39**	Plate Screws, Crowned		
20	Frame	**40**	Plate Screw, Flat Head		

Model 34 and 35 Revolver

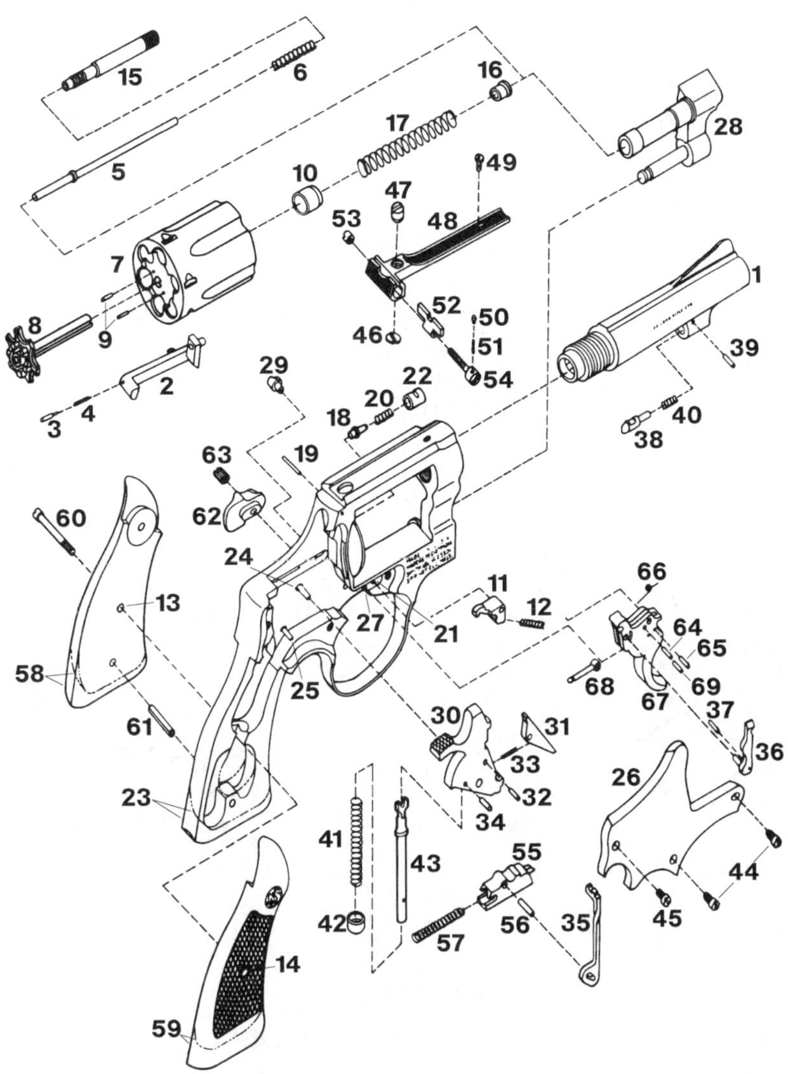

1	Barrel
2	Bolt
3	Bolt Plunger
4	Bolt Plunger Spring
5	Center Pin
6	Center Pin Spring
7	Cylinder
8	Extractor
9	Extractor Pins
10	Gas Ring
11	Cylinder Stop
12	Cylinder Stop Spring
13	Escutcheon
14	Escutcheon Nut
15	Extractor Rod
16	Extractor Rod Collar
17	Extractor Spring
18	Firing Pin
19	Firing Pin Bushing Pin
20	Firing Pin Spring
21	Cylinder Stop Stud
22	Firing Pin Bushing
23	Frame
24	Hammer Stud
25	Rebound Slide Stud
26	Sideplate
27	Trigger Stud
28	Yoke
29	Frame Lug
30	Hammer
31	Sear
32	Sear Pin
33	Sear Spring
34	Stirrup Pin
35	Hammer Block
36	Hand
37	Hand Pin
38	Locking Bolt
39	Locking Bolt Pin
40	Locking Bolt Spring
41	Mainspring
42	Mainspring Rod Swivel
43	Mainspring Stirrup
44	Plate Screws, Crowned
45	Plate Screw, Flat Head
46	Rear Sight Elevation Click Plug
47	Rear Sight Elevation Screw
48	Rear Sight Leaf
49	Rear Sight Leaf Screw
50	Rear Sight Plunger
51	Rear Sight Plunger Spring
52	Rear Sight Slide
53	Rear Sight Windage Nut
54	Rear Sight Windage Screw
55	Rebound Slide
56	Rebound Slide Pin
57	Rebound Slide Spring
58	Stock, Left
59	Stock, Right
60	Stock Screw
61	Stock Pin
62	Thumb-Piece
63	Thumb-Piece Nut
64	Hand Spring Pin
65	Hand Spring Torsion Pin
66	Hand Torsion Spring
67	Trigger
68	Trigger Lever
69	Trigger Lever Pin
Parts Not Shown	
	Barrel Pin

Model 35 Auto

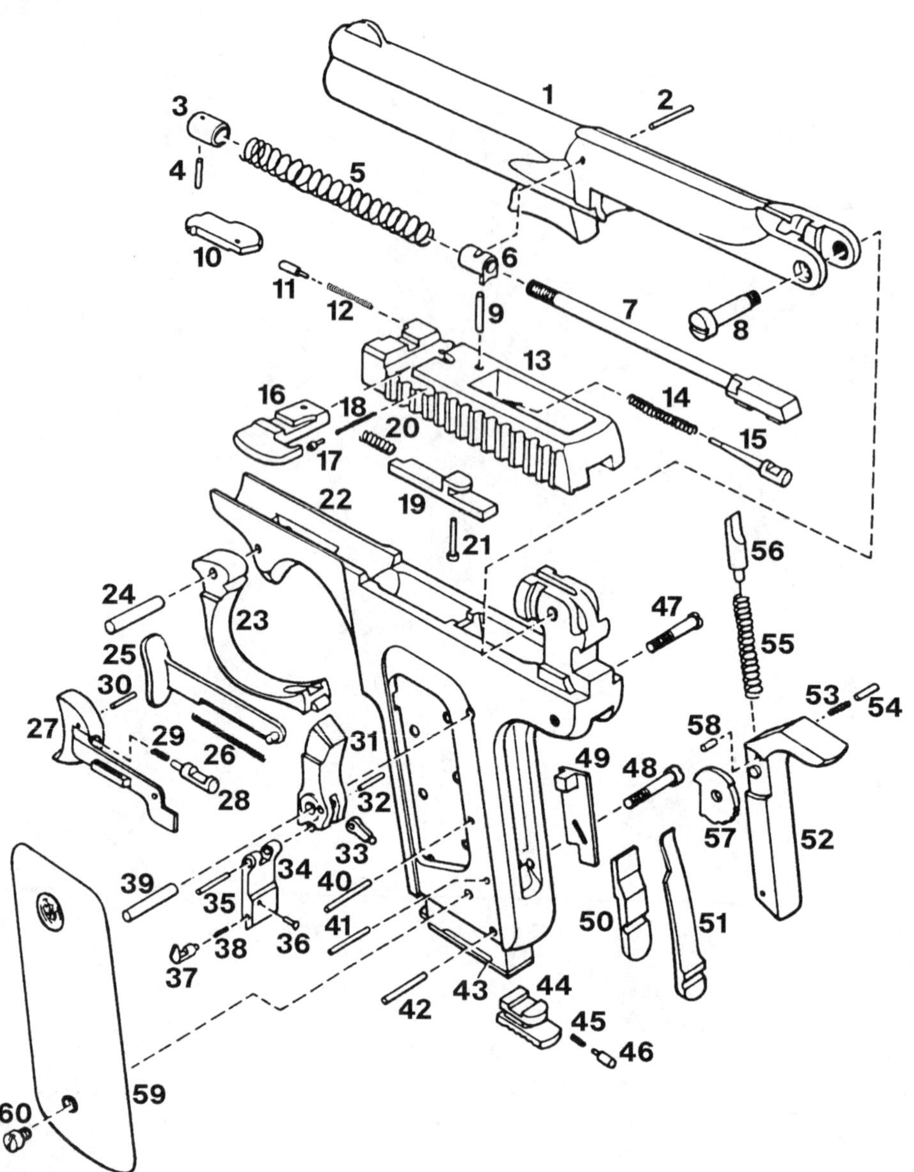

1	Barrel	21	Ejector Pin	41	Sear Spring Pin
2	Bushing Retaining Pin	22	Frame	42	Magazine Catch Pin
3	Recoil Spring Cap	23	Trigger Guard	43	Magazine
4	Cap Retaining Pin	24	Trigger Guard Pivot	44	Magazine Catch
5	Recoil Spring	25	Grip Safety	45	Magazine Catch Spring
6	Spring Rod Bushing	26	Grip Safety Spring	46	Magazine Catch Plunger
7	Recoil Spring Rod	27	Trigger	47	Upper Backstrap Screw
8	Pivot Screw	28	Trigger Plunger	48	Lower Backstrap Screw
9	Firing Pin Retaining Pin	29	Trigger Plunger Spring	49	Safety Slide
10	Extractor	30	Trigger Plunger Pin	50	Notch Plate
11	Extractor Plunger	31	Hammer	51	Sear Spring
12	Extractor Spring	32	Hammer Strut Pin	52	Backstrap
13	Slide	33	Hammer Strut	53	Safety Catch Spring
14	Firing Pin Spring	34	Sear	54	Plunger Retaining Pin
15	Firing Pin	35	Sear Hinge Pin	55	Mainspring
16	Bolt Release Catch	36	Sear Plunger Pin	56	Mainspring Plunger
17	Bolt Release Catch Spring Plunger	37	Sear Plunger	57	Safety Catch
18	Bolt Release Catch Spring	38	Sear Plunger Spring	58	Safety Catch Plunger
19	Ejector	39	Hammer Pin	59	Grip
20	Ejector Spring	40	Notch Plate Pin	60	Grip Screw

Model 36 Revolver

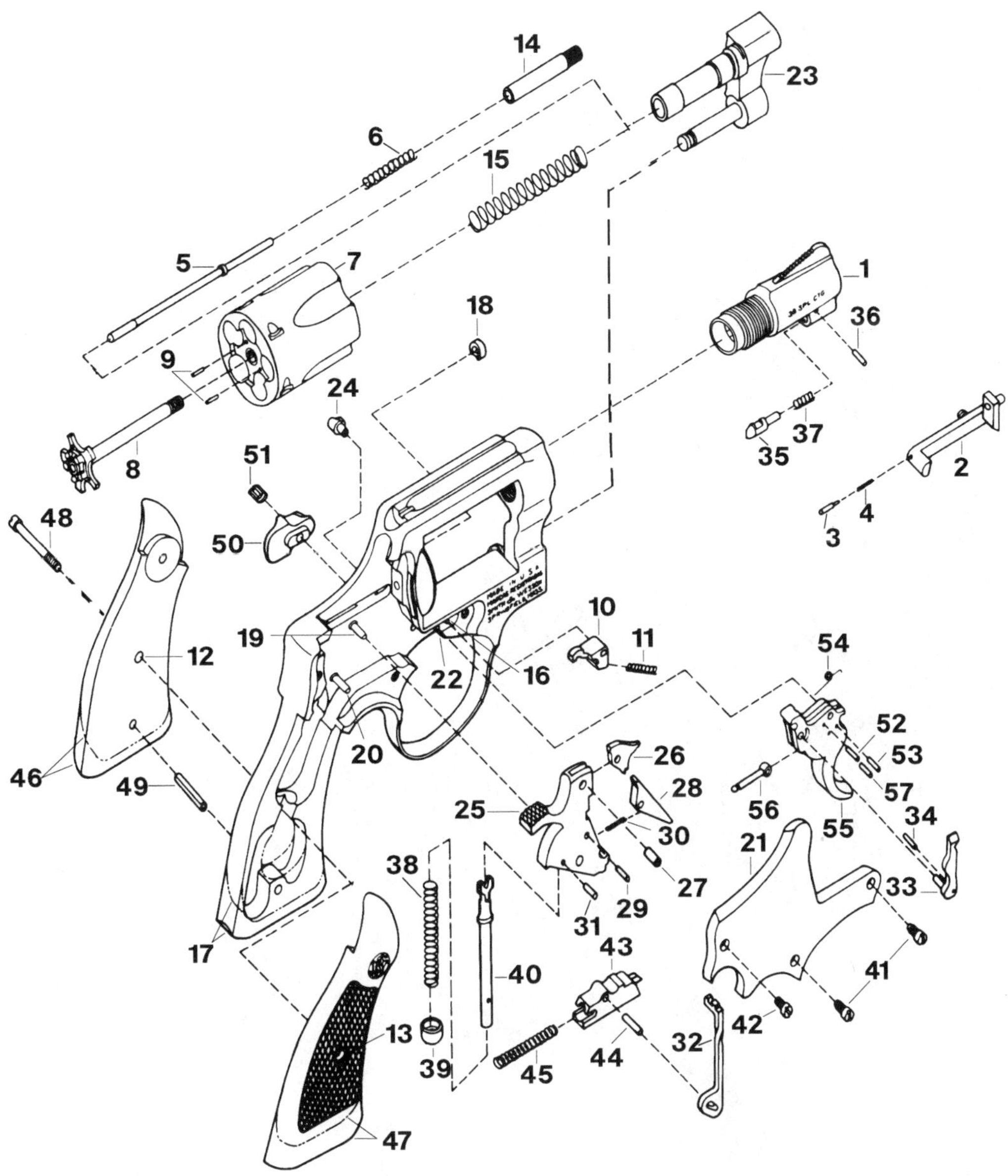

1	Barrel	**20**	Rebound Slide Stud	**39**	Mainspring Rod Swivel
2	Bolt	**21**	Slideplate	**40**	Mainspring Stirrup
3	Bolt Plunger	**22**	Trigger Stud	**41**	Plate Screws, Crowned
4	Bolt Plunger Spring	**23**	Yoke	**42**	Plate Screw, Flat Head
5	Center Pin	**24**	Frame Lug	**43**	Rebound Slide
6	Center Pin Spring	**25**	Hammer	**44**	Rebound Slide Pin
7	Cylinder	**26**	Hammer Nose	**45**	Rebound Slide Spring
8	Extractor	**27**	Hammer Nose Rivet	**46**	Stock, Left
9	Extractor Pins	**28**	Sear	**47**	Stock, Right
10	Cylinder Stop	**29**	Sear Pin	**48**	Stock Screw
11	Cylinder Stop Spring	**30**	Sear Spring	**49**	Stock Pin
12	Escutcheon	**31**	Stirrup Pin	**50**	Thumb-Piece
13	Escutcheon Nut	**32**	Hammer Block	**51**	Thumb-Piece Nut
14	Extractor Rod	**33**	Hand	**52**	Hand Spring Pin
15	Extractor Spring	**34**	Hand Pin	**53**	Hand Spring Torsion Pin
16	Cylinder Stop Stud	**35**	Locking Bolt	**54**	Hand Torsion Spring
17	Frame	**36**	Locking Bolt Pin	**55**	Trigger
18	Hammer Nose Bushing	**37**	Locking Bolt Spring	**56**	Trigger Lever
19	Hammer Stud	**38**	Mainspring	**57**	Trigger Lever Pin

Model 37 Revolver

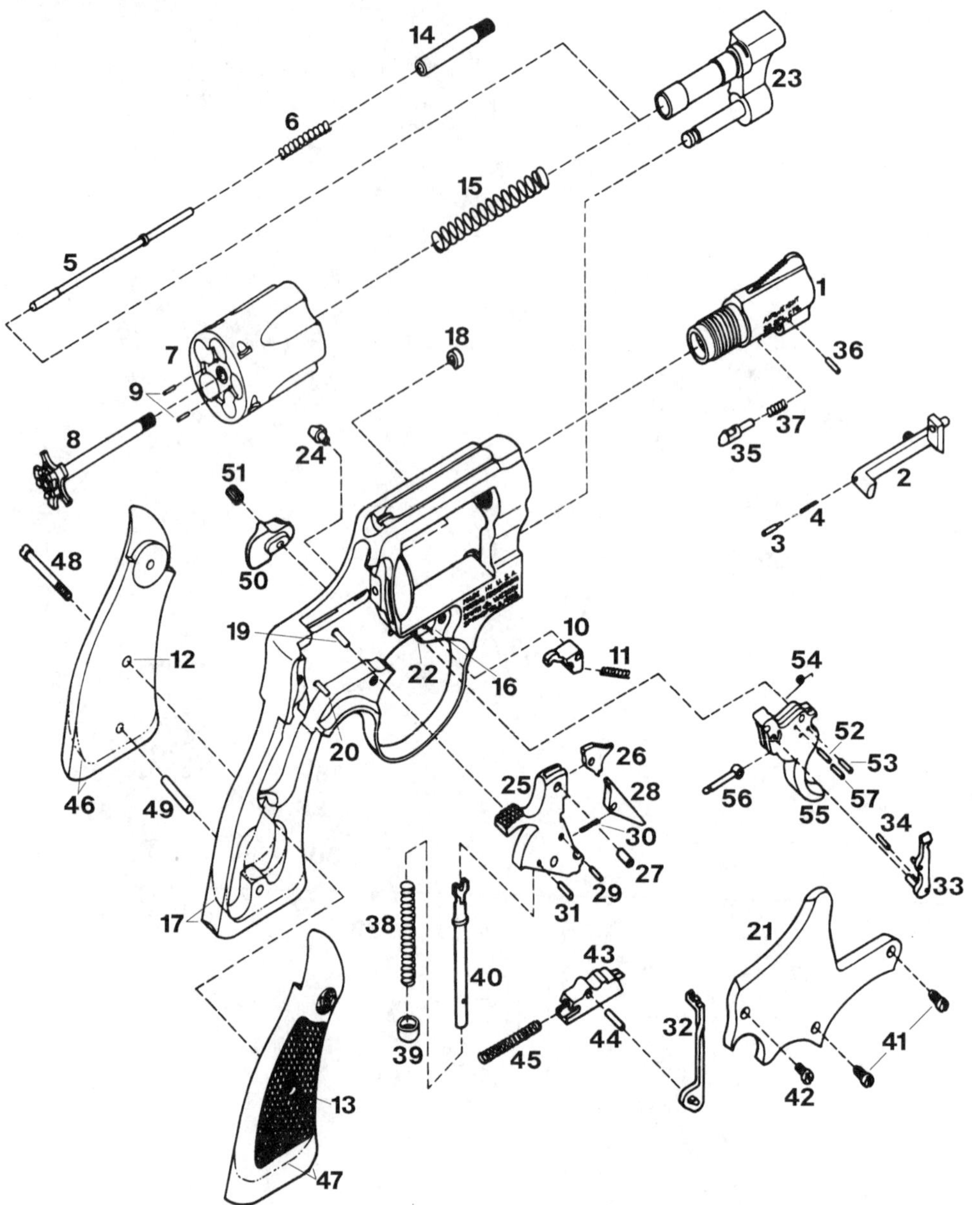

1	Barrel	**20**	Rebound Slide Stud	**39**	Mainspring Rod Swivel
2	Bolt	**21**	Sideplate	**40**	Mainspring Stirrup
3	Bolt Plunger	**22**	Trigger Stud	**41**	Plate Screws, Crowned
4	Bolt Plunger Spring	**23**	Yoke	**42**	Plate Screw, Flat Head
5	Center Pin	**24**	Frame Lug	**43**	Rebound Slide
6	Center Pin Spring	**25**	Hammer	**44**	Rebound Slide Pin
7	Cylinder	**26**	Hammer Nose	**45**	Rebound Slide Spring
8	Extractor	**27**	Hammer Nose Rivet	**46**	Stock, Left
9	Extractor Pins	**28**	Sear	**47**	Stock, Right
10	Cylinder Stop	**29**	Sear Pin	**48**	Stock Screw
11	Cylinder Stop Spring	**30**	Sear Spring	**49**	Stock Pin
12	Escutcheon	**31**	Stirrup Pin	**50**	Thumb-Piece
13	Escutcheon Nut	**32**	Hammer Block	**51**	Thumb-Piece Nut
14	Extractor Rod	**33**	Hand	**52**	Hand Spring Pin
15	Extractor Spring	**34**	Hand Pin	**53**	Hand Spring Torsion Pin
16	Cylinder Stop Stud	**35**	Locking Bolt	**54**	Hand Torsion Spring
17	Frame	**36**	Locking Bolt Pin	**55**	Trigger
18	Hammer Nose Bushing	**37**	Locking Bolt Spring	**56**	Trigger Lever
19	Hammer Stud	**38**	Mainspring	**57**	Trigger Lever Pin

Model 38 Revolver

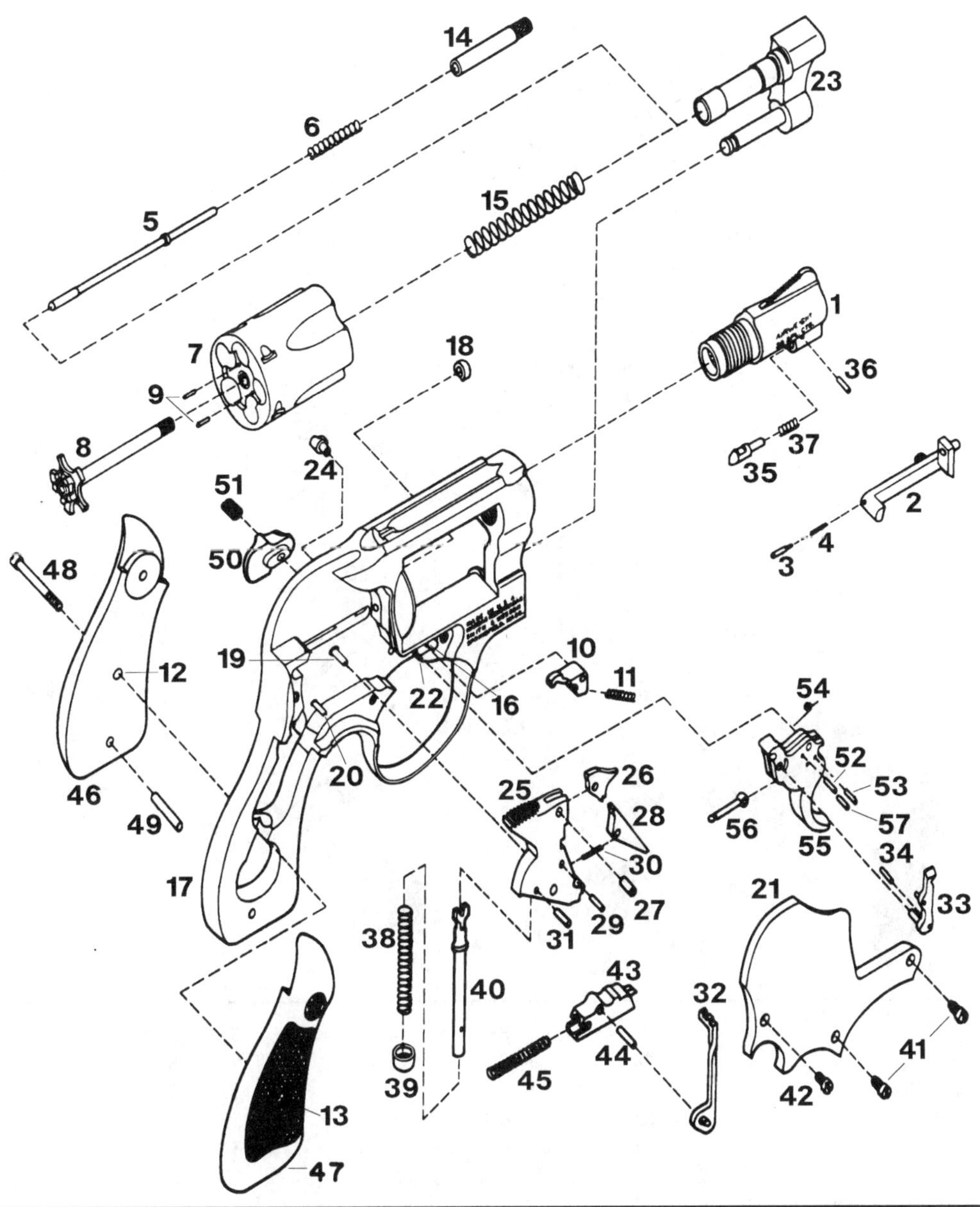

1	Barrel	20	Rebound Slide Stud	39	Mainspring Rod Swivel
2	Bolt	21	Sideplate	40	Mainspring Stirrup
3	Bolt Plunger	22	Trigger Stud	41	Plate Screws, Crowned
4	Bolt Plunger Spring	23	Yoke	42	Plate Screw, Flat Head
5	Center Pin	24	Frame Lug	43	Rebound Slide
6	Center Pin Spring	25	Hammer	44	Rebound Slide Pin
7	Cylinder	26	Hammer Nose	45	Rebound Slide Spring
8	Extractor	27	Hammer Nose Rivet	46	Stock, Left
9	Extractor Pins	28	Sear	47	Stock, Right
10	Cylinder Stop	29	Sear Pin	48	Stock Screw
11	Cylinder Stop Spring	30	Sear Spring	49	Stock Pin
12	Escutcheon	31	Stirrup Pin	50	Thumb-Piece
13	Escutcheon Nut	32	Hammer Block	51	Thumb-Piece Nut
14	Extractor Rod	33	Hand	52	Hand Spring Pin
15	Extractor Spring	34	Hand Pin	53	Hand Spring Torsion Pin
16	Cylinder Stop Stud	35	Locking Bolt	54	Hand Torsion Spring
17	Frame	36	Locking Bolt Pin	55	Trigger
18	Hammer Nose Bushing	37	Locking Bolt Spring	56	Trigger Lever
19	Hammer Stud	38	Mainspring	57	Trigger Lever Pin

Model 39 Auto

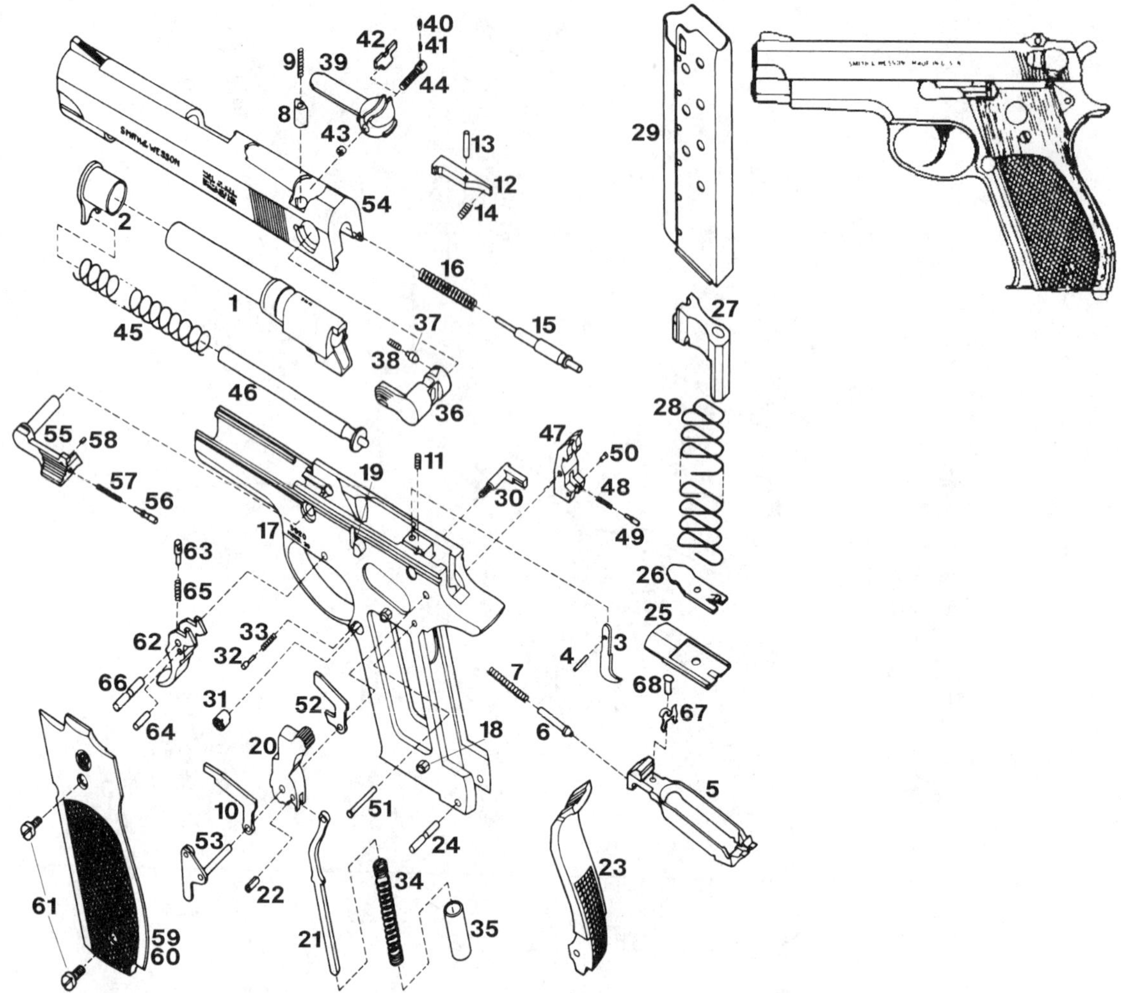

1	Barrel	27	Magazine Follower	53	Sideplate
2	Barrel Bushing	28	Magazine Spring	54	Slide
3	Disconnector	29	Magazine Tube	55	Slide Stop
4	Disconnector Pin	30	Magazine Catch	56	Slide Stop Plunger
5	Drawbar	31	Magazine Catch Nut	57	Slide Stop Plunger Spring
6	Drawbar Plunger	32	Magazine Catch Plunger	58	Slide Stop Spiral Pin
7	Drawbar Plunger Spring	33	Magazine Catch Plunger Spring	59	Stock, Left
8	Ejector Depressor Plunger	34	Mainspring	60	Stock, Right
9	Ejector Depressor Plunger Spring	35	Mainspring Plunger	61	Stock Screws
10	Ejector Magazine Depressor	36	Manual Safety	62	Trigger
11	Ejector Spring	37	Manual Safety Plunger	63	Trigger Plunger
12	Extractor	38	Manual Safety Plunger Spring	64	Trigger Plunger Pin
13	Extractor Pin	39	Rear Sight Body	65	Trigger Plunger Spring
14	Extractor Spring	40	Rear Sight Plunger	66	Trigger Pin
15	Firing Pin	41	Rear Sight Plunger Spring	67	Trigger Play Spring
16	Firing Pin Spring	42	Rear Sight Slide	68	Trigger Play Spring Rivet
17	Frame	43	Rear Sight Windage Nut	**Parts Not Shown**	
18	Frame Stud	44	Rear Sight Windage Screw		Recoil Spring Guide
19	Slide Stop Button	45	Recoil Spring		Recoil Spring Guide Bushing
20	Hammer	46	Recoil Spring Guide Assembly		Recoil Spring Guide Plunger
21	Stirrup	47	Sear		Recoil Spring Guide Plunger Spring
22	Stirrup Pin	48	Sear Spring		Hammer Pin
23	Insert	49	Sear Spring Plunger		Sideplate Button
24	Insert Pin	50	Sear Spring Plunger Pin		
25	Magazine Buttplate	51	Sear Pin		
26	Magazine Buttplate Catch	52	Sear Release Lever		

Model 40 and 42 Revolver

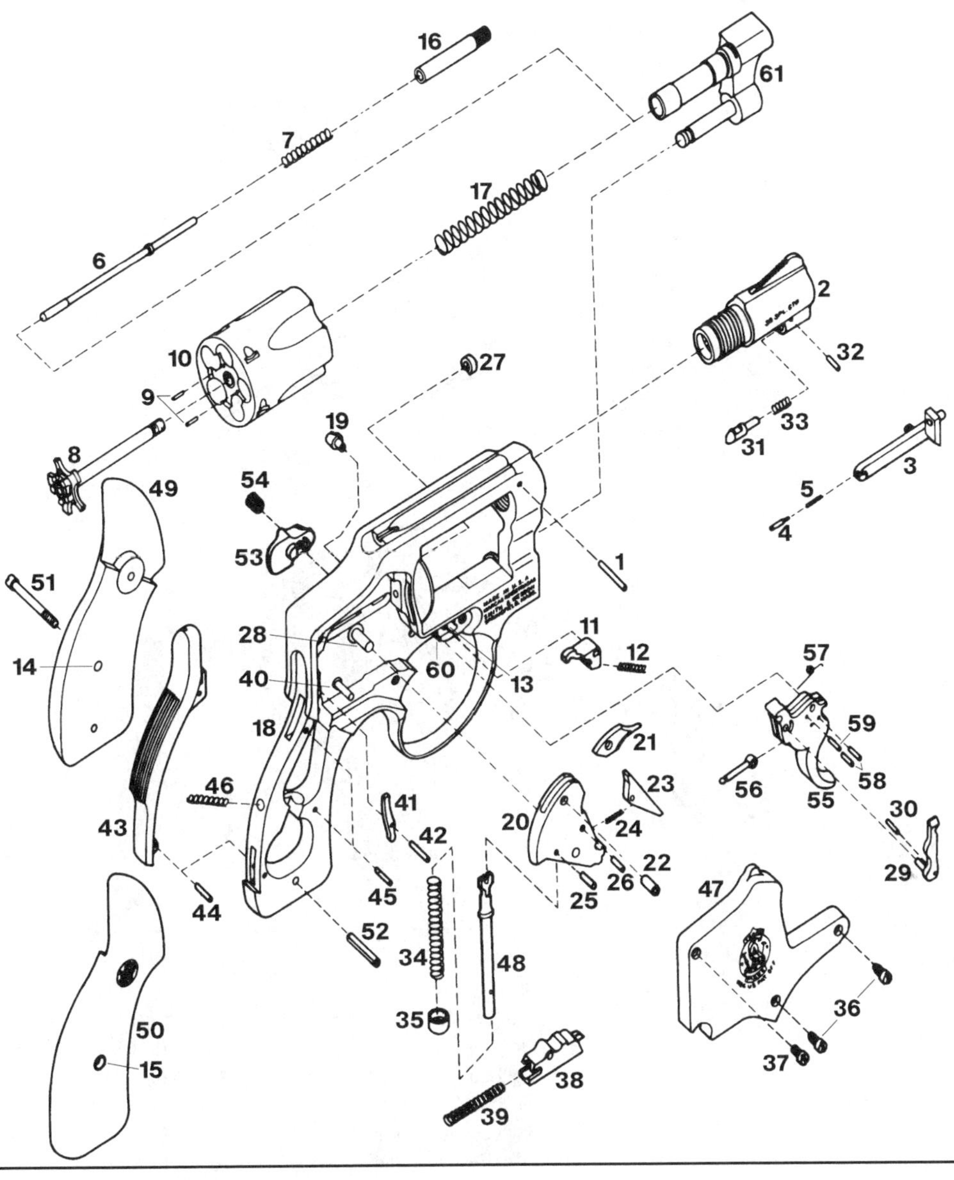

1	Barrel Pin	**21**	Hammer Nose	**41**	Safety Latch
2	Barrel	**22**	Hammer Nose Rivet	**42**	Safety Latch Pin
3	Bolt	**23**	Sear	**43**	Safety-Lever
4	Bolt Plunger	**24**	Sear Spring	**44**	Safety-Lever Disengaging Pin
5	Bolt Plunger Spring	**25**	Stirrup Pin	**45**	Safety-Lever Pin
6	Center Pin	**26**	Sear Pin	**46**	Safety-Lever Spring
7	Center Pin Spring	**27**	Hammer Nose Bushing	**47**	Sideplate
8	Extractor Assembly	**28**	Hammer Stud	**48**	Stirrup
9	Extractor Pins	**29**	Hand	**49**	Left Grip
10	Cylinder	**30**	Hand Pin	**50**	Right Grip
11	Cylinder Stop	**31**	Locking Bolt	**51**	Grip Screw
12	Cylinder Stop Spring	**32**	Locking Bolt Pin	**52**	Grip Locator Pin
13	Cylinder Stop Stud	**33**	Locking Bolt Spring	**53**	Thumb-Piece
14	Grip Escutcheon	**34**	Mainspring	**54**	Thumb-Piece Nut
15	Grip Escutcheon Nut	**35**	Mainspring Rod Swivel	**55**	Trigger
16	Extractor Rod	**36**	Sideplate Screws, Crowned	**56**	Trigger Lever
17	Extractor Spring	**37**	Sideplate Screw, Flat Head	**57**	Hand Torsion Spring
18	Frame	**38**	Rebound Slide Assembly	**58**	Trigger Lever and Hand Spring Pins
19	Frame Lug	**39**	Rebound Slide Spring	**59**	Hand Spring Torsion Pin
20	Hammer	**40**	Rebound Slide Stud	**60**	Trigger Stud

Model 41 Auto

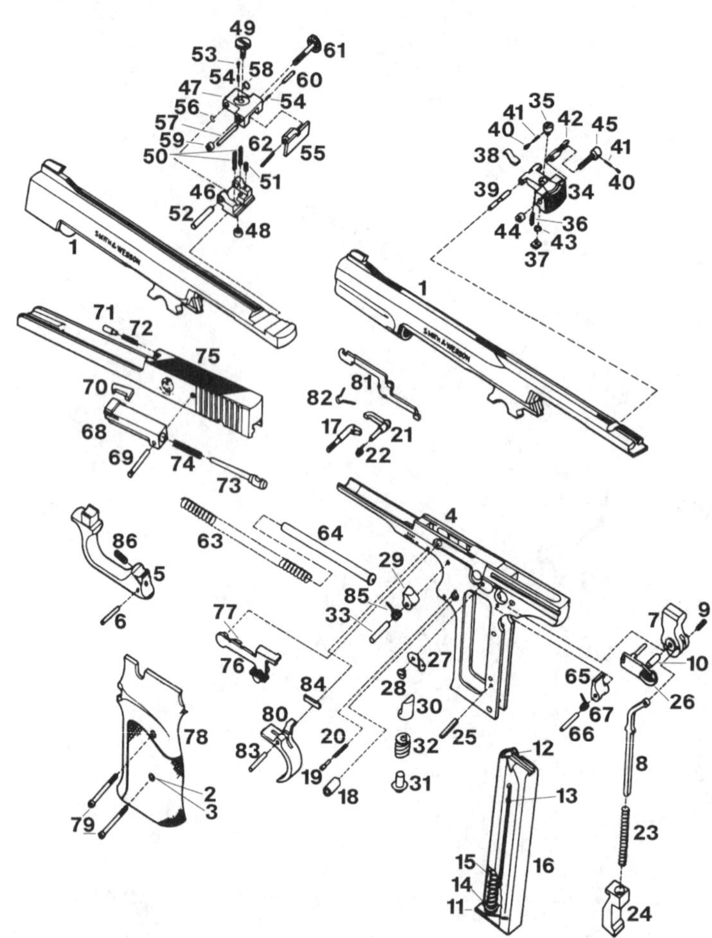

1	Barrel, 5 1/2" Heavy, 7"	30	Pawl Cam	59	Rear Sight Windage Nut
2	Grip Escutcheon	31	Pawl Cam Plunger	60	Rear Sight Windage Plunger
3	Grip Escutcheon Nut	32	Pawl Cam Spring	61	Rear Sight Windage Screw
4	Frame	33	Pawl Pin	62	Rear Sight Windage Spring
5	Trigger Guard	34	Rear Sight Body	63	Recoil Spring
6	Trigger Guard Pin	35	Rear Sight Elevation Nut	64	Recoil Spring Guide
7	Hammer	36	Rear Sight Elevation Spring	65	Sear
8	Stirrup	37	Rear Sight Elevation Stud	66	Sear Pin
9	Stirrup Pin	38	Rear Sight Pivot Clip	67	Sear Spring
10	Hammer Pin	39	Rear Sight Pivot Pin	68	Bolt
11	Magazine Base Plate	40	Rear Sight Plungers	69	Bolt Pin
12	Magazine Follower	41	Rear Sight Plunger Springs	70	Extractor
13	Magazine Pin	42	Rear Sight Slide	71	Extractor Plunger
14	Magazine Plunger	43	Rear Sight Spring Clip	72	Extractor Spring
15	Magazine Spring	44	Rear Sight Windage Nut	73	Firing Pin
16	Magazine Body	45	Rear Sight Windage Screw	74	Firing Pin Spring
17	Magazine Catch	46	Rear Sight Base	75	Slide
18	Magazine Catch Nut	47	Rear Sight Body	76	Slide Stop and Ejector
19	Magazine Catch Plunger	48	Rear Sight Elevation Nut	77	Slide Stop Spring
20	Magazine Catch Spring	49	Rear Sight Elevation Screw	78	Grip
21	Magazine Disconnector	50	Rear Sight Elevation Springs	79	Stock Screws
22	Magazine Disconnector Spring	51	Rear Sight Lock Screw	80	Trigger
23	Mainspring	52	Rear Sight Pivot Pin	81	Trigger Bar
24	Mainspring Retainer	53	Rear Sight Plunger	82	Trigger Bar Spring
25	Mainspring Retainer Pin	54	Rear Sight Plunger Springs	83	Trigger Pin
26	Manual Safety	55	Rear Sight Slide	84	Trigger Pull Adjusting Lever
27	Manual Safety Spring Plate	56	Rear Sight Spring Clip	85	Trigger Spring
28	Manual Safety Spring Plate Screw	57	Rear Sight Traverse Pin	86	Trigger Stop Screw
29	Pawl	58	Rear Sight Wavy Washer		

Model 43 and 51 Revolver

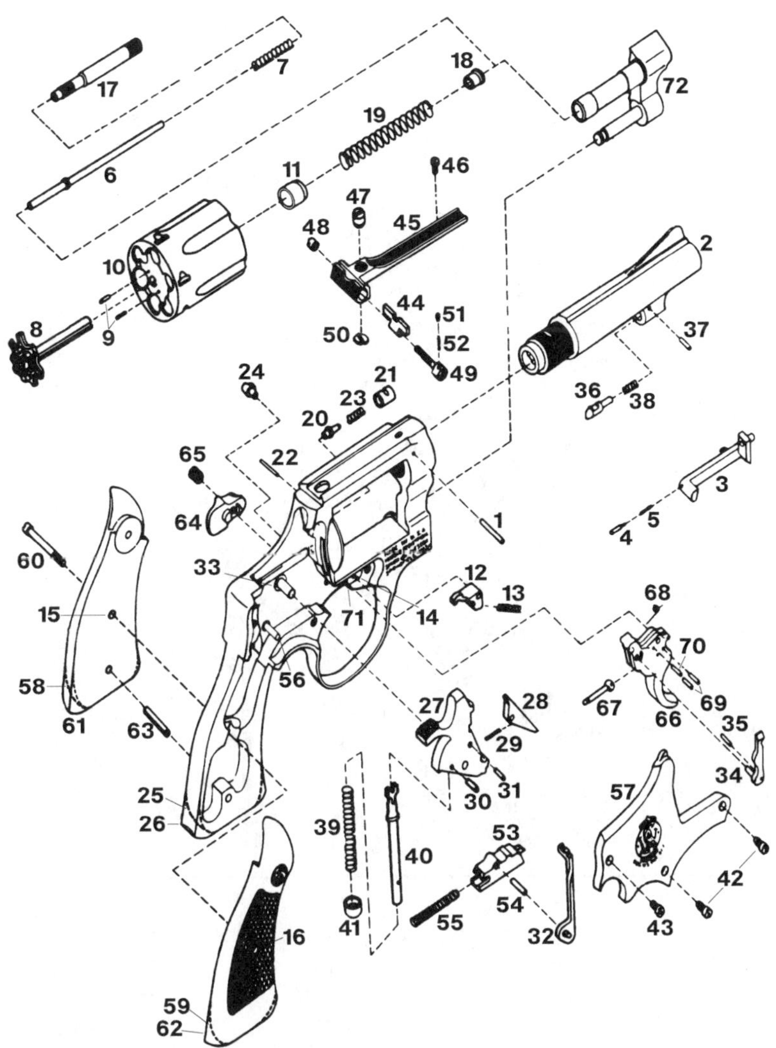

1	Barrel Pin	25	Frame, Round (Model 51)	49	Rear Sight Windage Screw
2	Barrel	26	Frame, Square (Model 43, 51)	50	Rear Sight Elevation Click Plug
3	Bolt	27	Hammer	51	Rear Sight Plunger
4	Bolt Plunger	28	Sear	52	Rear Sight Plunger Spring
5	Bolt Plunger Spring	29	Sear Spring	53	Rebound Slide Assembly
6	Center Pin	30	Stirrup Pin	54	Rebound Slide Pin
7	Center Pin Spring	31	Sear Pin	55	Rebound Slide Spring
8	Extractor Assembly	32	Hammer Block	56	Rebound Slide Stud
9	Extractor Pins	33	Hammer Stud	57	Sideplate
10	Cylinder	34	Hand	58	Left Grip, Round Butt
11	Gas Ring	35	Hand Pin	59	Right Grip, Round Butt
12	Cylinder Stop	36	Locking Bolt	60	Grip Screw
13	Cylinder Stop Spring	37	Locking Bolt Pin	61	Left Grip, Square Butt
14	Cylinder Stop Stud	38	Locking Bolt Spring	62	Right Grip, Square Butt
15	Grip Escutcheon	39	Mainspring	63	Grip Locator Pin
16	Grip Escutcheon Nut	40	Mainspring Stirrup	64	Thumb-Piece
17	Extractor Rod	41	Mainspring Swivel	65	Thumb-Piece Nut
18	Extractor Rod Collar	42	Sideplate Screws, Crowned	66	Trigger
19	Extractor Spring	43	Sideplate Screw, Flat Head	67	Trigger Lever
20	Firing Pin	44	Rear Sight Slide	68	Hand Torsion Spring
21	Firing Pin Bushing	45	Rear Sight Leaf	69	Trigger Lever and Hand Spring Pins
22	Firing Pin Bushing Pin	46	Rear Sight Leaf Screw	70	Hand Torsion Spring Pin
23	Firing Pin Spring	47	Rear Sight Elevation Screw	71	Trigger Stud
24	Frame Lug	48	Rear Sight Windage Nut	72	Yoke

SMITH & WESSON

Model 46 Auto

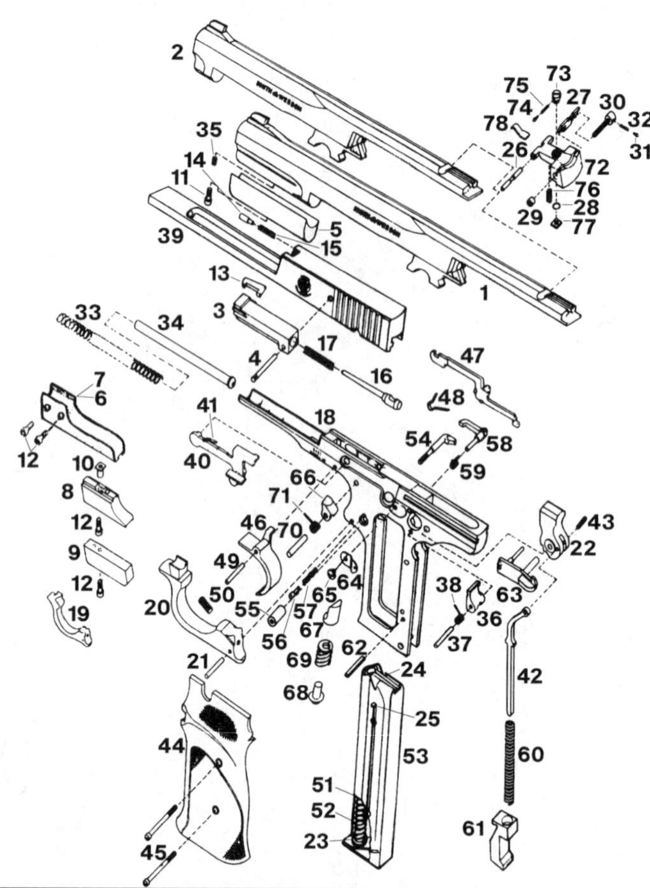

1	Barrel, 7"
2	Barrel, 5"
3	Bolt
4	Bolt Pin
5	Counterweight, 2 oz.
6	Counterweight Upper Section, Steel, 7 1/4 oz.
7	Counterweight Upper Section, Aluminum, 3 oz.
8	Counterweight Middle Section, 4 1/4 oz.
9	Counterweight Lower Section, 4 oz.
10	Counterweight Nut
11	Counterweight Screw
12	Counterweight Screws
13	Extractor
14	Extractor Plunger
15	Extractor Spring
16	Firing Pin
17	Firing Pin Spring
18	Frame
19	Guard Accessory
20	Guard
21	Guard Pin
22	Hammer
23	Magazine Base Plate
24	Magazine Follower
25	Magazine Pin
26	Rear Sight Pivot Pin
27	Rear Sight Slide
28	Rear Sight Spring Clip
29	Rear Sight Windage Nut
30	Rear Sight Windage Screw
31	Rear Sight Windage Screw Plunger
32	Rear Sight Windage Screw Plunger Spring
33	Recoil Spring
34	Recoil Spring Guide
35	Counterweight Hole Screw
36	Sear
37	Sear Pin
38	Sear Spring
39	Slide
40	Slide Stop and Ejector Assembly
41	Slide Stop Spring
42	Stirrup
43	Stirrup Pin
44	Left Grip with Escutcheon
45	Grip Screws
46	Trigger
47	Trigger Bar
48	Trigger Bar Spring
49	Trigger Pin
50	Trigger Stop Screw
51	Magazine Spring
52	Magazine Spring Plunger
53	Magazine Body
54	Magazine Catch
55	Magazine Catch Nut
56	Magazine Catch Plunger
57	Magazine Catch Spring
58	Magazine Disconnector Assembly
59	Magazine Disconnector Spring
60	Mainspring
61	Mainspring Retainer
62	Mainspring Retainer Pin
63	Manual Safety Assembly
64	Manual Safety Spring Plate
65	Manual Safety Spring Plate Screw
66	Pawl
67	Pawl Cam
68	Pawl Cam Plunger
69	Pawl Cam Spring
70	Pawl Pin
71	Pawl and Trigger Spring
72	Rear Sight Base
73	Rear Sight Elevating Nut
74	Rear Sight Elevating Nut Plunger
75	Rear Sight Elevating Nut Plunger Spring
76	Rear Sight Elevating Spring
77	Rear Sight Elevating Stud
78	Rear Sight Pivot Clip

Parts Not Shown

Right Grip with Escutcheon

Model 48 Revolver

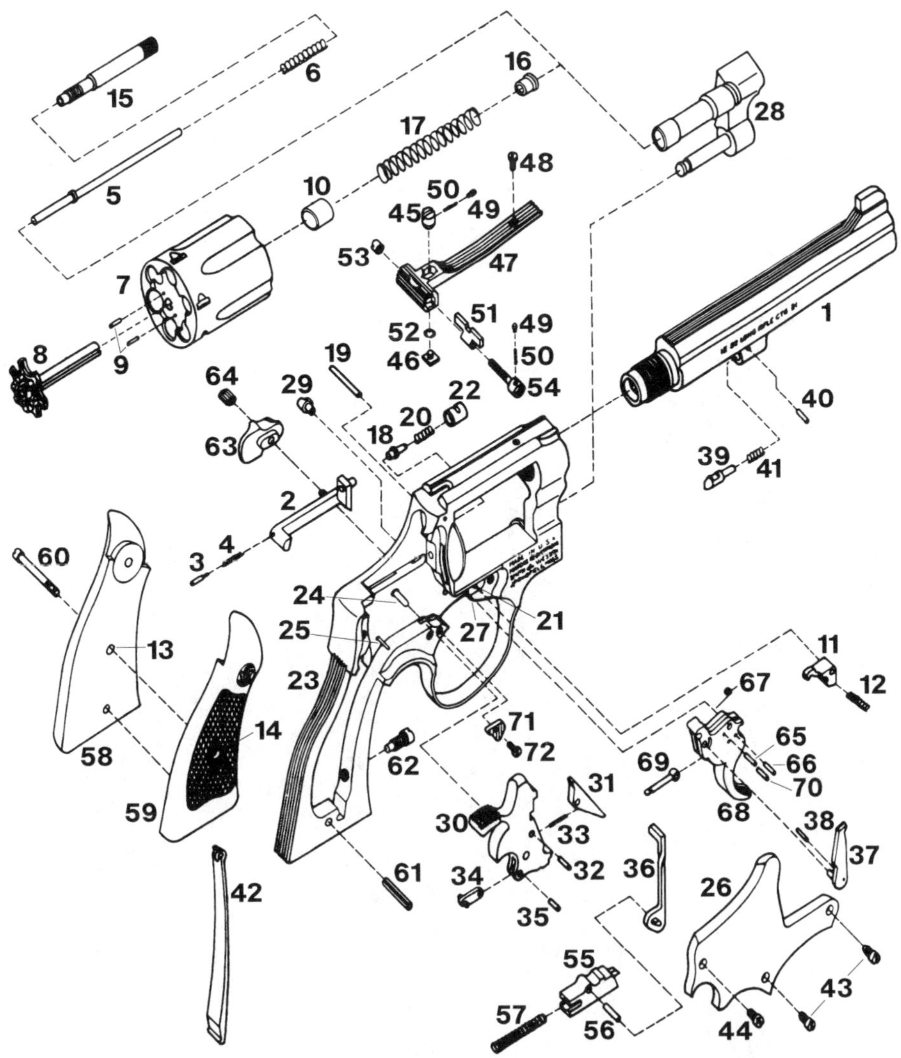

1	Barrel	**25**	Rebound Slide Stud	**49**	Rear Sight Plungers
2	Bolt	**26**	Sideplate	**50**	Rear Sight Plunger Springs
3	Bolt Plunger	**27**	Trigger Stud	**51**	Rear Sight Slide
4	Bolt Plunger Spring	**28**	Yoke	**52**	Rear Sight Spring Clip
5	Center Pin	**29**	Frame Lug	**53**	Rear Sight Windage Nut
6	Center Pin Spring	**30**	Hammer	**54**	Rear Sight Windage Screw
7	Cylinder	**31**	Sear	**55**	Rebound Slide
8	Extractor	**32**	Sear Pin	**56**	Rebound Slide Pin
9	Extractor Pins	**33**	Sear Spring	**57**	Rebound Slide Spring
10	Gas Ring	**34**	Stirrup	**58**	Left Grip
11	Cylinder Stop	**35**	Stirrup Pin	**59**	Right Grip
12	Cylinder Stop Spring	**36**	Hammer Block	**60**	Grip Screw
13	Grip Escutcheon	**37**	Hand	**61**	Grip Locator Pin
14	Grip Escutcheon Nut	**38**	Hand Pin	**62**	Strain Screw
15	Extractor Rod	**39**	Locking Bolt	**63**	Thumb-Piece
16	Extractor Rod Collar	**40**	Locking Bolt Pin	**64**	Thumb-Piece Nut
17	Extractor Spring	**41**	Locking Bolt Spring	**65**	Hand Spring Pin
18	Firing Pin	**42**	Mainspring	**66**	Hand Spring Torsion Pin
19	Firing Pin Bushing Pin	**43**	Sideplate Screws, Crowned	**67**	Hand Torsion Spring
20	Firing Pin Spring	**44**	Sideplate Screw, Flat Head	**68**	Trigger
21	Cylinder Stop Stud	**45**	Rear Sight Elevation Nut	**69**	Trigger Lever
22	Firing Pin Bushing	**46**	Rear Sight Elevation Stud	**70**	Trigger Lever Pin
23	Frame	**47**	Rear Sight Leaf	**71**	Trigger Stop
24	Hammer Stud	**48**	Rear Sight Leaf Screw	**72**	Trigger Stop Screw

Model 49 Revolver

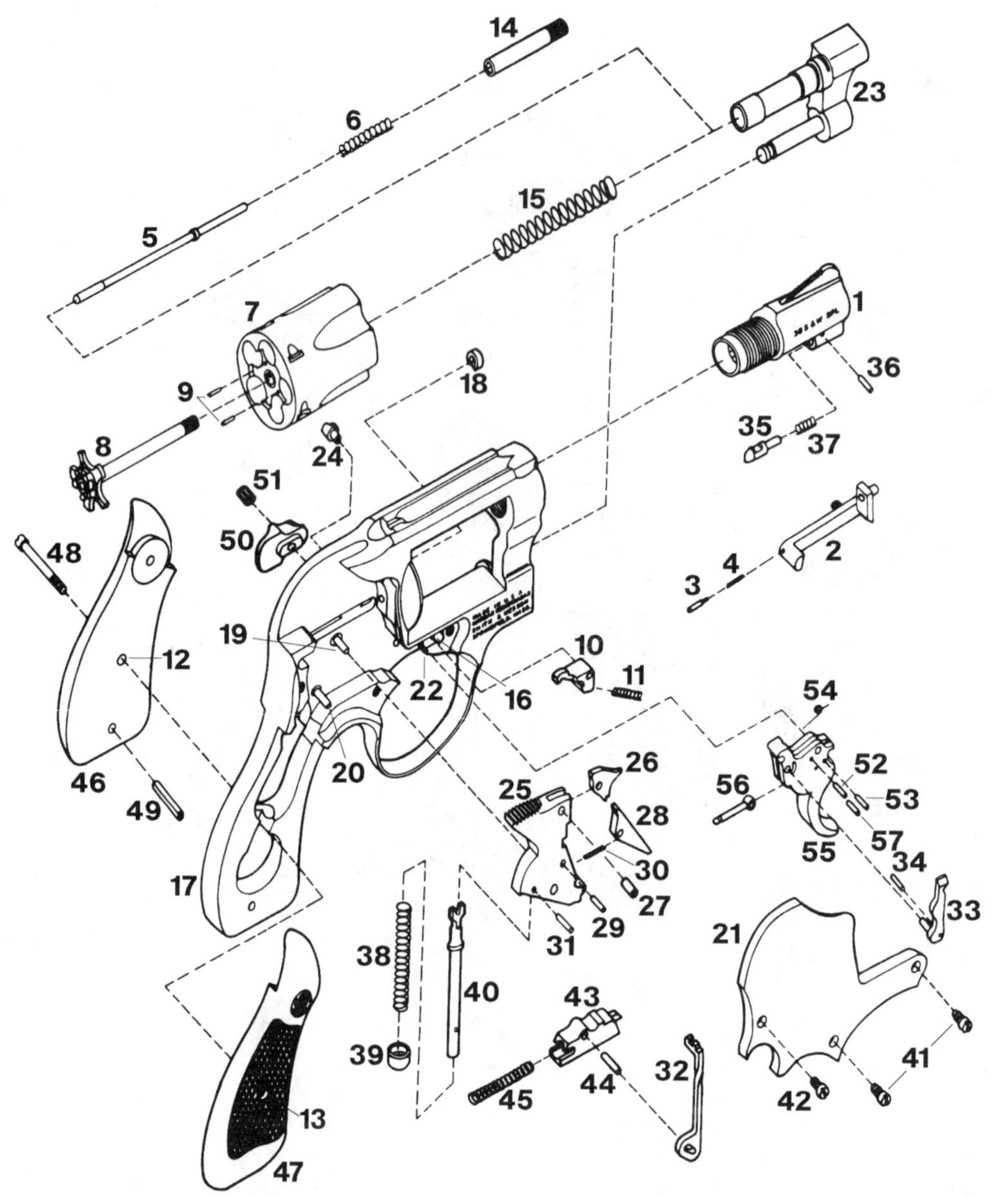

1	Barrel	20	Rebound Slide Stud	39	Mainspring Rod Swivel
2	Bolt	21	Sideplate	40	Mainspring Stirrup
3	Bolt Plunger	22	Trigger Stud	41	Sideplate Screws, Crowned
4	Bolt Plunger Spring	23	Yoke	42	Sideplate Screw, Flat Head
5	Center Pin	24	Frame Lug	43	Rebound Slide
6	Center Pin Spring	25	Hammer	44	Rebound Slide Pin
7	Cylinder	26	Hammer Nose	45	Rebound Slide Spring
8	Extractor	27	Hammer Nose Rivet	46	Left Grip
9	Extractor Pins	28	Sear	47	Right Grip
10	Cylinder Stop	29	Sear Pin	48	Grip Screw
11	Cylinder Stop Spring	30	Sear Spring	49	Grip Locator Pin
12	Grip Escutcheon	31	Stirrup Pin	50	Thumb-Piece
13	Grip Escutcheon Nut	32	Hammer Block	51	Thumb-Piece Nut
14	Extractor Rod	33	Hand	52	Hand Spring Pin
15	Extractor Spring	34	Hand Pin	53	Hand Spring Torsion Pin
16	Cylinder Stop Stud	35	Locking Bolt	54	Hand Torsion Spring
17	Frame	36	Locking Bolt Pin	55	Trigger
18	Hammer Nose Bushing	37	Locking Bolt Spring	56	Trigger Lever
19	Hammer Stud	38	Mainspring	57	Trigger Lever Pin

Model 52 Auto

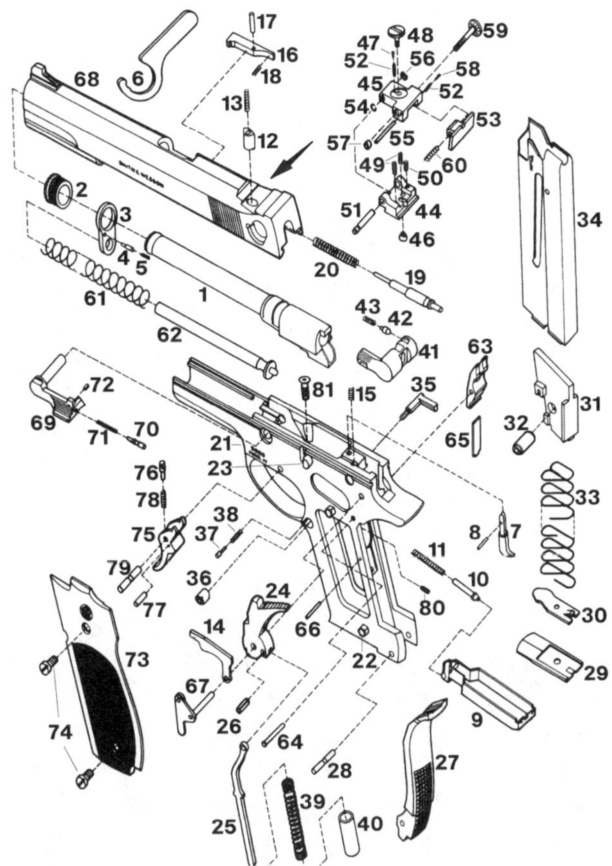

1	Barrel	32	Magazine Follower Pin	63	Sear
2	Barrel Bushing	33	Magazine Spring	64	Sear Pin
3	Barrel Bushing Plate	34	Magazine Body	65	Sear Spring
4	Barrel Bushing Plunger	35	Magazine Catch	66	Sear Spring Retaining Pin
5	Barrel Bushing Plunger Spring	36	Magazine Catch Nut	67	Sideplate Assembly
6	Barrel Bushing Wrench	37	Magazine Catch Plunger	68	Slide
7	Disconnector	38	Magazine Catch Spring	69	Slide Stop
8	Disconnector Pin	39	Mainspring	70	Slide Stop Plunger
9	Drawbar	40	Mainspring Plunger	71	Slide Stop Plunger Spring
10	Drawbar Plunger	41	Manual Safety	72	Slide Stop Spiral Pin
11	Drawbar Plunger Spring	42	Manual Safety Plunger	73	Grip
12	Ejector Depressor Plunger	43	Manual Safety Plunger Spring	74	Grip Screws
13	Ejector Depressor Plunger Spring	44	Rear Sight Base	75	Trigger
14	Ejector Magazine Depressor	45	Rear Sight Body	76	Trigger Plunger
15	Ejector Spring	46	Rear Sight Elevation Nut	77	Trigger Plunger Pin
16	Extractor	47	Rear Sight Elevation Plunger	78	Trigger Plunger Spring
17	Extractor Pivot Pin	48	Rear Sight Elevation Screw	79	Trigger Pin
18	Extractor Spring	49	Rear Sight Elevation Springs	80	Lower Trigger Stop Screw
19	Firing Pin	50	Rear Sight Lock Screw	81	Upper Trigger Stop Screw
20	Firing Pin Spring	51	Rear Sight Pivot Pin	**Parts Not Shown**	
21	Frame	52	Rear Sight Plunger Spring		Hammer Pin
22	Frame Stud	53	Rear Sight Slide		Recoil Spring Guide
23	Slide Stop Button	54	Rear Sight Spring Clip		Recoil Spring Guide Bushing
24	Hammer	55	Rear Sight Traverse Pin		Recoil Spring Guide Plunger
25	Stirrup	56	Rear Sight Wavey Washer		Recoil Spring Guide Spring
26	Stirrup Pin	57	Rear Sight Windage Nut		Sideplate
27	Frame Insert	58	Rear Sight Windage Plunger		Sideplate Button
28	Frame Insert Pin	59	Rear Sight Windage Screw		
29	Magazine Floorplate	60	Rear Sight Windage Spring		
30	Magazine Floorplate Catch	61	Recoil Spring		
31	Magazine Follower	62	Recoil Spring Guide Assembly		

Model 53 Revolver

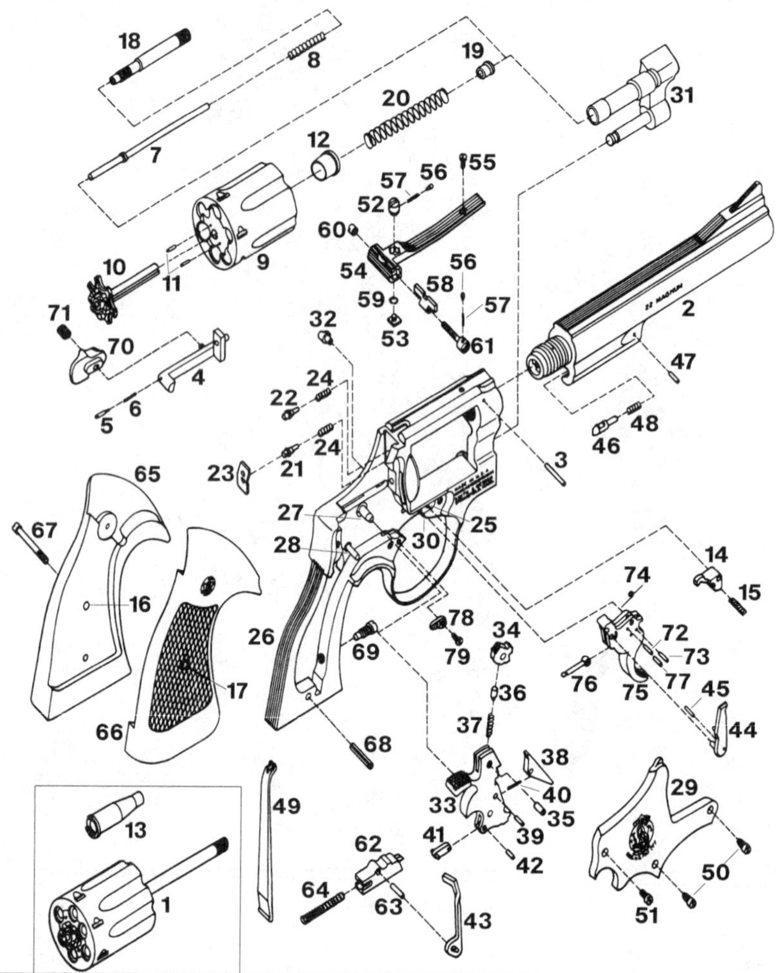

1	Auxiliary 22LR Cylinder
2	Barrel
3	Barrel Pin
4	Bolt
5	Bolt Plunger
6	Bolt Plunger Spring
7	Center Pin
8	Center Pin Spring
9	Cylinder, 22 WMR
10	Extractor
11	Extractor Pins
12	Gas Ring
13	Cylinder Insert
14	Cylinder Stop
15	Cylinder Stop Spring
16	Grip Escutcheon
17	Grip Escutcheon Nut
18	Extractor Rod
19	Extractor Rod Collar
20	Extractor Spring
21	Lower Firing Pin
22	Upper Firing Pin
23	Firing Pin Retainer
24	Firing Pin Springs
25	Cylinder Stop Stud
26	Frame
27	Hammer Stud
28	Rebound Slide Stud
29	Sideplate
30	Trigger Stud
31	Yoke
32	Frame Lug
33	Hammer
34	Hammer Nose
35	Hammer Nose Rivet
36	Hammer Nose Plunger
37	Hammer Nose Plunger Spring
38	Sear
39	Sear Pin
40	Sear Spring
41	Stirrup
42	Stirrup Pin
43	Hammer Block
44	Hand
45	Hand Pin
46	Locking Bolt
47	Locking Bolt Pin
48	Locking Bolt Spring
49	Mainspring
50	Sideplate Screws, Crowned
51	Sideplate Screw, Flat Head
52	Rear Sight Elevation Nut
53	Rear Sight Elevation Stud
54	Rear Sight Leaf
55	Rear Sight Leaf Screw
56	Rear Sight Plungers
57	Rear Sight Plunger Spring
58	Rear Sight Slide
59	Rear Sight Spring Clip
60	Rear Sight Windage Nut
61	Rear Sight Windage Screw
62	Rebound Slide
63	Rebound Slide Pin
64	Rebound Slide Spring
65	Left Grip
66	Right Grip
67	Grip Screw
68	Grip Locator Pin
69	Strain Screw
70	Thumb-Piece
71	Thumb-Piece Nut
72	Hand Spring Pin
73	Hand Spring Torsion Pin
74	Hand Torsion Spring
75	Trigger
76	Trigger Lever
77	Trigger Lever Pin
78	Trigger Stop
79	Trigger Stop Screw

Model 57 Revolver

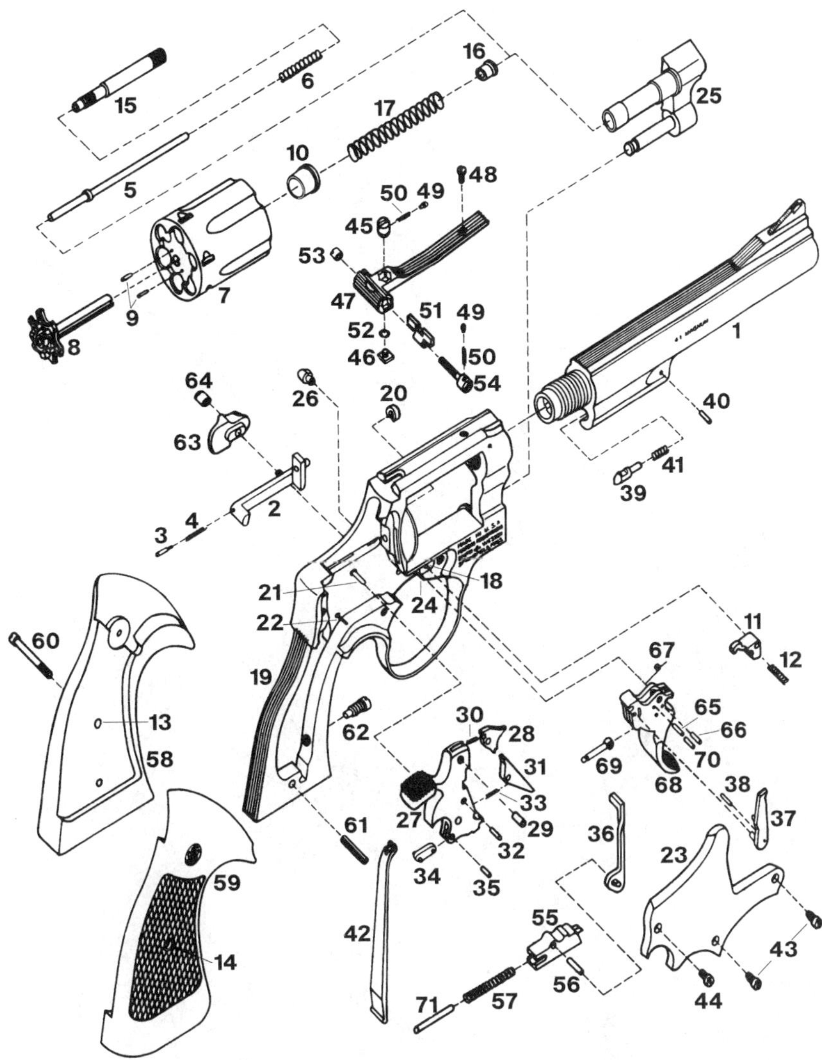

1	Barrel	**25**	Yoke	**49**	Rear Sight Plunger
2	Bolt	**26**	Frame Lug	**50**	Rear Sight Plunger Spring
3	Bolt Plunger	**27**	Hammer	**51**	Rear Sight Slide
4	Bolt Plunger Spring	**28**	Hammer Nose	**52**	Rear Sight Spring Clip
5	Center Pin	**29**	Hammer Nose Rivet	**53**	Rear Sight Windage Nut
6	Center Pin Spring	**30**	Hammer Nose Spring	**54**	Rear Sight Windage Screw
7	Cylinder	**31**	Sear	**55**	Rebound Slide
8	Extractor	**32**	Sear Pin	**56**	Rebound Slide Pin
9	Extractor Pins	**33**	Sear Spring	**57**	Rebound Slide Spring
10	Gas Ring	**34**	Stirrup	**58**	Left Grip
11	Cylinder Stop	**35**	Stirrup Pin	**59**	Right Grip
12	Cylinder Stop Spring	**36**	Hammer Block	**60**	Grip Screw
13	Grip Escutcheon	**37**	Hand	**61**	Grip Locator Pin
14	Grip Escutcheon Nut	**38**	Hand Pin	**62**	Strain Screw
15	Extractor Rod	**39**	Locking Bolt	**63**	Thumb-Piece
16	Extractor Rod Collar	**40**	Locking Bolt Pin	**64**	Thumb-Piece Nut
17	Extractor Spring	**41**	Locking Bolt Spring	**65**	Hand Spring Pin
18	Cylinder Stop Stud	**42**	Mainspring	**66**	Hand Spring Torsion Pin
19	Frame	**43**	Sideplate Screws, Crowned	**67**	Hand Torsion Spring
20	Hammer Nose Bushing	**44**	Sideplate Screw, Flat Head	**68**	Trigger
21	Hammer Stud	**45**	Rear Sight Elevation Nut	**69**	Trigger Lever
22	Rebound Slide Stud	**46**	Rear Sight Elevation Stud	**70**	Trigger Lever Pin
23	Sideplate	**47**	Rear Sight Leaf	**71**	Trigger Stop Rod
24	Trigger Stud	**48**	Rear Sight Leaf Screw		

Model 58 Revolver

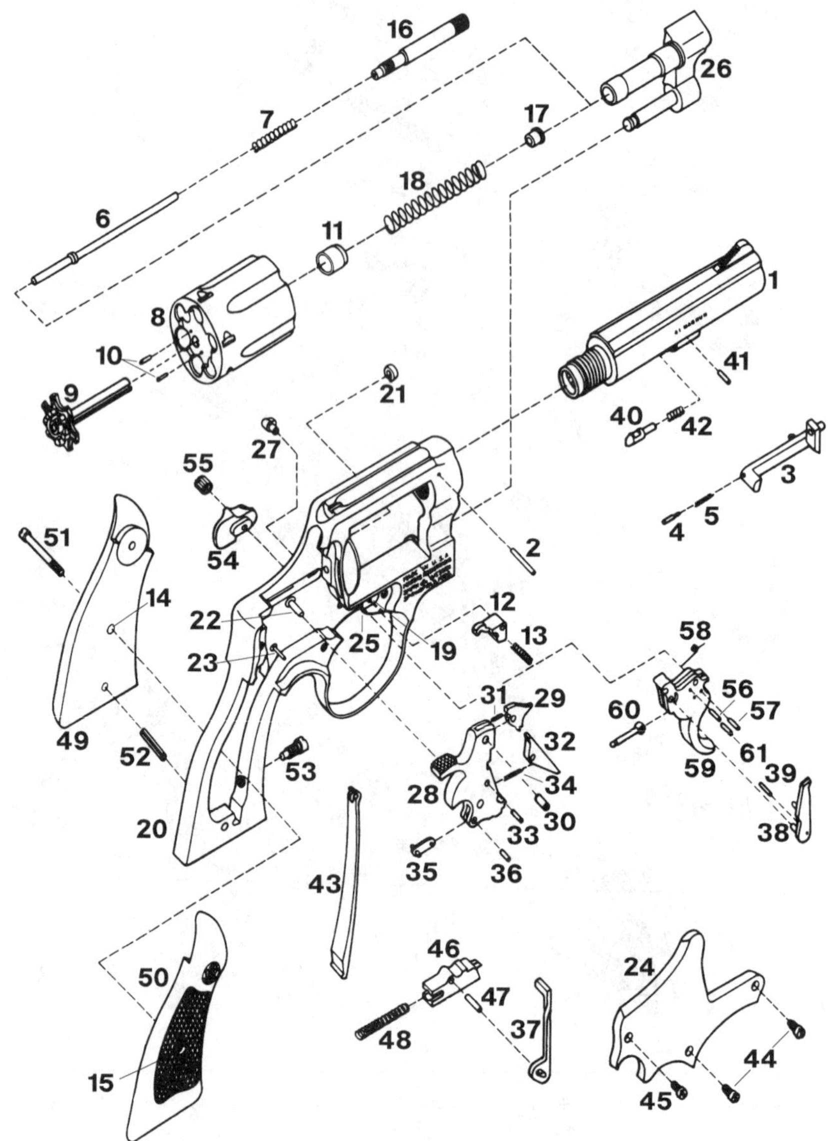

1	Barrel	**22**	Hammer Stud	**43**	Mainspring
2	Barrel Pin	**23**	Rebound Slide Stud	**44**	Sideplate Screws, Crowned
3	Bolt	**24**	Sideplate	**45**	Sideplate Screw, Flat Head
4	Bolt Plunger	**25**	Trigger Stud	**46**	Rebound Slide
5	Bolt Plunger Spring	**26**	Yoke	**47**	Rebound Slide Pin
6	Center Pin	**27**	Frame Lug	**48**	Rebound Slide Spring
7	Center Pin Spring	**28**	Hammer	**49**	Left Grip
8	Cylinder	**29**	Hammer Nose	**50**	Right Grip
9	Extractor	**30**	Hammer Nose Rivet	**51**	Grip Screw
10	Extractor Pins	**31**	Hammer Nose Spring	**52**	Grip Locator Pin
11	Gas Ring	**32**	Sear	**53**	Strain Screw
12	Cylinder Stop	**33**	Sear Pin	**54**	Thumb-Piece
13	Cylinder Stop Spring	**34**	Sear Spring	**55**	Thumb-Piece Nut
14	Grip Escutcheon	**35**	Stirrup	**56**	Hand Spring Pin
15	Grip Escutcheon Nut	**36**	Stirrup Pin	**57**	Hand Spring Torsion Pin
16	Extractor Rod	**37**	Hammer Block	**58**	Hand Torsion Spring
17	Extractor Rod Collar	**38**	Hand	**59**	Trigger
18	Extractor Spring	**39**	Hand Pin	**60**	Trigger Lever
19	Cylinder Stop Stud	**40**	Locking Bolt	**61**	Trigger Lever Pin
20	Frame	**41**	Locking Bolt Pin		
21	Hammer Nose Bushing	**42**	Locking Bolt Spring		

Model 59 Auto

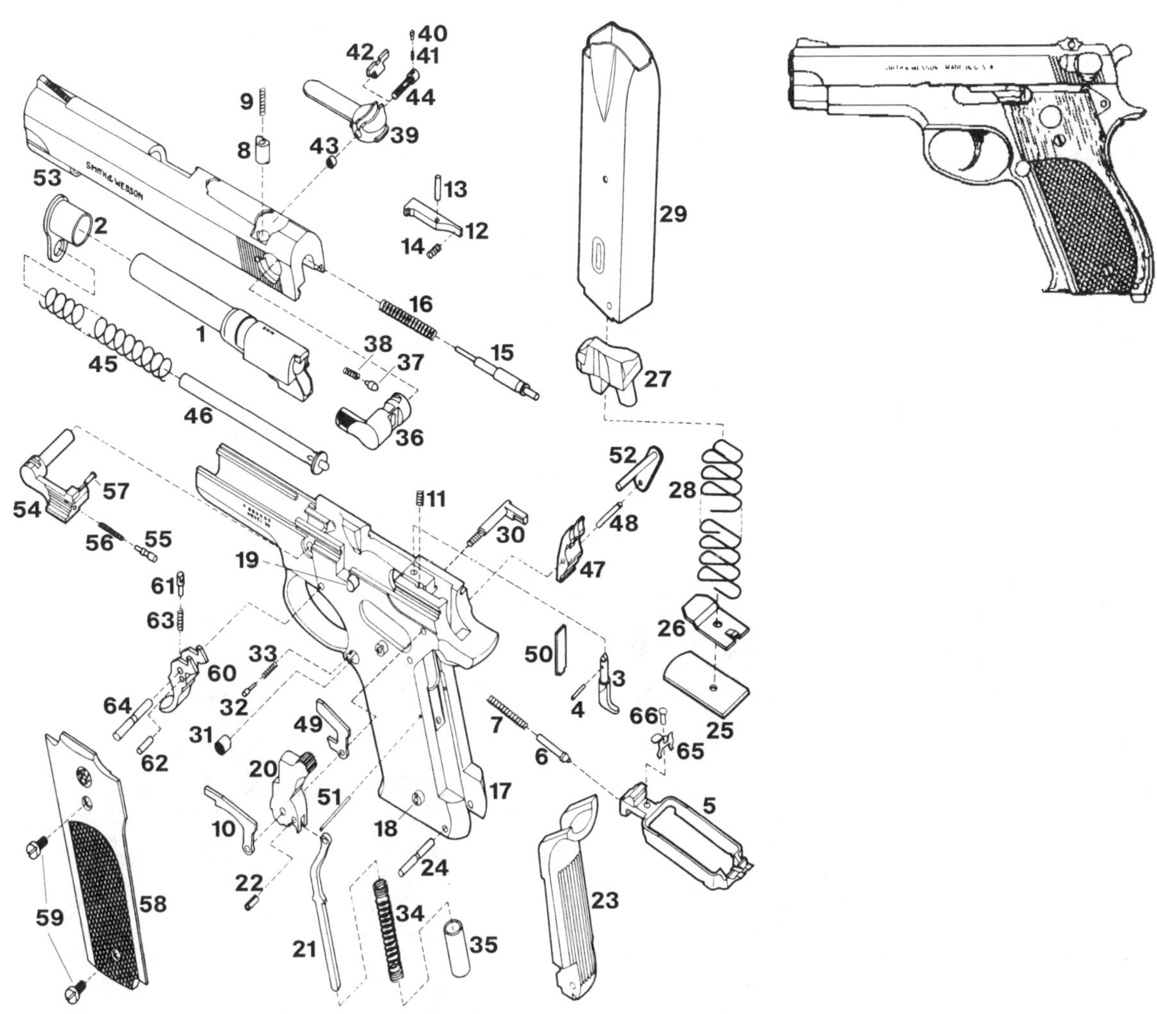

1	Barrel	**26**	Magazine Base Plate Catch	**51**	Sear Spring Retaining Pin
2	Barrel Bushing	**27**	Magazine Follower	**52**	Sideplate
3	Disconnector	**28**	Magazine Spring	**53**	Slide
4	Disconnector Pin	**29**	Magazine Body	**54**	Slide Stop
5	Drawbar	**30**	Magazine Catch	**55**	Slide Stop Plunger
6	Drawbar Plunger	**31**	Magazine Catch Nut	**56**	Slide Stop Plunger Spring
7	Drawbar Plunger Spring	**32**	Magazine Catch Plunger	**57**	Slide Stop Spiral Pin
8	Ejector Depressor Plunger	**33**	Magazine Catch Plunger Spring	**58**	Left Grip
9	Ejector Depressor Plunger Spring	**34**	Mainspring	**59**	Stock Screws
10	Ejector Magazine Depressor	**35**	Mainspring Plunger	**60**	Trigger
11	Ejector Spring	**36**	Manual Safety	**61**	Trigger Plunger
12	Extractor	**37**	Manual Safety Plunger	**62**	Trigger Plunger Pin
13	Extractor Pin	**38**	Manual Safety Plunger Spring	**63**	Trigger Plunger Spring
14	Extractor Spring	**39**	Rear Sight Leaf	**64**	Trigger Pin
15	Firing Pin	**40**	Rear Sght Plunger	**65**	Trigger Play Spring
16	Firing Pin Spring	**41**	Rear Sight Plunger Spring	**66**	Trigger Play Rivet
17	Frame	**42**	Rear Sight Slide	**Parts Not Shown**	
18	Frame Stud	**43**	Rear Sight Windage Nut		Hammer Pin
19	Slide Stop Button	**44**	Rear Sight Windage Screw		Recoil Spring Guide
20	Hammer	**45**	Recoil Spring		Recoil Spring Guide Bushing
21	Stirrup	**46**	Recoil Spring Guide Assembly		Recoil Spring Guide Plunger
22	Stirrup Pin	**47**	Sear		Recoil Spring Guide Plunger Spring
23	Frame Insert	**48**	Sear Pin		Right Grip
24	Frame Insert Pin	**49**	Sear Release Lever		Sideplate Button
25	Magazine Base Plate	**50**	Sear Spring		

Model 60 Revolver

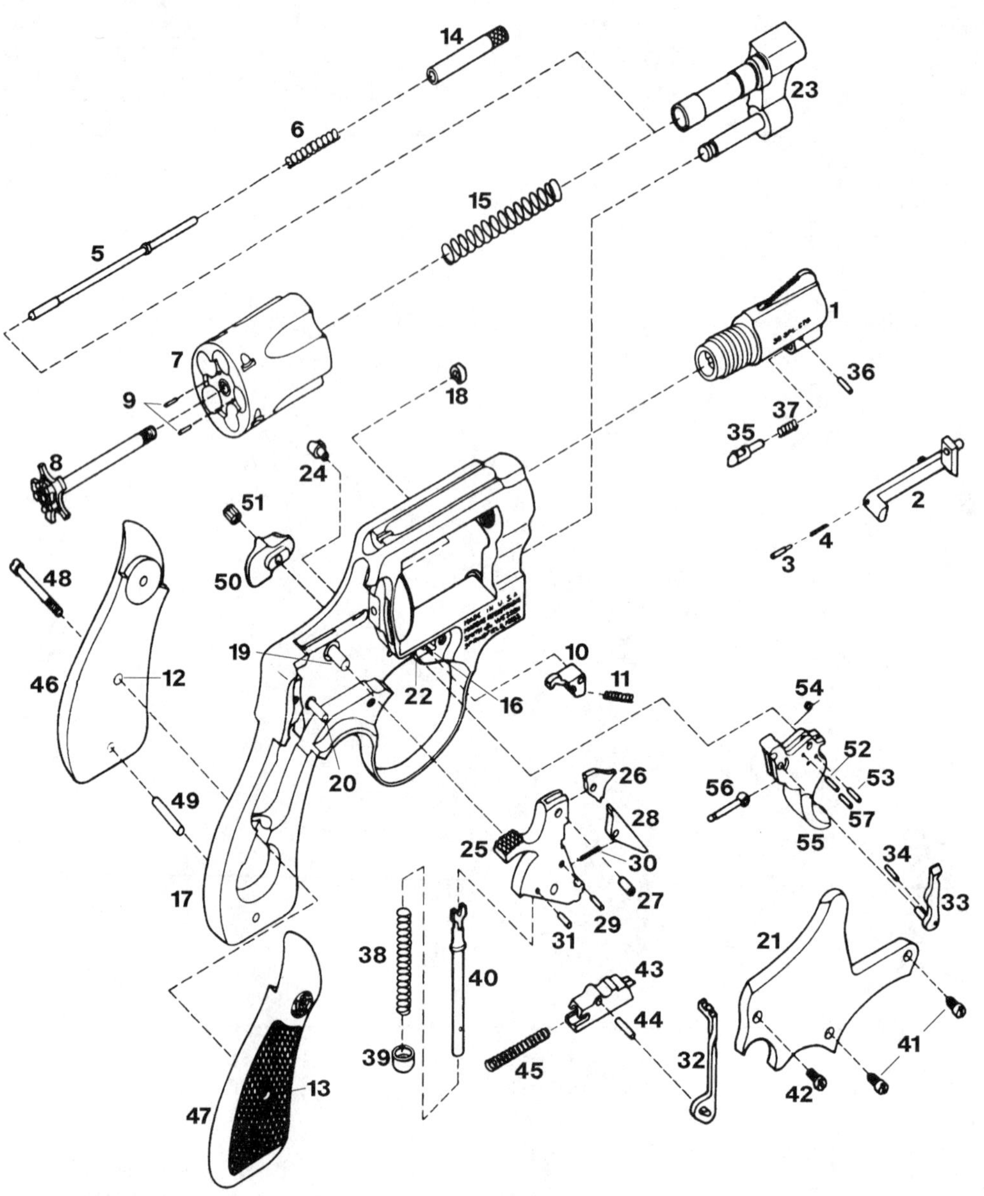

1	Barrel	**20**	Rebound Slide Stud	**39**	Mainspring Rod Swivel
2	Bolt	**21**	Sideplate	**40**	Mainspring Stirrup
3	Bolt Plunger	**22**	Trigger Stud	**41**	Sideplate Screws, Crowned
4	Bolt Plunger Spring	**23**	Yoke	**42**	Sideplate Screw, Flat Head
5	Center Pin	**24**	Frame Lug	**43**	Rebound Slide
6	Center Pin Spring	**25**	Hammer	**44**	Rebound Slide Pin
7	Cylinder	**26**	Hammer Nose	**45**	Rebound Slide Spring
8	Extractor	**27**	Hammer Nose Rivet	**46**	Left Grip
9	Extractor Pins	**28**	Sear	**47**	Right Grip
10	Cylinder Stop	**29**	Sear Pin	**48**	Grip Screw
11	Cylinder Stop Spring	**30**	Sear Spring	**49**	Grip Locator Pin
12	Grip Escutcheon	**31**	Stirrup Pin	**50**	Thumb-Piece
13	Grip Escutcheon Nut	**32**	Hammer Block	**51**	Thumb-Piece Nut
14	Extractor Rod	**33**	Hand	**52**	Hand Spring Pin
15	Extractor Spring	**34**	Hand Pin	**53**	Hand Spring Torsion Pin
16	Cylinder Stop Stud	**35**	Locking Bolt	**54**	Hand Torsion Spring
17	Frame	**36**	Locking Bolt Pin	**55**	Trigger
18	Hammer Nose Bushing	**37**	Locking Bolt Spring	**56**	Trigger Lever
19	Hammer Stud	**38**	Mainspring	**57**	Trigger Lever Pin

Model 61 Auto

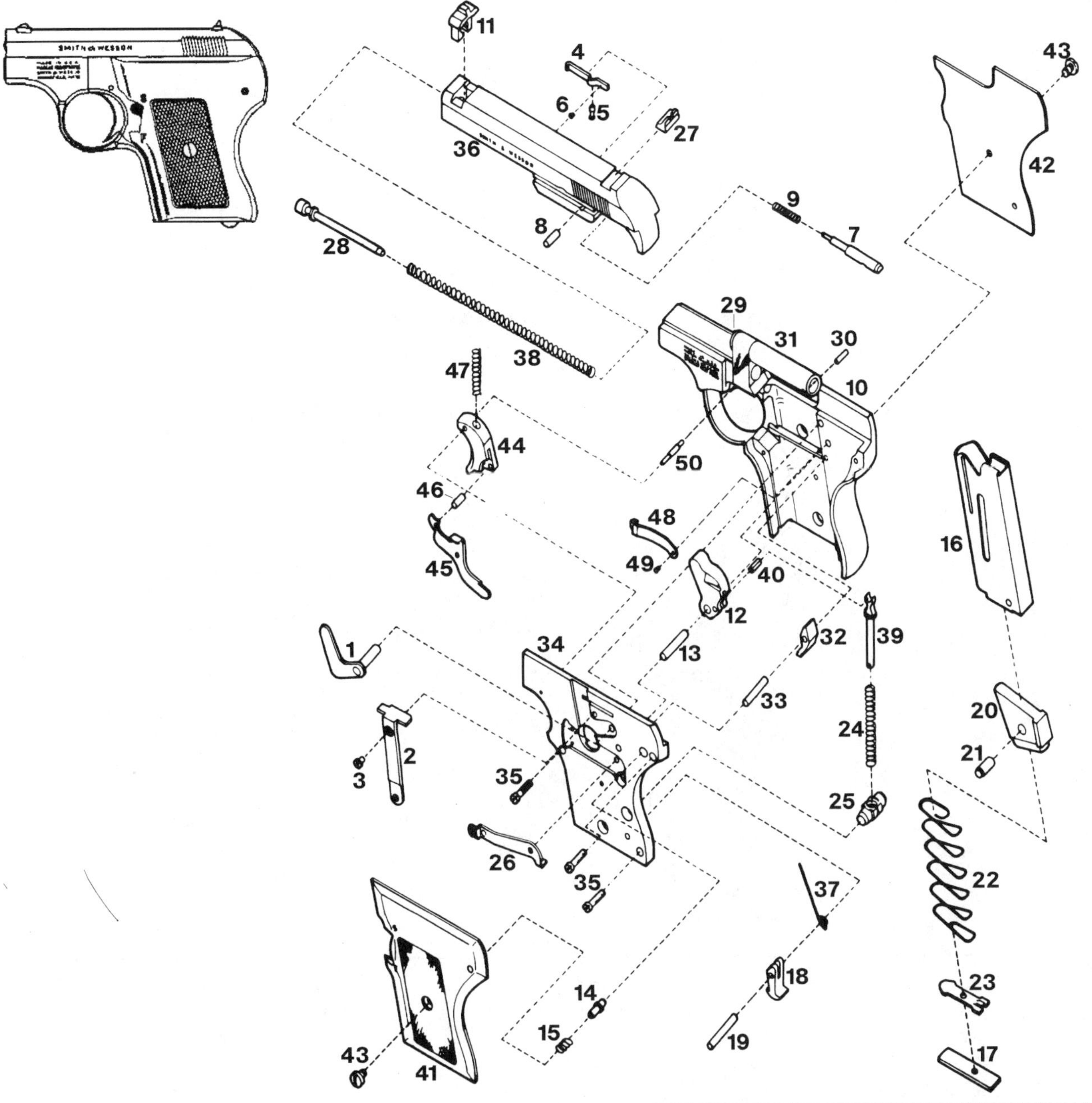

1	Disconnector	18	Magazine Catch	35	Sideplate Screws
2	Ejector	19	Magazine Catch Pin	36	Slide
3	Ejector Screw	20	Magazine Follower	37	Magazine Catch and Sear Spring
4	Extractor	21	Magazine Follower Pin	38	Recoil Spring
5	Extractor Pin	22	Magazine Spring	39	Stirrup
6	Extractor Spring	23	Magazine Spring Plate	40	Stirrup Pin
7	Firing Pin	24	Mainspring	41	Left Grip
8	Firing Pin Retaining Pin	25	Mainspring Retainer	42	Right Grip
9	Firing Pin Spring	26	Manual Safety-Lever	43	Grip Screws
10	Frame	27	Rear Sight Blade	44	Trigger
11	Front Sight	28	Recoil Spring Guide	45	Trigger Bar
12	Hammer	29	Recoil Spring Guide Tube	46	Trigger Bar Pin
13	Hammer Pin	30	Recoil Spring Stop Pin	47	Trigger Bar Spring
14	Indicator Plunger	31	Retainer Tube	48	Trigger Block
15	Indicator Plunger Spring	32	Sear	49	Trigger Block Rivet
16	Magazine Body	33	Sear Pin	50	Trigger Pin
17	Magazine Base Plate	34	Sideplate		

Model 63 Revolver

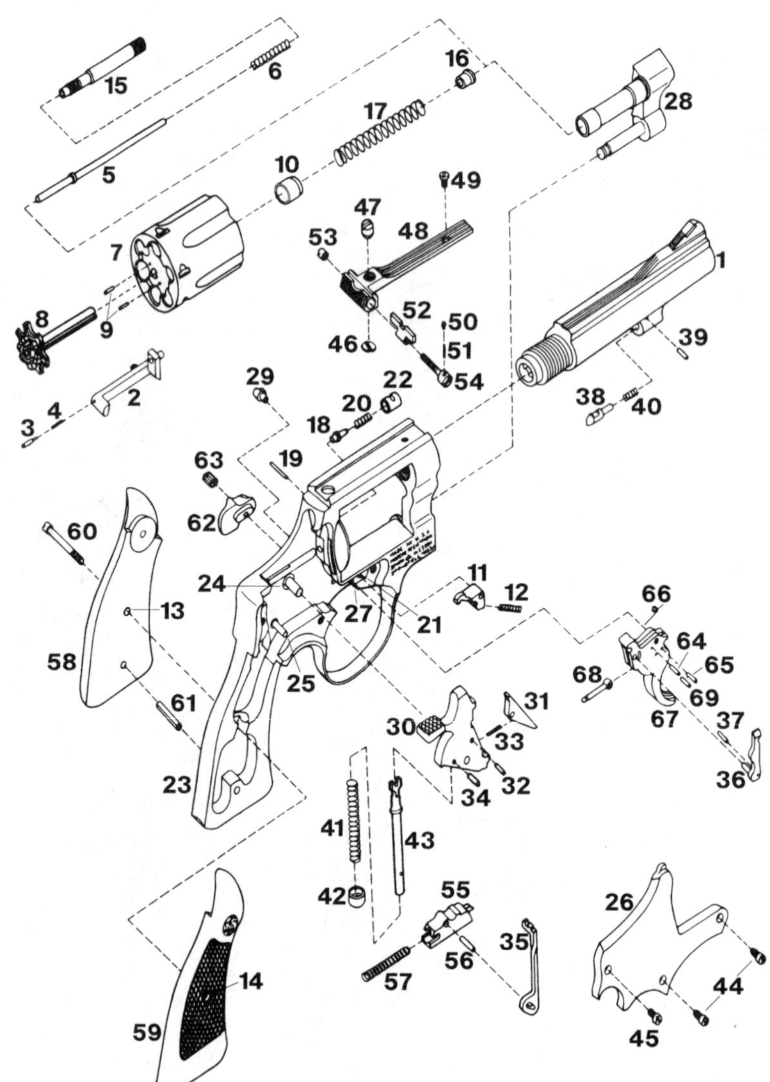

1	Barrel	24	Hammer Stud	47	Rear Sight Elevation Screw
2	Bolt	25	Rebound Slide Stud	48	Rear Sight Leaf
3	Bolt Plunger	26	Sideplate	49	Rear Sight Leaf Screw
4	Bolt Plunger Spring	27	Trigger Stud	50	Rear Sight Plunger
5	Center Pin	28	Yoke	51	Rear Sight Plunger Spring
6	Center Pin Spring	29	Frame Lug	52	Rear Sight Slide
7	Cylinder	30	Hammer	53	Rear Sight Windage Nut
8	Extractor	31	Sear	54	Rear Sight Windage Screw
9	Extractor Pins	32	Sear Pin	55	Rebound Slide
10	Gas Ring	33	Sear Spring	56	Rebound Slide Pin
11	Cylinder Stop	34	Stirrup Pin	57	Rebound Slide Spring
12	Cylinder Stop Spring	35	Hammer Block	58	Left Grip
13	Grip Escutcheon	36	Hand	59	Right Grip
14	Grip Escutcheon Nut	37	Hand Pin	60	Grip Screw
15	Extractor Rod	38	Locking Bolt	61	Grip Locator Pin
16	Extractor Rod Collar	39	Locking Bolt Pin	62	Thumb-Piece
17	Extractor Spring	40	Locking Bolt Spring	63	Thumb-Piece Nut
18	Firing Pin	41	Mainspring	64	Hand Spring Pin
19	Firing Pin Bushing Pin	42	Mainspring Rod Swivel	65	Hand Spring Torsion Pin
20	Firing Pin Spring	43	Mainspring Stirrup	66	Hand Torsion Spring
21	Cylinder Stop Stud	44	Sideplate Screws, Crowned	67	Trigger
22	Firing Pin Bushing	45	Sideplate Screw, Flat Head	68	Trigger Lever
23	Frame	46	Rear Sight Elevation Click Plug	69	Trigger Lever Pin

Model 64 Revolver

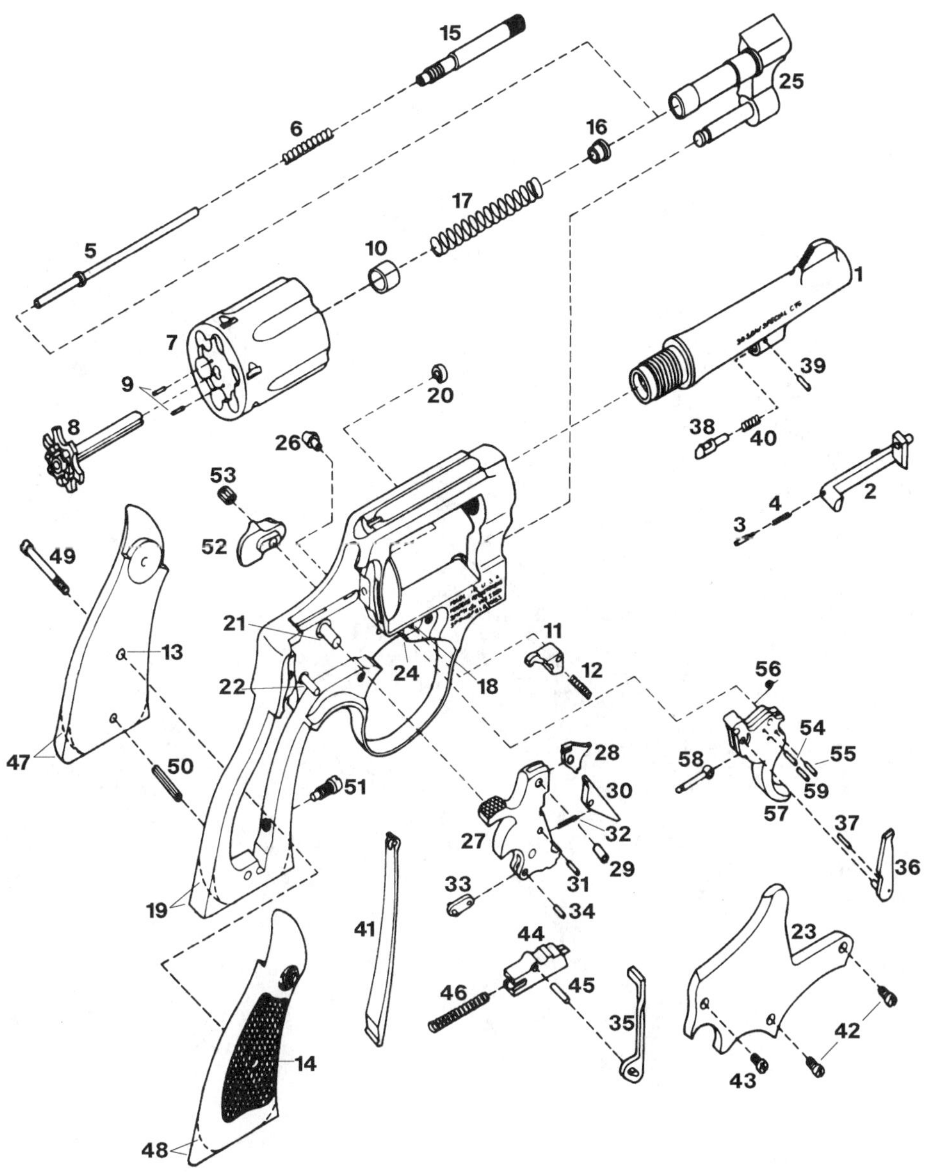

1	Barrel	21	Hammer Stud	41	Mainspring
2	Bolt	22	Rebound Slide Stud	42	Sideplate Screws, Crowned
3	Bolt Plunger	23	Sideplate	43	Sideplate Screw, Flat Head
4	Bolt Plunger Spring	24	Trigger Stud	44	Rebound Slide
5	Center Pin	25	Yoke	45	Rebound Slide Pin
6	Center Pin Spring	26	Frame Lug	46	Rebound Slide Spring
7	Cylinder	27	Hammer	47	Left Grip
8	Extractor	28	Hammer Nose	48	Right Grip
9	Extractor Pins	29	Hammer Nose Rivet	49	Grip Screw
10	Gas Ring	30	Sear	50	Grip Locator Pin
11	Cylinder Stop	31	Sear Pin	51	Strain Screw
12	Cylinder Stop Spring	32	Sear Spring	52	Thumb-Piece
13	Grip Escutcheon	33	Stirrup	53	Thumb-Piece Nut
14	Grip Escutcheon Nut	34	Stirrup Pin	54	Hand Spring Pin
15	Extractor Rod	35	Hammer Block	55	Hand Spring Torsion Pin
16	Extractor Rod Collar	36	Hand	56	Hand Torsion Spring
17	Extractor Spring	37	Hand Pin	57	Trigger
18	Cylinder Stop Stud	38	Locking Bolt	58	Trigger Lever
19	Frame	39	Locking Bolt Pin	59	Trigger Lever Pin
20	Hammer Nose Bushing	40	Locking Bolt Spring		

Model 65 Revolver

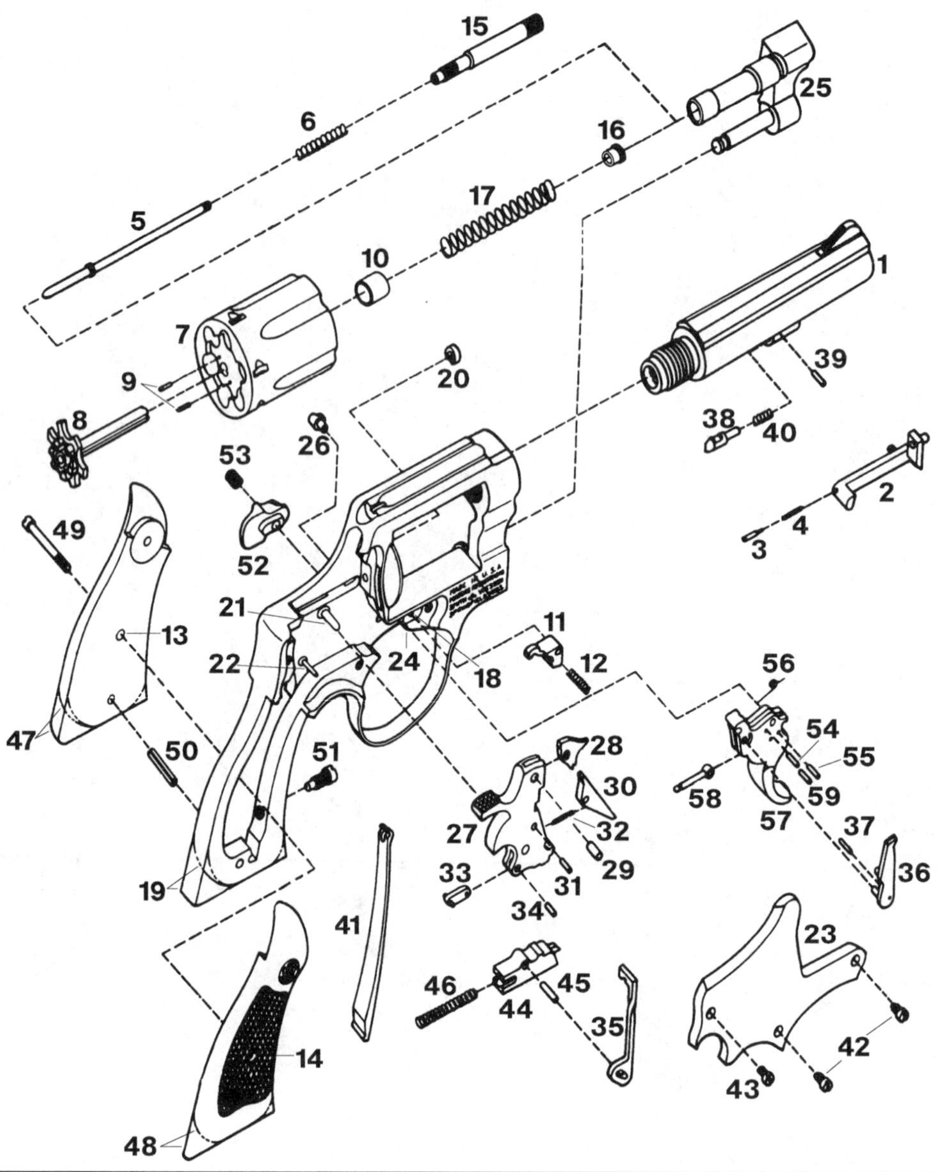

1	Barrel	21	Hammer Stud	41	Mainspring
2	Bolt	22	Rebound Slide Stud	42	Sideplate Screws, Crowned
3	Bolt Plunger	23	Sideplate	43	Sideplate Screw, Flat Head
4	Bolt Plunger Spring	24	Trigger Stud	44	Rebound Slide
5	Center Pin	25	Yoke	45	Rebound Slide Pin
6	Center Pin Spring	26	Frame Lug	46	Rebound Slide Spring
7	Cylinder	27	Hammer	47	Left Grip
8	Extractor	28	Hammer Nose	48	Right Grip
9	Extractor Pins	29	Hammer Nose Rivet	49	Grip Screw
10	Gas Ring	30	Sear	50	Grip Locator Pin
11	Cylinder Stop	31	Sear Pin	51	Strain Screw
12	Cylinder Stop Spring	32	Sear Spring	52	Thumb-Piece
13	Grip Escutcheon	33	Stirrup	53	Thumb-Piece Nut
14	Grip Escutcheon Nut	34	Stirrup Pin	54	Hand Spring Pin
15	Extractor Rod	35	Hammer Block	55	Hand Spring Torsion Pin
16	Extractor Rod Collar	36	Hand	56	Hand Torsion Spring
17	Extractor Spring	37	Hand Pin	57	Trigger
18	Cylinder Stop Stud	38	Locking Bolt	58	Trigger Lever
19	Frame	39	Locking Bolt Pin	59	Trigger Lever Pin
20	Hammer Nose Bushing	40	Locking Bolt Spring		

Model 66 Revolver

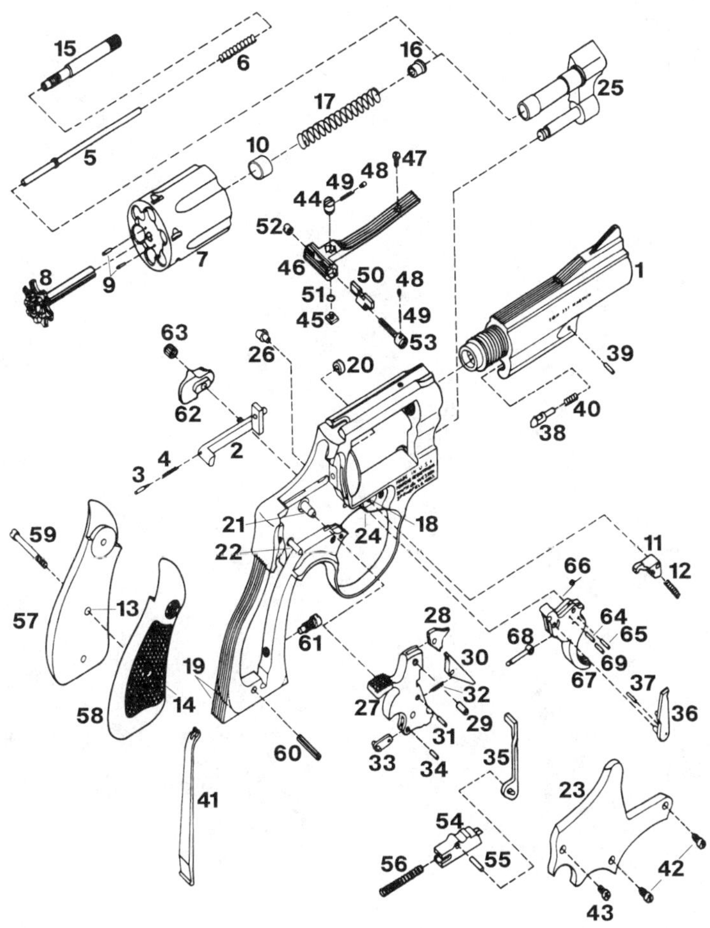

1	Barrel	24	Trigger Stud	47	Rear Sight Leaf Screw
2	Bolt	25	Yoke	48	Rear Sight Plungers
3	Bolt Plunger	26	Frame Lug	49	Rear Sight Plunger Springs
4	Bolt Plunger Spring	27	Hammer	50	Rear Sight Slide
5	Center Pin	28	Hammer Nose	51	Rear Sight Clip
6	Center Pin Spring	29	Hammer Nose Rivet	52	Rear Sight Windage Nut
7	Cylinder	30	Sear	53	Rear Sight Windage Screw
8	Extractor	31	Sear Pin	54	Rebound Slide
9	Extractor Pins	32	Sear Spring	55	Rebound Slide Pin
10	Gas Ring	33	Stirrup	56	Rebound Slide Spring
11	Cylinder Stop	34	Stirrup Pin	57	Left Grip, Round Butt
12	Cylinder Stop Spring	35	Hammer Block	58	Right Grip, Round Butt
13	Grip Escutcheon	36	Hand	59	Grip Screw
14	Grip Escutcheon Nut	37	Hand Pin	60	Grip Locator Pin
15	Extractor Rod	38	Locking Bolt	61	Strain Screw
16	Extractor Rod Collar	39	Locking Bolt Pin	62	Thumb-Piece
17	Extractor Spring	40	Locking Bolt Spring	63	Thumb-Piece Nut
18	Cylinder Stop Stud	41	Mainspring	64	Hand Spring Pin
19	Frame	42	Sideplate Screws, Crowned	65	Hand Spring Torsion Pin
20	Hammer Nose Bushing	43	Sideplate Screw, Flat Head	66	Hand Torsion Spring
21	Hammer Stud	44	Rear Sight Elevation Nut	67	Trigger
22	Rebound Slide Stud	45	Rear Sight Elevation Stud	68	Trigger Lever
23	Sideplate	46	Rear Sight Leaf	69	Trigger Lever Pin

Model 67 Revolver

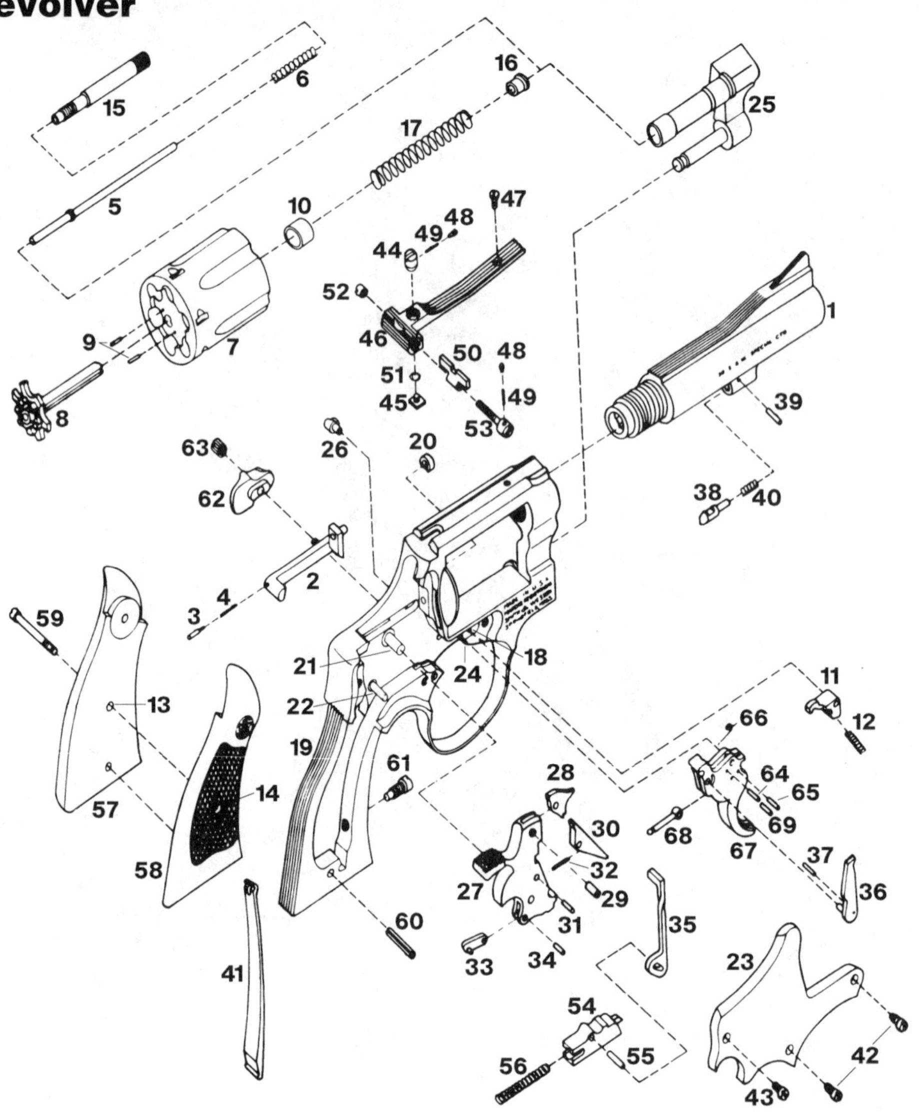

1	Barrel
2	Bolt
3	Bolt Plunger
4	Bolt Plunger Spring
5	Center Pin
6	Center Pin Spring
7	Cylinder
8	Extractor
9	Extractor Pins
10	Gas Ring
11	Cylinder Stop
12	Cylinder Stop Spring
13	Grip Escutcheon
14	Grip Escutcheon Nut
15	Extractor Rod
16	Extractor Rod Collar
17	Extractor Spring
18	Cylinder Stop Stud
19	Frame
20	Hammer Nose Bushing
21	Hammer Stud
22	Rebound Slide Stud
23	Sideplate
24	Trigger Stud
25	Yoke
26	Frame Lug
27	Hammer
28	Hammer Nose
29	Hammer Nose Rivet
30	Sear
31	Sear Pin
32	Sear Spring
33	Stirrup
34	Stirrup Pin
35	Hammer Block
36	Hand
37	Hand Pin
38	Locking Bolt
39	Lockng Bolt Pin
40	Locking Bolt Spring
41	Mainspring
42	Sideplate Screws, Crowned
43	Sideplate Screw, Flat Head
44	Rear Sight Elevation Nut
45	Rear Sight Elevation Stud
46	Rear Sight Leaf
47	Rear Sight Leaf Screw
48	Rear Sight Plungers
49	Rear Sight Plunger Springs
50	Rear Sight Slide
51	Rear Sight Spring Clip
52	Rear Sight Windage Nut
53	Rear Sight Windage Screw
54	Rebound Slide
55	Rebound Slide Pin
56	Rebound Slide Spring
57	Left Grip
58	Right Grip
59	Grip Screw
60	Grip Locator Pin
61	Strain Screw
62	Thumb-Piece
63	Thumb-Piece Nut
64	Hand Spring Pin
65	Hand Spring Torsion Pin
66	Hand Torsion Spring
67	Trigger
68	Trigger Lever
69	Trigger Lever Pin

Model 422 Auto

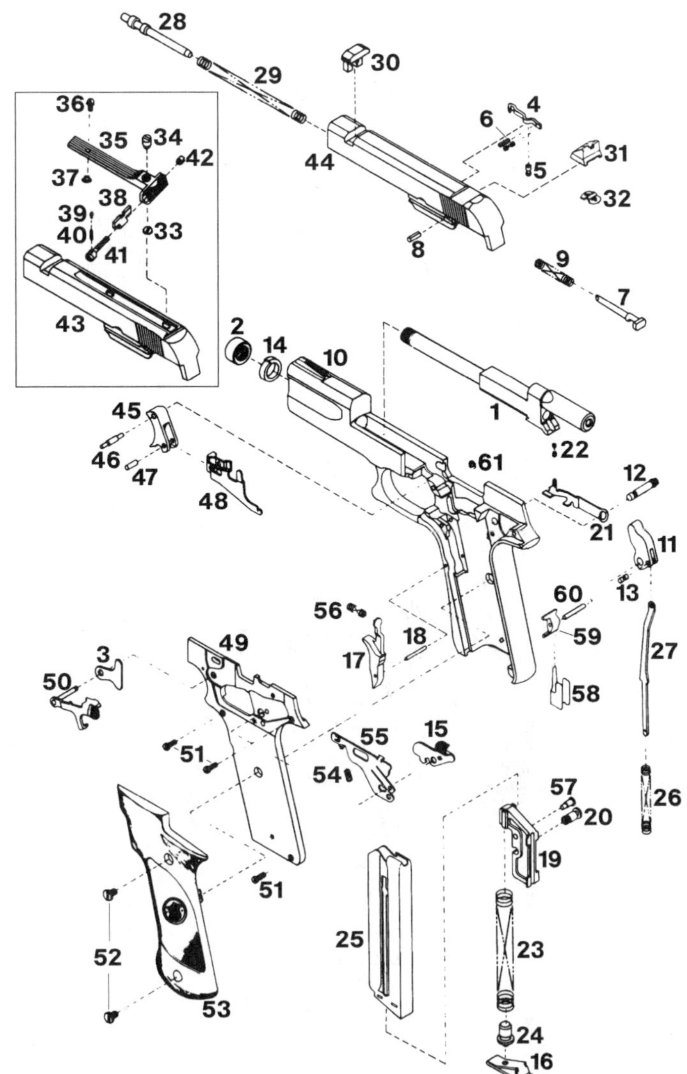

1 Barrel
2 Barrel Nut
3 Disconnector
4 Extractor
5 Extractor Pin
6 Extractor Springs
7 Firing Pin
8 Firing Pin Retaining Pin
9 Firing Pin Spring
10 Frame
11 Hammer
12 Hammer Pin
13 Hammer Stirrup Pin
14 Barrel Nut Lock Washer
15 Safety Catch
16 Magazine Base Plate
17 Magazine Catch
18 Magazine Catch Pin
19 Magazine Follower
20 Magazine Follower Pin
21 Magazine Safety
22 Magazine Safety Pin
23 Magazine Spring
24 Magazine Spring Plunger
25 Magazine Body
26 Mainspring
27 Hammer Strut
28 Recoil Spring Guide
29 Recoil Spring
30 Recoil Spring Guide Plug
31 Rear Sight Body
32 Rear Sight Recoil Bushing
33 Rear Sight Elevation Screw<R>Retainer
34 Rear Sight Elevation Screw, Target
35 Rear Sight Leaf, Target
36 Rear Sight Leaf Screw, Target
37 Rear Sight Retainer Nut, Target
38 Rear Sight Leaf, Target
39 Rear Sight Wind. Screw Plunger, Target
40 Rear Sight Windage Screw Spring, Target
41 Rear Sight Windage Screw, Target
42 Rear Wind. Screw Nut, Target
43 Slide, Target
44 Slide, 4 1/2"
45 Trigger
46 Trigger Pin
47 Trigger Bar Pin
48 Trigger Bar
49 Sideplate
50 Slide Stop/Ejector Assembly
51 Sideplate Screws
52 Grip Screws
53 Left Grip
54 Slide Stop Spring
55 Safety Catch Spring Plate
56 Trigger and Magazine Catch Spring
57 Slide Stop Stud
58 Sear Spring
59 Sear
60 Sear Pin
61 Trigger Pin Retainer

Parts Not Shown

Right Grip

Model 439 Auto

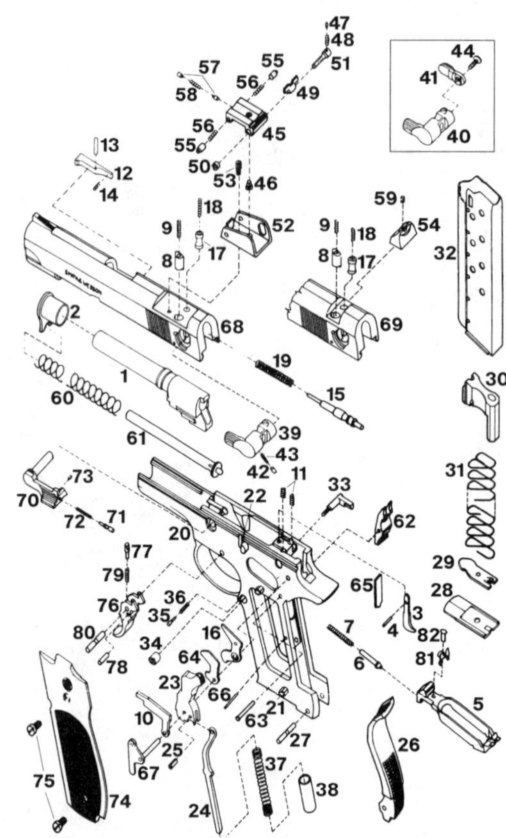

1	Barrel	**32**	Magazine Body	**63**	Sear Pin
2	Barrel Bushing	**33**	Magazine Catch	**64**	Sear Release Lever
3	Disconnector	**34**	Magazine Catch Nut	**65**	Sear Spring
4	Disconnector Pin	**35**	Magazine Catch Plunger	**66**	Sear Spring Retaining Pin
5	Drawbar	**36**	Magazine Catch Plunger Spring	**67**	Sideplate
6	Drawbar Plunger	**37**	Mainspring	**68**	Slide, Adjustable Sight
7	Drawbar Plunger Spring	**38**	Mainspring Plunger	**69**	Slide, Fixed Sight
8	Ejector Depressor Plunger	**39**	Manual Safety	**70**	Slide Stop
9	Ejector Depressor Plunger Spring	**40**	Ambidextrous Manual Safety	**71**	Slide Stop Plunger
10	Ejector Magazine Depressor	**41**	Manual Safety Right Side Lever	**72**	Slide Stop Plunger Spring
11	Ejector Springs	**42**	Manual Safety Plunger	**73**	Slide Stop Spiral Pin
12	Extractor	**43**	Manual Safety Plunger Spring	**74**	Left Grip
13	Extractor Pin	**44**	Manual Safety Screw	**75**	Stock Screws
14	Extractor Spring	**45**	Rear Sight Body	**76**	Trigger
15	Firing Pin	**46**	Rear Sight Elevation Screw	**77**	Trigger Plunger
16	Firing Pin Safety-Lever	**47**	Rear Sight Plunger	**78**	Trigger Plunger Pin
17	Firing Pin Safety-Lever Plunger	**48**	Rear Sight Plunger Spring	**79**	Trigger Plunger Spring
18	Firing Pin Safty-Lever Spring	**49**	Rear Sight Slide	**80**	Trigger Pin
19	Firing Pin Spring	**50**	Rear Sight Windage Nut	**81**	Trigger Play Spring
20	Frame	**51**	Rear Sight Windage Screw	**82**	Trigger Play Spring Rivet
21	Frame Stud	**52**	Rear Sight Base	**Parts Not Shown**	
22	Slide Stop Button	**53**	Rear Sight Base Screw		Hammer Pin
23	Hammer	**54**	Rear Sight Body, Fixed Sight		Recoil Spring Guide
24	Stirrup	**55**	Rear Sight Body Plungers		Recoil Spring Guide Bushing
25	Stirrup Pin	**56**	Rear Sight Body Plunger Springs		Recoil Spring Guide Plunger
26	Frame Insert	**57**	Rear Sight Elevation Plungers		Recoil Spring Guide Plunger Spring
27	Frame Insert Pin	**58**	Rear Sight Elevation Spring		Right Grip
28	Magazine Base Plate	**59**	Rear Sight Set Screw, Fixed Sight		Slide Stop Pin
29	Magazine Base Plate Catch	**60**	Recoil Spring		
30	Magazine Follower	**61**	Recoil Spring Guide Assembly		
31	Magazine Spring	**62**	Sear		

Model 459 Auto

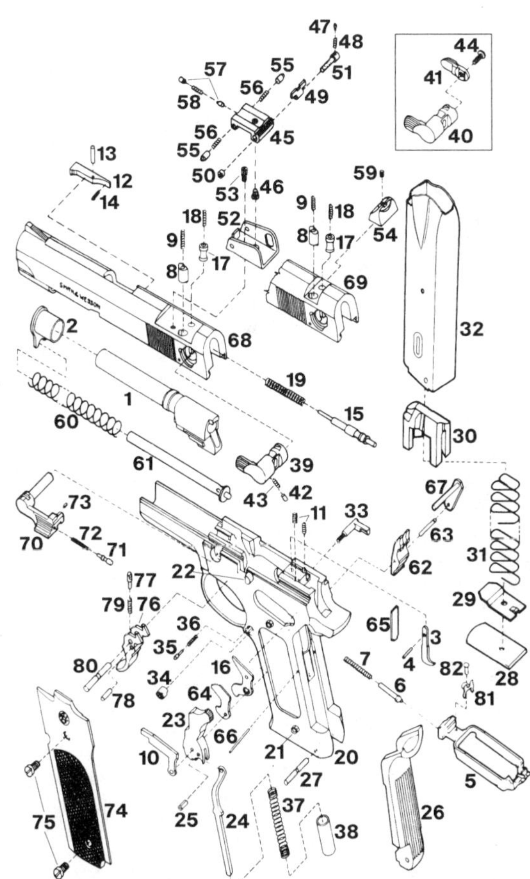

1 Barrel
2 Barrel Bushing
3 Disconnector
4 Disconnector Pin
5 Drawbar
6 Drawbar Plunger
7 Drawbar Plunger Spring
8 Ejector Depressor Plunger
9 Ejector Depressor Plunger Spring
10 Ejector Magazine Depressor
11 Ejector Springs
12 Extractor
13 Extractor Pin
14 Extractor Spring
15 Firing Pin
16 Firing Pin Safety-Lever
17 Firing Pin Safety-Lever Plunger
18 Firing Pin Safety-Lever Spring
19 Firing Pin Spring
20 Frame
21 Frame Stud
22 Slide Stop Button
23 Hammer
24 Stirrup
25 Stirrup pin
26 Frame Insert
27 Frame Insert Pin
28 Magazine Base Plate
29 Magazine Base Plate Catch
30 Magazine Follower
31 Magazine Spring
32 Magazine Body
33 Magazine Catch
34 Magazine Catch Nut
35 Magazine Catch Plunger
36 Magazine Catch Plunger Spring
37 Mainspring
38 Mainspring Plunger
39 Manual Safety
40 Ambidextrous Manual Safety
41 Manual Safety Right Side Lever
42 Manual Safety Plunger
43 Manual Safety Plunger Spring
44 Manual Safety Screw
45 Rear Sight Body
46 Rear Sight Elevation Screw
47 Rear Sight Plunger
48 Rear Sight Plunger Spring
49 Rear Sight Slide
50 Rear Sight Windage Nut
51 Rear Sight Windage Screw
52 Rear Sight Base
53 Rear Sight Base Screw
54 Rear Sight Body, Fixed Sight
55 Rear Sight Body Plungers
56 Rear Sight Body Plunger Springs
57 Rear Sight Elevation Plungers
58 Rear Sight Elevation Plunger Spring
59 Rear Sight Set Screw, Fixed Sight
60 Recoil Spring
61 Recoil Spring Guide Assembly
62 Sear
63 Sear Pin
64 Sear Release Lever
65 Sear Spring
66 Sear Spring Retaining Pin
67 Sideplate
68 Slide, Adjustable Sight
69 Slide, Fixed Sight
70 Slide Stop
71 Slide Stop Plunger
72 Slide Stop Plunger Spring
73 Slide Stop Spiral Pin
74 Left Grip
75 Grip Screws
76 Trigger
77 Trigger Plunger
78 Trigger Plunger Pin
79 Trigger Plunger Spring
80 Trigger Pin
81 Trigger Play Spring
82 Trigger Play Spring Rivet

Parts Not Shown

Hammer Pin
Recoil Spring Guide
Recoil Spring Guide Bushing
Recoil Spring Guide Plunger
Recoil Spring Guide Plunger Spring
Right Grip

Model 469 Auto

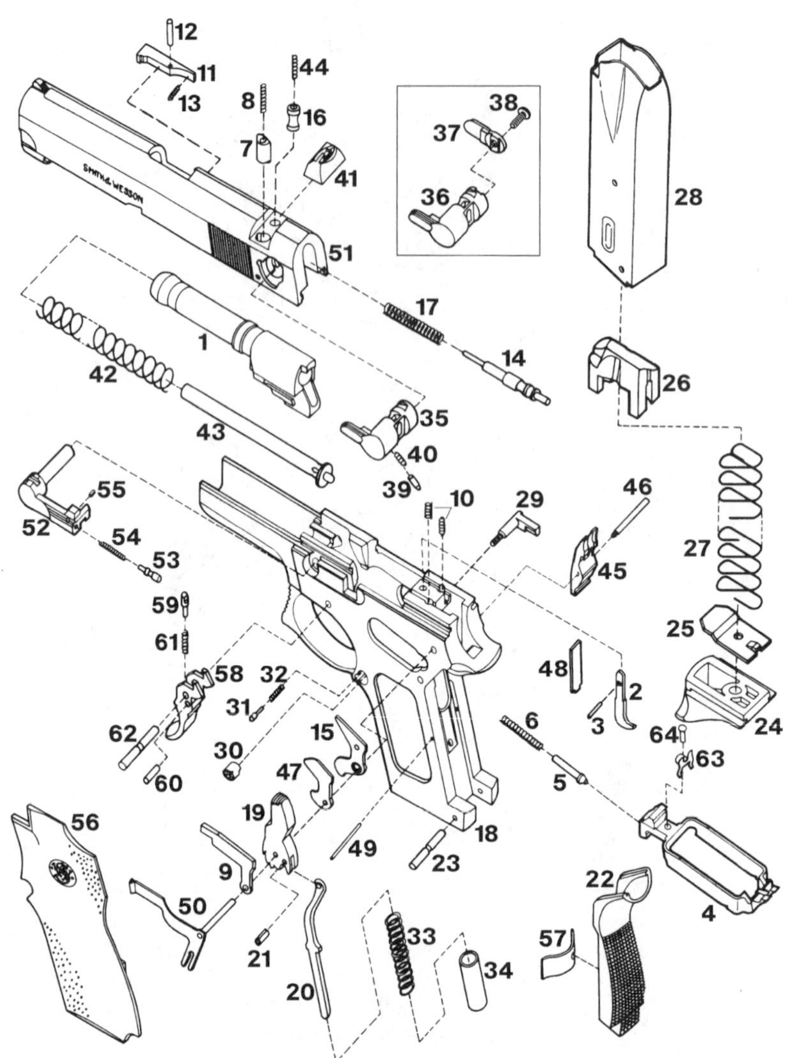

1	Barrel	**25**	Magazine Base Plate Catch	**48**	Sear Spring
2	Disconnector	**26**	Magazine Follower	**49**	Sear Spring Retaining Pin
3	Disconnector Pin	**27**	Magazine Spring	**50**	Sideplate
4	Drawbar	**28**	Magazine Body	**51**	Slide
5	Drawbar Plunger	**29**	Magazine Catch	**52**	Slide Stop
6	Drawbar Plunger Spring	**30**	Magazine Catch Nut	**53**	Slide Stop Plunger
7	Ejector Depressor Plunger	**31**	Magazine Catch Plunger	**54**	Slide Stop Plunger Spring
8	Ejector Depressor Plunger Spring	**32**	Magazine Catch Plunger Spring	**55**	Slide Stop Spiral Pin
9	Ejector Magazine Depressor	**33**	Mainspring	**56**	Left Grip
10	Ejector Springs	**34**	Mainspring Plunger	**57**	Grip Retaining Spring
11	Extractor	**35**	Manual Safety	**58**	Trigger
12	Extractor Pin	**36**	Ambidextrous Manual Safety	**59**	Trigger Plunger
13	Extractor Spring	**37**	Ambidextrous Manual Safety-Lever	**60**	Trigger Plunger Pin
14	Firing Pin	**38**	Ambidextrous Manual Safety-Lever Screw	**61**	Trigger Plunger Spring
15	Firing Pin Safety-Lever			**62**	Trigger Pin
16	Firing Pin Safety Plunger	**39**	Manual Safety Plunger	**63**	Trigger Play Spring
17	Firing Pin Spring	**40**	Manual Safety Plunger Spring	**64**	Trigger Play Spring Rivet
18	Frame	**41**	Rear Sight	**Parts Not Shown**	
19	Hammer	**42**	Recoil Spring		Hammer Pin
20	Stirrup	**43**	Recoil Spring Guide Assembly		Recoil Spring Guide
21	Stirrup Pin	**44**	Safety-Lever Plunger Spring		Recoil Spring Guide Bushing
22	Frame Insert	**45**	Sear		Recoil Spring Guide Plunger
23	Frame Insert Pin	**46**	Sear Pin		Recoil Spring Guide Plunger Spring
24	Magazine Base Plate	**47**	Sear Release Lever		

Model 539 Auto

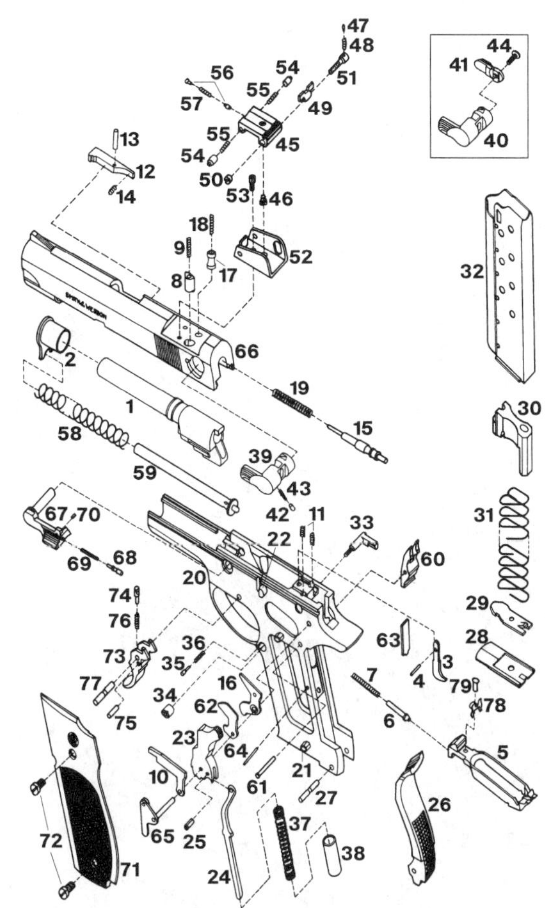

1	Barrel
2	Barrel Bushing
3	Disconnector
4	Disconnector Pin
5	Drawbar
6	Drawbar Plunger
7	Drawbar Plunger Spring
8	Ejector Depressor Plunger
9	Ejector Depressor Plunger Spring
10	Ejector Magazine Depressor
11	Ejector Springs
12	Extractor
13	Extractor Pin
14	Extractor Spring
15	Firing Pin
16	Firing Pin Safety-Lever
17	Firing Pin Safety-Lever Plunger
18	Firing Pin Safety-Lever Spring
19	Firing Pin Spring
20	Frame
21	Frame Stud
22	Slide Stop Button
23	Hammer
24	Stirrup
25	Stirrup Pin
26	Frame Insert
27	Frame Insert Pin
28	Magazine Base Plate
29	Magazine Base Plate Catch
30	Magazine Follower
31	Magazine Spring
32	Magazine Body
33	Magazine Catch
34	Magazine Catch Nut
35	Magazine Catch Plunger
36	Magazine Catch Plunger Spring
37	Mainspring
38	Mainspring Plunger
39	Manual Safety
40	Manual Safety, Ambidextrous
41	Manual Safety Right Side Lever
42	Manual Safety Plunger
43	Manual Safety Plunger Spring
44	Manual Safety Screw
45	Rear Sight Body
46	Rear Sight Elevation Screw
47	Rear Sight Plunger
48	Rear Sight Plunger Spring
49	Rear Sight Slide
50	Rear Sight Windage Nut
51	Rear Sight Windage Screw
52	Rear Sight Base
53	Rear Sight Base Screw
54	Rear Sight Body Plungers
55	Rear Sight Body Plunger Springs
56	Rear Sight Elevation Plungers
57	Rear Sight Elevation Spring
58	Recoil Spring
59	Recoil Spring Guide Assembly
60	Sear
61	Sear Pin
62	Sear Release Lever
63	Sear Spring
64	Sear Spring Retaining Pin
65	Sideplate
66	Slide
67	Slide Stop
68	Slide Stop Plunger
69	Slide Stop Plunger Spring
70	Slide Stop Spiral Pin
71	Grip
72	Grip Screws
73	Trigger
74	Trigger Plunger
75	Trigger Plunger Pin
76	Trigger Plunger Spring
77	Trigger Pin
78	Trigger Play Spring
79	Trigger Play Spring Rivet

Parts Not Shown

- Hammer Pin
- Recoil Spring Guide
- Recoil Spring Guide Bushing
- Recoil Spring Guide Plunger
- Recoil Spring Guide Plunger Spring
- Slide Stop Pin

Model 547 Revolver

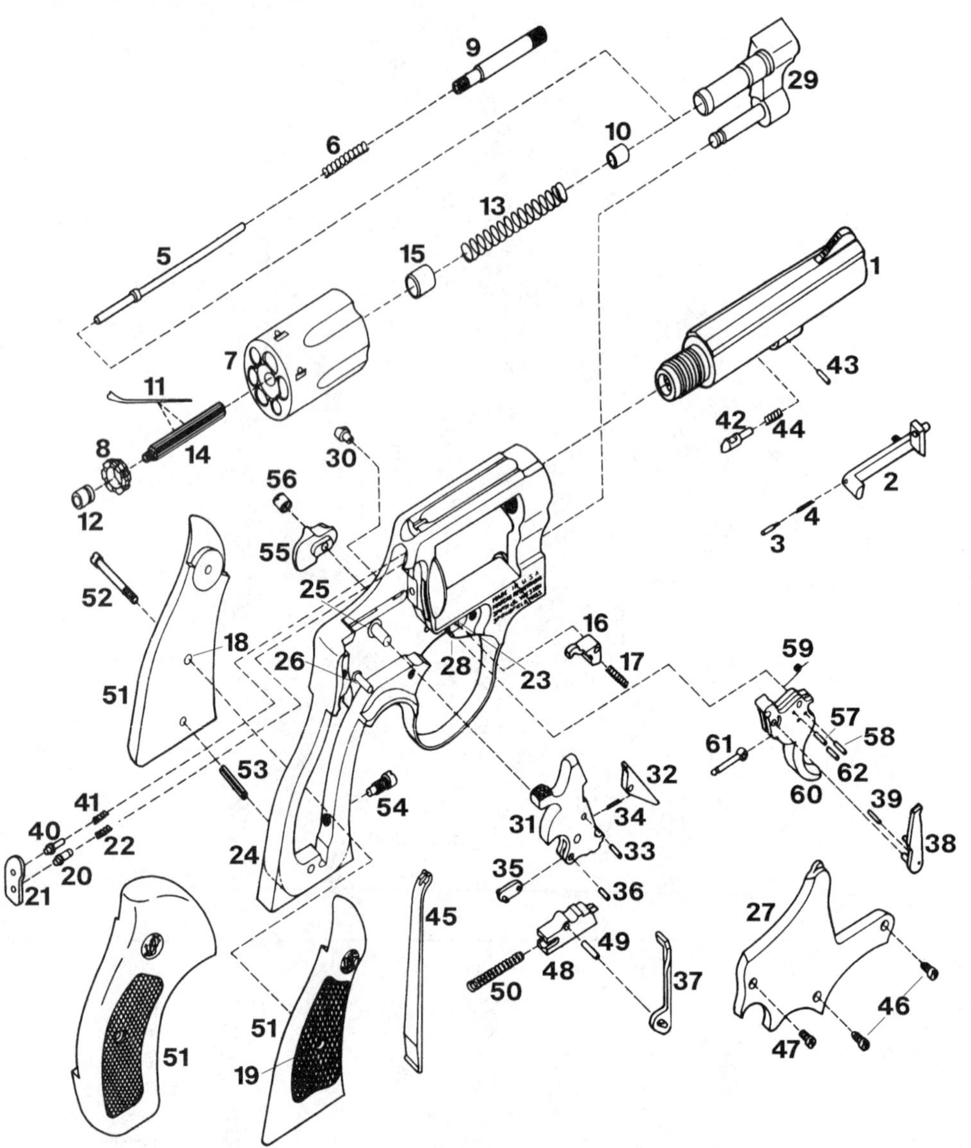

1	Barrel	22	Firing Pin Spring	43	Locking Bolt Pin
2	Bolt	23	Cylinder Stop Stud	44	Locking Bolt Spring
3	Bolt Plunger	24	Frame	45	Mainspring
4	Bolt Plunger Spring	25	Hammer Stud	46	Sideplate Screws, Crowned
5	Center Pin	26	Rebound Slide Stud	47	Sideplate Screw, Flat Head
6	Center Pin Spring	27	Sideplate	48	Rebound Slide
7	Cylinder	28	Trigger Stud	49	Rebound Slide Pin
8	Extractor Head	29	Yoke	50	Rebound Slide Spring
9	Extractor Rod	30	Frame Lug	51	Grips
10	Extractor Rod Collar	31	Hammer	52	Grip Screw
11	Extractor Segment	32	Sear	53	Grip Locator Pin
12	Extractor Shear Nut	33	Sear Pin	54	Strain Screw
13	Extractor Spring	34	Sear Spring	55	Thumb-Piece
14	Extractor Stem	35	Stirrup	56	Thumb-Piece Nut
15	Gas Ring	36	Stirrup Pin	57	Hand Spring Pin
16	Cylinder Stop	37	Hammer Block	58	Hand Spring Torsion Pin
17	Cylinder Stop Spring	38	Hand	59	Hand Torsion Spring
18	Grip Escutcheon	39	Hand Pin	60	Trigger
19	Grip Escutcheon Nut	40	Limit Pin	61	Trigger Lever
20	Firing Pin	41	Limit Pin Spring	62	Trigger Lever Pin
21	Firing Pin Retainer	42	Locking Bolt		

Model 559 Auto

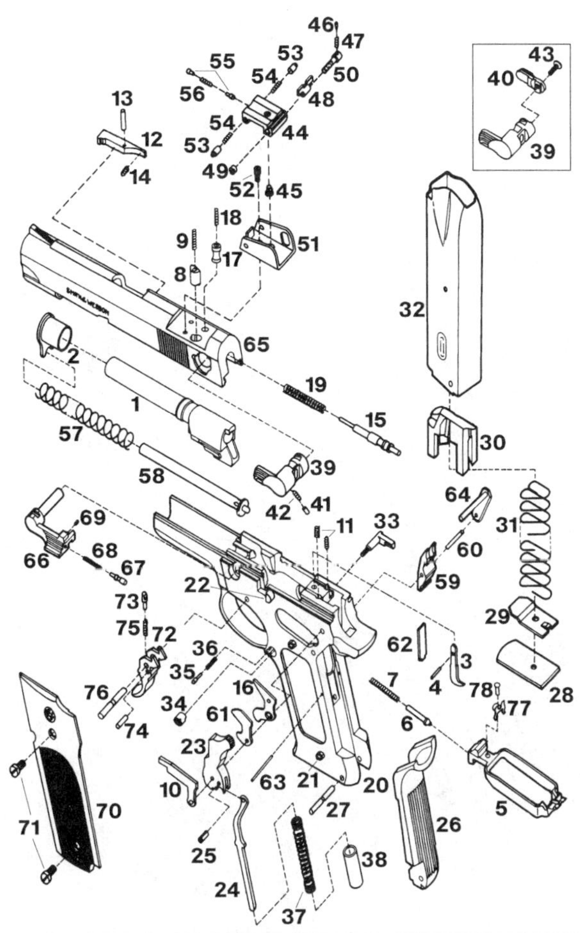

No.	Part	No.	Part	No.	Part
1	Barrel	30	Magazine Follower	59	Sear
2	Barrel Bushing	31	Magazine Spring	60	Sear Pin
3	Disconnector	32	Magazine Body	61	Sear Release Lever
4	Disconnector Pin	33	Magazine Catch	62	Sear Spring
5	Drawbar	34	Magazine Catch Nut	63	Sear Spring Retaining Pin
6	Drawbar Plunger	35	Magazine Catch Plunger	64	Sideplate
7	Drawbar Plunger Spring	36	Magazine Catch Plunger Spring	65	Slide, Adjustable Sight
8	Ejector Depressor Plunger	37	Mainspring	66	Slide Stop
9	Ejector Depressor Plunger Spring	38	Mainspring Plunger	67	Slide Stop Plunger
10	Ejector Magazine Depressor	39	Manual Safety	68	Slide Stop Plunger Spring
11	Ejector Springs	40	Manual Safety Right Side Lever	69	Slide Stop Spiral Pin
12	Extractor	41	Manual Safety Plunger	70	Left Grip
13	Extractor Pin	42	Manual Safety Plunger Spring	71	Grip Screws
14	Extractor Spring	43	Manual Safety Screw	72	Trigger
15	Firing Pin	44	Rear Sight Body	73	Trigger Plunger
16	Firing Pin Safety-Lever	45	Rear Sight Elevation Screw	74	Trigger Plunger Pin
17	Firing Pin Safety-Lever Plunger	46	Rear Sight Plunger	75	Trigger Plunger Spring
18	Firing Pin Safety-Lever Spring	47	Rear Sight Plunger Spring	76	Trigger Pin
19	Firing Pin Spring	48	Rear Sight Slide	77	Trigger Play Spring
20	Frame	49	Rear Sight Windage Nut	78	Trigger Play Spring Rivet
21	Frame Stud	50	Rear Sight Windage Screw		
22	Slide Stop Button	51	Rear Sight Base		
23	Hammer	52	Rear Sight Base Screw		
24	Stirrup	53	Rear Sight Body Plungers		
25	Stirrup Pin	54	Rear Sight Body Plunger Springs		
26	Frame Insert	55	Rear Sight Elevation Plungers		
27	Frame Insert Pin	56	Rear Sight Elevation Spring		
28	Magazine Base Plate	57	Recoil Spring		
29	Magazine Base Plate Catch	58	Recoil Spring Guide Assembly		

Parts Not Shown

- Hammer Pin
- Recoil Spring Guide
- Recoil Spring Guide Bushing
- Recoil Spring Guide Plunger
- Recoil Spring Guide Plunger Spring

Model 581 Revolver

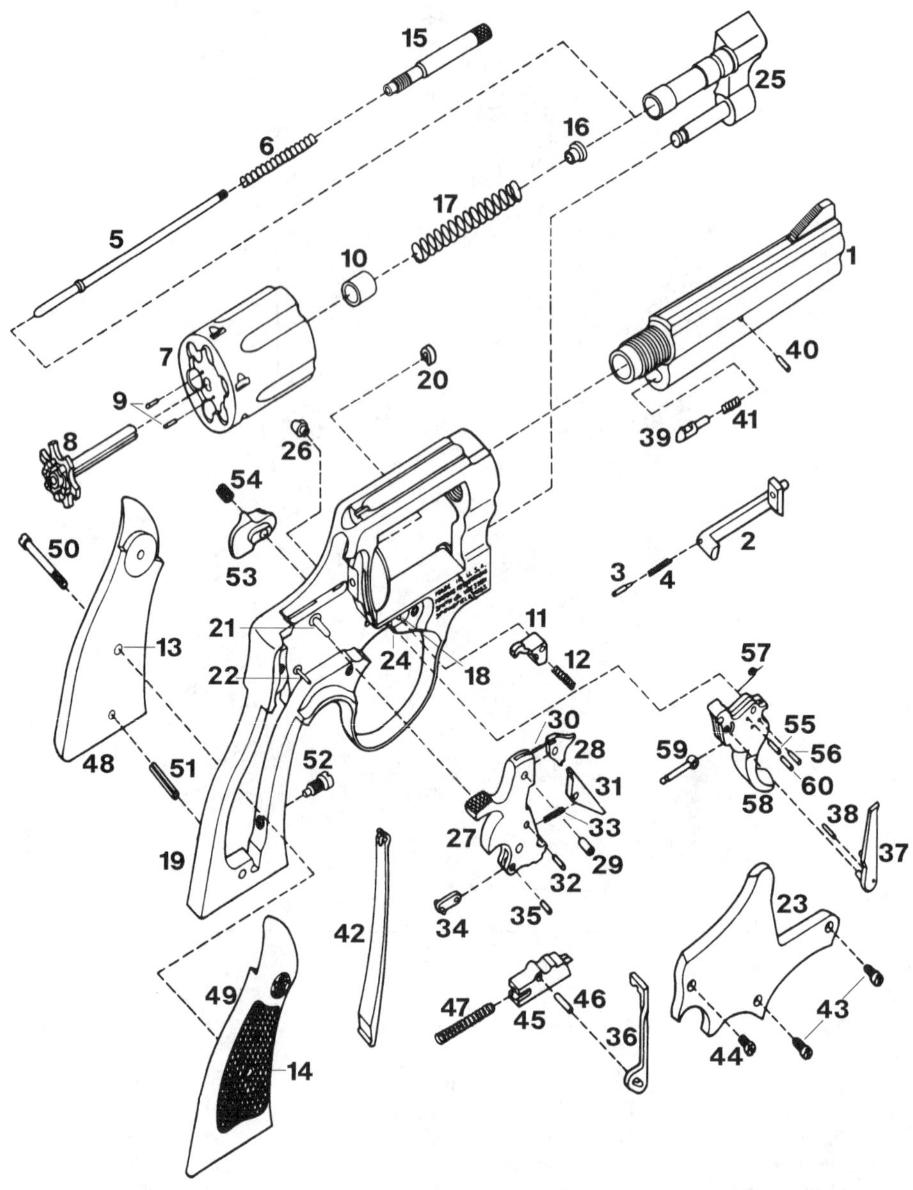

1	Barrel	**21**	Hammer Stud	**41**	Locking Bolt Spring
2	Bolt	**22**	Rebound Slide Stud	**42**	Mainspring
3	Bolt Plunger	**23**	Sideplate	**43**	Sideplate Screws, Crowned
4	Bolt Plunger Spring	**24**	Trigger Stud	**44**	Sideplate Screw, Flat Head
5	Center Pin	**25**	Yoke	**45**	Rebound Slide
6	Center Pin Spring	**26**	Frame Lug	**46**	Rebound Slide Pin
7	Cylinder	**27**	Hammer	**47**	Rebound Slide Spring
8	Extractor	**28**	Hammer Nose	**48**	Left Grip
9	Extractor Pins	**29**	Hammer Nose Rivet	**49**	Right Grip
10	Gas Ring	**30**	Hammer Nose Spring	**50**	Grip Screw
11	Cylinder Stop	**31**	Sear	**51**	Grip Locator Pin
12	Cylinder Stop Spring	**32**	Sear Pin	**52**	Strain Screw
13	Grip Escutcheon	**33**	Sear Spring	**53**	Thumb-Piece
14	Grip Escutcheon Nut	**34**	Stirrup	**54**	Thumb-Piece Nut
15	Extractor Rod	**35**	Stirrup Pin	**55**	Hand Spring Pin
16	Extractor Rod Collar	**36**	Hammer Block	**56**	Hand Spring Torsion Pin
17	Extractor Spring	**37**	Hand	**57**	Hand Torsion Spring
18	Cylinder Stop Stud	**38**	Hand Pin	**58**	Trigger
19	Frame	**39**	Locking Bolt	**59**	Trigger Lever
20	Hammer Nose Bushing	**40**	Locking Bolt Pin	**60**	Trigger Lever Pin

Model 586 Revolver

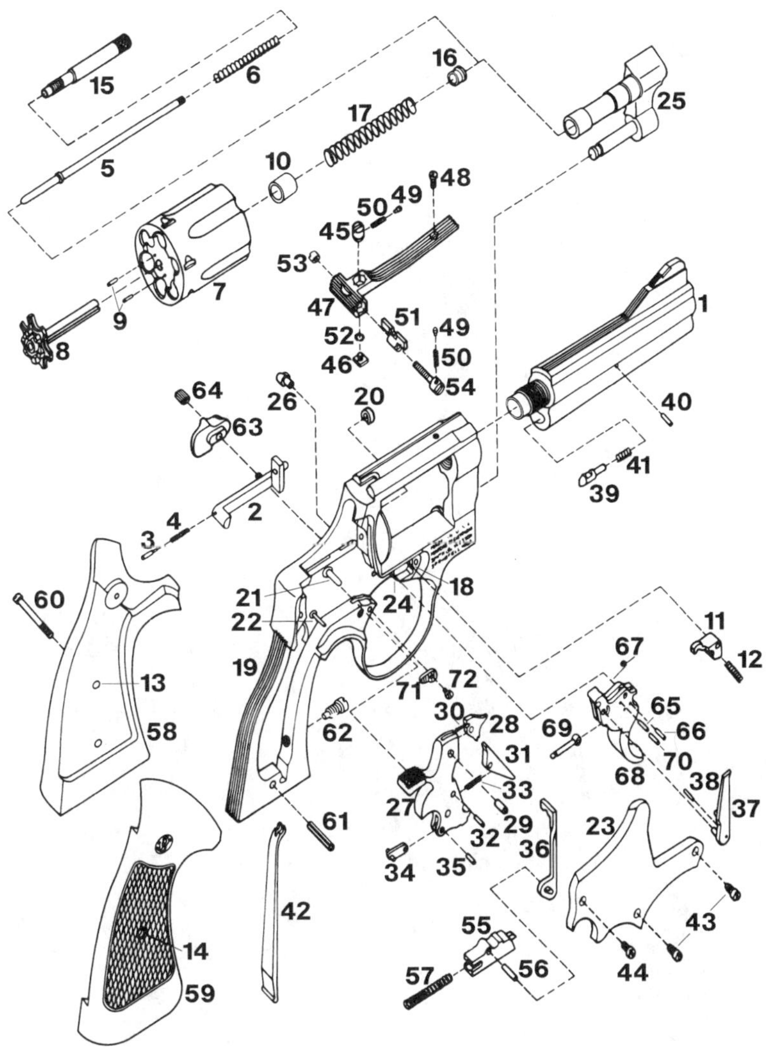

1	Barrel	25	Yoke	49	Rear Sight Plungers
2	Bolt	26	Frame Lug	50	Rear Sight Plunger Springs
3	Bolt Plunger	27	Hammer	51	Rear Sight Slide
4	Bolt Plunger Spring	28	Hammer Nose	52	Rear Sight Spring Clip
5	Center Pin	29	Hammer Nose Rivet	53	Rear Sight Windage Nut
6	Center Pin Spring	30	Hammer Nose Spring	54	Rear Sight Windage Screw
7	Cylinder	31	Sear	55	Rebound Slide
8	Extractor	32	Sear Pin	56	Rebound Slide Pin
9	Extractor Pins	33	Sear Spring	57	Rebound Slide Spring
10	Gas Ring	34	Stirrup	58	Left Grip
11	Cylinder Stop	35	Stirrup Pin	59	Right Grip
12	Cylinder Stop Spring	36	Hammer Block	60	Grip Screw
13	Grip Escutcheon	37	Hand	61	Grip Locator Pin
14	Grip Escutcheon Nut	38	Hand Pin	62	Strain Screw
15	Extractor Rod	39	Locking Bolt	63	Thumb-Piece
16	Extractor Rod Collar	40	Locking Bolt Pin	64	Thumb-Piece Nut
17	Extractor Spring	41	Locking Bolt Spring	65	Hand Spring Pin
18	Cylinder Stop Stud	42	Mainspring	66	Hand Spring Torsion Pin
19	Frame	43	Sideplate Screws, Crowned	67	Hand Torsion Spring
20	Hammer Nose Bushing	44	Sideplate Screw, Flat Head	68	Trigger
21	Hammer Stud	45	Rear Sight Elevation Nut	69	Trigger Lever
22	Rebound Slide Stud	46	Rear Sight Elevation Stud	70	Trigger Lever Pin
23	Sideplate	47	Rear Sight Leaf	71	Trigger Stop
24	Trigger Stud	48	Rear Sight Leaf Screw	72	Trigger Stop Screw

Model 624 Revolver

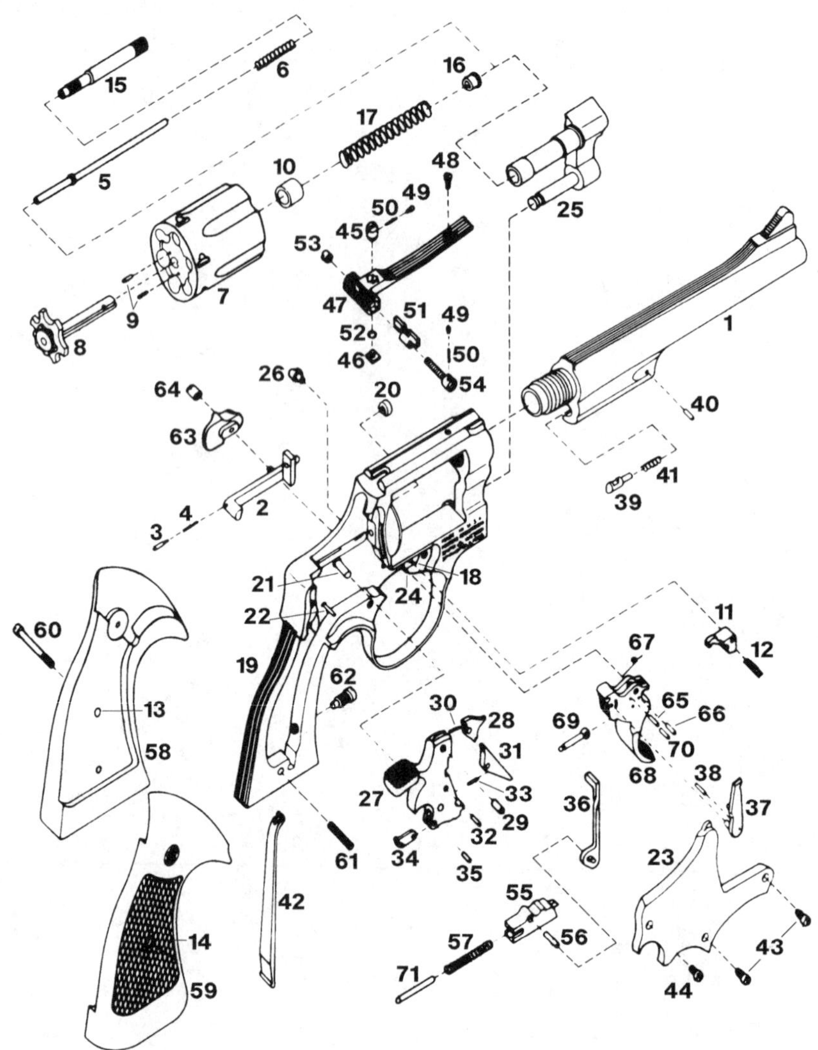

1	Barrel	**25**	Yoke	**49**	Rear Sight Plungers
2	Bolt	**26**	Frame Lug	**50**	Rear Sight Plunger Springs
3	Bolt Plunger	**27**	Hammer	**51**	Rear Sight Slide
4	Bolt Plunger Spring	**28**	Hammer Nose	**52**	Rear Sight Spring Clip
5	Center Pin	**29**	Hammer Nose Rivet	**53**	Rear Sight Windage Nut
6	Center Pin Spring	**30**	Hammer Nose Spring	**54**	Rear Sight Windage Screw
7	Cylinder	**31**	Sear	**55**	Rebound Slide
8	Extractor	**32**	Sear Pin	**56**	Rebound Slide Pin
9	Extractor Pins	**33**	Sear Spring	**57**	Rebound Slide Spring
10	Gas Ring	**34**	Stirrup	**58**	Left Grip
11	Cylinder Stop	**35**	Stirrup Pin	**59**	Right Grip
12	Cylinder Stop Spring	**36**	Hammer Block	**60**	Grip Screw
13	Grip Escutcheon	**37**	Hand	**61**	Grip Locator Pin
14	Grip Escutcheon Nut	**38**	Hand Pin	**62**	Strain Screw
15	Extractor Rod	**39**	Locking Bolt	**63**	Thumb-Piece
16	Extractor Rod Collar	**40**	Locking Bolt Pin	**64**	Thumb-Piece Nut
17	Extractor Spring	**41**	Locking Bolt Spring	**65**	Hand Spring Pin
18	Cylinder Stop Stud	**42**	Mainspring	**66**	Hand Spring Torsion Pin
19	Frame	**43**	Sideplate Screws, Crowned	**67**	Hand Torsion Spring
20	Hammer Nose Bushing	**44**	Sideplate Screw, Flat Head	**68**	Trigger
21	Hammer Stud	**45**	Rear Sight Elevation Nut	**69**	Trigger Lever
22	Rebound Slide Stud	**46**	Rear Sight Elevation Stud	**70**	Trigger Level Pin
23	Sideplate	**47**	Rear Sight Leaf	**71**	Trigger Stop Rod
24	Trigger Stud	**48**	Rear Sight Leaf Screw		

Model 629-1 Revolver

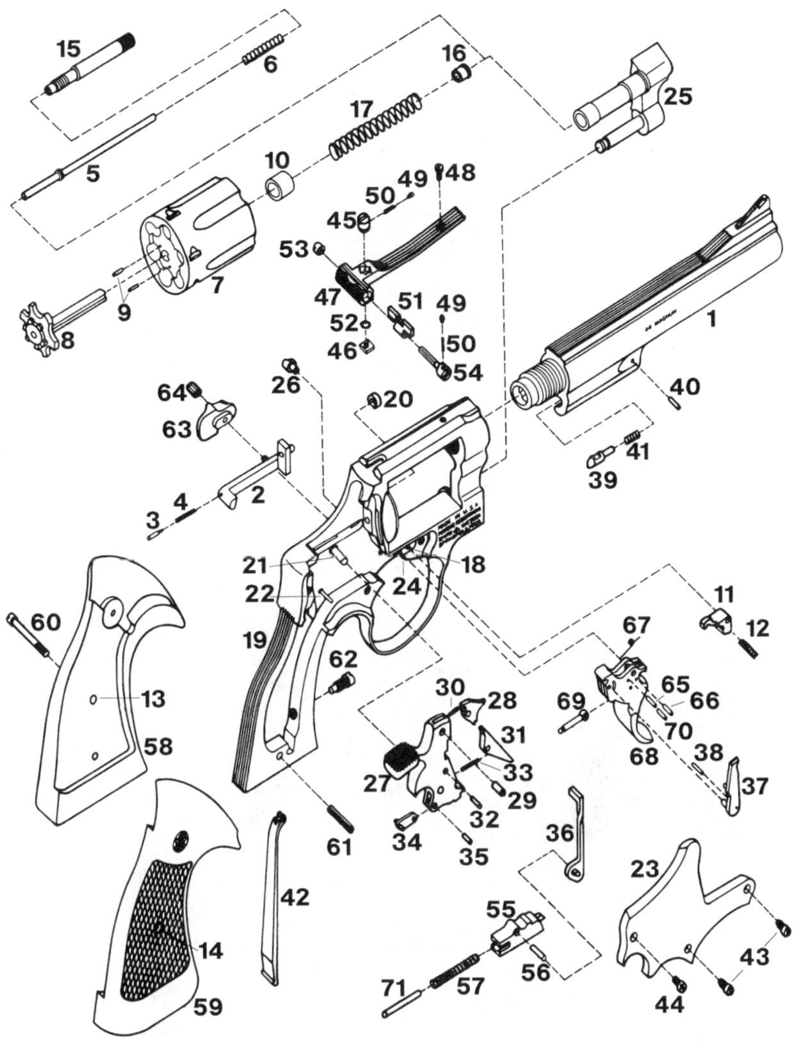

1	Barrel
2	Bolt
3	Bolt Plunger Pin
4	Bolt Plunger Spring
5	Center Pin
6	Center Pin Spring
7	Cylinder
8	Extractor
9	Extractor Pins
10	Gas Ring
11	Cylinder Stop
12	Cylinder Stop Spring
13	Grip Escutcheon
14	Grip Escutcheon Nut
15	Extractor Rod
16	Extractor Rod Collar
17	Extractor Spring
18	Cylinder Stop Stud
19	Frame
20	Hammer Nose Bushing
21	Hammer Stud
22	Rebound Slide Stud
23	Sideplate
24	Trigger Stud
25	Yoke
26	Frame Lug
27	Hammer
28	Hammer Nose
29	Hammer Nose Rivet
30	Hammer Nose Spring
31	Sear
32	Sear Pin
33	Sear Spring
34	Stirrup
35	Stirrup Pin
36	Hammer Block
37	Hand
38	Hand Pin
39	Locking Bolt
40	Locking Bolt Pin
41	Locking Bolt Spring
42	Mainspring
43	Sideplate Screws, Crowned
44	Sideplate Screw, Flat Head
45	Rear Sight Elevation Nut
46	Rear Sight Elevation Stud
47	Rear Sight Leaf
48	Rear Sight Leaf Screw
49	Rear Sight Plungers
50	Rear Sight Plunger Springs
51	Rear Sight Slide
52	Rear Sight Spring Clip
53	Rear Sight Windage Nut
54	Rear Sight Windage Screw
55	Rebound Slide
56	Rebound Slide Pin
57	Rebound Slide Spring
58	Left Grip
59	Right Grip
60	Grip Screw
61	Grip Locator Pin
62	Strain Screw
63	Thumb-Piece
64	Thumb-Piece Nut
65	Hand Spring Pin
66	Hand Spring Torsion Pin
67	Hand Torsion Spring
68	Trigger
69	Trigger Lever
70	Trigger Lever Pin
71	Trigger Stop Rod

Parts Not Shown

Barrel Pin

Model 639 Auto

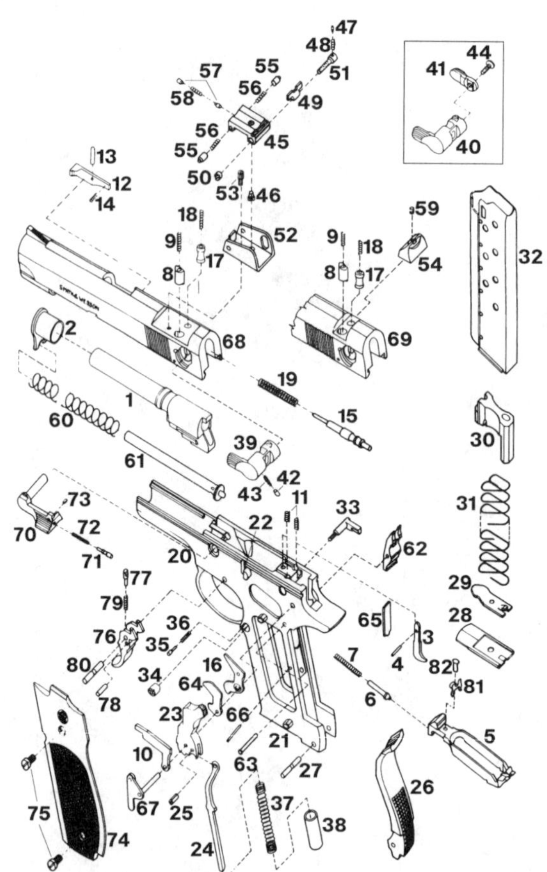

1	Barrel
2	Barrel Bushing
3	Disconnector
4	Disconnector Pin
5	Drawbar
6	Drawbar Plunger
7	Drawbar Plunger Spring
8	Ejector Depressor Plunger
9	Ejector Depressor Plunger Spring
10	Ejector Magazine Depressor
11	Ejector Springs
12	Extractor
13	Extractor Pin
14	Extractor Spring
15	Firing Pin
16	Firing Pin Safety-Lever
17	Firing Pin Safety-Lever Plunger
18	Firing Pin Safety-Lever Spring
19	Firing Pin Spring
20	Frame
21	Frame Stud
22	Slide Stop Button
23	Hammer
24	Stirrup
25	Stirrup Pin
26	Frame Insert
27	Frame Insert Pin
28	Magazine Base Plate
29	Magazine Base Plate Catch
30	Magazine Follower
31	Magazine Spring
32	Magazine Body
33	Magazine Catch
34	Magazine Catch Nut
35	Magazine Catch Plunger
36	Magazine Catch Plunger Spring
37	Mainspring
38	Mainspring Plunger
39	Manual Safety
40	Manual Safety, Ambidextrous
41	Manual Safety Right Side Lever
42	Manual Safety Plunger
43	Manual Safety Plunger Spring
44	Manual Safety Screw
45	Rear Sight Body
46	Rear Sight Elevation Screw
47	Rear Sight Plunger
48	Rear Sight Plunger Spring
49	Rear Sight Slide
50	Rear Sight Windage Nut
51	Rear Sight Windage Screw
52	Rear Sight Base
53	Rear Sight Base Screw
54	Rear Sight Body, Fixed Sight
55	Rear Sight Body Plungers
56	Rear Sight Body Plunger Springs
57	Rear Sight Elevation Plungers
58	Rear Sight Elevation Spring
59	Rear Sight Set Screw, Fixed Sight
60	Recoil Spring
61	Recoil Spring Guide Assembly
62	Sear
63	Sear Pin
64	Sear Release Lever
65	Sear Spring
66	Sear Spring Retaining Pin
67	Sideplate
68	Slide, Adjustable Sight
69	Slide, Fixed Sight
70	Slide Stop
71	Slide Stop Plunger
72	Slide Stop Plunger Spring
73	Slide Stop Spiral Pin
74	Left Grip
75	Grip Screws
76	Trigger
77	Trigger Plunger
78	Trigger Plunger Pin
79	Trigger Plunger Spring
80	Trigger Pin
81	Trigger Play Spring
82	Trigger Play Spring Rivet

Parts Not Shown

Hammer Pin
Recoil Spring Guide
Recoil Spring Guide Bushing
Recoil Spring Guide Plunger
Recoil Spring Guide Plunger Spring
Right Grip
Slide Stop Bar

Model 645 Auto

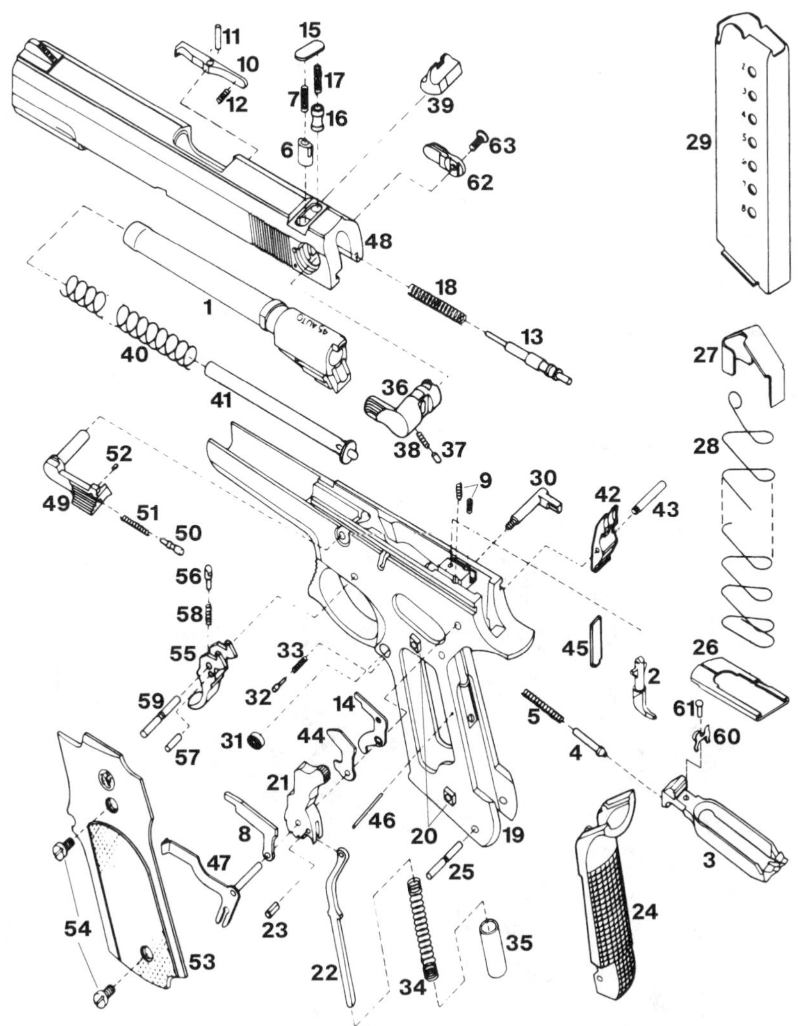

1	Barrel	**25**	Frame Insert Pin	**49**	Slide Stop
2	Disconnector	**26**	Magazine Base Plate	**50**	Slide Stop Plunger
3	Drawbar	**27**	Magazine Follower	**51**	Slide Stop Plunger Spring
4	Drawbar Plunger	**28**	Magazine Spring	**52**	Slide Stop Spiral Pin
5	Drawbar Plunger Spring	**29**	Magazine Tube	**53**	Left Grip
6	Ejector Depressor Plunger	**30**	Magazine Catch	**54**	Grip Screws
7	Ejector Depressor Plunger Spring	**31**	Magazine Catch Nut	**55**	Trigger
8	Ejector Magazine Depressor	**32**	Magazine Catch Plunger	**56**	Trigger Plunger
9	Ejector Springs	**33**	Magazine Catch Plunger Spring	**57**	Trigger Plunger Pin
10	Extractor	**34**	Mainspring	**58**	Trigger Plunger Spring
11	Extractor Pin	**35**	Mainspring Plunger	**59**	Trigger Pin
12	Extractor Spring	**36**	Manual Safety	**60**	Trigger Play Spring
13	Firing Pin	**37**	Manual Safety Plunger	**61**	Trigger Play Spring Rivet
14	Firing Pin Safety-Lever	**38**	Manual Safety Plunger Spring	**62**	Ambidextrous Manual Safety Right Side Lever
15	Safety-Lever Spring Retainer	**39**	Rear Sight Body, Fixed	**63**	Ambidextrous Manual Safety Screw
16	Firing Pin Safety-Lever Plunger	**40**	Recoil Spring	**Parts Not Shown**	
17	Firing Pin Safety-Lever Plunger Spring	**41**	Recoil Spring Guide Assembly		Hammer Pin
18	Firing Pin Spring	**42**	Sear		Recoil Spring Guide
19	Frame	**43**	Sear Pin		Recoil Spring Guide Bushing
20	Frame Studs	**44**	Sear Release Lever		Recoil Spring Guide Plunger
21	Hammer	**45**	Sear Spring		Recoil Spring Guide Plunger Spring
22	Stirrup	**46**	Sear Spring Retaining Pin		Right Grip
23	Stirrup Pin	**47**	Sideplate		
24	Frame Insert	**48**	Slide		

Model 649 Revolver

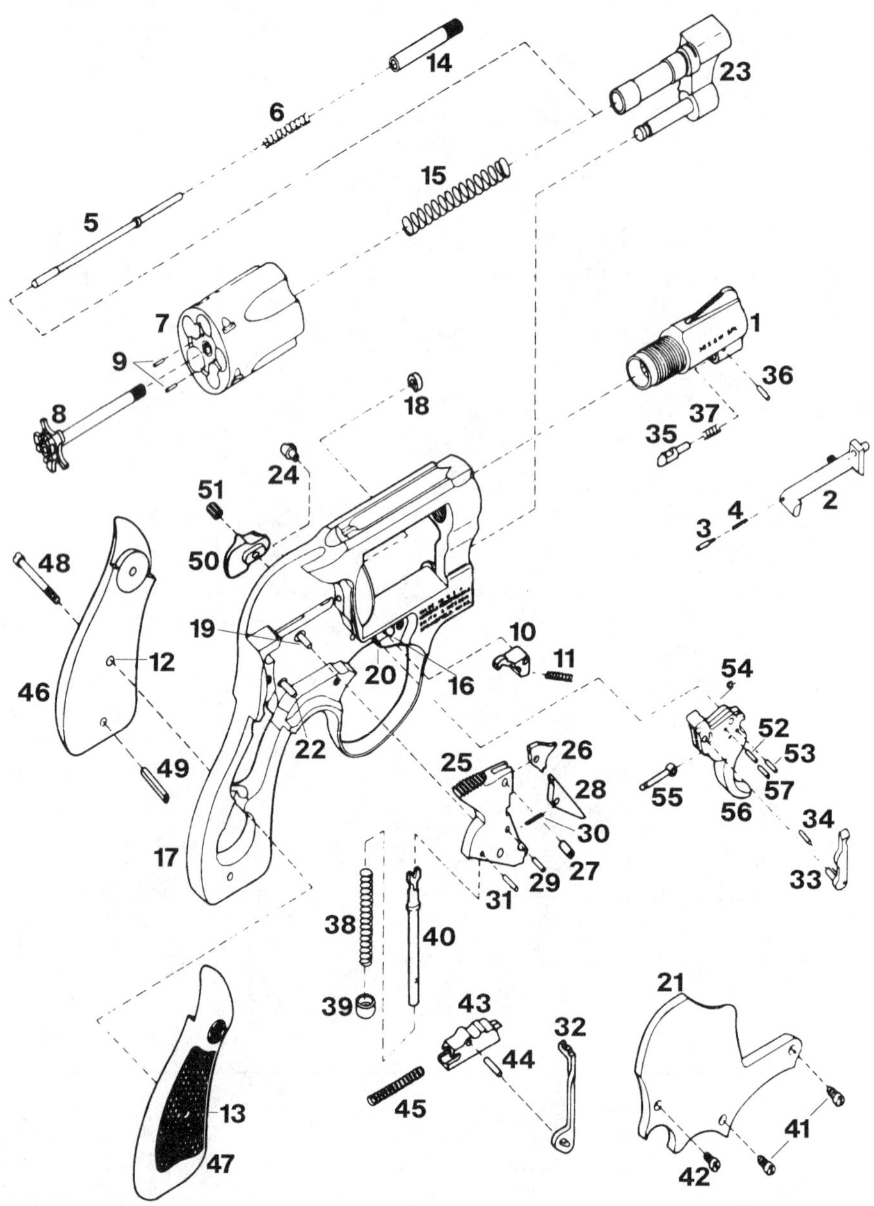

1	Barrel	20	Trigger Stud	39	Mainspring Swivel
2	Bolt	21	Sideplate	40	Mainspring Stirrup
3	Bolt Plunger	22	Rebound Slide Stud	41	Sideplate Screws, Crowned
4	Bolt Plunger Spring	23	Yoke	42	Sideplate Screw, Flat
5	Center Pin	24	Frame Lug	43	Rebound Slide
6	Center Pin Spring	25	Hammer	44	Rebound Slide Pin
7	Cylinder	26	Hammer Nose	45	Rebound Slide Spring
8	Extractor	27	Hammer Nose Rivet	46	Left Grip
9	Extractor Pins	28	Sear	47	Right Grip
10	Cylinder Stop	29	Sear Pin	48	Grip Pin
11	Cylinder Stop Spring	30	Sear Spring	49	Grip Locator Pin
12	Grip Escutcheon	31	Stirrup Pin	50	Thumb-Piece
13	Grip Escutcheon Nut	32	Hammer Block	51	Thumb-Piece Nut
14	Extractor Rod	33	Hand	52	Hand Torsion Spring Pin
15	Extractor Spring	34	Hand Pin	53	Hand Spring Pin
16	Cylinder Stop Stud	35	Locking Bolt	54	Hand Spring
17	Frame	36	Locking Bolt Pin	55	Trigger Lever
18	Hammer Nose Bushing	37	Locking Bolt Spring	56	Trigger
19	Hammer Stud	38	Mainspring	57	Trigger Lever Pin

Model 650 Revolver

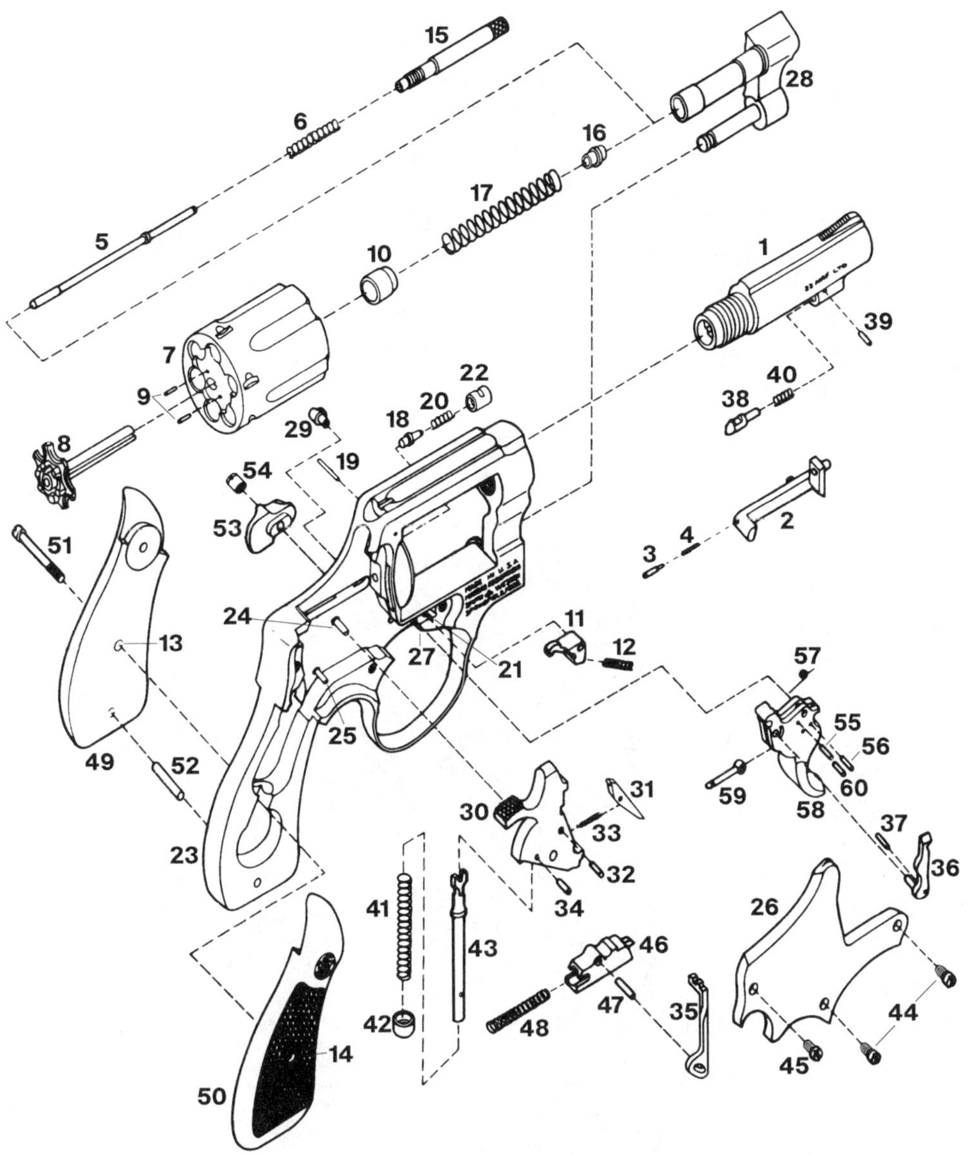

1	Barrel	21	Cylinder Stop Stud	41	Mainspring
2	Bolt	22	Firing Pin Bushing	42	Mainspring Rod Swivel
3	Bolt Plunger	23	Frame	43	Mainspring Stirrup
4	Bolt Plunger Spring	24	Hammer Stud	44	Sideplate Screws, Crowned
5	Center Pin	25	Rebound Slide Stud	45	Sideplate Screw, Flat Head
6	Center Pin Spring	26	Sideplate	46	Rebound Slide
7	Cylinder	27	Trigger Stud	47	Rebound Slide Pin
8	Extractor	28	Yoke	48	Rebound Slide Spring
9	Extractor Pins	29	Frame Lug	49	Left Grip
10	Gas Ring	30	Hammer	50	Right Grip
11	Cylinder Stop	31	Sear	51	Stock Screw
12	Cylinder Stop Spring	32	Sear Pin	52	Stock Pin
13	Escutcheon	33	Sear Spring	53	Thumb-Piece
14	Escutcheon Nut	34	Stirrup Pin	54	Thumb-Piece Nut
15	Extractor Rod	35	Hammer Block	55	Hand Spring Pin
16	Extractor Rod Collar	36	Hand	56	Hand Spring Torsion Pin
17	Extractor Spring	37	Hand Pin	57	Hand Torsion Spring
18	Firing Pin	38	Locking Bolt	58	Trigger
19	Firing Pin Bushing Pin	39	Locking Bolt Pin	59	Trigger Lever
20	Firing Pin Spring	40	Locking Bolt Spring	60	Trigger Lever Pin

Model 651 Revolver

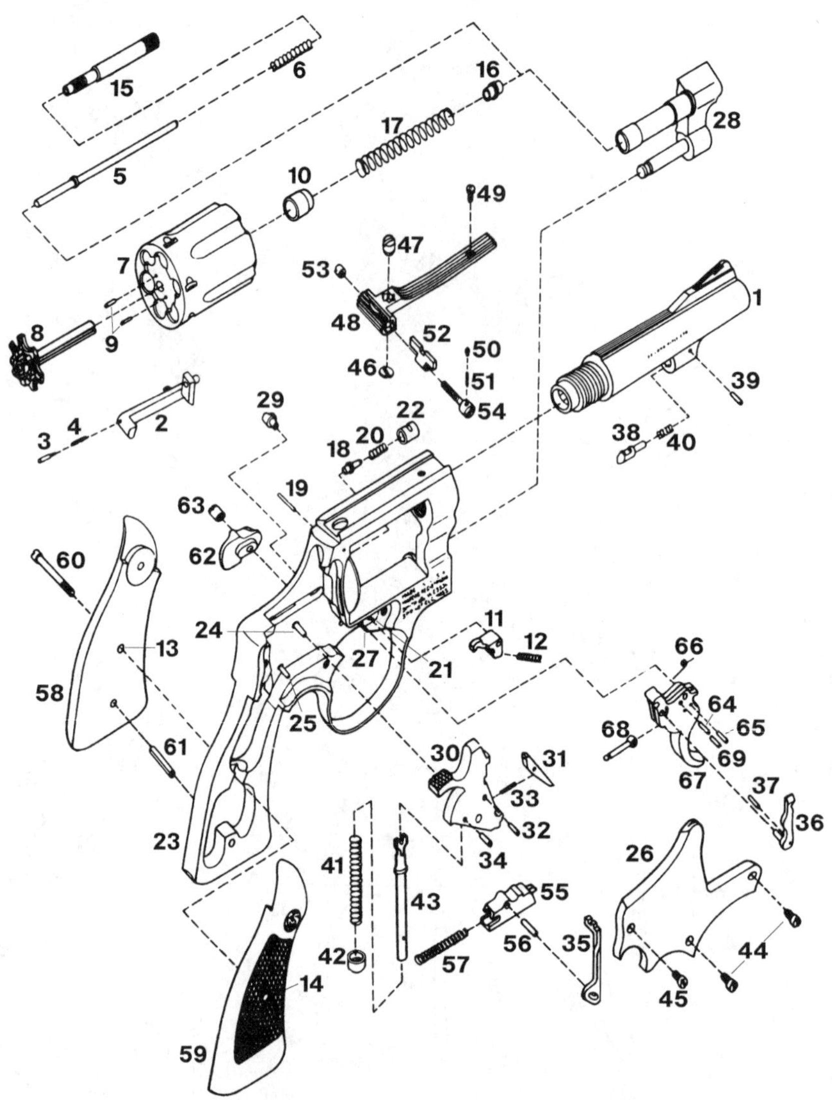

1	Barrel	**24**	Hammer Stud	**47**	Rear Sight Elevation Screw
2	Bolt	**25**	Rebound Slide Stud	**48**	Rear Sight Leaf
3	Bolt Plunger	**26**	Sideplate	**49**	Rear Sight Leaf Screw
4	Bolt Plunger Spring	**27**	Trigger Stud	**50**	Rear Sight Plunger
5	Center Pin	**28**	Yoke	**51**	Rear Sight Plunger Spring
6	Center Pin Spring	**29**	Frame Lug	**52**	Rear Sight Slide
7	Cylinder	**30**	Hammer	**53**	Rear Sight Windage Nut
8	Extractor	**31**	Sear	**54**	Rear Sight Windage Screw
9	Extractor Pins	**32**	Sear Pin	**55**	Rebound Slide
10	Gas Ring	**33**	Sear Spring	**56**	Rebound Slide Pin
11	Cylinder Stop	**34**	Stirrup Pin	**57**	Rebound Slide Spring
12	Cylinder Stop Spring	**35**	Hammer Block	**58**	Left Grip
13	Grip Escutcheon	**36**	Hand	**59**	Right Grip
14	Grip Escutcheon Nut	**37**	Hand Pin	**60**	Grip Screw
15	Extractor Rod	**38**	Locking Bolt	**61**	Grip Locator Pin
16	Extractor Rod Collar	**39**	Locking Bolt Pin	**62**	Thumb-Piece
17	Extractor Spring	**40**	Locking Bolt Spring	**63**	Thumb-Piece Nut
18	Firing Pin	**41**	Mainspring	**64**	Hand Spring Pin
19	Firing Pin Bushing Pin	**42**	Mainspring Rod Swivel	**65**	Hand Spring Torsion Pin
20	Firing Pin Spring	**43**	Mainspring Stirrup	**66**	Hand Torsion Spring
21	Cylinder Stop Stud	**44**	Sideplate Screws, Crowned	**67**	Trigger
22	Firing Pin Bushing	**45**	Sideplate Screw, Flat Head	**68**	Trigger Lever
23	Frame	**46**	Rear Sight Elevation Click Plug	**69**	Trigger Lever Pin

Model 657 Revolver

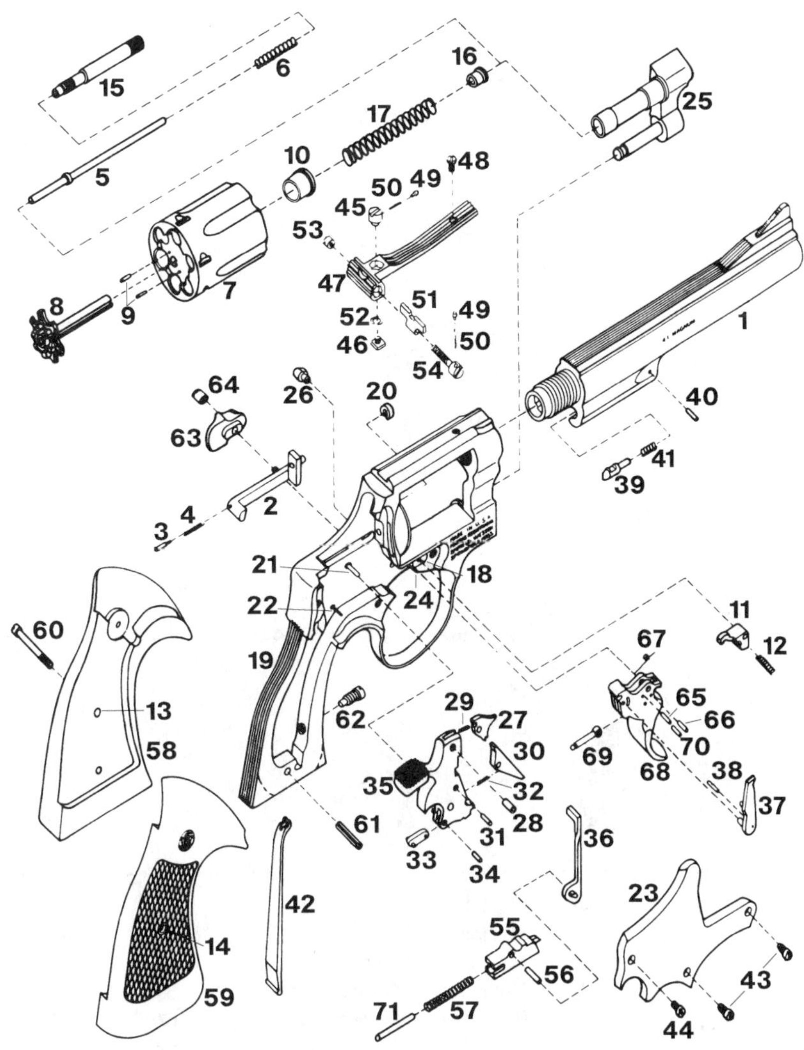

1	Barrel	**25**	Yoke	**49**	Rear Sight Plungers
2	Bolt	**26**	Frame Lug	**50**	Rear Sight Plunger Springs
3	Bolt Plunger	**27**	Hammer Nose	**51**	Rear Sight Slide
4	Bolt Plunger Spring	**28**	Hammer Nose Rivet	**52**	Rear Sight Spring Clip
5	Center Pin	**29**	Hammer Nose Spring	**53**	Rear Sight Windage Nut
6	Center Pin Spring	**30**	Sear	**54**	Rear Sight Windage Screw
7	Cylinder	**31**	Sear Pin	**55**	Rebound Slide
8	Extractor	**32**	Sear Spring	**56**	Rebound Slide Pin
9	Extractor Pins	**33**	Stirrup	**57**	Rebound Slide Spring
10	Gas Ring	**34**	Stirrup Pin	**58**	Left Grip
11	Cylinder Stop	**35**	Hammer	**59**	Right Grip
12	Cylinder Stop Spring	**36**	Hammer Block	**60**	Grip Screw
13	Grip Escutcheon	**37**	Hand	**61**	Grip Locator Pin
14	Grip Escutcheon Nut	**38**	Hand Pin	**62**	Strain Screw
15	Extractor Rod	**39**	Locking Bolt	**63**	Thumb-Piece
16	Extractor Rod Collar	**40**	Locking Bolt Pin	**64**	Thumb-Piece Nut
17	Extractor Spring	**41**	Locking Bolt Spring	**65**	Hand Spring Pin
18	Cylinder Stop Stud	**42**	Mainspring	**66**	Hand Spring Torsion Pin
19	Frame	**43**	Sideplate Screws, Crowned	**67**	Hand Torsion Spring
20	Hammer Nose Bushing	**44**	Sideplate Screw, Flat Head	**68**	Trigger
21	Hammer Stud	**45**	Rear Sight Elevation Nut	**69**	Trigger Lever
22	Rebound Slide Stud	**46**	Rear Sight Elevation Stud	**70**	Trigger Lever Pin
23	Sideplate	**47**	Rear Sight Leaf	**71**	Trigger Stop Rod
24	Trigger Stud	**48**	Rear Sight Leaf Screw		

Model 659 Auto

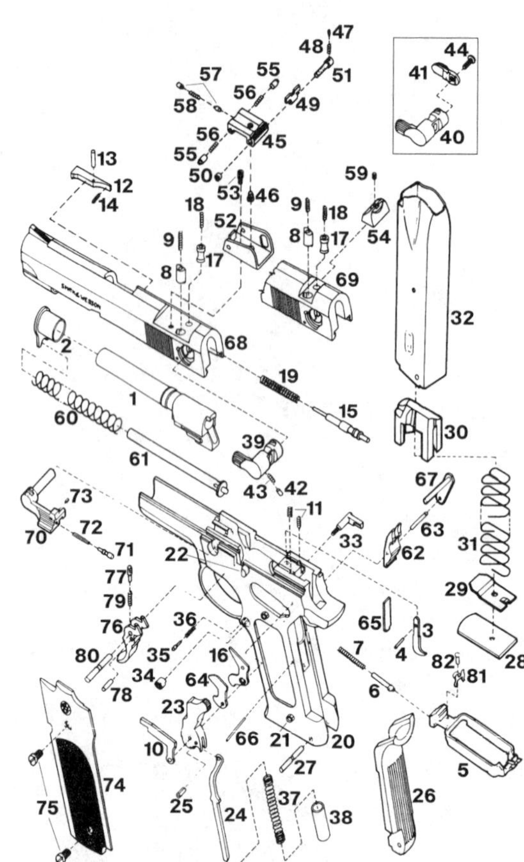

1	Barrel
2	Barrel Bushing
3	Disconnector
4	Disconnector Pin
5	Drawbar
6	Drawbar Plunger
7	Drawbar Plunger Spring
8	Ejector Depressor Plunger
9	Ejector Depressor Plunger Spring
10	Ejector Magazine Depressor
11	Ejector Springs
12	Extractor
13	Extractor Pin
14	Extractor Spring
15	Firing Pin
16	Firing Pin Safety-Lever
17	Firing Pin Safety-Lever Plunger
18	Firing Pin Safety-Lever Spring
19	Firing Pin Spring
20	Frame
21	Frame Stud
22	Slide Stop Button
23	Hammer
24	Stirrup
25	Stirrup Pin
26	Frame Insert
27	Frame Insert Pin
28	Magazine Base Plate
29	Magazine Base Plate Catch
30	Magazine Follower
31	Magazine Spring
32	Magazine Tube
33	Magazine Catch
34	Magazine Catch Nut
35	Magazine Catch Plunger
36	Magazine Catch Plunger Spring
37	Mainspring
38	Mainspring Plunger
39	Manual Safety
40	Manual Safety, Ambidextrous
41	Manual Safety Right Side Lever
42	Manual Safety Plunger
43	Manual Safety Plunger Spring
44	Manual Safety Screw
45	Rear Sight Body
46	Rear Sight Elevation Screw
47	Rear Sight Plunger
48	Rear Sight Plunger Spring
49	Rear Sight Slide
50	Rear Sight Windage Nut
51	Rear Sight Windage Screw
52	Rear Sight Base
53	Rear Sight Base Screw
54	Rear Sight Body, Fixed Sight
55	Rear Sight Body Plungers
56	Rear Sight Body Plunger Springs
57	Rear Sight Elevation Plungers
58	Rear Sight Elevation Spring
59	Rear Sight Set Screw, Fixed Sight
60	Recoil Spring
61	Recoil Spring Guide Assembly
62	Sear
63	Sear Pin
64	Sear Release Lever
65	Sear Spring
66	Sear Spring Retaining Pin
67	Sideplate
68	Slide, Adjustable Sight
69	Slide, Fixed Sight
70	Slide Stop
71	Slide Stop Plunger
72	Slide Stop Plunger Spring
73	Slide Stop Spiral Pin
74	Left Grip
75	Grip Screws
76	Trigger
77	Trigger Plunger
78	Trigger Plunger Pin
79	Trigger Plunger Spring
80	Trigger Pin
81	Trigger Play Spring
82	Trigger Play Spring Rivet

Parts Not Shown

- Hammer Pin
- Recoil Spring Guide
- Recoil Spring Guide Bushing
- Recoil Spring Guide Plunger
- Recoil Spring Guide Plunger Spring
- Slide Stop Pin
- Right Grip

Model 669 Auto

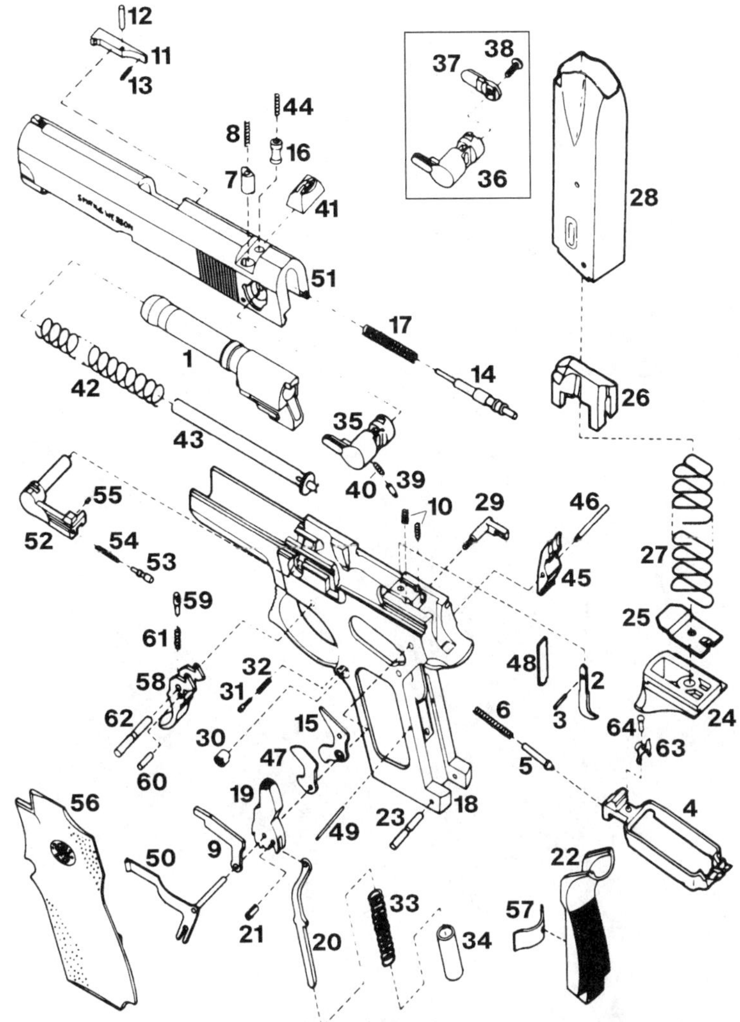

1	Barrel	**26**	Magazine Follower	**48**	Sear Spring
2	Disconnector	**27**	Magazine Spring	**49**	Sear Spring Retaining Pin
3	Disconnector Pin	**28**	Magazine Tube	**50**	Sideplate
4	Drawbar	**29**	Magazine Catch	**51**	Slide
5	Drawbar Plunger	**30**	Magazine Catch Nut	**52**	Slide Stop
6	Drawbar Plunger Spring	**31**	Magazine Catch Plunger	**53**	Slide Stop Plunger
7	Ejector Depressor Plunger	**32**	Magazine Catch Plunger Spring	**54**	Slide Stop Plunger Spring
8	Ejector Depressor Plunger Spring	**33**	Mainspring	**55**	Slide Stop Spiral Pin
9	Ejector Magazine Depressor	**34**	Mainspring Plunger	**56**	Left Grip
10	Ejector Springs	**35**	Manual Safety	**57**	Stock Retaining Spring
11	Extractor	**36**	Manual Safety, Ambidextrous	**58**	Trigger
12	Extractor Pin	**37**	Manual Safety-Lever,<R>Ambidextrous	**59**	Trigger Plunger
13	Extractor Spring	**38**	Manual Safety-Lever Screw,<R>Ambidextrous	**60**	Trigger Plunger Pin
14	Firing Pin	**39**	Manual Safety Plunger	**61**	Trigger Plunger Spring
15	Firing Pin Safety-Lever	**40**	Manual Safety Plunger Spring	**62**	Trigger Pin
16	Firing Pin Safety Plunger	**41**	Rear Sight	**63**	Trigger Play Spring
17	Firing Pin Spring	**42**	Recoil Spring	**64**	Trigger Play Spring Rivet
18	Frame	**43**	Recoil Spring Guide Assembly		
19	Hammer	**44**	Safety-Lever Plunger Spring		
20	Stirrup	**45**	Sear		
21	Stirrup Pin	**46**	Sear Pin		
22	Frame Insert	**47**	Sear Release Lever		
23	Frame Insert Pin				
24	Magazine Base Plate				
25	Magazine Base Plate Catch				

Parts Not Shown

Recoil Spring Guide
Recoil Spring Guide Bushing
Recoil Spring Guide Plunger
Recoil Spring Guide Plunger Spring
Right Grip

Model 681 Revolver

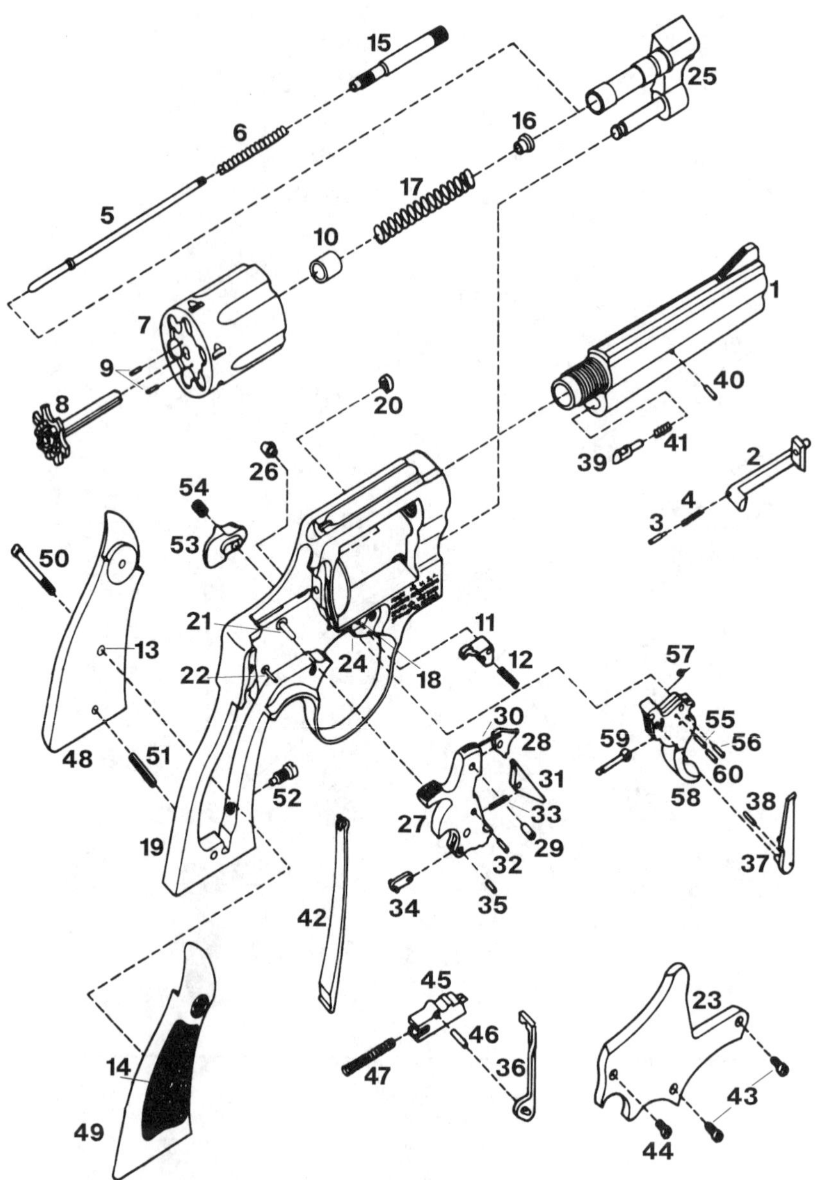

1	Barrel	21	Hammer Stud	41	Locking Bolt Spring
2	Bolt	22	Rebound Slide Stud	42	Mainspring
3	Bolt Plunger	23	Sideplate	43	Sideplate Screws, Crowned
4	Bolt Plunger Spring	24	Trigger Stud	44	Sideplate Screw, Flat Head
5	Center Pin	25	Yoke	45	Rebound Slide
6	Center Pin Spring	26	Frame Lug	46	Rebound Slide Pin
7	Cylinder	27	Hammer	47	Rebound Slide Spring
8	Extractor	28	Hammer Nose	48	Left Grip
9	Extractor Pins	29	Hammer Nose Rivet	49	Right Grip
10	Gas Ring	30	Hammer Nose Spring	50	Grip Screw
11	Cylinder Stop	31	Sear	51	Grip Locator Pin
12	Cylinder Stop Spring	32	Sear Pin	52	Strain Screw
13	Grip Escutcheon	33	Sear Spring	53	Thumb-Piece
14	Grip Escutcheon Nut	34	Stirrup	54	Thumb-Piece Nut
15	Extractor Rod	35	Stirrup Pin	55	Hand Spring Pin
16	Extractor Rod Collar	36	Hammer Block	56	Hand Spring Torsion Pin
17	Extractor Spring	37	Hand	57	Hand Torsion Spring
18	Cylinder Stop Stud	38	Hand Pin	58	Trigger
19	Frame	39	Locking Bolt	59	Trigger Lever
20	Hammer Nose Bushing	40	Locking Bolt Pin	60	Trigger Lever Pin

Model 686 Revolver

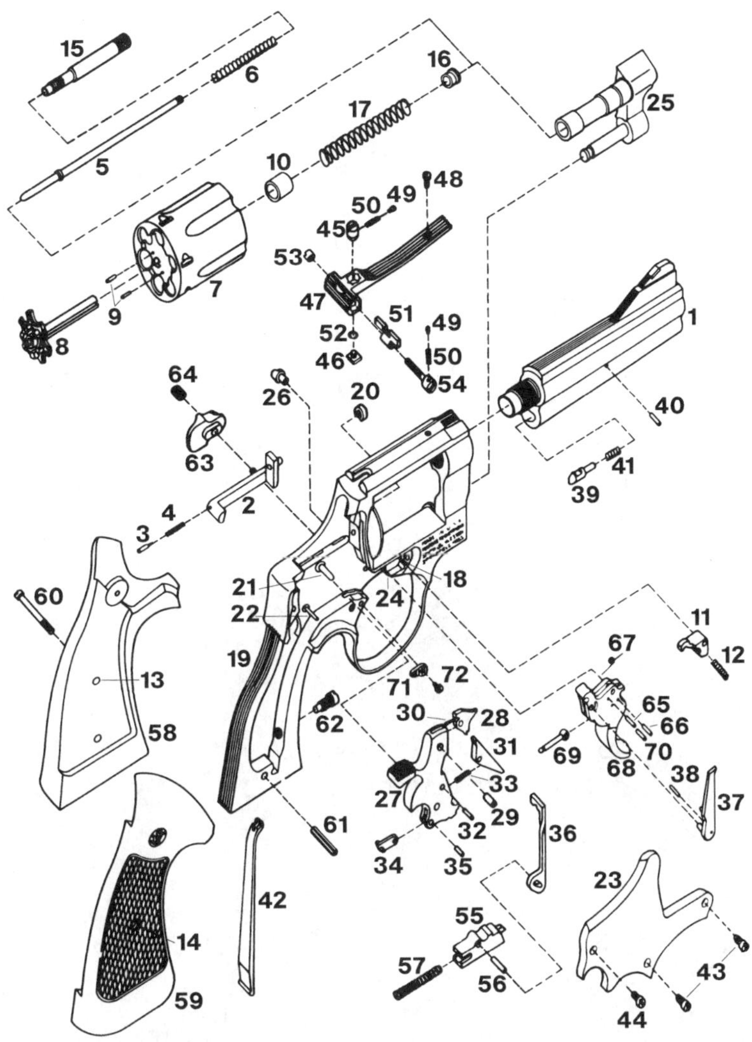

1	Barrel	**26**	Frame Lug	**51**	Rear Sight Slide
2	Bolt	**27**	Hammer	**52**	Rear Sight Spring Clip
3	Bolt Plunger	**28**	Hammer Nose	**53**	Rear Sight Windage Nut
4	Bolt Plunger Spring	**29**	Hammer Nose Rivet	**54**	Rear Sight Windage Screw
5	Center Pin	**30**	Hammer Nose Spring	**55**	Rebound Slide
6	Center Pin Spring	**31**	Sear	**56**	Rebound Slide Pin
7	Cylinder	**32**	Sear Pin	**57**	Rebound Slide Spring
8	Extractor	**33**	Sear Spring	**58**	Left Grip
9	Extractor Pins	**34**	Stirrup	**59**	Right Grip
10	Gas Ring	**35**	Stirrup Pin	**60**	Grip Screw
11	Cylinder Stop	**36**	Hammer Block	**61**	Grip Locator Pin
12	Cylinder Stop Spring	**37**	Hand	**62**	Strain Screw
13	Grip Escutcheon	**38**	Hand Pin	**63**	Thumb-Piece
14	Grip Escutcheon Nut	**39**	Locking Bolt	**64**	Thumb-Piece Nut
15	Extractor Rod	**40**	Locking Bolt Pin	**65**	Hand Spring Pin
16	Extractor Rod Collar	**41**	Locking Bolt Spring	**66**	Hand Spring Torsion Pin
17	Extractor Spring	**42**	Mainspring	**67**	Hand Torsion Spring
18	Cylinder Stop Stud	**43**	Sideplate Screws, Crowned	**68**	Trigger
19	Frame	**44**	Sideplate Screw, Flat Head	**69**	Trigger Lever
20	Hammer Nose Bushing	**45**	Rear Sight Elevation Nut	**70**	Trigger Lever Pin
21	Hammer Stud	**46**	Rear Sight Elevation Stud	**71**	Trigger Stop
22	Rebound Slide Stud	**47**	Rear Sight Leaf	**72**	Trigger Stop Screw
23	Sideplate	**48**	Rear Sight Screw	**Parts Not Shown**	
24	Trigger Stud	**49**	Rear Sight Plungers		Front Sight Blade
25	Yoke	**50**	Rear Sight Plunger Springs		

Model 745 Auto

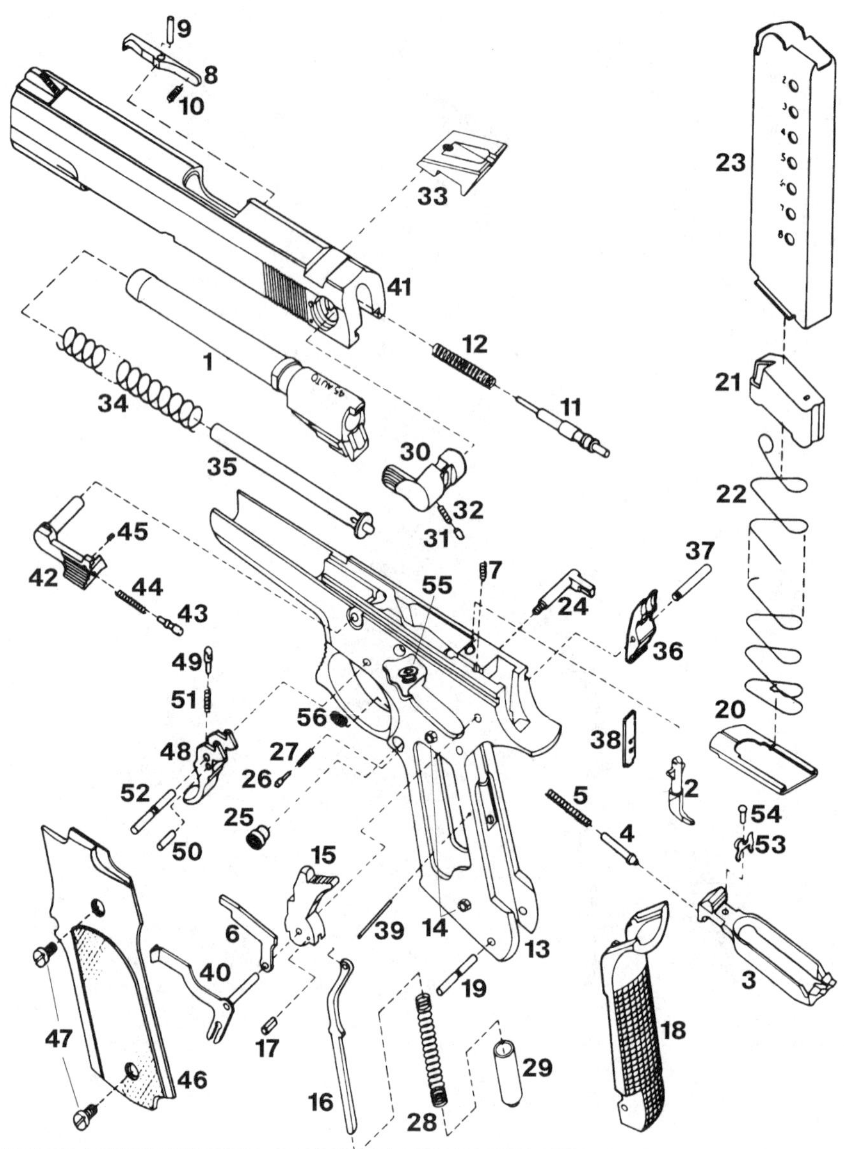

1	Barrel
2	Disconnector
3	Drawbar
4	Drawbar Plunger
5	Drawbar Plunger Spring
6	Ejector Magazine Depressor
7	Ejector Spring
8	Extractor
9	Extractor Pin
10	Extractor Spring
11	Firing Pin
12	Firing Pin Spring
13	Frame
14	Frame Studs
15	Hammer
16	Stirrup
17	Stirrup Pin
18	Frame Insert
19	Frame Insert Pin
20	Magazine Base Plate
21	Magazine Follower
22	Magazine Spring
23	Magazine Tube
24	Magazine Catch
25	Magazine Catch Nut
26	Magazine Catch Plunger
27	Magazine Catch Plunger Spring
28	Mainspring
29	Mainspring Plunger
30	Manual Safety
31	Manual Safety Plunger
32	Manual Safety Plunger Spring
33	Rear Sight Body Fixed
34	Recoil Spring
35	Recoil Spring Guide Assembly
36	Sear
37	Sear Pin
38	Sear Spring
39	Sear Spring Retaining Pin
40	Sideplate
41	Slide
42	Slide Stop
43	Slide Stop Plunger
44	Slide Stop Plunger Spring
45	Slide Stop Spiral Pin
46	Left Grip
47	Grip Screws
48	Trigger
49	Trigger Plunger
50	Trigger Plunger Pin
51	Trigger Plunger Spring
52	Trigger Pin
53	Trigger Play Spring
54	Trigger Play Spring Rivet
55	Upper Lock-Out Screw
56	Adjustable Trigger Stop

Parts Not Shown

Recoil Spring Guide
Recoil Spring Guide Bushing
Recoil Spring Guide Plunger
Recoil Spring Guide Plunger Spring
Right Grip

Tip-Up 32 Revolver

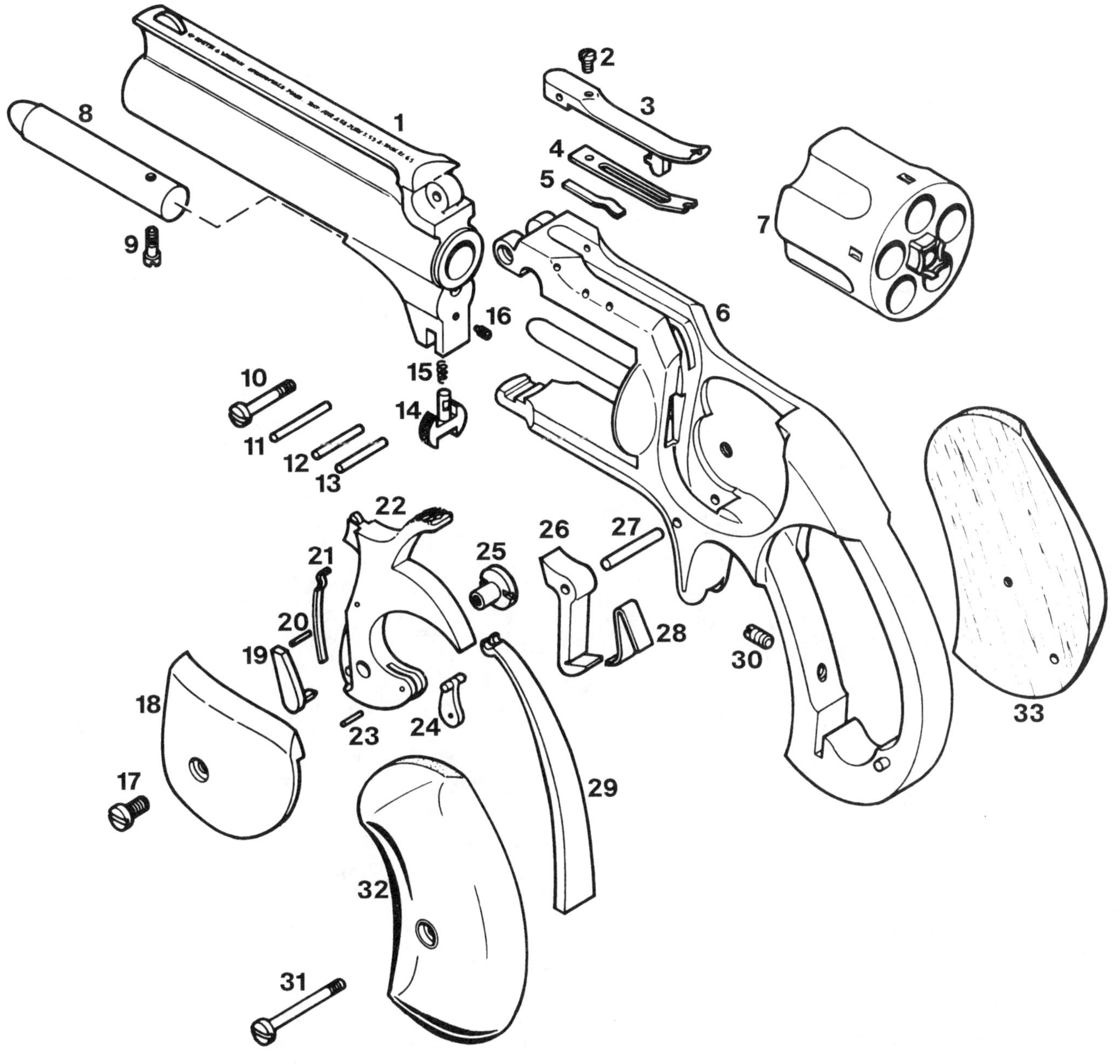

1	Barrel
2	Cylinder Stop Screw
3	Cylinder Stop and Rear Sight
4	Cylinder Stop Striker
5	Cylinder Stop Spring
6	Frame
7	Cylinder
8	Ejector Rod
9	Ejector Rod Screw
10	Barrel Hinge Pin
11	Cylinder Stop Pin
12	Cylinder Stop Spring Pin
13	Cylinder Stop Striker Pin
14	Barrel Latch
15	Barrel Latch Spring
16	Barrel Latch Screw
17	Sideplate Screw
18	Sideplate
19	Cylinder Hand
20	Cylinder Hand Spring Pin
21	Cylinder Hand Spring
22	Hammer
23	Hammer Stirrup Pin
24	Hammer Stirrup
25	Hammer Stud
26	Trigger
27	Trigger Pin
28	Trigger Spring
29	Mainspring
30	Mainspring Strain Screw
31	Grip Screw
32	Left Grip Panel
33	Right Grip Panel

1911-A2 Auto

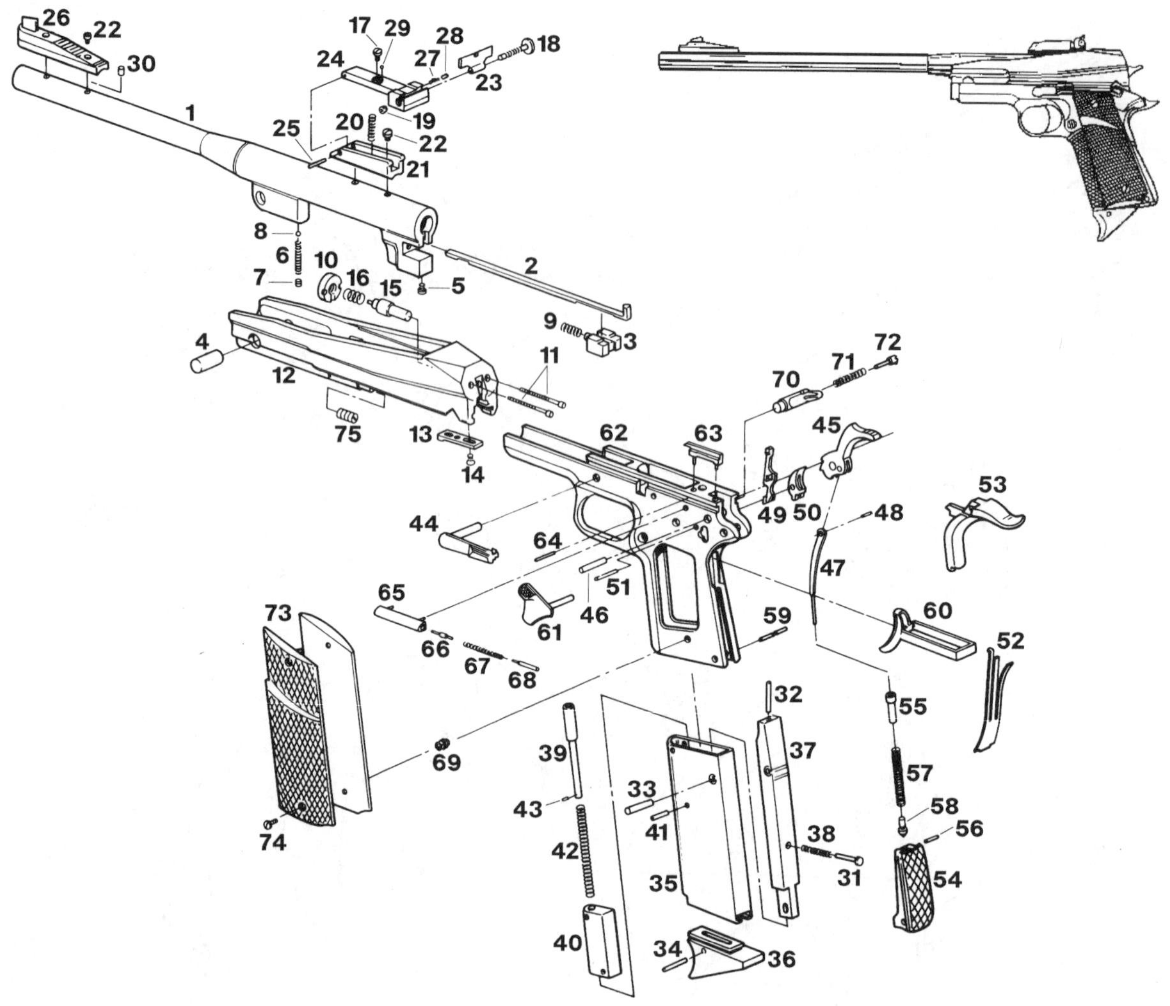

1	Barrel	26	Front Sight	51	Sear Pin
2	Extractor	27	Rear Sight Windage Spring	52	Sear Spring
3	Barrel Lock	28	Rear Sight Windage Plunger	53	Grip Safety
4	Pivot Pin	29	Rear Sight Ball Bearing	54	Mainspring Housing
5	Barrel Lock Screw	30	Sight Plug Screw	55	Mainspring Cap
6	Extractor Detent Spring	31	Release Lever Return Spring Guide	56	Mainspring Cap Pin
7	Extractor Detent Screw	32	Release Lever Unlocking Pin	57	Mainspring
8	Extractor Detent Bearing	33	Release Housing Lever Pivot Pin	58	Housing Pin Retainer
9	Barrel Lock Spring	34	Release Lever Trigger Pin	59	Mainspring Housing Pin
10	Recoil Plate	35	Release Housing	60	Trigger
11	Recoil Plate Screws	36	Release Lever Trigger	61	Safety Lock
12	Slide	37	Release Housing Lever	62	Frame
13	Disconnector Interface	38	Release Lever Return Spring	63	Ejector
14	Disconnector Interface Screw	39	Release Housing Plunger	64	Ejector Pin
15	Firing Pin	40	Release Plunger Housing	65	Plunger Tube
16	Firing Pin Spring	41	Release Plunger Pin	66	Slide Stop Plunger
17	Elevation Screw	42	Release Housing Plunger Spring	67	Plunger Spring
18	Windage Screw	43	Release Housing Plunger Pin	68	Safety Lock Plunger
19	Windage Cap	44	Slide Stop	69	Grip Screw Bushing
20	Elevation Spring	45	Hammer	70	Magazine Catch
21	Rear Sight Base	46	Hammer Pin	71	Magazine Catch Spring
22	Front and Rear Sight Screws	47	Hammer Strut	72	Magazine Catch Lock
23	Rear Sight Aperture	48	Hammer Strut Pin	73	Wraparound Grip
24	Rear Sight Leaf	49	Disconnector	74	Grip Screw
25	Rear Sight Pin	50	Sear	75	Recoil Lug Adjustment Screw

Omega Auto

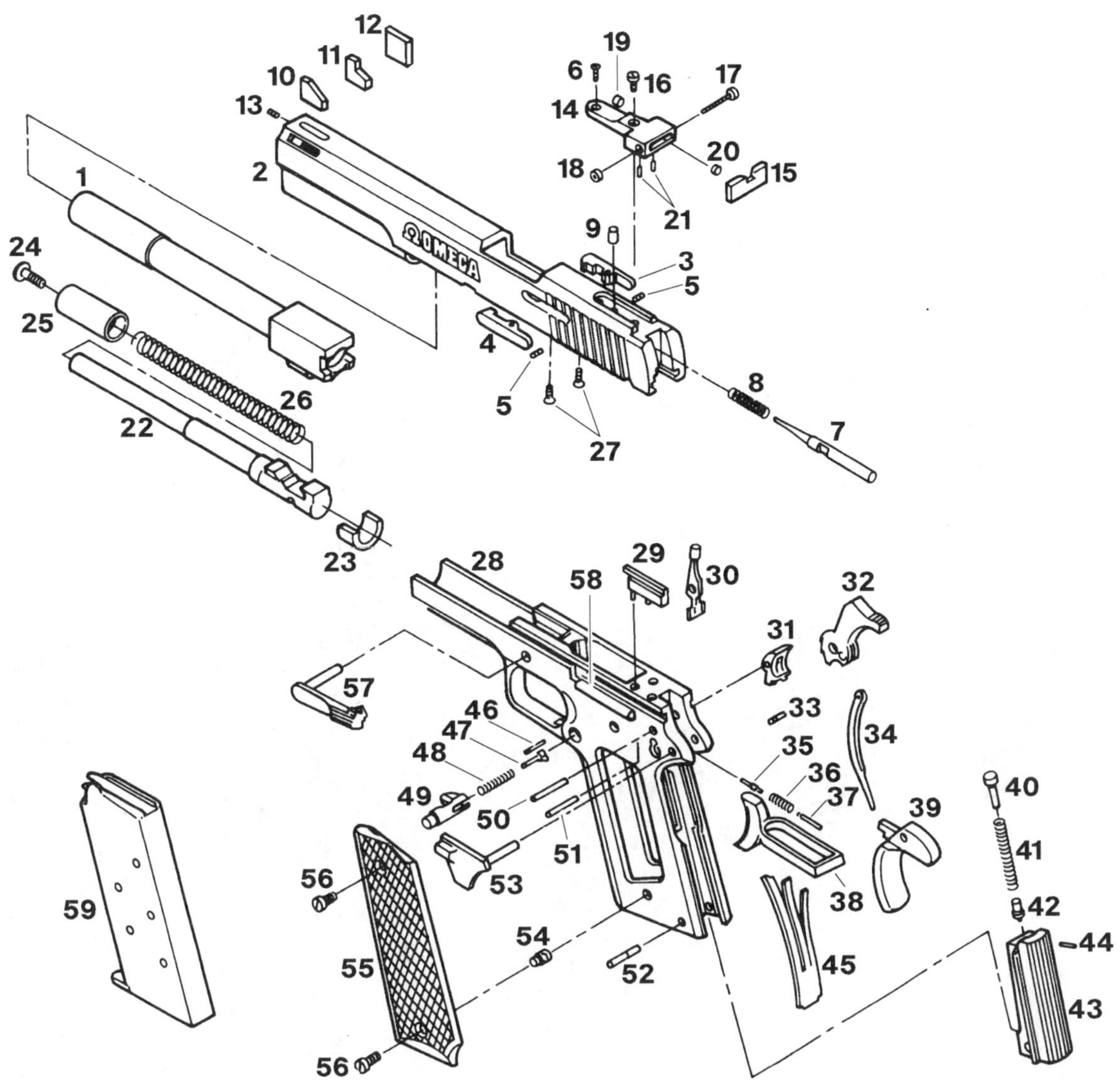

No.	Part	No.	Part	No.	Part
1	Barrel	21	Rear Sight Springs	40	Mainspring Cap
2	Slide	22	Recoil Spring Guide	41	Mainspring
3	Extractor	23	Buffer	42	Mainspring Retainer
4	Extractor/Pusher	24	Recoil Spring Guide Retaining Screw	43	Mainspring Housing
5	Extractor Springs	25	Recoil Spring Guide Plug	44	Mainspring Cap Retaining Pin
6	Rear Sight Screw	26	Recoil Spring	45	Sear Spring
7	Firing Pin	27	Extractor Screws	46	Ejector Pin
8	Firing Pin Spring	28	Frame	47	Magazine Catch Cock
9	Firing Pin Retainer	29	Ejector	48	Magazine Catch Spring
10	Front Sight, Ramp Style	30	Disconnector	49	Magazine Catch
11	Front Sight, Patridge Style	31	Sear	50	Hammer Pin
12	Front Sight, Blank	32	Hammer	51	Sear Pin
13	Front Sight Screw	33	Hammer Strut Pin	52	Mainspring Housing Retaining Pin
14	Rear Sight Housing	34	Hammer Strut	53	Safety Cock
15	Rear Sight Blade	35	Slide Lock Plunger	54	Escutcheon
16	Elevation Screw	36	Plunger Spring	55	Grip Panel
17	Windage Screw	37	Safety Lock Plunger	56	Grip Screws
18	Windage Screw Nut	38	Trigger	57	Slide Lock
19	Front Spring Housing	39	Grip Safety	58	Plunger
20	Rear Spring Housing			59	Magazine

P9 Auto

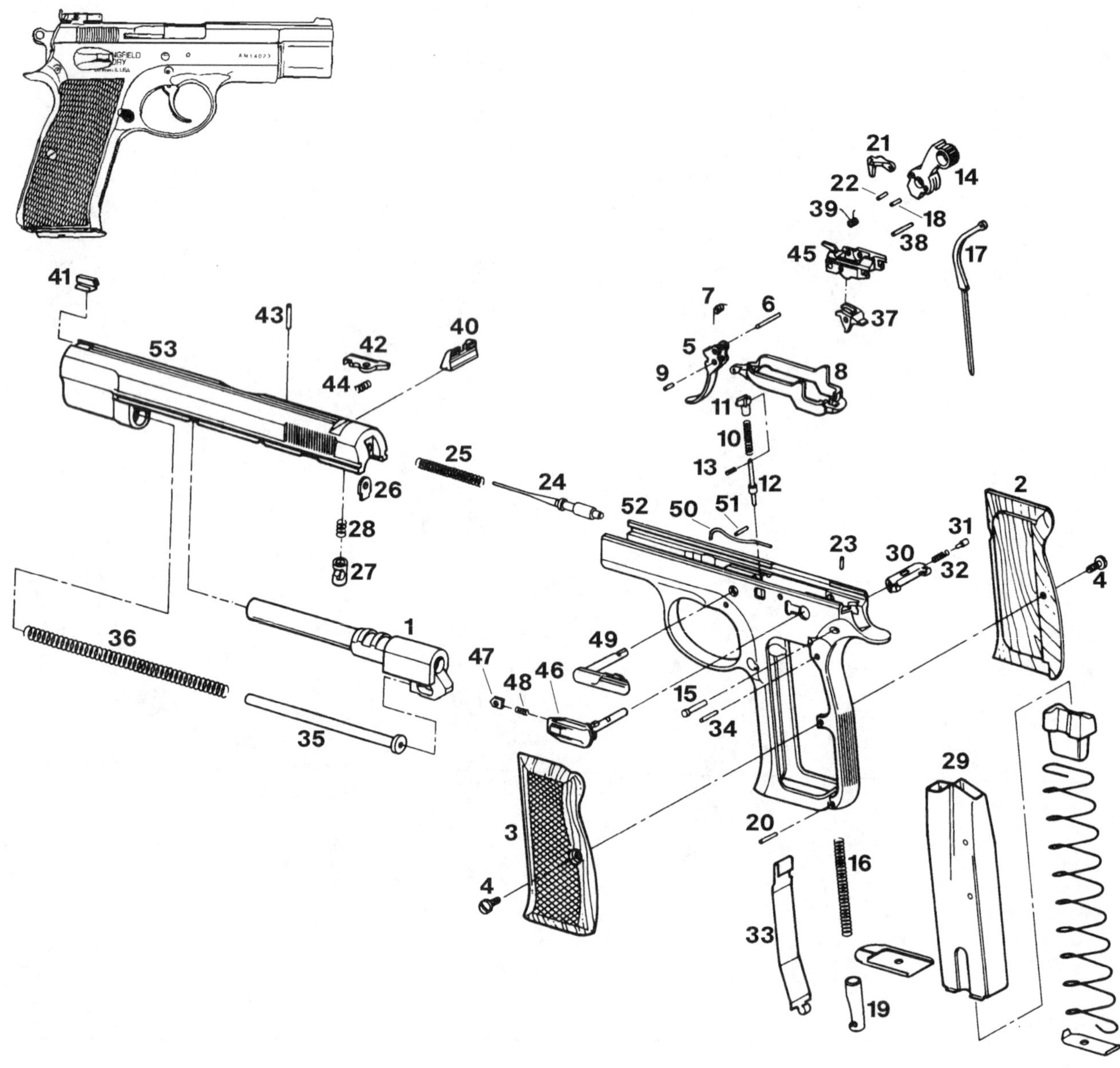

1	Barrel	19	Hammer Spring Cup	37	Sear
2	Right Grip	20	Hammer Spring Cup Pin	38	Sear Pin
3	Left Grip	21	Interruptor	39	Sear Spring
4	Grip Screws	22	Interruptor Pin	40	Rear Sight
5	Trigger	23	Hammer Pin Retaining Pin	41	Front Sight
6	Trigger Pin	24	Firing Pin	42	Extractor
7	Trigger Spring	25	Firing Pin Spring	43	Extractor Pin
8	Trigger Bar	26	Firing Pin Retainer Plate	44	Extractor Spring
9	Trigger Bar Pin	27	Firing Pin Safety	45	Sear Assembly Housing with Ejector
10	Trigger Bar Spring	28	Firing Pin Safety Spring	46	Sear Safety
11	Trigger Bar Guide	29	Magazine	47	Sear Safety Retainer Plate
12	Trigger Bar Plunger	30	Magazine Catch	48	Sear Safety Spring
13	Trigger Bar Plunger Pin	31	Magazine Catch Spring Plunger	49	Slide Stop Pin
14	Hammer	32	Magazine Catch Spring	50	Slide Stop Pin Spring
15	Hammer Pin	33	Magazine Security Spring Plate	51	Slide Stop Pin Spring Pin
16	Hammer Spring	34	Magazine Security Spring Plate Pin	52	Frame
17	Hammer Strut	35	Recoil Spring Guide	53	Slide
18	Hammer Strut Pin	36	Recoil Spring		

30PK Auto

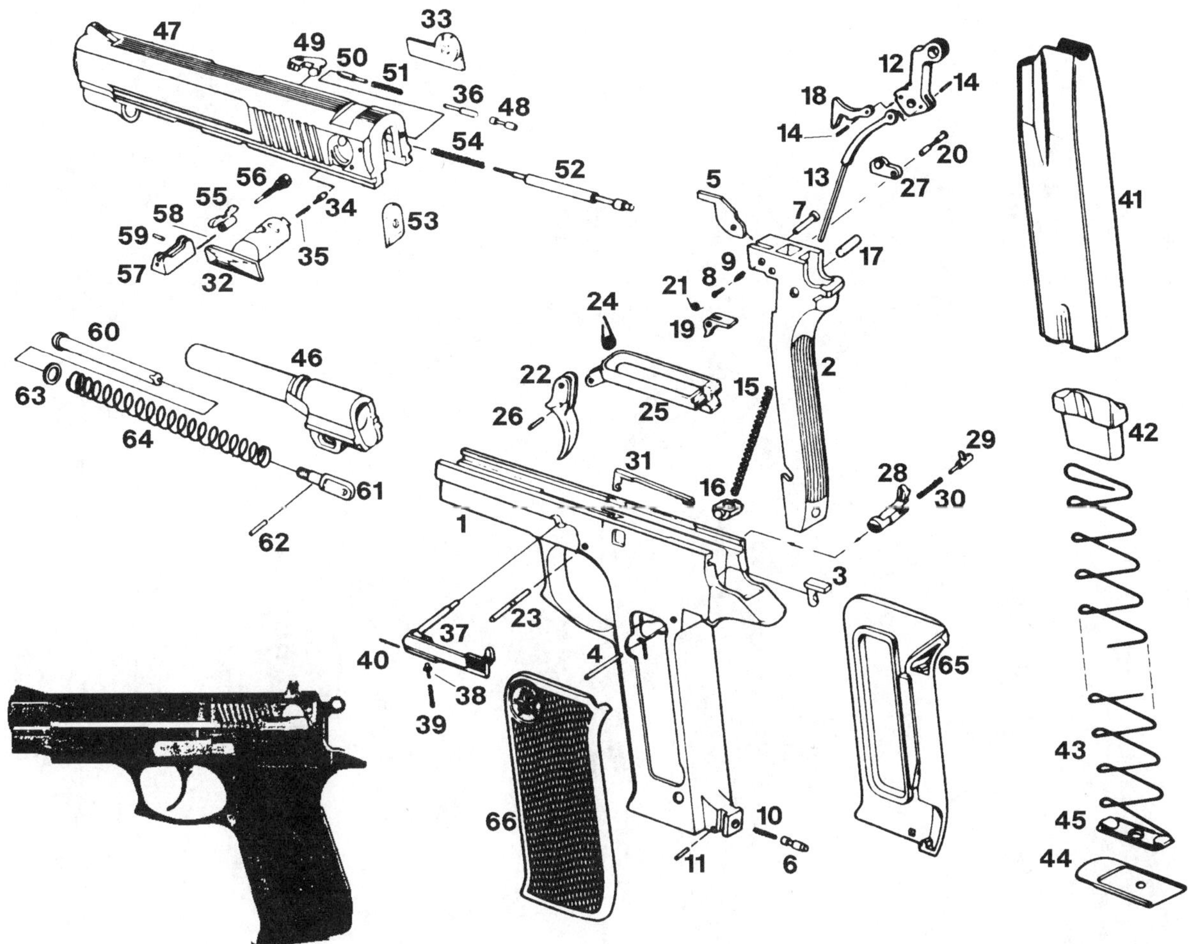

1	Frame	**25**	Trigger Bar	**44**	Magazine Floorplate
2	Backstrap	**26**	Trigger Bar Pin	**45**	Magazine Floorplate Catch
3	Hammer Lock Sliding Way	**27**	Interruptor	**46**	Barrel
4	Hammer Lock Sliding Way Retaining Pin	**28**	Magazine Catch	**47**	Slide
5	Ejector	**29**	Magazine Catch Lock	**48**	Plunger Housing Plug
6	Backstrap Retaining Plunger	**30**	Magazine Catch Lock Spring	**49**	Extractor
7	Ejector Pin	**31**	Magazine Safety	**50**	Extractor Plunger
8	Ejector Friction Plunger	**32**	Ambidextrous Thumb Safety	**51**	Extractor Plunger Spring
9	Ejector Friction Plunger Spring	**33**	Ambidextrous Thumb Safety Wing, Right	**52**	Firing Pin
10	Backstrap Retaining Plunger Spring	**34**	Ambidextrous Thumb Safety Retaining Plunger	**53**	Firing Pin Retainer
11	Backstrap Retaining Plunger Pin	**35**	Ambidextrous Thumb Safety Retaining Plunger Spring	**54**	Firing Pin Spring
12	Hammer	**36**	Ambidextrous Thumb Safety Positioning Plunger	**55**	Rear Sight
13	Hammer Bar	**37**	Slide Stop	**56**	Rear Sight Windage Spindle
14	Hammer Pins	**38**	Slide Stop Plunger	**57**	Rear Sight Base
15	Hammer Spring	**39**	Slide Stop Plunger Spring	**58**	Rear Sight Windage Spindle Spring
16	Hammer Spring Support	**40**	Slide Stop Plunger Elastic Retaining Pin	**59**	Rear Sight Windage Spindle Retaining Pin
17	Hammer Axis	**41**	Magazine Tube	**60**	Recoil Spring Guide
18	Hammer Lock	**42**	Magazine Follower	**61**	Recoil Spring Guide Coupling
19	Sear	**43**	Magazine Follower Spring	**62**	Recoil Spring Guide Coupling Locking Pin
20	Sear Axis			**63**	Recoil Spring Guide Washer
21	Sear Spring			**64**	Recoil Spring
22	Trigger			**65**	Grip, Right
23	Trigger Pin			**66**	Grip, Left
24	Trigger Spring				

BKS Starlight Auto

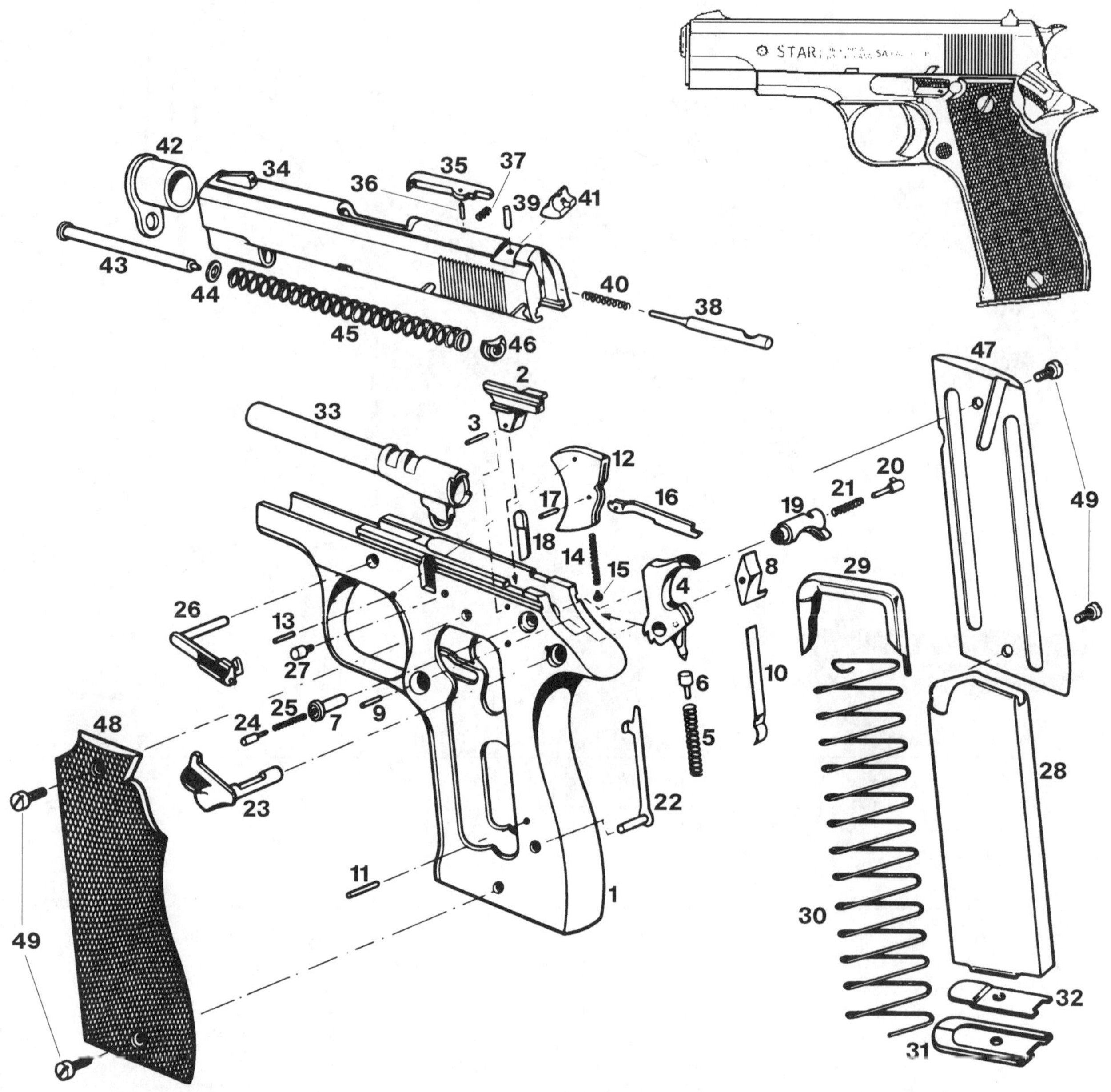

1	Frame	**18**	Interrupter	**35**	Extractor
2	Ejector	**19**	Magazine Catch	**36**	Extractor Pin
3	Ejector Pin	**20**	Magazine Catch Lock	**37**	Extractor Spring
4	Hammer with Strut and Pin	**21**	Magazine Catch Spring	**38**	Firing Pin
5	Hammer Spring	**22**	Magazine Safety	**39**	Firing Pin Retaining Pin
6	Hammer Spring Plunger	**23**	Thumb Safety	**40**	Firing Pin Spring
7	Hammer Pin	**24**	Safety Plunger	**41**	Rear Sight
8	Sear	**25**	Safety Spring	**42**	Barrel Bushing
9	Sear Pin	**26**	Slide Stop	**43**	Recoil Spring Guide
10	Sear Spring	**27**	Slide Stop Screw Button	**44**	Recoil Spring Guide Washer
11	Sear Spring Retaining Pin	**28**	Magazine Tube	**45**	Recoil Spring
12	Trigger	**29**	Magazine Follower	**46**	Recoil Spring Guide Head
13	Trigger Pin	**30**	Magazine Spring	**47**	Grip, Right
14	Trigger Plunger Spring	**31**	Magazine Floorplate	**48**	Grip, Left
15	Trigger Plunger	**32**	Magazine Floorplate Catch	**49**	Grip Screws
16	Sear Bar	**33**	Barrel		
17	Sear Bar Pin	**34**	Slide		

BM and BKM Auto

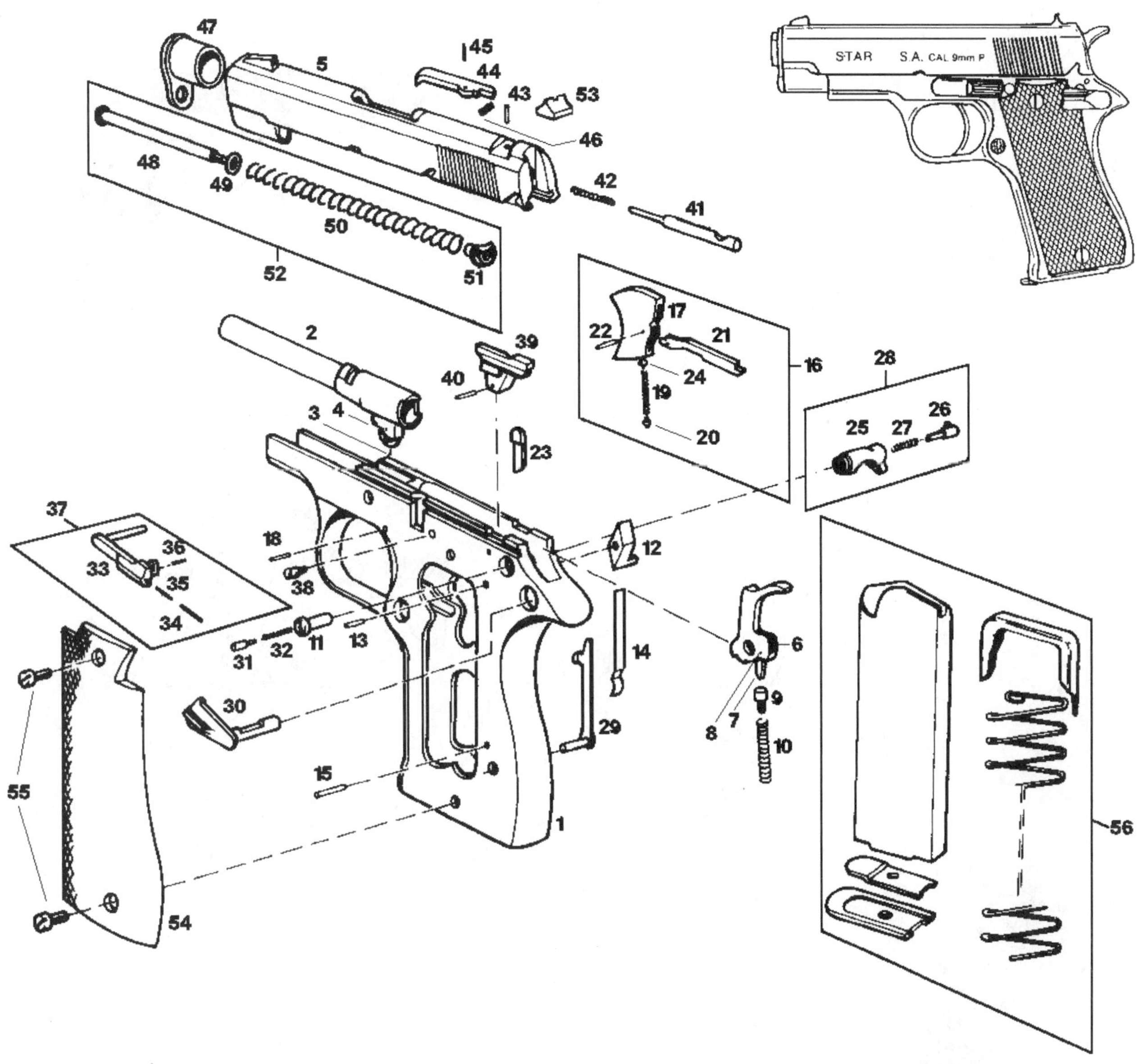

1	Frame	20	Trigger Plunger	39	Ejector
2	Barrel	21	Sear Bar	40	Ejector Pin
3	Barrel Link	22	Sear Bar Pin	41	Firing Pin
4	Barrel Link Pin	23	Disconnector	42	Firing Pin Spring
5	Slide	24	Trigger Pin Retaining Plunger	43	Firing Pin Retaining Pin
6	Hammer	25	Magazine Catch	44	Extractor
7	Hammer Strut	26	Magazine Catch Lock	45	Extractor Pin
8	Hammer Strut Pin	27	Magazine Catch Lock Spring	46	Extractor Spring
9	Hammer Spring Plunger	28	Magazine Catch Assembly	47	Barrel Bushing
10	Hammer Spring	29	Magazine Satety	48	Recoil Spring Guide
11	Hammer Pin	30	Thumb Safety	49	Recoil Spring Guide Washer
12	Sear	31	Thumb Safety Plunger	50	Recoil Spring
13	Sear Pin	32	Thumb Safety Plunger Spring	51	Recoil Spring Guide Head
14	Sear Spring	33	Slide Stop	52	Recoil Spring Assembly
15	Sear Spring Retaining Pin	34	Slide Stop Plunger	53	Rear Sight
16	Trigger Assembly	35	Slide Stop Plunger Spring	54	Grips
17	Trigger	36	Slide Stop Plunger Pin	55	Grip Screws
18	Trigger Pin	37	Slide Stop Assembly	56	Magazine Assembly
19	Trigger Plunger Spring	38	Slide Stop Screw Button		

BS Auto

Courtesy of Dennis Riordan

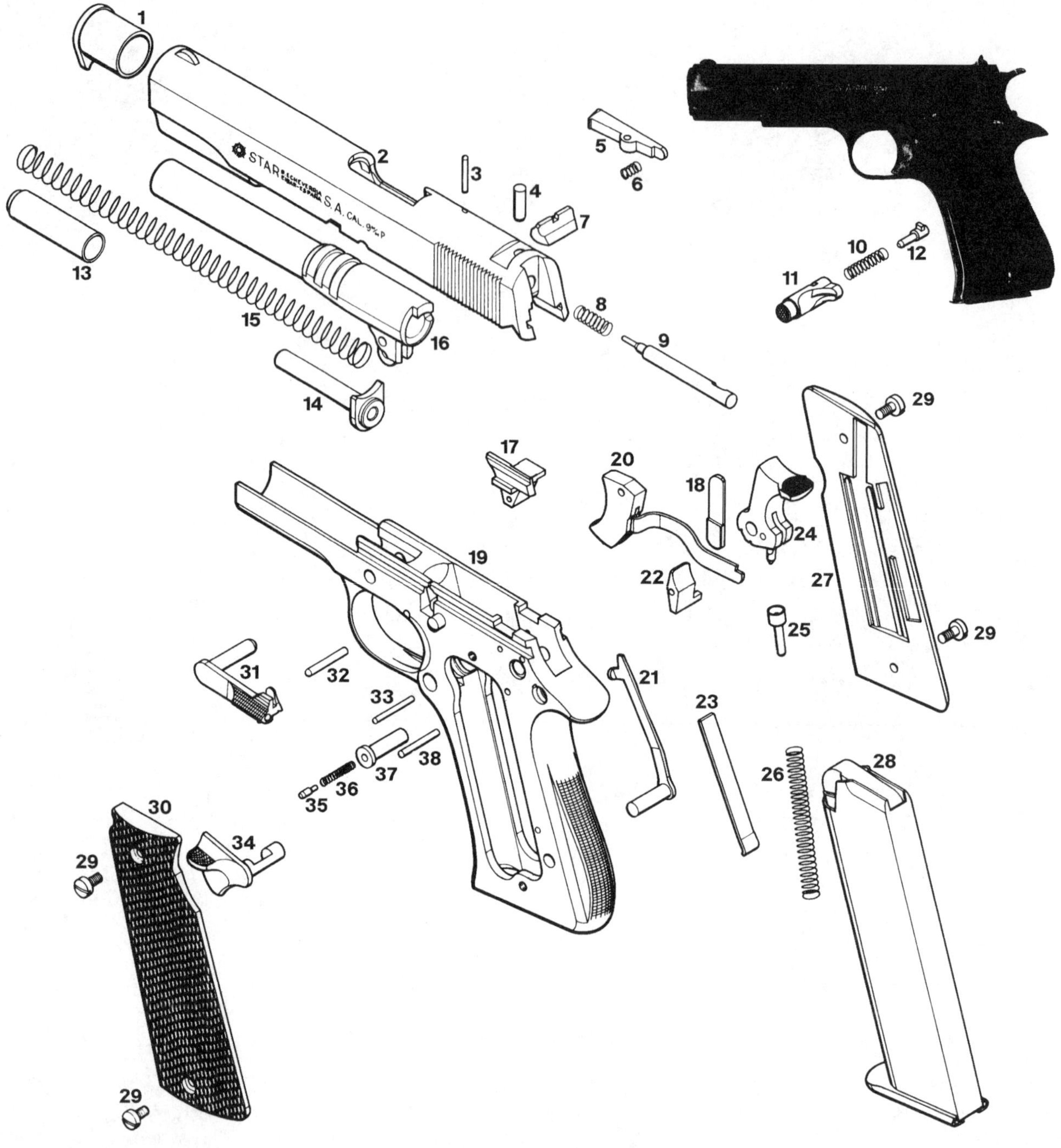

No.	Part	No.	Part	No.	Part
1	Barrel Bushing	14	Recoil Spring Guide	27	Grip, Right
2	Slide	15	Recoil Spring	28	Magazine Assembly
3	Extractor Pin	16	Barrel with Link and Pin	29	Grip Screws
4	Firing Pin Retaining Pin	17	Ejector	30	Grip, Left
5	Extractor	18	Disconnector	31	Slide Stop
6	Extractor Spring	19	Frame	32	Trigger Pin
7	Rear Sight	20	Trigger with Sear Bar	33	Ejector Pin
8	Firing Pin Spring	21	Magazine Safety	34	Thumb Safety
9	Firing Pin	22	Sear	35	Safety Plunger
10	Magazine Catch Lock Spring	23	Sear Spring	36	Safety Spring
11	Magazine Catch	24	Hammer with Strut and Pin	37	Hammer Pin
12	Magazine Catch Lock	25	Hammer Spring Plunger	38	Sear Pin
13	Recoil Spring Plug	26	Hammer Spring		

Firestar Auto

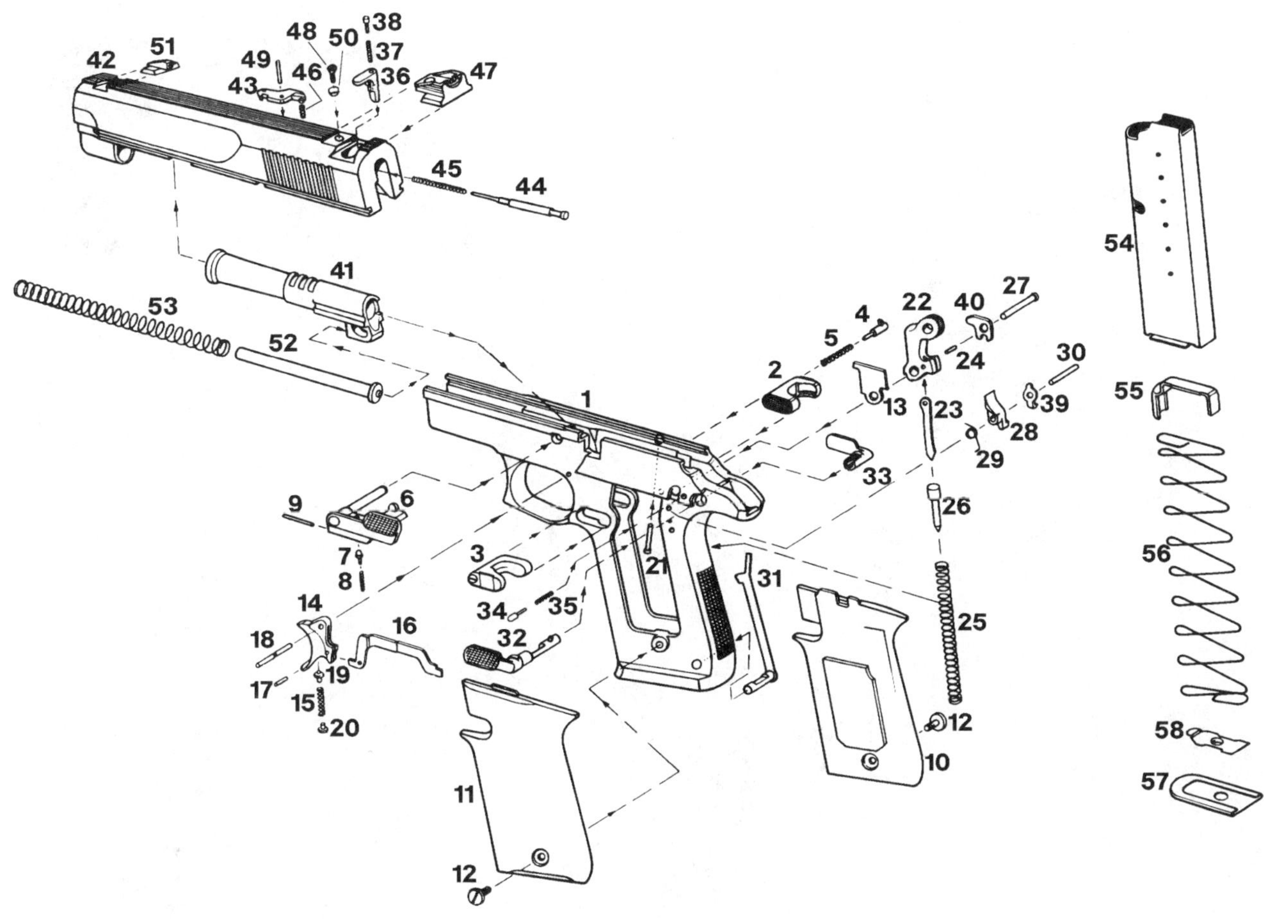

1	Frame	**21**	Interruptor	**41**	Barrel
2	Magazine Catch Body, Right	**22**	Hammer Body	**42**	Slide
3	Magazine Catch Body, Left	**23**	Hammer Bar	**43**	Extractor
4	Magazine Catch Lock	**24**	Hammer Bar Axis	**44**	Firing Pin
5	Magazine Catch Spring	**25**	Hammer Spring	**45**	Firing Pin Spring
6	Slide Stop	**26**	Hammer Spring Plunger	**46**	Extractor Spring
7	Slide Stop Plunger	**27**	Hammer Axis	**47**	Rear Sight
8	Slide Stop Plunger Spring	**28**	Sear	**48**	Rear Sight Screw
9	Slide Stop Plunger Retaining Pin	**29**	Sear Spring	**49**	Extractor Axis
10	Grip, Right	**30**	Sear Axis	**50**	Rear Sight Screw Washer
11	Grip, Left	**31**	Magazine Safety	**51**	Front Sight
12	Grip Screws	**32**	Thumb Safety	**52**	Recoil Spring Guide
13	Ejector	**33**	Thumb Safety Wing	**53**	Recoil Spring
14	Trigger Body	**34**	Thumb Safety Plunger	**54**	Magazine Tube
15	Trigger Spring	**35**	Thumb Safety Plunger Spring	**55**	Magazine Follower
16	Trigger Bar	**36**	Firing Pin Safety	**56**	Magazine Follower Spring
17	Trigger Bar Pin	**37**	Firing Pin Safety Spring	**57**	Magazine Floorplate
18	Trigger Axis	**38**	Firing Pin Safety Spring Plunger	**58**	Magazine Floorplate Catch
19	Trigger Axis Clip	**39**	Sear Pusher		
20	Trigger Plunger	**40**	Firing Pin Safety Pusher		

Model F Auto

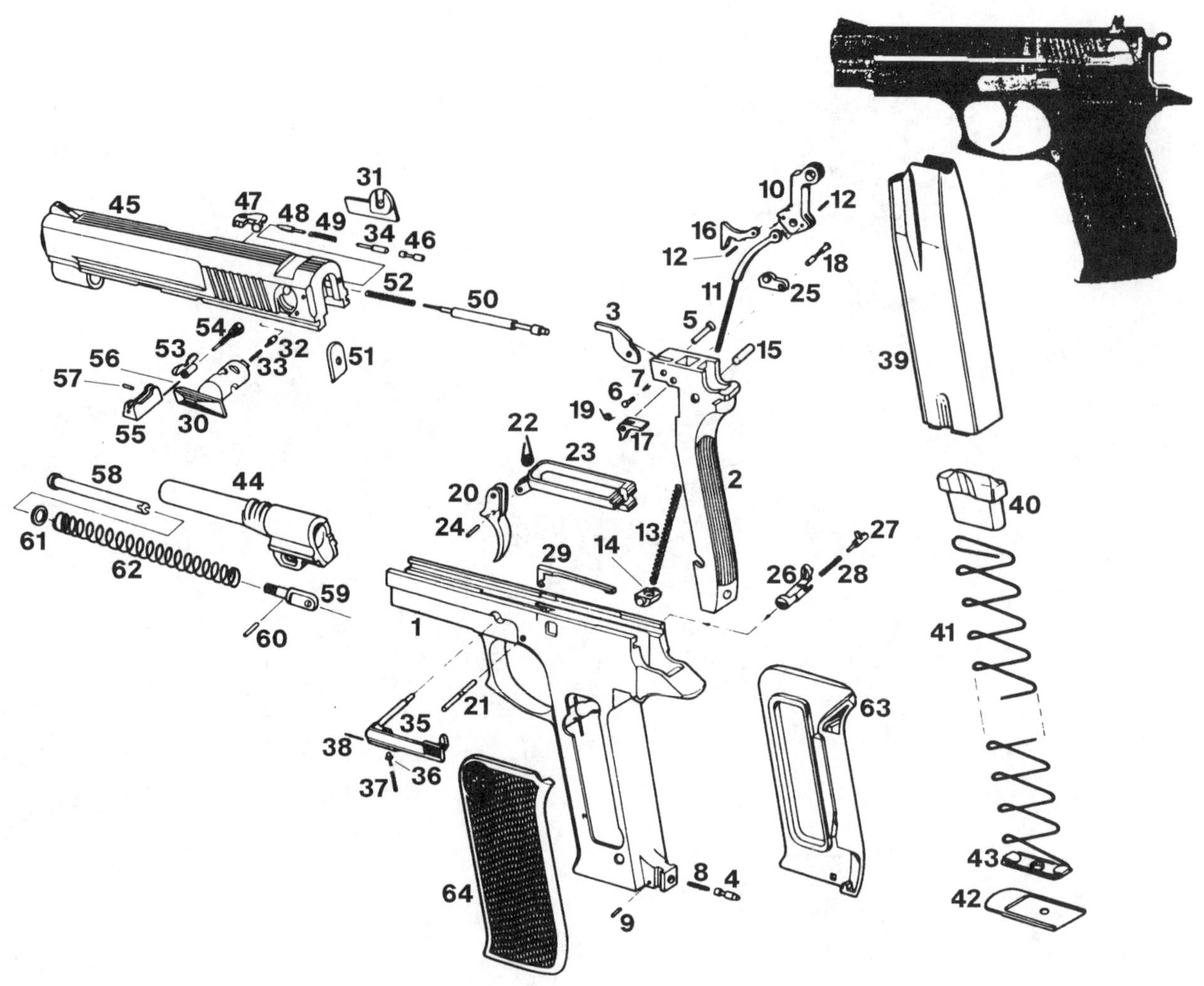

1	Frame	**25**	Interruptor	**43**	Magazine Floorplate Catch
2	Backstrap	**26**	Magazine Catch	**44**	Barrel
3	Ejector	**27**	Magazine Catch Lock	**45**	Slide
4	Backstrap Retaining Plunger	**28**	Magazine Catch Lock Spring	**46**	Housing Plug Plunger
5	Ejector Pin	**29**	Magazine Safety	**47**	Extractor
6	Ejector Friction Plunger	**30**	Ambidextrous Thumb Safety	**48**	Extractor Plunger
7	Ejector Friction Plunger Spring	**31**	Ambidextrous Thumb Safety Wing, Right	**49**	Extractor Plunger Spring
8	Backstrap Retaining Plunger Spring	**32**	Ambidextrous Thumb Safety Retaining Plunger	**50**	Firing Pin
9	Backstrap Retaining Plunger Pin	**33**	Ambidextrous Thumb Safety Retaining Plunger Spring	**51**	Firing Pin Retainer
10	Hammer	**34**	Ambidextrous Thumb Safety Positioning Plunger	**52**	Firing Pin Spring
11	Hammer Bar	**35**	Slide Stop	**53**	Rear Sight
12	Hammer Pins	**36**	Slide Stop Plunger	**54**	Rear Sight Windage Spindle
13	Hammer Spring	**37**	Slide Stop Plunger Spring	**55**	Rear Sight Base
14	Hammer Spring Support	**38**	Slide Stop Plunger Elastic Retaining Pin	**56**	Rear Sight Windage Spindle Spring
15	Hammer Axis	**39**	Magazine Tube	**57**	Rear Sight Windage Spindle Retaining Pin
16	Hammer Lock	**40**	Magazine Follower	**58**	Recoil Spring Guide
17	Sear	**41**	Magazine Follower Spring	**59**	Recoil Spring Guide Coupling
18	Sear Axis	**42**	Magazine Floorplate	**60**	Recoil Spring Guide Coupling Locking Pin
19	Sear Spring			**61**	Recoil Spring Guide Washer
20	Trigger			**62**	Recoil Spring
21	Trigger Pin			**63**	Grip, Right
22	Trigger Spring			**64**	Grip, Left
23	Trigger Bar				
24	Trigger Bar Pin				

Model 30M Auto

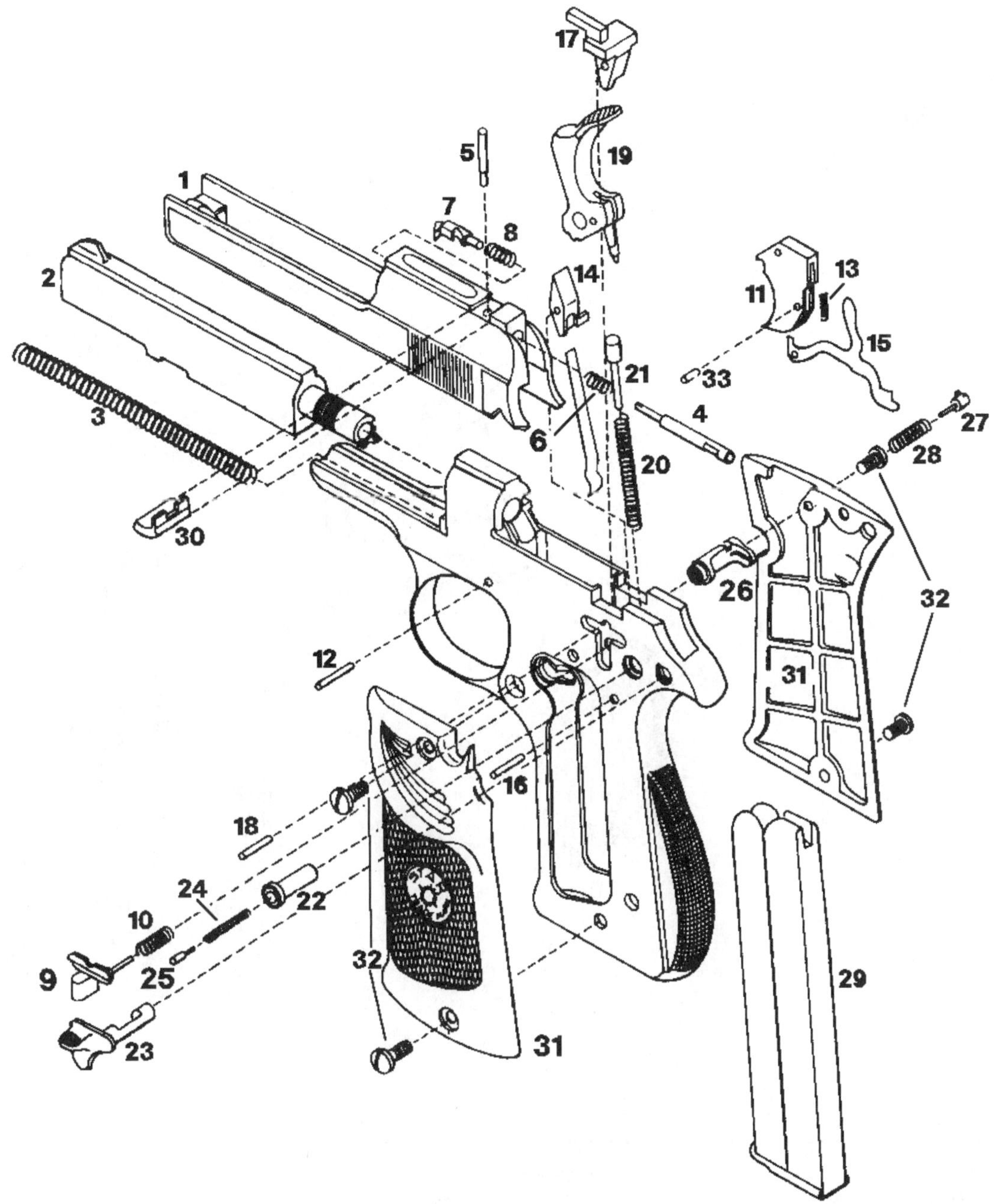

1	Slide	**16**	Sear Pin	**31**	Grip
2	Barrel with Front Sight	**17**	Ejector	**32**	Grip Screws
3	Recoil Spring	**18**	Ejector Pin	**33**	Sear Bar Pin
4	Firing Pin	**19**	Hammer with Strut and Pin	**Parts Not Shown**	
5	Firing Pin Retaining Pin	**20**	Hammer Spring		Extractor Plunger
6	Firing Pin Spring	**21**	Hammer Spring Plunger		Front Sight Screw
7	Extractor	**22**	Hammer Pin		Hammer Strut
8	Extractor Spring	**23**	Thumb Safety		Hammer Strut Pin
9	Slide Retainer	**24**	Safety Spring		Rear Sight Screw
10	Slide Retainer Spring	**25**	Safety Plunger		Sear Spring
11	Trigger	**26**	Magazine Catch		Slide Stop
12	Trigger Pin	**27**	Magazine Catch Lock		Trigger Plunger
13	Trigger Plunger Spring	**28**	Magazine Catch Lock Spring		
14	Sear	**29**	Magazine Assembly		
15	Sear Bar	**30**	Rear Sight		

Model FM Auto

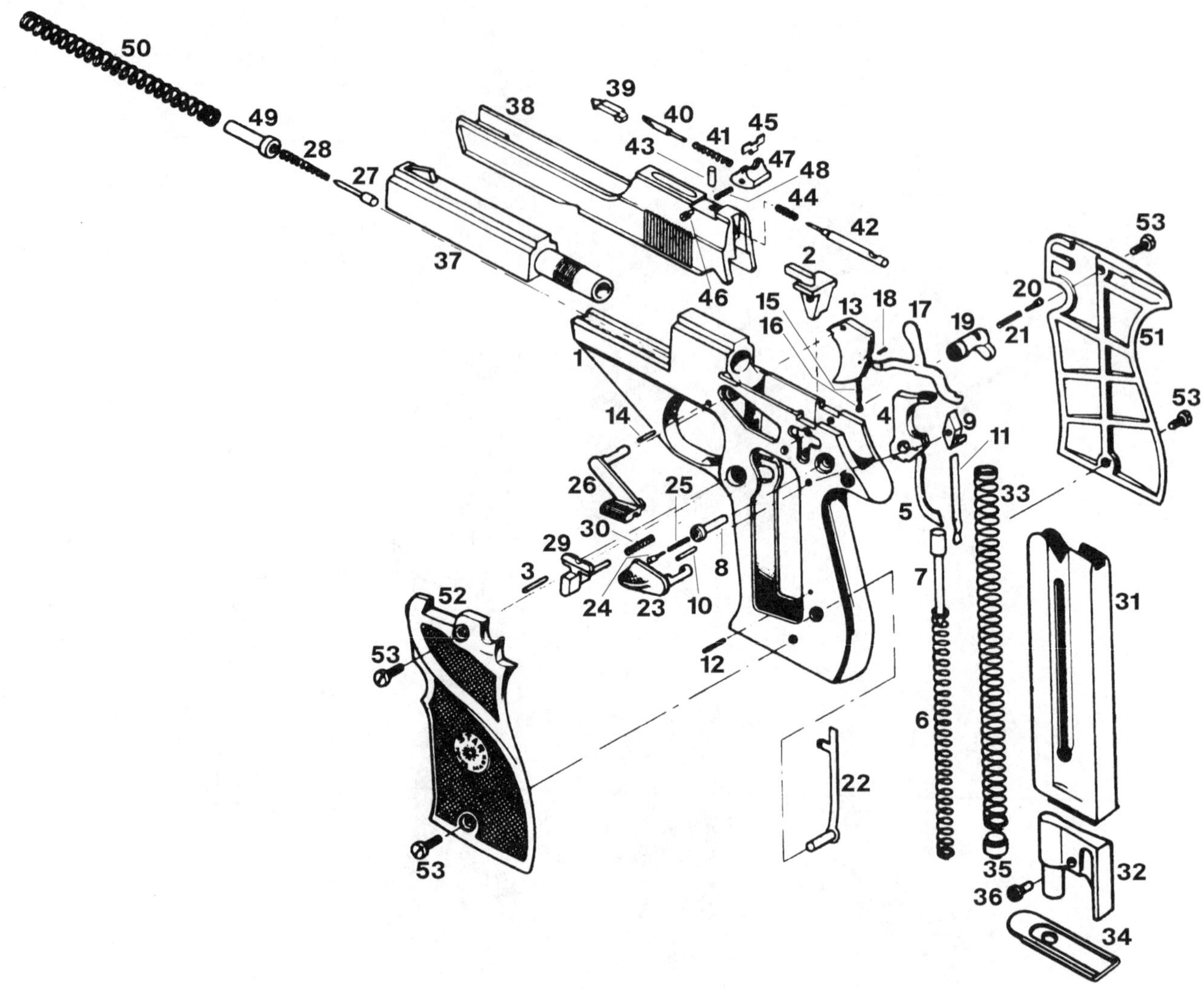

1	Frame	**19**	Magazine Catch	**37**	Barrel
2	Ejector	**20**	Magazine Catch Lock	**38**	Slide
3	Ejector Pin	**21**	Magazine Catch Spring	**39**	Extractor
4	Hammer with Strut and Pin	**22**	Magazine Safety	**40**	Extractor Plunger
5	Hammer Strut	**23**	Thumb Safety	**41**	Extractor Plunger Spring
6	Hammer Spring	**24**	Safety Plunger	**42**	Firing Pin
7	Hammer Spring Plunger	**25**	Safety Spring	**43**	Firing Pin Retaining Pin
8	Hammer Spring Guide	**26**	Slide Stop	**44**	Firing Pin Spring
9	Sear	**27**	Slide Stop Plunger	**45**	Rear Sight Blade
10	Sear Pin	**28**	Slide Stop Plunger Spring	**46**	Rear Sight Screw
11	Sear Spring	**29**	Slide Retainer	**47**	Rear Sight Base
12	Sear Spring Retaining Pin	**30**	Slide Retainer Spring	**48**	Rear Sight Spring
13	Trigger	**31**	Magazine Tube	**49**	Recoil Spring Guide
14	Trigger Pin	**32**	Magazine Follower	**50**	Recoil Spring
15	Trigger Plunger Spring	**33**	Magazine Follower Spring	**51**	Grip, Right
16	Trigger Plunger	**34**	Magazine Floorplate	**52**	Grip, Left
17	Sear Bar	**35**	Magazine Floorplate Release	**53**	Grip Screws
18	Sear Bar Pin	**36**	Magazine Follower Button		

Model P, A and B Auto

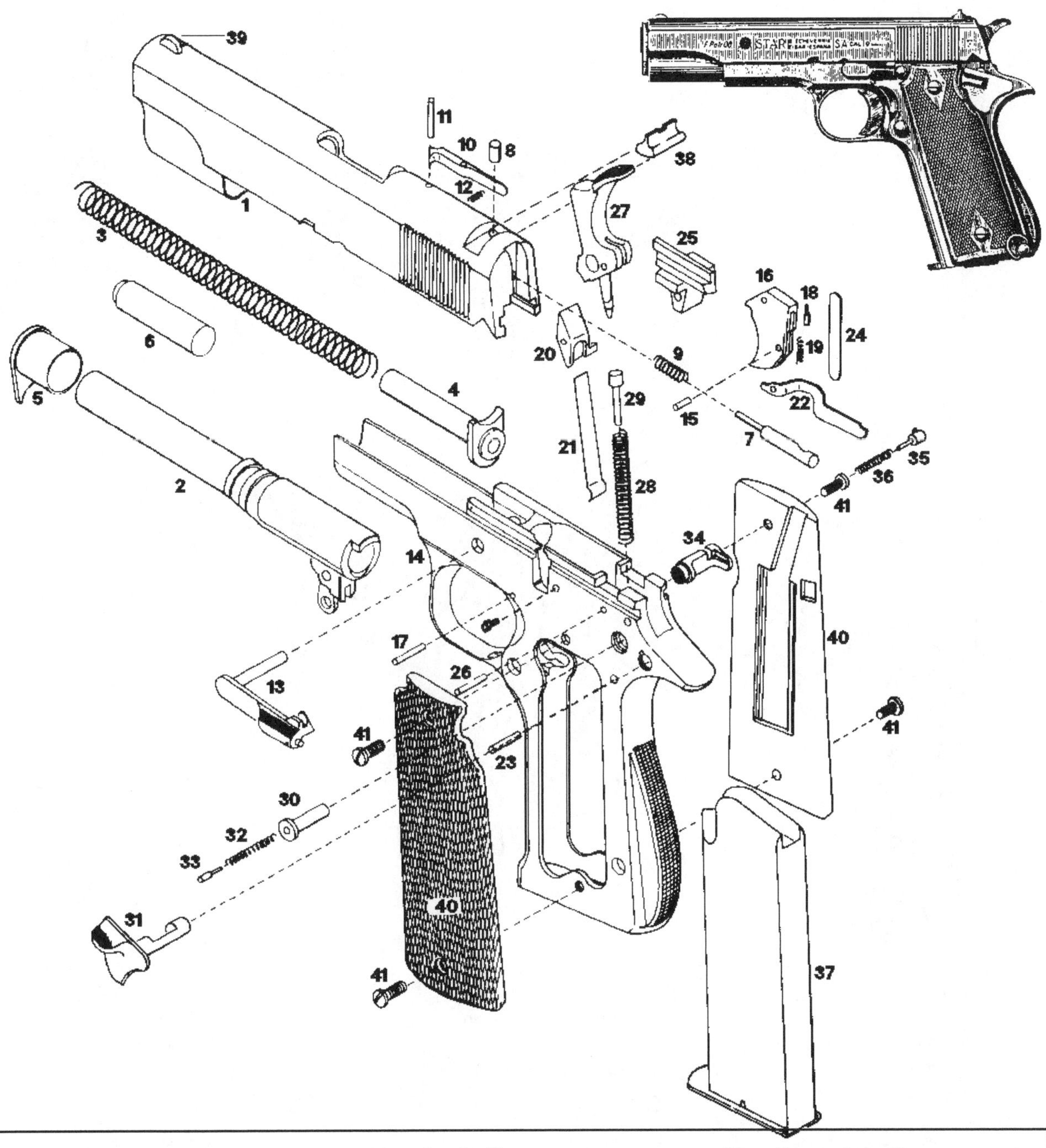

1	Slide	**15**	Sear Bar Pin	**29**	Hammer Spring Plunger
2	Barrel with Link and Pin	**16**	Trigger	**30**	Hammer Pin
3	Recoil Spring	**17**	Trigger Pin	**31**	Thumb Safety
4	Recoil Spring Guide	**18**	Trigger Plunger	**32**	Safety Spring
5	Barrel Bushing	**19**	Trigger Plunger Spring	**33**	Safety Plunger
6	Recoil Spring Plug	**20**	Sear	**34**	Magazine Catch
7	Firing Pin	**21**	Sear Spring	**35**	Magazine Catch Lock
8	Firing Pin Retaining Pin	**22**	Sear Bar	**36**	Magazine Catch Lock Spring
9	Firing Pin Spring	**23**	Sear Pin	**37**	Magazine Assembly
10	Extractor	**24**	Disconnector	**38**	Rear Sight
11	Extractor Pin	**25**	Ejector	**39**	Front Sight
12	Extractor Spring	**26**	Ejector Pin	**40**	Grips
13	Slide Stop	**27**	Hammer with Strut and Pin	**41**	Grip Screws
14	Slide Stop Plunger Screw	**28**	Hammer Spring		

PD Auto

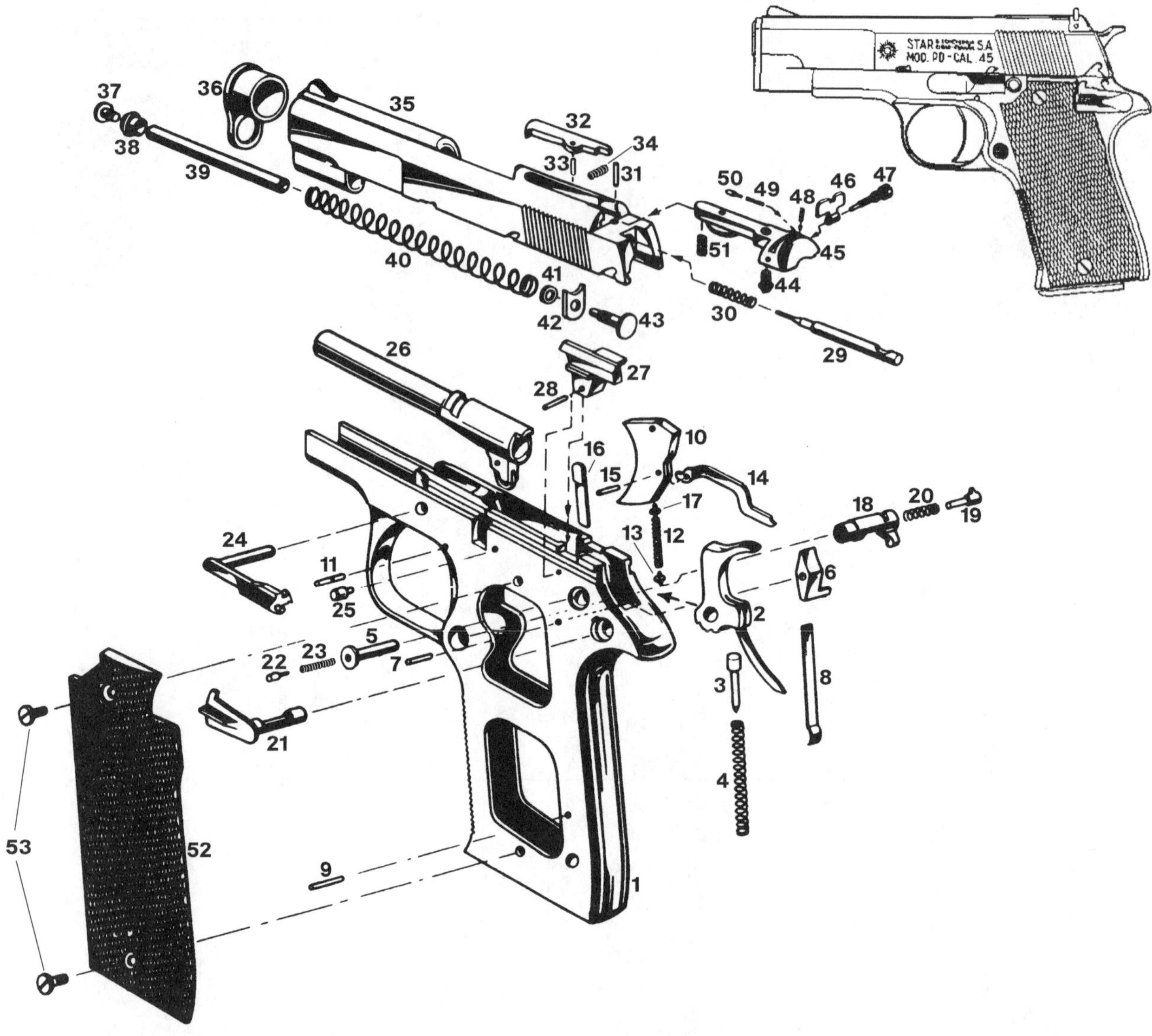

1	Frame	**22**	Thumb Safety Plunger	**42**	Recoil Spring Guide Buffer
2	Hammer and Strut	**23**	Safety Plunger Spring	**43**	Recoil Spring Guide Head
3	Hammer Spring Plunger	**24**	Slide Stop	**44**	Rear Sight Elevation Screw
4	Hammer Spring	**25**	Slide Stop Screw Button	**45**	Rear Sight Base
5	Hammer Pin	**26**	Barrel with Link and Pin	**46**	Rear Sight Leaf
6	Sear	**27**	Ejector	**47**	Rear Sight Windage Spindle
7	Sear Pin	**28**	Ejector Pin	**48**	Rear Sight Windage Spindle Retaining Pin
8	Sear Spring	**29**	Firing Pin	**49**	Rear Sight Windage Spindle Plunger Spring
9	Sear Spring Retaining Pin	**30**	Firing Pin Spring	**50**	Rear Sight Windage Spindle Plunger
10	Trigger	**31**	Firing Pin Retaining Pin	**51**	Rear Sight Elevation Spring
11	Trigger Pin	**32**	Extractor	**52**	Grips
12	Trigger Plunger Spring	**33**	Extractor Pin	**53**	Grip Screws
13	Trigger Plunger	**34**	Extractor Spring		**Parts Not Shown**
14	Sear Bar	**35**	Slide with Front Sight		Slide Stop Plunger
15	Sear Bar Pin	**36**	Barrel Bushing		Slide Stop Plunger Spring
16	Disconnector	**37**	Recoil Spring Guide Plug		Slide Stop Plunger Pin
17	Trigger Pin Retaining Plunger	**38**	Recoil Spring Guide Washer		
18	Magazine Catch	**39**	Recoil Spring Guide		
19	Magazine Catch Lock	**40**	Recoil Spring		
20	Magazine Catch Lock Spring	**41**	Recoil Spring Guide Buffer Bearing Washer		
21	Thumb Safety				

Starfire Auto (also Firearms International Model D)

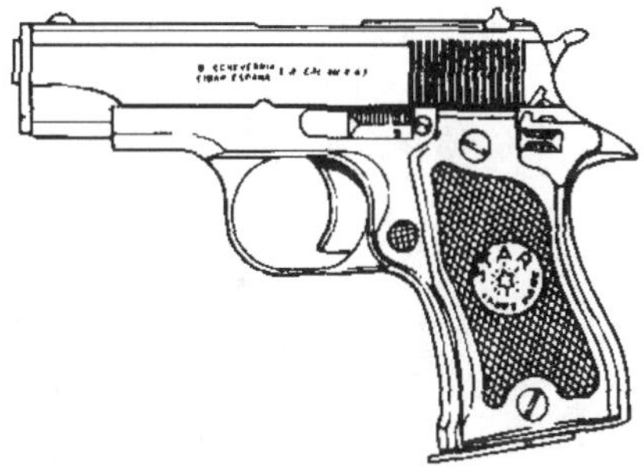

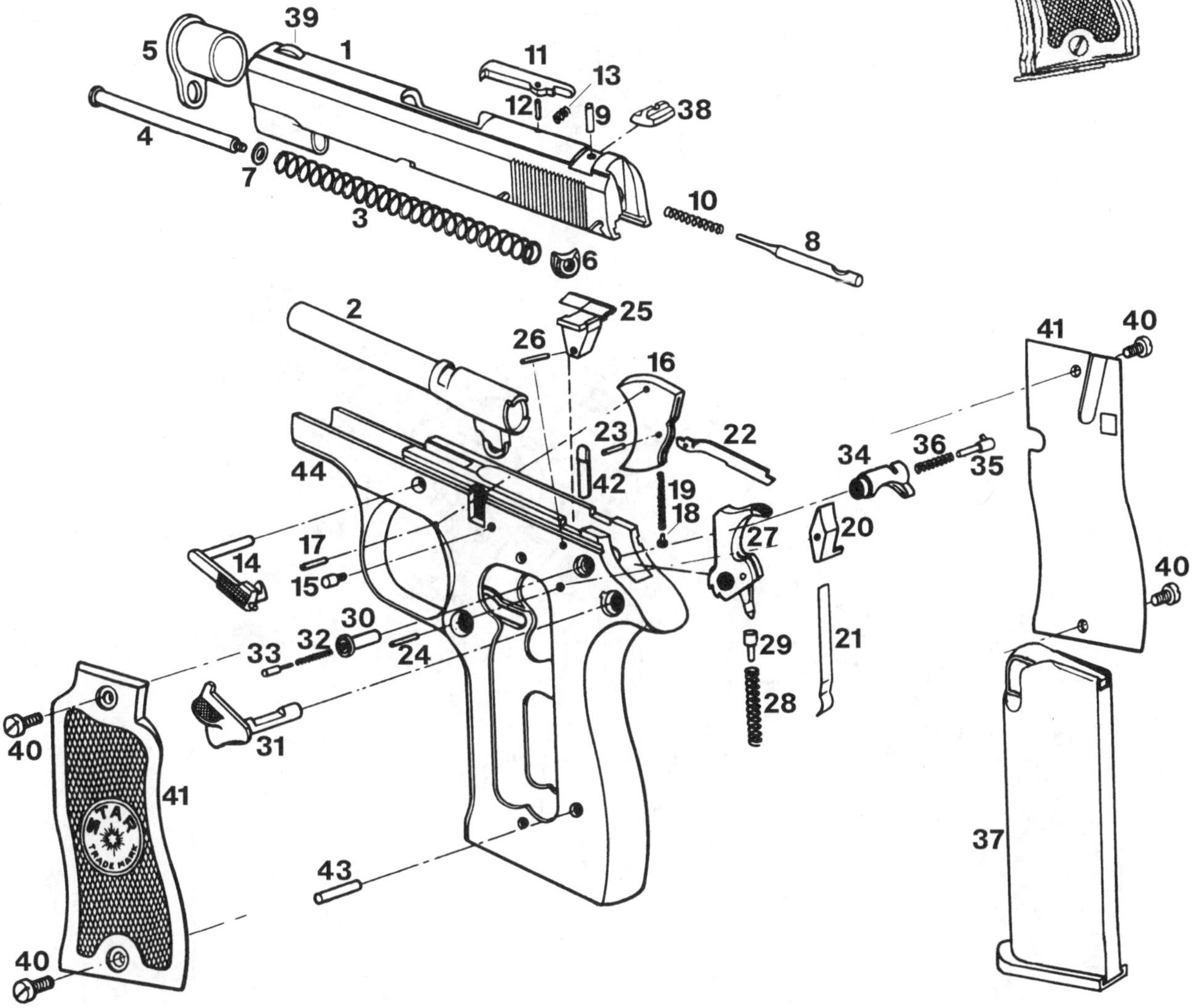

1	Slide	**16**	Trigger	**31**	Thumb Safety
2	Barrel with Link and Pin	**17**	Trigger Pin	**32**	Safety Spring
3	Recoil Spring	**18**	Trigger Plunger	**33**	Safety Plunger
4	Recoil Spring Guide	**19**	Trigger Plunger Spring	**34**	Magazine Catch
5	Barrel Bushing	**20**	Sear	**35**	Magazine Catch Lock
6	Recoil Spring Guide Head	**21**	Sear Spring	**36**	Magazine Catch Lock Spring
7	Recoil Spring Guide Washer	**22**	Sear Bar	**37**	Magazine Assembly
8	Firing Pin	**23**	Sear Bar Pin	**38**	Rear Sight
9	Firing Pin Retaining Pin	**24**	Sear Pin	**39**	Front Sight
10	Firing Pin Spring	**25**	Ejector	**40**	Grip Screws
11	Extractor	**26**	Ejector Pin	**41**	Grips
12	Extractor Pin	**27**	Hammer with Strut and Pin	**42**	Disconnector
13	Extractor Spring	**28**	Hammer Spring	**43**	Sear Spring Retaining Pin
14	Slide Stop	**29**	Hammer Spring Plunger	**44**	Frame
15	Slide Stop Plunger Screw	**30**	Hammer Pin		

Starlet Auto

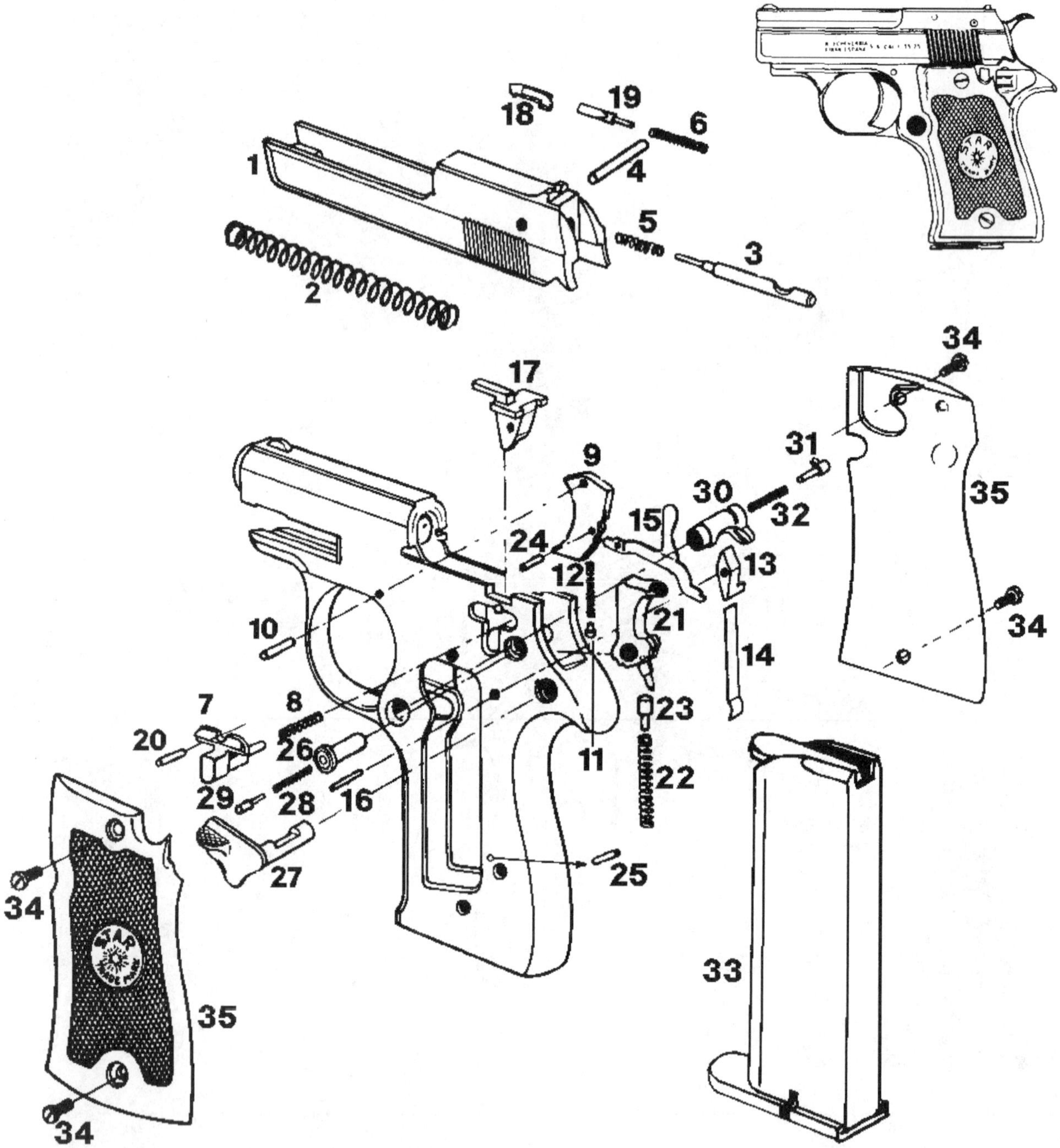

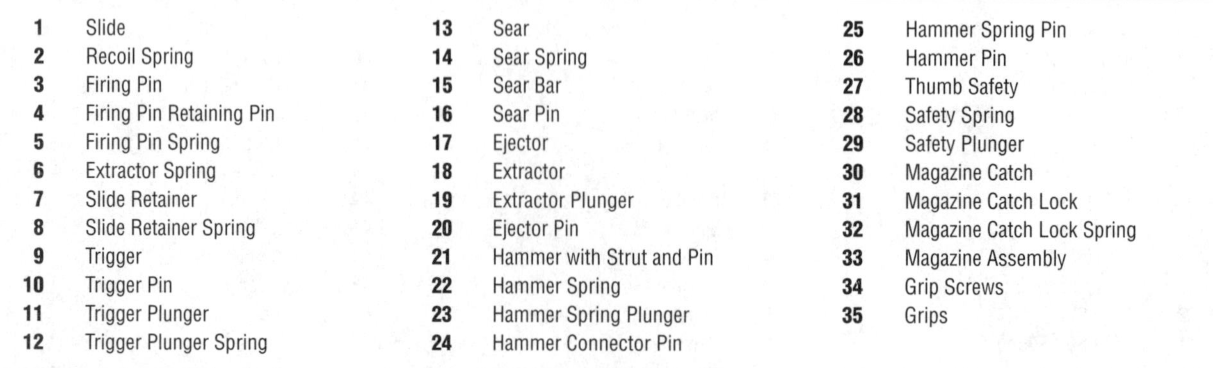

No.	Part	No.	Part	No.	Part
1	Slide	13	Sear	25	Hammer Spring Pin
2	Recoil Spring	14	Sear Spring	26	Hammer Pin
3	Firing Pin	15	Sear Bar	27	Thumb Safety
4	Firing Pin Retaining Pin	16	Sear Pin	28	Safety Spring
5	Firing Pin Spring	17	Ejector	29	Safety Plunger
6	Extractor Spring	18	Extractor	30	Magazine Catch
7	Slide Retainer	19	Extractor Plunger	31	Magazine Catch Lock
8	Slide Retainer Spring	20	Ejector Pin	32	Magazine Catch Lock Spring
9	Trigger	21	Hammer with Strut and Pin	33	Magazine Assembly
10	Trigger Pin	22	Hammer Spring	34	Grip Screws
11	Trigger Plunger	23	Hammer Spring Plunger	35	Grips
12	Trigger Plunger Spring	24	Hammer Connector Pin		

Model 400 Mk. II Auto

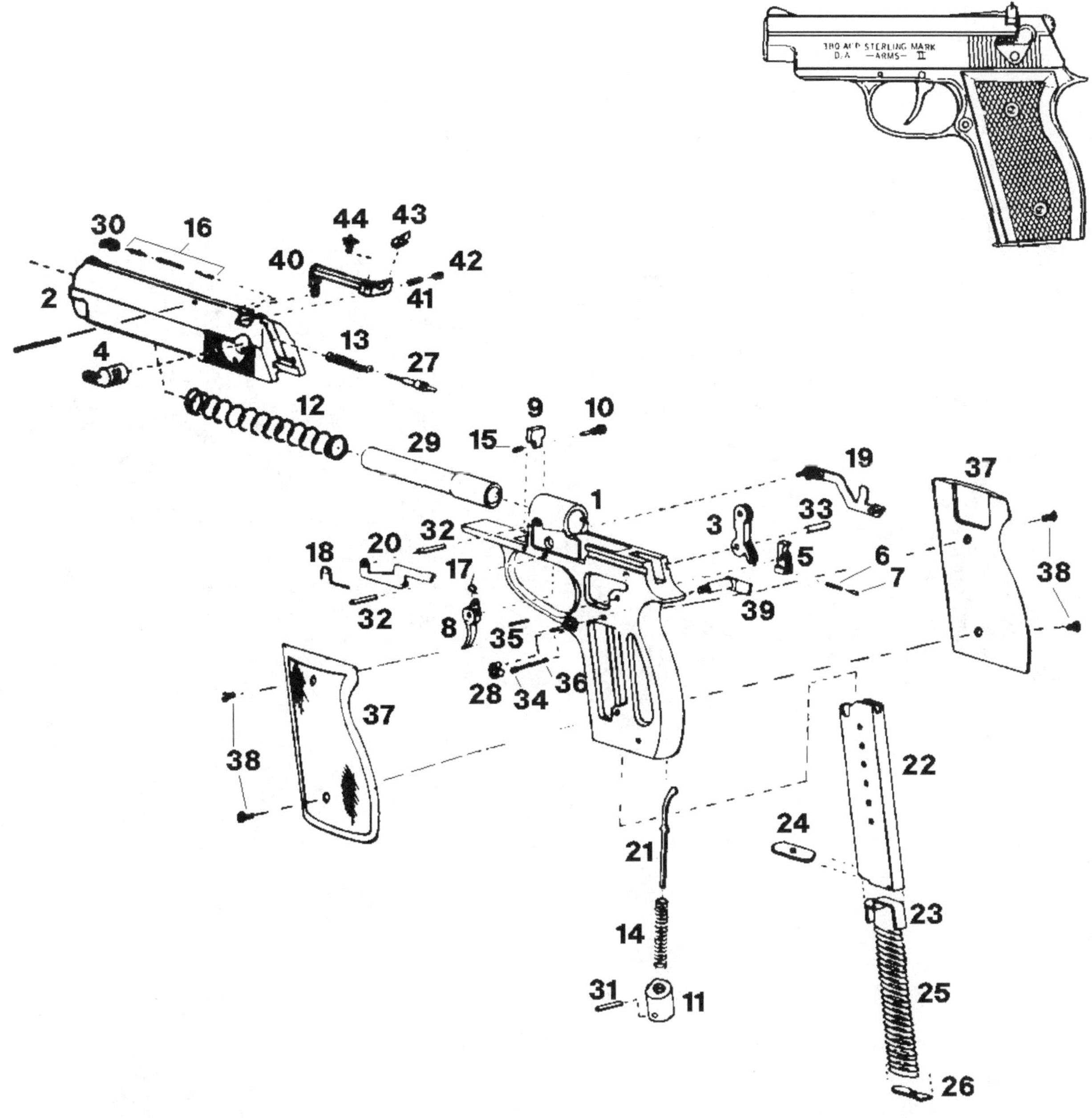

No.	Part	No.	Part	No.	Part
1	Frame	17	Trigger Bar Spring	33	Hammer Pin
2	Slide	18	Hold-Open Spring	34	Magazine Release Button Plunger
3	Hammer	19	Trigger Bar	35	Sear Pin
4	Safety	20	Hold-Open/Ejector	36	Magazine Release Button Plunger Spring
5	Sear	21	Hammer Strut	37	Grips
6	Sear Spring	22	Magazine	38	Grip Screws
7	Follower	23	Magazine Follower	39	Magazine Release Arm and Stud Assembly
8	Trigger	24	Magazine Floorplate Catch	40	Rear Sight Base
9	Takedown Block	25	Magazine Spring	41	Rear Sight Windage Spring
10	Takedown Shaft	26	Magazine Floorplate	42	Rear Sight Windage Screw
11	Mainspring Seat	27	Firing Pin	43	Rear Sight Blade
12	Recoil Spring	28	Magazine Release Button	44	Rear Sight Elevation Screw
13	Firing Pin Spring	29	Barrel		
14	Mainspring	30	Extractor		
15	Takedown Spring	31	Mainspring Seat Pin		
16	Extractor Spring and Followers	32	Trigger Pin		

Model 300 and 302 Auto

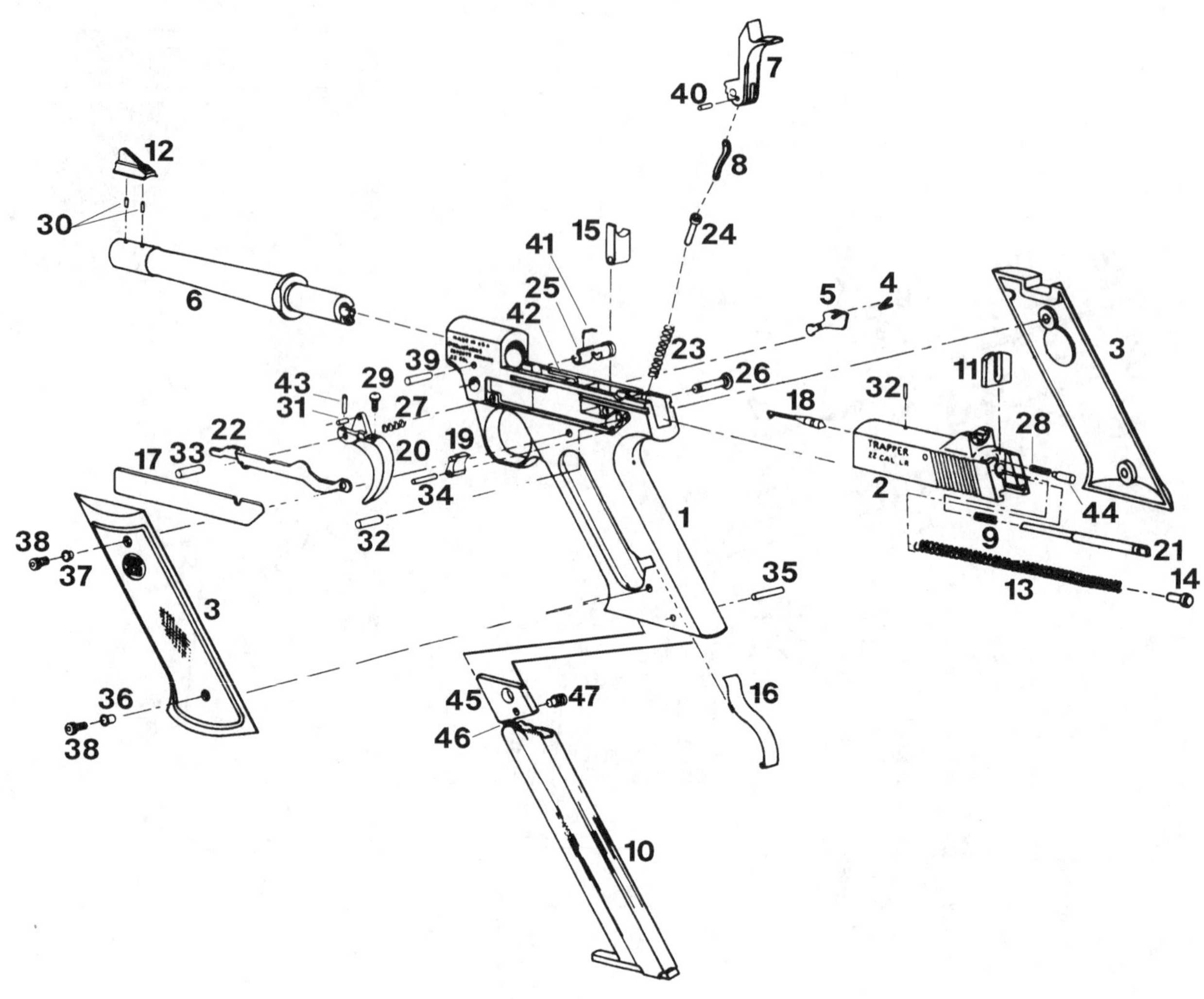

1	Receiver	**17**	Sideplate	**32**	Hammer
2	Slide	**18**	Extractor	**33**	Trigger Pin
3	Grips	**19**	Sear	**34**	Sear
4	Slide Hold-Open Latch Spring	**20**	Trigger	**35**	Magazine Locating Pins
5	Slide Hold-Open Latch	**21**	Firing Pin	**36**	Grip Screw Bushings, Lower
6	Barrel	**22**	Trigger Bar	**37**	Grip Screw Bushings, Upper
7	Hammer	**23**	Hammer Spring	**38**	Grip Screws
8	Hammer Strut	**24**	Hammer Spring Follower	**39**	Banner Receiver Pin
9	Firing Pin Spring	**25**	Safety Pin	**40**	Hammer Strut Pin
10	Magazine Body	**26**	Stop Lug Pin	**41**	Safety Friction Pin
11	Hammer Plate	**27**	Trigger	**42**	Ejector
12	Front Sight	**28**	Hammer Plate Springs	**43**	Trigger Bar Support Pin
13	Recoil Spring	**29**	Front Trigger Adjustable Screw	**44**	Hammer Plate Pin
14	Recoil Spring Follower	**30**	Front Sight Pins	**45**	Magazine Follower
15	Stop Lug	**31**	Trigger Disconnector and Extractor Pins	**46**	Magazine Follower Spring
16	Magazine Retainer Spring			**47**	Magazine Follower Pin

Model 285 Auto

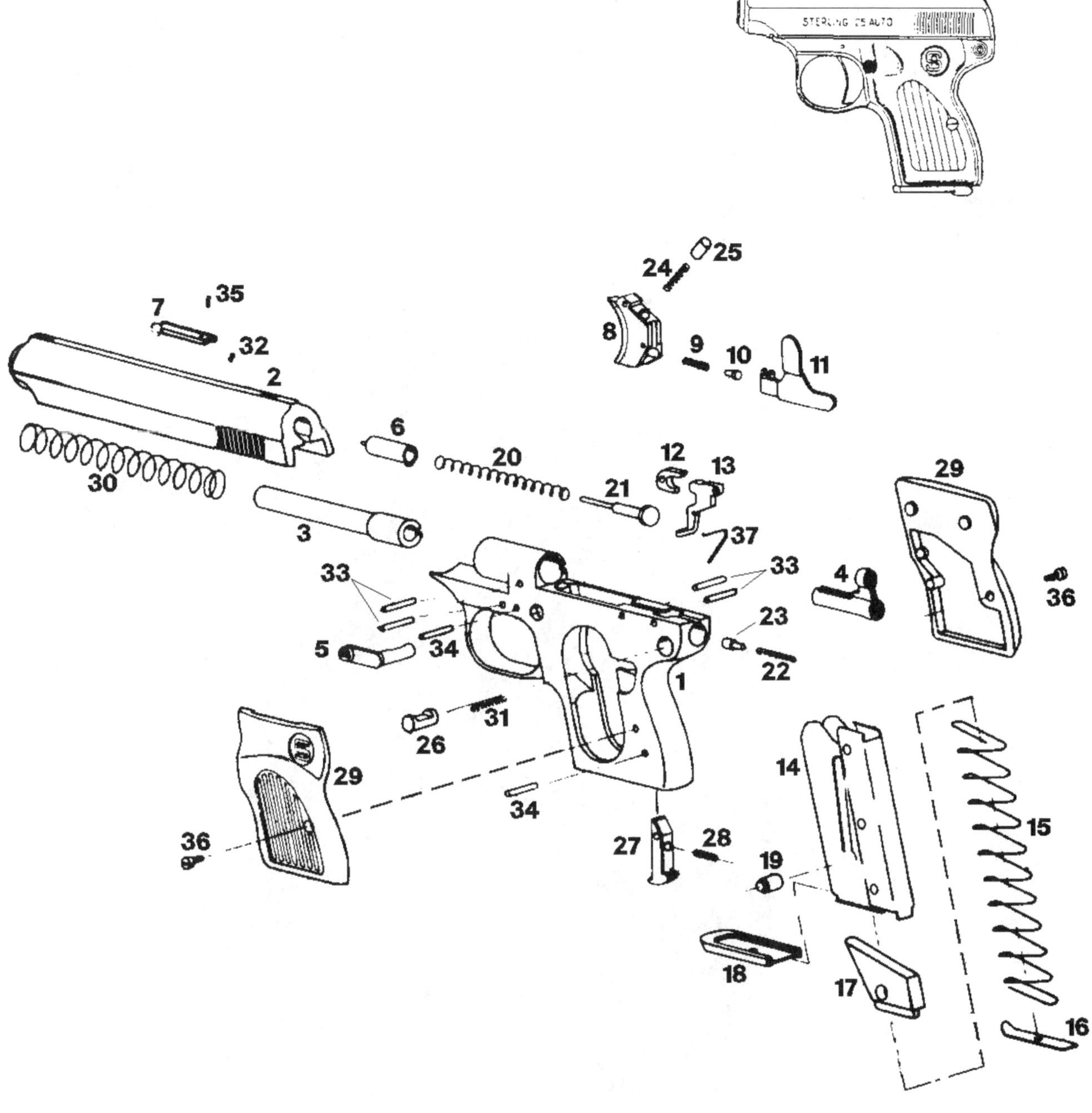

1	Frame	**14**	Magazine Body	**26**	Disconnector Button
2	Slide	**15**	Magazine Spring	**27**	Magazine Retainer
3	Barrel	**16**	Magazine Spring Follower Locking Plate	**28**	Magazine Retainer Spring
4	Hammer			**29**	Grips
5	Safety	**17**	Magazine Follower	**30**	Barrel Spring
6	Firing Pin	**18**	Magazine Floorplate	**31**	Disconnect Button Spring
7	Extractor	**19**	Magazine Loading Button	**32**	Extractor Spring
8	Trigger	**20**	Firing Pin Spring	**33**	Dowel Pins
9	Trigger Spring	**21**	Firing Pin Follower	**34**	Magazine Retainer Pin
10	Trigger Spring Plunger	**22**	Sear Cam Spring	**35**	Extractor Pin
11	Trigger Bar	**23**	Sear Cam Follower	**36**	Grip Screws
12	Sear	**24**	Safety Spring	**37**	Sear Spring
13	Sear Cam	**25**	Safety Follower		

Model 1912 Auto

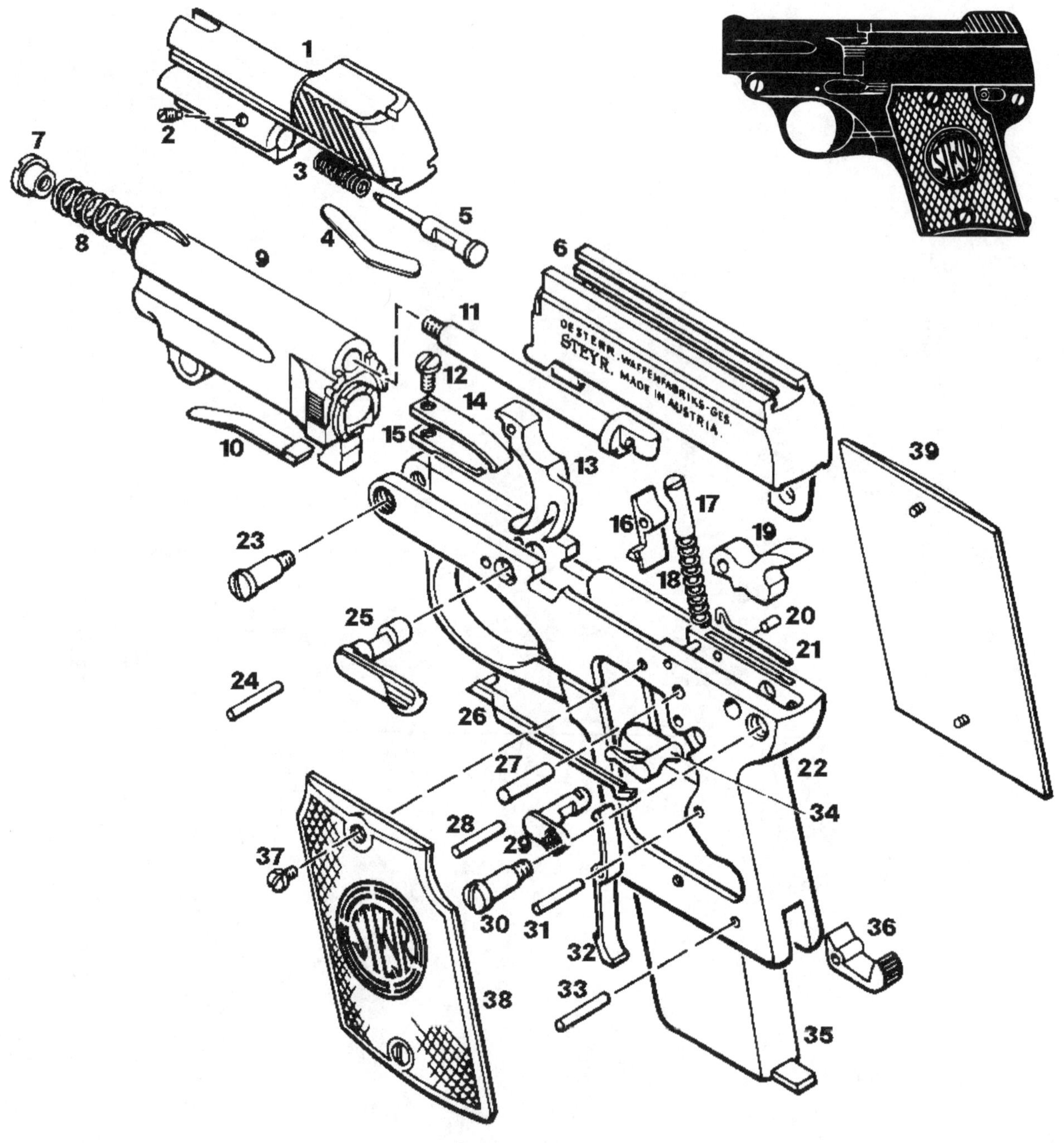

1	Breechblock	14	Barrel Latch Spring	27	Hammer Pivot
2	Firing Pin Retainer	15	Trigger Spring	28	Sear Pivot
3	Firing Pin Spring	16	Sear	29	Safety
4	Breechblock Tension Spring	17	Hammer Spring Assembly	30	Upper Frame Retainer
5	Firing Pin	18	Hammer Spring	31	Sear/Magazine Catch Spring Pin
6	Upper Frame	19	Hammer	32	Sear/Magazine Catch Spring
7	Recoil Spring Retainer	20	Safety Spring Retainer	33	Magazine Catch Pivot
8	Recoil Spring	21	Safety Spring	34	Disconnector
9	Barrel	22	Frame	35	Magazine Assembly
10	Barrel Spring	23	Barrel Pivot	36	Magazine Catch
11	Recoil Spring Guide	24	Trigger Pin	37	Grip Screws
12	Spring Retainer	25	Barrel Latch	38	Left Grip Panel
13	Trigger	26	Trigger Bar	39	Right Grip Panel

Model 1908 Auto

Courtesy of Blacksmith Corporation

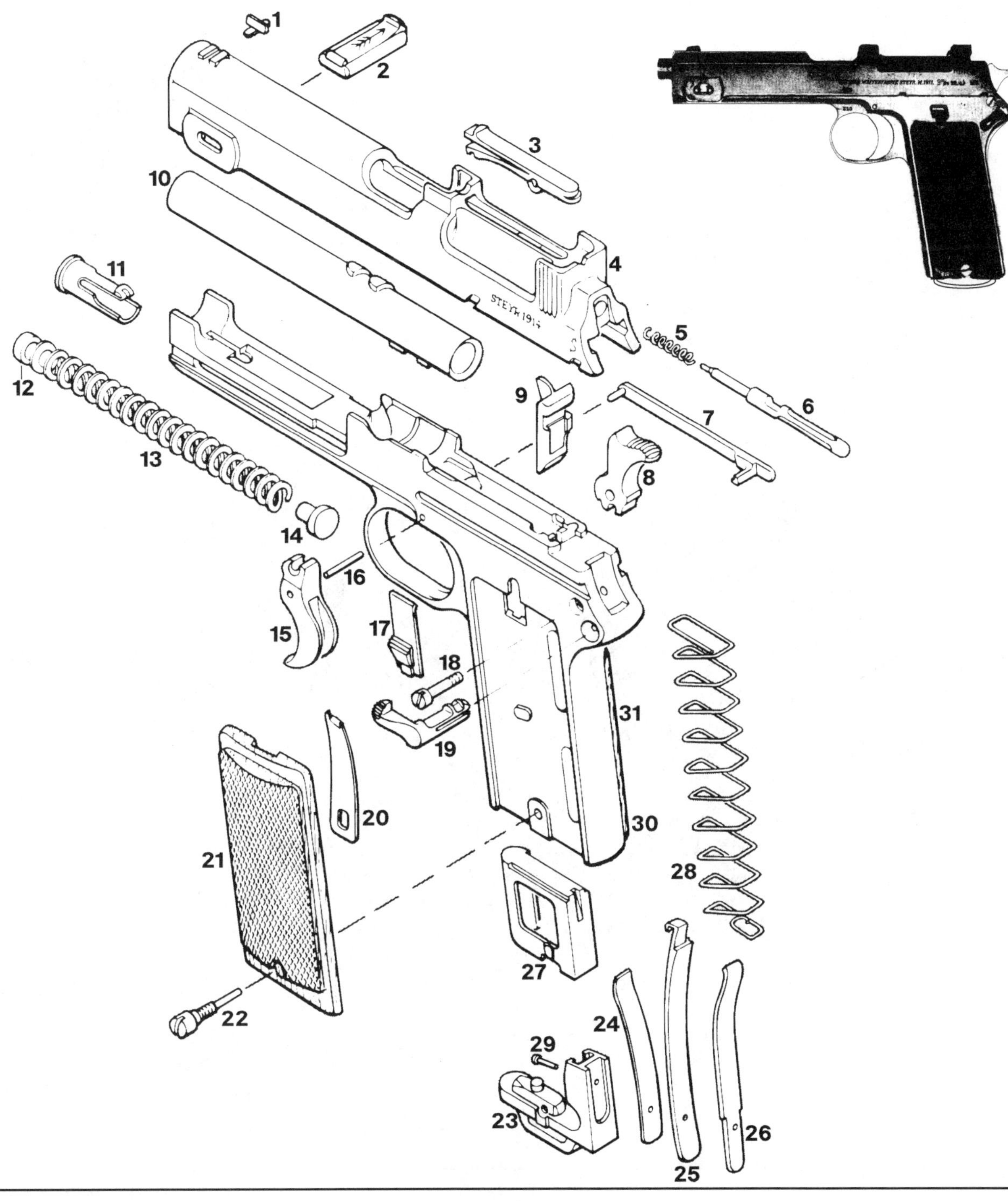

1	Front Sight	12	Front Recoil Spring Cap	23	Floorplate
2	Wedge	13	Recoil Spring	24	Disconnector Spring
3	Extractor	14	Rear Recoil Spring Cap	25	Sear and Sear Spring
4	Slide	15	Trigger	26	Hammer Spring
5	Firing Pin Spring	16	Trigger Pin	27	Magazine Follower
6	Firing Pin	17	Cartridge Release	28	Magazine Spring
7	Trigger Bar	18	Hammer Screw	29	Spring Retainer Pin
8	Hammer	19	Safety	30	Receiver
9	Ejector and Disconnector	20	Cartridge Release Spring	31	Right Grip
10	Barrel	21	Left Grip		
11	Recoil Spring Retainer	22	Grip and Floorplate Screw		

Model SP Auto

Courtesy of Blacksmith Corporation

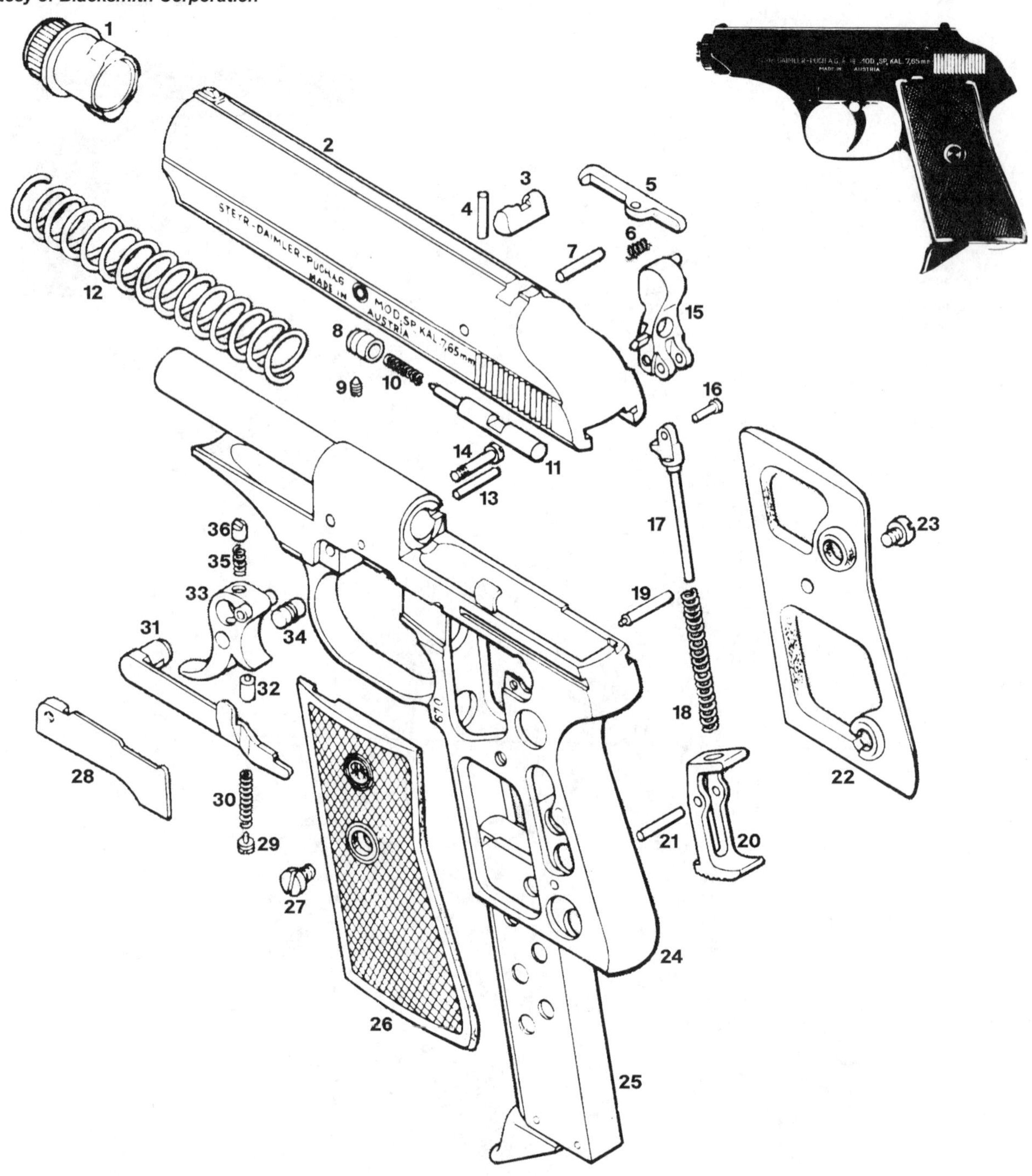

No.	Part	No.	Part	No.	Part
1	Barrel Bushing	**13**	Trigger Pin	**25**	Magazine Assembly
2	Slide	**14**	Sideplate Screw	**26**	Left Grip
3	Rear Sight	**15**	Hammer	**27**	Left Grip Screw
4	Extractor Pin	**16**	Hammer Strut Pin	**28**	Sideplate
5	Extractor	**17**	Hammer Strut	**29**	Trigger Spring Retaining Screw
6	Extractor Spring	**18**	Hammer Spring	**30**	Trigger Spring
7	Firing Pin Retaining Pin	**19**	Hammer Hinge Pin	**31**	Trigger Bar
8	Firing Pin Bushing	**20**	Magazine Catch	**32**	Trigger Spring Follower
9	Firing Pin Bushing Lock Screw	**21**	Magazine Catch Pin	**33**	Trigger
10	Firing Pin Spring	**22**	Right Grip Panel	**34**	Safety Catch
11	Firing Pin	**23**	Right Grip Screw	**35**	Safety Catch Spring
12	Recoil Spring	**24**	Frame	**36**	Safety Catch Detent

Model 1911 Auto

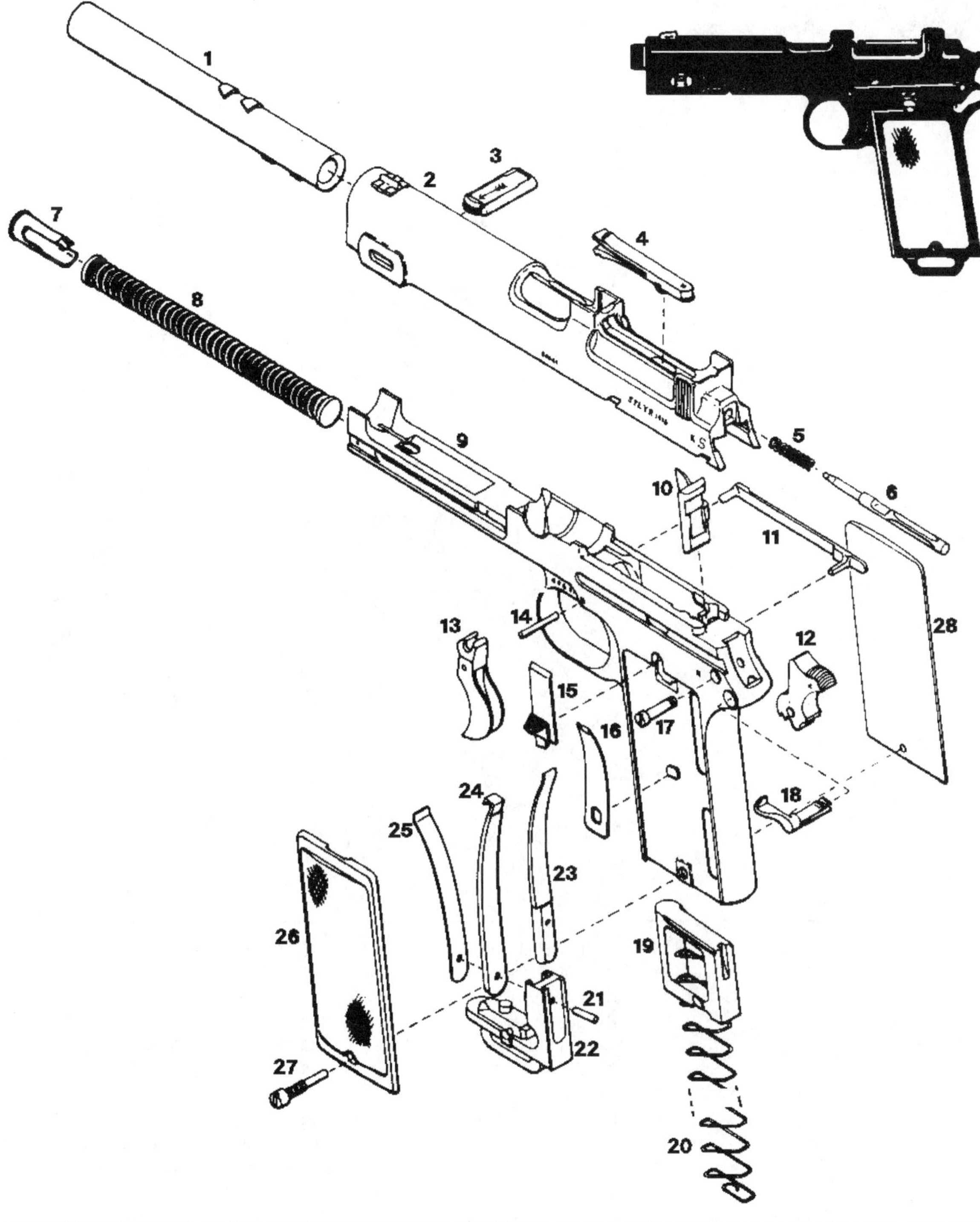

1	Barrel	11	Trigger Bar	21	Spring Retainer Pin
2	Slide	12	Hammer	22	Magazine Floorplate
3	Slide Wedge	13	Trigger	23	Hammer Spring
4	Extractor	14	Trigger Pin	24	Sear and Sear Spring
5	Firing Pin Spring	15	Cartridge Release	25	Disconnector Spring
6	Firing Pin	16	Cartridge Release Spring	26	Left Grip Panel
7	Recoil Spring Retainer	17	Hammer Screw	27	Grip Screw
8	Recoil Spring with Caps	18	Safety	28	Right Grip Panel
9	Frame	19	Magazine Follower		
10	Ejector and Disconnector	20	Magazine Spring		

Luger Auto

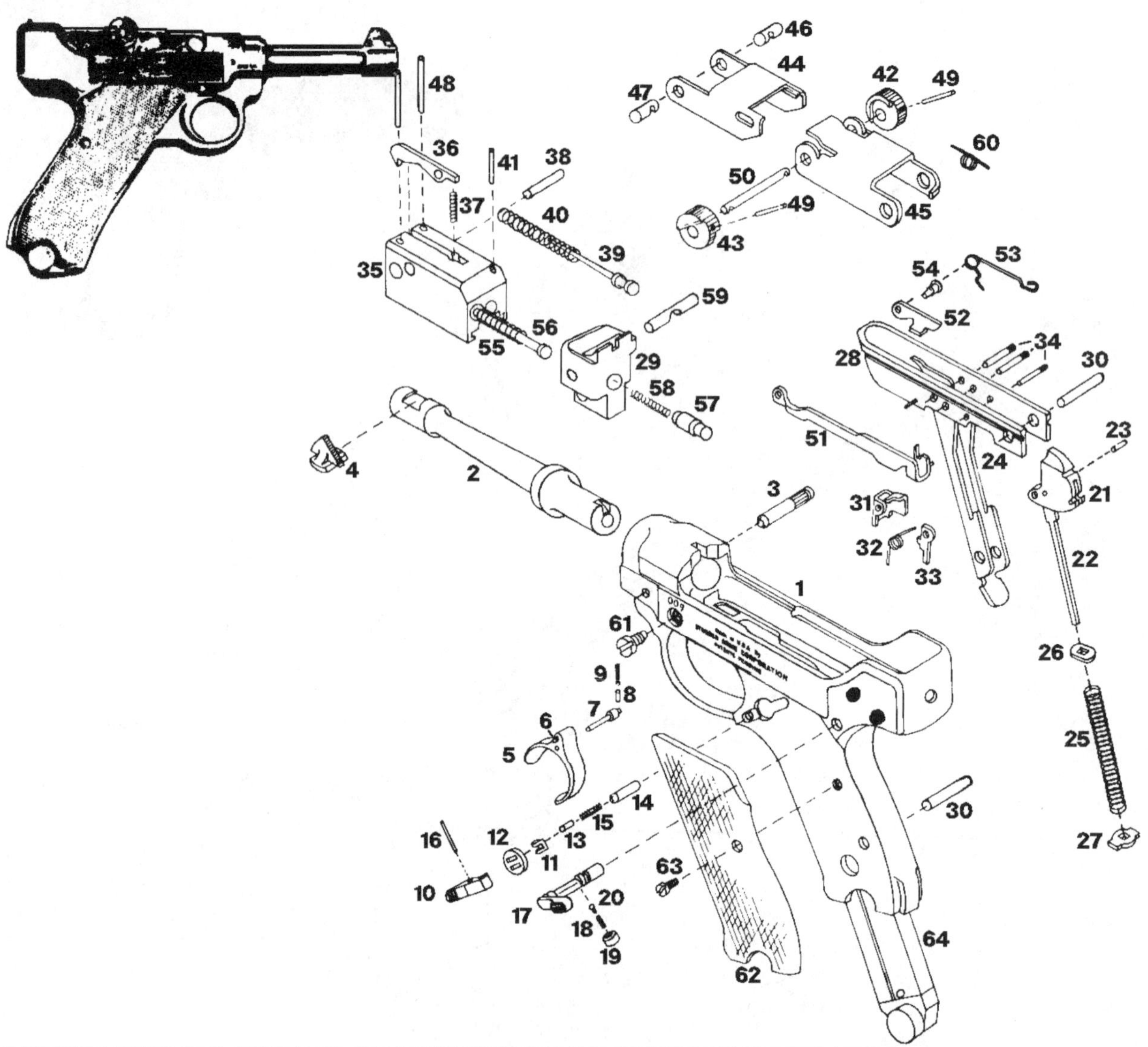

1	Frame	**23**	Hammer Strut Pin	**45**	Rear Toggle
2	Barrel	**24**	Magazine Guide	**46**	Right Front Toggle Pin
3	Barrel Retaining Pin	**25**	Hammer Spring	**47**	Left Front Toggle Pin
4	Front Sight	**26**	Hammer Spring Washer	**48**	Front Toggle Retaining Pins
5	Trigger	**27**	Hammer Strut Anchor Plate	**49**	Toggle Grip Retaining Pins
6	Trigger Roll Pin	**28**	Boltways	**50**	Toggle Link Pin
7	Trigger Pin	**29**	Boltways Block	**51**	Sear Bar
8	Trigger Plunger	**30**	Main Frame and Block Pins	**52**	Bolt Stop
9	Trigger Pin Plunger Spring	**31**	Sear	**53**	Bolt Stop Spring
10	Magazine Catch	**32**	Sear Spring	**54**	Bolt Stop Retainer
11	Magazine Catch Anchor	**33**	Safety Shoe	**55**	Recoil Spring
12	Magazine Catch Anchor Plunger	**34**	Swagged Pins	**56**	Recoil Spring Guide
13	Magazine Catch Plunger	**35**	Bolt	**57**	Takedown Plunger
14	Magazine Catch Plunger Guide	**36**	Extractor	**58**	Takedown Plunger Spring
15	Magazine Catch Spring	**37**	Extractor Spring	**59**	Rear Toggle Pivot Pin
16	Magazine Catch Pin	**38**	Extractor Pin	**60**	Rear Toggle Spring
17	Safety Lever	**39**	Firing Pin	**61**	Sear Bar Retaining Screw
18	Safety Spring	**40**	Firing Pin Spring	**62**	Left Grip Panel
19	Safety Housing (Old Style)	**41**	Firing Pin Retaining Pin	**63**	Grip Screws
20	Safety Detent Plunger	**42**	Right Toggle Grip	**64**	Magazine Assembly
21	Hammer	**43**	Left Toggle Grip	**Parts Not Shown**	
22	Hammer Strut	**44**	Front Toggle		Right Grip Panel

Lahti Auto

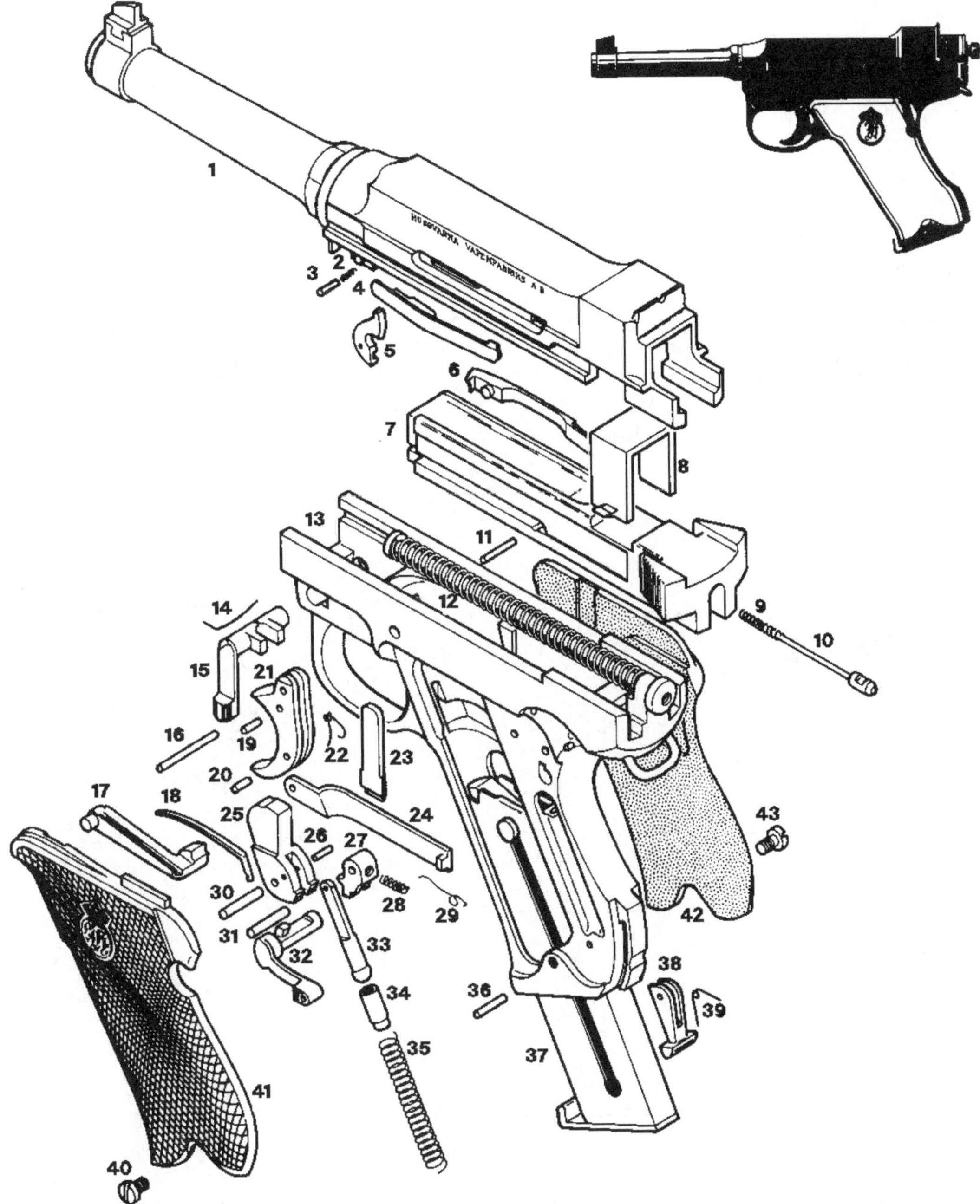

No.	Part	No.	Part	No.	Part
1	Barrel and Barrel Extension	16	Trigger Pin	31	Sear Pin
2	Accelerator Retaining Spring	17	Hold-Open Catch	32	Safety
3	Accelerator Retaining Pin	18	Hold-Open Catch Spring	33	Hammer Strut
4	Ejector	19	Trigger Spring Pin	34	Hammer Strut Plunger
5	Accelerator	20	Trigger Bar Pin	35	Hammer Spring
6	Extractor	21	Trigger	36	Magazine Catch Pin
7	Bolt	22	Trigger Spring	37	Magazine Assembly
8	Locking Block	23	Disconnector	38	Magazine Catch
9	Firing Pin Spring	24	Trigger Bar	39	Magazine Catch Spring
10	Firing Pin	25	Hammer	40	Left Grip Screw
11	Firing Pin Retaining Pin	26	Hammer Strut Pin	41	Left Grip Panel
12	Recoil Spring and Guide	27	Sear	42	Right Grip Panel
13	Frame	28	Sear Spring	43	Right Grip Screw
14	Takedown Catch Spring	29	Trigger Bar Spring		
15	Takedown Catch	30	Hammer Pin		

BTA90 Auto

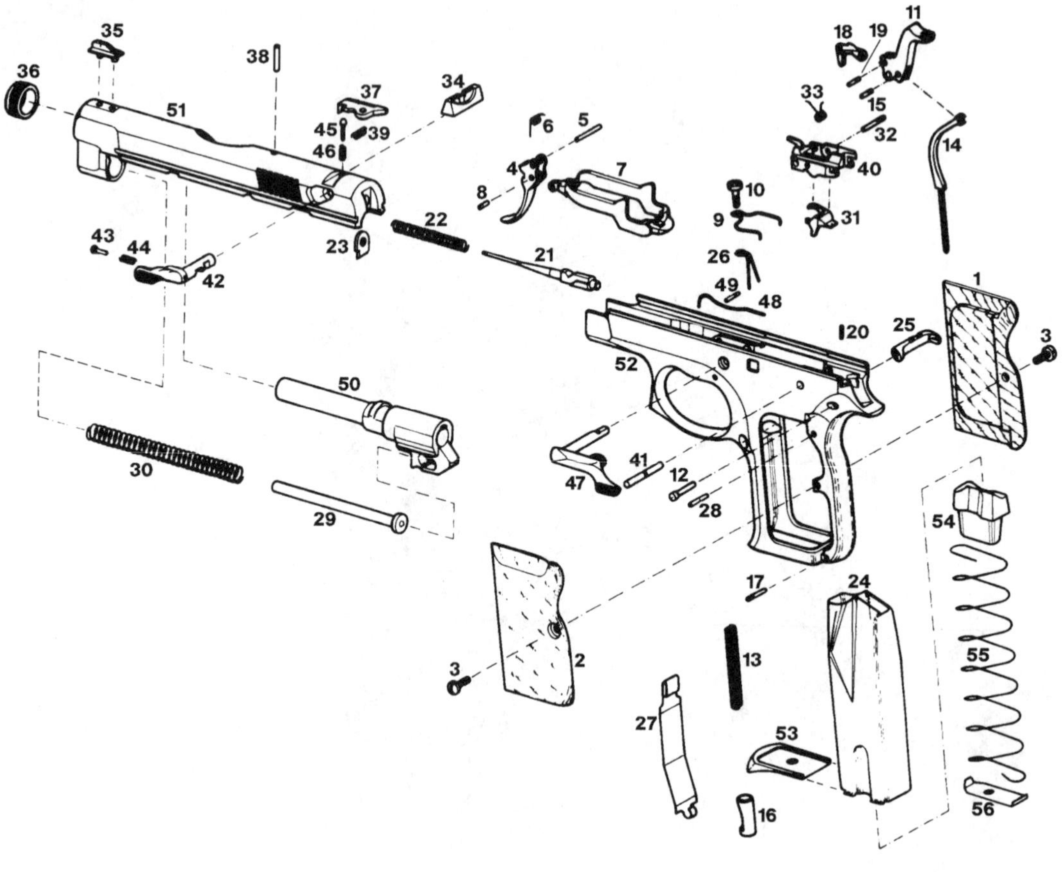

1	Right Grip	**19**	Interruptor Pin	**38**	Extractor Pin
2	Left Grip	**20**	Hammer Pin Retaining Pin	**39**	Extractor Spring
3	Grip Screws	**21**	Firing Pin	**40**	Sear Assembly Housing with Ejector
4	Trigger	**22**	Firing Pin Spring	**41**	Sear Assembly Housing Pin
5	Trigger Pin	**23**	Firing Pin Retainer Plate	**42**	Safety-Lever
6	Trigger Spring	**24**	Magazine Body	**43**	Safety-Lever Plunger
7	Trigger Bar	**25**	Magazine Catch	**44**	Safety-Lever Spring
8	Trigger Bar Pin	**26**	Magazine Catch Spring	**45**	Sear Safety
9	Trigger Bar Spring	**27**	Magazine Spring Plate	**46**	Sear Safety Spring
10	Trigger Bar and Magazine Catch Spring Screw	**28**	Magazine Spring Plate Pin	**47**	Slide Stop
11	Hammer	**29**	Recoil Spring Guide	**48**	Slide Stop Spring
12	Hammer Pin	**30**	Recoil Spring	**49**	Slide Stop Spring Pin
13	Mainspring	**31**	Sear	**50**	Barrel
14	Hammer Strut	**32**	Sear Pin	**51**	Slide
15	Hammer Strut Pin	**33**	Sear Spring	**52**	Frame
16	Hammer Spring Cup	**34**	Rear Sight	**53**	Magazine Base Plate
17	Hammer Spring Cup Pin	**35**	Front Sight	**54**	Magazine Follower
18	Interruptor	**36**	Barrel Bushing	**55**	Magazine Spring
		37	Extractor	**56**	Magazine Base Plate Retainer

TA38S Derringer

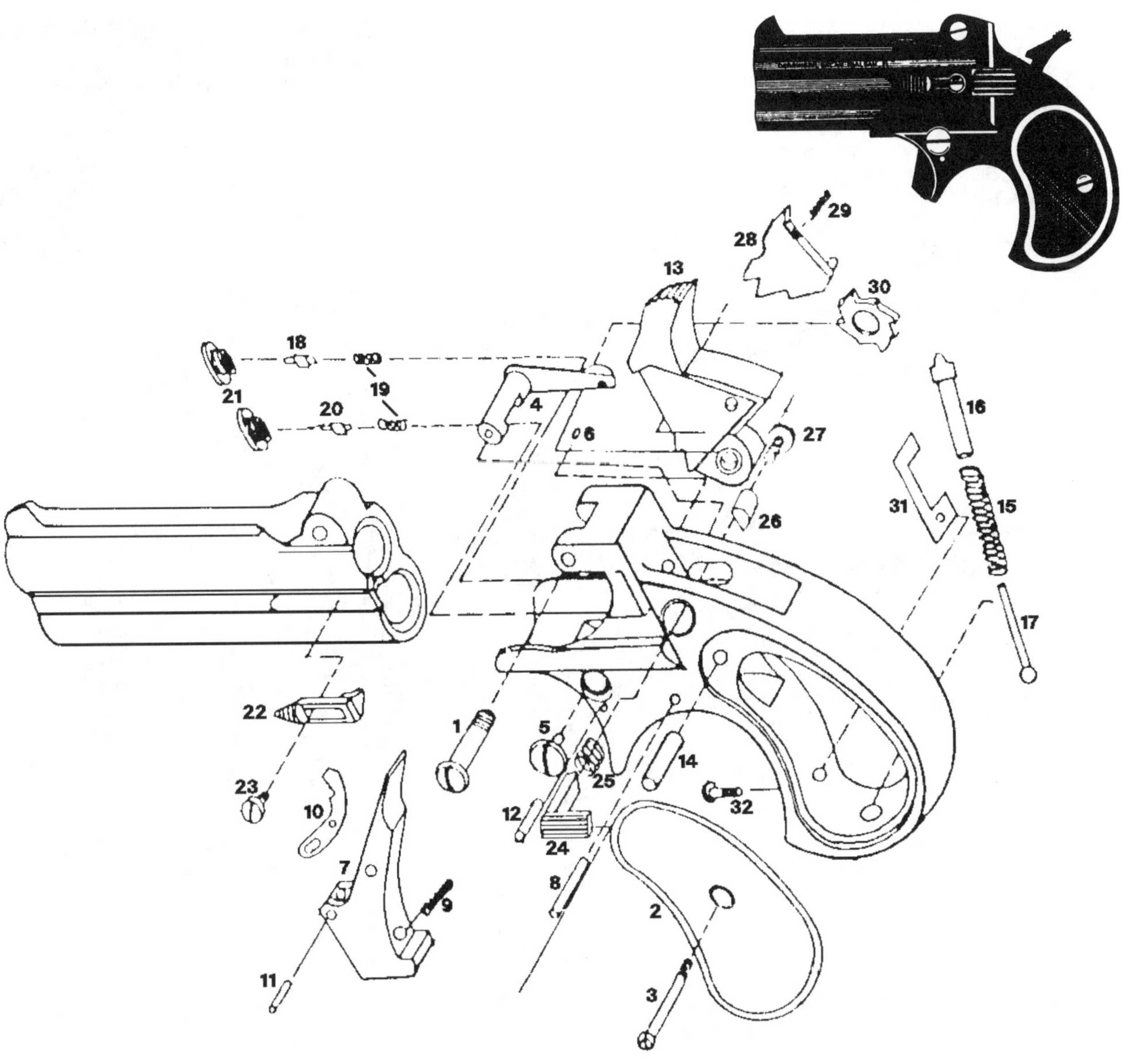

1	Barrel Screw	**13**	Hammer	**25**	Safety-Lever Spring
2	Left Grip	**14**	Hammer Pin	**26**	Safety Insert
3	Grip Screw	**15**	Mainspring	**27**	Safety Screw
4	Barrel Latch	**16**	Mainspring Plunger	**28**	Barrel Selector
5	Barrel Latch Screw	**17**	Mainspring Guide	**29**	Selector Spring
6	Barrel Latch Stop	**18**	Upper Firing Pin	**30**	Selector Cam
7	Trigger	**19**	Firing Pin Springs	**31**	Selector Cam Spring
8	Trigger Pin	**20**	Lower Firing Pin	**32**	Selector Cam Spring Screw
9	Trigger Spring	**21**	Recoil Plates	**Parts Not Shown**	
10	Barrel Interlock	**22**	Extractor		Right Grip
11	Interlock Pin	**23**	Extractor Screw		Selector Spring Screw Nut
12	Pivot Pin	**24**	Safety-Lever		

TA90 Auto

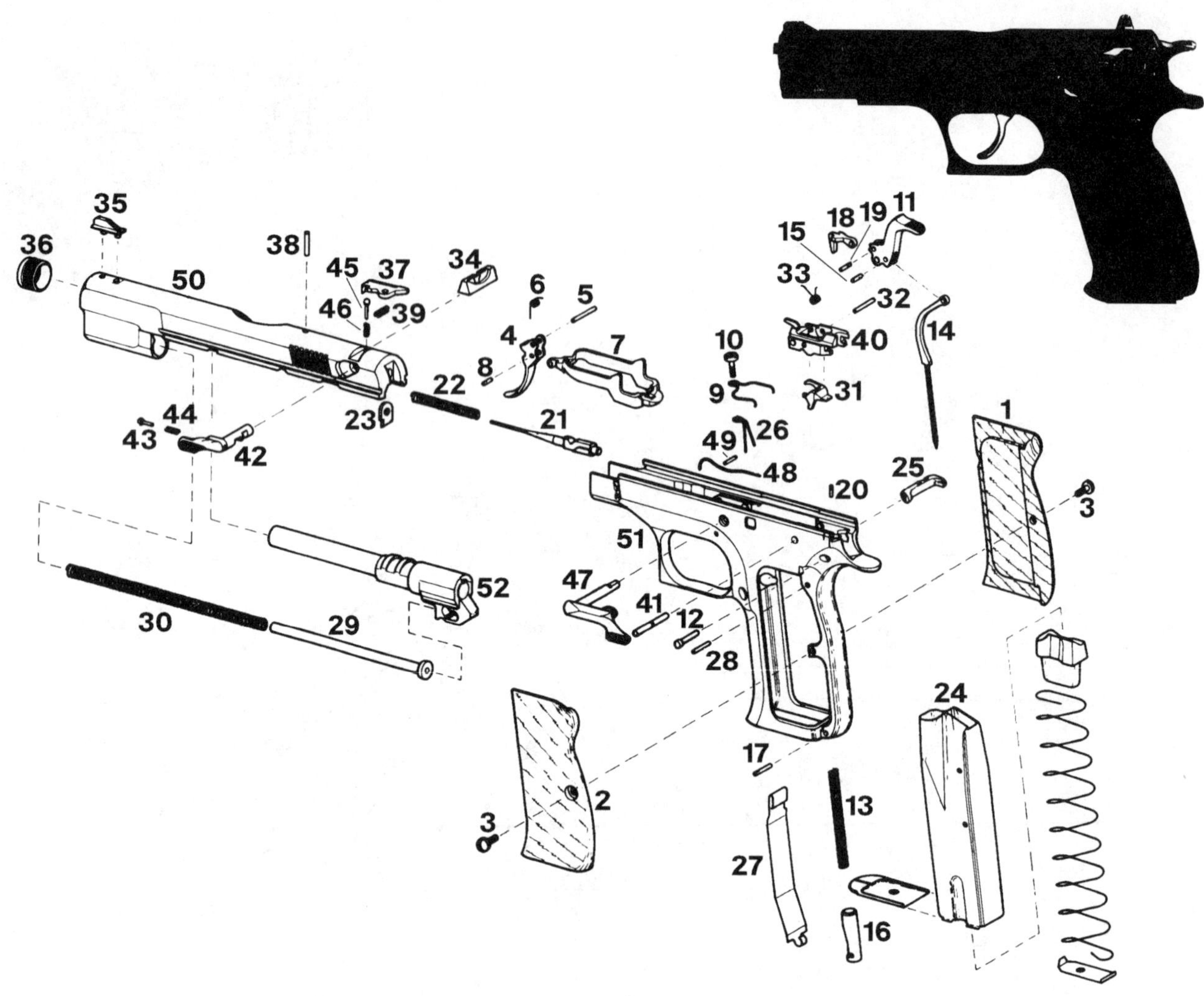

1	Right Grip	18	Interruptor	36	Barrel Bushing
2	Left Grip	19	Interruptor Pin	37	Extractor
3	Grip Screws	20	Hammer Pin Retaining Pin	38	Extractor Pin
4	Trigger	21	Firing Pin	39	Extractor Spring
5	Trigger Pin	22	Firing Pin Spring	40	Sear Assembly Housing with Ejector
6	Trigger Spring	23	Firing Pin Retaining Plate	41	Sear Assembly Housing Pin
7	Trigger Bar	24	Magazine	42	Firing Pin Safety
8	Trigger Bar Pin	25	Magazine Catch	43	Firing Pin Safety Plunger
9	Trigger Bar Spring	26	Magazine Catch Spring	44	Firing Pin Safety Spring
10	Trigger Bar and Magazine Catch Spring Screws	27	Magzine Security Spring Plate	45	Sear Safety
11	Hammer	28	Magazine Security Spring Plate Pin	46	Sear Safety Spring
12	Hammer Pin	29	Recoil Spring Guide	47	Slide Stop Pin
13	Hammer Spring	30	Recoil Spring	48	Slide Stop Spring
14	Hammer Strut	31	Sear	49	Slide Stop Spring Pin
15	Hammer Strut Pin	32	Sear Pin	50	Slide
16	Hammer Spring Cup	33	Sear Spring	51	Frame
17	Hammer Spring Cup Interruptor	34	Rear Sight	52	Barrel
		35	Front Sight		

GT26 Auto

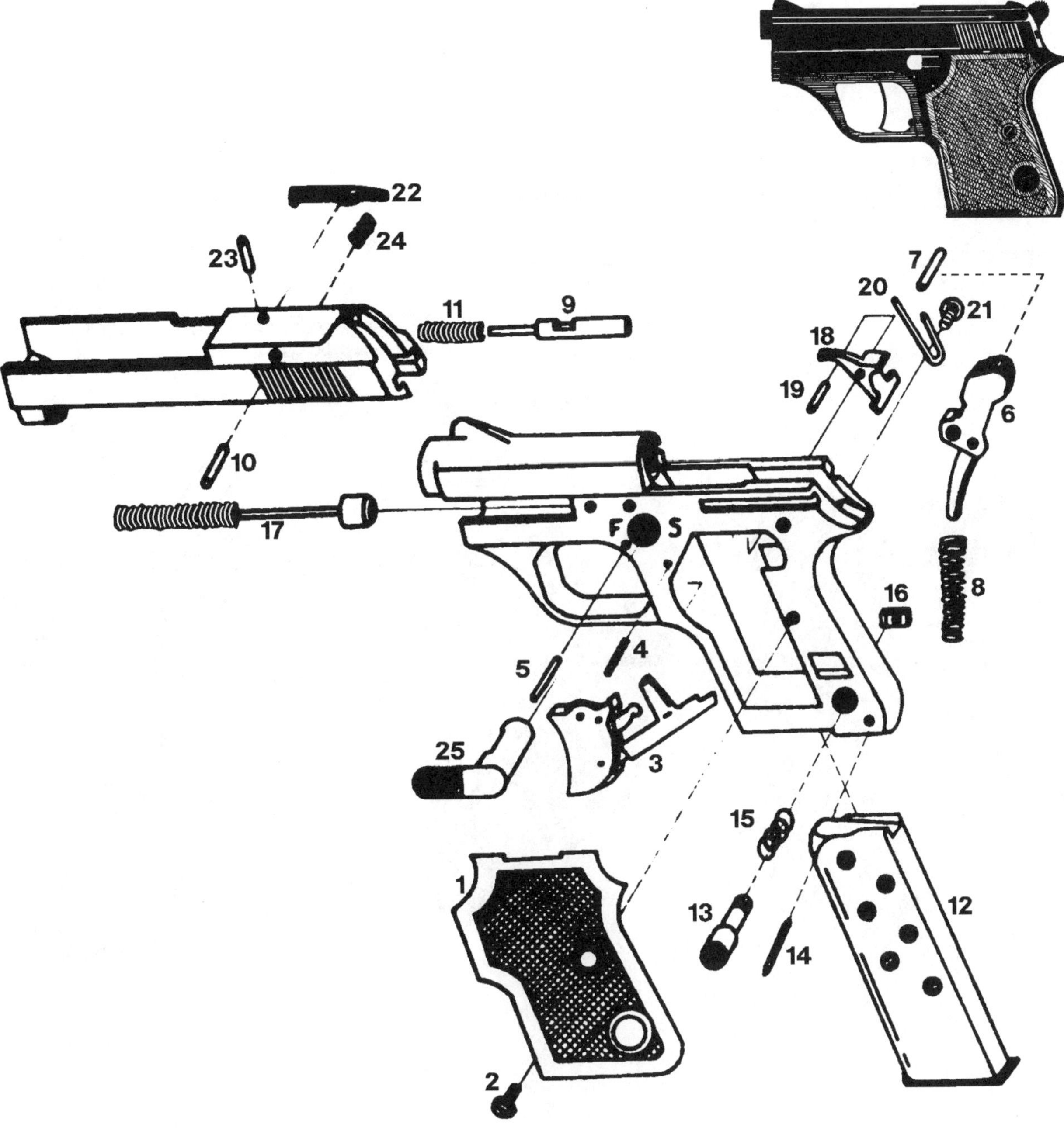

1	Grip	**14**	Grip Retaining Pin
2	Grip Screw	**15**	Magazine Catch Spring
3	Trigger Assembly	**16**	Magazine Catch Nut
4	Trigger Pin	**17**	Recoil Spring Assembly
5	Safety Pin	**18**	Sear/Ejector Lever
6	Hammer Assembly	**19**	Sear Pin
7	Hammer Pin	**20**	Sear Spring
8	Mainspring	**21**	Sear Spring Screw
9	Firing Pin	**22**	Extractor
10	Firing Pin Retaining Pin	**23**	Extractor Pin
11	Firing Pin Spring	**24**	Extractor Spring
12	Magazine Assembly	**25**	Thumb Safety-Lever
13	Magazine Catch		

GT27B and GT27C Auto

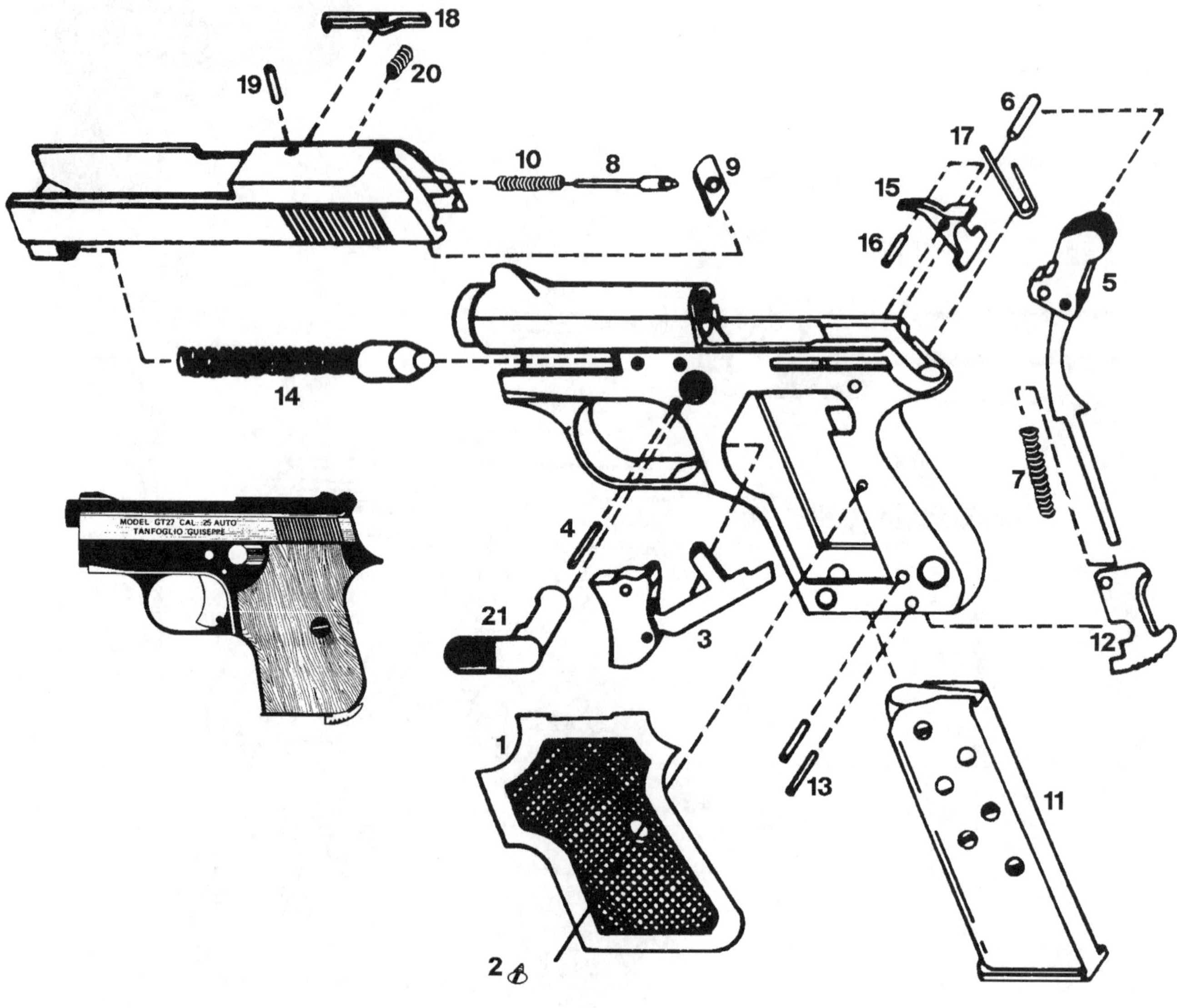

1	Grip	**13**	Catch Pins
2	Grip Screw	**14**	Recoil Assembly
3	Trigger Assembly	**15**	Sear/Ejector
4	Trigger Pin	**16**	Sear Pin
5	Hammer Assembly	**17**	Sear Spring
6	Hammer Pin	**18**	Extractor
7	Mainspring	**19**	Extractor Pin
8	Firing Pin	**20**	Extractor Spring
9	Retaining Plate	**21**	Thumb Safety-Lever
10	Firing Pin Spring	**Parts Not Shown**	
11	Magazine Assembly		Sear Spring Screw
12	Magazine Catch		

Model 65 Revolver

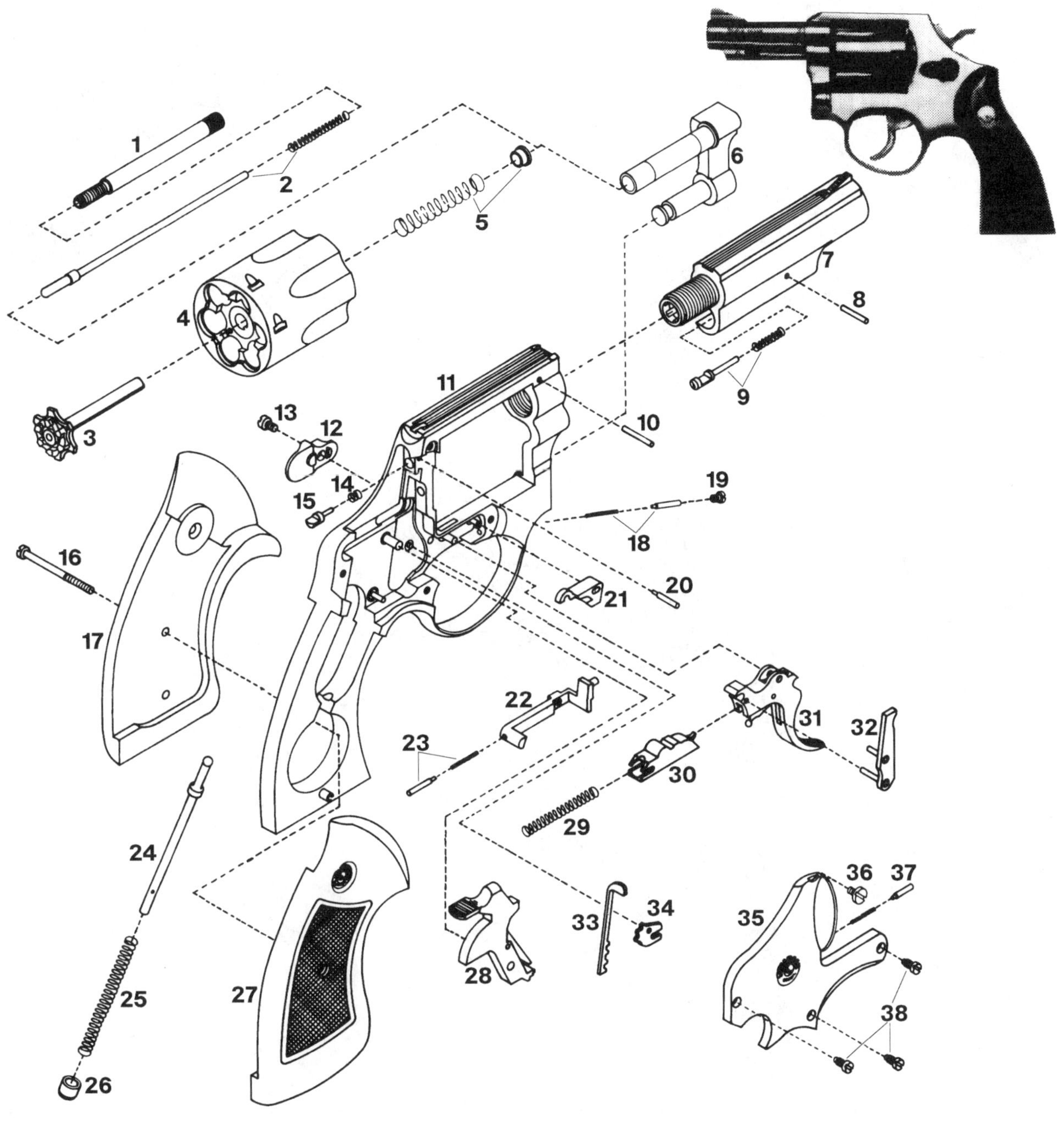

1	Extractor Rod	14	Firing Pin Spring	27	Right Stock
2	Center Pin with Spring	15	Firing Pin	28	Hammer
3	Extractor	16	Stock Screw	29	Trigger Spring
4	Cylinder	17	Left Stock	30	Rebound Slide
5	Extractor Spring with Rod Collar	18	Cylinder Stop Plunger with Spring	31	Trigger
6	Yoke	19	Cylinder Stop Screw	32	Hand
7	Barrel	20	Firing Pin Retaining Pin	33	Hammer Block
8	Locking Bolt Pin	21	Cylinder Stop	34	Gear
9	Locking Bolt with Spring	22	Bolt	35	Sideplate
10	Barrel Pin	23	Bolt Pin with Spring	36	Sideplate Short Screw
11	Frame	24	Mainspring Center Pin	37	Hand Pin with Spring
12	Thumb-Piece	25	Mainspring	38	Sideplate Long Screws
13	Thumb-Piece Screw	26	Mainspring Bushing		

Model 66 Revolver

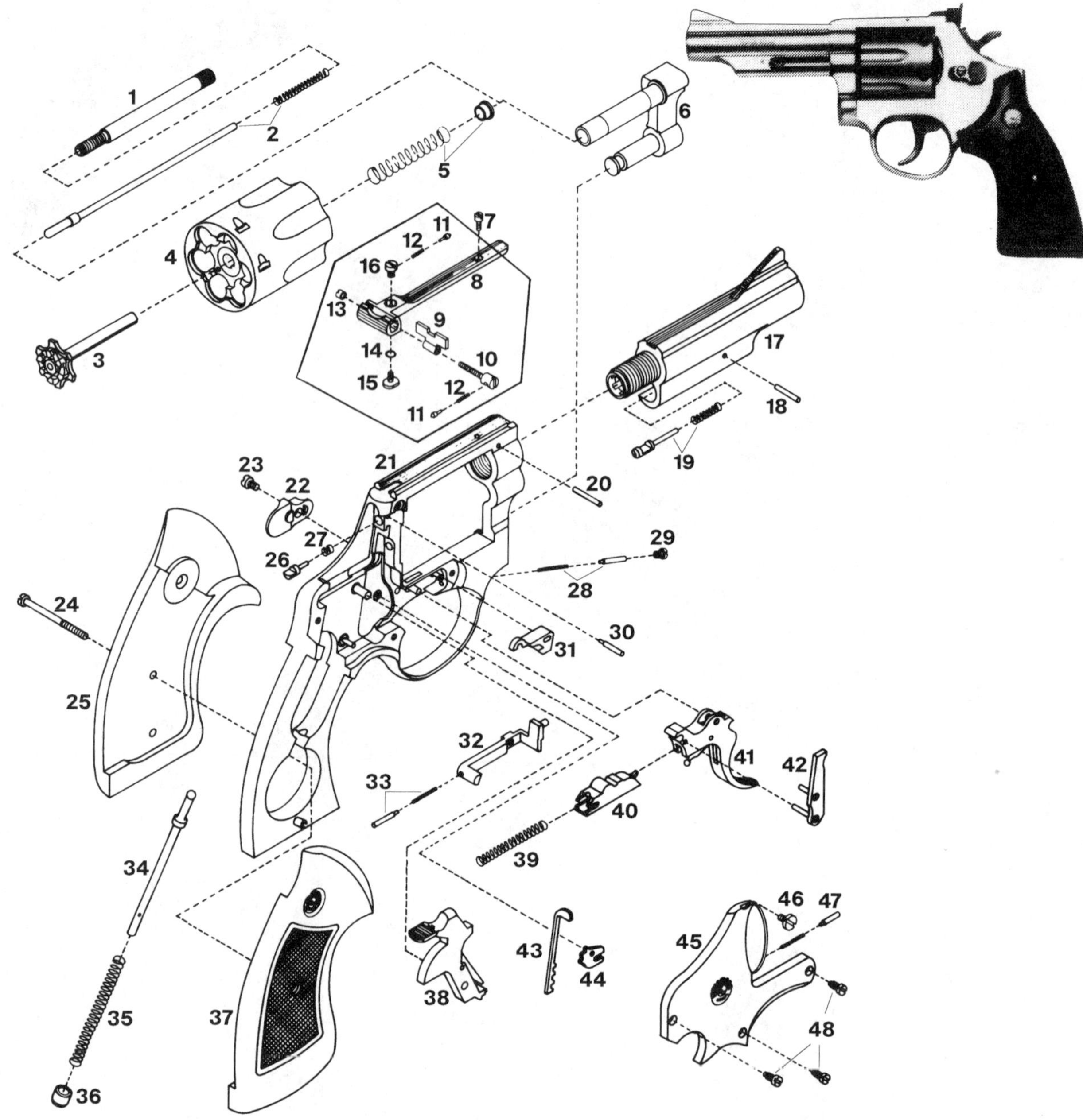

1	Extractor Rod	**17**	Barrel	**33**	Bolt Pin with Spring
2	Center Pin with Spring	**18**	Locking Bolt Pin	**34**	Mainspring Center Pin
3	Extractor	**19**	Locking Bolt with Spring	**35**	Mainspring
4	Cylinder	**20**	Barrel Pin	**36**	Mainspring Bushing
5	Extractor Spring with Rod Collar	**21**	Frame	**37**	Right Stock
6	Yoke	**22**	Thumb-Piece	**38**	Hammer
7	Rear Sight Screw	**23**	Thumb-Piece Screw	**39**	Trigger Spring
8	Rear Sight Leaf	**24**	Stock Screw	**40**	Rebound Slide
9	Rear Sight Blade	**25**	Left Stock	**41**	Trigger
10	Rear Sight Windage Screw	**26**	Firing Pin	**42**	Hand
11	Click Pin	**27**	Firing Pin Spring	**43**	Hammer Block
12	Click Pin Spring	**28**	Cylinder Stop Plunger with Spring	**44**	Gear
13	Windage Nut	**29**	Cylinder Stop Screw	**45**	Sideplate
14	Safety Ring	**30**	Firing Pin Retaining Pin	**46**	Sideplate Short Screw
15	Rear Sight Elevation Screw	**31**	Cylinder Stop	**47**	Hand Pin with Spring
16	Elevation Nut	**32**	Bolt	**48**	Sideplate Long Screws

Model 67 Revolver

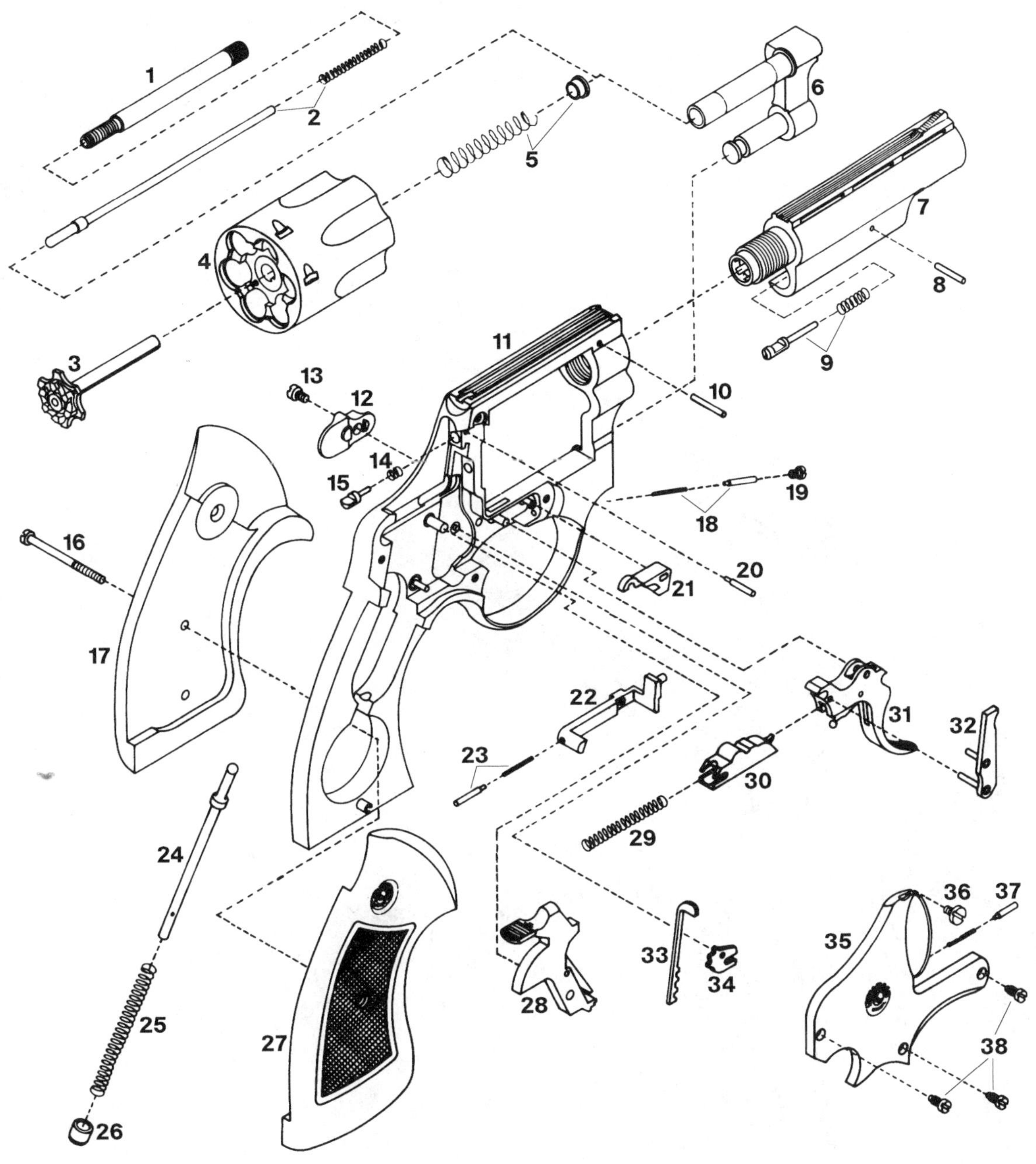

1	Extractor Rod	**14**	Firing Pin Spring	**27**	Right Stock
2	Center Pin with Spring	**15**	Firing Pin	**28**	Hammer
3	Extractor	**16**	Stock Screw	**29**	Trigger Spring
4	Cylinder	**17**	Left Stock	**30**	Rebound Slide
5	Extractor Spring with Rod Collar	**18**	Cylinder Stop Plunger with Spring	**31**	Trigger
6	Yoke	**19**	Cylinder Stop Screw	**32**	Hand
7	Barrel	**20**	Firing Pin Retaining Pin	**33**	Hammer Block
8	Locking Bolt Pin	**21**	Cylinder Stop	**34**	Gear
9	Locking Bolt with Spring	**22**	Bolt	**35**	Sideplate
10	Barrel Pin	**23**	Bolt Pin with Spring	**36**	Sideplate Short Screw
11	Frame	**24**	Mainspring Center Pin	**37**	Hand Pin with Spring
12	Thumb-Piece	**25**	Mainspring	**38**	Sideplate Long Screws
13	Thumb-Piece Screw	**26**	Mainspring Bushing		

Model 689 Revolver

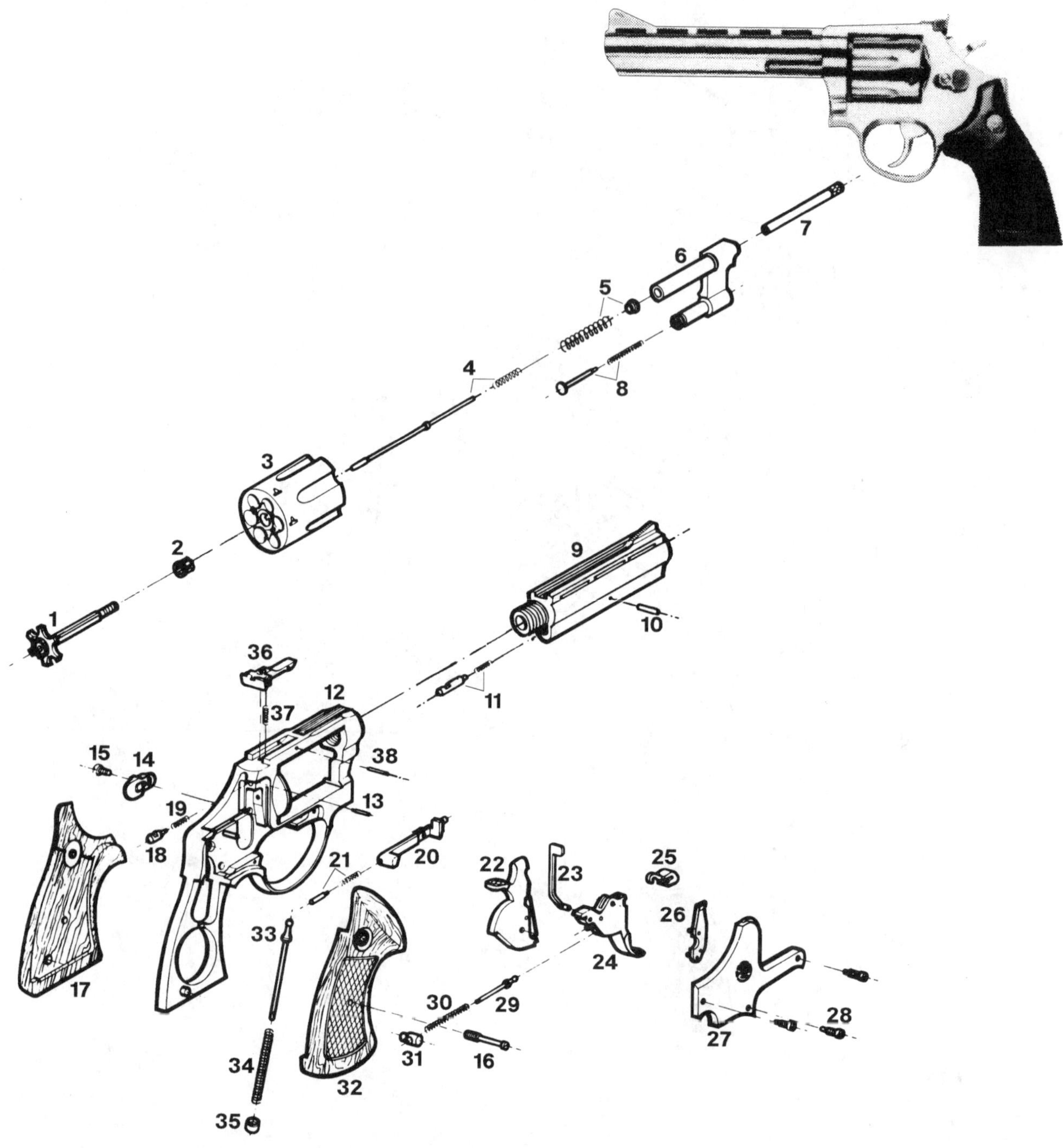

1	Extractor	14	Thumb-Piece	27	Sideplate
2	Cylinder Retaining Bushing	15	Thumb-Piece Screw	28	Sideplate Screws
3	Cylinder	16	Stock Screw	29	Trigger Spring Center Pin
4	Center Pin with Spring	17	Left Stock	30	Trigger Spring
5	Extractor Spring with Rod Collar	18	Firing Pin	31	Trigger Spring Swivel
6	Yoke	19	Firing Pin Spring	32	Right Stock
7	Extractor Rod	20	Bolt	33	Mainspring Center Pin
8	Cylinder Stop Plunger with Spring	21	Bolt Plunger with Spring	34	Mainspring
9	Barrel	22	Hammer	35	Mainspring Bushing
10	Locking Bolt Pin	23	Transfer Bar	36	Rear Sight
11	Locking Bolt with Spring	24	Trigger	37	Rear Sight Spring
12	Frame	25	Cylinder Stop	38	Rear Sight Pin
13	Firing Pin Retaining Pin	26	Hand		

Model 70 Revolver

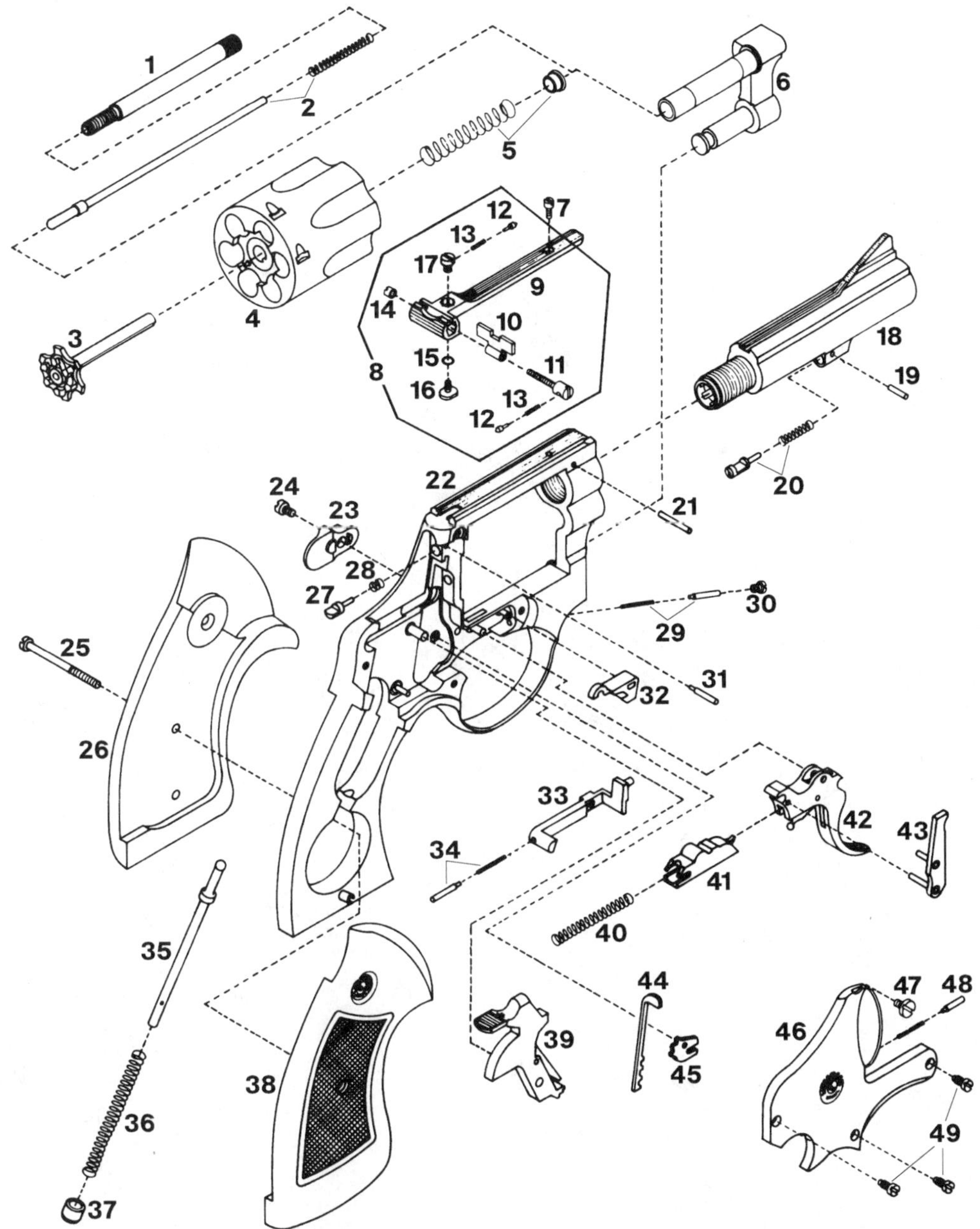

1	Extractor Rod	18	Barrel	35	Mainspring Center Pin
2	Center Pin with Spring	19	Locking Bolt Pin	36	Mainspring
3	Extractor	20	Locking Bolt with Spring	37	Mainspring Bushing
4	Cylinder	21	Barrel Pin	38	Right Stock
5	Extractor Spring with Rod Collar	22	Frame	39	Hammer
6	Yoke	23	Thumb-Piece	40	Trigger Spring
7	Rear Sight Screw	24	Thumb-Piece Screw	41	Rebound Slide
8	Rear Sight Assembly	25	Stock Screw	42	Trigger
9	Rear Sight Leaf	26	Left Stock	43	Hand
10	Rear Sight Blade	27	Firing Pin	44	Hammer Block
11	Rear Sight Windage Screw	28	Firing Pin Spring	45	Gear
12	Click Pin	29	Cylinder Stop Plunger with Spring	46	Sideplate
13	Click Pin Spring	30	Cylinder Stop Screw	47	Sideplate Short Screw
14	Windage Nut	31	Firing Pin Retaining Pin	48	Hand Pin with Spring
15	Safety Ring	32	Cylinder Stop	49	Sideplate Long Screws
16	Rear Sight Elevation Screw	33	Bolt		
17	Elevation Nut	34	Bolt Pin with Spring		

Model 71 Revolver

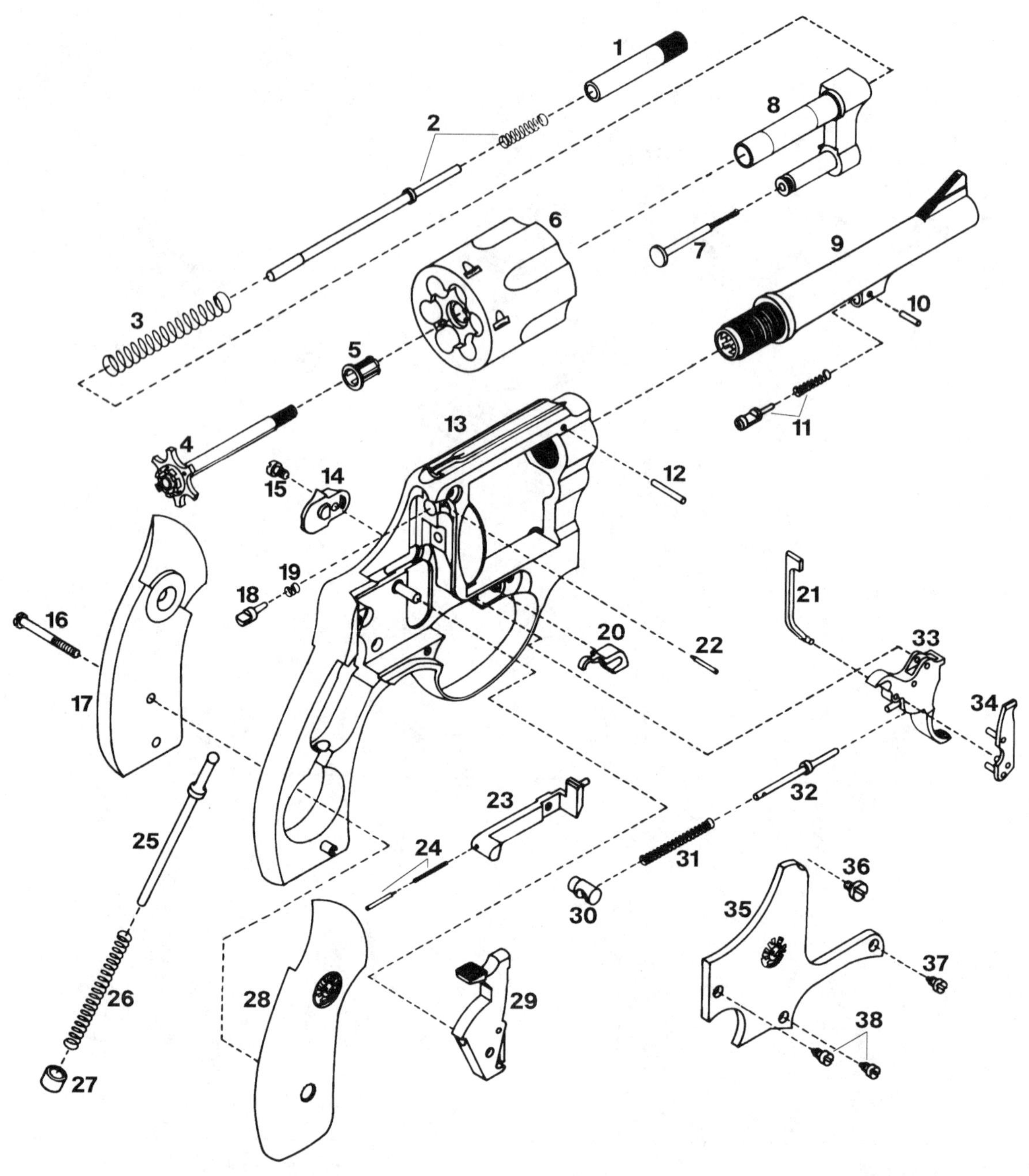

1	Extractor Rod	14	Thumb-Piece	27	Mainspring Bushing
2	Center Pin with Spring	15	Thumb-Piece Screw	28	Right Stock
3	Extractor Spring	16	Stock Screw	29	Hammer
4	Extractor	17	Left Stock	30	Trigger Spring Swivel
5	Cylinder Retaining Bushing	18	Firing Pin	31	Trigger Spring
6	Cylinder	19	Firing Pin Spring	32	Trigger Spring Center Pin
7	Cylinder Stop Plunger with Spring	20	Cylinder Stop	33	Trigger
8	Yoke	21	Transfer Bar	34	Hand
9	Barrel	22	Firing Pin Retaining Pin	35	Sideplate
10	Locking Bolt Pin	23	Bolt	36	Sideplate Short Screw
11	Locking Bolt with Spring	24	Bolt Plunger with Spring	37	Sideplate and Yoke Screw
12	Barrel Pin	25	Mainspring Center Pin	38	Sideplate Long Screws
13	Frame	26	Mainspring		

Model 73 Revolver

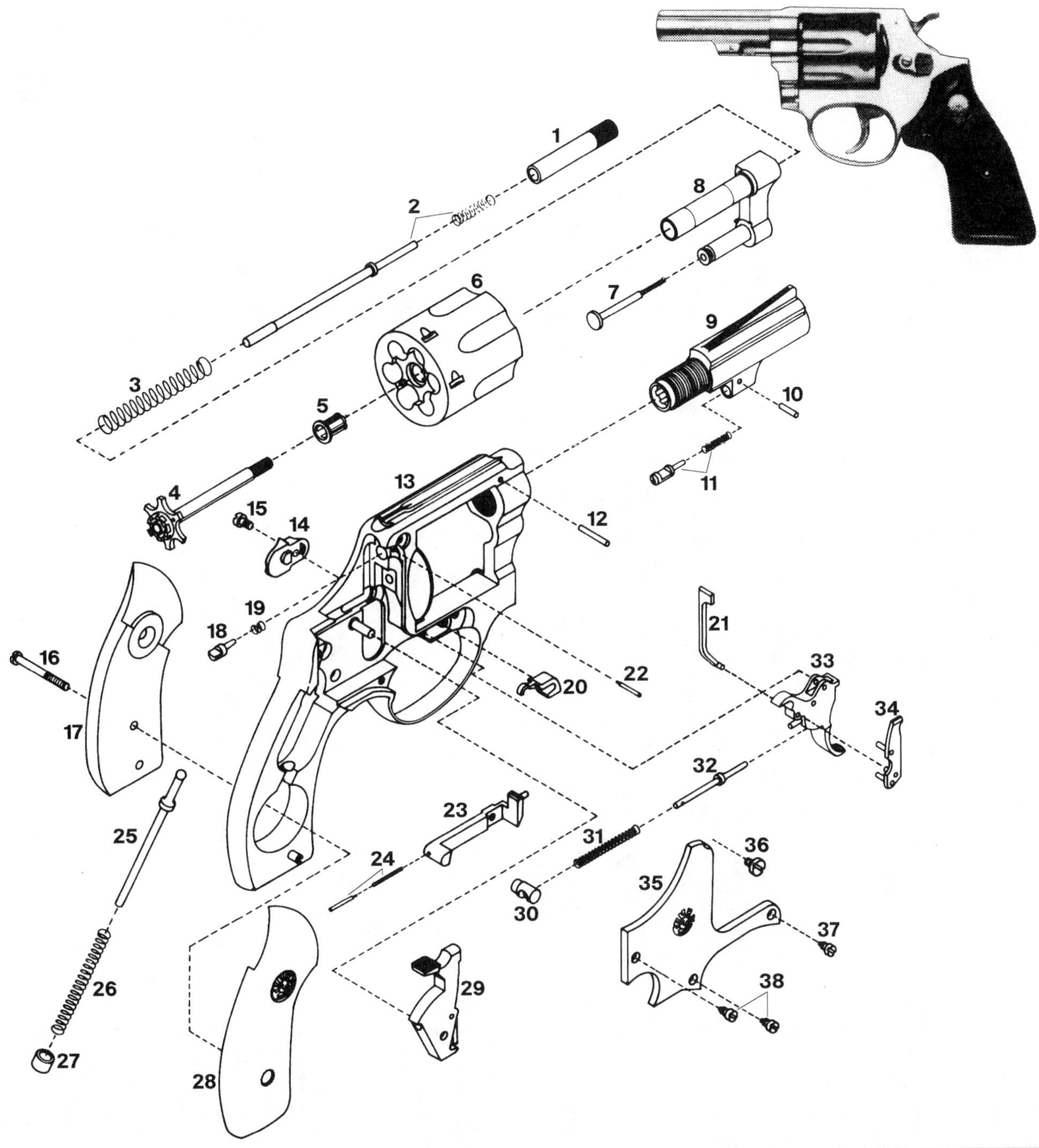

1	Extractor Rod	**14**	Thumb-Piece	**27**	Mainspring Bushing
2	Center Pin with Spring	**15**	Thumb-Piece Screw	**28**	Right Stock
3	Extractor Spring	**16**	Stock Screw	**29**	Hammer
4	Extractor	**17**	Left Stock	**30**	Trigger Spring Swivel
5	Cylinder Retaining Bushing	**18**	Firing Pin	**31**	Trigger Spring
6	Cylinder	**19**	Firing Pin Spring	**32**	Trigger Spring Center Pin
7	Cylinder Stop Plunger with Spring	**20**	Cylinder Stop	**33**	Trigger
8	Yoke	**21**	Transfer Bar	**34**	Hand
9	Barrel	**22**	Firing Pin Retaining Pin	**35**	Sideplate
10	Locking Bolt Pin	**23**	Bolt	**36**	Sideplate Short Screw
11	Locking Bolt with Spring	**24**	Bolt Plunger with Spring	**37**	Sideplate and Yoke Screw
12	Barrel Pin	**25**	Mainspring Center Pin	**38**	Sideplate Long Screws
13	Frame	**26**	Mainspring		

Model 76 Revolver

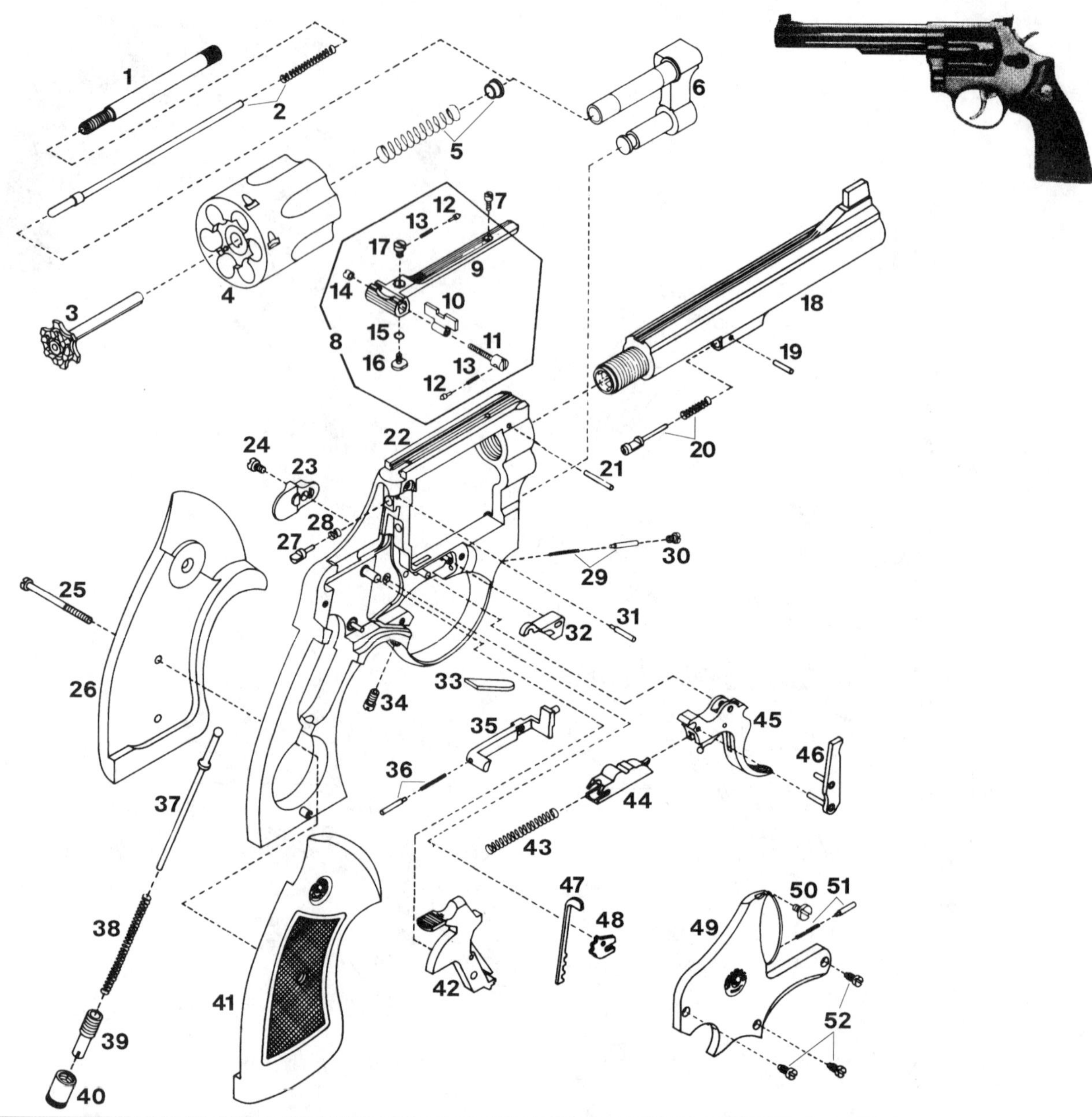

1	Extractor Rod	19	Locking Bolt Pin	37	Mainspring Center Pin
2	Center Pin with Spring	20	Locking Bolt with Spring	38	Mainspring
3	Extractor	21	Barrel Pin	39	Mainspring Adjustable Bushing
4	Cylinder	22	Frame	40	Mainspring Fixed Bushing
5	Extractor Spring with Rod Collar	23	Thumb-Piece	41	Right Stock
6	Yoke	24	Thumb-Piece Screw	42	Hammer
7	Rear Sight Screw	25	Stock Screw	43	Trigger Spring
8	Rear Sight Assembly	26	Left Stock	44	Rebound Slide
9	Rear Sight Leaf	27	Firing Pin	45	Trigger
10	Rear Sight Blade	28	Firing Pin Spring	46	Hand
11	Rear Sight Windage Screw	29	Cylinder Stop Plunger with Spring	47	Hammer Block
12	Click Pins	30	Cylinder Stop Screw	48	Gear
13	Click Pin Springs	31	Firing Pin Retaining Pin	49	Sideplate
14	Windage Nut	32	Cylinder Stop	50	Sideplate Short Screw
15	Safety Ring	33	Trigger Stop	51	Hand Pin with Spring
16	Rear Sight Elevation Screw	34	Trigger Stop Screw	52	Sideplate Long Screws
17	Elevation Nut	35	Bolt		
18	Barrel	36	Bolt Pin with Spring		

Model 80 Revolver

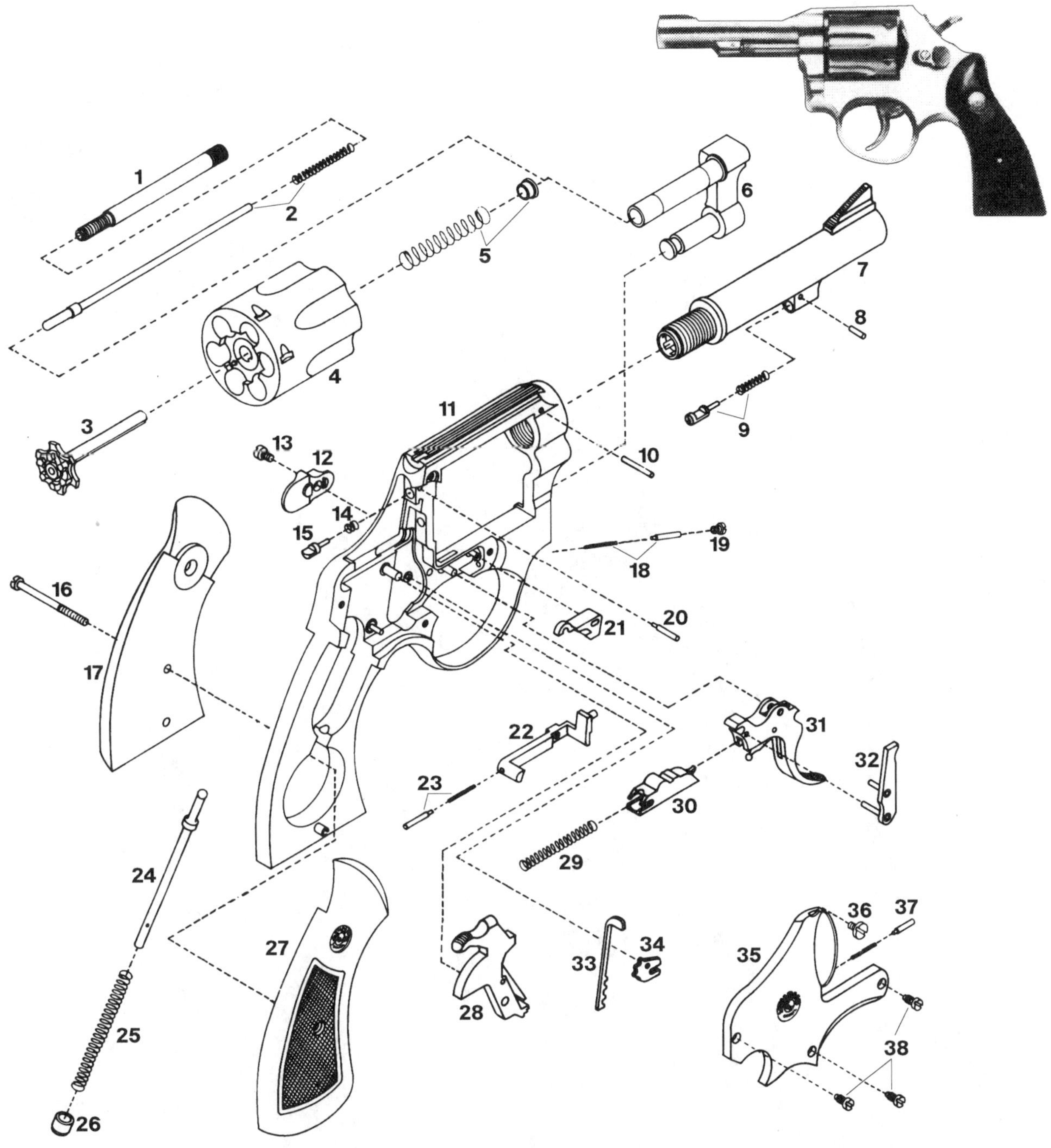

1	Extractor Rod	**14**	Firing Pin Spring	**26**	Mainspring Bushing
2	Center Pin with Spring	**15**	Firing Pin	**27**	Right Stock
3	Extractor	**16**	Stock Screw	**28**	Hammer
4	Cylinder	**17**	Left Stock	**29**	Trigger Spring
5	Extractor Spring with Rod Collar	**18**	Cylinder Stop Plunger with Spring	**30**	Rebound Slide
6	Yoke	**19**	Cylinder Stop Screw	**31**	Trigger
7	Barrel	**20**	Firing Pin Retaining Pin	**32**	Hand
8	Locking Bolt Pin	**21**	Cylinder Stop	**33**	Hammer Block
9	Locking Bolt with Spring	**22**	Bolt	**34**	Gear
10	Barrel Pin	**23**	Bolt Pin with Spring	**35**	Sideplate
11	Frame	**24**	Mainspring Center Pin	**36**	Sideplate Short Screw
12	Thumb-Piece	**25**	Mainspring	**37**	Hand Pin with Spring
13	Thumb-Piece Screw			**38**	Sideplate Long Screws

Model 82 and 82S Revolver

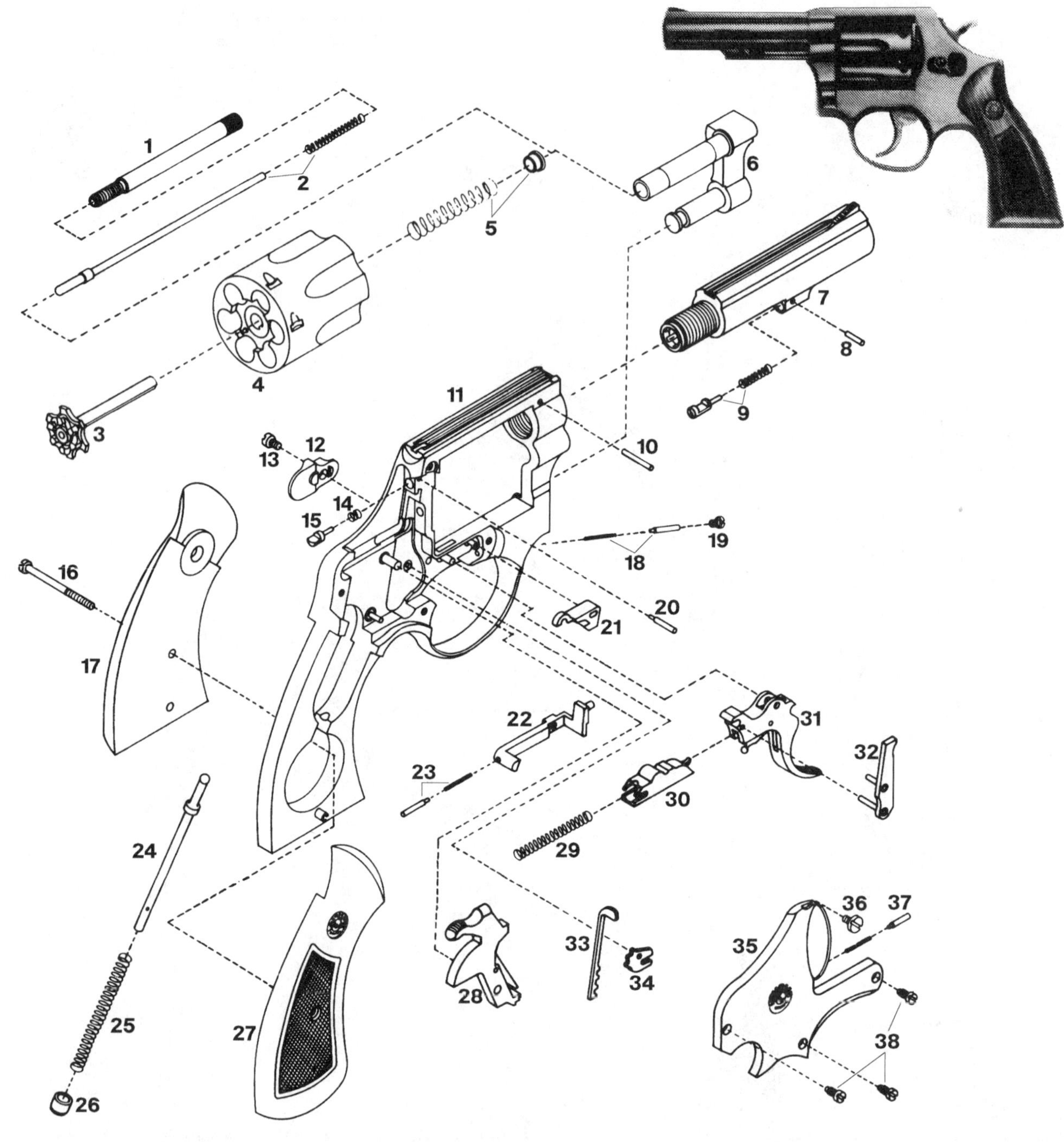

1	Extractor Rod	**14**	Firing Pin Spring	**27**	Right Stock
2	Center Pin with Spring	**15**	Firing Pin	**28**	Hammer
3	Extractor	**16**	Stock Screw	**29**	Trigger Spring
4	Cylinder	**17**	Left Stock	**30**	Rebound Slide
5	Extractor Spring with Rod Collar	**18**	Cylinder Stop Plunger with Spring	**31**	Trigger
6	Yoke	**19**	Cylinder Stop Screw	**32**	Hand
7	Barrel	**20**	Firing Pin Retaining Pin	**33**	Hammer Block
8	Locking Bolt Pin	**21**	Cylinder Stop	**34**	Gear
9	Locking Bolt with Spring	**22**	Bolt	**35**	Sideplate
10	Barrel Pin	**23**	Bolt Pin with Spring	**36**	Sideplate Short Screw
11	Frame	**24**	Mainspring Center Pin	**37**	Hand Pin with Spring
12	Thumb-Piece	**25**	Mainspring	**38**	Sideplate Long Screws
13	Thumb-Piece Screw	**26**	Mainspring Bushing		

Model 83 and 83S Revolver

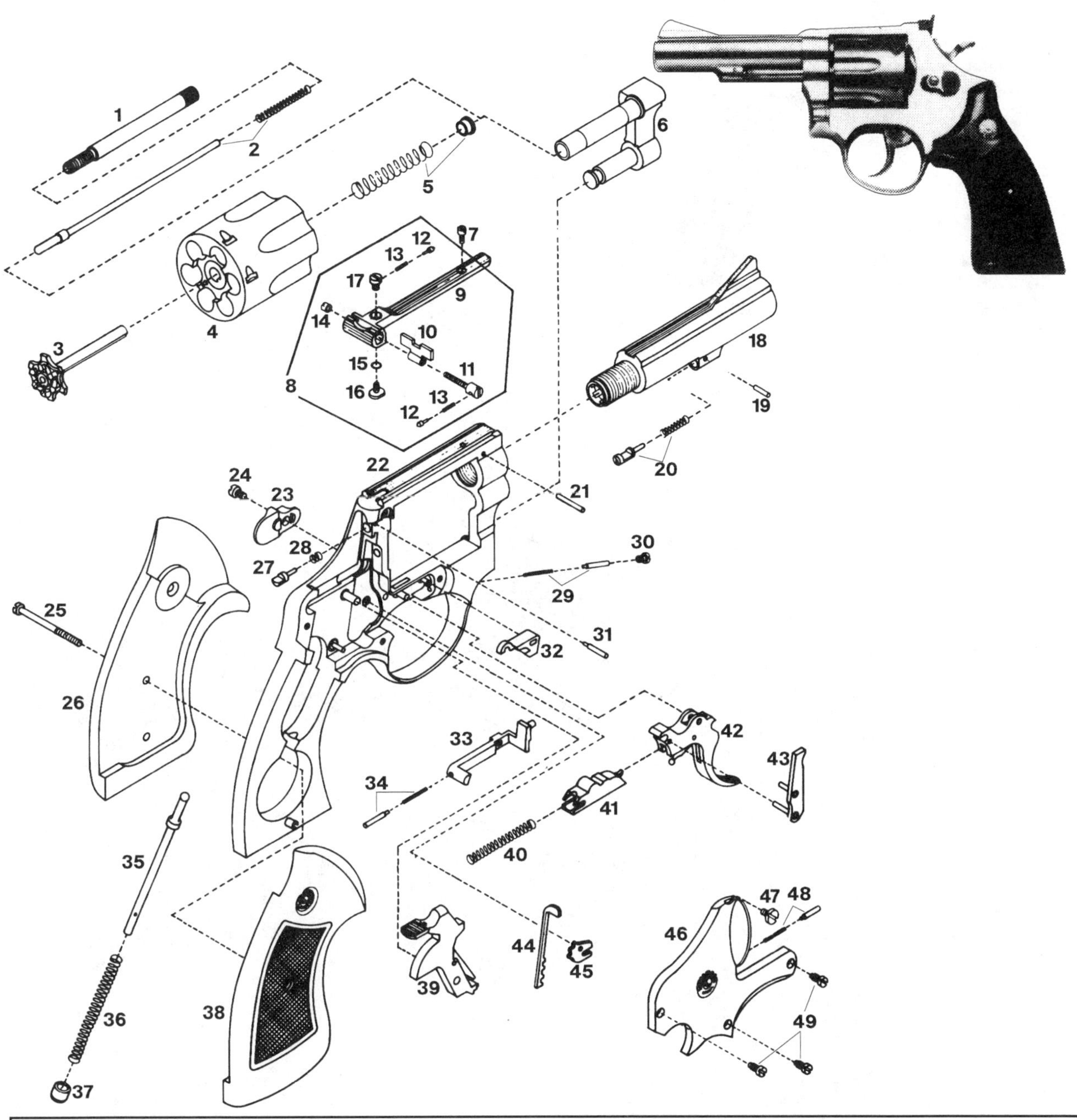

1	Extractor Rod	18	Barrel	35	Mainspring Center Pin
2	Center Pin with Spring	19	Locking Bolt Pin	36	Mainspring
3	Extractor	20	Locking Bolt with Spring	37	Mainspring Bushing
4	Cylinder	21	Barrel Pin	38	Right Stock
5	Extractor Spring with Rod Collar	22	Frame	39	Hammer
6	Yoke	23	Thumb-Piece	40	Trigger Spring
7	Rear Sight Screw	24	Thumb-Piece Screw	41	Rebound Slide
8	Rear Sight Assembly	25	Stock Screw	42	Trigger
9	Rear Sight Leaf	26	Left Stock	43	Hand
10	Rear Sight Blade	27	Firing Pin	44	Hammer Block
11	Rear Sight Windage Screw	28	Firing Pin Spring	45	Gear
12	Click Pins	29	Cylinder Stop Plunger with Spring	46	Sideplate
13	Click Pin Springs	30	Cylinder Stop Screw	47	Sideplate Short Screw
14	Windage Nut	31	Firing Pin Retaining Pin	48	Hand Pin with Spring
15	Safety Ring	32	Cylinder Stop	49	Sideplate Long Screws
16	Rear Sight Elevation Screw	33	Bolt		
17	Elevation Nut	34	Bolt Pin with Spring		

Model 85 and 85S Revolver

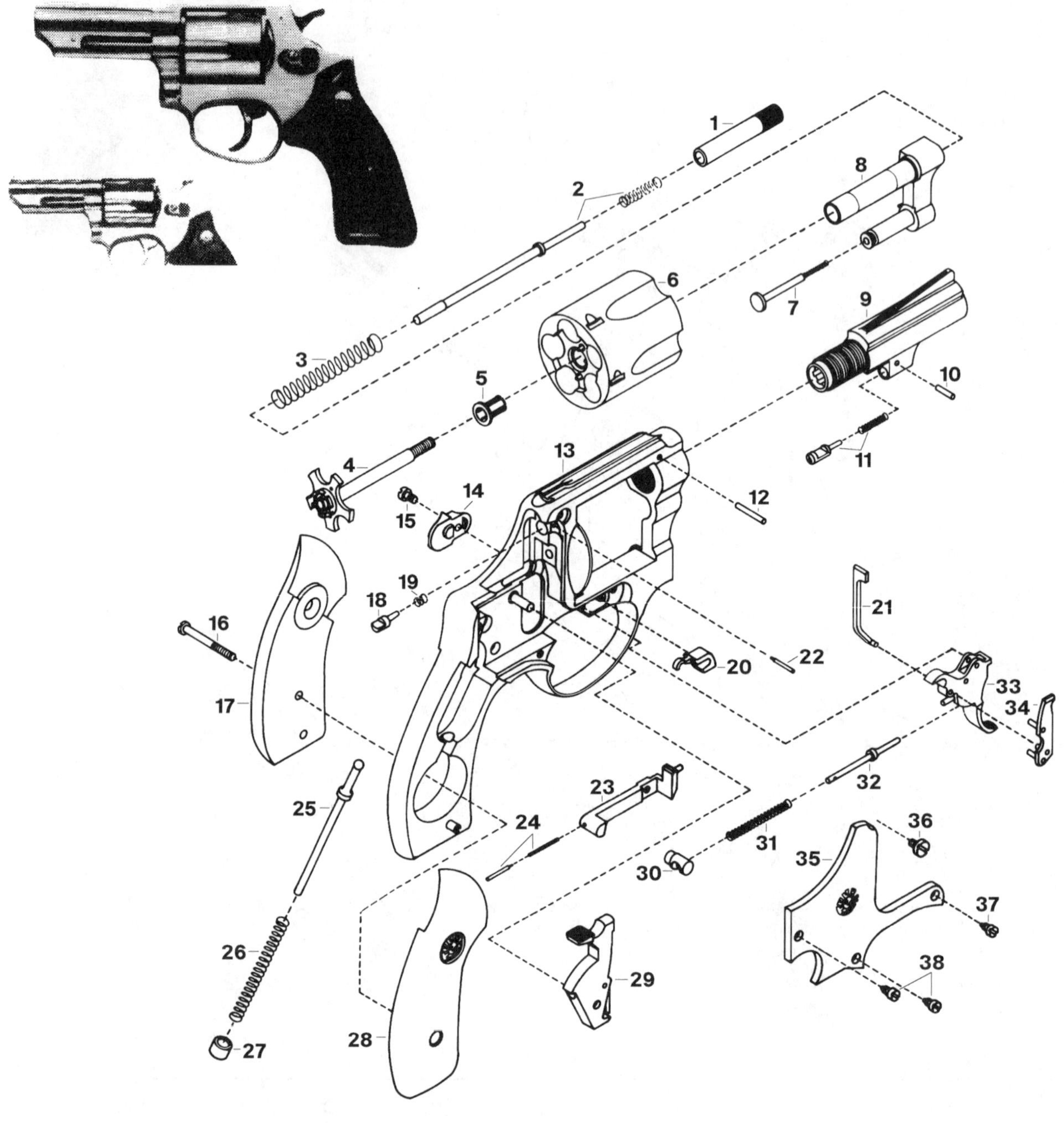

1	Extractor Rod	14	Thumb-Piece	27	Mainspring Bushing
2	Center Pin with Spring	15	Thumb-Piece Screw	28	Right Stock
3	Extractor Spring	16	Stock Screw	29	Hammer
4	Extractor	17	Left Stock	30	Trigger Spring Swivel
5	Cylinder Retaining Bushing	18	Firing Pin	31	Trigger Spring
6	Cylinder	19	Firing Pin Spring	32	Trigger Spring Center Pin
7	Cylinder Stop Plunger with Spring	20	Cylinder Stop	33	Trigger
8	Yoke	21	Transfer Bar	34	Hand
9	Barrel	22	Firing Pin Retaining Pin	35	Sideplate
10	Locking Bolt Pin	23	Bolt	36	Sideplate Short Screw
11	Locking Bolt with Spring	24	Bolt Plunger with Spring	37	Sideplate and Yoke Screw
12	Barrel Pin	25	Mainspring Center Pin	38	Sideplate Long Screws
13	Frame	26	Mainspring		

Model 85S Stainless Revolver

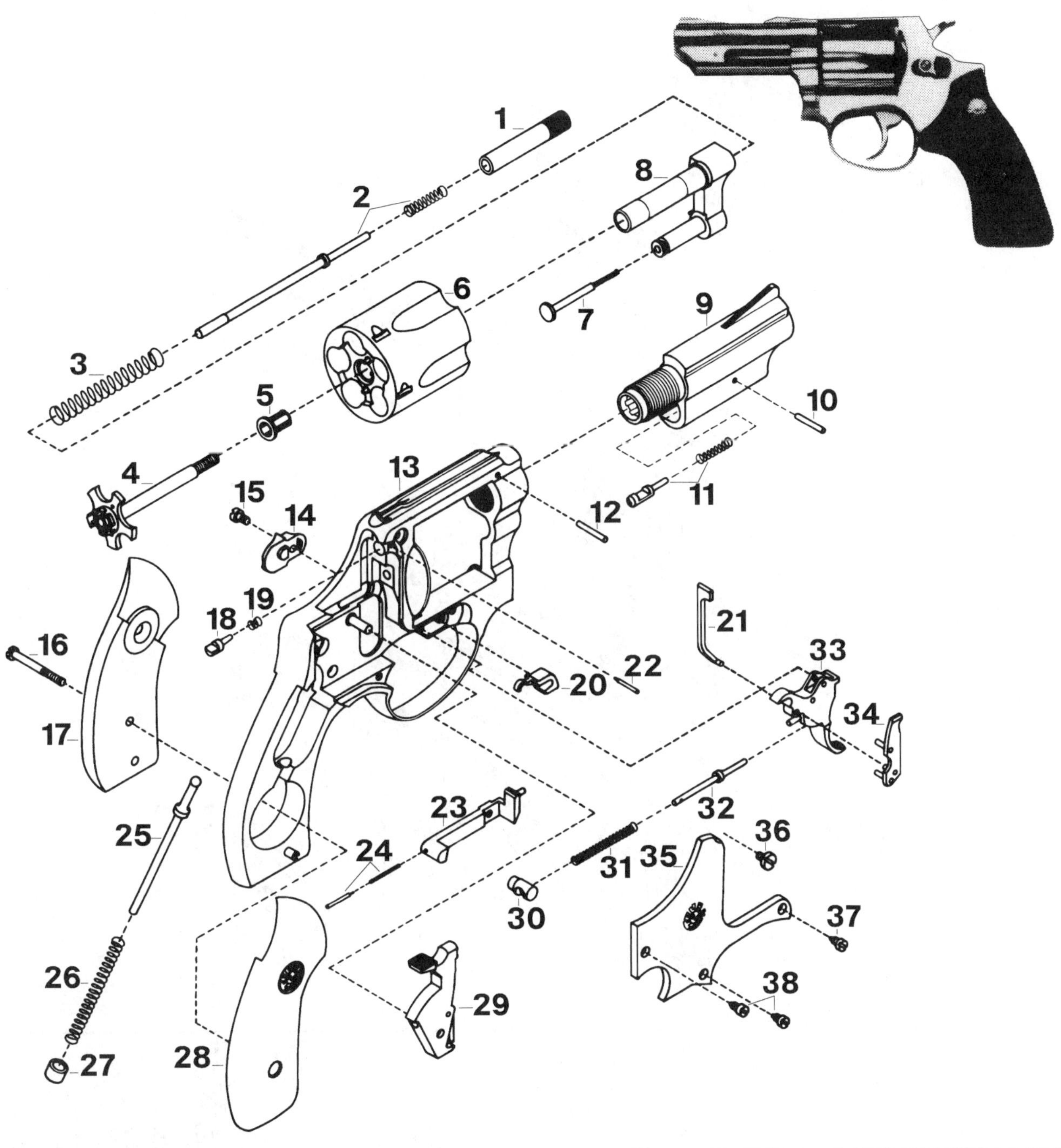

1	Extractor Rod
2	Center Pin with Spring
3	Extractor Spring
4	Extractor
5	Cylinder Retaining Bushing
6	Cylinder
7	Cylinder Stop Plunger with Spring
8	Yoke
9	Barrel
10	Locking Bolt Pin
11	Locking Bolt with Spring
12	Barrel Pin
13	Frame
14	Thumb-Piece
15	Thumb-Piece Screw
16	Stock Screw
17	Left Stock
18	Firing Pin
19	Firing Pin Spring
20	Cylinder Stop
21	Transfer Bar
22	Firing Pin Retaining Pin
23	Bolt
24	Bolt Plunger with Spring
25	Mainspring Center Pin
26	Mainspring
27	Mainspring Bushing
28	Right Stock
29	Hammer
30	Trigger Spring Swivel
31	Trigger Spring
32	Trigger Spring Center Pin
33	Trigger
34	Hand
35	Sideplate
38	Sideplate Short Screw
37	Sideplate and Yoke Screw
38	Sideplate Long Screws

Model 86 Revolver

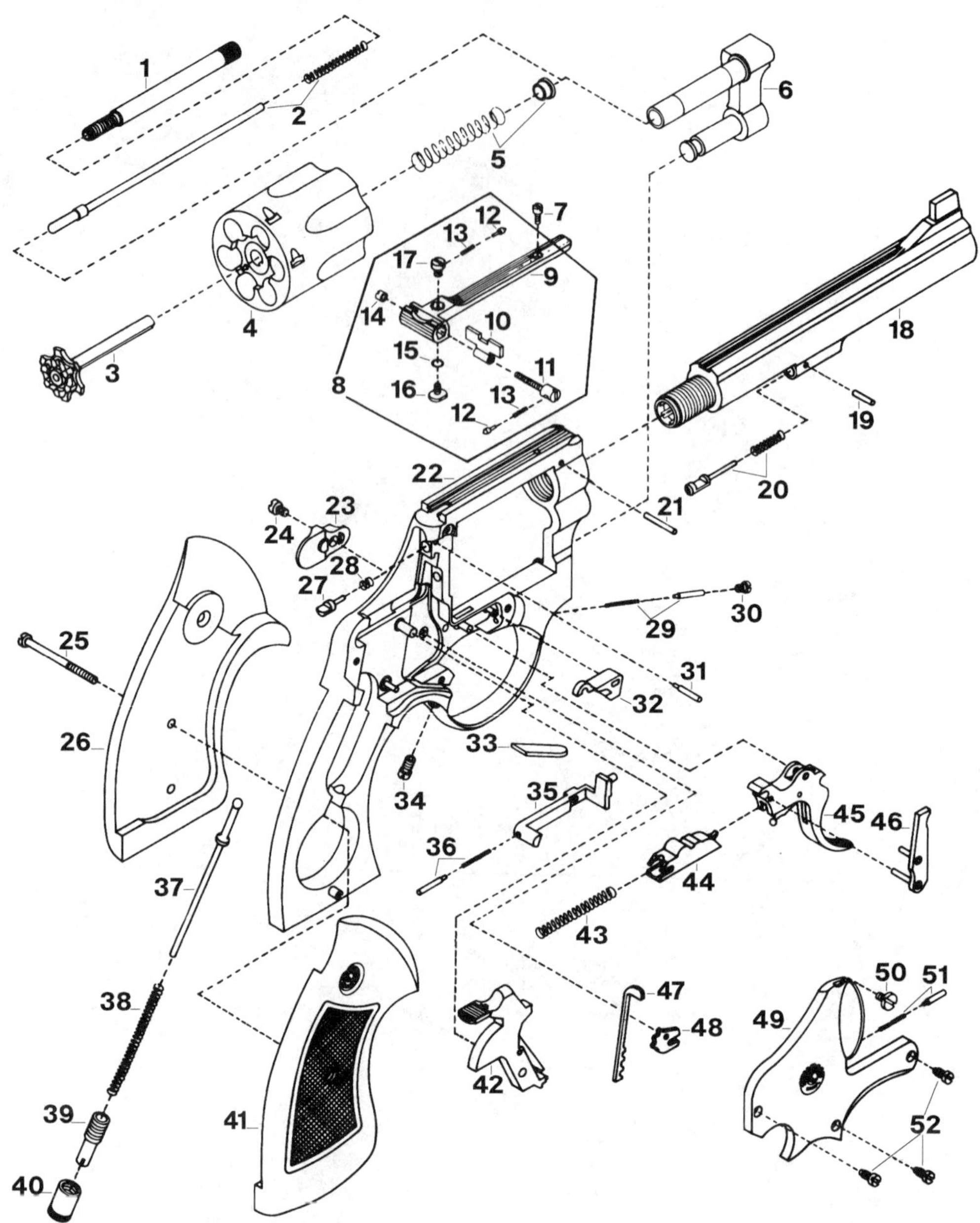

1	Extractor Rod	**19**	Locking Bolt Pin	**37**	Mainspring Center Pin
2	Center Pin with Spring	**20**	Locking Bolt with Spring	**38**	Mainspring
3	Extractor	**21**	Barrel Pin	**39**	Mainspring Adjustable Bushing
4	Cylinder	**22**	Frame	**40**	Mainspring Fixed Bushing
5	Extractor Spring with Rod Collar	**23**	Thumb-Piece	**41**	Right Stock
6	Yoke	**24**	Thumb-Piece Screw	**42**	Hammer
7	Rear Sight Screw	**25**	Stock Screw	**43**	Trigger Spring
8	Rear Sight Assembly	**26**	Left Stock	**44**	Rebound Slide
9	Rear Sight Leaf	**27**	Firing Pin	**45**	Trigger
10	Rear Sight Blade	**28**	Firing Pin Spring	**46**	Hand
11	Rear Sight Windage Screw	**29**	Cylinder Stop Plunger with Spring	**47**	Hammer Block
12	Click Pins	**30**	Cylinder Stop Screw	**48**	Gear
13	Click Pin Springs	**31**	Firing Pin Retaining Pin	**49**	Sideplate
14	Windage Nut	**32**	Cylinder Stop	**50**	Sideplate Short Screw
15	Safety Ring	**33**	Trigger Stop	**51**	Hand Pin with Spring
16	Rear Sight Elevation Screw	**34**	Trigger Stop Screw	**52**	Sideplate Long Screws
17	Elevation Nut	**35**	Bolt		
18	Barrel	**36**	Bolt Pin with Spring		

Model 87 Revolver

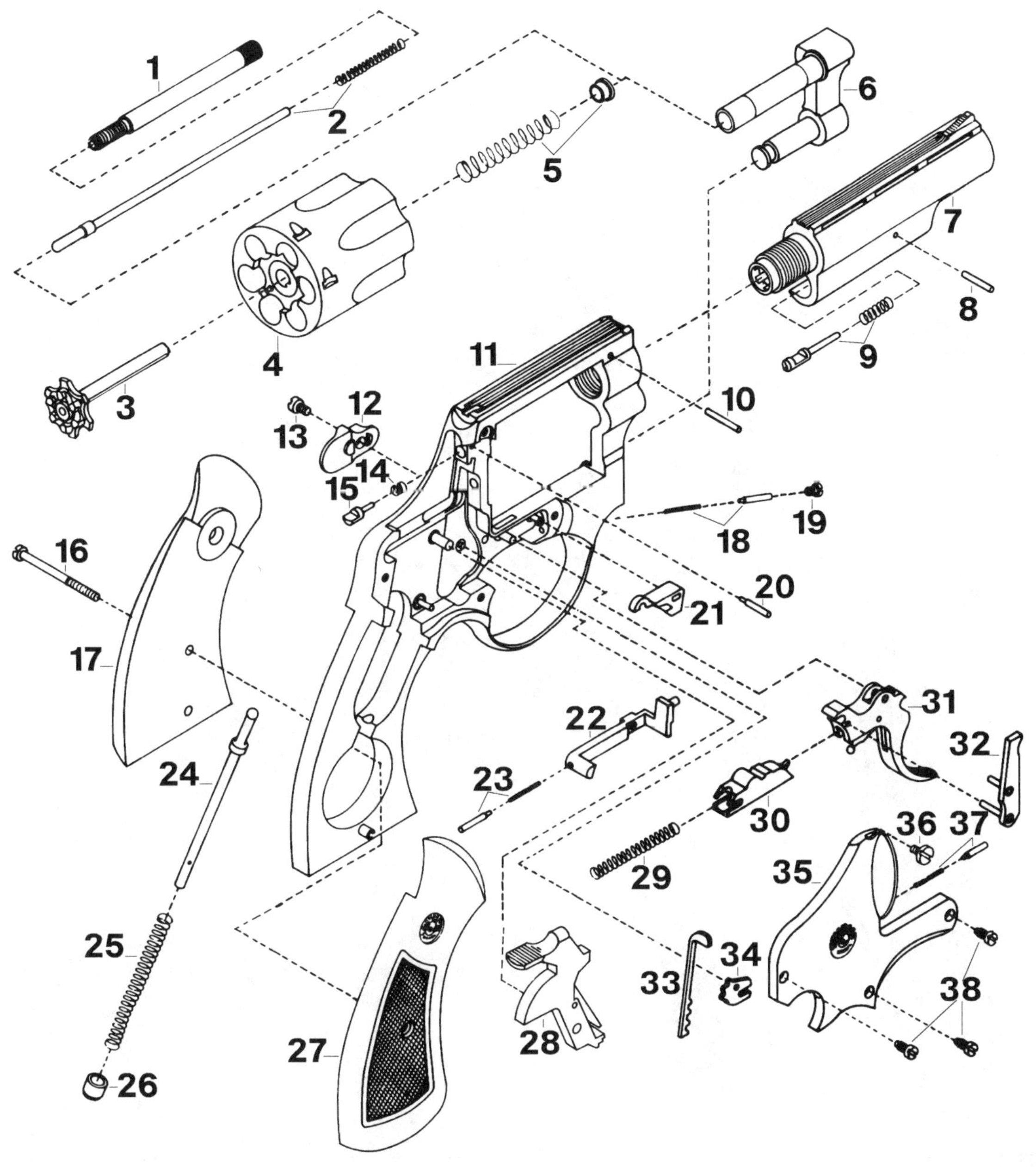

1	Extractor Rod	**14**	Firing Pin Spring	**27**	Right Stock
2	Center Pin with Spring	**15**	Firing Pin	**28**	Hammer
3	Extractor	**16**	Stock Screw	**29**	Trigger Spring
4	Cylinder	**17**	Left Stock	**30**	Rebound Slide
5	Extractor Spring with Rod Collar	**18**	Cylinder Stop Plunger with Spring	**31**	Trigger
6	Yoke	**19**	Cylinder Stop Screw	**32**	Hand
7	Barrel	**20**	Firing Pin Retaining Pin	**33**	Hammer Block
8	Locking Bolt Pin	**21**	Cylinder Stop	**34**	Gear
9	Locking Bolt with Spring	**22**	Bolt	**35**	Sideplate
10	Barrel Pin	**23**	Bolt Pin with Spring	**36**	Sideplate Short Screw
11	Frame	**24**	Mainspring Center Pin	**37**	Hand Pin with Spring
12	Thumb-Piece	**25**	Mainspring	**38**	Sideplate Long Screws
13	Thumb-Piece Screw	**26**	Mainspring Bushing		

Model 88 and 889 Revolver

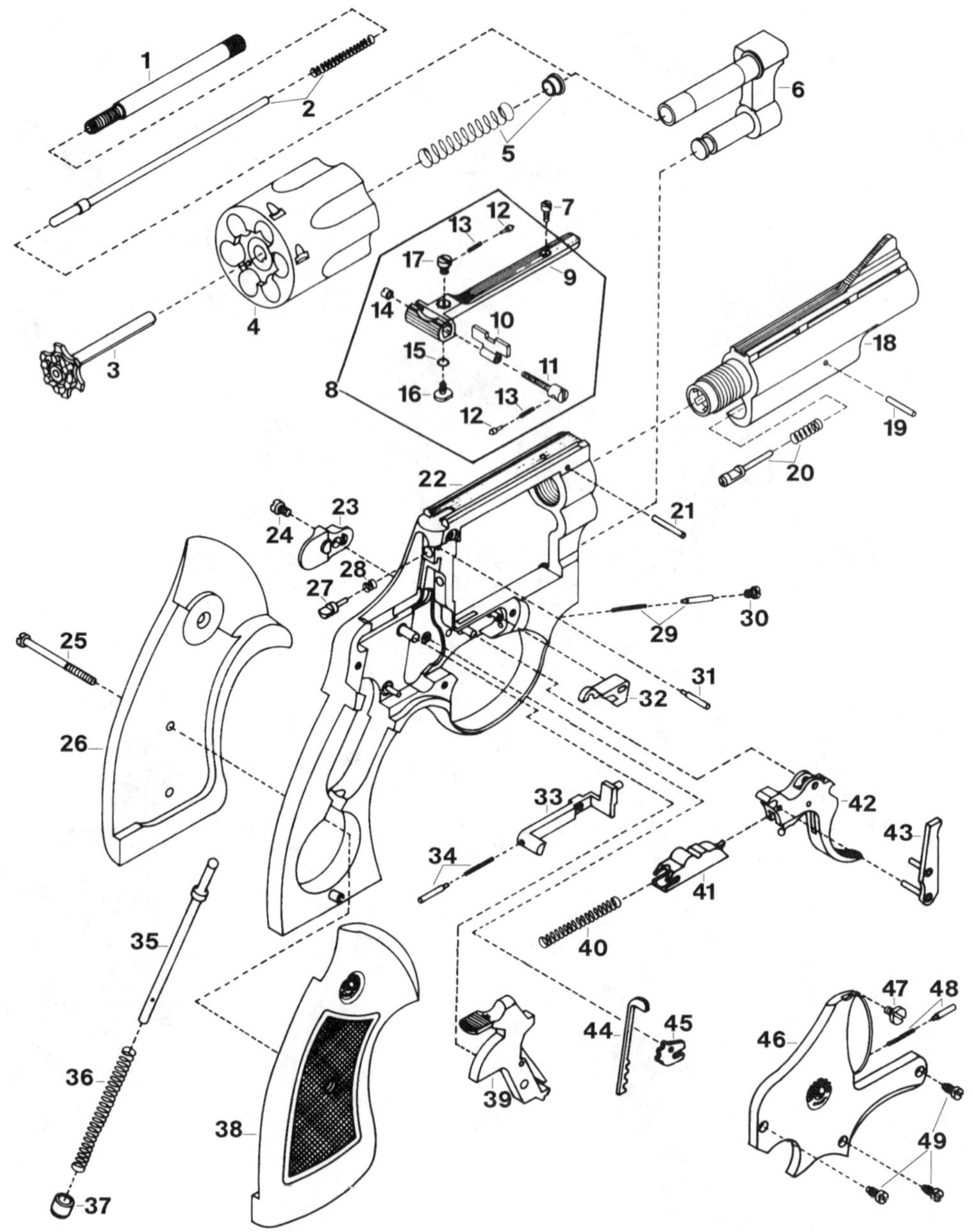

1	Extractor Rod	**18**	Barrel	**35**	Mainspring Center Pin
2	Center Pin with Spring	**19**	Locking Bolt Pin	**36**	Mainspring
3	Extractor	**20**	Locking Bolt With Spring	**37**	Mainspring Bushing
4	Cylinder	**21**	Barrel Pin	**38**	Right Stock
5	Extractor Spring with Rod Collar	**22**	Frame	**39**	Hammer
6	Yoke	**23**	Thumb-Piece	**40**	Trigger Spring
7	Rear Sight Screw	**24**	Thumb-Piece Screw	**41**	Rebound Slide
8	Rear Sight Assembly	**25**	Stock Screw	**42**	Trigger
9	Rear Sight Leaf	**26**	Left Stock	**43**	Hand
10	Rear Sight Blade	**27**	Firing Pin	**44**	Hammer Block
11	Rear Sight Windage Screw	**28**	Firing Pin Spring	**45**	Gear
12	Click Pins	**29**	Cylinder Stop Plunger with Spring	**46**	Sideplate
13	Click Pin Springs	**30**	Cylinder Stop Screw	**47**	Sideplate Short Screw
14	Windage Nut	**31**	Firing Pin Retaining Pin	**48**	Hand Pin with Spring
15	Safety Ring	**32**	Cylinder Stop	**49**	Sideplate Long Screws
16	Rear Sight Elevation Screw	**33**	Bolt		
17	Elevation Nut	**34**	Bolt Pin with Spring		

Model 90 Revolver

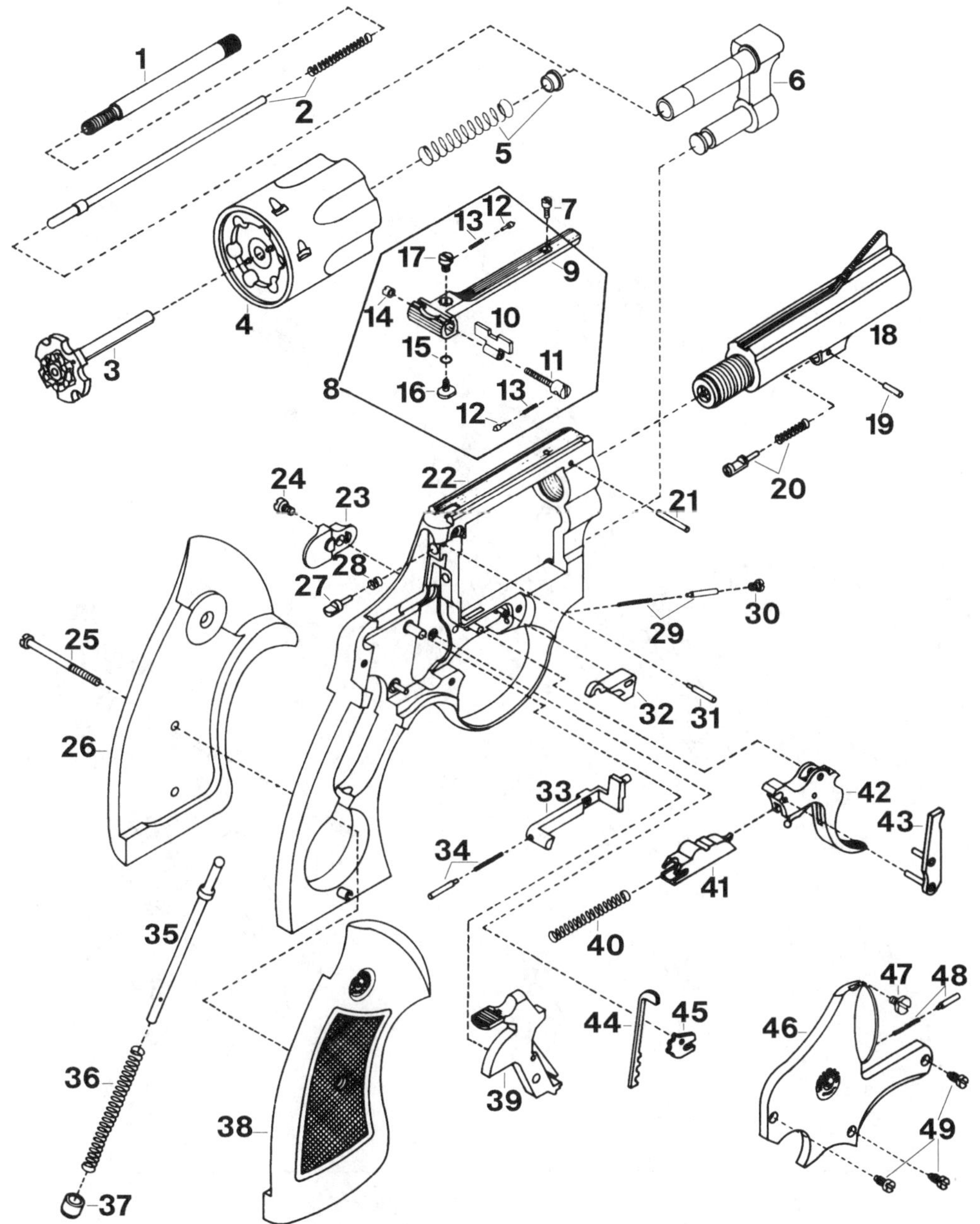

1	Extractor Rod	18	Barrel	35	Mainspring Center Pin
2	Center Pin with Spring	19	Locking Bolt Pin	36	Mainspring
3	Extractor	20	Locking Bolt with Spring	37	Mainspring Bushing
4	Cylinder	21	Barrel Pin	38	Right Stock
5	Extractor Spring with Rod Collar	22	Frame	39	Hammer
6	Yoke	23	Thumb-Piece	40	Trigger Spring
7	Rear Sight Screw	24	Thumb-Piece Screw	41	Rebound Slide
8	Rear Sight Assembly	25	Stock Screw	42	Trigger
9	Rear Sight Leaf	26	Left Stock	43	Hand
10	Rear Sight Blade	27	Firing Pin	44	Hammer Block
11	Rear Sight Windage Screw	28	Firing Pin Spring	45	Gear
12	Click Pins	29	Cylinder Stop Plunger with Spring	46	Sideplate
13	Click Pin Springs	30	Cylinder Stop Screw	47	Sideplate Short Screw
14	Windage Nut	31	Firing Pin Retaining Pin	48	Hand Pin with Spring
15	Safety Ring	32	Cylinder Stop	49	Sideplate Long Screws
16	Rear Sight Elevation Screw	33	Bolt		
17	Elevation Nut	34	Bolt Pin with Spring		

Model 93 Revolver

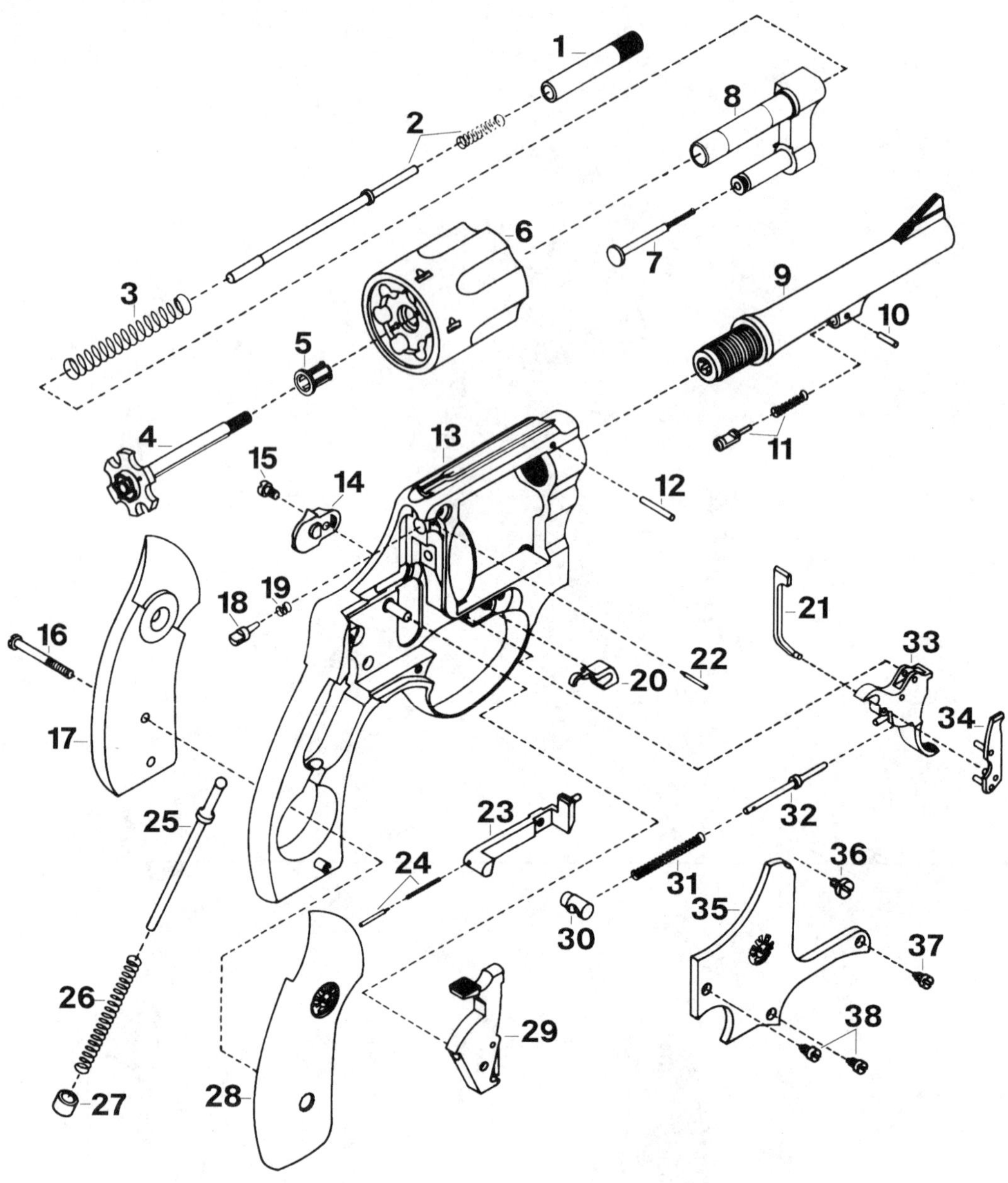

1	Extractor Rod	20	Cylinder Stop
2	Center Pin with Spring	21	Transfer Bar
3	Extractor Spring	22	Firing Pin Retaining Pin
4	Extractor	23	Bolt
5	Cylinder Retaining Bushing	24	Bolt Plunger with Spring
6	Cylinder	25	Mainspring Center Pin
7	Cylinder Stop Plunger With Spring	26	Mainspring
8	Yoke	27	Mainspring Bushing
9	Barrel	28	Right Stock
10	Locking Bolt Pin	29	Hammer
11	Locking Bolt with Spring	30	Trigger Spring Swivel
12	Barrel Pin	31	Trigger Spring
13	Frame	32	Trigger Spring Center Pin
14	Thumb-Piece	33	Trigger
15	Thumb-Piece Screw	34	Hand
16	Stock Screw	35	Sideplate
17	Left Stock	36	Sideplate Short Screw
18	Firing Pin	37	Sideplate and Yoke Screw
19	Firing Pin Spring	38	Sideplate Long Screws

Model 94 Revolver

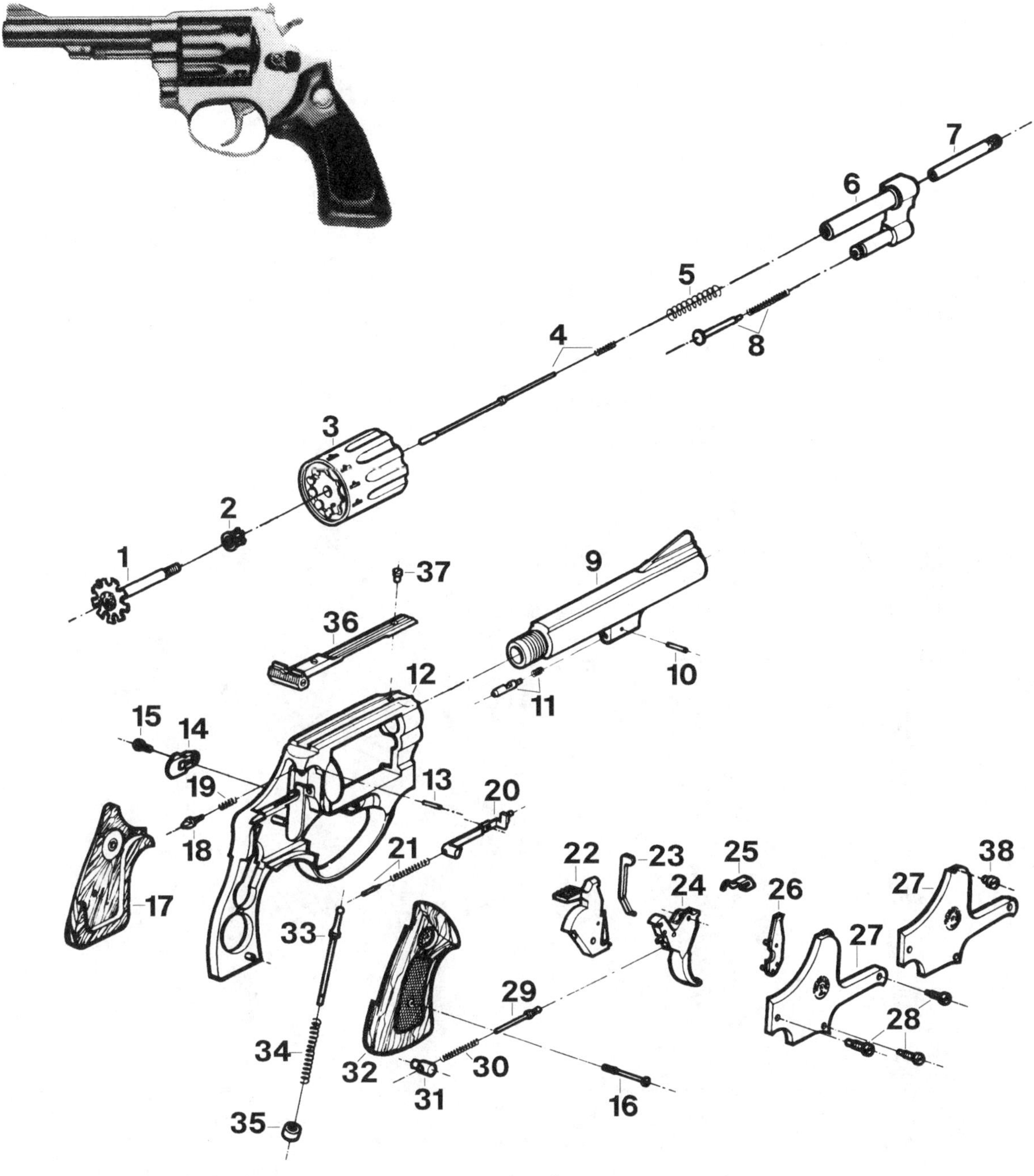

1	Extractor	14	Thumb-Piece	27	Sideplate
2	Cylinder Retaining Bushing	15	Thumb-Piece Screw	28	Sideplate Screws
3	Cylinder	16	Stock Screw	29	Trigger Spring Center Pin
4	Center Pin with Spring	17	Left Stock	30	Trigger Spring
5	Extractor Spring	18	Firing Pin	31	Trigger Spring Swivel
6	Yoke	19	Firing Pin Spring	32	Right Stock
7	Extractor Rod	20	Bolt	33	Mainspring Center Pin
8	Cylinder Stop Plunger with Spring	21	Bolt Plunger with Spring	34	Mainspring
9	Barrel	22	Hammer	35	Mainspring Bushing
10	Locking Bolt Pin	23	Transfer Bar	36	Rear Sight
11	Locking Bolt with Spring	24	Trigger	37	Rear Sight Screw
12	Frame	25	Cylinder Stop	38	Sideplate Short Screw
13	Firing Pin Retaining Pin	26	Hand		

Model 96 Revolver

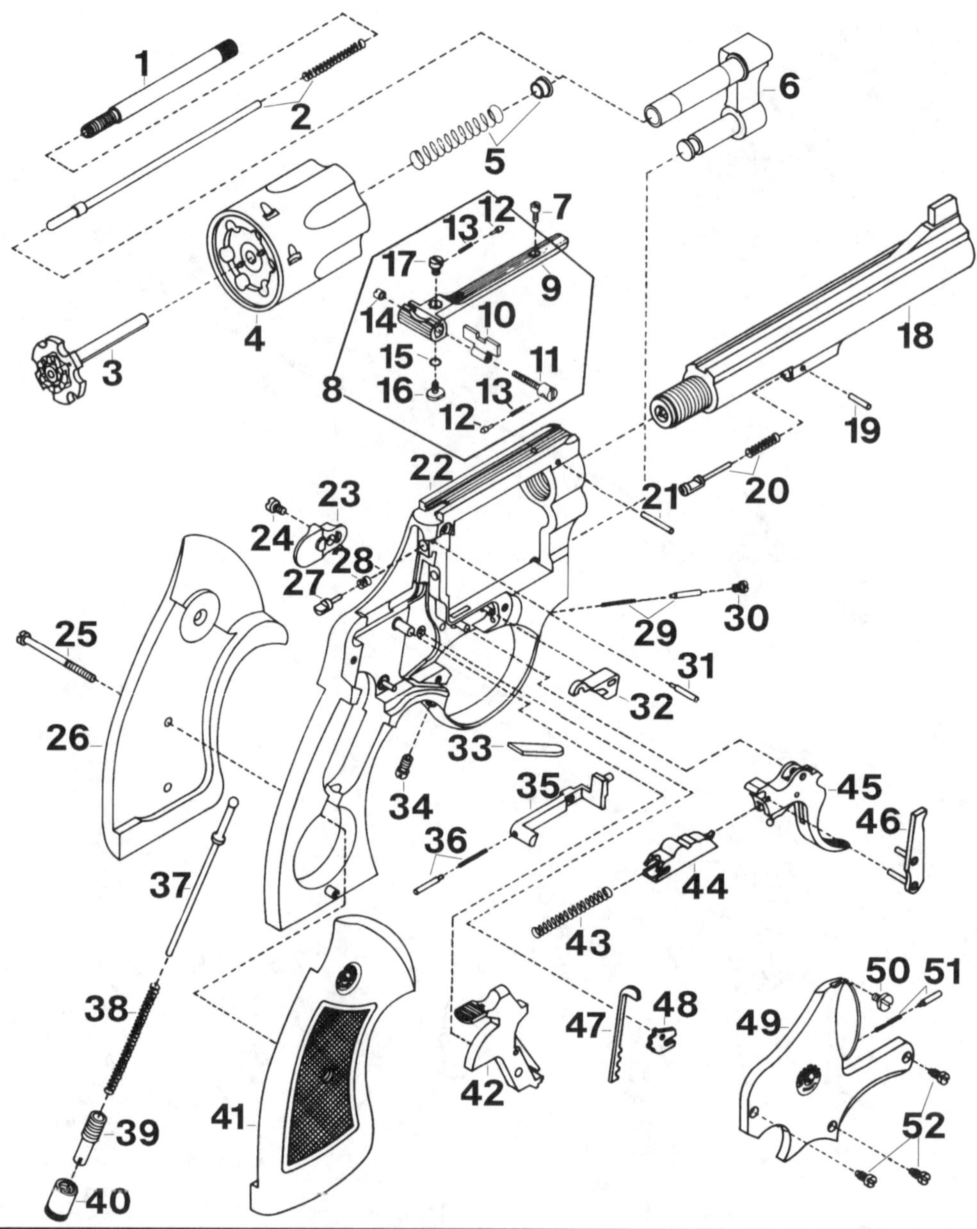

1	Extractor Rod	19	Locking Bolt Pin	37	Mainspring Center Pin
2	Center Pin with Spring	20	Locking Bolt with Spring	38	Mainspring
3	Extractor	21	Barrel Pin	39	Mainspring Adjustable Bushing
4	Cylinder	22	Frame	40	Mainspring Fixed Bushing
5	Extractor Spring with Rod Collar	23	Thumb-Piece	41	Right Stock
6	Yoke	24	Thumb-Piece Screw	42	Hammer
7	Rear Sight Screw	25	Stock Screw	43	Trigger Spring
8	Rear Sight Assembly	26	Left Stock	44	Rebound Slide
9	Rear Sight Leaf	27	Firing Pin	45	Trigger
10	Rear Sight Blade	28	Firing Pin Spring	46	Hand
11	Rear Sight Windage Screw	29	Cylinder Stop Plunger with Spring	47	Hammer Block
12	Click Pins	30	Cylinder Stop Screw	48	Gear
13	Click Pin Springs	31	Firing Pin Retaining Pin	49	Sideplate
14	Windage Nut	32	Cylinder Stop	50	Sideplate Short Screw
15	Safety Ring	33	Trigger Stop	51	Hand Pin with Spring
16	Rear Sight Elevation Screw	34	Trigger Stop Screw	52	Sideplate Long Screws
17	Elevation Nut	35	Bolt		
18	Barrel	36	Bolt Pin with Spring		

Model PT-22 Auto

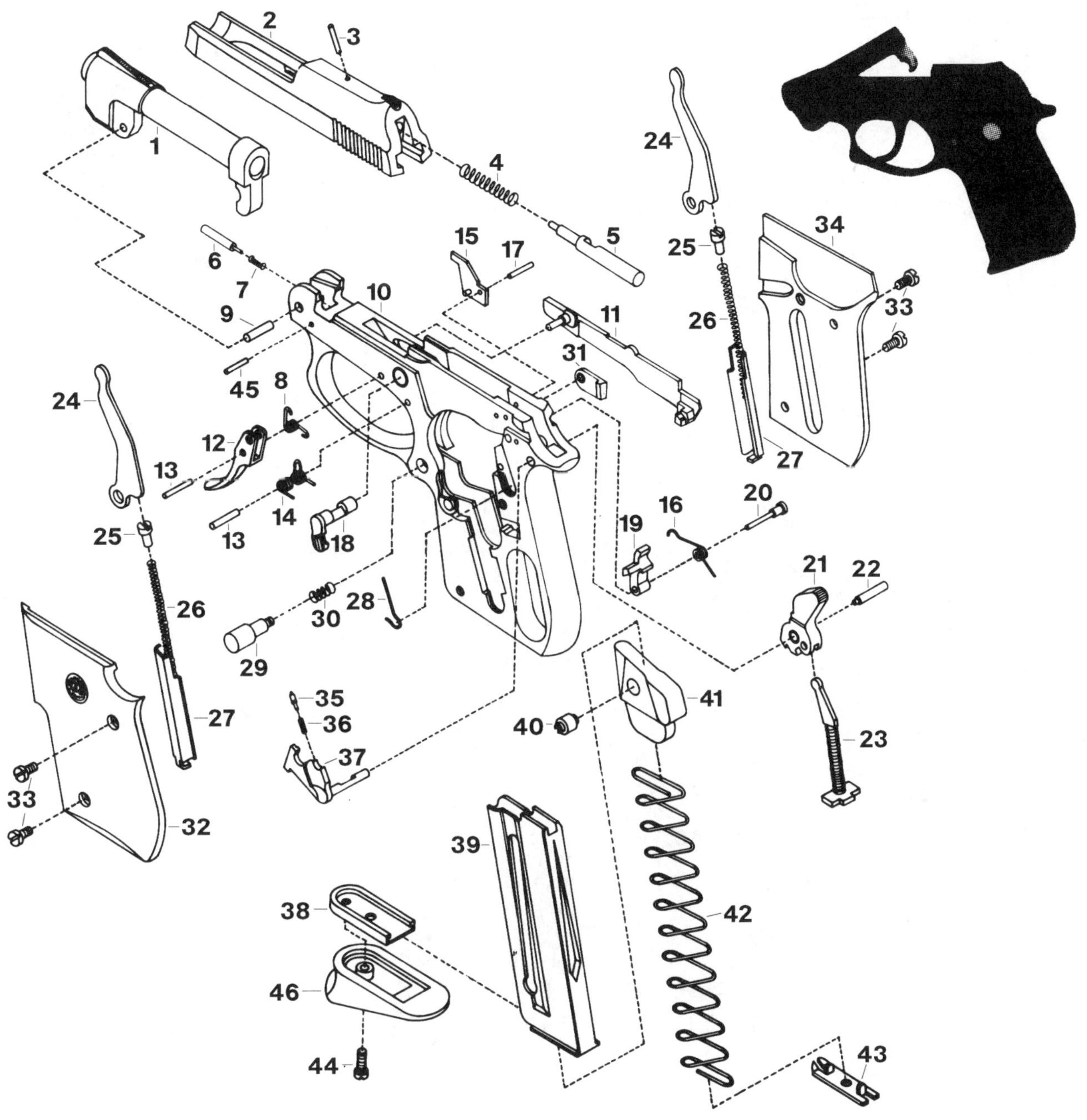

1	Barrel	**17**	Ejector Pin	**33**	Grip Screws
2	Slide	**18**	Barrel Release	**34**	Right Grip
3	Firing Pin Elastic Pin	**19**	Sear	**35**	Safety Spring Pin
4	Firing Pin Spring	**20**	Sear Pin	**36**	Safety Spring
5	Firing Pin	**21**	Hammer	**37**	Safety
6	Barrel Spring Pin	**22**	Hammer Pin	**38**	Magazine Bottom
7	Barrel Spring	**23**	Hammer Spring Assembly	**39**	Magazine
8	Trigger Spring	**24**	Slide Lever	**40**	Magazine Follower Bushing
9	Barrel Stud	**25**	Slide Spring Pin	**41**	Magazine Follower
10	Frame	**26**	Slide Spring	**42**	Magazine Spring
11	Trigger Bar	**27**	Slide Spring Case	**43**	Magazine Bottom Plate
12	Trigger	**28**	Sear Spring	**44**	Magazine Lengthening Screw
13	Pin	**29**	Magazine Release Button	**45**	Pin
14	Barrel Release Spring	**30**	Magazine Release Spring	**46**	Magazine Lengthening
15	Ejector	**31**	Magazine Release		
16	Trigger Bar Spring	**32**	Left Grip		

Model PT-25 Auto

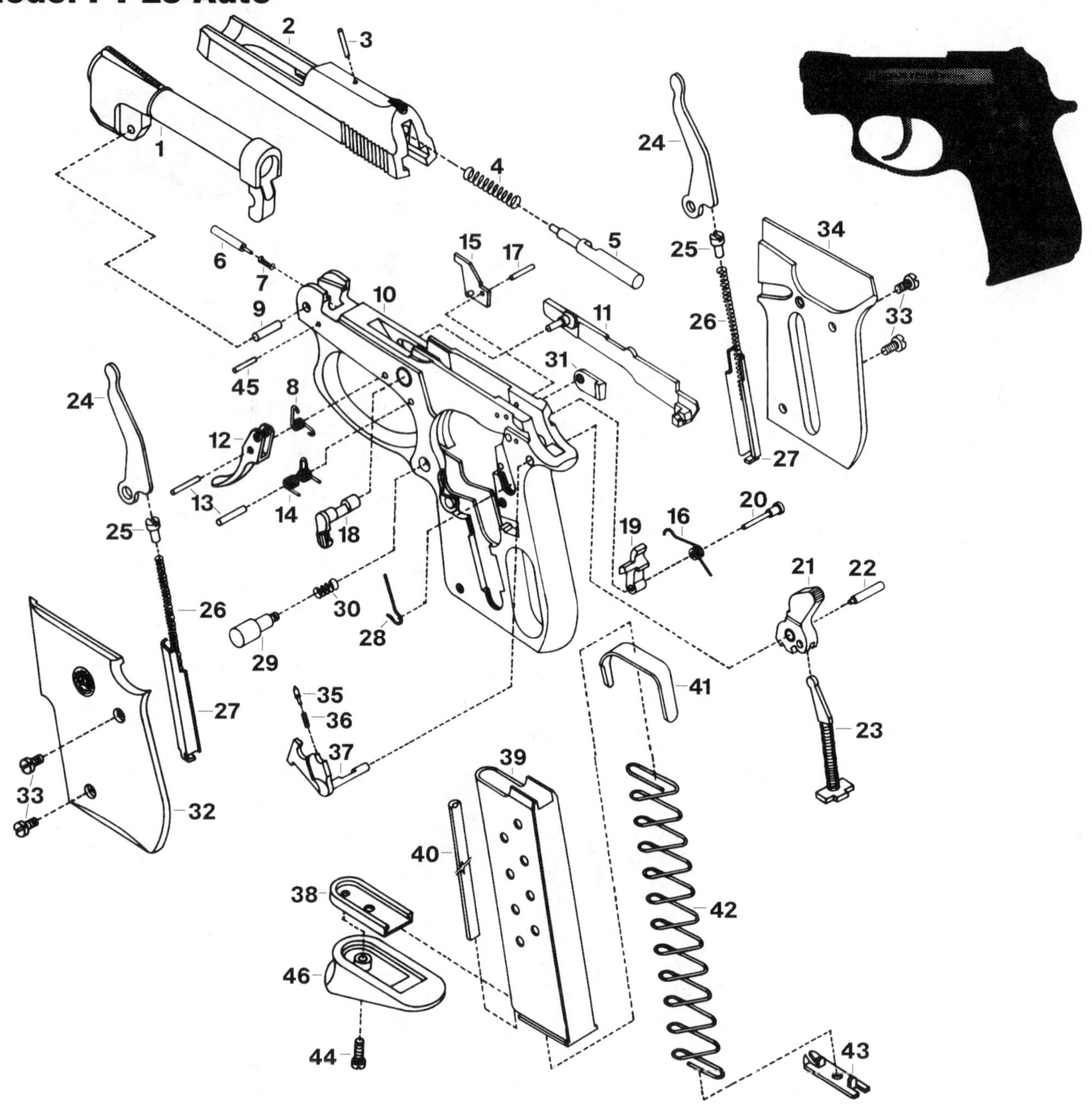

1	Barrel	**17**	Ejector Pin	**33**	Grip Screws
2	Slide	**18**	Barrel Release	**34**	Right Grip
3	Firing Pin Elastic Pin	**19**	Sear	**35**	Safety Spring Pin
4	Firing Pin Spring	**20**	Sear Pin	**36**	Safety Spring
5	Firing Pin	**21**	Hammer	**37**	Safety
6	Barrel Spring Pin	**22**	Hammer Pin	**38**	Magazine Bottom
7	Barrel Spring	**23**	Hammer Spring Assembly	**39**	Magazine
8	Trigger Spring	**24**	Slide Lever	**40**	Magazine Reducer
9	Barrel Stud	**25**	Slide Spring Pin	**41**	Magazine Follower
10	Frame	**26**	Slide Spring	**42**	Magazine Spring
11	Trigger Bar	**27**	Slide Spring Case	**43**	Magazine Bottom Plate
12	Trigger	**28**	Sear Spring	**44**	Magazine Lengthening Screw
13	Trigger Pins	**29**	Magazine Release Button	**45**	Pin
14	Barrel Release Spring	**30**	Magazine Release Spring	**46**	Magazine Lengthening
15	Ejector	**31**	Magazine Release		
16	Trigger Bar Spring	**32**	Left Grip		

Model PT-51 Auto

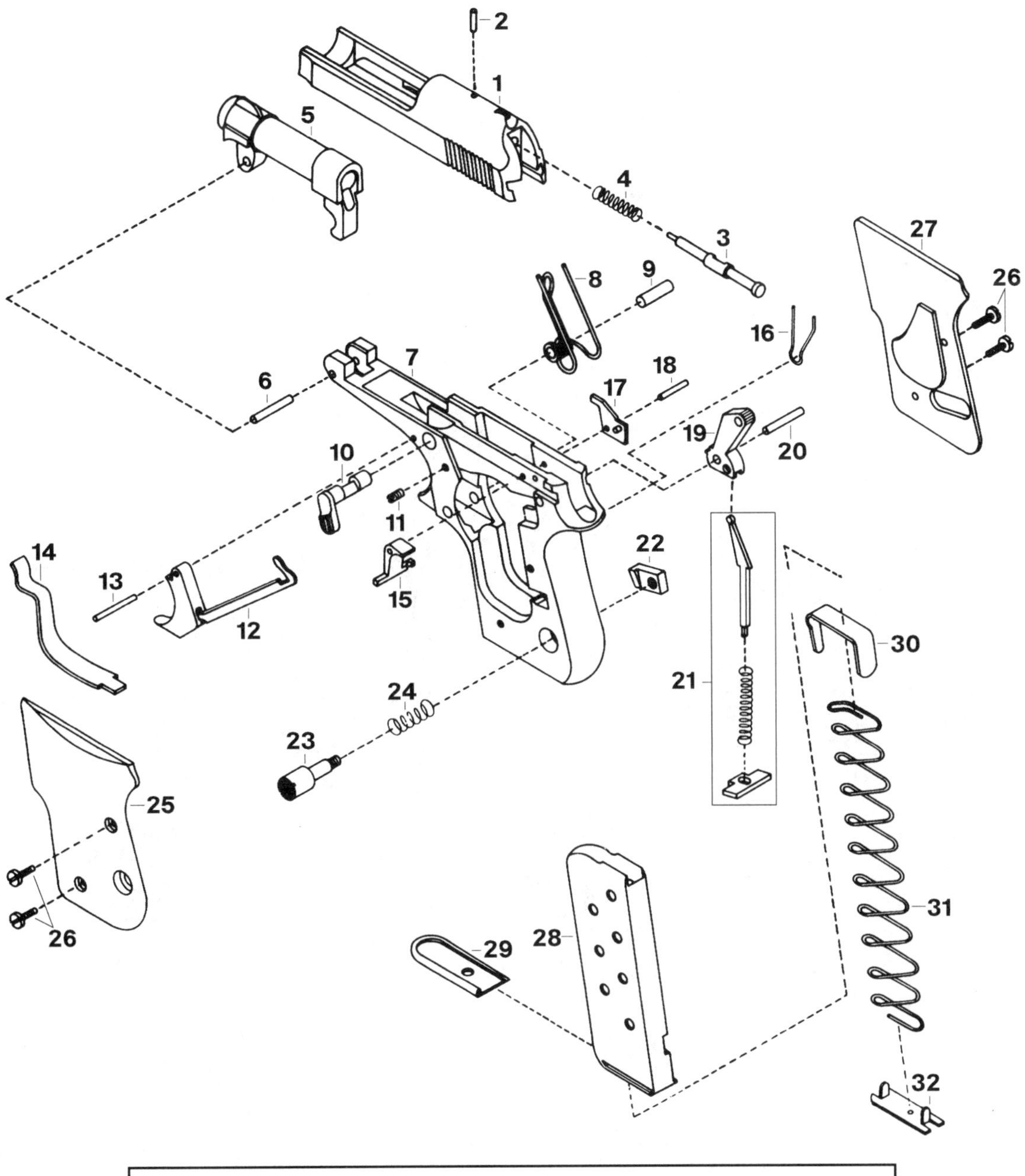

1	Slide	17	Ejector
2	Firing Pin Retaining Pin	18	Ejector Pin and Sear Pin
3	Firing Pin	19	Hammer
4	Firing Pin Spring	20	Hammer Pin
5	Barrel	21	Hammer Spring Assembly
6	Barrel Pin	22	Magazine Release
7	Frame	23	Magazine Release Button
8	Recoil Spring	24	Magazine Release Spring
9	Recoil Spring Pin	25	Left Grip
10	Barrel Release	26	Grip Screws
11	Barrel Release Screw	27	Right Grip
12	Trigger	28	Magazine
13	Trigger Pin	29	Magazine Bottom
14	Trigger Guard	30	Magazine Follower
15	Sear	31	Magazine Spring
16	Sear Spring	32	Magazine Spring Plate

Model PT-53 Auto

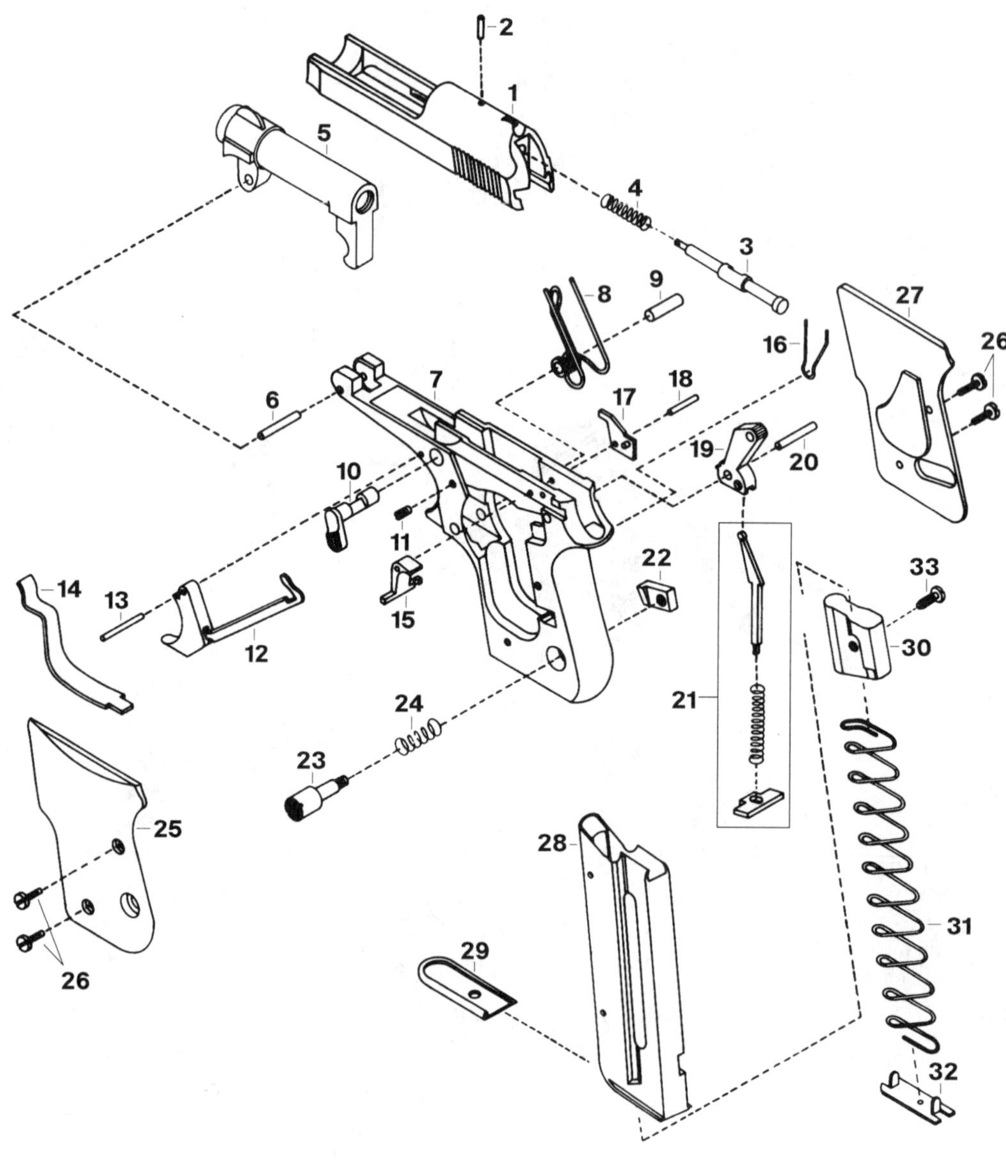

1	Slide	**18**	Ejector Pin and Sear Pin
2	Firing Pin Retaining Pin	**19**	Hammer
3	Firing Pin	**20**	Hammer Pin
4	Firing Pin Spring	**21**	Hammer Spring Assembly
5	Barrel	**22**	Magazine Release
6	Barrel Pin	**23**	Magazine Release Button
7	Frame	**24**	Magazine Release Spring
8	Recoil Spring	**25**	Left Grip
9	Recoil Spring Pin	**26**	Grip Screws
10	Barrel Release	**27**	Right Grip
11	Barrel Release Screw	**28**	Magazine
12	Trigger	**29**	Magazine Bottom
13	Trigger Pin	**30**	Magazine Follower
14	Trigger Guard	**31**	Magazine Spring
15	Sear	**32**	Magazine Spring Plate
16	Sear Spring	**33**	Magazine Follower Screw
17	Ejector		

Model PT-55 Auto

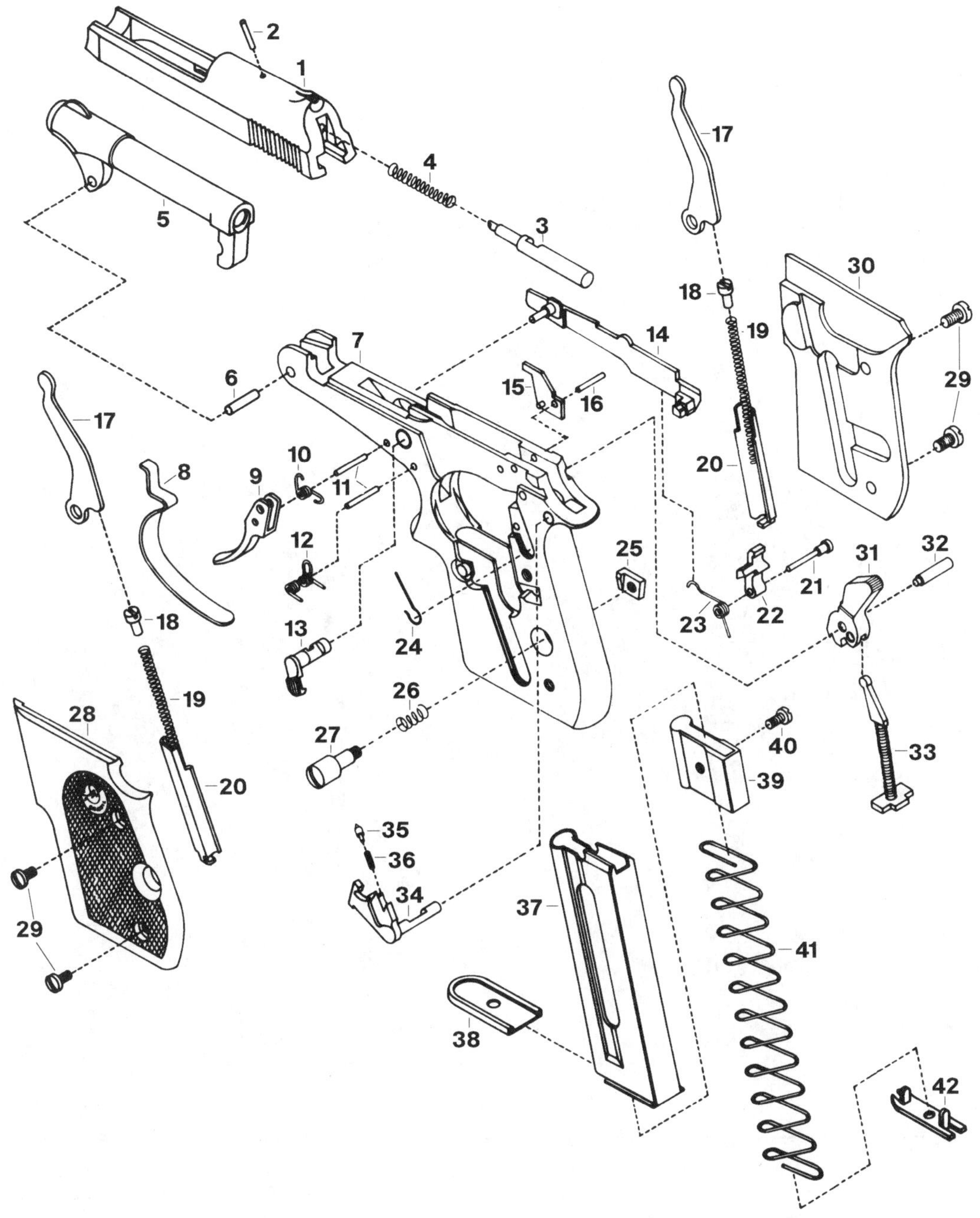

1	Slide	**15**	Ejector	**29**	Grip Screws
2	Firing Pin Retaining Pin	**16**	Ejector Pin	**30**	Right Grip
3	Firing Pin	**17**	Slide Lever	**31**	Hammer
4	Firing Pin Spring	**18**	Slide Spring Pin	**32**	Hammer Pin
5	Barrel	**19**	Slide Spring	**33**	Hammer Spring Assembly
6	Barrel Pin	**20**	Slide Spring Case	**34**	Safety
7	Frame	**21**	Sear Pin	**35**	Safety Spring Pin
8	Trigger Guard	**22**	Sear	**36**	Safety Spring
9	Trigger	**23**	Trigger Bar Spring	**37**	Magazine
10	Trigger Spring	**24**	Sear Spring	**38**	Magazine Bottom
11	Trigger Pins	**25**	Magazine Release	**39**	Magazine Follower
12	Barrel Release Spring	**26**	Magazine Release Spring	**40**	Magazine Follower Screw
13	Barrel Release	**27**	Magazine Release Button	**41**	Magazine Spring
14	Trigger Bar	**28**	Left Grip	**42**	Magazine Spring Plate

Model PT-57 S Auto

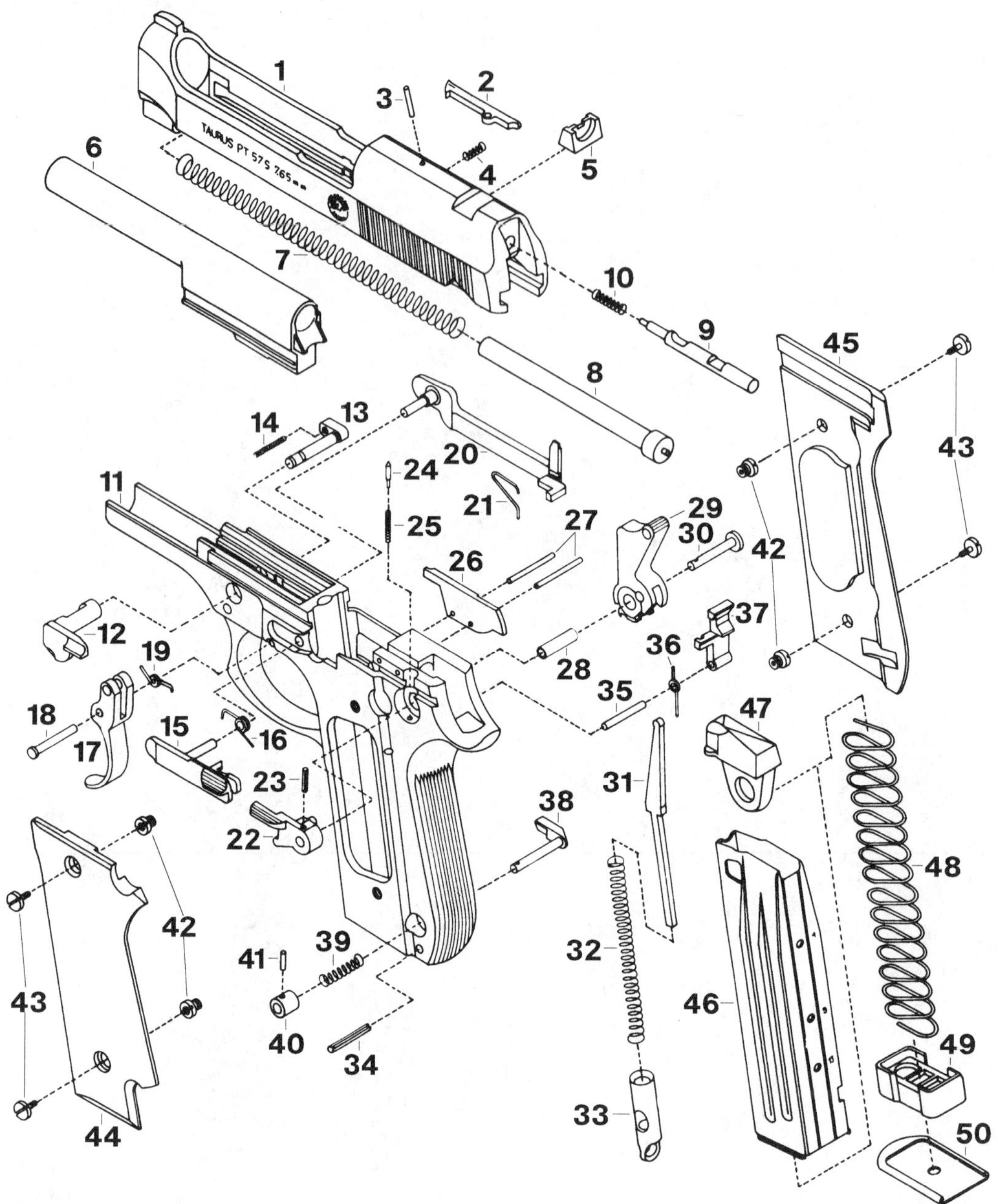

1	Slide	17	Trigger	34	Hammer Strut Guide Pin
2	Extractor	18	Trigger Pin	35	Sear Pin
3	Extractor Pin	19	Trigger Spring	36	Sear Spring
4	Extractor Spring	20	Trigger Bar	37	Sear
5	Rear Sight	21	Trigger Bar Spring	38	Magazine Release Button
6	Barrel	22	Safety	39	Magazine Release Button Spring
7	Recoil Spring	23	Safety Elastic Pin	40	Magazine Release Button Bushing
8	Recoil Spring Guide	24	Safety Spring Pin	41	Magazine Release Button Pin
9	Firing Pin	25	Safety Spring	42	Grip Bushings
10	Firing Pin Spring	26	Ejector	43	Grip Screws
11	Frame	27	Ejector Pins	44	Left Grip
12	Disassembling Latch	28	Hammer Bushing	45	Right Grip
13	Disassembling Latch Release	29	Hammer	46	Magazine Box
14	Disassembling Latch Release<R>Spring	30	Safety Pin	47	Magazine Follower
		31	Hammer Spring Strut	48	Magazine Spring
15	Slide Catch	32	Hammer Spring	49	Magazine Plate
16	Slide Catch Spring	33	Hammer Strut Guide	50	Magazine Bottom

Model PT-57 TA Auto

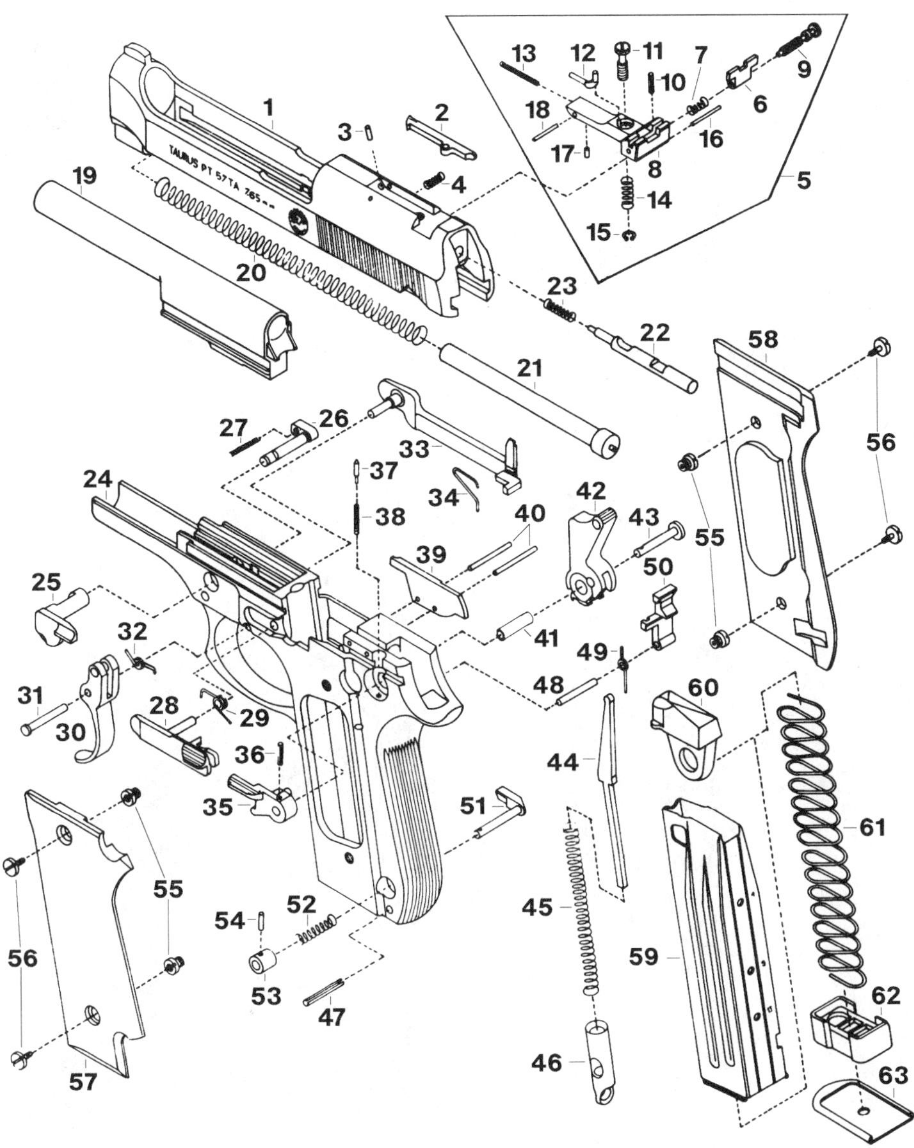

1	Slide	**22**	Firing Pin	**43**	Safety Pin
2	Extractor	**23**	Firing Pin Spring	**44**	Hammer Spring Strut
3	Extractor Pin	**24**	Frame	**45**	Hammer Spring
4	Extractor Spring	**25**	Disassembling Latch	**46**	Hammer Strut Guide
5	Rear Sight Complete	**26**	Disassembling Latch Release	**47**	Hammer Strut Guide Pin
6	Rear Sight Blade	**27**	Disassembling Latch Release Spring	**48**	Sear Pin
7	Rear Sight Spring	**28**	Slide Catch	**49**	Sear Spring
8	Rear Sight Leaf	**29**	Slide Catch Spring	**50**	Sear
9	Rear Sight Windage Screw	**30**	Trigger	**51**	Magazine Release Button
10	Rear Sight Windage Screw Pin	**31**	Trigger Pin	**52**	Magazine Release Button Spring
11	Rear Sight Elevation Screw	**32**	Trigger Spring	**53**	Magazine Release Button Bushing
12	Rear Sight Elevation Pin	**33**	Trigger Bar	**54**	Magazine Release Button Pin
13	Rear Sight Elevation Pin Spring	**34**	Trigger Bar Spring	**55**	Grip Bushings
14	Rear Sight Leaf Elevation Spring	**35**	Safety	**56**	Grip Screws
15	Rear Sight Ring	**36**	Safety Elastic Pin	**57**	Left Grip
16	Rear Sight Windage Pin	**37**	Safety Spring Pin	**58**	Right Grip
17	Rear Sight Spring Limiting Pin	**38**	Safety Spring	**59**	Magazine Box
18	Rear Sight Pin	**39**	Ejector	**60**	Magazine Follower
19	Barrel	**40**	Ejector Pins	**61**	Magazine Spring
20	Recoil Spring	**41**	Hammer Bushing	**62**	Magazine Plate
21	Recoil Spring Guide	**42**	Hammer	**63**	Magazine Bottom

Model PT-92 Auto

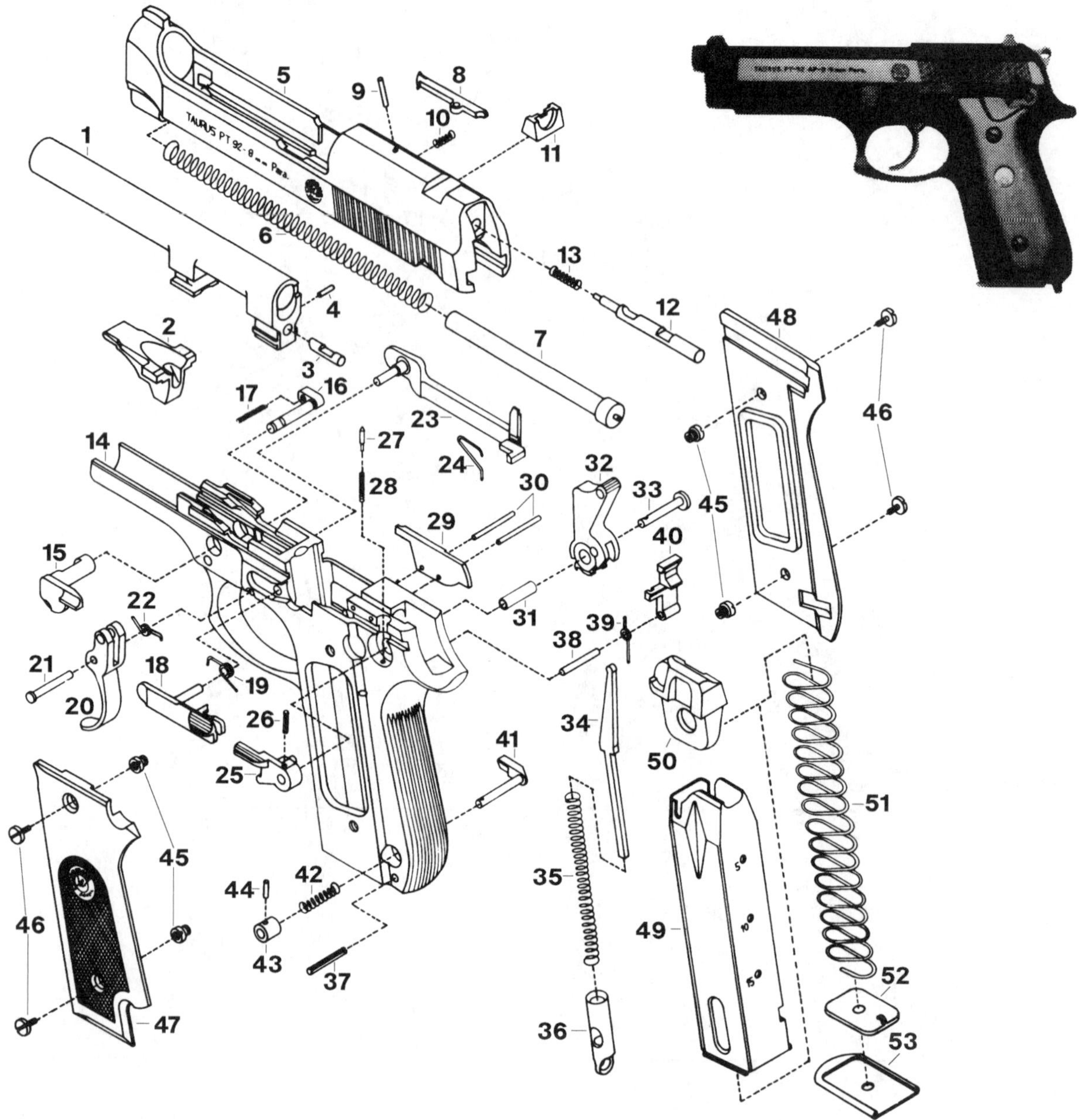

1	Barrel	19	Slide Catch Spring	37	Hammer Strut Guide Pin
2	Locking Block	20	Trigger	38	Sear Pin
3	Locking Block Plunger	21	Trigger Pin	39	Sear Spring
4	Locking Block Plunger Pin	22	Trigger Spring	40	Sear
5	Slide	23	Trigger Bar	41	Magazine Release Button
6	Recoil Spring	24	Trigger Bar Spring	42	Magazine Release Button Spring
7	Recoil Spring Guide	25	Safety	43	Magazine Release Button Bushing
8	Extractor	26	Safety Elastic Pin	44	Magazine Release Button Pin
9	Extractor Pin	27	Safety Spring Pin	45	Grip Bushings
10	Extractor Spring	28	Safety Spring	46	Grip Screws
11	Rear Sight	29	Ejector	47	Left Grip
12	Firing Pin	30	Ejector Pins	48	Right Grip
13	Firing Pin Spring	31	Hammer Bushing	49	Magazine Box
14	Frame	32	Hammer	50	Magazine Follower
15	Diasasembling Latch	33	Safety Pin	51	Magazine Spring
16	Disassembling Latch Release	34	Hammer Spring Strut	52	Magazine Plate
17	Latch Release Spring	35	Hammer Spring	53	Magazine Bottom
18	Slide Catch	36	Hammer Strut Guide		

Model PT-92 AF Auto

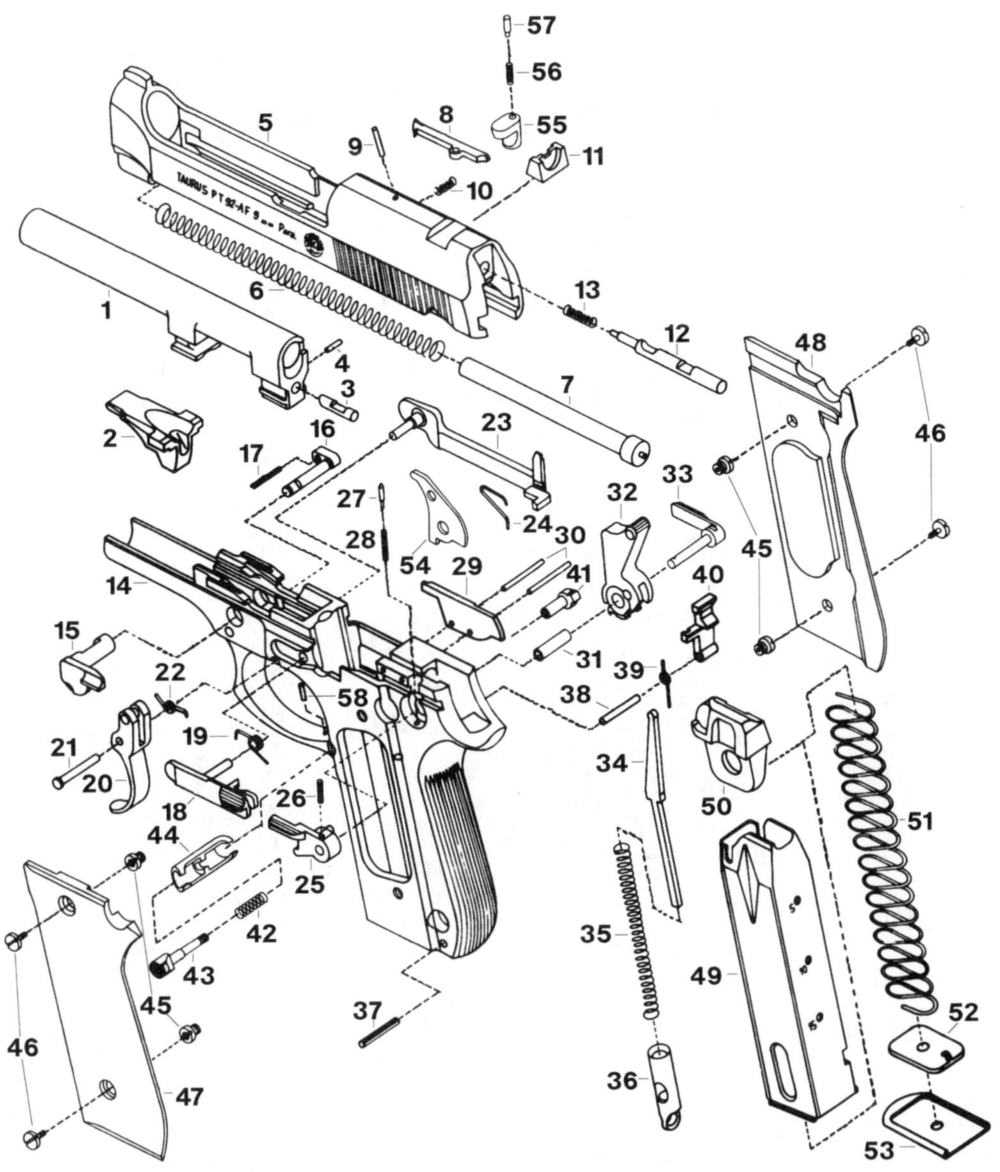

1	Barrel	21	Trigger Pin	41	Magazine Release
2	Locking Block	22	Trigger Spring	42	Magazine Release Spring
3	Locking Block Plunger	23	Trigger Bar	43	Magazine Release Button
4	Locking Block Plunger Pin	24	Trigger Bar Spring	44	Magazine Release Case
5	Slide	25	Safety	45	Grip Bushings
6	Recoil Spring	26	Safety Elastic Pin	46	Grip Screws
7	Recoil Spring Guide	27	Safety Spring Pin	47	Left Grip
8	Extractor	28	Safety Spring	48	Right Grip
9	Extractor Pin	29	Ejector	49	Magazine Box
10	Extractor Spring	30	Ejector Pins	50	Magazine Follower
11	Rear Sight	31	Hammer Bushing	51	Magazine Spring
12	Firing Pin	32	Hammer	52	Magazine Plate
13	Firing Pin Spring	33	Safety	53	Magazine Bottom
14	Frame	34	Hammer Spring Strut	54	Firing Pin Block Lever
15	Disassembling Latch	35	Hammer Spring	55	Firing Pin Block
16	Disassembling Latch Release	36	Hammer Strut Guide	56	Firing Pin Block Spring
17	Disassembling Latch Release Spring	37	Hammer Strut Guide Pin	57	Firing Pin Block Pin
18	Slide Catch	38	Sear Pin	58	Magazine Release Case Pin
19	Slide Catch Spring	39	Sear Spring		
20	Trigger	40	Sear		

Model PT-99 Auto

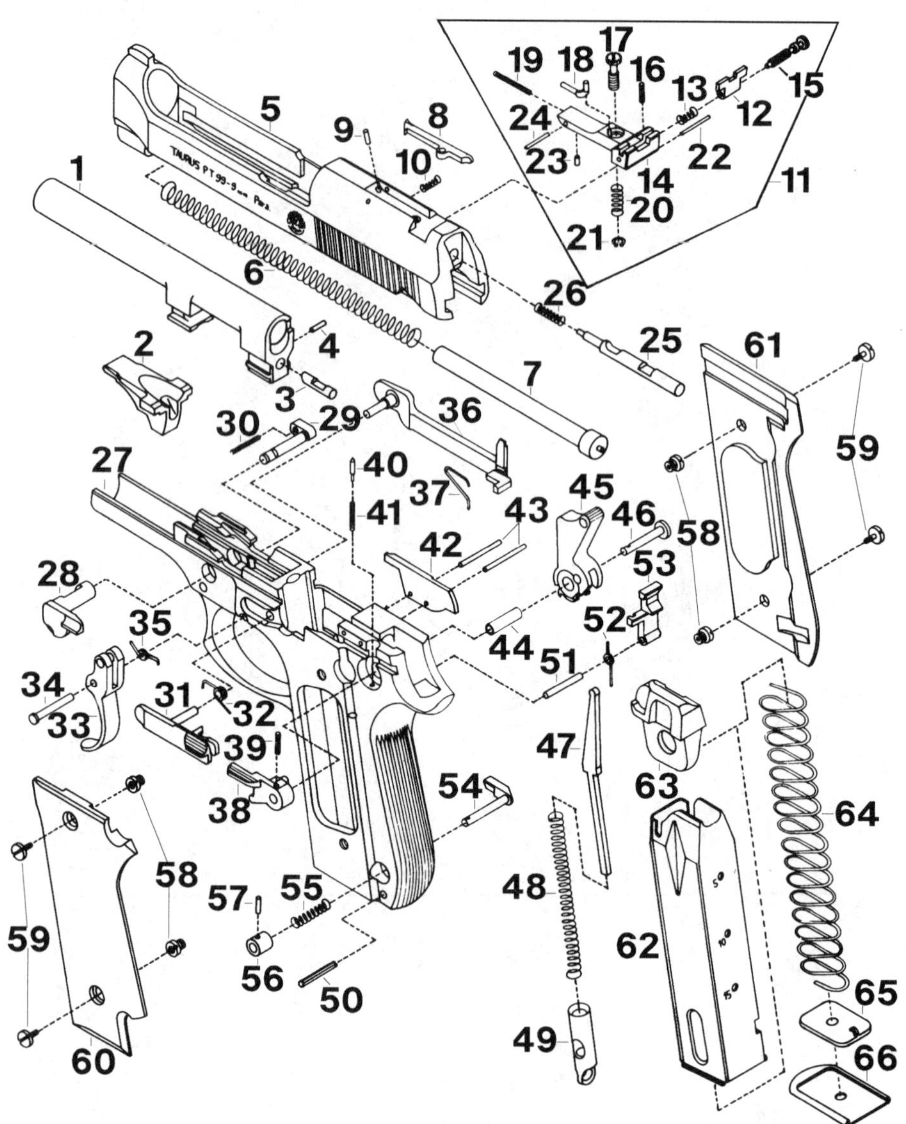

1	Barrel	23	Rear Sight Spring Limiting Pin	45	Hammer
2	Locking Block	24	Rear Sight Pin	46	Safety Pin
3	Locking Block Plunger	25	Firing Pin	47	Hammer Spring Strut
4	Locking Block Plunger Pin	26	Firing Pin Spring	48	Hammer Spring
5	Slide	27	Frame	49	Hammer Strut Guide
6	Recoil Spring	28	Disassembling Latch	50	Hammer Strut Guide Pin
7	Recoil Spring Guide	29	Disassembling Latch Release	51	Sear Pin
8	Extractor	30	DIsassembling Latch Release Spring	52	Sear Spring
9	Extractor Pin	31	Slide Catch	53	Sear
10	Extractor Spring	32	Slide Catch Spring	54	Magazine Release Button
11	Rear Sight Assembly	33	Trigger	55	Magazine Release Button Spring
12	Rear Sight Blade	34	Trigger Pin	56	Magazine Release Button Bushing
13	Rear Sight Spring	35	Trigger Spring	57	Magazine Release Button Pin
14	Rear Sight Leaf	36	Trigger Bar	58	Grip Bushings
15	Rear Sight Windage Screw	37	Trigger Bar Spring	59	Grip Screws
16	Rear Sight Windage Screw Pin	38	Safety	60	Left Grip
17	Rear Sight Elevation Screw	39	Safety Elastic Pin	61	Right Grip
18	Rear Sight Elevation Pin	40	Safety Spring Pin	62	Magazine Box
19	Rear Sight Elevation Pin Spring	41	Safety Spring	63	Magazine Follower
20	Rear Sight Leaf Elevation Spring	42	Ejector	64	Magazine Spring
21	Rear Sight Ring	43	Ejector Pins	65	Magazine Plate
22	Sight Windage Pin	44	Hammer Bushing	66	Magazine Bottom

Model PT-99 AF Auto

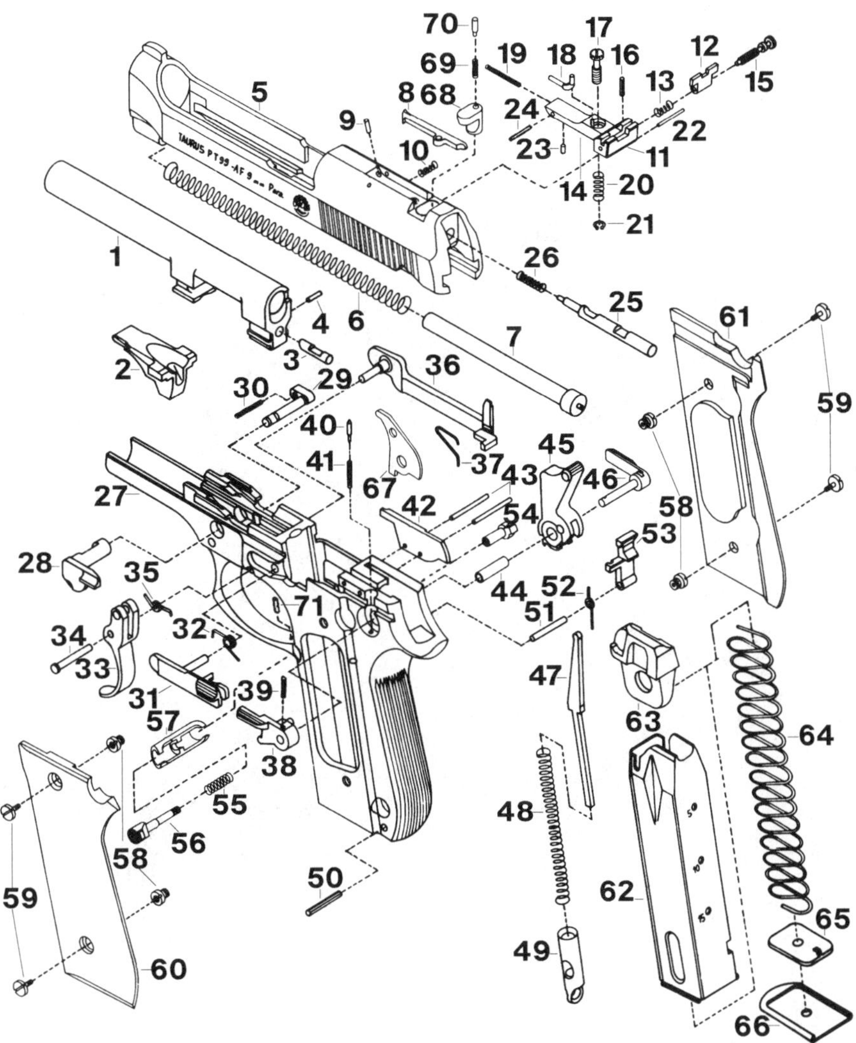

No.	Part	No.	Part	No.	Part
1	Barrel	25	Firing Pin	48	Hammer Spring
2	Locking Block	26	Firing Pin Spring	49	Hammer Strut Guide
3	Locking Block Plunger	27	Frame	50	Hammer Strut Guide Pin
4	Locking Block Plunger Pin	28	Disassembling Latch	51	Sear Pin
5	Slide	29	Disassembling Latch Release	52	Sear Spring
6	Recoil Spring	30	Disassembling Latch Release Spring	53	Sear
7	Recoil Spring Guide	31	Slide Catch	54	Magazine Release
8	Extractor	32	Slide Catch Spring	55	Magazine Release Spring
9	Extractor Pin	33	Trigger	56	Magazine Release Button
10	Extractor Spring	34	Trigger Pin	57	Magazine Release Case
11	Rear Sight Complete	35	Trigger Spring	58	Grip Bushings
12	Rear Sight Blade	36	Trigger Bar	59	Grip Screws
13	Rear Sight Spring	37	Trigger Bar Spring	60	Left Grip
14	Rear Sight Leaf	38	Safety	61	Right Grip
15	Rear Sight Windage Screw	39	Safety Elastic Pin	62	Magazine Box
16	Rear Sight Windage Screw Pin	40	Safety Spring Pin	63	Magazine Follower
17	Rear Sight Elevation Screw	41	Safety Spring	64	Magazine Spring
18	Rear Sight Elevation Pin	42	Ejector	65	Magazine Plate
19	Rear Sight Elevation Pin Spring	43	Ejector Pins	66	Magazine Bottom
20	Rear Sight Leaf Elevation Spring	44	Hammer Bushing	67	Firing Pin Block Lever
21	Rear Sight Ring	45	Hammer	68	Firing Pin Block
22	Rear Sight Windage Pin	46	Safety Pin	69	Firing Pin Block Spring
23	Rear Sight Spring Limiting Pin	47	Hammer Spring Strut	70	Firing Pin Block Pin
24	Rear Sight Pin			71	Magazine Release Case Pin

Single-Action Revolver

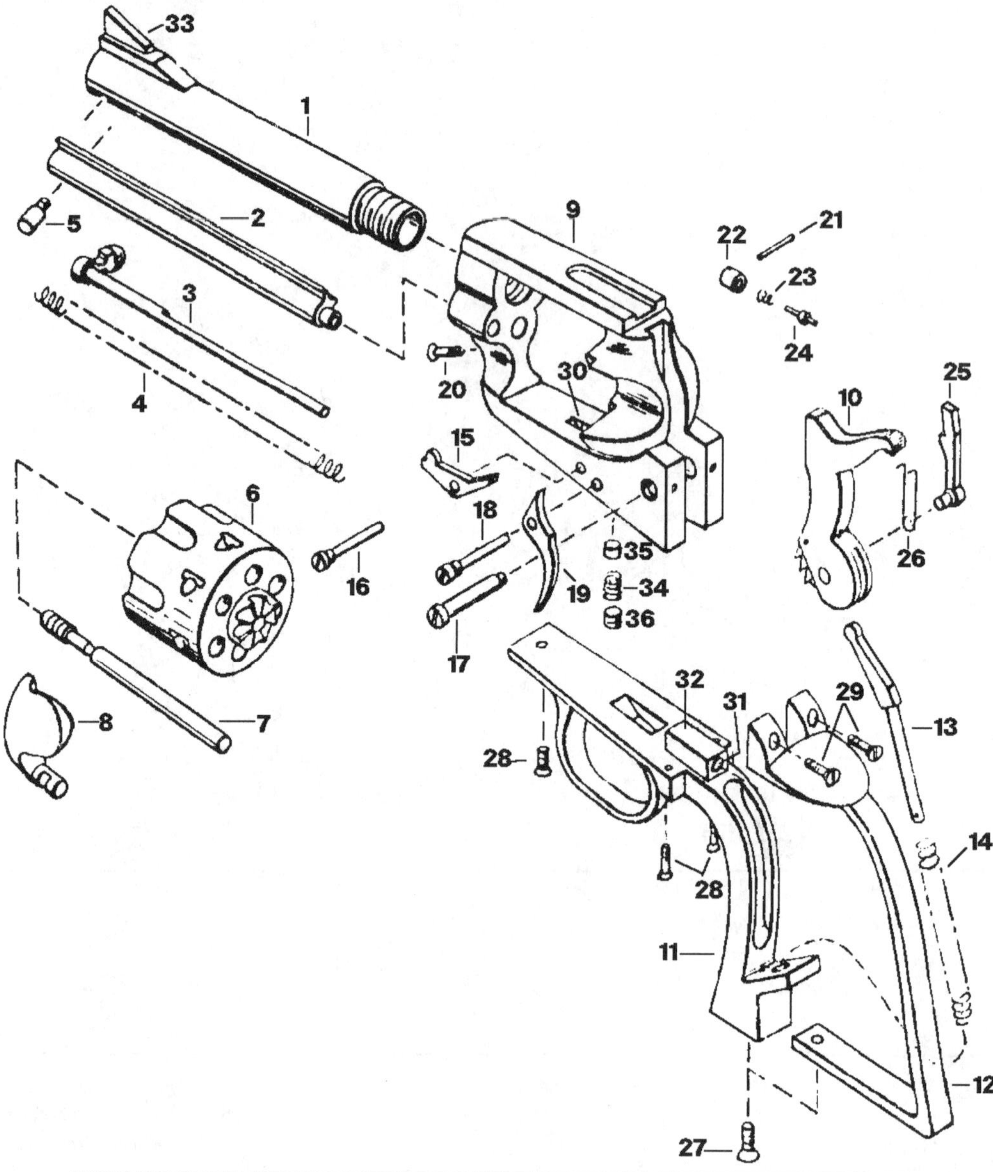

1	Barrel	21	Recoil Retaining Screw
2	Ejector Housing	22	Recoil Plate
3	Ejector Rod	23	Firing Pin Spring
4	Ejector Spring	24	Firing Pin
5	Ejector Housing Screw	25	Hand
6	Cylinder	26	Hand Spring
7	Cylinder Pin	27	Lower Backstrap Screw
8	Loading Gate	28	Trigger Guard Screws
9	Frame	29	Upper Backstrap Screws
10	Hammer	30	Bolt Window
11	Trigger Guard	31	Trigger Spring Adjustment Hole
12	Backstrap	32	Trigger Spring Block
13	Hammer Strut	33	Front Sight
14	Mainspring	34	Loading Gate Spring
15	Cylinder Bolt	35	Loading Gate Plunger
16	Cylinder Bolt Screw	36	Loading Gate Screw
17	Hammer Pivot Screw	**Parts Not Shown**	
18	Trigger Pivot Screw		Rear Sight
19	Trigger		Grips
20	Cylinder Pin Screw		

Contender (Old Style)

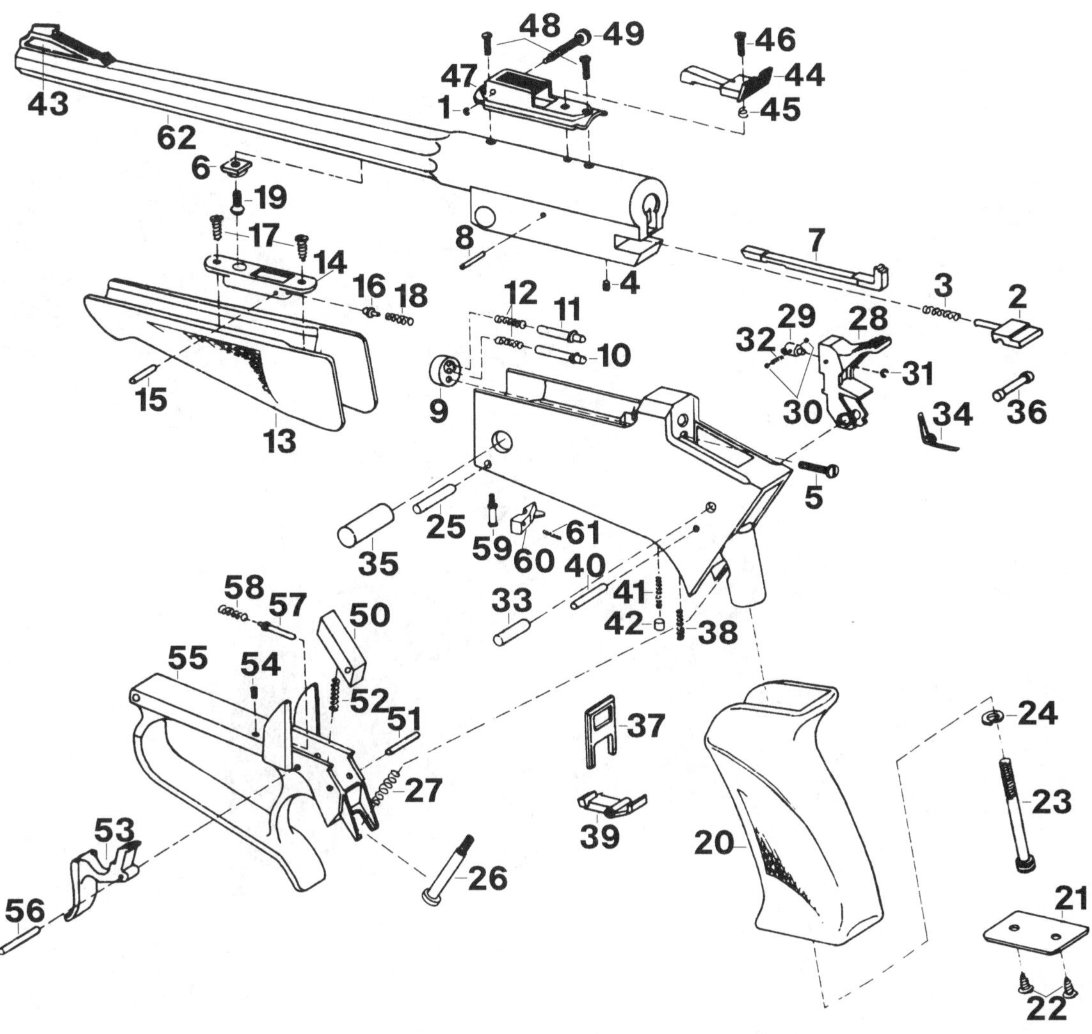

No.	Part	No.	Part	No.	Part
1	Adjusting Screw Snap Ring	23	Grip Screw	45	Rear Sight Elevating Spring
2	Bolt	24	Grip Screw Washer	46	Rear Sight Elevation Adjusting<R>Screw
3	Bolt Spring	25	Guard Pin	47	Rear Sight Housing
4	Bolt Stop Screw	26	Guard Stop Screw	48	Rear Sight Screws
5	Bushing Screw	27	Guard Stop Spring	49	Rear Sight Windage Adjusting<R>Screw
6	Dovetail Lock	28	Hammer	50	Striker
7	Extractor	29	Hammer Nose	51	Striker Pin
8	Extractor Stop Pin	30	Hammer Nose Detents	52	Striker Spring
9	Firing Pin Bushing	31	Hammer Nose Snap Ring	53	Trigger
10	Firing Pin, Centerfire	32	Hammer Nose Spring	54	Trigger Adjusting Screw
11	Firing Pin, Rimfire	33	Hammer Pin	55	Trigger Guard
12	Firing Pin Springs	34	Hammer Spring	56	Trigger Pin
13	Forend	35	Hinge Pin	57	Trigger Return Plunger
14	Forend Catch	36	Roller	58	Trigger Spring
15	Forend Catch Pin	37	Safety	59	Safety Screw
16	Forend Catch Plunger	38	Safety Spring	60	Interlock Safety
17	Forend Catch Screws	39	Sear	61	Safety Screw
18	Forend Catch Spring	40	Sear Pin	62	Barrel
19	Forend Lug	41	Sear Spring		
20	Grip	42	Sear Plunger		
21	Grip Cap	43	Front Sight		
22	Grip Cap Screws	44	Rear Sight Blade		

TYPICAL FLINTLOCK PISTOL

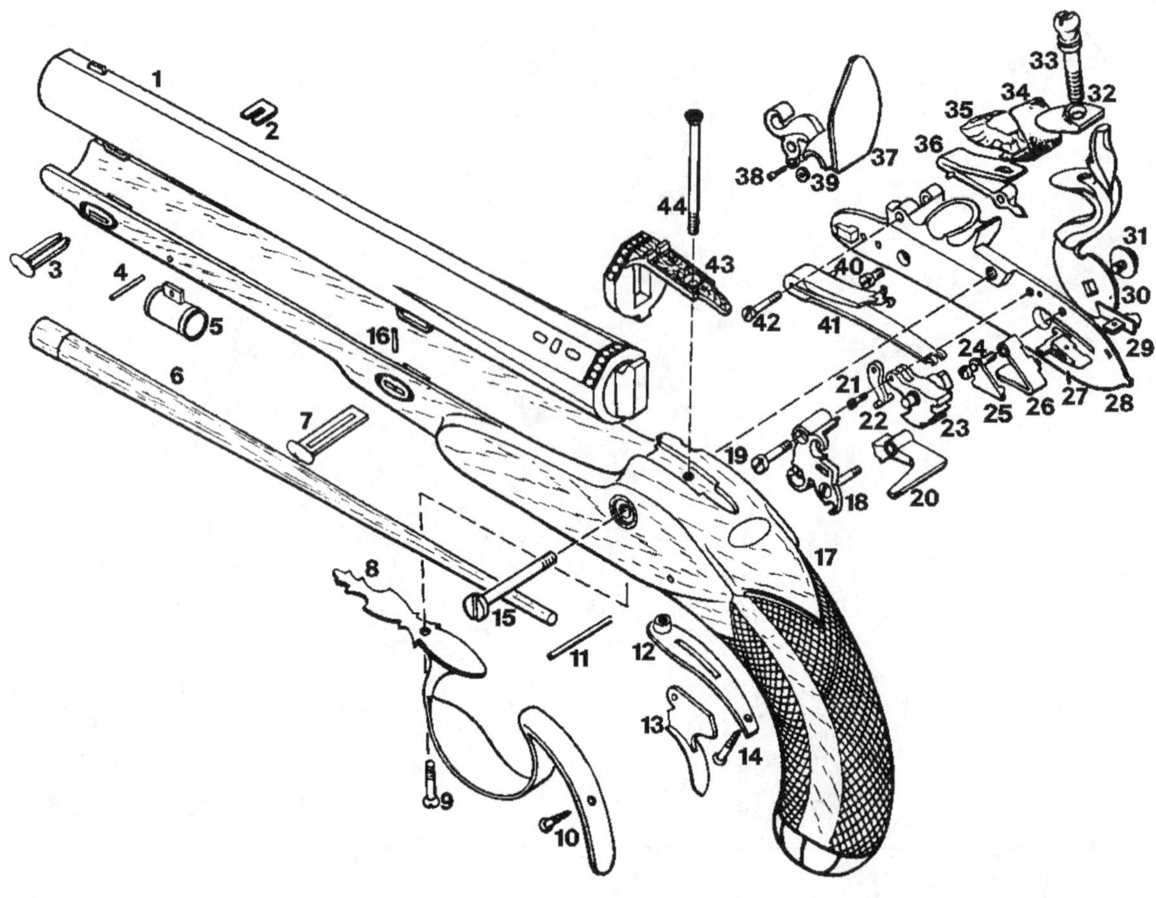

1	Barrel	**23**	Tumbler
2	Barrel Wedge Key	**24**	Sear Cover Screw
3	Barrel Wedge	**25**	Sear Spring Cover
4	Thimble Pin	**26**	Sear Spring
5	Thimble	**27**	Safety-Lever Pin
6	Ramrod	**28**	Lockplate
7	Rear Barrel Wedge	**29**	Hammer Safety-Lever
8	Trigger Guard	**30**	Hammer
9	Trigger Guard/Plate Screw	**31**	Hammer Screw
10	Rear Guard Screw	**32**	Top Jaw
11	Trigger Pin	**33**	Jaw Screw
12	Trigger Plate	**34**	Flint Leather
13	Trigger	**35**	Flint
14	Rear Trigger Plate Screw	**36**	Frizzen Spring
15	Lock Plate Screw	**37**	Frizzen
16	Escutcheon Plate Pin	**38**	Frizzen Screw
17	Stock	**39**	Frizzen Bushing
18	Bridle	**40**	Frizzen Spring Screw
19	Bridle Screw	**41**	Mainspring
20	Sear	**42**	Frizzen Spring Screw
21	Stirrup Screw	**43**	Tang
22	Stirrup	**44**	Tang Screw

1849 Pocket Revolver

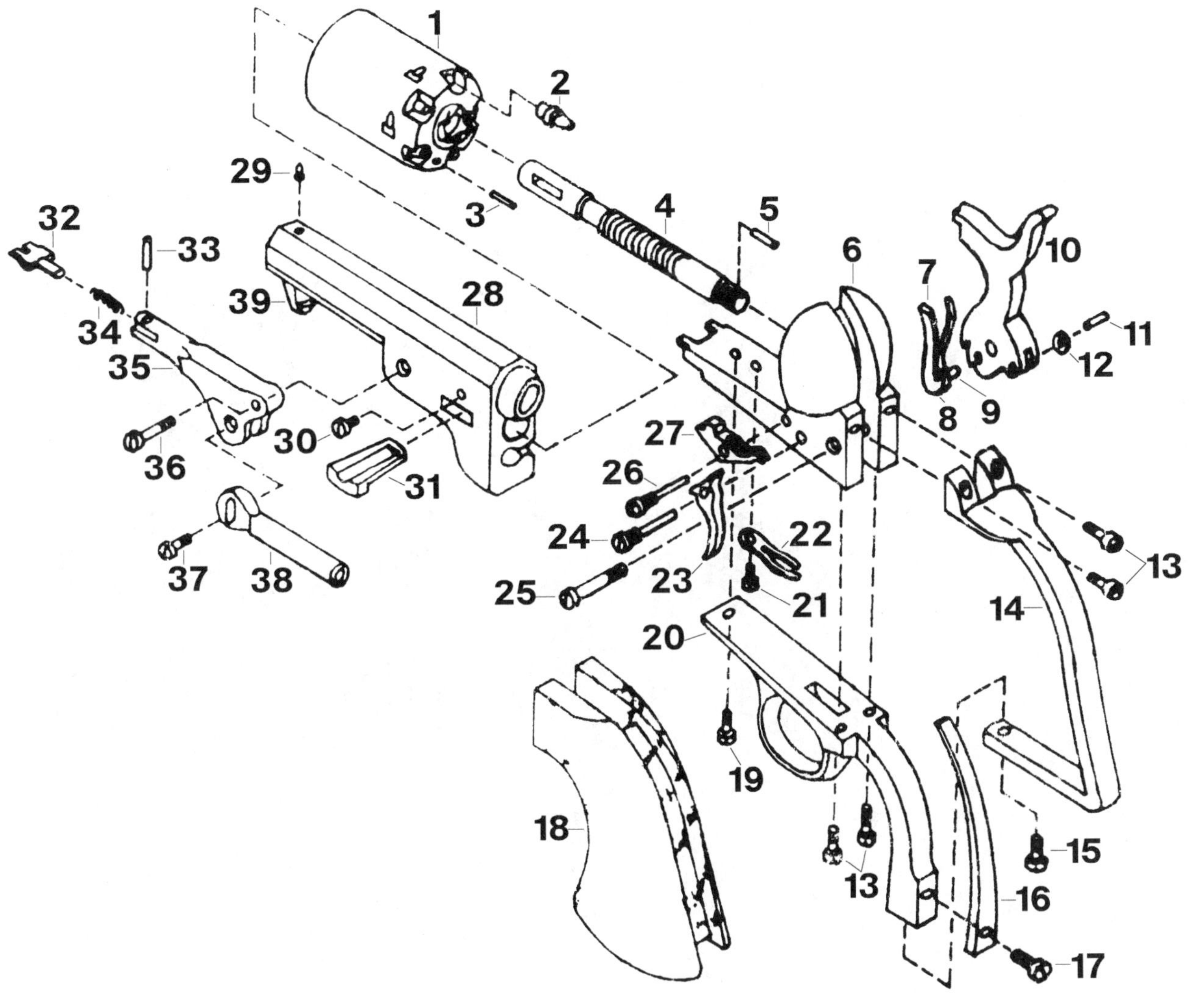

1	Cylinder	**21**	Trigger Bolt Spring Screw
2	Nipple	**22**	Trigger Bolt Spring
3	Safety Pin	**23**	Trigger
4	Base Pin	**24**	Trigger Screw
5	Cylinder Pin Lock Pin	**25**	Hammer Screw
6	Frame	**26**	Bolt Screw
7	Hand Spring	**27**	Bolt
8	Hand	**28**	Barrel
9	Hand Spring Pin	**29**	Sight
10	Hammer	**30**	Wedge Screw
11	Roller Pin	**31**	Wedge
12	Roller	**32**	Loading Lever Latch
13	Rear Backstrap Screws	**33**	Loading Lever Latch Pin
14	Backstrap	**34**	Loading Lever Latch Spring
15	Rear Trigger Guard Screw	**35**	Loading Lever
16	Mainspring	**36**	Loading Lever Screw
17	Mainspring Screw	**37**	Plunger Screw
18	Grip	**38**	Plunger
19	Front Trigger Guard Screw	**39**	Barrel Stud
20	Trigger Guard		

1860 Army Revolver

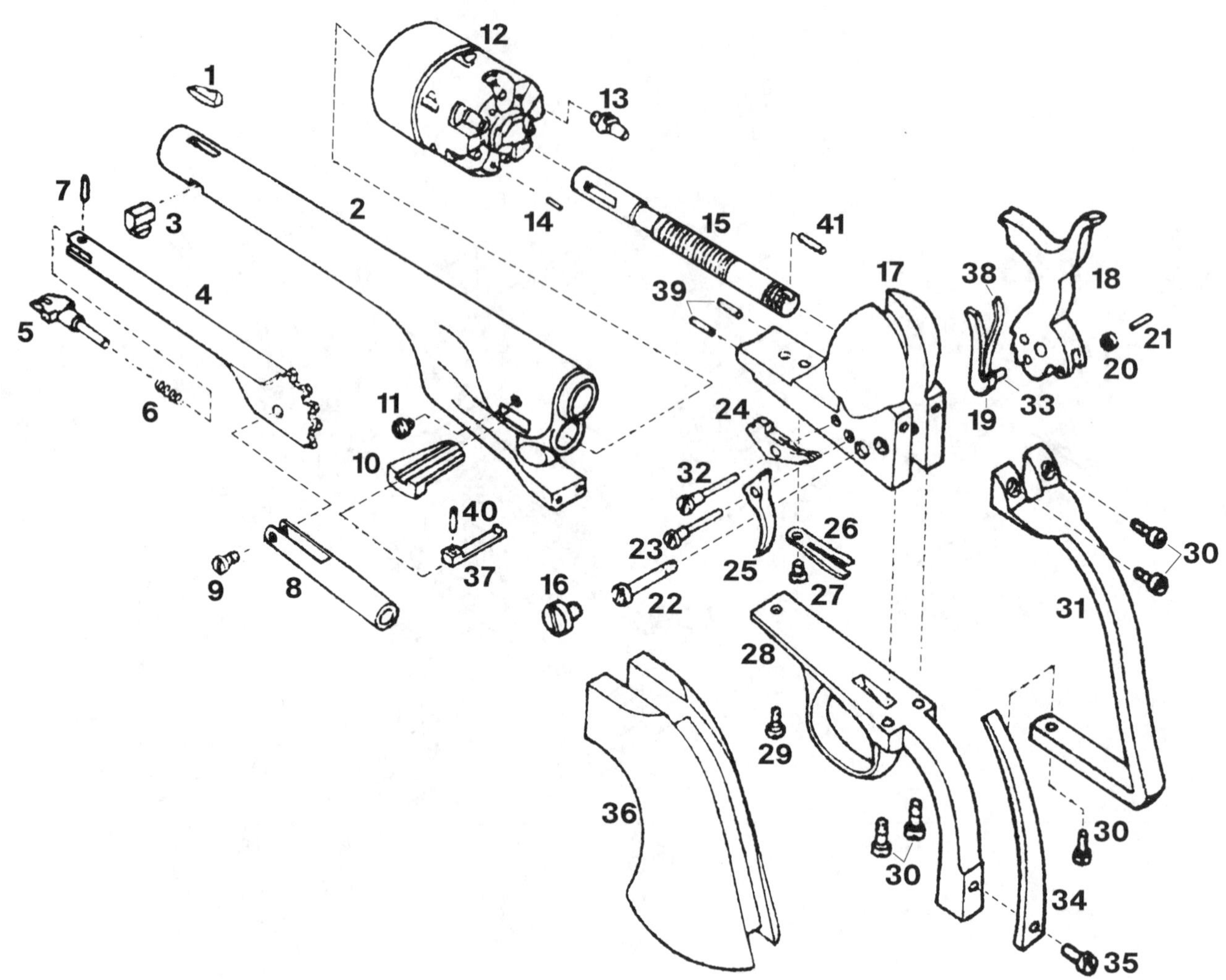

1	Front Sight	22	Hammer Screw
2	Barrel	23	Trigger Screw
3	Barrel Stud	24	Bolt
4	Loading Lever	25	Trigger
5	Loading Lever Latch	26	Trigger Bolt Spring
6	Loading Lever Latch Spring	27	Trigger Bolt Spring Screw
7	Loading Lever Latch Pin	28	Trigger Guard
8	Plunger	29	Front Trigger Guard Screw
9	Plunger Screw	30	Rear Backstrap Screws
10	Wedge	31	Backstrap
11	Wedge Screw	32	Bolt Screw
12	Cylinder	33	Hand Spring Pin
13	Nipple	34	Mainspring
14	Safety Pins	35	Mainspring Screw
15	Base Pin	36	Grip
16	Stock Screw	37	Wedge Spring
17	Frame With Pin	38	Hand Spring
18	Hammer	39	Barrel Guide Pins
19	Hand	40	Wedge Pin
20	Roller	41	Cylinder Pin Lock Pin
21	Roller Pin		

1861 Navy Revolver

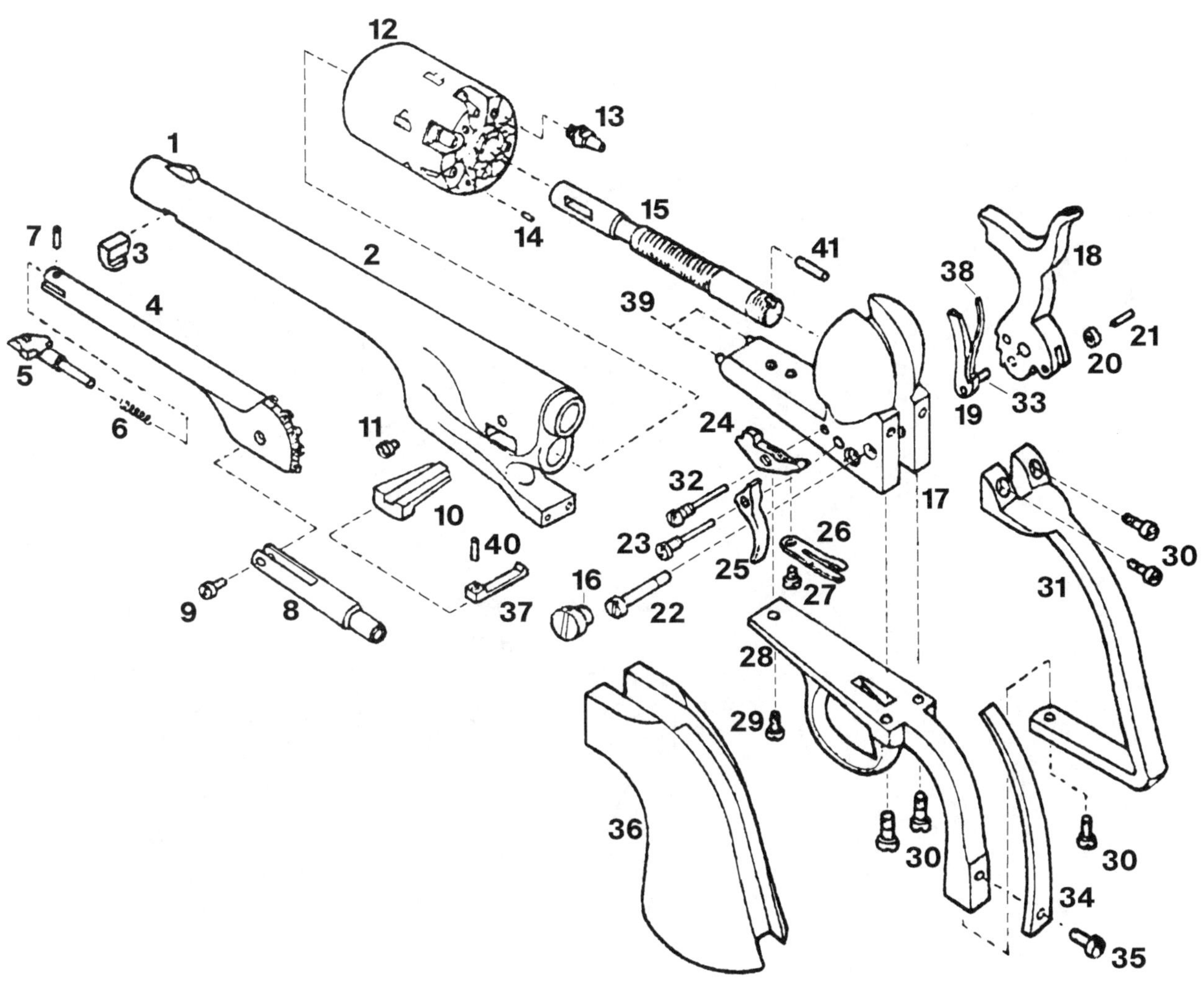

1	Front Sight	22	Hammer Screw
2	Barrel	23	Trigger Screw
3	Barrel Stud	24	Bolt
4	Loading Lever	25	Trigger
5	Loading Lever Latch	26	Trigger Bolt Spring
6	Loading Lever Latch Spring	27	Trigger Bolt Spring Screw
7	Loading Lever Latch Pin	28	Trigger Guard
8	Plunger	29	Front Trigger Guard Screw
9	Plunger Screw	30	Rear Backstrap Screws
10	Wedge	31	Backstrap
11	Wedge Screw	32	Bolt Screw
12	Cylinder	33	Hand Spring Pin
13	Nipple	34	Mainspring
14	Safety Pin	35	Mainspring Screw
15	Base Pin	36	Grip
16	Stock Screw	37	Wedge Spring
17	Frame With Pin	38	Hand Spring
18	Hammer	39	Barrel Guide Pin
19	Hand With Spring	40	Wedge Pin
20	Roller	41	Cylinder Pin Lock Pin
21	Roller Pin		

1862 Navy Pocket Revolver

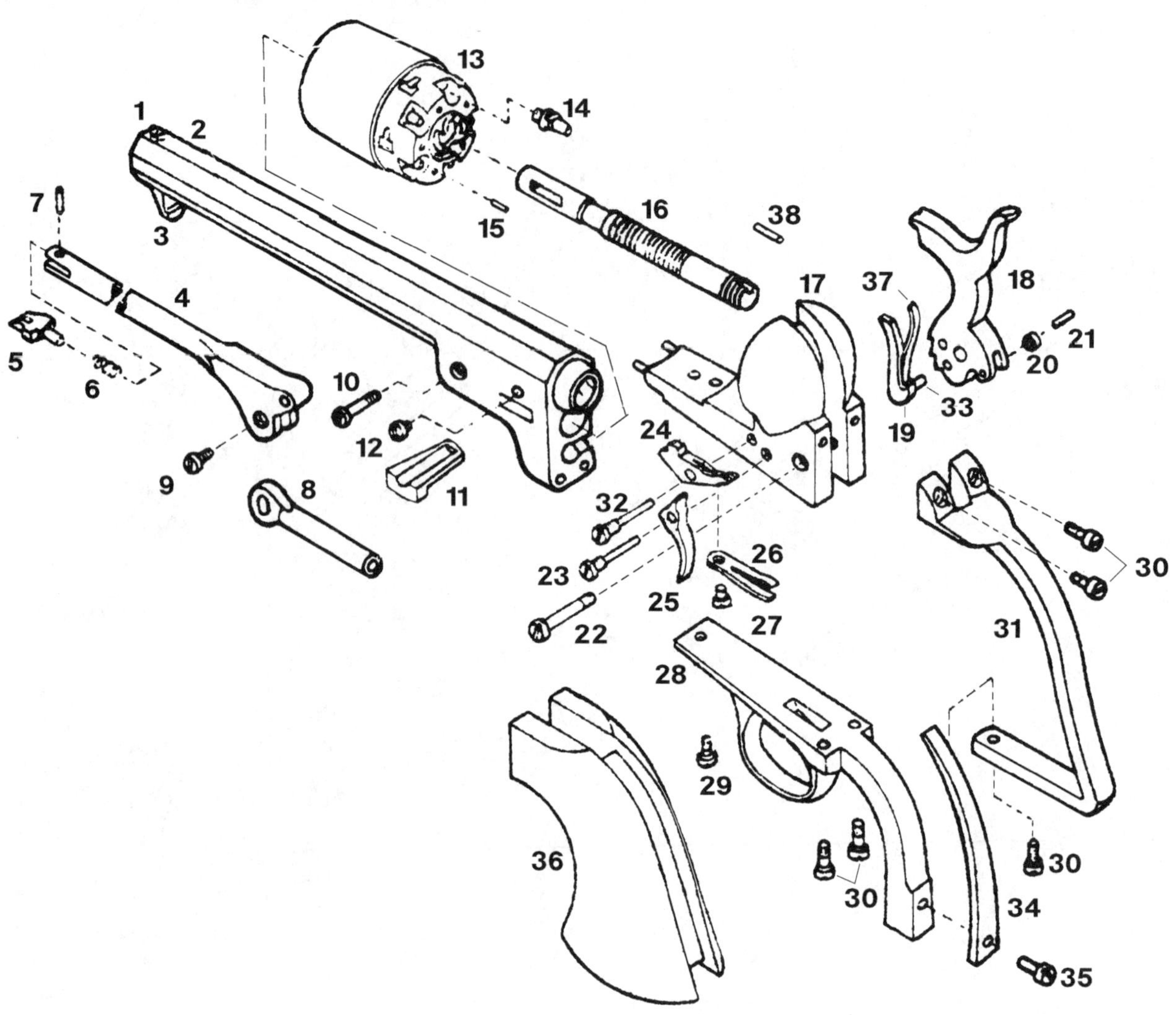

1	Front Sight	20	Roller
2	Barrel	21	Roller Pin
3	Barrel Stud	22	Hammer Screw
4	Loading Lever	23	Trigger Screw
5	Loading Lever Latch	24	Bolt
6	Loading Lever Latch Spring	25	Trigger
7	Loading Lever Latch Pin	26	Trigger Bolt Spring
8	Plunger	27	Trigger Bolt Spring Screw
9	Plunger Screw	28	Trigger Guard
10	Loading Lever Screw	29	Front Trigger Guard Screw
11	Wedge	30	Rear Backstrap Screws
12	Wedge Screw	31	Backstrap
13	Cylinder	32	Bolt Screw
14	Nipple	33	Hand Spring Pin
15	Safety Pins	34	Mainspring
16	Base Pin	35	Mainspring Screw
17	Frame Assembly	36	Grip
18	Hammer	37	Hand Spring
19	Hand With Spring	38	Cylinder Lock Pin

1862 Police Revolver

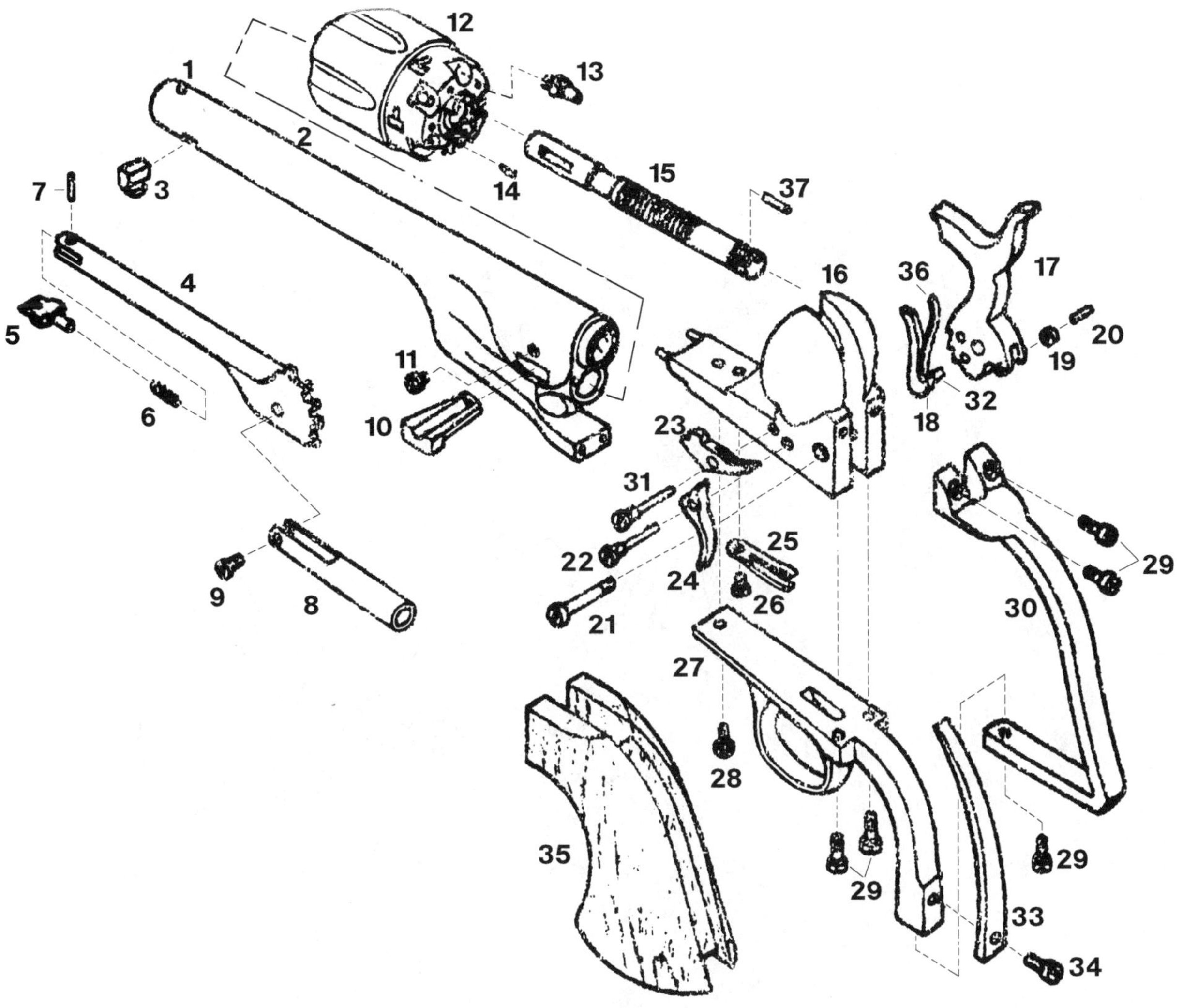

1	Front Sight	20	Roller pin
2	Barrel	21	Hammer Screw
3	Barrel Stud	22	Trigger Screw
4	Loading Lever	23	Bolt
5	Loading Lever Latch	24	Trigger
6	Loading Lever Latch Spring	25	Trigger Bolt Spring
7	Loading Lever Latch Pin	26	Trigger and Cylinder Stop Spring Screw
8	Plunger	27	Trigger Guard
9	Plunger Screw	28	Front Trigger Guard Screw
10	Wedge	29	Rear Backstrap Screws
11	Wedge Screw	30	Backstrap
12	Cylinder	31	Cylinder Stop Screw
13	Nipple	32	Hand Spring Pin
14	Safety Pins	33	Mainspring
15	Base Pin	34	Mainspring Screw
16	Frame	35	Grip
17	Hammer	36	Hand Spring
18	Hand With Spring	37	Cylinder Lock Pin
19	Roller		

1875 Remington Revolver

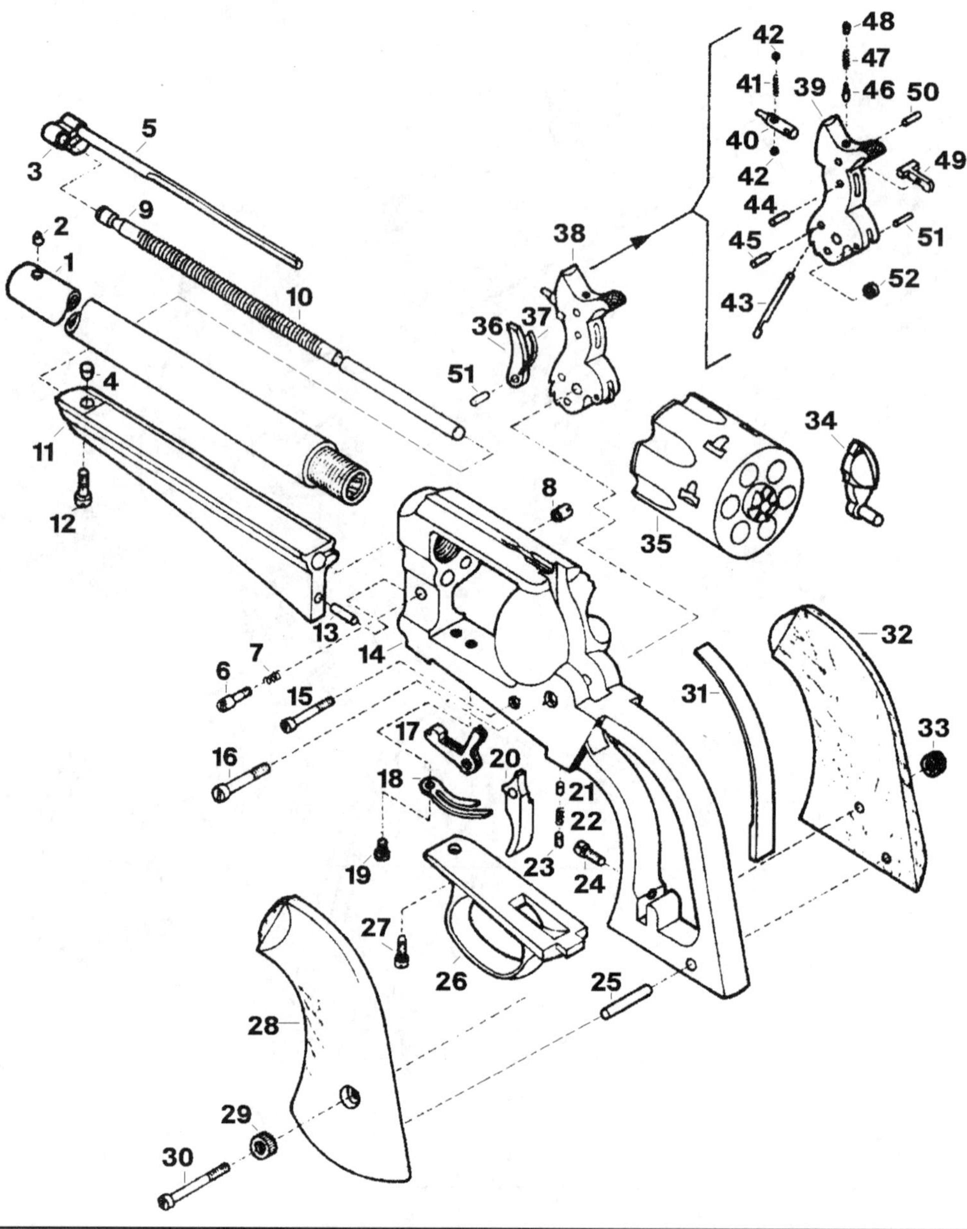

1	Barrel	**19**	Trigger Cylinder Stop Spring Screw	**37**	Hand Spring
2	Front Sight	**20**	Trigger	**38**	Hammer Assembly
3	Ejector Nut	**21**	Gate Catch	**39**	Hammer
4	Ejector Support Screw Nut	**22**	Gate Spring	**40**	Firing Pin
5	Ejector	**23**	Gate Catch Screw	**41**	Firing Pin Spring
6	Base Pin Screw	**24**	Mainspring Screw	**42**	Firing Pin Spheres
7	Base Pin Spring	**25**	Grip Pin	**43**	Bottom Piston
8	Base Pin Nut	**26**	Trigger Guard	**44**	Hammer Safety-Lever Pin
9	Base Pin	**27**	Trigger Guard Screw	**45**	Bottom Piston Stop Pin
10	Ejector Spring	**28**	Left Grip	**46**	Push Lever Pin
11	Support Ejector	**29**	Left Grip Nut	**47**	Push Lever Spring
12	Support Ejector Screw	**30**	Grip Screw	**48**	Stop Spring Screw for Push
13	Support Ejector Pin	**31**	Mainspring	**49**	Hammer Safety-Lever
14	Frame	**32**	Right Grip	**50**	Firing Pin Roll
15	Trigger Screw	**33**	Right Grip Nut	**51**	Hammer Roller Pin
16	Hammer Screw	**34**	Gate	**52**	Hammer Roller
17	Cylinder Stop	**35**	Cylinder		
18	Trigger Cylinder Stop Spring	**36**	Hand		

1st and 2nd Model Dragoon Revolver

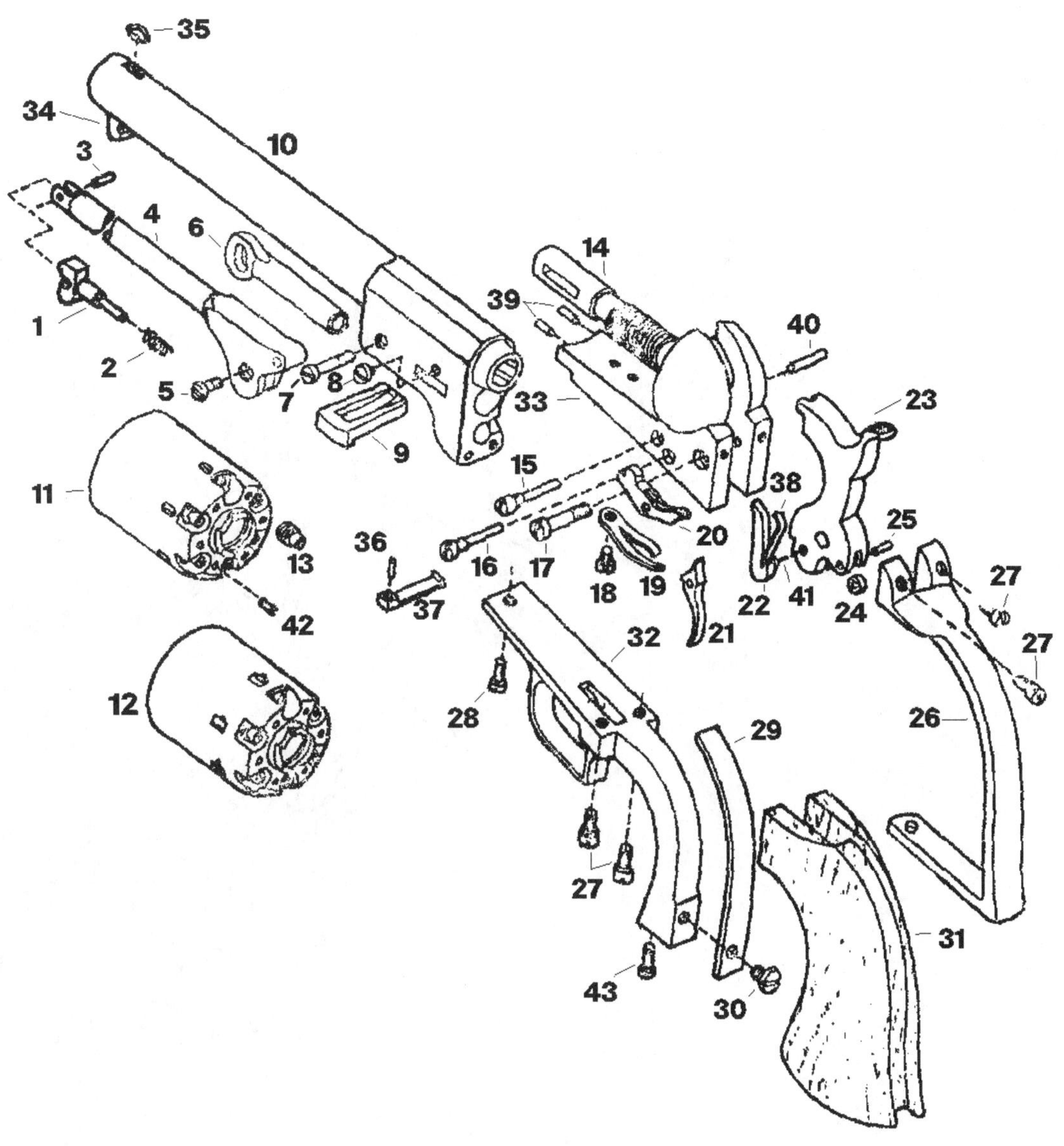

1	Loading Lever Catch	**16**	Trigger Screw	**31**	Grip
2	Loading Lever Latch Spring	**17**	Hammer Screw	**32**	Trigger Guard Square
3	Loading Lever Latch Pin	**18**	Trigger Bolt Spring Screw	**33**	Frame with Pin
4	Loading Lever	**19**	Trigger Bolt Spring	**34**	Barrel Stud
5	Plunger Screw	**20**	Bolt	**35**	Front Sight
6	Plunger	**21**	Trigger	**36**	Wedge Pin
7	Loading Lever Screw	**22**	Hand Assembly	**37**	Wedge Spring
8	Wedge Screw	**23**	Hammer	**38**	Hand Spring
9	Wedge	**24**	Roller	**39**	Barrel Guide Pins
10	Barrel	**25**	Roller Pin	**40**	Cylinder Pin Lock Pin
11	Cylinder (1st Model)	**26**	Backstrap	**41**	Hand Spring Pin
12	Cylinder (2nd Model)	**27**	Rear Backstrap Screws	**42**	Safety Pin
13	Nipple	**28**	Front Trigger Guard Screw	**43**	Rear Trigger Guard Screw
14	Base Pin	**29**	Mainspring		
15	Bolt Screw	**30**	Mainspring Screw		

3rd Model Dragoon Revolver

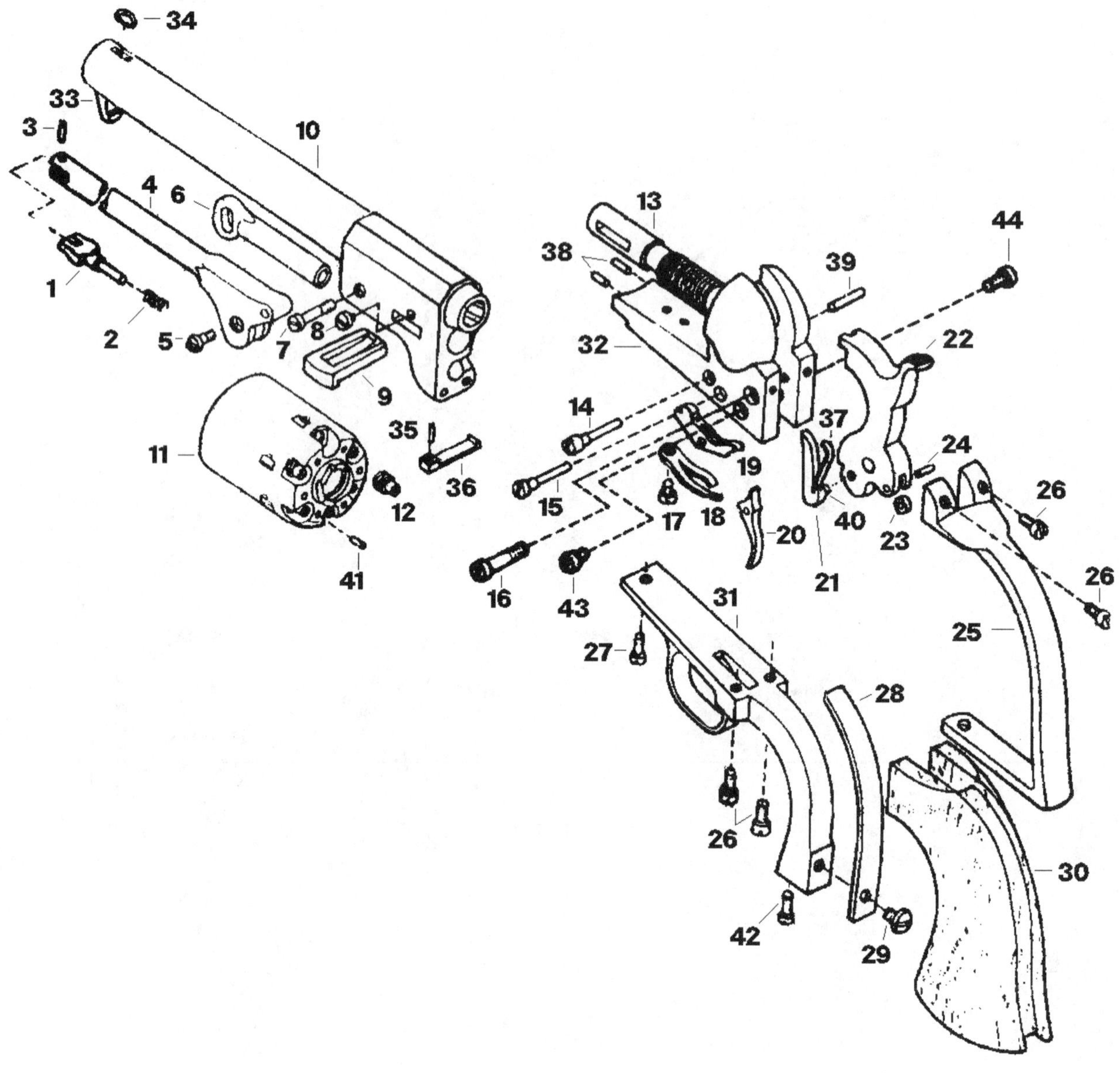

1	Loading Lever Latch	**16**	Hammer Screw	**31**	Trigger Guard Oval
2	Loading Lever Latch Spring	**17**	Trigger Bolt Spring Screw	**32**	Frame with Pin
3	Loading Lever Latch Pin	**18**	Trigger Bolt Spring	**33**	Barrel Stud
4	Loading Lever	**19**	Bolt	**34**	Sight
5	Plunger Screw	**20**	Trigger	**35**	Wedge Pin
6	Plunger	**21**	Hand with Spring	**36**	Wedge Spring
7	Loading Lever Screw	**22**	Hammer	**37**	Hand Spring
8	Wedge Screw	**23**	Roller	**38**	Barrel Guide Pins
9	Wedge	**24**	Roller Pin	**39**	Cylinder Pin Lock Pin
10	Barrel	**25**	Backstrap	**40**	Hand Spring Pin
11	Cylinder	**26**	Rear Backstrap Screws	**41**	Safety Pin
12	Nipple	**27**	Front Trigger Guard Screw	**42**	Rear Trigger Guard Screw
13	Base Pin	**28**	Mainspring	**43**	Left Stock Screw
14	Bolt Screw	**29**	Mainspring Screw	**44**	Right Stock Screw
15	Trigger Screw	**30**	Grip		

Buckhorn Revolver

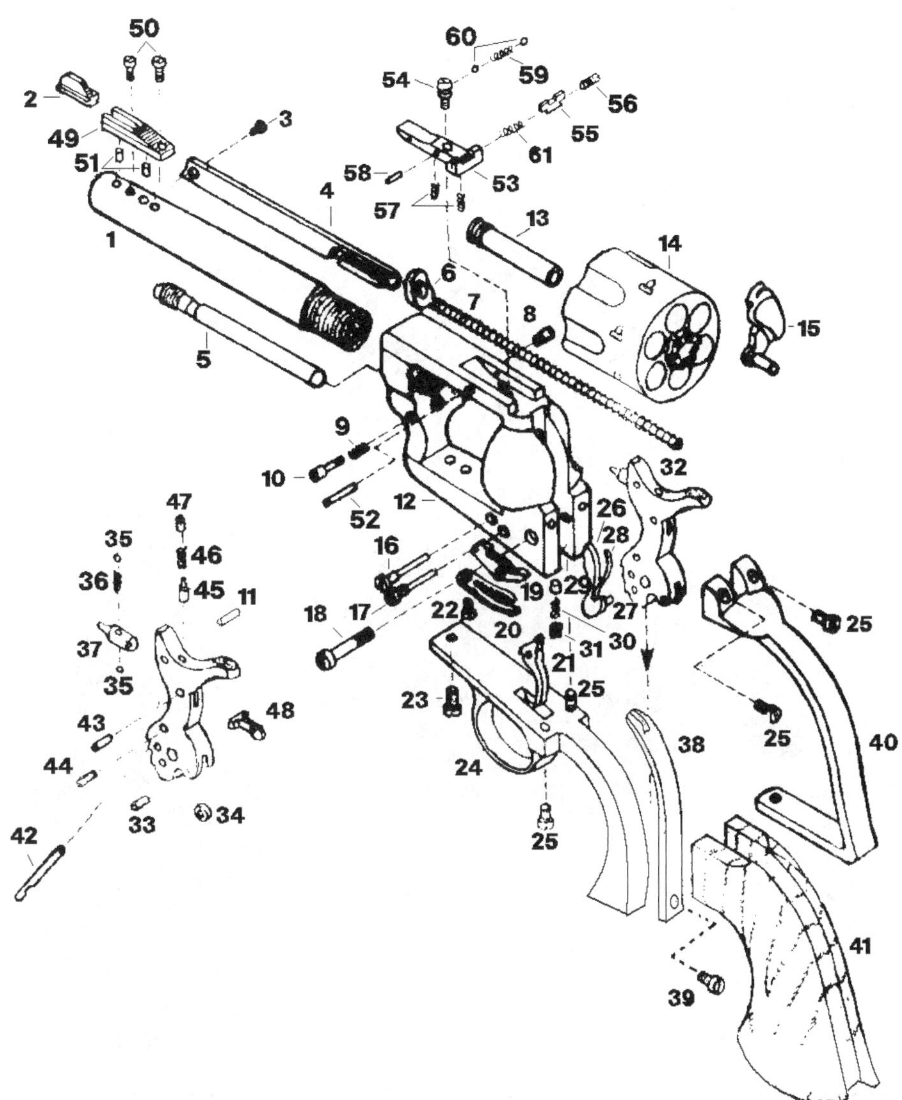

1 Barrel
2 Sight
3 Ejector Rod Tube Screw
4 Ejector Rod Tube
5 Base Pin
6 Ejector
7 Ejector Spring
8 Base Pin Nut
9 Base Pin Spring
10 Base Pin Screw
11 Firing Pin Retaining Pin
12 Frame
13 Base Pin Bushing
14 Cylinder
15 Gate
16 Bolt Screw
17 Trigger Screw
18 Hammer Screw
19 Bolt
20 Sear and Bolt Spring
21 Trigger
22 Bolt Spring Screw
23 Trigger Guard Screw
24 Trigger Guard
25 Trigger Guard Backstrap Screws
26 Hand Assembly
27 Hand Pin
28 Hand Spring
29 Gate Catch
30 Gate Spring
31 Gate Catch Screw
32 Hammer
33 Hammer Roll Pin
34 Hammer Roll
35 Firing Pin Spheres
36 Firing Pin Spring
37 Firing Pin
38 Mainspring
39 Mainspring Screw
40 Backstrap
41 Grips
42 Hammer Safety Plunger
43 Hammer Safety Bar Pin
44 Hammer Safety Plunger Pin
45 Hammer Safety Pin
46 Hammer Safety Spring
47 Hammer Safety Stop Screw
48 Hammer Safety Bar
49 Front Sight Ramp
50 Front Sight Ramp Retaining Screws
51 Front Sight Ramp Pins
52 Rear Sight Retaining Screw
53 Rear Sight
54 Rear Sight Elevation Screw
55 Rear Sight Blade
56 Rear Sight Windage Screw
57 Rear Sight Springs
58 Rear Screw
59 Rear Spring
60 Rear Spheres
61 Rear Sight Blade Spring

Parts Not Shown

Rear Sight Elevation Screw Pin

Cattleman SA Revolver

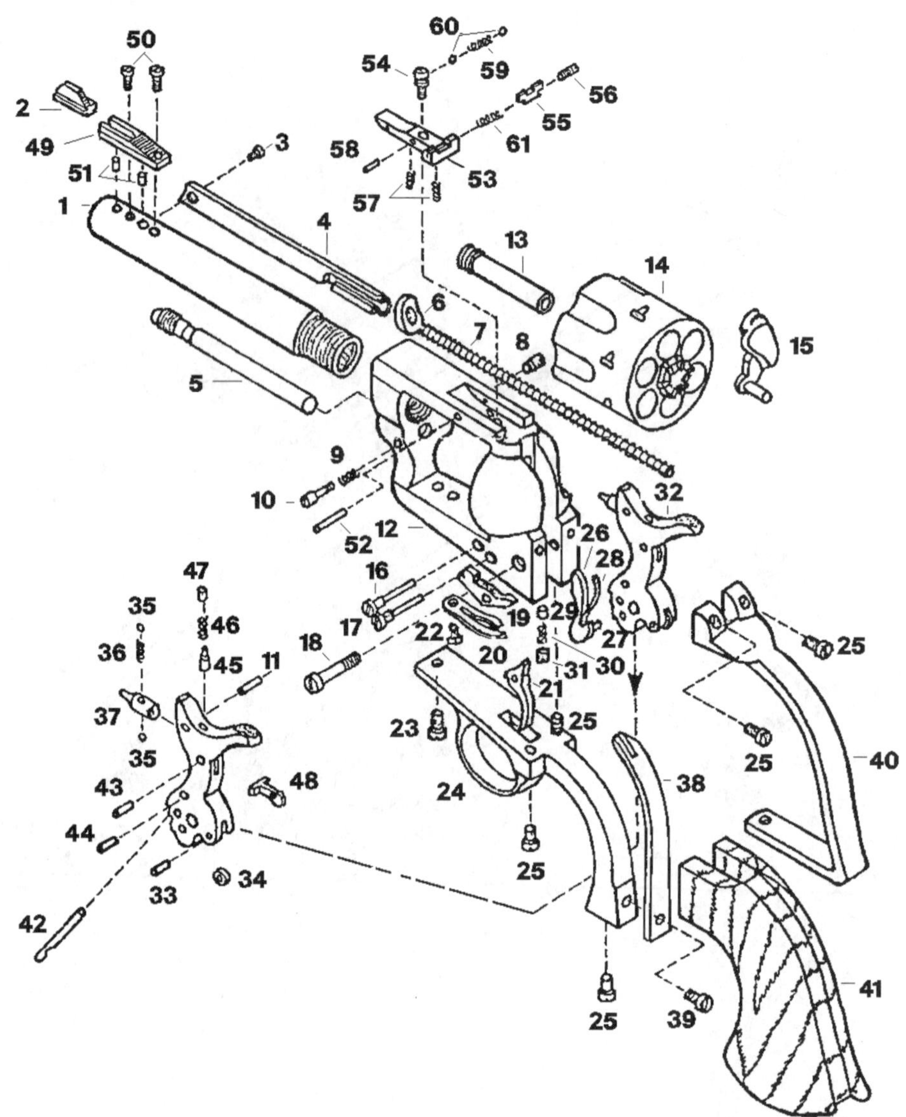

1	Barrel	**23**	Trigger Guard Screw	**45**	Hammer Safety Pin
2	Front Sight	**24**	Trigger Guard	**46**	Hammer Safety Spring
3	Ejector Rod Tube Screw	**25**	Trigger Guard Backstrap Screws	**47**	Hammer Safety Stop Screw
4	Ejector Rod Tube	**26**	Hand Assembly	**48**	Hammer Safety Bar
5	Base Pin	**27**	Hand Pin	**49**	Front Sight Ramp
6	Ejector	**28**	Hand Spring	**50**	Front Sight Ramp Retaining Screws
7	Ejector Spring	**29**	Gate Catch	**51**	Front Sight Ramp Pins
8	Base Pin Nut	**30**	Gate Spring	**52**	Rear Sight Retaining Screw
9	Base Pin Spring	**31**	Gate Catch Screw	**53**	Rear Sight
10	Base Pin Screw	**32**	Hammer	**54**	Rear Sight Elevation Screw
11	Firing Pin Retaining Pin	**33**	Hammer Roll Pin	**55**	Rear Sight Blade
12	Frame	**34**	Hammer Roll	**56**	Rear Sight Windage Screw
13	Base Pin Bushing	**35**	Firing Pin Spheres	**57**	Rear Sight Springs
14	Cylinder	**36**	Firing Pin Spring	**58**	Rear Sight Screw
15	Gate	**37**	Firing Pin	**59**	Rear Sight Sphere Spring
16	Bolt Screw	**38**	Mainspring	**60**	Rear Sight Spheres
17	Trigger Screw	**39**	Mainspring Screw	**61**	Rear Sight Blade Spring
18	Hammer Screw	**40**	Backstrap	**Parts Not Shown**	
19	Bolt	**41**	Grip		Ejector Rod Tube Screw Nut
20	Sear and Bolt Spring	**42**	Hammer Safety Plunger		Rear Sight Elevation Screw Pin
21	Trigger	**43**	Hammer Safety Bar Pin		
22	Bolt Spring Screw	**44**	Hammer Safety Plunger Pin		

Rolling Block Single Shot

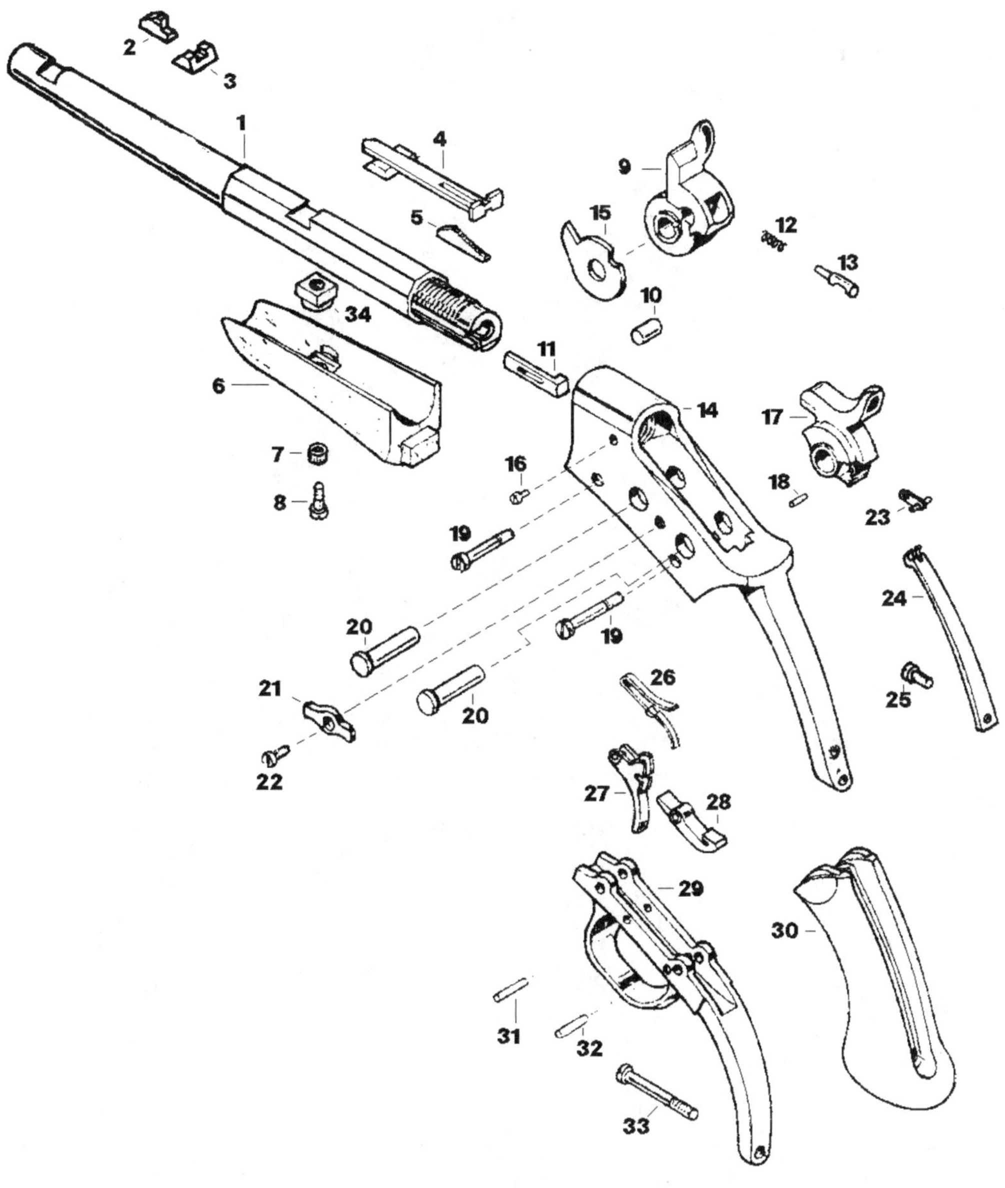

1	Barrel	**18**	Stirrup Pin
2	Front Sight	**19**	Trigger Guard Screws
3	Front Sight Ramp	**20**	Block Pin and Rammer
4	Rear Sight	**21**	Pin Plate
5	Rear Sight Windage Ramp	**22**	Plate Screw
6	Forend	**23**	Stirrup
7	Forend Cap	**24**	Mainspring
8	Forend Screw	**25**	Mainspring Screw
9	Stop Block	**26**	Sear Spring
10	Firing Pin Roller	**27**	Trigger
11	Extractor	**28**	Sear
12	Firing Pin Spring	**29**	Trigger Guard
13	Firing Pin	**30**	Grips
14	Frame	**31**	Trigger Pin
15	Extractor Cam	**32**	Sear Pin
16	Stopping Extractor Screw	**33**	Tang Screw
17	Hammer	**34**	Tenon

Stallion Revolver

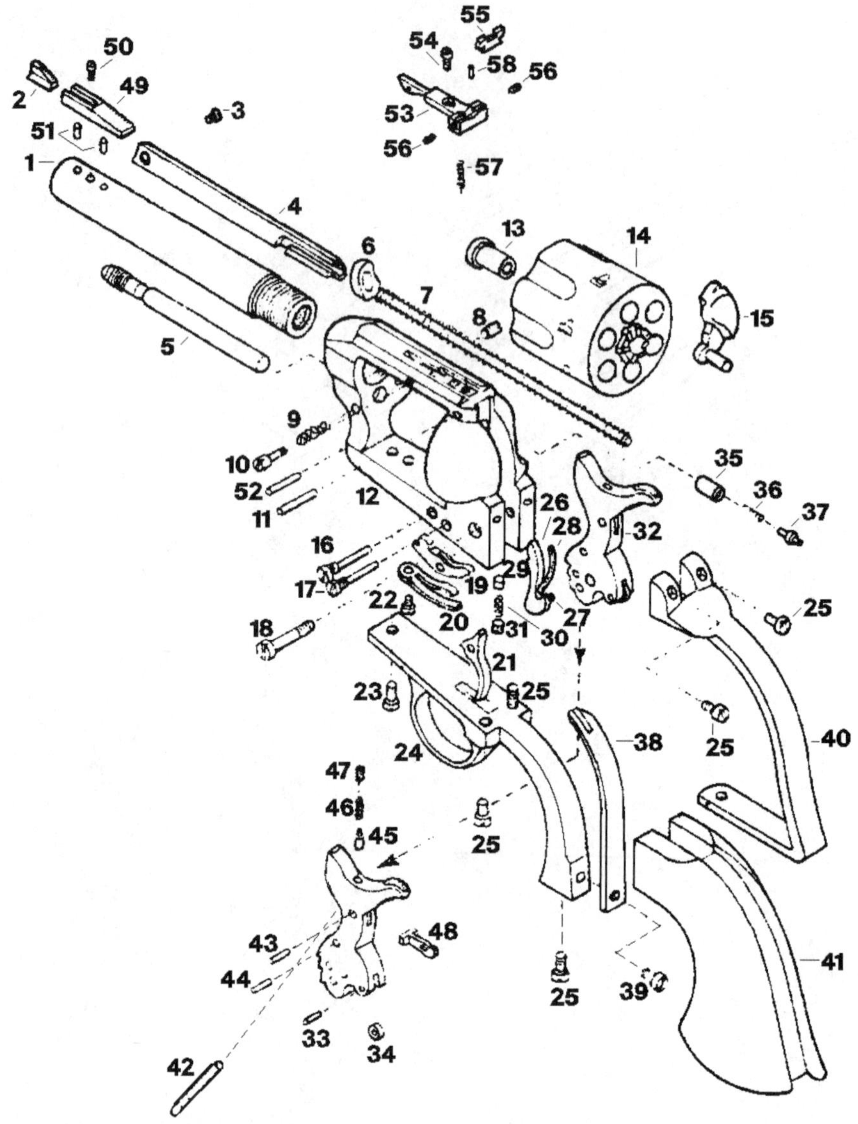

1	Barrel	**21**	Trigger	**41**	Grip
2	Sight	**22**	Bolt Spring Screw	**42**	Hammer Safety Plunger
3	Ejector Rod Tube Screw	**23**	Trigger Guard Screw	**43**	Hammer Safety Bar Pin
4	Ejector Rod Tube	**24**	Trigger Guard	**44**	Hammer Safety Plunger Pin
5	Base Pin	**25**	Trigger Guard Backstrap Screws	**45**	Hammer Safety Pin
6	Ejector	**26**	Hand Assembly	**46**	Hammer Safety Spring
7	Ejector Spring	**27**	Hand Pin	**47**	Hammer Safety Stop Screw
8	Base Pin Nut	**28**	Hand Spring	**48**	Hammer Safety Bar
9	Base Pin Spring	**29**	Gate Catch	**49**	Front Sight Ramp
10	Base Pin Screw	**30**	Gate Spring	**50**	Front Sight Ramp Retaining Screw
11	Firing Pin Retaining Pin	**31**	Gate Catch Screw	**51**	Front Sight Ramp Pins
12	Frame	**32**	Hammer	**52**	Rear Sight Retaining Screw
13	Base Pin Bushing	**33**	Hammer Roll Pin	**53**	Rear Sight
14	Cylinder	**34**	Hammer Roll	**54**	Rear Sight Elevation Screw
15	Gate	**35**	Firing Pin Bearing	**55**	Rear Sight Blade
16	Bolt Screw	**36**	Firing Pin Spring	**56**	Rear Sight Windage Screws
17	Trigger Screw	**37**	Firing Pin	**57**	Rear Sight Elevation Spring
18	Hammer Screw	**38**	Mainspring	**58**	Rear Sight Lock Pin
19	Bolt	**39**	Mainspring Screw		
20	Sear and Bolt Spring	**40**	Backstrap		

Walker Revolver

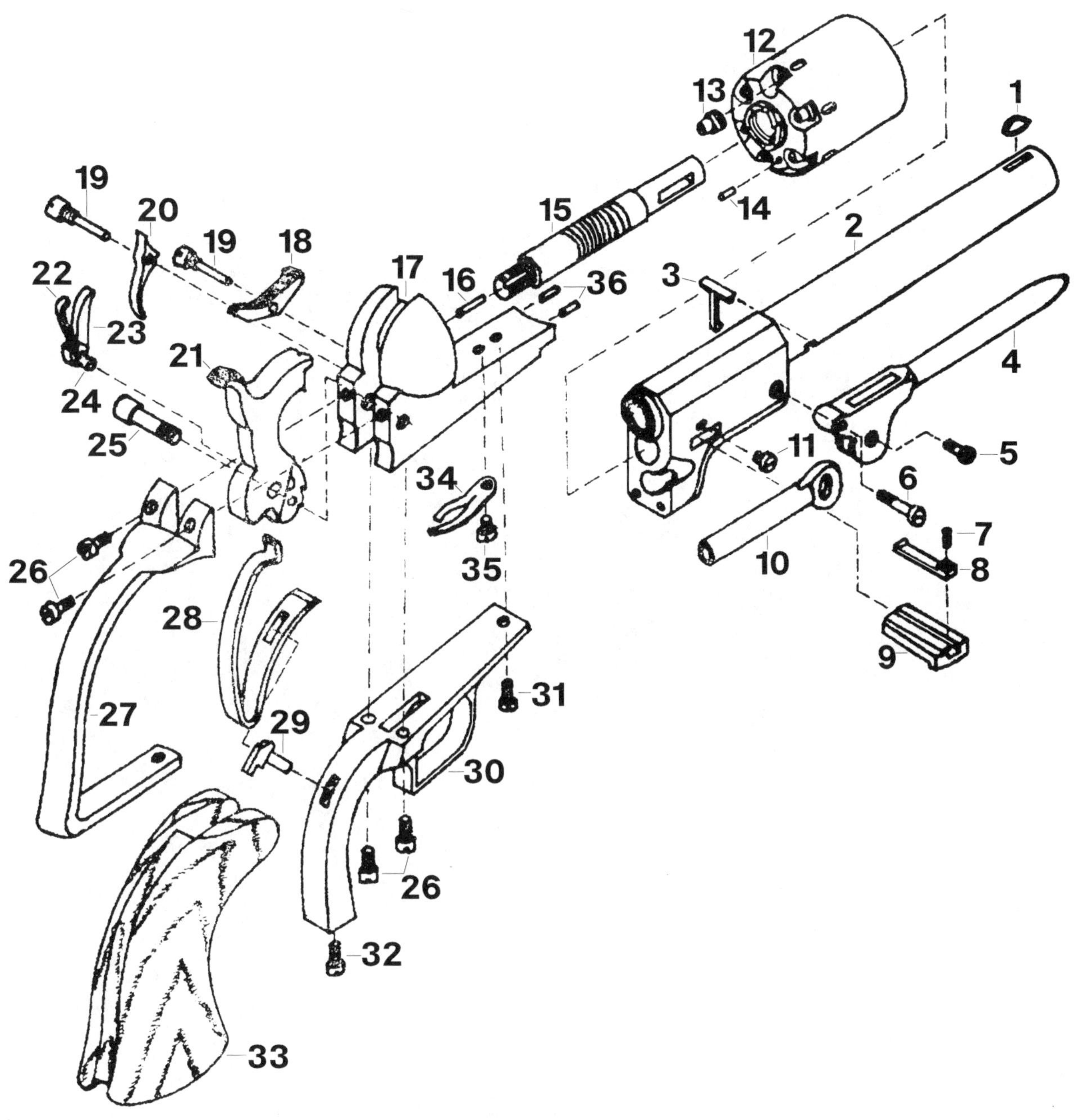

1	Front Sight	**13**	Nipple	**25**	Hammer Screw
2	Barrel	**14**	Safety Pin	**26**	Rear Backstrap Screws
3	Loading Lever Latch	**15**	Base Pin	**27**	Backstrap
4	Loading Lever	**16**	Cylinder Pin Lock Pin	**28**	Mainspring
5	Plunger Screw	**17**	Frame	**29**	Latch Hooking Mainspring
6	Loading Lever Screw	**18**	Bolt	**30**	Trigger Guard
7	Wedge Pin	**19**	Bolt Screws	**31**	Front Trigger Guard Screw
8	Wedge Spring	**20**	Trigger	**32**	Rear Trigger Guard Screw
9	Wedge	**21**	Hammer	**33**	Grip
10	Plunger	**22**	Hand Spring	**34**	Trigger Bolt Spring
11	Wedge Screw	**23**	Hand	**35**	Trigger Bolt Spring Screw
12	Cylinder	**24**	Hand Pin	**36**	Barrel Guide Pins

Wells Fargo Revolver

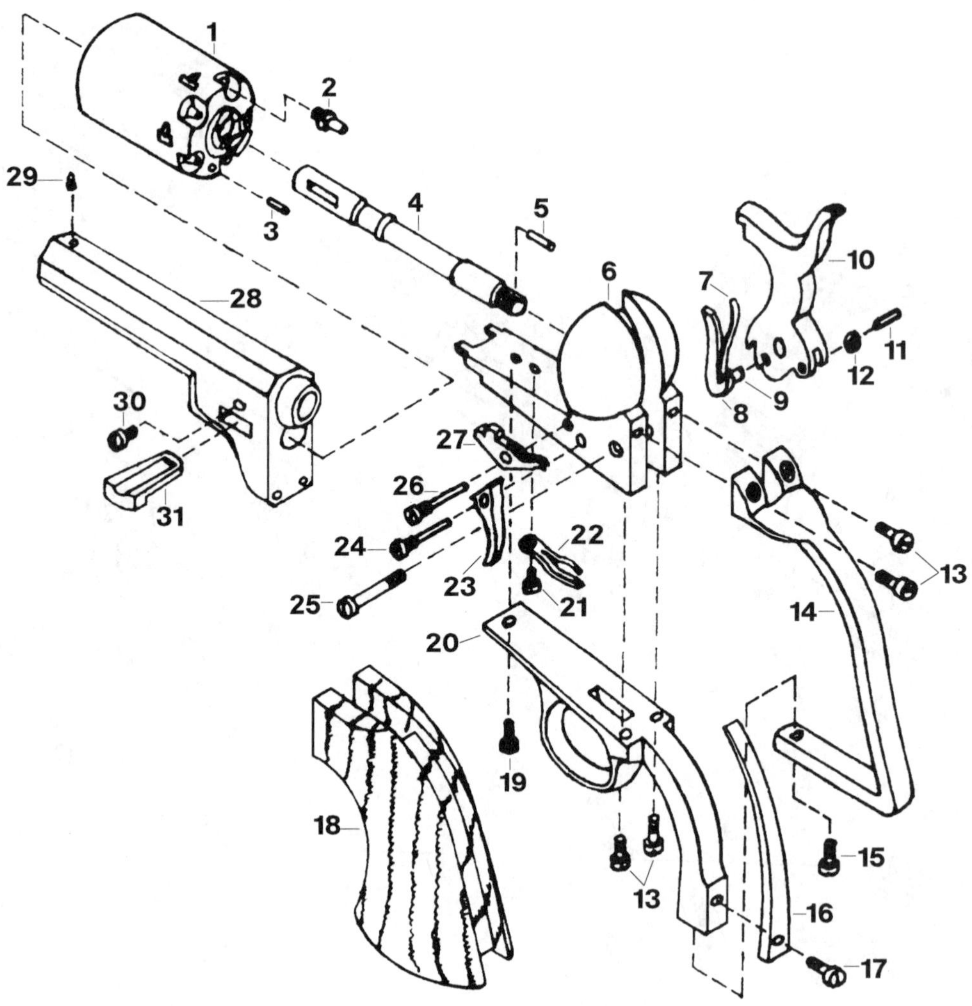

1	Cylinder	**17**	Mainspring Screw
2	Nipple	**18**	Grip
3	Safety Pin	**19**	Front Trigger Guard Screw
4	Base Pin	**20**	Trigger Guard
5	Cylinder Pin Lock Pin	**21**	Trigger Bolt Spring Screw
6	Frame	**22**	Trigger Bolt Spring
7	Hand Spring	**23**	Trigger
8	Hand	**24**	Trigger Screw
9	Hand Spring Pin	**25**	Hammer Screw
10	Hammer	**26**	Bolt Screw
11	Roller Pin	**27**	Bolt
12	Roller	**28**	Barrel
13	Rear Backstrap Screws	**29**	Front Sight
14	Backstrap	**30**	Wedge Screw
15	Rear Trigger Guard Screw	**31**	Wedge
16	Mainspring		

823 U Auto

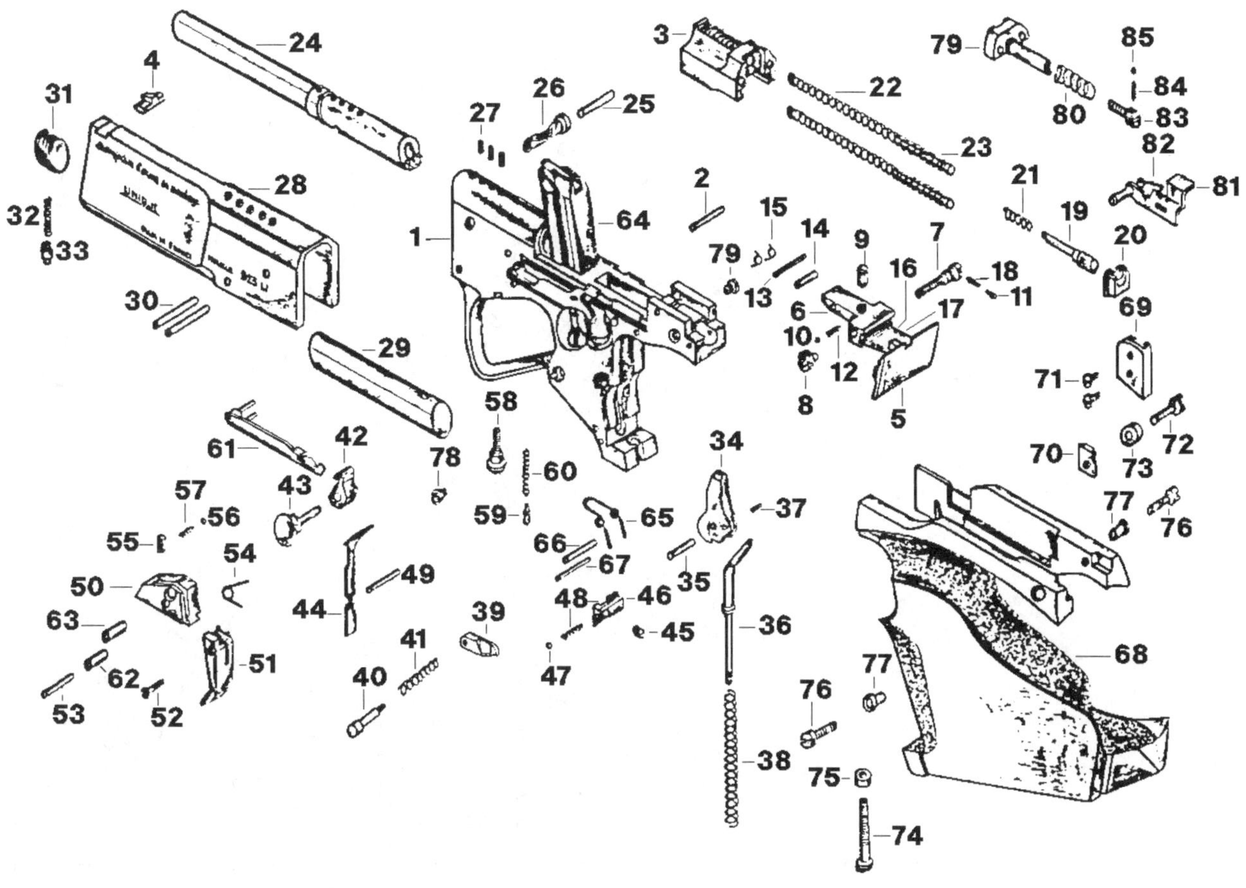

1	Frame	**31**	Counterweight Screw Cap	**61**	Trigger Bar
2	Pin	**32**	Retaining Button Spring	**62**	Trigger Axis Pin Bushing
3	Slide	**33**	Retaining Button	**63**	Trigger Bar Pin Bushing
4	Front Sight	**34**	Hammer	**64**	Magazine
5	Rear Sight Blade	**35**	Hammer Axis Pin	**65**	Magazine Ejector Spring
6	Rear Sight Base	**36**	Hammer Strut	**66**	Magazine Ejector Spring Pivot Pin
7	Lateral Sight Adjustment Screw	**37**	Hammer Strut Pin	**67**	Magazine Ejector Spring Retaining Pin
8	Locknut	**38**	Hammer Spring	**68**	Grip
9	Vertical Adjustment Screw	**39**	Magazine Catch	**69**	Hand Rest Notch
10	Adjustment Screw Ball Click	**40**	Magazine Catch Button	**70**	Notch Support
11	Piston Click	**41**	Magazine Catch Spring	**71**	Hand Rest Fixing Screws
12	Ball Spring	**42**	Sear	**72**	Notch Support Screw
13	Rear Sight Axis Pin	**43**	Sear Axis Pin	**73**	Notch Support Washer
14	Rear Sight Bushing	**44**	Sear Spring	**74**	Grip Screw
15	Vertical Adjustment Spring	**45**	Sear Regulating Screw	**75**	Grip Screw Bushing
16	Ball Bearing	**46**	Sear Screw Stand	**76**	Upper Grip Screw
17	Ball Bearing Spring	**47**	Sear Screw Ball Click	**77**	Upper Grip Screw Bushing
18	Piston Click Spring	**48**	Sear Screw Springs	**78**	Upper Grip Screw Frame Bushing
19	Firing Pin	**49**	Sear Spring Retaining Screw	**79**	Slide Recoil Buffer/Dry Firing Stop
20	Firing Pin Stop	**50**	Trigger Block	**80**	Shock Absorber Spring
21	Firing Pin Spring	**51**	Trigger	**81**	Slide Stop
22	Slide Recoil Spring	**52**	Trigger Overtravel Screw	**82**	Slide Stop Spring
23	Recoil Spring Guide	**53**	Trigger Axis Pin	**83**	Dry Firing Stop
24	Barrel	**54**	Trigger Spring	**84**	Dry Firing Stop Spring
25	Barrel Pin	**55**	Sear Engagement Regulating Screw	**85**	Spring Ball Click
26	Barrel Bushing	**56**	Sear Engagement Screw Ball Click	**Parts Not Shown**	
27	Gas Escape Port Screws	**57**	Ball Click Spring		Movable Hand Rest
28	Barrel Sheath	**58**	Backlash Regulating Screw		
29	Additional Counterweight	**59**	Backlash Screw Ball Click		
30	Barrel Sheath Pins	**60**	Backlash Screw Ball Click Spring		

2000 U Auto

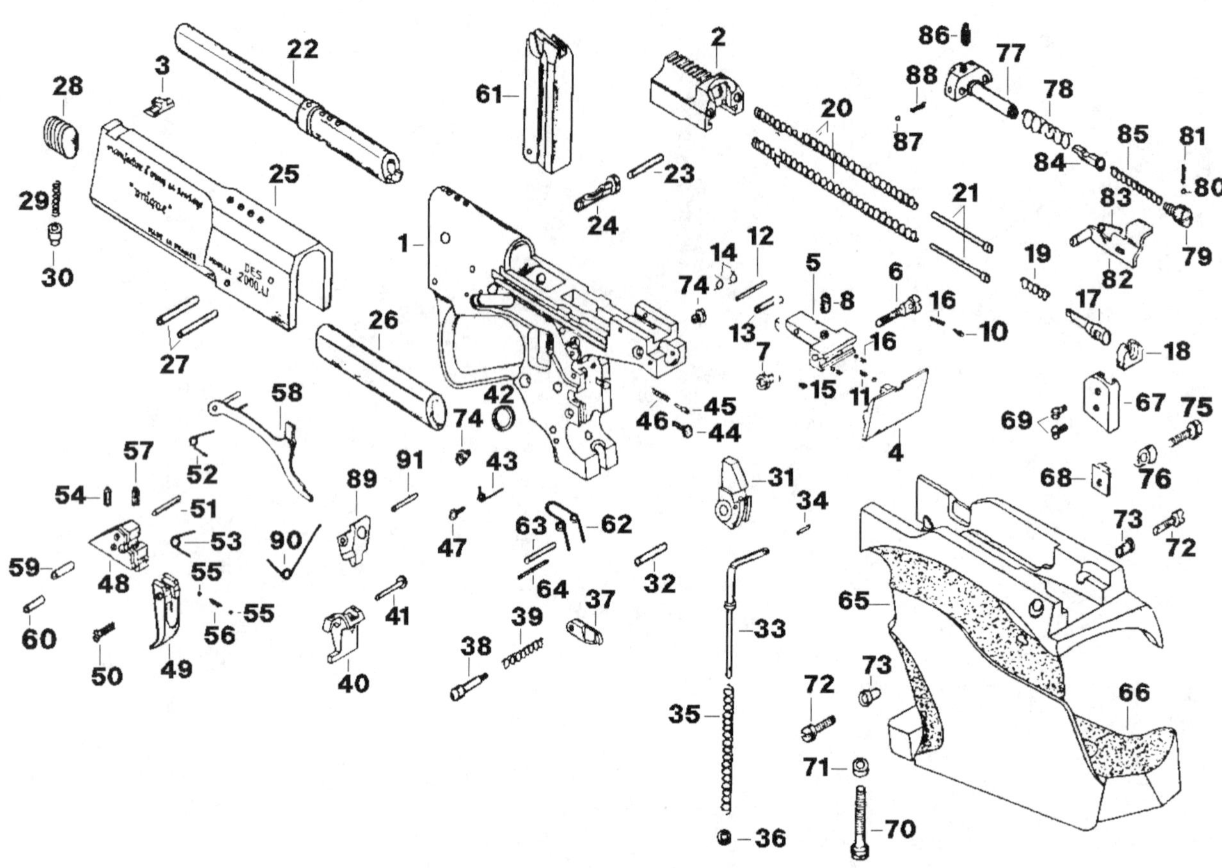

1	Frame
2	Slide
3	Front Sight
4	Rear Sight Blade
5	Rear Sight Base
6	Lateral Sight Adjustment Screw
7	Adjustment Screw Locknut
8	Vertical Sight Adjustment Screw
9	Adjustment Screw Ball Click
10	Adjustment Screw Piston Click
11	Adjustment Screw Ball Spring
12	Rear Sight Axis Pin
13	Axis Pin Bushing
14	Vertical Adjustment Springs
15	Rear Sight Ball Bearing
16	Springs
17	Firing Pin
18	Firing Pin and Hammer Stop
19	Firing Pin Spring
20	Slide Recoil Spring
21	Recoil Spring Guides
22	Barrel
23	Barrel Pin
24	Barrel Pin Bushing
25	Barrel Sheath
26	Additional Counterweight
27	Barrel Sheath Pins
28	Screw Cap
29	Screw Cap Retaining Button Spring
30	Screw Cap Retaining Button
31	Hammer
32	Hammer Axis Pin
33	Hammer Strut
34	Hammer Strut Pin
35	Hammer Spring
36	Hammer Spring Stop
37	Magazine Catch
38	Magazine Catch Button
39	Magazine Catch Spring
40	Sear
41	Sear Axis Pin
42	Trigger Bar Cam Ring
43	Sear Spring
44	Sear Regulating Screw
45	Screw Stand
46	Screw Ball Click
47	Sear Spring Retaining Screw
48	Trigger Block
49	Trigger
50	Trigger Screw
51	Trigger Axis Pin
52	Trigger Spring
53	Trigger Bar Spring
54	Sear Engagement Regulating Screw
55	Ball Click Screws
56	Ball Click Spring
57	Backlash Regulating Screw
58	Trigger Bar
59	Trigger Axis Pin Bushing
60	Trigger Bar Pin Bushing
61	Magazine
62	Magazine Ejector Spring
63	Magazine Ejector Spring Pivot Pin
64	Magazine Ejector Spring Retaining Pin
65	Grip
66	Movable Hand Rest
67	Hand Rest Notch
68	Notch Support
69	Fixing Screws
70	Grip Screw
71	Grip Screw Bushing
72	Upper Grip Screw
73	Upper Grip Screw Bushing
74	Upper Grip Screw Frame Bushings
75	Notch Support Screw
76	Notch Support Bushing
77	Slide Recoil Buffer
78	Shock Absorber Spring
79	Buffer Retaining Screw
80	Buffer Screw Ball Click
81	Ball Click Spring
82	Slide Stop
83	Slide Stop Spring
84	Dry Firing Stop
85	Stop Spring
86	Stop Lock Screw
87	Screw Ball Click
88	Ball Click Spring
89	Intermediate Sear
90	Intermediate Sear Spring
91	Intermediate Sear Spring Pin

Escort and Corsair Auto

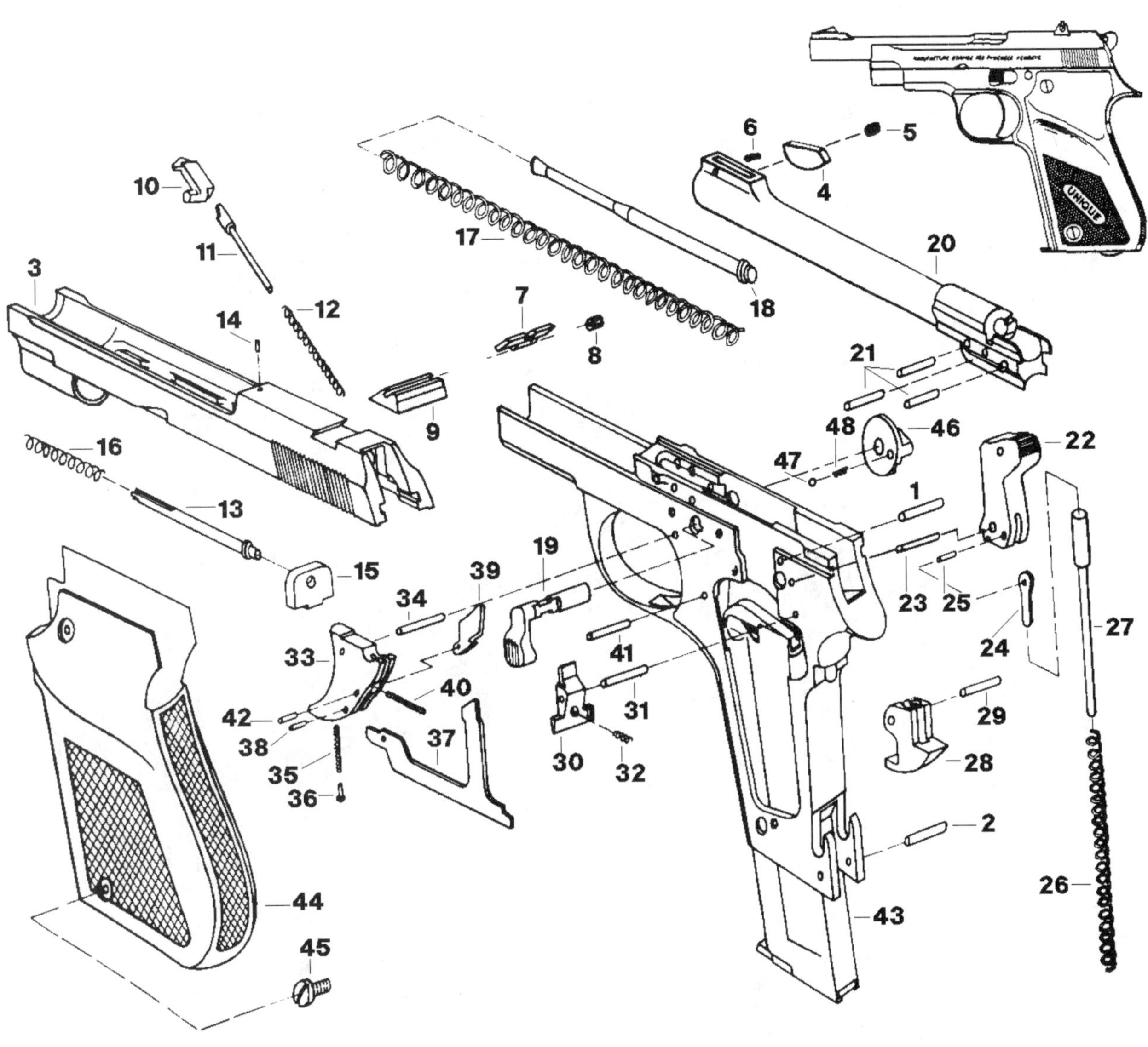

1	Hammer Stop	18	Recoil Spring Guide	34	Trigger Axis Pin
2	Magazine Catch Stop	19	Safety	35	Trigger Spring
3	Slide	20	Barrel	36	Trigger Spring Guide
4	Front Sight	21	Barrel Rivets	37	Trigger Bar and Disconnector
5	Front Sight Screw	22	Hammer with Guide and Pin Complete	38	Trigger Pin
6	Front Sight Pin	23	Hammer Axis Pin	39	Magazine Safety
7	Rear Sight	24	Hammer Guide	40	Magazine Safety Spring
8	Rear Sight Screw	25	Hammer Guide Pin	41	Magazine Safety Stop
9	Rear Sight Base	26	Hammer Spring	42	Magazine Safety Pin
10	Extractor	27	Hammer Spring Guide	43	Magazine Complete
11	Extractor Spring Guide	28	Magazine Catch	44	Grips
12	Extractor Spring	29	Magazine Catch Axis Pin	45	Grip Screws
13	Firing Pin	30	Sear	46	Dismantling Stud
14	Firing Pin Stop	31	Sear Axis Pin	47	Dismantling Stud Ball Catch
15	Firing Pin Guide	32	Sear Spring	48	Dismantling Stud Ball Catch Spring
16	Firing Pin Spring	33	Trigger	**Parts Not Shown**	
17	Recoil Spring				Rear Sight Spring

Model Bcf 66 Auto

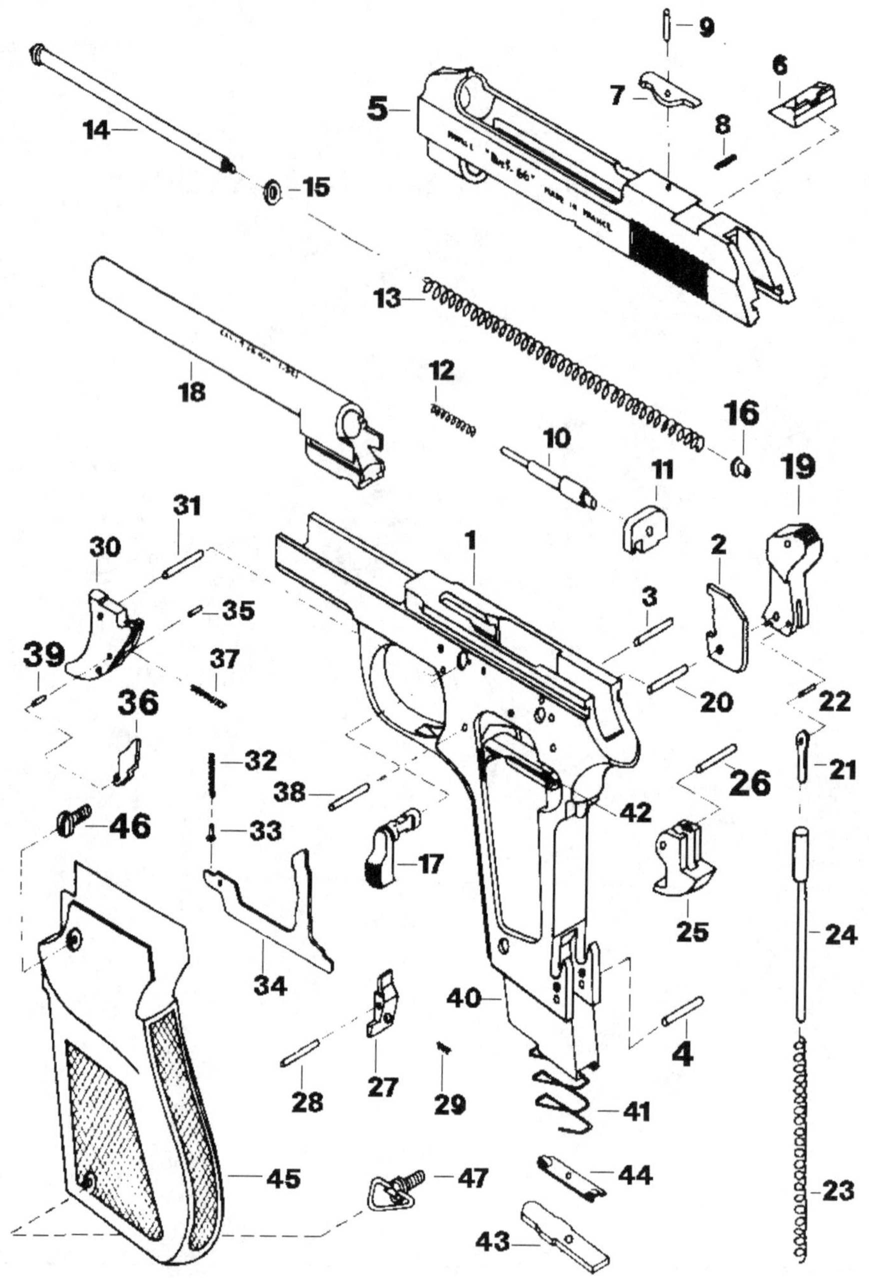

1	Frame	**17**	Safety	**33**	Trigger Bar Guide
2	Ejector	**18**	Barrel	**34**	Trigger Bar
3	Hammer Stop	**19**	Hammer	**35**	Trigger Bar Pin
4	Magazine Catch Stop	**20**	Hammer Pin	**36**	Magazine Safety
5	Slide	**21**	Hammer Link	**37**	Magazine Safety Spring
6	Rear Sight	**22**	Hammer Link Pin	**38**	Magazine Safety Stop
7	Extractor	**23**	Hammer Spring	**39**	Magazine Safety Pin
8	Extractor Spring	**24**	Hammer Spring Guide	**40**	Magazine Body
9	Extractor Pin	**25**	Magazine Catch	**41**	Magazine Spring
10	Firing Pin	**26**	Magazine Catch Pin	**42**	Magazine Follower
11	Firing Pin Stop	**27**	Sear	**43**	Magazine Bottom Plate
12	Firing Pin Spring	**28**	Sear Pin	**44**	Magazine Spring Bottom Plate
13	Recoil Spring	**29**	Sear Spring	**45**	Grip
14	Recoil Spring Guide	**30**	Trigger	**46**	Grip Screw
15	Recoil Spring Guide Washer	**31**	Trigger Pin	**47**	Lanyard Ring
16	Recoil Spring Guide Screw Nut	**32**	Trigger Bar Spring		

Model 1842 Percussion

Courtesy of Blacksmith Corporation

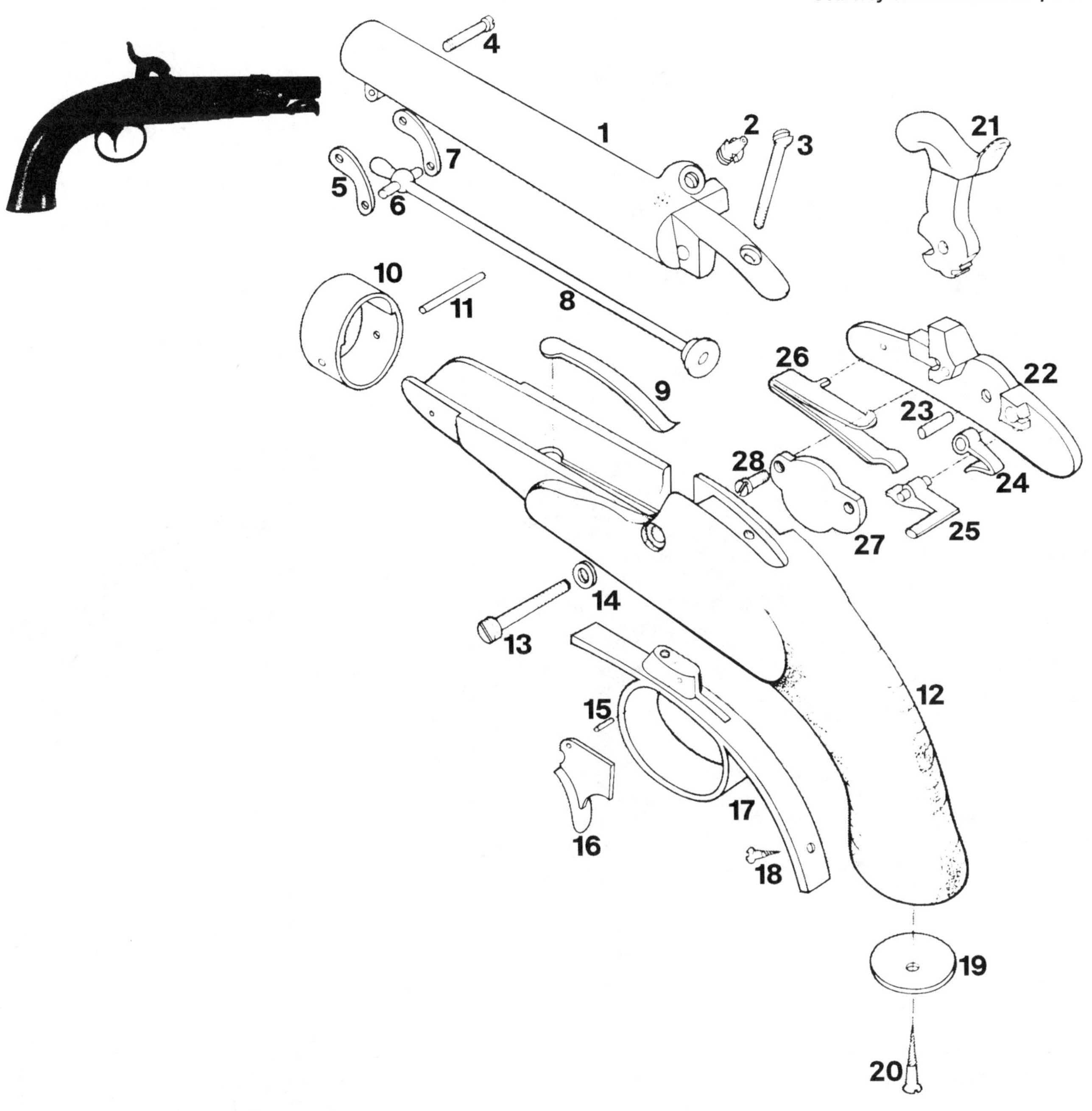

1	Barrel	15	Trigger Pin
2	Cone	16	Trigger
3	Barrel Screw	17	Trigger Guard
4	Swivel Screw	18	Trigger Guard Screw
5	Left Ramrod Swivel	19	Buttcap
6	Ramrod Guide	20	Buttcap Screw
7	Right Ramrod Swivel	21	Hammer
8	Ramrod	22	Lockplate
9	Ramrod Spring	23	Hammer Pin
10	Band	24	Sear Spring
11	Band Cross Pin	25	Sear
12	Stock	26	Mainspring
13	Lock Retaining Screw	27	Bridle
14	Washer	28	Bridle Screws

Auto

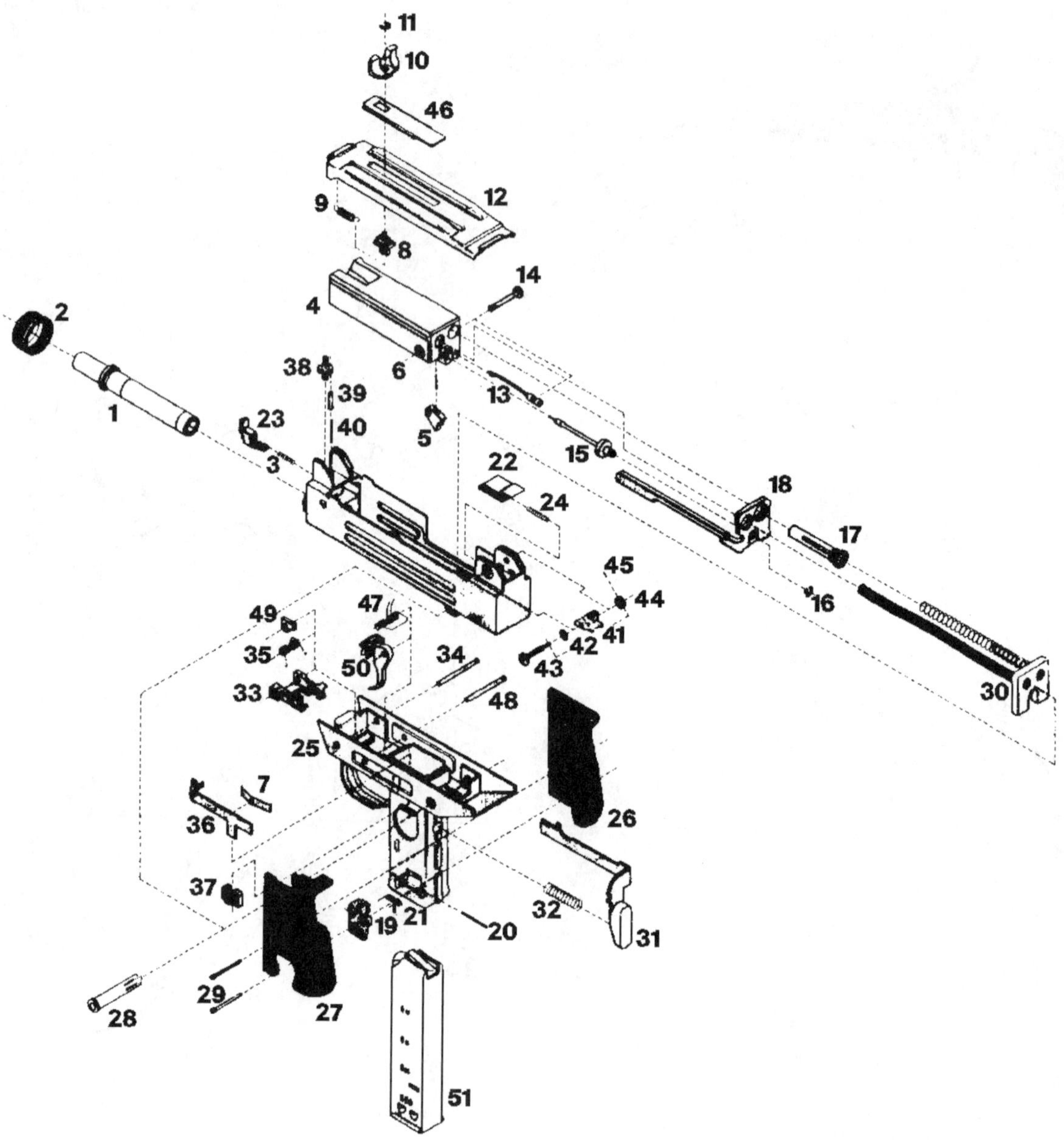

1	Barrel		**18**	Striker Guide		**35**	Sear Spring
2	Barrel Retaining Nut		**19**	Magazine Catch		**36**	Fire Selector Lever
3	Barrel Retaining Nut Spring		**20**	Magazine Catch Pin		**37**	Fire Selector Button
4	Bolt		**21**	Magazine Catch Spring		**38**	Front Sight
5	Blocking Latch		**22**	Cover Catch		**39**	Front Sight Detent
6	Blocking Latch Spring		**23**	Barrel Return Nut Catch		**40**	Front Sight Spring
7	Lever Spring		**24**	Cover Catch Spring		**41**	Rear Sight
8	Cocking Lug		**25**	Frame		**42**	Rear Sight Spring Washer
9	Cocking Lug Spring		**26**	Right Grip		**43**	Rear Sight Axis
10	Cocking Knob		**27**	Left Grip		**44**	Rear Sight Windage Drum
11	Cocking Knob Retainer		**28**	Grip Pin		**45**	Windage Drum Pin
12	Receiver Cover Plate		**29**	Grip Screws		**46**	Slot Cover Plate
13	Extractor		**30**	Return Spring Assembly		**47**	Trigger Spring
14	Extractor Pin		**31**	Grip Safety		**48**	Trigger Pin
15	Firing Pin		**32**	Safety Spring		**49**	Dog Stop
16	Firing Pin Return Ring		**33**	Sear		**50**	Trigger Assembly
17	Firing Pin Spring Seat		**34**	Sear Pin		**51**	Magazine Assembly

Dragoon Revolver

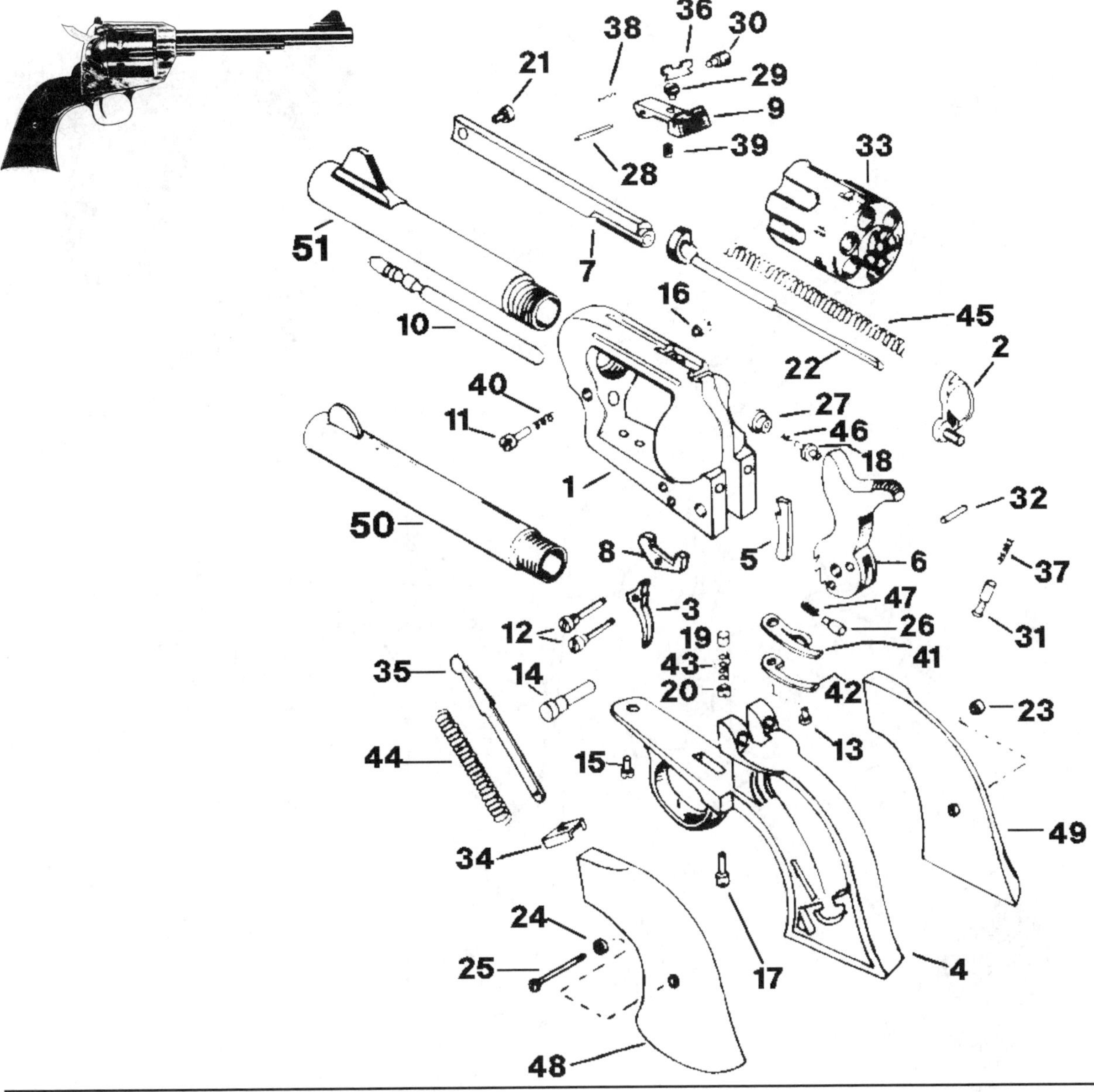

1	Frame
2	Gate
3	Trigger
4	Grip Frame
5	Hand
6	Hammer
7	Ejector Tube
8	Bolt
9	Rear Sight Block
10	Base Pin
11	Base Pin Screw
12	Trigger and Bolt Pivots
13	Bolt Spring Screw
14	Hammer Pivot
15	Front Trigger Guard Screw
16	Base Pin Nut
17	Trigger Guard Screws
18	Firing Pin
19	Gate Catch
20	Gate Screw
21	Ejector Tube Screw
22	Ejector Rod Assembly
23	Grip Nut
24	Grip Bushing
25	Grip Screw
26	Hand Spring Plunger
27	Firing Pin Bushing
28	Rear Sight Pivot Pin
29	Rear Sight Elevation Screw
30	Rear Sight Windage Adjustment Screw
31	Kicker
32	Kicker Retaining Pin
33	Cylinder
34	Hammer Spring Retainer
35	Hammer Push Rod
36	Rear Sight Blade
37	Kicker Spring
38	Rear Sight Windage Spring
39	Rear Sight Elevation Spring
40	Base Pin Spring
41	Bolt and Trigger Spring
42	Bolt and Trigger Backer Spring
43	Gate Spring
44	Hammer Spring
45	Ejector Spring
46	Firing Pin Spring
47	Hand Spring
48	Left-Hand Grip
49	Right-Hand Grip
50	Barrel-Field Sights
51	Barrel-Adjustable Sights

Parts Not Shown

Base Pin Catch Assembly
Mainspring Assembly
Ejector Rod

Model 1 Auto

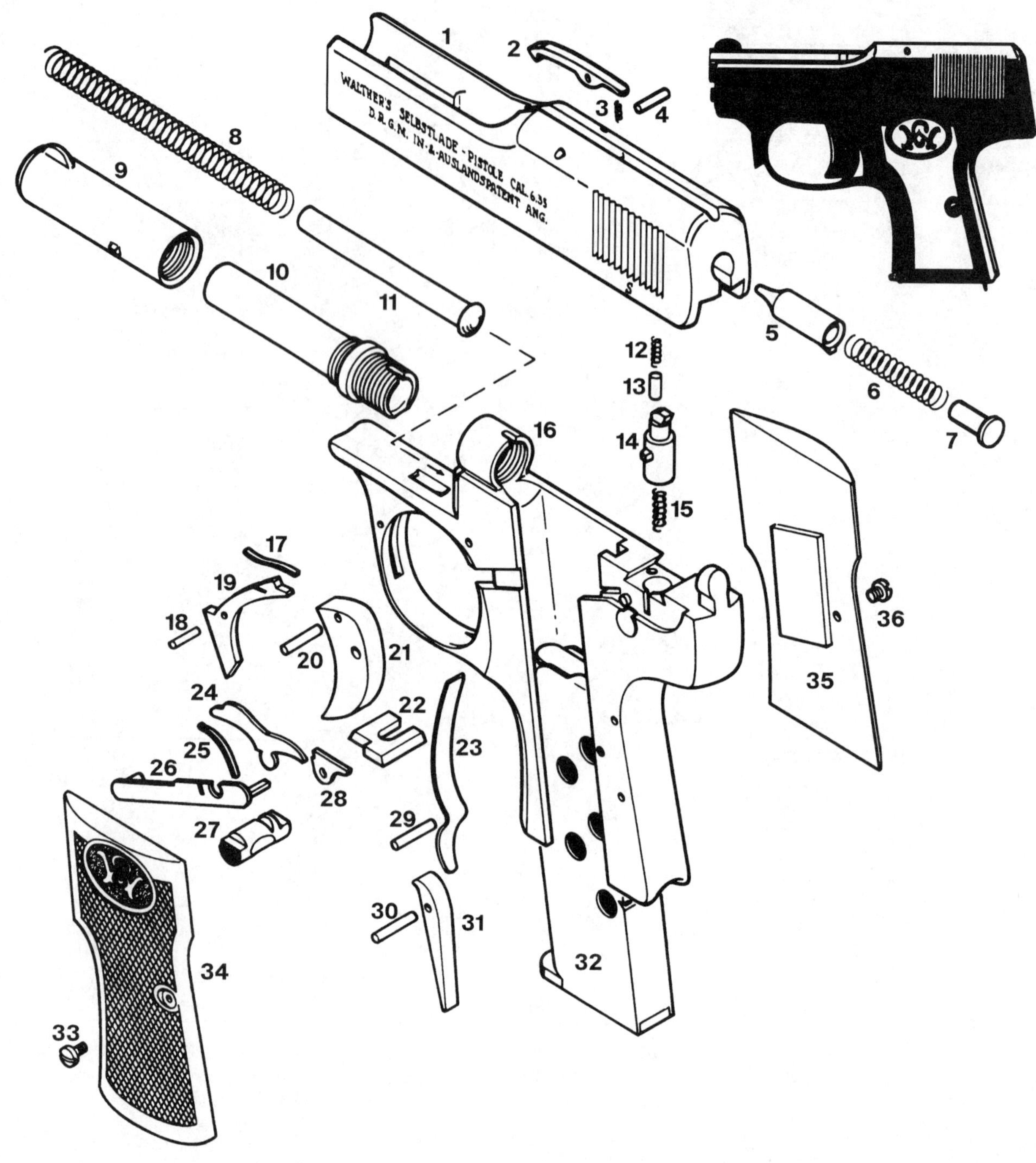

1	Slide	**13**	Safety Plunger	**25**	Disconnector Spring
2	Extractor	**14**	Sear	**26**	Trigger Bar
3	Extractor Spring	**15**	Sear Spring	**27**	Safety
4	Extractor Pin	**16**	Frame	**28**	Sear Lever
5	Firing Pin	**17**	Slide Lock Spring	**29**	Magazine Catch Spring Pin
6	Firing Pin Spring	**18**	Slide Lock Pin	**30**	Magazine Catch Pin
7	Firing Pin Spring Guide	**19**	Slide Lock	**31**	Magazine Catch
8	Recoil Spring	**20**	Trigger Pin	**32**	Magazine
9	Barrel Cover	**21**	Trigger	**33**	Left Grip Screw
10	Barrel	**22**	Sear Retainer	**34**	Left Grip Panel
11	Recoil Spring Guide	**23**	Trigger/Magazine Catch Spring	**35**	Right Grip Screw
12	Safety Plunger Spring	**24**	Disconnector	**36**	Right Grip Panel

Model 4 Auto

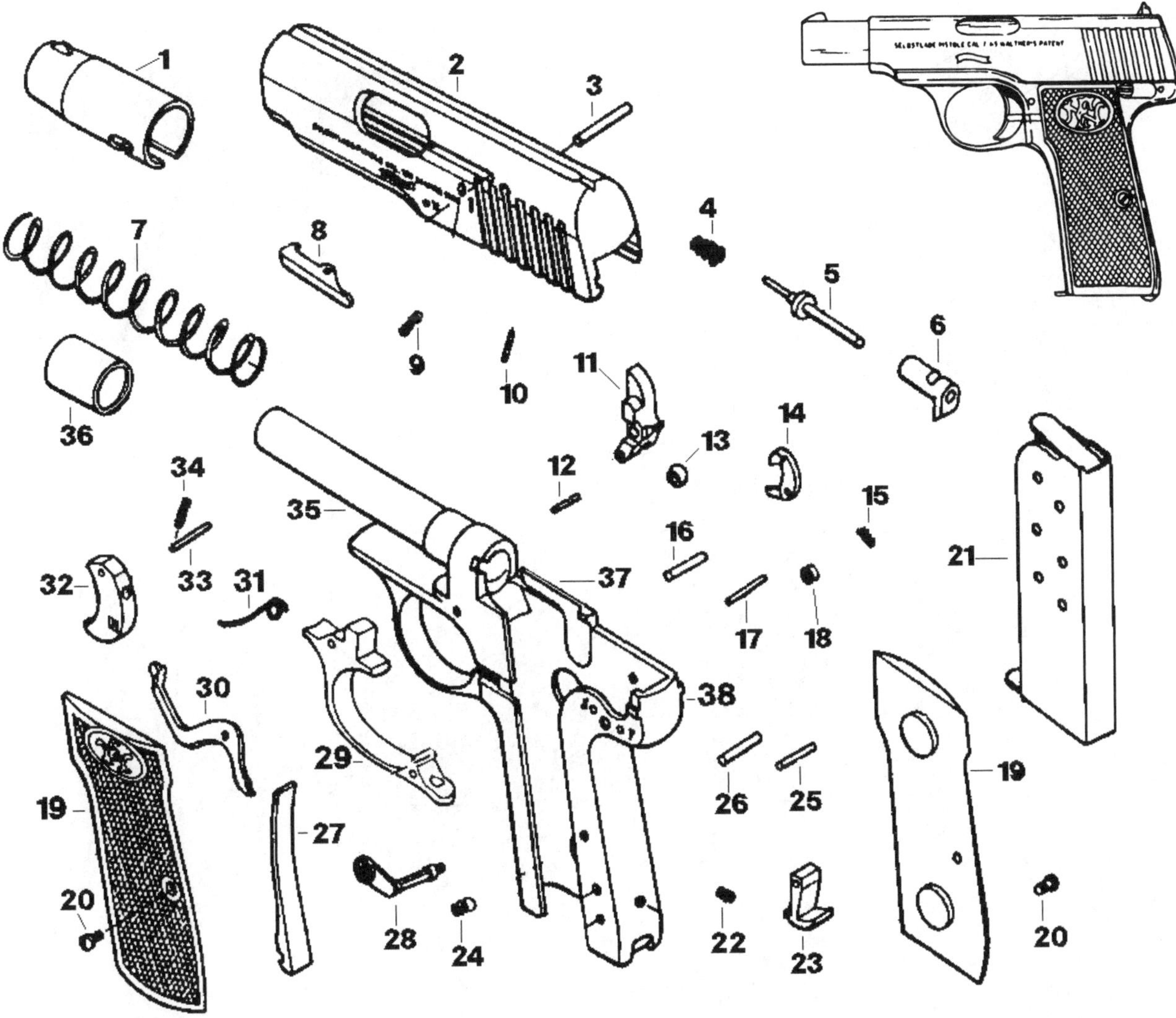

1	Slide Extension	20	Grip Screws
2	Slide	21	Magazine
3	Firing Pin Retainer	22	Mainspring Retainer Screw
4	Firing Pin Spring	23	Magazine Catch
5	Firing Pin	24	Magazine Catch Spring
6	Firing Pin Extension	25	Magazine Catch Pin
7	Recoil Spring	26	Mainspring Pin
8	Extractor	27	Mainspring
9	Extractor Spring	28	Safety Catch
10	Extractor Pin	29	Trigger Guard
11	Hammer	30	Trigger Bar
12	Hammer Roller Pin	31	Trigger Bar Spring
13	Hammer Roller	32	Trigger
14	Sear	33	Trigger Pin
15	Sear Spring	34	Trigger Spring
16	Hammer Pin	35	Barrel
17	Sear Pin	36	Recoil Spring Bushing
18	Safety Catch Nut	37	Ejector
19	Grips	38	Frame

Model 8 Auto

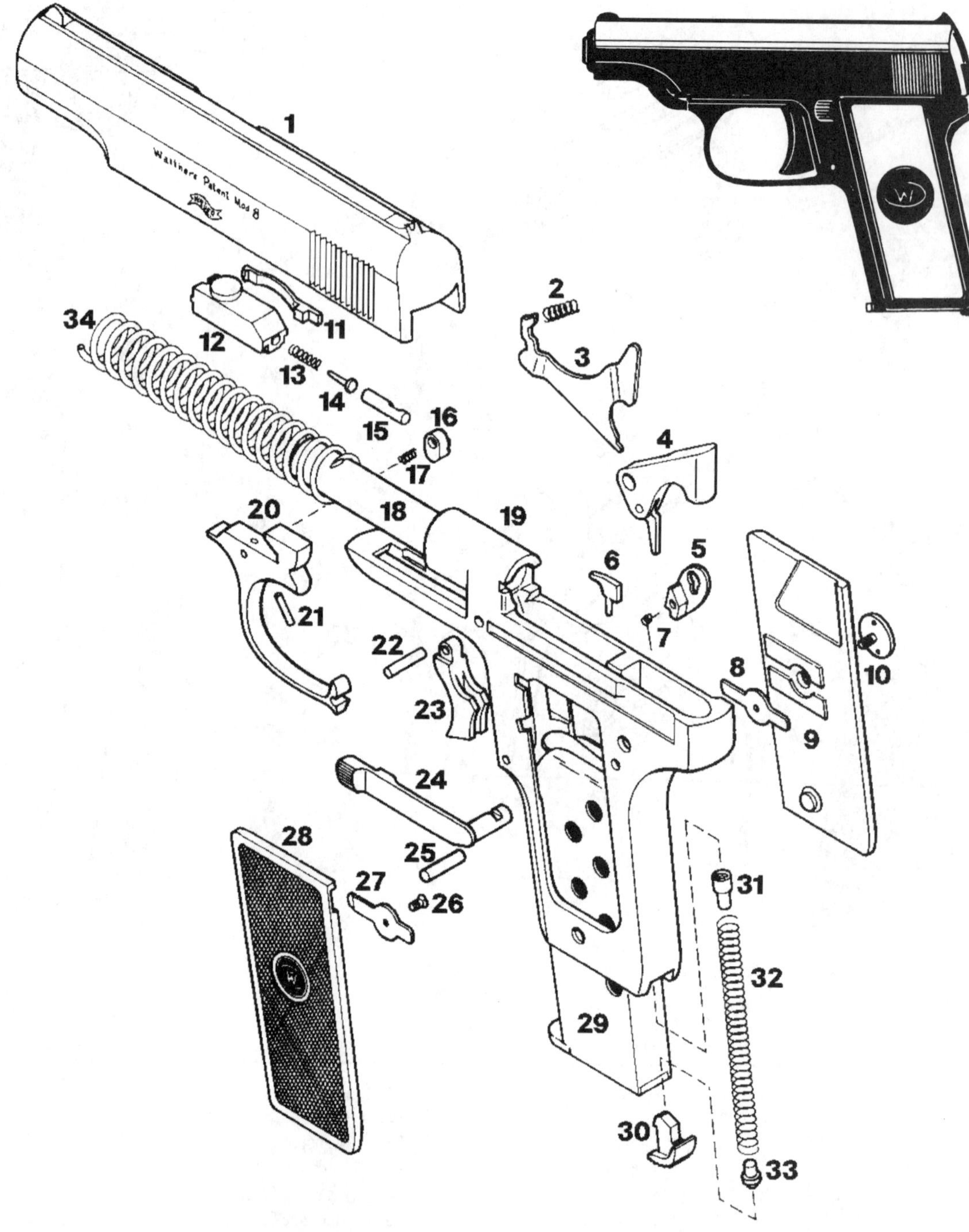

1 Slide
2 Trigger Bar Spring
3 Trigger Bar
4 Hammer
5 Sear
6 Ejector
7 Sear Spring
8 Right Grip Retainer
9 Right Grip Panel
10 Right Grip Panel Screw
11 Extractor
12 Breechblock
13 Firing Pin Spring
14 Firing Pin
15 Firing Pin Extension
16 Takedown Latch
17 Takedown Latch Spring
18 Barrel
19 Frame
20 Trigger Guard
21 Takedown Latch Pin
22 Trigger Pin
23 Trigger
24 Safety
25 Sear Pin
26 Left Grip Retainer Screw
27 Left Grip Retainer
28 Left Grip Panel
29 Magazine
30 Magazine Catch
31 Mainspring Plunger
32 Mainspring
33 Magazine Catch Plunger
34 Recoil Spring

Model 9 Auto

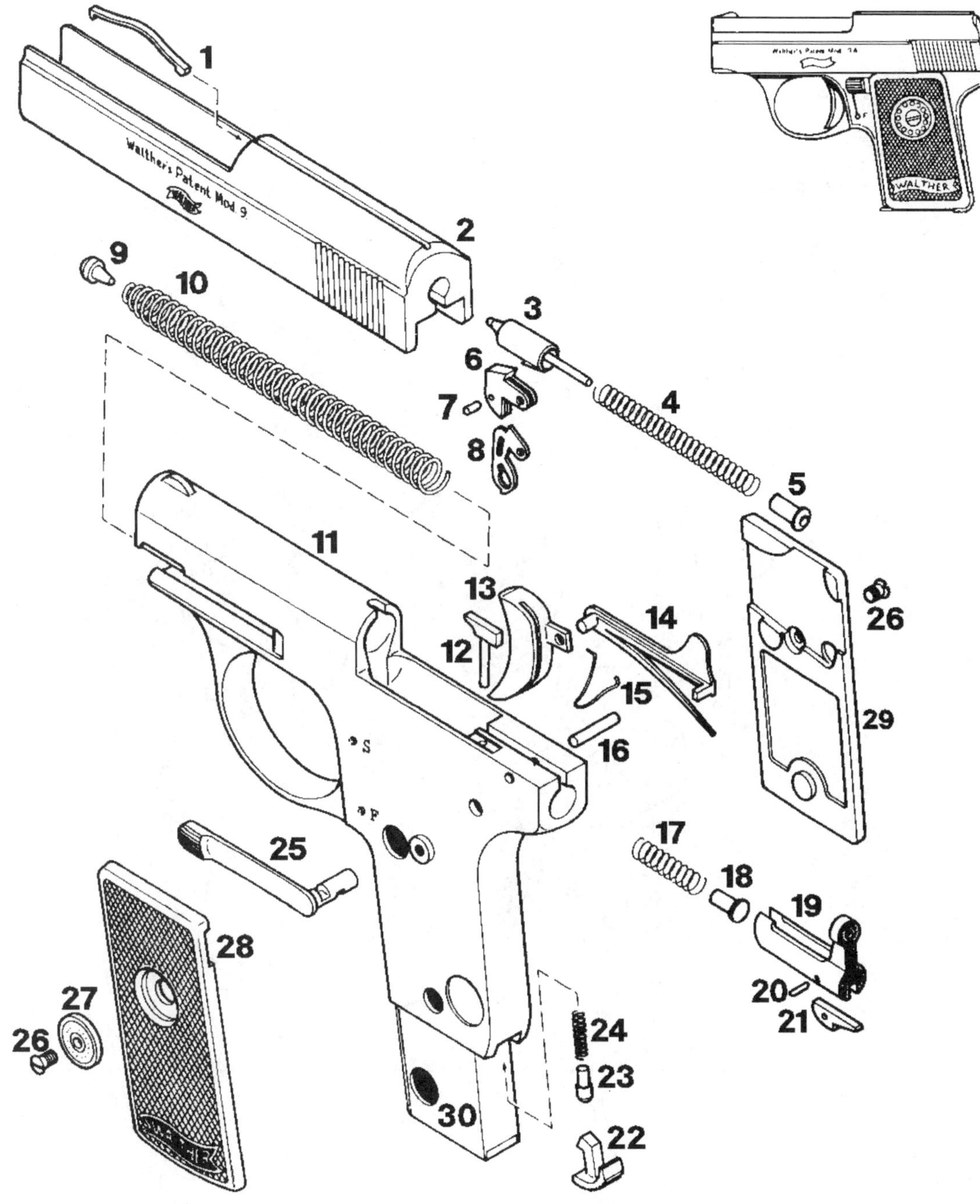

1	Extractor	**11**	Barrel and Frame Assembly	**21**	Latch Release Lever
2	Slide	**12**	Ejector	**22**	Magazine Catch
3	Firing Pin	**13**	Trigger	**23**	Magazine Catch Spring Plunger
4	Firing Pin Spring	**14**	Trigger Bar/Disconnector	**24**	Magazine Catch Spring
5	Firing Pin Spring Guide	**15**	Trigger Return Spring	**25**	Safety
6	Sear	**16**	Sear Pin	**26**	Grip Screws
7	Sear Connector Pin	**17**	Takedown Latch Spring	**27**	Grip Escutcheons
8	Sear Lever	**18**	Takedown Latch Spring Plunger	**28**	Left Grip Panel
9	Recoil Spring Guide	**19**	Takedown Latch	**29**	Right Grip Panel
10	Recoil Spring	**20**	Latch Release Pin	**30**	Magazine

Olympia-Pistole Auto

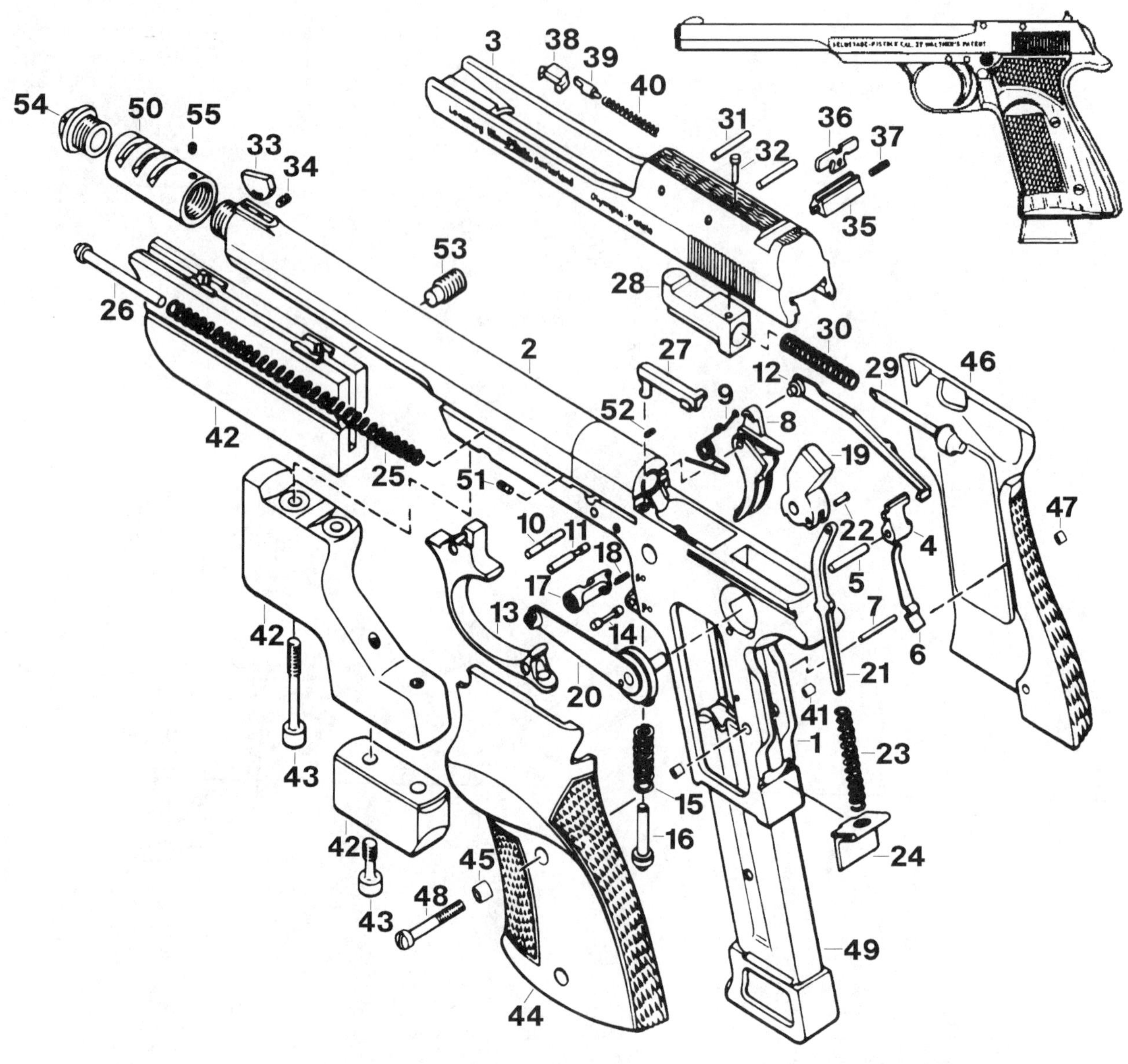

1	Frame	20	Safety	39	Extractor Bolt
2	Barrel	21	Hammer Spring Plunger	40	Extractor Spring
3	Slide	22	Hammer Spring Plunger Pin	41	Grip Screw Sleeve
4	Sear	23	Hammer Spring	42	Weights
5	Sear Pin	24	Hammer Spring Bearing	43	Weight Screws
6	Sear Spring	25	Recoil Spring	44	Grip, Left
7	Sear Pin Spring	26	Recoil Spring Pin	45	Escutcheon
8	Trigger	27	Ejector	46	Grip, Right
9	Trigger Spring	28	Firing Pin Support	47	Grip Nut
10	Trigger Pin	29	Firing Pin	48	Grip Screw
11	Trigger Striking Pin	30	Firing Pin Spring	49	Magazine
12	Trigger Sear Bar	31	Firing Pin Support Pin	50	Muzzlebrake
13	Trigger Guard	32	Firing Pin Lock Pin	51	Trigger Adjusting Screw
14	Trigger Guard Pin	33	Front Sight	52	Lock Screw
15	Trigger Guard Spring	34	Front Sight Screw	53	Weight Screw
16	Trigger Guard Spring Pin	35	Rear Sight Base	54	Muzzlebrake Cover
17	Magazine Release	36	Rear Sight Blade	55	Muzzlebrake Lock Screw
18	Magazine Release Spring	37	Rear Sight Blade Screw		
19	Hammer	38	Extractor		

Olympia Rapid-Fire Auto

Courtesy of Blacksmith Corporation

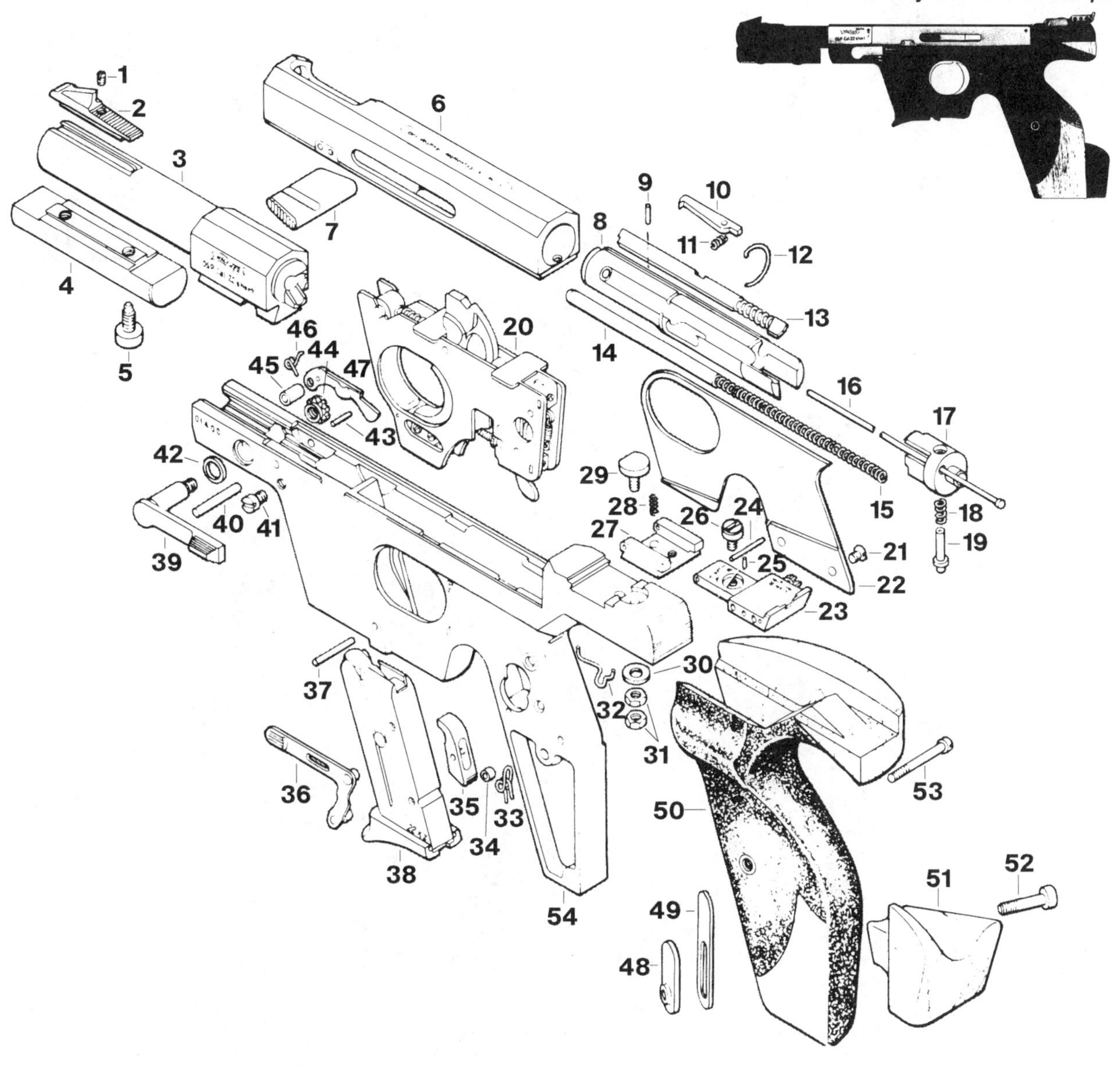

1	Sight Lock Screw	**19**	Stop Retaining Plunger	**37**	Magazine Catch Pin
2	Front Sight	**20**	Trigger Assembly	**38**	Magazine
3	Barrel	**21**	Sideplate Screw	**39**	Barrel Lock
4	Weight	**22**	Sideplate	**40**	Hold-Open Latch Pin
5	Weight Screw	**23**	Rear Sight Leaf Assembly	**41**	Barrel Lock Stop Screw
6	Receiver	**24**	Sight Leaf Pin	**42**	Barrel Lock Bushing
7	Cocking Piece	**25**	Click Pin	**43**	Lock Nut Pin
8	Bolt	**26**	Sight Elevation Screw	**44**	Lock Nut
9	Extractor Pin	**27**	Rear Sight Base	**45**	Spacer
10	Extractor	**28**	Rear Sight Spring	**46**	Hold-Open Latch Spring
11	Extractor Spring	**29**	Sight Retainer Screw	**47**	Hold-Open Latch
12	Firing Pin Retainer	**30**	Washer	**48**	Adjusting Screw Nut
13	Firing Pin and Spring	**31**	Sight Retainer Nuts	**49**	Slide Plate
14	Recoil Spring Housing	**32**	Safety Catch Spring	**50**	Grip
15	Recoil Spring	**33**	Magazine Catch Spring	**51**	Palm Rest
16	Recoil Spring Guide	**34**	Magazine Catch Bushing	**52**	Adjusting Screw
17	Bolt Stop	**35**	Magazine Catch	**53**	Grip Screw
18	Plunger Spring	**36**	Safety Catch	**54**	Frame

P-38 Auto

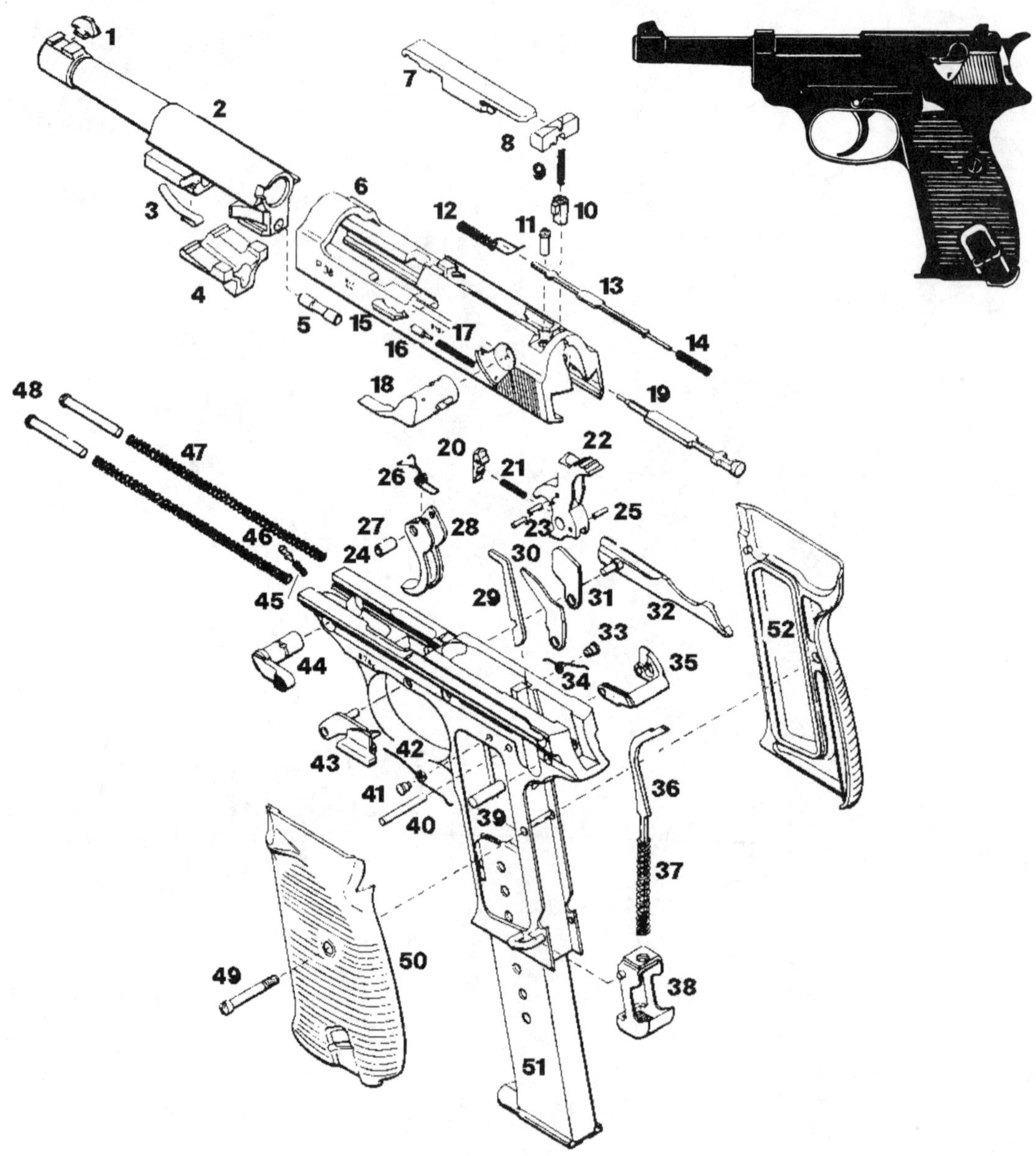

1	Front Sight	19	Firing Pin	37	Hammer Spring
2	Barrel	20	Hammer Lever	38	Magazine Catch
3	Locking-Block Retainer Spring	21	Hammer Lever Spring	39	Hammer Pin
4	Locking Block	22	Hammer	40	Sear Pin
5	Locking-Block Operating Pin	23	Hammer Lever Pins	41	Slide Stop Return Spring Stud
6	Slide	24	Frame	42	Slide Stop Return Spring
7	Firing Pin and Indicator Cover	25	Strut Axle Pin	43	Slide Stop
8	Rear Sight	26	Trigger Spring	44	Takedown Lever
9	Automatic Firing Pin Lock Spring	27	Trigger Bushing	45	Retainer Latch Plunger Spring
10	Automatic Firing Pin Lock	28	Trigger	46	Retainer Latch Plunger
11	Firing Pin Retainer Pin	29	Ejector	47	Recoil Springs
12	Firing Pin Spring	30	Safety Hammer Lowering Lever	48	Recoil Spring Guides
13	Cartridge Indicator Pin	31	Firing Pin Lock Lifter	49	Grip Screw
14	Cartridge Indicator Spring	32	Trigger Bar	50	Left Grip Panel
15	Extractor	33	Trigger Bar Spring Stud	51	Magazine
16	Extractor Plunger	34	Trigger Bar Spring	52	Right Grip Panel
17	Extractor Plunger Spring	35	Sear		
18	Safety	36	Hammer Strut		

Mark IV Revolver

Courtesy of Dennis Riordan

1	Barrel	**17**	Grip Pins	**33**	Bolt
2	Extractor Nut	**18**	Frame	**34**	Bolt Catch Pin
3	Extractor Spring	**19**	Lanyard Ring	**35**	Bolt Spring
4	Cylinder Retaining Cam	**20**	Trigger	**36**	Bolt Pin
5	Cylinder Cam Screws	**21**	Hand	**37**	Barrel Catch Screw
6	Cylinder	**22**	Trigger Guard	**38**	Cam Lever Lock Screw
7	Extractor	**23**	Trigger Guard Screws	**39**	Cam Lever
8	Hammer	**24**	Mainspring Lever	**40**	Cam Lever Screw
9	Barrel Catch Spring	**25**	Mainspring	**41**	Recoil Shield Screw
10	Barrel Catch	**26**	Hammer Screw	**42**	Hinge Pin
11	Hammer Catch	**27**	Trigger Screw	**43**	Extractor Lever Spring
12	Hammer Catch Spring	**28**	Recoil Shield	**44**	Extractor Lever Roller
13	Hammer Swivel Screw	**29**	Left-Hand Grip	**45**	Extractor Lever
14	Hammer Swivel	**30**	Grip Screw	**46**	Hinge Pin Screw
15	Hammer Catch Screw	**31**	Bolt Catch		
16	Right-Hand Grip	**32**	Bolt Catch Spring		

Metropolitan Police Auto

Courtesy of Dennis Riordan

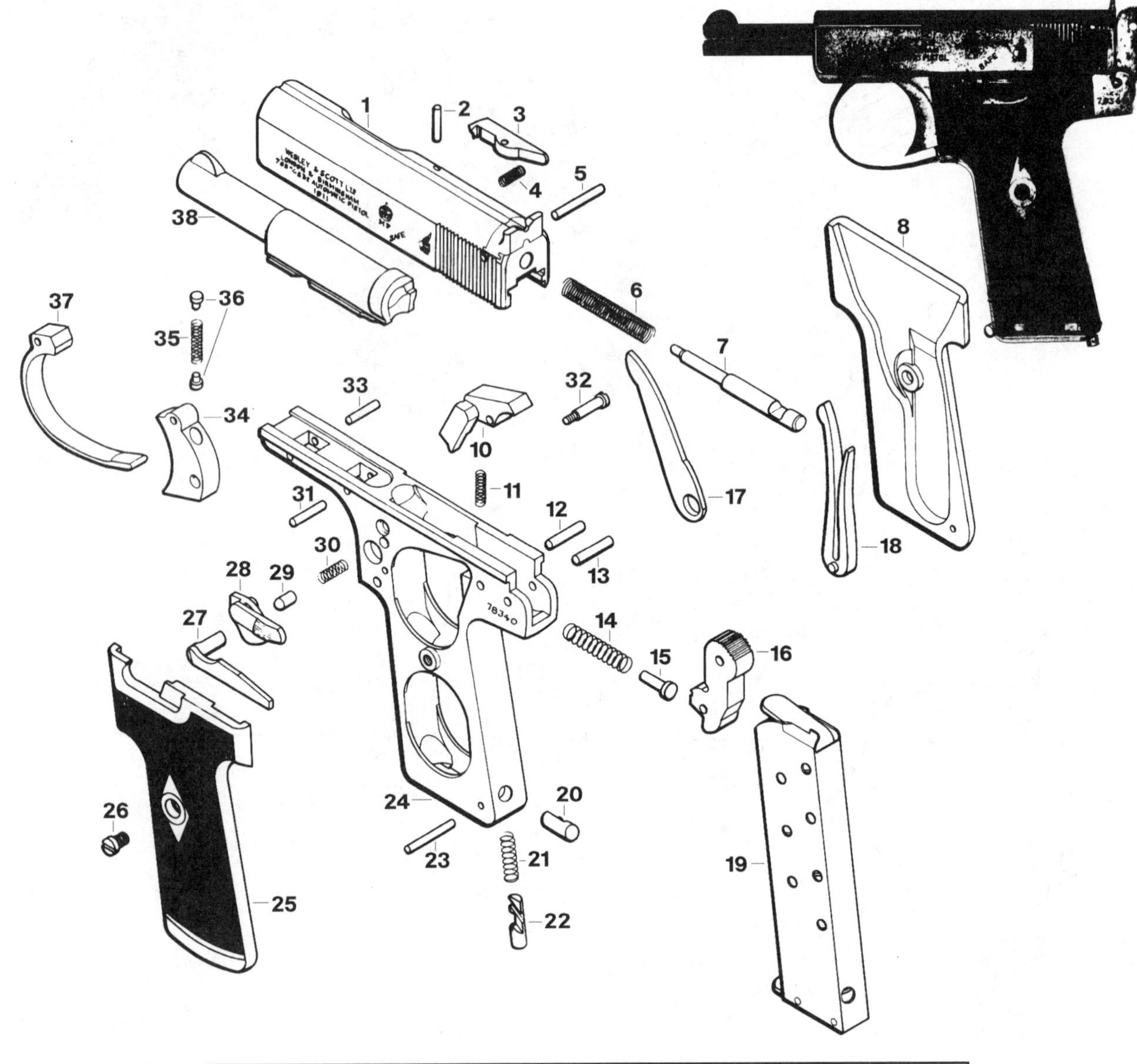

No.	Part	No.	Part
1	Slide	20	Magazine Catch
2	Extractor Pin	21	Magazine Catch Spring
3	Extractor	22	Magazine Release Button
4	Extractor Spring	23	Magazine Catch Pin
5	Firing Pin Retaining Pin	24	Frame
6	Firing Pin Spring	25	Left Grip
7	Firing Pin	26	Left Grip Screw (Short)
8	Right Grip	27	Trigger Bar
9	Right Grip Screw (Long)	28	Safety
10	Sear	29	Safety Detent
11	Sear Spring	30	Safety Detent Spring
12	Sear Pin	31	Trigger Pin
13	Hammer Pin	32	Safety Screw
14	Hammer Spring	33	Trigger Guard Pin
15	Hammer Spring Plunger	34	Trigger
16	Hammer	35	Trigger Spring
17	Recoil Arm	36	Trigger Spring Plungers
18	Recoil Spring	37	Trigger Guard
19	Magazine	38	Barrel

455 Auto

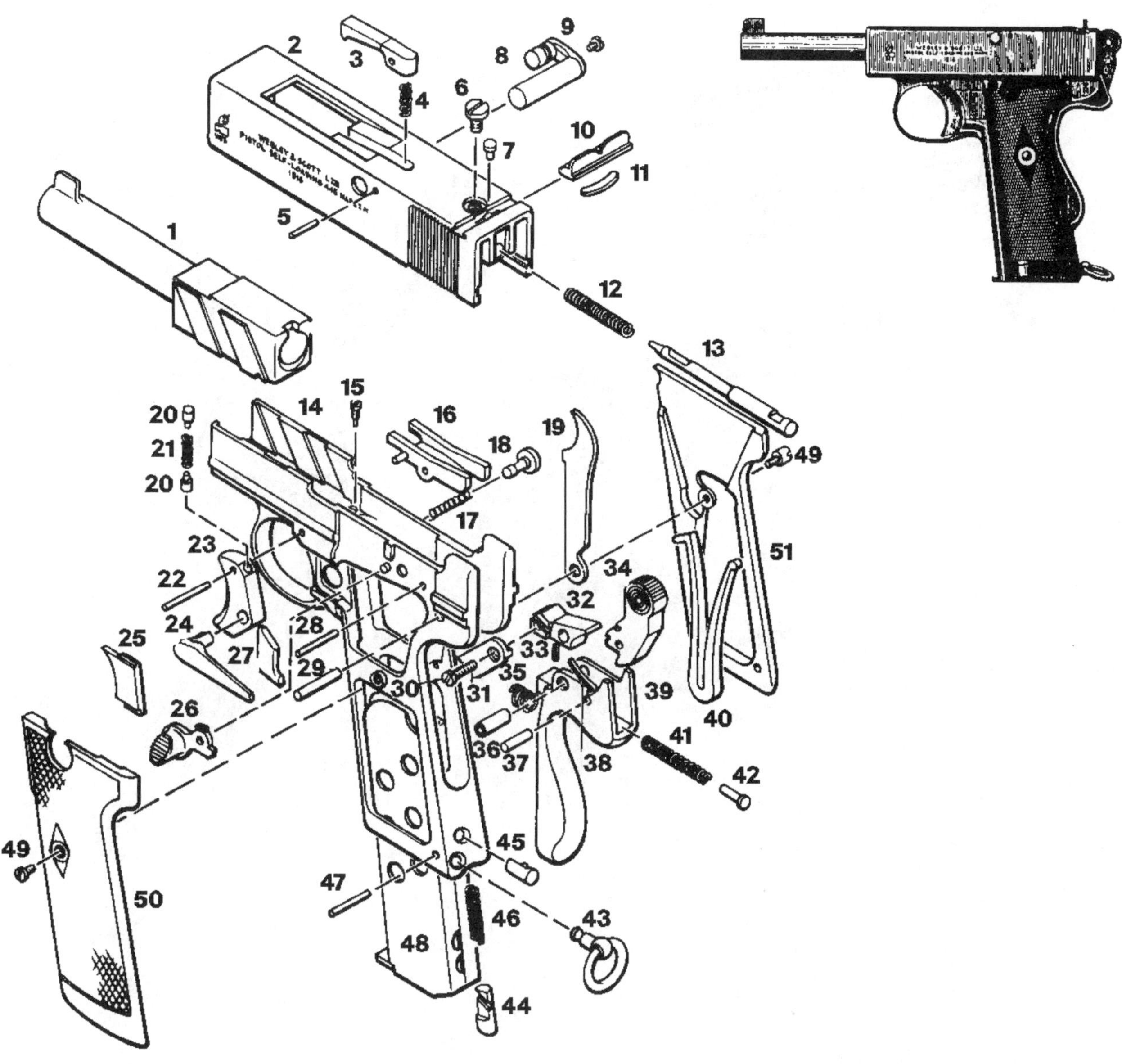

1	Barrel	18	Recoil Lever Stop	35	Grip Safety Spring
2	Slide	19	Recoil Spring Lever	36	Grip Safety Pivot
3	Extractor	20	Trigger Spring Plungers	37	Hammer Pin
4	Extractor Spring	21	Trigger Spring	38	Slide Latch Spring
5	Extractor Pin	22	Trigger Pivot Pin	39	Grip Safety
6	Rear Sight Screw	23	Trigger	40	Recoil Spring
7	Firing Pin Retainer	24	Trigger Bar	41	Hammer Spring
8	Takedown Block	25	Trigger Plate	42	Hammer Spring Plunger
9	Takedown Block Screw	26	Slide Latch	43	Lanyard Loop
10	Rear Sight	27	Trigger Auxiliary Lever	44	Magazine Catch Button
11	Firing Pin Retainer Spring	28	Slide Hold-Open Pin	45	Magazine Catch
12	Firing Pin Spring	29	Grip Safety Pin	46	Magazine Catch Spring
13	Firing Pin	30	Sear Lever Screw	47	Lanyard Loop Pin
14	Frame	31	Sear Lever	48	Magazine
15	Trigger Pin Screw	32	Sear	49	Grip Screws
16	Slide Latch	33	Sear Spring	50	Left Grip Panel
17	Recoil Lever Stop Spring	34	Hammer	51	Right Grip Panel

Wolverine 22 Auto

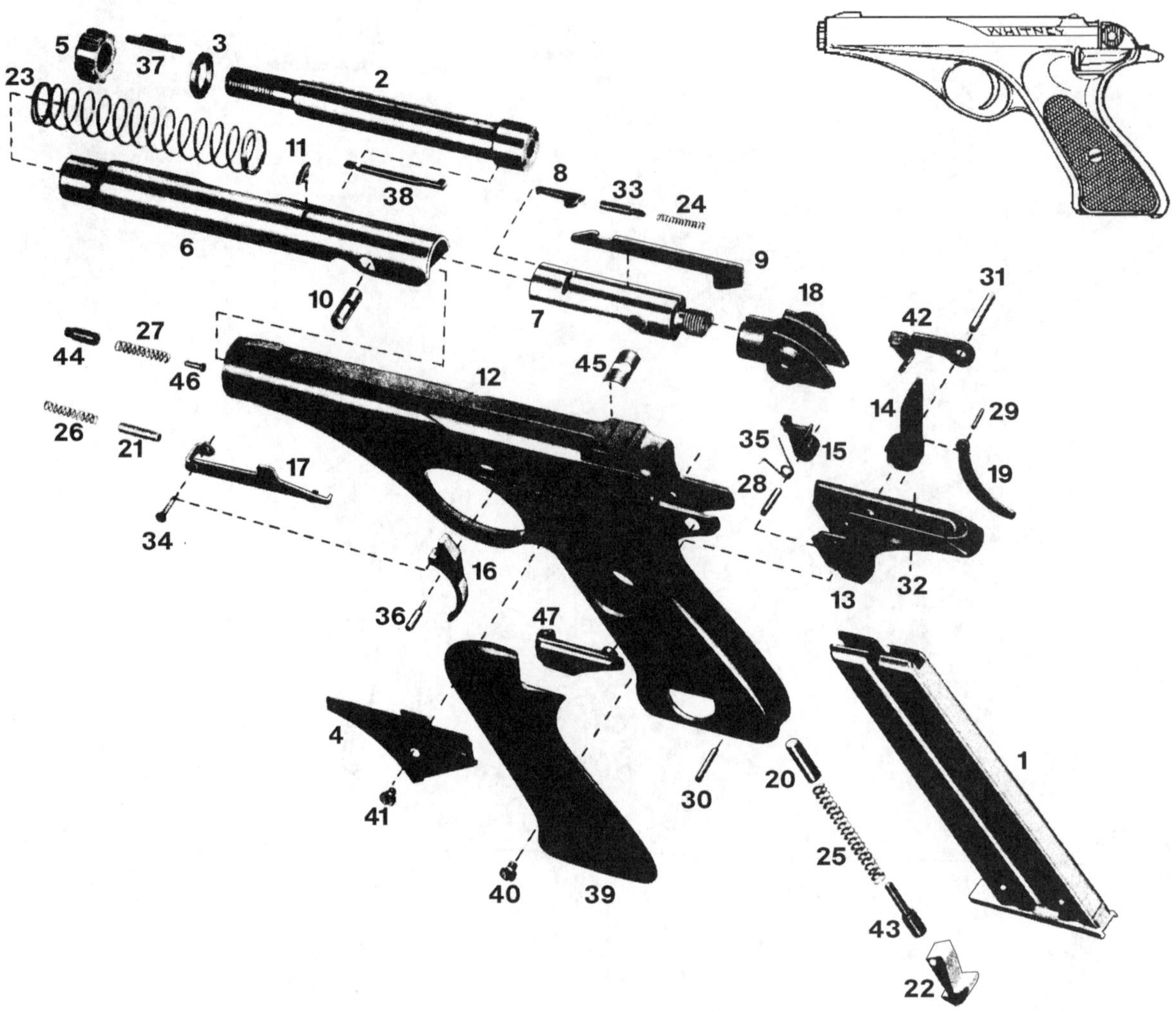

No.	Part	No.	Part
1	Magazine Assembly	25	Hammer Spring
2	Barrel	26	Trigger Spring
3	Barrel Seat	27	Locking Plunger Spring
4	Sideplate	28	Sear Pin
5	Nut	29	Strut Pin
6	Tube	30	Magazine Catch Pin
7	Breechblock	31	Hammer Pin
8	Extractor	32	Safety Lock Pin
9	Firing Pin	33	Extractor Plunger
10	Breech Pin	34	Trigger Connector
11	Firing Pin Lock	35	Sear Spring
12	Frame	36	Trigger Pin
13	Action Frame	37	Barrel Key
14	Hammer	38	Ejector
15	Sear	39	Pistol Grips
16	Trigger	40	Pistol Grip Screw
17	Sear Bar	41	Sideplate Screw
18	Cocking Piece	42	Magazine Disconnector Safety
19	Strut	43	Hammer Spring Seat
20	Hammer Spring Plunger	44	Barrel Locking Plunger
21	Trigger Spring Plunger	45	Rear Sight
22	Magazine Catch	46	Spring Seat
23	Mainspring	47	Safety
24	Extractor Spring		

Linda Auto

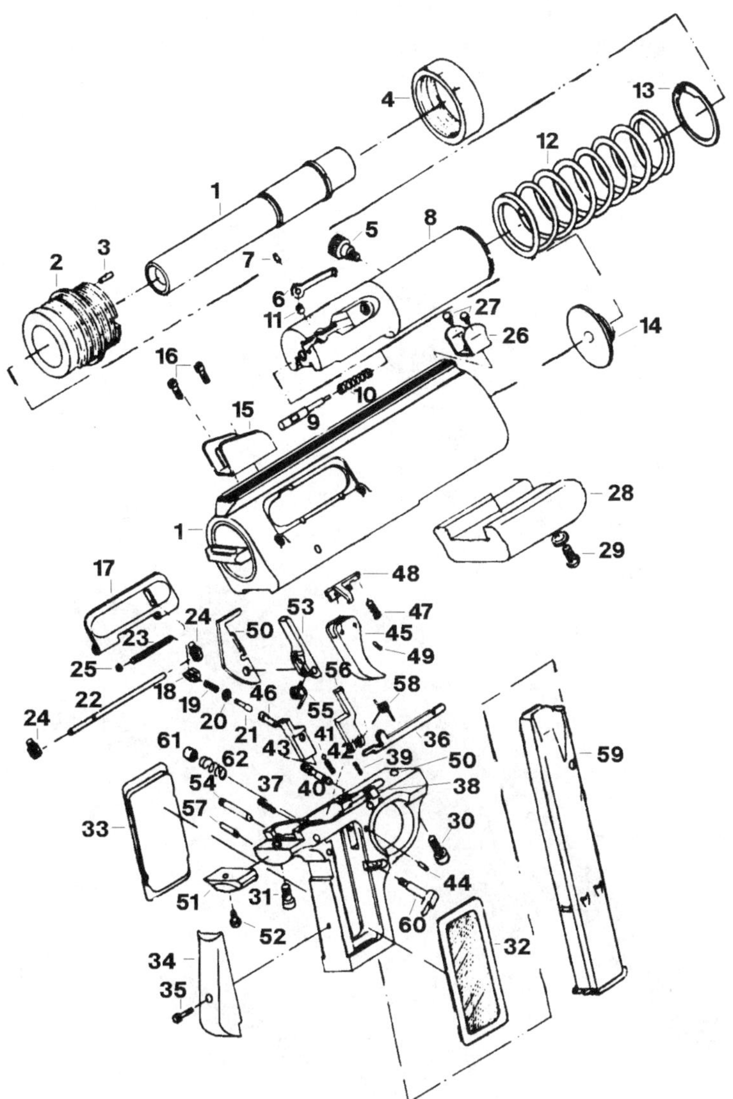

1	Barrel
2	Barrel Support Sleeve
3	Barrel Support Sleeve Pin
4	Barrel Retaining Nut
5	Cocking Knob
6	Extractor
7	Extractor Pin
8	Bolt
9	Firing Pin
10	Firing Pin Spring
11	Firing Pin Retaining Button
12	Recoil Spring
13	Recoil Spring C-Clip
14	Recoil Buffer Pad
15	Peep Sight
16	Peep Sight Screws
17	Trap Door
18	Trap Door Button
19	Trap Door Spring
20	Trap Door C-Clip
21	Trap Door Plunger
22	Trap Door Rod
23	Trap Door Rod Spring
24	Trap Door Studs
25	Trap Door Rod C-Clip
26	Front Sight
27	Front Sight Screws
28	Fore Grip
29	Fore Grip Screw
30	Front Trigger Group Screw
31	Rear Trigger Group Screw
32	Right Grip
33	Left Grip
34	Grip Retainer
35	Grip Retainer Screw
36	Disconnect
37	Disconnect Spring
38	Disconnect Guide
39	Disconnect Guide Spring
40	Safety
41	Safety Retainer
42	Safety Retainer Spring
43	Feed Ramp
44	Feed Ramp Pin
45	Trigger
46	Trigger Pin
47	Trigger Spring
48	Connector
49	Connector Pin
50	Trigger Group
51	Trigger Group Rear Insert
52	Trigger Group Rear Insert Screw
53	Hammer
54	Hammer Pin
55	Hammer Spring
56	Sear
57	Sear Pin
58	Sear Spring
59	Magazine
60	Magazine Catch
61	Magazine Catch Button
62	Magazine Catch Spring

Parts Not Shown

Ejector

Trap Door Buffer Pad

EXPLODED LONG GUN DRAWINGS

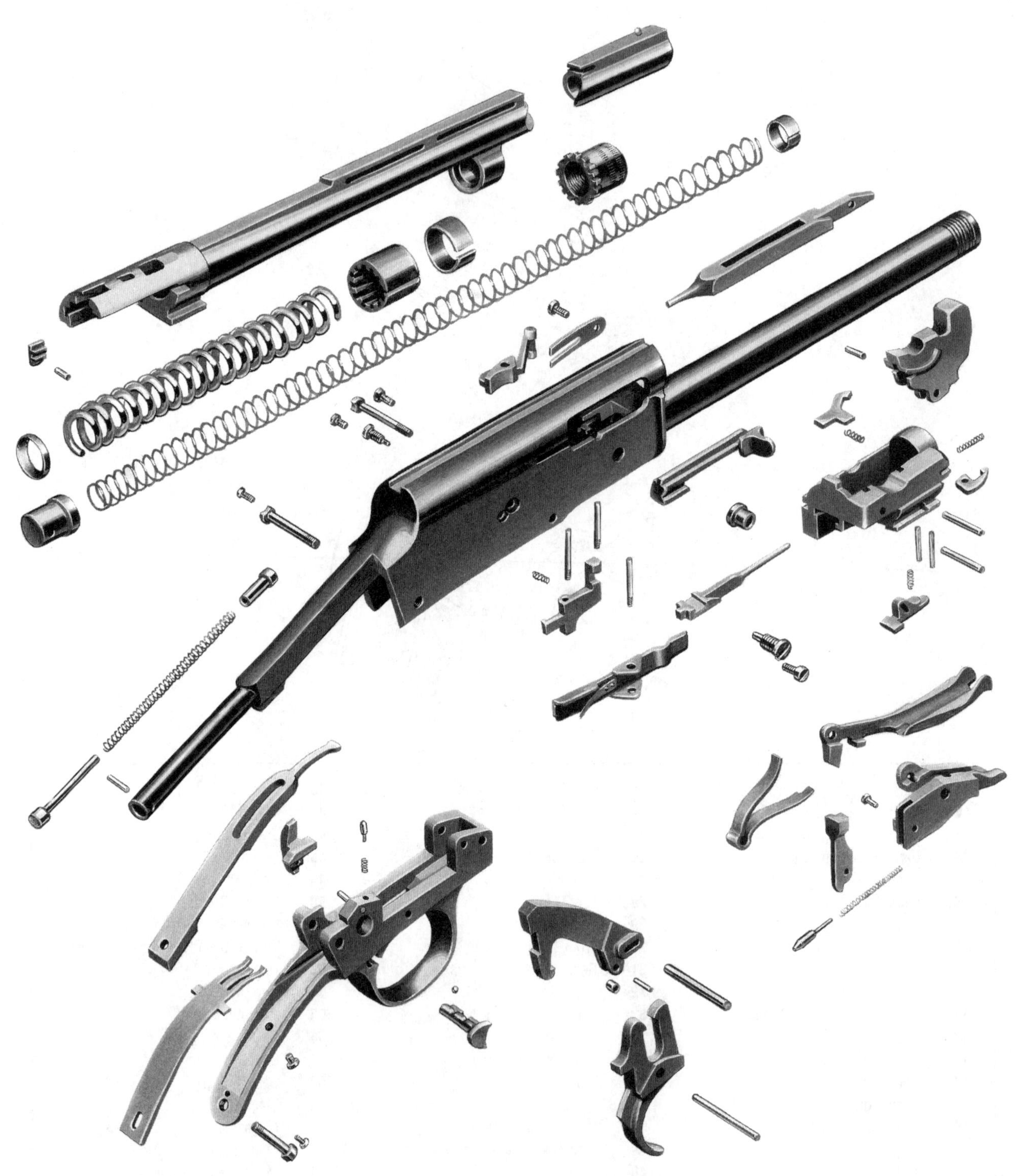

Timber Wolf Slide-Action Rifle

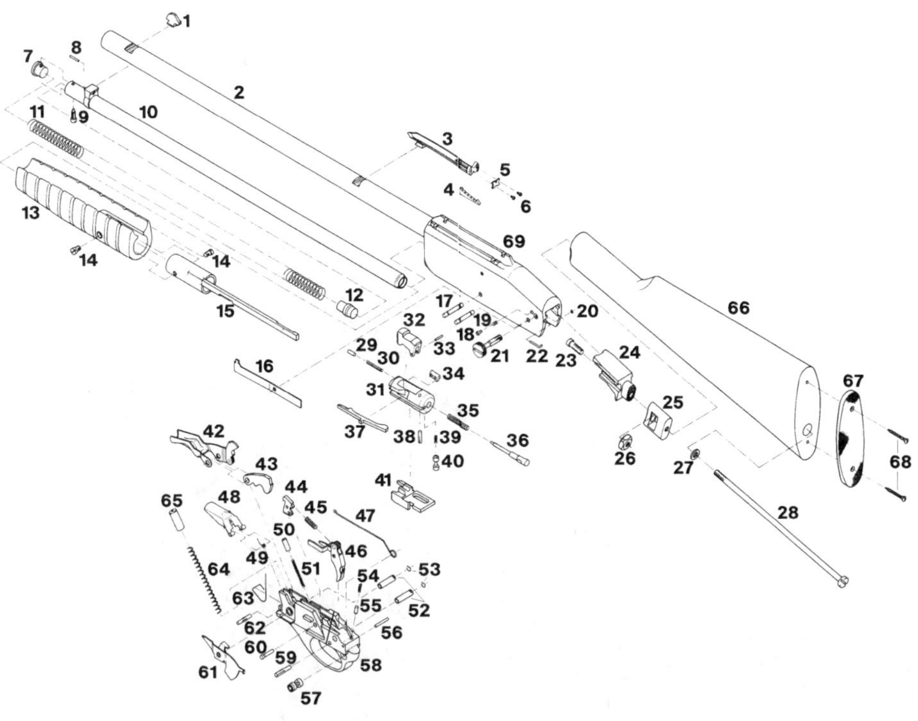

1	Front Sight	36	Firing Pin
2	Barrel	37	Ejector
3	Rear Sight	38	Firing Pin Retaining Pin
4	Rear Sight Elevator	39	Firing Pin Blocking Pin Spring
5	Rear Sight Plate	40	Firing Pin Blocking Pin
6	Rear Sight Screws	41	Bolt Slide
7	Magazine Plug	42	Carrier
8	Magazine Cap Pin	43	Hammer
9	Magazine Plug Screw	44	Sear
10	Magazine Tube	45	Trigger Sear Spring
11	Magazine Spring	46	Trigger Assembly
12	Magazine Follower	47	Firing Pin Blocking Rod
13	Forend	48	Loading Tray
14	Forend Tube Screws	49	Loading Tray Spring
15	Forend Tube	50	Carrier Spring Housing
16	Shell Latch	51	Carrier Spring
17	Trigger Plate Pin	52	Trigger Plate Pin Bushings
18	Locking Plunger	53	Trigger Plate Pin Detent Springs
19	Locking Plunger Spring	54	Safety Spring
20	Locking Plunger Retaining Ring	55	Safety Plunger
21	Takedown Screw	56	Safety Spring Pin
22	Takedown Screw Pin	57	Safety
23	Adjusting Screw, Buttstock	58	Trigger Plate
24	Buttstock Base	59	Trigger Pin
25	Adjusting Block, Buttstock	60	Sear Pin
26	Adjusting Screw Nut, Buttstock	61	Slide Latch
27	Stock Bolt Washer	62	Loading Tray Pin
28	Stock Bolt	63	Slide Latch Spring
29	Extractor Plunger	64	Hammer Spring
30	Extractor Spring	65	Hammer Spring Housing
31	Bolt	66	Buttstock
32	Bolt Locking Block	67	Buttplate
33	Bolt Locking Block Pin	68	Buttplate Screws
34	Extractor	69	Receiver
35	Firing Pin Spring		

AKY and AKF 39 Autoloading Rifle

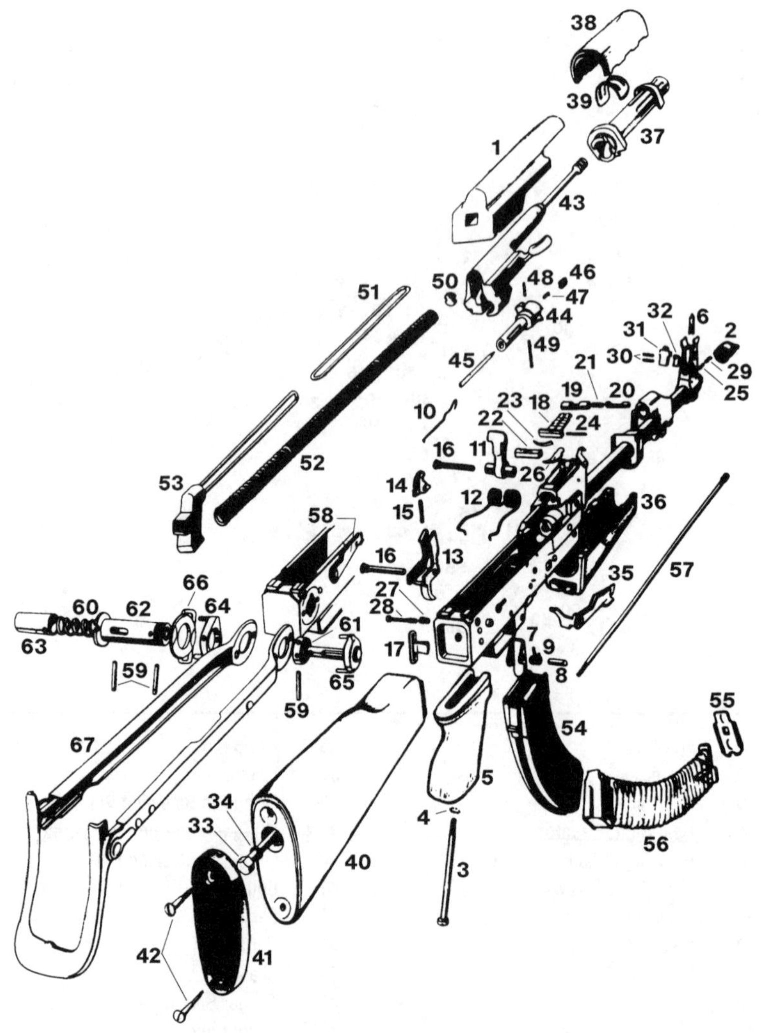

1	Receiver Cover	**23**	Rear Night Sight Spring	**45**	Firing Pin
2	Compensator	**24**	Pin	**46**	Extractor
3	Handgrip Screw	**25**	Muzzle Protecting Ring Spring	**47**	Extractor Spring
4	Washer	**26**	Rear Sight Leaf Spring	**48**	Extractor Locking Pin
5	Hand Grip	**27**	Recoil Spring Guide Rod<R>Lock Spring	**49**	Firing Pin Locking Pin
6	Front Sight	**28**	Recoil Spring Rod Lock	**50**	Locking Ring Recoil Spring
7	Magazine Catch	**29**	Protecting Ring Safety Pin	**51**	Front Guide Spring
8	Magazine Catch Pin	**30**	Front Night Sight Pins	**52**	Recoil Spring
9	Magazine Catch spring	**31**	Front Night Sight	**53**	Rear Guide Spring
10	Securing Pin	**32**	Front Night Sight Spring	**54**	Magazine Body
11	Striker	**33**	Butt Screw	**55**	Bottom Plate
12	Striker Spring	**34**	Ring Spring Washer	**56**	Follower Subassembly
13	Trigger	**35**	Fire Selector	**57**	Cleaning Rod
14	Cocking Piece	**36**	Forehand	**58**	Fire Selector (AKF 39)
15	Cocking Spring	**37**	Piston	**59**	Pins (AKF 39)
16	Trigger, Strike and Full-Automatic Sear Shaft	**38**	Cylinder Handguard	**60**	Plunger Spring (AKF 39)
17	Rear Swivel	**39**	Spring	**61**	Guide Nut (AKF 39)
18	Rear Sight Leaf	**40**	Stock	**62**	Guide (AKF 39)
19	Slide Rear Sight	**41**	Buttplate Rubber	**63**	Plunger (AKF 39)
20	Rear Sight Leaf Slide Catch	**42**	Butt Screws	**64**	Left Abutment (AKF 39)
21	Slide Catch Spring	**43**	Bolt Carrier with Piston	**65**	Right Abutment (AKF 39)
22	Rear Night Sight	**44**	Bolt Body	**66**	Rear Swivel (AKF 39)
				67	Metal Folding Stock (AKF 39)

Black Magic Autoloading Shotgun

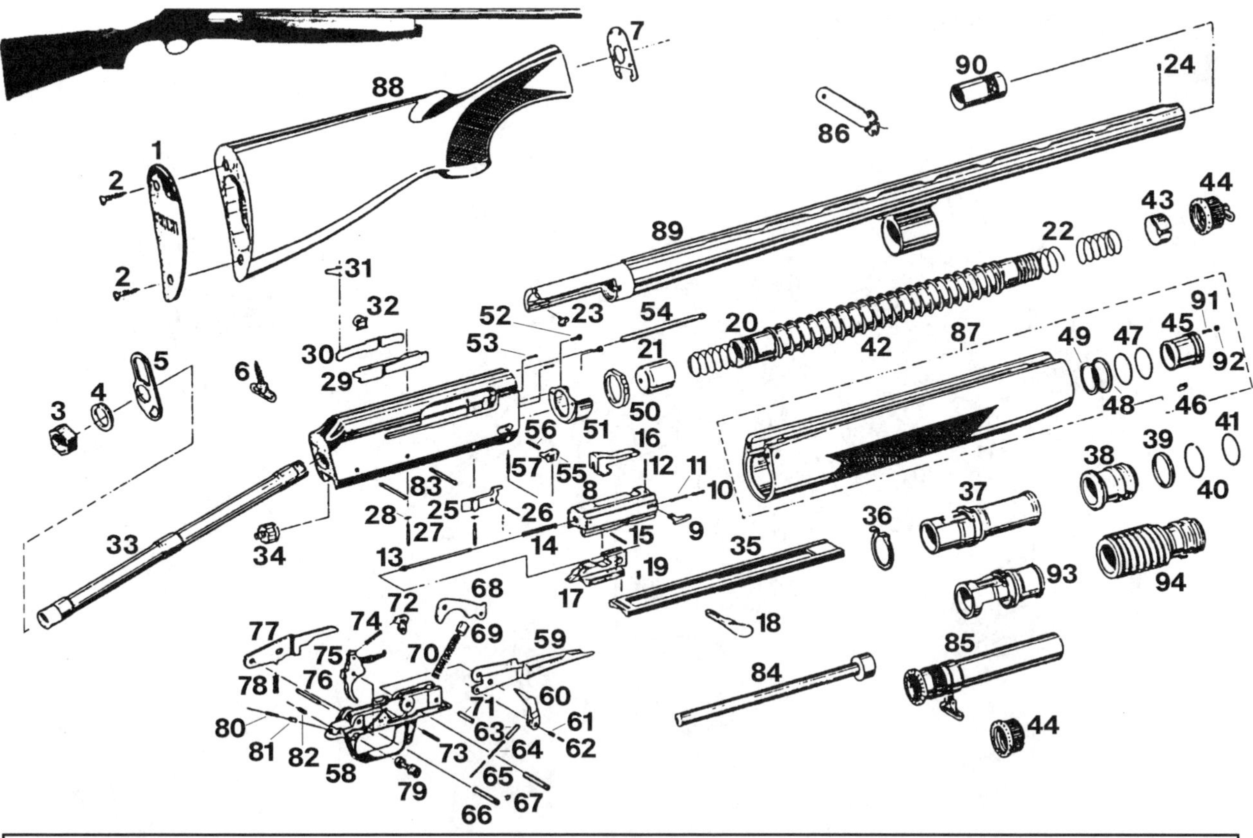

1	Rubber Buttplate	33	Stock Fastening Tube	63	Breechblock Latch Spring Follower
2	Buttplate Screws	34	Receiver Stock Absorber	64	Carrier Main Spring
3	Stock Plug	35	Cocking Rod	65	Carrier Auxiliary Spring
4	Stock Elastic Washer	36	Cocking Rod Retaining Spring	66	Trigger Guard Pin Bushings
5	Internal Buffer	37	Cocking Rod Support	67	Trigger Guard Pin Bushing Spring
6	Stock Swivel	38	Piston	68	Hammer
7	Stock Buffer	39	Piston Bushing	69	Hammer Spring Follower
8	Breechblock	40	Piston Bushing Snap Ring	70	Hammer Spring
9	Extractor	41	Cylinder Rubber Guide	71	Hammer Pin
10	Extractor Plunger	42	Action Spring	72	Sear
11	Extractor Spring	43	Magazine Spring Retaining Ring	73	Sear Pin
12	Extractor Pin	44	Forend Cap	74	Sear Spring
13	Firing Pin	45	Forend Front Support	75	Trigger Assembly
14	Firing Pin Spring	46	Key	76	Trigger Pin
15	Firing Pin Elastic Stop	47	Rubber Rings	77	Automatic Safety-Lever
16	Locking Block	48	Bearing Washer	78	Automatic Safety Spring
17	Breechblock Slide	49	Forend Front Support Retaining Ring	79	Hand Safety
18	Operating Handle			80	Hand Safety Spring
19	Operating Handle Spring	50	Support Shock Absorber	81	Hand Safety Spring Follower
20	Magazine Tube	51	Forend Rear Support	82	Hand Safety Spring Retaining Pin
21	Magazine Follower	52	Forend Support Screws	83	Trigger Plate Pins
22	Magazine Spring	53	Forend Dowels	84	Plug Reducer
23	Ejector	54	Locking Block Shoe	85	Magazine Extension
24	Front Sight	55	Magazine Cut-Off Button	86	Franchok Key
25	Magazine Shell Latch	56	Magazine Cut-Off Button Spring	87	Forend Assembly
26	Magazine Shell Latch Spring	57	Magazine Cut-Off Button Pin	88	Stock
27	Latch Pin	58	Trigger Plate	89	Barrel Extension
28	Latch Pin Retaining Spring	59	Carrier	90	Internal Choke
29	Carrier Latch	60	Breechblock Latch	91	Magazine Cap Retaining Pin Spring
30	Auxiliary Magazine Latch	61	Breechblock Latch Pin	92	Magazine Cap Retaining Pin
31	Carrier Latch Spring	62	Breechblock Latch Internal Pin	93	Cocking Rod Support
32	Carrier Latch Button			94	Piston Assembly

Brittany Side-by-Side Shotgun

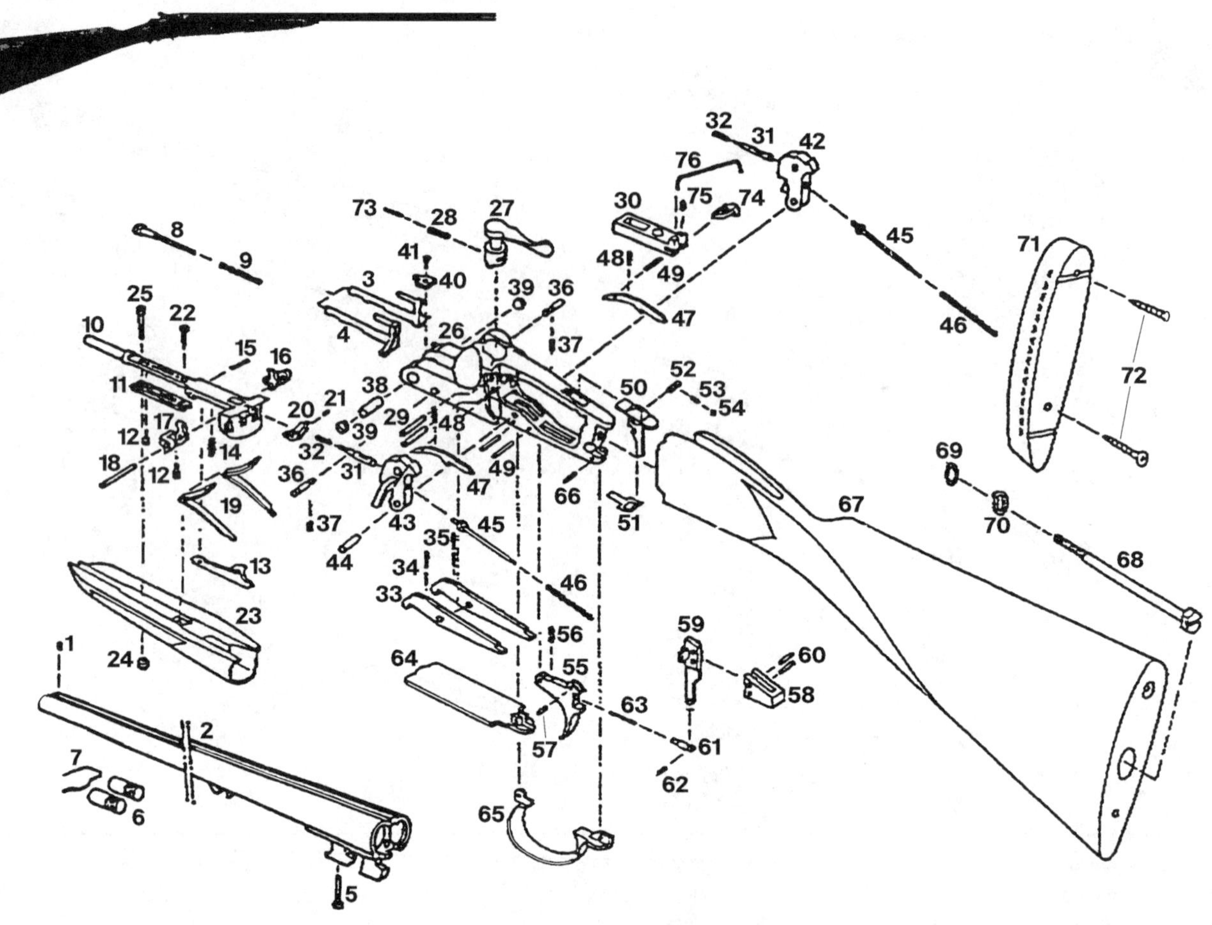

1 Front Sight Bead
2 Barrels
3 Right Ejector
4 Left Ejector
5 Ejector Retaining Screw
6 Choke Tubes
7 Choke Tube Key
8 Forend Catch Button
9 Forend Catch Spring
10 Forend Iron
11 Forend Catch
12 Forend Catch Screws
13 Ejector Kicker Elevator
14 Ejector Kicker Elevator Spring
15 Ejector Kicker Elevator Pin
16 Right Ejector Kicker
17 Left Ejector Kicker
18 Ejector Kicker Pin
19 Ejector Spring
20 Ejector Activator
21 Ejector Activator Screw
22 Forend Mount Screw
23 Forend
24 Forend Nut
25 Forend Screw
26 Receiver
27 Top Opening Lever
28 Top Opening Lever Spring
29 Retaining Pins for Top Lever and Firing Pins
30 Barrel Locking Bolt
31 Firing Pins
32 Firing Pin Springs
33 Cocking Levers
34 Cocking Lever Springs
35 Cocking Lever Spring Pin
36 Cocking Lever Pins
37 Cocking Lever Pin Retaining<R>Screw
38 Barrel Pivot Pin
39 Barrel Pivot Pin Caps
40 Activator for Ejector Kicker Elevator
41 Activator Screw for Ejector Kicker Elevator
42 Right Hammer
43 Left Hammer
44 Ejector Kickers Pin
45 Hammer Springs
46 Hammer Spring Guides
47 Sears
48 Sear Springs
49 Sear and Trigger Plate Pins
50 Selective Safety
51 Safety Spring
52 Safety Guide
53 Selector Spring
54 Selector Spring Ball
55 Single Selective Trigger
56 Single Selective Trigger Spring
57 Single Selective Trigger Plate Screw
58 Inertia Block
59 Single Selective Trigger Plate
60 Inertia Block Roll Pins
61 Trigger Plate Hinged Guide
62 Hinged Guide Pin
63 Hinged Guide Spring
64 Trigger Plate
65 Trigger Guard
66 Trigger Guard Pin
67 Stock
68 Stock Screw
69 Stock Screw Washer
70 Stock Screw Lock Washer
71 Recoil Pad
72 Recoil Pad Screws
73 Top Opening Lever Spring Plunger
74 Locking Bolt Piece
75 Locking Bolt Detent
76 Locking Bolt Spring

Eagle Over/Under Shotgun

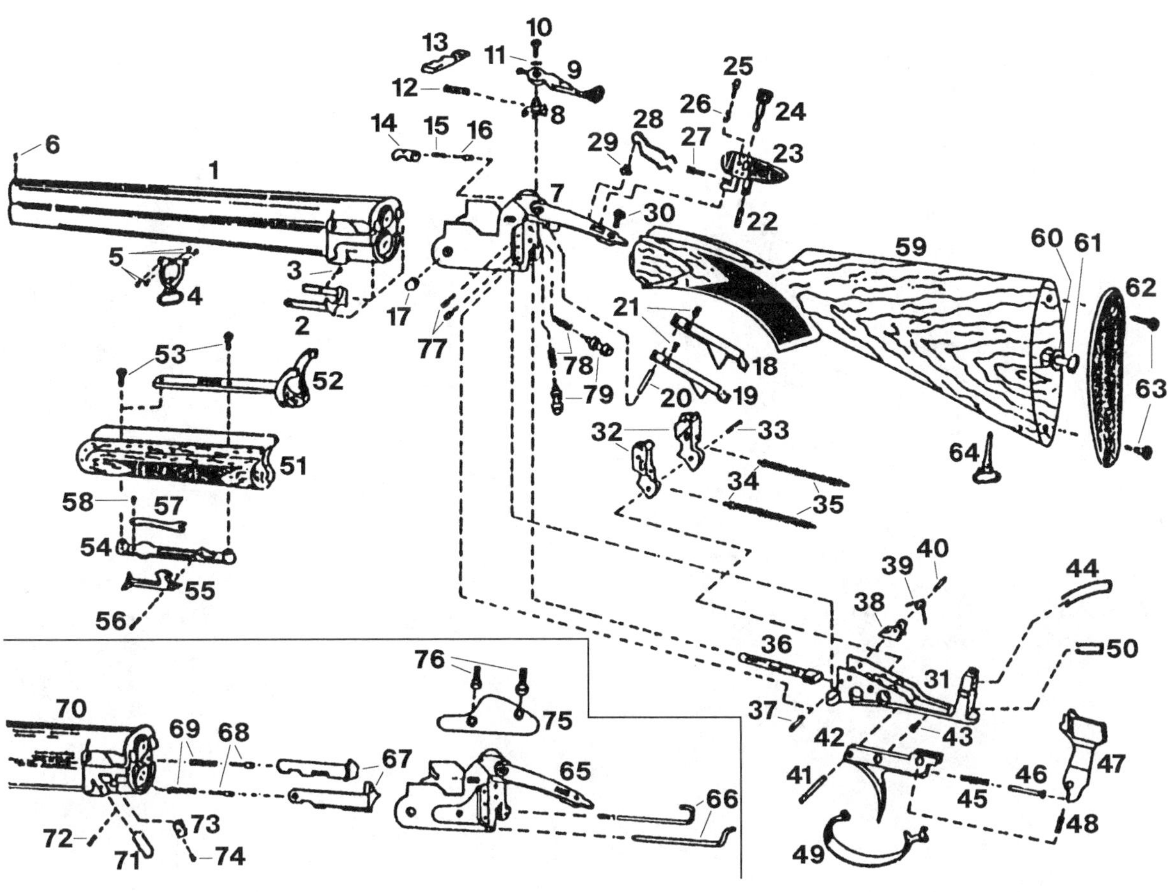

1	Barrel
2	Extractor
3	Retaining Extractor Screw
4	Sling Swivel
5	Sling Swivel Screws
6	Bead
7	Action
8	Top Lever Key
9	Top Lever
10	Top Lever Screw
11	Top Lever Washer
12	Top Lever Spring
13	Barrel Locking Bolt
14	Locking Bolt Retaining
15	Locking Bolt Retaining Spring
16	Locking Bolt Retaining Guide Spring
17	Barrel Pivot Axe
18	Right Sear
19	Left Sear
20	Sear Pivot
21	Sear Springs
22	Safety Pivot
23	Safety Button
24	Selective Catch
25	Selective Spring Guide
26	Selective Catch Spring
27	Selective Catch Retaining Screw
28	Safety Spring
29	Safety Spring Retaining Screw
30	Floorplate Retaining Screw
31	Floorplate
32	Hammers
33	Hammer Pivot
34	Mainspring Guides
35	Mainsprings
36	Cocking Lever Rod
37	Floorplate/Action Retaining Pivot Pin
38	Cocking Lever
39	Cocking Lever Spring
40	Cocking Lever Pivot Pin
41	Trigger Pivot Pin
42	Trigger
43	Trigger Buttscrew
44	Trigger Spring
45	Cam Spring
46	Cam Spring Guide
47	Cam
48	Cam Retaining Screw
49	Trigger Guard
50	Trigger Guard Retaining Spring
51	Wood Forend
52	Metal Forend
53	Forend Screws
54	Forend Catch
55	Forend Handle
56	Forend Handle Pin
57	Forend Handle Spring
58	Forend Handle Spring Retaining
59	Stock
60	Stock Screw Washer
61	Stock/Action Retaining Screw
62	Recoil Pad
63	Recoil Pad Retaining Screws
64	Sling Swivel
65	Action
66	Ejector Rods
67	Ejectors
68	Ejector Spring Guides
69	Ejector Springs
70	Barrel
71	Ejector Sear
72	Ejector Sear Spring
73	Ejector Sear Retaining Plate
74	Ejector Retaining Plate Screw
75	Sideplate
76	Sideplate Screws
77	Firing Pin Retaining Screws
78	Firing Pin Return Springs
79	Firing Pins

Silver I Over/Under Shotgun

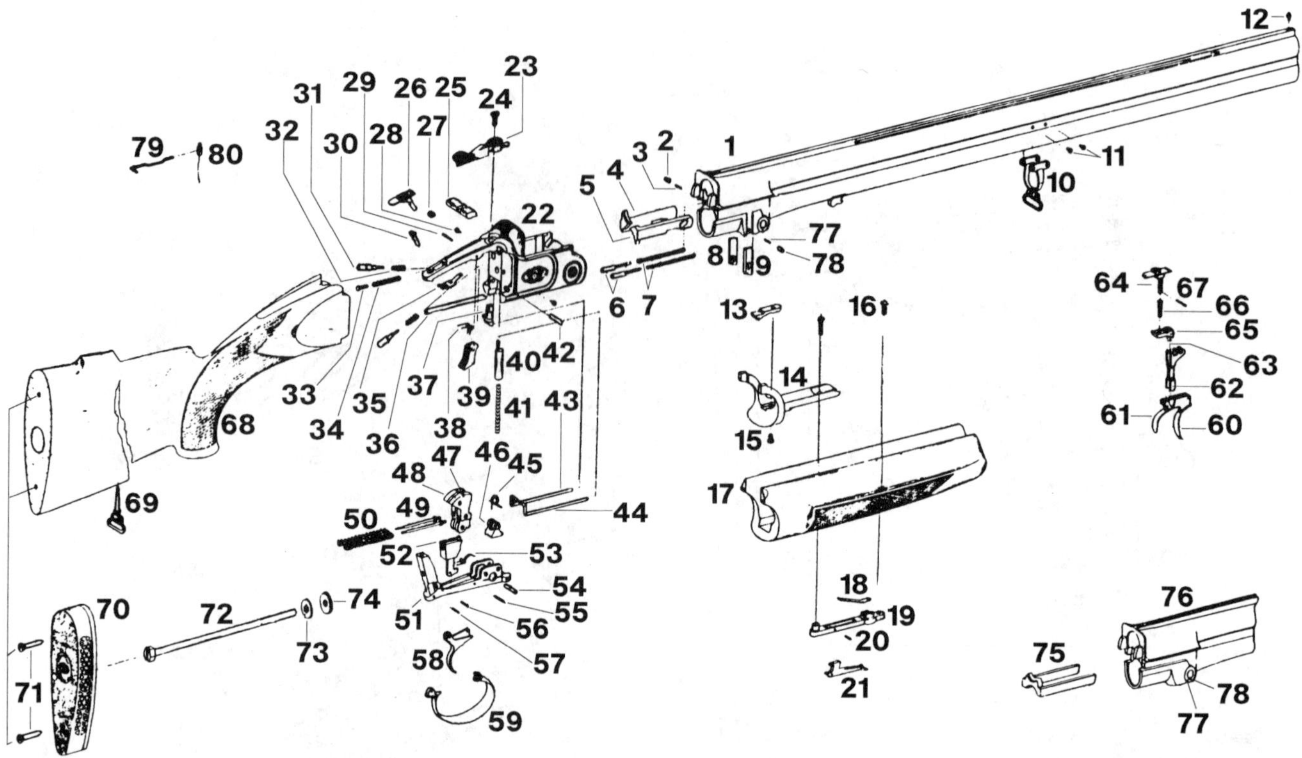

1 Barrels
2 Catch Plate Stop Piston
3 Catch Plate Stop Piston Spring
4 Left Extractor
5 Right Extractor
6 Extractor Spring Guides
7 Extractor Springs
8 Left Extractor Catch Plate
9 Right Extractor Catch Plate
10 Front Sling Swivel
11 Sling Swivel Screws
12 Front Sight
13 Cocking Hook
14 Forend Iron
15 Cocking Hook Screw
16 Forend Iron Screws
17 Forearm Wood
18 Forearm Catch Plate Spring
19 Forearm Catch Plate
20 Forearm Catch Pin
21 Forearm Catch
22 Frame
23 Top Lever
24 Top Lever Screw
25 Cross Bolt
26 Safety
27 Safety Guide Plate
28 Firing Pin Stop Screw
29 Sear Pin
30 Tang Screw
31 Firing Pin
32 Firing Pin Springs
33 Top Lever Spring Guide
34 Top Lever Spring
35 Safety Spring
36 Cocking Bar
37 Spindle
38 Sear Spring
39 Sear
40 Cross Bolt Stop Piston
41 Cross Bolt Stop Piston Spring
42 Cocking Toggle Pin
43 Left Ejector Control Rod
44 Right Ejector Control Rod
45 Cocking Toggle Spring
46 Cocking Toggle
47 Left Hammer
48 Right Hammer
49 Hammer Strut
50 Hammer Spring
51 Trigger Plate
52 Inertia Block
53 Inertia Block Spring
54 Hammer Pin
55 Trigger Pin
56 Inertia Block Spring Pin
57 Trigger Guard Stop Pin
58 Single Trigger
59 Trigger Guard
60 Right Trigger
61 Left Trigger
62 Right Trigger Plate
63 Left Trigger Plate
64 Safety
65 Safety Plate
66 Safety Spring
67 Safety Spring Pin
68 Stock
69 Sling Swivel
70 Buttplate
71 Buttplate Screws
72 Stock Bolt
73 Stock Lock Washer
74 Stock Washer
75 Normal Extractor
76 Barrels
77 Washer Lump
78 Washer Lump Lock Screw
79 Automatic Safety Bar
80 Automatic Safety Bar Screw

Silver I and II, Sterling, Bristol and Charles Daly Over/Under Shotgun

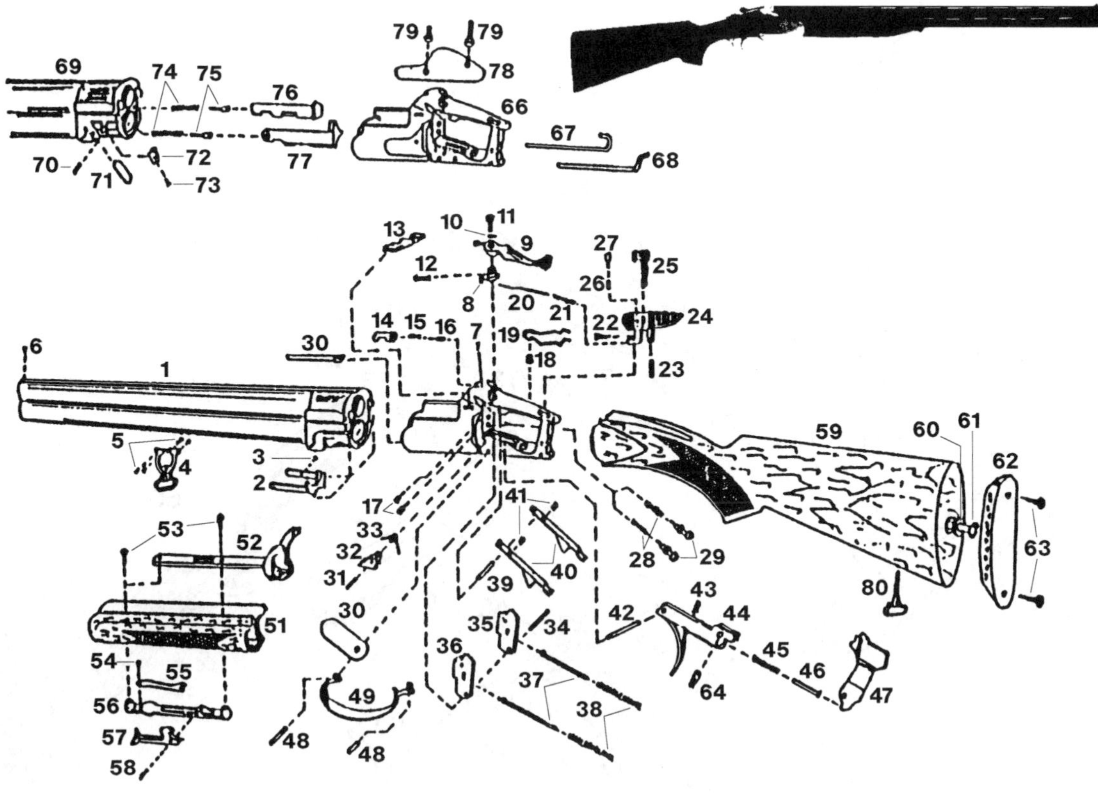

1 Barrel
2 Extractor
3 Retaining Extractor Screw
4 Sling Swivel
5 Sling Swivel Screws
6 Bead
7 Action
8 Top Lever Key
9 Top Lever
10 Top Lever Washer
11 Top Lever Screw
12 Top Lever Spring
13 Barrel Locking Bolt
14 Locking Bolt Retaining
15 Locking Bolt Retaining Spring
16 Locking Bolt Retaining Guide Spring
17 Firing Pin Retaining
18 Safety Spring Retaining Screw
19 Safety Spring
20 Automatic Safety Rod
21 Automatic Safety Rod Spring
22 Selective Catch Retaining Screw
23 Safety Pivot
24 Safety Button
25 Selective Catch
26 Selective Catch Spring
27 Selective Spring Guide
28 Firing Pin Return Springs
29 Firing Pins
30 Cocking Lever Rod
31 Cocking Lever Pivot Pin
32 Cocking Lever
33 Cocking Lever Spring
34 Hammer Pivot
35 Right Hammer
36 Left Hammer
37 Mainspring Guides
38 Mainsprings
39 Sear Pivot
40 Sears
41 Sear Springs
42 Trigger Pivot
43 Trigger Spring
44 Trigger
45 Cam Spring
46 Cam Spring Guide
47 Cam
48 Trigger Guard Pins
49 Trigger Guard
50 Floorplate
51 Wood Forend
52 Metal Forend
53 Forend Screws
54 Forend Hand Spring Screw
55 Forend Handle Spring
56 Forend Catch
57 Forend Handle
58 Forend Handle Pin
59 Stock
60 Stock Screw Washer
61 Stock/Action Retaining Screw
62 Recoil Pad
63 Recoil Pad Screws
64 Cam Retaining Screw
65 Safety
66 Ejection Action
67 Ejector Rod, Right
68 Ejector Rod, Left
69 Ejector Barrel
70 Ejector Sear Spring
71 Ejector Sear
72 Ejector Retaining Plate
73 Ejector Retaining Plate Screw
74 Ejector Springs
75 Ejector Spring Guides
76 Right Automatic Ejector
77 Left Automatic Ejector
78 Sideplate
79 Sideplate Screws
80 Sling Swivel

Waterfowl Special and Turkey Special Side-by-Side Shotgun

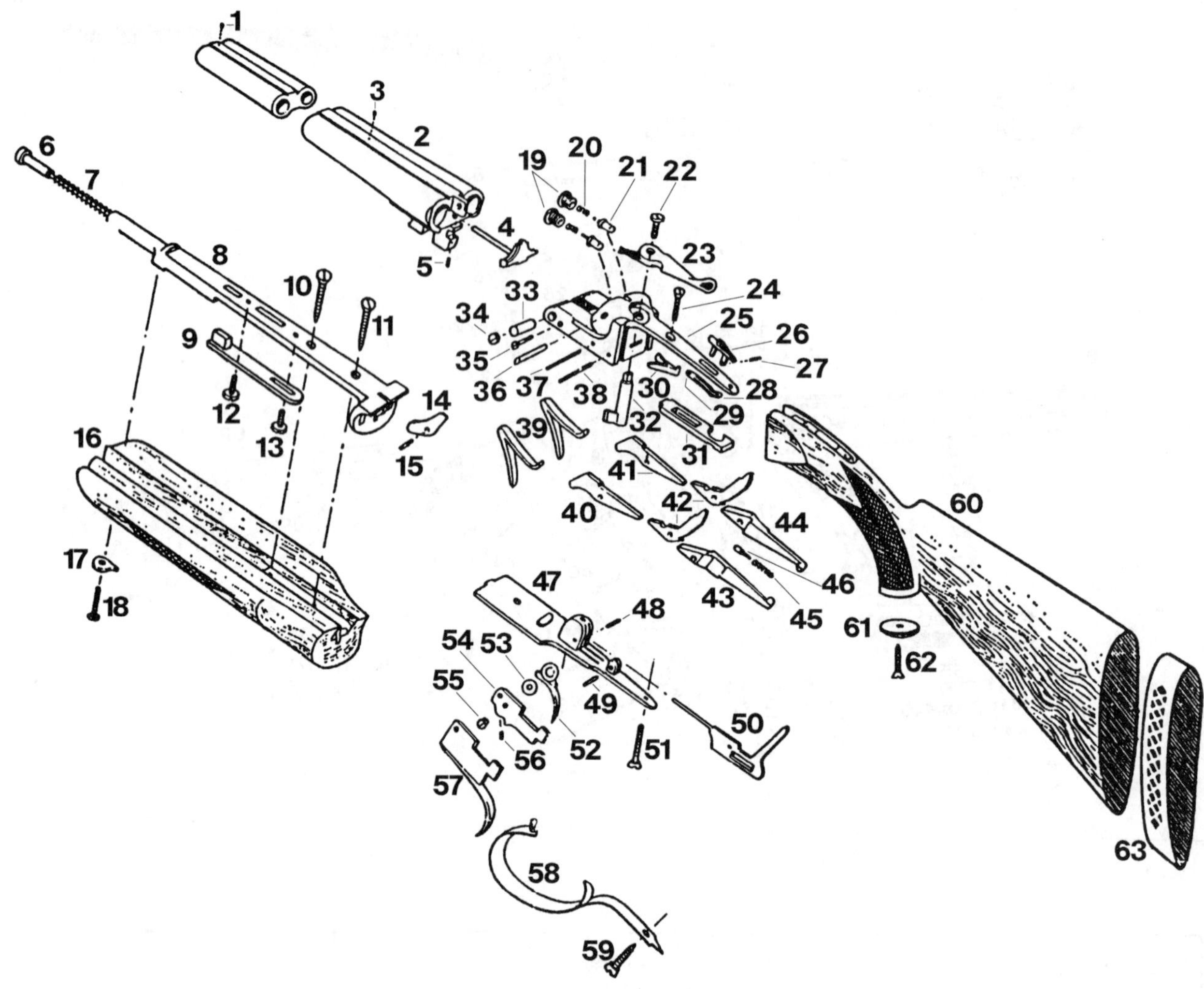

1 Front Sight Bead
2 Barrels
3 Rear Sight Bead
4 Extractor
5 Extractor Retaining Screw
6 Forend Catch Button
7 Forend Catch Spring
8 Forend Iron
9 Forend Catch
10 Forend Mount Screw, Front
11 Forend Mount Screw, Rear
12 Forend Catch Screw, Front
13 Forend Catch Screw, Rear
14 Extractor Hammer Cocking Lever Activator
15 Extractor Hammer Cocking Lever Screw
16 Forend Wood
17 Forend Escutcheon
18 Forend Escutcheon Mounting Screw
19 Firing Pin Bushings
20 Firing Pin Springs
21 Firing Pins
22 Top Lever Screw
23 Top Lever
24 Upper Tang Screw
25 Breech Assembly
26 Safety Button
27 Safety Button Pin
28 Safety Spring
29 Safety Spring Screw
30 Top Lever Spring
31 Horizontal Bolt
32 Vertical Bolt
33 Barrel Pivot Pin
34 Barrel Pivot Pin Cap
35 Cocking Lever Pivot Screw
36 Round Cross-Bolt
37 Hammer Pivot Pin
38 Sear Pivot Pin
39 Hammer Springs
40 Cocking Lever, Left
41 Cocking Lever, Right
42 Hammers
43 Sear, Left
44 Sear, Right
45 Sear Springs
46 Sear Spring Guides
47 Trigger Plate
48 Trigger Pin
49 Safety Square Pin
50 Safety Activator
51 Trigger Plate Screw, Rear
52 Front Trigger, Lower
53 Front Trigger Rivet Plate
54 Front Trigger Sear
55 Front Trigger Screw
56 Front Trigger Hinge Spring
57 Rear Trigger
58 Trigger Guard
59 Trigger Guard Screw
60 Stock
61 Grip Cap
62 Grip Cap Screw
63 Rubber Recoil Pad

Waterfowl Special and Turkey Special Single Shotgun

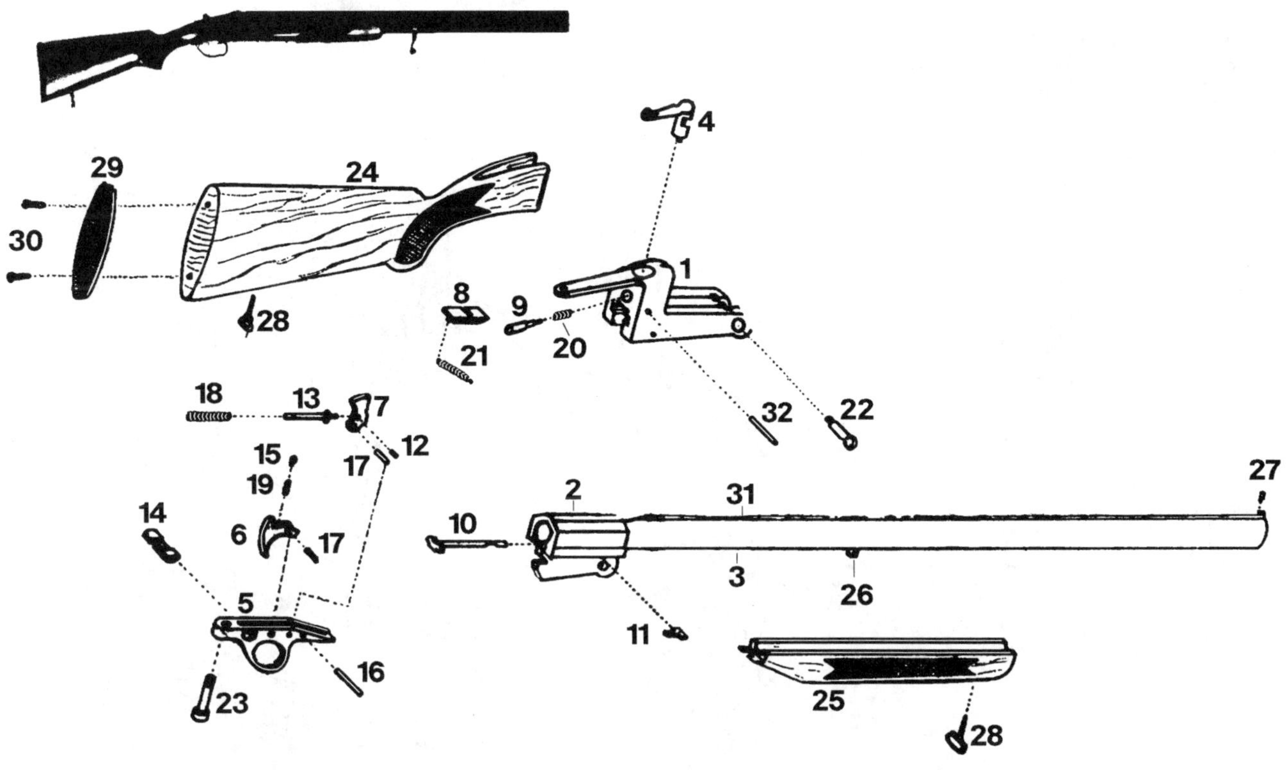

1	Frame	**17**	Hammer and Trigger Pin
2	Coupling Box	**18**	Hammer Spring
3	Barrel	**19**	Trigger Spring
4	Top Lever	**20**	Firing Spring
5	Trigger Guard	**21**	Crossbolt Spring
6	Trigger	**22**	Hinge Screw
7	Hammer	**23**	Tang Screw
8	Cross Bolt	**24**	Stock
9	Firing Pin	**25**	Forearm
10	Extractor	**26**	Forend Holder
11	Extractor Plate	**27**	Front Sight
12	Spring Guide Pin	**28**	Sling Swivels
13	Spring Guide	**29**	Buttplate
14	Safety	**30**	Buttplate Screws
15	Safety Top Spring	**31**	Ventilated Rib
16	Trigger Guard Retaining Pin	**32**	Firing Pin Retaining Pin

Waterfowl Special and Turkey Special Over/Under Shotgun

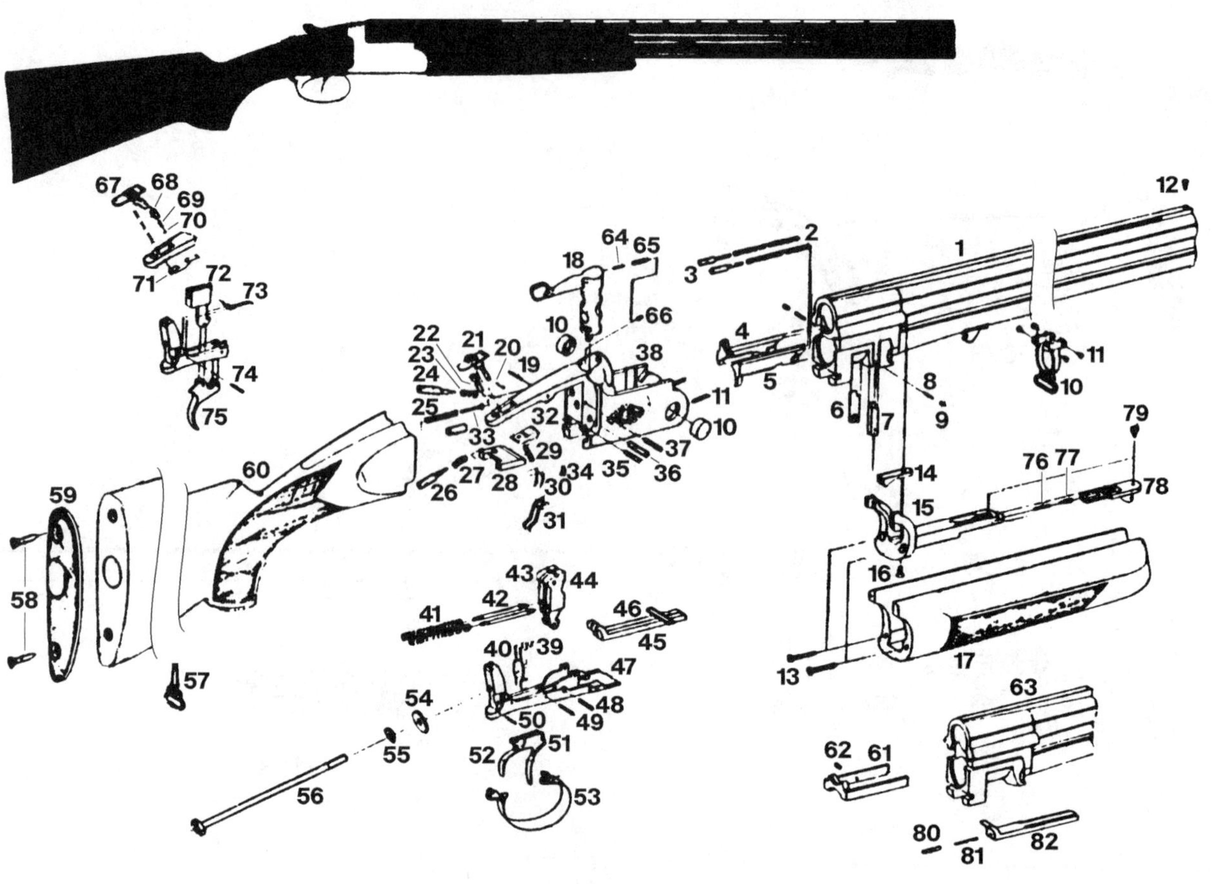

1	Barrels	29	Safety Spring	57	Swing Swivel, Rear
2	Extractor Springs	30	Sear Spring	58	Buttplate Screws
3	Extractor Spring Guides	31	Sear	59	Buttplate
4	Left Extractor	32	Safety Guide Plate	60	Stock
5	Right Extractor	33	Top Lever Spring Guide	61	Normal Extractor
6	Left Extractor Catch Plate	34	Screw Contrast Spring Top Lever	62	Screw Extractor
7	Right Extractor Catch Plate	35	Trigger Plate Forearm Catch Pin	63	Barrels
8	Catch Plate Stop Piston Spring	36	Top Lever Forearm Catch Pin	64	Top Lever Spring
9	Catch Plate Stop Piston	37	Firing Pin Forearm Catch Pin	65	Top Lever Plunger
10	Front Swing Swivel	38	Frame	66	Top Lever Detent
11	Sling Swivel Screws	39	Right Trigger Plate	67	Barrel Selector/Safety
12	Front Sight	40	Left Trigger Plate	68	Barrel Selector/Safety Plunger
13	Forearm Wood Screws	41	Hammer Spring	69	Barrel Selector/Safety Spring
14	Cocking Hook	42	Hammer Strut	70	Barrel Selector/Safety Detent
15	Forend Iron	43	Left Hammer	71	Barrel Selector/Safety Plate
16	Cocking Hook Screw	44	Right Hammer	72	Safety Connector
17	Forearm	45	Cocking Bar, Right	73	Trigger Spring
18	Top Lever	46	Cocking Bar, Left	74	Trigger Accessory Pin
19	Sear Pin	47	Trigger Plate	75	Single Selective Trigger
20	Forearm Spring Safety	48	Hammer Pin	76	Forend Catch Spring
21	Safety	49	Trigger Pin	77	Forend Catch Plunger
22	Tang Screw	50	Trigger Guard Stop Pin	78	Forend Catch
23	Firing Pin Springs	51	Right Trigger	79	Forend Latch Screw
24	Right Firing Pin	52	Left Trigger	80	Lifter Plunger
25	Top Lever Spring	53	Trigger Guard	81	Lifter Spring
26	Left Firing Pin	54	Stock Washer	82	Extractor Lifter
27	Firing Pin Spring	55	Stock Lock Washer		
28	Cross Bolt	56	Stock Bolt		

Achiever Bolt-Action Rifle

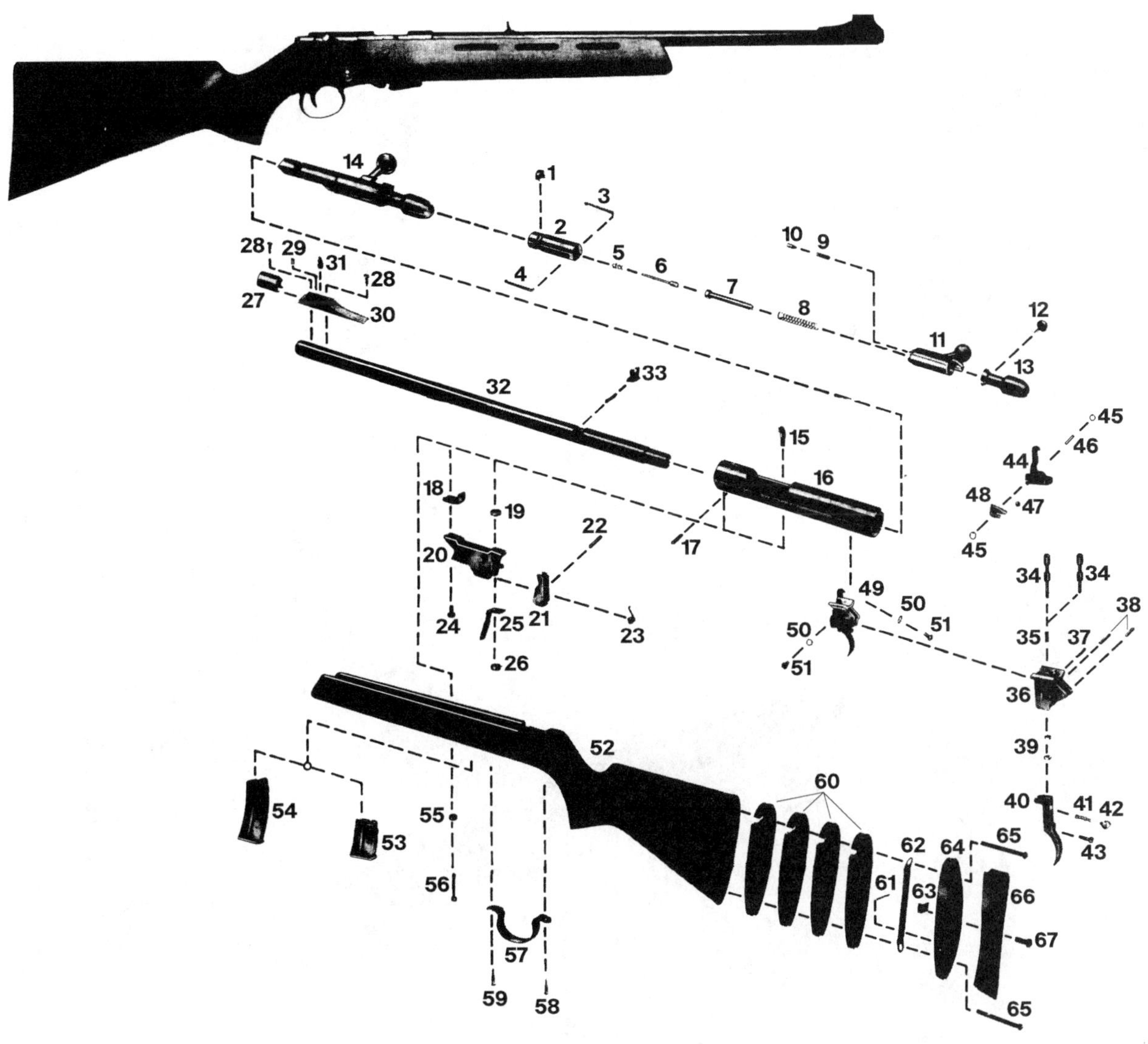

1	Spring Clamp	24	Pan Head Screw	47	Detent Balls
2	Bolt Head	25	Guide Tongue	48	Leaf Spring
3	Extractor	26	Ejector Nut	49	Two-Stage Trigger Assembly
4	Cartridge Retainer	27	Front Sight Hood	50	Toothed Lock Washers
5	Firing Pin Spring	28	Countersunk Flat-Head Screws	51	Pan Head Screws
6	Firing Pin	29	Clamping Piece	52	Stock
7	Striker Pin	30	Front Sight Base	53	5-Shot Magazine Assembly
8	Striker Spring	31	Front Sight Bead	54	10-Shot Magazine Assembly
9	Catch Bolt Spring	32	Barrel	55	Threaded Sleeve
10	Catch Bolt	33	Folding Sight	56	Pan Head Screw
11	Bolt with Handle	34	Release Plungers	57	Trigger Guard
12	Guide Bolt	35	Release Plunger Spring	58	Countersunk Oval Head Wood Screw
13	Cocking Piece	36	Trigger Housing	59	Screw
14	Bolt Assembly	37	Clamping Pin	60	Spacers
15	Ejector Screw	38	Cylindrical Pins	61	Cylindrical Pin
16	Receiver	39	Hexagon Nuts	62	Cover Plate
17	Cylindrical Pin	40	Trigger	63	Nut
18	Intermediate Piece	41	Trigger Spring	64	Guide Plate
19	Distance Ring	42	Bolt Spring	65	Screws
20	Magazine Guide	43	Pan Head Screw	66	Buttplate
21	Magazine Catch	44	Safety-Lever	67	Screw
22	Cylindrical Pin	45	Retaining Collars		
23	Torsional Spring	46	Pin		

Mark 2000 and 2000 D Bolt-Action Rifle

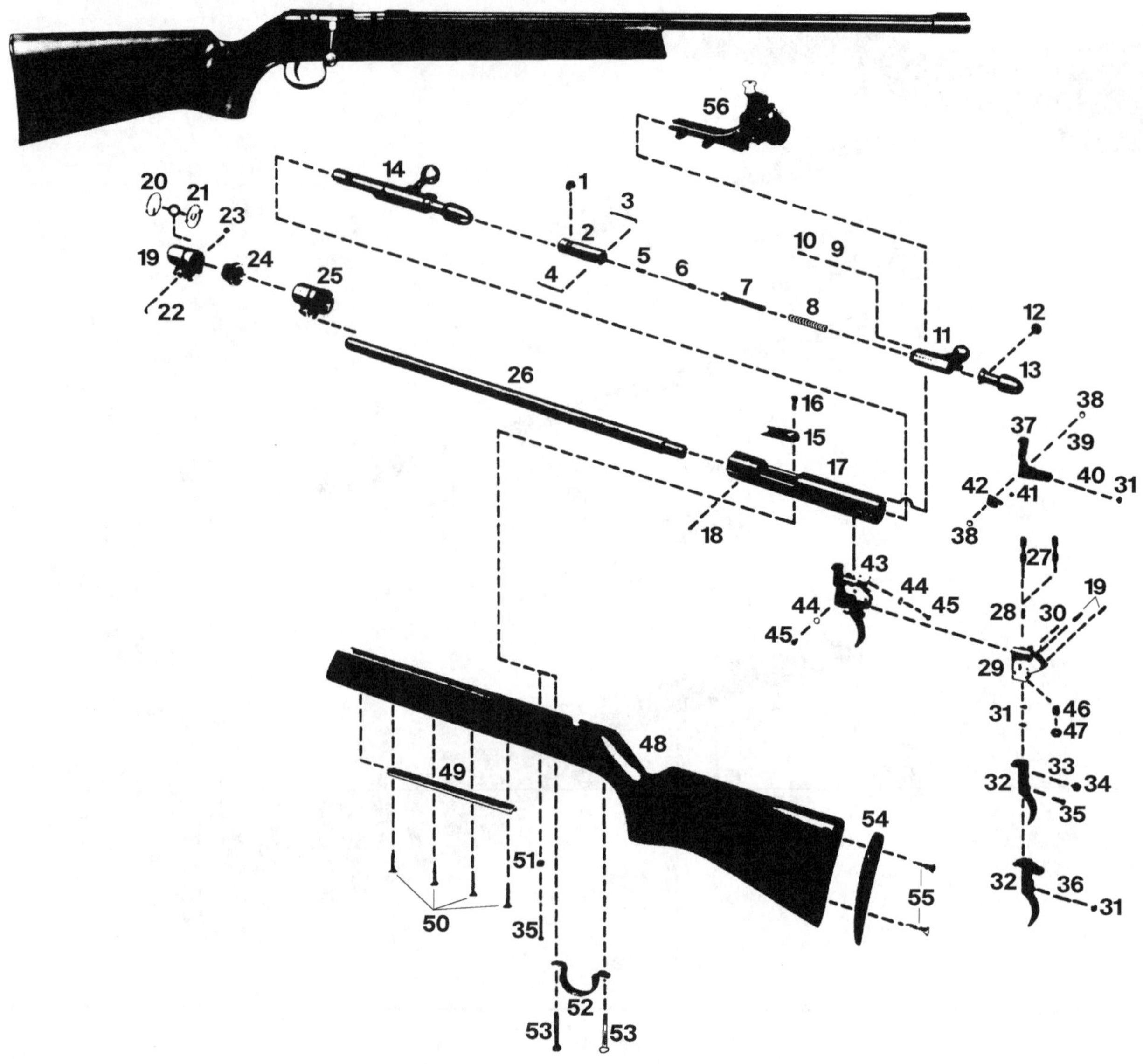

1	Bolt Head Spring Clamp	**20**	Post Insert	**39**	Retaining Collar Pin
2	Bolt Head	**21**	Aperture Insert	**40**	Retaining Collar Set Screw
3	Extractor	**22**	Hook Screw	**41**	Detent Ball
4	Cartridge Retainer	**23**	Nut	**42**	Leaf Spring
5	Firing Pin Spring	**24**	Clamp Ring	**43**	Two-Stage Trigger Assembly
6	Firing Pin	**25**	Front Sight, Complete	**44**	Toothed Lock Washers
7	Striker Pin	**26**	Barrel	**45**	Single-Stage Trigger Pan Head Screws
8	Striker Spring	**27**	Release Plungers	**46**	Threaded Sleeve
9	Catch Bolt Spring	**28**	Release Plunger Spring	**47**	Flat Nut
10	Catch Bolt	**29**	Trigger Housing	**48**	Stock with Buttplate
11	Bolt with Handle	**30**	Clamping Sleeve	**49**	Front Swivel Rail
12	Guide Bolt	**31**	Hexagon Nuts	**50**	Front Swivel Rail Screws
13	Cocking Piece	**32**	Triggers	**51**	Sleeve
14	Bolt Assembly	**33**	Trigger Spring	**52**	Trigger Guard
15	Loading Platform	**34**	Spring Bolt	**53**	Trigger Guard Screws
16	Loading Platform Screw	**35**	Pan Head Screws	**54**	Buttplate
17	Receiver	**36**	Set Screw	**55**	Buttplate Screws
18	Cylindrical Pins	**37**	Safety-Lever	**56**	Micrometer Rear Sight
19	Front Sight Hood	**38**	Retaining Collars		

Model 1415, 1415 D, 1416, 1416 D, 1515 D and 1516 D Deluxe Bolt-Action Rifle

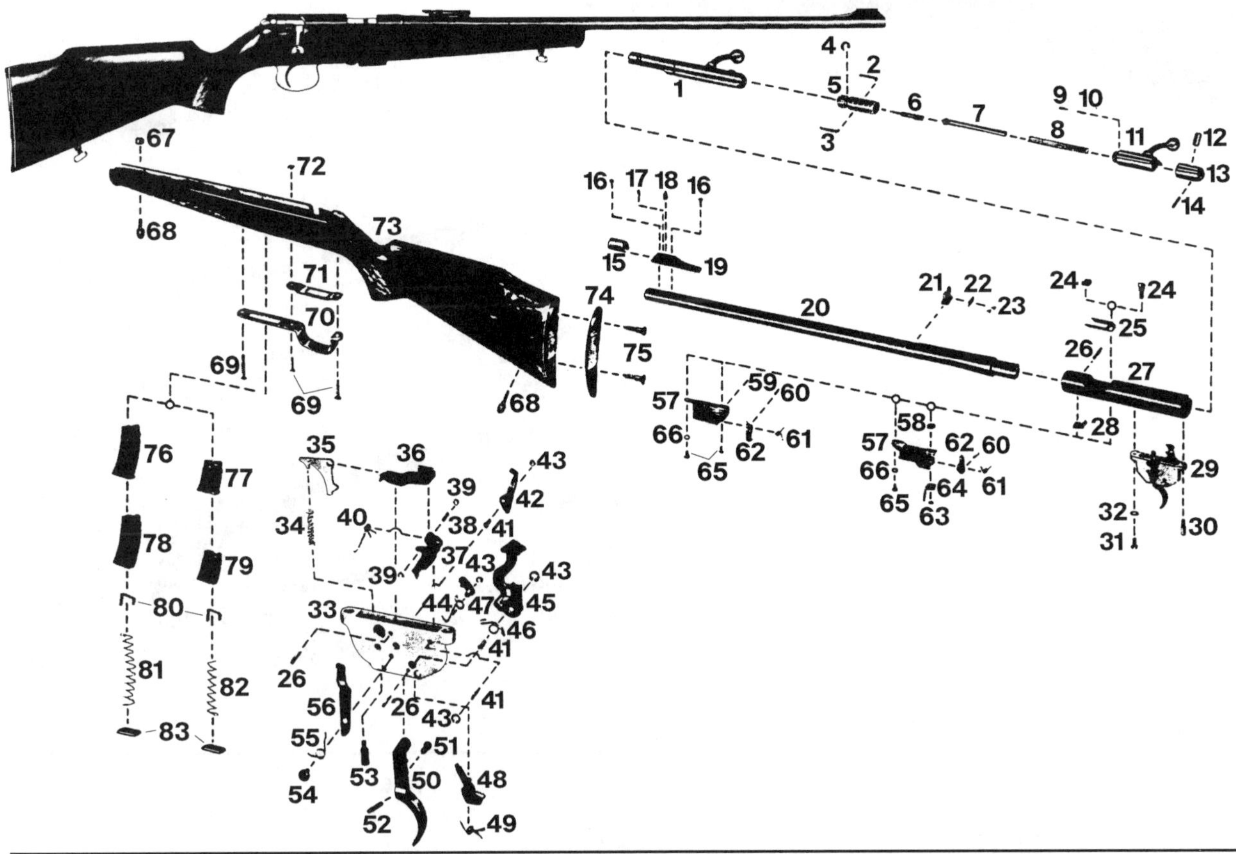

No.	Part	No.	Part	No.	Part
1	Bolt Assembly	31	Trigger Assembly Screw	60	Magazine Retainer Pin
2	Extractor	32	Trigger Assembly Toothed Lock Washer	61	Torsional Spring
3	Cartridge Retainer	33	Trigger Housing	62	Magazine Retainer
4	Spring Clamp	34	Trigger Spring	63	Guide Tongue Nut
5	Bolt Head	35	Cam Lever	64	Guide Tongue
6	Firing Pin	36	Release Plunger	65	Magazine Guide Screw
7	Striker Pin	37	Catch Link	66	Spring Washer
8	Striker Spring	38	Catch Link Pin	67	Swivel Nut
9	Catch Bolt	39	Catch Link Retaining Collar	68	Swivels
10	Catch Bolt Spring	40	Torsional Spring	69	Trigger Guard Screws
11	Bolt with Handle	41	Pivots	70	Trigger Guard
12	Guide Bolt	42	Bolt Pawl	71	Cover Plate
13	Cocking Piece	43	Retaining Collars	72	Square Nut
14	Cocking Piece Pin	44	Spring	73	Stock
15	Front Sight Hood	45	Safety-Lever	74	Buttplate
16	Front Sight Bar Screws	46	Safety-Lever Spring	75	Buttplate Screws
17	Safety Plug	47	Catch Lever	76	Magazine, 10-Shot
18	Front Sight Bead	48	Release Latch	77	Magazine, 5-Shot
19	Front Sight Base	49	Torsional Spring	78	Magazine Housing, 10-Shot
20	Barrel	50	Trigger	79	Magazine Housing, 5-Shot
21	Folding Sight	51	Adjusting Screw	80	Magazine Followers
22	Rear Sight Blade	52	Set-Screw	81	Follower Spring, 10-Shot
23	Rear Sight Blade Screws	53	Adjusting Screw	82	Follower Spring, 5-Shot
24	Ejectors	54	Shoulder Screw	83	Magazine Floor
25	Bolt Guide	55	Torsional Spring	**Parts Not Shown**	
26	Cylindrical Pins	56	Bolt Release Lever		Sight Elevator
27	Receiver	57	Magazine Guides		Sight Elevator Screws
28	Cartridge Guide	58	Distance Ring		Pointer
29	Two-Stage Trigger Assembly	59	Magazine Guide Pin		Intermediate Plate
30	Hexagon Threaded Bolt				Rear Sight Blade

Model 1418 D and 1518 D Deluxe Bolt-Action Rifle

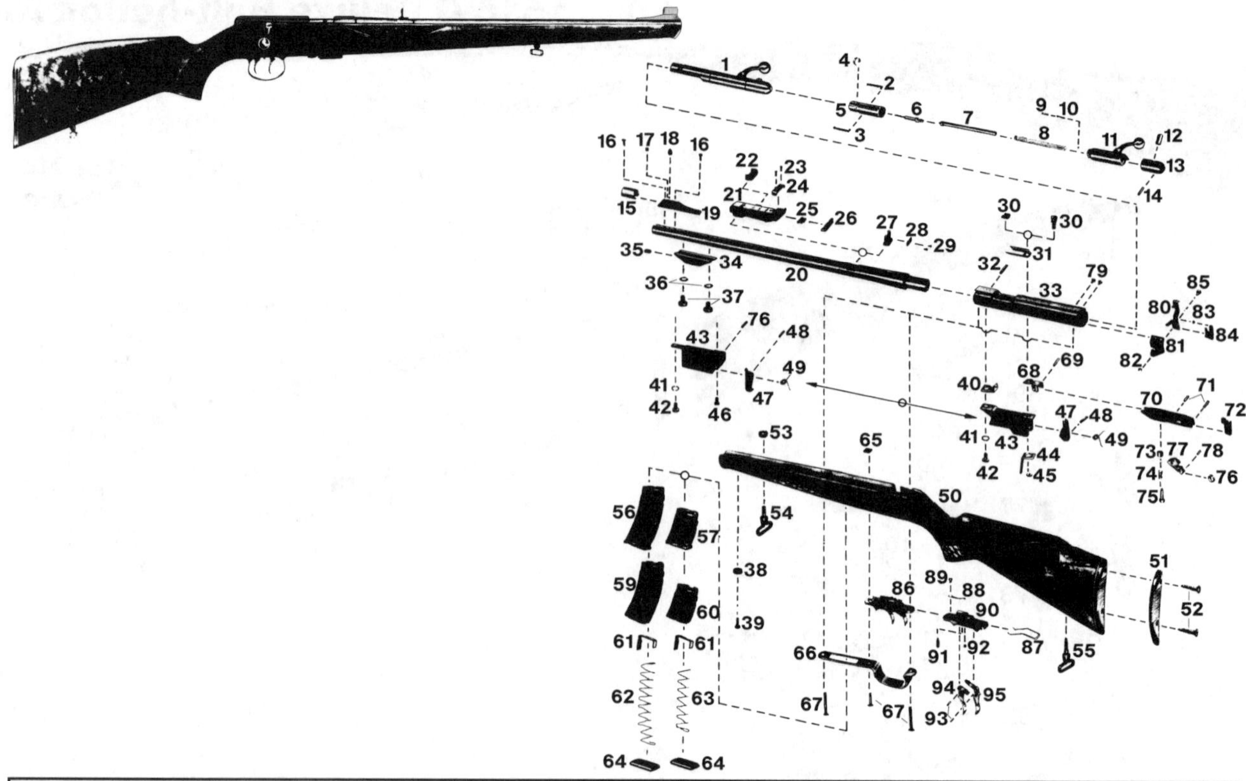

1	Bolt Assembly
2	Extractor
3	Cartridge Retainer
4	Spring Clamp
5	Bolt Head
6	Firing Pin
7	Striker Pin
8	Striker Spring
9	Catch Bolt
10	Catch Bolt Spring
11	Bolt with Handle
12	Guide Bolt
13	Cocking Piece
14	Parallel Pin
15	Front Sight Hood
16	Countersunk Head Screws
17	Safety Plug
18	Bead
19	Front Sight Base
20	Barrel
21	Tangent Sight
22	Sight Elevator
23	Pan Head Screws
24	Pointer
25	Intermediate Plate
26	Rear Sight Blade
27	Folding Sight
28	Rear Sight Blade
29	Pan Head Screws
30	Ejector
31	Bolt Guide
32	Parallel Pin
33	Receiver
34	Retainer
35	Screw Nut
36	Toothed Lock Washers
37	Cheese Head Screws
38	Bushing
39	Pan Head Screw
40	Cartridge Guide
41	Spring Lock Washer
42	Cheese Head Screw
43	Magazine Guide
44	Guide Tongue
45	Screw Nut
46	Cheese Head Screw
47	Magazine Retainer
48	Parallel Pin
49	Torsional Spring
50	Stock with Partial Fittings
51	Buttplate
52	Countersunk Oval Head Wood Screws
53	Screw Nut
54	Front Swivel
55	Rear Swivel
56	Magazine, 10-Shot
57	Magazine, 5-Shot, 22 Mag.
58	Magazine, 4-Shot
59	Magazine Housing, 10-Shot
60	Magazine Housing, 5-Shot, 22 Mag.
61	Magazine Follower
62	Follower Spring, 10-Shot
63	Follower Spring, 5-Shot, 22 Mag.
64	Magazine Floor
65	Square Nut
66	Trigger Guard
67	Countersunk Oval Head Screws
68	Bearing Piece
69	Parallel Pin
70	Trigger Bracket
71	Parallel Pins
72	Release Plunger
73	Spring Sleeve
74	Trigger Bracket Spring
75	Shoulder Screw
76	Roller
77	Release Lever
78	Parallel Pin
79	Countersunk Oval Head Screws
80	Safety-Lever
81	Bracket
82	Retaining Collar
83	Detent Ball
84	Leaf Spring
85	Bearing Pin
86	Double-Set Trigger Assembly
87	Double-Set Trigger Spring
88	Trigger Spring
89	Cheese Head Screw
90	Set Trigger Housing
91	Adjusting Screw
92	Safety Plug
93	Parallel Pins
94	Front Trigger
95	Rear Trigger

Parts Not Shown

- Rear Swivel Stud
- Front Swivel Stud
- Trigger Bracket (Complete)
- Safety (Complete)
- Barrelled Action (Complete)

Model 1422 D and 1522 D Classic Bolt-Action Rifle

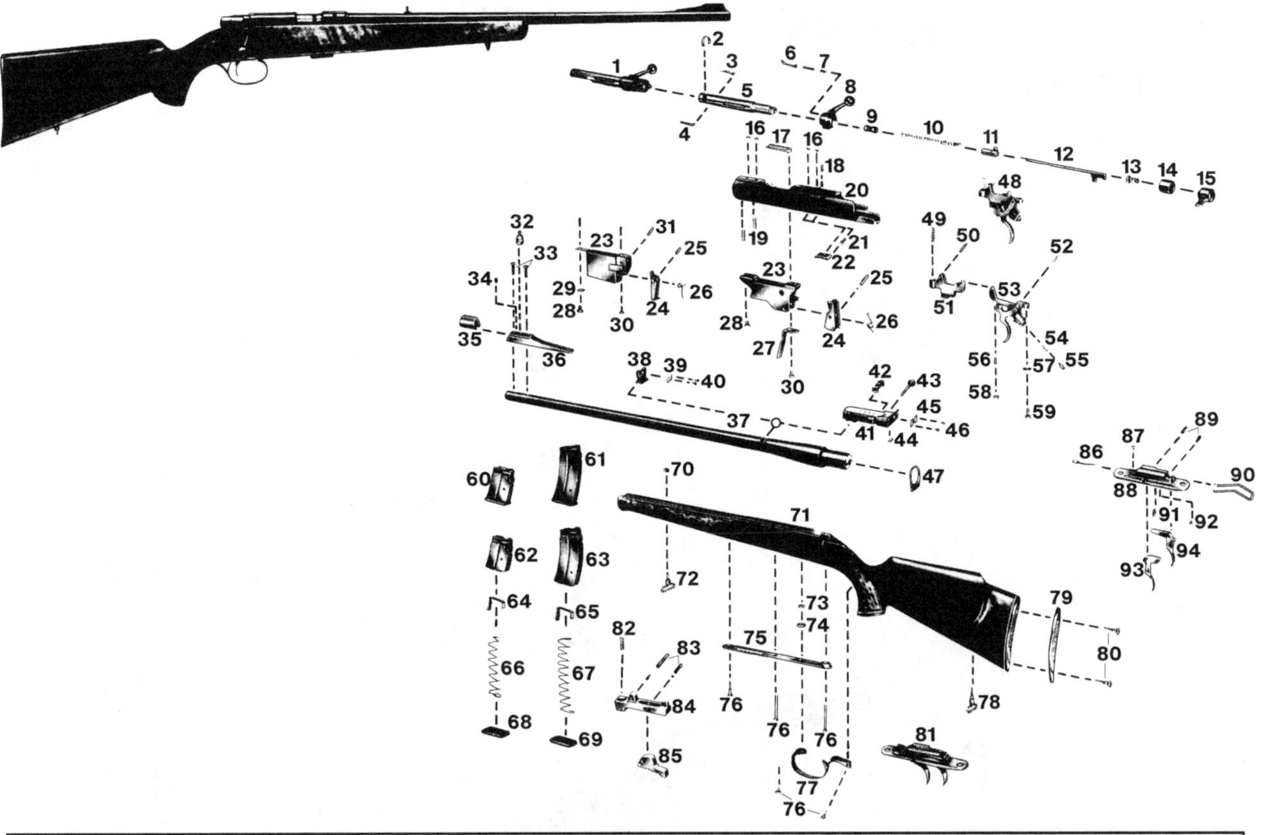

1	Bolt Assembly
2	Spring Clamp
3	Extractor
4	Cartridge Retainer
5	Bolt Body
6	Catch Bolt
7	Catch Bolt Spring
8	Bolt Handle
9	Spring Support, Front
10	Firing Pin Spring
11	Spring Support, Rear
12	Firing Pin
13	Signal Pin with Spring
14	Cover Sleeve
15	Safety
16	Dummy Screws
17	Bolt Guide
18	Grooved Pin
19	Parallel Pins
20	Receiver
21	Compression Spring
22	Bolt Stop
23	Magazine Guide
24	Magazine Retainer
25	Parallel Pin
26	Torsional Spring
27	Guide Tongue
28	Cheese Head Screw
29	Toothed Lock Washer
30	Shoulder Screw
31	Parallel Pin
32	Bead
33	Countersunk Head Screws
34	Safety Plug
35	Front Sight Hood
36	Front Sight Base
37	Barrel
38	Folding Sight
39	Rear Sight Blade
40	Pan Head Screws
41	Tangent Sight
42	Sight Elevator
43	Adjusting Screw
44	Sleeve
45	Rear Sight Blade
46	Pan Head Screws
47	Abutment
48	Trigger Assembly
49	Compression Spring
50	Parallel Pin
51	Trigger Bracket
52	Round Head Rivet
53	Trigger Support with Trigger
54	Compression Spring
55	Adjusting Screw
56	Set Screw
57	Toothed Lock Washer
58	Hexagon Nut
59	Cheese Head Screw
60	Magazine-4—, 5- Shot
61	Magazine—10-Shot
62	Magazine Housing—4-, 5-Shot
63	Magazine Housing—10-Shot
64	Magazine Follower—4-, 5-Shot
65	Magazine Follower—10-Shot
66	Follower Spring—4-, 5-Shot
67	Follower Spring—10-Shot
68	Magazine Floor—4-, 5-Shot
69	Magazine Floor—10-Shot
70	Screw Nut
71	Stock with Partial Fittings
72	Front Swivel
73	Hexagon Nut
74	Toothed Lock Washer
75	Floorplate
76	Raised Countersunk Head Screws
77	Trigger Guard
78	Rear Swivel
79	Buttplate
80	Countersunk Oval Head Wood Screws
81	Double-Set Trigger Assembly
82	Compression Spring
83	Parallel Pins
84	Trigger Bracket
85	Release Lever
86	Trigger Spring
87	Cheese Head Screw
88	Set-Trigger Housing
89	Parallel Pins
90	Double-Set Trigger Spring
91	Adjusting Screw
92	Safety Plug
93	Front Trigger
94	Rear Trigger

Model 1449, 1449D, 1450 and 1450D Bolt-Action Rifle

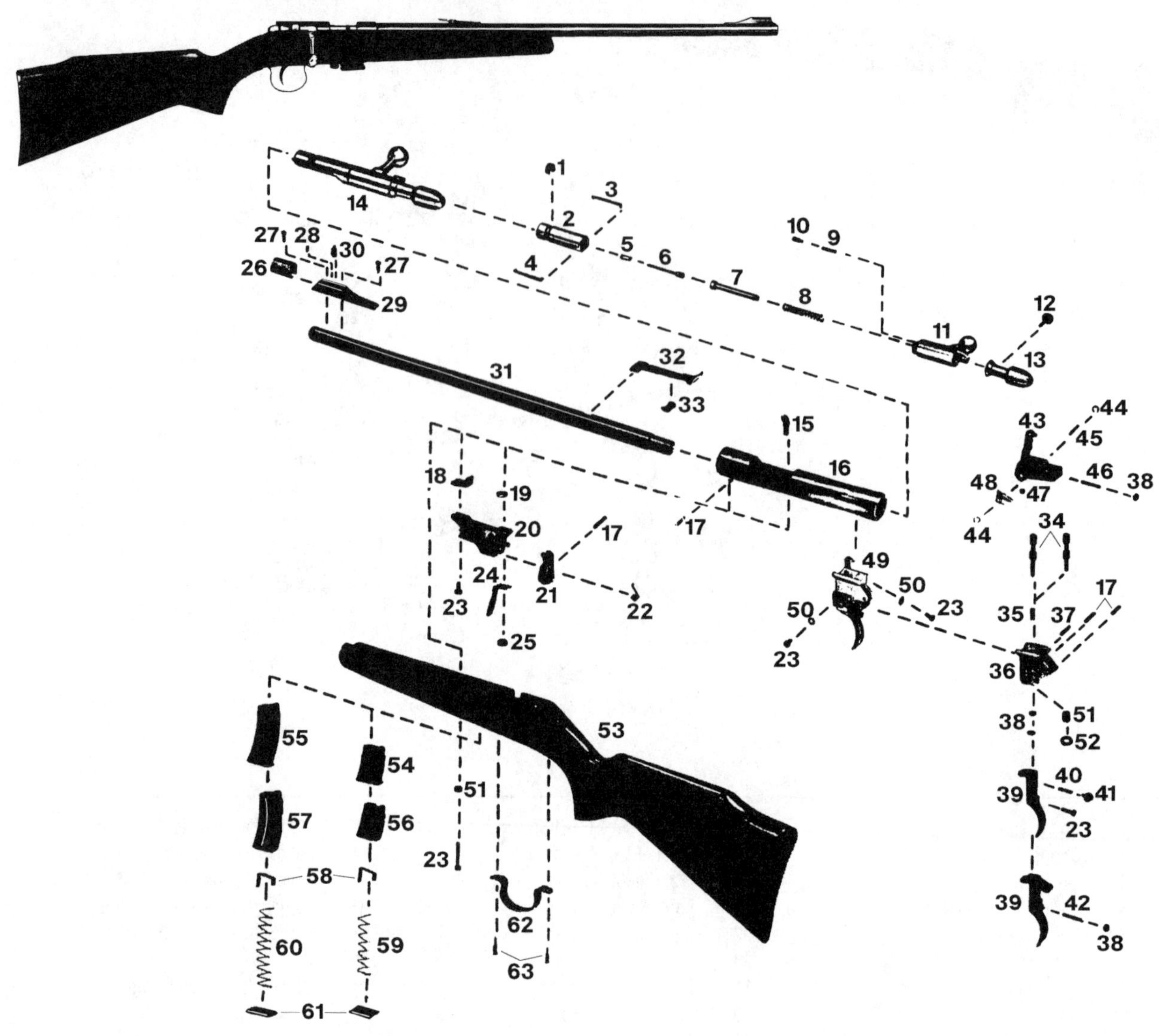

1	Spring Clamp	23	Pan Head Screws	45	Pin
2	Bolt Head	24	Guide Tongue	46	Set Screw
3	Extractor	25	Ejector Nut	47	Detent Ball
4	Cartridge Retainer	26	Front Sight Hood	48	Leaf Spring
5	Firing Pin Spring	27	Countersunk Flat Head Screws	49	Trigger Assembly
6	Firing Pin	28	Clamping Piece	50	Toothed Lock Washers (2)
7	Striker Pin	29	Front Sight Base	51	Threaded Sleeves
8	Striker Spring	30	Bead Front Sight	52	Flat Nut
9	Catch Bolt Spring	31	Barrel	53	Stock with Buttplate
10	Catch Bolt	32	Sight Leaf	54	5-Shot Magazine Assembly
11	Bolt with Handle	33	Sight Adjustor	55	10-Shot Magazine Assembly
12	Guide Bolt	34	Release Plungers	56	5-Shot Magazine Tube
13	Cocking Piece	35	Release Plunger Spring	57	10-Shot Magazine Tube
14	Bolt Assembly	36	Trigger Housing	58	Magazine Follower
15	Ejector Screw	37	Clamping Sleeve	59	5-Shot Magazine Follower Spring
16	Receiver	38	Hexagon Nuts	60	10-Shot Magazine Follower Spring
17	Cylindrical Pins	39	Triggers	61	Magazine Floor
18	Intermediate Piece	40	Trigger Spring	62	Trigger Guard
19	Distance Ring	41	Spring Bolt	63	Countersunk Oval Head Wood Screws
20	Magazine Guide	42	Set Screw		**Parts Not Shown**
21	Magazine Catch	43	Safety-Lever		Buttplate
22	Torsional Spring	44	Retaining Collar		

Model 1803, 1803 D, 1803 L and 1803 LD Bolt-Action Rifle

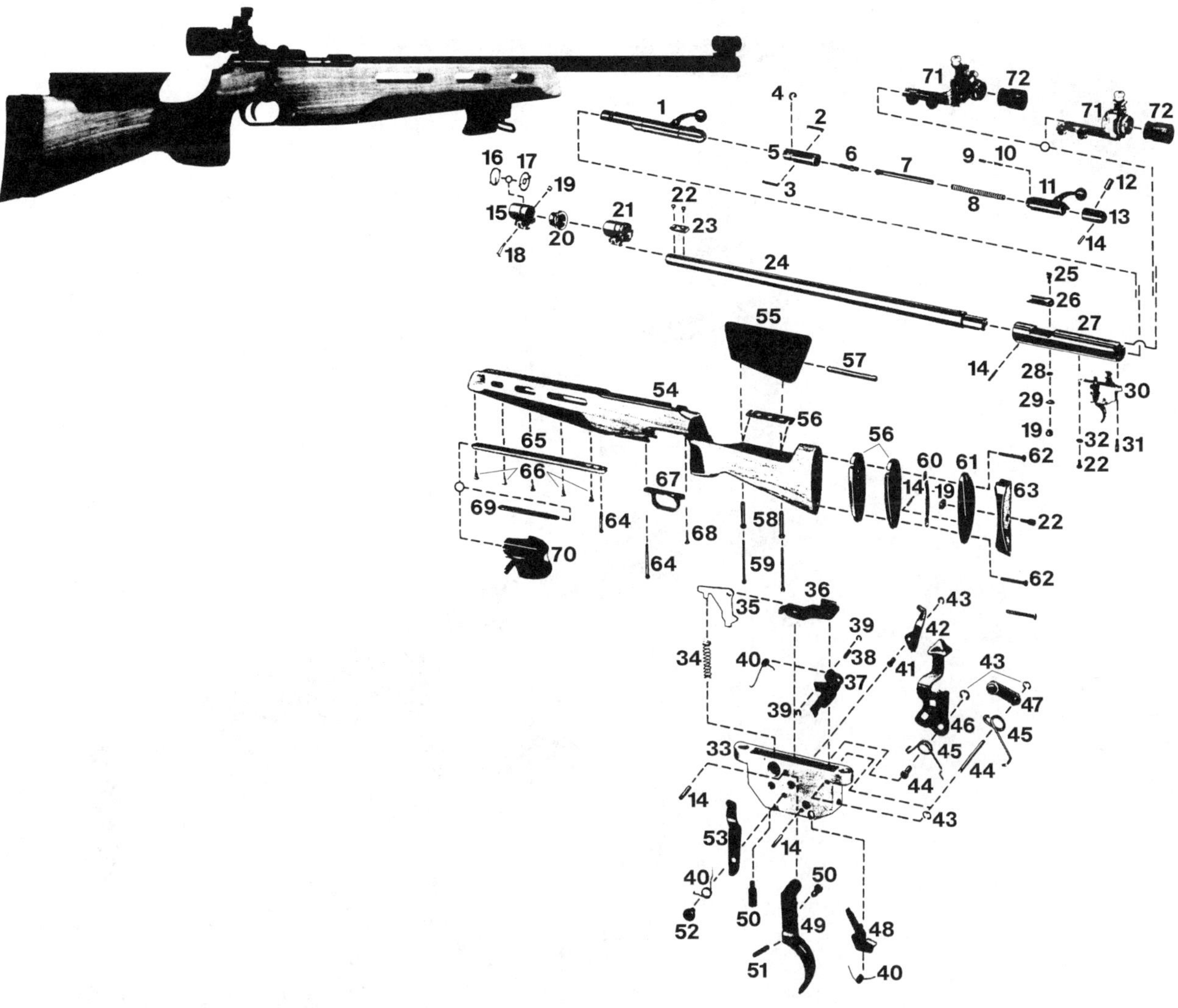

1	Bolt Assembly	25	Ejector	49	Trigger
2	Extractor	26	Loading Platform	50	Adjusting Screw
3	Cartridge Retainer	27	Receiver	51	Set-Screw
4	Spring Clamp	28	Distance Ring	52	Shoulder Screw
5	Bolt Head	29	Spring Washer	53	Bolt Release Lever
6	Firing Pin	30	Trigger Assembly	54	Stock with Partial Fittings
7	Striker Pin	31	Hexagon Threaded Bolt	55	Cheekpiece
8	Striker Spring	32	Toothed Lock Washer	56	Spacers
9	Catch Bolt	33	Trigger Housing	57	Bolt
10	Catch Bolt Spring	34	Trigger Spring	58	Bushings
11	Bolt with Handle	35	Cam Lever	59	Socket-Head Screws
12	Guide Bolt	36	Release Plunger	60	Cover Plate
13	Cocking Piece	37	Catch Link	61	Guide Plate
14	Cylindrical Pins	38	Pin	62	Raised Cheese Head Screws
15	Front Sight Hood	39	Retaining Collars	63	Buttplate
16	Post Insert	40	Torsional Springs	64	Screws
17	Aperture Insert	41	Pivot	65	Front Swivel Rail
18	Hook Screw	42	Bolt Pawl	66	Countersunk Head Wood Screws
19	Nuts	43	Retaining Collars	67	Trigger Guard
20	Clamp Ring	44	Pivots	68	Raised Countersunk Wood Screw
21	Front Sight, Complete	45	Springs	69	Swivel Rail Filler
22	Pan Head Screws	46	Safety-Lever	70	Handstop Sling Swivel Complete
23	Base	47	Catch-Lever	71	Peep Sight, Complete
24	Barrel	48	Release Latch	72	Rubber Eyeshade

Model 525 Autoloading Rifle

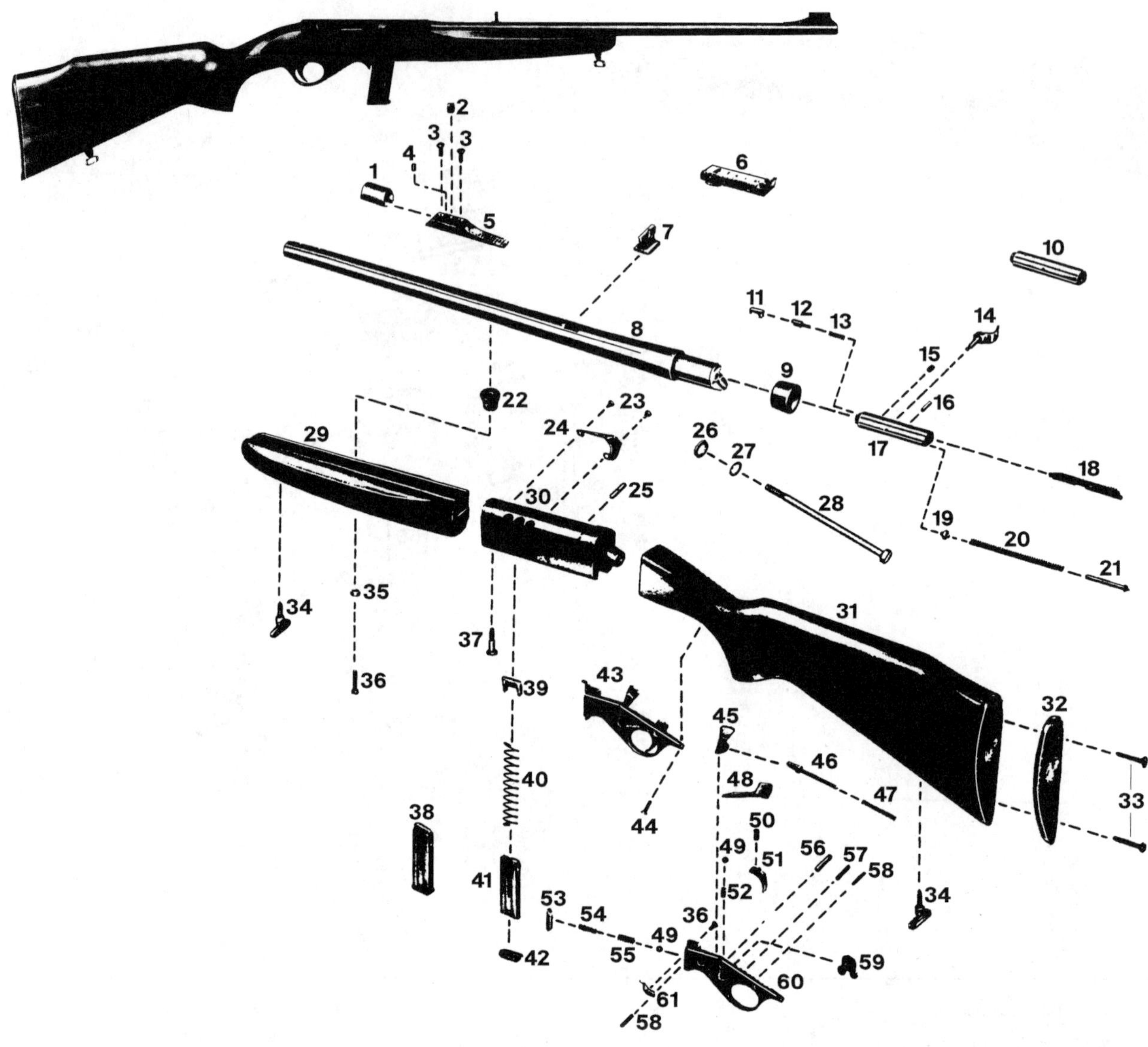

No.	Part	No.	Part	No.	Part
1	Front Sight Hood	**22**	Barrel Stud	**43**	Trigger Guard with Trigger Assembly
2	Front Sight Bead	**23**	Pan Head Screws	**44**	Raised Countersunk Head Screw
3	Front Sight Base Screws	**24**	Deflector	**45**	Hammer
4	Safety Plug	**25**	Trigger Guard Retaining Pin	**46**	Hammer Spring Bolt
5	Front Sight Base	**26**	Washer	**47**	Hammer Spring
6	Tangent Rear Sight	**27**	Lock Washer	**48**	Catch Link
7	Folding Leaf Rear Sight	**28**	Stock Assembly Screw	**49**	Steel Balls
8	Barrel	**29**	Forend	**50**	Trigger Spring
9	Intermediate Ring	**30**	Receiver	**51**	Trigger
10	Bolt Assembly, Complete	**31**	Stock with Partial Fittings	**52**	Safety Spring
11	Extractor	**32**	Buttplate	**53**	Magazine Retainer
12	Spring Bolt	**33**	Buttplate Screws	**54**	Magazine Retaining Spring, Large
13	Extractor Spring	**34**	Sling Swivels	**55**	Magazine Retaining Spring, Small
14	Bolt Handle	**35**	Bushing	**56**	Hammer Pin
15	Threaded Pin	**36**	Cheese Head Screws	**57**	Catch Link Pin
16	Firing Pin Retaining Pin	**37**	Barrel Assembly Screw	**58**	Cylindrical Pins
17	Bolt Body	**38**	Magazine Assembly, Complete	**59**	Safety
18	Firing Pin	**39**	Magazine Follower	**60**	Trigger Guard
19	Catch Bolt	**40**	Magazine Follower Spring	**61**	Ejector
20	Recoil Spring	**41**	Magazine Housing		
21	Spring Bolt	**42**	Magazine Bottom		

Model 1927 A-1 and M1 Autoloading Rifle

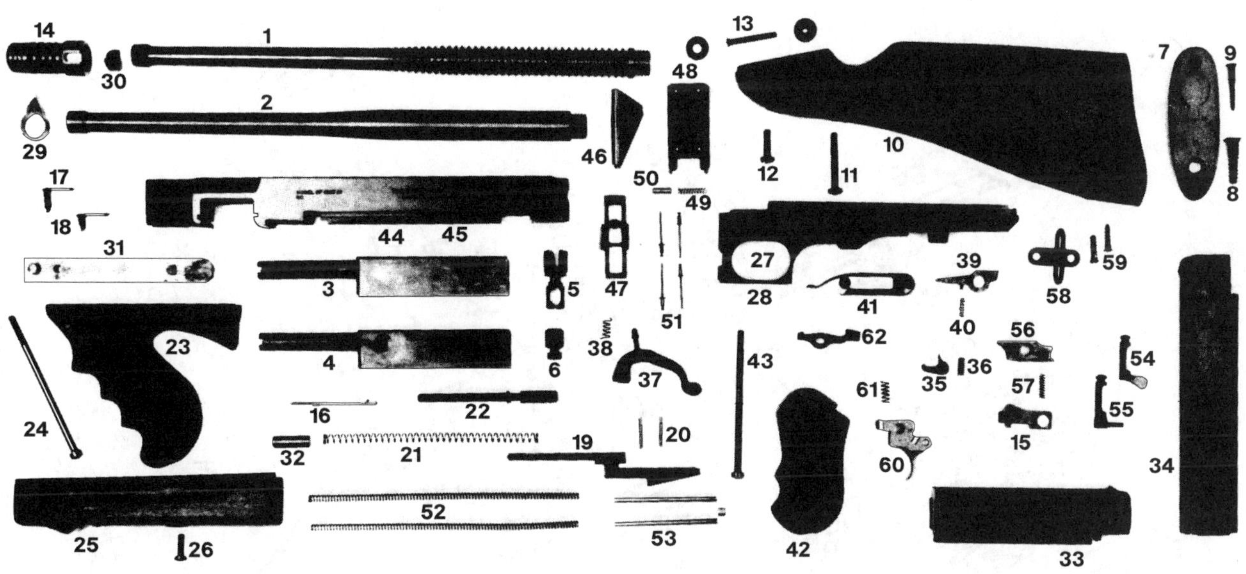

1 Barrel, Finned and Threaded
2 Barrel, Smooth
3 Bolt
4 Bolt (M1)
5 Bolt Handle
6 Bolt Handle (M1)
7 Buttplate
8 Buttplate Screw, Large
9 Buttplate Screw, Small
10 Buttstock
11 Buttstock Retaining Screw, Large
12 Buttstock Retaining Screw, Small
13 Buttstock Reinforcing Nut and Bolt
14 Compensator
15 Disconnector
16 Extractor
17 Ejector
18 Ejector (M1)
19 Firing Pin
20 Firing Pin Retaining Pins
21 Firing Pin Spring
22 Firing Pin Pilot
23 Foregrip, Vertical
24 Foregrip, Vertical Screw
25 Foregrip, Horizontal
26 Foregrip, Horizontal Screw
27 Frame
28 Frame (M1)
29 Front Sight
30 Front Sight for Compensator
31 Grip Mount
32 Hammer
33 Magazine, 20-Round
34 Magazine, 30-Round
35 Lifter
36 Lifter Spring
37 Magazine Catch
38 Magazine Catch Spring
39 Pawl
40 Pawl Spring
41 Pivot Plate
42 Rear Grip
43 Rear Grip Screw
44 Receiver
45 Receiver (M1)
46 Rear Sight (M1)
47 Rear Sight Leaf Complete
48 Rear Sight Base
49 Rear Sight Plunger Spring
50 Rear Sight Plunger
51 Rear Sight Rivets
52 Recoil Spring
53 Recoil Spring Pilot and Plate
54 Safety-Lever
55 Safety-Lever (M1)
56 Sear Block
57 Sear Block Spring
58 Sling Swivel
59 Sling Swivel Screws
60 Trigger
61 Trigger Spring
62 Trip

Parts Not Shown

Firing Pin Retracting Pin
Frame Latch
Frame Latch Spring

Model 1 Side-by-Side Shotgun

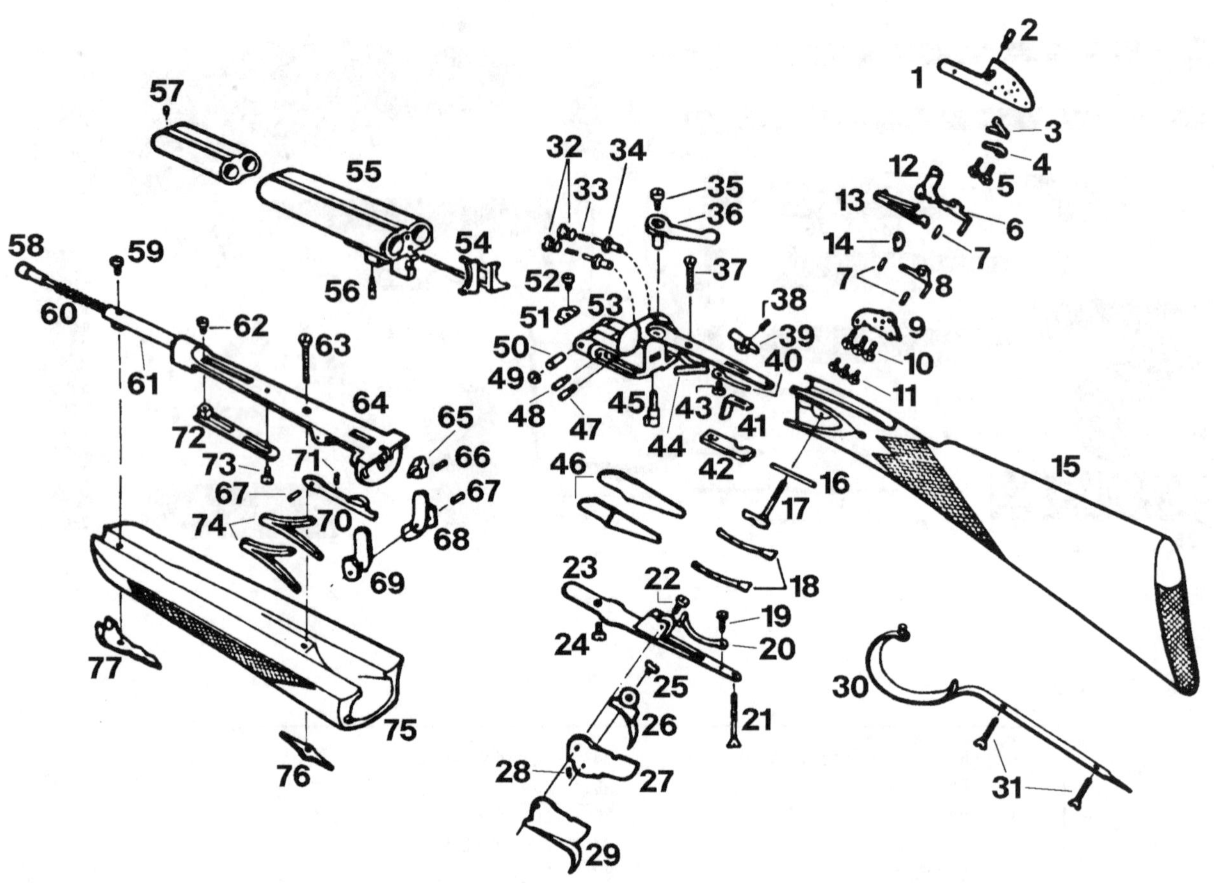

1	Sideplate
2	Sideplate Screw
3	Sear Spring
4	Sear Lever
5	Sear Spring Screws
6	Sear, Right
7	Sear Pins
8	Sear, Left
9	Bridle
10	Bridle Screws, Long
11	Bridle Screws, Short
12	Hammer
13	Hammer Spring
14	Hammer Spring Stirrup
15	Buttstock
16	Safety Rod
17	Sideplate Lever
18	Locking Lever Springs
19	Trigger Spring Screw
20	Trigger Spring
21	Trigger Plate Screw, Rear
22	Trigger Screw, Right
23	Trigger Plate
24	Trigger Plate Screw, Front
25	Trigger Screw, Left
26	Trigger, Right
27	Right Trigger Lever
28	Trigger Lever Pin
29	Trigger, Left
30	Trigger Guard
31	Trigger Guard Screws
32	Firing Pin Bushings
33	Firing Pin Springs
34	Firing Pins
35	Top Lever Screw
36	Top Lever
37	Top Tang Screw
38	Safety Thumb-Piece Screw
39	Safety Thumb-Piece
40	Safety Spring
41	Safety
42	Locking Block
43	Safety Spring Screw
44	Barrel Latch Lever Spring
45	Locking Block Actuator
46	Cocking Levers
47	Frame Pin
48	Cocking Lever Pivot
49	Pivot Pin Retainer
50	Pivot Pin
51	Receiver Insert Plate
52	Insert Plate Screw
53	Receiver
54	Extractors
55	Barrels
56	Extractor Screw
57	Front Sight
58	Forend Release Thumb-Piece
59	Forend Release Tube Screw
60	Forend Release Thumb-Piece Spring
61	Forend Release Tube
62	Forend Iron Screw, Front
63	Forend Iron Screw, Rear
64	Forend Iron
65	Ejector
66	Ejector Pin
67	Ejector Hammer Pins
68	Ejector Hammer, Right
69	Ejector Hammer, Left
70	Forend Release
71	Forend Release Spring
72	Forend Plate
73	Forend Plate Screw
74	Ejector Hammer Springs
75	Forend
76	Forend Escutcheon, Rear
77	Forend Escutcheon, Front

Model 2 Side-by-Side Shotgun

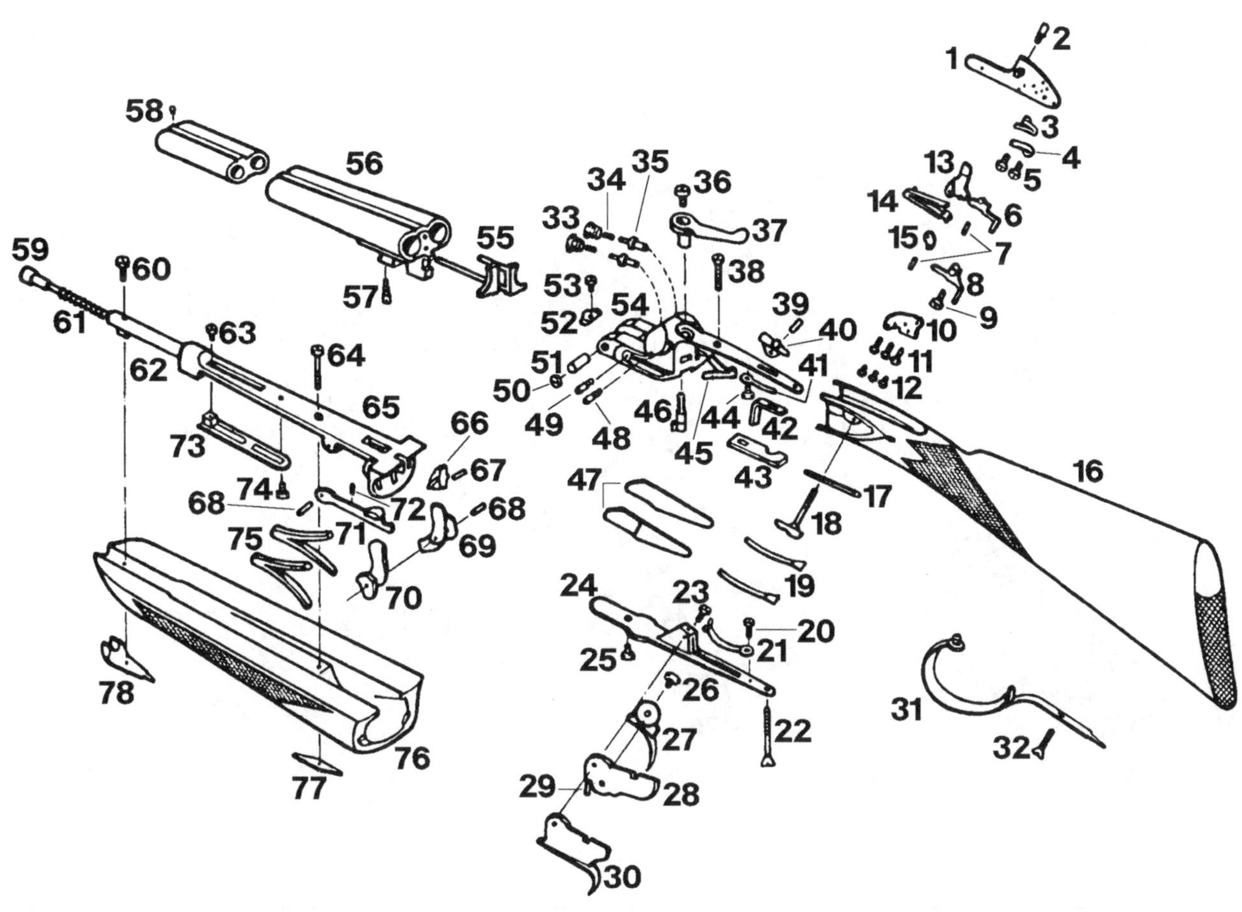

1	Sideplate	**28**	Right Trigger Lever	**55**	Extractors
2	Sideplate Screw	**29**	Trigger Lever Pin	**56**	Barrels
3	Sear Spring	**30**	Trigger, Left	**57**	Extractor Screw
4	Sear Lever	**31**	Trigger Guard	**58**	Front Sight
5	Sear Spring Screws	**32**	Trigger Guard Screw	**59**	Forend Release Thumb-Piece
6	Sear, Right	**33**	Firing Pin Bushings	**60**	Forend Release Tube Screw
7	Sear Pins	**34**	Firing Pin Springs	**61**	Forend Release Thumb-Piece Spring
8	Sear, Left	**35**	Firing Pins	**62**	Forend Release Tube
9	Sear Screw	**36**	Top Lever Screw	**63**	Forend Iron Screw, Front
10	Bridle	**37**	Top Lever	**64**	Forend Iron Screw, Rear
11	Bridle Screws, Long	**38**	Top Tang Screw	**65**	Forend Iron
12	Bridle Screws, Short	**39**	Safety Thumb-Piece Screw	**66**	Ejector
13	Hammer	**40**	Safety Thumb-Piece	**67**	Ejector Pin
14	Hammer Spring	**41**	Safety Spring	**68**	Ejector Hammer Pins
15	Hammer Spring Stirrup	**42**	Safety	**69**	Ejector Hammer, Right
16	Buttstock	**43**	Locking Block	**70**	Ejector Hammer, Left
17	Safety Rod	**44**	Safety Spring Screw	**71**	Forend Release
18	Sideplate Lever	**45**	Barrel Latch Lever Spring	**72**	Forend Release Spring
19	Locking Lever Springs	**46**	Locking Block Actuator	**73**	Forend Plate
20	Trigger Spring Screw	**47**	Cocking Levers	**74**	Forend Plate Screw
21	Trigger Spring	**48**	Frame Pin	**75**	Ejector Hammer Springs
22	Trigger Plate Screw, Rear	**49**	Cocking Lever Pivot	**76**	Forend
23	Trigger Screw, Right	**50**	Pivot Pin Retainer	**77**	Forend Escutcheon, Rear
24	Trigger Plate	**51**	Pivot Pin	**78**	Forend Escutcheon, Front
25	Trigger Plate Screw, Front	**52**	Receiver Insert Plate		
26	Trigger Screw, Left	**53**	Insert Plate Screw		
27	Trigger, Right	**54**	Receiver		

Model 37 Over/Under Shotgun

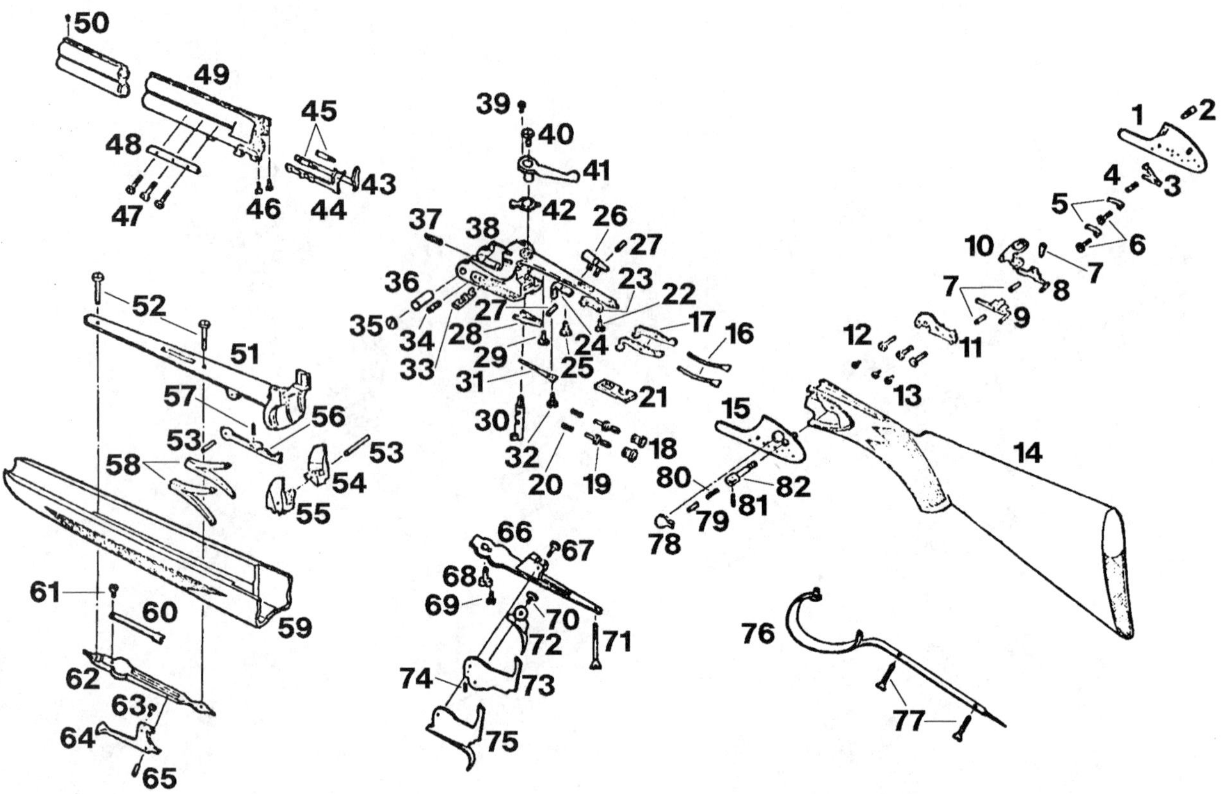

1	Sideplate, Right	**29**	Safety Rod Bracket Screw	**57**	Forend Release Spring
2	Sideplate Screw	**30**	Locking Block Actuator	**58**	Ejector Hammer Springs
3	Sear Spring	**31**	Safety Rod	**59**	Forend
4	Sear Spring Pin	**32**	Safety Rod Retaining Screw	**60**	Forend Latch Spring
5	Sear Lever Trips	**33**	Barrel Lock Cross Piece	**61**	Latch Spring Screw
6	Sear Spring Screws	**34**	Cocking Lever Pivot	**62**	Forend Latch Housing
7	Sear Pins	**35**	Pivot Pin Retainer	**63**	Latch Housing Screw
8	Sear, Upper	**36**	Pivot Pin	**64**	Forend Latch
9	Sear, Lower	**37**	Top Lever Trip Pin	**65**	Latch Pivot Pin
10	Hammer	**38**	Receiver	**66**	Trigger Plate
11	Bridle	**39**	Top Lever Lock Screw	**67**	Trigger Screw, Upper
12	Bridle Screws, Long	**40**	Top Lever Screw	**68**	Trigger Plate Screw, Front
13	Bridle Screws, Short	**41**	Top Lever	**69**	Trigger Plate Lock Screw
14	Buttstock	**42**	Top Lever Bushing	**70**	Trigger Screw, Lower
15	Sideplate, Left	**43**	Ejector, Upper	**71**	Trigger Plate Screw, Rear
16	Cocking Lever Springs	**44**	Ejector, Lower	**72**	Trigger, Right
17	Cocking Levers	**45**	Ejector Retainer	**73**	Right Trigger Lever
18	Firing Pin Bushings	**46**	Ejector Screws	**74**	Lever Pin
19	Firing Pins	**47**	Rib Screws	**75**	Left Trigger
20	Firing Pin Spring	**48**	Spacer Rib	**76**	Trigger Guard
21	Locking Plate	**49**	Barrels	**77**	Trigger Guard Screws
22	Safety Spring Screw	**50**	Front Sight	**78**	Sideplate Lever
23	Safety Spring	**51**	Forend Iron	**79**	Lever Plunger
24	Safety	**52**	Forend Iron Screws	**80**	Plunger Spring
25	Safety Screw	**53**	Ejector Hammer Pin	**81**	Lever Shaft Pin
26	Safety Thumb-Piece	**54**	Ejector Hammer, Upper	**82**	Lever Shaft
27	Safety Thumb-Piece Pins	**55**	Ejector Hammer, Lower		
28	Safety Rod Bracket	**56**	Forend Release		

Model 53 Side-by-Side Shotgun

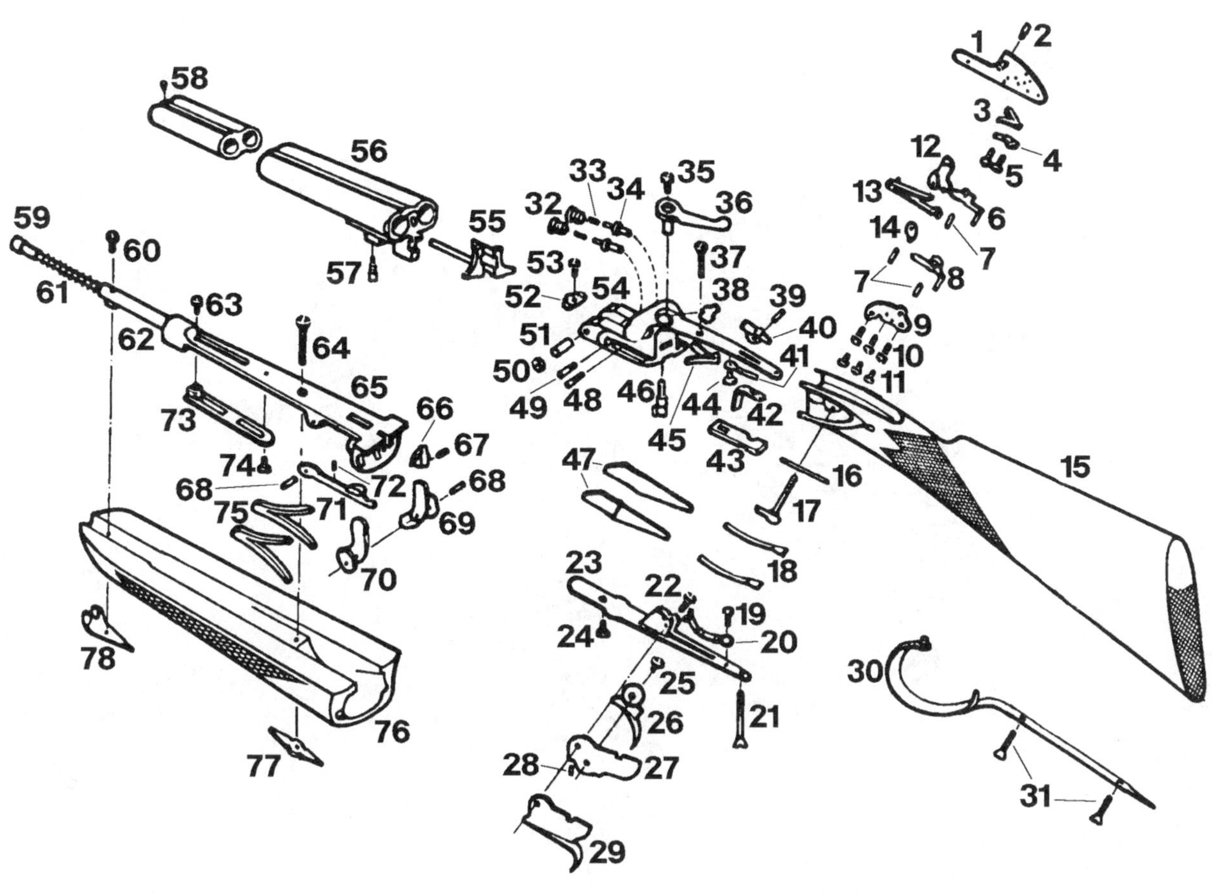

1	Sideplate	28	Trigger Lever Pin	55	Extractors
2	Sideplate Screw	29	Trigger, Left	56	Barrels
3	Sear Spring	30	Trigger Guard	57	Extractor Screw
4	Sear Lever	31	Trigger Guard Screws	58	Front Sight
5	Sear Spring Screws	32	Firing Pin Bushings	59	Forend Release Thumb-Piece
6	Sear, Right	33	Firing Pin Springs	60	Forend Release Tube Screw
7	Sear Pins	34	Firing Pins	61	Forend Release Thumb-Piece Spring
8	Sear, Left	35	Top Lever Screw	62	Forend Release Tube
9	Bridle	36	Top Lever	63	Forend Iron Screw, Front
10	Bridle Screws, Long	37	Top Tang Screw	64	Forend Iron Screw, Rear
11	Bridle Screws, Short	38	Top Lever Bushing	65	Forend Iron
12	Hammer	39	Safety Thumb-Piece Screw	66	Ejector
13	Hammer Spring	40	Safety Thumb-Piece	67	Ejector Pin
14	Hammer Spring Stirrup	41	Safety Spring	68	Ejector Hammer Pins
15	Buttstock	42	Safety	69	Ejector Hammers, Right
16	Safety Rod	43	Locking Block	70	Ejector Hammer, Left
17	Sideplate Lever	44	Safety Spring Screw	71	Forend Release
18	Cocking Lever Springs	45	Barrel Latch Lever Spring	72	Forend Release Spring
19	Trigger Spring Screw	46	Locking Block Actuator	73	Forend Plate
20	Trigger Spring	47	Cocking Levers	74	Forend Plate Screw
21	Trigger Plate Screw, Rear	48	Frame Pin	75	Ejector Hammer Springs
22	Trigger Screw, Right	49	Cocking Lever Pivot	76	Forend Wood
23	Trigger Plate	50	Pivot Pin Retainer	77	Forend Escutcheon, Rear
24	Trigger Plate Screw, Front	51	Pivot Pin	78	Forend Escutcheon, Front
25	Trigger Screw, Left	52	Receiver Insert Plate		
26	Trigger, Right	53	Insert Plate Screw		
27	Right Trigger Lever	54	Receiver		

Model 56 Side-by-Side Shotgun

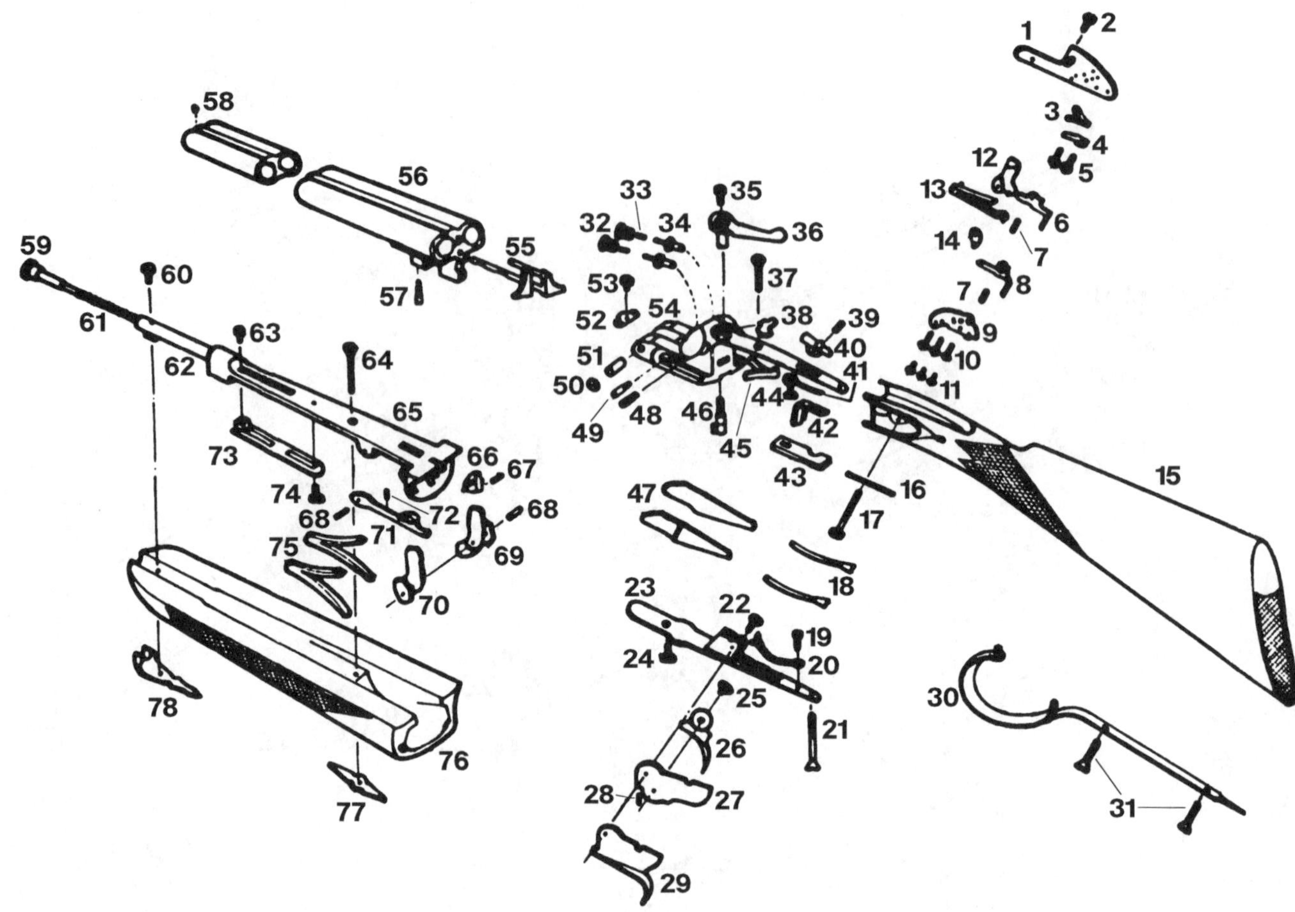

1	Sideplate	**28**	Trigger Lever Pin	**55**	Extractors
2	Sideplate Screw	**29**	Trigger, Left	**56**	Barrels
3	Sear Spring	**30**	Trigger Guard	**57**	Extractor Screw
4	Sear Lever	**31**	Trigger Guard Screw	**58**	Front Sight
5	Sear Spring Screws	**32**	Firing Pin Bushings	**59**	Forend Release Thumb-Piece
6	Sear, Right	**33**	Firing Pin Springs	**60**	Forend Release Tube Screw
7	Sear Pins	**34**	Firing Pins	**61**	Forend Release Thumb-Piece Spring
8	Sear, Left	**35**	Top Lever Screw	**62**	Forend Release Tube
9	Bridle	**36**	Top Lever	**63**	Forend Iron Screw, Front
10	Bridle Screws, Long	**37**	Top Tang Screw	**64**	Forend Iron Screw, Rear
11	Bridle Screws, Short	**38**	Top Lever Bushing	**65**	Forend Iron
12	Hammer	**39**	Safety Thumb-Piece Screw	**66**	Ejector
13	Hammer Spring	**40**	Safety Thumb-Piece	**67**	Ejector Pin
14	Hammer Spring Stirrup	**41**	Safety Spring	**68**	Ejector Hammer Pins
15	Buttstock	**42**	Safety	**69**	Ejector Hammer, Right
16	Safety Rod	**43**	Locking Block	**70**	Ejector Hammer, Left
17	Sideplate Lever	**44**	Safety Spring Screw	**71**	Forend Release
18	Cocking Lever Springs	**45**	Barrel Latch Lever Spring	**72**	Forend Release Spring
19	Trigger Spring Screw	**46**	Locking Block Actuator	**73**	Forend Plate
20	Trigger Spring	**47**	Cocking Levers	**74**	Forend Plate Screw
21	Trigger Plate Screw, Rear	**48**	Frame Pin	**75**	Ejector Hammer Springs
22	Trigger Screw, Right	**49**	Cocking Lever Pivot	**76**	Forend Wood
23	Trigger Plate	**50**	Pivot Pin Retainer	**77**	Forend Escutcheon, Rear
24	Trigger Plate Screw, Front	**51**	Pivot Pin	**78**	Forend Escutcheon, Front
25	Trigger Screw, Left	**52**	Receiver Insert Plate		
26	Trigger, Right	**53**	Insert Plate Screw		
27	Right Trigger Lever	**54**	Receiver		

Model XXV Side-by-Side Shotgun

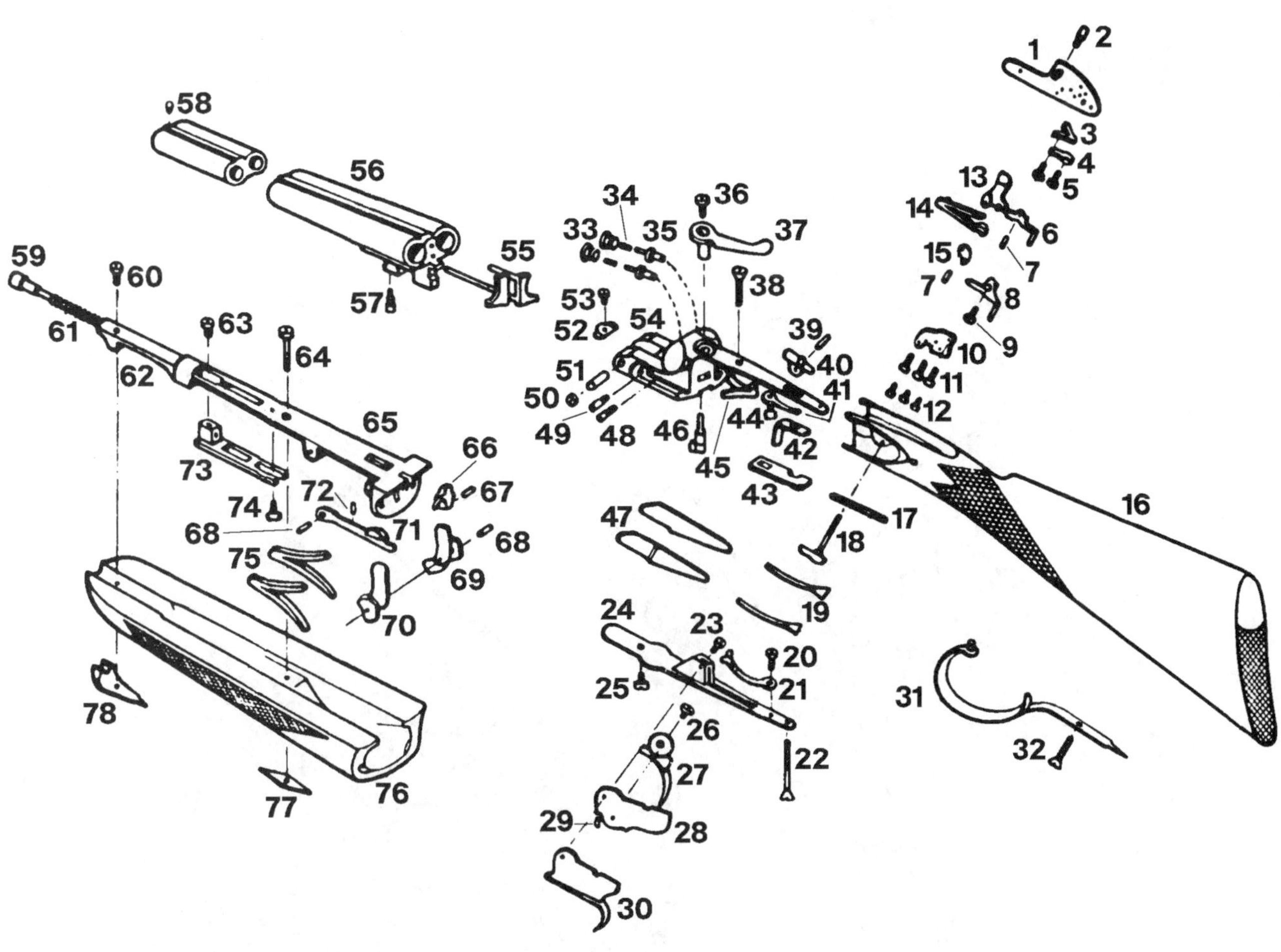

1	Sideplate	**27**	Trigger, Right	**53**	Insert Plate Screw
2	Sideplate Screw	**28**	Right Trigger Lever	**54**	Receiver
3	Sear Spring	**29**	Trigger Lever Pin	**55**	Extractors
4	Sear Lever	**30**	Trigger, Left	**56**	Barrels
5	Sear Spring Screws	**31**	Trigger Guard	**57**	Extractor Screw
6	Sear, Right	**32**	Trigger Guard Screw	**58**	Front Sight
7	Sear Pins	**33**	Firing Pin Bushings	**59**	Forend Release Thumb-Piece
8	Sear, Left	**34**	Firing Pin Springs	**60**	Forend Release Tube Screw
9	Sear Screw	**35**	Firing Pins	**61**	Forend Release Thumb-Piece Spring
10	Bridle	**36**	Top Lever Screw	**62**	Forend Release Tube
11	Bridle Screws, Long	**37**	Top Lever	**63**	Forend Iron Screw, Front
12	Bridle Screws, Short	**38**	Top Tang Screw	**64**	Forend Iron Screw, Rear
13	Hammer	**39**	Safety Thumb-Piece Screw	**65**	Forend Iron
14	Hammer Spring	**40**	Safety Thumb-Piece	**66**	Ejector
15	Hammer Spring Stirrup	**41**	Safety Spring	**67**	Ejector Pin
16	Buttstock	**42**	Safety	**68**	Ejector Hammer Pins
17	Safety Rod	**43**	Locking Block	**69**	Ejector Hammer, Right
18	Sideplate Lever	**44**	Safety Spring Screw	**70**	Ejector Hammer, Left
19	Cocking Lever Springs	**45**	Barrel Latch Lever Spring	**71**	Forend Release
20	Trigger Spring Screw	**46**	Locking Block Actuator	**72**	Forend Release Spring
21	Trigger Spring	**47**	Cocking Levers	**73**	Forend Plate
22	Trigger Plate Screw, Rear	**48**	Frame Pin	**74**	Forend Plate Screw
23	Trigger Screw, Right	**49**	Cocking Lever Pivot	**75**	Ejector Hammer Springs
24	Trigger Plate	**50**	Pivot Pin Retainer	**76**	Forend Wood
25	Trigger Plate Screw, Front	**51**	Pivot Pin	**77**	Forend Escutcheon, Rear
26	Trigger Screw, Left	**52**	Receiver Insert Plate	**78**	Forend Escutcheon, Front

Single-Shot Rifle

Courtesy of Thomas E. Wessel

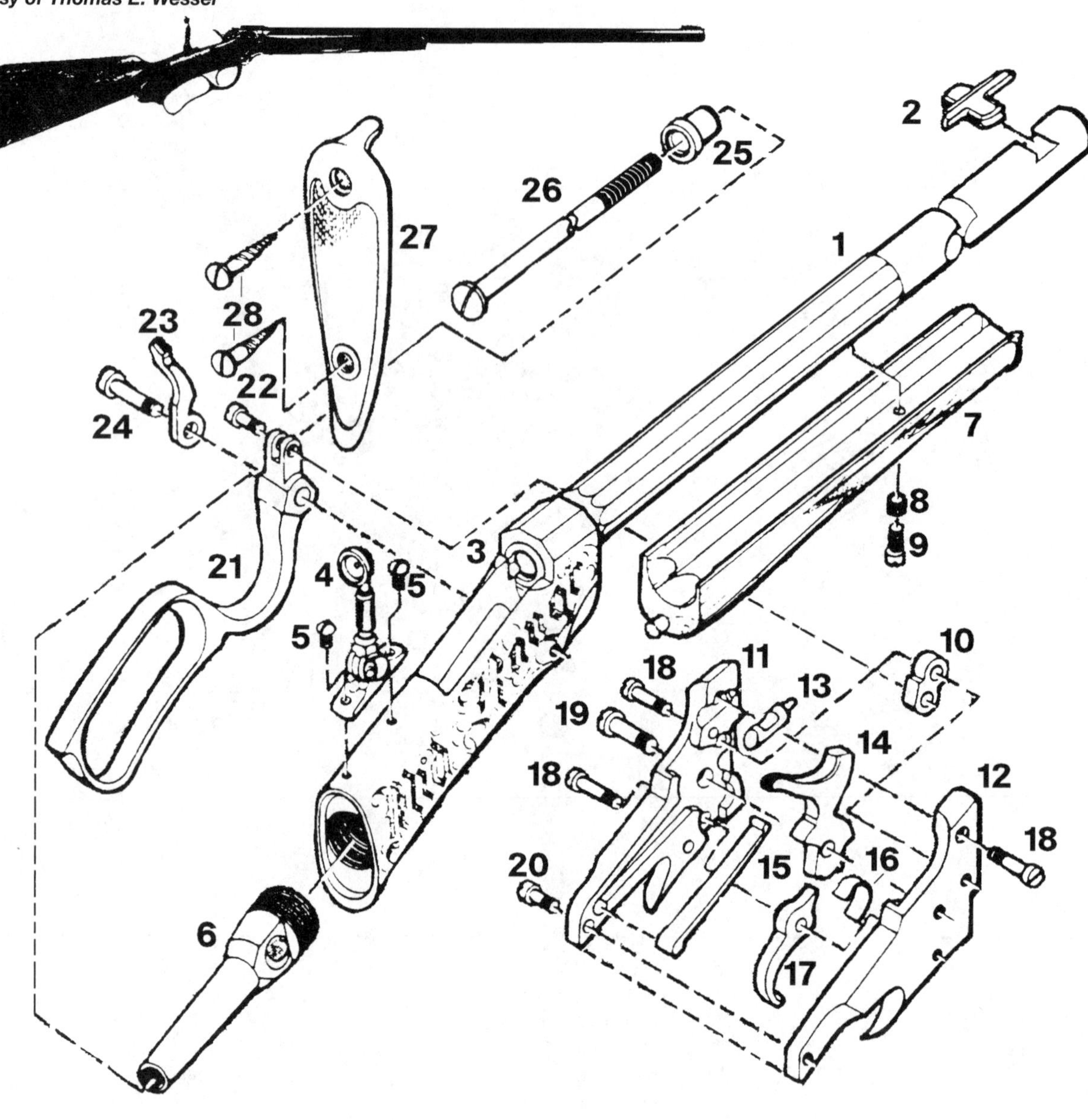

1	Barrel	16	Trigger Spring
2	Front Sight	17	Trigger
3	Receiver	18	Block Screws
4	Rear Sight	19	Hammer Screw
5	Rear Sight Screws	20	Rear Block Screw
6	Stock Lug	21	Finger Lever
7	Forearm	22	Lever Link Screw
8	Forearm Insert	23	Extractor
9	Forearm Screw	24	Lever Screw
10	Lever Link	25	Stock Insert
11	Breechblock, Left	26	Stock Bolt
12	Breechblock, Right	27	Buttplate
13	Firing Pin	28	Buttplate Screws
14	Hammer	**Parts Not Shown**	
15	Mainspring		Stock

M1 Super 90 Autoloading Shotgun

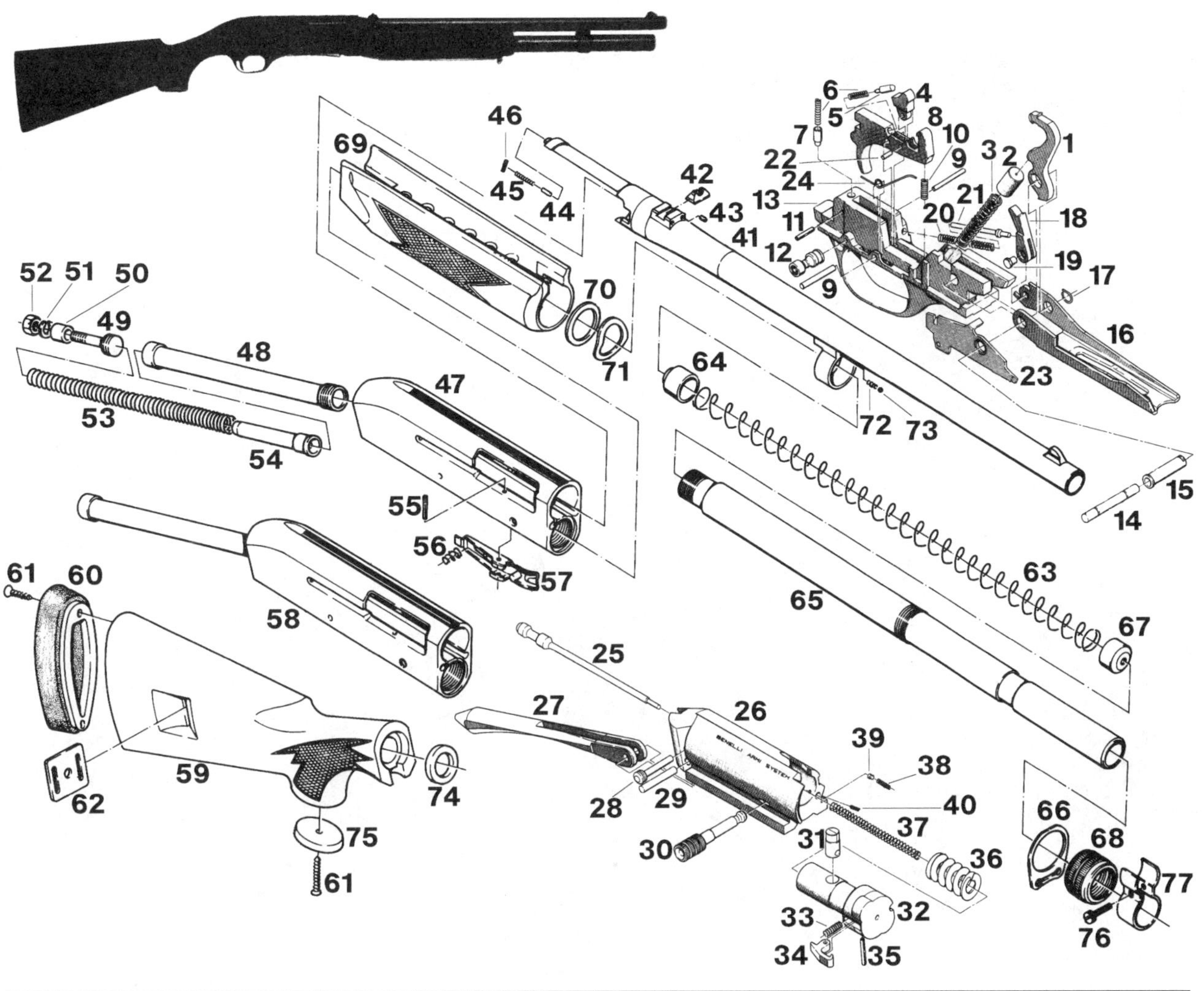

1	Hammer	**26**	Bolt	**50**	Spacer
2	Hammer Spring Cap	**27**	Link	**51**	Elastic Washer
3	Hammer Spring	**28**	Firing Pin Retaining Pin	**52**	Stock Retaining Nut
4	Disconnector	**29**	Link Pin	**53**	Recoil Spring
5	Disconnector Plunger	**30**	Bolt Handle	**54**	Recoil Spring Plunger
6	Safety Plunger Springs	**31**	Locking Head Pin	**55**	Carrier Latch Pin
7	Hand Safety Plunger	**32**	Locking Head	**56**	Carrier Latch
8	Trigger	**33**	Extractor Spring	**57**	Carrier Latch Spring
9	Trigger Pin	**34**	Extractor	**58**	Receiver Assembly
10	Trigger Spring	**35**	Extractor Pin	**59**	Stock
11	Safety Spring Retaining Pin	**36**	Inertia Spring	**60**	Buttplate
12	Hand Safety	**37**	Firing Pin Spring	**61**	Self-Threaded Screw
13	Trigger Guard	**38**	Bolt Handle Retaining Spring	**62**	Swivel Plate
14	Trigger Guard Pin	**39**	Bolt Handle Pin	**63**	Magazine Spring
15	Trigger Pin Bush	**40**	Bolt Handle Spring Retaining Pin	**64**	Magazine Follower
16	Carrier	**41**	Breech and Barrel Assembly	**65**	Magazine Tube
17	Trigger Guard Pin Spring	**42**	Front Sight	**66**	Ring
18	Breech Bolt Latch	**43**	Front Sight Screw	**67**	Magazine Tube Plug
19	Breech Bolt Latch Pin	**44**	Ejector Pin	**68**	Forend Cap
20	Carrier Spring	**45**	Ejector Pin Spring	**69**	Forend
21	Carrier Spring Plunger	**46**	Ejector Spring Retaining Pin	**70**	Washer
22	Disconnector Pin	**47**	Receiver	**71**	Spring Washer
23	Cartridge Drop Lever	**48**	Recoil Spring Tube	**72**	Cap Retaining Ball Spring
24	Cartridge Drop Lever Spring	**49**	Stock Retaining Nut Screw	**73**	Cap Retaining Ball
25	Firing Pin			**74**	Ring

Montefeltro Super 90 Autoloading Shotgun

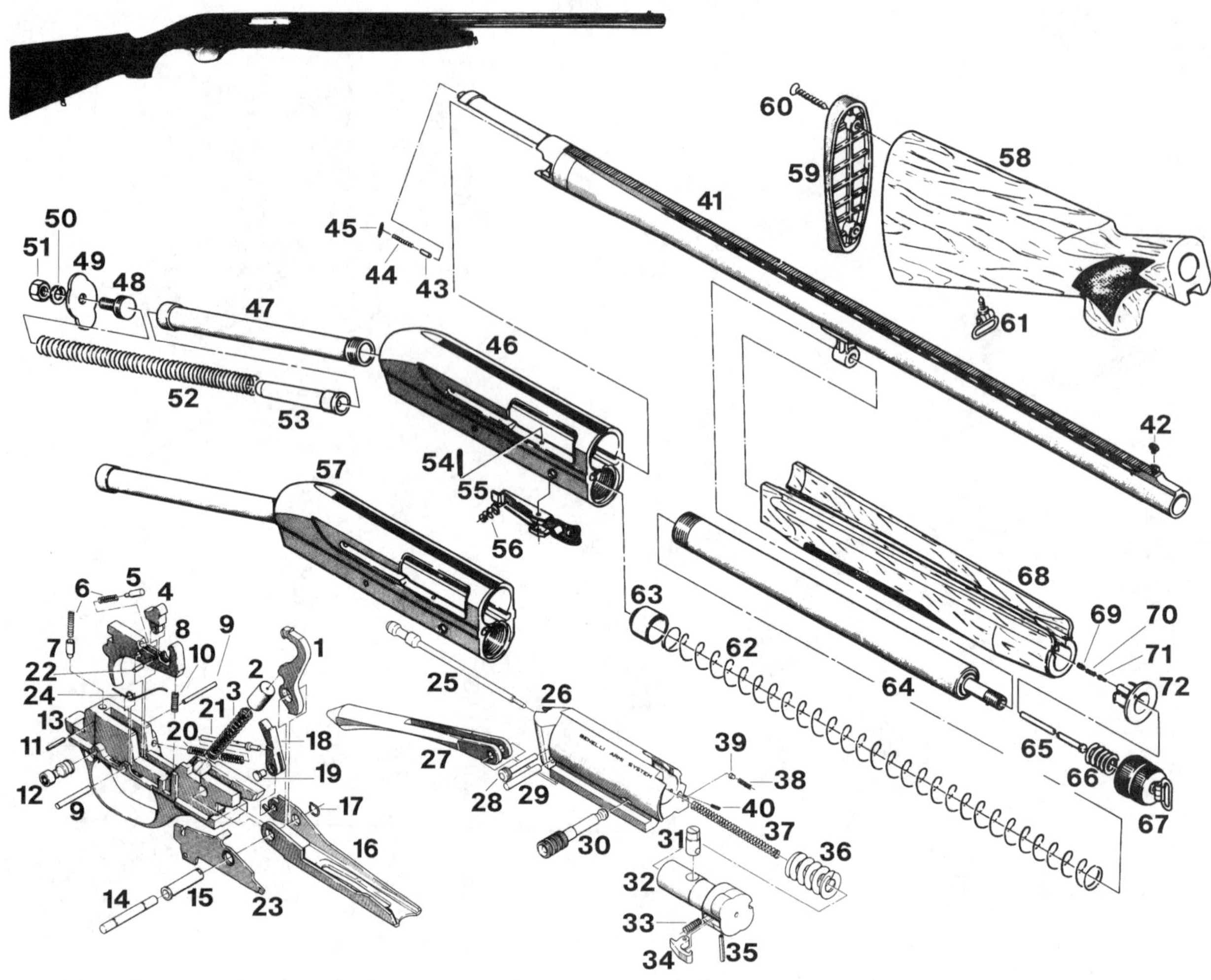

1	Hammer	**25**	Firing Pin	**49**	Locking Plate
2	Hammer Spring Cap	**26**	Bolt	**50**	Elastic Washer
3	Hammer Spring	**27**	Link	**51**	Stock Retaining Nut
4	Disconnector	**28**	Firing Pin Retaining Pin	**52**	Recoil Spring
5	Disconnector Plunger	**29**	Link Pin	**53**	Recoil Spring Plunger
6	Safety Plunger Springs	**30**	Bolt Handle	**54**	Carrier Latch Pin
7	Hand Safety Plunger	**31**	Locking Head Pin	**55**	Carrier Latch
8	Trigger	**32**	Locking Head	**56**	Carrier Latch Spring
9	Trigger Pin	**33**	Extractor Spring	**57**	Receiver Assembly
10	Trigger Spring	**34**	Extractor	**58**	Stock
11	Safety Spring Retaining Pin	**35**	Extractor Pin	**59**	Buttplate
12	Hand Safety	**36**	Inertia Spring	**60**	Buttplate Screw
13	Trigger Guard	**37**	Firing Pin Spring	**61**	Stock Swivel
14	Trigger Guard Pin	**38**	Bolt Handle Retaining Spring	**62**	Magazine Spring
15	Trigger Pin Bushing	**39**	Bolt Handle Pin	**63**	Magazine Follower
16	Carrier	**40**	Bolt Handle Spring Retaining Pin	**64**	Magazine Tube
17	Trigger Guard Pin Spring	**41**	Breech and Barrel Assembly	**65**	Shot Plug
18	Breech Bolt Latch	**42**	Front Sight	**66**	Forend Cap Spring
19	Breech Bolt Latch Pin	**43**	Ejector Pin	**67**	Forend Cap
20	Carrier Spring	**44**	Ejector Pin Spring	**68**	Forend
21	Carrier Spring Plunger	**45**	Ejector Spring Retaining Pin	**69**	Cap Retaining Pin Screw
22	Disconnector Pin	**46**	Receiver	**70**	Cap Retaining Pin Spring
23	Cartridge Drop Lever	**47**	Recoil Spring Tube	**71**	Cap Retaining Pin
24	Cartridge Drop Lever Spring	**48**	Stock Retaining Nut Screw	**72**	Cap Retaining Pin Bushing

Model A300, A301, A302 and A303 Autoloading Shotgun

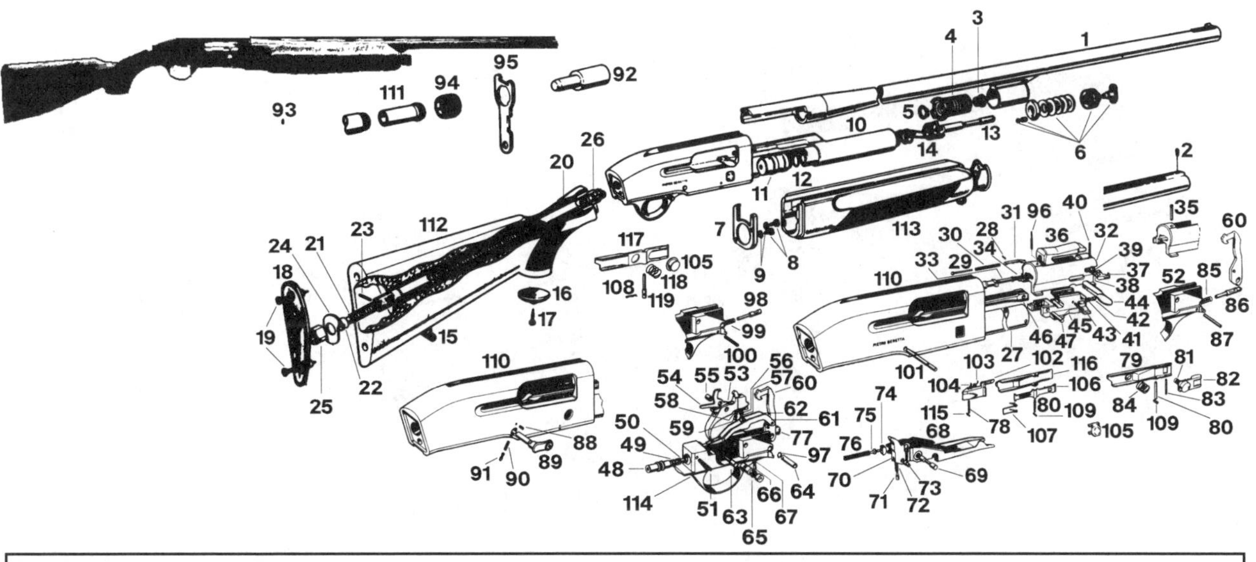

1	Barrel
2	Front Sight
3	Piston Bush
4	Piston
5	Piston Bush Snap Ring
6	Forend Cap with Swivel
7	Forend Cover
8	Forend Cover Screws
9	Spring Washers
10	Operating Rod
11	Magazine Follower
12	Magazine Spring
13	Magazine Tube Cap
14	Magazine Tube Cap Spring
15	Stock Swivel
16	Cap with Escutcheon
17	Cap Screw
18	Buttplate
19	Buttplate Screws
20	Stock Bolt Tube
21	Recoil Spring
22	Recoil Spring Cap
23	Recoil Spring Cap Pin
24	Spacer
25	Stock Bolt Nut
26	Recoil Spring Guide
27	Magazine Tube
28	Ejector Spring Pin
29	Ejector Spring Guide
30	Ejector Spring
31	Ejector
32	Breechbolt
33	Firing Pin
34	Firing Pin Spring
35	Firing Pin Retaining Pin
36	Locking Block
37	Extractor
38	Extractor Plunger
39	Extractor Spring
40	Extractor Pin
41	Cocking Handle Plunger Spring
42	Cocking Handle Plunger
43	Cocking Handle Plunger Retaining Spring Pin
44	Cocking Handle
45	Breechbolt Slide
46	Connecting Rod
47	Connecting Rod Pin
48	Hammer Spring Guide
49	Hammer Spring
50	Hammer Spring Guide Plunger
51	Hammer Spring Guide Spring Pin
52	Trigger Plate
53	Trigger
54	Sear
55	Trigger Bush
56	Trigger Spring
57	Trigger Spring Guide Plunger
58	Sear Spring
59	Sear Plunger
60	Hammer
61	Right Brace
62	Left Brace
63	Trigger Pin
64	Hammer Bush
65	Safety
66	Safety Spring Plunger
67	Safety Spring
68	Carrier
69	Carrier Pin
70	Carrier Lever
71	Carrier Lever Spring Guide Plunger
72	Carrier Lever Spring
73	Carrier Lever Pin
74	Carrier Swivel Joint
75	Carrier Spring Guide
76	Carrier Spring
77	Carrier Guide Swivel Joint
78	Cartridge Lever Pin
79	Cartridge Latch Body
80	Cartridge Lever Pin
81	Cartridge Latch Spring
82	Cartridge Latch
83	Cartridge Latch Pin
84	Cartridge Latch Body Spring
85	Carrier Catch Plunger Spring
86	Carrier Catch Plunger
87	Carrier Catch Plunger Pin
88	Trigger Plate Retaining Lever Plunger Spring Pin
89	Trigger Plate Retaining Lever
90	Trigger Plate Retaining Lever Plunger Spring
91	Trigger Plate Retaining Lever Plunger
92	Magazine Tube Capacity Reducer
93	Intermediate Sight
94	Mobilchoke Tightening Ring
95	Mobilchoke Ring Spanner
96	Firing Pin Spring Pin Assembly
97	Trigger Plate Pin Snap Ring
98	Safety Locking Plunger
99	Safety Locking Plunger Spring
100	Safety Locking Plunger Retaining Spring Pin
101	Trigger Plate Retaining Pin
102	Cartridge Latch
103	Cartridge Latch Spring
104	Cartridge Latch Spring Spring Pin
105	Cartridge Latch Button
106	Cartridge Latch Spring Lever
107	Cartridge Latch Spring
108	Cartridge Latch Pin Retaining Spring
109	Cartridge Lever Pin Retaining Spring Pin
110	Receiver
111	Mobilchoke Tube
112	Buttstock
113	Forend Assembly
114	Trigger Group Body
115	Carrier Latch Lock Pin
116	Cartridge Stop
117	Cartridge Stop/Carrier Latch
118	Carrier Latch Spring
119	Carrier Latch Pivot

Model AR70 Autoloading Rifle

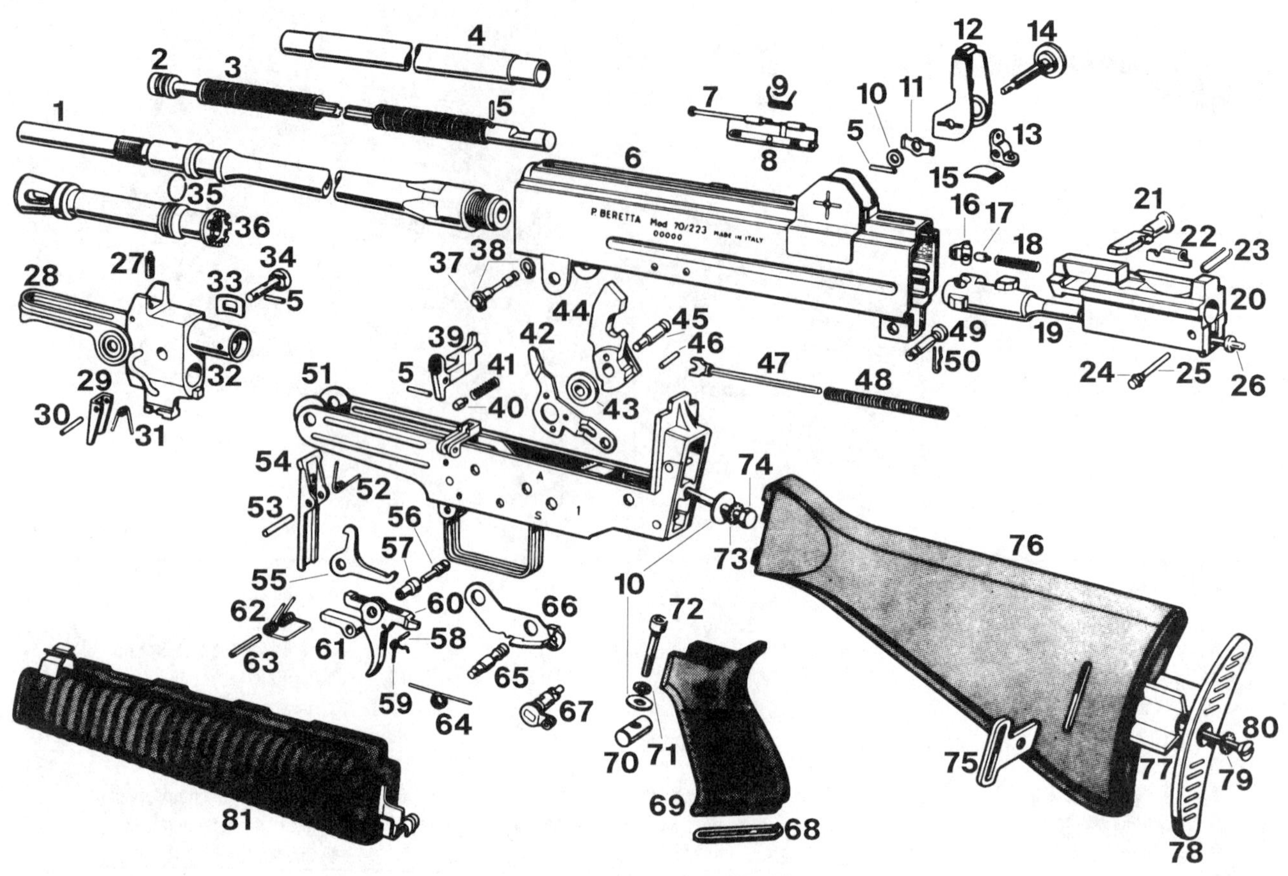

1	Barrel
2	Operating Rod
3	Recoil Spring
4	Operating Rod Tube
5	Split Pins
6	Frame
7	Dust Cover Pin
8	Dust Cover Assembly
9	Dust Cover Spring
10	Washers
11	Aperture Sight Adjusting Screw Spring
12	Grenade Launcher Sight
13	Aperture Sight
14	Aperture Sight Adjusting Screw
15	Aperture Sight Spring
16	Extractor
17	Extractor Pin
18	Extractor Spring
19	Bolt
20	Bolt Carrier
21	Charging Handle
22	Charging Handle Latch
23	Charging Handle Latch Spring
24	Firing Pin Retaining Ring Pin
25	Firing Pin Retaining Pin
26	Firing Pin
27	Front Sight
28	Spindle Valve Lever
29	Grenade Launcher Latch
30	Stop Lever Pin
31	Grenade Launcher Stop Lever Spring
32	Gas Cylinder
33	Spindle Valve Spring
34	Spindle Valve
35	Grenade Retaining Ring
36	Grenade Launcher
37	Hinge Pin
38	Two-Piece Hinge Pin Ring
39	Bolt Hold-Open
40	Bolt Hold-Open Pin
41	Bolt Hold-Open Spring
42	Automatic Fire Lever
43	Hammer Bushing
44	Hammer
45	Hammer Pin
46	Hammer Spring Pin
47	Hammer Spring Guide
48	Hammer Spring
49	Receiver Retaining Pin
50	Receiver Retaining Pin Spring
51	Trigger Housing
52	Magazine Latch Spring
53	Magazine Latch Pin
54	Magazine Latch
55	Pawl
56	Trigger Pin
57	Trigger Bushing
58	Pawl Spring Split Pin
59	Pawl Spring
60	Trigger
61	Automatic Fire Lever Tooth
62	Trigger Spring
63	Trigger Spring Split Pin
64	Automatic Fire Lever Spring
65	Automatic Fire Lever Pin
66	Pin Retaining Plate
67	Safety Assembly
68	Pistol Grip Bottom
69	Pistol Grip
70	Pistol Grip Cotter
71	Pistol Spring Washer
72	Pistol Grip Screw
73	Spring Washer
74	Tie Rod
75	Stock Swivel
76	Stock
77	Stock Spacer
78	Buttplate
79	Buttplate Spring Washer
80	Buttplate Screw
81	Hand Guard Assembly

Model 680, 682, 685, 686 and 687 Over/Under Shotgun

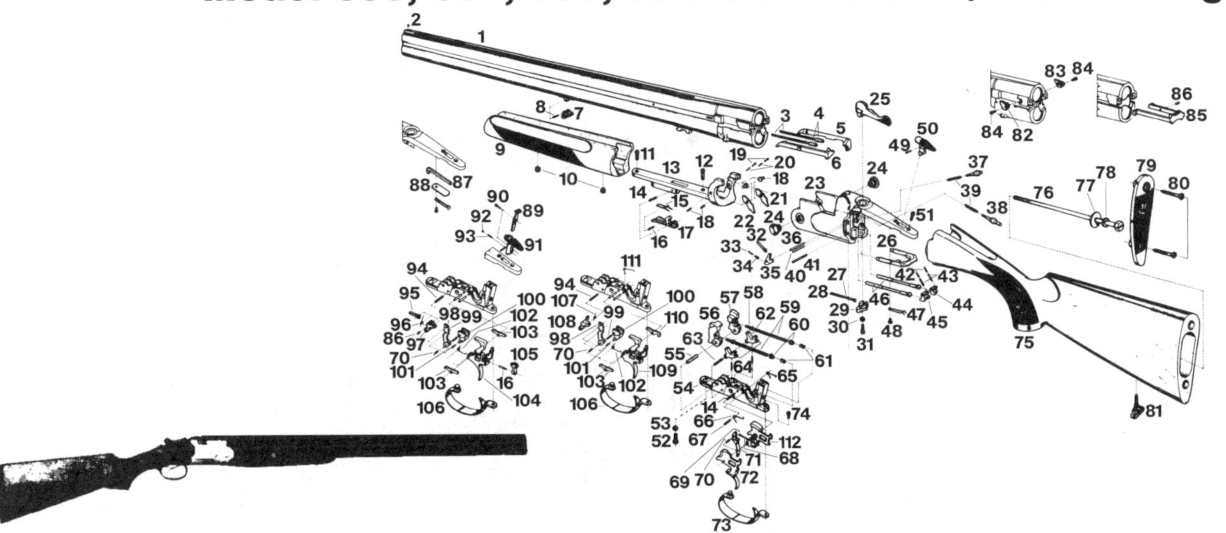

1	Barrel
2	Ventilated Rib Front Sight
3	Extractor Springs
4	Extractor Pins
5	Lower Extractor, Right
6	Upper Extractor, Left
7	Swivel Ring
8	Swivel Ring Spring Pin
9	Forend
10	Forend Washers
11	Forend Iron Front Screw
12	Forend Iron Rear Screw
13	Forend Iron
14	Trigger and Forend Iron Catch Pin
15	Forend Iron Catch Spring
16	Forend Iron Catch and Selector Pawl Pin
17	Forend Iron Catch
18	Forend Iron Lever Screws
19	Forend Iron Lever Pins
20	Forend Iron Lever Springs
21	Forend Iron Lever, Right
22	Forend Iron Lever, Left
23	Frame
24	Hinge Pins
25	Top Lever
26	Locking Latch
27	Top Lever Spring Pin
28	Top Lever Spring
29	Top Lever Dog
30	Top Lever Screw Spring Washer
31	Top Lever Screw
32	Locking Latch Release Pin
33	Locking Latch Clamping Lever Spring
34	Locking Latch Clamping Lever Pin
35	Locking Latch Clamping Lever
36	Locking Latch Clamping Lever Pin
37	Lower Firing Pin, Right
38	Upper Firing Pin, Left
39	Firing Pin Springs
40	Firing Pin Stop Spring Pin
41	Cocking Lever Pin
42	Cocking Lever Spring
43	Cocking Lever Spring Pin
44	Right-Hand Cocking Lever
45	Left-Hand Cocking Lever
46	Cocking Rods
47	Safety Spring
48	Safety Spring Screw
49	Safety Pin
50	Safety
51	Stock Bolt Plate Screw
52	Trigger Plate Screw
53	Trigger Plate Screw Spring Washer
54	Trigger Plate
55	Hammer Pin
56	Left-Hand Hammer
57	Right-Hand Hammer
58	Hammer Spring Guides
59	Hammer Springs
60	Hammer Spring Guide Bushings
61	Hammer Spring Guide Nuts
62	Sears
63	Sear Pin
64	Sear Springs
65	Trigger Spring, Right
66	Trigger Spring, Left
67	Connecting Lever and Trigger Spring Pin
68	Inertia Block Spring
69	Inertia Block Spring Plunger
70	Single Selective Trigger Inertia Block and Right Trigger Pin
71	Gold Plated Trigger, Right
72	Gold Plated Trigger, Left
73	Dougle Trigger—Trigger Guard
74	Trigger Guard Screw
75	Buttstock
76	Stock Bolt Screw
77	Stock Washer
78	Stock Spring Washer
79	Buttplate
80	Buttplate Screws
81	Stock Swivel
82	Left Sideplate Retainer
83	Right Sideplate Retainer
84	Sideplate Retainer Screws
85	Extractor
86	Extractor Stop Spring Pin
87	Automatic Safety Rod
88	Automatic Safety Spring Washer
89	Single Selective Trigger Selector Lever
90	Single Selective Trigger Selector Lever Pin
91	Single Selective Trigger Safety
92	Single Selective Trigger Ball
93	Single Selective Trigger Selector Lever Spring
94	Single Selective Trigger Inertia Block Pin
95	Single Selective Trigger Inertia Block Lever Pawl
96	Single Selective Trigger Inertia Block Lever Spring
97	Single Selective Trigger Inertia Block Lever
98	Single Selective Trigger Inertia Block Rest
99	Single Selective Trigger Inertia Block Spring Pin
100	Single Selective Trigger Inertia Block
101	Single Selective Trigger Inertia Block Spring Pin
102	Single Selective Trigger Inertia Block Spring
103	Single Selective Trigger Connecting Lever
104	Single Selective Trigger, Gold Plated
105	Single Selective Trigger Selector Pawl
106	Single Trigger Trigger Guard
107	Single Trigger Inertia Block Lever Spring
108	Single Trigger Inertia Block Lever
109	Single Trigger
110	Single Trigger Connecting Lever
111	Single Trigger Trigger Spring
112	Right Trigger Safety Connector

New Model Over/Under Shotgun

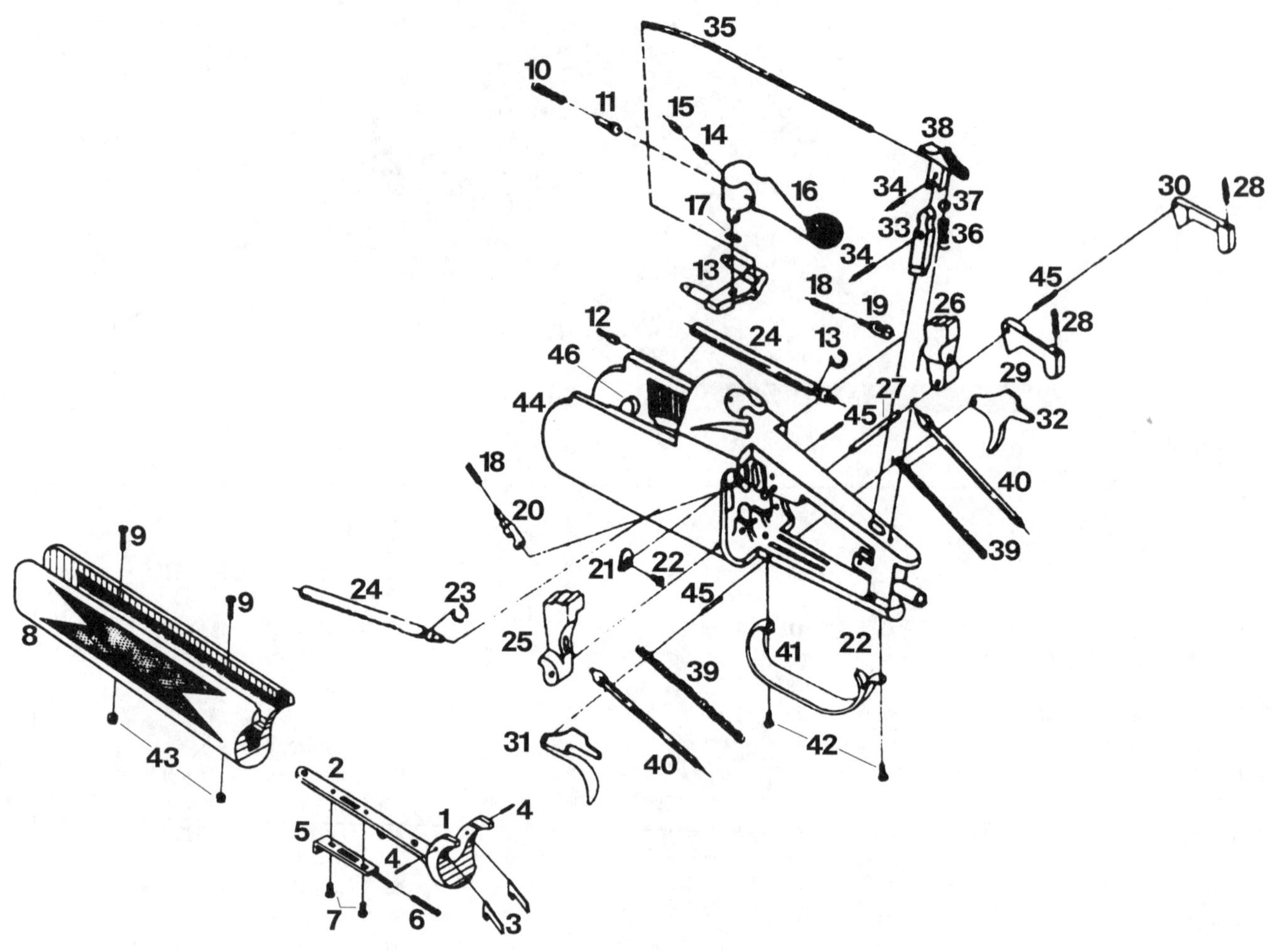

1	Forend Iron Assembly	**20**	Upper Firing Pin	**39**	Hammer Springs
2	Forend Iron	**21**	Firing Pin Limiter	**40**	Hammer Impellers
3	Ejector Levers	**22**	Fixing Screws	**41**	Trigger Guard
4	Ejector Lever Pins	**23**	Cocking Lever Pin	**42**	Trigger Guard Screws
5	Forend Lock	**24**	Cocking Lever	**43**	Forend Screw Nuts
6	Forend Lock Spring	**25**	Hammer, Left	**44**	Frame
7	Forend Lock Screws	**26**	Hammer, Right	**45**	Transverse Pins
8	Forend	**27**	Hammer Pin	**46**	Frame Lug
9	Forend Screws	**28**	Sear Springs	**Parts Not Shown**	
10	Lever Spring	**29**	Sear, Left		Buttplate
11	Lever Pin	**30**	Sear, Right		Buttplate Screws
12	Lever Impeller Pin	**31**	Trigger, Left		Buttplate Spacer
13	Lock Retainer	**32**	Trigger, Right		Buttstock Screw
14	Lock Retainer Springs	**33**	Sear Lock Lever		Front Sight
15	Lock Retainer Pin	**34**	Safety Retainer Pins		Grip Cap
16	Top Lever	**35**	Safety Impeller		Spacer
17	Lever Retainer Pin	**36**	Safety Spring		Washer
18	Firing Pin Springs	**37**	Safety Motion Limiting Ball		
19	Lower Firing Pin	**38**	Safety Thumb-Piece		

Side-by-Side Shotgun

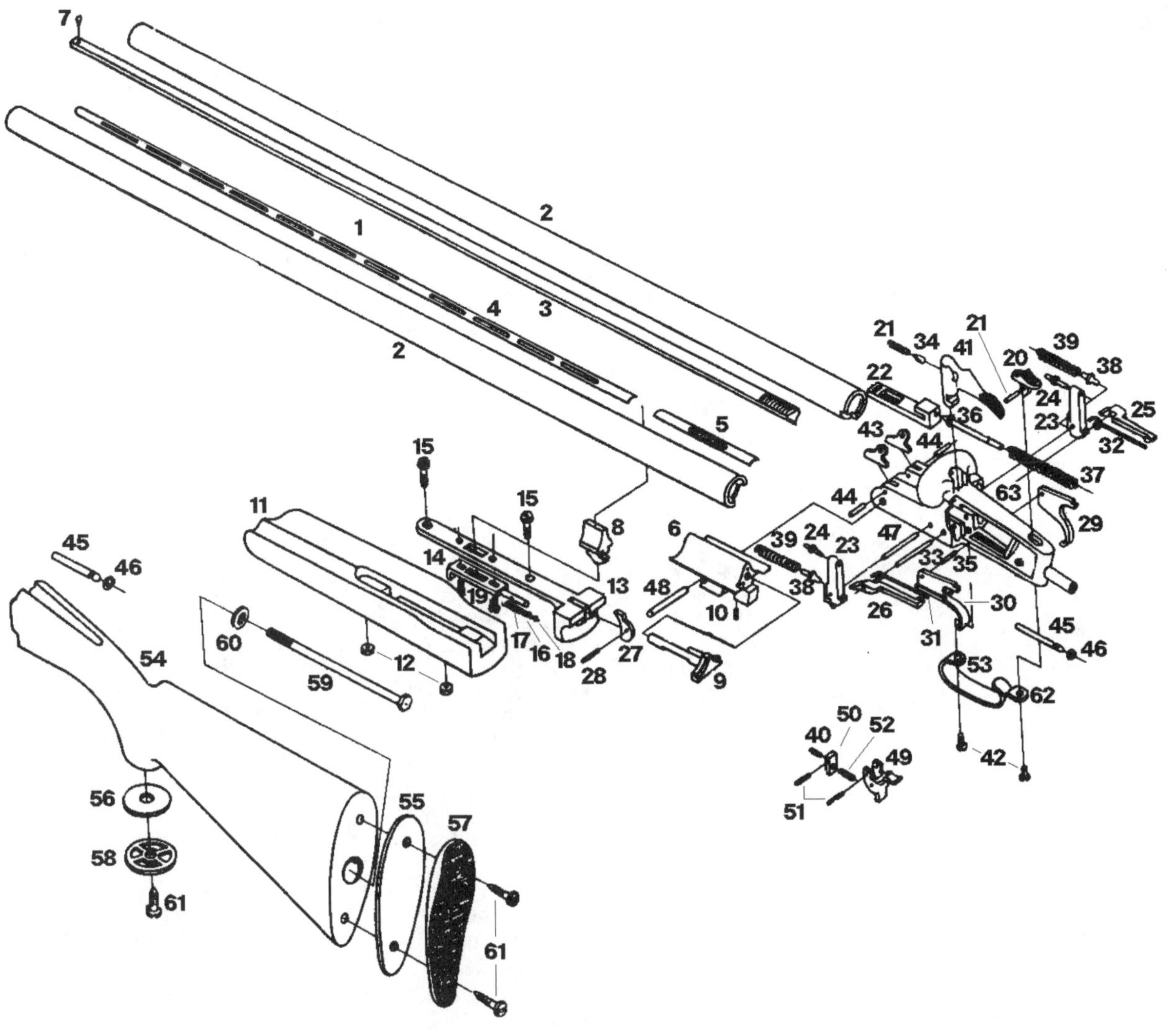

1	Barrel Assembly	22	Latch Lock	43	Cocking Levers
2	Barrel	23	Hammer	44	Cocking Lever Pins
3	Solid Barrel Rib	24	Firing Pins	45	Cocking Lever Rod
4	Under Rib	25	Right Sear	46	Cocking Lever Rod Ring
5	Under Rib Extension	26	Left Sear	47	Hammer Pin
6	Barrel Lug Unit	27	Actuator Extractor	48	Hinge Pin
7	Front Sight	28	Actuator Extractor Pin	49	Actuator
8	Forend Latch Lug	29	Right Trigger	50	Safety Guide
9	Extractor Assembly	30	Left Trigger	51	Safety Pins
10	Limiter Screw	31	Left Sear Spring	52	Trigger Lock Spring
11	Forend	32	Right Sear Spring	53	Trigger Guard
12	Fastening Nuts	33	Sear Pin	54	Stock
13	Forend Iron Assembly	34	Ball Headed Pin	55	White Spacer
14	Lock	35	Trigger Pin	56	Grip Cap Spacer
15	Screws	36	Top Lever Spring Guide	57	Buttplate
16	Forend Iron Spring	37	Top Lever Spring	58	Grip Cap
17	Forend Latch	38	Firing Pin Spring Guides	59	Butt Screw
18	Activating Pin Guide	39	Firing Pin Springs	60	Butt Screw Washer
19	Forend Lock Screws	40	Trigger Lock Spring	61	Screws
20	External Lock	41	Top Lever	62	Trigger Guard Extension
21	External Lock Pins	42	Trigger Guard Screws	63	Frame

Mark II Autoloading Shotgun

Courtesy of Thomas E. Wessel

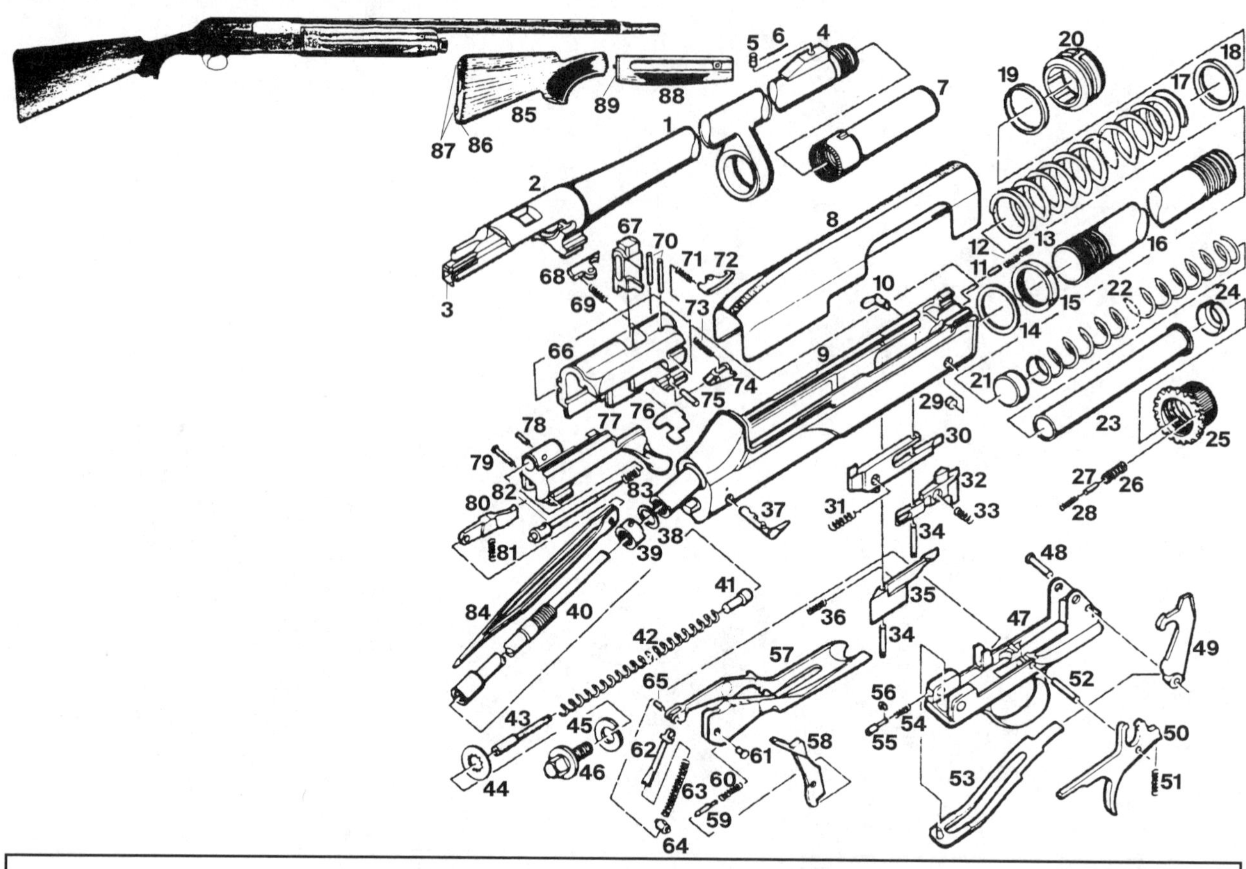

1	Barrel
2	Barrel Extension
3	Ejector
4	Front Sight Base
5	Front Sight
6	Choking Tube Retaining Spring
7	Choking Tube
8	Receiver Cover
9	Receiver
10	Magazine Cut-Off Lever
11	Magazine Cut-Off Plunger
12	Magazine Cut-Off Plunger Spring
13	Magazine Cut-Off Plunger Spring Screw
14	Magazine Ring Washer
15	Magazine Ring
16	Magazine Tube
17	Recoil Spring
18	Recoil Spring Washer
19	Beveled Brake Ring
20	Bronze Friction Brake
21	Magazine Spring Follower
22	Magazine Spring
23	Magazine Reducer
24	Magazine Spring Retainer
25	Magazine Cap
26	Magazine Cap Retainer Screw
27	Magazine Cap Plunger
28	Magazine Cap Retainer Spring
29	Carrier Latch Button
30	Carrier Latch Lever
31	Carrier Latch Spring
32	Right Magazine Shell Latch Lever
33	Right Magazine Shell Latch Spring
34	Shell Latch—Carrier Latch Pins
35	Left Magazine Shell Latch Lever
36	Left Latch Spring
37	Reversible Safety-Lever Disassembly Pin
38	Action Spring Tube Lock Washer
39	Action Spring Tube Lock Nut
40	Action Spring Tube
41	Action Spring Follower
42	Action Spring
43	Action Spring Guide
44	Stock Lock Washer
45	Stock Spring Washer
46	Action Spring Tube Plug
47	Trigger Guard
48	Hammer Pin
49	Hammer
50	Trigger
51	Trigger Spring
52	Trigger Pin
53	Hammer Spring
54	Safety Plunger Spring
55	Safety Plunger
56	Safety Plunger Plastic Washer
57	Carrier
58	Carrier Dog
59	Carrier Dog Plunger
60	Carrier Dog Spring
61	Carrier Dog Pin
62	Carrier Rocker Arm
63	Carrier Rocker Spring
64	Carrier Rocker Pivot
65	Carrier Rocker Pin
66	Bolt
67	Locking Block
68	Left Extractor
69	Left Extractor Spring
70	Extractor Pins
71	Right Extractor Spring
72	Right Extractor
73	Bolt Pawl Spring
74	Bolt Pawl
75	Bolt Pawl Pin
76	Bolt Plate
77	Operating Handle
78	Firing Pin Retaining Pin
79	Link Pin
80	Operating Handle Latch
81	Link Spring
82	Firing Pin
83	Firing Pin Spring
84	Bolt Link
85	Pistol Grip Stock
86	Buttplate
87	Buttplate Screws
88	Forend
89	Forend Yoke

Single Shot Shotgun

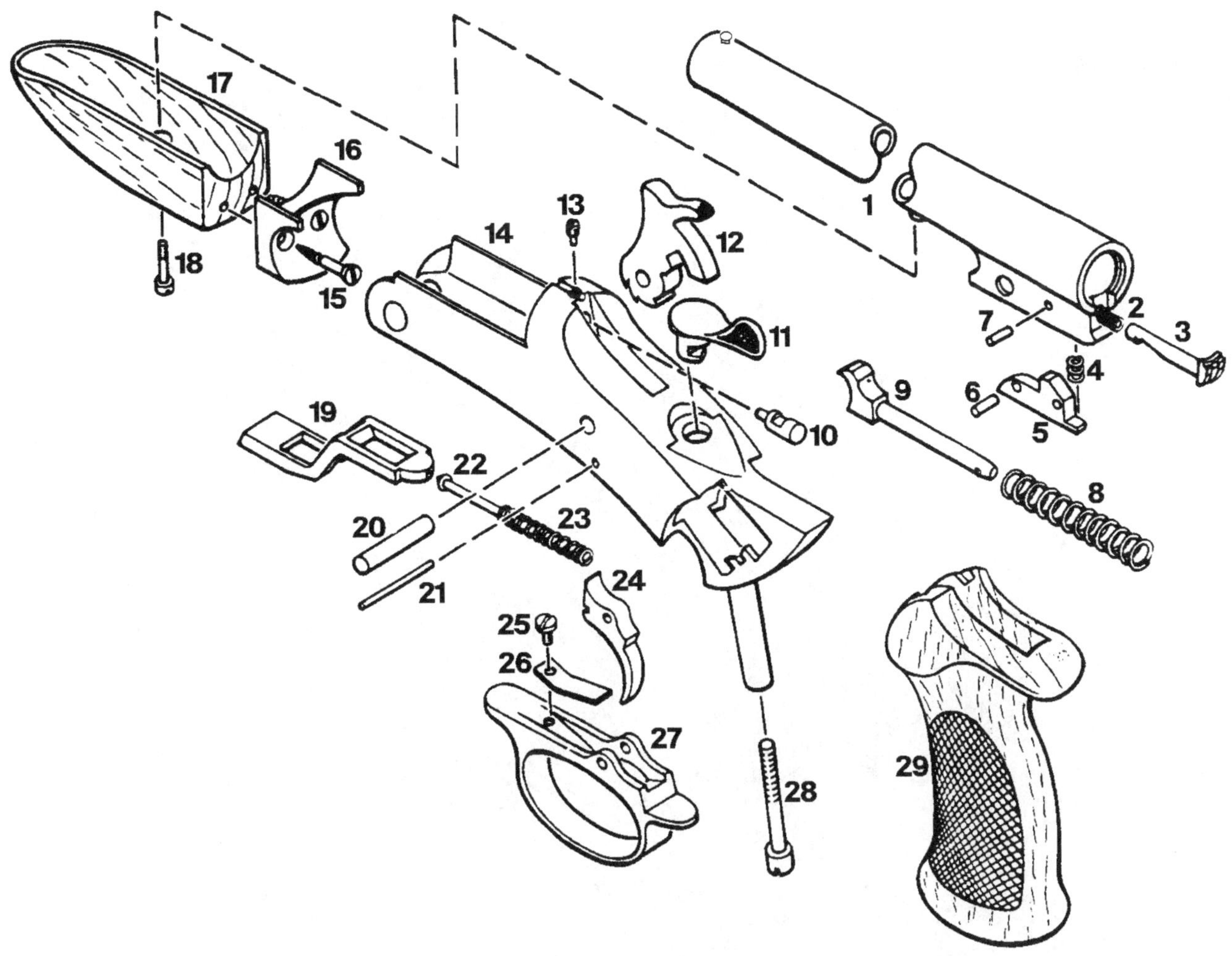

1	Barrel	**16**	Forend Iron
2	Ejector Spring	**17**	Forend
3	Ejector	**18**	Forend Screw
4	Ejector Sear Spring	**19**	Barrel Latch
5	Ejector Sear	**20**	Hammer Pin
6	Ejector Sear Trip Pin	**21**	Trigger Pin
7	Ejector Sear Pivot	**22**	Barrel Latch Plunger
8	Hammer Spring	**23**	Barrel Latch Spring
9	Hammer Strut	**24**	Trigger
10	Firing Pin	**25**	Trigger Spring Screw
11	Barrel Latch Lever	**26**	Trigger Spring
12	Hammer	**27**	Trigger Guard
13	Firing Pin Retaining Screw	**28**	Grip Screw
14	Frame	**29**	Grip
15	Forend Iron Screw		

No. 1, Mark III (SMLE) Bolt-Action Rifle

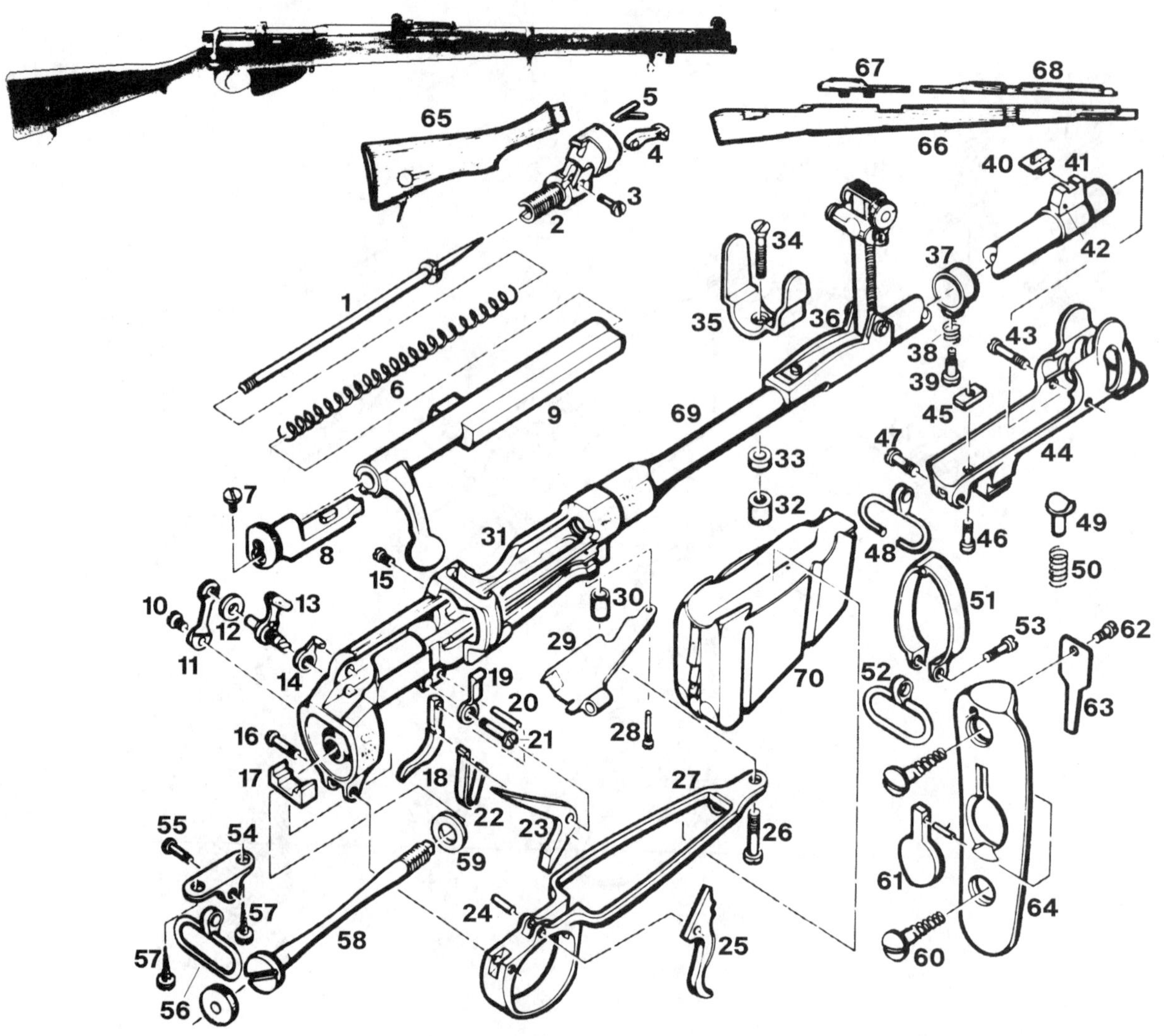

1	Firing Pin	25	Trigger	49	Forend Stud
2	Bolt Head, Stripped	26	Front Guard Screw	50	Forend Stud Spring
3	Extractor Screw	27	Trigger Guard	51	Swivel Band
4	Extractor	28	Cut-Off Screw	52	Front Swivel
5	Extractor Spring	29	Cut-Off	53	Swivel Screw
6	Firing Pin Spring	30	Guard Screw Bushing	54	Butt Swivel Base
7	Firing Pin Screw	31	Receiver	55	Swivel Base Screw
8	Cocking Piece	32	Protector Nut	56	Buttstock Swivel
9	Bolt Body	33	Forend Collar	57	Butt Swivel Screws
10	Safety Spring Screw	34	Rear Sight Protector Screw	58	Stock Bolt
11	Safety Spring	35	Rear Sight Protector	59	Stock Bolt Washer
12	Safety Catch Washer	36	Rear Sight Assembly with Base	60	Buttplate Screw
13	Locking Bolt	37	Inner Band	61	Trapdoor Buttplate
14	Safety Catch	38	Inner Band Spring	62	Trapdoor Spring Screw
15	Ejector	39	Inner Band Screw	63	Trapdoor Spring
16	Rear Trigger Guard Screw	40	Front Sight Blade	64	Buttplate
17	Stock Bolt Plate	41	Front Sight Base	65	Buttstock
18	Magazine Catch	42	Front Sight Pin	66	Forestock
19	Bolt Head Retaining Spring	43	Front Nosecap Screw	67	Rear Hand Guard
20	Magazine Catch Pin	44	Nosecap	68	Front Hand Guard
21	Retaining Spring Screw	45	Nosecap Nut	69	Barrel
22	Sear Spring	46	Rear Nosecap Screw	70	Magazine
23	Sear	47	Stacking Swivel Screw		
24	Trigger Pin	48	Stacking Swivel		

No. 4, Mark I* (SMLE) Bolt Action Rifle

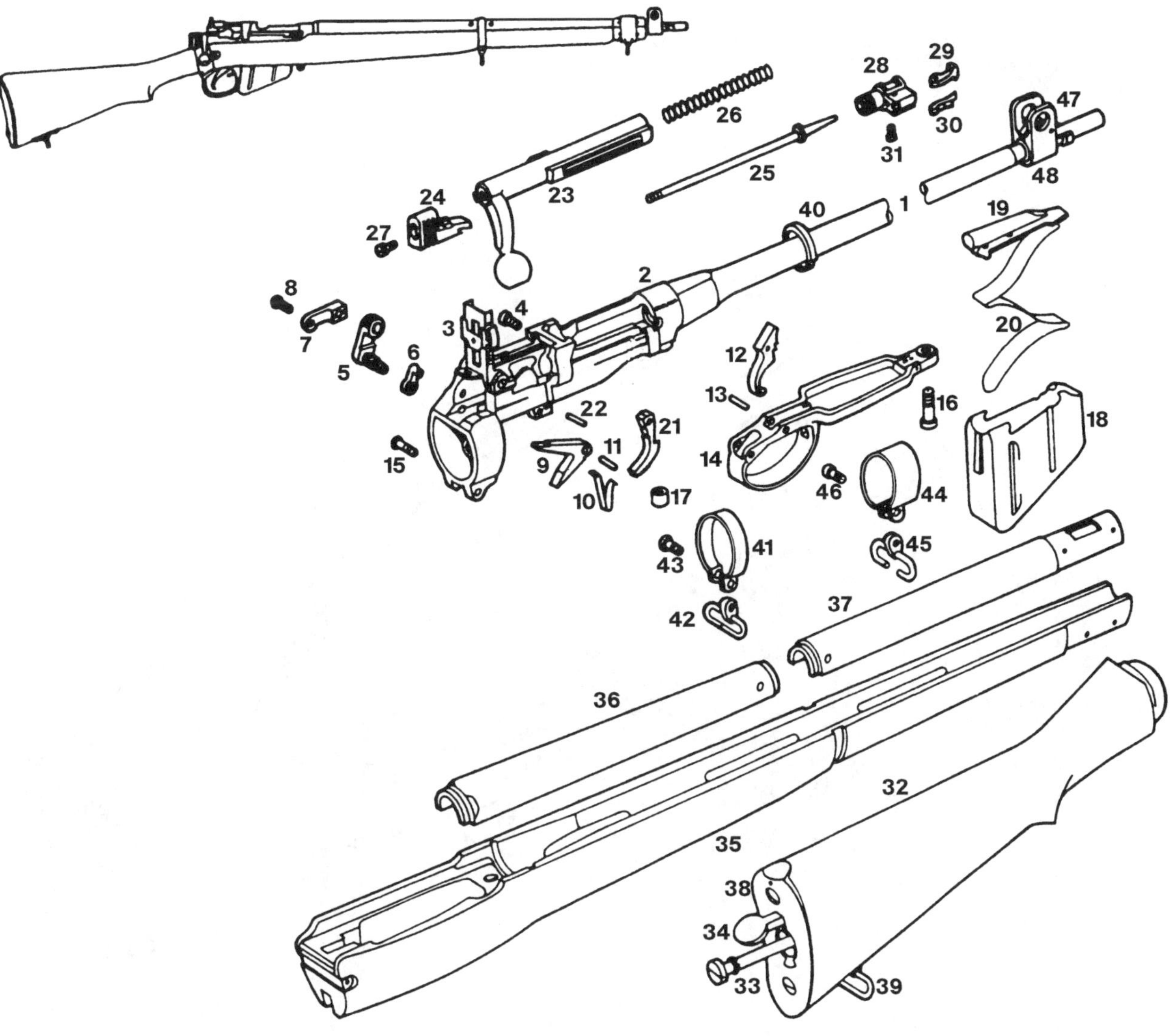

1	Barrel	**22**	Magazine Catch Pin	**43**	Front Sling Swivel Screw
2	Receiver	**23**	Bolt	**44**	Front Stock Band
3	Rear Sight	**24**	Cocking Piece	**45**	Stacking Swivel
4	Ejector Screw	**25**	Firing Pin	**46**	Stacking Swivel Screw
5	Safety Bolt	**26**	Firing Pin Spring	**47**	Front Sight Guard
6	Safety Catch	**27**	Firing Pin Stop Screw	**48**	Front Sight Base and Guard Screw
7	Safety Bolt Spring	**28**	Bolt Head	**Parts Not Shown**	
8	Safety Bolt Spring Screw	**29**	Extractor		Bolt Head Release
9	Sear	**30**	Extractor Spring		Bolt Head Release Spring
10	Sear Spring	**31**	Extractor Screw		Bolt Head Release Stop
11	Sear Pin	**32**	Buttstock		Bolt Head Release Stop Screw
12	Trigger	**33**	Stock Bolt		Front Sight Base
13	Trigger Pin	**34**	Stock Bolt Washer		Front Sight Blades
14	Trigger Guard	**35**	Forestock		Rear Sight Base Pin
15	Rear Guard Screw	**36**	Rear Hand Guard		Rear Sight Plunger
16	Front Guard Screw	**37**	Front Hand Guard		Rear Sight Plunger Spring
17	Front Guard Screw Bushing	**38**	Buttplate		Stripper Clips
18	Magazine, Complete	**39**	Butt Sling Swivel Assembly		
19	Follower	**40**	Rear Stock Band		
20	Follower Spring	**41**	Middle Stock Band		
21	Magazine Catch	**42**	Front Sling Swivel		

1885 Lever-Action Rifle

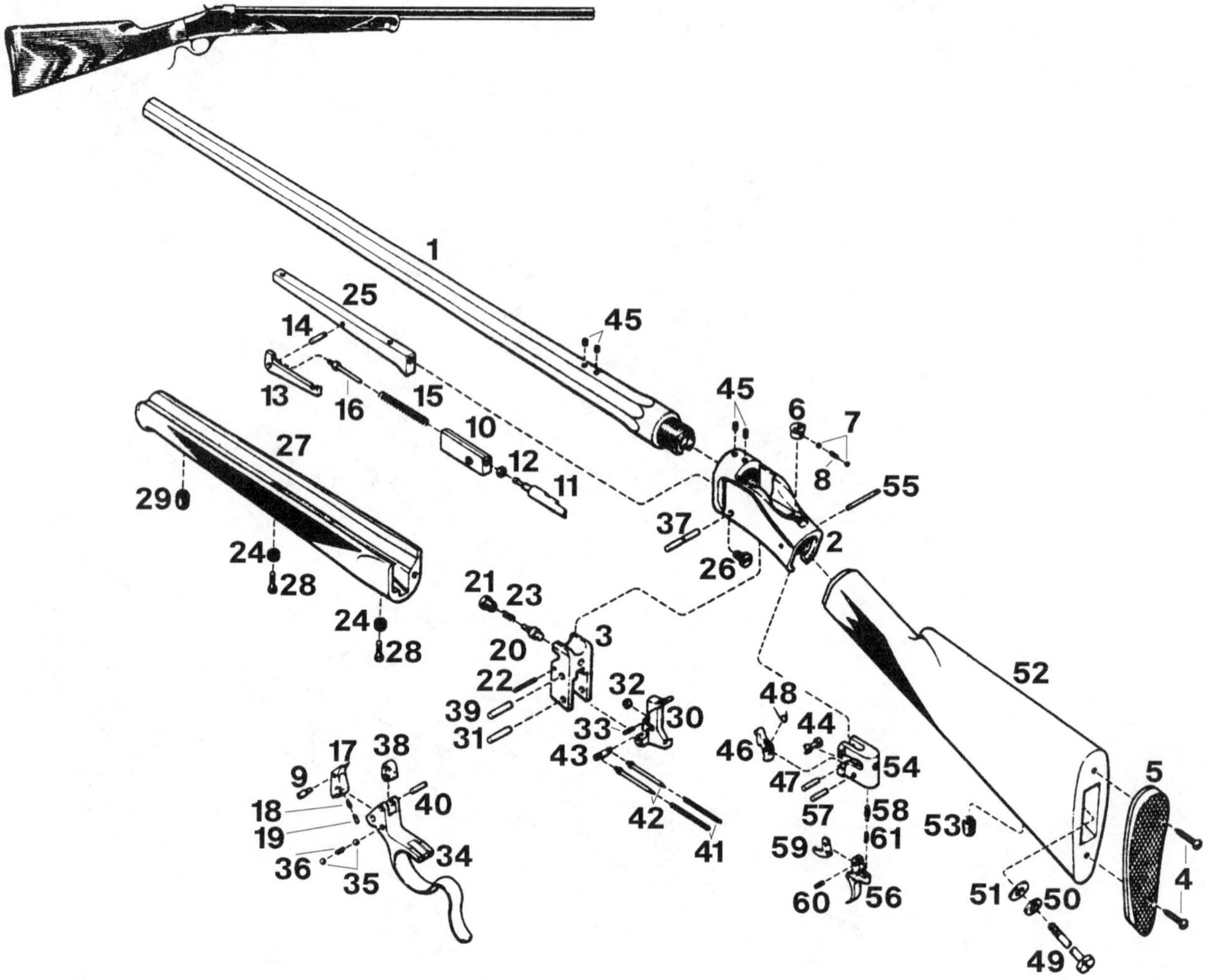

1	Barrel
2	Receiver
3	Breech Block
4	Buttplate Screws
5	Buttplate
6	Deflector
7	Deflector Balls
8	Deflector Ball Spring
9	Ejector Connecting Pin
10	Ejector Hammer
11	Ejector Hammer Extension
12	Ejector Hammer Extension Washer
13	Ejector Hammer Sear
14	Ejector Hammer Sear Pin
15	Ejector Hammer Spring
16	Ejector Hammer Spring Guide
17	Extractor
18	Extractor Spring
19	Extractor Spring Plunger
20	Firing Pin
21	Firing Pin Bushing
22	Firing Pin Bushing Pin
23	Firing Pin Spring
24	Forearm Escutcheons
25	Forearm Hanger
26	Forearm Hanger Bolt
27	Forearm
28	Forearm Screws
29	Forearm Swivel Base
30	Hammer
31	Hammer Pin
32	Hammer Roller
33	Hammer Roller Rivet
34	Lever
35	Lever Latch Balls
36	Lever Latch Ball Spring
37	Lever Pin
38	Link
39	Link Breech Block Pin
40	Link Lever Pin
41	Mainsprings
42	Mainspring Guides
43	Mainspring Pin
44	Mainspring Pin, Rear
45	Scope Mount Filler Screw
46	Sear
47	Sear Pin
48	Sear Spring
49	Stock Bolt
50	Stock Bolt Spring Washer
51	Stock Bolt Washer
52	Stock
53	Stock Swivel Base
54	Trigger Housing
55	Trigger Housing Pin
56	Trigger
57	Trigger Pin
58	Trigger Pull Adjusting Screw
59	Trigger Sear
60	Trigger Sear Pin
61	Trigger Spring

Parts Not Shown

Front Sight

Rear Sight

1886 Lever-Action Rifle

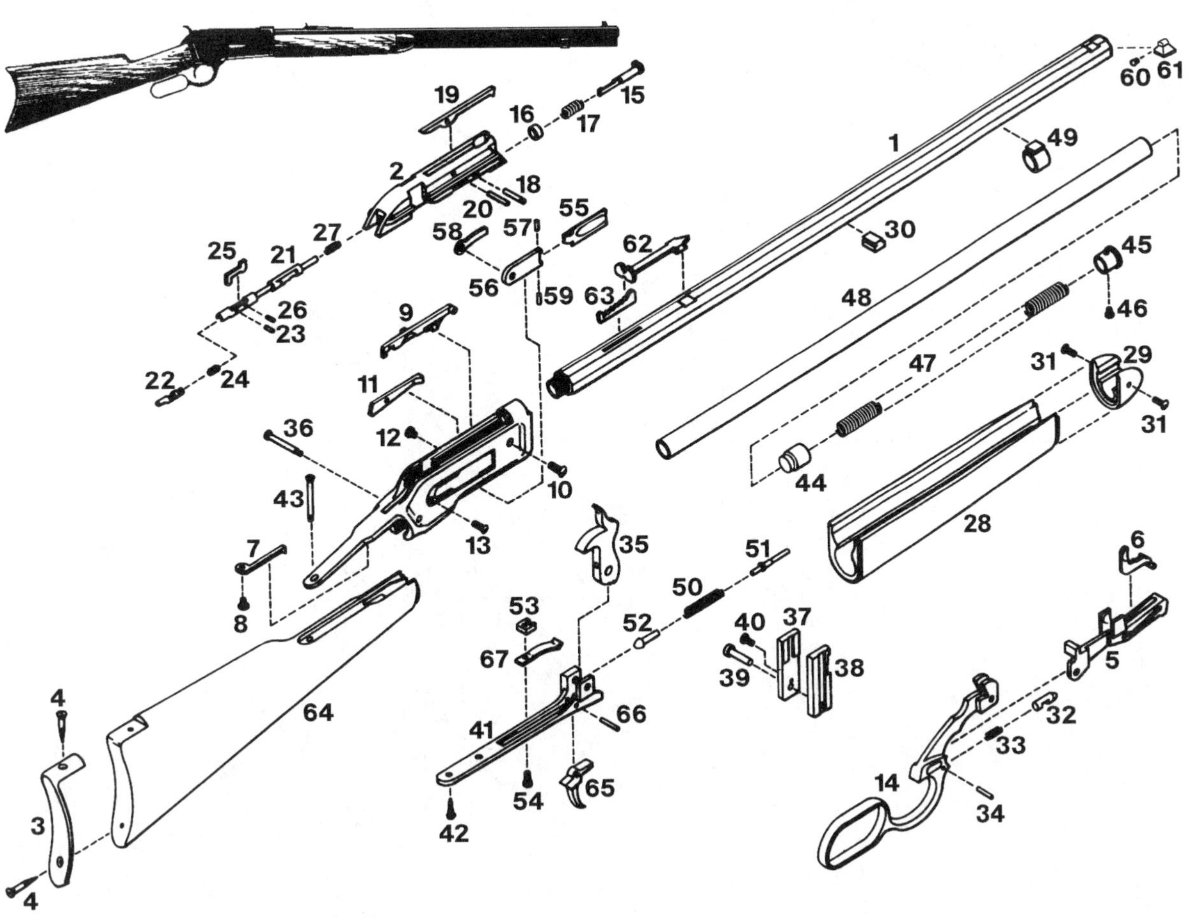

1	Barrel with Receiver
2	Breech Bolt
3	Buttplate
4	Buttplate Screws
5	Carrier
6	Carrier Link
7	Carrier Spring
8	Carrier Spring Screw
9	Cartridge Guide
10	Cartridge Guide Screw
11	Cartridge Guide Stop
12	Cartridge Guide Stop Screw
13	Receiver Spring Cover Screw
14	Cocking Lever
15	Ejector
16	Ejector Collar
17	Ejector Spring
18	Ejector Stop Pin
19	Extractor
20	Extractor Pin and Mainspring Abutment Pin
21	Firing Pin
22	Firing Pin Inertia Slide
23	Firing Pin Inertia Slide Pin
24	Firing Pin Inertia Slide Spring
25	Firing Pin Safety Lock
26	Firing Pin Safety Lock Pin
27	Firing Pin Spring
28	Forearm
29	Forearm Tip
30	Forearm Tip Tenon
31	Forearm Tip Screws
32	Friction Stud
33	Friction Stud Spring
34	Friction Stud Stop Pin
35	Hammer
36	Hammer Screw
37	Left Locking Bolt
38	Right Locking Bolt
39	Locking Bolt Stop Pin
40	Locking Bolt Stop Pin Stop Screw
41	Lower Tang
42	Lower Tang Screw
43	Lower Tang Stock Screw
44	Magazine Follower
45	Magazine Plug
46	Magazine Plug Screw
47	Magazine Spring
48	Magazine Tube
49	Magazine Tube Retainer Ring
50	Mainspring
51	Inner Mainspring Guide
52	Outer Mainspring Guide
53	Mainspring Guide Stud
54	Mainspring Guide Stud Screw
55	Receiver Spring Cover
56	Receiver Spring Cover Base
57	Receiver Spring Cover Pin
58	Receiver Spring Cover Spring
59	Receiver Spring Cover Stop Pin
60	Front Sight Bead
61	Front Sight
62	Rear Sight
63	Rear Sight Elevator
64	Stock
65	Trigger
66	Trigger Pin
67	Trigger Spring

1895 Lever-Action Rifle

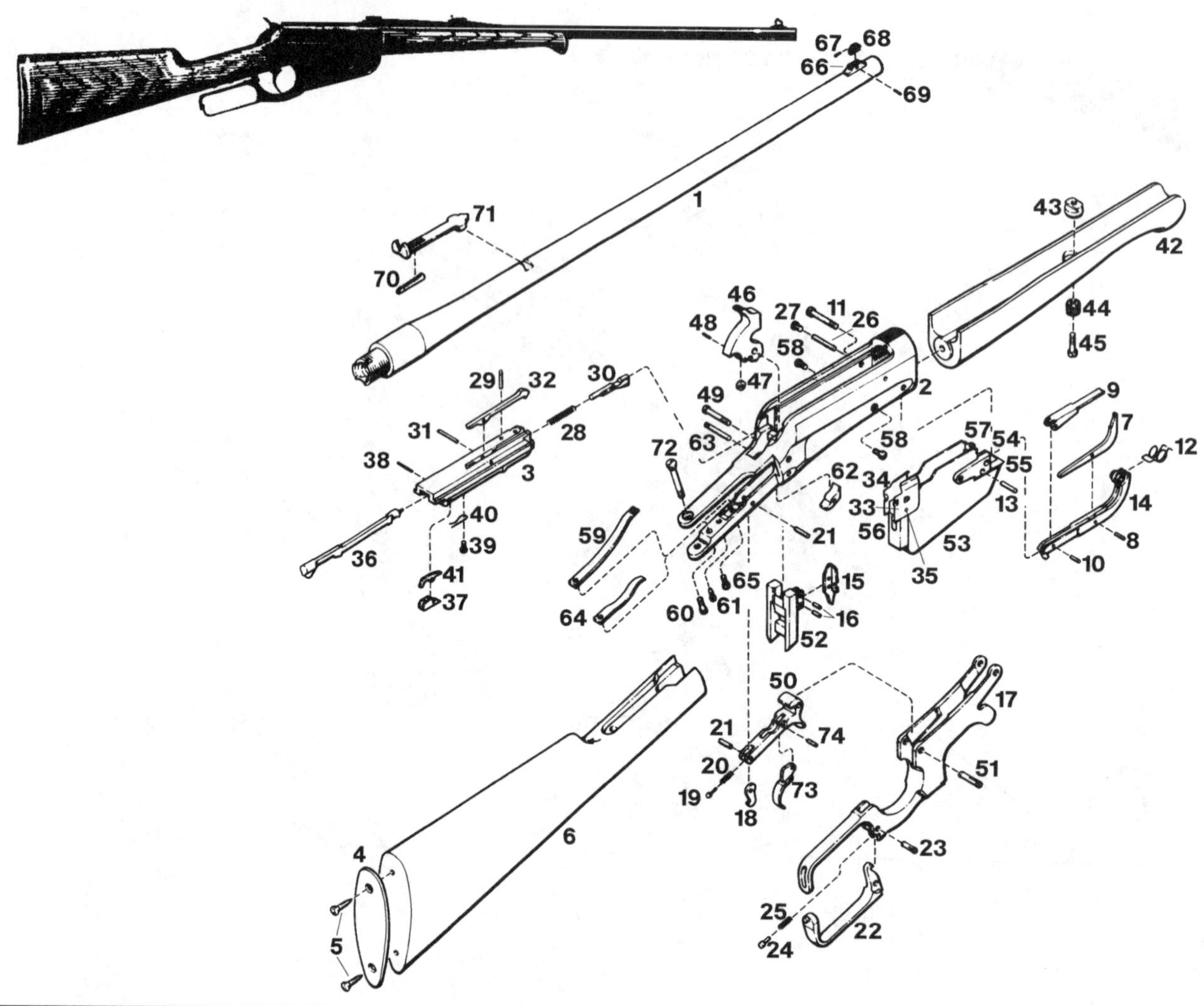

1	Barrel	**26**	Cocking Lever Pin	**50**	Link
2	Receiver	**27**	Cocking Lever Pin Stop Screw	**51**	Link Pin
3	Breech Bolt	**28**	Ejector Spring	**52**	Locking Bolt
4	Buttplate	**29**	Ejector Stop Pin	**53**	Magazine Body
5	Buttplate Screws	**30**	Ejector	**54**	Magazine Bracket
6	Buttstock	**31**	Extractor Pin	**55**	Magazine Follower
7	Carrier Cam Lever	**32**	Extractor	**56**	Magazine Rib
8	Carrier Cam Lever Pin	**33**	Feed Guide, Left	**57**	Magazine Rib, Front
9	Carrier Cradle	**34**	Feed Guide, Right	**58**	Magazine Tip Screws
10	Carrier Cradle Pin	**35**	Feed Guide Set Pin	**59**	Mainspring
11	Carrier Screw	**36**	Firing Pin	**60**	Mainspring Screw
12	Carrier Spring	**37**	Firing Pin Lock	**61**	Mainspring Strain Screw
13	Carrier Stop Pin	**38**	Firing Pin Lock and Firing Pin Recoil Lock Pin	**62**	Sear
14	Carrier			**63**	Sear Pin
15	Cartridge Stop	**39**	Firing Pin Lock and Recoil Lock Screw	**64**	Sear Spring
16	Cartridge Stop Pins	**40**	Firing Pin Lock and Recoil Lock Spring	**65**	Sear Spring Screw
17	Cocking Lever	**41**	Firing Pin Recoil Lock	**66**	Front Sight Base
18	Cocking Lever Catch	**42**	Forearm	**67**	Front Sight Bead
19	Cocking Lever Catch Plunger	**43**	Forearm Stud	**68**	Front Sight Blade
20	Cocking Lever Catch Plunger Spring	**44**	Forearm Stud Escutcheon	**69**	Front Sight Blade Pin
21	Cocking Lever Link Pin	**45**	Forearm Stud Screw	**70**	Rear Sight Elevator
22	Cocking Lever Lock	**46**	Hammer	**71**	Rear Sight
23	Cocking Lever Lock Joint Pin	**47**	Hammer Roll	**72**	Upper Tang Screw
24	Cocking Lever Lock Plunger	**48**	Hammer Roll Pin	**73**	Trigger
25	Cocking Lever Lock Plunger Spring	**49**	Hammer Screw	**74**	Trigger Pin

Auto-22 Autoloading Rifle

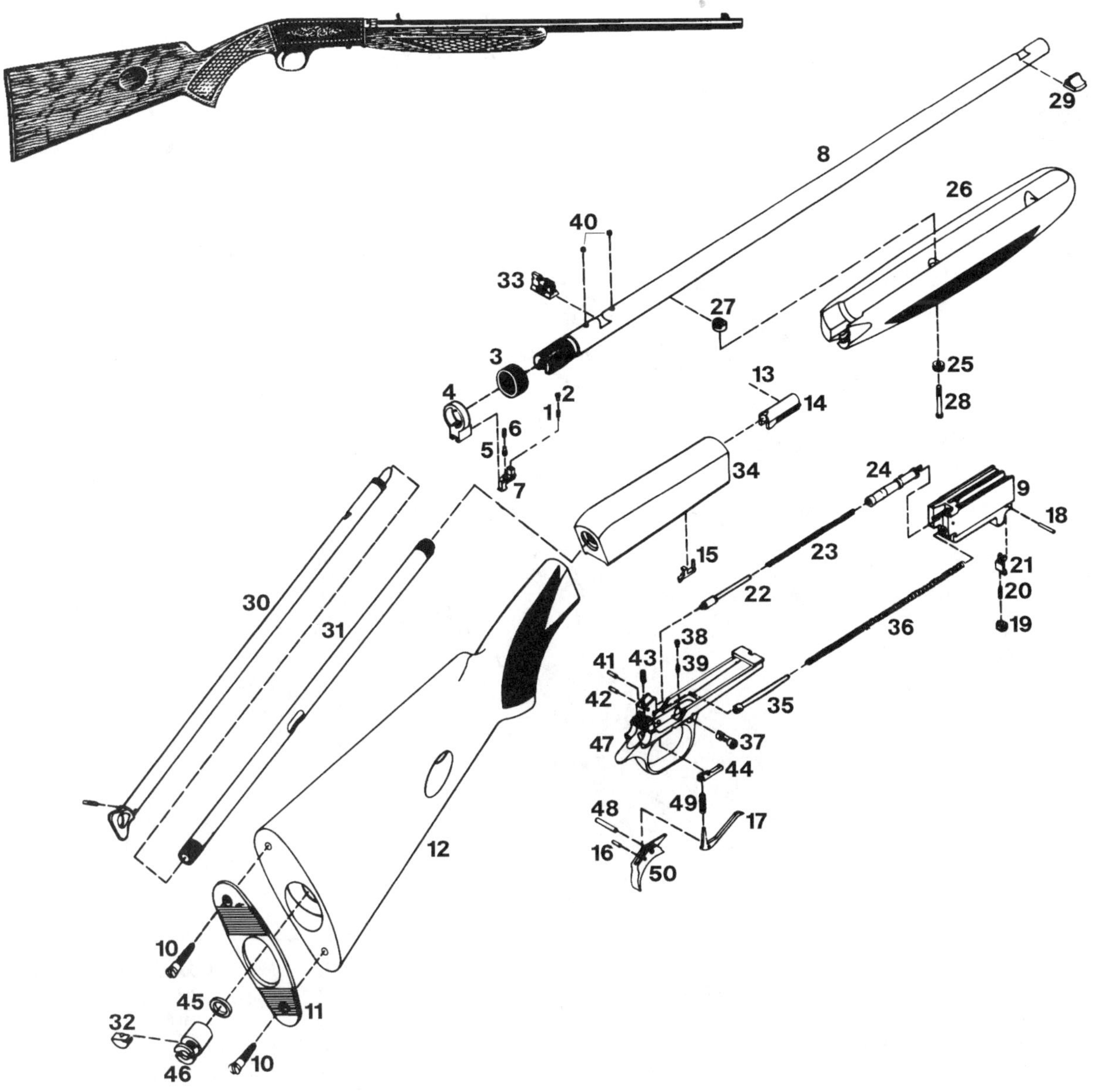

1	Barrel Adjusting Ring Follower Spring	**17**	Disconnector	**34**	Receiver
2	Barrel Adjusting Ring Follower	**18**	Extractor Spring Retainer Pin	**35**	Recoil Spring Guide
3	Barrel Adjusting Ring	**19**	Extractor Spring Retainer	**36**	Recoil Spring
4	Barrel Lock Ring	**20**	Extractor Spring	**37**	Safety Button
5	Barrel Lock Spring Plunger	**21**	Extractor	**38**	Safety Spring Plunger
6	Barrel Lock Spring	**22**	Firing Pin Spring Guide	**39**	Safety Spring
7	Barrel Lock	**23**	Firing Pin Spring	**40**	Scope Mount Base Filler Screws
8	Barrel	**24**	Firing Pin	**41**	Sear Pin
9	Breechblock	**25**	Forend Escutcheon	**42**	Sear Spring Pin
10	Buttplate Screws	**26**	Forend	**43**	Sear Spring
11	Buttplate	**27**	Forend Retainer Stud	**44**	Sear
12	Buttstock	**28**	Forend Screw	**45**	Stock Nut Washer
13	Cartridge Guide Spring	**29**	Front Sight	**46**	Stock Nut
14	Cartridge Guide	**30**	Inner Magazine Tube Assembly	**47**	Trigger Guard
15	Cartridge Stop	**31**	Outer Magazine Tube	**48**	Trigger Pin
16	Disconnector Pin	**32**	Magazine Tube Stop Spring	**49**	Trigger Spring
		33	Rear Sight Assembly	**50**	Trigger

Auto-5 Autoloading Shotgun

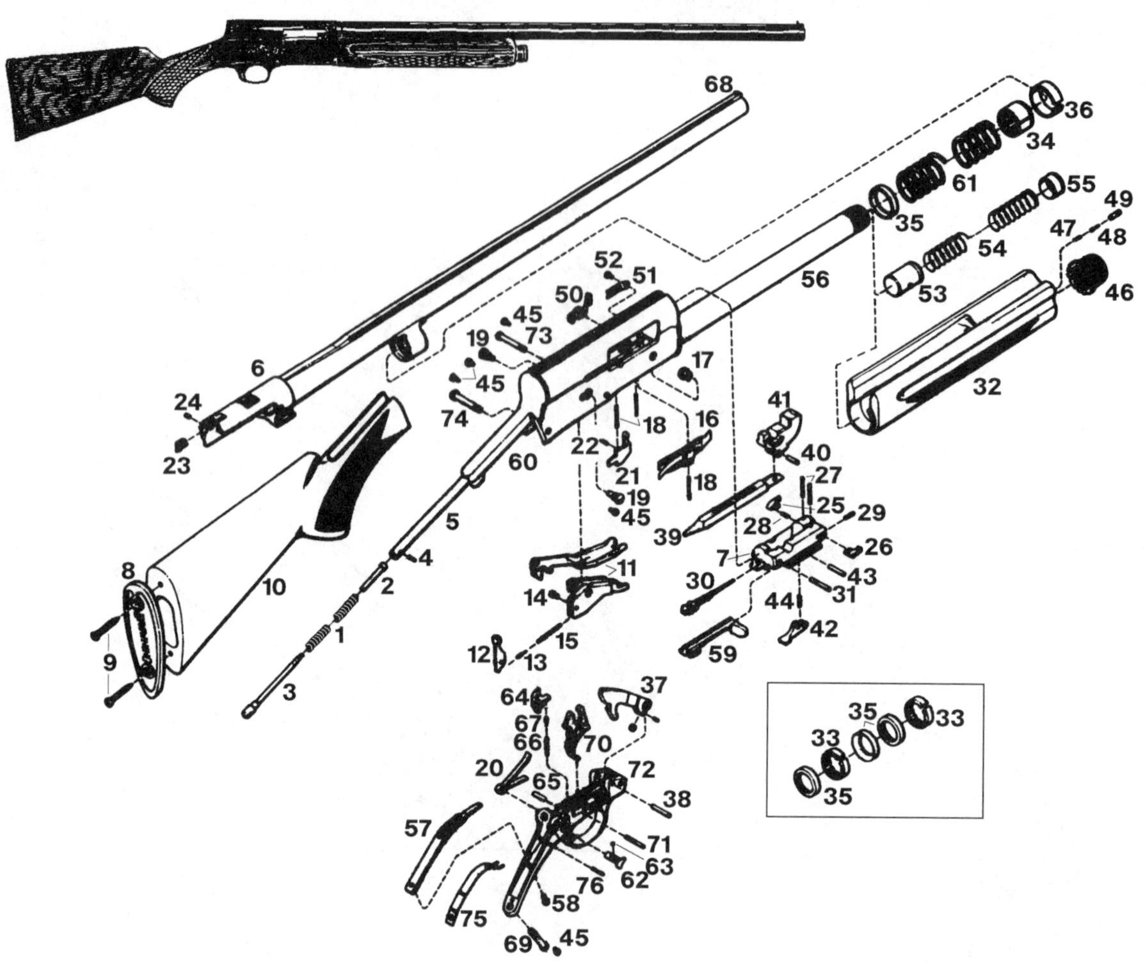

1	Action Spring	26	Extractor, Right	51	Magazine Cutoff Spring
2	Action Spring Follower	27	Extractor Pins	52	Magazine Cutoff Spring Screw
3	Action Spring Plug	28	Extractor Spring, Left	53	Magazine Follower
4	Action Spring Plug Pin	29	Extractor Spring, Right	54	Magazine Spring
5	Action Spring Tube	30	Firing Pin	55	Magazine Spring Retainer
6	Barrel Extension Assembly	31	Firing Pin Stop Pin	56	Magazine Tube
7	Breechblock	32	Forend	57	Mainspring
8	Buttplate	33	Friction Piece, Magnum	58	Mainspring Screw
9	Buttplate Screws	34	Friction Piece	59	Operating Handle
10	Buttstock	35	Friction Ring	60	Receiver
11	Carrier Assembly (Two-Piece)	36	Friction Spring	61	Recoil Spring
12	Carrier Dog	37	Hammer Assembly	62	Safety Crossbolt
13	Carrier Dog Follower	38	Hammer Pin	63	Safety Ball
14	Carrier Dog Pin	39	Link	64	Safety Sear
15	Carrier Dog Spring	40	Link Pin	65	Safety Sear Pin
16	Carrier Latch Assembly	41	Locking Block	66	Safety Sear Spring
17	Carrier Latch Button	42	Locking Block Latch Two-Piece Carrier	67	Safety Sear Spring Follower
18	Cartridge Stop/Carrier Latch/ Magazine Cutoff Pins	43	Locking Block Latch Pin	68	Sight Bead
19	Carrier Screw	44	Locking Block Latch Spring	69	Tang Screw
20	Carrier Spring Trigger Plate	45	Lock Screw	70	Trigger
21	Cartridge Stop	46	Magazine Cap	71	Trigger Pin
22	Cartridge Stop Spring	47	Magazine Cap Detent Spring	72	Trigger Plate
23	Ejector	48	Magazine Cap Detent	73	Front Trigger Plate Screw
24	Ejector Rivet	49	Magazine Cap Detent Housing	74	Rear Trigger Plate Screw
25	Extractor, Left	50	Magazine Cutoff	75	Trigger Spring Pin Retainer
				76	Trigger Spring Retaining Pin

A-500 R Autoloading Shotgun

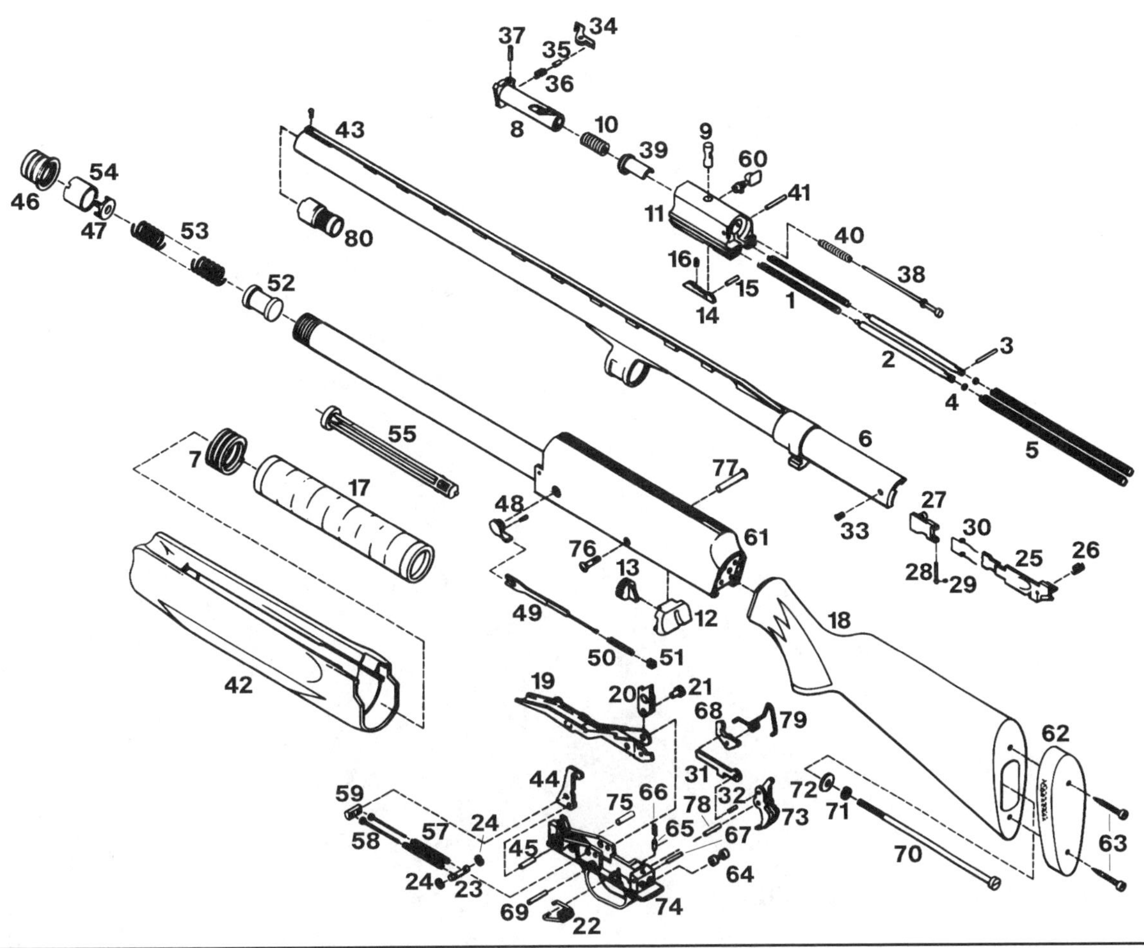

1 Front Action Springs
2 Action Spring Guides
3 Action Spring Guide Pin
4 Action Spring Guide Washers
5 Rear Action Springs
6 Barrel Extension
7 Barrel Spring
8 Bolt
9 Bolt Cam Pin
10 Bolt Spring
11 Breechblock
12 Breechblock Buffer
13 Breechblock Buffer Core
14 Breechblock Lever
15 Breechblock Lever Pin
16 Breechblock Lever Spring
17 Buffer Rings
18 Buttstock
19 Carrier
20 Carrier Dog
21 Carrier Dog Pin
22 Carrier and Carrier Dog Spring
23 Carrier Pin
24 Carrier Pin Circlips
25 Carrier Latch
26 Carrier Latch Spring
27 Cartridge Stop
28 Cartridge Stop and Carrier Latch Pin
29 Cartridge Stop and Carrier Latch Pin Clip
30 Cartridge Stop Spring
31 Disconnector
32 Disconnector Pin
33 Ejector
34 Extractor
35 Inner Extractor Spring
36 Outer Extractor Spring
37 Extractor Pin
38 Firing Pin
39 Firing Pin Cover
40 Firing Pin Spring
41 Firing Pin Stop Pin
42 Forend
43 Front Sight
44 Hammer
45 Hammer Pin
46 Magazine Cap
47 Magazine Cap Retainer
48 Magazine Cutoff and Pin
49 Magazine Cutoff Plunger, Spring<R>and Retainer
50 Magazine Cutoff Plunger Spring
51 Magazine Cutoff Plunger Spring Retainer
52 Magazine Follower
53 Magazine Spring
54 Magazine Spring Retainer
55 Magazine Three-Shot Adaptor
56 Magazine Tube
57 Mainsprings
58 Mainspring Guides
59 Mainspring Guide Pin Hammer
60 Operating Handle
61 Receiver
62 Recoil Pad
63 Recoil Pad Screws
64 Safety
65 Safety Plunger
66 Safety Plunger Spring
67 Safety Spring Stop Pin
68 Sear
69 Sear Pin
70 Stock Screw
71 Stock Screw Lock Washer
72 Stock Screw Washer
73 Trigger
74 Trigger Guard
75 Trigger Guard Pin Sleeve
76 Trigger Guard Retaining Screw
77 Trigger Guard Retaining Screw Nut
78 Trigger Pin
79 Trigger Spring
80 Choke Tube

A-Bolt Bolt-Action Rifle

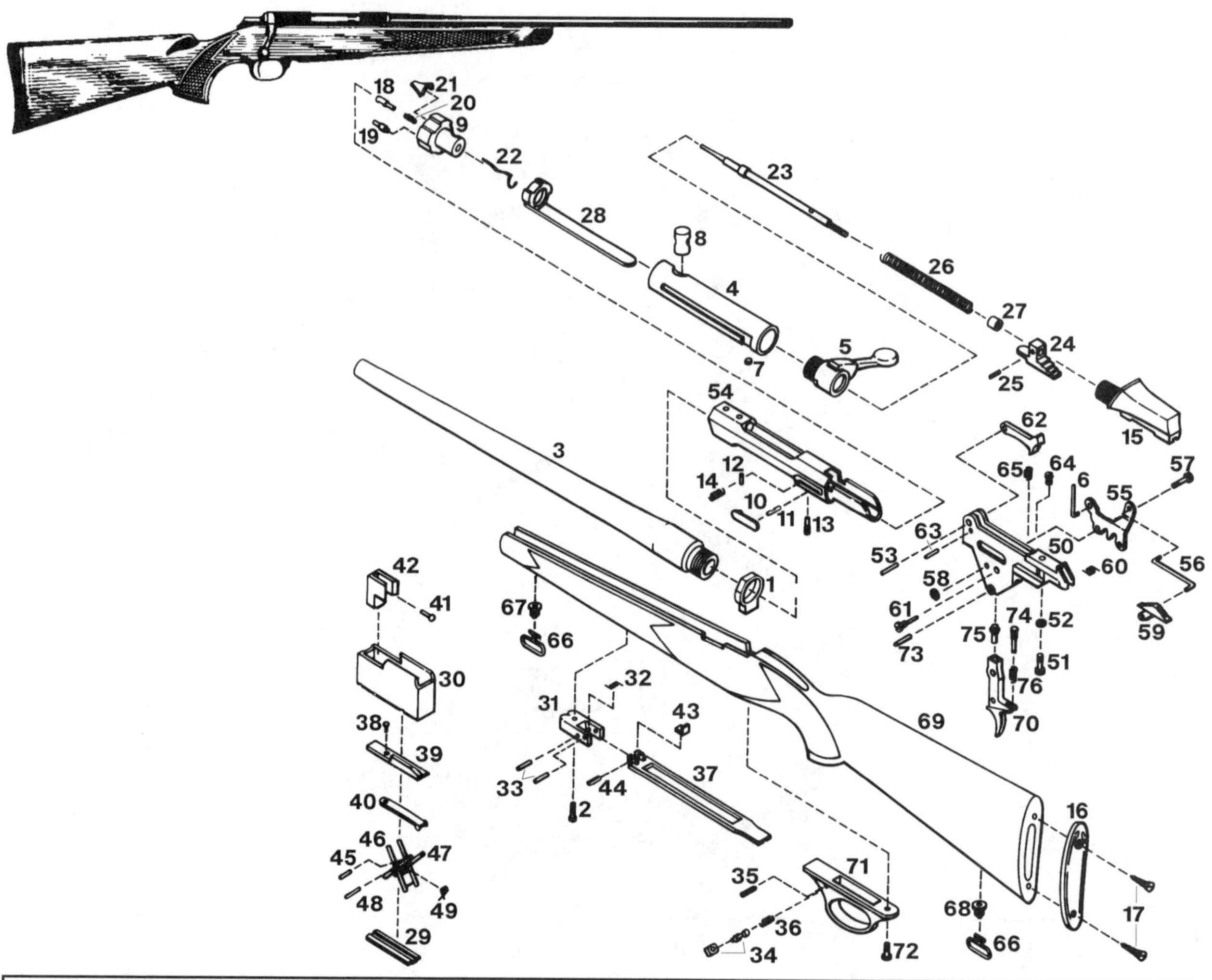

1	Barrel Mounting Block
2	Barrel Mounting Screw
3	Barrel
4	Bolt Body
5	Bolt Handle
6	Bolt Handle Lock
7	Bolt Handle Pin
8	Bolt Head Key Pin
9	Bolt Head
10	Bolt Retainer
11	Bolt Retainer Guide Pin
12	Bolt Retainer Pin
13	Bolt Retainer Screw
14	Bolt Retainer Spring
15	Bolt Shroud
16	Buttplate
17	Buttplate Screws
18	Ejector
19	Ejector Pin
20	Ejector Spring
21	Extractor
22	Extractor Spring
23	Firing Pin
24	Firing Pin Sear
25	Firing Pin Sear Pin
26	Firing Pin Spring
27	Firing Pin Washer
28	Gas Stop Assembly
29	Magazine Base
30	Magazine Body
31	Magazine Floorplate Hinge
32	Magazine Floorplate Hinge Spring
33	Magazine Floorplate Hinge Pins
34	Magazine Floorplate Latch Assembly
35	Magazine Floorplate Latch Pin
36	Magazine Floorplate Latch Spring
37	Magazine Floorplate
38	Magazine Follower Rivet
39	Magazine Follower
40	Magazine Follower Spring
41	Magazine Ramp Rivet
42	Magazine Ramp
43	Magazine Retainer Spring
44	Magazine Retainer Spring Pin
45	Magazine Spring Pin
46	Inner Magazine Spring Strut
47	Outer Magazine Spring Strut
48	Magazine Strut Pin
49	Magazine Strut Spring
50	Mechanism Housing
51	Mechanism Housing Screw
52	Mechanism Housing Screw Washer
53	Mechanism Housing Set Pin
54	Receiver
55	Safety
56	Safety Link
57	Safety Pin
58	Safety Pin Snap Ring
59	Safety Selector
60	Safety Spring
61	Safety Stud
62	Sear
63	Sear Pin
64	Sear Screw
65	Sear Spring
66	Sling Swivels
67	Swing Swivel Base, Front
68	Swing Swivel Base, Rear
69	Stock
70	Trigger
71	Trigger Guard
72	Trigger Guard Screw
73	Trigger Pin
74	Trigger Pull Adjusting Screw
75	Trigger Sear
76	Trigger Spring

A-Bolt 22 Bolt-Action Rifle

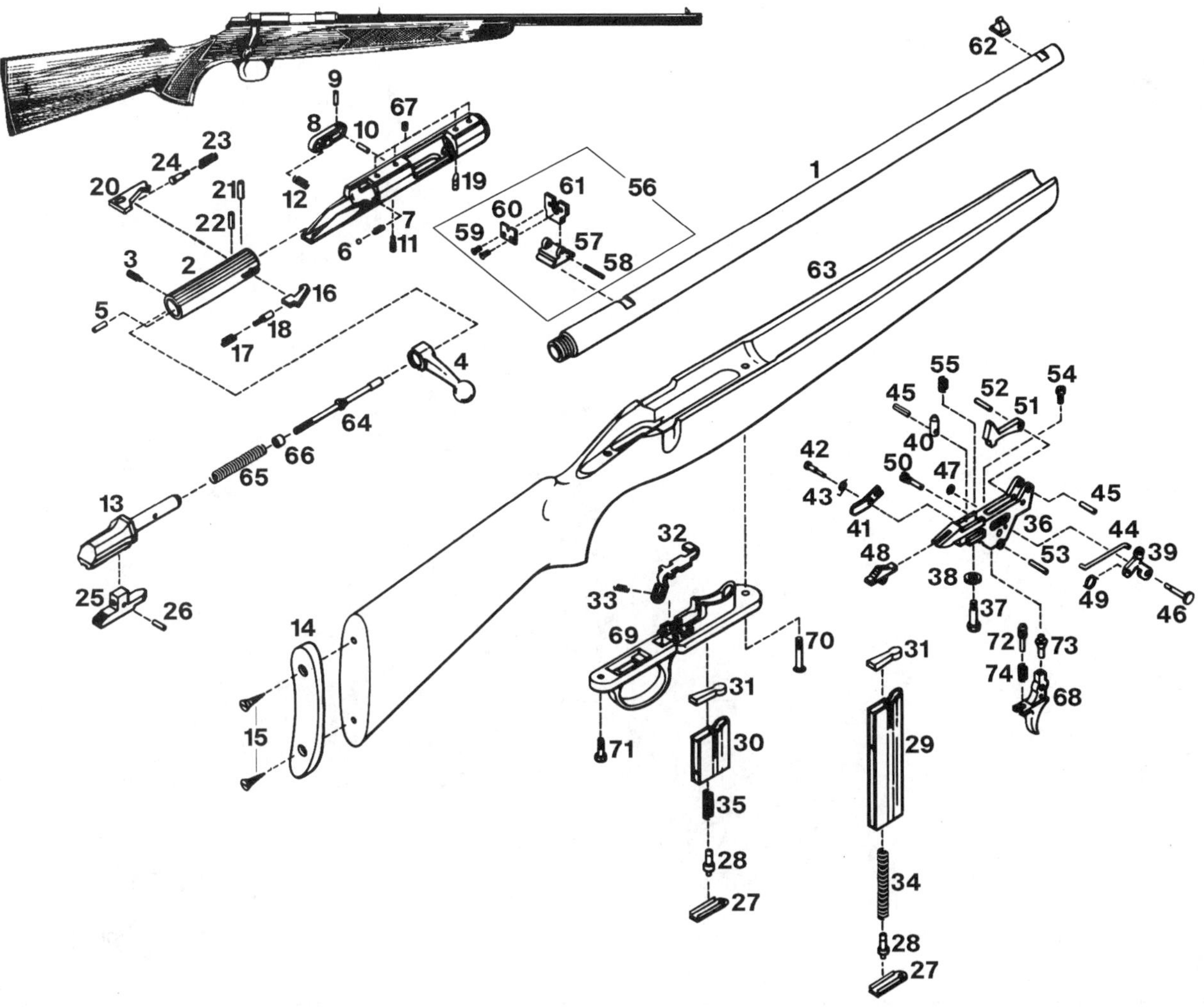

1	Barrel	26	Firing Pin Sear Pin	51	Sear
2	Bolt	27	Magazine Base	52	Sear Pin
3	Bolt Assembly Screw	28	Magazine Base Retainer	53	Trigger Pin
4	Bolt Handle	29	Magazine Body, 15 Shot	54	Sear Screw
5	Bolt Handle Pin	30	Magazine Body, 5 Shot	55	Sear Spring
6	Bolt Handle Stop Ball	31	Magazine Follower Guide	56	Rear Sight Assembly
7	Bolt Handle Stop Spring	32	Magazine Latch	57	Sight Base
8	Bolt Retainer	33	Magazine Latch Spring	58	Sight Pin
9	Bolt Retainer Pin	34	Magazine Spring, 15 Shot	59	Sight Elevation Screws
10	Bolt Retainer Pin Guide	35	Magazine Spring, 5 Shot	60	Sight Elevation Leaf
11	Bolt Retainer Screw	36	Mechanism Housing	61	Sight Leaf
12	Bolt Retainer Spring	37	Mechanism Housing Screw	62	Front Sight
13	Bolt Shroud	38	Mechanism Housing Screw Washer	63	Stock
14	Buttplate	39	Safety	64	Striker
15	Buttplate Screws	40	Safety Blocking Pin	65	Striker Spring
16	Extractor	41	Safety-Lever	66	Striker Spring Washer
17	Extractor Spring	42	Safety-Lever Pin	67	Telescope Mount Filler Screws
18	Extractor Spring Follower	43	Safety-Lever Spring	68	Trigger
19	Feed Ramp	44	Safety Link	69	Trigger Guard
20	Firing Pin Ejector	45	Safety Link Roll Pins	70	Trigger Guard Screw, Front
21	Firing Pin Ejector Pin	46	Safety Pin	71	Trigger Guard Screw, Rear
22	Firing Pin Ejector Relief Pin	47	Safety Pin Snap Ring	72	Trigger Pull Adjusting Screw
23	Firing Pin Ejector Spring	48	Safety Selector	73	Trigger Sear
24	Firing Pin Ejector Spring Follower	49	Safety Spring	74	Trigger Spring
25	Firing Pin Sear	50	Safety Stud		

BAR Standard and Magnum Autoloading Rifle

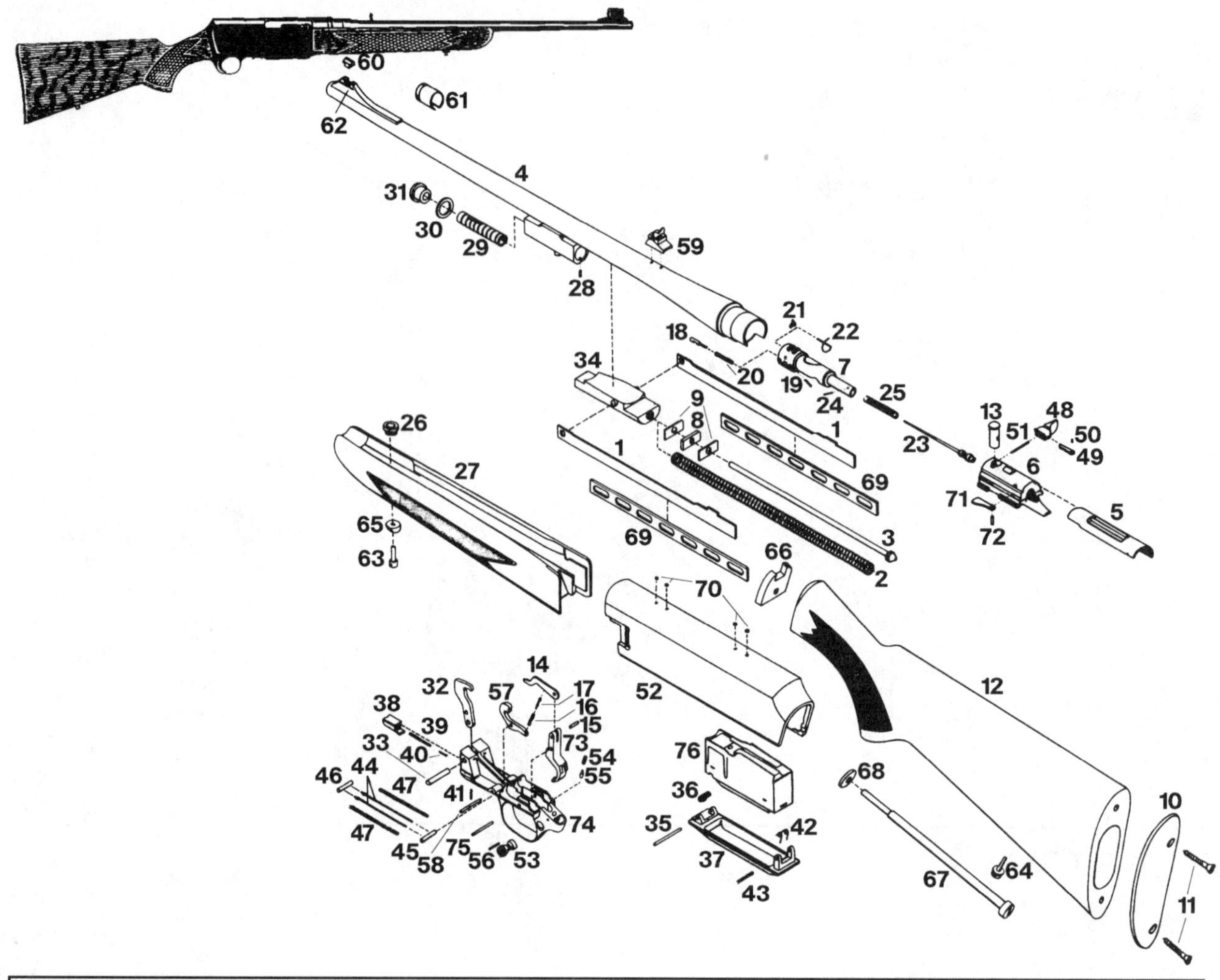

1	Action Rod
2	Action Spring
3	Action Spring Guide
4	Barrel
5	Bolt Cover
6	Bolt Sleeve
7	Bolt
8	Buffer
9	Buffer Plates
10	Buttplate
11	Buttplate Screws
12	Buttstock
13	Cam Pin
14	Disconnector
15	Disconnector Pin
16	Disconnector Spring
17	Disconnector Spring Plunger
18	Ejector
19	Ejector Retaining Pin
20	Ejector Spring
21	Extractor
22	Extractor Spring
23	Firing Pin
24	Firing Pin Retaining Pin
25	Firing Pin Spring
26	Forend Escutcheon
27	Forend
28	Gas Cylinder
29	Gas Piston
30	Gas Regulator Gasket
31	Gas Regulator
32	Hammer
33	Hammer Pin
34	Inertia Piece
35	Magazine Floorplate Pivot Pin
36	Magazine Floorplate Spring
37	Magazine Floorplate
38	Magazine Latch
39	Magazine Latch Spring
40	Magazine Latch Spring Plunger
41	Magazine Latch Stop Pin
42	Magazine Retaining Spring
43	Magazine Retaining Spring Pin
44	Mainspring Guides
45	Mainspring Pin Hammer
46	Mainspring Pin Trigger Guard
47	Mainsprings
48	Operating Handle
49	Operating Handle Lock
50	Operating Handle Lock Pin
51	Operating Handle Lock Spring
52	Receiver
53	Safety Cross Bolt
54	Safety Spring
55	Safety Spring Plunger
56	Safety Spring Retaining Pin
57	Sear
58	Sear Pin
59	Sight Assembly
60	Sight Bead
61	Sight Hood
62	Sight Ramp
63	Sling Eyelet, Front
64	Sling Eyelet, Rear
65	Sling Eyelet Washer
66	Stock Bolt Plate
67	Stock Bolt
68	Stock Bolt Washer
69	Support Rails
70	Telescope Mount Filler Screws
71	Timing Latch
72	Timing Latch Retaining Pin
73	Trigger
74	Trigger Guard
75	Trigger Pin
76	Magazine Assembly

BAR-22 Type II Autoloading Rifle

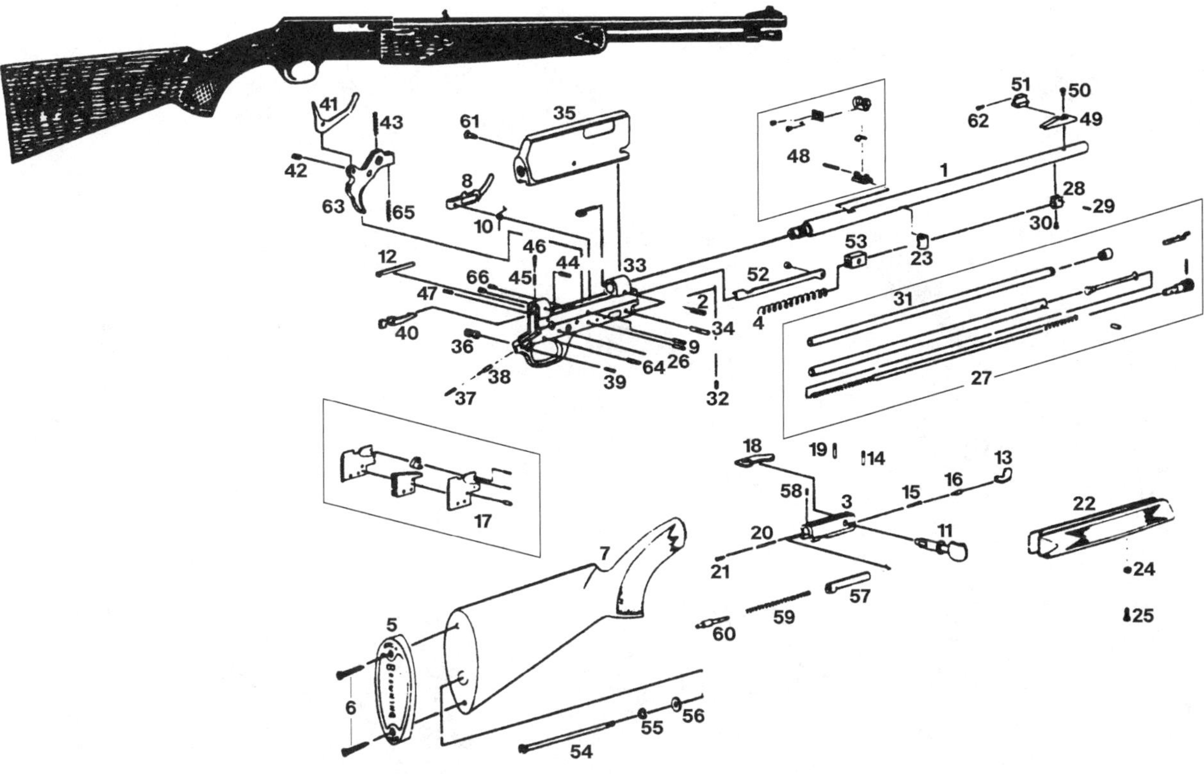

1	Barrel	**34**	Mechanism Housing Pin
2	Barrel Pin	**35**	Receiver
3	Bolt	**36**	Safety
4	Bolt Return Spring	**37**	Safety Spring
5	Buttplate	**38**	Safety Spring Follower
6	Buttplate Screws	**39**	Safety Spring Pin
7	Buttstock	**40**	Sear
8	Carrier	**41**	Sear Lever
9	Carrier Pin	**42**	Sear Lever Pin
10	Carrier Spring	**43**	Sear Lever Spring
11	Cocking Handle	**44**	Sear Pin
12	Ejector Bar	**45**	Sear Spring
13	Extractor	**46**	Sear Spring Screw
14	Extractor Pin	**47**	Sear Stop Pin
15	Extractor Spring	**48**	Rear Sight Assembly
16	Extractor Spring Follower	**49**	Front Sight Base
17	Feed Guide Assembly	**50**	Front Sight Base Screw
18	Firing Pin Ejector	**51**	Front Sight
19	Firing Pin Ejector Pin	**52**	Slide Arm with Rivet
20	Firing Pin Ejector Spring	**53**	Slide Arm Weight
21	Firing Pin Ejector Spring Follower	**54**	Stock Bolt
22	Forearm	**55**	Stock Bolt Lock Washer
23	Forearm Bracket	**56**	Stock Bolt Washer
24	Forearm Escutcheon	**57**	Striker
25	Forearm Screw	**58**	Striker Guide Pin
26	Lock Pin	**59**	Striker Spring
27	Inner Magazine Assembly	**60**	Striker Spring Guide
28	Magazine Tube Bracket	**61**	Takedown Screw
29	Magazine Tube Bracket Pin	**62**	Front Sight Pin
30	Magazine Tube Bracket Screw	**63**	Trigger
31	Outer Magazine Tube	**64**	Trigger Pin
32	Magazine Tube Retaining Screw	**65**	Trigger Spring
33	Mechanism Housing	**66**	Feed Guide Retaining Screws

BAR-22 Type III Autoloading Rifle

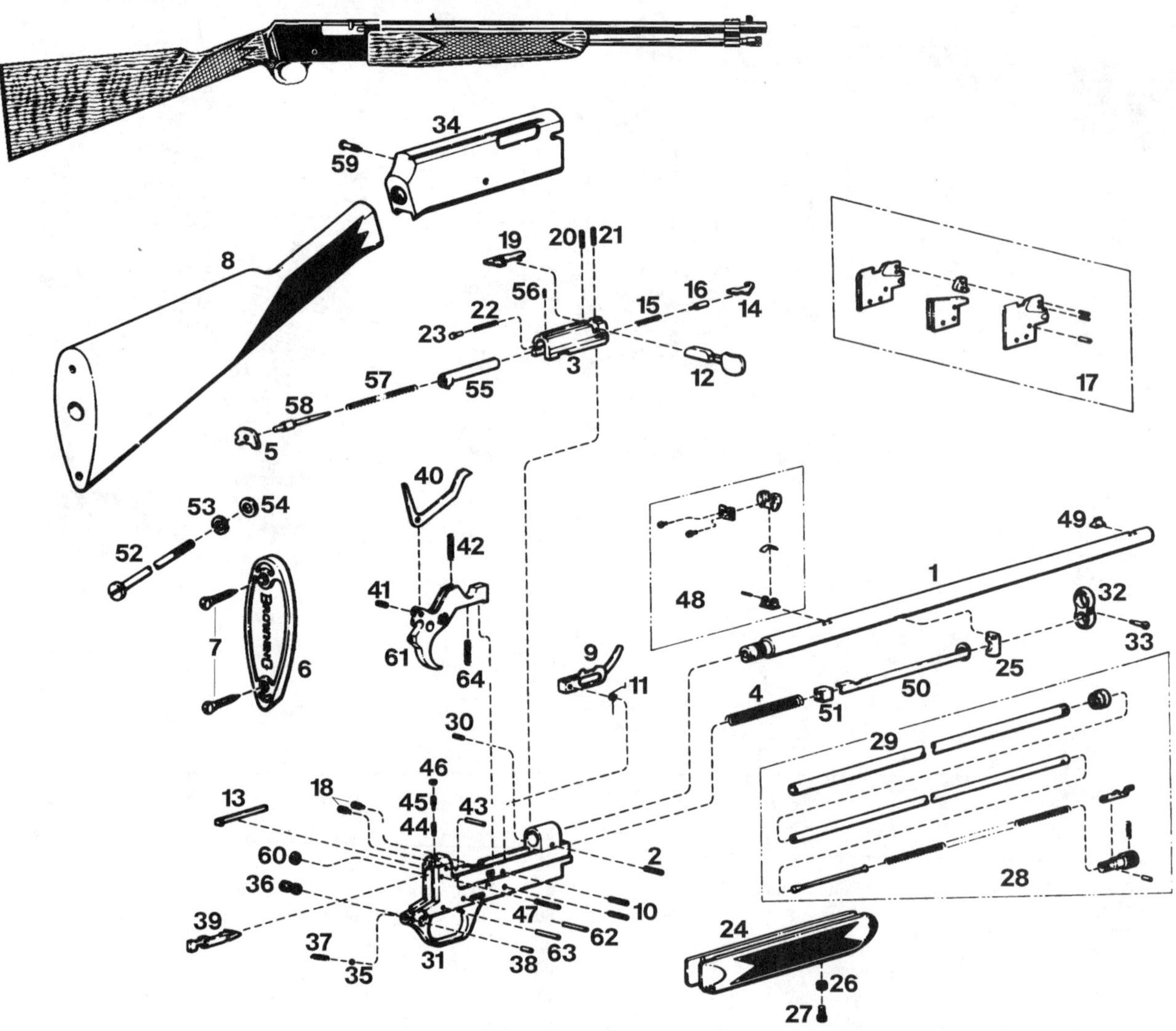

1	Barrel	23	Firing Pin Ejector Spring Follower	45	Sear Spring Screw
2	Barrel Pin	24	Forearm	46	Sear Spring Screw Nut
3	Bolt	25	Forearm Bracket	47	Sear Stop Pin
4	Bolt Return Spring	26	Forearm Escutcheon	48	Rear Sight Assembly
5	Buffer	27	Forearm Screw	49	Front Sight
6	Buttplate	28	Inner Magazine Assembly	50	Slide Arm with Rivet
7	Buttplate Screws	29	Outer Magazine Tube	51	Slide Arm Weight
8	Buttstock	30	Magazine Tube Retaining Screw	52	Stock Bolt
9	Carrier	31	Mechanism Housing	53	Stock Bolt Lock Washer
10	Carrier Pins	32	Muzzle Clamp	54	Stock Bolt Washer
11	Carrier Spring	33	Muzzle Clamp Screw	55	Striker
12	Cocking Handle	34	Receiver	56	Striker Guide Pin
13	Ejector Bar	35	Safety Ball	57	Striker Spring
14	Extractor	36	Safety	58	Striker Spring Guide
15	Extractor Spring	37	Safety Spring	59	Takedown Screw
16	Extractor Spring Follower	38	Safety Spring Pin	60	Takedown Screw Washer
17	Feed Guide Assembly	39	Sear	61	Trigger
18	Feed Guide Retaining Screws	40	Sear Lever	62	Trigger Pin
19	Firing Pin Ejector	41	Sear Lever Pin	63	Trigger Set Pin
20	Firing Pin Ejector Pin	42	Sear Lever Spring	64	Trigger Spring
21	Firing Pin Ejector Relief Pin	43	Sear Pin		
22	Firing Pin Ejector Spring	44	Sear Spring		

BBR Bolt-Action Rifle

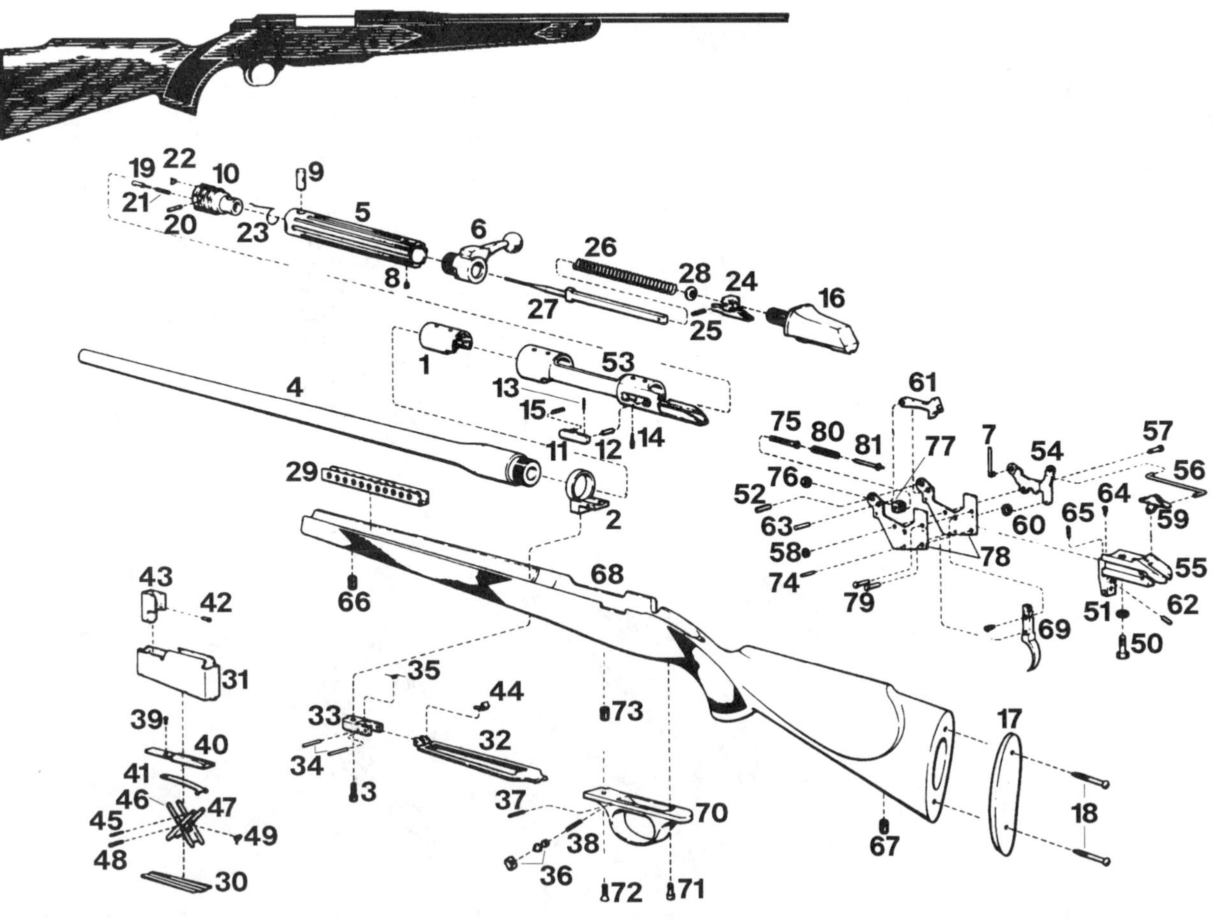

1	Barrel Extension	29	Forearm Insert	57	Safety Pin
2	Barrel Mounting Block	30	Magazine Base	58	Safety Pin Snap Ring
3	Barrel Mounting Screw	31	Magazine Body	59	Safety Selector
4	Barrel	32	Magazine Floorplate	60	Safety Spring
5	Bolt Body	33	Magazine Floorplate Hinge	61	Sear
6	Bolt Handle	34	Magazine Floorplate Hinge Pins	62	Sear Adjusting Screw
7	Bolt Handle Lock	35	Magazine Floorplate Hinge Spring	63	Sear Pin
8	Bolt Handle Pin	36	Magazine Floorplate Latch Assembly	64	Sear Screw
9	Bolt Head Key Pin	37	Magazine Floorplate Latch Pin	65	Sear Spring
10	Bolt Head	38	Magazine Floorplate Latch Spring	66	Sling Swivel Base, Front
11	Bolt Retainer	39	Magazine Follower Rivet	67	Sling Swivel Base, Rear
12	Bolt Retainer Guide Pin	40	Magazine Follower	68	Stock
13	Bolt Retainer Pin	41	Magazine Follower Spring	69	Trigger
14	Bolt Retainer Screw	42	Magazine Ramp Rivet	70	Trigger Guard
15	Bolt Retainer Spring	43	Magazine Ramp	71	Rear Trigger Guard Screw
16	Bolt Shroud	44	Magazine Retainer Spring	72	Front Trigger Guard Screw
17	Buttplate	45	Magazine Spring Pin	73	Helicoil Trigger Guard Screw
18	Buttplate Screws	46	Inner Magazine Spring Strut	74	Trigger Pin
19	Ejector	47	Outer Magazine Spring Strut	75	Trigger Pull Adjusting Screw
20	Ejector Pin	48	Magazine Strut Pin	76	Trigger Pull Adjustment Screw Lock Nut
21	Ejector Spring	49	Magazine Strut Spring	77	Trigger Pull Adjustment Swivel
22	Extractor	50	Mechanism Housing Screw	78	Trigger Sideplates
23	Extractor Spring	51	Mechanism Housing Screw Washer	79	Trigger Sideplate Rivets
24	Firing Pin Sear	52	Mechanism Housing Set Pin	80	Trigger Spring
25	Firing Pin Sear Pin	53	Mechanism Housing	81	Trigger Spring Rod
26	Firing Pin Spring	54	Safety		
27	Firing Pin	55	Safety Block		
28	Firing Pin Washer	56	Safety Link		

BLR and Model '81 BLR Lever-Action Rifle

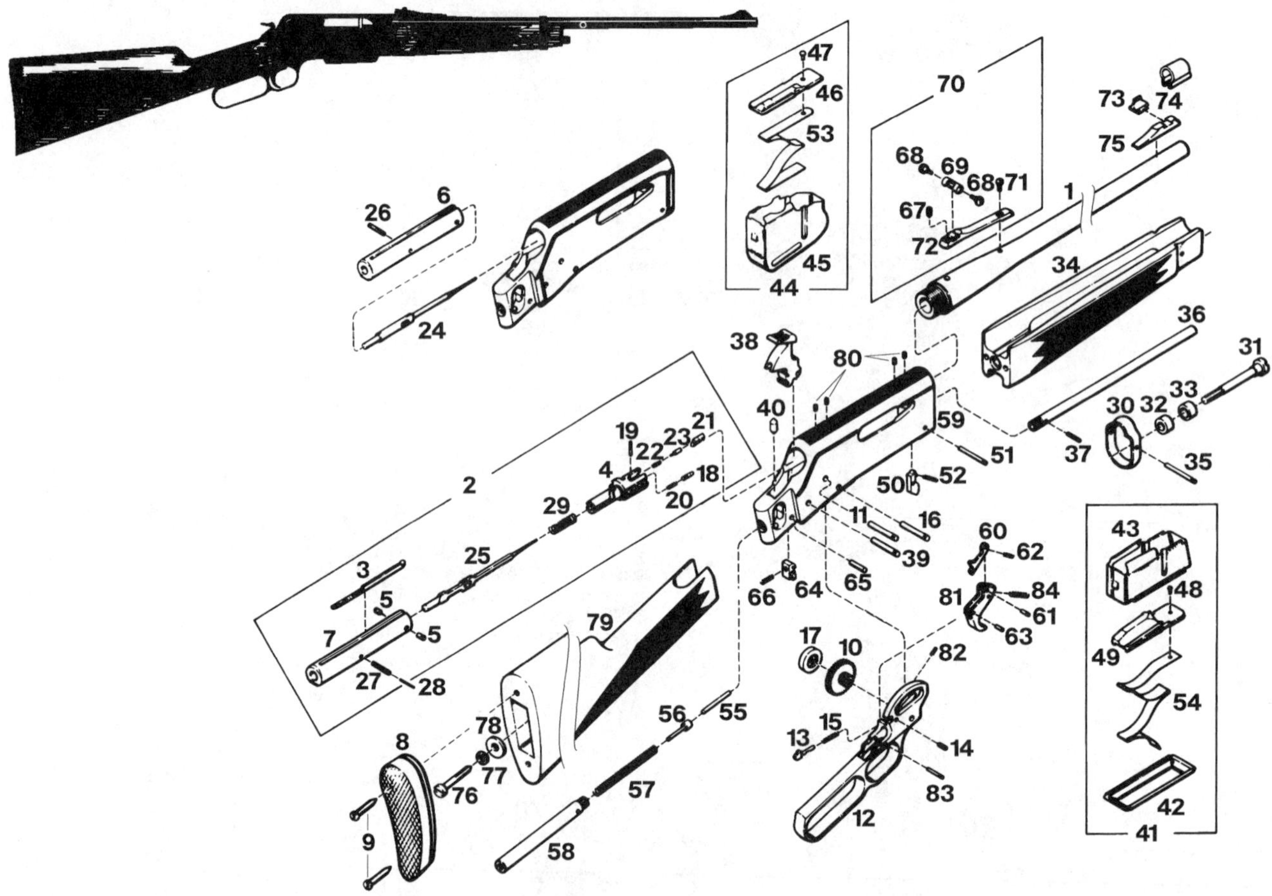

1	Barrel	30	Forearm Band	59	Receiver
2	Bolt Assembly	31	Forearm Bolt	60	Sear Link
3	Breech Bolt Guide	32	Forearm Bolt Spacer, Inner	61	Sear Link Pin
4	Breech Bolt Lock	33	Forearm Bolt Spacer, Outer	62	Sear Link Spring
5	Breech Bolt Pins	34	Forearm	63	Sear Link Stop Pin
6	Breech Bolt Slide (BLR)	35	Forearm Pin	64	Sear
7	Breech Bolt Slide (M'81)	36	Forearm Tube	65	Sear Pin
8	Buttplate	37	Forearm Tube Pin	66	Sear Spring
9	Buttplate Screws	38	Hammer	67	Rear Sight Elevation Adjusting Screw
10	Cocking Gear	39	Hammer Pin	68	Rear Sight Windage Adjusting Screws
11	Cocking Gear Pin	40	Hammer Stop	69	Rear Sight Aperture
12	Cocking Lever	41	Magazine Assembly (M'81)	70	Rear Sight Assembly
13	Cocking Lever Latch	42	Magazine Base (M'81)	71	Rear Sight Base Mounting Screw
14	Cocking Lever Latch Pin	43	Magazine Body (M'81)	72	Rear Sight Base
15	Cocking Lever Latch Spring	44	Magazine Assembly (BLR)	73	Front Sight
16	Cocking Lever Pin	45	Magazine Body (BLR)	74	Front Sight Hood
17	Cocking Lever Stop	46	Magazine Follower (BLR)	75	Front Sight Ramp
18	Ejector	47	Magazine Follower Rivet (BLR)	76	Stock Bolt
19	Ejector Pin	48	Magazine Follower Rivet (M'81)	77	Stock Bolt Lock Washer
20	Ejector Spring	49	Magazine Follower (M'81)	78	Stock Bolt Washer
21	Extractor	50	Magazine Latch	79	Stock
22	Extractor Spring	51	Magazine Latch Pin	80	Telescope Mount Filler Screws
23	Extractor Spring Follower	52	Magazine Latch Spring	81	Trigger
24	Firing Pin (BLR)	53	Magazine Spring (BLR)	82	Trigger Adjusting Screw
25	Firing Pin (M'81)	54	Magazine Spring (M'81)	83	Trigger Pin
26	Firing Pin Retaining Pin	55	Mainspring Follower	84	Trigger Spring
27	Inner Firing Pin Retaining Pin	56	Mainspring Guide	**Parts Not Shown**	
28	Outer Firing Pin Retaining Pin	57	Mainspring		Front Sling Eyelet
29	Firing Pin Spring	58	Mainspring Tube		Rear Sling Eyelet

BPS Slide-Action Shotgun

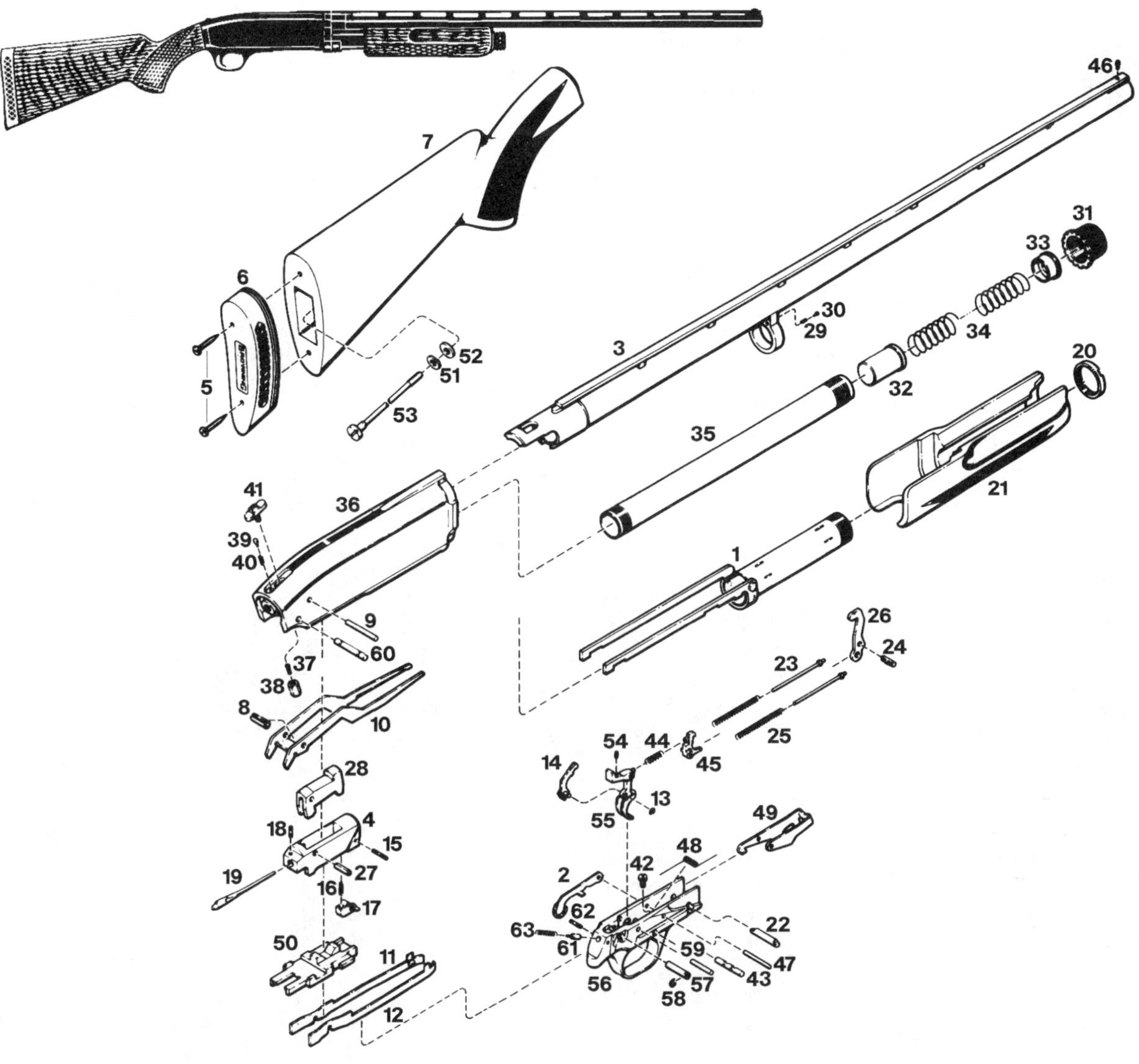

1	Action Bar Assembly	**22**	Hammer Pin	**43**	Sear Pin
2	Action Slide Lock Release	**23**	Hammer Spring Guides	**44**	Sear Spring
3	Barrel Extension	**24**	Hammer Spring Pin	**45**	Sear
4	Bolt	**25**	Hammer Springs	**46**	Front Sight Bead
5	Buttplate Screws	**26**	Hammer	**47**	Slide Lock Pin
6	Buttplate	**27**	Lock Pin	**48**	Slide Lock Spring
7	Buttstock	**28**	Lock	**49**	Slide Lock Stop
8	Carrier Pin Retainer	**29**	Magazine Cap Stop Spring	**50**	Slide
9	Carrier Pin	**30**	Magazine Cap Stopper	**51**	Stock Bolt Lock Washer
10	Carrier	**31**	Magazine Cap	**52**	Stock Bolt Washer
11	Cartridge Stop, Left	**32**	Magazine Follower	**53**	Stock Bolt
12	Cartridge Stop, Right	**33**	Magazine Spring Retainer	**54**	Trigger Adjusting Screw
13	Disconnector Assembly Retainer	**34**	Magazine Spring	**55**	Trigger
14	Disconnector Assembly	**35**	Magazine Tube	**56**	Trigger Guard
15	Extractor Pin	**36**	Receiver	**57**	Trigger Guide Bushing
16	Extractor Spring	**37**	Safety Adjusting Screw	**58**	Trigger Guide Bushing Spring
17	Extractor	**38**	Safety Nut	**59**	Trigger Pin
18	Firing Pin Retaining Pin	**39**	Safety Plunger	**60**	Trigger Guide Pin
19	Firing Pin	**40**	Safety Spring	**61**	Trigger Spring Follower
20	Forearm Screw	**41**	Safety	**62**	Trigger Spring Pin
21	Forearm	**42**	Sear Adjusting Screw	**63**	Trigger Spring

B-2000 Autoloading Shotgun

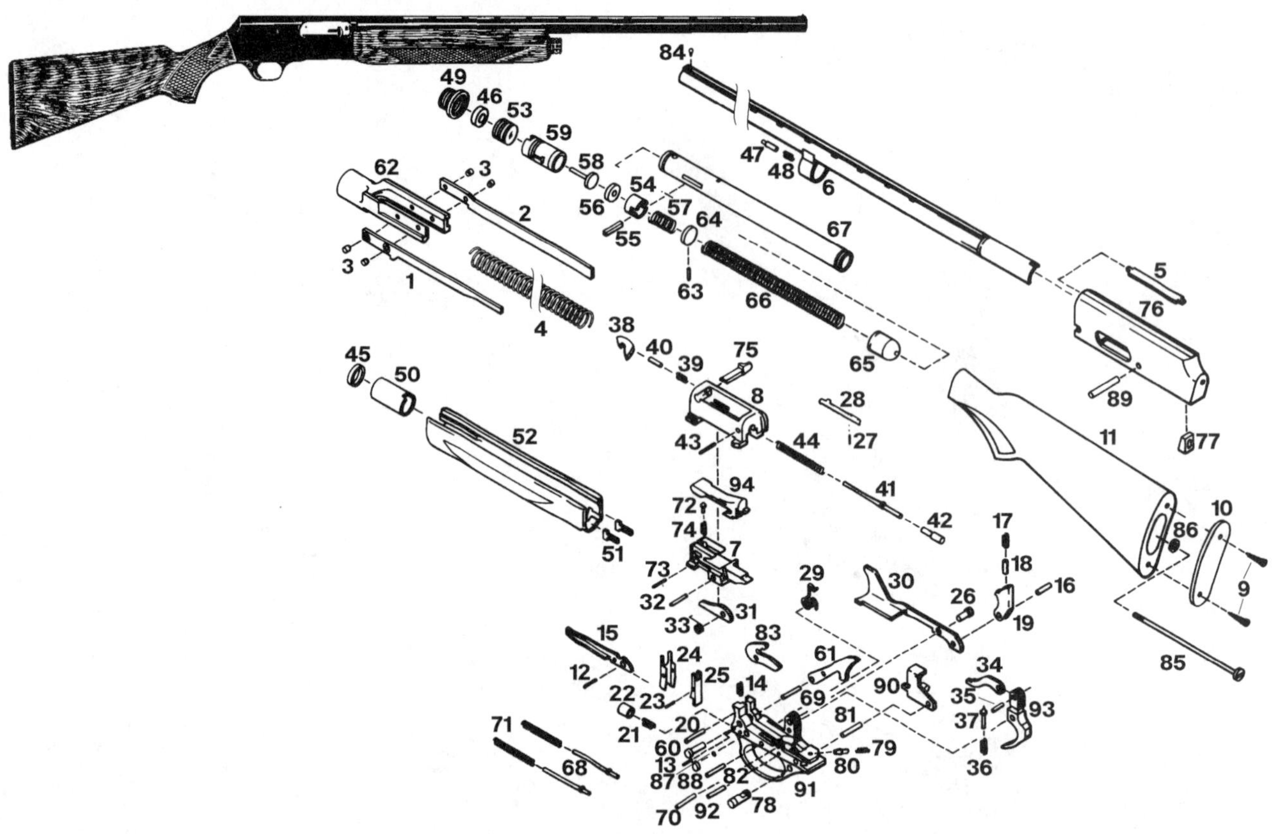

1	Action Bar, Left	**33**	Cartridge Stop Spring	**65**	Magazine Follower
2	Action Bar, Right	**34**	Disconnector	**66**	Magazine Spring
3	Action Bar Rivets	**35**	Disconnector Pin	**67**	Magazine Tube
4	Action Spring	**36**	Disconnector Spring	**68**	Mainspring Guides
5	Barrel Guide	**37**	Disconnector Spring Plunger	**69**	Mainspring Hammer Pin
6	Barrel Ring	**38**	Extractor	**70**	Mainspring Trigger Guard Pin
7	Bolt Slide	**39**	Extractor Spring	**71**	Mainsprings
8	Bolt	**40**	Extractor Spring Plunger	**72**	Operating Handle Retainer
9	Buttplate Screws	**41**	Firing Pin	**73**	Operating Handle Retaining Pin
10	Buttplate	**42**	Firing Pin Bushing	**74**	Operating Handle Retaining Spring
11	Buttstock	**43**	Firing Pin Bushing Pin	**75**	Operating Handle
12	Carrier Cartridge Limit Pin	**44**	Firing Pin Spring	**76**	Receiver Assembly
13	Carrier Cartridge Pin	**45**	Forearm Bushing	**77**	Receiver Buffer
14	Carrier Cartridge Spring	**46**	Forearm Cap Buffer	**78**	Safety Crossbolt
15	Carrier Cartridge Stop	**47**	Forearm Cap Plunger	**79**	Safety Spring
16	Carrier Dog Pin	**48**	Forearm Cap Plunger Spring	**80**	Safety Spring Plunger
17	Carrier Dog Spring	**49**	Forearm Cap	**81**	Safety Spring Retaining Pin
18	Carrier Dog Spring Guide	**50**	Forearm Liner	**82**	Sear Pin
19	Carrier Dog	**51**	Forearm Tabs	**83**	Sear
20	Carrier Latch Pin	**52**	Forearm	**84**	Front Sight Bead
21	Carrier Latch Spring	**53**	Gas Cylinder Plug	**85**	Stock Bolt
22	Carrier Latch Spring Plunger	**54**	Gas Piston Bar Guide	**86**	Stock Bolt Washer
23	Carrier Latch Trip Pin	**55**	Gas Piston Bar	**87**	Trigger Guard Retaining Pin Bushing
24	Carrier Latch Trip	**56**	Gas Piston Buffer	**88**	Trigger Guard Retaining Pin Spring
25	Carrier Latch	**57**	Gas Piston Spring	**89**	Trigger Guard Retaining Pin
26	Carrier Pin	**58**	Gas Piston Valve	**90**	Trigger Guard Shield
27	Carrier Release Pin	**59**	Gas Piston	**91**	Trigger Guard
28	Carrier Release	**60**	Hammer Pin	**92**	Trigger Pin
29	Carrier Spring	**61**	Hammer	**93**	Trigger
30	Carrier	**62**	Inertia Piece with Action Bars	**94**	Locking Block
31	Cartridge Stop	**63**	Magazine Base Pin		
32	Cartridge Stop Pin	**64**	Magazine Base		

B-27 Over/Under Shotgun

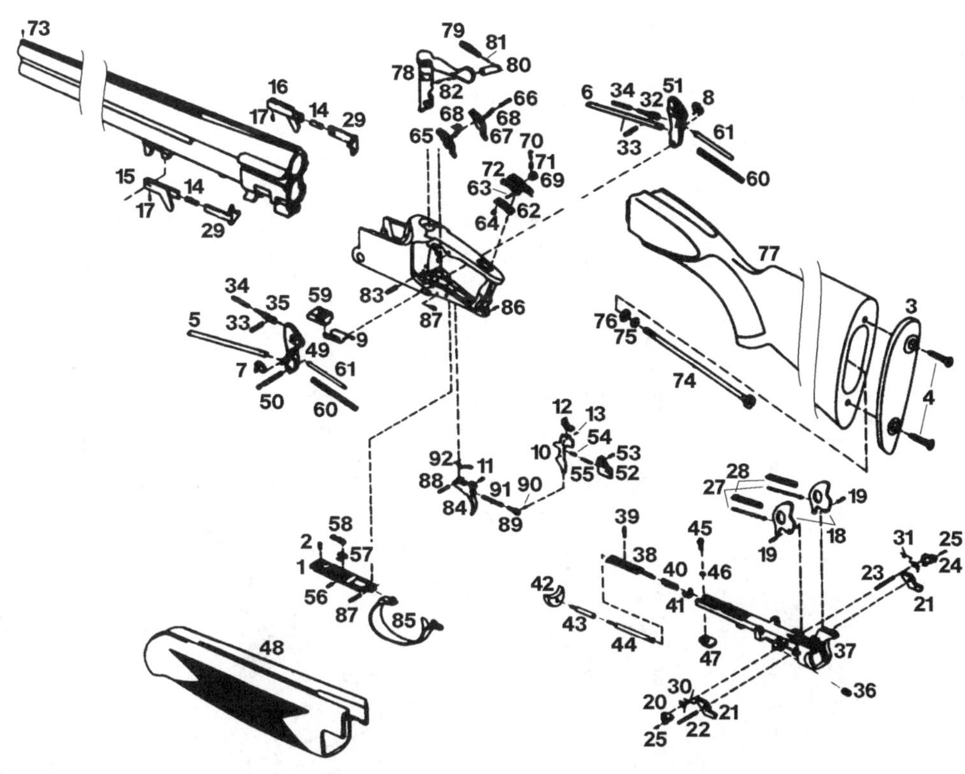

1	Bottom Plate	33	Firing Pin Pin	61	Mainspring Guide
2	Bottom Plate Screw	34	Firing Pin Spring	62	Safety Spring
3	Buttplate	35	Firing Pin, Upper	63	Safety Spring Pin
4	Buttplate Screws	36	Forearm Bracket Adjusting Screw	64	Safety Spring Screw
5	Cocking Rod, Left	37	Forearm Bracket	65	Sear, Left
6	Cocking Rod, Right	38	Forearm Bracket Lock	66	Sear Pin
7	Cocking Rod Spring, Left	39	Forearm Bracket Lock Pin	67	Sear, Right
8	Cocking Rod Spring, Right	40	Forearm Bracket Lock Spring	68	Sear Spring
9	Connector Cam	41	Forearm Bracket Lock Spring Retaining Plate	69	Selector Block
10	Connector	42	Forearm Bracket Release Button	70	Selector Block Spring Guide
11	Connector Pin	43	Forearm Bracket Release Button Push Rod, Front	71	Selector Block Spring
12	Connector Selector	44	Forearm Bracket Release Button Push Rod, Rear	72	Selector Safety
13	Connector Selector Pin	45	Forearm Bracket Screw, Front	73	Front Sight Bead Field
14	Ejector Connectors	46	Forearm Bracket Screw Washer, Front	74	Stock Bolt
15	Ejector Extension, Left	47	Forearm Bracket Screw Plate	75	Stock Bolt Lock Washer
16	Ejector Extension, Right	48	Forearm	76	Stock Bolt Washer
17	Ejector Extension Stop Pins	49	Hammer, Left	77	Stock
18	Ejector Hammers	50	Hammer Pivot Pin	78	Top Lever
19	Ejector Hammer Pins	51	Hammer, Right	79	Top Lever Spring
20	Ejector Hammer Sear, Left	52	Inertia Block	80	Top Lever Spring Retainer
21	Ejector Hammer Sear Lever	53	Inertia Block Pin	81	Top Lever Spring Retainer Pin
22	Ejector Hammer Sear Lever Pin	54	Inertia Block Spring Guide	82	Top Lever Spring Retainer Spring
23	Ejector Hammer Sear Pin	55	Inertia Block Spring	83	Top Lever Stop Pin
24	Ejector Hammer Sear, Right	56	Lock Open Latch Pin	84	Trigger
25	Ejector Hammer Sear Spring Pins	57	Lock Open Latch Spring	85	Trigger Guard
26	Ejector Hammer Sear Spring	58	Lock Open Latch	86	Rear Trigger Guard Pin
27	Ejector Hammer Spring Guides	59	Locking Bolt	87	Trigger Guard/Bottom Plate Pin
28	Ejector Hammer Springs	60	Mainspring	88	Trigger Pin
29	Ejector			89	Trigger Piston
30	Ejector Sear Spring, Left			90	Trigger Piston Pin
31	Ejector Sear Spring, Right			91	Trigger Piston Spring
32	Firing Pin, Lower			92	Trigger Spring

B-78 Single Shot Rifle

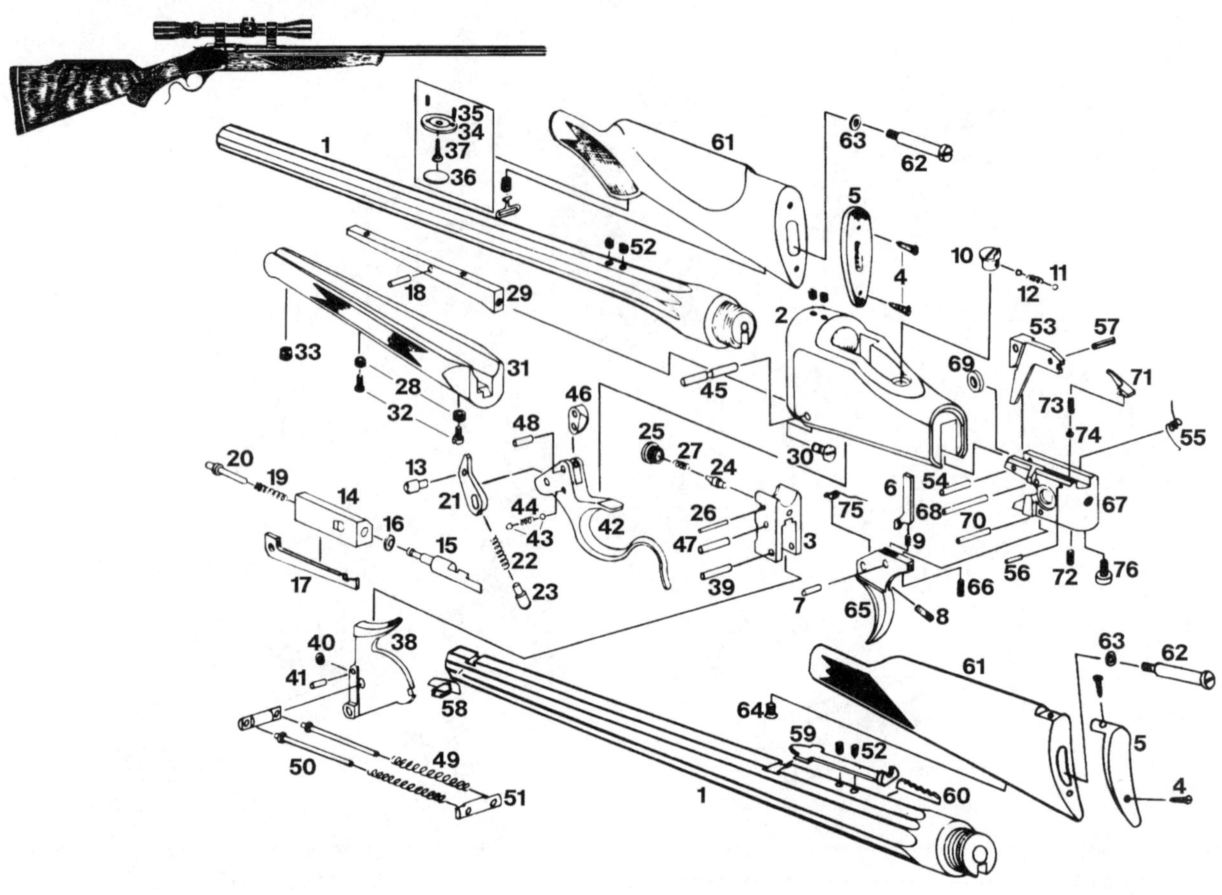

1	Barrel
2	Receiver
3	Breechblock
4	Buttplate Screws
5	Buttplate
6	Connector
7	Connector Pin
8	Connector Screw
9	Connector Spring
10	Deflector
11	Deflector Ball
12	Deflector Ball Spring
13	Ejector Connecting Pin
14	Ejector Hammer
15	Ejector Hammer Extension
16	Ejector Hammer Extension Washer
17	Ejector Hammer Sear
18	Ejector Hammer Sear Pin
19	Ejector Hammer Spring
20	Ejector Hammer Spring Guide
21	Extractor
22	Extractor Spring
23	Extractor Spring Plunger
24	Firing Pin
25	Firing Pin Bushing
26	Firing Pin Bushing Pin
27	Firing Pin Spring
28	Forearm Escutcheons
29	Forearm Hanger
30	Forearm Hanger Bolt
31	Forearm
32	Forearm Screws
33	Forearm Swivel Base
34	Grip Cap
35	Grip Cap Pin
36	Grip Cap Plate
37	Grip Cap Screw
38	Hammer
39	Hammer Pin
40	Hammer Roller
41	Hammer Roller Rivet
42	Lever
43	Lever Latch Balls
44	Lever Latch Ball Spring
45	Lever Pin
46	Link
47	Link Breech Block Pin
48	Link Lever Pin
49	Mainsprings
50	Mainspring Guides
51	Mainspring Pins
52	Scope Mount Filler Screws
53	Sear
54	Sear Pin
55	Sear Spring
56	Sear Spring Pin
57	Sear Spring Rest Pin
58	Front Sight Assembly
59	Rear Sight
60	Rear Sight Step
61	Stock
62	Stock Bolt
63	Stock Bolt Washer
64	Stock Swivel Base
65	Trigger
66	Trigger Backlash Adjusting Screw
67	Trigger Housing
68	Trigger Housing Pin
69	Trigger Housing Spacer
70	Trigger Pin
71	Trigger Pull Adjusting Lever
72	Trigger Pull Adjusting Screw
73	Trigger Pull Adjusting Spring
74	Trigger Pull Adjusting Spring Follower
75	Trigger Spring
76	Trigger Take-Up Screw

B-80 Autoloading Shotgun

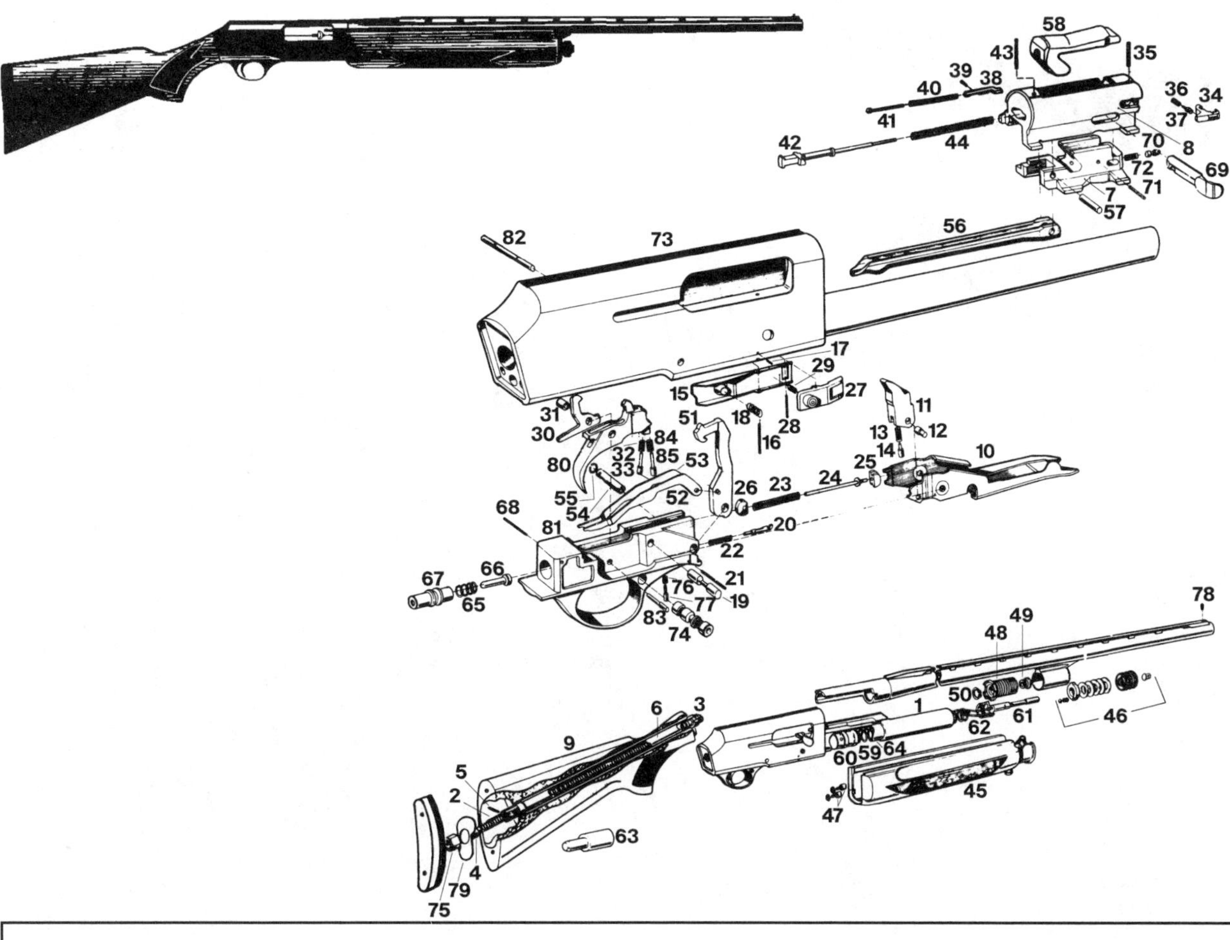

1	Action Bar and Sleeve	30	Disconnector	59	Magazine Spring
2	Action Spring	31	Disconnector Pin	60	Magazine Spring Follower
3	Action Spring Follower	32	Disconnector Spring	61	Magazine Spring Retainer and Forearm Cap Stud
4	Action Spring Plug	33	Disconnector Spring Guide	62	Magazine Spring Retainer Lock Spring
5	Action Spring Plug Pin	34	Extractor	63	Magazine Three-Shot Adaptor
6	Action Tube	35	Extractor Pin	64	Magazine Tube
7	Bolt Slide	36	Extractor Spring	65	Mainspring
8	Breechbolt	37	Extractor Spring Plunger	66	Mainspring Guide
9	Buttstock	38	Ejector	67	Mainspring Support
10	Carrier	39	Ejector Pin	68	Mainspring Support Pin
11	Carrier Dog	40	Ejector Spring	69	Operating Handle
12	Carrier Dog Pin	41	Ejector Spring Follower	70	Operating Handle Retainer
13	Carrier Dog Spring	42	Firing Pin	71	Operating Handle Retainer Pin
14	Carrier Dog Spring Follower	43	Firing Pin Retaining Pin	72	Operating Handle Retainer Spring
15	Carrier Latch	44	Firing Pin Spring	73	Receiver
16	Carrier Latch Pin	45	Forearm	74	Safety
17	Carrier Latch Lock Pin	46	Forearm Cap Assembly with Eyelet	75	Recoil Pad
18	Carrier Latch Spring	47	Forearm Guide Screws	76	Safety Spring
19	Carrier Pin	48	Gas Piston	77	Safety Spring Follower
20	Carrier Release	49	Gas Piston Seal	78	Front Sight Bead
21	Carrier Release Pin	50	Gas Pin Seal Retaining Ring	79	Stock Retaining Plate
22	Carrier Release Spring	51	Hammer	80	Trigger
23	Carrier Spring	52	Hammer Bar, Right	81	Trigger Guard
24	Carrier Spring Guide	53	Hammer Bar, Left	82	Trigger Guard Retaining Pin
25	Carrier Spring Guide Pivot, Front	54	Hammer Pin	83	Trigger Pin
26	Carrier Spring Guide Pivot, Rear	55	Hammer Pin Circlip	84	Trigger Spring
27	Cartridge Stop Button	56	Link	85	Trigger Spring Plunger
28	Cartridge Stop Pin	57	Link Pin		
29	Cartridge Stop Spring	58	Locking Bolt		

B-92 Lever-Action Rifle

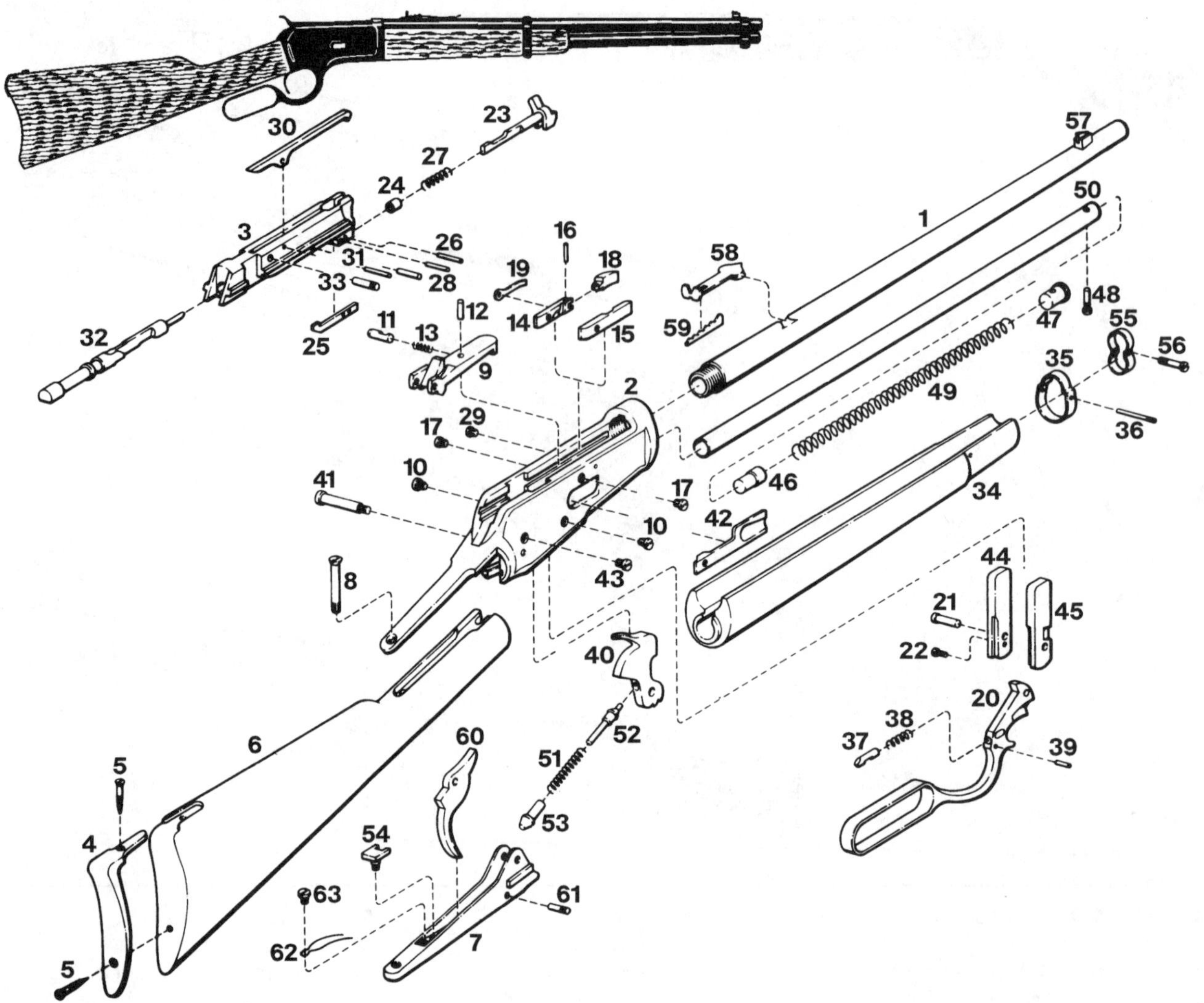

1	Barrel	**22**	Cocking Lever Stop Screw	**43**	Loading Gate Cover Screw
2	Receiver	**23**	Ejector	**44**	Locking Bolt, Left
3	Breechbolt	**24**	Ejector Collar	**45**	Locking Bolt, Right
4	Buttplate	**25**	Ejector Collar Stop	**46**	Magazine Follower
5	Buttplate Screws	**26**	Ejector Collar Stop Pin	**47**	Magazine Plug
6	Buttstock	**27**	Ejector Spring	**48**	Magazine Plug Screw
7	Buttstock Lower Tang	**28**	Ejector Stop Pin	**49**	Magazine Spring
8	Buttstock Tang Screw	**29**	Ejector Stop Pin Plug Screw	**50**	Magazine Tube
9	Carrier	**30**	Extractor	**51**	Mainspring
10	Carrier Screw	**31**	Extractor Pin	**52**	Mainspring Guide, Inner
11	Carrier Striker	**32**	Firing Pin	**53**	Mainspring Guide, Outer
12	Carrier Striker Pin	**33**	Firing Pin Stop Pin	**54**	Mainspring Guide Stud
13	Carrier Striker Spring	**34**	Forearm	**55**	Muzzle Clamp
14	Cartridge Guide, Left	**35**	Forearm Band	**56**	Muzzle Clamp Screw
15	Cartridge Guide, Right	**36**	Forearm Band Pin	**57**	Front Sight Assembly
16	Cartridge Guide Pin	**37**	Friction Stud	**58**	Rear Sight
17	Cartridge Guide Screw	**38**	Friction Stud Spring	**59**	Rear Sight Elevator
18	Cartridge Stop	**39**	Friction Stud Stop Pin	**60**	Trigger
19	Cartridge Stop Spring	**40**	Hammer	**61**	Trigger Pin
20	Cocking Lever	**41**	Hammer Screw	**62**	Trigger Spring
21	Cocking Lever Pin	**42**	Loading Gate Cover	**63**	Trigger Spring Screw

B-SS Side-by-Side Shotgun

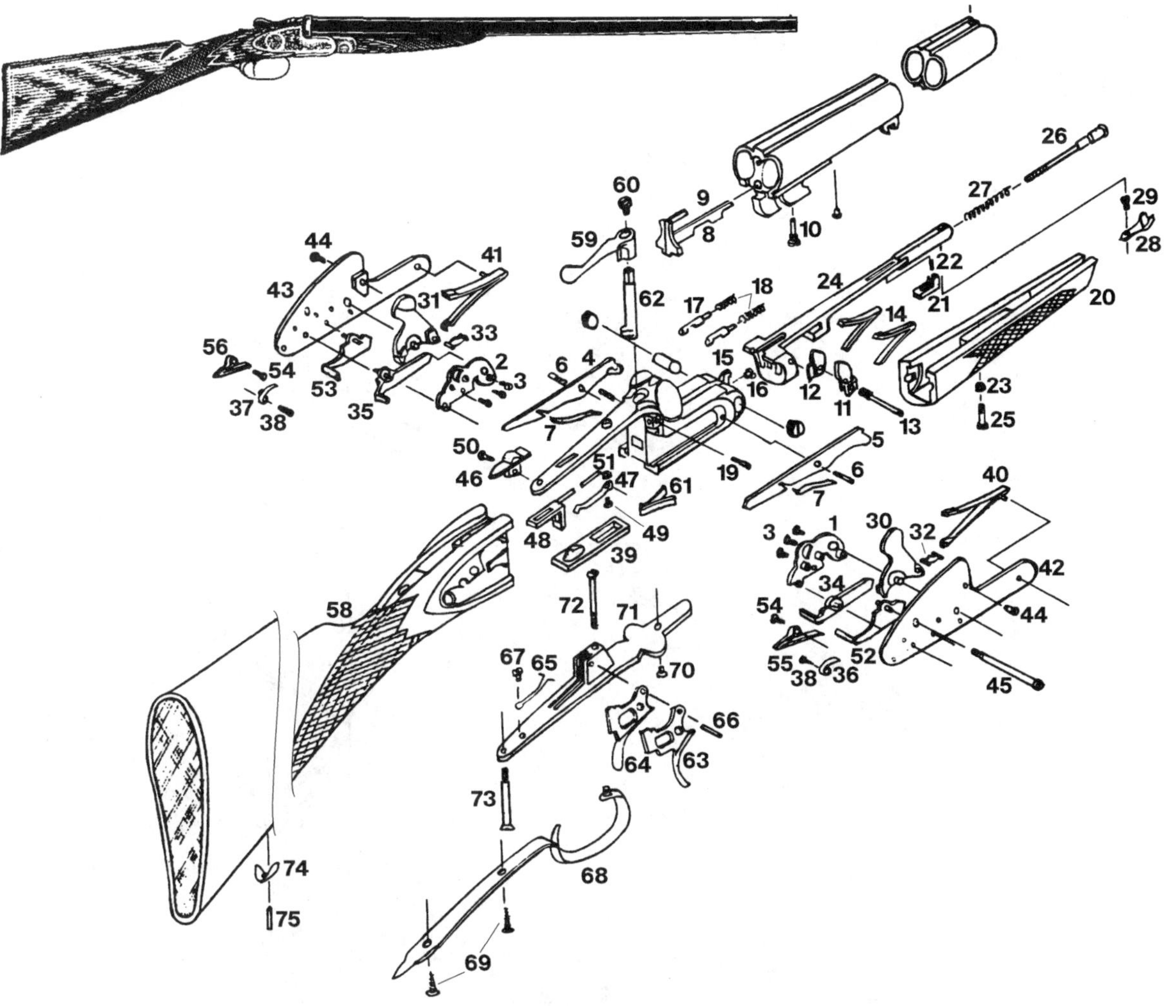

1	Bridle, Right	**26**	Forearm Push Down Rod	**51**	Safety Washer
2	Bridle, Left	**27**	Forearm Push Down Spring	**52**	Sear, Right
3	Bridle Screws	**28**	Forearm Tip	**53**	Sear, Left
4	Cocking Lever, Left	**29**	Forearm Tip Screw	**54**	Sear Spring Screw
5	Cocking Lever, Right	**30**	Hammer, Right	**55**	Sear Spring, Right
6	Cocking Lever Screws	**31**	Hammer, Left	**56**	Sear Spring, Left
7	Cocking Lever Springs	**32**	Hammer/Mainspring Connector, Right	**57**	Front Sight
8	Ejector, Right	**33**	Hammer/Mainspring Connector, Left	**58**	Stock
9	Ejector, Left	**34**	Intercepting Safety, Right	**59**	Top Lever
10	Ejector Stop Screw	**35**	Intercepting Safety, Left	**60**	Top Lever Screw
11	Ejector Hammer, Right	**36**	Intercepting Safety Spring, Right	**61**	Top Lever Spring
12	Ejector Hammer, Left	**37**	Intercepting Safety Spring, Left	**62**	Top Lever Dog Shaft
13	Ejector Hammer Pin	**38**	Intercepting Safety Spring Screws	**63**	Trigger, Right
14	Ejector Hammer Springs	**39**	Locking Bolt	**64**	Trigger, Left
15	Ejector Trip	**40**	Mainspring, Right	**65**	Trigger Spring
16	Ejector Trip Screw	**41**	Mainspring, Left	**66**	Trigger Pin
17	Firing Pins	**42**	Sideplate, Right	**67**	Trigger Spring Screw
18	Firing Pin Springs	**43**	Sideplate, Left	**68**	Trigger Guard
19	Firing Pin Screw	**44**	Sideplate Screws, Short	**69**	Trigger Guard Screws
20	Forearm	**45**	Sideplate Screw, Long	**70**	Trigger Plate Screw, Front
21	Forearm Catch	**46**	Safety	**71**	Trigger Plate
22	Forearm Catch Screw	**47**	Safety Spring	**72**	Trigger Plate Screw, Center
23	Forearm Escutcheon	**48**	Safety-Lever	**73**	Trigger Plate Screw, Rear
24	Forearm Bracket	**49**	Safety Spring Screw	**74**	Initial Plate
25	Forearm Bracket Screw	**50**	Safety-Lever Screw	**75**	Initial Plate Pin

BT-99 Single Shot Shotgun

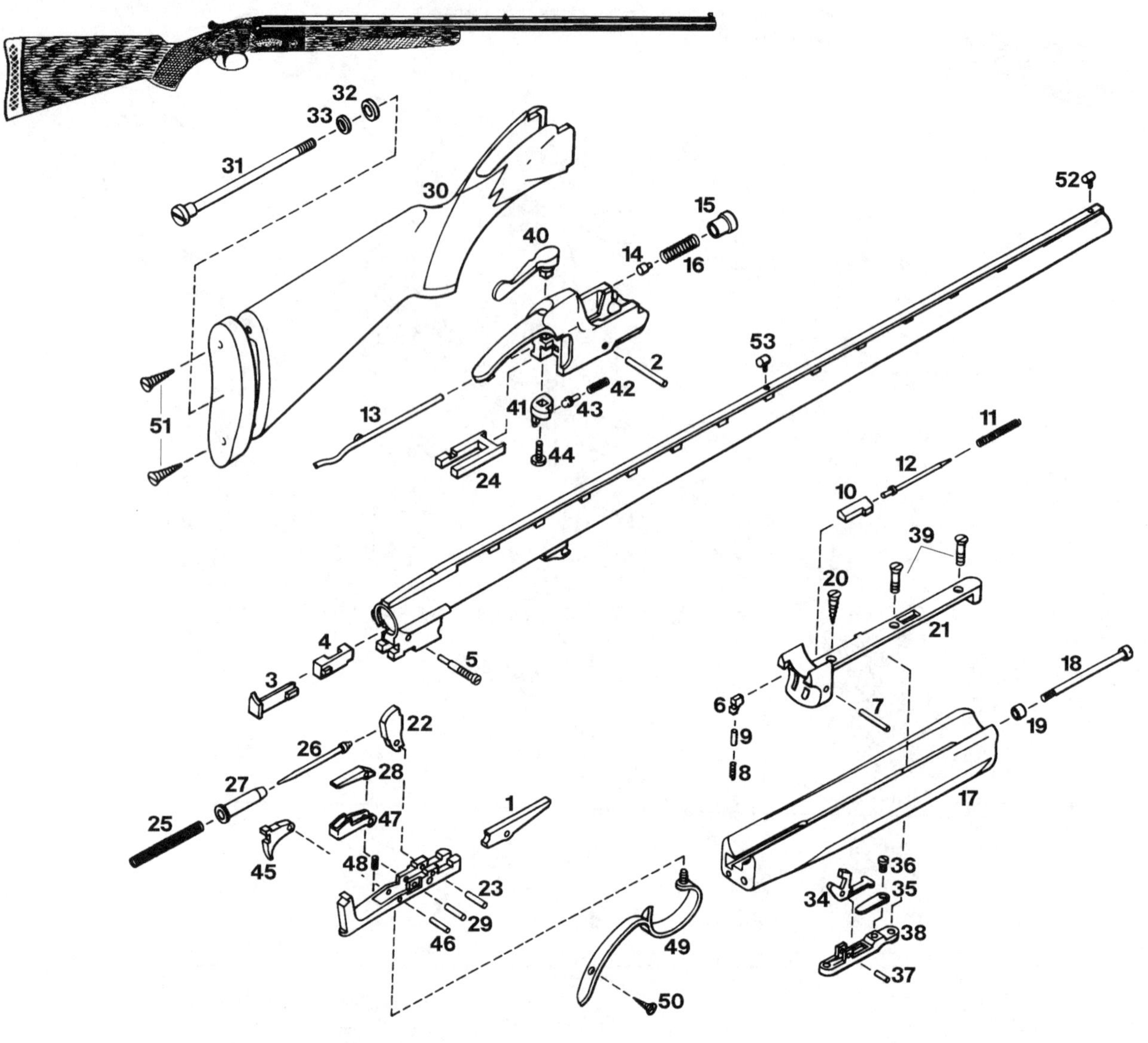

1	Cocking Lever
2	Cocking Lever Pin
3	Ejector
4	Ejector Extension
5	Ejector Stop Screw
6	Ejector Sear
7	Ejector Sear Pin
8	Ejector Sear Spring
9	Ejector Sear Spring Follower
10	Ejector Hammer
11	Ejector Hammer Spring
12	Ejector Hammer Spring Guide
13	Ejector Trip Rod
14	Firing Pin
15	Firing Pin Bushing
16	Firing Pin Spring
17	Forearm
18	Forearm Bolt
19	Forearm Bolt Escutcheon
20	Forearm Screw
21	Forearm Bracket
22	Hammer
23	Hammer Pin
24	Locking Bolt
25	Mainspring
26	Mainspring Guide
27	Mainspring Sleeve
28	Sear
29	Sear Pin
30	Stock Trap with Buttpad
31	Stock Bolt
32	Stock Bolt Washer
33	Stock Bolt Lock Washer
34	Takedown Lever
35	Takedown Lever Spring
36	Takedown Lever Spring Screw
37	Takedown Lever Pin
38	Takedown Lever Bracket
39	Takedown Lever Bracket Screws
40	Top Lever
41	Top Lever Dog
42	Top Lever Dog Spring
43	Top Lever Dog Spring Guide
44	Top Lever Screw
45	Trigger
46	Trigger Pin
47	Trigger Safety
48	Trigger Spring
49	Trigger Guard
50	Trigger Guard Screw
51	Buttpad Screws
52	Front Sight
53	Middle Sight

Parts Not Shown

Sear Spring

Tang Piece

Citori Original Over/Under Shotgun

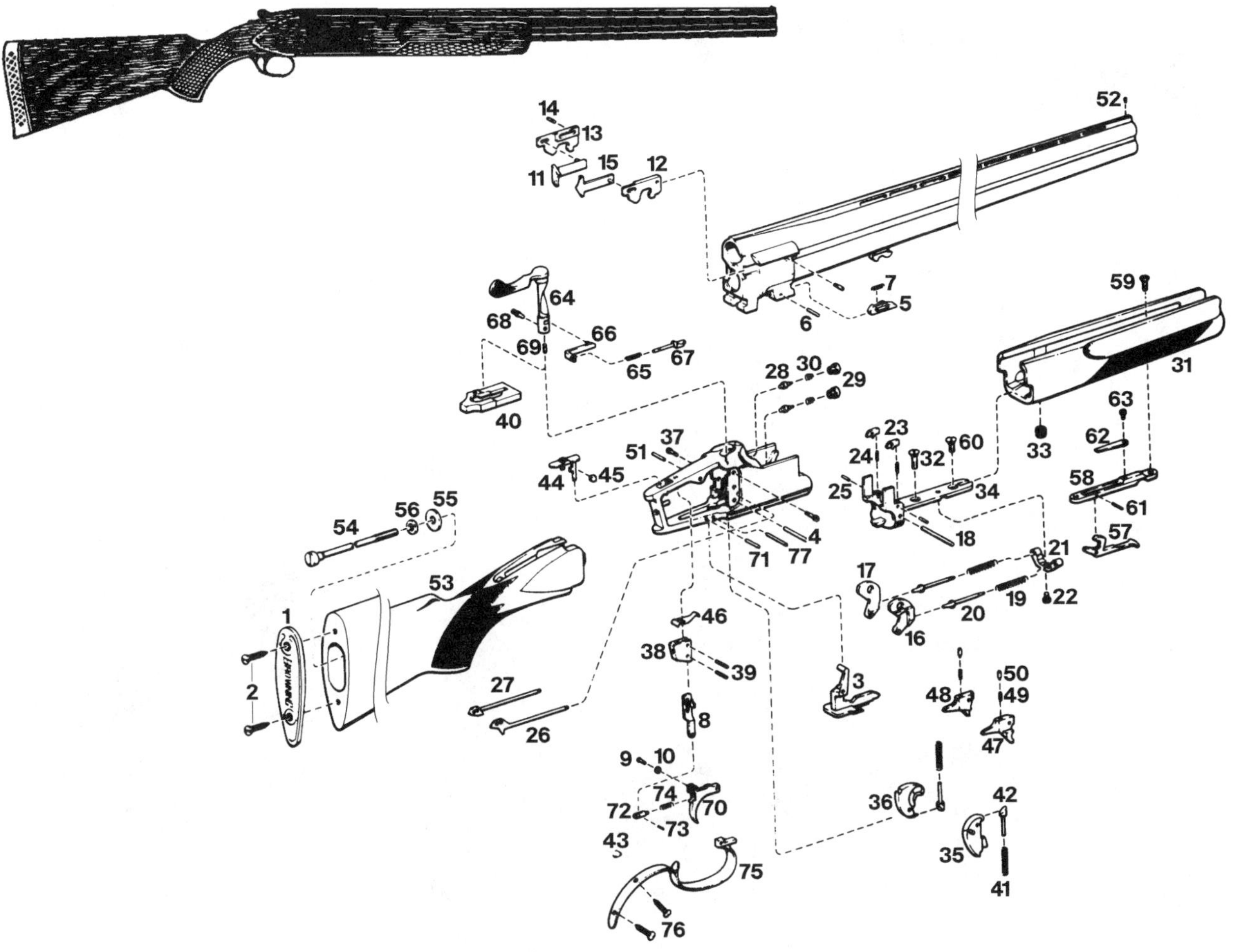

1	Buttplate	**26**	Ejector Trip Rod, Right	**52**	Front Sight Bead
2	Buttplate Screws	**27**	Ejector Trip Rod, Left	**53**	Stock
3	Cocking Lever	**28**	Firing Pins	**54**	Stock Bolt
4	Cocking Lever Pin	**29**	Firing Pin Bushings	**55**	Stock Bolt Washer
5	Cocking Lever Lifter	**30**	Firing Pin Springs	**56**	Stock Bolt Lock Washer
6	Cocking Lever Lifter Pin	**31**	Forearm	**57**	Takedown Lever
7	Cocking Lever Lifter Spring	**32**	Forearm Screw	**58**	Takedown Lever Bracket
8	Connector	**33**	Forearm Screw Escutcheon	**59**	Takedown Lever Bracket Screw, Front
9	Connector Pin	**34**	Forearm Bracket	**60**	Takedown Lever Bracket Screw, Rear
10	Connector Pin Retaining Ring	**35**	Hammer, Right	**61**	Takedown Lever Pin
11	Ejector	**36**	Hammer, Left	**62**	Takedown Lever Spring
12	Ejector Extension, Right	**37**	Hammer Pins	**63**	Takedown Lever Spring Screw
13	Ejector Extension, Left	**38**	Inertia Block	**64**	Top Lever
14	Ejector Extension Screw	**39**	Inertia Block Pins	**65**	Top Lever Spring
15	Ejector Retaining Pin	**40**	Locking Bolt	**66**	Top Lever Spring Retainer
16	Ejector Hammer, Right	**41**	Mainsprings	**67**	Top Lever Spring Plunger
17	Ejector Hammer, Left	**42**	Mainspring Plungers	**68**	Top Lever Dog
18	Ejector Hammer Pin	**43**	Mainspring Receiver	**69**	Top Lever Dog Screw
19	Ejector Hammer Springs	**44**	Selector Safety	**70**	Trigger
20	Ejector Hammer Spring Plungers	**45**	Selector Block	**71**	Trigger Pin
21	Ejector Hammer Spring Receiver	**46**	Selector Spring	**72**	Trigger Piston
22	Ejector Hammer Spring Receiver Screw	**47**	Sear, Right	**73**	Trigger Piston Pin
		48	Sear, Left	**74**	Trigger Piston Spring
23	Ejector Sears	**49**	Sear Springs	**75**	Trigger Guard
24	Ejector Sear Springs	**50**	Sear Spring Plungers	**76**	Trigger Guard Screws
25	Ejector Sear Pins	**51**	Sear Pin	**77**	Trigger Guard Pin

Citori Types 1, 2 and 3 Over/Under Shotgun

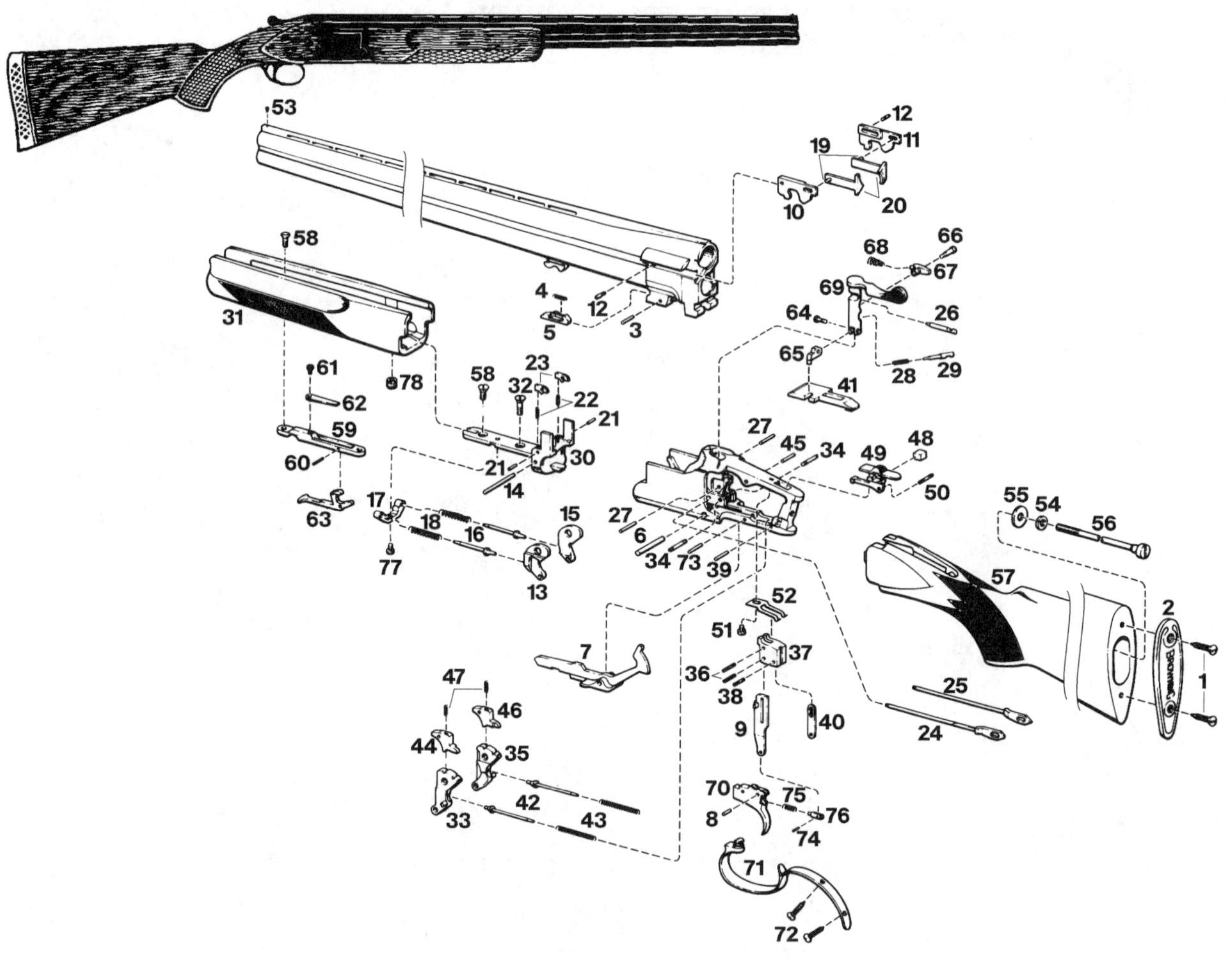

1	Buttplate Screws	**28**	Firing Pin Spring	**55**	Stock Bolt Washer
2	Buttplate	**29**	Firing Pin, Under	**56**	Stock Bolt
3	Cocking Lever Lifter Pin	**30**	Forearm Bracket	**57**	Stock
4	Cocking Lever Lifter Spring	**31**	Forearm	**58**	Takedown Lever Bracket Screw
5	Cocking Lever Lifter	**32**	Forearm Screw	**59**	Takedown Lever Bracket
6	Cocking Lever Pin	**33**	Hammer, Left	**60**	Takedown Lever Pin
7	Cocking Lever	**34**	Hammer Pin	**61**	Takedown Lever Spring Screw
8	Connector Stop Pin	**35**	Hammer, Right	**62**	Takedown Lever Spring
9	Connector	**36**	Inertia Block Pins	**63**	Takedown Lever
10	Ejector Extension, Left	**37**	Inertia Block	**64**	Top Lever Dog Screw
11	Ejector Extension, Right	**38**	Inertia Block Link Pin	**65**	Top Lever Dog
12	Ejector Extension Screws	**39**	Receiver Link Pin	**66**	Top Lever Spring Retainer Screw
13	Ejector Hammer, Left	**40**	Link	**67**	Top Lever Spring Retainer
14	Ejector Hammer Pin	**41**	Locking Bolt	**68**	Top Lever Spring
15	Ejector Hammer, Right	**42**	Mainspring Guides	**69**	Top Lever
16	Ejector Hammer Spring Plungers	**43**	Mainsprings	**70**	Trigger
17	Ejector Hammer Spring Receiver	**44**	Sear, Left	**71**	Trigger Guard
18	Ejector Hammer Springs	**45**	Sear Pin	**72**	Trigger Guard Screws
19	Ejector Retaining Pins	**46**	Sear, Right	**73**	Trigger Pin
20	Ejectors	**47**	Sear Springs	**74**	Trigger Piston Pin
21	Ejector Sear Pins	**48**	Selector Block	**75**	Trigger Piston Spring
22	Ejector Sear Springs	**49**	Selector Safety	**76**	Trigger Piston
23	Ejector Sears	**50**	Selector Spring Detent Pin	**77**	Ejector Hammer Spring Receiver Screw
24	Ejector Trip Rod, Left	**51**	Selector Spring Screw	**78**	Forearm Screw Nut
25	Ejector Trip Rod, Right	**52**	Selector Spring		
26	Firing Pin, Over	**53**	Sight Bead Front		
27	Firing Pin Retaining Pins	**54**	Stock Bolt Lock Washer		

Double Automatic Shotgun

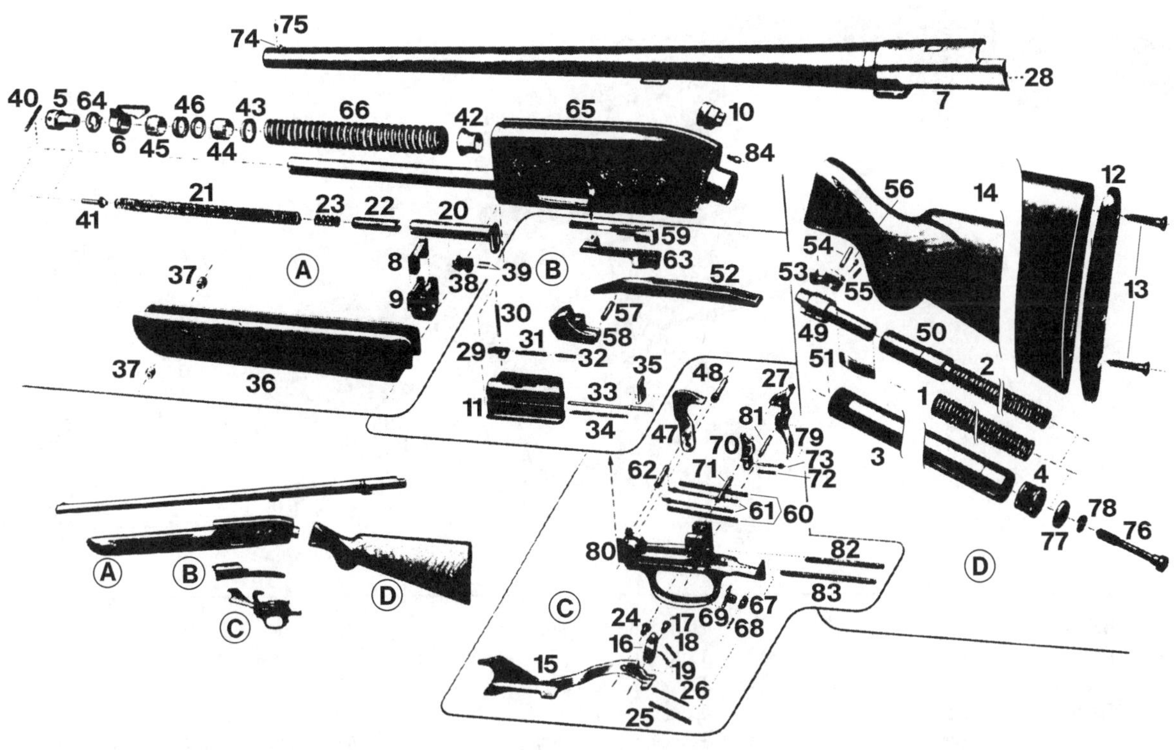

1	Action Spring, Inside
2	Action Spring, Outside
3	Action Spring Tube
4	Action Spring Tube Cap
5	Adjusting Cap
6	Barrel Guide
7	Barrel Extension
8	Barrel Lock
9	Barrel Lock Guide
10	Breechblock Buffer
11	Breechblock
12	Buttplate
13	Buttplate Screws
14	Buttstock
15	Carrier
16	Carrier Dog
17	Carrier Dog Pin
18	Carrier Dog Spring
19	Carrier Dog Spring Guide
20	Carrier Latch
21	Carrier Latch Spring
22	Carrier Latch Stabilizer
23	Carrier Latch Stabilizer Spring
24	Carrier Pin
25	Carrier Spring
26	Carrier Spring Guide
27	Disconnector
28	Ejector
29	Extractor
30	Extractor Pin
31	Extractor Spring
32	Extractor Spring Guide
33	Firing Pin
34	Firing Pin Spring
35	Firing Pin Stop Plate
36	Forend
37	Forend Escutcheons
38	Forend Latch
39	Forend Latch Springs
40	Forend Pivot Pin
41	Forend Pivot Pin Stop
42	Friction Brake Bronze, Buffer
43	Friction Brake Ring
44	Friction Brake Bronze, Rear
45	Friction Brake Bronze, Front
46	Friction Brake Washers
47	Hammer
48	Hammer Pin
49	Inertia Block Core
50	Inertia Block
51	Inertia Block Core Spring
52	Link
53	Link Hook
54	Link Hook Pin
55	Link Hook Spring
56	Link Hook Spring Plunger
57	Link Pin
58	Locking Block
59	Locking Block Latch
60	Mainsprings
61	Mainspring Guides
62	Mainspring Yoke
63	Operating Handle
64	Orienting Ring
65	Receiver
66	Recoil Spring
67	Safety Finger Piece
68	Safety Retaining Pin
69	Safety Spring Assembly
70	Sear
71	Sear Pivot
72	Sear Spring
73	Sear Spring Guide
74	Sight Base
75	Sight Bead
76	Stock Bolt
77	Stock Bolt Washer
78	Stock Bolt Lock Washer
79	Trigger
80	Trigger Guard
81	Trigger Pin
82	Trigger Guard Fastening Guide, Right
83	Trigger Guard Fastening Guide, Left
84	Sleeve/Buttstock Bolt

Parts Not Shown

- Carrier Latch Guide Pin
- Disconnector Pin
- Disconnector Spring
- Disconnector Spring Plunger
- Locking Block Latch Rivet
- Recoil Spring Tube
- Recoil Spring Tube Pin

FAL Standard Autoloading Rifle

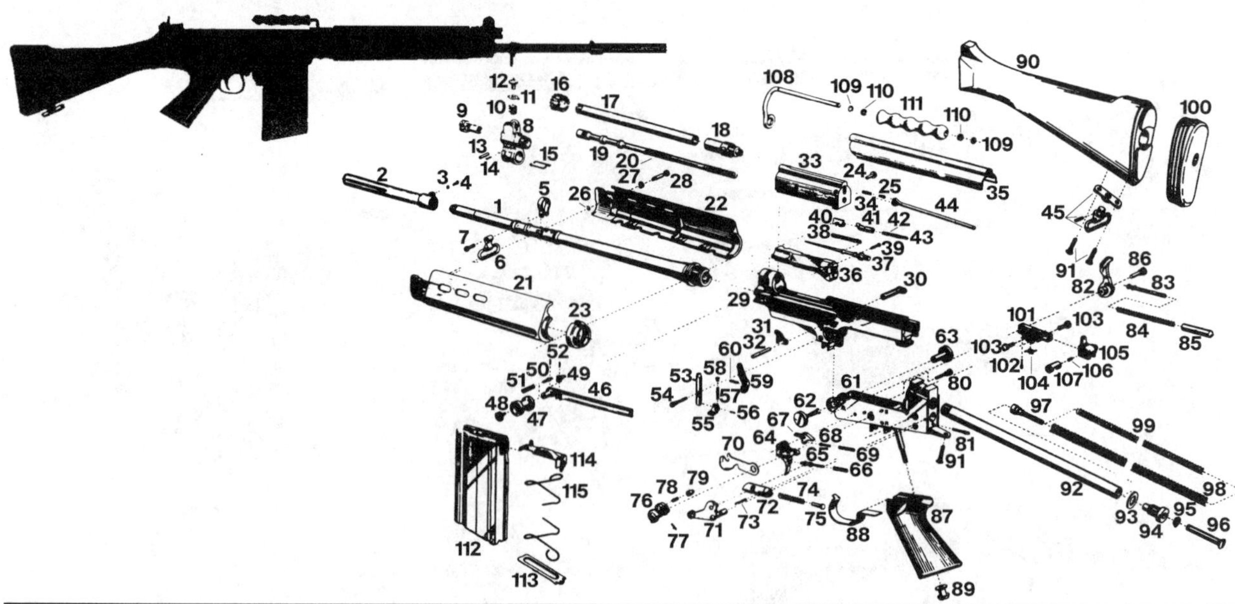

1	Barrel Body	**39**	Firing Pin Retaining Pin	**77**	Pin
2	Flash Hider	**40**	Extractor	**78**	Lever Spring
3	Washer	**41**	Extractor Plunger	**79**	Plunger
4	Flash Hider Retaining Screw	**42**	Extractor Spring	**80**	Trigger and Sear Axis Pin
5	Band, Front Sling Swivel	**43**	Extractor Spring Buffer	**81**	Locking Catch Lever Retaining Screw
6	Front Sling Swivel	**44**	Slide Rod	**82**	Hammer
7	Front Sling Swivel Retaining Screw	**45**	Rear Sling Swivel Assembly	**83**	Hammer Spring Rod
8	Gas Block	**46**	Cocking Handle Body	**84**	Hammer Spring
9	Gas Cylinder Plug	**47**	Cocking Handle Lug	**85**	Hammer Spring Housing
10	Foresight Retaining Spring	**48**	Cocking Handle Stud	**86**	Hammer Pin
11	Foresight Plate	**49**	Lug	**87**	Pistol Grip
12	Foresight	**50**	Cocking Handle Detent	**88**	Trigger Guard
13	Gas Block Retaining Pin	**51**	Cocking Handle Detent Spring	**89**	Pistol Grip Retaining Nut
14	Retaining Pin	**52**	Lug and Cocking Handle Detent Retaining Pins	**90**	Buttstock Body
15	Gas Regulator Sleeve Spring			**91**	Rear Sling Swivel Screws
16	Gas Regulator Sleeve	**53**	Hold-Open Device Assembly	**92**	Return Spring Tube
17	Gas Cylinder	**54**	Magazine Catch Axis Pin	**93**	Butt Screw Washer
18	Gas Cylinder Bush	**55**	Thumb-Piece	**94**	Butt Retaining Screw
19	Piston	**56**	Thumb-Piece Retaining Rivet	**95**	Buttplate Screw Washer
20	Piston Spring	**57**	Spring	**96**	Buttplate Screw
21	Hand Guard, Left	**58**	Spring Plunger	**97**	Return Spring Plunger
22	Hand Guard, Right	**59**	Magazine Catch	**98**	Outer Return Spring
23	Hand Guard Rear Socket	**60**	Magazine Catch Spring	**99**	Inner Return Spring
24	Slide Rod Pin	**61**	Trigger Mechanism Assembly	**100**	Rubber Plate Screw
25	Slide Rod Plunger	**62**	Pivot Butt Retaining Pin	**101**	Rear Sight Support
26	Securing Ring, Hand Guard Retaining Screw	**63**	Pivot Butt	**102**	Retaining Pin for Rear Sight
		64	Trigger	**103**	Rear Sight Support Adjusting Screws
27	Grower Washer for Hand Guard Retaining Screw	**65**	Trigger Plunger	**104**	Rear Sight Support Adjusting Screw Spring
		66	Trigger Spring		
28	Hand Guard Retaining Screw	**67**	Sear	**105**	Rear Sight Cursor
29	Receiver Body	**68**	Sear Spring Plunger	**106**	Rear Sight Catch Spring
30	Breechblock Support	**69**	Sear Spring	**107**	Rear Sight Catch
31	Ejector	**70**	Locating Plate for Hammer and Trigger Axis Pin	**108**	Carrying Handle Axis
32	Ejector Pin			**109**	Washer Springs
33	Slide Body	**71**	Locking Latch Lever Assembly	**110**	Carrying Handle Washers
34	Slide Rod Spring	**72**	Locking Catch Body	**111**	Carrying Handle Body
35	Slide Rod Spring Plunger	**73**	Locking Latch Pin	**112**	Magazine Body
36	Breechblock	**74**	Spring	**113**	Bottom Plate
37	Firing Pin	**75**	Spring Plunger	**114**	Platform
38	Firing Pin Spring	**76**	Axis and Arm Assembly	**115**	Platform Spring

High-Power Bolt-Action Rifle

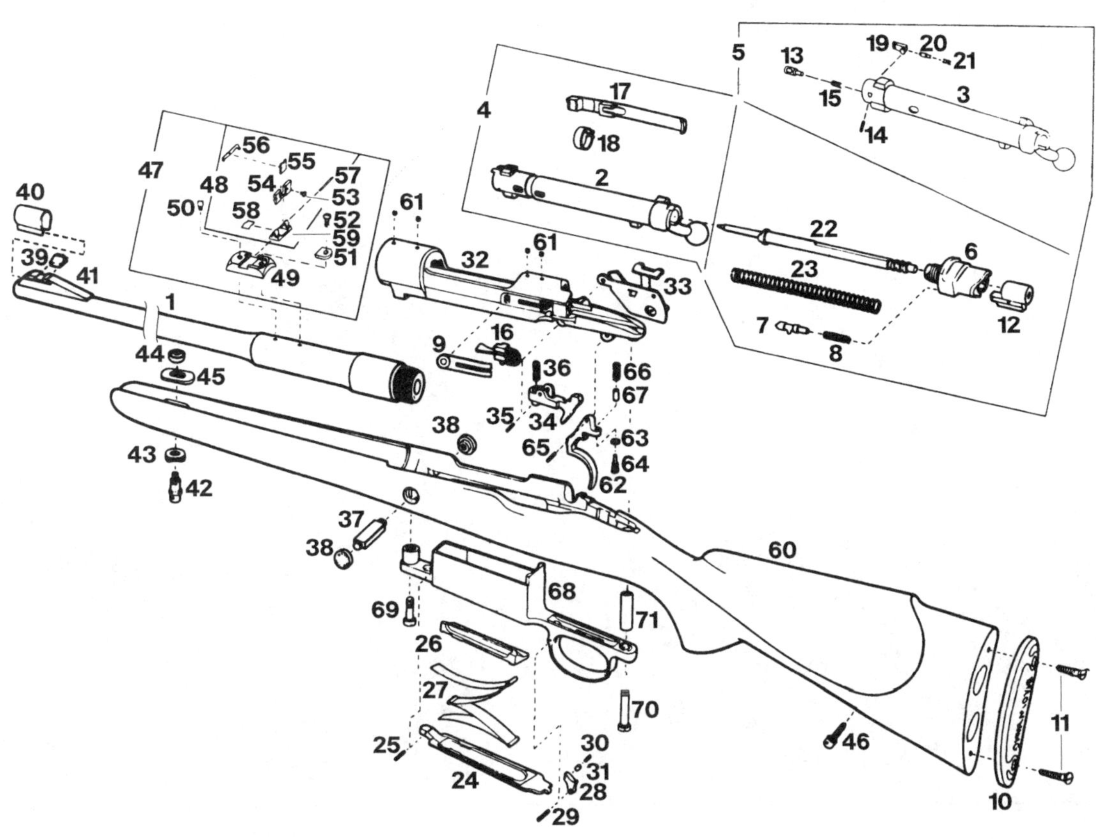

1	Barrel
2	Bolt, Regular
3	Bolt, Magnum
4	Bolt Assembly, Regular
5	Bolt Assembly, Magnum
6	Bolt Sleeve
7	Bolt Sleeve Lock Plunger
8	Bolt Sleeve Lock Plunger Spring
9	Bolt Stop Spring Assembly
10	Buttplate
11	Buttplate Screws
12	Cocking Piece
13	Ejector, Magnum
14	Ejector Pin, Magnum
15	Ejector Spring, Magnum
16	Ejector and Bolt Stop Assembly
17	Extractor
18	Extractor Collar
19	Extractor, Magnum
20	Extractor Plunger, Magnum
21	Extractor Spring, Magnum
22	Firing Pin
23	Firing Pin Spring
24	Magazine Floorplate
25	Magazine Floorplate Pin
26	Magazine Follower
27	Magazine Spring
28	Magazine Floorplate Latch
29	Magazine Floorplate Latch Pin
30	Magazine Floorplate Latch Spring
31	Magazine Floorplate Latch Spring Follower
32	Receiver
33	Safety Assembly
34	Sear
35	Sear Pin
36	Sear Spring
37	Recoil Lug
38	Recoil Lug Screw
39	Sight Bead, Front
40	Sight Hood, Front
41	Sight Ramp, Front
42	Sling Eyelet, Front
43	Sling Eyelet Base Washer, Front
44	Sling Eyelet Base Nut, Front
45	Sling Eyelet Base Plate, Front
46	Sling Eyelet, Rear
47	Sight Assembly
48	Folding Leaf Assembly
49	Sight Base
50	Sight Base Screw, Front
51	Windage Adjustment Plate
52	Sight Base and Windage Adjustment Plate Lock Screw
53	Sight Aperture - Elevation Lock Screw
54	Folding Leaf
55	Sight Elevation Plate
56	Sight Elevation Ratchet
57	Folding Leaf Pin
58	Windage Adjustable Plate
59	Folding Leaf Base
60	Stock
61	Telescopic Mount and Rear Sight Base Filler Screws
62	Trigger
63	Trigger Backlash Adjustment Nut
64	Trigger Backlash Adjustment Screw
65	Trigger Pin
66	Trigger Spring
67	Trigger Spring Guide
68	Trigger Guard
69	Trigger Guard Screw, Front
70	Trigger Guard Screw, Rear
71	Trigger Guard Screw Bushing, Rear

Liege Over/Under Shotgun

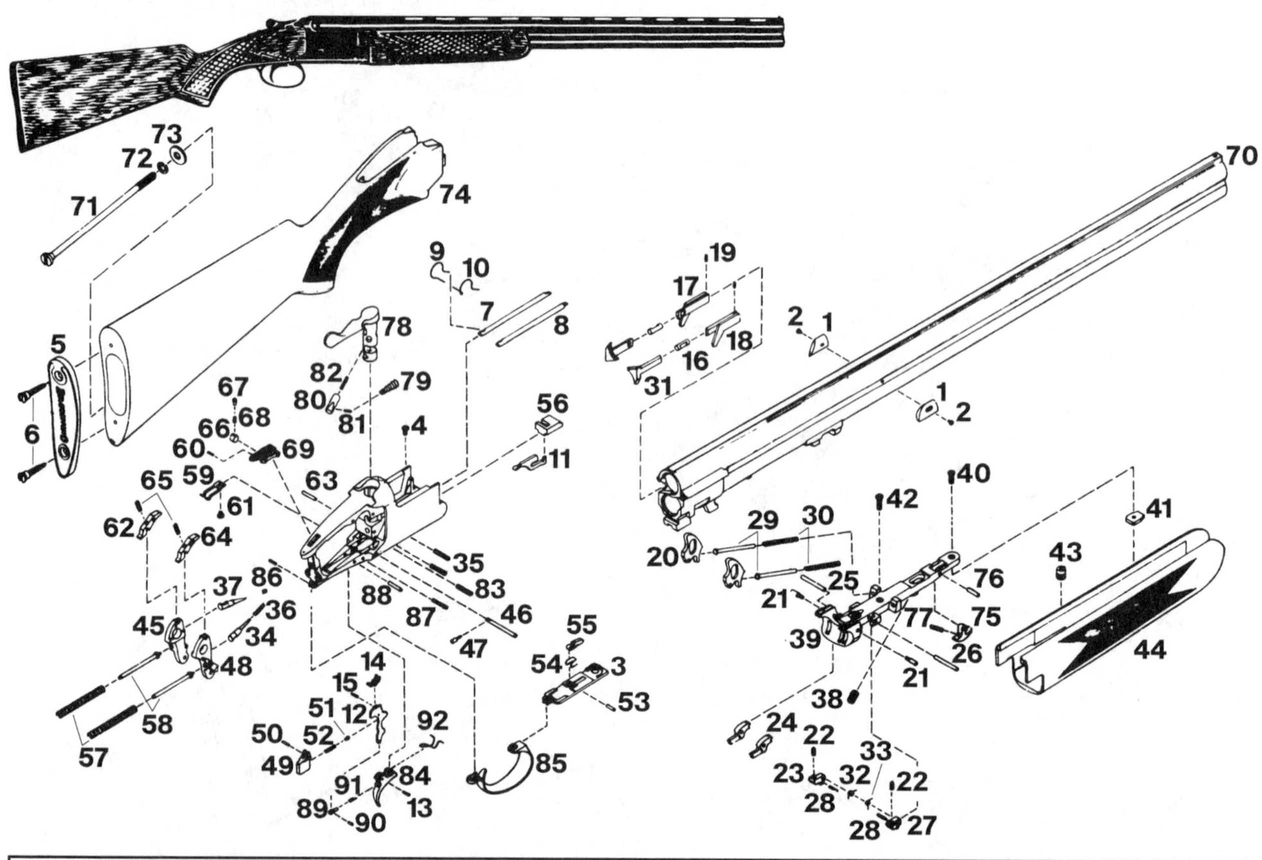

1	Barrel Sideplates	31	Ejectors	62	Sear, Left
2	Barrel Sideplate Screws	32	Ejector Sear Spring, Left	63	Sear Pin
3	Bottom Plate	33	Ejector Sear Spring, Right	64	Sear, Right
4	Bottom Plate Screw	34	Firing Pin, Lower	65	Sear Springs
5	Buttplate	35	Firing Pin Retaining Pins	66	Selector Block
6	Buttplate Screws	36	Firing Pin Spring	67	Selector Block Spring Guide
7	Cocking Rod, Left	37	Firing Pin, Upper	68	Selector Block Spring
8	Cocking Rod, Right	38	Forearm Bracket Adjusting Screw	69	Selector Safety
9	Cocking Rod Spring, Left	39	Forearm Bracket	70	Sight Bead, Front
10	Cocking Rod Spring, Right	40	Forearm Bracket Screw, Front	71	Stock Bolt
11	Connector Cam	41	Forearm Bracket Screw Plate	72	Stock Bolt Lock Washer
12	Connector	42	Forearm Bracket Screw, Rear	73	Stock Bolt Washer
13	Connector Pin	43	Forearm Insert Escutcheon	74	Stock
14	Connector Selector	44	Forearm	75	Takedown Latch
15	Connector Selector Pin	45	Hammer, Left	76	Takedown Latch Pin
16	Ejector Connectors	46	Hammer Pin	77	Takedown Latch Spring
17	Ejector Extension, Left	47	Hammer Pin Screw	78	Top Lever
18	Ejector Extension, Right	48	Hammer, Right	79	Top Lever Spring
19	Ejector Extension Stop Pins	49	Inertia Block	80	Top Lever Spring Retainer
20	Ejector Hammers	50	Inertia Block Pin	81	Top Lever Spring Retainer Pin
21	Ejector Hammer Pins	51	Inertia Block Spring Guide	82	Top Lever Spring Retainer Spring
22	Ejector Hammer Sear Adjusting Screws	52	Inertia Block Spring	83	Top Lever Stop Pin
		53	Lock Open Latch Pin	84	Trigger
23	Ejector Hammer Sear, Left	54	Lock Open Latch Spring	85	Trigger Guard
24	Ejector Hammer Sear Levers	55	Lock Open Latch	86	Trigger Guard Pin, Rear
25	Ejector Hammer Sear Lever Pin	56	Locking Bolt	87	Trigger Guard/Bottom Plate Pin
26	Ejector Hammer Sear Pin	57	Mainsprings	88	Trigger Pin
27	Ejector Hammer Sear, Right	58	Mainspring Guides	89	Trigger Piston
28	Ejector Hammer Sear Spring Pins	59	Safety Spring	90	Trigger Piston Pin
29	Ejector Hammer Spring Guides	60	Safety Spring Pin	91	Trigger Piston Spring
30	Ejector Hammer Springs	61	Safety Spring Screw	92	Trigger Spring

Model 12 Slide-Action Shotgun

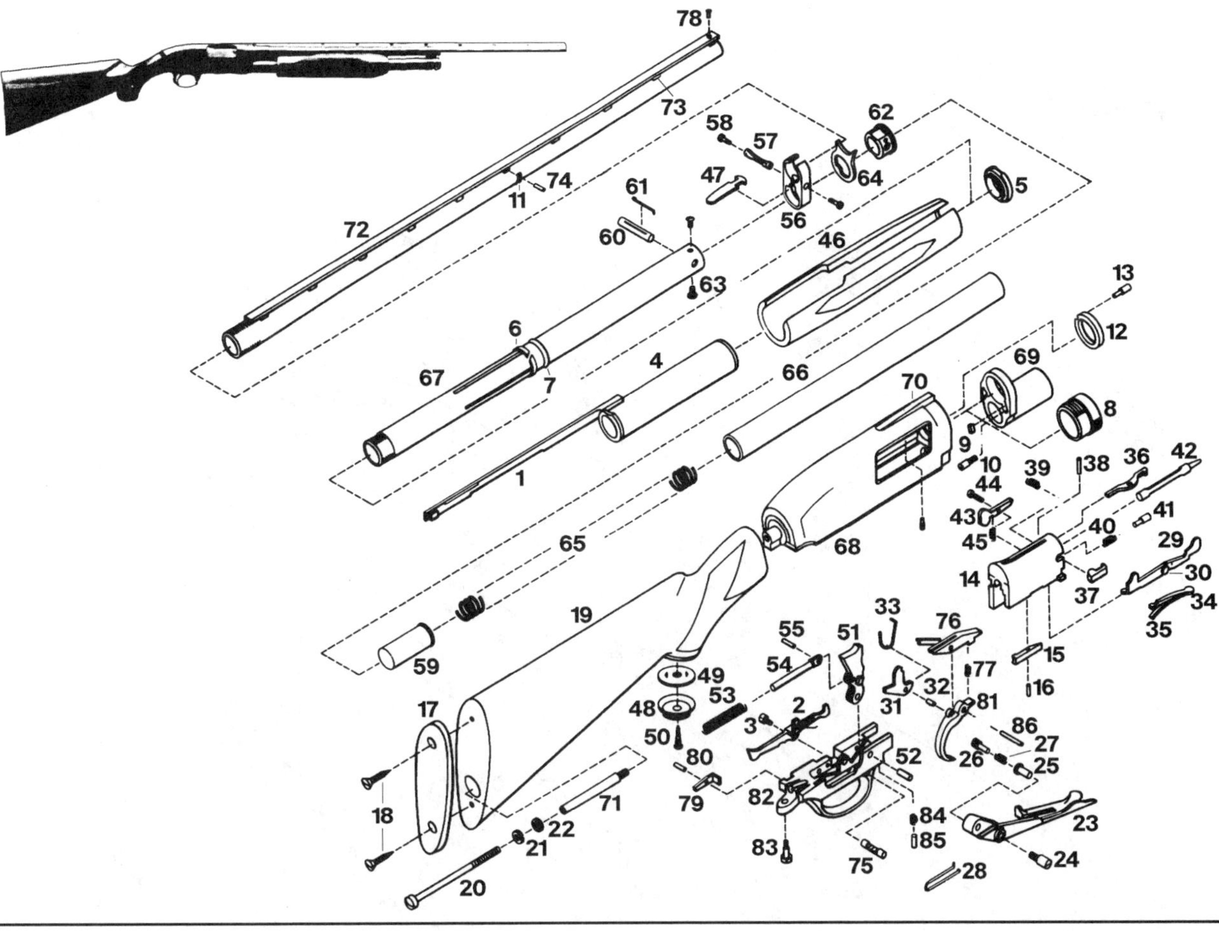

1 Action Slide Bar
2 Action Slide Lock
3 Action Slide Lock Pivot
4 Action Slide Sleeve
5 Action Slide Sleeve Screw Cap
6 Action Slide Spring
7 Action Slide Spring Stop Ring
8 Adjusting Sleeve
9 Adjusting Sleeve Lock
10 Adjusting Sleeve Lock Screw
11 Barrel Band
12 Barrel Chamber Ring
13 Barrel Chamber Ring Screw
14 Breechbolt
15 Breechbolt Retaining Lever
16 Breechbolt Retaining Lever Pin
17 Buttplate
18 Buttplate Screws
19 Buttstock
20 Buttstock Bolt
21 Buttstock Bolt Lock Washer
22 Buttstock Bolt Washer
23 Carrier
24 Carrier Pivot
25 Carrier Plunger
26 Carrier Plunger Screw
27 Carrier Plunger Spring
28 Carrier Spring
29 Cartridge Cutoff
30 Cartridge Cutoff Boss
31 Disconnector
32 Disconnector Pin
33 Disconnector Spring
34 Ejector
35 Ejector Spring
36 Extractor, Left
37 Extractor, Right
38 Extractor Pin
39 Extractor Spring, Left
40 Extractor Spring, Right
41 Extractor Spring Plunger, Right
42 Firing Pin
43 Firing Pin Retractor
44 Firing Pin Retractor Screw
45 Firing Pin Retractor Spring
46 Forearm
47 Forearm Retaining Spring
48 Grip Cap
49 Grip Cap Retainer
50 Grip Cap Screw
51 Hammer
52 Hammer Pin
53 Hammer Spring
54 Hammer Spring Guide
55 Hammer Spring Guide Pin
56 Magazine Band
57 Magazine Band Bushing
58 Magazine Band Bushing Screw
59 Magazine Follower
60 Magazine Locking Pin
61 Magazine Locking Pin Spring
62 Magazine Plug
63 Magazine Plug Screw
64 Magazine Plug Stop
65 Magazine Spring
66 Magazine Three-Shot Adapter
67 Magazine Tube
68 Receiver
69 Receiver Extension
70 Receiver Rib Ramp
71 Receiver Shank
72 Rib
73 Rib Post
74 Rib Retaining Pin
75 Safety
76 Sear
77 Sear Spring
78 Sight Bead, Front
79 Transfer Lever
80 Transfer Lever Pin
81 Trigger
82 Trigger Guard
83 Trigger Guard Screw
84 Trigger Lock Plunger
85 Trigger Lock Plunger Spring
86 Trigger Pin

Model 65 Lever-Action Rifle

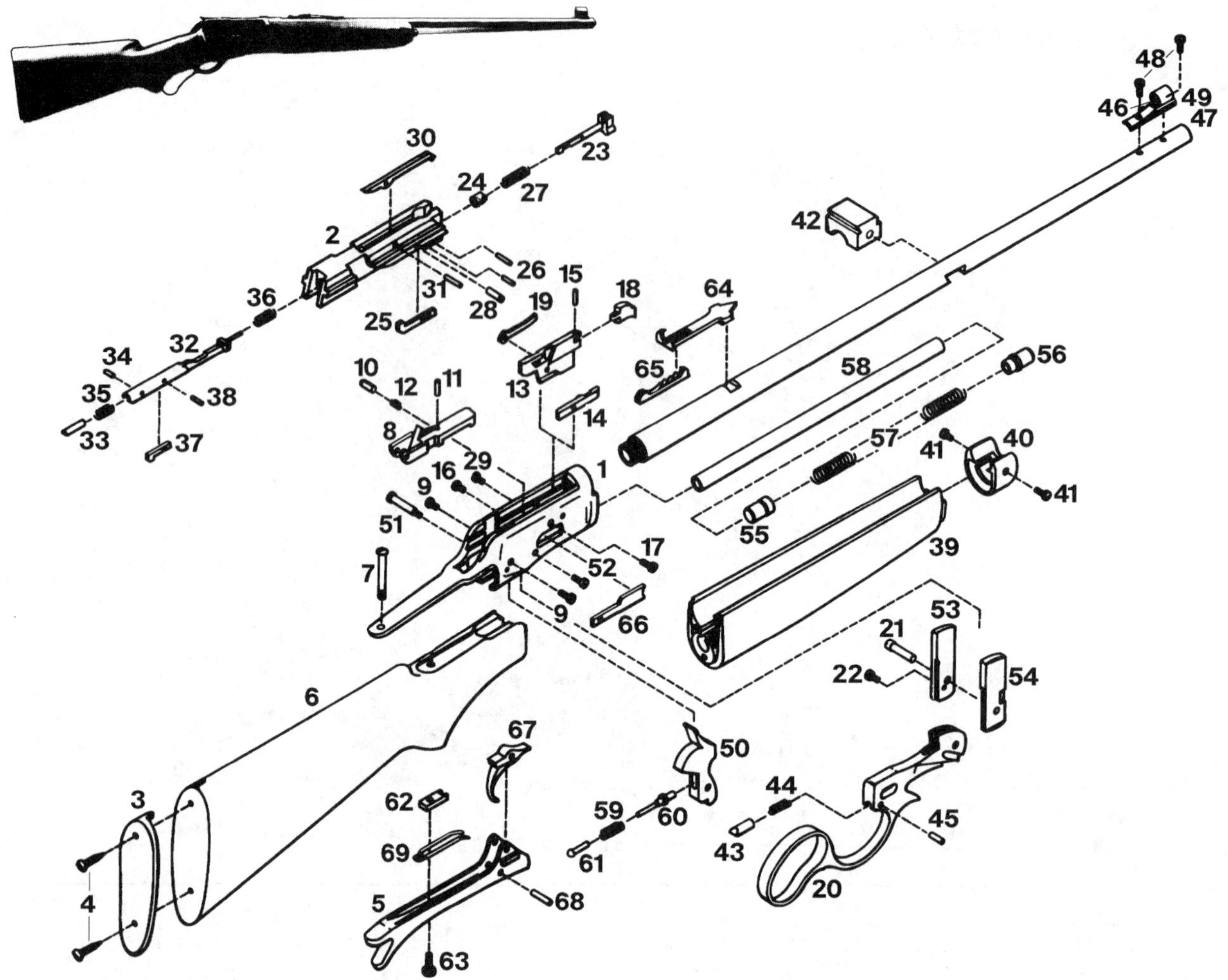

1	Barrel/Receiver	**24**	Ejector Collar	**47**	Front Sight Base
2	Breechbolt	**25**	Ejector Collar Stop	**48**	Front Sight Base Screws
3	Buttplate	**26**	Ejector Collar Stop Pins	**49**	Front Sight Hood
4	Buttplate Screws	**27**	Ejector Spring	**50**	Hammer
5	Buttstock Lower Tang	**28**	Ejector Stop Pin	**51**	Hammer Screw
6	Buttstock	**29**	Ejector Stop Pin Plug Screw	**52**	Loading Gate Cover Screw
7	Buttstock Tang Screw	**30**	Extractor	**53**	Locking Bolt, Left
8	Carrier	**31**	Extractor Pin	**54**	Locking Bolt, Right
9	Carrier Screws	**32**	Firing Pin	**55**	Magazine Follower
10	Carrier Striker	**33**	Firing Pin Inertia Slide	**56**	Magazine Muzzle Plug
11	Carrier Striker Pin	**34**	Firing Pin Inertia Slide Pin	**57**	Magazine Spring
12	Carrier Striker Spring	**35**	Firing Pin Inertia Slide Spring	**58**	Magazine Tube
13	Cartridge Guide, Left	**36**	Firing Pin Spring	**59**	Mainspring
14	Cartridge Guide, Right	**37**	Firing Pin Safety Lock	**60**	Mainspring Guide, Inner
15	Cartridge Guide Pin	**38**	Firing Pin Safety Lock Pin	**61**	Mainspring Guide, Outer
16	Cartridge Guide Screw	**39**	Forearm	**62**	Mainspring Guide Stud
17	Mainspring Guide Stud Screw	**40**	Forearm Tip	**63**	Mainspring Guide Stud Screw
18	Cartridge Stop	**41**	Forearm Tip Screws	**64**	Rear Sight
19	Cartridge Stop Spring	**42**	Forearm Tip Tenon	**65**	Rear Sight Elevator
20	Cocking Lever	**43**	Friction Stud	**66**	Receiver Spring Cover
21	Cocking Lever Pin	**44**	Friction Stud Spring	**67**	Trigger
22	Cocking Lever Stop Screw	**45**	Friction Stud Stop Pin	**68**	Trigger Pin
23	Ejector	**46**	Front Sight	**69**	Trigger Spring

Model 71 Lever-Action Rifle

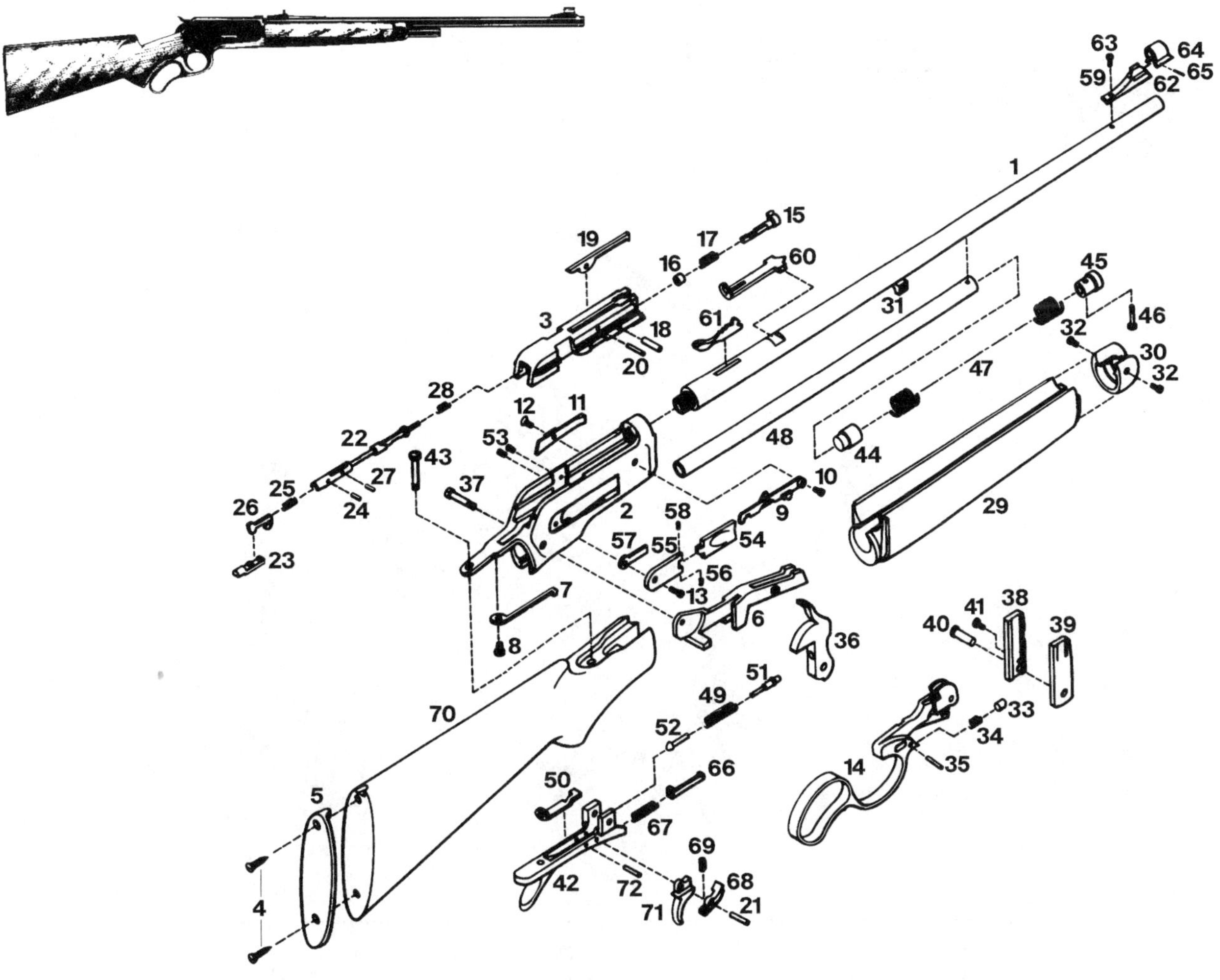

1	Barrel	**25**	Firing Pin Inertia Slide Spring	**49**	Mainspring
2	Receiver	**26**	Firing Pin Safety Lock	**50**	Mainspring Abutment
3	Breechbolt	**27**	Firing Pin Safety Lock Pin	**51**	Mainspring Guide, Inner
4	Buttplate Screws	**28**	Firing Pin Spring	**52**	Mainspring Guide, Outer
5	Buttplate	**29**	Forearm	**53**	Receiver Sight Filler Screws
6	Carrier	**30**	Forearm Tip	**54**	Receiver Spring Cover
7	Carrier Spring	**31**	Forearm Tip Tenon	**55**	Receiver Spring Cover Base
8	Carrier Spring Screw	**32**	Forearm Tip Screws	**56**	Receiver Spring Cover Pin
9	Cartridge Guide	**33**	Friction Stud	**57**	Receiver Spring Cover Spring
10	Cartridge Guide Screw	**34**	Friction Stud Spring	**58**	Receiver Spring Cover Stop Pin
11	Cartridge Guide Stop	**35**	Friction Stud Stop Pin	**59**	Front Sight
12	Cartridge Guide Stop Screw	**36**	Hammer	**60**	Rear Sight
13	Receiver Spring Cover Screw	**37**	Hammer Screw	**61**	Rear Sight Elevator
14	Cocking Lever	**38**	Locking Bolt, Left	**62**	Front Sight Base
15	Ejector	**39**	Locking Bolt, Right	**63**	Front Sight Base Screw
16	Ejector Collar	**40**	Locking Bolt Stop Pin	**64**	Front Sight Hood
17	Ejector Spring	**41**	Locking Bolt Stop Pin Stop Screw	**65**	Sight Hood Pin
18	Ejector Stop Pin	**42**	Lower Tang	**66**	Safety Slide
19	Extractor	**43**	Lower Tang Stock Screw	**67**	Safety Slide Spring
20	Extractor Pin	**44**	Magazine Follower	**68**	Sear
21	Mainspring Abutment Pin	**45**	Magazine Plug	**69**	Sear Spring
22	Firing Pin	**46**	Magazine Plug Screw	**70**	Stock
23	Firing Pin Inertia Slide	**47**	Magazine Spring	**71**	Trigger
24	Firing Pin Inertia Slide Pin	**48**	Magazine Tube	**72**	Trigger Pin

Model BL-22 Lever-Action Rifle

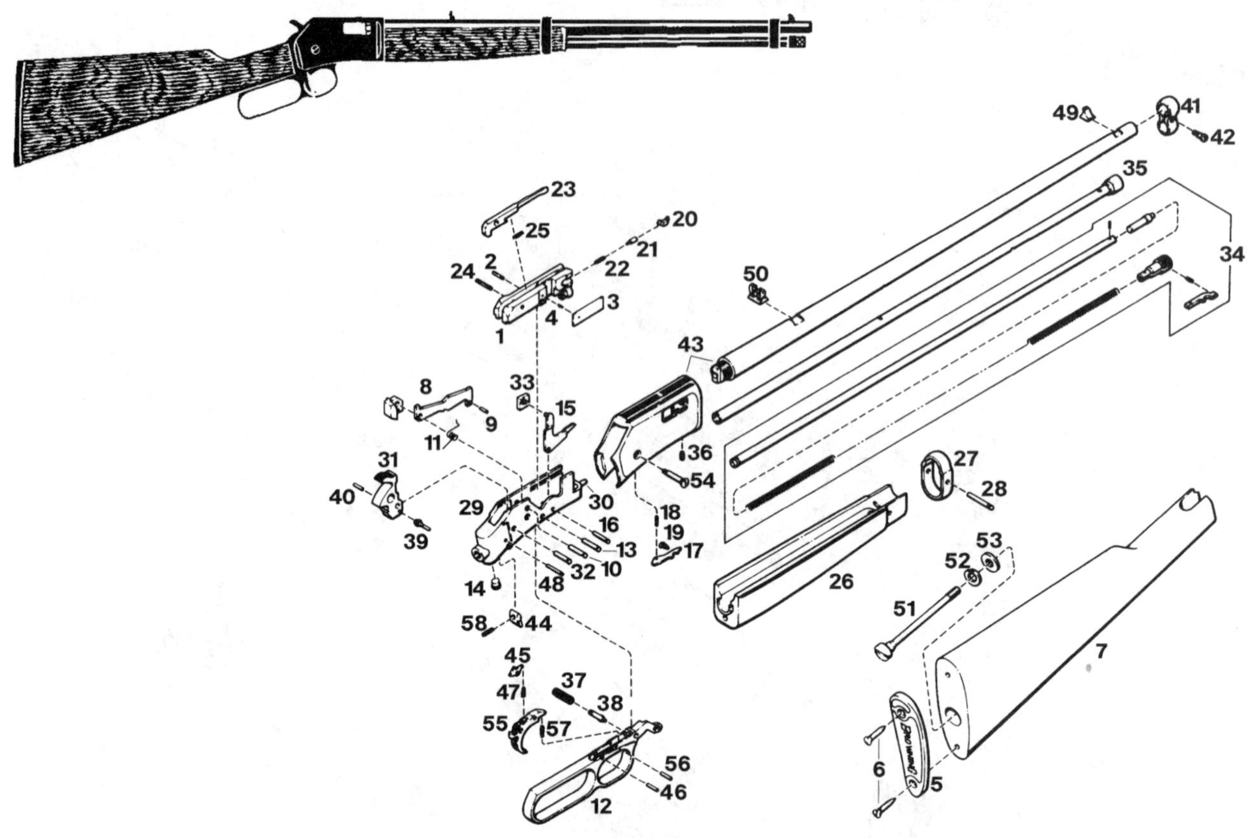

1	Bolt	30	Frame Insert Pin
2	Bolt Actuating Pin	31	Hammer
3	Bolt Cover Plate	32	Hammer Pin
4	Bolt Cover Pin	33	Locking Block
5	Buttplate	34	Magazine Assembly
6	Buttplate Screws	35	Outer Magazine Tube
7	Buttstock	36	Magazine Tube Retaining Screw
8	Carrier Assembly	37	Mainspring
9	Carrier Guide Pin	38	Mainspring Follower
10	Carrier Pin	39	Mainspring Guide
11	Carrier Spring	40	Mainspring Guide Pin
12	Cocking Lever	41	Muzzle Clamp
13	Cocking Lever Pin	42	Muzzle Clamp Screw
14	Cocking Lever Stop Screw	43	Receiver with Fitted Barrel
15	Cocking Lever Link	44	Sear
16	Cocking Lever Link Pin	45	Sear Link
17	Ejector	46	Sear Link Pin
18	Ejector Pin	47	Sear Link Spring
19	Ejector Spring	48	Sear Pin
20	Extractor	49	Front Sight
21	Extractor Plunger	50	Rear Sight Assembly
22	Extractor Spring	51	Stock Bolt
23	Firing Pin	52	Stock Bolt Lock Washer
24	Firing Pin Retaining Pin	53	Stock Bolt Washer
25	Firing Pin Spring	54	Takedown Screw
26	Forearm	55	Trigger
27	Forearm Band	56	Trigger Pin
28	Forearm Band Pin	57	Trigger Spring
29	Frame	58	Sear Spring

Percussion Mountain Rifle

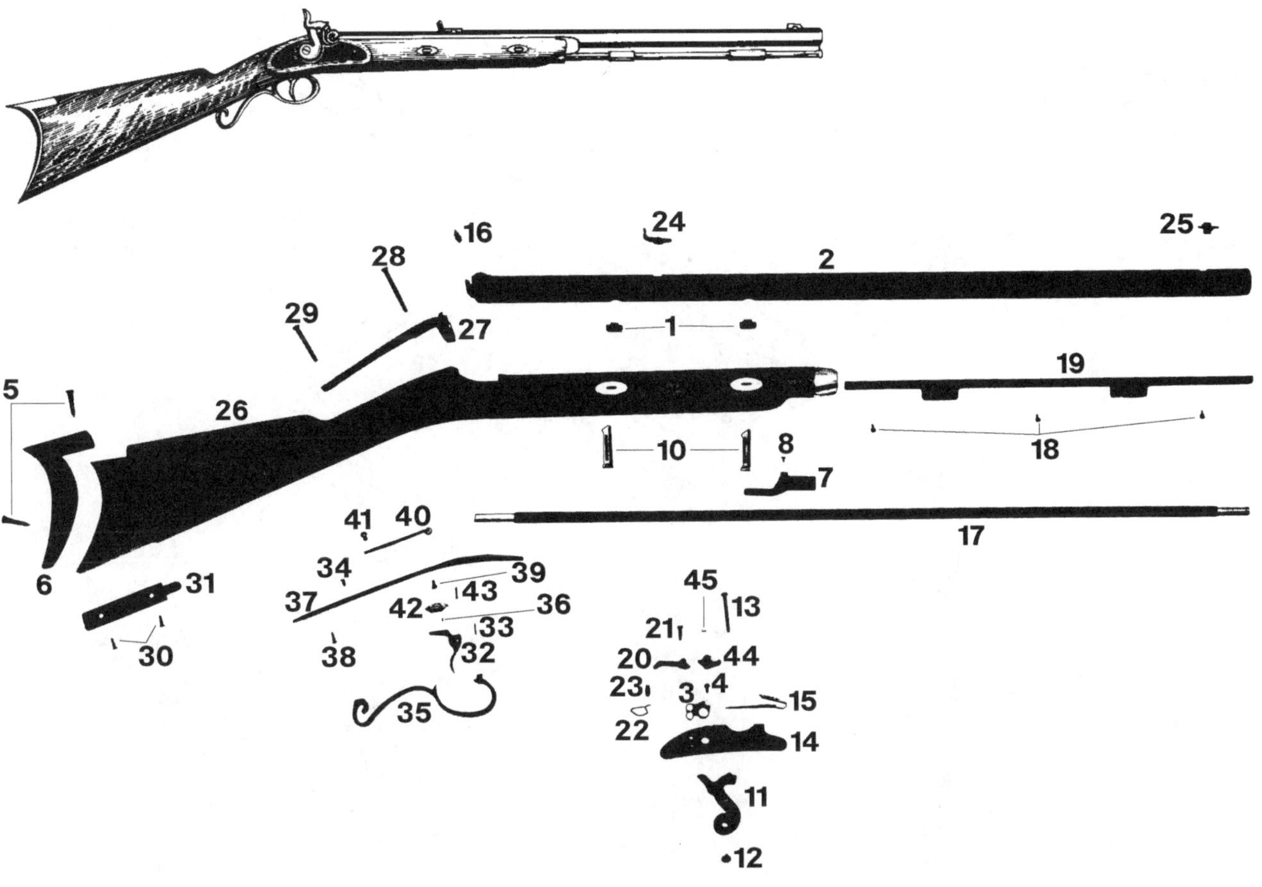

1	Barrel Lugs	25	Front Sight
2	Barrel with Breech Plug, Breech Housing and Clean-Out Screw	26	Stock Assembly with Forend Tip, Forend Tip Screw, Lockplate Screw Escutcheon, Wedge Plates and Wedge Plate Screws
3	Bridle	27	Tang
4	Bridle Screw	28	Tang Screw, Front
5	Buttplate Screws	29	Tang Screw, Rear
6	Buttplate	30	Toe Plate Screws
7	Forend Body and Thimble	31	Toe Plate
8	Forend Thimble Body Screw	32	Trigger
9	Forend Tip Screw	33	Trigger Guard Pin
10	Forend Wedges	34	Trigger Guard Screw
11	Hammer	35	Trigger Guard
12	Hammer Screw	36	Trigger Pin
13	Lockplate Screw	37	Trigger Plate
14	Lockplate with Bolster	38	Trigger Plate Screw
15	Mainspring	39	Trigger Pull Adjustment Screw
16	Nipple	40	Trigger Spring Assembly with Roller and Roller Pin
17	Ramrod, Complete with Brass Ends	41	Trigger Spring Screw
18	Rib Screws	42	Trigger Strut
19	Rib with Thimbles	43	Trigger Strut Pin
20	Sear	44	Tumbler Assembly with Roller and Roller Pin
21	Sear Screw	45	Tumbler Fly
22	Sear Spring		
23	Sear Spring Pin		
24	Sight Assembly Complete		

Superposed Over/Under Shotgun

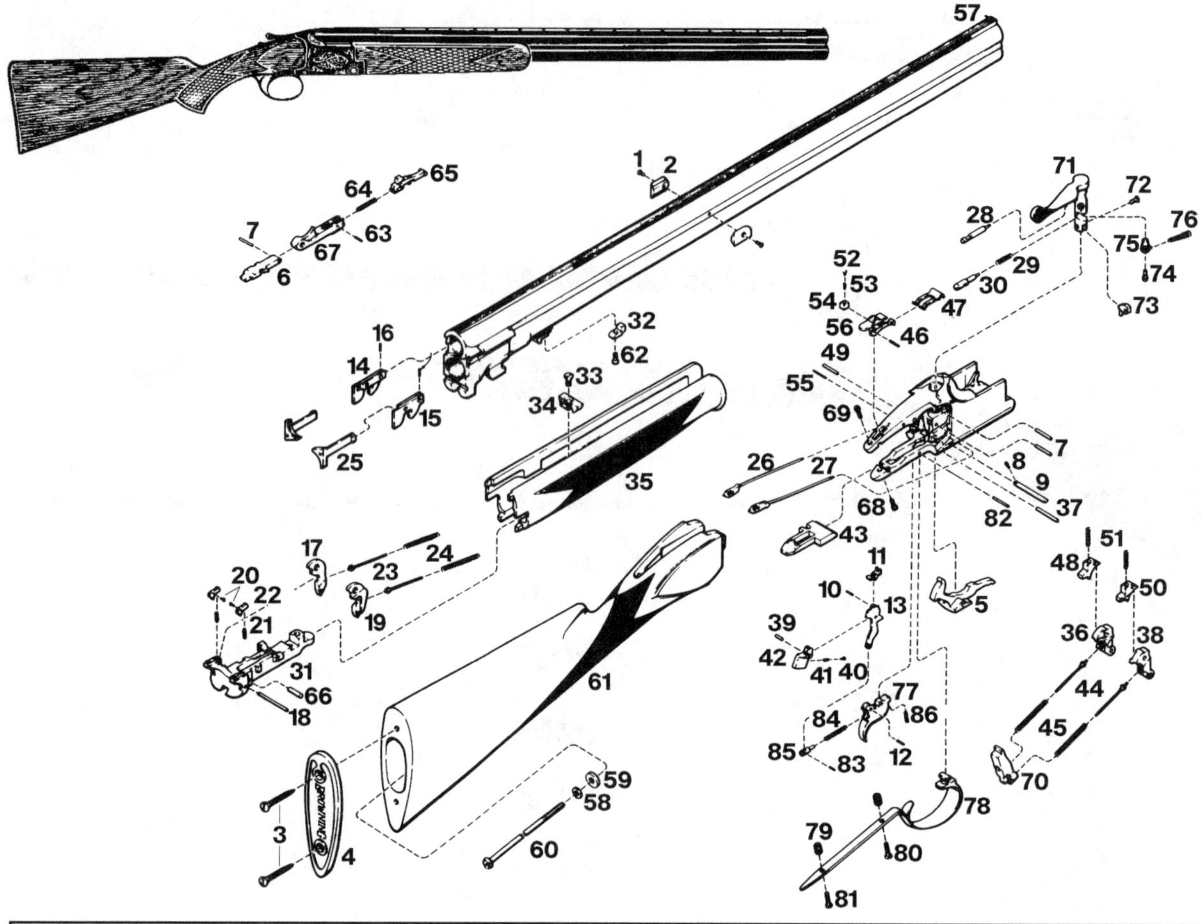

No.	Part	No.	Part	No.	Part
1	Barrel Plate Screws	30	Firing Pin, Under	59	Stock Bolt Washer
2	Barrel Plate Wood	31	Forearm Bracket	60	Stock Bolt
3	Buttplate Screw	32	Forearm Bracket Stop Block	61	Stock
4	Buttplate	33	Forearm Retaining Clamp Screw	62	Stop Block Retaining Screw
5	Cocking Lever	34	Forearm Retaining Clamp	63	Takedown Lever Latch Pin
6	Cocking Lever Lifter	35	Forearm	64	Takedown Lever Latch Spring
7	Cocking Lever Lifter Pin	36	Hammer, Left	65	Takedown Lever Latch
8	Cocking Lever Pin Retaining Screw	37	Hammer Pin	66	Takedown Lever Pin
9	Cocking Lever Pin	38	Hammer, Right	67	Takedown Lever
10	Connector Selector Pin	39	Inertia Block Pin	68	Tang Piece Screw, Bottom
11	Connector Selector	40	Inertia Block Spring Guide	69	Tang Piece Screw, Top
12	Connector Stop Pin	41	Inertia Block Spring	70	Tang Piece
13	Connector	42	Inertia Block	71	Top Lever
14	Ejector Extension, Left	43	Locking Bolt	72	Top Lever Dog Screw
15	Ejector Extension, Right	44	Mainspring Guides	73	Top Lever Dog
16	Ejector Extension Stop Pin	45	Mainsprings	74	Top Lever Spring Retainer Screw
17	Ejector Hammer, Left	46	Safety Spring Pin	75	Top Lever Spring Retainer
18	Ejector Hammer Pin	47	Safety Spring	76	Top Lever Spring
19	Ejector Hammer, Right	48	Sear, Left	77	Trigger
20	Ejector Hammer Sear Pins	49	Sear Pin	78	Trigger Guard
21	Ejector Hammer Sear Spring	50	Sear, Right	79	Trigger Guard Screw Escutcheons
22	Ejector Hammer Sear	51	Sear Springs	80	Trigger Guard Screw, Front
23	Ejector Hammer Spring Guides	52	Selector Block Spring Follower	81	Trigger Guard Screw, Rear
24	Ejector Hammer Springs	53	Selector Block Spring	82	Trigger Pin
25	Ejectors, Right and Left	54	Selector Block	83	Trigger Piston Pin
26	Ejector Trip Rod, Left	55	Selector Safety Spring Retaining Pin	84	Trigger Piston Spring
27	Ejector Trip Rod, Right	56	Selector Safety	85	Trigger Piston
28	Firing Pin, Over	57	Sight Bead	86	Trigger Spring
29	Firing Pin Spring, Under	58	Stock Bolt Lock Washer		

T-Bolt Bolt-Action Rifle

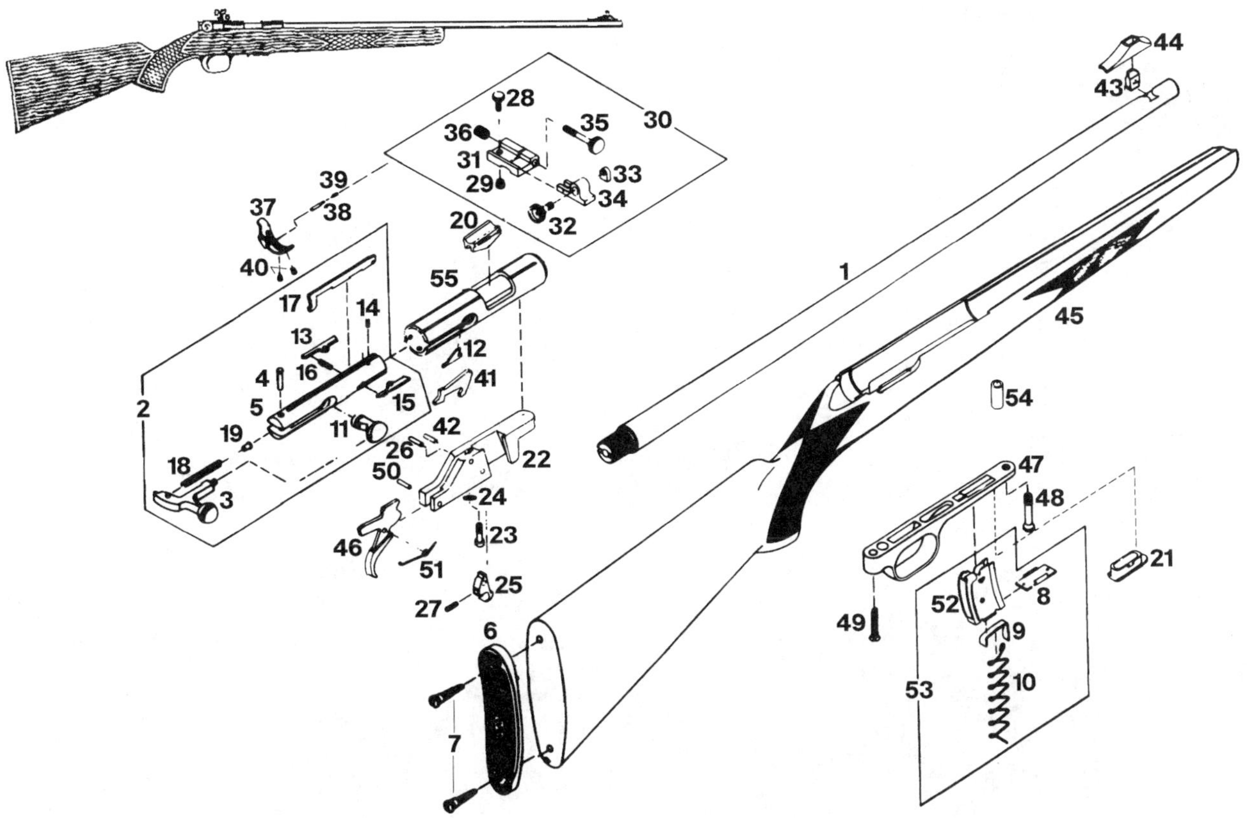

1	Barrel
2	Bolt Assembly
3	Bolt Handle
4	Bolt Handle Pin
5	Breechbolt
6	Buttplate
7	Buttplate Screws
8	Clip Magazine Floorplate
9	Clip Magazine Follower
10	Clip Magazine Follower Spring
11	Cross Bolt
12	Ejector
13	Extractor, Left
14	Extractor Pin
15	Extractor, Right
16	Extractor Spring
17	Firing Pin
18	Firing Pin Spring
19	Firing Pin Spring Follower
20	Loading Ramp
21	Magazine Enclosure
22	Magazine Housing
23	Magazine Housing Screw
24	Magazine Housing Screw Lock Washer
25	Magazine Latch
26	Magazine Latch Pin
27	Magazine Latch Spring
28	Receiver Sight Adjusting Screw, Horizontal
29	Receiver Sight Adjusting Screw Bushing, Horizontal
30	Receiver Sight Assembly Complete
31	Receiver Sight Base
32	Receiver Sight Eyepiece
33	Receiver Sight Eyepiece Adjusting Bushing, Vertical
34	Receiver Sight Eyepiece Housing
35	Receiver Sight Mounting Screw
36	Receiver Sight Mounting Screw Bushing
37	Safety Body
38	Safety Click Pin
39	Safety Click Pin Spring
40	Safety Screws
41	Sear
42	Sear Pin
43	Front Sight Blade
44	Front Sight Ramp
45	Stock T-Bolt
46	Trigger
47	Trigger Guard
48	Front Takedown Screw
49	Rear Trigger Guard Screw
50	Trigger Pin
51	Trigger Spring
52	Magazine Body
53	Magazine Assembly
54	Takedown Screw
55	Receiver

CF2 High-Power Autoloading Rifle

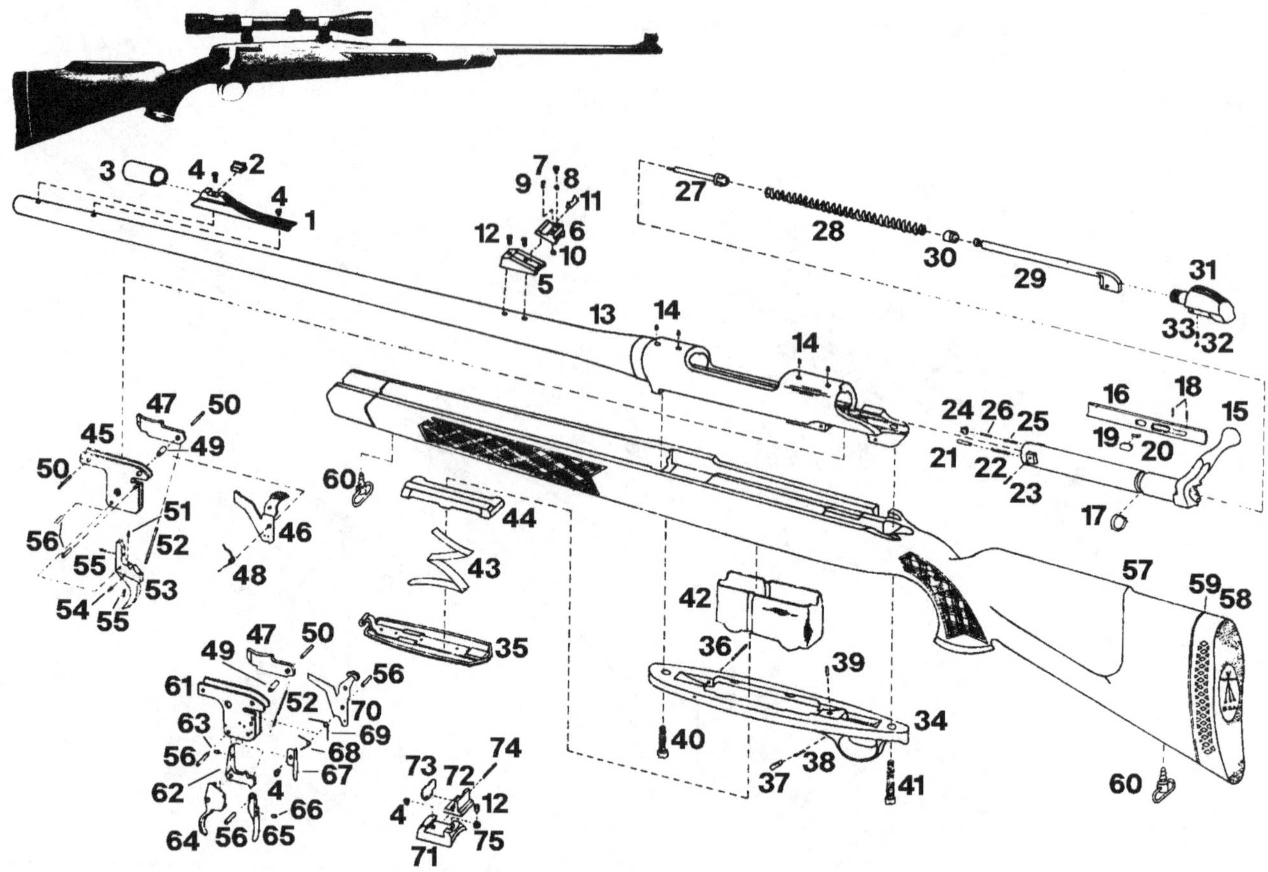

1 Front Sight Ramp
2 Front Sight Blade
3 Front Sight Hood
4 Fixing Screws
5 Rear Sight Base
6 Rear Sight Elevating Slide
7 Gib Screw Blade
8 Gib Blade
9 Gib Screw Elevating Slide
10 Gib Elevating Slide
11 Rear Sight Blade
12 Rear Sight Locking Screws
13 Barrel and Receiver
14 Scope Mount Filler Screws
15 Bolt
16 Bolt Rib
17 Bolt Rib Clip
18 Bolt Rib Pins
19 Bolt Rib Plunger
20 Bolt Rib Plunger Spring
21 Ejector
22 Ejector Spring
23 Ejector Retaining Pin
24 Extractor
25 Extractor Spring
26 Extractor Plunger
27 Striker
28 Striker Spring
29 Cocking Piece
30 Guide Bushing
31 Cocking Piece Housing
32 Indicator
33 Indicator Spring
34 Trigger Guard
35 Magazine Floorplate
36 Magazine Floorplate Pin
37 Magazine Floorplate Catch
38 Magazine Floorplate Catch Spring
39 Magazine Floorplate Catch Retaining Pin
40 Front Trigger Guard Screw
41 Rear Trigger Guard Screw
42 Magazine Box
43 Magazine Follower Spring
44 Magazine Follower
45 Trigger Mechanism Housing
46 Safety
47 Sear
48 Sear Spring
49 Sear Axis Bushing
50 Trigger Mechanism Retaining Pin
51 Trigger Spring
52 Trigger and Sear Coupling Rod
53 Trigger
54 Trigger Locking Plug
55 Trigger Spring Screws
56 Trigger Axis Pins
57 Stock
58 Recoil Pad
59 Recoil Pad Spacer
60 Sling Swivels

For Optional Set-Trigger

61 Trigger Housing Mechanism
62 Trigger Sear
63 Trigger Sear Adjusting Screw
64 Set-Trigger
65 Firing Trigger
66 Firing Trigger Adjustment Screw
67 Trigger Spring
68 Hammer Spring
69 Sear Spring
70 Safety

Optional Rear Sight Parts

71 Rear Sight Base
72 Rear Sight Fixed Leaf
73 Folding Leaf
74 Folding Leaf Axis Pin
75 Rear Sight Gib

Carbine

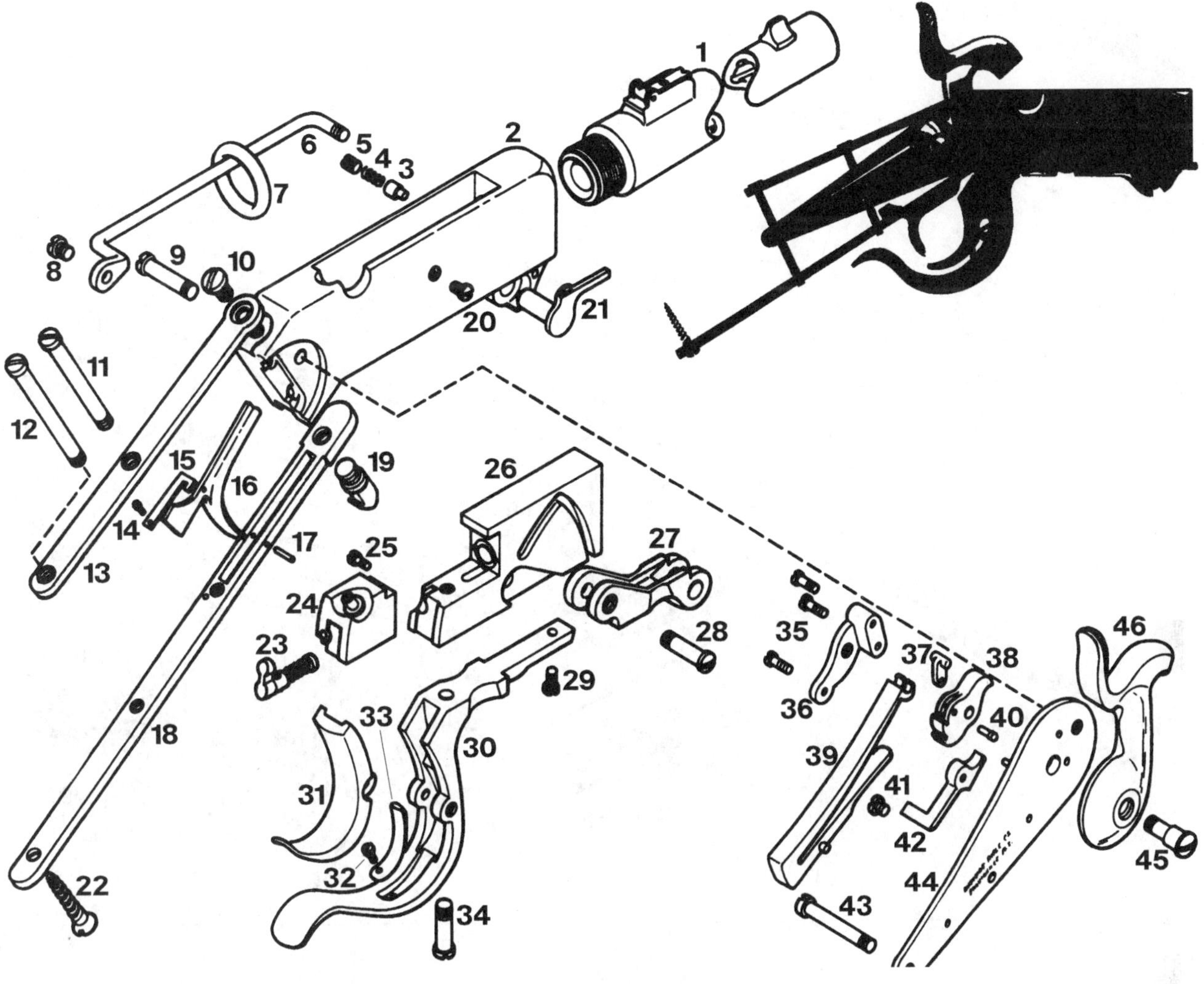

1	Barrel	25	Nipple Block Plunger Retaining Screw
2	Frame	26	Breechblock
3	Takedown Lever Plunger	27	Breechblock Link
4	Takedown Lever Plunger Spring	28	Breechblock Link Screw
5	Takedown Lever Spring Plunger	29	Lever Retaining Screw
6	Saddle Ring Bar	30	Finger Lever
7	Saddle Ring	31	Lever Latch
8	Saddle Ring Bar Screw	32	Lever Latch Spring Screw
9	Front Lockplate Screw	33	Lever Latch Spring
10	Upper Tang Screw	34	Main Lever Retaining Screw
11	Front Tang Screw	35	Bridle Screws
12	Rear Tang Screw	36	Bridle
13	Upper Tang	37	Stirrup
14	Trigger Spring Screw	38	Tumbler
15	Trigger Spring	39	Mainspring
16	Trigger	40	Stirrup Pin
17	Trigger Pin	41	Mainspring Stop Screw
18	Trigger Plate	42	Sear
19	Finger Lever Latch Lock	43	Rear Lockplate Screw
20	Cam Screw	44	Lockplate
21	Takedown Lever	45	Hammer Screw
22	Trigger Plate Screw	46	Hammer
23	Nipple Block Spring and Plunger		
24	Nipple Block		

12-Gauge Autoloading Shotgun

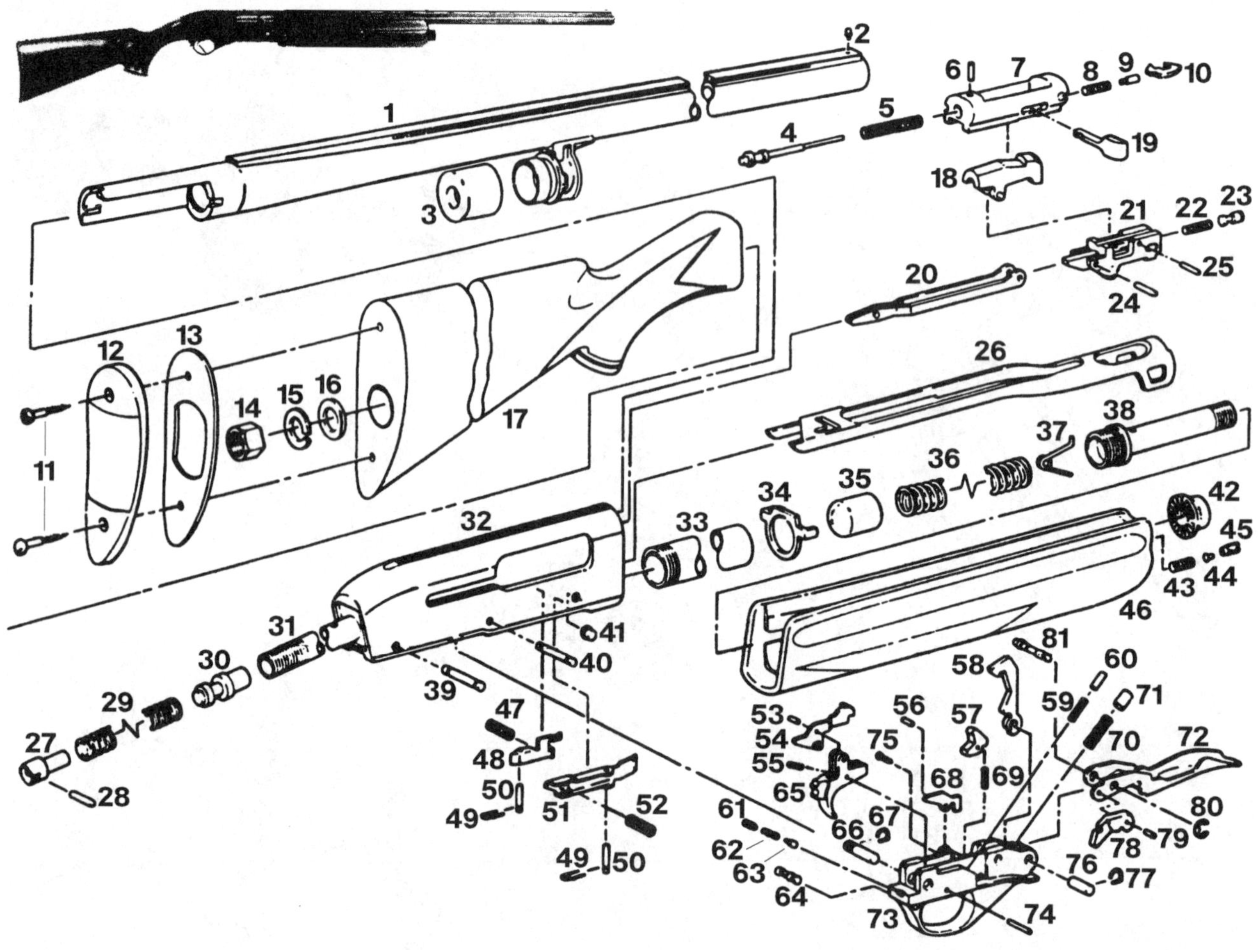

1	Barrel Assembly	28	Action Spring Plug Pin	55	Trigger Spring
2	Front Sight	29	Action Spring	56	Release Lever Pin
3	Piston	30	Action Spring Follower	57	Sear
4	Firing Pin	31	Action Spring Tube	58	Hammer
5	Firing Pin Spring	32	Receiver	59	Lifter Pawl Spring
6	Firing Pin Stop Pin	33	Magazine Tube	60	Lifter Pawl Plunger
7	Breechbolt Assembly	34	Forend Support	61	Safety Plunger Screw
8	Extractor Spring	35	Magazine Follower	62	Safety Plunger Spring
9	Extractor Plunger	36	Magazine Follower Spring	63	Safety Plunger
10	Extractor	37	Magazine Extension Retaining Spring	64	Safety
11	Buttplate Screws	38	Magazine Tube Extension	65	Trigger
12	Buttplate	39	Trigger Guard Pin, Rear	66	Trigger Guard Pin Bushing, Rear
13	Buttplate Liner	40	Trigger Guard Pin, Front	67	Trigger Guard Pin Retainer, Rear
14	Stock Retaining Nut	41	Release Button	68	Release Lever
15	Stock Bolt Lock Washer	42	Magazine Cap	69	Sear Spring
16	Stock Bolt Washer	43	Magazine Cap Stop Spring	70	Mainspring
17	Stock Assembly	44	Magazine Cap Stop Plunger	71	Mainspring Plunger
18	Locking Bolt	45	Magazine Cap Stop	72	Lifter
19	Operating Handle	46	Forend	73	Trigger Guard
20	Link Assembly	47	Cartridge Stop Spring	74	Trigger Pin
21	Slide	48	Cartridge Stop	75	Sear Pin
22	Operating Handle Plunger Spring	49	Retaining Spring, Small	76	Hammer Bushing
23	Operating Handle Plunger	50	Cartridge Stop Pins	77	Trigger Guard Pin Retainer, Front
24	Link Pin	51	Lifter Latch	78	Lifter Pawl
25	Operating Handle Plunger Pin	52	Lifter Latch Spring	79	Lifter Pawl Pin
26	Action Bar	53	Sear Trip Pin	80	Lifter Pin Retainer
27	Action Spring Plug	54	Sear Trip	81	Lifter Pin

AR-7 and AR-7S Explorer Autoloading Rifle

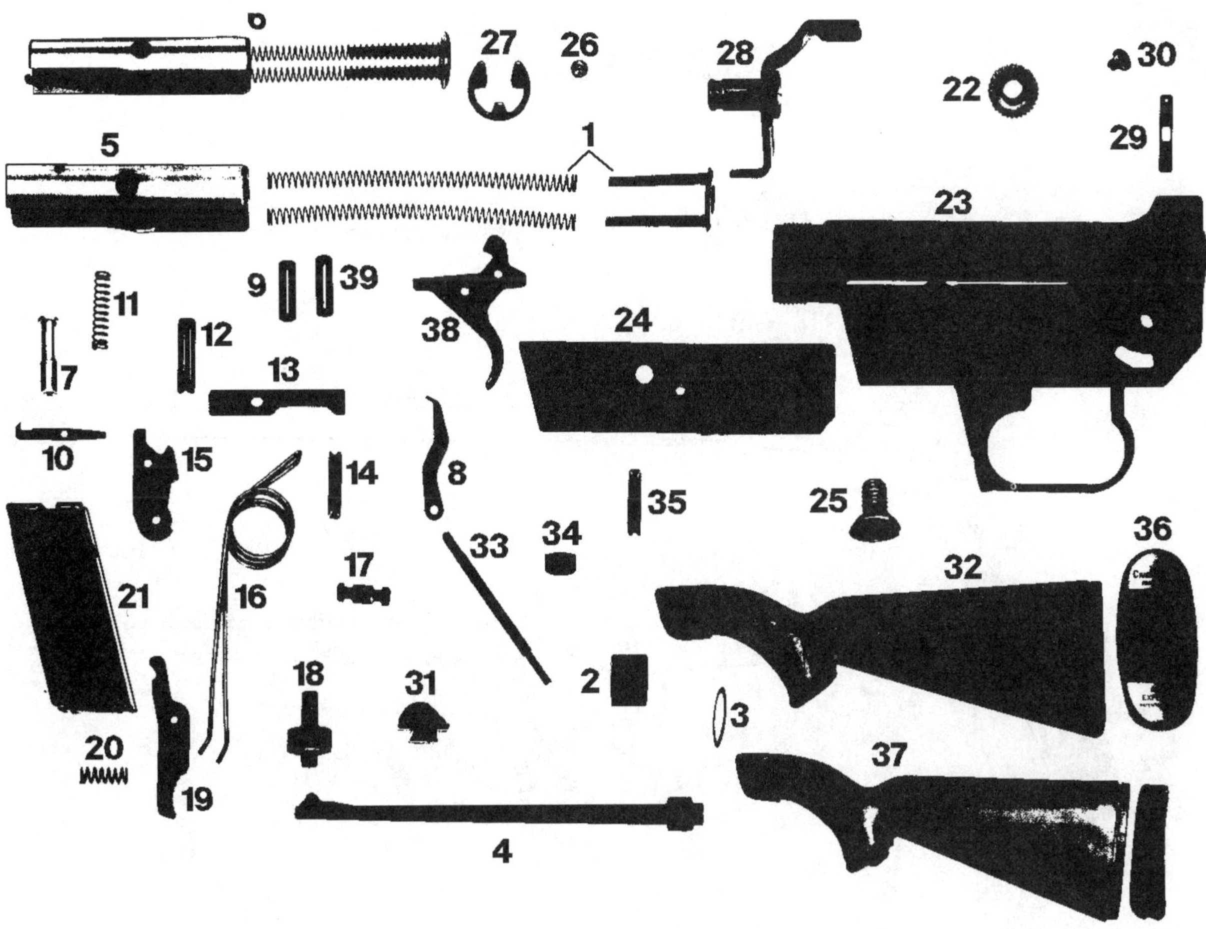

1	Action Springs and Guide	**21**	Magazine, Complete
2	Barrel Nut	**22**	Rear Sight Press Nut
3	Barrel Nut Lock Washer	**23**	Receiver
4	Barrel Assembly	**24**	Receiver Sideplate
5	Bolt	**25**	Receiver Sideplate Screw
6	Bolt Assembly	**26**	Safety Detent Ball
7	Charging Handle	**27**	Safety Snap Ring
8	Ejector	**28**	Safety
9	Ejector Pin	**29**	Sight, Rear
10	Extractor	**30**	Rear Sight Screw
11	Extractor Spring	**31**	Sight, Front
12	Extractor Assembly Pin	**32**	Stock
13	Firing Pin	**33**	Stock Takedown Screw
14	Firing Pin Assembly Pin	**34**	Stock Takedown Screw Nut
15	Hammer	**35**	Stock Takedown Screw Nut Roll Pin
16	Hammer and Trigger Spring	**36**	Stock Outer Buttcap
17	Hammer and Trigger Spring Support Pin	**37**	Stock Assembly
18	Hammer Pivot Pin	**38**	Trigger
19	Magazine Latch	**39**	Trigger Pivot Pin
20	Magazine Latch Spring		

Single Shot Rifle

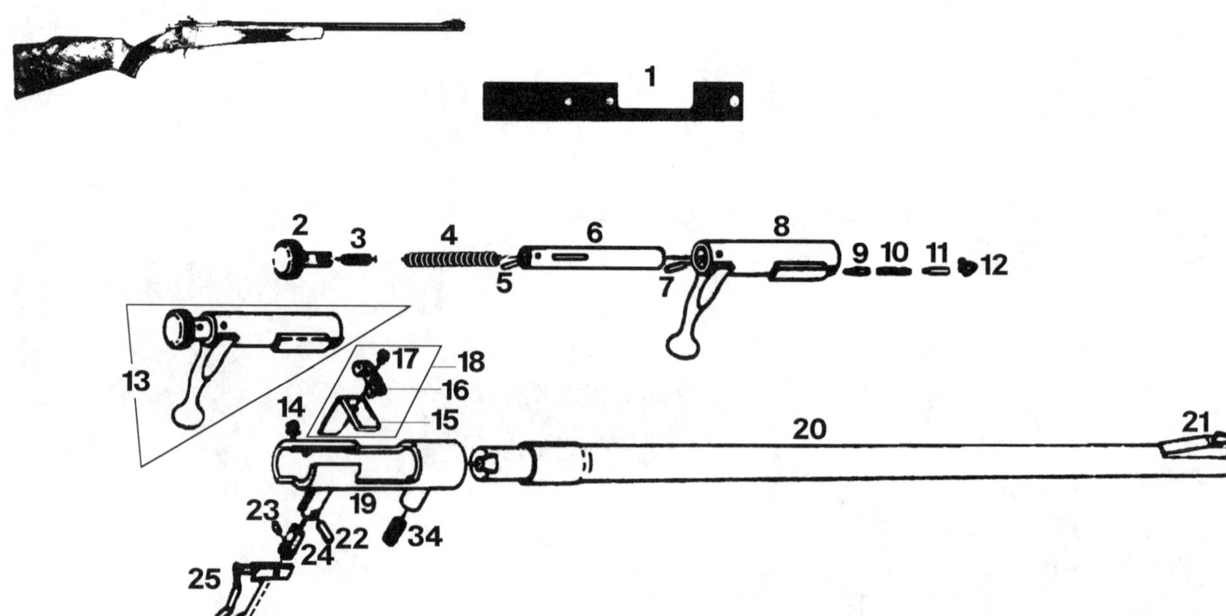

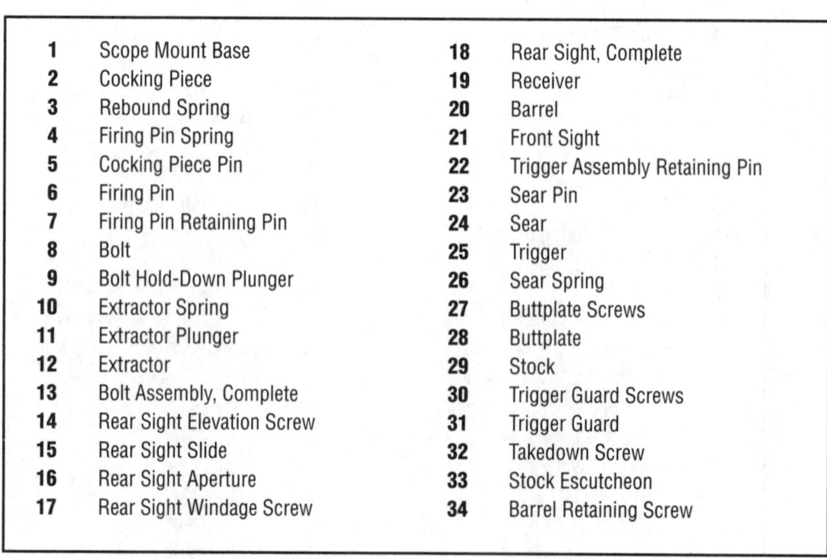

1	Scope Mount Base	**18**	Rear Sight, Complete
2	Cocking Piece	**19**	Receiver
3	Rebound Spring	**20**	Barrel
4	Firing Pin Spring	**21**	Front Sight
5	Cocking Piece Pin	**22**	Trigger Assembly Retaining Pin
6	Firing Pin	**23**	Sear Pin
7	Firing Pin Retaining Pin	**24**	Sear
8	Bolt	**25**	Trigger
9	Bolt Hold-Down Plunger	**26**	Sear Spring
10	Extractor Spring	**27**	Buttplate Screws
11	Extractor Plunger	**28**	Buttplate
12	Extractor	**29**	Stock
13	Bolt Assembly, Complete	**30**	Trigger Guard Screws
14	Rear Sight Elevation Screw	**31**	Trigger Guard
15	Rear Sight Slide	**32**	Takedown Screw
16	Rear Sight Aperture	**33**	Stock Escutcheon
17	Rear Sight Windage Screw	**34**	Barrel Retaining Screw

Bolt-Action Rifle

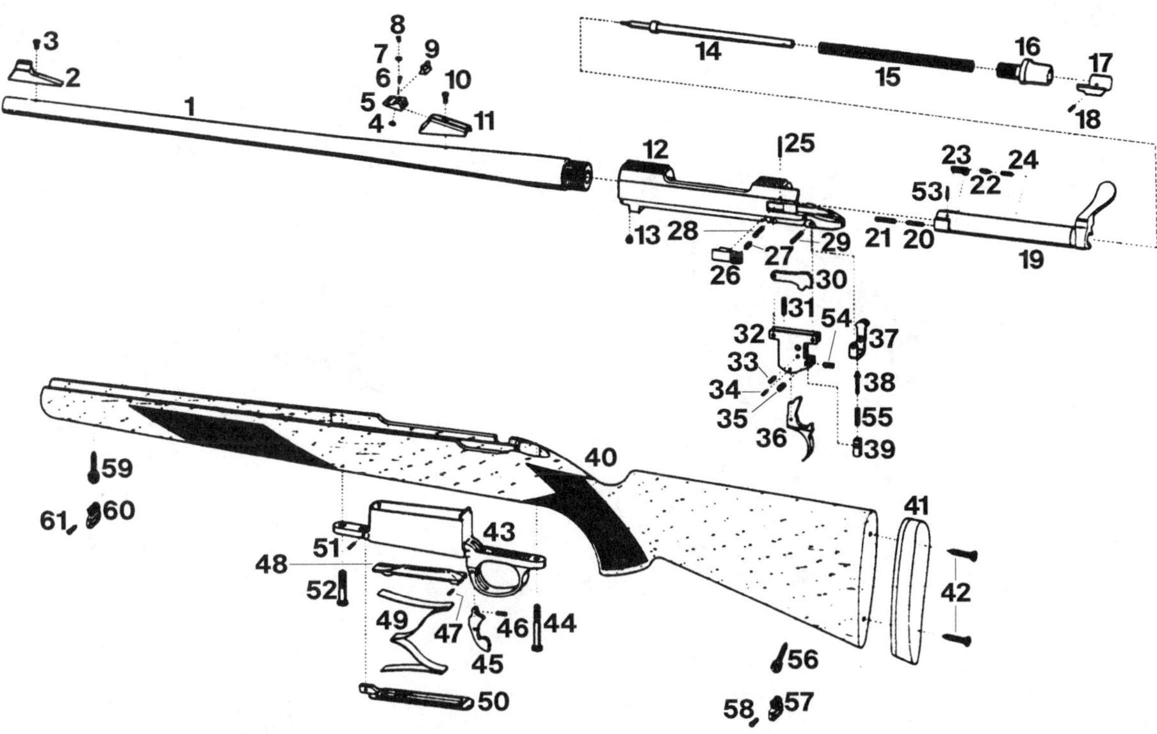

1	Barrel	32	Trigger Housing
2	Front Sight	33	Trigger Stop Pin
3	Front Sight Screw	34	Trigger Pin
4	Elevation Nut	35	Safety-Lever Pin
5	Rear Sight Slide	36	Trigger
6	Elevation Screw	37	Safety Button
7	Windage Washer	38	Safety Spring Plunger
8	Windage Screw	39	Safety-Lever
9	Rear Sight Aperture	40	Stock
10	Base Screw	41	Recoil Pad
11	Rear Sight Base	42	Recoil Pad Screws
12	Action Receiver	43	Trigger Guard/Magazine Case
13	Stop Barrel Screw	44	Rear Guard Assembly Screw
14	Firing Pin	45	Floorplate Catch
15	Firing Pin Spring	46	Floorplate Catch Spring
16	Bolt Sleeve	47	Floorplate Pin
17	Cocking Piece	48	Magazine Follower
18	Firing Pin Retaining Pin	49	Magazine Spring
19	Bolt Body	50	Floorplate
20	Ejector Spring	51	Floorplate Pin
21	Ejector	52	Front Guard Assembly Screw
22	Extractor Pin	53	Ejector Stop Pin
23	Extractor	54	Trigger Spring
24	Extractor Spring	55	Safety Spring
25	Bolt Stop Pin	56	Rear Swivel Stud
26	Bolt Stop	57	Rear Swivel
27	Bolt Stop Spring	58	Rear Swivel Screw
28	Sear Pin	59	Front Swivel Stud
29	Safety Pin	60	Front Swivel
30	Sear	61	Front Swivel Screw
31	Sear Spring		

Over/Under Shotgun

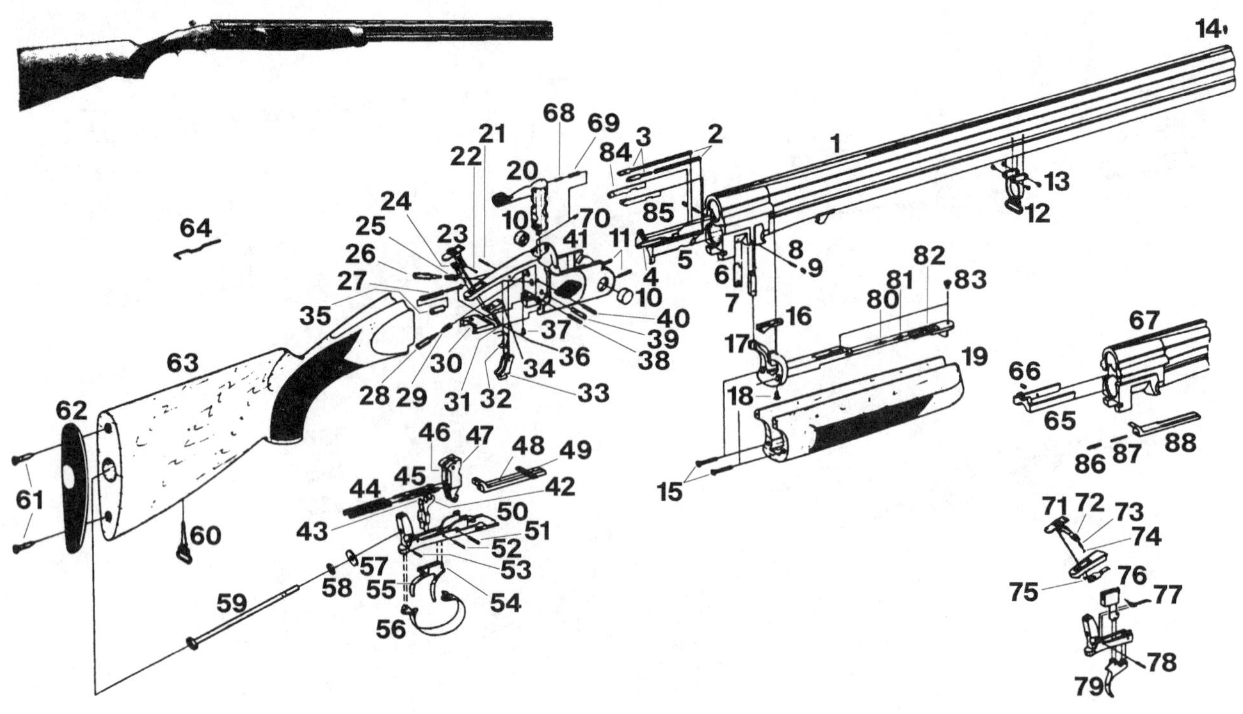

No.	Part	No.	Part	No.	Part
1	Barrels	31	Safety Spring	61	Buttplate Screws
2	Ejector Springs	32	Sear Springs	62	Buttplate
3	Ejector Spring Guides	33	Sear	63	Stock
4	Left Ejector	34	Safety Plate	64	Automatic Safety Bar
5	Right Ejector	35	Top Lever Spring Guide, Outside	65	Extractor
6	Left Ejector Catch Plate	36	Top Lever Spring Guide, Inside	66	Extractor Stop Screw
7	Right Ejector Catch Plate	37	Top Lever Spring Contrast Screw	67	Barrels
8	Catch Plate Stop Piston Spring	38	Trigger Plate Assembly Pin	68	Top Lever Stop Spring
9	Catch Plate Stop Piston	39	Top Lever Stop Pin	69	Top Lever Stop Pin
10	Joint Pin	40	Firing Pin Stop Pin	70	Top Lever Releasing Pin
11	Joint Pin Stop Pins	41	Frame	71	Single Trigger Safety
12	Front Sling Swivel	42	Right Trigger Plate	72	Safety Block
13	Swing Swivel Screws	43	Left Trigger Plate	73	Block Spring
14	Front Sight	44	Hammer Springs	74	Safety Position Ball
15	Forend Hinge Screws	45	Hammer Spring Guides	75	Single Trigger Safety Spring
16	Cocking Hook	46	Left Hammer	76	Inertia Block
17	Forend Iron	47	Right Hammer	77	Inertia Block Spring
18	Cocking Hook Screw	48	Right Cocking Bar	78	Single Trigger Pin
19	Forearm	49	Left Cocking Bar	79	Single Trigger
20	Top Lever	50	Trigger Plate	80	Forearm Catch Spring
21	Sear Pin	51	Hammer Pin	81	Forearm Catch Spring Guide
22	Safety Spring Pin	52	Trigger Pin	82	Forearm Catch
23	Safety Slide	53	Trigger Guard Stop Pin	83	Forearm Catch Screw
24	Strap Screw	54	Right Trigger	84	Left Ejector Hammer
25	Firing Pin Spring	55	Left Trigger	85	Right Ejector Hammer
26	Lower Firing Pin	56	Trigger Guard	86	Cocking Bar Spring Guide
27	Top Lever Spring	57	Stock Washer	87	Cocking Bar Spring
28	Upper Firing Pin	58	Stock Lock Washer	88	Cocking Bar
29	Firing Pin Spring	59	Stock Bolt		
30	Locking Bolt	60	Stock Sling Swivel		

Side-by-Side Shotgun

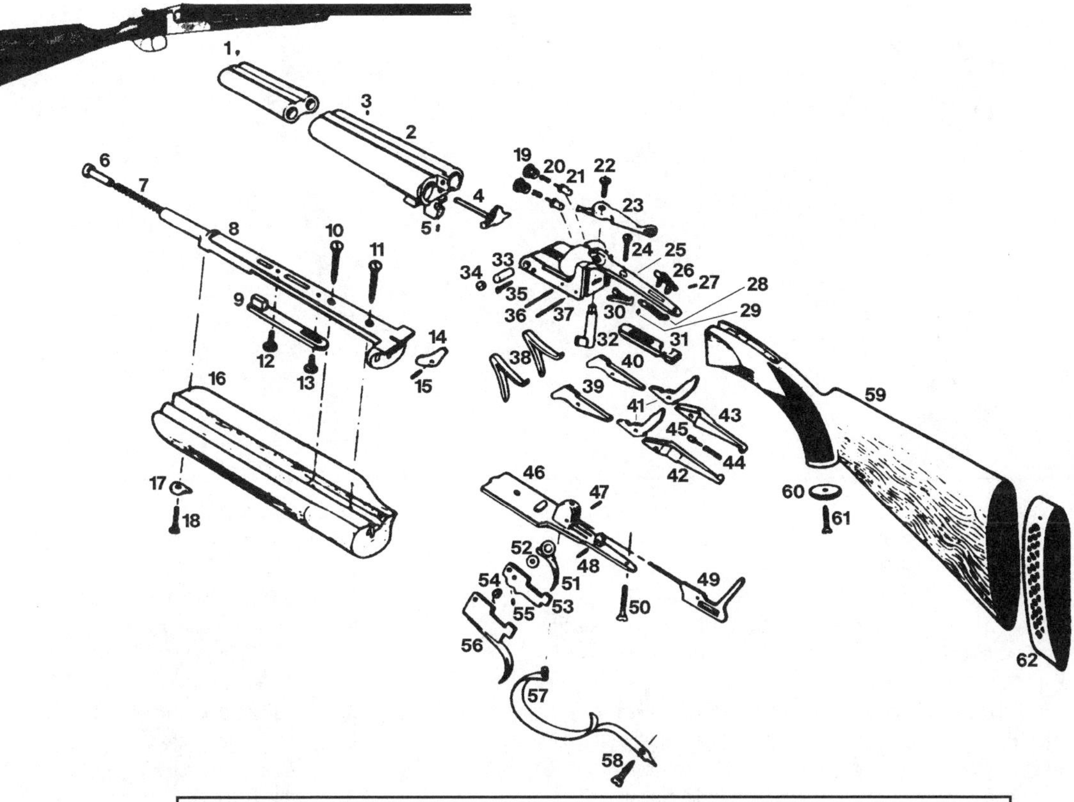

1	Front Sight Bead	30	Top Lever Spring
2	Barrels	31	Horizontal Bolt
3	Rear Sight Bead	32	Vertical Bolt
4	Extractor	33	Barrel Pivot Pin
5	Extractor Retaining Screw	34	Barrel Pivot Pin Cap
6	Forend Catch Button	35	Cocking Lever Pivot Screw
7	Forend Catch Spring	36	Hammer Pivot Pin
8	Forend Iron	37	Sear Pivot Pin
9	Forend Catch	38	Hammer Springs
10	Forend Mount Screw, Front	39	Cocking Lever, Left
11	Forend Mount Screw, Rear	40	Cocking Lever, Right
12	Forend Catch Screw, Front	41	Hammers
13	Forend Catch Screw, Rear	42	Sear, Left
14	Extractor Hammer Cocking Lever Activator	43	Sear, Right
		44	Sear Springs
15	Extractor Hammer Cocking Lever Screw	45	Sear Spring Guides
		46	Trigger Plate
16	Forend Wood	47	Trigger Pin
17	Forend Escutcheon	48	Safety Square Pin
18	Forend Escutcheon Mounting Screw	49	Safety Activator
		50	Trigger Plate Screw, Rear
19	Firing Pin Bushings	51	Front Trigger
20	Firing Pin Springs	52	Trigger Roller
21	Firing Pins	53	Trigger Housing
22	Top Lever Screw	54	Front Trigger Screw
23	Top Lever	55	Front Trigger Hinge Spring
24	Upper Tang Screw	56	Rear Trigger
25	Breech Assembly	57	Trigger Guard
26	Safety Button	58	Trigger Guard Screw
27	Safety Button Pin	59	Stock
28	Safety Spring	60	Grip Cap
29	Safety Spring Screw	61	Grip Cap Screw
		62	Buttplate

AR15-A2 Sporter Autoloading Rifle

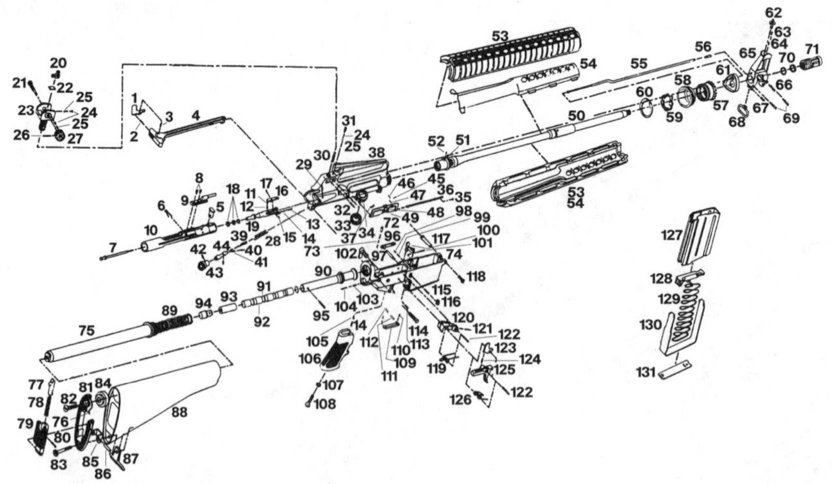

No.	Part	No.	Part	No.	Part
1	Charging Handle Latch	**44**	Forward Assist Plunger	**88**	Buttstock
2	Charging Handle Latch Spring	**45**	Cover Latch Retaining Pin	**89**	Action Spring
3	Charging Handle Latch Roll Pin	**46**	Cover Latch	**90**	Buffer Body
4	Charging Handle	**47**	Cover Latch Spring	**91**	Buffer Disc
5	Cam Pin	**48**	Cover Latch Housing	**92**	Buffer Weight
6	Firing Pin Retaining Pin	**49**	Ejection Slot Cover	**93**	Buffer Spacer
7	Firing Pin	**50**	Barrel	**94**	Buffer Bumper
8	Socket Head Cap Screws	**51**	Barrel Extension	**95**	Buffer Bumper Pin
9	Bolt Carrier Key	**52**	Barrel Indexing Pin	**96**	Magazine Catch Plate
10	Bolt Carrier	**53**	Handguard	**97**	Magazine Catch Shaft
11	Extractor Spring Insert	**54**	Handguard Liner	**98**	Bolt Catch Plunger
12	Extractor Spring	**55**	Gas Tube	**99**	Bolt Catch Spring
13	Ejector	**56**	Gas Tube Plug	**100**	Bolt Catch
14	Ejector and Safety Detent Spring	**57**	Barrel Nut	**101**	Bolt Catch Roll Pin
15	Ejector Roll Pin	**58**	Handguard Slip Ring	**102**	Safety Selector Lever
16	Extractor	**59**	Handguard	**103**	Takedown Pin Detent
17	Bolt Ring	**60**	Handguard Snap Ring	**104**	Takedown Pin Spring Detent
18	Extractor Pins	**61**	Handguard Cap	**105**	Safety Detent
19	Bolt	**62**	Front Sight Post	**106**	Pistol Grip
20	Rear Sight Aperture	**63**	Front Sight Detent	**107**	Lock Washer
21	Rear Sight Windage Screw	**64**	Front Sight Detent Spring	**108**	Pistol Grip Screw
22	Rear Sight Flat Spring	**65**	Front Sight	**109**	Trigger Guard
23	Rear Sight Base	**66**	Gas Tube Roll Pin	**110**	Roll Pin
24	Rear Sight Ball Bearing	**67**	Front Sling Swivel Rivet	**111**	Trigger Guard Plunger
25	Rear Sight Helical Spring	**68**	Front Sling Swivel	**112**	Trigger Guard Spring
26	Rear Sight Windage Knob Spring Pin	**69**	Front Sight Taper Pins	**113**	Trigger Guard Pivot Pin Roll Pin
		70	Compensator Spacer	**114**	Takedown Pin
27	Rear Sight Windage Knob	**71**	Flash Suppressor	**115**	Magazine Catch Spring
28	Forward Assist Assembly Spring	**72**	Buffer Retainer	**116**	Magazine Release Button
29	Forward Assist Spring Pin	**73**	Buffer Retainer Spring	**117**	Receiver Pivot Pin
30	Rear Sight Elevation Spring	**74**	Lower Receiver	**118**	Receiver Pivot Pin Screw
31	Index Screw	**75**	Receiver Extension	**119**	Hammer Spring
32	Rear Sight Elevation Spring Pin	**76**	Buttplate Insert	**120**	Hammer
33	Rear Sight Elevation Knob	**77**	Door Assembly Plunger	**121**	Hammer Pin Retainer
34	Rear Sight Elevation Index	**78**	Door Assembly Plunger Spring	**122**	Hammer and Trigger Pin
35	Cover Hinge Pin Snap Ring	**79**	Door Assembly Door	**123**	Disconnector
36	Cover Hinge Pin	**80**	Door Assembly Door Pin	**124**	Disconnector Spring
37	Cover Spring	**81**	Buttcap	**125**	Trigger
38	Upper Receiver	**82**	Buttcap Screw	**126**	Trigger Spring
39	Forward Assist Pawl	**83**	Rear Swivel Screw	**127**	Magazine Box
40	Forward Assist Pawl Detent	**84**	Buttcap Spacer	**128**	Magazine Follower
41	Forward Assist Detent Spring	**85**	Swivel Hinge	**129**	Magazine Spring
42	Forward Assist Cap Pin	**86**	Rear Swivel Pin	**130**	Magazine Spacer
43	Forward Assist Cap	**87**	Rear Sling Swivel	**131**	Magazine Bottom Plate

AR15-A2 Autoloading Rifle

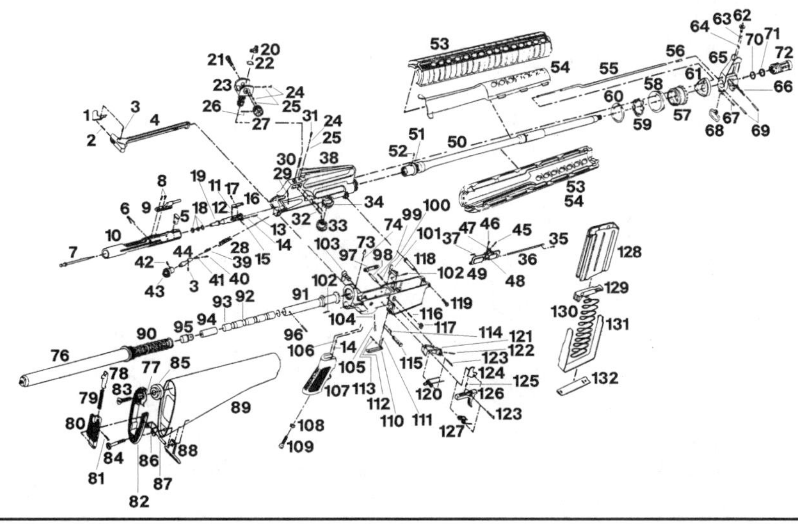

No.	Part	No.	Part	No.	Part
1	Charging Handle Latch	45	Cover Latch Retaining Pin	89	Buttstock
2	Charging Handle Latch Spring	46	Cover Latch	90	Action Spring
3	Charging Handle Latch Roll Pin	47	Cover Latch Spring	91	Buffer Body
4	Charging Handle	48	Cover Latch Housing	92	Buffer Disc
5	Cam Pin	49	Ejection Slot Cover	93	Buffer Weight
6	Firing Pin Retaining Pin	50	Barrel	94	Buffer Spacer
7	Firing Pin	51	Barrel Extension	95	Buffer Bumper
8	Socket Head Cap Screws	52	Barrel Indexing Pin	96	Buffer Bumper Pin
9	Bolt Carrier Key	53	Handguard	97	Magazine Catch Plate
10	Bolt Carrier	54	Handguard Liner	98	Magazine Catch Shaft
11	Extractor Spring Insert	55	Gas Tube	99	Bolt Catch Plunger
12	Extractor Spring	56	Gas Tube Plug	100	Bolt Catch Spring
13	Ejector	57	Barrel Nut	101	Bolt Catch
14	Ejector and Safety Detent Spring	58	Handguard Slip Ring	102	Bolt Catch Roll Pin
15	Ejector Roll Pin	59	Handguard	103	Safety Selector Lever
16	Extractor	60	Handguard Snap Ring	104	Takedown Pin Detent
17	Bolt Ring	61	Handguard Cap	105	Takedown Pin Spring Detent
18	Extractor Pins	62	Front Sight Post	106	Safety Detent
19	Bolt	63	Front Sight Detent	107	Pistol Grip
20	Rear Sight Aperture	64	Front Sight Detent Spring	108	Lock Washer
21	Rear Sight Windage Screw	65	Front Sight	109	Pistol Grip Screw
22	Rear Sight Flat Spring	66	Gas Tube Roll Pin	110	Trigger Guard
23	Rear Sight Base	67	Front Sling Swivel Rivet	111	Roll Pin
24	Rear Sight Ball Bearings	68	Front Sling Swivel	112	Trigger Guard Plunger
25	Rear Sight Helical Springs	69	Front Sight Taper Pins	113	Trigger Guard Spring
26	Rear Sight Windage Knob Spring Pin	70	Compensator Spacer	114	Trigger Guard Pivot Pin Roll Pin
27	Rear Sight Windage Knob	71	Compensator Spacer	115	Takedown Pin
28	Forward Assist Assembly Spring	72	Flash Suppressor	116	Magazine Catch Spring
29	Forward Assist Spring Pin	73	Buffer Retainer	117	Magazine Release Button
30	Rear Sight Elevation Spring	74	Buffer Retainer Spring	118	Receiver Pivot Pin
31	Index Screw	75	Lower Receiver	119	Receiver Pivot Pin Screw
32	Rear Sight Elevation Spring Pin	76	Receiver Extension	120	Hammer Spring
33	Rear Sight Elevation Knob	77	Buttplate Insert	121	Hammer
34	Rear Sight Elevation Index	78	Door Assembly Plunger	122	Hammer Pin Retainer
35	Cover Hinge Pin Snap Ring	79	Door Assembly Plunger Spring	123	Hammer and Trigger Pin
36	Cover Hinge Pin	80	Door Assembly Door	124	Disconnector
37	Cover Spring	81	Door Assembly Door Pin	125	Disconnector Spring
38	Upper Receiver	82	Buttcap	126	Trigger
39	Forward Assist Pawl	83	Buttcap Screw	127	Trigger Spring
40	Forward Assist Pawl Detent	84	Rear Swivel Screw	128	Magazine Box
41	Forward Assist Detent Spring	85	Buttcap Spacer	129	Magazine Follower
42	Forward Assist Cap Pin	86	Swivel Hinge	130	Magazine Spring
43	Forward Assist Cap	87	Rear Swivel Pin	131	Magazine Spacer
44	Forward Assist Plunger	88	Rear Sling Swivel	132	Magazine Bottom Plate

Colteer, Courier and Stagecoach Autoloading Rifle

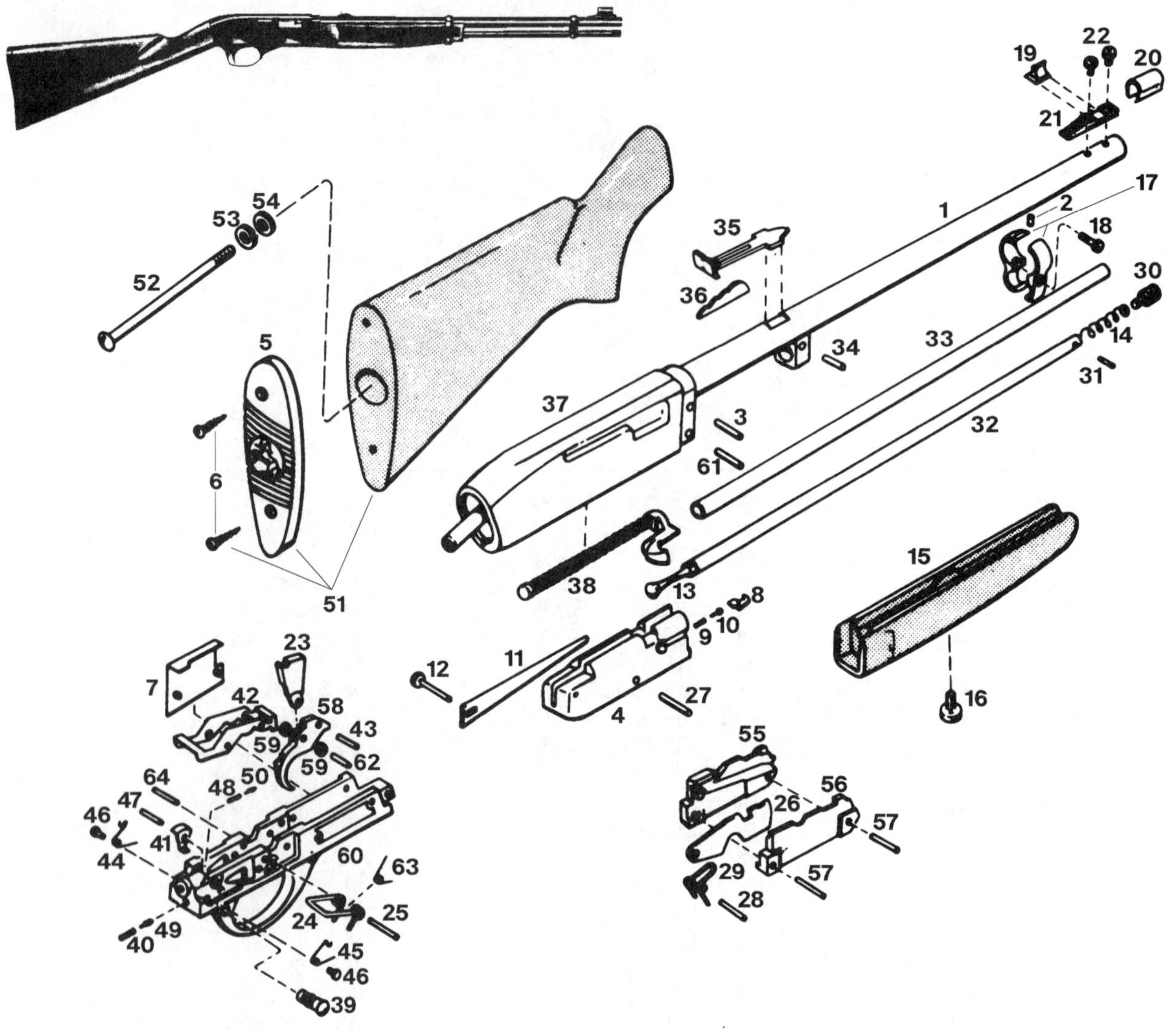

1	Barrel	**23**	Hammer	**45**	Sear Bar Spring, Right
2	Barrel Band Pin	**24**	Hammer Spring	**46**	Sear Bar Spring Pins
3	Barrel Retaining Pin	**25**	Hammer Spring Pin	**47**	Sear and Sear Bar Retaining Pin
4	Bolt	**26**	Lifter	**48**	Sear Detent Spring
5	Buttplate	**27**	Lifter Cam Pin	**49**	Safety Spring Detent
6	Buttplate Screws	**28**	Lifter Pin	**50**	Sear Spring Detent
7	Ejector Assembly	**29**	Lifter Spring	**51**	Stock
8	Extractor	**30**	Magazine Tube Cap	**52**	Stock Bolt
9	Extractor Spring	**31**	Magazine Tube Cap Pin	**53**	Stock Bolt Lock Washer
10	Extractor Spring Plunger	**32**	Magazine Tube, Inner	**54**	Stock Bolt Washer
11	Firing Pin	**33**	Magazine Tube, Outer	**55**	Throat, Left
12	Firing Pin Retaining Pin	**34**	Magazine Tube Retaining Pin	**56**	Throat, Right
13	Follower	**35**	Rear Sight Leaf	**57**	Throat Pins
14	Follower Spring	**36**	Rear Sight Elevator	**58**	Trigger
15	Forearm	**37**	Receiver	**59**	Trigger Bushings
16	Forearm Screw	**38**	Recoil Spring Assembly	**60**	Trigger Guard
17	Front Band	**39**	Safety	**61**	Trigger Guard Pin
18	Front Band Screw	**40**	Safety Detent Spring	**62**	Trigger Pin
19	Front Sight Bead	**41**	Sear	**63**	Trigger Spring
20	Front Sight Hood	**42**	Sear Bar	**64**	Trigger Stop Pin
21	Front Sight	**43**	Sear Bar Pin		
22	Front Sight Screws	**44**	Sear Bar Spring, Left		

Lightning Slide-Action Rifle

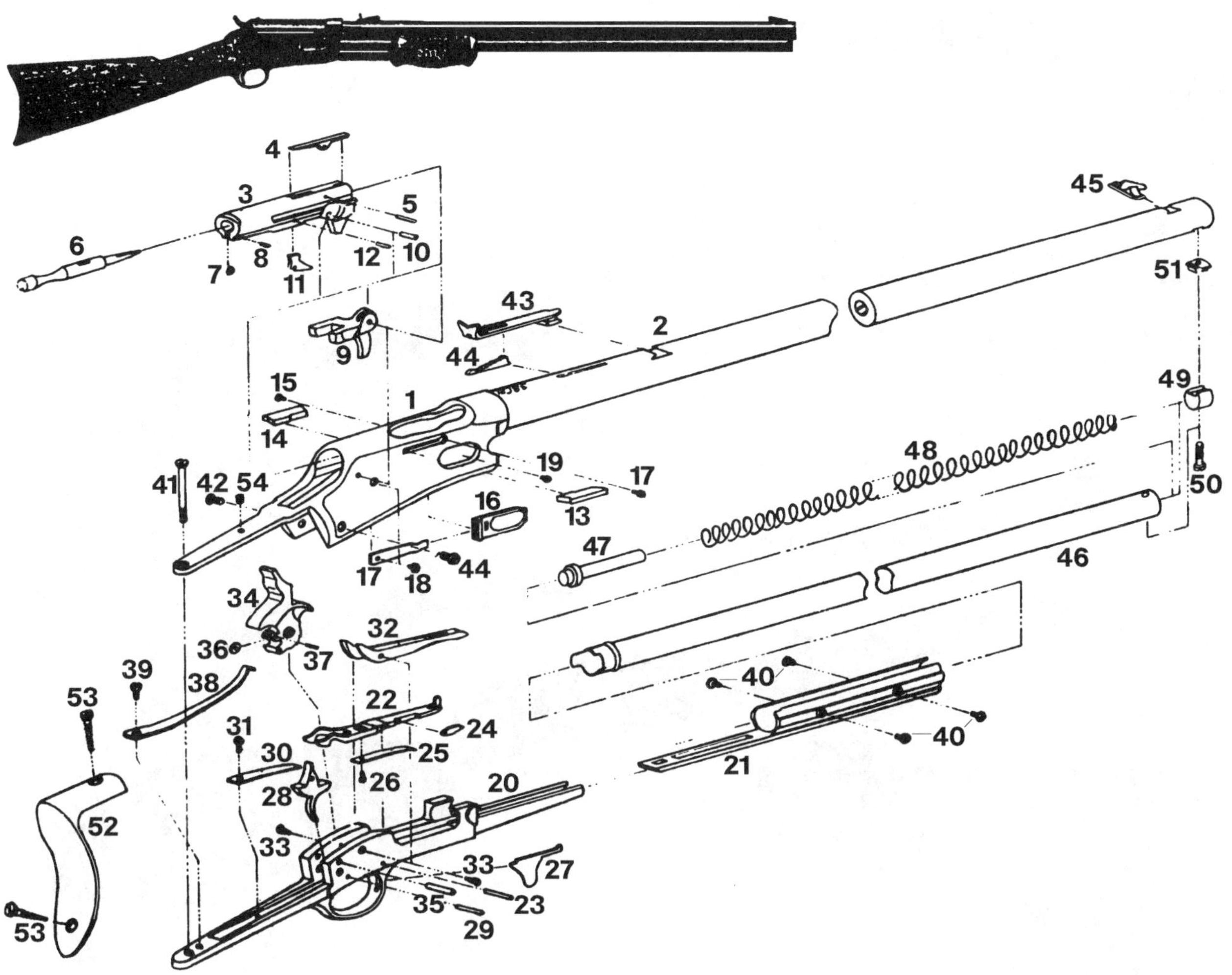

1	Receiver
2	Barrel
3	Bolt
4	Extractor
5	Extractor Pin
6	Firing Pin
7	Bolt Roller Bearing
8	Bolt Roller Bearing Pin
9	Locking Brace
10	Locking Brace Pin
11	Firing Pin Lever
12	Firing Pin Lever Pin
13	Ejector/Bolt Guide
14	Ejector/Bolt
15	Ejector/Bolt Guide Screw
16	Magazine Gate Latch
17	Magazine Gate Latch Spring
18	Magazine Gate Spring Screw
19	Magazine Guide Screw
20	Trigger Guard
21	Slide
22	Magazine Gate
23	Magazine Gate Pin
24	Magazine Gate Locking Latch
25	Magazine Gate Spring
26	Magazine Gate Spring Screw
27	Slide Lock
28	Trigger
29	Trigger Pin
30	Trigger Spring
31	Trigger Spring Screw
32	Cartridge Carrier
33	Cartridge Carrier Screws
34	Hammer
35	Hammer Pin
36	Mainspring Roller Bearing
37	Mainspring Roller Bearing Pin
38	Mainspring
39	Mainspring Screw
40	Slide Arm Screws
41	Tang Screw
42	Receiver Screws
43	Rear Sight
44	Rear Sight Elevator
45	Front Sight
46	Magazine Tube
47	Magazine Follower
48	Magazine Spring
49	Magazine Tube Cap
50	Magazine Tube Cap Screw
51	Magazine Barrel Lug
52	Buttplate
53	Buttplate Screws
54	Blank Tang Screws

Parts Not Shown

- Set Hammer
- Set-Trigger
- Set Lock Hammer Fly
- Set Lock Sear
- Set Lock Adjusting Screw
- Set Lock Sear Pin
- Top Cover
- Top Cover Screw

Bolt-Action Rifle

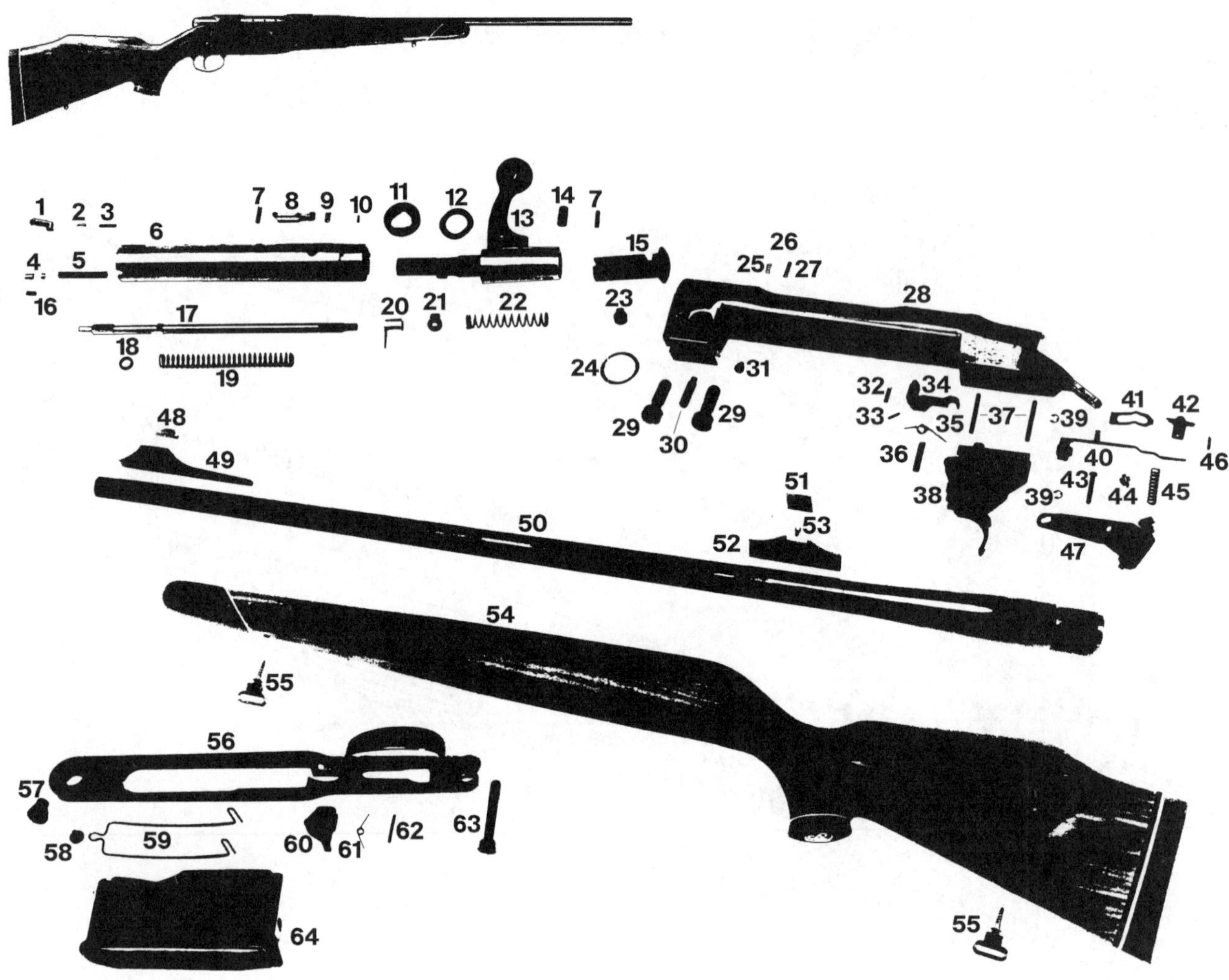

1	Extractor
2	Extractor Pin
3	Extractor Spring
4	Ejector
5	Ejector Spring
6	Bolt Body
7	Bolt Body Lock Pins
8	Bolt Body Lock
9	Bolt Body Lock Spring
10	Lug Pin
11	Closing Cam Ring
12	Spring Ring
13	Bolt Locking Head
14	Pressure Pin
15	Lock
16	Ejector Pin
17	Firing Pin Assembly
18	Firing Pin Ring
19	Firing Pin Spring
20	Cocking Piece
21	Firing Pin Key
22	Mainspring
23	Bolt Cap Pin
24	Headspacer Ring
25	Indicator Spring
26	Indicator Snap Ring
27	Indicator
28	Receiver
29	Receiver Lock Screws
30	Thread Screw
31	Safety Screw
32	Bolt Lock Pin
33	Receiver Lock Pin
34	Bolt Catch
35	Bolt Catch Spring
36	Bolt Catch Pin
37	Trigger Mechanism Pins
38	Trigger Assembly
39	Bolt Stop Link Pin Snap Rings
40	Safety Connector
41	Safety Slide Spring
42	Safety Slide
43	Bolt Stop Link Pin
44	Safety Link
45	Safety Link Spring
46	Safety Slide Pin
47	Bolt Stop Link
48	Front Sight
49	Front Sight Base
50	Barrel
51	Rear Sight
52	Rear Sight Base
53	Rear Sight Screw
54	Stock
55	Swivel Assembly
56	Trigger Guard
57	Trigger Guard Screw, Front
58	Magazine Ejector Screw
59	Magazine Ejector Spring
60	Magazine Latch
61	Magazine Latch Spring
62	Magazine Latch Pin
63	Trigger Guard Screw, Rear
64	Magazine

Derby Side-by-Side Shotgun

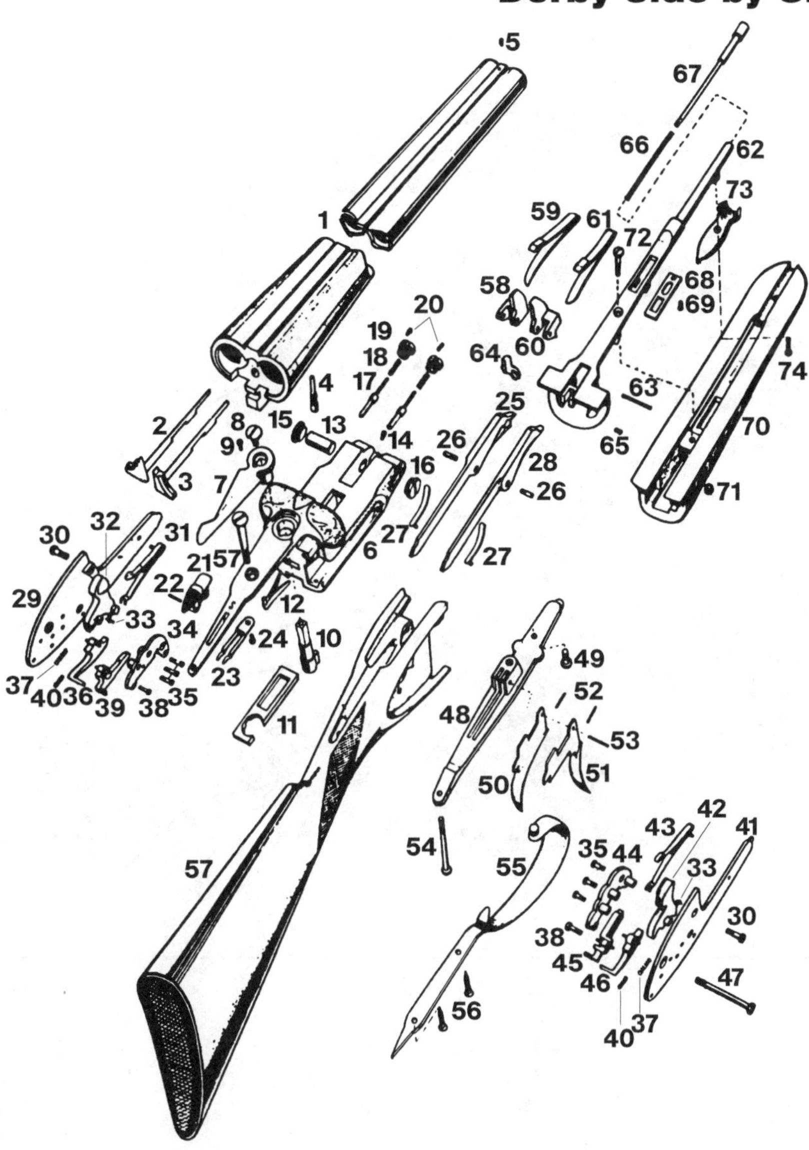

1	Barrel
2	Left Ejector
3	Right Ejector
4	Ejector Retaining Screw
5	Front Sight Bead
6	Receiver
7	Top Lever
8	Top Lever Screw
9	Screw
10	Vertical Bolt
11	Horizontal Bolt
12	Top Lever Spring
13	Barrel Pivot Pin
14	Barrel Pivot Pin Retainer
15	Barrel Pivot Pin Cap
16	Barrel Pivot Pin Cap
17	Firing Pins
18	Firing Pin Springs
19	Firing Pin Bushings
20	Firing Pin Bushing Lock Screws
21	Safety Button
22	Safety Button Pin
23	Safety Spring
24	Safety Spring Screw
25	Left Cocking Lever
26	Cocking Lever Screws
27	Cocking Lever Springs
28	Right Cocking Lever
29	Left Sidelock
30	Sidelock Front Screw
31	Left Hammer Spring
32	Left Hammer
33	Stirrup
34	Hammer and Sear Ledge, Left
35	Ledge Screws
36	Sear
37	Sear Springs
38	Sear Screw
39	Double Safety Sear
40	Safety Sear Springs
41	Right Sidelock
42	Right Hammer
43	Right Hammer Spring
44	Hammer and Sear Ledge, Right
45	Double Safety Sear
46	Sear
47	Rear Sidelock Screw
48	Trigger Plate
49	Trigger Plate Screw
50	Rear Trigger
51	Front Trigger
52	Trigger Return Springs
53	Trigger Pin
54	Trigger Plate Screw
55	Trigger Guard
56	Trigger Guard Screws
57	Stock
58	Left Ejector Latch
59	Left Ejector Spring
60	Right Ejector Latch
61	Right Ejector Spring
62	Forearm Iron
63	Forearm Latch Screw
64	Extractor Hammer Cocking Lever Activator

Silver, Lince and Bristol Over/Under Shotgun

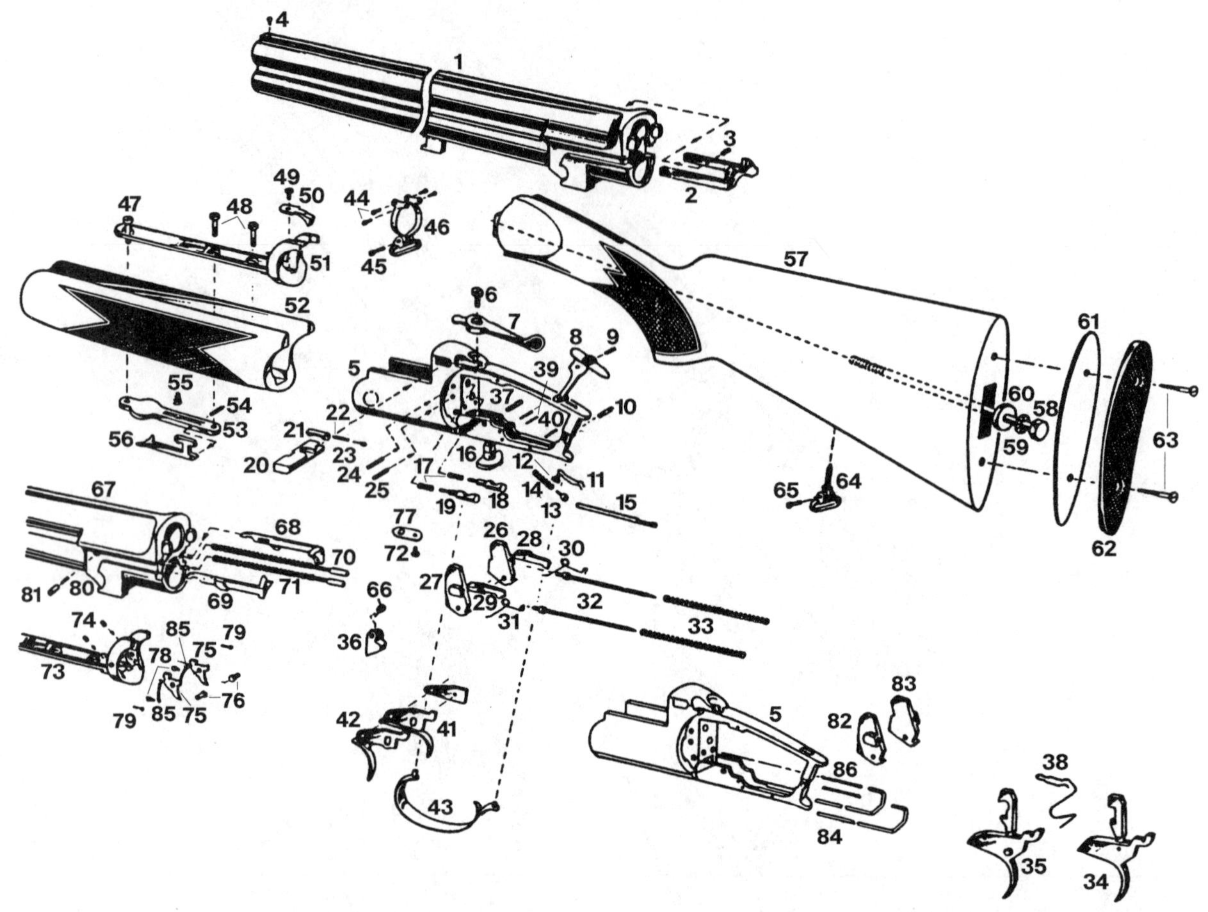

No.	Part	No.	Part	No.	Part
1	Barrels	**30**	Right Sear Spring	**59**	Stock Mounting Bolt Lock Washer
2	Extractors	**31**	Left Sear Spring	**60**	Stock Mounting Bolt Washer
3	Extractor Screw	**32**	Hammer Plungers	**61**	Buttplate Spacer
4	Front Side Bead	**33**	Main Hammer Springs	**62**	Plastic Buttplate
5	Receiver	**34**	Single Non-Selective Trigger	**63**	Buttplate Screws
6	Top Lever Screw	**35**	Single Selective Trigger	**64**	Rear Sling Swivel
7	Top Lever	**36**	Cocking Block	**65**	Rear Sling Swivel Screw
8	Safety Button	**37**	Hammer Pin	**66**	Cocking Block Spring
9	Safety Button Pin	**38**	Trigger Return Spring	**67**	Barrels
10	Trigger Guard Retaining Pin	**39**	Sear Pins	**68**	Lower Ejector
11	Safety Spring	**40**	Trigger Pin	**69**	Upper Ejector
12	Safety Spring Screw	**41**	Rear Trigger	**70**	Ejector Spring Plungers
13	Bolt Lever Spring Guide	**42**	Front Trigger	**71**	Ejector Springs
14	Bolt Lever Spring	**43**	Trigger Guard	**72**	Cocking Rod Retaining Screw
15	Cocking Rod	**44**	Front Sling Swivel Screws, Top	**73**	Forearm Iron
16	Bolt Lever	**45**	Front Sling Swivel Screws, Bottom	**74**	Ejector Latch Springs
17	Firing Pin Spring	**46**	Front Sling Swivel	**75**	Ejector Latches
18	Lower Firing Pin	**47**	Forearm Screws, Front	**76**	Ejector Latch Pins
19	Upper Firing Pin	**48**	Forearm Screws, Rear	**77**	Cocking Rod Retainer
20	Bolt	**49**	Cocking Log Screw	**78**	Screws
21	Bolt Detent	**50**	Cocking Log Screw	**79**	Ejector Latch Pin Retainers
22	Bolt Detent Spring	**51**	Forearm Iron	**80**	Spring
23	Bolt Detent Spring Guide	**52**	Forearm Stock	**81**	Ejector Retainer
24	Upper Firing Pin Retainer	**53**	Takedown Lever Bracket	**82**	Lower Hammer
25	Lower Firing Pin Retainer	**54**	Takedown Lever Pin	**83**	Upper Hammer
26	Lower Hammer	**55**	Takedown Lever Spring	**84**	Ejector Operating Rods
27	Upper Hammer	**56**	Takedown Lever	**85**	Ejector Latch Springs
28	Right Sear	**57**	Stock	**86**	Ejector Rod Springs
29	Left Sear	**58**	Stock Mounting Bolt		

York and Shogun Side-by-Side Shotgun

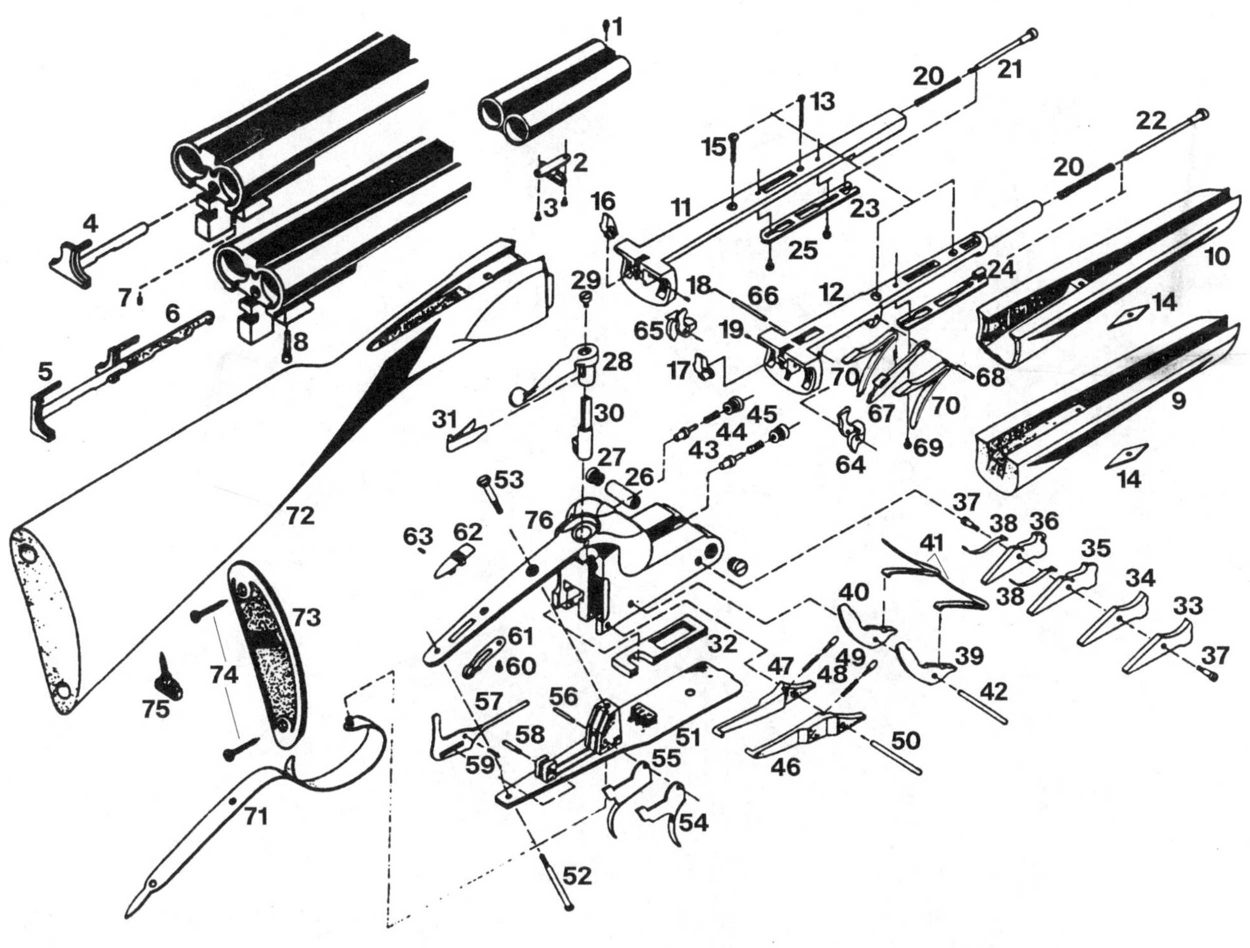

1	Front Sight Bead	**23**	Forearm Catch, Extractor Model	**51**	Trigger Plate
2	Front Sling Swivel	**24**	Forearm Catch, Ejector Model	**52**	Trigger Plate Screw
3	Front Sling Swivel Screws	**25**	Forearm Catch Screws	**53**	Upper Tang Screw
4	Extractor	**26**	Barrel Pivot Pin	**54**	Front Trigger
5	Right Ejector	**27**	Barrel Pivot Pin Cap	**55**	Rear Trigger
6	Left Ejector	**28**	Top Lever	**56**	Trigger Pin
7	Extractor Retaining Screw	**29**	Top Lever Screw	**57**	Safety Activator
8	Ejector Retaining Screw	**30**	Vertical Bolt	**58**	Safety Square Pin
9	Forearm, Extractor Model	**31**	Top Lever Spring	**59**	Safety Bar
10	Forearm, Ejector Model	**32**	Locking Bar	**60**	Safety Spring Screw
11	Forearm Iron, Extractor Model	**33**	Cocking Lever, Right	**61**	Safety Spring
12	Forearm Iron, Ejector Model	**34**	Cocking Lever, Left	**62**	Safety Button
13	Forearm Mounting Screw	**35**	Cocking Lever, Right	**63**	Safety Button Pin
14	Forearm Escutcheon	**36**	Cocking Lever, Left	**64**	Right Ejector Latch
15	Forearm Mounting Screw	**37**	Cocking Lever Retaining Screws	**65**	Left Ejector Latch
16	Hammer Cocking Lever Activator, Extractor Model	**38**	Cocking Lever Return Spring	**66**	Ejector Latch Pin
17	Hammer Cocking Lever Activator, Ejector Model	**39**	Right Hammer	**67**	Hammer Cocking Lever Activator, Ejector Model
18	Hammer Cocking Lever Activator Retaining Screw, Extractor Model	**40**	Left Hammer	**68**	Hammer Cocking Lever Activator Pin
19	Hammer Cocking Lever Activator Retaining Screw, Ejector Model	**41**	Hammer Spring	**69**	Set Screw
20	Forearm Catch Spring	**42**	Hammer Pin	**70**	Ejector Springs
21	Forearm Catch Button, Extractor Model	**43**	Firing Pins	**71**	Trigger Guard
22	Forearm Catch Button, Ejector	**44**	Firing Pin Return Spring	**72**	Stock
		45	Firing Pin Bushing	**73**	Plastic Buttplate
		46	Right Sear	**74**	Buttplate Screws
		47	Left Sear	**75**	Rear Sling Swivel
		48	Sear Springs	**76**	Receiver
		49	Sear Spring Guides		
		50	Sear Pin		

Autoloading Carbine

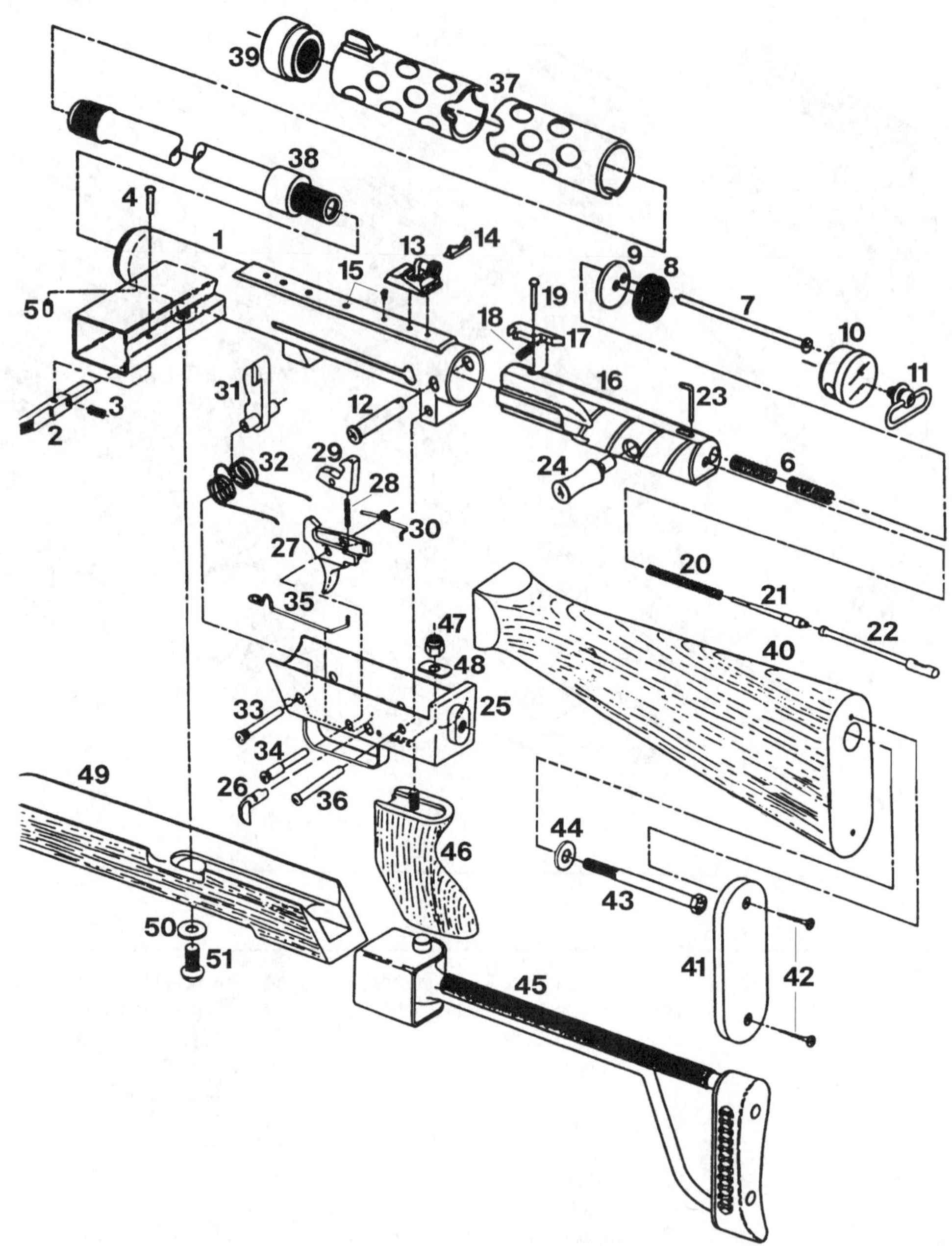

1	Receiver	18	Extractor Spring	35	Safety Pin Clip
2	Magazine Catch	19	Extractor Pin	36	Trigger Housing Pin
3	Magazine Catch Spring	20	Firing Pin Spring	37	Shroud
4	Magazine Catch Pin	21	Firing Pin	38	Barrel
5	Shroud Locator Pin	22	Firing Pin Extension	39	Barrel End Cap
6	Recoil Spring	23	Firing Pin Extension Clip	40	Buttstock
7	Recoil Spring Guide	24	Operating Handle	41	Buttplate
8	Recoil Buffer, Rubber	25	Trigger Housing	42	Buttplate Screws
9	Recoil Buffer, Steel	26	Safety-Lever	43	Buttstock Bolt
10	Receiver End Cap	27	Trigger	44	Buttstock Bolt Washers
11	Pistol Sling Swivel	28	Disconnector Spring	45	Folding Stock
12	Receiver End Cap Pin	29	Disconnector	46	Pistol Grip
13	Rear Sight, Peep	30	Trigger Return Spring	47	Pistol Grip Nut
14	Rear Sight, Blade	31	Hammer	48	Pistol Grip Washer
15	Filler Screws	32	Hammer Spring	49	Forend
16	Bolt	33	Hammer Pin	50	Forend Washer
17	Extractor	34	Trigger Pin	51	Forend Bolt

Model 1917 Bolt-Action Rifle

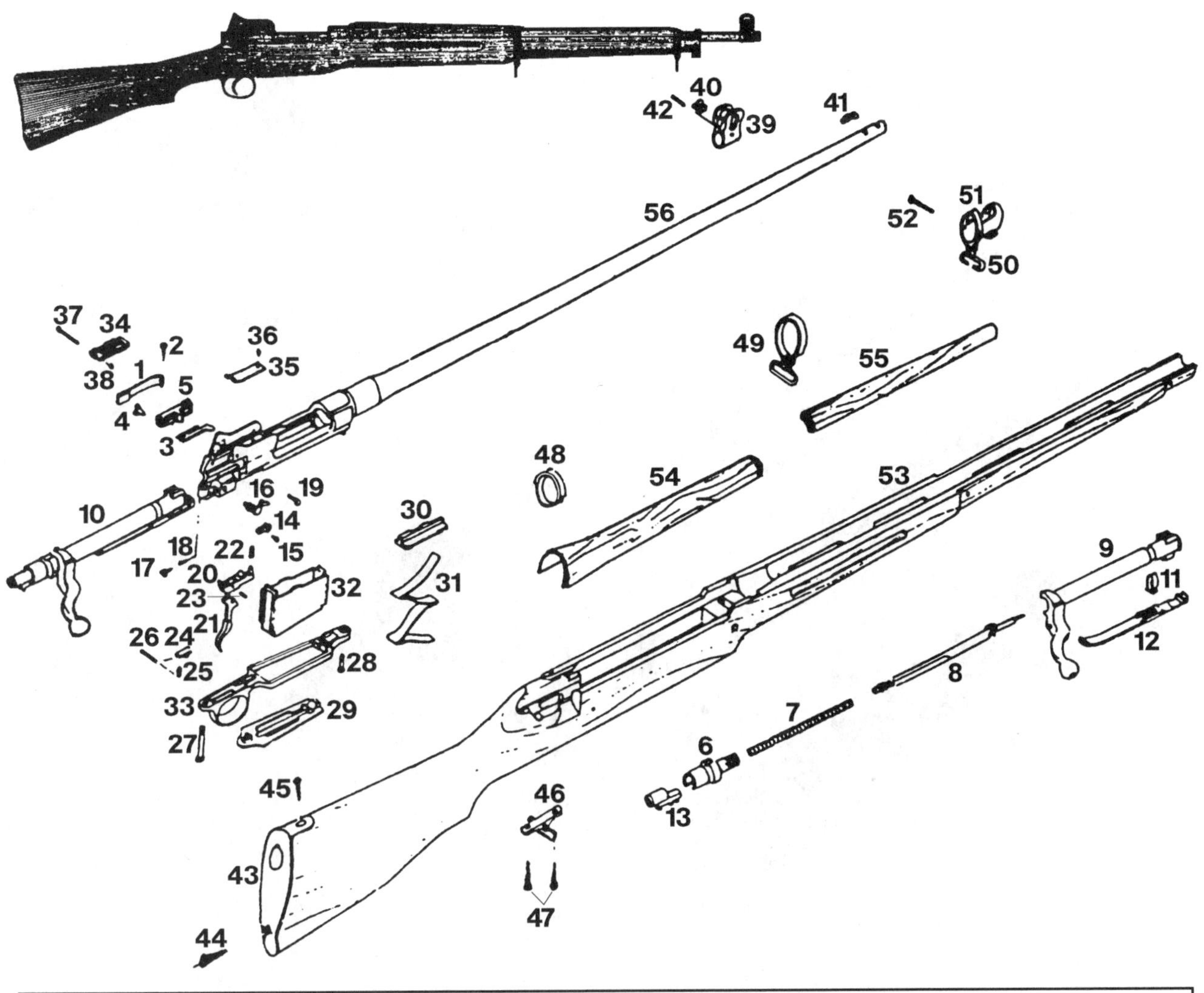

1	Bolt Stop Spring	**25**	Floorplate Catch Spring	**49**	Lower Band Assembly
2	Bolt Stop Screw	**26**	Floorplate Catch Pin	**50**	Stacking Swivel
3	Ejector	**27**	Rear Guard Screw	**51**	Upper Band
4	Bolt Stop Spring Rest	**28**	Front Guard Screw	**52**	Upper Band Screw
5	Bolt Stop	**29**	Floorplate	**53**	Stock
6	Bolt Sleeve	**30**	Follower	**54**	Handguard, Lower
7	Mainspring	**31**	Magazine Spring	**55**	Handguard, Upper
8	Firing Pin	**32**	Magazine Box	**56**	Barrel
9	Bolt, Stripped	**33**	Trigger Guard	**Parts Not Shown**	
10	Bolt, Complete	**34**	Rear Sight		Follower Depressor
11	Extractor Collar	**35**	Rear Sight Base Spring		Front Guard Screw Bushing
12	Extractor	**36**	Rear Sight Base Screw		Lower Band
13	Cocking Piece	**37**	Rear Sight Axis Screw		Lower Band Screw
14	Safety Lock Holder	**38**	Rear Sight Axis Nut		Plate Spring
15	Safety Lock Holder Screw	**39**	Front Sight Carrier		Rear Guard Screw Bushing
16	Safety	**40**	Front Sight Blade		Rear Sight Slide
17	Safety Lock Plunger	**41**	Front Sight Spline		Rear Sight Slide Spring
18	Safety Lock Plunger Spring	**42**	Front Sight Pin		Rear Swivel Base
19	Sear Pin	**43**	Buttplate		Sling Swivel
20	Sear	**44**	Buttplate Screw, Large		Stacking Swivel Screw
21	Trigger	**45**	Buttplate Screw, Small		
22	Sear Spring	**46**	Rear Swivel Assembly		
23	Trigger Pin	**47**	Rear Swivel Base Screws		
24	Floorplate Catch	**48**	Handguard Ring		

EG 722 Autoloading Rifle

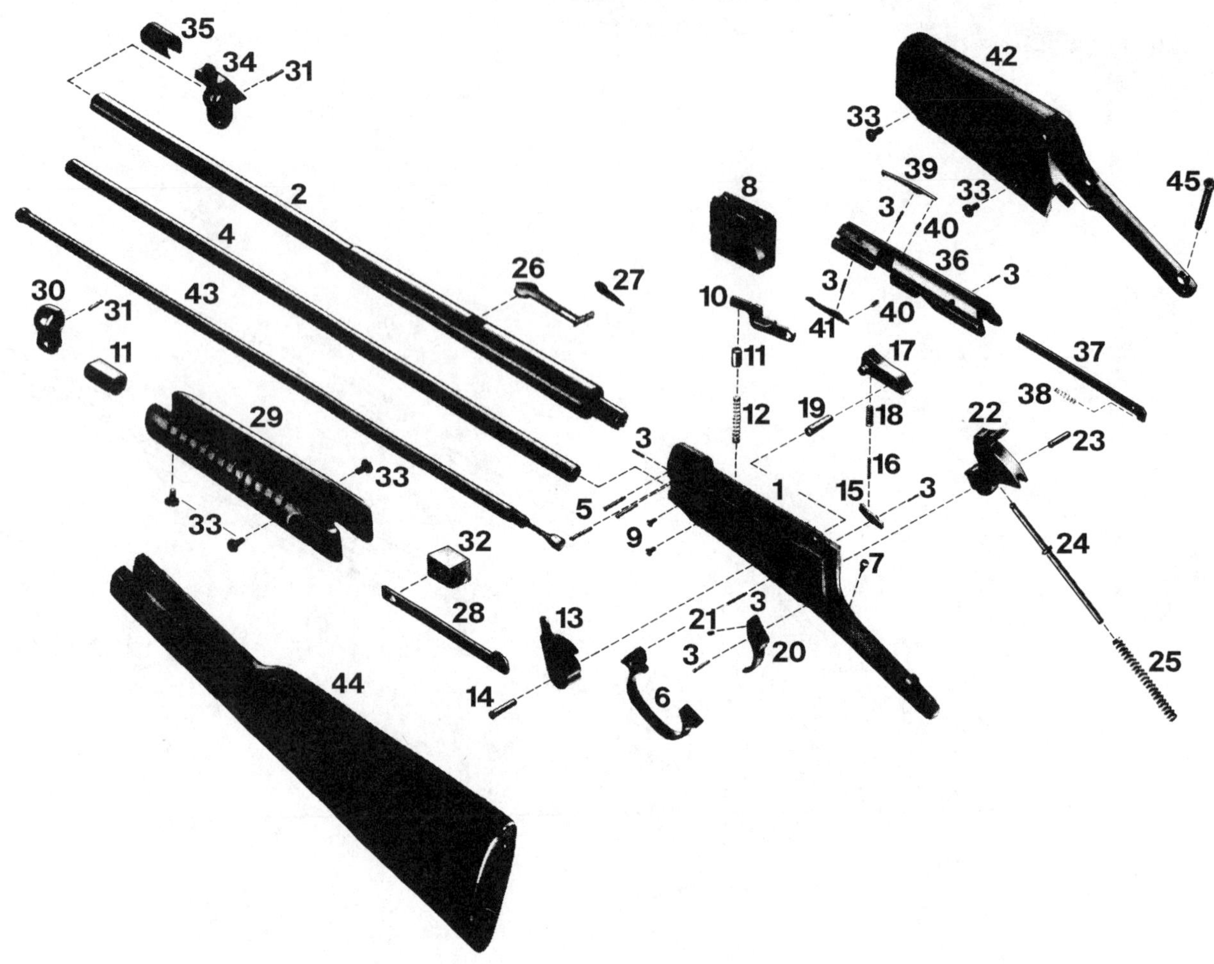

1	Frame	**24**	Mainspring Guide
2	Barrel	**25**	Mainspring
3	Cylindrical Pins	**26**	Rear Sight
4	Magazine Tube, Outside	**27**	Rear Sight Elevator
5	Tapered Pins	**28**	Operating Slide
6	Trigger Guard	**29**	Forearm
7	Screw	**30**	Intermediate Band
8	Carrier	**31**	Conical Pin
9	Countersunk Screws	**32**	Bushing Guide
10	Carrier Lever	**33**	Set Screws with Disk
11	Sleeve	**34**	Front Sight
12	Carrier Spring	**35**	Front Sight Cover
13	Action Lever	**36**	Breechbolt
14	Action Lever Pin	**37**	Firing Pin
15	Detent	**38**	Firing Pin Spring
16	Detent Spring	**39**	Extractor
17	Locking Bar	**40**	Extractor Spring
18	Locking Bar Spring	**41**	Ejector
19	Locking Bar Pin	**42**	Receiver
20	Trigger	**43**	Magazine
21	Trigger Spring	**44**	Buttstock, Complete
22	Hammer	**45**	Upper Tang Screw
23	Hammer Pin		

EG 73 Lever-Action Rifle

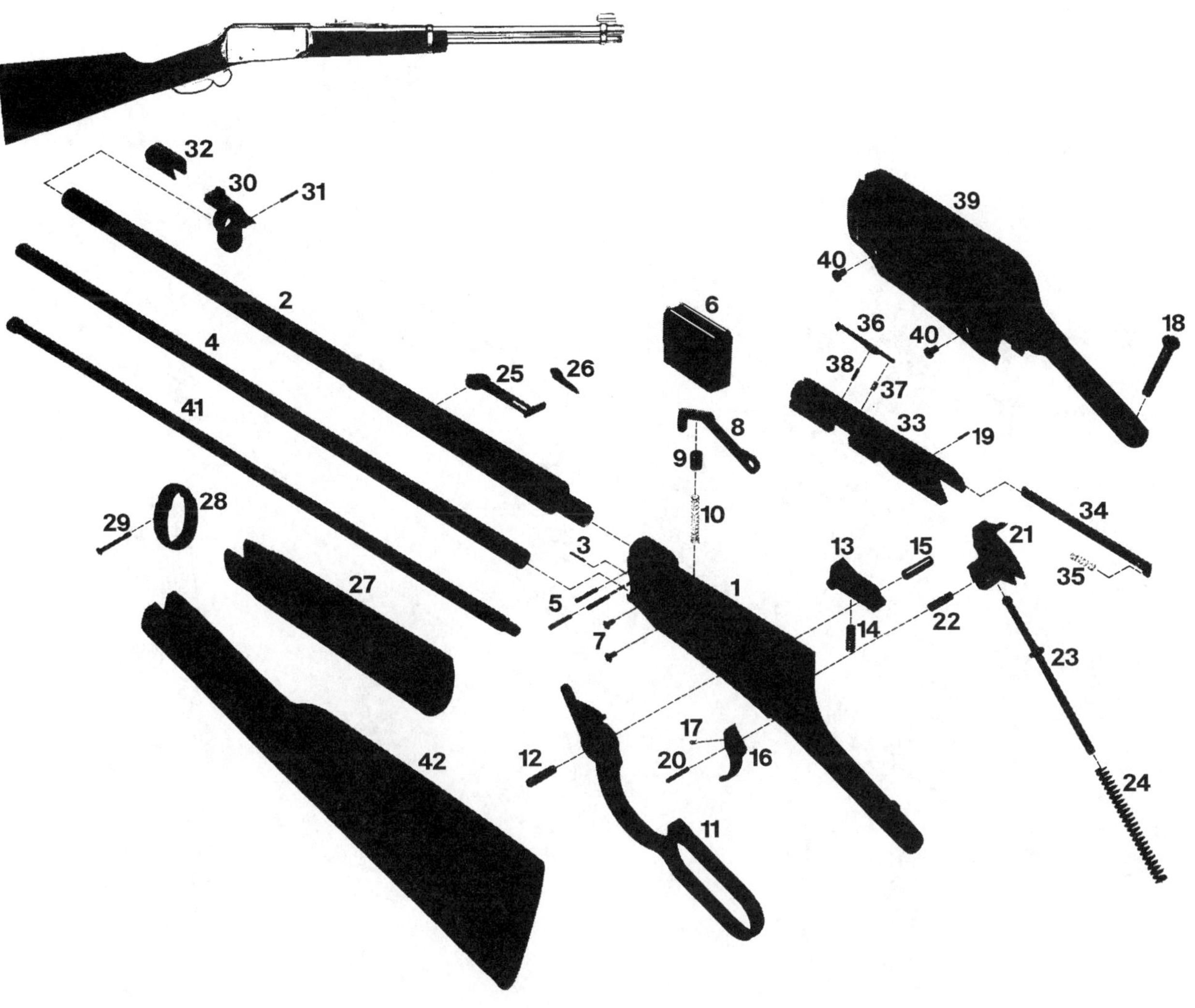

1	Frame	**21**	Hammer
2	Barrel	**22**	Hammer Pin
3	Locating Pin	**23**	Mainspring Guide
4	Magazine Tube, Outside	**24**	Mainspring
5	Magazine Tube and Barrel Retaining Pins	**25**	Rear Sight
		26	Rear Sight Elevator
6	Carrier	**27**	Forend
7	Action Set Screws	**28**	Rear Barrel Band
8	Carrier Lever	**29**	Rear Barrel Band Screw
9	Carrier Spring Plunger	**30**	Front Sight
10	Carrier Spring	**31**	Upper Barrel Band Pin
11	Finger Lever	**32**	Front Sight Hood
12	Finger Lever Axis Pin	**33**	Breechbolt
13	Locking Bar	**34**	Firing Pin
14	Locking Bar Spring	**35**	Firing Pin Spring
15	Locking Bar Pin	**36**	Extractor
16	Trigger	**37**	Extractor Spring
17	Trigger Spring	**38**	Extractor Pivot Pin
18	Upper Tang Screw	**39**	Receiver
19	Firing Pin Retaining Pin	**40**	Receiver Screws
20	Trigger Pivot Pin	**41**	Magazine Tube
		42	Buttstock

EM1 Autoloading Rifle

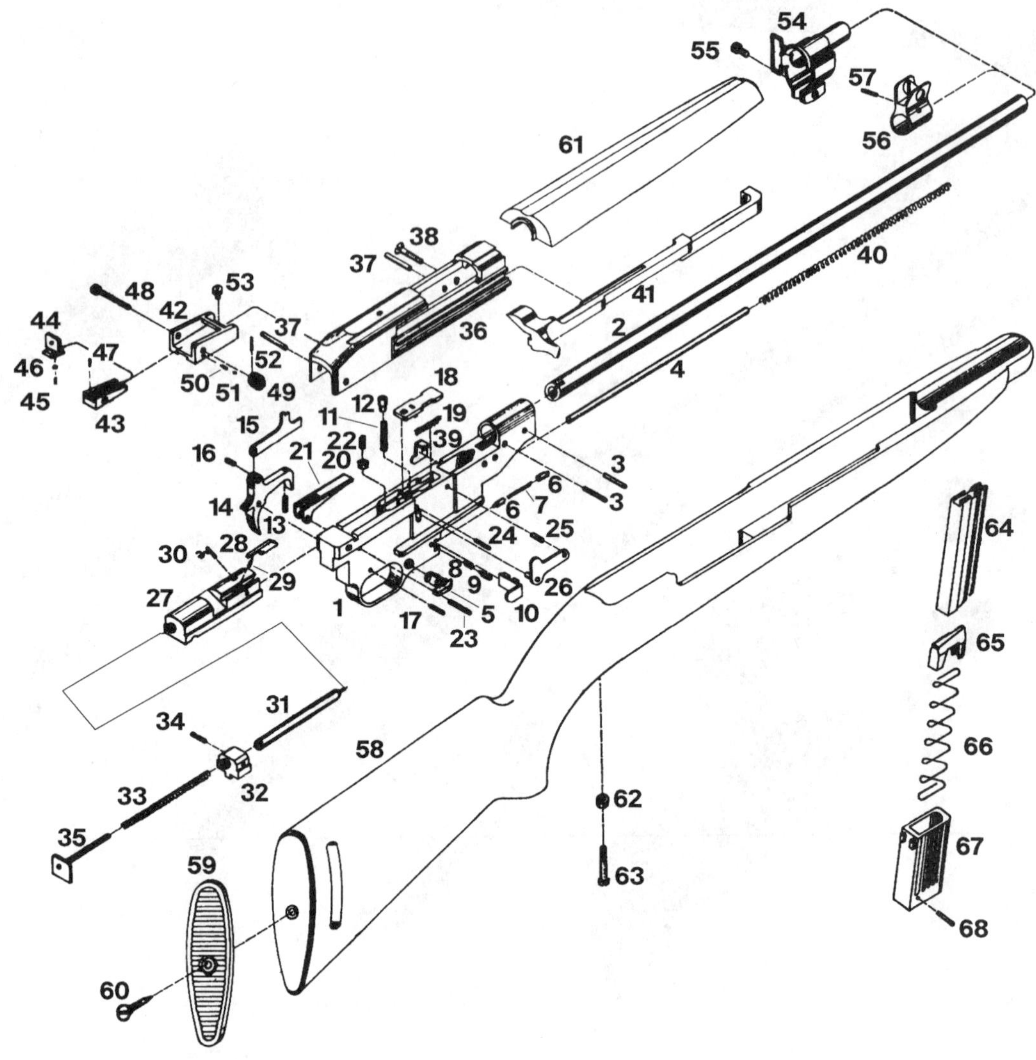

1	Trigger Housing	**24**	Sear Release Plate Pin	**47**	Rear Sight Ramp Pin
2	Barrel	**25**	Sear Release Pin	**48**	Rear Sight Windage Screw
3	Barrel Pins	**26**	Sear Release	**49**	Rear Sight Windage Knob
4	Operating Slide Spring Guide	**27**	Bolt	**50**	Windage Stop Spring
5	Safety-Lever	**28**	Extractor	**51**	Windage Stop Ball
6	Safety Detent Plungers	**29**	Extractor Spring	**52**	Windage Stop Pin
7	Safety Detent Plunger Spring	**30**	Extractor Pin	**53**	Rear Sight Base Screw
8	Magazine Catch Spring	**31**	Firing Pin	**54**	Front Band Assembly
9	Magazine Catch Spring Plunger	**32**	Firing Pin Collar	**55**	Front Band Screw
10	Magazine Catch	**33**	Firing Pin Spring	**56**	Front Sight Assembly
11	Trigger Bar Spring	**34**	Firing Pin Collar Pin	**57**	Front Sight Pin
12	Trigger Bar Spring Plunger	**35**	Recoil Plate	**58**	Stock
13	Trigger Spring	**36**	Receiver	**59**	Buttplate
14	Trigger	**37**	Trigger Housing Retaining Pins	**60**	Buttplate Screw
15	Trigger Bar	**38**	Receiver Screw	**61**	Handguard
16	Trigger Bar Pin	**39**	Ejector	**62**	Rear Guard Screw Escutcheon
17	Trigger Pin	**40**	Operating Slide Spring	**63**	Rear Guard Screw
18	Sear Release Plate	**41**	Operating Slide	**64**	Magazine Body
19	Sear Release Plate Spring	**42**	Rear Sight Base	**65**	Magazine Follower
20	Sear Spring Plunger	**43**	Rear Sight Ramp	**66**	Magazine Spring
21	Sear	**44**	Rear Sight Aperture	**67**	Magazine Body Housing
22	Sear Spring	**45**	Rear Sight Aperture Spring	**68**	Magazine Body Housing Pin
23	Sear Retaining Pin	**46**	Rear Sight Aperture Spring Ball		

ESG 22 Autoloading Rifle

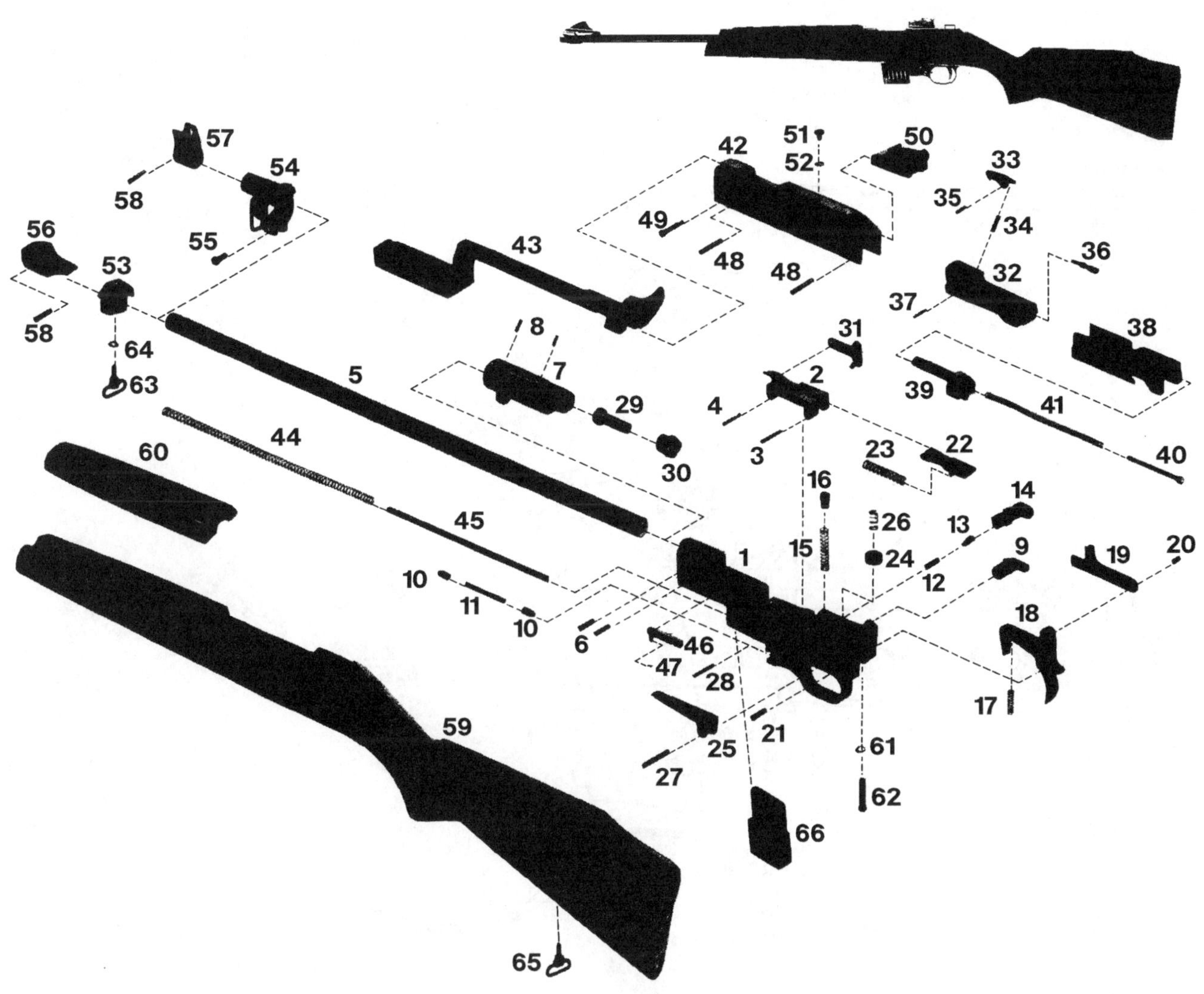

1	Trigger Housing	**24**	Sear Spring Plunger	**47**	Bolt Catch Plunger Spring
2	Sear Block	**25**	Sear	**48**	Trigger Housing Retaining Pins
3	Long Sear Block Pin	**26**	Sear Spring	**49**	Receiver Screw
4	Short Sear Block Pin	**27**	Sear Pin	**50**	Rear Sight Assembly
5	Barrel	**28**	Sear Release Plate Pin	**51**	Rear Sight Mounting Screw
6	Barrel Pins	**29**	Gas Piston	**52**	Rear Sight Mounting Screw Washer
7	Gas Cylinder	**30**	Gas Piston Screw	**53**	Front Band Assembly
8	Gas Cylinder Locking Pins	**31**	Sear Release	**54**	Front Band Assembly (M1 type)
9	Safety-Lever	**32**	Bolt	**55**	Front Band Screw (M1 type)
10	Safety Detent Plungers	**33**	Extractor	**56**	Front Sight Assembly
11	Safety Detent Plunger Spring	**34**	Extractor Spring	**57**	Front Sight Assembly (M1 type)
12	Magazine Catch Spring	**35**	Extractor Pin	**58**	Front Sight Assembly Pin
13	Magazine Catch Spring Plunger	**36**	Firing Pin	**59**	Stock
14	Magazine Catch	**37**	Firing Pin Retaining Pin	**60**	Handguard
15	Trigger Bar Spring	**38**	Bolt Carrier	**61**	Rear Guard Screw Washer
16	Trigger Bar Spring Plunger	**39**	Firing Pin Striker	**62**	Rear Guard Screw
17	Trigger Spring	**40**	Firing Pin Striker Spring Guide	**63**	Sling Swivel, Front
18	Trigger	**41**	Firing Pin Striker Spring	**64**	Sling Swivel Washer
19	Trigger Bar	**42**	Receiver	**65**	Sling Swivel, Rear
20	Trigger Bar Pin	**43**	Operating Slide	**66**	Magazine
21	Trigger Pin	**44**	Operating Slide Spring		
22	Sear Release Plate	**45**	Operating Slide Spring Guide		
23	Sear Release Plate Spring	**46**	Bolt Catch Plunger		

Senator SOUF41, SOUF20 and SOUF12 Over/Under Shotgun

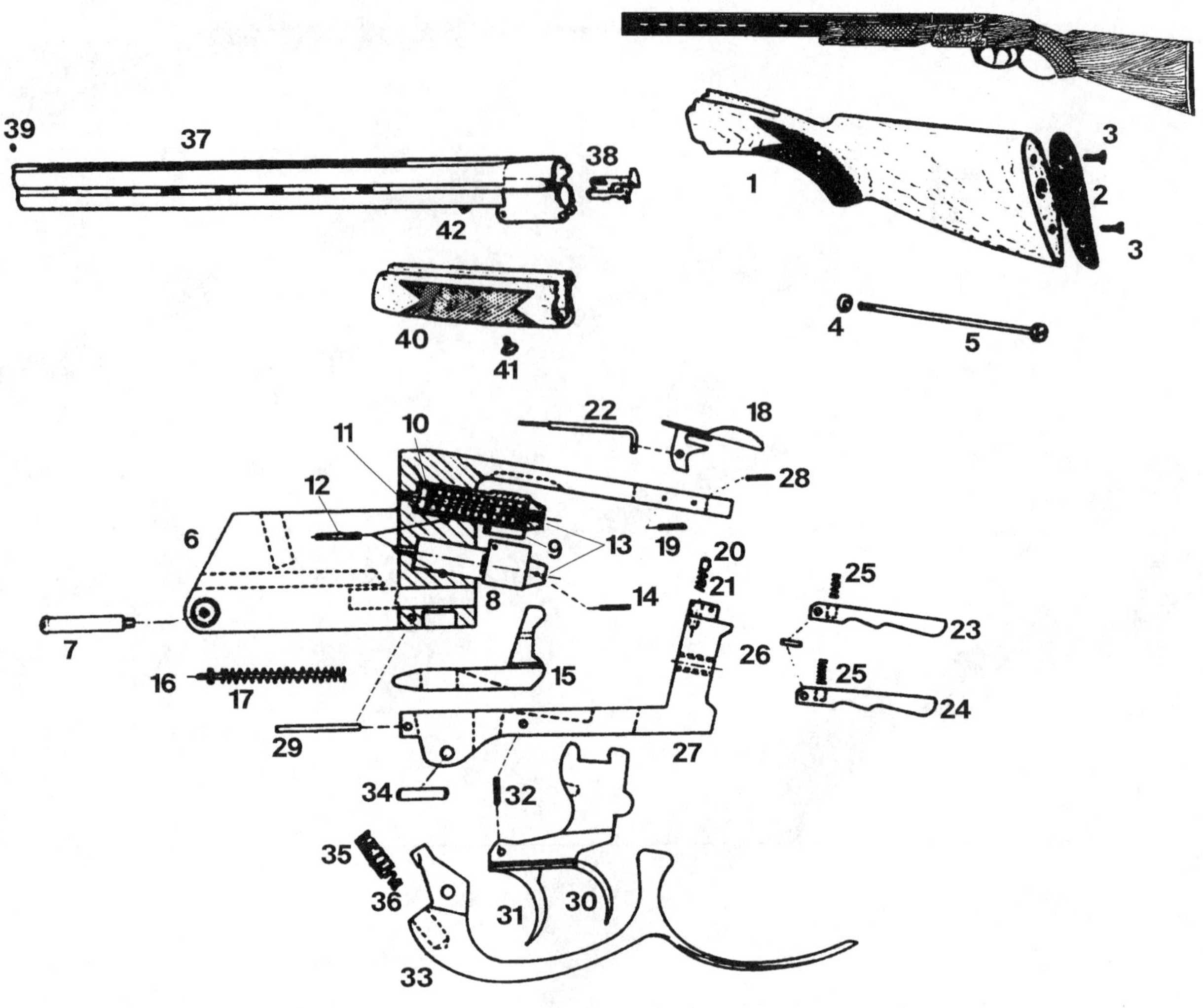

1	Buttstock	22	Safety Actuating Rod
2	Buttplate	23	Sear Lever, Upper
3	Buttplate Screws	24	Sear Lever, Lower
4	Stock Bolt Washer	25	Sear Lever Springs
5	Stock Bolt	26	Sear Lever Pins
6	Receiver	27	Floorplate
7	Barrel Hinge Screw	28	Floorplate Tang Pin
8	Firing Pin Housing, Lower	29	Floorplate Receiver Pin
9	Firing Pin Housing, Upper	30	Rear Trigger, Upper
10	Firing Pin Springs	31	Front Trigger, Lower
11	Firing Pins	32	Trigger Retaining Pin
12	Firing Pin Retaining Pins	33	Cocking Lever
13	Firing Pin Collars	34	Cocking Lever Pin
14	Firing Pin Collar Retaining Pins	35	Cocking Lever Plunger
15	Locking Block	36	Cocking Lever Plunger Spring
16	Locking Block Spring Guide	37	Barrel Assembly
17	Locking Block Spring	38	Extractors
18	Safety-Lever	39	Sight Bead
19	Safety-Lever Pin	40	Forend
20	Safety Detent	41	Forend Screw
21	Safety Detent Spring	42	Forend Screw Lug

1949 Autoloading Rifle

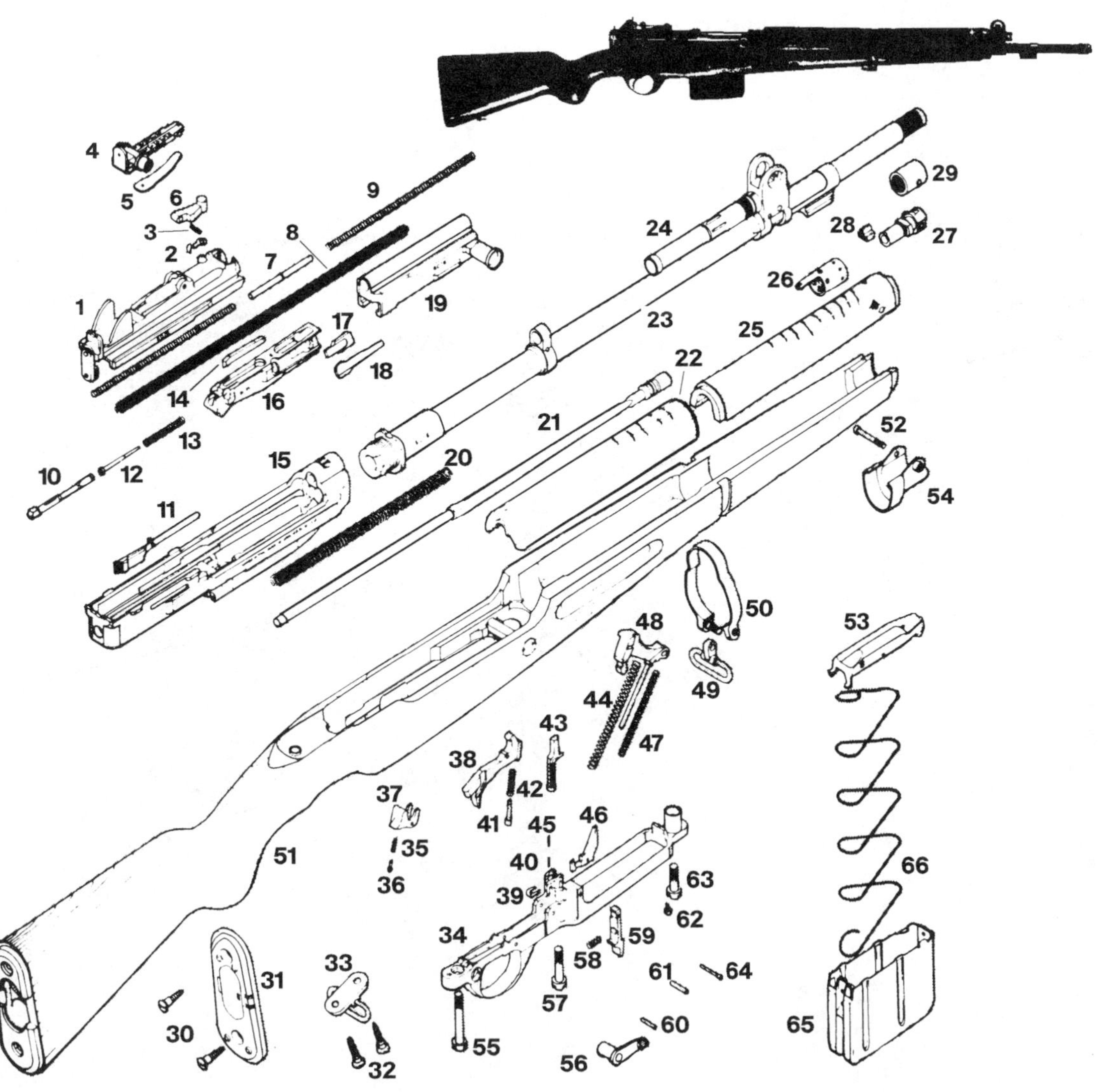

1	Receiver Cover Assembly	**23**	Barrel	**45**	Bolt Stop Retainer Plunger
2	Bolt Carrier Catch Stop	**24**	Gas Cylinder	**46**	Ejector
3	Bolt Carrier Catch Spring	**25**	Front Handguard	**47**	Inner Hammer Spring
4	Rear Sight	**26**	Gas Adjusting Sleeve	**48**	Hammer and Hammer Spring Guide
5	Rear Sight Spring	**27**	Gas Cylinder Plug	**49**	Lower Band Swivel
6	Bolt Carrier Catch	**28**	Front Sight	**50**	Lower Band
7	Inner Recoil Spring Guide	**29**	Muzzle Cap	**51**	Stock
8	Outer Recoil Spring	**30**	Buttplate Screws	**52**	Stock End Cap Screw
9	Inner Recoil Springs	**31**	Buttplate	**53**	Magazine Follower
10	Firing Pin Extension	**32**	Butt Swivel Screws	**54**	Stock End Cap
11	Sliding Dust Cover	**33**	Butt Swivel	**55**	Rear Guard Screw
12	Firing Pin	**34**	Trigger Guard	**56**	Safety
13	Firing Pin Spring	**35**	Auxiliary Sear Spring	**57**	Center Guard Screw
14	Firing Pin Safety Stop	**36**	Auxiliary Sear Spring Plunger	**58**	Magazine Catch Spring
15	Receiver	**37**	Auxiliary Sear	**59**	Magazine Catch
16	Bolt	**38**	Trigger	**60**	Trigger Pin
17	Extractor	**39**	Bolt Stop Retainer	**61**	Hammer Pin
18	Extractor Spring	**40**	Bolt Stop Retainer Plunger Spring	**62**	Guard Screw Stop Screws
19	Bolt Carrier	**41**	Trigger Spring Plunger	**63**	Front Guard Screw
20	Piston Spring	**42**	Trigger Spring	**64**	Magazine Catch Pin
21	Piston	**43**	Bolt Stop Assembly	**65**	Magazine Box
22	Rear Handguard	**44**	Outer Hammer Spring	**66**	Magazine Follower Spring

Supreme Bolt-Action Rifle

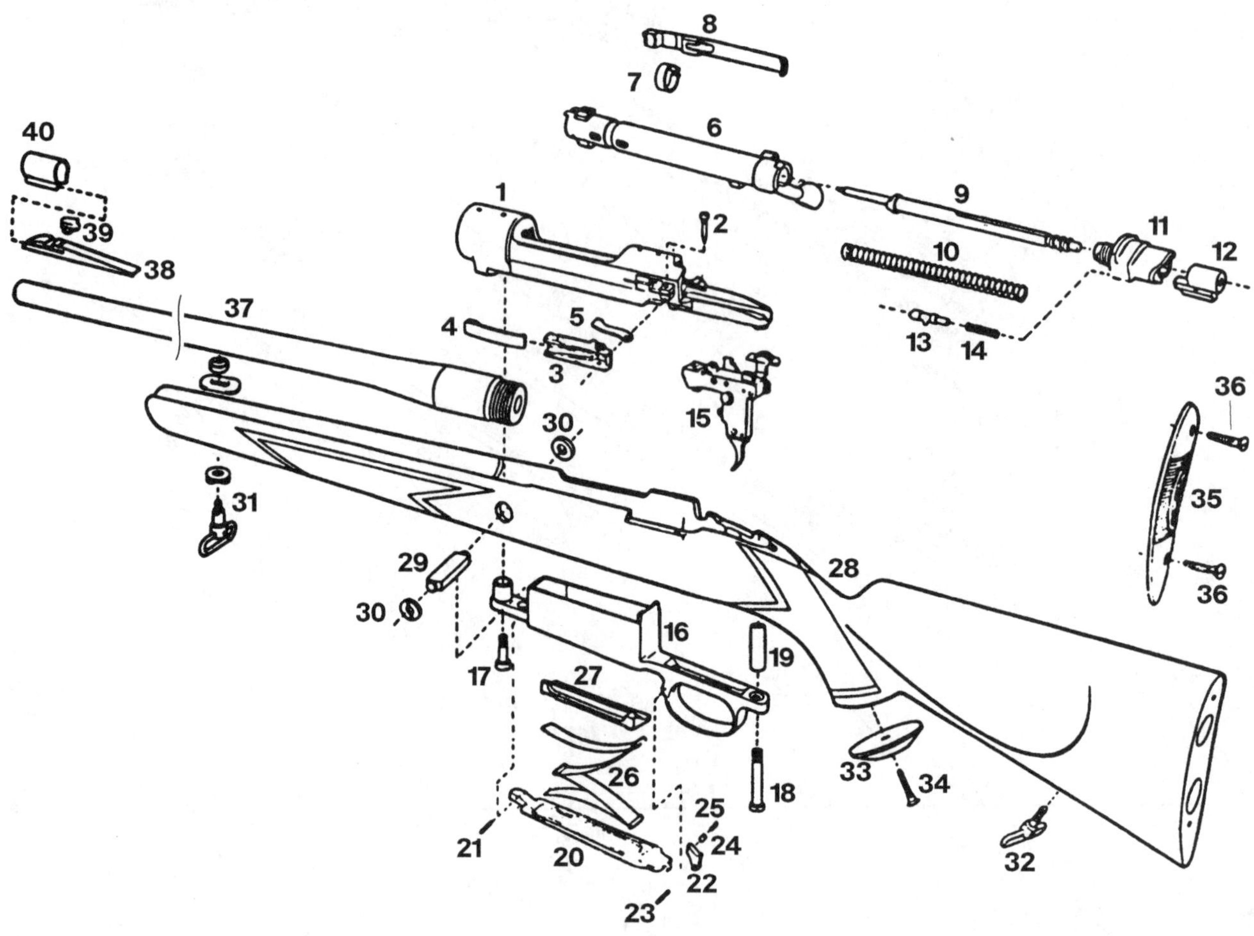

1	Receiver	**21**	Floorplate Pivot Pin
2	Bolt Stop Screw	**22**	Floorplate Catch
3	Bolt Stop	**23**	Floorplate Catch Pin
4	Bolt Stop Spring	**24**	Floorplate Catch Plunger
5	Ejector	**25**	Floorplate Catch Plunger Spring
6	Bolt Body	**26**	Follower Spring
7	Extractor Collar	**27**	Follower
8	Extractor	**28**	Stock
9	Firing Pin	**29**	Stock Crossbolt
10	Firing Pin Spring	**30**	Stock Crossbolt Nuts
11	Bolt Sleeve	**31**	Front Sling Swivel
12	Cocking Piece	**32**	Rear Sling Swivel
13	Bolt Sleeve Lock Plunger	**33**	Grip Cap
14	Bolt Sleeve Lock Spring	**34**	Grip Cap Screw
15	Trigger Assembly	**35**	Buttplate
16	Trigger Guard	**36**	Buttplate Screws
17	Front Guard Screw	**37**	Barrel
18	Rear Guard Screw	**38**	Front Sight Ramp
19	Rear Guard Screw Bushing	**39**	Front Sight
20	Floorplate	**40**	Front Sight Cover

Model B Side-by-Side Shotgun

Courtesy of Thomas E. Wessel

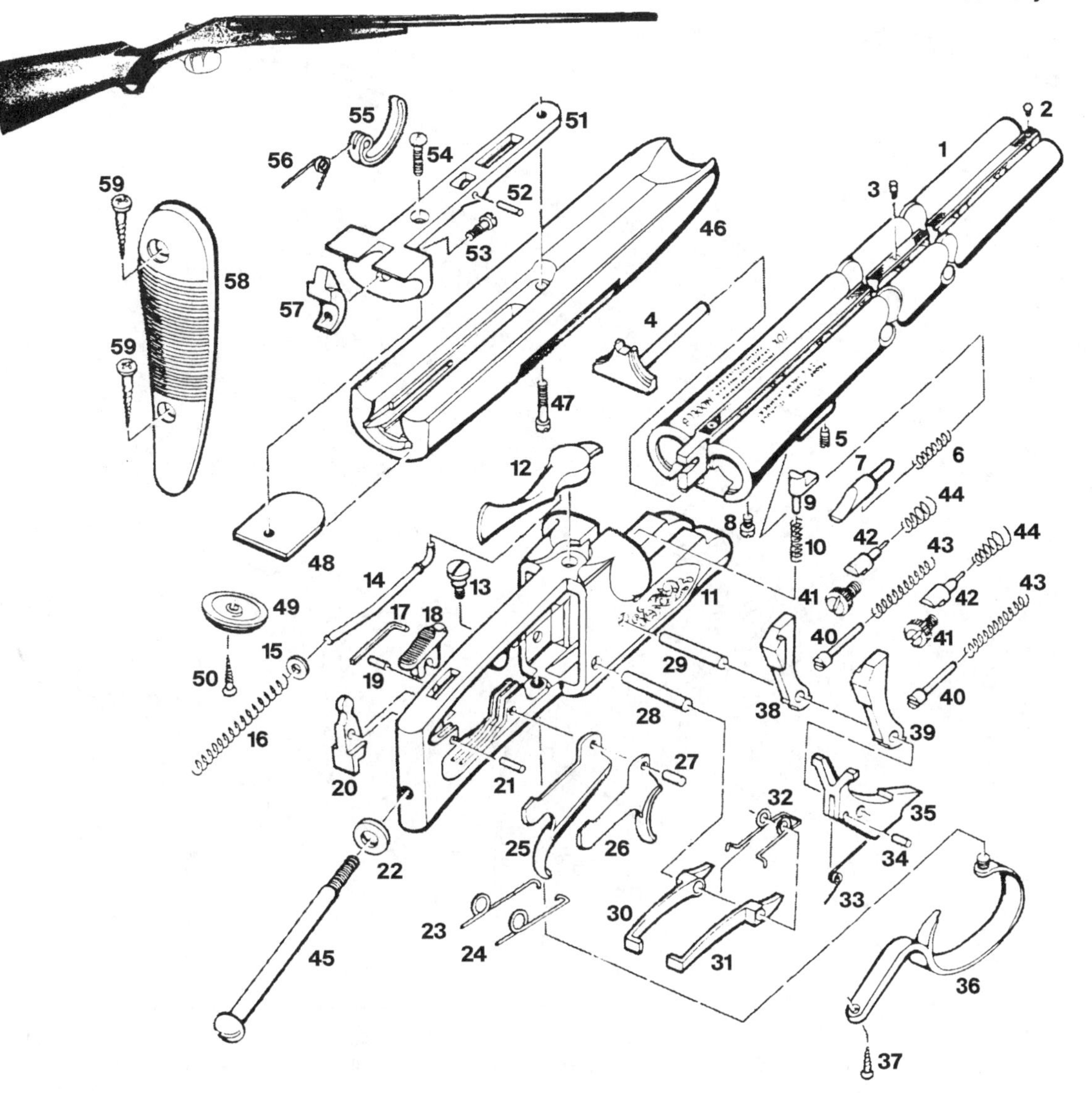

1	Barrel Assembly	**22**	Stock Bolt Washer	**43**	Mainsprings
2	Front Sight	**23**	Trigger Spring, Left	**44**	Firing Pin Springs
3	Rear Sight	**24**	Trigger Spring, Right	**45**	Stock Bolt
4	Extractor	**25**	Trigger, Left	**46**	Forend
5	Cocking Plunger Retaining Screw	**26**	Trigger, Right	**47**	Forend Screw, Front
6	Cocking Plunger Spring	**27**	Trigger Pin	**48**	Forend Insert
7	Cocking Plunger	**28**	Sear Pin	**49**	Pistol Grip Cap
8	Extractor Screw	**29**	Cocking Lever and Hammer Pin	**50**	Pistol Grip Cap Screw
9	Top Snap Trip	**30**	Sear, Left	**51**	Forend Iron
10	Top Snap Trip Spring	**31**	Sear, Right	**52**	Forend Spring Pin
11	Frame	**32**	Sear Spring	**53**	Ejector Screw
12	Top Snap	**33**	Cocking Lever Spring	**54**	Forend Screw, Rear
13	Top Snap Screw	**34**	Cocking Lever Spring Pin	**55**	Forend Spring
14	Top Snap Plunger	**35**	Cocking Lever	**56**	Forend Spring Spring
15	Top Snap Plunger Collar	**36**	Trigger Guard	**57**	Ejector
16	Top Snap Plunger Spring	**37**	Trigger Guard Screw	**58**	Buttplate
17	Safety Spring	**38**	Hammer, Left	**59**	Buttplate Screws
18	Safety Button	**39**	Hammer, Right	**Parts Not Shown**	
19	Safety Plunger	**40**	Mainspring Plungers		Stock
20	Safety-Lever	**41**	Firing Pin Retaining Screws		
21	Safety-Lever Pin	**42**	Firing Pins		

Model B-SE Side-by-Side Shotgun

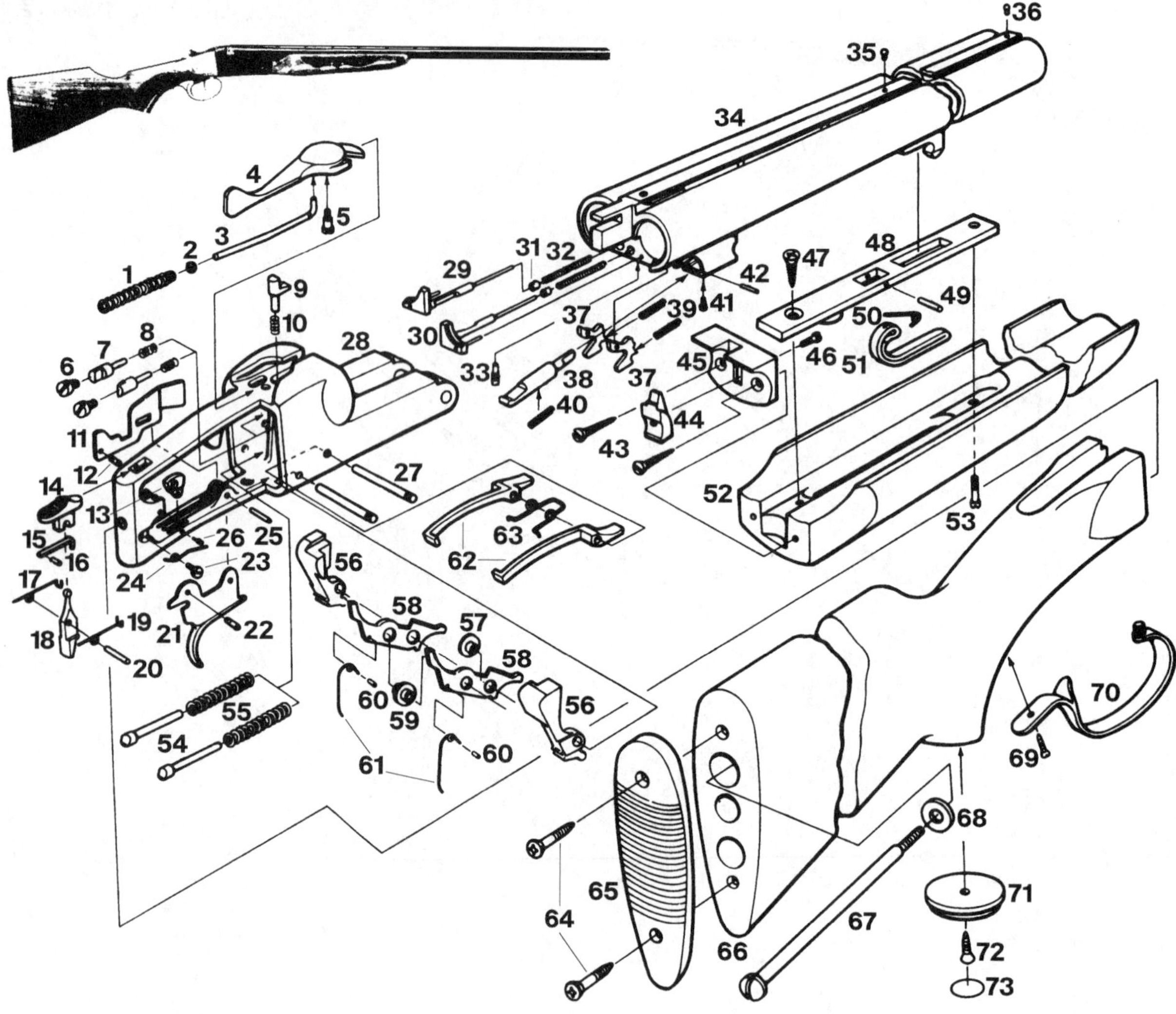

1	Top Snap Plunger Spring	26	Inertia Block Pin	49	Forend Spring Pin
2	Mainspring Retaining Collar	27	Sear Pin and Cocking Lever/ Hammer Pin	50	Forend Spring Spring
3	Top Snap Plunger	28	Frame	51	Forend Spring
4	Top Snap	29	Extractor, Left	52	Forend Wood
5	Top Snap Screw	30	Extractor, Right	53	Forend Screw, Front
6	Firing Pin Retaining Screws	31	Ejector Collars	54	Mainspring Plungers
7	Firing Pins	32	Ejector Springs	55	Mainsprings
8	Firing Pin Springs	33	Extractor Screw	56	Hammers
9	Top Snap Trip	34	Barrels	57	Cocking Lever Spacer
10	Top Snap Trip Spring	35	Rear Sight	58	Cocking Levers
11	Slide	36	Front Sight	59	Cocking Lever Bushing
12	Trigger Stud	37	Ejector Sear	60	Cocking Lever Spring Pins
13	Inertia Block	38	Cocking Plunger	61	Cocking Lever Springs
14	Safety Button	39	Ejector Sear Spring	62	Sears
15	Safety Spring	40	Cocking Plunger Spring	63	Sear Spring
16	Safety Plunger	41	Cocking Plunger Retaining Screw	64	Buttplate Screws
17	Slide Spring	42	Ejector Sear Pin	65	Buttplate
18	Safety-Lever	43	Forend Iron Head Screws	66	Stock
19	Trigger Spring	44	Ejector	67	Stock Bolt
20	Safety-Lever Pin	45	Forend Iron Head	68	Stock Bolt Washer
21	Trigger	46	Ejector Screw	69	Trigger Guard Screw
22	Trigger Stud	47	Forend Screw, Rear	70	Trigger Guard
23	Inertia Block Spring Screw	48	Forend Spring Housing	71	Pistol Grip Cap
24	Inertia Block Spring			72	Pistol Grip Cap Screw
25	Trigger Pin			73	Medallion

Model BDE, BSE-C, BSE-D, BSE-E and BSE Series F and H Side-by-Side Shotgun

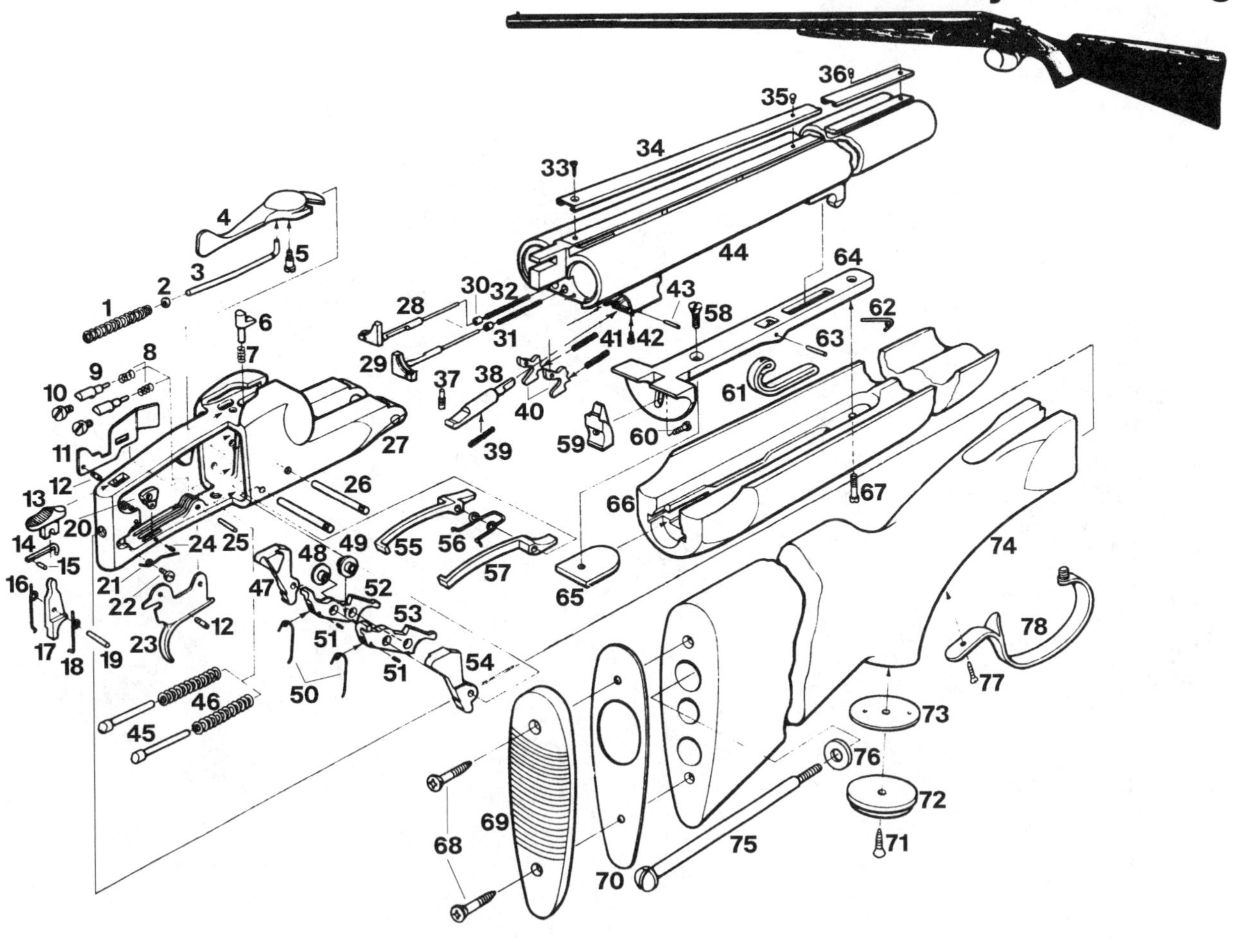

1	Top Snap Plunger Spring	27	Frame	54	Hammer, Right
2	Top Snap Plunger Collar	28	Extractor, Left	55	Sear, Left
3	Top Snap Plunger	29	Extractor, Right	56	Sear Spring
4	Top Snap	30	Ejector Collar, Left	57	Sear, Right
5	Top Snap Screw	31	Ejector Collar, Right	58	Forend Screw, Rear
6	Top Snap Trip	32	Ejector Springs	59	Ejector
7	Top Snap Trip Spring	33	Top Rib Lock Screw	60	Ejector Screw
8	Firing Pin Springs	34	Top Rib	61	Forend Spring
9	Firing Pins	35	Rear Sight	62	Forend Spring Spring
10	Firing Pin Retaining Screws	36	Front Sight	63	Forend Spring Pin
11	Slide	37	Extractor Screw	64	Forend Iron
12	Trigger Studs	38	Cocking Plunger	65	Forend Insert
13	Safety Button	39	Cocking Plunger Spring	66	Forend Wood
14	Safety Spring	40	Ejector Sears	67	Forend Screw, Front
15	Safety Plunger	41	Ejector Sear Springs	68	Buttplate Screws
16	Slide Spring	42	Cocking Plunger Retaining Screw	69	Buttplate
17	Safety-Lever	43	Ejector Sear Pin	70	Buttplate Liner
18	Trigger Spring	44	Barrel	71	Pistol Grip Cap Screw
19	Safety-Lever Pin	45	Mainspring Plungers	72	Pistol Grip Cap
20	Inertia Block	46	Mainsprings	73	Pistol Grip Cap Liner
21	Inertia Block Spring	47	Hammer, Left	74	Stock
22	Inertia Block Spring Screw	48	Cocking Lever Spacer	75	Stock Bolt
23	Trigger	49	Cocking Lever Bushing	76	Stock Bolt Washer
24	Inertia Block Pin	50	Cocking Lever Springs	77	Trigger Guard Screw
25	Trigger Pin	51	Cocking Lever Spring Pin	78	Trigger Guard
26	Sear Pin and Cocking Lever/ Hammer Pin	52	Cocking Lever, Left		
		53	Cocking Lever, Right		

Model BST, B-C, B-D, B-E and B Series F Side-by-Side Shotgun

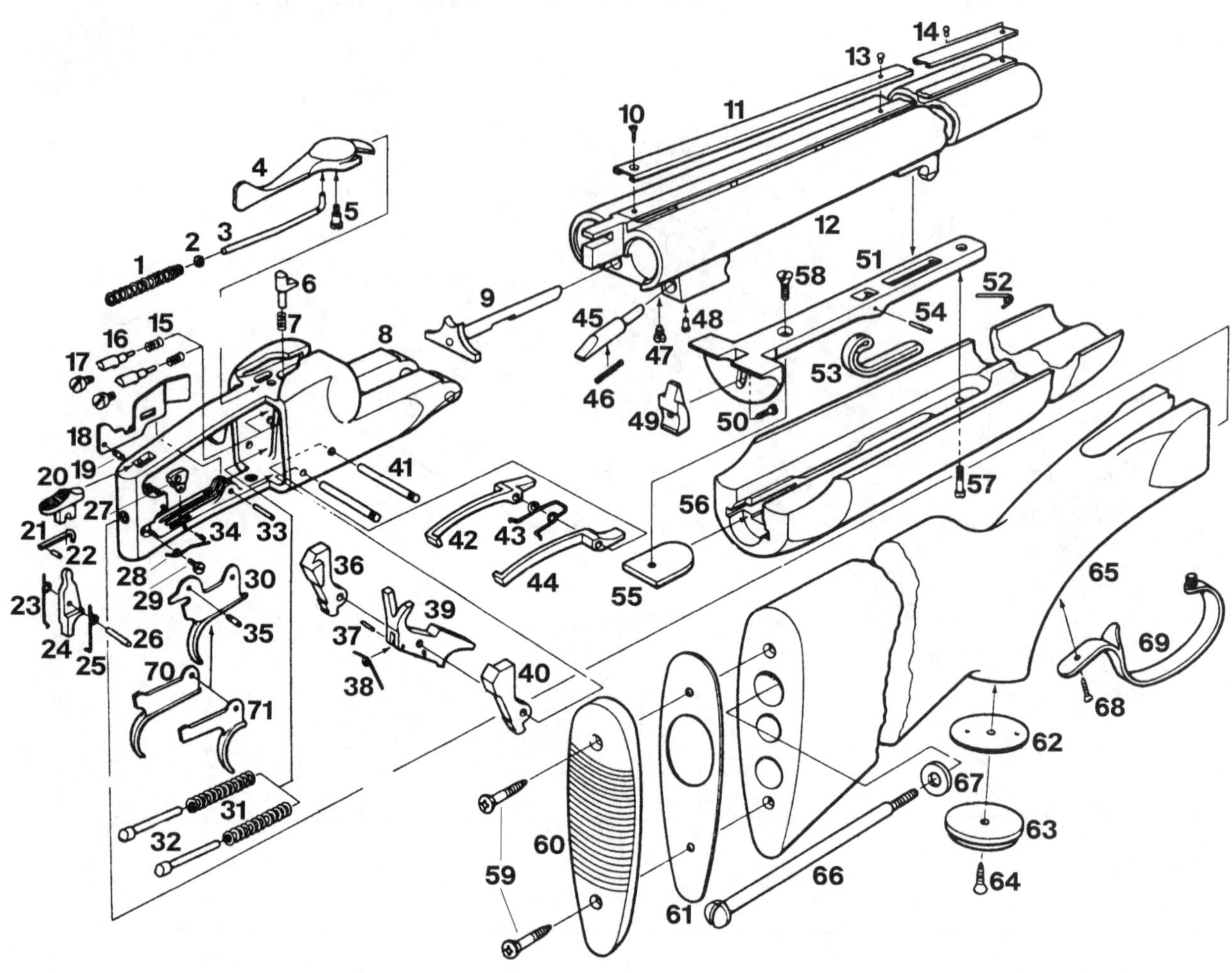

No.	Part	No.	Part	No.	Part
1	Top Snap Plunger Spring	25	Trigger Spring (BST)	48	Cocking Plunger Retaining Screw
2	Top Snap Plunger Collar	26	Safety-Lever Pin	49	Ejector
3	Top Snap Plunger	27	Inertia Block (BST)	50	Ejector Screw
4	Top Snap	28	Inertia Block Spring (BST)	51	Forend Iron
5	Top Snap Screw	29	Inertia Block Spring Screw (BST)	52	Forend Spring Spring
6	Top Snap Trip	30	Trigger (BST)	53	Forend Spring
7	Top Snap Trip Spring	31	Mainsprings	54	Forend Spring Pin
8	Frame	32	Mainspring Plungers	55	Forend Insert
9	Extractor	33	Trigger Pin	56	Forend Wood
10	Top Rib Lock Screw	34	Inertia Block Screw (BST)	57	Forend Screw, Front
11	Top Rib	35	Trigger Stud (BST)	58	Forend Screw, Rear
12	Barrel	36	Hammer, Left	59	Buttplate Screws
13	Rear Sight	37	Cocking Lever Spring Pin	60	Buttplate
14	Front Sight	38	Cocking Lever Spring	61	Buttplate Liner
15	Firing Pin Springs	39	Cocking Lever	62	Pistol Grip Cap Liner
16	Firing Pins	40	Hammer, Right	63	Pistol Grip Cap
17	Firing Pin Retaining Screws	41	Sear Pin and Cocking Lever/ Hammer Pin	64	Pistol Grip Cap Screw
18	Slide (BST)	42	Sear, Left	65	Stock
19	Stud (BST)	43	Sear Spring	66	Stock Bolt
20	Safety Button	44	Sear, Right	67	Stock Bolt Washer
21	Safety Spring	45	Cocking Plunger	68	Trigger Guard Screw
22	Safety Plunger	46	Cocking Plunger Spring	69	Trigger Guard
23	Slide Spring (BST)	47	Extractor Screw	70	Trigger, Right
24	Safety-Lever			71	Trigger, Left

Autoloading Shotgun

Courtesy of Thomas E. Wessel

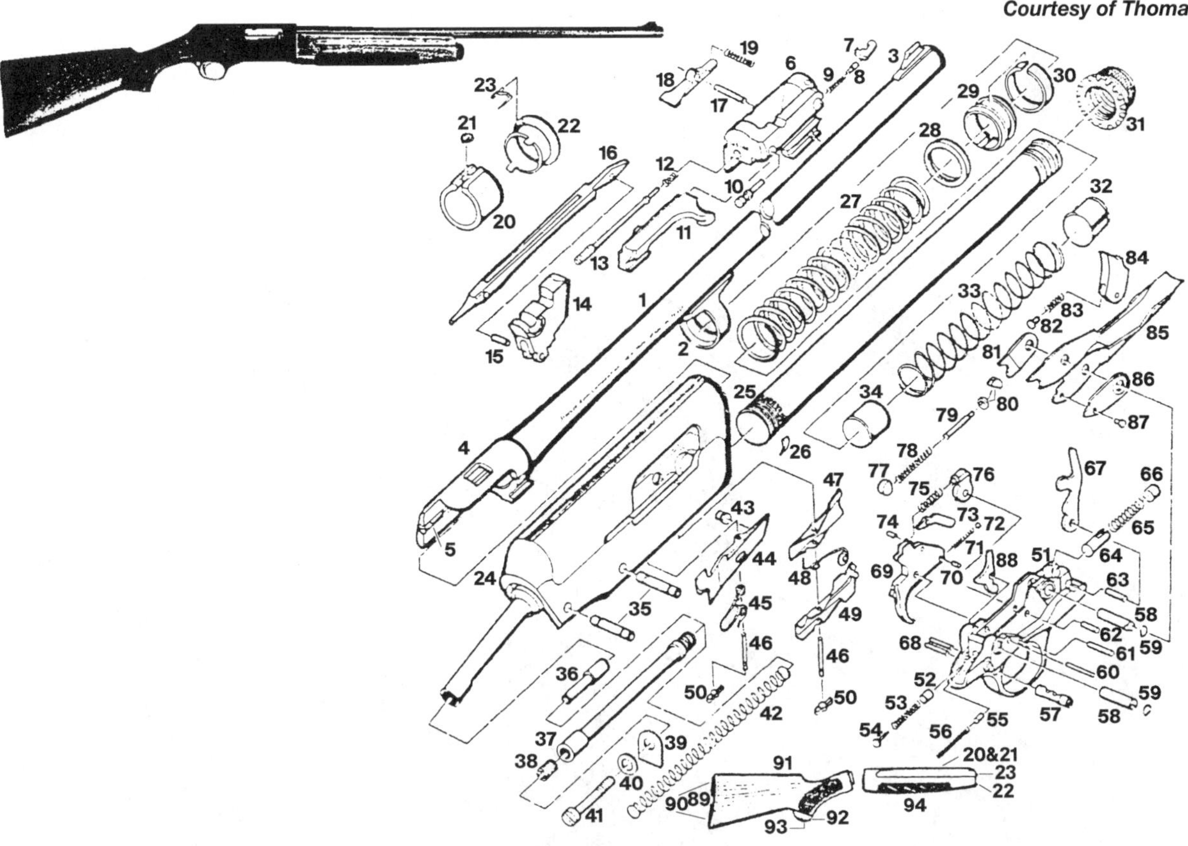

1	Barrel	33	Magazine Spring	64	Hammer Spring Tube
2	Barrel Ring	34	Magazine Follower	65	Hammer Spring
3	Front Sight and Base	35	Trigger Guard Pins	66	Hammer Spring Follower
4	Barrel Extension	36	Action Spring Follower	67	Hammer
5	Ejector	37	Action Spring Tube	68	Hand Safety Retaining Pins
6	Breechbolt	38	Action Spring Tube Fastener	69	Trigger
7	Extractor	39	Eccentric Washer	70	Trigger Lever Retaining Pin
8	Extractor Plunger	40	Elastic Washer	71	Trigger Lever Spring
9	Extractor Spring	41	Stock Retaining Screw	72	Trigger Lever Spring Ball
10	Firing Pin Limit Stop	42	Action Spring	73	Trigger Lever
11	Operating Handle	43	Carrier Latch Button	74	Trigger Lever Pin
12	Firing Pin Spring	44	Carrier Latch	75	Sear Spring
13	Firing Pin	45	Carrier Latch Spring	76	Sear
14	Locking Block	46	Pins	77	Carrier Spring Stem Pivot Point
15	Link Pin	47	Auxiliary Shell Latch	78	Carrier Spring
16	Link	48	Magazine Shell Latch and Auxiliary Shell Latch Spring	79	Carrier Spring Stem
17	Locking Block Lever Pin	49	Magazine Shell Latch	80	Carrier Spring Retaining Washer and Detent
18	Locking Block Lever	50	Detents	81	Left Carrier Plate
19	Locking Block Lever Spring	51	Trigger Guard	82	Carrier Dog Spring Follower
20	Rear Nylon Ring	52	Auto Safety Spring Plunger	83	Carrier Dog Spring
21	Rear Nylon Ring Spring	53	Auto Safety Spring	84	Carrier Dog
22	Front Nylon Ring	54	Auto Safety Spring Guide	85	Carrier
23	Forend Cap Retaining Spring	55	Hand Safety Spring Follower	86	Right Carrier Plate
24	Receiver	56	Hand Safety Spring	87	Carrier Dog Spring Guide Pin
25	Magazine Tube	57	Hand Safety	88	Auto Safety
26	Magazine Tube Blocking Spring	58	Trigger Guard Pins, Large	89	Buttplate
27	Recoil Spring	59	Trigger Guard Pin Detents	90	Buttplate Screws
28	Friction Ring	60	Trigger Pin	91	Pistol Grip Stock
29	Friction Piece	61	Auto Safety Pin	92	Pistol Grip Cap
30	Friction Spring	62	Sear Pin	93	Pistol Grip Cap Screw
31	Forend Cap	63	Hammer Pin	94	Forend
32	Magazine Spring Retaining Ring				

MAS 1936 Bolt-Action Rifle

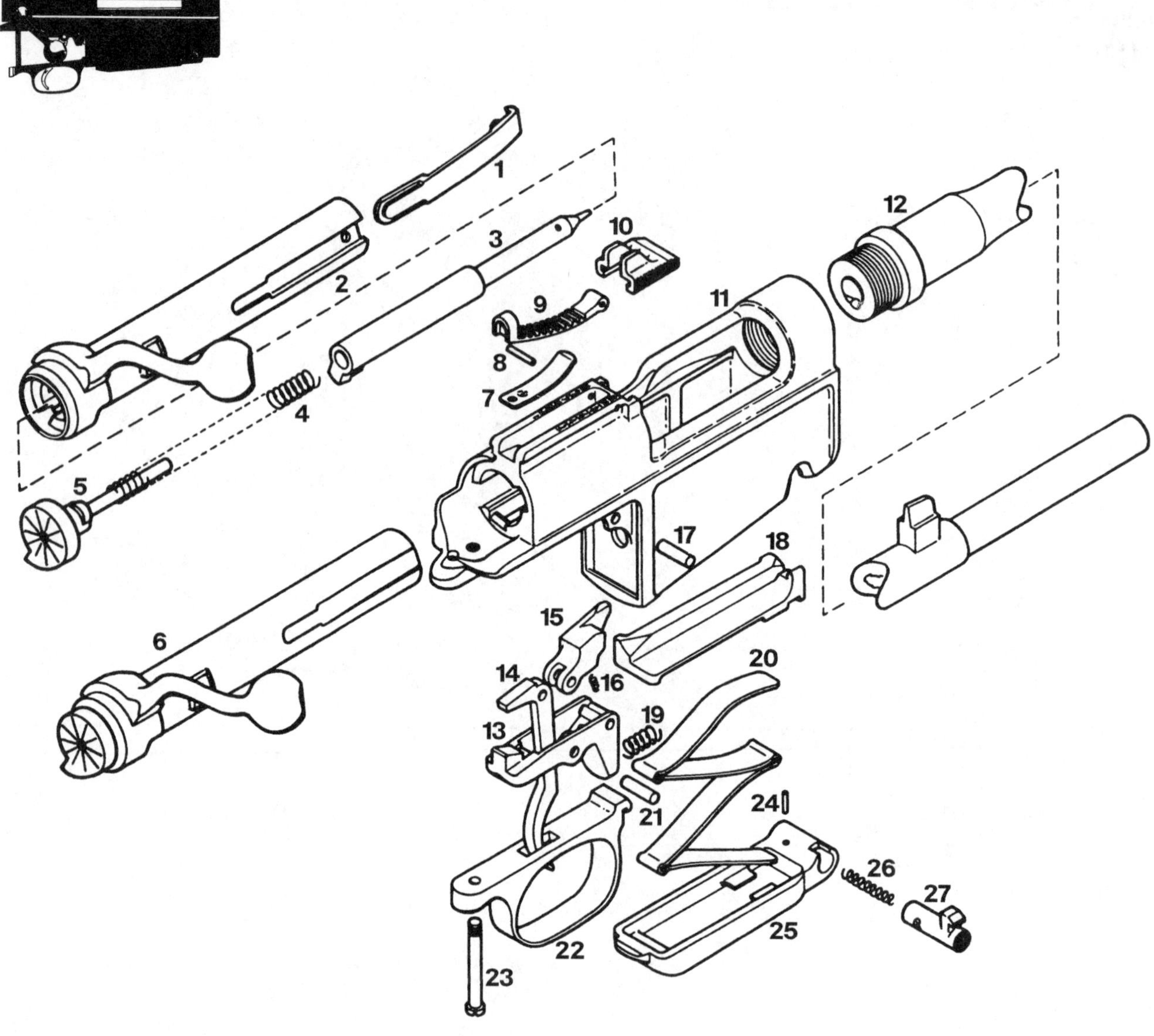

1	Extractor	15	Ejector and Bolt Stop
2	Bolt Body	16	Bolt Stop/Ejector Spring
3	Firing Pin	17	Sear Pin
4	Firing Pin Spring	18	Magazine Follower
5	Cocking Piece	19	Sear Spring
6	Bolt Assembly	20	Magazine Spring
7	Rear Sight Tension Spring	21	Trigger Pin
8	Rear Sight Pin	22	Trigger Guard
9	Rear Sight	23	Trigger Guard Screw
10	Rear Sight Slide	24	Floorplate Catch Pin
11	Receiver	25	Floorplate
12	Barrel	26	Floorplate Catch Spring
13	Sear	27	Floorplate Catch
14	Trigger		

Model 1874 Gras Bolt-Action Rifle

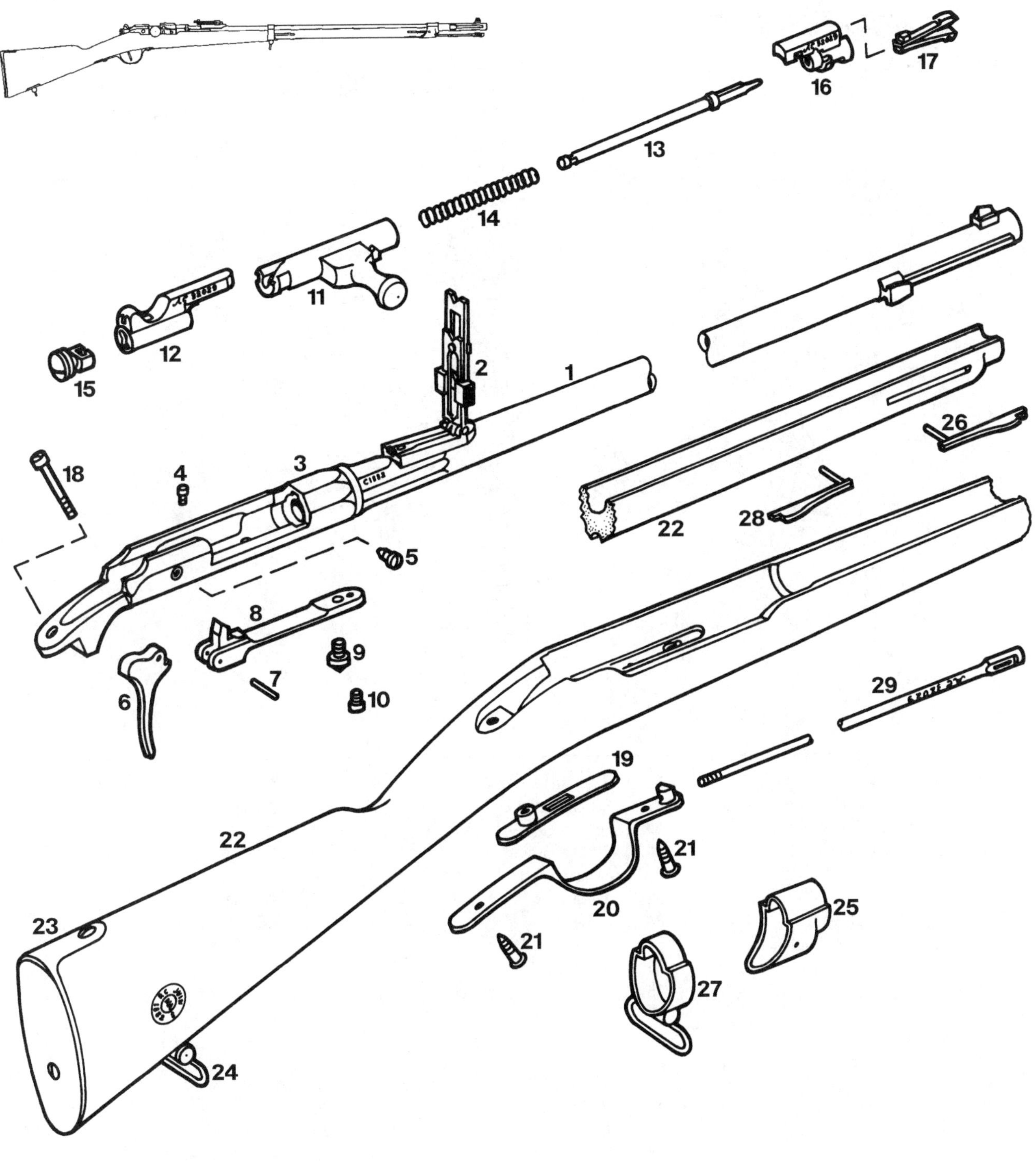

1	Barrel	11	Bolt	21	Trigger Guard Screws
2	Rear Sight	12	Cocking Piece	22	Stock
3	Receiver	13	Firing Pin	23	Buttplate
4	Ejector Screw	14	Firing Pin Spring	24	Rear Sling Swivel
5	Bolt Stop Screw	15	Firing Pin Nut	25	Front Barrel Band
6	Trigger	16	Bolt Head	26	Front Barrel Band Spring
7	Trigger Pin	17	Extractor	27	Rear Barrel Band
8	Trigger Spring and Sear	18	Tang Screw	28	Rear Barrel Band Spring
9	Trigger Spring Screw	19	Tang Screw Plate	29	Cleaning Rod
10	Trigger Spring Set Screw	20	Trigger Guard		

GALIL

308 AR Autoloading Rifle

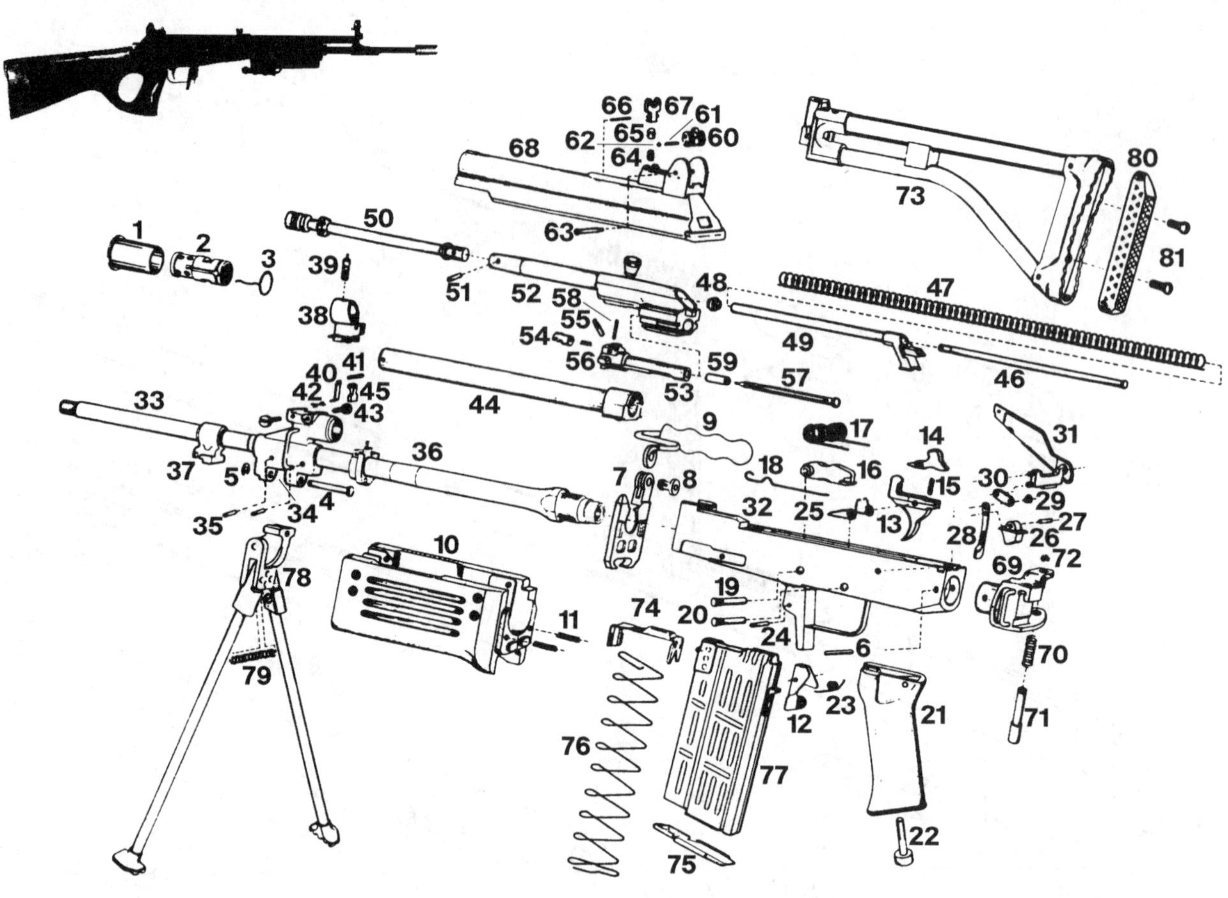

1	Muzzle Cup
2	Flash Suppressor
3	Suppressor Retaining Ring
4	Bipod Suppressor Pivot Pin
5	Bipod Connector Pin Retaining Ring
6	Stock Spring Pin
7	Handguard Holder, Rear
8	Carrying Handle Pin
9	Carrying Handle
10	Handguard
11	Handguard Springs
12	Magazine Catch
13	Trigger
14	Disconnector
15	Disconnector Spring
16	Hammer
17	Hammer Spring
18	Sear Spring
19	Hammer Pivot Pin
20	Sear and Trigger Pivot Pin
21	Pistol Grip
22	Pistol Grip Screw
23	Magazine Catch Spring
24	Magazine Catch Pivot Pin
25	Trigger Spring
26	Pistol Grip Base
27	Pistol Grip Base Pin
28	Selector Lever, Left
29	Selector Link Rivet, Left
30	Selector Lever Link
31	Selector Lever, Right
32	Receiver
33	Barrel
34	Gas Block
35	Gas Block Pin
36	Handguard Front Holder
37	Bayonet Catch
38	Front Sight Base
39	Front Sight Post
40	Front Night Sight Spring
41	Front Sight Pin
42	Spring
43	Front Sight Set Screw
44	Gas Cylinder
45	Front Night Sight
46	Guide Rod
47	Return Spring
48	Guide Rod Ring
49	Buffer Retainer
50	Gas Piston
51	Gas Piston Pin
52	Bolt Carrier
53	Bolt
54	Extractor
55	Extractor Pin
56	Extractor Spring
57	Firing Pin
58	Bolt Pin
59	Firing Pin Buffer
60	Rear Sight
61	Rear Sight Spring
62	Rear Sight Ball
63	Rear Sight Pivot Screw
64	Rear Night Sight Spring
65	Rear Night Sight Plunger
66	Rear Night Sight Pin
67	Rear Night Sight
68	Cover
69	Stock Base
70	Stock Spring
71	Stock Pivot Pin
72	Stock Retaining Ring
73	Stock
74	Follower
75	Magazine Bottom Plate
76	Magazine Spring
77	Magazine, 25-Round
78	Bipod
79	Bipod Spring
80	Recoil Pad
81	Recoil Pad Screws

Bronco Single Shot Shotgun

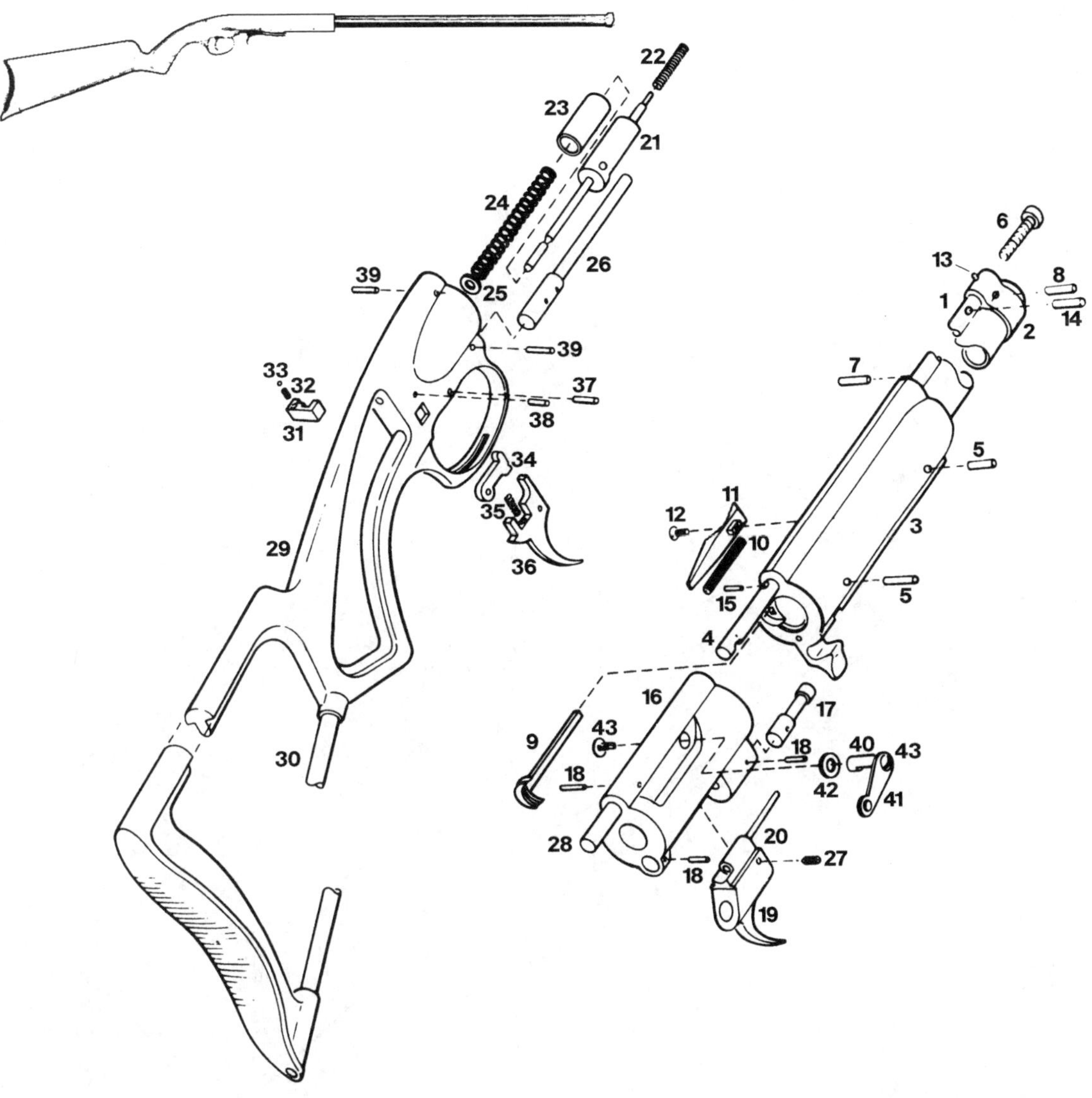

1	Barrel	**23**	Firing Pin Spring Bushing
2	Front Link	**24**	Firing Pin Spring
3	Barrel Sleeve	**25**	Firing Pin Washer
4	Barrel Support Rod	**26**	Cocking Lever Guide Rod
5	Barrel Sleeve Pins	**27**	Cocking Lever Screw
6	Front Link Adjustment Screw	**28**	Breech Body Support Rod
7	Support Rod Pins	**29**	Stock/Receiver
8	Front Link Pin	**30**	Stock Rod
9	Extractor	**31**	Safety
10	Extractor Spring	**32**	Safety Spring
11	Extractor Slide	**33**	Safety Ball
12	Extractor Screw	**34**	Sear
13	Bead Sight	**35**	Trigger Spring
14	Barrel Stop Pin	**36**	Trigger
15	Support Rod Position Pin	**37**	Trigger Pin
16	Breech Body with Insert Bushing	**38**	Sear Pin
17	Lock Shaft	**39**	Stock Pins
18	Breech Body Pins	**40**	Support Rod Locking Bolt
19	Cocking Lever Assembly	**41**	Support Rod Locking Arm with Knob
20	Locking Pin	**42**	Locking Bolt Spring Washer
21	Firing Pin	**43**	Locking Bolt Screws
22	Cocking Lever Spring		

Model 43 Bolt-Action Rifle

Courtesy of Blacksmith Corporation

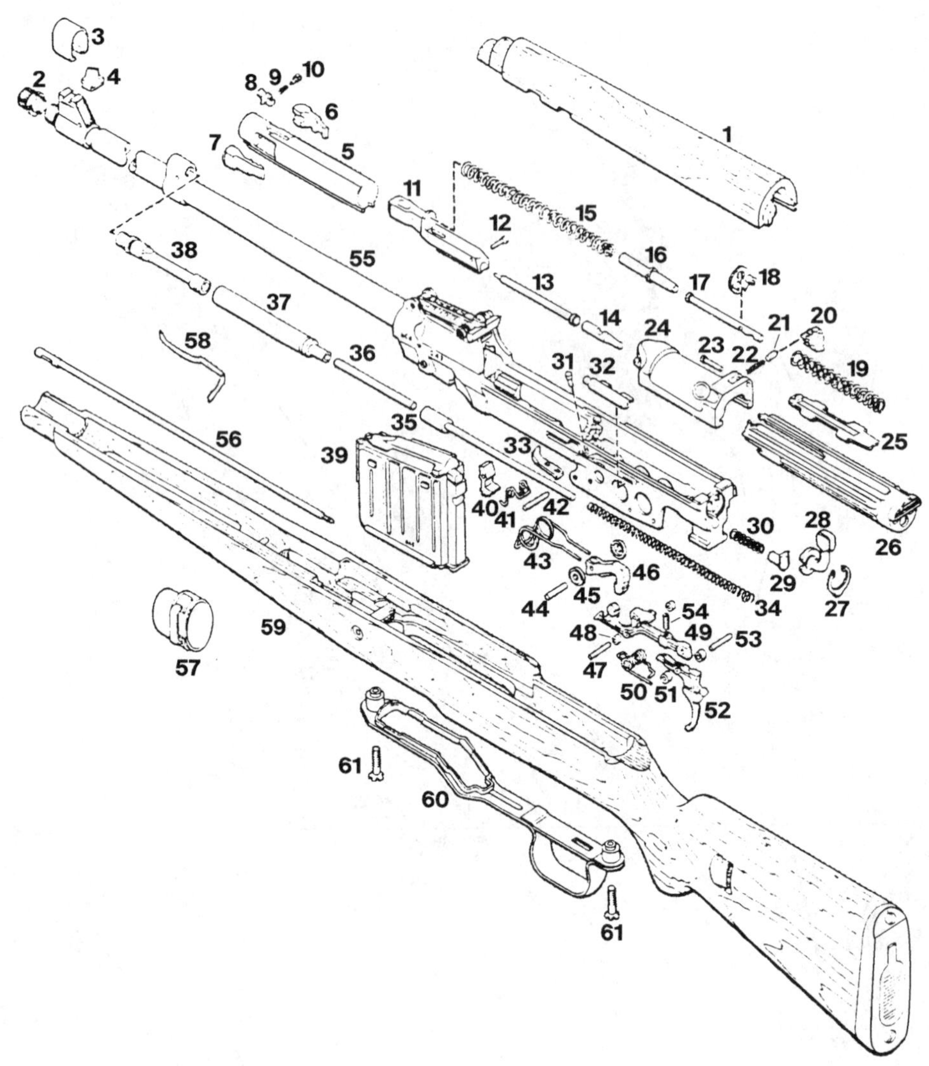

1	Handguard	**22**	Latch Spring	**43**	Hammer Spring
2	Thread Protector	**23**	Bolt Carrier Latch Pin	**44**	Hammer Pin
3	Sight Hood	**24**	Bolt Carrier	**45**	Hammer Washers
4	Front Sight	**25**	Sliding Dust Cover	**46**	Hammer
5	Bolt	**26**	Bolt Housing	**47**	Sear Pin
6	Locking Lug, Right	**27**	Safety Retainer	**48**	Sear Spacers
7	Locking Lug, Left	**28**	Safety	**49**	Sear
8	Extractor	**29**	Safety Plunger	**50**	Sear Spring
9	Extractor Spring	**30**	Safety Spring	**51**	Trigger Spacers
10	Extractor Retainer	**31**	Ejector Pin	**52**	Trigger
11	Firing Pin Housing	**32**	Ejector Spring Housing	**53**	Trigger Pin
12	Firing Pin Retainer	**33**	Ejector	**54**	Trigger Adjusting Screw
13	Firing Pin	**34**	Actuator Rod Spring	**55**	Barrel and Receiver
14	Firing Pin Extension	**35**	Actuator Rod	**56**	Cleaning Rod
15	Recoil Spring, Front	**36**	Connecting Rod	**57**	Barrel Band
16	Spring Guide, Front	**37**	Gas Cylinder	**58**	Band Retainer
17	Recoil Spring Guide, Rear	**38**	Gas Piston	**59**	Stock
18	Bolt Housing Retainer	**39**	Magazine	**60**	Trigger Guard
19	Recoil Spring, Rear	**40**	Magazine Catch	**61**	Trigger Guard Screws
20	Bolt Carrier Latch	**41**	Magazine Catch Spring		
21	Latch Plunger	**42**	Magazine Catch Pin		

Model 15 and 15 Youth Bolt-Action Rifle

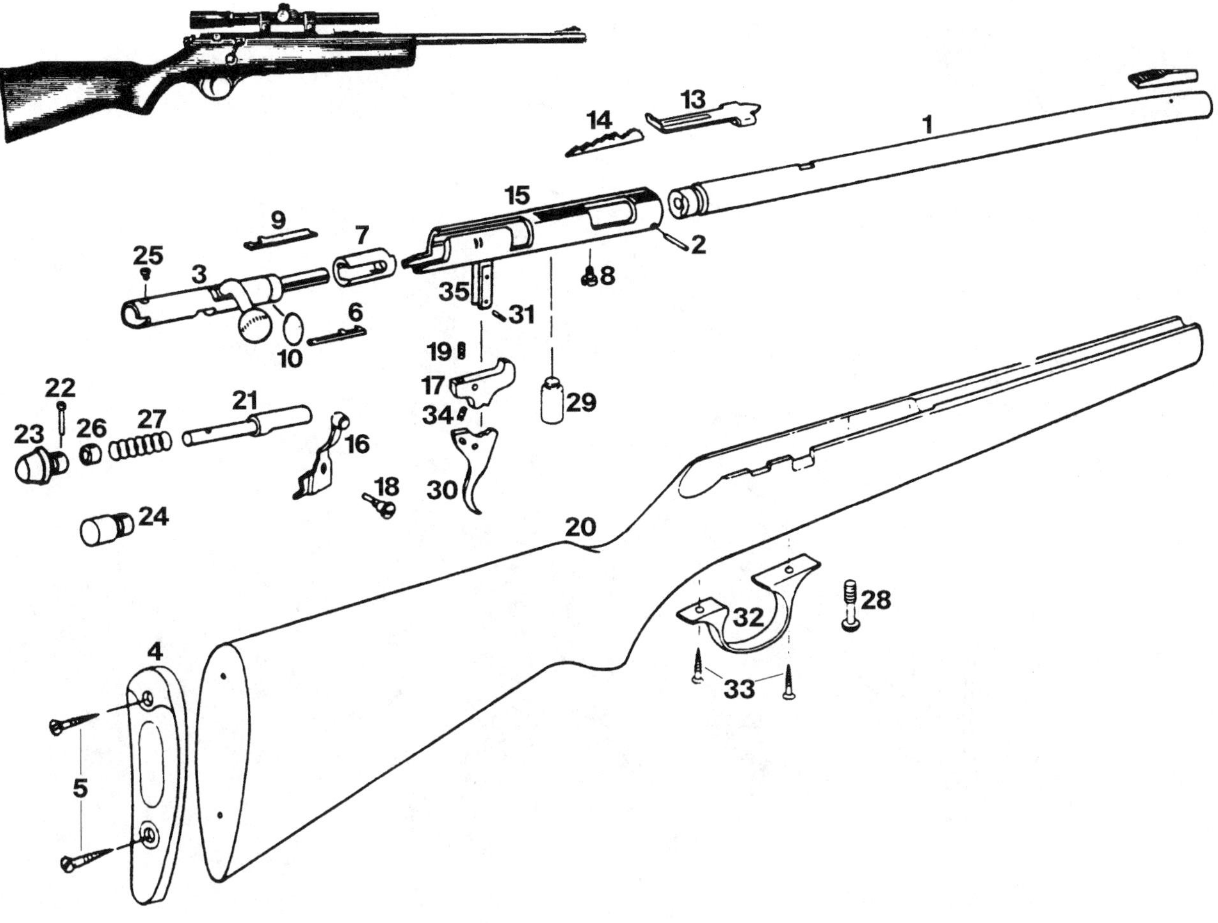

1	Barrel	**19**	Sear Spring
2	Barrel Retaining Pin	**20**	Stock with Buttplate
3	Breechbolt	**21**	Striker
4	Buttplate	**22**	Striker Cam Pin
5	Buttplate Screws	**23**	Striker Knob
6	Extractor	**24**	Striker Knob, Old Style
7	Feed Throat	**25**	Striker Retaining Screw
8	Feed Throat Screw	**26**	Striker Sleeve
9	Firing Pin	**27**	Striker Spring
10	Firing Pin Retaining Spring	**28**	Takedown Screw
11	Front Sight	**29**	Takedown Screw Stud
12	Front Sight Screw	**30**	Trigger Assembly
13	Rear Sight with Elevator	**31**	Trigger Pin
14	Rear Sight Elevator	**32**	Trigger Guard
15	Receiver	**33**	Trigger Guard Screws
16	Safety	**34**	Trigger Spring
17	Sear	**35**	Trigger Stud
18	Sear and Safety Pivot Screw		

Model 30A and 30AS Lever-Action Shotgun

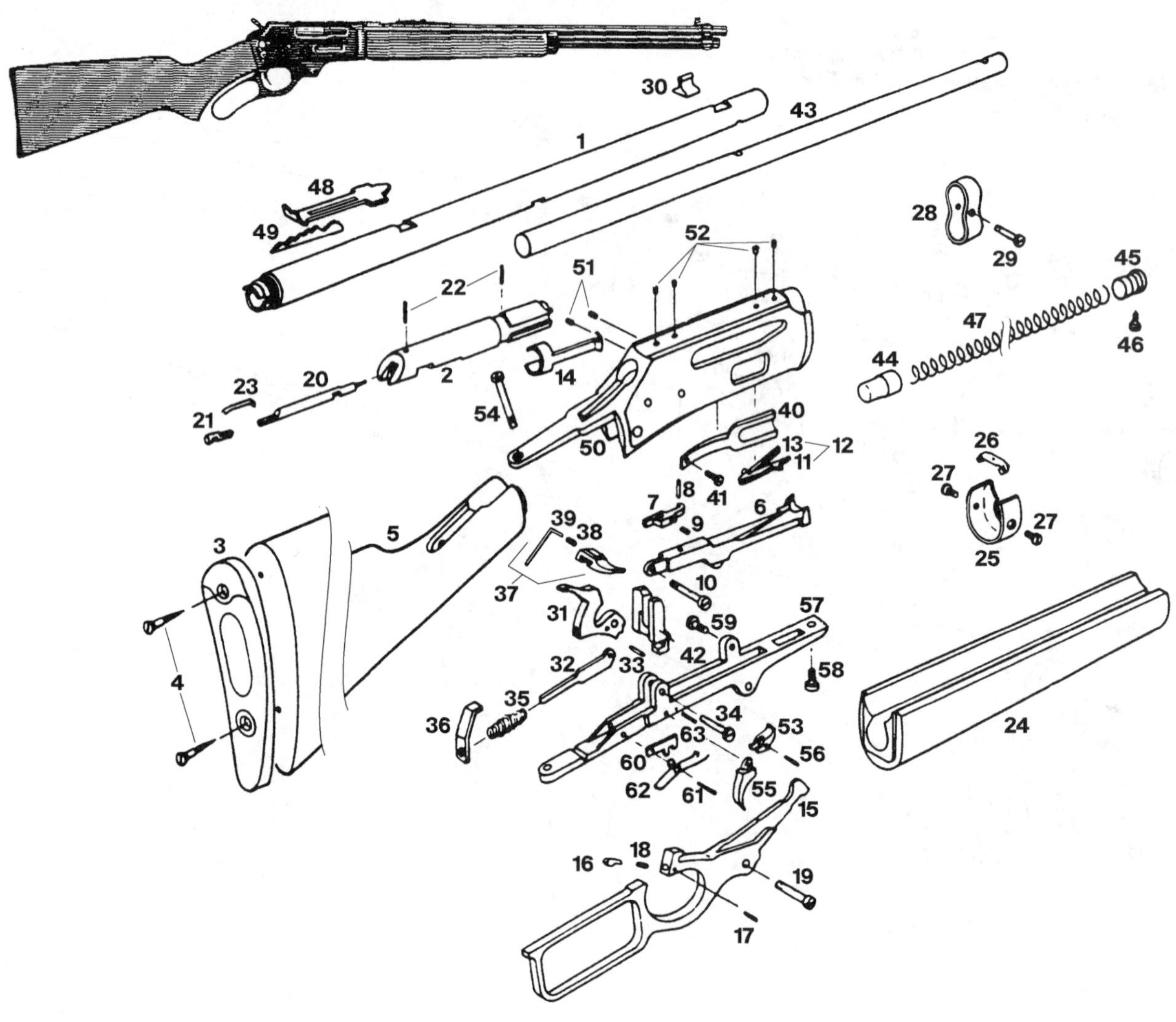

1	Barrel	22	Firing Pin Retaining Pins	43	Magazine Tube
2	Breechbolt	23	Firing Pin Spring	44	Magazine Tube Follower
3	Buttplate	24	Forearm	45	Magazine Tube Plug
4	Buttplate Screws	25	Forearm Tip	46	Magazine Tube Plug Screw
5	Buttstock	26	Forearm Tip Tenon	47	Magazine Tube Spring
6	Carrier	27	Forearm Tip Tenon Screws	48	Rear Sight with Elevator
7	Carrier Rocker	28	Front Band	49	Rear Sight Elevator
8	Carrier Rocker Pin	29	Front Band Screw	50	Receiver
9	Carrier Rocker Spring	30	Front Sight with Brass Bead	51	Peep Sight Dummy Screws
10	Carrier Screw	31	Hammer	52	Scope Mount Dummy Screws
11	Ejector	32	Hammer Strut	53	Sear
12	Ejector with Spring	33	Hammer Strut Pin	54	Tang Screw
13	Ejector Spring	34	Hammer Screw	55	Trigger
14	Extractor	35	Hammer Spring	56	Trigger and Sear Pin
15	Finger Lever	36	Hammer Spring Adjusting Plate	57	Trigger Guard Plate
16	Finger Lever Plunger	37	Hammer Spur, Complete	58	Trigger Guard Plate Screw
17	Finger Lever Plunger Pin	38	Hammer Spur Screw	59	Trigger Guard Plate Support Screw
18	Finger Lever Plunger Spring	39	Hammer Spur Wrench	60	Trigger Safety Block
19	Finger Lever Screw	40	Loading Spring	61	Trigger Safety Block Pin
20	Firing Pin, Front	41	Loading Spring Screw	62	Trigger Safety Block Spring
21	Firing Pin, Rear	42	Locking Bolt	63	Trigger Guard Plate Latch Pin

Model 50 Bolt-Action Shotgun

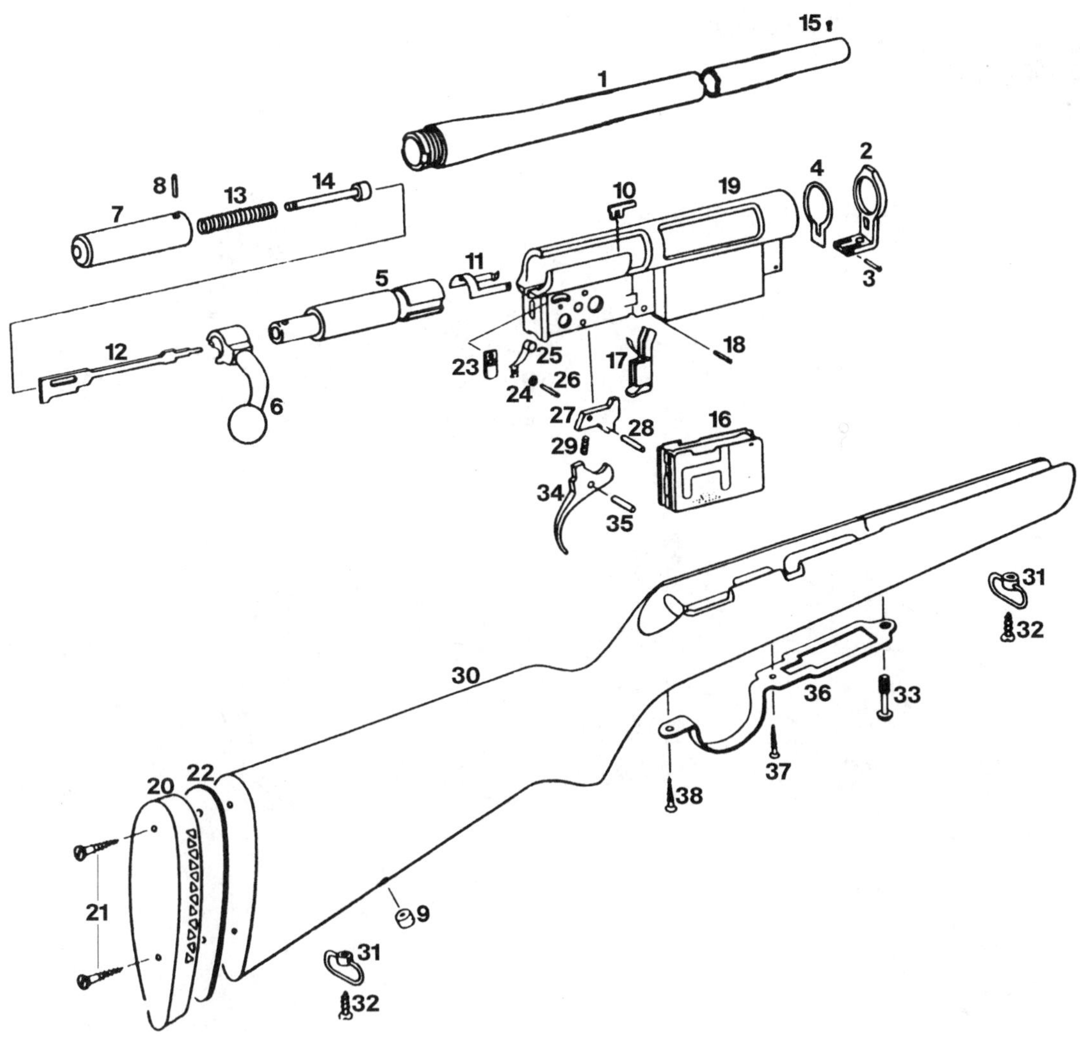

1	Barrel	**20**	Recoil Pad
2	Barrel Collar	**21**	Recoil Pad Screws
3	Barrel Collar Pin	**22**	Recoil Pad Spacer
4	Barrel Washer	**23**	Safety Blade
5	Breech Bolt, Front	**24**	Safety Blade Spacer
6	Breech Bolt Handle	**25**	Safety-Lever
7	Breech Bolt, Rear	**26**	Safety Pin
8	Breech Bolt Assembly Pin	**27**	Sear
9	Bullseye	**28**	Sear Pin
10	Ejector	**29**	Sear and Trigger Spring
11	Extractor	**30**	Stock
12	Firing Pin	**31**	Swivels
13	Firing Pin Spring	**32**	Swivel Screws
14	Firing Pin Spring Guide	**33**	Takedown Screw
15	Front Sight	**34**	Trigger
16	Magazine	**35**	Trigger Pin
17	Magazine Catch	**36**	Trigger Guard Plate
18	Magazine Catch Pin	**37**	Trigger Guard Plate Screw, Front
19	Receiver	**38**	Trigger Guard Plate Screw, Rear

Model 088 and 099 Single Shot Shotgun

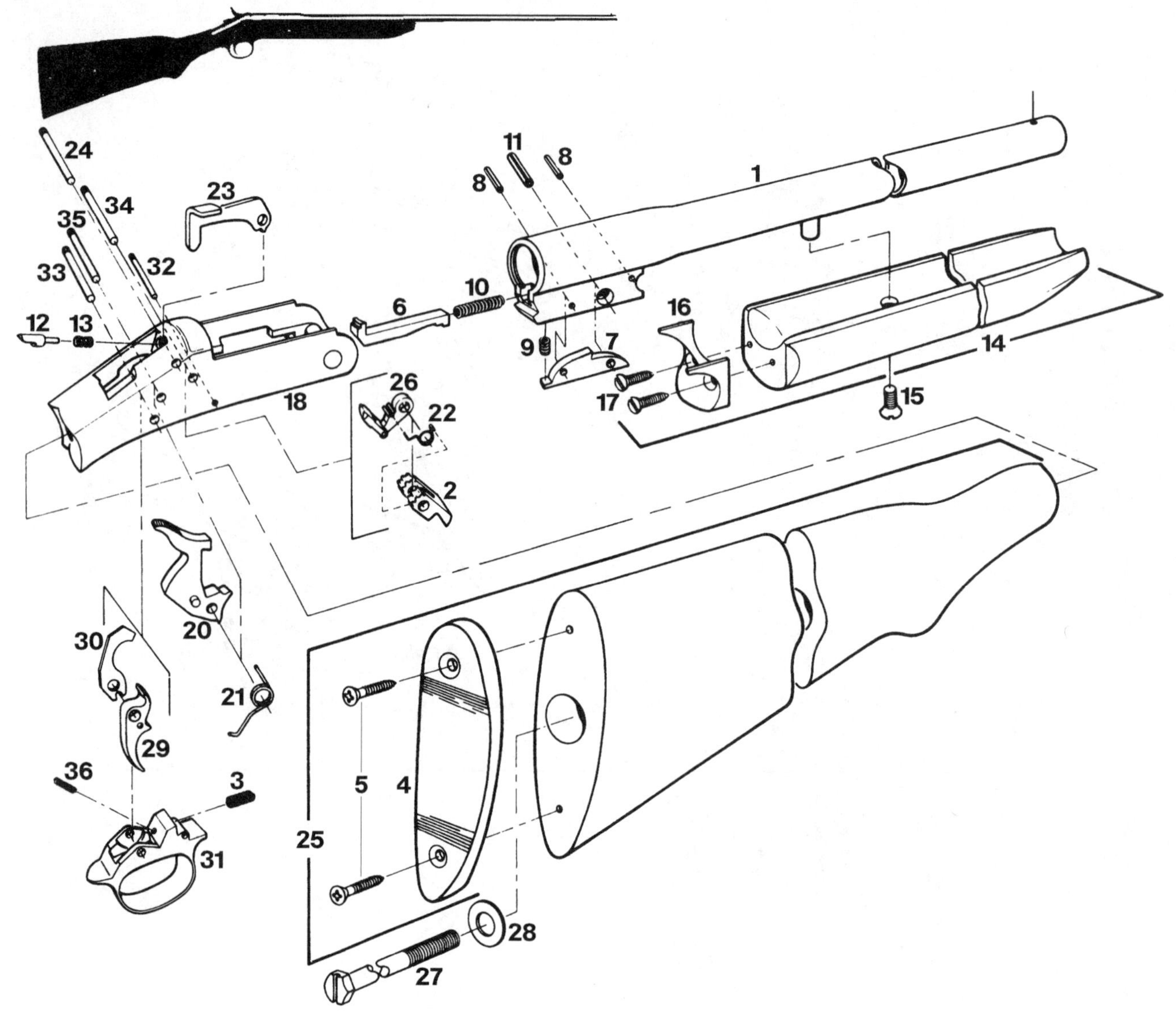

1	Barrel	19	Front Sight
2	Barrel Catch	20	Hammer
3	Barrel Catch Spring	21	Hammer Spring
4	Buttplate	22	Lifter Spring
5	Buttplate Screws	23	Release Lever
6	Ejector	24	Release Lever and Firing Pin Retaining Pin
7	Ejector Latch	25	Stock Assembly
8	Ejector Latch and Ejector Spring Stop Pin	26	Striker and Lifter Assembly
9	Ejector Latch Spring	27	Tang Screw
10	Ejector Spring	28	Tang Screw Washer
11	Ejector Stop Pin	29	Trigger
12	Firing Pin	30	Trigger Extension
13	Firing Pin Spring	31	Trigger Guard
14	Forend	32	Trigger Guard Pin, Front
15	Forend Screw	33	Trigger Guard Pin, Rear
16	Forend Spacer	34	Barrel Catch Pin
17	Forend Spacer Screws	35	Hammer Pin
18	Frame	36	Trigger Spring

Model 360 Autoloading Rifle

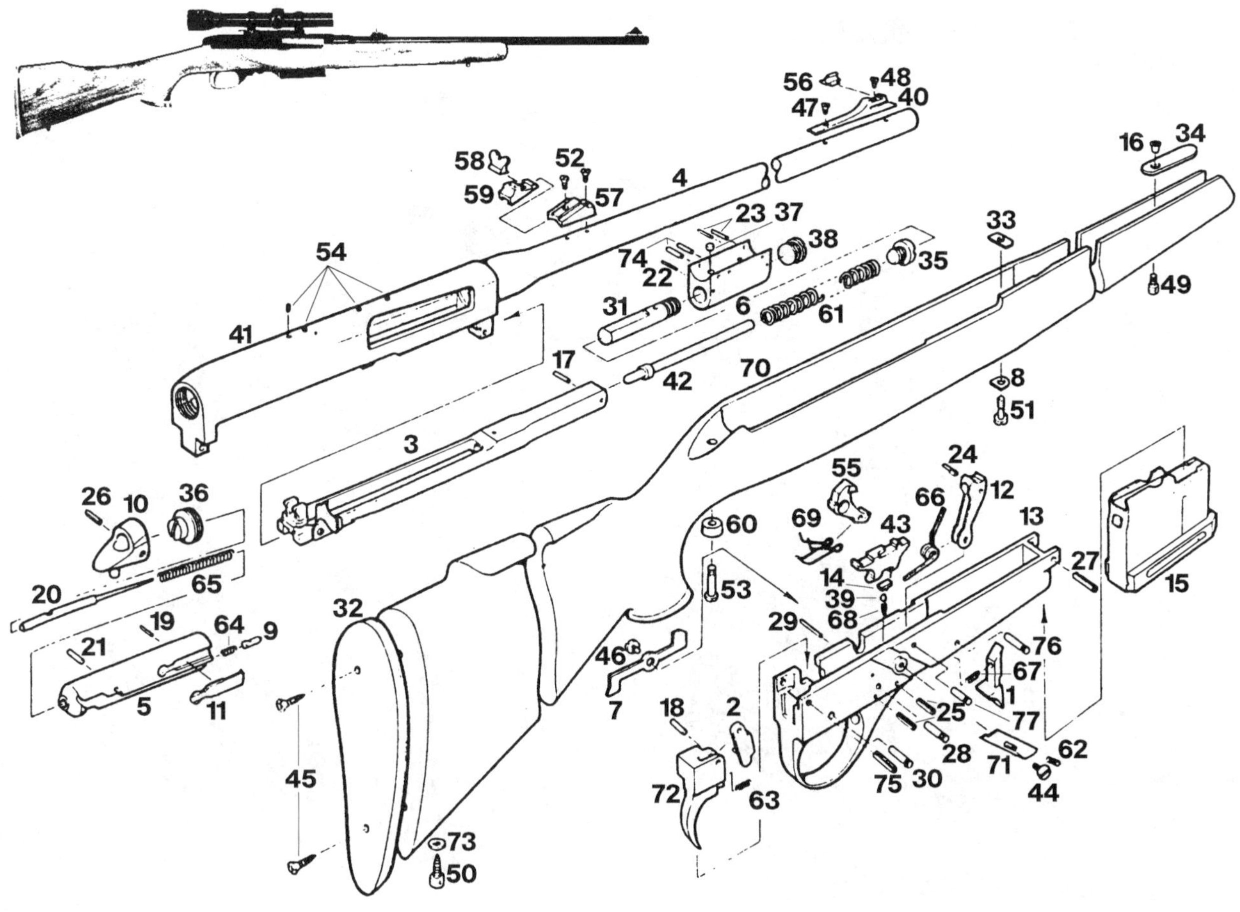

1	Magazine Latch Adapter	**28**	Sear Pin	**55**	Sear
2	Disconnector Arm	**29**	Sear Stop Pin	**56**	Front Sight Blade
3	Action Bar	**30**	Trigger Pin	**57**	Rear Sight Base
4	Barrel	**31**	Gas Piston	**58**	Rear Sight Blade
5	Bolt	**32**	Buttplate	**59**	Rear Sight Slide
6	Gas Cylinder	**33**	Stock Bedding Plate	**60**	Rear Takedown Sleeve
7	Disconnector	**34**	Swivel Tie-Down Plate	**61**	Action Bar Spring
8	Front Takedown Escutcheon Plate	**35**	Action Bar Plug	**62**	Bolt Stop Spring
9	Ejector	**36**	Bumper Plug	**63**	Disconnector Arm Spring
10	Receiver Extension	**37**	Gas Cylinder Location Plug	**64**	Ejector Spring
11	Extractor	**38**	Gas Plug	**65**	Firing Pin Spring
12	Hammer	**39**	Safety Spring Plunger	**66**	Hammer Spring
13	Trigger Housing	**40**	Front Sight Ramp	**67**	Magazine Latch Adapter Spring
14	Safety Insert	**41**	Receiver	**68**	Safety Plunger Spring
15	Magazine	**42**	Action Bar Retaining Spring Rod	**69**	Sear Return Spring
16	Swivel Tie-Down Nut	**43**	Safety	**70**	Stock
17	Action Bar Plug Retaining Pin	**44**	Bolt Stop Screw	**71**	Bolt Stop
18	Disconnector Arm Pin	**45**	Buttplate Screws	**72**	Trigger
19	Ejector Stop Pin	**46**	Disconnector Screw	**73**	Stock and Swivel Washer
20	Firing Pin	**47**	Front Ramp Screw, Rear	**74**	Gas Cylinder Retaining Pins
21	Firing Pin Stop Pin	**48**	Front Ramp Screw, Front	**75**	Trigger Housing Pin
22	Gas Piston Alignment Pin	**49**	Front Swivel Screw with Swivel	**76**	Magazine Latch Adapter Pin
23	Gas Plug Retaining Pins	**50**	Rear Swivel Screw with Swivel	**77**	Hammer Pin
24	Hammer Stop Pin	**51**	Front Takedown Screw	**Parts Not Shown**	
25	Safety Retaining Pins	**52**	Rear Sight Base Screws		Safety and Sear Adjustment Screw
26	Receiver Extension Pin	**53**	Rear Tie-Down Screw		Gas Piston Retaining Ring
27	Receiver Pin	**54**	Scope Mount Filler Screws		

Model 440 Slide-Action Shotgun

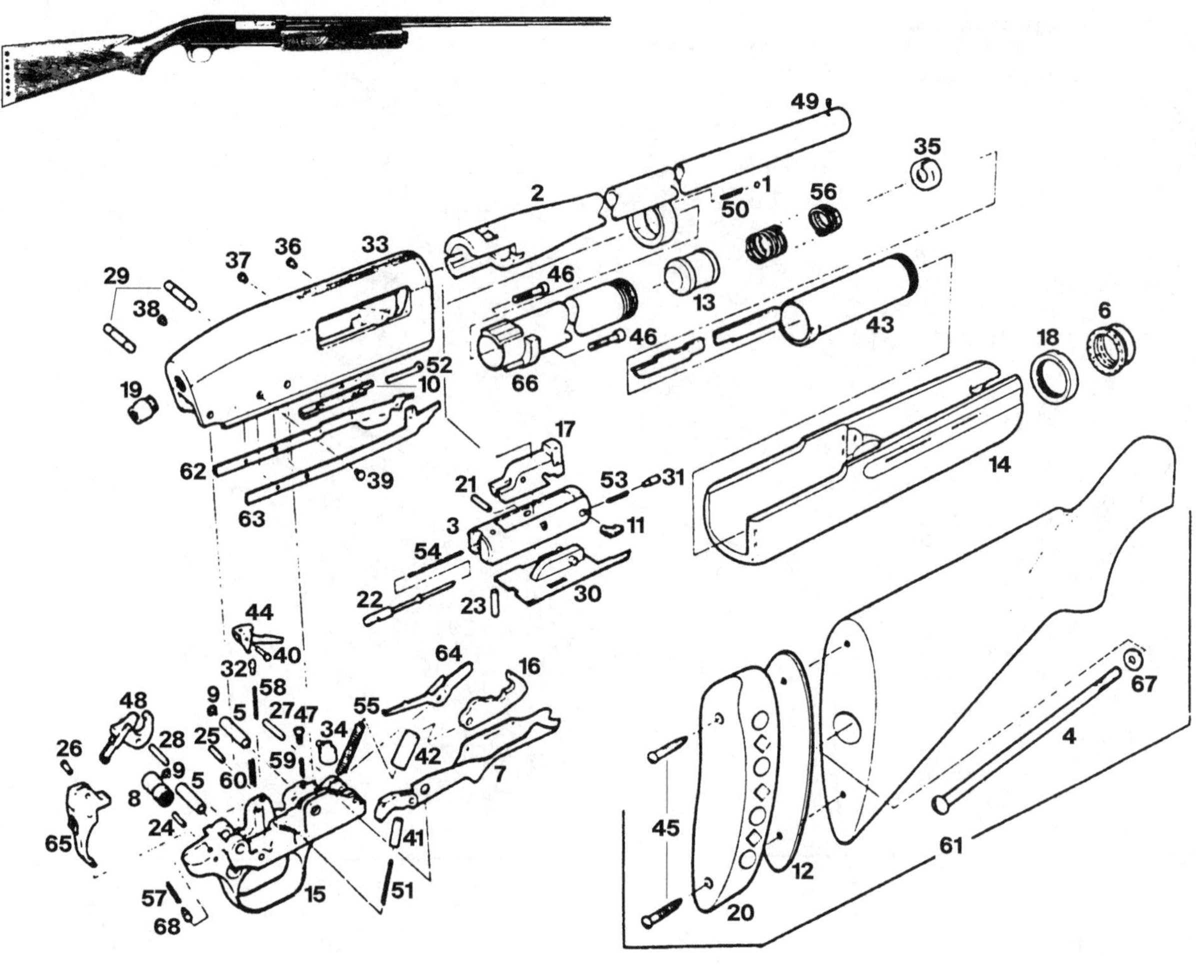

1	Ball Barrel Ring	**24**	Safety Catch Stop Pin	**47**	Slide Stop Spring Screw
2	Barrel	**25**	Sear Pin	**48**	Sear and Operating Rod
3	Bolt	**26**	Sear Operating Rod Pin	**49**	Sight, Front
4	Stock Mounting Bolt	**27**	Slide Stop and Hammer Pin	**50**	Barrel Ring Spring
5	Trigger Housing Pin Bushings	**28**	Trigger Pin	**51**	Carrier Spring
6	Magazine Cap	**29**	Trigger Housing Pins	**52**	Ejector Spring
7	Carrier	**30**	Bolt Lock Operating Plate	**53**	Extractor Spring
8	Safety Catch	**31**	Extractor Plunger	**54**	Firing Pin Return Spring
9	Trigger Housing Pins	**32**	Sear Safety Plunger	**55**	Hammer Spring
10	Ejector	**33**	Receiver	**56**	Magazine Spring
11	Extractor	**34**	Slide Stop Release	**57**	Safety Catch Spring
12	Plastic Filler	**35**	Magazine Spring Ring	**58**	Sear Safety Spring
13	Magazine Follower	**36**	Ejector Rivet, Front	**59**	Slide Stop Spring
14	Forend	**37**	Ejector Rivet, Rear	**60**	Trigger Spring
15	Trigger Guard	**38**	Cartridge Stop Rivet, Left	**61**	Stock Assembly
16	Hammer	**39**	Cartridge Stop Rivet, Right	**62**	Cartridge Stop, Left
17	Bolt Lock	**40**	Sear Safety Rivet	**63**	Cartridge Stop, Right
18	Forend Nut	**41**	Carrier Push Rod	**64**	Slide Stop
19	Stock Mounting Nut	**42**	Hammer Push Rod	**65**	Trigger
20	Recoil Pad	**43**	Operating Rod	**66**	Magazine Tube
21	Bolt Pin	**44**	Sear Safety	**67**	Stock Mounting Washer
22	Firing Pin	**45**	Recoil Pad Screws	**68**	Safety Catch Plunger
23	Firing Pin Stop Pin	**46**	Magazine Screws		

Model 480 and 580 Topper Jr. Single Shot Shotgun

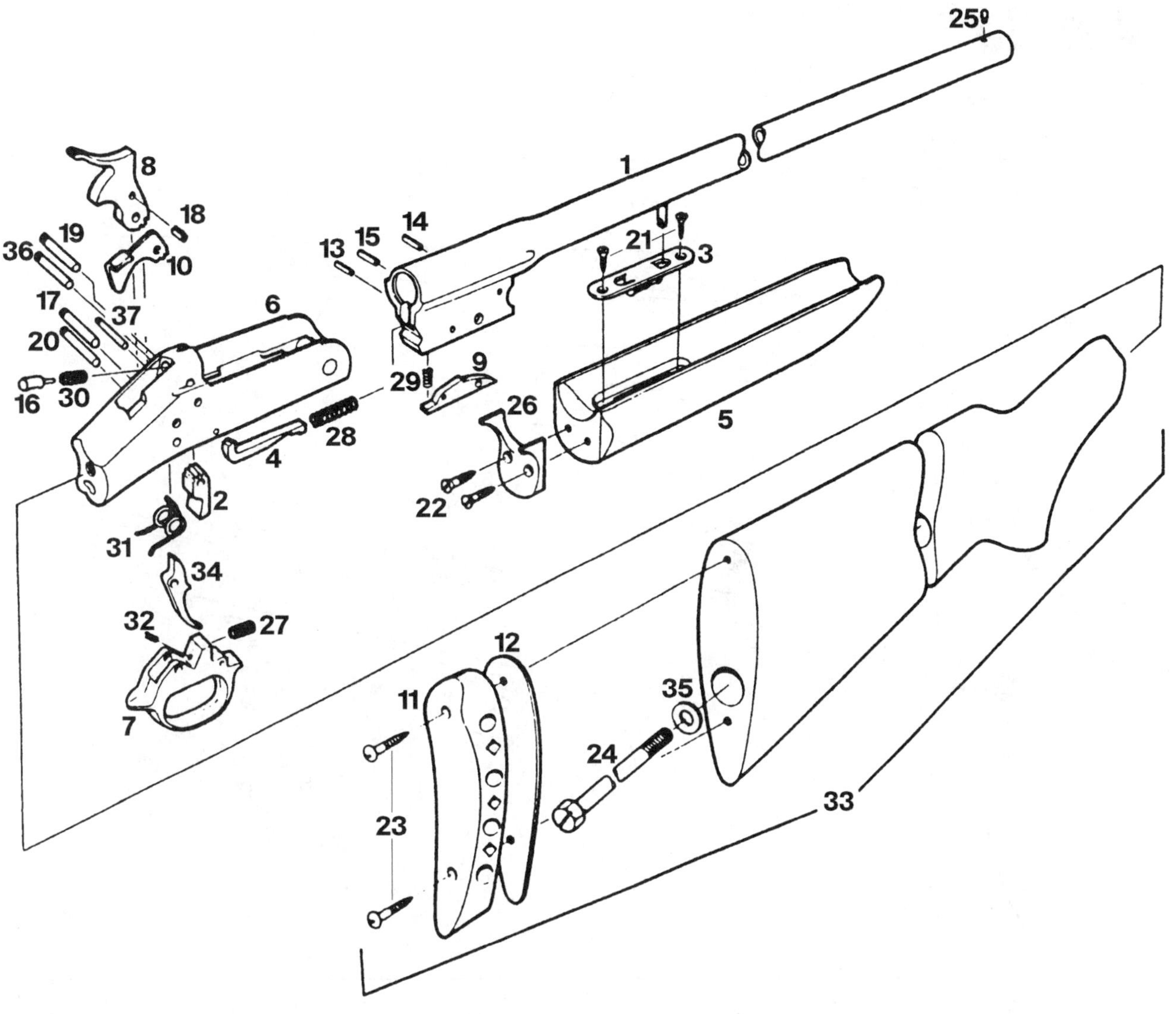

1	Barrel	**20**	Trigger Pin
2	Barrel Catch	**21**	Forend Catch Screws
3	Forend Catch	**22**	Forend Spacer Screws
4	Ejector	**23**	Recoil Pad Screws
5	Forend	**24**	Tang Screw
6	Frame	**25**	Front Sight
7	Trigger Guard	**26**	Forend Spacer
8	Hammer	**27**	Barrel Catch Spring
9	Ejector Latch	**28**	Ejector Spring
10	Release Lever	**29**	Ejector Latch Spring
11	Recoil Pad	**30**	Firing Pin Spring
12	Recoil Filler Pad	**31**	Hammer Spring
13	Ejector Latch Pin	**32**	Trigger Spring
14	Ejector Spring Stop Pin	**33**	Stock
15	Ejector Stop Pin	**34**	Trigger
16	Firing Pin	**35**	Tang Screw Washer
17	Hammer Barrel Catch Pin	**36**	Barrel Catch Pin
18	Hammer Safety Pin	**37**	Trigger Guard Pin
19	Release Lever Pin		

Model 700 and 700 Deluxe Autoloading Rifle

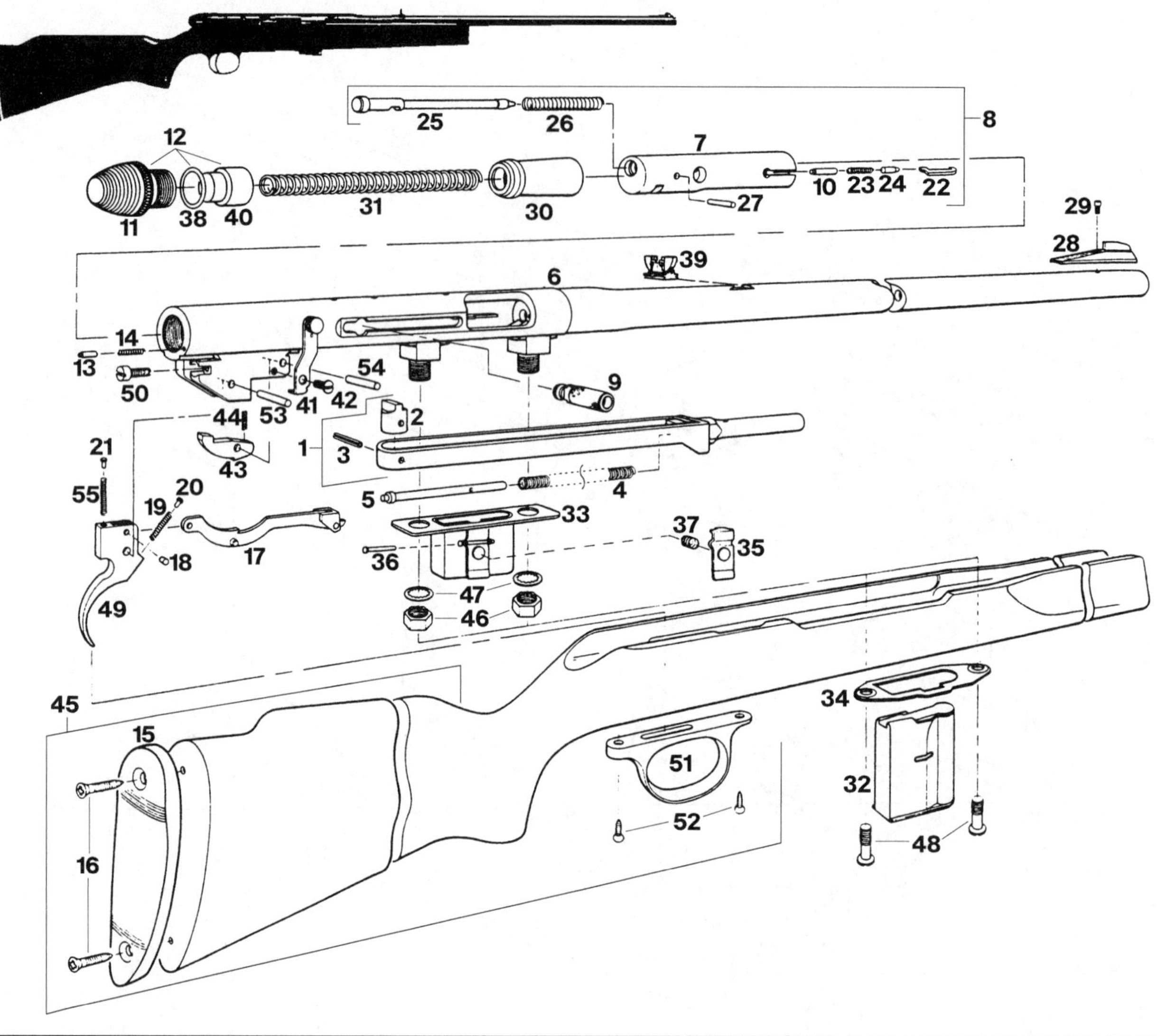

1	Action Bar Assembly	**23**	Extractor Spring	**44**	Sear Spring
2	Action Bar Lug	**24**	Extractor Spring Plunger	**45**	Stock Assembly
3	Action Bar Lug Pin	**25**	Firing Pin	**46**	Stud Nuts
4	Action Bar Spring	**26**	Firing Pin Spring	**47**	Stud Nut Lock Washers
5	Action Bar Spring Guide	**27**	Firing Pin Retaining Pin	**48**	Takedown Screws
6	Barrel	**28**	Front Sight	**49**	Trigger
7	Bolt	**29**	Front Sight Screw	**50**	Trigger Adjusting Screw
8	Bolt Assembly	**30**	Hammer	**51**	Trigger Guard
9	Bolt Handle	**31**	Hammer Spring	**52**	Trigger Guard Screws
10	Bolt Handle Plunger	**32**	Magazine Assembly	**53**	Trigger Pin
11	Bumper Plug	**33**	Magazine Guide Box and Release Lever Assembly	**54**	Sear Pin
12	Bumper Plug Assembly	**34**	Magazine Guide Plate	**55**	Trigger Spring
13	Bumper Plug Plunger	**35**	Magazine Release Lever	**Parts Not Shown**	
14	Bumper Plug Plunger Spring	**36**	Magazine Release Lever Pin		Bullet Ramp
15	Buttplate	**37**	Magazine Release Lever Spring		Ejector
16	Buttplate Screws	**38**	O Ring		Front Sight
17	Disconnector and Cam Assembly	**39**	Rear Sight		Front Sight Ramp
18	Disconnector Pin	**40**	Recoil Buffer		Magazine Guide Box Assembly
19	Disconnector Spring	**41**	Safety-Lever		Trigger Adjusting Screw Lock Screw
20	Disconnector Spring Plunger	**42**	Safety-Lever Screw		Trigger Housing
21	Trigger Spring Plunger	**43**	Sear		
22	Extractor				

Model 750 and 751 Pioneer Bolt-Action Rifle

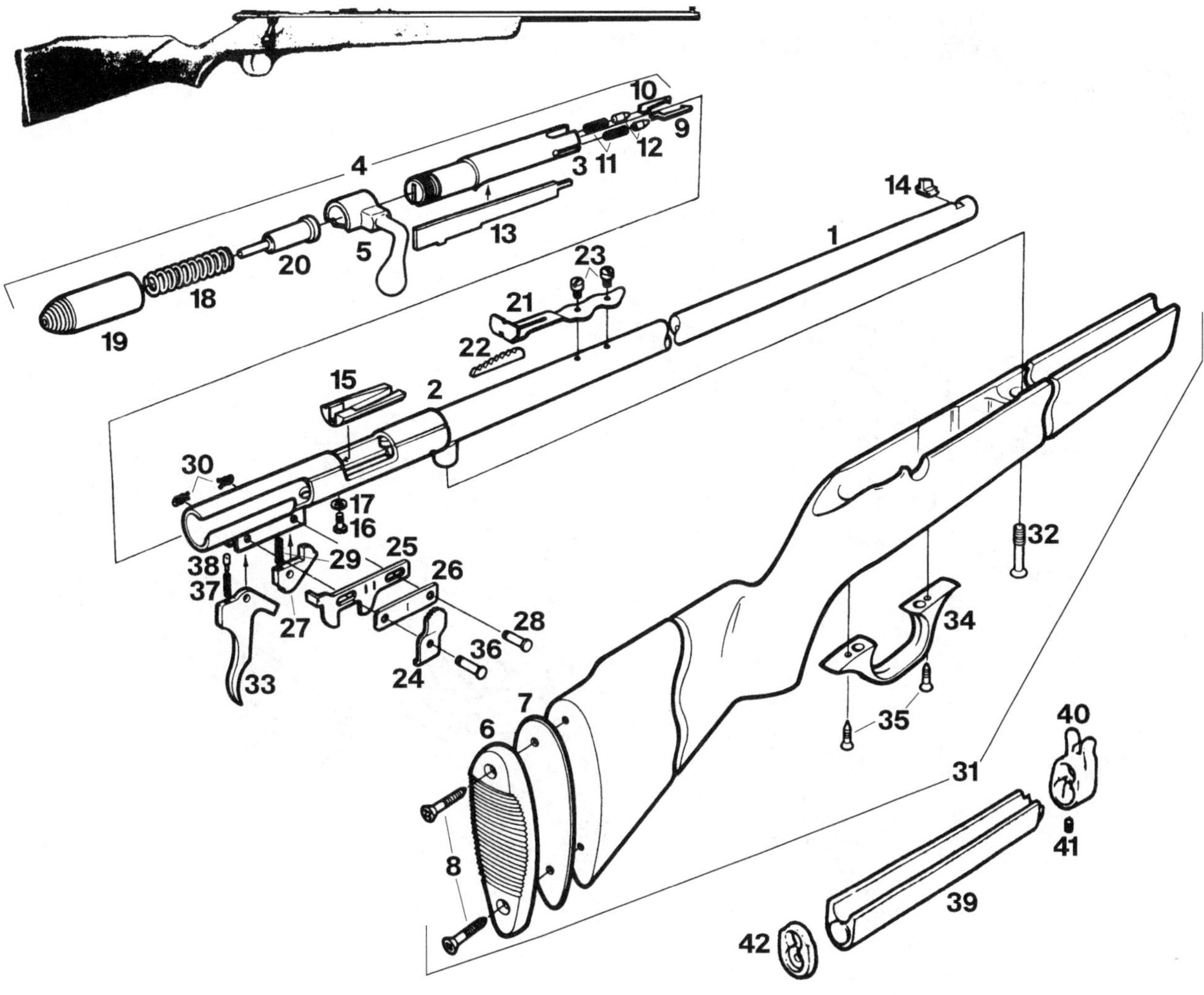

1	Barrel	22	Rear Sight Elevator
2	Barrel and Receiver Assembly	23	Rear Sight Screws
3	Bolt, Front	24	Safety-Lever
4	Bolt Assembly, Complete	25	Safety-Lever Slide
5	Bolt Cocking Cam Assembly	26	Safety-Lever Spring
6	Buttplate	27	Sear
7	Buttplate Filler	28	Sear Pin
8	Buttplate Screws	29	Sear Spring
9	Extractor, Right	30	Sear and Trigger Pin Clip
10	Extractor, Left	31	Stock Assembly, Complete
11	Extractor Springs	32	Takedown Screw
12	Extractor Spring Plungers	33	Trigger
13	Firing Pin	34	Trigger Guard
14	Front Sight	35	Trigger Guard Screws
15	Loading Platform	36	Trigger Pin
16	Loading Platform Screw	37	Trigger Spring
17	Loading Platform Screw Washer	38	Trigger Spring Plunger
18	Mainspring	39	Forend
19	Mainspring Housing	40	Front Sight
20	Mainspring Plunger with Safety Pin	41	Front Sight Screw
21	Rear Sight	42	Stock Band

Model 755 and 760 Sahara Single Shot Rifle

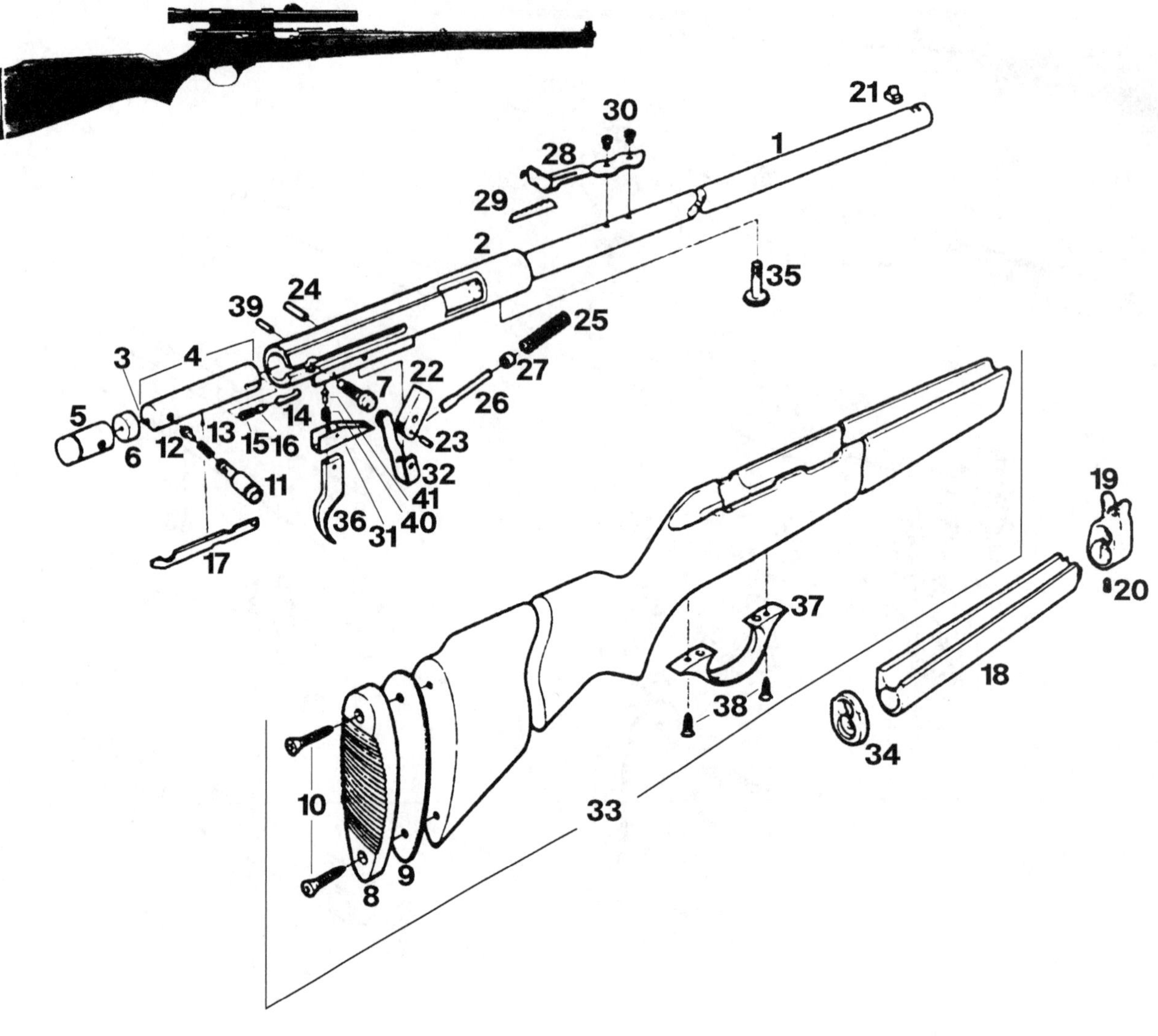

1	Barrel	**22**	Hammer
2	Barrel and Receiver Assembly	**23**	Hammer Cross Pin
3	Bolt	**24**	Hammer Pivot Pin
4	Bolt Assembly	**25**	Hammer Spring
5	Bumper Plug	**26**	Hammer Spring Guide
6	Bumper Plug Insert	**27**	Hammer Spring Guide Sleeve
7	Bumper Plug Screw	**28**	Rear Sight
8	Buttplate	**29**	Rear Sight Elevator
9	Buttplate Filler	**30**	Rear Sight Screws
10	Buttplate Screws	**31**	Sear
11	Cocking Handle	**32**	Safety Assembly
12	Cocking Handle Plunger	**33**	Stock Assembly
13	Cocking Handle Plunger Spring	**34**	Stock Band
14	Extractor	**35**	Takedown Screw
15	Extractor Spring	**36**	Trigger
16	Extractor Spring Plunger	**37**	Trigger Guard
17	Firing Pin	**38**	Trigger Guard Screws
18	Forend	**39**	Trigger Pin
19	Front Sight (755)	**40**	Trigger Spring
20	Front Sight Screw	**41**	Trigger Spring Plunger
21	Front Sight (760)		

Topper Model 158 Combo and Mustang Model 163 Single Shot Rifle

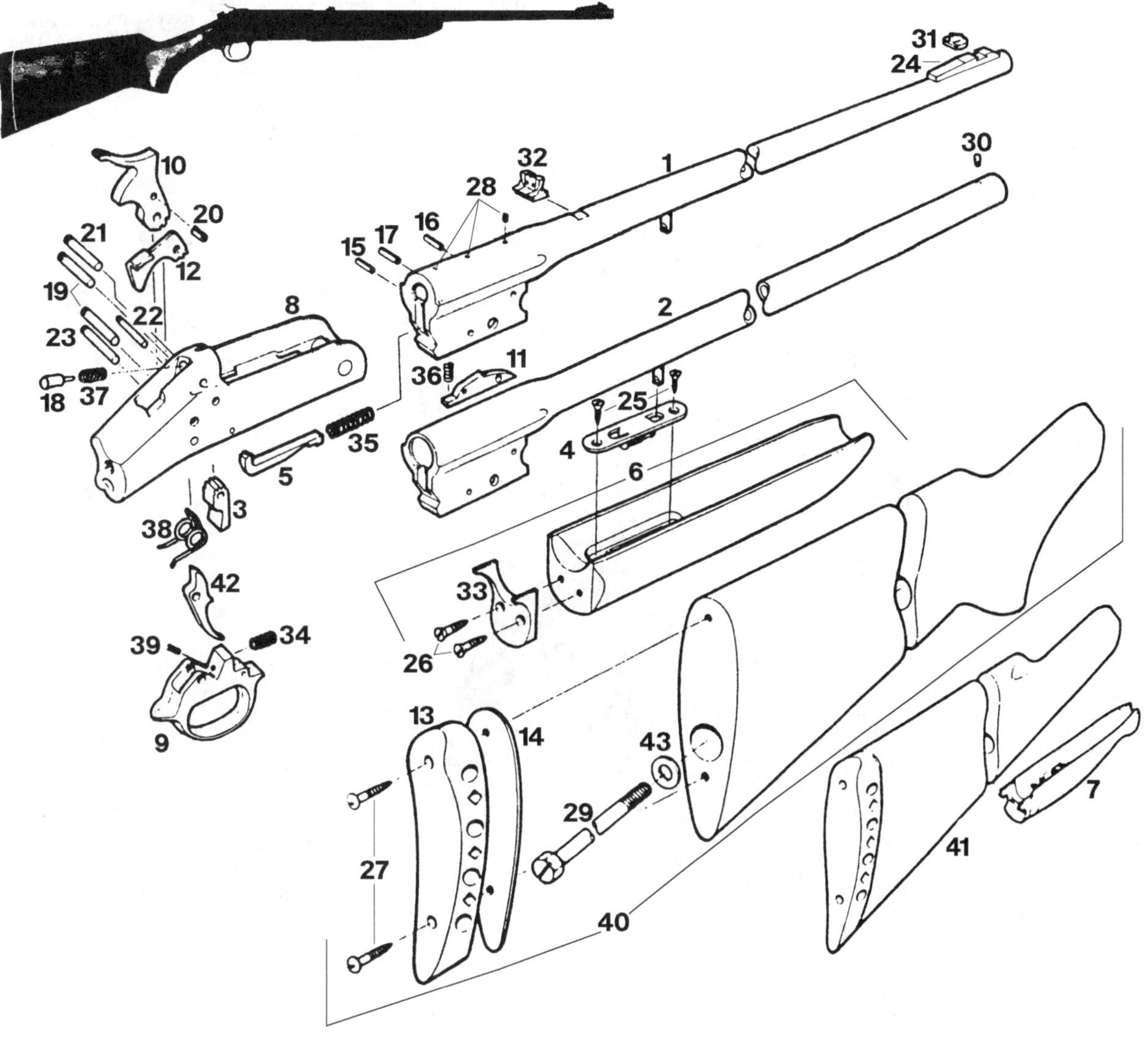

1	Barrel Assembly (Rifle)	**22**	Front Guard Pin
2	Barrel Assembly (Shotgun)	**23**	Trigger and Guard Pin, Rear
3	Barrel Catch	**24**	Front Sight Ramp
4	Forend Assembly Catch	**25**	Forend Catch Screw
5	Ejector	**26**	Forend Spacer Screws
6	Forend Assembly (Model 158)	**27**	Recoil Pad Screw
7	Forend Assembly (Model 163)	**28**	Sight Base Plug Screws
8	Frame	**29**	Tang Screw
9	Trigger Guard	**30**	Front Sight (Shotgun)
10	Hammer	**31**	Front Sight (Rifle)
11	Ejector Latch	**32**	Rear Sight (Rifle)
12	Release Lever	**33**	Forend Spacer
13	Recoil Pad	**34**	Barrel Catch Spring
14	Plastic Recoil Filler Pad	**35**	Ejector Spring
15	Ejector Latch Pin	**36**	Ejector Latch Spring
16	Ejector Spring Stop Pin	**37**	Firing Pin Spring
17	Ejector Stop Pin	**38**	Hammer Spring
18	Firing Pin	**39**	Trigger Spring
19	Hammer and Barrel Catch Pins	**40**	Stock Assembly (Model 158)
20	Hammer Safety Pin	**41**	Stock Assembly (Model 163)
21	Release Lever and Firing Pin Retainer Pin	**42**	Trigger
		43	Tang Screw Washer

300 Autoloading Rifle

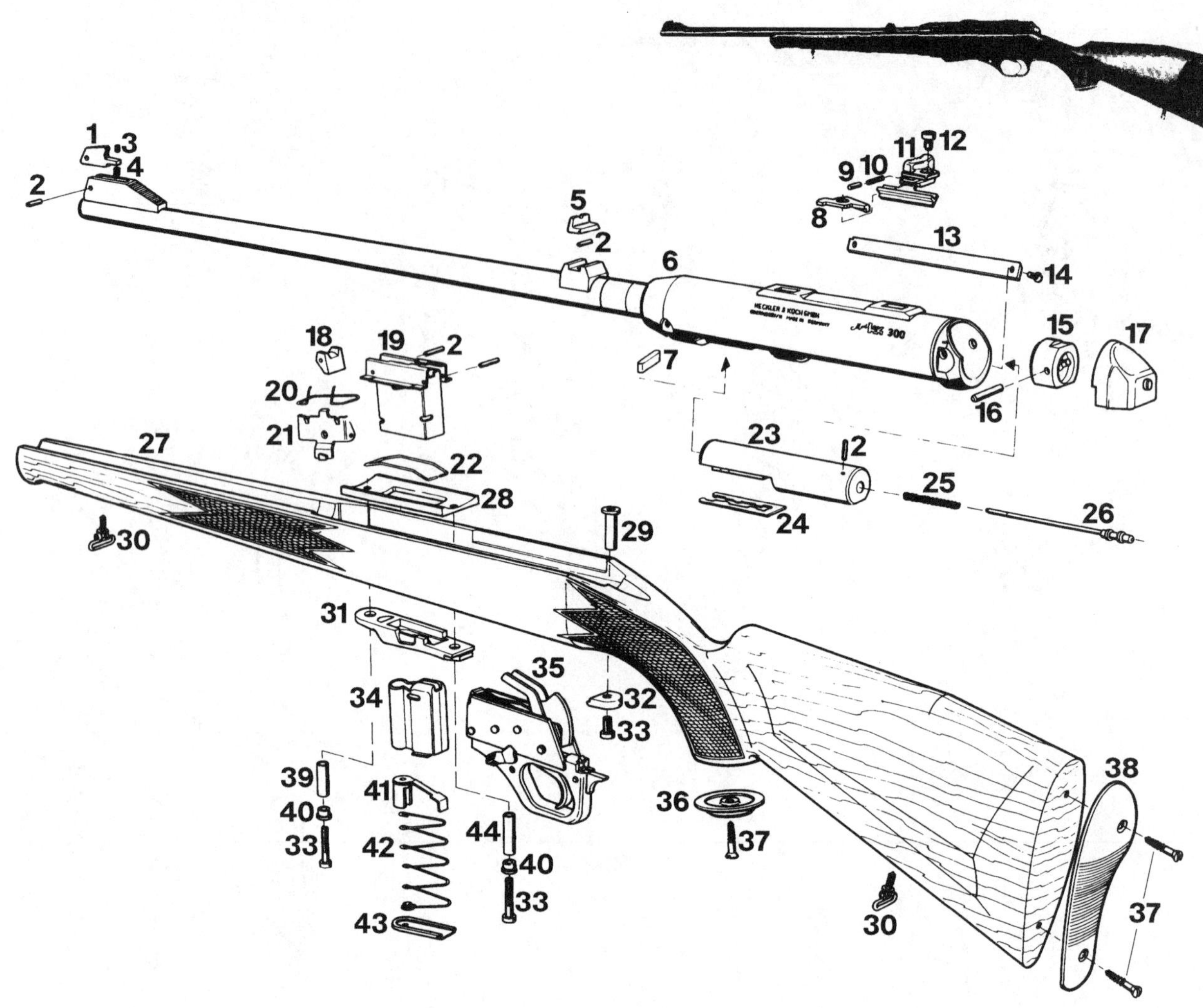

1	Front Sight	24	Extractor
2	Clamping Sleeves	25	Firing Pin Spring
3	Threaded Pin	26	Firing Pin
4	Compression Spring for Ball Catch	27	Stock
5	Rear Sight	28	Supporting Plate
6	Receiver with Barrel	29	Threaded Bush
7	Parallel Key	30	Sling Swivel Hook
8	Catch Lever	31	Base Plate
9	Cylindrical Pin	32	Retaining Plate
10	Cocking Lever Spring	33	Cylinder Head Screws
11	Cocking Lever with Slide	34	Magazine Housing
12	Cylindrical Screw	35	Trigger Assembly, Complete
13	Cover Plate	36	Cap
14	Countersunk Screw	37	Lens Head Countersunk Wood Screws
15	Buffer	38	Buttcap
16	Retaining Pin	39	Spacer, Front
17	Back Plate, Complete	40	Spacer Ring
18	Feed Ramp	41	Follower
19	Magazine Well	42	Follower Spring Assembly
20	Magazine Catch Spring	43	Magazine Floorplate
21	Magazine Catch	44	Spacer
22	Retaining Spring		
23	Bolt Head		

33 Full-Auto Rifle

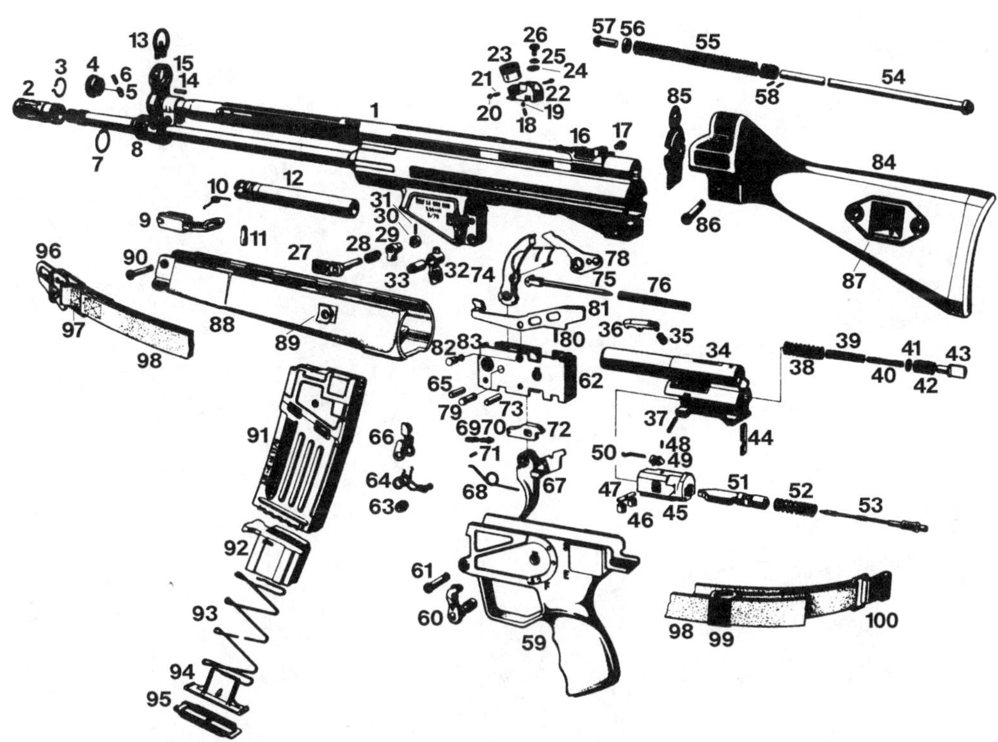

1	Barreled Receiver	**35**	Bolt Head Locking Lever Spring	**69**	Trigger Bolt Compression Spring
2	Flash Suppressor	**36**	Bolt Head Locking Lever	**70**	Trigger Bolt
3	Retaining Spring	**37**	Cylindrical Pin	**71**	Retaining Pin
4	Cap	**38**	Outer Buffer Spring	**72**	Sear
5	Compression Bolt for Cap	**39**	Center Buffer Spring	**73**	Trigger Pivot Pin
6	Pressure Spring for Cap	**40**	Inner Buffer Spring	**74**	Hammer
7	Spring Ring	**41**	Disc	**75**	Pressure Shank
8	Eye Bolt	**42**	Brake Spring	**76**	Pressure Spring
9	Cocking Lever	**43**	Buffer Bolt	**77**	Rivet
10	Cocking Lever Elbow Spring	**44**	Buffer Stop	**78**	Release Lever
11	Cocking Lever Pivot Pin	**45**	Bolt Head	**79**	Hammer Pivot Pin
12	Cocking Lever Support	**46**	Locking Rollers	**80**	Ejector Pressure Spring
13	Front Sight	**47**	Locking Roller Retainer	**81**	Ejector
14	Retaining Pin	**48**	Retaining Pin	**82**	Ejector Pivot Pin
15	Front Sight Holder	**49**	Extractor	**83**	Spring Ring
16	Sight Base	**50**	Extractor Spring	**84**	Buttstock
17	Adjusting Screw	**51**	Locking Piece	**85**	Back Plate
18	Ball Catch Compression Spring	**52**	Firing Pin Spring	**86**	Buttstock Locking Pin
19	Ball	**53**	Firing Pin	**87**	Carrying Sling Support
20	Catch Bolt	**54**	Recoil Spring Guide Rod	**88**	Handguard
21	Catch Bolt Spring	**55**	Recoil Spring	**89**	Hook
22	Sight Support	**56**	Recoil Spring Guide Ring	**90**	Handguard Locking Pin
23	Sight Cylinder	**57**	Stop Pin	**91**	Magazine Housing
24	Fix Plate	**58**	Rivets	**92**	Follower
25	Locking Washer	**59**	Grip	**93**	Follower Spring
26	Binding Screw	**60**	Safety	**94**	Floorplate Spring
27	Magazine Catch	**61**	Grip Locking Pin	**95**	Magazine Floorplate
28	Compression Spring	**62**	Trigger Housing	**96**	Carbine Hook
29	Contact Piece	**63**	Catch Spacer Sleeve	**97**	Double Eye
30	Push Button	**64**	Elbow Spring with Roller	**98**	Carrying Sling
31	Retaining Pin	**65**	Catch	**99**	Sling Buckle
32	Magazine Release Lever	**66**	Catch Pivot Pin	**100**	Spring Hook
33	Magazine Release Lever Bushing	**67**	Trigger		
34	Bolt Head Carrier	**68**	Trigger Spring		

630, 770 and 940 Autoloading Rifle

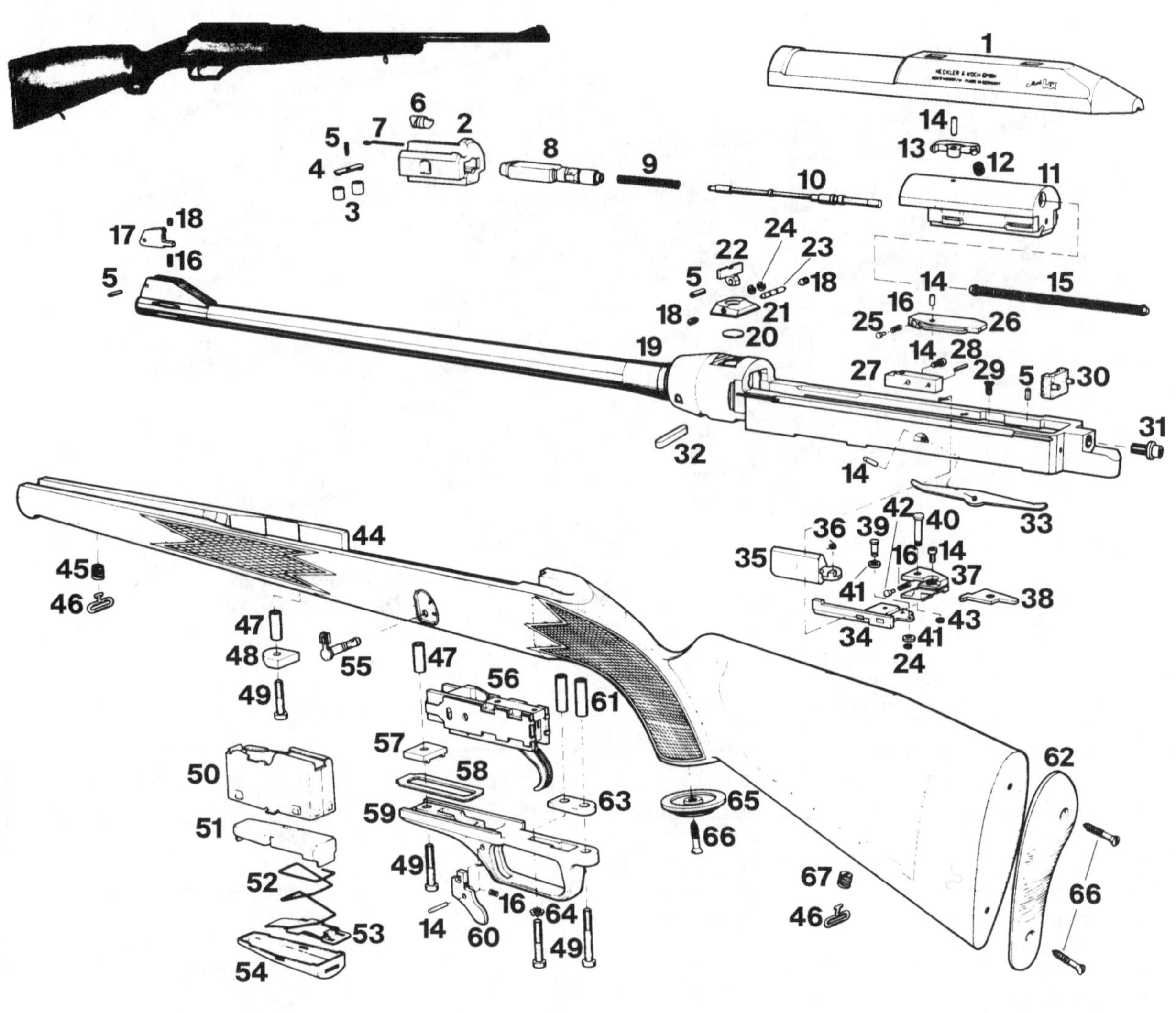

1	Upper Receiver, Complete	21	Rear Sight Base	45	Threaded Bush, Front
2	Bolt Head	22	Rear Sight	46	Sling Swivels
3	Locking Rollers	23	Rear Sight Axle	47	Bushings, Center
4	Holder for Locking Rollers	24	Lock Washer	48	Cover
5	Clamping Sleeves	25	Pressure Bolt	49	Cylinder Head Screw
6	Extractor	26	Support Lever	50	Magazine
7	Extractor Spring	27	Ramp	51	Follower
8	Locking Piece	28	Retaining Pin	52	Follower Spring
9	Firing Pin Spring	29	Raised Countersunk Head Screw	53	Locking Plate
10	Firing Pin	30	Buffer Plate	54	Floorplate
11	Bolt Head Carrier	31	Spindle	55	Safety
12	Compression Spring for Bolt Head Locking Lever	32	Feather Key	56	Trigger Assembly Housing, Complete
13	Bolt Head Locking Lever, Complete	33	Ejector	57	Retaining Unit
14	Cylindrical Pins	34	Cocking Slide	58	Latch
15	Recoil Spring Assembly	35	Cocking Lever, Complete	59	Trigger Guard, Assembled
16	Compression Spring for Ball Catch	36	Elbow Spring	60	Magazine Catch
17	Front Sight	37	Bearing Plate	61	Center Bushings
18	Threaded Pins	38	Catch Lever	62	Buttcap
19	Receiver with Barrel	39	Axle for Support Roller	63	Intermediate Plate
20	Leaf Spring	40	Axle for Cocking Lever	64	Toothed Lock Washer
		41	Support Roller	65	Cap
		42	Stop Pin	66	Oval Head Wood Screws
		43	Lock Washer	67	Threaded Bushing, Rear
		44	Stock, Complete		

91A2 Autoloading Rifle

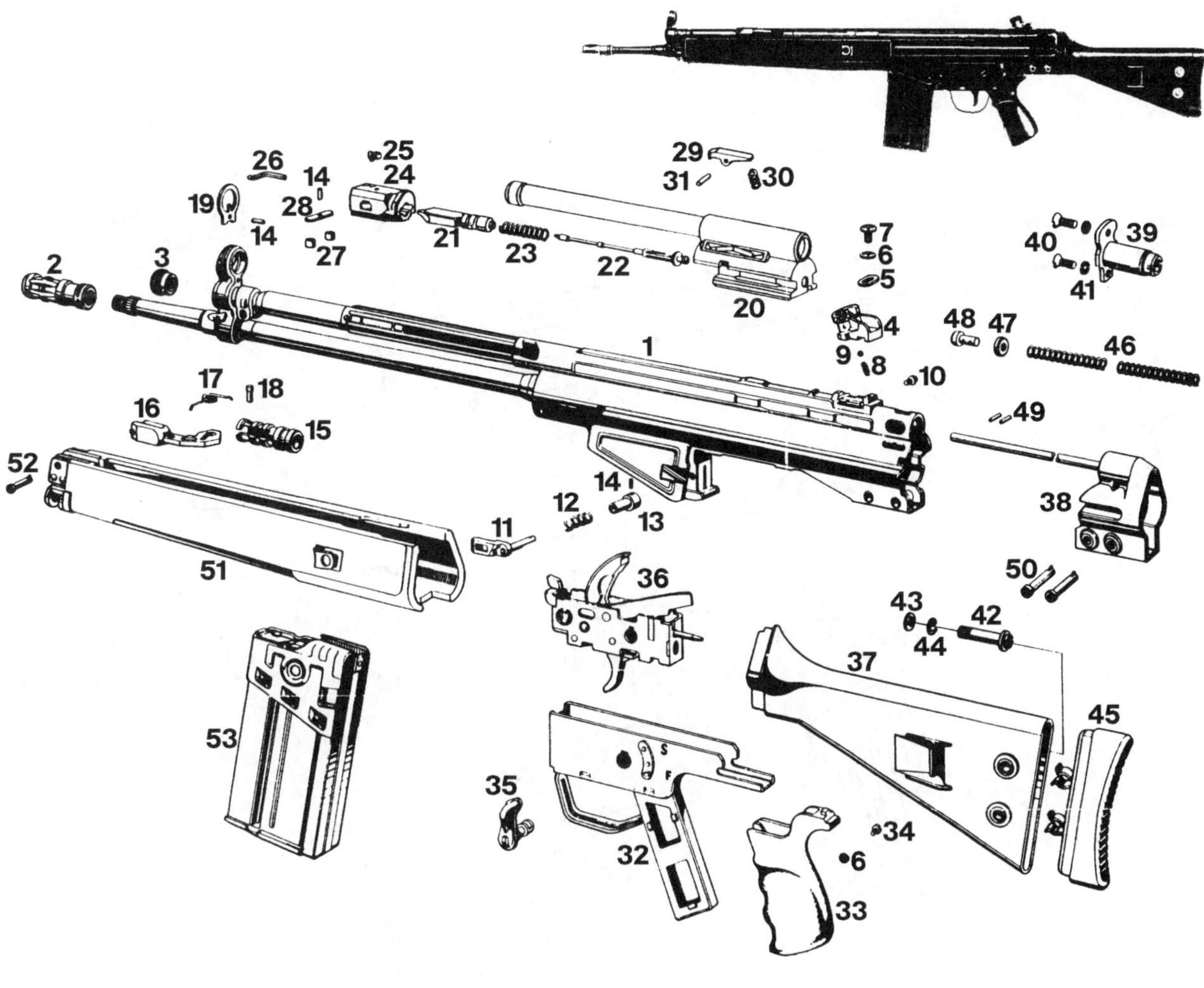

- **1** Receiver with Barrel and Cocking Lever Housing
- **2** Flash Hider, Complete
- **3** Cap, Complete
- **4** Rotary Rear Sight
- **5** Washer
- **6** Toothed Lock Washer
- **7** Clamping Screw
- **8** Compression Springs for Ball Catch
- **9** Balls
- **10** Windage Adjusting Screw
- **11** Magazine Catch, Complete
- **12** Compression Spring for Magazine Catch
- **13** Push Button for Magazine Catch
- **14** Clamping Sleeve
- **15** Support for Cocking Lever
- **16** Cocking Lever
- **17** Elbow Spring for Cocking Lever
- **18** Cocking Lever Axle
- **19** Front Sight
- **20** Bolt Head Carrier
- **21** Locking Piece
- **22** Firing Pin
- **23** Firing Pin Spring
- **24** Bolt Head, Complete
- **25** Extractor
- **26** Extractor Spring
- **27** Locking Rollers
- **28** Holder for Locking Rollers
- **29** Bolt Head Locking Lever
- **30** Compression Spring for Bolt Head Locking Lever
- **31** Cylindrical Pin
- **32** Pistol Grip
- **33** Grip
- **34** Lens Head Cylindrical Screw
- **35** Safety, Complete
- **36** Trigger Housing, Complete
- **37** Buttstock
- **38** Back Plate, Complete
- **39** Buffer
- **40** Countersunk Screws for Buffer
- **41** Lock Washers
- **42** Buffer Screw
- **43** Lock Washer
- **44** Spring Ring
- **45** Buttplate
- **46** Recoil Spring
- **47** Recoil Spring Guide Ring
- **48** Recoil Spring Stop Pin
- **49** Riveted Pins
- **50** Buttstock Locking Pins
- **51** Handguard
- **52** Handguard Locking Pin
- **53** Magazine

93A2 Autoloading Rifle

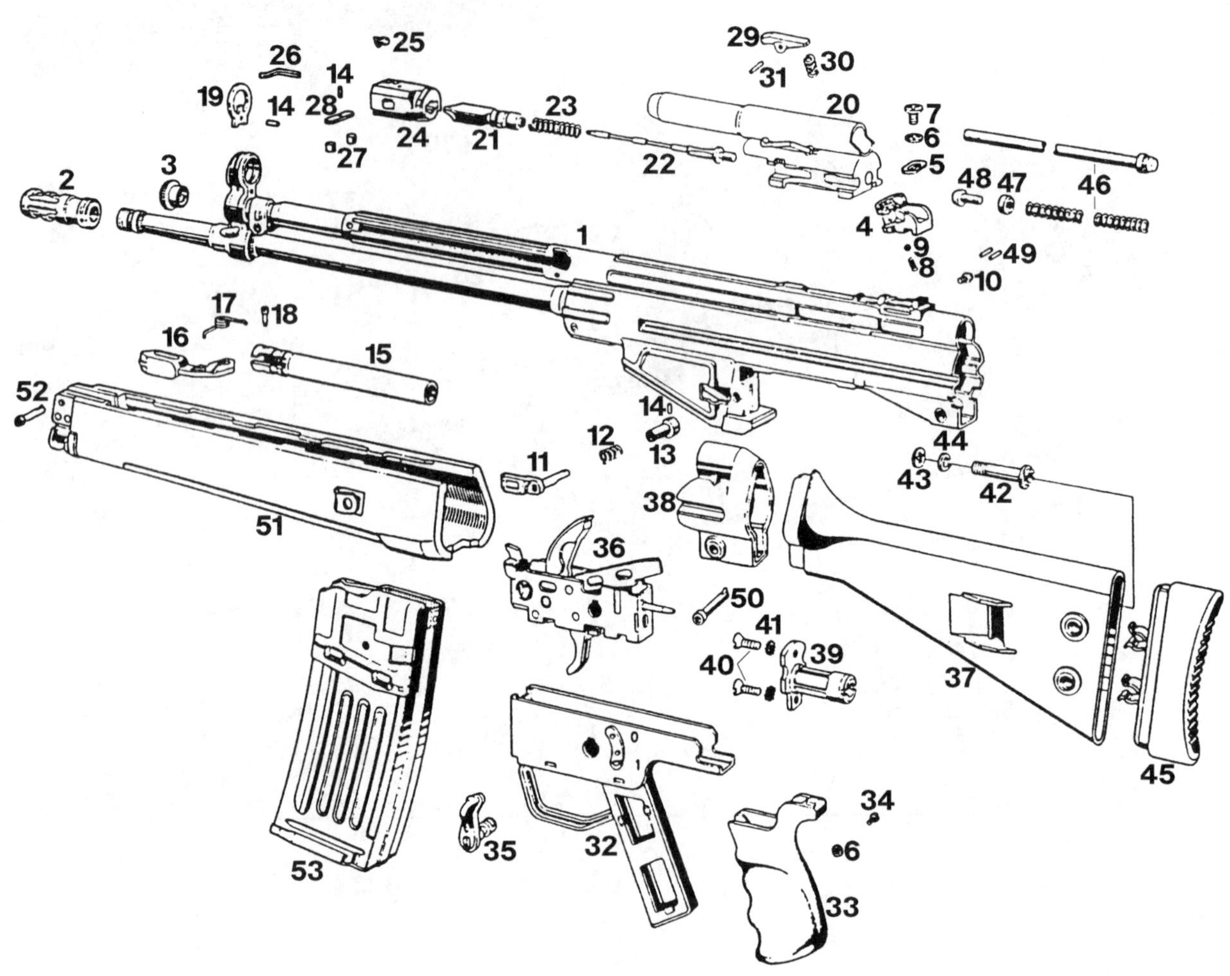

1	Receiver with Barrel and Cocking Lever Housing	**17**	Elbow Spring for Cocking Lever	**35**	Safety, Complete
2	Flash Hider, Complete	**18**	Cocking Lever Axle	**36**	Trigger Housing, Complete
3	Cap, Complete	**19**	Front Sight	**37**	Buttstock
4	Rotary Rear Sight	**20**	Bolt Head Carrier	**38**	Back Plate, Complete
5	Washer	**21**	Locking Piece	**39**	Buffer
6	Toothed Lock Washer	**22**	Firing Pin	**40**	Countersunk Screws for Buffer
7	Clamping Screw	**23**	Firing Pin Spring	**41**	Lock Washers
8	Compression Springs for Ball Catch	**24**	Bolt Head, Complete	**42**	Buffer Screw
9	Balls	**25**	Extractor	**43**	Lock Washer
10	Windage Adjusting Screw	**26**	Extractor Spring	**44**	Spring Ring
11	Magazine Catch, Complete	**27**	Locking Rollers	**45**	Buttplate
12	Compression Spring for Magazine Catch	**28**	Holder for Locking Rollers	**46**	Recoil Spring Assembly
13	Push Button for Magazine Catch	**29**	Bolt Head Locking Lever	**47**	Recoil Spring Guide Ring
14	Clamping Sleeve	**30**	Compression Spring for Bolt Head Locking Lever	**48**	Recoil Spring Stop Pin
15	Support for Cocking Lever	**31**	Cylindrical Pin	**49**	Riveted Pins
16	Cocking Lever	**32**	Pistol Grip	**50**	Buttstock Locking Pins
		33	Grip	**51**	Handguard
		34	Lens Head Cylindrical Screw	**52**	Handguard Locking Pin
				53	Magazine

MP 5A2/A3 Full-Auto Rifle

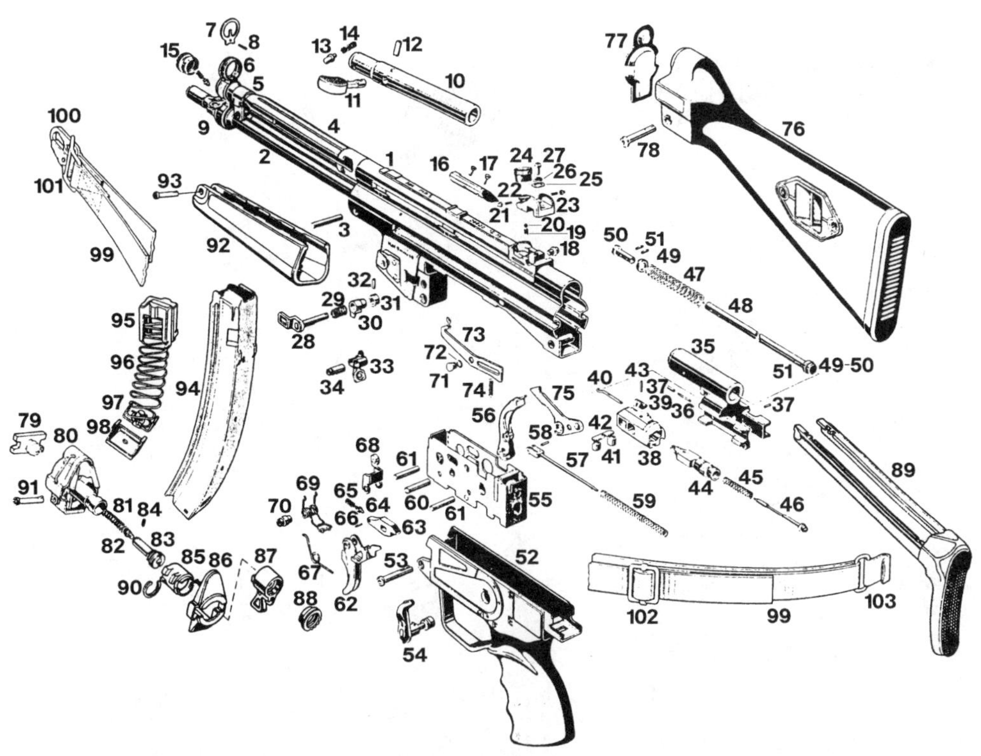

1	Receiver	**36**	Stop Pin	**71**	Axle for Ejector
2	Barrel	**37**	Clamping Sleeve	**72**	Spring Ring
3	Dowel Pin	**38**	Bolt Head	**73**	Ejector
4	Cocking Lever Housing	**39**	Extractor	**74**	Ejector Spring
5	Retaining Clip with Bush	**40**	Extractor Spring	**75**	Release Lever
6	Front Sight Holder	**41**	Locking Rollers	**76**	Buttstock
7	Front Sight	**42**	Holder for Locking Rollers	**77**	Back Plate
8	Clamping Sleeve	**43**	Clamping Sleeve	**78**	Locking Pin for Buttstock
9	Eye Bolt	**44**	Locking Piece	**79**	Buffer
10	Cocking Lever Support with Collar	**45**	Firing Pin Spring	**80**	Back Plate
11	Cocking Lever	**46**	Firing Pin	**81**	Compression Spring
12	Axle for Cocking Lever	**47**	Recoil Spring	**82**	Compression Bolt
13	Catch Bolt	**48**	Recoil Spring Guide Rod	**83**	Buffer Screw
14	Spring for Catch Bolt	**49**	Guide Ring for Recoil Spring	**84**	Clamping Sleeve
15	Cap	**50**	Stop Pin for Recoil Spring	**85**	Ratchet
16	Cartridge Case Deflector	**51**	Riveting Pin	**86**	Protective Cover with Plug
17	Rivets for Cartridge Case Deflector	**52**	Pistol Grip	**87**	Clamping Lever
18	Adjusting Screw	**53**	Locking Pin for Pistol Grip	**88**	Spring Ring with Catch
19	Compression Spring	**54**	Selector Lever	**89**	Buttstock, Retractable
20	Ball	**55**	Trigger Housing	**90**	Circlip
21	Catch Bolt	**56**	Hammer	**91**	Locking Pin, Complete
22	Spring for Catch Bolt	**57**	Pressure Shank for Hammer	**92**	Handguard
23	Rear Sight Support	**58**	Riveting Pin for Pressure Shank	**93**	Locking Pin for Handguard
24	Rear Sight Cylinder	**59**	Compression Spring for Hammer	**94**	Magazine Housing
25	Washer	**60**	Axle for Hammer	**95**	Follower
26	Toothed Lock Washer	**61**	Axle for Trigger and Catch	**96**	Follower Spring
27	Clamping Screw	**62**	Trigger	**97**	Spring Floorplate
28	Magazine Catch	**63**	Sear	**98**	Magazine Floorplate
29	Spring for Magazine Catch	**64**	Trigger Bolt	**99**	Carrying Sling
30	Contact Piece	**65**	Spring for Trigger Bolt	**100**	Carbine Hook
31	Push Button	**66**	Clamping Sleeve	**101**	Double Eye
32	Clamping Sleeve	**67**	Elbow Spring for Trigger	**102**	Buckle
33	Magazine Release Lever	**68**	Catch	**103**	Spring Hook
34	Bush for Magazine Release Lever	**69**	Elbow Spring with Roller for Catch		
35	Bolt Head Carrier	**70**	Distance Sleeve		

SL6 and SL7 Autoloading Rifle

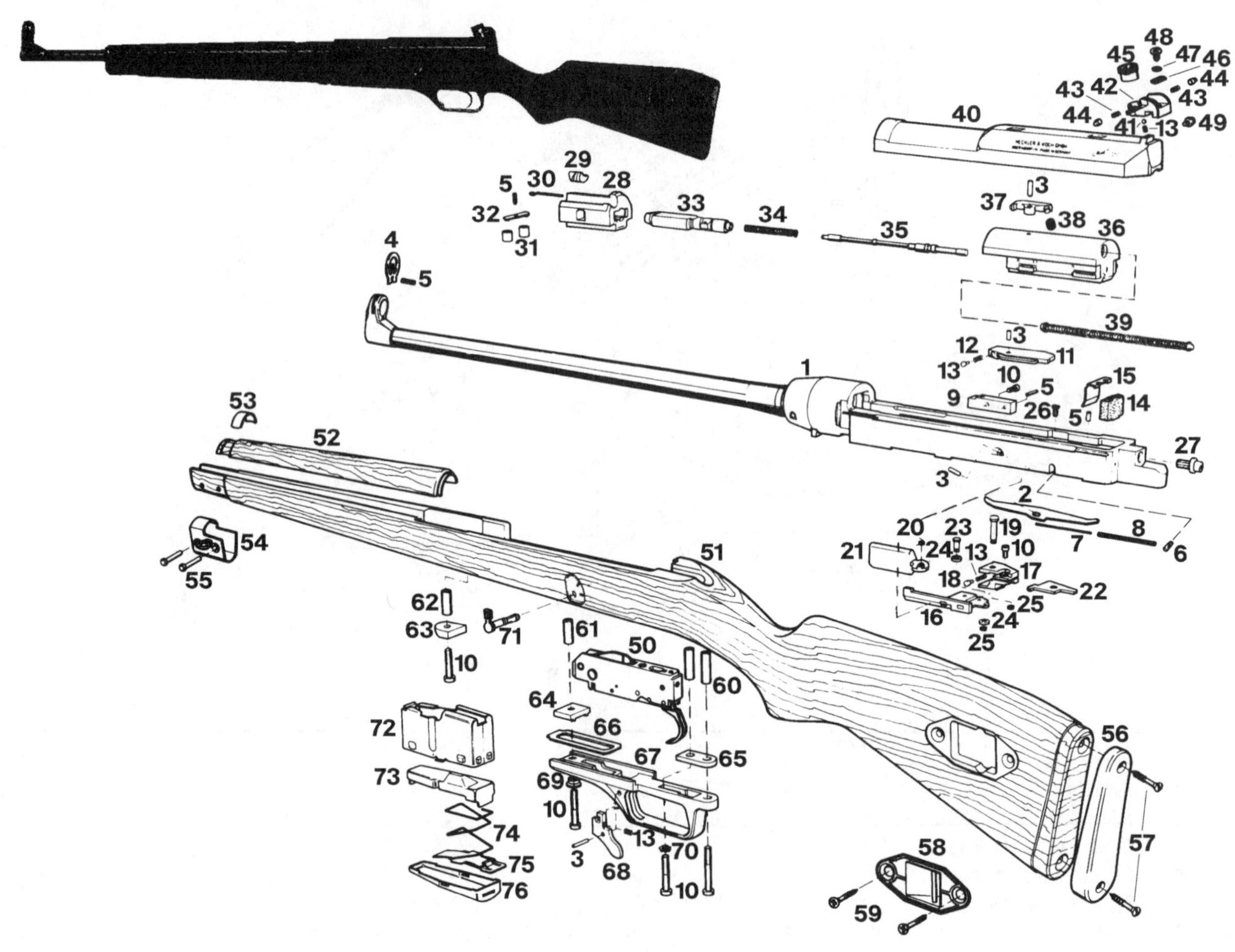

No.	Part	No.	Part	No.	Part
1	Receiver with Barrel	27	Spindle	51	Stock
2	Ejector	28	Bolt Head	52	Handguard
3	Cylindrical Pin	29	Extractor	53	Spacer Clip
4	Front Sight	30	Extractor Spring	54	Band
5	Clamping Sleeves	31	Locking Rollers	55	Retaining Bolts
6	Spring Holder	32	Holder for Locking Rollers	56	Buttcap
7	Spring Guide	33	Locking Piece	57	Wood Screws
8	Ejector Spring	34	Firing Pin Return Spring	58	Holder for Carrying Sling
9	Ramp	35	Firing Pin	59	Wood Screws
10	Cylinder Head Screws	36	Bolt Head Carrier	60	Bushings, Long
11	Support Lever	37	Bold Head Locking Lever	61	Bushing, Medium
12	Compression Spring for Ball Catch	38	Compression Spring for Bolt Head Locking Lever	62	Bushing, Short
13	Pressure Bolts			63	Cover
14	Buffer Plate	39	Recoil Spring	64	Retaining Unit
15	Buffer Sheet	40	Upper Receiver	65	Intermediate Plate
16	Cocking Slide	41	Ball	66	Magazine Catch
17	Cocking Lever Support	42	Rear Sight Support	67	Trigger Guard
18	Stop Pin	43	Compression Springs	68	Magazine Release Lever
19	Cocking Lever Axle	44	Catch Bolts	69	Spacer Ring
20	Elbow Spring	45	Rear Sight Cylinder	70	Toothed Lock Washer
21	Cocking Lever, Complete	46	Washer	71	Safety
22	Catch Lever	47	Serrated Lock Washer	72	Magazine Housing
23	Axle for Slide Roller	48	Clamping Screw	73	Follower
24	Slide Rollers	49	Windage Adjustment Screw	74	Follower Spring
25	Retaining Washers	50	Trigger Housing, Complete	75	Locking Plate
26	Raised Countersunk Head Screw			76	Magazine Floorplate

Model 33N Drilling

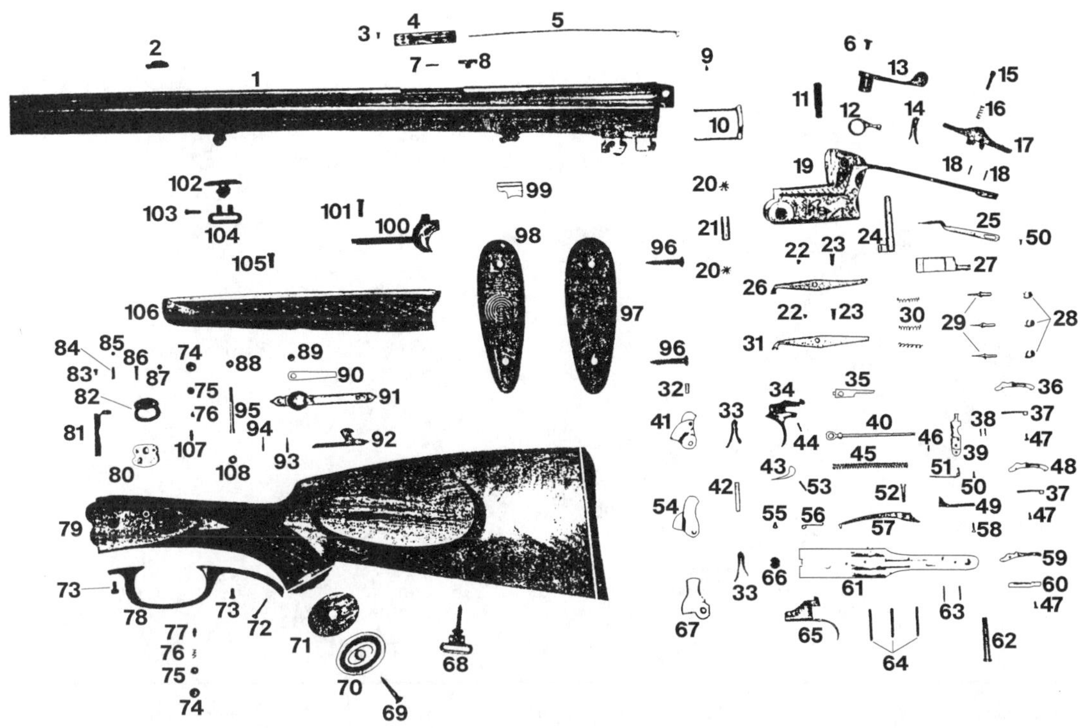

1	Barrel Unit
2	Front Sight
3	Rear Sight Screw
4	Rear Sight Base
5	Rear Sight Actuator Rod
6	Top Lever Screw
7	Rear Sight Pivot Pin
8	Rear Sight
9	Rear Sight Rod Screw
10	Ejector Unit
11	Barrel Crossbolt Shaft
12	Top Lever Connector, Crossbolt Shaft
13	Top Lever
14	Top Lever Spring
15	Safety Plunger
16	Safety Plunger Spring
17	Safety
18	Safety Pins
19	Receiver
20	Barrel Pivot Cap Screws
21	Barrel Pivot
22	Cocking Lever Lock Screws
23	Cocking Lever Pivot Screws
24	Top Lever Shaft
25	Rifle Change Lever
26	Cocking Lever, Left
27	Locking Block
28	Firing Pin Retainers
29	Firing Pins
30	Firing Pin Springs
31	Cocking Lever, Right
32	Sear Pin
33	Sear Spring
34	Trigger Extension
35	Set Trigger Spring
36	Sear, Right
37	Right Sear Spring
38	Safety Bearings
39	Safety Connector
40	Hammer Spring Guide
41	Hammer, Right
42	Hammer Pivot Pin
43	Set Trigger Sear
44	Trigger, Right
45	Hammer Spring
46	Cocking Knob Frame
47	Sear Spring Screw
48	Sear, Rifle
49	Safety Connector Bar
50	Connector Bar Screw
51	Connector Spring
52	Trigger Spring
53	Set Trigger Sear Spring
54	Hammer, Rifle
55	Trigger Spring Screw
56	Trigger Spring
57	Safety Actuator
58	Actuator Screw
59	Sear, Left
60	Left Trigger Sear Spring
61	Trigger Plate
62	Stock Screw
63	Trigger Pins
64	Sear Pins
65	Trigger, Left
66	Large Trigger Plate Screw
67	Hammer, Left
68	Rear Sling Loop
69	Grip Cap Screw
70	Grip Cap
71	Grip Cap Spacer
72	Rear Guard Screw
73	Guard Screws
74	Large Cocking Indicator Pin Grommet
75	Small Cocking Indicator Pin Grommet
76	Cocking Indicator Pin Spring
77	Short Cocking Indicator Pin
78	Guard
79	Stock
80	Change Lever Plate
81	Change Lever
82	Change Lever Cover Plate
83	Cover Plate Screws
84	Ball Detent Spring
85	Ball Detent
86	Safety Screw
87	Threaded Safety Pin
88	Stock Bolt Grommet
89	Forend Latch Spring Screw
90	Forend Latch Spring
91	Forend Latch Housing
92	Forend Latch
93	Forend Latch Pivot Pin
94	Forend Latch Pivot Limit Pin
95	Change Lever Screw
96	Buttplate Screws
97	Buttplate Spacer
98	Buttplate
99	Ejector Actuator
100	Forend Base
101	Forend Base Screw
102	Sling Loop Base
103	Sling Loop Screw
104	Sling Loop
105	Forend Base Screw
106	Forend

Model 37 Drilling

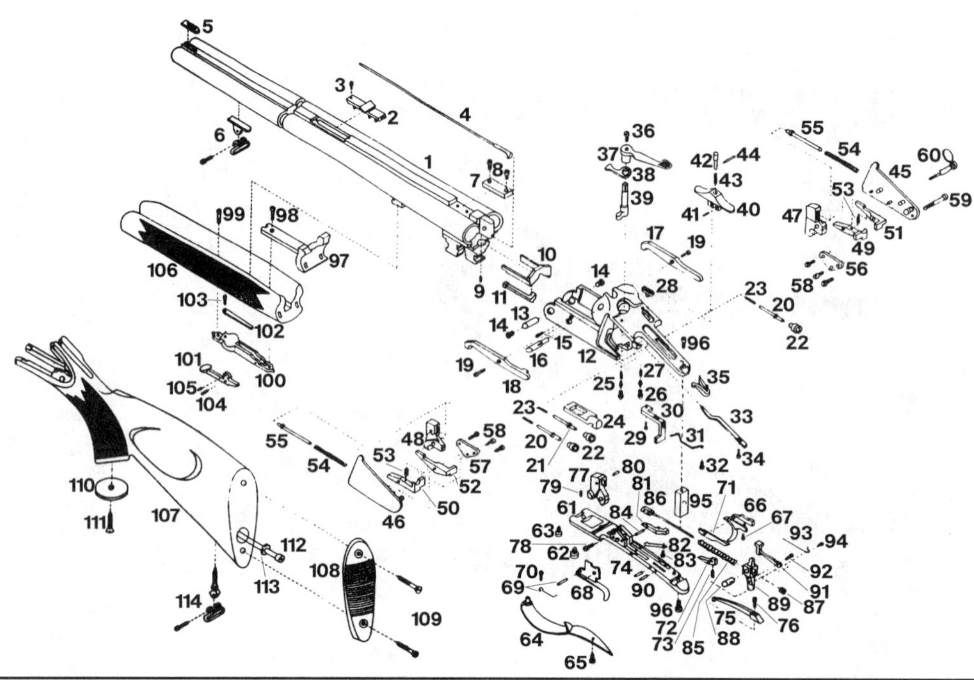

1	Barrel Unit	**39**	Top Lever Shaft	**77**	Hammer, Rifle
2	Rear Sight Base	**40**	Safety Button	**78**	Hammer Pivot
3	Sight Base Screw	**41**	Safety Pin	**79**	Set Screw
4	Sight Actuator Rod	**42**	Safety Plunger	**80**	Spring Guide Pin
5	Front Sight	**43**	Plunger Spring	**81**	Hammer Sear, Rifle
6	Sling Loop Assembly	**44**	Plunger Retaining Pin	**82**	Sear Spring
7	Rib Spacer Plate	**45**	Sideplate, Right	**83**	Spring Screw
8	Plate Screws	**46**	Sideplate, Left	**84**	Sear Pin
9	Sight Actuator Rod Screw	**47**	Hammer, Right	**85**	Hammer Spring, Rifle
10	Ejector	**48**	Hammer, Left	**86**	Spring Guide
11	Ejector Actuator	**49**	Sear, Right	**87**	Guide Seat
12	Receiver	**50**	Sear, Left	**88**	Safety Crosspiece
13	Barrel Unit Pivot	**51**	Sear Lever, Right	**89**	Safety
14	Pivot Cap Screws	**52**	Sear Lever, Left	**90**	Safety Pin
15	Lock Screw	**53**	Sear Springs	**91**	Safety Connector
16	Barrel Unit Crossbolt	**54**	Hammer Springs	**92**	Connector Screw
17	Cocking Lever, Right	**55**	Hammer Spring Guides	**93**	Safety Spring
18	Cocking Lever, Left	**56**	Sideplate Yoke, Right	**94**	Spring Screw
19	Cocking Lever Pivot Screws	**57**	Sideplate Yoke, Left	**95**	Frame Post
20	Firing Pins, Left and Right	**58**	Yoke Screws	**96**	Post Screws
21	Firing Pin, Rifle	**59**	Sideplate Screw	**97**	Forend Base
22	Firing Pin Retainers	**60**	Sideplate Lever	**98**	Base Screw
23	Firing Pin Springs	**61**	Trigger Plate	**99**	Latch Housing Screw
24	Barrel Unit Locking Bolt	**62**	Plate Screw	**100**	Forend Latch Housing
25	Cocking Indicators, Left and Right	**63**	Plate Screw	**101**	Forend Latch
26	Cocking Indicator Retainers	**64**	Guard	**102**	Latch Spring
27	Cocking Indicator Springs	**65**	Guard Screw	**103**	Spring Screw
28	Rifle Change Button	**66**	Trigger, Right	**104**	Latch Pivot Pin
29	Button Screw	**67**	Trigger Limit Screw	**105**	Latch Limit Pin
30	Button Connector	**68**	Trigger, Left	**106**	Forend
31	Connector Spring	**69**	Trigger Spring and Pin	**107**	Stock
32	Spring Screw	**70**	Trigger Spring Screw	**108**	Buttplate
33	Safety Actuator	**71**	Right Trigger Bar	**109**	Buttplate Screws
34	Actuator Screw	**72**	Set-Trigger Lever	**110**	Grip Cap
35	Top Lever Spring	**73**	Trigger Lever Spring	**111**	Grip Cap Screw
36	Top Lever Screw	**74**	Trigger Lever Pin	**112**	Stock Bolt
37	Top Lever	**75**	Set-Trigger Spring	**113**	Stock Bolt Washer
38	Crossbolt Actuator	**76**	Spring Screw	**114**	Sling Loop Assembly

Model SR 20 Bolt-Action Rifle

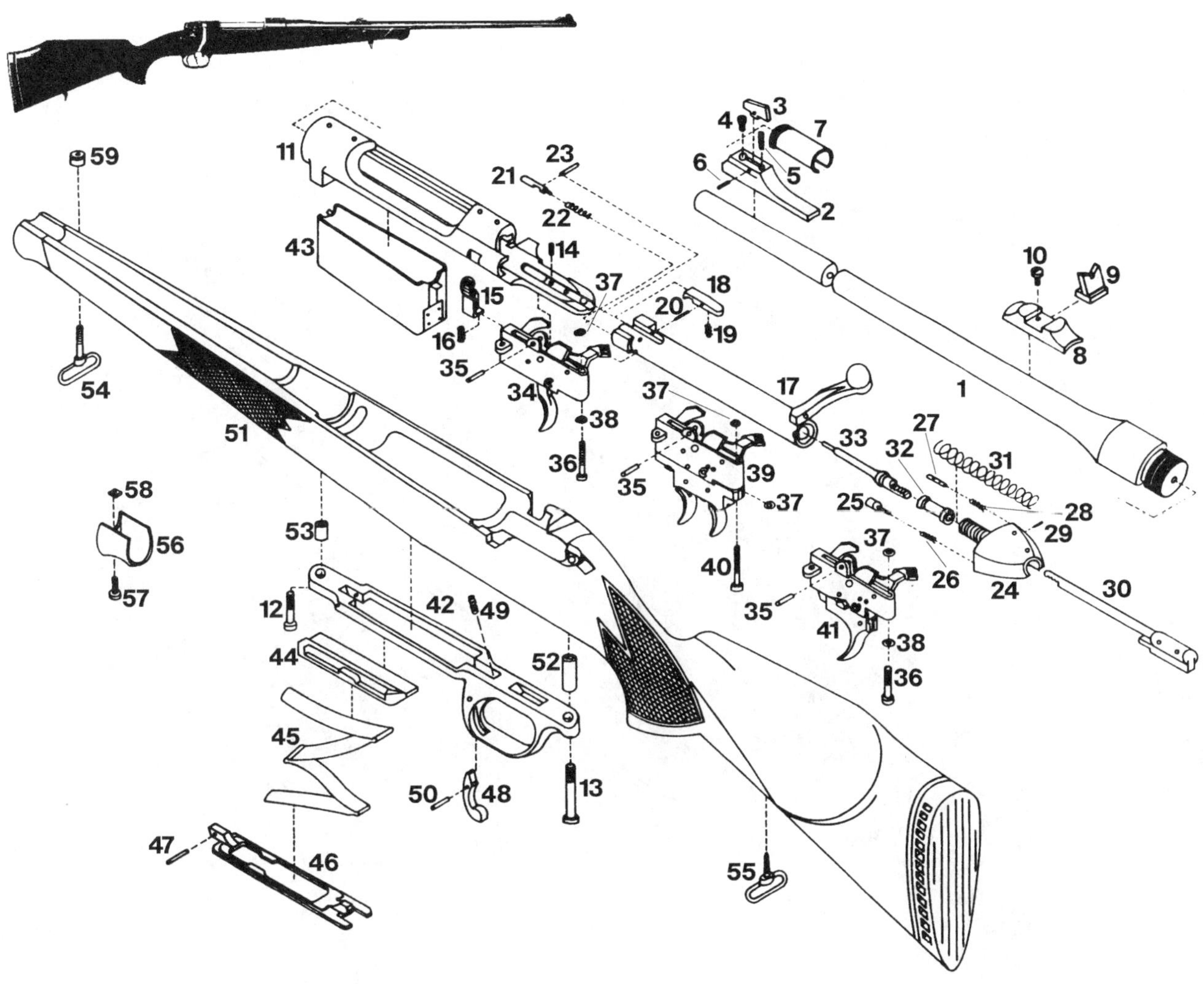

1	Barrel	21	Ejector	41	Single-Set Trigger Assembly
2	Front Sight Base	22	Ejector Spring	42	Trigger Guard Unit
3	Front Sight	23	Ejector Pin	43	Magazine Housing
4	Sight Screw	24	Bolt End Piece	44	Magazine Follower
5	Sight Spring	25	End Piece Lock	45	Magazine Spring
6	Sight Pin	26	Lock Spring	46	Magazine Floorplate
7	Sight Hood	27	Bolt Handle Lock	47	Floorplate Pin
8	Rear Sight Base	28	Bolt Handle Lock Spring	48	Floorplate Latch
9	Rear Sight	29	Bolt Handle Lock Pin	49	Latch Spring
10	Sight Base Screw	30	Striker	50	Latch Pin
11	Receiver	31	Striker Spring	51	Stock
12	Front Guard Screw	32	Connector	52	Rear Guard Screw Sleeve
13	Rear Guard Screw	33	Firing Pin	53	Front Guard Screw Sleeve
14	Bolt Stop Pin	34	Trigger Assembly	54	Sling Loop, Front
15	Bolt Stop	35	Trigger Assembly Pin	55	Sling Loop, Rear
16	Bolt Stop Spring	36	Trigger Assembly Screw	56	Stock End Cap
17	Bolt	37	Trigger Assembly Screw Spacers	57	End Cap Screw
18	Extractor	38	Trigger Assembly Screw Spacer	58	End Cap Nut
19	Extractor Spring	39	Double-Set Trigger Assembly	59	Front Sling Loop Nut
20	Extractor Pin	40	Double-Set Trigger Assembly Screw		

12-Gauge Slide-Action Shotgun

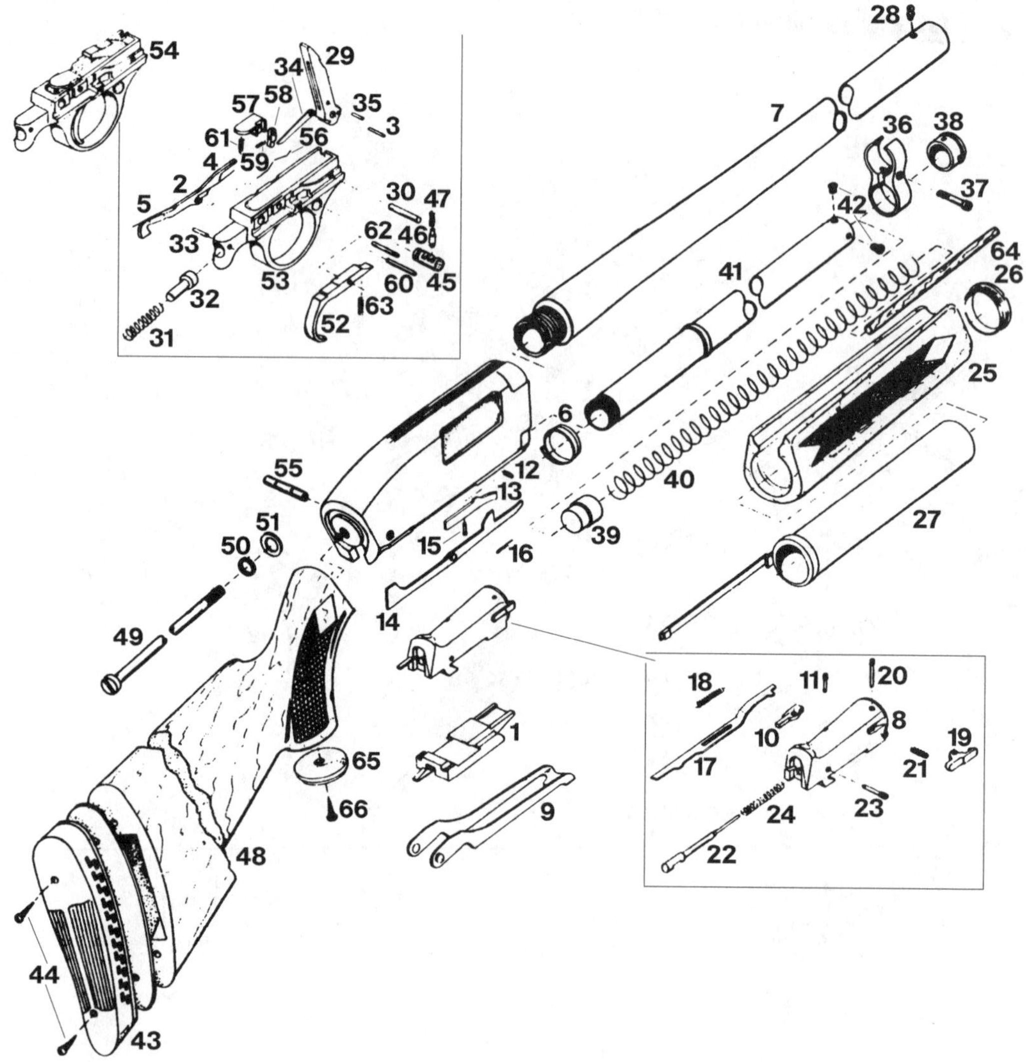

1	Action Slide	21	Extractor Spring, Right	44	Recoil Pad Screws
2	Action Slide Release Lever	22	Firing Pin	45	Safety Button, Right
3	Action Slide Release Lever Operating Pin	23	Firing Pin Retaining Pin	46	Safety Plunger
4	Action Slide Release Lever Spring	24	Firing Pin Spring	47	Safety Plunger Spring
5	Action Slide Release Lever Spring, Rear	25	Forehand Operating Handle	48	Stock
6	Action Slide Spring	26	Forehand Operating Sleeve Front Nut	49	Stock Bolt
7	Barrel	27	Forehand Operating Tube Assembly	50	Stock Bolt Lock Washer
8	Bolt	28	Front Sight	51	Stock Bolt Washer
9	Carrier Assembly	29	Hammer	52	Trigger
10	Carrier Operating Cam	30	Hammer Hinge Pin	53	Trigger Guard
11	Carrier Operating Cam Retaining Pin	31	Hammer Spring	54	Trigger Guard Assembly
12	Cartridge Stop Spring	32	Hammer Spring Guide	55	Trigger Guard Retaining Pin
13	Cartridge Stop, Left	33	Hammer Spring Retaining Pin	56	Trigger Guard Retaining Pin Spring
14	Cartridge Stop, Right	34	Hammer Strut	57	Trigger Lock
15	Cartridge Stop Pin	35	Hammer Strut Pin	58	Trigger Lock Pawl
16	Cartridge Stop Pin Retaining Clip	36	Magazine Band	59	Trigger Lock Pawl Spring
17	Ejector	37	Magazine Band Screw	60	Trigger Lock Pin
18	Ejector Spring	38	Magazine Cap	61	Trigger Lock Spring
19	Extractor, Right	39	Magazine Follower	62	Trigger Pin
20	Extractor Hinge Pin	40	Magazine Spring	63	Trigger Spring
		41	Magazine Tube	64	Wood Plug
		42	Magazine Tube Locking Screws	65	Pistol Grip Cap
		43	Recoil Pad	66	Pistol Grip Cap Screw

Flite King Slide-Action Shotgun

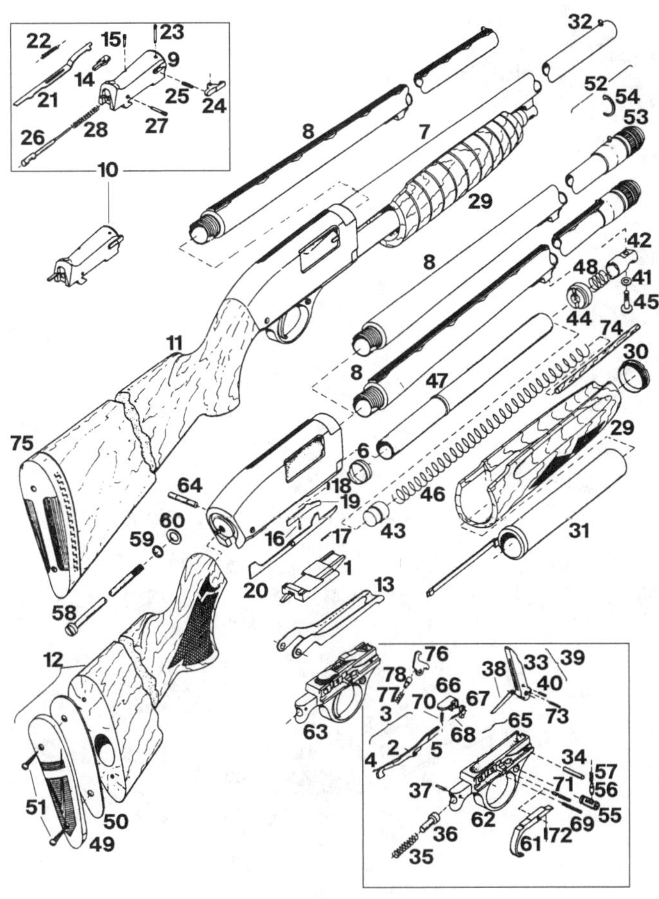

1	Slide Action	**23**	Extractor Hinge Pin	**51**	Buttplate Screws
2	Slide Action Release Lever	**24**	Extractor, Right	**52**	Choke Assembly
3	Slide Action Release Lever Assembly	**25**	Extractor Spring, Right	**53**	Choke Cap
4	Slide Action Release Lever Spring, Rear	**26**	Firing Pin	**54**	Choke Click Spring
5	Slide Action Release Lever Spring, Front	**27**	Firing Pin Retaining Pin	**55**	Safety Button
6	Slide Action Spring	**28**	Firing Pin Spring	**56**	Safety Plunger
7	Barrel	**29**	Forehand Operating Handle	**57**	Safety Plunger Spring
8	Alternate Barrel	**30**	Forehand Operating Sleeve Front Nut	**58**	Stock Bolt
9	Bolt	**31**	Forehand Operating Tube Assembly	**59**	Stock Bolt Lock Washer
10	Bolt Assembly	**32**	Front Sight Bead	**60**	Stock Bolt Washer
11	Stock Assembly, Plain with Recoil Pad	**33**	Hammer	**61**	Trigger
12	Stock Assembly, with Checkering, Buttplate and Trim	**34**	Hammer Hinge Pin	**62**	Trigger Guard
13	Carrier Assembly	**35**	Hammer Spring	**63**	Trigger Guard Assembly
14	Carrier Operating Cam	**36**	Hammer Spring Guide	**64**	Trigger Guard Retaining Pin
15	Carrier Operating Cam Retaining Pin	**37**	Hammer Spring Retaining Pin	**65**	Trigger Guard Retaining Pin Spring
16	Cartridge Stop Pin	**38**	Hammer Strut	**66**	Trigger Lock
17	Cartridge Stop Pin Retaining Clip	**39**	Hammer and Strut Assembly	**67**	Trigger Lock Pawl
18	Cartridge Stop Spring	**40**	Hammer Strut Pin	**68**	Trigger Lock Pawl Spring
19	Cartridge Stop, Left	**41**	Magazine Cap Screw Lock Washer	**69**	Trigger Lock Pin
20	Cartridge Stop, Right	**42**	Magazine Cap Support	**70**	Trigger Lock Spring
21	Extractor/Ejector	**43**	Magazine Follower	**71**	Trigger Pin
22	Extractor/Ejector Spring	**44**	Magazine Cap	**72**	Trigger Spring
		45	Magazine Cap Screw	**73**	Slide Action Release Lever Operating Pin
		46	Magazine Spring	**74**	Wood Plug
		47	Magazine Tube Assembly	**75**	Recoil Pad
		48	Magazine Cap Spring	**76**	Escapement Hook
		49	Buttplate	**77**	Escapement Hook Spring
		50	Buttplate Trim	**78**	Escapement Hook Spring Plunger

Model 10A Autoloading Shotgun

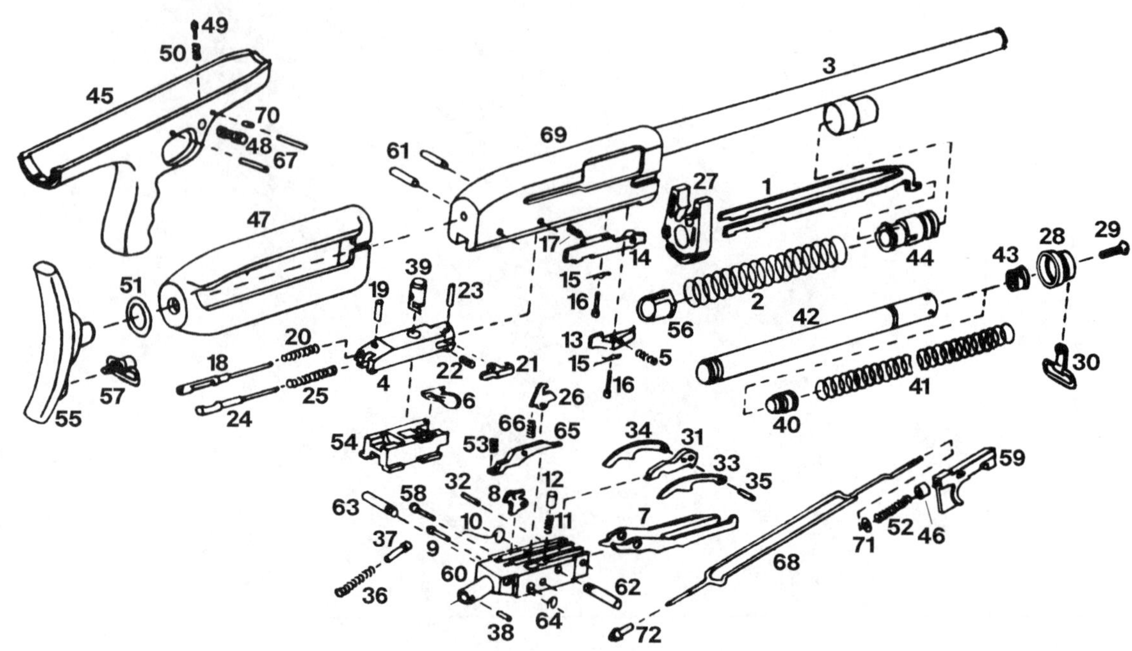

1	Action Bar	**24**	Firing Pin	**50**	Safety Spring
2	Action Spring	**25**	Firing Pin Retracting Spring	**51**	Shoulder Yoke Spring
3	Barrel and Cylinder Assembly with Front Sight Threads	**26**	Escapement Hook	**52**	Trigger Return Spring
4	Bolt	**27**	Housing Coupling	**53**	Sear Set Screw
5	Cartridge Stop Spring, Right	**28**	Forehand Cap	**54**	Slide
6	Cocking Handle	**29**	Forehand Cap Screw	**55**	Shoulder Yoke
7	Cartridge Lifter	**30**	Front Swivel Assembly	**56**	Shoulder Yoke Bolt
8	Cartridge Lifter Actuator Assembly	**31**	Hammer	**57**	Rear Swivel Assembly
9	Cartridge Lifter Actuator Hinge Pin	**32**	Hammer Hinge Pin	**58**	Rear Swivel Nut
10	Cartridge Lifter Actuator Spring	**33**	Hammer Strut, Right	**59**	Trigger
11	Cartridge Lifter Spring	**34**	Hammer Strut, Left	**60**	Guard
12	Cartridge Lifter Spring Plunger	**35**	Hammer Strut Pin	**61**	Guard Retracting Pins
13	Cartridge Stop, Right	**36**	Hammer Spring	**62**	Guard Retracting Pin Bushing, Front
14	Cartridge Stop, Left	**37**	Hammer Spring Guide	**63**	Guard Retracting Pin Bushing, Rear
15	Cartridge Stop Pin Retaining Clips	**38**	Hammer Spring Retracting Pin	**64**	Guard Retracting Pin Bushing Retracting Spring
16	Cartridge Stop Pins	**39**	Locking Pin	**65**	Sear
17	Cartridge Stop Spring, Left	**40**	Magazine Follower	**66**	Escapement Hook Spring
18	Ejector	**41**	Magazine Spring	**67**	Trigger Retracting Pins
19	Firing Pin and Ejector Retracting Pin	**42**	Magazine Tube	**68**	Trigger Rod
20	Ejector Retracting Spring	**43**	Magazine Tube Cap	**69**	Receiver
21	Extractor, Right	**44**	Piston	**70**	Trigger Rod Lock Nut
22	Extractor Spring, Right	**45**	Pistol Grip Housing	**71**	Rod Washer
23	Extractor Hinge Pin	**46**	Pistol Grip Sling Pin	**72**	Base Spring Plug
		47	Receiver Housing		
		48	Safety Button		
		49	Safety Spring Plunger		

Model 200 Slide-Action Shotgun

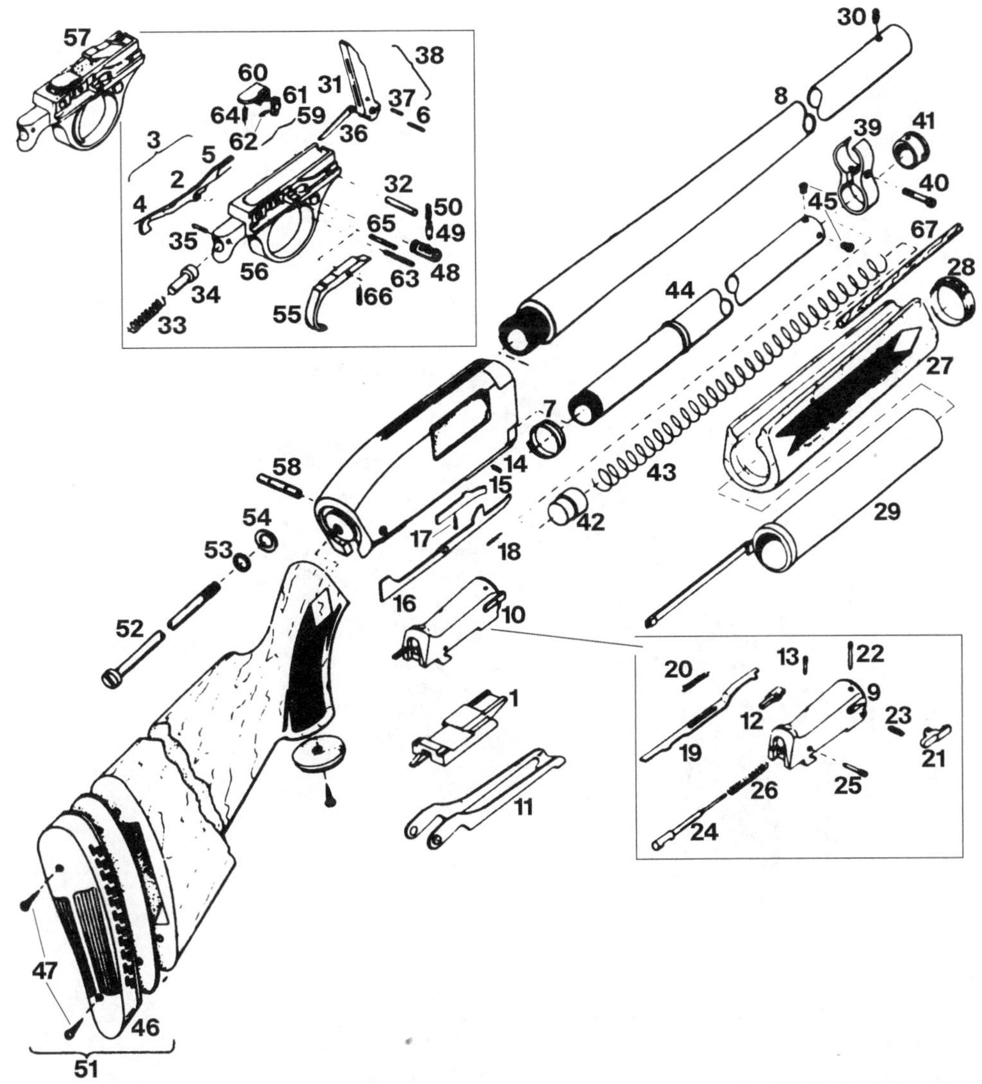

1	Slide Action	**21**	Extractor, Right	**45**	Magazine Tube Locking Screws
2	Slide Action Release Lever	**22**	Extractor Hinge Pin	**46**	Recoil Pad
3	Slide Action Release Lever Assembly	**23**	Extractor Spring, Right	**47**	Recoil Pad Screws
4	Slide Action Release Lever Spring, Rear	**24**	Firing Pin	**48**	Safety Button
5	Slide Action Release Lever Spring, Front	**25**	Firing Pin Retaining Pin	**49**	Safety Plunger
6	Slide Action Release Lever Operating Pin	**26**	Firing Pin Spring	**50**	Safety Plunger Spring
7	Slide Action Spring	**27**	Forehand Operating Handle	**51**	Stock Assembly
8	Barrel	**28**	Forehand Operating Sleeve Front Nut	**52**	Stock Bolt
9	Bolt	**29**	Forehand Operating Tube Assembly	**53**	Stock Bolt Lock Washer
10	Bolt Assembly	**30**	Front Sight	**54**	Stock Bolt Washer
11	Carrier Assembly	**31**	Hammer	**55**	Trigger
12	Carrier Operating Cam	**32**	Hammer Hinge Pin	**56**	Trigger Guard
13	Carrier Operating Cam Retaining Pin	**33**	Hammer Spring	**57**	Trigger Guard Assembly
14	Cartridge Stop Spring	**34**	Hammer Spring Guide	**58**	Trigger Guard Retaining Pin
15	Cartridge Stop, Left	**35**	Hammer Spring Retaining Pin	**59**	Trigger Guard Retaining Pin Spring
16	Cartridge Stop, Right	**36**	Hammer Strut	**60**	Trigger Lock
17	Cartridge Stop Pin	**37**	Hammer Strut Pin	**61**	Trigger Lock Pawl
18	Cartridge Stop Pin Retaining Clip	**38**	Hammer and Strut Assembly	**62**	Trigger Lock Pawl Spring
19	Extractor/Ejector	**39**	Magazine Band	**63**	Trigger Lock Pin
20	Extractor/Ejector Spring	**40**	Magazine Band Screw	**64**	Trigger Lock Spring
		41	Magazine Cap	**65**	Trigger Pin
		42	Magazine Follower	**66**	Trigger Spring
		43	Magazine Spring	**67**	Wood Plug
		44	Magazine Tube		

Model 514 Bolt-Action Shotgun

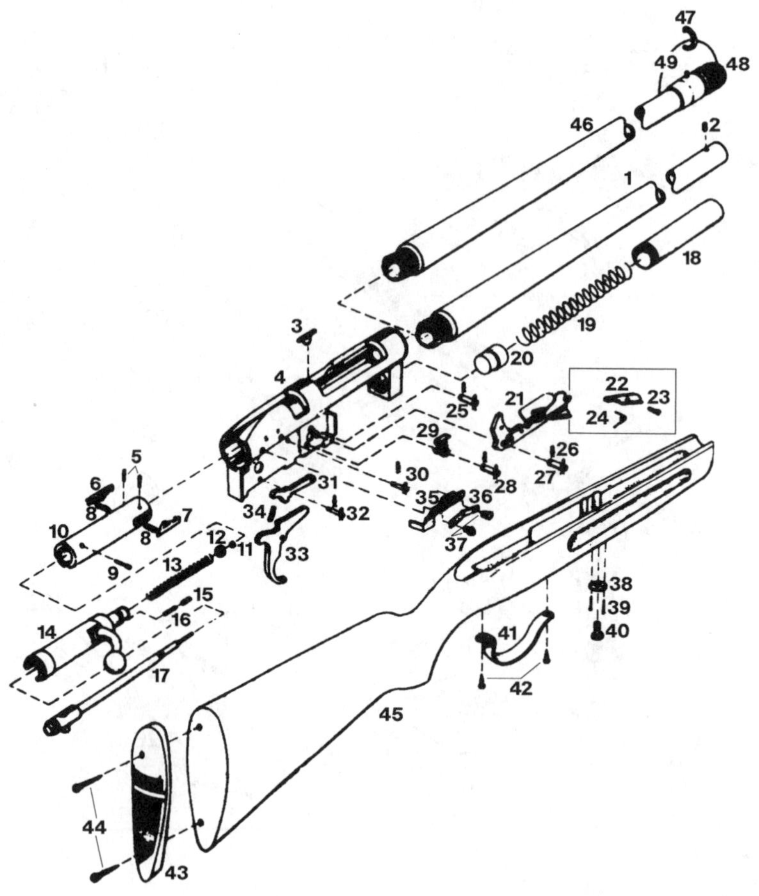

No.	Part	No.	Part
1	Barrel	25	Cartridge Lifter Stop Pin
2	Front Sight	26	Retaining Spring Pin
3	Ejector	27	Cartridge Lifter Pin
4	Receiver	28	Cartridge Lifter Spring Pin
5	Extractor Retaining Pin	29	Cartridge Lifter Spring
6	Extractor, Left	30	Sear Pin
7	Extractor, Right	31	Sear
8	Extractor Springs	32	Trigger Pin
9	Bolt Head Retaining Pin	33	Trigger
10	Bolt Head	34	Trigger Spring
11	Firing Pin Spring Retaining Sleeve Stop Ring	35	Safety
		36	Safety Spring
12	Firing Pin Spring Retaining Sleeve	37	Safety Screws
13	Firing Pin Spring	38	Takedown Escutcheon
14	Bolt Handle and Bolt Body Assembly	39	Takedown Escutcheon Pins
		40	Takedown Screw
15	Bolt Head Detent	41	Trigger Guard
16	Bolt Head Detent Spring	42	Trigger Guard Screws
17	Firing Pin and Head Assembly	43	Buttplate
18	Magazine Tube Assembly	44	Buttplate Screws
19	Magazine Spring	45	Stock Assembly
20	Magazine Follower	46	Barrel with Adjustable Choke Assembly
21	Cartridge Lifter Assembly		
22	Cartridge Stop and Lifter	47	Choke Click Spring
23	Cartridge Stop and Lifter Pin	48	Choke Cap
24	Cartridge Stop and Lifter Spring	49	Choke Assembly

Sport King and Higgins 25 A101 Autoloading Carbine

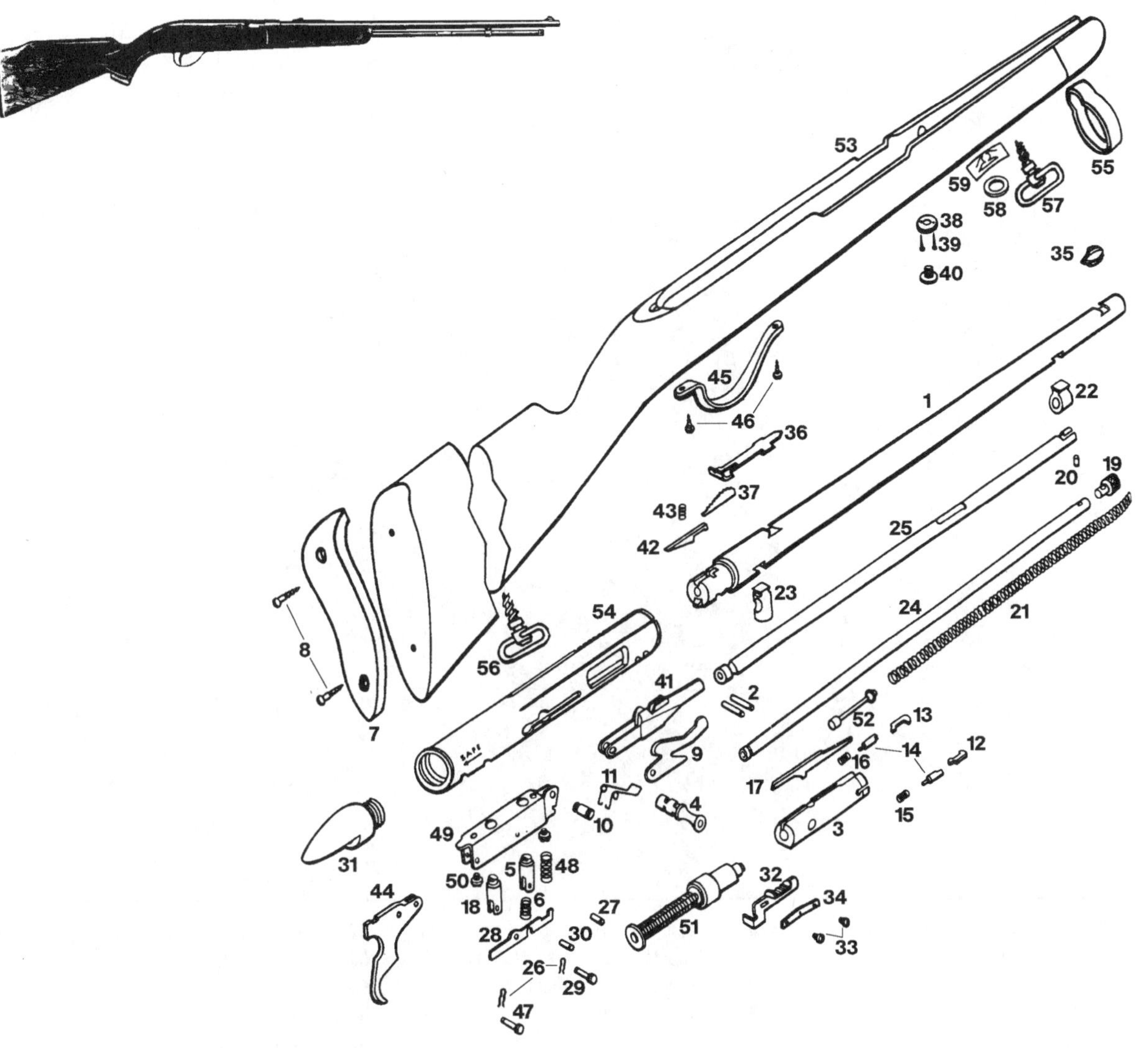

1	Barrel	21	Magazine Spring	41	Throat
2	Barrel Pins	22	Magazine Support, Front	42	Top Ramp
3	Bolt	23	Magazine Support, Rear	43	Top Ramp Spring
4	Bolt Handle	24	Magazine Tube, Inner	44	Trigger
5	Bolt Plunger	25	Magazine Tube, Outer	45	Trigger Guard
6	Bolt Plunger Spring	26	Retaining Spring Pins	46	Trigger Guard Screws
7	Buttplate	27	Plunger Assembly Pin	47	Trigger Pin
8	Buttplate Screws	28	Plunger Connector	48	Trigger Return Spring
9	Cartridge Lifter	29	Plunger Connector Pin	49	Underbody
10	Cartridge Lifter Pin	30	Plunger Connector Stop Pin	50	Underbody Screws
11	Cartridge Lifter Spring	31	Receiver Plug, Rear	51	Hammer Assembly
12	Extractor, Right	32	Safety	52	Magazine Follower Assembly
13	Extractor, Left	33	Safety Screws	53	Stock Assembly
14	Extractor Plungers	34	Safety Spring	54	Breechbolt
15	Extractor Spring, Right	35	Front Sight	55	Stock Band
16	Extractor Spring, Left	36	Rear Sight	56	Rear Swivel
17	Firing Pin	37	Rear Sight Elevator	57	Front Swivel
18	Hammer Plunger	38	Takedown Escutcheon	58	Front Swivel Washer
19	Magazine Cap	39	Takedown Escutcheon Pins	59	Front Swivel Speed Nut
20	Magazine Cap Pin	40	Takedown Screw		

Supermatic Deluxe Model C-1200 and C-1211 Autoloading Shotgun

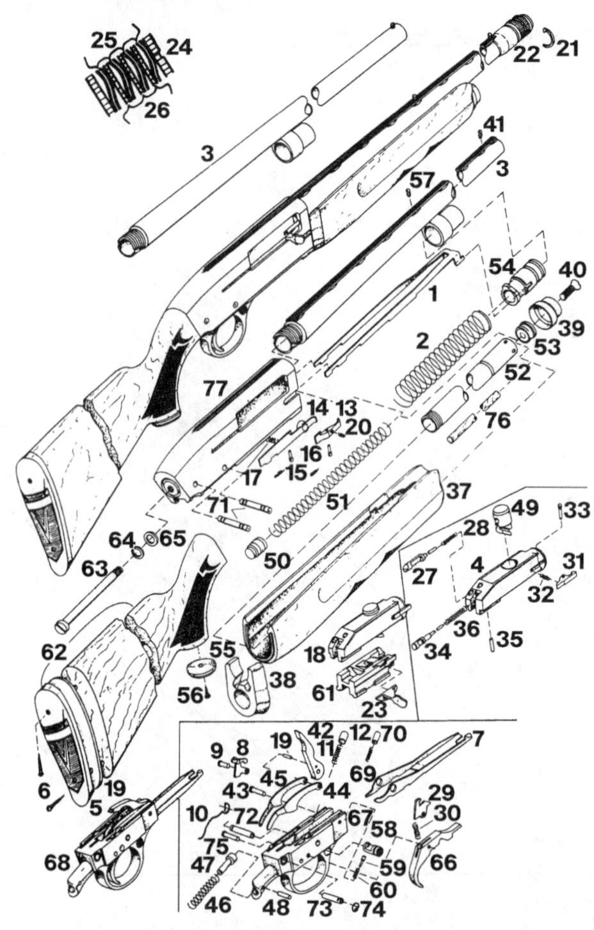

1	Action Bar
2	Action Spring
3	Barrel
4	Bolt
5	Buttplate
6	Buttplate Screws
7	Cartridge Lifter
8	Cartridge Lifter Actuator Assembly
9	Cartridge Lifter Actuator Hinge Pin
10	Cartridge Lifter Actuator Spring
11	Cartridge Lifter Spring
12	Cartridge Lifter Spring Plunger
13	Cartridge Stop, Right
14	Cartridge Stop, Left
15	Cartridge Stop Pin Retaining Clips
16	Cartridge Stop Pins
17	Cartridge Stop Spring, Left
18	Bolt Assembly
19	Buttplate Trim
20	Cartridge Stop Spring, Right
21	Choke Click Spring
22	Choke Cap Assembly
23	Cocking Handle
24	Cylinder Nut
25	Cylinder Wavy Springs
26	Cylinder Spacer Washers
27	Ejector
28	Ejector Retracting Spring
29	Escapement Hook
30	Escapement Hook Spring
31	Extractor, Right
32	Extractor Spring, Right
33	Extractor Pivot Pin
34	Firing Pin
35	Firing Pin Retracting Pin and Ejector Retracting Pin
36	Firing Pin Retracting Spring
37	Forehand Assembly
38	Forehand Base
39	Forehand Cap
40	Forehand Cap Screw
41	Front Sight
42	Hammer
43	Hammer Hinge Pin
44	Hammer Strut, Right
45	Hammer Strut, Left
46	Hammer Spring
47	Hammer Spring Guide
48	Hammer Spring Retracting Pin
49	Locking Pin
50	Magazine Follower
51	Magazine Spring
52	Magazine Tube
53	Magazine Tube Cap
54	Piston
55	Pistol Grip Cap
56	Pistol Grip Cap Screw
57	Rear Sight
58	Safety Button
59	Safety Spring Plunger
60	Safety Spring
61	Slide
62	Stock Assembly
63	Stock Bolt
64	Stock Bolt Lock Washer
65	Stock Bolt Washer
66	Trigger
67	Trigger Guard
68	Trigger Guard Assembly
69	Trigger Spring
70	Trigger Spring Plunger
71	Trigger Guard Retaining Pins
72	Trigger Guard Retaining Pin Bushing, Front
73	Trigger Guard Retaining Pin Bushing, Rear
74	Trigger Guard Retaining Pin Bushing Retaining Spring
75	Trigger Hinge Pin
76	Wood Plug
77	Receiver

Parts Not Shown

Choke Cap

Cylinder Washer

Hammer Strut Pin

Series 1500 Bolt-Action Rifle

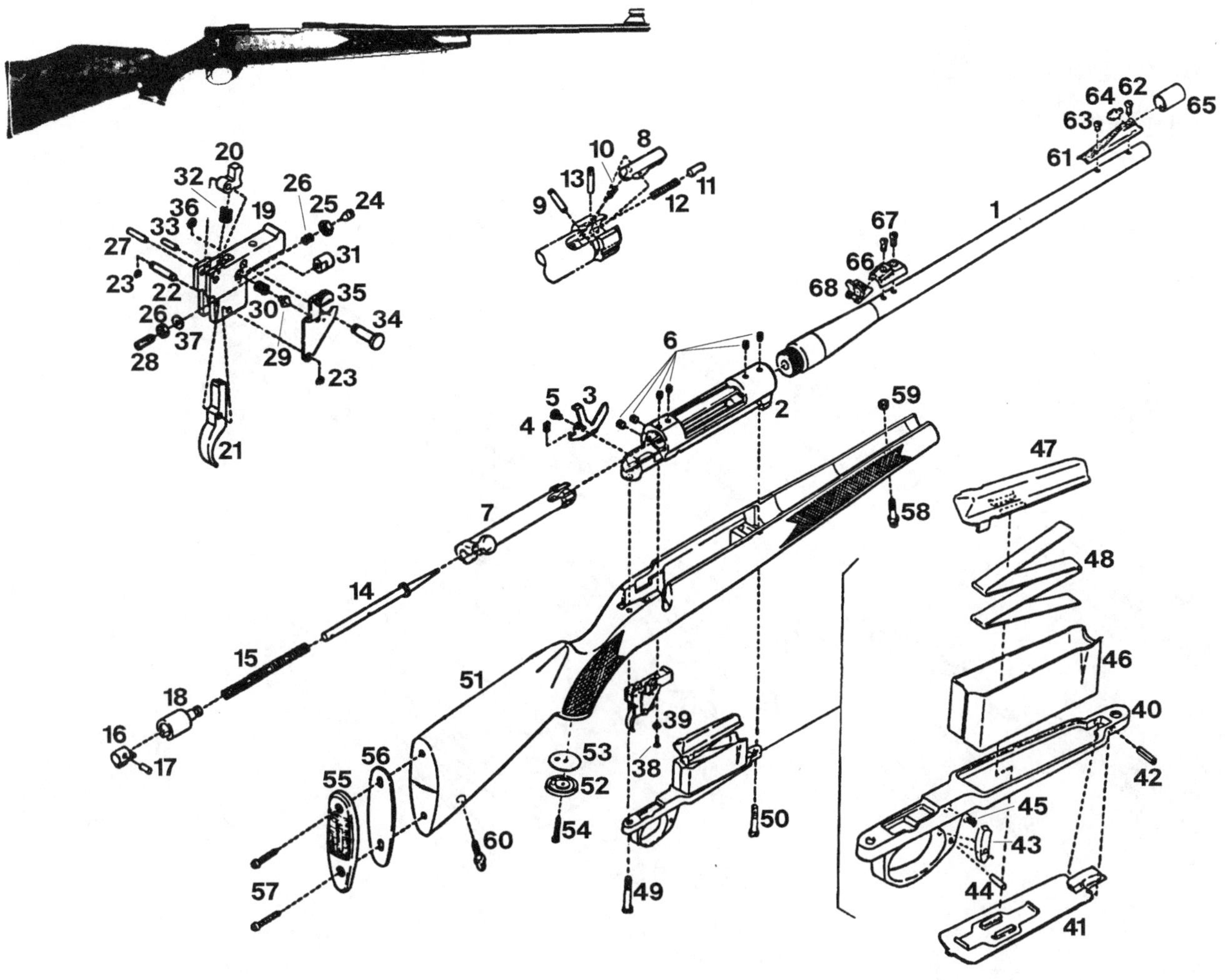

1	Barrel	**24**	Trigger Adjusting Screw, Front	**47**	Magazine Follower
2	Receiver	**25**	Trigger Spring	**48**	Magazine Spring
3	Bolt Stop	**26**	Lock Nut	**49**	Rear Guard Screw
4	Bolt Stop Spring	**27**	Sear Pin	**50**	Front Guard Screw
5	Bolt Stop Screw	**28**	Trigger Adjusting Screw, Rear	**51**	Stock Body
6	Receiver Plug Screw	**29**	Safety Plunger	**52**	Grip Cap
7	Bolt Body	**30**	Safety Plunger Spring	**53**	Grip Cap White Spacer
8	Extractor	**31**	Block	**54**	Grip Cap Screw
9	Extractor Pin	**32**	Sear Spring	**55**	Buttplate
10	Extractor Spring	**33**	Sear Stop Pin	**56**	Buttplate White Spacer
11	Ejector	**34**	Safety Guide Pin	**57**	Buttplate Screws
12	Ejector Spring	**35**	Safety	**58**	Front Swivel Screw
13	Ejector Pin	**36**	Retaining Ring Safety Guide Pin	**59**	Front Swivel Nut
14	Firing Pin	**37**	Washer	**60**	Rear Swivel Screw
15	Mainspring	**38**	Trigger Housing Screw	**61**	Front Sight Ramp
16	Cocking Piece	**39**	Star Washer	**62**	Front Sight Screw, Long
17	Firing Pin Retaining Pin	**40**	Trigger Guard	**63**	Front Sight Screw, Short
18	Bolt Sleeve	**41**	Floorplate	**64**	Front Sight
19	Trigger Housing	**42**	Floorplate Pin	**65**	Front Sight Hood
20	Sear	**43**	Floorplate Catch	**66**	Rear Sight Base
21	Trigger	**44**	Floorplate Catch Pin	**67**	Rear Sight Base Screws
22	Trigger Pin	**45**	Floorplate Catch Spring	**68**	Rear Sight
23	Retaining Ring Trigger Pin	**46**	Magazine		

Model 98/40 Bolt-Action Rifle

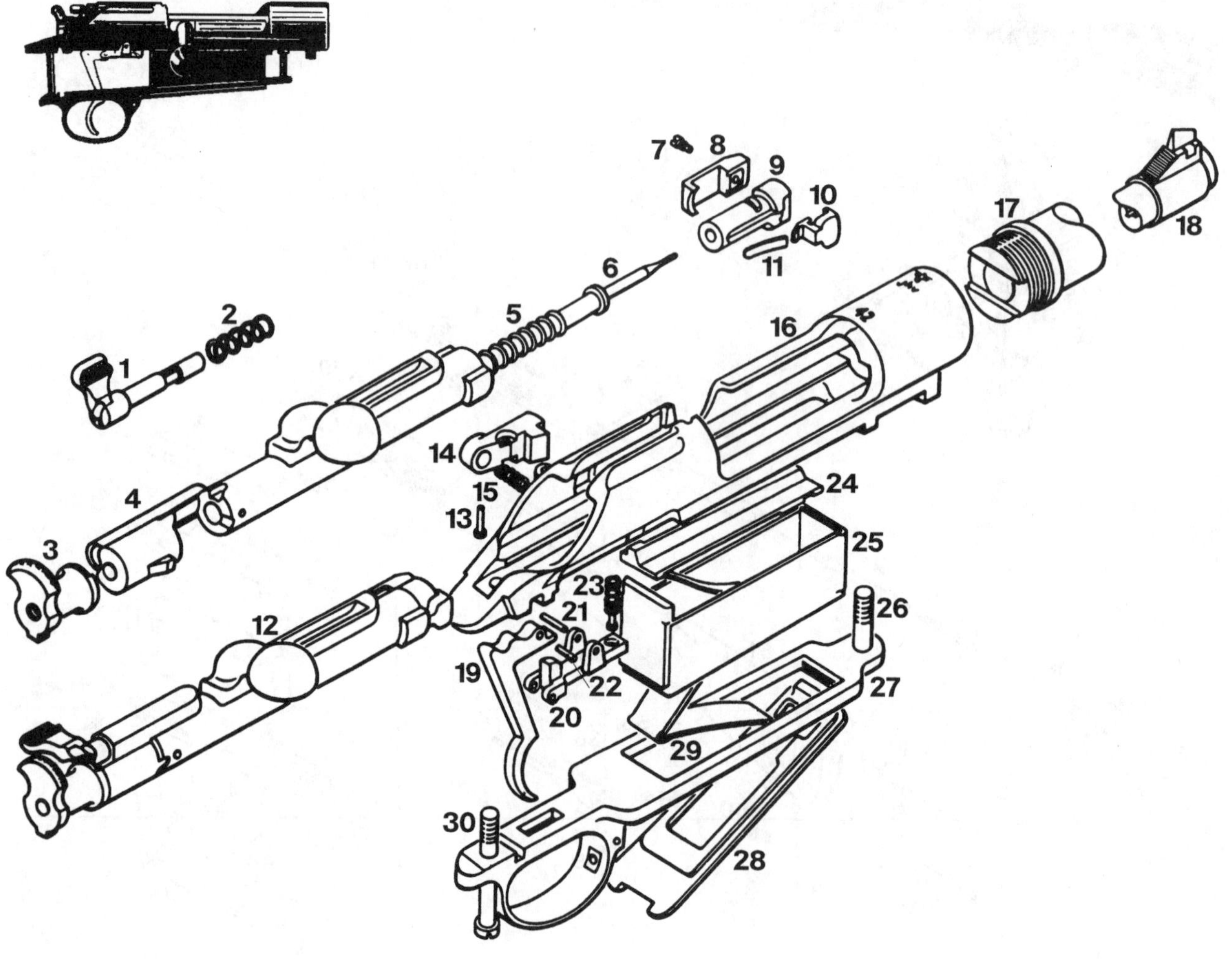

1	Safety	**16**	Receiver
2	Safety Spring	**17**	Barrel
3	Firing Pin Nut	**18**	Front Sight
4	Cocking Piece	**19**	Trigger
5	Firing Pin Spring	**20**	Sear
6	Firing Pin	**21**	Sear Pivot Pin
7	Ejector Screw	**22**	Trigger Pin
8	Ejector	**23**	Sear Spring and Safety Pin
9	Bolt Head	**24**	Magazine Follower
10	Extractor	**25**	Magazine Box
11	Extractor Spring	**26**	Front Guard Screw
12	Bolt Assembly	**27**	Trigger Guard
13	Bolt Stop Pin	**28**	Floorplate
14	Bolt Stop	**29**	Magazine Spring
15	Bolt Stop Spring	**30**	Rear Guard Screw

Over/Under Shotgun

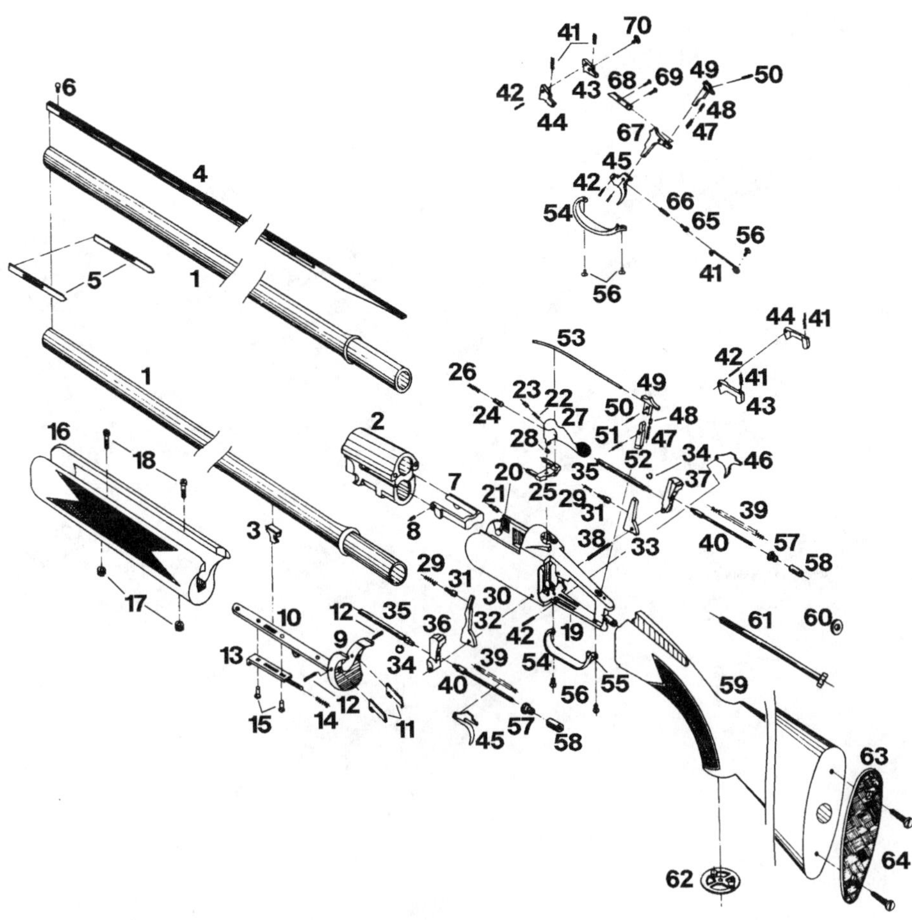

1	Barrels
2	Monobloc
3	Forend Iron Catch
4	Top Ventilated Rib
5	Side Ventilated Rib
6	Front Sight
7	Extractor
8	Limited Screw
9	Forend Iron Assembly
10	Forend Bar
11	Ejector Levers
12	Ejector Lever Pins
13	Forend Lock
14	Forend Lock Spring
15	Forend Lock Screws
16	Forend Wood
17	External Fastening Nuts
18	Forend Iron Screws
19	Tail
20	Trunnion Pin
21	Top Lever Release Pin
22	Top Lever Pin Spring
23	Top Lever Pin
24	Lever Impeller Pin
25	Lock Fastener
26	Lever Impeller Spring
27	Top Lever
28	Retainer Pin
29	Firing Pin Springs
30	Frame
31	Firing Pins
32	Top Firing Pin Plunger
33	Bottom Firing Pin Plunger
34	Locking Lever Rings
35	Cocking Levers
36	Hammer, Left
37	Hammer, Right
38	Hammer Pin
39	Hammer Springs
40	Hammer Spring Guides
41	Sear Springs
42	Sear and Trigger Pins
43	Sear, Left
44	Sear, Right
45	Trigger, Left
46	Trigger, Right
47	Safety Spring
48	Safety Travel Control Pin
49	Safety Catch
50	Safety Catch Pin
51	Safety Catch Lever Pin
52	Safety Catch Lever
53	Safety Impeller
54	Trigger Guard
55	Trigger Guard Internal Arch
56	Trigger Guard Screws
57	Hammer Activator Guide
58	Limiter Nut
59	Buttstock
60	Washer
61	Buttscrew
62	Grip Cap
63	Buttplate
64	Buttplate Screws
65	Selective Mechanism Block Pin
66	Selective Mechanism Block Spring
67	Selective Mechanism Block
68	Sear Impulsor
69	Fixing Pins
70	Pin

Side-by-Side Shotgun

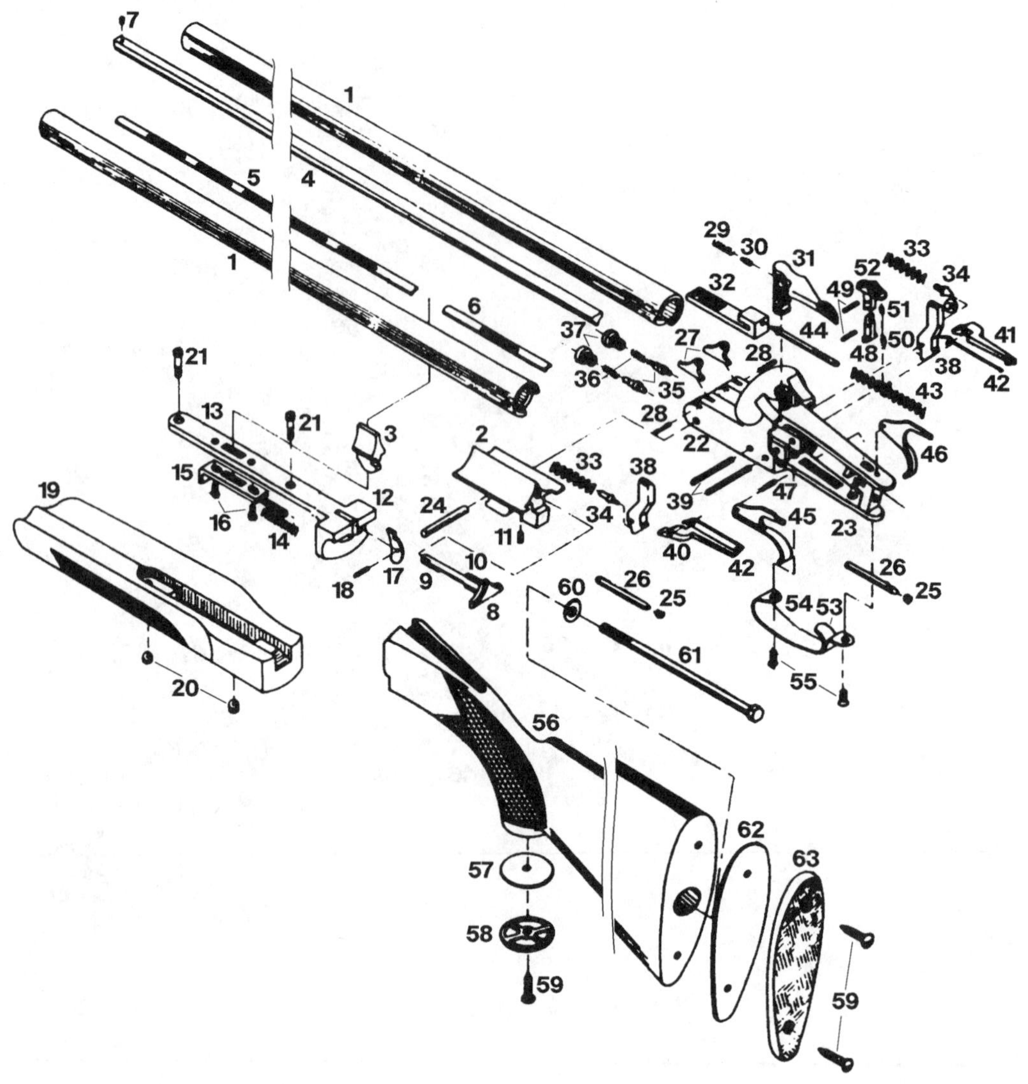

1	Barrels	**22**	Frame	**43**	Top Lever Spring
2	Latch Supporting Piece	**23**	Receiver	**44**	Top Lever Spring Guide
3	Forend Iron Catch	**24**	Pin	**45**	Trigger, Left
4	Top Ventilated Rib	**25**	Cocking Lever Rod Ring	**46**	Trigger, Right
5	Bottom Ventilated Rib, Long	**26**	Cocking Lever Rod	**47**	Trigger Pin
6	Bottom Ventilated Rib, Short	**27**	Cocking Levers	**48**	Trigger Lock Lever
7	Front Sight	**28**	Cocking Lever Pins	**49**	Trigger Lock Lever Pins
8	Extractor	**29**	Lever Lock Spring	**50**	Trigger Lock Spring
9	Extractor Pin	**30**	Lever Lock Pin	**51**	Trigger Lock Ball Pin
10	Guide Pin	**31**	Top Lever	**52**	Trigger Lock
11	Limiter Screw	**32**	Latch Lock	**53**	Trigger Guard Arch
12	Forend Iron	**33**	Hammer Impeller Springs	**54**	Trigger Guard
13	Forend Bar	**34**	Hammer Impellers	**55**	Trigger Guard Screws
14	Forend Iron Spring	**35**	Firing Pins	**56**	Stock
15	Forend Lock	**36**	Firing Pin Springs	**57**	Pistol Grip Cap Spacer
16	Forend Fastening Screws	**37**	Firing Pin Fixing Bolts	**58**	Grip Cap
17	Actuator Extractor	**38**	Hammers	**59**	Screws
18	Actuator Extractor Pin	**39**	Hammer Pins	**60**	Buttscrew Washer
19	Forend	**40**	Sear, Left	**61**	Buttscrew
20	Forend Fastening Nuts	**41**	Sear, Right	**62**	Buttplate Trim
21	Forend Lock Screws	**42**	Sear Springs	**63**	Buttplate

Single Barrel Shotgun

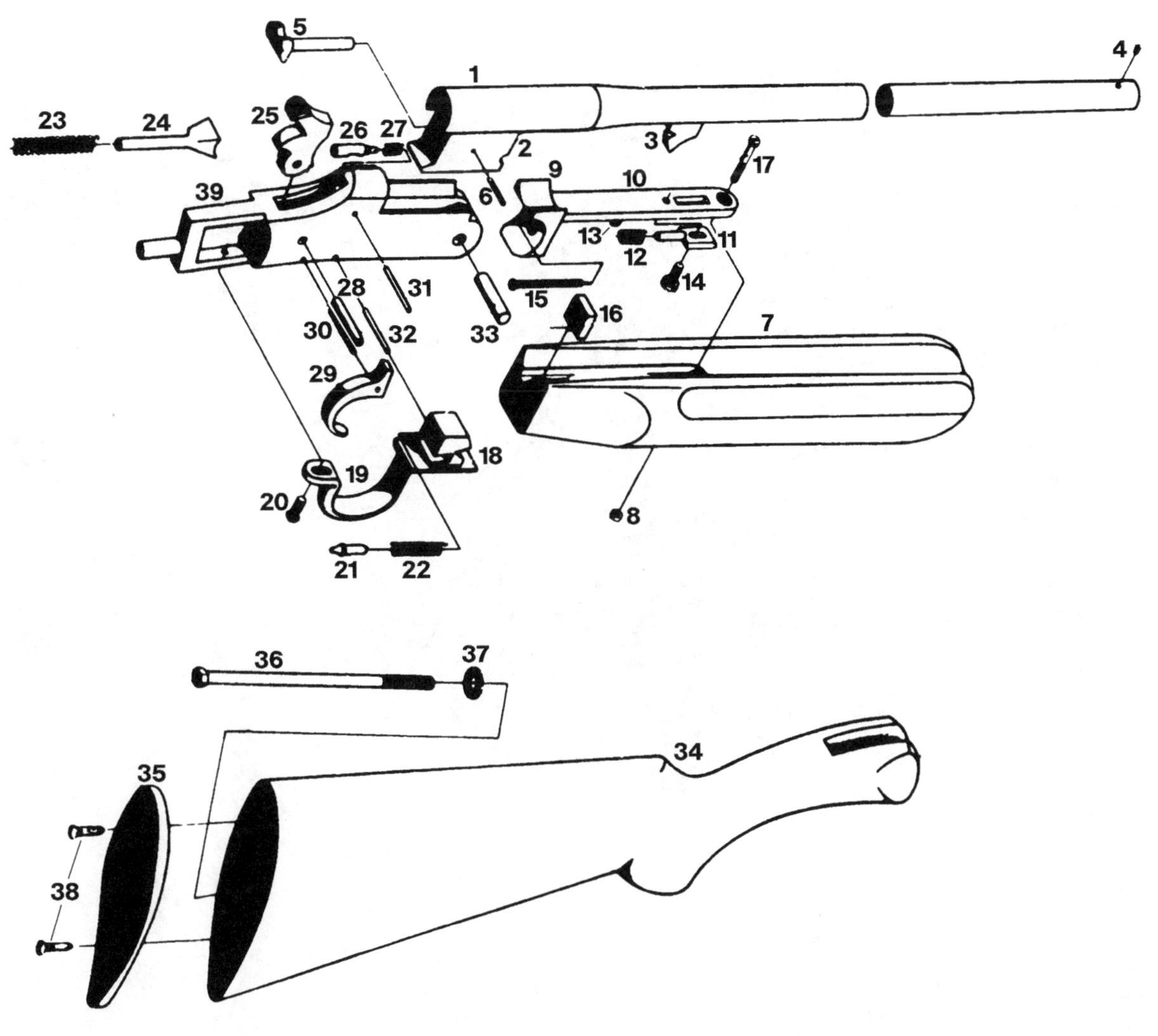

1	Barrel	**14**	Forend Retainer Pin Screw	**27**	Firing Pin Spring
2	Barrel Latch	**15**	Forend Iron Screw	**28**	Hammer Pin
3	Forend Iron Catch	**16**	Forend Nut	**29**	Trigger
4	Front Sight	**17**	Forend Rod Screw	**30**	Trigger Pin
5	Extractor	**18**	Trigger Guard and Locking Bolt	**31**	Firing Pin Retaining Pin
6	Extractor Pin	**19**	Trigger Guard Arc	**32**	Trigger Guard Pin
7	Forend	**20**	Trigger Guard Screw	**33**	Block Pin
8	Fixing Screw	**21**	Spring Guide Pin	**34**	Stock
9	Forend Iron	**22**	Spring	**35**	Buttplate
10	Forend Rod	**23**	Cocking Lever Spring	**36**	Stock Bolt
11	Forend Retainer Pin	**24**	Cocking Lever	**37**	Washer
12	Forend Iron Spring	**25**	Hammer	**38**	Buttplate Screws
13	Forend Iron Spring Catch	**26**	Firing Pin	**39**	Frame

Mark X Bolt-Action Rifle

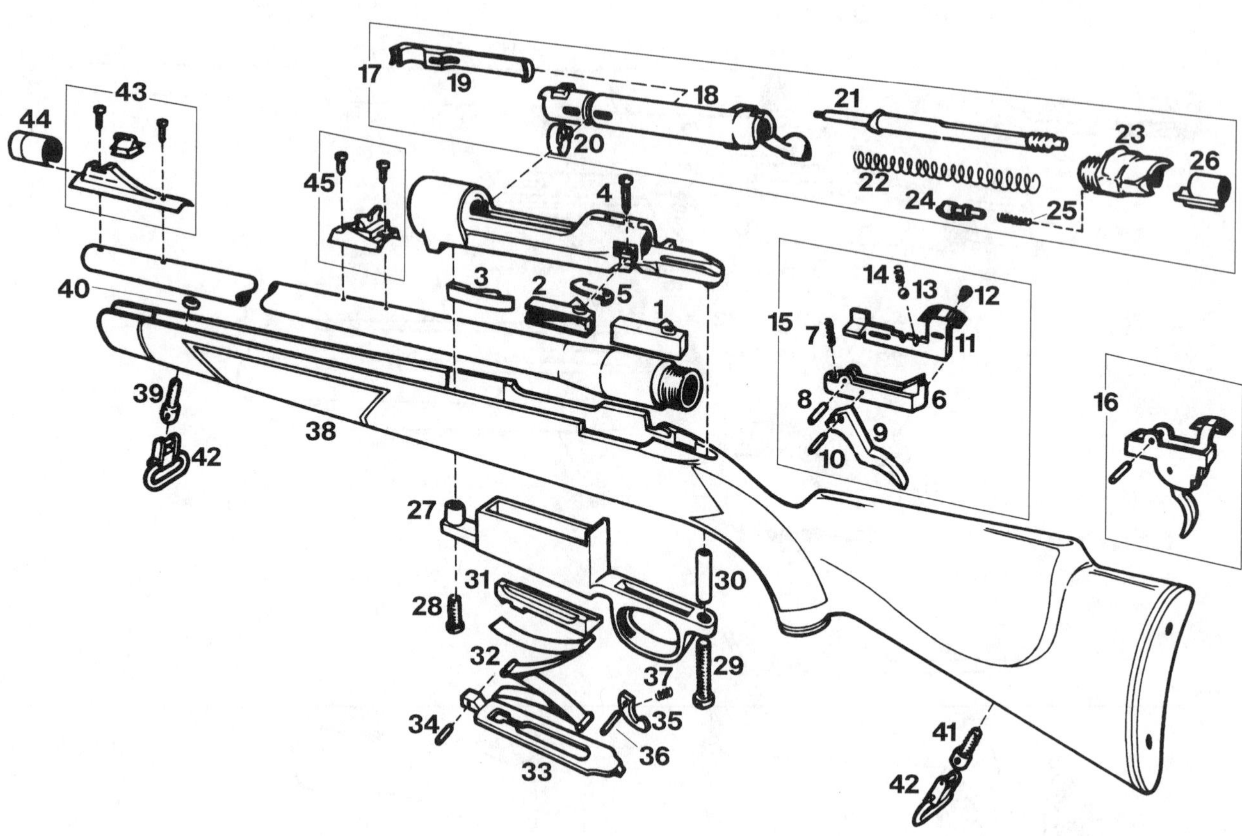

1	Bolt Stop/Ejector Assembly	24	Bolt Sleeve Lock
2	Bolt Stop	25	Bolt Sleeve Lock Spring
3	Bolt Stop Spring	26	Cocking Piece
4	Bolt Stop Screw	27	Trigger Guard Assembly
5	Ejector	28	Front Guard Screw
6	Sear	29	Rear Guard Screw
7	Sear Spring	30	Bushing
8	Sear Pin	31	Follower
9	Trigger	32	Follower Spring
10	Trigger Pin	33	Floorplate
11	Safety	34	Floorplate Pin
12	Safety Screw	35	Floorplate Latch
13	Safety Detent	36	Floorplate Latch Pin
14	Safety Detent Spring	37	Latch Spring
15	Standard Trigger Assembly	38	Stock
16	Adjustable Trigger Assembly	39	Front Swivel Screw
17	Bolt Assembly	40	Front Swivel Screw Nut
18	Bolt Body	41	Rear Swivel Screw
19	Extractor	42	Detachable Sling Swivels
20	Extractor Collar	43	Front Sight Assembly
21	Firing Pin	44	Front Sight Hood
22	Firing Pin Spring	45	Rear Sight Assembly
23	Bolt Sleeve		

1891 Bolt-Action Rifle

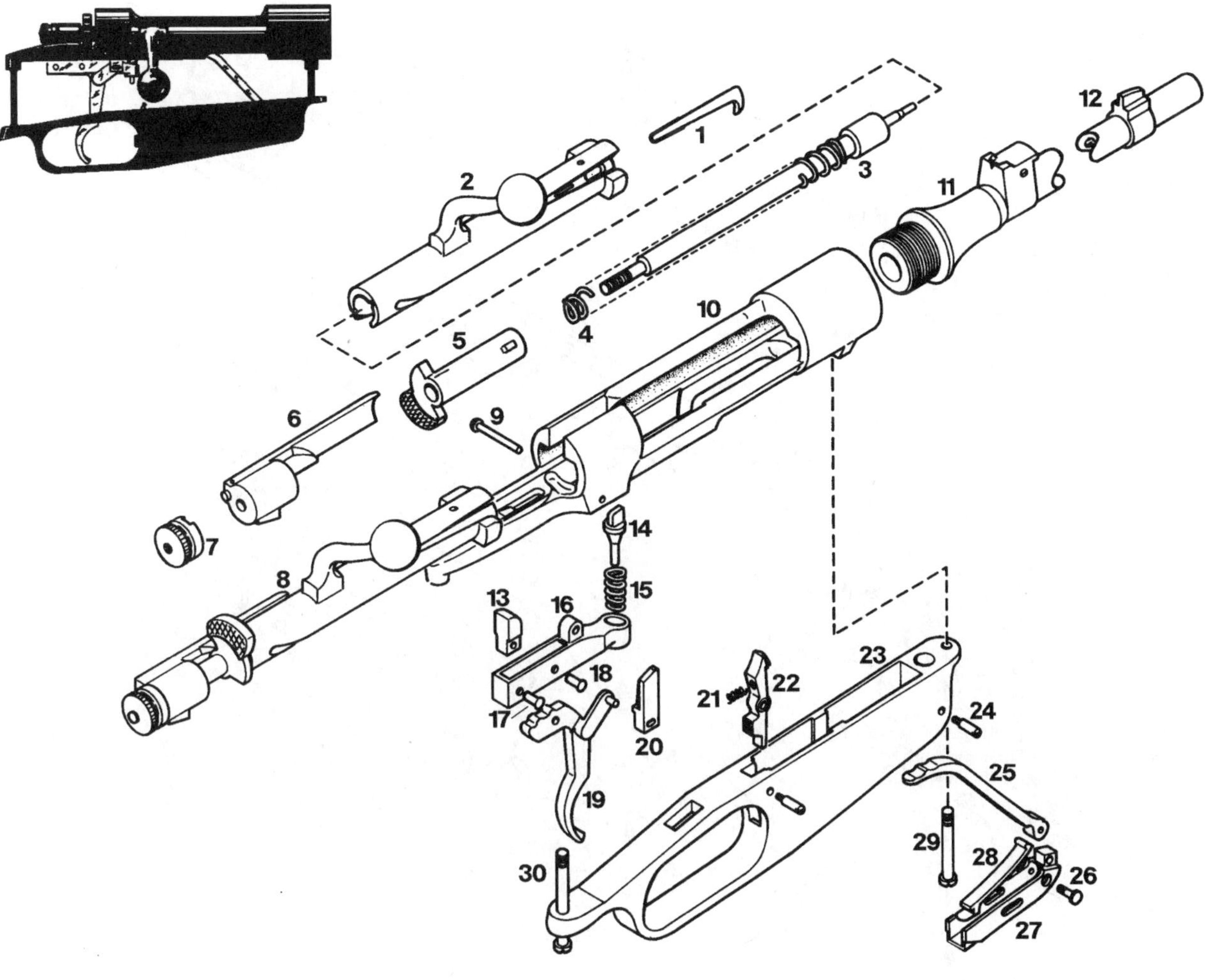

1	Extractor	**16**	Sear Housing
2	Bolt Body	**17**	Sear Retaining Pin
3	Firing Pin	**18**	Trigger Pin
4	Firing Pin Spring	**19**	Trigger
5	Safety	**20**	Bolt Stop
6	Cocking Piece	**21**	Clip Latch Spring
7	Cocking Piece Nut	**22**	Clip Latch
8	Bolt Assembly	**23**	Trigger Guard
9	Sear Pin	**24**	Housing Retainer Screw
10	Receiver	**25**	Cartridge Follower
11	Barrel	**26**	Follower Hinge Pin
12	Front Sight	**27**	Follower Housing
13	Sear	**28**	Follower Spring
14	Ejector	**29**	Front Guard Screw
15	Sear Spring	**30**	Rear Guard Screw

LSA-65 Bolt-Action Rifle

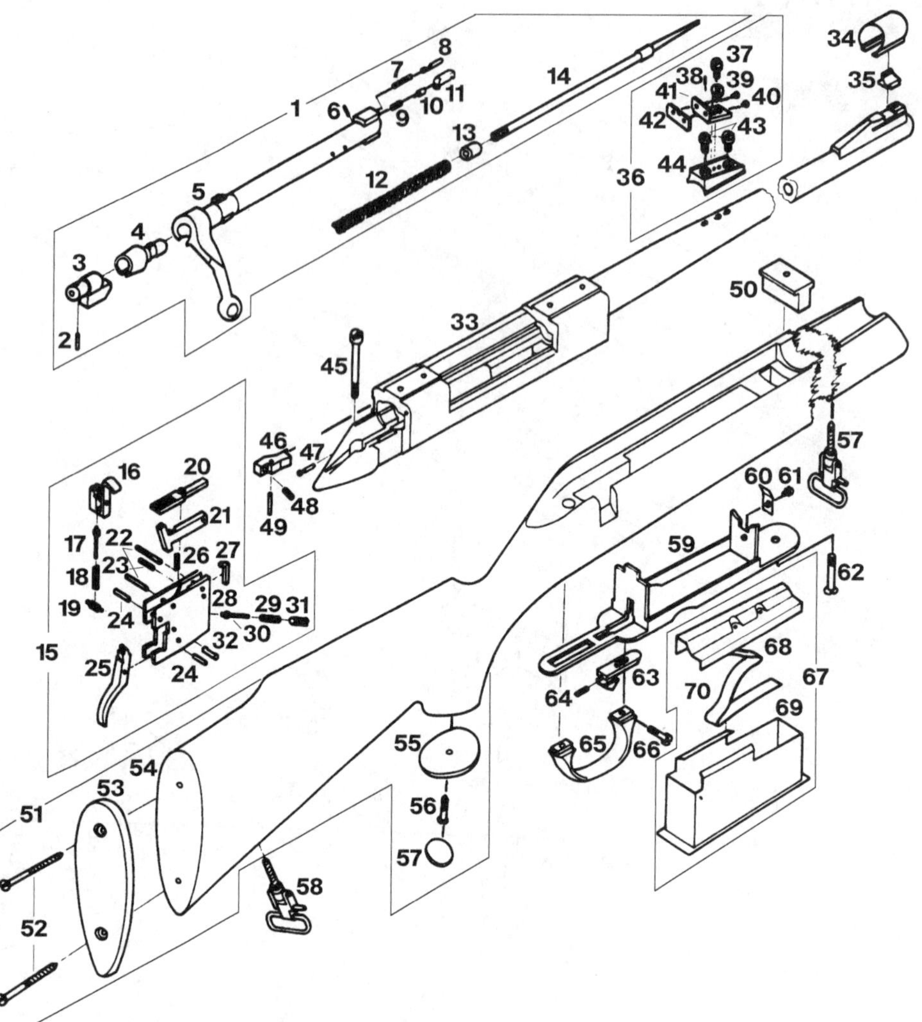

1	Breechbolt Assembly	23	Sear Pin	47	Detaching Pin
2	Firing Pin Nut Pin	24	Thumb Safety Pins	48	Bolt Stop Spring
3	Firing Pin Nut	25	Trigger	49	Bolt Stop Pin
4	Breechbolt Sleeve	26	Sear Spring	50	Recoil Shoulder
5	Bolt Body	27	Safety Bar	51	Stock Assembly
6	Ejector Retainer Pin	28	Trigger Housing	52	Buttplate Screws
7	Ejector Spring	29	Trigger Spring	53	Buttplate
8	Ejector	30	Trigger Spring Plunger	54	Stock
9	Extractor Spring	31	Trigger Adjusting Screw	55	Pistol Grip Cap
10	Extractor Spring Plunger	32	Trigger Adjusting Pin	56	Grip Cap Screw
11	Extractor	33	Barreled Receiver	57	Grip Cap Screw Cap
12	Firing Pin Spring	34	Front Sight Hood	58	Swivel Assembly
13	Firing Pin Collar	35	Front Sight	59	Floorplate
14	Firing Pin	36	Rear Sight Assembly	60	Magazine Support Spring
15	Trigger Assembly	37	Rear Sight Adjusting Screw	61	Magazine Support Spring Screw
16	Thumb Safety	38	Rear Sight Base Locking Pin	62	Front Stock Screw
17	Safety Spring Guide	39	Rear Sight Adjusting Screw Washer	63	Magazine Lock
18	Safety Spring	40	Rear Sight Leaf Adjusting Screws	64	Magazine Lock Spring
19	Safety Spring Support	41	Rear Sight Elevator	65	Trigger Guard
20	Safety Slide	42	Rear Sight Leaf	66	Trigger Guard Screw
21	Sear	43	Rear Sight Base Screws	67	Magazine Assembly
22	Trigger Plate Assembly Attaching Pins	44	Rear Sight Base	68	Magazine Follower
		45	Rear Stock Screw	69	Magazine Body
		46	Bolt Stop	70	Magazine Spring

Mag 10 Autoloading Shotgun

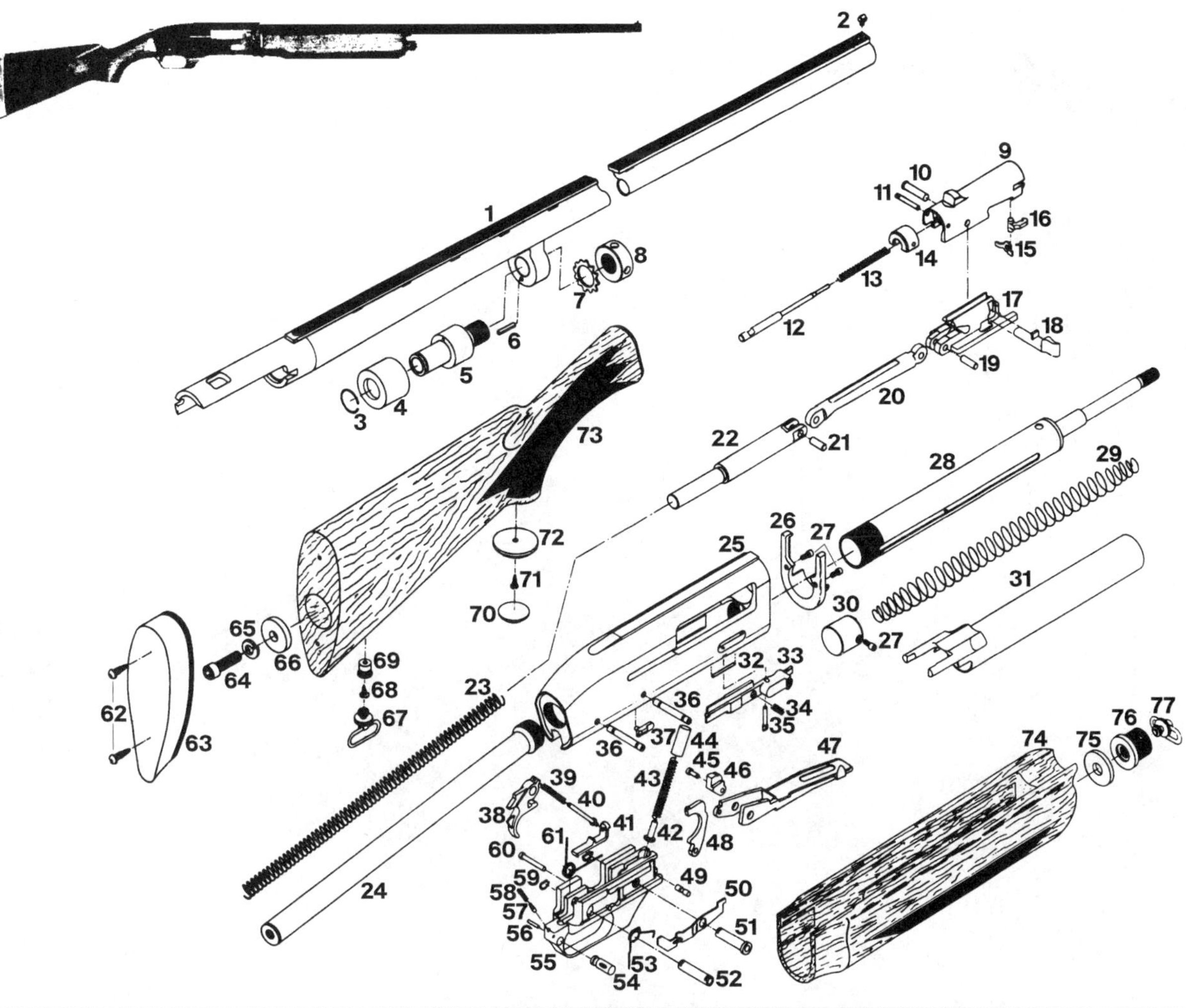

1	Barrel Assembly	27	Collar and Magazine Cup Cap Screws	53	Lever Spring
2	Front Sight	28	Magazine Sub-Assembly	54	Safety
3	Gas Cylinder Retainer	29	Magazine Spring	55	Trigger Housing
4	Gas Cylinder	30	Magazine Cup	56	Safety Detent Pin
5	Gas Piston	31	Slide Extension Assembly	57	Safety Detent
6	Gas Piston Lug Pin	32	Shell Stop Pivot Retainer	58	Safety Spring
7	Gas Piston Lock Washer	33	Shell Stop	59	Retainer Clips
8	Gas Piston Nut	34	Shell Stop Spring	60	Trigger Bar Pin
9	Bolt Body	35	Shell Stop Pivot	61	Carrier Spring
10	Cam Pin	36	Trigger Housing Retainer Pins	62	Recoil Pad Screws
11	Firing Pin Retainer	37	Ejector	63	Recoil Pad
12	Firing Pin	38	Trigger	64	Stock Bolt
13	Firing Pin Spring	39	Trigger Spring	65	Stock Bolt Lock Washer
14	Bolt Buffer	40	Trigger Bar Spring Guide	66	Stock Bolt Washer
15	Extractor Retainer	41	Trigger Bar	67	Stock Swivel
16	Extractor	42	Hammer Spring Guide	68	Swivel Screw
17	Slide	43	Hammer Spring	69	Swivel Base
18	Charging Handle	44	Hammer Spring Cap	70	Grip Cap Insert
19	Slide Pivot	45	Carrier Cam Pivot	71	Grip Cap Screw
20	Slide Link	46	Carrier Cam	72	Grip Cap Spacer
21	Plunger Pivot	47	Carrier	73	Buttstock
22	Action Spring Plunger	48	Hammer	74	Forend
23	Action Spring	49	Hammer Pivot	75	Forend Washer
24	Stock Tube Assembly	50	Release Lever	76	Forend Nut
25	Receiver	51	Carrier Pivot	77	Front Swivel
26	Receiver Collar	52	Trigger Pivot		

Model 37 Featherweight Slide-Action Shotgun

Courtesy of Blacksmith Corporation

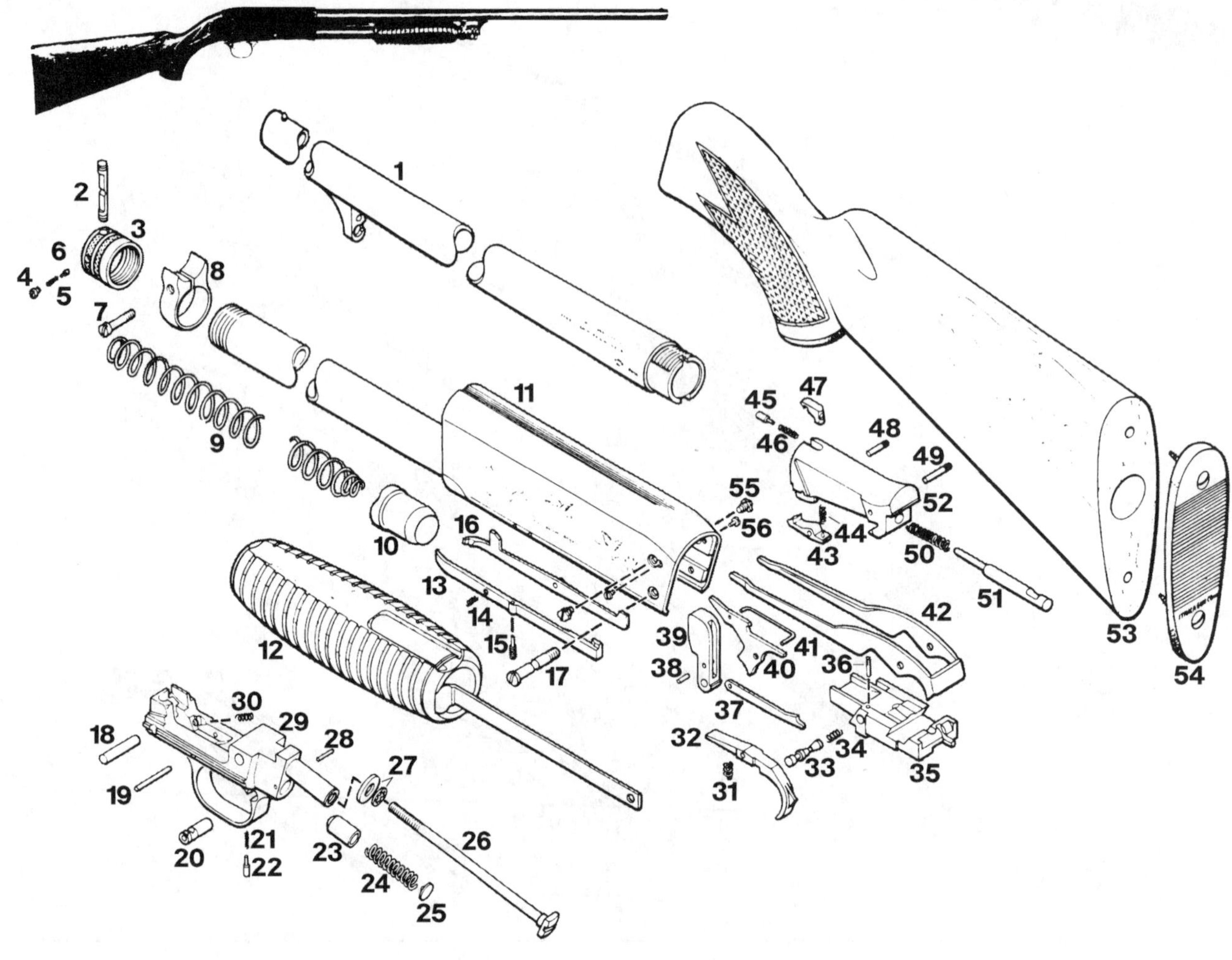

1	Barrel
2	Magazine Nut Pin*
3	Magazine Nut
4	Magazine Nut Pin Retainer Screw*
5	Magazine Nut Pin Catch Spring*
6	Magazine Nut Pin Retainer Spring Cap*
7	Yoke Screw
8	Yoke
9	Magazine Spring
10	Magazine Spring Cup
11	Receiver and Magazine Tube Assembly
12	Slide Handle Assembly
13	Spring Shell Stop, Left
14	Spring Shell Stop Spring
15	Spring Shell Stop Screw
16	Positive Shell Stop, Right
17	Trigger Plate Screw
18	Hammer Pin
19	Trigger Pin
20	Safety
21	Safety Catch Spring
22	Safety Catch
23	Mainspring Cup
24	Mainspring
25	Mainspring Cap
26	Stock Bolt
27	Stock Washers
28	Mainspring Stop Pin
29	Trigger Housing
30	Slide Stop Spring, Bottom
31	Trigger Spring
32	Trigger
33	Slide Pin
34	Slide Pin Spring
35	Slide
36	Slide Pin Retainer Pin
37	Hammer Bar
38	Hammer Bar Pin
39	Hammer
40	Slide Stop
41	Slide Stop Release Spring, Top
42	Carrier
43	Bottom Extractor
44	Bottom Extractor Spring
45	Positive Extractor Spring Cap
46	Positive Extractor Spring
47	Positive Extractor, Top
48	Extractor Hinge Pin, Bottom
49	Firing Pin Retainer Pin
50	Firing Pin Spring
51	Firing Pin
52	Breechblock
53	Stock
54	Buttplate and Screws
55	Carrier Screws
56	Carrier Screw Lock Screws

***Not used in guns made after 1954.**

Model 51 Featherlight Autoloading Shotgun

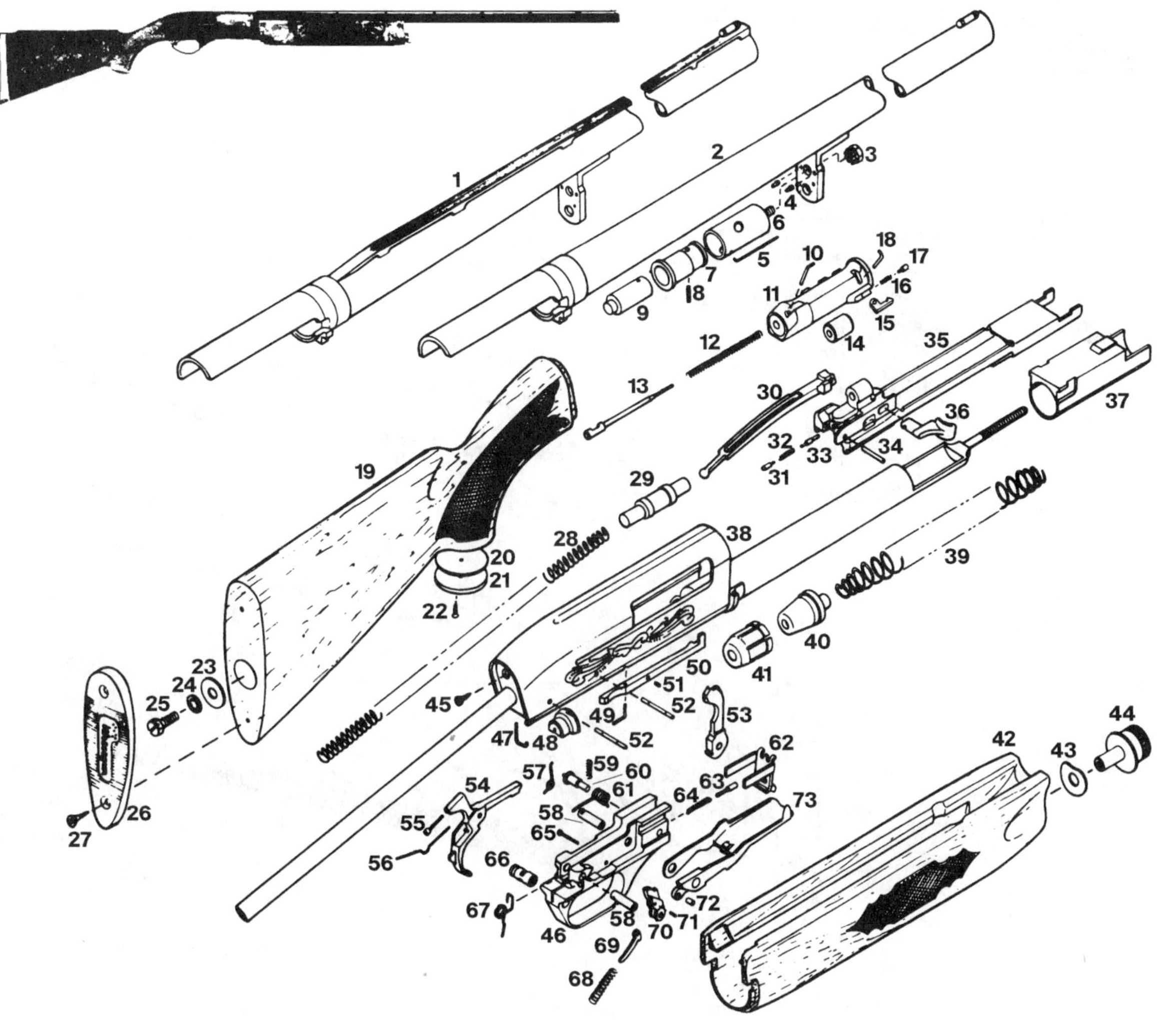

1	Barrel, Ventilated Rib	**26**	Buttplate	**51**	Cartridge Stop Spring
2	Barrel, Plain	**27**	Buttplate Screws	**52**	Trigger Guard Pins
3	Gas Cylinder Nut	**28**	Action Spring	**53**	Hammer
4	Gas Cylinder Lug Pins	**29**	Action Spring Plunger	**54**	Trigger
5	Gas Piston Retainer	**30**	Link	**55**	Disconnector Plunger
6	Gas Cylinder	**31**	Link Plunger	**56**	Carrier Pivot Retainer Spring
7	Gas Piston	**32**	Charging Handle and Link Spring	**57**	Disconnector Spring
8	Gas Piston Pin	**33**	Charging Handle Plunger	**58**	Safety Spring and Carrier Pivots
9	Gas Piston Buffer	**34**	Link Pivot Pin	**59**	Trigger Spring
10	Firing Pin Retainer	**35**	Slide Action Assembly	**60**	Hammer Pivot
11	Bolt	**36**	Charging Handle	**61**	Hammer Spring
12	Firing Pin Spring	**37**	Rail Extension Tube	**62**	Carrier Release
13	Firing Pin	**38**	Receiver	**63**	Carrier Release Plunger
14	Bolt Buffer	**39**	Magazine Spring	**64**	Carrier Release Spring
15	Extractor	**40**	Inner Magazine Cup	**65**	Trigger Pivot Pin
16	Extractor Spring	**41**	Outer Magazine Cup	**66**	Safety
17	Extractor Plunger	**42**	Forend	**67**	Safety Spring
18	Extractor Pivot Pin	**43**	Forend Washer	**68**	Carrier Spring
19	Buttstock	**44**	Forend Nut	**69**	Carrier Spring Guide
20	Grip Cap Spacer	**45**	Receiver Buffer Screw	**70**	Carrier Cam
21	Grip Cap	**46**	Trigger Housing	**71**	Carrier Spring Guide Pivot
22	Grip Cap Screw	**47**	Action Spring Retainer Pin	**72**	Carrier Cam Pin
23	Stock Bolt Washer	**48**	Receiver Buffer	**73**	Carrier
24	Stock Bolt Lock Washer	**49**	Cartridge Stop Pivot		
25	Stock Bolt	**50**	Cartridge Stop		

Model 66 Supersingle Single Shot Lever-Action Shotgun

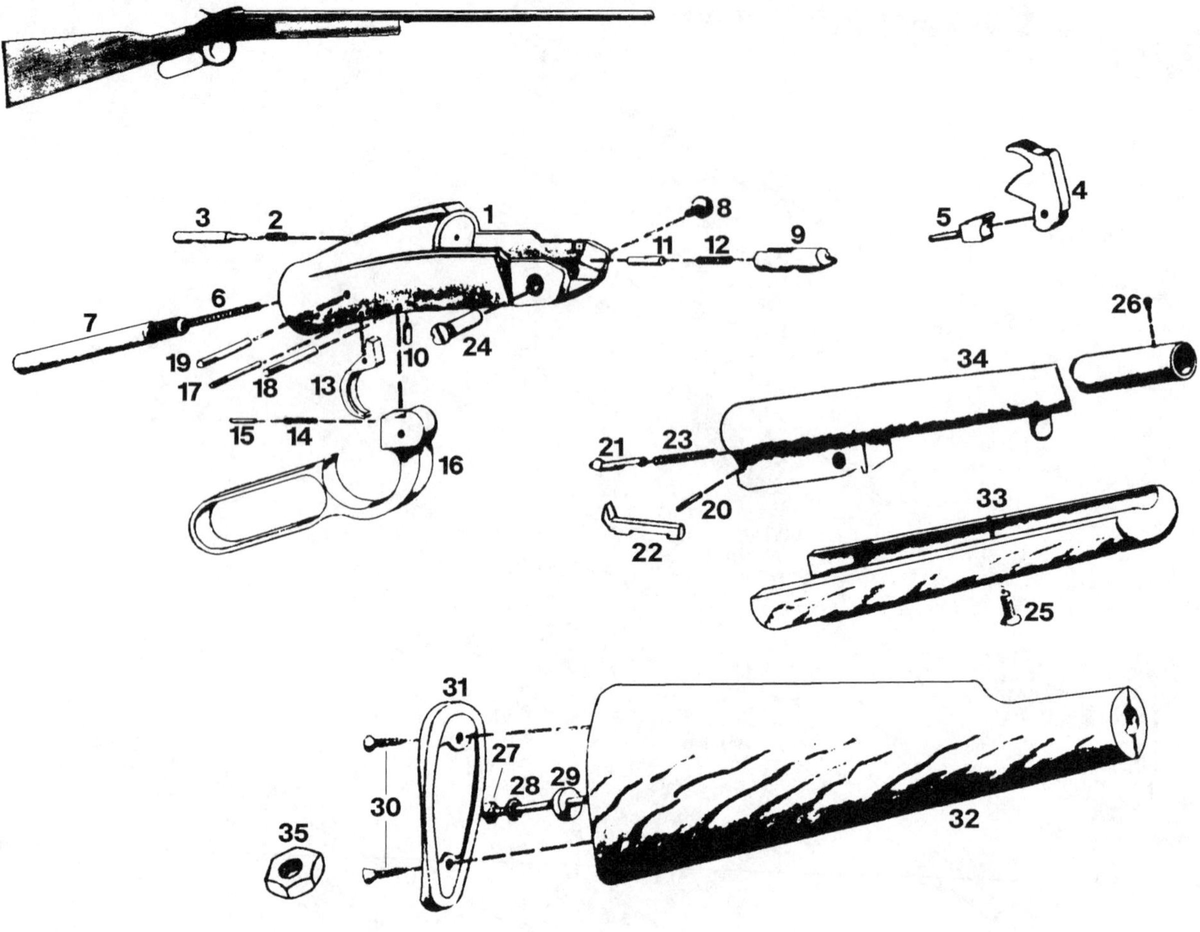

1	Receiver	**19**	Hammer Pin
2	Firing Pin Spring	**20**	Extractor Pin
3	Firing Pin	**21**	Extractor (Old Style, round shank)
4	Hammer	**22**	Extractor (New Style, square shank)
5	Rebound Cam	**23**	Extractor Spring
6	Hammer Spring	**24**	Hinge Pin
7	Stock Stud	**25**	Forend Screw
8	Hinge Pin Screw	**26**	Front Sight
9	Action Bolt	**27**	Stock Bolt
10	Firing Pin Retainer Pin	**28**	Stock Bolt Lock Washer
11	Bolt Spring Plunger	**29**	Stock Bolt Flat Washer
12	Bolt Spring	**30**	Buttplate Screws
13	Trigger	**31**	Buttplate
14	Lever Spring	**32**	Buttstock
15	Lever Spring Plunger	**33**	Forend
16	Lever	**34**	Barrel
17	Trigger Pin	**35**	Stock Stud Nut
18	Lever Pin		

Model 72 Lever-Action Rifle

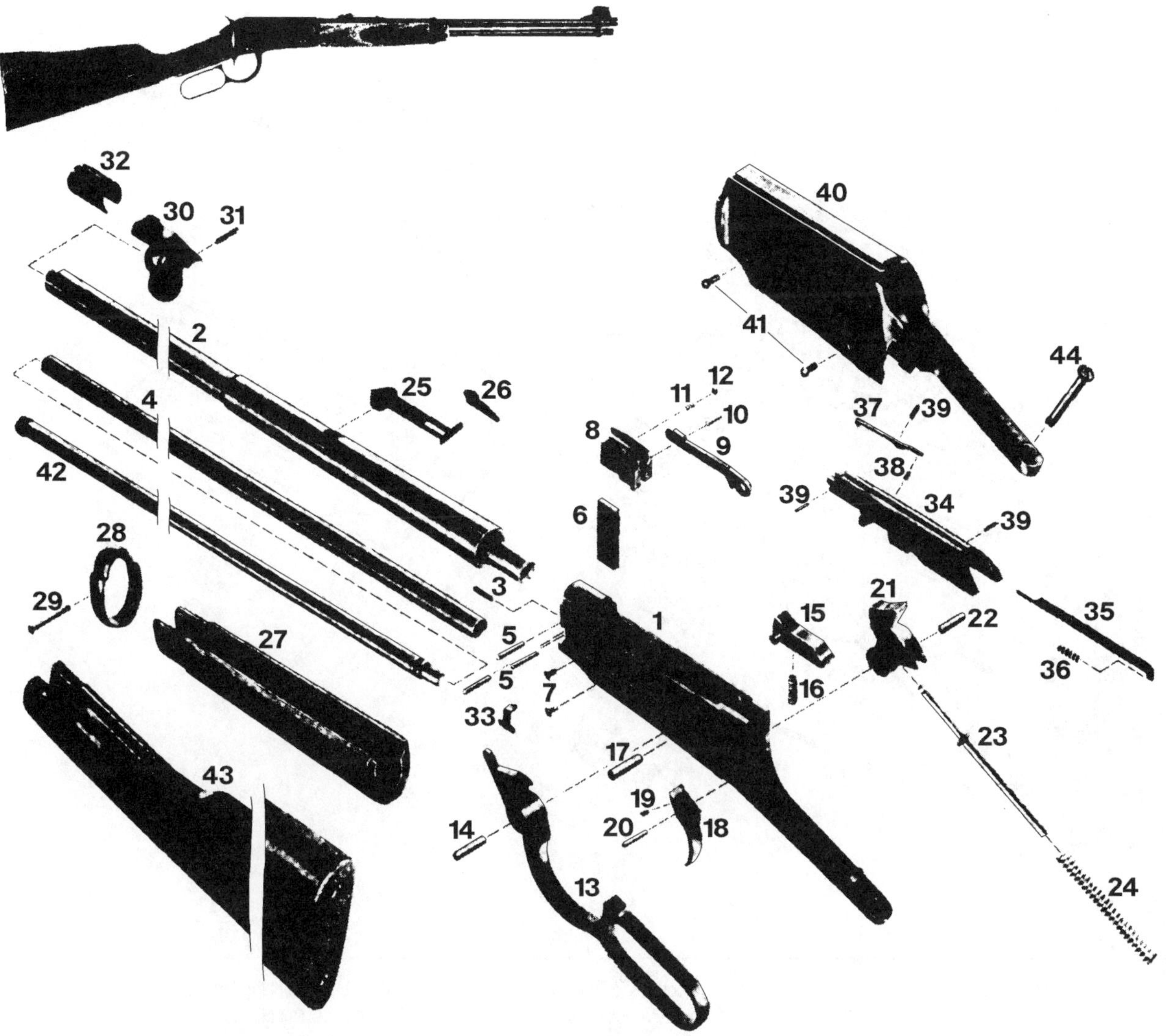

1	Frame	**23**	Mainspring Guide
2	Barrel	**24**	Mainspring
3	Barrel Alignment Pin	**25**	Rear Sight
4	Outer Magazine Tube	**26**	Rear Sight Elevator
5	Barrel Retaining Pins	**27**	Forend
6	Cartridge Guide	**28**	Rear Barrel Band
7	Cartridge Guide Screws	**29**	Barrel Band Screw
8	Carrier	**30**	Front Sight
9	Carrier Lever	**31**	Front Sight Pin
10	Carrier Lever Pivot Pin	**32**	Front Sight Hood
11	Carrier Spring	**33**	Ejector
12	Carrier Detent Ball	**34**	Breechbolt
13	Finger Lever	**35**	Firing Pin
14	Finger Lever Pivot Pin	**36**	Firing Pin Spring
15	Locking Bolt	**37**	Extractor
16	Locking Bolt Spring	**38**	Extractor Spring
17	Locking Bolt Pin	**39**	Extractor Pivot Pins
18	Trigger	**40**	Receiver
19	Trigger Spring	**41**	Receiver Sideplate Screws
20	Trigger Pivot Pin	**42**	Inner Magazine Assembly
21	Hammer	**43**	Buttstock
22	Hammer Pivot Pin	**44**	Tang Screw

Perazzi Single Barrel Trap Shotgun

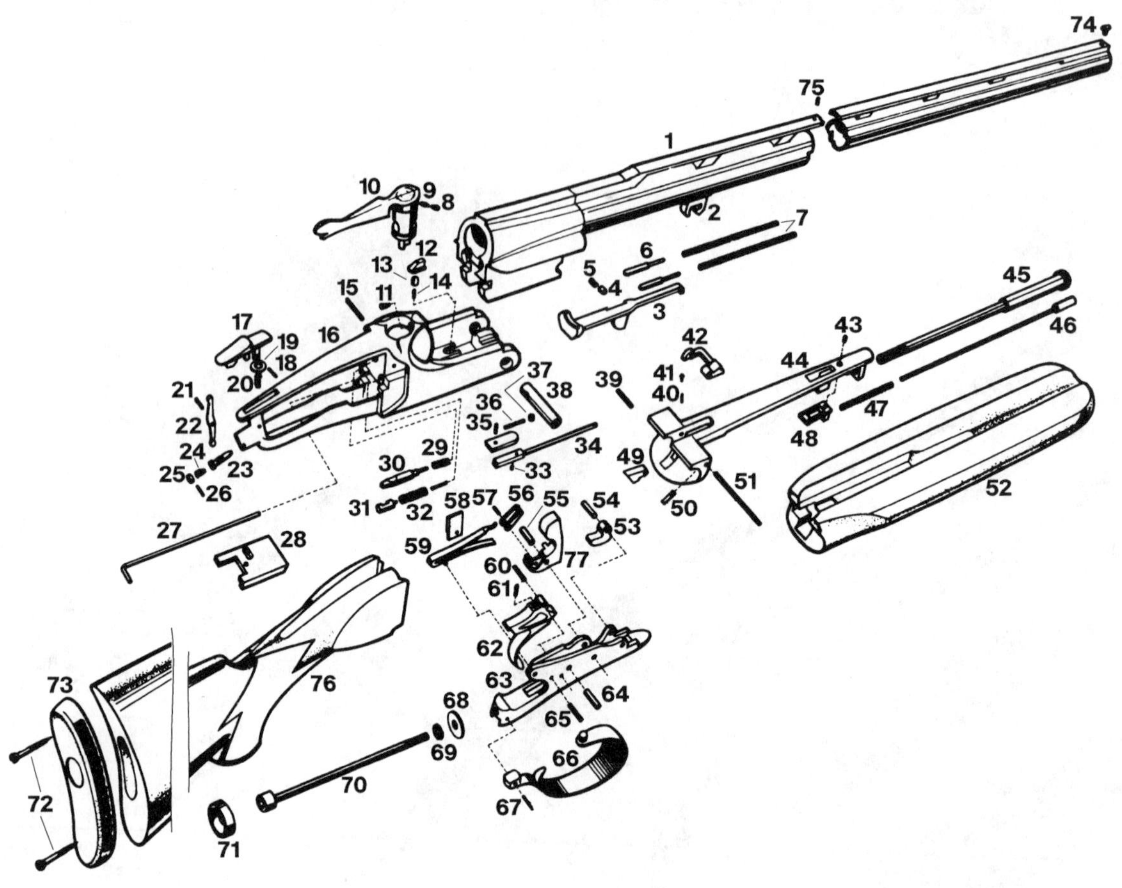

1	Barrel	**27**	Ejector Trip Rod	**53**	Cocking Foot
2	Barrel Lug	**28**	Action Locking Bolt	**54**	Cocking Foot Pivot Pin
3	Ejector	**29**	Firing Pin Spring	**55**	Hammer Pivot Pin
4	Ejector Retainer	**30**	Firing Pin	**56**	Bridle
5	Ejector Retainer Spring	**31**	Top Lever Retainer	**57**	Bridle Pin
6	Ejector Spring Plungers	**32**	Top Lever Retainer Spring, Large	**58**	Hammer Spring Retainer
7	Ejector Springs	**33**	Cocking Rod Screw	**59**	Hammer Spring
8	Top Lever Trip Plunger	**34**	Cocking Rod	**60**	Trigger Pivot Pin
9	Top Lever Trip Spring	**35**	Cocking Rod Spring Guide Plate Pin	**61**	Trigger Return Spring
10	Top Lever	**36**	Cocking Rod Return Spring	**62**	Trigger/Sear
11	Top Lever Trip	**37**	Cocking Rod Screw Collar	**63**	Trigger Plate
12	Ejector Stop	**38**	Hinge Pin	**64**	Trigger Plate Pin
13	Ejector Stop Retainer	**39**	Cocking Cam Pin	**65**	Trigger Spring Pin
14	Ejector Stop Retainer Spring	**40**	Ejector Sear Spring	**66**	Trigger Guard
15	Firing Pin Retainer Pin	**41**	Ejector Sear Spring Plunger	**67**	Trigger Guard Pin
16	Frame	**42**	Ejector Sear	**68**	Stock Bolt Washer, Plain
17	Safety Button	**43**	Forend Retainer Screw	**69**	Stock Bolt Washer, Lock
18	Safety Button Retaining Pin	**44**	Forend Iron	**70**	Stock Bolt
19	Safety Button Retainer	**45**	Forend Push Rod Guide	**71**	Stock Bolt Retainer
20	Safety Button Spring	**46**	Forend Push Release Rod	**72**	Recoil Pad Screws
21	Trigger Plate Release Lever Pin	**47**	Forend Push Rod Spring	**73**	Recoil Pad
22	Trigger Plate Release Lever	**48**	Forend Locking Block	**74**	Front Sight
23	Trigger Plate Lock	**49**	Cocking Cam	**75**	Middle Sight
24	Trigger Plate Lock Spring	**50**	Frame Stop	**76**	Buttstock
25	Trigger Plate Lock Cap	**51**	Ejector Sear Pin	**77**	Hammer
26	Trigger Plate Lock Pin	**52**	Forend		

XL-300 and XL-900 Autoloading Shotgun

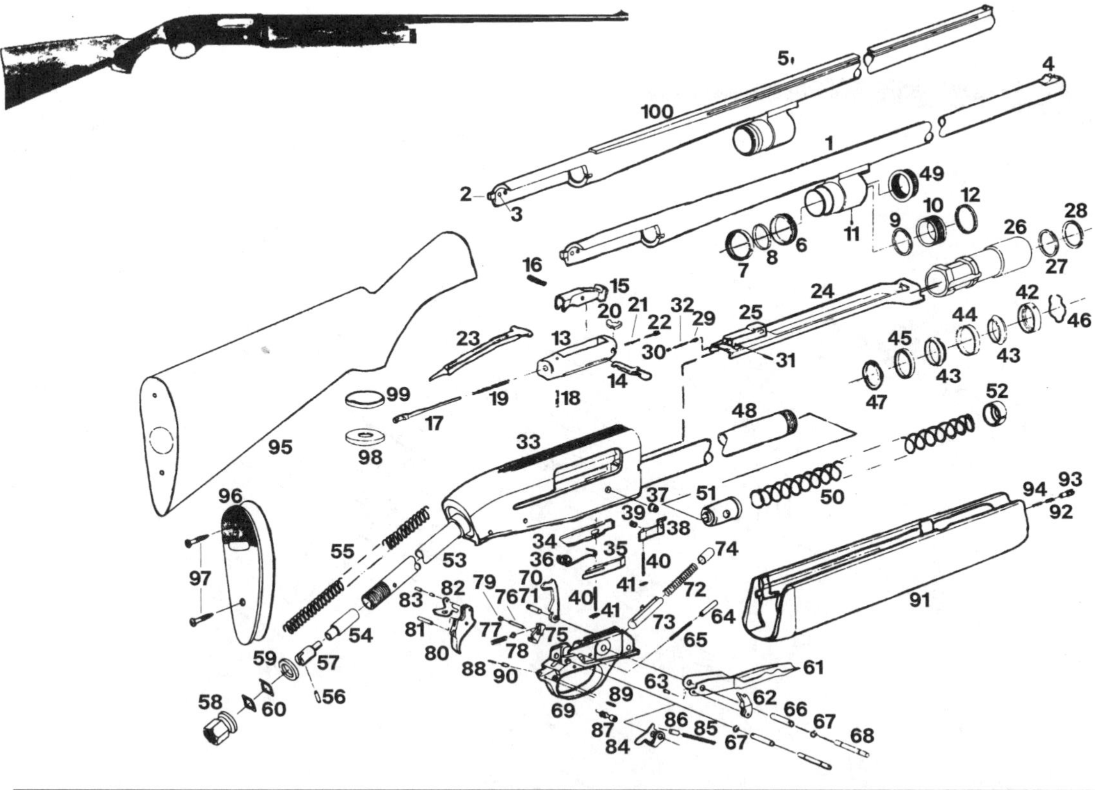

1	Barrel, Plain	**35**	Shell Latch, Right	**69**	Trigger Plate
2	Ejector	**36**	Carrier Latch Spring	**70**	Hammer
3	Ejector Rivet	**37**	Carrier Latch Button	**71**	Hammer Pin
4	Front Sight	**38**	Shell Latch, Left	**72**	Hammer Spring
5	Middle Sight	**39**	Shell Latch Spring	**73**	Hammer Spring Case
6	Piston Ring	**40**	Latch Pins	**74**	Hammer Spring Plunger
7	Piston Ring Retainer	**41**	Latch Pin Snaps	**75**	Sear
8	Piston Ring Spring	**42**	Cushion Ring Retainer	**76**	Sear Pin
9	Barrel Ring Packing	**43**	Inner Cushion Rings	**77**	Sear Spring
10	Barrel Ring Bushing	**44**	Outer Cushion Ring	**78**	Sear Spring Retainer
11	Barrel Bushing Retaining Screw	**45**	Cushion Ring Follower	**79**	Sear Pin Snap
12	Bushing Packing	**46**	Cushion Ring Spring	**80**	Trigger
13	Breechbolt	**47**	Cushion Ring Spacer	**81**	Trigger Pin
14	Charging Handle	**48**	Magazine Tube	**82**	Trigger Lever
15	Locking Block	**49**	Magazine Cap	**83**	Trigger Lever Pin
16	Locking Block Pin	**50**	Magazine Spring	**84**	Safety, Auto
17	Firing Pin	**51**	Magazine Spring Follower	**85**	Auto Safety Spring
18	Firing Pin Stop	**52**	Magazine Spring Retainer	**86**	Auto Safety Spring Plunger
19	Firing Pin Spring	**53**	Action Tube	**87**	Safety, Hand
20	Extractor	**54**	Action Spring Follower	**88**	Hand Safety Spring
21	Extractor Spring	**55**	Action Spring	**89**	Hand Safety Retaining Pin
22	Extractor Spring Plunger	**56**	Action Spring Plug Pin	**90**	Hand Safety Spring Plunger
23	Link	**57**	Action Spring Plug	**91**	Forend
24	Action Bar	**58**	Stock Bolt	**92**	Cap Stop Locking Pin
25	Slide Block	**59**	Washer	**93**	Cap Stop Locking Pin Cylinder
26	Action Bar Sleeve	**60**	Lock Washers	**94**	Cap Stop Locking Pin Spring
27	Cylinder Ring	**61**	Carrier	**95**	Buttstock
28	Cylinder Ring Retainer	**62**	Carrier Dog	**96**	Buttplate
29	Charging Handle Plunger	**63**	Carrier Dog Pin	**97**	Buttplate Screws
30	Slide Plunger	**64**	Carrier Dog Plunger	**98**	Pistol Grip Cap
31	Slide Plunger Pin	**65**	Carrier Dog Spring	**99**	Pistol Grip Cap Spacer
32	Slide Plunger Spring	**66**	Bushing Guide	**100**	Barrel, Ventilated Rib
33	Receiver	**67**	Trigger Plate Pin Snap		
34	Carrier Latch	**68**	Trigger Plate Pin		

Arisaka Model 1905 Bolt-Action Carbine

Courtesy of Blacksmith Corporation

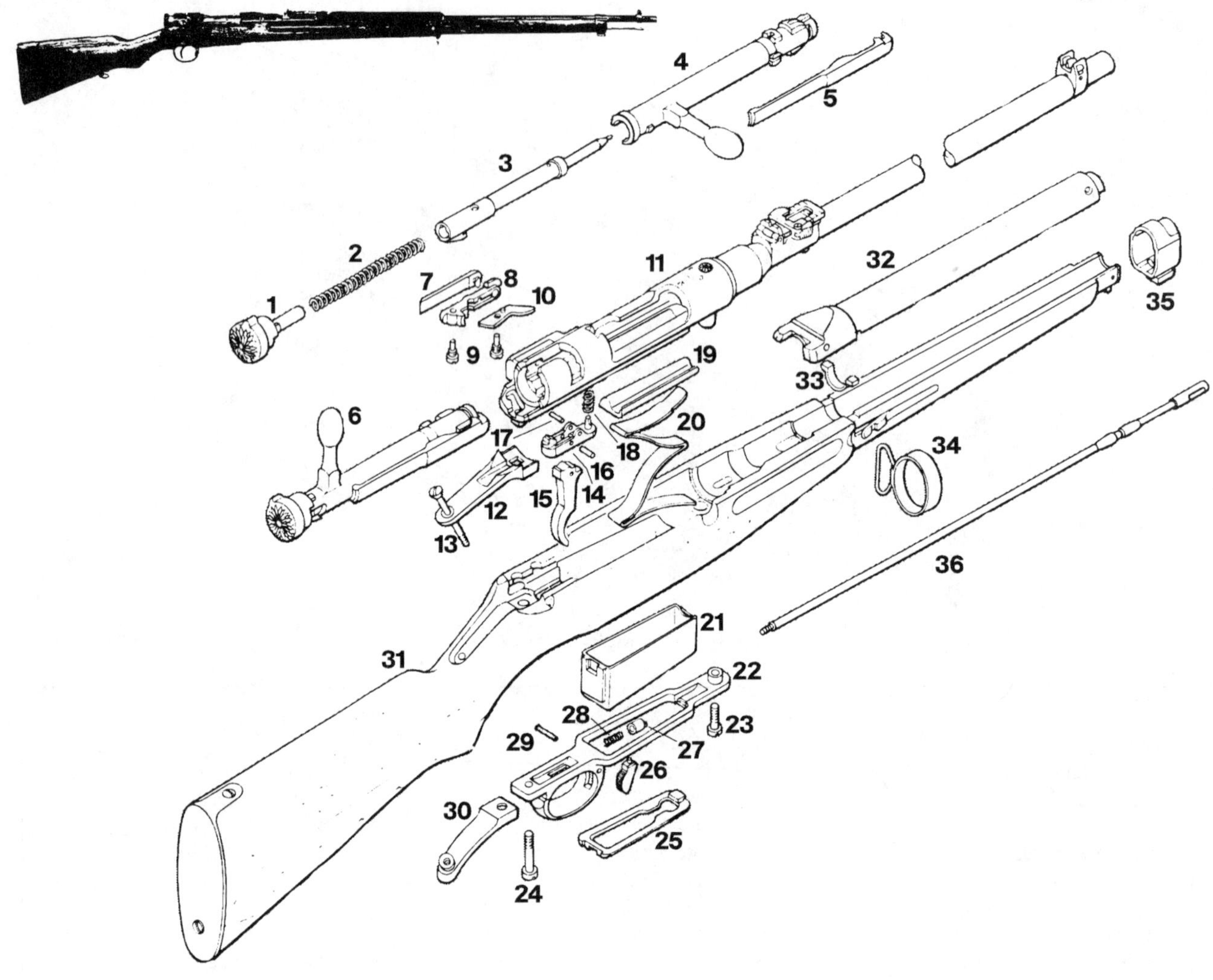

1	Safety Catch	**19**	Magazine Follower
2	Firing Pin Spring	**20**	Magazine Spring
3	Firing Pin	**21**	Magazine Box
4	Bolt	**22**	Trigger Guard
5	Extractor	**23**	Front Guard Screw
6	Bolt Assembly	**24**	Rear Guard Screw
7	Bolt Stop Spring	**25**	Floorplate
8	Bolt Stop	**26**	Floorplate Release
9	Bolt Stop and Ejector Screws	**27**	Floorplate Catch
10	Ejector	**28**	Floorplate Catch Spring
11	Carbine Receiver and Barrel	**29**	Floorplate Release Pin
12	Upper Tang	**30**	Lower Tang
13	Tang Screw	**31**	Carbine Stock
14	Sear	**32**	Upper Handguard
15	Trigger	**33**	Barrel Seat
16	Trigger Pin	**34**	Lower Band
17	Sear Pin	**35**	Front Band
18	Sear Spring	**36**	Cleaning Rod

Arisaka Type 38 Bolt-Action Rifle

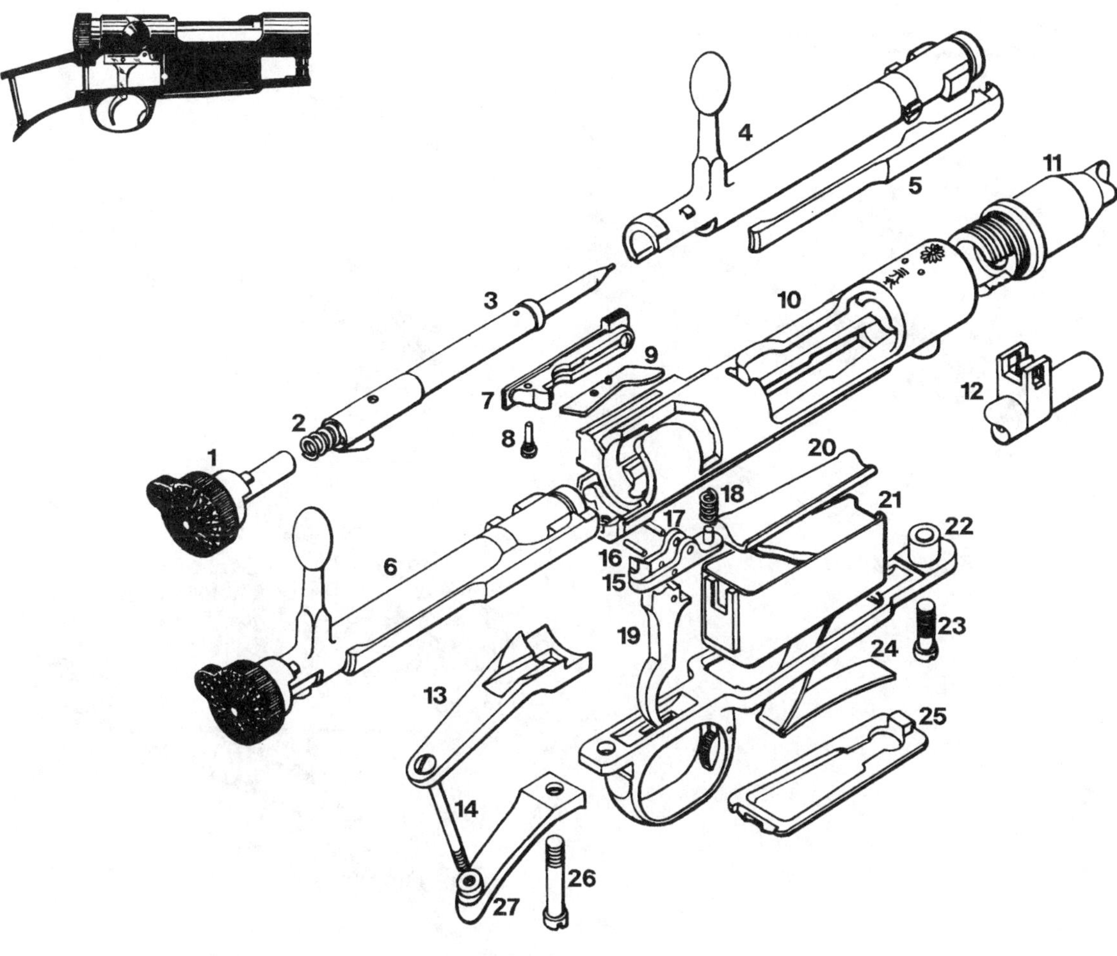

1	Safety	**15**	Sear
2	Firing Pin Spring	**16**	Trigger Pin
3	Firing Pin	**17**	Sear Pin
4	Bolt Body	**18**	Sear Spring
5	Extractor	**19**	Trigger
6	Bolt Assembly	**20**	Magazine Follower
7	Bolt Stop Assembly	**21**	Magazine Box
8	Bolt Stop and Ejector Screw	**22**	Trigger Guard
9	Ejector	**23**	Front Guard Screw
10	Receiver	**24**	Magazine Spring
11	Barrel	**25**	Floorplate
12	Front Sight	**26**	Rear Guard Screw
13	Upper Tang	**27**	Lower Tang
14	Tang Screw		

Model 10 Bolt-Action Shotgun

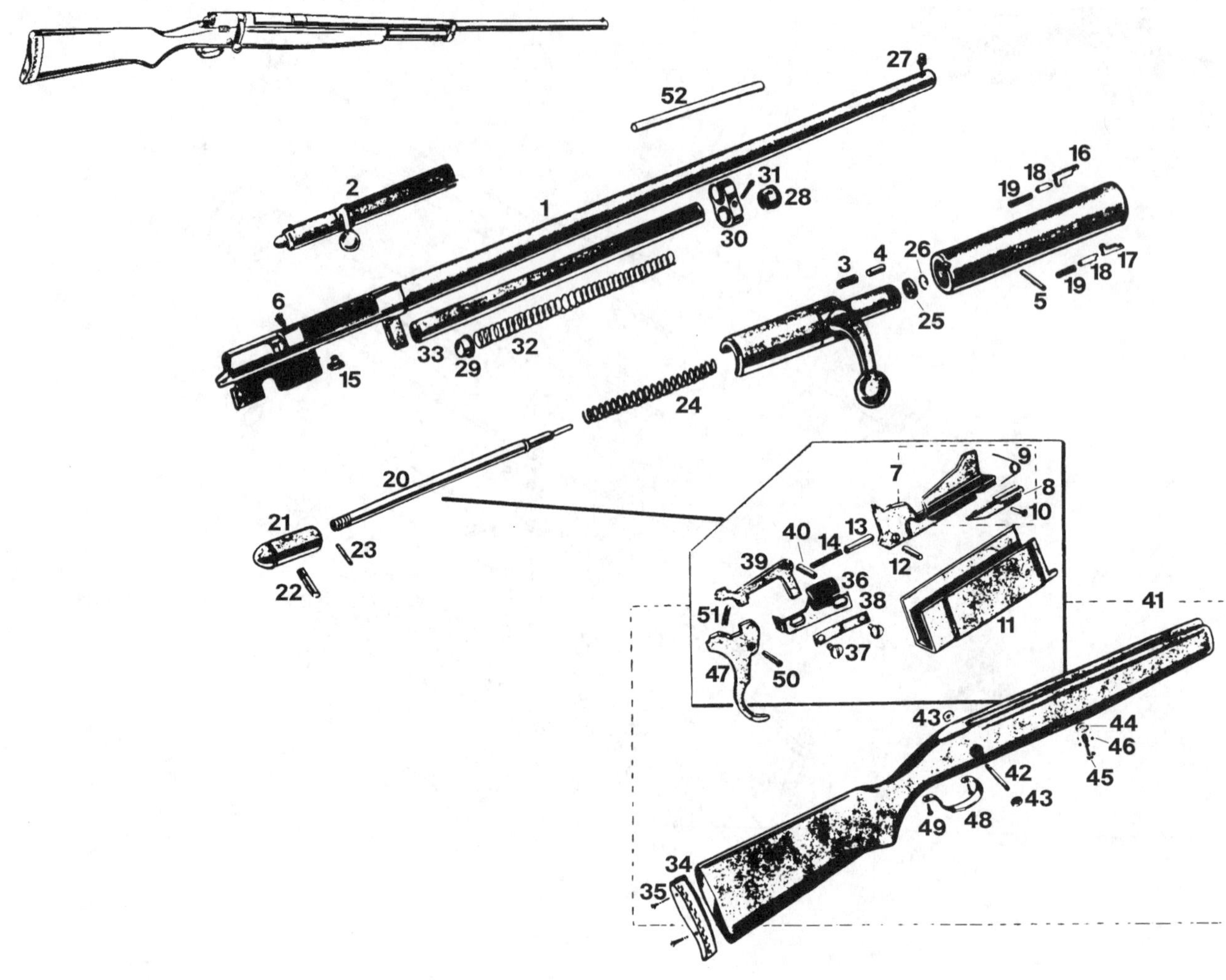

1	Barrel	**19**	Extractor Springs	**35**	Recoil Pad Screws
2	Bolt Assembly	**20**	Firing Pin	**36**	Safety
3	Bolt Handle Aligning Plunger Spring	**21**	Firing Pin Head	**37**	Safety Screws
4	Bolt Handle Aligning Plunger	**22**	Firing Pin Head Cross Pin	**38**	Safety Spring
5	Bolt Head Retaining Pin	**23**	Firing Pin Head Lock Pin	**39**	Sear
6	Bolt Stop Screw	**24**	Firing Pin Spring	**40**	Sear Pin
7	Carrier Assembly	**25**	Firing Pin Spring Retaining Sleeve	**41**	Stock Assembly
8	Cartridge Stop	**26**	Firing Pin Spring Retaining Sleeve Stop Ring	**42**	Stock Binding Stud
9	Cartridge Stop Spring	**27**	Front Sight	**43**	Stock Binding Stud Nuts
10	Cartridge Stop Rivet	**28**	Magazine Cap	**44**	Takedown Escutcheon
11	Carrier Housing	**29**	Magazine Follower	**45**	Takedown Screw
12	Carrier Pin	**30**	Magazine Front Band	**46**	Takedown Escutcheon Pins
13	Carrier Plunger	**31**	Magazine Front Band Binding Screw	**47**	Trigger
14	Carrier Plunger Spring	**32**	Magazine Spring	**48**	Trigger Guard
15	Ejector	**33**	Magazine Tube	**49**	Trigger Guard Screw
16	Extractor, Left	**34**	Recoil Pad Assembly	**50**	Trigger Pin
17	Extractor, Right			**51**	Trigger Spring
18	Extractor Plungers			**52**	Wood Plug

Model 20 Slide-Action Shotgun

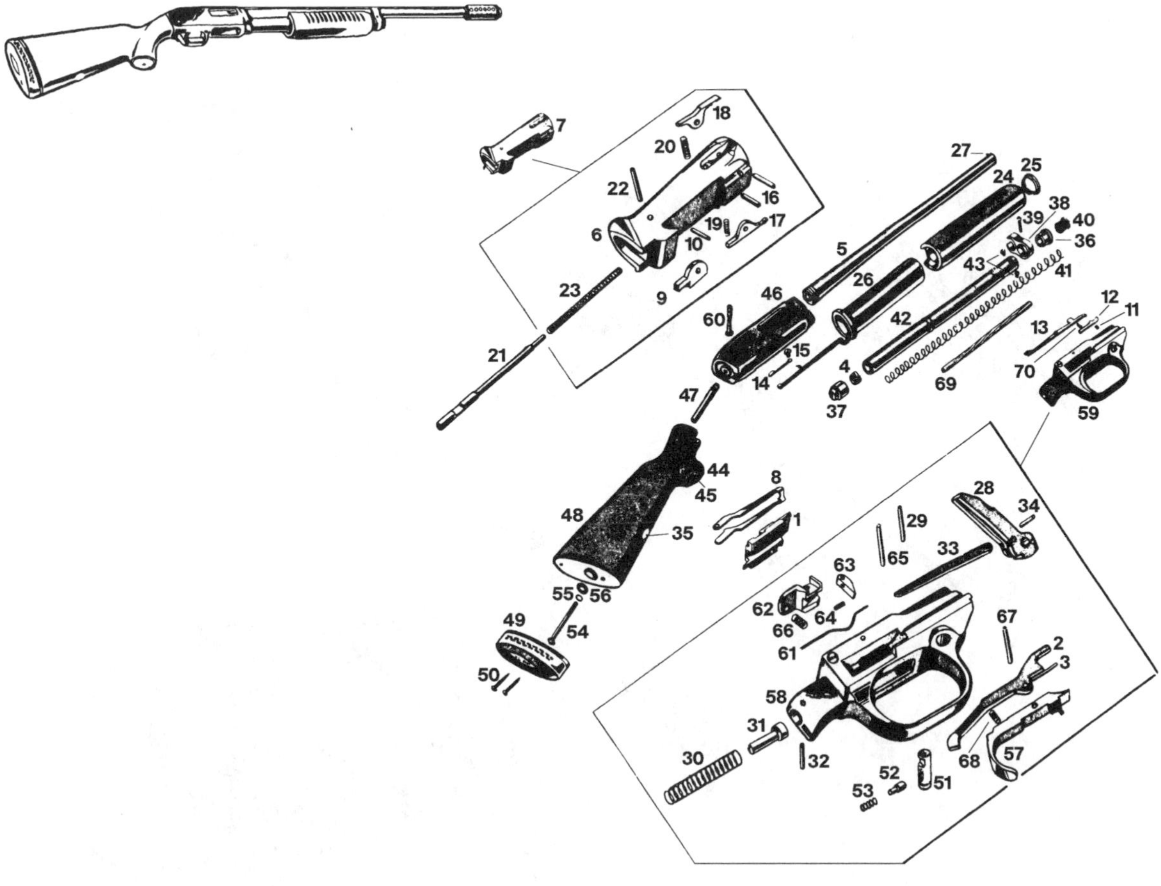

1	Slide Action	26	Forehand Operating Tube and Action Bar Assembly	51	Safety Button
2	Slide Action Release Lever			52	Safety Plunger
3	Slide Action Release Lever Spring	27	Front Sight	53	Safety Plunger Spring
4	Slide Action Spring	28	Hammer	54	Stock Bolt
5	Barrel	29	Hammer Hinge Pin	55	Stock Bolt Lock Washer
6	Bolt	30	Hammer Spring	56	Stock Bolt Washer
7	Bolt Assembly	31	Hammer Spring Guide	57	Trigger
8	Carrier	32	Hammer Spring Retaining Pin	58	Trigger Guard
9	Carrier Operating Cam	33	Hammer Strut	59	Trigger Guard Assembly
10	Carrier Operating Cam Retaining Pin	34	Hammer Strut Pin	60	Trigger Guard Retaining Pin
11	Cartridge Stop Spring	35	Initial Plate	61	Trigger Guard Retaining Pin Spring
12	Cartridge Stop, Left	36	Magazine Cap	62	Trigger Lock
13	Cartridge Stop, Right	37	Magazine Follower	63	Trigger Lock Pawl
14	Ejector	38	Magazine Band	64	Trigger Lock Pawl Spring
15	Ejector Screw	39	Magazine Band Screw	65	Trigger Lock Pin
16	Extractor Hinge Pins	40	Magazine Plug Filler Screw	66	Trigger Lock Spring
17	Extractor, Left	41	Magazine Spring	67	Trigger Pin
18	Extractor, Right	42	Magazine Tube and Ring Assembly	68	Trigger Spring
19	Extractor Spring, Left	43	Magazine Tube Locking Screws	69	Wood Plug
20	Extractor Spring, Right	44	Pistol Grip Cap	70	Cartridge Stop Pin
21	Firing Pin	45	Pistol Grip Cap Screw	**Parts Not Shown**	
22	Firing Pin Retaining Pin	46	Receiver Assembly		Action Slide Release Lever
23	Firing Pin Spring	47	Receiver Tang		Operating Pin
24	Forehand Operating Handle	48	Buttstock		Cartridge Stop Pin
25	Forehand Operating Handle Sleeve Front Nut	49	Recoil Pad		Hammer Spacer
		50	Recoil Pad Screws		Trigger Lock Pawl Screw

Model 31, 28, 29 and 30 Autoloading Rifle

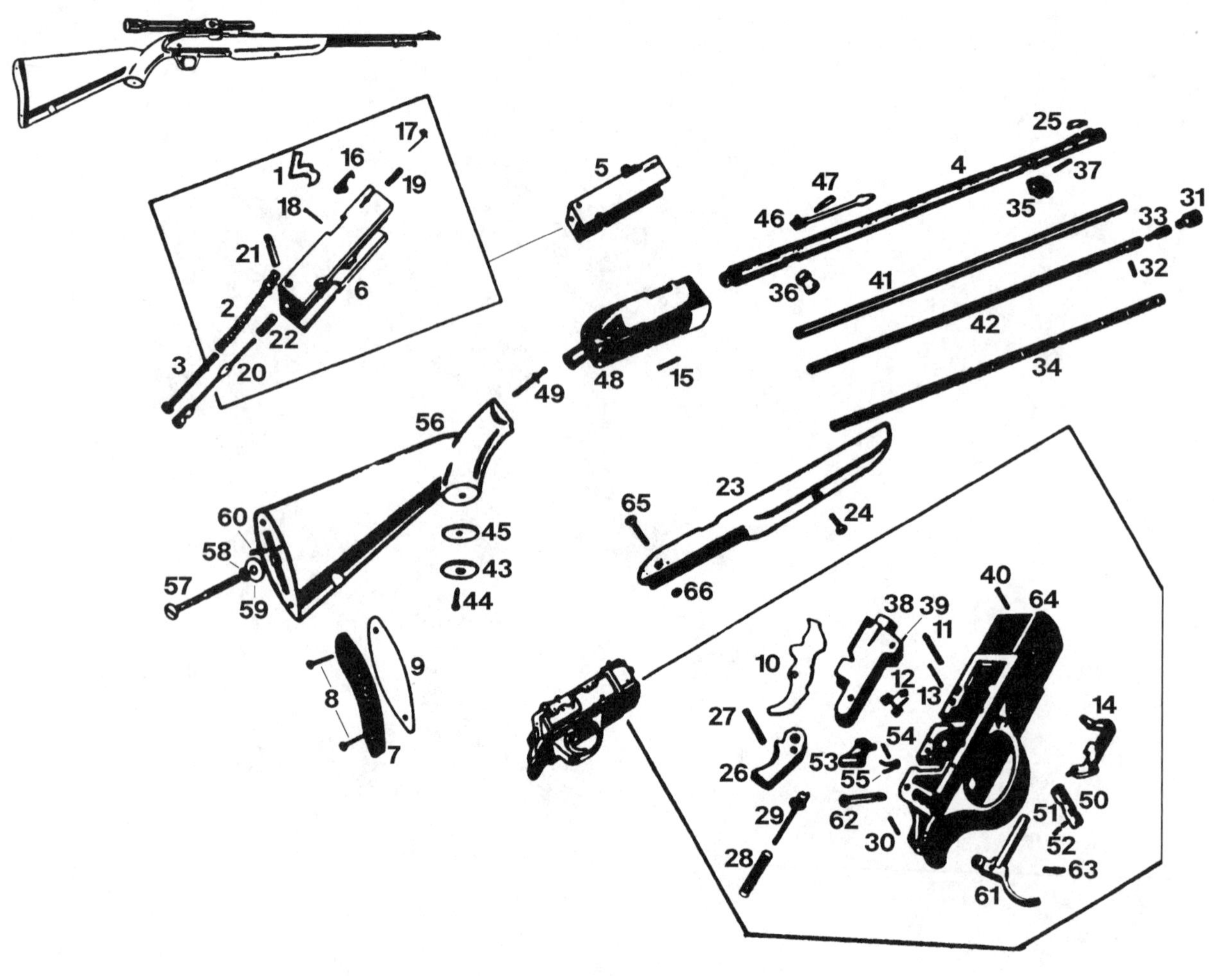

1	Bolt Operating Handle	**25**	Front Sight	**49**	Receiver Tang
2	Driving Spring	**26**	Hammer	**50**	Safety Button
3	Driving Spring Guide	**27**	Hammer Pin	**51**	Safety Button Plunger
4	Barrel and Ramp Assembly	**28**	Hammer Spring	**52**	Safety Button Plunger Spring
5	Bolt Assembly	**29**	Hammer Spring Guide	**53**	Sear
6	Bolt	**30**	Hammer Spring Pin	**54**	Sear Pin
7	Buttplate	**31**	Magazine Cap	**55**	Sear Spring
8	Buttplate Screws	**32**	Magazine Cap Pin	**56**	Stock Assembly
9	Buttplate Trim	**33**	Magazine Follower	**57**	Stock Bolt
10	Cartridge Lifter	**34**	Magazine Spring	**58**	Stock Bolt Lock Washer
11	Cartridge Lifter Pin	**35**	Magazine Support, Front	**59**	Stock Bolt Washer
12	Cartridge Lifter Spring	**36**	Magazine Support, Rear	**60**	Stock Washer
13	Lifter Spring Retaining Pin	**37**	Magazine Support Pin	**61**	Trigger and Trigger Extension Assembly
14	Disconnector Assembly	**38**	Magazine Throat, Right	**62**	Trigger Pin
15	Ejector	**39**	Magazine Throat, Left	**63**	Trigger Spring
16	Extractor	**40**	Magazine Throat Retaining Pin	**64**	Trigger Guard
17	Disconnector Spring	**41**	Magazine Tube, Outside	**65**	Trigger Guard Retaining Screw
18	Extractor Spring Retaining Pin	**42**	Magazine Tube, Inside	**66**	Trigger Guard Retaining Screw Nut
19	Extractor Spring	**43**	Pistol Grip Cap		**Parts Not Shown**
20	Firing Pin	**44**	Pistol Grip Cap Screw		Extractor Retaining Pin
21	Firing Pin Retaining Pin	**45**	Pistol Grip Cap Trim		Extractor Plunger
22	Firing Pin Spring	**46**	Rear Sight		
23	Forearm	**47**	Rear Sight Elevator		
24	Forearm Retaining Screw	**48**	Receiver		

Model 60 Autoloading Shotgun

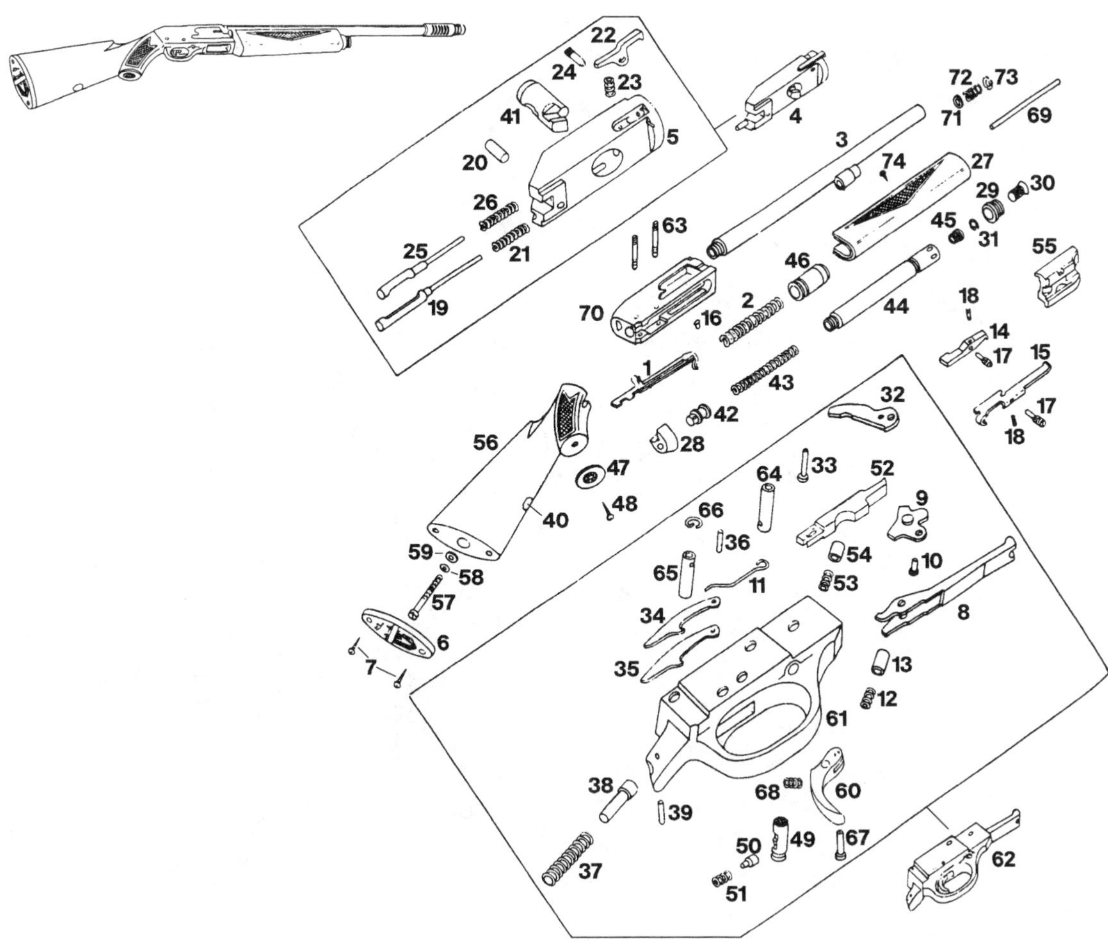

1	Action Bar Assembly	**27**	Forehand Assembly	**52**	Sear
2	Action Spring	**28**	Forehand Base	**53**	Sear Spring
3	Barrel and Cylinder	**29**	Forehand Cap	**54**	Sear Spring Plunger
4	Bolt Assembly	**30**	Forehand Cap Screw	**55**	Slide
5	Bolt	**31**	Forehand Cap Screw Retaining Ring	**56**	Stock Assembly
6	Buttplate	**32**	Hammer	**57**	Stock Bolt
7	Buttplate Screws	**33**	Hammer Hinge Pin	**58**	Stock Bolt Lock Washer
8	Cartridge Lifter	**34**	Hammer Strut, Right	**59**	Stock Bolt Washer
9	Cartridge Lifter Actuator Assembly	**35**	Hammer Strut, Left	**60**	Trigger
10	Cartridge Lifter Actuator Hinge Pin	**36**	Hammer Strut Pin	**61**	Trigger Guard
11	Cartridge Lifter Actuator Spring	**37**	Hammer Spring	**62**	Trigger Guard Assembly
12	Cartridge Lifter Spring	**38**	Hammer Spring Guide	**63**	Trigger Guard Retaining Pins
13	Cartridge Lifter Spring Plunger	**39**	Hammer Spring Retaining Pin	**64**	Trigger Guard Retaining Pin Bushing, Front
14	Cartridge Stop, Right	**40**	Initial Plate	**65**	Trigger Guard Retaining Pin Bushing, Rear
15	Cartridge Stop, Left	**41**	Locking Pin	**66**	Trigger Guard Retaining Pin Bushing Retaining Spring
16	Cartridge Stop Button	**42**	Magazine Follower	**67**	Trigger Hinge Pin
17	Cartridge Stop Pins	**43**	Magazine Spring	**68**	Trigger Spring
18	Cartridge Stop Springs	**44**	Magazine Tube	**69**	Wood Plug
19	Ejector	**45**	Magazine Tube Cap	**70**	Receiver
20	Ejector and Firing Pin Retaining Pin	**46**	Piston	**71**	Washer
21	Ejector Retracting Spring	**47**	Pistol Grip Cap	**72**	Spring
22	Extractor, Right	**48**	Pistol Grip Cap Screw	**73**	Lock Washer
23	Extractor Spring, Right	**49**	Safety Button	**74**	Takedown Screw
24	Extractor Pivot Pin	**50**	Safety Spring Plunger		
25	Firing Pin	**51**	Safety Spring		
26	Firing Pin Retracting Spring				

Autoloading Rifle

Courtesy of Blacksmith Corporation

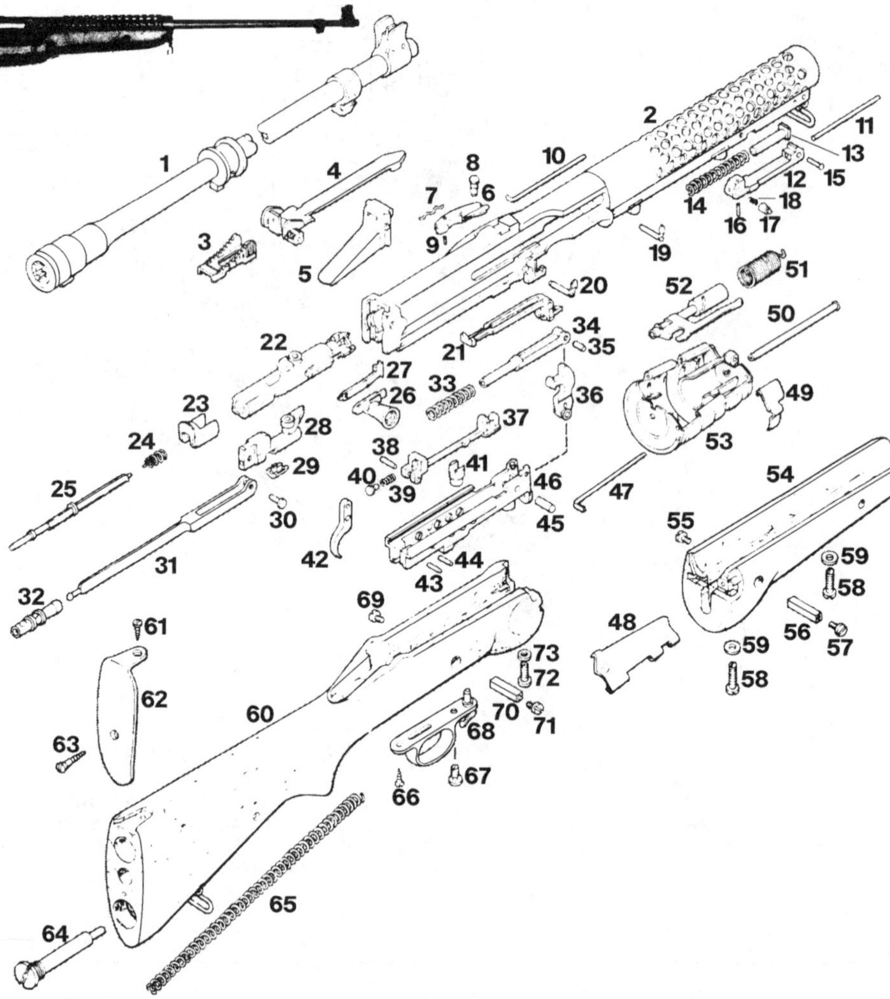

1	Barrel and Collar
2	Receiver
3	Rear Sight Elevator
4	Rear Sight Assembly
5	Bolt Stop Plate and Plunger
6	Ejector
7	Ejector Pin Retainer Spring
8	Ejector Hinge Pin
9	Spring Retaining Pin
10	Magazine Retainer Pin
11	Latch Spring Guide
12	Barrel Latch
13	Return Spring Plunger
14	Barrel Return Spring
15	Latch Hinge Pin
16	Detent Retainer Pin
17	Detent
18	Detent Spring
19	Cross Pin, Front
20	Cross Pin, Rear
21	Bolt Catch
22	Bolt
23	Bolt Stop
24	Firing Pin Spring
25	Firing Pin
26	Operating Handle
27	Extractor
28	Locking Cam Unit
29	Firing Pin Stop
30	Hinge Pin
31	Link
32	Mainspring Follower
33	Hammer Spring
34	Hammer Strut
35	Hammer Strut Pin
36	Hammer
37	Sear
38	Trigger Pin Link Pin
39	Trigger Spring
40	Spring Plunger
41	Safety Catch Cam
42	Trigger
43	Trigger Pin
44	Sear Stop Pin
45	Hammer Hinge Pin
46	Sear Housing
47	Magazine Cover Hinge Pin
48	Magazine Cover
49	Magazine Cover Spring
50	Magazine Axis
51	Magazine Spring
52	Magazine Follower
53	Magazine Housing
54	Forend
55	Recoil Stop Screw
56	Recoil Stop
57	Recoil Stop Screw
58	Forend Screws
59	Washers
60	Buttstock
61	Upper Buttplate Screw
62	Buttplate
63	Buttplate Screw
64	Mainspring Tube Cap and Buffer Assembly
65	Mainspring
66	Trigger Guard Wood Screw
67	Trigger Guard Screw
68	Trigger Guard and Safety Assembly
69	Recoil Stop Screw
70	Recoil Stop
71	Recoil Stop Screw
72	Stock Screw
73	Washer

Omega Over/Under Shotgun

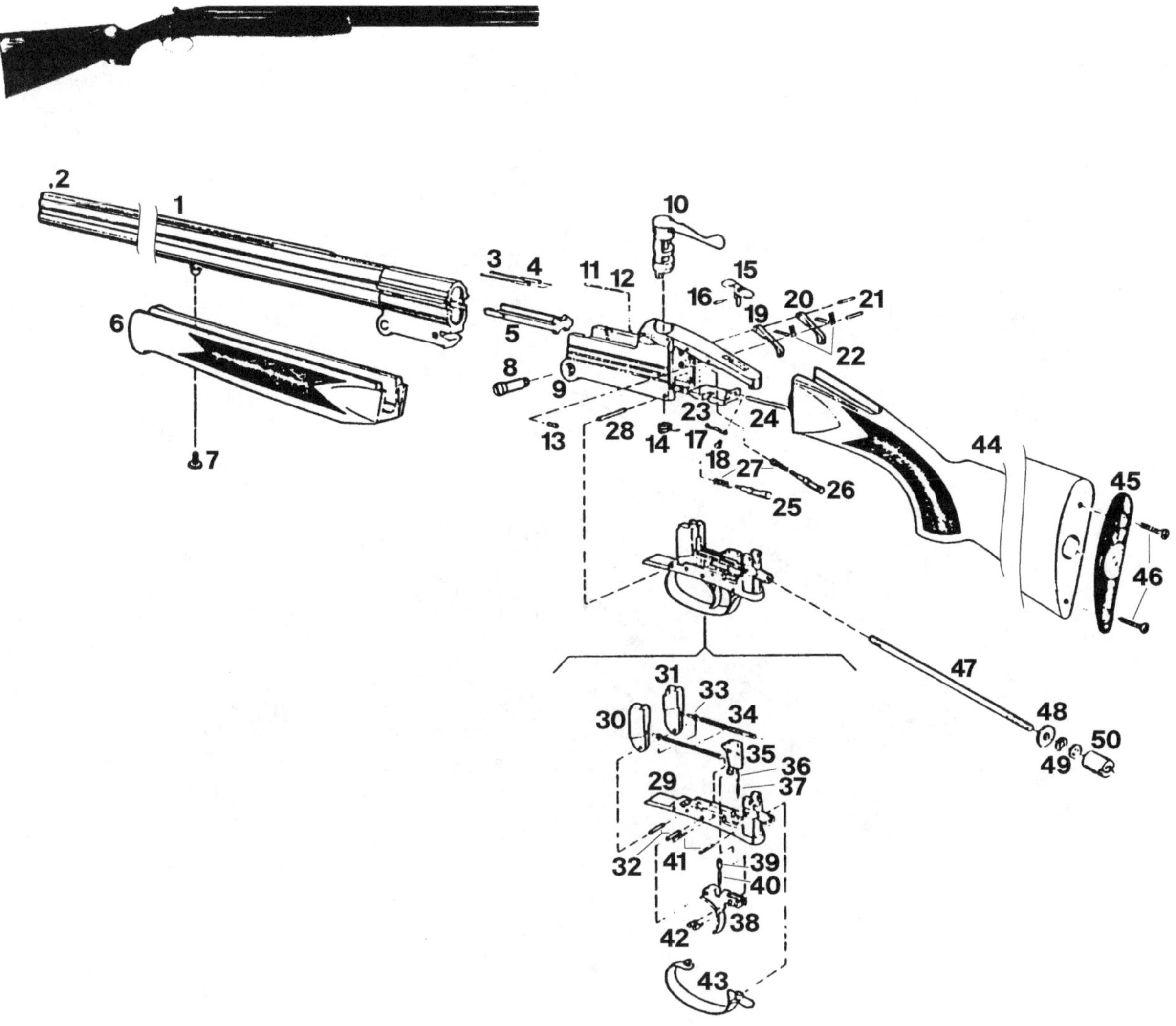

1	Barrel	**18**	Safety Spring Screw	**35**	Inertia Block
2	Front Sight	**19**	Left Sear	**36**	Inertia Block Spring
3	Extractor Spring	**20**	Right Sear	**37**	Inertia Block Spring Guide
4	Extractor Spring Guide	**21**	Sear and Sear Spring Pins	**38**	Trigger
5	Extractor	**22**	Sear Springs	**39**	Trigger Spring Plunger
6	Forend	**23**	Crossbolt	**40**	Trigger Spring
7	Forend Screw	**24**	Automatic Safety Activator Pin	**41**	Trigger Spring and Trigger Guard Retaining Pins
8	Receiver Screw	**25**	Lower Firing Pin	**42**	Inertia Block Retaining Screws
9	Action	**26**	Upper Firing Pin	**43**	Trigger Guard
10	Top Opening Lever	**27**	Firing Pin Springs	**44**	Stock
11	Lock Release Button	**28**	Trigger Plate Pin	**45**	Buttplate
12	Lock Release Button Spring	**29**	Trigger Plate	**46**	Buttplate Screws
13	Top Lever Retaining Screw	**30**	Hammer, Left	**47**	Stock Bolt
14	Top Lever Spring Release	**31**	Hammer, Right	**48**	Stock Bolt Washer
15	Safety	**32**	Hammer and Trigger Pins	**49**	Plastic Stock Bolt Washers
16	Safety Pin	**33**	Mainspring Guides	**50**	Stock Bolt Nut
17	Safety Spring	**34**	Mainsprings		

Omega Single Shot Shotgun

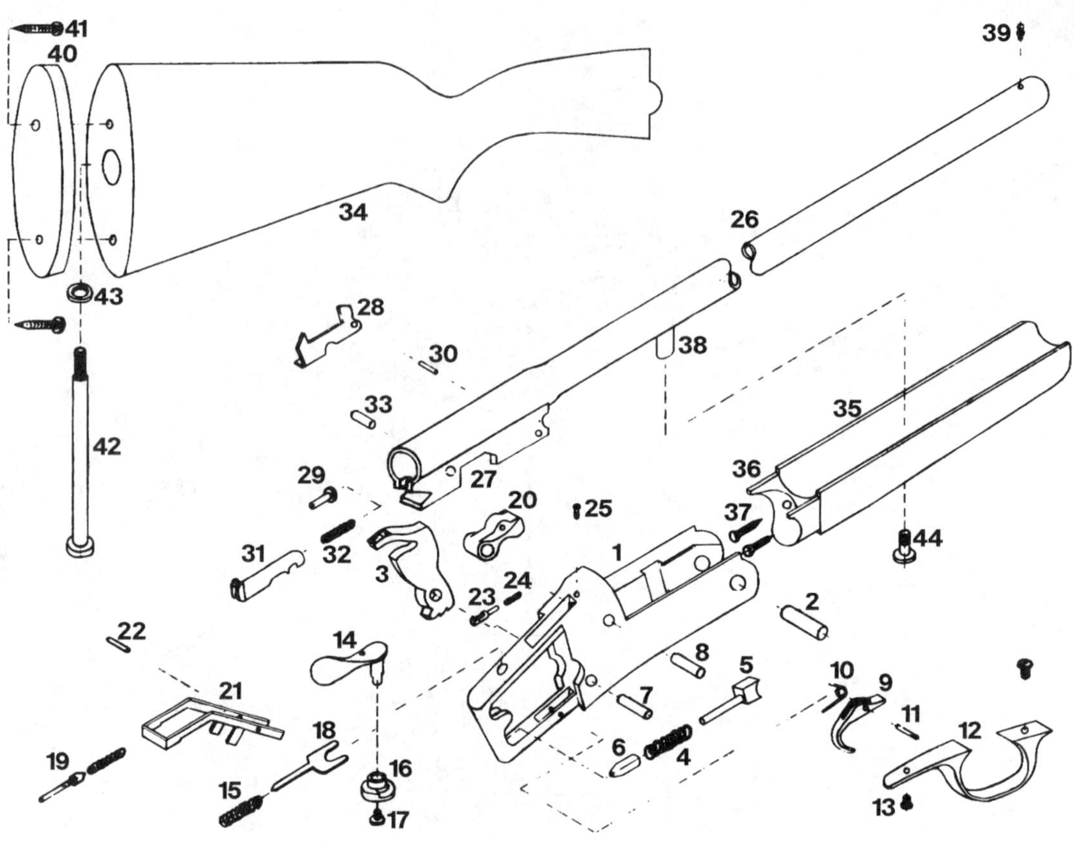

1	Receiver	**23**	Firing Pin
2	Receiver Connection Pin	**24**	Firing Pin Spring
3	Hammer	**25**	Firing Pin Bolt
4	Mainspring	**26**	Barrel
5	Mainspring Guide	**27**	Barrel Connector
6	Mainspring Retainer	**28**	Ejector Extension
7	Hammer Pin	**29**	Shotshell Retaining Pin
8	Barrel Fixing Pin	**30**	Ejector Extension Pin
9	Trigger	**31**	Ejector
10	Trigger Spring	**32**	Ejector Spring
11	Trigger Pin	**33**	Ejector Pin
12	Trigger Guard	**34**	Stock
13	Trigger Guard Screw	**35**	Forearm
14	Top Lever	**36**	Forearm Bracket
15	Top Lever Spring	**37**	Forearm Bracket Bolts
16	Top Lever Cam	**38**	Forearm Nut
17	Top Lever Cam Bolt	**39**	Sight
18	Top Lever Spring Guide Plate	**40**	Buttplate
19	Top Lever Spring Guide	**41**	Buttplate Screws
20	Barrel Fixture	**42**	Stock Bolt
21	Barrel Fixture Connector	**43**	Stock Bolt Washer
22	Barrel Fixture Connector Pin		

Regent VI Side-by-Side Shotgun

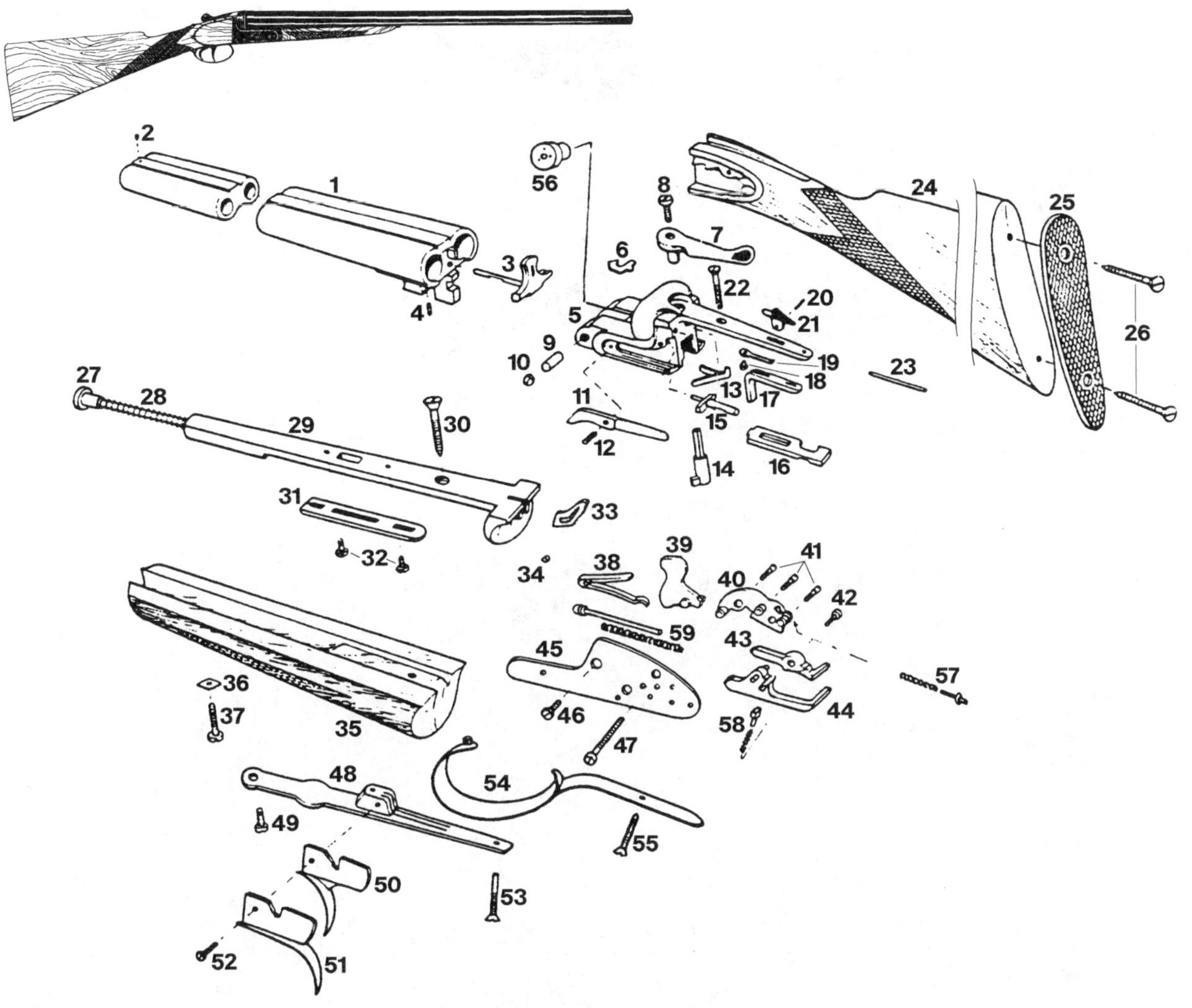

1	Barrels	22	Upper Tang Screw	40	Hammer and Sear Ledge
2	Sight Bead	23	Safety Activator Pin	41	Ledge Screws
3	Extractor	24	Stock	42	Sear Screw
4	Extractor Retaining Screw	25	Buttplate	43	Double Safety Sear
5	Breech Assembly	26	Buttplate Screw	44	Sear
6	Purdey Lock	27	Forend Catch Button	45	Sidelock
7	Top Lever	28	Forend Catch Spring	46	Front Sidelock Screw
8	Top Lever Screw	29	Forend Iron	47	Rear Sidelock Screw
9	Barrel Pivot Pin	30	Forend Mount Screw	48	Trigger Pate
10	Barrel Pivot Pin Cap	31	Forend Catch	49	Trigger Plate Screw
11	Cocking Lever Pivot	32	Forend Catch Screw	50	Front Trigger
12	Cocking Lever Pivot Screw	33	Extractor Hammer Cocking Lever Activator	51	Rear Trigger
13	Top Lever Spring	34	Extractor Hammer Cocking Lever Screw	52	Trigger Pin
14	Vertical Bolt	35	Forend Wood	53	Rear Trigger Plate Screw
15	Firing Pin	36	Forend Escutcheon	54	Trigger Guard
16	Horizontal Bolt	37	Forend Escutcheon Mounting Screw	55	Trigger Guard Screw
17	Safety Activator	38	Hammer Spring	56	Firing Pin Bushing
18	Safety Spring Screw	39	Hammer	57	Ledge Spring and Plunger
19	Safety Spring			58	Sear Spring and Plunger
20	Safety Button Pin			59	Safety Sear Spring and Plunger
21	Safety Button				

Model 82 U.S. Government Bolt-Action Rifle

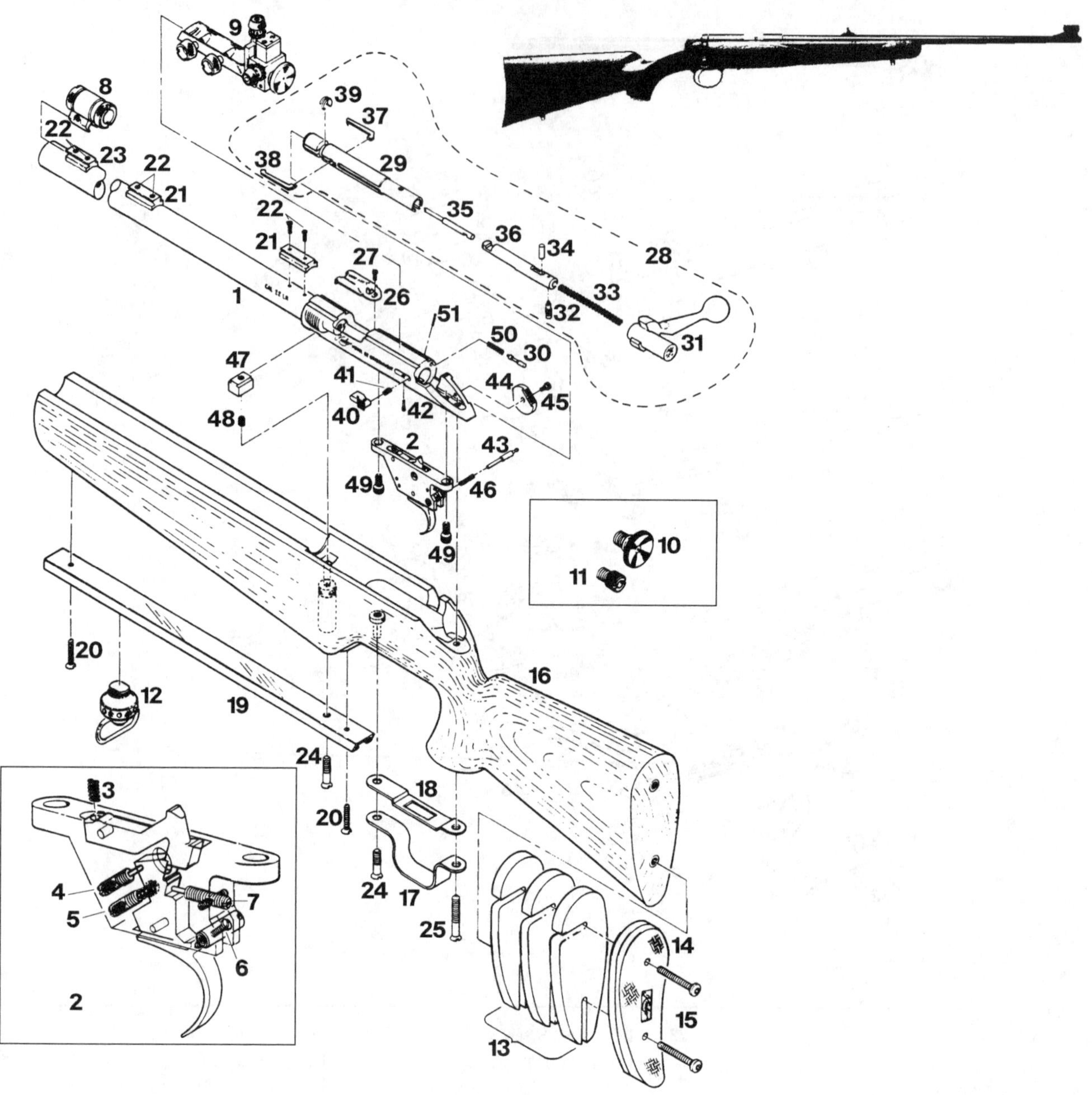

1	Receiver and Barrel Assembly	**18**	Trigger Guard Plate	**35**	Firing Pin
2	Trigger Group Assembly	**19**	Hand Stop Rail	**36**	Striker
3	Sear Spring	**20**	Hand Stop Rail Screws	**37**	Extractor
4	Overtravel Screw	**21**	Scope Mount Bases	**38**	Helper
5	Trigger Adjustment Screw	**22**	Base Screws	**39**	Extractor Spring
6	Safety Adjustment Screw	**23**	Front Sight Base	**40**	Bolt-Stop
7	Sear Engagement Screw	**24**	Front Takedown Screws	**41**	Bolt-Stop Spring
8	Front Sight Assembly	**25**	Rear Takedown Screw	**42**	Bolt-Stop Screw
9	Rear Sight Assembly	**26**	Loading Platform/Ejector	**43**	Safety Pin
10	Rear Sight Aperture	**27**	Loading Platform Screw	**44**	Safety Disc
11	Rear Sight Adaptor	**28**	Bolt Assembly	**45**	Safety Disc Screw
12	Hand Stop Assembly	**29**	Bolt Head	**46**	Safety Pin Spring
13	Buttplate Spacers	**30**	Bolt Locking Plunger	**47**	Recoil Lug
14	Buttplate	**31**	Bolt Handle	**48**	Recoil Lug Set Screw
15	Buttplate Screws	**32**	Cocking Stud	**49**	Trigger Housing Screws
16	Stock Assembly	**33**	Mainspring	**50**	Bolt Locking Spring
17	Trigger Guard	**34**	Mainspring Pin	**51**	Bolt Locking Plunger Retaining Pin

Model 1892-99 Bolt-Action Rifle

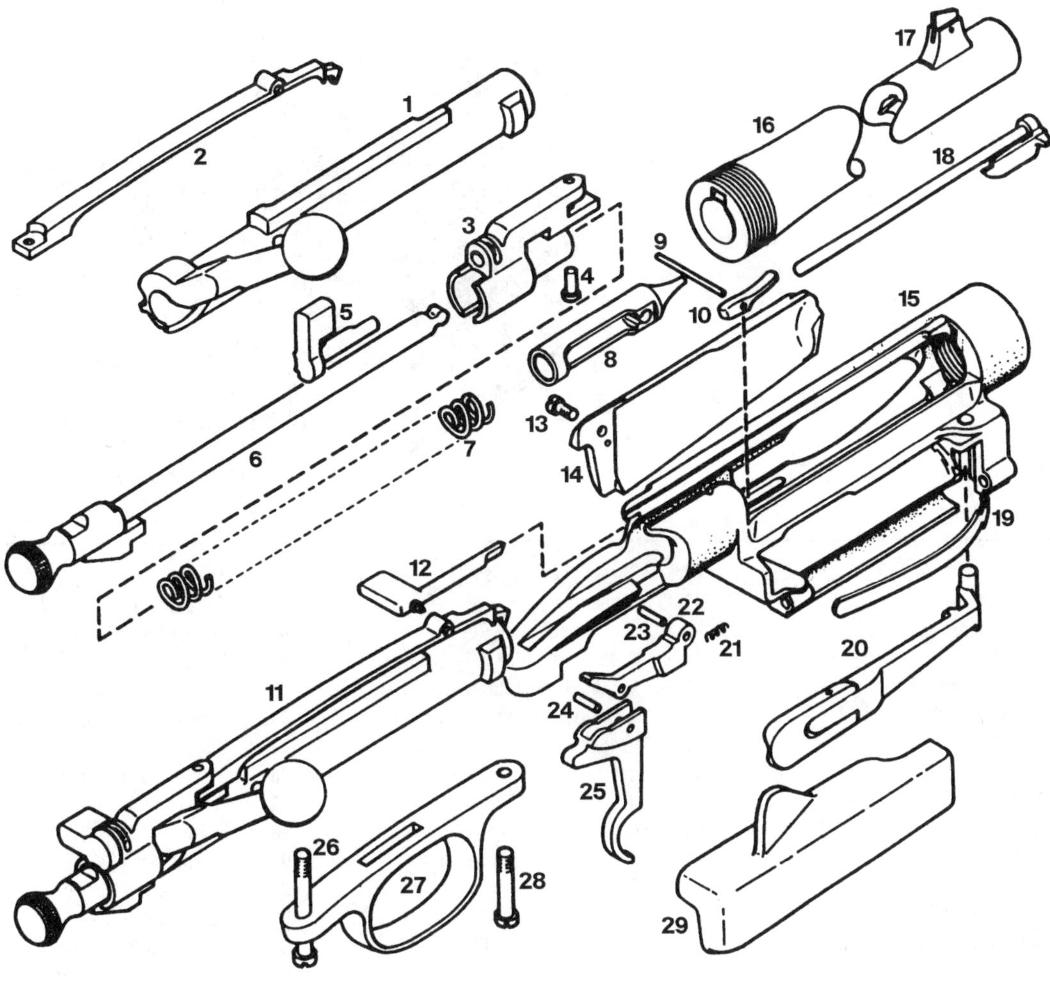

1	Bolt Body	**16**	Barrel
2	Extractor	**17**	Front Sight
3	Bolt Sleeve	**18**	Hinge Bar
4	Extractor Rivet	**19**	Magazine Spring
5	Safety	**20**	Carrier and Follower Assembly
6	Firing Pin Assembly	**21**	Sear Spring
7	Mainspring	**22**	Sear
8	Striker	**23**	Sear Pin
9	Ejector Pin	**24**	Trigger Pin
10	Ejector	**25**	Trigger
11	Bolt Assembly	**26**	Rear Guard Screw
12	Magazine Cutoff	**27**	Trigger Guard
13	Sideplate Screw	**28**	Front Guard Screw
14	Sideplate	**29**	Magazine Gate
15	Receiver		

KREIGHOFF

K-32 Over/Under Shotgun

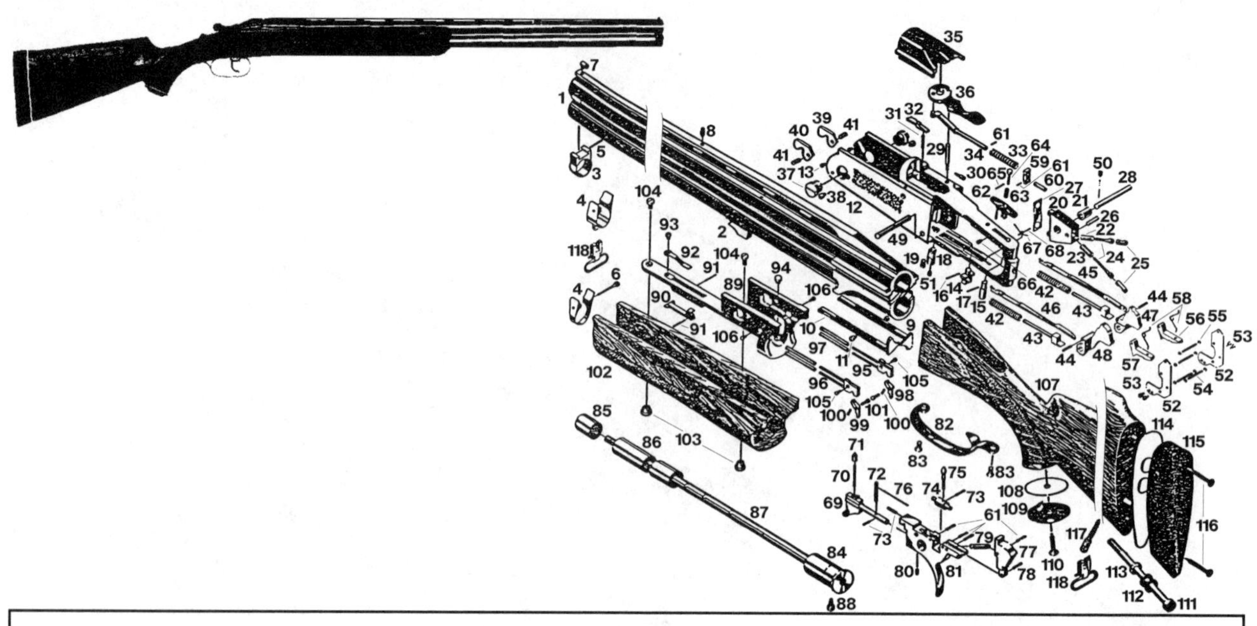

1	Barrels
2	Barrel Lug
3	Front Hanger
4	Rear Hanger
5	Front Hanger Pin
6	Rear Hanger Screw
7	Front Sight
8	Middle Sight
9	Ejector, Bottom
10	Ejector, Top
11	Ejector Screws
12	Receiver
13	Impact Pins
14	Top Lever Spring Rod Support
15	Safety Stud
16	Support Pin
17	Safety Stud Pin
18	Pivot Pin Stud
19	Hammer Pivot Pin Stud Lock Screw
20	Firing Pin Housing
21	Bushing
22	Firing Pin Spring, Bottom
23	Firing Pin Spring, Top
24	Firing Pins, Front
25	Firing Pins, Rear
26	Firing Pin Retaining Pin
27	Distance Piece
28	Firing Pins Housing Pin
29	Pin
30	Pin Lock Screw
31	Catch Spring
32	Catch
33	Top Lever Spring
34	Top Lever Spring Rod
35	Top Latch
36	Top Lever
37	Hinge Screw
38	Hinge Screw Lock Screw
39	Cocking Lever, Bottom
40	Cocking Lever, Top
41	Cocking Lever Pins
42	Mainsprings
43	Mainspring Guide Rods
44	Cocking Rod Pins
45	Cocking Rod, Bottom
46	Cocking Rod, Top
47	Hammer, Bottom
48	Hammer, Top
49	Hammer Pivot Pin
50	Firing Pin Housing Set Screw
51	Hammer Pivot Pin Set Screw
52	Sideplates
53	Sideplate Screws
54	Pivot and Spacing Pins
55	Circlips
56	Sear, Bottom
57	Sear, Top
58	Sear Springs
59	Safety Block
60	Safety Block Bolt
61	Drive Pins
62	Safety Slide
63	Push Button Spring
64	Push Button
65	Push Button Pin
66	Stop Screw
67	Trigger Spring
68	Trigger Spring Drive Pin
69	Barrel Selector
70	Barrel Selector Spring
71	Barrel Selector Stop
72	Barrel Selector Pin
73	Retaining Pins
74	Sear Selector Axle
75	Sear Selector
76	Sear Spring
77	Inertia Block
78	Inertia Block Pin
79	Inertia Block Spring
80	Trigger Set Screw
81	Trigger
82	Trigger Guard
83	Trigger Guard Screws
84	Snap Cap
85	Threaded Bushing
86	Threaded Bushing Weights
87	Spacing Bushing
88	Snap Cap Lock Screw
89	Forearm Iron
90	Forend Catch
91	Forend Catch Pin
92	Forend Catch Spring
93	Forend Catch Screw
94	Forend Stop
95	Ejector Hammer, Bottom
96	Ejector Hammer, Top
97	Ejector Springs
98	Ejector Sear, Bottom
99	Ejector Sear, Top
100	Ejector Sear Springs
101	Ejector Sear Pins
102	Forearm Wood
103	Forearm Rosettes
104	Forearm Screws
105	Ejector Hammer Pins
106	Forend Stop Pins
107	Stock
108	Pistol Grip Spacer
109	Pistol Grip Cap
110	Stock Screw
111	Guide Sleeve
112	Plate Spring
113	Spring Washer
114	Buttplate Spacer
115	Buttplate
116	Buttplate Screws
117	Phillips Head Screw
118	Sling Swivels

K-80 Over/Under Shotgun

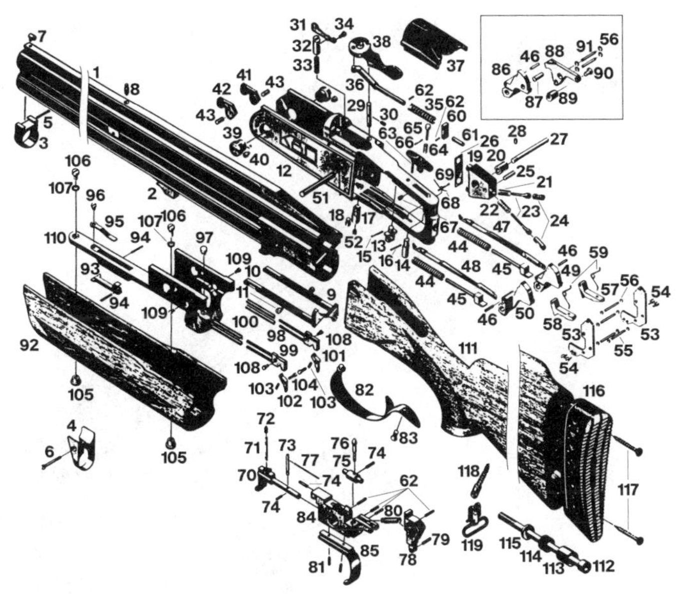

1	Barrel
2	Barrel Lug
3	Front Hanger
4	Rear Hanger
5	Front Hanger Pin
6	Rear Hanger Screw
7	Front Sight
8	Middle Sight
9	Ejector, Bottom
10	Ejector, Top
11	Ejector Screws
12	Receiver
13	Top Lever Spring Rod Support
14	Safety Stud
15	Support Pin
16	Safety Stud Pin
17	Hammer Pivot Pin Stud
18	Hammer Pivot Pin Stud Lock Screw
19	Firing Pin Housing
20	Bushing
21	Firing Pin Spring, Bottom
22	Firing Pin Spring, Top
23	Firing Pins, Front
24	Firing Pins, Rear
25	Firing Pin Retaining Pin
26	Distance Piece
27	Firing Pin Housing Pin
28	Housing Pin Lock Screw
29	Pin
30	Pin Lock Screw
31	Catch
32	Catch Pin
33	Catch Spring
34	Catch Screw
35	Top Lever Spring
36	Top Lever Spring Rod
37	Top Latch
38	Top Lever
39	Hinge Screw
40	Hinge Screw Lock Screw
41	Cocking Lever, Bottom
42	Cocking Lever, Top
43	Cocking Lever Pins
44	Mainsprings
45	Guide Rods
46	Cocking Rod Pins
47	Cocking Rod, Bottom
48	Cocking Rod, Top
49	Hammer, Bottom
50	Hammer, Top
51	Pivot Pin
52	Pivot Pin Set Screw
53	Sideplates
54	Sideplate Screws
55	Pivot and Spacing Pins
56	Circlips
57	Sear, Bottom
58	Sear, Top
59	Sear Springs
60	Safety Block
61	Safety Block Bolt
62	Drive Pins
63	Safety Slide
64	Push Button Spring
65	Push Button
66	Pin
67	Stop Screw
68	Trigger Spring
69	Trigger Spring Drive Pin
70	Barrel Selector
71	Barrel Selector Spring
72	Barrel Selector Stop
73	Barrel Selector Pin
74	Pins
75	Sear Selector Axle
76	Selector Sear
77	Spring
78	Inertia Block
79	Inertia Block Pin
80	Inertia Block Spring
81	Set Screw
82	Trigger Guard
83	Trigger Guard Screw
84	Trigger Housing
85	Trigger
86	Hammer
87	Hammer Pin
88	Release Plate
89	Eccentric Bushing
90	Countersunk Screw
91	Release Pins
92	Forearm
93	Forend Catch
94	Forend Catch Pins
95	Forend Catch Spring
96	Forend Catch Screw
97	Forend Stop
98	Ejector Hammer, Bottom
99	Ejector Hammer, Top
100	Ejector Springs
101	Ejector Sear, Bottom
102	Ejector Sear, Top
103	Ejector Sear Springs
104	Ejector Sear Pins
105	Rosettes
106	Forearm Screws
107	Forearm Washers
108	Pin
109	Stop Pin
110	Forearm Iron
111	Stock
112	Guide Sleeve
113	Guide Sleeve Collar
114	Plate Spring
115	Spring Washer
116	Buttplate
117	Buttplate Screws
118	Phillips Head Screw
119	Sling Swivel

KS-5 Single Shot Shotgun

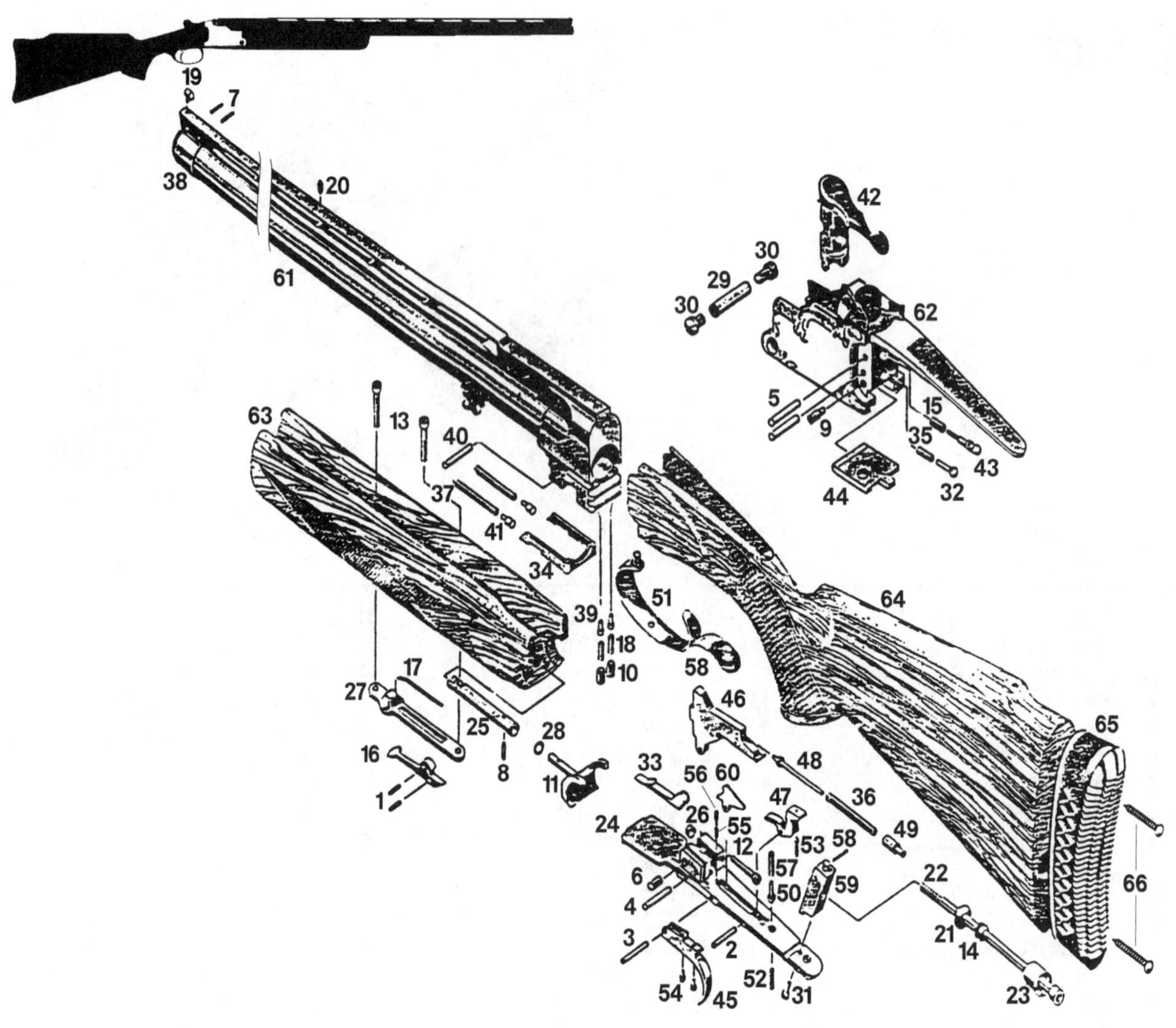

1	Forend Catch Pins	23	Guiding Bushing	45	Trigger
2	Pin	24	Forend Iron	46	Hammer
3	Trigger Pin	25	Forend Iron End	47	Sear
4	Hammer Pin	26	Trigger Floorplate Washer	48	Mainspring Guiding Rod
5	Firing Pin and Top Lever Pins	27	Forend Catch Housing	49	Guiding Rod Bushing
6	Top Lever Release Bolt Pin	28	Forend Spacer	50	Bushing Pin
7	Front Hanger Pins	29	Hinge Pin	51	Trigger Guard
8	Forearm Pin	30	Hinge Screws	52	Threaded Pin
9	Top Lever Threaded Pin	31	Allen Screw	53	Pin
10	Ejector Bolt Threaded Pins	32	Top Lever Roll Pin	54	Trigger Adjustment Screws
11	Top Lever Catch Spring	33	Top Lever Release	55	Disconnector Spring
12	Trigger Floorplate Screw	34	Ejector	56	Disconnector Spring Guide Pin
13	Forearm Screws	35	Top Lever Spring	57	Bushing Spring
14	Spring Washer for Stock Bolt	36	Mainspring	58	Support Pins
15	Firing Pin Spring	37	Ejector Springs	59	Rear Support Block
16	Forend Catch	38	Front Hanger	60	Disconnector
17	Forend Catch Spring	39	Ejector Locking Pins	61	Barrel
18	Release and Ejector Springs	40	Ejector Pin	62	Receiver
19	Front Sight	41	Ejector Hammers	63	Forearm
20	Middle Sight	42	Top Lever	64	Buttstock
21	Stock Washer	43	Firing Pin	65	Buttplate
22	Stock Bolt	44	Locking Bolt	66	Buttplate Screws

Model 844 ST Over/Under Shotgun

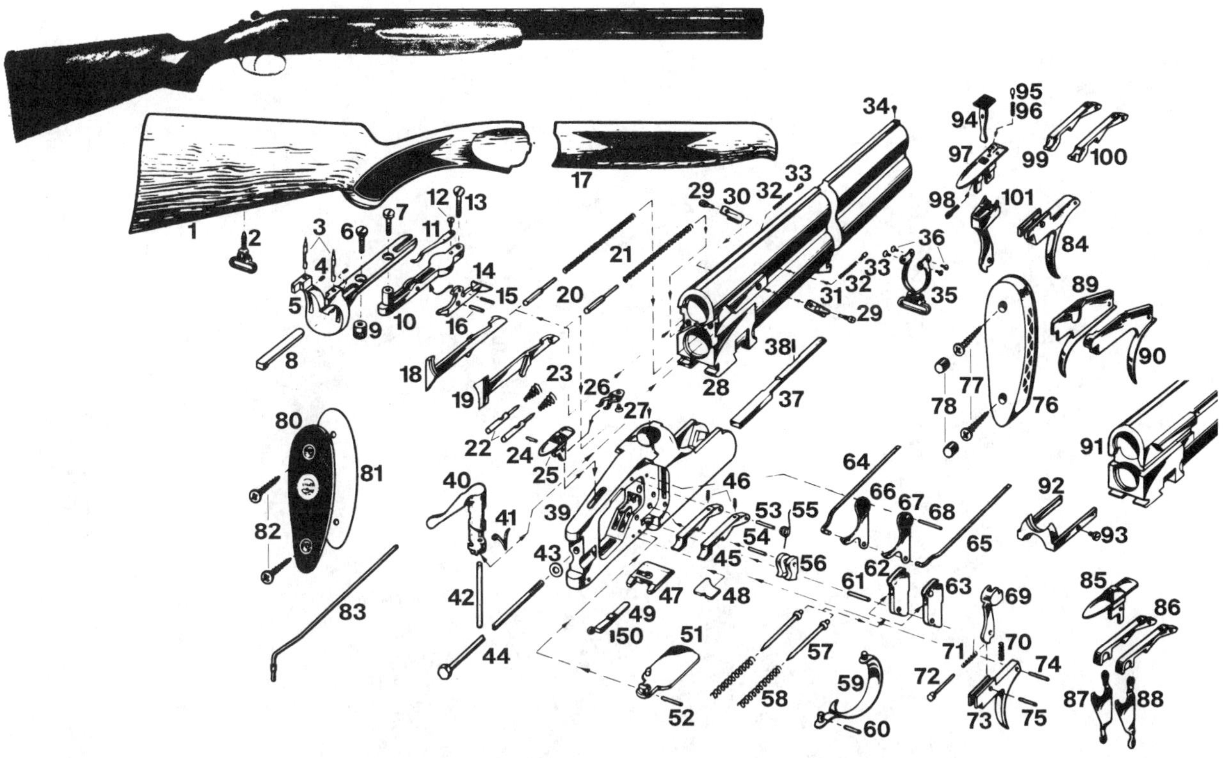

1	Stock
2	Swivel
3	Ejector Trip Lifters
4	Ejector Trip Stop Pins
5	Forend Iron
6	Forend Wood Retaining Pin
7	Forend Catch Retaining Pin
8	Cocking Stud
9	Retaining Pin Bushing
10	Delay Catch Frame
11	Delay Catch Spring
12	Spring Retaining Screw
13	Forend Catch Retaining Pin
14	Delay Catch
15	Catch Stop Pin
16	Catch Retaining Pin
17	Forend Wood
18	Top Ejector
19	Bottom Ejector
20	Ejector Plungers
21	Ejector Springs
22	Strikers
23	Striker Return Springs
24	Safety Button Retaining Pin
25	Safety Button
26	Safety Spring
27	Safety Spring Retaining Pin
28	Barrels
29	Ejector Trip Retaining Pins
30	Ejector Trip, Top
31	Ejector Trip, Bottom
32	Ejector Trip Springs
33	Ejector Trip Plungers
34	Bead Sight
35	Barrel Swivel
36	Barrel Swivel Retaining Pins
37	Cocking Rod
38	Cocking Rod Retaining Pin
39	Action Body
40	Top Lever
41	Top Lever Spring
42	Striker Retaining Rod
43	Stock Bolt Washer
44	Stock Bolt
45	Sears
46	Sear Springs
47	Bolt
48	Striker Lifter
49	Top Lever Trip
50	Top Lever Trip Spring
51	Cover Plate
52	Cover Plate Retaining Pin
53	Sear Retaining Pin
54	Cocking Cam Retaining Pin
55	Cocking Cam Return Spring
56	Cocking Cam
57	Mainspring Guides
58	Mainsprings
59	Trigger Guard
60	Trigger Guard Retaining Pin
61	Tumbler Retaining Pin
62	Top Barrel Tumbler
63	Bottom Barrel Tumbler
64	Top Ejector Rod
65	Bottom Ejector Rod
66	Top Ejector Cam
67	Bottom Ejector Cam
68	Ejector Cam Retaining Pin
69	Inertia Block
70	Trigger Return Spring
71	Inertia Block Spring
72	Inertia Block Plunger
73	Trigger
74	Trigger Retaining Pin
75	Inertia Block Retaining Pin
76	Recoil Pad
77	Recoil Pad Screws
78	Recoil Pad Plugs
80	Buttplate
81	White Spacer
82	Buttplate Screws
83	Auto Safe Rod
84	Selective Trigger
85	Safe Button
86	Sears
87	Top Barrel Sear Lifter
88	Bottom Barrel Sear Lifter
89	Back Trigger
90	Front Trigger
91	Barrels
92	Extractors
93	Extractor Stop Pin
94	Selector
95	Selector Spring Plunger
96	Selector Spring
97	Selective Safe Button
98	Selector Retaining Pin
99	Top Barrel Sear
100	Bottom Barrel Sear
101	Selective Inertia Block

82 Over/Under Shotgun

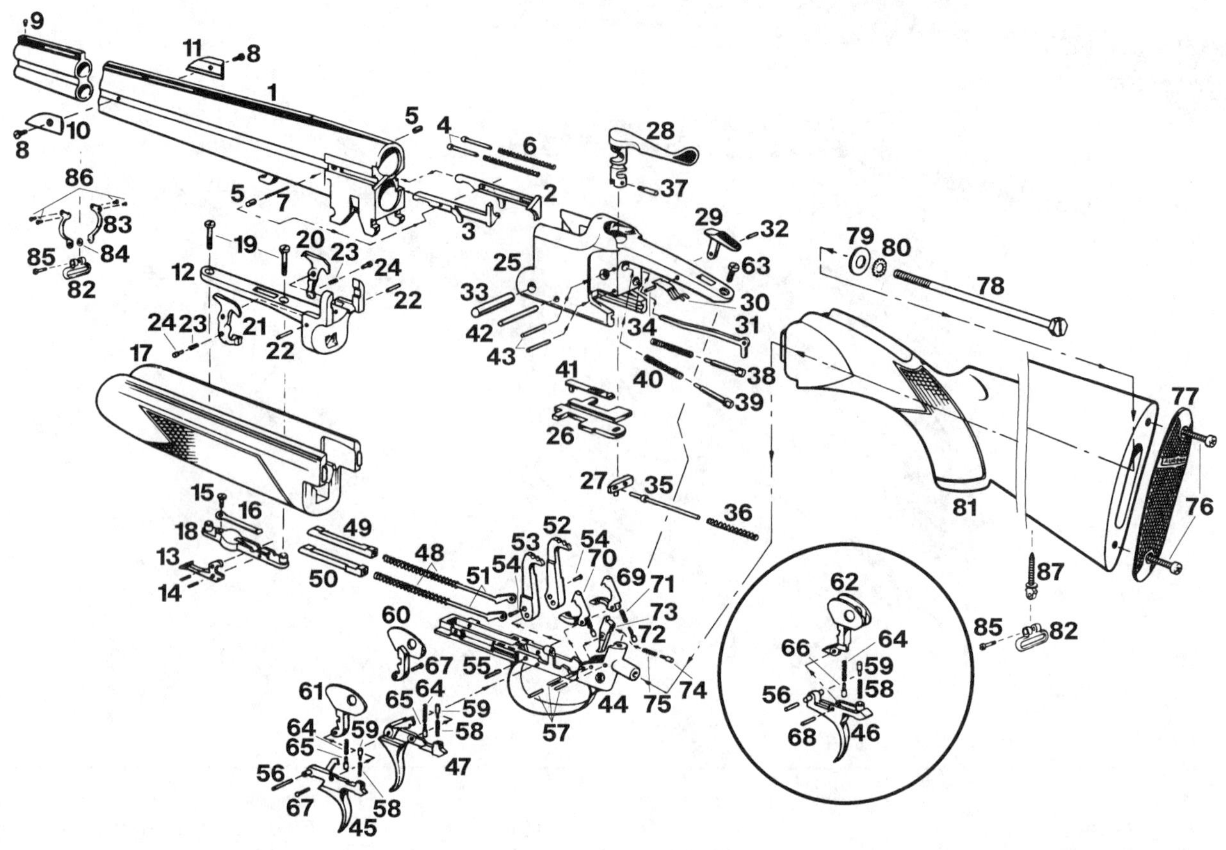

1	Barrels with Ventilated Rib
2	Right Ejector
3	Left Ejector
4	Ejector Spring Pins
5	Ejector Retaining Pins
6	Ejector Springs
7	Ejector Retainer Springs
8	Forend Plate Screws
9	Front Sight
10	Forend Plate, Left
11	Forend Plate, Right
12	Forend Bracket
13	Takedown Lever
14	Takedown Lever Latch Pins
15	Takedown Lever Latch Spring Screw
16	Takedown Lever Latch Spring
17	Forend Wood
18	Takedown Lever Latch
19	Forend Screws
20	Right Ejector Lever
21	Left Ejector Lever
22	Ejector Lever Retaining Pins
23	Ejector Lever Springs
24	Ejector Lever Plungers
25	Frame
26	Locking Plate
27	Top Lever Cam
28	Top Lever
29	Safety Catch
30	Safety Catch Spring
31	Safety Converting Rod
32	Safety Pin
33	Hinge Pin
34	Safety Spring Pin
35	Top Lever Stud Spring Guide
36	Top Lever Stud Spring
37	Top Lever Screw
38	Firing Pin, Lower Barrel
39	Firing Pin, Top Barrel
40	Firing Pin Springs
41	Locking Plate Retainer
42	Trigger Guard Pin
43	Firing Pin Retaining Pins
44	Trigger Guard
45	Rear Twin Trigger
46	Non-Selective Single Trigger
47	Front Twin Trigger
48	Trigger Springs
49	Hammer Rod Nut, Right
50	Hammer Rod Nut, Left
51	Hammer Rods
52	Hammer, Right
53	Hammer, Left
54	Hammer Rod Pins
55	Hammer Pin
56	Trigger Pin
57	Trigger Guard Pins
58	Trigger Spring, Left
59	Trigger Plunger Pin
60	Trigger Inertia Block, Right
61	Trigger Inertia Block, Left
62	Single Trigger Inertia Block
63	Tang Screw
64	Inertia Block Spring
65	Twin Trigger Inertia Block Plunger Pin
66	Single Trigger Inertia Block Plunger Pin
67	Twin Trigger Inertia Block Pins
68	Single Trigger Inertia Block Pin
69	Sear, Right
70	Sear, Left
71	Sear Spring
72	Sear Plunger
73	Safety Lever
74	Safety Lever Pin
75	Safety Lever Spring
76	Buttplate Screws
77	Buttplate
78	Buttstock Bolt
79	Buttstock Bolt Flat Washer
80	Stock Bolt Lock Washer
81	Stock
82	Barrel Band Swivels
83	Barrel Swivel Bands
84	Stock Swivel Band Spacing Washer
85	Stock Swivel Screws
86	Barrel Swivel Band Retaining Screws
87	Stock Swivel Supporting Screw

85 Over/Under Shotgun

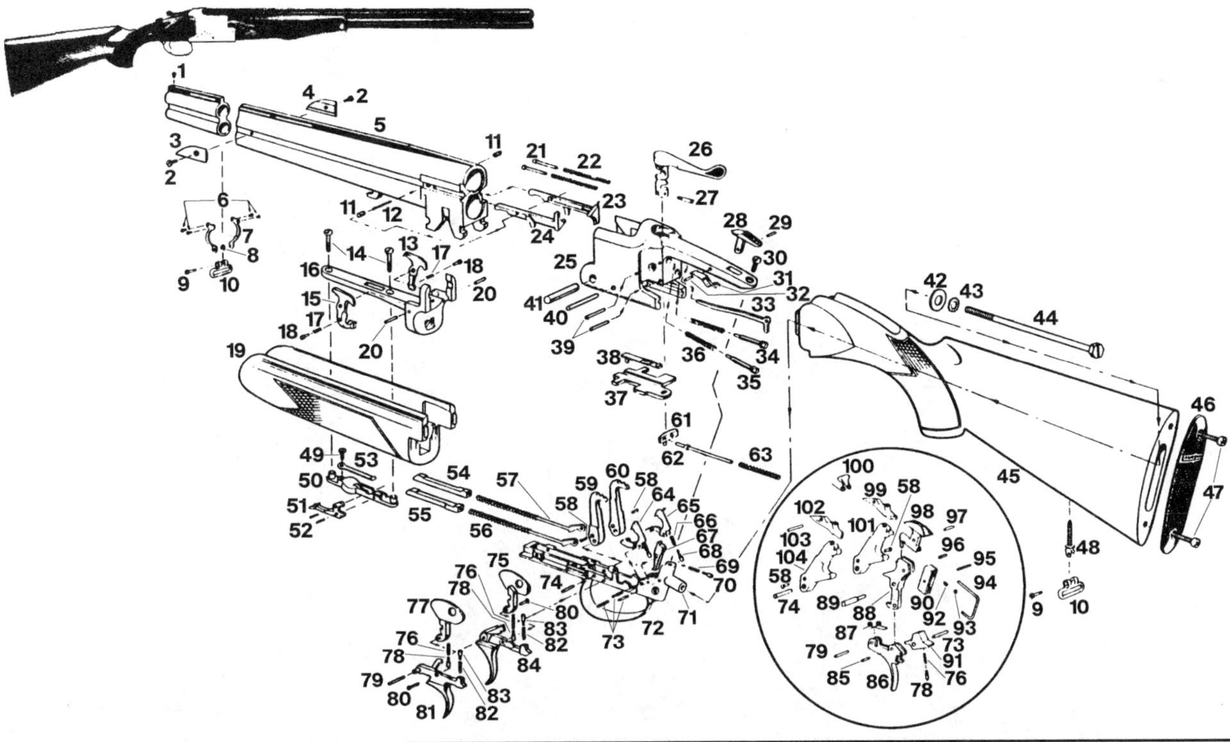

1	Front Bead Sight	36	Firing Pin Springs	71	Stock Bolt Boss
2	Barrel Plate Screws	37	Locking Block	72	Trigger Housing
3	Left Barrel Plate	38	Locking Block Slide	73	Sear and Safety Block Pins
4	Right Barrel Plate	39	Firing Pin Retaining Pins	74	Hammer Pivot Pin
5	Barrels	40	Trigger Group Pin	75	Sear Connector, Lower
6	Bracket Screws	41	Barrel Pivot Pin	76	Sear Connector Springs
7	Swivel Brackets	42	Stock Bolt Washer	77	Sear Connector, Upper
8	Swivel Washer	43	Stock Bolt Lock Washer	78	Sear Connector Spring Plunger
9	Swivel Screws	44	Stock Bolt	79	Trigger Pivot Pin
10	Sling Swivels	45	Stock	80	Sear Connector Pin
11	Ejector Retainers	46	Buttplate	81	Upper Trigger
12	Retainer Spring	47	Buttplate Screws	82	Trigger Springs
13	Right Ejector Hammer	48	Sling Swivel Stud	83	Trigger Spring Plungers
14	Forend Iron Screws	49	Forend Release Latch Spring Screw	84	Lower Trigger
15	Left Ejector Hammer	50	Forend Release Housing	85	Inertia Block Pivot
16	Forend Iron	51	Forend Release Lever	86	Single Selective Trigger
17	Ejector Hammer Plunger Springs	52	Forend Release Lever Pins	87	Trigger Spring
18	Ejector Hammer Plungers	53	Forend Release Lever Spring	88	Inertia Block
19	Forend Wood	54	Right Hammer Spring Seat	89	Inertia Block Shaft
20	Ejector Hammer Pivot Pins	55	Left Hammer Spring Seat	90	Inertia Block Collar
21	Ejector Tip Rods	56	Hammer Springs	91	Safety Block
22	Ejector Trip Rod Springs	57	Hammer Spring Guides	92	Block Collar Spring
23	Top Ejector	58	Hammer Spring Guide Pins	93	Spring Ball
24	Bottom Ejector	59	Upper Hammer	94	Safety Retainer
25	Receiver	60	Lower Hammer	95	Collar Pin
26	Top Lever	61	Locking Block Lever	96	Connector Pin
27	Top Lever Retaining Pin	62	Block Lever Spring Guide	97	Safety Button Pin
28	Safety Button	63	Block Lever Spring	98	Safety Button/Barrel Selector
29	Safety Button Pin	64	Lower Hammer Sear	99	Sear, Lower
30	Top Tang Screw	65	Upper Hammer Sear	100	Sear Spring
31	Safety Button Spring	66	Sear Springs	101	Lower Hammer
32	Safety Button Spring Pin	67	Safety Block	102	Sear, Upper
33	Barrel Selector Rod	68	Sear Spring Plungers	103	Sear Pivot
34	Lower Firing Pin	69	Safety Block Plunger Spring	104	Upper Hammer
35	Upper Firing Pin	70	Safety Block Plunger		

Double Side-by-Side Shotgun

Courtesy of Thomas E. Wessel

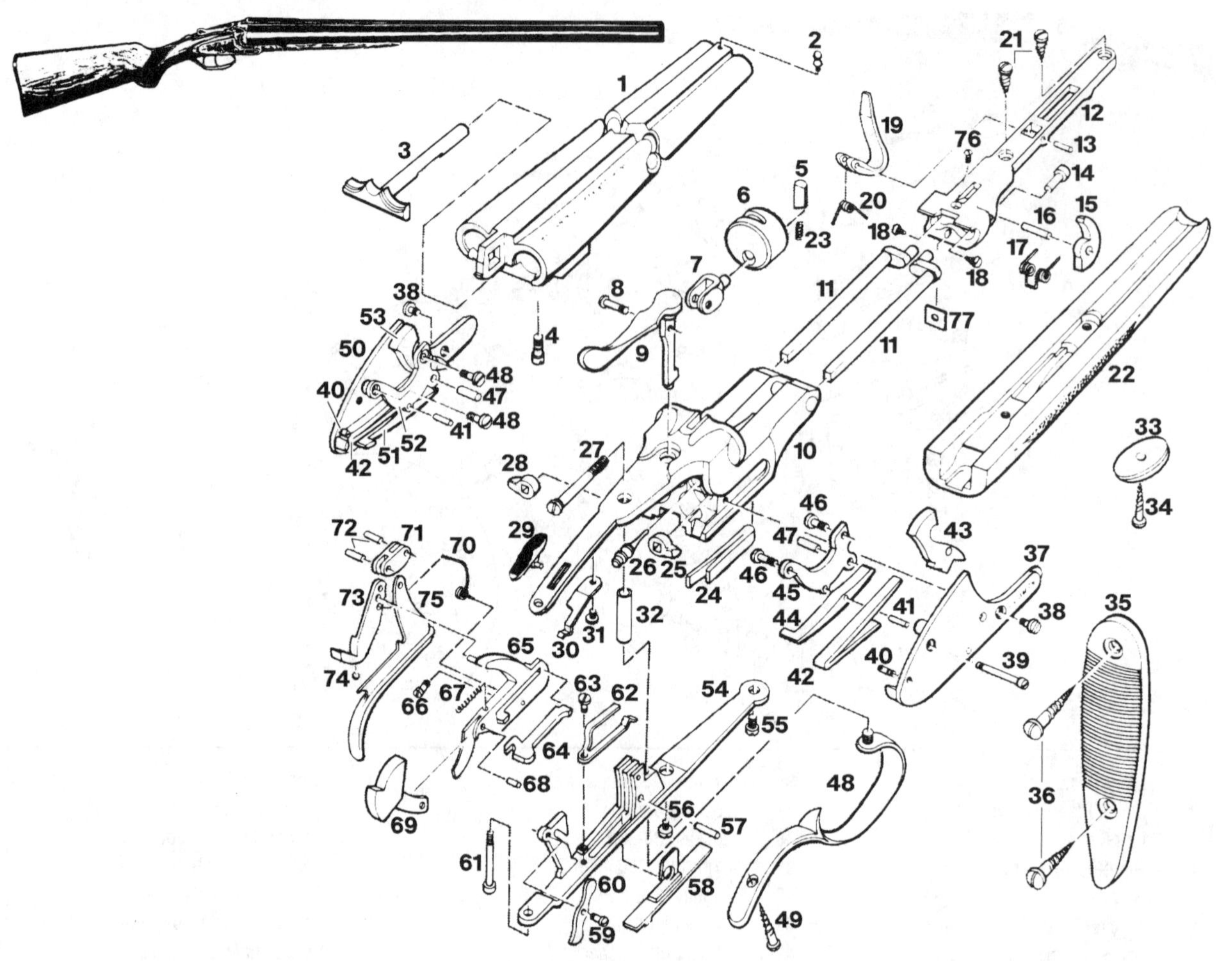

1	Barrel	**28**	Left Lifter	**55**	Trigger Plate Retaining Screw, Front
2	Front Sight	**29**	Safety Button and Pin	**56**	Top-Lever Screw
3	Extractor	**30**	Safety Spring	**57**	Trigger Pin
4	Extractor Screw	**31**	Safety Spring Screw	**58**	Selector
5	Trip	**32**	Trigger Plate Screw Bushing	**59**	Safety Stud Screw
6	Bolt	**33**	Grip Cap	**60**	Safety Stud
7	Coupler	**34**	Grip Cap Screw	**61**	Trigger Plate Retaining Screw, Rear
8	Coupler Screw	**35**	Buttplate	**62**	Selector Spring
9	Top-Lever	**36**	Buttplate Screws	**63**	Selector Spring Screw
10	Frame	**37**	Lockplate, Right	**64**	Sear Plate
11	Cocking Rods	**38**	Lockplate Retaining Screws	**65**	Firing Plate
12	Forend Iron	**39**	Lockplate Connector Screw	**66**	Spur Spring Screw
13	Forend Spring Pin	**40**	Mainspring Retaining Screw	**67**	Recoil Weight Spring
14	Extractor Actuator Bar	**41**	Sear Pins	**68**	Recoil Weight Pin
15	Extractor Actuator	**42**	Mainsprings	**69**	Recoil Weight
16	Extractor Actuator Pin	**43**	Hammer, Right	**70**	Spur Spring
17	Extractor Actuator Spring	**44**	Sear, Right	**71**	Spur Link
18	Rear Forend Screws	**45**	Bridle, Right	**72**	Spur Link Pins
19	Forend Spring	**46**	Bridle Screws	**73**	Spur
20	Forend Spring Retracting Spring	**47**	Hammer Pins	**74**	Spur Ball
21	Forend Screws	**48**	Trigger Guard	**75**	Trigger
22	Forend	**49**	Trigger Guard Screw	**76**	Cocking Plate Screw
23	Trip Spring	**50**	Lockplate, Left	**77**	Cocking Plate
24	Bolt Spring	**51**	Sear, Left	**Parts Not Shown**	
25	Right Lifter	**52**	Bridle, Left		Stock
26	Firing Pins	**53**	Hammer, Left		
27	Trigger Plate Screw	**54**	Trigger Plate		

Straight-Pull Single Shot Rifle

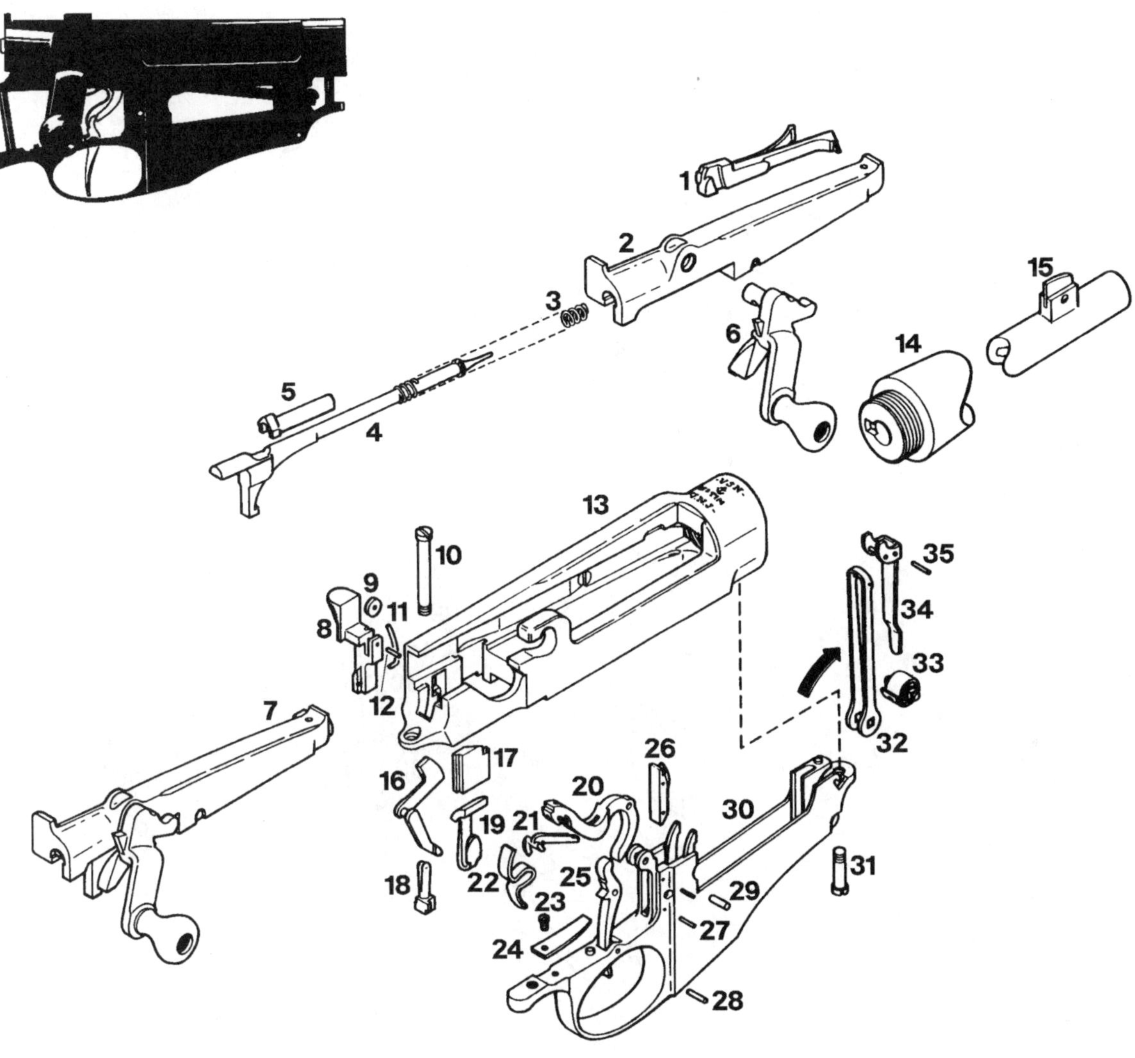

1	Extractor	19	Bolt Stop Thumb-Piece
2	Bolt Body	20	Sear
3	Firing Pin Spring	21	Sear Fly
4	Firing Pin	22	Sear Spring
5	Firing Pin Collar	23	Trigger Spring Screw
6	Bolt Handle	24	Trigger Spring
7	Bolt Assembly	25	Trigger
8	Safety Thumb-Piece	26	Clip Guide
9	Bolt Stop Roller	27	Clip Guide Rivets
10	Rear Action Screw	28	Trigger Pin
11	Bolt Stop Spring	29	Sear Axis Pin
12	Bolt Stop Pin	30	Trigger Guard
13	Receiver	31	Trigger Guard Screw
14	Barrel	32	Elevator Arm
15	Front Sight Blade	33	Elevator Spring
16	Bolt Stop Release	34	Follower
17	Bolt Stop	35	Follower/Elevator Pin
18	Lock Pin		

Model 1958 Bolt-Action Rifle

Courtesy of Dennis Riordan

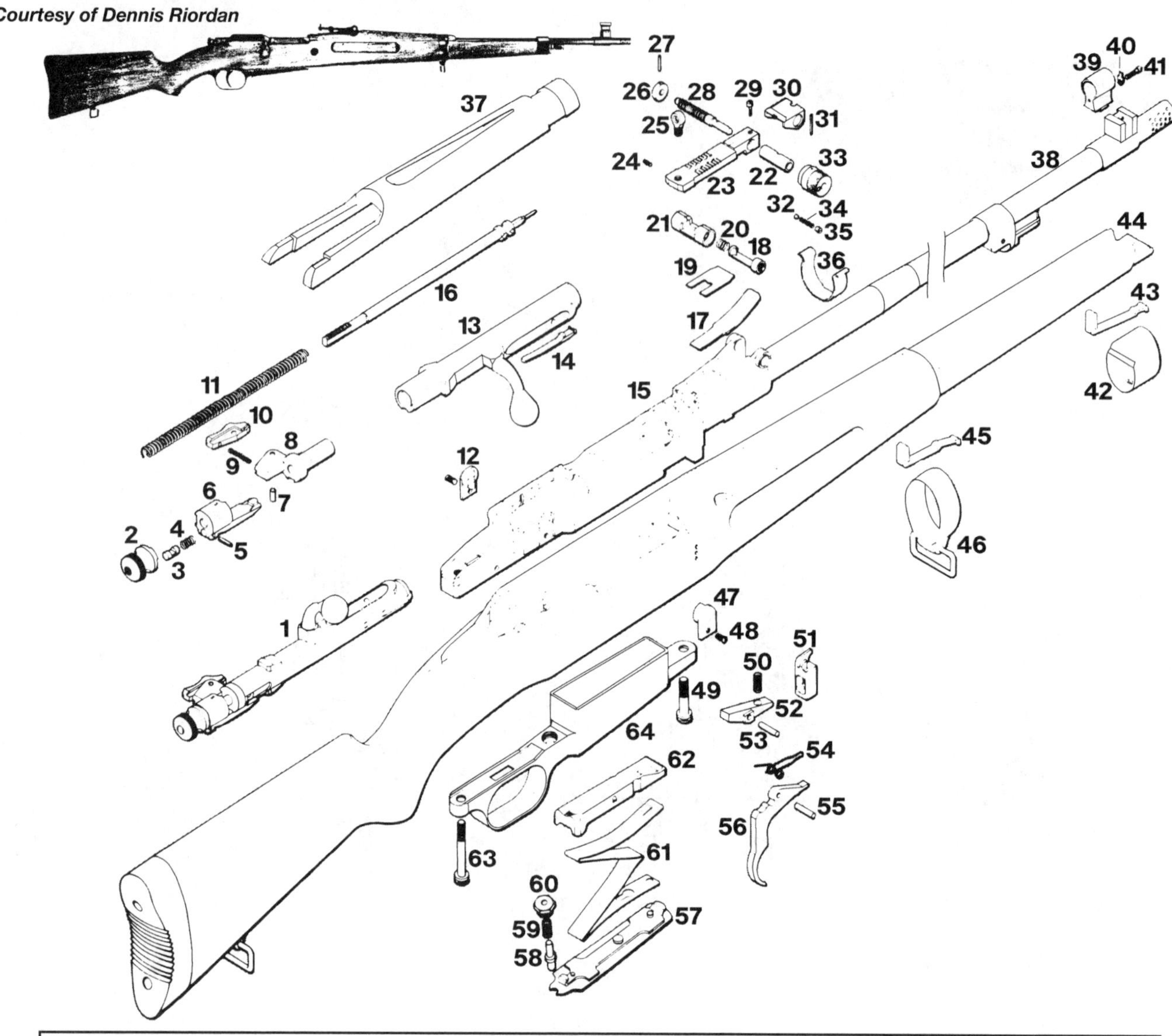

1	Assembled Bolt	**23**	Sight Leaf	**45**	Lower Band Spring
2	Firing Pin Nut	**24**	Aperture Set Screw	**46**	Lower Band
3	Nut Retainer	**25**	Aperture	**47**	Right Locking Seat
4	Nut Retainer Spring	**26**	Windage Screw Flange	**48**	Locking Seat Screws
5	Nut Retainer Pin	**27**	Flange Pin	**49**	Front Guard Screw
6	Cocking Piece	**28**	Windage Screw	**50**	Sear Spring
7	Safety Catch Pin	**29**	Leaf Bushing Lock Screw	**51**	Ejector Bolt Stop
8	Safety	**30**	Windage Scale	**52**	Sear
9	Safety Catch Spring	**31**	Windage Knob Pin	**53**	Sear Pin
10	Safety Catch	**32**	Windage Index Ball	**54**	Ejector Spring
11	Firing Pin Spring	**33**	Windage Knob	**55**	Trigger Pin
12	Left Locking Seat	**34**	Index Spring	**56**	Trigger
13	Bolt	**35**	Index Spring Plug	**57**	Magazine Floorplate
14	Extractor	**36**	Handguard Clamp	**58**	Floorplate Catch
15	Receiver	**37**	Handguard	**59**	Floorplate Catch Spring
16	Firing Pin	**38**	Barrel	**60**	Floorplate Catch Guide Bushing
17	Rear Sight Leaf Spring	**39**	Front Sight Hood	**61**	Magazine Spring
18	Sight Slide Catch	**40**	Sight Post	**62**	Magazine Follower
19	Left Spring Keeper	**41**	Sight Post Lock Screw	**63**	Rear Guard Screw
20	Sight Slide Spring	**42**	Upper Band	**64**	Trigger Guard
21	Sight Slide	**43**	Upper Band Spring		
22	Sight Leaf Bushing	**44**	Stock		

Model 1903, 1905, 1908 and 1910 Bolt-Action Rifle

Courtesy of Blacksmith Corporation

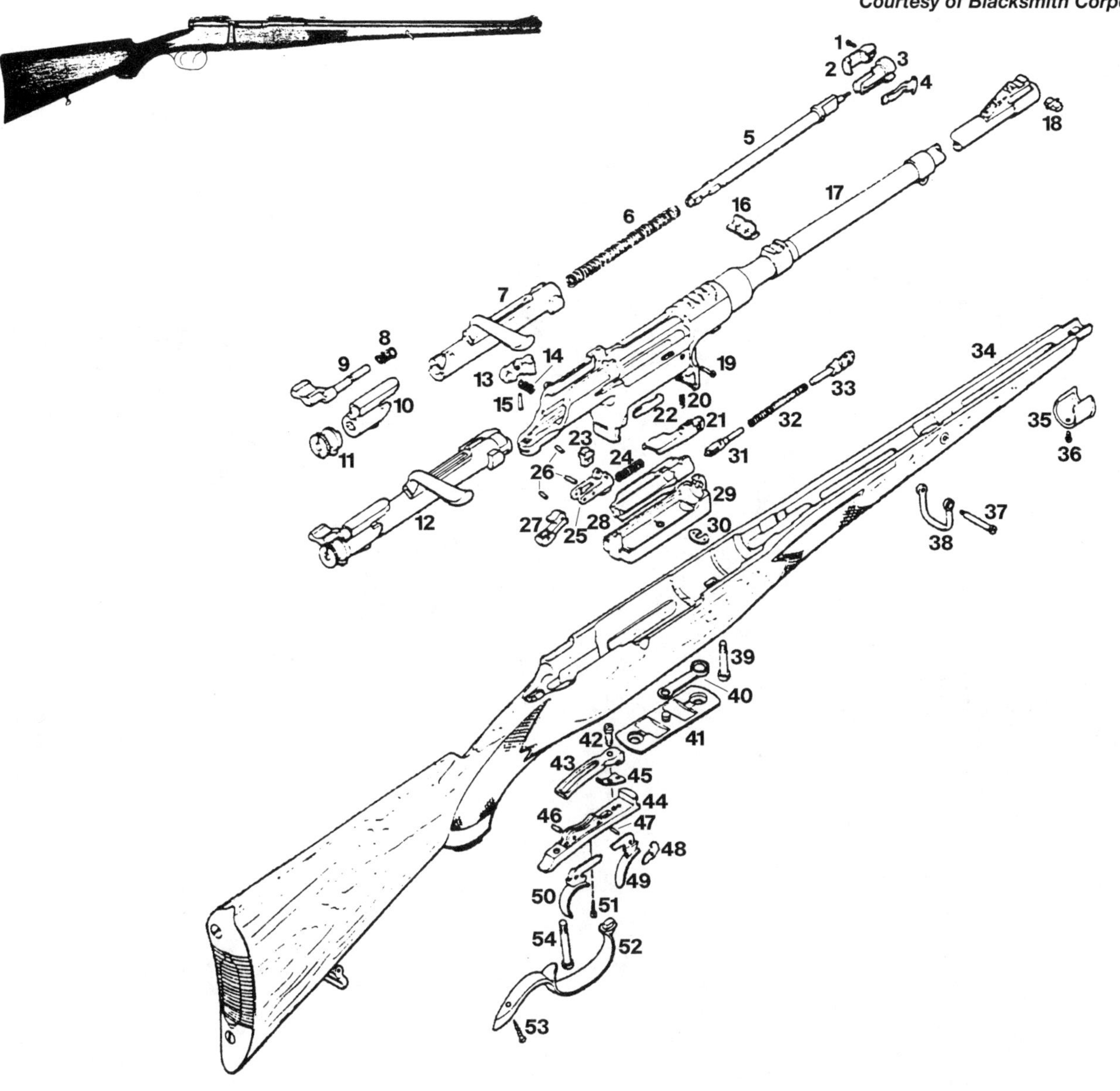

1	Ejector Screw	**19**	Cartridge Stop Screw	**37**	Front Swivel Screw
2	Ejector	**20**	Cartridge Stop Spring	**38**	Front Swivel
3	Bolt Head	**21**	Cartridge Stop	**39**	Front Receiver Screw
4	Extractor	**22**	Bolt Tension Spring	**40**	Floorplate Spring
5	Firing Pin	**23**	Sear	**41**	Floorplate
6	Firing Pin Spring	**24**	Sear Spring	**42**	Set Trigger Mainspring Screw
7	Bolt	**25**	Sear Carrier	**43**	Set Trigger Mainspring
8	Safety Catch Spring	**26**	Sear Pins	**44**	Set Trigger Housing
9	Safety Catch	**27**	Trigger Connection	**45**	Set Trigger Sear Spring
10	Cocking Piece	**28**	Magazine Follower	**46**	Trigger Pin, Rear
11	Firing Pin Nut	**29**	Magazine Box	**47**	Trigger Pin, Front
12	Bolt	**30**	Floorplate Spring Retainer	**48**	Trigger Sear
13	Bolt Stop	**31**	Rear Magazine Bearing	**49**	Front Trigger
14	Bolt Stop Spring	**32**	Magazine Spring	**50**	Rear Trigger
15	Bolt Stop Pin	**33**	Front Magazine Bearing	**51**	Adjusting Screw
16	Rear Sight	**34**	Carbine Stock	**52**	Trigger Guard
17	Barrel and Receiver	**35**	Forend Cap	**53**	Trigger Guard Screw
18	Front Sight	**36**	Forend Cap Screw	**54**	Rear Receiver Screw

Model 10 Bolt-Action Rifle

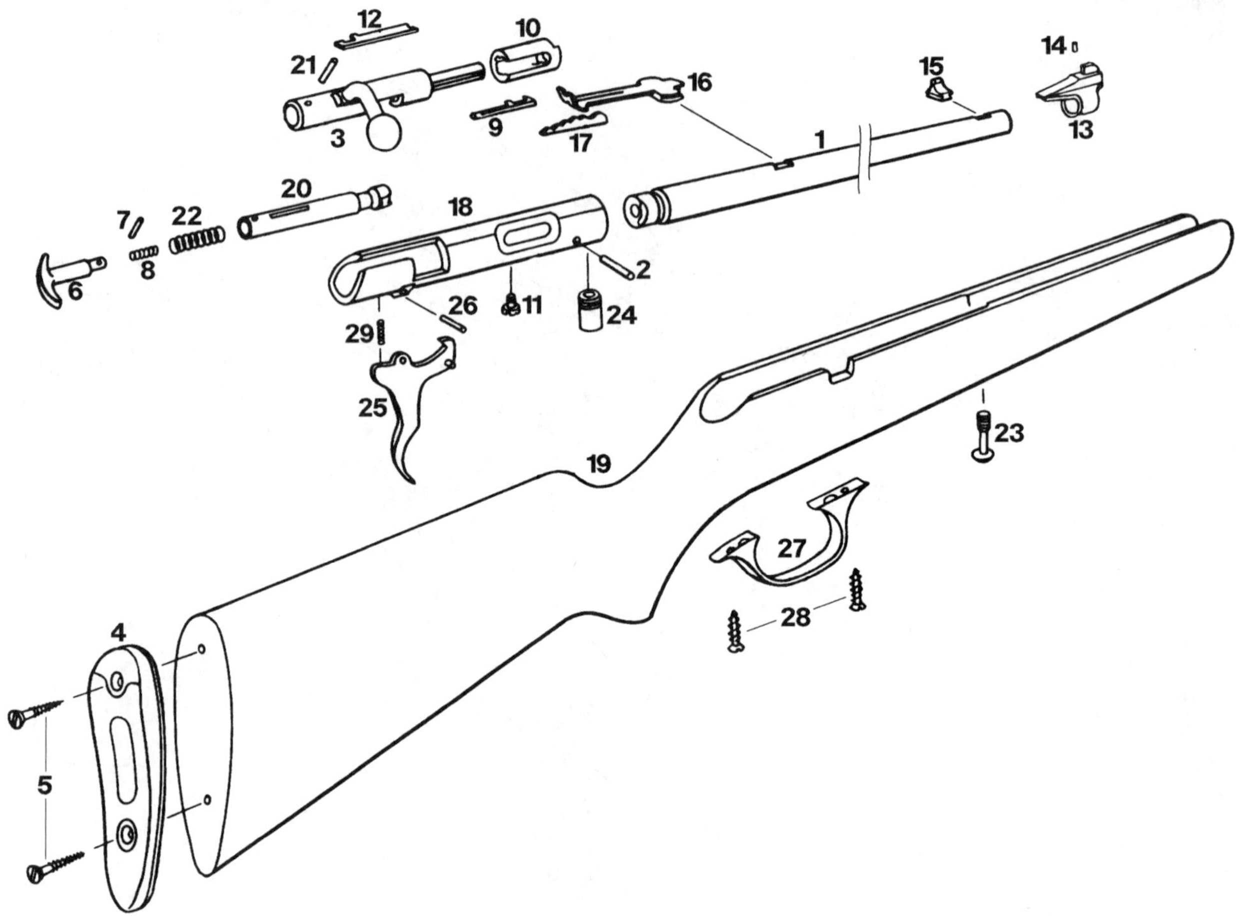

1	Barrel	**16**	Rear Sight with Elevator
2	Barrel Retaining Pin	**17**	Rear Sight Elevator
3	Breechbolt	**18**	Receiver
4	Buttplate	**19**	Stock
5	Buttplate Screws	**20**	Striker
6	Cocking Knob	**21**	Striker Pin
7	Cocking Knob Pin	**22**	Striker Spring
8	Cocking Knob Spring	**23**	Takedown Screw
9	Extractor	**24**	Takedown Screw Stud
10	Feed Throat	**25**	Trigger
11	Feed Throat Screw	**26**	Trigger Pin
12	Firing Pin	**27**	Trigger Guard
13	Front Sight Complete	**28**	Trigger Guard Screws
14	Front Sight Binding Screw	**29**	Trigger Spring
15	Front Sight		

Model 101 and Glenfield 10 Bolt-Action Rifle

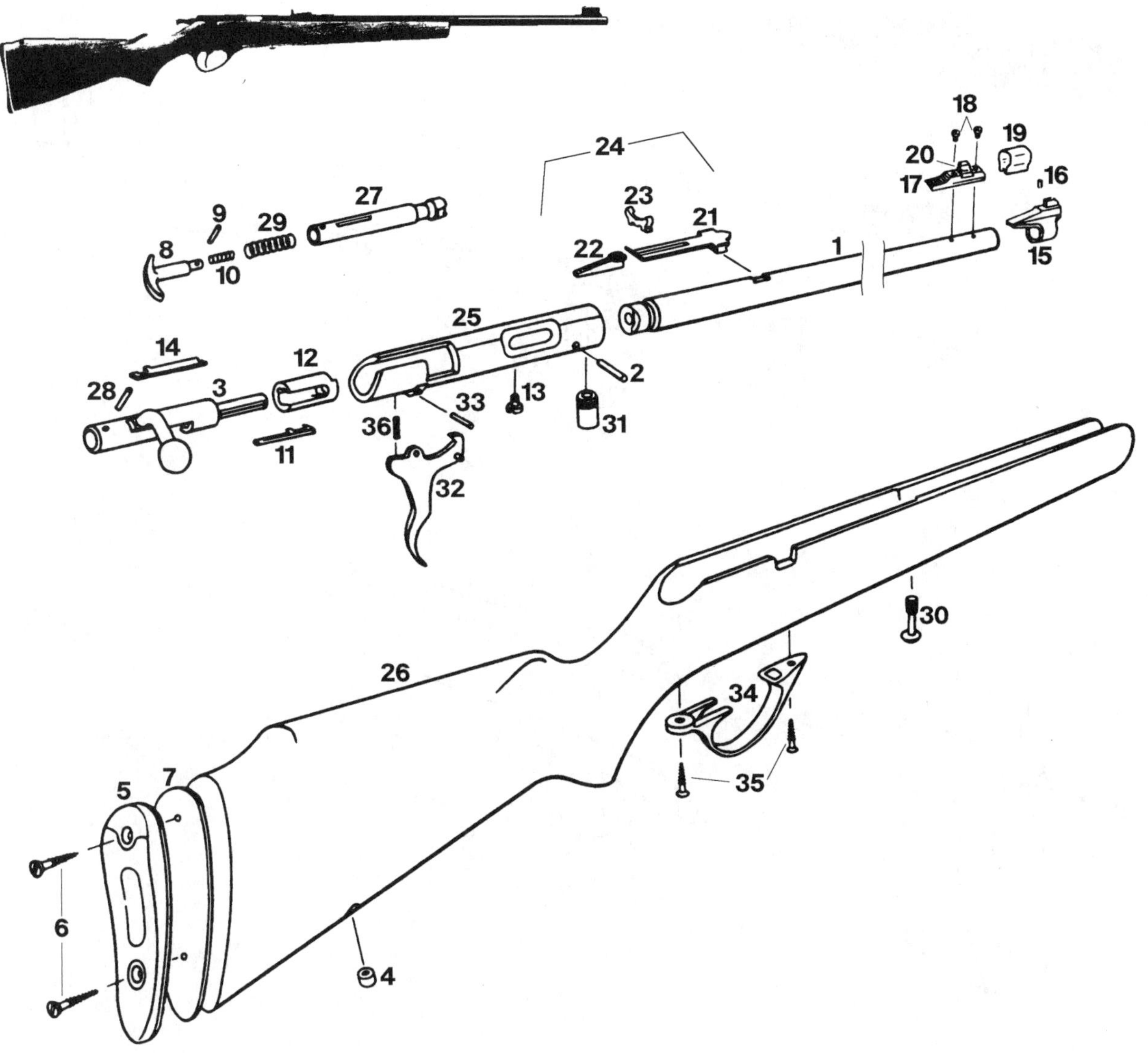

1	Barrel	**13**	Feed Throat Screw	**25**	Receiver
2	Barrel Retaining Pin	**14**	Firing Pin	**26**	Stock
3	Breech Bolt	**15**	Front Sight	**27**	Striker
4	Bullseye	**16**	Front Sight Binding Screw	**28**	Striker Pin
5	Buttplate with Spacer	**17**	Front Sight Base	**29**	Striker Spring
6	Buttplate Screws	**18**	Front Sight Base Screws	**30**	Takedown Screw
7	Buttplate Spacer	**19**	Front Sight Hood	**31**	Takedown Screw Stud
8	Cocking Knob	**20**	Front Sight Insert	**32**	Trigger
9	Cocking Knob Pin	**21**	Rear Sight Base	**33**	Trigger Pin
10	Cocking Knob Spring	**22**	Rear Sight Elevator	**34**	Trigger Guard
11	Extractor	**23**	Rear Sight Folding Leaf	**35**	Trigger Guard Screws
12	Feed Throat	**24**	Rear Sight Complete	**36**	Trigger Spring

Model 15YN Little Buckaroo Bolt-Action Rifle

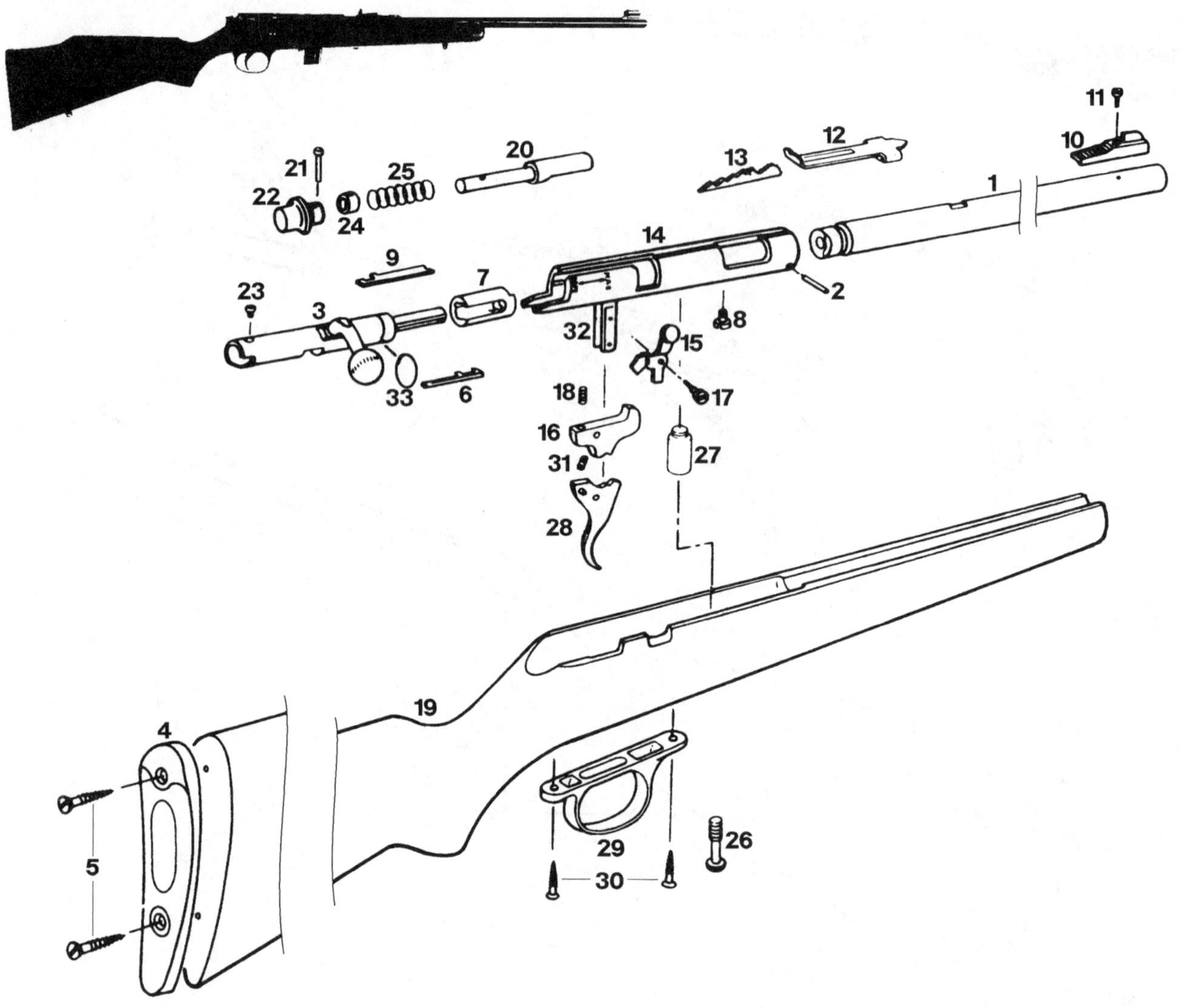

1	Barrel	18	Sear Spring
2	Barrel Retaining Pin	19	Stock
3	Breechbolt	20	Striker
4	Buttplate	21	Striker Cam Pin
5	Buttplate Screws	22	Striker Knob
6	Extractor	23	Striker Retaining Screw
7	Feed Throat	24	Striker Sleeve
8	Feed Throat Screw	25	Striker Spring
9	Firing Pin	26	Takedown Screw
10	Front Sight	27	Takedown Screw Stud
11	Front Sight Screw	28	Trigger
12	Rear Sight Complete	29	Trigger Guard
13	Rear Sight Elevator	30	Trigger Guard Screws
14	Receiver	31	Trigger Spring
15	Safety Assembly	32	Trigger Stud
16	Sear	33	Firing Pin Retaining Spring
17	Sear and Safety Pivot Screw		

Model 1881 Lever-Action Rifle

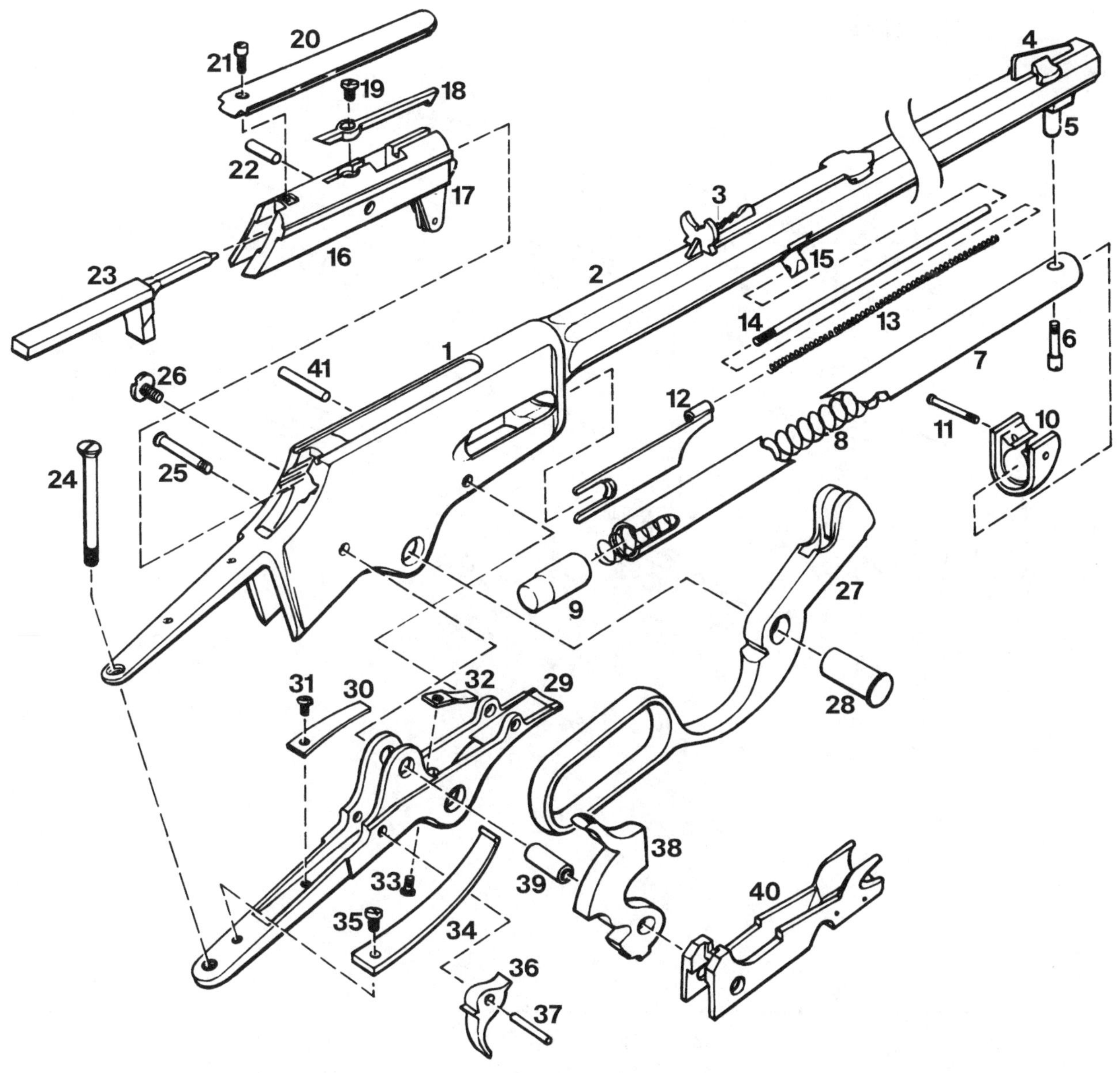

1	Receiver	**17**	Ejector	**33**	Lever Spring Screw
2	Barrel	**18**	Extractor	**34**	Mainspring
3	Rear Sight Assembly	**19**	Extractor Screw	**35**	Mainspring Screw
4	Front Sight	**20**	Dust Cover	**36**	Trigger
5	Magazine Tube Stud	**21**	Dust Cover Screw	**37**	Trigger Pin
6	Magazine Tube Stud Screw	**22**	Firing Pin Retaining Pin	**38**	Hammer
7	Magazine Tube	**23**	Firing Pin	**39**	Hammer Bushing
8	Magazine Spring	**24**	Tang Screw	**40**	Carrier Block Assembly
9	Magazine Follower	**25**	Hammer Screw	**41**	Trigger Strap Pin
10	Forend Tip	**26**	Lever Pin Screw	**Parts Not Shown**	
11	Forend Tip Screw	**27**	Lever		Buttstock
12	Loading Port Cover	**28**	Lever Pin		Buttplate
13	Cover Spring	**29**	Trigger Strap		Buttplate Screws
14	Cover Spring Guide	**30**	Trigger Spring		Forend
15	Cover Spring Abutment	**31**	Trigger Spring Screw		
16	Bolt	**32**	Lever Spring		

Model 1894, 1894C, 1894CS and 1894S Lever-Action Carbine

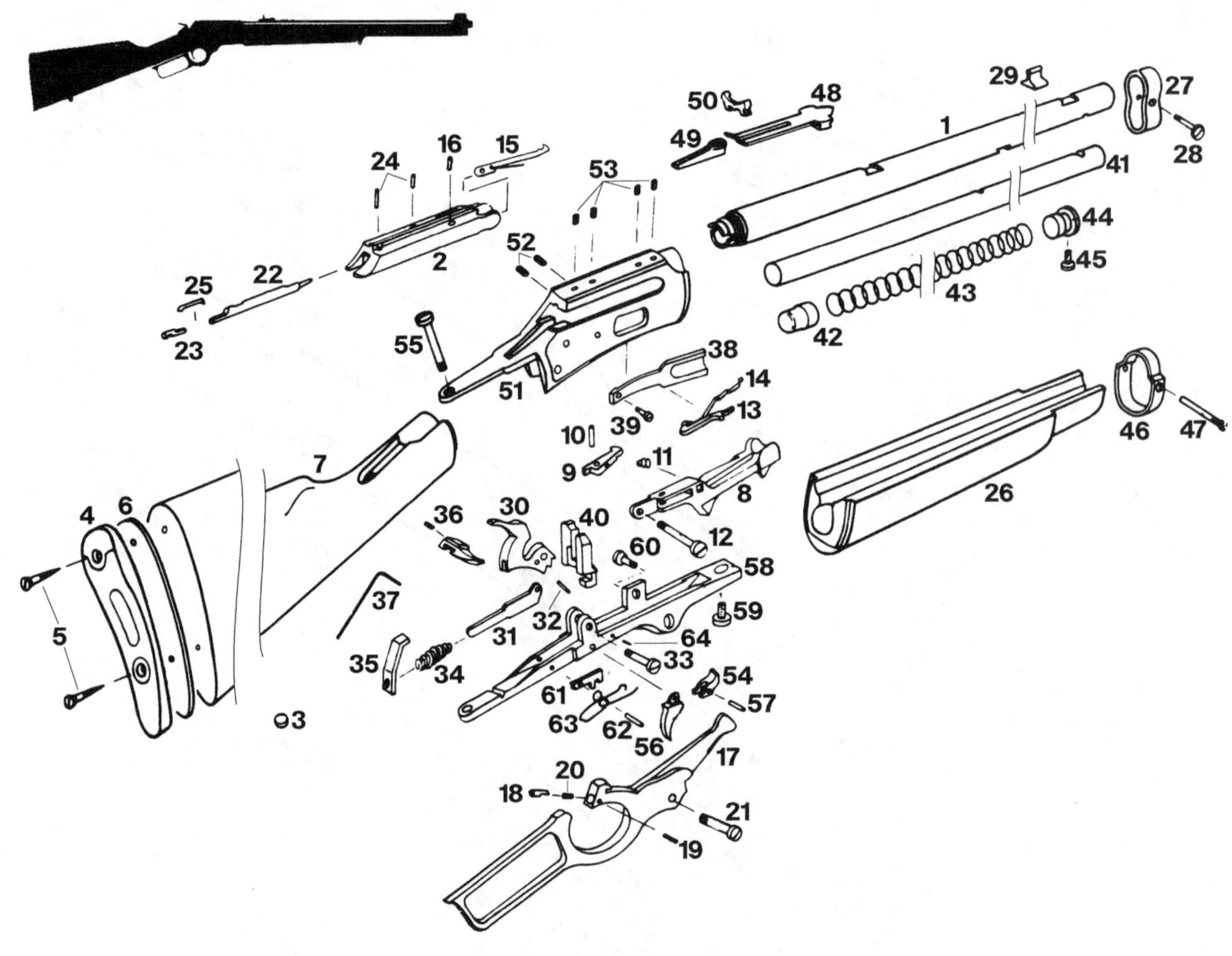

1	Barrel
2	Breechbolt
3	Bullseye
4	Buttplate
5	Buttplate Screws
6	Buttplate Spacer
7	Buttstock Complete
8	Carrier
9	Carrier Rocker
10	Carrier Rocker Pin
11	Carrier Rocker Spring
12	Carrier Screw
13	Ejector
14	Ejector Spring
15	Extractor with Spring
16	Extractor Retaining Pin
17	Finger Lever
18	Finger Lever Plunger
19	Finger Lever Plunger Pin
20	Finger Lever Plunger Spring
21	Finger Lever Screw
22	Firing Pin, Front
23	Firing Pin, Rear
24	Firing Pin Retaining Pins
25	Firing Pin Spring
26	Forearm
27	Front Band
28	Front Band Screw
29	Front Sight with Brass Bead
30	Hammer
31	Hammer Strut
32	Hammer Strut Pin
33	Hammer Screw
34	Hammer Spring
35	Hammer Spring Adjusting Plate
36	Hammer Spur Screw
37	Hammer Spur Wrench
38	Loading Spring
39	Loading Spring Screw
40	Locking Bolt
41	Magazine Tube
42	Magazine Tube Follower
43	Magazine Tube Follower Spring
44	Magazine Tube Plug
45	Magazine Tube Plug Screw
46	Rear Band
47	Rear Band Screw
48	Rear Sight Base
49	Rear Sight Elevator
50	Rear Sight Folding Leaf
51	Receiver
52	Peep Sight Dummy Screws
53	Scope Mount Dummy Screws
54	Sear
55	Tang Screw
56	Trigger
57	Trigger and Sear Pin
58	Trigger Guard Plate
59	Trigger Guard Plate Screw
60	Trigger Guard Plate Support Screw
61	Trigger Safety Block
62	Trigger Safety Block Pin
63	Trigger Safety Block Spring
64	Trigger Guard Plate Latch Pin

Model 1894M Lever-Action Rifle

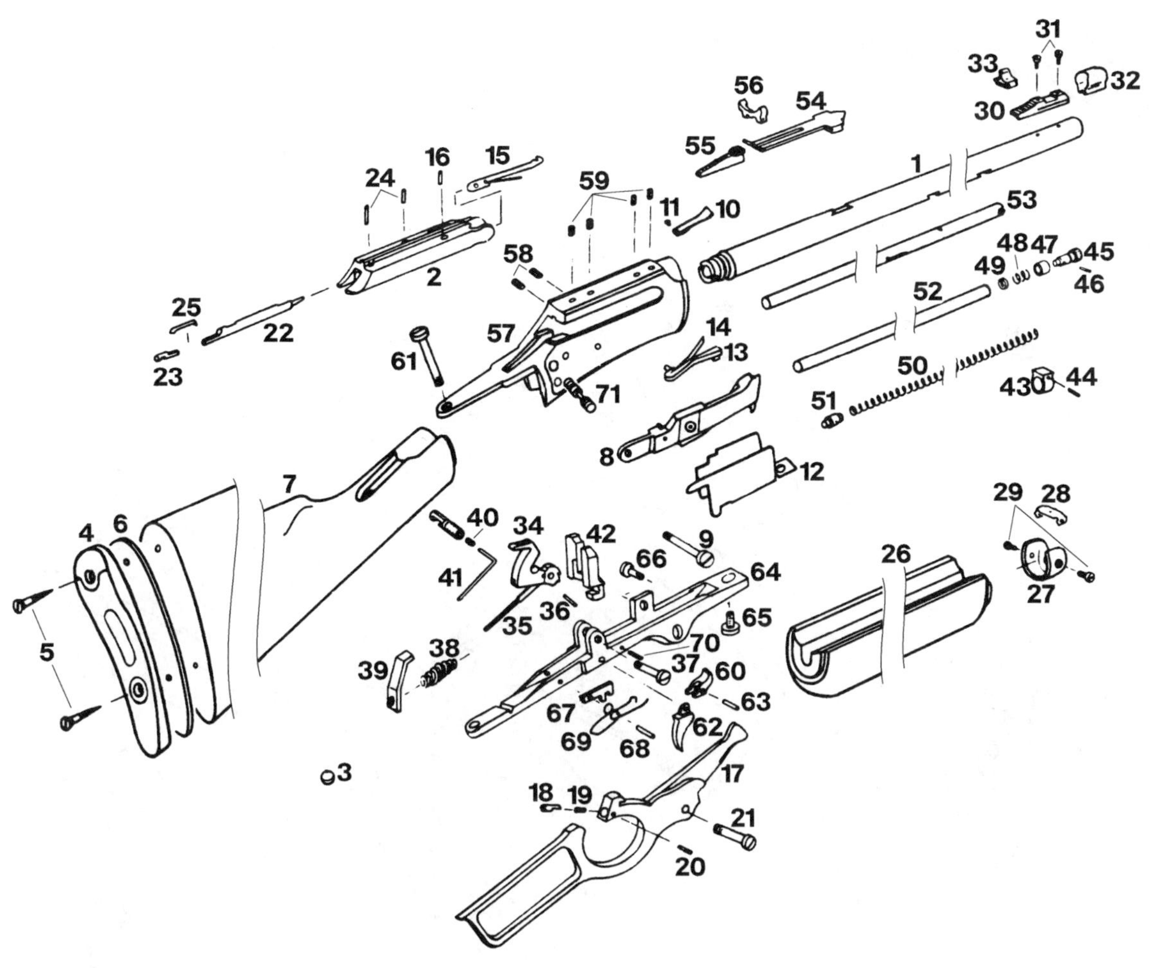

1	Barrel	**25**	Firing Pin Spring	**49**	Magazine Tube Plug Bushing
2	Breechbolt	**26**	Forearm	**50**	Magazine Tube Spring
3	Bullseye	**27**	Forearm Tip	**51**	Magazine Tube Follower
4	Buttplate with Spacer	**28**	Forearm Tip Tenon	**52**	Inside Magazine Tube
5	Buttplate Screws	**29**	Forearm Tip Tenon Screws	**53**	Outside Magazine Tube
6	Buttplate Spacer	**30**	Front Sight Ramp Base	**54**	Rear Sight Base
7	Buttstock Assembly	**31**	Front Sight Ramp Base Screws	**55**	Rear Sight Elevator
8	Carrier Assembly	**32**	Front Sight Ramp Hood	**56**	Rear Sight Folding Leaf
9	Carrier Screw	**33**	Front Sight Ramp Insert	**57**	Receiver
10	Cartridge Guide, Upper	**34**	Hammer	**58**	Peep Sight Dummy Screws
11	Cartridge Guide Screw, Upper	**35**	Hammer Strut	**59**	Scope Mount Dummy Screws
12	Cartridge Guide, Inner	**36**	Hammer Strut Pin	**60**	Sear
13	Ejector	**37**	Hammer Screw	**61**	Tang Screw
14	Ejector Spring	**38**	Mainspring	**62**	Trigger
15	Extractor with Spring	**39**	Hammer Spring Adjusting Plate	**63**	Trigger and Sear Pin
16	Extractor Retaining Pin	**40**	Hammer Spur Screw	**64**	Trigger Guard Plate
17	Finger Lever	**41**	Hammer Spur Wrench	**65**	Trigger Guard Plate Screw
18	Finger Lever Plunger	**42**	Locking Bolt	**66**	Trigger Guard Plate Support Screw
19	Finger Lever Plunger Spring	**43**	Magazine Tube Band	**67**	Trigger Safety Block
20	Finger Lever Plunger Pin	**44**	Magazine Tube Band Pin	**68**	Trigger Safety Block Pin
21	Finger Lever Screw	**45**	Magazine Tube Plug	**69**	Trigger Safety Block Spring
22	Firing Pin, Front	**46**	Magazine Tube Plug Pin	**70**	Trigger Guard Plate Latch Pin
23	Firing Pin, Rear	**47**	Magazine Tube Plug Cap	**71**	Safety Button Assembly
24	Firing Pin, Retaining Pins	**48**	Magazine Tube Plug Spring		

Model 1895 Lever-Action Rifle

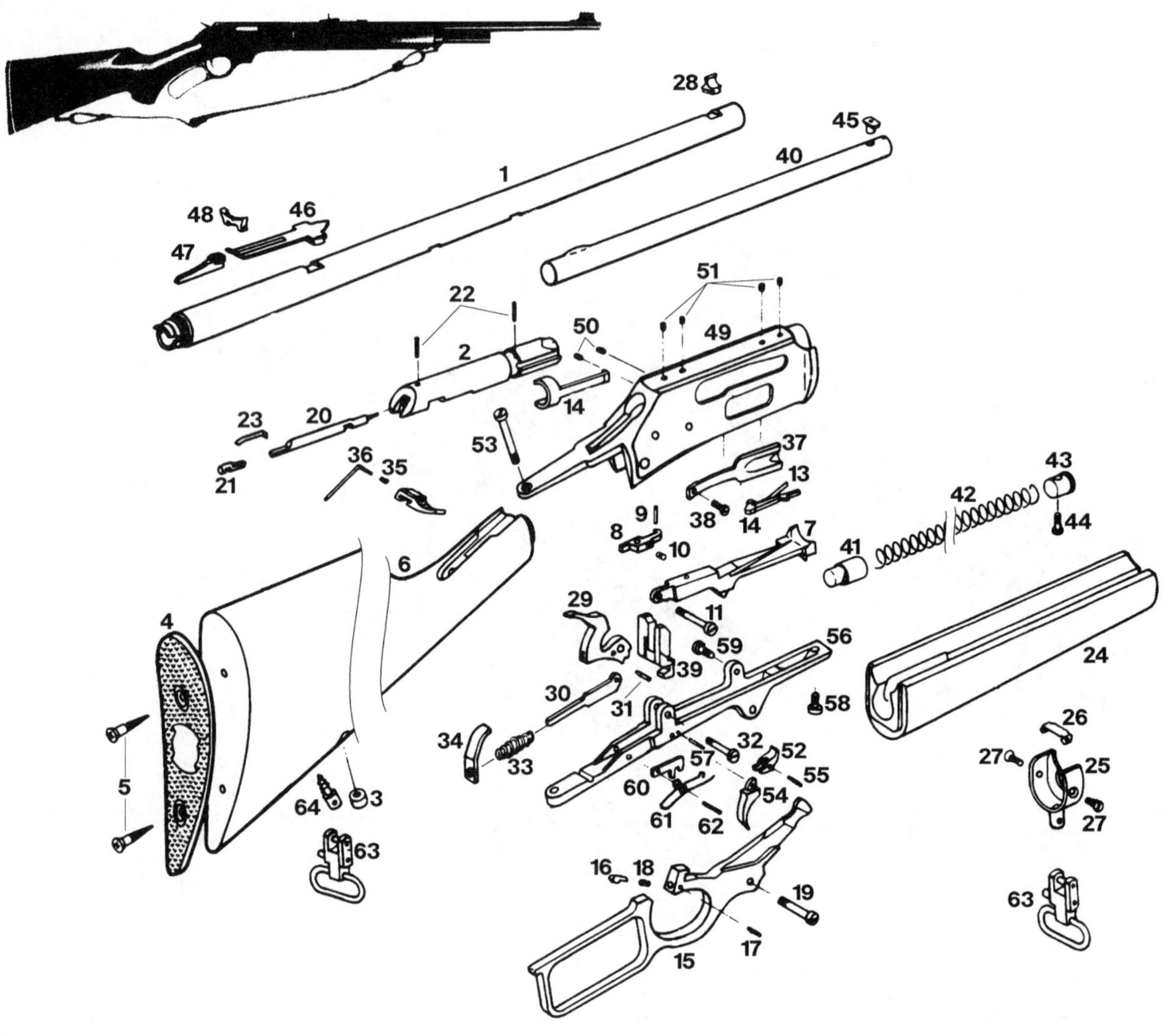

1	Barrel
2	Breechbolt
3	Bullseye
4	Buttplate
5	Buttplate Screws
6	Buttstock Complete
7	Carrier
8	Carrier Rocker
9	Carrier Rocker Pin
10	Carrier Rocker Spring
11	Carrier Screw
12	Ejector
13	Ejector Spring
14	Extractor
15	Finger Lever
16	Finger Lever Plunger
17	Finger Lever Plunger Pin
18	Finger Lever Plunger Spring
19	Finger Lever Screw
20	Firing Pin, Front
21	Firing Pin, Rear
22	Firing Pin Retaining Pins
23	Firing Pin Spring
24	Forearm
25	Forearm Tip with Swivel Stud
26	Forearm Tip Tenon
27	Forearm Tip Tenon Screws
28	Front Sight with Brass Bead
29	Hammer
30	Hammer Strut
31	Hammer Strut Pin
32	Hammer Screw
33	Mainspring
34	Hammer Spring Adjusting Plate
35	Hammer Spur Screw
36	Hammer Spur Wrench
37	Loading Spring
38	Loading Spring Screw
39	Locking Bolt
40	Magazine Tube
41	Magazine Tube Follower
42	Magazine Tube Follower Spring
43	Magazine Tube Plug
44	Magazine Tube Plug Screw
45	Magazine Tube Stud
46	Rear Sight Base
47	Rear Sight Elevator
48	Rear Sight Folding Leaf
49	Receiver
50	Peep Sight Dummy Screws
51	Scope Mount Dummy Screws
52	Sear
53	Tang Screw
54	Trigger
55	Trigger and Sear Pin
56	Trigger Guard Plate
57	Trigger Guard Plate Latch Pin
58	Trigger Guard Plate Screw
59	Trigger Guard Plate Support Screw
60	Trigger Safety Block
61	Trigger Safety Spring
62	Trigger Safety Block Pin
63	Swivels
64	Swivel Stud

Model 1895S and 1895SS Lever-Action Rifle

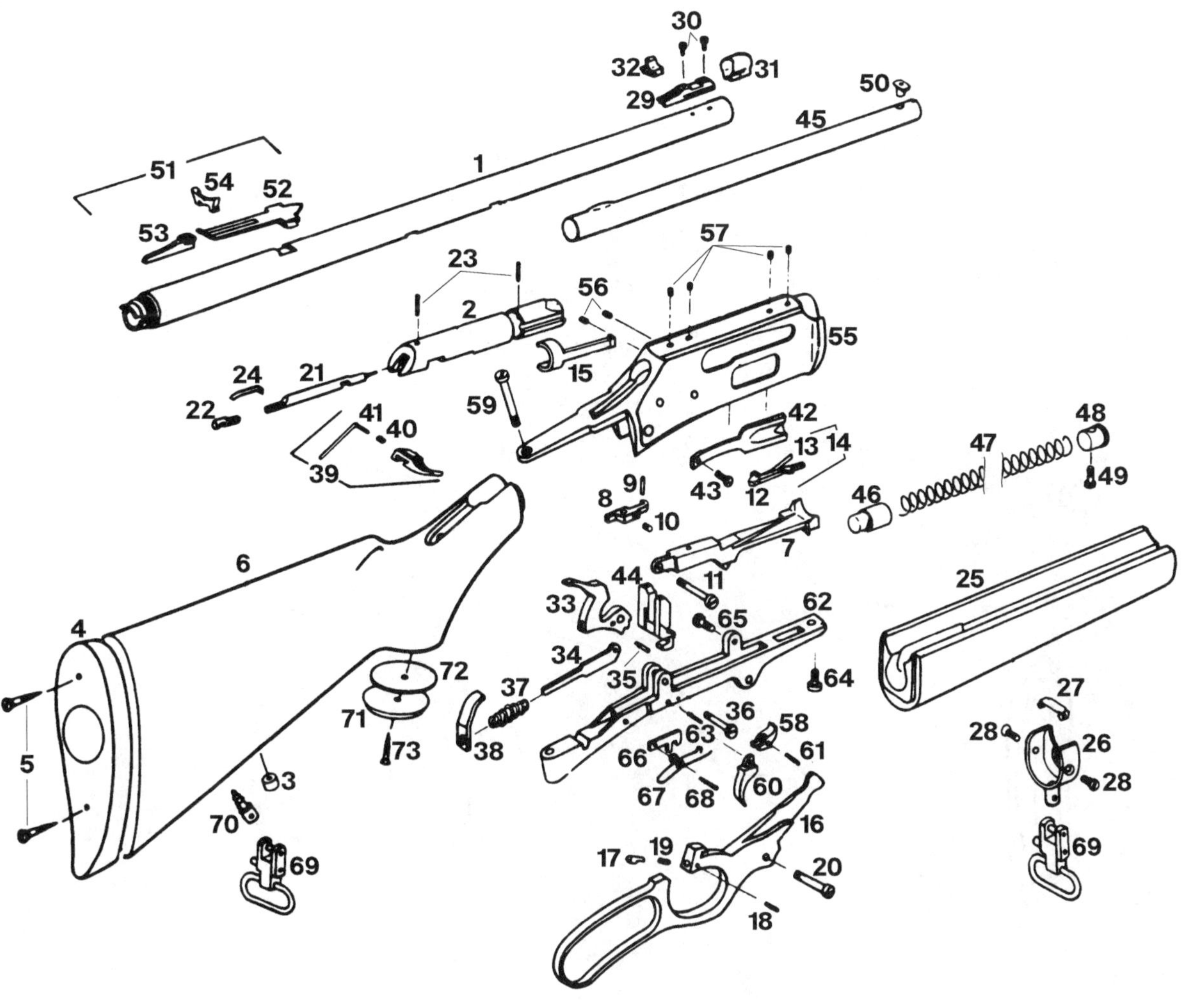

1	Barrel	**26**	Forearm Tip with Swivel Stud	**51**	Rear Sight Complete
2	Breechbolt	**27**	Forearm Tip Tenon	**52**	Rear Sight Base
3	Bullseye	**28**	Forearm Tip Tenon Screws	**53**	Rear Sight Elevator
4	Buttpad with Spacers	**29**	Front Sight Base	**54**	Rear Sight Folding Leaf
5	Buttpad Screws	**30**	Front Sight Base Screws	**55**	Receiver
6	Buttstock	**31**	Front Sight Hood	**56**	Peep Sight Dummy Screws
7	Carrier	**32**	Front Sight Insert	**57**	Scope Mount Dummy Screws
8	Carrier Rocker	**33**	Hammer	**58**	Sear
9	Carrier Rocker Pin	**34**	Hammer Strut	**59**	Tang Screw
10	Carrier Rocker Spring	**35**	Hammer Strut Pin	**60**	Trigger
11	Carrier Screw	**36**	Hammer Screw	**61**	Trigger and Sear Pin
12	Ejector	**37**	Hammer Spring	**62**	Trigger Guard Plate
13	Ejector Spring	**38**	Hammer Spring Adjusting Plate	**63**	Trigger Guard Plate Latch Pin
14	Ejector with Spring	**39**	Hammer Spur	**64**	Trigger Guard Plate Screw
15	Extractor	**40**	Hammer Spur Screw	**65**	Trigger Guard Plate Support Screw
16	Finger Lever	**41**	Hammer Spur Wrench	**66**	Trigger Safety Block
17	Finger Lever Plunger	**42**	Loading Spring	**67**	Trigger Safety Spring
18	Finger Lever Plunger Pin	**43**	Loading Spring Screw	**68**	Trigger Spring Pin
19	Finger Lever Plunger Spring	**44**	Locking Bolt	**69**	Swivels
20	Finger Lever Screw	**45**	Magazine Tube	**70**	Swivel Stud
21	Firing Pin, Front	**46**	Magazine Tube Follower	**71**	Pistol Grip Cap
22	Firing Pin, Rear	**47**	Magazine Tube Follower Spring	**72**	Pistol Grip Cap Spacer
23	Firing Pin Retaining Pins	**48**	Magazine Tube Plug	**73**	Pistol Grip Cap Screw
24	Firing Pin Spring	**49**	Magazine Tube Plug Screw		
25	Forearm	**50**	Magazine Tube Stud		

Model 25MN Bolt-Action Rifle

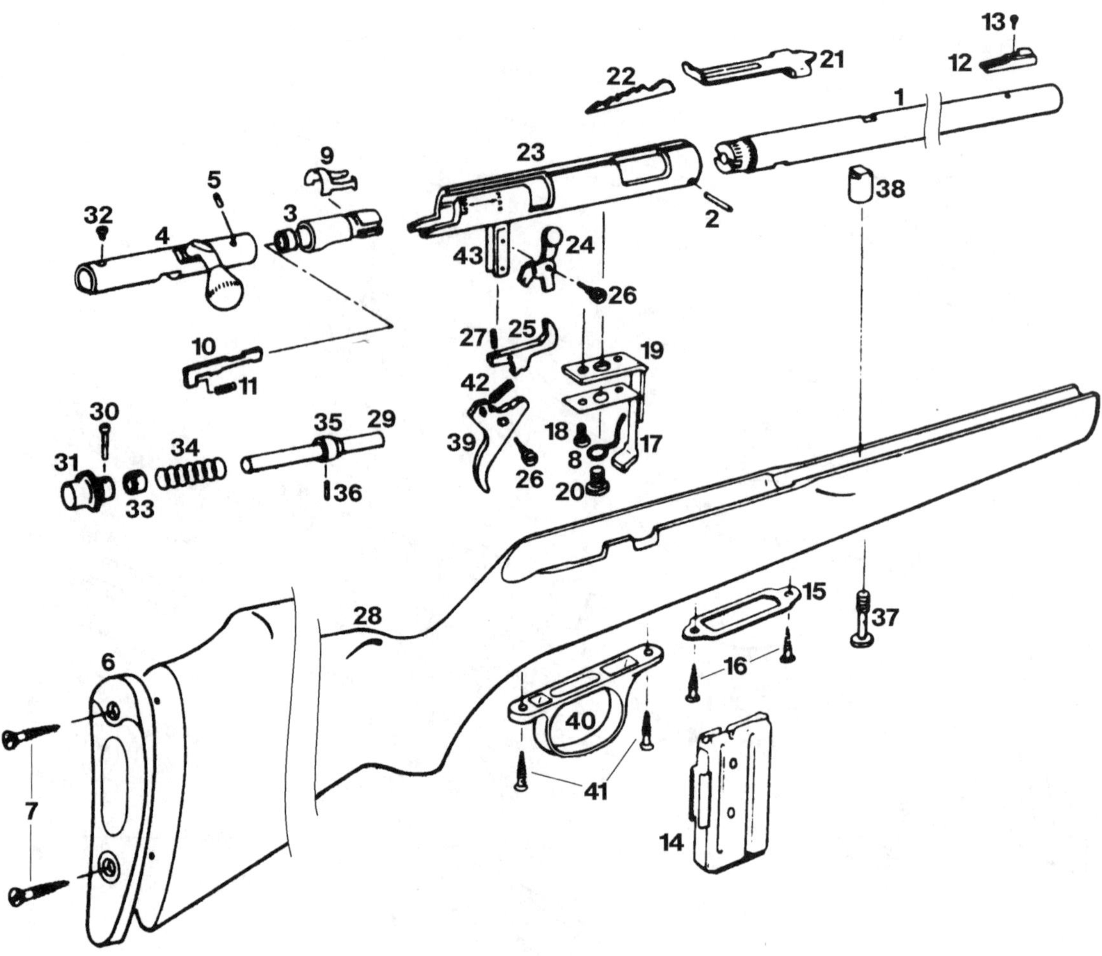

1	Barrel	22	Rear Sight Elevator
2	Barrel Retaining Pin	23	Receiver
3	Breechbolt, Front	24	Safety Assembly
4	Breechbolt, Rear	25	Sear
5	Breechbolt Assembly Pin	26	Trigger and Safety Pivot Screws
6	Buttplate	27	Sear Spring
7	Buttplate Screws	28	Stock
8	Ejector	29	Striker
9	Extractor	30	Striker Cam Pin
10	Firing Pin	31	Striker Knob
11	Firing Pin Spring	32	Striker Retaining Screw
12	Front Sight	33	Striker Sleeve
13	Front Sight Screw	34	Striker Spring
14	Magazine	35	Striker Cam Bushing
15	Magazine Guard Plate	36	Striker Assembly Pin
16	Magazine Guard Plate Screws	37	Takedown Screw
17	Magazine Latch	38	Takedown Screw Stud
18	Magazine Latch Screw	39	Trigger
19	Magazine Mounting Bracket	40	Trigger Guard
20	Magazine Mounting Bracket Screw	41	Trigger Guard Screws
		42	Trigger Spring
21	Rear Sight	43	Trigger Stud

Model 25N Bolt-Action Rifle

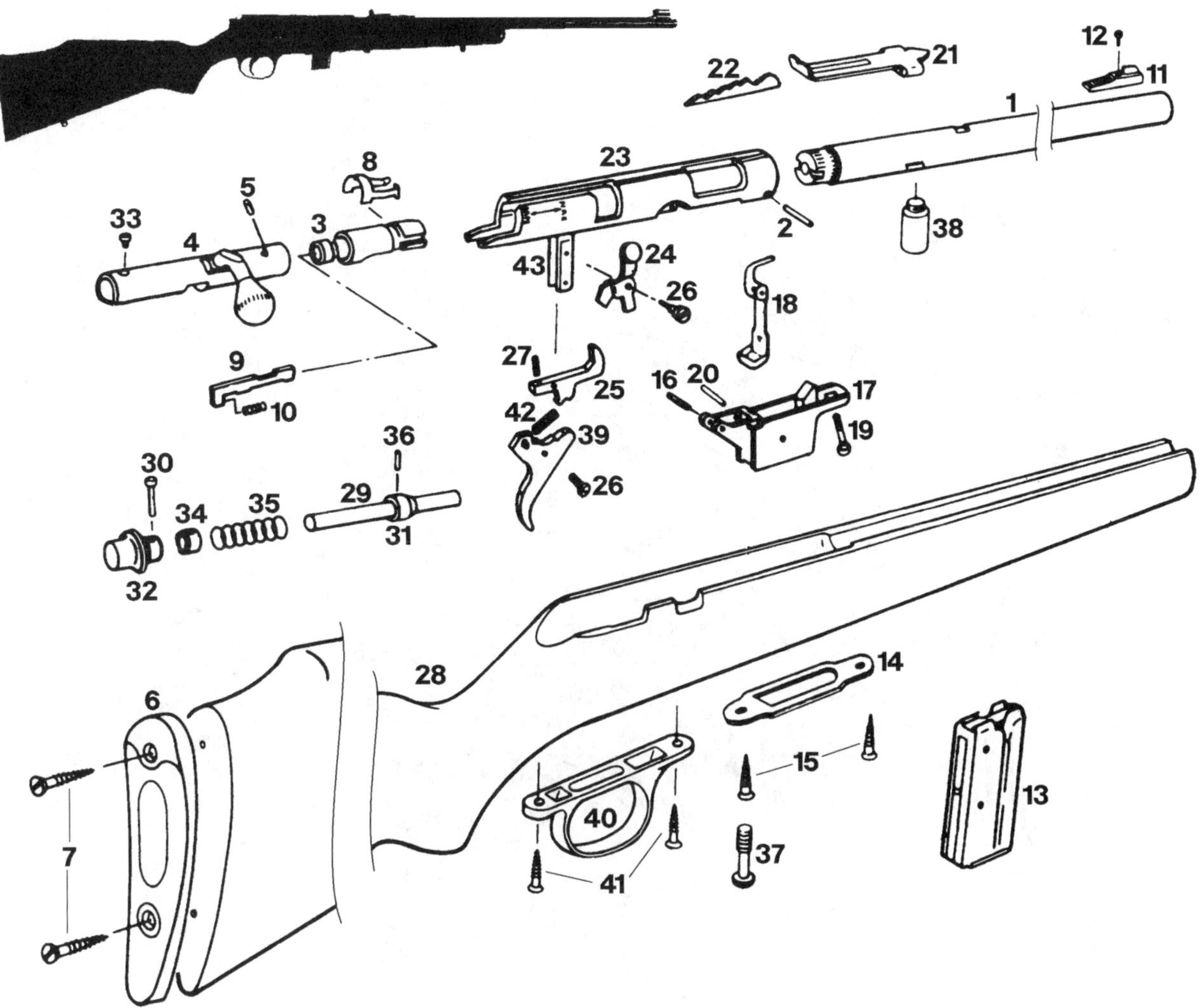

1	Barrel	**22**	Rear Sight Elevator
2	Barrel Retaining Pin	**23**	Receiver
3	Breechbolt, Front	**24**	Safety Assembly
4	Breechbolt, Rear	**25**	Sear
5	Breechbolt Assembly Pin	**26**	Sear and Safety Pivot Screws
6	Buttplate	**27**	Sear Spring
7	Buttplate Screws	**28**	Stock
8	Extractor	**29**	Striker
9	Firing Pin	**30**	Striker Cam Pin
10	Firing Pin Spring	**31**	Striker Cam Bushing
11	Front Sight	**32**	Striker Knob
12	Front Sight Screw	**33**	Striker Retaining Screw
13	Magazine	**34**	Striker Sleeve
14	Magazine Guide Plate	**35**	Striker Spring
15	Magazine Guide Plate Screws	**36**	Striker Assembly Pin
16	Magazine Guide and Latch Assembly Pin	**37**	Takedown Screw
17	Magazine Guide	**38**	Takedown Screw Stud
18	Magazine Latch and Ejector	**39**	Trigger
19	Magazine Guide Screw	**40**	Trigger Guard
20	Magazine Guide Pivot Pin	**41**	Trigger Guard Screws
21	Rear Sight	**42**	Trigger Spring
		43	Trigger Stud

Model 30 and 30AS Lever-Action Rifle

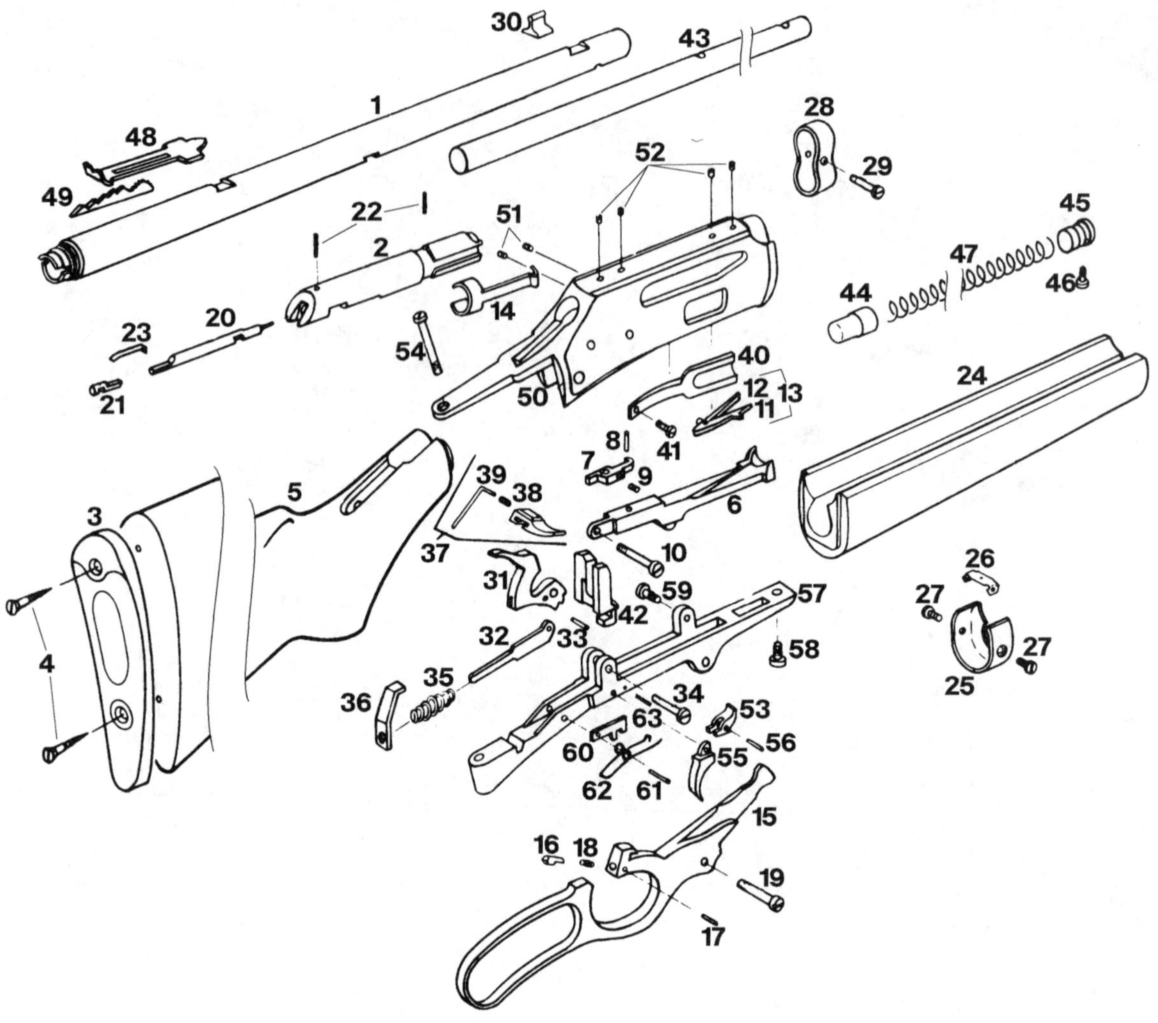

1	Barrel	23	Firing Pin Spring	45	Magazine Tube Plug
2	Breechbolt	24	Forearm	46	Magazine Tube Plug Screw
3	Buttplate	25	Forearm Tip	47	Magazine Tube Spring
4	Buttplate Screws	26	Forearm Tip Tenon	48	Rear Sight
5	Buttstock	27	Forearm Tip Tenon Screws	49	Rear Sight Elevator
6	Carrier	28	Front Band	50	Receiver
7	Carrier Rocker	29	Front Band Screw	51	Peep Sight Dummy Screws
8	Carrier Rocker Pin	30	Front Sight with Brass Bead	52	Scope Mount Dummy Screws
9	Carrier Rocker Spring	31	Hammer	53	Sear
10	Carrier Screw	32	Hammer Strut	54	Tang Screw
11	Ejector	33	Hammer Strut Pin	55	Trigger
12	Ejector Spring	34	Hammer Screw	56	Trigger and Sear Pin
13	Ejector with Spring	35	Hammer Spring	57	Trigger Guard Plate
14	Extractor	36	Hammer Spring Adjusting Plate	58	Trigger Guard Plate Screw
15	Finger Lever	37	Hammer Spur	59	Trigger Guard Plate Support Screw
16	Finger Lever Plunger	38	Hammer Spur Screw	60	Trigger Safety Block
17	Finger Lever Plunger Pin	39	Hammer Spur Wrench	61	Trigger Safety Block Pin
18	Finger Lever Plunger Spring	40	Loading Spring	62	Trigger Safety Block Spring
19	Finger Lever Screw	41	Loading Spring Screw	63	Trigger Guard Plate Latch Pin
20	Firing Pin, Front	42	Locking Bolt		
21	Firing Pin, Rear	43	Magazine Tube		
22	Firing Pin Retaining Pins	44	Magazine Tube Follower		

Model 336A Lever-Action Rifle

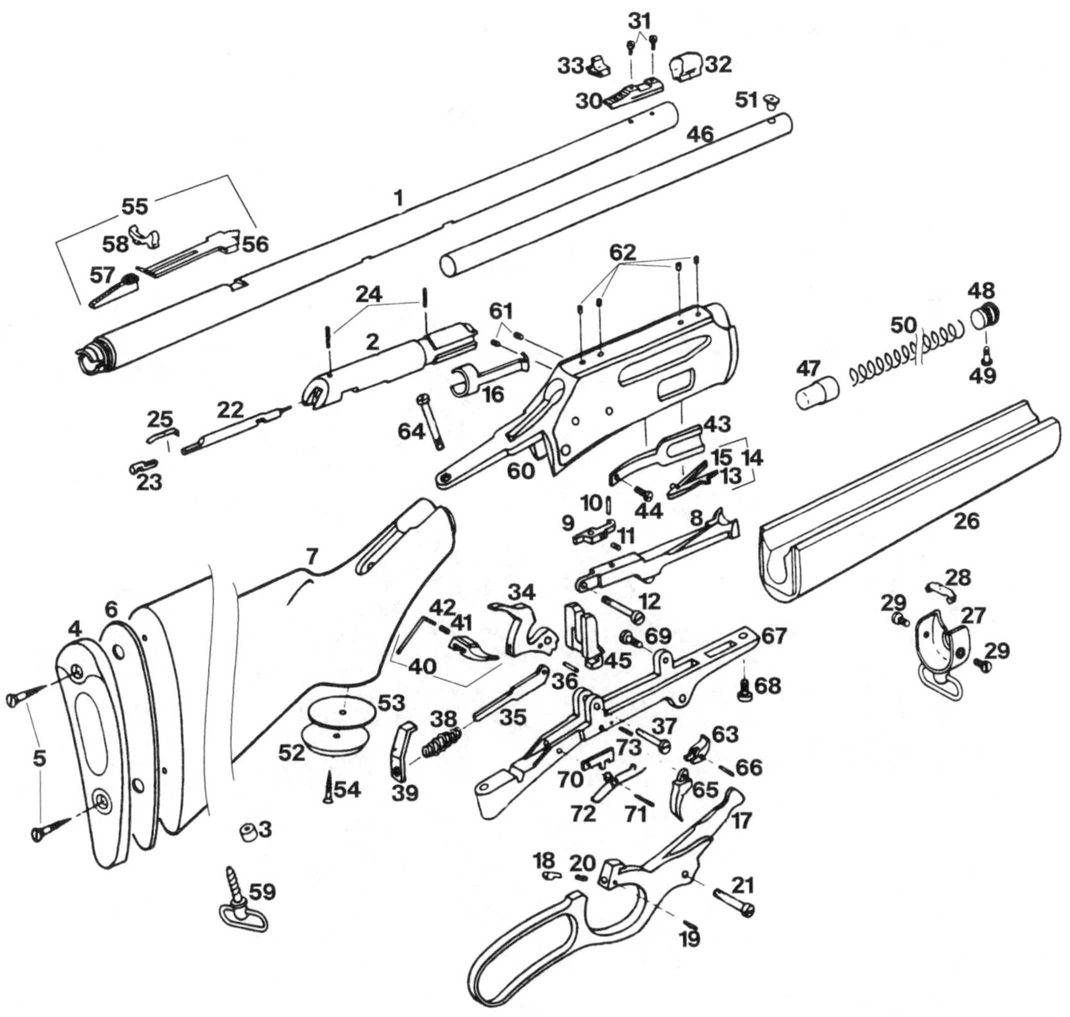

1	Barrel	**26**	Forearm	**51**	Magazine Tube Stud
2	Breechbolt	**27**	Forearm Tip with Swivel	**52**	Pistol Grip Cap
3	Bullseye	**28**	Forearm Tip Tenon	**53**	Pistol Grip Cap Spacer
4	Buttplate with Spacer	**29**	Forearm Tip Tenon Screws	**54**	Pistol Grip Cap Screw
5	Buttplate Screws	**30**	Front Sight Base	**55**	Rear Sight Assembly
6	Buttplate Spacer	**31**	Front Sight Base Screws	**56**	Rear Sight Base
7	Buttstock	**32**	Front Sight Hood	**57**	Rear Sight Elevator
8	Carrier	**33**	Front Sight Insert	**58**	Rear Sight Folding Leaf
9	Carrier Rocker	**34**	Hammer	**59**	Rear Swivel
10	Carrier Rocker Pin	**35**	Hammer Strut	**60**	Receiver
11	Carrier Rocker Spring	**36**	Hammer Strut Pin	**61**	Peep Sight Dummy Screws
12	Carrier Screw	**37**	Hammer Screw	**62**	Scope Mount Dummy Screws
13	Ejector	**38**	Hammer Spring	**63**	Sear
14	Ejector with Spring	**39**	Hammer Spring Adjusting Plate	**64**	Tang Screw
15	Ejector Spring	**40**	Hammer Spur	**65**	Trigger
16	Extractor	**41**	Hammer Spur Screw	**66**	Trigger and Sear Pin
17	Finger Lever	**42**	Hammer Spur Wrench	**67**	Trigger Guard Plate
18	Finger Lever Plunger	**43**	Loading Spring	**68**	Trigger Guard Plate Screw
19	Finger Lever Plunger Pin	**44**	Loading Spring Screw	**69**	Trigger Guard Plate Support Screw
20	Finger Lever Plunger Spring	**45**	Locking Bolt	**70**	Trigger Safety Block
21	Finger Lever Screw	**46**	Magazine Tube	**71**	Trigger Safety Block Pin
22	Firing Pin, Front	**47**	Magazine Tube Follower	**72**	Trigger Safety Block Spring
23	Firing Pin, Rear	**48**	Magazine Tube Plug	**73**	Trigger Guard Plate Latch Pin
24	Firing Pin Retaining Pins	**49**	Magazine Tube Plug Screw		
25	Firing Pin Spring	**50**	Magazine Tube Spring		

Model 336CS Lever-Action Rifle

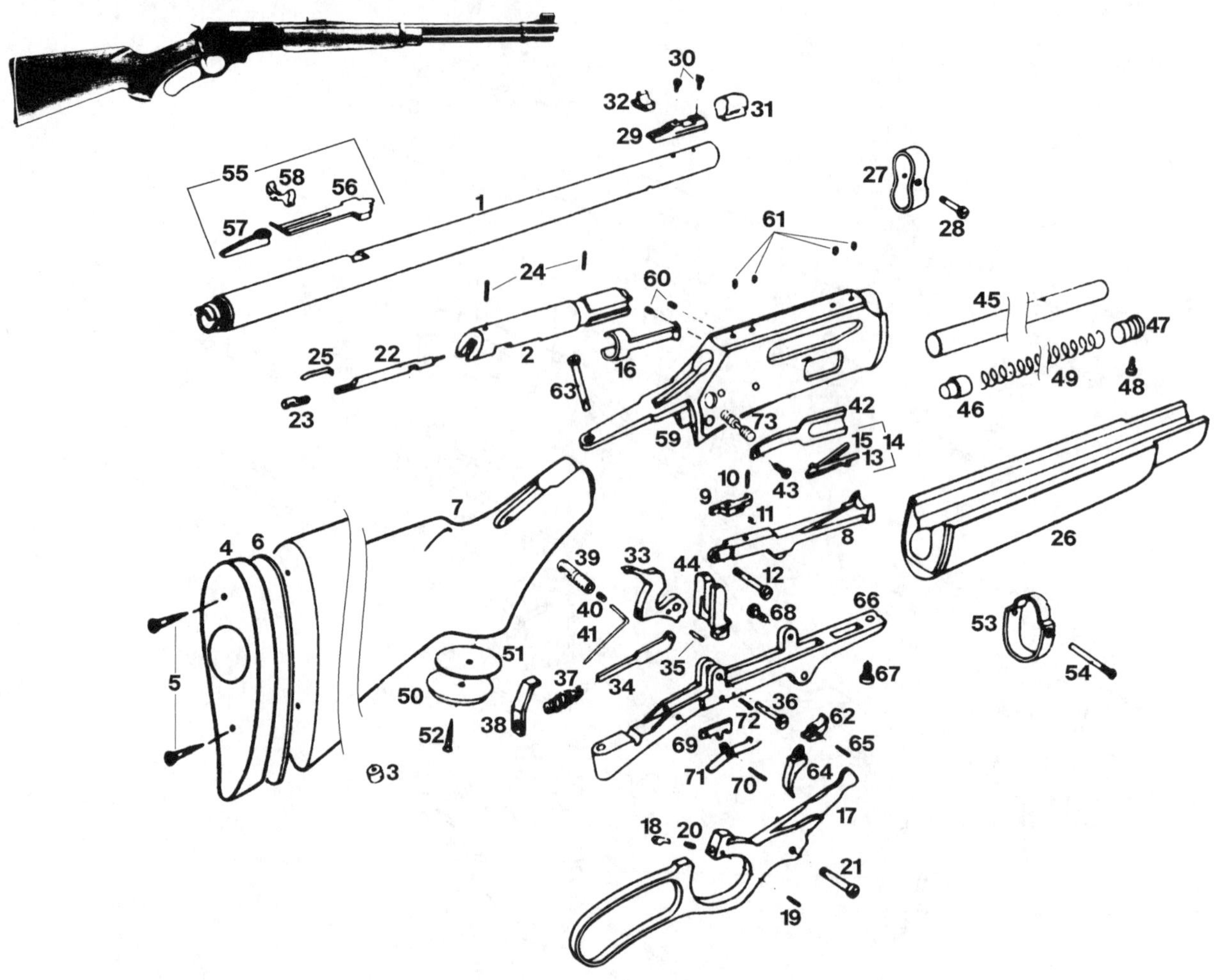

1	Barrel
2	Breechbolt
3	Bullseye
4	Buttpad
5	Buttpad Screws
6	Buttpad Spacer
7	Buttstock
8	Carrier
9	Carrier Rocker
10	Carrier Rocker Pin
11	Carrier Rocker Spring
12	Carrier Screw
13	Ejector
14	Ejector with Spring
15	Ejector Spring
16	Extractor
17	Finger Lever
18	Finger Lever Plunger
19	Finger Lever Plunger Pin
20	Finger Lever Plunger Spring
21	Finger Lever Screw
22	Firing Pin, Front
23	Firing Pin, Rear
24	Firing Pin Retaining Pins
25	Firing Pin Spring
26	Forearm
27	Front Band
28	Front Band Screw
29	Front Sight Base
30	Front Sight Base Screws
31	Front Sight Hood
32	Front Sight Insert
33	Hammer
34	Hammer Strut
35	Hammer Strut Pin
36	Hammer Screw
37	Hammer Spring
38	Hammer Spring Adjusting Plate
39	Hammer Spur
40	Hammer Spur Screw
41	Hammer Spur Wrench
42	Loading Spring
43	Loading Spring Screw
44	Locking Bolt
45	Magazine Tube
46	Magazine Tube Follower
47	Magazine Tube Plug
48	Magazine Tube Plug Screw
49	Magazine Tube Spring
50	Pistol Grip Cap
51	Pistol Grip Cap Spacer
52	Pistol Grip Cap Screw
53	Rear Band
54	Rear Band Screw
55	Rear Sight Assembly
56	Rear Sight Base
57	Rear Sight Elevator
58	Rear Sight Folding Leaf
59	Receiver
60	Peep Sight Dummy Screws
61	Scope Mount Dummy Screws
62	Sear
63	Tang Screw
64	Trigger
65	Trigger and Sear Pin
66	Trigger Guard Plate
67	Trigger Guard Plate Screw
68	Trigger Guard Plate Support Screw
69	Trigger Safety Block
70	Trigger Safety Block Pin
71	Trigger Safety Block Spring
72	Trigger Guard Plate Latch Pin
73	Safety Button Assembly

Model 375 and 375S Lever-Action Rifle

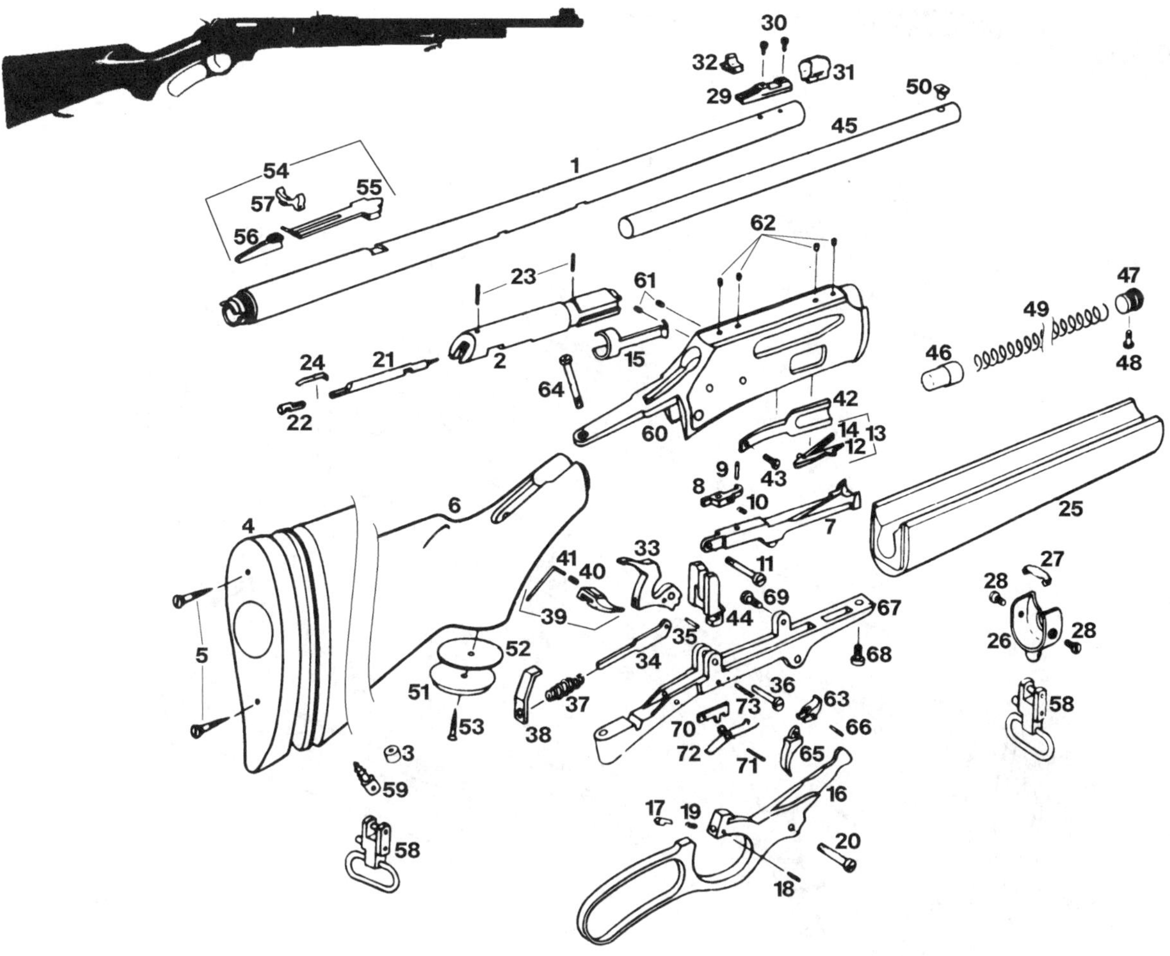

1	Barrel	**26**	Forearm Tip with Swivel Stud	**51**	Pistol Grip Cap
2	Breechbolt	**27**	Forearm Tip Tenon	**52**	Pistol Grip Cap Spacer
3	Bullseye	**28**	Forearm Tip Tenon Screws	**53**	Pistol Grip Cap Screw
4	Buttpad and Spacers	**29**	Front Sight Base	**54**	Rear Sight Assembly
5	Buttpad Screws	**30**	Front Sight Base Screws	**55**	Rear Sight Base
6	Buttstock	**31**	Front Sight Hood	**56**	Rear Sight Elevator
7	Carrier	**32**	Front Sight Insert	**57**	Rear Sight Folding Leaf
8	Carrier Rocker	**33**	Hammer	**58**	Swivels
9	Carrier Rocker Pin	**34**	Hammer Strut	**59**	Swivel Stud
10	Carrier Rocker Spring	**35**	Hammer Strut Pin	**60**	Receiver
11	Carrier Screw	**36**	Hammer Screw	**61**	Peep Sight Dummy Screws
12	Ejector	**37**	Hammer Spring	**62**	Scope Mount Dummy Screws
13	Ejector with Spring	**38**	Hammer Spring Adjusting Plate	**63**	Sear
14	Ejector Spring	**39**	Hammer Spur	**64**	Tang Screw
15	Extractor	**40**	Hammer Spur Screw	**65**	Trigger
16	Finger Lever	**41**	Hammer Spur Wrench	**66**	Trigger and Sear Pin
17	Finger Lever Plunger	**42**	Loading Spring	**67**	Trigger Guard Plate
18	Finger Lever Plunger Pin	**43**	Loading Spring Screw	**68**	Trigger Guard Plate Screw
19	Finger Lever Plunger Spring	**44**	Locking Bolt	**69**	Trigger Guard Plate Support Screw
20	Finger Lever Screw	**45**	Magazine Tube	**70**	Trigger Safety Block
21	Firing Pin, Front	**46**	Magazine Tube Follower	**71**	Trigger Safety Block Pin
22	Firing Pin, Rear	**47**	Magazine Tube Plug	**72**	Trigger Safety Block Spring
23	Firing Pin Retaining Pins	**48**	Magazine Tube Plug Screw	**73**	Trigger Guard Plate Latch Pin
24	Firing Pin Spring	**49**	Magazine Tube Spring		
25	Forearm	**50**	Magazine Tube Stud		

Model 39A Lever-Action Rifle

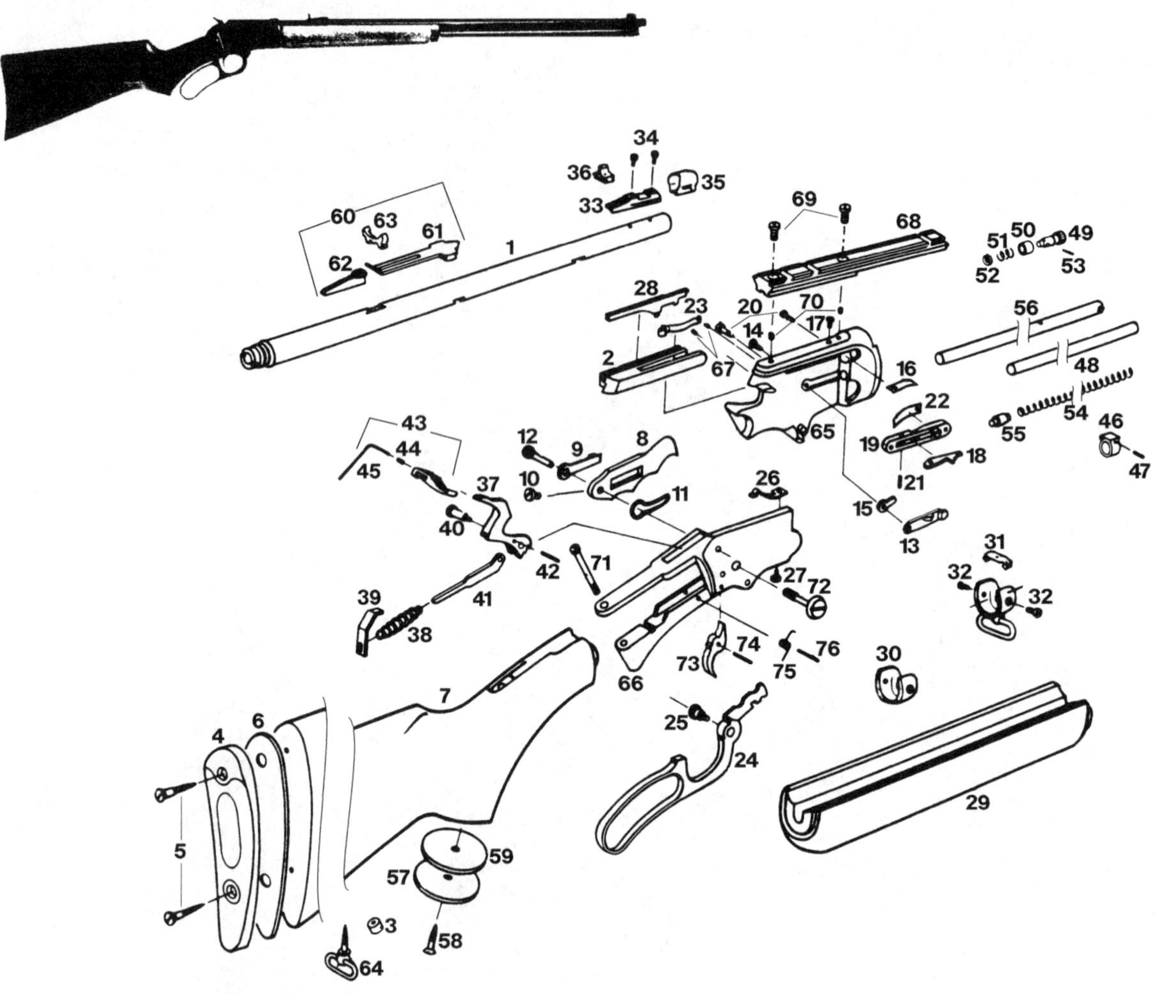

1	Barrel
2	Breechbolt
3	Bullseye
4	Buttplate
5	Buttplate Screws
6	Buttplate Spacer
7	Buttstock
8	Carrier
9	Carrier Rocker
10	Carrier Rocker Screw
11	Carrier Rocker Spring
12	Carrier Screw
13	Cartridge Cutoff
14	Cartridge Cutoff Screw
15	Cartridge Cutoff Spacer
16	Cartridge Guide Spring
17	Cartridge Guide Spring Screw
18	Ejector
19	Ejector Base with Rivet
20	Ejector Base Screws
21	Ejector Pin
22	Ejector Spring
23	Extractor
24	Finger Lever
25	Finger Lever Screw
26	Finger Lever Spring
27	Finger Lever Spring Screw
28	Firing Pin
29	Forearm
30	Forearm Tip Assembly
31	Forearm Tip Tenon
32	Forearm Tip Tenon Screws
33	Front Sight Ramp Base
34	Front Sight Ramp Base Screws
35	Front Sight Ramp Hood
36	Front Sight Ramp Insert
37	Hammer
38	Hammer Spring
39	Hammer Spring Adjusting Plate
40	Hammer Screw
41	Hammer Strut
42	Hammer Strut Pin
43	Hammer Spur Assembly
44	Hammer Spur Screw
45	Hammer Spur Wrench
46	Magazine Tube Band
47	Magazine Tube Band Pin
48	Magazine Tube, Inside
49	Magazine Tube Plug
50	Magazine Tube Plug Cap
51	Magazine Tube Plug Spring
52	Magazine Tube Plug Bushing
53	Magazine Tube Plug Pin
54	Magazine Tube Spring
55	Magazine Tube Follower
56	Magazine Tube, Outside
57	Pistol Grip Cap
58	Pistol Grip Cap Screw
59	Pistol Grip Cap Spacer
60	Rear Sight
61	Rear Sight Base
62	Rear Sight Elevator
63	Rear Sight Folding Leaf
64	Rear Swivel
65	Receiver
66	Receiver Tang
67	Peep Sight Dummy Screws
68	Scope Adapter Base with Screws
69	Scope Adapter Base Screws
70	Scope Mount Dummy Screws
71	Tang Screw
72	Thumb Screw
73	Trigger
74	Trigger Pin
75	Trigger Spring
76	Trigger Spring Pin

Model 39AS Lever-Action Rifle

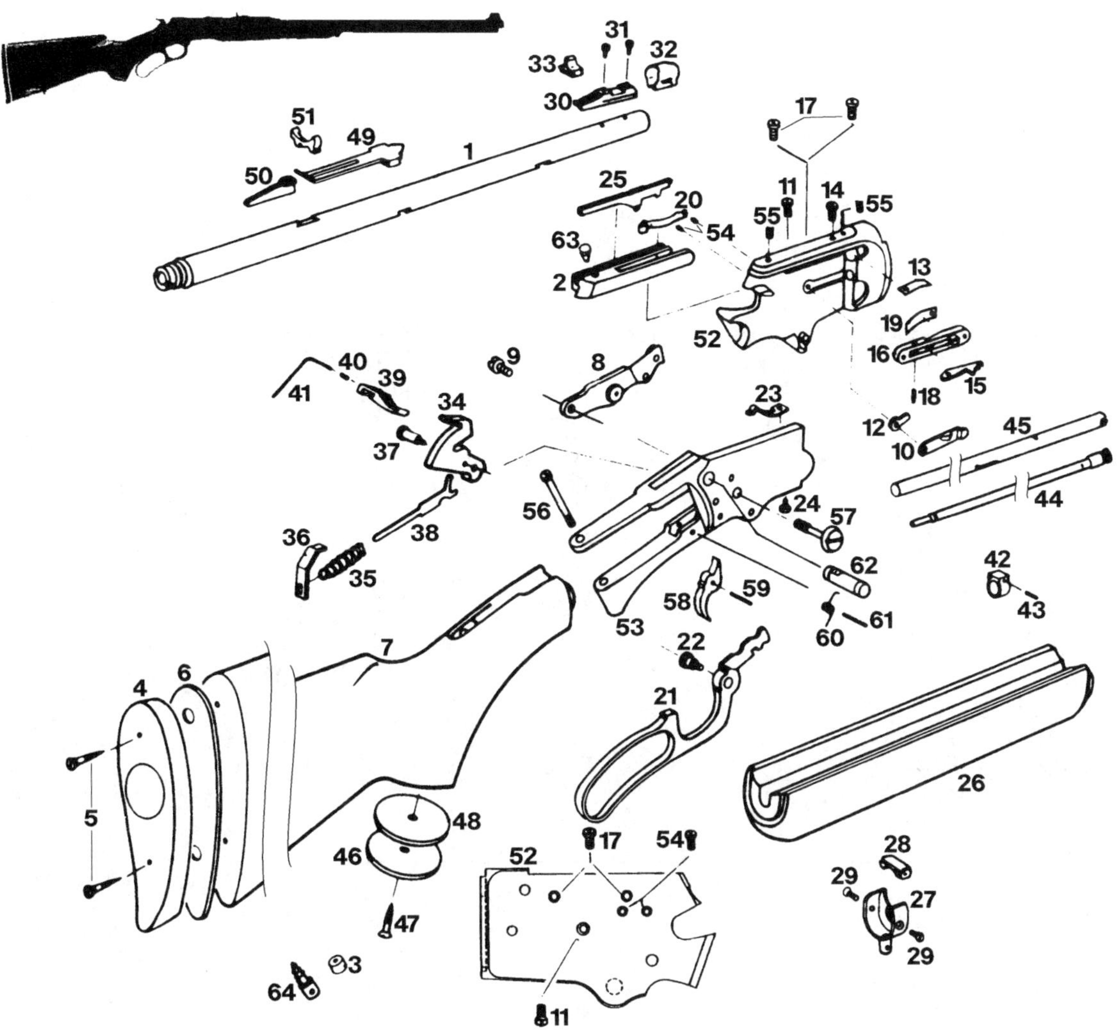

1	Barrel	**24**	Finger Lever Spring Screw	**47**	Pistol Grip Cap Screw
2	Breechbolt	**25**	Firing Pin	**48**	Pistol Grip Cap Spacer
3	Bullseye	**26**	Forearm	**49**	Rear Sight Base
4	Buttpad	**27**	Forearm Tip with Stud	**50**	Rear Sight Elevator
5	Buttpad Screws	**28**	Forearm Tip Tenon	**51**	Rear Sight Folding Leaf
6	Buttpad Spacer	**29**	Forearm Tip Tenon Screws	**52**	Receiver
7	Buttstock	**30**	Front Sight Ramp Base	**53**	Receiver Tang
8	Carrier Assembly	**31**	Front Sight Ramp Base Screws	**54**	Receiver Sight Dummy Screws
9	Carrier Screw	**32**	Front Sight Ramp Hood	**55**	Scope Mount Dummy Screws
10	Cartridge Cutoff	**33**	Front Sight Ramp Insert	**56**	Tang Screw
11	Cartridge Cutoff Screw	**34**	Hammer	**57**	Thumb Screw
12	Cartridge Cutoff Spacer	**35**	Hammer Spring	**58**	Trigger
13	Cartridge Guide Spring	**36**	Hammer Spring Adjusting Plate	**59**	Trigger Pin
14	Cartridge Guide Spring Screw	**37**	Hammer Screw	**60**	Trigger Spring
15	Ejector	**38**	Rebound Strut	**61**	Trigger Spring Pin
16	Ejector Base with Rivet	**39**	Hammer Spur Assembly	**62**	Safety Assembly
17	Ejector Base Screws	**40**	Hammer Spur Screw	**63**	Firing Pin Retaining Stud
18	Ejector Pin	**41**	Hammer Spur Wrench	**64**	Rear Swivel Stud
19	Ejector Spring	**42**	Magazine Tube Band	**Parts Not Shown**	
20	Extractor	**43**	Magazine Tube Band Pin		Scope Adapter Base with Screws
21	Finger Lever	**44**	Magazine Tube Assembly		
22	Finger Lever Screw	**45**	Magazine Tube, Outside		
23	Finger Lever Spring	**46**	Pistol Grip Cap		

Model 39TDS Lever-Action Carbine

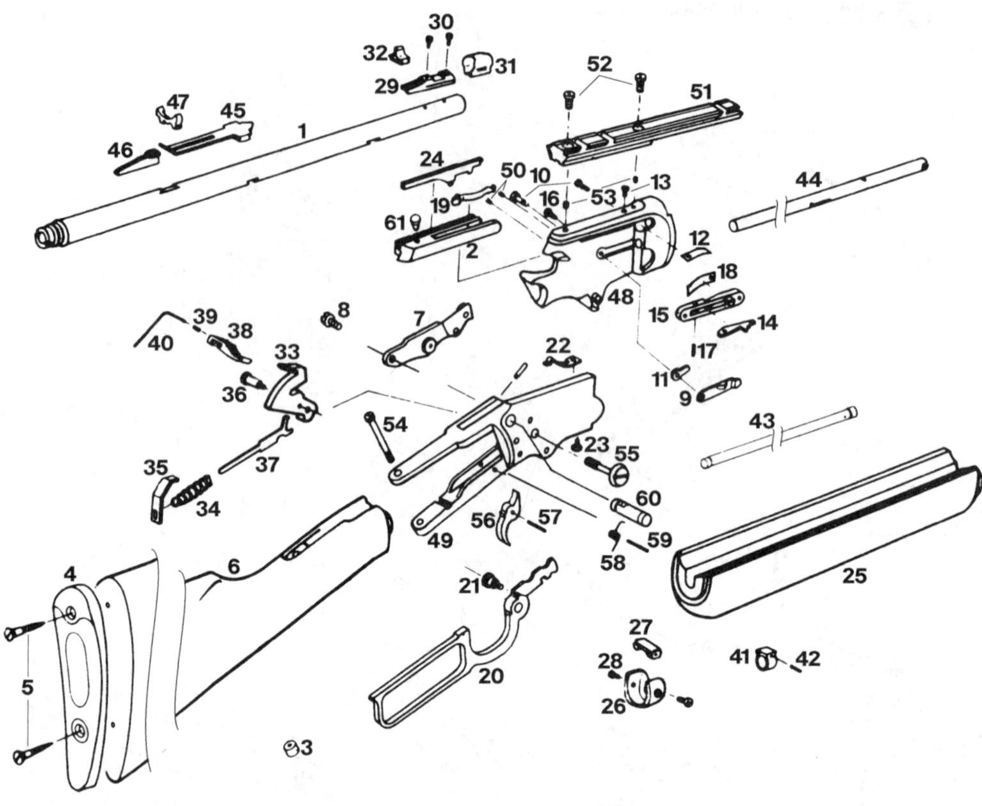

1	Barrel	32	Front Sight Ramp Insert
2	Breechbolt	33	Hammer
3	Bullseye	34	Hammer Spring
4	Buttplate	35	Hammer Spring Adjusting Plate
5	Buttplate Screws	36	Hammer Screw
6	Buttstock	37	Hammer Rebound Strut
7	Carrier Assembly	38	Hammer Spur Assembly
8	Carrier Screw	39	Hammer Spur Screw
9	Cartridge Cutoff	40	Hammer Spur Wrench
10	Cartridge Cutoff Screws	41	Magazine Tube Band
11	Cartridge Cutoff Spacer	42	Magazine Tube Band Pin
12	Cartridge Guide Spring	43	Magazine Tube, Inside
13	Cartridge Guide Spring Screw	44	Magazine Tube, Outside
14	Ejector	45	Rear Sight Base
15	Ejector Base with Rivet	46	Rear Sight Elevator
16	Ejector Base Screws	47	Rear Sight Folding Leaf
17	Ejector Pin	48	Receiver, Left
18	Ejector Spring	49	Receiver, Right
19	Extractor	50	Receiver Sight Dummy Screws
20	Finger Lever	51	Scope Adapter Base with Screws
21	Finger Lever Screw	52	Scope Adapter Base Screws
22	Finger Lever Spring	53	Scope Mount Dummy Screws
23	Finger Lever Spring Screw	54	Tang Screw
24	Firing Pin	55	Thumb Screw
25	Forearm	56	Trigger
26	Forearm Tip	57	Trigger Pin
27	Forearm Tip Tenon	58	Trigger Spring
28	Forearm Tip Tenon Screws	59	Trigger Spring Pin
29	Front Sight Ramp Base	60	Safety Assembly
30	Front Sight Ramp Base Screws	61	Firing Pin Retaining Stud
31	Front Sight Ramp Hood		

Model 444, 444S and 444SS Lever-Action Rifle

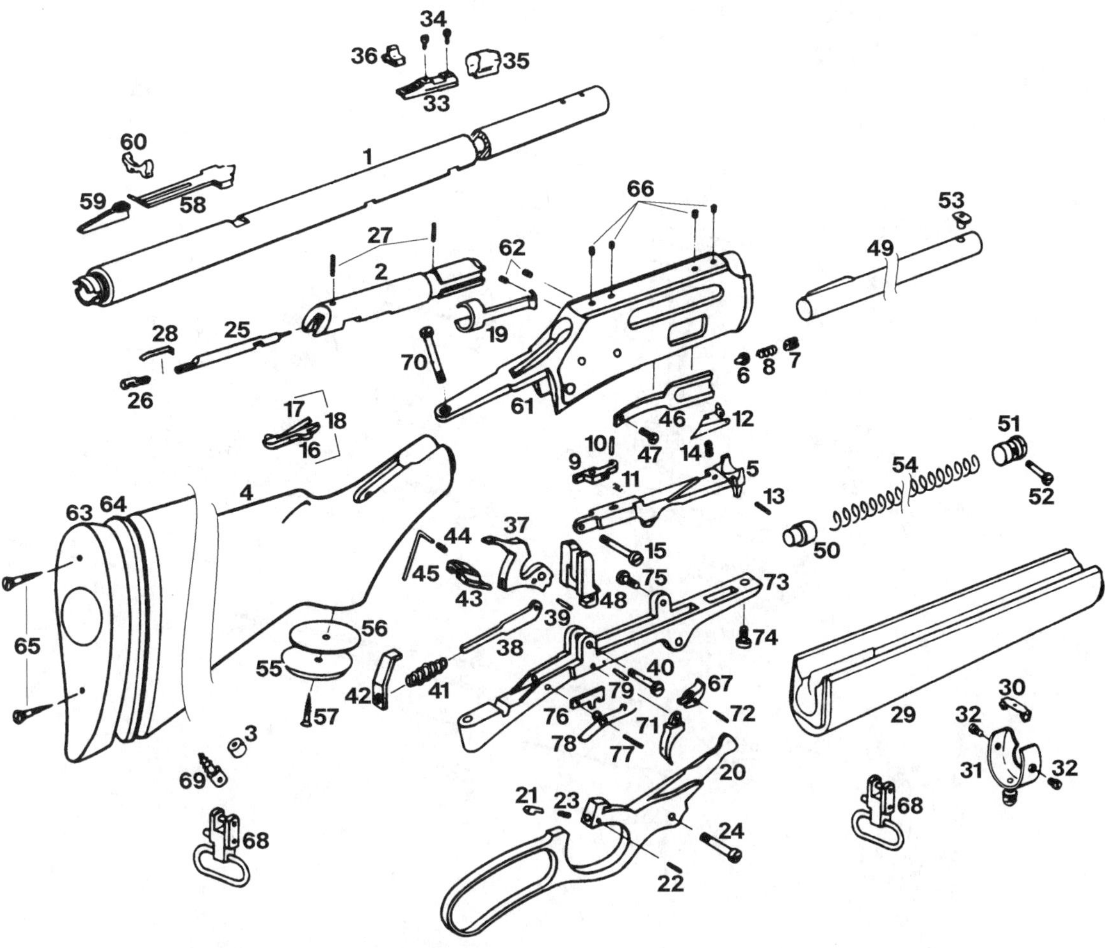

No.	Part	No.	Part	No.	Part
1	Barrel	28	Firing Pin Spring	55	Pistol Grip Cap
2	Breechbolt	29	Forearm	56	Pistol Grip Cap Spacer
3	Bullseye	30	Forearm Tip Tenon	57	Pistol Grip Cap Screw
4	Buttstock	31	Forearm Tip and Swivel Stud	58	Rear Sight Base
5	Carrier	32	Forearm Tip Screws	59	Rear Sight Elevator
6	Carrier Detent	33	Front Sight Base	60	Rear Sight Folding Leaf
7	Carrier Detent Screw	34	Front Sight Base Screws	61	Receiver
8	Carrier Detent Spring	35	Front Sight Hood	62	Peep Sight Dummy Screws
9	Carrier Rocker	36	Front Sight Insert	63	Buttpad with Spacers
10	Carrier Rocker Pin	37	Hammer	64	Buttpad Spacer
11	Carrier Rocker Spring	38	Hammer Strut	65	Buttpad Screws
12	Cartridge Leveler	39	Hammer Strut Pin	66	Scope Mount Dummy Screws
13	Cartridge Leveler Pivot Pin	40	Hammer Screw	67	Sear
14	Cartridge Leveler Spring	41	Hammer Spring	68	Swivels
15	Carrier Screw	42	Hammer Spring Adjusting Plate	69	Rear Swivel Stud
16	Ejector	43	Hammer Spur	70	Tang Screw
17	Ejector Spring	44	Hammer Spur Screw	71	Trigger
18	Ejector with Spring	45	Hammer Spur Wrench	72	Trigger and Sear Pin
19	Extractor	46	Loading Spring	73	Trigger Guard Plate
20	Finger Lever	47	Loading Spring Screw	74	Trigger Guard Plate Screw
21	Finger Lever Plunger	48	Locking Bolt	75	Trigger Guard Plate Support Screw
22	Finger Lever Plunger Pin	49	Magazine Tube	76	Trigger Safety Block
23	Finger Lever Plunger Spring	50	Magazine Tube Follower	77	Trigger Safety Block Pin
24	Finger Lever Screw	51	Magazine Tube Plug	78	Trigger Safety Block Spring
25	Firing Pin, Front	52	Magazine Tube Plug Screw	79	Trigger Guard Plate Latch Pin
26	Firing Pin, Rear	53	Magazine Tube Stud		
27	Firing Pin Retaining Pin (2)	54	Magazine Tube Spring		

Model 45 Autoloading Carbine

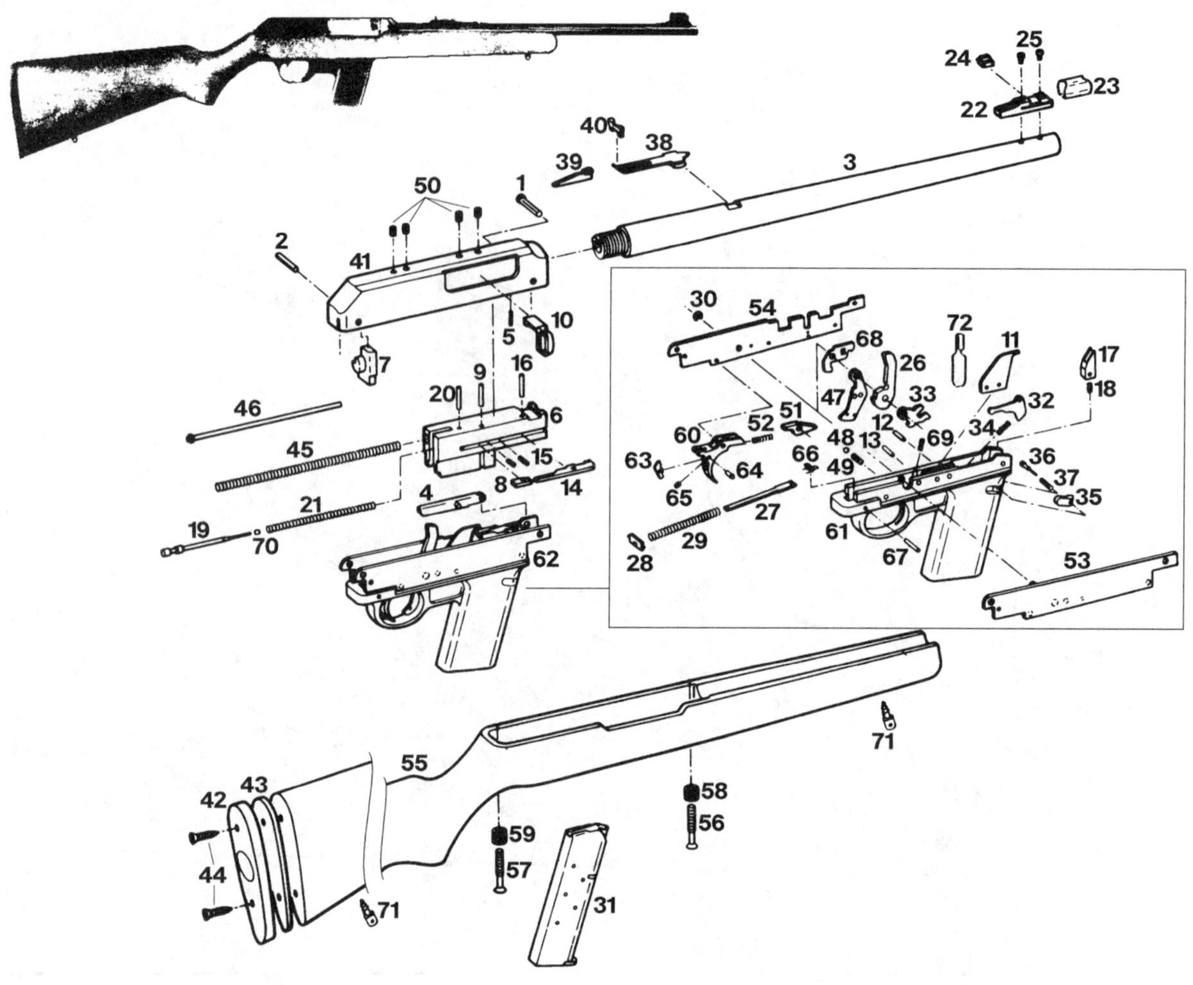

1	Action Assembly Pin, Front
2	Action Assembly Pin, Rear
3	Barrel
4	Bolt Stop
5	Bolt Stop Spring
6	Breechbolt
7	Buffer
8	Cartridge Indicator
9	Cartridge Indicator Assembly Pin
10	Charging Handle
11	Ejector
12	Ejector/Magazine Disconnector Pin
13	Ejector Pin, Rear
14	Extractor
15	Extractor/Cartridge Indicator Springs
16	Extractor Pin
17	Feed Ramp
18	Feed Ramp Spring
19	Firing Pin
20	Firing Pin Assembly Pin
21	Firing Pin Spring
22	Front Ramp Sight Base
23	Front Ramp Sight Cutaway Hood
24	Front Ramp Sight Red Insert
25	Front Ramp Sight Screws
26	Hammer
27	Hammer Strut
28	Hammer Strut Bridge
29	Hammer Strut Spring
30	Hammer Pivot Pin Retaining Ring
31	Magazine
32	Magazine Disconnector
33	Magazine Disconnector Trigger Block
34	Magazine Disconnector Spring
35	Magazine Latch
36	Magazine Latch Retaining Screw
37	Magazine Latch Retaining Spring
38	Rear Sight Base
39	Rear Sight Elevator
40	Rear Sight Leaf
41	Receiver
42	Recoil Pad
43	Recoil Pad Spacer
44	Recoil Pad Screws
45	Recoil Spring
46	Recoil Spring Rod
47	Safety
48	Safety Detent Ball
49	Safety Detent Spring
50	Scope Mount Dummy Screws
51	Sear
52	Sear Spring
53	Sideplate, Right
54	Sideplate, Left
55	Stock
56	Takedown Screw, Front
57	Takedown Screw, Rear
58	Takedown Screw Bushing, Front
59	Takedown Screw Bushing, Rear
60	Trigger
61	Trigger Guard
62	Trigger Guard/Action Assembly
63	Trigger Disconnector
64	Trigger Disconnector Pin
65	Trigger Disconnector Spring
66	Trigger Return Spring
67	Trigger Return Spring Pin
68	Trigger Block
69	Trigger Block Spring
70	Firing Pin Bushing
71	Swivel Studs
72	Manual Hold-Open

Model 50 Bolt-Action Rifle

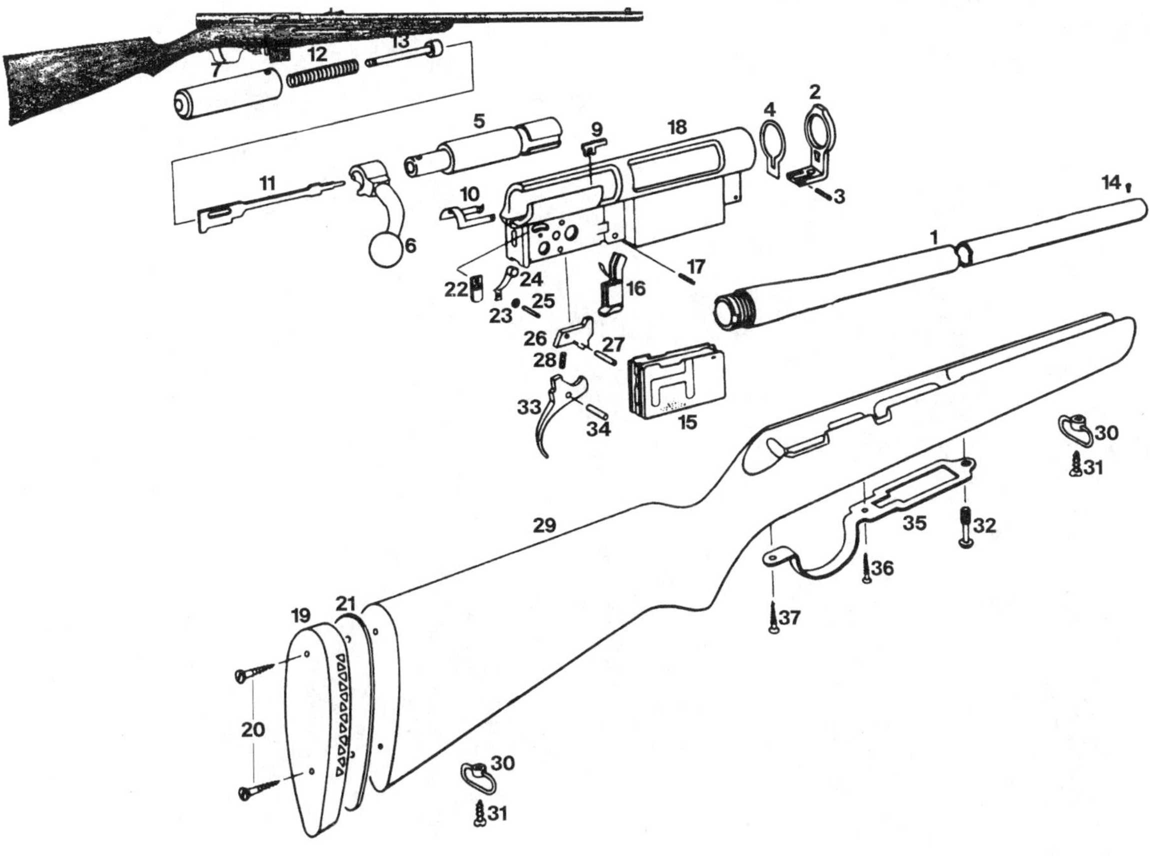

1	Barrel	20	Recoil Pad Screws
2	Barrel Collar	21	Recoil Pad Spacer
3	Barrel Collar Pin	22	Safety Blade
4	Barrel Washer	23	Safety Blade Spacer
5	Breechbolt, Front	24	Safety-Lever
6	Breechbolt Handle	25	Safety Pin
7	Breechbolt, Rear	26	Sear
8	Breechbolt Assembly Pin	27	Sear Pin
9	Ejector	28	Sear and Trigger Spring
10	Extractor	29	Stock
11	Firing Pin	30	Swivels
12	Firing Pin Spring	31	Swivel Screws
13	Firing Pin Spring Guide	32	Takedown Screw
14	Front Sight	33	Trigger
15	Magazine	34	Trigger Pin
16	Magazine Catch	35	Trigger Guard Plate
17	Magazine Catch Pin	36	Trigger Guard Plate Screw, Front
18	Receiver	37	Trigger Guard Plate Screw, Rear
19	Recoil Pad		

Model 5510 Supergoose Bolt-Action Shotgun

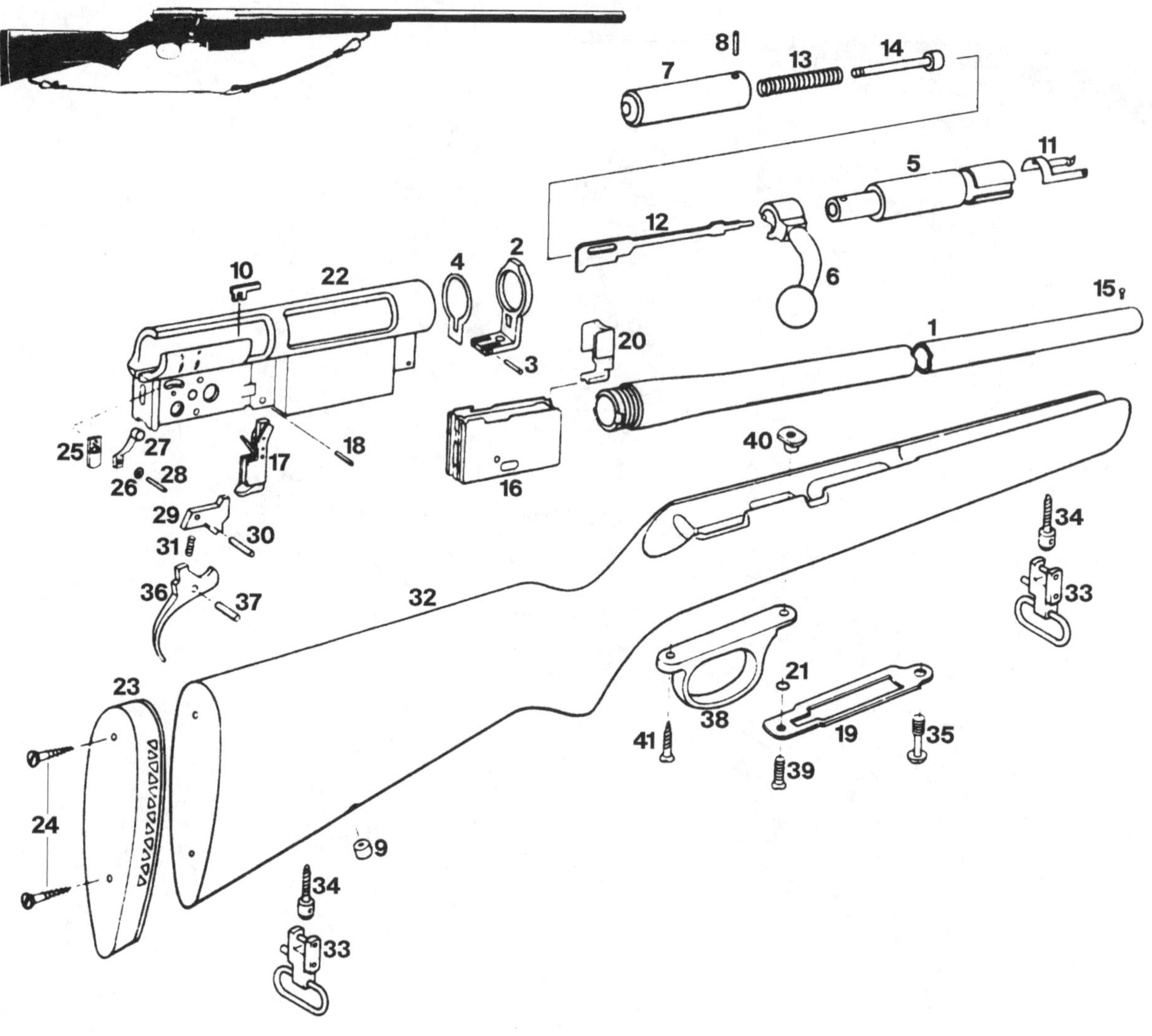

1	Barrel	22	Receiver
2	Barrel Collar	23	Recoil Pad
3	Barrel Collar Pin	24	Recoil Pad Screws
4	Barrel Washer	25	Safety Blade
5	Breechbolt, Front	26	Safety Blade Spacer
6	Breechbolt Handle	27	Safety-Lever
7	Breechbolt, Rear	28	Safety Pin
8	Breechbolt Assembly Pin	29	Sear
9	Bullseye	30	Sear Pin
10	Ejector	31	Sear and Trigger Spring
11	Extractor	32	Stock
12	Firing Pin	33	Swivels
13	Firing Pin Spring	34	Swivel Studs
14	Firing Pin Spring Guide	35	Takedown Screw
15	Front Sight	36	Trigger
16	Magazine	37	Trigger Pin
17	Magazine Catch	38	Trigger Guard
18	Magazine Catch Pin	39	Trigger Guard/Plate Screw
19	Magazine Guard Plate	40	Trigger Guard/Plate Screw Nut
20	Magazine Spacer	41	Rear Trigger Guard Screw
21	Magazine Guard Plate "O" Ring		

Model 56 Lever-Action Rifle

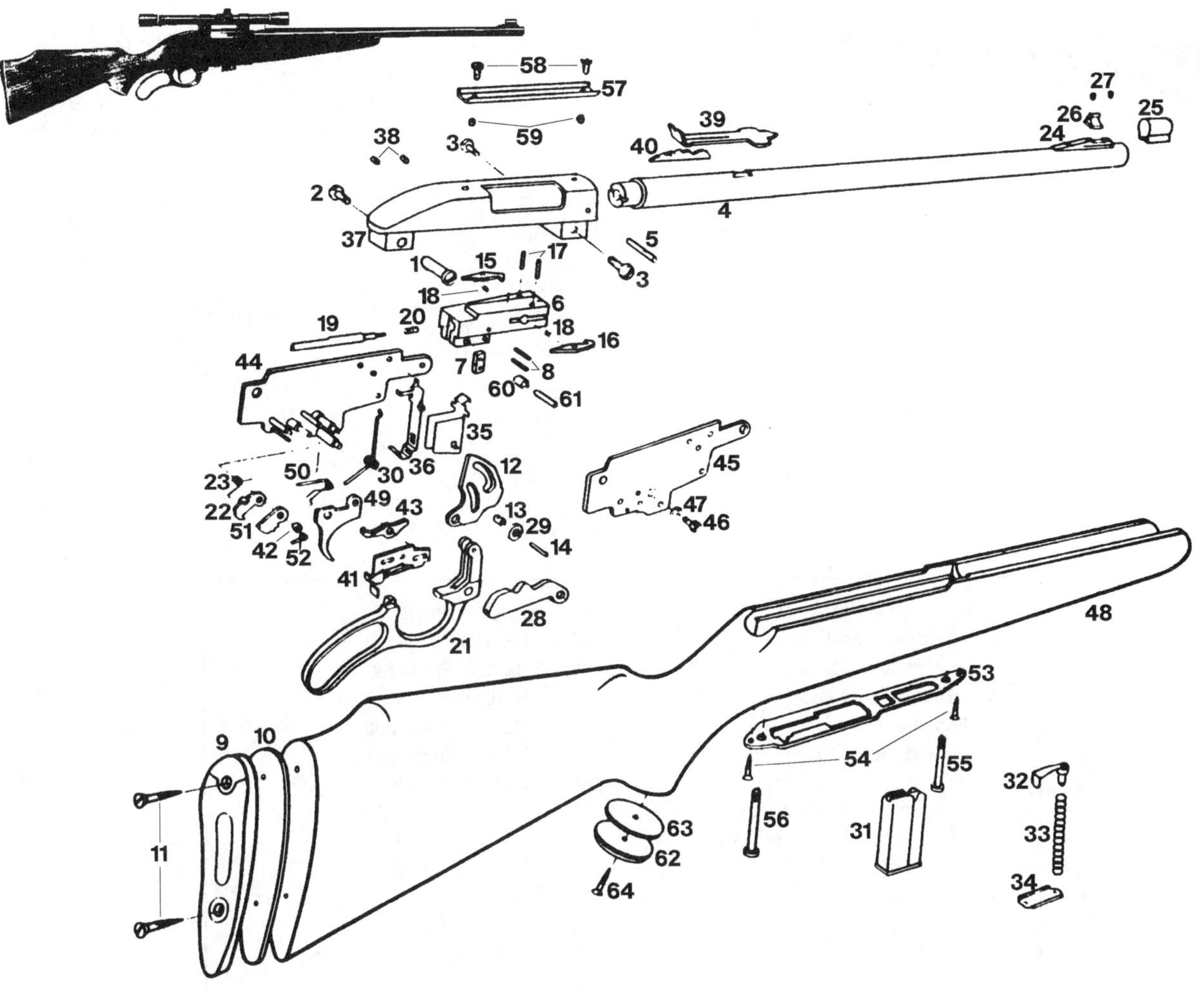

1	Assembly Post	23	Finger Lever Latch Spring	45	Right Sideplate
2	Assembly Post Screw	24	Front Ramp Sight Base	46	Sideplate Assembly Screw
3	Assembly Screws, Front	25	Front Sight Hood	47	Sideplate Assembly Screw Lock Washer
4	Barrel	26	Front Sight Insert	48	Stock
5	Barrel Retaining Pin	27	Front Sight Ramp Screws	49	Trigger
6	Breechbolt	28	Hammer	50	Trigger and Sear Spring
7	Breechbolt Bearing Insert	29	Hammer Cocking Roller	51	Trigger Block
8	Breechbolt Bearing Insert Pins	30	Hammer Spring	52	Trigger Block Spring
9	Buttplate	31	Magazine	53	Trigger Plate
10	Buttplate Spacer	32	Magazine Follower	54	Trigger Plate Screws
11	Buttplate Screws	33	Magazine Follower Spring	55	Takedown Screw, Front
12	Cam Lever	34	Magazine Bottom Plate	56	Takedown Screw, Rear
13	Cam Roller	35	Magazine Guide, Front	57	Scope Adapter Base with Screws
14	Cam Roller Pin	36	Magazine Latch and Ejector	58	Scope Adapter Base Screws
15	Extractor, Left	37	Receiver	59	Scope Adapter Base Dummy Screws
16	Extractor, Right	38	Receiver Peep Sight Dummy Screws	60	Breechbolt Cam Roller
17	Extractor Pins	39	Rear Sight	61	Breechbolt Cam Roller Pin
18	Extractor Springs	40	Rear Sight Elevator	62	Pistol Grip Cap
19	Firing Pin	41	Safety Slide	63	Pistol Grip Cap Spacer
20	Firing Pin Spring	42	Safety Slide Spacing Sleeve	64	Pistol Grip Cap Screw
21	Finger Lever	43	Sear		
22	Finger Lever Latch	44	Left Sideplate with Pins		

Model 57 Lever-Action Rifle

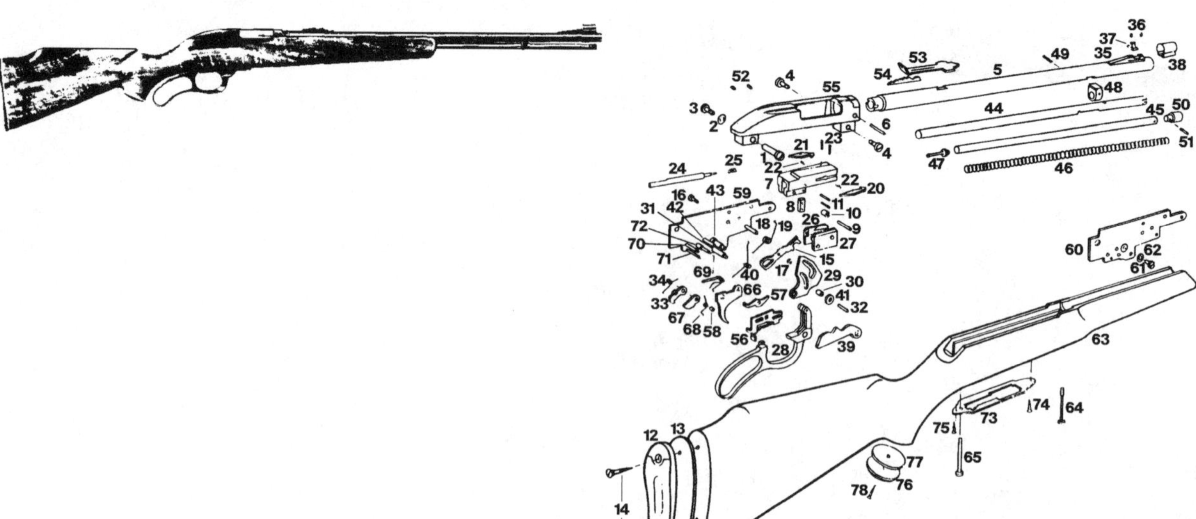

1	Assembly Post, Rear	40	Hammer Spring
2	Assembly Post Washer	41	Hammer Cocking Roller
3	Assembly Post Screw	42	Hammer Spring Mounting Pin
4	Assembly Screws	43	Hammer Pivot Pin
5	Barrel	44	Magazine Tube, Outside
6	Barrel Retaining Pin	45	Magazine Tube, Inside
7	Breechbolt	46	Magazine Tube Spring
8	Breechbolt Bearing Insert	47	Magazine Tube Follower
9	Breechbolt Cam Roller Pin	48	Magazine Tube Band
10	Breechbolt Cam Roller	49	Magazine Tube Band Pin
11	Breechbolt Bearing Inserts	50	Magazine Tube Plug
12	Buttplate	51	Magazine Tube Plug Pin
13	Buttplate Spacer	52	Peep Sight Dummy Screws
14	Buttplate Screws	53	Rear Sight
15	Cartridge Lifter	54	Rear Sight Elevator
16	Cartridge Lifter Pivot Stud	55	Receiver
17	Cartridge Lifter Stud Ring	56	Safety Slide
18	Cartridge Lifter Spring Mounting Pin	57	Sear
19	Cartridge Lifter Spring	58	Spacing Sleeve
20	Extractor, Right	59	Sideplate Assembly, Left
21	Extractor, Left	60	Sideplate, Right
22	Extractor Springs	61	Sideplate Assembly Screw
23	Extractor Pins	62	Sideplate Assembly Screw Lock Washer
24	Firing Pin	63	Stock
25	Firing Pin Spring	64	Takedown Screw, Front
26	Feed Throat, Left	65	Takedown Screw, Rear
27	Feed Throat, Right	66	Trigger
28	Finger Lever	67	Trigger Block
29	Finger Lever Cam	68	Trigger Block Spring
30	Finger Lever Cam Roller	69	Trigger and Sear Spring
31	Finger Lever Pivot Pin	70	Trigger Block Pivot Pin
32	Finger Lever Cam Roller Pin	71	Trigger Stop Pin
33	Finger Lever Latch	72	Trigger and Sear Pivot Pin
34	Finger Lever Latch Spring	73	Trigger Plate
35	Front Sight Ramp	74	Trigger Plate Screw, Front
36	Front Sight Ramp Screws	75	Trigger Plate Screw, Rear
37	Front Sight Ramp Insert	76	Pistol Grip Cap
38	Front Sight Ramp Hood	77	Pistol Grip Cap Spacer
39	Hammer	78	Pistol Grip Cap Screw

Model 59 and 60G Bolt-Action Shotgun

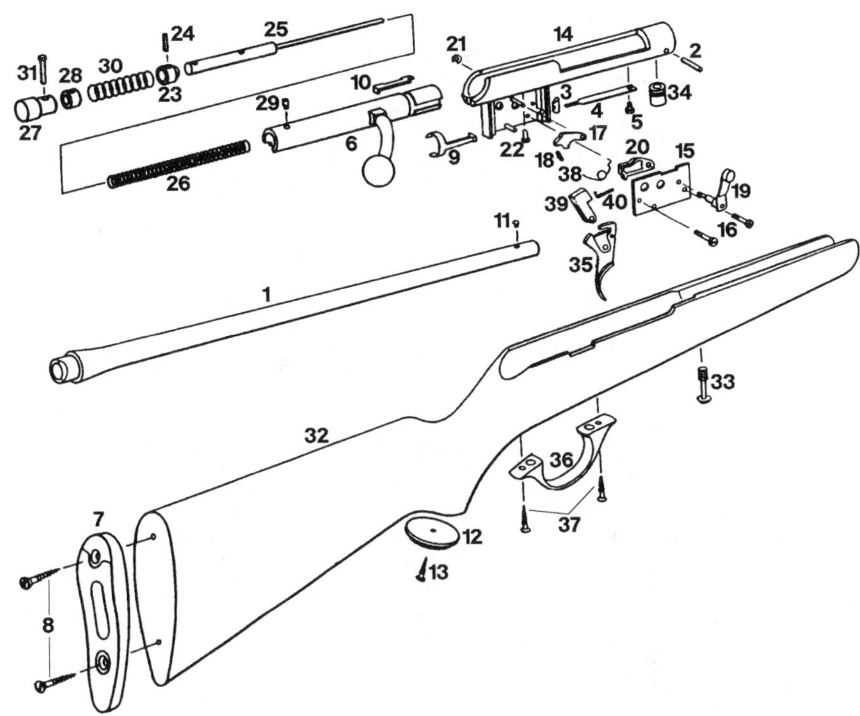

1	Barrel	**21**	Safety Lever Lock Ring
2	Barrel Retaining Pin	**22**	Safety Plunger
3	Bolt Stop	**23**	Striker Bushing
4	Bolt Stop Spring	**24**	Striker Bushing Pin
5	Bolt Stop Spring Screw	**25**	Striker
6	Breechbolt	**26**	Striker Guide Spring
7	Buttplate	**27**	Striker Knob
8	Buttplate Screws	**28**	Striker Sleeve
9	Extractor	**29**	Striker Sleeve Screw
10	Ejector	**30**	Striker Spring
11	Front Sight	**31**	Striker Cam Pin
12	Pistol Grip Cap	**32**	Stock
13	Pistol Grip Cap Screw	**33**	Takedown Screw
14	Receiver	**34**	Takedown Screw Stud
15	Receiver Extension Plate	**35**	Trigger
16	Receiver Extension Plate Screws	**36**	Trigger Guard
17	Sear	**37**	Trigger Guard Screws
18	Sear Spring	**38**	Trigger Spring
19	Safety-Lever	**39**	Trigger Yoke
20	Safety Lever Blade	**40**	Trigger Yoke Spring

Model 60 Autoloading Rifle

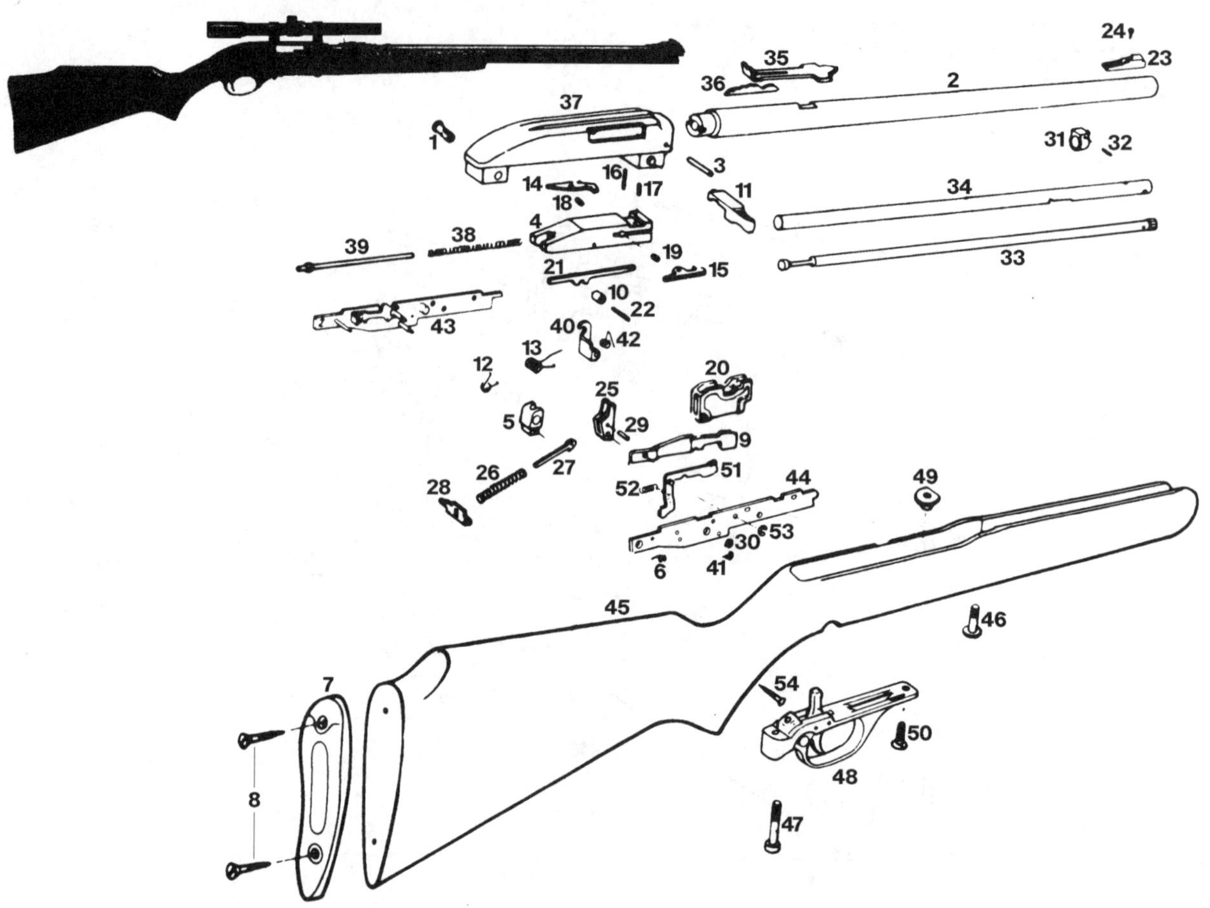

1	Assembly Post	**28**	Hammer Strut Bridge
2	Barrel	**29**	Hammer Strut Pin
3	Barrel Retaining Pin	**30**	Hammer Lifter Pin Ring
4	Breechbolt	**31**	Magazine Tube Band
5	Buffer	**32**	Magazine Tube Band Pin
6	Buffer Pin Ring	**33**	Magazine Tube, Inner
7	Buttplate	**34**	Magazine Tube, Outer
8	Buttplate Screws	**35**	Rear Sight
9	Cartridge Lifter	**36**	Rear Sight Elevator
10	Cartridge Lifter Roller	**37**	Receiver
11	Charging Handle	**38**	Recoil Spring
12	Disconnector Spring	**39**	Recoil Spring Guide
13	Ejector Lifter Spring	**40**	Sear
14	Left Extractor	**41**	Sear Pin Ring
15	Right Extractor	**42**	Sear Spring
16	Extractor Pin, Left	**43**	Sideplate Assembly, Left
17	Extractor Pin, Right	**44**	Sideplate, Right
18	Extractor Spring, Left	**45**	Stock
19	Extractor Spring, Right	**46**	Takedown Screw, Front
20	Feed Throat	**47**	Takedown Screw, Rear
21	Firing Pin	**48**	Trigger Guard Assembly
22	Firing Pin Retaining Pin	**49**	Trigger Guard Nut
23	Front Sight	**50**	Trigger Guard Screw
24	Front Sight Screw	**51**	Bolt Release Lever
25	Hammer	**52**	Extension Spring
26	Hammer Spring	**53**	Lever Retaining Ring
27	Hammer Strut	**54**	Stock Reinforcement Screw

Model 70HC Autoloading Rifle

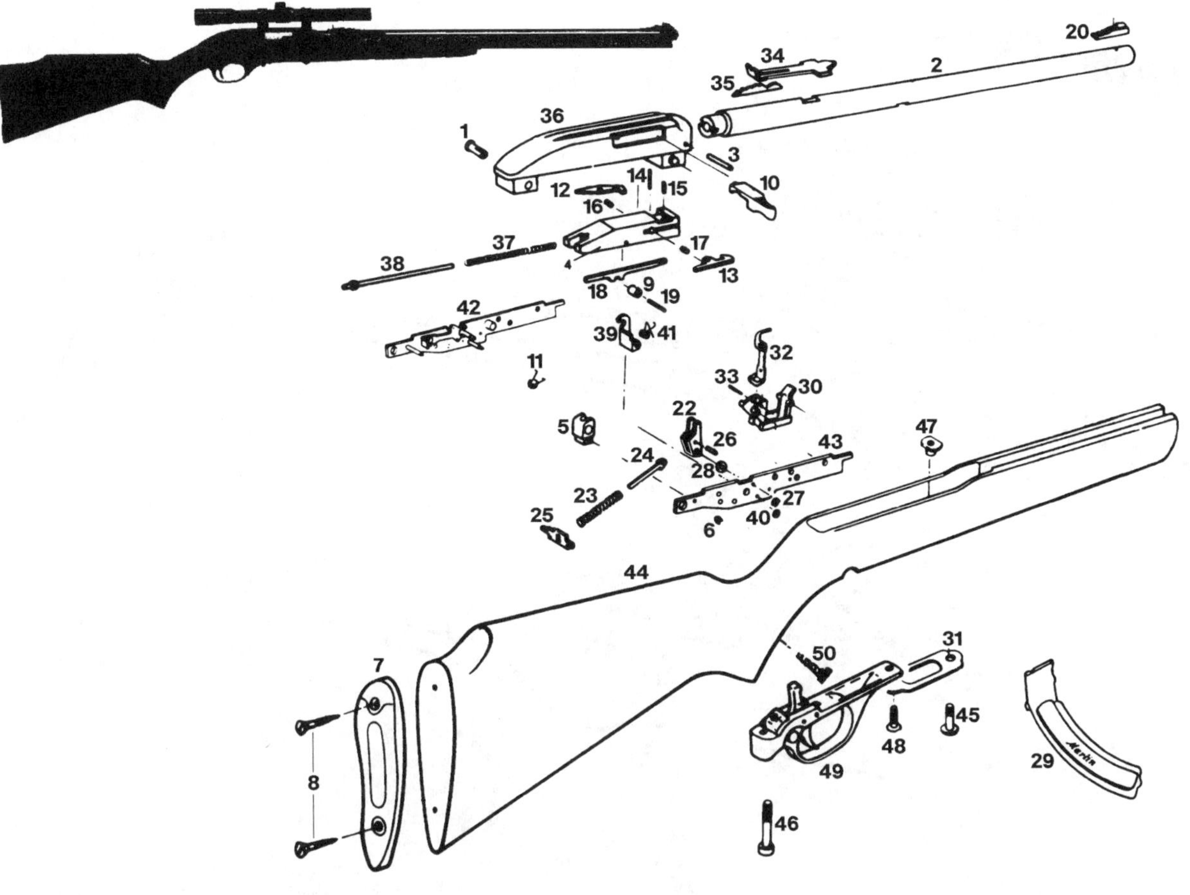

1	Assembly Post	26	Hammer Strut Pin
2	Barrel	27	Hammer Pin Ring
3	Barrel Retaining Pin	28	Hammer Spacer
4	Breechbolt	29	Magazine
5	Buffer	30	Magazine Guide
6	Buffer Pin Ring	31	Magazine Guard Plate
7	Buttplate	32	Magazine Latch and Ejector
8	Buttplate Screws	33	Magazine Latch Pin
9	Cartridge Lifter Roller	34	Rear Sight
10	Charging Handle	35	Rear Sight Elevator
11	Disconnector Spring	36	Receiver
12	Extractor, Left	37	Recoil Spring
13	Extractor, Right	38	Recoil Spring Guide
14	Extractor Pin, Left	39	Sear
15	Extractor Pin, Right	40	Sear Pin Ring
16	Extractor Spring, Left	41	Sear Spring
17	Extractor Spring, Right	42	Sideplate, Left
18	Firing Pin	43	Sideplate, Right
19	Firing Pin Retaining Pin	44	Stock
20	Front Sight	45	Takedown Screw, Front
21	Front Sight Screw	46	Takedown Screw, Rear
22	Hammer	47	Trigger Guard Nut
23	Hammer Spring	48	Trigger Guard Screw
24	Hammer Strut	49	Trigger Guard
25	Hammer Strut Bridge	50	Stock Reinforcement Screw

Model 70P Autoloading Carbine

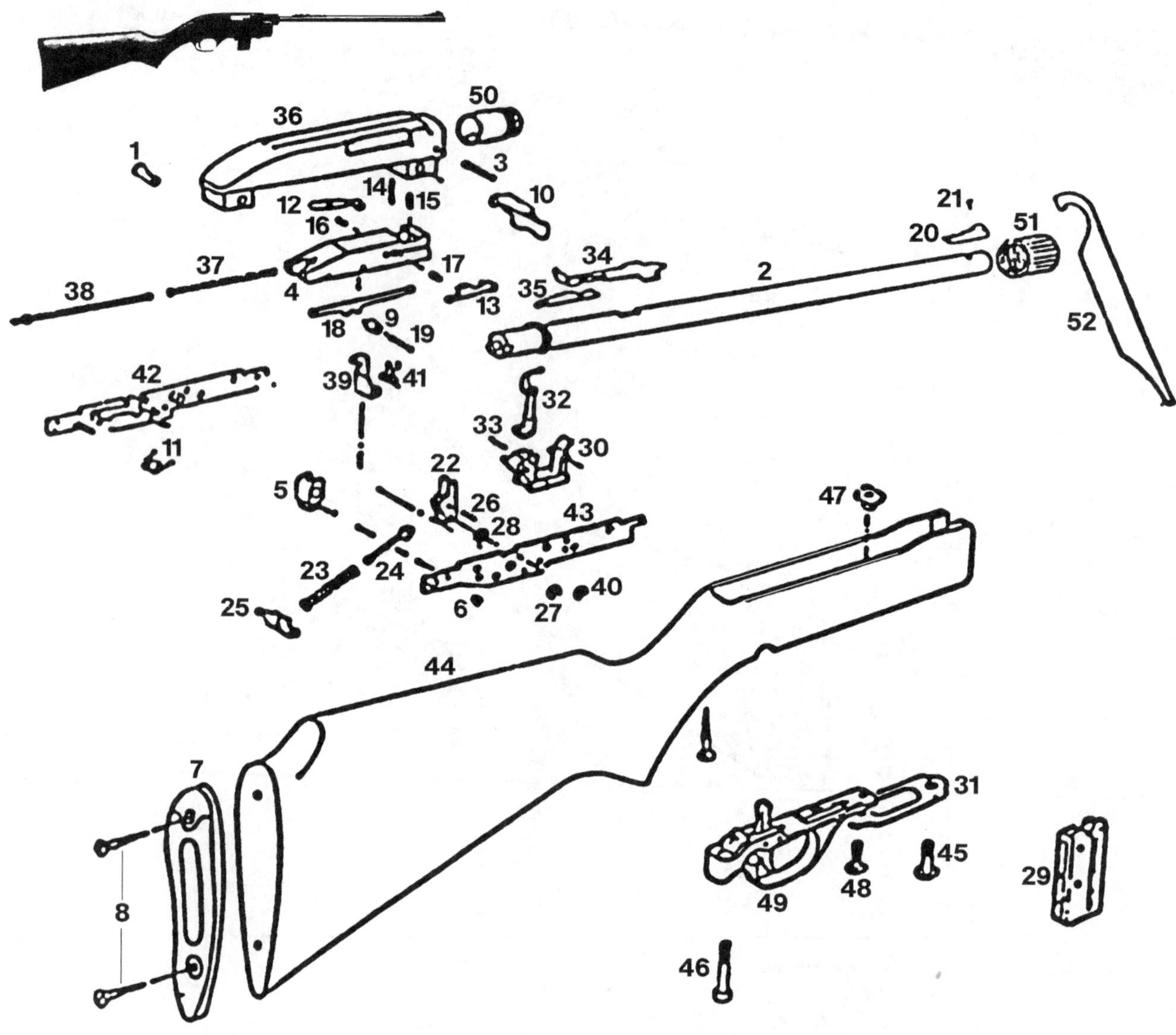

1	Assembly Post	**19**	Firing Pin Retaining Pin	**37**	Recoil Spring
2	Barrel	**20**	Front Sight	**38**	Recoil Spring Guide
3	Barrel Retaining Pin	**21**	Front Sight Screw	**39**	Sear
4	Breechbolt	**22**	Hammer	**40**	Sear Pin Ring
5	Buffer	**23**	Hammer Spring	**41**	Sear Spring
6	Buffer Pin Ring	**24**	Hammer Strut	**42**	Sideplate, Left
7	Buttplate	**25**	Hammer Strut Bridge	**43**	Sideplate, Right
8	Buttplate Screws	**26**	Hammer Strut Pin	**44**	Stock
9	Cartridge Lifter Roller	**27**	Hammer Pin Ring	**45**	Takedown Screw, Front
10	Charging Handle	**28**	Hammer Spacer	**46**	Takedown Screw, Rear
11	Disconnector Spring	**29**	Magazine	**47**	Trigger Guard Nut
12	Extractor, Left	**30**	Magazine Guide	**48**	Trigger Guard Screw, Front
13	Extractor, Right	**31**	Magazine Guide Plate	**49**	Trigger Guard
14	Extractor Pin, Left	**32**	Magazine Latch and Ejector	**50**	Receiver Adapter
15	Extractor Pin, Right	**33**	Magazine Latch Pin	**51**	Takedown Nut
16	Extractor Spring, Left	**34**	Rear Sight Base	**52**	Spanner Wrench
17	Extractor Spring, Right	**35**	Rear Sight Elevator		
18	Firing Pin	**36**	Receiver		

Model 75 and 75C Autoloading Carbine

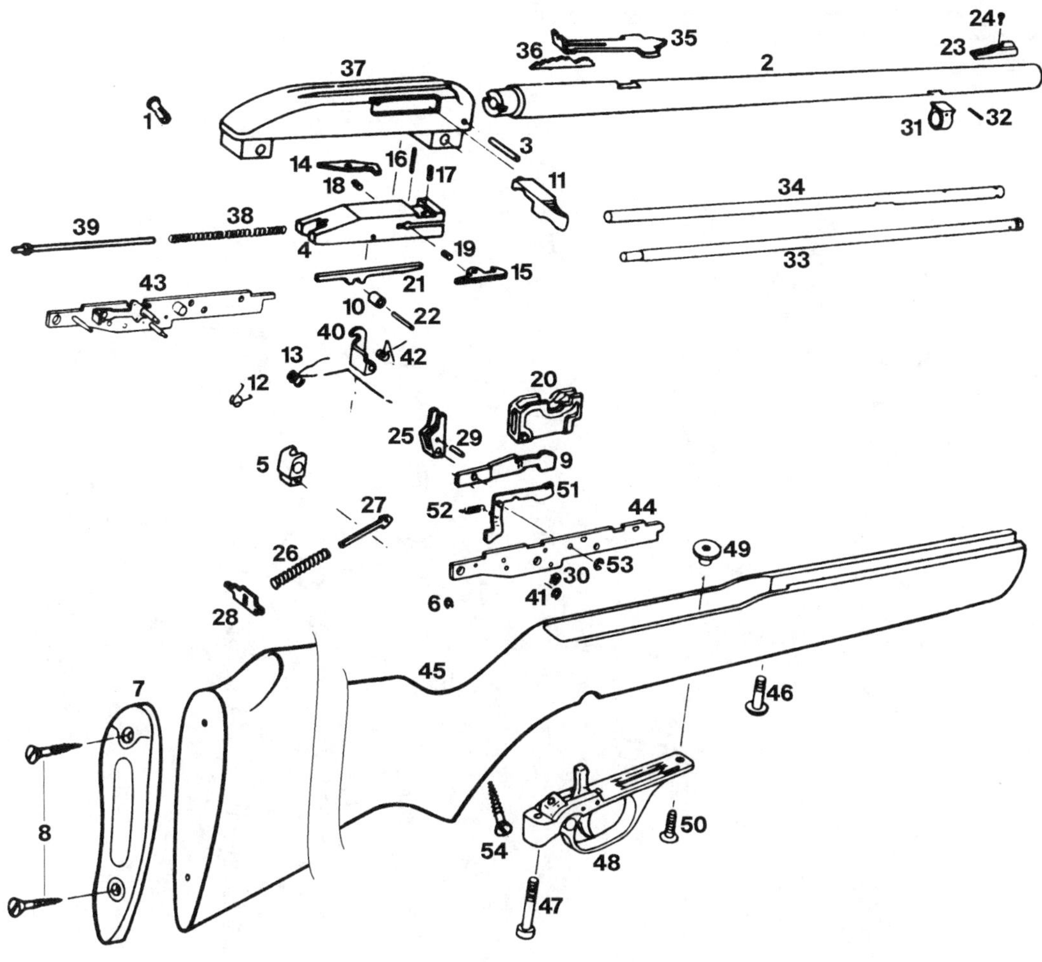

1	Assembly Post	**28**	Hammer Strut Bridge
2	Barrel	**29**	Hammer Strut Pin
3	Barrel Retaining Pin	**30**	Hammer/Lifter Pin Ring
4	Breechbolt	**31**	Magazine Tube Band
5	Buffer	**32**	Magazine Tube Band Pin
6	Buffer Pin Ring	**33**	Magazine Tube, Inside
7	Buttplate	**34**	Magazine Tube, Outside
8	Buttplate Screws	**35**	Rear Sight
9	Cartridge Lifter	**36**	Rear Sight Elevator
10	Cartridge Lifter Roller	**37**	Receiver
11	Charging Handle	**38**	Recoil Spring
12	Disconnector Spring	**39**	Recoil Spring Guide
13	Ejector/Lifter Spring	**40**	Sear
14	Extractor, Left	**41**	Sear Pin Ring
15	Extractor, Right	**42**	Sear Spring
16	Extractor Pin, Left	**43**	Sideplate Assembly, Left
17	Extractor Pin, Right	**44**	Sideplate, Right
18	Extractor Spring, Left	**45**	Stock
19	Extractor Spring, Right	**46**	Takedown Screw, Front
20	Feed Throat	**47**	Takedown Screw, Rear
21	Firing Pin	**48**	Trigger Guard Assembly
22	Firing Pin Retaining Pin	**49**	Trigger Guard Nut, Front
23	Front Sight	**50**	Trigger Guard Screw, Front
24	Front Sight Screw	**51**	Stop/Release Lever Assembly
25	Hammer	**52**	Extension Spring
26	Hammer Spring	**53**	Lever Retaining Ring
27	Hammer Strut	**54**	Stock Reinforcement Screw

Model 778 and 120 and Glenfield Model 778 Slide-Action Shotgun

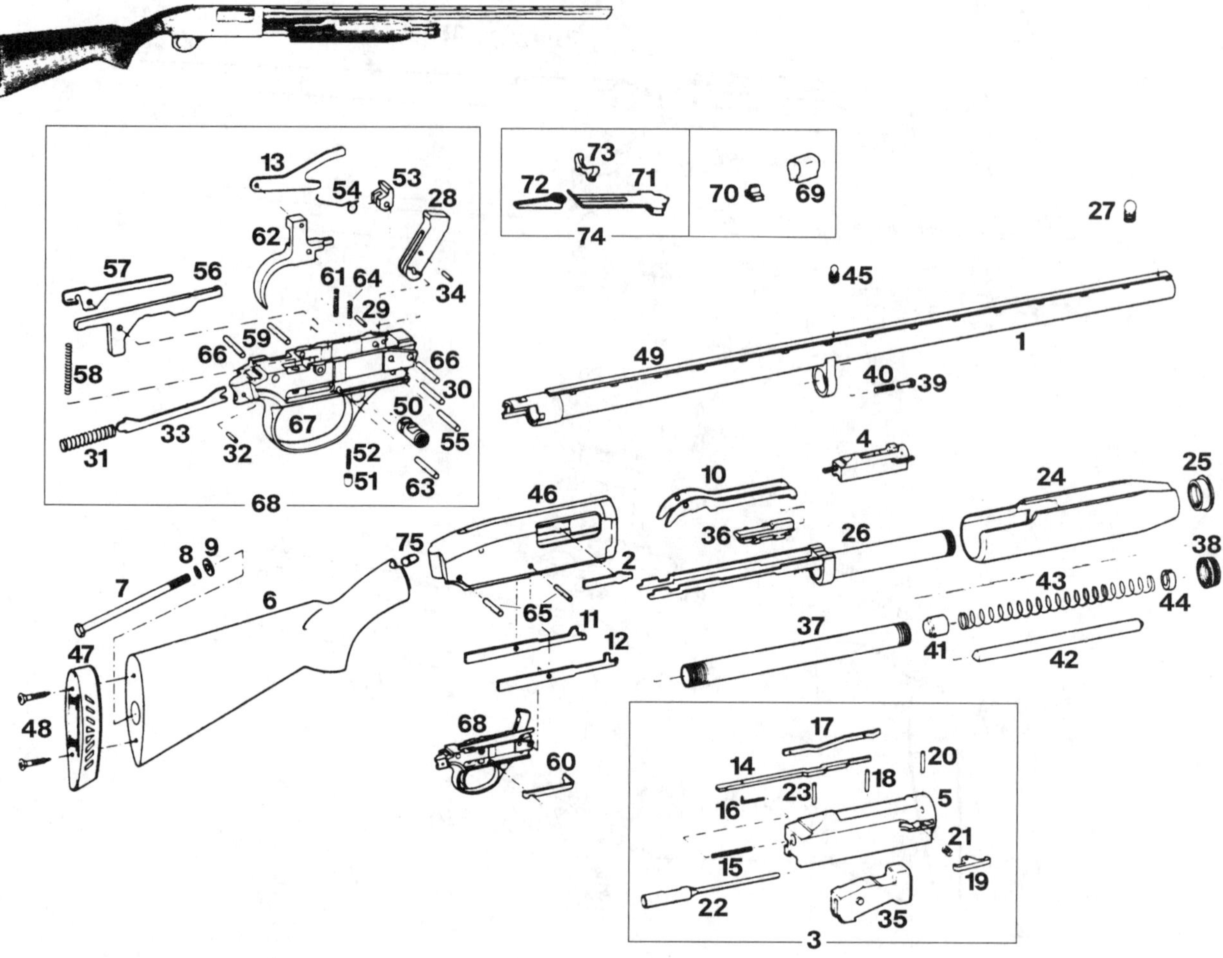

No.	Part	No.	Part	No.	Part
1	Barrel Assembly	27	Front Sight Bead	53	Sear
2	Barrel Locator	28	Hammer	54	Sear and Disconnector Spring
3	Breechbolt Complete	29	Hammer Location Pin	55	Sear Pin
4	Breechbolt Assembly	30	Hammer Pin	56	Slide Lock
5	Breechbolt	31	Hammer Spring	57	Slide Lock Actuator
6	Buttstock	32	Hammer Spring Pin	58	Slide Lock Actuator Spring
7	Buttstock Bolt	33	Hammer Strut	59	Slide Lock Pin
8	Buttstock Bolt Lock Washer	34	Hammer Strut Pin	60	Slide Lock Release
9	Buttstock Bolt Washer	35	Locking Bolt	61	Slide Lock Spring
10	Carrier	36	Lock Bolt Slide	62	Trigger
11	Cartridge Cutoff, Left	37	Magazine Tube	63	Trigger Pin
12	Cartridge Cutoff, Right	38	Magazine Tube Cap	64	Trigger Spring
13	Disconnector	39	Magazine Tube Cap Detent	65	Trigger Guard Retaining Pins
14	Ejector	40	Magazine Tube Cap Detent Spring	66	Trigger Guard Retaining Pin<R>Bushings
15	Ejector Spring	41	Magazine Tube Follower	67	Trigger Housing
16	Ejector Spring Retainer	42	Magazine Tube Plug	68	Trigger Housing Complete
17	Extractor, Left	43	Magazine Tube Spring	69	Front Sight Hood
18	Extractor Pin, Left	44	Magazine Tube Spring Retainer	70	Front Sight Insert
19	Extractor, Right	45	Middle Sight Bead	71	Rear Sight Base
20	Extractor Pin, Right	46	Receiver	72	Rear Sight Elevator
21	Extractor Spring, Right	47	Recoil Pad	73	Rear Sight Folding Leaf
22	Firing Pin	48	Recoil Pad Screws	74	Rear Sight Complete
23	Firing Pin Retaining Pin	49	Rib	75	Sleeve/Buttstock Bolt
24	Forearm	50	Safety		
25	Forearm Retaining Nut	51	Safety Plunger		
26	Forearm Liner Assembly	52	Safety Plunger Spring		

Model 780 and Glenfield Model 20 and 25 Bolt-Action Rifle

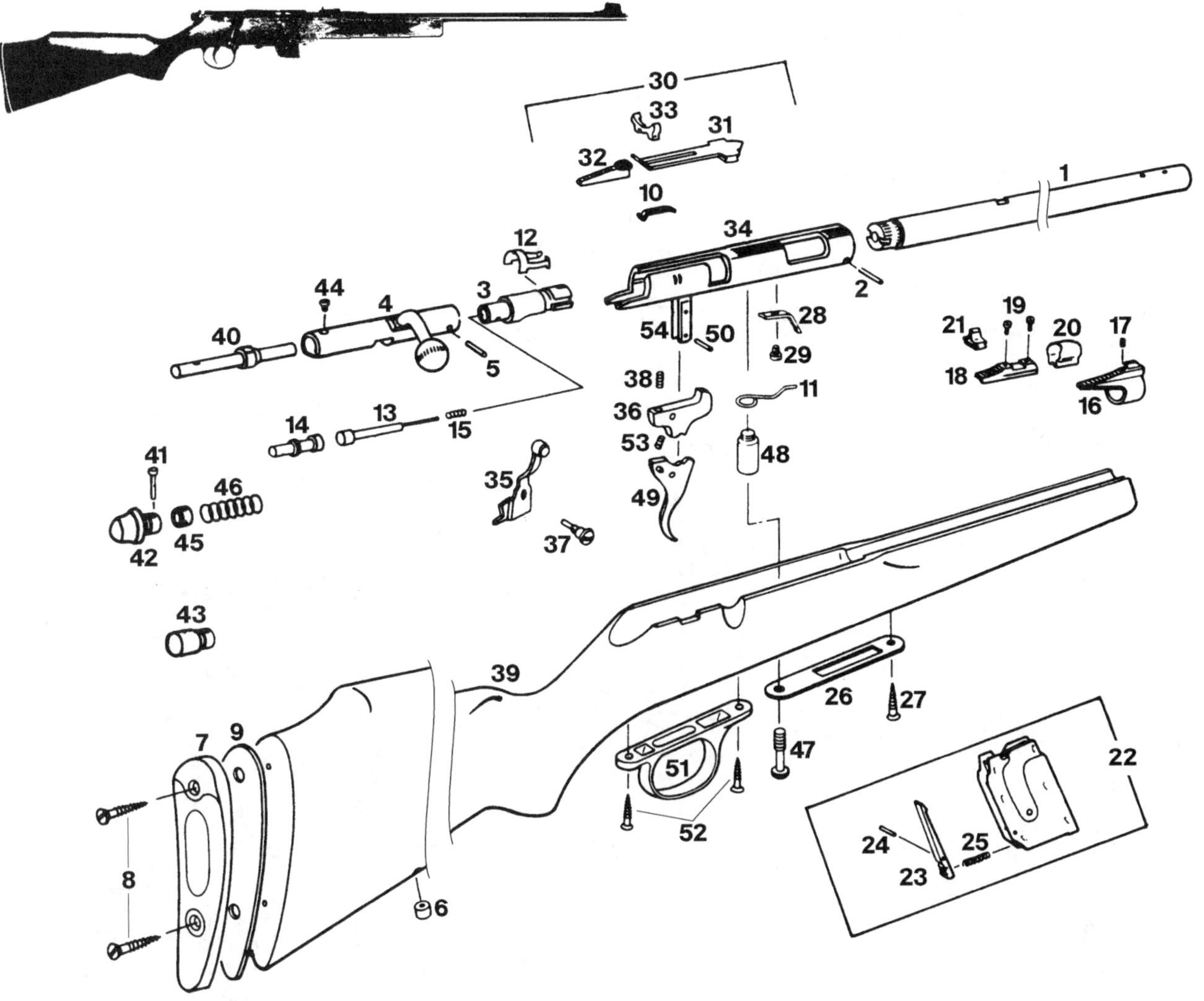

1	Barrel	**21**	Front Sight Ramp Insert	**42**	Striker Knob (Old Style)
2	Barrel Retaining Pin	**22**	Magazine Complete	**43**	Striker Knob
3	Breechbolt, Front	**23**	Magazine Catch	**44**	Striker Retaining Screw
4	Breechbolt, Rear	**24**	Magazine Catch Pin	**45**	Striker Sleeve
5	Breechbolt Retaining Pin	**25**	Magazine Catch Spring	**46**	Striker Spring
6	Bullseye	**26**	Magazine Guard Plate	**47**	Takedown Screw
7	Buttplate	**27**	Magazine Guard Plate Screw	**48**	Takedown Screw Stud
8	Buttplate Screws	**28**	Magazine Receiver Catch	**49**	Trigger
9	Buttplate Spacer	**29**	Magazine Receiver Catch Screw	**50**	Trigger Pin
10	Cartridge Guide Spring	**30**	Rear Sight Complete (New Style)	**51**	Trigger Guard
11	Ejector	**31**	Rear Sight Base	**52**	Trigger Guard Screws
12	Extractor	**32**	Rear Sight Elevator	**53**	Trigger Spring
13	Firing Pin, Front	**33**	Rear Sight Folding Leaf	**54**	Trigger Stud
14	Firing Pin, Rear	**34**	Receiver	**Parts Not Shown**	
15	Firing Pin Spring	**35**	Safety		Rear Sight (Old Style)
16	Front Sight Assembly (Old Style)	**36**	Sear		Sear (Old Style)
17	Front Sight Binding Screw (Old Style)	**37**	Sear and Safety Pivot Screw		Sear Spring (Old Style)
18	Front Sight Ramp Base	**38**	Sear Spring		Trigger (Old Style)
19	Front Sight Ramp Base Screws	**39**	Stock		Trigger Spring (Old Style)
20	Front Sight Ramp Hood	**40**	Striker		
		41	Striker Cam Pin		

Model 80C and 80DL Bolt-Action Rifle

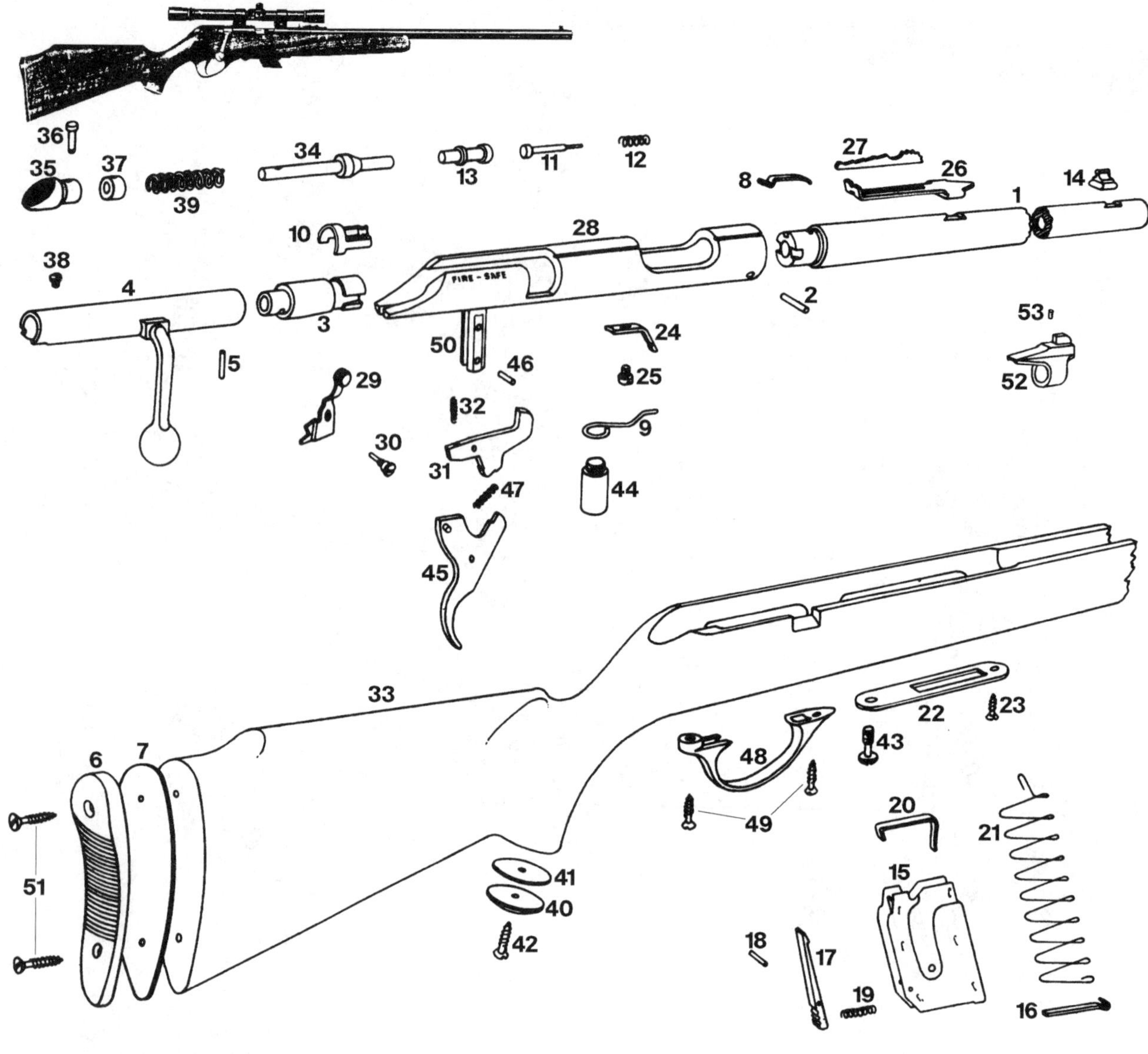

1	Barrel	20	Magazine Follower	39	Striker Spring
2	Barrel Retaining Pin	21	Magazine Follower Spring	40	Pistol Grip Cap
3	Breechbolt, Front	22	Magazine Guard Plate	41	Pistol Grip Cap Spacer
4	Breechbolt, Rear	23	Magazine Guard Plate Screw	42	Pistol Grip Cap Screw
5	Breechbolt Retaining Pin	24	Magazine Receiver Catch	43	Takedown Screw
6	Buttplate	25	Magazine Receiver Catch Screw	44	Takedown Screw Stud
7	Buttplate Spacer	26	Rear Sight	45	Trigger
8	Cartridge Guide Spring	27	Rear Sight Elevator	46	Trigger Pin
9	Ejector	28	Receiver	47	Trigger Spring
10	Extractor	29	Safety	48	Trigger Guard
11	Firing Pin, Front	30	Safety Pivot Screw	49	Trigger Guard Screws
12	Firing Pin Spring, Front	31	Sear	50	Trigger Stud
13	Firing Pin, Rear	32	Sear Spring	51	Buttplate Screws
14	Front Sight	33	Stock	52	Front Ramp Sight
15	Magazine	34	Striker	53	Front Sight Screw
16	Magazine Bottom Plate	35	Striker Knob	**Parts Not Shown**	
17	Magazine Catch	36	Striker Cam Pin		Sear Pin
18	Magazine Catch Pin	37	Striker Sleeve		
19	Magazine Catch Spring	38	Striker Sleeve Screw		

Model 880 Bolt-Action Rifle

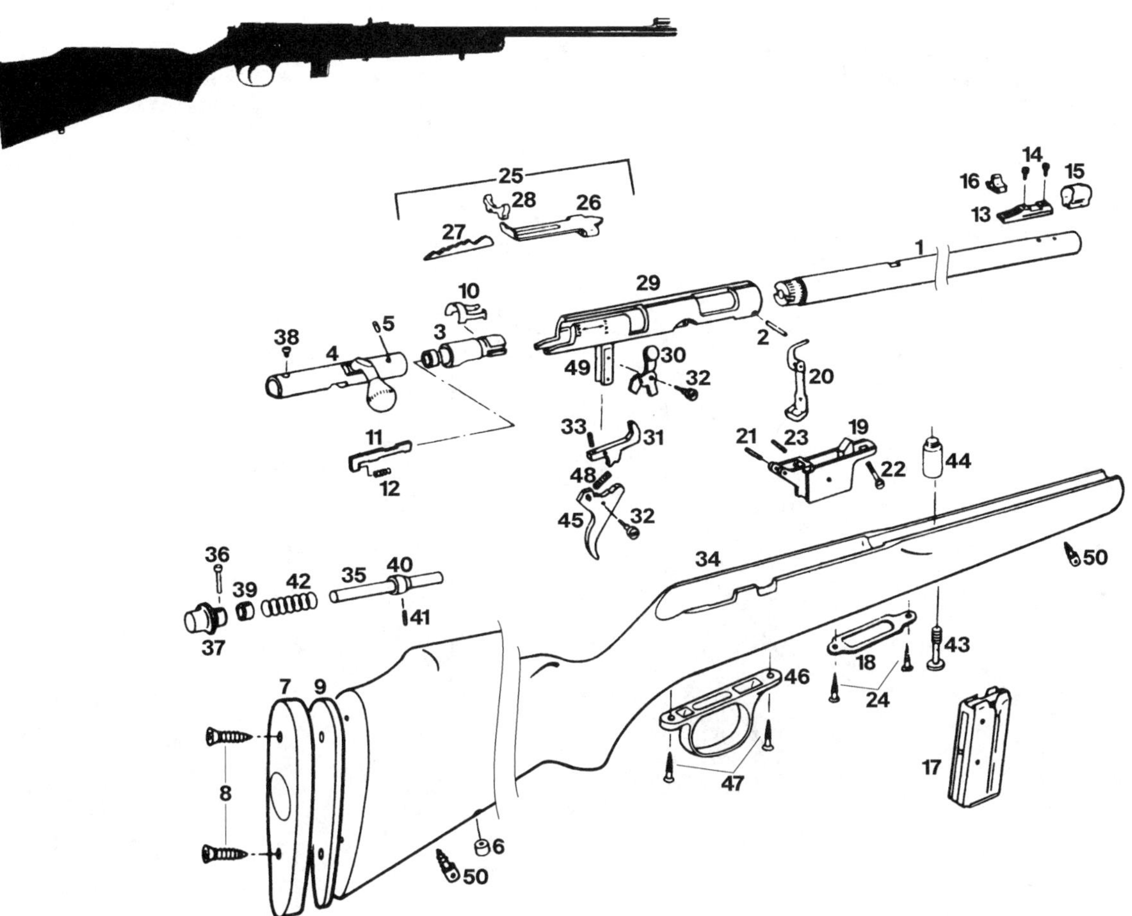

1	Barrel	26	Rear Sight Base
2	Barrel Retaining Pin	27	Rear Sight Elevator
3	Breechbolt, Front	28	Rear Sight Folding Leaf
4	Breechbolt, Rear	29	Receiver
5	Breechbolt Assembly Pin	30	Safety Assembly
6	Bullseye	31	Sear
7	Buttpad	32	Trigger Safety Screws
8	Buttpad Screws	33	Sear Spring
9	Buttpad Spacer	34	Stock
10	Extractor	35	Striker
11	Firing Pin	36	Striker Cam Pin
12	Firing Pin Spring	37	Striker Knob
13	Front Sight Ramp Base	38	Striker Retaining Screw
14	Front Sight Ramp Base Screws	39	Striker Sleeve
15	Front Sight Ramp Hood	40	Striker Cam Bushing
16	Front Sight Ramp Insert	41	Striker Assembly Pin
17	Magazine Complete	42	Striker Spring
18	Magazine Guide Plate	43	Takedown Screw
19	Magazine Guide	44	Takedown Screw Stud
20	Magazine Latch and Ejector	45	Trigger
21	Magazine Guide and Latch Assembly Pin	46	Trigger Guard
		47	Trigger Guard Screws
22	Magazine Guide Screw	48	Trigger Spring
23	Magazine Guide Pivot Pin	49	Trigger Stud
24	Magazine Guide Plate Screws	50	Swivel Studs
25	Rear Sight Complete		

Model 883 Bolt-Action Rifle

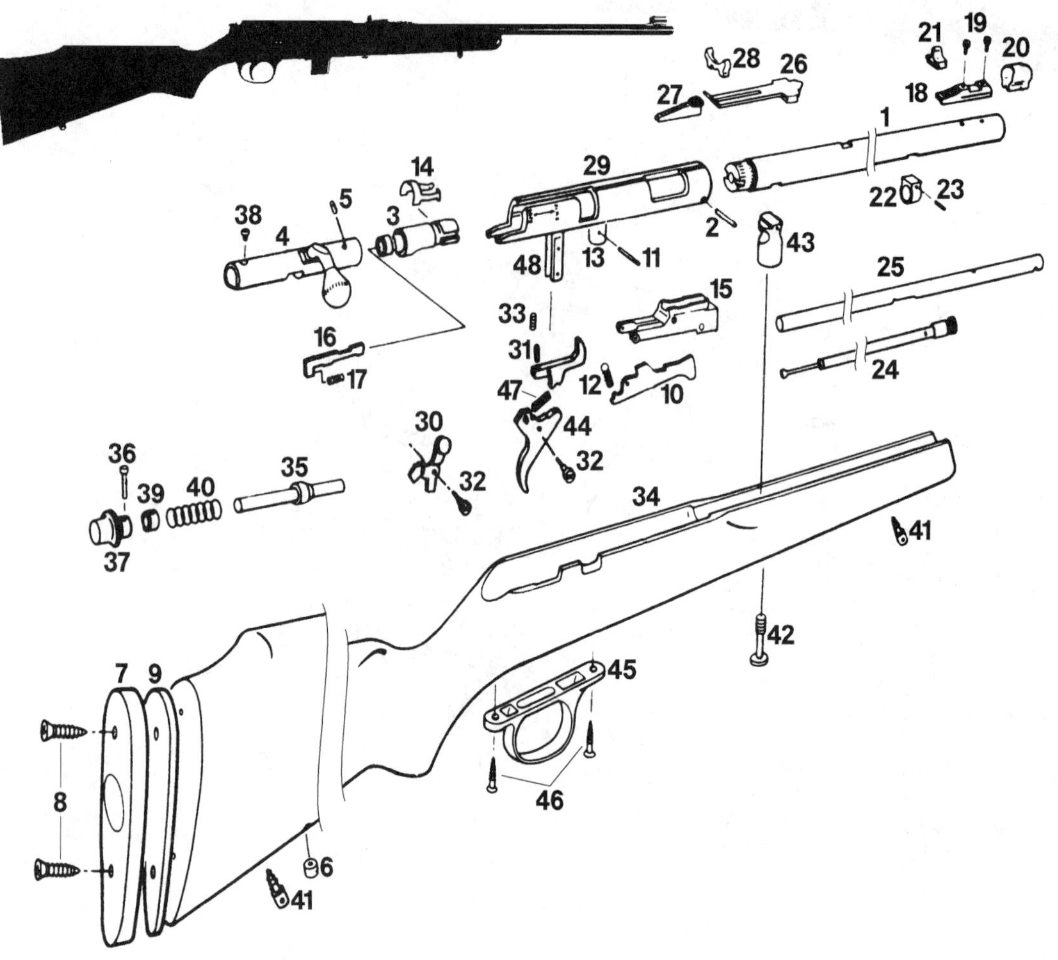

1	Barrel	25	Magazine Tube, Outside
2	Barrel Retaining Pin	26	Rear Sight Base
3	Breechbolt, Front	27	Rear Sight Elevator
4	Breechbolt, Rear	28	Rear Sight Folding Leaf
5	Breechbolt Assembly Pin	29	Receiver
6	Bullseye	30	Safety Assembly
7	Buttpad	31	Sear
8	Buttpad Screws	32	Trigger Safety Pivot Screws
9	Buttpad Spacer	33	Sear Spring
10	Cartridge Lifter	34	Stock
11	Cartridge Lifter Pivot Pin	35	Striker
12	Cartridge Lifter Spring	36	Striker Cam Pin
13	Cartridge Lifter Stud	37	Striker Knob
14	Extractor	38	Striker Retaining Screw
15	Feed Throat	39	Striker Sleeve
16	Firing Pin	40	Striker Spring
17	Firing Pin Spring	41	Swivel Studs
18	Front Sight Base	42	Takedown Screw
19	Front Sight Base Screws	43	Takedown Screw Stud
20	Front Sight Hood	44	Trigger
21	Front Sight Insert	45	Trigger Guard
22	Magazine Tube Band	46	Trigger Guard Screws
23	Magazine Tube Band Pin	47	Trigger Spring
24	Magazine Tube, Inside	48	Trigger Stud

Model 9 Autoloading Carbine

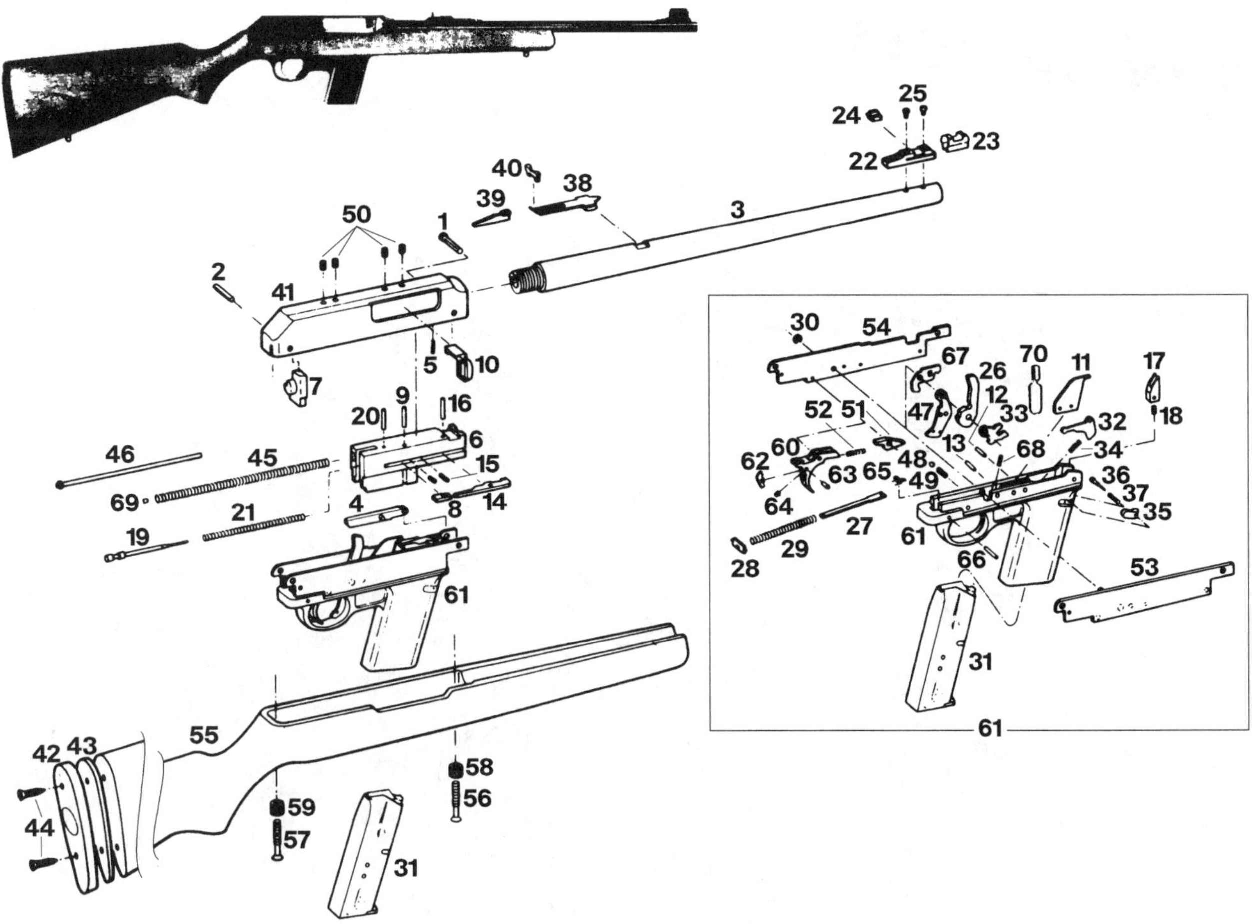

1	Action Assembly Pin, Front
2	Action Assembly Pin, Rear
3	Barrel
4	Bolt Stop
5	Bolt Stop Spring
6	Breechbolt
7	Buffer
8	Cartridge Indicator
9	Cartridge Indicator Assembly Pin
10	Charging Handle
11	Ejector
12	Ejector/Magazine Disconnector Pin
13	Ejector Pin, Rear
14	Extractor
15	Extractor/Cartridge Indicator Springs
16	Extractor Pin
17	Feed Ramp
18	Feed Ramp Spring
19	Firing Pin
20	Firing Pin Assembly Pin
21	Firing Pin Spring
22	Front Sight Ramp Base
23	Front Sight Ramp Cutaway Hood
24	Front Sight Ramp Red Insert
25	Front Sight Ramp Screws
26	Hammer
27	Hammer Strut
28	Hammer Strut Bridge
29	Hammer Strut Spring
30	Hammer Pivot Pin Retaining Ring
31	Magazine
32	Magazine Disconnector
33	Magazine Disconnector Trigger Block
34	Magazine Disconnector Spring
35	Magazine Latch
36	Magazine Latch Retaining Screw
37	Magazine Latch Retaining Spring
38	Rear Sight Base
39	Rear Sight Elevator
40	Rear Sight Leaf
41	Receiver
42	Recoil Pad
43	Recoil Pad Spacer
44	Recoil Pad Screws
45	Recoil Spring
46	Recoil Spring Rod
47	Safety
48	Safety Plunger Ball
49	Safety Plunger Spring
50	Scope Mount Dummy Screws
51	Sear
52	Sear Spring
53	Sideplate, Right
54	Sideplate, Left
55	Stock
56	Takedown Screw, Front
57	Takedown Screw, Rear
58	Takedown Screw Bushing, Front
59	Takedown Screw Bushing, Rear
60	Trigger
61	Trigger Guard
62	Trigger Disconnector
63	Trigger Disconnector Pin
64	Trigger Disconnector Spring
65	Trigger Return Spring
66	Trigger Return Spring Pin
67	Trigger Block
68	Trigger Block Spring
69	Firing Pin Bushing
70	Manual Hold-Open Lever

Model 989M2 Autoloading Carbine

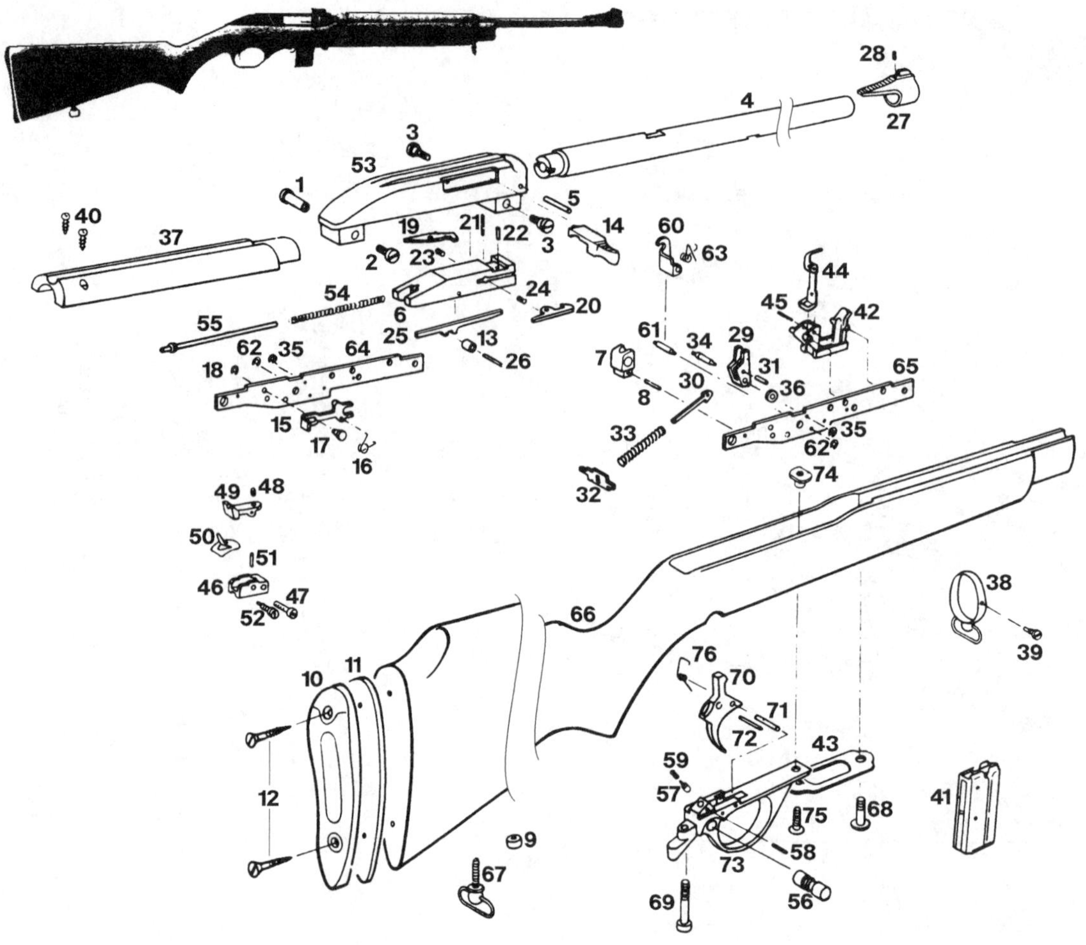

1	Assembly Post	**27**	Front Sight Complete	**53**	Receiver
2	Assembly Post Screw	**28**	Front Sight Binding Screw	**54**	Recoil Spring
3	Assembly Screws, Front	**29**	Hammer	**55**	Recoil Spring Guide
4	Barrel	**30**	Hammer Strut	**56**	Safety
5	Barrel Retaining Pin	**31**	Hammer Strut Pin	**57**	Safety Plunger
6	Breechbolt	**32**	Hammer Strut Bridge	**58**	Safety Plunger Pin
7	Buffer	**33**	Hammer Spring	**59**	Safety Plunger Spring
8	Buffer Pin	**34**	Hammer Pin	**60**	Sear
9	Bullseye	**35**	Hammer Pin Ring	**61**	Sear Pin
10	Buttplate	**36**	Hammer Spacer	**62**	Sear Pin Ring
11	Buttplate Spacer	**37**	Handguard	**63**	Sear Spring
12	Buttplate Screws	**38**	Handguard Band with Swivel	**64**	Sideplate, Left
13	Cartridge Lifter Roller	**39**	Handguard Band Screw	**65**	Sideplate, Right
14	Charging Handle	**40**	Handguard Screws	**66**	Stock
15	Disconnector	**41**	Magazine Complete	**67**	Swivel, Rear
16	Disconnector Spring	**42**	Magazine Guide	**68**	Takedown Screw, Front
17	Disconnector Stud	**43**	Magazine Guard Plate	**69**	Takedown Screw, Rear
18	Disconnector Stud Ring	**44**	Magazine Latch and Ejector	**70**	Trigger
19	Extractor, Left	**45**	Magazine Latch Pin	**71**	Trigger Pin
20	Extractor, Right	**46**	Rear Sight Base	**72**	Trigger Stop Pin
21	Extractor Pin, Left	**47**	Rear Sight Binding Screw	**73**	Trigger Guard
22	Extractor Pin, Right	**48**	Rear Sight Elevator Screw	**74**	Trigger Guard Nut, Front
23	Extractor Spring, Left	**49**	Rear Sight Leaf	**75**	Trigger Guard Screw, Front
24	Extractor Spring, Right	**50**	Rear Sight Leaf Spring	**76**	Trigger Spring
25	Firing Pin	**51**	Rear Sight Pin		
26	Firing Pin Retaining Pin	**52**	Rear Sight Windage Screw		

Model 995 Autoloading Carbine

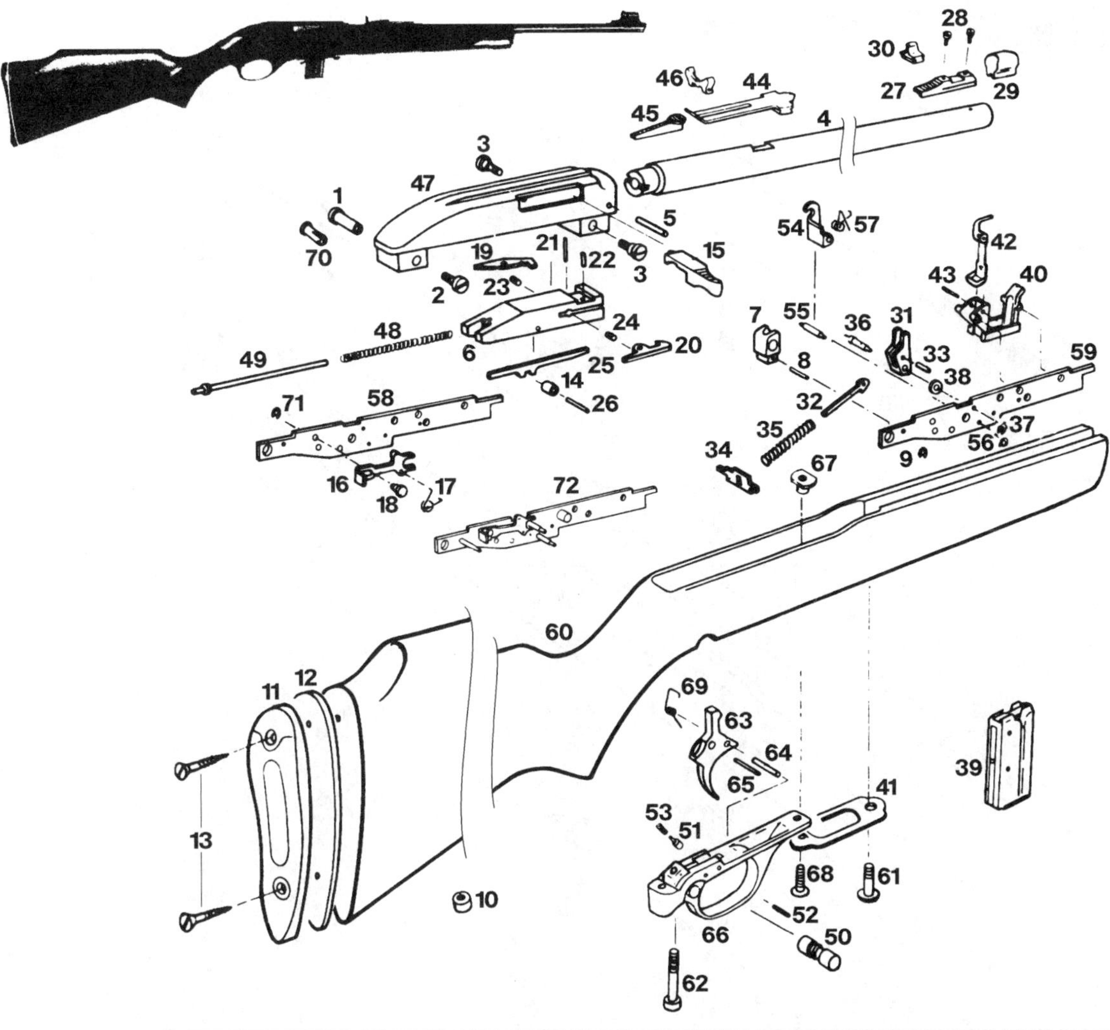

1	Assembly Post (Old Style)
2	Assembly Post Screw (Old Style)
3	Assembly Screws, Front (Old Style)
4	Barrel
5	Barrel Retaining Pin
6	Breechbolt
7	Buffer
8	Buffer Pin (Old Style)
9	Buffer Pin Ring
10	Bullseye
11	Buttplate
12	Buttplate Spacer
13	Buttplate Screws
14	Cartridge Lifter Roller
15	Charging Handle
16	Disconnector
17	Disconnector Spring
18	Disconnector Stud (Old Style)
19	Extractor, Left
20	Extractor, Right
21	Extractor Pin, Left
22	Extractor Pin, Right
23	Extractor Spring, Left
24	Extractor Spring, Right
25	Firing Pin
26	Firing Pin Retaining Pin
27	Front Sight Ramp Base
28	Front Sight Ramp Base Screws
29	Front Sight Ramp Hood
30	Front Sight Ramp Insert
31	Hammer
32	Hammer Strut
33	Hammer Strut Pin
34	Hammer Strut Bridge
35	Hammer Spring
36	Hammer Pin (Old Style)
37	Hammer Pin Ring
38	Hammer Spacer
39	Magazine Complete
40	Magazine Guide
41	Magazine Guard Plate
42	Magazine Latch and Ejector
43	Magazine Latch Pin
44	Rear Sight Base
45	Rear Sight Elevator
46	Rear Sight Folding Leaf
47	Receiver
48	Recoil Spring
49	Recoil Spring Guide
50	Safety
51	Safety Plunger
52	Safety Plunger Pin
53	Safety Plunger Spring
54	Sear
55	Sear Pin (Old Style)
56	Sear Pin Ring
57	Sear Spring
58	Sideplate, Left
59	Sideplate, Right
60	Stock
61	Takedown Screw, Front
62	Takedown Screw, Rear
63	Trigger
64	Trigger Pin
65	Trigger Stop Pin
66	Trigger Guard
67	Trigger Guard Nut, Front
68	Trigger Guard Screw, Front
69	Trigger Spring
70	Assembly Post (New Style)
71	Disconnector Stud Ring
72	Sideplate Sub-Assembly, Left

Model 1888 Commission Bolt-Action Rifle

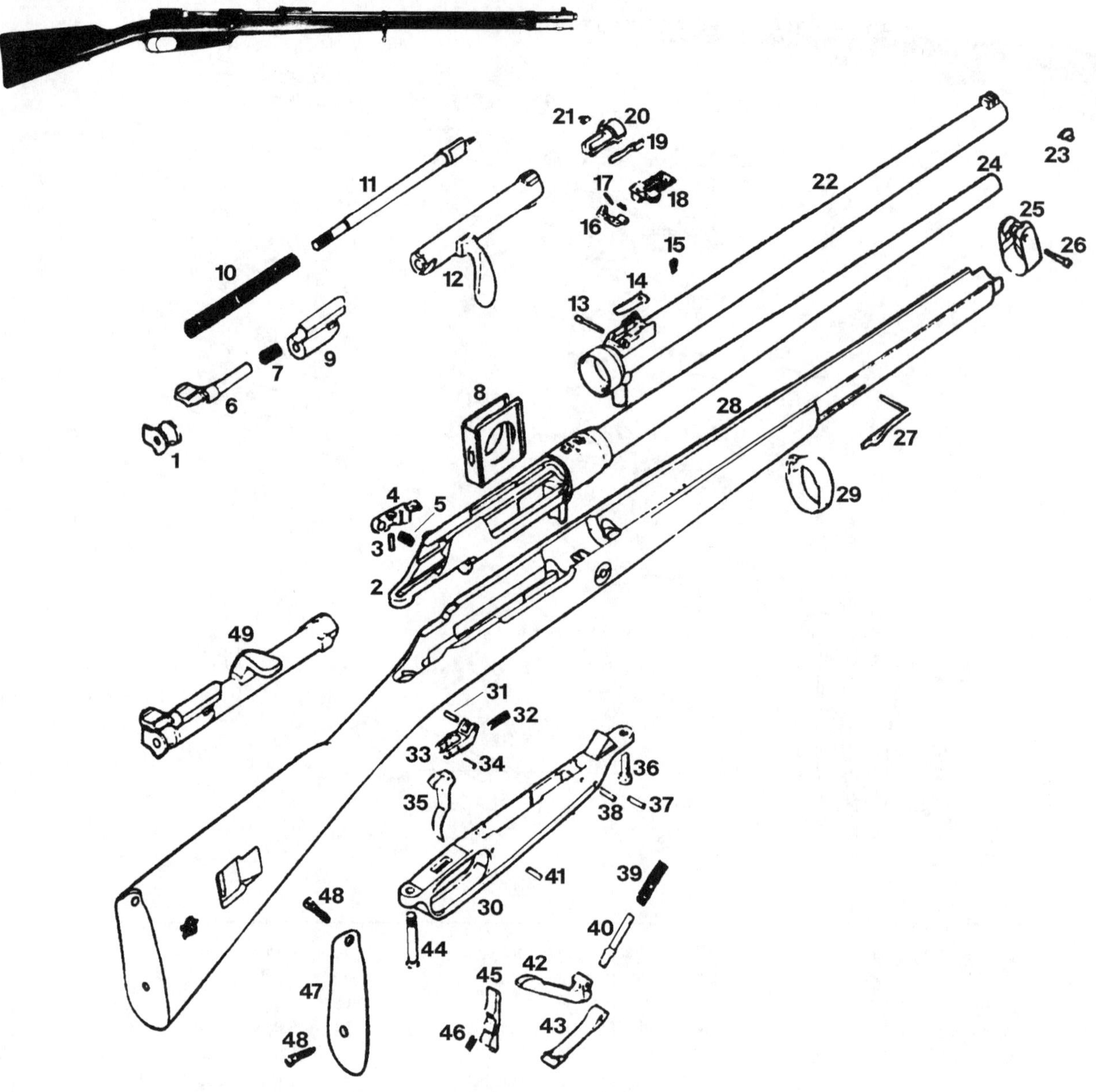

1	Firing Pin Nut	18	Adjustable Range Leaf and Slide	35	Trigger
2	Receiver	19	Extractor	36	Front Guard Screw
3	Bolt Stop Pin	20	Bolt Head	37	Dust Cover Screw
4	Bolt Stop	21	Ejector	38	Follower Axle Screw
5	Bolt Stop Spring	22	Barrel Jacket	39	Follower Spring
6	Safety	23	Front Sight	40	Follower Spring Guide
7	Safety Spring	24	Barrel	41	Clip Latch Screw
8	Stripper Clip	25	Upper Band	42	Magazine Follower
9	Cocking Piece	26	Upper Band Screw	43	Magazine Bottom, Front
10	Firing Pin Spring	27	Lower Band Spring	44	Rear Guard Screw
11	Firing Pin	28	Stock	45	Clip Latch
12	Bolt	29	Lower Band	46	Clip Latch Spring
13	Rear Sight Hinge Pin	30	Trigger Guard	47	Buttplate
14	Sight Spring	31	Sear Pin	48	Buttplate Screws
15	Sight Spring Screw	32	Sear Spring	49	Assembled Bolt Complete
16	Fixed Range Leaf	33	Sear		
17	Fixed Range Leaf Spring	34	Trigger Pin		

Model 1891 Argentine Bolt-Action Rifle

Courtesy of Thomas E. Wessel

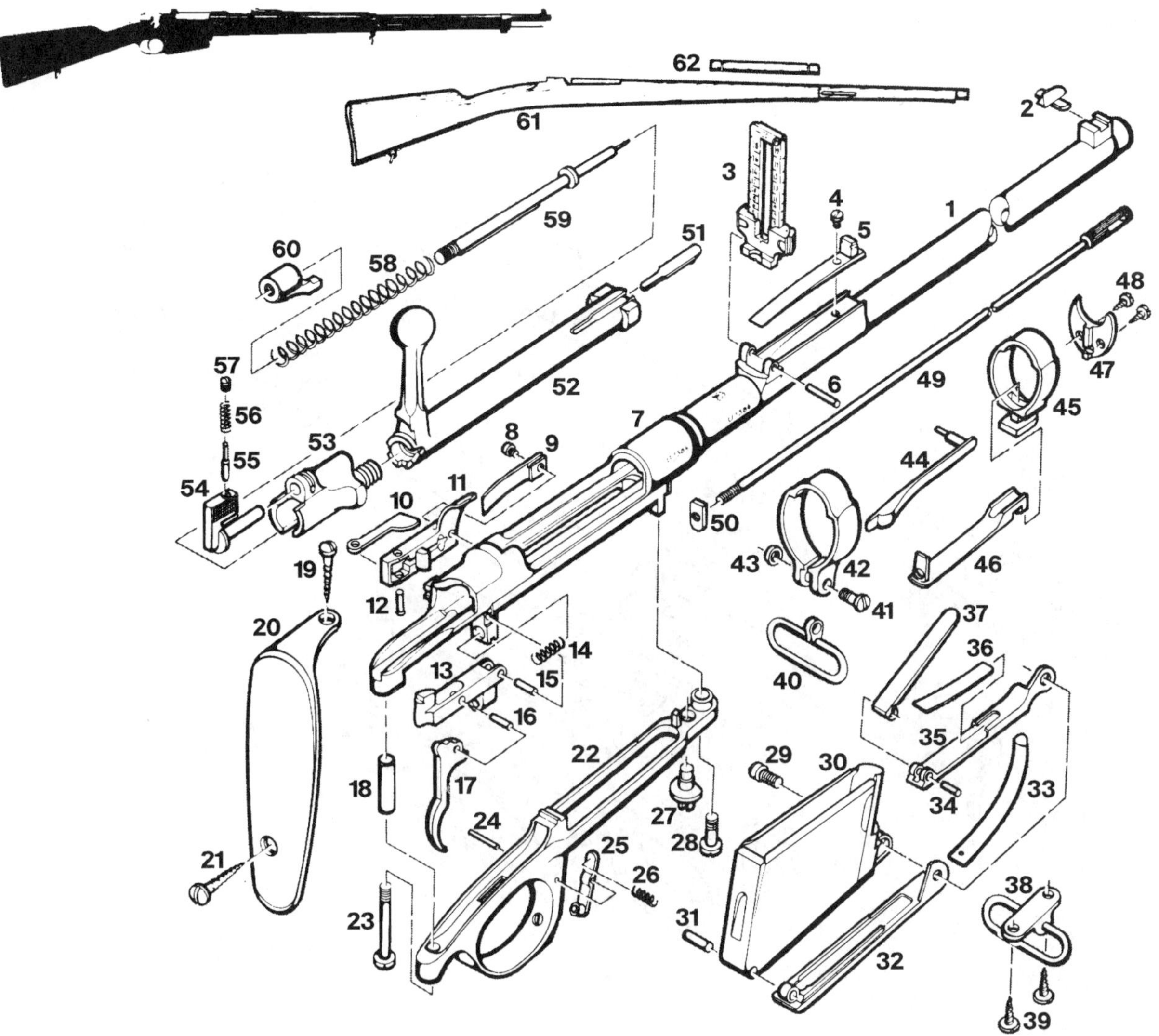

1	Barrel	22	Trigger Guard	43	Front Swivel Nut
2	Front Sight	23	Rear Guard Screw	44	Lower Band Spring
3	Rear Sight	24	Magazine Latch Pin	45	Upper Band
4	Rear Sight Spring Screw	25	Magazine Latch	46	Upper Band Spring
5	Rear Sight Spring	26	Magazine Latch Spring	47	Front Plate
6	Rear Sight Pin	27	Magazine Catch	48	Front Plate Screws
7	Receiver	28	Front Guard Screw	49	Cleaning Rod
8	Bolt Stop Spring Screw	29	Follower Screw	50	Cleaning Rod Stop
9	Bolt Stop Spring	30	Magazine	51	Extractor
10	Ejector	31	Floorplate Pin	52	Bolt
11	Bolt Stop	32	Floorplate	53	Bolt Sleeve
12	Bolt Stop Pin	33	Floorplate Spring	54	Safety
13	Sear	34	Follower Pin	55	Safety Detent
14	Sear Spring	35	Follower Arm	56	Safety Detent Spring
15	Sear Pin	36	Follower Spring	57	Safety Detent Screw
16	Trigger Pin	37	Magazine Follower	58	Mainspring
17	Trigger	38	Rear Swivel	59	Firing Pin
18	Rear Guard Screw Bushing	39	Rear Swivel Screws	60	Cocking Piece
19	Top Buttplate Screw	40	Front Swivel	61	Stock
20	Buttplate	41	Front Swivel Screw	62	Handguard
21	Rear Buttplate Screw	42	Lower Band		

Model 1893 Bolt-Action Rifle

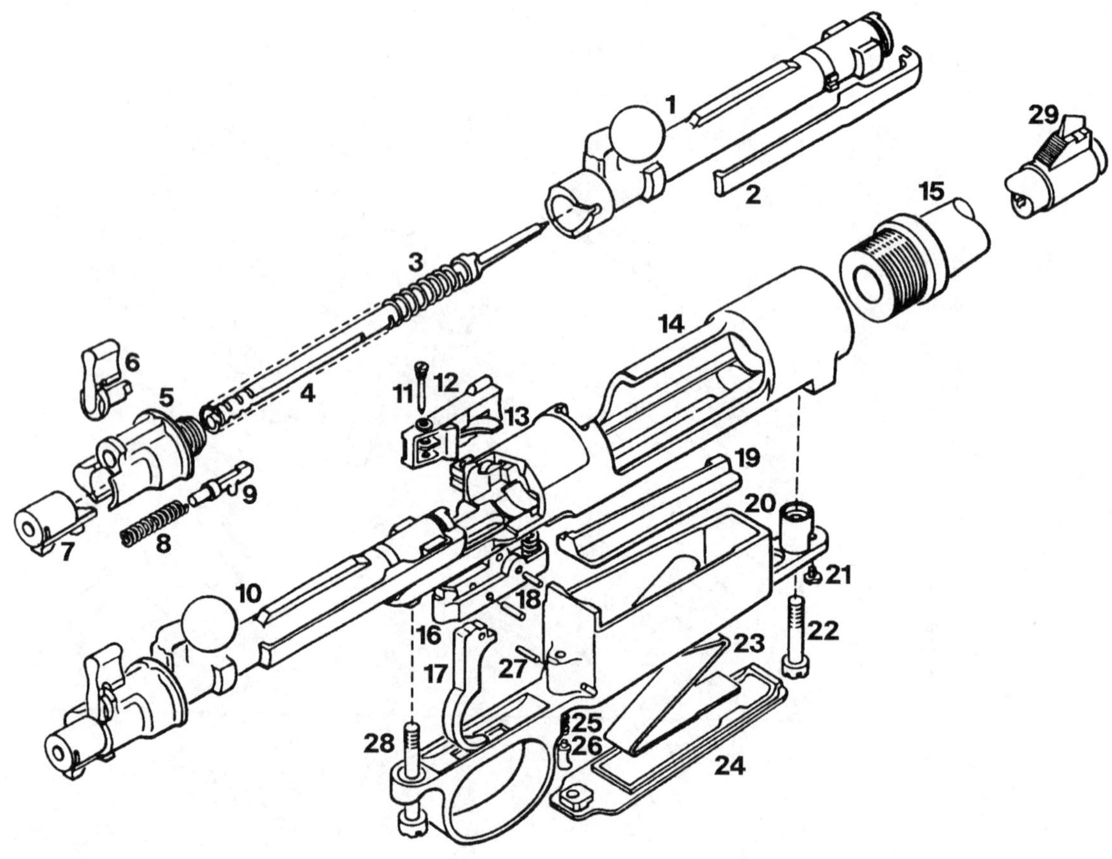

1	Bolt Body	20	Trigger Guard
2	Extractor	21	Lock Screw
3	Firing Pin Spring	22	Front Guard Screw
4	Firing Pin	23	Magazine Spring
5	Bolt Sleeve	24	Floorplate
6	Safety Catch	25	Floorplate Latch Spring
7	Cocking Piece	26	Floorplate Latch
8	Bolt Sleeve Stop Spring	27	Floorplate Latch Pin
9	Bolt Sleeve Stop	28	Rear Guard Screw
10	Bolt Assembly	29	Front Sight
11	Bolt Stop Screw	**Parts Not Shown**	
12	Bolt Stop and Spring		Bolt Stop
13	Ejector		Bolt Stop Assembly
14	Receiver		Bolt Stop Spring
15	Barrel		Ejector Spring
16	Sear		Extractor Collar
17	Trigger		Sear Spring
18	Sear and Trigger Pins		
19	Magazine Follower		

Model 1894 Bolt-Action Rifle

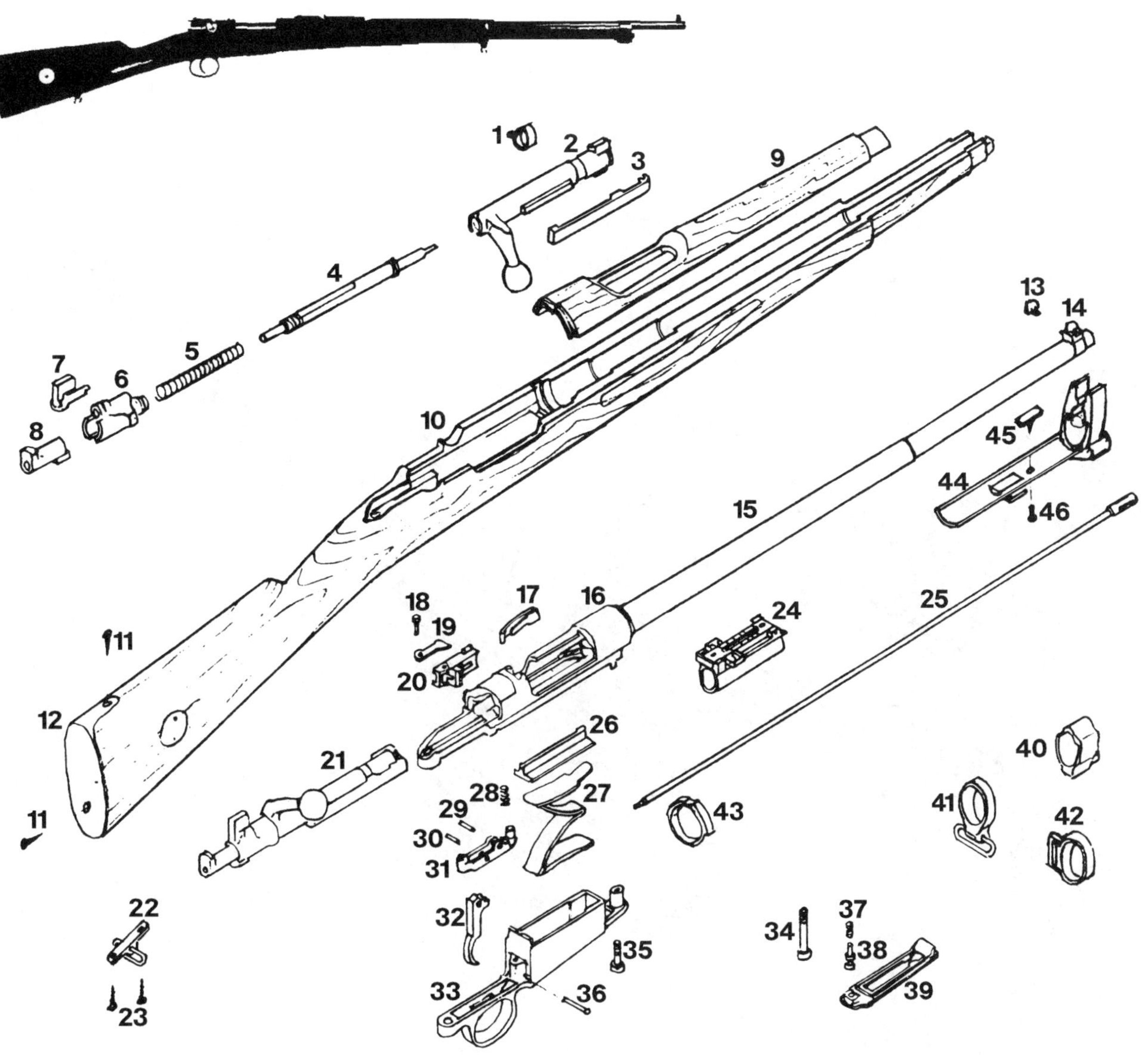

1	Extractor Collar	**17**	Ejector Spring	**33**	Trigger Guard Stripped
2	Bolt Stripped	**18**	Ejector Screw	**34**	Rear Guard Screw
3	Extractor	**19**	Ejector	**35**	Front Guard Screw
4	Firing Pin	**20**	Ejector Box Complete	**36**	Floorplate Catch Pin
5	Firing Pin Spring	**21**	Bolt Complete	**37**	Floorplate Catch Spring
6	Bolt Sleeve	**22**	Rear Swivel	**38**	Floorplate Catch
7	Safety	**23**	Rear Swivel Screws	**39**	Floorplate
8	Cocking Piece	**24**	Rear Sight Complete	**40**	Bayonet Stud, Short
9	Handguard	**25**	Cleaning Rod	**41**	Handguard Band with Swivel
10	Stock	**26**	Follower	**42**	Handguard Band
11	Buttplate Screws	**27**	Follower Spring	**43**	Handguard Ring, Rear
12	Buttplate	**28**	Sear Spring	**44**	Bayonet Stud, Long
13	Front Sight	**29**	Sear Pin	**45**	Bayonet Stud Nut
14	Front Sight Band	**30**	Trigger Pin	**46**	Bayonet Stud Screw
15	Barrel	**31**	Sear		
16	Receiver	**32**	Trigger		

Model 1896 Bolt-Action Rifle

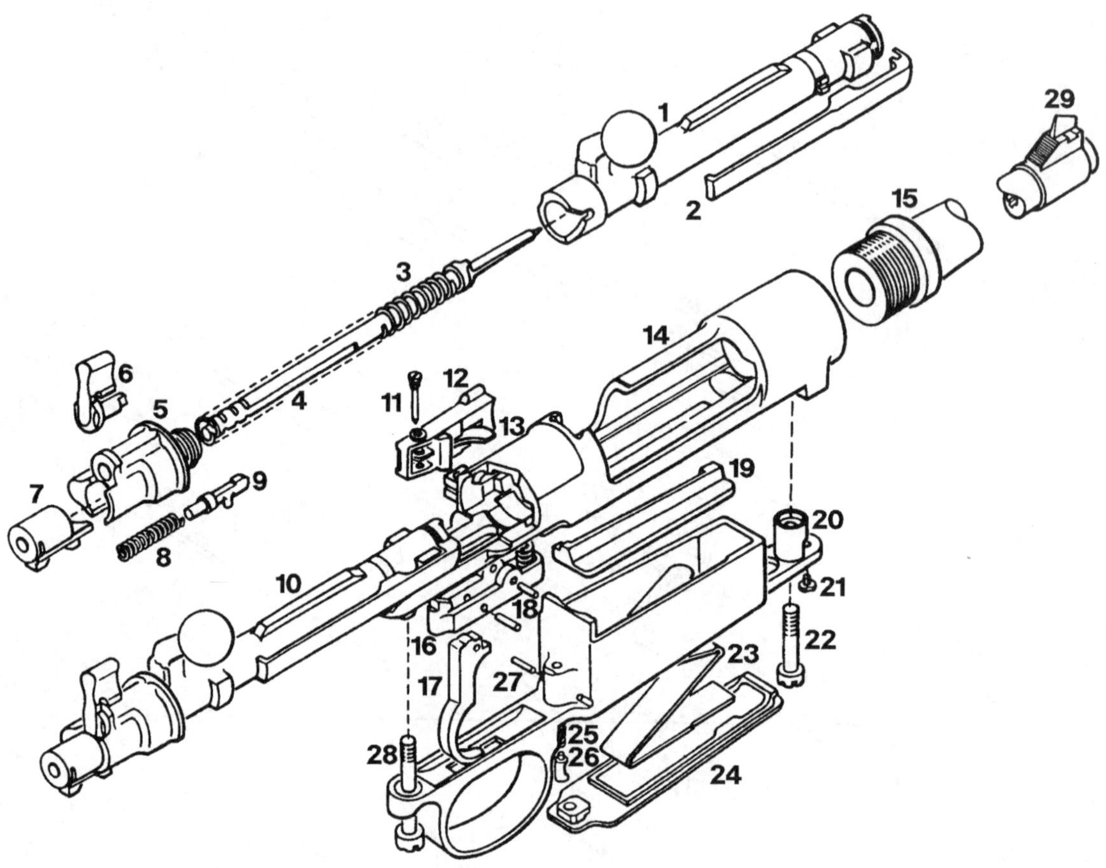

1	Bolt Body
2	Extractor
3	Firing Pin Spring
4	Firing Pin
5	Bolt Sleeve
6	Safety Catch
7	Cocking Piece
8	Bolt Sleeve Stop Spring
9	Bolt Sleeve Stop
10	Bolt Assembly
11	Bolt Stop Screw
12	Bolt Stop and Spring
13	Ejector
14	Receiver
15	Barrel
16	Sear
17	Trigger
18	Sear And Trigger Pins
19	Magazine Follower
20	Trigger Guard
21	Lock Screw
22	Front Guard Screw
23	Magazine Spring
24	Floorplate
25	Floorplate Latch Spring
26	Floorplate Latch
27	Floorplate Latch Pin
28	Rear Guard Screw
29	Front Sight

Parts Not Shown

Bolt Stop
Bolt Stop Assembly
Bolt Stop Spring
Ejector Spring
Extractor Collar
Sear Spring

Model 71/84 Bolt-Action Rifle

Courtesy of Blacksmith Corporation

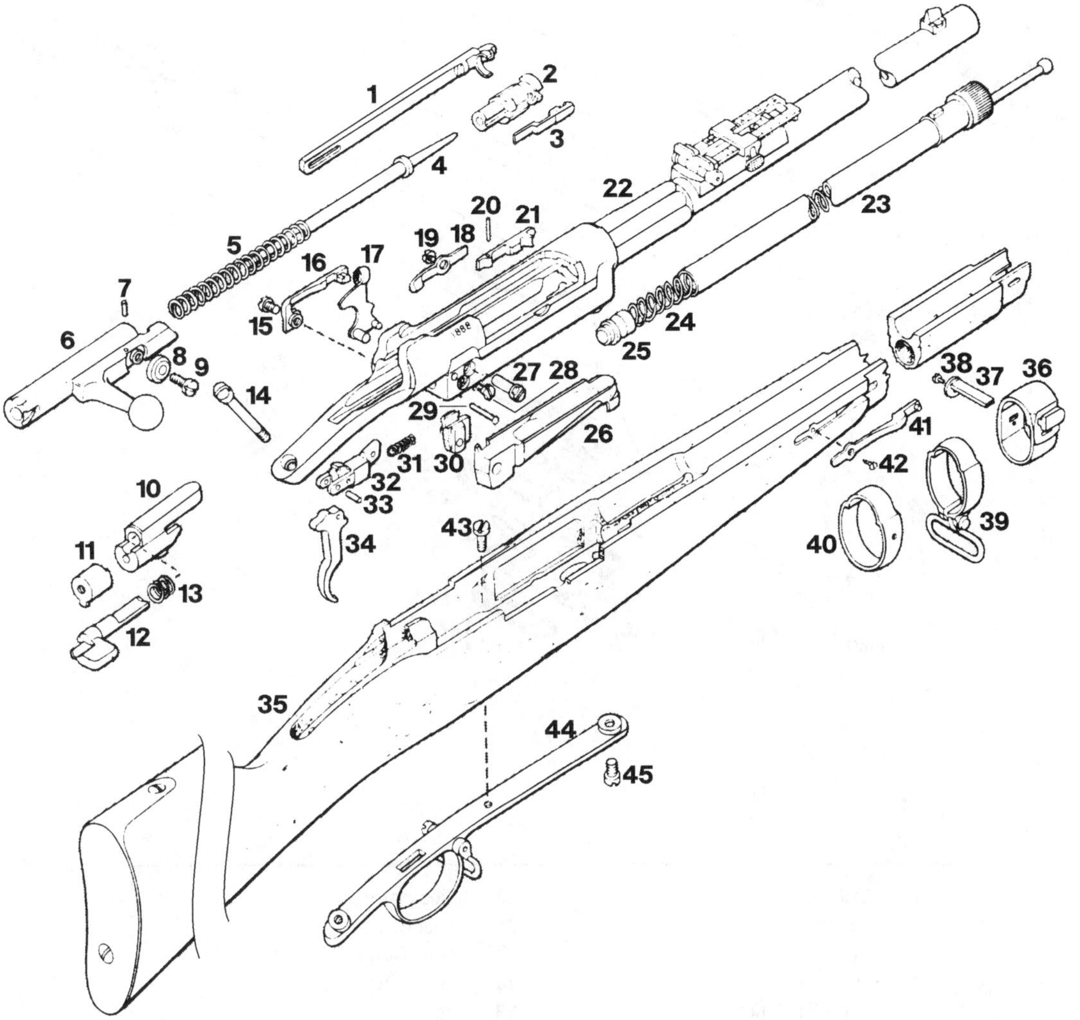

1	Ejector	**16**	Cutoff Spring	**31**	Sear Spring
2	Bolt Head	**17**	Cutoff Lever	**32**	Sear
3	Extractor	**18**	Cartridge Lifter Detent	**33**	Trigger Pin
4	Firing Pin	**19**	Detent Retainer Screw	**34**	Trigger
5	Firing Pin Spring	**20**	Cartridge Stop Pin	**35**	Stock
6	Bolt Body	**21**	Cartridge Stop	**36**	Forward Band
7	Retainer Pin	**22**	Barrel and Receiver	**37**	Cross KEY
8	Bolt Stop	**23**	Magazine Tube	**38**	KEY Retaining Screw
9	Bolt Stop Screw	**24**	Magazine Spring	**39**	Middle Band
10	Cocking Piece	**25**	Magazine Follower	**40**	Rear Band
11	Firing Pin Nut	**26**	Cartridge Lifter	**41**	Band Spring
12	Safety Catch	**27**	Cartridge Lifter Hinge	**42**	Band Spring Screw
13	Safety Catch Spring	**28**	Hinge Lock Screw	**43**	Center Trigger Guard Screw
14	Rear Guard Screw	**29**	Sear Hinge Pin	**44**	Trigger Guard
15	Cutoff Spring Screw	**30**	Cutoff Cam	**45**	Front Guard Screw

Model 98 Bolt-Action Rifle

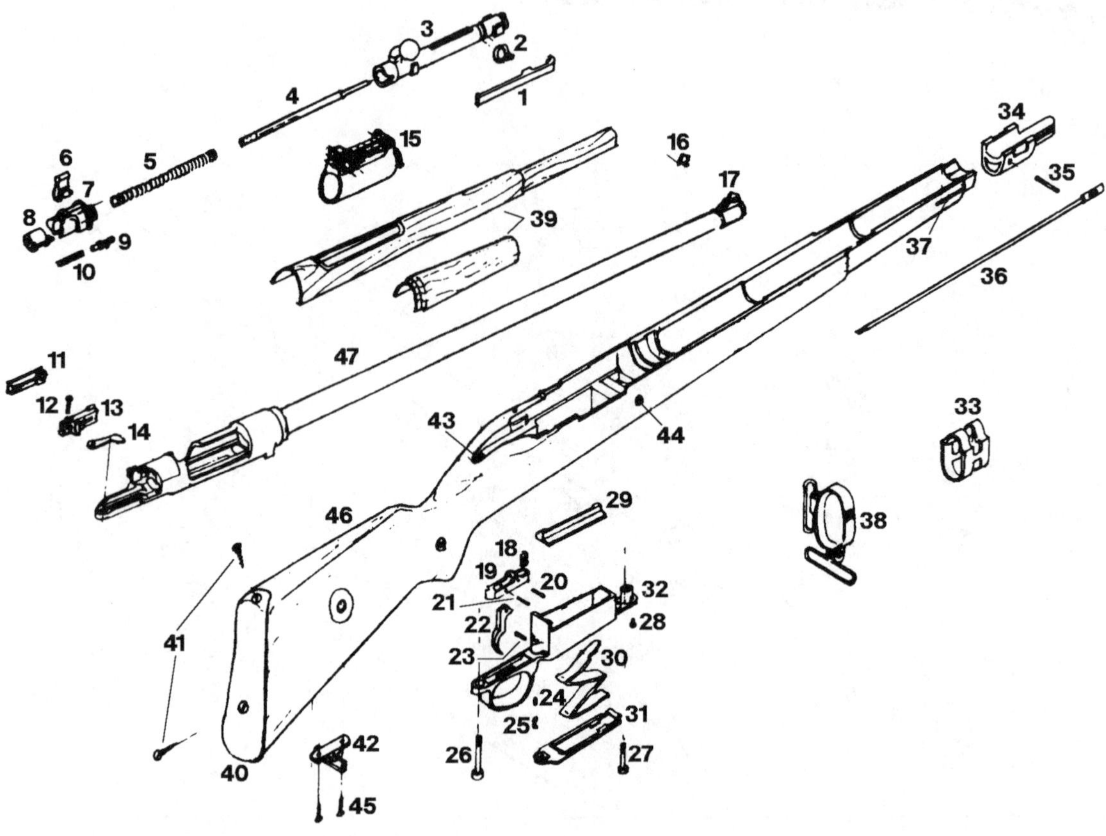

1	Extractor
2	Extractor Collar
3	Stripped Bolt
4	Firing Pin
5	Firing Pin Spring
6	Safety
7	Bolt Sleeve
8	Cocking Piece
9	Bolt Sleeve Catch
10	Bolt Sleeve Catch Spring
11	Ejector Spring and Bolt Stop Assembly
12	Bolt Stop Screw
13	Bolt Stop
14	Ejector
15	Rear Sight Complete
16	Front Sight Blade
17	Front Sight Complete
18	Sear Spring
19	Sear
20	Sear Pin
21	Trigger Pin
22	Trigger
23	Floorplate Catch Pin
24	Floorplate Catch Spring
25	Floorplate Catch
26	Rear Guard Screw
27	Front Guard Screw
28	Lock Screw
29	Follower
30	Magazine Spring
31	Floorplate
32	Trigger Guard
33	Front Band
34	Bayonet Stud
35	Bayonet Stud Pin
36	Cleaning Rod
37	Front Band Spring
38	Lower Band with Side and Bottom Swivels
39	Handguard
40	Buttplate
41	Butt Screws
42	Rear Swivel
43	Rear Guard Screw Bushing
44	Recoil Lug Assembly
45	Rear Swivel Screws
46	Stock
47	Barrel

AK-22 Autoloading Rifle

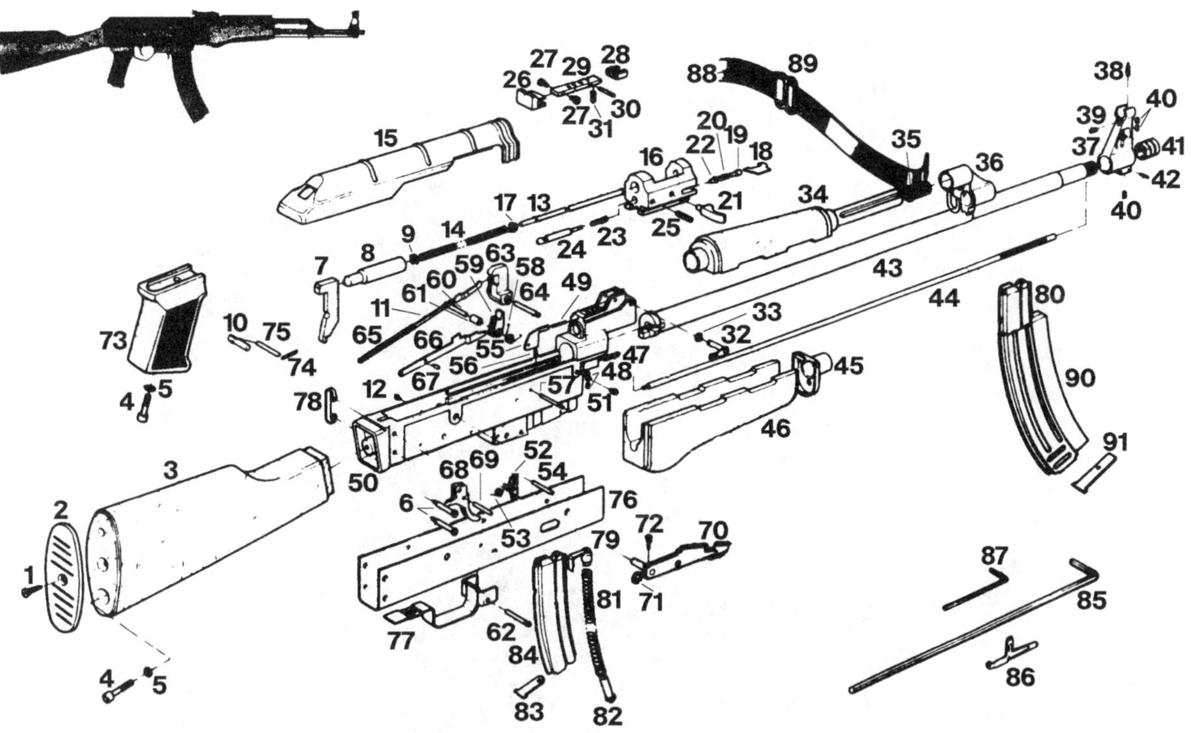

1	Buttplate Screw
2	Buttplate
3	Stock
4	Grip Screws
5	Washers
6	Rear Link Screws
7	Recoil Spring Support
8	Limiting Device
9	Recoil Spring Stop Ring
10	Hammer Spring Holding Pin
11	Hammer Spring Guide
12	Scope Mount Filler Screws
13	Recoil Spring Guide
14	Recoil Spring
15	Upper Cover
16	Bolt
17	Recoil Spring Guide Bushing
18	Extractor
19	Extractor Pin
20	Extractor Spring
21	Cocking Lever
22	Cocking Lever Catch Pin
23	Firing Pin Spring
24	Striker
25	Striker Pin
26	Rear Sight Blade
27	Rear Sight Adjusting Screws
28	Rear Sight Elevator
29	Rear Sight Base
30	Rear Sight Pin
31	Rear Sight Spring
32	Upper Handguard Catch
33	Handguard Catch Ring
34	Front Handguard Holder, Upper
35	Upper Handguard Spring
36	Upper Handguard Support
37	Front Sight Ramp and Hood
38	Front Sight
39	Front Sight Stop Screw
40	Front Sight Ramp Stop Screws
41	Barrel Cap
42	Front Sight Ramp and Hood Pin
43	Barrel
44	Cleaning Rod
45	Lower Handguard Support
46	Lower Handguard
47	Cleaning Rod Spring
48	Barrel Catch Screws
49	Cover Catch Pin
50	Frame
51	Frame Cover Catch Screw
52	Magazine Catch
53	Magazine Catch Spring
54	Magazine Catch Pin
55	Ejector
56	Ejector Spring
57	Ejector Pin
58	Sear Spring
59	Sear
60	Sear Pin
61	Sear Spacer
62	Trigger Guard Pin
63	Hammer
64	Hammer Pin
65	Hammer Spring
66	Sear Lever
67	Sear Lever Pin
68	Trigger
69	Trigger Pin
70	Safety
71	Safety Holding Ring
72	Safety Screw
73	Grip
74	Trigger Spring
75	Trigger Spring Pin
76	Frame Cover
77	Trigger Guard
78	Rear Link
79	Magazine Follower
80	Long Magazine Box
81	Magazine Spring
82	Magazine Spring Guide Pin
83	Short Magazine Box Base
84	Short Magazine Box
85	Stock Set Screw Wrench
86	Front Sight Adjustment Tool
87	Front Sight Set Screw Wrench
88	Sling
89	Sling Buckle
90	Long Magazine Body
91	Long Magazine Base

AK-47 Autoloading Rifle

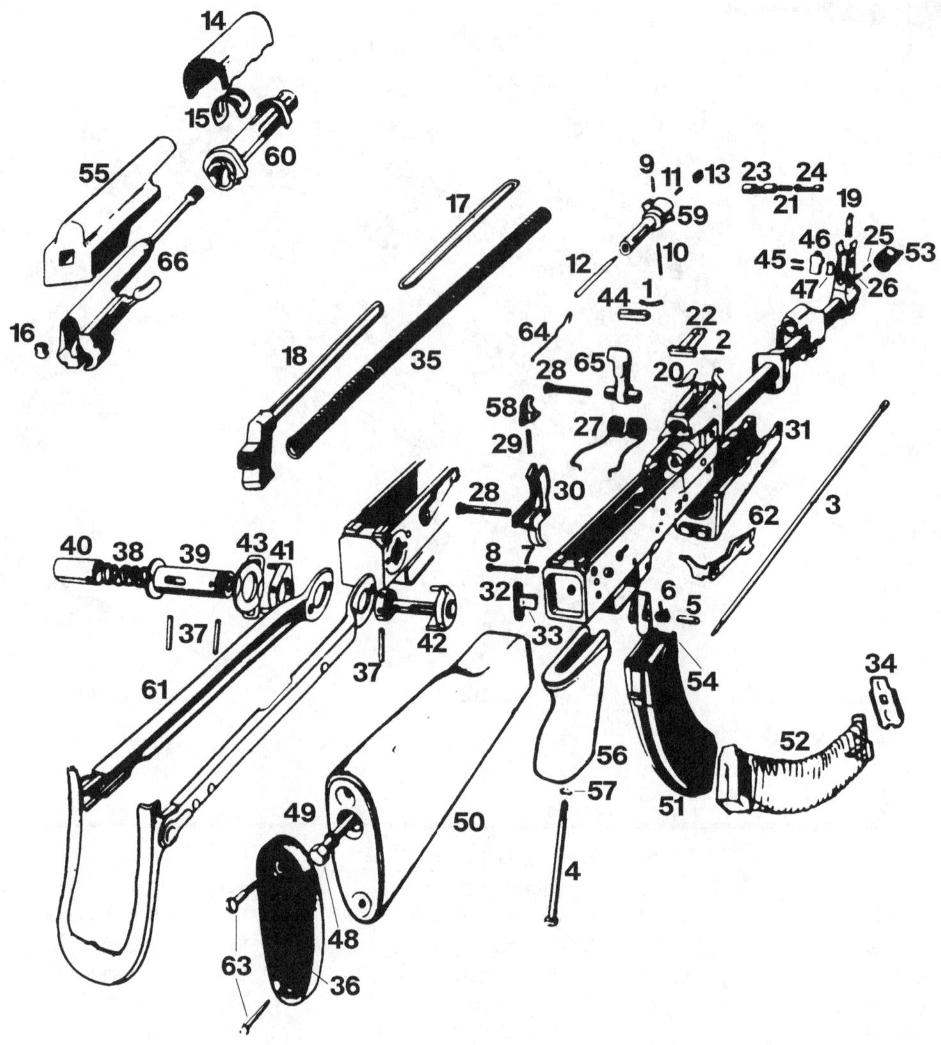

1	Rear Night Sight Spring	**23**	Rear Sight Slide	**45**	Front Night Sight Pins
2	Rear Night Sight Pin	**24**	Rear Sight Leaf Slide Catch	**46**	Front Night Sight
3	Cleaning Rod	**25**	Muzzle Brake Plunger	**47**	Front Night Sight Spring
4	Handgrip Bolt	**26**	Muzzle Brake Plunger Spring	**48**	Stock Bolt
5	Magazine Latch Pin	**27**	Hammer Spring	**49**	Stock Bolt Washer
6	Magazine Latch Spring	**28**	Hammer and Trigger Pin	**50**	Buttstock
7	Cover Latch Lock Spring	**29**	Disconnector Spring	**51**	Magazine Body
8	Cover Lock Plunger	**30**	Trigger	**52**	Magazine Follower
9	Extractor Pin	**31**	Forend, Lower	**53**	Muzzle Brake
10	Extractor Pin Spring	**32**	Rear Sling Swivel	**54**	Magazine Latch
11	Extractor Spring	**33**	Rear Sling Swivel Base	**55**	Upper Receiver Cover
12	Firing Pin	**34**	Magazine Floorplate	**56**	Handgrip
13	Extractor	**35**	Recoil Spring	**57**	Handgrip Bolt Washer
14	Forend, Upper	**36**	Recoil Pad	**58**	Disconnector
15	Forend Support	**37**	Folding Stock Hinge Pins	**59**	Bolt
16	Recoil Spring Securing Ring	**38**	Folding Stock Plunger Spring	**60**	Gas Tube
17	Recoil Spring Guide, Front	**39**	Folding Stock Stock Hinge	**61**	Folding Buttstock Sub-Assembly
18	Recoil Spring Rear Assembly	**40**	Folding Stock Plunger	**62**	Safety-Lever
19	Front Sight Post	**41**	Folding Stock Base	**63**	Recoil Pad Screws
20	Rear Sight Leaf Spring	**42**	Folding Stock Receiver	**64**	Securing Pin
21	Slide Catch Spring	**43**	Folding Stock Base Washer	**65**	Hammer
22	Rear Sight Blade Sub-Assembly	**44**	Rear Night Sight Sub-Assembly	**66**	Bolt Carrier

M-16 Autoloading Rifle

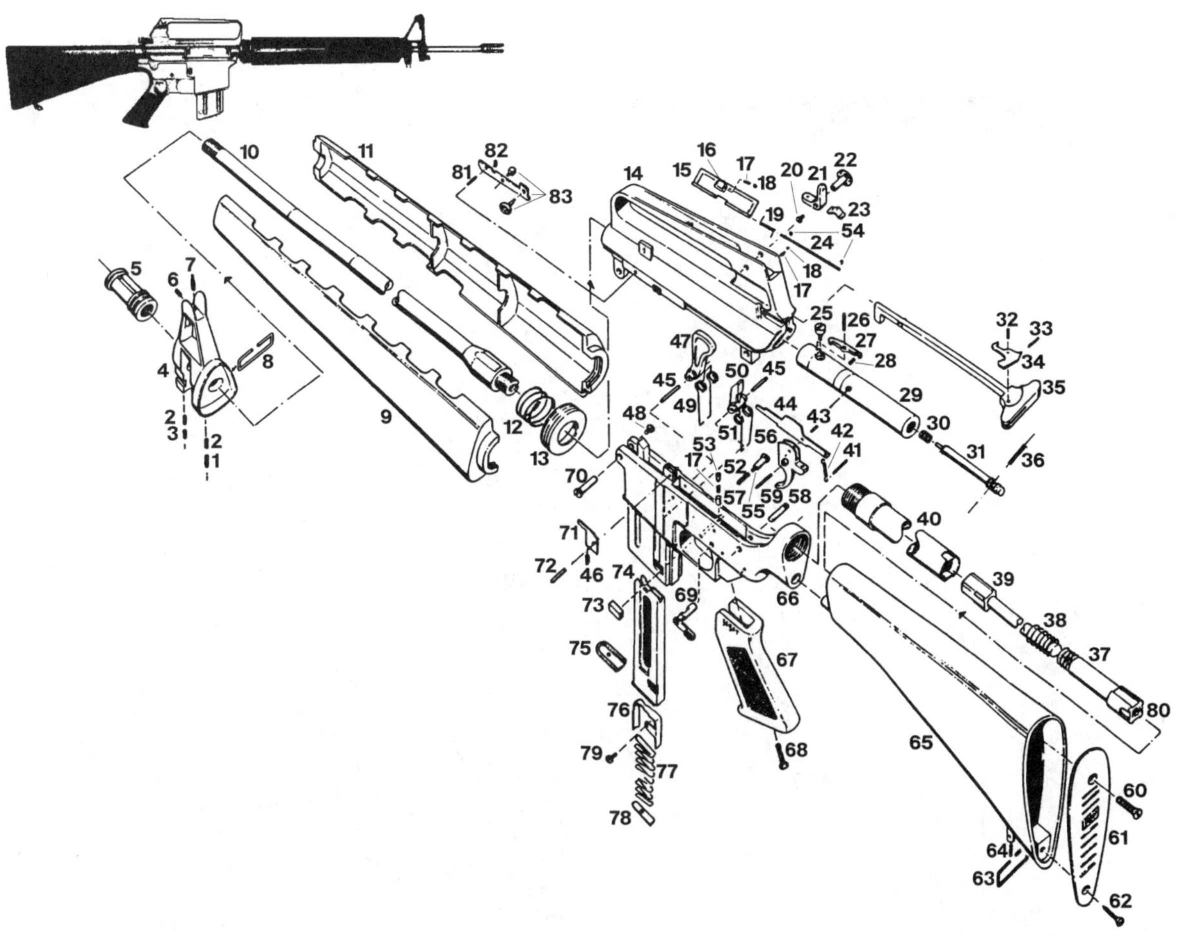

No.	Part	No.	Part	No.	Part
1	Front Link Screw	28	Extractor Spring	56	Trigger
2	Stop Ramp Screws	29	Bolt	57	Safety Pin
3	Ramp Screw	30	Firing Pin Spring	58	Frame/Receiver Pin
4	Front Sight Ramp and Hood	31	Firing Pin	59	Trigger Pin
5	Stop Flame	32	Lever Bolt Pin	60	Tube Screw
6	Front Flame Retaining Screw	33	Lever Bolt Screw	61	Buttplate
7	Front Sight	34	Stop Lever Bolt	62	Buttplate Screw
8	Front Link	35	Bolt Button	63	Link, Rear
9	Grip, Left	36	Firing Pin Pin	64	Link Pin, Rear
10	Barrel	37	Spring Guide, Rear	65	Stock
11	Grip, Right	38	Recoil Spring	66	Frame
12	Stock Spring	39	Spring Guide, Front	67	Grip
13	Stop Link Grip	40	Tube Stock	68	Grip Screw
14	Receiver	41	Sear Spring Pin	69	Safety
15	Door	42	Trigger Spring	70	Frame/Receiver Pin
16	Door Link	43	Sear Lever Pin	71	Ejector
17	Receiver Sight Disc and Safety Springs	44	Sear Lever	72	Ejector Pin
18	Sphere Receiver Sight Disc	45	Sear and Hammer Pins	73	Magazine Catch
19	Door Screw	46	Ejector Spring	74	Magazine
20	Receiver Sight Screw	47	Hammer	75	Magazine Bottom Plate
21	Receiver Sight Disc	48	Frame/Receiver Screw	76	Follower
22	Disc Pin	49	Hammer Spring	77	Magazine Spring
23	Receiver Sight Disc Spring	50	Sear	78	Stop Plate
24	Door Pin	51	Sear Screw	79	Follower Screw
25	Breechbolt Screw	52	Magazine Catch Spring	80	Spring Guide Stop
26	Concealed Hammer Pin	53	Safety Screw	81	Bolt Stop Pin
27	Extractor	54	Door Pin Stops	82	Bolt Stop Spring
		55	Magazine Screw	83	Bolt Stop

Model 144-LS Bolt-Action Rifle

Courtesy of James M. Triggs

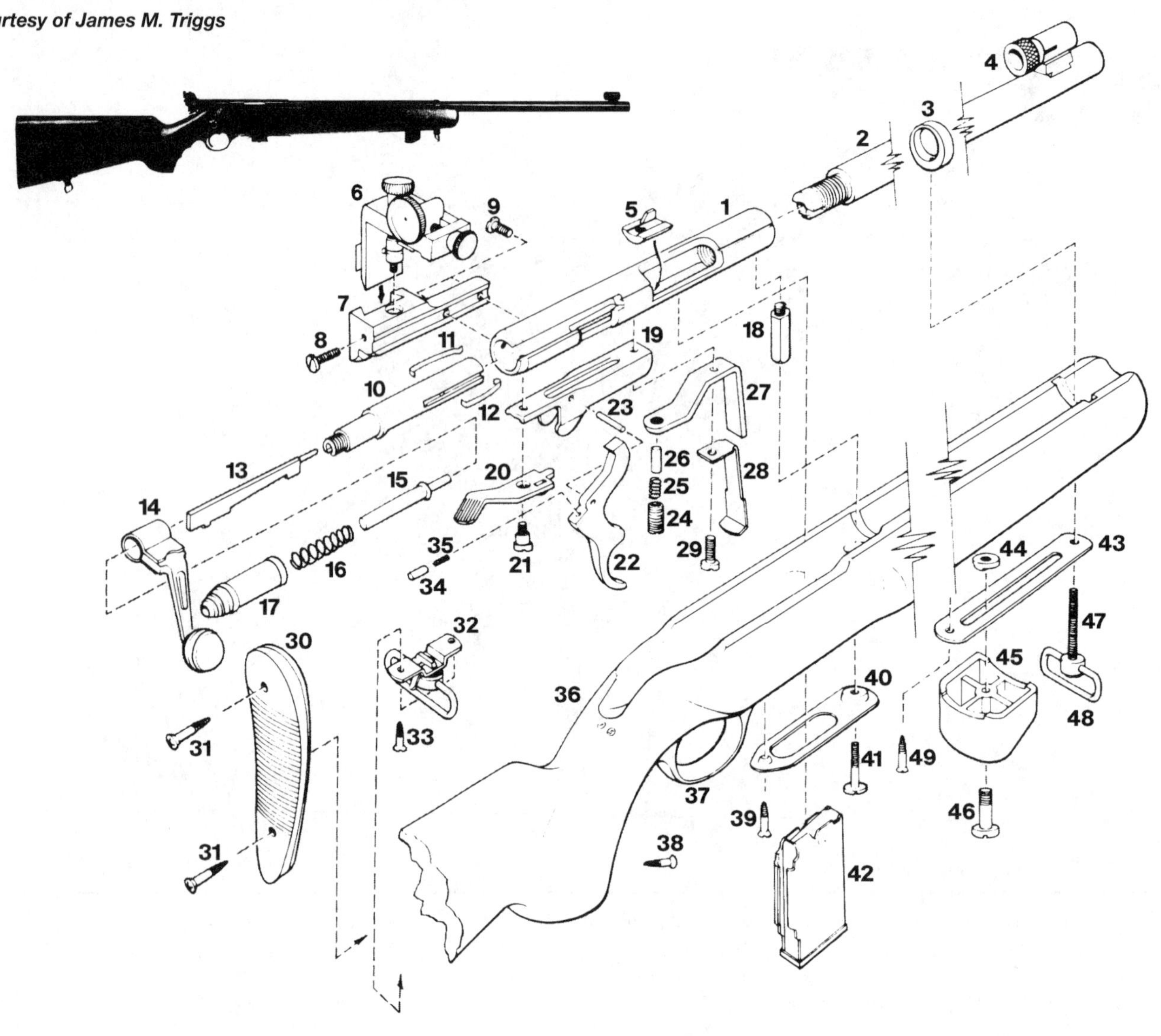

1	Receiver	**16**	Mainspring	**33**	Butt Swivel Screws
2	Barrel	**17**	Mainspring Cap	**34**	Trigger Spring Plunger
3	Barrel Band	**18**	Takedown Stud	**35**	Trigger Spring
4	Front Sight Assembly	**19**	Bracket	**36**	Stock
5	Ejector	**20**	Safety	**37**	Trigger Guard
6	Receiver Peep Sight Assembly	**21**	Safety Screw	**38**	Rear Trigger Guard Screw
7	Receiver Sight Base	**22**	Trigger	**39**	Front Trigger Guard Screw
8	Receiver Sight Lock Screw	**23**	Trigger Pin	**40**	Magazine Stock Plate
9	Receiver Sight Base Mounting Screws	**24**	Trigger Pull Adjusting Screw	**41**	Takedown Screw
10	Bolt Body	**25**	Trigger Pull Adjusting Spring	**42**	Magazine Assembly
11	Extractor, Left	**26**	Trigger Pull Adjusting Plunger	**43**	Adjustable Forearm Plate
12	Extractor, Right	**27**	Angle Bar and Adjusting Bracket	**44**	Adjustable Forearm Stop Nut
13	Firing Pin	**28**	Magazine Latch	**45**	Adjustable Forearm Stop
14	Bolt Lever	**29**	Bracket Screw	**46**	Adjustable Forearm Stop Screw
15	Mainspring Plunger	**30**	Buttplate	**47**	Forearm Swivel Screw
		31	Buttplate Screws	**48**	Forearm Swivel
		32	Butt Swivel Assembly	**49**	Adjustable Forearm Plate Screw

Model 183K, 183T, 184T and 184TY Bolt-Action Shotgun

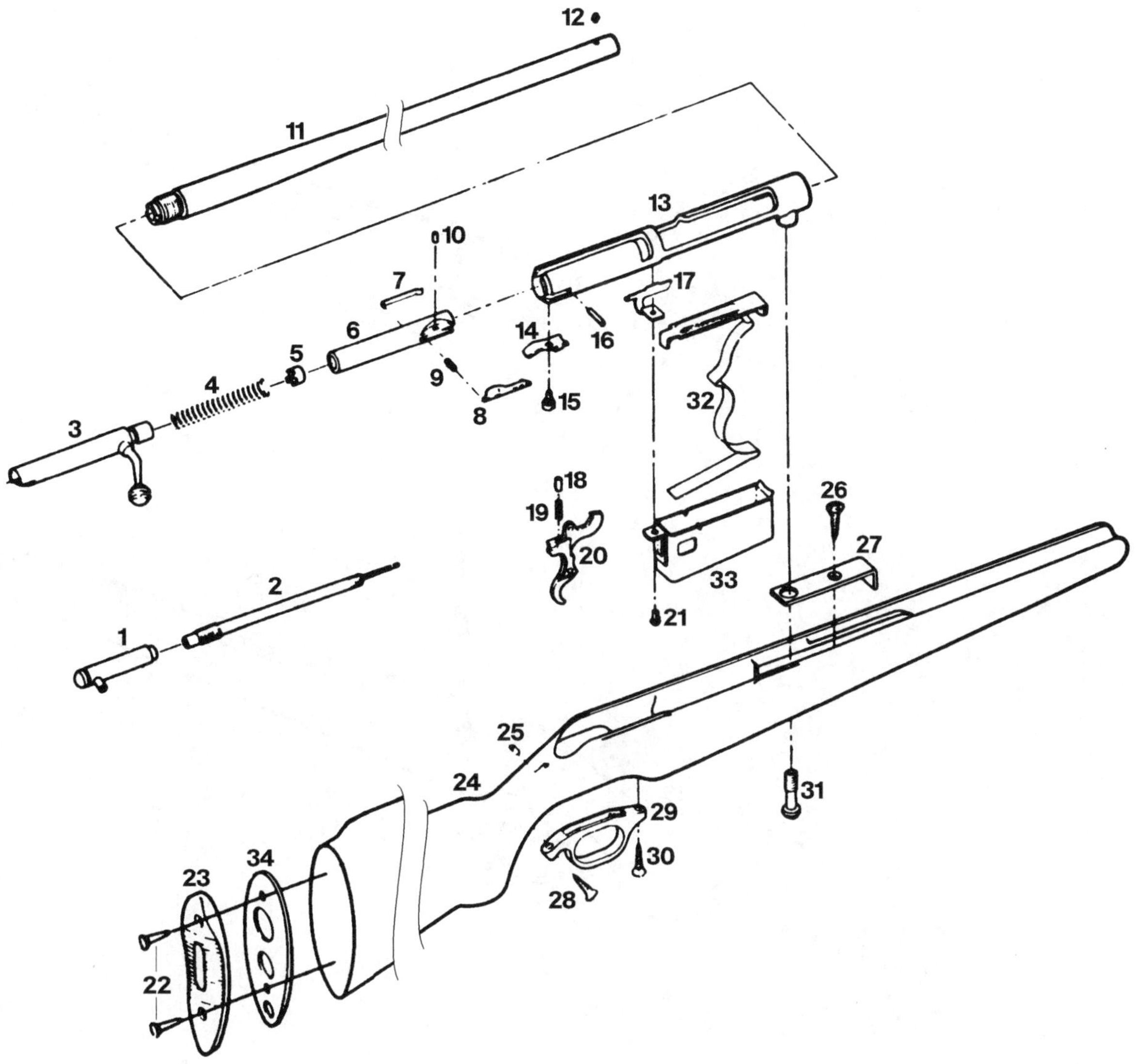

1	Striker Assembly	19	Trigger Spring
2	Firing Pin	20	Trigger Assembly
3	Bolt Body Sub-Assembly	21	Magazine Screw
4	Mainspring	22	Buttplate Screws
5	Firing Pin Nut	23	Recoil Pad
6	Bolt Head	24	Stock Complete
7	Extractor, Left	25	Safety Button
8	Extractor, Right	26	Recoil Plate Screw
9	Extractor Spring, Right	27	Recoil Plate
10	Extractor Pin, Right	28	Trigger Guard Screw, Rear
11	Barrel	29	Trigger Guard
12	Front Sight	30	Trigger Guard Screw, Front
13	Receiver Assembly	31	Takedown Screw
14	Safety-Lever	32	Magazine Spring Assembly
15	Safety-Lever Screw	33	Magazine Shell and Bracket Assembly
16	Trigger Pin	34	Buttplate Spacer
17	Ejector		
18	Trigger Spring Plunger		

Model 183KE and 283T Bolt-Action Shotgun

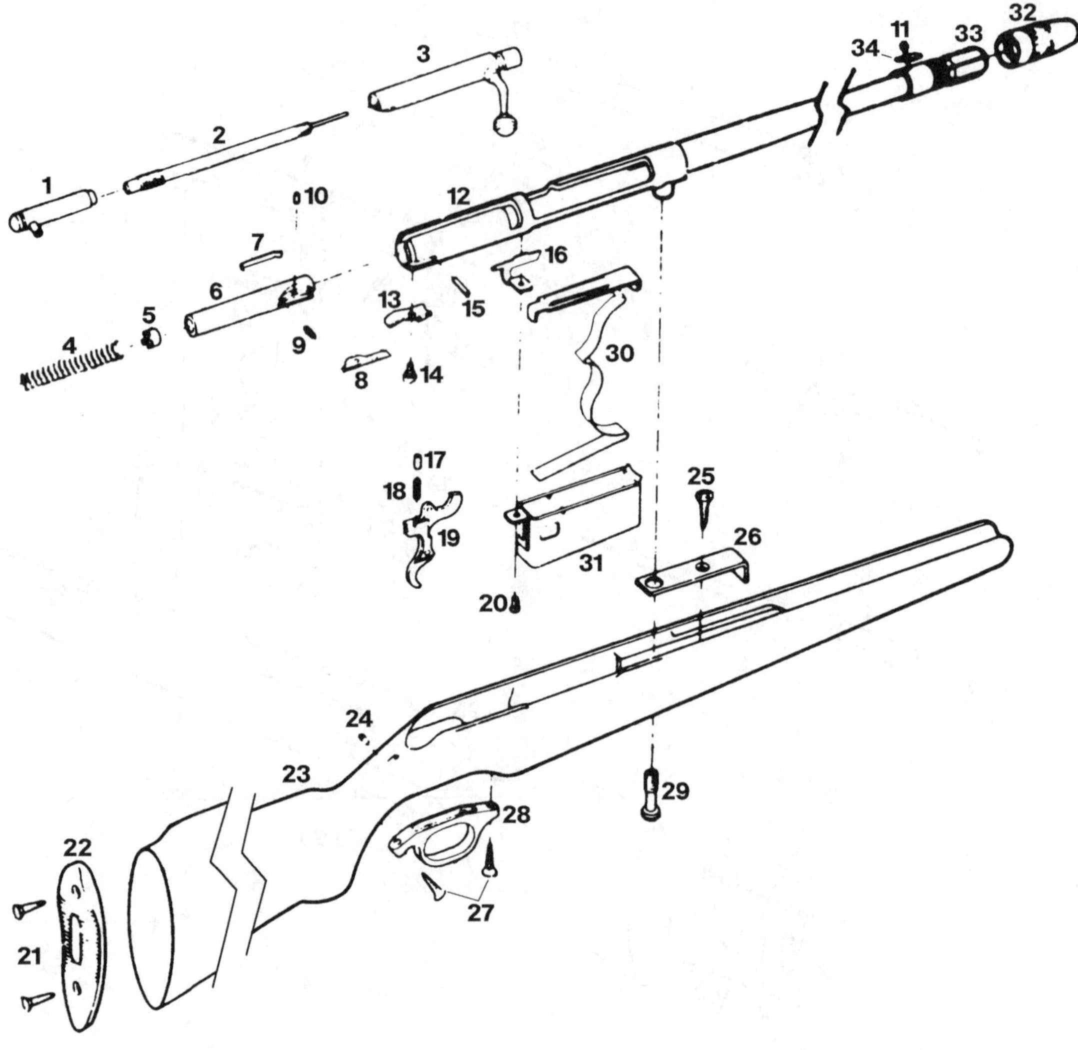

1	Striker Assembly	17	Trigger Spring Plunger
2	Firing Pin	18	Trigger Spring
3	Bolt Body Sub-Assembly	19	Trigger Assembly
4	Mainspring	20	Magazine Screw
5	Firing Pin Nut	21	Buttplate Screws
6	Bolt Head	22	Buttplate
7	Extractor, Left	23	Stock Complete
8	Extractor, Right	24	Safety Button
9	Extractor Spring, Right	25	Recoil Plate Screw
10	Extractor Pin, Right	26	Recoil Plate
11	Front Sight	27	Trigger Guard Screws
12	Barrel and Receiver Sub-Assembly	28	Trigger Guard
13	Safety-Lever	29	Takedown Screw
14	Safety-Lever Screw	30	Magazine Spring Assembly
15	Trigger Pin	31	Magazine Shell Assembly
16	Ejector	32	Choke Sleeve
		33	Choke Tube
		34	Choke Index Plate

Model 340B, 340K and 341 Bolt-Action Rifle

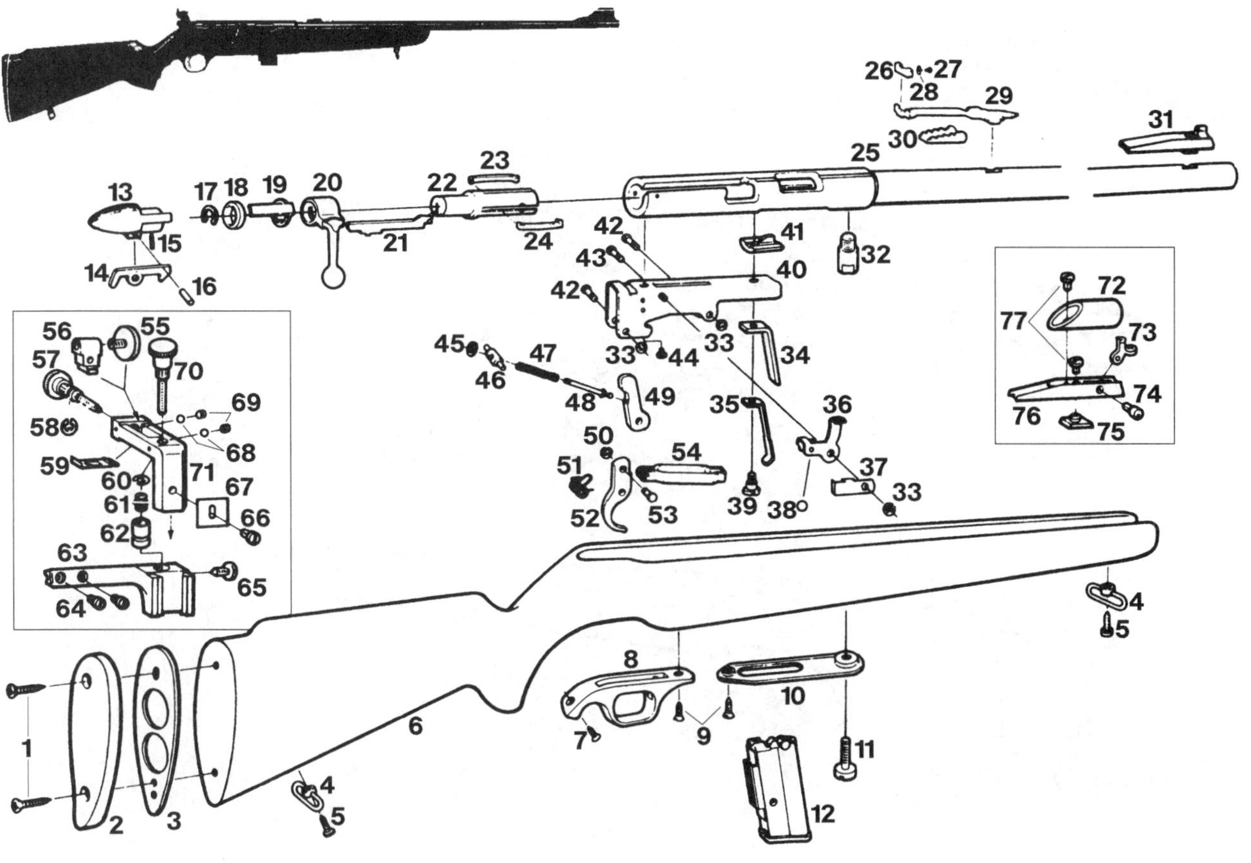

1	Buttplate Screws	**28**	Washer	**52**	Trigger
2	Buttplate	**29**	Base	**53**	Sear Pin
3	Buttplate Spacer	**30**	Elevation Slide	**54**	Sear
4	Swivel Loop and Bushing	**31**	Beaded Front Sight	**55**	Peep Disc
5	Swivel Screw	**32**	Takedown Stud	**56**	Windage Slide
6	Stock	**33**	Retaining Rings for Hammer Pin, Safety Pin and Trigger Pin	**57**	Windage Screw
7	Trigger Guard Screw	**34**	Angle Bar	**58**	Retaining Ring
8	Trigger Guard	**35**	Magazine Latch	**59**	Windage Clip
9	Stock Plate Screws	**36**	Safety	**60**	Retaining Ring
10	Stock Plate	**37**	Click Plate	**61**	Elevation Spring
11	Takedown Screw	**38**	Click Ball	**62**	Elevation Nut
12	Magazine	**39**	Bracket Screw, Front	**63**	Base
13	Receiver Cap	**40**	Bracket	**64**	Base Screws
14	Receiver Cap Latch	**41**	Ejector	**65**	Elevation Lock Screw
15	Receiver Cap Spring	**42**	Trigger Pin and Hammer Pin	**66**	Indicator Plate Screw
16	Receiver Cap Pin	**43**	Safety Pin	**67**	Indicator Plate
17	Bolt Retaining Ring	**44**	Bracket Screw, Rear	**68**	Click Balls
18	Bolt Collar	**45**	Retaining Ring for Hammer Plunger	**69**	Click Springs
19	Bolt Plate	**46**	Hammer Plunger Guide	**70**	Elevation Screw
20	Bolt Lever	**47**	Hammer Spring	**71**	Windage and Elevation Bracket
21	Firing Pin	**48**	Hammer Plunger	**72**	Hood
22	Bolt	**49**	Hammer	**73**	Bead and Aperture
23	Extractor, Left	**50**	Retaining Ring for Sear Pin	**74**	Bead and Aperture Screw
24	Extractor, Right	**51**	Trigger Spring	**75**	Sight Base
25	Barrel and Receiver Assembly			**76**	Ramp Base
26	Windage Plate			**77**	Base Screws
27	Windage Plate Screw				

Model 346KB Bolt-Action Rifle

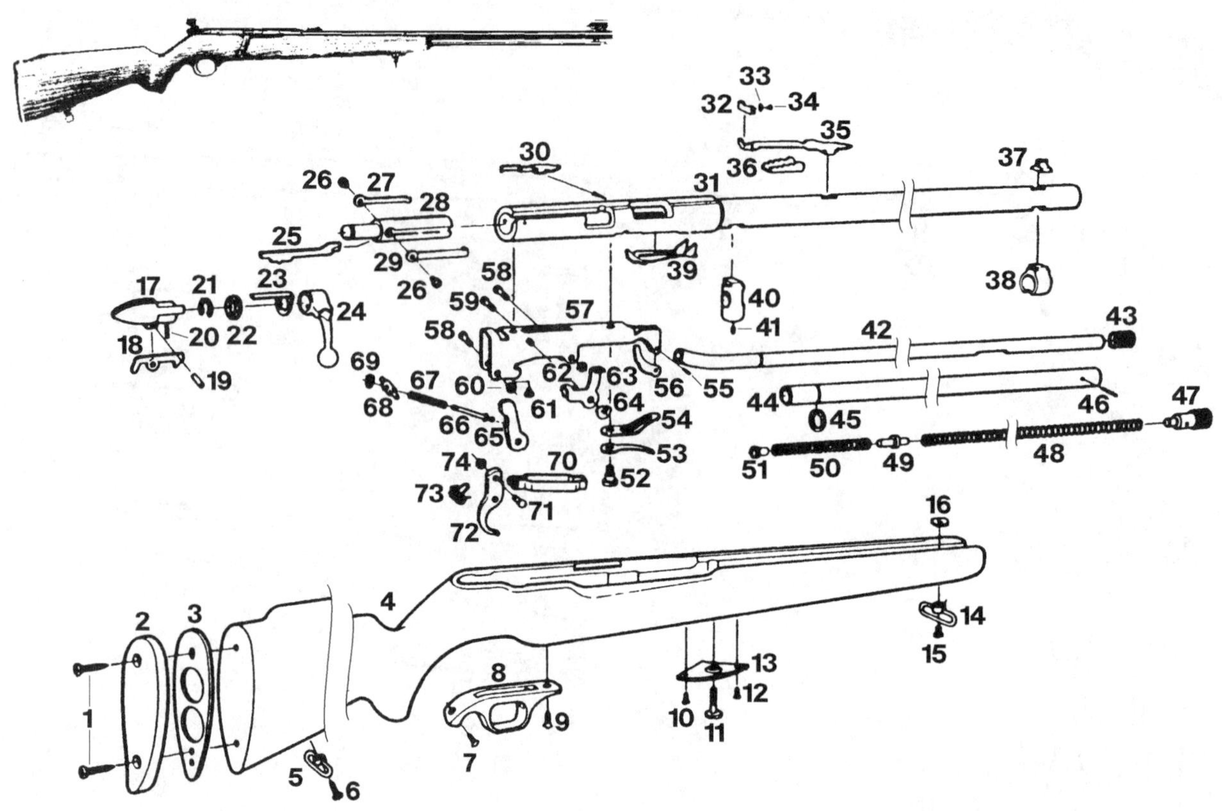

1	Buttplate Screws	26	Extractor Screws	51	Follower
2	Buttplate	27	Extractor, Left	52	Bracket Screw, Front
3	Buttplate Spacer	28	Bolt	53	Elevator Spring
4	Stock	29	Extractor, Right	54	Cartridge Stop Spring
5	Loop and Bushing, Rear	30	Ejector	55	Elevator Pin
6	Swivel Screw, Rear	31	Barrel and Receiver Assembly	56	Elevator
7	Trigger Guard Screw, Rear	32	Windage Plate	57	Bracket
8	Trigger Guard	33	Washer	58	Hammer and Trigger Pins
9	Trigger Guard Screw, Front	34	Windage Plate Screw	59	Safety Pin
10	Escutcheon Plate Screw, Rear	35	Base	60	Retaining Ring
11	Takedown Screw	36	Elevation Slide	61	Bracket Screw, Rear
12	Escutcheon Plate Screw, Front	37	Front Sight	62	Retaining Ring
13	Escutcheon Plate	38	Magazine Mount	63	Safety
14	Loop and Bushing, Front	39	Cartridge Stop	64	Retaining Ring
15	Swivel Screw, Front	40	Takedown Mount	65	Hammer
16	Swivel Nut	41	Retaining Screw	66	Hammer Plunger
17	Receiver Cap	42	Magazine Tube, Inside	67	Hammer Spring
18	Receiver Cap Latch	43	Magazine Tube Tension Spring	68	Hammer Plunger Guide
19	Receiver Cap Pin	44	Magazine Tube, Outside	69	Retaining Ring
20	Receiver Cap Spring	45	Retaining Ring	70	Sear
21	Retaining Ring	46	Magazine Pin	71	Sear Pin
22	Bolt Collar	47	Magazine Knob	72	Trigger
23	Bolt Plate	48	Magazine Spring	73	Trigger Spring
24	Bolt Lever	49	Feed Spring Plunger	74	Retaining Ring
25	Firing Pin	50	Feed Spring		

Model 350KC Autoloading Rifle

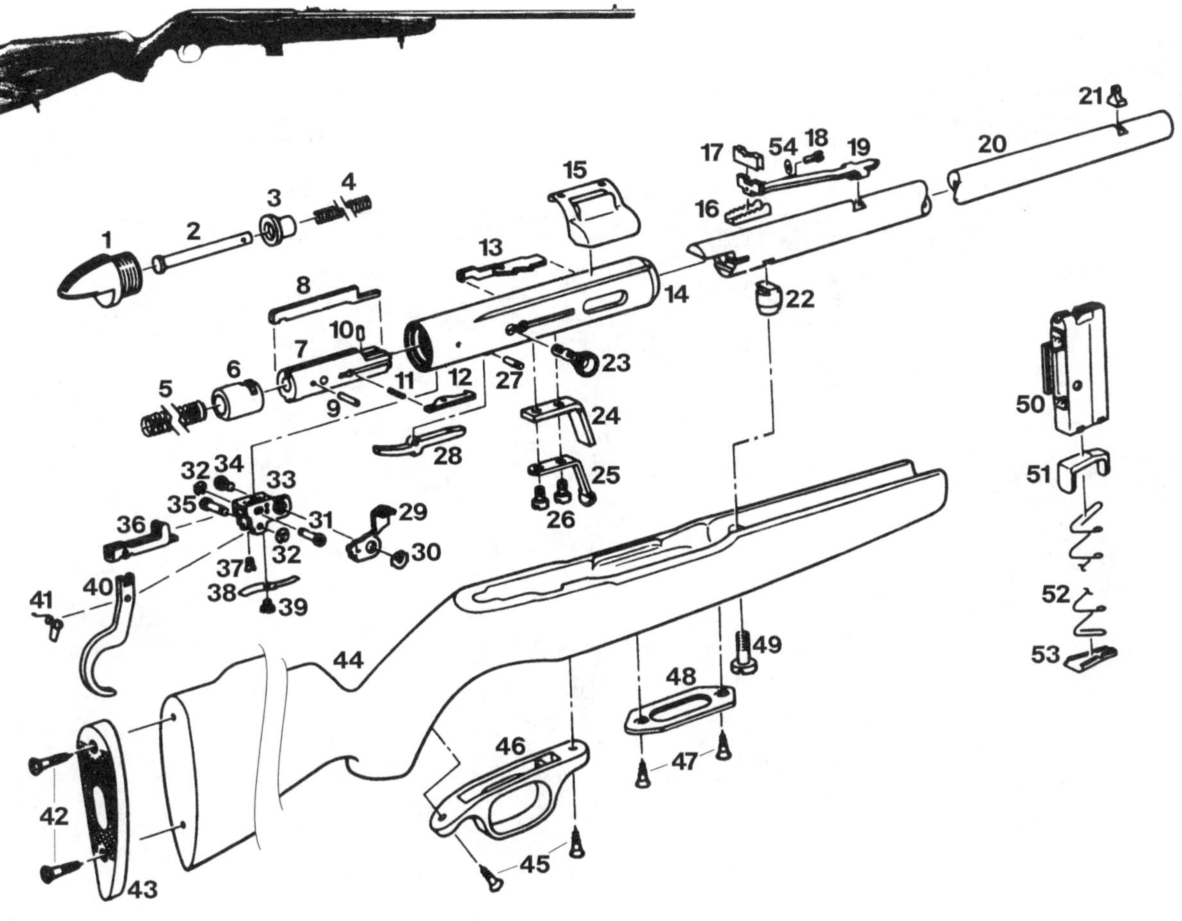

1	Breech Plug	**28**	Sear
2	Retracting Spring Plunger	**29**	Safety-Lever
3	Retracting Spring Bushing	**30**	Retaining Ring
4	Retracting Spring	**31**	Disconnector Pin
5	Mainspring	**32**	Retaining Ring
6	Hammer	**33**	Disconnector Bracket
7	Bolt	**34**	Safety Pin
8	Firing Pin	**35**	Trigger Pin
9	Retaining Pin	**36**	Disconnector
10	Extractor Pin	**37**	Disconnector Bracket Screw
11	Extractor Spring	**38**	Disconnector Spring
12	Extractor	**39**	Disconnector Spring Screw
13	Ejector	**40**	Trigger
14	Receiver	**41**	Trigger Spring
15	Deflector	**42**	Buttplate Screws
16	Elevation Slide	**43**	Buttplate
17	Windage Plate	**44**	Stock
18	Windage Plate Screw	**45**	Trigger Guard Screws
19	Base	**46**	Trigger Guard
20	Barrel	**47**	Stock Plate Screws
21	Beaded Front Sight	**48**	Magazine Stock Plate
22	Takedown Stud	**49**	Takedown Screw
23	Cocking Knob	**50**	Magazine Shell and Channel
24	Angle Bar	**51**	Magazine Follower
25	Magazine Latch	**52**	Magazine Spring
26	Angle Bar Screws	**53**	Magazine Bottom Plate
27	Sear Pin	**54**	Windage Plate Washer

Model 385K Bolt-Action Shotgun

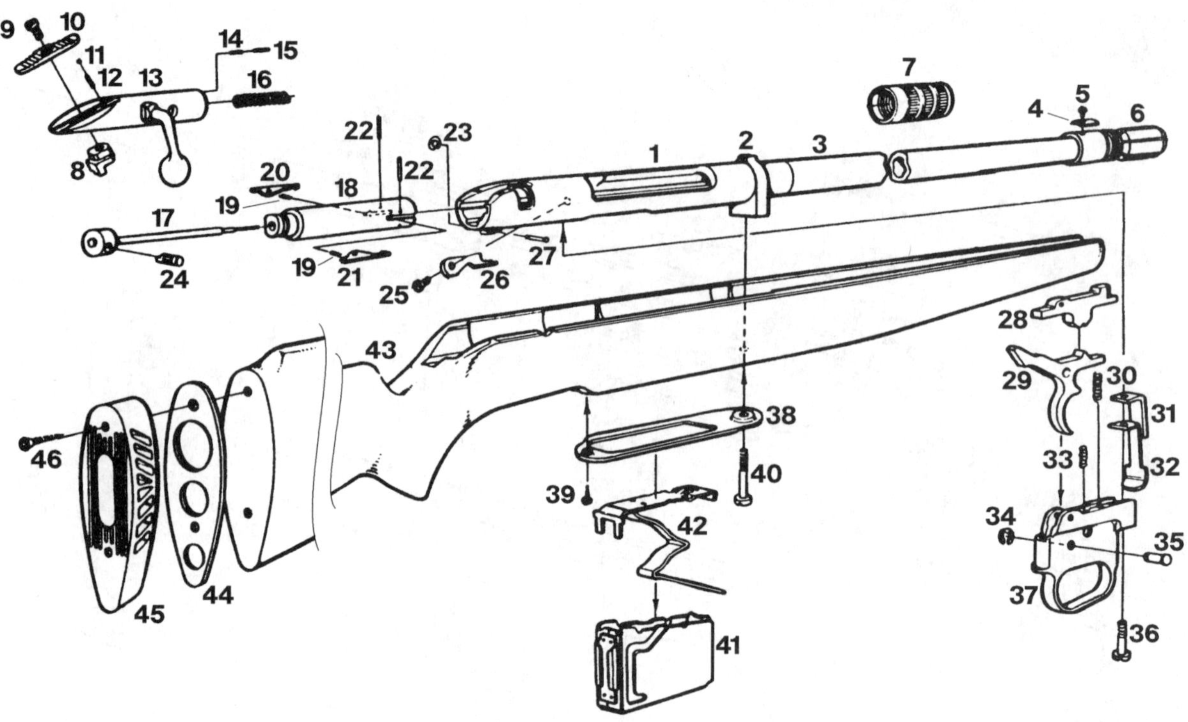

1	Receiver	25	Ejector Screw
2	Recoil Plate	26	Ejector
3	Barrel	27	Sear and Trigger Housing Retaining Pin
4	Choke Index Plate	28	Sear
5	Front Sight	29	Trigger
6	Choke Tube	30	Sear Spring
7	Choke Adjusting Sleeve	31	Angle Bar
8	Safety Lock	32	Magazine Latch
9	Safety Button Screw	33	Trigger Spring
10	Safety Button	34	Trigger Retaining Ring
11	Safety Click Ball	35	Trigger Pin
12	Safety Click Ball Spring	36	Trigger Housing Screw
13	Bolt	37	Trigger Housing
14	Bolt Index Plunger Spring	38	Stock Plate
15	Bolt Index Plunger	39	Stock Plate Screw and Nut
16	Striker Spring	40	Takedown Screw
17	Firing Pin	41	Magazine
18	Bolt Head	42	Magazine Spring Assembly
19	Extractor Springs	43	Stock
20	Extractor, Left	44	Recoil Pad Spacer
21	Extractor, Right	45	Recoil Pad
22	Extractor Pins	46	Recoil Pad Screw
23	Pin Retaining Ring		
24	Sear Pin		

Model 385KB and 485T Bolt-Action Shotgun

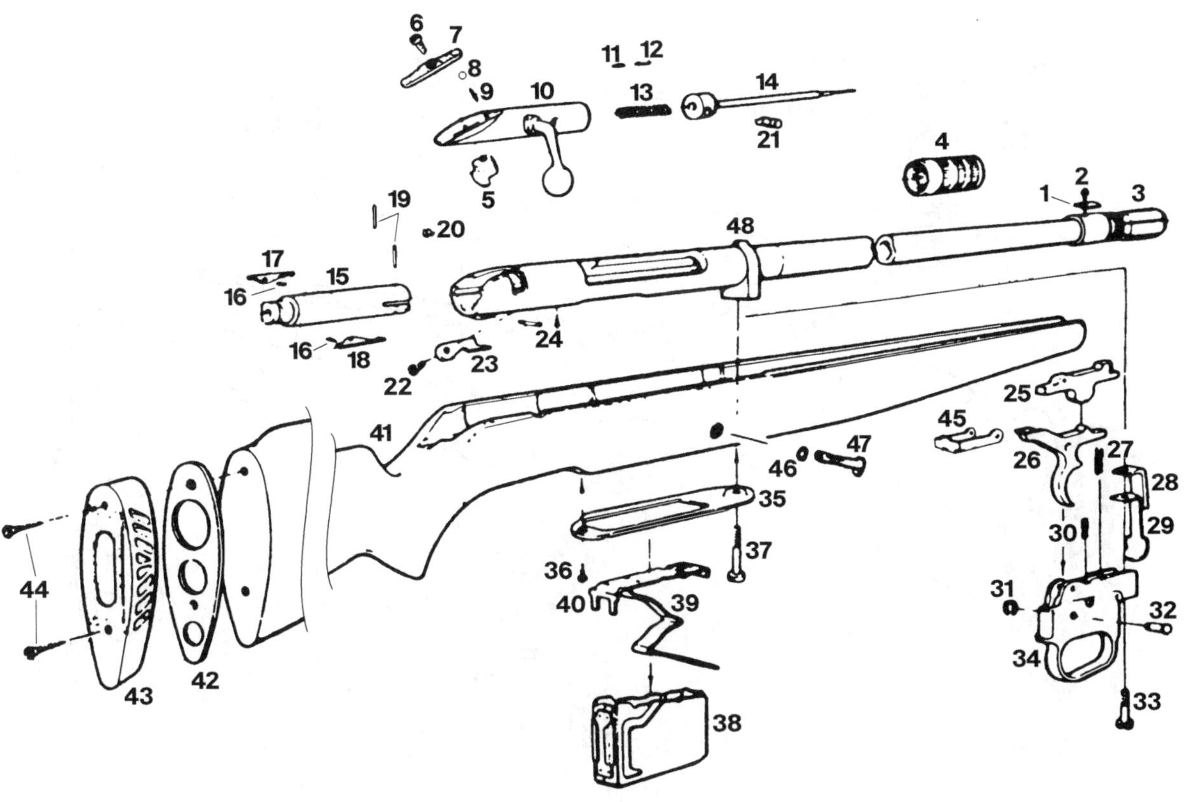

1	Choke Index Plate	**26**	Trigger
2	Front Sight	**27**	Sear Spring
3	Choke Tube	**28**	Angle Bar
4	Choke Adjusting Sleeve	**29**	Magazine Latch
5	Safety Lock	**30**	Trigger Spring
6	Safety Button Screw	**31**	Trigger Retaining Ring
7	Safety Button	**32**	Trigger Pin
8	Safety Click Ball	**33**	Trigger Housing Screw
9	Safety Click Ball Spring	**34**	Trigger Housing
10	Bolt Complete	**35**	Stock Plate
11	Bolt Index Plunger Spring	**36**	Stock Plate Screw
12	Bolt Index Plunger	**37**	Takedown Screw
13	Striker Spring	**38**	Magazine Shell
14	Firing Pin Assembly	**39**	Magazine Spring
15	Bolt Head	**40**	Magazine Follower
16	Extractor Springs	**41**	Stock Complete
17	Extractor, Left	**42**	Recoil Pad Spacer
18	Extractor, Right	**43**	Recoil Pad
19	Extractor Pins	**44**	Recoil Pad Screw
20	Sear and Trigger Housing Retaining Ring	**45**	Safety Adapter
		46	Cross-Bolt Screw
21	Sear Pin	**47**	Cross-Bolt Nut
22	Ejector Screw	**48**	Barrel and Receiver
23	Ejector	**Parts Not Shown**	
24	Sear and Trigger Housing Retaining Pin		Safety Detent Plate
			Stock Plate Nut
25	Sear		

Model 390KA Bolt-Action Shotgun

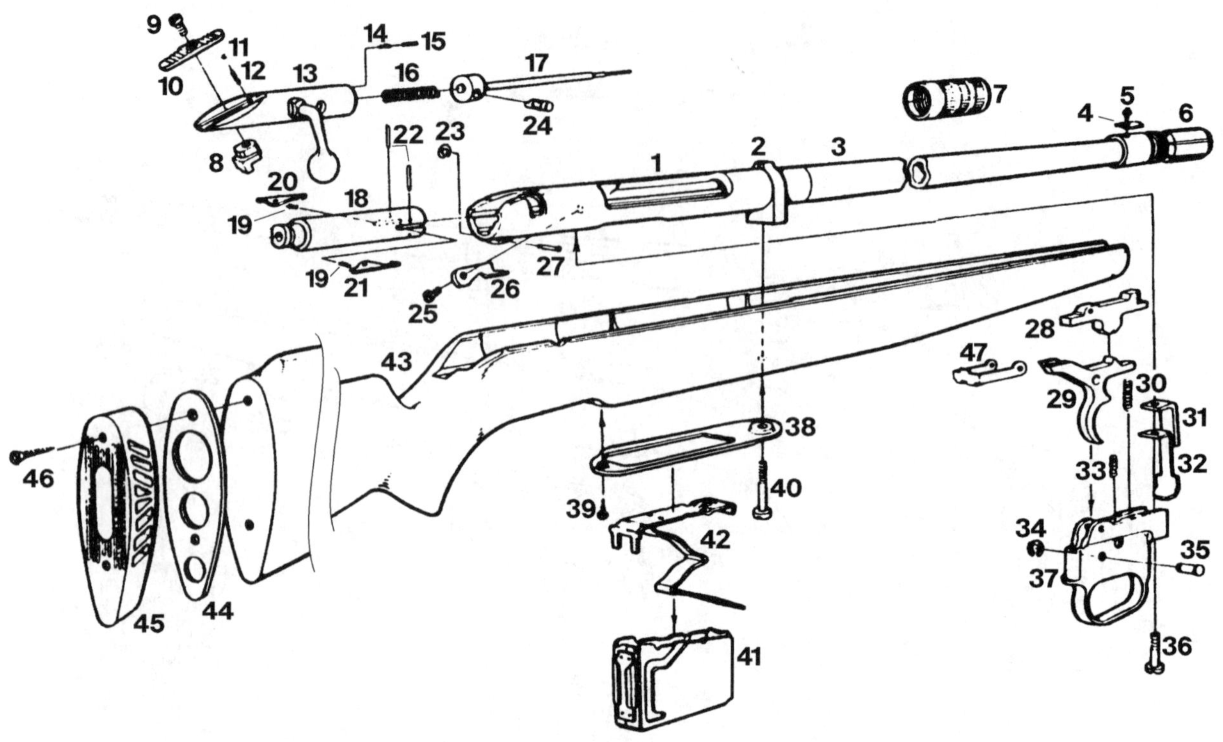

1	Receiver	**25**	Ejector Screw
2	Recoil Pad	**26**	Ejector
3	Barrel	**27**	Sear and Trigger Housing Retaining Pin
4	Choke Index Plate	**28**	Sear
5	Front Sight	**29**	Trigger
6	Choke Tube	**30**	Sear Spring
7	Choke Adjusting Sleeve	**31**	Angle Bar
8	Safety Lock	**32**	Magazine Latch
9	Safety Button Screw	**33**	Trigger Spring
10	Safety Button	**34**	Trigger Retaining Ring
11	Safety Click Ball	**35**	Trigger Pin
12	Safety Click Ball Spring	**36**	Trigger Housing Screw
13	Bolt	**37**	Trigger Housing
14	Bolt Index Plunger Spring	**38**	Stock Plate
15	Bolt Index Plunger	**39**	Stock Plate Screw and Nut
16	Striker Spring	**40**	Takedown Screw
17	Firing Pin	**41**	Magazine
18	Bolt Head	**42**	Magazine Spring Assembly
19	Extractor Springs	**43**	Stock
20	Extractor, Left	**44**	Recoil Pad Spacer
21	Extractor, Right	**45**	Recoil Pad
22	Extractor Pins	**46**	Recoil Pad Screw
23	Sear and Trigger Housing Retaining Ring	**47**	Safety Adapter
24	Sear Pin		

Model 395K and 395KA Bolt-Action Shotgun

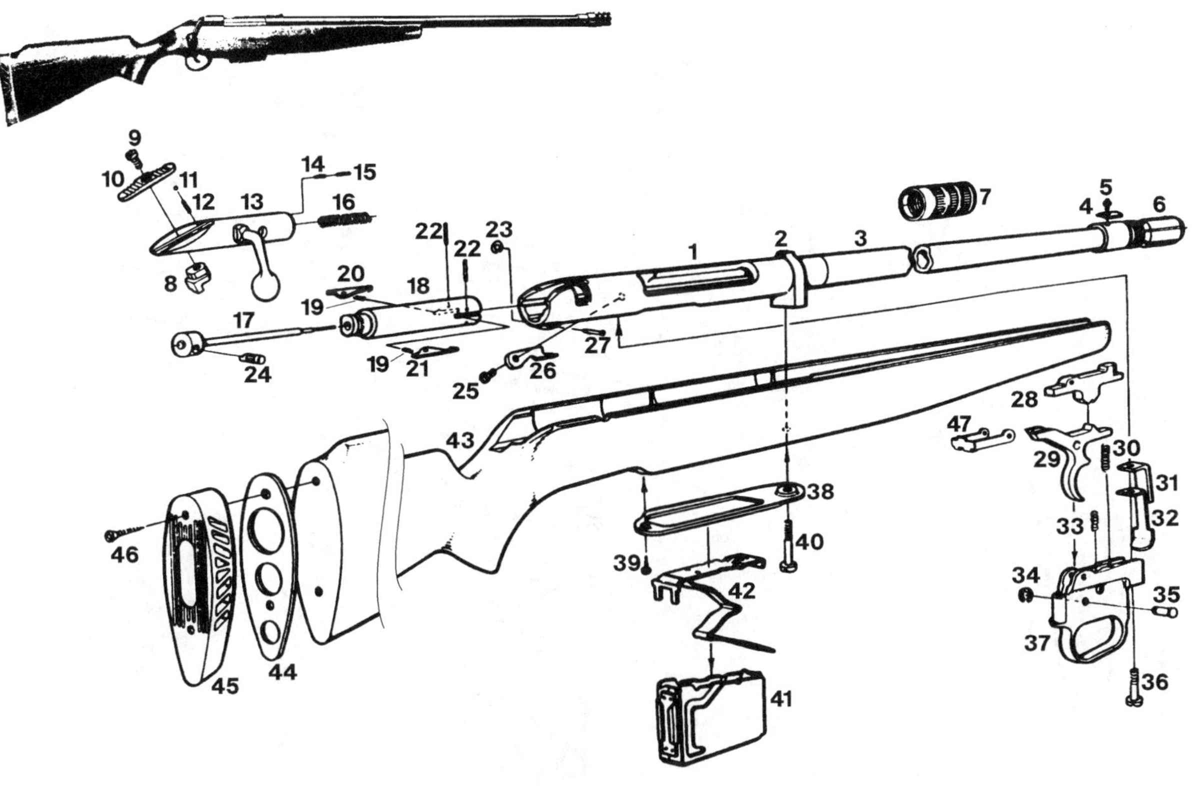

1	Receiver	**25**	Ejector Screw
2	Recoil Plate	**26**	Ejector
3	Barrel	**27**	Sear and Trigger Housing Retaining Pin
4	Choke Index Plate	**28**	Sear
5	Front Sight	**29**	Trigger
6	Choke Tube	**30**	Sear Spring
7	Choke Adjusting Sleeve	**31**	Angle Bar
8	Safety Lock	**32**	Magazine Latch
9	Safety Button Screw	**33**	Trigger Spring
10	Safety Button	**34**	Trigger Retaining Ring
11	Safety Click Ball	**35**	Trigger Pin
12	Safety Click Ball Spring	**36**	Trigger Housing Screw
13	Bolt	**37**	Trigger Housing
14	Bolt Index Plunger Spring	**38**	Stock Plate
15	Bolt Index Plunger	**39**	Stock Plate Screw and Nut
16	Striker Spring	**40**	Takedown Screw
17	Firing Pin	**41**	Magazine
18	Bolt Head	**42**	Magazine Spring Assembly
19	Extractor Springs	**43**	Stock
20	Extractor, Left	**44**	Recoil Pad Spacer
21	Extractor, Right	**45**	Recoil Pad
22	Extractor Pins	**46**	Recoil Pad Screw
23	Sear and Trigger Housing Retaining Pin	**47**	Safety Adapter
24	Sear Pin		

Model 395KB and 495T Bolt-Action Rifle

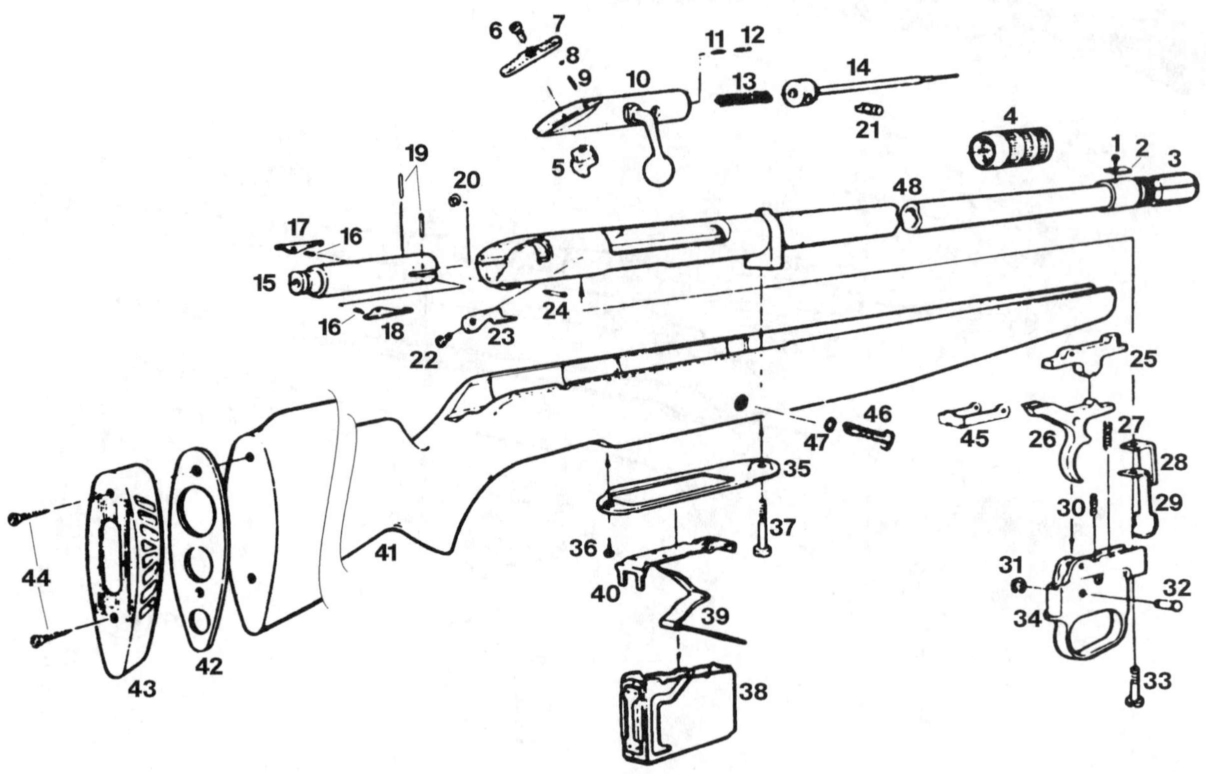

1	Front Sight	**26**	Trigger
2	Choke Index Plate	**27**	Sear Spring
3	Choke Tube	**28**	Angle Bar
4	Choke Adjusting Sleeve	**29**	Magazine Latch
5	Safety Lock	**30**	Trigger Spring
6	Safety Button Screw	**31**	Trigger Retaining Ring
7	Safety Button	**32**	Trigger Pin
8	Safety Click Ball	**33**	Trigger Housing Screw
9	Safety Click Ball Spring	**34**	Trigger Housing
10	Bolt Body	**35**	Stock Plate
11	Bolt Index Plunger Spring	**36**	Stock Plate Screw
12	Bolt Index Plunger	**37**	Takedown Screw
13	Striker Spring	**38**	Magazine Shell Assembly
14	Firing Pin Assembly	**39**	Magazine Spring Assembly
15	Bolt Head	**40**	Magazine Follower
16	Extractor Springs	**41**	Stock Complete
17	Extractor, Left	**42**	Recoil Pad Spacer
18	Extractor, Right	**43**	Recoil Pad
19	Extractor Pins	**44**	Recoil Pad Screws
20	Sear and Trigger Housing Retaining Ring	**45**	Safety Adapter
21	Sear Pin	**46**	Cross Bolt Screw
22	Ejector Screw	**47**	Cross Bolt Nut
23	Ejector	**48**	Barrel and Receiver
24	Sear and Trigger Housing Retaining Pin	**Parts Not Shown**	
25	Sear		Safety Detent Plate
			Stock Plate Nut

Model 472PRA and 472PCA Lever-Action Rifle

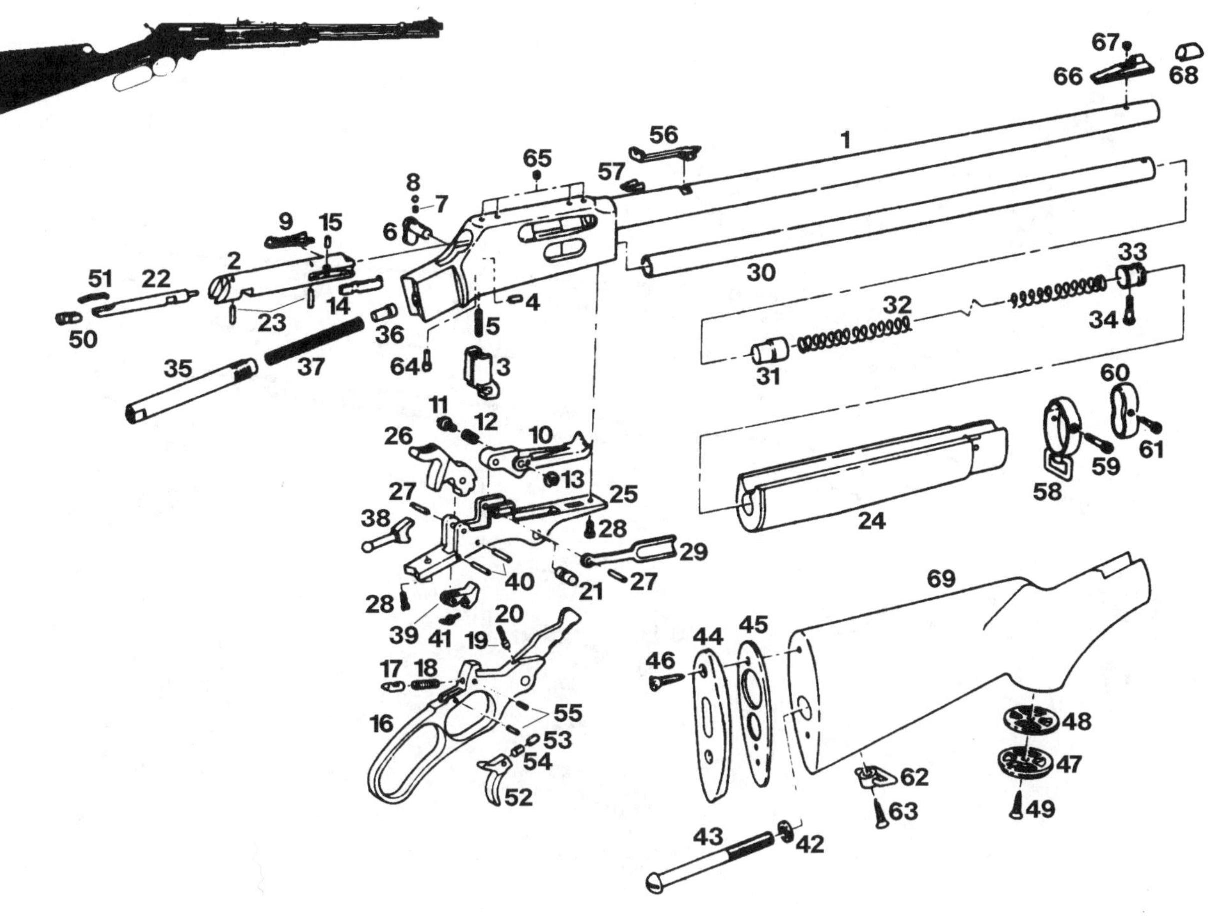

1	Barrel and Receiver Assembly	**23**	Firing Pin Retaining Pins	**47**	Grip Cap
2	Bolt	**24**	Forearm	**48**	Grip Cap Spacer
3	Bolt Lock	**25**	Hammer Housing	**49**	Grip Cap Screw
4	Bolt Lock Pin	**26**	Hammer	**50**	Striker
5	Bolt Lock Spring	**27**	Hammer Pins	**51**	Striker Retracting Spring
6	Safety	**28**	Hammer Housing Screws	**52**	Trigger
7	Safety Click Spring	**29**	Loading Ramp	**53**	Trigger Plunger
8	Safety Click Ball	**30**	Magazine Tube	**54**	Trigger Plunger Return Spring
9	Ejector Assembly	**31**	Magazine Tube Follower	**55**	Trigger Housing Plunger Pins
10	Elevator	**32**	Magazine Spring	**56**	Rear Sight
11	Elevator Plunger	**33**	Magazine Tube End Cap	**57**	Rear Sight Elevation Slide
12	Elevator Plunger Spring	**34**	Magazine Tube End Cap Screw	**58**	Rear Barrel Band
13	Elevator Plunger Retaining Ring	**35**	Mainspring Tube	**59**	Rear Barrel Band Screw
14	Extractor	**36**	Mainspring Guide	**60**	Forward Barrel Band
15	Extractor Pin	**37**	Mainspring	**61**	Forward Barrel Band Screw
16	Finger Lever	**38**	Rebound Lever	**62**	Loop and Bushing
17	Finger Lever Retaining Plunger	**39**	Sear	**63**	Swivel Screw
18	Finger Lever Retaining Plunger Spring	**40**	Sear Pins	**64**	Safety Retaining Screw
19	Finger Lever Pin Retaining Plunger	**41**	Sear Spring	**65**	Dummy Screws
20	Spring	**42**	Stock Washer	**66**	Front Sight
21	Finger Lever Pin	**43**	Stock Bolt	**67**	Screw
22	Firing Pin	**44**	Recoil Pad	**68**	Front Sight Hood
		45	Buttplate Spacer	**69**	Stock
		46	Buttplate Screws		

Model 485 Bolt-Action Shotgun

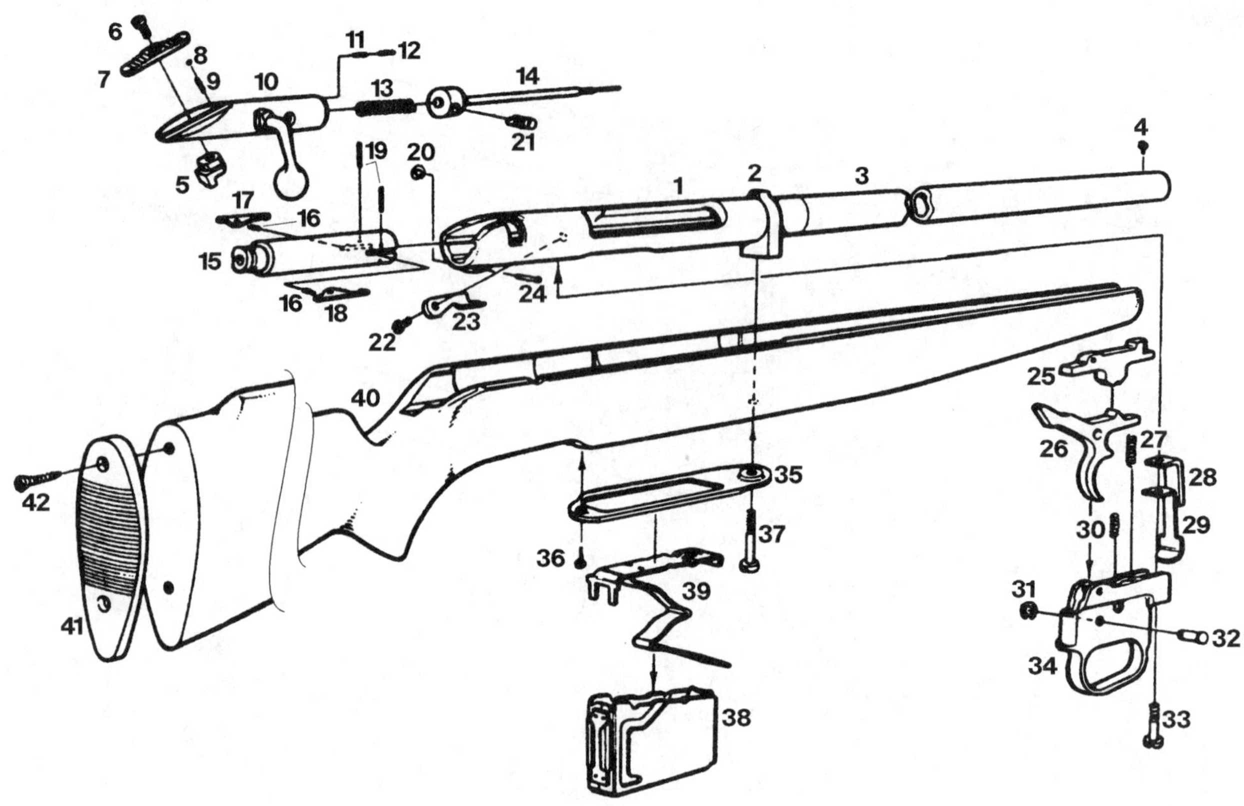

1	Receiver	**22**	Ejector Screw
2	Recoil Plate	**23**	Ejector
3	Barrel	**24**	Sear and Trigger Housing Retaining Pin
4	Front Sight	**25**	Sear
5	Safety Lock	**26**	Trigger
6	Safety Button Screw	**27**	Sear Spring
7	Safety Button	**28**	Angle Bar
8	Safety Click Ball	**29**	Magazine Latch
9	Safety Click Spring	**30**	Trigger Spring
10	Bolt	**31**	Trigger Retaining Ring
11	Bolt Index Plunger Spring	**32**	Trigger Pin
12	Bolt Index Plunger	**33**	Trigger Housing Screw
13	Striker Spring	**34**	Trigger Housing
14	Firing Pin	**35**	Stock Plate
15	Bolt Head	**36**	Stock Plate Screw and Nut
16	Extractor Springs	**37**	Takedown Screw
17	Left Extractor	**38**	Magazine
18	Right Extractor	**39**	Magazine Spring Assembly
19	Extractor Pins	**40**	Stock
20	Sear and Trigger Housing Retaining Ring	**41**	Buttplate
21	Sear Pin	**42**	Buttplate Screw

Model 490A and 495A Bolt-Action Shotgun

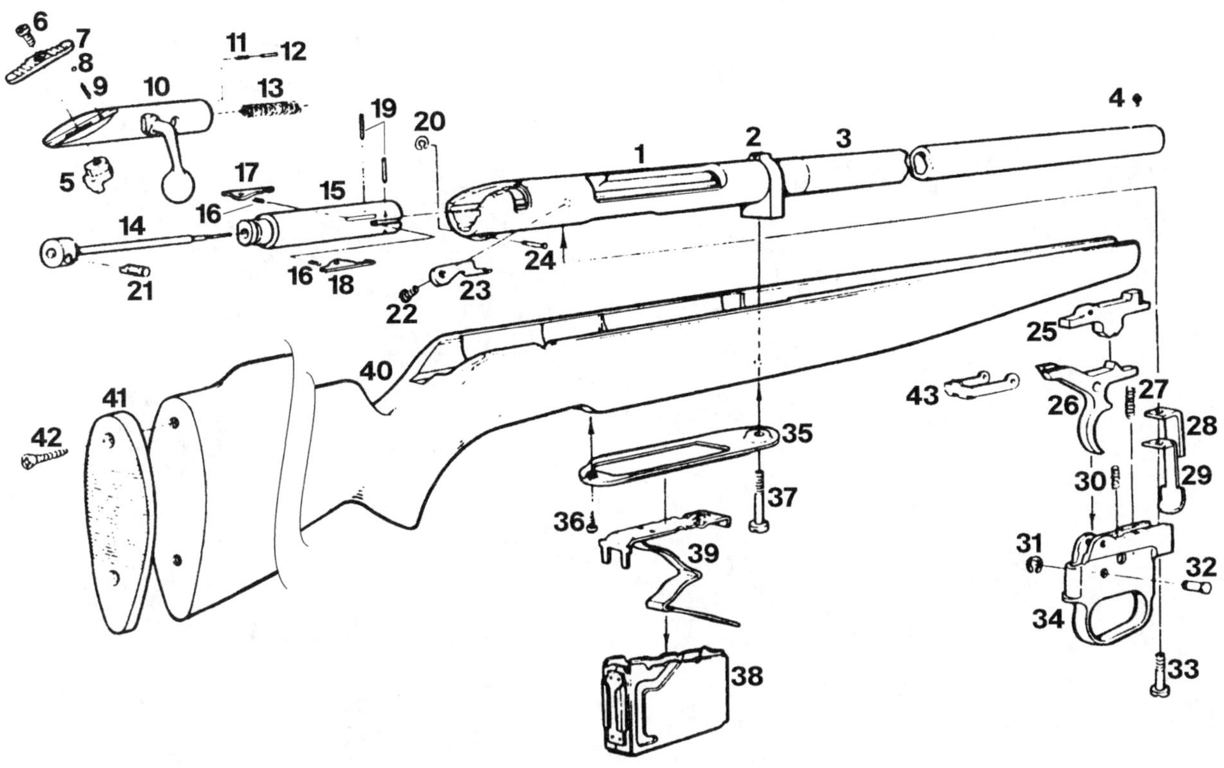

1	Receiver	16	Extractor Springs	29	Magazine Latch
2	Recoil Plate	17	Extractor, Left	30	Trigger Spring
3	Barrel	18	Extractor, Right	31	Trigger Retaining Ring
4	Front Sight	19	Extractor Pins	32	Trigger Pin
5	Safety Lock	20	Sear and Trigger Housing Retaining Ring	33	Trigger Housing Screw
6	Safety Button Screw	21	Sear Pin	34	Trigger Housing
7	Safety Button	22	Ejector Screw	35	Stock Plate
8	Safety Click Ball	23	Ejector	36	Stock Plate Screw and Nut
9	Safety Click Spring	24	Sear and Trigger Housing Retaining Pin	37	Takedown Screw
10	Bolt	25	Sear	38	Magazine
11	Bolt Index Plunger Spring	26	Trigger	39	Magazine Spring Assembly
12	Bolt Index Plunger	27	Sear Spring	40	Stock
13	Striker Spring	28	Angle Bar	41	Buttplate
14	Firing Pin			42	Buttplate Screw
15	Bolt Head			43	Safety Adapter

Model 500 Bullpup Slide-Action Shotgun

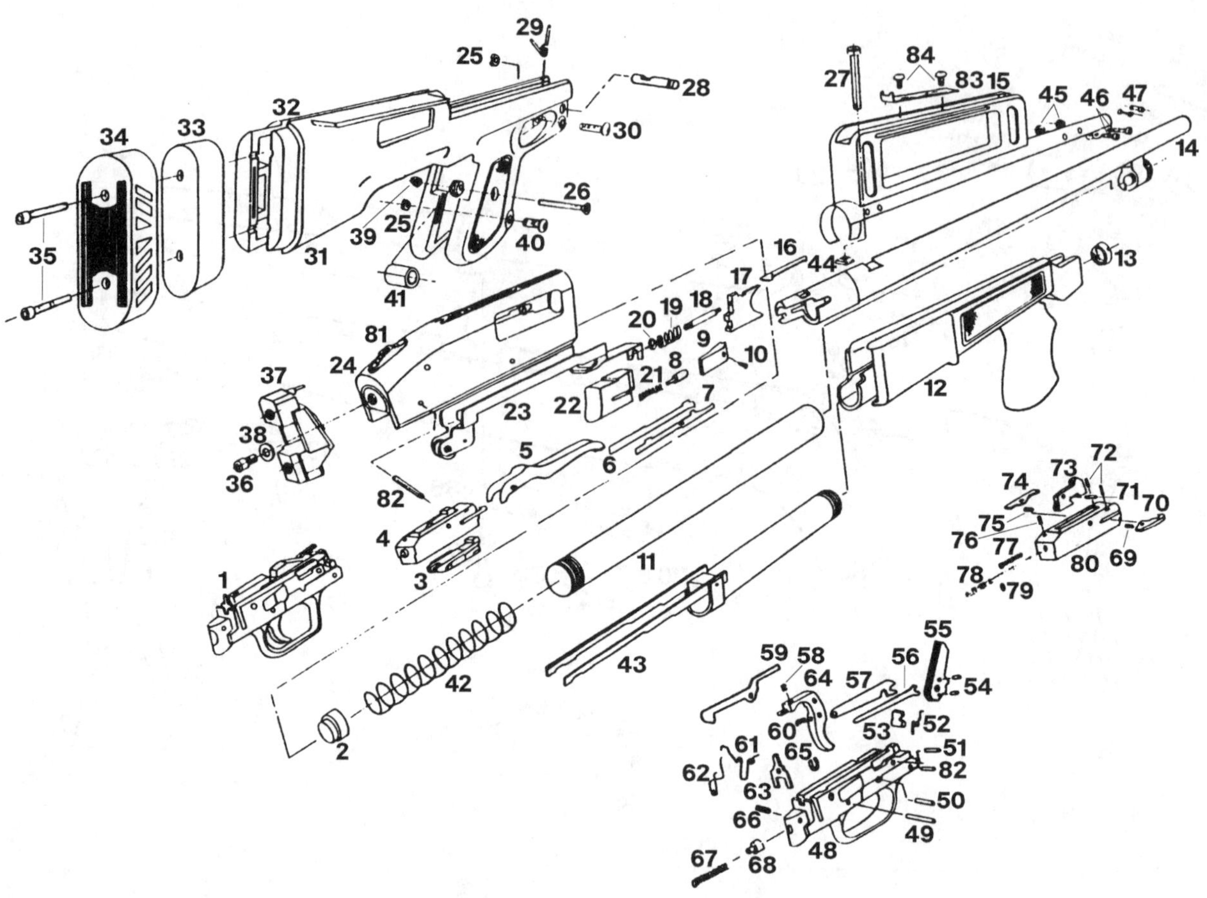

1 Trigger Housing Assembly
2 Magazine Follower
3 Bolt Slide
4 Bolt Assembly
5 Elevator Assembly
6 Cartridge Stop
7 Cartridge Interrupter Assembly
8 Grip Safety Plunger
9 Trigger Block
10 Trigger Block Spring
11 Magazine Tube
12 Forend Assembly
13 Retaining Ring
14 Barrel Assembly
15 Handle Sight Assembly
16 Trigger Extension
17 Primary Trigger
18 Trigger Pin
19 Trigger Return Spring
20 Trigger Pin Washer
21 Safety Grip Spring
22 Grip Safety
23 Trigger Connector Assembly
24 Receiver Assembly
25 Stock Bolt Nuts
26 Stock Screw
27 Handle Sight Retaining Screw
28 Crossbolt Safety
29 Crossbolt Safety Spring
30 Stock Bolt, Long
31 Pistol Grip Stock, Right
32 Pistol Grip Stock, Left
33 Cup Plate
34 Recoil Pad
35 Recoil Pad Screws
36 Recoil Beam Retaining Screw
37 Recoil Beam Assembly
38 Recoil Beam Washer
39 Stock Screw Lock Nut
40 Stock Bolt, Short
41 Support Spacer
42 Magazine Spring
43 Slide Action Assembly
44 Retaining Base
45 Retaining Nuts
46 Screws
47 Spacers
48 Trigger Housing
49 Trigger Pin
50 Action Lock Pin
51 Hammer Pivot Pin
52 Sear Spring
53 Sear
54 Mainspring Guide Pins
55 Hammer
56 Mainspring Guide
57 Disconnector
58 Trigger Stop
59 Action Lock
60 Trigger Spring
61 Action Lock Disc Spring
62 Action Lock Hammer Spring
63 Connector
64 Trigger
65 Trigger Housing Pin Retaining<R>Spring
66 Mainspring Retaining Pin
67 Mainspring
68 Mainspring Plunger
69 Extractor Spring, Right
70 Extractor, Right
71 Bolt Lock Pin
72 Extractor Retaining Pins
73 Bolt Lock
74 Extractor, Left
75 Extractor Spring, Left
76 Firing Pin Retaining Pin
77 Firing Pin Spring
78 Firing Pin
79 Firing Pin Washer
80 Bolt
81 Safety Button
82 Sear Pin
83 Sight
84 Sight Screws

Model 500 Slide-Action Shotgun

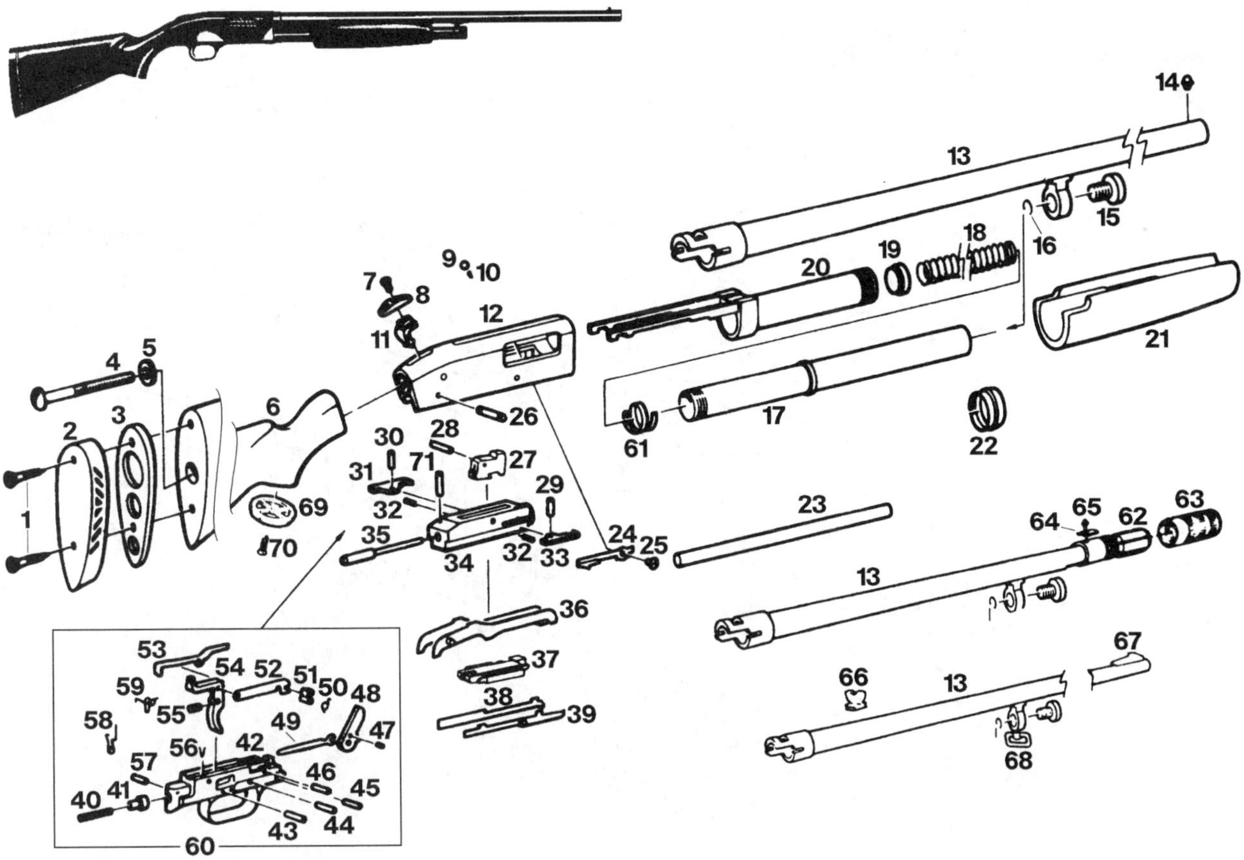

1	Recoil Pad Screws	**26**	Trigger Housing Pin	**51**	Sear
2	Recoil Pad	**27**	Bolt Lock	**52**	Disconnector
3	Black Spacer	**28**	Bolt Lock Pin	**53**	Action Lock
4	Stock Bolt	**29**	Extractor Retaining Pin, Right	**54**	Trigger
5	Stock Bolt Washer	**30**	Extractor Retaining Pin, Left	**55**	Trigger Spring
6	Stock	**31**	Extractor, Left	**56**	Trigger Housing Pin Retaining<R>Spring
7	Safety Button Screw	**32**	Extractor Springs	**57**	Mainspring Retaining Pin
8	Safety Button	**33**	Extractor, Right	**58**	Lock Action Hammer Spring
9	Safety Click Ball	**34**	Bolt	**59**	Lock Action Disconnector Spring
10	Safety Click Spring	**35**	Firing Pin	**60**	Trigger Housing
11	Safety Lock	**36**	Elevator Assembly	**61**	Slide Action Spring
12	Receiver	**37**	Bolt Slide	**62**	Choke Tube
13	Barrel	**38**	Cartridge Stop	**63**	Choke Sleeve
14	Front Sight	**39**	Cartridge Interruptor Assembly	**64**	Index Plate
15	Takedown Screw	**40**	Mainspring	**65**	Front Sight
16	Retaining Ring	**41**	Mainspring Plunger	**66**	Rear Sight Assembly
17	Magazine Tube Assembly	**42**	Trigger Housing	**67**	Front Sight
18	Magazine Spring	**43**	Trigger Pin	**68**	Front Swivel
19	Magazine Follower	**44**	Action Lock Pin	**69**	Grip Cap
20	Slide Action Assembly	**45**	Sear Pin	**70**	Grip Cap Screw
21	Forend	**46**	Hammer Pin	**71**	Firing Pin Retaining Pin
22	Slide Action Tube Nut	**47**	Mainspring Guide Pin		
23	Magazine Wood Plug	**48**	Hammer		
24	Ejector	**49**	Mainspring Guide		
25	Ejector Screw	**50**	Sear Spring		

Model 5500 Mark II Autoloading Shotgun

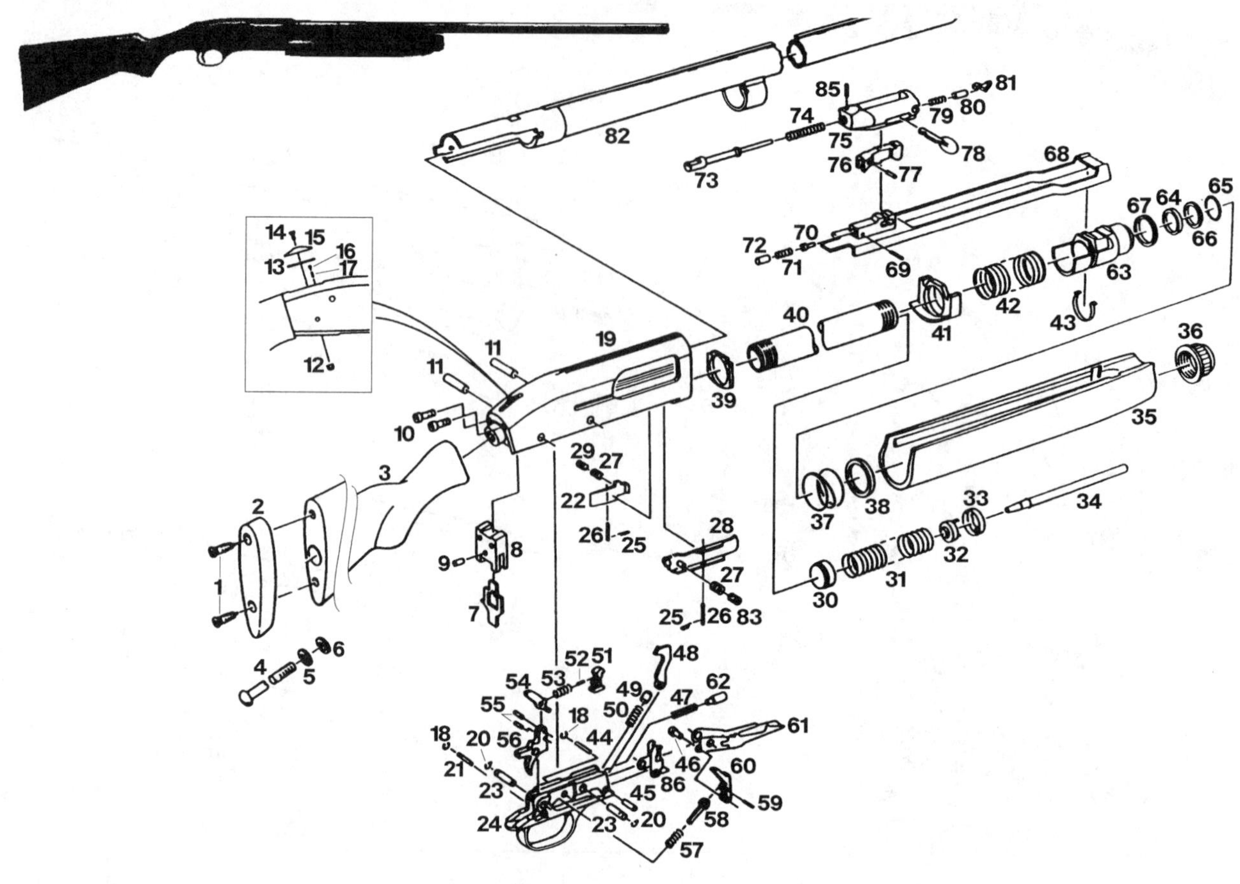

1	Recoil Pad Screws	**30**	Magazine Follower	**59**	Elevator Pawl Strut Pin
2	Recoil Pad	**31**	Magazine Spring	**60**	Elevator Pawl
3	Stock	**32**	Forend Cap Detent	**61**	Elevator
4	Stock Bolt	**33**	Magazine Spring Retainer	**62**	Bolt Release Spring Plunger
5	Stock Bolt Lock Washer	**34**	Magazine Plug	**63**	Inertia Weight
6	Stock Bolt Washer	**35**	Forend	**64**	Inner Piston Ring
7	Safety Connector	**36**	Forend Cap	**65**	O Ring
8	Bolt Buffer	**37**	Recoil Spring	**66**	Forward Seal Ring
9	Safety Connector Retaining Pin	**38**	Recoil Washer	**67**	Outer Piston Ring
10	Bolt Buffer Screws	**39**	Receiver Insert	**68**	Action Bar Sub-Assembly
11	Trigger Housing Pins	**40**	Magazine Tube	**69**	Retaining Pin
12	Safety Lock	**41**	Inertia Weight Buffer	**70**	Operating Handle Plunger
13	Detent Plate	**42**	Action Spring	**71**	Operating Handle Plunger Spring
14	Safety Button Screw	**43**	Action Bar Spring Retainer	**72**	Slide Block Buffer
15	Safety Button	**44**	Sear Pin	**73**	Firing Pin
16	Safety Detent Ball	**45**	Hammer Pin	**74**	Firing Pin Spring
17	Safety Detent Spring	**46**	Elevator Pawl Pin	**75**	Bolt
18	Trigger Housing Pin Retainers	**47**	Bolt Release Spring	**76**	Bolt Lock
19	Receiver	**48**	Hammer	**77**	Bolt Lock Pin
20	Retaining Rings	**49**	Hammer Spring Plunger	**78**	Operating Handle
21	Trigger Pin	**50**	Hammer Spring	**79**	Extractor Spring
22	Shell Stop, Left	**51**	Sear	**80**	Extractor Plunger
23	Trigger Housing Pin Bushings	**52**	Sear Spring Pin	**81**	Extractor
24	Trigger Housing	**53**	Sear Disconnector Spring	**82**	Barrel Assembly
25	Pivot Pin Retaining Clips	**54**	Disconnector	**83**	Cartridge Stop Buffer, Right
26	Shell Stop Pivot Pins	**55**	Disconnector Pins	**84**	Front Sight
27	Shell Stop Springs	**56**	Trigger	**85**	Firing Pin Retaining Pin
28	Shell Stop Assembly, Right	**57**	Elevator Pawl Spring	**86**	Bolt Release
29	Cartridge Stop Buffer, Left	**58**	Elevator Pawl Strut		

Model 800 Bolt-Action Rifle

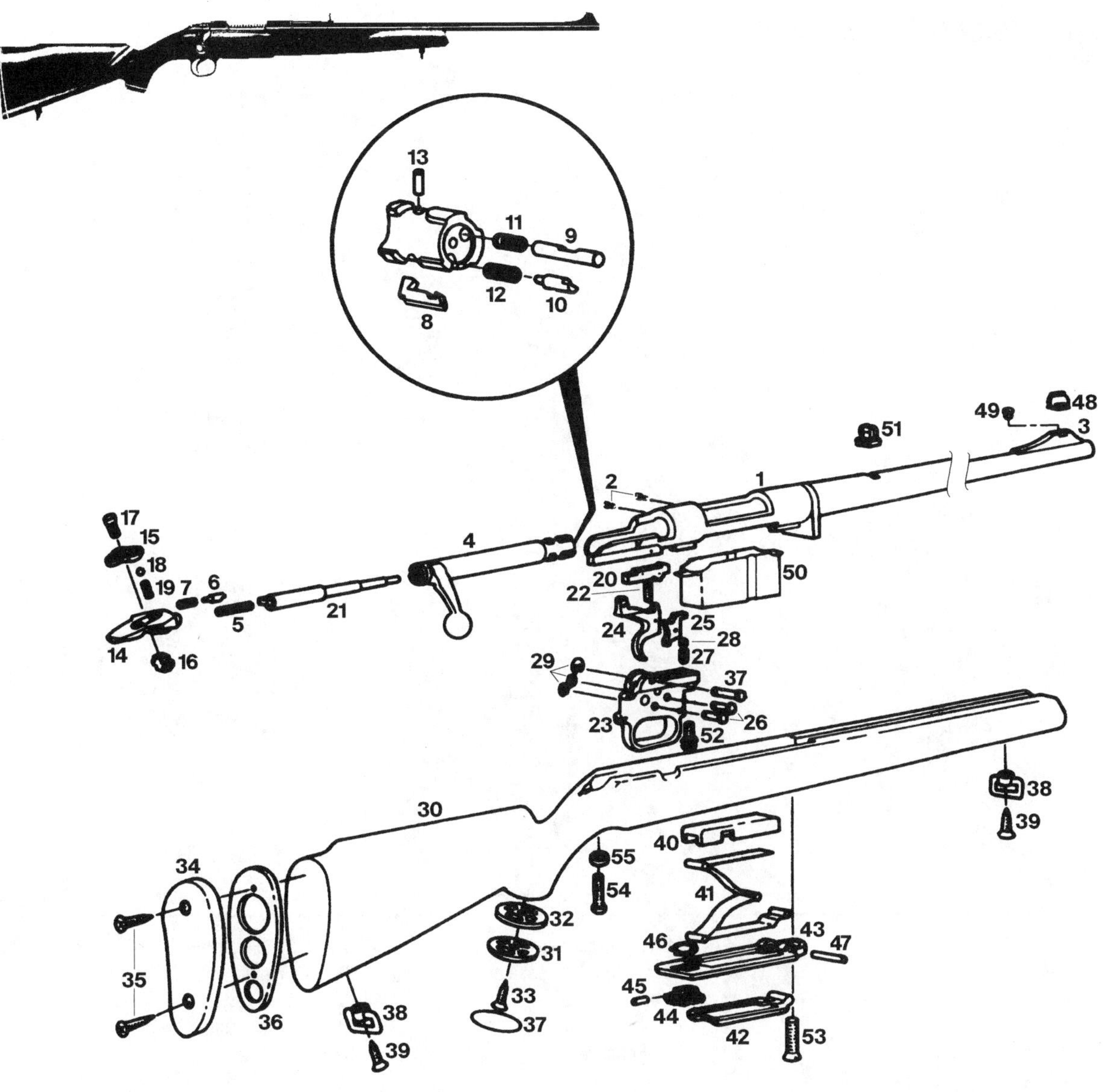

1	Barrel and Receiver Assembly	**20**	Sear	**38**	Swivel Loop and Bushing Assembly
2	Dummy Screws	**21**	Firing Pin	**39**	Swivel Screws
3	Front Sight Ramp	**22**	Sear and Trigger Spring	**40**	Magazine Follower
4	Bolt	**23**	Trigger Housing	**41**	Magazine Spring
5	Striker Spring	**24**	Trigger	**42**	Magazine Floorplate
6	Safety Cap Lock Plunger	**25**	Trigger Sear	**43**	Magazine Stock Plate
7	Safety Cap Lock Spring	**26**	Trigger and Sear Pins	**44**	Magazine Latch
8	Extractor	**27**	Trigger Sear Spring	**45**	Magazine Latch Spring
9	Ejector	**28**	Trigger Sear Plunger	**46**	Magazine Latch Retaining Ring
10	Extractor Plunger	**29**	Retaining Rings	**47**	Magazine Floorplate Pin
11	Ejector Spring	**30**	Stock	**48**	Front Sight
12	Extractor Spring	**31**	Grip Cap	**49**	Front Sight Screw
13	Ejector Retaining Pin	**32**	Grip Cap Spacer	**50**	Magazine Shell
14	Safety Cap	**33**	Grip Cap Screw	**51**	Rear Sight
15	Safety Button	**34**	Buttplate	**52**	Trigger Housing Screw
16	Safety Lock	**35**	Buttplate Screws	**53**	Front Takedown Screw
17	Safety Button Screw	**36**	Buttplate Spacer	**54**	Rear Takedown Screw
18	Safety Click Ball	**37**	Housing Pin	**55**	Escutcheon
19	Safety Click Spring				

Model 835 Ulti-Mag Slide-Action Shotgun

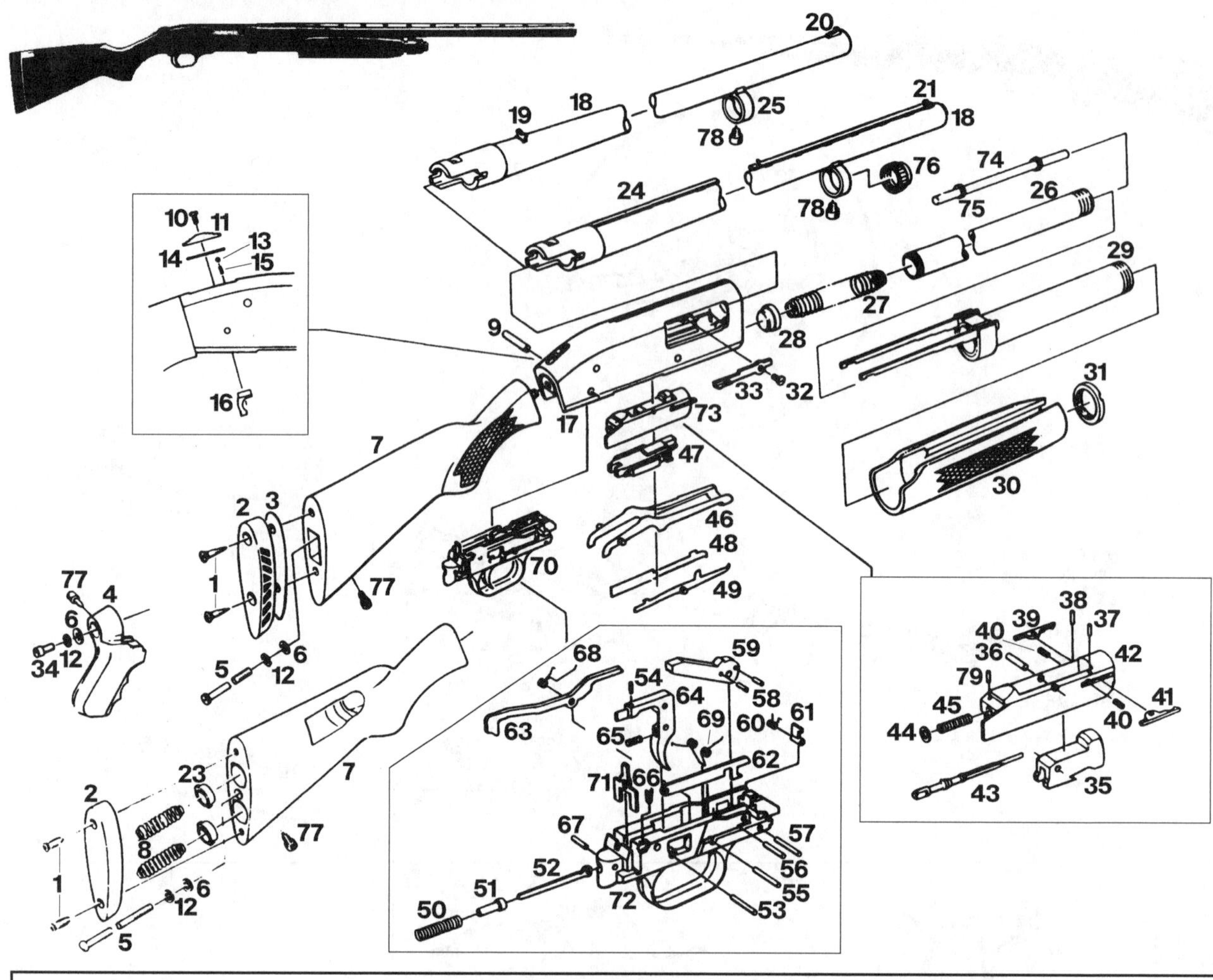

1	Recoil Pad Screws
2	Recoil Pad
3	Spacer
4	Cruiser Grip
5	Stock Bolt
6	Stock Bolt Washers
7	Stock
8	Follower Springs
9	Trigger Housing Pin
10	Safety Button Screw
11	Safety Button
12	Stock Bolt Lock Washer
13	Safety Detent Ball
14	Safety Detent Plate
15	Safety Detent Spring
16	Safety Block
17	Receiver
18	Barrel Assembly
19	Rear Sight Assembly
20	Front Sight Ramp
21	Bead Sight
22	Middle Sight
23	Followers
24	Ventilated Rib
25	Takedown Screw Assembly
26	Magazine Tube
27	Magazine Tube Spring
28	Magazine Follower
29	Slide Action Tube Assembly
30	Forearm
31	Action Slide Tube Nut
32	Ejector Screw
33	Ejector
34	Pistol Grip Stock Bolt
35	Bolt Lock
36	Bolt Lock Pin
37	Extractor Retaining Pin, Right
38	Extractor Retaining Pin, Left
39	Extractor, Left
40	Extractor Springs
41	Extractor, Right
42	Bolt
43	Firing Pin
44	Firing Pin Washer
45	Firing Pin Spring
46	Elevator Assembly
47	Bolt Slide
48	Cartridge Stop
49	Cartridge Interruptor Assembly
50	Mainspring
51	Mainspring Plunger
52	Mainspring Guide
53	Trigger Pin
54	Trigger Stop
55	Action Lock Pin
56	Hammer Pin
57	Sear Pin
58	Mainspring Guide Pins
59	Hammer
60	Sear Spring
61	Sear
62	Disconnector
63	Action Lock Lever
64	Trigger
65	Trigger Spring
66	Trigger Housing Pin Retaining<R>Spring
67	Mainspring Retaining Pin
68	Lock Action Hammer Spring
69	Lock Action Disconnector Spring
70	Trigger Housing Assembly
71	Connector
72	Trigger Housing
73	Bolt Assembly
74	Dowel
75	O Rings
76	Magazine Cap
77	Stud, Rear
78	Stud, Front
79	Firing Pin Retaining Pin

1866 Henry Military Lever-Action Rifle

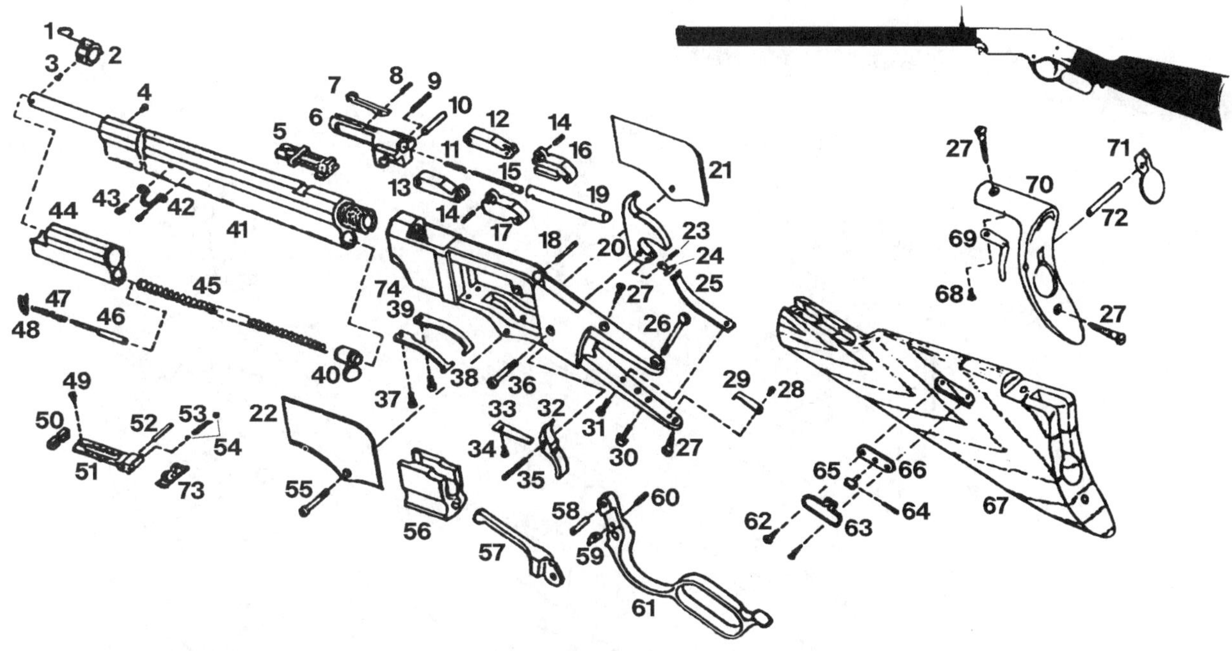

1	Front Sight Blade	38	Left Lever Spring
2	Front Sight Ring	39	Right Lever Spring
3	Front Sight Ring Screw	40	Magazine Follower
4	Sleeve Stop Screw	41	Barrel
5	Rear Sight Assembly	42	Sling Loop
6	Bolt	43	Sling Loop Screws
7	Extractor	44	Barrel Sleeve
8	Extractor Pin	45	Magazine Spring
9	Extension Pin	46	Magazine Detent
10	Front Link Pin	47	Magazine Detent Spring
11	Firing Pin Spring	48	Magazine Detent Head
12	Right Front Link	49	Rear Sight Ladder Screw
13	Left Front Link	50	Rear Sight Notch
14	Link Pins	51	Rear Sight Ladder
15	Firing Pin	52	Rear Sight Pin
16	Right Rear Link	53	Rear Sight Spring
17	Left Rear Link	54	Rear Sight Windage Screws
18	Firing Pin Retaining Pin	55	Sideplate Screw
19	Firing Pin Extension	56	Carrier Block
20	Hammer	57	Lifter Arm
21	Right Sideplate	58	Lever Pin
22	Left Sideplate	59	Lifter Arm Spacer
23	Hammer Link Pin	60	Lifter Arm Spacer Pin
24	Hammer Link	61	Lever
25	Mainspring	62	Sling Swivel Screws
26	Main Tang Screw	63	Sling Swivel
27	Buttplate and Tang Screws	64	Sling Swivel Base Pin
28	Lever Lock Spring Screw	65	Sling Swivel Base
29	Lever Lock Spring	66	Sling Swivel Plate
30	Lever Lock	67	Buttstock
31	Mainspring Screw	68	Trap Spring Screw
32	Trigger	69	Trap Spring
33	Trigger Spring	70	Buttplate
34	Trigger Spring Screw	71	Buttplate Trap
35	Trigger Pin	72	Buttplate Trap Pin
36	Hammer Screw	73	Rear Sight Base
37	Lever Spring Screws	74	Receiver

1873 Trapdoor Springfield Rifle

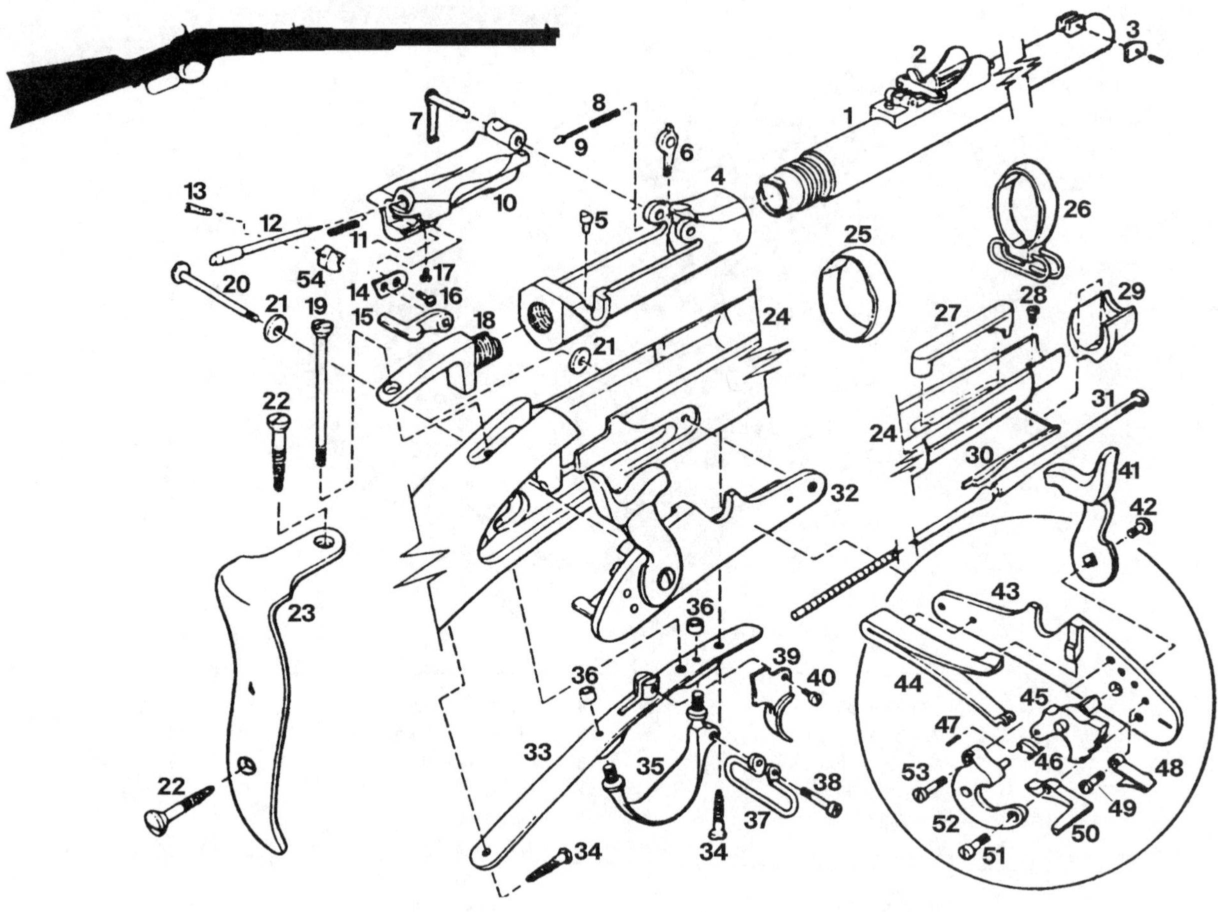

1	Barrel	28	Stock Tip Screw
2	Rear Sight Assembly	29	Stock Tip
3	Front Sight and Pin	30	Band Springs
4	Breech	31	Ramrod
5	Ejector Stud	32	Lock
6	Extractor	33	Guard Plate
7	Hinge Pin	34	Guard Screws
8	Ejector Spring	35	Guard Bow
9	Spindle	36	Guard Bow Nuts
10	Breechblock	37	Guard Bow Swivel
11	Cam Latch Spring	38	Guard Bow Swivel Screw
12	Firing Pin	39	Trigger
13	Cam Latch Screw	40	Trigger Screw
14	Breechblock Cap	41	Hammer
15	Thumb-Piece	42	Tumbler Screw
16	Breechblock Cap Screw	43	Lock Plate
17	Firing Pin Screw	44	Mainspring
18	Breech Screw	45	Tumbler
19	Tang Screw	46	Mainspring Swivel
20	Side Screws	47	Mainspring Swivel Pin
21	Side Screw Washers	48	Sear Spring
22	Buttplate Screws	49	Sear Spring Screw
23	Buttplate	50	Sear
24	Stock	51	Sear Screw
25	Lower Band	52	Bridle
26	Upper Band	53	Bridle Screw
27	Ramrod Stop	54	Cam Latch

Pardner Single Shot Shotgun

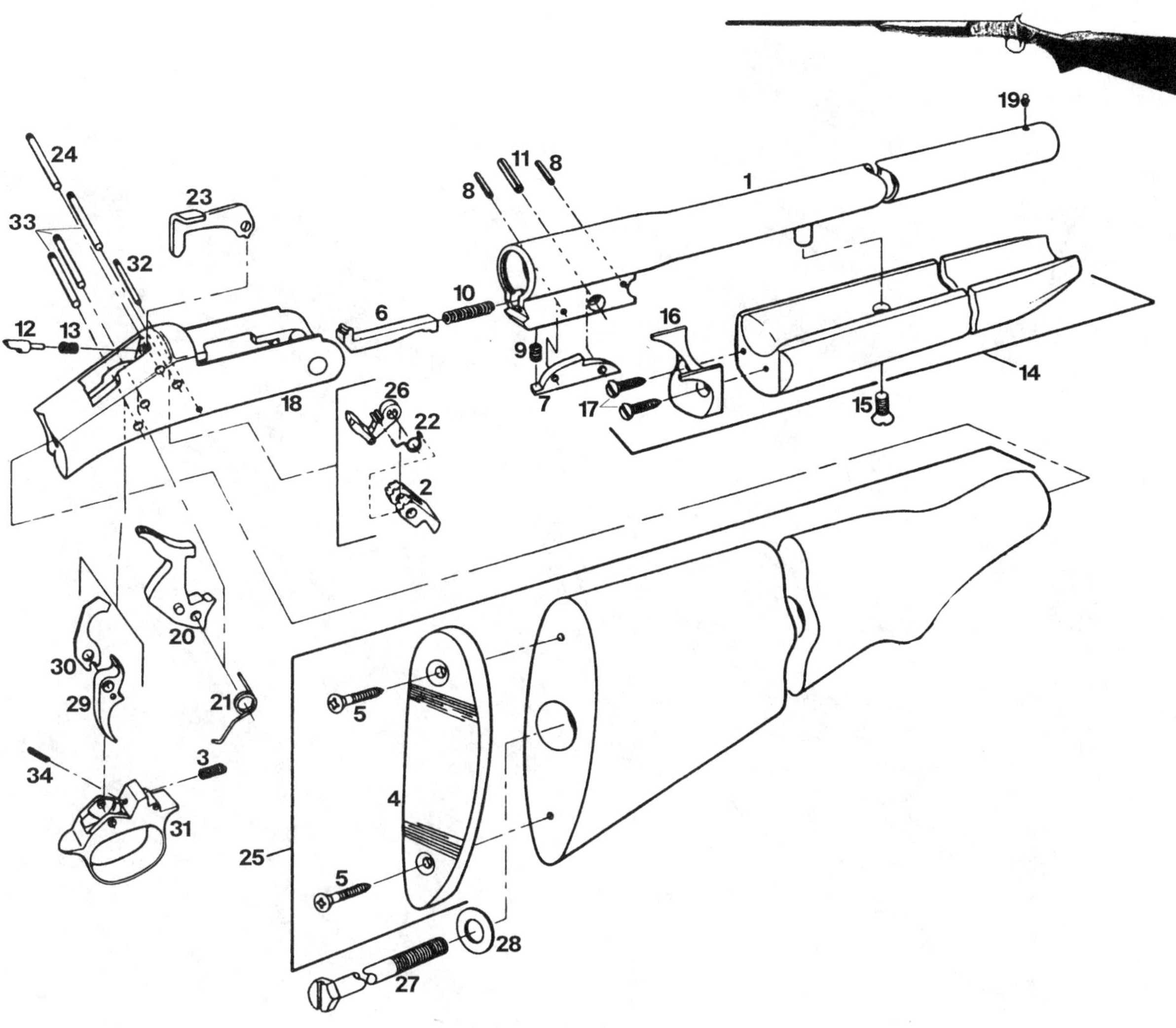

1	Barrel	**18**	Frame
2	Barrel Catch	**19**	Front Sight
3	Barrel Catch Spring	**20**	Hammer
4	Buttplate	**21**	Hammer Spring
5	Buttplate Screws	**22**	Lifter Spring
6	Ejector	**23**	Release Lever
7	Ejector Latch	**24**	Release Lever and Firing Pin Retaining Pin
8	Ejector Latch and Ejector Spring Stop Pins	**25**	Stock Assembly
9	Ejector Latch Spring	**26**	Striker and Lifter Assembly
10	Ejector Spring	**27**	Stock Screw
11	Ejector Stop Pin	**28**	Stock Screw Washer
12	Firing Pin	**29**	Trigger
13	Firing Pin Spring	**30**	Trigger Extension
14	Forend Assembly	**31**	Trigger Guard
15	Forend Screw	**32**	Trigger Guard Pin, Front
16	Forend Spacer	**33**	Trigger Guard Pins, Rear
17	Forend Spacer Screws	**34**	Trigger Spring

Bolt-Action Rifle

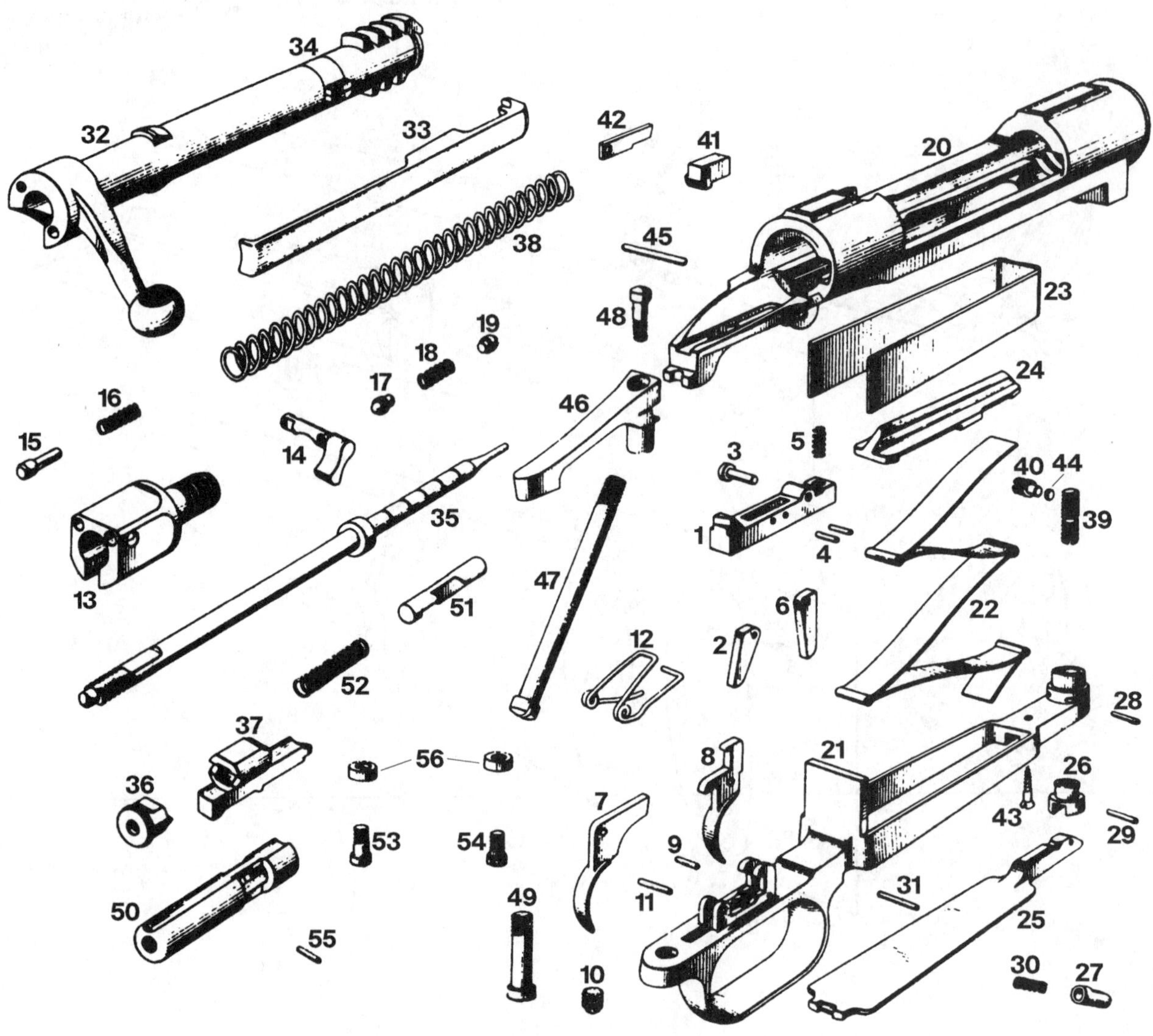

1	Sear	20	Receiver	39	Front Receiver Screw
2	Rear Knockoff	21	Trigger Guard	40	Front Receiver Screw Binding Screw
3	Sear Pin	22	Magazine Spring	41	Bolt Stop
4	Knockoff Pins	23	Magazine Box	42	Ejector
5	Sear Spring	24	Magazine Follower	43	Front Guard Screw
6	Front Knockoff	25	Magazine Floorplate	44	Front Receiver Screw Binding Screw Plug
7	Set-Trigger	26	Front Receiver Screw Nut	45	Bolt Stop Pin
8	Front Trigger	27	Magazine Floorplate Catch	46	Upper Tang
9	Front Trigger Pin	28	Front Receiver Screw Nut Pin	47	Upper Tang Truss Bolt
10	Trigger Adjusting Screw	29	Magazine Floorplate Pin	48	Upper Tang Adjusting Screw
11	Rear Trigger Pin	30	Magazine Floorplate Catch Spring	49	Rear Receiver Screw
12	Set-Trigger Spring	31	Magazine Floorplate Catch Pin	50	Forearm Snap Body
13	Sleeve	32	Bolt	51	Forearm Snap Bolt
14	Safety	33	Extractor	52	Forearm Snap Spring
15	Sleeve Locking Bolt	34	Extractor Collar	53	Forearm Snap Rear Screw
16	Sleeve Locking Bolt Spring	35	Firing Pin	54	Forearm Snap Front Screw
17	Rear Sleeve Poppet	36	Firing Pin Nut	55	Forearm Snap Pin
18	Sleeve Poppet Spring	37	Cocking Head	56	Forearm Snap Screw Escutcheons
19	Front Sleeve Poppet	38	Mainspring		

Model 60, 60AF, 160 and 65 Slide-Action Shotgun

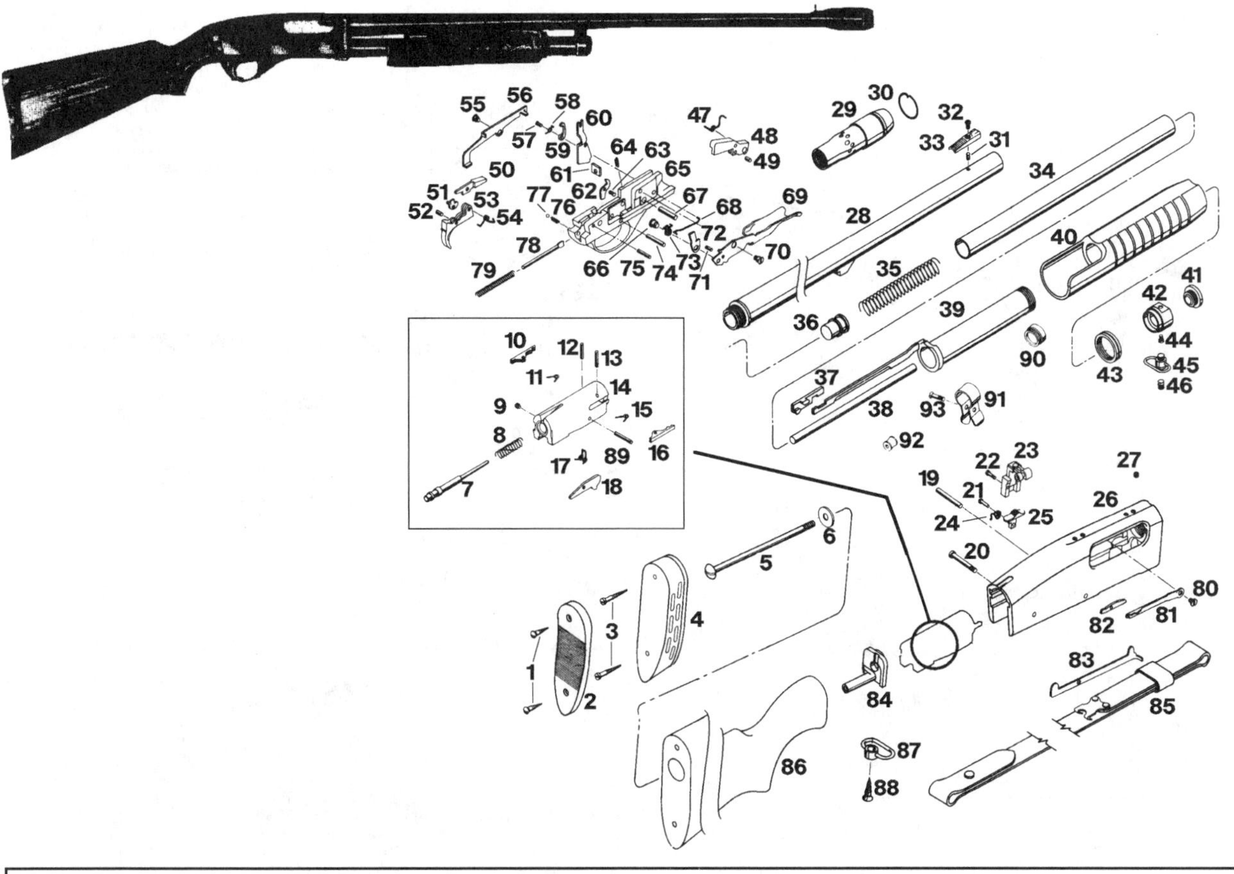

1	Buttplate Screws	32	Front Sight Screw	63	Detent Pin
2	Hard Rubber Buttplate	33	Ramp Front Sight	64	Release Lever Booster Spring
3	Recoil Pad Screws	34	Magazine Tube	65	Trigger Plate
4	Recoil Pad	35	Magazine Spring	66	Lifter Pawl Stud
5	Stock Bolt	36	Magazine Spring Follower	67	Hammer Pin
6	Stock Bolt Washer	37	Bolt Slide	68	Lifter Spring
7	Firing Pin	38	Wood Plug	69	Lifter
8	Firing Pin Spring	39	Handle Bar Tube Assembly	70	Pivot Screw Lifter
9	Firing Pin Retainer Screw	40	Forend Wood	71	Lifter Pawl Spring Post
10	Extractor, Left	41	Magazine Plug Dummy	72	Lifter Pawl
11	Extractor Spring, Left	42	Magazine Mount Plug	73	Lifter Pawl Spring
12	Extractor Pin, Left	43	Forend Retainer, Front	74	Trigger Pin
13	Extractor Pin, Right	44	Magazine Mount Plug Screw	75	Top Safe Pivot Pin
14	Breechbolt	45	Top Swivel with Screw	76	Safety Click Ball Spring
15	Extractor Spring, Right	46	Magazine Mount Plug Dummy Screw	77	Safety Click Ball
16	Extractor, Right	47	Release Lever Actuator Spring	78	Mainspring Follower
17	Cartridge Stop Spring	48	Hammer	79	Mainspring
18	Cartridge Stop	49	Mainspring Follower Pin	80	Ejector Screw
19	Trigger Plate Pin	50	Sear	81	Ejector
20	Trigger Plate Screw	51	Detent Trip	82	Shell Bumper
21	Safety Button Spring Retainer	52	Detent Trip Pin	83	Cartridge Cuttoff
22	Sight Screw	53	Trigger	84	Stock Retainer
23	Sight	54	Trigger Spring	85	Gun Carry Strap
24	Safety Button Spring	55	Pivot Screw Release	86	Stock
25	Top Safety Button	56	Release Lever	87	Bottom Swivel
26	Receiver	57	Release Latch Spring Pin	88	Bottom Swivel Screw
27	Dummy Screw	58	Release Latch Spring	89	Cartridge Stop Pin
28	Barrel	59	Release Latch	90	Magazine Cap
29	Choke	60	Top Safe Lever	91	Magazine Mount Band
30	Choke Click Spring	61	Mainspring Bridge	92	Barrel Mount Spacer
31	Front Sight Bead	62	Detent	93	Magazine Mount KEY Retaining Screw

Model 60G and 65G Slide-Action Shotgun

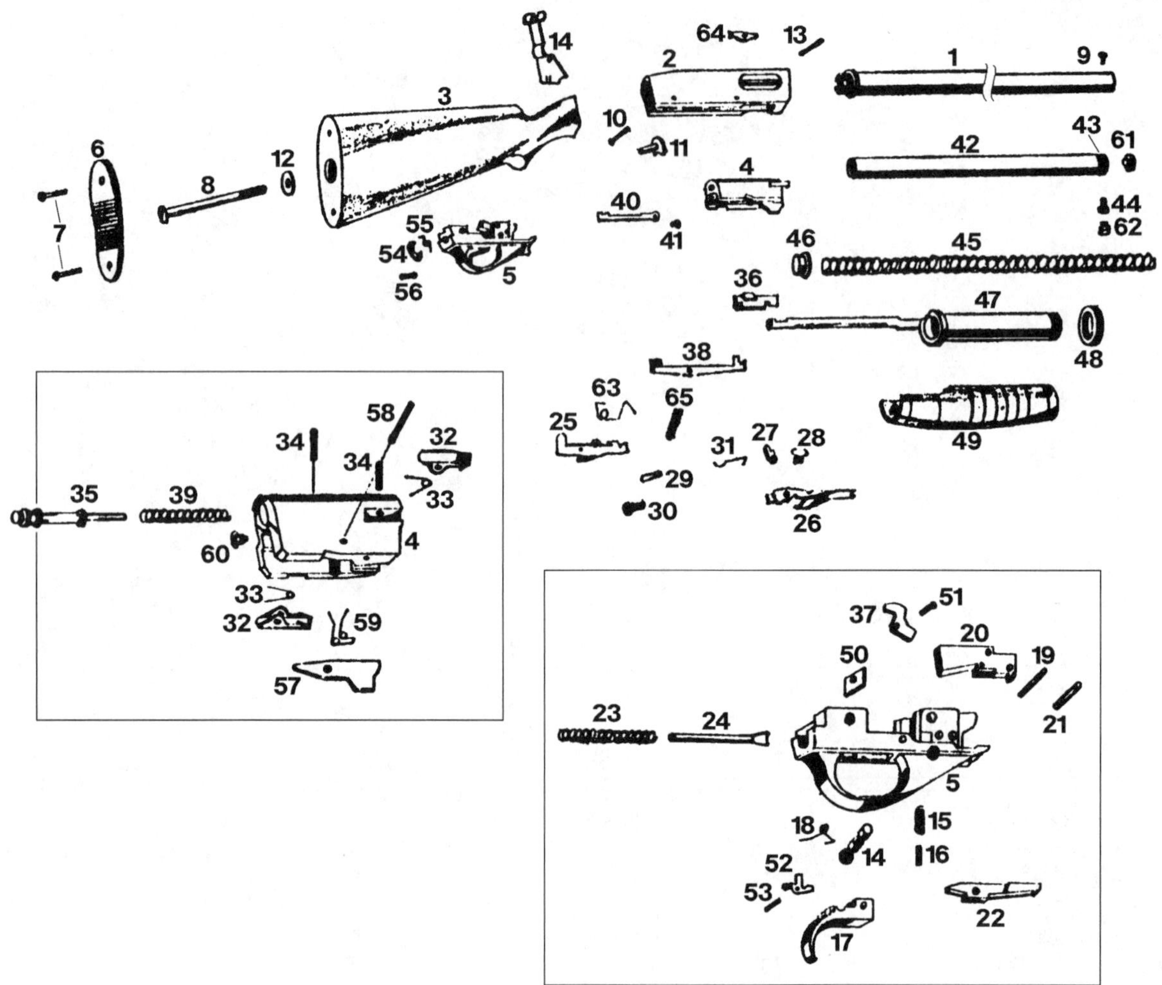

No.	Part	No.	Part	No.	Part
1	Barrel	23	Mainspring	45	Magazine Spring
2	Receiver	24	Mainspring Follower	46	Magazine Spring Follower
3	Stock	25	Release Lever	47	Operating Bar and Tube Assembly
4	Breechbolt	26	Lifter	48	Forend Retainer, Front
5	Trigger Guard	27	Lifter Pawl	49	Forend Wood
6	Buttplate	28	Lifter Pawl Spring	50	Mainspring Bridge
7	Buttplate Screws	29	Lifter Pawl Spring Post	51	Detent Pin
8	Stock Bolt	30	Lifter Pawl Stud	52	Detent Trip
9	Front Sight	31	Lifter Spring	53	Detent Trip Pin
10	Trigger Plate Screw	32	Extractors	54	Release Latch
11	Stock Retainer	33	Extractor Springs	55	Release Latch Spring
12	Stock Bolt Washer	34	Extractor Pins	56	Release Latch Spring Pin
13	Trigger Plate Pin	35	Firing Pin	57	Cartridge Stop
14	Safety Button	36	Bolt Slide	58	Cartridge Stop Pin
15	Safety Button Spring	37	Detent	59	Cartridge Stop Spring
16	Safety Spring Plunger	38	Cartridge Cutoff	60	Firing Pin Retaining Screw
17	Trigger	39	Firing Pin Spring	61	Magazine Plug Dummy
18	Trigger Spring	40	Ejector	62	Magazine Mount Plug Dummy Screw
19	Trigger Pin	41	Ejector Screw	63	Release Actuator Spring
20	Hammer	42	Magazine Tube	64	Shell Bumper
21	Hammer Pin	43	Magazine Mount Plug	65	Release Lever Booster Spring
22	Sear	44	Magazine Mount Plug Screw		

Model 70G and 72G Slide-Action Shotgun

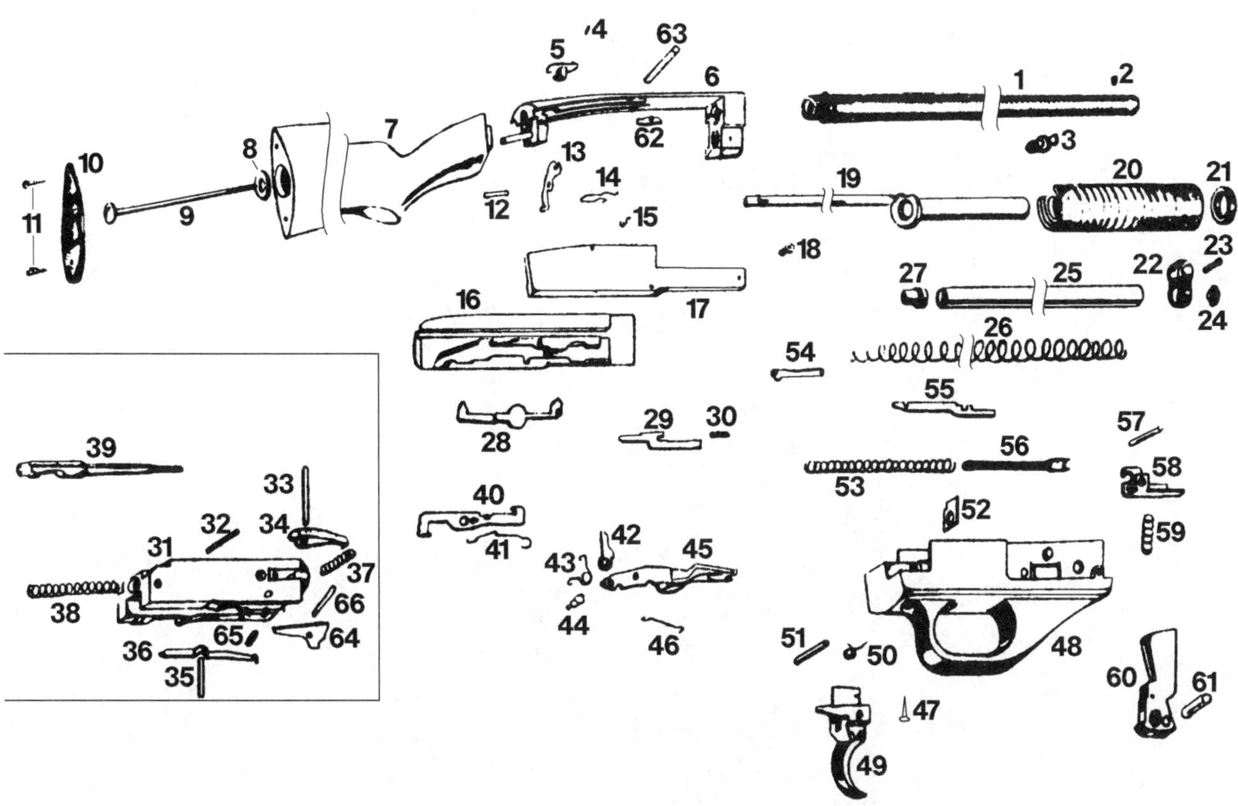

1	Barrel	**23**	Magazine Mount Key Retaining Screw	**45**	Lifter
2	Front Sight	**24**	Magazine Plug Dummy	**46**	Lifter Spring
3	Magazine Mount Key	**25**	Magazine Tube	**47**	Rear Trigger Guard Screw
4	Safety Button Pin	**26**	Magazine Spring	**48**	Trigger Guard
5	Safety Button	**27**	Magazine Follower	**49**	Trigger
6	Frame	**28**	Cartridge Cutoff	**50**	Trigger Spring
7	Stock	**29**	Ejector	**51**	Trigger Pin
8	Stock Bolt Washer	**30**	Ejector Spring	**52**	Mainspring Bridge
9	Stock Bolt	**31**	Bolt	**53**	Mainspring
10	Buttplate	**32**	Firing Pin Retaining Pin	**54**	Trip Spring
11	Buttplate Screw	**33**	Right Extractor Pin	**55**	Sear Trip
12	Safety Pin	**34**	Right Extractor	**56**	Mainspring Follower
13	Safety Lever	**35**	Left Extractor Pin	**57**	Sear Pin
14	Safety Button Spring	**36**	Left Extractor	**58**	Sear
15	Sideplate Screws	**37**	Right Extractor Spring	**59**	Sear Spring
16	Left Sideplate	**38**	Firing Pin Spring	**60**	Hammer
17	Right Sideplate	**39**	Firing Pin	**61**	Hammer Pin
18	Front Sideplate Screws	**40**	Release Lever	**62**	Shell Bumper
19	Handle Bar Tube Assembly	**41**	Release Lever Spring	**63**	Front Trigger Guard Screw
20	Forend	**42**	Lifter Pawl	**64**	Latch Cartridge Stop
21	Forend Retainer, Front	**43**	Lifter Pawl Spring	**65**	Latch Cartridge Stop Spring
22	Magazine Mount	**44**	Lifter Pawl Pin	**66**	Cartridge Stop Pin

Side-by-Side Shotgun

Courtesy of Thomas E. Wessel

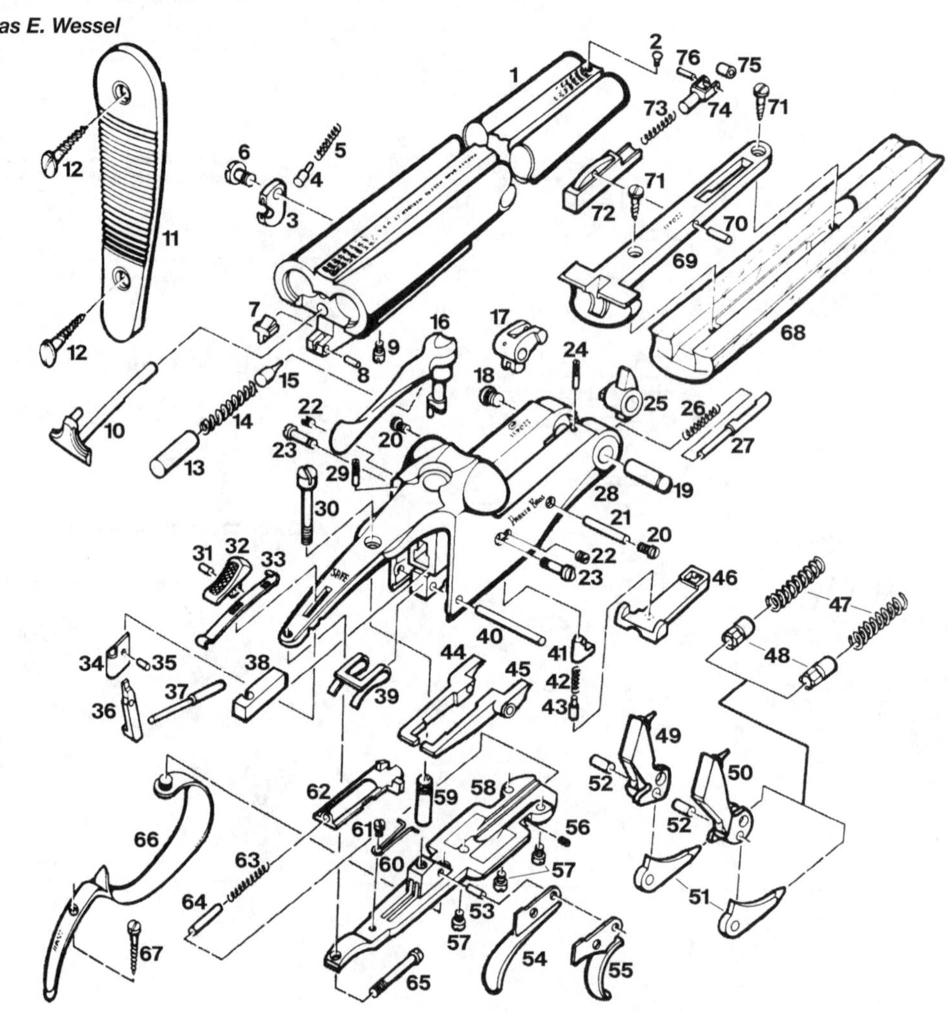

1	Barrels
2	Front Sight
3	Cocking Link
4	Cocking Link Spring Pin
5	Cocking Link Spring
6	Cocking Link Screw
7	Bolt Plate
8	Bolt Plate Retaining Pin
9	Extractor Screw
10	Extractor
11	Buttplate
12	Buttplate Screws
13	Top-Lever Spring Shell
14	Top-Lever Spring
15	Top-Lever Spring Plunger
16	Top-Lever
17	Cocking Crank
18	Joint Pin Screw
19	Joint Pin
20	Cocking Crank Pin Stop Screws
21	Cocking Crank Pin
22	Hammer Fastening Screws
23	Hammer Screws
24	Unhooking Pin Screw
25	Joint Roll
26	Unhooking Pin Spring
27	Unhooking Pin
28	Receiver
29	Top-Lever Retaining Screw
30	Tang Screw, Front
31	Safety Slide Pin
32	Safety Slide
33	Safety Slide Spring
34	Safety-Lever Jacket
35	Safety-Lever Pin
36	Safety-Lever
37	Safety Pin
38	Bolt
39	Sear Spring
40	Sear Pin
41	Trip
42	Trip Spring
43	Trip Spring Plunger
44	Sear, Left
45	Sear, Right
46	Cocking Slide
47	Mainsprings
48	Mainspring Plungers
49	Hammer, Left
50	Hammer, Right
51	Hammer Stirrups
52	Mainspring Pins
53	Trigger Pin
54	Trigger, Left
55	Trigger, Right
56	Unhooking Slide Screw
57	Trigger Plate Screws
58	Trigger Plate
59	Tang Screw Sleeve
60	Trigger Spring
61	Trigger Spring Screw
62	Unhooking Slide
63	Unhooking Slide Spring
64	Unhooking Slide Plunger
65	Tang Screw, Rear
66	Guard Bow
67	Guard Bow Screw
68	Forend
69	Forend Iron
70	Forend Plunger Box Pin
71	Forend Screws
72	Forend Plunger Box
73	Forend Plunger Spring
74	Forend Plunger
75	Forend Plunger Roll
76	Forend Plunger Roll Pin

1200, 1100 and 1000 Series Bolt-Action Rifle

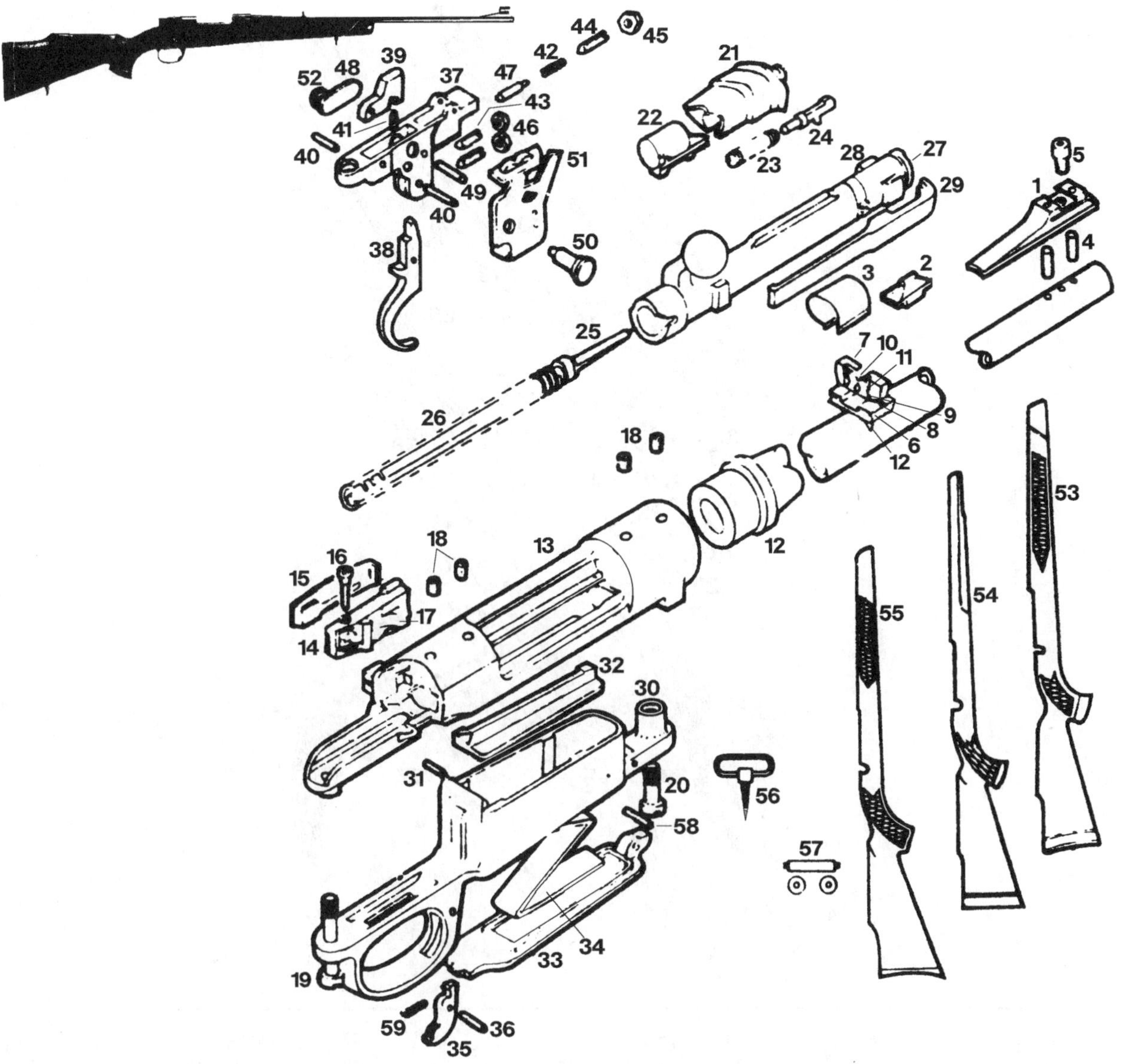

1	Front Sight Ramp	21	Bolt Plug	41	Sear Spring
2	Front Sight Blade	22	Cocking Piece	42	Trigger Spring
3	Protector	23	Bolt Plug Spring	43	Trigger Screws
4	Front Sight Dowels	24	Bolt Plug Plunger	44	Spring Screw
5	Front Sight Screw	25	Striker	45	Spring Screw Nut
6	Slide	26	Striker Spring	46	Trigger Nuts
7	Leaf	27	Bolt	47	Plunger
8	Gib Spring	28	Bolt Ring	48	Detent Pin Spring
9	Pivot Pin	29	Extractor	49	Detent Pin
10	Scale Plate	30	Trigger Guard and Magazine Box	50	Axis Pin
11	Scale Plate Screw	31	Trigger Assembly Pin	51	Safety Catch
12	Barrel	32	Magazine Platform	52	Washer Axis Pin
13	Action	33	Floorplate	53	Stock (1200)
14	Bolt Stop	34	Magazine Spring	54	Stock (1100)
15	Bolt Stop Spring	35	Magazine Catch	55	Stock (1000)
16	Bolt Stop Screw	36	Magazine Catch Pin	56	Swivel
17	Ejector	37	Frame	57	Recoil Bar Nuts
18	Grub Screws	38	Trigger	58	Floorplate Pin
19	Rear Trigger Guard Screw	39	Sear	59	Magazine Catch Spring
20	Front Trigger Guard Screw	40	Trigger and Sear Pins		

600 Side-by-Side Shotgun

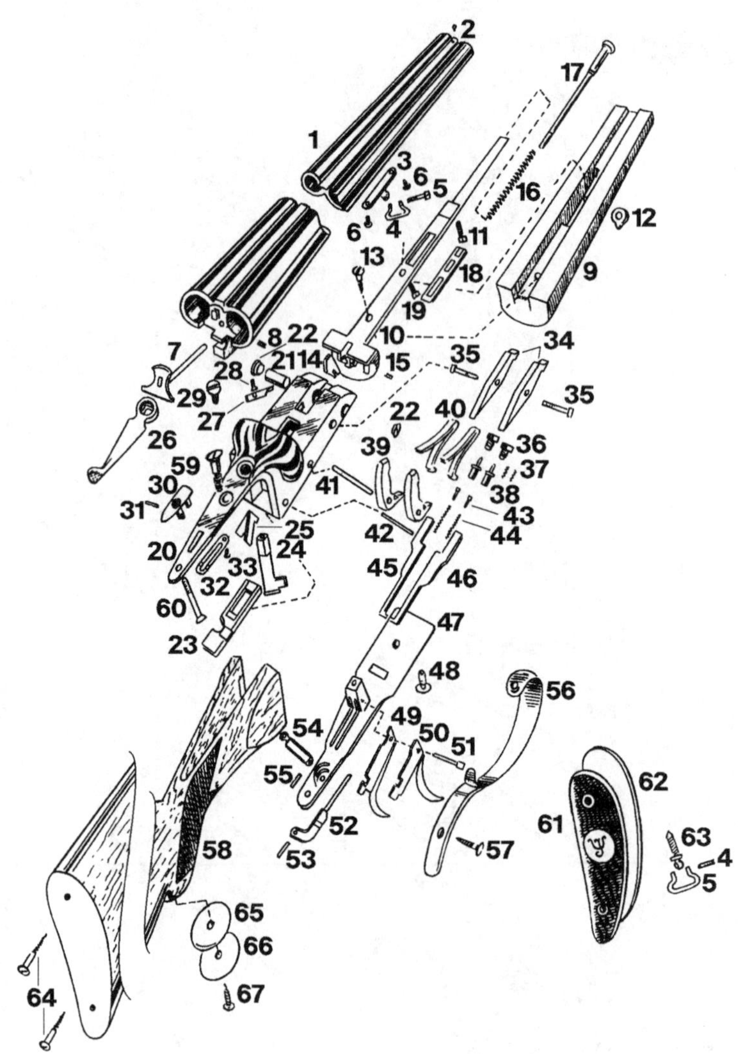

1	Barrels
2	Front Sight
3	Swivel Base
4	Swivel Clamps
5	Swivel Pins
6	Swivel Base Screws
7	Extractor
8	Extractor Stop Screw
9	Forend Wood
10	Forend Iron
11	Forend Screw, Front
12	Forend Nut
13	Forend Screw, Rear
14	Extractor Cam
15	Extractor Cam Screw
16	Forend Latch Rod Spring
17	Forend Release Rod
18	Forend Latch Bolt
19	Pin Screw
20	Action
21	Cross Pin
22	Screw Plug
23	Cross Bolt
24	Spindle
25	Top-Lever Spring
26	Top-Lever
27	Treble Cross Bolt
28	Cross Bolt Screw
29	Top-Lever Screw
30	Safety Button
31	Safety Button Pin
32	Safety Spring
33	Safety Spring Screw
34	Cocking Levers
35	Cocking Lever Screws
36	Firing Pin Bushings
37	Firing Pin Springs
38	Firing Pins
39	Hammers
40	Mainsprings
41	Hammer Cross Pin
42	Sear Pin
43	Spring Spouts
44	Spiral Springs
45	Sear, Left
46	Sear, Right
47	Trigger Plate
48	Frame Top-Plate Screw
49	Trigger, Left
50	Trigger, Right
51	Cross Pin Screw
52	Safety Square
53	Square Pin
54	Swing Bar
55	Swing Bar Pin
56	Trigger Guard
57	Trigger Guard Screw
58	Stock
59	Frame Screw, Rear
60	Frame Top-Plate Screw, Rear
61	Buttplate
62	Buttplate Spacer
63	Swivel Stock Screw
64	Buttplate Screws
65	Pistol Grip Cap Spacer
66	Pistol Grip Cap
67	Pistol Grip Cap Screw

Rifle

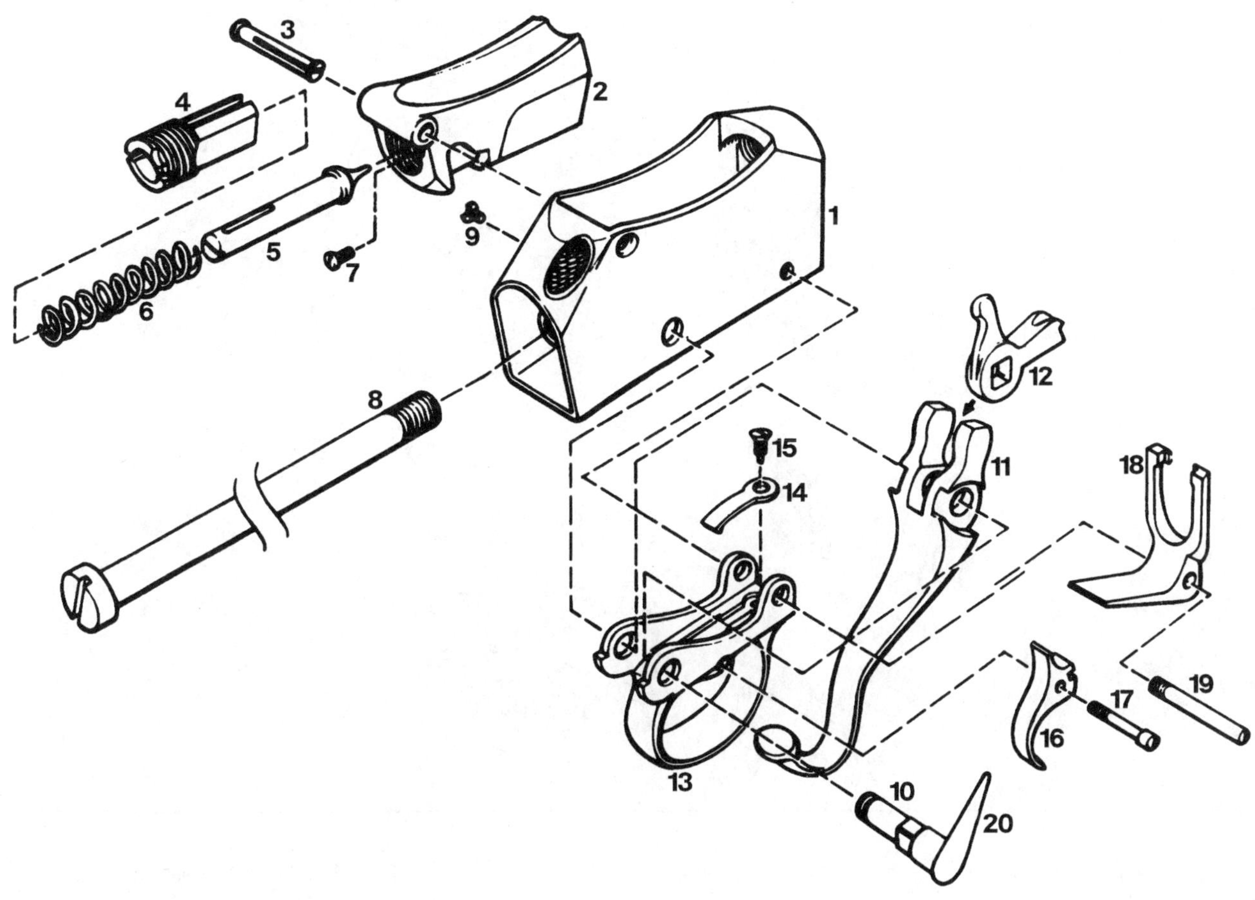

1	Receiver	**16**	Trigger
2	Breechblock	**17**	Trigger Axis Screw
3	Breechblock Axis Pin	**18**	Extractor
4	Stop Nut	**19**	Extractor Axis Screw
5	Firing Pin	**20**	Lever and Tumbler Axis Pin Indicator
6	Firing Pin Spring	**Parts Not Shown**	
7	Stop Nut Keeper Screw		Barrel
8	Stock Bolt		Buttstock
9	Lever and Tumbler Axis Pin Keeper Screw		Buttplate
10	Lever and Tumbler Axis Pin		Buttplate Screws
11	Lever		Forend
12	Tumbler		Front Sight
13	Guard		Rear Sight
14	Trigger Spring		
15	Trigger Spring Screw		

Grade MT6 Model MS80 and DB81E Over/Under Shotgun

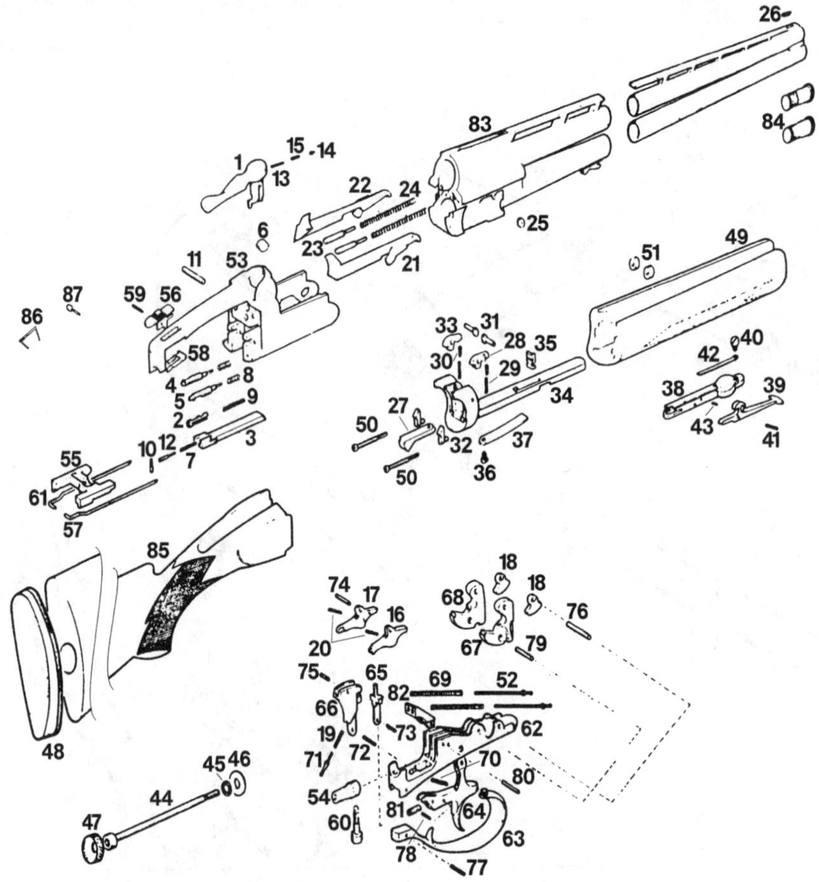

1	Top Lever
2	Top Lever Locking Piece
3	Cocking Bar
4	Top Firing Pin
5	Bottom Firing Pin
6	Pivot
7	Cocking Bar Spring
8	Firing Pin Return Springs
9	Top Lever Return Spring
10	Cocking Bar Screw Check
11	Firing Pin Lock Cam Trip
12	Plunger Trip
13	Top Lever Spring
14	Top Lever Release Trip
15	Top Lever Lock Trip
16	Right Sear
17	Left Sear
18	Cocking Feet
19	Connector Spring
20	Sear Springs
21	Right Ejector
22	Left Ejector
23	Ejector Spring Plungers
24	Ejector Springs
25	Ejector Lock
26	Front Sight
27	Cocking Bar Cam
28	Right Ejector Sear
29	Ejector Sear Springs
30	Ejector Sear Plungers
31	Ejector Sear Pins
32	Ejector Trips
33	Left Ejector Sear
34	Iron Forend
35	Catch Bolt
36	Cocking Bar Cam Lock Screw
37	Catch Bolt Spring
38	Latch Plate
39	Latch Plate Lever
40	Latch Plate Lever Spring Lock Screw
41	Latch Plate Pin
42	Latch Plate Lever Return Spring
43	Latch Plate Lever Lock Pin
44	Stock Bolt
45	Lock Washer
46	Plain Washer
47	Retainer Guide
48	Recoil Pad
49	Forend
50	Forend Lock Screw
51	Forend Lock Bolts
52	Hammer Spring Plungers
53	Action Frame
54	Stock Bolt Lock
55	Action Bolt
56	Safety
57	Right Ejector Trip Rod
58	Safety Spring
59	Safety Retaining Pin
60	Lock Bolt Nut Retainer Screw
61	Left Ejector Trip Rod
62	Trigger Plate
63	Trigger Guard
64	Trigger
65	Sear Tip
66	Connector Block
67	Right Hammer
68	Left Hammer
69	Hammer Spring
70	Trigger Spring
71	Connector Block Plunger
72	Connector Block Pivot Pin
73	Sear Trip Pivot Pin
74	Pivot Sear Pin
75	Safety Pin
76	Cocking Foot Pin
77	Trigger Guard Pin
78	Link Retainer Pin
79	Hammer Pin
80	Pivot Sear Trip
81	Link Sear Trip
82	Spring File
83	Barrels
84	Chokes
85	Stock
86	Safety Button Locking Piece
87	Selective Lever Locking Pin

Mirage MX8 and DB81 and Grand America SC3 and SCO Over\Under Shotgun

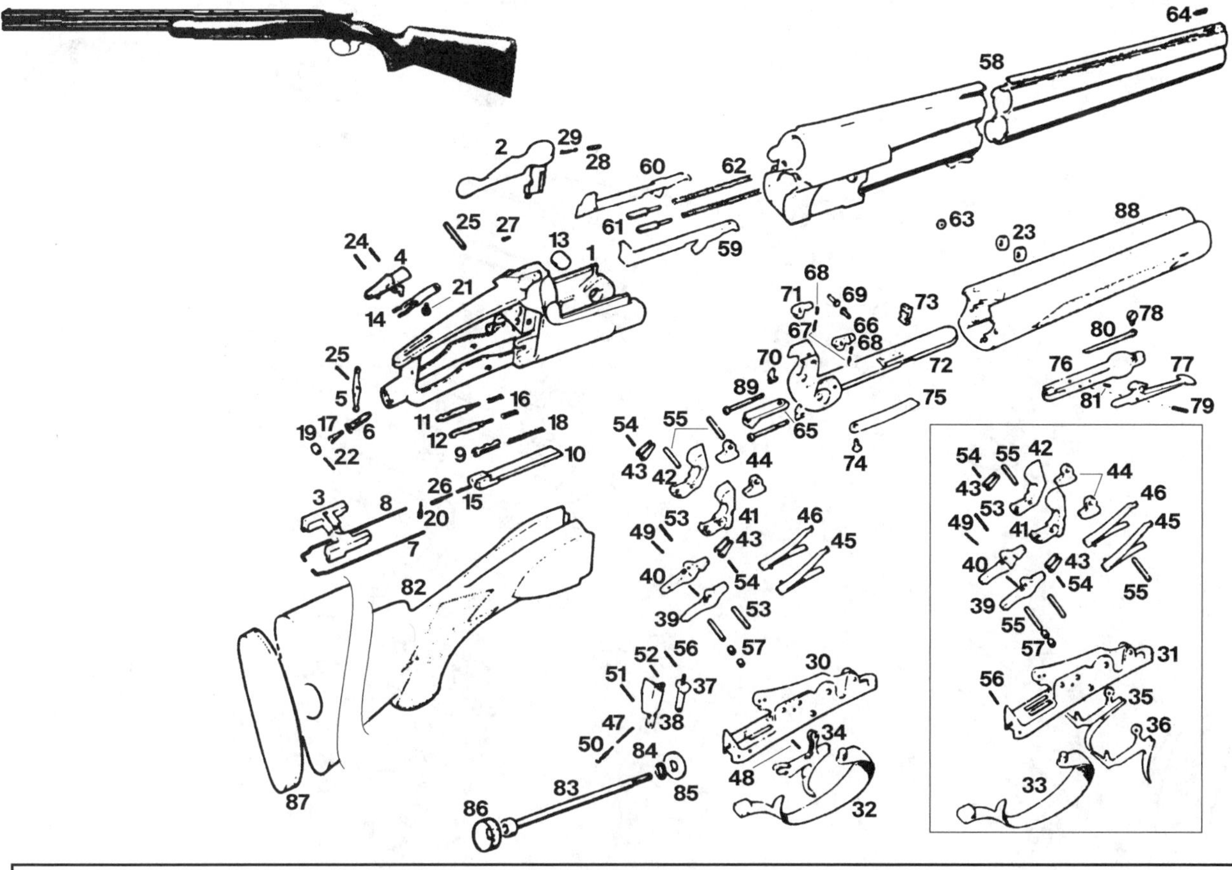

No.	Part	No.	Part	No.	Part
1	Action Frame	31	Trigger Plate (Double)	61	Ejector Spring Plungers
2	Top Lever	32	Trigger Guard	62	Ejector Springs
3	Action Bolt	33	Trigger Guard (Double)	63	Ejector Lock
4	Safety	34	Trigger	64	Front Sight
5	Link Trigger Release	35	Left Trigger	65	Cocking Bar Cam
6	Lock Trigger Plate	36	Right Trigger	66	Right Ejector Sear
7	Right Ejector Trip Rod	37	Release	67	Ejector Sear Springs
8	Left Ejector Trip Rod	38	Connector	68	Ejector Sear Plungers
9	Locking Piece Top Lever	39	Right Sear	69	Sear Pins
10	Cocking Bar	40	Left Sear	70	Ejector Trip
11	Top Firing Pin	41	Right Hammer	71	Left Ejector Trip
12	Bottom Firing Pin	42	Left Hammer	72	Iron Forend
13	Pivot	43	Bridle	73	Catch Bolt
14	Safety Spring	44	Cocking Foot	74	Cocking Bar Cam Lock Screw
15	Cocking Bar Spring	45	Right Hammer Spring	75	Catch Bolt Spring
16	Firing Pin Return Springs	46	Left Hammer Spring	76	Latch Plate
17	Trigger Plate Lock Spring	47	Connector Spring	77	Latch Plate Lever
18	Top Lever Return Spring	48	Trigger Spring	78	Latch Plate Lever Spring Lock Screw
19	Trigger Plate Lock Cap	49	Sear Spring	79	Latch Plate Pin
20	Cocking Bar Screw Check	50	Connector Plunger	80	Return Spring Latch Plate Lever
21	Safety Spring Screw	51	Connector Pin	81	Latch Plate Lever Lock Pin
22	Trigger Plate Lock Pin	52	Connector Post Pin	82	Stock
23	Forend Lock Bolts	53	Sear Pin	83	Stock Bolt
24	Safety Button Pins	54	Bridle Pin	84	Lock Washer
25	Firing Pin Lock Pin Trip Cam	55	Sear Retainer Pins	85	Plain Washer
26	Plunger Trip	56	Trigger Guard Pin	86	Retainer Guide
27	Top Lever Release Trip	57	Sear Retainer Sleeve	87	Recoil Pad
28	Top Lever Lock Trip	58	Barrels	88	Forend
29	Top Lever Release Spring	59	Right (Bottom) Ejector	89	Forend Lock Screw
30	Trigger Plate	60	Left (Top) Ejector		

Model TM1 and TMX Single Shot Shotgun

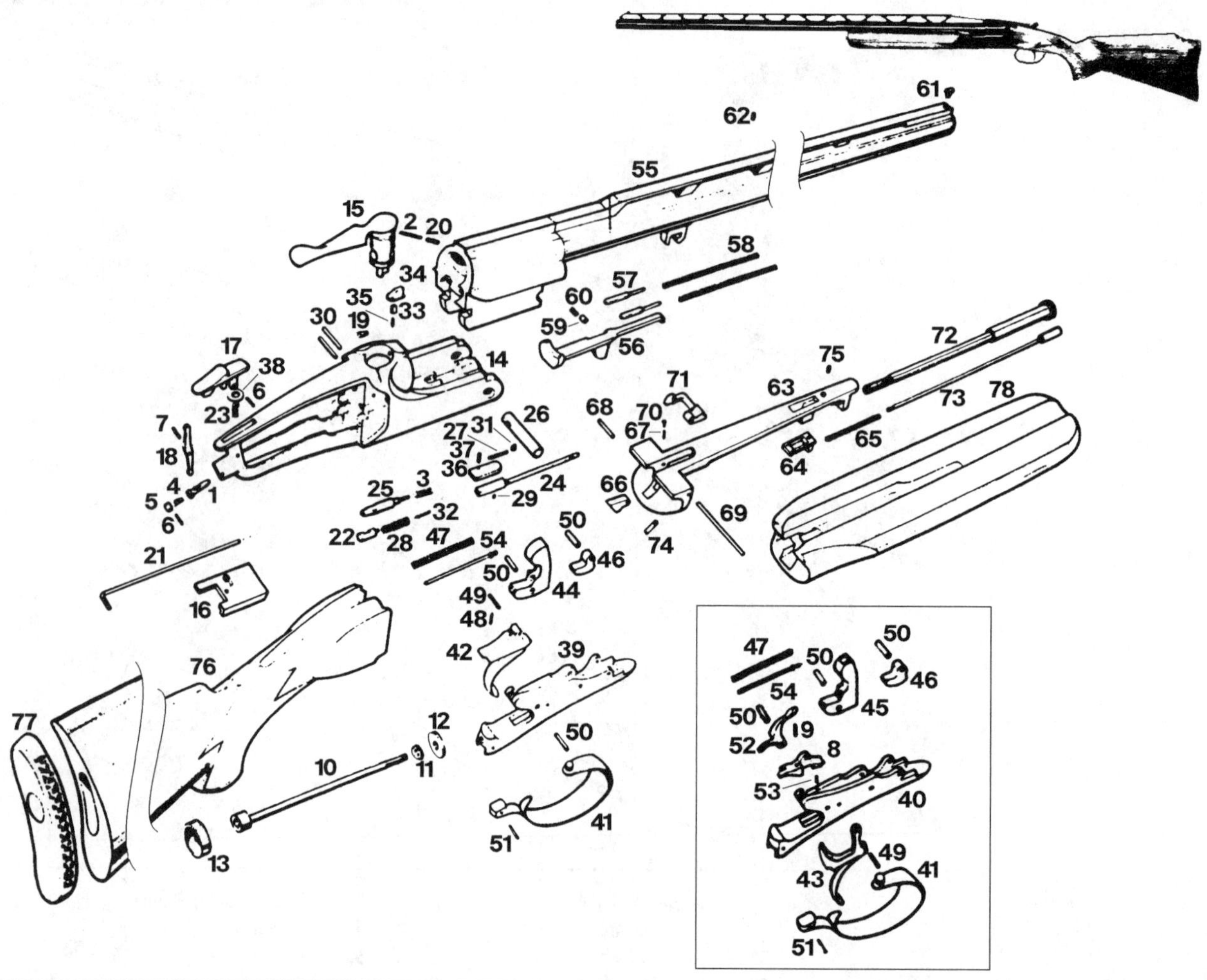

No.	Part	No.	Part	No.	Part
1	Trigger Plate Lock	27	Cocking Bar Spring	53	Release Sear Retaining Spring
2	Top Lever Pin Spring	28	Top Lever Return Spring	54	Hammer Spring Guide
3	Firing Pin Return Spring	29	Cocking Bar Screw Check	55	Barrels
4	Trigger Plate Lock Spring	30	Firing Lock Cam Pin Trips	56	Ejector
5	Trigger Plate Lock Cap	31	Plunger Trip	57	Ejector Spring Plungers
6	Trigger Plate Lock Pin	32	Top Lever Spring	58	Ejector Springs
7	Link Pin	33	Spring Guide	59	Ejector Lock
8	Left Sear	34	Top Lever Release Trip	60	Ejector Retaining Spring
9	Sear Spring	35	Top Lever Lock Trip	61	Front Sight
10	Stock Bolt	36	Cocking Bar Piece	62	Middle Sight
11	Lock Washer	37	Pin	63	Iron Forend
12	Plain Washer	38	Washer	64	Forend Latch
13	Retainer Guide	39	Trigger Plate	65	Forend Plate Guide Spring
14	Action Frame	40	Trigger Plate Release	66	Cocking Bar Cam
15	Top Lever	41	Trigger Guard	67	Ejector Sear Spring
16	Action Bolt	42	Trigger	68	Cocking Rod Boss Screw
17	Safety Button	43	Trigger Release	69	Ejector Lock Pin
18	Link Trigger Release	44	Hammer	70	Ejector Sear Plunger
19	Frame Top Lever Pin	45	Hammer Release	71	Ejector Sear
20	Top Lever Pin	46	Cocking Foot	72	Forend Operating Button Guide
21	Ejector Trip Rod	47	Hammer Spring	73	Forend Opening Button
22	Top Lever Locking Piece	48	Trigger Spring	74	Pin
23	Safety Spring	49	Trigger Pin	75	Iron Forend Tension Bushing
24	Cocking Bar	50	Cocking Foot Pins	76	Stock
25	Firing Pin	51	Trigger Guard Pin	77	Recoil Pad
26	Pivot	52	Sear Release	78	Forend

Model 11 Autoloading Shotgun

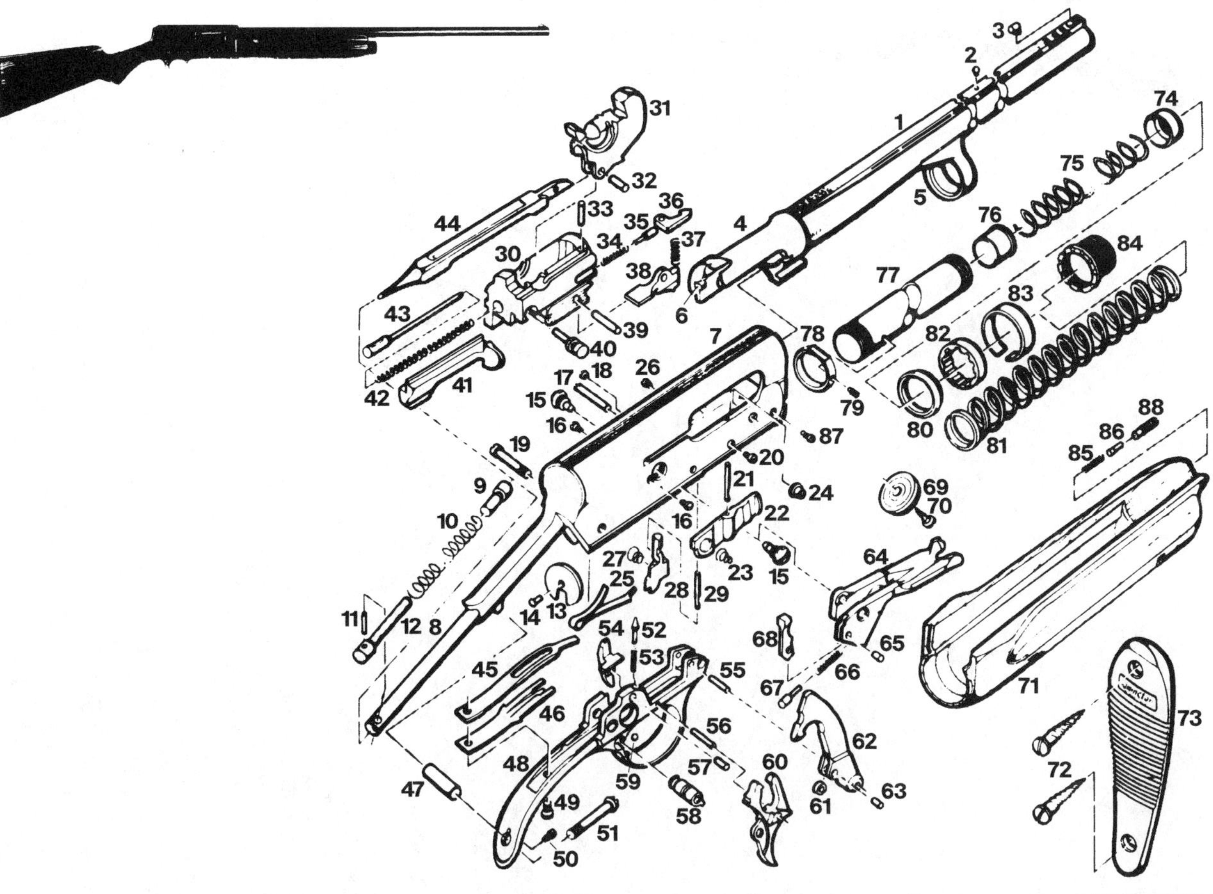

No.	Part	No.	Part	No.	Part
1	Barrel	**31**	Locking Bolt	**61**	Hammer Roll
2	Bead Sight	**32**	Link Pin	**62**	Hammer
3	Front Sight Base	**33**	Extractor Pin	**63**	Hammer Roll Pin
4	Barrel Extension	**34**	Extractor Spring	**64**	Carrier
5	Barrel Guide	**35**	Extractor Plunger	**65**	Carrier Dog Pin
6	Ejector	**36**	Extractor	**66**	Carrier Dog Spring
7	Receiver	**37**	Locking Block Latch Spring	**67**	Carrier Dog Spring Follower
8	Action Spring Tube	**38**	Locking Block Latch	**68**	Carrier Dog
9	Action Spring Follower	**39**	Locking Block Latch Pin	**69**	Pistol Grip Cap
10	Action Spring	**40**	Firing Pin Retaining Pin	**70**	Pistol Grip Cap Screw
11	Action Spring Plug Pin	**41**	Operating Handle	**71**	Forend
12	Action Spring Plug	**42**	Firing Pin Retractor Spring	**72**	Buttplate Screws
13	Fiber Cushion	**43**	Firing Pin	**73**	Buttplate
14	Fiber Cushion Rivet	**44**	Link	**74**	Magazine Spring Retainer
15	Carrier Screws	**45**	Mainspring	**75**	Magazine Spring
16	Carrier Screw Locking Screws	**46**	Trigger Spring	**76**	Magazine Follower
17	Trigger Plate Pin	**47**	Tang Screw Bushing	**77**	Magazine Tube
18	Trigger Plate Pin Locking Screw	**48**	Trigger Plate	**78**	Forend Guide Ring
19	Trigger Plate Screw	**49**	Mainspring Screw	**79**	Forend Guide Ring Screw
20	Carrier Latch Pin Locking Screw	**50**	Tang Screw Locking Screw	**80**	Friction Ring
21	Carrier Latch Pin	**51**	Tang Screw	**81**	Recoil Spring
22	Carrier Latch	**52**	Safety Sear Spring Follower	**82**	Friction Piece
23	Carrier Latch Spring	**53**	Safety Sear Spring	**83**	Friction Spring
24	Carrier Latch Button	**54**	Safety Sear	**84**	Magazine Cap
25	Carrier Spring	**55**	Hammer Pin	**85**	Magazine Cap Stop Plunger Spring
26	Cartridge Stop Pin Lock Screw	**56**	Trigger Pin	**86**	Magazine Cap Stop Plunger
27	Cartridge Stop Spring	**57**	Safety Sear Pin	**87**	Magazine Stop Screw
28	Cartridge Stop	**58**	Safety	**88**	Magazine Cap Stop Plunger Tube
29	Cartridge Stop Pin	**59**	Safety Ball		
30	Bolt	**60**	Trigger		

Model 11-48 Autoloading Shotgun

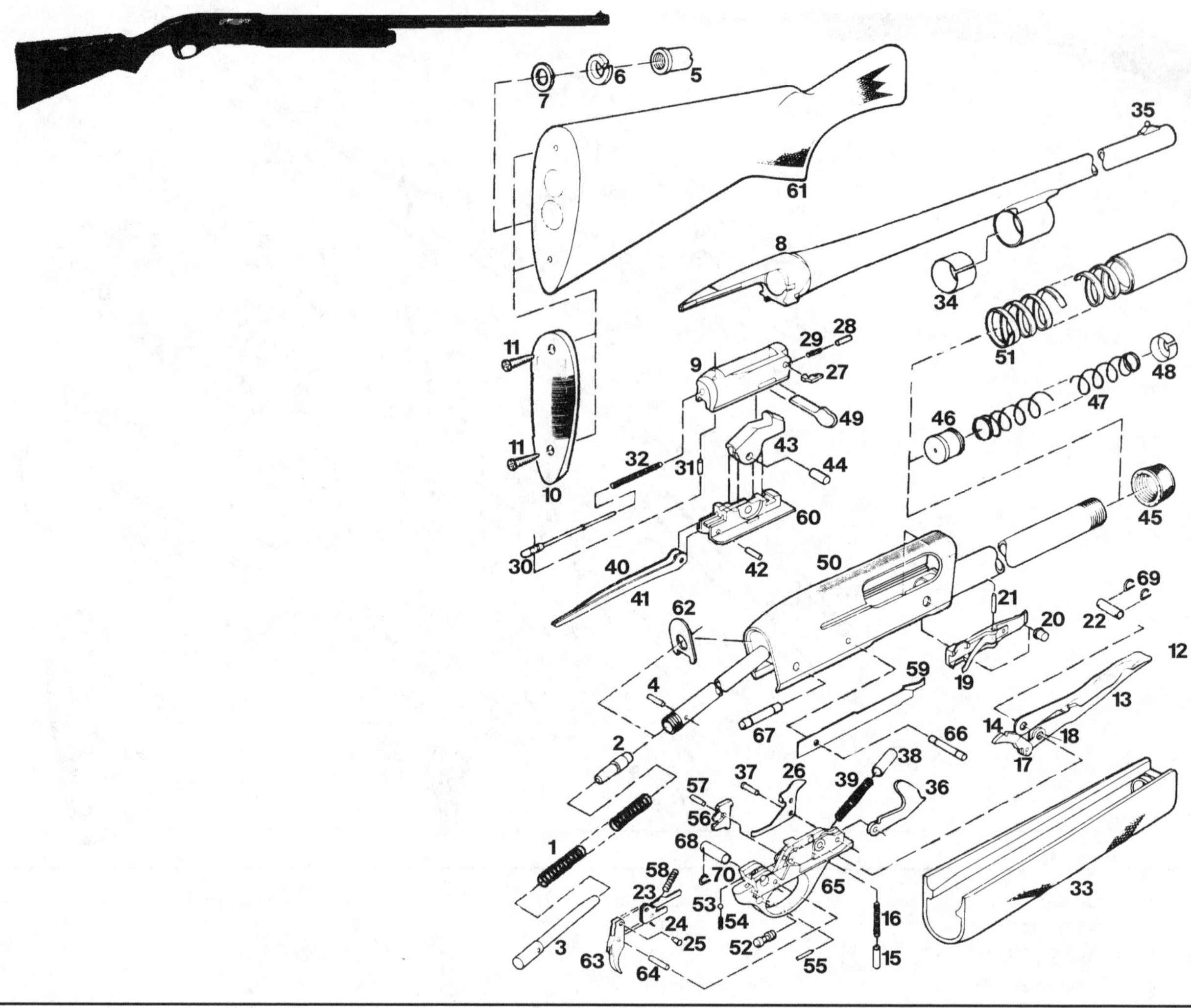

1	Action Spring	**25**	Connector Pin	**50**	Receiver
2	Action Spring Follower	**26**	Disconnector	**51**	Recoil Spring and Ring Assembly
3	Action Spring Plug	**27**	Extractor	**52**	Safety
4	Action Spring Plug Pin	**28**	Extractor Plunger	**53**	Safety Detent Ball
5	Action Spring Tube Nut	**29**	Extractor Spring	**54**	Safety Spring
6	Action Spring Tube Nut Lock Washer	**30**	Firing Pin	**55**	Safety Spring Retaining Pin
7	Action Spring Tube Nut Washer	**31**	Firing Pin Retaining Pin	**56**	Sear
8	Barrel Assembly	**32**	Firing Pin Retractor Spring	**57**	Sear Pin
9	Breechbolt	**33**	Forend	**58**	Sear Spring
10	Buttplate	**34**	Friction Piece	**59**	Shell Latch
11	Buttplate Screws	**35**	Front Sight	**60**	Slide
12	Carrier Assembly	**36**	Hammer	**61**	Stock
13	Carrier	**37**	Hammer Pin	**62**	Stock Bearing Plate
14	Carrier Dog	**38**	Hammer Plunger	**63**	Trigger
15	Carrier Dog Follower	**39**	Hammer Spring	**64**	Trigger Pin
16	Carrier Dog Follower Spring	**40**	Link, Left	**65**	Trigger Plate, Right
17	Carrier Dog Pin	**41**	Link, Right	**66**	Trigger Plate Pin, Front
18	Carrier Dog Washer	**42**	Link Pin	**67**	Trigger Plate Pin, Rear
19	Carrier Latch Assembly	**43**	Locking Block	**68**	Trigger Plate Pin Bushing
20	Carrier Latch Button	**44**	Locking Block Pin	**69**	Trigger Plate Pin Detent Springs, Front
21	Carrier Latch Pin	**45**	Magazine Cap	**70**	Trigger Plate Pin Detent Spring, Rear
22	Carrier Pivot Tube	**46**	Magazine Follower		
23	Connector, Left	**47**	Magazine Spring		
24	Connector, Right	**48**	Magazine Spring Retainer		
		49	Operating Handle		

Model 11-87 Autoloading Shotgun

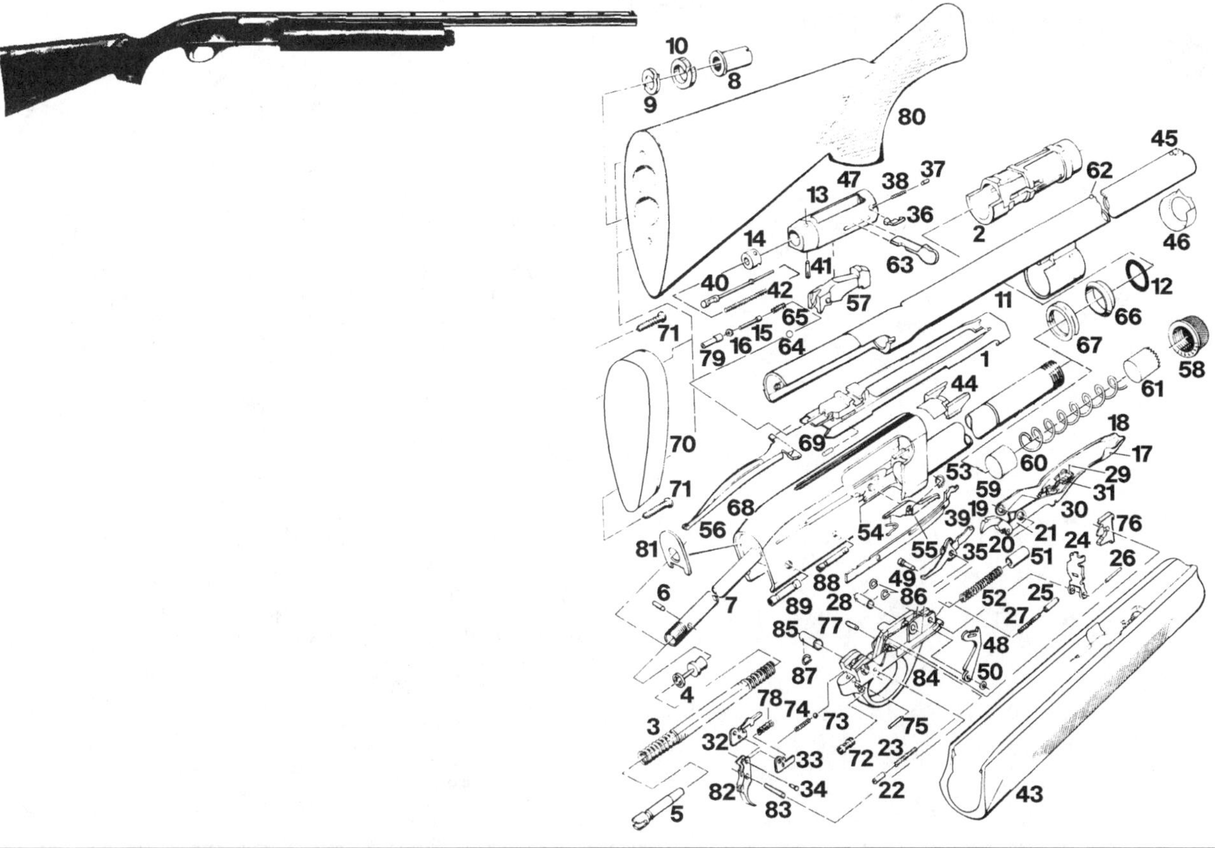

1	Action Bar Assembly	**30**	Carrier Release Pin	**61**	Magazine Spring Retainer
2	Action Bar Sleeve	**31**	Carrier Release Spring	**62**	Middle Sight
3	Action Spring	**32**	Connector, Left	**63**	Operating Handle
4	Action Spring Follower	**33**	Connector, Right	**64**	Operating Handle Detent Ball
5	Action Spring Plug	**34**	Connector Pin	**65**	Operating Handle Detent Spring
6	Action Spring Plug Pin	**35**	Disconnector	**66**	Piston
7	Action Spring Tube	**36**	Extractor	**67**	Piston Seal
8	Action Spring Tube Nut	**37**	Extractor Plunger	**68**	Receiver Assembly
9	Action Spring Tube Nut Washer	**38**	Extractor Spring	**69**	Return Plunger Retaining Pin
10	Action Spring Tube Nut Lock Washer	**39**	Feed Latch	**70**	Recoil Pad
11	Barrel Assembly	**40**	Firing Pin	**71**	Recoil Pad Screws
12	Barrel Seal	**41**	Firing Pin Retaining Pin	**72**	Safety Switch
13	Breechbolt	**42**	Firing Pin Retractor Spring	**73**	Safety Switch Detent Ball
14	Breechbolt Buffer	**43**	Forend Assembly	**74**	Safety Switch Spring
15	Breechbolt Return Plunger	**44**	Forend Support	**75**	Safety Switch Spring Retaining Pin
16	Breechbolt Return Plunger Retaining Ring	**45**	Front Sight	**76**	Sear
17	Carrier	**46**	Gas Cylinder Collar	**77**	Sear Pin
18	Carrier Assembly	**47**	Grip Cap	**78**	Sear Spring
19	Carrier Dog	**48**	Hammer	**79**	Slide Block Buffer
20	Carrier Dog Pin	**49**	Hammer Pin	**80**	Stock Assembly
21	Carrier Dog Washer	**50**	Hammer Pin Washer	**81**	Stock Bearing Plate
22	Carrier Dog Follower	**51**	Hammer Plunger	**82**	Trigger
23	Carrier Dog Follower Spring	**52**	Hammer Spring	**83**	Trigger Pin
24	Carrier Latch	**53**	Interceptor Latch Retainer	**84**	Trigger Plate Safety
25	Carrier Latch Follower	**54**	Interceptor Latch Spring	**85**	Trigger Plate Pin
26	Carrier Latch Pin	**55**	Interceptor Latch	**86**	Trigger Plate Pin Detent Springs, Front
27	Carrier Latch Spring	**56**	Link	**87**	Trigger Plate Pin Detent Spring, Rear
28	Carrier Pivot Tube	**57**	Locking Block Assembly	**88**	Trigger Plate Pin, Front
29	Carrier Release	**58**	Magazine Cap	**89**	Trigger Plate Pin, Rear
		59	Magazine Follower		
		60	Magazine Spring		

Model 1100 Autoloading Shotgun

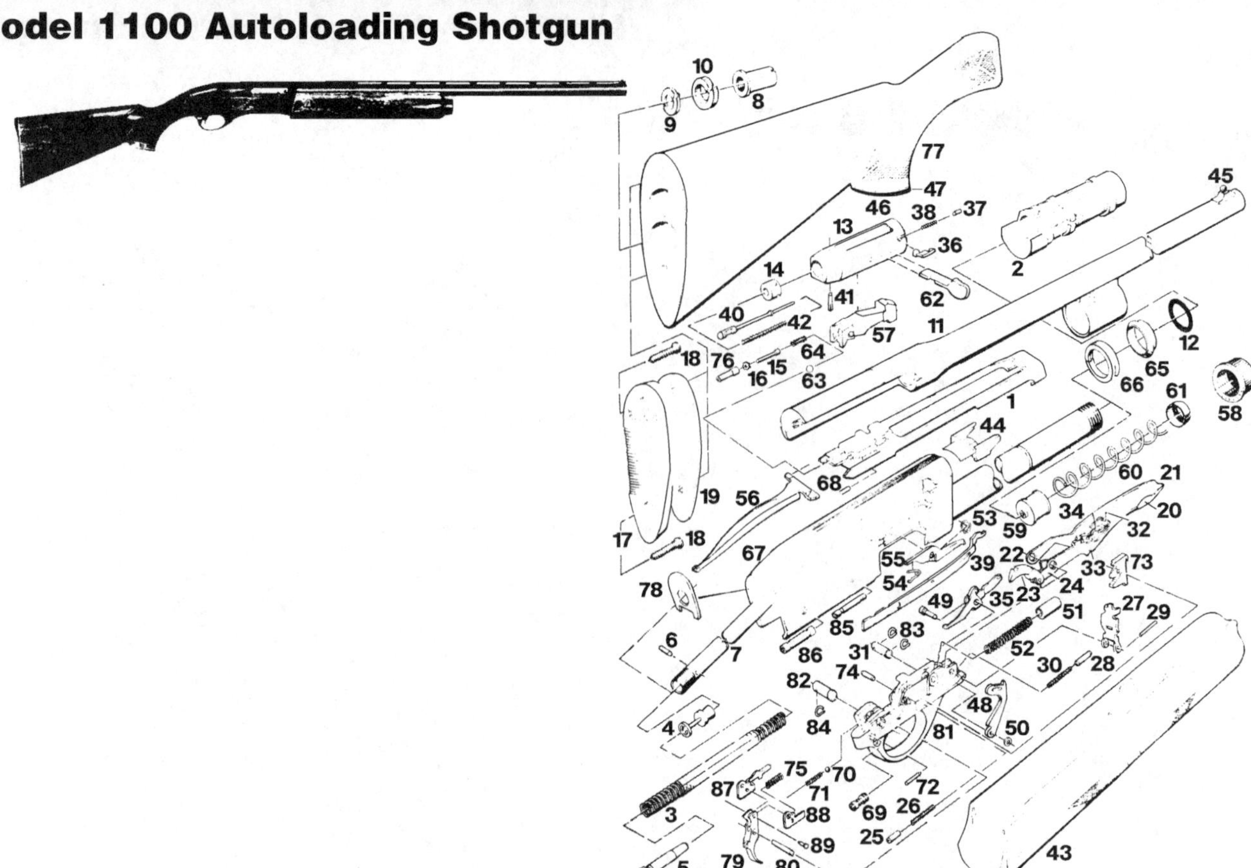

1 Action Bar Assembly
2 Action Bar Sleeve
3 Action Spring
4 Action Spring Follower
5 Action Spring Plug
6 Action Spring Plug Pin
7 Action Spring Tube
8 Action Spring Tube Nut
9 Action Spring Tube Nut Washer
10 Action Spring Tube Nut Lock Washer
11 Barrel Assembly
12 Barrel Seal
13 Breechbolt
14 Breechbolt Buffer
15 Breechbolt Return Plunger
16 Breechbolt Return Plunger Retaining Ring
17 Buttplate
18 Buttplate Screws
19 Buttplate Spacer
20 Carrier
21 Carrier Assembly
22 Carrier Dog
23 Carrier Dog Pin
24 Carrier Dog Washer
25 Carrier Dog Follower
26 Carrier Dog Follower Spring
27 Carrier Latch
28 Carrier Latch Follower
29 Carrier Latch Pin
30 Carrier Latch Spring
31 Carrier Pivot Tube
32 Carrier Release
33 Carrier Release Pin
34 Carrier Release Spring
35 Disconnector
36 Extractor
37 Extractor Plunger
38 Extractor Spring
39 Feed Latch
40 Firing Pin
41 Firing Pin Retaining Pin
42 Firing Pin Retractor Spring
43 Forend Assembly
44 Forend Support
45 Front Sight
46 Grip Cap
47 Grip Cap Spacer
48 Hammer
49 Hammer Pin
50 Hammer Pin Washer
51 Hammer Plunger
52 Hammer Spring
53 Interceptor Latch Retainer
54 Interceptor Latch Spring
55 Interceptor Latch
56 Link
57 Locking Block Assembly
58 Magazine Cap
59 Magazine Follower
60 Magazine Spring
61 Magazine Spring Retainer
62 Operating Handle
63 Operating Handle Detent Ball
64 Operating Handle Detent Spring
65 Piston
66 Piston Seal
67 Receiver Assembly
68 Return Plunger Retaining Pin
69 Safety Switch
70 Safety Switch Detent Ball
71 Safety Switch Spring
72 Safety Switch Spring Retaining Pin
73 Sear
74 Sear Pin
75 Sear Spring
76 Slide Block Buffer
77 Stock Assembly
78 Stock Bearing Plate
79 Trigger Assembly
80 Trigger Pin
81 Trigger Plate Safety
82 Trigger Plate Pin Bushing
83 Trigger Plate Pin Detent Spring, Front
84 Trigger Plate Pin Detent Spring, Rear
85 Trigger Plate Pin, Front
86 Trigger Plate Pin, Rear
87 Connector, Left
88 Connector, Right
89 Connector Pin

Model 12 Slide-Action Rifle

Courtesy of Dennis Riordan

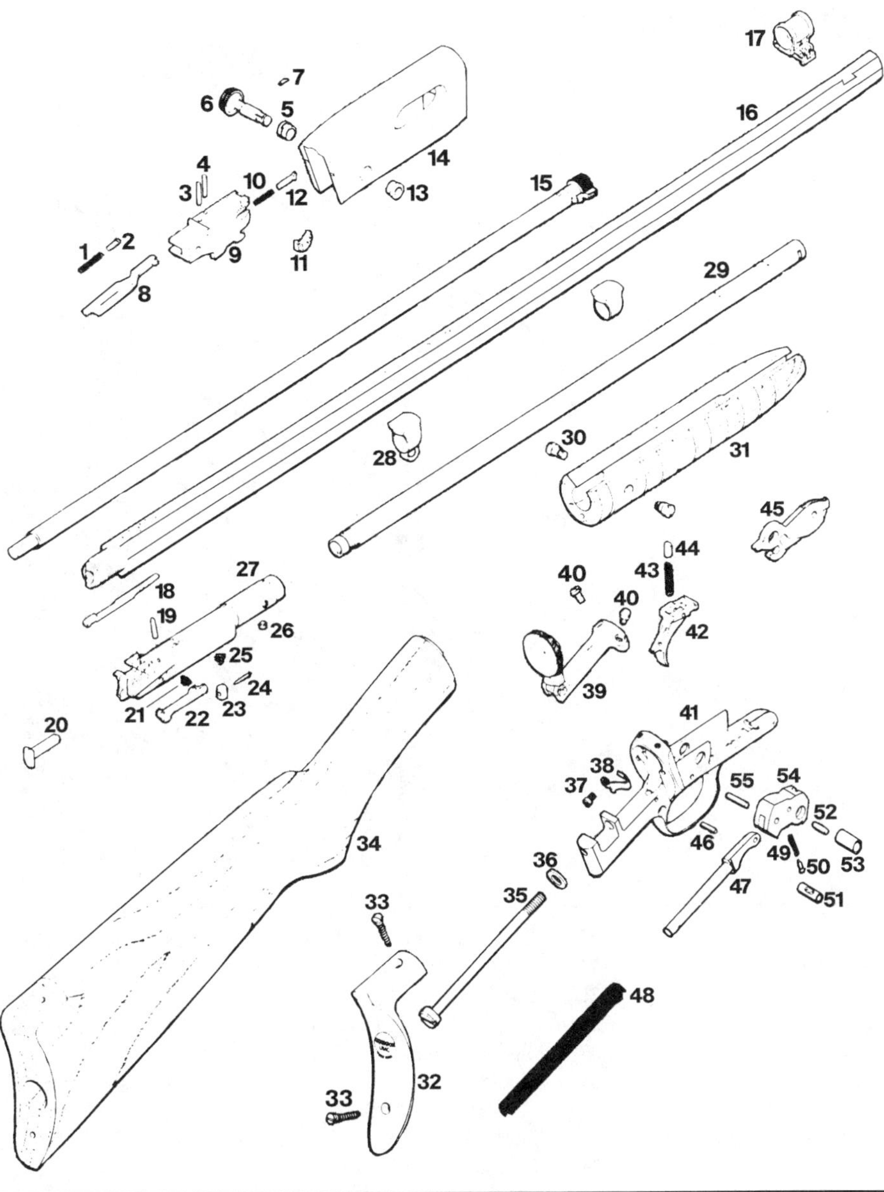

1	Firing Pin Spring	**20**	Cartridge Stop	**39**	Rear Sight
2	Firing Pin Spring Guide	**21**	Carrier Dog Spring	**40**	Rear Sight Screws
3	Firing Pin Pin	**22**	Carrier Dog	**41**	Guard
4	Ejector Pin	**23**	Action Bar Plunger	**42**	Trigger
5	Receiver Bushing	**24**	Action Bar Plunger Pin	**43**	Trigger Spring
6	Takedown Screw	**25**	Action Bar Spring	**44**	Trigger Spring Case
7	Takedown Screw Retainer	**26**	Magazine Screw	**45**	Carrier
8	Firing Pin	**27**	Action Bar	**46**	Safety Plunger Pin
9	Breechblock	**28**	Magazine Rings	**47**	Mainspring Rod
10	Extractor Spring	**29**	Magazine Tube, Outer	**48**	Mainspring
11	Extractor	**30**	Forend Screws	**49**	Safety Spring
12	Extractor Plunger	**31**	Forend	**50**	Safety Plunger
13	Receiver Bushing, Threaded	**32**	Buttplate	**51**	Safety
14	Receiver	**33**	Buttplate Screws	**52**	Hammer Pin
15	Magazine Tube, Inner	**34**	Stock	**53**	Hammer Bushing
16	Barrel	**35**	Stock Bolt	**54**	Hammer
17	Front Sight	**36**	Stock Bolt Washer	**55**	Trigger Pin
18	Cartridge Retainer	**37**	Ejector Spring Screw		
19	Carrier Dog Pin	**38**	Ejector Spring		

Model 31 Slide-Action Shotgun

Courtesy of Thomas E. Wessel

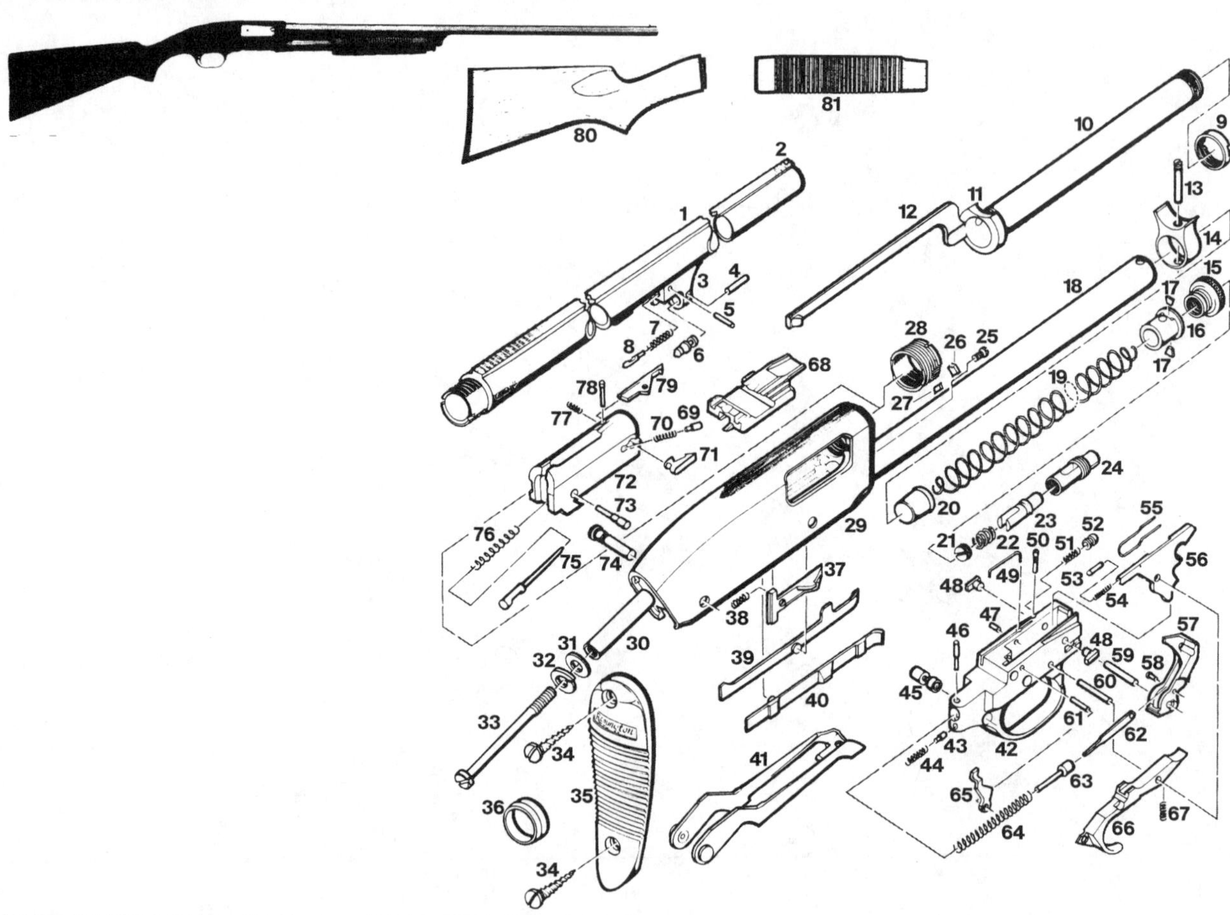

1	Barrel	**26**	Barrel Adjusting Bushing Lock	**53**	Trigger Lock Plunger
2	Front Sight	**27**	Magazine Lock	**54**	Trigger Lock Spring
3	Barrel Lug	**28**	Barrel Adjusting Bushing	**55**	Action Bar Lock Spring
4	Barrel Lug Stud Pin	**29**	Receiver	**56**	Action Bar Lock
5	Barrel Lock Nut Stop Plunger Pin	**30**	Stock Bolt Stud	**57**	Hammer
6	Barrel Lug Stud	**31**	Stock Bolt Washer	**58**	Hammer Link Pin
7	Barrel Lock Nut Stop Plunge Spring	**32**	Stock Bolt Lock Washer	**59**	Hammer Pin
8	Barrel Lock Nut Stop Plunger	**33**	Stock Bolt	**60**	Trigger Pin
9	Forend Tube Nut	**34**	Buttplate Screws	**61**	Trigger Lock Pin
10	Forend Tube	**35**	Buttplate	**62**	Hammer Link
11	Forend Tube Cap	**36**	Stock Reinforcement Ring	**63**	Mainspring Follower
12	Action Bar	**37**	Ejector	**64**	Mainspring
13	Magazine Guide Screw	**38**	Ejector Spring	**65**	Trigger Lock
14	Magazine Guide	**39**	Right Cartridge Stop	**66**	Trigger
15	Barrel Lock Nut	**40**	Left Cartridge Stop	**67**	Trigger Spring
16	Magazine Plug	**41**	Carrier	**68**	Slide
17	Barrel Lock Nut Keys	**42**	Trigger Plate	**69**	Extractor Plunger
18	Magazine Tube	**43**	Safety Plunger	**70**	Right Extractor Spring
19	Magazine Spring	**44**	Safety Spring	**71**	Right Extractor
20	Magazine Follower	**45**	Safety	**72**	Breechblock
21	Barrel Lock Compensator Screw	**46**	Mainspring Pin	**73**	Firing Pin Retaining Pin
22	Barrel Lock Spring	**47**	Trigger Plate Pin Spring Pin	**74**	Trigger Plate Pin
23	Barrel Lock Compensator	**48**	Trigger Plate Studs	**75**	Firing Pin
24	Barrel Lock	**49**	Trigger Plate Pin Spring	**76**	Firing Pin Spring
25	Barrel Adjusting Bushing Lock Screw	**50**	Left Cartridge Stop Plunger Screw	**77**	Left Extractor Spring
		51	Left Cartridge Stop Spring	**78**	Extractor Pin
		52	Left Cartridge Stop Plunger	**79**	Left Extractor
				80	Stock
				81	Forend

Model 3200 Over/Under Shotgun

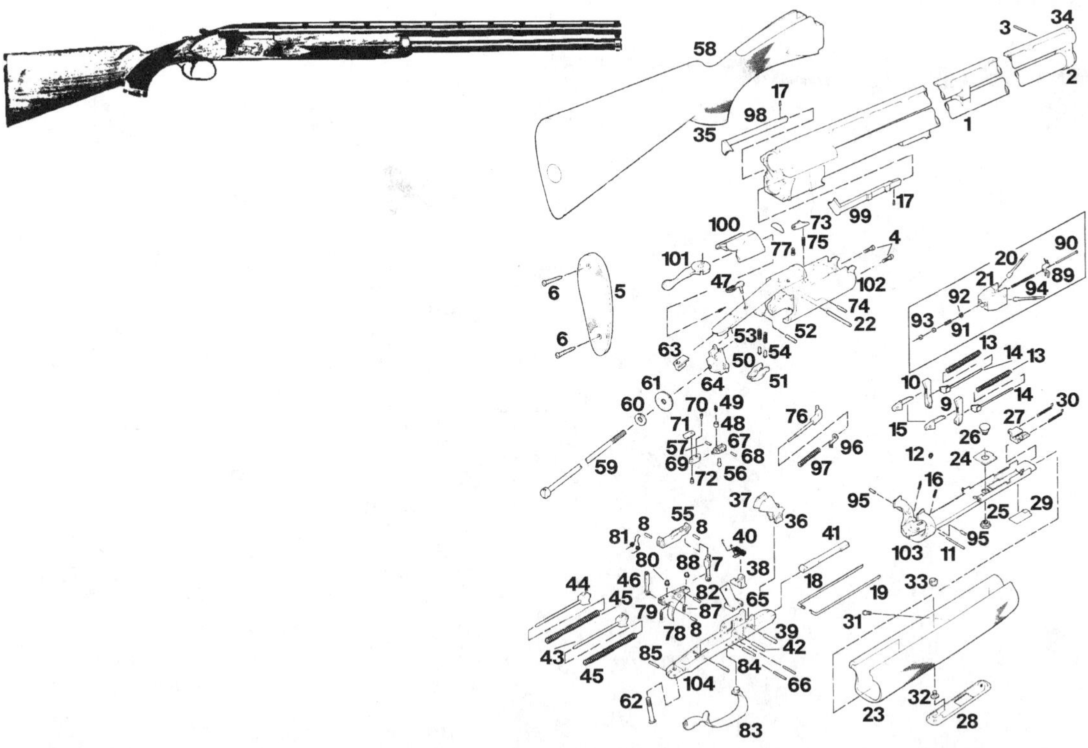

1	Barrel
2	Barrel Band
3	Barrel Band Lock Pin
4	Bottom Tang Screws
5	Buttplate
6	Buttplate Screws
7	Connector
8	Connector Pin
9	Ejector Hammer, Right
10	Ejector Hammer, Left
11	Ejector Hammer Pin
12	Ejector Hammer Pivot Ring
13	Ejector Hammer Springs
14	Ejector Plungers
15	Ejector Sears
16	Ejector Sear Springs
17	Ejector Stop Pins
18	Ejector Trip Rod, Left
19	Ejector Trip Rod, Right
20	Firing Pin
21	Firing Pin Housing
22	Firing Pin Housing Assembly Pin
23	Forend
24	Forend Adjuster Plate
25	Forend Adjuster Plate Lock Nut
26	Forend Adjuster Plate Stud
27	Forend Latch
28	Forend Latch Cover
29	Forend Latch Finger Piece
30	Forend Latch Springs
31	Forend Screw, Front
32	Forend Screw, Rear
33	Forend Screw Nut
34	Front Sight
35	Grip Cap
36	Hammer Assembly, Right
37	Hammer Assembly, Left
38	Hammer Cocking Cam
39	Hammer Cocking Cam Pin
40	Hammer Cocking Cam Spring
41	Hammer Cocking Rod
42	Hammer Pin
43	Hammer Plunger Assembly, Right
44	Hammer Plunger Assembly, Left
45	Main Hammer Spring
46	Rear Connector Link
47	Safety Selector Assembly
48	Safety Selector Detent
49	Safety Selector Detent Spring
50	Sear, Left
51	Sear, Right
52	Sear Pin
53	Sear Spring
54	Sear Spring Plunger
55	Selector Block
56	Selector Block Guide
57	Selector Block Guide Pin
58	Stock Assembly
59	Stock Bolt
60	Stock Bolt Lock Washer
61	Stock Bolt Washer
62	Tang Block Screw
63	Tang Block Slot Nut
64	Tang Connecting Block
65	Tang Strut
66	Tang Strut Pin
67	Toggle Block
68	Toggle Block Retaining Pin
69	Toggle Link
70	Toggle Link Screw
71	Toggle Slide Block
72	Toggle Slide Block Stud
73	Top Lock Latch
74	Top Lock Latch Pin
75	Top Lock Latch Spring
76	Top Lock Lever Plunger Assembly
77	Top Lock Lever Screw
78	Trigger
79	Trigger Adjusting Screw
80	Trigger Adjusting Screw Nut
81	Trigger Connector Spring
82	Trigger Connector Spring Pin
83	Trigger Guard
84	Trigger Guard Pin, Front
85	Trigger Guard Pin, Rear
86	Trigger Pin
87	Trigger Stop Screw
88	Trigger Stop Screw Nut
89	Yoke
90	Yoke Rod
91	Yoke Rod Buffer Spring
92	Yoke Rod Buffer Spring Washer
93	Yoke Rod Nut
94	Yoke Rod Spring
95	Ejector Sear Pins
96	Firing Pin Retractor
97	Top Lock Lever Spring
98	Ejector, Left
99	Ejector, Right
100	Top Lock
101	Top Lock Lever
102	Frame
103	Forend Iron Assembly
104	Bottom Tang

Model 37 Rangemaster Bolt-Action Rifle

Courtesy of James M. Triggs

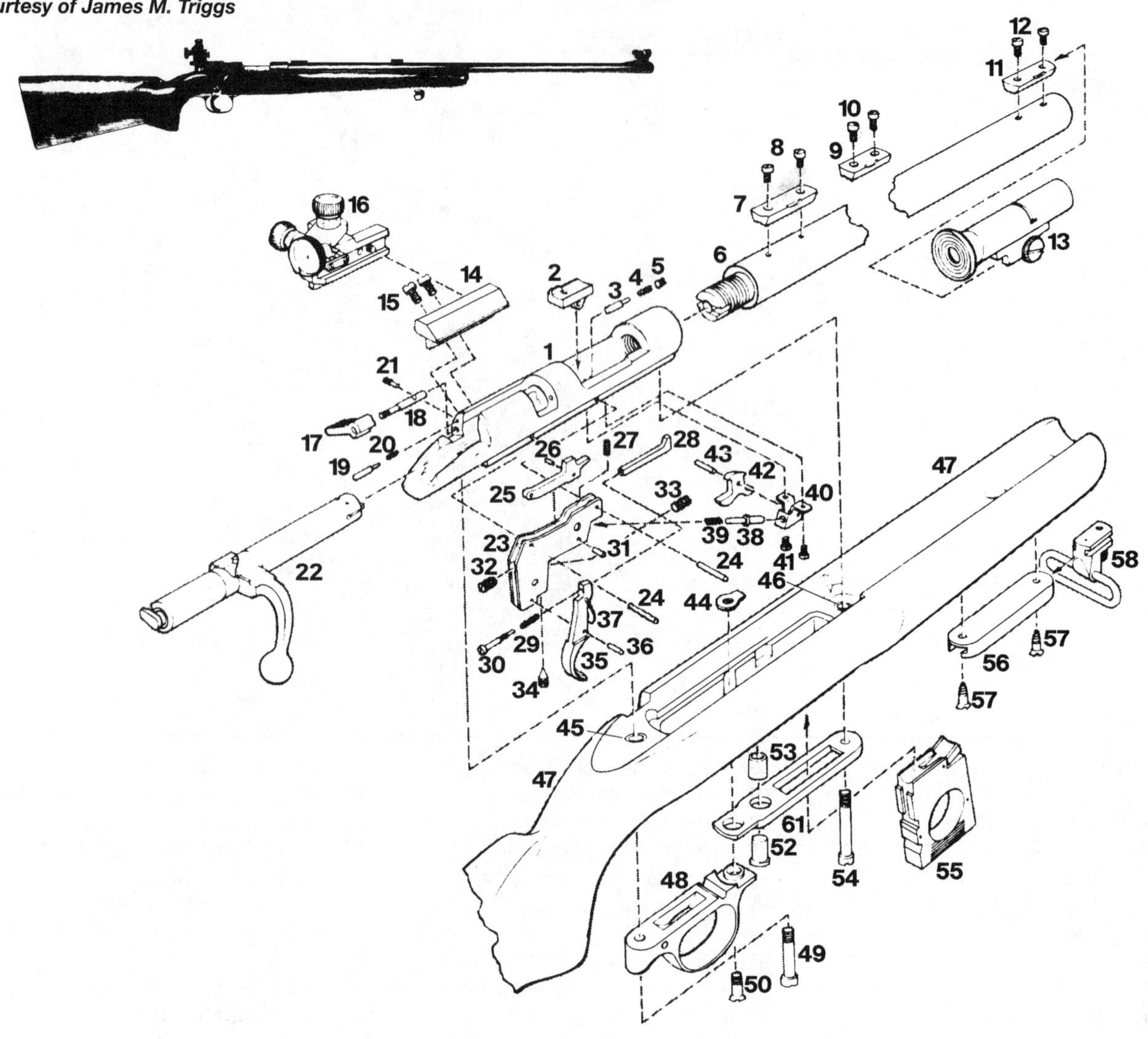

1	Receiver
2	Ejector
3	Bolt Handle Detent Plunger
4	Bolt Handle Detent Spring
5	Bolt Handle Detent Screw
6	Barrel
7	Telescope Base, Rear
8	Telescope Base Screws, Rear
9	Telescope Base, Front
10	Telescope Base Screws, Front
11	Front Sight Base
12	Front Sight Base Screws
13	Front Sight Assembly
14	Receiver Sight Base
15	Receiver Sight Base Screws
16	Receiver Sight
17	Safety
18	Safety Shaft
19	Safety Detent
20	Safety Detent Spring
21	Safety Shaft Lock Screw
22	Bolt Assembly
23	Trigger Housing
24	Trigger Housing Pins
25	Bolt Stop
26	Bolt Stop Pin
27	Bolt Stop Spring
28	Sear
29	Sear Spring
30	Sear Screw
31	Sear Guide Pin
32	Trigger Adjusting Screw, Rear
33	Trigger Adjusting Screw, Front
34	Trigger Adjusting Screw
35	Trigger
36	Trigger Pin
37	Trigger Spring
38	Magazine Lock Plunger
39	Magazine Lock Plunger Spring
40	Magazine Lock Bracket
41	Magazine Lock Bracket Screws
42	Magazine Lock
43	Magazine Lock Pin
44	Front Guard Bow Screw Nut
45	Rear Guard Bow Screw Bushing
46	Front Guard Bow Extension Screw Bushing
47	Stock
48	Guard Bow
49	Rear Guard Bow Screw
50	Front Guard Bow Screw
51	Guard Bow Extension
52	Magazine Lock Button
53	Magazine Lock Button Bushing
54	Front Guard Bow Extension Screw
55	Magazine Assembly
56	Swivel Base Guide
57	Swivel Base Guide Screws
58	Front Swivel Assembly

Parts Not Shown

Rear Swivel
Buttplate
Buttplate Screws

Model 40-XB Centerfire Bolt-Action Rifle

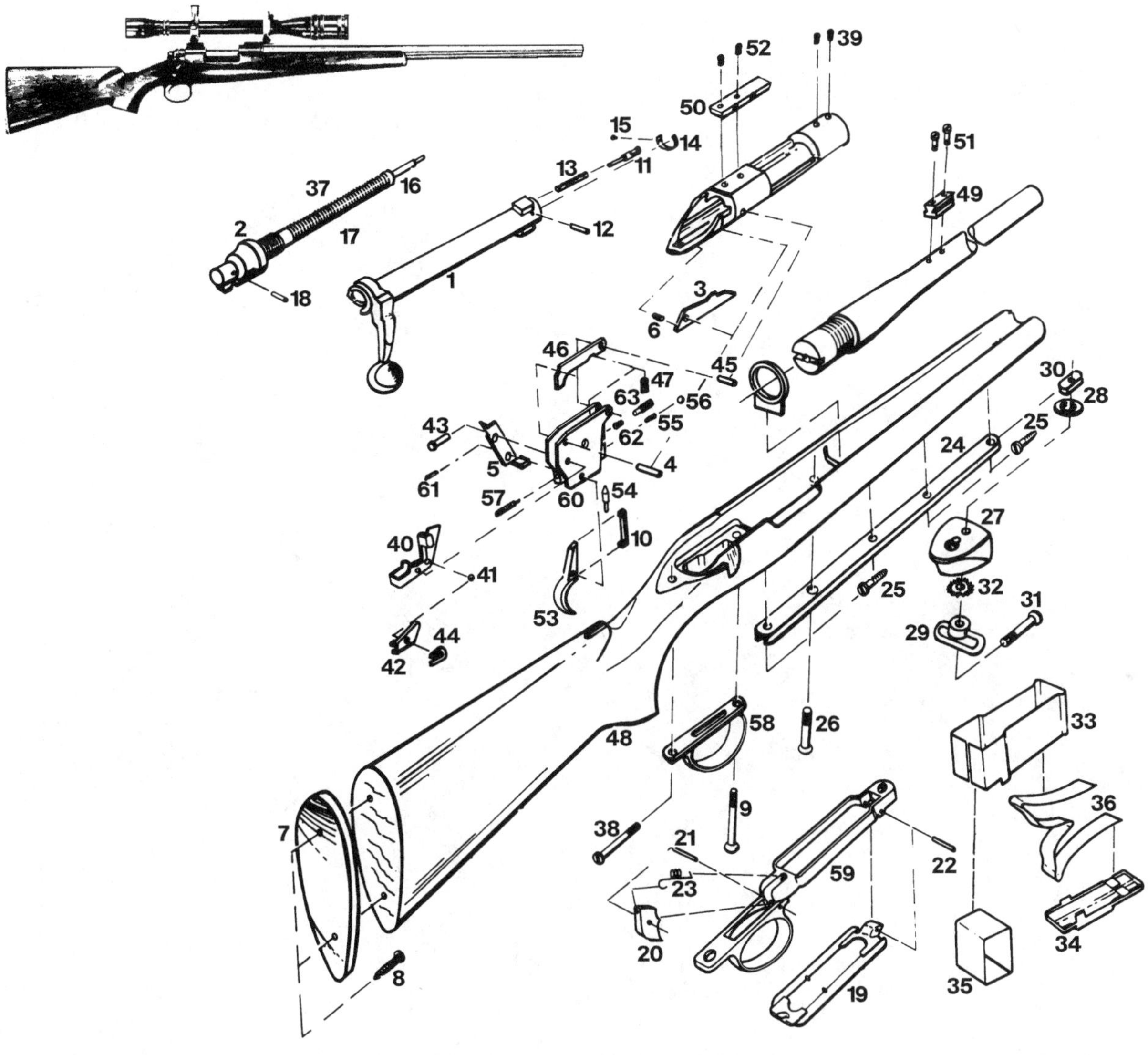

1	Bolt Assembly	**23**	Floorplate Latch Spring	**45**	Sear Pin
2	Bolt Plug	**24**	Forend Rail	**46**	Sear Safety Cam
3	Bolt Stop	**25**	Forend Rail Screws	**47**	Sear Spring
4	Bolt Stop Pin	**26**	Front Guard Screw	**48**	Stock
5	Bolt Stop Release	**27**	Front Swivel Block	**49**	Telescope Base, Front
6	Bolt Stop Spring	**28**	Front Swivel Block Washer	**50**	Telescope Base, Rear
7	Buttplate	**29**	Front Swivel with Bushing	**51**	Telescope Base Screws, Front
8	Buttplate Screws	**30**	Front Swivel Nut	**52**	Telescope Base Screws, Rear
9	Center Guard Screw	**31**	Front Swivel Screw	**53**	Trigger
10	Connector	**32**	Front Swivel Washer	**54**	Trigger Adjusting Screw
11	Ejector	**33**	Magazine	**55**	Trigger Adjusting Spring
12	Ejector Pin	**34**	Magazine Follower	**56**	Trigger Adjusting Ball
13	Ejector Spring	**35**	Magazine Spacer	**57**	Trigger Engagement Screw
14	Extractor	**36**	Magazine Spring	**58**	Trigger Guard
15	Extractor Rivet	**37**	Mainspring	**59**	Trigger Guard and Magazine Guide
16	Firing Pin	**38**	Rear Guard Screw	**60**	Trigger Housing Assembly
17	Firing Pin Assembly	**39**	Receiver Plug Screws	**61**	Trigger Pin
18	Firing Pin Cross Pin	**40**	Safety Assembly	**62**	Trigger Spring
19	Floorplate	**41**	Safety Detent Ball	**63**	Trigger Stop Screw
20	Floorplate Latch	**42**	Safety Detent Spring		
21	Floorplate Latch Pin	**43**	Safety Pivot Pin		
22	Floorplate Pivot Pin	**44**	Safety Snap Washer		

Model 40-XB Rimfire Bolt-Action Rifle

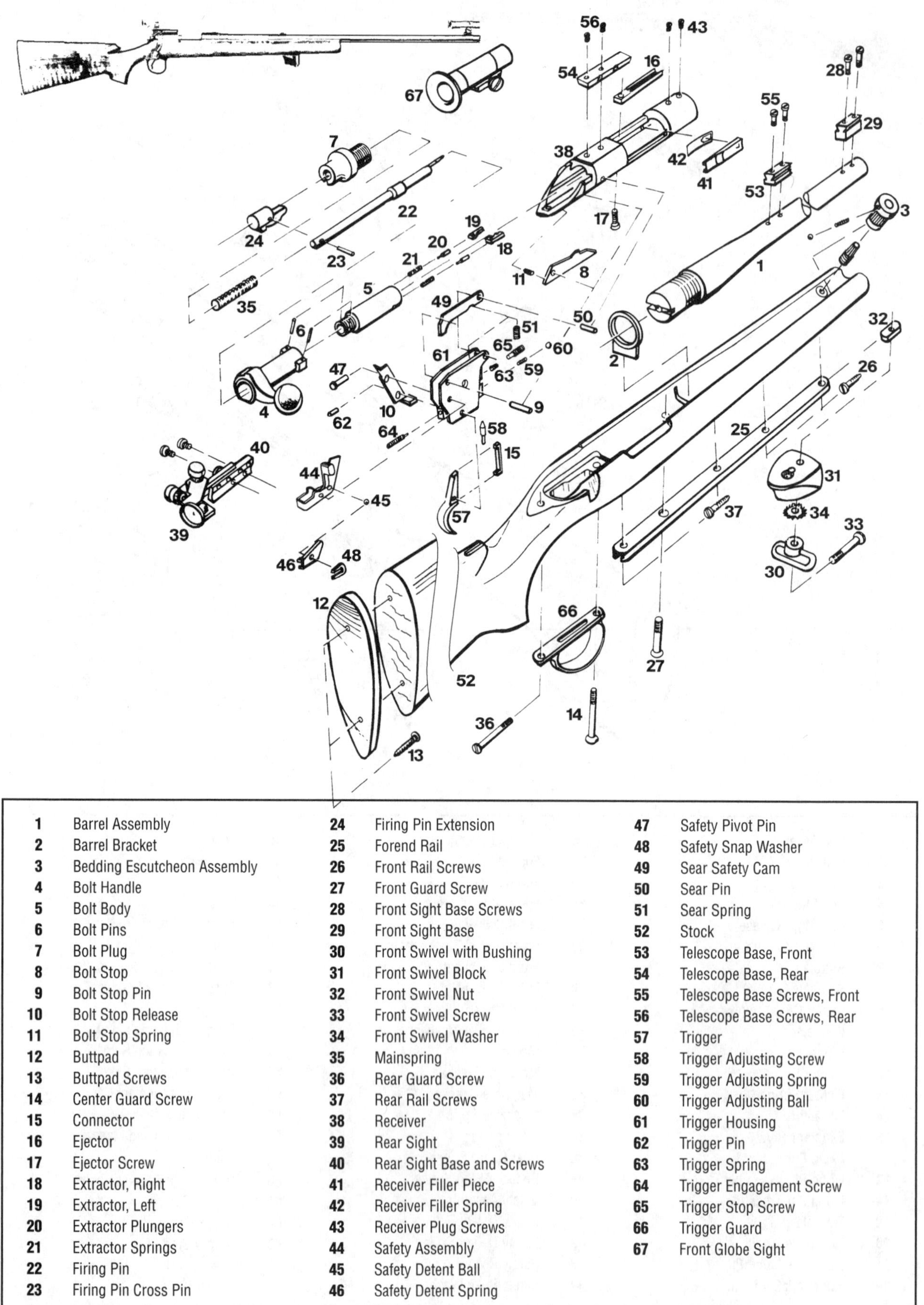

1	Barrel Assembly	24	Firing Pin Extension	47	Safety Pivot Pin
2	Barrel Bracket	25	Forend Rail	48	Safety Snap Washer
3	Bedding Escutcheon Assembly	26	Front Rail Screws	49	Sear Safety Cam
4	Bolt Handle	27	Front Guard Screw	50	Sear Pin
5	Bolt Body	28	Front Sight Base Screws	51	Sear Spring
6	Bolt Pins	29	Front Sight Base	52	Stock
7	Bolt Plug	30	Front Swivel with Bushing	53	Telescope Base, Front
8	Bolt Stop	31	Front Swivel Block	54	Telescope Base, Rear
9	Bolt Stop Pin	32	Front Swivel Nut	55	Telescope Base Screws, Front
10	Bolt Stop Release	33	Front Swivel Screw	56	Telescope Base Screws, Rear
11	Bolt Stop Spring	34	Front Swivel Washer	57	Trigger
12	Buttpad	35	Mainspring	58	Trigger Adjusting Screw
13	Buttpad Screws	36	Rear Guard Screw	59	Trigger Adjusting Spring
14	Center Guard Screw	37	Rear Rail Screws	60	Trigger Adjusting Ball
15	Connector	38	Receiver	61	Trigger Housing
16	Ejector	39	Rear Sight	62	Trigger Pin
17	Ejector Screw	40	Rear Sight Base and Screws	63	Trigger Spring
18	Extractor, Right	41	Receiver Filler Piece	64	Trigger Engagement Screw
19	Extractor, Left	42	Receiver Filler Spring	65	Trigger Stop Screw
20	Extractor Plungers	43	Receiver Plug Screws	66	Trigger Guard
21	Extractor Springs	44	Safety Assembly	67	Front Globe Sight
22	Firing Pin	45	Safety Detent Ball		
23	Firing Pin Cross Pin	46	Safety Detent Spring		

Model 510-X, 511-X and 512-X Bolt-Action Rifle

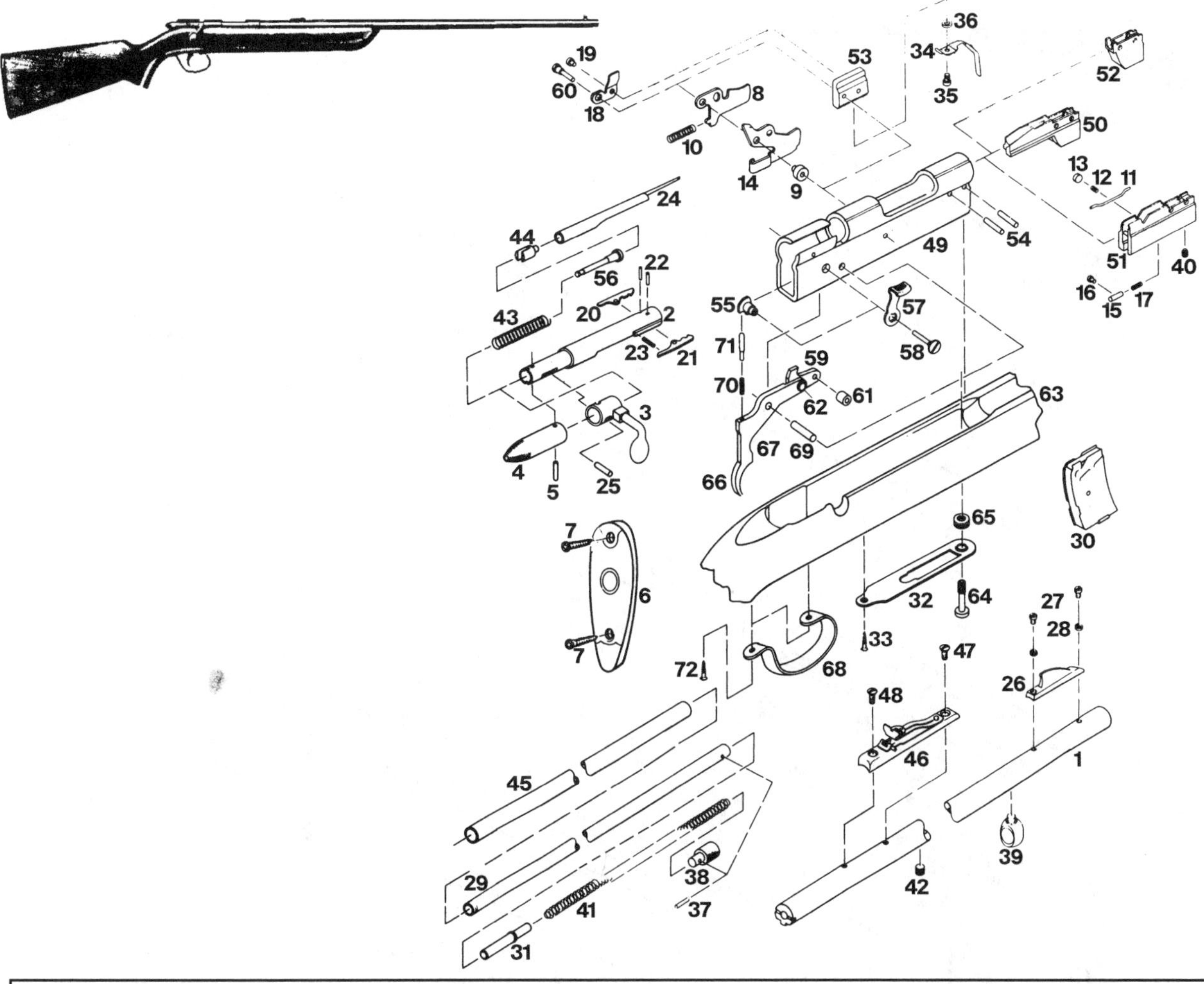

1 Barrel (510-X)
2 Bolt
3 Bolt Handle
4 Bolt Sleeve
5 Bolt Sleeve Pin
6 Buttplate
7 Buttplate Screws
8 Carrier (512-X)
9 Carrier Spacer Bushing (512-X)
10 Carrier Tension Spring (512-X)
11 Cartridge Retainer (512-X)
12 Cartridge Retainer Spring (512-X)
13 Cartridge Retainer Spring Screw (512-X)
14 Cartridge Stop (512-X)
15 Cartridge Stop Plunger (512-X)
16 Cartridge Stop Plunger Screw (512-X)
17 Cartridge Stop Plunger Spring (512-X)
18 Ejector (510-X and 512-X)
19 Ejector Screw (510-X and 512-X)
20 Extractor, Left
21 Extractor, Right
22 Extractor Pins
23 Extractor Spring
24 Firing Pin
25 Firing Pin Cam Pin
26 Front Sight
27 Front Sight Screws
28 Front Sight Washers
29 Inner Magazine Tube (512-X)
30 Magazine Assembly
31 Magazine Follower (512-X)
32 Magazine Guide Plate (511-X)
33 Magazine Guide Plate Screw (511-X)
34 Magazine Lock (511-X)
35 Magazine Lock Screw (511-X)
36 Magazine Lock Spacer (511-X)
37 Magazine Pin (512-X)
38 Magazine Plug (512-X)
39 Magazine Ring (512-X)
40 Magazine Screw (512-X)
41 Magazine Spring (512-X)
42 Magazine Tube Support Screw (512-X)
43 Mainspring
44 Mainspring Plunger
45 Outer Magazine Tube (512-X)
46 Rear Sight Assembly
47 Rear Sight Screw, Front
48 Rear Sight Screw, Rear
49 Receiver (510-X and 511-X)
50 Receiver Insert (510-X)
51 Receiver Insert (512-X)
52 Receiver Insert, Front (511-X)
53 Receiver Insert, Rear (511-X)
54 Receiver Insert Retaining Pins
55 Safety (510-X)
56 Safety Indicator
57 Safety-Lever
58 Safety Screw
59 Sear
60 Sear Pivot Screw
61 Sear Spacing Collar (510-X)
62 Sear Stud
63 Stock
64 Takedown Screw (511-X)
65 Takedown Screw Escutcheon
66 Trigger
67 Trigger Assembly
68 Trigger Guard
69 Trigger Pin
70 Trigger Spring
71 Trigger Spring Plunger
72 Trigger Guard Screw

Model 514 Single Shot Bolt-Action Rifle

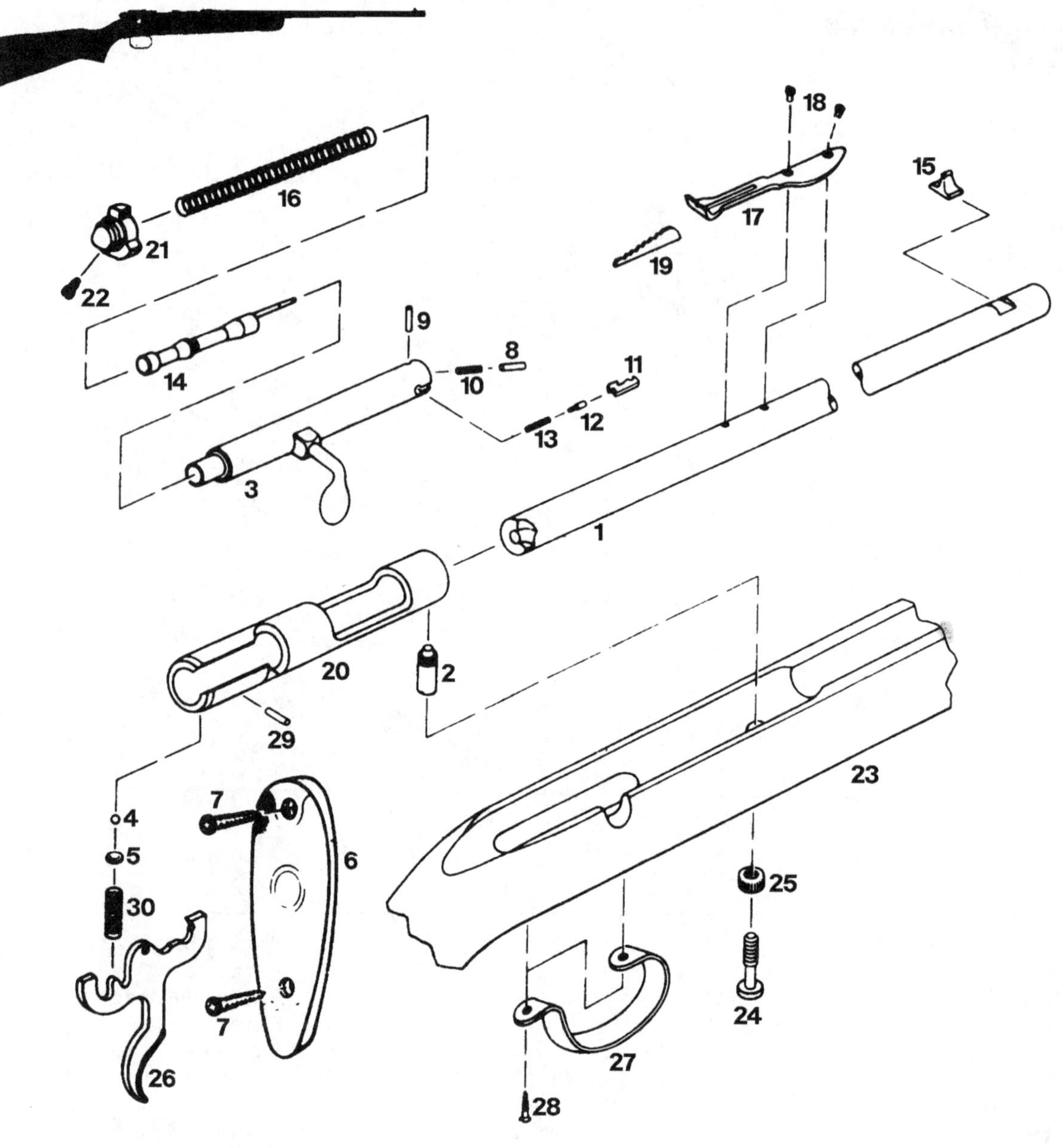

1	Barrel	16	Mainspring
2	Barrel Lock Screw	17	Open Sight Leaf
3	Bolt Body with Handle	18	Open Sight Screws
4	Bolt Detent Ball	19	Open Sight Step
5	Bolt Detent Retainer	20	Receiver
6	Buttplate	21	Safety
7	Buttplate Screws	22	Safety Screw
8	Ejector	23	Stock
9	Ejector Pin	24	Takedown Screw
10	Ejector Spring	25	Takedown Screw Escutcheon
11	Extractor	26	Trigger
12	Extractor Plunger	27	Trigger Guard
13	Extractor Spring	28	Trigger Guard Screws
14	Firing Pin	29	Trigger Pin
15	Front Sight	30	Trigger Spring

Model 521-T Single Shot Bolt-Action Rifle

Courtesy of Thomas E. Wessel

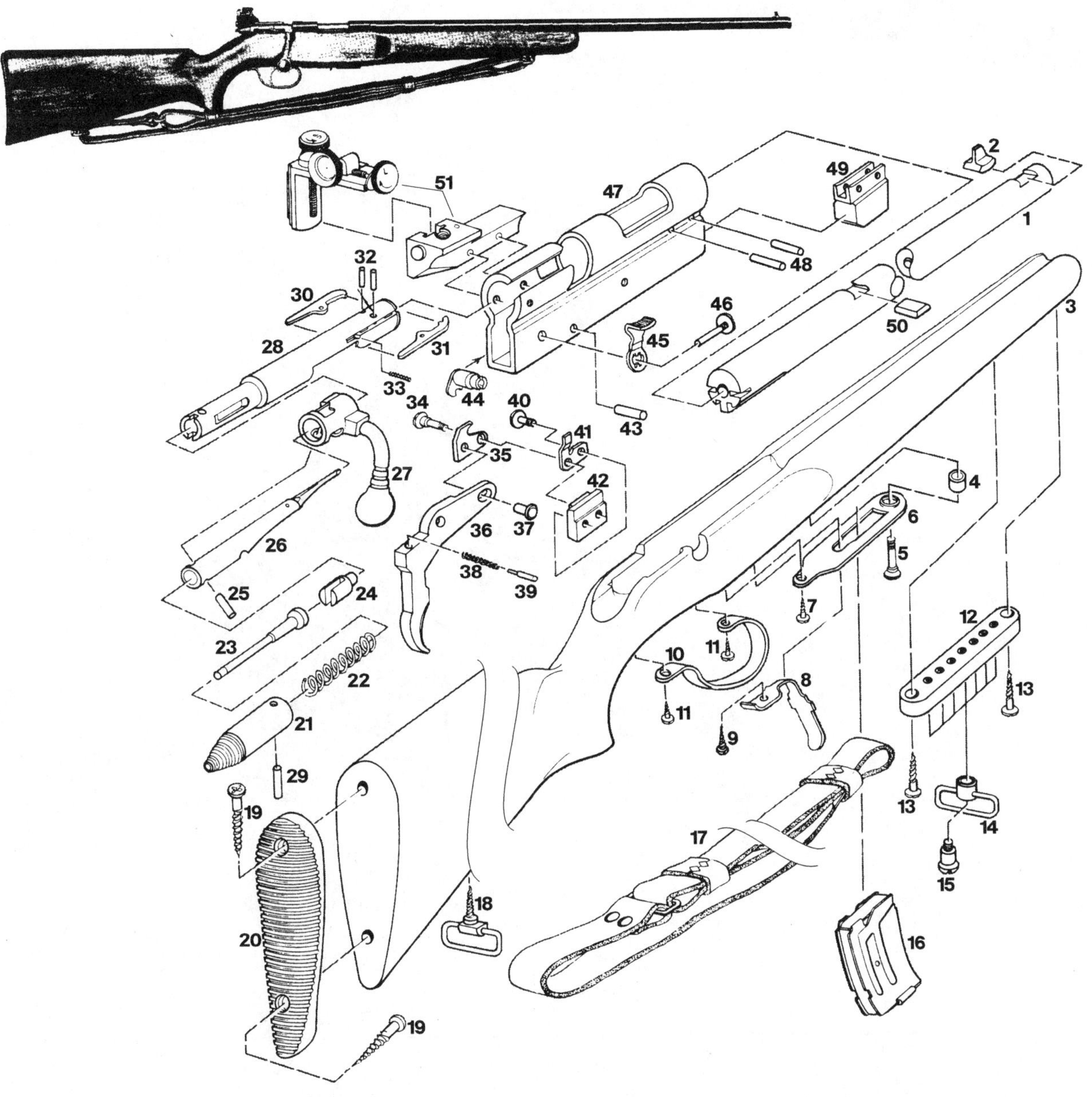

1	Barrel	**18**	Rear Swivel	**35**	Sear
2	Front Sight	**19**	Buttplate Screws	**36**	Trigger
3	Stock	**20**	Buttplate	**37**	Sear Stud
4	Takedown Screw Escutcheon	**21**	Bolt Sleeve	**38**	Trigger Spring
5	Takedown Screw	**22**	Mainspring	**39**	Trigger Spring Plunger
6	Magazine Guide Plate	**23**	Safety Indicator	**40**	Ejector Screw
7	Magazine Guide Plate Screw	**24**	Mainspring Plunger	**41**	Ejector
8	Magazine Lock	**25**	Firing Pin Cam Pin	**42**	Receiver Insert, Rear
9	Magazine Lock Screw	**26**	Firing Pin	**43**	Trigger Pin
10	Trigger Guard	**27**	Bolt Handle	**44**	Safety
11	Trigger Guard Screws	**28**	Bolt	**45**	Safety-Lever
12	Front Swivel Base	**29**	Bolt Sleeve Pin	**46**	Safety Screw
13	Front Swivel Base Screws	**30**	Extractor, Left	**47**	Receiver
14	Front Swivel	**31**	Extractor, Right	**48**	Barrel Lock Pins
15	Front Swivel Screw	**32**	Extractor Pins	**49**	Receiver Insert, Front
16	Magazine Assembly	**33**	Extractor Spring	**50**	Barrel Filler Block
17	Sling Strap Assembly	**34**	Sear Pivot Screw	**51**	Rear Micrometer Sight

Model 540-X Single Shot Bolt-Action Rifle

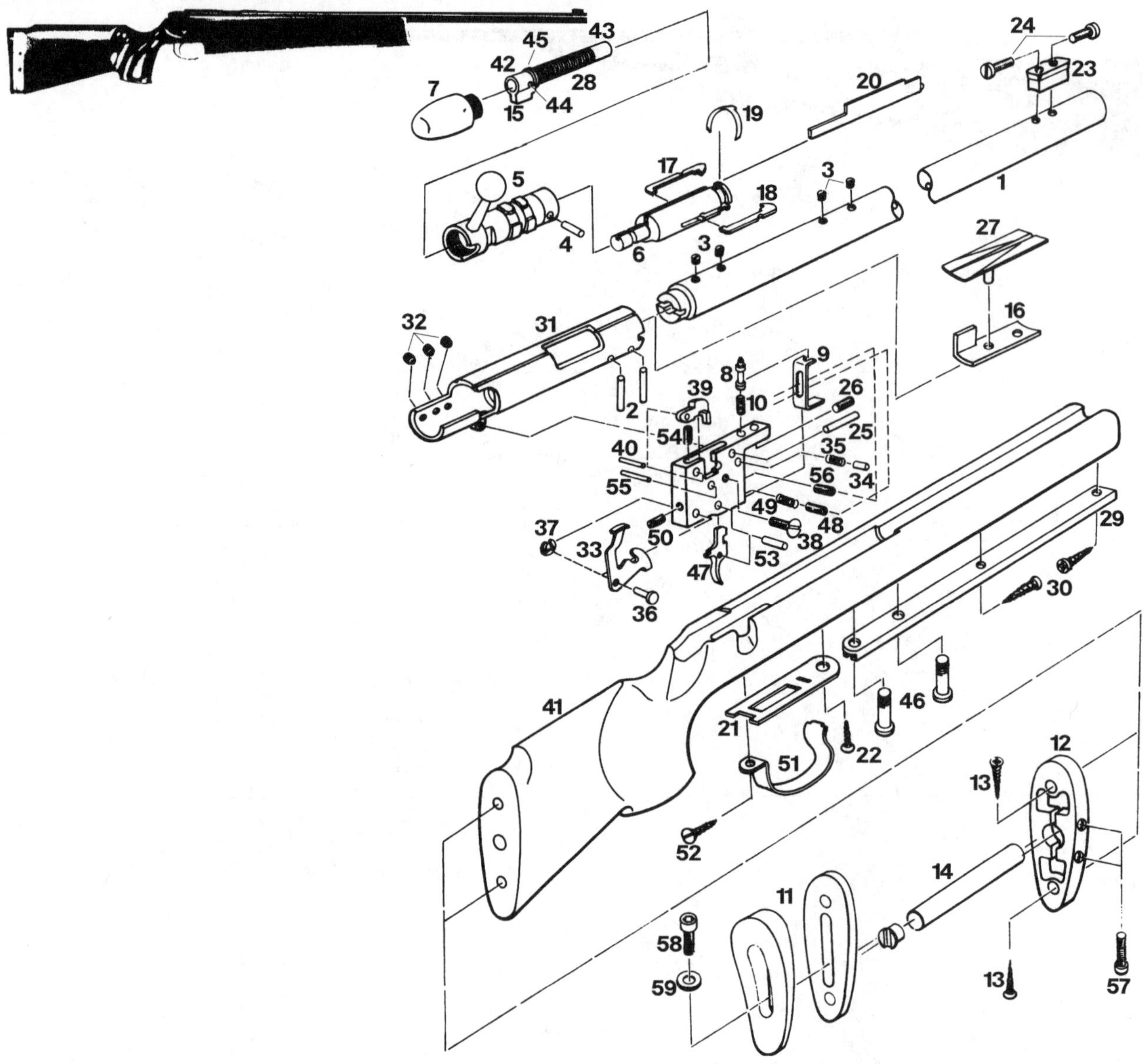

1	Barrel	21	Floorplate	40	Sear Pin
2	Barrel Assembly Pins	22	Floorplate Screw	41	Stock
3	Barrel Plug Screws	23	Front Sight Base	42	Striker Assembly
4	Bolt Assembly Pin	24	Front Sight Base Screws	43	Striker
5	Bolt Body	25	Housing Pin	44	Striker Cross Pin
6	Bolt Head	26	Housing Lock Screw	45	Striker Washer
7	Bolt Plug	27	Loading Platform	46	Takedown Screws
8	Bolt Stop	28	Mainspring	47	Trigger
9	Bolt Stop Release	29	Rail	48	Trigger Adjustment Screw
10	Bolt Stop Spring	30	Rail Screws	49	Trigger Adjustment Spring
11	Buttplate Assembly	31	Receiver	50	Trigger Engagement Screw
12	Buttplate Base	32	Receiver Plug Screws	51	Trigger Guard
13	Buttplate Plate Screws	33	Safety	52	Trigger Guard Screw
14	Buttplate Tube Assembly	34	Safety Detent	53	Trigger Pin
15	Cocking Piece	35	Safety Detent Spring	54	Trigger Spring
16	Ejector	36	Safety Pivot Pin	55	Trigger Spring Retaining Pin
17	Extractor, Left	37	Safety Pivot Pin Retaining Washer	56	Trigger Stop Screw
18	Extractor, Right	38	Safety Retainer Screw	57	Tube Clamp Screws
19	Extractor Spring	39	Sear	58	Tube Screw
20	Firing Pin			59	Tube Screw Washer

Model 541-S Bolt-Action Rifle

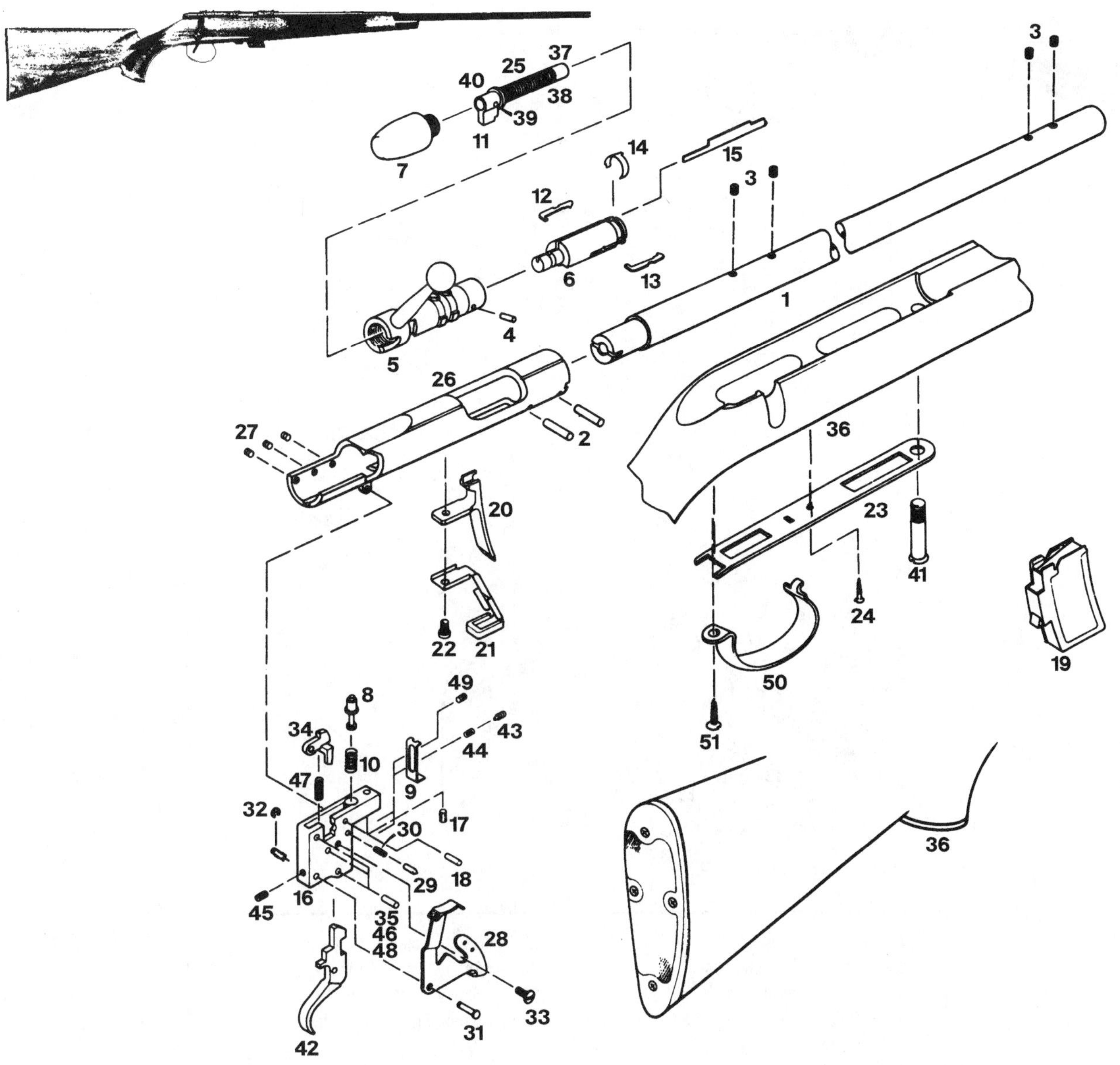

1	Barrel	18	Housing Pin	35	Sear Pin
2	Barrel Assembly Pins	19	Magazine Assembly	36	Stock Assembly
3	Barrel Plug Screws	20	Magazine Guide	37	Striker Assembly
4	Bolt Assembly Pin	21	Magazine Latch Assembly	38	Striker
5	Bolt Body Assembly	22	Magazine Latch Screw	39	Striker Cross Pin
6	Bolt Head	23	Magazine Plate	40	Striker Washer
7	Bolt Plug	24	Magazine Plate Screw	41	Takedown Screw
8	Bolt Stop	25	Mainspring	42	Trigger
9	Bolt Stop Release	26	Receiver Assembly	43	Trigger Adjusting Screw
10	Bolt Stop Spring	27	Receiver Plug Screws	44	Trigger Adjusting Spring
11	Cocking Piece	28	Safety	45	Trigger Engagement Screw
12	Extractor, Left	29	Safety Detent	46	Trigger Pin
13	Extractor, Right	30	Safety Detent Spring	47	Trigger Spring
14	Extractor Spring	31	Safety Pivot Pin	48	Trigger Spring Retaining Pin
15	Firing Pin	32	Safety Pivot Pin Washer	49	Trigger Stop Screw
16	Trigger Housing	33	Safety Retainer Screw	50	Trigger Guard
17	Housing Lock Screw	34	Sear	51	Trigger Guard Screw

Model 541-T and 581-S Bolt-Action Rifle

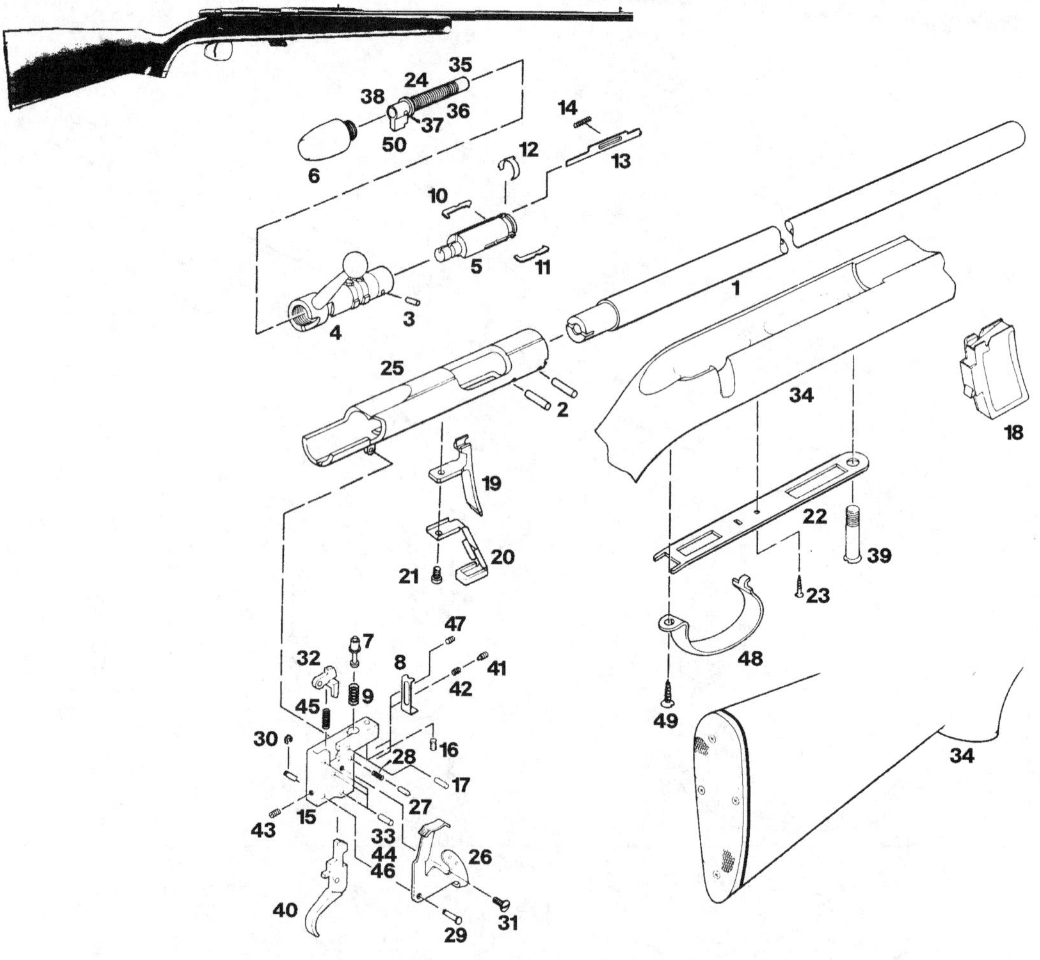

1	Barrel	**27**	Safety Detent
2	Barrel Assembly Pins	**28**	Safety Detent Spring
3	Bolt Assembly Pin	**29**	Safety Pivot Pin
4	Bolt Body Assembly	**30**	Safety Pivot Pin Retaining Washer
5	Bolt Head	**31**	Safety Retainer Screw
6	Bolt Plug	**32**	Sear
7	Bolt Stop	**33**	Sear Pin
8	Bolt Stop Release	**34**	Stock Assembly
9	Bolt Stop Spring	**35**	Striker Assembly
10	Extractor, Left	**36**	Striker
11	Extractor, Right	**37**	Striker Cross Pin
12	Extractor Spring	**38**	Striker Washer
13	Firing Pin	**39**	Takedown Screw
14	Firing Pin Return Spring	**40**	Trigger
15	Trigger Housing	**41**	Trigger Adjustment Screw
16	Housing Lock Screw	**42**	Trigger Adjustment Spring
17	Housing Pin	**43**	Trigger Engagement Screw
18	Magazine Assembly	**44**	Trigger Pin
19	Magazine Guide	**45**	Trigger Spring
20	Magazine Latch Assembly	**46**	Trigger Spring Retaining Pin
21	Magazine Latch Screw	**47**	Trigger Stop Screw
22	Magazine Plate	**48**	Trigger Guard
23	Magazine Plate Screw	**49**	Trigger Guard Screw
24	Mainspring	**50**	Cocking Piece
25	Receiver Assembly		
26	Safety		

Model 550-1 Autoloading Rifle

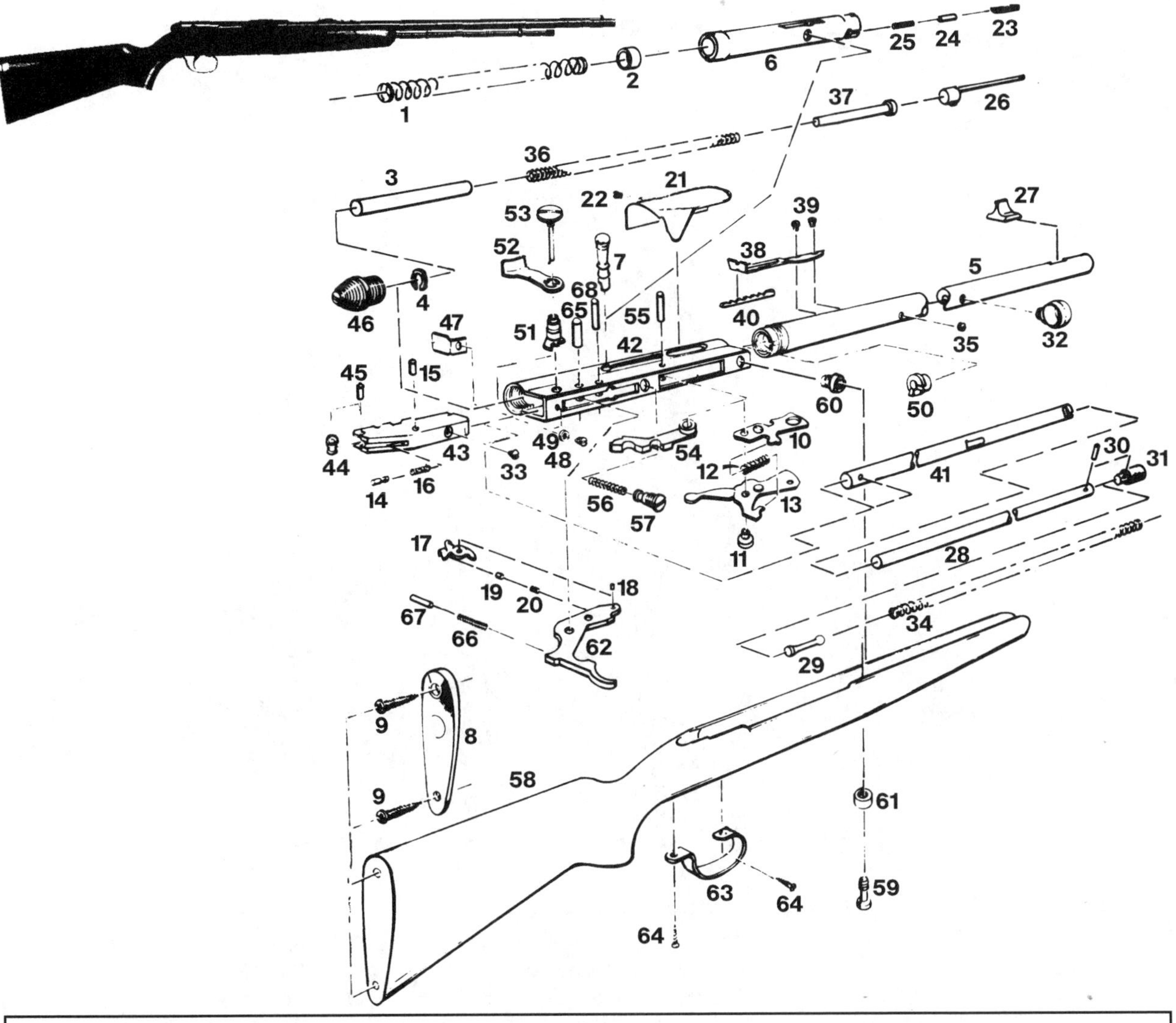

1	Action Spring	**24**	Extractor Plunger	**47**	Receiver Plug Retainer
2	Action Spring Bushing	**25**	Extractor Spring	**48**	Receiver Plug Retainer Screw
3	Action Spring Guide	**26**	Firing Pin	**49**	Receiver Plug Retainer Screw Lock Washer
4	Action Spring Guide Retainer	**27**	Front Sight		
5	Barrel	**28**	Inner Magazine Tube	**50**	Recoiling Chamber
6	Bolt	**29**	Magazine Follower	**51**	Safety
7	Bolt Handle	**30**	Magazine Pin	**52**	Safety-Lever
8	Buttplate	**31**	Magazine Plug	**53**	Safety Screw
9	Buttplate Screws	**32**	Magazine Ring	**54**	Sear Assembly
10	Carrier	**33**	Magazine Screw	**55**	Sear Pin
11	Carrier Spacer Bushing	**34**	Magazine Spring	**56**	Sear Spring
12	Carrier Tension Spring	**35**	Magazine Tube Support Screw	**57**	Sear Spring Case
13	Cartridge Stop	**36**	Mainspring	**58**	Stock
14	Cartridge Stop Detent	**37**	Mainspring Plunger	**59**	Takedown Screw
15	Cartridge Stop Detent Pin	**38**	Open Sight Leaf	**60**	Takedown Screw Bushing
16	Cartridge Stop Detent Spring	**39**	Open Sight Screws	**61**	Takedown Screw Escutcheon
17	Connector	**40**	Open Sight Step	**62**	Trigger
18	Connector Pin	**41**	Outer Magazine Tube	**63**	Trigger Guard
19	Connector Plunger	**42**	Receiver Assembly	**64**	Trigger Guard Screws
20	Connector Spring	**43**	Receiver Insert	**65**	Trigger Pin
21	Deflector	**44**	Receiver Insert Spacer	**66**	Trigger Spring
22	Deflector Screw	**45**	Receiver Insert Spacer Pin	**67**	Trigger Spring Plunger
23	Extractor	**46**	Receiver Plug	**68**	Trigger Stop Pin

Model 552 and 552 BDL Autoloading Rifle

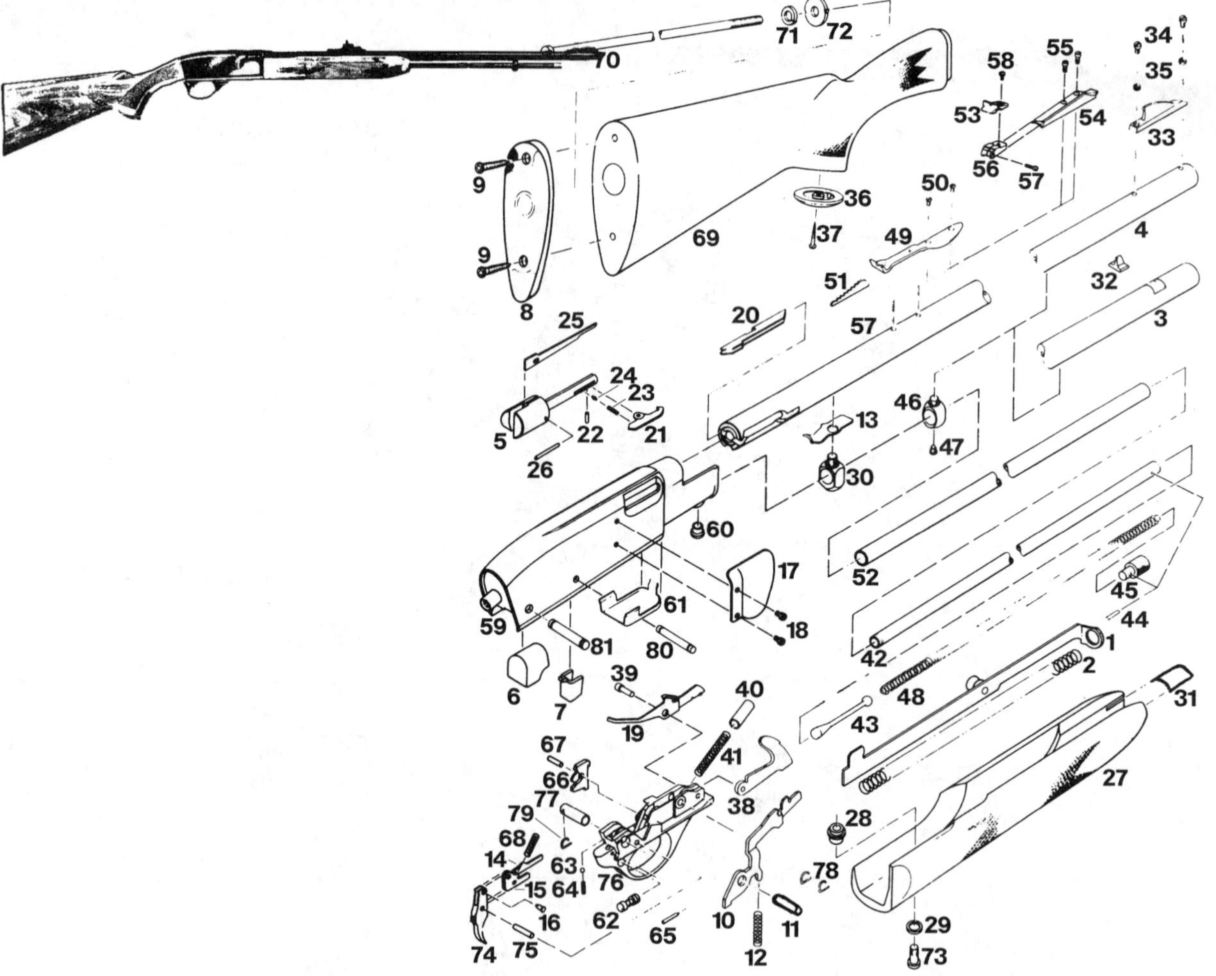

1	Action Bar Assembly	**28**	Forend Escutcheon	**55**	Rear Sight Base Screws (BDL)
2	Action Spring	**29**	Forend Escutcheon Nut	**56**	Rear Sight Slide (BDL)
3	Barrel	**30**	Forend Hanger	**57**	Elevation Screw (BDL)
4	Barrel (BDL)	**31**	Forend Support	**58**	Windage Screw (BDL)
5	Bolt	**32**	Front Sight	**59**	Receiver
6	Buffer Pad	**33**	Front Sight (BDL)	**60**	Receiver Bushing
7	Bolt Buffer	**34**	Front Sight Screws	**61**	Receiver Cover
8	Buttplate	**35**	Front Sight Washers	**62**	Safety
9	Buttplate Screws	**36**	Grip Cap (BDL)	**63**	Safety Detent Ball
10	Carrier	**37**	Grip Cap Screw	**64**	Safety Spring
11	Carrier Pivot Tube	**38**	Hammer	**65**	Safety Spring Retaining Pin
12	Carrier Spring	**39**	Hammer Pin	**66**	Sear
13	Cartridge Ramp	**40**	Hammer Plunger	**67**	Sear Pin
14	Connector, Left	**41**	Hammer Spring	**68**	Sear Spring
15	Connector, Right	**42**	Inner Magazine Tube	**69**	Stock Assembly (BDL)
16	Connector Pin	**43**	Magazine Follower	**70**	Stock Bolt
17	Deflector	**44**	Magazine Pin	**71**	Stock Bolt Lock Washer
18	Deflector Screws	**45**	Magazine Plug	**72**	Stock Bolt Washer
19	Disconnector	**46**	Magazine Ring	**73**	Takedown Screw
20	Ejector	**47**	Magazine Screw	**74**	Trigger
21	Extractor	**48**	Magazine Spring	**75**	Trigger Pin
22	Extractor Pin	**49**	Open Sight Leaf	**76**	Trigger Plate
23	Extractor Spring	**50**	Open Sight Screws	**77**	Trigger Plate Pin Bushing, Rear
24	Extractor Spring Seat	**51**	Open Sight Step	**78**	Trigger Plate Pin Detent Springs, Front
25	Firing Pin	**52**	Outer Magazine Tube	**79**	Trigger Plate Pin Detent Spring, Rear
26	Firing Pin Retaining Pin	**53**	Rear Sight Aperture (BDL)	**80**	Trigger Plate Pin, Front
27	Forend Assembly	**54**	Rear Sight Base (BDL)	**81**	Trigger Plate Pin, Rear

Model 572 and 572 BDL Autoloading Rifle

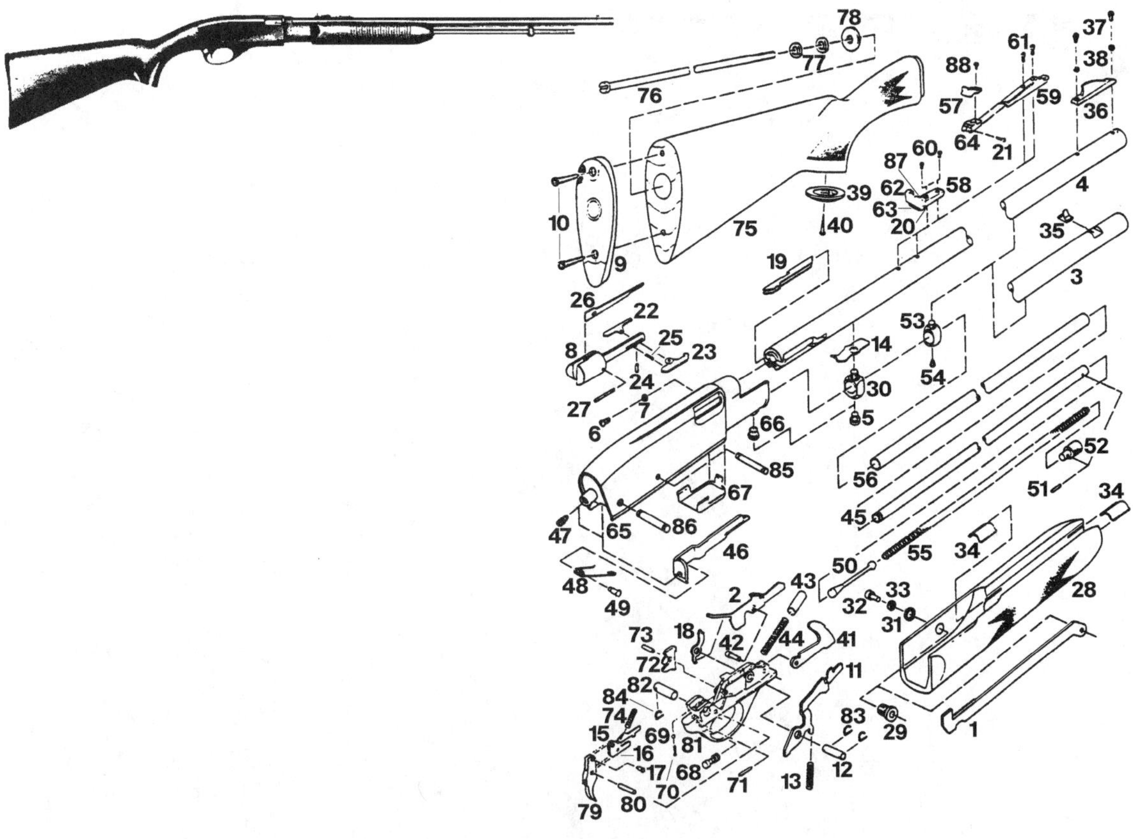

1 Action Bar
2 Action Bar Lock
3 Barrel
4 Barrel (BDL)
5 Barrel Lock Screw
6 Barrel Dowel Screw
7 Barrel Dowel Screw Washer
8 Bolt Assembly
9 Buttplate
10 Buttplate Screws
11 Carrier
12 Carrier Pivot Tube
13 Carrier Spring
14 Cartridge Ramp
15 Connector, Left
16 Connector, Right
17 Connector Pin
18 Disconnector
19 Ejector
20 Elevation Screw
21 Elevation Screw (BDL)
22 Extractor, Left
23 Extractor, Right
24 Extractor Pin
25 Extractor Spring
26 Firing Pin
27 Firing Pin Retaining Pin
28 Forend Assembly
29 Forend Escutcheon
30 Forend Hanger
31 Forend Nut
32 Forend Screw
33 Forend Screw Lock Washer
34 Forend Supports
35 Front Sight
36 Front Sight (BDL)
37 Front Sight Screws (BDL)
38 Front Sight Washers (BDL)
39 Grip Cap (BDL)
40 Grip Cap Screw
41 Hammer
42 Hammer Pin
43 Hammer Plunger
44 Hammer Spring
45 Inner Magazine Tube
46 Locking Bar
47 Locking Bar Retaining Screw
48 Locking Bar Spring
49 Locking Bar Spring Stud
50 Magazine Follower
51 Magazine Pin
52 Magazine Plug
53 Magazine Ring
54 Magazine Screw
55 Magazine Spring
56 Outer Magazine Tube
57 Rear Sight Aperture (BDL)
58 Rear Sight Base
59 Rear Sight Base (BDL)
60 Rear Sight Base Screws
61 Rear Sight Base Screws (BDL)
62 Rear Sight Eyepiece
63 Rear Sight Leaf
64 Rear Sight Slide (BDL)
65 Receiver
66 Receiver Bushing
67 Receiver Cover
68 Safety Switch
69 Safety Switch Detent Ball
70 Safety Switch Spring
71 Safety Switch Spring Retaining Pin
72 Sear
73 Sear Pin
74 Sear Spring
75 Stock Assembly (BDL)
76 Stock Bolt
77 Stock Bolt Lock Washers
78 Stock Bolt Washer
79 Trigger Assembly
80 Trigger Pin
81 Trigger Plate Assembly
82 Trigger Plate Pin Bushing, Rear
83 Trigger Plate Pin Detent Springs, Front
84 Trigger Plate Pin Detent Spring, Rear
85 Trigger Plate Pin, Front
86 Trigger Plate Pin, Rear
87 Windage Screw
88 Windage Screw (BDL)

Model 580, 581 and 582 Bolt-Action Rifle

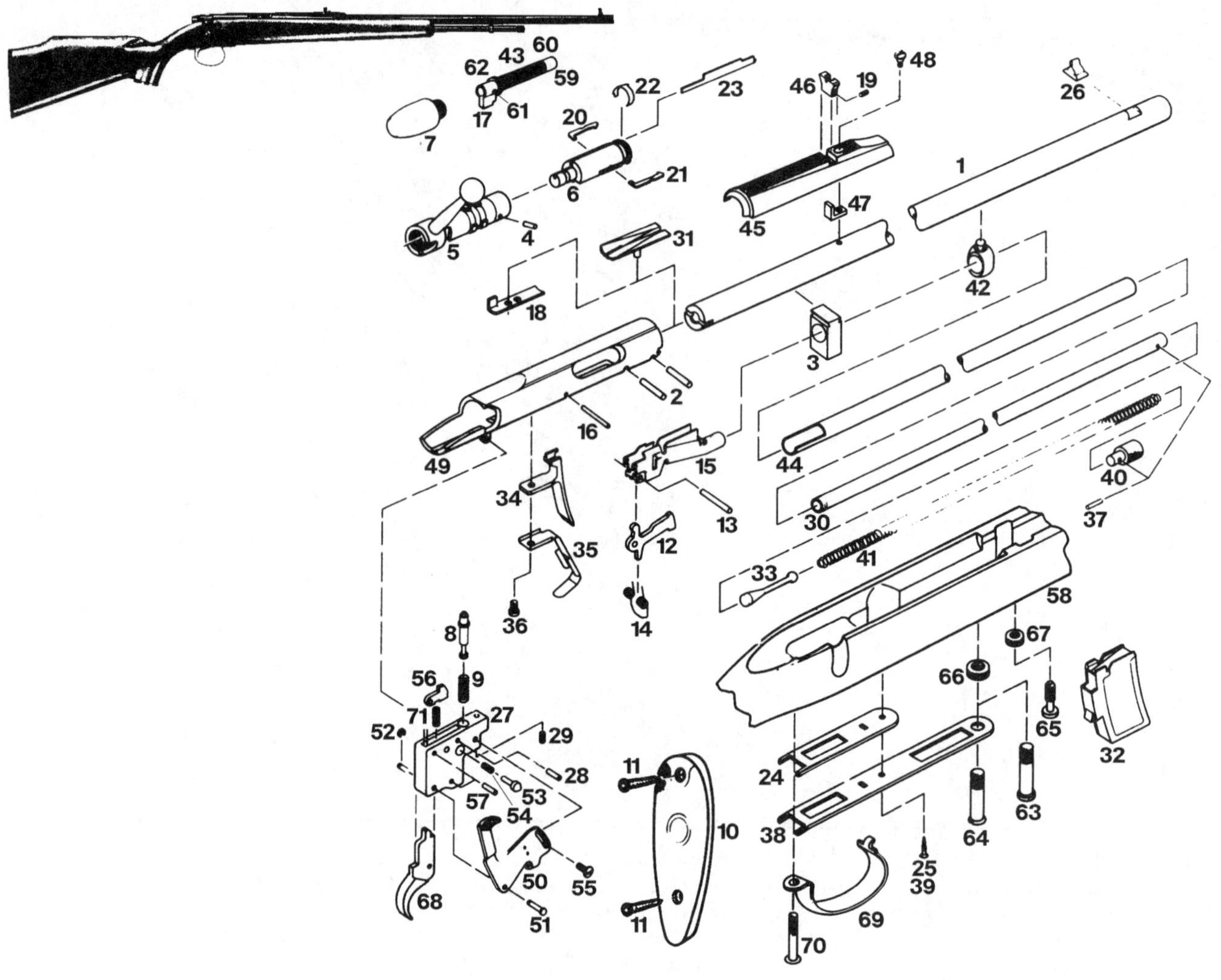

1	Barrel	26	Front Sight	51	Safety Pivot Pin
2	Barrel Assembly Pins	27	Trigger Housing	52	Safety Pivot Pin Retaining Washer
3	Barrel Bracket	28	Housing Pin	53	Safety Plunger
4	Bolt Assembly Pin	29	Housing Lock Screw	54	Safety Plunger Spring
5	Body Bolt Assembly	30	Inner Magazine Tube	55	Safety Retaining Screw
6	Bolt Head	31	Loading Platform	56	Sear
7	Bolt Plug	32	Magazine Assembly (581)	57	Sear Pin
8	Bolt Stop	33	Magazine Follower	58	Stock Assembly
9	Bolt Stop Spring	34	Magazine Guide	59	Striker Assembly
10	Buttplate	35	Magazine Latch	60	Striker
11	Buttplate Screws	36	Magazine Latch Screw	61	Striker Cross Pin
12	Carrier	37	Magazine Pin	62	Striker Washer
13	Carrier Pin	38	Magazine Plate (581)	63	Takedown Screw (580)
14	Carrier Spring	39	Magazine Plate Screw	64	Takedown Screw (581)
15	Cartridge Feed Insert	40	Magazine Plug	65	Takedown Screw (582)
16	Cartridge Feed Insert Pin	41	Magazine Spring	66	Takedown Screw Escutcheon
17	Cocking Piece	42	Magazine Ring	67	Takedown Screw Escutcheon (582)
18	Ejector	43	Mainspring	68	Trigger
19	Elevation Screw	44	Outer Magazine Tube	69	Trigger Guard
20	Extractor, Left	45	Rear Sight Base	70	Trigger Guard Screw
21	Extractor, Right	46	Rear Sight Aperture	71	Trigger Spring
22	Extractor Spring	47	Rear Sight Leaf		
23	Firing Pin	48	Rear Sight Screw		
24	Floorplate	49	Receiver Assembly		
25	Floorplate Screw	50	Safety		

Model 600 Bolt-Action Carbine

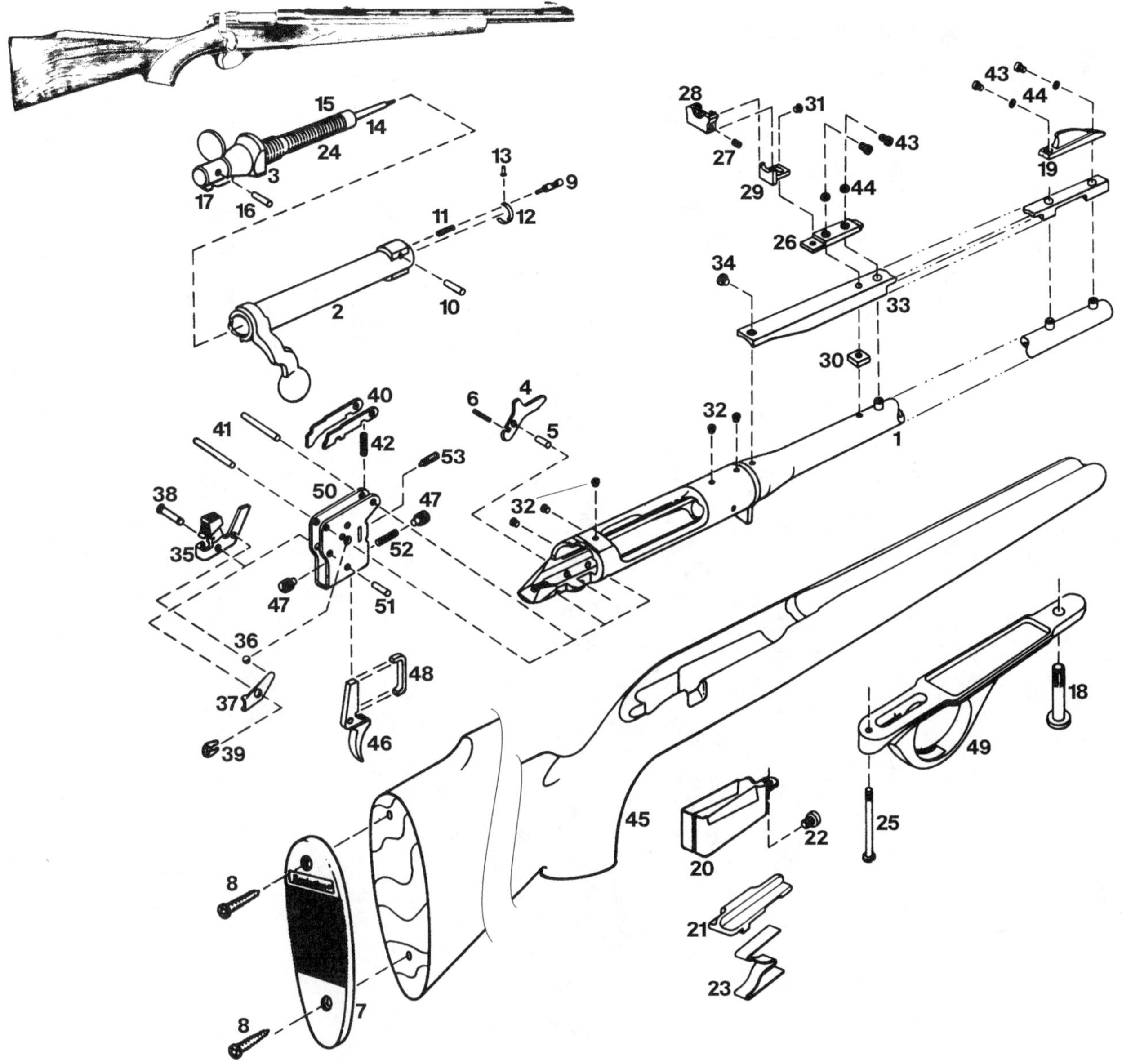

1	Barrel	**19**	Front Sight Assembly	**37**	Safety Detent Spring
2	Bolt Assembly	**20**	Magazine	**38**	Safety Pivot Pin
3	Bolt Plug	**21**	Magazine Follower	**39**	Safety Snap Washer
4	Bolt Stop	**22**	Magazine Housing Screw	**40**	Sear Safety Cam
5	Bolt Stop Pin	**23**	Magazine Spring	**41**	Sear Pins
6	Bolt Stop Spring	**24**	Mainspring	**42**	Sear Spring
7	Buttplate	**25**	Rear Guard Screw	**43**	Sight Screws
8	Buttplate Screws	**26**	Rear Sight Base	**44**	Sight Washers
9	Ejector	**27**	Rear Sight Elevation Screw	**45**	Stock
10	Ejector Pin	**28**	Rear Sight Eyepiece	**46**	Trigger
11	Ejector Spring	**29**	Rear Sight Leaf	**47**	Trigger Adjusting Screws
12	Extractor	**30**	Rear Sight Nut	**48**	Trigger Connector
13	Extractor Rivet	**31**	Rear Sight Windage Screw	**49**	Trigger Guard
14	Firing Pin	**32**	Receiver Plug Screws	**50**	Trigger Housing
15	Firing Pin Assembly	**33**	Rib	**51**	Trigger Pin
16	Firing Pin Cross Pin	**34**	Rib Screw	**52**	Trigger Spring
17	Firing Pin Head	**35**	Safety Assembly	**53**	Trigger Stop Screw
18	Front Guard Screw	**36**	Safety Detent Ball		

Model 700 New Model Bolt-Action Rifle

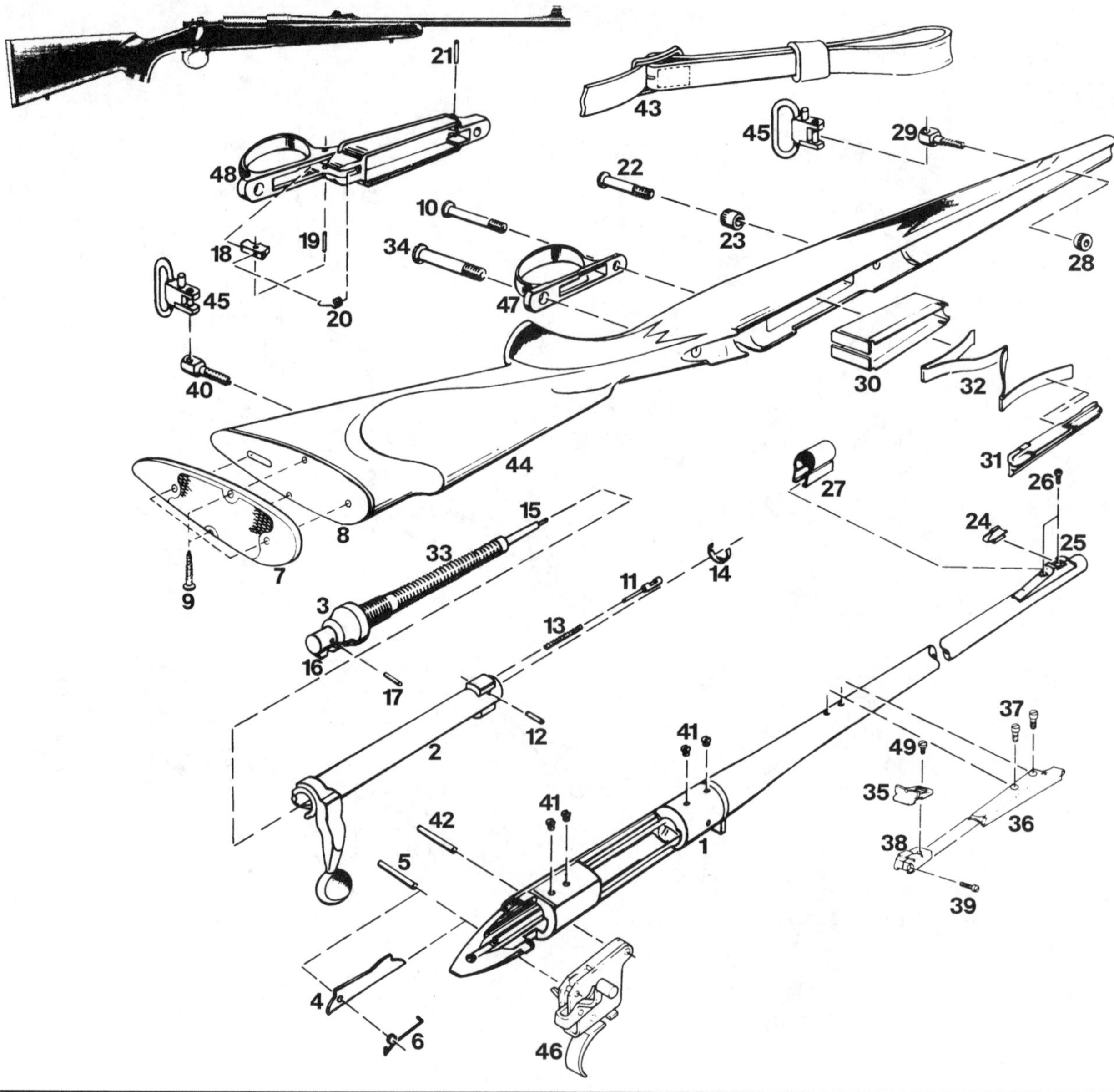

1	Barrel Assembly	**20**	Floorplate Latch Spring	**39**	Elevation Screw
2	Bolt Assembly	**21**	Floorplate Pivot Pin	**40**	Rear Swivel Screw
3	Bolt Plug	**22**	Front Guard Screw	**41**	Receiver Plug Screws
4	Bolt Stop	**23**	Front Guard Screw Bushing	**42**	Sear Pin
5	Bolt Stop Pin	**24**	Front Sight	**43**	Sling Strap Assembly
6	Bolt Stop Spring	**25**	Front Sight Ramp	**44**	Stock Assembly
7	Buttplate	**26**	Front Sight Ramp Screws	**45**	Swivel Assembly
8	Buttplate Spacer	**27**	Front Sight Hood	**46**	Trigger Assembly
9	Buttplate Screws	**28**	Front Swivel Bushing	**47**	Trigger Guard
10	Center Guard Screw	**29**	Front Swivel Screw	**48**	Trigger Guard Assembly
11	Ejector	**30**	Magazine	**49**	Windage Screw
12	Ejector Pin	**31**	Magazine Follower	**Parts Not Shown**	
13	Ejector Spring	**32**	Magazine Spring		Grip Cap
14	Extractor	**33**	Mainspring		Grip Cap ScrewGrip Cap Screw
15	Firing Pin	**34**	Rear Guard Screw		Grip Cap Spacer
16	Firing Pin Assembly	**35**	Rear Sight Aperture		Magazine Tab Screw
17	Firing Pin Cross Pin	**36**	Rear Sight Base		Stock Reinforcing Screw
18	Floorplate Latch	**37**	Rear Sight Base Screws		Stock Reinforcing Screw Dowel
19	Floorplate Latch Pin	**38**	Rear Sight Slide		

Model 700 Old Style Bolt-Action Rifle

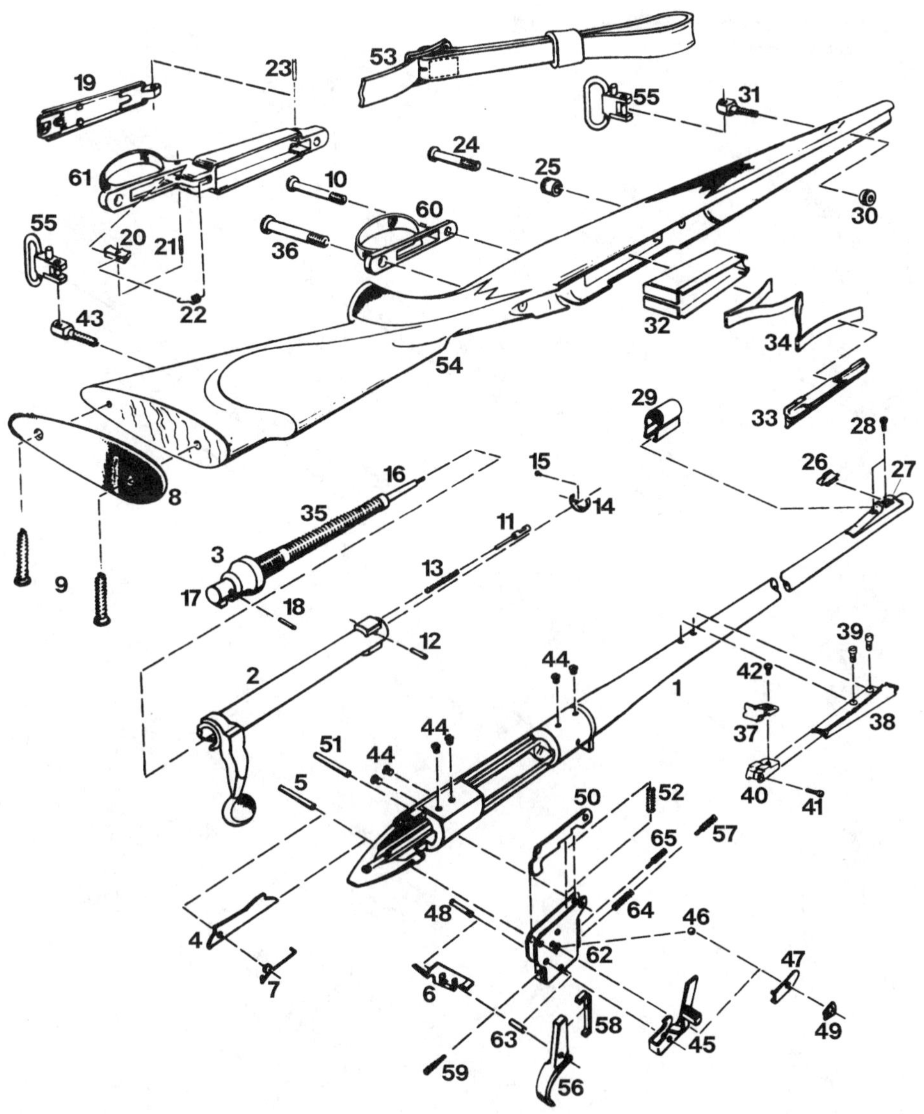

1	Barrel Assembly	**23**	Floorplate Pivot Pin	**45**	Safety Assembly
2	Bolt Assembly	**24**	Front Guard Screw	**46**	Safety Detent Ball
3	Bolt Plug	**25**	Front Guard Screw Bushing	**47**	Safety Detent Spring
4	Bolt Stop	**26**	Front Sight	**48**	Safety Pivot Pin
5	Bolt Stop Pin	**27**	Front Sight Ramp	**49**	Safety Snap Washer
6	Bolt Stop Release	**28**	Front Sight Ramp Screws	**50**	Sear Safety Cam
7	Bolt Stop Spring	**29**	Front Sight Hood	**51**	Sear Pin
8	Buttplate	**30**	Front Swivel Nut	**52**	Sear Spring
9	Buttplate Screws	**31**	Front Swivel Screw	**53**	Sling Strap Assembly
10	Center Guard Screw	**32**	Magazine	**54**	Stock
11	Ejector	**33**	Magazine Follower	**55**	Swivel Assembly
12	Ejector Pin	**34**	Magazine Spring	**56**	Trigger
13	Ejector Spring	**35**	Mainspring	**57**	Trigger Adjusting Screw
14	Extractor	**36**	Rear Guard Screw	**58**	Trigger Connector
15	Extractor Rivet	**37**	Rear Sight Aperture	**59**	Trigger Engagement Screw
16	Firing Pin	**38**	Rear Sight Base	**60**	Trigger Guard
17	Firing Pin Assembly	**39**	Rear Sight Base Screws	**61**	Trigger Guard (BDL)
18	Firing Pin Cross Pin	**40**	Rear Sight Slide	**62**	Trigger Housing Assembly
19	Floorplate	**41**	Elevation Screw	**63**	Trigger Pin
20	Floorplate Latch	**42**	Windage Screw	**64**	Trigger Spring
21	Floorplate Latch Pin	**43**	Rear Swivel Screw	**65**	Trigger Stop Screw
22	Floorplate Latch Spring	**44**	Receiver Plug Screws		

721 and 722 Bolt-Action Rifle

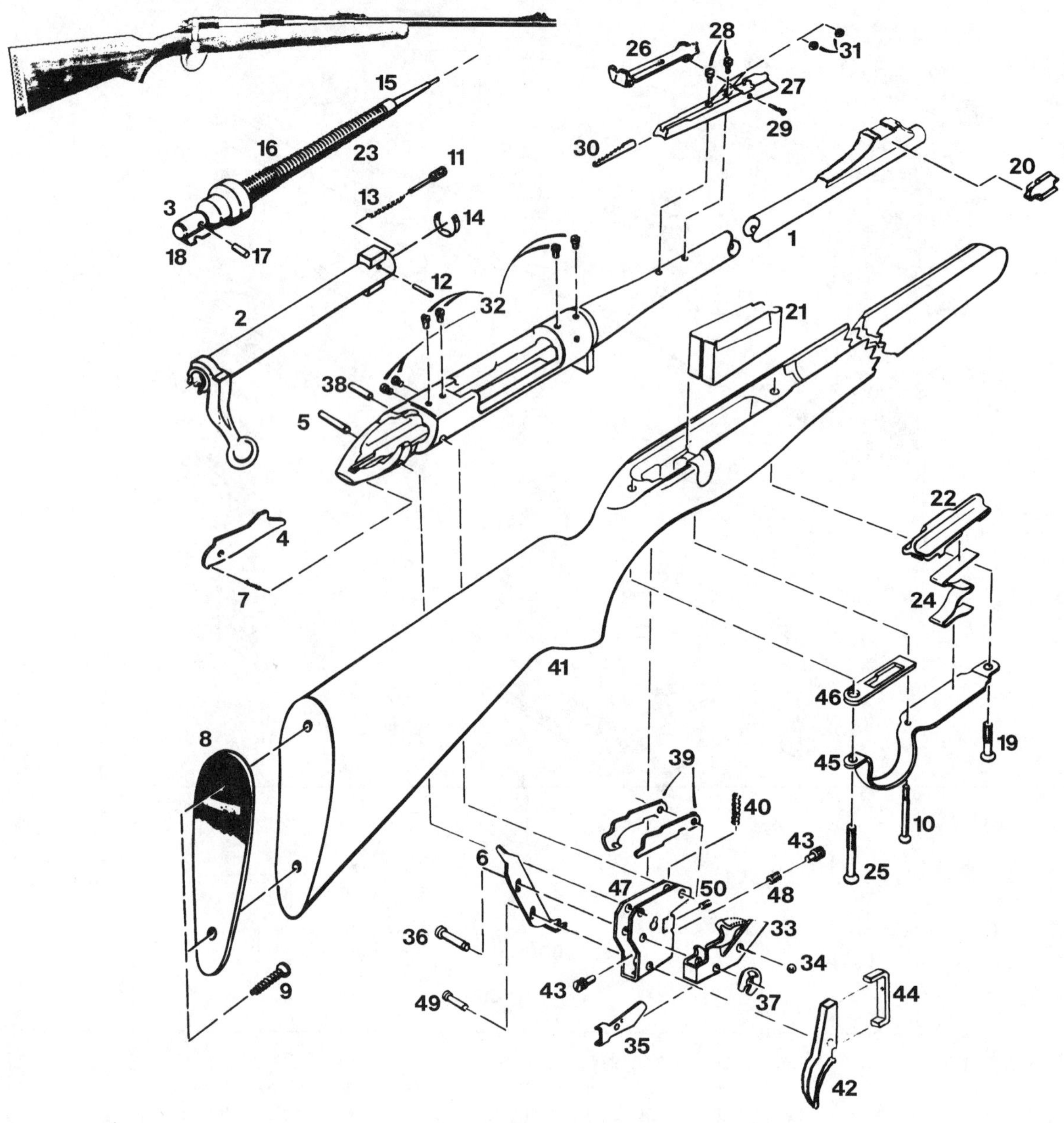

1	Barrel	**18**	Firing Pin Head	**35**	Safety Detent Spring
2	Bolt Assembly	**19**	Front Guard Screw	**36**	Safety Detent Pivot Pin
3	Bolt Plug	**20**	Front Sight	**37**	Safety Snap Washer
4	Bolt Stop	**21**	Magazine	**38**	Sear Pin
5	Bolt Stop Pin	**22**	Magazine Follower	**39**	Sear and Safety Cam Assembly
6	Bolt Stop Release	**23**	Mainspring	**40**	Sear Spring
7	Bolt Stop Spring	**24**	Magazine Spring	**41**	Stock
8	Buttplate	**25**	Rear Guard Screw	**42**	Trigger
9	Buttplate Screws	**26**	Rear Sight Assembly	**43**	Trigger Adjusting Screw
10	Center Guard Screw	**27**	Rear Sight Base	**44**	Trigger Connector
11	Ejector	**28**	Rear Sight Base Screws	**45**	Trigger Guard
12	Ejector Pin	**29**	Rear Sight Screw	**46**	Trigger Guard Plate
13	Ejector Spring	**30**	Rear Sight Step	**47**	Trigger Housing
14	Extractor	**31**	Rear Sight Washers	**48**	Trigger Spring
15	Firing Pin	**32**	Receiver Plug Screws	**49**	Trigger Pin
16	Firing Pin Assembly	**33**	Safety	**50**	Trigger Stop Screw
17	Firing Pin Cross Pin	**34**	Safety Detent Ball		

Model 742 Autoloading Rifle

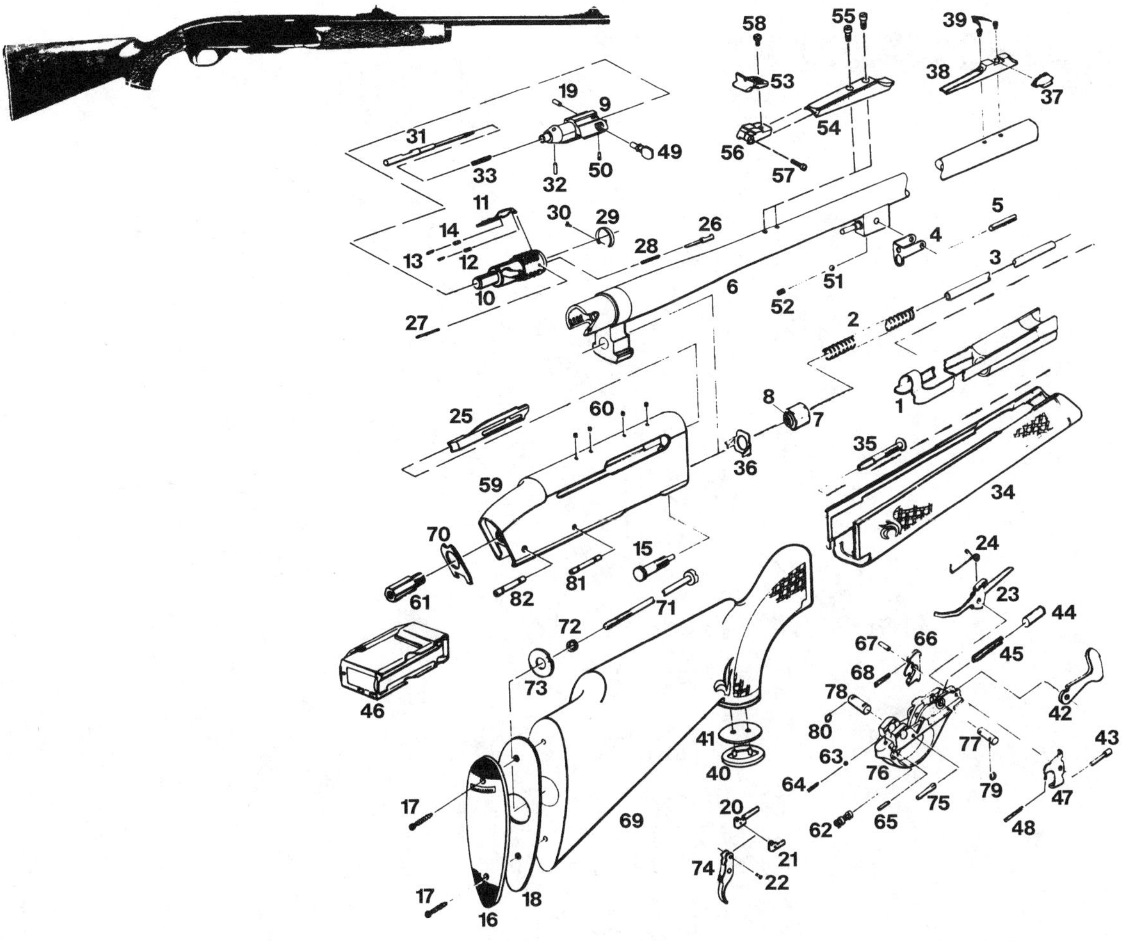

1	Action Bar Assembly	29	Extractor	57	Elevation Screw
2	Action Spring	30	Extractor Rivet	58	Windage Screw
3	Action Tube	31	Firing Pin	59	Receiver Assembly
4	Action Tube Support	32	Firing Pin Retaining Pin	60	Receiver Plug Screws
5	Action Tube Support Pin	33	Firing Pin Retractor Spring	61	Receiver Stud
6	Barrel Assembly	34	Forend Assembly	62	Safety
7	Barrel Takedown Nut	35	Forend Screw	63	Safety Detent Ball
8	Barrel Takedown Nut Washer	36	Forend Spring	64	Safety Spring
9	Bolt Carrier	37	Front Sight	65	Safety Spring Retaining Pin
10	Breechbolt Assembly	38	Front Sight Ramp	66	Sear
11	Bolt Latch	39	Front Sight Ramp Screws	67	Sear Pin
12	Bolt Latch Pivot	40	Grip Cap	68	Sear Spring
13	Bolt Latch Springs	41	Grip Cap Spacer	69	Stock
14	Bolt Latch Spring Plunger	42	Hammer	70	Stock Bearing Plate
15	Breech Ring Bolt	43	Hammer Pin	71	Stock Bolt
16	Buttplate	44	Hammer Plunger	72	Stock Bolt Lock Washer
17	Buttplate Screws	45	Hammer Spring	73	Stock Bolt Washer
18	Buttplate Spacer	46	Magazine Assembly	74	Trigger
19	Cam Pin	47	Magazine Latch	75	Trigger Pin
20	Connector, Left	48	Magazine Latch Spring	76	Trigger Plate
21	Connector, Right	49	Operating Handle	77	Trigger Plate Pin Bushing, Front
22	Connector Pin	50	Operating Handle Retaining Pin	78	Trigger Plate Pin Bushing, Rear
23	Disconnector	51	Orifice Ball	79	Trigger Plate Pin Detent Spring, Front
24	Disconnector Spring	52	Orifice Screw	80	Trigger Plate Pin Detent Spring, Rear
25	Ejector Port Cover	53	Rear Sight Aperture	81	Trigger Plate Pin, Front
26	Ejector	54	Rear Sight Base	82	Trigger Plate Pin, Rear
27	Ejector Retaining Pin	55	Rear Sight Base Screws		
28	Ejector Spring	56	Rear Sight Slide		

Model 760 Slide-Action Rifle

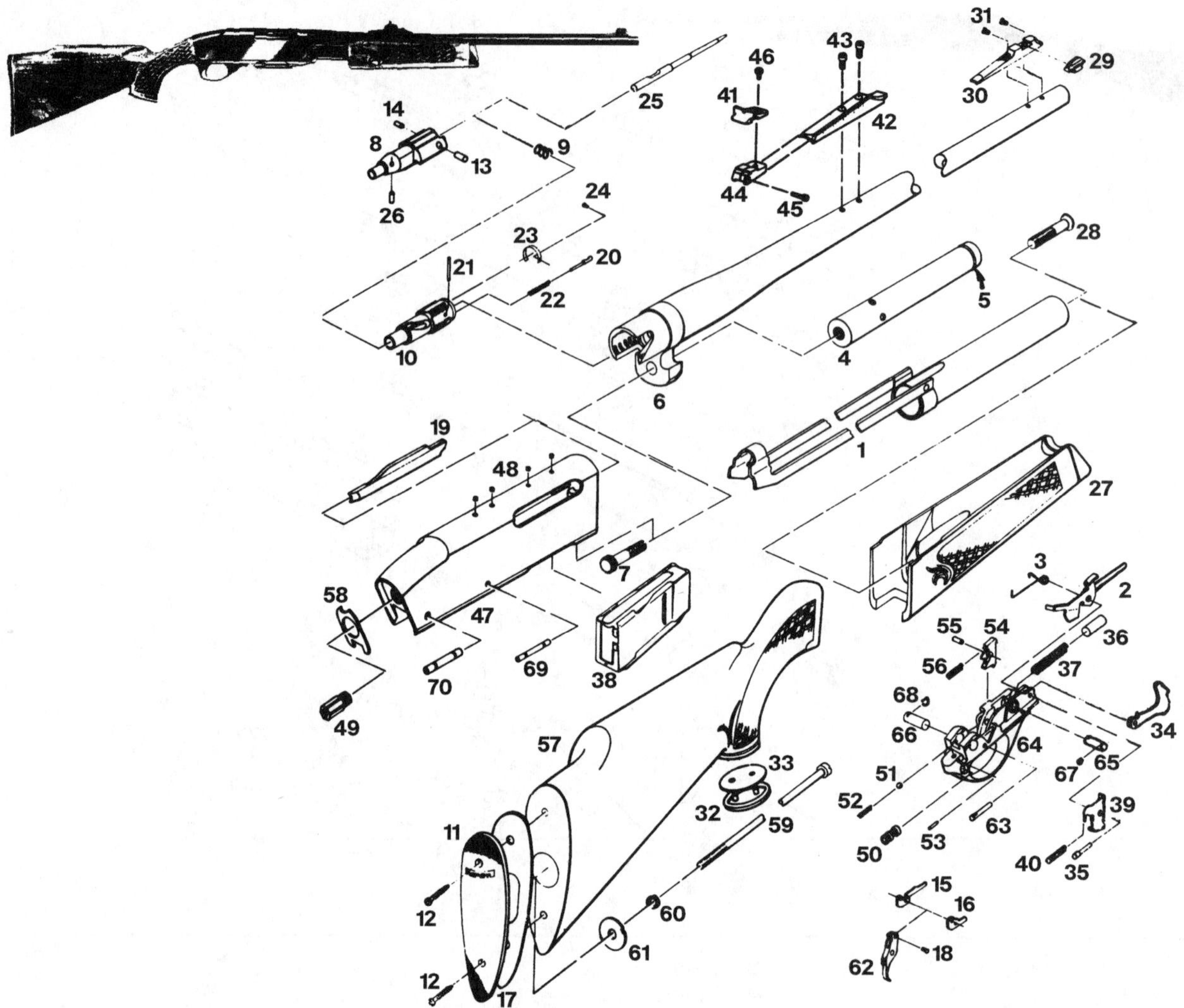

1	Action Bar Assembly
2	Action Bar Lock
3	Action Bar Lock Spring
4	Action Tube Assembly
5	Action Tube Ring
6	Barrel Assembly
7	Barrel Bracket Bolt
8	Bolt Carrier
9	Bolt Carrier Spring
10	Breechbolt Assembly
11	Buttplate
12	Buttplate Screws
13	Cam Pin (Large)
14	Cam Pin (Small)
15	Connector, Left
16	Connector, Right
17	Buttplate Spacer
18	Connector Pin
19	Ejection Port Cover
20	Ejector
21	Ejector Retaining Pin
22	Ejector Spring
23	Extractor
24	Extractor Rivet
25	Firing Pin
26	Firing Pin Retaining Pin
27	Forend Assembly
28	Forend Cap Screw
29	Front Sight
30	Front Sight Ramp
31	Front Sight Ramp Screws
32	Grip Cap
33	Grip Cap Spacer
34	Hammer
35	Hammer Pin
36	Hammer Plunger
37	Hammer Spring
38	Magazine Assembly
39	Magazine Latch
40	Magazine Latch Spring
41	Rear Sight Aperture
42	Rear Sight Base
43	Rear Sight Base Screws
44	Rear Sight Slide
45	Elevation Screw
46	Windage Screw
47	Receiver Assembly
48	Receiver Plug Screws
49	Receiver Stud
50	Safety
51	Safety Detent Ball
52	Safety Spring
53	Safety Spring Retaining Pin
54	Sear
55	Sear Pin
56	Sear Spring
57	Stock
58	Stock Bearing Plate
59	Stock Bolt
60	Stock Bolt Lock Washer
61	Stock Bolt Washer
62	Trigger
63	Trigger Pin
64	Trigger Plate
65	Trigger Plate Pin Bushing, Front
66	Trigger Plate Pin Bushing, Rear
67	Trigger Plate Pin Detent Spring, Front
68	Trigger Plate Pin Detent Spring, Rear
69	Trigger Plate Pin, Front
70	Trigger Plate Pin, Rear

Model 7600 Slide-Action Rifle

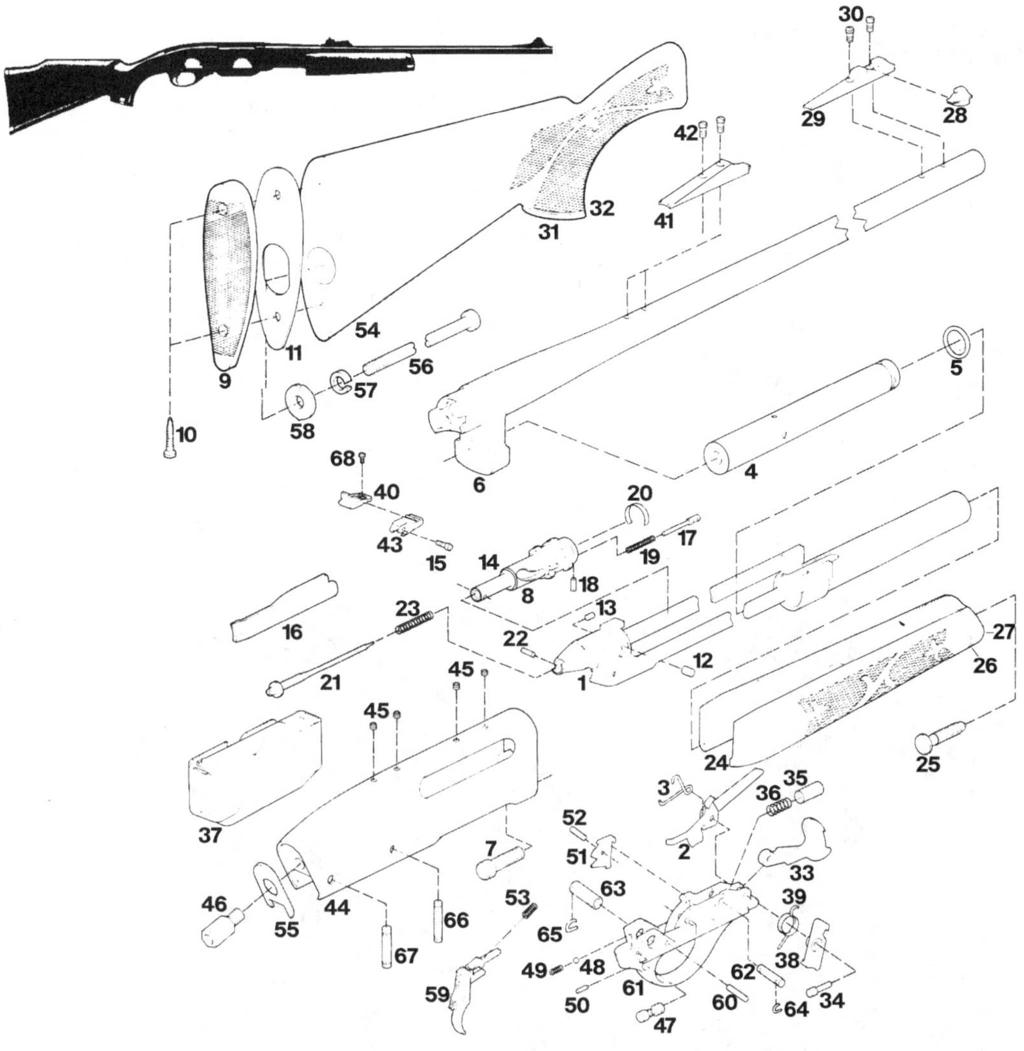

1	Action Bar Assembly	25	Forend Screw	49	Safety Switch Spring
2	Action Bar Lock	26	Forend Spacer	50	Safety Switch Spring Retaining Pin
3	Action Bar Lock Spring	27	Forend Tip	51	Sear
4	Action Tube Assembly	28	Front Sight	52	Sear Pin
5	Action Tube Ring	29	Front Sight Ramp	53	Sear Spring
6	Barrel Assembly	30	Front Sight Screws	54	Stock
7	Barrel Extension Bolt	31	Grip Cap	55	Stock Bearing Plate
8	Breechbolt	32	Grip Cap Spacer	56	Stock Bolt
9	Buttplate	33	Hammer	57	Stock Bolt Lock Washer
10	Buttplate Screws	34	Hammer Pin	58	Stock Bolt Washer
11	Buttplate Spacer	35	Hammer Plunger	59	Trigger Assembly
12	Cam Pin (Large)	36	Hammer Spring	60	Trigger Pin
13	Cam Pin (Small)	37	Magazine Assembly	61	Trigger Plate
14	Curve Spring Washer	38	Magazine Latch	62	Trigger Plate Pin Bushing, Front
15	Elevation Screw	39	Magazine Latch Spring	63	Trigger Plate Pin Bushing, Rear
16	Ejection Port Cover	40	Rear Sight Aperture	64	Trigger Plate Pin Detent Spring, Front
17	Ejector	41	Rear Sight Base	65	Trigger Plate Pin Detent Spring, Rear
18	Ejector Retaining Pin	42	Rear Sight Base Screws	66	Trigger Plate Pin, Front
19	Ejector Spring	43	Rear Sight Slide	67	Trigger Plate Pin, Rear
20	Extractor	44	Receiver	68	Windage Screw
21	Firing Pin	45	Receiver Plug Screws		
22	Firing Pin Retaining Pin	46	Receiver Stud		
23	Firing Pin Retractor Spring	47	Safety Switch		
24	Forend Assembly	48	Safety Switch Detent Ball		

Model 788 Bolt-Action Rifle

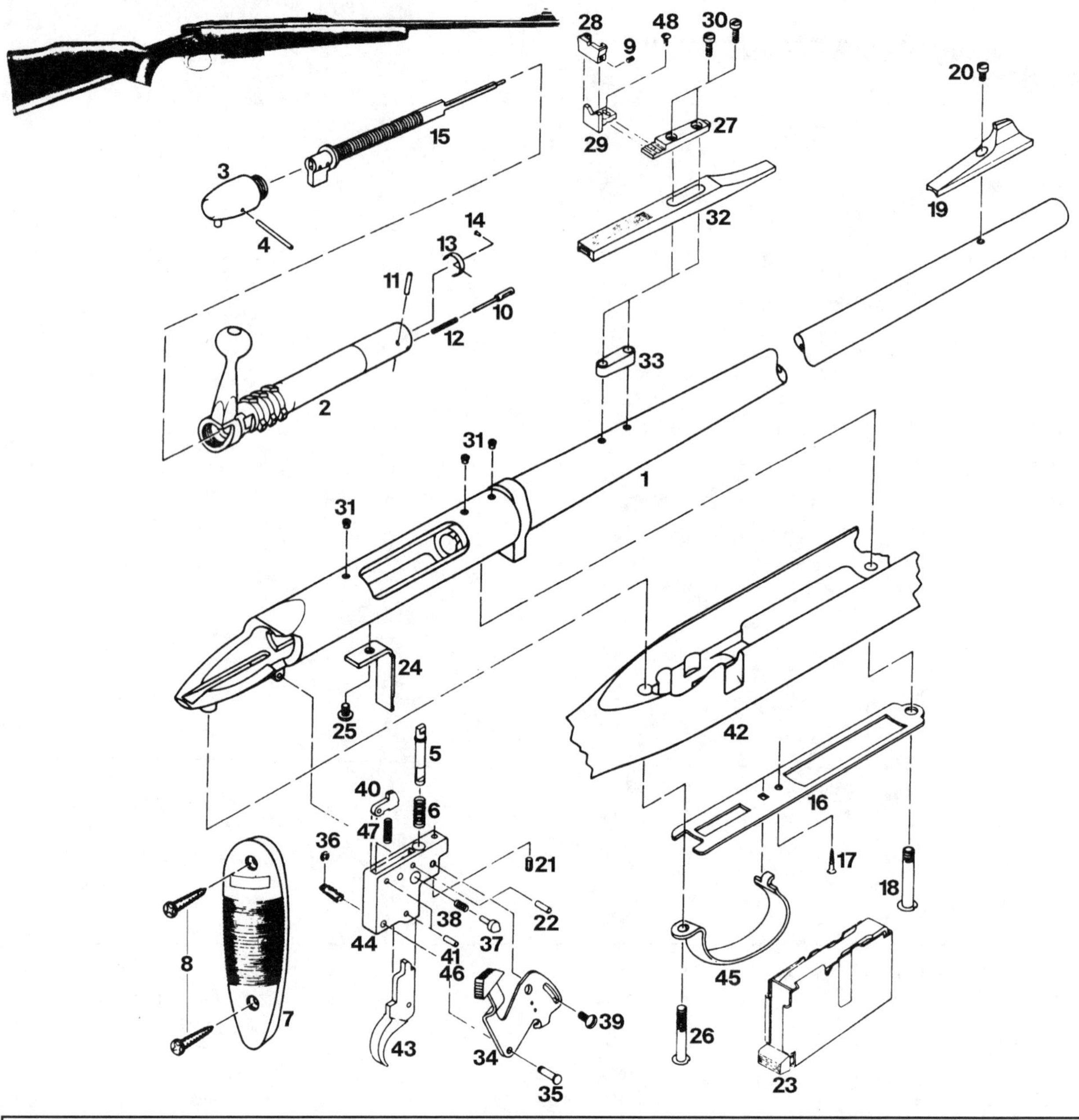

1	Barrel Assembly	**18**	Front Guard Screw	**35**	Safety Pivot Pin
2	Bolt Assembly	**19**	Front Sight	**36**	Safety Pivot Pin Retaining Washer
3	Bolt Plug	**20**	Front Sight Screw	**37**	Safety Plunger
4	Bolt Plug Pin	**21**	Housing Lock Screw	**38**	Safety Plunger Spring
5	Bolt Stop	**22**	Housing Pin	**39**	Safety Retaining Screw
6	Bolt Stop Spring	**23**	Magazine Assembly	**40**	Sear
7	Buttplate	**24**	Magazine Guide Bar	**41**	Sear Pin
8	Buttplate Screws	**25**	Magazine Guide Bar Screw	**42**	Stock Assembly
9	Elevation Screw	**26**	Rear Guard Screw	**43**	Trigger
10	Ejector	**27**	Rear Sight Base	**44**	Trigger Housing
11	Ejector Pin	**28**	Rear Sight Aperture	**45**	Trigger Guard
12	Ejector Spring	**29**	Rear Sight Leaf	**46**	Trigger Pin
13	Extractor	**30**	Rear Sight Screws	**47**	Trigger Spring
14	Extractor Rivet	**31**	Receiver Plug Screws	**48**	Windage Screw
15	Firing Pin Assembly	**32**	Rib (Rear Sight)		
16	Floorplate	**33**	Rib Spacer (Rear Sight)		
17	Floorplate Screw	**34**	Safety Assembly		

Model 8 and 81 Autoloading Rifle

Courtesy of James M. Triggs

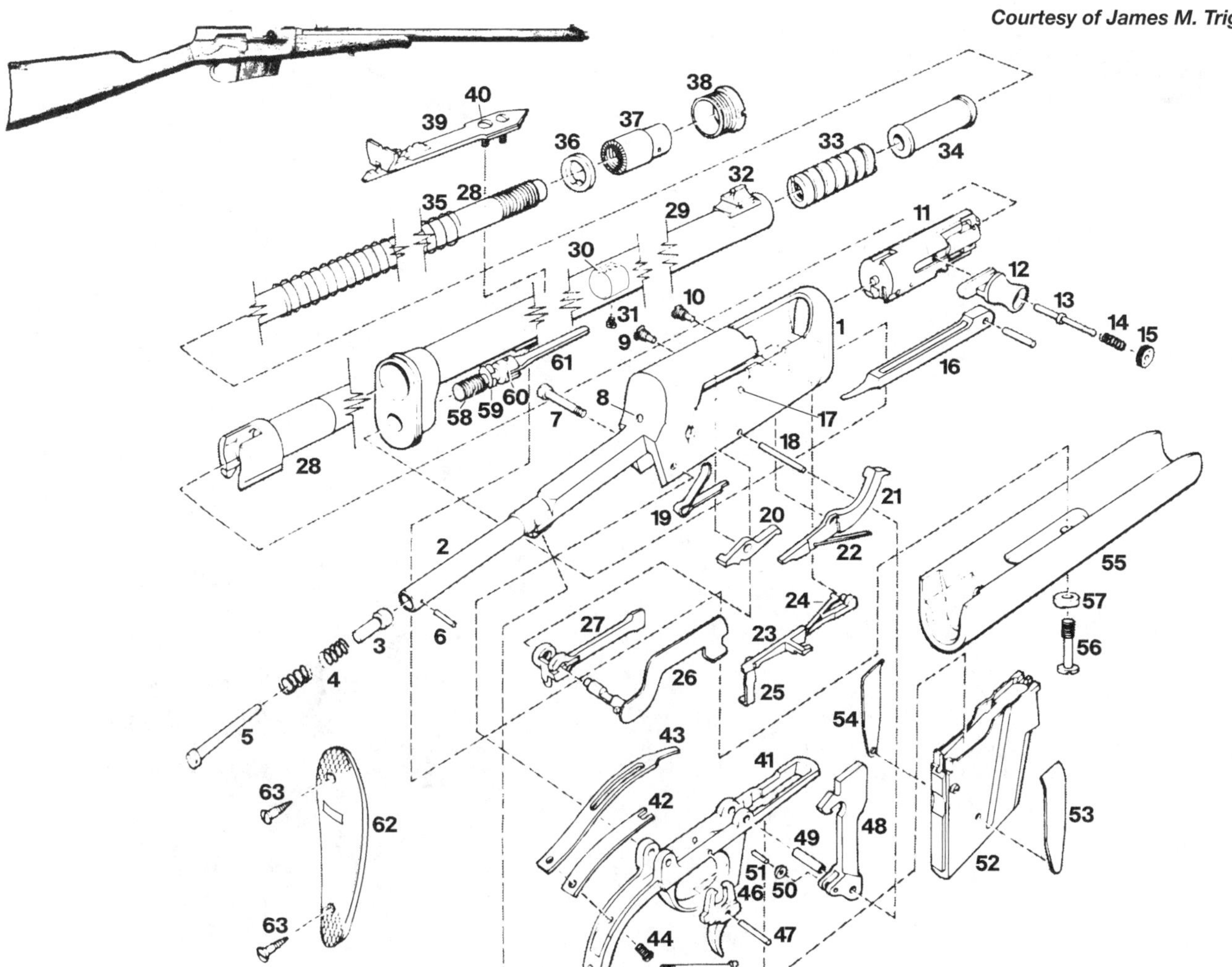

1	Receiver
2	Action Spring Tube
3	Action Spring Follower
4	Action Spring
5	Action Spring Plug
6	Action Spring Plug Pin
7	Trigger Plate Screw
8	Peep Sight Plug Screw
9	Bolt Carrier Latch Screw
10	Barrel Lock Screw
11	Bolt Assembly
12	Operating Handle
13	Operating Handle Plunger
14	Operating Handle Plunger Spring
15	Operating Handle Bushing
16	Link
17	Safety Detent Ball
18	Hammer Pin
19	Bolt Carrier Latch Spring
20	Bolt Carrier Latch
21	Barrel Lock
22	Barrel Lock Spring
23	Magazine Indicator
24	Magazine Indicator Spring
25	Magazine Indicator Thumb-Piece
26	Safety
27	Safety Rocker
28	Barrel
29	Barrel Jacket
30	Barrel Jacket Plug
31	Barrel Jacket Plug Screw
32	Front Sight Assembly
33	Buffer Spring
34	Recoil Spring Case
35	Recoil Spring
36	Barrel Nut Washer
37	Barrel Nut
38	Barrel Jacket Bushing
39	Bar Sight Assembly
40	Bar Sight Mounting Screws
41	Trigger Plate
42	Trigger Spring
43	Mainspring
44	Mainspring Screw
45	Tang Screw
46	Trigger
47	Trigger Pin
48	Hammer
49	Hammer Bushing
50	Hammer Roll
51	Hammer Roll Pin
52	Magazine Assembly
53	Magazine Side Spring, Right
54	Magazine Side Spring, Left
55	Forend
56	Forend Screw
57	Forend Escutcheon
58	Takedown Screw
59	Takedown Screw Washers
60	Takedown Lever Pin
61	Takedown Lever
62	Buttplate
63	Buttplate Screws

Parts Not Shown

Buttstock

Safety Rocker Stop Screw

Model 870 Slide-Action Shotgun

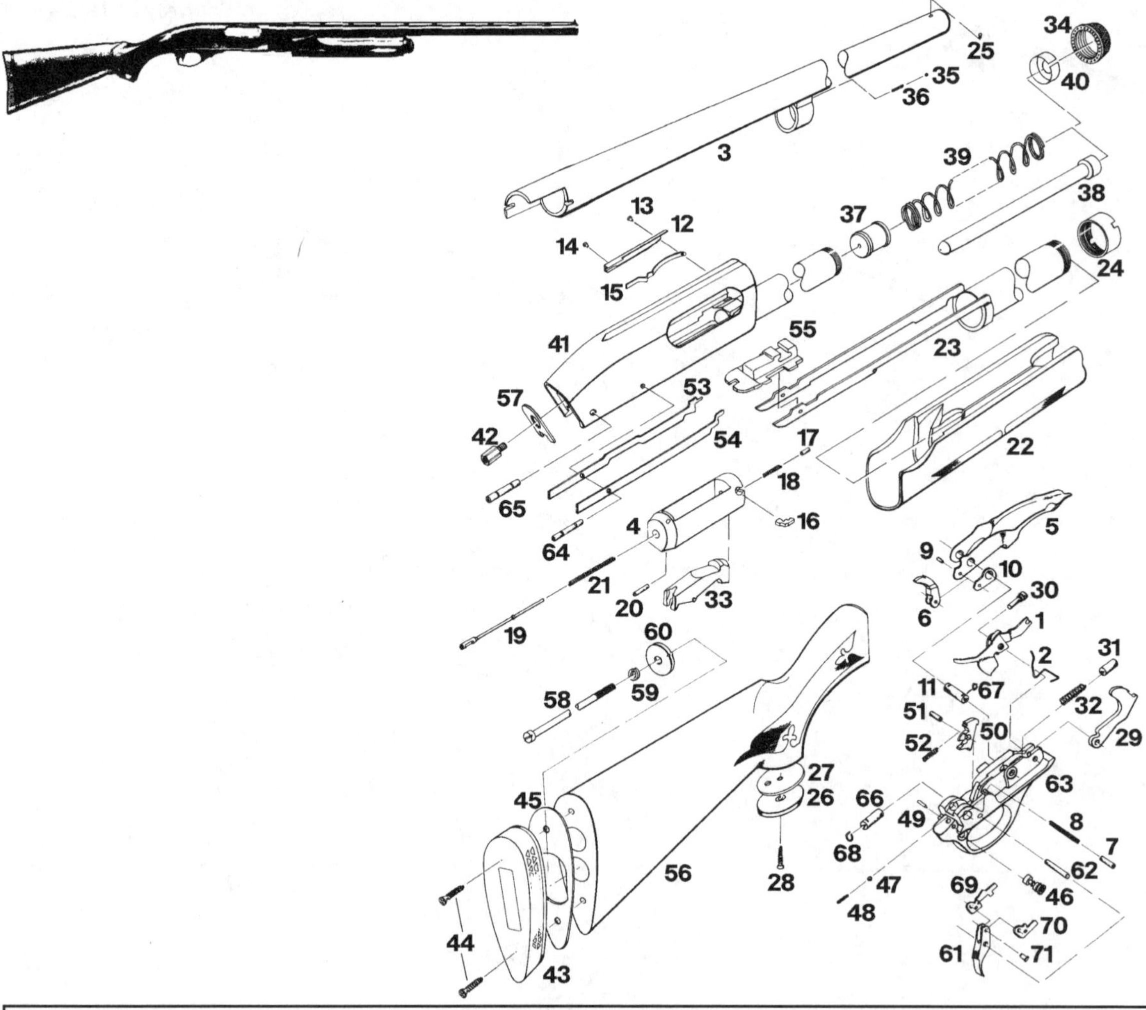

1	Action Bar Lock
2	Action Bar Lock Spring
3	Barrel Assembly
4	Breechbolt
5	Carrier
6	Carrier Dog
7	Carrier Dog Follower
8	Carrier Dog Follower Spring
9	Carrier Dog Pin
10	Carrier Dog Washer
11	Carrier Pivot Tube
12	Ejector
13	Ejector Rivet, Front
14	Ejector Rivet, Rear
15	Ejector Spring
16	Extractor
17	Extractor Plunger
18	Extractor Spring
19	Firing Pin
20	Firing Pin Retaining Pin
21	Firing Pin Retractor Spring
22	Forend Wood
23	Forend Tube Assembly
24	Forend Tube Nut
25	Front Sight
26	Grip Cap
27	Grip Cap Spacer
28	Grip Cap Screw
29	Hammer
30	Hammer Pin
31	Hammer Plunger
32	Hammer Spring
33	Locking Block Assembly
34	Magazine Cap
35	Magazine Cap Detent
36	Magazine Cap Detent Spring
37	Magazine Follower
38	Magazine Plug
39	Magazine Spring
40	Magazine Spring Retainer
41	Receiver Assembly
42	Receiver Stud
43	Recoil Pad
44	Recoil Pad Screws
45	Recoil Pad Spacer
46	Safety Switch
47	Safety Switch Detent Ball
48	Safety Switch Spring
49	Safety Switch Spring Retaining Pin
50	Sear
51	Sear Pin
52	Sear Spring
53	Shell Latch, Left
54	Shell Latch, Right
55	Slide Assembly
56	Stock Assembly
57	Stock Bearing Plate
58	Stock Bolt
59	Stock Bolt Lock Washer
60	Stock Bolt Washer
61	Trigger Assembly
62	Trigger Pin
63	Trigger Plate
64	Trigger Plate Pin, Front
65	Trigger Plate Pin, Rear
66	Trigger Plate Pin Bushing
67	Trigger Plate Pin Detent Spring, Front
68	Trigger Plate Pin Detent Spring, Rear
69	Connector, Left
70	Connector, Right
71	Connector Pin

Parts Not Shown

Hammer Pin Washer

Locking Block Retainer

Model 878 Autoloading Shotgun

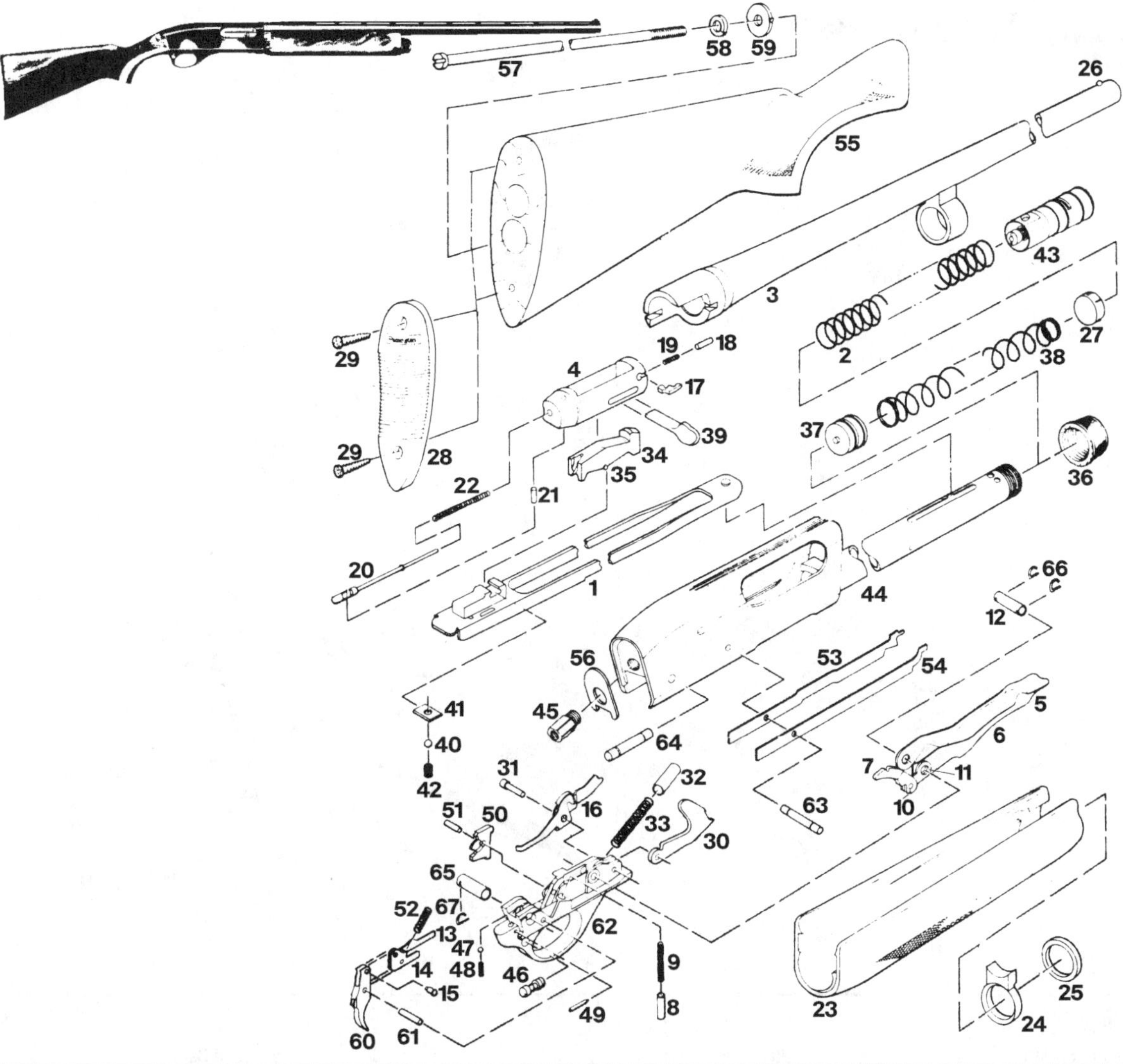

1	Action Bar Lock	**24**	Forend Ring	**47**	Safety Detent Ball
2	Action Spring	**25**	Forend Ring Washer	**48**	Safety Spring
3	Barrel	**26**	Front Sight	**49**	Safety Spring Retaining Pin
4	Breechbolt	**27**	Action Spring Stop	**50**	Sear
5	Carrier Assembly	**28**	Buttplate	**51**	Sear Pin
6	Carrier	**29**	Buttplate Screws	**52**	Sear Spring
7	Carrier Dog	**30**	Hammer	**53**	Shell Latch, Left
8	Carrier Dog Follower	**31**	Hammer Pin	**54**	Shell Latch, Right
9	Carrier Dog Follower Spring	**32**	Hammer Plunger	**55**	Stock
10	Carrier Dog Pin	**33**	Hammer Spring	**56**	Stock Bearing Plate
11	Carrier Dog Washer	**34**	Locking Block Assembly	**57**	Stock Bolt
12	Carrier Pivot Tube	**35**	Locking Block Stud	**58**	Stock Bolt Lock Washer
13	Connector, Left	**36**	Magazine Cap	**59**	Stock Bolt Washer
14	Connector, Right	**37**	Magazine Follower	**60**	Trigger
15	Connector Pin	**38**	Magazine Spring	**61**	Trigger Pin
16	Disconnector	**39**	Operating Handle	**62**	Trigger Plate
17	Extractor	**40**	Operating Handle Plunger	**63**	Trigger Plate Pin, Front
18	Extractor Plunger	**41**	Operating Handle Plunger Retainer	**64**	Trigger Plate Pin, Rear
19	Extractor Spring	**42**	Operating Handle Spring	**65**	Trigger Plate Pin Bushing
20	Firing Pin	**43**	Piston Assembly	**66**	Trigger Plate Pin Detent Springs, Front
21	Firing Pin Retaining Pin	**44**	Receiver		
22	Firing Pin Retractor Spring	**45**	Receiver Stud	**67**	Trigger Plate Pin Detent Springs, Rear
23	Forend	**46**	Safety		

Model Four Autoloading Rifle

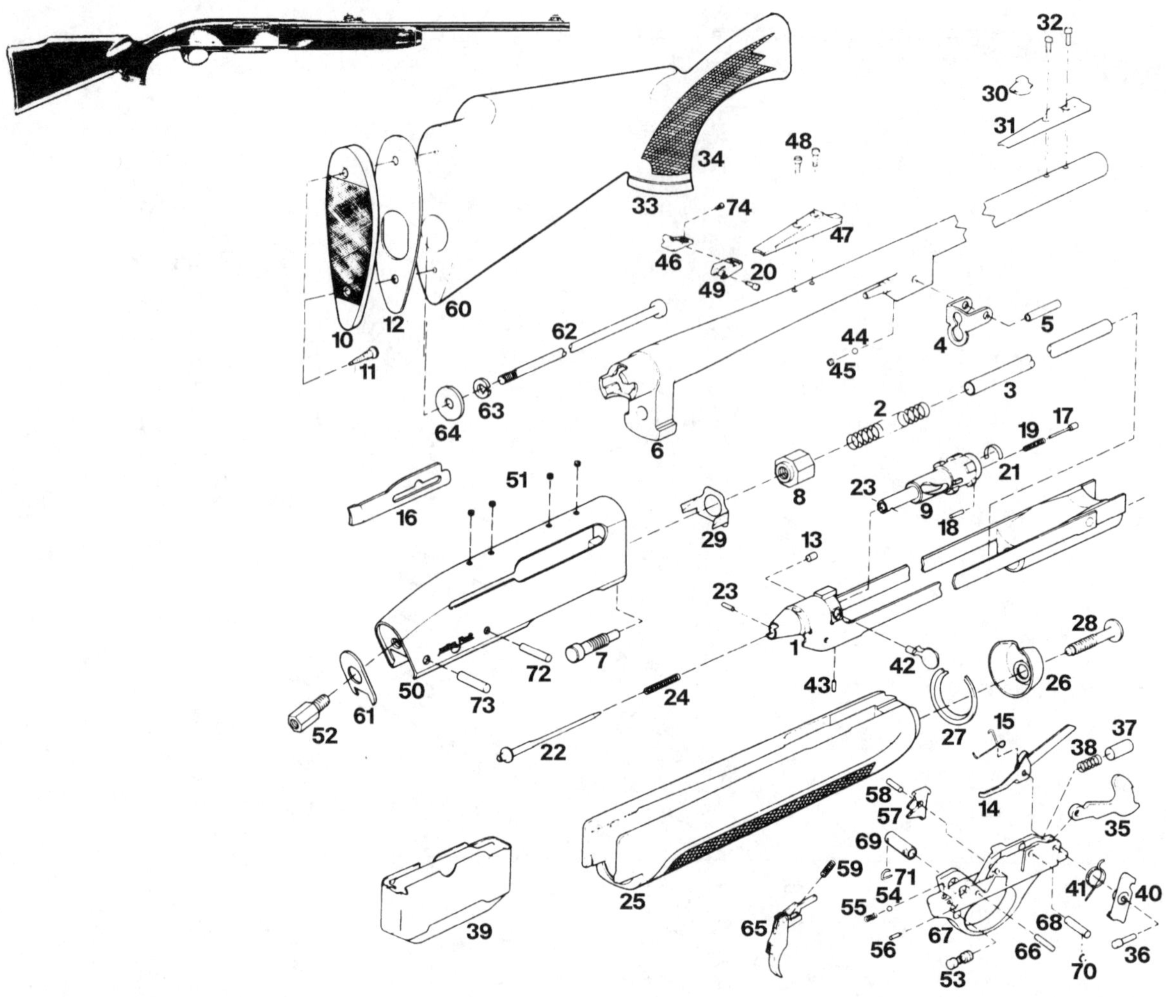

1	Action Bar Assembly	**27**	Forend Cap Spacer	**53**	Safety
2	Action Spring	**28**	Forend Screw	**54**	Safety Detent Ball
3	Action Tube	**29**	Forend Spring	**55**	Safety Spring
4	Action Tube Support	**30**	Front Sight	**56**	Safety Spring Retaining Pin
5	Action Tube Support Pin	**31**	Front Sight Ramp	**57**	Sear
6	Barrel Assembly	**32**	Front Sight Ramp Screws	**58**	Sear Pin
7	Barrel Extension Bolt	**33**	Grip Cap	**59**	Sear Spring
8	Barrel Takedown Nut	**34**	Grip Cap Spacer	**60**	Stock Assembly
9	Breechbolt	**35**	Hammer	**61**	Stock Bearing Plate
10	Buttplate	**36**	Hammer Pin	**62**	Stock Bolt
11	Buttplate Screw	**37**	Hammer Plunger	**63**	Stock Bolt Lock Washer
12	Buttplate Spacer	**38**	Hammer Spring	**64**	Stock Bolt Washer
13	Cam Pin	**39**	Magazine Assembly	**65**	Trigger Assembly
14	Disconnector	**40**	Magazine Latch	**66**	Trigger Pin
15	Disconnector Spring	**41**	Magazine Latch Spring	**67**	Trigger Plate
16	Ejection Port Cover	**42**	Operating Handle	**68**	Trigger Plate Pin Bushing, Front
17	Ejector	**43**	Operating Handle Retaining Pin	**69**	Trigger Plate Bushing, Rear
18	Ejector Retaining Pin	**44**	Orifice Ball	**70**	Trigger Plate Pin Detent Spring, Front
19	Ejector Spring	**45**	Orifice Screw	**71**	Trigger Plate Pin Detent Spring, Rear
20	Elevation Screw	**46**	Rear Sight Aperture	**72**	Trigger Plate Pin, Front
21	Extractor	**47**	Rear Sight Base	**73**	Trigger Plate Pin, Rear
22	Firing Pin	**48**	Rear Sight Base Screws	**74**	Windage Screw
23	Firing Pin Retaining Pins	**49**	Rear Sight Slides		
24	Firing Pin Retracting Pin	**50**	Receiver		
25	Forend Assembly	**51**	Receiver Plug Screws		
26	Forend Cap	**52**	Receiver Stud		

Model Seven Bolt-Action Rifle

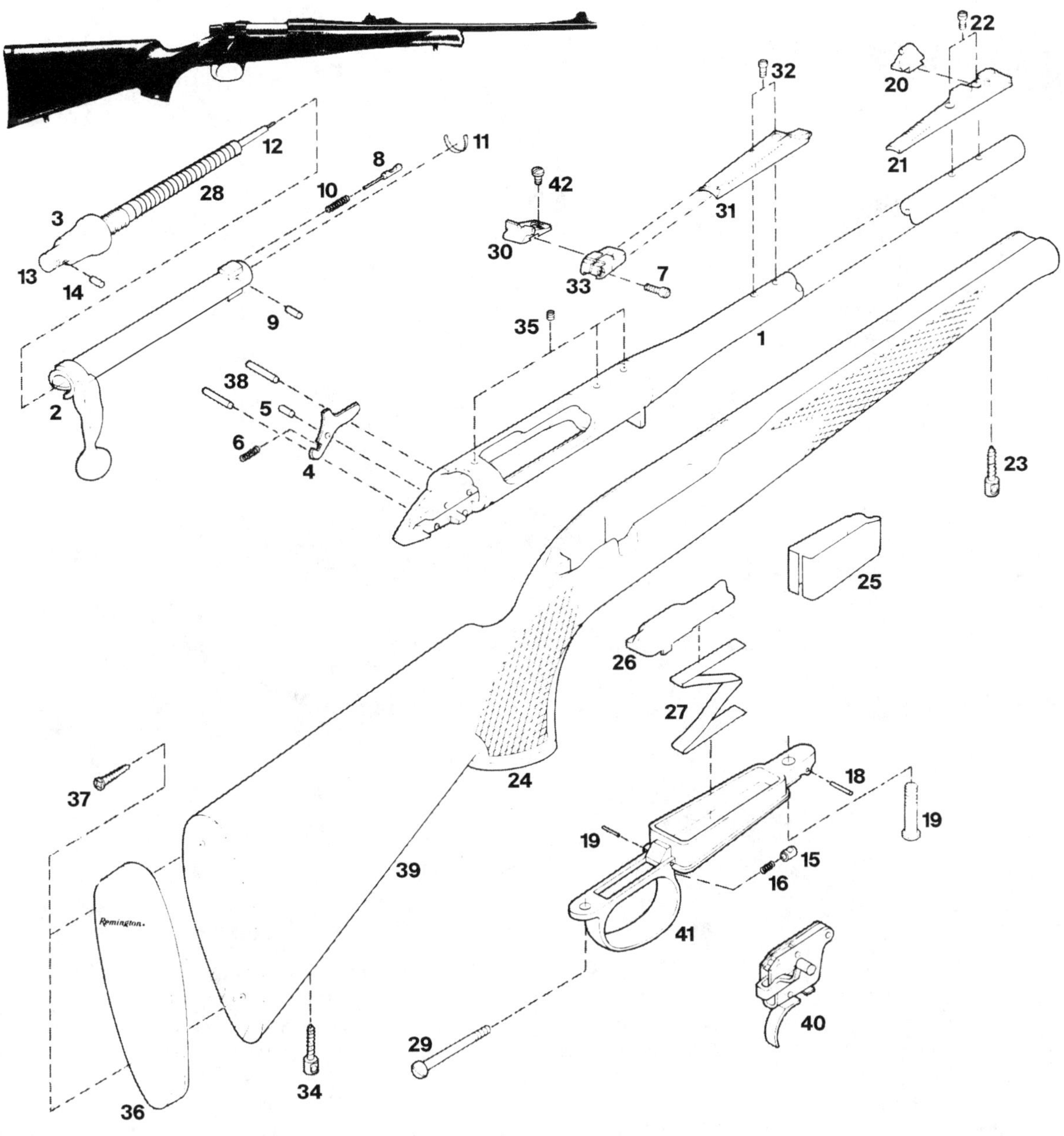

1	Barrel Assembly	**17**	Floorplate Latch Pin	**33**	Rear Sight Slide
2	Bolt Assembly	**18**	Floorplate Pivot Pin	**34**	Rear Swivel Screw
3	Bolt Plug	**19**	Front Guard Screw	**35**	Receiver Plug Screw
4	Bolt Stop	**20**	Front Sight	**36**	Recoil Pad
5	Bolt Stop Pin	**21**	Front Sight Ramp	**37**	Recoil Pad Screw
6	Bolt Stop Spring	**22**	Front Sight Ramp Screw	**38**	Sear Pins
7	Elevation Screw	**23**	Front Swivel Screw	**39**	Stock Assembly
8	Ejector	**24**	Grip Cap	**40**	Trigger Assembly
9	Ejector Pin	**25**	Magazine	**41**	Trigger Guard Assembly
10	Ejector Spring	**26**	Magazine Follower	**42**	Windage Screw
11	Extractor	**27**	Magazine Spring	**Parts Not Shown**	
12	Firing Pin	**28**	Mainspring		Grip Cap Insert
13	Firing Pin Assembly	**29**	Rear Guard Screw		Grip Cap Screw
14	Firing Pin Cross Pin	**30**	Rear Sight Aperture		Magazine Spacer
15	Floorplate Latch	**31**	Rear Sight Base		
16	Floorplate Latch Spring	**32**	Rear Sight Base Screw		

Model Six Autoloading Rifle

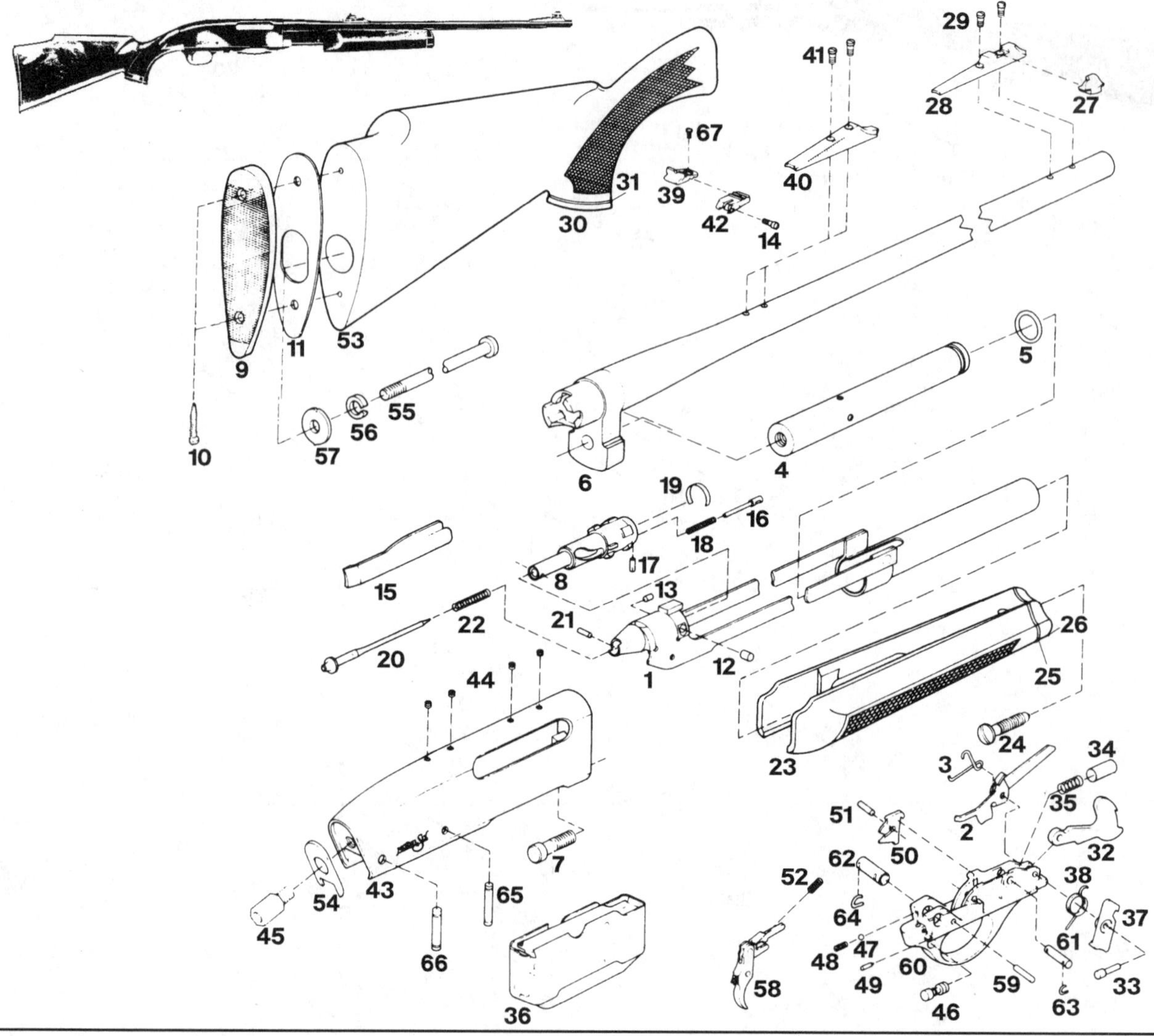

1	Action Bar Assembly
2	Action Bar Lock
3	Action Bar Lock Spring
4	Action Tube Assembly
5	Action Tube Ring
6	Barrel Assembly
7	Barrel Extension Bolt
8	Breechbolt
9	Buttplate
10	Buttplate Screws
11	Buttplate Spacer
12	Cam Pin, Large
13	Cam Pin, Small
14	Elevation Screw
15	Ejection Port Cover
16	Ejector
17	Ejector Retaining Pin
18	Ejector Spring
19	Extractor
20	Firing Pin
21	Firing Pin Retaining Pin
22	Firing Pin Retractor Spring
23	Forend Assembly
24	Forend Screw
25	Forend Spacer
26	Forend Tip
27	Front Sight
28	Front Sight Ramp
29	Front Sight Screws
30	Grip Cap
31	Grip Cap Spacer
32	Hammer
33	Hammer Pin
34	Hammer Plunger
35	Hammer Spring
36	Magazine Assembly
37	Magazine Latch
38	Magazine Latch Spring
39	Rear Sight Aperture
40	Rear Sight Base
41	Rear Sight Base Screws
42	Rear Sight Slide
43	Receiver
44	Receiver Plug Screws
45	Receiver Stud
46	Safety
47	Safety Detent Ball
48	Safety Spring
49	Safety Spring Retaining Pin
50	Sear
51	Sear Pin
52	Sear Spring
53	Stock
54	Stock Bearing Plate
55	Stock Bolt
56	Stock Bolt Lock Washer
57	Stock Bolt Washer
58	Trigger Assembly
59	Trigger Pin
60	Trigger Plate
61	Trigger Plate Pin Bushing, Front
62	Trigger Plate Pin Bushing, Rear
63	Trigger Plate Pin Detent Spring, Front
64	Trigger Plate Pin Detent Spring, Rear
65	Trigger Assembly Pin, Front
66	Trigger Assembly Pin, Rear
67	Windage Screw

Nylon 66 Autoloading Rifle

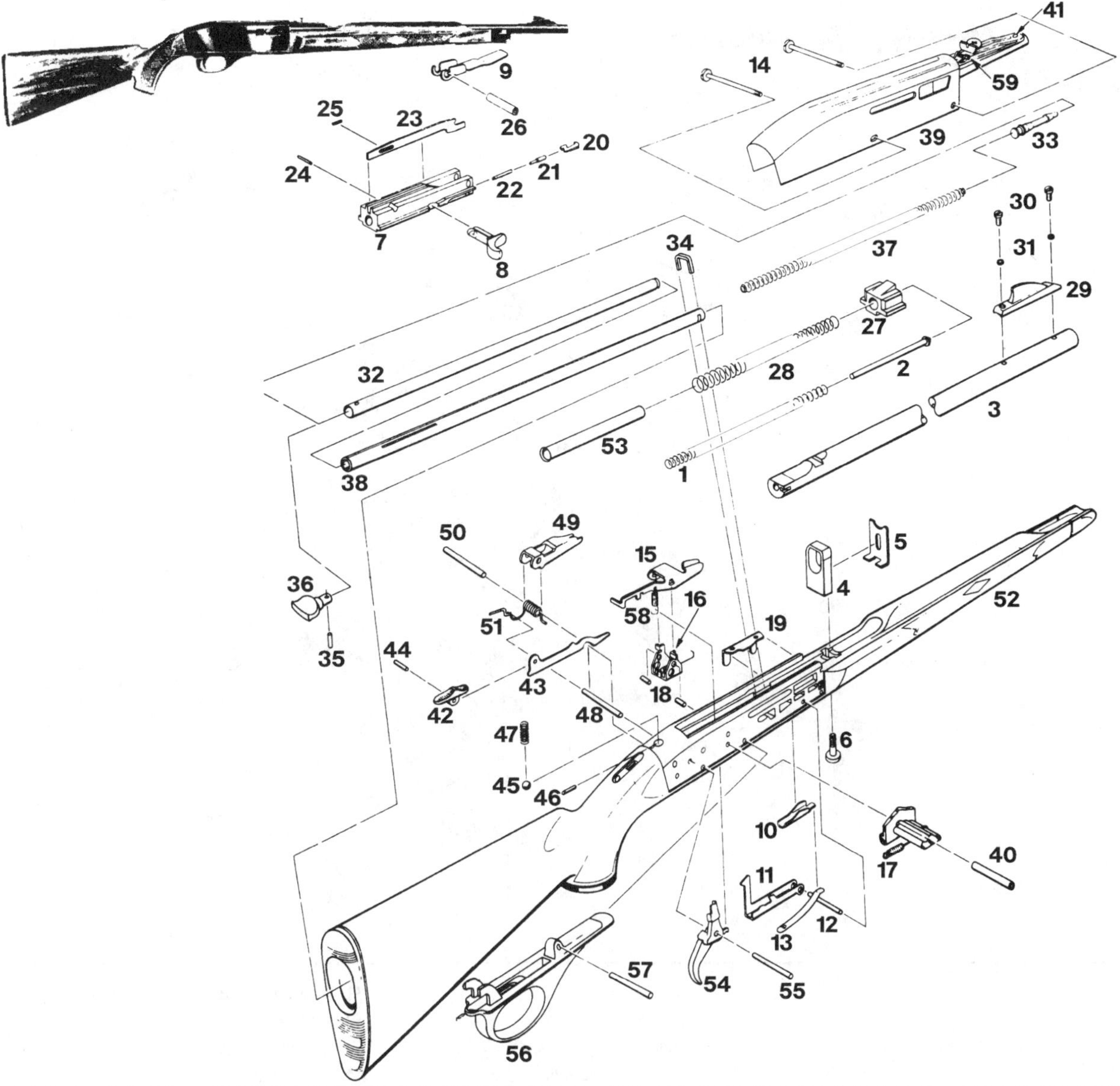

1	Action Spring	**21**	Extractor Plunger	**41**	Rear Sight Rivet
2	Action Spring Plunger	**22**	Extractor Spring	**42**	Safety
3	Barrel	**23**	Firing Pin	**43**	Safety-Lever
4	Barrel Bracket	**24**	Firing Pin Retaining Pin	**44**	Safety-Lever Pin
5	Barrel Support	**25**	Firing Pin Retractor Spring	**45**	Safety Detent Ball
6	Barrel Lock Screw	**26**	Firing Pin Stop Pin	**46**	Safety Detent Retaining Pin
7	Bolt	**27**	Firing Pin Striker	**47**	Safety Detent Spring
8	Bolt Handle	**28**	Firing Pin Striker Spring	**48**	Safety-Lever Cam Pin
9	Cartridge Feed Guide	**29**	Front Sight	**49**	Sear
10	Cartridge Feed Insert	**30**	Front Sight Screws	**50**	Sear Assembly Pin
11	Cartridge Stop	**31**	Front Sight Washers	**51**	Sear Spring
12	Cartridge Stop Pin	**32**	Inner Magazine Tube	**52**	Stock Assembly
13	Cartridge Stop Spring	**33**	Magazine Follower	**53**	Striker Spring Sleeve
14	Cover Screws	**34**	Magazine Lock	**54**	Trigger Complete
15	Disconnector	**35**	Magazine Pin	**55**	Trigger Assembly Pin
16	Disconnector Pivot	**36**	Magazine Plug	**56**	Trigger Guard
17	Disconnector Pivot Spring	**37**	Magazine Spring	**57**	Trigger Guard Assembly Pin
18	Disconnector Pivot Pins	**38**	Outer Magazine Tube	**58**	Trigger Spring
19	Ejector	**39**	Receiver Cover Assembly	**59**	Windage Screw
20	Extractor	**40**	Rear Cover Screw Bushing		

Nylon 76 Lever-Action Rifle

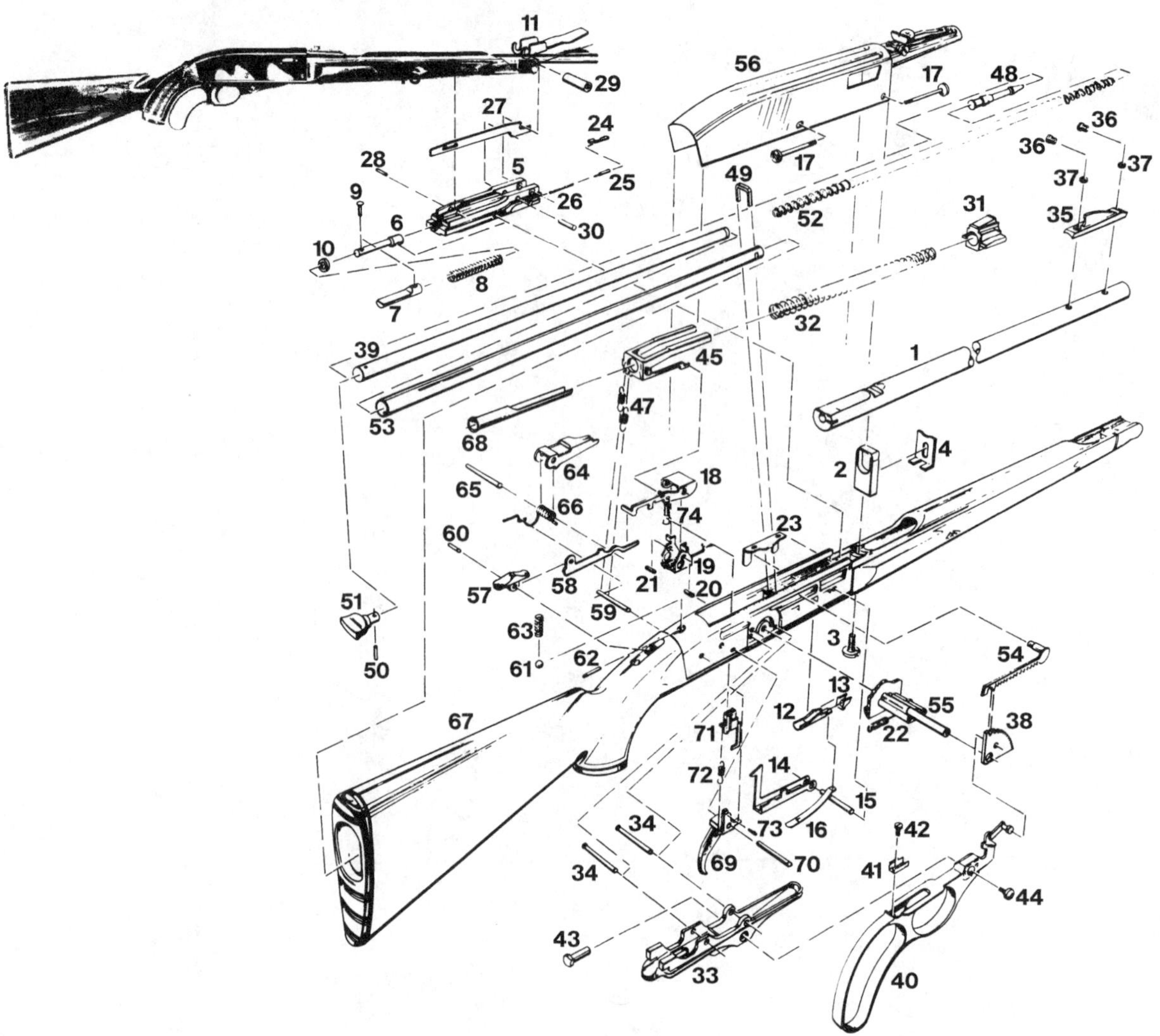

1	Barrel
2	Barrel Bracket
3	Barrel Lock Screw
4	Barrel Support
5	Bolt
6	Bolt Push Rod
7	Bolt Push Rod Extension
8	Bolt Push Rod Spring
9	Bolt Push Rod Stud
10	Bolt Push Rod Washer
11	Cartridge Feed Guide
12	Cartridge Feed Insert
13	Cartridge Feed Insert Spring
14	Cartridge Stop
15	Cartridge Stop Pin
16	Cartridge Stop Spring
17	Cover Screws
18	Disconnector
19	Disconnector Pivot
20	Disconnector Pivot Pin, Right
21	Disconnector Pivot Pin, Left
22	Disconnector Pivot Spring
23	Ejector
24	Extractor
25	Extractor Plunger
26	Extractor Spring
27	Firing Pin
28	Firing Pin Retaining Pin
29	Firing Pin Stop Pin, Front
30	Firing Pin Stop Pin, Rear
31	Firing Pin Striker
32	Firing Pin Striker Spring
33	Floorplate
34	Floorplate Retaining Pins
35	Front Sight
36	Front Sight Screws
37	Front Sight Washers
38	Gear
39	Inner Magazine Tube
40	Lever Assembly
41	Lever Latch
42	Lever Latch Screw
43	Lever Pivot Bushing
44	Lever Pivot Screw
45	Locking Bar
46	Locking Bar Release Lever
47	Locking Bar Springs
48	Magazine Follower
49	Magazine Lock
50	Magazine Pin
51	Magazine Plug
52	Magazine Spring
53	Outer Magazine Tube
54	Rack
55	Rear Cover Screw Bushing
56	Receiver Cover Assembly
57	Safety
58	Safety-Lever
59	Safety-Lever Cam Pin
60	Safety-Lever Pin
61	Safety Detent Ball
62	Safety Detent Retaining Pin
63	Safety Detent Spring
64	Sear
65	Sear Assembly Pin
66	Sear Spring
67	Stock Assembly
68	Striker Spring Sleeve
69	Trigger
70	Trigger Assembly Pin
71	Trigger Cap
72	Trigger Cap Spring
73	Trigger Cap Retaining Pin
74	Trigger Spring

Nylon 77 Autoloading Rifle

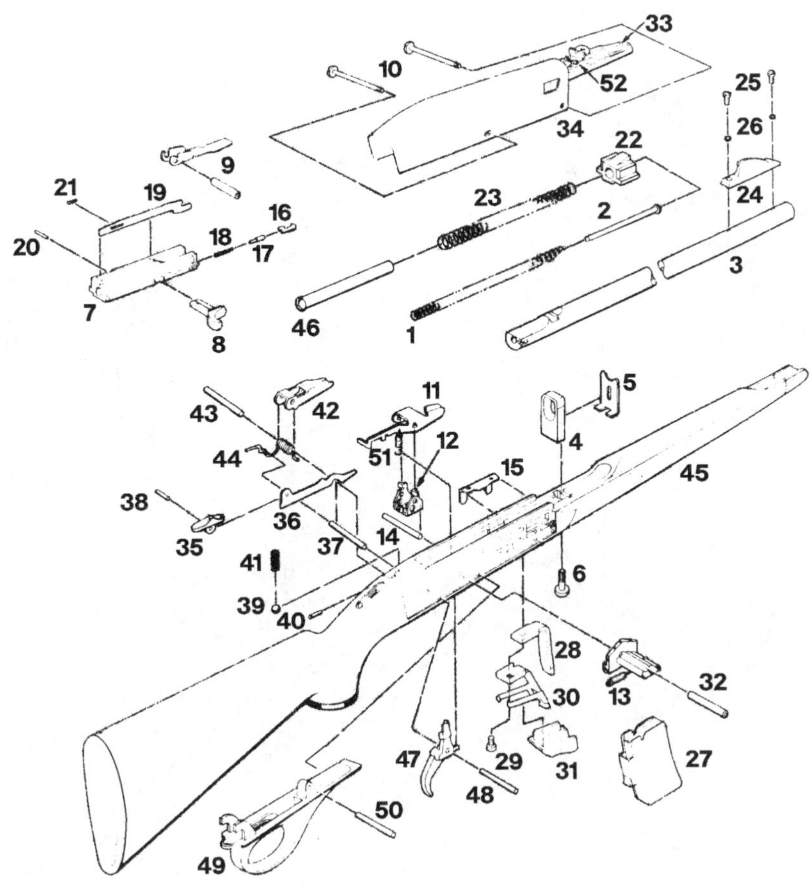

1	Action Spring	27	Magazine Assembly
2	Action Spring Plunger	28	Magazine Guide
3	Barrel	29	Magazine Guide Screw
4	Barrel Bracket	30	Magazine Latch
5	Barrel Support	31	Magazine Latch Thumb-Piece
6	Barrel Lock Screw	32	Rear Cover Screw Bushing
7	Bolt Sub-Assembly	33	Rear Sight Rivet
8	Bolt Handle	34	Receiver Cover
9	Cartridge Feed Guide	35	Safety
10	Cover Screws	36	Safety-Lever
11	Disconnector	37	Safety-Lever Cam Pin
12	Disconnector Pivot	38	Safety-Lever Pin
13	Disconnector Pivot Spring	39	Safety Detent Ball
14	Disconnector Pivot Pin	40	Safety Detent Retaining Pin
15	Ejector	41	Safety Detent Spring
16	Extractor	42	Sear
17	Extractor Plunger	43	Sear Assembly Pin
18	Extractor Spring	44	Sear Spring
19	Firing Pin	45	Stock Assembly
20	Firing Pin Retaining Pin	46	Striker Spring Sleeve
21	Firing Pin Retractor Spring	47	Trigger
22	Firing Pin Striker	48	Trigger Assembly Pin
23	Firing Pin Striker Spring	49	Trigger Guard
24	Front Sight	50	Trigger Guard Assembly Pin
25	Front Sight Screws	51	Trigger Spring
26	Front Sight Washers	52	Windage Screw

Rolling Block Rifle

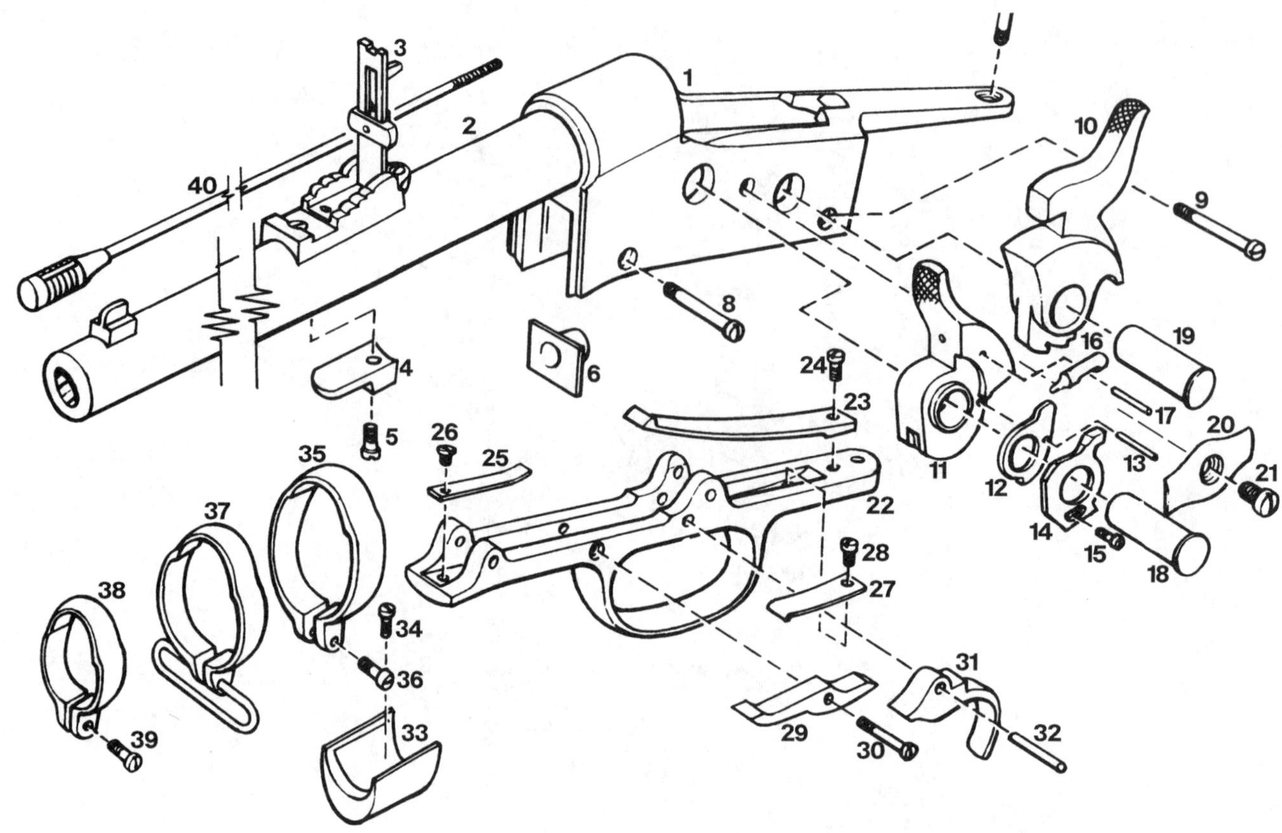

1	Receiver	**25**	Lever Spring
2	Barrel	**26**	Lever Spring Screw
3	Rear Sight	**27**	Trigger Spring
4	Recoil Stud	**28**	Trigger Spring Screw
5	Recoil Stud Screw	**29**	Locking Lever
6	Ramrod Stop	**30**	Locking Lever Screw
7	Tang Screw	**31**	Trigger
8	Front Guard Plate Screw	**32**	Trigger Pin
9	Rear Guard Plate Screw	**33**	Stock Tip
10	Hammer	**34**	Stock Tip Screw
11	Breechblock	**35**	Rear Band
12	Firing Pin Retractor	**36**	Rear Band Screw
13	Retractor Pin	**37**	Middle Band and Screw
14	Extractor	**38**	Front Band
15	Extractor Screw	**39**	Front Band Screw
16	Firing Pin	**40**	Ramrod
17	Firing Pin Limit Pin	**Parts Not Shown**	
18	Breechblock Pin		Buttstock
19	Hammer Pin		Buttplate
20	Button		Buttplate Screws
21	Button Screw		Rear Stock Swivel
22	Guard Plate		Rear Stock Swivel Screws
23	Mainspring		
24	Mainspring Screw		

SP-10 Magnum Autoloading Shotgun

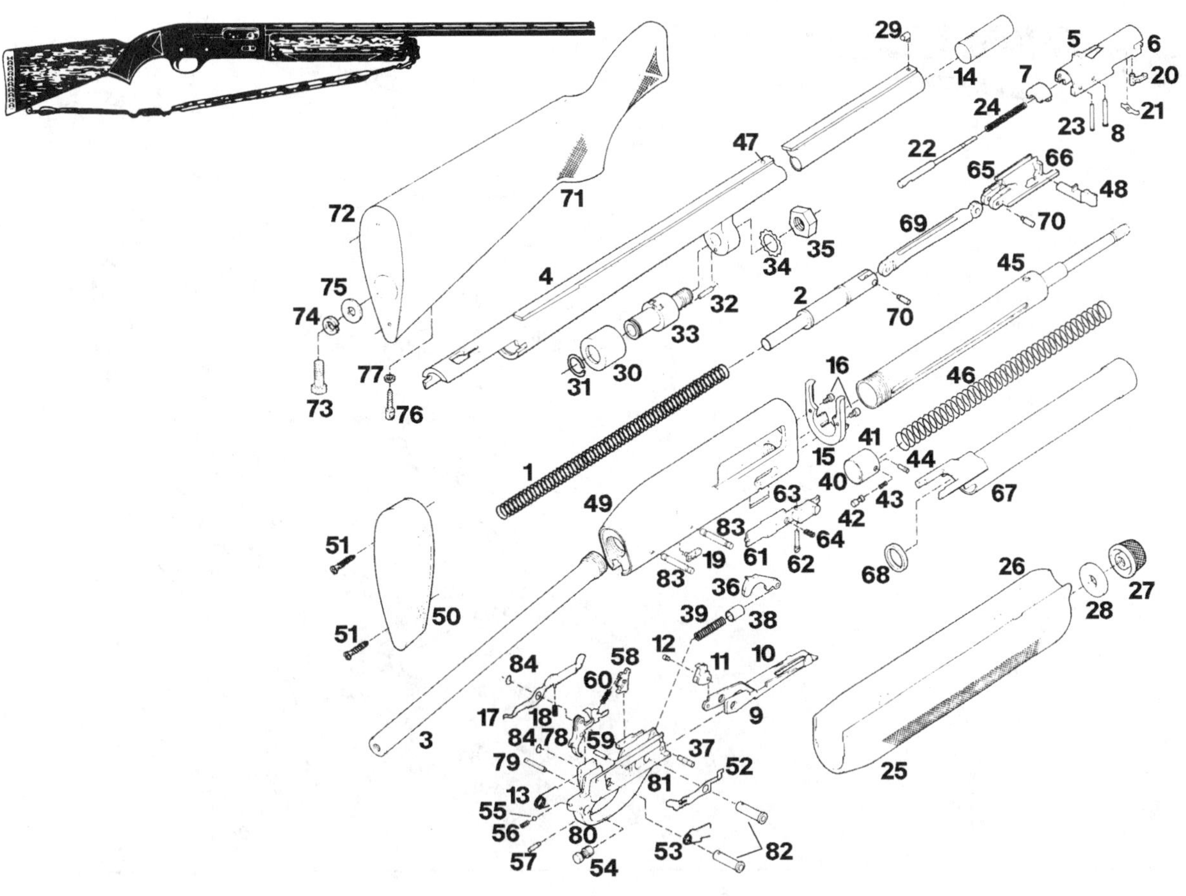

1	Action Spring
2	Action Spring Plunger
3	Action Spring Tube Assembly
4	Barrel Assembly
5	Bolt
6	Bolt Assembly
7	Bolt Buffer
8	Bolt Cam Pin
9	Carrier
10	Carrier Assembly
11	Carrier Dog
12	Carrier Dog Pin
13	Carrier Dog Spring
14	Choke Tube
15	Collar
16	Collar Screws
17	Disconnector
18	Disconnector Spring
19	Ejector
20	Extractor
21	Extractor Retainer
22	Firing Pin
23	Firing Pin Retaining Pin
24	Firing Pin Spring
25	Forend
26	Forend Assembly
27	Forend Cap Assembly
28	Forend Washer
29	Front Sight
30	Gas Cylinder
31	Gas Cylinder Retainer
32	Gas Lug Pin
33	Gas Piston
34	Gas Piston Lock Washer
35	Gas Piston Nut
36	Hammer
37	Hammer Pivot Pin
38	Hammer Plunger
39	Hammer Spring
40	Magazine Follower
41	Magazine Follower Assembly
42	Magazine Follower Plunger
43	Magazine Follower Plunger Spring
44	Magazine Follower Plunger Retaining Pin
45	Magazine Tube Sub-Assembly
46	Magazine Spring
47	Middle Sight
48	Operating Handle
49	Receiver Sub-Assembly
50	Recoil Pad
51	Recoil Pad Screws
52	Release Lever
53	Release Lever Spring
54	Safety Switch
55	Safety Switch Detent Ball
56	Safety Switch Spring
57	Safety Switch Spring Retaining Pin
58	Sear
59	Sear Pivot Pin
60	Sear Spring
61	Shell Stop
62	Shell Stop Pivot
63	Shell Stop Pivot Retainer
64	Shell Stop Spring
65	Slide
66	Slide Assembly
67	Slide Extension Assembly
68	Slide Extension Buffer
69	Slide Link
70	Slide Link Pivots
71	Stock
72	Stock Assembly
73	Stock Bolt
74	Stock Bolt Lock Washer
75	Stock Bolt Washer
76	Stock Swivel Screw
77	Stock Swivel Screw Spacer
78	Trigger Assembly
79	Trigger Pivot Pin
80	Trigger Plate Sub-Assembly
81	Trigger Plate Assembly
82	Trigger Plate Pin Bushings
83	Trigger Plate Pins
84	Trigger Plate Pin Detent Springs

Sportsman 12 Autoloading Shotgun

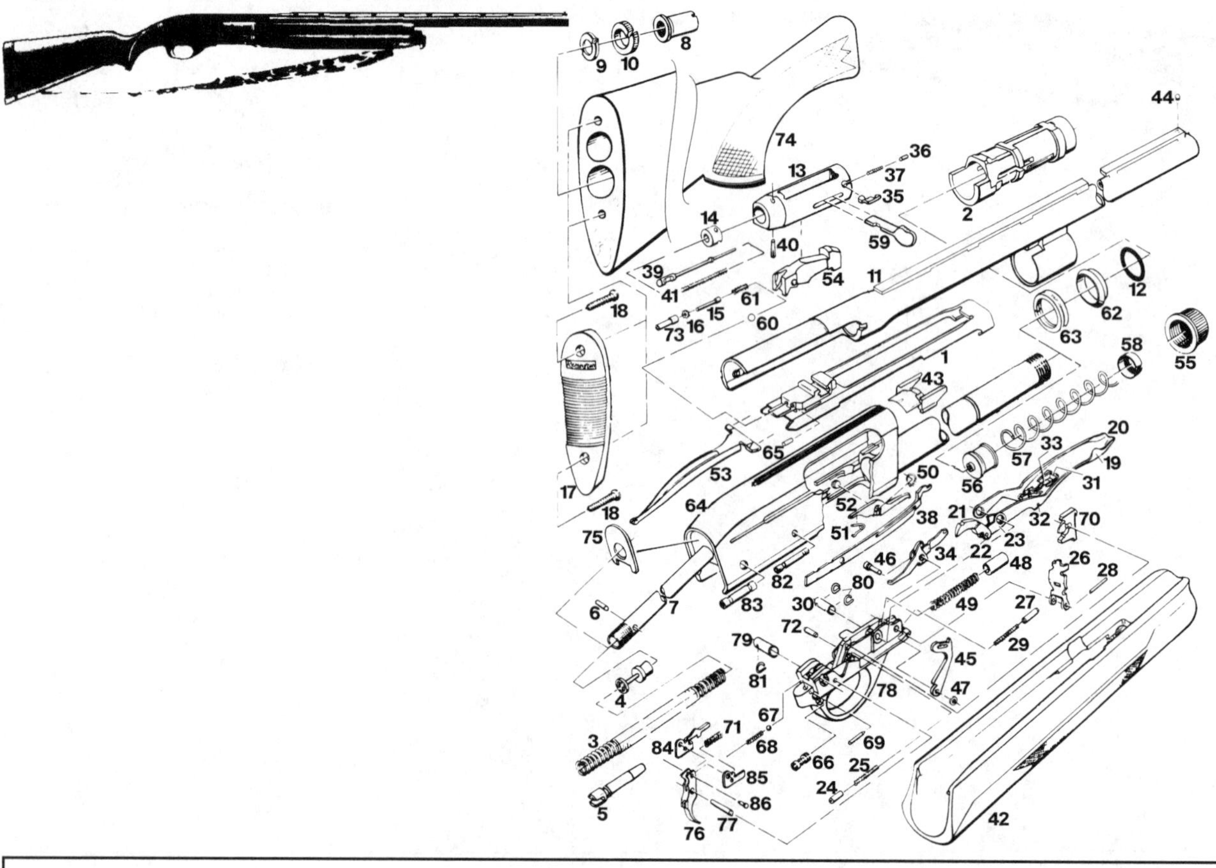

1	Action Bar Assembly	**29**	Carrier Latch Spring	**60**	Operating Handle Detent Ball
2	Action Bar Sleeve	**30**	Carrier Pivot Tube	**61**	Operating Handle Detent Spring
3	Action Spring	**31**	Carrier Release	**62**	Piston
4	Action Spring Follower	**32**	Carrier Release Pin	**63**	Piston Seal
5	Action Spring Plug	**33**	Carrier Release Spring	**64**	Receiver Assembly
6	Action Spring Plug Pin	**34**	Disconnector	**65**	Return Plunger Retaining Pin
7	Action Spring Tube	**35**	Extractor	**66**	Safety Switch
8	Action Spring Tube Nut	**36**	Extractor Plunger	**67**	Safety Switch Detent Ball
9	Action Spring Tube Nut Washer	**37**	Extractor Spring	**68**	Safety Switch Spring
10	Action Spring Tube Nut Lock Washer	**38**	Feed Latch	**69**	Safety Switch Spring Retaining Pin
		39	Firing Pin	**70**	Sear
11	Barrel Assembly	**40**	Firing Pin Retaining Pin	**71**	Sear Spring
12	Barrel Seal	**41**	Firing Pin Retractor Spring	**72**	Sear Pin
13	Breechbolt	**42**	Forend Assembly	**73**	Slide Block Buffer
14	Breechbolt Buffer	**43**	Forend Support	**74**	Stock Assembly
15	Breechbolt Return Plunger	**44**	Front Sight	**75**	Stock Bearing Plate
16	Breechbolt Return Plunger Retaining Ring	**45**	Hammer	**76**	Trigger Assembly
		46	Hammer Pin	**77**	Trigger Pin
17	Buttplate	**47**	Hammer Pin Washer	**78**	Trigger Plate
18	Buttplate Screws	**48**	Hammer Plunger	**79**	Trigger Plate Pin Bushing, Rear
19	Carrier	**49**	Hammer Spring	**80**	Trigger Plate Pin Detent Springs, Front
20	Carrier Assembly	**50**	Interceptor Latch Retainer		
21	Carrier Dog	**51**	Interceptor Latch Spring	**81**	Trigger Plate Detent Spring, Rear
22	Carrier Dog Pin	**52**	Interceptor Latch	**82**	Trigger Plate Pin, Front
23	Carrier Dog Washer	**53**	Link	**83**	Trigger Plate Pin, Rear
24	Carrier Dog Follower	**54**	Locking Block Assembly	**84**	Connector, Left
25	Carrier Dog Follower Spring	**55**	Magazine Cap	**85**	Connector, Right
26	Carrier Latch	**56**	Magazine Follower	**86**	Connector Pin
27	Carrier Latch Follower	**57**	Magazine Spring	**Parts Not Shown**	
28	Carrier Latch Pin	**58**	Magazine Spring Retainer		Magazine Plug
		59	Operating Handle		

Sportsman 12 Slide-Action Shotgun

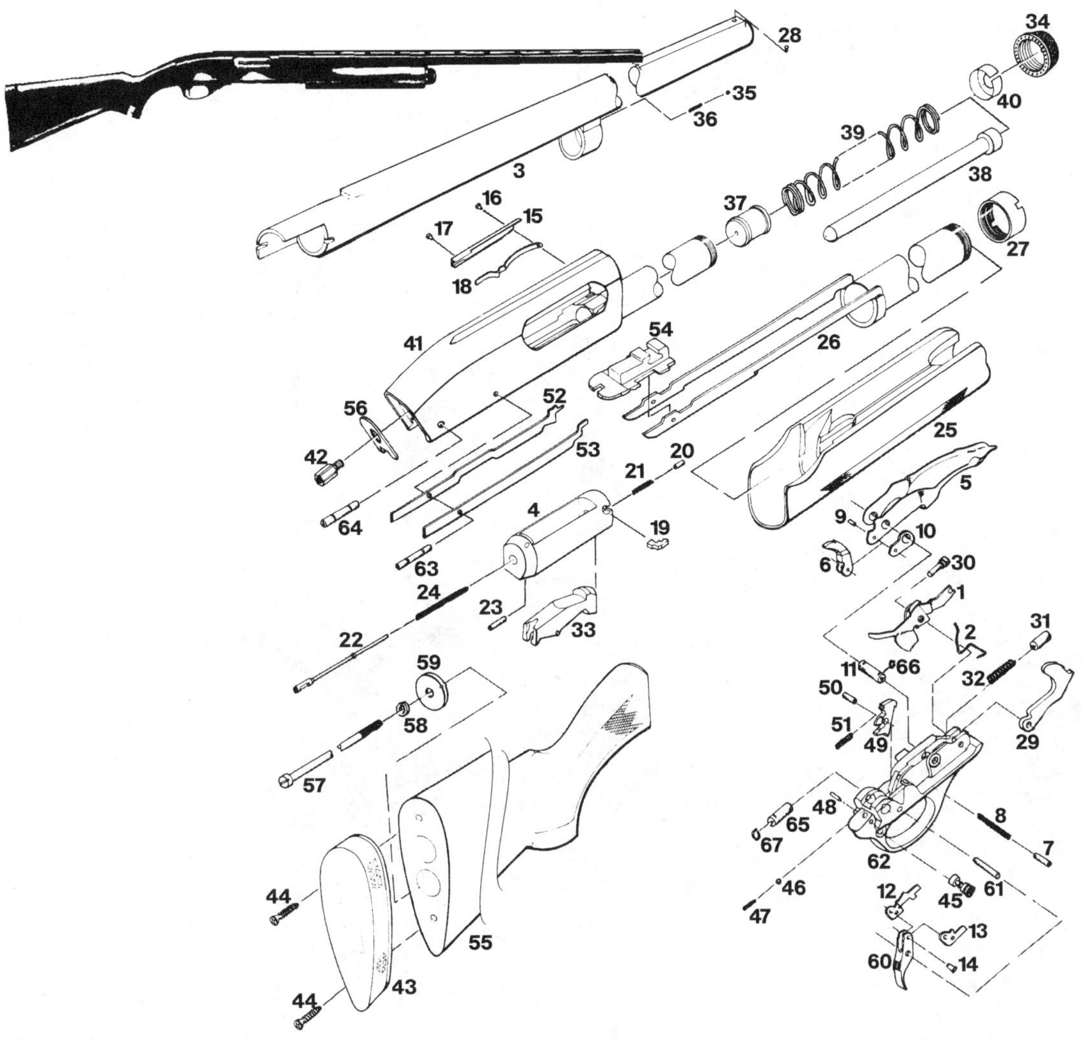

1	Action Bar Lock	25	Forend Assembly	49	Sear
2	Action Bar Lock Spring	26	Forend Tube Assembly	50	Sear Pin
3	Barrel Assembly	27	Forend Tube Nut	51	Sear Spring
4	Breechbolt	28	Front Sight Bead	52	Shell Latch, Left
5	Carrier	29	Hammer	53	Shell Latch, Right
6	Carrier Dog	30	Hammer Pin	54	Slide Assembly
7	Carrier Dog Follower	31	Hammer Plunger	55	Stock Assembly
8	Carrier Dog Follower Spring	32	Hammer Spring	56	Stock Bearing Plate
9	Carrier Dog Pin	33	Locking Block Assembly	57	Stock Bolt
10	Carrier Dog Washer	34	Magazine Cap	58	Stock Bolt Lock Washer
11	Carrier Pivot Tube	35	Magazine Cap Detent	59	Stock Bolt Washer
12	Connector, Left	36	Magazine Cap Detent Spring	60	Trigger
13	Connector, Right	37	Magazine Follower	61	Trigger Pin
14	Connector Pin	38	Magazine Plug	62	Trigger Plate
15	Ejector	39	Magazine Spring	63	Trigger Plate Pin, Front
16	Ejector Rivet, Front	40	Magazine Spring Retainer	64	Trigger Plate Pin, Rear
17	Ejector Rivet, Rear	41	Receiver Assembly	65	Trigger Plate Pin Bushing, Rear
18	Ejector Spring	42	Receiver Stud	66	Trigger Plate Pin Detent Spring, Front
19	Extractor	43	Recoil Pad	67	Trigger Plate Pin Detent Spring, Rear
20	Extractor Plunger	44	Recoil Pad Screws	**Parts Not Shown**	
21	Extractor Spring	45	Safety Switch		Hammer Pin Washer
22	Firing Pin	46	Safety Switch Detent Ball		
23	Firing Pin Retaining Pin	47	Safety Switch Spring		
24	Firing Pin Retainer Spring	48	Safety Switch Spring Retaining Pin		

Model 200, 202 and 711 Side-by-Side Shotgun

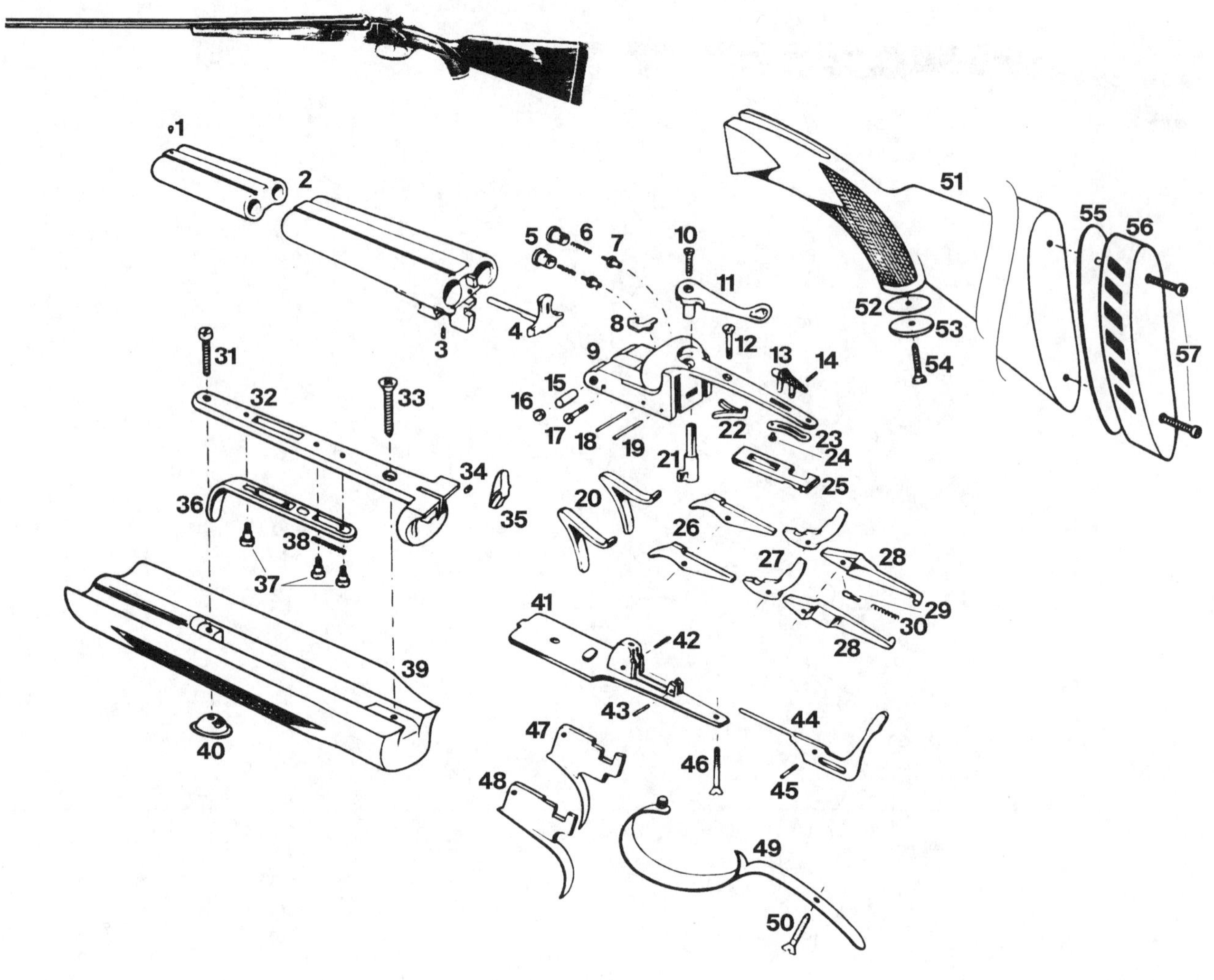

1	Front Sight Bead	20	Hammer Springs	39	Forend
2	Barrels	21	Vertical Bolt	40	Forend Pan
3	Extractor Retaining Screw	22	Top Lever Spring	41	Trigger Plate
4	Extractor	23	Safety Spring	42	Trigger Pin
5	Firing Pin Bushings	24	Safety Spring Screw	43	Safety Square Pin
6	Firing Pin Springs	25	Horizontal Bolt	44	Safety Activator
7	Firing Pins	26	Cocking Levers	45	Safety Activator Screw
8	Purdey Bolt	27	Hammers	46	Trigger Plate Screw, Rear
9	Receiver	28	Right and Left Sear	47	Right Trigger
10	Top Lever Screw	29	Sear Spring Guide	48	Left Trigger
11	Top Lever	30	Sear Spring	49	Trigger Guard
12	Upper Tang Screw	31	Forend Screw, Front	50	Trigger Guard Screw
13	Safety Button	32	Iron Forend	51	Buttstock
14	Safety Button Pin	33	Forend Screw, Rear	52	Pistol Grip Spacer
15	Hinge Bolt	34	Extractor Cam Screw	53	Pistol Grip Cap
16	Hinge Bolt Cover Screw	35	Extractor Cam	54	Pistol Grip Cap Screw
17	Cocking Lever Pivot Screw	36	Forend Catch	55	Stock Spacer
18	Hammer Pivot Pin	37	Forend Catch Screws	56	Recoil Pad
19	Sear Pivot Pin	38	Forend Catch Spring	57	Recoil Pad Screws

Models 59, 62SA and 62SAC Slide-Action Rifle

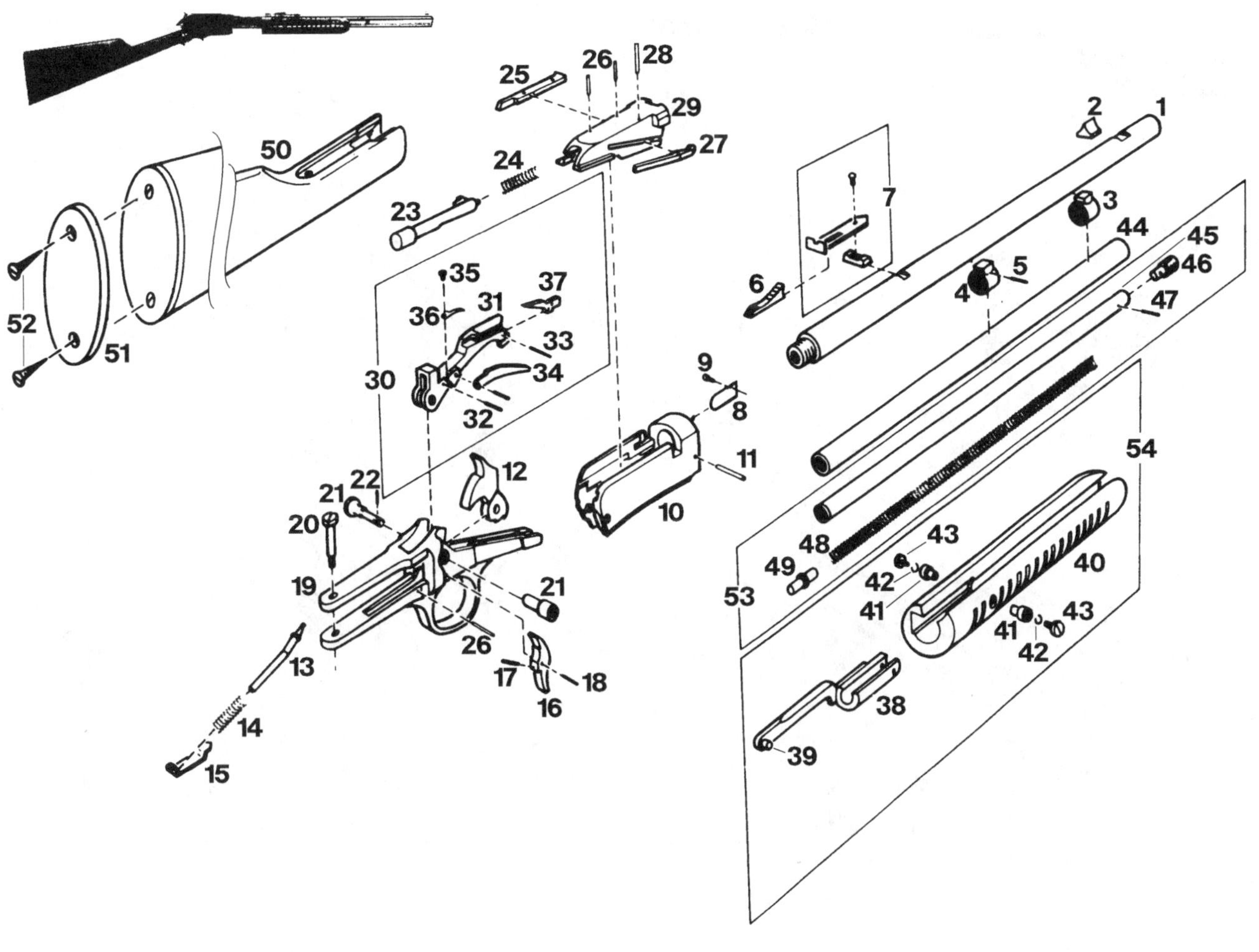

1	Barrel	**19**	Trigger Guard	**37**	Cartridge Stop
2	Front Sight	**20**	Tang Screw	**38**	Action Slide
3	Front Magazine Ring	**21**	Assembly Screw Bushing	**39**	Action Slide Stud
4	Rear Magazine Ring	**22**	Assembly Screw Stop Pin	**40**	Forend
5	Rear Magazine Ring Pin	**23**	Firing Pin	**41**	Forend Bushings
6	Elevator	**24**	Firing Pin Spring	**42**	Forend Pressure Washers
7	Rear Sight Assembly	**25**	Firing Pin Stop	**43**	Forend Screws
8	Sideplate	**26**	Firing Pin Stop Pins	**44**	Magazine Tube, Outside
9	Sideplate Screw	**27**	Extractor	**45**	Magazine Tube, Inside
10	Receiver	**28**	Extractor Pin	**46**	Magazine Plug
11	Barrel Pin	**29**	Breechbolt	**47**	Magazine Plug Pin
12	Hammer	**30**	Carrier Assembly	**48**	Magazine Spring
13	Hammer Spring Guide Rod	**31**	Carrier	**49**	Magazine Follower
14	Hammer Spring	**32**	Carrier Lever Pins	**50**	Stock
15	Hammer Spring Stop	**33**	Cartridge Stop Pin	**51**	Buttplate
16	Trigger	**34**	Carrier Lever	**52**	Buttplate Screws
17	Trigger Spring	**35**	Carrier Lever Spring Screw	**53**	Inner Magazine Tube Assembly
18	Trigger Pin	**36**	Carrier Lever Spring	**54**	Forend Assembly

Model 92SRC Lever-Action Carbine

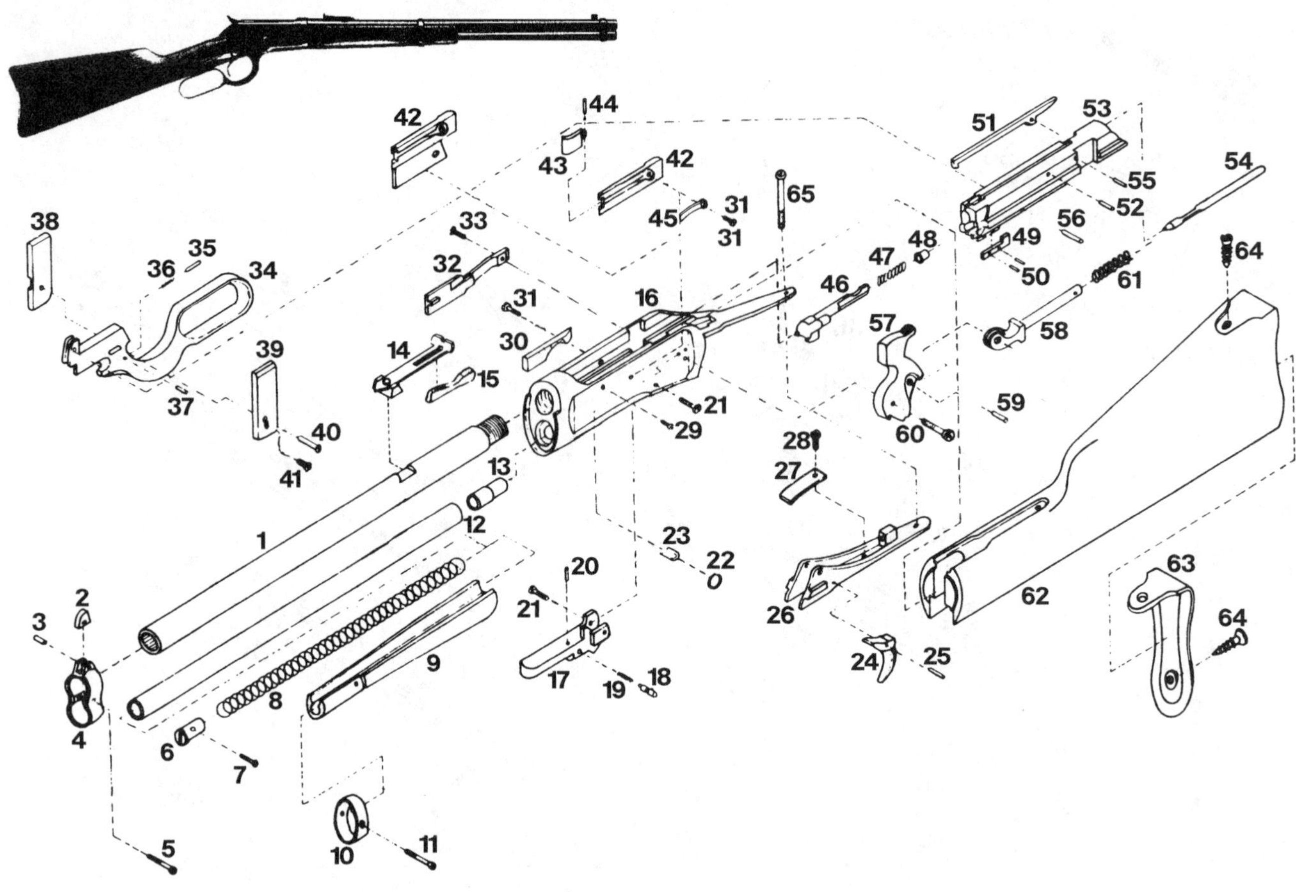

1	Barrel	**23**	Saddle Ring Support	**44**	Cartridge Stop Joint Pin
2	Front Sight	**24**	Trigger	**45**	Cartridge Stop Spring
3	Front Sight Pin	**25**	Trigger Pin	**46**	Ejector
4	Upper Band	**26**	Lower Tang	**47**	Ejector Spring
5	Upper Band Screw	**27**	Trigger Spring	**48**	Ejector Collar
6	Magazine Plug	**28**	Trigger Spring Screw	**49**	Ejector Spring Stop
7	Magazine Plug Screw	**29**	Lever and Breechbolt Pin Hole Plug Screw	**50**	Ejector Spring Stop Pins
8	Magazine Spring	**30**	Cartridge Guide, Right	**51**	Extractor
9	Forend	**31**	Cartridge Guide Screw	**52**	Extractor Pin
10	Lower Band	**32**	Spring Cover	**53**	Breechbolt
11	Lower Band Screw	**33**	Spring Cover Screw	**54**	Firing Pin
12	Magazine Tube	**34**	Finger Lever	**55**	Firing Pin Stop Pin
13	Magazine Follower	**35**	Friction Stud	**56**	Lever and Breechbolt Pin
14	Rear Sight	**36**	Friction Stud Spring	**57**	Hammer
15	Elevator	**37**	Friction Stud Stop Pin	**58**	Mainspring Rod
16	Receiver	**38**	Locking Bolt, Right	**59**	Mainspring Rod Pin
17	Carrier	**39**	Locking Bolt, Left	**60**	Hammer Screw
18	Carrier Stop	**40**	Locking Bolt Pin	**61**	Mainspring
19	Carrier Stop Spring	**41**	Locking Bolt Pin Stop Screw	**62**	Stock
20	Carrier Stop Pin	**42**	Cartridge Guide, Left	**63**	Buttplate
21	Carrier Screws	**43**	Cartridge Stop	**64**	Buttplate Screws
22	Saddle Ring			**65**	Upper Tang Screw

Overland Side-by-Side Shotgun

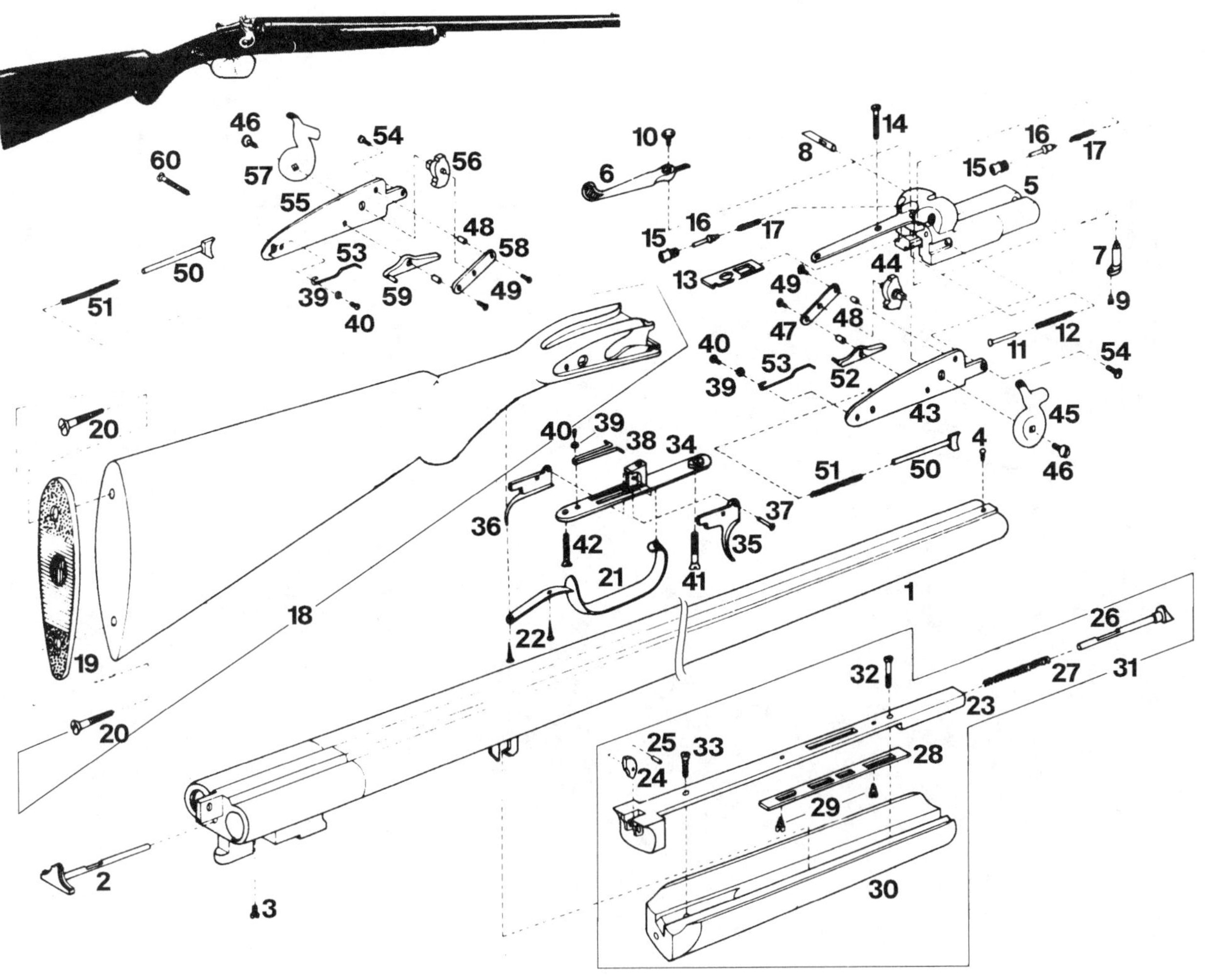

1	Barrel Assembly	**22**	Trigger Guard Screws	**43**	Right Plate
2	Extractor Assembly	**23**	Forend Iron	**44**	Right Locking Nut
3	Extractor Screw	**24**	Extractor Lever	**45**	Right Hammer
4	Front Sight	**25**	Extractor Lever Pin	**46**	Hammer Screws
5	Breech Assembly	**26**	Forend Rod	**47**	Right Holding Plate
6	Top Lever	**27**	Forend Spring	**48**	Holding Plate Bushings
7	Top Lever Stud	**28**	Forend Catch	**49**	Holding Plate Screws
8	Locking Pin	**29**	Forend Catch Screws	**50**	Hammer Spring Rods
9	Top Lever Stud Screw	**30**	Forend Wood	**51**	Hammer Springs
10	Top Lever Screw	**31**	Forend Assembly	**52**	Right Sear
11	Top Lever Spring Pin	**32**	Forend Anterior Screw	**53**	Sear Springs
12	Top Lever Spring	**33**	Forend Posterior Screw	**54**	Plate Screws
13	Locking Plate	**34**	Trigger Plate	**55**	Left Plate
14	Breech Trigger Plate Screw	**35**	Right Trigger	**56**	Left Locking Nut
15	Firing Pin Carriers	**36**	Left Trigger	**57**	Left Hammer
16	Firing Pins	**37**	Trigger Pin	**58**	Left Holding Plates
17	Firing Pin Springs	**38**	Trigger Spring	**59**	Left Sear
18	Stock	**39**	Trigger Nuts	**60**	Plate and Stock Screw
19	Buttplate	**40**	Trigger Spring Locking Screws	**Parts Not Shown**	
20	Buttplate Screws	**41**	Breech Plate Anterior Screw		Breech Trigger Plate Locking Pin
21	Trigger Guard	**42**	Breech Plate Posterior Screw		Plate Bushing

Single Shot Shotgun

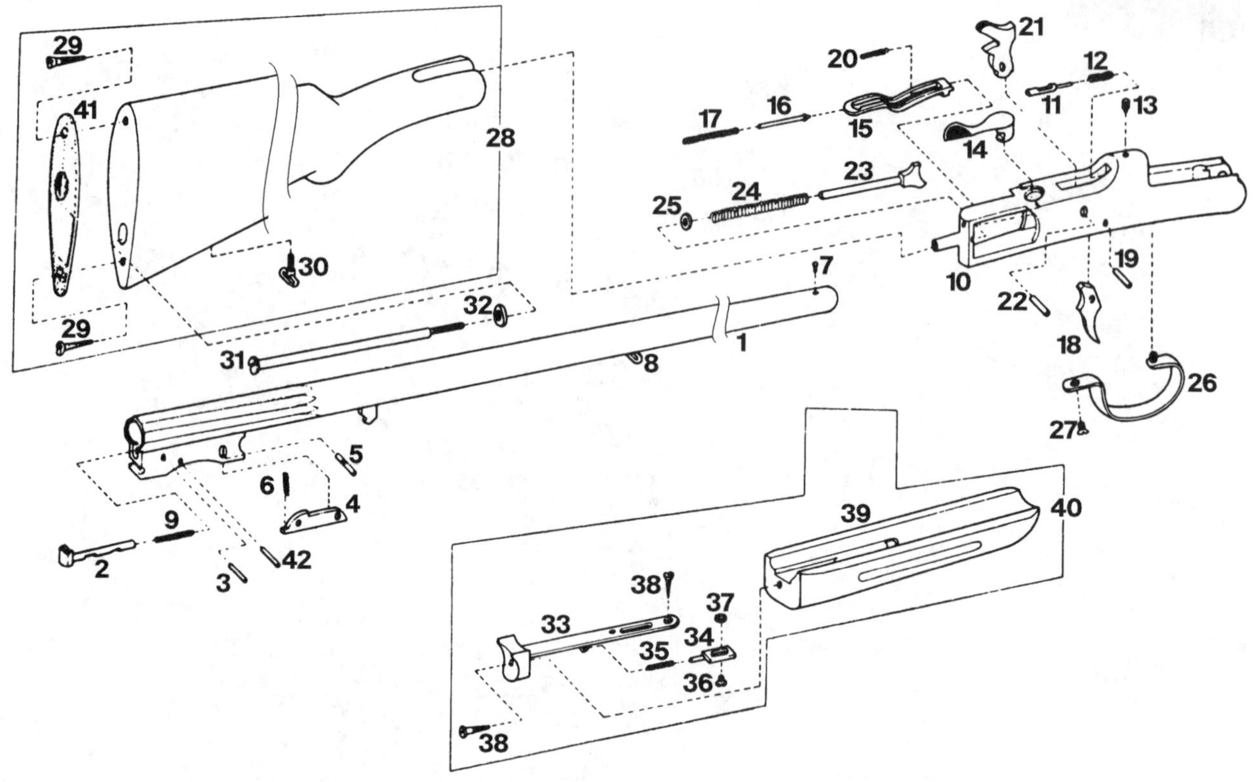

1	Barrel Assembly	22	Hammer Pin
2	Extractor Assembly	23	Hammer Spring Pin
3	Extractor Pin	24	Hammer Spring
4	Ejector Lever	25	Hammer Spring Washer
5	Ejector Lever Pin	26	Trigger Guard
6	Ejector Lever Spring	27	Trigger Guard Screw
7	Front Sight Bead	28	Stock Assembly
8	Front Swivel	29	Buttplate Screws
9	Extractor Spring	30	Rear Swivel
10	Frame	31	Frame Stock Screw
11	Firing Pin	32	Frame Stock Screw Washer
12	Firing Pin Spring	33	Forend Iron
13	Firing Pin Screw	34	Forend Catch
14	Top Lever	35	Forend Spring
15	Locking Plate	36	Forend Catch Screw
16	Locking Plate Spring Rod	37	Forend Catch Washer
17	Locking Plate Spring	38	Rear Forend Iron Screws
18	Trigger	39	Forend
19	Trigger Pin	40	Forend Assembly
20	Trigger Spring	41	Buttplate
21	Hammer	42	Barrel Pin

Squire Side-by-Side Shotgun

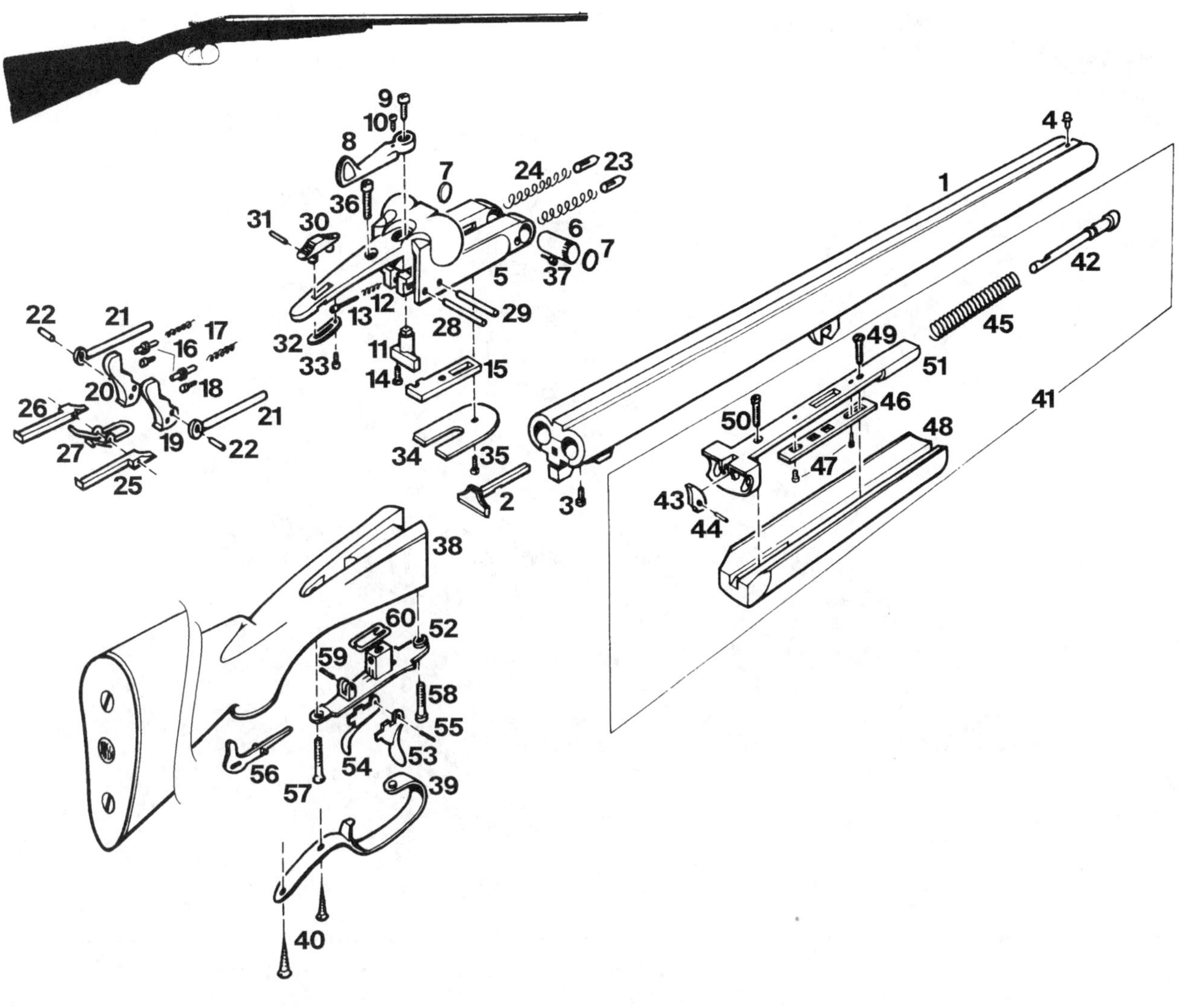

1	Barrel Assembly	**22**	Hammer Spring Rod Pins	**41**	Forend Assembly
2	Extractor	**23**	Hammer Spring Rod Heads	**42**	Forend Rod
3	Extractor Screw	**24**	Hammer Springs	**43**	Extractor Lever
4	Front Sight	**25**	Right Sear	**44**	Extractor Lever Pin
5	Breech Assembly	**26**	Left Sear	**45**	Forend Rod Spring
6	Hinge Pin	**27**	Sear Spring	**46**	Forend Catch
7	Hinge Pin Caps	**28**	Sear Pin	**47**	Forend Catch Screws
8	Top Lever	**29**	Hammer Pin	**48**	Forend Wood
9	Top Lever Screw	**30**	Safety	**49**	Front Forend Screw
10	Locking Screw	**31**	Safety Pin	**50**	Rear Forend Screw
11	Top Lever Stud	**32**	Safety Spring	**51**	Forend Iron
12	Top Lever Stud Spring	**33**	Safety Spring Screw	**52**	Trigger Plate
13	Top Lever Spring Plunger	**34**	Breech Plate	**53**	Right Trigger
14	Top Lever Stud Screw	**35**	Breech Plate Screw	**54**	Left Trigger
15	Locking Plate	**36**	Upper Tang Screw	**55**	Trigger Pin
16	Firing Pins	**37**	Hinge Pin Cap Screw	**56**	Safety-Lever
17	Firing Pin Springs	**38**	Stock Assembly with Buttplate and Screws	**57**	Rear Tang Screw
18	Firing Pin Screws			**58**	Front Trigger Plate Breech Screw
19	Hammer, Right	**39**	Trigger Guard Assembly	**59**	Safety-Lever Retainer Pin
20	Hammer, Left	**40**	Trigger Guard Screws	**60**	Trigger Spring
21	Hammer Spring Rods				

44 Autoloading Carbine

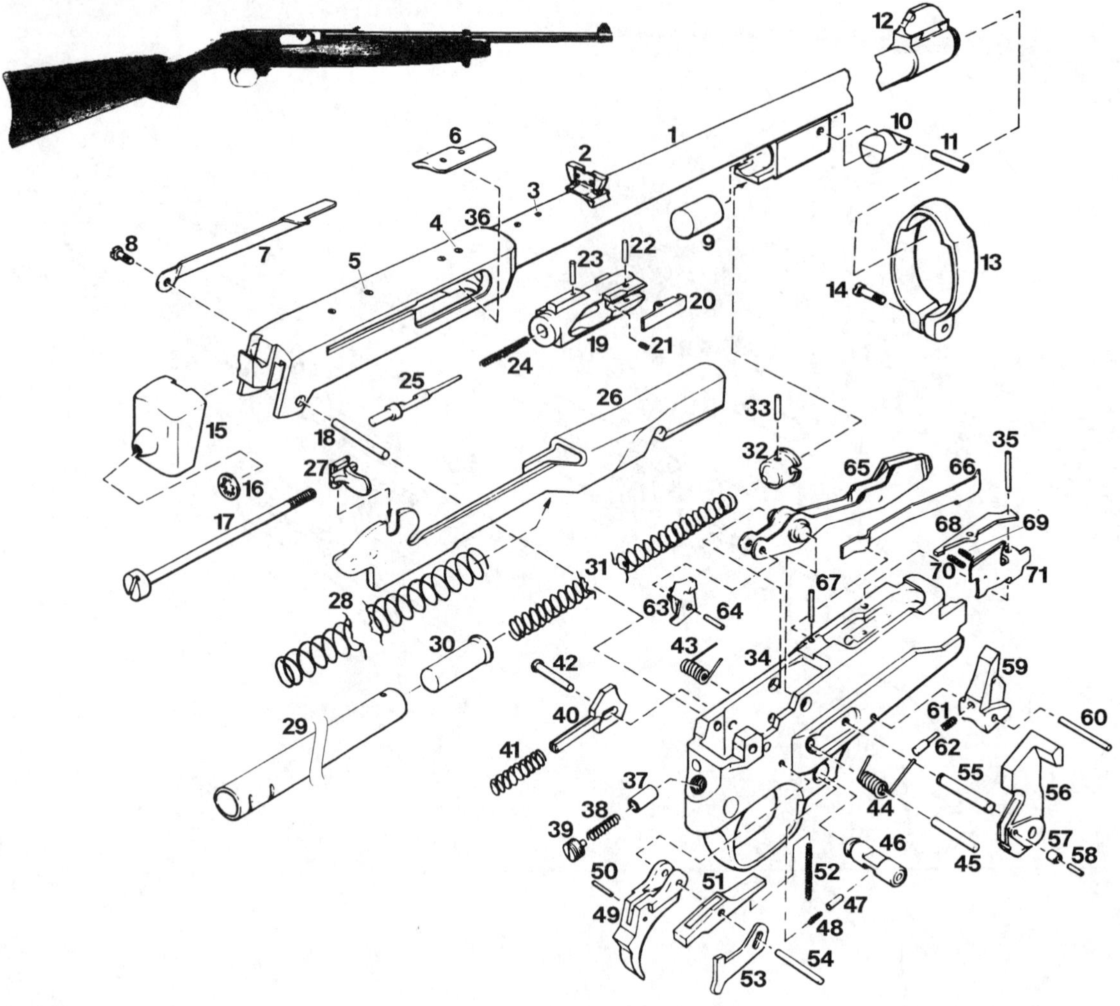

1 Barrel
2 Rear Sight
3 Scope Mount Filler Screws
4 Ejector Screws
5 Scope Mount Filler Screws
6 Ejector
7 Cartridge Guide Plate
8 Cartridge Guide Plate Screw
9 Piston
10 Piston Block Plug
11 Piston Block Plug Retaining Pin
12 Front Sight
13 Barrel Band
14 Barrel Band Screw
15 Recoil Block
16 Recoil Block Bolt Washer
17 Recoil Block Bolt
18 Receiver Cross Pin
19 Bolt
20 Extractor
21 Extractor Spring
22 Extractor Pivot Pin
23 Firing Pin Retaining Pin
24 Firing Pin Retaining Spring
25 Firing Pin
26 Slide
27 Slide Handle
28 Slide Spring
29 Magazine Tube
30 Magazine Follower
31 Magazine Spring
32 Magazine Plug
33 Magazine Plug Cross Pin
34 Trigger Guard and Housing
35 Cartridge Stop Pivot Pin
36 Receiver
37 Disconnector Plunger
38 Disconnector Plunger Spring
39 Disconnector Plunger Spring Screw
40 Lifter Cam
41 Lifter Cam Spring
42 Lifter Cam Pin
43 Hammer Spring, Left
44 Hammer Spring, Right
45 Hammer Spring Retaining Pin
46 Safety
47 Safety Detent Plunger
48 Safety Detent Plunger Spring
49 Trigger
50 Trigger Cross Pin
51 Sear
52 Sear Spring
53 Disconnector
54 Trigger Pivot Pin
55 Hammer Pivot Pin
56 Hammer
57 Hammer Roller
58 Hammer Roller Pivot Pin
59 Lifter Latch
60 Lifter Latch Pivot Pin
61 Lifter Latch Spring
62 Lifter Latch Plunger
63 Lifter Dog
64 Lifter Dog Pivot Pin
65 Lifter Assembly
66 Cartridge Stop Flat Spring
67 Retaining Pin
68 Cartridge Stop
69 Flapper Spring
70 Cartridge Stop Coil Spring
71 Flapper

Parts Not Shown

Buttstock
Buttpad
Screws
Forend

Mini-14 Autoloading Rifle (180-Prefix)

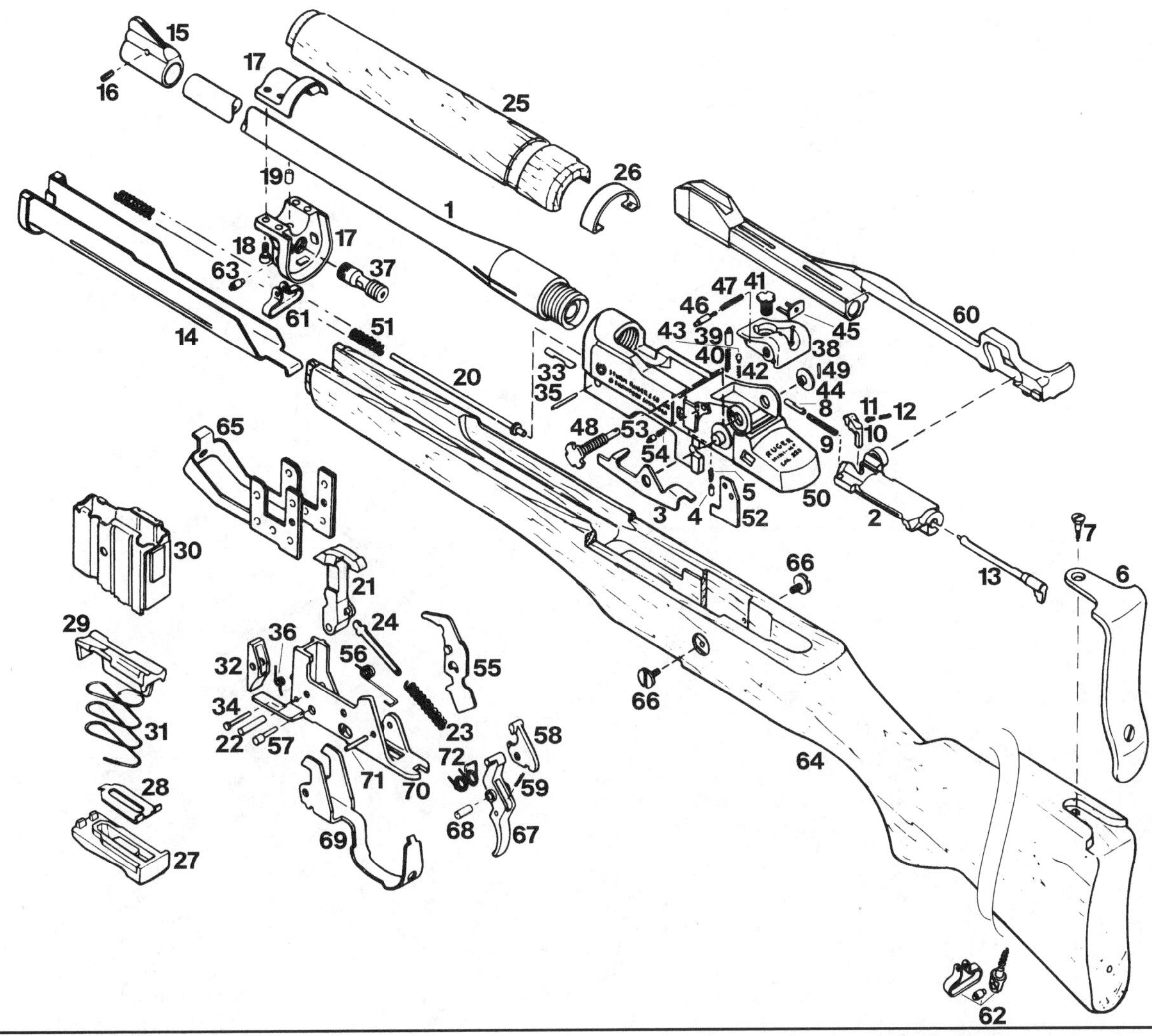

1	Barrel	**25**	Handguard	**49**	Rear Sight Windage Screw Pin
2	Bolt and Roller Assembly	**26**	Handguard Clip	**50**	Receiver
3	Bolt Lock	**27**	Magazine Bottom	**51**	Recoil Spring
4	Bolt Lock Plunger	**28**	Magazine Bottom Retainer	**52**	Retainer Plate
5	Bolt Lock Plunger Spring	**29**	Magazine Follower	**53**	Retainer Plate Plunger
6	Buttplate	**30**	Magazine Shell	**54**	Retainer Plate Plunger Spring
7	Buttplate Screws	**31**	Magazine Spring	**55**	Safety Assembly
8	Ejector	**32**	Magazine Latch	**56**	Safety Detent Spring
9	Ejector Spring	**33**	Magazine Catch	**57**	Safety Spring Retaining Pin
10	Extractor	**34**	Magazine Latch Pivot Pin	**58**	Secondary Sear
11	Extractor Plunger	**35**	Magazine Catch Retaining Pin	**59**	Secondary Sear Spring
12	Extractor Spring	**36**	Magazine Latch Spring	**60**	Slide
13	Firing Pin	**37**	Piston	**61**	Sling Swivel, Front
14	Forend Liner and Stock Cap Assembly	**38**	Rear Sight Base	**62**	Sling Swivel, Rear
15	Front Sight	**39**	Rear Sight Elevation Detent Plunger	**63**	Sling Swivel Pin, Front
16	Front Sight Cross Pin	**40**	Rear Sight Elevation Detent Plunger Spring	**64**	Stock
17	Gas Block, Top and Bottom	**41**	Rear Sight Elevation Screw	**65**	Stock Reinforcement
18	Gas Block Screws	**42**	Rear Sight Elevation Plunger Spring	**66**	Stock Reinforcement Screws
19	Gas Port Bushing	**43**	Rear Sight Elevation Plunger	**67**	Trigger
20	Guide Rod	**44**	Rear Sight Nut	**68**	Trigger Bushing
21	Hammer	**45**	Rear Sight Peep	**69**	Trigger Guard
22	Hammer Pivot Pin	**46**	Rear Sight Windage Detent Plunger	**70**	Trigger Housing
23	Hammer Spring	**47**	Rear Sight Windage Detent Spring	**71**	Trigger Pivot
24	Hammer Strut	**48**	Rear Sight Windage Screw	**72**	Trigger Spring

Mini-14 Autoloading Rifle (181-184 Prefix)

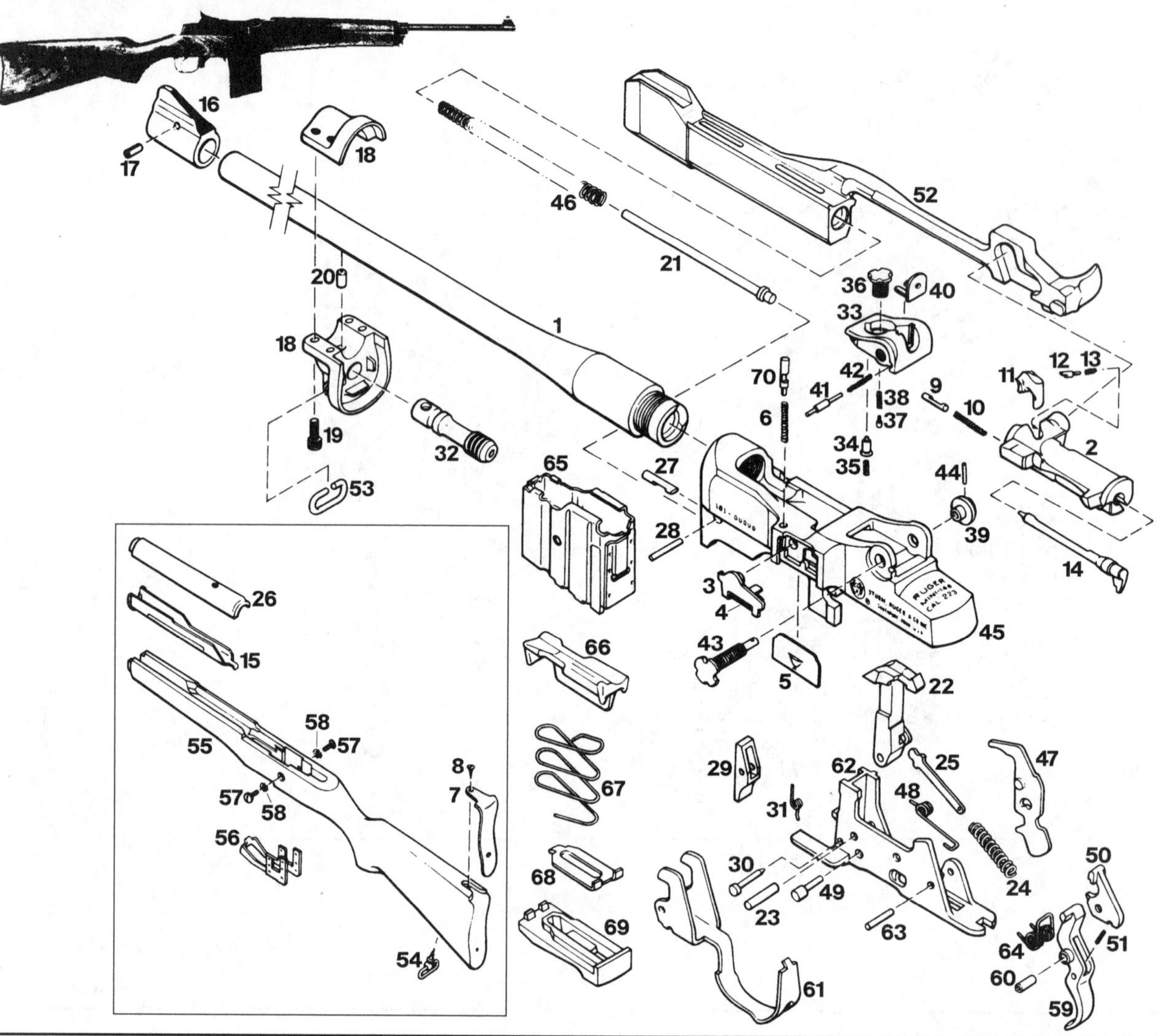

1	Barrel	**23**	Hammer Pivot Pin	**47**	Safety Assembly
2	Bolt	**24**	Hammer Spring	**48**	Safety Detent Spring
3	Bolt Lock Assembly	**25**	Hammer Strut	**49**	Safety Spring Retaining Pin
4	Bolt Lock Buffer Spring	**26**	Handguard	**50**	Secondary Sear
5	Bolt Lock Cover Plate	**27**	Magazine Catch, Front	**51**	Secondary Sear Spring
6	Bolt Lock Plunger Spring	**28**	Magazine Catch Retaining Pin	**52**	Slide Assembly
7	Buttplate	**29**	Magazine Latch	**53**	Sling Swivel, Front
8	Buttplate Screws	**30**	Magazine Latch Pivot Pin	**54**	Sling Swivel Assembly, Rear
9	Ejector	**31**	Magazine Latch Spring	**55**	Stock
10	Ejector Spring	**32**	Piston (Gas Pipe)	**56**	Stock Reinforcement
11	Extractor	**33**	Rear Sight Base	**57**	Stock Reinforcement Screws
12	Extractor Plunger	**34**	Rear Sight Elevation Detent Plunger	**58**	Stock Reinforcement Lock Washers
13	Extractor Spring	**35**	Rear Sight Elevation Detent Spring	**59**	Trigger
14	Firing Pin	**36**	Rear Sight Elevation Screw	**60**	Trigger Bushing
15	Forend Liner and Stock Cap Assembly	**37**	Rear Sight Elevation Plunger	**61**	Trigger Guard
16	Front Sight	**38**	Rear Sight Elevation Plunger Spring	**62**	Trigger Housing
17	Front Sight Cross Pin	**39**	Rear Sight Nut	**63**	Trigger Pivot Pin
18	Gas Block	**40**	Rear Sight Peep	**64**	Trigger Spring
19	Gas Block Screws	**41**	Rear Sight Windage Detent Plunger	**65**	Magazine Box
20	Gas Port Bushing	**42**	Rear Sight Windage Detent	**66**	Magazine Follower
21	Guide Rod	**43**	Rear Sight Windage Screw	**67**	Magazine Spring
22	Hammer	**44**	Rear Sight Windage Screw Pin	**68**	Magazine Spring Retainer
		45	Receiver	**69**	Magazine Floorplate
		46	Recoil Spring	**70**	Bolt Lock Plunger

Mini-14 Ranch Autoloading Rifle

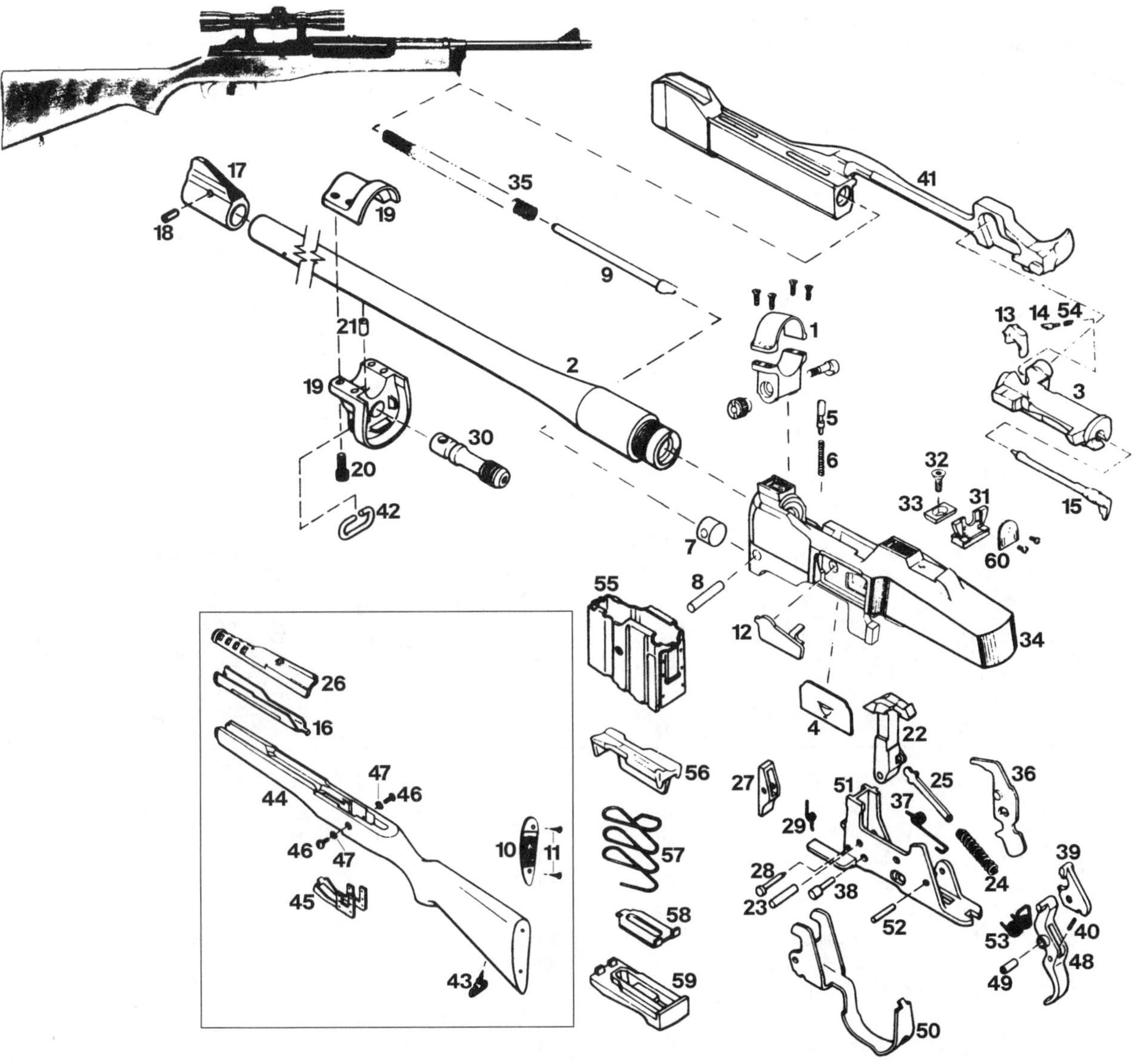

1	Scope Rings
2	Barrel
3	Bolt
4	Bolt Lock Cover Plate
5	Bolt Lock Plunger
6	Bolt Lock Plunger Spring
7	Buffer Bushing
8	Buffer Cross Pin
9	Buffer Guide Rod
10	Buttplate
11	Buttplate Screws
12	Ejector Bolt Stop
13	Extractor
14	Extractor Plunger
15	Firing Pin
16	Forend Liner and Stock Cap Assembly
17	Front Sight
18	Front Sight Cross Pin
19	Gas Block, Top and Bottom
20	Gas Block Screws
21	Gas Port Bushing
22	Hammer
23	Hammer Pivot Pin
24	Hammer Spring
25	Hammer Strut
26	Handguard Assembly
27	Magazine Latch
28	Magazine Latch Pivot Pin
29	Magazine Latch Spring
30	Piston (Gas Pipe)
31	Rear Sight Assembly
32	Rear Sight Windage Lock Screw
33	Rear Sight Windage Lock
34	Receiver
35	Recoil Spring
36	Safety Assembly
37	Safety Detent Spring
38	Safety Spring Retaining Pin
39	Secondary Sear
40	Secondary Sear Spring
41	Slide Assembly
42	Sling Swivel, Front
43	Sling Swivel Assembly, Rear
44	Stock
45	Stock Reinforcement
46	Stock Reinforcement Screws
47	Stock Reinforcement Lock Washers
48	Trigger
49	Trigger Bushing
50	Trigger Guard
51	Trigger Housing
52	Trigger Pivot Pin
53	Trigger Spring
54	Extractor Spring
55	Magazine Box
56	Magazine Follower
57	Magazine Spring
58	Magazine Spring Retainer
59	Magazine Floorplate
60	Rear Sight Peep and Screws

Mini-Thirty Autoloading Rifle

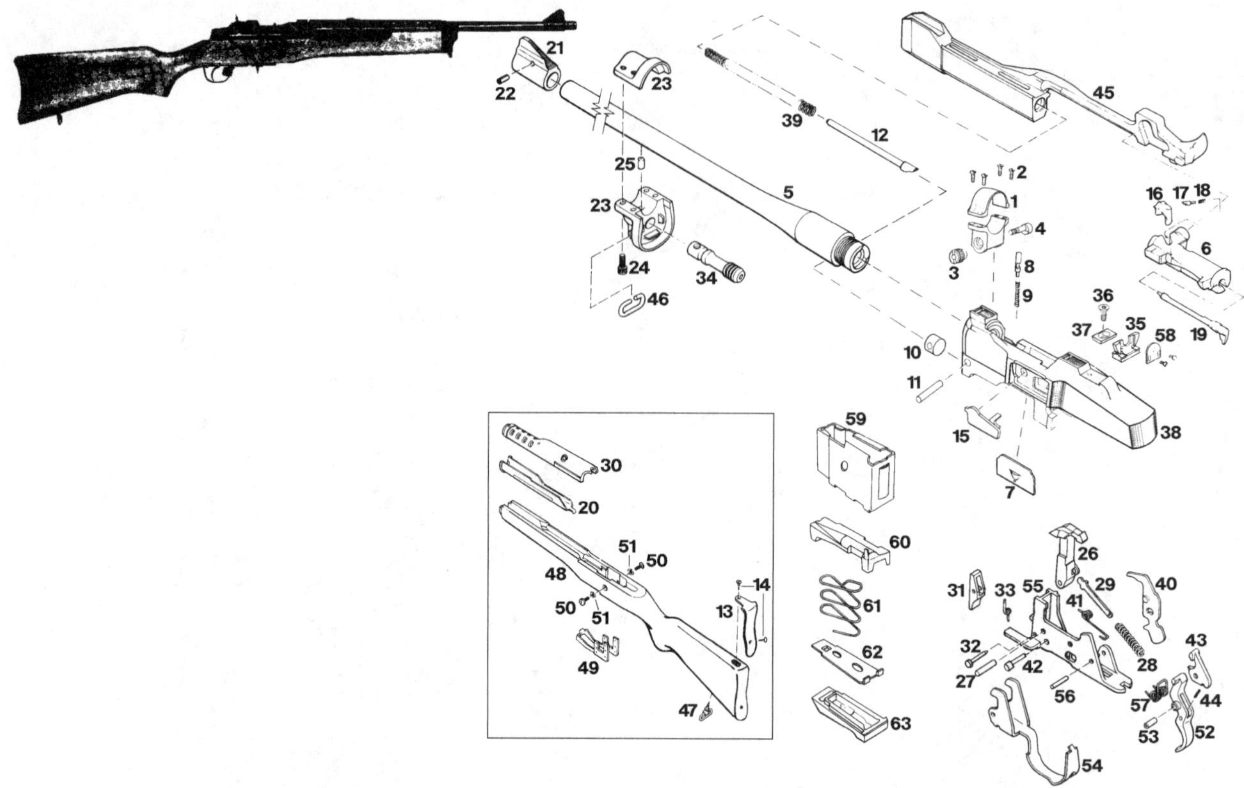

1	Scope Rings	33	Magazine Latch Spring
2	Scope Ring Screws	34	Piston (Gas Pipe)
3	Scope Ring Nut	35	Rear Sight Assembly, Complete
4	Scope Ring Clamp	36	Rear Sight Windage Lock Screw
5	Barrel	37	Rear Sight Windage Lock
6	Bolt	38	Receiver
7	Bolt Lock Cover Plate	39	Recoil Spring
8	Bolt Lock Plunger	40	Safety Assembly
9	Bolt Lock Plunger Spring	41	Safety Detent Spring
10	Buffer Bushing	42	Safety Spring Retaining Pin
11	Buffer Cross Pin	43	Secondary Sear
12	Buffer Guide Rod	44	Secondary Sear Spring
13	Buttplate	45	Slide Assembly
14	Buttplate Screws	46	Sling Swivel, Front
15	Ejector Bolt Stop	47	Sling Swivel Assembly, Rear
16	Extractor	48	Stock with Buttplate
17	Extractor Plunger	49	Stock Reinforcement Assembly
18	Extractor Spring	50	Stock Reinforcement Screws
19	Firing Pin	51	Stock Reinforcement Lock Washers
20	Forearm Liner and Stock Cap Assembly	52	Trigger
21	Front Sight	53	Trigger Bushing
22	Front Sight Cross Pin	54	Trigger Guard
23	Gas Block, Top and Bottom	55	Trigger Housing
24	Gas Block Screws	56	Trigger Pivot Pin
25	Gas Port Bushing	57	Trigger Spring
26	Hammer	58	Rear Sight Peep and Screws
27	Hammer Pivot Pin	59	Magazine Box
28	Hammer Spring	60	Magazine Follower
29	Hammer Strut	61	Magazine Spring
30	Handguard Assembly	62	Magazine Spring Retainer
31	Magazine Latch	63	Magazine Floorplate
32	Magazine Latch Pivot Pin		

Model 10/22 Autoloading Rifle

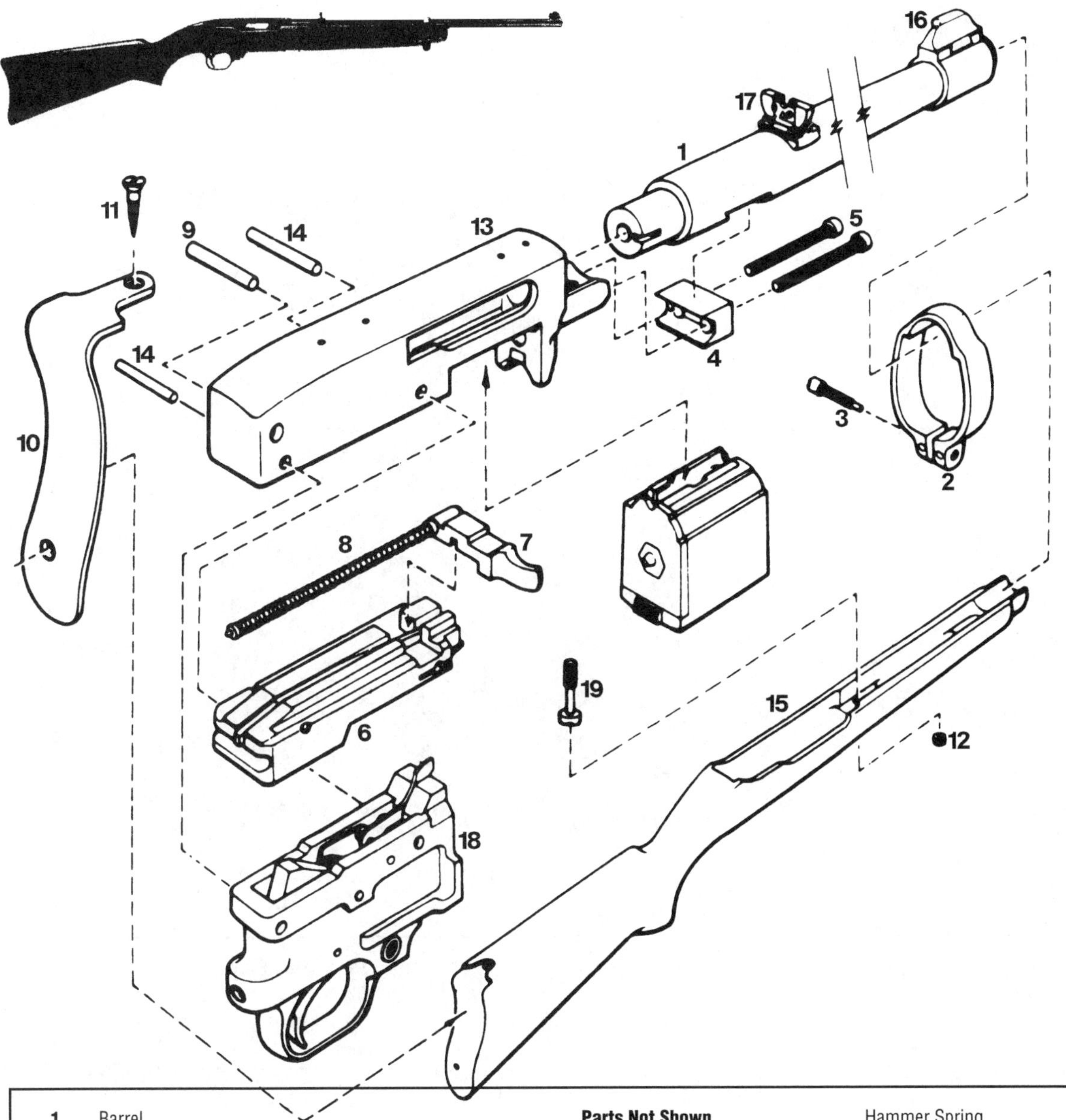

1	Barrel
2	Barrel Band
3	Barrel Band Screw
4	Barrel Retainer
5	Barrel Retainer Screws
6	Bolt Assembly
7	Bolt Handle
8	Guide Rod and Recoil Spring Assembly
9	Bolt Stop Pin
10	Buttplate
11	Buttplate Screws
12	Stock Escutcheon
13	Receiver
14	Receiver Cross Pins
15	Stock
16	Front Sight Bead
17	Open Rear Sight
18	Trigger Guard Assembly
19	Takedown Screw

Parts Not Shown

Bolt Lock
Bolt Lock Spring
Disconnector
Disconnector Pivot Pin
Ejector
Ejector Pins
Extractor
Extractor Plunger
Extractor Spring
Firing Pin
Firing Pin Rebound Spring
Firing Pin Stop Pin
Hammer
Hammer Bushings
Hammer Pivot Pin
Hammer Spring
Hammer Strut
Hammer Strut Washer
Magazine Assembly
Magazine Cap
Magazine Cap Nut
Magazine Latch
Magazine Latch Pivot Pin
Magazine Latch Plunger
Magazine Latch Plunger Spring
Magazine Rotor
Magazine Rotor Spring
Magazine Screw
Magazine Shell
Magazine Throat

Model 77 Bolt-Action Rifle

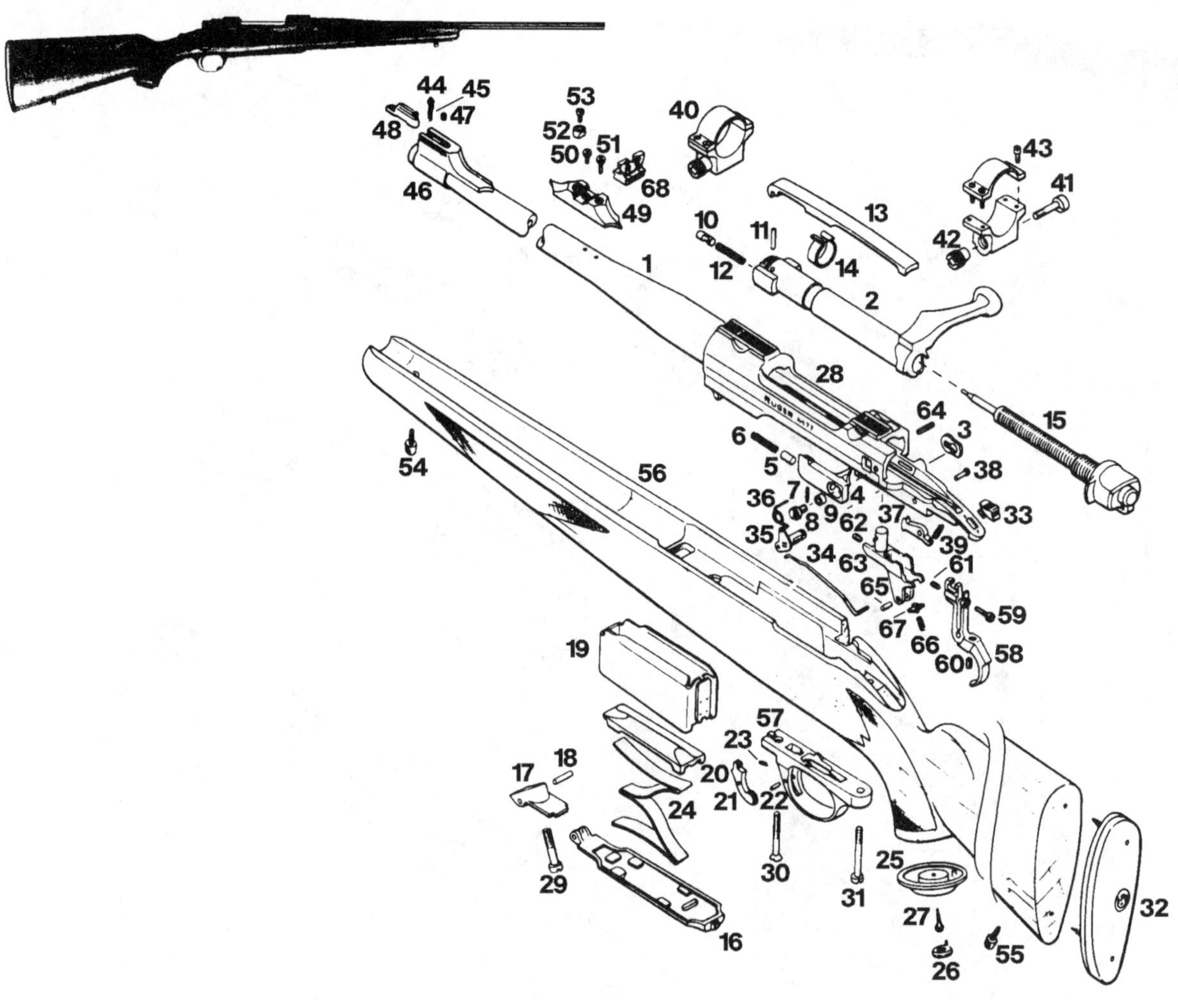

1	Barrel	**25**	Pistol Grip Cap	**51**	Rear Sight Base Rear Screw
2	Bolt Body	**26**	Pistol Grip Cap Medallion	**52**	Williams Gib Lock
3	Bolt Lock	**27**	Pistol Grip Cap Screw	**53**	Williams Gib Lock Screw
4	Bolt Stop	**28**	Receiver	**54**	Sling Swivel Front Screw with Nut
5	Bolt Stop Plunger	**29**	Receiver Mounting Screw, Front	**55**	Sling Swivel Rear Mounting Stud
6	Bolt Stop Plunger Spring	**30**	Receiver Mounting Screw, Center	**56**	Stock
7	Bolt Stop Plunger Spring Retaining Pin	**31**	Receiver Mounting Screw, Rear	**57**	Trigger Guard
		32	Recoil Pad	**58**	Trigger
8	Bolt Stop Screw Stud	**33**	Safety Button	**59**	Trigger Engagement Screw
9	Bolt Stop Stud Bushing	**34**	Safety Link	**60**	Trigger Weight of Pull Screw
10	Ejector	**35**	Safety Shaft Assembly	**61**	Trigger Over Travel Screw
11	Ejector Retaining Pin	**36**	Safety Spring	**62**	Trigger Over Travel Set Screw
12	Ejector Spring	**37**	Sear	**63**	Trigger Housing
13	Extractor	**38**	Sear Pivot Pin	**64**	Trigger Housing Cross Pin
14	Extractor Band	**39**	Sear Spring	**65**	Trigger Pivot Pin
15	Firing Pin Assembly	**40**	Scope Ring Assembly	**66**	Trigger Return Spring
16	Floorplate	**41**	Scope Ring Clamp	**67**	Trigger Return Spring Seat
17	Floorplate Hinge	**42**	Scope Ring Nut	**68**	Rear Sight Blade
18	Floorplate Pivot Pin	**43**	Scope Ring Screw	**Parts Not Shown**	
19	Magazine Box	**44**	Front Sight Plunger		Forend Escutcheons
20	Magazine Follower	**45**	Front Sight Plunger Spring		Stock Cross Bolt
21	Magazine Latch	**46**	Front Sight Base		Stock Cross Bolt Nut
22	Magazine Latch Pin	**47**	Front Sight Base Set Screw		Stock Reinforcement Assembly
23	Magazine Latch Spring	**48**	Front Sight Blade		Stock Reinforcement Screw
24	Magazine Spring	**49**	Rear Sight Base		
		50	Rear Sight Base Center Screw		

Model 77/22 Bolt-Action Rifle

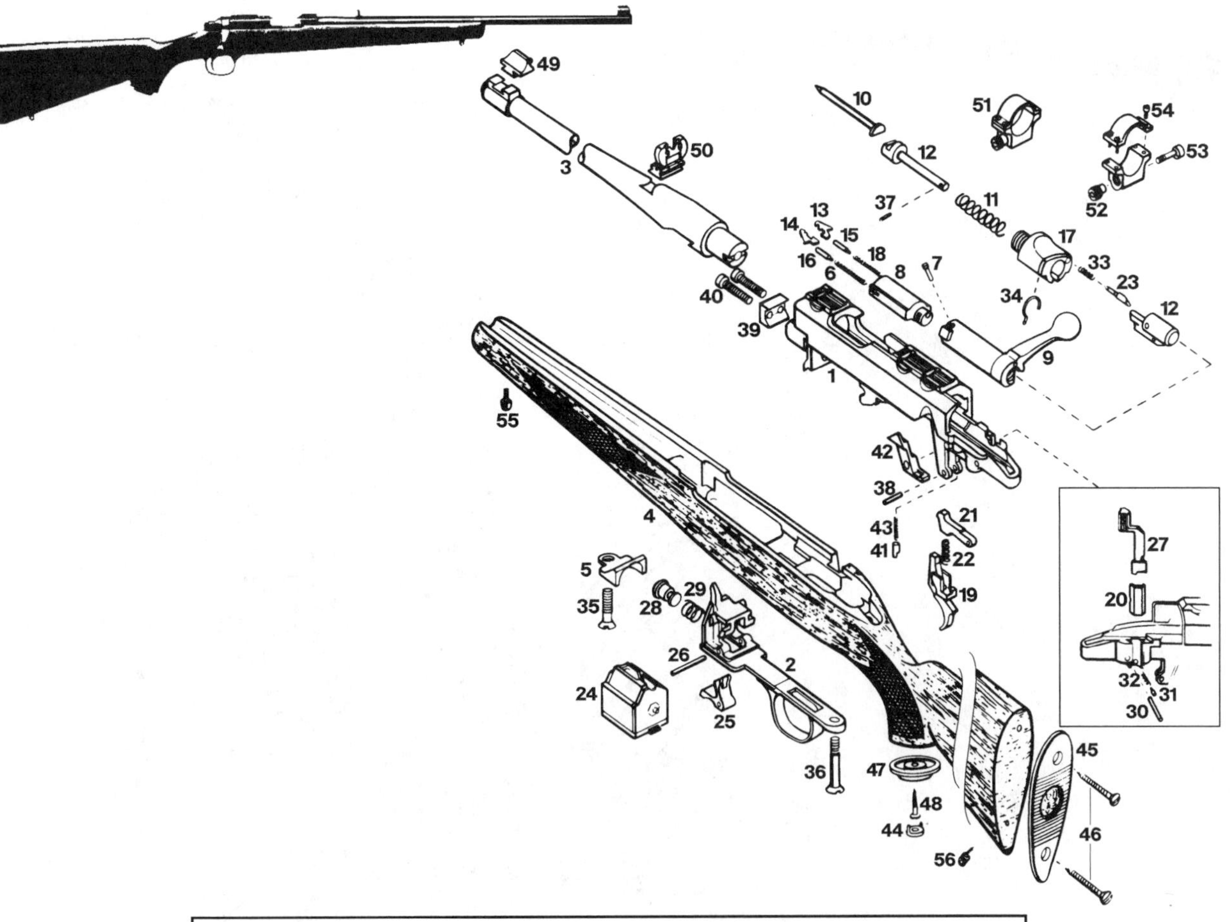

1	Receiver	**30**	Sear Pivot Pin
2	Trigger Guard Assembly	**31**	Safety Selector Detent
3	Barrel	**32**	Safety Selector Detent Spring
4	Stock	**33**	Bolt Lock Plunger Spring
5	Magazine Well Liner	**34**	Bolt Lock Plunger Retainer
6	Cartridge Support Spring	**35**	Front Mounting Screw
7	Breechblock Retainer	**36**	Rear Mounting Screw
8	Breechblock	**37**	Striker Cross Pin
9	Bolt	**38**	Trigger Pivot Pin
10	Firing Pin	**39**	Barrel Retainer
11	Striker Spring	**40**	Barrel Retainer Screws
12	Striker/Cocking Piece Assembly	**41**	Bolt Stop Plunger
13	Extractor	**42**	Bolt Stop
14	Cartridge Support	**43**	Bolt Stop Plunger Spring
15	Extractor Plunger	**44**	Pistol Grip Cap Medallion
16	Cartridge Support Plunger	**45**	Buttplate
17	Bolt Sleeve	**46**	Buttplate Screws
18	Extractor Spring	**47**	Pistol Grip Cap
19	Trigger	**48**	Pistol Grip Cap Screw
20	Safety Selector Retainer	**49**	Front Sight
21	Sear	**50**	Rear Sight
22	Trigger/Sear Spring	**51**	Scope Ring
23	Bolt Lock Plunger	**52**	Scope Ring Nut
24	Magazine Complete	**53**	Scope Ring Clamp
25	Magazine Latch	**54**	Scope Ring Screw
26	Magazine Latch Pivot Pin	**55**	Sling Swivel Front Screw with Nut
27	Safety Selector		
28	Magazine Latch Plunger	**56**	Sling Swivel Rear Mounting Stud
29	Magazine Latch Plunger Spring		

M-77 Mark II Bolt-Action Rifle

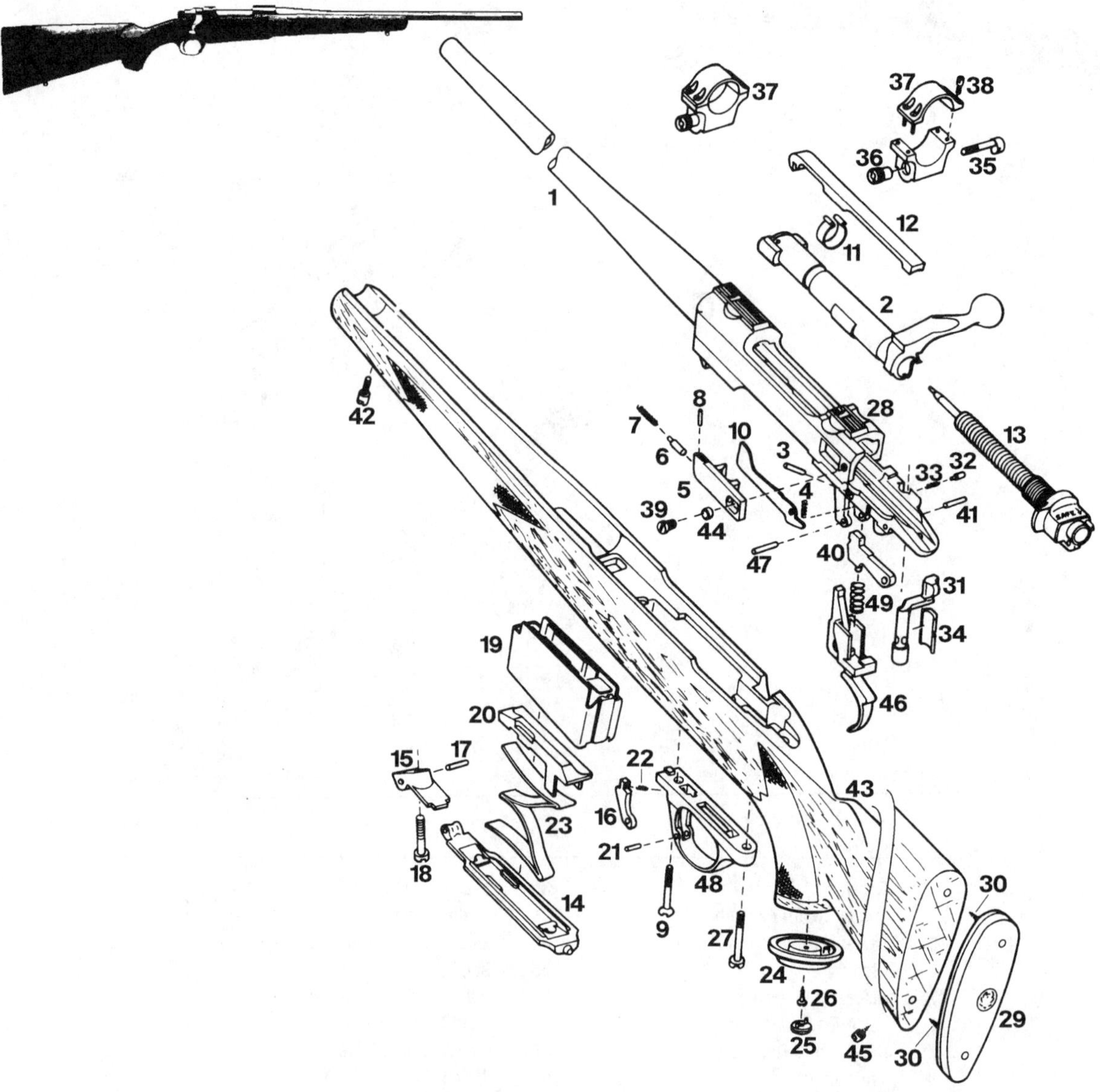

1	Barrel	**19**	Magazine Box	**39**	Screw Stud
2	Bolt and Bolt Key	**20**	Magazine Follower	**40**	Sear
3	Bolt Lock Plunger	**21**	Magazine Latch Pin	**41**	Sear Pivot Pin
4	Bolt Lock Plunger Spring	**22**	Magazine Latch Spring	**42**	Sling Swivel Screw
5	Bolt Stop	**23**	Magazine Spring	**43**	Stock
6	Bolt Stop Plunger	**24**	Pistol Grip Cap	**44**	Stud Bushing
7	Bolt Stop Plunger Spring	**25**	Pistol Grip Cap Medallion	**45**	Swivel Mounting Screw
8	Bolt Stop Plunger Spring Retaining Pin	**26**	Pistol Grip Cap Screw	**46**	Trigger
		27	Rear Mounting Screw	**47**	Trigger Pivot Pin
9	Center Mounting Screw	**28**	Receiver	**48**	Trigger Guard
10	Ejector	**29**	Recoil Pad	**49**	Trigger/Sear Spring
11	Extractor Band	**30**	Recoil Pad Screws	**Parts Not Shown**	
12	Extractor	**31**	Safety Selector		Bolt Lock Plunger Retainer
13	Firing Pin Assembly	**32**	Safety Selector Detent		Bolt Sleeve
14	Floorplate Assembly	**33**	Safety Selector Detent Spring		Cocking Piece
15	Floorplate Hinge	**34**	Safety Selector Retainer		Ejector Spring
16	Floorplate Latch	**35**	Scope Base Clamp		Ejector Pivot Pin
17	Floorplate Pivot Pin	**36**	Scope Base Nut		Firing Pin Cross Pin
18	Front Mounting Screw	**37**	Scope Ring Assembly		
		38	Scope Ring Screws		

No. 1 Single Shot Rifle

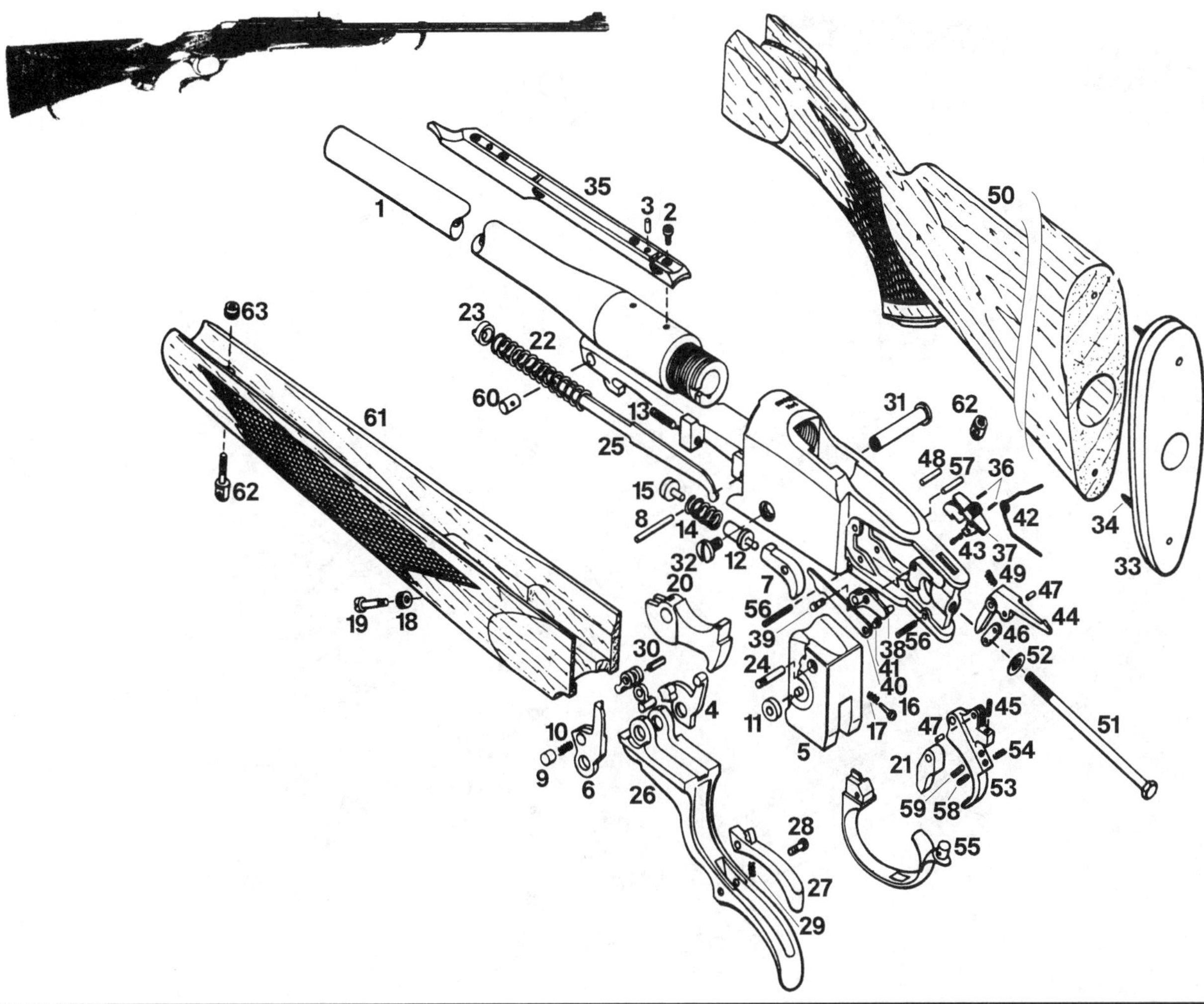

1	Barrel	**27**	Lever Latch	**53**	Trigger
2	Barrel Rib Screws	**28**	Lever Latch Pivot Pin	**54**	Trigger Adjustment Spring
3	Barrel Rib Dowels	**29**	Lever Latch Spring	**55**	Trigger Guard
4	Breechblock Arm	**30**	Lever Link and Pin Assemblies	**56**	Trigger Guard Retaining Pins
5	Breechblock	**31**	Lever Pivot Pin	**57**	Trigger Pivot Pin
6	Ejector	**32**	Lever Pivot Screw	**58**	Trigger Spring Adjustment Screw
7	Ejector Cam	**33**	Recoil Pad	**59**	Trigger Stop Screw
8	Ejector Cam Pivot Pin	**34**	Recoil Pad Screws	**60**	Forend Takedown Nut
9	Ejector Plunger	**35**	Rib	**61**	Forend
10	Ejector Plunger Spring	**36**	Roll Pins for Safety Thumb-Piece	**62**	Sling Swivel Screws
11	Ejector Roller	**37**	Safety	**63**	Sling Swivel Escutcheon
12	Ejector Strut	**38**	Safety Arm	**Parts Not Shown**	
13	Ejector Strut Adjusting Screw	**39**	Safety Arm Pivot Pin		Front Sight Base
14	Ejector Strut Spring	**40**	Safety Bar		Front Sight Base Set Screw
15	Ejector Strut Swivel	**41**	Safety Bar Pivot Pin		Front Sight Blade
16	Firing Pin	**42**	Safety Detent Spring		Front Sight Plunger Spring
17	Firing Pin Spring	**43**	Safety Detent Spring Pin		Front Sight Retaining Plunger
18	Forend Escutcheon	**44**	Sear		Lever Pilot Groove Pin
19	Forend Takedown Screw	**45**	Sear Adjustment Screw		Medallion
20	Hammer	**46**	Sear Link		Pistol Grip Cap
21	Hammer Transfer Block	**47**	Sear Link Pins		Pistol Grip Cap Screw
22	Hammer Spring	**48**	Sear Pivot Pin		Rear Sight
23	Hammer Spring Retaining Washer	**49**	Sear Spring		
24	Hammer Transfer Block Pivot Pin	**50**	Buttstock		
25	Hammer Strut	**51**	Stock Bolt		
26	Lever	**52**	Stock Bolt Washer		

No. 3 Single Shot Carbine

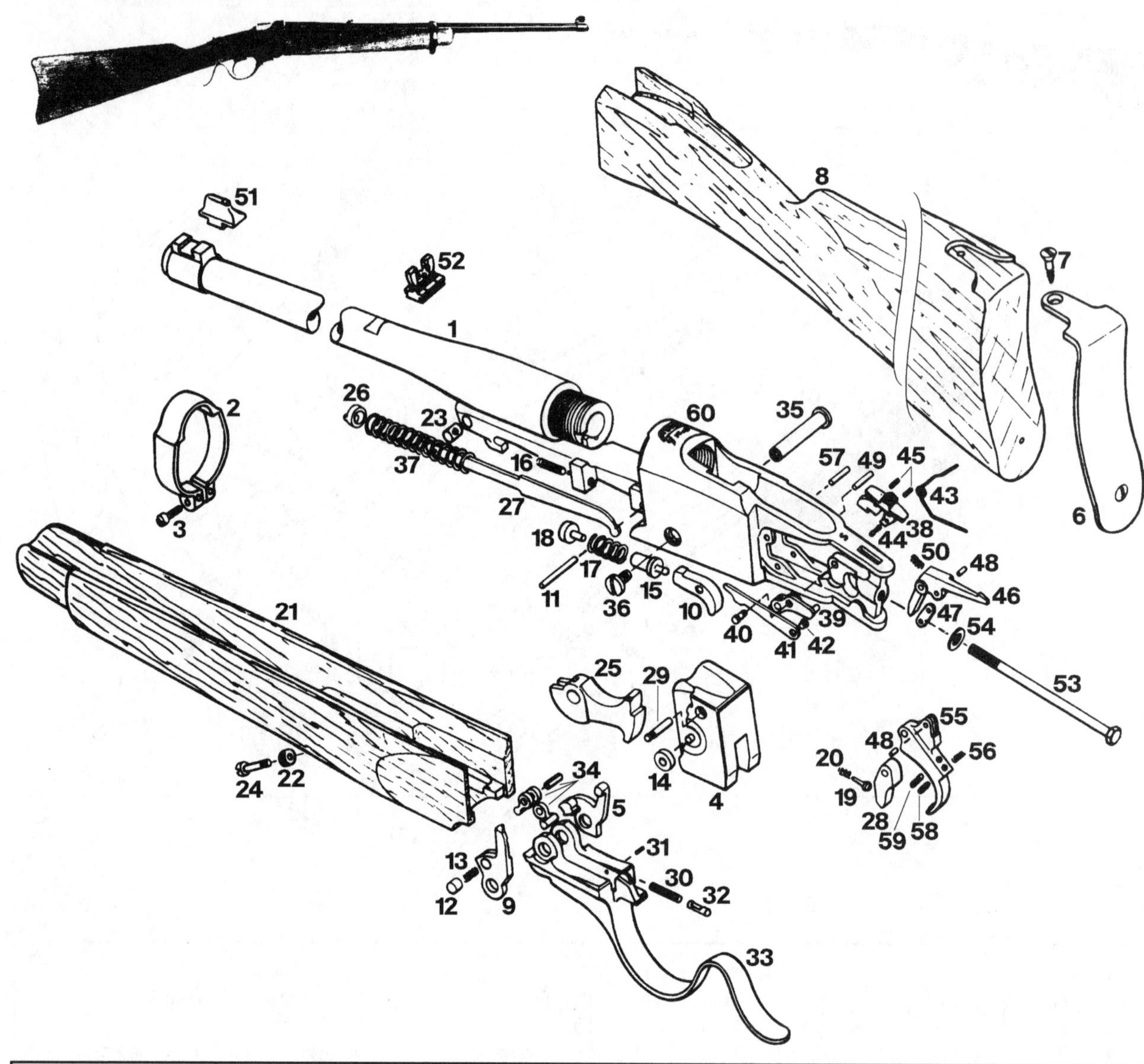

1	Barrel	**22**	Forend Escutcheon	**41**	Safety Bar
2	Barrel Band	**23**	Forend Takedown Nut	**42**	Safety Bar Pivot Pin
3	Barrel Band Screw	**24**	Forend Takedown Screw	**43**	Safety Detent Spring
4	Breechblock	**25**	Hammer	**44**	Safety Detent Spring Pin
5	Breechblock Arm	**26**	Hammer Spring Retainer Washer	**45**	Safety Retaining Pins
6	Buttplate	**27**	Hammer Strut	**46**	Sear
7	Buttplate Screws	**28**	Hammer Transfer Block	**47**	Sear Link
8	Buttstock	**29**	Hammer Transfer Block Pivot Pin	**48**	Sear Link Pins
9	Ejector	**30**	Latch Plunger Spring	**49**	Sear Pivot Pin
10	Ejector Cam	**31**	Latch Plunger Set Screw	**50**	Sear Spring
11	Ejector Cam Pivot Pin	**32**	Latch Plunger	**51**	Front Sight
12	Ejector Plunger	**33**	Lever	**52**	Rear Sight
13	Ejector Plunger Spring	**34**	Lever and Arm Link Assembly	**53**	Stock Bolt
14	Ejector Roller	**35**	Lever Pivot Pin	**54**	Stock Bolt Washer
15	Ejector Strut	**36**	Lever Pivot Screw	**55**	Trigger
16	Ejector Strut Adjustment Screw	**37**	Mainspring	**56**	Trigger Adjustment Spring
17	Ejector Strut Spring	**38**	Safety	**57**	Trigger Pivot Pin
18	Ejector Strut Swivel	**39**	Safety Arm	**58**	Trigger Spring Adjustment Screw
19	Firing Pin	**40**	Safety Arm Pivot Pin	**59**	Trigger Stop Screw
20	Firing Pin Spring			**60**	Receiver
21	Forend				

Red Label Over/Under Shotgun

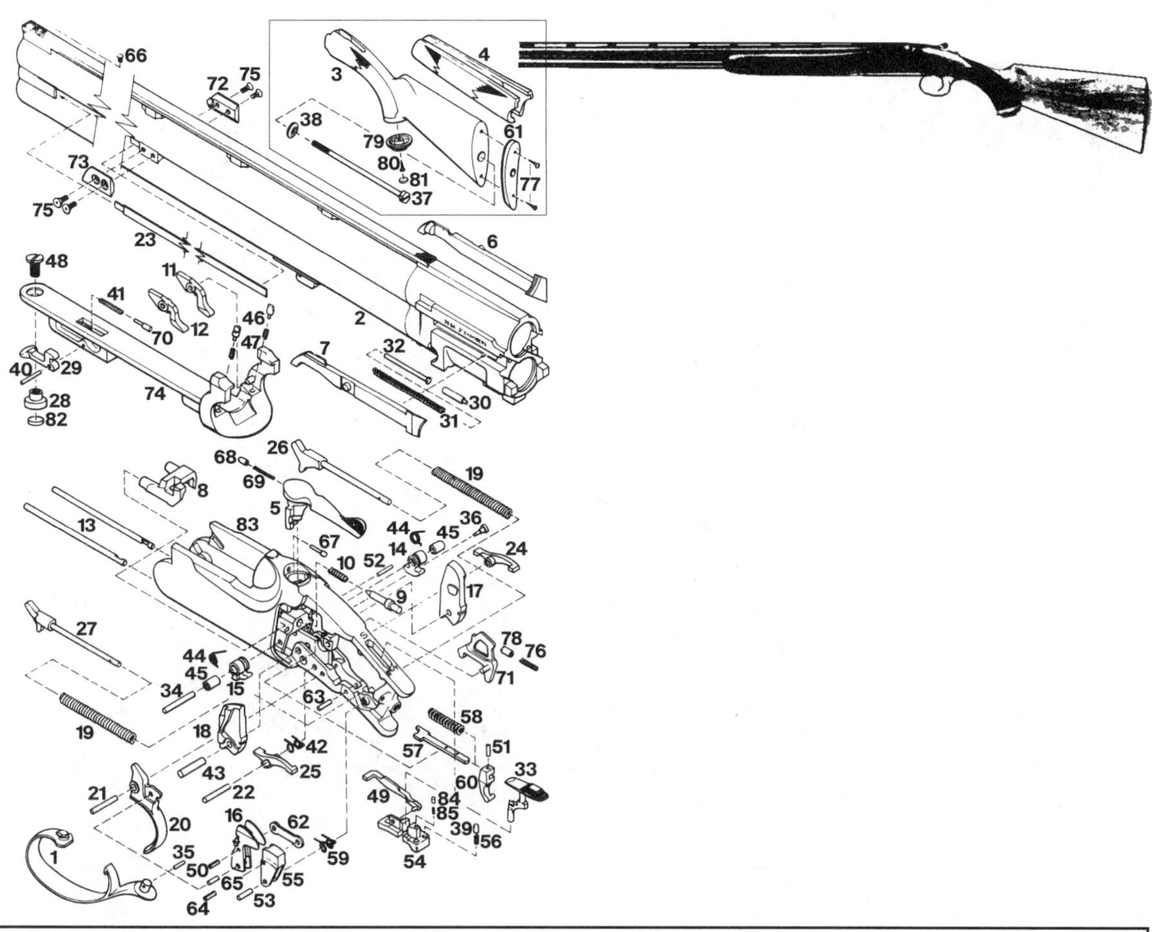

1	Trigger Guard	**30**	Ejector Plungers	**58**	Top Lever Spring
2	Barrel Assembly	**31**	Ejector Springs	**59**	Inertia Weight Spring
3	Stock	**32**	Ejector Spring Guides	**60**	Sear Selector Actuator
4	Forend	**33**	Safety Thumb-Piece	**61**	Recoil Pad
5	Top Lever	**34**	Cocking Cam Pivot Pin	**62**	Link
6	Ejector, Right	**35**	Trigger Guard Retaining Pin	**63**	Trigger Stop Pin
7	Ejector, Left	**36**	Blocking Bar Retaining Pin	**64**	Link Retaining Pin
8	Locking Bolt	**37**	Stock Bolt	**65**	Sear Selector Pivot Pin
9	Firing Pins	**38**	Stock Bolt Washer	**66**	Front Sight
10	Firing Pin Springs	**39**	Safety Detent Plunger	**67**	Top Lever Trip
11	Sear Ejector, Right	**40**	Forend Latch Lever Pin	**68**	Top Lever Trip Plunger
12	Sear Ejector, Left	**41**	Forend Latch Spring	**69**	Top Lever Trip Plunger Spring
13	Cocking Rods	**42**	Sear Spring	**70**	Forend Latch Plunger
14	Cocking Cam, Right	**43**	Hammer Pivot Pin	**71**	Hammer Interrupter
15	Cocking Cam, Left	**44**	Cocking Cam Springs	**72**	Forend Filler Block, Right
16	Sear Selector	**45**	Cocking Cam Sleeves	**73**	Forend Filler Block, Left
17	Hammer, Right	**46**	Ejector Sear Plungers	**74**	Forend Iron Sub-Assembly
18	Hammer, Left	**47**	Ejector Sear Plunger Springs	**75**	Forend Filler Screws
19	Hammer Springs	**48**	Forend Iron Escutcheon Screw	**76**	Interrupter Plunger Spring
20	Trigger	**49**	Blocking Bar	**77**	Recoil Pad Screws
21	Trigger Pin	**50**	Sear Selector Pivot Pin	**78**	Interrupter Plunger
22	Sear Pivot Pin	**51**	Sear Selector Actuator Retaining Pin	**79**	Pistol Grip Cap
23	Barrel Filler Strip	**52**	Firing Pin Retaining Pin	**80**	Pistol Grip Cap Screw
24	Sear, Right	**53**	Inertia Weight Pivot Pins	**81**	Pistol Grip Cap Medallion
25	Sear, Left	**54**	Safety Block	**82**	Forend Escutcheon Medallion
26	Hammer Strut Assembly, Right	**55**	Inertia Weight	**83**	Receiver
27	Hammer Strut Assembly, Left	**56**	Safety Detent Springs	**84**	Safety Thumb-Piece Detent
28	Forend Iron Escutcheon	**57**	Top Lever Spring Strut	**85**	Safety Thumb-Piece Detent Spring
29	Forend Latch Lever				

Red Label Over/Under Shotgun

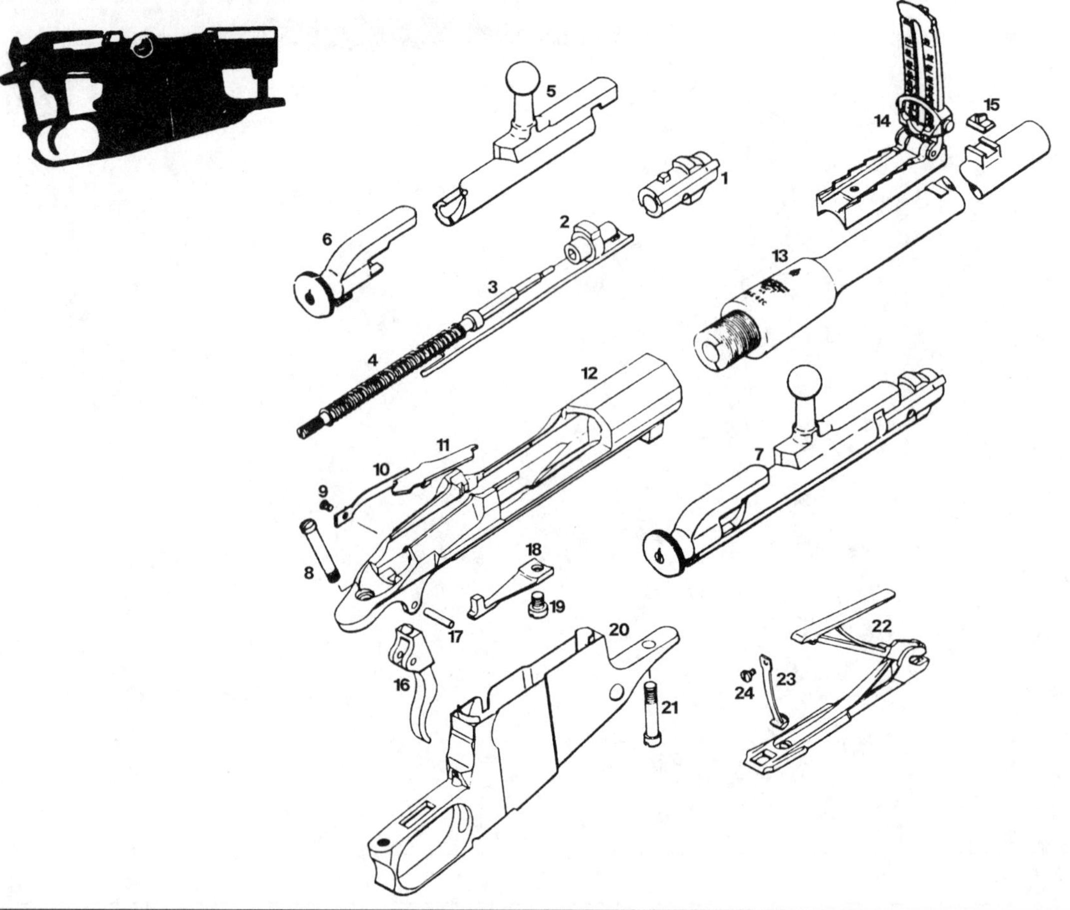

1 Trigger Guard
2 Barrel Assembly
3 Stock
4 Forend
5 Top Lever
6 Ejector, Right
7 Ejector, Left
8 Locking Bolt
9 Firing Pins
10 Firing Pin Springs
11 Sear Ejector, Right
12 Sear Ejector, Left
13 Cocking Rods
14 Cocking Cam, Right
15 Cocking Cam, Left
16 Sear Selector
17 Hammer, Right
18 Hammer, Left
19 Hammer Springs
20 Trigger
21 Trigger Pin
22 Sear Pivot Pin
23 Barrel Filler Strip
24 Sear, Right
25 Sear, Left
26 Hammer Strut Assembly, Right
27 Hammer Strut Assembly, Left
28 Forend Iron Escutcheon
29 Forend Latch Lever
30 Ejector Plungers
31 Ejector Springs
32 Ejector Spring Guides
33 Safety Thumb-Piece
34 Cocking Cam Pivot Pin
35 Trigger Guard Retaining Pin
36 Blocking Bar Retaining Pin
37 Stock Bolt
38 Stock Bolt Washer
39 Safety Detent Plunger
40 Forend Latch Lever Pin
41 Forend Latch Spring
42 Sear Spring
43 Hammer Pivot Pin
44 Cocking Cam Springs
45 Cocking Cam Sleeves
46 Ejector Sear Plungers
47 Ejector Sear Plunger Springs
48 Forend Iron Escutcheon Screw
49 Blocking Bar
50 Sear Selector Pivot Pin
51 Sear Selector Actuator Retaining Pin
52 Firing Pin Retaining Pin
53 Inertia Weight Pivot Pins
54 Safety Block
55 Inertia Weight
56 Safety Detent Springs
57 Top Lever Spring Strut
58 Top Lever Spring
59 Inertia Weight Spring
60 Sear Selector Actuator
61 Recoil Pad
62 Link
63 Trigger Stop Pin
64 Link Retaining Pin
65 Sear Selector Pivot Pin
66 Front Sight
67 Top Lever Trip
68 Top Lever Trip Plunger
69 Top Lever Trip Plunger Spring
70 Forend Latch Plunger
71 Hammer Interrupter
72 Forend Filler Block, Right
73 Forend Filler Block, Left
74 Forend Iron Sub-Assembly
75 Forend Filler Screws
76 Interrupter Plunger Spring
77 Recoil Pad Screws
78 Interrupter Plunger
79 Pistol Grip Cap
80 Pistol Grip Cap Screw
81 Pistol Grip Cap Medallion
82 Forend Escutcheon Medallion
83 Receiver
84 Safety Thumb-Piece Detent
85 Safety Thumb-Piece Detent Spring

Finnbear and Forrester Bolt-Action Rifle

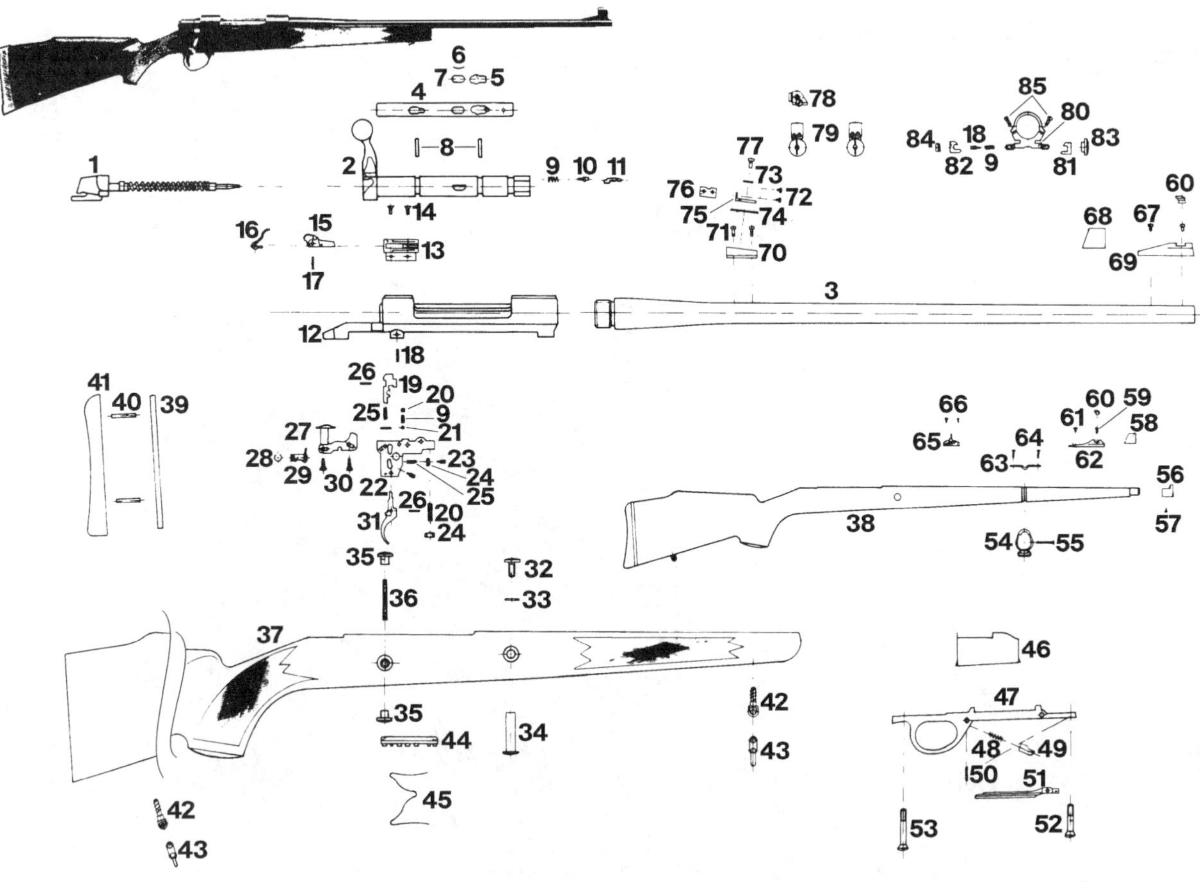

1	Firing Pin Assembly
2	Bolt
3	Barrel
4	Bolt Guide
5	Bolt Guide Stop Plate
6	Bolt Guide Stop Plate Spring
7	Bolt Guide Stop Spring
8	Bolt Guide Mounting Rings
9	Springs
10	Extractor Plunger
11	Extractor
12	Receiver
13	Bolt Stop Body
14	Bolt Stop Mounting Screws
15	Bolt Stop
16	Bolt Stop Spring
17	Bolt Stop Pin
18	Pins
19	Cocking Piece
20	Set Screws
21	Ball
22	Trigger Mechanism Body
23	Adjusting Screw
24	Hexagon Nut
25	Trigger Spring
26	Spring Pin
27	Knob Plate
28	Stop Ring
29	Safety Shaft Assembly
30	Knob Plate Screws
31	Trigger
32	Recoil Lug Screw, Front
33	Recoil Lug Spacer
34	Recoil Lug Nut, Front
35	Recoil Lug Nuts, Rear
36	Recoil Lug Screw, Rear
37	Stock Complete, Rifle
38	Stock Complete, Carbine
39	Buttplate Base
40	Mounting Screws
41	Buttplate
42	Swivel Screws
43	Swivels
44	Magazine Follower
45	Magazine Spring
46	Magazine Box
47	Trigger Guard
48	Floorplate Catch Spring
49	Floorplate Catch
50	Spring Pin
51	Floorplate
52	Front Fastening Screw
53	Rear Fastening Screw
54	Stock Band
55	Stock Band Screw
56	Muzzle Cap
57	Muzzle Cap Screw
58	Front Sight Hood
59	Front Mounting Screw
60	Beads
61	Rear Mounting Screw
62	Sight Base
63	Connecting Plate
64	Connecting Plate Screws
65	Rear Sight
66	Rear Sight Mounting Screws
67	Sight Base Mounting Screws
68	Front Sight Hood
69	Front Sight Base
70	Rear Sight Base
71	Mounting Screws
72	Sight Body Mounting Screws
73	Washer
74	Covering Plate
75	Sight Body
76	Sight Blade
77	Mounting Screw
78	Peep Sight Complete
79	Scope Mount Complete
80	Scope Mount Base
81	Scope Mount Locking Piece
82	Scope Mount Adjusting Piece
83	Tightening Screw
84	Tightening Screw
85	Fastening Screws

Finnwolf Lever-Action Rifle

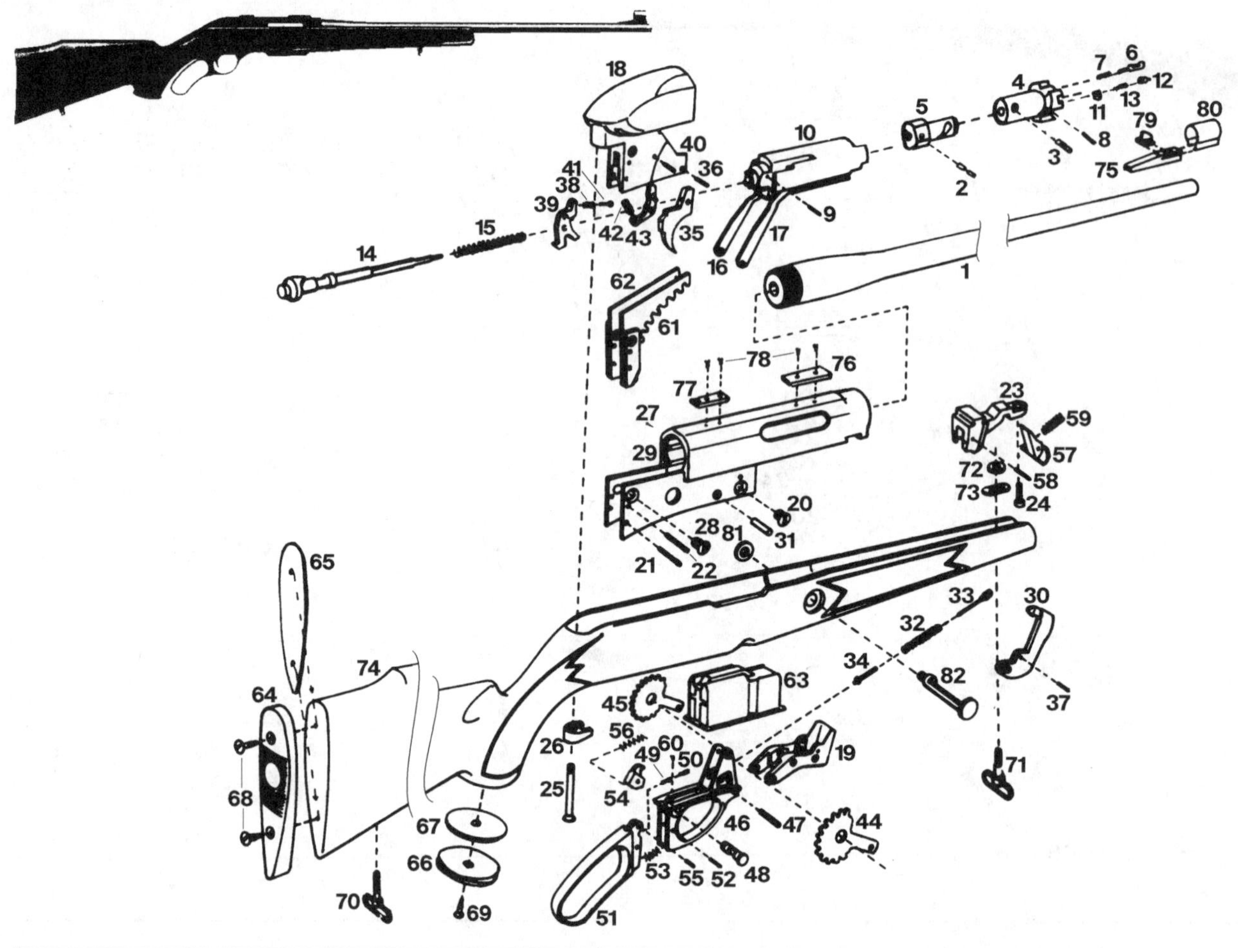

1	Barrel
2	Connector Link Pin
3	Bolt Guide Pin
4	Breechbolt
5	Slide
6	Ejector
7	Ejector Spring
8	Ejector Pin
9	Firing Pin Dowel
10	Bolt Body
11	Extractor
12	Extractor Guide
13	Extractor Spring
14	Firing Pin
15	Firing Pin Spring
16	Connector Link, Left
17	Connector Link, Right
18	Receiver Rear Piece
19	Magazine Rear Stop
20	Sideplate Screw
21	Sideplate Pin
22	Sideplate Dowel Pin
23	Magazine Catch Body
24	Front Guard Screw
25	Rear Guard Screw
26	Rear Guard Screw Base
27	Plug Screw
28	Rear Tie Screw
29	Receiver
30	Hammer
31	Hammer Pin
32	Hammer Spring
33	Hammer Spring Guide Rod
34	Hammer Spring Guide
35	Trigger
36	Trigger Pin
37	Hammer Spring and Guide Rod Pin
38	Trigger Spring
39	Front Safety
40	Front Safety Pin
41	Trigger Spring Rod
42	Hammer Catch Spring
43	Hammer Catch Complete
44	Rack Lever, Right
45	Rack Lever, Left
46	Trigger Guard
47	Trigger Guard Pin
48	Safety
49	Safety Spring
50	Safety Button
51	Finger Lever
52	Finger Lever Pin
53	Finger Lever Spring
54	Finger Lever Catch
55	Finger Lever Catch Pin
56	Finger Lever Catch Spring
57	Magazine Catch
58	Magazine Catch Pin
59	Magazine Catch Spring
60	Safety Guide Screw
61	Rack, Right
62	Rack, Left
63	Magazine Complete
64	Buttplate
65	Buttplate Spacer
66	Pistol Grip Cap
67	Pistol Grip Cap Spacer
68	Buttplate Screws
69	Pistol Grip Cap Screw
70	Stock Swivel
71	Upper Swivel
72	Upper Swivel Nut
73	Upper Swivel Bottom Plate
74	Stock
75	Front Sight Ramp
76	Front Scope Block
77	Rear Scope Block
78	Scope Block Screws
79	Front Sight Bead
80	Sight Hood
81	Recoil Bolt Nut
82	Recoil Bolt

Vixen Bolt-Action Rifle

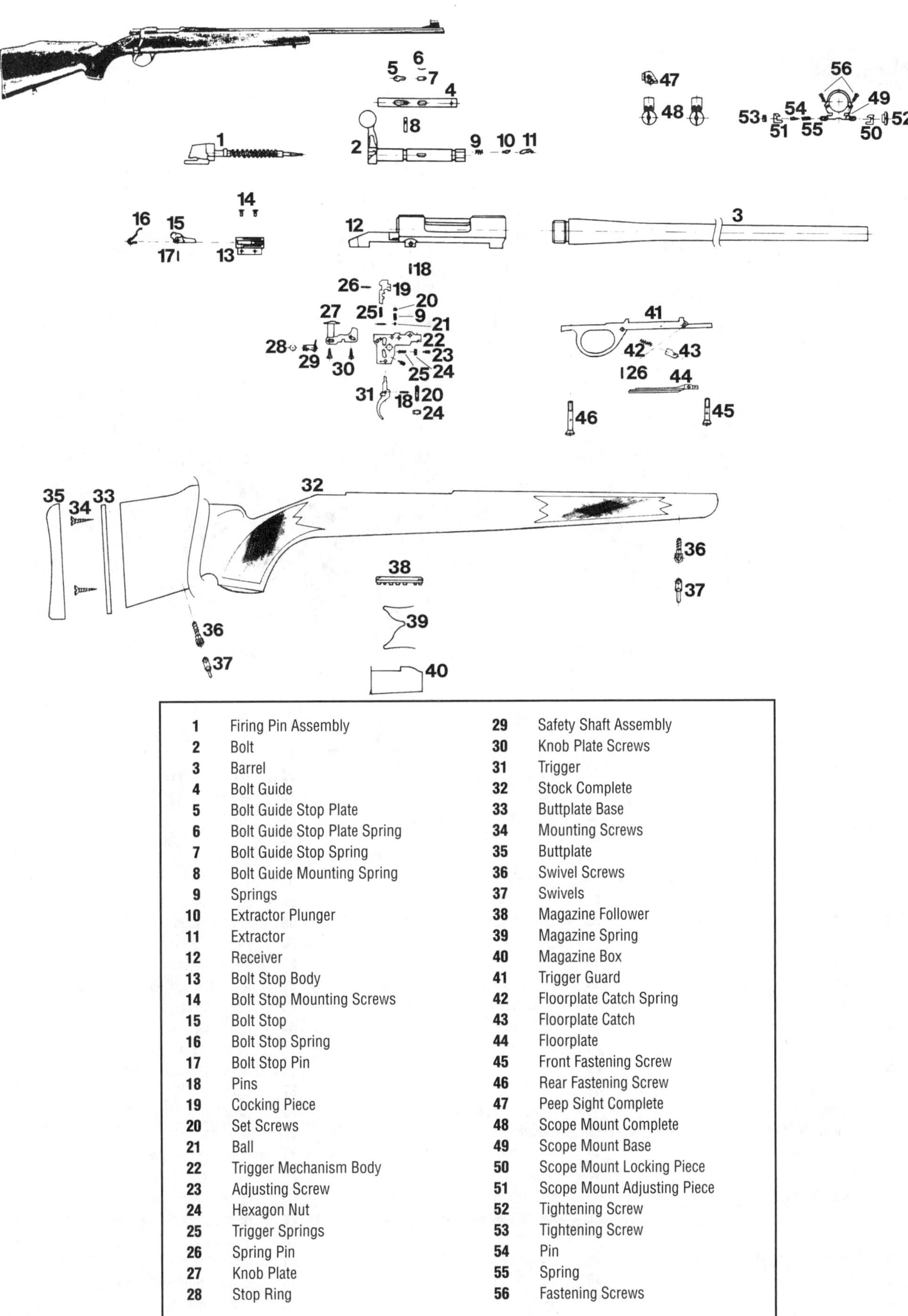

1	Firing Pin Assembly	29	Safety Shaft Assembly
2	Bolt	30	Knob Plate Screws
3	Barrel	31	Trigger
4	Bolt Guide	32	Stock Complete
5	Bolt Guide Stop Plate	33	Buttplate Base
6	Bolt Guide Stop Plate Spring	34	Mounting Screws
7	Bolt Guide Stop Spring	35	Buttplate
8	Bolt Guide Mounting Spring	36	Swivel Screws
9	Springs	37	Swivels
10	Extractor Plunger	38	Magazine Follower
11	Extractor	39	Magazine Spring
12	Receiver	40	Magazine Box
13	Bolt Stop Body	41	Trigger Guard
14	Bolt Stop Mounting Screws	42	Floorplate Catch Spring
15	Bolt Stop	43	Floorplate Catch
16	Bolt Stop Spring	44	Floorplate
17	Bolt Stop Pin	45	Front Fastening Screw
18	Pins	46	Rear Fastening Screw
19	Cocking Piece	47	Peep Sight Complete
20	Set Screws	48	Scope Mount Complete
21	Ball	49	Scope Mount Base
22	Trigger Mechanism Body	50	Scope Mount Locking Piece
23	Adjusting Screw	51	Scope Mount Adjusting Piece
24	Hexagon Nut	52	Tightening Screw
25	Trigger Springs	53	Tightening Screw
26	Spring Pin	54	Pin
27	Knob Plate	55	Spring
28	Stop Ring	56	Fastening Screws

200 Bolt-Action Rifle

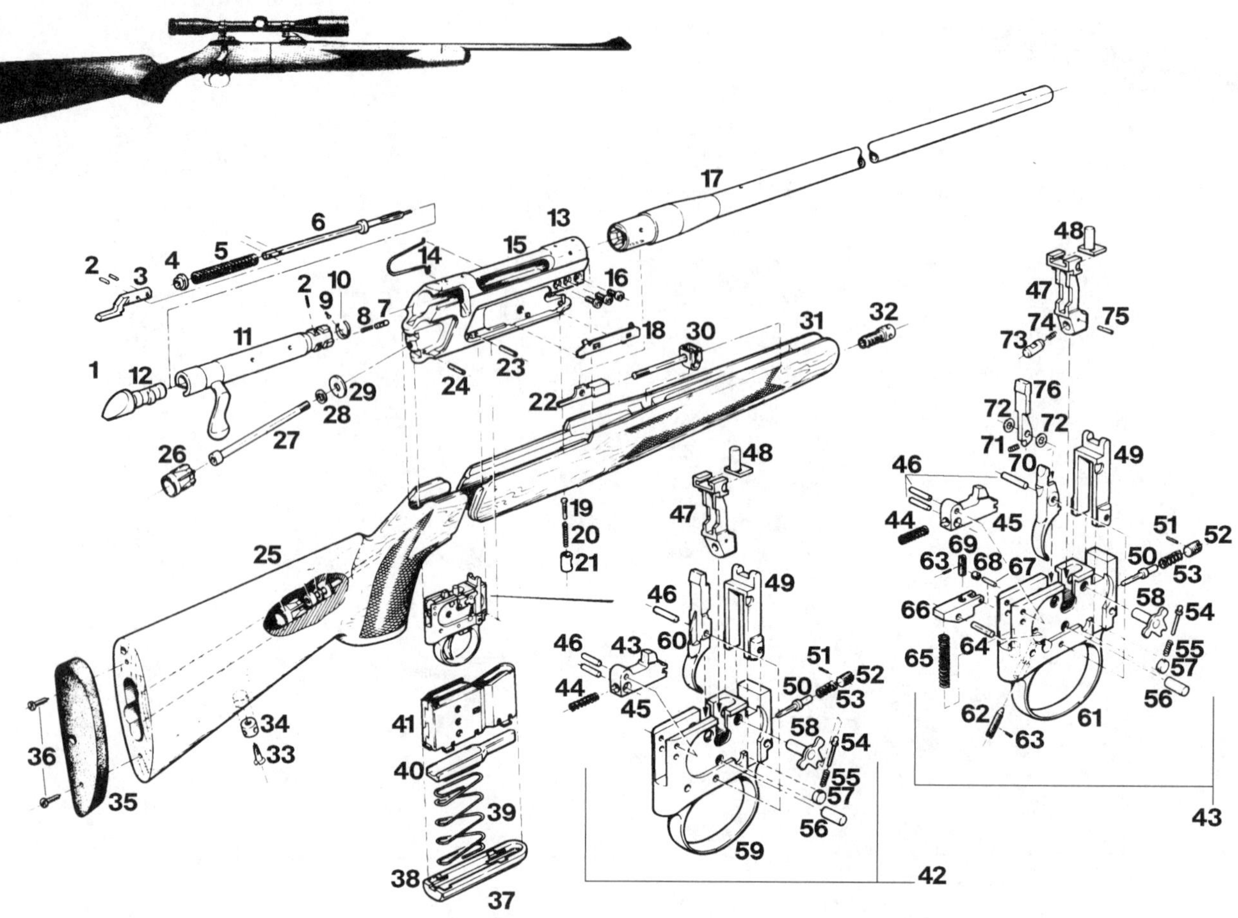

No.	Part	No.	Part	No.	Part
1	Bolt Assembly	26	Retaining Bushing	52	Adjusting Screw for Trigger Spring
2	Slotted Spring Pins	27	Buttstock Screw	53	Compression Spring
3	Firing Pin Nut	28	Washer	54	Spring Pin
4	Collar Bushing	29	Serrated Washer	55	Rocker Arm Spring
5	Firing Pin Spring	30	Forend Screw	56	Cylindrical Pin
6	Firing Pin	31	Forend	57	Spring Support
7	Ejector Pin	32	Sling Swivel Socket for Forend	58	Rocker Arm
8	Compression Spring for Ejector	33	Countersunk-Head Wood Screw	59	Trigger Housing
9	Extractor Rivet	34	Sling Swivel Bushing	60	Direct Trigger
10	Extractor	35	Butt Cap	61	Trigger Housing
11	Bolt Body	36	Butt Cap Screws	62	Adjusting Screw for Set Trigger
12	Cocking Sleeve	37	Magazine	63	Screw Locks
13	Receiver/Barrel	38	Magazine Base	64	Cylindrical Pin
14	Magazine Ejector Spring	39	Magazine Spring	65	Compression Spring for Set Trigger
15	Receiver	40	Feeder	66	Striking Lever for Set Trigger
16	Clamping Screws	41	Magazine Box	67	Cylindrical Pin
17	Barrel	42	Direct Trigger Assembly	68	Roller
18	Magazine Catch	43	Double-Set Trigger Assembly	69	Discharge Screw
19	Guide Pin	44	Compression Spring for Sear	70	Double-Set Trigger
20	Compression Spring for Magazine Catch	45	Sear	71	Compression Spring for Finger Lever
21	Locking Catch	46	Cylindrical Pins	72	Shims
22	Insert	47	Safety Release Catch	73	Spring Pin
23	Slotted Spring Pin, Front	48	Action Catch Pin	74	Spring
24	Slotted Spring Pin, Rear	49	Safety Catch	75	Connex Slotted Spring Pin
25	Buttstock	50	Spring Pin	76	Trigger Bar
		51	Screw Lock		

Model 110, 110E, 110M, 110P and 110PE Bolt-Action Rifle

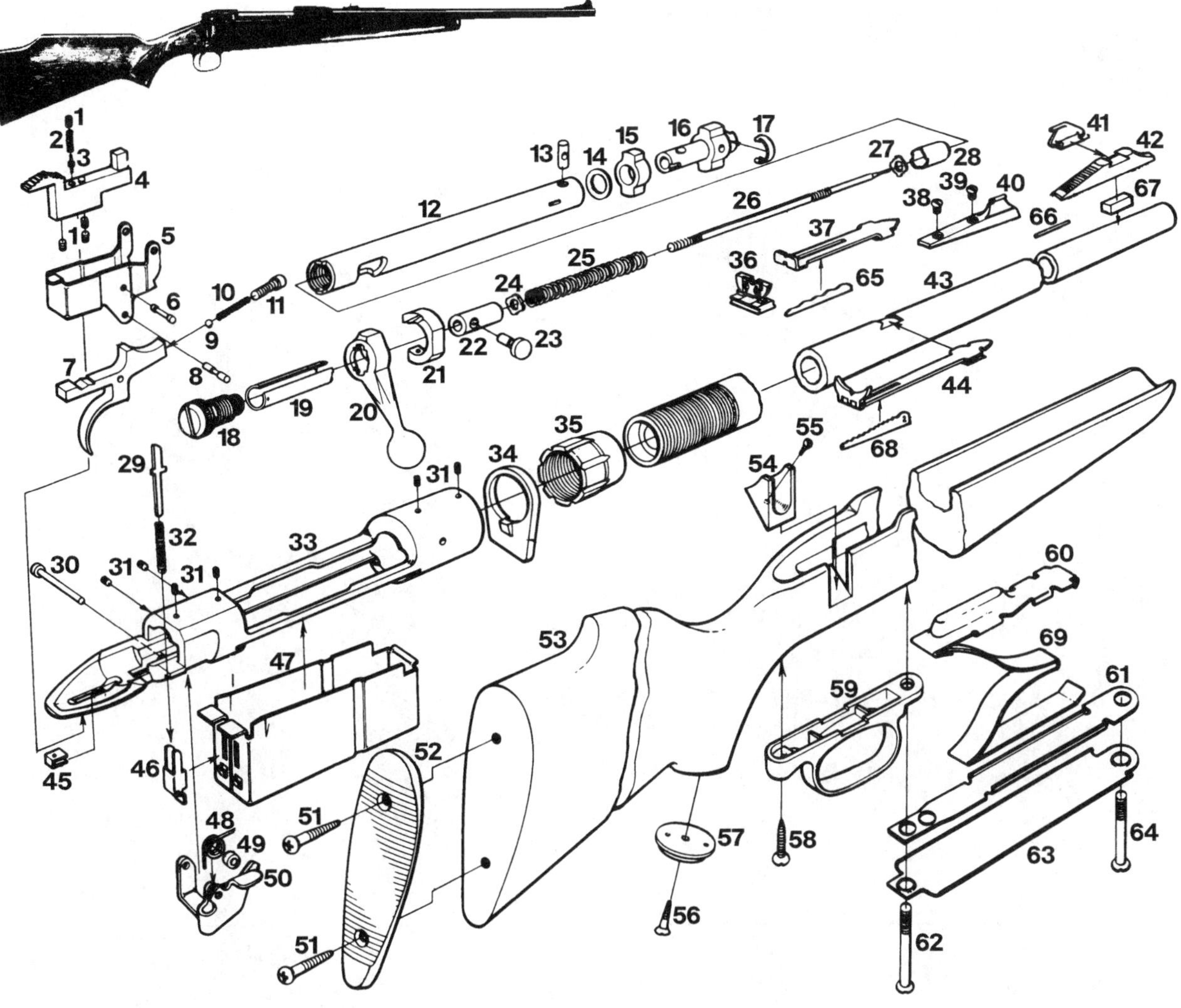

1	Trigger Pull Adjusting Screws
2	Trigger Spring
3	Trigger Spring Plunger
4	Safety
5	Trigger Bracket
6	Safety Bearing Pin
7	Trigger
8	Trigger Pin
9	Steel Ball
10	Trigger Pin Retaining Spring
11	Trigger Engagement Adjusting Screw
12	Bolt Body
13	Bolt Head Retaining Pin
14	Front Baffle Friction Washer
15	Front Baffle
16	Bolt Head
17	Extractor
18	Bolt Assembly Screw
19	Cocking Piece Sleeve
20	Bolt Handle
21	Rear Baffle
22	Cocking Piece
23	Cocking Piece Pin
24	Cocking Piece Lock Washer
25	Mainspring
26	Firing Pin
27	Firing Pin Stop Nut Lock Washer
28	Firing Pin Stop Nut
29	Ejector
30	Sear Pin
31	Dummy Screws
32	Ejector Spring
33	Receiver
34	Recoil Lug
35	Barrel Lock Nut
36	Rear Sight
37	Rear Sight Step
38	Front Sight Screw, Short
39	Front Sight Screw, Long
40	Front Sight
41	Front Sight Blade
42	Front Sight and Base Assembly
43	Barrel
44	Rear Sight and Step
45	Trigger Adjusting Screw Cover
46	Magazine Latch
47	Magazine Box
48	Sear Spring
49	Sear Bushing
50	Sear
51	Buttplate Screws
52	Buttplate
53	Stock
54	Bolt Handle Slot Liner
55	Bolt Handle Slot Liner Screw
56	Pistol Grip Cap Screw
57	Pistol Grip Cap
58	Trigger Guard Screw
59	Trigger Guard
60	Magazine Follower
61	Floorplate Insert
62	Floorplate Screw, Rear
63	Floorplate
64	Floorplate Screw, Front
65	Rear Sight Step
66	Front Sight Pin
67	Front Sight Dovetail Block
68	Rear Sight Step
69	Magazine Spring

Model 110B, 110C, 110D and 110E Series J and K Bolt-Action Rifle

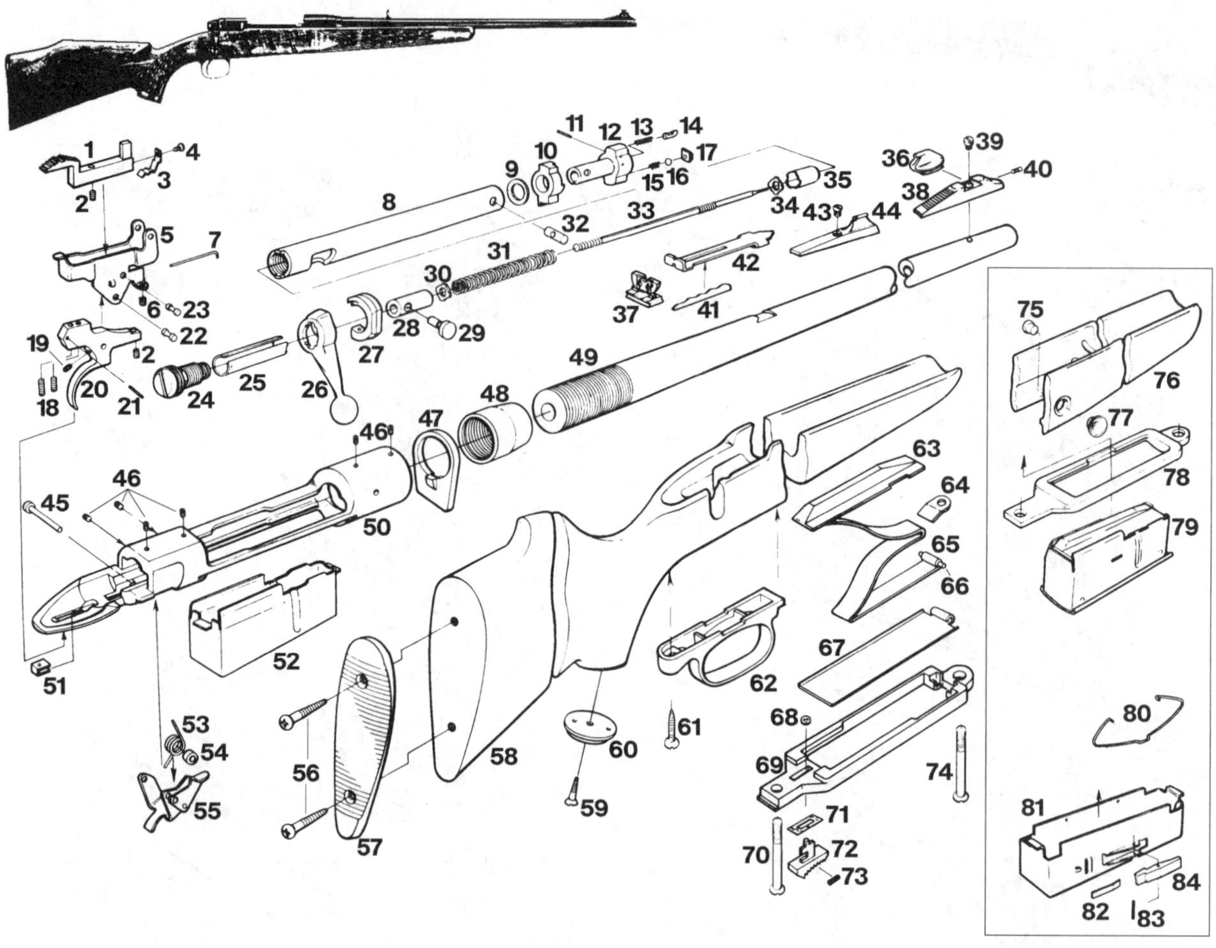

No.	Part	No.	Part	No.	Part
1	Safety	29	Cocking Piece Pin	57	Buttplate
2	Trigger Pull Adjusting Screw	30	Cocking Piece Link Washer	58	Stock
3	Safety Detent Spring	31	Mainspring	59	Pistol Grip Cap Screw
4	Safety Detent Spring Screw	32	Bolt Head Retaining Pin	60	Pistol Grip Cap
5	Trigger Bracket	33	Firing Pin Assembly	61	Trigger Guard Screw
6	Trigger Pull Adjusting Screw	34	Firing Pin Stop Nut Washer	62	Trigger Guard
7	Trigger Pull Adjusting Spring	35	Firing Pin Stop Nut	63	Magazine Follower Assembly
8	Bolt Body	36	Front Sight	64	Hinge Plate Spring
9	Front Baffle Friction Washer	37	Rear Sight	65	Magazine Spring
10	Front Baffle	38	Front Sight Base	66	Hinge Pin
11	Ejector Retaining Pin	39	Front Sight Screw	67	Hinged Plate
12	Bolt Head Assembly	40	Front Sight Adjusting Screw	68	Magazine Latch Retaining Ring
13	Ejector Spring	41	Rear Sight Step	69	Floorplate
14	Ejector	42	Rear Sight	70	Floorplate Screw, Rear
15	Extractor Spring	43	Front Sight Screw	71	Magazine Latch Spacer
16	Steel Ball	44	Front Sight Assembly	72	Magazine Latch
17	Extractor	45	Sear Pin	73	Magazine Latch Spring
18	Trigger Travel Adjusting Screws	46	Dummy Screw	74	Floorplate Screw, Front
19	Trigger Pin Retaining Screws	47	Recoil Lug	75	Magazine Latch Button
20	Trigger	48	Barrel Lock Nut	76	Stock
21	Trigger Spring Pin	49	Barrel	77	Escutcheon
22	Trigger Pin	50	Receiver	78	Floorplate
23	Safety Bearing Pin	51	Trigger Adjusting Screw Cover	79	Magazine Assembly
24	Bolt Assembly Screw	52	Magazine Box	80	Magazine Ejector Spring
25	Cocking Piece Sleeve	53	Sear Spring	81	Magazine Guide
26	Bolt Handle	54	Sear Bushing	82	Magazine Latch Spring
27	Rear Baffle Assembly	55	Sear Assembly	83	Magazine Latch Pin
28	Cocking Piece	56	Buttplate Screws	84	Magazine Latch

Model 110C and 110CL Bolt-Action Rifle

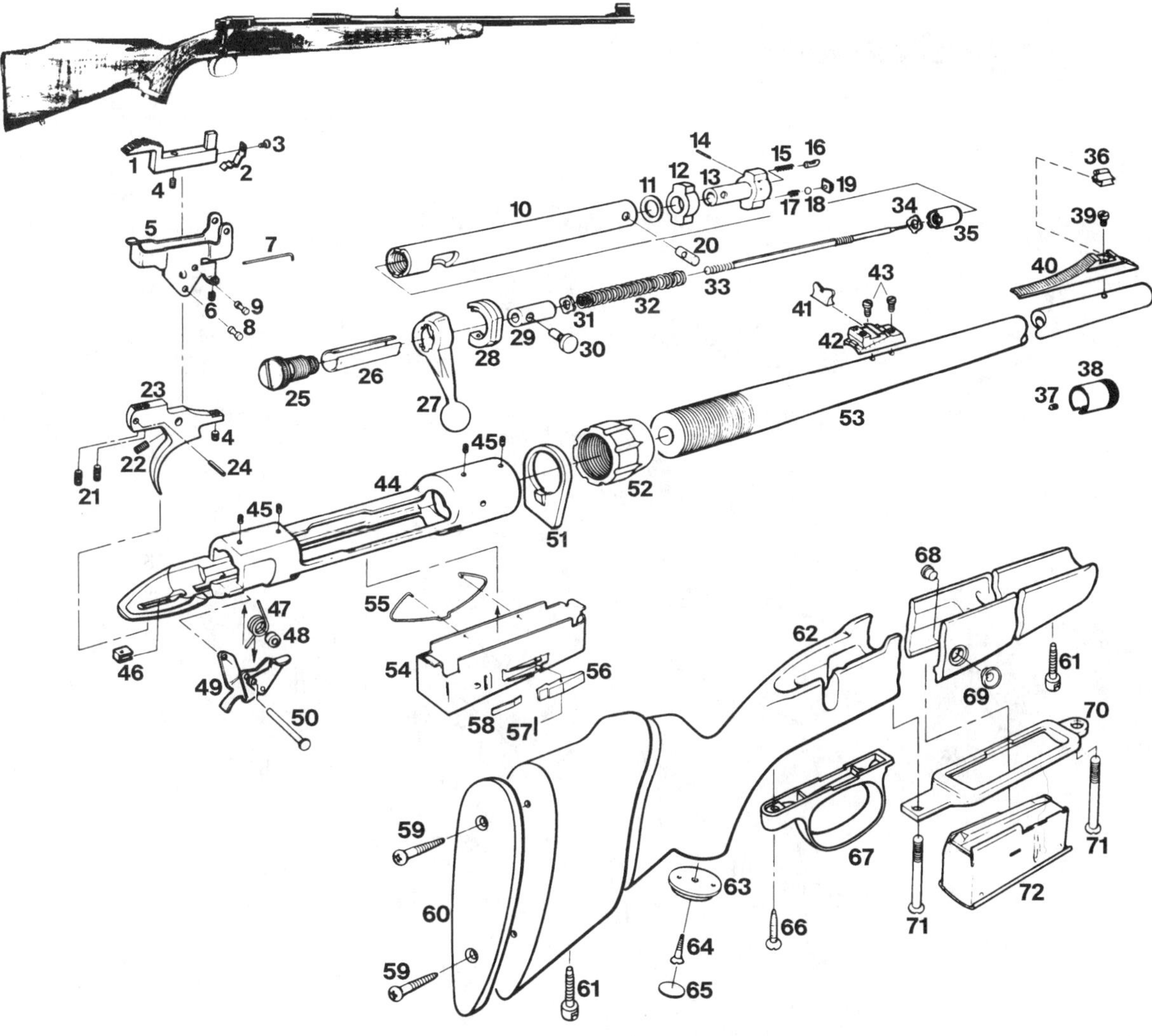

1	Safety
2	Safety Detent Spring
3	Safety Detent Spring Screw
4	Trigger Pull Adjusting Screw
5	Trigger Bracket
6	Trigger Pull Adjusting Screw
7	Trigger Pull Adjusting Spring
8	Trigger Pin
9	Safety Bearing Pin
10	Bolt Body
11	Front Baffle Friction Washer
12	Front Baffle
13	Bolt Head Assembly
14	Ejector Retaining Pin
15	Ejector Spring
16	Ejector
17	Extractor Spring
18	Steel Ball
19	Extractor
20	Bolt Head Retaining Pin
21	Trigger Travel Adjusting Screws
22	Trigger Pin Retaining Screw
23	Trigger
24	Trigger Spring Pin
25	Bolt Assembly Screw
26	Cocking Piece Sleeve
27	Bolt Handle
28	Rear Baffle Assembly
29	Cocking Piece
30	Cocking Piece Pin
31	Cocking Piece Link Washer
32	Mainspring
33	Firing Pin Assembly
34	Firing Pin Stop Nut Washer
35	Firing Pin Stop Nut
36	Front Sight
37	Front Sight Pin
38	Front Sight Hood
39	Front Sight Screw
40	Front Sight Ramp
41	Rear Sight Blade
42	Rear Sight Base
43	Rear Sight Screws
44	Receiver
45	Dummy Screws
46	Trigger Adjusting Screw Cover
47	Sear Spring
48	Sear Bushing
49	Sear Assembly
50	Sear Pin
51	Recoil Lug
52	Barrel Lock Nut
53	Barrel
54	Magazine Guide
55	Magazine Ejector Spring
56	Magazine Latch
57	Magazine Latch Pin
58	Magazine Latch Spring
59	Buttplate Screws
60	Buttplate
61	Swivel Studs
62	Stock
63	Pistol Grip Cap
64	Pistol Grip Cap Screw
65	Medallion
66	Trigger Guard Screw
67	Trigger Guard
68	Magazine Latch Button
69	Escutcheon
70	Floorplate
71	Floorplate Screws
72	Magazine Box

Model 110E, 110B, 110F and 110V Bolt-Action Rifle

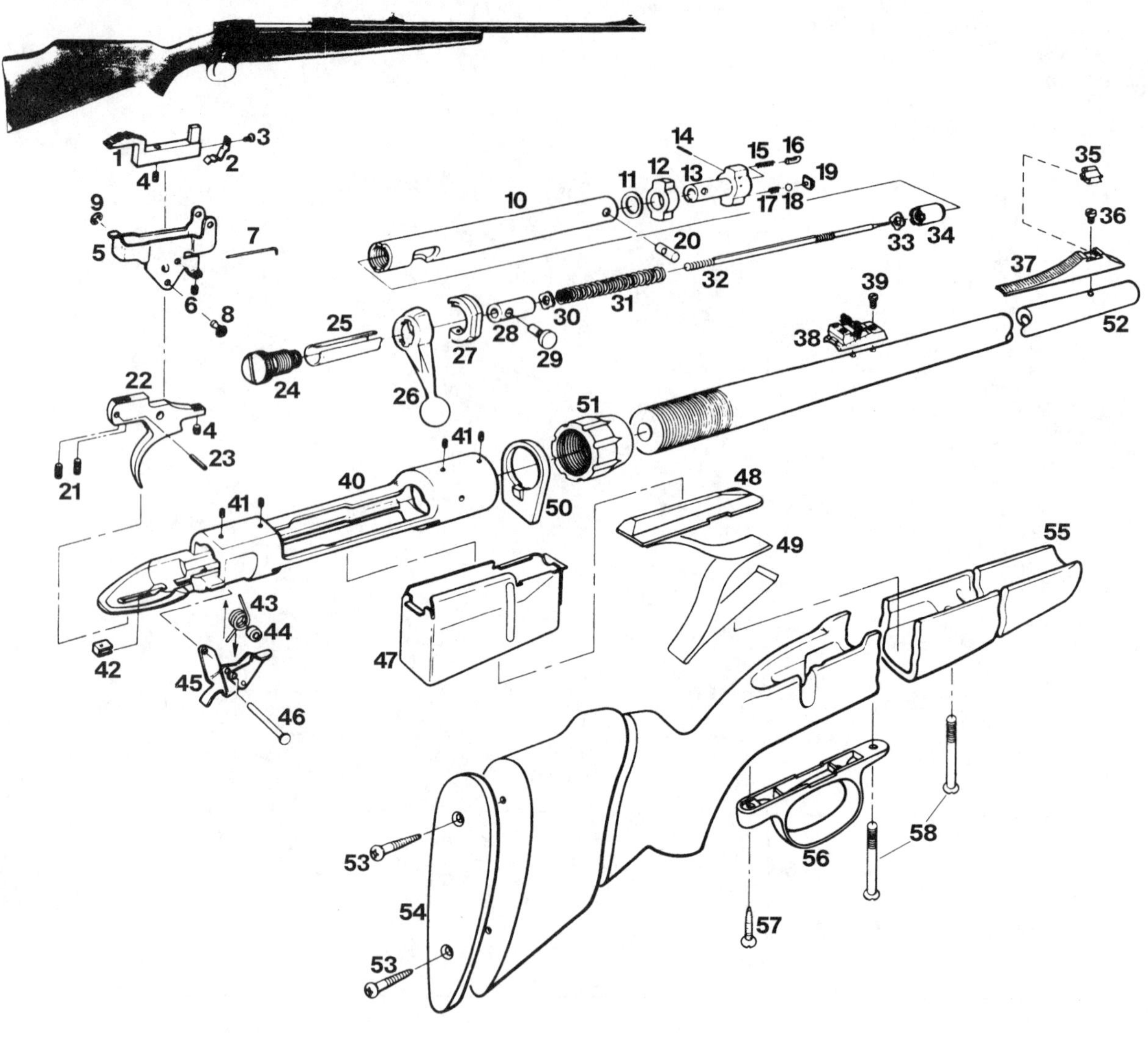

1	Safety	21	Trigger Travel Adjusting Screws	41	Dummy Screws
2	Safety Detent Spring	22	Trigger	42	Trigger Adjusting Screw Lever
3	Safety Detent Spring Screw	23	Trigger Spring Pin	43	Sear Spring
4	Trigger Pull Adjusting Screw	24	Bolt Assembly Screw	44	Sear Bushing
5	Trigger Bracket	25	Cocking Piece Sleeve	45	Sear Assembly
6	Trigger Pull Adjusting Screw	26	Bolt Handle	46	Sear Pin
7	Trigger Pull Adjusting Spring	27	Rear Baffle Assembly	47	Magazine Guide
8	Trigger Pin	28	Cocking Piece	48	Magazine Follower
9	Trigger Pin Clip	29	Cocking Piece Pin	49	Magazine Spring
10	Bolt Body	30	Cocking Piece Link Washer	50	Recoil Lug
11	Front Baffle Friction Washer	31	Mainspring	51	Barrel Lock Nut
12	Front Baffle	32	Firing Pin Assembly	52	Barrel
13	Bolt Head Assembly	33	Firing Pin Stop Nut Washer	53	Buttplate Screws
14	Ejector Retaining Pin	34	Firing Pin Stop Nut	54	Buttplate
15	Ejector Spring	35	Front Sight	55	Stock
16	Ejector	36	Front Sight Screw	56	Trigger Guard
17	Extractor Spring	37	Front Sight Ramp	57	Trigger Guard Screw
18	Steel Ball	38	Rear Sight	58	Floorplate Screws
19	Extractor	39	Rear Sight Screw		
20	Bolt Head Retaining Pin	40	Receiver		

Model 111 Series J Bolt-Action Rifle

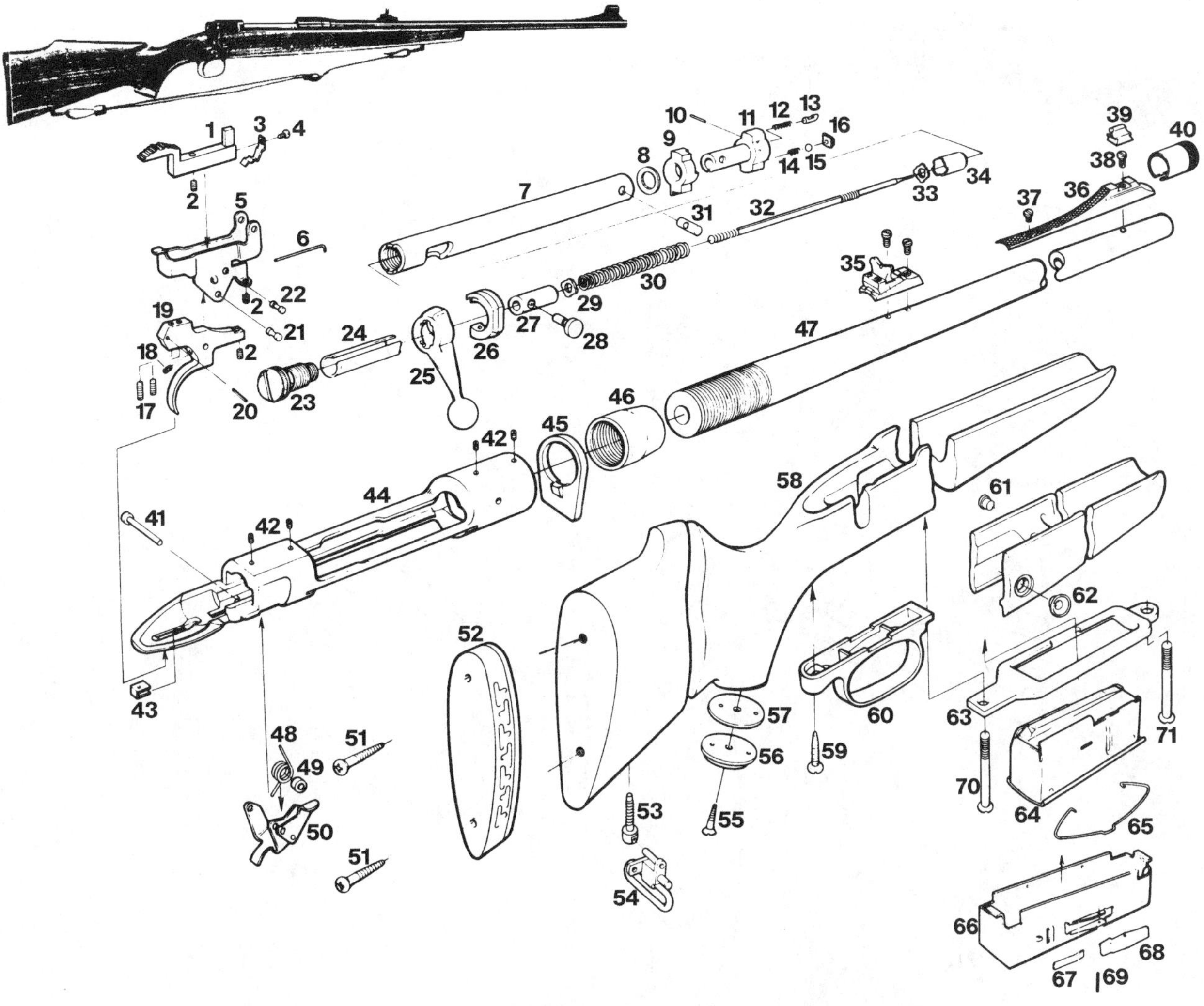

1	Safety
2	Trigger Pull Adjusting Screws
3	Safety Detent Spring
4	Safety Detent Spring Screw
5	Trigger Bracket
6	Trigger Pull Adjusting Spring
7	Bolt Body
8	Front Baffle Friction Washer
9	Front Baffle
10	Ejector Retaining Pin
11	Bolt Head
12	Ejector Spring
13	Ejector
14	Extractor Spring
15	Steel Ball
16	Extractor
17	Trigger Travel Adjusting Screws
18	Trigger Pin Retaining Screw
19	Trigger
20	Trigger Spring Pin
21	Trigger Pin
22	Safety Bearing Pin
23	Bolt Assembly Screw
24	Cocking Piece Sleeve
25	Bolt Handle
26	Rear Baffle Assembly
27	Cocking Piece
28	Cocking Piece Pin
29	Cocking Piece Link Washer
30	Mainspring
31	Bolt Head Retaining Pin
32	Firing Pin
33	Firing Pin Stop Nut Washer
34	Firing Pin Stop Nut
35	Rear Sight Assembly
36	Front Sight Base
37	Front Sight Screw, Short
38	Front Sight Screw, Long
39	Front Sight
40	Front Sight Hood
41	Sear Pin
42	Dummy Screws
43	Trigger Adjusting Screw Cover
44	Receiver
45	Recoil Lug
46	Barrel Lock Nut
47	Barrel
48	Sear Spring
49	Sear Bushing
50	Sear Assembly
51	Buttplate Screws
52	Buttplate
53	Swivel Stud
54	Swivel
55	Pistol Grip Cap Screw
56	Pistol Grip Cap
57	Pistol Grip Cap Liner
58	Stock
59	Trigger Guard Screw
60	Trigger Guard
61	Magazine Latch Button
62	Escutcheon
63	Floorplate
64	Magazine Assembly
65	Magazine Ejector Spring
66	Magazine Guide
67	Magazine Latch Spring
68	Magazine Latch
69	Magazine Latch Pin
70	Floorplate Screw, Rear
71	Floorplate Screw, Front

Model 112 Series J Bolt-Action Rifle

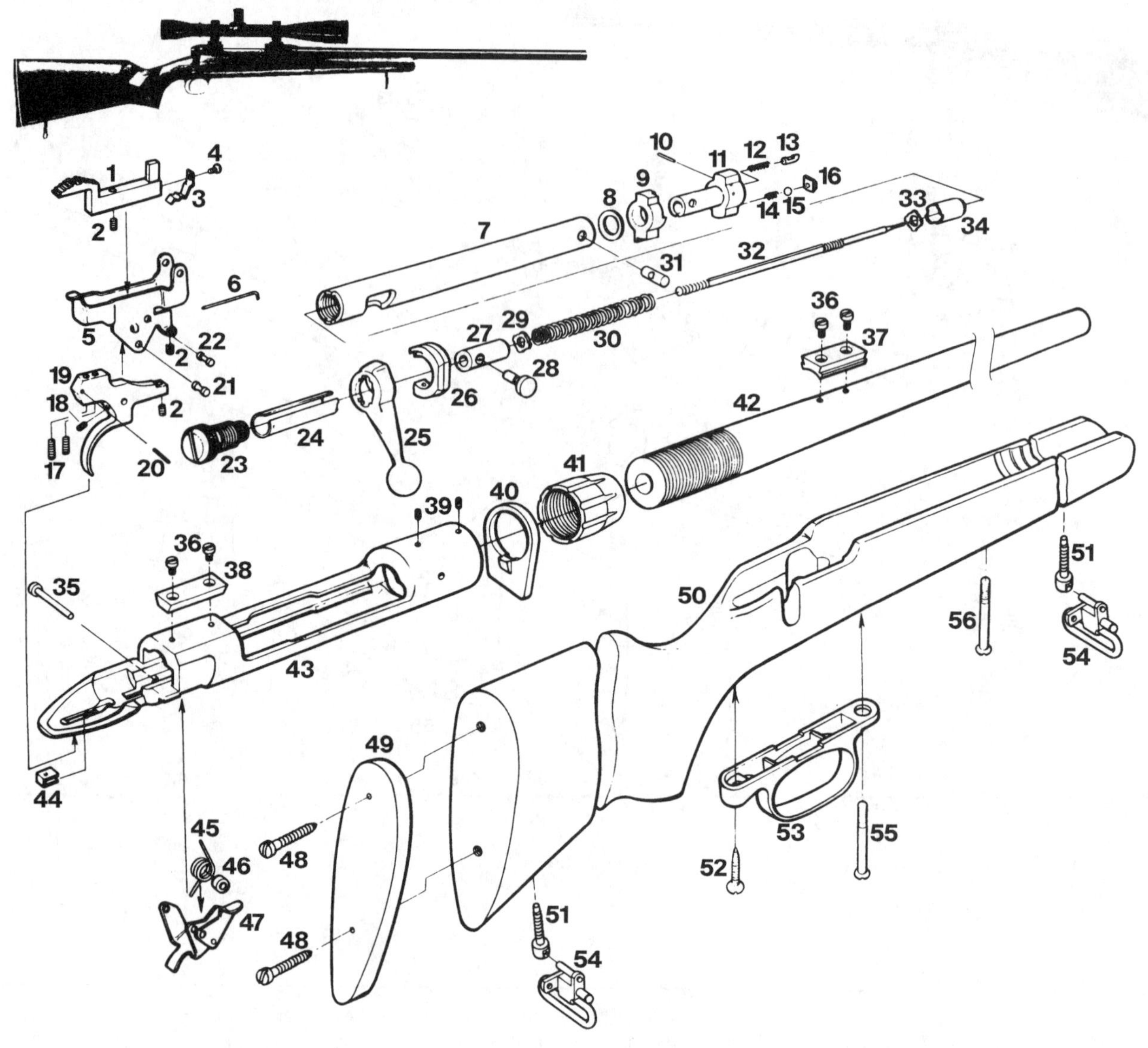

1	Safety	20	Trigger Spring Pin	39	Dummy Screws
2	Trigger Pull Adjusting Screws	21	Trigger Pin	40	Recoil Lug
3	Safety Detent Spring	22	Safety Bearing Pin	41	Barrel Lock Nut
4	Safety Detent Spring Screw	23	Bolt Assembly Screw	42	Barrel
5	Trigger Bracket	24	Cocking Piece Sleeve	43	Receiver
6	Trigger Pull Adjusting Spring	25	Bolt Handle	44	Trigger Pull Adjusting Screw Cover
7	Bolt Body	26	Rear Baffle Assembly	45	Sear Spring
8	Front Baffle Friction Washer	27	Cocking Piece	46	Sear Bushing
9	Front Baffle	28	Cocking Piece Pin	47	Sear
10	Ejector Retaining Pin	29	Cocking Piece Link Washer	48	Recoil Pad Screws
11	Bolt Head	30	Mainspring	49	Recoil Pad
12	Ejector Spring	31	Bolt Head Retaining Pin	50	Stock
13	Ejector	32	Firing Pin	51	Swivel Studs
14	Extractor Spring	33	Firing Pin Stop Nut Washer	52	Trigger Guard Screw
15	Steel Ball	34	Firing Pin Stop Nut	53	Trigger Guard
16	Extractor	35	Sear Pin	54	Swivel Loops
17	Trigger Travel Adjusting Screws	36	Scope Block Screws	55	Floorplate Screw, Rear
18	Trigger Pin Retaining Screw	37	Scope Block, Front	56	Floorplate Screw, Front
19	Trigger	38	Scope Block, Rear		

Model 170 and 170C Series A and B Slide-Action Rifle

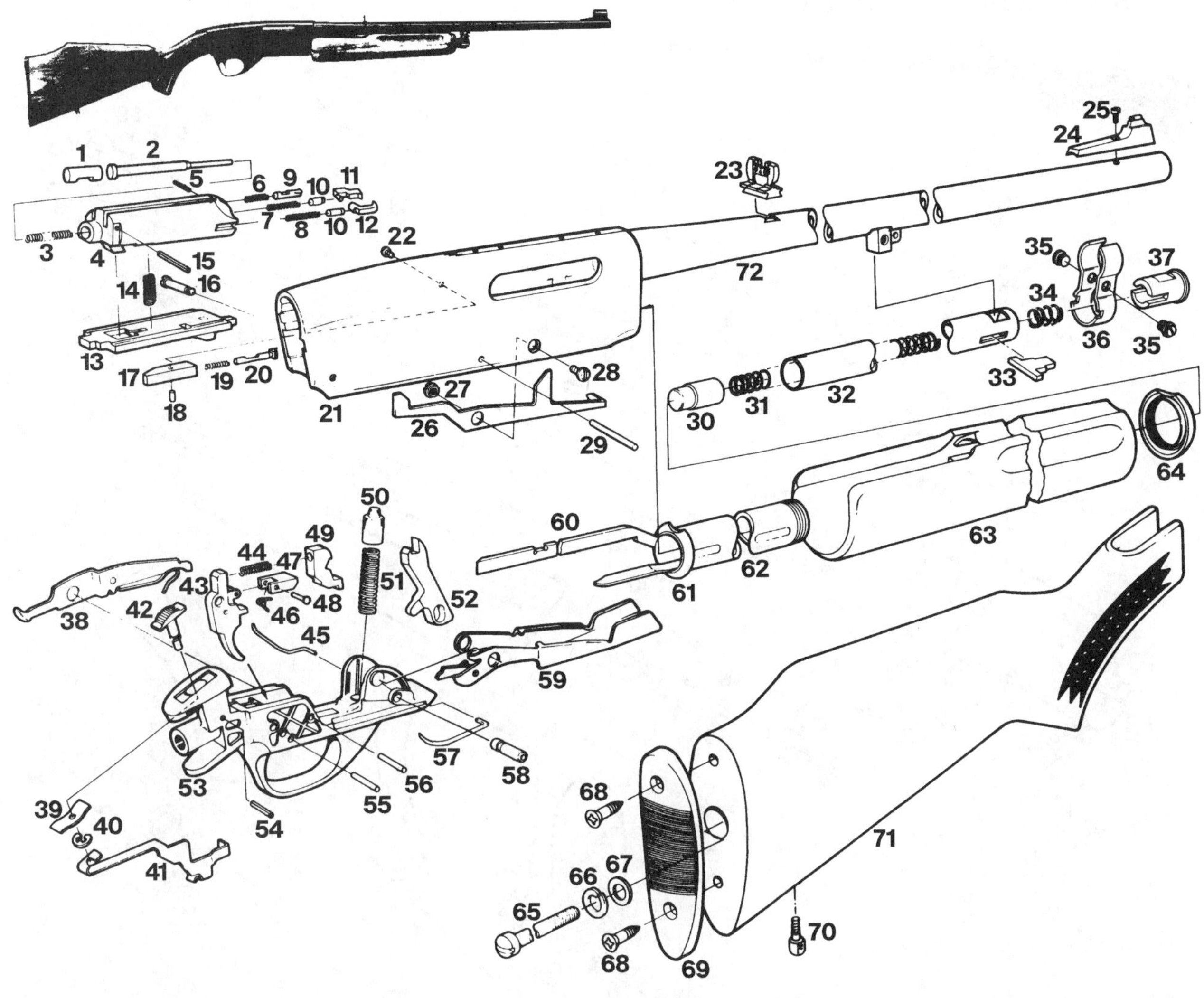

1	Firing Pin Extension	25	Front Sight Screw, Long	49	Sear
2	Firing Pin	26	Cartridge Stop	50	Mainspring Plunger
3	Firing Pin Spring	27	Cartridge Stop Pivot Nut	51	Mainspring
4	Breechbolt	28	Cartridge Stop Pivot Screw	52	Hammer
5	Shell Stop Retaining Pin	29	Trigger Guard Pin	53	Trigger Guard
6	Shell Stop Spring	30	Magazine Follower	54	Safety-Lever Retaining Pin
7	Extractor Spring, Left	31	Magazine Spring	55	Trigger Pin
8	Extractor Spring, Right	32	Magazine Tube	56	Sear Pin
9	Shell Stop	33	Damper	57	Lifter Spring
10	Extractor Plungers	34	Damper Spring	58	Hammer Bushing
11	Extractor, Left	35	Magazine Tube Screws	59	Lifter
12	Extractor, Right	36	Magazine Tube Yoke	60	Operating Handle Bar
13	Slide	37	Magazine Plug	61	Operating Handle Collar, Rear
14	Bolt Support Spring	38	Slide Lock Assembly	62	Operating Handle Tube
15	Firing Pin Stop Pin	39	Safety Spring	63	Operating Handle
16	Trigger Guard Screw	40	Safety Retaining Ring	64	Operating Handle Collar, Front
17	Ejector Assembly	41	Safety-Lever	65	Stock Bolt
18	Ejector Pin	42	Safety	66	Stock Bolt Lock Washer
19	Ejector Spring	43	Trigger Assembly	67	Stock Bolt Washer
20	Ejector Plunger	44	Trigger Spring	68	Buttplate Screws
21	Receiver	45	Slide Lock Release Spring	69	Buttplate
22	Ejector Screw	46	Sear Trip Spring	70	Swivel Stud
23	Rear Sight	47	Sear Trip	71	Stock
24	Front Sight	48	Sear Trip Pin	72	Barrel

Model 219L and 219LD Single Shot Rifle and Model 220L and 220LD Single Shot Shotgun

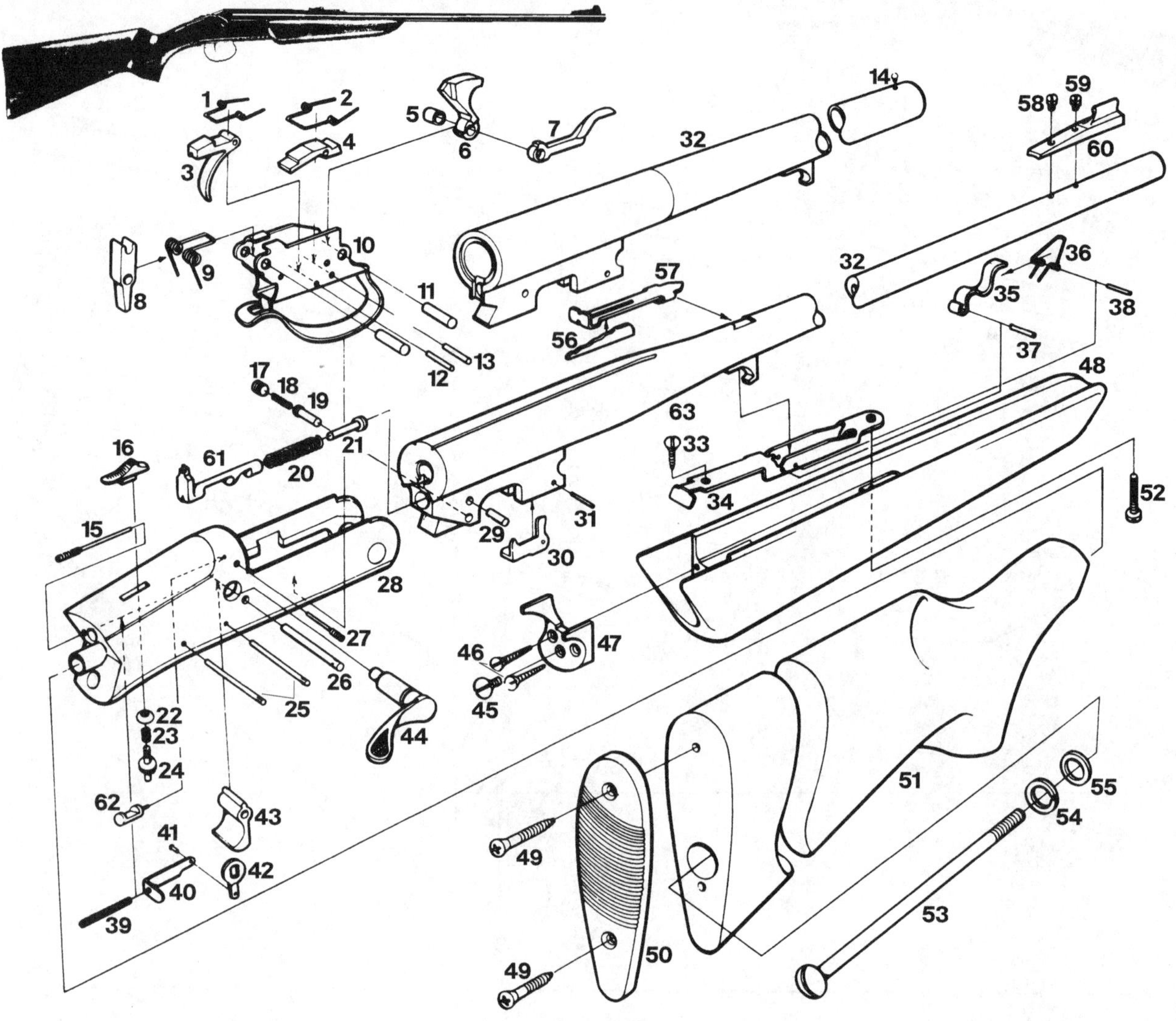

1	Trigger Spring	23	Safety Spring	45	Forend Iron Stop Screw
2	Sear Spring	24	Safety Adjusting Screw	46	Forend Iron Head Screws
3	Trigger	25	Trigger Bracket Pins	47	Forend Iron Head
4	Sear	26	Locking Bolt Pin	48	Forend
5	Hammer Spacer	27	Firing Pin Screw	49	Buttplate Screws
6	Hammer	28	Frame	50	Buttplate
7	Cocking Lever	29	Extractor Stop Pin	51	Stock
8	Safety-Lever	30	Ejector Hook	52	Forend Screw
9	Hammer Spring	31	Extractor Lever Pin	53	Stock Bolt
10	Trigger Bracket	32	Barrel	54	Stock Bolt Lock Washer
11	Hammer Pin and Safety-Lever Pin	33	Forend Spring Housing Screw	55	Stock Bolt Washer
12	Trigger Pin	34	Forend Spring Housing	**Parts for 219L and 219LD Only**	
13	Sear Pin	35	Forend Spring	56	Rear Sight Step
14	Front Sight	36	Forend Spring Spring	57	Rear Sight
15	Safety Slide Spring Pin	37	Forend Spring Pin	58	Front Sight Screw, Short
16	Safety Button	38	Forend Spring Spring Pin	59	Front Sight Screw, Long
17	Cocking Plunger Spring Screw	39	Safety Slide Spring	60	Front Sight
18	Cocking Plunger Spring	40	Safety Slide	61	Extractor
19	Cocking Plunger	41	Safety Slide Rivet	62	Firing Pin
20	Ejector Spring	42	Safety Slide Arm	63	Barrel
21	Ejector Starter Pin	43	Locking Bolt		
22	Safety Washer	44	Lever		

Model 23B, 23C and 23D-19H Bolt-Action Rifle

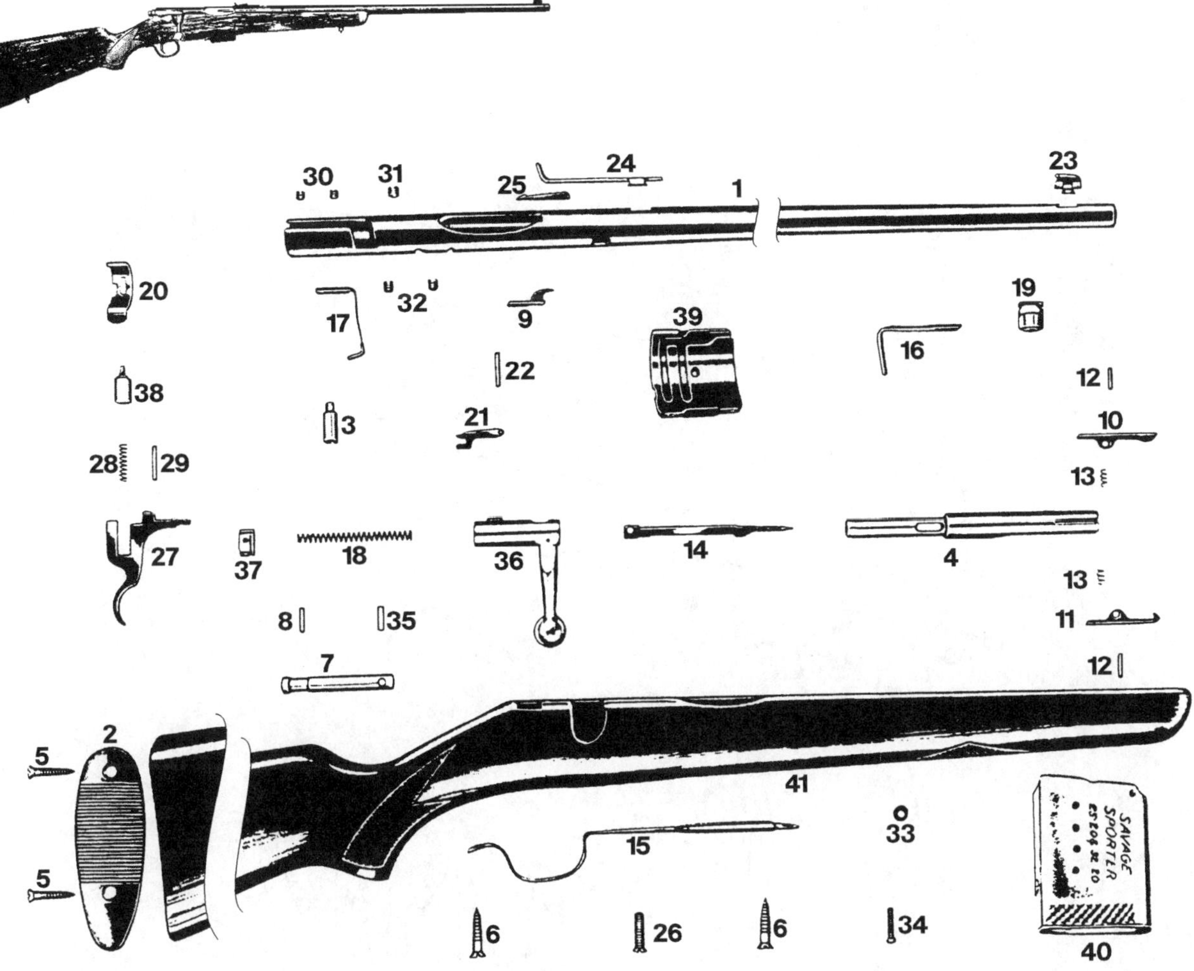

1	Barrel	**22**	Sear Pin
2	Buttplate	**23**	Front Sight
3	Barrel Stud	**24**	Rear Sight
4	Bolt Head	**25**	Rear Sight Step
5	Buttplate Screws	**26**	Takedown Screw, Rear
6	Trigger Guard Wood Screw	**27**	Trigger
7	Cocking Piece	**28**	Trigger Spring
8	Cocking Piece Pin	**29**	Trigger Pin
9	Ejector	**30**	Sight Dummy Screw, Small
10	Extractor, Left	**31**	Sight Dummy Screw, Large
11	Extractor, Right	**32**	Telescope Dummy Screws
12	Extractor Pins	**33**	Escutcheon
13	Extractor Springs	**34**	Takedown Screw, Front
14	Firing Pin	**35**	Bolt Pin
15	Trigger Guard	**36**	Bolt Sleeve
16	Magazine Retainer, Front	**37**	Bolt Sleeve Retaining Collar
17	Magazine Retainer, Rear	**38**	Trigger Spring Box
18	Mainspring	**39**	Magazine Assembly (Model 23D-19H)
19	Recoil Lug	**40**	Magazine Assembly (Old Style)
20	Safety	**41**	Stock
21	Sear		

Model 24, 24C and 24D Series M, P and S Combo

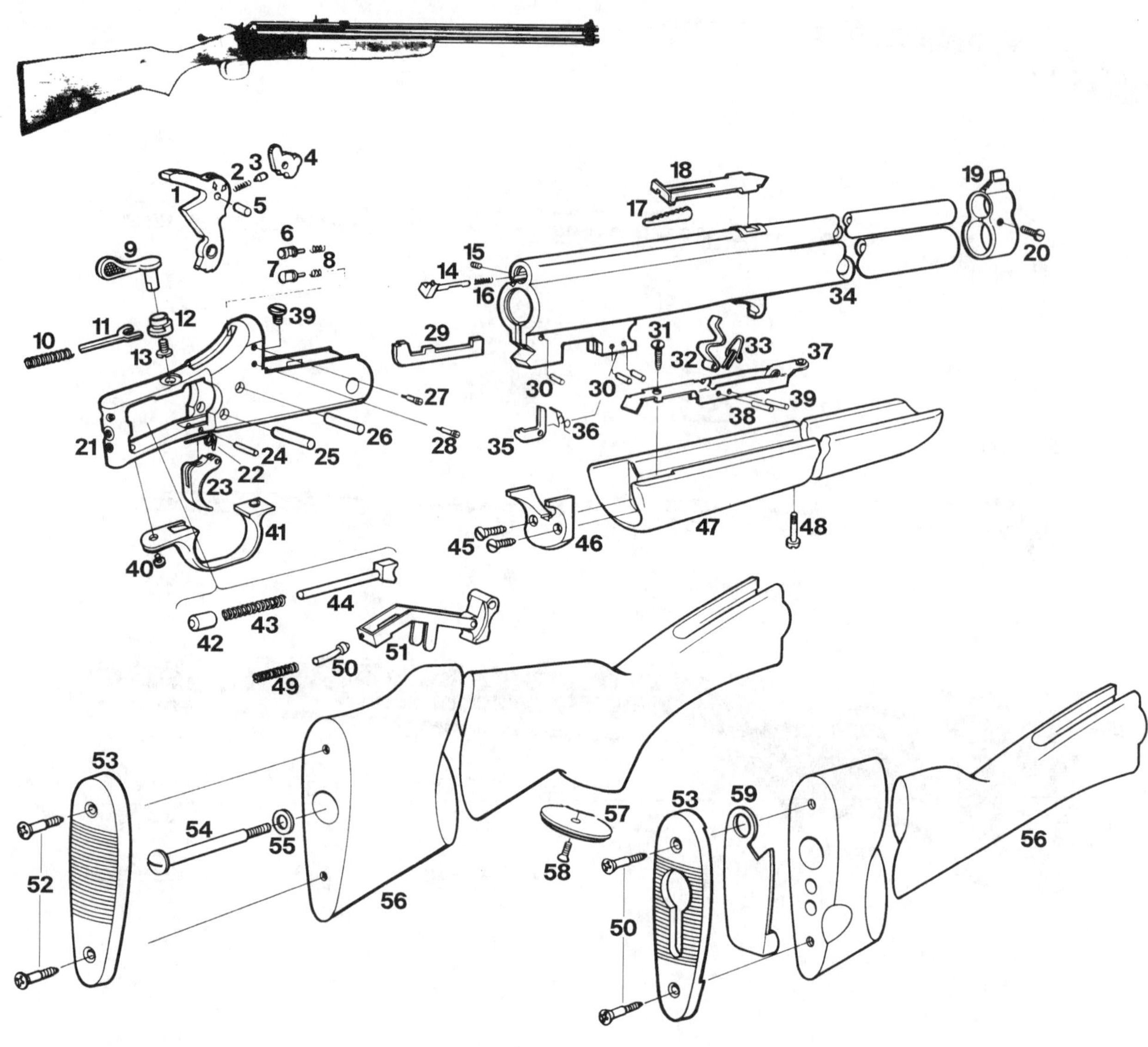

1	Hammer Assembly	21	Frame	40	Trigger Guard Screw
2	Selector Plunger Spring	22	Trigger Spring	41	Trigger Guard
3	Selector Plunger	23	Trigger	42	Mainspring Plunger Seat
4	Selector	24	Trigger Pin	43	Mainspring
5	Selector Pin	25	Hammer Pin	44	Mainspring Plunger Assembly
6	Firing Pin (Rifle)	26	Locking Bolt Pin	45	Forend Iron Head Screws
7	Firing Pin (Shotgun)	27	Firing Pin Screw (Shotgun)	46	Forend Pivot Plate
8	Firing Pin Springs	28	Firing Pin Screw (Rifle)	47	Forend Wood
9	Top Snap	29	Ejector	48	Forend Screw
10	Top Snap Spring	30	Extractor Lever Pin and Lever Spring Pin and Stop Pin	49	Locking Bolt Spring
11	Top Snap Plunger	31	Forend Spring Housing Screw	50	Locking Bolt Plunger
12	Top Snap Sleeve	32	Forend Spring	51	Locking Bolt Assembly
13	Top Snap/Trigger Guard Screw	33	Forend Spring Spring	52	Buttplate Screws
14	Extractor	34	Barrels	53	Buttplate
15	Extractor Screw	35	Extractor Lever	54	Stock Bolt
16	Extractor Spring	36	Extractor Lever Spring	55	Stock Bolt Washer
17	Rear Sight Step	37	Forend Spring Housing	56	Stock
18	Rear Sight	38	Forend Spring Pin	57	Pistol Grip Cap
19	Barrel Band and Front Sight	39	Forend Spring Spring Pin	58	Pistol Grip Cap Screw
20	Barrel Band Screw			59	Trap Cover

Model 2400 Combo

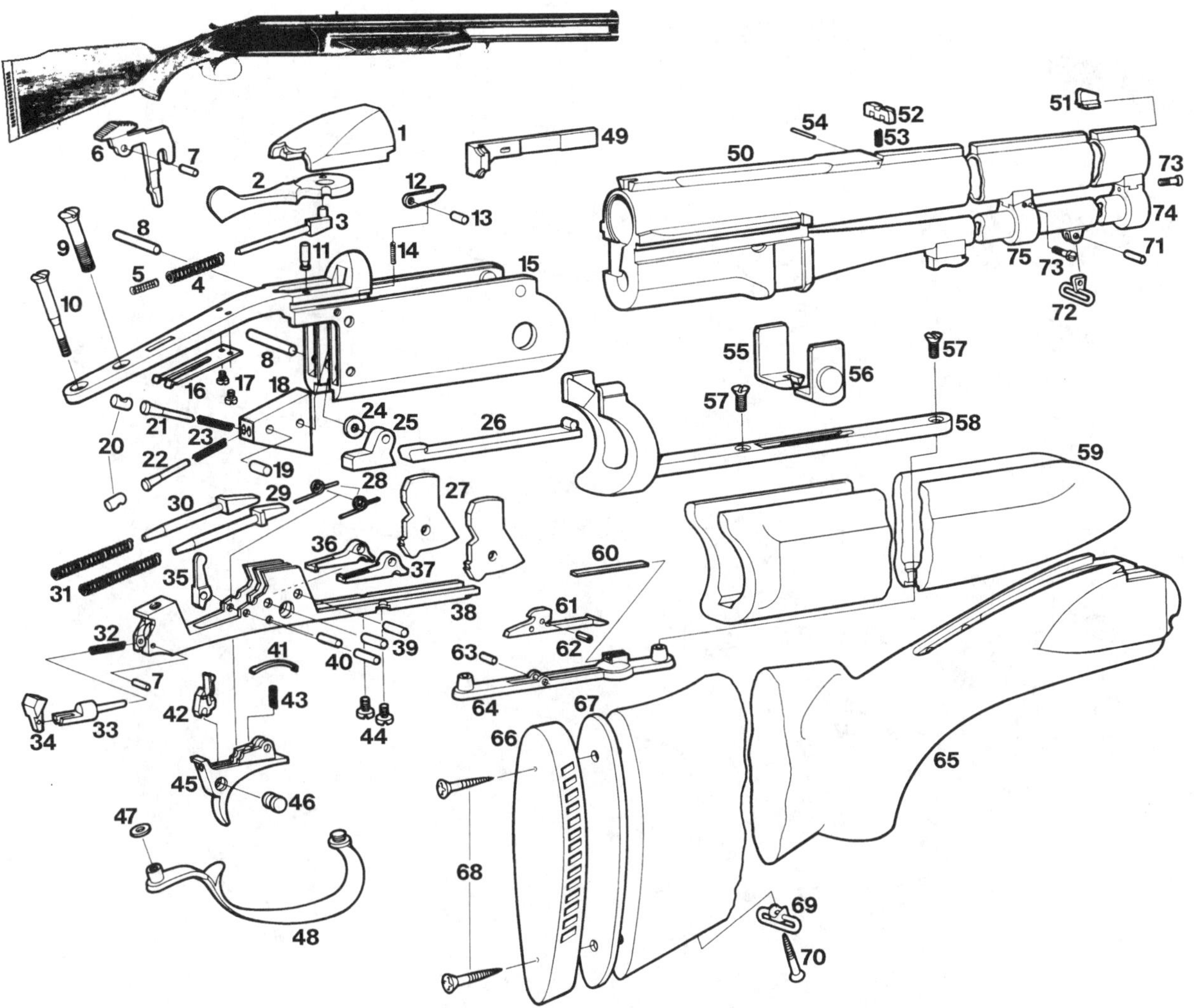

1	Locking Bolt	26	Cocking Slide	51	Front Sight
2	Top Snap	27	Hammers	52	Front Sight Plate
3	Top Snap Plunger	28	Sear Springs	53	Rear Sight Spring
4	Top Snap Spring	29	Mainspring Plunger, Right	54	Rear Sight Pin
5	Safety Plunger Spring	30	Mainspring Plunger, Left	55	Barrel Pivot Pin, Left
6	Safety Button	31	Mainsprings	56	Barrel Pivot Pin, Right
7	Safety Detent and Inertia Block Pin	32	Inertia Block Spring	57	Forend Snap Housing Screws
8	Firing Pin Block and Cocking Pins	33	Inertia Block Plunger	58	Forend Iron
9	Top Tang Screw, Front	34	Inertia Block	59	Forend Wood
10	Top Tang Screw, Rear	35	Safety-Lever	60	Forend Snap Spring
11	Top Snap Pin	36	Sear, Left	61	Forend Snap
12	Top Slide Trip	37	Sear, Right	62	Forend Snap Stop Pin
13	Top Slide Trip Pin	38	Trigger Plate	63	Forend Snap Pin
14	Top Slide Trip Spring	39	Sear Pin and Hammer Pin	64	Forend Snap Housing
15	Frame	40	Trigger Pin and Safety-Lever Pin	65	Stock Complete
16	Safety Slide	41	Selector Spring	66	Recoil Pad
17	Safety Slide Screws	42	Selector Lever	67	Buttplate Liner
18	Firing Pin Block	43	Trigger Spring	68	Recoil Pad Screws
19	Striker Pin	44	Trigger Plate Screws	69	Swivel Bow Assembly
20	Strikers	45	Trigger	70	Swivel Screw
21	Firing Pin, Shotgun	46	Selector Button	71	Swivel Pin, Front
22	Firing Pin, Rifle	47	Trigger Guard Washer	72	Swivel Bow, Front
23	Firing Pin Springs	48	Trigger Guard	73	Barrel Locking Screw
24	Cocking Lever Spring	49	Extractor	74	Barrel Locking Ring, Front
25	Cocking Crank	50	Barrel Assembly	75	Barrel Locking Ring, Rear

Model 242 Series C and D Over/Under Shotgun

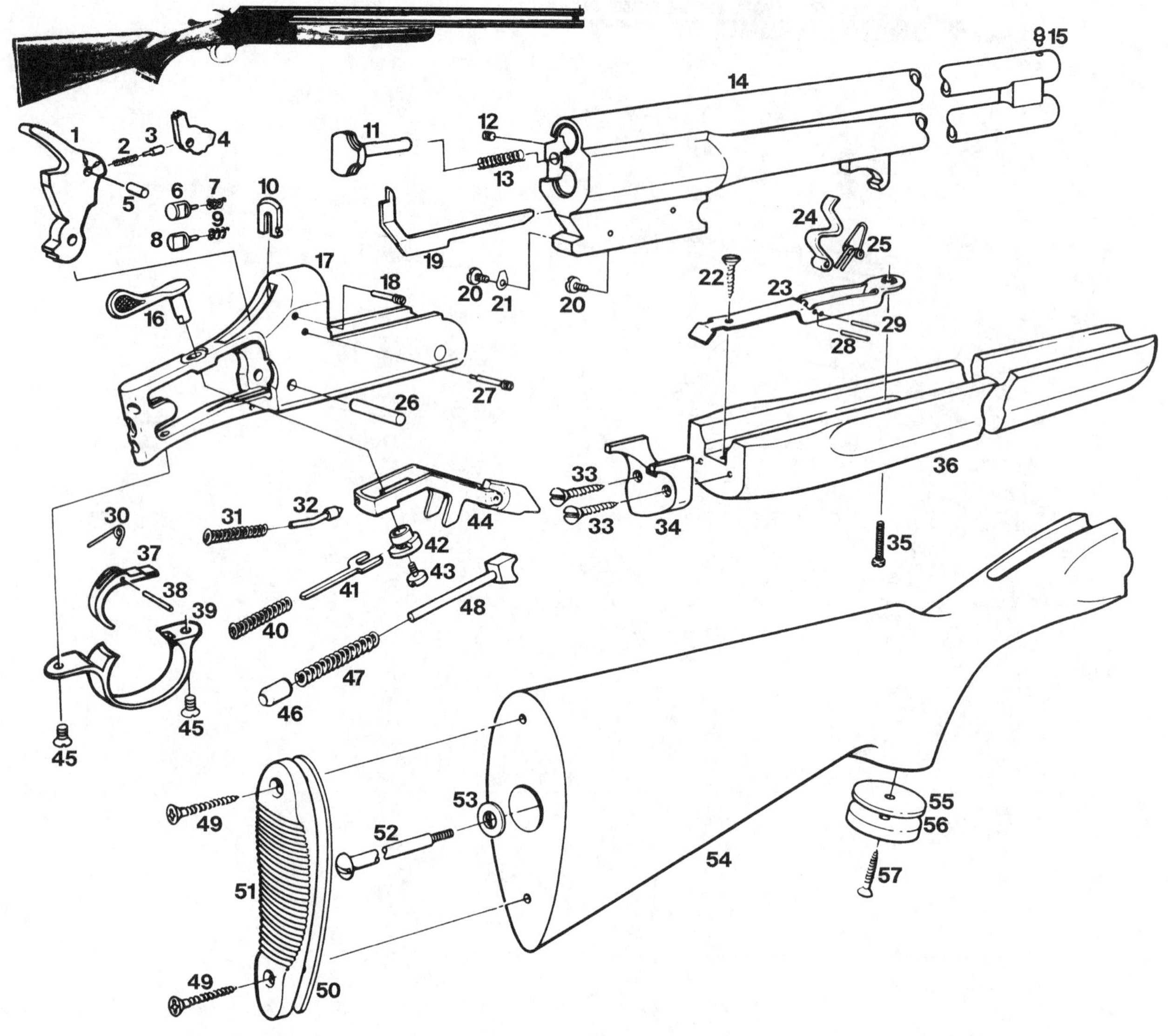

1	Hammer	21	Extractor Lever Guide	41	Top Snap Plunger
2	Selector Plunger Spring	22	Forend Spring Housing Screw	42	Top Snap Sleeve
3	Selector Plunger	23	Forend Spring Housing	43	Top Snap Screw
4	Selector	24	Forend Spring	44	Locking Bolt Assembly
5	Selector Pin	25	Forend Spring Spring	45	Trigger Guard Screw and Lifter Housing Screws
6	Firing Pin, Upper	26	Locking Bolt/Hammer Pin	46	Mainspring Plunger Seat
7	Firing Pin Spring, Upper	27	Firing Pin Screw	47	Mainspring
8	Firing Pin, Lower	28	Forend Spring Pin	48	Mainspring Plunger Head Assembly
9	Firing Pin Spring, Lower	29	Forend Spring Spring Pin	49	Buttplate Screws
10	Firing Pin Return Plate	30	Trigger Spring	50	Buttplate Liner
11	Extractor	31	Locking Bolt and Yoke Spring	51	Buttplate
12	Extractor Screw	32	Locking Bolt Plunger	52	Stock Bolt
13	Extractor Spring	33	Forend Iron Head Screws	53	Stock Bolt Washer
14	Barrel Assembly	34	Forend Pivot Plate	54	Stock Assembly
15	Front Sight	35	Forend Screw	55	Pistol Grip Cap Liner
16	Top Snap	36	Forend Wood	56	Pistol Grip Cap
17	Frame	37	Trigger	57	Pistol Grip Cap Screw
18	Firing Pin Return Screw	38	Trigger Pin		
19	Extractor Lever	39	Trigger Guard		
20	Extractor Lever Screws	40	Top Snap/Locking Bolt Spring		

Model 24S, 24SD, 24SE, 24MS, 24MSD and 24MSE Over/Under Combo

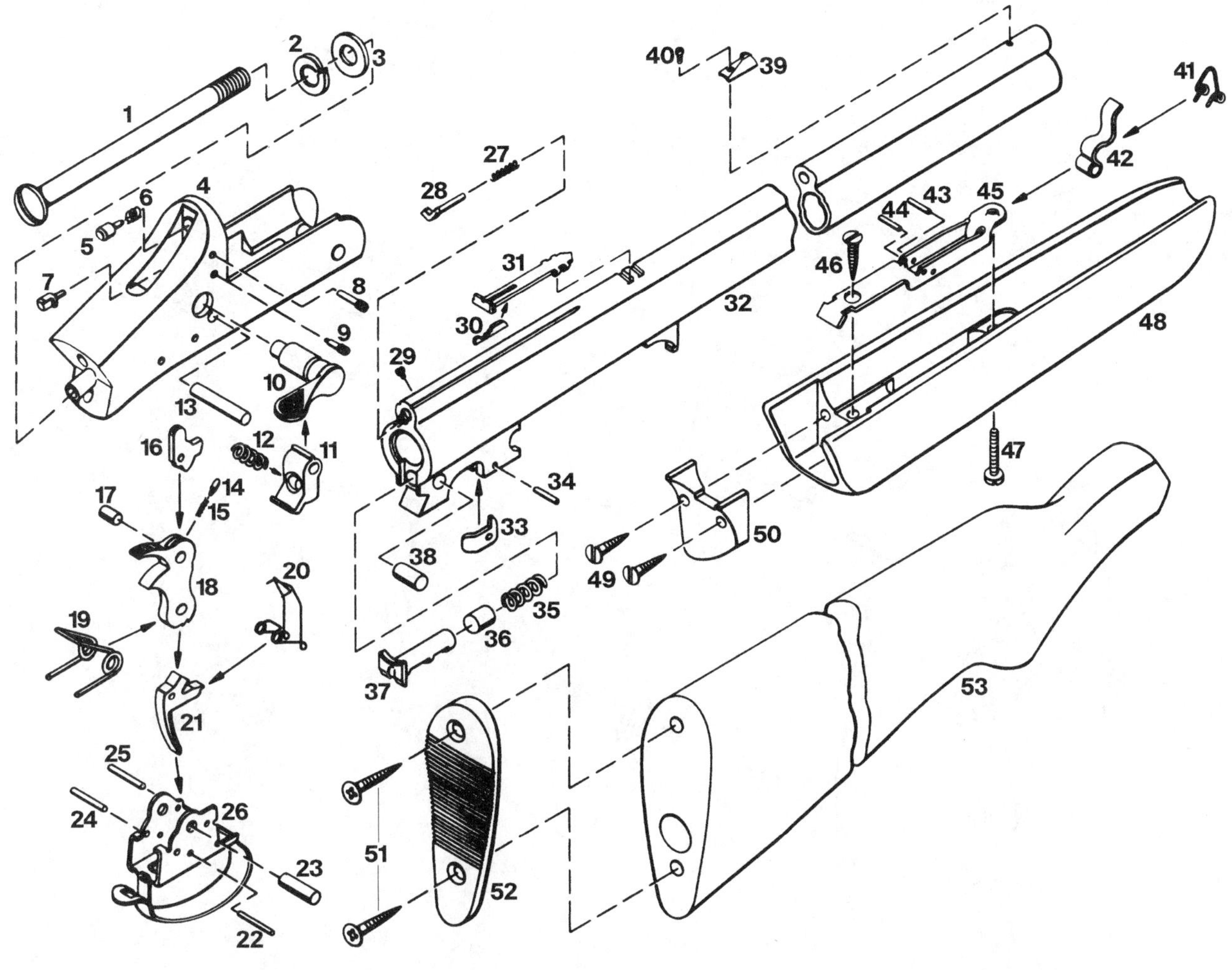

1	Stock Bolt	**19**	Hammer Spring	**37**	Extractor
2	Stock Bolt Lock Washer	**20**	Trigger Spring	**38**	Extractor Stop Pin
3	Stock Bolt Washer	**21**	Trigger	**39**	Front Sight
4	Frame	**22**	Trigger Bracket Pin	**40**	Front Sight Screw
5	Firing Pin (Rifle)	**23**	Hammer Pin	**41**	Forend Spring Spring
6	Firing Pin Spring (Rifle)	**24**	Trigger Bracket Pin	**42**	Forend Spring
7	Firing Pin (Shotgun)	**25**	Trigger Pin	**43**	Forend Spring Spring Pin
8	Firing Pin Screw (Rifle)	**26**	Trigger Guard	**44**	Forend Spring Pin
9	Firing Pin Screw (Shotgun)	**27**	Extractor Spring	**45**	Forend Spring Housing
10	Lever	**28**	Extractor	**46**	Forend Spring Housing Screw
11	Locking Bolt	**29**	Extractor Screw	**47**	Forend Screw
12	Locking Bolt Spring	**30**	Rear Sight Step	**48**	Forend
13	Locking Bolt Pin	**31**	Rear Sight	**49**	Forend Iron Head Screws
14	Selector Plunger	**32**	Barrel	**50**	Forend Iron Head
15	Selector Plunger Spring	**33**	Extractor Lever	**51**	Buttplate Screws
16	Selector	**34**	Extractor Lever Pin	**52**	Buttplate
17	Selector Pin	**35**	Extractor Lever Spring	**53**	Stock
18	Hammer	**36**	Extractor Stem		

Model 24V and 24V-A Combo

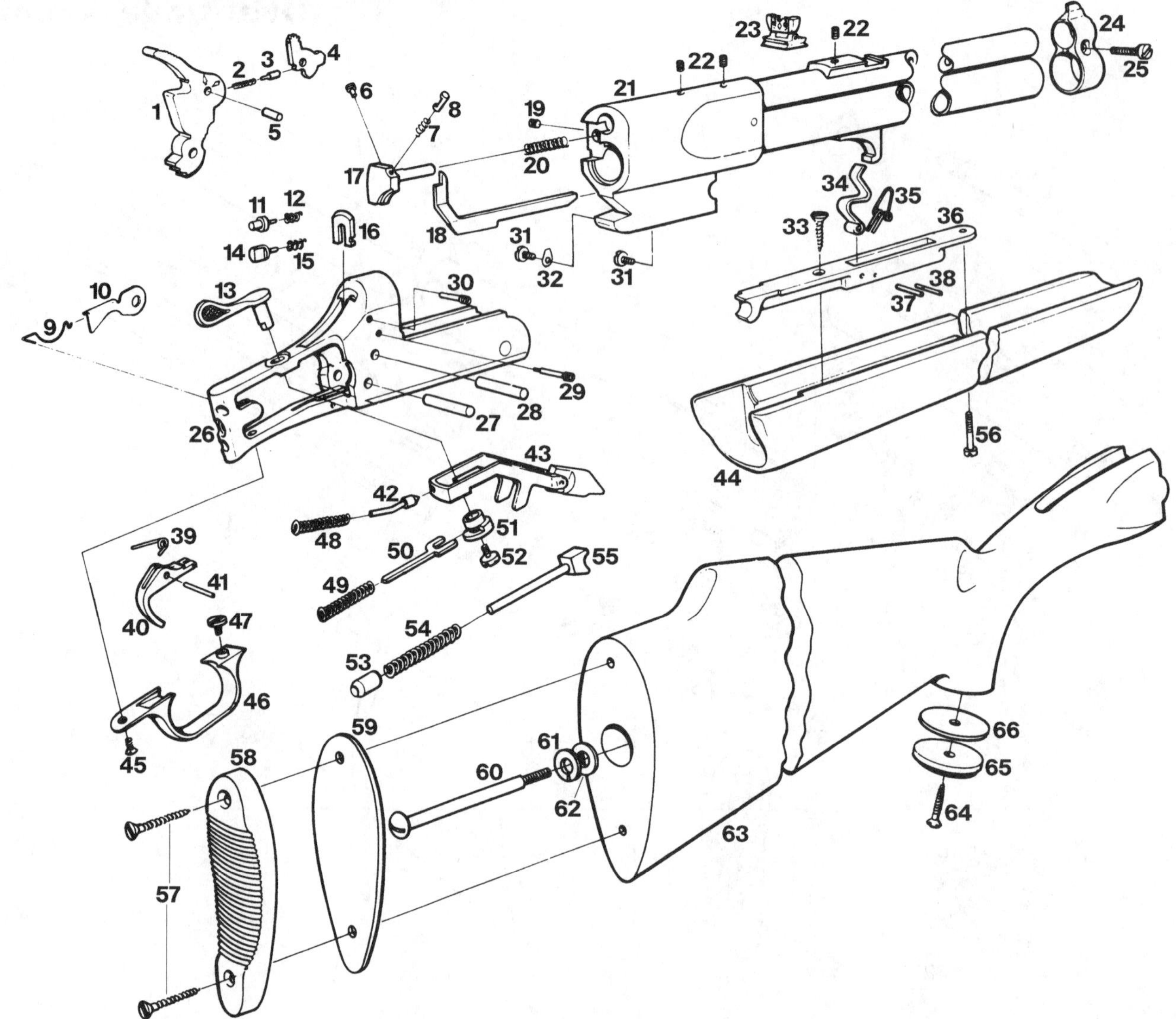

No.	Part	No.	Part	No.	Part
1	Hammer Assembly	24	Barrel Band and Front Sight	45	Trigger Guard Screw
2	Selector Plunger Spring	25	Barrel Band Screw	46	Trigger Guard
3	Selector Plunger	26	Frame	47	Trigger Guard Screw, Front
4	Selector	27	Hammer Pin	48	Locking Bolt Plunger Spring
5	Selector Pin	28	Locking Bolt Pin	49	Top Snap Plunger Spring
6	Extractor Plunger Screw	29	Firing Pin Retaining Screw	50	Top Snap Plunger
7	Extractor Plunger Spring	30	Firing Pin Retaining Plate Screw	51	Top Snap Sleeve
8	Extractor Plunger	31	Extractor Lever Retaining Screws	52	Top Snap Screw
9	Yoke Stop Spring	32	Extractor Lever Guide	53	Mainspring Plunger Seat
10	Yoke Stop	33	Forend Iron Screw	54	Mainspring
11	Firing Pin (Rifle)	34	Forend Spring	55	Mainspring Plunger
12	Firing Pin Spring (Rifle)	35	Forend Spring Spring	56	Forend Screw
13	Top Snap	36	Forend Iron	57	Buttplate Screws
14	Firing Pin (Shotgun)	37	Forend Spring Pin	58	Buttplate
15	Firing Pin Spring (Shotgun)	38	Forend Spring Spring Pin	59	Buttplate Liner
16	Firing Pin Retaining Plate	39	Trigger Spring	60	Stock Bolt
17	Extractor Plate	40	Trigger	61	Stock Bolt Lock Washer
18	Extractor Lever	41	Trigger Pin	62	Stock Bolt Washer
19	Extractor Screw	42	Locking Bolt Plunger	63	Stock
20	Extractor Spring	43	Locking Bolt Assembly	64	Pistol Grip Cap Screw
21	Barrel	44	Forend	65	Pistol Grip Cap
22	Dummy Screws			66	Pistol Grip Cap Liner
23	Rear Sight				

Model 30 Series D, E and F Slide-Action Shotgun

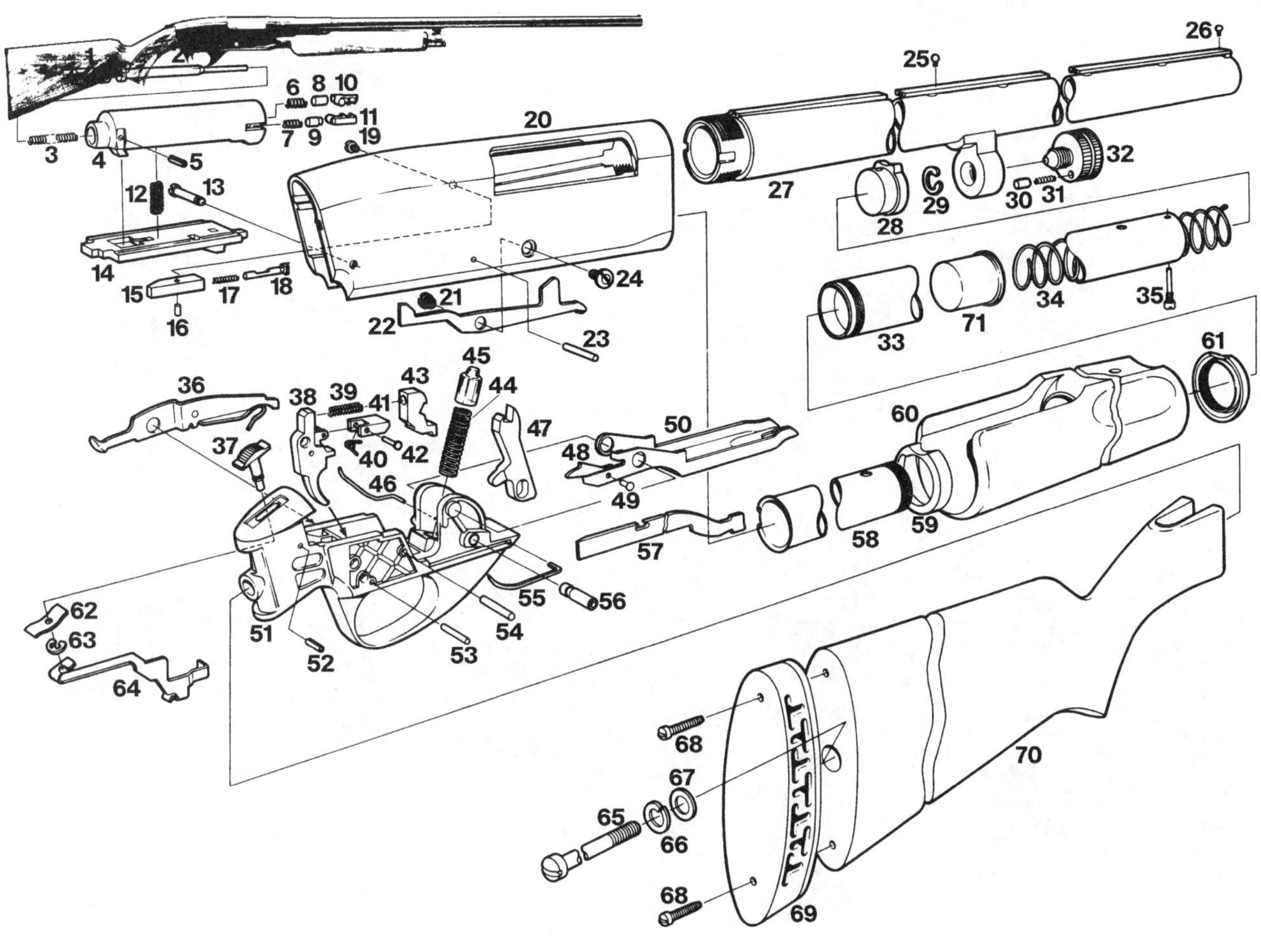

1	Firing Pin Extension
2	Firing Pin
3	Firing Pin Spring
4	Breechbolt
5	Firing Pin Stop Pin
6	Extractor Spring, Left
7	Extractor Spring, Right
8	Extractor Plunger, Left
9	Extractor Plunger, Right
10	Extractor, Left
11	Extractor, Right
12	Bolt Support Spring
13	Trigger Guard Screw
14	Slide Assembly
15	Ejector Assembly
16	Ejector Pin
17	Ejector Spring
18	Ejector Plunger
19	Ejector Screw
20	Receiver
21	Cartridge Stop Pivot Nut
22	Cartridge Stop
23	Trigger Guard Pin
24	Cartridge Stop Pivot Screw
25	Rear Sight
26	Front Sight
27	Barrel
28	Magazine Plug
29	Takedown Screw Retaining Ring
30	Takedown Screw Plunger
31	Takedown Screw Plunger Spring
32	Takedown Screw
33	Magazine Tube
34	Magazine Spring
35	Magazine Plug Screw
36	Slide Lock Assembly
37	Safety
38	Trigger Assembly
39	Trigger Spring
40	Sear Trip Spring
41	Sear Trip
42	Sear Trip Pin
43	Sear
44	Mainspring
45	Mainspring Plunger
46	Slide Lock Release Spring
47	Hammer
48	Lifter Pawl
49	Lifter Pawl Pin
50	Lifter
51	Trigger Guard
52	Safety-Lever Retaining Pin
53	Trigger Pin
54	Sear Pin
55	Lifter Spring
56	Hammer Bushing
57	Operating Handle Bar
58	Operating Handle Tube
59	Operating Handle Collar, Rear
60	Operating Handle Wood
61	Operating Handle Collar, Front
62	Safety Spring
63	Safety Retaining Ring
64	Safety-Lever
65	Stock Bolt
66	Stock Bolt Lock Washer
67	Stock Bolt Washer
68	Recoil Pad Screws
69	Recoil Pad
70	Stock
71	Magazine Follower

Model 30, Stevens Model 77 and Springfield Model 67 Slide-Action Shotgun

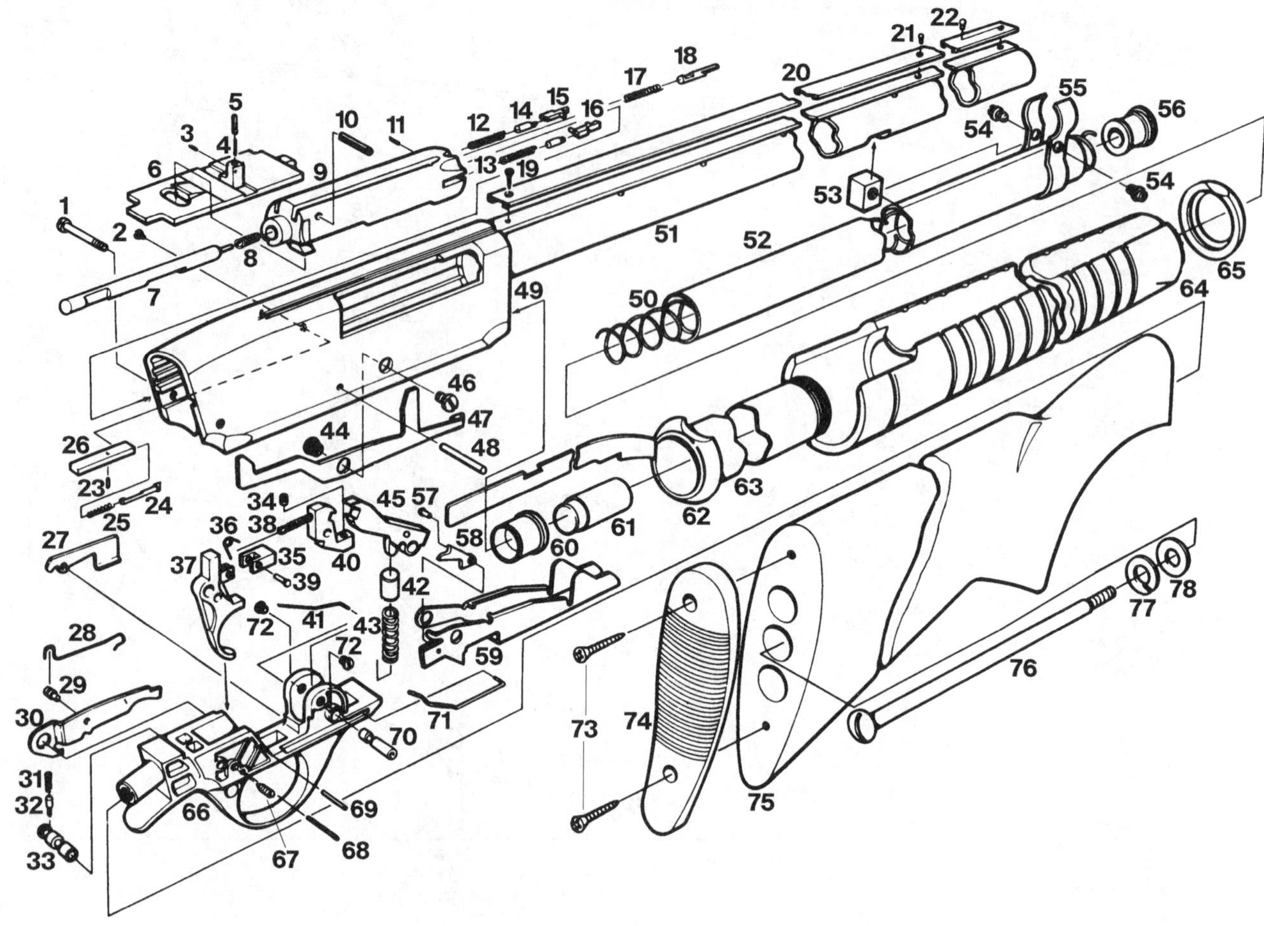

1	Trigger Guard Screw
2	Ejector Screw
3	Firing Pin Retractor Plunger Pin
4	Firing Pin Retractor Plunger Spring
5	Firing Pin Retractor Plunger
6	Slide Assembly
7	Firing Pin
8	Firing Pin Spring
9	Breechbolt
10	Firing Pin Stop Pin
11	Shell Stop Retaining Pin
12	Extractor Spring, Left
13	Extractor Spring, Right
14	Extractor Plungers
15	Extractor, Left
16	Extractor, Right
17	Shell Stop Spring
18	Shell Stop
19	Top Rib Support Screw
20	Top Rib Sleeve
21	Rear Sight
22	Front Sight
23	Ejector Pin
24	Ejector Plunger
25	Ejector Spring
26	Ejector Assembly
27	Slide Lock Release
28	Slide Lock Spring
29	Slide Lock Spring Stud
30	Slide Lock and Spring Assembly
31	Safety Spring
32	Safety Spring Plunger
33	Safety
34	Sear Adjusting Screw
35	Sear Trip
36	Sear Trip Spring
37	Trigger
38	Trigger Spring
39	Sear Trip Pin
40	Sear
41	Slide Lock Release Spring
42	Mainspring Plunger
43	Mainspring
44	Cartridge Stop Pivot Screw Nut
45	Hammer
46	Cartridge Stop Pivot Screw
47	Cartridge Stop
48	Trigger Guard Pin
49	Receiver
50	Magazine Spring
51	Barrel
52	Magazine Tube
53	Filling Block
54	Magazine Tube Yoke Screws
55	Magazine Tube Yoke
56	Magazine Plug
57	Lifter Pawl Pin
58	Lifter Pawl
59	Lifter Assembly
60	Magazine Tube Adapter
61	Magazine Follower
62	Operating Handle Bar Collar, Rear
63	Operating Handle Bar Assembly
64	Operating Handle Wood
65	Operating Handle Bar Collar, Front
66	Trigger Guard
67	Trigger Adjusting Screw
68	Trigger Pin
69	Sear Pin
70	Hammer Bushing
71	Lifter Spring
72	Lifter Screws
73	Buttplate Screws
74	Buttplate
75	Stock
76	Stock Bolt
77	Stock Bolt Lock Washer
78	Stock Bolt Washer

Model 30D, 30E, 30H and 30T Slide-Action Shotgun

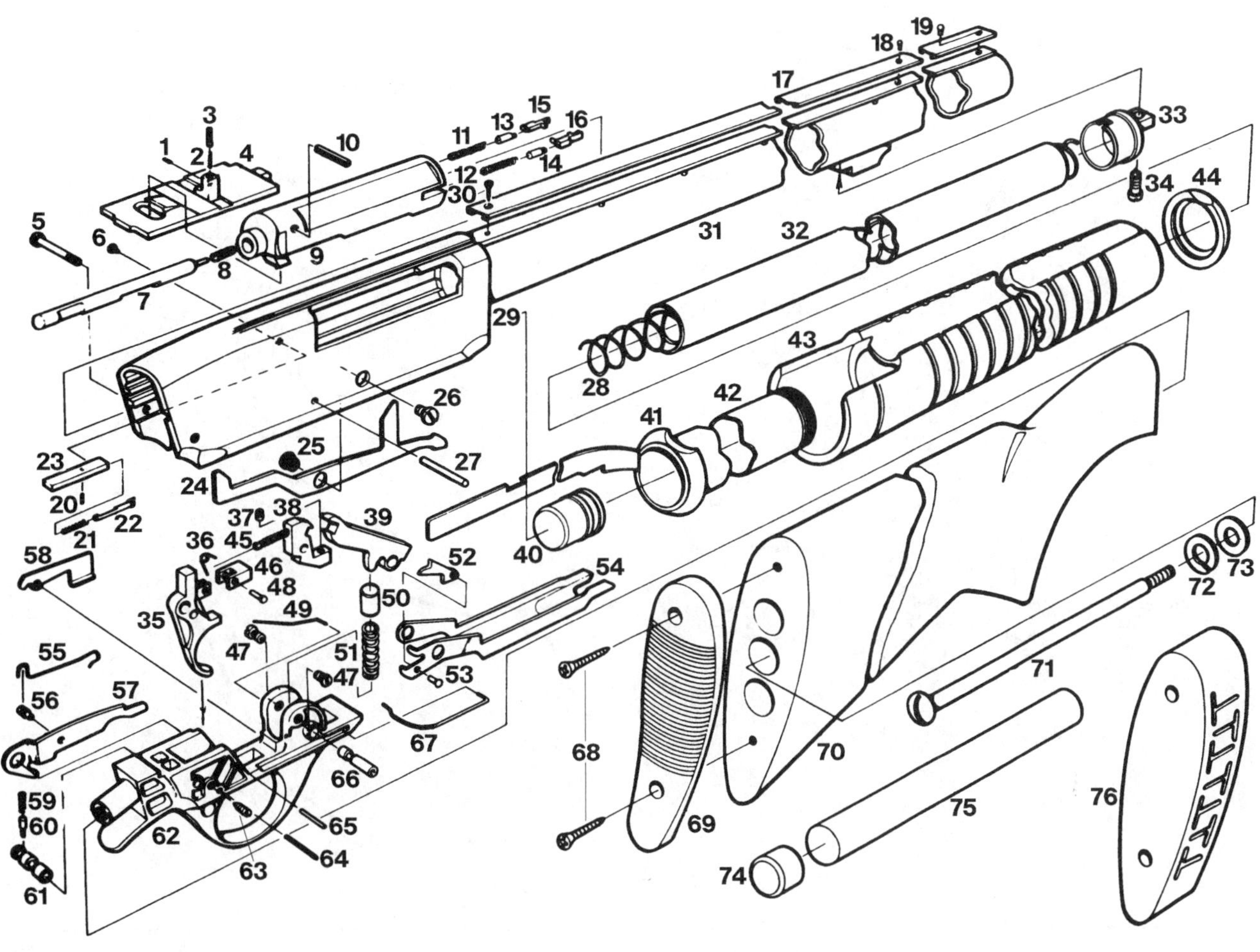

1	Firing Pin Retractor Plunger Pin
2	Firing Pin Retractor Plunger Spring
3	Firing Pin Retractor Plunger
4	Slide Assembly
5	Trigger Guard Screw
6	Ejector Screw
7	Firing Pin
8	Firing Pin Spring
9	Breechbolt
10	Firing Pin Stop Pin
11	Extractor Spring, Left
12	Extractor Spring, Right
13	Extractor Plunger, Left
14	Extractor Plunger, Right
15	Extractor, Left
16	Extractor, Right
17	Top Rib Sleeve
18	Middle Sight
19	Front Sight
20	Ejector Pin
21	Ejector Spring
22	Ejector Plunger
23	Ejector Assembly
24	Cartridge Stop
25	Cartridge Stop Pivot Nut
26	Cartridge Stop Pivot Screw
27	Trigger Guard Pin
28	Magazine Spring
29	Receiver
30	Rib Screw
31	Barrel
32	Magazine Tube
33	Magazine Plug
34	Magazine Plug Screw
35	Trigger
36	Sear Trip Spring
37	Sear Adjustment Screw
38	Sear
39	Hammer
40	Magazine Follower
41	Operating Handle Collar, Rear
42	Operating Handle Bar Assembly
43	Operating Handle
44	Operating Handle Collar, Front
45	Trigger Spring
46	Sear Trip
47	Lifter Screws
48	Sear Trip Pin
49	Slide Lock Release Spring
50	Mainspring Plunger
51	Mainspring
52	Lifter Pawl
53	Lifter Pawl Pin
54	Lifter Assembly
55	Slide Lock Spring
56	Slide Lock Spring Stud
57	Slide Lock Assembly
58	Slide Lock Release
59	Safety Spring
60	Safety Spring Plunger
61	Safety
62	Trigger Guard
63	Trigger Adjusting Screw
64	Trigger Pin
65	Sear Pin
66	Hammer Bushing
67	Lifter Spring
68	Buttplate Screws
69	Buttplate
70	Stock
71	Stock Bolt
72	Stock Bolt Lock Washer
73	Stock Bolt Washer
74	Recoil Weight Buffer (30T only)
75	Recoil Weight (30T only)
76	Recoil Pad (30T only)

Model 30J, 30K and 30T Series A, B and C Slide-Action Shotgun

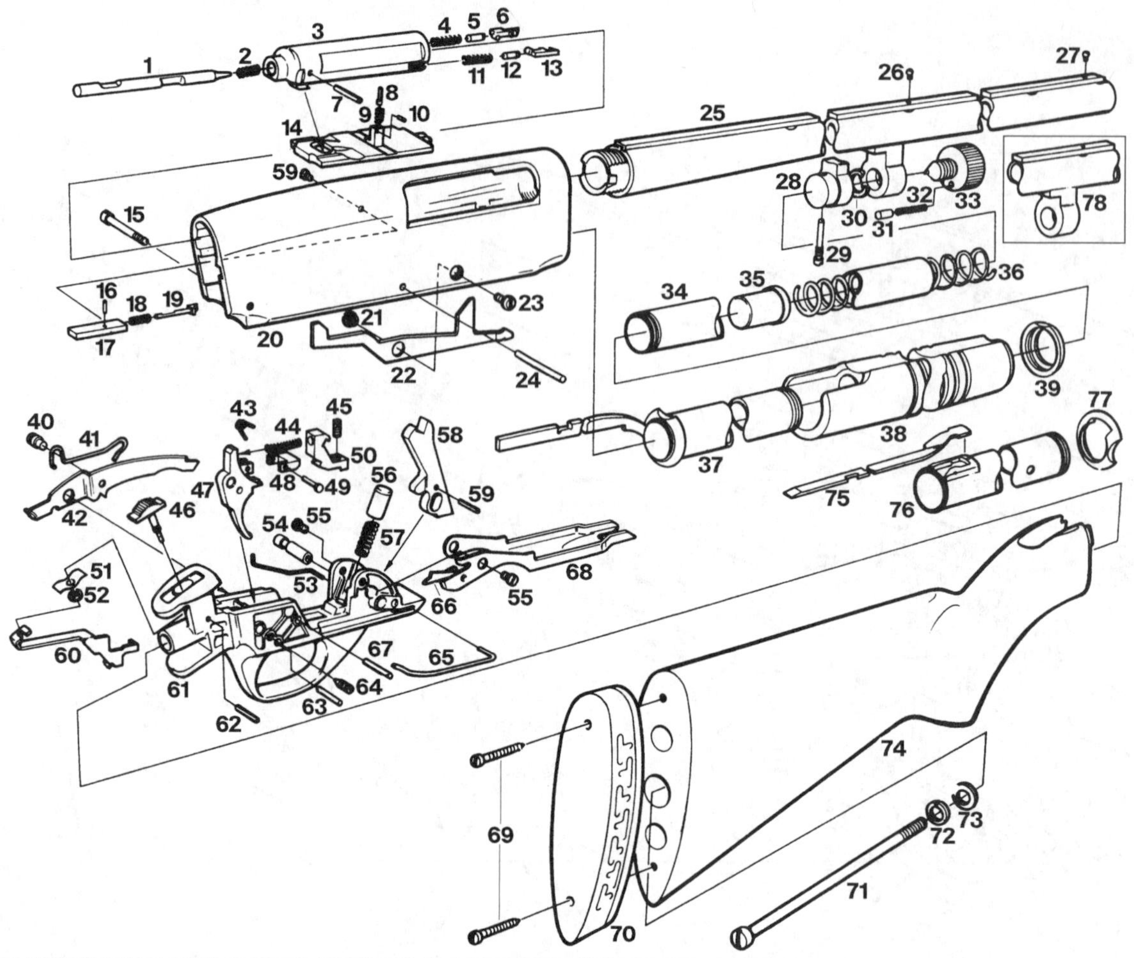

1	Firing Pin	**28**	Magazine Plug	**55**	Lifter Screw
2	Firing Pin Spring	**29**	Magazine End Plug Screw	**56**	Mainspring Plunger
3	Breechbolt	**30**	Takedown Screw Retaining Ring	**57**	Mainspring
4	Extractor Spring, Left	**31**	Takedown Screw Plunger	**58**	Hammer
5	Extractor Plunger, Left	**32**	Takedown Screw Plunger Spring	**59**	Ejector Screw
6	Extractor, Left	**33**	Takedown Screw	**60**	Safety-Lever
7	Firing Pin Stop Pin	**34**	Magazine Tube	**61**	Trigger Guard
8	Firing Pin Retractor Plunger	**35**	Magazine Follower	**62**	Safety-Lever Retaining Pin
9	Firing Pin Retractor Spring	**36**	Magazine Spring	**63**	Trigger Pin
10	Firing Pin Retractor Plunger Pin	**37**	Operating Handle Bar Assembly	**64**	Safety Adjustment Screw
11	Extractor Spring, Right	**38**	Operating Handle Wood	**65**	Lifter Spring
12	Extractor Plunger, Right	**39**	Operating Handle Collar, Front	**66**	Lifter Pawl
13	Extractor, Right	**40**	Slide Lock Spring Stud	**67**	Sear Pin
14	Slide Assembly	**41**	Slide Lock Spring	**68**	Lifter Assembly
15	Trigger Guard Screw	**42**	Slide Lock Assembly	**69**	Recoil Pad Screws
16	Ejector Pin	**43**	Sear Trip Spring	**70**	Recoil Pad
17	Ejector Assembly	**44**	Trigger Spring	**71**	Stock Bolt
18	Ejector Spring	**45**	Sear Engagement Screw	**72**	Stock Bolt Lock Washer
19	Ejector Plunger	**46**	Safety	**73**	Stock Bolt Washer
20	Receiver	**47**	Trigger	**74**	Stock
21	Cartridge Stop Pivot Nut	**48**	Sear Trip	**75**	Operating Handle Bar (Series C only)
22	Cartridge Stop	**49**	Sear Trip Pin	**76**	Operating Handle Tube Assembly (Series C only)
23	Cartridge Stop Pivot Screw	**50**	Sear	**77**	Operating Handle Collar, Rear (Series C only)
24	Trigger Guard Pin	**51**	Safety Spring	**78**	Barrel with Ventilated Rib (Series B, C only)
25	Barrel with Ventilated Rib	**52**	Safety Retainer Ring		
26	Middle Sight	**53**	Slide Lock Release Spring		
27	Front Sight	**54**	Hammer Bushing		

Model 312 Over/Under Shotgun

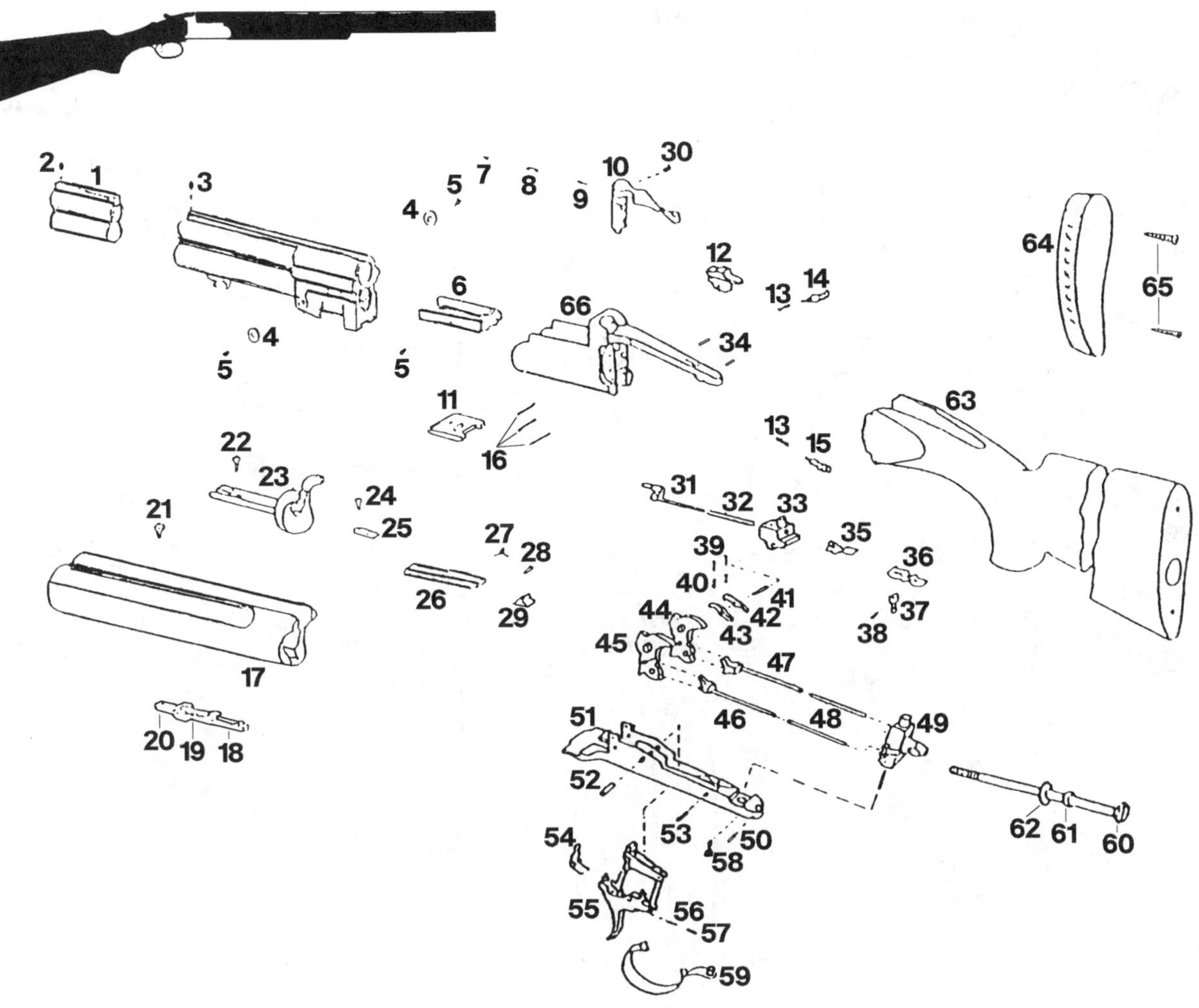

1	Barrel	**24**	Cocking Piece Screw	**47**	Mainspring Plunger, Left
2	Front Sight	**25**	Cocking Piece	**48**	Mainspring
3	Rear Sight	**26**	Cocking Plunger	**49**	Action Spring Plug
4	Barrel Trunnions	**27**	Cocking Lever Spring	**50**	Action Spring Plunger Pin
5	Barrel Trunnion Screws	**28**	Cocking Lever Pin	**51**	Trigger Housing
6	Extractor	**29**	Cocking Lever	**52**	Hammer Pin
7	Top Snap Trip	**30**	Top Snap Retaining Screw	**53**	Trigger Pin
8	Lever Lock	**31**	Top Snap Plunger	**54**	Sear Trip Spring
9	Top Snap Trip Spring	**32**	Top Snap Plunger Spring	**55**	Trigger/Sear Trip Assembly
10	Top Snap	**33**	Top Snap Plunger Guide	**56**	Trigger Spring
11	Locking Bolt	**34**	Top Snap Plunger Guide Pins	**57**	Trigger Spring Plunger
12	Safety	**35**	Safety Plunger	**58**	Trigger Guard Housing Screw, Rear
13	Firing Pin Springs	**36**	Safety Detent Spring	**59**	Trigger Guard
14	Firing Pin, Lower	**37**	Safety-Lever	**60**	Stock Bolt
15	Firing Pin, Upper	**38**	Safety-Lever Pin	**61**	Stock Bolt Lock Washer
16	Firing Pin Retaining Pins	**39**	Sear Springs	**62**	Stock Bolt Washer
17	Forend	**40**	Sear Plungers	**63**	Stock Assembly
18	Forend Latch	**41**	Sear Pin	**64**	Recoil Pad
19	Forend Latch Spring	**42**	Sear, Right	**65**	Recoil Pad Screws
20	Forend Insert	**43**	Sear, Left	**66**	Receiver
21	Forend Screw	**44**	Hammer, Right		
22	Forend Iron Screw	**45**	Hammer, Left		
23	Forend Iron	**46**	Mainspring Plunger, Right		

Model 330 Over/Under Shotgun

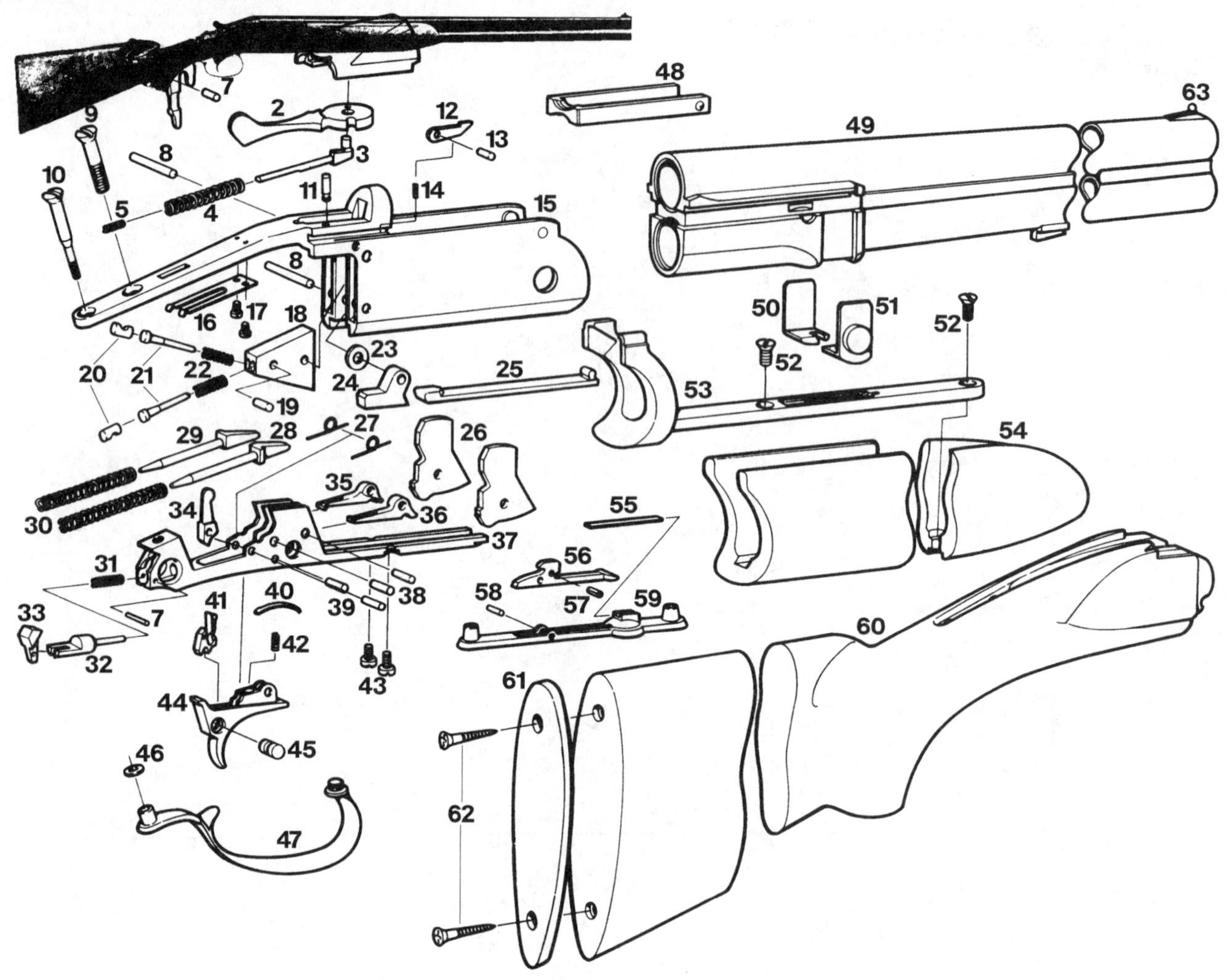

1	Locking Bolt	**20**	Strikers	**42**	Trigger Spring
2	Top Snap	**21**	Firing Pins	**43**	Trigger Plate Screws
3	Top Snap Plunger	**22**	Firing Pin Springs	**44**	Trigger
4	Top Snap Spring	**23**	Cocking Lever Spacer	**45**	Selector Button
5	Safety Plunger Spring	**24**	Cocking Crank	**46**	Trigger Guard Washer
6	Safety Button	**25**	Cocking Slide	**47**	Trigger Guard
7	Safety Detent and Inertia Block Pins	**26**	Hammers	**48**	Extractor
8	Firing Pin Block and Cocking Crank Pins	**27**	Sear Springs	**49**	Barrel
9	Top Tang Screw, Front	**28**	Mainspring Plunger, Right	**50**	Barrel Pivot Pin, Left
10	Top Tang Screw, Rear	**29**	Mainspring Plunger, Left	**51**	Barrel Pivot Pin, Right
11	Top Snap Pin	**30**	Mainsprings	**52**	Forend Snap Housing Screws
12	Top Slide Trip	**31**	Inertia Block Spring	**53**	Forend Iron
13	Top Slide Trip Pin	**32**	Inertia Block Plunger	**54**	Forend Wood
14	Top Slide Trip Spring	**33**	Inertia Block	**55**	Forend Snap Spring
15	Frame	**34**	Safety-Lever	**56**	Forend Snap
16	Safety Spring	**35**	Sear, Left	**57**	Forend Snap Stop Pin
17	Safety Spring Screws	**36**	Sear, Right	**58**	Forend Snap Pin
18	Firing Pin Block	**37**	Trigger Plate	**59**	Forend Snap Housing
19	Striker Pin	**38**	Sear Pin and Hammer Pin	**60**	Stock Complete
		39	Trigger Pin and Safety-Lever Pin	**61**	Buttplate
		40	Selector Spring	**62**	Buttplate Screws
		41	Selector Lever	**63**	Front Sight Bead

Model 333 Over/Under Shotgun

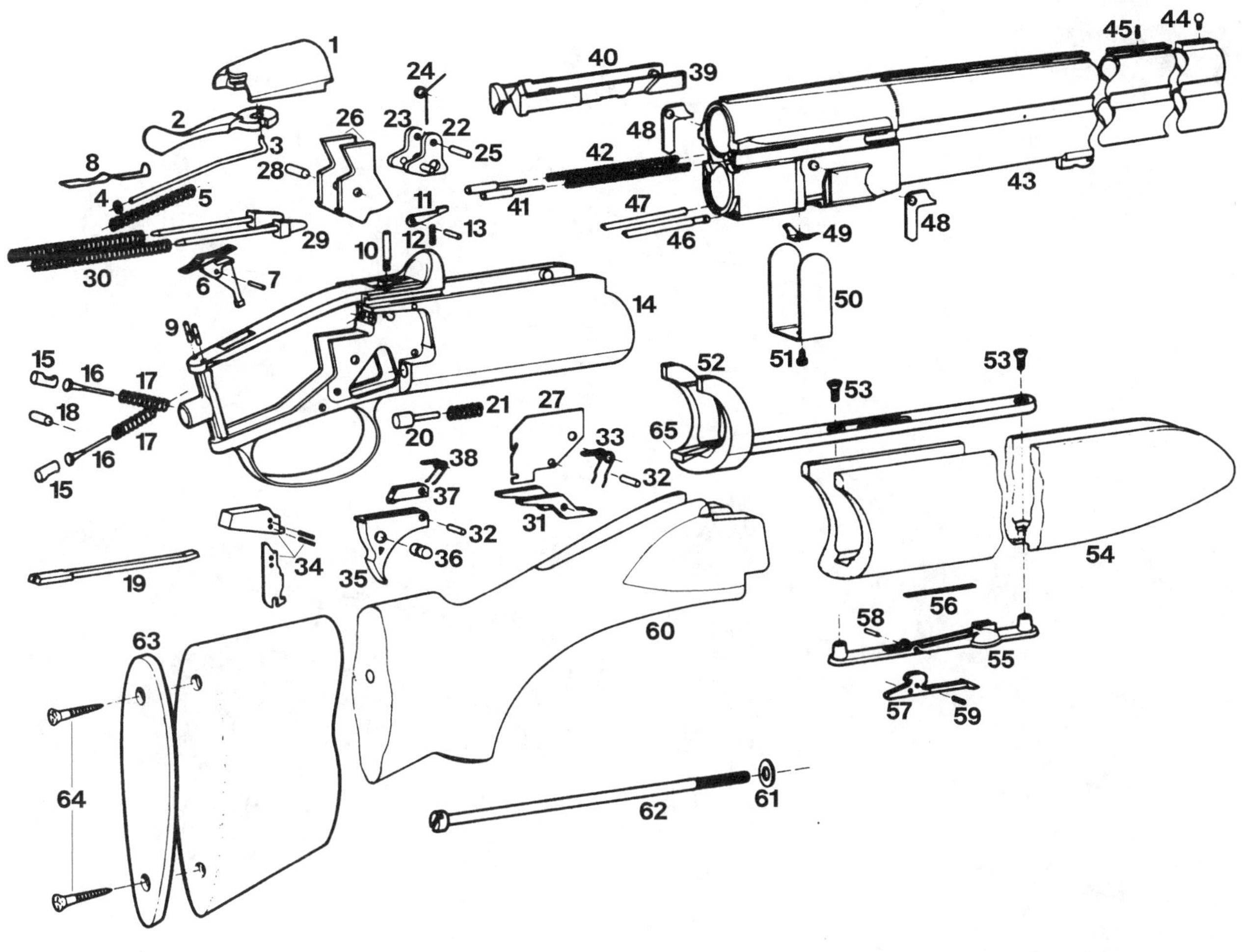

1 Locking Bolt
2 Top Snap
3 Top Snap Plunger
4 Top Snap Plunger Washer
5 Top Snap Spring
6 Safety Button
7 Safety Pin
8 Safety Spring
9 Indicators
10 Top Snap Pin
11 Top Slide Trip
12 Top Slide Trip Spring
13 Top Slide Trip Pin
14 Frame
15 Strikers
16 Firing Pins
17 Firing Pin Springs
18 Striker Pin
19 Cocking Slide
20 Ejector Operating Pin
21 Ejector Operating Pin Spring
22 Cocking Crank, Right
23 Cocking Crank, Left
24 Cocking Slide Spring
25 Cocking Crank Pin
26 Hammers
27 Support Plate
28 Hammer Pin
29 Mainspring Plungers
30 Mainsprings
31 Sears
32 Trigger Pin
33 Sear Springs
34 Inertia Block Assembly
35 Trigger
36 Selector Button
37 Selector Cam
38 Selector Cam Spring
39 Extractor, Right
40 Extractor, Left
41 Ejector Spring Plungers
42 Ejector Springs
43 Barrel
44 Front Sight Bead
45 Rear Sight Bead
46 Ejector Operating Rod, Right
47 Ejector Operating Rod, Left
48 Ejector Trip
49 Ejector Trip Spring
50 Covering Plate
51 Covering Plate Screw
52 Forend Iron
53 Forend Screws
54 Forend Wood
55 Forend Snap Housing
56 Forend Snap Spring
57 Forend Snap
58 Forend Snap Pin
59 Forend Snap Stop Pin
60 Stock
61 Stock Bolt Washer
62 Stock Bolt
63 Buttplate
64 Buttplate Screws
65 Cocking Lug

Model 34, 34M, 65 and 65M Bolt-Action Rifle

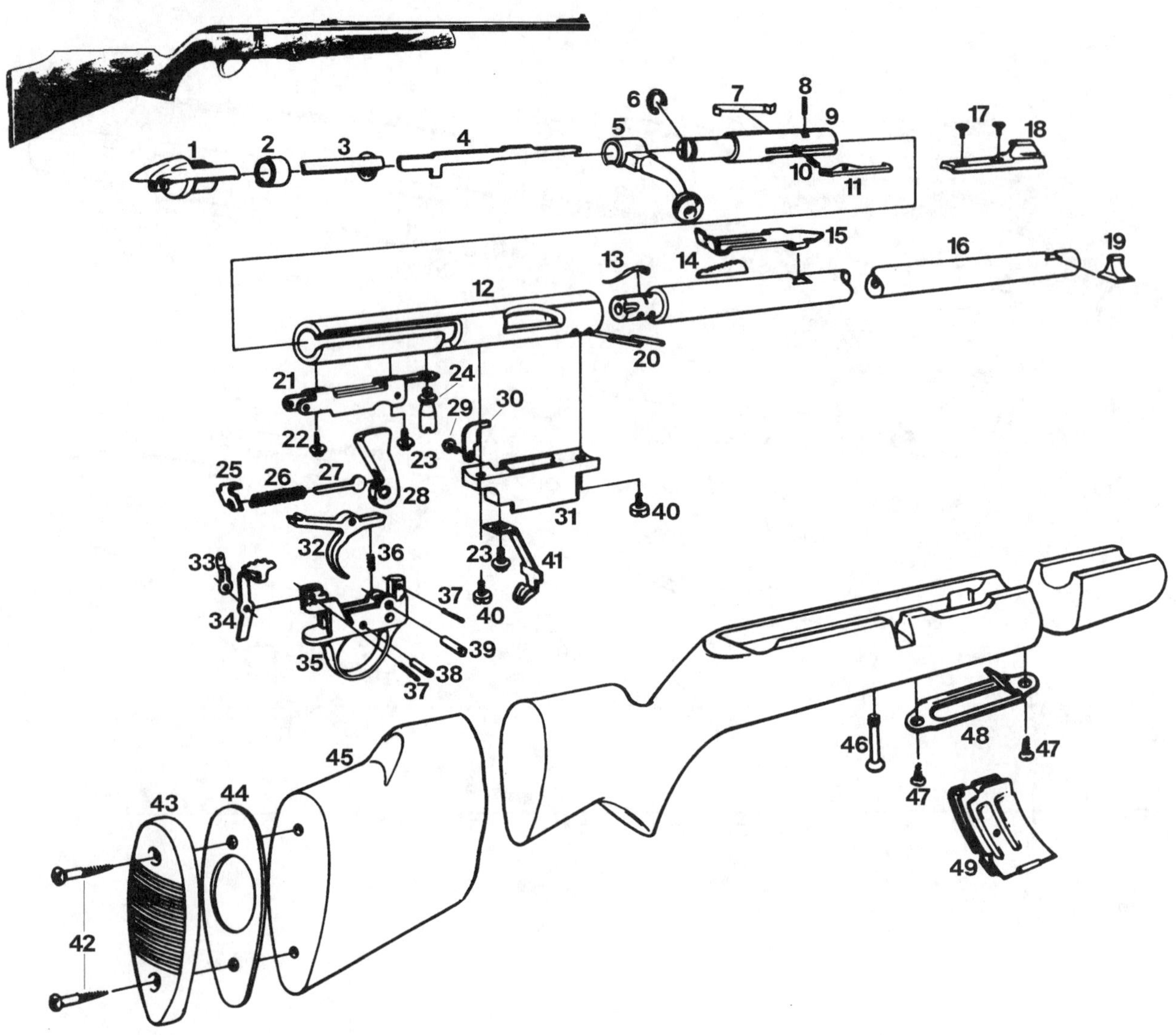

1	Receiver Extension	**18**	Front Sight	**34**	Safety
2	Bolt Handle Retaining Collar	**19**	Front Sight (34M only)	**35**	Trigger Guard
3	Breechbolt Key	**20**	Barrel Pins	**36**	Trigger Spring
4	Firing Pin	**21**	Trigger Guard Housing	**37**	Safety Pin and Trigger Guard Pin
5	Bolt Handle	**22**	Trigger Guard Housing Screw	**38**	Trigger Pin
6	Bolt Handle Snap Ring	**23**	Trigger Guard Housing Screw and Magazine Retainer Screw	**39**	Hammer Pin
7	Extractor, Left	**24**	Takedown Stud	**40**	Magazine Housing Screws
8	Extractor Pin	**25**	Mainspring Plunger Bridge	**41**	Magazine Retainer
9	Breechbolt	**26**	Mainspring	**42**	Buttplate Screws
10	Extractor Spring	**27**	Mainspring Plunger	**43**	Buttplate
11	Extractor, Right	**28**	Hammer	**44**	Buttplate Spacer
12	Receiver	**29**	Ejector Screw	**45**	Stock
13	Bumper	**30**	Ejector	**46**	Takedown Screw
14	Rear Sight Step	**31**	Magazine Housing	**47**	Floorplate Screws
15	Rear Sight	**32**	Trigger	**48**	Floorplate
16	Barrel	**33**	Safety Detent	**49**	Magazine
17	Front Sight Screws				

Model 340, 340B, 340C, 340D and 340V Bolt-Action Rifle

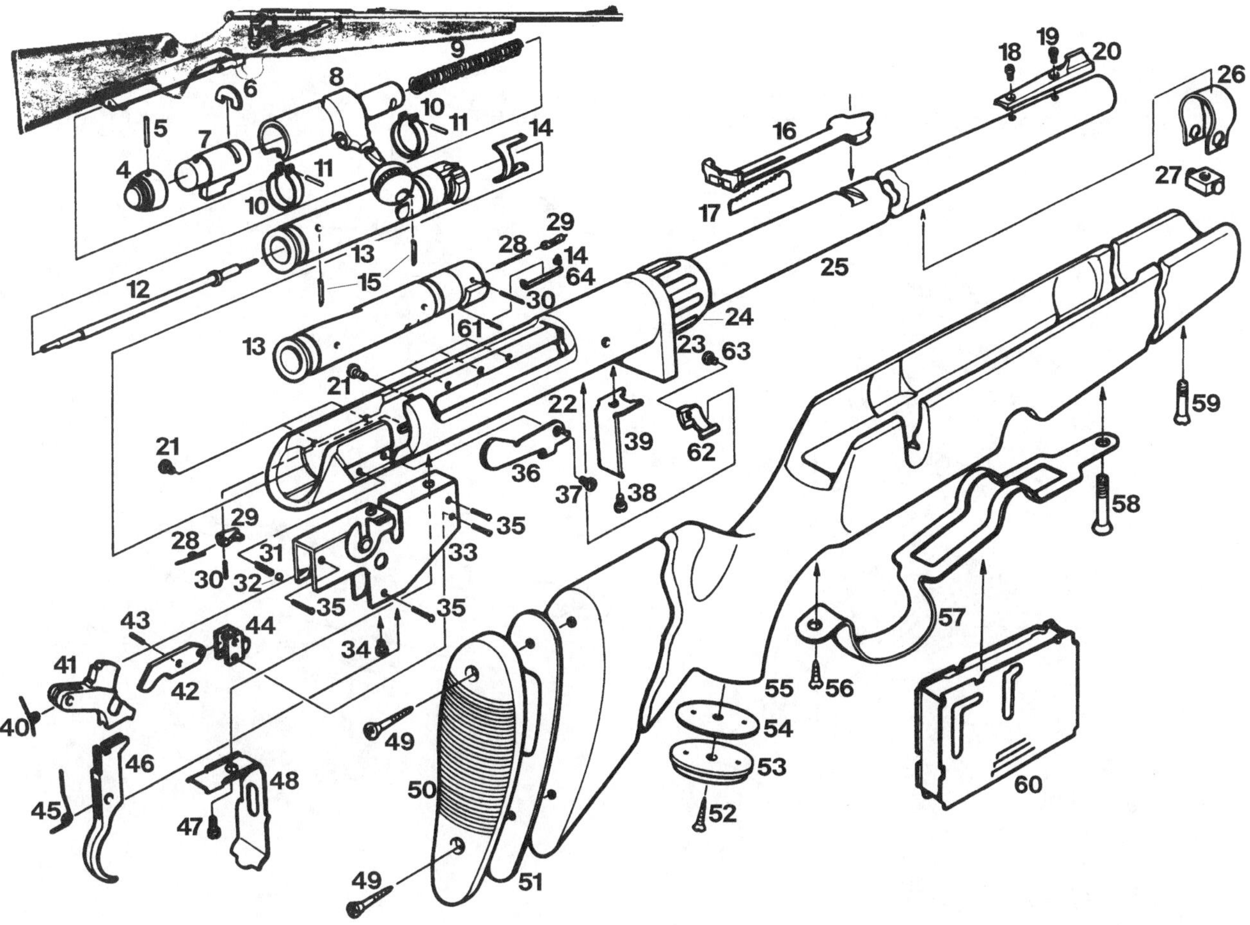

1	Gas Shield Key	23	Barrel Lug	45	Trigger Spring
2	Gas Shield Key Spring	24	Barrel Lock Nut	46	Trigger
3	Gas Shield	25	Barrel	47	Trigger Bracket Screw
4	Cocking Piece Cap	26	Barrel Band	48	Magazine Retainer Spring, Rear
5	Cocking Piece Cap Pin	27	Barrel Band Nut	49	Buttplate Screws
6	Cocking Piece Key	28	Ejector Spring	50	Buttplate
7	Cocking Piece	29	Ejector	51	Buttplate Spacer
8	Bolt Body and Handle	30	Ejector Pin	52	Pistol Grip Cap Screw
9	Mainspring	31	Safety Spring	53	Pistol Grip Cap
10	Gas Shield Clips	32	Safety Plunger Ball	54	Pistol Grip Cap Spacer
11	Gas Shield Clip Pins	33	Trigger Bracket	55	Stock
12	Firing Pin	34	Trigger Bracket Screw, Short	56	Trigger Guard Screw, Rear
13	Bolt Head	35	Sear Pins	57	Trigger Guard
14	Extractor	36	Safety	58	Recoil Lug Screw
15	Bolt Head Retaining Pins	37	Safety Screw	59	Barrel Band Screw
16	Rear Sight	38	Magazine Retainer Screw	60	Magazine Assembly
17	Rear Sight Step	39	Magazine Retainer Spring, Front	61	Extractor Spring Pin
18	Front Sight Screw, Short	40	Sear Spring	62	Baffle Block
19	Front Sight Screw, Long	41	Sear	63	Baffle Block Screw
20	Front Sight	42	Sear Lever	64	Extractor Spring
21	Dummy Screws	43	Sear Cam Pin		
22	Receiver	44	Magazine Stop		

Model 35 and 35M Bolt-Action Rifle

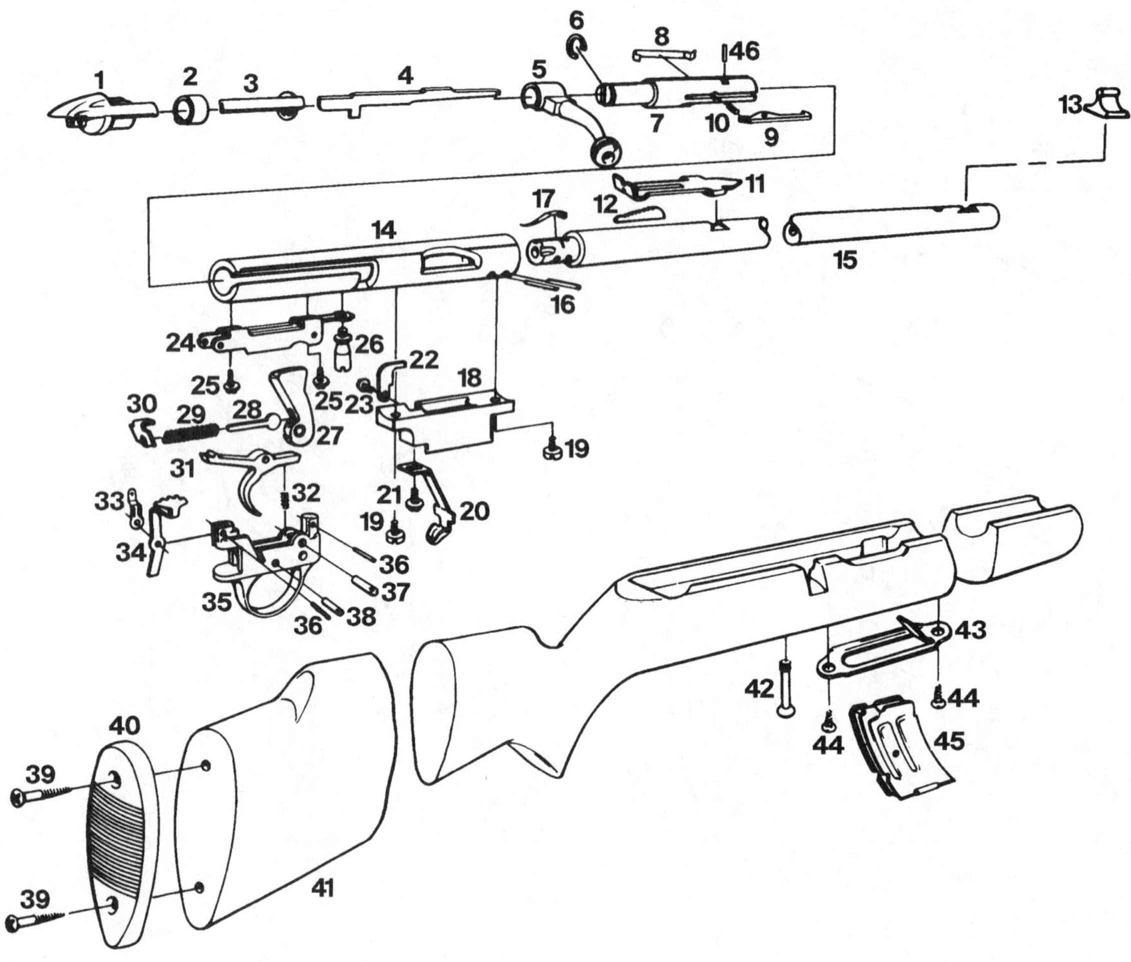

1	Receiver Extension	24	Trigger Guard Housing
2	Bolt Collar	25	Trigger Guard Housing Screws
3	Firing Pin Extension	26	Takedown Stud
4	Firing Pin	27	Hammer
5	Bolt Handle	28	Mainspring Guide Rod
6	Bolt Retaining Clip	29	Mainspring
7	Bolt Housing	30	Mainspring Seat
8	Left Extractor	31	Trigger
9	Right Extractor	32	Trigger Spring
10	Extractor Spring	33	Safety Detent
11	Rear Sight	34	Safety
12	Rear Sight Ramp	35	Trigger Guard
13	Front Sight	36	Trigger Guard Pins
14	Receiver	37	Hammer Pin
15	Barrel	38	Trigger Pin
16	Barrel Retaining Screws	39	Buttplate Screws
17	Barrel Bumper	40	Buttplate
18	Magazine Housing	41	Stock
19	Magazine Housing Screws	42	Takedown Screw
20	Magazine Retainer	43	Floorplate
21	Magazine Retainer Screw	44	Floorplate Screws
22	Magazine Ejector	45	Magazine Assembly
23	Magazine Ejector Screw	46	Extractor Pin

Model 440, 440A and 440T Over/Under Shotgun

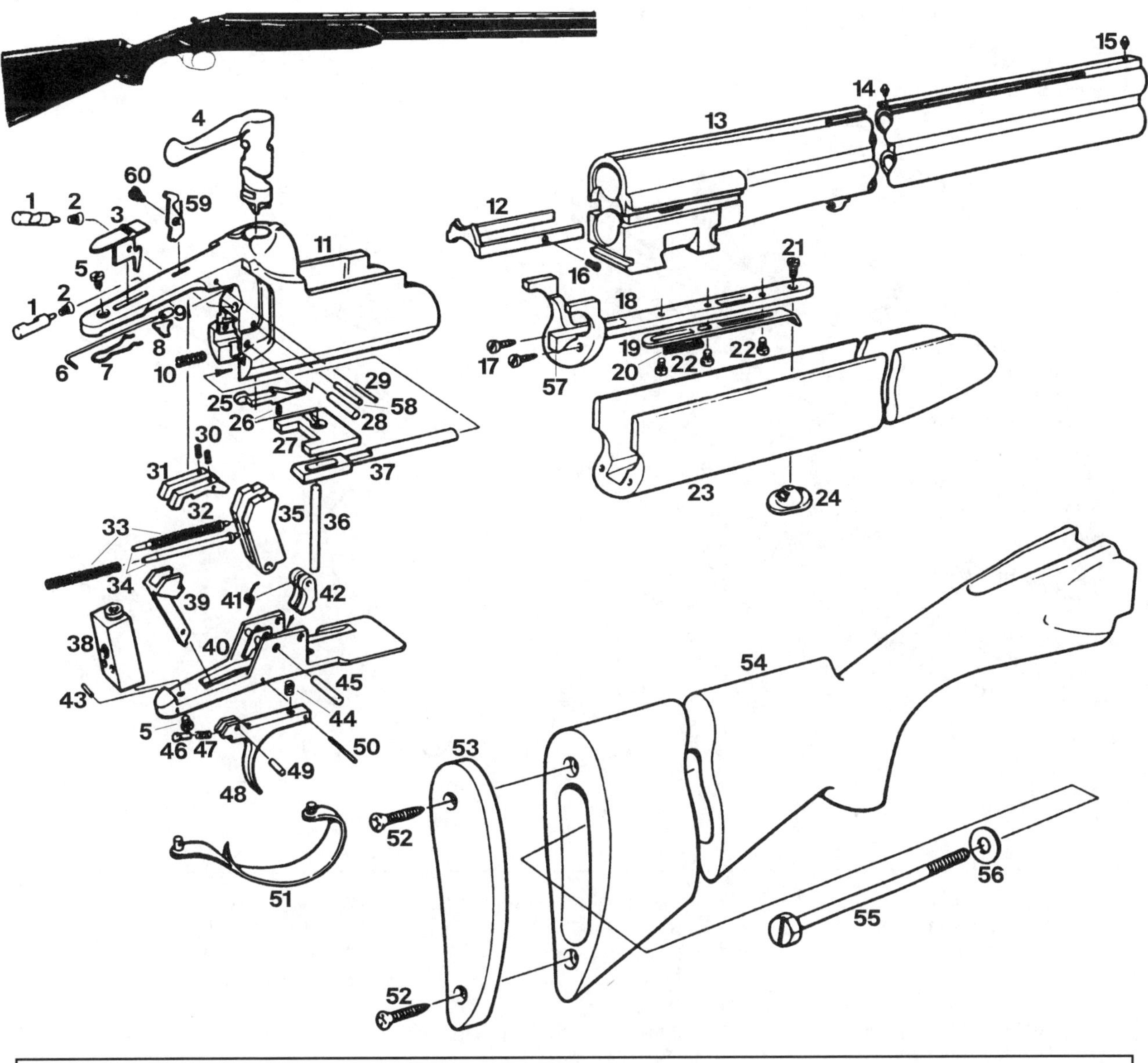

1	Firing Pins	21	Forend Screw	41	Cocking Lever Spring
2	Firing Pin Springs	22	Forend Latch Screws	42	Cocking Lever
3	Safety	23	Forend Wood	43	Trigger Guard Pin
4	Top Lever	24	Escutcheon	44	Trigger Spring
5	Receiver Tang Screws	25	Top Snap Trip	45	Hammer Pin
6	Top Snap Plunger	26	Top Snap Trip Spring	46	Rocker Arm Spring Plunger
7	Safety Spring	27	Bolt	47	Inertia Block Spring
8	Hammer Retractor	28	Cocking Lever Pin	48	Trigger
9	Top Snap Plunger Collar	29	Sear Pin	49	Rocker Arm Pin
10	Top Lever Spring	30	Sear Springs	50	Trigger Pin
11	Receiver	31	Sear, Left	51	Trigger Guard
12	Extractor	32	Sear, Right	52	Buttplate Screws
13	Barrel	33	Hammer Springs	53	Buttplate
14	Rear Sight	34	Mainspring Plungers	54	Stock
15	Front Sight	35	Hammer	55	Stock Bolt
16	Extractor Screw	36	Top Lever Spindle	56	Stock Bolt Washer
17	Forend Iron Head Screws	37	Cocking Rod	57	Cocking Lug
18	Forend Iron	38	Receiver Space Block	58	Firing Pin Retaining Pin
19	Forend Latch	39	Inertia Block	59	Selector Assembly (440A only)
20	Forend Latch Spring	40	Trigger Plate	60	Selector Screw (440A only)

Model 550 Side-by-Side Shotgun

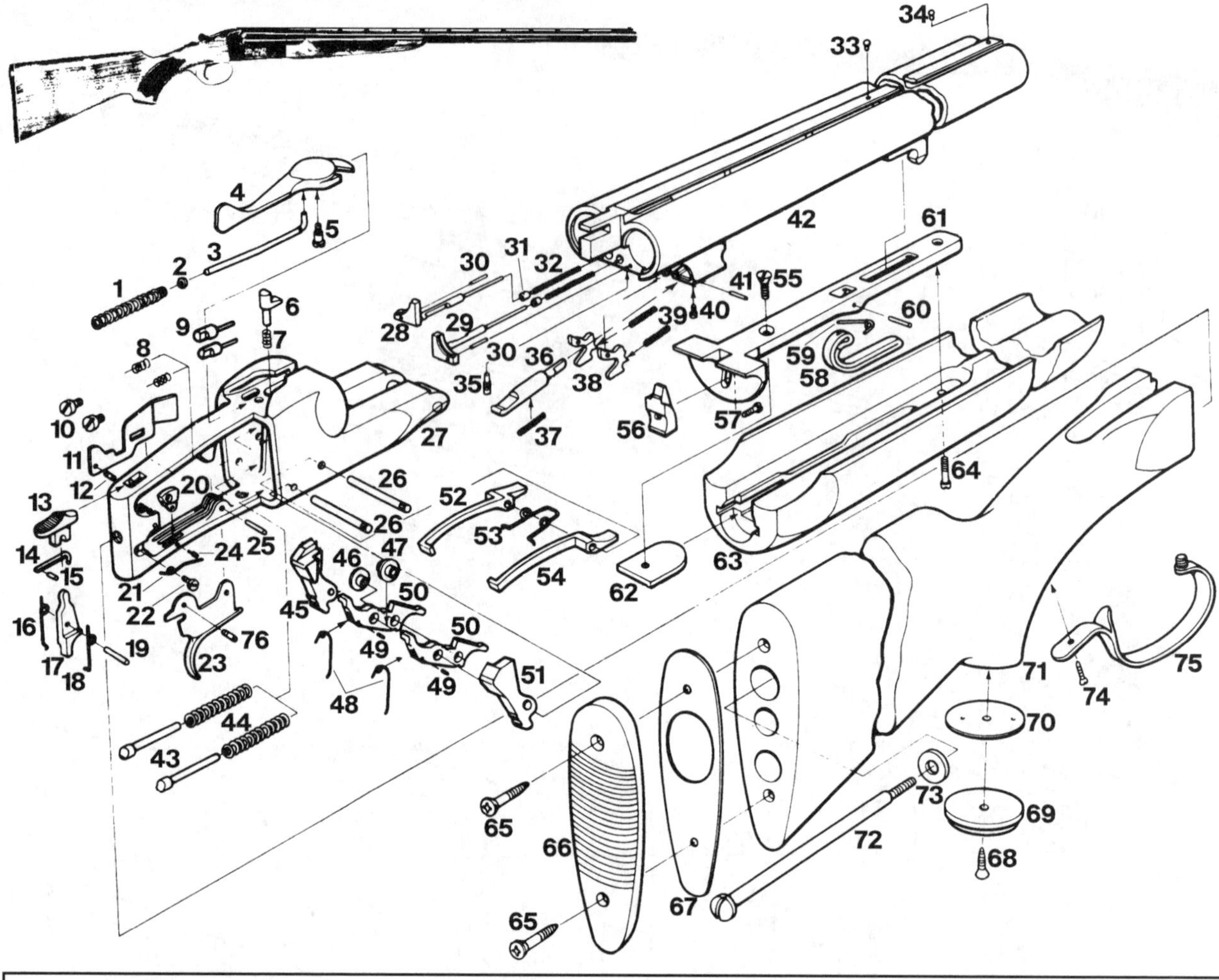

1	Top Snap Plunger Spring
2	Top Snap Plunger Collar
3	Top Snap Plunger
4	Top Snap
5	Top Snap Screw
6	Top Snap Trip
7	Top Snap Trip Spring
8	Firing Pin Springs
9	Firing Pins
10	Firing Pin Retaining Screws
11	Slide
12	Trigger Stud
13	Safety Button
14	Safety Spring
15	Safety Plunger
16	Slide Spring
17	Safety-Lever
18	Trigger Spring
19	Safety-Lever Pin
20	Inertia Block
21	Inertia Block Spring
22	Inertia Block Spring Screw
23	Trigger
24	Inertia Block Pin
25	Trigger Pin
26	Sear Pin and Cocking Lever and Hammer Pin
27	Frame
28	Extractor, Left
29	Extractor, Right
30	Extractor Guide Pins
31	Ejector Collars
32	Ejector Springs
33	Rear Sight
34	Front Sight
35	Extractor Screw
36	Cocking Plunger
37	Cocking Plunger Spring
38	Ejector Sears
39	Ejector Sear Springs
40	Cocking Plunger Retaining Screw
41	Ejector Sear Pin
42	Barrel
43	Mainspring Plungers
44	Mainsprings
45	Hammer, Left
46	Cocking Lever Spacer
47	Cocking Lever Bushing
48	Cocking Lever Springs
49	Cocking Lever Spring Pins
50	Cocking Levers
51	Hammer, Right
52	Sear, Left
53	Sear Spring
54	Sear, Right
55	Forend Screw, Rear
56	Ejector
57	Ejector Screw
58	Forend Spring
59	Forend Spring Spring
60	Forend Spring Pin
61	Forend Iron
62	Forend Insert
63	Forend Wood
64	Forend Screw, Front
65	Buttplate Screws
66	Buttplate
67	Buttplate Liner
68	Pistol Grip Cap Screw
69	Pistol Grip Cap
70	Pistol Grip Cap Liner
71	Stock
72	Stock Bolt
73	Stock Bolt Washer
74	Trigger Guard Screw
75	Trigger Guard
76	Trigger Stop Pin

Model 6J, 6M, 6N, 6JDL and 6P, Stevens Model 87J, 87M and 87N, and Springfield Model 187J, 187M and 187N Autoloading Rifle

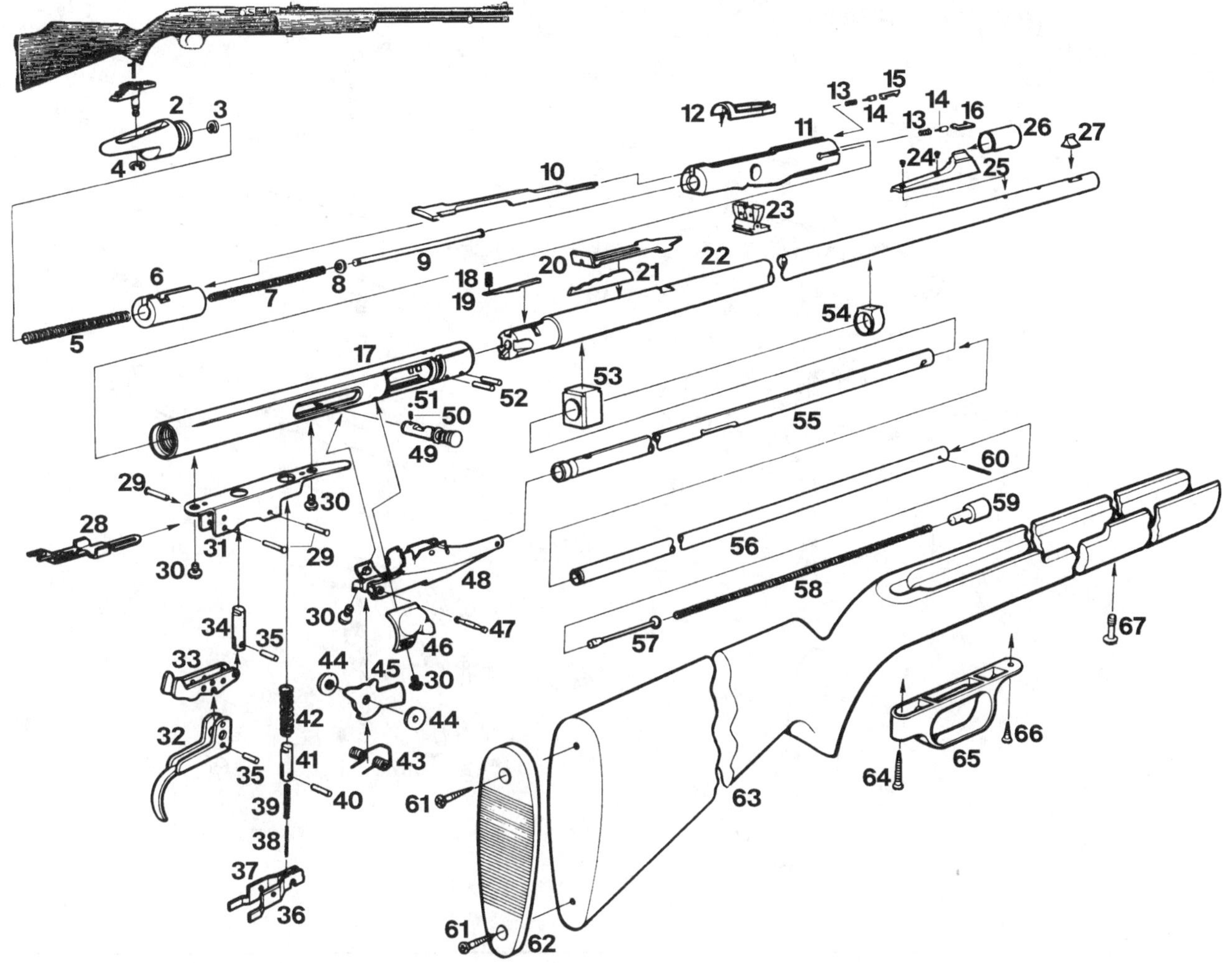

1	Safety Button	24	Front Sight Screws	45	Lifter
2	Recoil Plug Assembly	25	Front Sight Complete	46	Deflector
3	Hammer Spring Washer	26	Front Sight Hood	47	Lifter Pin
4	Safety Button Retaining Ring	27	Front Sight	48	Magazine Guide
5	Hammer Spring	28	Safety Slide	49	Locking Bolt
6	Hammer	29	Trigger, Detent and Release Lever Pins	50	Locking Bolt Plunger Ball Spring
7	Breechbolt Spring			51	Locking Bolt Plunger Ball
8	Breechbolt Spring Washer	30	Release Housing and Magazine Guide Screws	52	Barrel Pins
9	Breechbolt Spring Rod			53	Magazine Mount, Rear
10	Firing Pin	31	Release Housing	54	Magazine Mount, Front
11	Breechbolt	32	Trigger	55	Outside Magazine Tube
12	Extractor	33	Release Lever	56	Inside Magazine Tube
13	Extractor Plunger Springs	34	Release Plunger	57	Magazine Follower
14	Extractor Plungers	35	Trigger and Detent Plunger Pins	58	Magazine Follower Spring
15	Extractor, Left	36	Detent Lever, Right	59	Magazine Plug
16	Extractor, Right	37	Detent Lever, Left	60	Magazine Plug Pin
17	Receiver	38	Detent Plunger Inner Spring	61	Buttplate Screws
18	Bumper Spring	39	Detent Plunger Spring	62	Buttplate
19	Bumper	40	Release Plunger Pin	63	Stock
20	Rear Sight	41	Detent Plunger	64	Trigger Guard Screw, Long
21	Rear Sight Step	42	Release Spring	65	Trigger Guard
22	Barrel	43	Lifter Spring	66	Trigger Guard Screw, Short
23	Rear Sight	44	Lifter Spacers	67	Takedown Screw

Model 60 and 90, and Stevens and Springfield Model 88 and 388 Autoloading Rifle

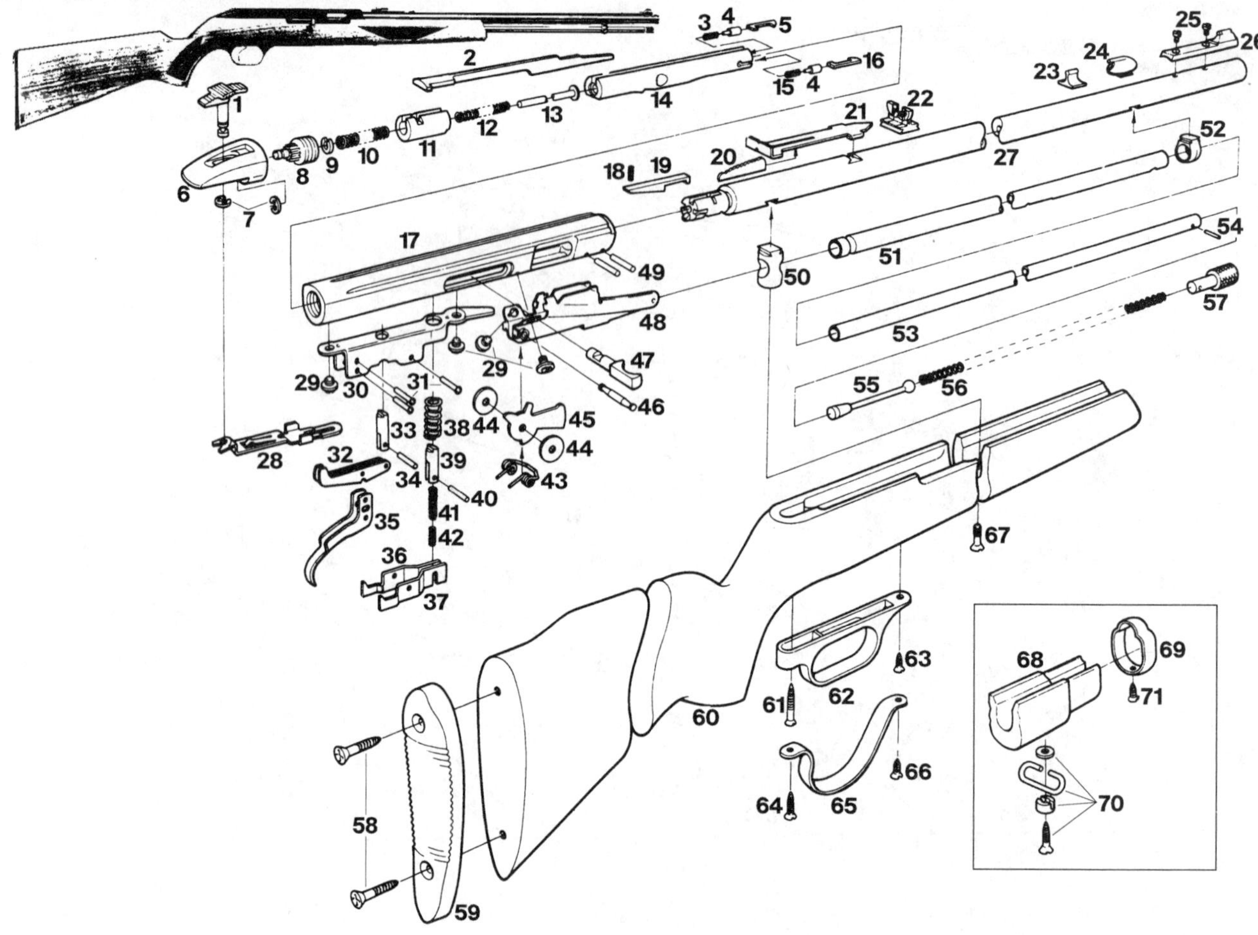

1	Safety Button	**26**	Front Sight Base	**50**	Magazine Mount, Rear
2	Firing Pin	**27**	Barrel	**51**	Outside Magazine Tube
3	Extractor Plunger Spring, Left	**28**	Safety Slide	**52**	Magazine Mount, Front
4	Extractor Plungers	**29**	Release Housing Screw	**53**	Inside Magazine Tube
5	Extractor, Left	**30**	Release Housing	**54**	Magazine Plug Pin
6	Recoil Plug Assembly	**31**	Trigger, Detent and Release Lever Pins	**55**	Magazine Follower
7	Safety Button Retaining Rings	**32**	Release Lever	**56**	Magazine Follower Spring
8	Recoil Plug Insert	**33**	Release Plunger	**57**	Magazine Plug
9	Hammer Spring Washer	**34**	Trigger Pin	**58**	Buttplate Screws
10	Hammer Spring	**35**	Trigger	**59**	Buttplate
11	Hammer	**36**	Detent Lever, Left	**60**	Stock
12	Breechbolt Spring	**37**	Detent Lever, Right	**61**	Trigger Guard Screw, Long
13	Breechbolt Spring Rod	**38**	Release Spring	**62**	Trigger Guard
14	Breechbolt	**39**	Detent Plunger	**63**	Trigger Guard Screw, Short
15	Extractor Plunger Spring, Right	**40**	Release Plunger Pin	**64**	Trigger Guard Screw, Rear (Model 88 and 388)
16	Extractor, Right	**41**	Detent Plunger Spring	**65**	Trigger Guard (Model 88 and 388)
17	Receiver	**42**	Detent Plunger Inner Spring	**66**	Trigger Guard Screw, Front (Model 88 and 388)
18	Bumper Spring	**43**	Lifter Spring	**67**	Takedown Screw
19	Bumper	**44**	Lifter Spacers	**68**	Stock (Model 90)
20	Rear Sight Step	**45**	Lifter	**69**	Barrel Band (Model 90 and 388)
21	Rear Sight	**46**	Lifter Pin	**70**	Swivel Assembly
22	Rear Sight (Model 90)	**47**	Locking Bolt	**71**	Barrel Band Screw
23	Front Sight (Model 88 and 388)	**48**	Magazine Guide		
24	Front Sight (Model 90)	**49**	Barrel Pins		
25	Front Sight Screws				

Model 67 Series C and E Slide-Action Shotgun

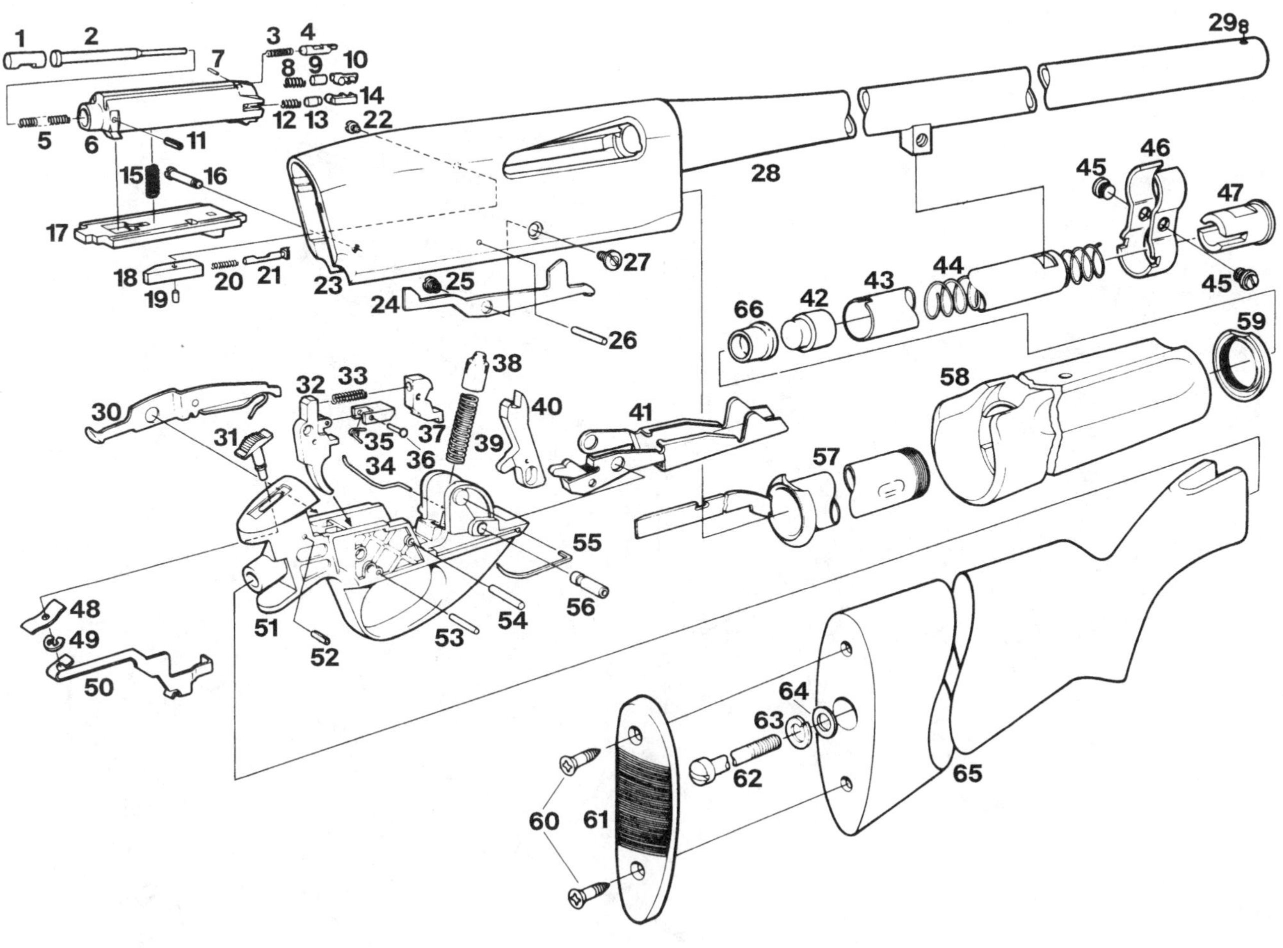

1	Firing Pin Extension	**23**	Receiver	**45**	Magazine House/Tube Screws
2	Firing Pin	**24**	Cartridge Stop	**46**	Magazine Tube Yoke
3	Shell Stop Spring	**25**	Cartridge Stop Pivot Nut	**47**	Magazine Plug
4	Shell Stop	**26**	Trigger Guard Pin	**48**	Safety Spring
5	Firing Pin Spring	**27**	Cartridge Stop Pivot Screw	**49**	Safety Return Ring
6	Breechbolt	**28**	Barrel	**50**	Safety-Lever
7	Shell Stop Retaining Pin	**29**	Front Sight	**51**	Trigger Guard
8	Extractor Spring, Left	**30**	Slide Lock Assembly	**52**	Safety-Lever Return Pin
9	Extractor Plunger, Left	**31**	Safety	**53**	Trigger Pin
10	Extractor, Left	**32**	Trigger Assembly	**54**	Sear Pin
11	Firing Pin Stop Pin	**33**	Trigger Spring	**55**	Lifter Spring
12	Extractor Spring, Right	**34**	Slide Lock Release Spring	**56**	Hammer Bushing
13	Extractor Plunger, Right	**35**	Sear Trip and Spring	**57**	Operating Handle Bar Assembly
14	Extractor, Right	**36**	Sear Trip Pin	**58**	Operating Handle Wood
15	Bolt Support Spring	**37**	Sear	**59**	Operating Handle Collar Front
16	Trigger Guard Screw	**38**	Mainspring Plunger	**60**	Buttplate Screws
17	Slide Assembly (Series C Only)	**39**	Mainspring	**61**	Buttplate
18	Ejector	**40**	Hammer Assembly	**62**	Stock Bolt
19	Ejector Pin	**41**	Lifter Assembly	**63**	Stock Bolt Lock Washer
20	Ejector Spring	**42**	Magazine Follower	**64**	Stock Bolt Washer
21	Ejector Plunger	**43**	Magazine Tube	**65**	Stock Assembly
22	Ejector Screw	**44**	Magazine Spring	**66**	Magazine Tube Adapter

Model 71 and Stevens Favorite Single Shot Rifle

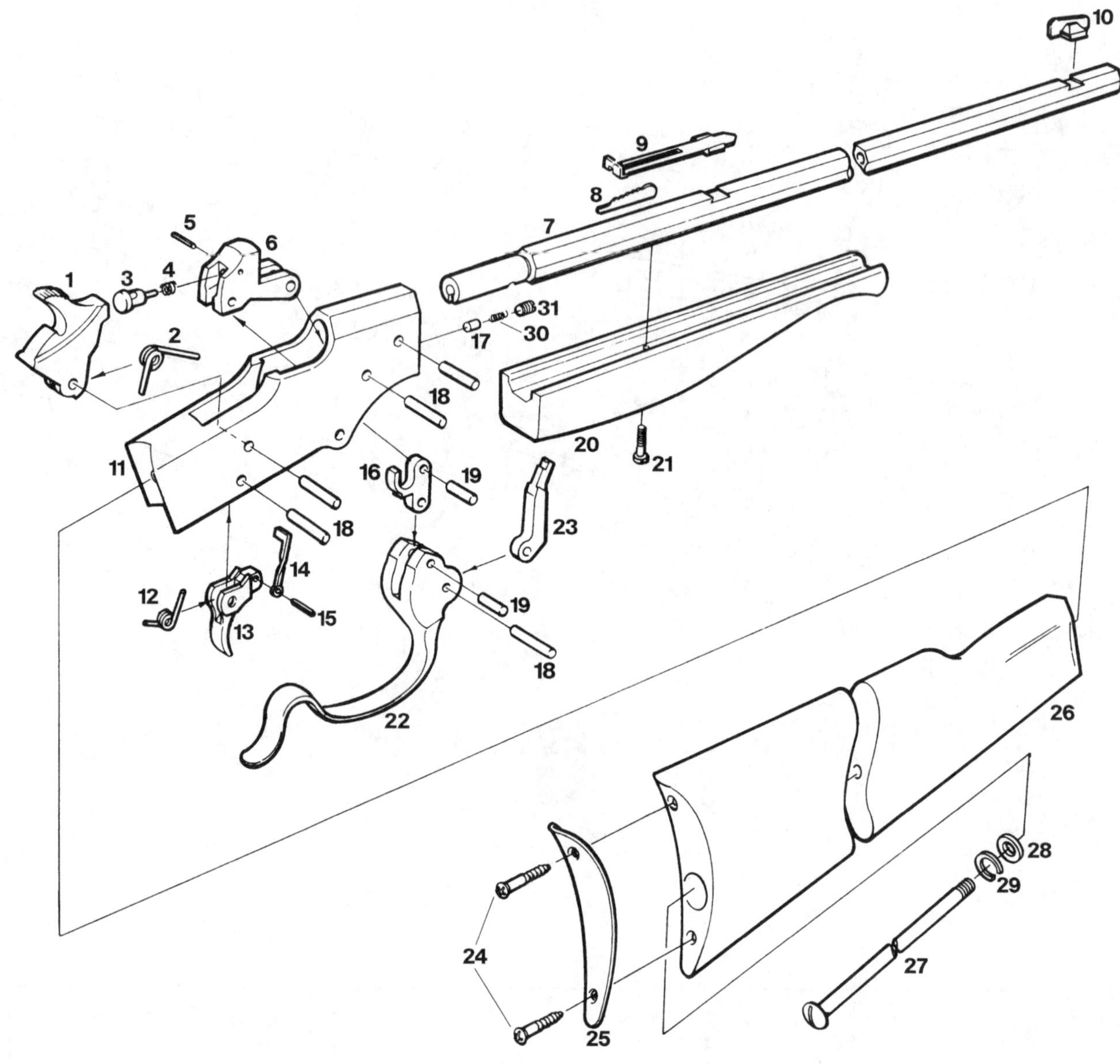

1	Hammer	**18**	Hammer, Breechblock and Trigger Pins
2	Hammer Spring	**19**	Link Pin
3	Firing Pin	**20**	Forend
4	Firing Pin Spring	**21**	Forend Screw
5	Firing Pin Retaining Pin	**22**	Lever
6	Breechblock	**23**	Extractor
7	Barrel	**24**	Buttplate Screws
8	Rear Sight Step	**25**	Buttplate
9	Rear Sight	**26**	Stock
10	Front Sight Assembly	**27**	Stock Bolt
11	Frame	**28**	Stock Bolt Washer
12	Trigger Spring	**29**	Stock Bolt Lock Washer
13	Trigger	**30**	Breechblock Plunger Spring
14	Hammer Block	**31**	Breechblock Plunger Retaining Screw
15	Hammer Block Pin		
16	Link		
17	Breechblock Plunger		

Model 72 and 74 Single Shot Rifle

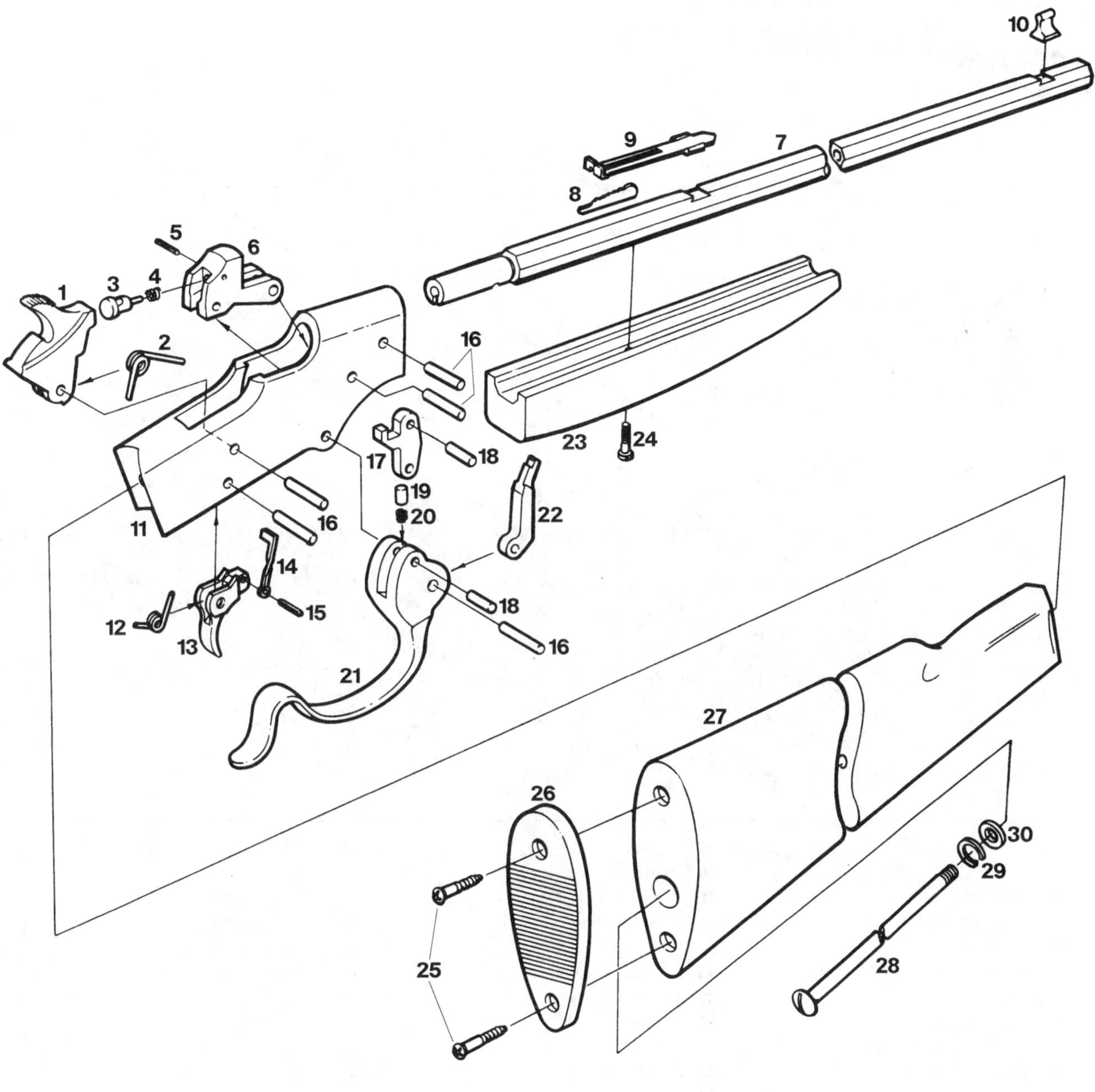

1	Hammer	**16**	Hammer, Breechblock and Trigger Pins
2	Hammer Spring	**17**	Link
3	Firing Pin	**18**	Link Pins
4	Firing Pin Spring	**19**	Detent Plunger
5	Firing Pin Securing Pin	**20**	Detent Plunger Spring
6	Breechblock	**21**	Lever
7	Barrel	**22**	Extractor
8	Rear Sight Step	**23**	Forend
9	Rear Sight	**24**	Forend Screw
10	Front Sight	**25**	Buttplate Screws
11	Frame	**26**	Buttplate
12	Trigger Spring	**27**	Stock
13	Trigger	**28**	Stock Bolt
14	Hammer Block	**29**	Stock Bolt Washer
15	Hammer Block Pin	**30**	Stock Bolt Lock Washer

Model 720, 745, 750 and 750C and Springfield 745B and 745C Autoloading Shotgun

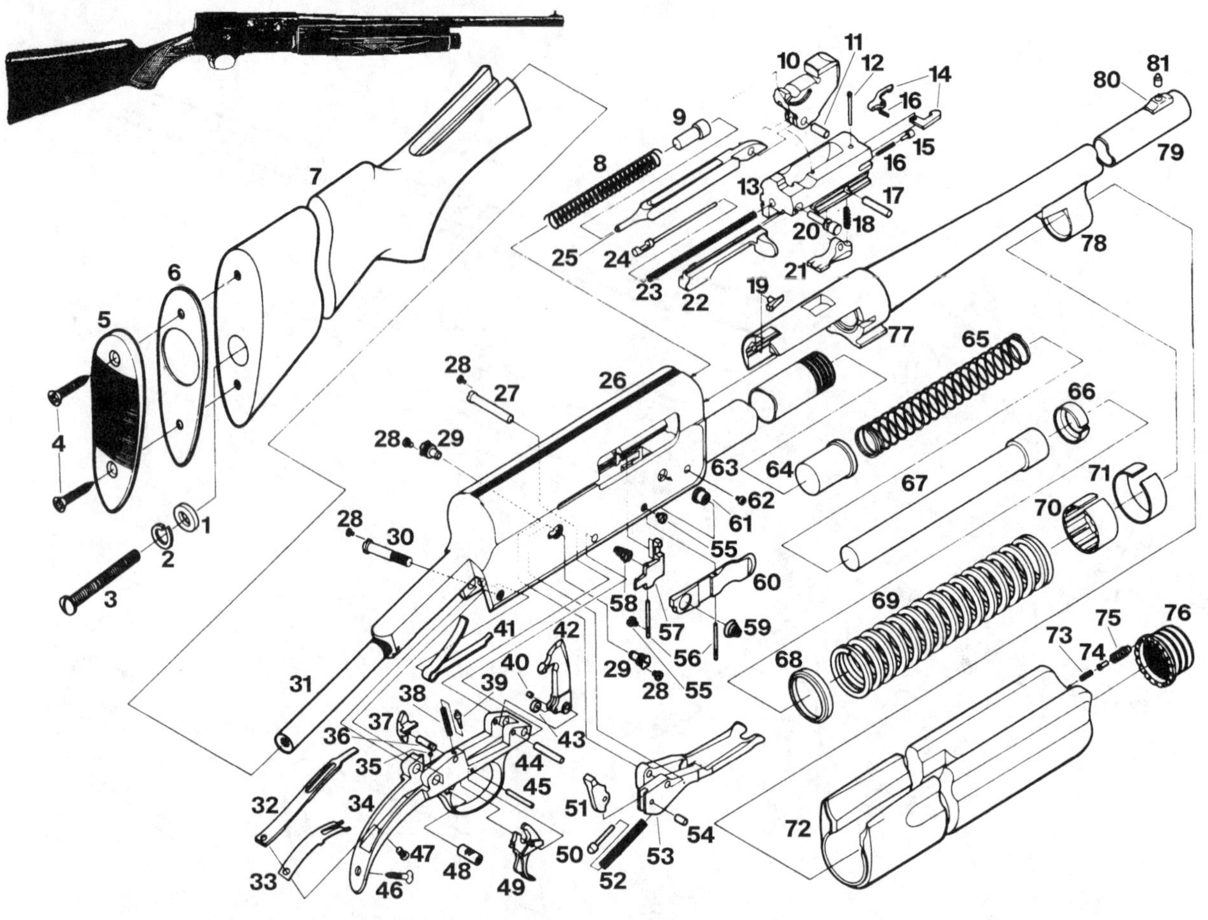

1	Stock Bolt Washer
2	Stock Bolt Lock Washer
3	Stock Bolt
4	Buttplate Screws
5	Buttplate
6	Buttplate Liner
7	Stock
8	Action Spring
9	Action Spring Follower
10	Locking Bolt
11	Link Pin
12	Extractor Pin
13	Breechblock
14	Extractors
15	Extractor Plunger
16	Extractor Springs
17	Locking Bolt Latch Pin
18	Locking Bolt Latch Spring
19	Ejector
20	Firing Pin Stop Pin
21	Locking Bolt Latch
22	Slide Action
23	Firing Pin Spring
24	Firing Pin
25	Link
26	Receiver
27	Trigger Guard Pin
28	Locking Screws
29	Lifter Screws
30	Trigger Guard Screw
31	Action Spring Tube
32	Mainspring
33	Trigger Spring
34	Trigger Guard
35	Safety Plunger Ball
36	Safety Sear Pin
37	Sear
38	Safety Sear Spring
39	Safety Sear Follower
40	Hammer Roll Pin
41	Lifter Spring
42	Hammer
43	Hammer Roll
44	Hammer Pin
45	Trigger Pin
46	Tang Screw
47	Mainspring Screw
48	Safety
49	Trigger
50	Lifter Pawl Plunger
51	Lifter Pawl
52	Lifter Pawl Spring
53	Lifter
54	Lifter Pawl Pin
55	Locking Screws
56	Lifter Latch and Cocking Stop Pins
57	Cartridge Stop
58	Cartridge Stop Spring
59	Lifter Latch Spring
60	Lifter Latch
61	Lifter Latch Button
62	Magazine Screw
63	Magazine Tube
64	Magazine Follower
65	Magazine Spring
66	Magazine Spring Retainer
67	Magazine Plug Wood
68	Friction Ring
69	Recoil Spring
70	Friction Piece
71	Friction Spring
72	Forend
73	Magazine Cap Stop Spring
74	Magazine Cap Stop Plunger
75	Magazine Cap Stop
76	Magazine Cap
77	Barrel Extension
78	Barrel Guide
79	Barrel
80	Front Sight Base
81	Front Sight

Model 79, 79-T, 79VR and 79VR-T Slide-Action Shotgun

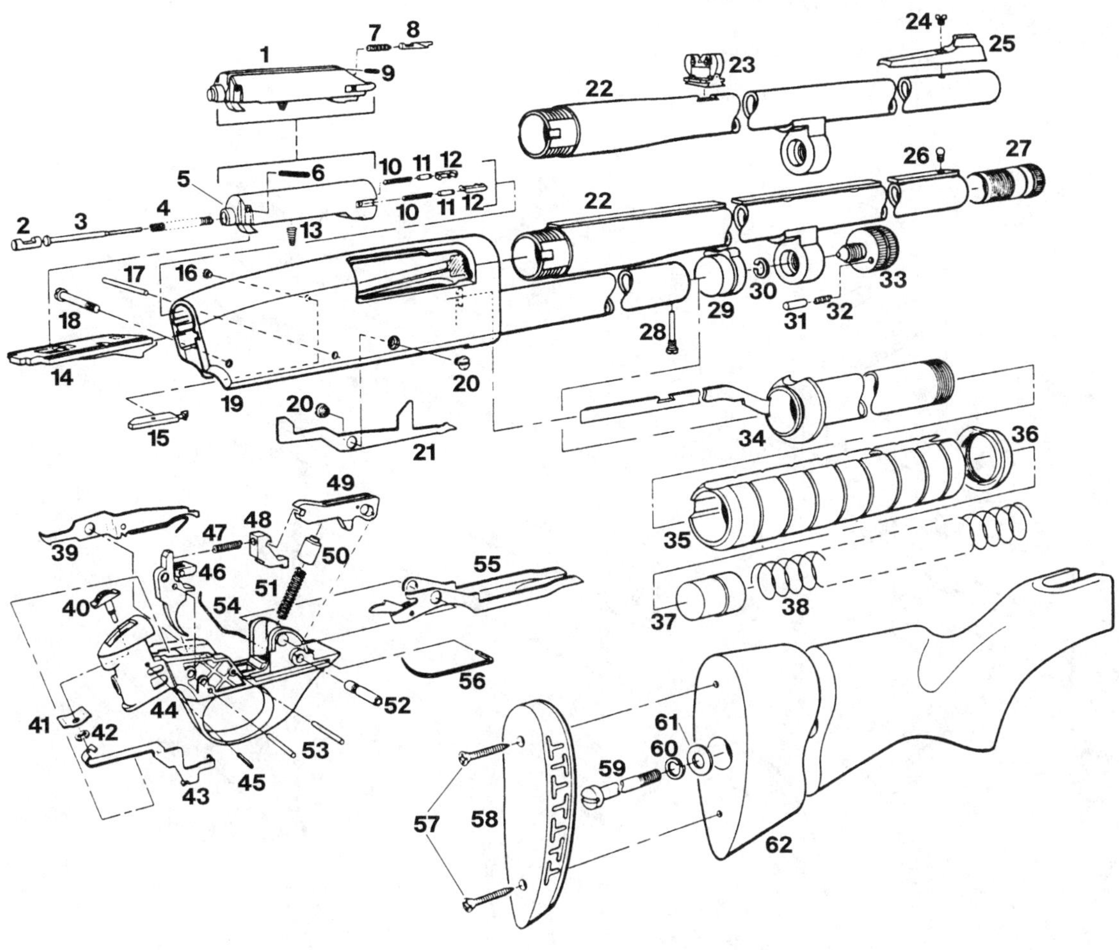

1	Bolt Assembly Complete	22	Barrel	43	Safety-Lever
2	Firing Pin Extension	23	Rear Sight, Slug Barrel	44	Trigger Guard and Housing
3	Firing Pin	24	Front Sight Screw, Slug Barrel	45	Safety Pin
4	Firing Pin Spring	25	Front Sight, Slug Barrel	46	Trigger
5	Bolt Body	26	Front Sight Bead	47	Sear Spring
6	Firing Pin Retaining Pin	27	Choke Tube	48	Sear
7	Shell Stop Spring	28	Magazine Plug Tube	49	Hammer
8	Shell Stop	29	Magazine Plug	50	Hammer Spring Plunger
9	Shell Stop Pin	30	Takedown Screw Lock Washer	51	Hammer Spring
10	Extractor Springs	31	Takedown Screw Spring Pin	52	Hammer Pins
11	Extractor Plungers	32	Takedown Screw Spring	53	Trigger Pins
12	Extractors	33	Takedown Screw	54	Slide Lock Spring
13	Bolt Support Spring	34	Operating Handle Bar Assembly	55	Lifter
14	Slide Assembly	35	Operating Handle	56	Lifter Spring
15	Ejector	36	Operating Handle Collar	57	Buttpad Screws
16	Ejector Screw	37	Magazine Follower	58	Buttpad
17	Trigger Guard Pin	38	Magazine Spring	59	Stock Bolt
18	Trigger Guard Screw	39	Slide Lock	60	Lock Washer
19	Receiver	40	Safety Switch	61	Washer
20	Cartridge Stop Screws	41	Safety Bushing	62	Stock
21	Cartridge Stop	42	Safety Lock Washer		

Model 99, 99A and 358 Series A Lever-Action Rifle

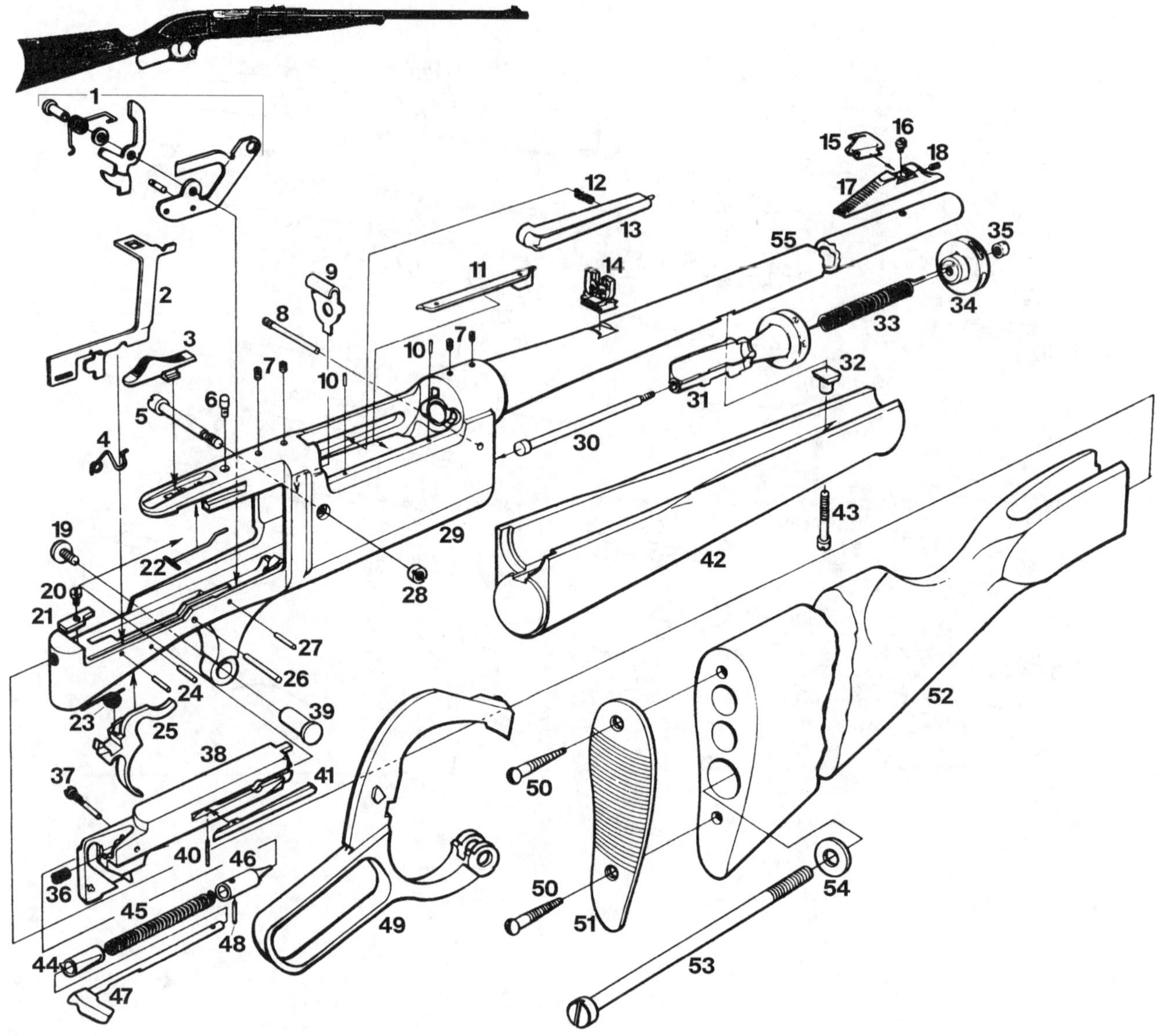

1	Sear Bracket Assembly	20	Breechbolt Stop Screw	37	Hammer Bushing Screw
2	Safety Slide	21	Breechbolt Stop	38	Breechbolt
3	Safety Button	22	Hammer Indicator Spring	39	Lever Bushing
4	Safety Slide Spring	23	Trigger Spring	40	Extractor Pin
5	Sear Screw	24	Safety Slide Spring and Stop Pins	41	Extractor
6	Hammer Indicator			42	Forend
7	Dummy Screws	25	Trigger	43	Forend Screw
8	Carrier Spindle Head Screw	26	Trigger Pin	44	Hammer Bushing
9	Carrier Spindle Support	27	Sear Bracket Pin	45	Mainspring
10	Cartridge Guide Pins	28	Sear Screw Nut	46	Firing Pin
11	Cartridge Guide	29	Receiver	47	Hammer
12	Automatic Cutoff Spring	30	Carrier Spindle	48	Firing Pin Securing Pin
13	Automatic Cutoff	31	Carrier	49	Lever
14	Rear Sight	32	Barrel Stud	50	Buttplate Screws
15	Front Sight	33	Carrier Spring	51	Buttplate
16	Front Sight Screw	34	Carrier Spindle Head	52	Stock
17	Front Sight Base	35	Carrier Spindle Nut	53	Stock Bolt
18	Front Sight Adjusting Screw	36	Hammer Retractor Spring	54	Stock Bolt Washer
19	Lever Bushing Screw			55	Barrel

Model 99C Lever-Action Rifle

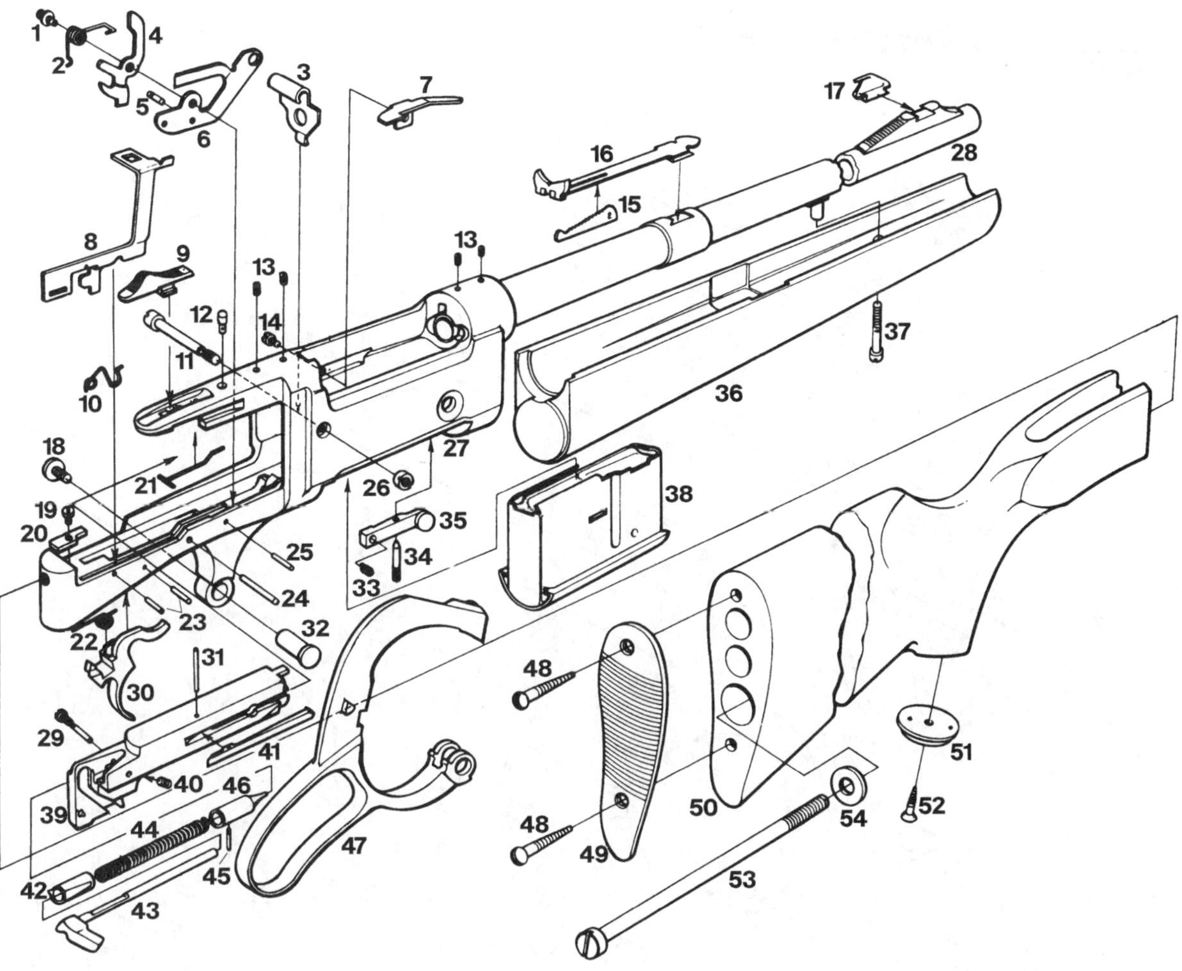

1	Sear Stop Stud
2	Sear Spring
3	Filler Block
4	Sear
5	Sear Pivot Stud
6	Sear Bracket
7	Ejector
8	Safety Slide
9	Safety Button
10	Safety Slide Spring
11	Sear Screw
12	Hammer Indicator
13	Dummy Screws
14	Ejector Screw
15	Rear Sight Step
16	Rear Sight
17	Front Sight
18	Lever Bushing Screw
19	Breechbolt Stop Screw
20	Breechbolt Stop
21	Hammer Indicator Spring
22	Trigger Spring
23	Safety Slide Pins
24	Trigger Pin
25	Sear Bracket Pin
26	Sear Screw Nut
27	Receiver
28	Barrel
29	Hammer Bushing Screw
30	Trigger
31	Extractor Pin
32	Lever Bushing
33	Magazine Latch Spring
34	Magazine Latch Pin
35	Magazine Latch
36	Forend
37	Forend Screw
38	Magazine Assembly
39	Breechbolt
40	Hammer Retractor Spring
41	Extractor
42	Hammer Bushing
43	Hammer
44	Mainspring
45	Firing Pin Securing Pin
46	Firing Pin
47	Lever
48	Buttplate Screws
49	Buttplate
50	Stock
51	Pistol Grip Cap
52	Pistol Grip Cap Screw
53	Stock Bolt
54	Stock Bolt Washer

Model 99C, 99DL(M), 99E, 99F, 99DE and 99PE Series A Lever-Action Rifle (Serial No. 1,000,000+)

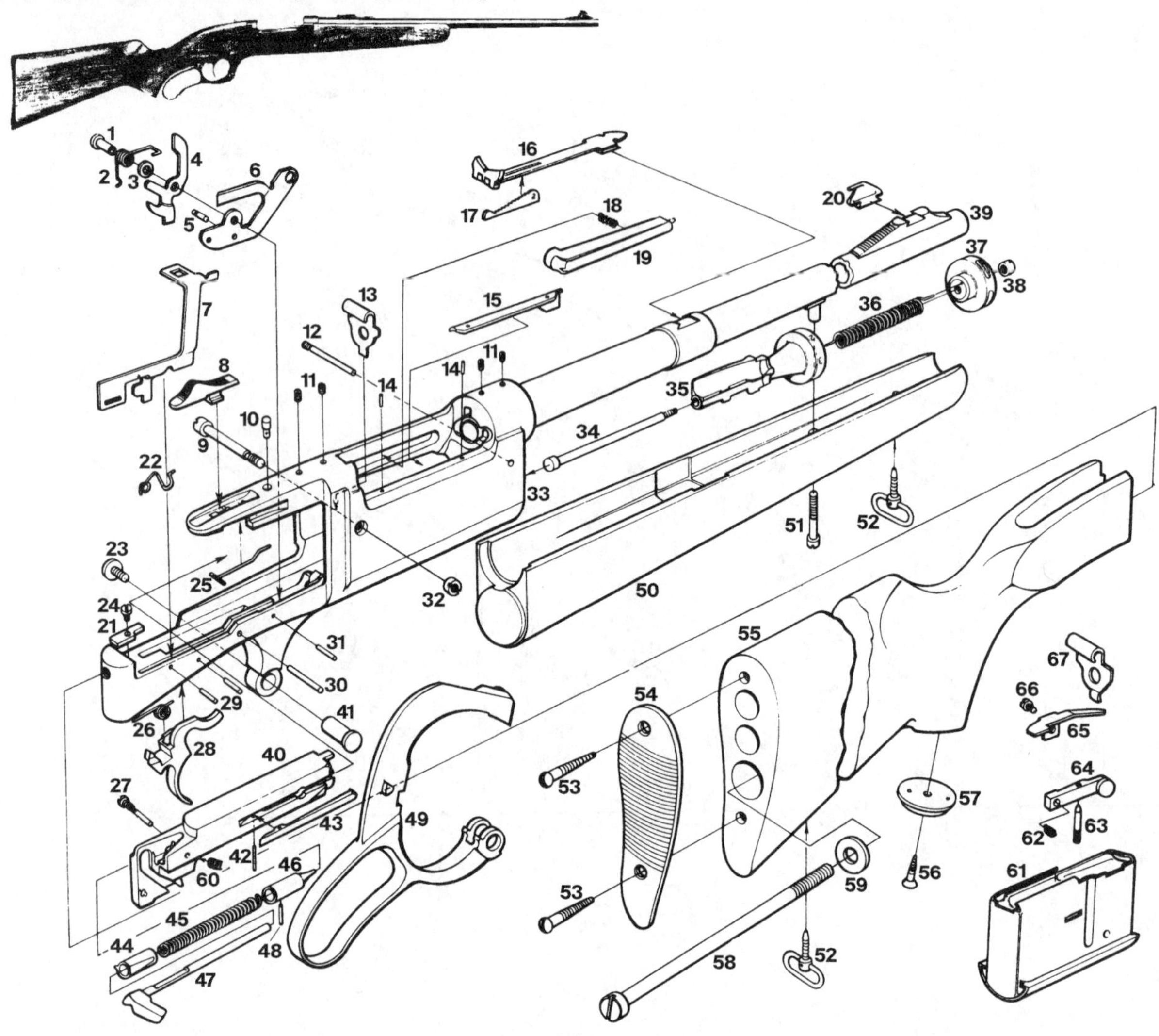

1	Sear Stop Stud	**24**	Breechbolt Stop Screw	**47**	Hammer
2	Sear Spring	**25**	Hammer Indicator Spring	**48**	Firing Pin Securing Pin
3	Washer	**26**	Trigger Spring	**49**	Lever
4	Sear	**27**	Hammer Bushing Screw	**50**	Forend
5	Sear Pivot Stud	**28**	Trigger	**51**	Forend Screw
6	Sear Bracket Assembly	**29**	Safety Slide Spring and Stop Pins	**52**	Swivel Screws
7	Safety Slide	**30**	Trigger Pin	**53**	Buttplate Screws
8	Safety Button	**31**	Sear Bracket Pin	**54**	Buttplate
9	Sear Screw	**32**	Sear Screw Nut	**55**	Stock
10	Hammer Indicator	**33**	Receiver	**56**	Pistol Grip Cap Screw
11	Dummy Screws	**34**	Carrier Spindle	**57**	Pistol Grip Cap
12	Carrier Spindle Head Screw	**35**	Carrier	**58**	Stock Bolt
13	Carrier Spindle Support	**36**	Carrier Spring	**59**	Stock Bolt Washer
14	Cartridge Guide Pins	**37**	Carrier Spindle Head	**60**	Hammer Retractor Spring
15	Cartridge Guide	**38**	Carrier Spindle Nut	**61**	Magazine Assembly (Model 99C only)
16	Rear Sight	**39**	Barrel	**62**	Magazine Latch Spring (Model 99C only)
17	Rear Sight Step	**40**	Breechbolt	**63**	Magazine Latch Pin (Model 99C only)
18	Automatic Cutoff Spring	**41**	Lever Bushing	**64**	Magazine Latch (Model 99C only)
19	Automatic Cutoff	**42**	Extractor Pin	**65**	Ejector (Model 99C only)
20	Front Sight	**43**	Extractor	**66**	Ejector Screw (Model 99C only)
21	Breechbolt Stop	**44**	Hammer Bushing	**67**	Filler Block (Model 99C only)
22	Safety Slide Spring	**45**	Mainspring		
23	Lever Bushing Screw	**46**	Firing Pin		

Model 99CD Series A Lever-Action Rifle

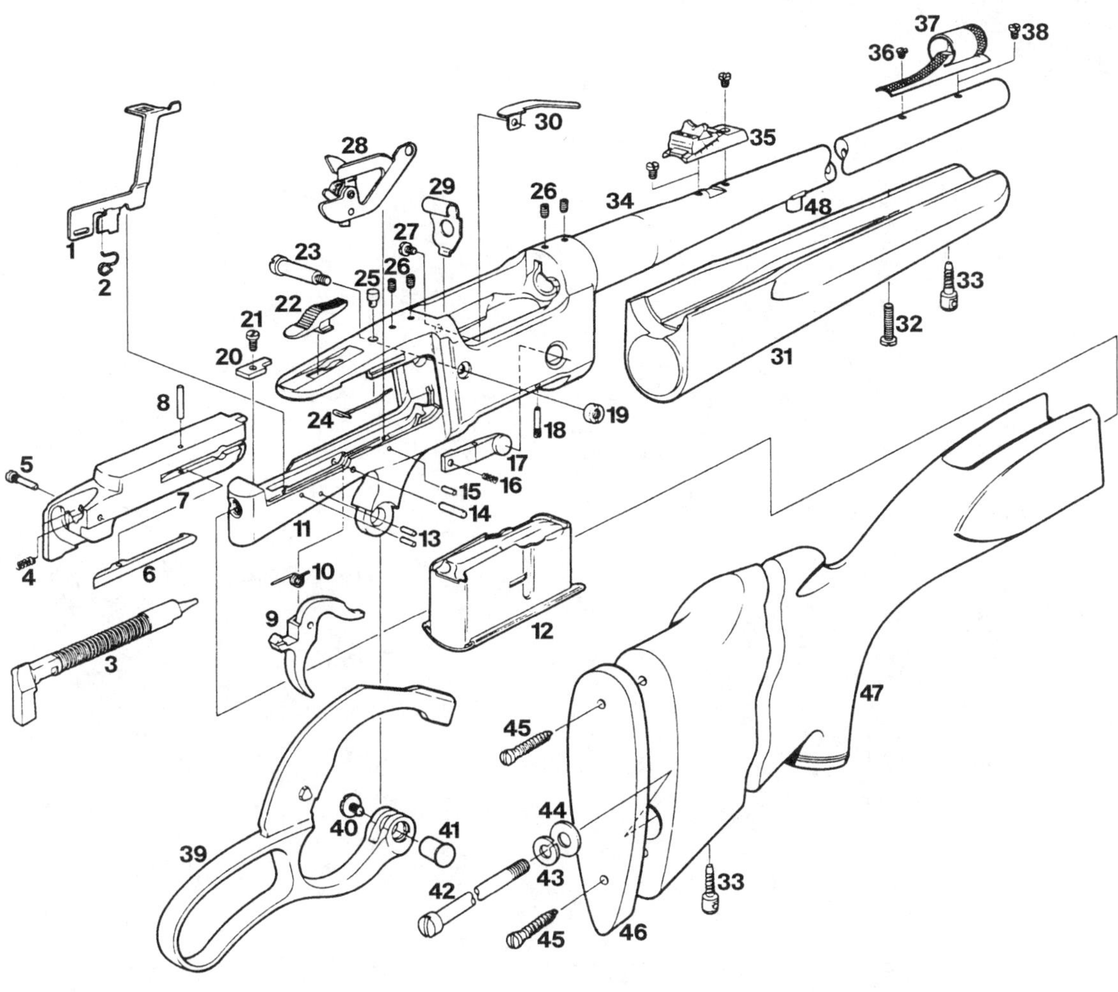

1	Safety Slide	24	Hammer Indicator Spring
2	Safety Slide Spring	25	Hammer Indicator
3	Hammer Assembly	26	Dummy Screws
4	Hammer Retractor Spring	27	Ejector Screw
5	Hammer Bushing Screw	28	Sear Bracket Assembly
6	Extractor	29	Filler Block
7	Breechbolt	30	Ejector
8	Extractor Pin	31	Forend
9	Trigger	32	Forend Screw
10	Trigger Spring	33	Swivel Stud
11	Receiver	34	Barrel
12	Magazine Assembly	35	Rear Sight Assembly and Screws
13	Safety Slide Stop and Spring Pins	36	Front Sight Screw, Short
		37	Front Sight Assembly
14	Trigger Pin	38	Front Sight Screw, Long
15	Sear Bracket Pin	39	Lever
16	Magazine Latch Spring	40	Lever Bushing Screw
17	Magazine Latch	41	Lever Bushing
18	Magazine Latch Pin	42	Stock Bolt
19	Sear Screw Nut	43	Stock Bolt Lock Washer
20	Breechbolt Stop	44	Stock Bolt Washer
21	Breechbolt Stop Screw	45	Recoil Pad Screws
22	Safety Button	46	Recoil Pad
23	Sear Screw	47	Stock Assembly
		48	Barrel Stud

Mark 12 Bolt-Action Rifle

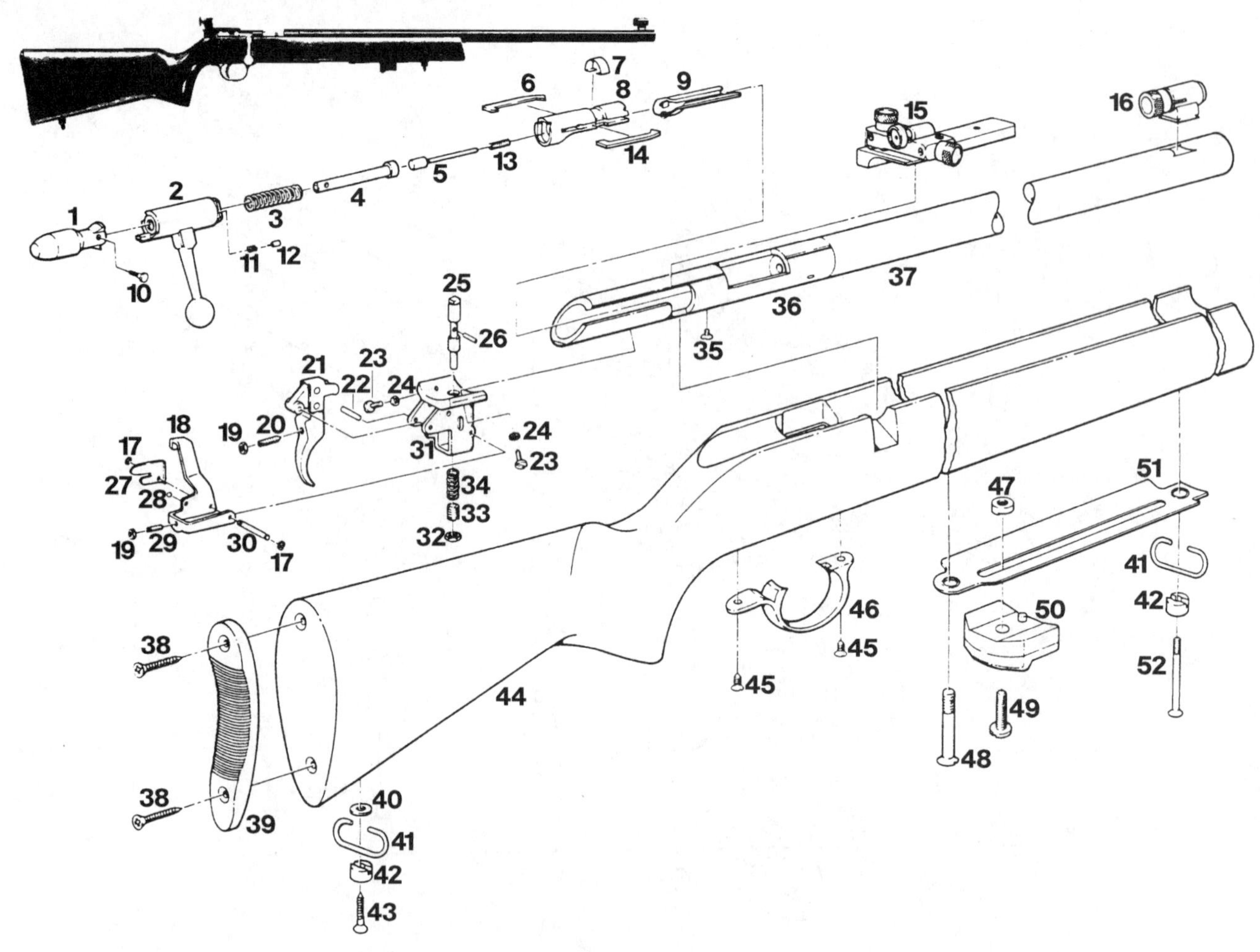

1	Bolt Nut	**27**	Safety Spring Clip
2	Bolt Body and Handle	**28**	Steel Ball
3	Mainspring	**29**	Safety Adjusting Screw
4	Hammer	**30**	Safety Pin
5	Firing Pin	**31**	Trigger Housing
6	Extractor, Left	**32**	Tension Screw Nut
7	Extractor Lock Ring	**33**	Release Plunger Tension Screw
8	Bolt Head	**34**	Sear Spring
9	Ejector Loading Platform	**35**	Loading Platform Screw
10	Plunger	**36**	Receiver
11	Bolt Lock Plunger Spring	**37**	Barrel
12	Bolt Lock Plunger	**38**	Buttplate Screws
13	Firing Pin Spring	**39**	Buttplate
14	Extractor, Right	**40**	Swivel Washer
15	Rear Sight Assembly	**41**	Swivel Loops
16	Front Sight Assembly	**42**	Swivel Collars
17	Safety Pin Clips	**43**	Swivel Screw
18	Safety	**44**	Stock
19	Adjusting Screw Safety Nuts	**45**	Trigger Guard Screws
20	Trigger Adjusting Screw	**46**	Trigger Guard
21	Trigger	**47**	Hand Stop Nut
22	Trigger Pin	**48**	Floorplate Screw, Rear
23	Trigger Housing Screws	**49**	Forend Screw
24	Trigger Housing Lock Washers	**50**	Hand Stop
25	Sear	**51**	Hand Stop Rail
26	Release Plunger Pin	**52**	Front Swivel Screw

Model 89 Lever-Action Rifle

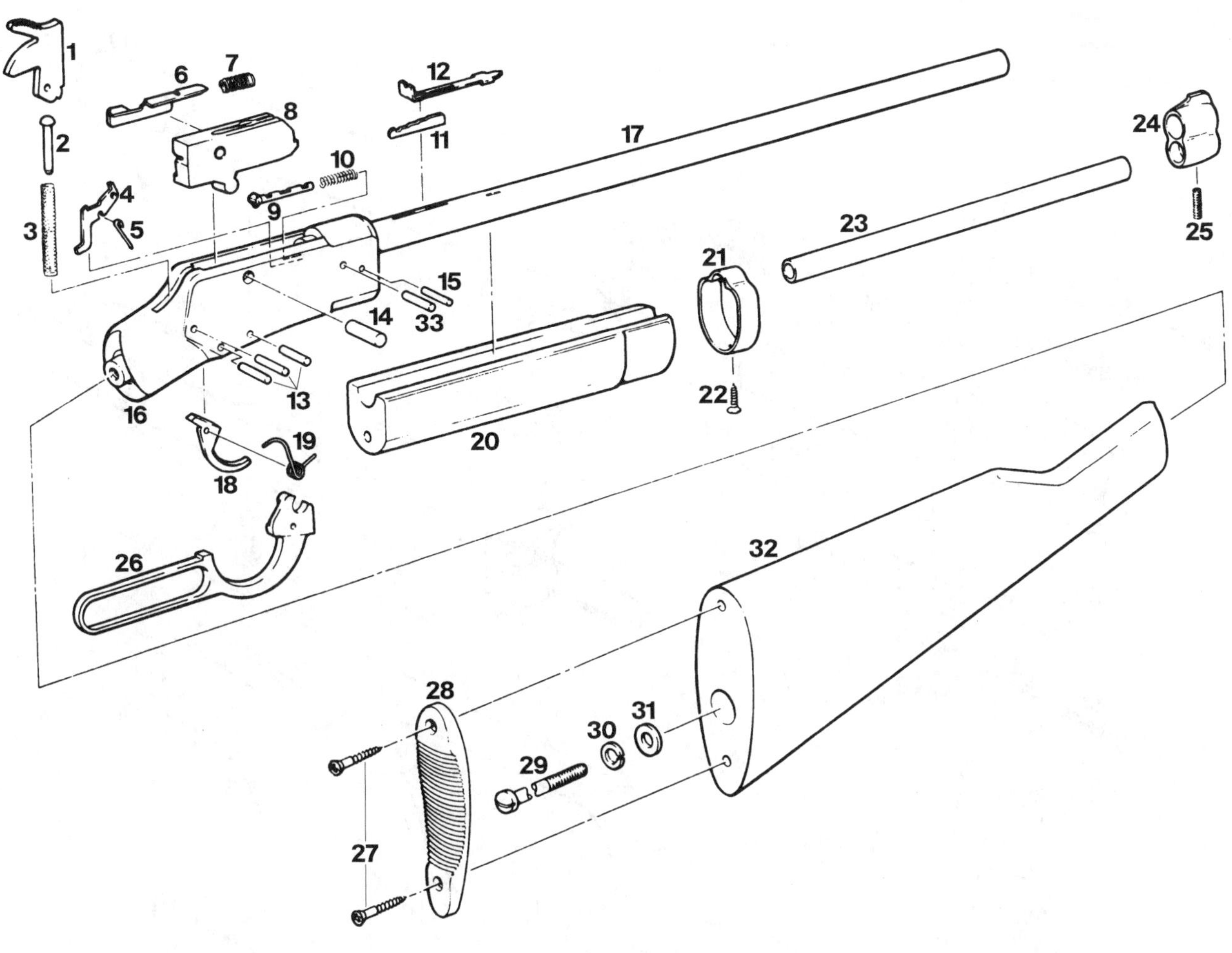

1	Hammer	**18**	Trigger
2	Mainspring Plunger	**19**	Trigger Spring
3	Mainspring	**20**	Forend
4	Ejector Sear	**21**	Forend Band
5	Ejector Sear Spring	**22**	Screw
6	Firing Pin	**23**	Magazine Tube
7	Firing Pin Spring	**24**	Front Sight and Barrel Band
8	Breechbolt	**25**	Barrel Band Screw
9	Ejector	**26**	Lever
10	Ejector Spring	**27**	Buttplate Screws
11	Rear Sight Step	**28**	Buttplate
12	Rear Sight	**29**	Stock Bolt
13	Hammer and Sear Pins	**30**	Stock Bolt Lock Washer
14	Joint Pin	**31**	Stock Bolt Washer
15	Ejector Pin	**32**	Stock
16	Frame	**33**	Barrel Retaining Pin
17	Barrel		

Model 94C and 94Y Series M Single Shot Shotgun

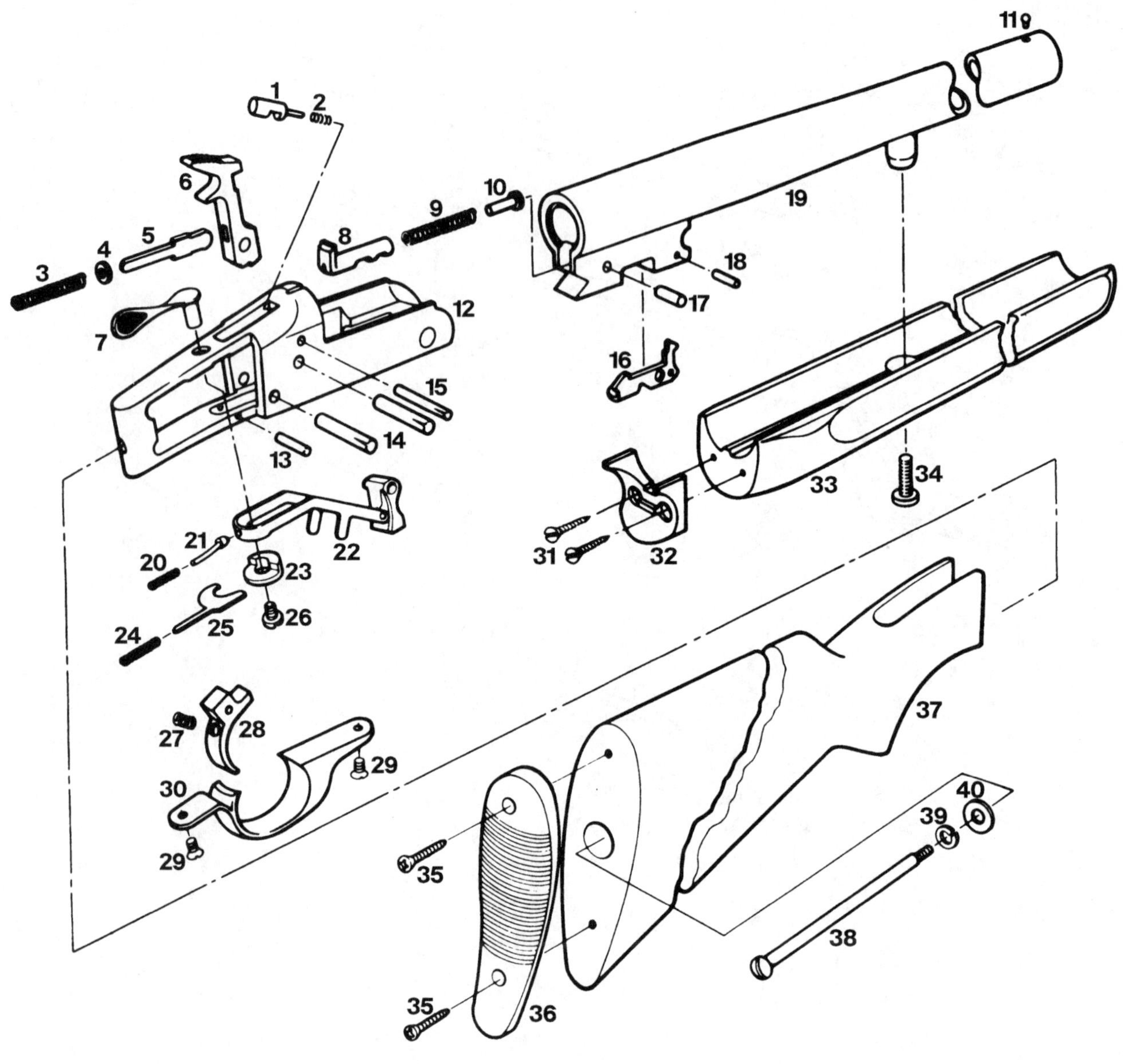

1	Firing Pin	**15**	Firing Pin Retaining Pin	**29**	Trigger Guard Screws
2	Firing Pin Spring	**16**	Ejector Hook	**30**	Trigger Guard
3	Mainspring	**17**	Extractor Stop Pin	**31**	Forend Iron Head Screws
4	Breechbolt Spring Washer	**18**	Extractor Lever and Spring Stop Pin	**32**	Forend Pivot Plate
5	Mainspring Plunger	**19**	Barrel Assembly	**33**	Forend
6	Hammer	**20**	Locking Bolt Spring	**34**	Forend Screw
7	Top Snap	**21**	Locking Bolt Plunger	**35**	Buttplate Screws
8	Extractor	**22**	Locking Bolt Assembly	**36**	Buttplate
9	Ejector Spring	**23**	Top Snap Sleeve	**37**	Stock Assembly
10	Ejector Starter Pin	**24**	Top Snap Plunger Spring	**36**	Stock Bolt
11	Front Sight	**25**	Top Snap Plunger	**39**	Stock Bolt Lock Washer
12	Frame	**26**	Top Snap Screw	**40**	Stock Bolt Washer
13	Trigger Pin	**27**	Trigger Spring		
14	Locking Bolt and Hammer Pins	**28**	Trigger		

Model 1889 and 1911 Straight-Pull Rifle

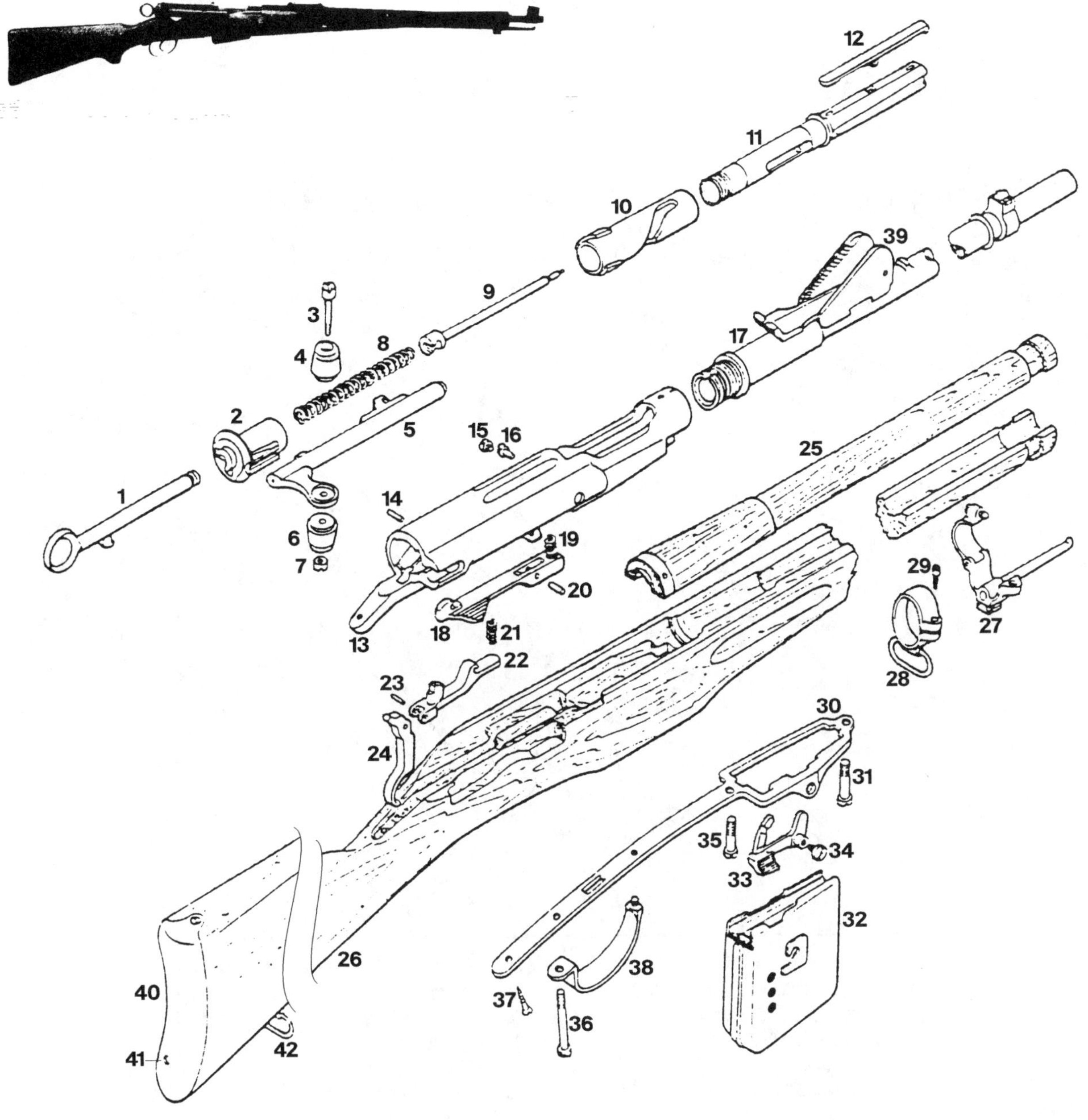

1	Cocking Piece	**16**	Ejector	**31**	Front Plate Screw
2	Bolt Plug	**17**	Barrel	**32**	Magazine
3	Bolt Knob Screw	**18**	Bolt Stop	**33**	Magazine Cutoff
4	Upper Bolt Knob	**19**	Bolt Stop Spring	**34**	Magazine Cutoff Screw
5	Bolt Cam Follower Rod	**20**	Bolt Stop Pin	**35**	Middle Plate Screw
6	Lower Bolt Knob	**21**	Trigger Spring	**36**	Rear Plate Screw
7	Knob Nut	**22**	Sear Arm	**37**	Trigger Plate Screw
8	Firing Pin Spring	**23**	Trigger Pin	**38**	Trigger Guard
9	Firing Pin	**24**	Trigger	**39**	Rear Sight Assembly
10	Bolt Locking Sleeve	**25**	Upper Handguard	**40**	Buttplate
11	Bolt	**26**	Stock	**41**	Buttplate Screws
12	Extractor	**27**	Front Band Complete	**42**	Rear Swivel
13	Receiver	**28**	Rear Band	**Parts Not Shown**	
14	Sear Hinge Pin	**29**	Band Screw		Barrel Collar
15	Ejector Lock Screw	**30**	Trigger and Magazine Plate		

Model 101.10041 Single Shot Shotgun

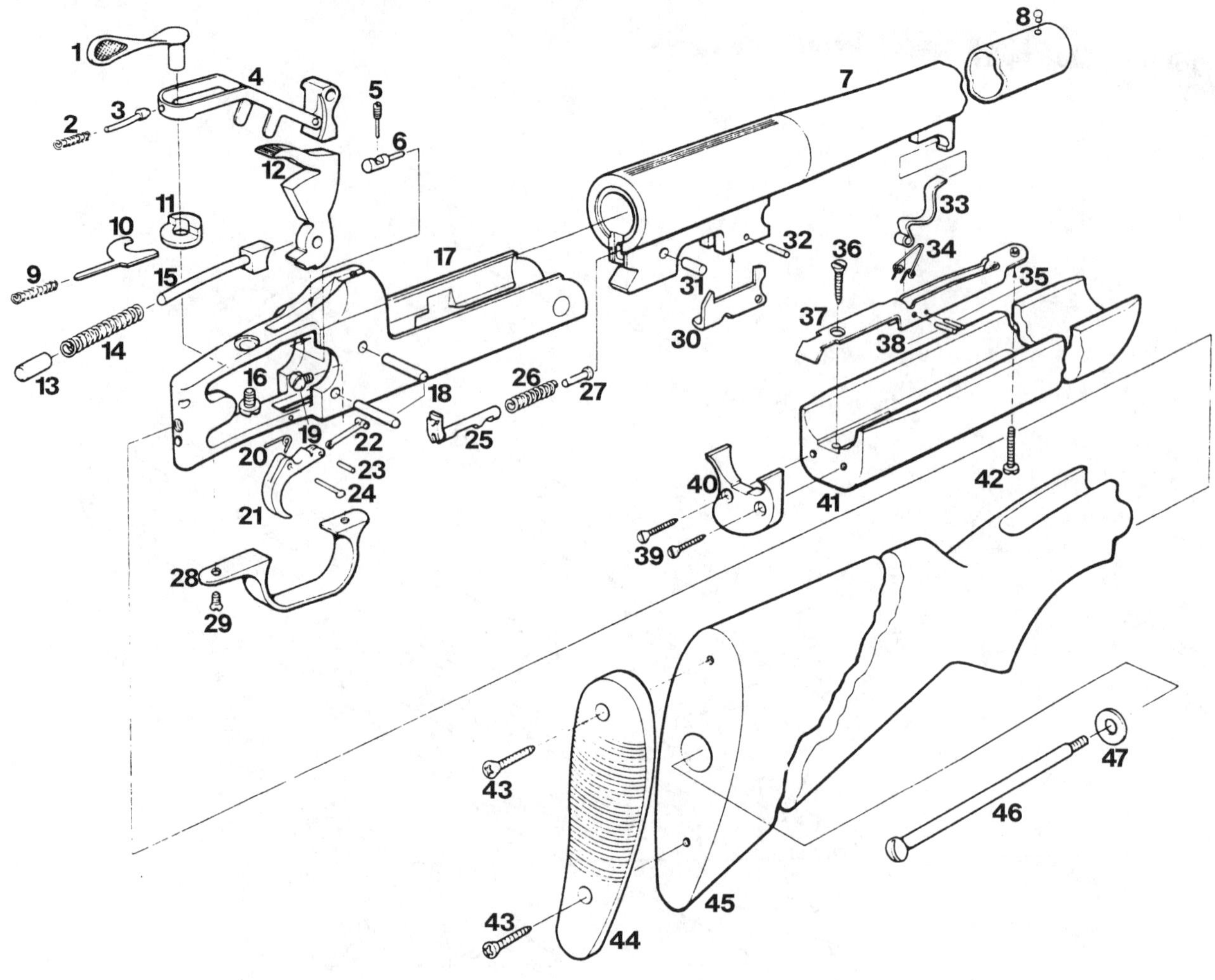

1	Top Snap	24	Trigger Pin
2	Locking Bolt Plunger Spring	25	Extractor
3	Locking Bolt Plunger	26	Ejector Spring
4	Locking Bolt Assembly	27	Ejector Starter Pin
5	Firing Pin Screw	28	Trigger Guard
6	Firing Pin	29	Trigger Guard Screw
7	Barrel Assembly	30	Ejector Hook
8	Front Sight	31	Extractor Stop Pin
9	Top Snap Plunger Spring	32	Extractor Lever Pin
10	Top Snap Plunger	33	Forend Spring
11	Top Snap Sleeve	34	Forend Spring Spring
12	Hammer	35	Forend Spring Spring Pin
13	Mainspring Plunger Seat	36	Forend Spring Housing Screw
14	Mainspring	37	Forend Spring Housing
15	Mainspring Plunger Head Assembly	38	Forend Spring Pin
16	Top Snap Screw	39	Forend Iron Head Screws
17	Frame	40	Forend Iron Head
18	Hammer and Locking Bolt Pins	41	Forend Wood
19	Trigger Guard Screw	42	Forend Screw
20	Trigger Spring	43	Buttplate Screws
21	Trigger	44	Buttplate
22	Hammer Stop Link Assembly	45	Stock Assembly
23	Link Pin	46	Stock Bolt
		47	Stock Bolt Washer

Model 101.1381 Bolt-Action Shotgun

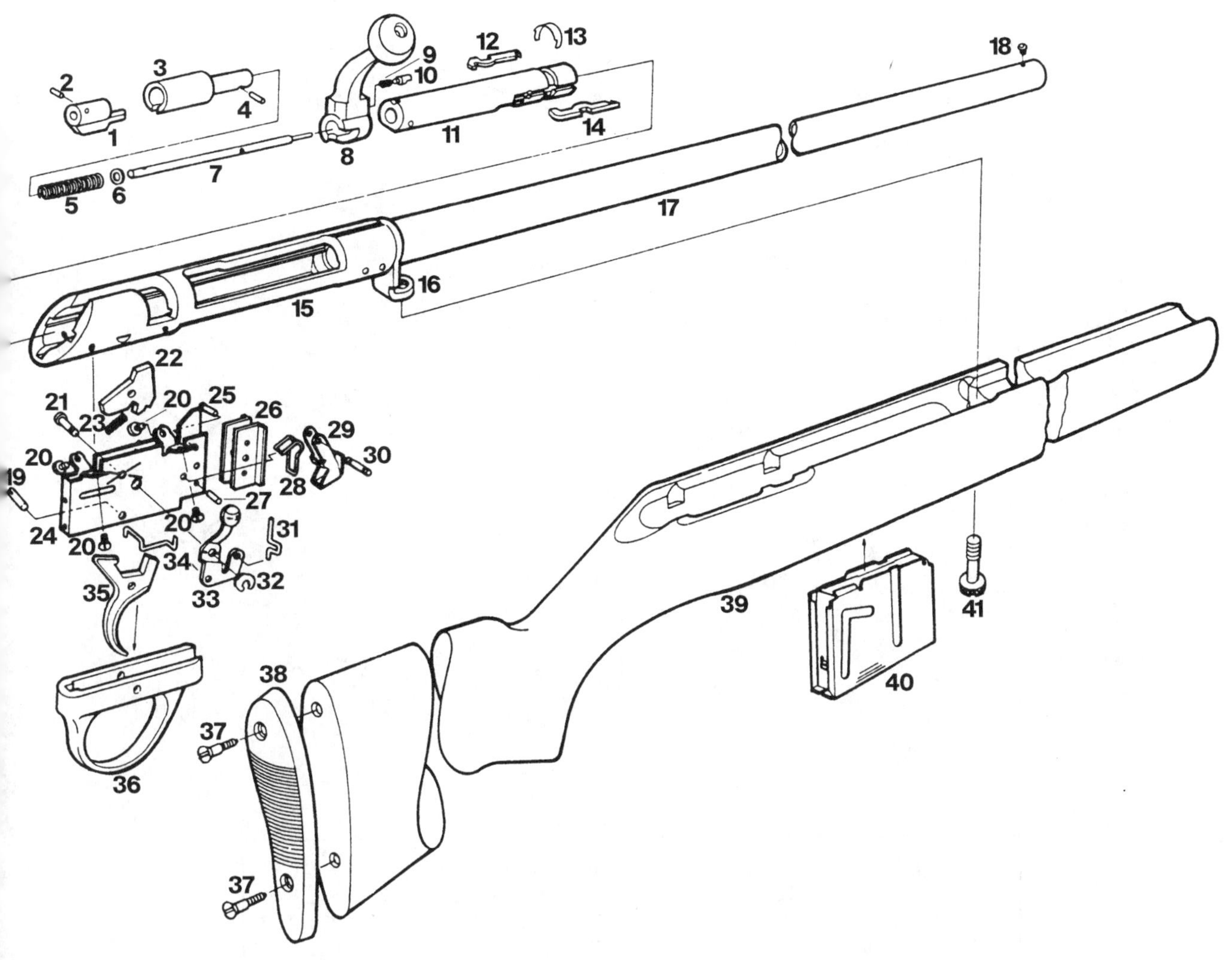

1	Cocking Piece	**23**	Trigger Spring
2	Cocking Piece Pin	**24**	Trigger Bracket
3	Breechbolt	**25**	Magazine Retainer Plate Pin, Upper
4	Bolt Head Retaining Pin	**26**	Magazine Retainer Plate
5	Mainspring	**27**	Magazine Retainer Plate Pin, Lower
6	Mainspring Washer	**28**	Magazine Latch Spring
7	Firing Pin	**29**	Magazine Latch
8	Bolt Handle	**30**	Magazine Latch Pin
9	Bolt Handle Plunger Spring	**31**	Bolt Head Stop Plunger
10	Bolt Handle Detent Plunger	**32**	Sear Pin Ring
11	Bolt Head	**33**	Safety
12	Extractor, Left	**34**	Safety-Lever
13	Extractor Spring	**35**	Trigger
14	Extractor, Right	**36**	Trigger Guard
15	Receiver	**37**	Buttplate Screws
16	Recoil Lug	**38**	Buttplate
17	Barrel	**39**	Stock Assembly
18	Front Sight	**40**	Magazine Assembly
19	Trigger and Trigger Guard Pin	**41**	Takedown Screw
20	Trigger Bracket Screws		
21	Sear Pin		
22	Sear		

Model 101.512220 and 101.512230 Side-by-Side Shotgun

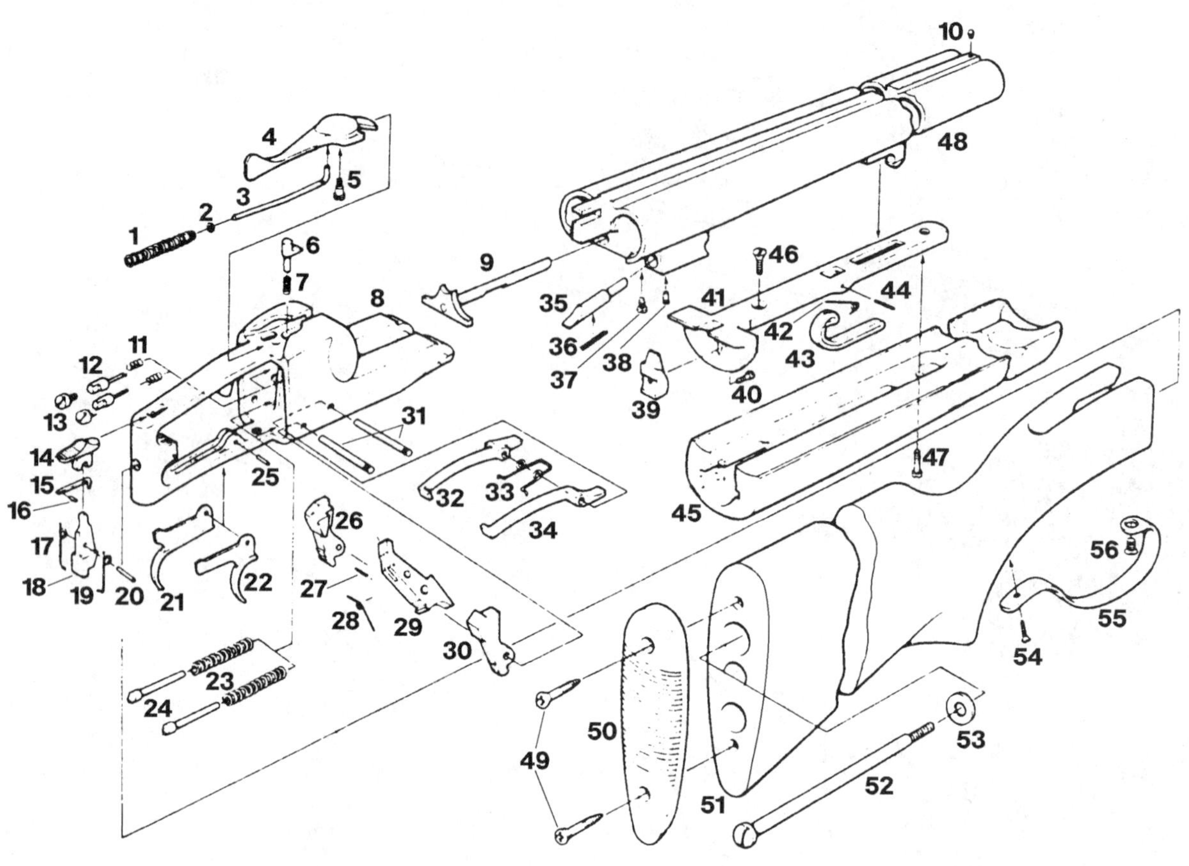

1	Top Snap Plunger Spring	30	Hammer, Right
2	Top Snap Plunger Collar	31	Sear and Cocking Lever Pins
3	Top Snap Plunger	32	Sear, Left
4	Top Snap	33	Sear Spring
5	Top Snap Screw	34	Sear, Right
6	Top Snap Trip	35	Cocking Plunger
7	Top Snap Trip Spring	36	Cocking Plunger Spring
8	Frame	37	Extractor Screw
9	Extractor Plate	38	Cocking Plunger Retaining Screw
10	Front Sight	39	Ejector
11	Firing Pin Springs	40	Ejector Screw
12	Firing Pins	41	Forend Iron
13	Firing Pin Retaining Screws	42	Forend Spring Spring
14	Safety Button	43	Forend Spring
15	Safety Spring	44	Forend Spring Pin
16	Safety Plunger	45	Forend
17	Trigger Spring, Left	46	Forend Screw, Rear
18	Safety-Lever	47	Forend Screw, Front
19	Trigger Spring, Right	48	Barrel
20	Safety-Lever Pin	49	Buttplate Screws
21	Trigger, Left	50	Buttplate
22	Trigger, Right	51	Stock Assembly
23	Mainsprings	52	Stock Bolt
24	Mainspring Plungers	53	Stock Bolt Washer
25	Trigger Pin	54	Trigger Guard Screw, Rear
26	Hammer, Left	55	Trigger Guard
27	Cocking Lever Spring Pin	56	Trigger Guard Screw, Front
28	Cocking Lever Spring		
29	Cocking Lever		

Model 66 Autoloading Shotgun

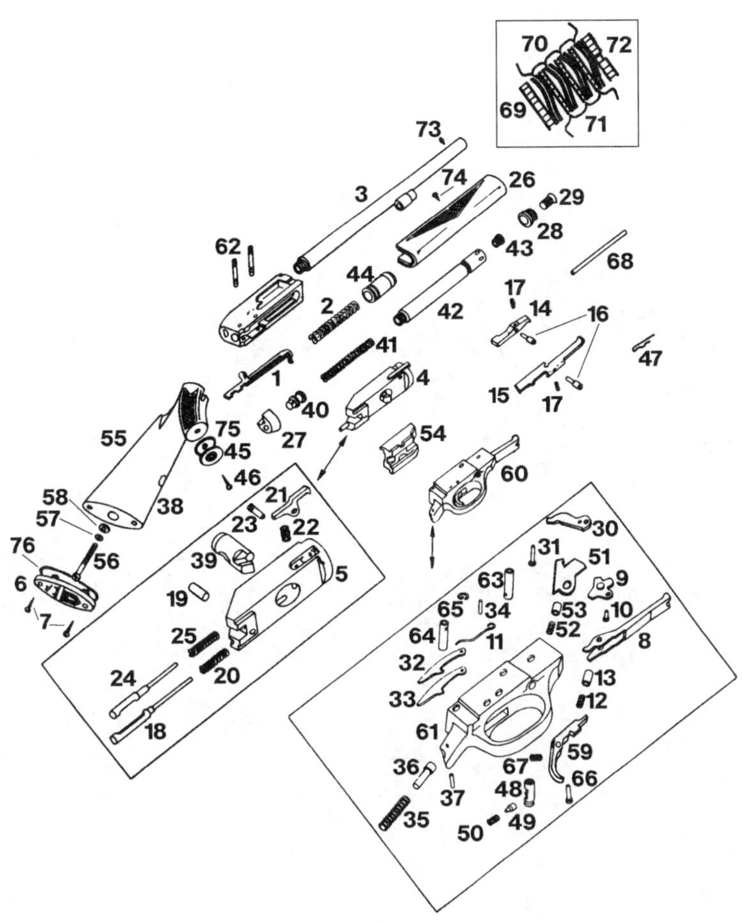

1	Action Bar
2	Action Spring
3	Barrel and Cylinder Assembly
4	Bolt Assembly
5	Bolt
6	Buttplate
7	Buttplate Screws
8	Cartridge Lifter
9	Cartridge Lifter Actuator Assembly
10	Cartridge Lifter Actuator Hinge Pin
11	Cartridge Lifter Actuator Spring
12	Cartridge Lifter Spring
13	Cartridge Lifter Spring Plunger
14	Cartridge Stop, Right
15	Cartridge Stop, Left
16	Cartridge Stop Pins
17	Cartridge Stop Springs
18	Ejector
19	Ejector and Firing Pin Retaining Pin
20	Ejector Retracting Spring
21	Extractor, Right
22	Extractor Spring, Right
23	Extractor Pivot Pin
24	Firing Pin
25	Firing Pin Retracting Spring
26	Forehand Assembly
27	Forehand Base
28	Forehand Cap
29	Forehand Cap Screw
30	Hammer
31	Hammer Hinge Pin
32	Hammer Strut, Right
33	Hammer Strut, Left
34	Hammer Strut Pin
35	Hammer Spring
36	Hammer Spring Guide
37	Hammer Spring Retaining Pin
38	Initial Plate
39	Locking Pin
40	Magazine Follower
41	Magazine Spring
42	Magazine Tube
43	Magazine Tube Cap
44	Piston
45	Pistol Grip Cap
46	Pistol Grip Screw
47	Cartridge Stop Pin Return Clips
48	Safety Button
49	Safety Spring Plunger
50	Safety Spring
51	Escapement Hook
52	Trigger Spring
53	Trigger Spring Plunger
54	Slide
55	Stock Assembly
56	Stock Bolt
57	Stock Bolt Lock Washer
58	Stock Bolt Washer
59	Trigger
60	Trigger Guard Assembly
61	Trigger Guard
62	Trigger Guard Retaining Pins
63	Trigger Guard Retaining Pin Bushing, Front
64	Trigger Guard Retaining Pin Bushing, Rear
65	Guard Bushing Retaining Spring
66	Trigger Hinge Pin
67	Escapement Hook Spring
68	Wood Plug
69	Cylinder Washer
70	Cylinder Wavy Springs
71	Cylinder Spacer Washers
72	Cylinder Nut
73	Front Sight
74	Drive Screw
75	Pistol Grip Cap Trim
76	Buttplate Trim

Model 1874 Creedmoore Rifle

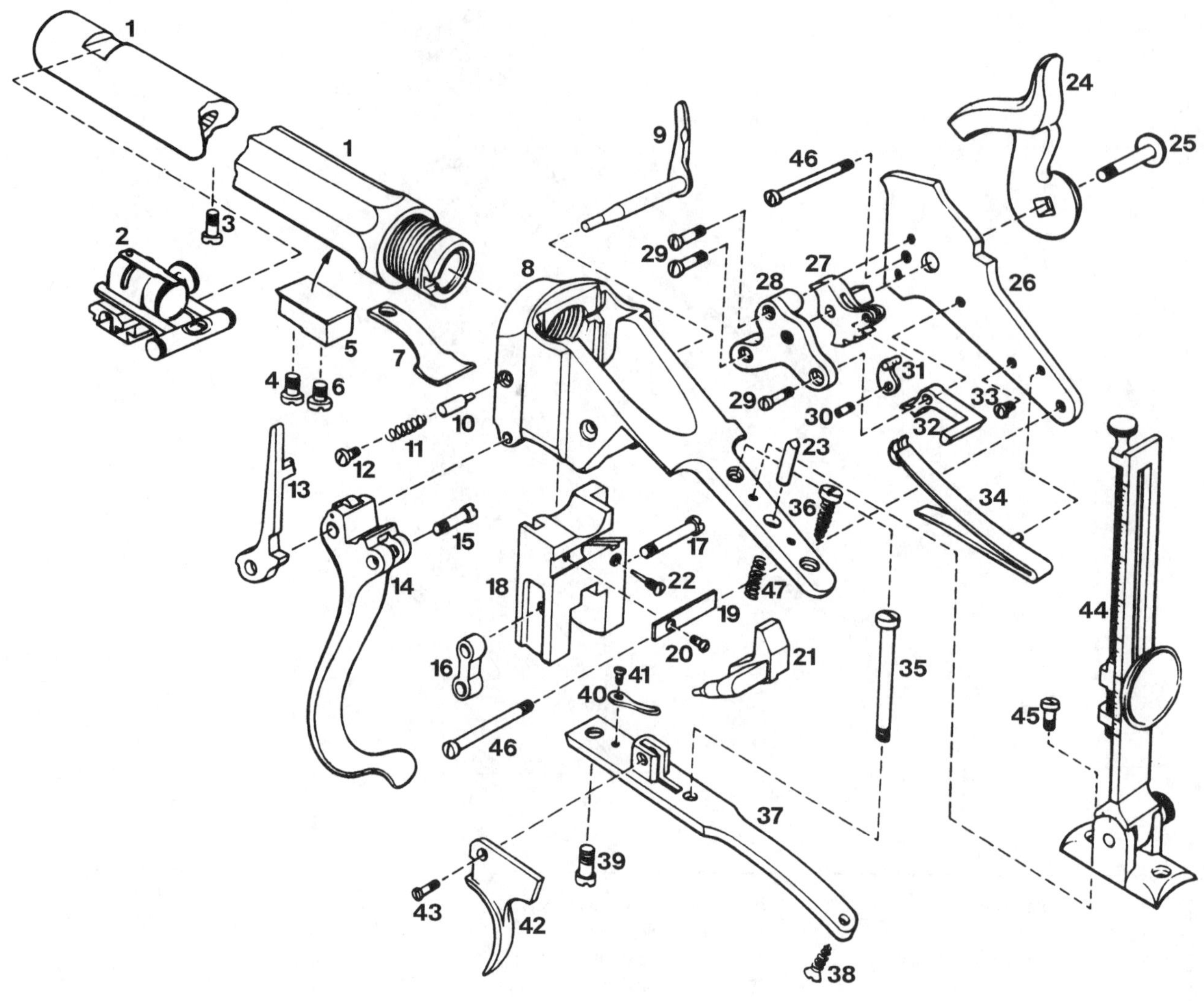

1	Barrel	**19**	Firing Pin Plate	**37**	Guard Plate
2	Front Sight Assembly	**20**	Firing Pin Plate Screw	**38**	Guard Plate Stock Screw
3	Front Forend Screw	**21**	Firing Pin	**39**	Guard Plate Receiver Screw
4	Rear Forend Screw	**22**	Firing Pin Screw	**40**	Trigger Spring
5	Barrel Stud	**23**	Rear Sight Detent	**41**	Trigger Spring Screw
6	Lever Spring Screw	**24**	Hammer	**42**	Trigger
7	Lever Spring	**25**	Tumbler Screw	**43**	Trigger Screw
8	Receiver	**26**	Lock Plate	**44**	Vernier Rear Sight Assembly
9	Lever Pin	**27**	Tumbler	**45**	Rear Sight Mounting Screws
10	Lever Pin Retainer Plunger	**28**	Bridle	**46**	Lockplate Screws
11	Lever Pin Retainer Spring	**29**	Bridle Screws	**47**	Rear Sight Detent Spring
12	Lever Pin Retainer Spring Screw	**30**	Stirrup Screw	**Parts Not Shown**	
13	Extractor	**31**	Stirrup		Forend
14	Lever	**32**	Sear		Buttstock
15	Lever Toggle Link Screw	**33**	Mainspring Screw		Buttplate
16	Lever Toggle Link	**34**	Mainspring		Buttplate Screws
17	Upper Toggle Link Screw	**35**	Front Guard Plate Screw		Lockplate Screw Washer
18	Breechblock	**36**	Rear Guard Plate Screw		

Mauser Bolt-Action Rifle

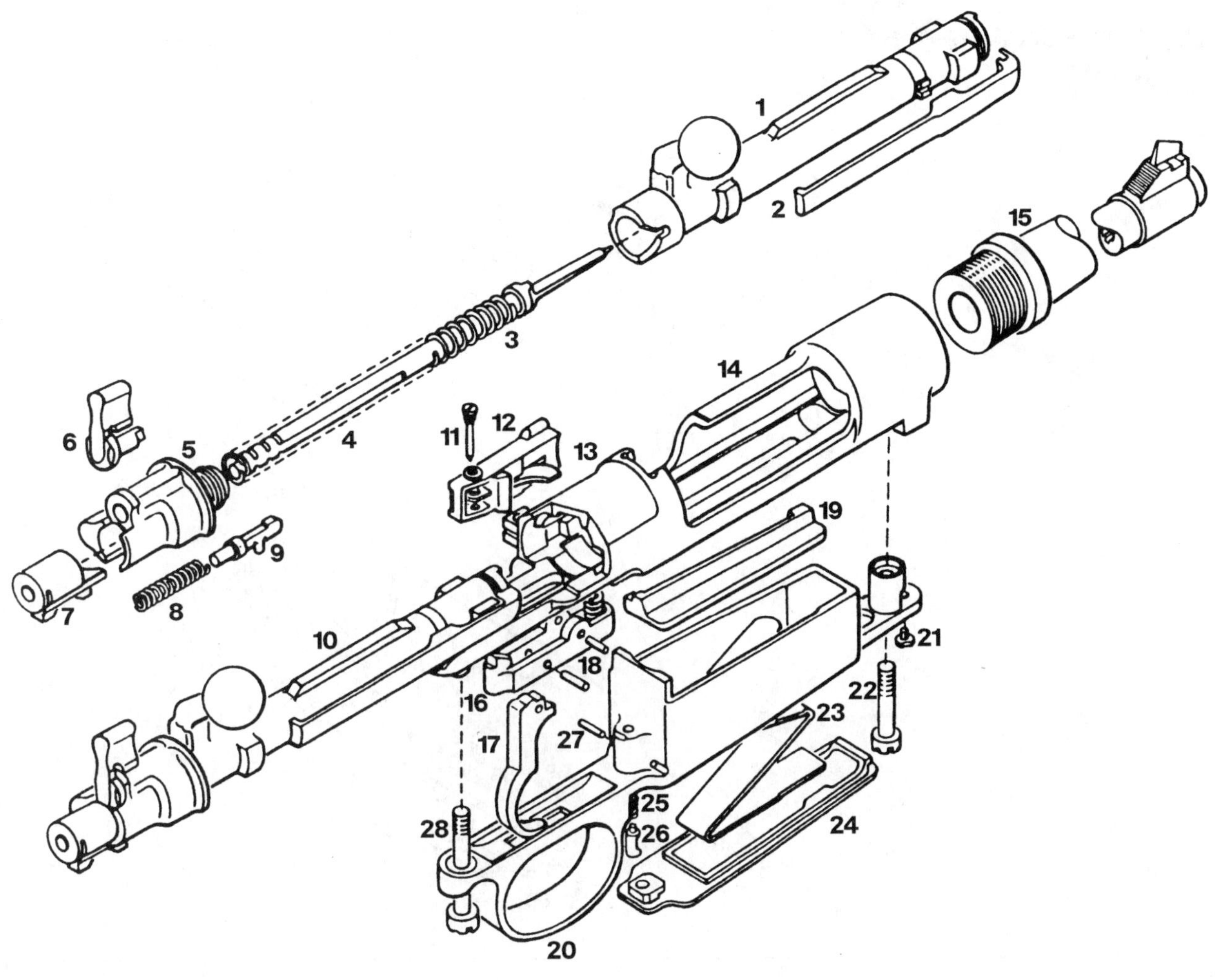

1	Bolt Body	**15**	Barrel
2	Extractor	**16**	Sear
3	Firing Pin Spring	**17**	Trigger
4	Firing Pin	**18**	Sear and Trigger Pins
5	Bolt Sleeve	**19**	Magazine Follower
6	Safety Catch	**20**	Trigger Guard
7	Cocking Piece	**21**	Lock Screw
8	Bolt Sleeve Stop Spring	**22**	Front Guard Screw
9	Bolt Sleeve Stop	**23**	Magazine Spring
10	Bolt Assembly	**24**	Floorplate
11	Bolt Stop Screw	**25**	Floorplate Latch Spring
12	Bolt Stop and Spring	**26**	Floorplate Latch
13	Ejector	**27**	Floorplate Latch Pin
14	Receiver	**28**	Rear Guard Screw

7.62x39mm Autoloading Carbine

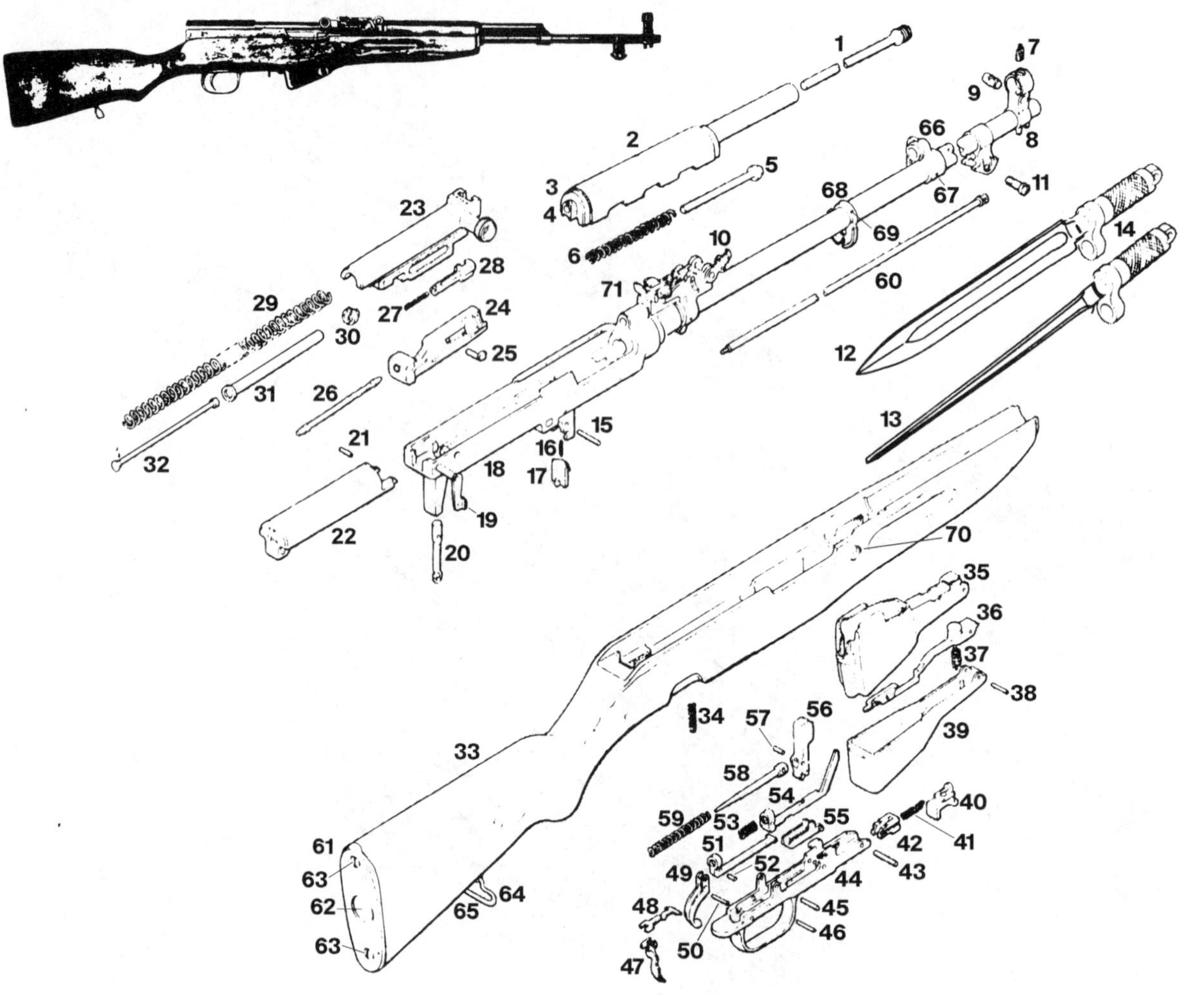

1	Piston
2	Handguard and Gas Cylinder
3	Handguard Ferrule
4	Handguard Ferrule Pin
5	Piston Extension
6	Piston Return Spring
7	Front Sight
8	Front Sight Base and Bayonet Lug
9	Front Sight Seat
10	Handguard Catch
11	Bayonet Screw
12	Bayonet, Blade
13	Bayonet, Spike
14	Bayonet Handle
15	Hold-Open Latch Pin
16	Hold-Open Latch Spring
17	Hold-Open Latch
18	Receiver and Barrel Assembly
19	Takedown Latch
20	Trigger Guard Latch
21	Latch Pin
22	Rear Housing
23	Bolt Carrier
24	Bolt, Stripped
25	Firing Pin Retainer
26	Firing Pin
27	Extractor Spring
28	Extractor
29	Recoil Spring
30	Spring Retainer
31	Large Spring Guide
32	Small Spring Guide
33	Stock
34	Trigger Guard Spring
35	Magazine
36	Magazine Follower
37	Magazine Follower Spring
38	Hinge Pin
39	Magazine Cover
40	Cover Latch
41	Latch Spring and Sear Spring
42	Sear
43	Latch Stop Pin
44	Trigger Guard
45	Disconnector Hinge Pin
46	Trigger Pin
47	Safety Catch
48	Safety Catch Spring
49	Trigger
50	Safety Catch Pin
51	Trigger Bar
52	Trigger Bar Pin
53	Trigger Spring
54	Disconnector
55	Rebound Disconnector
56	Hammer
57	Hammer Strut Pin
58	Hammer Strut
59	Hammer Spring
60	Cleaning Rod
61	Buttplate Assembly
62	Buttplate Trap Door Assembly
63	Buttplate Screws
64	Rear Swivel
65	Rear Swivel Screws
66	Gas Cylinder Front Bracket
67	Gas Cylinder Bracket Pin
68	Stock Ferrule
69	Stock Ferrule Pin
70	Recoil Lug Assembly
71	Rear Sight Assembly

Parts Not Shown

- Front Sight Base Pin, Front
- Front Sight Base Pin, Rear
- Bayonet Spring

Model 1000 and Mossberg Super 1000 Autoloading Shotgun

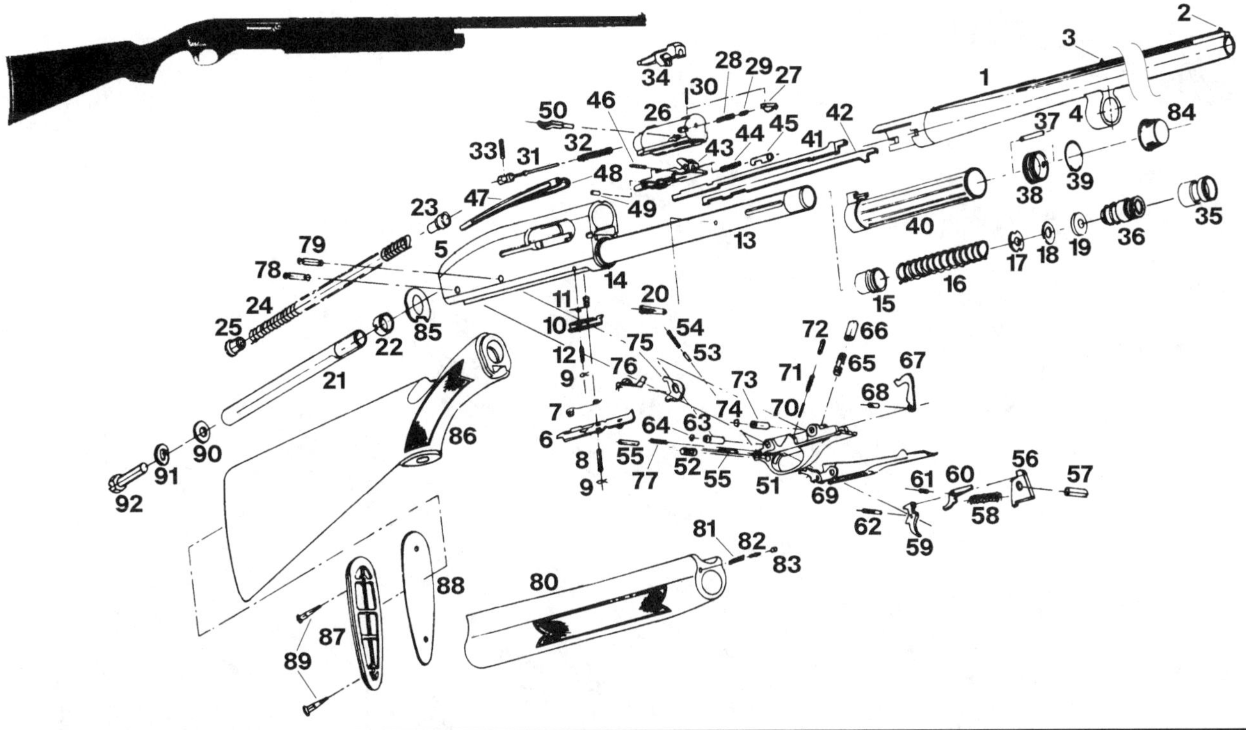

1	Barrel Assembly	35	Pressure Compensator Valve	67	Hammer
2	Front Sight	36	Piston	68	Hammer Pin
3	Middle Sight	37	Piston Pin	69	Carrier Assembly
4	Barrel Ring Guide	38	Piston Connector Ring	70	Carrier Spring Guide Pin
5	Receiver	39	Piston Connector Ring Spring	71	Carrier Spring
6	Carrier Latch Assembly	40	Action Bar Sleeve Assembly	72	Carrier Spring Sleeve
7	Latch Spring	41	Action Bar, Right	73	Trigger Plate Pin Bushing, Small
8	Latch Pin	42	Action Bar, Left	74	Trigger Plate Pin Stopper Spring, Small
9	Latch Pin Stopper Springs	43	Breechbolt Base	75	Auto Safety
10	Magazine Shell Stopper Plate	44	Plunger Spring	76	Auto Safety Spring
11	Shell Stopper Plate Spring	45	Plunger	77	Auto Safety Stopper Pin
12	Shell Stopper Plate Pin	46	Plunger Stopper Pin	78	Trigger Plate Pin, Large
13	Magazine Tube	47	Link, Right	79	Trigger Plate Pin, Small
14	Magazine Tube Nut	48	Link, Left	80	Forend Assembly
15	Magazine Follower	49	Link Pin	81	Forend Cap Spring
16	Magazine Spring	50	Operating Handle	82	Forend Cap Spring Plunger
17	Magazine Spring Retainer Washer	51	Trigger Plate	83	Forend Cap Pin
18	Shock Absorber Washer	52	Safety Button	84	Forend Cap
19	Piston Shock Absorber	53	Safety Button Spring Sleeve	85	Stock Spacer Plate
20	Capacity Reducing Pin	54	Safety Button Spring	86	Stock Assembly
21	Action Spring Tube	55	Safety Button Spring Stopper Pins	87	Buttplate
22	Action Spring Tube Nut	56	Sear	88	Buttplate Spacer
23	Action Spring Guide	57	Sear Pin	89	Buttplate Screws
24	Action Spring	58	Sear Spring	90	Stock Retainer Washer
25	Action Spring Retainer Screw	59	Trigger	91	Stock Retainer Spring Washer
26	Breechbolt	60	Trigger Connector Plate	92	Stock Retainer Bolt
27	Extractor	61	Trigger Connector Plate Pin	**Parts Not Shown**	
28	Extractor Spring	62	Trigger Pin		Ejector
29	Extractor Spring Plunger	63	Trigger Plate Pin Bushing, Large		Carrier
30	Extractor Pin	64	Trigger Plate Pin Stopper Spring, Large		Carrier Dog
31	Firing Pin	65	Hammer Spring		Carrier Dog Washer
32	Firing Pin Spring	66	Hammer Spring Sleeve		Carrier Dog Pin
33	Firing Pin Stopper Pin				
34	Locking Block				

Model 1500 Deluxe Bolt-Action Rifle

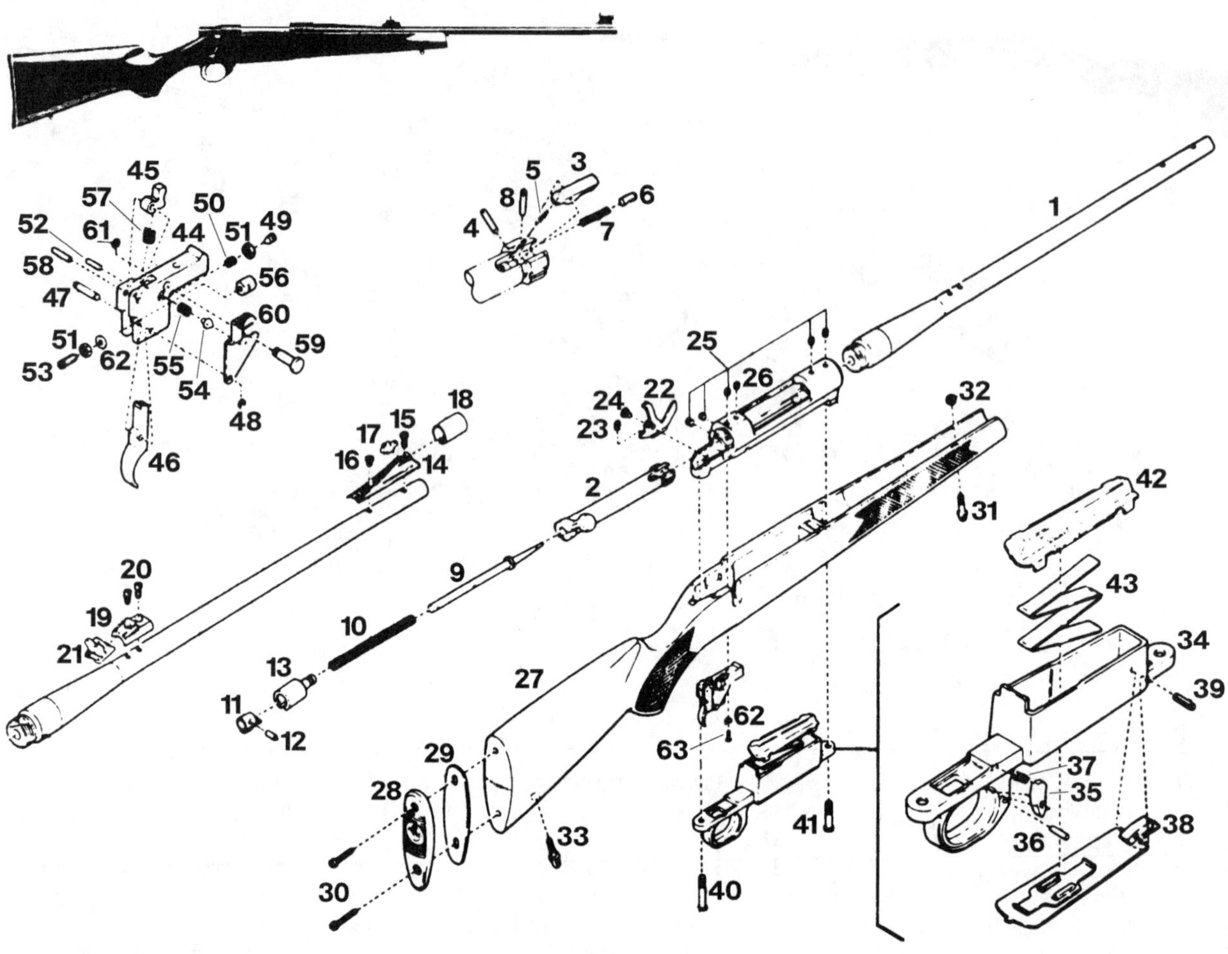

1	Barrel	**23**	Bolt Stop Spring	**45**	Sear
2	Bolt Body	**24**	Bolt Stop Screw	**46**	Trigger
3	Extractor	**25**	Receiver Plug Screws, Long	**47**	Trigger Pin
4	Extractor Pin	**26**	Receiver Plug Screw, Short	**48**	Retaining Ring Trigger Pin
5	Extractor Spring	**27**	Stock	**49**	Trigger Adjusting Screw, Front
6	Ejector	**28**	Buttplate	**50**	Trigger Spring
7	Ejector Spring	**29**	Buttplate White Spacer	**51**	Lock Nuts
8	Ejector Pin	**30**	Buttplate Screws	**52**	Sear Pin
9	Firing Pin	**31**	Front Swivel Screw	**53**	Trigger Adjusting Screw, Rear
10	Mainspring	**32**	Front Swivel Nut	**54**	Safety Plunger
11	Cocking Piece	**33**	Rear Swivel Screw	**55**	Safety Plunger Spring
12	Firing Pin Retaining Pin	**34**	Trigger Guard	**56**	Block
13	Bolt Sleeve	**35**	Floorplate Catch	**57**	Sear Spring
14	Front Sight Ramp	**36**	Floorplate Catch Pin	**58**	Sear Stop Pin
15	Front Sight Screw, Large	**37**	Floorplate Catch Spring	**59**	Safety Guide Pin
16	Front Sight Screw, Small	**38**	Floorplate	**60**	Safety
17	Front Sight	**39**	Floorplate Pin	**61**	Retaining Ring and Safety Guide Pin
18	Front Sight Hood	**40**	Rear Guard Screw	**62**	Washers
19	Rear Sight Base	**41**	Front Guard Screw	**63**	Trigger Housing Screw
20	Rear Sight Base Screws	**42**	Magazine Follower		
21	Rear Sight Blade	**43**	Magazine Spring		
22	Bolt Stop	**44**	Trigger Housing		

Model 3000 Slide-Action Shotgun

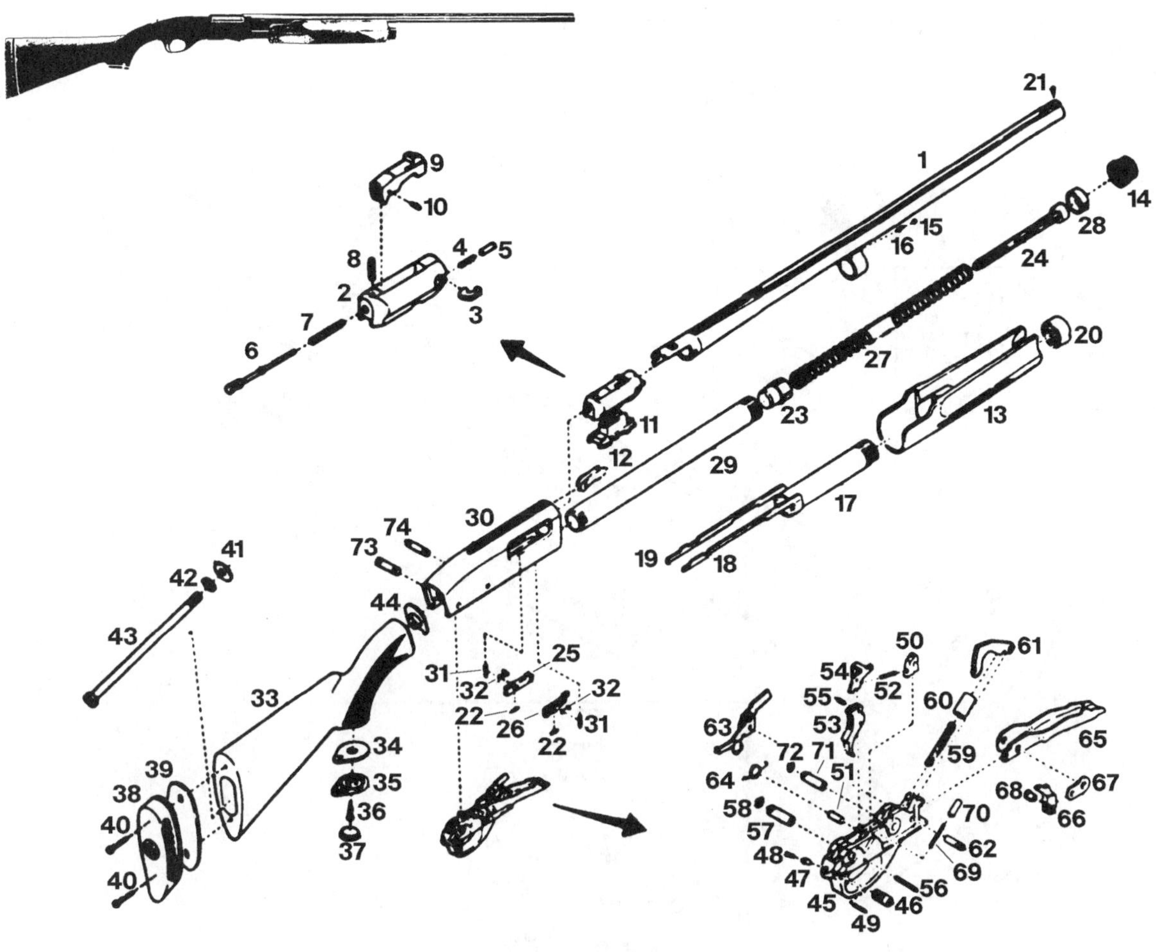

1	Barrel	**27**	Magazine Spring	**52**	Sear Spring
2	Breechbolt	**28**	Magazine Spring Retainer	**53**	Trigger
3	Extractor	**29**	Magazine Tube	**54**	Trigger Connector Plate
4	Extractor Spring	**30**	Receiver	**55**	Trigger Connector Plate Pin
5	Extractor Spring Plunger	**31**	Shell Stopper Pins	**56**	Trigger Pin
6	Firing Pin	**32**	Shell Stopper Plate Springs	**57**	Trigger Plate Pin Bushing, Large
7	Firing Pin Spring	**33**	Stock	**58**	Trigger Plate Pin Stopper Spring, Large
8	Firing Pin Retaining Pin	**34**	Grip Cap Spacer	**59**	Hammer Spring
9	Locking Block	**35**	Grip Cap	**60**	Hammer Spring Sleeve
10	Locking Block Stud	**36**	Grip Cap Screw	**61**	Hammer
11	Breechbolt Base	**37**	Grip Cap Inlay	**62**	Hammer Pin
12	Ejector	**38**	Recoil Pad	**63**	Action Bar Lock
13	Forend Assembly	**39**	Recoil Pad Spacer	**64**	Action Bar Lock Spring
14	Forend Cap	**40**	Recoil Pad Screws	**65**	Carrier
15	Forend Cap Ball	**41**	Stock Retainer Washer	**66**	Carrier Dog
16	Forend Cap Spring	**42**	Stock Retainer Spring Washer	**67**	Carrier Dog Washer
17	Forend Tube	**43**	Stock Retainer Bolt	**68**	Carrier Dog Pin
18	Action Bar, Right	**44**	Stock Spacer Plate	**69**	Carrier Spring
19	Action Bar, Left	**45**	Trigger Plate	**70**	Carrier Spring Sleeve
20	Forend Tube Nut	**46**	Safety Button	**71**	Trigger Plate Pin Bushing, Small
21	Front Sight	**47**	Safety Button Spring Sleeve	**72**	Trigger Plate Pin Bushing Spring, Small
22	Latch Pin Stopper Springs	**48**	Safety Button Spring	**73**	Trigger Plate Pin, Large
23	Magazine Follower	**49**	Safety Button Spring Stopper Pin	**74**	Trigger Plate Pin, Small
24	Magazine Plug	**50**	Sear		
25	Shell Stopper Plate, Left	**51**	Sear Pin		
26	Shell Stopper Plate, Right				

Model 916 Slide-Action Shotgun

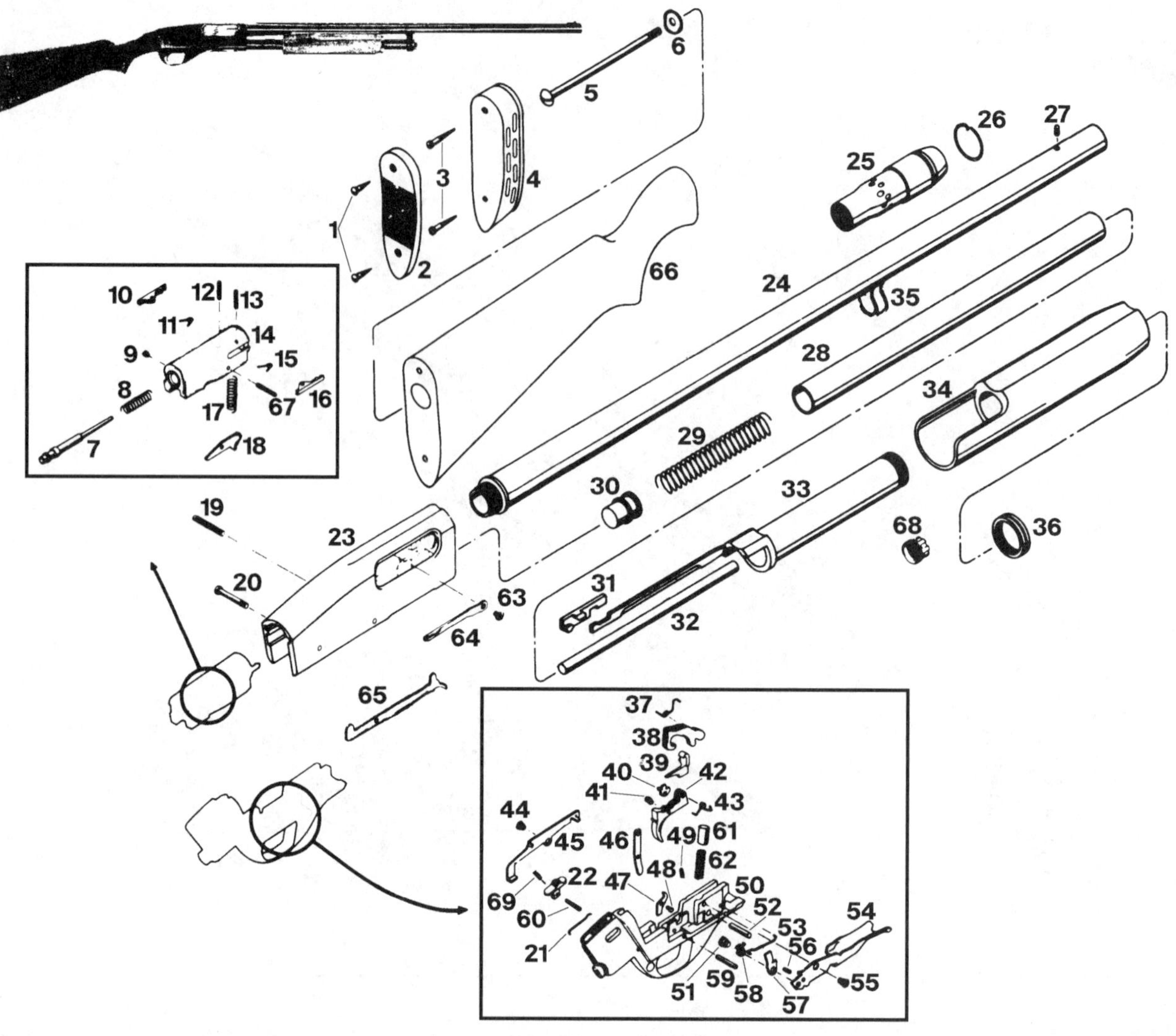

1	Buttplate Screws	24	Barrel	47	Detent
2	Buttplate	25	Vary Choke	48	Detent Pin
3	Recoil Pad Screws	26	Choke Click Spring	49	Release Lever Booster Spring
4	Rubber Recoil Pad	27	Front Sight	50	Trigger Plate
5	Stock Bolt	28	Magazine Tube	51	Lifter Pawl Stud
6	Stock Bolt Washer	29	Magazine Spring	52	Hammer Pin
7	Firing Pin	30	Magazine Spring Follower	53	Lifter Spring
8	Firing Pin Spring	31	Bolt Slide	54	Lifter
9	Firing Pin Retainer Screw	32	Wood Plug	55	Pivot Screw Lifter
10	Extractor, Left	33	Handle Bar Tube Assembly	56	Lifter Pawl Spring Post
11	Extractor Spring, Left	34	Forend	57	Lifter Pawl
12	Extractor Pin, Left	35	Magazine Mount	58	Lifter Pawl Spring
13	Extractor Pin, Right	36	Forend Retainer, Front	59	Trigger Pin
14	Breechbolt	37	Release Lever Actuator Spring	60	Top Safety Lever Pivot Pin
15	Extractor Spring, Right	38	Hammer	61	Mainspring Follower
16	Extractor, Right	39	Sear	62	Mainspring
17	Cartridge Stop Spring	40	Detent Trip	63	Ejector Screw
18	Cartridge Stop	41	Detent Trip Pin	64	Ejector
19	Trigger Plate Pin	42	Trigger	65	Cartridge Cutoff
20	Trigger Plate Screw	43	Trigger Spring	66	Stock
21	Safety Button Spring	44	Pivot Screw Release	67	Cartridge Stop Pin
22	Top Safety Button	45	Release Lever	68	Magazine Cap
23	Receiver	46	Top Safety Lever	69	Safety Button Pin

Model 1861 Musket

Courtesy of Thomas E. Wessel

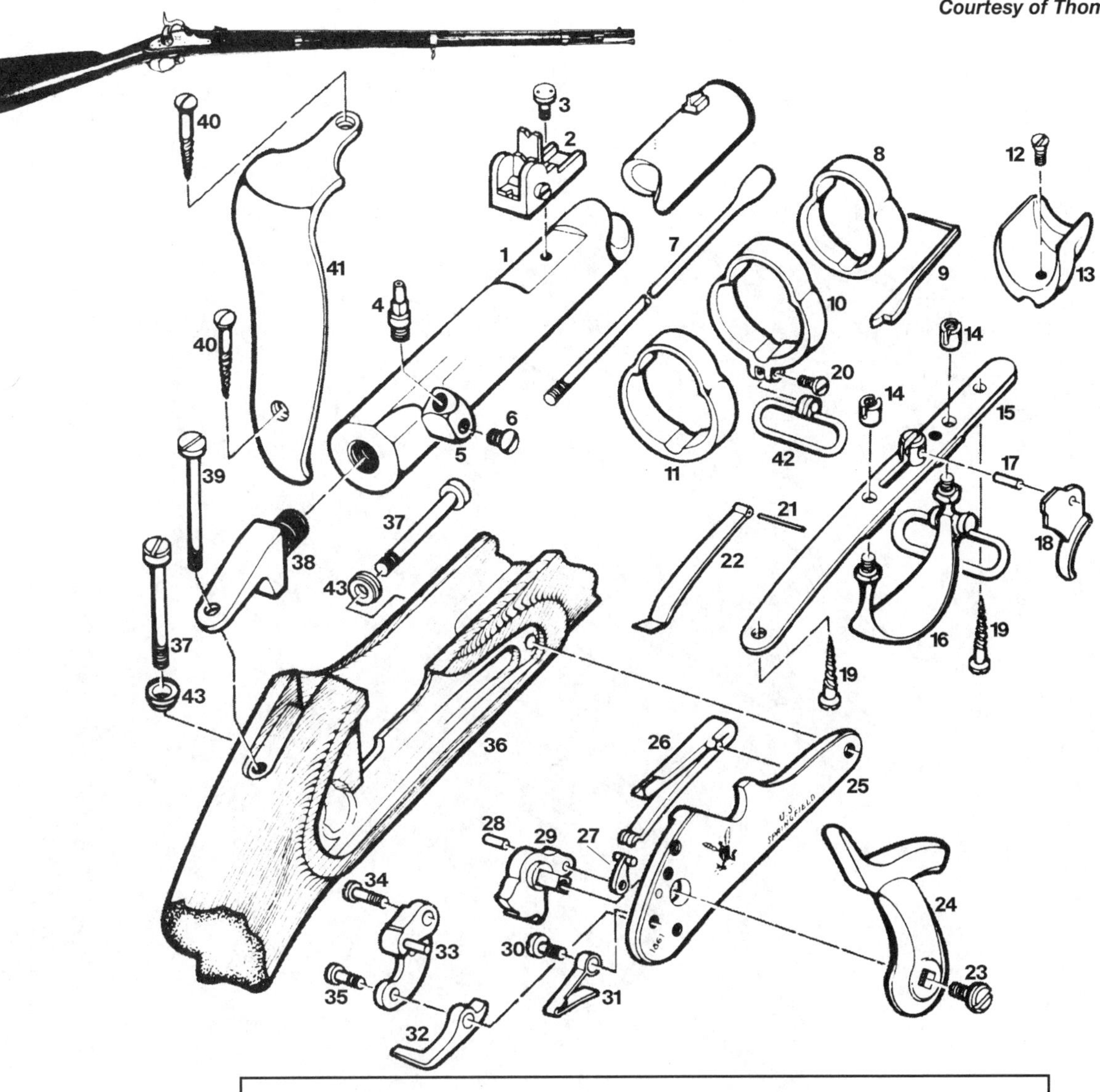

1	Barrel	23	Hammer Screw
2	Rear Sight	24	Hammer
3	Rear Sight Base Screw	25	Lockplate
4	Cone	26	Mainspring
5	Cone Seat	27	Mainspring Swivel
6	Cone Seat Screw	28	Tumbler Pin
7	Ramrod	29	Tumbler
8	Upper Band	30	Sear Spring Screw
9	Band Springs	31	Sear Spring
10	Middle Band	32	Sear
11	Lower Band	33	Bridle
12	Tip Screw	34	Bridle Screw
13	Tip	35	Sear Screw
14	Guard Nuts	36	Stock
15	Guard Plate	37	Side Screws
16	Guard Bow	38	Breech Screw
17	Trigger Pin	39	Tang Screw
18	Trigger	40	Buttplate Screws
19	Guard Plate Screws	41	Buttplate
20	Swivel Screw	42	Front Swivel
21	Rod Spring Pin	43	Side Screw Washers
22	Rod Spring		

Model 1873 Rifle

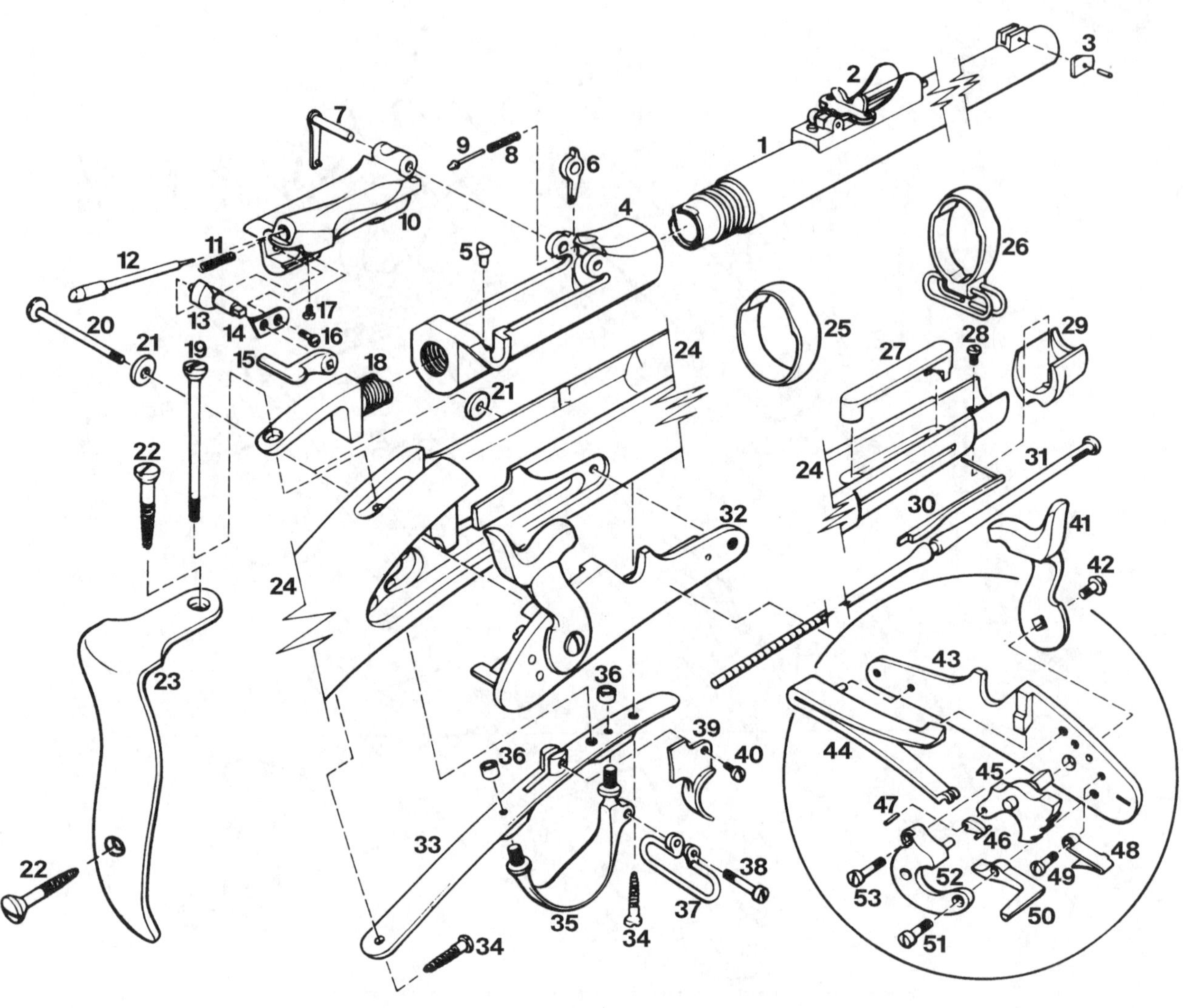

1	Barrel	**19**	Tang Screw	**37**	Guard Bow Swivel
2	Rear Sight Assembly	**20**	Side Screws	**38**	Guard Bow Swivel Screw
3	Front Sight and Pin	**21**	Side Screw Washers	**39**	Trigger
4	Breech	**22**	Buttplate Screws	**40**	Trigger Screw
5	Ejector Stud	**23**	Buttplate	**41**	Hammer
6	Extractor	**24**	Stock	**42**	Tumbler Screw
7	Hinge Pin	**25**	Lower Band	**43**	Lockplate
8	Ejector Spring	**26**	Upper Band	**44**	Mainspring
9	Spindle	**27**	Ramrod Stop	**45**	Tumbler
10	Breechblock	**28**	Stock Tip Screw	**46**	Mainspring Swivel
11	Cam Latch Spring	**29**	Stock Tip	**47**	Mainspring Swivel Pin
12	Firing Pin	**30**	Band Springs	**48**	Sear Spring
13	Cam Latch	**31**	Ramrod	**49**	Sear Spring Screw
14	Breechblock Cap	**32**	Lock, Complete	**50**	Sear
15	Thumb-Piece	**33**	Guard Plate	**51**	Sear Screw
16	Breechblock Cap Screw	**34**	Guard Screws	**52**	Bridle
17	Firing Pin Screw	**35**	Guard Bow	**53**	Bridle Screw
18	Breech Screw	**36**	Guard Bow Nuts		

Model 1903 A-1 and A-3 Bolt-Action Rifle

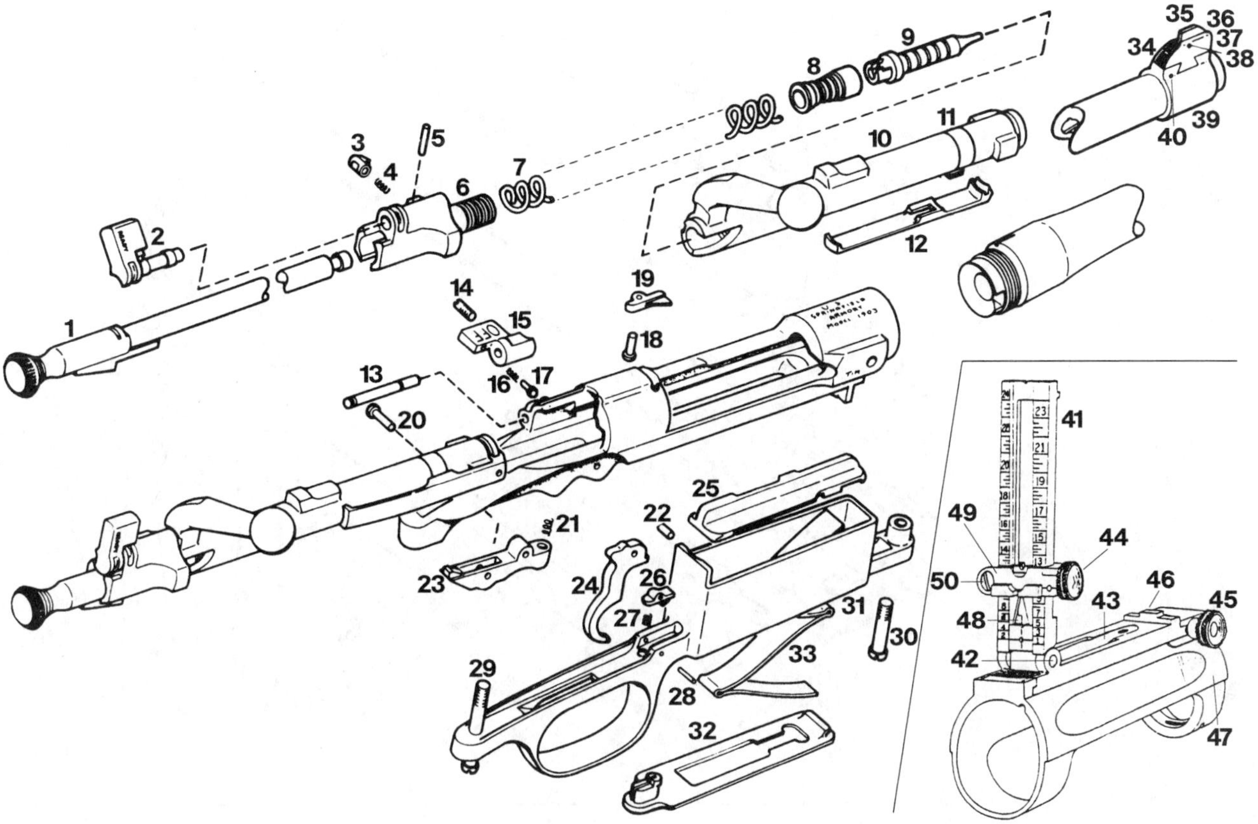

1	Firing Pin Rod	20	Sear Pin	39	Front Sight Band
2	Safety Lock Assembly	21	Sear Spring	40	Front Sight Base Pin
3	Bolt Sleeve Lock	22	Trigger Pin	41	Rear Sight Leaf
4	Bolt Sleeve Lock Spring	23	Sear	42	Leaf Hinge Pin
5	Bolt Sleeve Lock Pin	24	Trigger	43	Rear Sight Leaf Spring
6	Bolt Sleeve	25	Follower	44	Rear Sight Binding Knob, Elevation Slide
7	Mainspring	26	Floorplate Catch	45	Rear Sight Windage Knob Assembly
8	Striker Sleeve	27	Floorplate Catch Spring	46	Rear Sight Leaf Base
9	Striker	28	Floorplate Catch Pin	47	Rear Sight Base Collar
10	Bolt Complete	29	Rear Guard Screw	48	Rear Sight Drift
11	Extractor Collar	30	Front Guard Screw	49	Rear Sight Slide
12	Extractor	31	Trigger Guard	50	Rear Sight Slide Cap Screw
13	Cutoff Spindle	32	Floorplate	**Parts Not Shown**	
14	Cutoff Screw	33	Magazine Spring		Buttplate
15	Cutoff	34	Front Sight Base		Buttplate Trapdoor
16	Cutoff Plunger Spring	35	Front Sight Blade		
17	Cutoff Plunger	36	Front Sight Base Screw		
18	Ejector Pin	37	Front Sight Base Spline		
19	Ejector	38	Front Sight Blade Pin		

Model 1922 M2 Bolt-Action Rifle

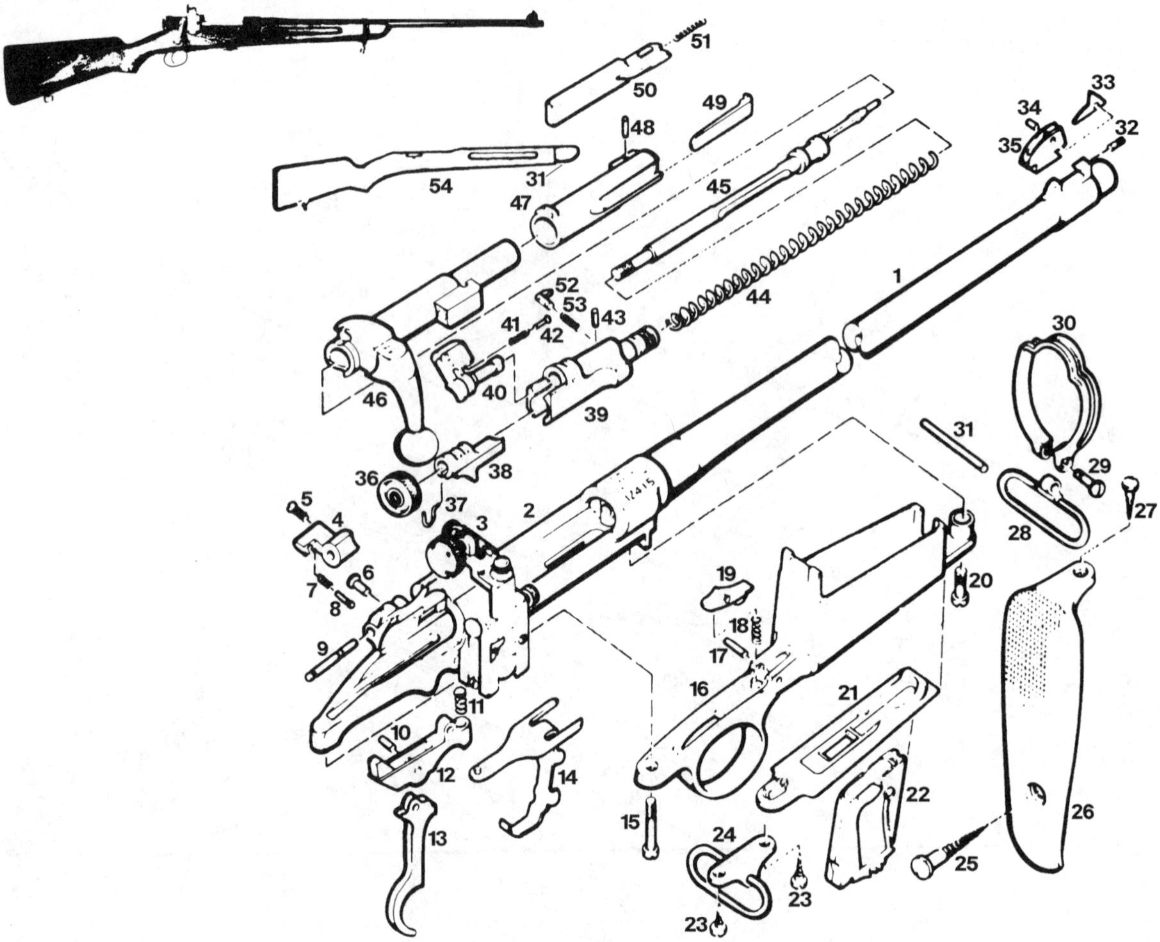

1	Barrel	28	Front Swivel
2	Receiver	29	Front Swivel Screw
3	Rear Sight Assembly	30	Front Band Assembly
4	Ejector Stop	31	Front Band Retaining Pin
5	Ejector Stop Screw	32	Sight Base Screw
6	Sear Retaining Pin	33	Front Sight
7	Ejector Stop Plunger Spring	34	Front Sight Pin
8	Ejector Stop Plunger	35	Movable Stud
9	Spindle	36	Firing Pin Nut
10	Trigger Pin	37	Firing Pin Nut Locking Spring
11	Sear Spring	38	Cocking Piece
12	Sear	39	Bolt Sleeve
13	Trigger	40	Safety Lock
14	Magazine Retaining Spring	41	Safety Lock Plunger Spring
15	Rear Guard Screw	42	Safety Lock Plunger
16	Trigger Guard	43	Bolt Sleeve Lock Pin
17	Floorplate Catch Pin	44	Mainspring
18	Floorplate Catch Spring	45	Firing Pin
19	Floorplate Catch	46	Bolt Handle
20	Front Guard Screw	47	Bolt Head
21	Floorplate	48	Ejector Retaining Pin
22	Magazine	49	Extractor
23	Butt Swivel Screws	50	Ejector
24	Butt Swivel	51	Ejector Spring
25	Lower Buttplate Screw	52	Bolt Sleeve Lock
26	Buttplate	53	Bolt Sleeve Lock Spring
27	Top Buttplate Screw	54	Stock

Model 511 Series A Side-by-Side Shotgun

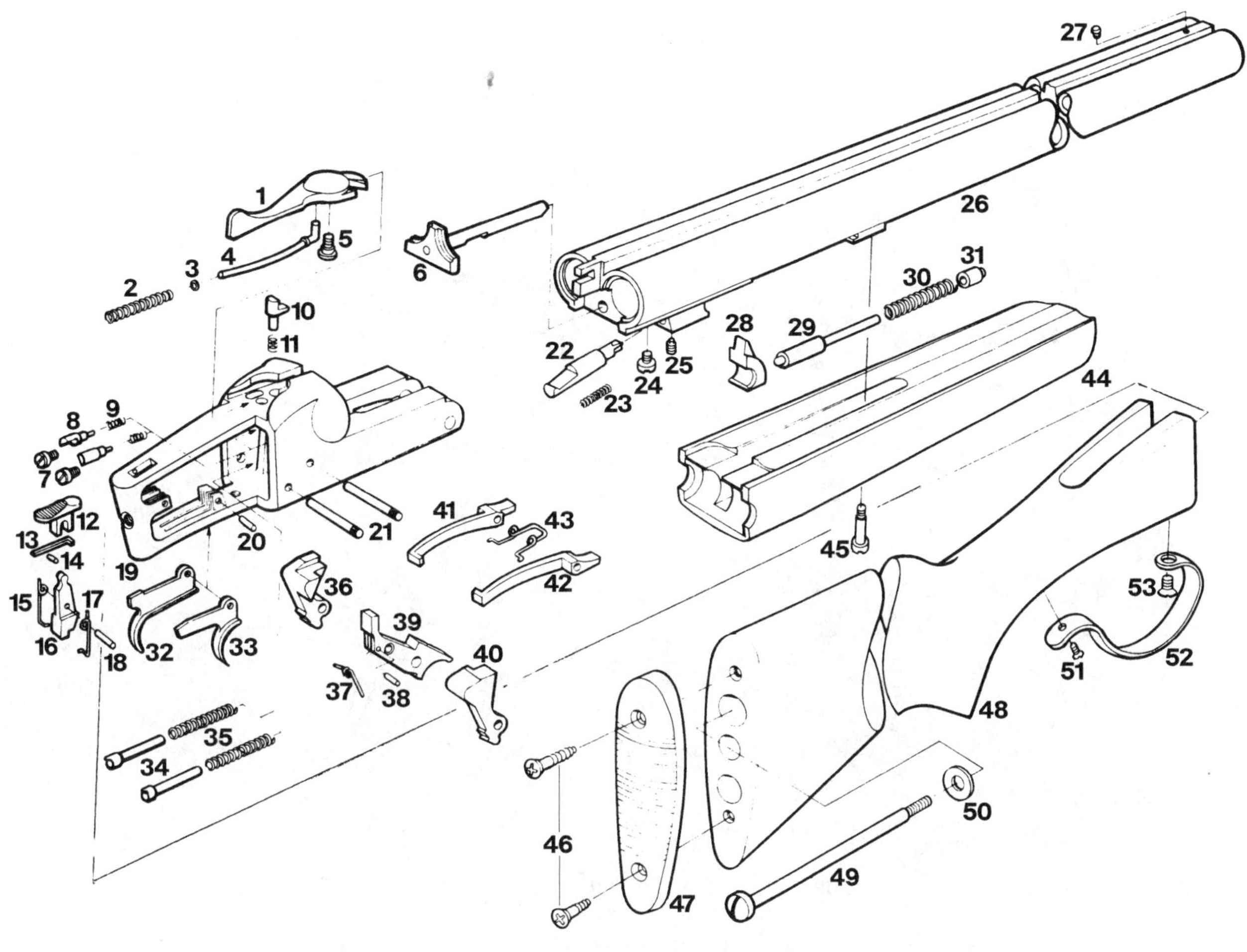

1	Top Snap	27	Front Sight
2	Top Snap Plunger Spring	28	Ejector
3	Mainspring Top Snap Washer	29	Ejector Rod
4	Top Snap Plunger	30	Ejector Rod Spring
5	Top Snap Screw	31	Ejector Rod Bushing
6	Extractor	32	Trigger, Left
7	Firing Pin Retaining Screws	33	Trigger, Right
8	Firing Pins	34	Mainspring Plungers
9	Firing Pin Springs	35	Mainsprings
10	Top Snap Trip	36	Hammer, Left
11	Top Snap Trip Spring	37	Cocking Lever Spring
12	Safety Button	38	Cocking Lever Spring Pin
13	Safety Spring	39	Cocking Lever
14	Safety Plunger	40	Hammer, Right
15	Trigger Spring, Left	41	Sear, Left
16	Safety-Lever	42	Sear, Right
17	Trigger Spring, Right	43	Sear Spring
18	Safety-Lever Pin	44	Forend
19	Frame	45	Forend Screw
20	Trigger Pin	46	Buttplate Screws
21	Sear Pin and Cocking Lever Pin	47	Buttplate
22	Cocking Plunger	48	Stock Assembly
23	Cocking Plunger Spring	49	Stock Bolt
24	Extractor Screw	50	Stock Bolt Washer
25	Cocking Plunger Retaining Screw	51	Trigger Guard Screw, Rear
		52	Trigger Guard
26	Barrel Assembly	53	Trigger Guard Screw, Front

Model 67, 67-T, 67VR and 67VR-T Slide-Action Shotgun

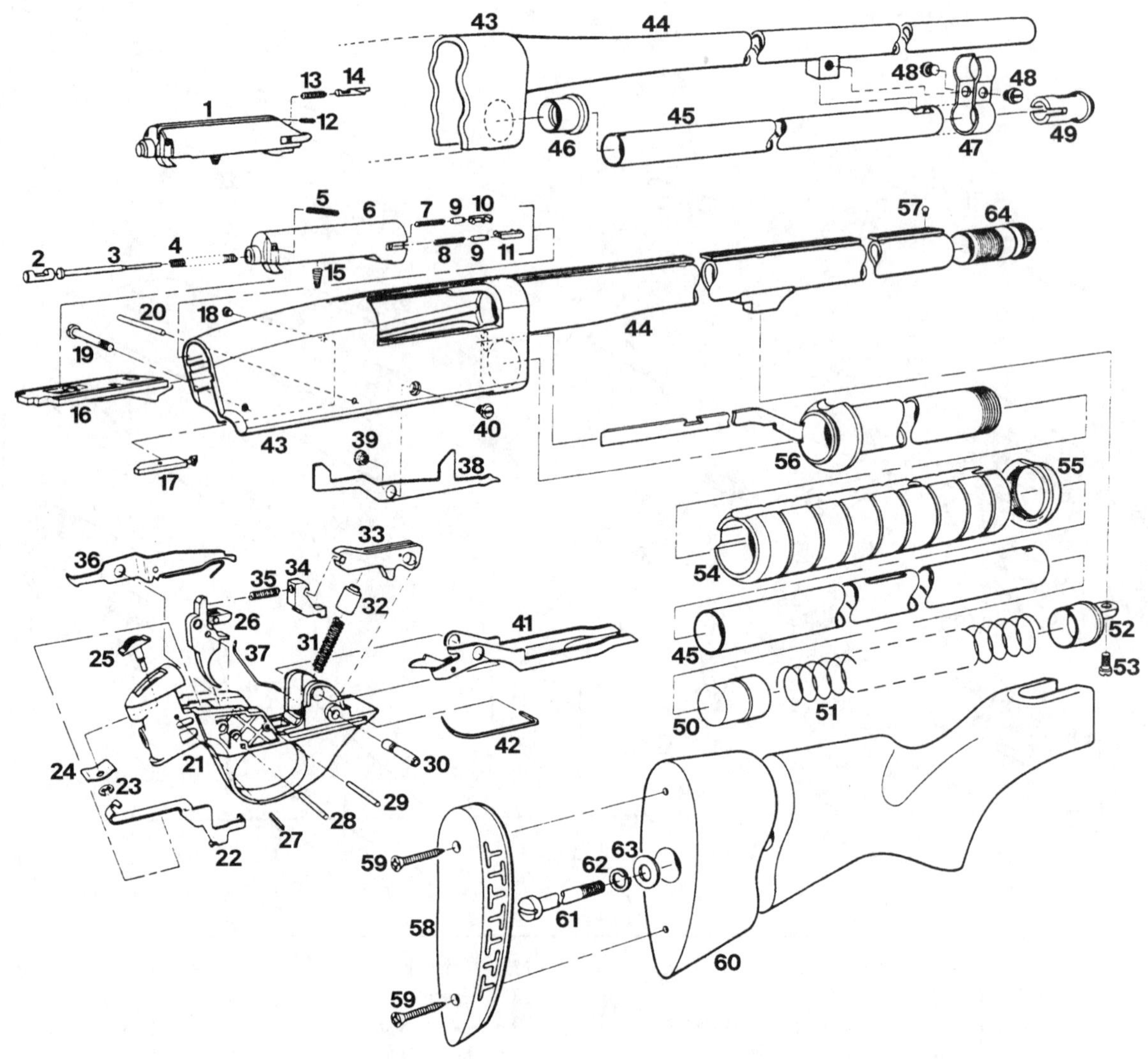

1	Bolt Assembly	23	Safety Retaining Ring	45	Magazine Tube
2	Firing Pin Extension	24	Safety Spring	46	Magazine Tube Adapter
3	Firing Pin	25	Safety	47	Magazine Tube Yoke
4	Firing Pin Spring	26	Trigger	48	Magazine Tube Screws
5	Firing Pin Stop Pin	27	Safety-Lever Retaining Pin	49	Magazine Plug
6	Bolt Body	28	Trigger Pin	50	Magazine Follower
7	Extractor Spring, Left	29	Sear Pin	51	Magazine Spring
8	Extractor Spring, Right	30	Hammer Bushing	52	Magazine Spring Seat
9	Extractor Plungers	31	Mainspring	53	Magazine Spring Seat Screw
10	Extractor, Left	32	Mainspring Plunger	54	Operating Handle
11	Extractor, Right	33	Hammer	55	Operating Handle Collar
12	Shell Stop Retaining Pin	34	Sear	56	Operating Handle Bar
13	Shell Stop Spring	35	Trigger Spring	57	Front Sight
14	Shell Stop	36	Slide Lock Assembly	58	Buttpad
15	Bolt Support Spring	37	Slide Lock Release Spring	59	Buttpad Screws
16	Slide	38	Cartridge Stop	60	Stock
17	Ejector	39	Cartridge Stop Pivot Nut	61	Stock Bolt
18	Ejector Screw	40	Cartridge Stop Pivot Screw	62	Stock Bolt Lock Washer
19	Trigger Guard Screw	41	Lifter	63	Stock Bolt Washer
20	Trigger Guard Pin	42	Lifter Spring	64	Choke Tube
21	Trigger Guard	43	Receiver		
22	Safety-Lever	44	Barrel		

Model 67 Series B Slide-Action Shotgun

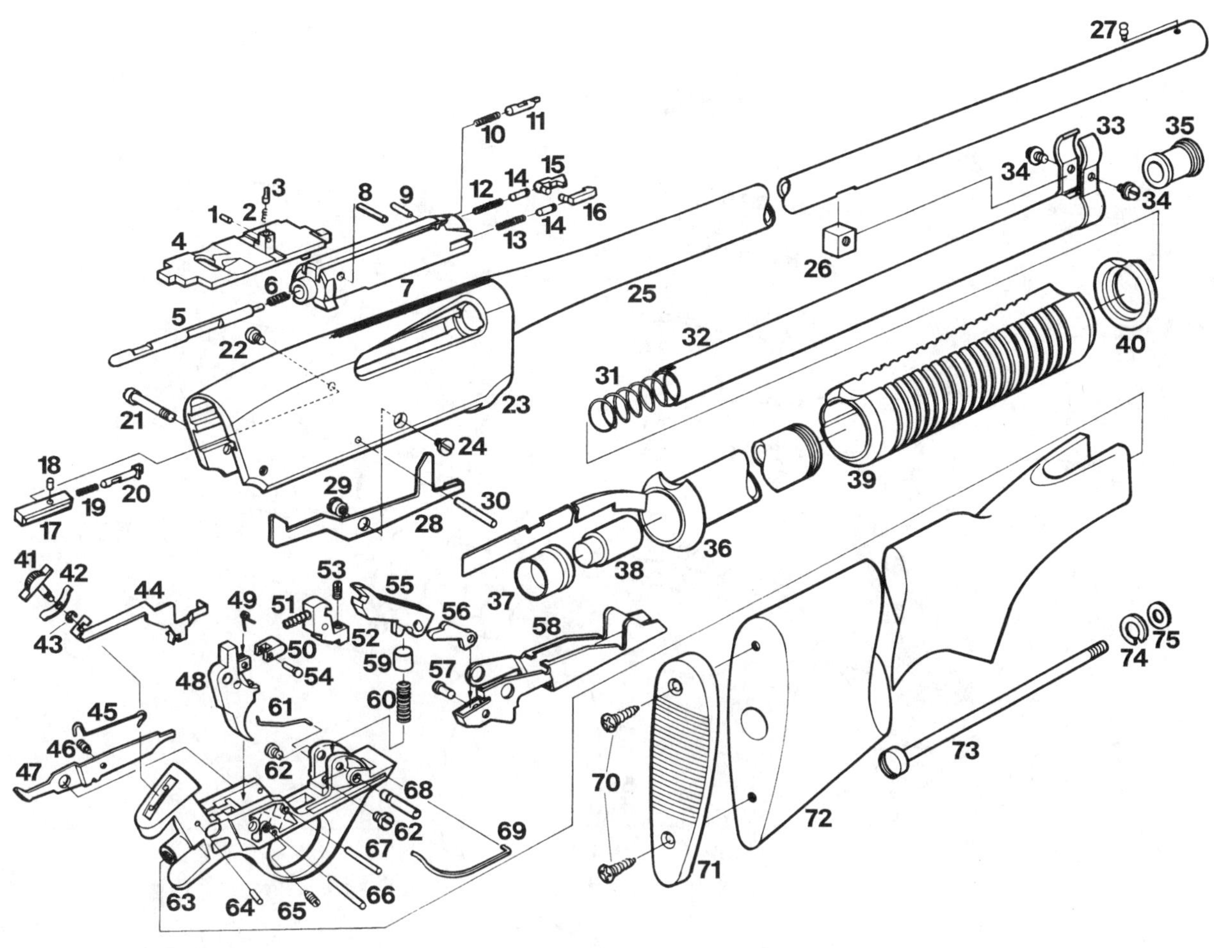

1	Firing Pin Retractor Plunger Pin
2	Firing Pin Retractor Plunger Spring
3	Firing Pin Retractor Plunger
4	Slide Assembly
5	Firing Pin
6	Firing Pin Spring
7	Breechbolt
8	Firing Pin Stop Pin
9	Shell Stop Retaining Pin
10	Shell Stop Spring
11	Shell Stop
12	Extractor Spring, Left
13	Extractor Spring, Right
14	Extractor Plungers
15	Extractor, Left
16	Extractor, Right
17	Ejector Assembly
18	Ejector Pin
19	Ejector Spring
20	Ejector Plunger
21	Trigger Guard Screw
22	Ejector Screw
23	Receiver
24	Cartridge Stop Pivot Screw
25	Barrel
26	Filler Block
27	Front Sight
28	Cartridge Stop
29	Cartridge Stop Pivot Nut
30	Trigger Guard Pin
31	Magazine Spring
32	Magazine Tube
33	Magazine Tube Yoke
34	Magazine Tube Yoke Screws
35	Magazine Plug
36	Operating Handle Bar Assembly
37	Magazine Tube Adapter
38	Magazine Follower
39	Operating Handle Wood
40	Operating Handle Bar Collar, Front
41	Safety
42	Safety Spring
43	Safety Retaining Ring
44	Safety-Lever
45	Slide Lock Spring
46	Slide Lock Spring Stud
47	Slide Lock and Spring Assembly
48	Trigger
49	Sear Trip Spring
50	Sear Trip
51	Trigger Spring
52	Sear
53	Sear Engagement Screw
54	Sear Trip Pin
55	Hammer Assembly
56	Lifter Pawl
57	Lifter Pawl Pin
58	Lifter Assembly
59	Mainspring Plunger
60	Mainspring
61	Slide Lock Release Spring
62	Lifter Screw
63	Trigger Guard
64	Safety-Lever Retaining Pin
65	Trigger Adjusting Screw
66	Trigger Pin
67	Sear Pin
68	Hammer Bushing
69	Lifter Spring
70	Buttplate Screws
71	Buttplate
72	Stock Assembly
73	Stock Bolt
74	Stock Bolt Lock Washer
75	Stock Bolt Washer

Model 67 Slug, 69N, 69R and 69RXL Slide-Action Shotgun

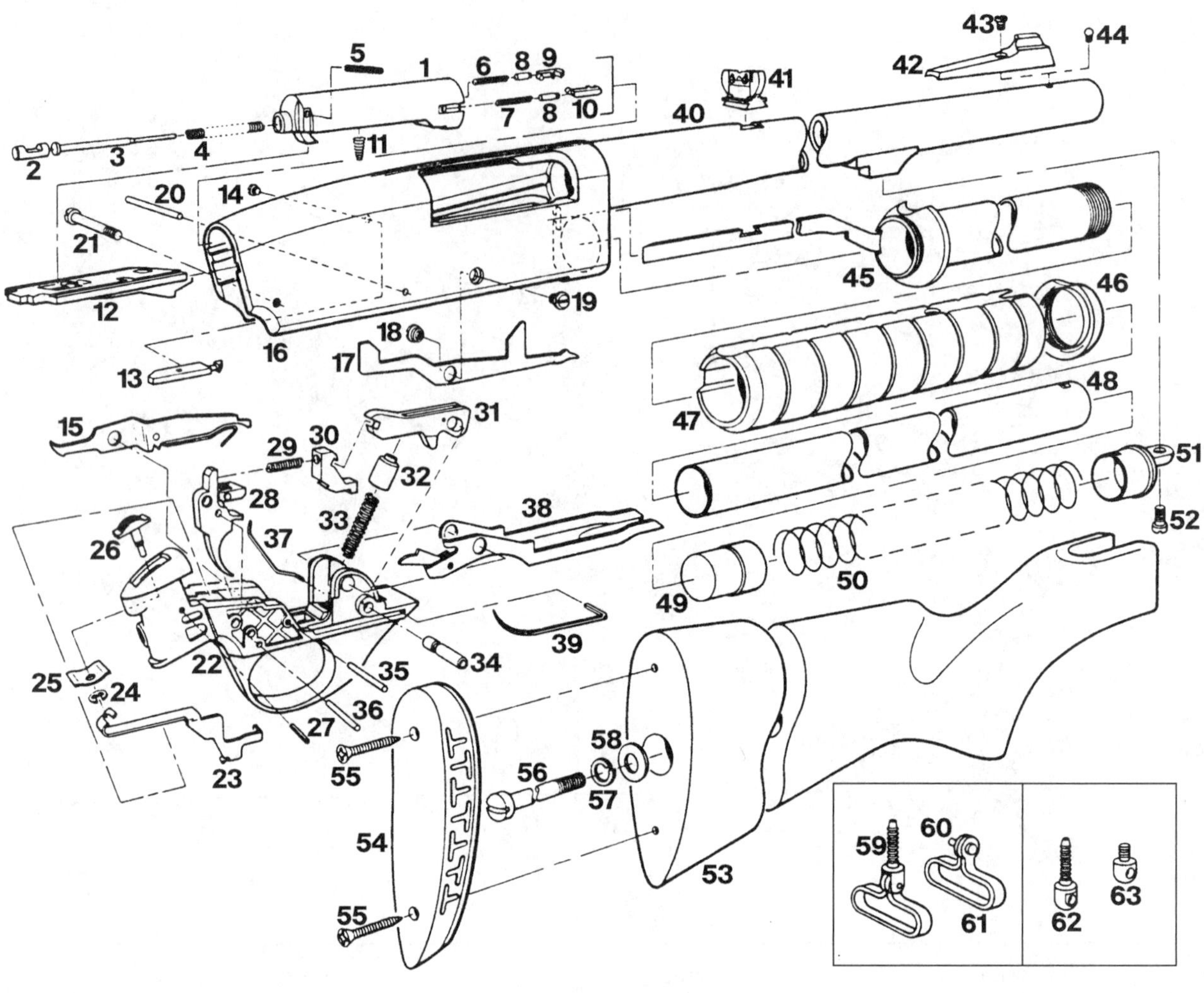

1	Bolt Assembly	**22**	Trigger Guard	**43**	Front Sight Screw
2	Firing Pin Extension	**23**	Safety-Lever	**44**	Front Bead
3	Firing Pin	**24**	Safety Retaining Ring	**45**	Operating Handle Bar
4	Firing Pin Spring	**25**	Safety Spring	**46**	Operating Handle Collar
5	Firing Pin Stop Pin	**26**	Safety	**47**	Operating Handle
6	Extractor Spring, Left	**27**	Safety-Lever Retaining Pin	**48**	Magazine Tube
7	Extractor Spring, Right	**28**	Trigger	**49**	Magazine Follower
8	Extractor Plungers	**29**	Trigger Spring	**50**	Magazine Spring
9	Extractor, Left	**30**	Sear	**51**	Magazine Spring Seat
10	Extractor, Right	**31**	Hammer	**52**	Magazine Spring Seat Screw
11	Bolt Support Spring	**32**	Mainspring Plunger	**53**	Stock
12	Slide Assembly	**33**	Mainspring	**54**	Buttpad
13	Ejector	**34**	Hammer Bushing	**55**	Buttpad Screws
14	Ejector Screw	**35**	Sear Pin	**56**	Stock Screw
15	Slide Lock Assembly	**36**	Trigger Pin	**57**	Stock Bolt Lock Washer
16	Receiver	**37**	Slide Lock Release Spring	**58**	Stock Bolt Washer
17	Cartridge Stop	**38**	Lifter	**59**	Stock Swivel Screw
18	Cartridge Stop Pivot Nut	**39**	Lifter Spring	**60**	Swivel Loop Rivet
19	Cartridge Stop Pivot Screw	**40**	Barrel	**61**	Swivel Loop
20	Trigger Guard Pin	**41**	Rear Sight	**62**	Swivel Stud, Wood Screw
21	Trigger Guard Screw	**42**	Front Sight	**63**	Swivel Stud, Machine Screw

Model 944 and 944Y Series A Single Shot Shotgun

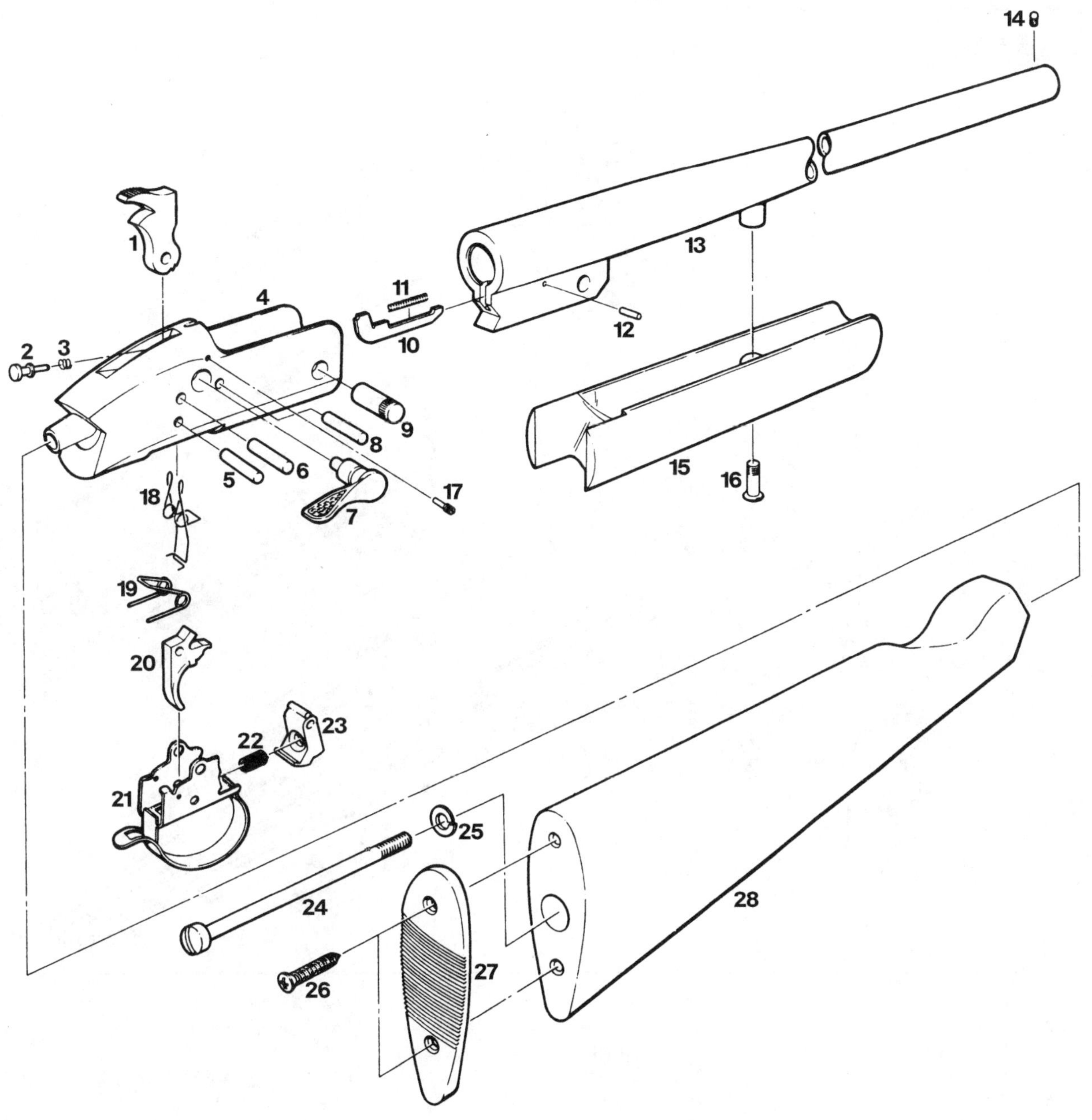

1	Hammer	15	Forend
2	Firing Pin	16	Takedown Screw
3	Firing Pin Spring	17	Firing Pin Retaining Screw
4	Frame	18	Trigger Spring
5	Trigger Pin	19	Hammer Spring
6	Hammer Pin	20	Trigger
7	Side Lever	21	Trigger Bracket
8	Lock Bolt Pin	22	Locking Bolt Spring
9	Joint Pin	23	Locking Bolt
10	Extractor	24	Stock Bolt
11	Extractor/Ejector Spring	25	Stock Bolt Lock Washer
12	Extractor/Ejector Spring Pin	26	Buttplate Screws
13	Barrel	27	Buttplate
14	Front Sight	28	Stock

SPRINGFIELD ARMORY

M1A Autoloading Rifle

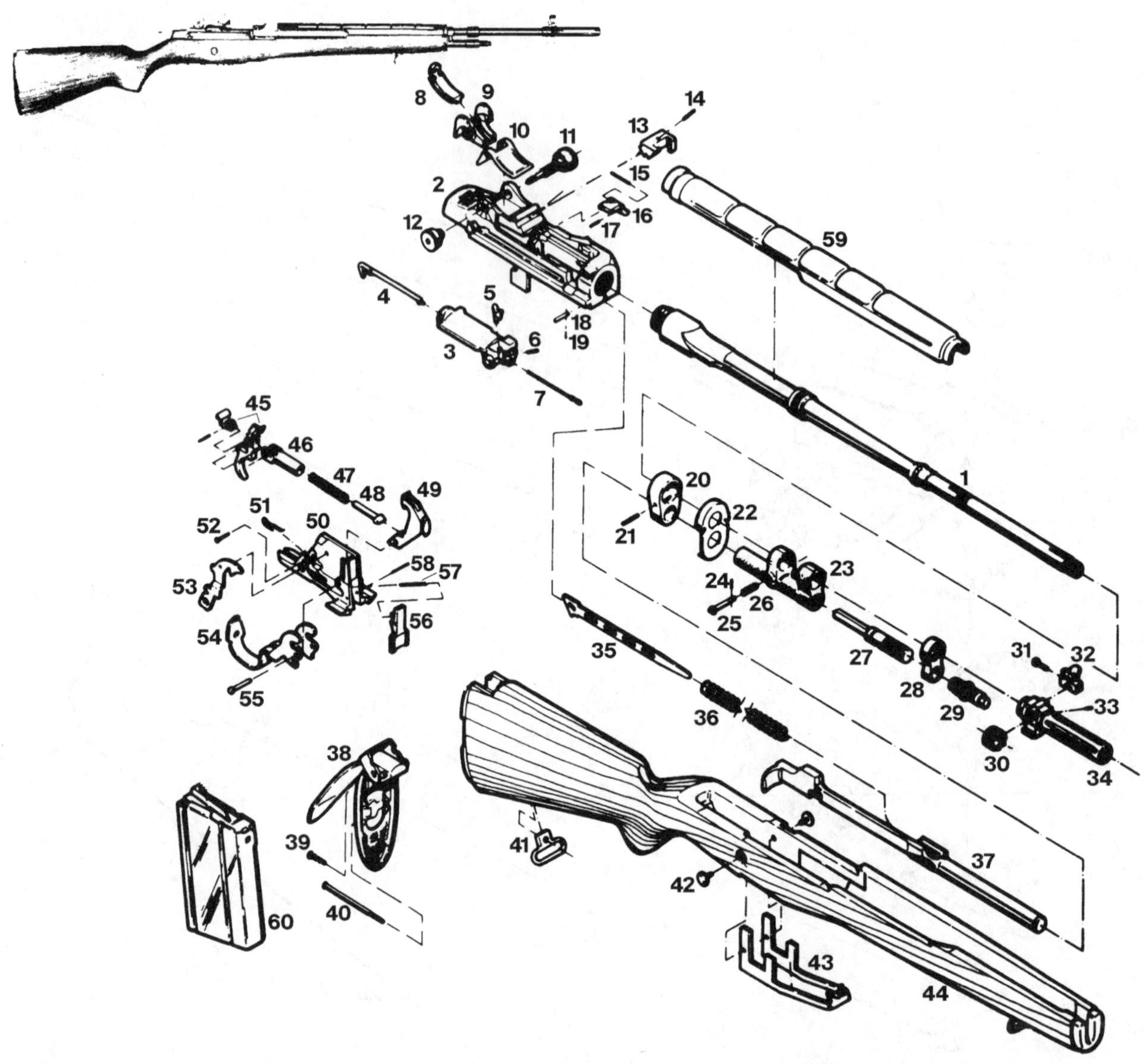

1	Barrel	**22**	Front Band	**42**	Stock Liner Screws
2	Receiver	**23**	Gas Cylinder	**43**	Stock Liner
3	Breech Bolt	**24**	Spring Pin	**44**	Stock
4	Firing Pin	**25**	Valve Spindle	**45**	Trigger and Sear Assembly
5	Extractor	**26**	Valve Spring	**46**	Hammer Spring Housing
6	Extractor Plunger with Spring	**27**	Gas Cylinder Piston	**47**	Helical Compression Spring
7	Ejector with Spring	**28**	Gas Cylinder Lock	**48**	Hammer Spring Plunger
8	Rear Sight Aperture	**29**	Gas Cylinder Plug	**49**	Hammer
9	Rear Sight Base	**30**	Flash Suppressor Nut	**50**	Trigger Housing
10	Rear Sight Cover	**31**	Front Sight Cap Socket Head Screw	**51**	Safety Spring
11	Elevating Pinion Assembly	**32**	Front Sight	**52**	Trigger Pin
12	Windage Knob Assembly	**33**	Set Screw	**53**	Safety
13	Cartridge Clip Guide	**34**	Flash Suppressor	**54**	Trigger Guard
14	Spring Pin	**35**	Operating Rod Spring Guide	**55**	Straight Headed Pin
15	Spring Pin	**36**	Operating Rod Spring	**56**	Magazine Latch
16	Bolt Lock	**37**	Operating Rod	**57**	Magazine Latch Spring
17	Bolt Lock Spring	**38**	Buttplate Assembly	**58**	Magazine Latch Pin
18	Connector Lock	**39**	Wood Screw	**59**	Handguard
19	Connector Lock Pin	**40**	Machine Screw	**60**	Magazine
20	Operating Rod Guide	**41**	Buttstock Swivel		
21	Spring Pin				

SAR-3 Autoloading Rifle

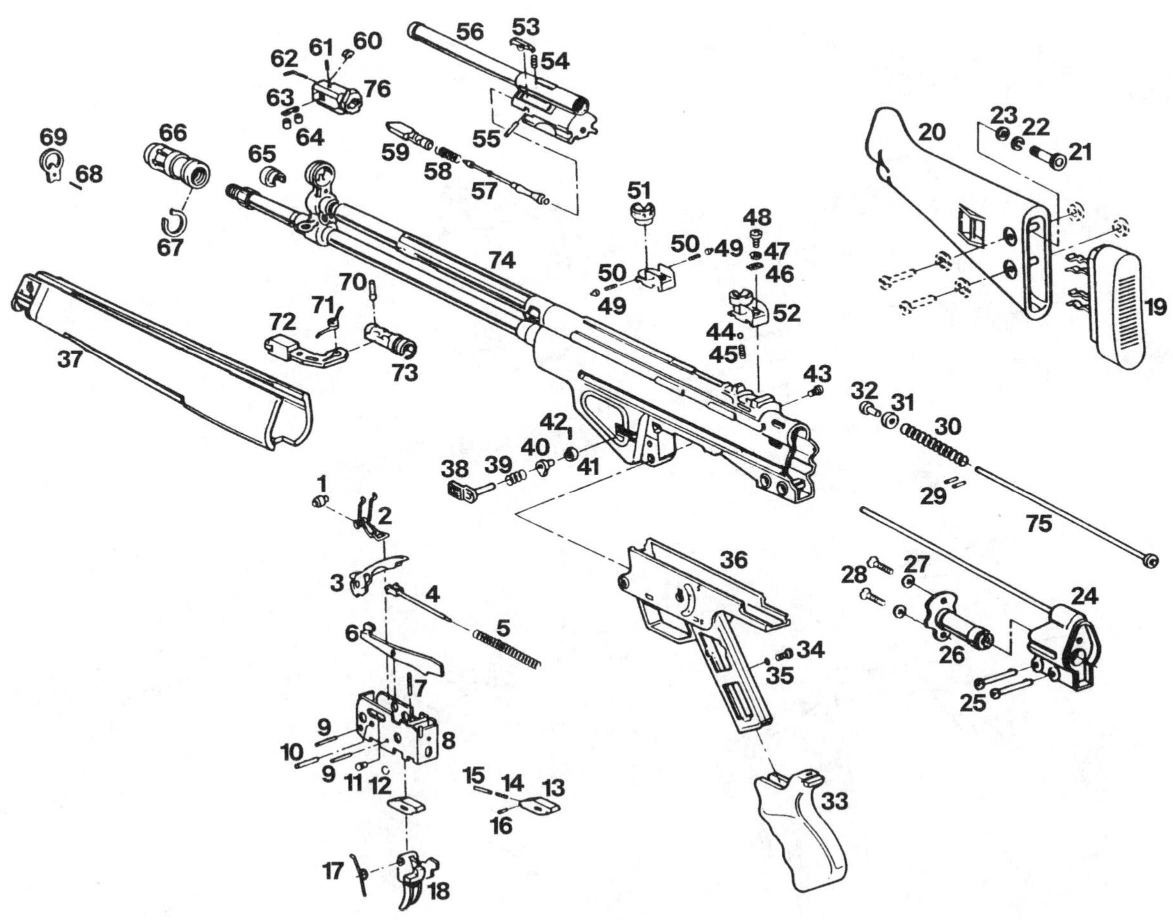

1	Distance Sleeve for Catch
2	Elbow Spring with Roller
3	Hammer
4	Hammer Pressure Shank
5	Hammer Compression Spring
6	Ejector
7	Ejector Compression Spring
8	Trigger Housing
9	Trigger Sear and Catch Axle
10	Hammer Axle
11	Ejector Axle
12	Ejector Axle Spring Ring
13	Sear
14	Sear Trigger Bolt
15	Sear Compression Spring
16	Bolt Head Clamping Sleeve
17	Trigger Elbow Spring
18	Trigger Complete
19	Buttplate with Stop Spring
20	Buttstock with Holder for Buffer Housing
21	Buffer Self-Locking Screw
22	Spring Washer
23	Locking Washer
24	Backplate Complete
25	Buttstock Locking Pins
26	Buffer
27	Locking Washers for Buffer
28	Self-Locking Buffer Screws
29	Stop Pin Rivets
30	Recoil Spring
31	Recoil Spring Guide Ring
32	Recoil Spring Stop Pin
33	Grip
34	Lens Head Cylindrical Screw
35	Toothed Washer for Grip Screw
36	Pistol Grip
37	Handguard Finished
38	Magazine Catch
39	Magazine Catch Compression Piece
40	Magazine Catch Contact Piece
41	Magazine Catch Push Button
42	Clamping Sleeve
43	Adjusting Screw
44	Ball
45	Ball Compression Spring
46	Rear Sight Washer
47	Locking Washer
48	Clamping Screw
49	Sight Catch Bolt
50	Catch Bolt Springs
51	Sight Cylinder
52	Sight Support
53	Bolt Head Locking Lever
54	Bolt Head Locking Lever Compression Spring
55	Cylindrical Pin
56	Bolt Head Carrier
57	Firing Pin
58	Firing Pin Piece
59	Locking Piece
60	Extractor
61	Clamping Sleeve Bolt Head
62	Extractor Spring
63	Locking Lever Holder
64	Locking Roller
65	Cap Complete
66	Flash Hider
67	Flash Hider Retaining Ring
68	Clamping Sleeve
69	Front Sight
70	Cocking Lever Axle
71	Cocking Lever Elbow Spring
72	Cocking Lever
73	Cocking Lever Support
74	Receiver with Barrel
75	Recoil Spring Guide Tube
76	Bolt Head Stripper

SAR-48 Autoadling Rifle

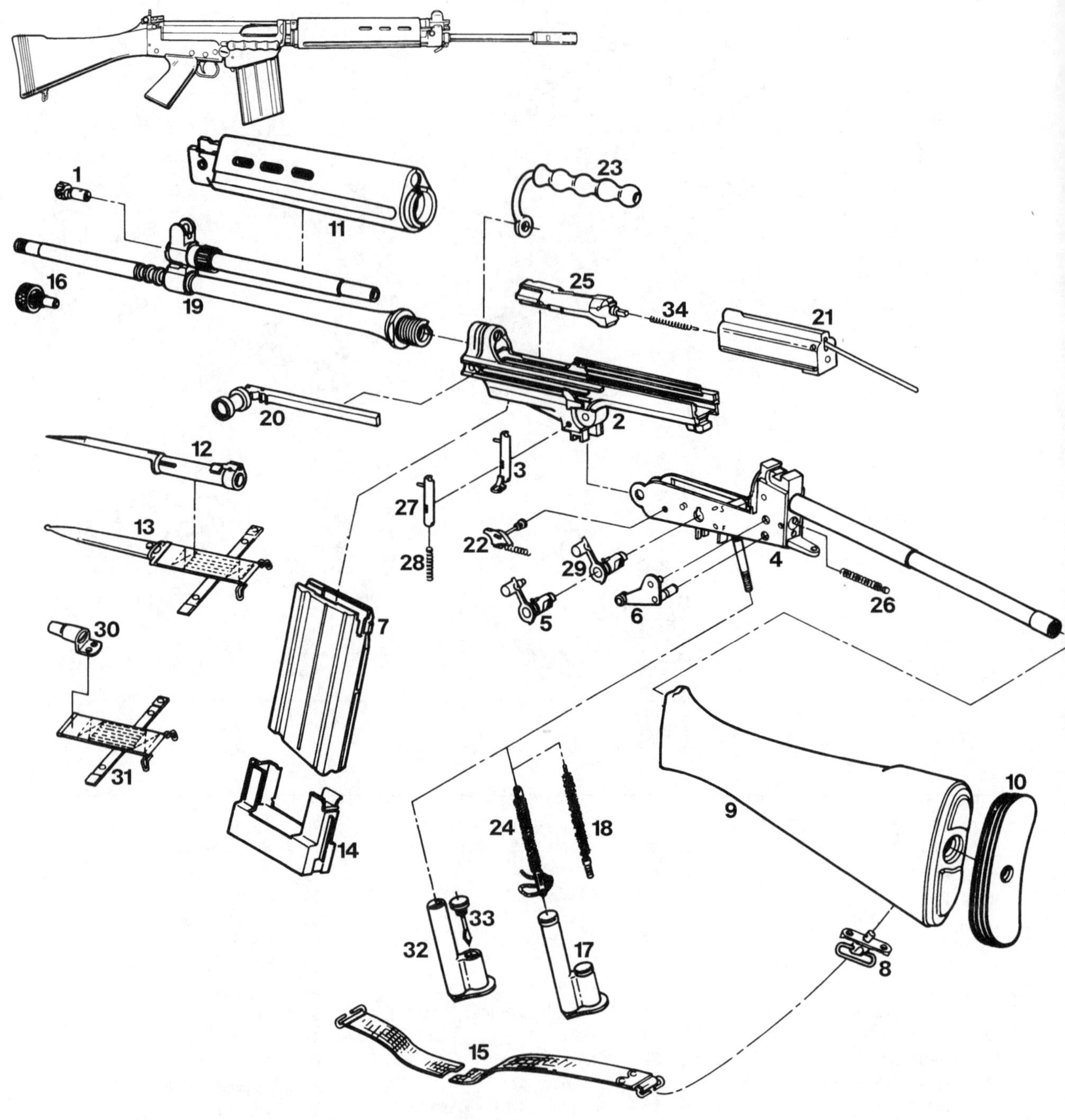

1	Gas Plug Assembly	**13**	Scabbard Assembly	**25**	Bolt and Slide Assembly
2	Receiver Assembly	**14**	Magazine Loader	**26**	Frame Lock Spring and Plunger Assembly
3	Bolt Catch	**15**	Shoulder Sling	**27**	Bolt Catch Body with Pin
4	Frame Assembly	**16**	Blank Firing Attachment	**28**	Bolt Catch Spring Plunger and Spring
5	Change Lever Assembly	**17**	Cleaning Case	**29**	Change Lever
6	Lock Lever Assembly	**18**	Pullthrough	**30**	Scabbard Collar and Spring
7	Magazine Assembly	**19**	Barrel and Bracket Assembly	**31**	Scabbard Holder
8	Rear Sling Swivel Assembly	**20**	Cocking Handle Assembly	**32**	Cleaning Device Body
9	Plastic Butt Assembly	**21**	Slide Assembly	**33**	Oil Can and Spoon
10	Buttplate	**22**	Safety Sear Assembly	**34**	Extractor Spring with Buffer
11	Handguard	**23**	Carrying Handle Assembly		
12	Bayonet Assembly	**24**	Cleaning Device		

Model 311 Side-by-Side Shotgun

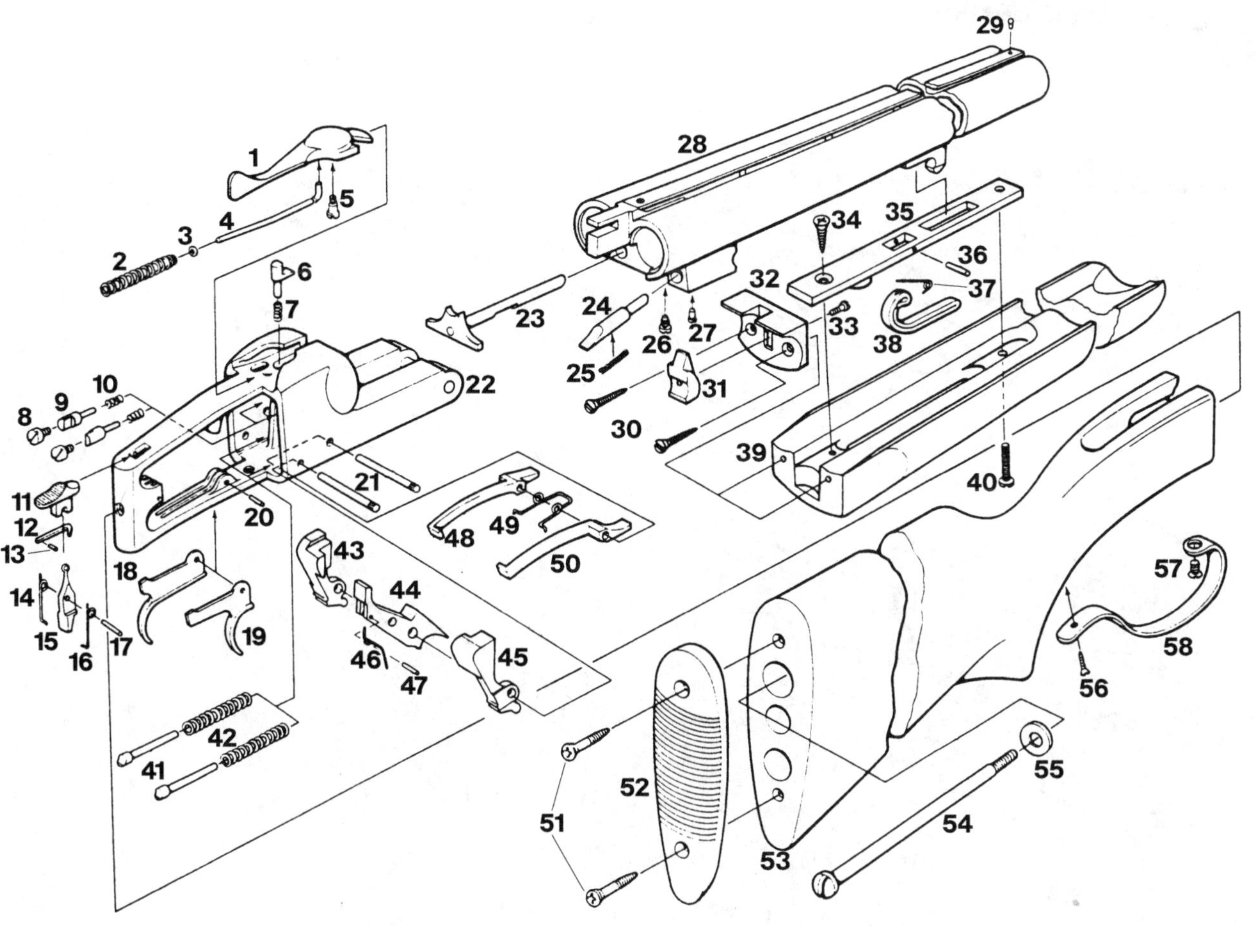

1	Top Snap	**21**	Cocking Lever, Hammer and Sear Pins	**39**	Forend Wood
2	Top Snap Plunger Spring	**22**	Frame	**40**	Forend Screw, Front
3	Mainspring Retaining Collar	**23**	Extractor Plate Assembly	**41**	Mainspring Plungers
4	Top Snap Plunger	**24**	Cocking Plunger	**42**	Mainsprings
5	Top Snap Screw	**25**	Cocking Plunger Spring	**43**	Hammer, Left
6	Top Snap Trip	**26**	Extractor Screw	**44**	Cocking Lever
7	Top Snap Trip Spring	**27**	Cocking Plunger Retaining Screw	**45**	Hammer, Right
8	Firing Pin Retaining Screws	**28**	Barrels	**46**	Cocking Lever Spring
9	Firing Pins	**29**	Front Sight	**47**	Cocking Lever Spring Pin
10	Firing Pin Springs	**30**	Forend Iron Head Screws	**48**	Sear, Left
11	Safety Button	**31**	Ejector	**49**	Sear Spring
12	Safety Spring	**32**	Forend Iron Head	**50**	Sear, Right
13	Safety Plunger	**33**	Ejector Screw	**51**	Buttplate Screws
14	Trigger Spring, Left	**34**	Forend Screw, Rear	**52**	Buttplate
15	Safety-Lever	**35**	Forend Spring Housing	**53**	Stock Assembly
16	Trigger Spring, Right	**36**	Forend Spring Pin	**54**	Stock Bolt
17	Safety-Lever Pin	**37**	Forend Spring Spring	**55**	Stock Bolt Washer
18	Trigger, Left	**38**	Forend Spring	**56**	Trigger Guard Screw, Rear
19	Trigger, Right			**57**	Trigger Guard Screw, Front
20	Trigger Pin			**58**	Trigger Guard

Model 39A, 59A, 59B and 59C Bolt-Action Shotgun

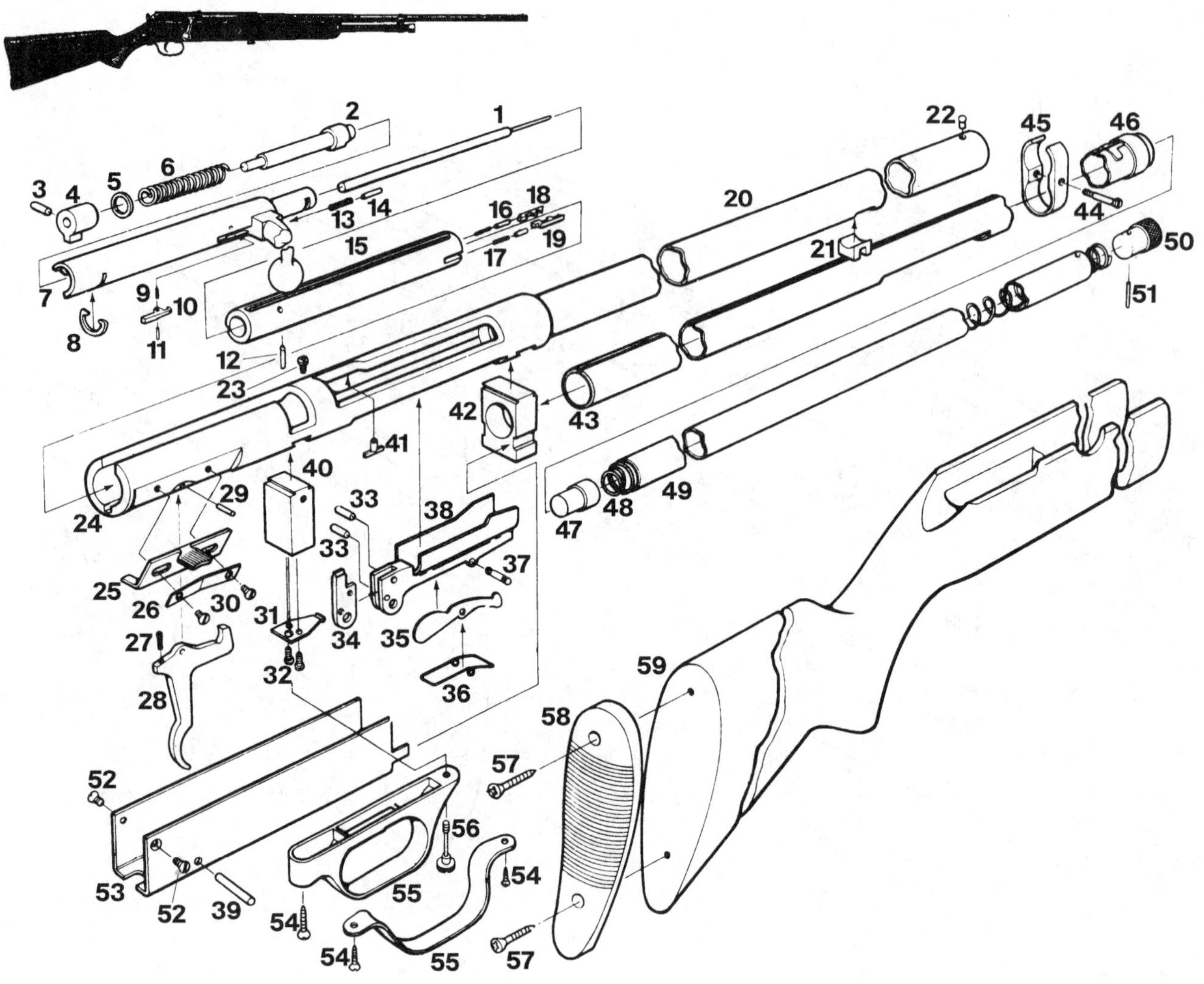

1	Firing Pin	21	Filler Block	41	Ejector
2	Striker	22	Front Sight	42	Dovetail Block, Front
3	Cocking Piece Pin	23	Bolt Stop Screw	43	Outside Magazine Tube
4	Cocking Piece	24	Receiver	44	Magazine Tube Yoke Screw
5	Striker Washer	25	Safety	45	Magazine Tube Yoke
6	Mainspring	26	Safety Spring	46	Magazine Tube Collar
7	Bolt Body and Handle	27	Trigger Spring	47	Magazine Follower
8	Mainspring Retainer	28	Trigger	48	Magazine Follower Spring
9	Safety Pawl Spring	29	Trigger Pin	49	Inside Magazine Tube
10	Safety Pawl	30	Safety Screws	50	Magazine Plug
11	Safety Pawl Pin	31	Lifter Spring	51	Magazine Plug Pin
12	Bolt Head Retaining Pin	32	Lifter Spring Screws	52	Lifter Housing Screws
13	Bolt Head Stop Plunger Spring	33	Lifter Pawl Pins	53	Lifter Housing
14	Bolt Head Stop Plunger	34	Lifter Pawl	54	Trigger Guard Screws
15	Bolt Head	35	Lifter Lever	55	Trigger Guard
16	Extractor Plungers	36	Lifter Lever Spring	56	Takedown Screw
17	Extractor Springs	37	Lifter Lever Pin	57	Buttplate Screws
18	Extractor, Left	38	Lifter Assembly	58	Buttplate
19	Extractor, Right	39	Lifter Pin	59	Stock
20	Barrel	40	Dovetail Block, Rear		

Model 44 and 44 1/2 Single Shot Rifle

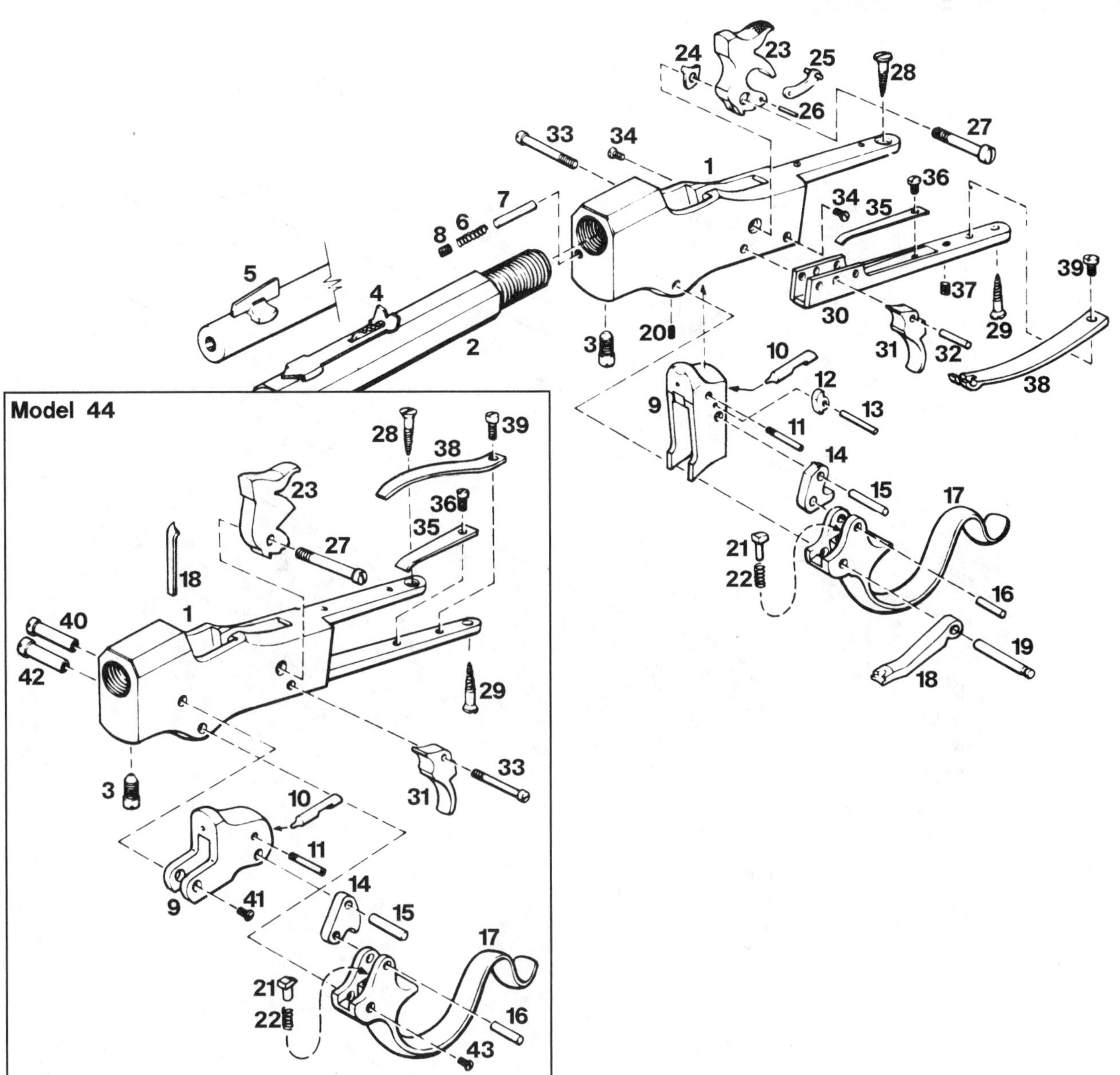

1	Frame	**18**	Extractor	**35**	Trigger Spring
2	Barrel	**19**	Lever Bolt	**36**	Trigger Spring Screw
3	Barrel Screw	**20**	Lever Bolt Screw	**37**	Filler Screw
4	Rear Sight	**21**	Lever Plunger	**38**	Mainspring
5	Front Sight	**22**	Lever Plunger Spring	**39**	Mainspring Screw
6	Breechblock Spring	**23**	Hammer	**40**	Breechblock Pivot
7	Breechblock Spring Plunger	**24**	Hammer Fly	**41**	Breechblock Pivot Screw
8	Breechblock Spring Screw	**25**	Hammer Stirrup	**42**	Lever Pivot
9	Breechblock	**26**	Hammer Stirrup Pin	**43**	Lever Pivot Screw
10	Firing Pin	**27**	Hammer Screw	**Parts Not Shown**	
11	Firing Pin Screw	**28**	Top Stock Screw		Forend
12	Firing Pin Lever	**29**	Bottom Stock Screw		Forend Screw
13	Firing Pin Lever Pin	**30**	Trigger Plate		Buttstock
14	Link	**31**	Trigger		Buttplate
15	Breechblock Link Pin	**32**	Trigger Pin		Buttplate Screws
16	Lever Link Pin	**33**	Trigger Plate Screw, Long		
17	Lever	**34**	Trigger Plate Screws, Short		

Model 51 and Springfield Model 951 and 951Y Bolt-Action Shotgun

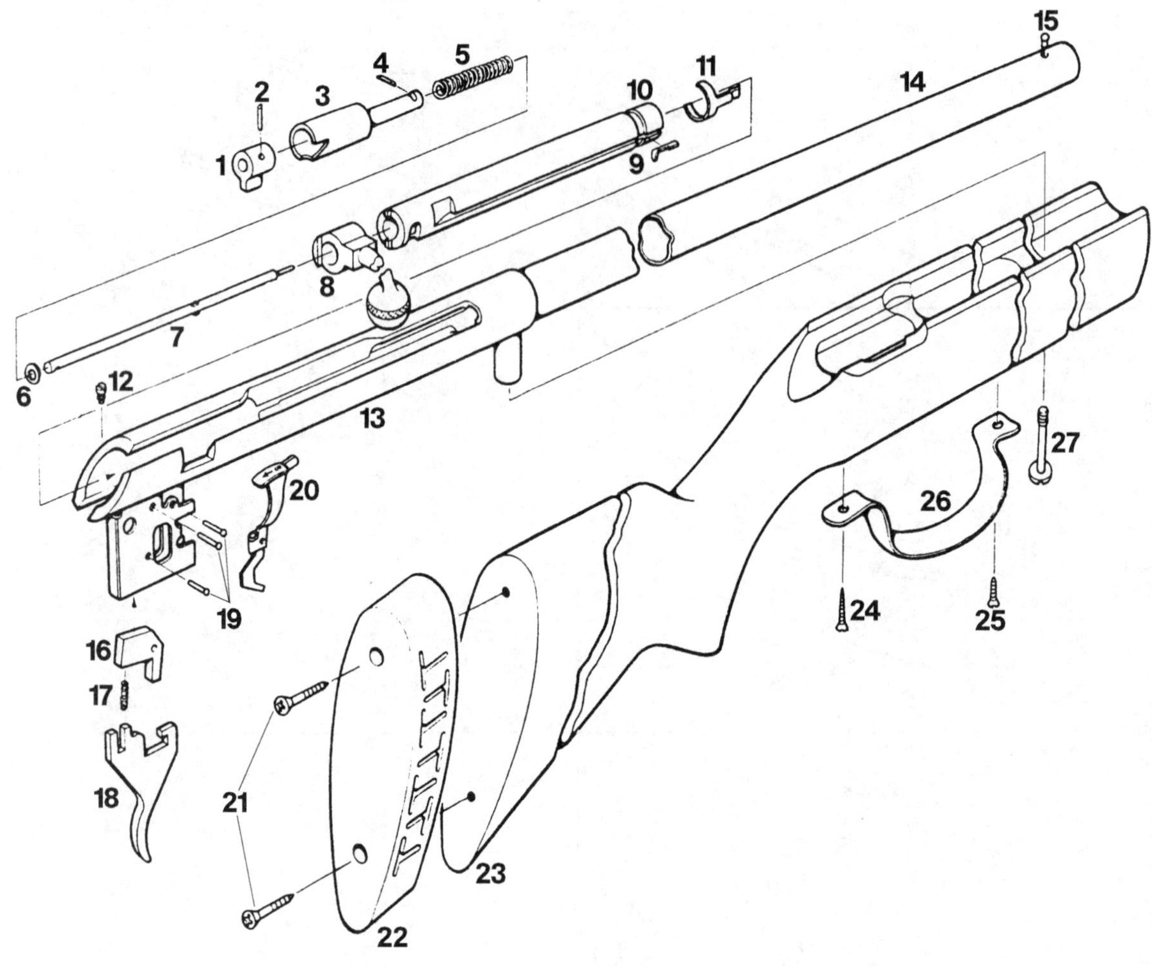

1	Cocking Piece	**15**	Front Sight
2	Cocking Piece Pin	**16**	Sear
3	Breechbolt	**17**	Trigger Spring
4	Bolt Hood Retaining Pin	**18**	Trigger
5	Mainspring	**19**	Trigger, Safety and Sear Pins
6	Breechbolt Spring Washer	**20**	Safety
7	Firing Pin	**21**	Recoil Pad Screws
8	Bolt Handle	**22**	Recoil Pad
9	Ejector	**23**	Stock Assembly
10	Bolt Hood	**24**	Trigger Guard Screw, Rear
11	Extractor	**25**	Trigger Guard Screw, Front
12	Bolt Stop Screw	**26**	Trigger Guard
13	Receiver	**27**	Takedown Screw
14	Barrel		

Model 5100, 530, 530A, 311, 311A, 311C, 311D, 311E and Series 311F Side-by-Side Shotgun

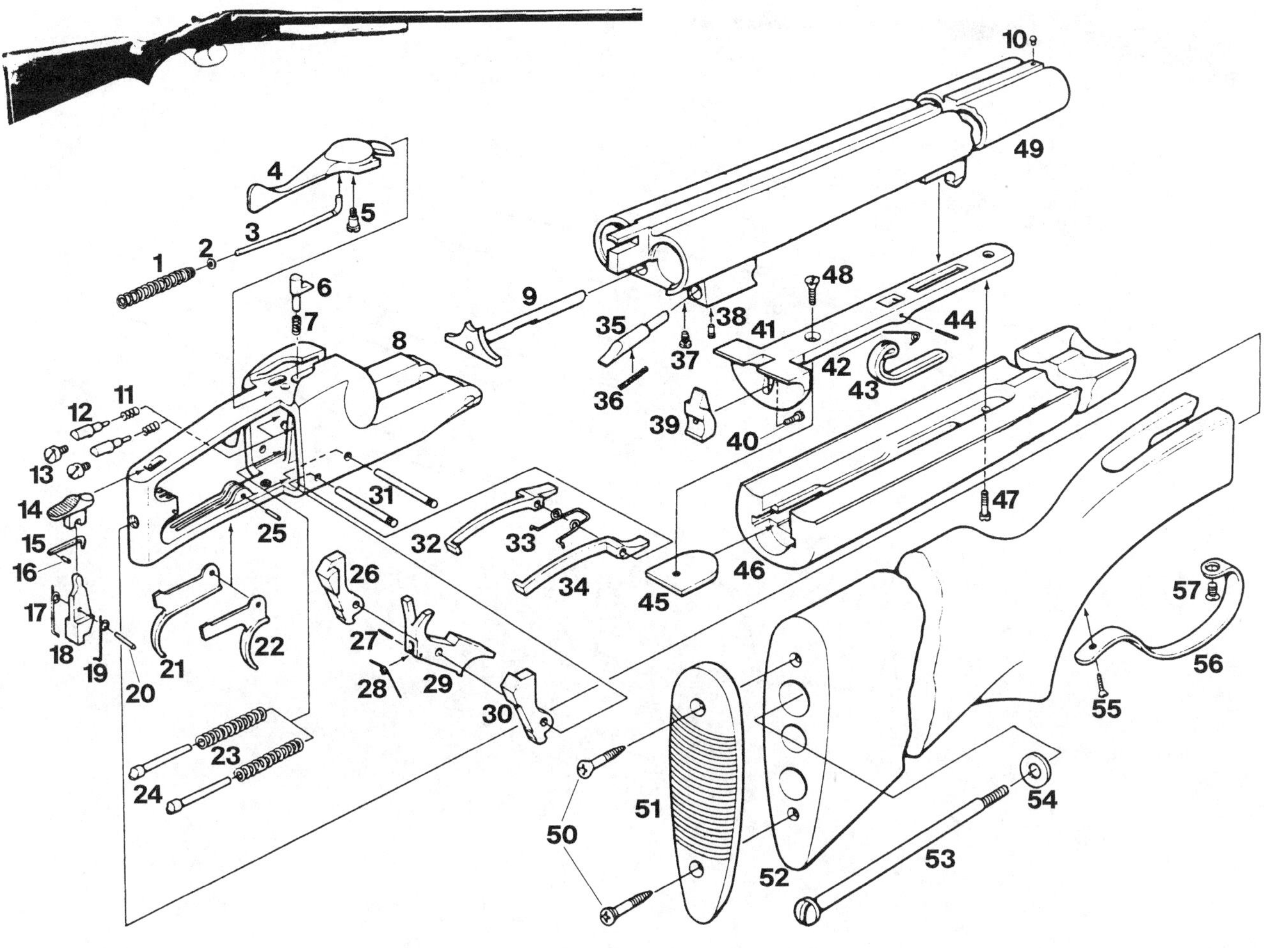

1	Top Snap Plunger Spring	21	Trigger, Left	40	Ejector Screw
2	Top Snap Plunger Collar	22	Trigger, Right	41	Forend Iron
3	Top Snap Plunger	23	Mainsprings	42	Forend Spring Spring
4	Top Snap	24	Mainspring Plungers	43	Forend Spring
5	Top Snap Screw	25	Trigger Pin	44	Forend Spring Pin
6	Top Snap Trip	26	Hammer, Left	45	Forend Insert
7	Top Snap Trip Spring	27	Cocking Lever Spring Pin	46	Forend Wood
8	Frame	28	Cocking Lever Spring	47	Forend Screw, Front
9	Extractor	29	Cocking Lever	48	Forend Screw, Rear
10	Front Sight	30	Hammer, Right	49	Barrel Assembly, Complete
11	Firing Pin Springs	31	Cocking Lever, Hammer and Sear Pins	50	Buttplate Screws
12	Firing Pins	32	Sear, Left	51	Buttplate
13	Firing Pin Retaining Screws	33	Sear Spring	52	Stock
14	Safety Button	34	Sear, Right	53	Stock Bolt
15	Safety Spring	35	Cocking Plunger	54	Stock Bolt Washer
16	Safety Plunger	36	Cocking Plunger Spring	55	Trigger Guard Screw, Rear
17	Trigger Spring, Left	37	Extractor Screw	56	Trigger Guard
18	Safety-Lever	38	Cocking Plunger Retaining Screw	57	Trigger Guard Screw, Front
19	Trigger Spring, Right	39	Ejector		
20	Safety-Lever Pin				

Model 58 and 51 Series E and F and Springfield Model 18 and 951 Series E and F Bolt-Action Shotgun

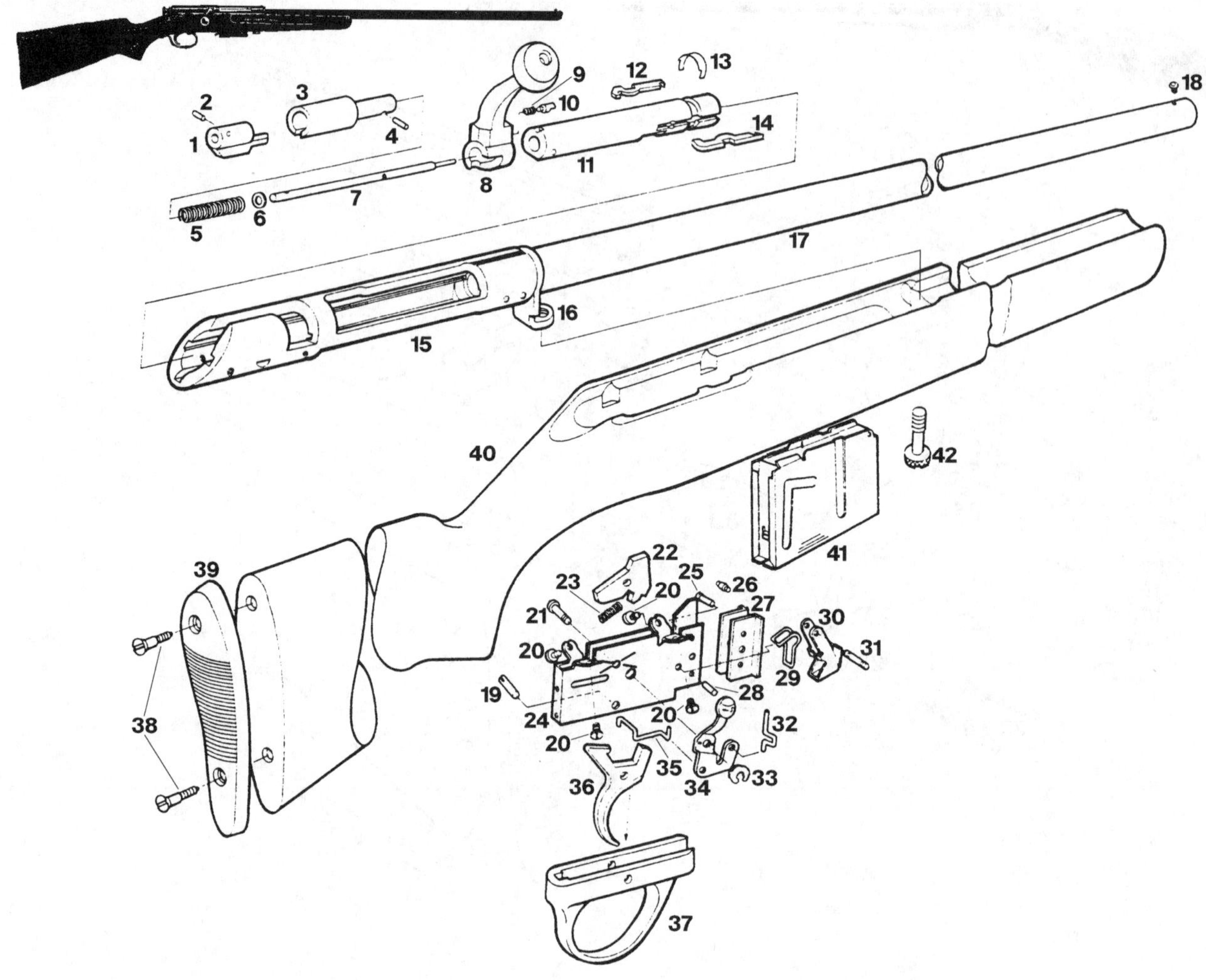

1	Cocking Piece	24	Trigger Bracket
2	Cocking Piece Pin	25	Magazine Retainer Plate Pin, Upper
3	Breechbolt	26	Trigger Bracket Spacer (51E only)
4	Bolt Head Retaining Pin	27	Magazine Retainer Plates
5	Mainspring	28	Magazine Retainer Plate Pin, Lower
6	Mainspring Washer	29	Magazine Latch Spring
7	Firing Pin	30	Magazine Latch
8	Bolt Handle	31	Magazine Latch Pin
9	Bolt Handle Plunger Spring	32	Bolt Head Stop Plunger
10	Bolt Handle Detent Plunger	33	Sear Pin Ring
11	Bolt Head	34	Safety
12	Extractor, Left	35	Safety-Lever
13	Extractor Spring	36	Trigger
14	Extractor, Right	37	Trigger Guard
15	Receiver	38	Buttplate Screws
16	Recoil Lug	39	Buttplate
17	Barrel	40	Stock Assembly
18	Front Sight	41	Magazine Assembly
19	Trigger and Trigger Guard Pin	42	Takedown Screw
20	Trigger Bracket Screws		
21	Sear Pin		
22	Sear		
23	Trigger Spring		

Model 58A, 58B, 58C, 38A and M-51 and Springfield Model 18C and M-951 Bolt-Action Shotgun

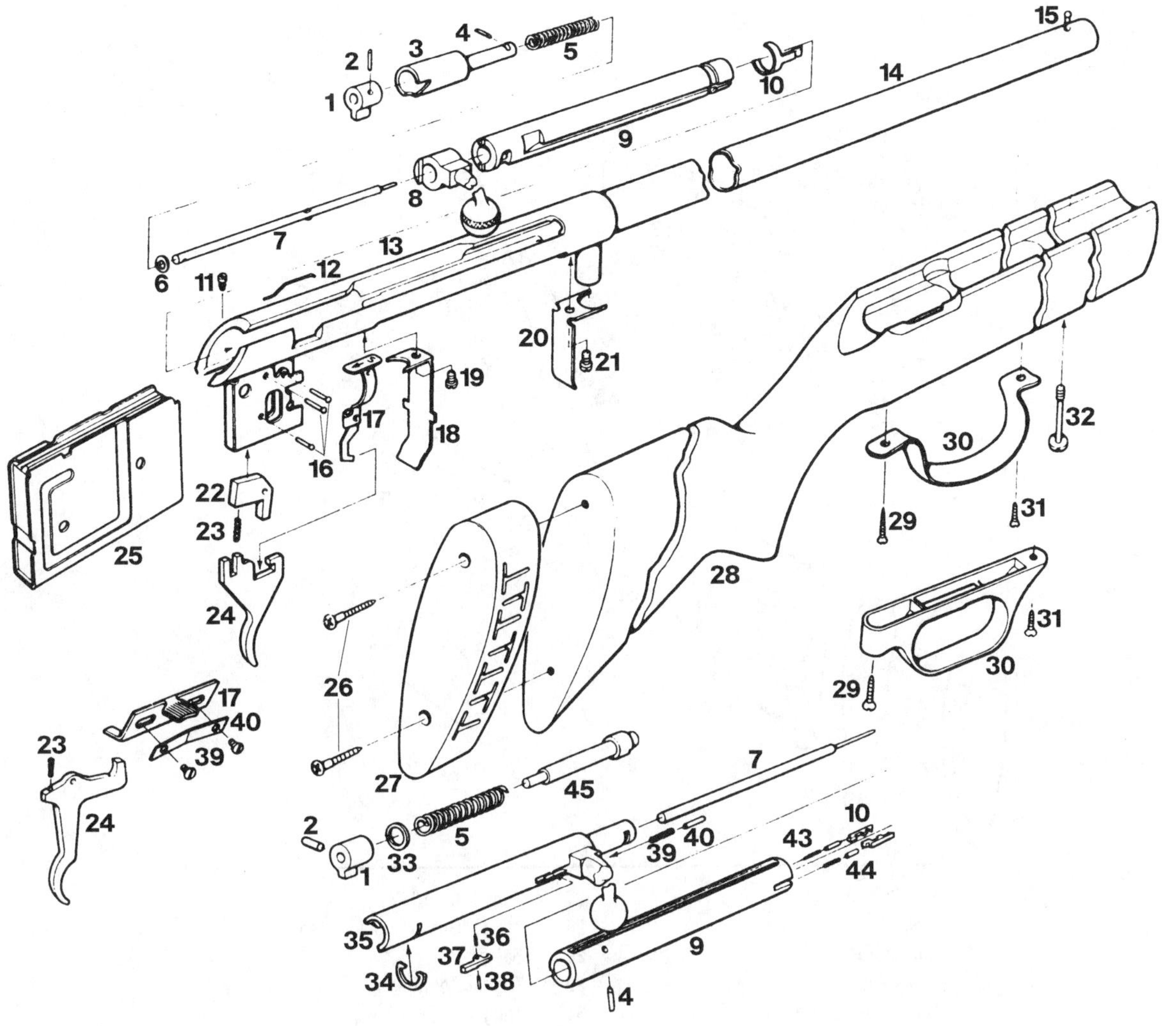

1	Cocking Piece	21	Magazine Retainer Screw, Front	36	Safety Pawl Spring (38A, 58A and 58B only)
2	Cocking Piece Pin	22	Sear	37	Safety Pawl (38A, 58A and 58B only)
3	Breechbolt	23	Trigger Spring	38	Safety Pawl Pin (38A, 58A and 58B only)
4	Bolt Head Retaining Pin	24	Trigger	39	Bolt Head Stop Plunger Spring (38A, 58A and 58B only)
5	Mainspring	25	Magazine Assembly	40	Bolt Head Stop Plunger (38A, 58A and 58B only)
6	Mainspring Washer	26	Recoil Pad Screws	41	Safety Screws (38A, 58A and 58B only)
7	Firing Pin	27	Recoil Pad	42	Safety Spring (38A, 58A and 58B only)
8	Bolt Handle	28	Stock	43	Extractor Springs (38A, 58A and 58B only)
9	Bolt Head	29	Trigger Guard Screw, Long	44	Extractor Plungers (38A, 58A and 58B only)
10	Extractor	30	Trigger Guard	45	Striker (58B only)
11	Bolt Stop Screw	31	Trigger Guard Screw, Short		
12	Ejector	32	Takedown Screw		
13	Receiver	33	Striker Washer (38A, 58A and 58B only)		
14	Barrel	34	Mainspring Retainer (38A, 58A and 58B only)		
15	Front Sight	35	Bolt Body and Handle (38A, 58A and 58B only)		
16	Safety, Sear and Trigger Pins				
17	Safety				
18	Magazine Retainer Spring, Rear				
19	Magazine Retainer Screw, Rear				
20	Magazine Retainer Spring, Front				

Model 58D, 58DAC, 18D and 18DAC Bolt-Action Shotgun

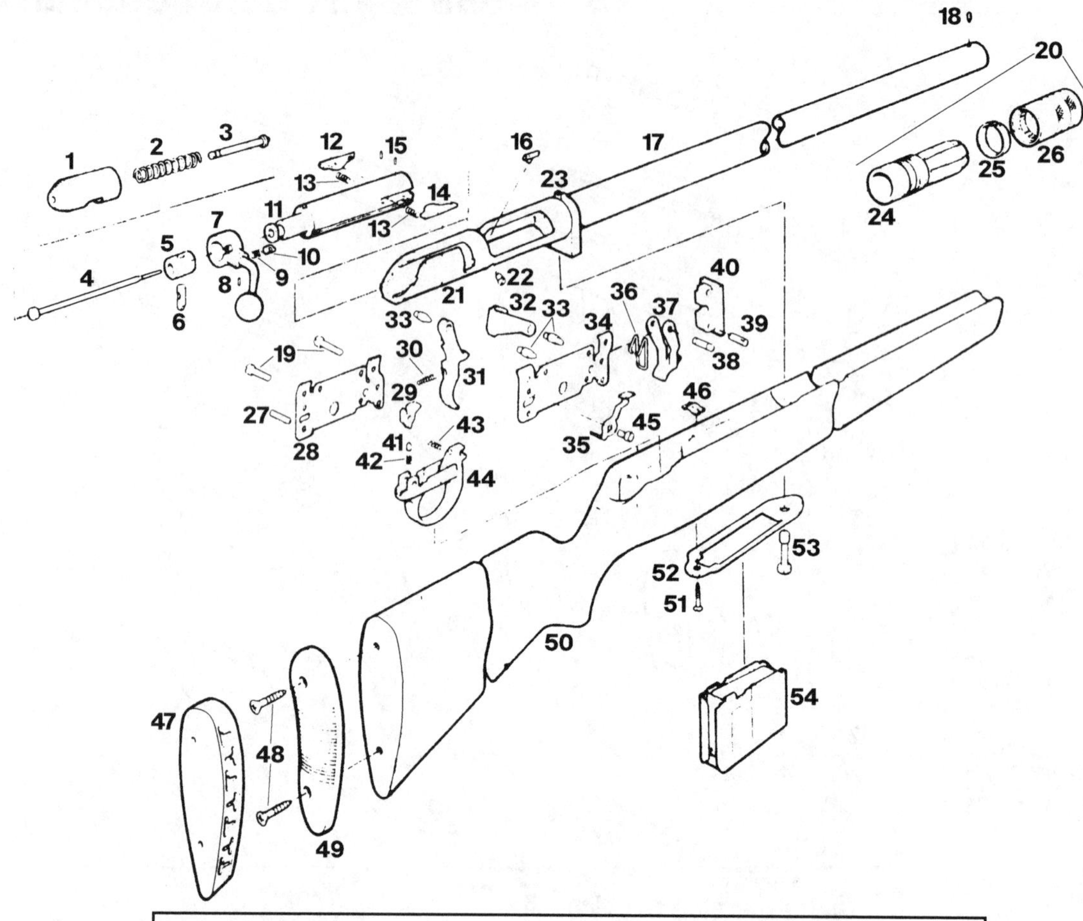

No.	Part	No.	Part
1	Bolt Cap	27	Trigger Guard Pin
2	Mainspring	28	Trigger Guard Housing, Left
3	Indicator Rod	29	Safety
4	Firing Pin	30	Trigger Spring
5	Cocking Piece Bushing	31	Trigger
6	Cocking Piece	32	Sear
7	Bolt Handle	33	Trigger Guard Housing Spacers
8	Bolt Handle Detent Plunger Pin	34	Trigger Guard Housing, Right
9	Bolt Handle Detent Plunger Spring	35	Safety
10	Bolt Handle Detent Plunger	36	Magazine Latch Spring
11	Bolt Head	37	Magazine Latch
12	Extractor, Left	38	Magazine Latch Pin
13	Extractor Springs	39	Magazine Plate Retaining Pin
14	Extractor, Right	40	Magazine Retaining Plate
15	Extractor Pins	41	Safety Detent Plunger
16	Ejector	42	Safety Detent Plunger Spring
17	Barrel	43	Sear Spring
18	Front Sight	44	Trigger Guard
19	Trigger Guard Housing Screws	45	Safety Screw
20	Choke Assembly	46	Floorplate Insert
21	Receiver	47	Recoil Pad
22	Bolt Stop Screw	48	Buttplate Screws (18D only)
23	Recoil Lug	49	Buttplate (18D only)
24	Inner Choke Sleeve (58DAC and 18DAC only)	50	Stock with Recoil Pad
25	Indicator Spring (58DAC and 18DAC only)	51	Floorplate Screw
26	Outer Choke Sleeve (58DAC and 18DAC only)	52	Floorplate
		53	Takedown Screw
		54	Magazine Assembly

Model 77D, 77E, 77EM, 77F, 77H and 77M Series A and Springfield Model 67D, 67E, 67F and 67H Series A Slide-Action Shotgun

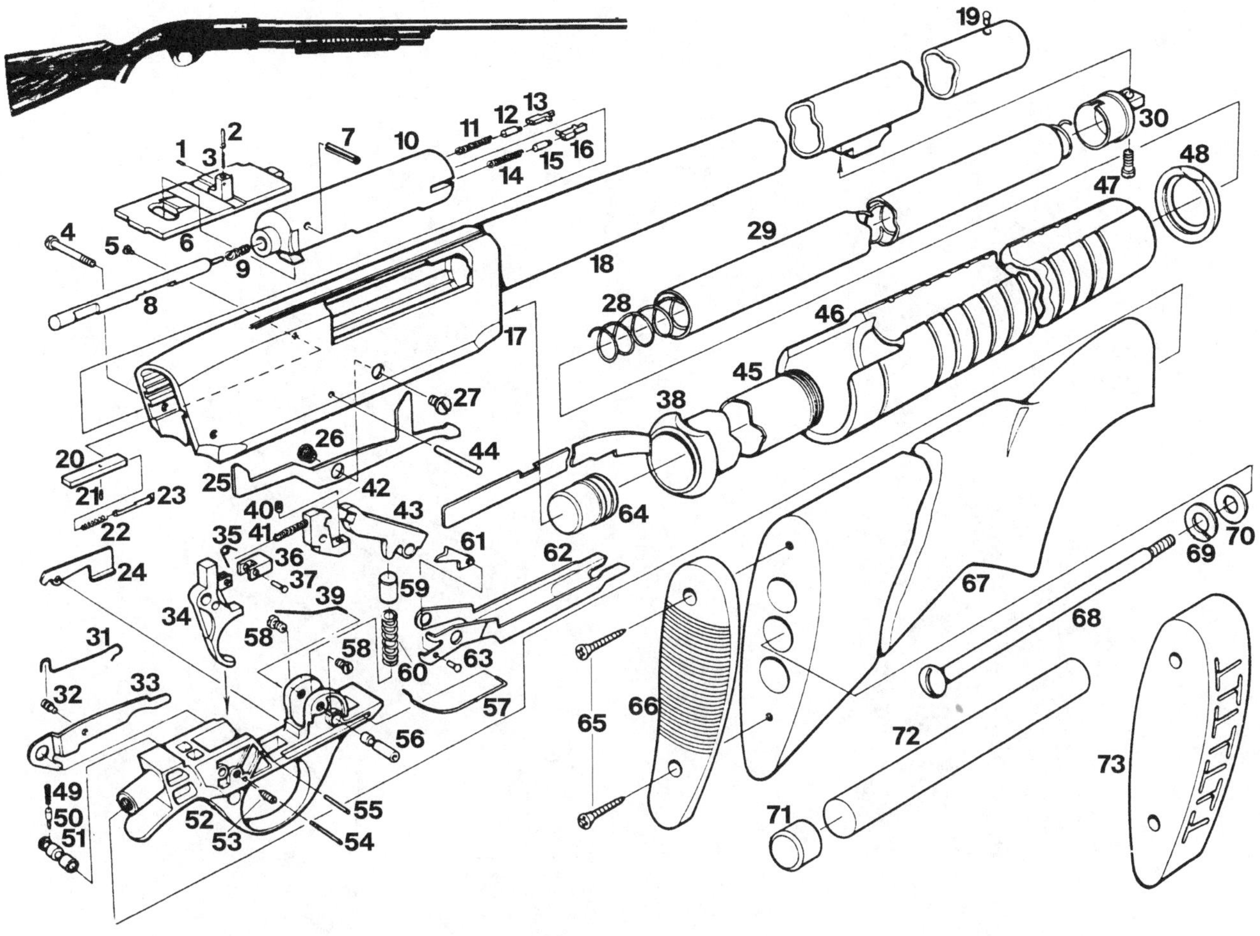

1	Firing Pin Retractor Plunger Pin	25	Cartridge Stop	50	Safety Spring Plunger
2	Firing Pin Retractor Plunger	26	Cartridge Stop Pivot Nut	51	Safety
3	Firing Pin Retractor Plunger Spring	27	Cartridge Stop Pivot Screw	52	Trigger Guard
4	Trigger Guard Screw	28	Magazine Spring	53	Trigger Adjusting Screw
5	Ejector Screw	29	Magazine Tube	54	Trigger Pin
6	Slide Assembly	30	Magazine Plug	55	Sear Pin
7	Firing Pin Stop Pin	31	Slide Lock Spring	56	Hammer Bushing
8	Firing Pin	32	Slide Lock Spring Stud	57	Lifter Spring
9	Firing Pin Spring	33	Slide Lock Assembly	58	Lifter Screw
10	Breechbolt	34	Trigger	59	Mainspring Plunger
11	Extractor Spring, Left	35	Sear Trip Spring	60	Mainspring
12	Extractor Plunger, Left	36	Sear Trip	61	Lifter Pawl
13	Extractor, Left	37	Sear Trip Pin	62	Lifter Assembly
14	Extractor Spring, Right	38	Operating Handle Collar, Rear	63	Lifter Pawl Pin
15	Extractor Plunger, Right	39	Slide Lock Release Spring	64	Magazine Follower
16	Extractor, Right	40	Sear Adjusting Screw	65	Buttplate Screws
17	Receiver	41	Trigger Spring	66	Buttplate
18	Barrel	42	Sear	67	Stock
19	Front Sight	43	Hammer	68	Stock Bolt
20	Ejector Assembly	44	Trigger Guard Pin	69	Stock Bolt Lock Washer
21	Ejector Pin	45	Operating Handle Bar Assembly	70	Stock Bolt Washer
22	Ejector Spring	46	Operating Handle	71	Recoil Weight Buffer
23	Ejector Plunger	47	Magazine Plug Screw	72	Recoil Weight
24	Slide Lock Release	48	Operating Handle Collar, Front	73	Recoil Pad
		49	Safety Spring		

Model 940, 940D, 940DY, 940E and 940EY and Springfield Model 947, 947D and 947E Single Shot Shotgun

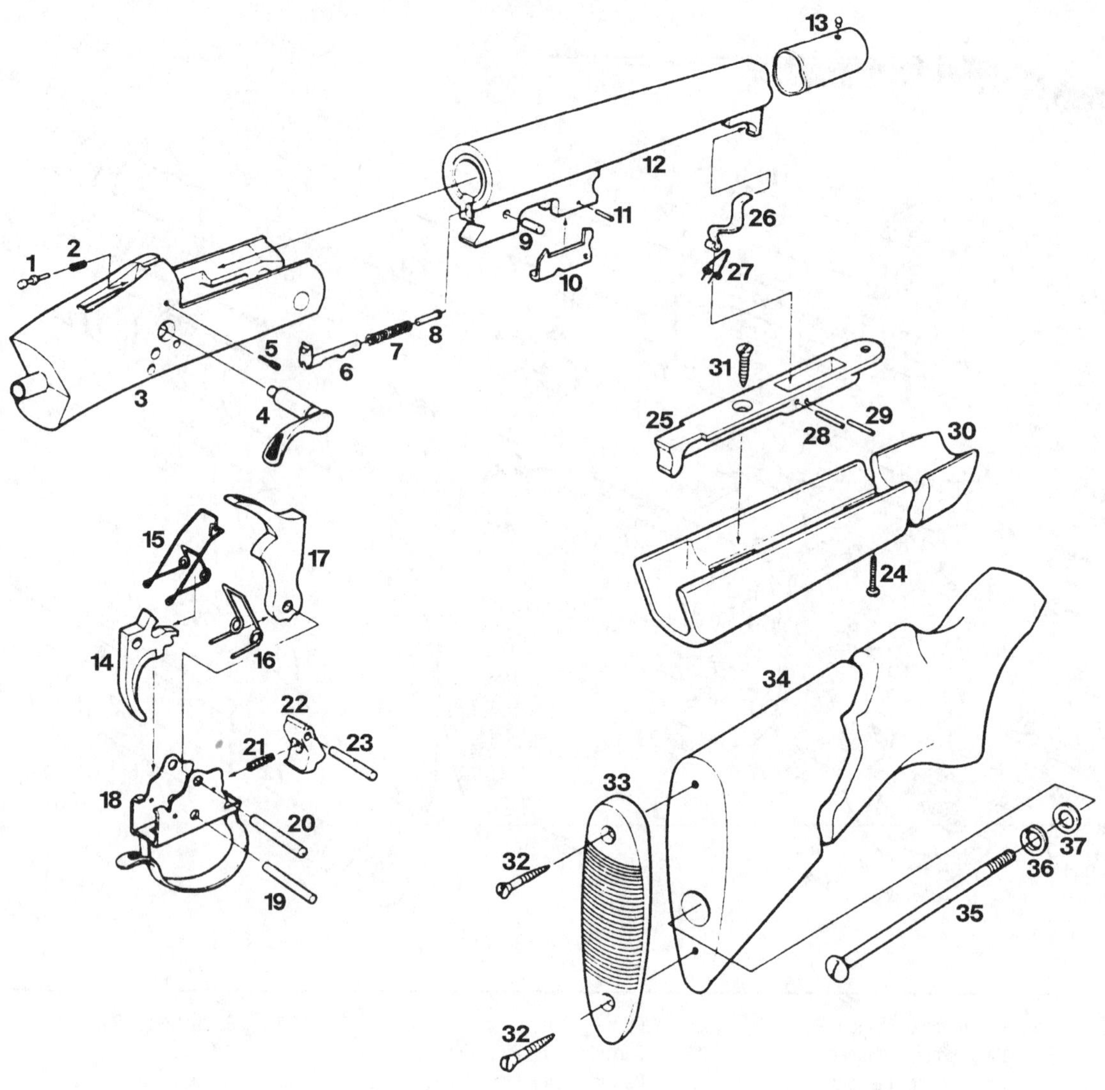

1	Firing Pin	**20**	Hammer Pin
2	Firing Pin Spring	**21**	Locking Bolt Spring
3	Frame	**22**	Locking Bolt
4	Side Lever	**23**	Locking Bolt Pin
5	Firing Pin Screw	**24**	Forend Screw
6	Extractor	**25**	Forend Iron
7	Ejector Spring	**26**	Forend Spring
8	Ejector Starter Pin	**27**	Forend Spring Spring
9	Extractor Stop Pin	**28**	Forend Spring Pin
10	Ejector Hook	**29**	Forend Spring Spring Pin
11	Extractor Lever Pin	**30**	Forend Wood
12	Barrel	**31**	Forend Iron Screw
13	Front Sight	**32**	Buttplate Screws
14	Trigger	**33**	Buttplate
15	Trigger Spring	**34**	Stock
16	Hammer Spring	**35**	Stock Bolt
17	Hammer	**36**	Stock Bolt Lock Washer
18	Trigger Guard	**37**	Stock Bolt Washer
19	Trigger Pin		

Model 9478 Single Shot Shotgun

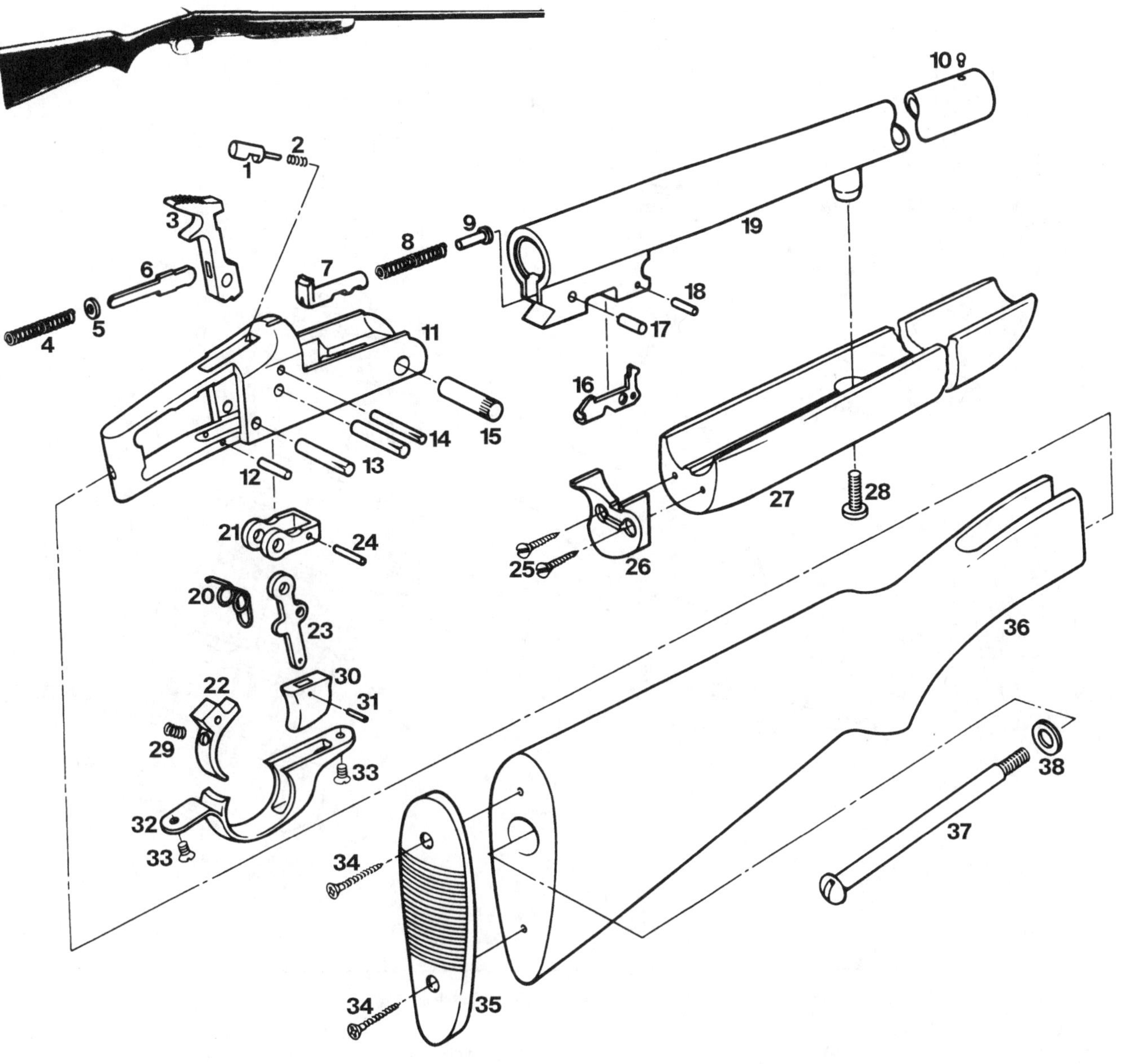

1	Firing Pin
2	Firing Pin Spring
3	Hammer
4	Mainspring
5	Breechbolt Spring Washer
6	Mainspring Plunger
7	Extractor
8	Ejector Spring
9	Ejector Starter Pin
10	Front Sight
11	Frame
12	Trigger Pin
13	Locking Bolt/Hammer Pin
14	Firing Pin Retaining Pin
15	Joint Pin
16	Ejector Hook
17	Extractor Stop Pin
18	Extractor Lever Spring/Stop Pin
19	Barrel
20	Locking Bolt Spring
21	Locking Bolt
22	Trigger
23	Locking Bolt Arm
24	Locking Bolt Arm Pin
25	Forend Head Screws
26	Forend Pivot Plate
27	Forend Wood
28	Forend Screw
29	Trigger Spring
30	Release Button
31	Release Button Pin
32	Trigger Guard
33	Trigger Guard Screws
34	Buttplate Screws
35	Buttplate
36	Stock Assembly
37	Stock Bolt
38	Stock Bolt Washer

Parts Not Shown

- Recoil Pad
- Recoil Weight
- Recoil Weight Buffer

Model 95, Savage M-96 and Sears 101.100 Single Shot Shotgun

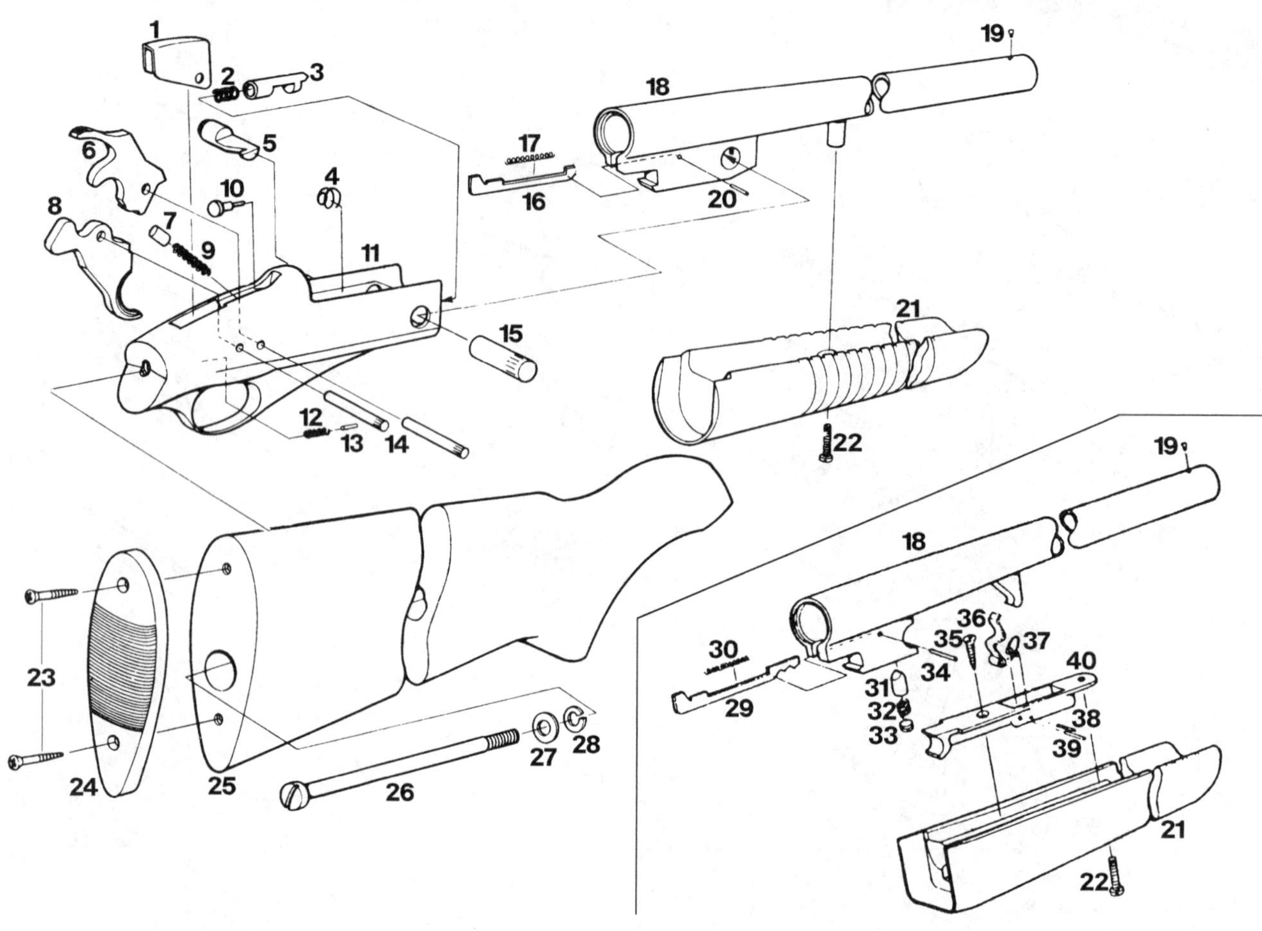

1	Cover Plate	**24**	Buttplate
2	Lock Spring	**25**	Stock
3	Lock	**26**	Stock Bolt
4	Lock Release Spring	**27**	Stock Bolt Washer
5	Lock Release	**28**	Stock Bolt Lock Washer
6	Hammer	**Models 96 and 101.100**	
7	Mainspring Plunger	**29**	Ejector
8	Trigger	**30**	Ejector Spring
9	Mainspring	**31**	Ejector Sear
10	Firing Pin	**32**	Ejector Sear Spring
11	Frame	**33**	Ejector Screw
12	Trigger Spring	**34**	Ejector Pin
13	Trigger Spring Plunger	**35**	Forend Iron Screw
14	Trigger Pin or Hammer Pins	**36**	Forend Spring
15	Joint Pin	**37**	Forend Spring Spring
16	Extractor	**38**	Forend Spring Pin
17	Extractor and Ejector Spring	**39**	Forend Spring Spring Pin
18	Barrel	**40**	Forend Iron
19	Front Sight	**Parts Not Shown**	
20	Extractor and Ejector Spring Pin		Ejector Activating Pin
21	Forend Wood		Firing Pin Spring
22	Forend Screw		Joint Locating Pin
23	Buttplate Screws		

Model 94B, 94BT, 94C, 94Y, 107, 107BT and 107C Single Shot Shotgun

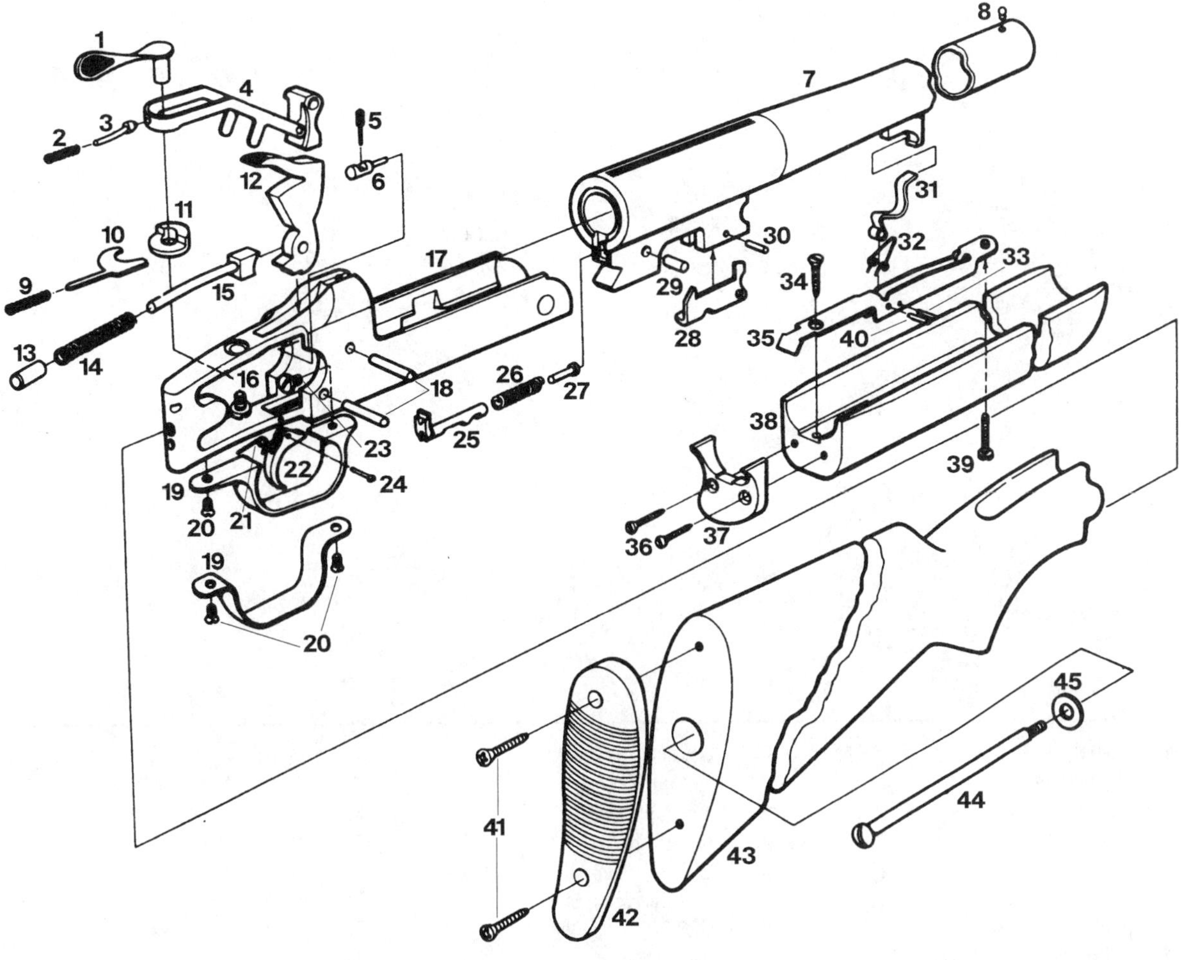

No.	Part	No.	Part
1	Top Snap	24	Trigger Pin
2	Locking Bolt Spring	25	Extractor
3	Locking Bolt Plunger	26	Ejector Spring
4	Locking Bolt Assembly	27	Ejector Starter Pin
5	Firing Pin Screw	28	Ejector Hook
6	Firing Pin	29	Extractor Stop Pin
7	Barrel	30	Extractor Lever Pin
8	Front Sight	31	Forend Spring
9	Top Snap Plunger Spring	32	Forend Spring Spring
10	Top Snap Plunger	33	Forend Spring Spring Pin
11	Top Snap Sleeve	34	Forend Spring Housing Screw
12	Hammer	35	Forend Spring Housing
13	Mainspring Plunger Seat	36	Forend Iron Head Screws
14	Mainspring	37	Forend Iron Head
15	Mainspring Plunger Assembly	38	Forend
16	Top Snap Screw	39	Forend Screw
17	Frame	40	Forend Spring Pin
18	Hammer Pins	41	Buttplate Screws
19	Trigger Guard	42	Buttplate
20	Trigger Guard Screws	43	Stock
21	Trigger Spring	44	Stock Bolt
22	Trigger	45	Stock Bolt Washer
23	Top Snap Screw		

AUG Autoloading Rifle

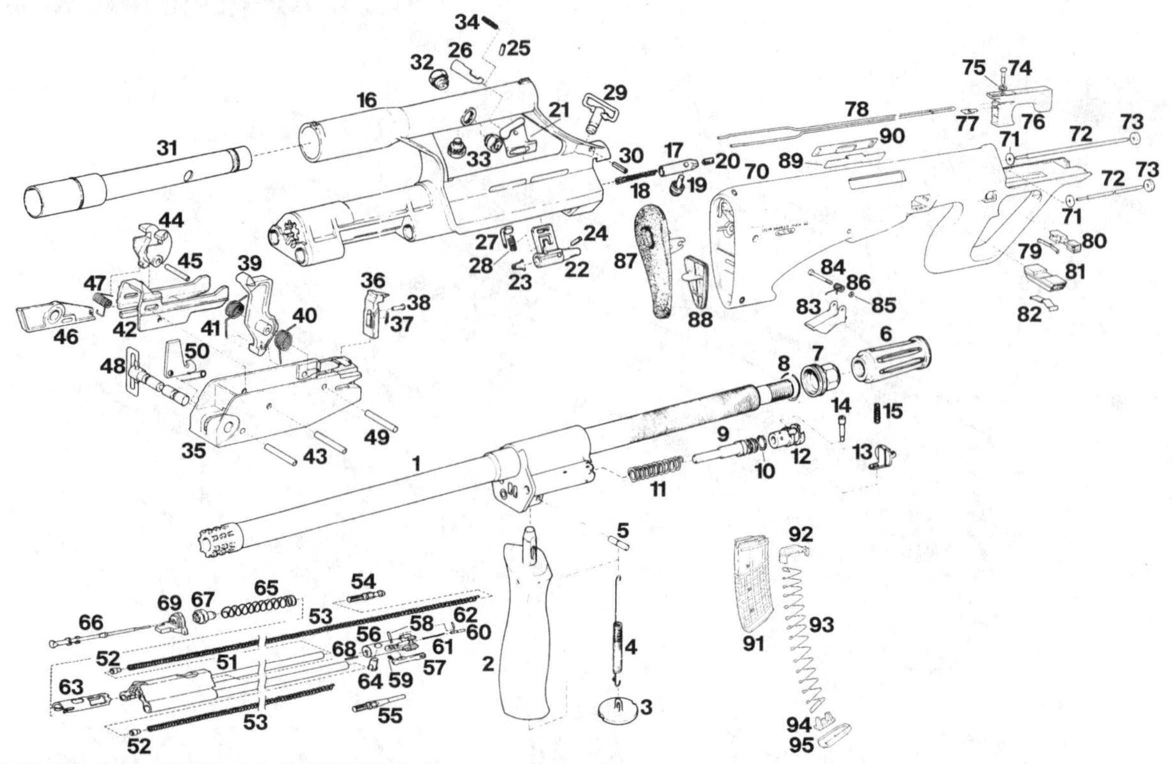

1	Barrel	33	Elevating and Windage Adjustment Screws	66	Firing Pin
2	Barrel Grip	34	Cocking Slide Knob Spring	67	Bolt Spring Sleeve
3	Barrel Grip Cap	35	Trigger Housing	68	Control Bolt Pin
4	Barrel Grip Spring	36	Lock Bolt Catch	69	Cocking Piece
5	Barrel Grip Pin	37	Lock Bolt Catch Spring	70	Stock
6	Flash Hider	38	Lock Bolt Catch Bolt	71	Buffer Plates
7	Flash Hider Nut	39	Hammer	72	Buffer Guide Rods
8	Flash Hider Nut Spring	40	Hammer Spring, Right	73	Buffers
9	Gas Piston	41	Hammer Spring, Left	74	Sear Lever Cap Screw
10	Gas Piston Ring	42	Slide	75	Sear Lever Cap Screw Washer
11	Gas Piston Spring	43	Pivot Pins	76	Trigger
12	Gas Plug Head	44	Disconnector Lever	77	Trigger Nut
13	Gas Plug Pressure Piece	45	Disconnector Lever Pin	78	Sear Lever
14	Gas Plug Plunger	46	Retaining Bolt Lock	79	Safety Button Spring
15	Gas Plug Spring	47	Trigger Spring	80	Safety Button
16	Receiver	48	Sling Swivel	81	Housing Latch
17	Barrel Lock Pin	49	Hammer Pivot Pin	82	Housing Latch Spring
18	Barrel Lock Pin Spring	50	Drop Safety	83	Magazine Release Button
19	Barrel Locking Catch	51	Slide Piece Body	84	Magazine Release Button Screw
20	Barrel Locking Catch Retaining Screw	52	Lock Spring Plunger	85	Magazine Release Button Screw Nut
21	Cocking Slide Knob	53	Lock Spring	86	Magazine Release Button Spring
22	Cocking Slide Body	54	Lock Spring Follower, Left	87	Buttplate
23	Cocking Slide Spring	55	Lock Spring Follower, Right	88	Cleaning Kit Compartment Lid
24	Cocking Slide Adaptor Sleeve	56	Right Ejection Bolt	89	Inner Ejection Port Cover
25	Cocking Slide Grip Adaptor Sleeve	57	Extractor	90	Outer Ejection Port Cover
26	Cocking Slide Grip Knob	58	Extractor Pin	91	Magazine Body
27	Cocking Slide Coupling Piece	59	Extractor Spring	92	Follower
28	Coupling Piece Spring	60	Ejector	93	Magazine Spring
29	Sling Swivel	61	Ejector Spring	94	Magazine Spring Lock
30	Sling Swivel Pin	62	Ejector Pin	95	Magazine Floorplate
31	Optical Tube	63	Locking Piece		
32	Optical Tube Retaining Screw	64	Control Bolt		
		65	Bolt Spring		

Luxus Model L and M Bolt-Action Rifle

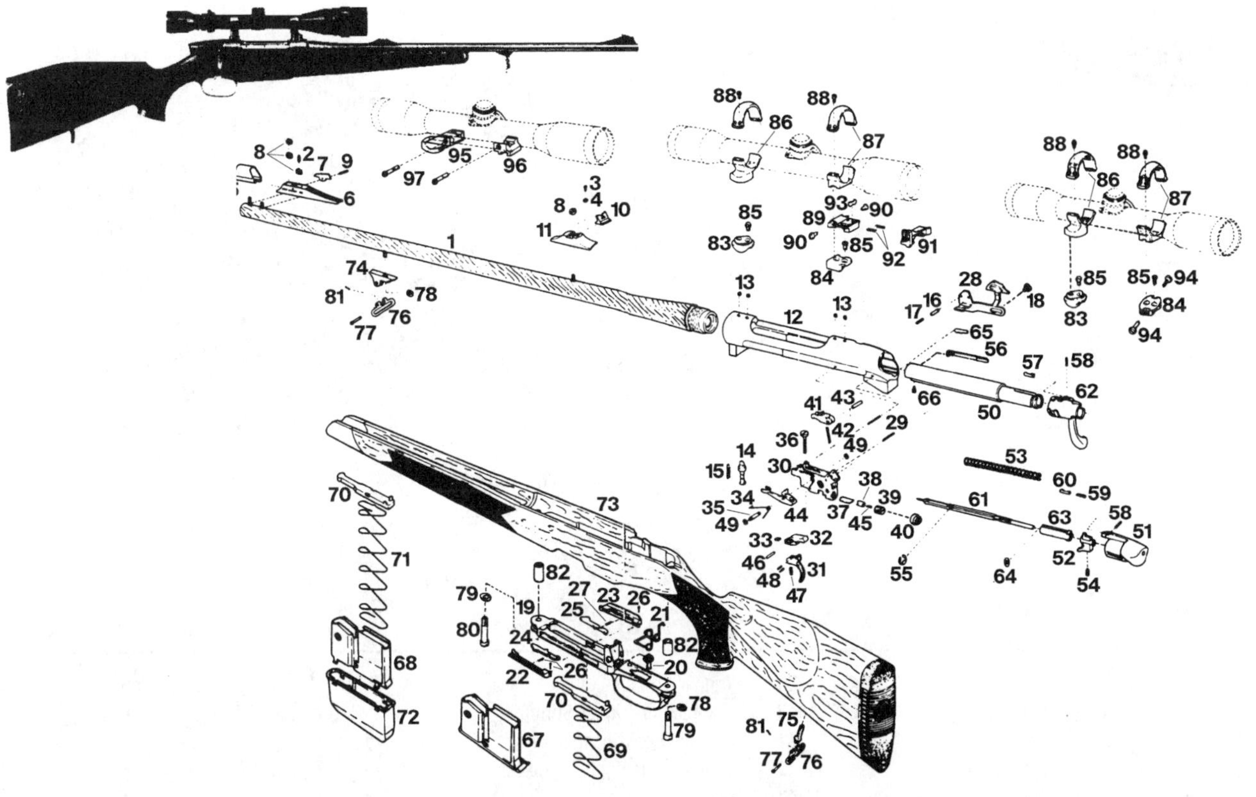

1	Barrel
2	Front Sight Blade Spring
3	Rear Sight Screw
4	Rear Sight Screw Lock Washer
5	Front Sight Hood
6	Front Sight Ramp
7	Front Sight Blade
8	Nuts
9	Front Sight Blade Pin
10	Rear Sight Leaf
11	Rear Sight Base
12	Receiver
13	Scope Mount Filler Screws
14	Stop bolt
15	Bolt Stop Spring
16	Safety Catch Detent
17	Safety Catch Detent Spring
18	Safety Catch Slide Retaining Screw
19	Trigger Guard
20	Trigger Guard Pin
21	Magazine Catch Spring
22	Left Magazine Catch Button
23	Right Magazine Catch Button
24	Left Magazine Catch
25	Right Magazine Catch
26	Blanking Screws
27	Spring
28	Safety Catch Slide
29	Trigger Housing Pins
30	Trigger Housing
31	Trigger
32	Rocker
33	Safety Screw
34	Spring
35	Pin
36	Trigger Adjusting Screw
37	Leaf Spring
38	Bolt Spring
39	Screw
40	Nut
41	Sear
42	Sear Spring
43	Sear Pivot
44	Sear Lever
45	Spring
46	Rocker Pivot
47	Blanking Screw
48	Trigger Pins
49	Circlip
50	Bolt Body
51	Bolt End Cap
52	Bolt Guide
53	Mainspring
54	Blanking Screw
55	Striker Circlip
56	Extractor
57	Bolt Handle Key
58	Bolt Handle Pin
59	Striker Sleeve Spring
60	Striker Sleeve Spring Plunger
61	Striker
62	Bolt Handle
63	Striker Sleeve
64	Striker Sleeve Spacer
65	Ejector
66	Ejector Screw
67	Magazine Body (3-shot)
68	Magazine Body (6-shot)
69	Magazine Spring (3-shot)
70	Magazine Folower
71	Magazine Spring (6-shot)
72	Magazine Extension (6-shot)
73	Stock
74	Swivel Base
75	Rear Swivel Base
76	Sling Swivels
77	Swivel Pivot Screws
78	Swivel Pivot Nut
79	Front Guard Screw Washer
80	Front Guard Screw
81	Swivel Pivot Spring Washers
82	Front Guard Screw Spacers
83	Front Scope Mount Base
84	Rear Scope Mount Base
85	Scope Mount Base Screws
86	Front Scope Rings
87	Rear Scope Rings
88	Scope Ring Screws
89	Windage Base
90	Windage Dovetail Screws
91	Windage Slide
92	Windage Slide Springs
93	Windage Slide Spring Key
94	Windage Screws
95	Front Mounting Rail Base
96	Rear Mounting Rail Base
97	Mounting Rail Screws

Model M, SL, L, S and S/T Bolt-Action Rifle

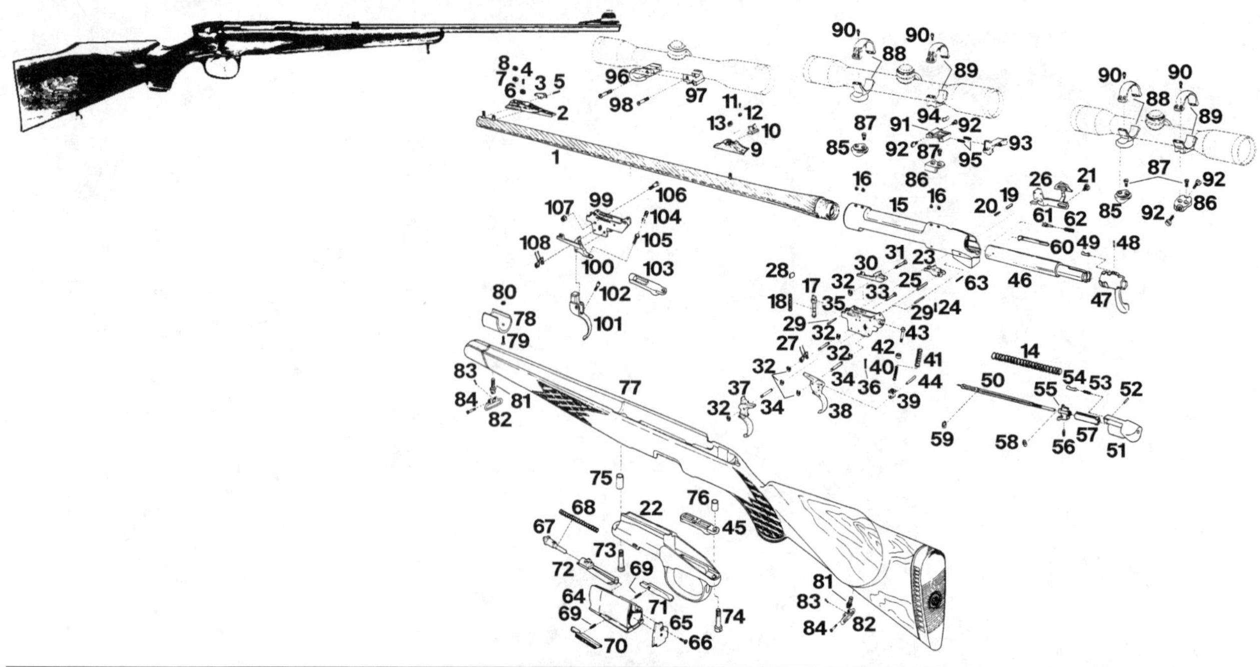

1	Barrel
2	Front Sight Ramp
3	Front Sight Blade
4	Front Sight Blade Spring
5	Front Sight Pin
6	Front Sight Blade Spring Nut
7	Front Sight Ramp Washer
8	Front Sight Ramp Nut
9	Rear Sight Base
10	Rear Sight Blade
11	Rear Sight Screw
12	Clamp Ring
13	Rear Sight Base Nut
14	Mainspring
15	Receiver
16	Scope Mount Filler Screws
17	Bolt Stop
18	Bolt Stop Spring
19	Safety Catch Detent
20	Safety Catch Defent Spring
21	Safety Catch Retaining Screw
22	Trigger Guard
23	Sear
24	Sear Spring
25	Sear Pin
26	Safety Catch Slide
27	Trigger Return Spring
28	Slide Leaf
29	Trigger Housing Pins
30	Set Trigger Sear Lever
31	Set Trigger Sear Lever Pin
32	Circlips
33	Trigger Stop Pin
34	Trigger Pins
35	Trigger Housing
36	Trigger Adjusting Screw
37	Standard Trigger
38	Set Trigger
39	Trigger Coupling Link
40	Internal Set Trigger Spring
41	External Set Trigger Spring
42	Trigger Coupling Link Spacer
43	Locking Screw
44	Trigger Coupling Pin
45	Set Trigger Insert
46	Bolt Body
47	Bolt Handle
48	Bolt Handle Pin
49	Bolt Handle Key
50	Striker
51	Bolt End Cap
52	Bolt End Cap Pin
53	Bolt End Cap Detent Spring
54	Bolt End Cap Detent
55	Bolt Guide
56	Blanking Screw
57	Bolt Guide Sleeve
58	Bolt Guide Washer
59	Striker Circlip
60	Extractor
61	Ejector
62	Ejector Spring
63	Ejector Pin
64	Magazine Body
65	Magazine End Cap
66	Magazine End Cap Screw
67	Magazine Rotor Axis Pin
68	Magazine Follower Spring
69	Magazine Catch Spring
70	Left Magazine Catch
71	Right Magazine Catch
72	Magazine Follower
73	Front Trigger Guard Screw
74	Rear Trigger Guard Screw
75	Front Trigger Guard Screw Bushing
76	Rear Trigger Guard Screw Bushing
77	Stock
78	Forend Tip
79	Forend Tip Screw
80	Forend Tip Screw Nut
81	Sling Swivel Stud
82	Sling Swivel
83	Swivel Spring Washer
84	Sling Swivel Screw
85	Front Scope Mount Base
86	Rear Scope Mount Base
87	Scope Mount Base Screws
88	Front Scope Rings
89	Rear Scope Rings
90	Scope Ring Screws
91	Windage Base
92	Windage Base Screws
93	Rear Scope Mount Slide
94	Windage Slide Spring
95	Rear Mount Slide Springs
96	Front Mounting Rail Base
97	Rear Mounting Rail Base
98	Dovetail Base Screws
99	Standard Trigger Housing
100	Standard Trigger Sear Lever
101	Single Trigger
102	Standard Trigger Set Screw
103	Standard Trigger Housing Insert
104	Standard Trigger Spring
105	Standard Trigger Adjusting Screw
106	Standard Trigger Eccentric Screw
107	Standard Trigger Eccentric Screw Nut
108	Standard Trigger Return Spring

Model 1895 Straight-Pull Rifle

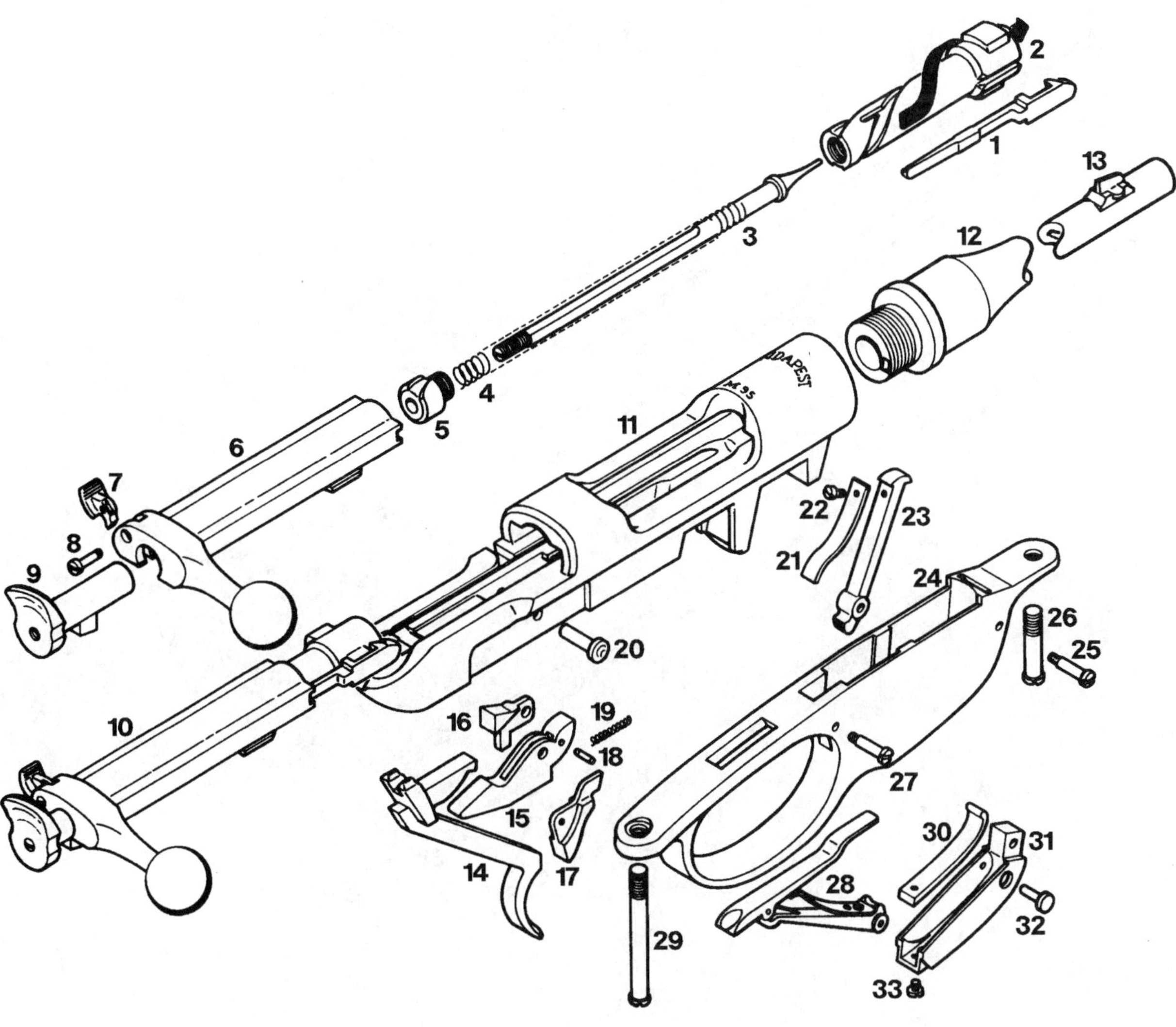

1	Extractor	**18**	Ejector Pin
2	Bolt Head	**19**	Sear Spring
3	Firing Pin	**20**	Sear Pin
4	Firing Pin Spring	**21**	Clip Latch Spring
5	Firing Pin Spring Retainer	**22**	Clip Latch Spring Screw
6	Bolt Body	**23**	Clip Latch
7	Safety	**24**	Trigger Guard
8	Safety Screw	**25**	Magazine Floorplate Screw
9	Cocking Piece	**26**	Front Guard Screw
10	Bolt Assembly	**27**	Clip Latch Screw
11	Receiver	**28**	Magazine Follower Assembly
12	Barrel	**29**	Rear Guard Screw
13	Front Sight	**30**	Magazine Spring
14	Trigger and Bolt Stop	**31**	Magazine Floorplate
15	Sear Lever	**32**	Follower Pivot Pin
16	Sear	**33**	Magazine Spring Screw
17	Ejector		

Condor I and II Over/Under Shotgun

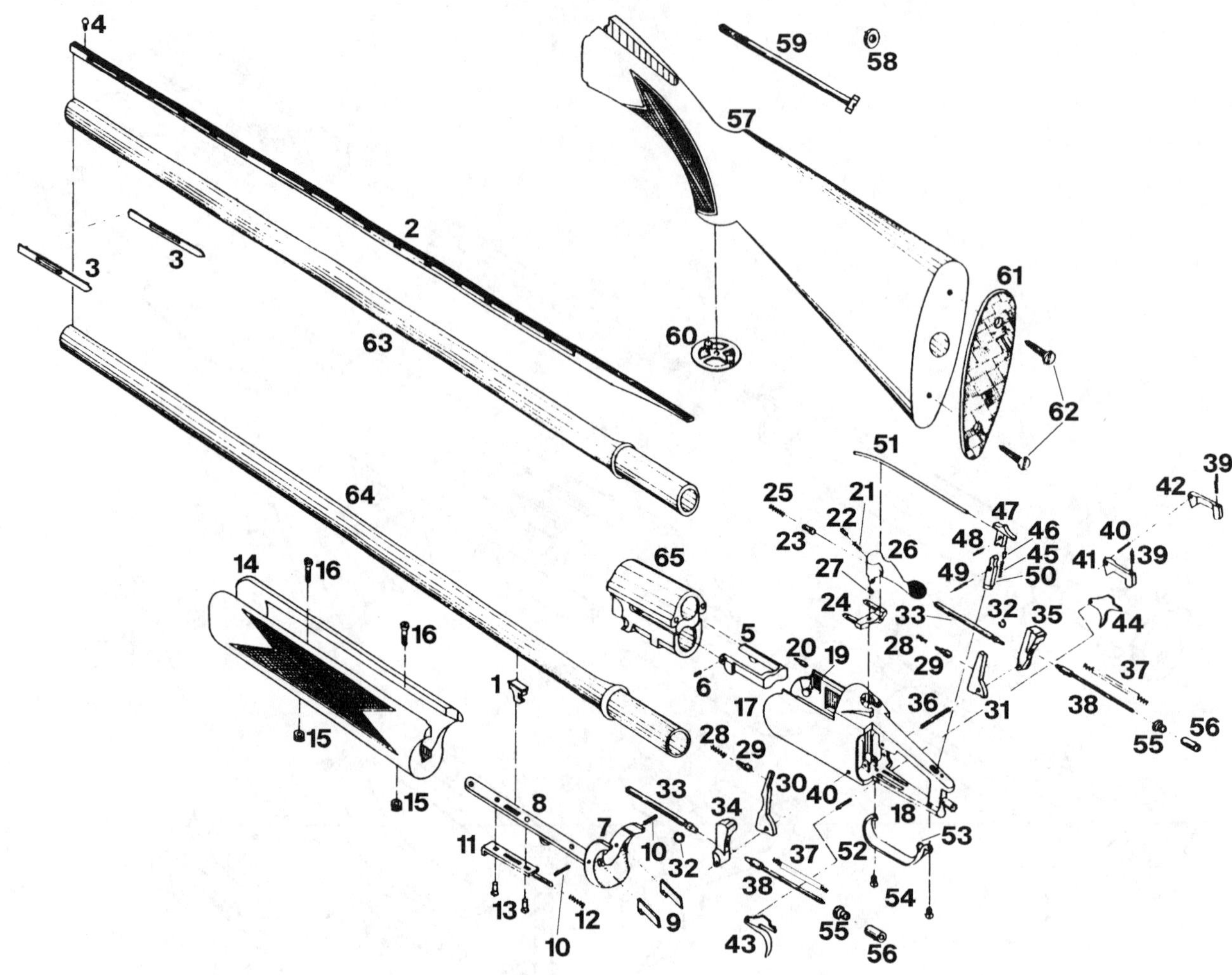

1	Forend Iron Catch
2	Top Ventilated Rib
3	Ventilated Side Ribs
4	Front Sight
5	Extractor
6	Extractor Limiter Screw
7	Forend Iron Assembly
8	Forend Bar
9	Ejector Levers
10	Ejector Lever Pins
11	Forend Latch
12	Forend Latch Spring
13	Forend Latch Screws
14	Forend
15	Forend Iron Nuts
16	Forend Iron Screws
17	Frame
18	Lower Tang
19	Trunnion Pin
20	Top Lever Release Pin
21	Top Lever Pin Spring
22	Top Lever Pin
23	Top lever Spring Plunger
24	Top Lever Lock Fastener
25	Top Lever Spring
26	Top Lever
27	Top Lever Retaining Pin
28	Firing Pin Springs
29	Firing Pins
30	Top Firing Pin Plunger
31	Bottom Firing Pin Plunger
32	Cocking Lever Rings
33	Cocking Levers
34	Left Hammer
35	Right Hammer
36	Hammer Pin
37	Hammer Springs
38	Hammer Spring Guides
39	Sear Springs
40	Sear and Trigger Pins
41	Left Sear
42	Right Sear
43	Left Trigger
44	Right Trigger
45	Safety Spring
46	Safety Limit Pin
47	Safety Catch
48	Safety Catch Pins
49	Safety Catch Lever Pin
50	Safety Catch Lever
51	Safety Bar
52	Trigger Guard
53	Trigger Guard Internal Arch
54	Trigger Guard Screws
55	Hammer Spring Guide Bushings
56	Hammer Spring Guide Limiter Nuts
57	Stock
58	Stock Bolt Washer
59	Stock Bolt
60	Grip Cap
61	Buttplate
62	Buttplate Screws
63	Upper Barrel
64	Lower Barrel
65	Barrel Monoblock

Uplander and Coachgun Side-by-Side Shotgun

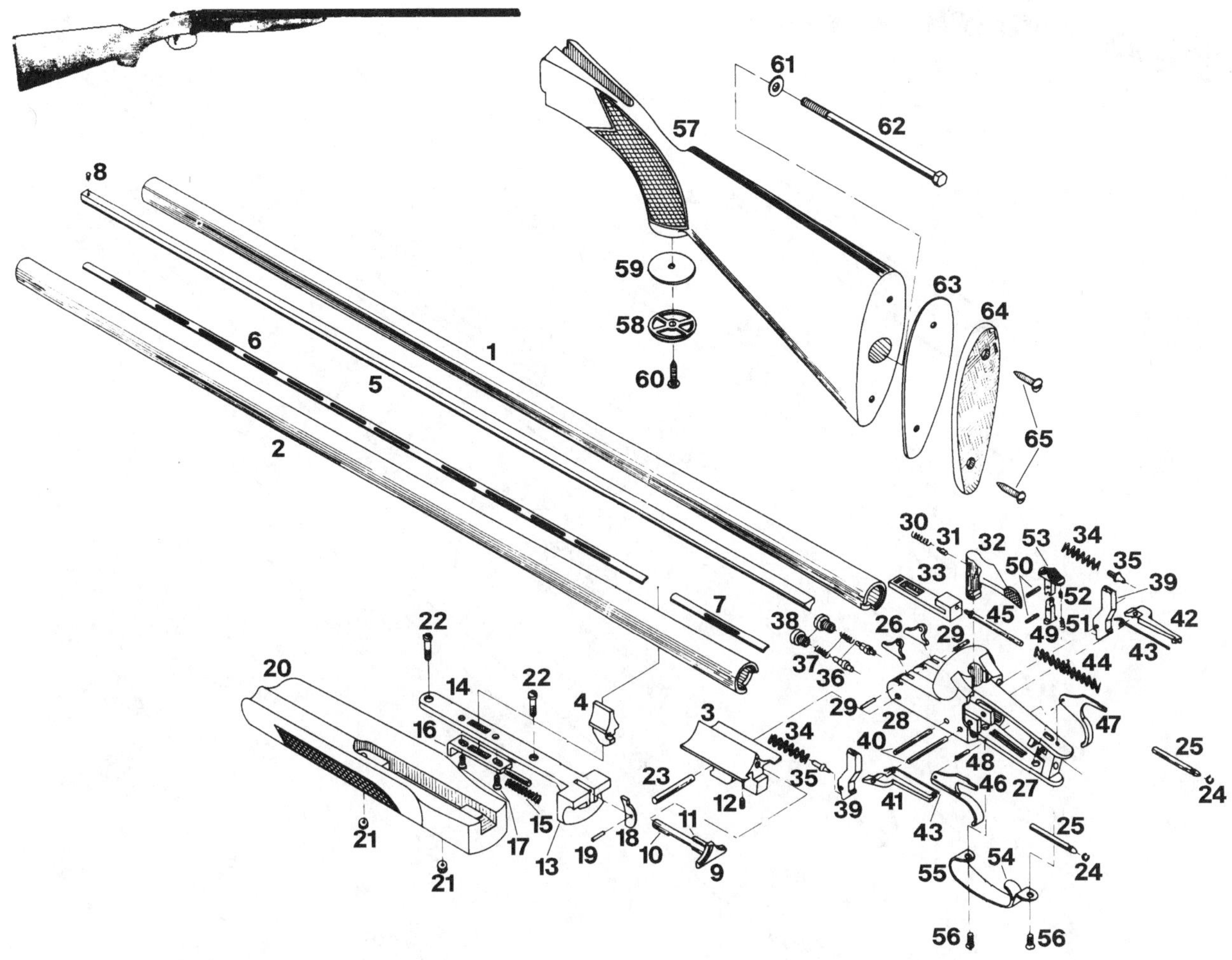

1	Right Barrel	**23**	Hinge Pin	**45**	Top Lever Spring Guide
2	Left Barrel	**24**	Cocking Lever Rod Circlips	**46**	Left Trigger
3	Forend Latch Supporting Piece	**25**	Cocking Lever Rods	**47**	Right Trigger
4	Forend Iron Catch	**26**	Cocking Levers	**48**	Trigger Pin
5	Top Rib	**27**	Lower Tang	**49**	Trigger Lock Lever
6	Long Bottom Rib	**28**	Frame	**50**	Trigger Lock Lever Pins
7	Short Bottom Rib	**29**	Cocking Lever Pins	**51**	Trigger Lock Spring
8	Front Sight	**30**	Top Lever Lock Spring	**52**	Trigger Lock Ball Pin
9	Extractor	**31**	Top Lever Lock Pin	**53**	Safety-Lever
10	Extractor Pin	**32**	Top Lever	**54**	Trigger Guard Arch
11	Extractor Guide Pin	**33**	Latch Lock	**55**	Trigger Guard
12	Extractor Limit Screw	**34**	Hammer Springs	**56**	Trigger Guard Screws
13	Forend Iron	**35**	Hammer Spring Plungers	**57**	Stock
14	Forend Bar	**36**	Firing Pins	**58**	Grip Cap
15	Forend Iron Spring	**37**	Firing Pin Springs	**59**	Grip Cap Spacer
16	Forend Latch	**38**	Firing Pin Bushings	**60**	Grip Cap Screw
17	Forend Iron Screws	**39**	Hammers	**61**	Stock Bolt Washer
18	Extractor Lever	**40**	Hammer Pins	**62**	Stock Bolt
19	Extractor Lever Pin	**41**	Left Sear	**63**	Buttplate Spacer
20	Forend	**42**	Right Sear	**64**	Buttplate
21	Forend Iron Fastening Nuts	**43**	Sear Springs	**65**	Buttplate Screws
22	Forend Lock Screws	**44**	Top Lever Spring		

Model 94 and 96 Bolt-Action Rifle

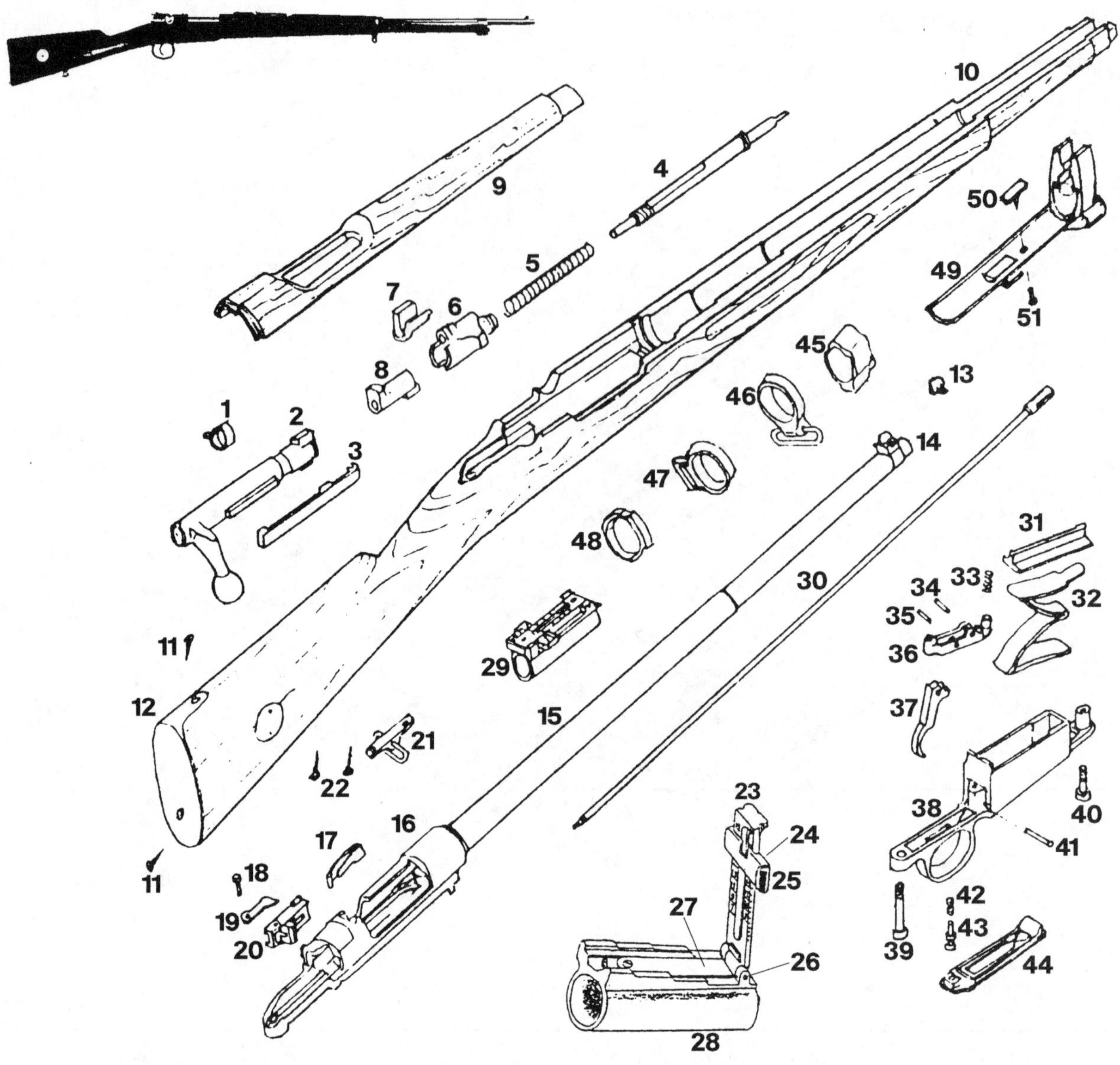

1	Extractor Collar	**21**	Rear Sling Swivel	**41**	Floor Plate Catch Pin
2	Bolt Body	**22**	Rear Swivel Screws	**42**	Floor Plate Catch Spring
3	Extractor	**23**	Rear Sight Ladder	**43**	Floor Plate Catch
4	Firing Pin	**24**	Rear Sight Slide	**44**	Floor Plate
5	Firing Pin Spring	**25**	Rear Sight Slide Catch	**45**	Front Barrel Band (Mod. 96)
6	Bolt Sleeve	**26**	Rear Sight Ladder Pivot	**46**	Rear Barrel Band (Mod. 96)
7	Safety	**27**	Rear Sight Ladder Spring	**47**	Front Barrel Band (Mod. 94)
8	Cocking Piece	**28**	Rear Sight Base	**48**	Rear Barrel Band (Mod. 94)
9	Handguard	**29**	Rear Sight Assembly	**49**	Nose Cap (Mod. 94)
10	Stock	**30**	Cleaning Rod (Mod. 96)	**50**	Nose Cap Nut (Mod. 94)
11	Buttplate Screws	**31**	Magazine Follower	**51**	Nose Cap Screw (Mod. 94)
12	Buttplate	**32**	Magazine Follower Spring	**Parts Not Shown**	
13	Front Sight	**33**	Sear Spring		Barrel Band Spring
14	Front Sight Band	**34**	Sear Pin		Bayonet Stud Spacer (Mod. 96)
15	Barrel	**35**	Trigger Pin		Bayonet Stud Spacer Pin (Mod. 96)
16	Receiver	**36**	Sear		Cleaning Rod Stud (Mod. 96)
17	Ejector Spring and Cover	**37**	Trigger		Rear Guard Screw Bushing
18	Ejector Screw	**38**	Trigger Guard		
19	Ejector	**39**	Rear Guard Screw		
20	Ejector and Bolt Release Housing	**40**	Front Guard Screw		

Model 1889 Straight-Pull Rifle

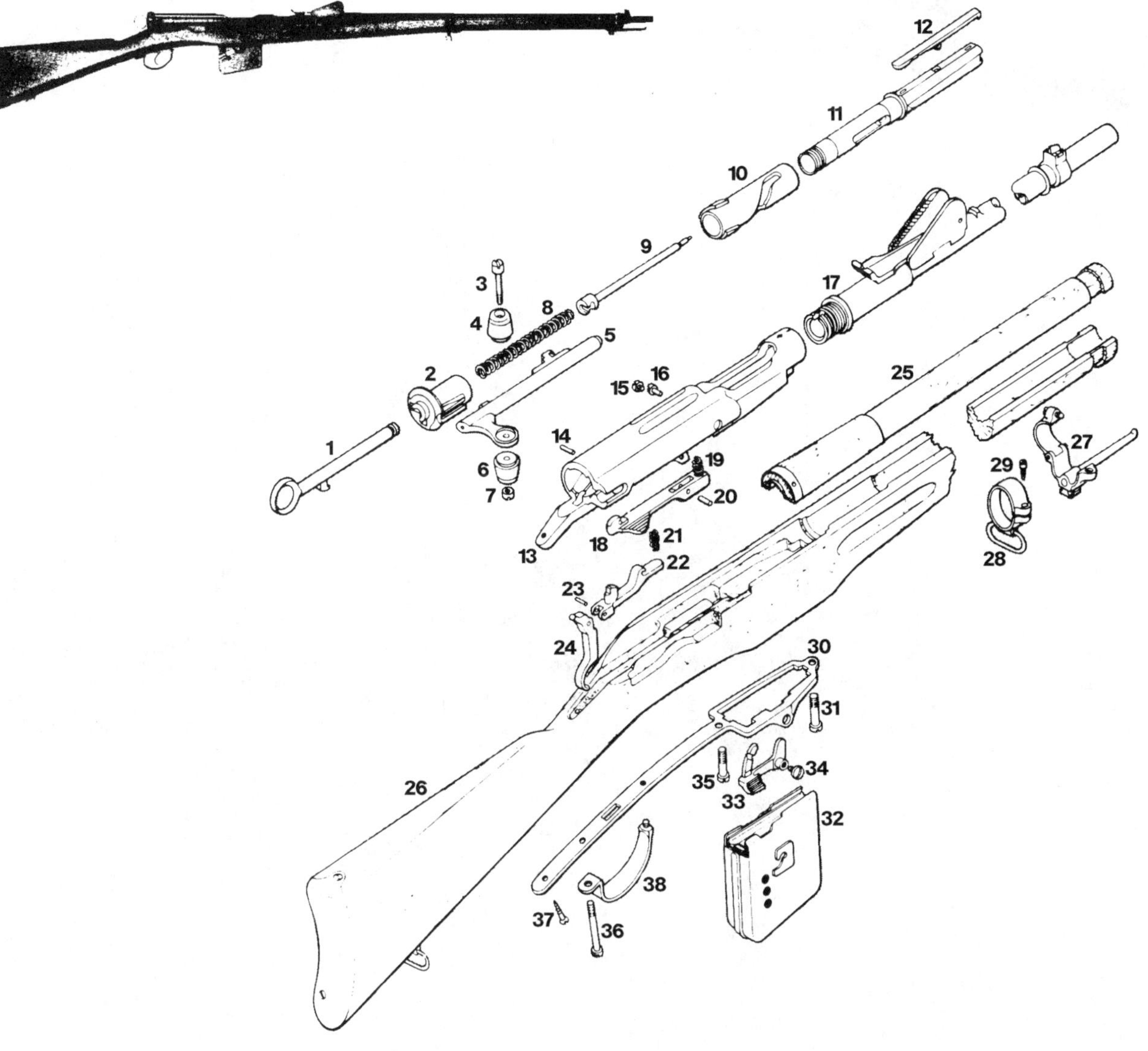

1	Cocking Piece	**20**	Bolt Stop Pin
2	Bolt Plug	**21**	Trigger Spring
3	Bolt Knob Screw	**22**	Sear Arm
4	Upper Bolt Knob	**23**	Trigger Pin
5	Bolt Cam Follower Rod	**24**	Trigger
6	Lower Bolt Knob	**25**	Upper Handguard
7	Knob Nut	**26**	Stock
8	Firing Pin Spring	**27**	Front Band
9	Firing Pin	**28**	Rear Band
10	Bolt Locking Sleeve	**29**	Band Screw
11	Bolt	**30**	Trigger and Magazine Plate
12	Extractor	**31**	Front Plate Screw
13	Receiver	**32**	Magazine
14	Sear Hinge Pin	**33**	Magazine Cut-Off
15	Ejector Lock Screw	**34**	Magazine Cut-Off Screw
16	Ejector	**35**	Middle Plate Screw
17	Barrel	**36**	Rear Guard Screw
18	Bolt Stop	**37**	Trigger Plate Screw
19	Bolt Stop Spring	**38**	Trigger Guard

Contender Single Shot Carbine

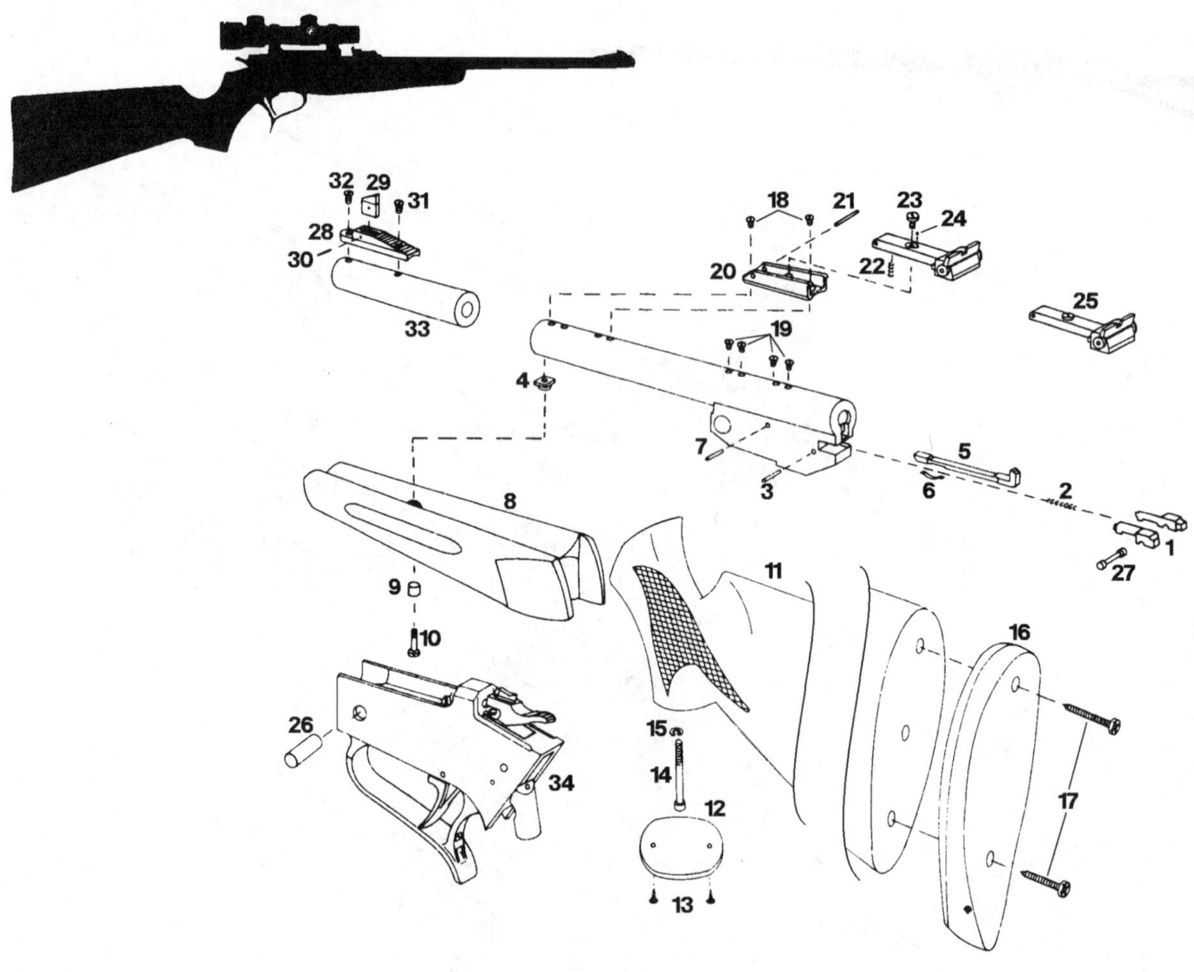

1	Two Piece Bolt	18	Rear Sight Mounting Screws
2	Bolt Spring	19	Filler Screws
3	Bolt Stop Pin	20	Rear Sight Base
4	Dovetail Lock	21	Rear Sight Sprial Pivot Pin
5	Extractor	22	Rear Sight Elevation Spring
6	Extractor Spring	23	Rear Sight Elevation Screw
7	Extractor Stop Pin	24	Rear Sight Detent Ball
8	Forend	25	Rear Sight Complete
9	Forend Bushing	26	Hinge Pin
10	Forend Screw	27	Roller
11	Buttstock	28	Front Sight Ramp
12	Grip Cap	29	Front Sight Blade
13	Grip Cap Screws	30	Front Sight Blade Pin
14	Grip Screw	31	Front Sight Screw, Rear
15	Grip Screw Lock Washer	32	Front Sight Screw, Front
16	Buttpad	33	Barrel
17	Buttpad Screws	34	Receiver

Model 38 and 40 Bolt-Action Rifle

Courtesy of Blacksmith Corporation

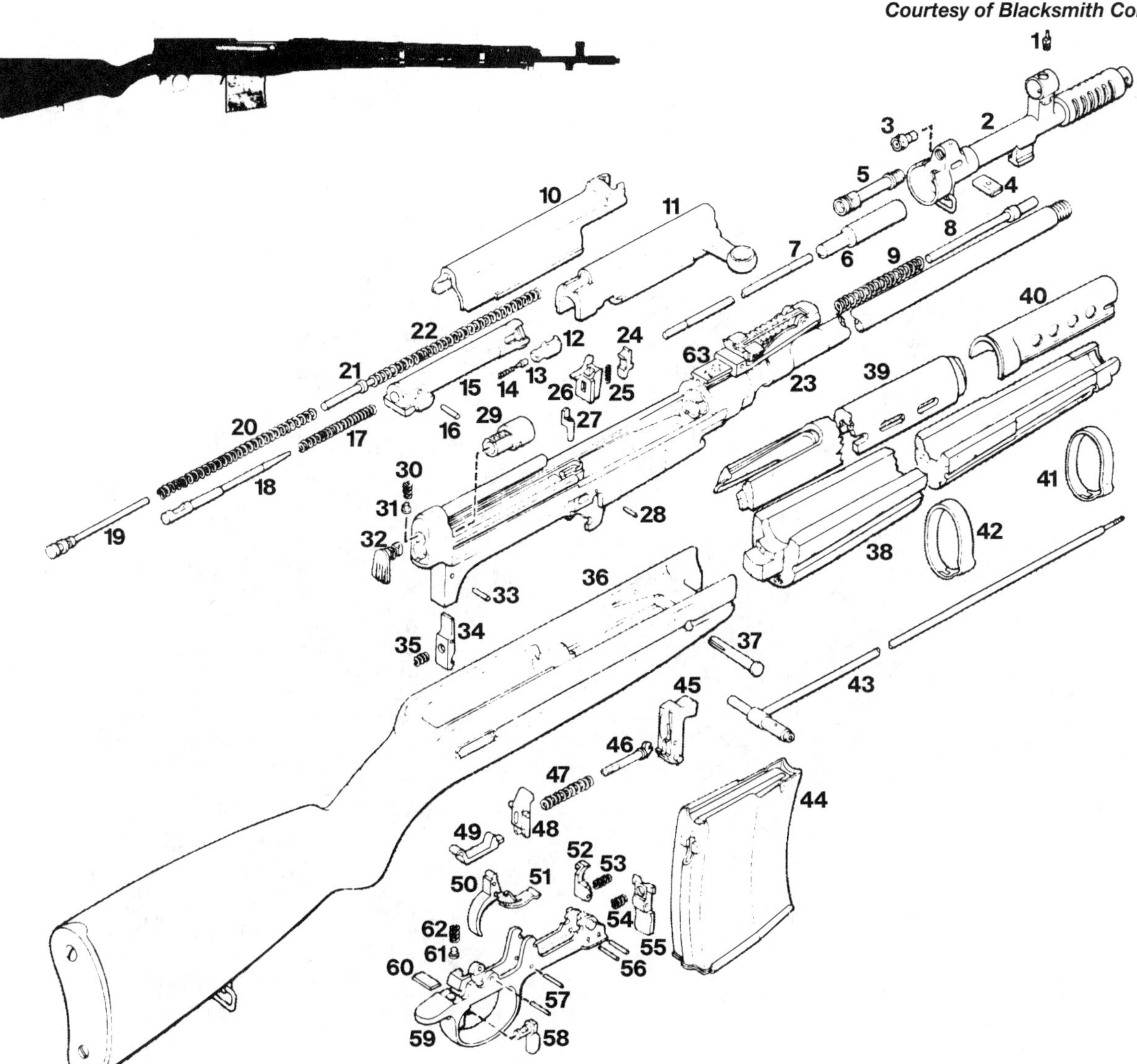

1	Front Sight	22	Forward Recoil Spring	43	Cleaning Rod
2	Muzzle Extension	23	Barrel and Receiver	44	Magazine
3	Gas Regulator	24	Hold-Open Latch	45	Hammer
4	Muzzle Extension Key	25	Hold-Open Latch Spring	46	Hammer Spring Guide
5	Gas Cylinder	26	Ejector	47	Hammer Spring
6	Gas Piston	27	Disconnector	48	Sear
7	Piston Rod	28	Ejector Pin	49	Trigger Bar
8	Piston Rod Extension	29	Trigger Guard Latch Plunger	50	Trigger
9	Piston Spring	30	Detent Spring	51	Trigger Spring
10	Bolt Cover	31	Detent	52	Disconnector Operated Sear
11	Bolt Carrier	32	Plunger Lock	53	Sear Spring
12	Extractor	33	Trigger Guard Latch Pin	54	Magazine Catch Spring
13	Extractor Plunger	34	Trigger Guard Latch	55	Magazine Catch
14	Extractor Spring	35	Trigger Guard Latch Spring	56	Magazine Catch and Sear Pins
15	Bolt	36	Buttstock	57	Trigger and Trigger Spring Pins
16	Firing Pin Retainer	37	Split Cross Pin	58	Safety Catch
17	Firing Pin Spring	38	Forestock	59	Trigger Guard
18	Firing Pin	39	Upper Handguard	60	Spring Cover
19	Rear Spring Guide	40	Piston Cover	61	Safety Catch Detent
20	Rear Recoil Spring	41	Front Band	62	Detent Spring
21	Middle Spring Guide	42	Rear Band	63	Rear Sight Assembly

TYPICAL AUSTRIAN

Side-by-Side Shotgun

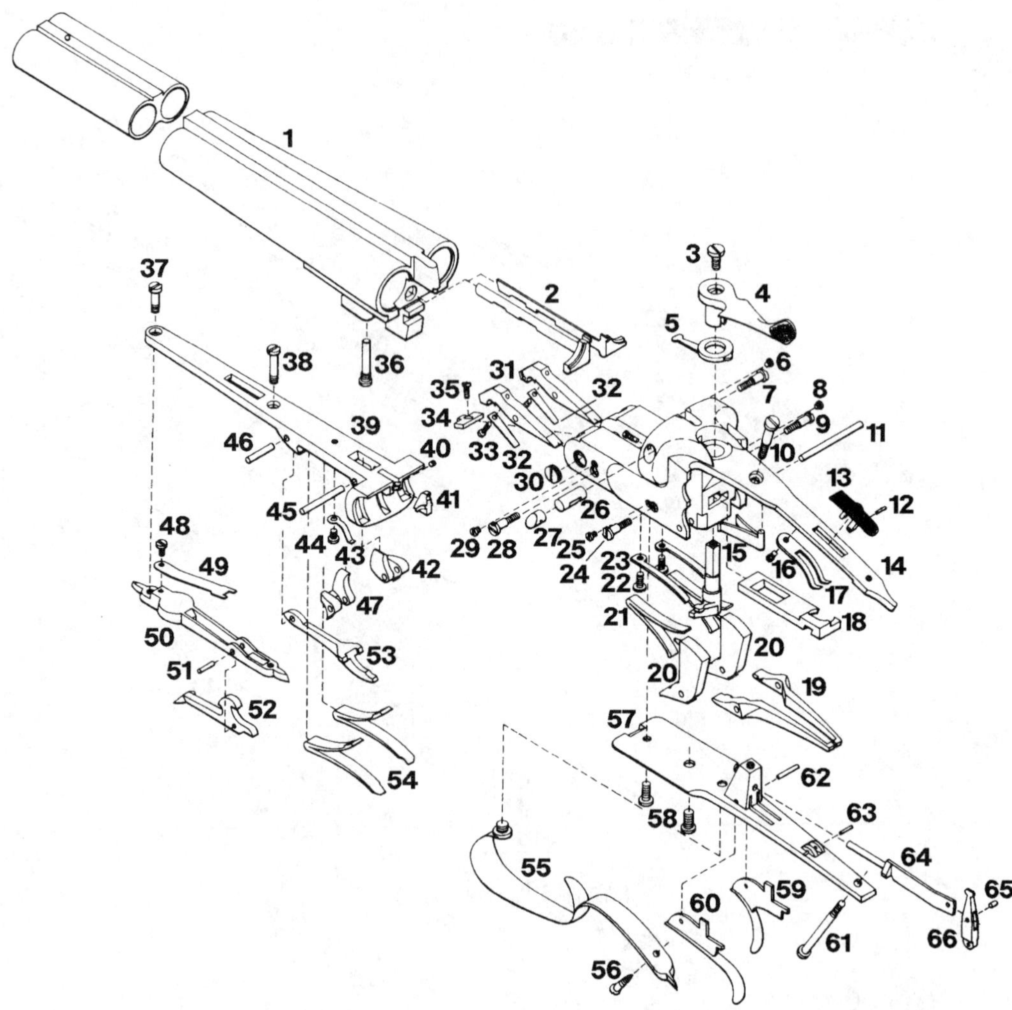

1	Barrel Assembly	**23**	Sear Springs	**45**	Ejector Sear Pivot
2	Extractors/Ejectors	**24**	Hammer Pivot Screw	**46**	Ejector Sear Lever Pin
3	Barrel Latch Lever Screw	**25**	Lock Screw	**47**	Left Ejector Trip
4	Barrel Latch Lever	**26**	Crossbolt	**48**	Forend Latch Spring Screw
5	Crossbolt Lever	**27**	Crossbolt Cap	**49**	Forend Latch Spring
6	Lock Screw	**28**	Cocking Lever Pivot Screw	**50**	Forend Latch Housing
7	Cocking Lever Pivot Screw	**29**	Lock Screw	**51**	Forend Latch Lever Pivot
8	Lock Screw	**30**	Barrel Hinge Cap Screw	**52**	Forend Latch Lever
9	Hammer Pivot Screw	**31**	Cocking Levers	**53**	Ejector Sear Lever
10	Top Trigger Plate Screw	**32**	Cocking Lever Springs	**54**	Ejector Trip Springs
11	Sear Pivot Pin	**33**	Cocking Lever Spring Screws	**55**	Trigger Guard
12	Safety Spring Bearing Pin	**34**	Receiver Insert	**56**	Trigger Guard Screw
13	Safety	**35**	Receiver Insert Screw	**57**	Trigger Plate
14	Receiver	**36**	Ejector Retaining Screw	**58**	Front Trigger Plate Screws
15	Barrel Latch Spring	**37**	Front Forend Latch Screw	**59**	Front Trigger
16	Safety Spring Screw	**38**	Rear Forend Latch Screw	**60**	Rear Trigger
17	Safety Spring	**39**	Forend Iron	**61**	Rear Trigger Plate Screw
18	Barrel Latch	**40**	Ejector Lever Screw	**62**	Trigger Pivot Pin
19	Right and Left Sears	**41**	Ejector Lever	**63**	Safety-Lever Pin
20	Hammers	**42**	Right Ejector Trip	**64**	Automatic Safety Actuator
21	Hammer Springs	**43**	Ejector Sear Spring	**65**	Actuator Connector Pin
22	Sear Spring Screws	**44**	Ejector Sear Spring Screw	**66**	Safety-Lever

TYPICAL PENNSYLVANIA
Flintlock Rifle

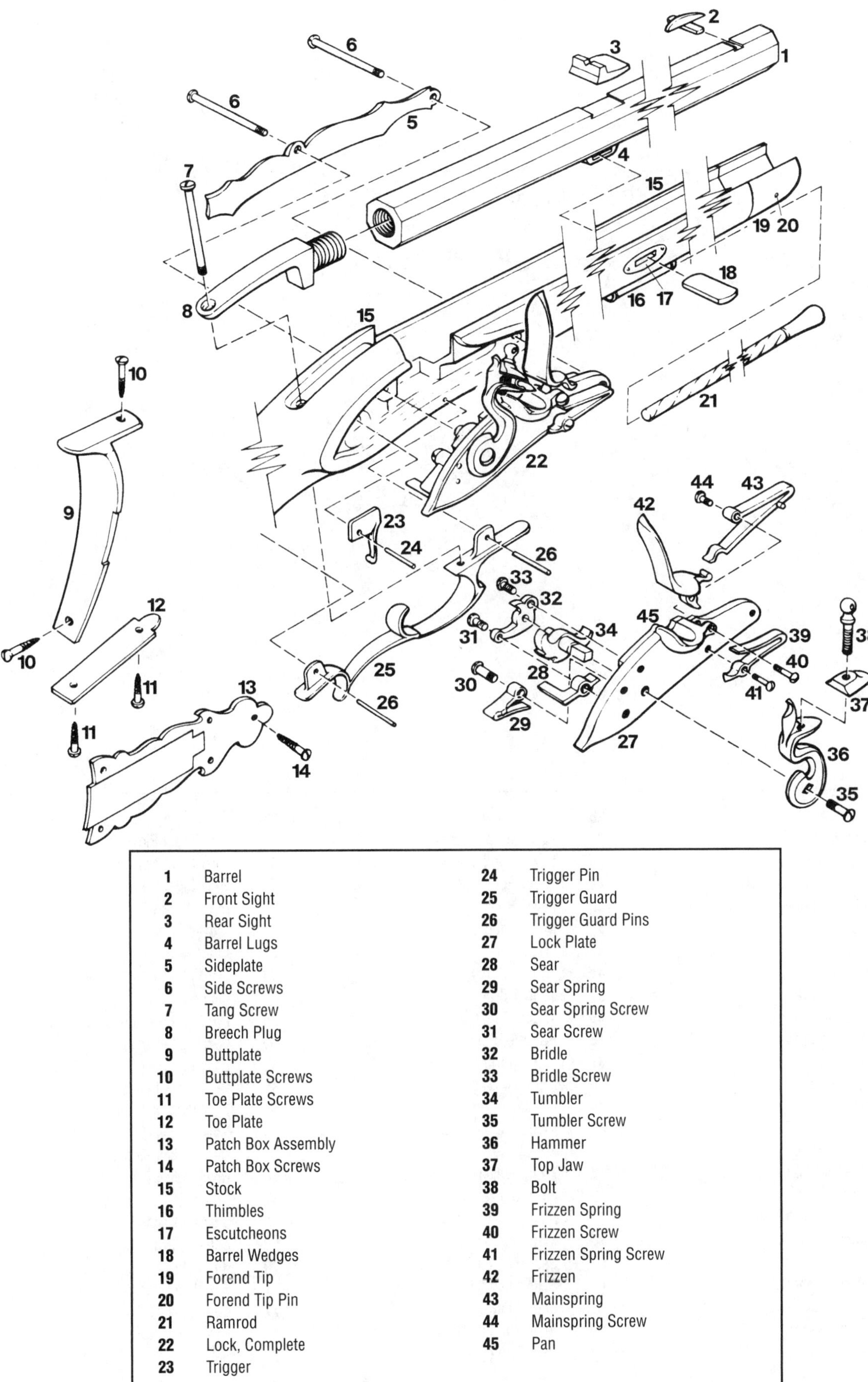

1	Barrel	**24**	Trigger Pin
2	Front Sight	**25**	Trigger Guard
3	Rear Sight	**26**	Trigger Guard Pins
4	Barrel Lugs	**27**	Lock Plate
5	Sideplate	**28**	Sear
6	Side Screws	**29**	Sear Spring
7	Tang Screw	**30**	Sear Spring Screw
8	Breech Plug	**31**	Sear Screw
9	Buttplate	**32**	Bridle
10	Buttplate Screws	**33**	Bridle Screw
11	Toe Plate Screws	**34**	Tumbler
12	Toe Plate	**35**	Tumbler Screw
13	Patch Box Assembly	**36**	Hammer
14	Patch Box Screws	**37**	Top Jaw
15	Stock	**38**	Bolt
16	Thimbles	**39**	Frizzen Spring
17	Escutcheons	**40**	Frizzen Screw
18	Barrel Wedges	**41**	Frizzen Spring Screw
19	Forend Tip	**42**	Frizzen
20	Forend Tip Pin	**43**	Mainspring
21	Ramrod	**44**	Mainspring Screw
22	Lock, Complete	**45**	Pan
23	Trigger		

Henry Lever-Action Carbine

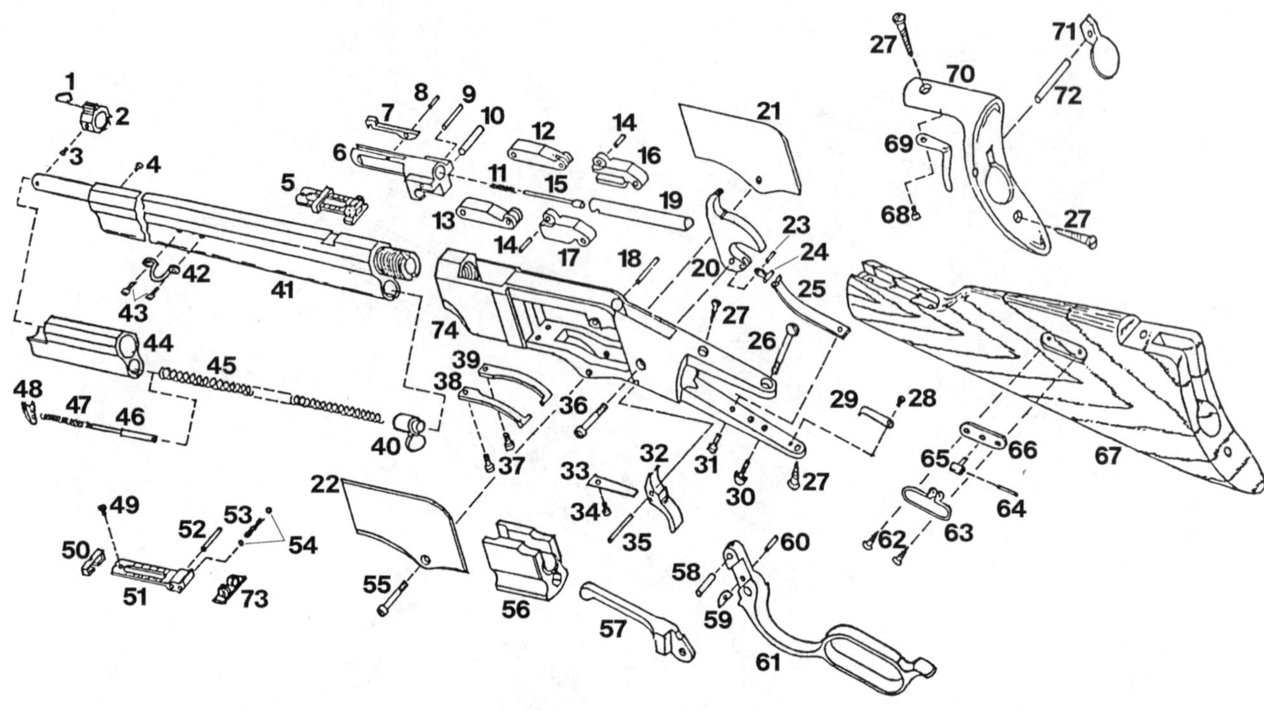

1	Sight	**26**	Tang Screw	**51**	Rear Sight
2	Front Band	**27**	Receiver and Stock Screws	**52**	Rear Sight Pin
3	Band Screw	**28**	Lever Hook Screw	**53**	Rear Sight Spring
4	Magazine Follower Stop Screw	**29**	Lever Hook Spring	**54**	Rear Sight Spheres
5	Sight Assembly	**30**	Lever Hook	**55**	Lever Screw
6	Breechblock	**31**	Mainspring Screw	**56**	Carrier Block
7	Extractor	**32**	Trigger	**57**	Lifter Arm
8	Extractor Pin	**33**	Trigger Spring	**58**	Loading Lever and Links Connection
9	Firing Pin Stop	**34**	Trigger Spring Screw	**59**	Loading Lever Cam
10	Breechblock Pin	**35**	Trigger Pin	**60**	Loading Lever Cam Pin
11	Firing Pin Spring	**36**	Hammer Pin Screw	**61**	Loading Lever
12	Left Front Link	**37**	Lever Spring Screws	**62**	Rear Swivel Base Screws
13	Right Front Link	**38**	Right Lever Spring	**63**	Rear Swivel
14	Link Pins	**39**	Left Lever Spring	**64**	Rear Swivel Pin
15	Firing Pin	**40**	Magazine Follower	**65**	Rear Swivel Pivot
16	Right Rear Link	**41**	Barrel	**66**	Rear Swivel Base
17	Left Rear Link	**42**	Front Swivel	**67**	Buttstock
18	Rear Link Pin	**43**	Front Swivel Screws	**68**	Buttstock Gate Spring Screw
19	Firing Pin Extension	**44**	Assembled Sleeve	**69**	Buttstock Gate Spring
20	Hammer	**45**	Magazine Spring	**70**	Buttplate
21	Right Sideplate	**46**	Sleeve Latch Rod	**71**	Buttplate Gate
22	Left Sideplate	**47**	Sleeve Latch Rod Spring	**72**	Buttplate Gate Pin
23	Hammer Link Pin	**48**	Sleeve Latch	**73**	Rear Base
24	Hammer Link	**49**	Rear Running Stop Screw	**74**	Receiver
25	Mainspring	**50**	Rear Running		

Model 1866 Yellowboy Lever-Action Rifle

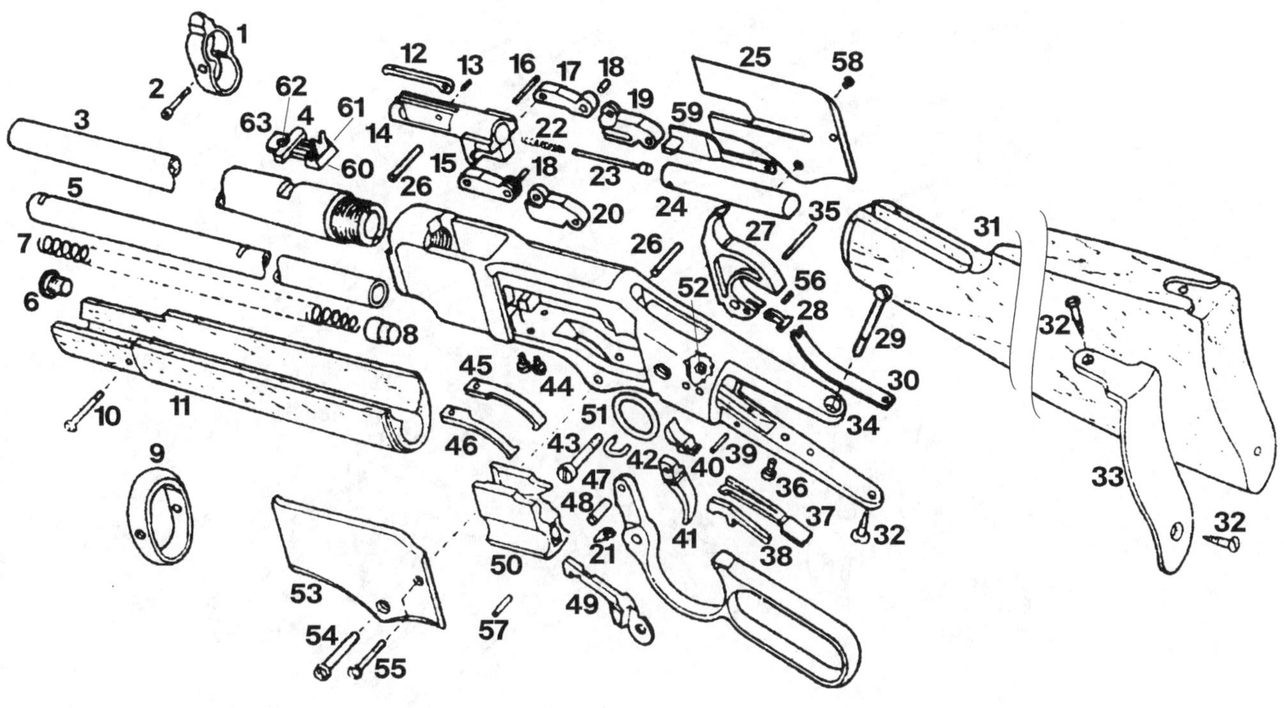

1	Front Band	**22**	Firing Pin Spring	**43**	Hammer Pin Screw
2	Band Screw	**23**	Firing Pin	**44**	Lever Spring Screws
3	Barrel	**24**	Firing Pin Extension	**45**	Right Lever Spring
4	Sight Assembly	**25**	Right Sideplate	**46**	Left Lever Spring
5	Magazine Tube	**26**	Rear Link Pin	**47**	Lever
6	Magazine Tube Plug	**27**	Hammer	**48**	Lever Pin
7	Magazine Spring	**28**	Hammer Link	**49**	Lifter Arm
8	Magazine Follower	**29**	Tang Screw	**50**	Carrier Block
9	Forend Band	**30**	Mainspring	**51**	Saddle Ring
10	Forend Screw	**31**	Buttstock	**52**	Saddle Ring Screw
11	Forend	**32**	Screws	**53**	Left Sideplate
12	Extractor	**33**	Buttplate	**54**	Lever Screw
13	Extractor Pin	**34**	Receiver	**55**	Plate Screw
14	Breechblock	**35**	Trigger Pin	**56**	Hammer Link Pin
15	Left Front Link	**36**	Mainspring Screw	**57**	Cam Lever Pin
16	Firing Pin Stop	**37**	Trigger and Safety Spring	**58**	Ladle Block Screw
17	Right Front Link	**38**	Safety Bar	**59**	Ladle
18	Link Pins	**39**	Safety Spring Pin	**60**	Rear Sight Base
19	Right Rear Link	**40**	Trigger (Upper Portion)	**61**	Rear Sight Blade
20	Left Rear Link	**41**	Trigger (Lower Portion)	**62**	Rear Sight Screw
21	Cam Lever	**42**	Saddle Ring Loop	**63**	Rear Sight Blade Pin

Model 1873 Lever-Action Carbine

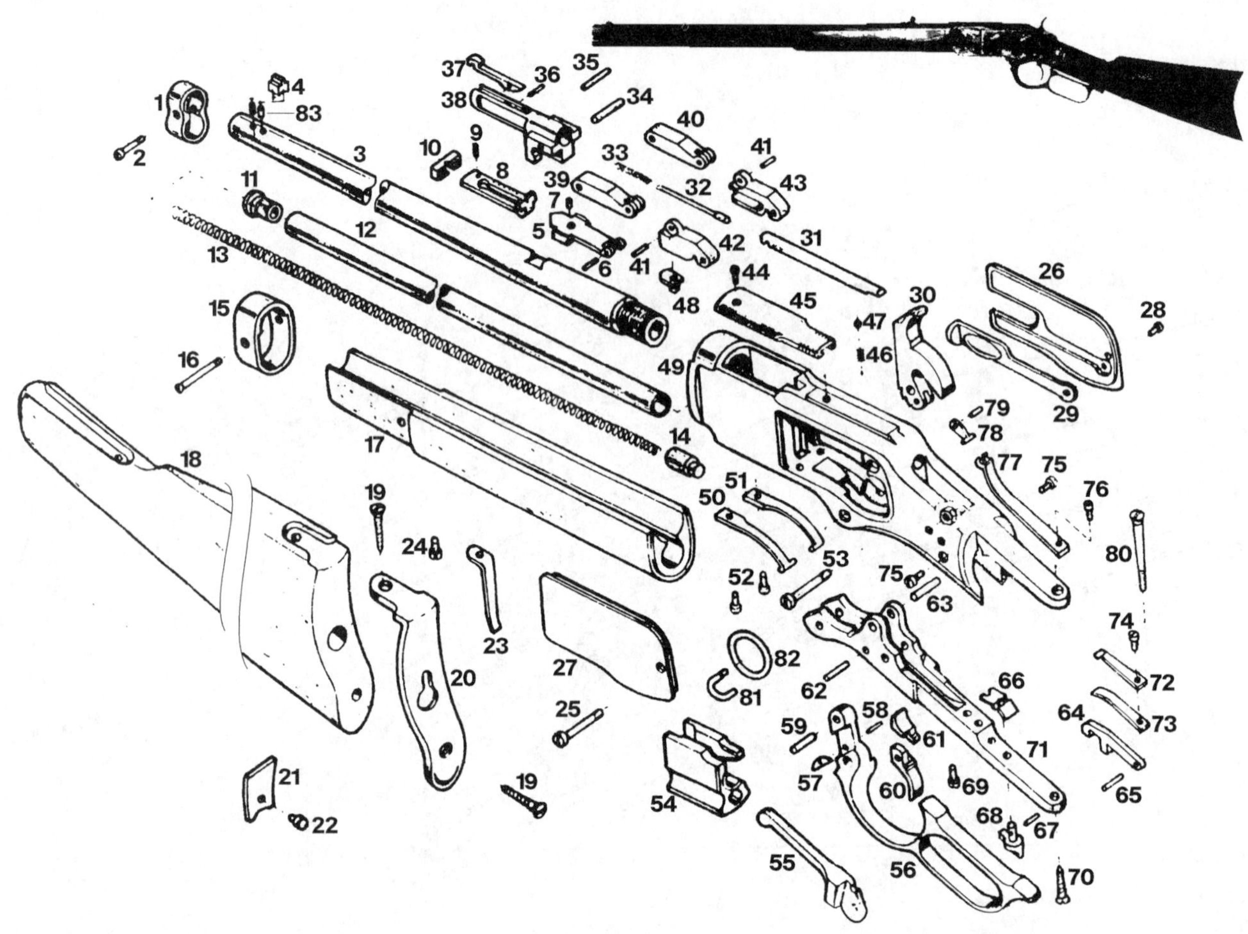

1	Front Band
2	Band Screw
3	Barrel
4	Front Sight
5	Rear Sight Base
6	Rear Sight Base Pin
7	Rear Sight Base Block Screw
8	Rear Sight
9	Rear Sight Elevator Screw
10	Rear Sight Elevator
11	Magazine Tube Plug
12	Magazine Tube
13	Magazine Spring
14	Magazine Follower
15	Forend Band
16	Forend Screw
17	Forend
18	Buttstock
19	Buttplate Screws
20	Buttplate
21	Buttplate Gate
22	Buttplate Gate Pin
23	Buttplate Gate Spring
24	Buttplate Gate Screw
25	Sideplate Screw
26	Right Sideplate
27	Left Sideplate
28	Ladle Block Screw
29	Ladle
30	Hammer
31	Firing Pin Extension
32	Firing Pin
33	Firing Pin Spring
34	Firing Pin Extension Stop Pin
35	Breechblock Pin
36	Extractor Pin
37	Extractor
38	Breechblock
39	Left Front Link
40	Right Front Link
41	Link Pins
42	Left Rear Link
43	Right Rear Link
44	Dust Cover Screw
45	Dust Cover
46	Dust Cover Detent Spring
47	Dust Cover Detent
48	Dust Cover Guide
49	Receiver
50	Left Lever Spring
51	Right Lever Spring
52	Lever Spring Screws
53	Lever Screw
54	Carrier Block
55	Lifter Arm
56	Lever
57	Lever Cam
58	Lever Cam Pin
59	Lever Pin
60	Trigger (Lower)
61	Trigger (Upper)
62	Trigger Pin
63	Hammer Pin
64	Safety Bar
65	Safety Spring Pin
66	Lever Spring Hook
67	Lever Pin Hook
68	Lever Hook
69	Mainspring Screw
70	Trigger Guard Screw
71	Trigger Guard
72	Safety Spring
73	Trigger Spring
74	Trigger Spring Screw
75	Trigger Guard Screws
76	Mainspring Screw
77	Mainspring
78	Hammer Link
79	Hammer Link Pin
80	Tang Screw
81	Saddle Ring Loop
82	Saddle Ring
83	Barrel Sight Pins

Model 1875 Remington Revolving Carbine

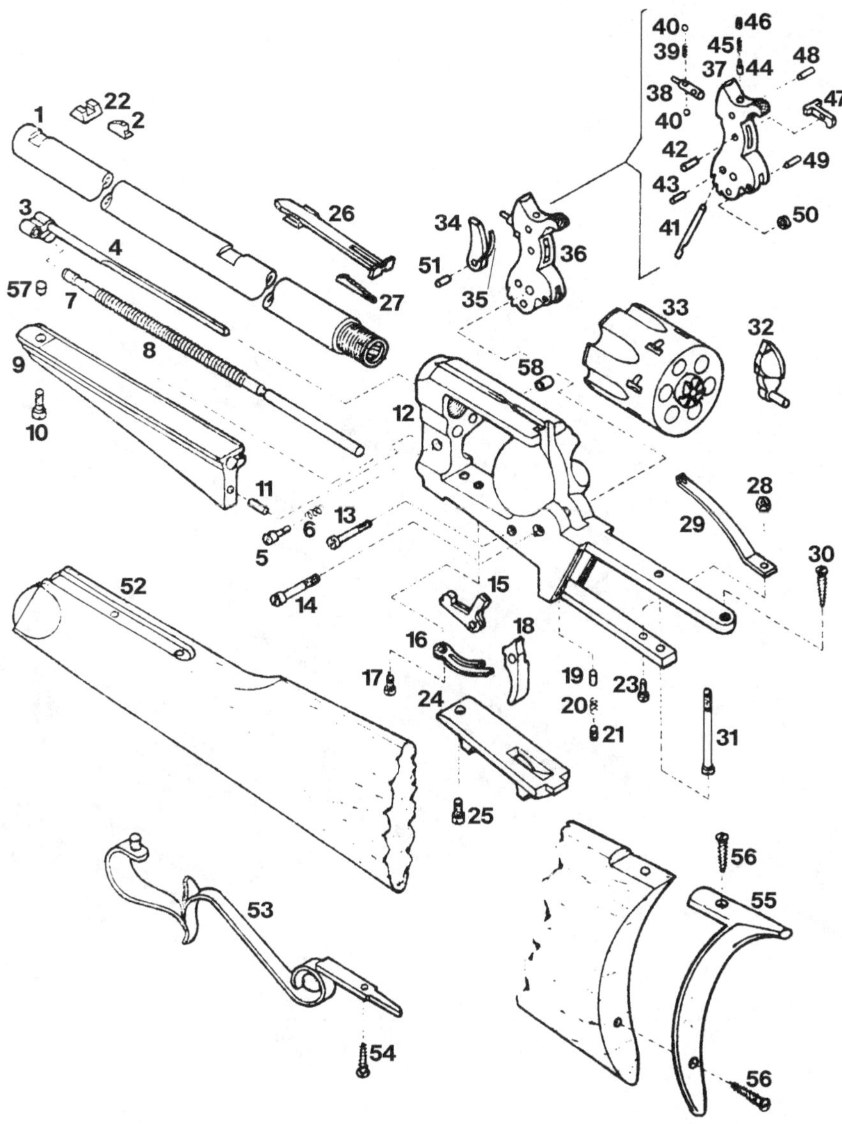

1	Barrel	**21**	Gate Catch Screw	**41**	Hammer Safety Plunger
2	Front Sight	**22**	Front Sight Ramp	**42**	Hammer Safety Bar Pin
3	Ejector Base	**23**	Mainspring Screw	**43**	Hammer Safety Plunger Pin
4	Ejector	**24**	Trigger Guard	**44**	Hammer Safety Pin
5	Base Pin Screw	**25**	Trigger Guard Screw	**45**	Hammer Safety Spring
6	Base Pin Spring	**26**	Rear Sight	**46**	Hammer Safety Stop Screw
7	Base Pin	**27**	Rear Sight Elevator	**47**	Hammer Safety Bar
8	Ejector Spring	**28**	Mainspring Loop Screw	**48**	Firing Pin Retaining Pin
9	Forend	**29**	Mainspring	**49**	Hammer Roller Pin
10	Forend Screw	**30**	Buttstock Screw	**50**	Hammer Roller
11	Forend Pin	**31**	Tang Screw	**51**	Carrier Block Screw
12	Frame	**32**	Gate	**52**	Buttstock
13	Trigger Screw	**33**	Cylinder	**53**	Trigger Guard
14	Hammer Screw	**34**	Hand	**54**	Trigger Guard Screw
15	Bolt	**35**	Hand Spring	**55**	Buttplate
16	Sear and Bolt Spring	**36**	Hammer Assembly	**56**	Buttplate Screws
17	Bolt Spring Screw	**37**	Hammer	**57**	Ejector Rod Tube Screw Nut
18	Trigger	**38**	Firing Pin	**58**	Base Pin Nut
19	Gate Nut	**39**	Firing Pin Spring		
20	Gate Spring	**40**	Firing Pin Spheres		

M-1 Autoloading Carbine

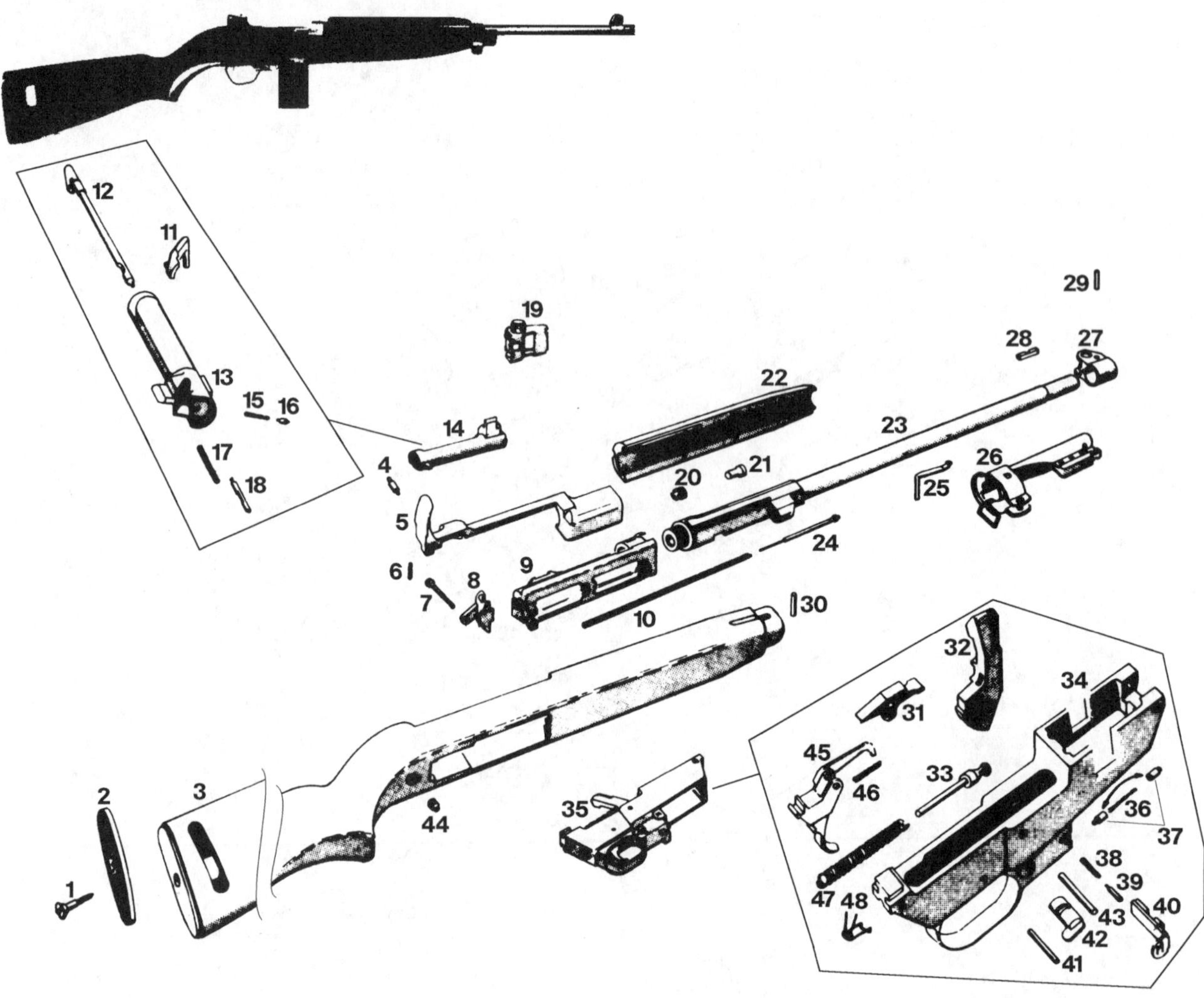

1	Buttplate Screw	**26**	Barrel Band with Swivel and Screw
2	Buttplate	**27**	Front Sight
3	Stock	**28**	Front Sight Key
4	Slide Lock	**29**	Front Sight Pin
5	Slide	**30**	Trigger Guard Pin
6	Slide Lock Spring	**31**	Sear
7	Recoil Plate Screw	**32**	Hammer
8	Recoil Plate	**33**	Hammer Spring Plunger
9	Receiver	**34**	Trigger Housing
10	Recoil Spring	**35**	Trigger Housing Complete
11	Extractor	**36**	Safety Spring
12	Firing Pin	**37**	Safety Spring Plungers
13	Bolt	**38**	Magazine Catch Spring
14	Bolt Complete	**39**	Magazine Catch Plunger
15	Extractor Spring	**40**	Magazine Catch
16	Extractor Spring Plunger	**41**	Trigger Pin
17	Ejector Spring	**42**	Safety
18	Ejector	**43**	Hammer Pin
19	Rear Sight	**44**	Stock Escutcheon
20	Gas Piston Nut	**45**	Trigger
21	Gas Piston	**46**	Sear Spring
22	Hand Guard	**47**	Hammer Spring
23	Barrel	**48**	Trigger Spring
24	Recoil Spring Guide		
25	Band Spring		

M-1 Garand Autoloading Rifle

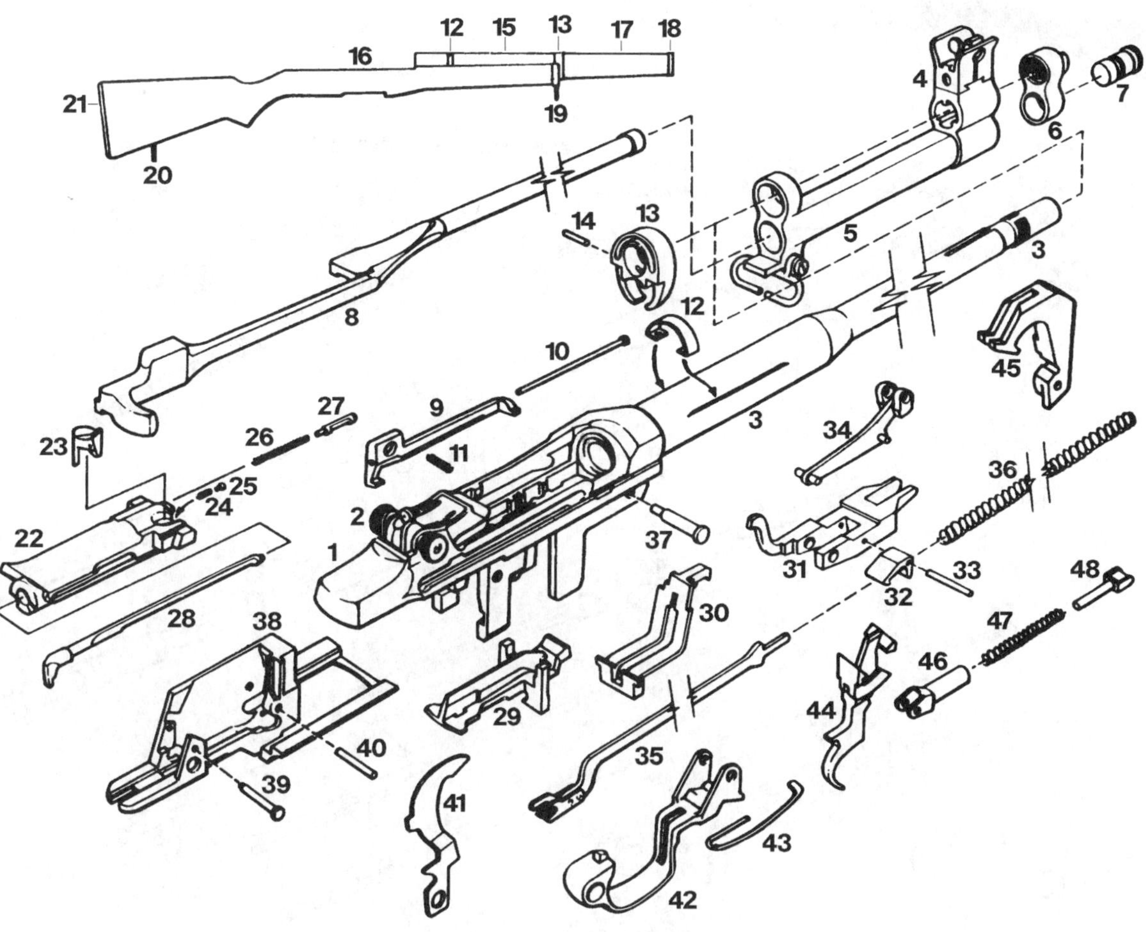

1	Receiver	**24**	Extractor Spring
2	Rear Sight Assembly	**25**	Extractor Plunger
3	Barrel	**26**	Ejector Spring
4	Front Sight	**27**	Ejector
5	Gas Cylinder with Stacking Swivel	**28**	Firing Pin
6	Gas Cylinder Lock	**29**	Slide and Follower
7	Gas Cylinder Lock Screw	**30**	Bullet Guide
8	Operating Rod	**31**	Operating Rod Catch
9	Clip Latch	**32**	Accelerator
10	Clip Latch Pin	**33**	Accelerator Pin
11	Clip Latch Spring	**34**	Follower Arm
12	Rear Handguard Band	**35**	Follower Rod
13	Lower Band	**36**	Operating Rod Spring
14	Lower Band Pin	**37**	Follower Arm Pin
15	Rear Handguard	**38**	Trigger Housing
16	Stock	**39**	Trigger Pin
17	Front Handguard	**40**	Hammer Pin
18	Front Handguard Ferrule	**41**	Safety
19	Stock Ferrule and Swivel	**42**	Trigger Guard
20	Buttstock Swivel	**43**	Clip Ejector
21	Buttplate and Screws	**44**	Trigger
22	Bolt	**45**	Hammer
23	Extractor	**46**	Hammer Spring Housing
		47	Hammer Spring
		48	Hammer Spring Plunger

M-14 Autoloading Rifle

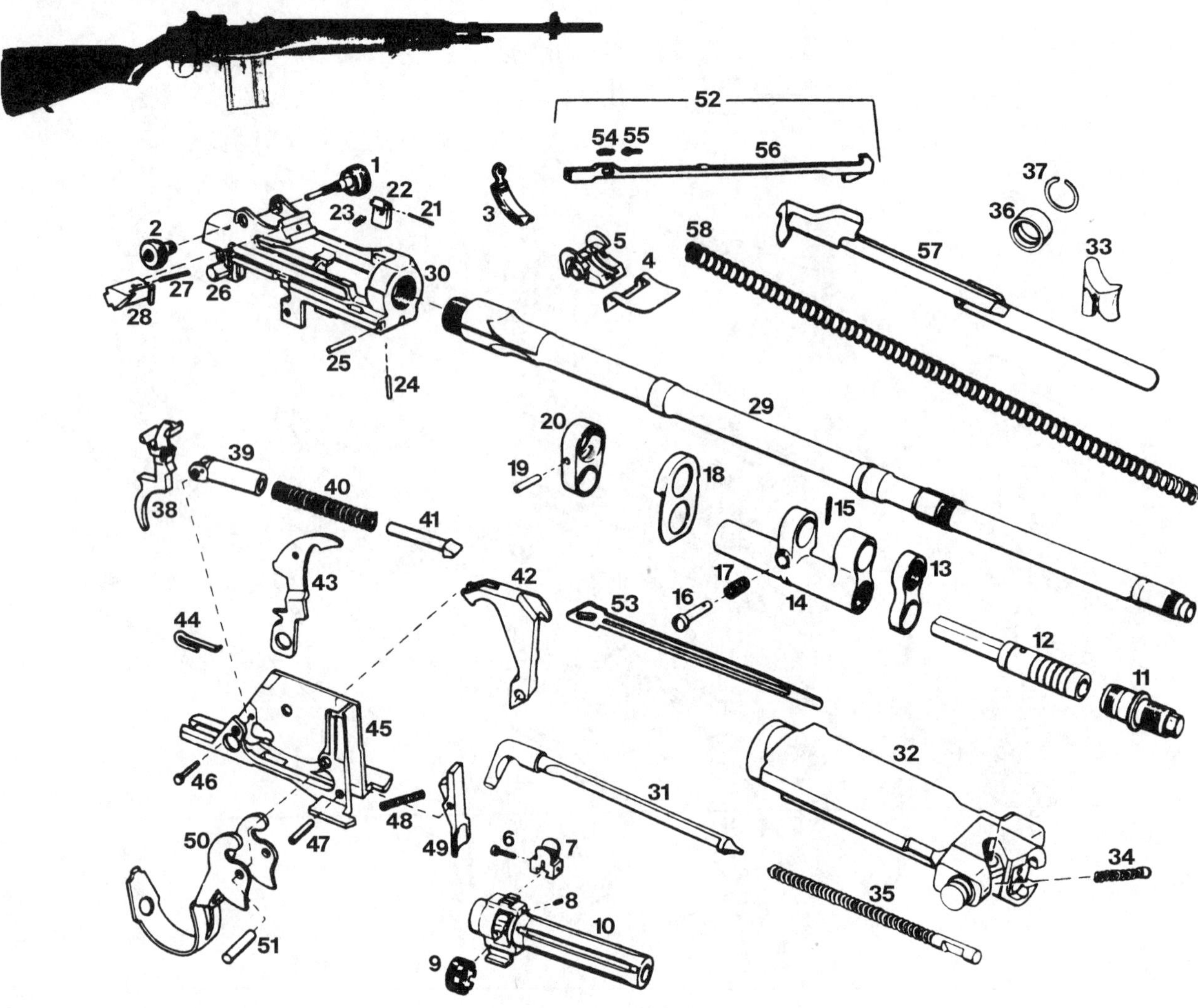

1	Rear Sight Elevation Pinion	**23**	Bolt Lock Spring	**45**	Trigger Housing
2	Windage Knob	**24**	Connector Lock Pin	**46**	Trigger Pin
3	Aperture Sight	**25**	Connector Lock	**47**	Magazine Latch Pin
4	Rear Sight Cover	**26**	Selector	**48**	Magazine Latch Spring
5	Rear Sight Base	**27**	Clip Guide Pin	**49**	Magazine Latch
6	Front Sight Screw	**28**	Cartridge Clip Guide	**50**	Trigger Guard
7	Front Sight	**29**	Barrel	**51**	Trigger Guard Pin
8	Flash Suppressor Set Screw	**30**	Receiver	**52**	Connector Rod Assembly
9	Flash Suppressor Nut	**31**	Firing Pin	**53**	Operating Rod Spring Guide
10	Flash Suppressor	**32**	Bolt Assembly	**54**	Connector Spring
11	Gas Cylinder Plug	**33**	Extractor	**55**	Connector Plunger
12	Gas Piston	**34**	Extractor Plunger and Spring	**56**	Connector Rod Body
13	Gas Cylinder Lock	**35**	Ejector and Spring	**57**	Operating Rod
14	Gas Cylinder	**36**	Bolt Roller	**58**	Operating Rod Spring
15	Gas Cylinder Pin	**37**	Bolt Roller Retainer	**Parts Not Shown**	
16	Gas Cylinder Valve Spindle	**38**	Trigger and Sear Assembly		Buttplate Assembly
17	Gas Cylinder Valve Spring	**39**	Hammer Spring Housing		Buttplate Screws
18	Front Band	**40**	Hammer Spring		Stock
19	Operating Rod Guide Spring Pin	**41**	Hammer Plunger		Rear Swivel
20	Operating Rod Guide	**42**	Hammer		Front Swivel
21	Bolt Lock Pin	**43**	Safety		Connector Rod Pin
22	Bolt Lock	**44**	Safety Spring		

Autoloading Carbine

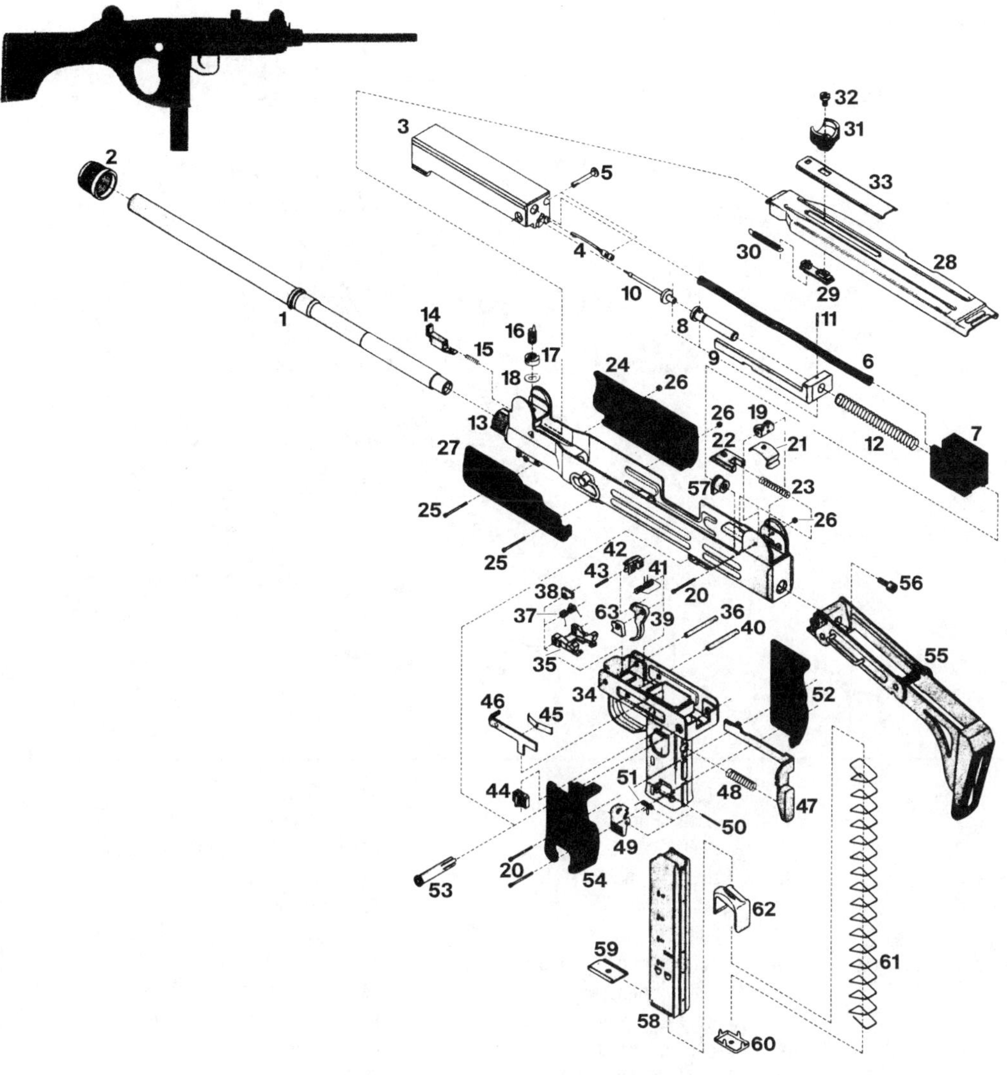

1	Barrel	**21**	Rear Sight Leaf Spring	**43**	Trigger Pin
2	Barrel Retaining Nut	**22**	Cover Catch	**44**	Change Lever Switch
3	Bolt	**23**	Cover Catch Spring	**45**	Change Lever Spring
4	Extractor	**24**	Handguard, Right	**46**	Change Lever
5	Extractor Pin	**25**	Handguard Screws	**47**	Safety Grip Lock Assembly
6	Return Spring Assembly	**26**	Handguard Screw Nuts	**48**	Safety Grip Lock Spring
7	Buffer	**27**	Handguard, Left	**49**	Magazine Catch
8	Firing Pin Spring Guide	**28**	Cover Body	**50**	Magazine Catch Pin
9	Firing Pin Carrier	**29**	Cocking Slide	**51**	Magazine Catch Spring
10	Firing Pin	**30**	Cocking Slide Spring	**52**	Pistol Grip, Right
11	Firing Pin Retaining Pin	**31**	Cocking Handle	**53**	Pistol Grip Split Bushing
12	Firing Pin Spring	**32**	Cocking Handle Screw	**54**	Pistol Grip, Left
13	Receiver	**33**	Slot Cover Plate	**55**	Folding Stock Assembly
14	Barrel Retaining Nut Catch	**34**	Grip Body (Trigger Housing)	**56**	Stock Screw
15	Barrel Retaining Nut Catch Spring	**35**	Sear	**57**	Stock Nut
16	Front Sight Screw	**36**	Sear Axis	**58**	Magazine
17	Front Sight Nut	**37**	Sear Spring	**59**	Magazine Floorplate
18	Front Sight Spring Washer	**38**	Stop Dog	**60**	Magazine Spring Retainer
19	Rear Sight Leaf	**39**	Trigger	**61**	Magazine Spring
20	Rear Sight Pivot Screw	**40**	Trigger Axis	**62**	Magazine Follower
		41	Trigger Spring	**63**	Trigger Plate
		42	Interruptor (Disconnector)		

412 Combo

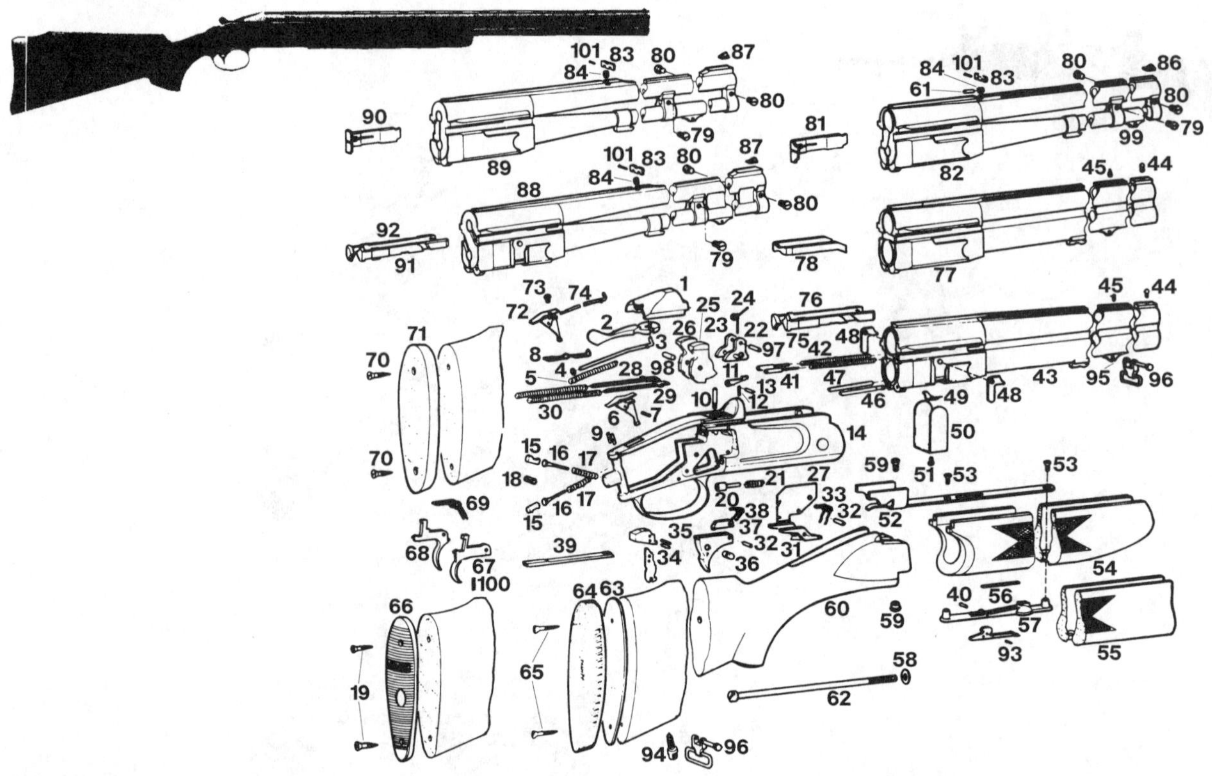

1	Locking Bolt
2	Top Snap
3	Top Snap Plunger
4	Top Snap Plunger Washer
5	Top Snap Spring
6	Safety Button
7	Safety Pin
8	Safety Spring
9	Indicator
10	Top Snap Pin
11	Top Slide Trip
12	Top Slide Trip Spring
13	Top Slide Trip Pin
14	Frame
15	Strikers
16	Firing Pins
17	Firing Pin Springs
18	Striker Pin
19	Screws
20	Ejector Operating Pin
21	Ejector Operating Pin Spring
22	Cocking Crank, Right
23	Cocking Crank, Left
24	Cocking Slide Spring
25	Hammer, Right
26	Hammer, Left
27	Support Plate
28	Mainspring Plunger, Left
29	Mainspring Plunger, Right
30	Mainsprings
31	Sear
32	Trigger Pins
33	Sear Spring
34	Inertia Block and Pins
35	Trigger
36	Selector Button
37	Selector Cam
38	Selector Cam Spring
39	Cocking Slide
40	Striker Pin
41	Ejector Spring Plungers
42	Ejector Springs
43	Barrels Complete, Shotgun
44	Front Sight Bead
45	Rear Sight Bead
46	Ejector Operating Rod, Right
47	Ejector Operating Rod, Left
48	Ejector Trips
49	Ejector Trip Spring
50	Covering Plate
51	Covering Plate Screw
52	Forend Iron
53	Forend Screws
54	Forend Wood
55	Forend Wood (Model Vainio)
56	Forend Snap Spring
57	Forend Snap Assembly
58	Stock Bolt Washer
59	Forend Nut
60	Stock
61	Snap Pin
62	Stock Bolt
63	Buttplate Spacer
64	Buttplate
65	Rubber Buttplate Screws
66	Buttplate VALMET
67	Rear Trigger
68	Front Trigger
69	Trigger Spring
70	Screws
71	Buttplate, Curled Birch Wood
72	Safety Button
73	Screw
74	Safety Spring
75	Extractor, Right
76	Extractor, Left
77	Barrels Complete, Shotgun
78	Extractor
79	Screw
80	Screws
81	Extractor
82	Barrels Complete, Combination
83	Sight Plate
84	Spring
85	Crank Pin
86	Sight Bead
87	Front Sight
88	Barrels Complete, Rifle
89	Barrels Complete, Rifle
90	Extractor
91	Extractor, Right
92	Extractor, Left
93	Spring Pin
94	Rear Swivel Bow Body
95	Front Swivel Bow Body
96	Swivel Bows
97	Cocking Crank Pin
98	Hammer Pin
99	Front Swivel Bow Body
100	Trigger Adjusting Screw
101	Sight Adjusting Screw

Hunter Autoloading Rifle

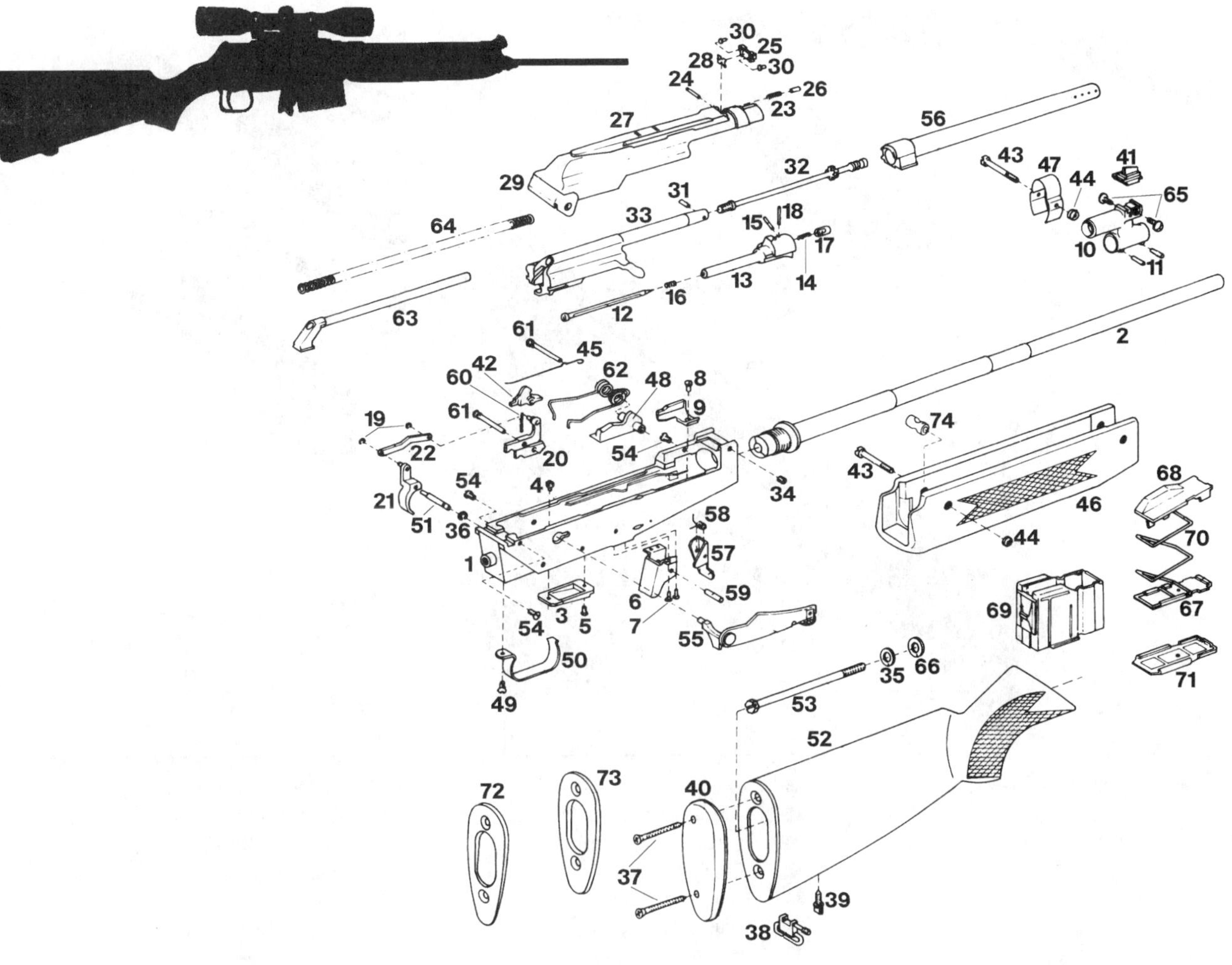

1	Receiver	**26**	Catch Pin	**51**	Trigger Pin
2	Barrel	**27**	Rib	**52**	Stock
3	Cover Plate	**28**	Sight Plate	**53**	Stock Screw
4	Trigger Stop	**29**	Cover, Complete	**54**	Cover Screws
5	Round Head Rivet	**30**	Sight Screws	**55**	Safety Assembly
6	Magazine Catch Body	**31**	Tension Pin	**56**	Gas Tube
7	Rivets	**32**	Gas Piston	**57**	Magazine Catch
8	Cam Plate Rivet	**33**	Slide	**58**	Magazine Catch Spring
9	Bolt Cam Plate	**34**	Retaining Screw	**59**	Magazine Catch Pin
10	Gas Block	**35**	Conical Spring Washer	**60**	Sear Spring
11	Taper Pins	**36**	Retaining Ring	**61**	Sear Pin
12	Firing Pin	**37**	Screws	**62**	Hammer Spring
13	Bolt (Carrier Assembly)	**38**	Sling Swivel	**63**	Recoil Spring Body
14	Extractor Spring	**39**	Sling Swivel Base	**64**	Recoil Spring
15	Extractor Pin	**40**	Buttplate	**65**	Front Sight Adjustment Screws
16	Firing Pin Spring	**41**	Front Sight Base	**66**	Washer
17	Extractor	**42**	Disconnector	**67**	Spring Plate Assembly
18	Firing Pin Retainer Pin	**43**	Forend Screw	**68**	Feeding Ramp Assembly
19	Retaining Rings	**44**	Forend Nut	**69**	Magazine Body Assembly
20	Sear, Complete	**45**	Pin Retainer Spring	**70**	Magazine Spring
21	Trigger, Complete	**46**	Forend	**71**	Bottom Plate
22	Trigger Bar	**47**	Forend Band	**72**	Angle Piece
23	Sight Spring	**48**	Hammer	**73**	Distance Piece, Straight
24	Sight Plate Pin	**49**	Trigger Guard Screw	**74**	Support Tube
25	Sight Plate Body	**50**	Trigger Guard		

Athena and Orion Over/Under Shotgun

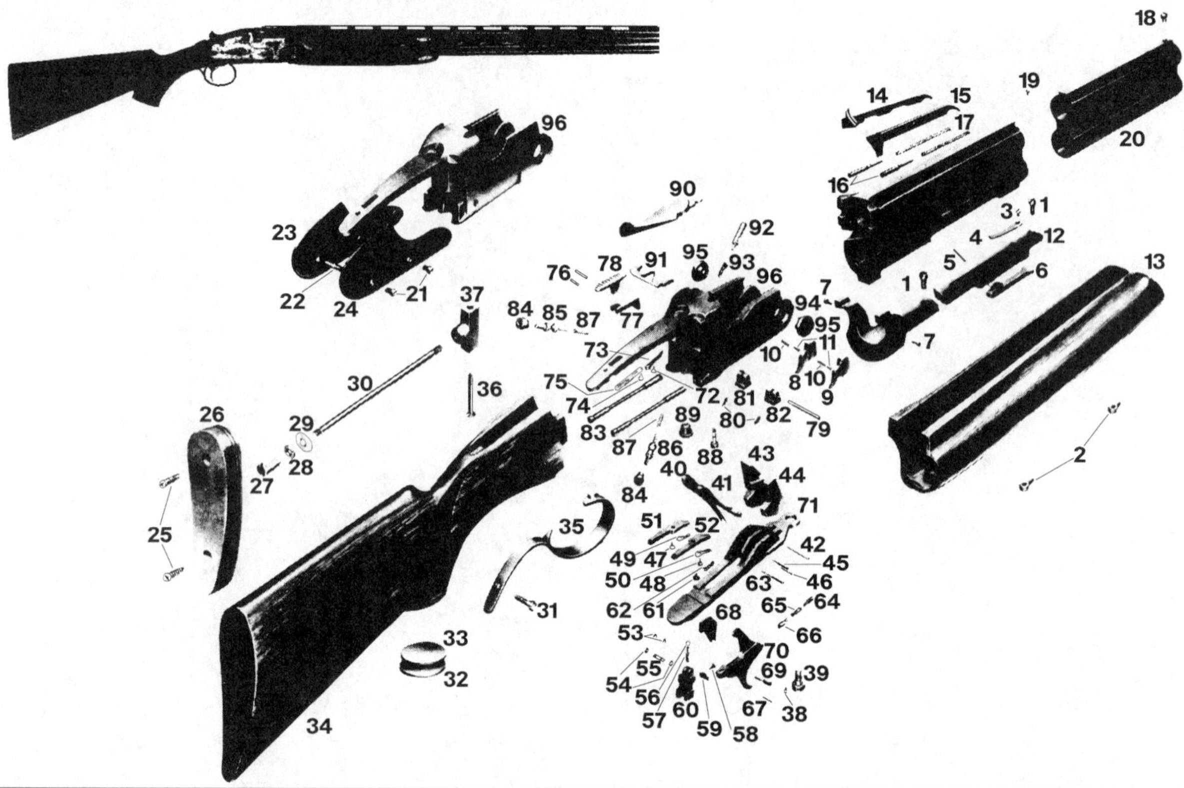

1	Forend Piece Screws
2	Forend Nuts
3	Forend Lever Spring Retaining Screw
4	Forend Lever Spring
5	Forend Lever Pin
6	Forend Lever
7	Cocking Lever Screw
8	Left Cocking Lever
9	Right Cocking Lever
10	Cocking Lever Springs
11	Cocking Lever Spring Plungers
12	Forend Piece
13	Forend
14	Ejector, Left
15	Ejector, Right
16	Ejector Spring Guides
17	Ejector Springs
18	Front Sight
19	Middle Sight
20	Barrel Assembly
21	Sideplate Screws
22	Sideplate Spacer Rod
23	Sideplate, Left
24	Sideplate, Right
25	Recoil Pad Screws
26	Recoil Pad
27	Stock Bolt Nut
28	Stock Bolt Spring Washer
29	Stock Bolt Washer
30	Stock Bolt
31	Trigger Guard Screw
32	Pistol Grip Cap
33	Spacer
34	Buttstock
35	Trigger Guard
36	Receiver Tang Screw
37	Receiver Shank
38	Trigger Plate Locking Screw
39	Trigger Plate Screw
40	Hammer Spring, Left
41	Hammer Spring, Right
42	Hammer Pin
43	Hammer, Left
44	Hammer, Right
45	Hammer Spring Retaining Pin
46	Sear Pin
47	Sear Spring Retaining Screw, Left
48	Sear Spring Retaining Screw, Right
49	Sear Spring, Left
50	Sear Spring, Right
51	Sear, Left
52	Sear, Right
53	Connector Pin Snap Rings
54	Connector Pin Washers
55	Connector Pin
56	Connector Spring Plunger
57	Connector Spring
58	Mechanical Switchover Screw
59	Mechanical Switchover
60	Connector
61	Trigger Spring Retaining Screw
62	Trigger Spring
63	Trigger Pin
64	Selector Spring Screw
65	Selector Spring
66	Selector Spring Plunger
67	Connector Guide Plate Pin
68	Connector Guide Plate
69	Selector Button
70	Trigger
71	Trigger Plate
72	Top Lever Spring Screw
73	Top Lever Spring
74	Safety Button Spring Retaining Screw
75	Safety Button Spring
76	Safety Button Pins
77	Trigger Block
78	Safety Button
79	Cocking Piece Pin
80	Cocking Piece Retractor Springs
81	Cocking Piece, Left
82	Cocking Piece, Right
83	Cocking Rods
84	Firing Pin Retainers
85	Firing Pin, Over (Long)
86	Firing Pin, Under (Short)
87	Firing Pin Retractor Springs
88	Top Lever Shaft Screw
89	Top Lever Shaft
90	Top Lever
91	Locking Piece
92	Locking Piece Retainer
93	Locking Piece Retainer Spring
94	Pivot Retainer Screw
95	Pivots
96	Receiver

Centurion Autoloading Shotgun

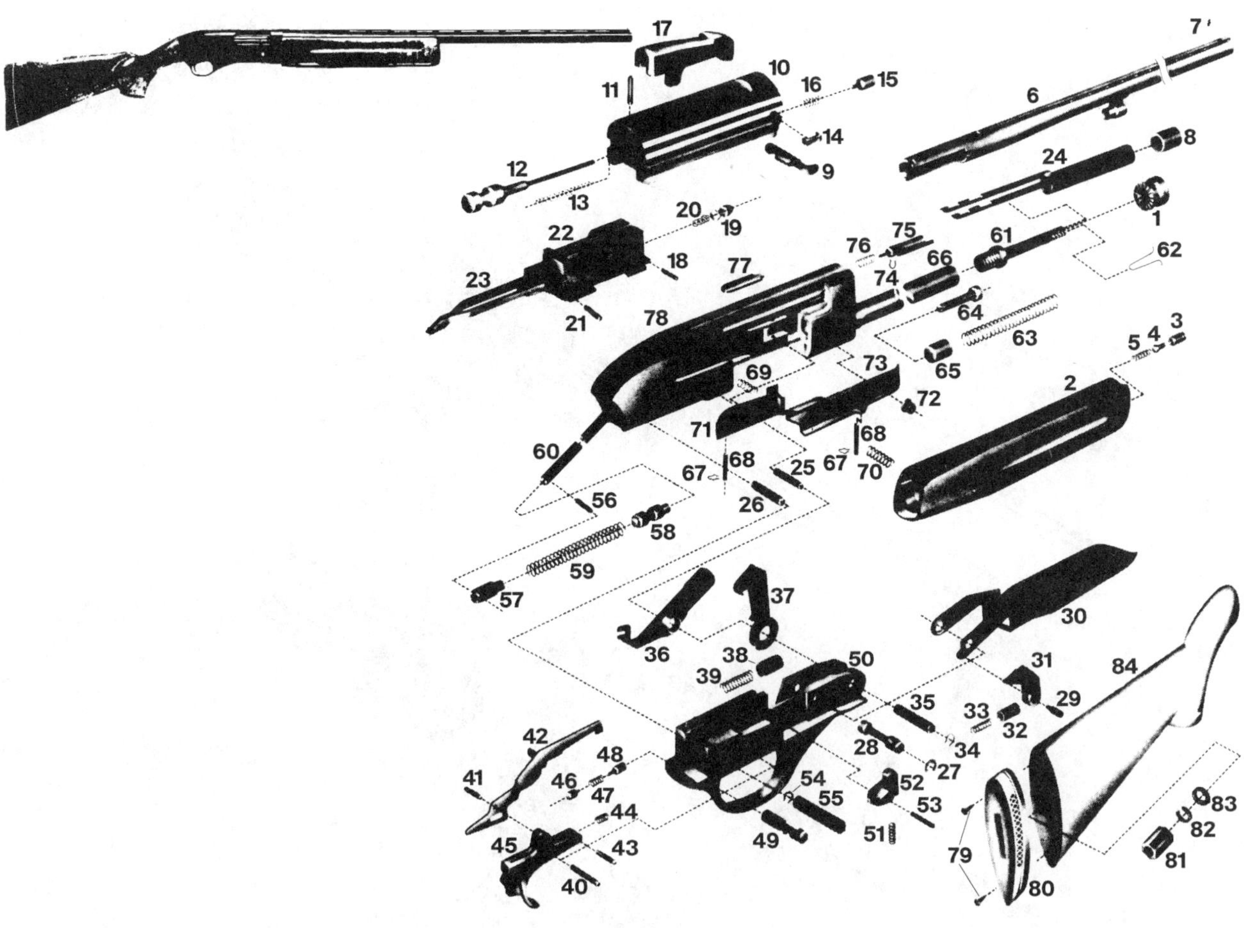

1	Forend Cap
2	Forend
3	Forend Cap Plunger Guide
4	Forend Cap Plunger
5	Plunger Spring
6	Barrel
7	Front Sight
8	Gas Piston
9	Operating Handle
10	Bolt
11	Retaining Pin
12	Firing Pin
13	Firing Pin Spring
14	Extractor
15	Extractor Plunger
16	Extractor Spring
17	Locking Block
18	Retaining Pin
19	Carrier Plunger
20	Plunger Spring
21	Carrier Extension Pin
22	Carrier
23	Carrier Extension Assembly
24	Slide
25	Front Trigger Frame Pin
26	Rear Trigger Frame Pin
27	Retaining Ring
28	Lifter Pivot
29	Lifter Dog Pin
30	Lifter
31	Lifter Dog
32	Dog Follower
33	Dog Follower Spring
34	Detent Spring
35	Hammer Pivot Tube
36	Lock Shaft Assembly
37	Hammer
38	Hammer Plunger
39	Hammer Plunger Spring
40	Trigger Pin
41	Disconnector Pin
42	Disconnector
43	Trigger Spring Pin
44	Trigger Spring
45	Trigger
46	Retainer Screw
47	Safety Spring
48	Safety Plunger
49	Safety Button
50	Trigger Frame
51	Sear Spring
52	Sear
53	Sear Pin
54	Detent Spring
55	Rear Trigger Frame Tube
56	Action Tube Plug Pin
57	Action Tube Plug
58	Action Tube Follower
59	Action Tube Spring
60	Action Tube
61	Magazine Extension
62	Extension Retainer
63	Magazine Spring
64	Magazine Plug
65	Magazine Follower
66	Magazine Tube
67	Latch Pin Retainers
68	Latch Pins
69	Latch Spring
70	Blocker Spring
71	Feed Latch
72	Bolt Release Button
73	Blocker Assembly
74	Ejector Retainer
75	Ejector
76	Ejector Spring
77	Receiver Insert
78	Receiver
79	Recoil Pad Screws
80	Recoil Pad
81	Action Tube Nut
82	Action Tube Lock Washer
83	Buttstock Washer
84	Buttstock

Mark V Bolt-Action Rifle

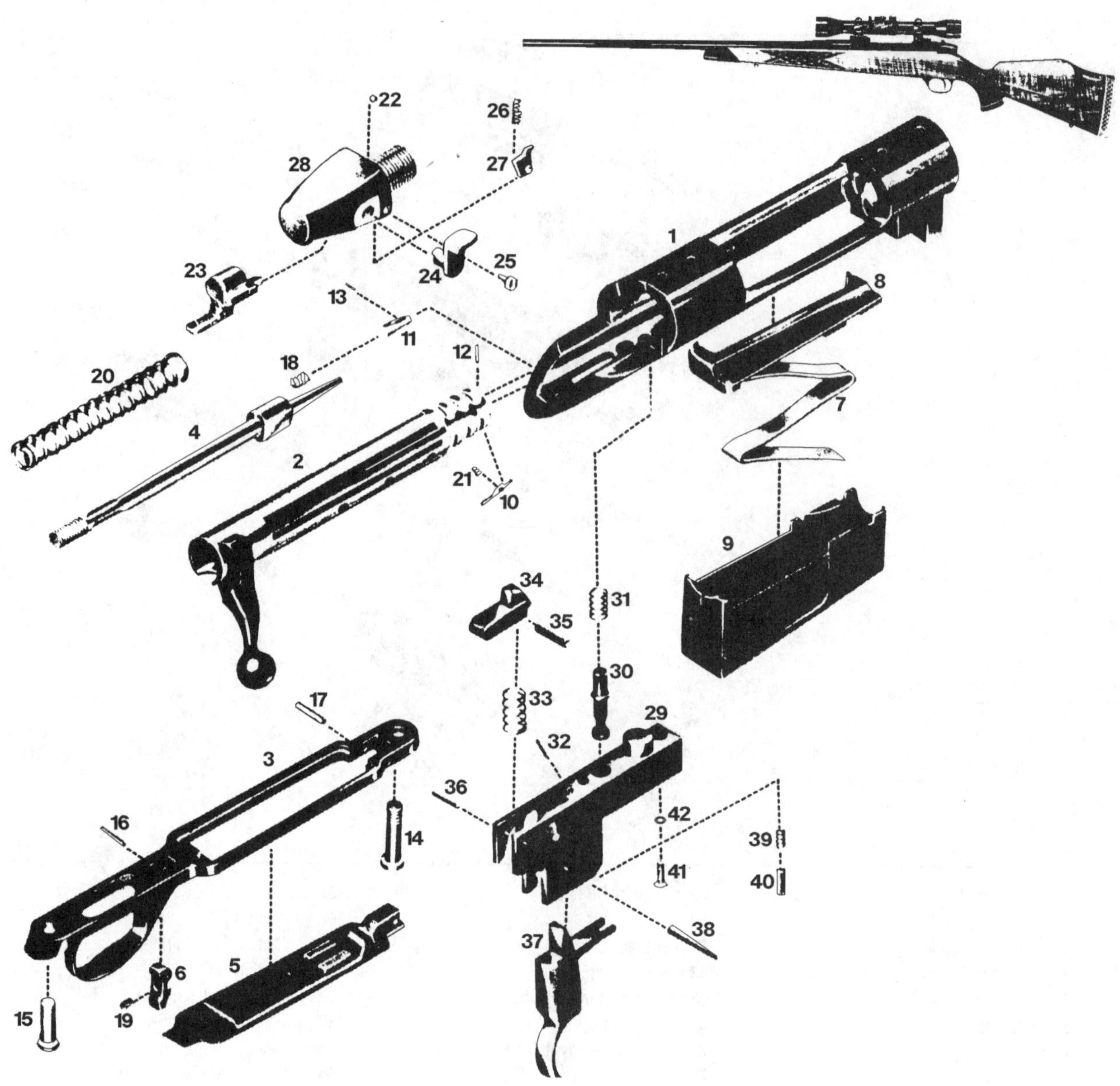

1	Receiver	**18**	Ejector Spring	**35**	Sear Lock Pin
2	Bolt Body	**19**	Floorplate Catch Spring	**36**	Sear Pin
3	Trigger Guard	**20**	Firing Pin Spring	**37**	Trigger
4	Firing Pin	**21**	Extractor Spring	**38**	Trigger Pin
5	Floorplate	**22**	Retainer Ball	**39**	Trigger Spring
6	Floorplate Catch	**23**	Cocking Piece	**40**	Pull Weight Adjustment Screw
7	Follower Spring	**24**	Safety-Lever	**41**	Trigger Housing Attachment Screw, Bottom
8	Magazine Follower	**25**	Safety Hook Screw	**42**	Star Washer, Bottom Attachment Screw
9	Magazine Box	**26**	Safety Spring		**Parts Not Shown**
10	Extractor	**27**	Safety Hook		Barrel
11	Ejector	**28**	Bolt Sleeve		Sear Spring Washer
12	Extractor Pin	**29**	Trigger Housing		Stock
13	Ejector Pin	**30**	Bolt Stop		Trigger Housing Attachment Screw, Top
14	Front Trigger Guard Screw	**31**	Bolt Stop Spring		
15	Rear Trigger Guard Screw	**32**	Creep Adjustment Screw		
16	Floorplate Catch Pin	**33**	Sear Spring		
17	Floorplate Pin	**34**	Sear		

Mark XXII (Clip) Autoloading Rifle

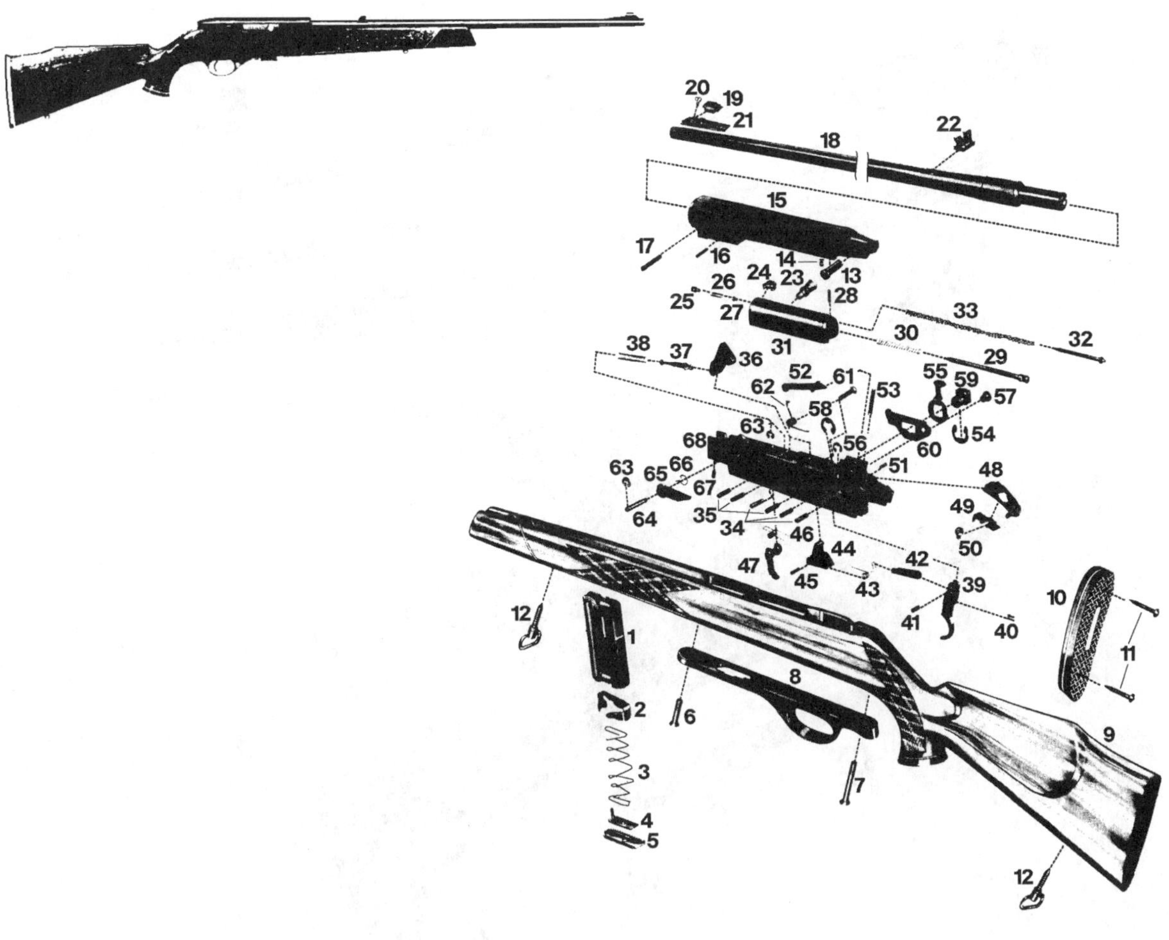

1	Magazine Box	**25**	Extractor Plunger	**47**	Magazine Release
2	Magazine Follower	**26**	Extractor Spring	**48**	Safety Tang Plate
3	Magazine Spring	**27**	Operating Handle Plunger	**49**	Safety Slide
4	Magazine Shoe Retainer	**28**	Firing Pin Retaining Pin	**50**	Safety Button
5	Magazine Shoe	**29**	Firing Pin	**51**	Safety-Lever Pin
6	Trigger Guard Screw, Front	**30**	Firing Pin Spring	**52**	Safety-Lever
7	Trigger Guard Screw, Rear	**31**	Bolt	**53**	Safety-Lever Spring
8	Trigger Guard	**32**	Recoil Spring Guide	**54**	Selector Stud Retaining Ring
9	Stock	**33**	Recoil Spring	**55**	Selector Lever
10	Buttpad	**34**	Hammer, Sear and Trigger Pins	**56**	Selector Lever Pin Retaining Ring
11	Buttpad Screws	**35**	Hammer Stop, Magazine Release and Sear Stop Pins	**57**	Selector Lever Plate Pin
12	Sling Swivel Assembly	**36**	Hammer	**58**	Selector Stud Lock Ring
13	Takedown Pin	**37**	Hammer Spring Guide	**59**	Selector Stud
14	Takedown Pin Spring	**38**	Hammer Spring	**60**	Selector Lever Plate
15	Receiver	**39**	Trigger	**61**	Trigger Assembly Cross Screw
16	Locating Pin	**40**	Trigger Spring	**62**	Selector Spring
17	Barrel Pin	**41**	Disconnector Pin	**63**	Bolt Lock Pin Retaining Ring
18	Barrel	**42**	Disconnector	**64**	Bolt Lock Pin
19	Front Sight	**43**	Disconnector Spring	**65**	Bolt Lock Lever
20	Front Sight Ramp Screw	**44**	Sear	**66**	Bolt Lock Spring
21	Front Sight Ramp	**45**	Disconnector Spring Pin	**67**	Tension Screw
22	Rear Sight	**46**	Magazine Release Spring	**68**	Trigger Frame Assembly
23	Operating Handle				
24	Extractor				

Mark XXII (Tube) Autoloading Rifle (Pre-1982)

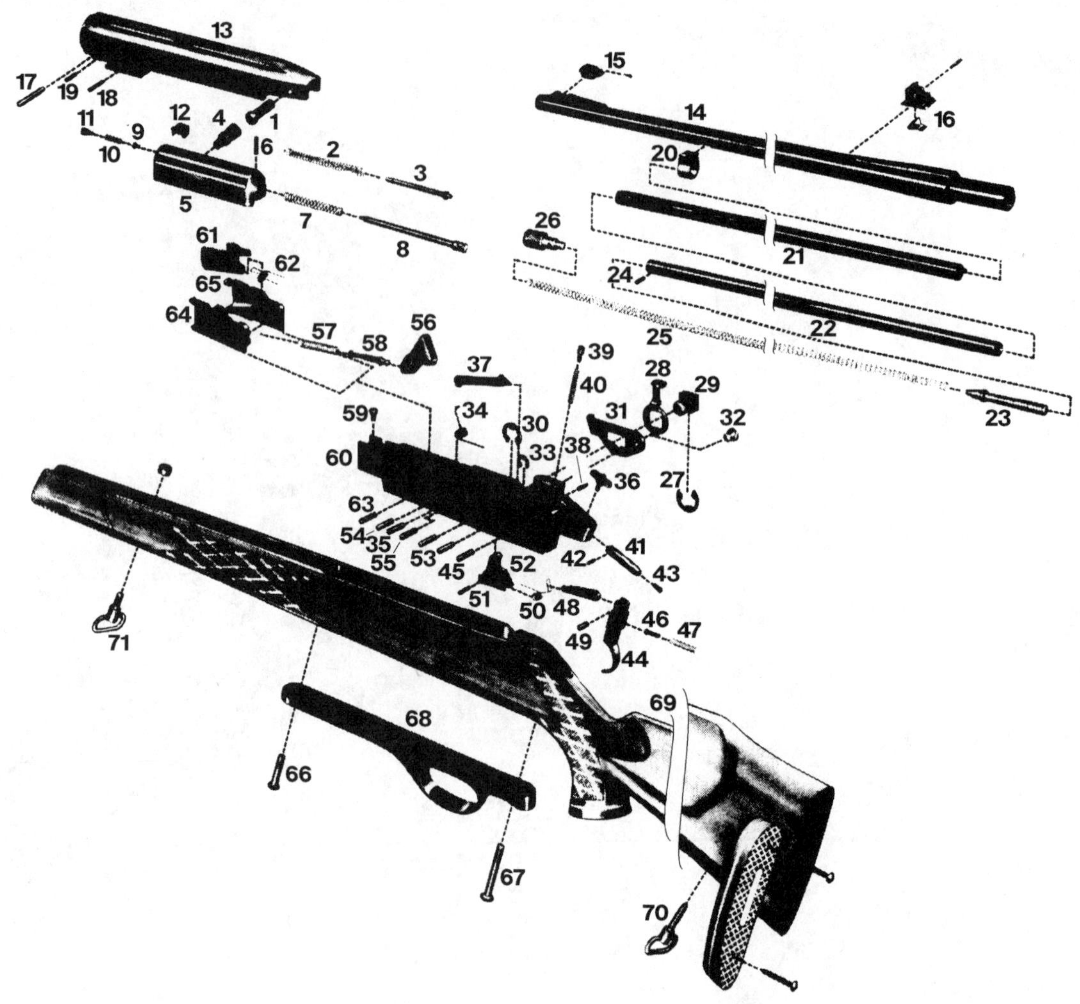

1	Takedown Pin	**25**	Magazine Spring	**48**	Disconnector
2	Recoil Spring	**26**	Magazine Plug	**49**	Disconnector Pin
3	Recoil Spring Guide	**27**	Selector Stud Retaining Ring	**50**	Disconnector Spring
4	Operating Handle	**28**	Selector Lever	**51**	Disconnector Spring Pin
5	Bolt	**29**	Selector Stud	**52**	Sear
6	Firing Pin Retaining Pin	**30**	Selector Stud Lock Ring	**53**	Sear Pin
7	Firing Pin Spring	**31**	Selector Lever Plate	**54**	Hammer Stop Pin
8	Firing Pin	**32**	Selector Lever Plate Pin	**55**	Hammer Pin
9	Operating Plunger	**33**	Selector Lever Pin Retaining Ring	**56**	Hammer
10	Extractor Spring			**57**	Hammer Spring
11	Extractor Plunger	**34**	Selector Spring	**58**	Hammer Spring Guide
12	Extractor	**35**	Selector Lever Spring Pin	**59**	Tension Screw
13	Receiver	**36**	Safety	**60**	Frame
14	Barrel	**37**	Safety-Lever	**61**	Lifter
15	Front Sight	**38**	Safety-Lever Pin	**62**	Lifter Spring
16	Rear Sight	**39**	Safety-Lever Plunger	**63**	Lifter Spring Pin
17	Barrel Pin	**40**	Safety-Lever Plunger Spring	**64**	Left Cartridge Guide
18	Retaining Pin	**41**	Safety Plunger	**65**	Right Cartridge Guide
19	Frame Retaining Pin	**42**	Safety Plunger Pin	**66**	Front Trigger Guard Screw
20	Magazine Ring	**43**	Safety Lock Screw	**67**	Rear Trigger Guard Screw
21	Outer Magazine Tube	**44**	Trigger	**68**	Trigger Guard
22	Inner Magazine Tube	**45**	Trigger Pin	**69**	Stock
23	Magazine Follower	**46**	Trigger Plunger	**70**	Rear Swivel
24	Magazine Plug Pin	**47**	Trigger Plunger Spring	**71**	Front Swivel

Mark XXII (Tube) Autoloading Rifle (Post-1982)

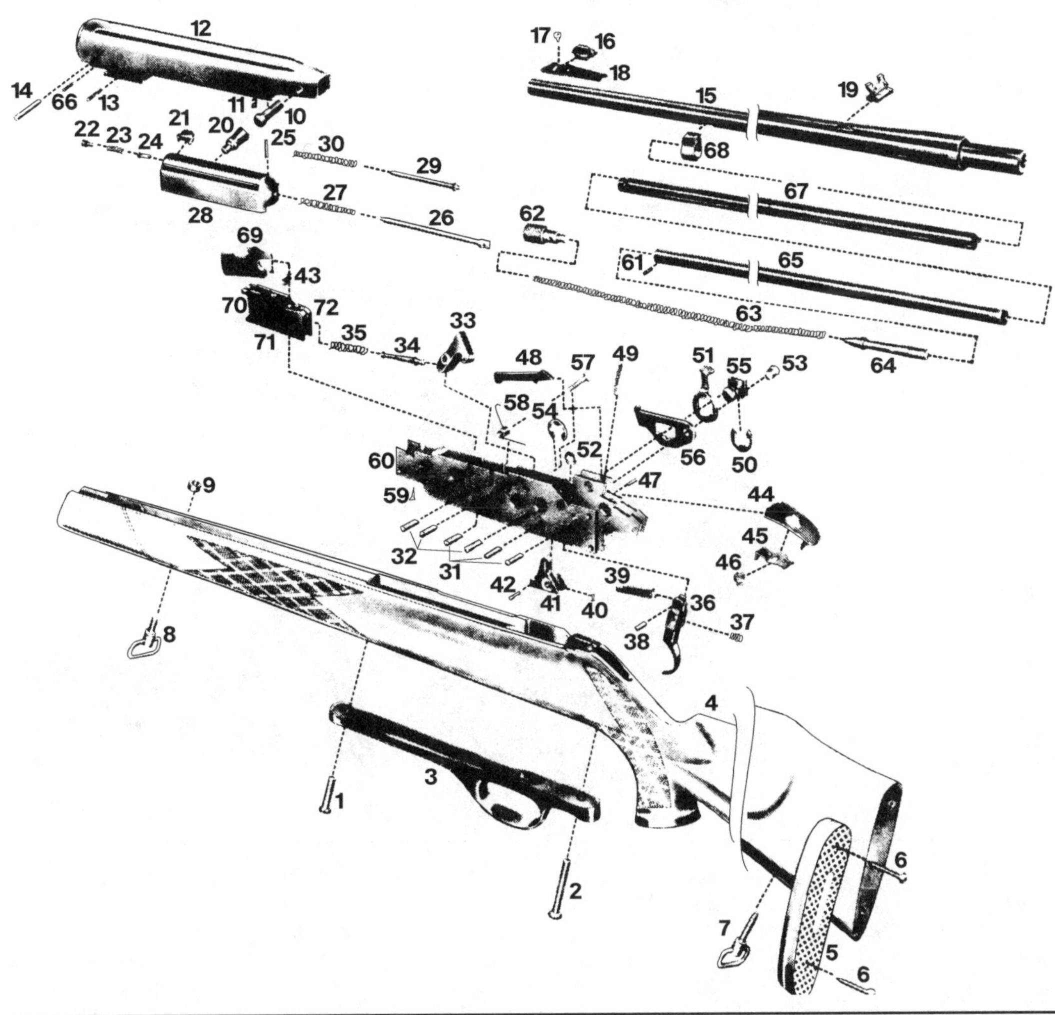

1 Front Trigger Guard Screw
2 Rear Trigger Guard Screw
3 Trigger Guard
4 Stock
5 Buttpad
6 Buttpad Screws
7 Rear Sling Swivel Assembly
8 Front Sling Swivel Assembly
9 Front Sling Swivel Nut
10 Takedown Pin
11 Takedown Pin Spring
12 Receiver
13 Locating Pin
14 Barrel Pin
15 Barrel
16 Front Sight
17 Front Sight Ramp Screw
18 Front Sight Ramp
19 Rear Sight
20 Operating Handle
21 Extractor
22 Extractor Plunger
23 Extractor Spring
24 Operating Handle Plunger
25 Firing Pin Retaining Pin
26 Firing Pin
27 Firing Pin Spring
28 Bolt
29 Recoil Spring Guide
30 Recoil Spring
31 Hammer, Sear and Trigger Pins
32 Hammer Stop, Sear Stop and Lifter Spring Pins
33 Hammer
34 Hammer Spring Guide
35 Hammer Spring
36 Trigger
37 Trigger Spring
38 Disconnector Pin
39 Disconnector
40 Disconnector Spring
41 Sear
42 Disconnector Spring Pin
43 Lifter Spring
44 Safety Tang Plate
45 Safety Slide
46 Safety Button
47 Safety-Lever Pin
48 Safety-Lever
49 Safety-Lever Spring
50 Selector Stud Retaining Ring
51 Selector Lever
52 Selector Lever Pin Retaining Ring
53 Selector Lever Plate Pin
54 Selector Stud Lock Ring
55 Selector Stud
56 Selector Lever Plate
57 Trigger Assembly Cross Screw
58 Selector Spring
59 Tension Screw
60 Trigger Frame Assembly
61 Magazine Plug Pin
62 Magazine Plug
63 Magazine Spring
64 Magazine Follower
65 Inner Magazine Tube
66 Magazine Tube Pin
67 Outer Magazine Tube
68 Magazine Ring
69 Lifter
70 Cartridge Guide Assembly
71 Left Cartridge Guide
72 Right Cartridge Guide

Model 82 Autoloading Shotgun

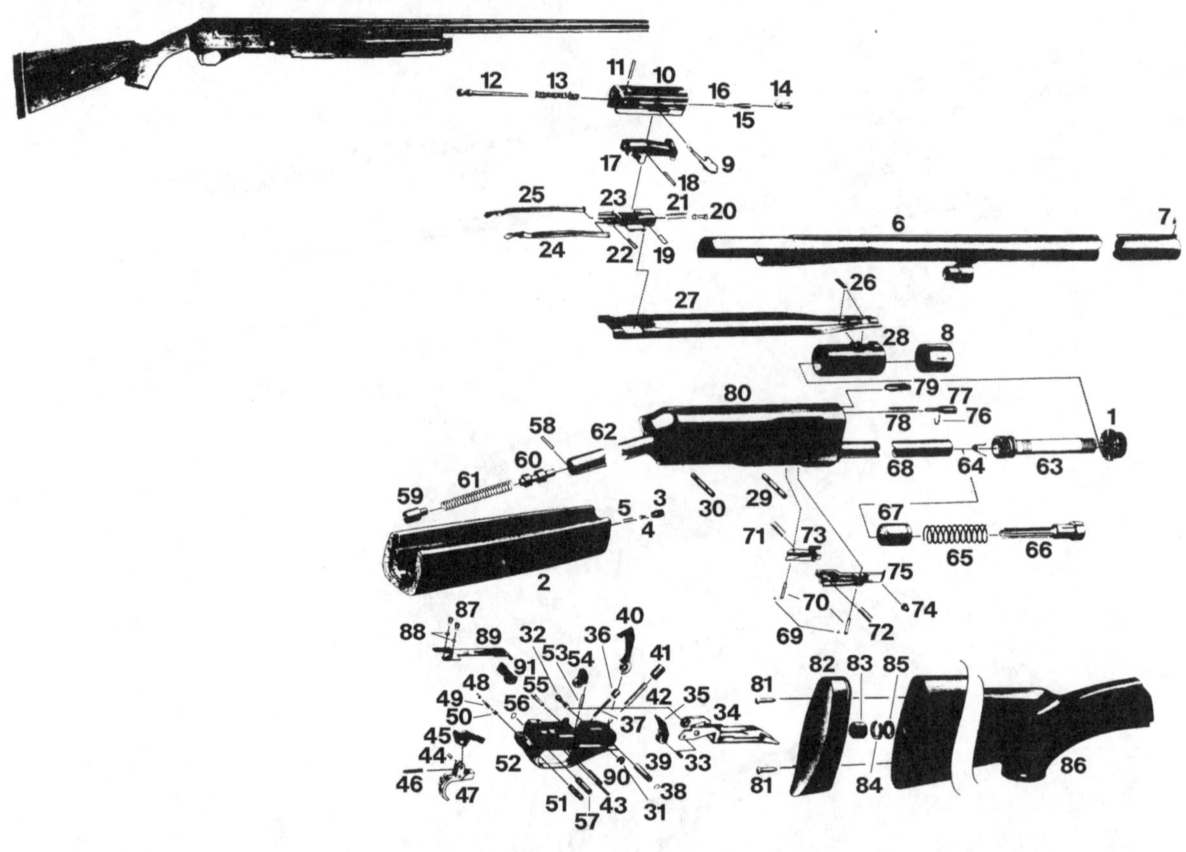

1	Forearm Cap	32	Lifter Pivot	63	Magazine Extension
2	Forearm	33	Lifter Dog Pin	64	Extension Retainer
3	Forearm Cap Plunger Guide	34	Lifter	65	Magazine Spring
4	Forearm Cap Plunger	35	Lifter Dog	66	Magazine Plug
5	Plunger Spring	36	Dog Follower	67	Magazine Follower
6	Barrel Assembly	37	Dog Follower Spring	68	Magazine Tube
7	Front Bead	38	Detent Spring	69	Latch Pin Retainers
8	Gas Piston	39	Hammer Pivot Tube	70	Latch Pins
9	Operating Handle	40	Hammer	71	Latch Spring
10	Bolt	41	Hammer Plunger	72	Blocker Spring
11	Firing Pin Retaining Pin	42	Hammer Plunger Spring	73	Feed Latch
12	Firing Pin	43	Trigger Pin	74	Bolt Release Button
13	Firing Pin Spring	44	Disconnector Pin	75	Blocker Assembly
14	Extractor	45	Disconnector	76	Ejector Retainer
15	Extractor Plunger	46	Trigger Spring	77	Ejector
16	Extractor Spring	47	Trigger	78	Ejector Spring
17	Locking Block	48	Retainer Screw	79	Receiver Insert
18	Locking Block Pin	49	Safety Spring	80	Receiver
19	Plunger Retaining Pin	50	Safety Plunger	81	Recoil Pad Screw
20	Carrier Plunger	51	Safety Button	82	Recoil Pad
21	Plunger Spring	52	Trigger Frame	83	Action Tube Nut
22	Carrier Extension Pin	53	Sear Spring	84	Action Tube Lock Washer
23	Bolt Carrier	54	Sear	85	Buttstock Washer
24	Carrier Extension, Right	55	Sear Pin	86	Buttstock
25	Carrier Extension, Left	56	Detent Spring	87	Protecting Cover Screws
26	Slide Tube Key	57	Rear Trigger Frame Tube	88	Lock Washers
27	Slide Bar	58	Action Tube Plug Pin	89	Protecting Cover
28	Slide Tube	59	Action Tube Plug	90	Disconnector Link Pin
29	Front Trigger Frame Pin	60	Action Tube Follower	91	Disconnector Link
30	Rear Trigger Frame Pin	61	Action Tube Spring		
31	Lifter Pivot Retaining Ring	62	Action Tube		

Model 92 Slide-Action Shotgun

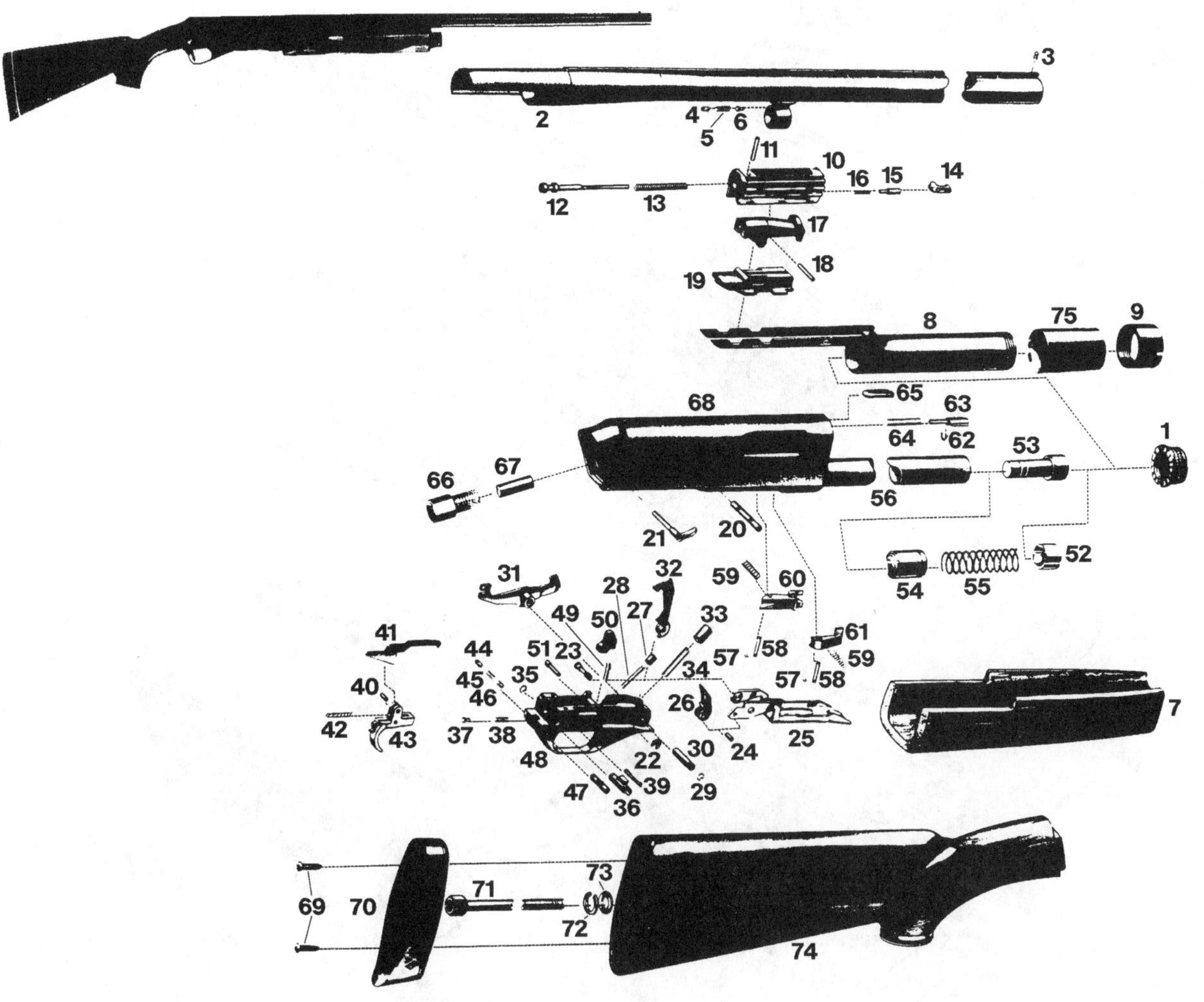

1	Forearm Cap	**26**	Lifter Dog	**51**	Sear Pin
2	Barrel Assembly	**27**	Dog Follower	**52**	Magazine Spring Retainer
3	Front Bead	**28**	Dog Follower Spring	**53**	Magazine Plug
4	Detent Screw	**29**	Detent Spring	**54**	Magazine Follower
5	Detent Spring	**30**	Hammer Pivot Tube	**55**	Magazine Spring
6	Detent Plunger	**31**	Lockshaft Assembly	**56**	Magazine Tube
7	Forearm	**32**	Hammer	**57**	Latch Pin Retainers
8	Slide Assembly	**33**	Hammer Plunger	**58**	Latch Pins
9	Forearm Tube Nut	**34**	Hammer Plunger Spring	**59**	Latch Springs
10	Bolt	**35**	Detent Spring	**60**	Feed Latch
11	Firing Pin Retaining Pin	**36**	Cam	**61**	Blocker
12	Firing Pin	**37**	Cam Plunger	**62**	Ejector Retainer
13	Firing Pin Spring	**38**	Cam Plunger Spring	**63**	Ejector
14	Extractor	**39**	Trigger Pin	**64**	Ejector Spring
15	Extractor Plunger	**40**	Disconnector Pin	**65**	Receiver Insert
16	Extractor Spring	**41**	Disconnector	**66**	Stock Bolt Adaptor
17	Locking Block	**42**	Trigger Spring	**67**	Buffer
18	Locking Block Pin	**43**	Trigger	**68**	Receiver
19	Bolt Carrier	**44**	Retainer Screw	**69**	Wood Screws
20	Front Trigger Frame Pin	**45**	Safety Spring	**70**	Recoil Pad
21	Forearm Release Lever	**46**	Safety Plunger	**71**	Stock Bolt
22	Retaining Ring	**47**	Safety Button	**72**	Lock Washer
23	Lifter Pivot	**48**	Trigger Frame	**73**	Buttstock Washer
24	Lifter Dog Pin	**49**	Sear Spring	**74**	Buttstock
25	Lifter	**50**	Sear	**75**	Spacer

Patrician Slide-Action Shotgun

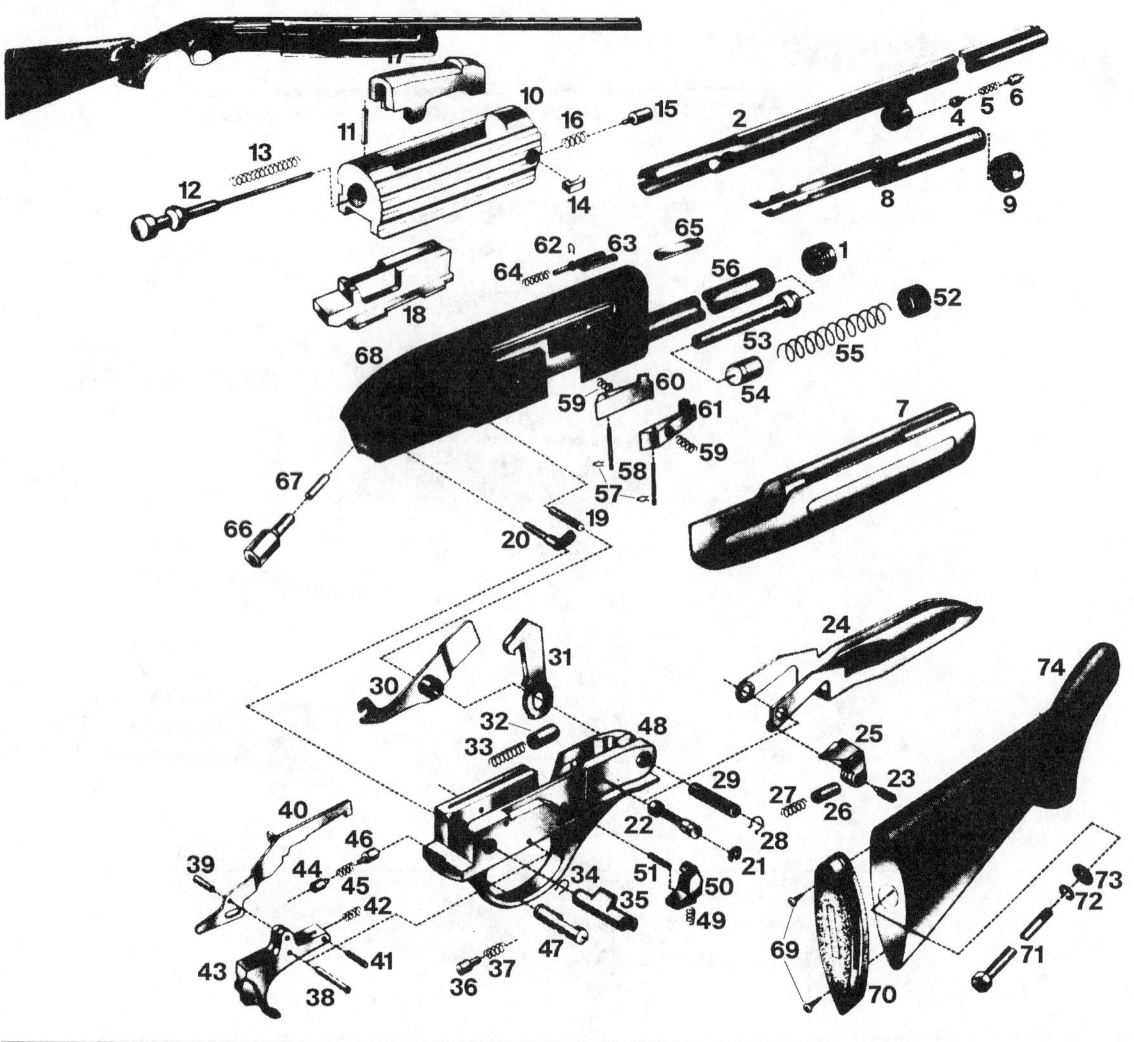

1	Forend Cap
2	Barrel
3	Front Sight
4	Detent Screw
5	Detent Spring
6	Detent Plunger
7	Forend
8	Slide
9	Forend Tube Nut
10	Bolt
11	Retaining Pin
12	Firing Pin
13	Firing Pin Spring
14	Extractor
15	Extractor Plunger
16	Extractor Spring
17	Locking Block
18	Carrier
19	Front Trigger Frame Pin
20	Forend Release Lever
21	Retaining Ring
22	Lifter Pivot
23	Lifter Dog Pin
24	Lifter
25	Lifter Dog
26	Dog Follower
27	Dog Follower Spring
28	Detent Spring
29	Hammer Pivot Tube
30	Lock Shaft Assembly
31	Hammer
32	Hammer Plunger
33	Hammer Plunger Spring
34	Detent Spring
35	Cam
36	Cam Plunger
37	Cam Plunger Spring
38	Trigger Pin
39	Disconnector Pin
40	Disconnector
41	Trigger Spring Pin
42	Trigger Spring
43	Trigger
44	Retainer Screw
45	Safety Spring
46	Safety Plunger
47	Safety Button
48	Trigger Frame
49	Sear Spring
50	Sear
51	Sear Pin
52	Magazine Spring Retainer
53	Magazine Plug
54	Magazine Follower
55	Magazine Spring
56	Magazine
57	Latch Pin Retainers
58	Latch Pins
59	Latch Springs
60	Feed Latch
61	Blocker
62	Ejector Retainer
63	Ejector
64	Ejector Spring
65	Receiver Insert
66	Stock Bolt Adaptor
67	Buffer
68	Receiver
69	Recoil Pad Screws
70	Recoil Pad
71	Stock Bolt
72	Lock Washer
73	Buttstock Washer
74	Buttstock

Vanguard Bolt-Action Rifle (Pre-1981)

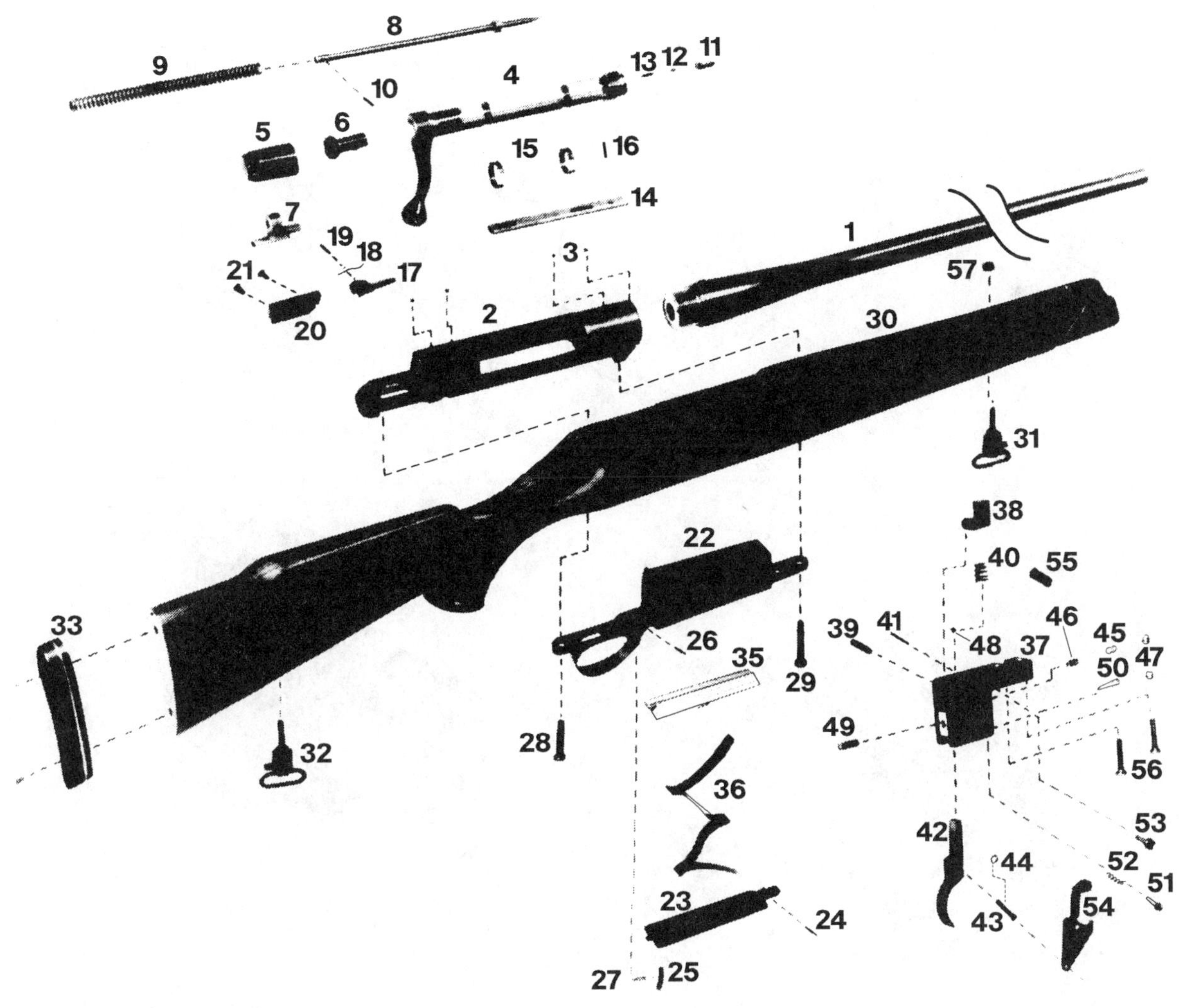

1	Barrel	**20**	Ejector Housing	**39**	Sear Pin
2	Receiver	**21**	Housing Screws	**40**	Sear Spring
3	Plug Screws	**22**	Trigger Guard	**41**	Sear Stopper Pin
4	Bolt	**23**	Floorplate	**42**	Trigger
5	Bolt Sleeve Body	**24**	Floorplate Hinge Pin	**43**	Trigger Pin
6	Bolt Sleeve Shank	**25**	Floorplate Catch	**44**	Retaining Ring
7	Cocking Piece	**26**	Floorplate Catch Pin	**45**	Trigger Spring Stopper
8	Firing Pin	**27**	Floorplate Catch Spring	**46**	Trigger Spring
9	Firing Pin Spring	**28**	Rear Trigger Guard Screw	**47**	Lock Nuts
10	Firing Pin Retaining Pin	**29**	Front Trigger Guard Screw	**48**	Lock Screw
11	Extractor	**30**	Stock	**49**	Rear Trigger Adjusting Screw
12	Extractor Plunger	**31**	Front Sling Swivel	**50**	Front Trigger Adjusting Screw
13	Extractor Spring	**32**	Rear Sling Swivel	**51**	Safety Plunger
14	Bolt Guide Plate	**33**	Buttplate	**52**	Safety Spring
15	Bolt Guide Plate Rings	**34**	Buttplate Screws	**53**	Safety-Lever Guide Screw
16	Stopper Spring	**35**	Magazine Follower	**54**	Safety-Lever
17	Ejector	**36**	Follower Spring	**55**	Trigger Housing Pin
18	Ejector Spring	**37**	Trigger Housing	**56**	Trigger Housing Screws
19	Ejector Pin	**38**	Sear	**57**	Forearm Escutcheon

Vanguard Bolt-Action Rifle (Post-1981)

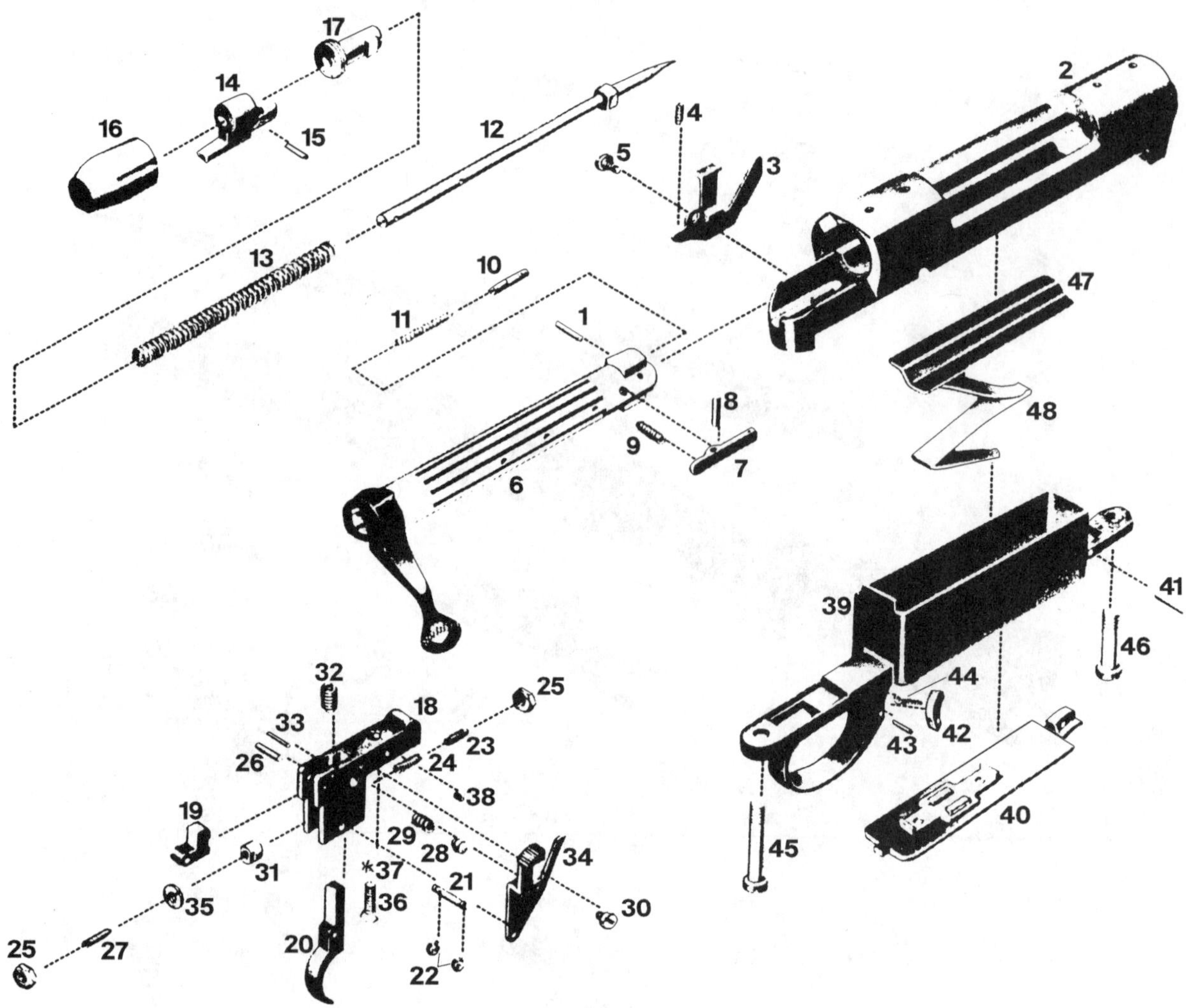

1 Ejector Pin
2 Receiver
3 Bolt Stop
4 Bolt Stop Spring
5 Bolt Stop Screw
6 Bolt Body
7 Extractor
8 Extractor Pin
9 Extractor Spring
10 Ejector
11 Ejector Spring
12 Firing Pin
13 Firing Pin Spring
14 Cocking Piece
15 Firing Pin Retaining Pin
16 Bolt Sleeve Body
17 Bolt Sleeve Shank
18 Trigger Housing
19 Sear
20 Trigger
21 Trigger Pin
22 Retaining Rings
23 Trigger Adjusting Screw, Pull Weight
24 Trigger Spring
25 Lock Nuts
26 Sear Pin
27 Trigger Adjusting Screw, Creep
28 Safety Plunger
29 Safety Spring
30 Safety-Lever Screw
31 Creep Screw Block
32 Sear Spring
33 Sear Stopper Pin
34 Safety-Lever
35 Creep Screw Washer
36 Trigger Housing Attachment Screw
37 Housing Screw Star Washer
38 Housing Screw Set Screw
39 Trigger Guard/Magazine
40 Floorplate
41 Floorplate Pin
42 Floorplate Catch
43 Floorplate Catch Pin
44 Floorplate Catch Spring
45 Trigger Guard Screw, Rear
46 Trigger Guard Screw, Front
47 Magazine Follower
48 Follower Spring

Model SB-100B Single Shot Shotgun

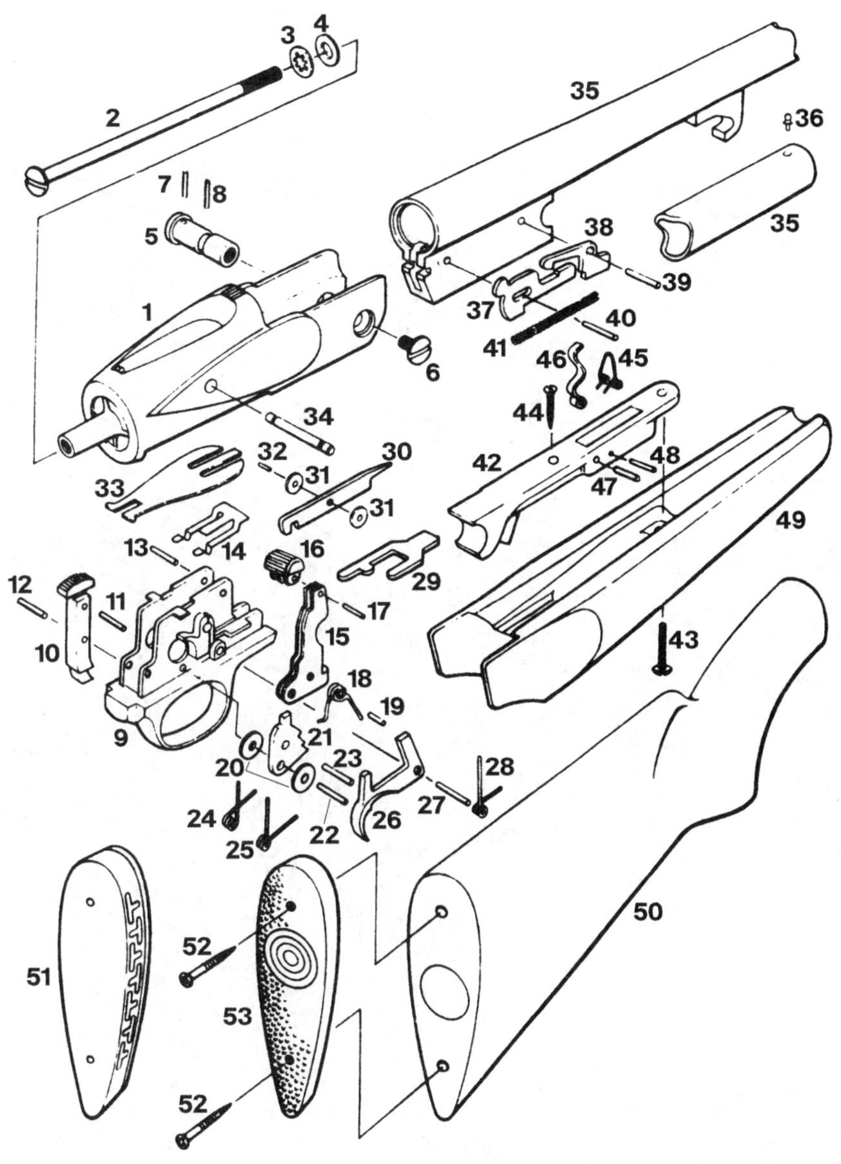

1	Frame	19	Release Lever Spring Pin	37	Ejector
2	Stock Bolt	20	Sear Washers	38	Ejector Sear
3	Stock Bolt Lock Washer	21	Sear	39	Ejector Sear Pin
4	Stock Bolt Washer	22	Sear Pin	40	Ejector Retaining Pin
5	Joint Pin	23	Sear Cross Pin	41	Ejector Spring
6	Joint Pin Screw	24	Sear Spring, Left	42	Forend Iron
7	Joint Locking Pin	25	Sear Spring, Right	43	Forend Screw
8	Ejector Actuating Pin	26	Trigger	44	Forend Iron Screw
9	Trigger Guard	27	Trigger Pin	45	Forend Spring Spring
10	Safety	28	Lock Spring	46	Forend Spring
11	Safety Detent Pin	29	Lock	47	Forend Spring Pin
12	Safety Pin	30	Firing Pin	48	Forend Spring Spring Pin
13	Firing Pin Guide Pin	31	Firing Pin Washers	49	Forend
14	Safety Detent Spring	32	Firing Pin Cross Pin	50	Stock
15	Release Lever	33	Cover Plate	51	Recoil Pad
16	Release Lever Thumb-Piece	34	Trigger Guard Pin	52	Buttplate Screws
17	Release Lever Thumb-Piece Pin	35	Barrel	53	Buttplate
18	Release Lever Spring	36	Front Sight		

Model SB-300 Side-by-Side Shotgun

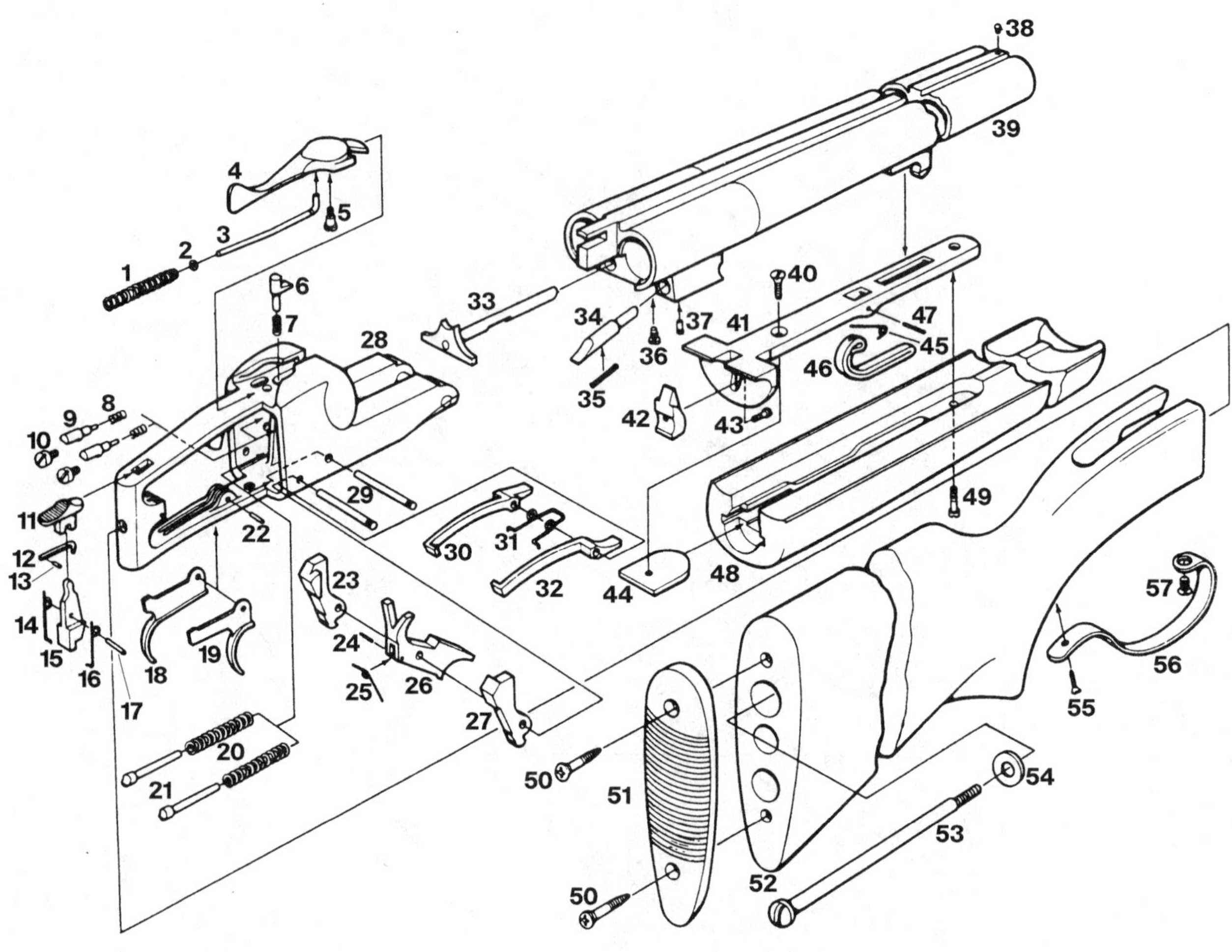

1	Top Snap Plunger Spring	21	Mainspring Plungers	38	Front Sight
2	Top Snap Plunger Collar	22	Trigger Pin	39	Barrel
3	Top Snap Plunger	23	Hammer, Left	40	Forend Screw, Rear
4	Top Snap	24	Cocking Lever Spring Pin	41	Forend Iron
5	Top Snap Screw	25	Cocking Lever Spring	42	Ejector
6	Top Snap Trip	26	Cocking Lever	43	Ejector Screw
7	Top Snap Trip Spring	27	Hammer, Right	44	Forend Insert
8	Firing Pin Springs	28	Frame	45	Forend Spring Spring
9	Firing Pins	29	Cocking Lever, Hammer and Sear Pins	46	Forend Spring
10	Firing Pin Retaining Screws	30	Sear, Left	47	Forend Spring Pin
11	Safety Button	31	Sear Spring	48	Forend Wood
12	Safety Spring	32	Sear, Right	49	Forend Screw, Front
13	Safety Plunger	33	Extractor	50	Buttplate Screws
14	Trigger Spring, Left	34	Cocking Plunger	51	Buttplate
15	Safety-Lever	35	Cocking Plunger Spring	52	Stock
16	Trigger Spring, Right	36	Extractor Screw	53	Stock Bolt
17	Safety-Lever Pin	37	Cocking Plunger Retaining Screw	54	Stock Bolt Washer
18	Trigger, Left			55	Trigger Guard Screw, Rear
19	Trigger, Right			56	Trigger Guard
20	Mainsprings			57	Trigger Guard Screw, Front

Model SB-312 Side-by-Side Shotgun

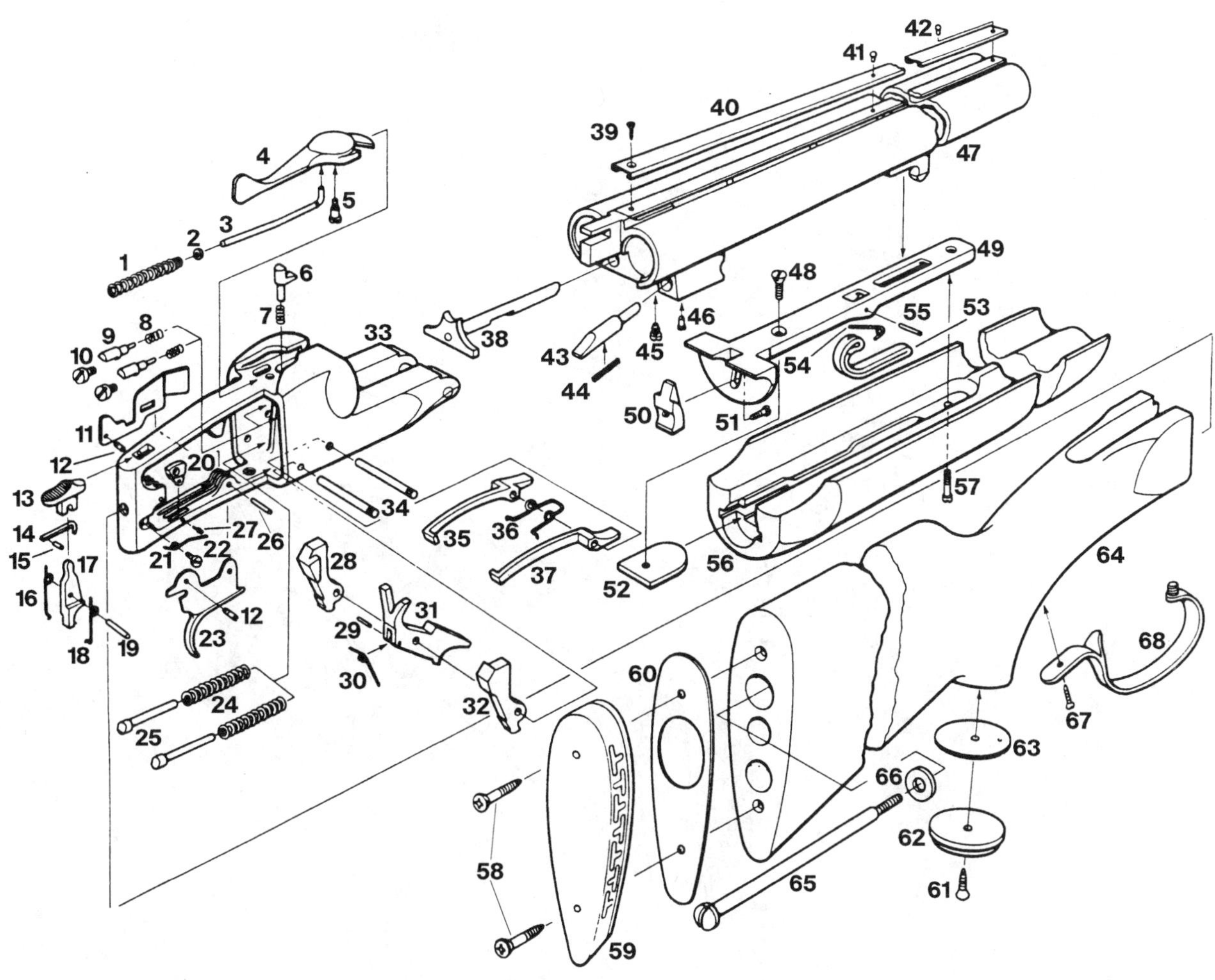

1	Top Snap Plunger Spring	**25**	Mainspring Plungers	**46**	Cocking Plunger Retaining Screw
2	Top Snap Plunger Collar	**26**	Trigger Pin	**47**	Barrel
3	Top Snap Plunger	**27**	Inertia Block Pin	**48**	Forend Screw, Rear
4	Top Snap	**28**	Hammer, Left	**49**	Forend Iron
5	Top Snap Screw	**29**	Cocking Lever Spring Pin	**50**	Ejector
6	Top Snap Trip	**30**	Cocking Lever Spring	**51**	Ejector Screw
7	Top Snap Trip Spring	**31**	Cocking Lever and Spring	**52**	Forend Insert
8	Firing Pin Springs	**32**	Hammer, Right	**53**	Forend Spring
9	Firing Pins	**33**	Frame	**54**	Forend Spring Spring
10	Firing Pin Retaining Screws	**34**	Cocking Lever, Hammer and Sear Pins	**55**	Forend Spring Pin
11	Slide	**35**	Sear, Left	**56**	Forend Wood
12	Trigger Stud	**36**	Sear Spring	**57**	Forend Screw, Front
13	Safety Button	**37**	Sear, Right	**58**	Recoil Pad Screws
14	Safety Spring	**38**	Extractor	**59**	Recoil Pad
15	Safety Plunger	**39**	Top Rib Lock Screw	**60**	Buttplate Liner
16	Slide Spring	**40**	Top Rib	**61**	Pistol Grip Cap Screw
17	Safety-Lever	**41**	Rear Sight	**62**	Pistol Grip Cap
18	Trigger Spring	**42**	Front Sight	**63**	Pistol Grip Cap Liner
19	Safety Lever Pin	**43**	Cocking Plunger	**64**	Stock
20	Inertia Block	**44**	Cocking Plunger Spring	**65**	Stock Bolt
21	Inertia Block Spring	**45**	Extractor Screw	**66**	Stock Bolt Washer
22	Inertia Block Spring Screw			**67**	Trigger Guard Screw
23	Trigger			**68**	Trigger Guard
24	Mainsprings				

Model SB-808C Autoloading Rifle

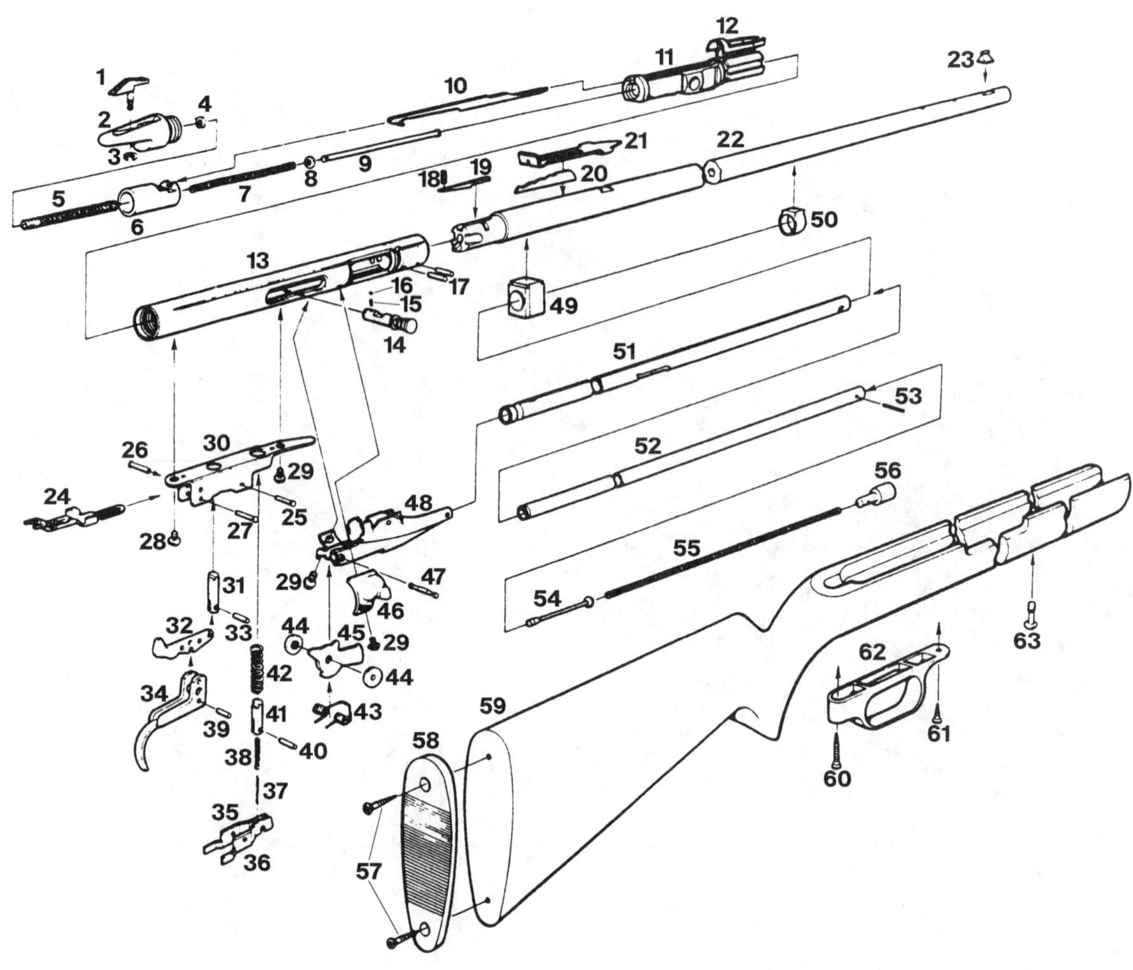

No.	Part	No.	Part	No.	Part
1	Safety Button	22	Barrel	43	Lifter Spring
2	Recoil Lug	23	Front Sight	44	Lifter Spacers
3	Safety Button Retaining Ring	24	Safety Slide	45	Lifter
4	Hammer Spring Washer	25	Detent Lever Pin	46	Deflector
5	Hammer Spring	26	Release Lever Pin	47	Lifter Pin
6	Hammer	27	Trigger Pin	48	Magazine Guide
7	Breechbolt Spring	28	Release Housing Screw	49	Magazine Mount, Rear
8	Breechbolt Spring Washer	29	Magazine Screw	50	Magazine Mount, Front
9	Breechbolt Spring Rod	30	Release Housing	51	Outside Magazine Tube
10	Firing Pin	31	Release Plunger	52	Inside Magazine Tube
11	Breechbolt	32	Release Lever	53	Magazine Plug Pin
12	Extractor	33	Release Plunger Pin	54	Magazine Follower
13	Receiver	34	Trigger	55	Magazine Follower Spring
14	Locking Bolt	35	Detent Lever, Left	56	Magazine Plug
15	Locking Bolt Plunger Ball Spring	36	Detent Lever, Right	57	Buttplate Screws
16	Locking Bolt Plunger Ball	37	Detent Plunger Inner Spring	58	Buttplate
17	Barrel Pins	38	Detent Plunger Spring	59	Stock Complete
18	Bumper Spring	39	Release Lever Actuating Pin	60	Trigger Guard Screw, Long
19	Bumper	40	Detent Plunger Pin	61	Trigger Guard Screw, Short
20	Rear Sight Step	41	Detent Plunger	62	Trigger Guard
21	Rear Sight	42	Release Spring	63	Takedown Screw

Model SB-836 Autoloading Rifle

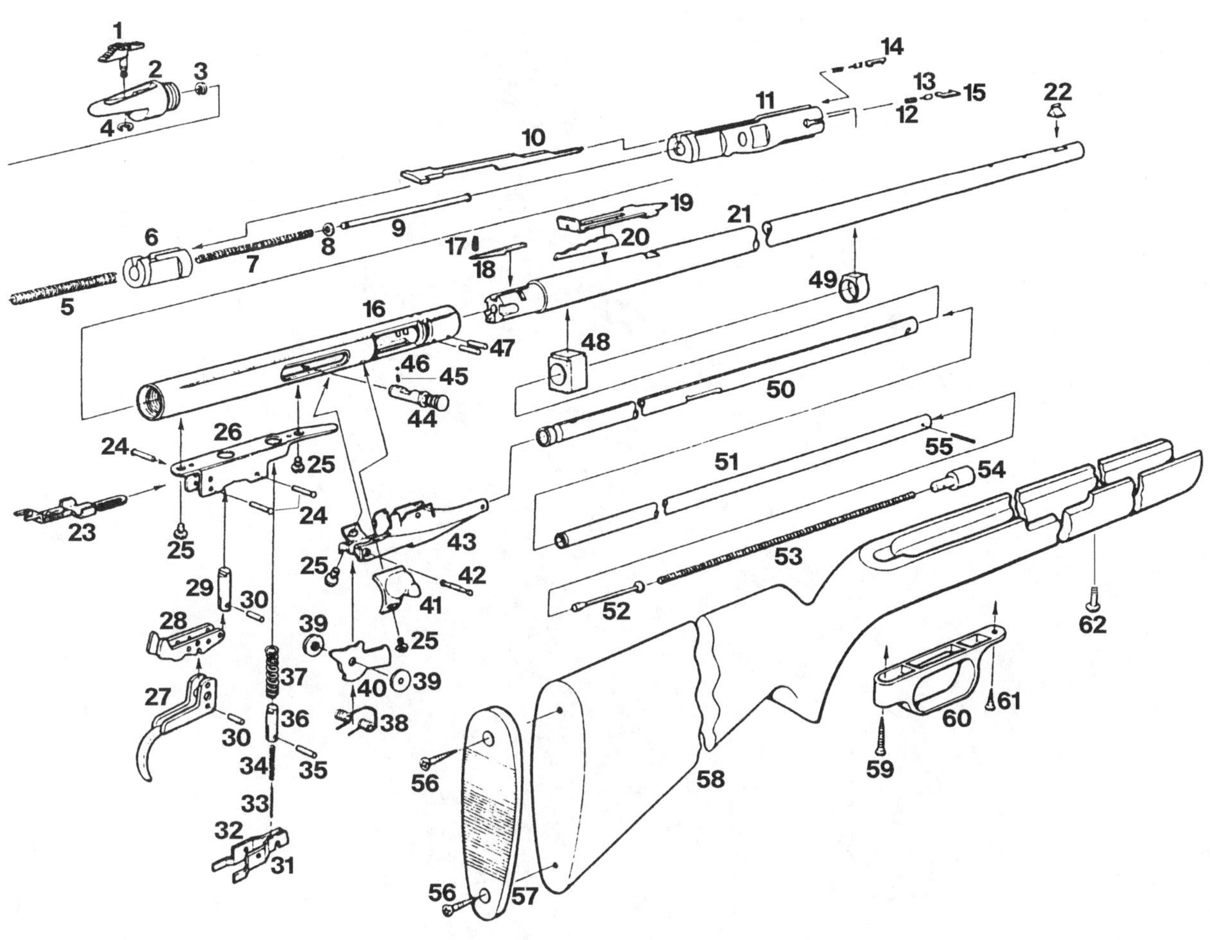

1	Safety Button	23	Safety Slide	41	Deflector
2	Recoil Plug Assembly	24	Trigger, Detent or Release Lever Pins	42	Lifter Pin
3	Hammer Spring Washer	25	Release Housing and Magazine Guide Screws	43	Magazine Guide
4	Safety Button Retaining Ring	26	Release Housing	44	Locking Bolt
5	Hammer Spring	27	Trigger	45	Locking Bolt Plunger Ball Spring
6	Hammer	28	Release Lever	46	Locking Bolt Plunger Ball
7	Breechbolt Spring	29	Release Plunger	47	Barrel Pins
8	Breechbolt Spring Washer	30	Trigger Pin or Detent Plunger Pin	48	Magazine Mount, Rear
9	Breechbolt Spring Rod	31	Detent Lever, Right	49	Magazine Mount, Front
10	Firing Pin	32	Detent Lever, Left	50	Outer Magazine Tube
11	Breechbolt	33	Detent Plunger Spring, Inner	51	Inner Magazine Tube
12	Extractor Plunger Spring	34	Detent Plunger Spring	52	Magazine Follower
13	Extractor Plunger	35	Release Plunger Pin	53	Magazine Follower Spring
14	Extractor, Left	36	Detent Plunger	54	Magazine Plug
15	Extractor, Right	37	Release Spring	55	Magazine Plug Pin
16	Receiver	38	Lifter Spring	56	Buttplate Screws
17	Bumper Spring	39	Lifter Spacers	57	Buttplate
18	Bumper	40	Lifter	58	Stock
19	Rear Sight			59	Trigger Guard Screw, Long
20	Rear Sight Step			60	Trigger Guard
21	Barrel			61	Trigger Guard Screw, Short
22	Front Sight			62	Takedown Screw

Terry Autoloading Carbine

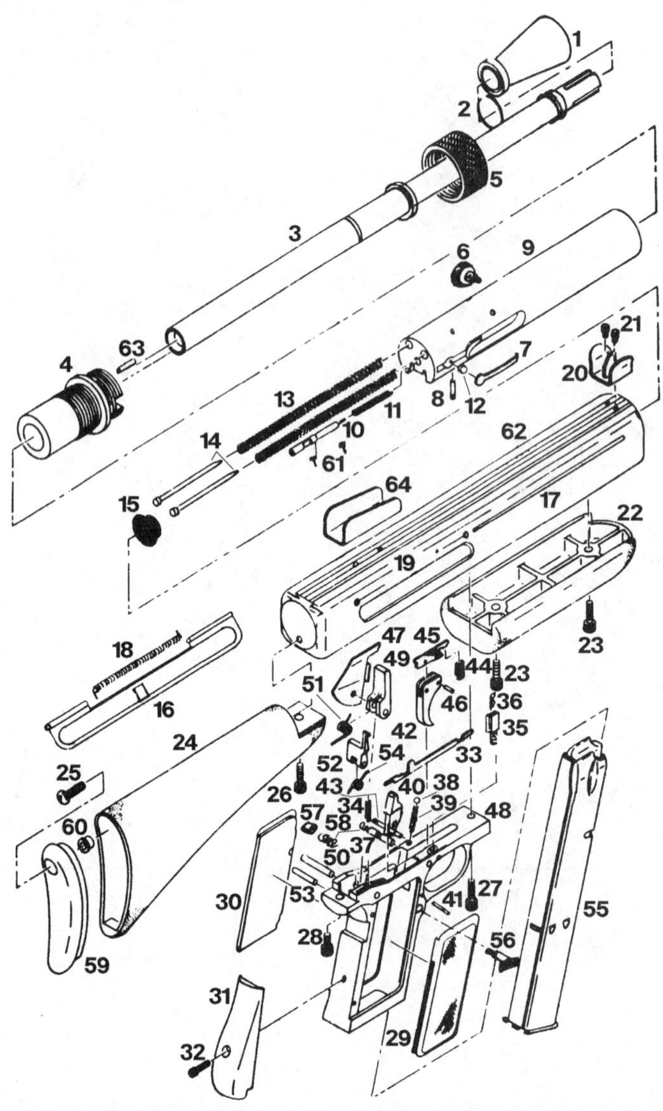

1	Flash Hider	**23**	Fore Grip Screw	**45**	Connector
2	Flash Hider Half Rings	**24**	Buttstock	**46**	Connector Pin
3	Barrel	**25**	Buttplate Screw	**47**	Ejector
4	Barrel Support Sleeve	**26**	Lower Buttstock Screw	**48**	Trigger Group Housing
5	Barrel Retaining Nut	**27**	Front Trigger Group Screw	**49**	Hammer
6	Cocking Knob	**28**	Rear Trigger Group Screw	**50**	Hammer Pin
7	Extractor	**29**	Right Grip	**51**	Hammer Spring
8	Extractor Retaining Pin	**30**	Left Grip	**52**	Sear
9	Bolt	**31**	Grip Retainer	**53**	Sear Pin
10	Firing Pin	**32**	Grip Retainer Screw	**54**	Sear Spring
11	Firing Pin Spring	**33**	Disconnector	**55**	Magazine
12	Firing Pin Button	**34**	Disconnector Spring	**56**	Magazine Catch
13	Recoil Springs	**35**	Disconnector Guide	**57**	Magazine Catch Button
14	Recoil Spring Guides	**36**	Disconnector Guide Spring	**58**	Magazine Catch Spring
15	Recoil Buffer Pad	**37**	Safety	**59**	Recoil Pad
16	Trapdoor	**38**	Safety Retainer	**60**	Upper Buttstock Nut
17	Trapdoor Rod	**39**	Safety Retainer Spring	**61**	Firing Pin Retaining Pins
18	Trapdoor Spring	**40**	Feed Ramp	**62**	Receiver
19	Trapdoor Studs	**41**	Feed Ramp Pin	**63**	Barrel Support Sleeve Pin
20	Front Sight	**42**	Trigger	**64**	Rear Sight Guard
21	Front Sight Screws	**43**	Trigger Pin		
22	Fore Grip	**44**	Trigger Spring		

Model 1 Super X Autoloading Shotgun

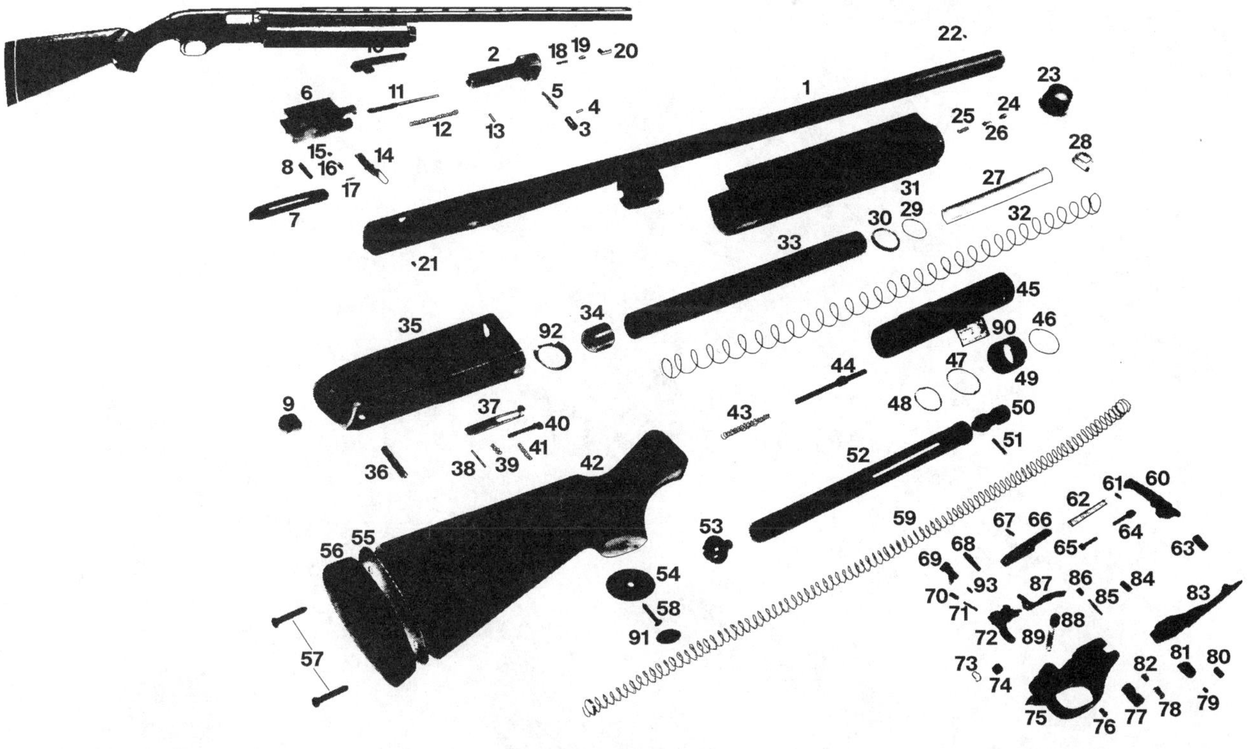

1	Barrel
2	Breechbolt
3	Breechbolt Beard
4	Breechbolt Beard Retaining Pin
5	Breechbolt Beard Spring
6	Bolt Slide
7	Bolt Slide Link
8	Bolt Slide Link Pin
9	Bolt Slide Buffer
10	Locking Bolt
11	Firing Pin
12	Firing Pin Spring
13	Firing Pin Retaining Pin
14	Cocking Handle
15	Cocking Handle Retainer
16	Cocking Handle Retainer Spring
17	Cocking Handle Retainer Spring Pin
18	Extractor Spring
19	Extractor Plunger
20	Extractor
21	Ejector
22	Front Sight
23	Magazine Cap
24	Magazine Cap Retainer Body
25	Magazine Cap Retainer Spring
26	Magazine Cap Retainer Plunger
27	Magazine Plug
28	Magazine Tube Plug
29	O-Ring
30	Gas Seal
31	Forend
32	Magazine Spring
33	Magazine Tube
34	Magazine Follower
35	Receiver
36	Trigger Guard Pin
37	Carrier Release
38	Carrier Release Pin
39	Carrier Release Spring
40	Cutoff
41	Cutoff Spring
42	Buttstock
43	Piston Rod Spring
44	Piston Rod
45	Piston Sleeve
46	Piston Ring, Outer
47	Piston Head Retaining Ring
48	Piston Ring, Inner
49	Piston Head
50	Return Spring Follower
51	Return Spring Follower Pin
52	Return Spring Tube
53	Buttstock Bolt
54	Pistol Grip Cap
55	Recoil Pad Spacer
56	Recoil Pad
57	Recoil Pad Screws
58	Pistol Grip Cap Screw
59	Return Spring
60	Hammer
61	Hammer Spring Guide Rivet, Inner
62	Hammer Spring, Single
63	Hammer Bushing
64	Hammer Spring Guide, Inner
65	Hammer Spring Guide, Outer
66	Disconnector Lever
67	Disconnector Lever Pin
68	Trigger Pin
69	Disconnector
70	Disconnector Plunger
71	Disconnector Spring
72	Trigger
73	Trigger Guard Pin Retaining Spring
74	Trigger Guard Pin Bushing
75	Trigger Guard
76	Trigger Guard Bushing
77	Safety
78	Safety Plunger Spring
79	Carrier Pawl Rivet
80	Carrier Pin, Right
81	Carrier Pawl
82	Safety Plunger
83	Carrier
84	Carrier Pin, Left
85	Sear Spring
86	Sear Spring Plunger
87	Sear
88	Carrier Plunger
89	Carrier Plunger Spring
90	Piston Sleeve Adjusting Decal
91	Pistol Grip Cap Insert
92	Magazine Tube Washer
93	Disconnector Pin

Parts Not Shown

Disconnector Rivet
Sear Screw
Shell Deflector
Trigger Bushing

Model 100 Autoloading Rifle

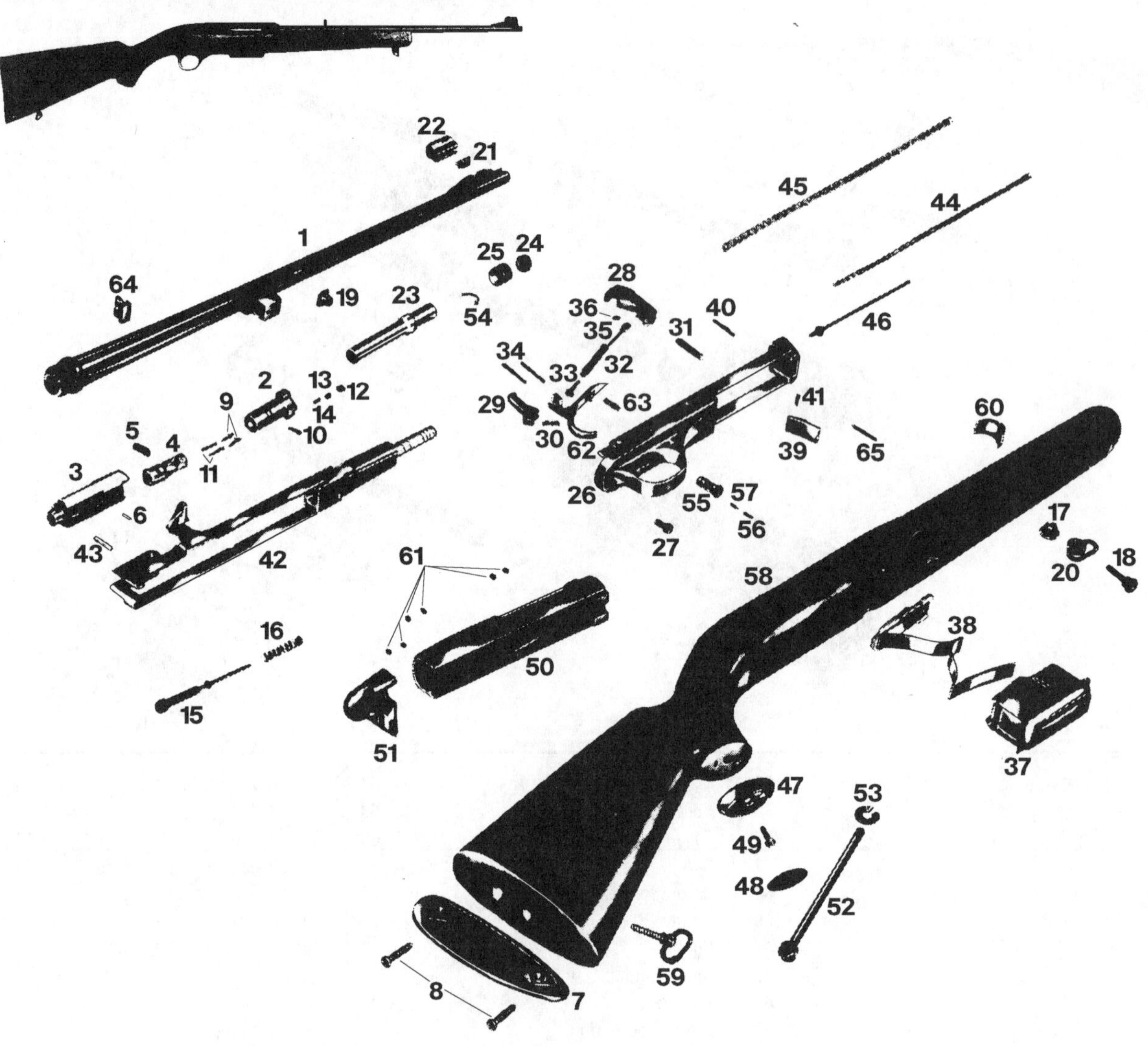

1	Barrel and Gas Cylinder Housing
2	Bolt Head
3	Bolt Sleeve
4	Bolt Sleeve Lock
5	Bolt Sleeve Lock Pin
6	Bolt Sleeve Pin
7	Buttplate
8	Buttplate Screws
9	Ejectors
10	Ejector Pin
11	Ejector Springs
12	Extractor
13	Extractor Plunger
14	Extractor Spring
15	Firing Pin
16	Firing Pin Spring
17	Forend Bushing
18	Forend Screw
19	Forend Stud
20	Forend Swivel
21	Front Sight
22	Front Sight Hood
23	Gas Cylinder
24	Gas Cylinder Plug
25	Gas Cylinder Sleeve
26	Guard Housing
27	Guard Screw
28	Hammer
29	Hammer Lock
30	Hammer Lock Spring
31	Hammer Pin
32	Hammer Spring
33	Hammer Spring Guide
34	Hammer Spring Guide Pins
35	Hammer Spring Guide Rod
36	Hammer Spring Guide Rod Pin
37	Magazine
38	Magazine Spring and Follower
39	Magazine Lock
40	Magazine Lock Pin
41	Magazine Lock Spring
42	Operating Slide Guide Assembly
43	Operating Slide Pin
44	Operating Slide Spring, Inner
45	Operating Slide Spring, Outer
46	Operating Slide Spring Guide
47	Pistol Grip Cap
48	Pistol Grip Cap Insert
49	Pistol Grip Cap Screw
50	Receiver
51	Recoil Block
52	Recoil Block Screw
53	Recoil Block Screw Washer
54	Retainer
55	Safety
56	Safety Spring
57	Safety Spring Plunger
58	Stock
59	Stock Swivel Bow
60	Stock Liner
61	Scope Mount Plug Screws
62	Trigger
63	Trigger Spring
64	Rear Sight
65	Trigger Pin

Model 101 Over/Under Shotgun

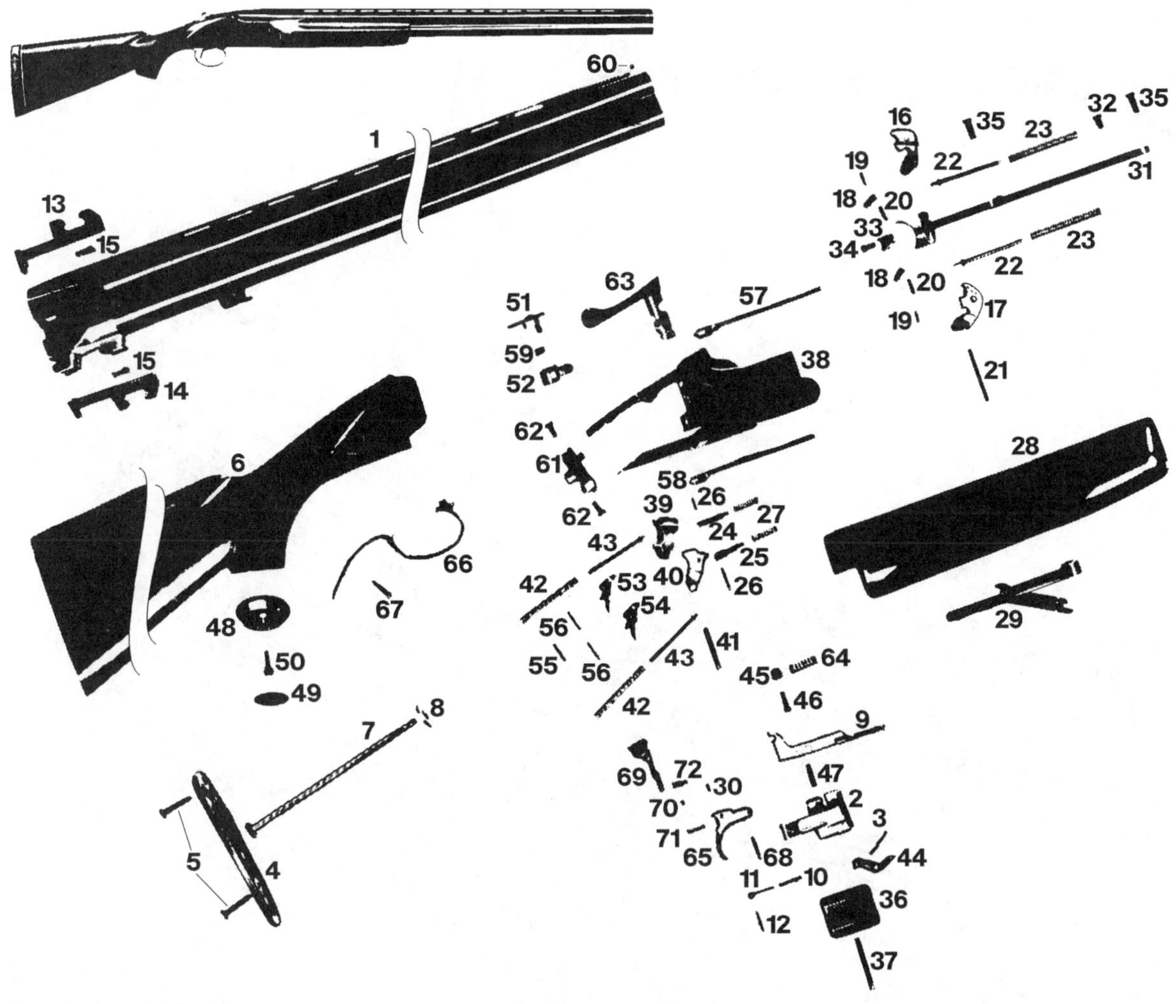

- **1** Barrels
- **2** Barrel Locking Plate
- **3** Barrel Locking Plate Latch Spring
- **4** Buttplate
- **5** Buttplate Screws
- **6** Buttstock
- **7** Buttstock Bolt
- **8** Buttstock Bolt Washer
- **9** Cocking Plate
- **10** Cocking Plate Spring
- **11** Cocking Plate Spring Guide Rod
- **12** Cocking Plate Spring Guide Rod Pin
- **13** Ejector, Left
- **14** Ejector, Right
- **15** Ejector Retaining Springs
- **16** Ejector Hammer, Left
- **17** Ejector Hammer, Right
- **18** Ejector Hammer Catches
- **19** Ejector Hammer Catch Pins
- **20** Ejector Hammer Catch Springs
- **21** Ejector Hammer Pin
- **22** Ejector Hammer Rods
- **23** Ejector Hammer Springs
- **24** Firing Pin, Upper
- **25** Firing Pin, Lower
- **26** Firing Pin Locking Pins
- **27** Firing Pin Springs
- **28** Forend
- **29** Forearm Latch
- **30** Trigger Swivel Plunger Stop Pin
- **31** Forend Iron
- **32** Forend Iron Screw, Short
- **33** Forend Hinge Block
- **34** Forend Hinge Block Screw
- **35** Forend Iron Screws, Long
- **36** Frame Plate, Bottom
- **37** Frame Plate Pin, Bottom
- **38** Frame
- **39** Hammer, Left
- **40** Hammer, Right
- **41** Hammer Pin
- **42** Hammer Springs
- **43** Hammer Spring Guide Rods
- **44** Locking Plate Latch
- **45** Locking Pin Catch
- **46** Locking Pin Screw
- **47** Pinion Screw
- **48** Pistol Grip Cap
- **49** Pistol Grip Cap Insert
- **50** Pistol Grip Cap Screw
- **51** Safety Button
- **52** Safety Button Spring
- **53** Sear, Left
- **54** Sear, Right
- **55** Sear Pin
- **56** Sear Springs
- **57** Selective Ejector Rod, Left
- **58** Selective Ejector Rod, Right
- **59** Selective Filler Block
- **60** Front Sight
- **61** Tang Spacer
- **62** Tang Spacer Screws
- **63** Top Lever
- **64** Top Lever Spring
- **65** Trigger
- **66** Trigger Guard
- **67** Trigger Guard Screw
- **68** Trigger Pin
- **69** Trigger Sear Catch
- **70** Trigger Sear Catch Pin
- **71** Trigger Spring
- **72** Trigger Swivel Plunger

Parts Not Shown

Trigger Recovery Spring

WINCHESTER

Model 12 Slide-Action Shotgun

Courtesy of James M. Triggs

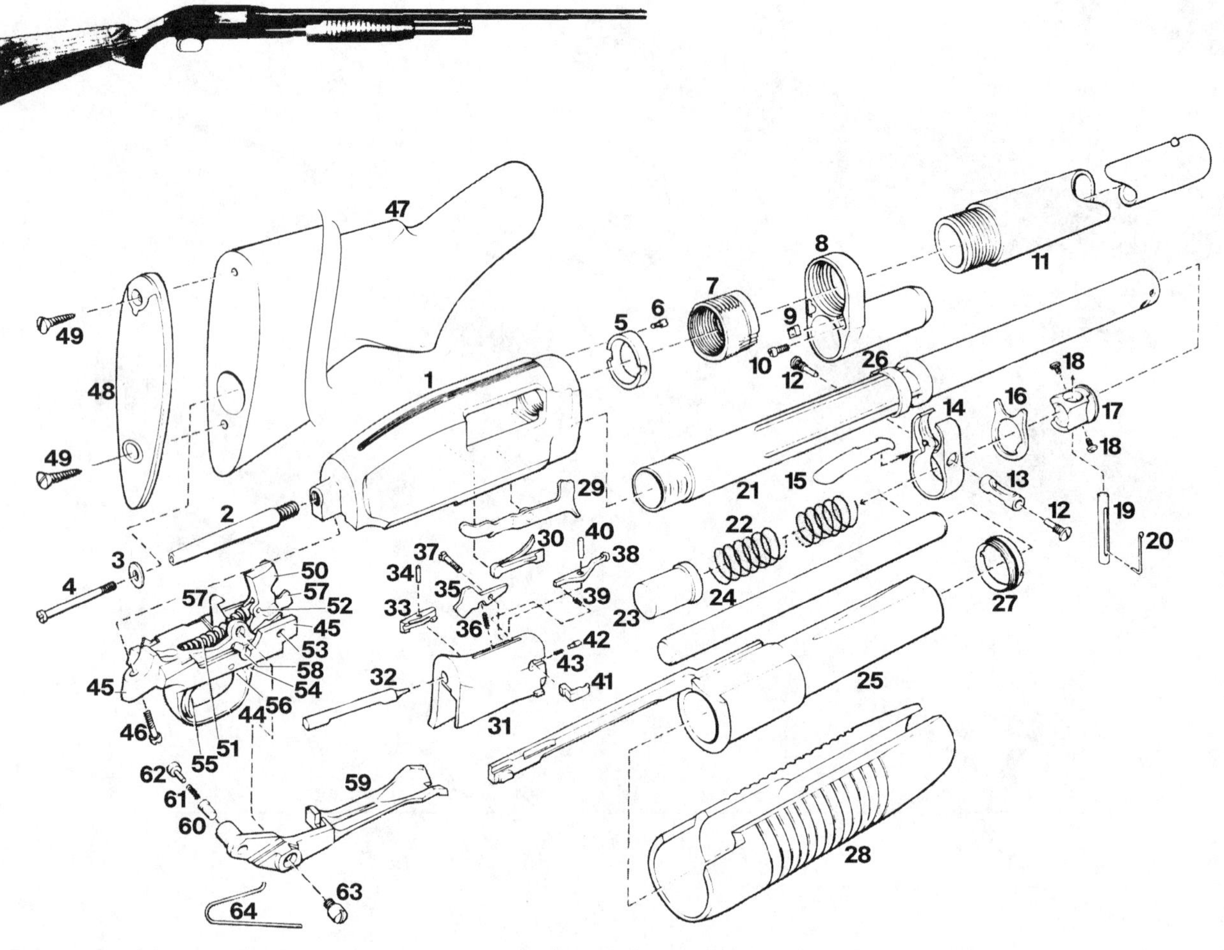

1	Receiver
2	Receiver Shank
3	Buttstock Bolt Washer
4	Buttstock Bolt
5	Barrel Chamber Ring
6	Barrel Chamber Ring Screw
7	Adjusting Sleeve
8	Receiver Extension
9	Adjusting Sleeve Lock
10	Adjusting Sleeve Lock Screw
11	Barrel
12	Magazine Band Bushing Screws
13	Magazine Band Bushing
14	Magazine Band
15	Action Slide Handle Retaining Spring
16	Magazine Plug Stop
17	Magazine Plug
18	Magazine Plug Screws
19	Magazine Locking Pin
20	Magazine Locking Pin Spring
21	Magazine Tube
22	Magazine Spring
23	Magazine Follower
24	Wooden Plug
25	Action Slide
26	Action Slide Spring
27	Action Slide Sleeve Screw Cap
28	Action Slide Handle
29	Cartridge Cutoff
30	Ejector and Ejector Spring
31	Breechbolt
32	Firing Pin
33	Breechbolt Retaining Lever
34	Breechbolt Retaining Lever Pin
35	Firing Pin Retractor
36	Firing Pin Retractor Spring
37	Firing Pin Retractor Screw
38	Extractor, Left
39	Extractor Spring
40	Extractor Pin, Left
41	Extractor, Right
42	Extractor Spring Plunger, Right
43	Extractor Spring, Right
44	Guard
45	Guard, Complete
46	Guard Screw
47	Buttstock
48	Buttplate
49	Buttplate Screws
50	Hammer
51	Hammer Spring and Guide Rod
52	Hammer Spring Guide Rod Pin
53	Hammer Pin
54	Trigger Lock Assembly
55	Trigger
56	Trigger Pin
57	Action Slide Lock and Spring
58	Action Slide Lock Pivot
59	Carrier
60	Carrier Plunger
61	Carrier Plunger Spring
62	Carrier Plunger Screw
63	Carrier Pivot
64	Carrier Spring
Parts Not Shown	
	Trigger Spring

Model 1200 Slide-Action Shotgun

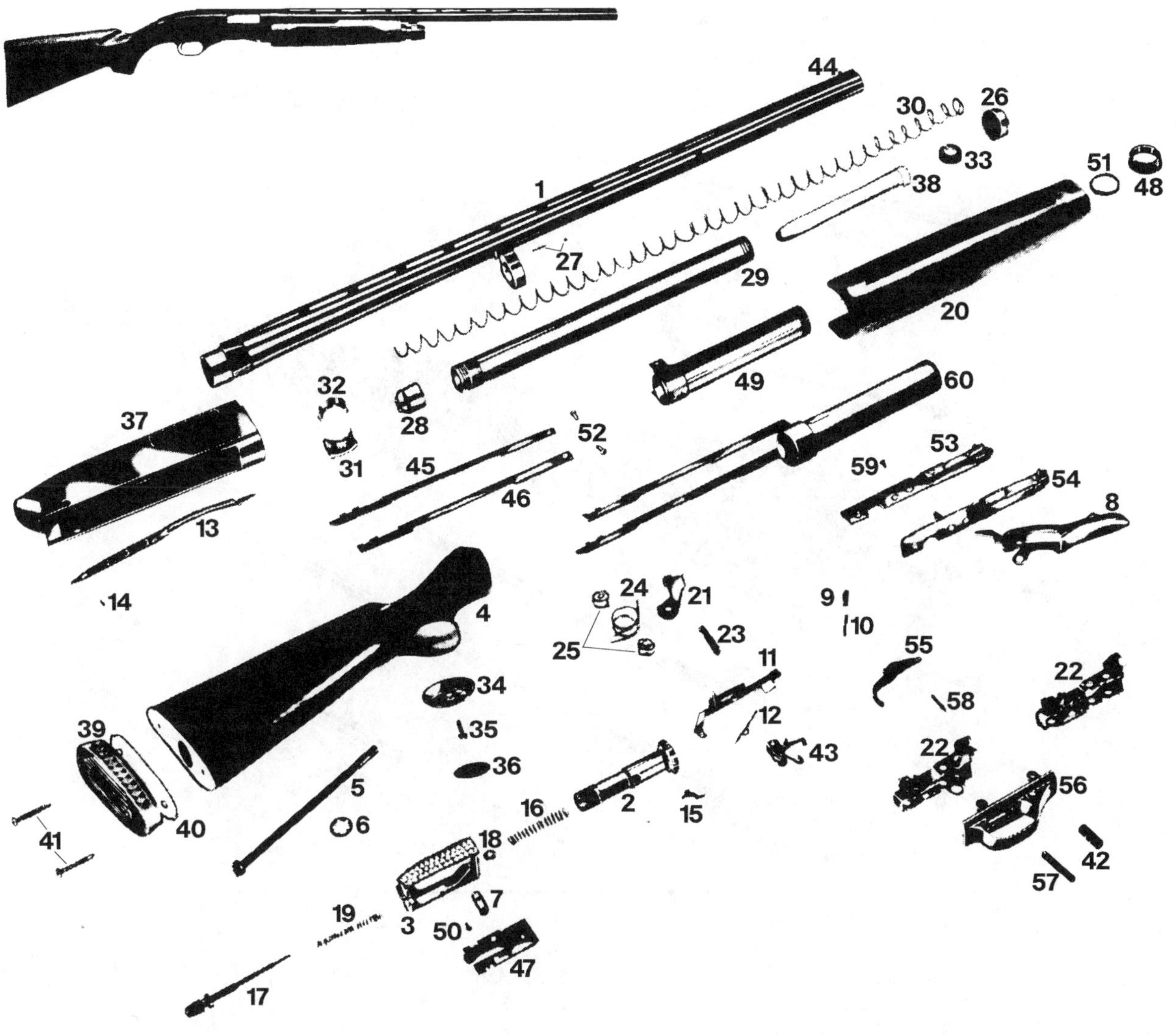

1	Barrel with Extension	**23**	Hammer Pin	**43**	Sear Assembly
2	Breechbolt	**24**	Hammer Spring	**44**	Front Sight
3	Breechbolt Slide	**25**	Hammer Spring Supports	**45**	Slide Arm, Left
4	Buttstock	**26**	Magazine Cap	**46**	Slide Arm, Right
5	Buttstock Bolt	**27**	Magazine Cap Retainer and Spring	**47**	Slide Arm Bridge
6	Buttstock Bolt Washer	**28**	Magazine Follower	**48**	Slide Arm Cap
7	Cam Pin	**29**	Magazine Tube	**49**	Slide Arm Extension
8	Carrier	**30**	Magazine Spring	**50**	Slide Arm Bridge Retaining Screw
9	Carrier Plunger	**31**	Magazine Throat, Lower	**51**	Slide Arm Extension Cap Ring
10	Carrier Spring	**32**	Magazine Throat, Upper	**52**	Slide Arm Pins
11	Disconnector	**33**	Magazine Tube Plug	**53**	Slide Support with Cutoff, Left
12	Disconnector Spring	**34**	Pistol Grip Cap	**54**	Slide Support with Cutoff, Right
13	Ejector	**35**	Pistol Grip Cap Screw	**55**	Trigger
14	Ejector Retainer Pin	**36**	Pistol Grip Cap Insert	**56**	Trigger Guard
15	Extractor	**37**	Receiver	**57**	Trigger Guard Pin
16	Extractor Spring	**38**	Magazine Plug	**58**	Trigger Pin
17	Firing Pin	**39**	Recoil Pad	**59**	Trigger Stop Pin Screw
18	Firing Pin Collar	**40**	Recoil Pad Spacer	**60**	Slide Arm Extension Assembly
19	Firing Pin Spring	**41**	Recoil Pad Screws	**Parts Not Shown**	
20	Forend	**42**	Safety		Spacer Ring
21	Hammer				
22	Hammer Housing				

Model 121 and 131 Bolt-Action Rifle

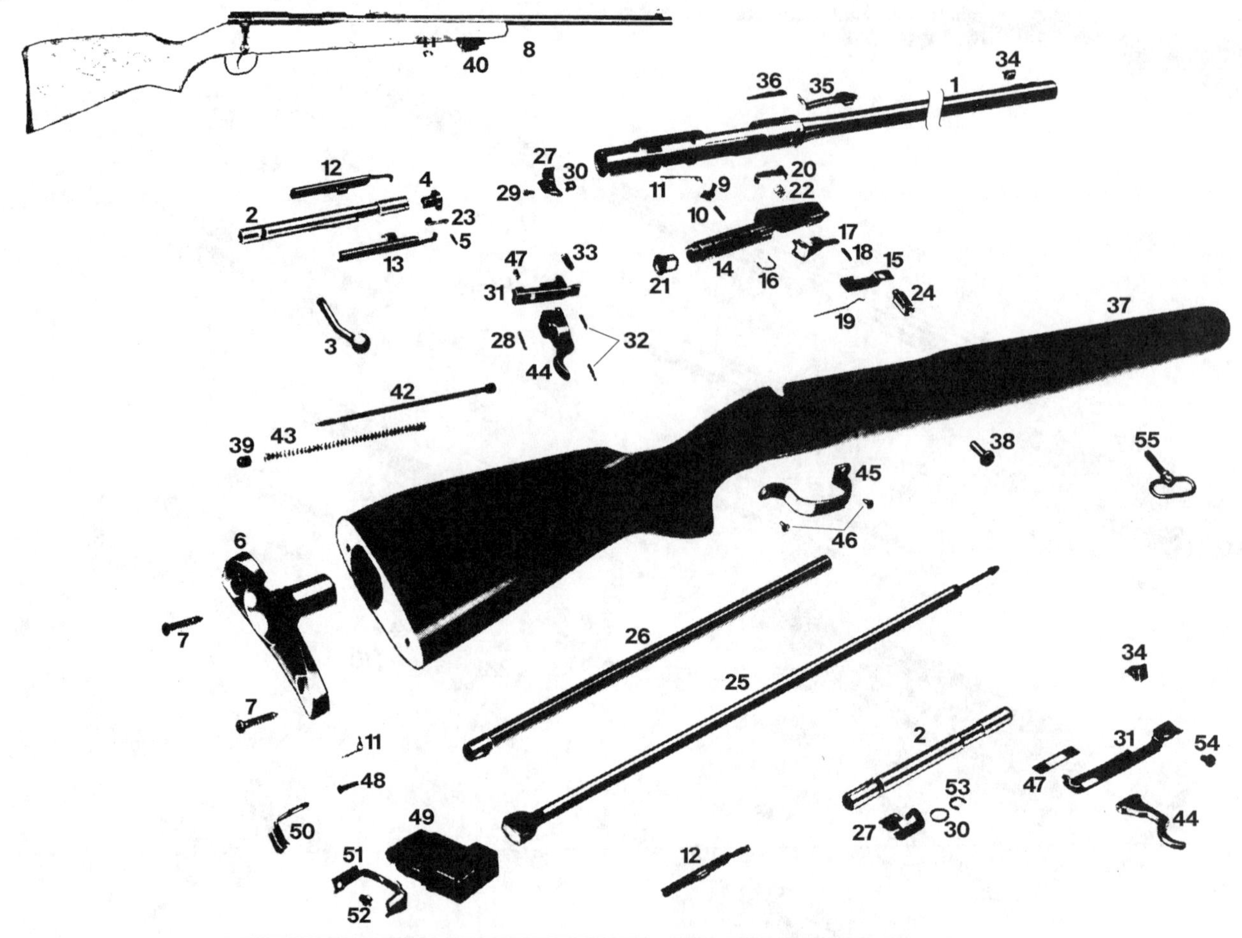

1	Barrel with Receiver Assembly
2	Bolt Body
3	Bolt Handle
4	Bolt Head
5	Bolt Head Pin
6	Buttplate
7	Buttplate Screws
8	Cocking Piece
9	Ejector
10	Ejector Pin
11	Ejector Spring
12	Extractor, Left
13	Extractor, Right
14	Feed Guides
15	Feed Guide Clip, Front
16	Feed Guide Clip, Rear
17	Feed Guide Cutoff
18	Feed Guide Cutoff Pin
19	Feed Guide Cutoff Spring
20	Feed Guide Ramp
21	Feed Guide Sleeve
22	Feed Ramp Spring
23	Firing Pin
24	Guide Stud
25	Inner Magazine Tube
26	Outer Magazine Tube
27	Safety
28	Safety Pin
29	Safety Screw and Washer
30	Safety Spring
31	Sear
32	Sear/Trigger Pins
33	Sear Spring
34	Front Sight
35	Rear Sight
36	Rear Sight Elevator
37	Stock
38	Stock Stud Screw
39	Striker Guide
40	Striker Head
41	Striker Retainer
42	Striker Rod
43	Striker Spring
44	Trigger
45	Trigger Guard
46	Trigger Guard Screws
47	Trigger Spring
48	Ejector Screw
49	Magazine Assembly
50	Magazine Guide
51	Magazine Latch
52	Magazine Latch Screw
53	Safety Retainer
54	Sear Screw
55	Swivel

Model 1300 XTR Slide-Action Shotgun

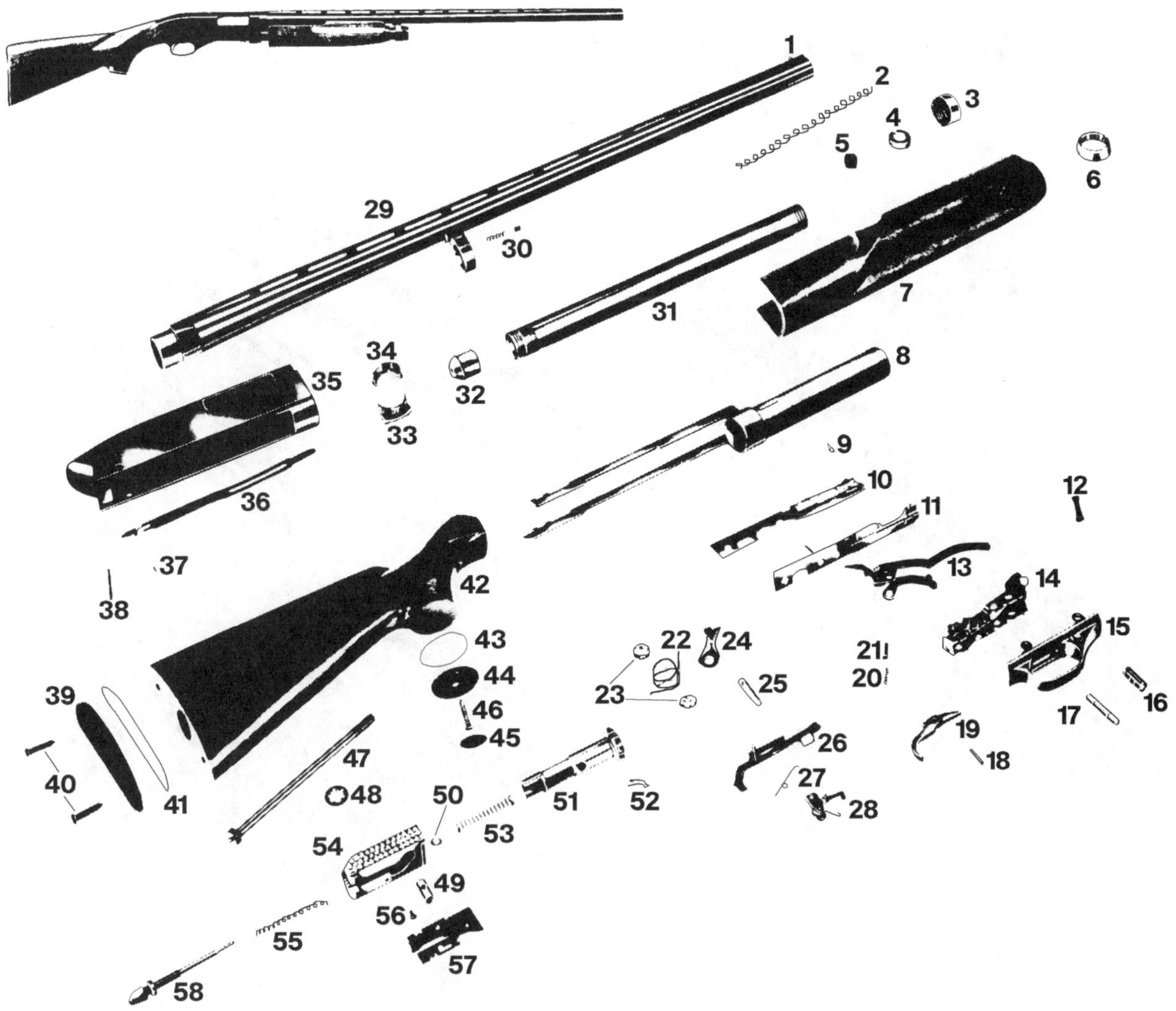

1	Front Sight	20	Carrier Spring	41	Buttplate Spacer
2	Magazine Spring	21	Carrier Plunger	42	Buttstock
3	Magazine Cap	22	Hammer Spring	43	Pistol Grip Cap Spacer
4	Magazine Tube Spring Retainer	23	Hammer Spring Supports	44	Pistol Grip Cap
5	Plug	24	Hammer	45	Pistol Grip Cap Insert
6	Slide Arm Cap with Ring	25	Hammer Pin	46	Pistol Grip Cap Screw
7	Forearm	26	Disconnector Assembly	47	Buttstock Bolt
8	Slide Arm Extension with Slide Arms	27	Disconnector Spring	48	Buttstock Bolt Washer
		28	Sear Assembly	49	Cam Pin
9	Trigger Stop Pin Screw	29	Barrel with Extension	50	Firing Pin Collar
10	Left Slide Support with Cutoff	30	Magazine Cap Retainer and Spring	51	Breechbolt
11	Right Slide Support with Cutoff	31	Magazine Tube	52	Extractor
12	Hammer Stop Pin	32	Magazine Follower	53	Extractor Spring
13	Carrier Assembly	33	Magazine Throat, Lower	54	Breechbolt Slide
14	Hammer Housing with Hammer Stop Pin	34	Magazine Throat, Upper	55	Firing Pin Spring
		35	Receiver	56	Slide Arm Bridge Retaining Screw
15	Trigger Guard	36	Ejector	57	Slide Arm Bridge
16	Safety	37	Ejector Retainer Pin	58	Firing Pin
17	Trigger Guard Pin	38	Ejector Spring	**Parts Not Shown**	
18	Trigger Pin	39	Buttplate		Barrel Rib Pins
19	Trigger	40	Buttplate Screws		Rear Sight

Model 1400, 1400 Mark II and Ranger Autoloading Shotgun

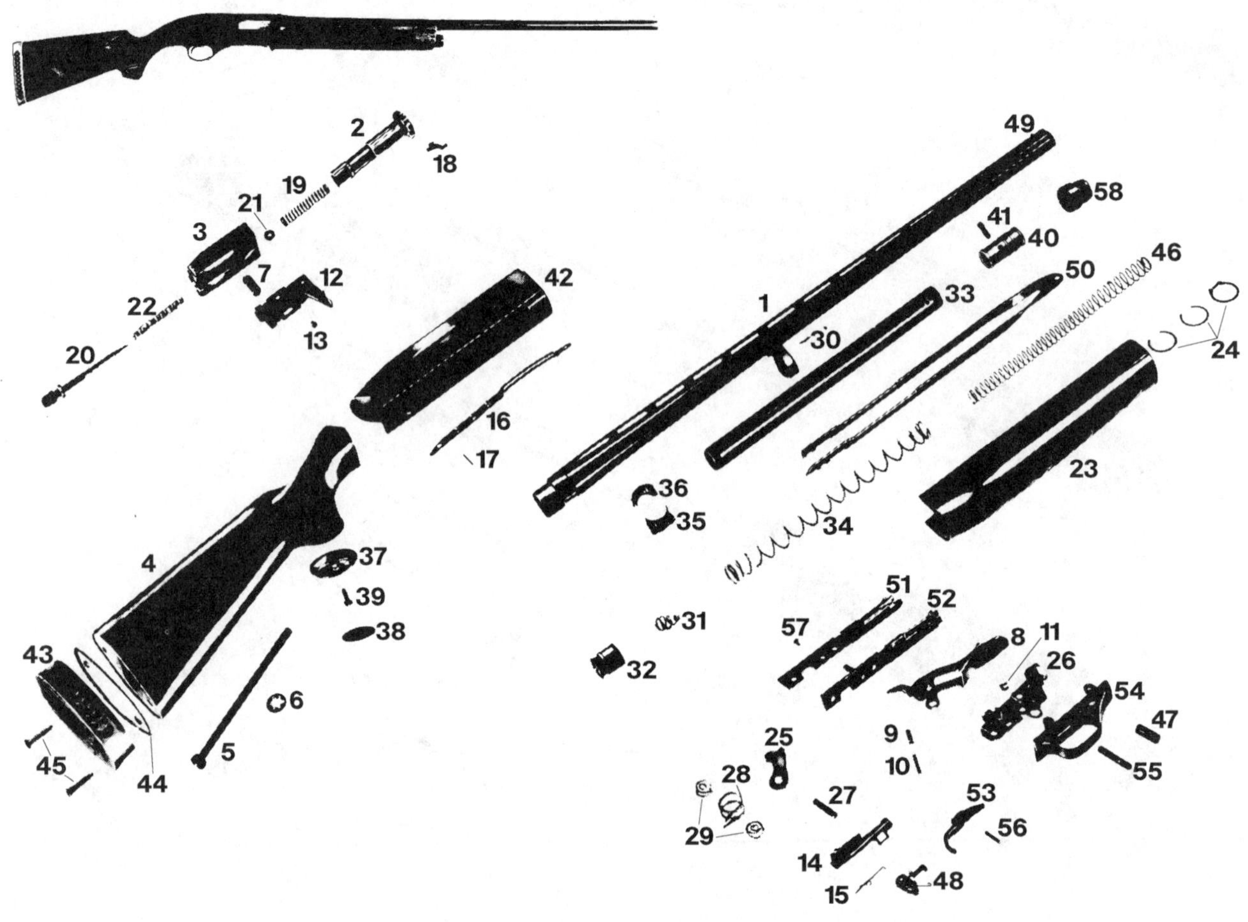

1	Barrel with Extension
2	Breechbolt
3	Breechbolt Slide
4	Buttstock
5	Buttstock Bolt
6	Buttstock Bolt Washer
7	Cam Pin
8	Carrier Assembly
9	Carrier Plunger
10	Carrier Spring
11	Carrier Support Spring
12	Cocking Handle Bridge
13	Cocking Handle Bridge Retaining Screw
14	Disconnector Assembly
15	Disconnector Spring
16	Ejector
17	Ejector Retainer Pin
18	Extractor
19	Extractor Spring
20	Firing Pin
21	Firing Pin Collar
22	Firing Pin Spring
23	Forend
24	Forend Spacers
25	Hammer
26	Hammer Housing
27	Hammer Pin
28	Hammer Spring
29	Hammer Spring Supports
30	Magazine Cap Retainer and Spring
31	Magazine Damper Spring
32	Magazine Follower
33	Magazine Tube
34	Magazine Spring
35	Magazine Throat, Lower
36	Magazine Throat, Upper
37	Pistol Grip Cap
38	Pistol Grip Cap Insert
39	Pistol Grip Cap Screw
40	Piston
41	Piston Pin
42	Receiver
43	Recoil Pad
44	Recoil Pad Spacer
45	Recoil Pad Screws
46	Return Spring
47	Safety
48	Sear Assembly
49	Front Sight
50	Slide Arm
51	Left Slide Support with Cutoff
52	Right Slide Support with Cutoff
53	Trigger
54	Trigger Guard
55	Trigger Guard Pin
56	Trigger Pin
57	Trigger Stop Pin Screw
58	Valve Cap Assembly

Model 141 Bolt-Action Rifle

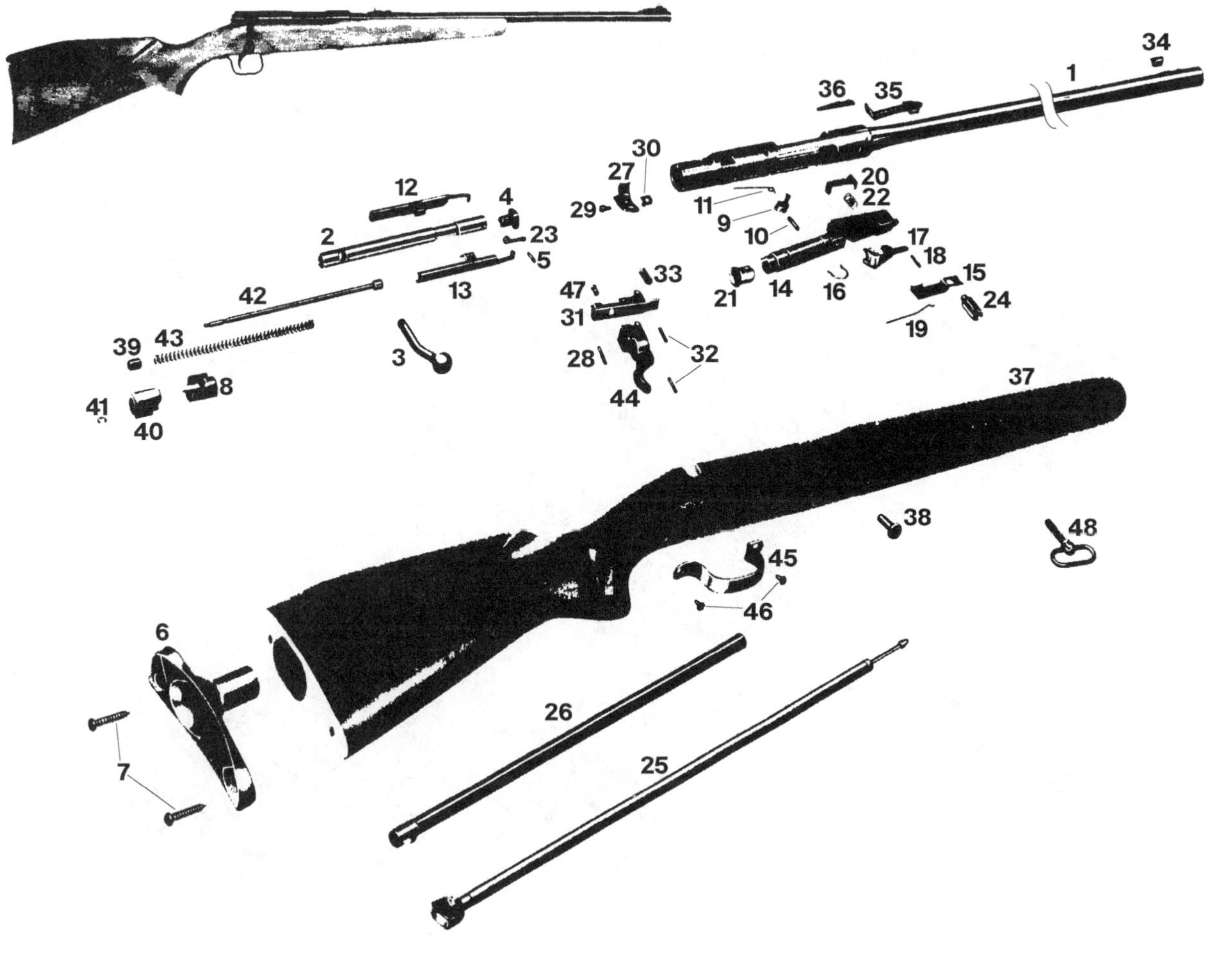

1	Barrel with Receiver Assembly	**25**	Inside Magazine Tube
2	Bolt Body	**26**	Outside Magazine Tube
3	Bolt Handle	**27**	Safety
4	Bolt Head	**28**	Safety Pin
5	Bolt Head Pin	**29**	Safety Screw and Washer
6	Buttplate	**30**	Safety Spring
7	Buttplate Screws	**31**	Sear
8	Cocking Piece	**32**	Sear and Trigger Pins
9	Ejector	**33**	Sear Spring
10	Ejector Pin	**34**	Front Sight
11	Ejector Spring	**35**	Rear Sight
12	Extractor, Left	**36**	Rear Sight Elevator
13	Extractor, Right	**37**	Stock
14	Feed Guides	**38**	Stock Stud Screw
15	Feed Guide Clip, Front	**39**	Striker Guide
16	Feed Guide Clip, Rear	**40**	Striker Head
17	Feed Guide Cutoff	**41**	Striker Retainer
18	Feed Guide Cutoff Pin	**42**	Striker Rod
19	Feed Guide Cutoff Spring	**43**	Striker Spring
20	Feed Guide Ramp	**44**	Trigger
21	Feed Guide Sleeve	**45**	Trigger Guard
22	Feed Ramp Spring	**46**	Trigger Guard Screws
23	Firing Pin	**47**	Trigger Spring
24	Guide Stud	**48**	Sling Swivel

Model 150 and 190 Lever-Action Rifle

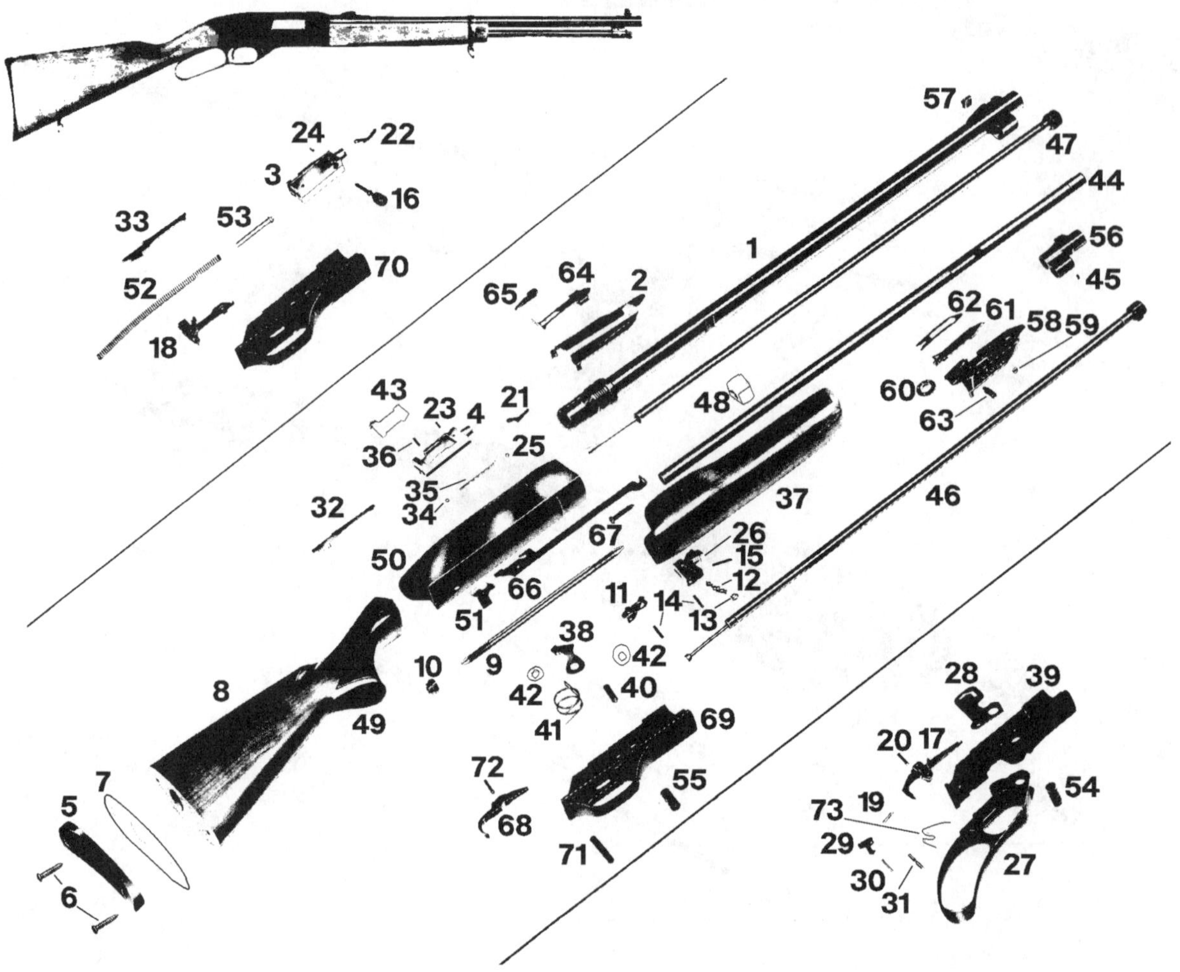

1	Barrel and Barrel Collar
2	Barrel Collar Cover
3	Breechbolt Complete (Model 190)
4	Breechbolt Complete (Model 150)
5	Buttplate
6	Buttplate Screws
7	Buttplate Spacer
8	Buttstock
9	Buttstock Bolt
10	Buttstock Nut with Washer
11	Carrier
12	Carrier Coil Spring
13	Carrier Coil Spring Plunger
14	Carrier Pins
15	Carrier Stop Pin
16	Cocking Handle
17	Disconnector and Sear Assembly (Model 150)
18	Disconnector and Sear Assembly (Model 190)
19	Disconnector Coil Spring
20	Disconnector Pin
21	Extractor (Model 150)
22	Extractor (Model 190)
23	Extractor Pin (Model 150)
24	Extractor Pin (Model 190)
25	Extractor Plunger
26	Feed Guide
27	Finger Lever
28	Finger Lever Arm
29	Finger Lever Latch
30	Finger Lever Latch Pin
31	Finger Lever Pin
32	Firing Pin (Model 150)
33	Firing Pin (Model 190)
34	Firing Pin Plunger
35	Firing Pin Spring
36	Firing Pin Stop Pin
37	Forearm
38	Hammer
39	Hammer Housing
40	Hammer Pin
41	Hammer Spring
42	Hammer Spring Supports
43	Locking Plate
44	Magazine Tube, Outside
45	Magazine Tube Retaining Pin, Outside
46	Magazine Tube, Inside Assembly (Rifle)
47	Magazine Tube, Inside Assembly
48	Magazine Tube Bracket
49	Pistol Grip Cap Assembly
50	Receiver
51	Recoil Plate
52	Return Spring
53	Return Spring Guide
54	Safety (Model 150)
55	Safety (Model 190)
56	Sight, Front (Plastic)
57	Sight, Front (Metal)
58	Sight Base, Rear
59	Sight Base Screw, Rear
60	Sight Elevator, Rear
61	Sight Leaf, Rear
62	Sight Spring, Rear
63	Sight Windage Screw, Rear
64	Rear Sight
65	Rear Sight Elevator
66	Slide Arm
67	Slide Arm Screw
68	Trigger Assembly
69	Trigger Guard
70	Trigger Guard (Model 190)
71	Trigger Guard Pin, Rear
72	Trigger Pin
73	Trigger Spring

Model 1500 XTR Autoloading Shotgun

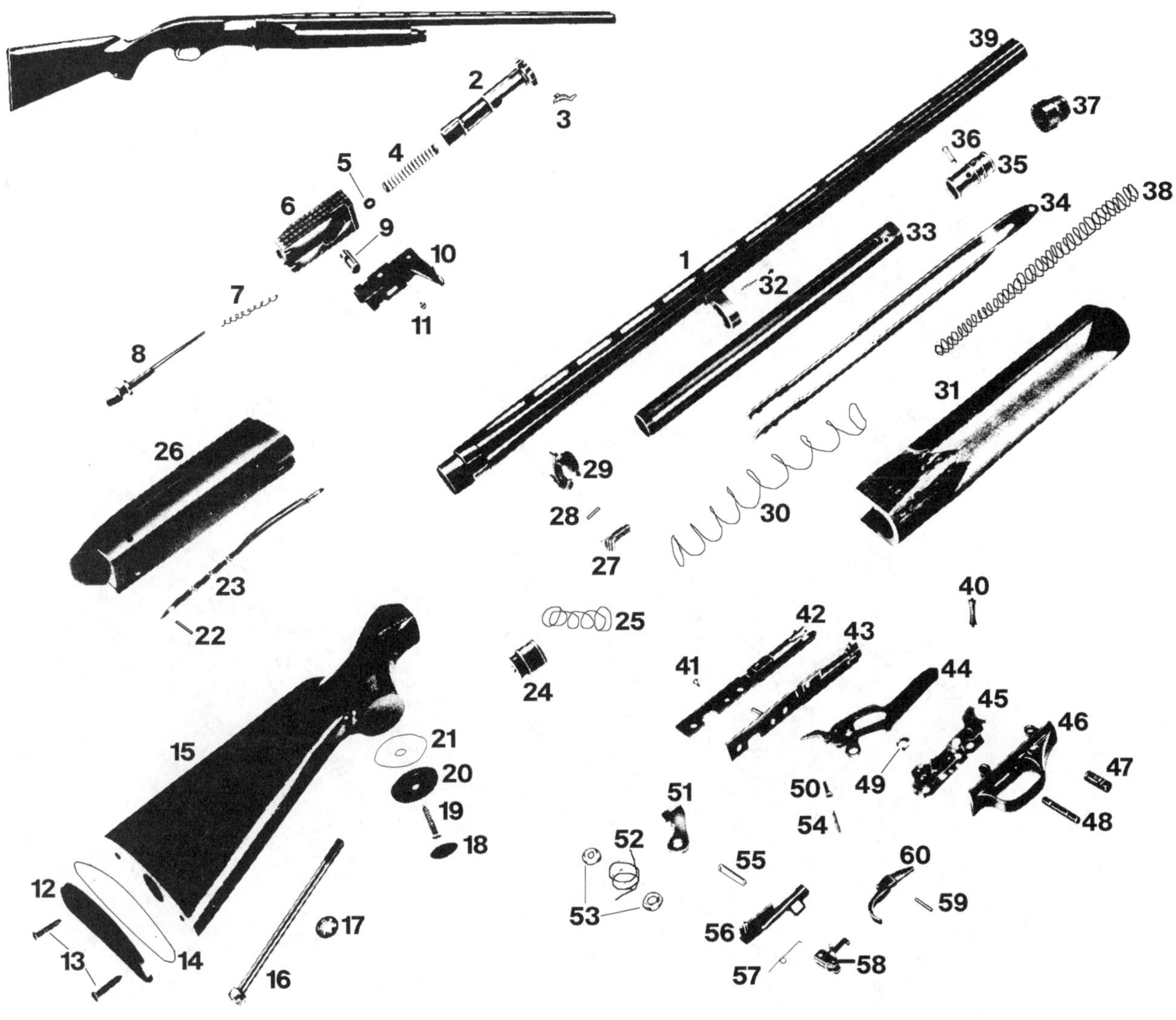

1	Barrel	21	Grip Cap Spacer	43	Right Slide Support with Cutoff
2	Breechbolt	22	Ejector Retainer Pin	44	Carrier Assembly
3	Extractor	23	Ejector	45	Hammer Housing
4	Extractor Spring	24	Magazine Follower	46	Trigger Guard
5	Firing Pin Collar	25	Magazine Damper Spring	47	Safety
6	Breechbolt Slide	26	Receiver	48	Trigger Guard Pin
7	Firing Pin Sleeve	27	Carrier Release	49	Carrier Support Spring
8	Firing Pin	28	Carrier Release Spring	50	Carrier Plunger
9	Cam Pin	29	Magazine Throat	51	Hammer
10	Cocking Handle Bridge	30	Magazine Spring	52	Hammer Spring
11	Cocking Handle Bridge Retaining Screw	31	Forend	53	Hammer Spring Supports
12	Buttplate	32	Magazine Cap Retainer and Spring	54	Carrier Spring
13	Buttplate Screws	33	Magazine Tube	55	Hammer Pin
14	Buttplate Spacer	34	Slide Arm	56	Disconnector Assembly
15	Buttstock	35	Piston	57	Disconnector Spring
16	Buttstock Bolt	36	Piston Pin	58	Sear Assembly
17	Buttstock Bolt Washer	37	Valve Cap Assembly	59	Trigger Pin
18	Grip Cap Insert	38	Return Spring	60	Trigger Assembly
19	Grip Cap Screw	39	Front Sight	**Parts Not Shown**	
20	Grip Cap	40	Hammer Stop Pin		Carrier Release Spring Retainer
		41	Trigger Stop Pin Screw		Forend Spacers
		42	Left Slide Support with Cutoff		

Model 1873 Lever-Action Rifle

Courtesy of James M. Triggs

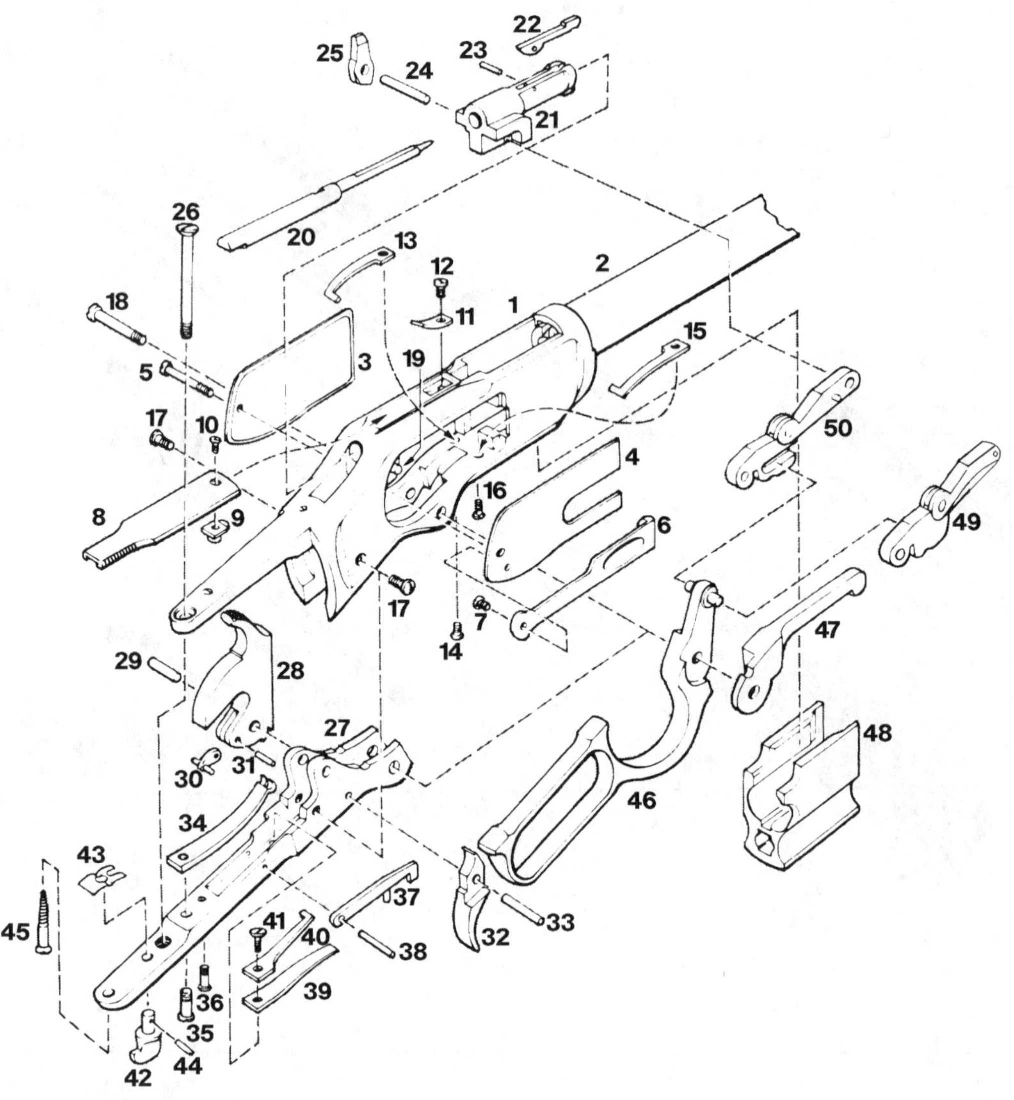

1	Receiver
2	Barrel
3	Sideplate, Left
4	Sideplate, Right
5	Sideplate Screw
6	Spring Cover
7	Spring Cover Screw
8	Mortise Cover
9	Mortise Cover Stop
10	Mortise Cover Stop Screw
11	Mortise Cover Spring
12	Mortise Cover Spring Screw
13	Finger Lever Spring
14	Finger Lever Spring Screw
15	Carrier Lever Spring
16	Carrier Lever Spring Screw
17	Slide Tang Screws
18	Finger Lever Screw
19	Rear Link Pin
20	Firing Pin
21	Breechblock
22	Extractor
23	Extractor Pin
24	Front Link Pin
25	Firing Pin Retractor
26	Upper Tang Screw
27	Lower Tang
28	Hammer
29	Hammer Pivot Pin
30	Stirrup
31	Stirrup Pin
32	Trigger
33	Trigger Pivot Pin
34	Mainspring
35	Mainspring Screw
36	Mainspring Tension Screw
37	Safety Catch
38	Safety Catch Pin
39	Trigger Spring
40	Safety Catch Spring
41	Trigger and Safety Catch Spring Screw
42	Lever Latch
43	Lever Latch Spring
44	Lever Latch Pin
45	Lower Tang Screw
46	Finger Lever
47	Carrier Lever
48	Carrier Block
49	Link Assembly, Right
50	Link Assembly, Left

Model 1885 Single Shot Rifle

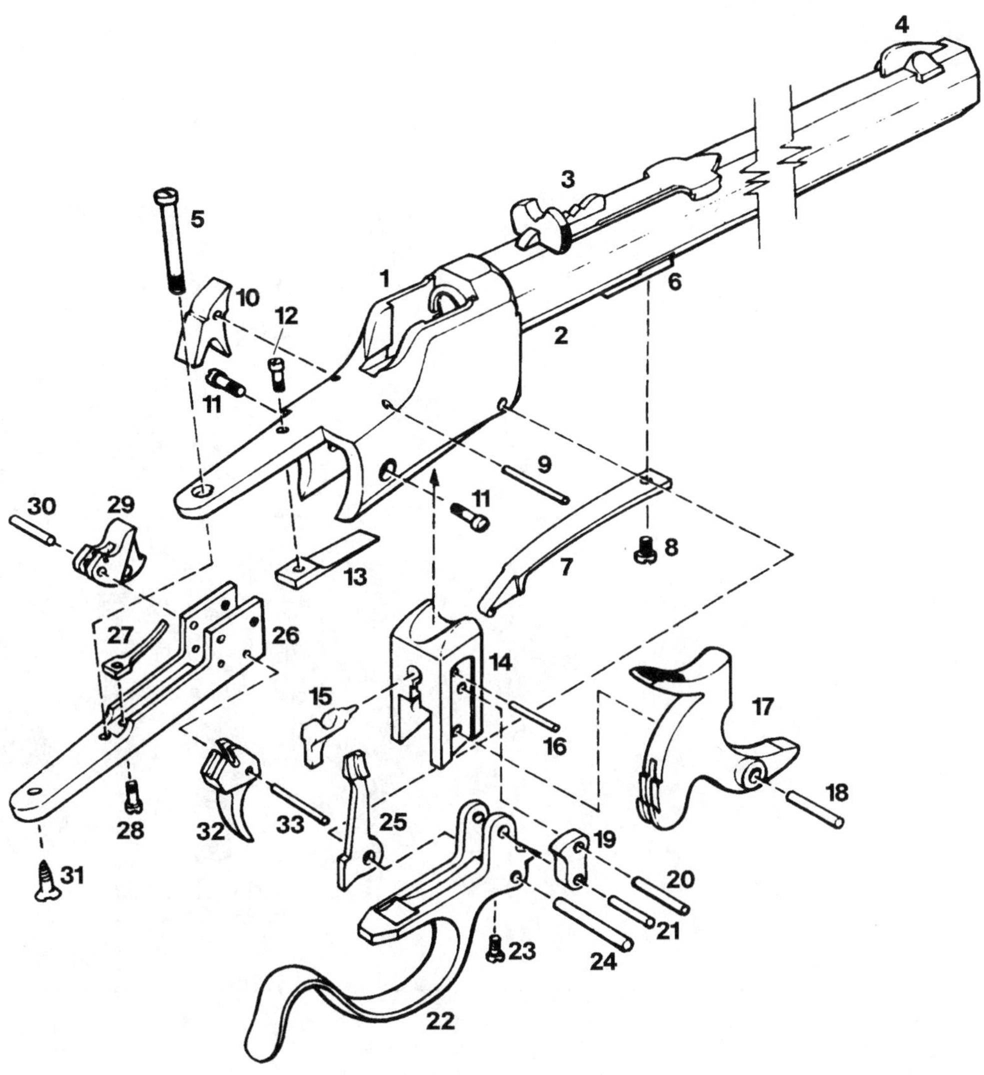

1	Receiver	**21**	Lever Link Pin, Short
2	Barrel	**22**	Finger Lever
3	Rear Sight	**23**	Finger Lever Pin Stop Screw
4	Front Sight	**24**	Finger Lever Pin
5	Upper Tang Screw	**25**	Extractor
6	Mainspring Base	**26**	Tang
7	Mainspring	**27**	Knock-Off Spring
8	Mainspring Screw	**28**	Knock-Off Spring Screw
9	Sear Pin	**29**	Knock-Off
10	Sear	**30**	Knock-Off Pin
11	Side Tang Screws	**31**	Lower Tang Screw
12	Sear Spring Screw	**32**	Trigger
13	Sear Spring	**33**	Trigger Pin
14	Breechblock	**Parts Not Shown**	
15	Firing Pin		Forend
16	Firing Pin Stop Pin		Forend Screw
17	Hammer		Buttstock
18	Hammer Pivot Pin		Buttplate
19	Lever Link		Buttplate Screws
20	Lever Link Pin, Long		

Model 1886 Lever-Action Rifle

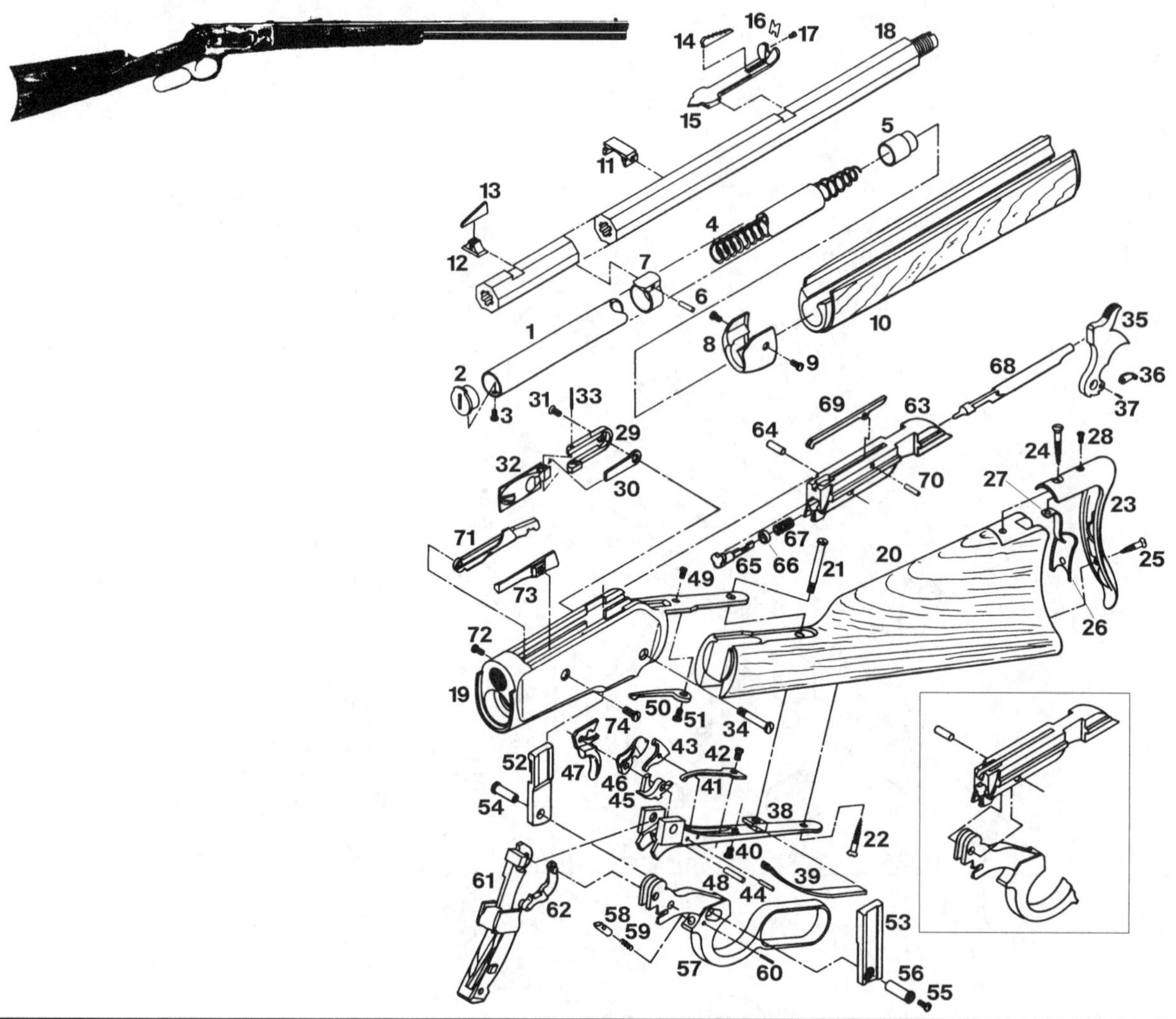

No.	Part	No.	Part	No.	Part
1	Magazine Tube	26	Buttplate Slide	51	Carrier Stop Screw
2	Magazine End Cap	27	Buttplate Slide Spring	52	Right Locking Bolt
3	Magazine End Cap Screw	28	Buttplate Slide Spring Screw	53	Left Locking Bolt
4	Magazine Spring	29	Spring Cover Base	54	Finger Lever Pin
5	Magazine Follower	30	Spring Cover Spring	55	Locking Block Bushing and Pin Screw
6	Magazine Ring Pin	31	Spring Cover Screw	56	Finger Lever Pin Bushing
7	Magazine Ring	32	Spring Cover Leaf	57	Finger Lever
8	Forend Tip	33	Spring Cover Leaf Pin	58	Friction Stud
9	Forend Tip and Tenon Screws	34	Receiver Screw	59	Friction Stud Spring
10	Forend	35	Hammer	60	Friction Stud Pin
11	Forend Tip Tenon	36	Hammer Stirrup	61	Carrier
12	Front Sight Base	37	Hammer Stirrup Pin	62	Carrier Hook
13	Front Sight	38	Lower Tang	63	Breechblock
14	Rear Sight Elevator	39	Mainspring	64	Lever and Breechblock Pin
15	Rear Sight	40	Mainspring Tension Screw	65	Ejector
16	Elevation Leaf	41	Sear and Trigger Spring	66	Ejector Collar
17	Elevation Leaf Screw	42	Sear and Trigger Spring Screw	67	Ejector Spring
18	Barrel	43	Sear Catch	68	Firing Pin
19	Receiver	44	Sear Catch Pin	69	Extractor
20	Stock	45	Sear	70	Extractor Pin
21	Upper Tang Stock Screw	46	Kick-Off for Set-Trigger	71	Cartridge Guide
22	Lower Tang Stock Screw	47	Trigger	72	Cartridge Guide Screw
23	Buttplate	48	Trigger, Sear and Kick-Off Pin	73	Cartridge Stop
24	Upper Buttplate Screw	49	Carrier Stop Tension Screw	74	Cartridge Stop Screw
25	Lower Buttplate Screw	50	Carrier Stop		

Model 1892 Lever-Action Rifle

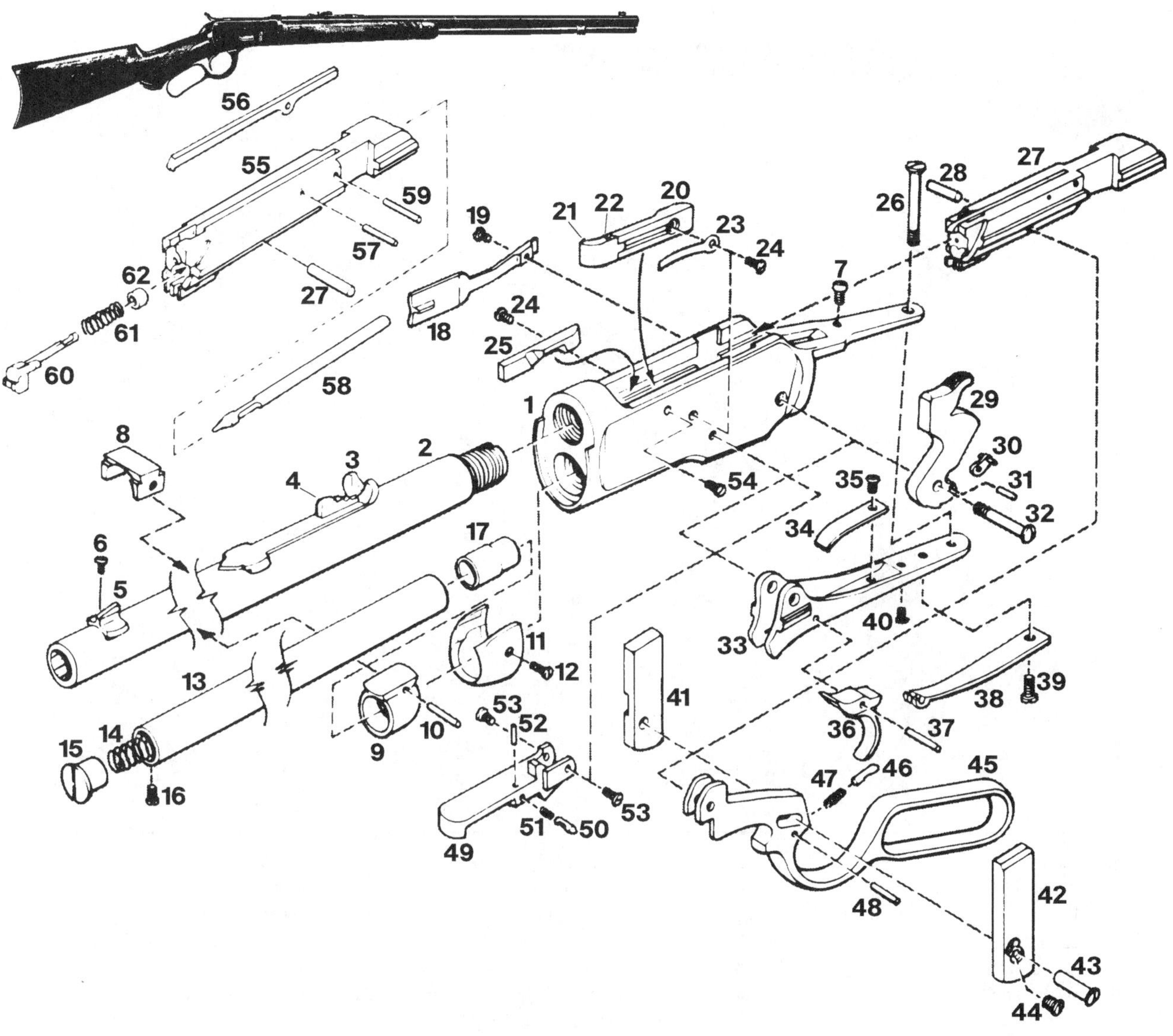

1	Receiver	**22**	Cartridge Stop Joint Pin	**43**	Locking Bolt Pin
2	Barrel	**23**	Cartridge Stop Spring	**44**	Locking Bolt Pin Screw
3	Rear Sight Assembly	**24**	Cartridge Guide Screws	**45**	Finger Lever
4	Rear Sight Elevator	**25**	Cartridge Guide, Right	**46**	Friction Plunger
5	Front Sight	**26**	Upper Tang Screw	**47**	Friction Plunger Spring
6	Front Sight Screw	**27**	Breechbolt	**48**	Friction Stud Stop Pin
7	Tang Sight Screw	**28**	Lever and Breechbolt Pin	**49**	Carrier Assembly
8	Forend Tip Tenon	**29**	Hammer	**50**	Carrier Stop
9	Magazine Ring	**30**	Hammer Stirrup	**51**	Carrier Stop Spring
10	Magazine Ring Pin	**31**	Hammer Stirrup Pin	**52**	Carrier Stop Pin
11	Forend Tip	**32**	Hammer Screw	**53**	Carrier Screws
12	Forend Tip Screw	**33**	Lower Tang	**54**	Lever and Breechblock Pin Hole Plug Screw
13	Magazine Tube	**34**	Trigger Spring	**55**	Breechbolt Assembly
14	Magazine Spring	**35**	Trigger Spring Screw	**56**	Extractor
15	Magazine End Cap	**36**	Trigger	**57**	Extractor Pin
16	Magazine End Cap Screw	**37**	Trigger Pin	**58**	Firing Pin
17	Magazine Follower	**38**	Mainspring	**59**	Firing Pin Stop Pin
18	Spring Cover	**39**	Mainspring Screw	**60**	Ejector
19	Spring Cover Screw	**40**	Mainspring Strain Screw	**61**	Ejector Spring
20	Cartridge Guide, Left	**41**	Locking Bolt, Right	**62**	Ejector Collar
21	Cartridge Stop	**42**	Locking Bolt, Left		

Model 1897 Slide-Action Shotgun

Courtesy of Thomas E. Wessel

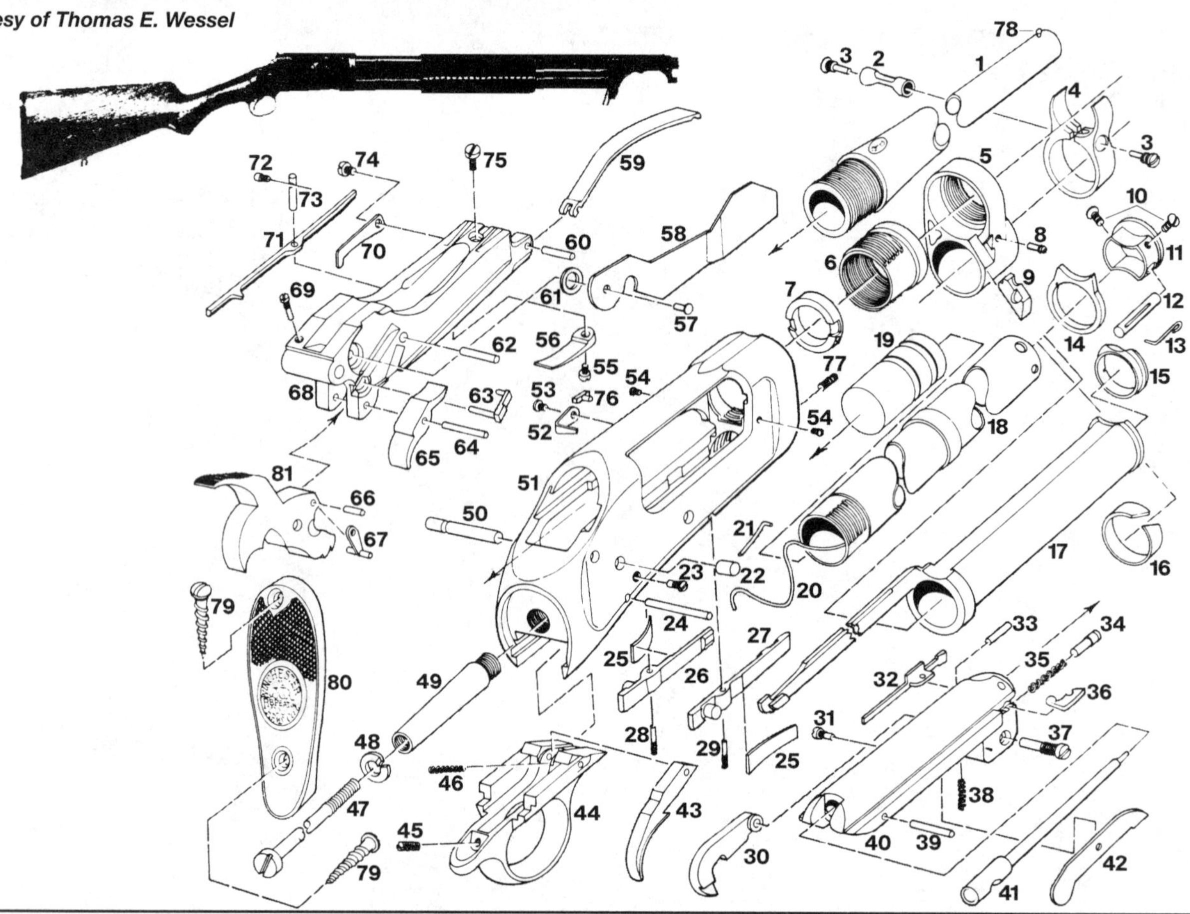

1	Barrel
2	Magazine Band Bushing
3	Magazine Band Bushing Screws
4	Magazine Band
5	Barrel Extension
6	Adjusting Sleeve
7	Barrel Chamber Ring
8	Adjusting Sleeve Lock Screw
9	Adjusting Sleeve Lock
10	Magazine Plug Screws
11	Magazine End Cap
12	Magazine Locking Pin
13	Magazine Locking Pin Spring
14	Magazine End Cap Stop
15	Action Slide Sleeve Screw Cap
16	Action Slide Spring
17	Action Slide
18	Magazine Tube
19	Magazine Follower
20	Magazine Spring
21	Action Slide Lock Release Plunger Pin Spring
22	Action Slide Lock Release Plunger Pin
23	Cartridge Guide Stop Screw
24	Trigger Pin
25	Cartridge Stop Springs
26	Cartridge Stop, Left
27	Cartridge Stop, Right
28	Cartridge Stop Screw, Left
29	Cartridge Stop Screw, Right
30	Action Slide Hook
31	Firing Pin Lock Screw
32	Extractor, Left
33	Extractor Pin, Left
34	Extractor Plunger, Right
35	Extractor Plunger Spring, Right
36	Extractor, Right
37	Action Slide Hook Screw
38	Firing Pin Lock Spring
39	Firing Pin Stop Pin
40	Breechbolt
41	Firing Pin
42	Firing Pin Lock
43	Trigger
44	Guard Bow
45	Trigger Stop Screw
46	Trigger Spring
47	Buttstock Bolt
48	Buttstock Bolt Washer
49	Receiver Shank
50	Carrier Pin
51	Receiver
52	Ejector Spring
53	Ejector Spring Screw
54	Barrel Chamber Ring Retaining Screws
55	Sear Spring Screw
56	Sear Spring
57	Cartridge Guide Rivet
58	Cartridge Guide
59	Mainspring
60	Mainspring Pin
61	Cartridge Guide Friction Spring
62	Hammer Pin
63	Action Slide Lock Release Plunger
64	Sear Pin
65	Sear
66	Hammer Stirrup Pin
67	Hammer Stirrup
68	Carrier
69	Carrier Pin Stop Screw
70	Action Slide Lock Spring
71	Action Slide Lock
72	Action Slide Lock Joint Pin Stop Screw
73	Action Slide Lock Joint Pin
74	Action Slide Lock Spring Screw
75	Mainspring Strain Screw
76	Ejector Pin
77	Extension Stop Screw
78	Front Sight
79	Buttplate Screws
80	Buttplate
81	Hammer

Parts Not Shown

Action Slide Handle

Buttstock

Model 1905 Autoloading Rifle

Courtesy of Blacksmith Corporation

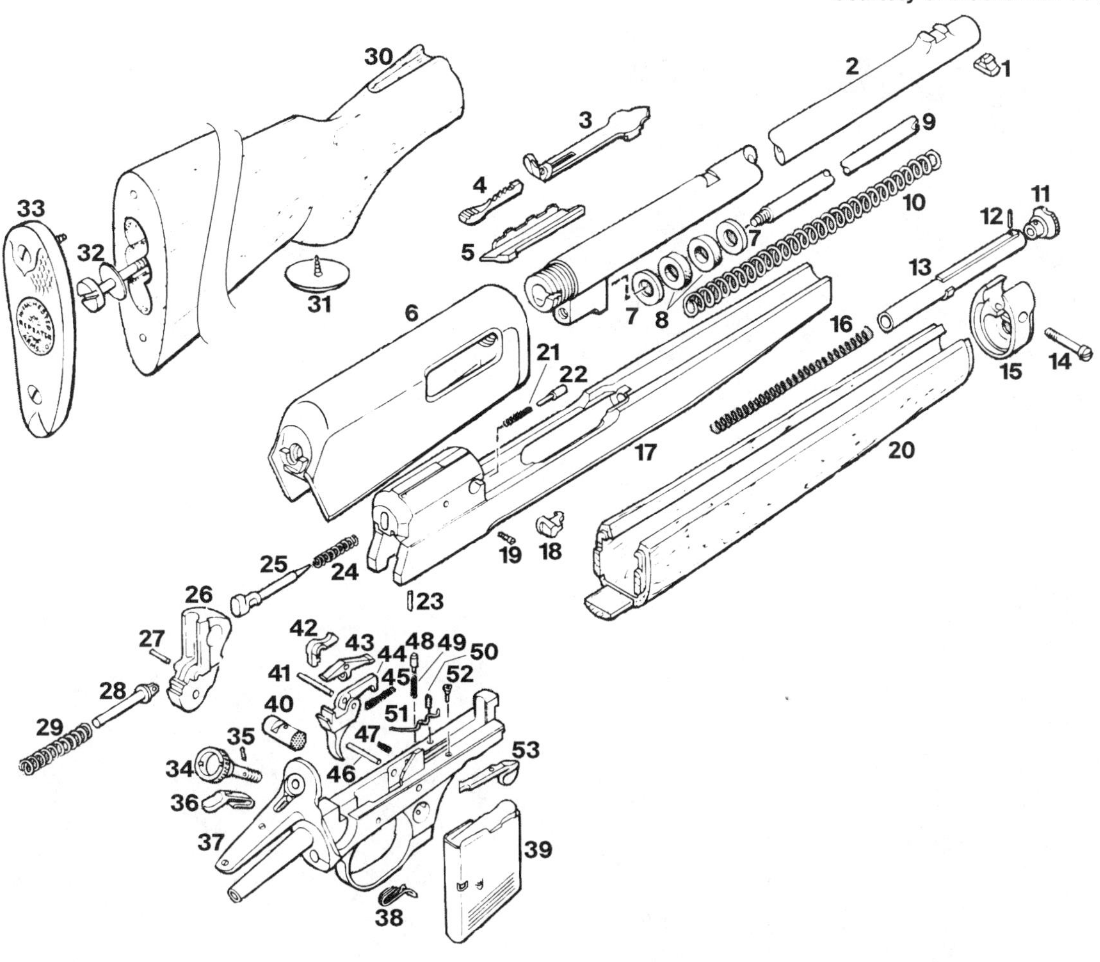

1	Front Sight	**28**	Hammer Strut
2	Barrel	**29**	Hammer Spring
3	Rear Sight	**30**	Buttstock
4	Rear Sight Elevator	**31**	Grip Cap
5	Ejector	**32**	Buttstock Bolt and Washer
6	Receiver	**33**	Buttplate
7	Steel Buffer Washers	**34**	Takedown Screw
8	Fiber Buffer Washers	**35**	Takedown Screw Stop Pin
9	Bolt Guide Rod	**36**	Takedown Screw Lock
10	Recoil Spring	**37**	Trigger Mechanism Housing
11	Operating Sleeve Tip	**38**	Trigger Spring
12	Operating Sleeve Tip Pin	**39**	Magazine
13	Operating Sleeve	**40**	Safety Catch
14	Forend Tip Screw	**41**	Trigger Pin
15	Forend Tip	**42**	Disconnector
16	Operating Sleeve Spring	**43**	Sear
17	Bolt	**44**	Trigger
18	Extractor	**45**	Sear Spring
19	Extractor Plunger Stop Screw	**46**	Hammer Pin
20	Forend	**47**	Magazine Catch Spring
21	Extractor Spring	**48**	Safety Catch Plunger
22	Extractor Plunger	**49**	Plunger Spring
23	Firing Pin Retainer Pin	**50**	Disconnector Spring Retainer
24	Firing Pin Spring	**51**	Disconnector Spring
25	Firing Pin	**52**	Magazine Catch Screw
26	Hammer	**53**	Magazine Catch
27	Hammer Strut Pin		

Model 1907 Autoloading Rifle

Courtesy of James M. Triggs

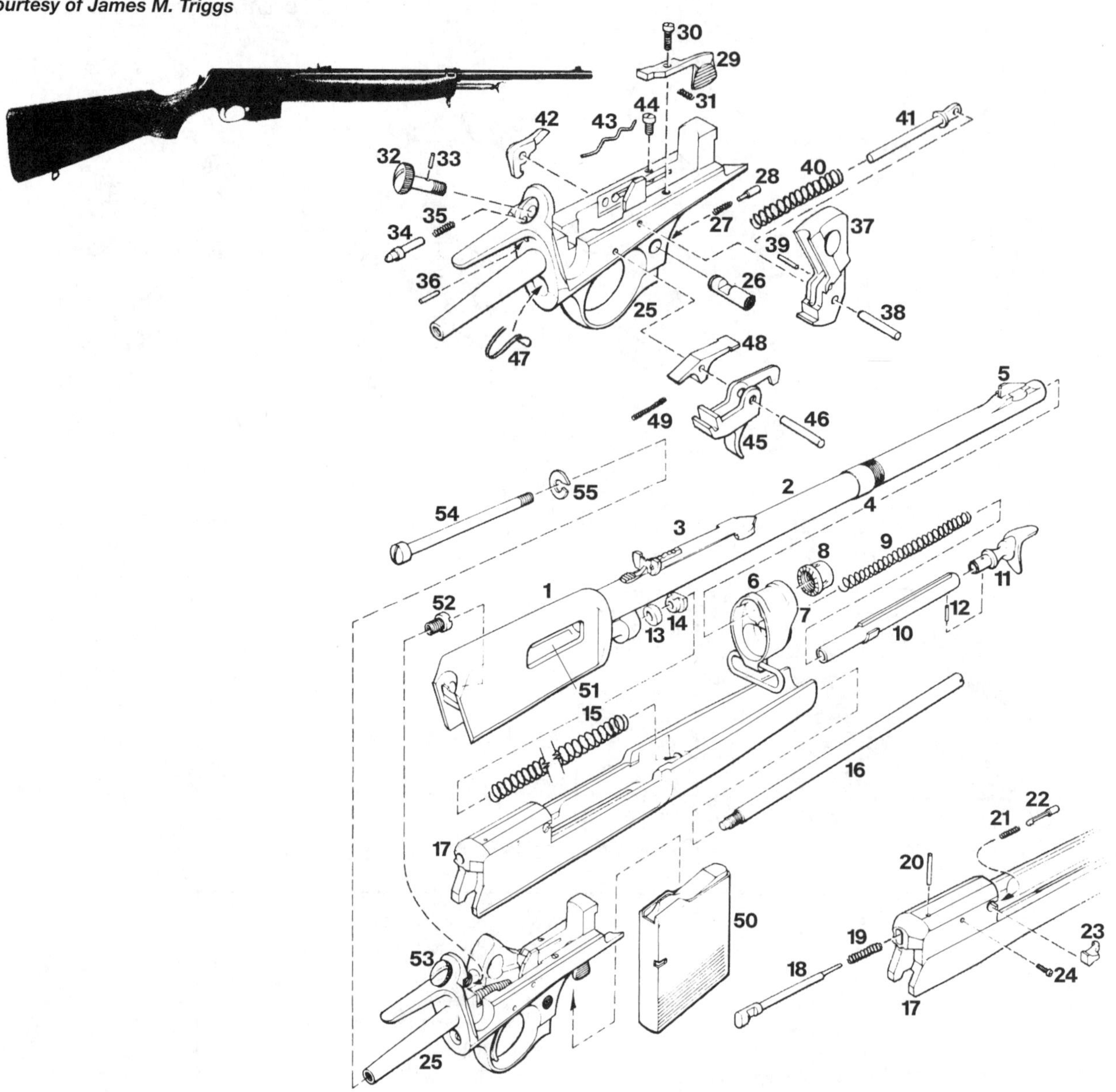

No.	Part	No.	Part	No.	Part
1	Receiver	18	Firing Pin	37	Hammer
2	Barrel	19	Firing Pin Spring	38	Hammer Pin
3	Rear Sight Assembly	20	Firing Pin Retaining Pin	39	Hammer Spring Guide Rod Pin
4	Forend Tip Key	21	Extractor Spring	40	Hammer Spring
5	Front Sight	22	Extractor Spring Plunger	41	Hammer Spring Guide Rod
6	Forend Tip (with Swivel)	23	Extractor	42	Timing Lever
7	Forend Tip Nut Plunger and Spring	24	Extractor Screw	43	Timing Lever Spring
8	Forend Tip Nut	25	Trigger Guard Housing	44	Timing Lever Spring Screw
9	Operating Sleeve Spring	26	Trigger Lock	45	Trigger
10	Operating Sleeve	27	Trigger Lock Plunger Spring	46	Trigger Pin
11	Operating Sleeve Tip	28	Trigger Lock Plunger	47	Trigger Spring
12	Operating Sleeve Tip Pin	29	Magazine Lock	48	Sear
13	Buffer Washers	30	Magazine Lock Screw	49	Sear Spring
14	Buffer	31	Magazine Lock Spring	50	Magazine
15	Bolt Spring	32	Takedown Screw	51	Ejector
16	Bolt Guide Rod	33	Takedown Screw Stop Pin	52	Takedown Screw Bushing
17	Bolt	34	Takedown Screw Lock	53	Takedown Screw
		35	Takedown Screw Lock Spring	54	Buttstock Bolt
		36	Takedown Screw Lock Pin	55	Buttstock Bolt Washer

Model 43 Bolt-Action Rifle

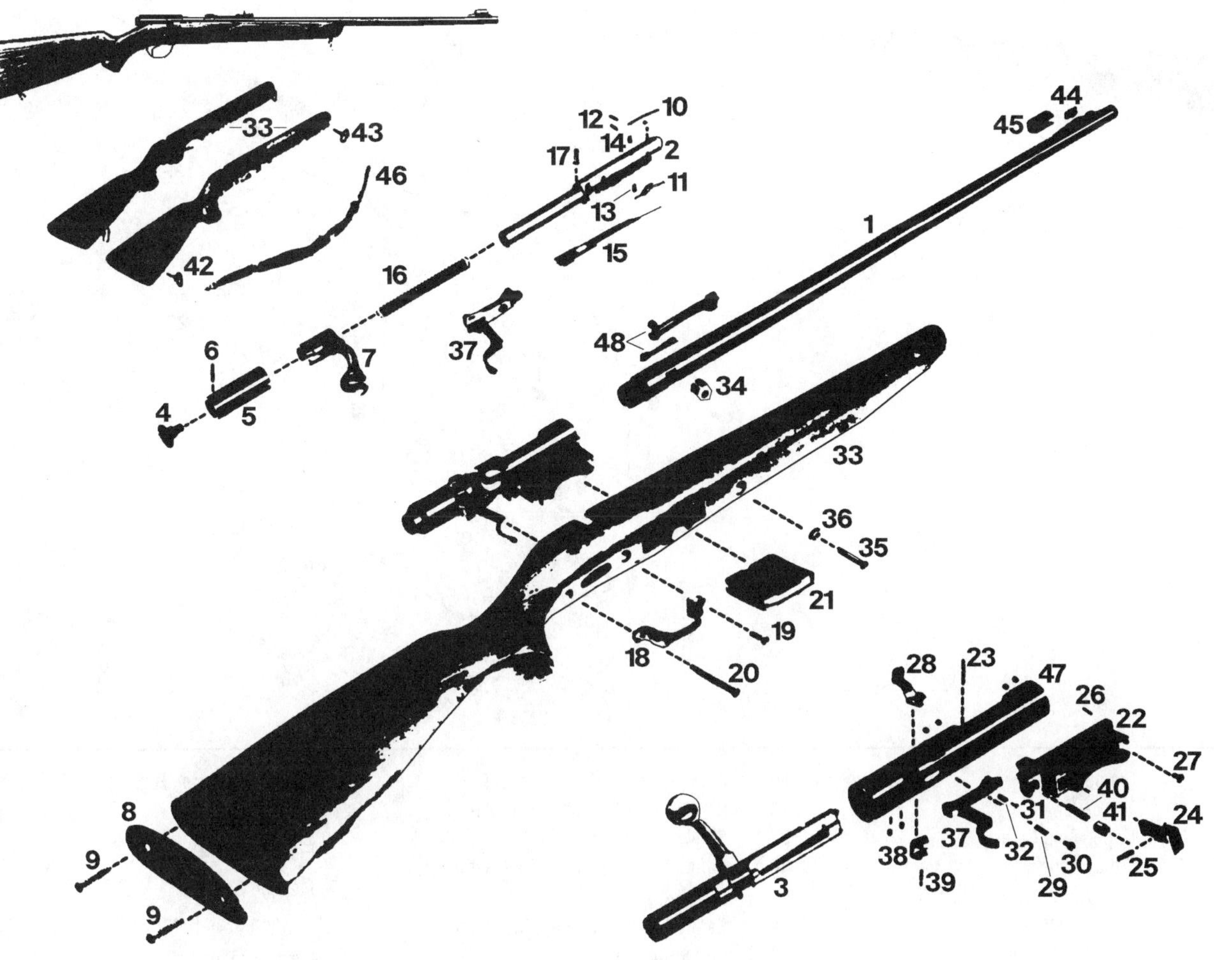

1	Barrel	**25**	Magazine Catch Spring
2	Breechbolt	**26**	Magazine Catch Pin
3	Breechbolt Complete	**27**	Magazine Holder Screw
4	Breechbolt Plug	**28**	Safety-Lever
5	Breechbolt Sleeve	**29**	Safety Lock
6	Breechbolt Sleeve Pin	**30**	Safety Lock Screw
7	Breechbolt Cocking Sleeve	**31**	Safety Lock Plunger
8	Buttplate	**32**	Safety Lock Plunger Spring
9	Buttplate Screws	**33**	Stock
10	Extractor, Left	**34**	Stock Stud
11	Extractor, Right	**35**	Stock Stud Screw
12	Extractor Pins	**36**	Stock Stud Screw Escutcheon
13	Extractor Spring, Right	**37**	Trigger
14	Extractor Spring, Left	**38**	Trigger Base
15	Firing Pin	**39**	Trigger Pin
16	Firing Pin Spring	**40**	Trigger Spring
17	Firing Pin Stop Pin	**41**	Trigger Spring Adjusting Screw
18	Guard	**42**	Rear Swivel
19	Guard Screw, Front	**43**	Front Swivel Assembly
20	Guard Screw, Rear	**44**	Front Sight
21	Magazine Complete	**45**	Front Sight Hood
22	Magazine Holder	**46**	Leather Sling
23	Magazine Holder Pin	**47**	Breechbolt Body
24	Magazine Catch	**48**	Front Sight with Elevator

Model 21 Side-by-Side Shotgun

Courtesy of James M. Triggs

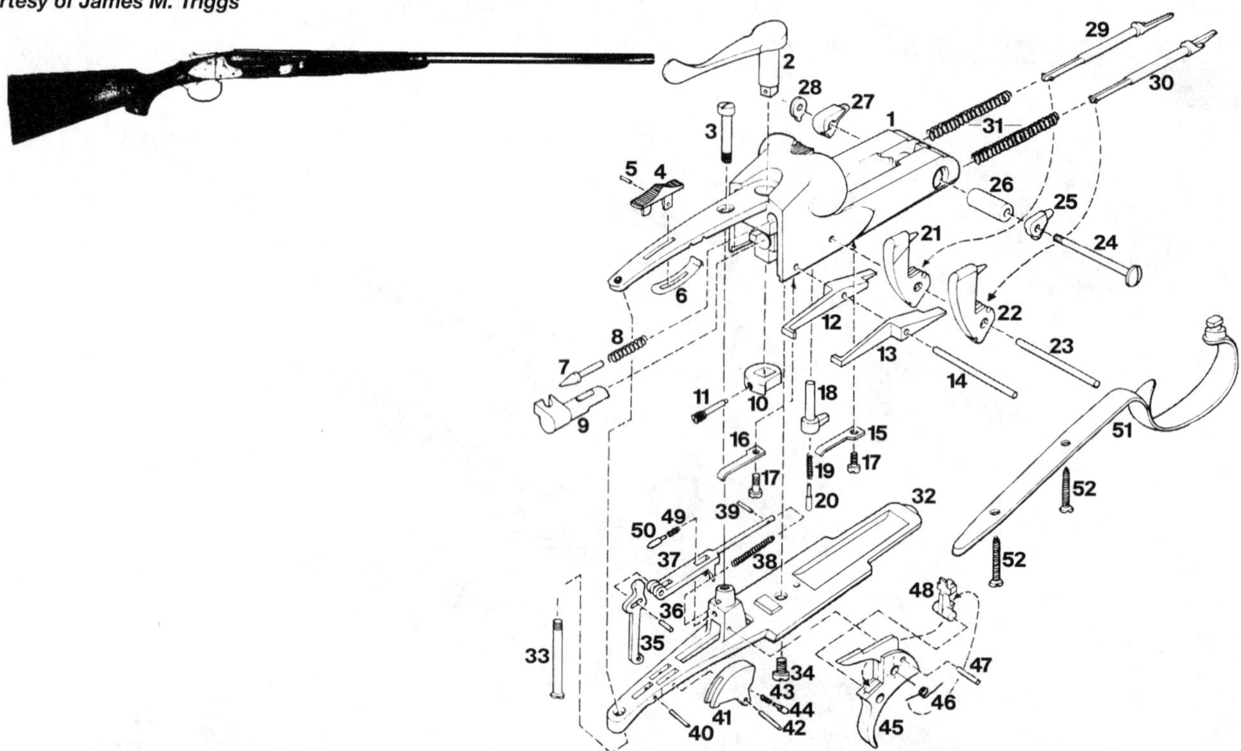

1	Frame
2	Top Lever
3	Upper Tang Screw
4	Safety Slide
5	Safety Slide Spring Stop Pin
6	Safety Slide Spring
7	Top-Lever Plunger
8	Top-Lever Spring
9	Locking Bolt
10	Locking Bolt Lever
11	Locking Bolt Lever Screw
12	Sear, Left
13	Sear, Right
14	Sear Pin
15	Sear Spring, Right
16	Sear Spring, Left
17	Sear Spring Screws
18	Locking Bolt Catch
19	Locking Bolt Catch Spring
20	Locking Bolt Catch Spring Plunger
21	Hammer, Left
22	Hammer, Right
23	Hammer Pin
24	Cocking Lever Screw
25	Cocking Lever, Right
26	Joint Pin
27	Cocking Lever, Left
28	Cocking Lever Screw Nut
29	Cocking Rod, Left
30	Cocking Rod, Right
31	Hammer Springs
32	Trigger Plate
33	Trigger Plate Tang Screw
34	Trigger Plate Screw
35	Safety-Lever
36	Safety-Lever Operating Rod Pin
37	Safety-Lever Operating Rod
38	Safety-Lever Operating Rod Returning Spring
39	Safety-Lever Operating Rod Returning Spring Pin
40	Safety-Lever Pivot Pin
41	Timing Weight
42	Timing Weight Pin
43	Timing Weight Plunger Spring
44	Timing Weight Plunger
45	Trigger Assembly
46	Shift Lever Spring
47	Trigger Pin
48	Shift Lever and Shift Lever Button
49	Trigger Spring
50	Trigger Spring Plunger
51	Guard Bow
52	Guard Bow Screws

Parts Not Shown

Barrel Stop
Barrel Stop Screw
Barrel Stop Spring
Barrels
Buttstock
Ejection Hammer Roll
Ejection Hammer Roll Pin
Ejection Hammer Spring Guide Rods
Ejection Hammer Springs
Ejection Hammer, Left
Ejection Hammer, Right
Ejection Sear Pin
Ejection Sear Spring
Ejection Sear, Left
Ejection Sear, Right
Extractor Plunger
Extractor Plunger Stop Pin
Extractor Stop Screw
Extractor, Left
Extractor, Right
Forearm
Forearm Catch
Forearm Catch Pin
Forearm Catch Plate
Forearm Catch Spring
Forearm Recoil Abutment
Forearm Recoil Screw
Forearm Retainer
Forearm Retainer Pin
Forearm Retainer Spring
Forearm Shoe
Front Forearm Screw
Front Sight
Locking Bolt Stop Screw
Rear Forearm Screw
Rear Sight
Upper Tang Screw Bushing

Model 23 XTR Side-by-Side Shotgun

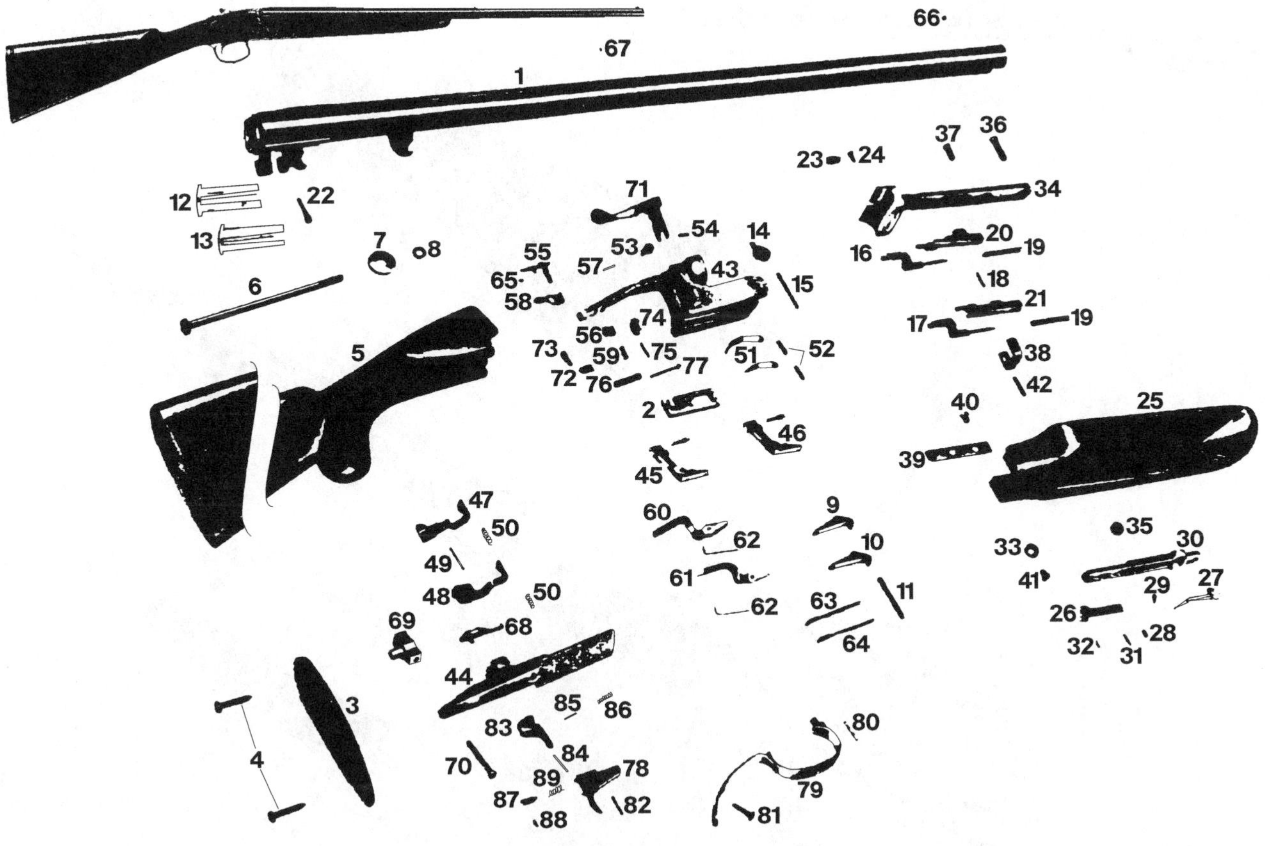

1	Barrels
2	Barrel Locking Plate
3	Buttplate
4	Buttplate Screws
5	Buttstock
6	Buttstock Bolt
7	Buttstock Bolt Washer (Flat)
8	Buttstock Bolt Washer (Lock)
9	Cocking Plate, Left
10	Cocking Plate, Right
11	Cocking Plate Pin
12	Ejector, Left
13	Ejector, Right
14	Ejector Cocking Lever
15	Ejector Cocking Lever Pin
16	Ejector Hammer, Left
17	Ejector Hammer, Right
18	Ejector Hammer Retaining Pin
19	Ejector Hammer Springs
20	Ejector Hammer Spring Housing, Left
21	Ejector Hammer Spring Housing, Right
22	Ejector Retaining Screw
23	Ejector Hammer Stopper
24	Ejector Hammer Stopper Screw, Front
25	Forearm
26	Forearm Catch
27	Forearm Catch Lock
28	Forearm Catch Lock Retaining Pin
29	Forearm Catch Lock Spring
30	Forearm Catch Plate Complete
31	Forearm Catch Retaining Pin
32	Forearm Catch Stop Pin
33	Forearm Escutcheon
34	Forearm Plate, Upper
35	Forearm Plate Escutcheon, Upper
36	Forearm Plate Screw, Upper Front
37	Forearm Plate Screw, Upper Middle
38	Forearm Spacer
39	Forearm Spacer Plate
40	Forearm Spacer Plate Retaining Screw
41	Forearm Spacer Plate Screw
42	Forearm Spacer Retaining Pin
43	Frame
44	Frame Plate, Lower
45	Hammer/Firing Pin Assembly, Left
46	Hammer/Firing Pin Assembly, Right
47	Hammer Catch, Left
48	Hammer Catch, Right
49	Hammer Catch Retaining Pin
50	Hammer Catch Springs
51	Hammer Springs
52	Hammer Spring Retaining Pins
53	Locking Plate Connecting Block
54	Locking Plate Connecting Block Pin
55	Safety
56	Safety-Lever Cam
57	Safety Retaining Pin
58	Safety Spring
59	Safety Stud
60	Sear, Left
61	Sear, Right
62	Sear Springs
63	Selective Ejector Rod, Left
64	Selective Ejector Rod, Right
65	Selective Filler Block
66	Sight, Front
67	Sight, Middle
68	Tang Sear Catch Plate
69	Tang Spacer
70	Tang Spacer Screw
71	Top Lever
72	Top Lever Locking Plate
73	Top Lever Locking Plate Screw
74	Top Lever Plunger Guide
75	Top Lever Plunger Guide Pin
76	Top Lever Spring
77	Top Lever Spring Plunger
78	Trigger
79	Trigger Guard
80	Trigger Guard Retaining Pin
81	Trigger Guard Screw
82	Trigger Pin
83	Trigger Sear Catch
84	Trigger Sear Catch Disconnector Pin
85	Trigger Sear Catch Pin
86	Trigger Spring
87	Trigger Swivel Plunger
88	Trigger Swivel Plunger Pin
89	Trigger Swivel Plunger Spring

Model 24 Side-by-Side Shotgun

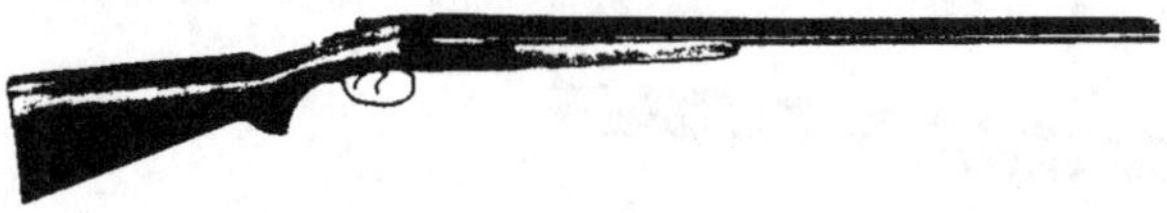

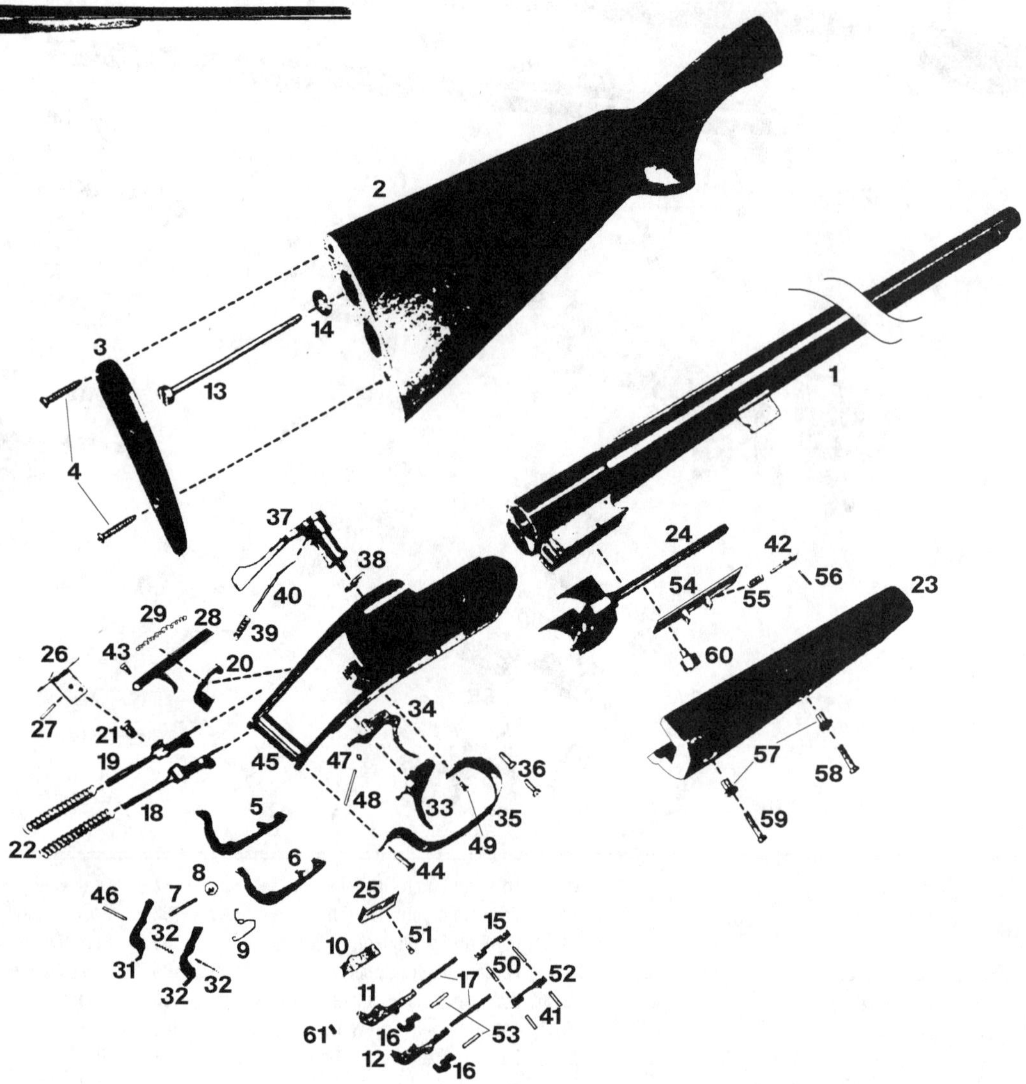

1	Barrel	22	Firing Pin Springs	43	Safety Slide Push Rod Screw
2	Buttstock	23	Forearm	44	Trigger Guard Screw, Rear
3	Buttplate	24	Forearm Shoe	45	Frame
4	Buttplate Screws	25	Locking Bolt	46	Sear Pin
5	Cocking Lever, Right	26	Safety Slide	47	Trigger Spacer
6	Cocking Lever, Left	27	Safety Slide Pin	48	Trigger Pin
7	Cocking Lever Pin	28	Safety Slide Push Rod	49	Trigger Guard Screw, Front
8	Cocking Lever Spacer	29	Safety Slide Spring	50	Extractor Guide Pins
9	Cocking Lever Spring	30	Sear, Right	51	Cocking Slide Retaining Screw
10	Cocking Slide	31	Sear, Left	52	Extractor Guide
11	Extractor, Right	32	Sear Springs	53	Extractor Lever Pins
12	Extractor, Left	33	Trigger, Right	54	Forearm Shoe Retainer
13	Buttstock Bolt	34	Trigger, Left	55	Forearm Shoe Retainer Spring
14	Buttstock Bolt Washer	35	Trigger Guard	56	Forearm Shoe Retainer Pin
15	Extractor Guide	36	Trigger Plate Screws	57	Forearm Escutcheons
16	Extractor Levers	37	Top Lever	58	Forearm Screw, Front
17	Extractor Springs	38	Top Lever Guide	59	Forearm Screw, Rear
18	Firing Pin Complete, Right	39	Top Lever Spring	60	Forearm Lug
19	Firing Pin Complete, Left	40	Top Lever Spring Guide Rod	61	Pin
20	Firing Pin Guide	41	Extractor Guide Pins		
21	Firing Pin Guide Screw	42	Forearm Retainer Shoe Plunger		

Model 25 Slide-Action Shotgun

Courtesy of Thomas E. Wessel

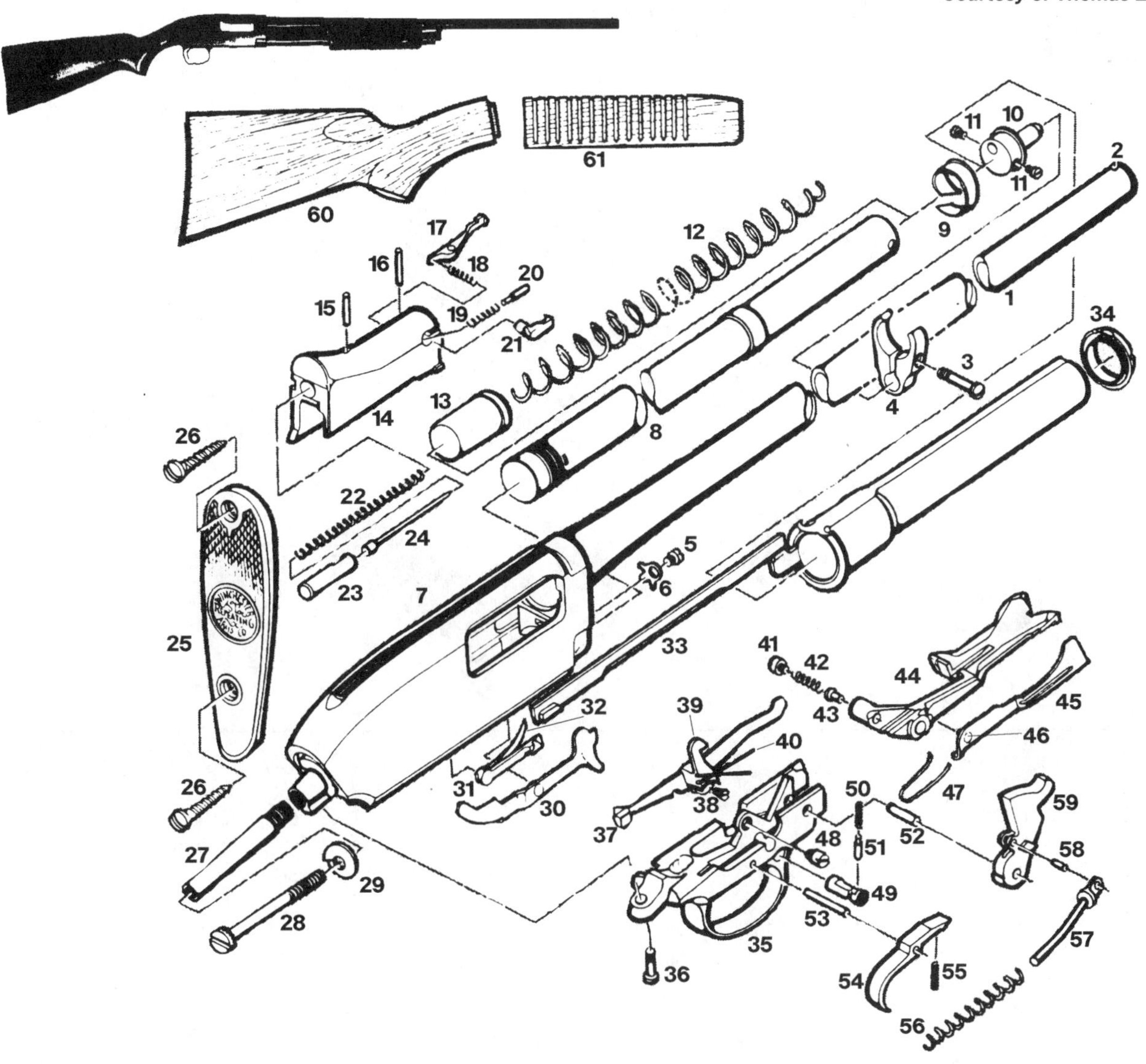

1	Barrel	**22**	Firing Pin Spring	**43**	Carrier Plunger
2	Front Sight	**23**	Firing Pin Striker	**44**	Carrier
3	Magazine Band Screw	**24**	Firing Pin	**45**	Cartridge Guide
4	Magazine Band	**25**	Buttplate	**46**	Cartridge Guide Pivot
5	Magazine Lock Screw	**26**	Buttplate Screws	**47**	Carrier Spring
6	Magazine Lock	**27**	Receiver Shank	**48**	Carrier Pivot
7	Receiver	**28**	Buttstock Bolt	**49**	Trigger Lock
8	Magazine	**29**	Buttstock Bolt Washer	**50**	Trigger Lock Plunger Spring
9	Action Slide Spring	**30**	Cartridge Cutoff	**51**	Trigger Lock Plunger
10	Magazine Plug	**31**	Ejector	**52**	Hammer Pin
11	Magazine Plug Screws	**32**	Ejector Spring	**53**	Trigger Pin
12	Magazine Spring	**33**	Action Slide	**54**	Trigger
13	Magazine Follower	**34**	Action Slide Sleeve Screw Cap	**55**	Trigger Spring
14	Breechbolt	**35**	Guard	**56**	Hammer Spring
15	Firing Pin Stop Pin	**36**	Guard Screw	**57**	Hammer Spring Guide Rod
16	Left Extractor Pin	**37**	Action Slide Lock	**58**	Hammer Spring Guide Pin
17	Left Extractor	**38**	Action Slide Lock Screw	**59**	Hammer
18	Left Extractor Spring	**39**	Action Slide Lock Pivot	**60**	Buttstock
19	Right Extractor Spring	**40**	Action Slide Lock Spring	**61**	Action Slide Handle
20	Right Extractor Spring Plunger	**41**	Carrier Plunger Screw		
21	Right Extractor	**42**	Carrier Plunger Spring		

Model 250, 255, 270, 275 and 290 Lever-Action Rifle

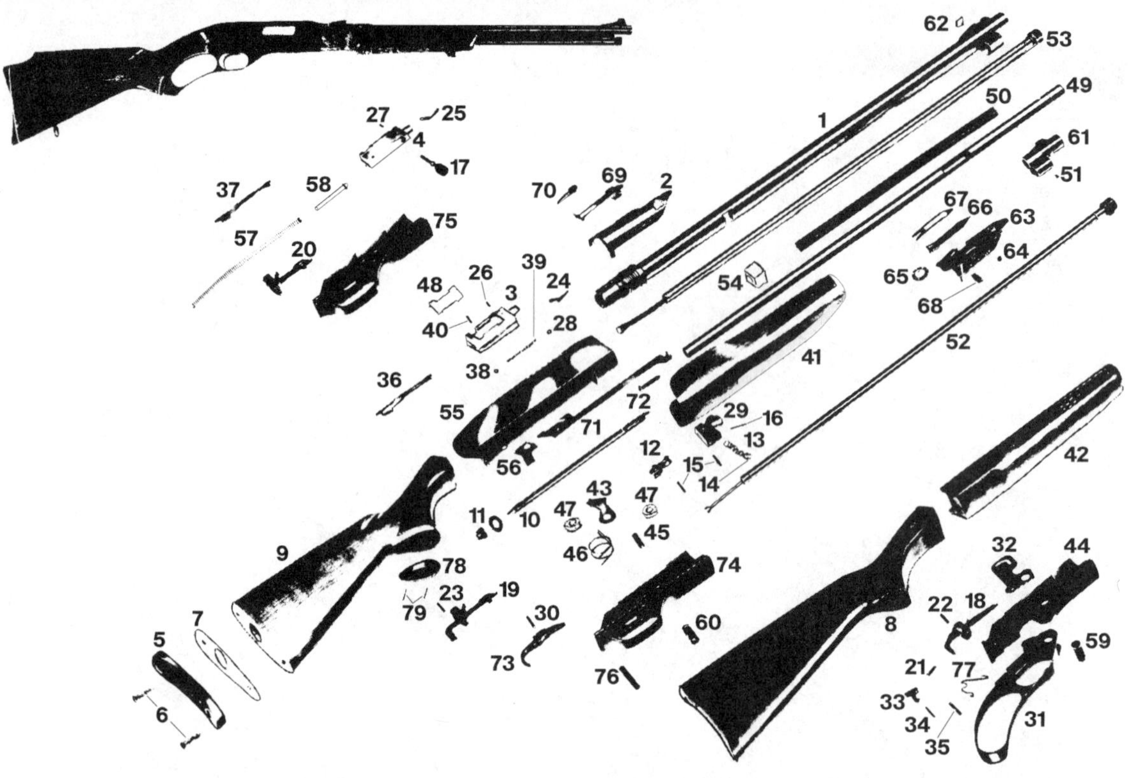

1	Barrel and Barrel Collar
2	Barrel Collar Cover
3	Breechbolt
4	Breechbolt (Model 290)
5	Buttplate
6	Buttplate Screws
7	Buttplate Spacer
8	Buttstock (Model 250 and 255)
9	Buttstock (Model 270, 275 and 290)
10	Buttstock Bolt
11	Buttstock Nut with Washer
12	Carrier
13	Carrier Coil Spring
14	Carrier Coil Spring Plunger
15	Carrier Pin and Trigger Pin
16	Carrier Stop Pin
17	Cocking Handle (Model 290)
18	Disconnector and Sear Assembly (Model 250 and 255)
19	Disconnector and Sear Assembly (Model 270 and 275)
20	Disconnector and Sear Assembly (Model 290)
21	Disconnector Coil Spring (Model 250 and 255)
22	Disconnector Pin (Model 250 and 255)
23	Disconnector Pin (Model 270 and 275)
24	Extractor (Model 250 and 270)
25	Extractor (Model 290)
26	Extractor Pin
27	Extractor Pin (Model 290)
28	Extractor Plunger
29	Feed Guide
30	Feed Guide Pin
31	Finger Lever (Model 250 and 255)
32	Finger Lever Arm (Model 250 and 255)
33	Finger Lever Latch (Model 250 and 255)
34	Finger Lever Latch Pin (Model 250 and 255)
35	Finger Lever Pin (Model 250 and 255)
36	Firing Pin (Model 250 and 270)
37	Firing Pin (Model 290)
38	Firing Pin Plunger
39	Firing Pin Spring
40	Firing Pin Stop Pin
41	Forend (Model 270 and 275)
42	Forend (Model 250, 255 and 290)
43	Hammer
44	Hammer Housing (Model 250 and 255)
45	Hammer Pin
46	Hammer Spring
47	Hammer Spring Supports
48	Locking Plate
49	Magazine Tube, Outside (old)
50	Magazine Tube, Outside
51	Magazine Tube Retaining Pin
52	Magazine Tube, Inside
53	Magazine Tube, Inside (Model 250, 270 and 290)
54	Magazine Tube Bracket
55	Receiver (Model 270)
56	Recoil Plate
57	Return Spring (Model 290)
58	Return Spring Guide (Model 290)
59	Safety (Model 250 and 255)
60	Safety (Model 270, 275 and 290)
61	Sight, Front (Plastic)
62	Sight, Front (Metal)
63	Sight Base, Rear (Model 270)
64	Sight Base Screw, Rear
65	Sight Elevator, Rear
66	Sight Leaf, Rear
67	Sight Spring, Rear
68	Sight Windage Screw, Rear
69	Sight, Rear
70	Sight Elevator, Rear
71	Slide Arm (Model 270 and 275)
72	Slide Arm Screw (Model 270 and 275)
73	Trigger Assembly
74	Trigger Guard (Model 270 and 275)
75	Trigger Guard (Model 290)
76	Trigger Guard Pin, Rear
77	Trigger Spring (Model 250 and 255)
78	Pistol Grip Cap
79	Pistol Grip Screws

Model 310 and 320 Bolt-Action Rifle

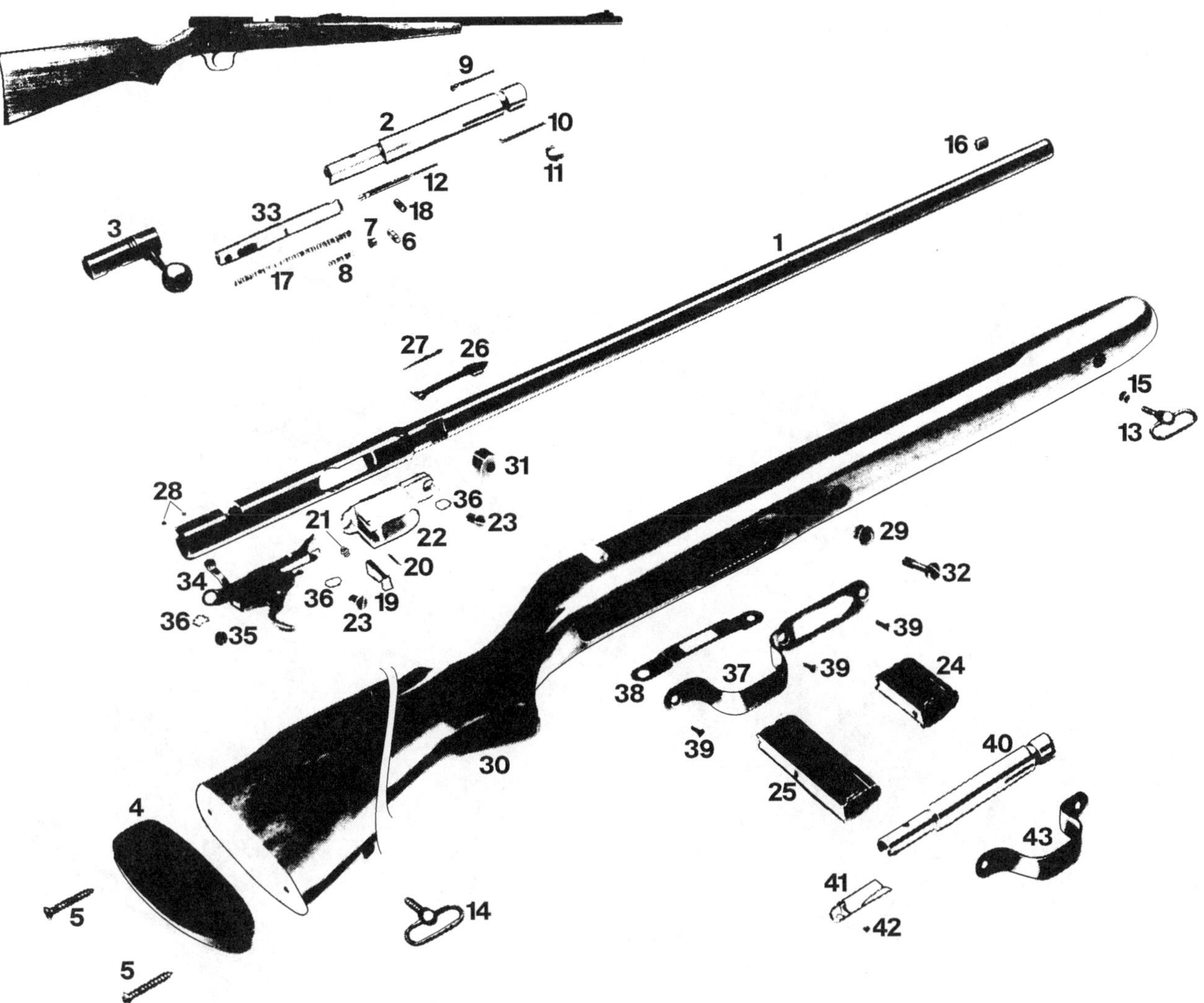

1. Barrel with Receiver Assembly
2. Breechbolt
3. Breechbolt Sleeve with Handle
4. Buttplate
5. Buttplate Screws
6. Cocking Stud
7. Cocking Stud Retainer
8. Cocking Stud Retainer Spring
9. Extractor, Left
10. Extractor, Right
11. Extractor Spring
12. Firing Pin
13. Forend Screw Eye Assembly
14. Buttstock Screw Eye Assembly
15. Forend Screw Eye Escutcheon
16. Front Sight
17. Mainspring
18. Mainspring Retaining Pin
19. Magazine Catch
20. Magazine Catch Pin
21. Magazine Catch Spring
22. Magazine Housing and Ejector
23. Magazine Housing Screws
24. Magazine Assembly, 5-Shot
25. Magazine Assembly, 10-Shot
26. Rear Sight
27. Rear Sight Elevator
28. Sight Base Plug Screws
29. Stock Escutcheon
30. Stock
31. Stock Stud
32. Stock Stud Screw
33. Striker
34. Trigger Housing Assembly
35. Trigger Housing Screw
36. Trigger and Magazine Housing Screw Washers
37. Trigger Guard
38. Trigger Guard Plate
39. Trigger Guard Screws
40. Breechbolt (Model 310)
41. Feed Ramp with Ejector (Model 310)
42. Feed Ramp Screw (Model 310)
43. Trigger Guard (Model 310)

Model 37A, 370 and 840 Single Shot Shotgun

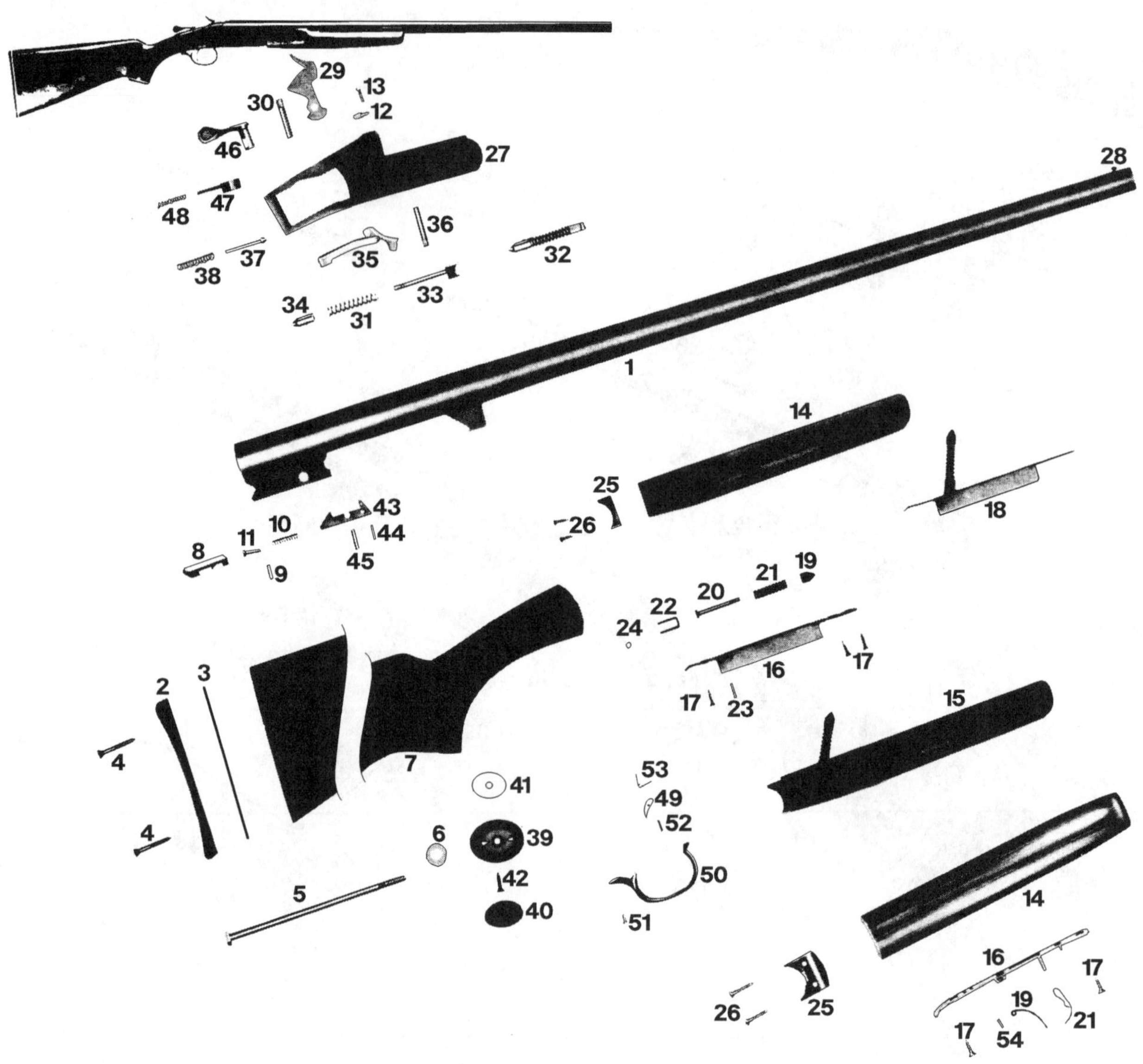

1	Barrel	**19**	Forearm Retainer	**37**	Locking Bolt Plunger
2	Buttplate	**20**	Forearm Retainer Rod	**38**	Locking Bolt Plunger Spring
3	Buttplate Spacer	**21**	Forearm Retainer Spring	**39**	Pistol Grip Cap
4	Buttplate Screws	**22**	Forearm Retainer Bracket	**40**	Pistol Grip Cap Insert
5	Buttstock Bolt	**23**	Forearm Retainer Bracket Pin	**41**	Pistol Grip Cap Spacer
6	Buttstock Bolt Washer	**24**	Forearm Retainer Bracket Spring	**42**	Pistol Grip Cap Screw
7	Buttstock Complete	**25**	Forearm Spacer	**43**	Extractor Sear
8	Extractor	**26**	Forearm Spacer Screws	**44**	Extractor Sear Pin
9	Extractor Pin	**27**	Frame	**45**	Extractor Sear Retaining Pin
10	Extractor Spring	**28**	Front Sight	**46**	Top Lever
11	Extractor Spring Plunger	**29**	Hammer	**47**	Top Lever Plunger
12	Firing Pin	**30**	Hammer Pin	**48**	Top Lever Plunger Spring
13	Firing Pin Retaining Screw	**31**	Hammer Spring	**49**	Trigger
14	Forearm	**32**	Hammer Spring Assembly	**50**	Trigger Guard
15	Forearm Complete	**33**	Hammer Spring Plunger	**51**	Trigger Guard Screw
16	Forearm Catch Plate	**34**	Hammer Spring Plunger Bushing	**52**	Trigger Pin
17	Forearm Catch Plate Screws	**35**	Locking Bolt and Connecting Rod	**53**	Trigger Spring
18	Forearm Catch Plate Assembly	**36**	Locking Bolt Pin	**54**	Forearm Catch Plate Pin

Model 490 Autoloading Rifle

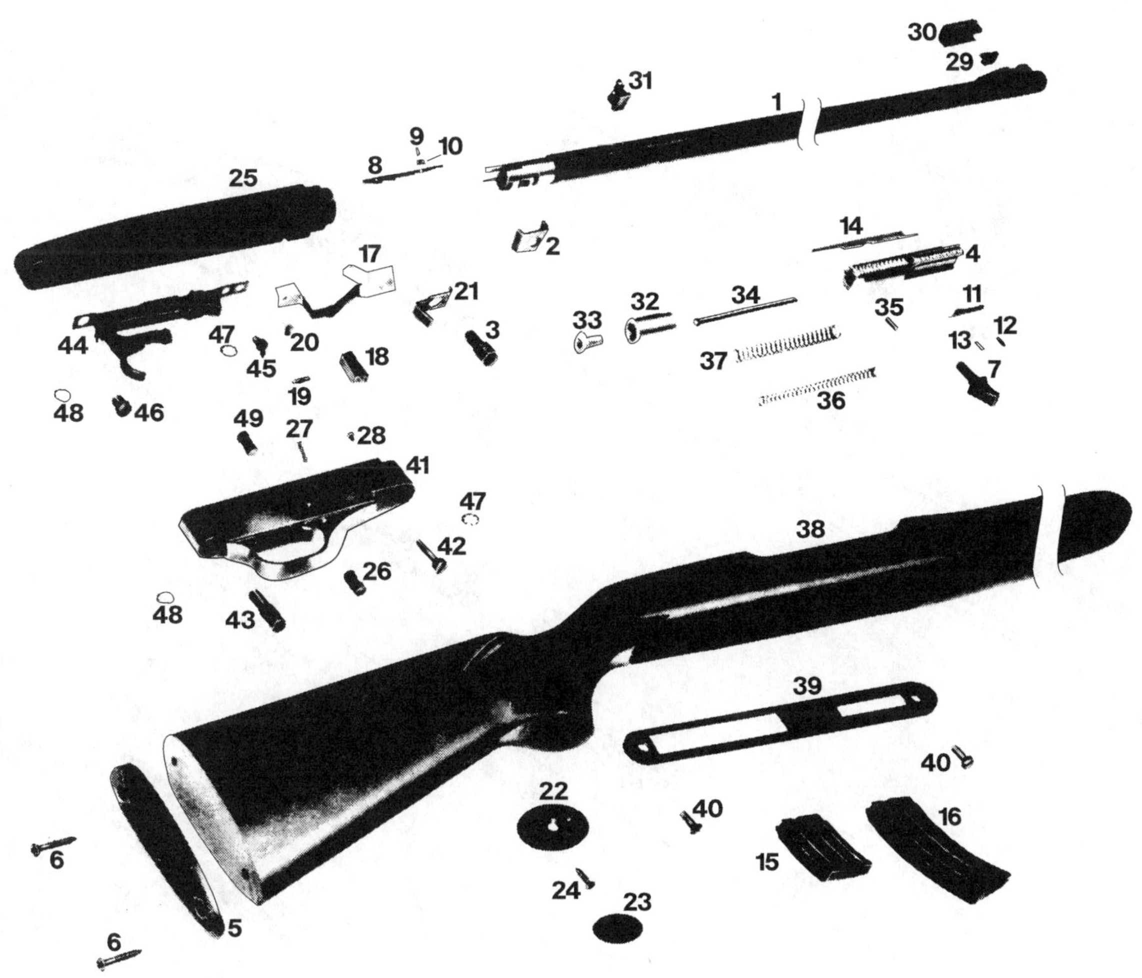

1	Barrel	18	Magazine Lock	35	Striker Rod Pin
2	Barrel Bracket	19	Magazine Lock Pin	36	Striker Spring, Inside
3	Barrel Bracket Stud	20	Magazine Lock Spring	37	Striker Spring, Outside
4	Breechbolt	21	Magazine Guide	38	Stock
5	Buttplate	22	Pistol Grip Cap	39	Stock Floorplate
6	Buttplate Screws	23	Pistol Grip Cap Insert	40	Stock Floorplate Screws
7	Cocking Handle	24	Pistol Grip Cap Screw	41	Trigger Guard
8	Ejector	25	Receiver	42	Front Trigger Guard Screw
9	Ejector Pin	26	Safety	43	Rear Trigger Guard Screw
10	Ejector Spring	27	Safety Spring	44	Trigger Housing Assembly
11	Extractor	28	Safety Spring Screw	45	Trigger Housing Screw, Front
12	Extractor Pin	29	Front Sight	46	Trigger Housing Screw, Rear
13	Extractor Spring	30	Front Sight Cover	47	Front Trigger Housing/Trigger Guard Screw Washers
14	Firing Pin	31	Rear Sight	48	Rear Trigger Housing/Guard Screw Washers
15	Magazine Assembly, 5 Shot	32	Striker	49	Trigger Stop Pin
16	Magazine Assembly, 10 Shot	33	Striker Retainer		
17	Magazine Housing	34	Striker Rod		

Model 50 and 59 Autoloading Shotgun

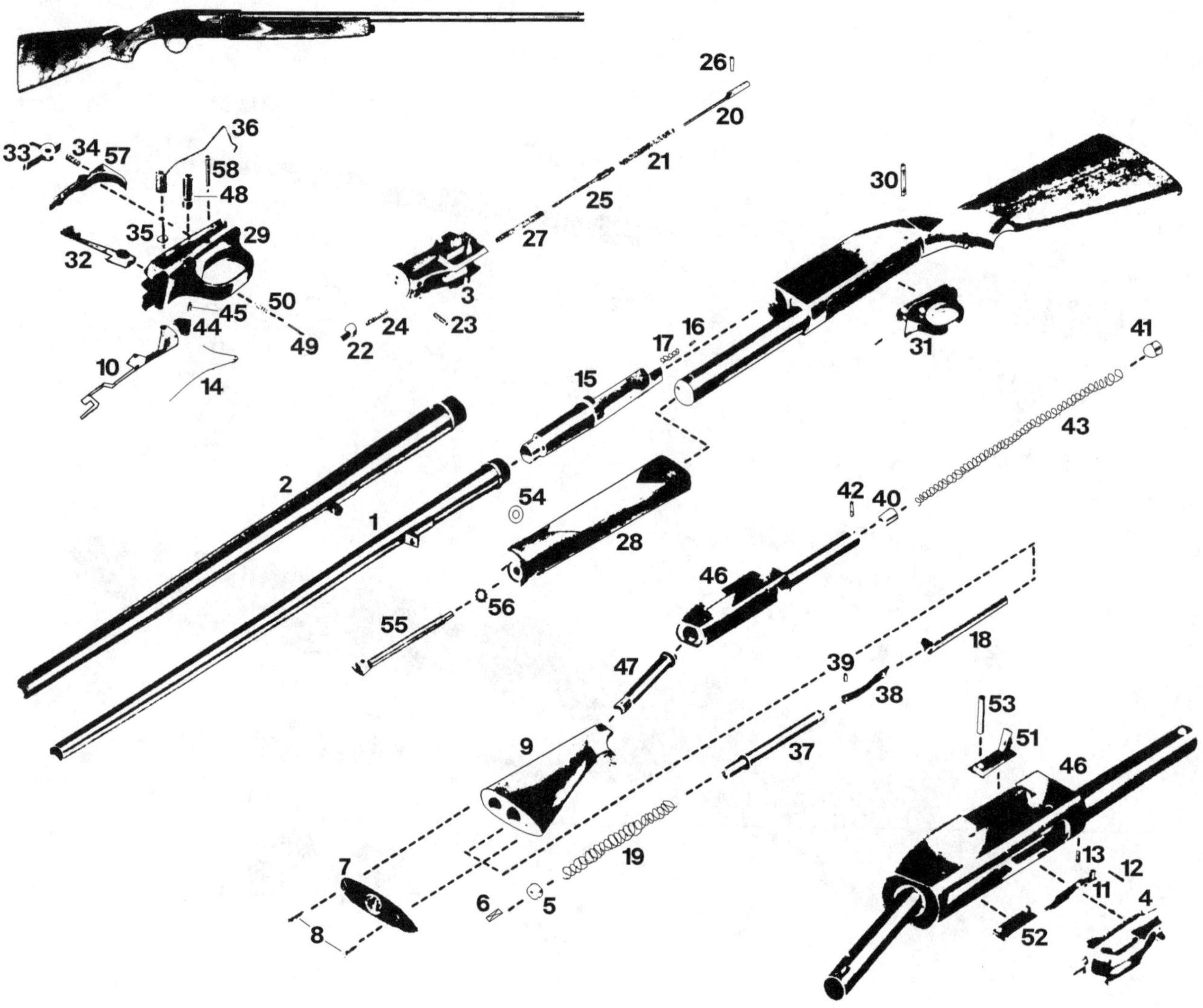

1	Barrel, Plain	**21**	Ejector Spring	**41**	Magazine Plug
2	Barrel, Ventilated Rib	**22**	Extractor	**42**	Magazine Plug Pin
3	Bolt	**23**	Extractor Pin	**43**	Magazine Spring
4	Bolt, Complete	**24**	Extractor Spring	**44**	Pawl
5	Buffer Plug	**25**	Firing Pin	**45**	Pawl Pin
6	Buffer Lock	**26**	Firing Pin Stop Pin	**46**	Receiver
7	Buttplate	**27**	Firing Pin Spring	**47**	Receiver Extension Tube
8	Buttplate Screws	**28**	Forearm	**48**	Safety
9	Buttstock	**29**	Trigger Guard	**49**	Safety Plunger
10	Carrier	**30**	Trigger Guard Pin	**50**	Safety Plunger Spring
11	Carrier Lock	**31**	Trigger Guard Complete	**51**	Slide, Right
12	Carrier Lock Screw	**32**	Hammer	**52**	Slide, Left
13	Carrier Lock Spring	**33**	Hammer Catch	**53**	Slide Pin
14	Carrier Spring	**34**	Hammer Catch Spring	**54**	Takedown Retaining Ring
15	Chamber	**35**	Hammer Pin	**55**	Takedown Screw
16	Chamber Plunger	**36**	Hammer Spring	**56**	Takedown Screw Washer
17	Chamber Plunger Spring	**37**	Inertia Rod	**57**	Trigger
18	Closing Spring Tube	**38**	Link	**58**	Trigger Pin
19	Closing Spring	**39**	Link Pin		
20	Ejector	**40**	Magazine Follower		

Model 52B Target and Sporting Bolt-Action Rifle

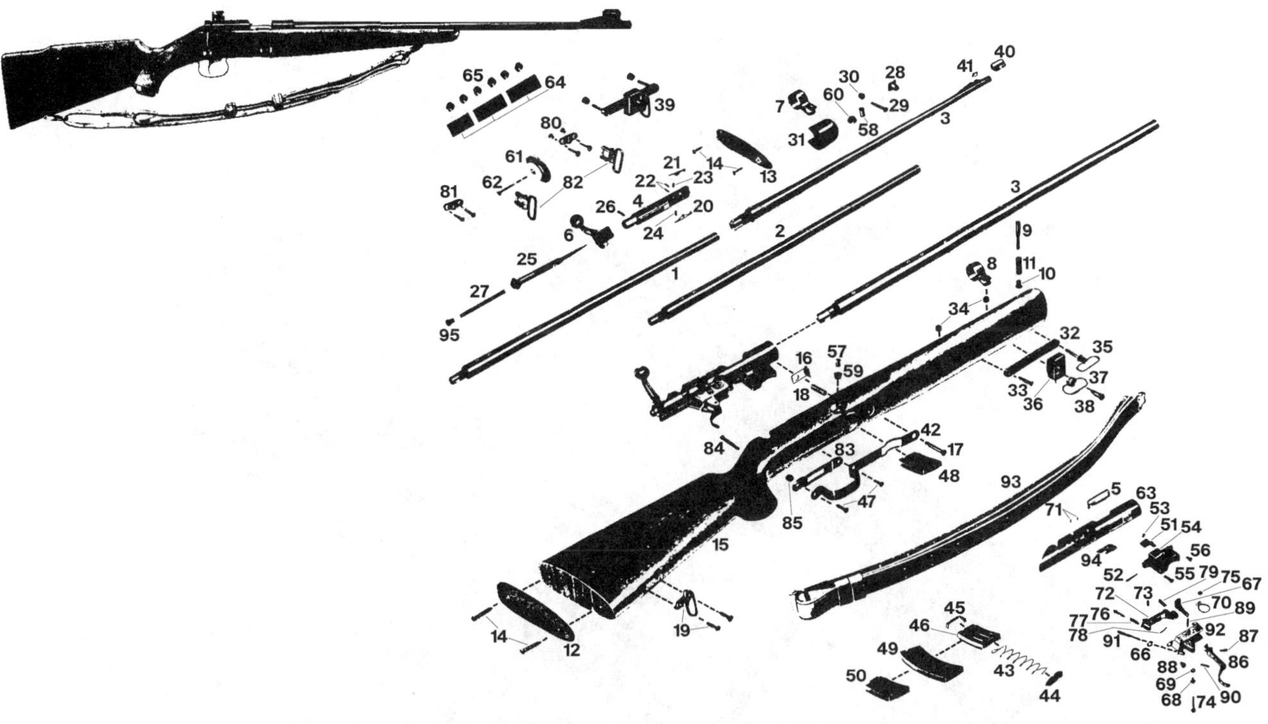

1	Barrel, Standard
2	Barrel, Heavy
3	Barrel, Bull
4	Breechbolt
5	Breechbolt Guide
6	Breechbolt Handle
7	Barrel Band for Standard Barrel
8	Barrel Band for Heavy Barrel
9	Barrel Band Screw
10	Barrel Band Screw Escutcheon
11	Barrel Band Screw Bushing
12	Buttplate
13	Buttplate, Sporting
14	Buttplate Screws
15	Buttstock
16	Buttstock Abutment Plate
17	Buttstock Screw
18	Buttstock Screw Bushing
19	Buttstock Swivel Base Complete
20	Extractor, Right
21	Extractor, Left
22	Extractor Pins
23	Extractor Spring, Left
24	Extractor Spring, Right
25	Firing Pin
26	Firing Pin Guide Pin
27	Firing Pin Spring
28	Forearm Stud
29	Forearm Stud Screw
30	Forearm Stud Screw Escutcheon
31	Forearm Tip
32	Forearm Adjustable Base
33	Forearm Adjustable Base Screw
34	Adjustable Screw Escutcheons
35	Forearm Adjustable Front Swivel Bow Complete
36	Forearm Adjusting Swivel Base
37	Forearm Adjusting Swivel Bow
38	Forearm Adjusting Swivel Bow Base Screw
39	Forearm Adjusting Base Complete
40	Front Sight Cover
41	Front Sight
42	Trigger Guard
43	Magazine Spring
44	Magazine Base
45	Magazine Follower
46	Magazine Box
47	Trigger Guard Screws, Rear
48	Magazine, 5-Shot
49	Magazine, 10-Shot
50	Single Loading Adapter
51	Magazine Catch
52	Magazine Catch Pin
53	Magazine Catch Spring
54	Magazine Holder
55	Rear Magazine Holder Screw, Long
56	Front Magazine Holder Screw, Short
57	Magazine Release Plunger, Standard
58	Magazine Release Plunger, Sporting
59	Magazine Release Plunger Escutcheon, Standard
60	Magazine Release Plunger Escutcheon, Sporting
61	Pistol Grip Cap
62	Pistol Grip Cap Screw
63	Receiver
64	Resilient Spacer (3 in set)
65	Resilient Spacer (6 in set)
66	Safety Washer
67	Safety-Lever
68	Safety-Lever Screw
69	Safety-Lever Screw Nut
70	Safety-Lever Spring
71	Safety Slide Pins
72	Sear and Pin
73	Sear Pin
74	Sear Screw
75	Sear Screw Nut
76	Sear Plunger
77	Sear Plunger Spring
78	Sear Plunger Pin
79	Sear Spring
80	Snap Swivel Base Complete (Forearm)
81	Snap Swivel Base Complete (Stock)
82	Sling Strap Snap Swivels
83	Trigger Guard Plate
84	Tang Screw
85	Tang Screw Escutcheon
86	Trigger
87	Trigger Adjusting Screw
88	Trigger Holder Screw
89	Trigger Pin
90	Trigger Spring
91	Trigger Spring Adjusting Screw
92	Trigger Housing
93	Sling
94	Safety Slide
95	Firing Pin Spring Plug

Model 52C Target and Sporting Bolt-Action Rifle

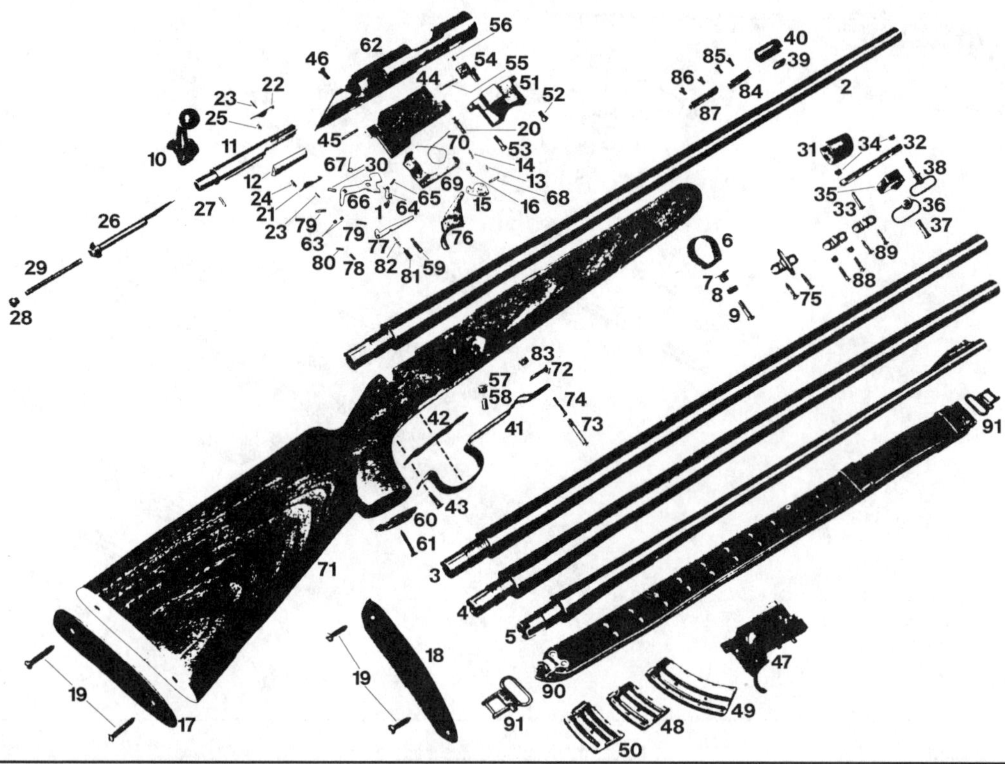

1	Adjustment Locking Screw	**32**	Forearm Adjustment Base	**61**	Pistol Grip Cap Screw
2	Barrel, Standard	**33**	Forearm Adjustment Base Screw, Rear	**62**	Receiver
3	Barrel, Heavy	**34**	Forearm Adjustment Base Screw Escutcheons	**63**	Receiver Sight Base Plug Screws
4	Barrel, Bull	**35**	Forearm Adjusting Swivel Base	**64**	Rocker
5	Barrel, Sporting	**36**	Forearm Adjusting Swivel Bow	**65**	Rocker Pin
6	Barrel Band	**37**	Forearm Adjusting Swivel Bow Base Screw	**66**	Sear
7	Barrel Band Lug	**38**	Forearm Adjustment Front Swivel Bow Complete, Front Screw	**67**	Sear Spring
8	Barrel Band Escutcheon	**39**	Front Sight Blank	**68**	Sear Pivot Pin
9	Barrel Band Screw	**40**	Front Sight Cover	**69**	Safety-Lever
10	Breechbolt Handle	**41**	Trigger Guard	**70**	Safety-Lever Spring
11	Breechbolt	**42**	Trigger Guard Plate	**71**	Stock
12	Breechbolt Guide	**43**	Trigger Guard Screw	**72**	Stock Abutment Plate
13	Breechbolt Handle Locking Plunger Pin	**44**	Trigger Housing	**73**	Stock Screw
14	Breechbolt Handle Locking Plunger Spring	**45**	Trigger Housing Retaining Pin	**74**	Stock Screw Bushing
15	Breechbolt Lock	**46**	Trigger Housing Screw	**75**	Stock Swivel Base Complete
16	Breechbolt Handle Locking Plunger	**47**	Trigger Housing Complete	**76**	Trigger
17	Buttplate	**48**	Magazine Complete, 5-Shot	**77**	Trigger Lever
18	Buttplate, Sporting	**49**	Magazine Complete, 10-Shot	**78**	Trigger Spring
19	Buttplate Screws	**50**	Magazine Single Shot Adapter	**79**	Trigger Lever Pins
20	Engagement Adjusting Screw Assembly	**51**	Magazine Holder	**80**	Trigger Pin
21	Extractor, Right	**52**	Magazine Holder Screw, Front	**81**	Trigger Pull Adjusting Screw
22	Extractor, Left	**53**	Magazine Holder Screw, Rear	**82**	Trigger Pull Adjusting Spring
23	Extractor Pins	**54**	Magazine Catch	**83**	Tang Screw Escutcheon
24	Extractor Spring, Right	**55**	Magazine Catch Pin	**84**	Telescope Front Mount Base Complete
25	Extractor Spring, Left	**56**	Magazine Catch Spring	**85**	Telescope Front Mount Base Screws
26	Firing Pin	**57**	Magazine Release Plunger	**86**	Telescope Rear Mount Base Complete
27	Firing Pin Guide Pin	**58**	Magazine Release Plunger Escutcheon	**87**	Telescope Rear Mount Base Screws
28	Firing Pin Plug	**59**	Overtravel Adjusting Screw	**88**	Snap Swivel Base Complete, Forearm
29	Firing Pin Spring	**60**	Pistol Grip Cap	**89**	Snap Swivel Base Complete, Stock
30	Forearm Stud Screw			**90**	Sling Strap
31	Forearm Tip			**91**	Sling Strap Snap Swivel

Model 52D Target Bolt-Action Rifle

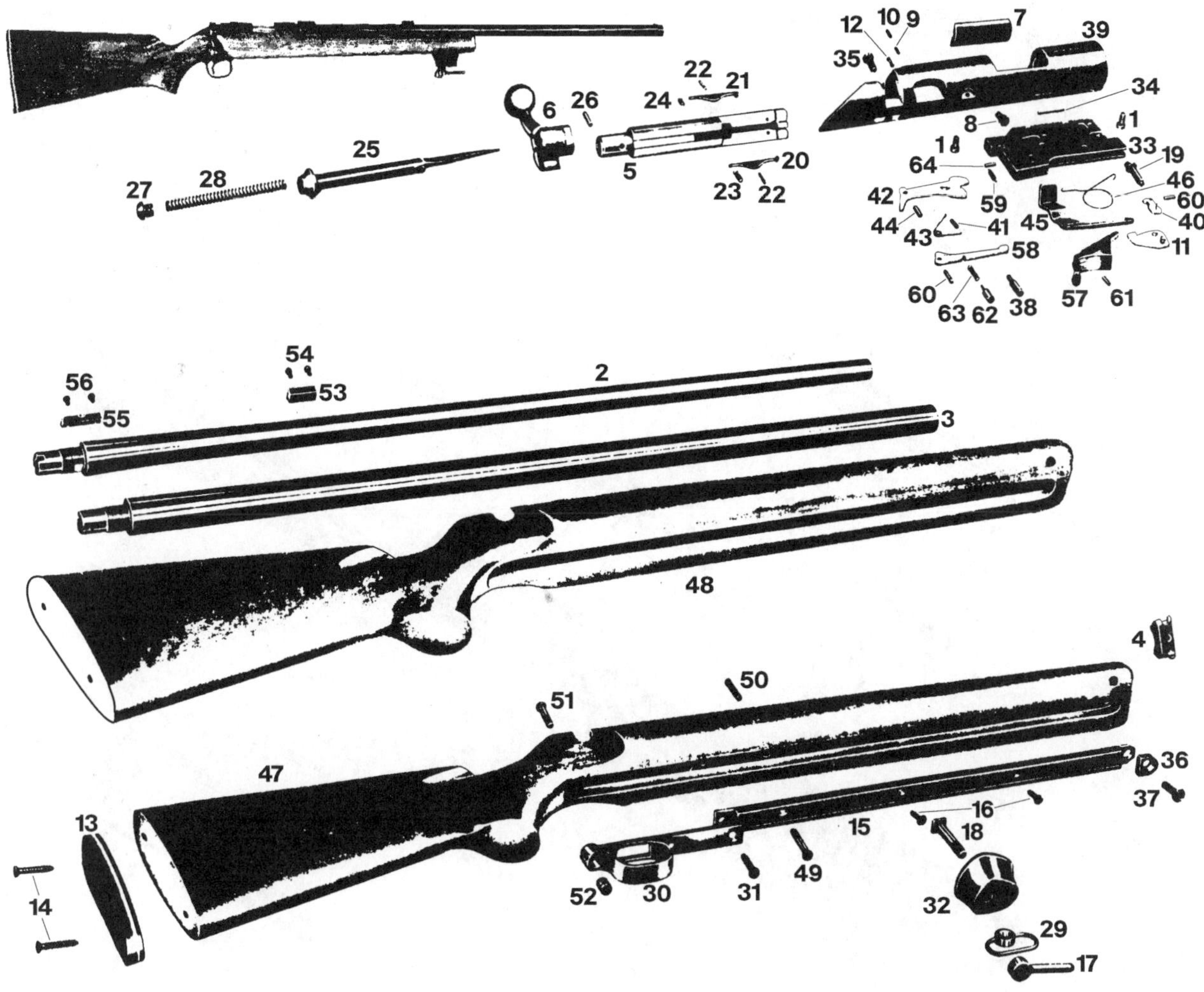

1	Adjustment Locking Screw	**22**	Extractor Pins	**45**	Safety-Lever
2	Barrel, Standard	**23**	Extractor Spring, Right	**46**	Safety-Lever Spring
3	Barrel, Heavy	**24**	Extractor Spring, Left	**47**	Stock, Standard
4	Bedding Screw Holder	**25**	Firing Pin	**48**	Stock, Heavy
5	Breechbolt	**26**	Firing Pin Guide Pin	**49**	Stock Screw
6	Breechbolt Handle	**27**	Firing Pin Plug	**50**	Stock Screw Bushing
7	Breechbolt Guide	**28**	Firing Pin Spring	**51**	Tang Screw
8	Breechbolt Guide Screw	**29**	Forend Swivel	**52**	Tang Screw Nut
9	Breechbolt Handle Locking Plunger Pin	**30**	Guard	**53**	Telescope Front Mount Base
10	Breechbolt Handle Locking Plunger Spring	**31**	Guard Screw	**54**	Telescope Front Mount Base Screws
11	Breechbolt Lock	**32**	Hand Stop	**55**	Telescope Front and Rear Sight Mount Base
12	Breechbolt Handle Locking Plunger	**33**	Trigger Housing	**56**	Telescope Rear Mount Base Screws
13	Rubber Non-Slip Buttplate	**34**	Trigger Housing Retaining Pin	**57**	Trigger
14	Buttplate Screws	**35**	Trigger Housing Screw	**58**	Trigger Lever
15	Channel	**36**	Insulator	**59**	Trigger Spring
16	Channel Screws	**37**	Insulator Screw	**60**	Trigger Lever Pins
17	Clamp Lever	**38**	Overtravel Adjusting Screw	**61**	Trigger Pin
18	Clamp Screw	**39**	Receiver	**62**	Trigger Pull Adjusting Screw
19	Engagement Adjusting Screw	**40**	Rocker	**63**	Trigger Pull Adjusting Spring
20	Extractor, Right	**41**	Rocker Pin	**64**	Trigger Spring Pin
21	Extractor, Left	**42**	Sear		
		43	Sear Spring		
		44	Sear Pivot Pin		

Model 55 Autoloading Rifle

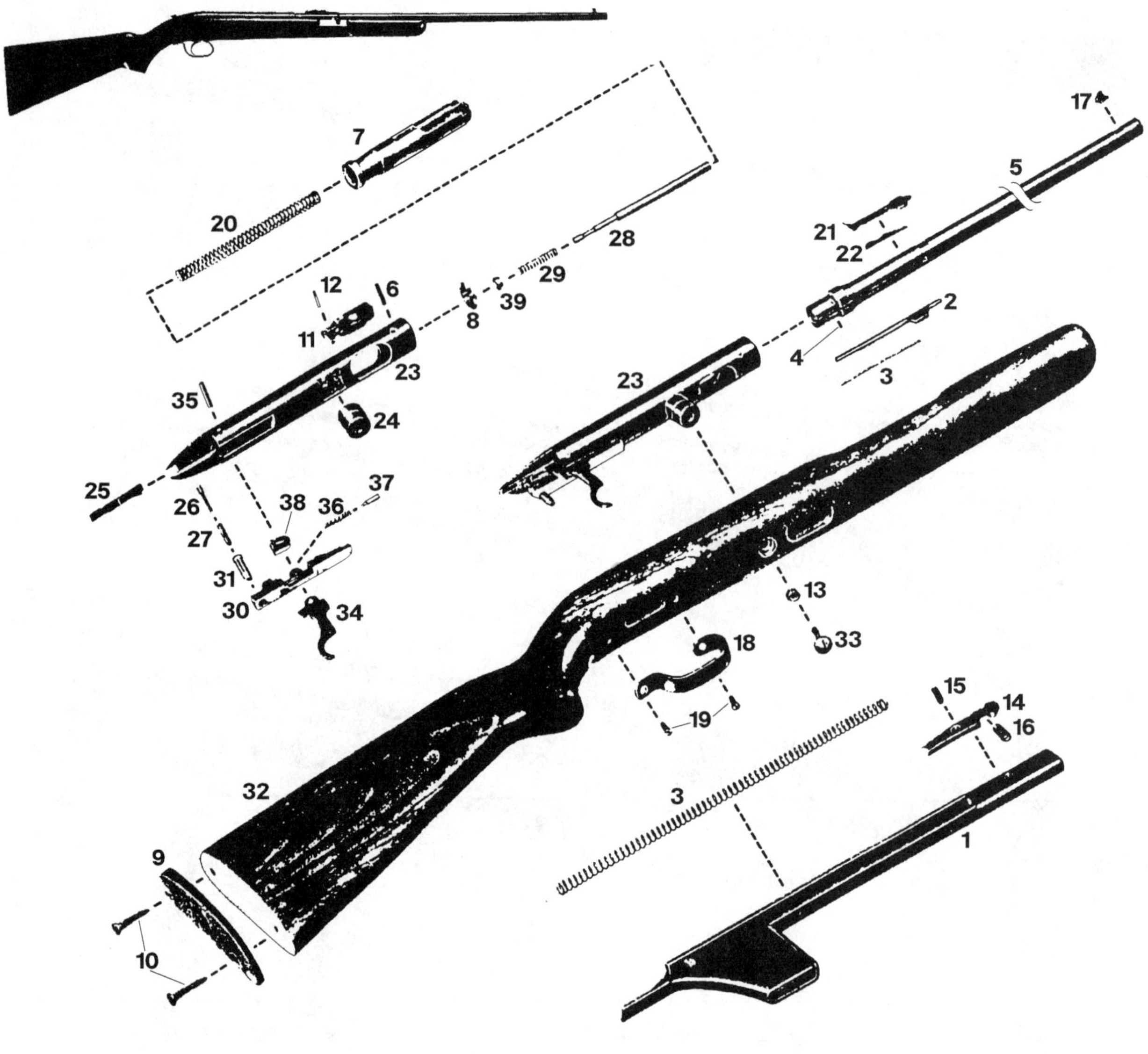

1	Action Slide	21	Rear Sight
2	Action Slide Complete	22	Rear Sight Elevator
3	Action Slide Spring	23	Receiver
4	Action Slide Stop Pin	24	Receiver Stud
5	Barrel	25	Safety
6	Barrel Locating Pin	26	Safety Plunger
7	Bolt	27	Safety Plunger Spring
8	Buffer Washer	28	Safety Rod
9	Buttplate	29	Safety Rod Spring
10	Buttplate Screws	30	Sear
11	Cover	31	Safety Sleeve
12	Cover Pin	32	Stock
13	Stock Screw Escutcheon	33	Stock Stud Screw
14	Extractor	34	Trigger
15	Extractor Pin	35	Trigger Pin
16	Extractor Spring	36	Trigger Spring
17	Front Sight	37	Trigger Spring Plunger
18	Trigger Guard	38	Trigger Top
19	Trigger Guard Bow Screws	39	Washer
20	Mainspring		

Model 61 Slide-Action Rifle

Courtesy of James M. Triggs

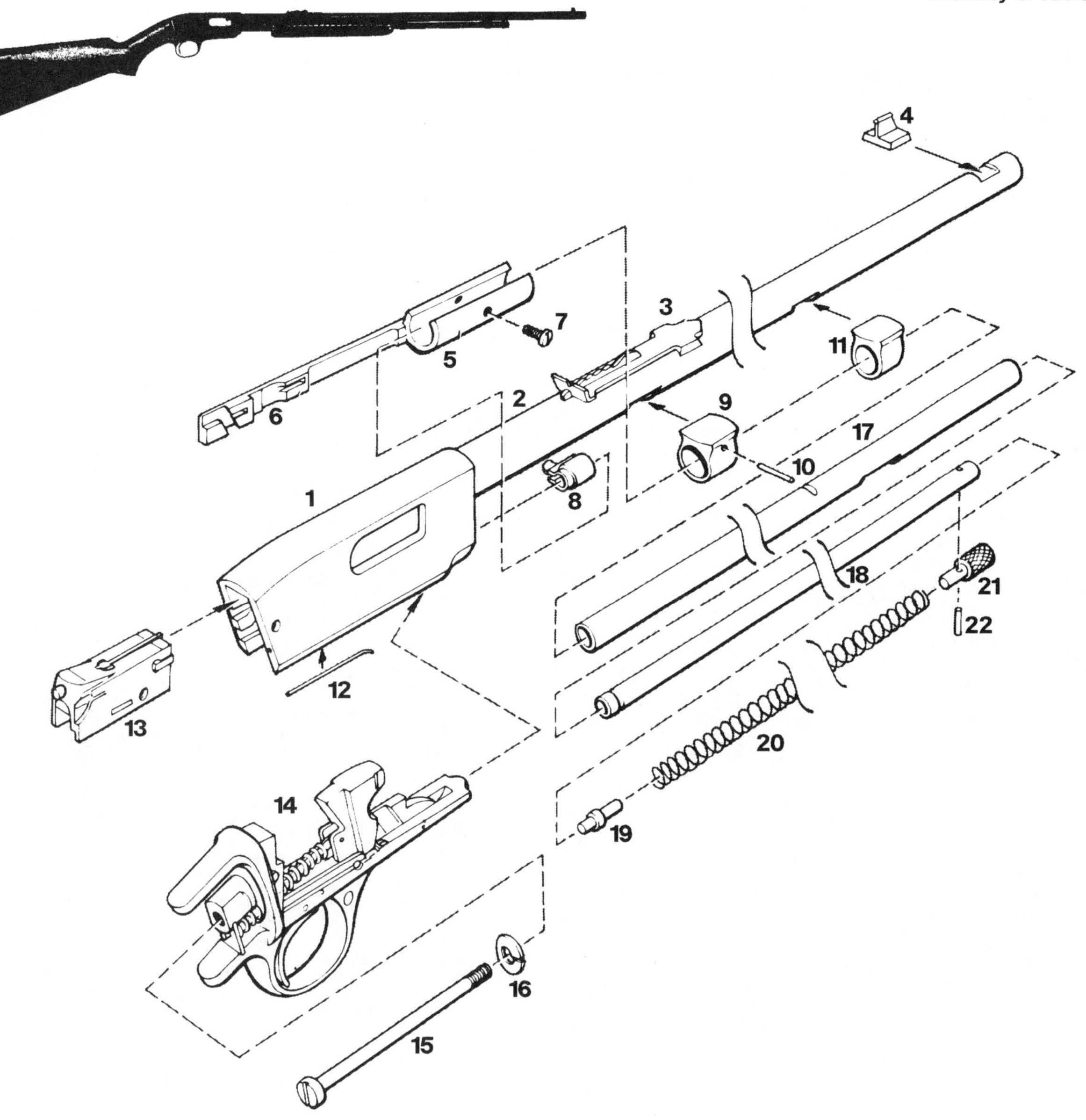

1	Receiver	**15**	Buttstock Bolt
2	Barrel	**16**	Buttstock Bolt Washer
3	Rear Sight and Elevator	**17**	Magazine Tube, Outer
4	Front Sight	**18**	Magazine Tube, Inner
5	Action Slide Sleeve	**19**	Magazine Follower
6	Action Slide Bar	**20**	Magazine Spring
7	Action Slide Handle Screws	**21**	Magazine Plug
8	Cartridge Cutoff Assembly	**22**	Magazine Plug Pin
9	Rear Magazine Ring	**Parts Not Shown**	
10	Rear Magazine Ring Pin		Action Handle Escutcheons
11	Front Magazine Ring		Buttplate
12	Breechbolt Retaining Spring		Buttplate Screws
13	Breechbolt Assembly		Buttstock
14	Trigger Guard Assembly		

Model 62A Slide-Action Rifle

Courtesy of Thomas E. Wessel

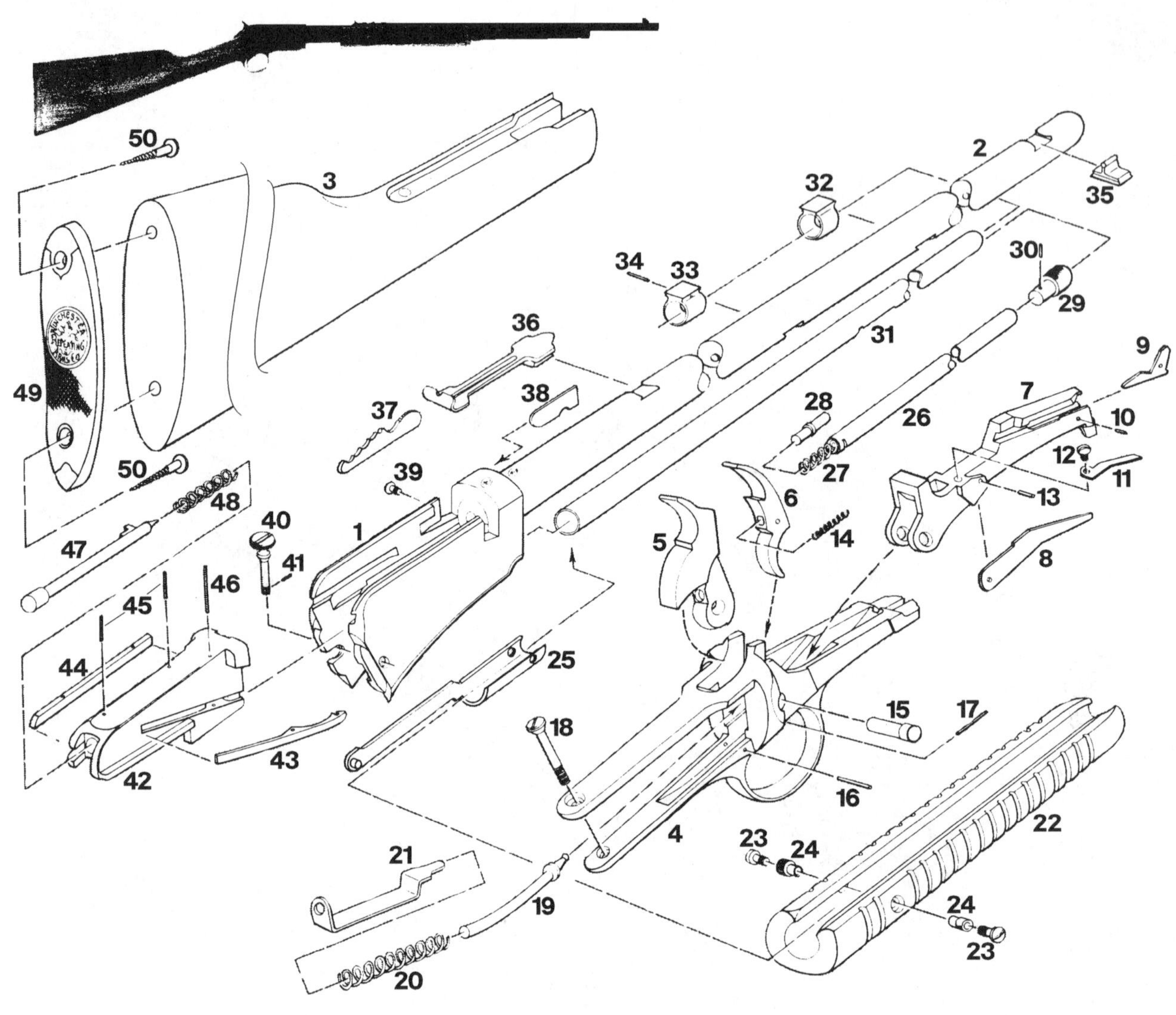

1	Receiver	**19**	Hammer Spring Abutment Guide Rod	**34**	Magazine Ring Pin, Rear
2	Barrel	**20**	Hammer Spring	**35**	Front Sight
3	Buttstock	**21**	Hammer Spring Abutment	**36**	Rear Sight
4	Trigger Guard	**22**	Action Slide Handle	**37**	Rear Sight Elevator
5	Hammer	**23**	Action Slide Handle Screws	**38**	Slide Cover
6	Trigger	**24**	Action Slide Handle Escutcheons	**39**	Slide Cover Stop Screw
7	Carrier	**25**	Action Slide	**40**	Assembling Screw
8	Carrier Lever	**26**	Magazine Tube, Inner	**41**	Assembling Screw Stop Pin
9	Cartridge Stop	**27**	Magazine Spring	**42**	Breechbolt
10	Cartridge Stop Pin	**28**	Magazine Follower	**43**	Extractor
11	Carrier Lever Spring	**29**	Magazine Plug	**44**	Firing Pin Stop
12	Carrier Lever Spring Screw	**30**	Magazine Plug Pin	**45**	Firing Pin Stop Pins
13	Carrier Lever Pin	**31**	Magazine Tube, Outer	**46**	Extractor Pin
14	Trigger Spring	**32**	Magazine Ring, Front	**47**	Firing Pin
15	Assembling Screw Bushing	**33**	Magazine Ring, Rear	**48**	Firing Pin Spring
16	Hammer Spring Abutment Pin			**49**	Buttplate
17	Trigger Pin			**50**	Buttplate Screws
18	Upper Tang Screw				

Model 63 Autoloading Rifle

Courtesy of James M. Triggs

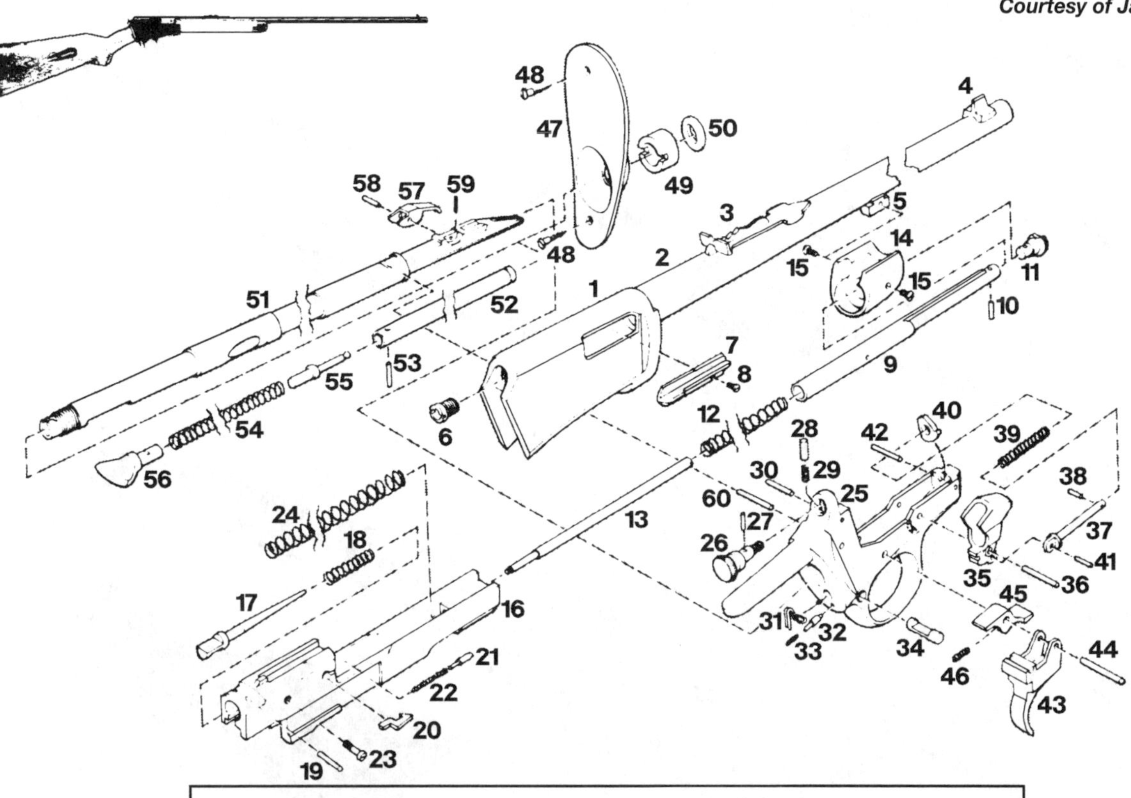

1	Receiver	**32**	Trigger Lock Plunger
2	Barrel	**33**	Trigger Lock Plunger Spring
3	Rear Sight	**34**	Trigger Lock
4	Front Sight	**35**	Hammer
5	Forearm Tip Tenon	**36**	Hammer Pin
6	Takedown Screw Bushing	**37**	Hammer Spring Guide Rod
7	Ejector	**38**	Slave Pin
8	Ejector Screw	**39**	Hammer Spring
9	Operating Sleeve	**40**	Hammer Spring Abutment
10	Operating Sleeve Tip Pin	**41**	Hammer Spring Guide Rod Pin
11	Operating Sleeve Tip	**42**	Hammer Spring Abutment Pin
12	Operating Sleeve Spring	**43**	Trigger
13	Bolt Guide Rod	**44**	Trigger Pin
14	Forearm Tip	**45**	Sear
15	Forearm Tip Screws	**46**	Sear Spring
16	Bolt	**47**	Buttplate
17	Firing Pin	**48**	Buttplate Screws
18	Firing Pin Spring	**49**	Buttstock Nut
19	Firing Pin Stop Pin	**50**	Buttstock Nut Washer
20	Extractor	**51**	Magazine Tube, Outer
21	Extractor Plunger	**52**	Magazine Tube, Inner
22	Extractor Plunger Spring	**53**	Magazine Plug Pin
23	Extractor Plunger Stop Screw	**54**	Magazine Spring
24	Bolt Spring	**55**	Magazine Follower
25	Trigger Housing	**56**	Magazine Plug
26	Takedown Screw	**57**	Cartridge Cutoff
27	Takedown Screw Stop Pin	**58**	Cartridge Cutoff Pin
28	Takedown Screw Lock Plunger	**59**	Cartridge Cutoff Spring
29	Takedown Screw Lock Plunger Spring	**60**	Throat Pin
30	Takedown Screw Lock Plunger Stop Pin	**Parts Not Shown**	
31	Trigger Spring		Forearm
			Stock

Model 64A Lever-Action Rifle

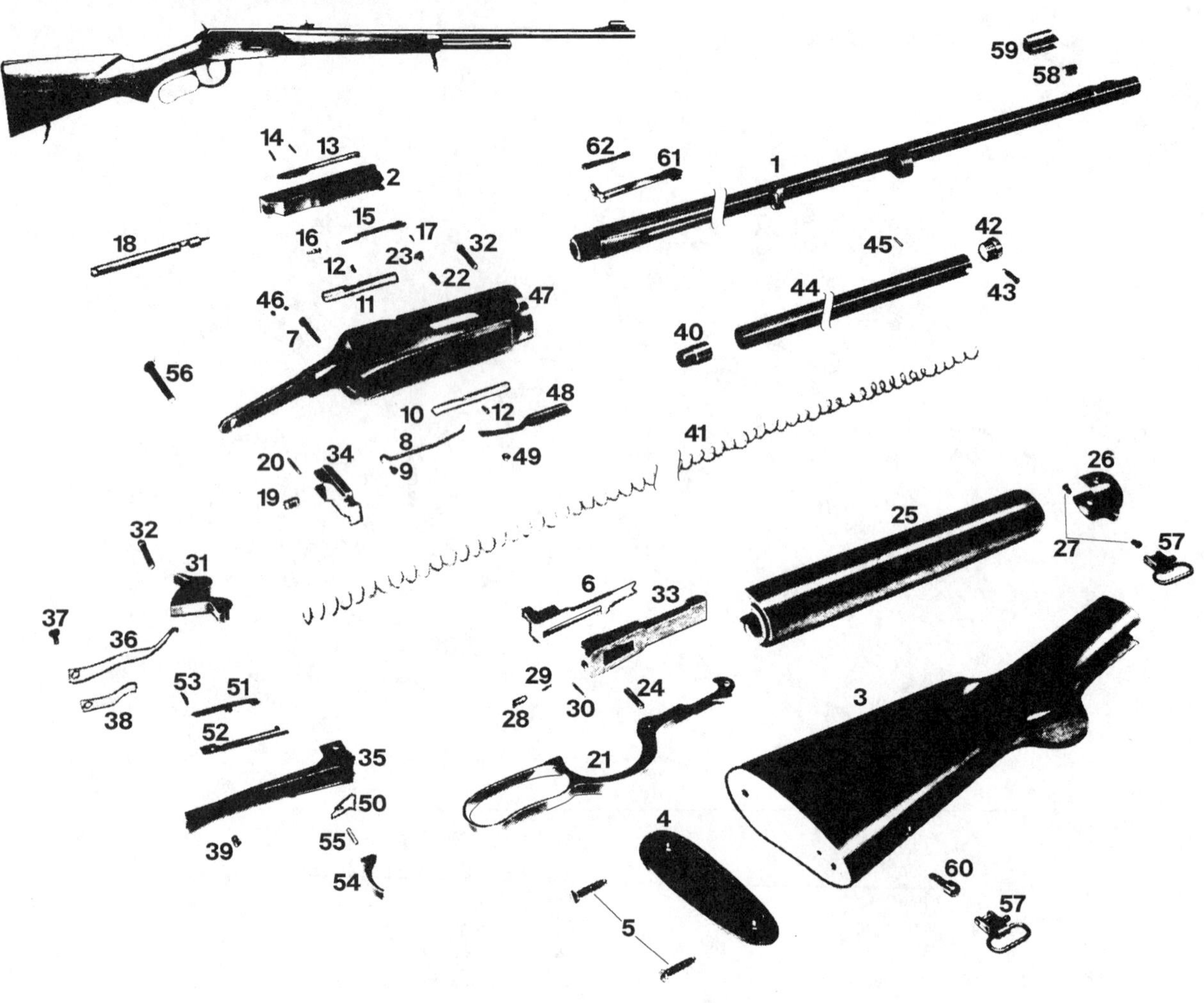

1	Barrel	**22**	Finger Lever Pin	**43**	Magazine Plug Screw
2	Breechbolt	**23**	Finger Lever Pin Stop Screw	**44**	Magazine Tube
3	Buttstock	**24**	Finger Lever Link Pin	**45**	Magazine Tube Bracket Pin
4	Buttplate	**25**	Forearm	**46**	Sight Plug Screws
5	Buttplate Screws	**26**	Forearm Cap	**47**	Receiver
6	Carrier	**27**	Forearm Cap Screws	**48**	Spring Cover
7	Carrier Screw	**28**	Friction Stud	**49**	Spring Cover Screw
8	Carrier Spring	**29**	Friction Stud Spring	**50**	Sear
9	Carrier Spring Screw	**30**	Friction Stud Stop Pin	**51**	Trigger Stop
10	Cartridge Guide, Right	**31**	Hammer	**52**	Trigger Stop Spring
11	Cartridge Guide, Left	**32**	Hammer Link Screw	**53**	Trigger Stop Pin
12	Cartridge Guide Screws	**33**	Link	**54**	Trigger
13	Extractor	**34**	Locking Bolt	**55**	Trigger Pin
14	Extractor Pins	**35**	Lower Tang	**56**	Upper Tang Screw
15	Ejector	**36**	Mainspring	**57**	Sling Swivels
16	Ejector Spring	**37**	Mainspring Screw	**58**	Front Sight
17	Ejector Stop Pin	**38**	Mainspring Base	**59**	Front Sight Cover
18	Firing Pin	**39**	Mainspring Strain Screw	**60**	Stock Swivel Stud
19	Firing Pin Striker	**40**	Magazine Follower	**61**	Rear Sight
20	Firing Pin Striker Pin	**41**	Magazine Spring	**62**	Rear Sight Elevator
21	Finger Lever	**42**	Magazine Plug		

Model 670A Bolt-Action Rifle

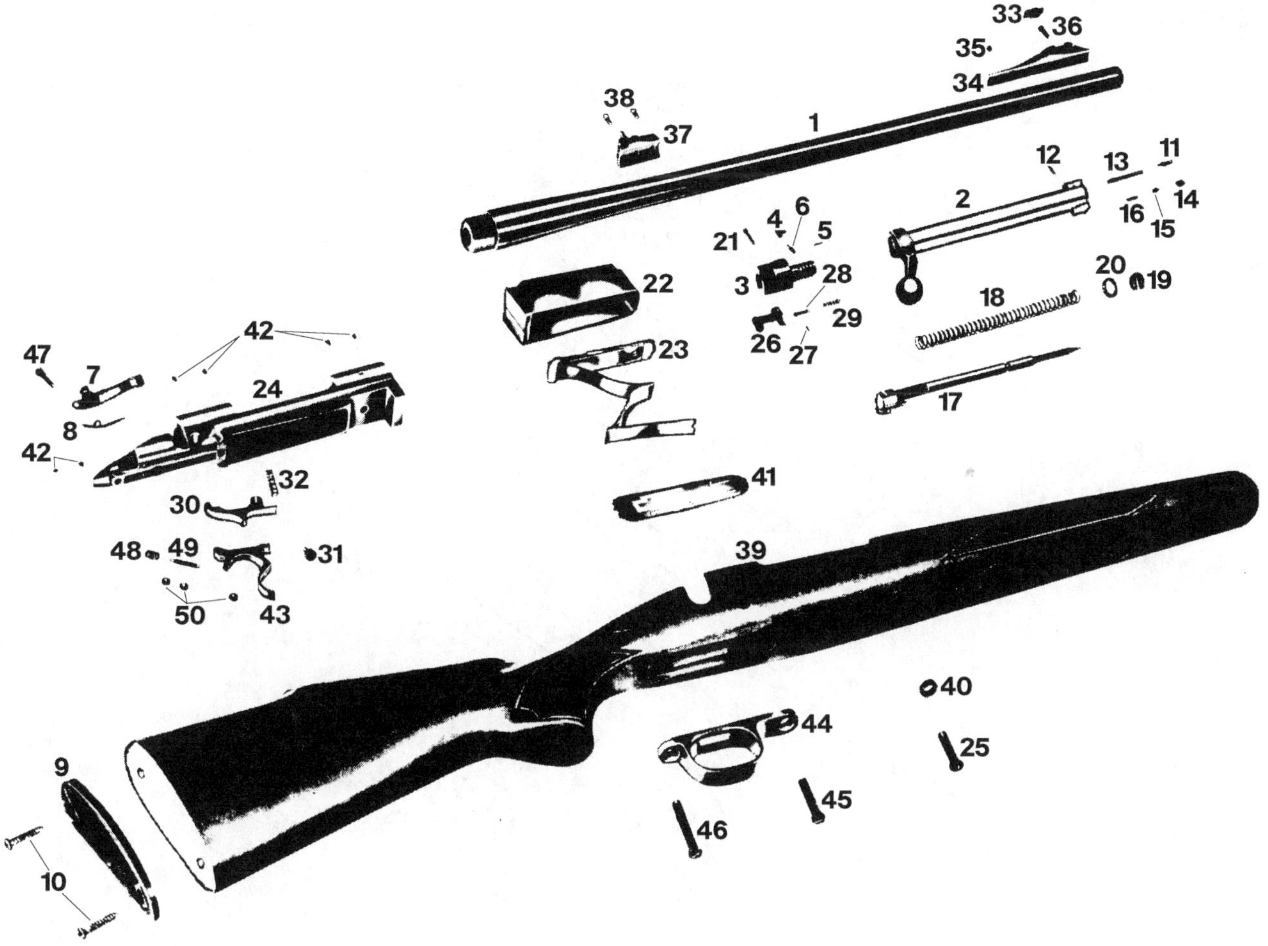

1	Barrel
2	Breechbolt
3	Breechbolt Sleeve
4	Breechbolt Sleeve Lock
5	Breechbolt Sleeve Lock Pin
6	Breechbolt Sleeve Lock Spring
7	Breechbolt Stop
8	Breechbolt Stop Spring
9	Buttplate
10	Buttplate Screws
11	Ejector
12	Ejector Pin
13	Ejector Spring
14	Extractor
15	Extractor Plunger
16	Extractor Spring
17	Firing Pin
18	Firing Pin Spring
19	Firing Pin Spring Retainer
20	Firing Pin Spring Retainer Washer
21	Firing Pin Stop Screw
22	Magazine
23	Magazine Follower and Spring Assembly
24	Receiver
25	Receiver Screw, Front
26	Safety
27	Safety Pin
28	Safety Plunger
29	Safety Plunger Spring
30	Sear
31	Sear Pin
32	Sear Spring
33	Front Sight
34	Front Sight Ramp
35	Front Sight Ramp Screw, Short
36	Front Sight Ramp Screw, Long
37	Rear Sight Assembly
38	Rear Sight Screws
39	Stock
40	Stock Escutcheon
41	Magazine Floorplate
42	Telescope Sight Base Plug Screws
43	Trigger
44	Trigger Guard
45	Trigger Guard Screw, Front
46	Trigger Guard Screw, Rear
47	Trigger Pin
48	Trigger Spring
49	Trigger Stop Screw
50	Trigger Stop Screw Nuts

Model 69A Bolt-Action Rifle

Courtesy of James M. Triggs

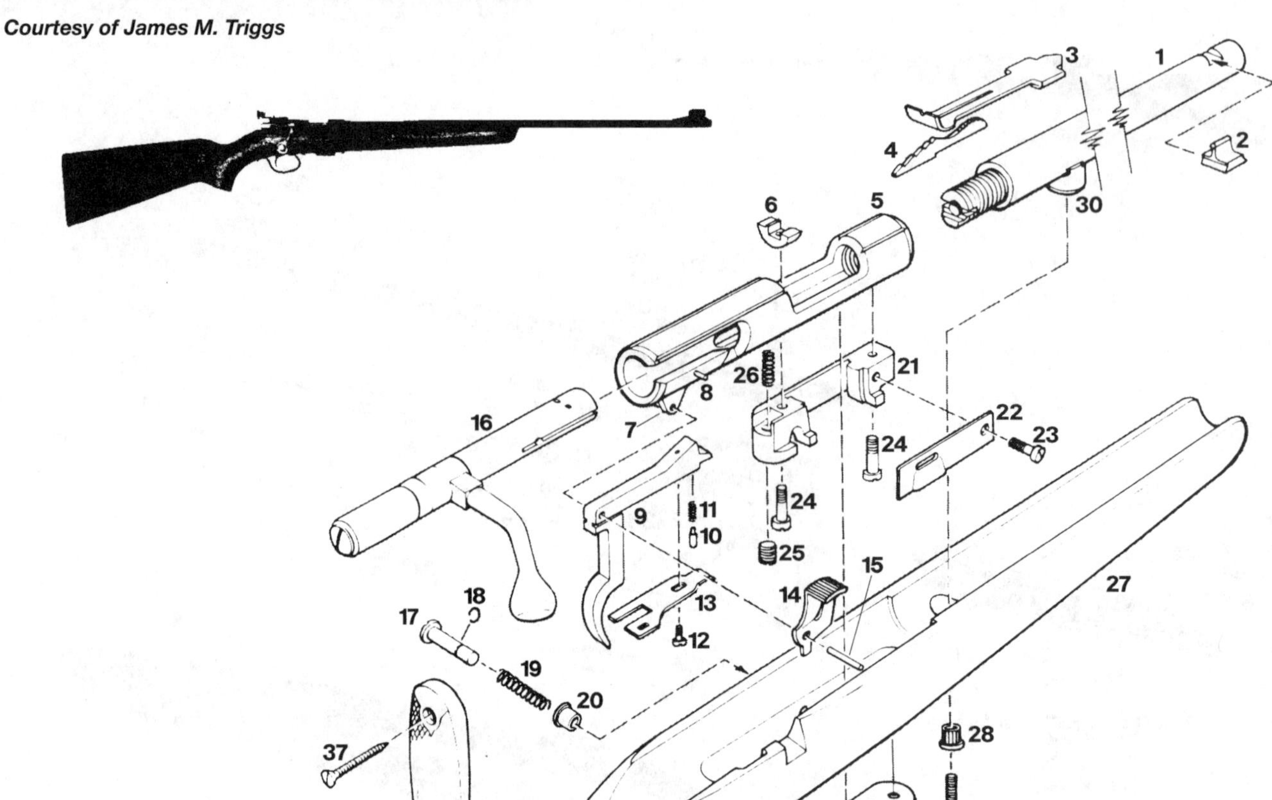

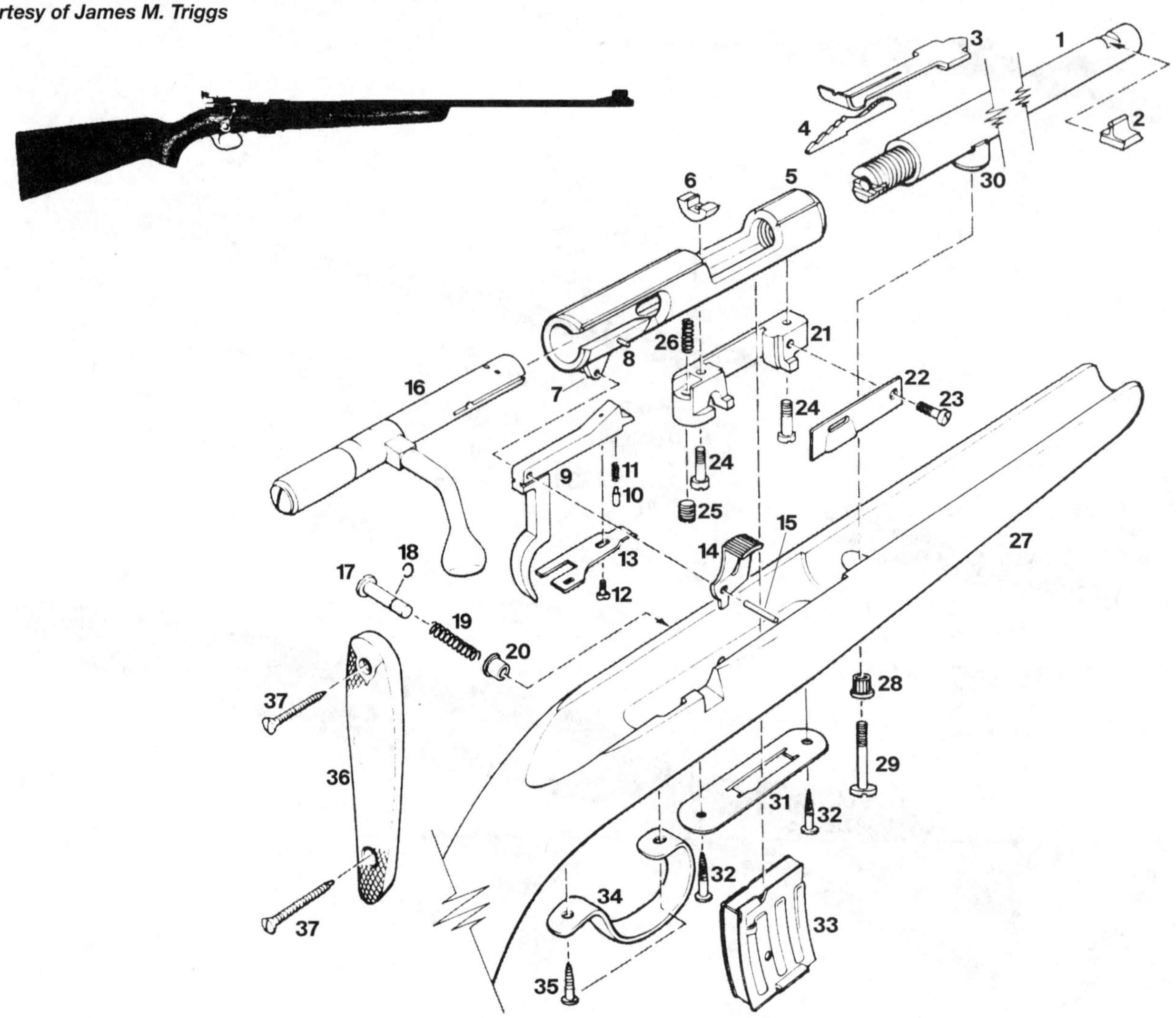

1	Barrel	**20**	Magazine Release Plunger Escutcheon
2	Front Sight	**21**	Magazine Holder
3	Rear Sight	**22**	Magazine Catch
4	Rear Sight Elevator	**23**	Magazine Catch Screw
5	Receiver	**24**	Magazine Holder Screws
6	Ejector	**25**	Trigger Spring Adjusting Screw
7	Trigger Base	**26**	Trigger Spring
8	Safety-Lever Stop Pin	**27**	Buttstock
9	Trigger	**28**	Stock Stud Screw Escutcheon
10	Safety Lock Plunger	**29**	Stock Stud Screw
11	Safety Lock Plunger Spring	**30**	Stock Stud
12	Safety Lock Screw	**31**	Magazine Plate
13	Safety Lock	**32**	Magazine Plate Screws
14	Safety-Lever	**33**	Magazine
15	Trigger Pin	**34**	Guard Bow
16	Breechbolt, Complete	**35**	Guard Bow Screws
17	Magazine Release Plunger	**36**	Buttplate
18	Magazine Release Plunger Stop	**37**	Buttplate Screws
19	Magazine Release Plunger Spring		

Model 70 and 70 Featherweight Bolt-Action Rifle

Courtesy of James M. Triggs

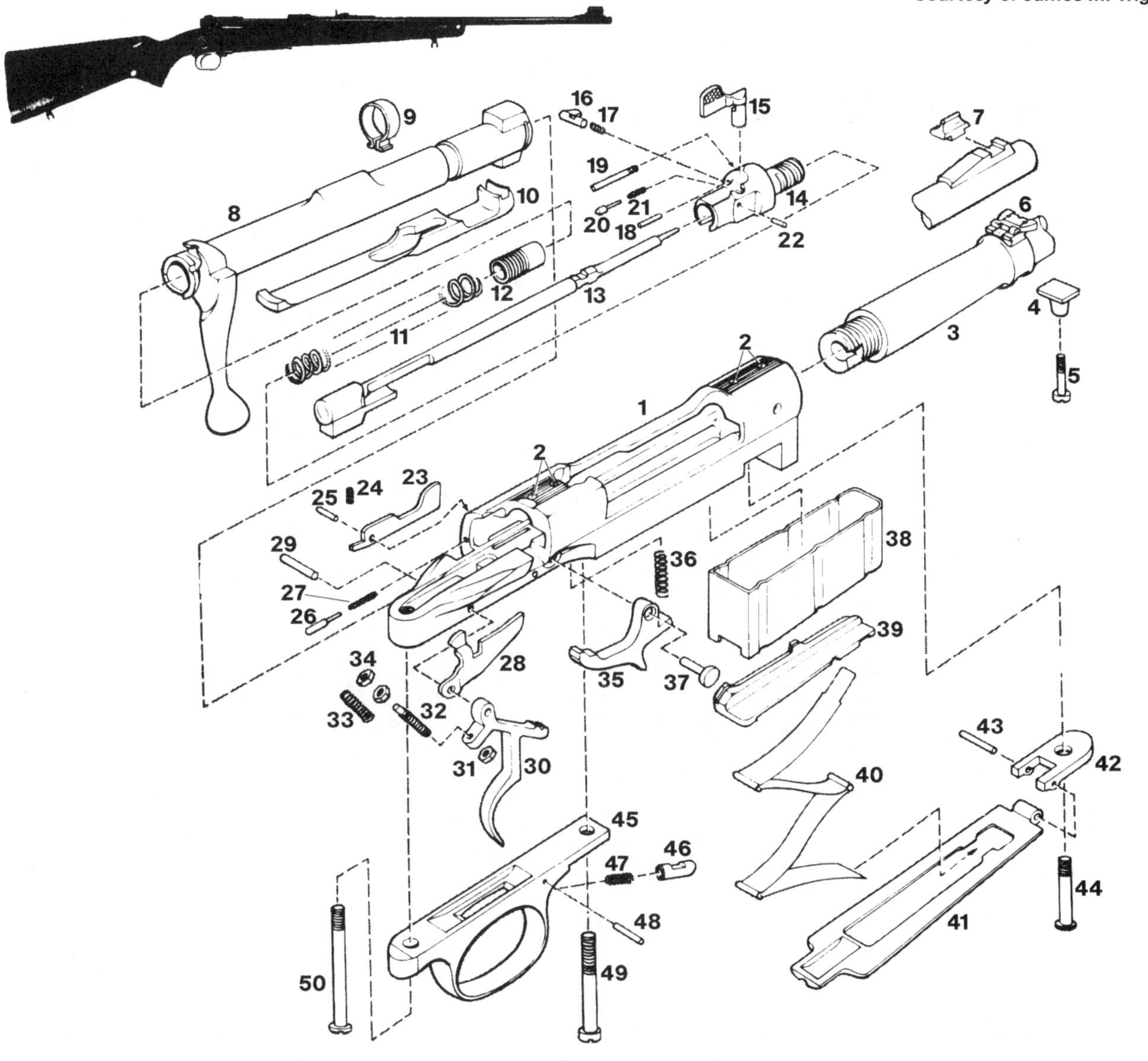

1	Receiver	**20**	Safety Lock Plunger	**39**	Magazine Follower
2	Receiver Plug Screws	**21**	Safety Lock Plunger Spring	**40**	Magazine Spring
3	Barrel	**22**	Safety Lock Stop Pin	**41**	Magazine Cover
4	Forearm Stud	**23**	Ejector	**42**	Magazine Cover Hinge Plate
5	Forearm Stud Screw	**24**	Ejector Spring	**43**	Magazine Cover Hinge Pin
6	Rear Sight Assembly	**25**	Ejector Pin	**44**	Magazine Cover Hinge Plate Screw
7	Front Sight	**26**	Bolt Stop Plunger	**45**	Guard Bow
8	Breechbolt	**27**	Bolt Stop Plunger Spring	**46**	Magazine Cover Catch
9	Extractor Ring	**28**	Bolt Stop	**47**	Magazine Cover Catch Spring
10	Extractor	**29**	Trigger Pin	**48**	Magazine Cover Catch Pin
11	Firing Pin Spring	**30**	Trigger	**49**	Front Guard Bow Screw
12	Firing Pin Sleeve	**31**	Trigger Stop Screw Nut	**50**	Rear Guard Bow Screw
13	Firing Pin	**32**	Trigger Stop Screw	**Parts Not Shown**	
14	Breechbolt Sleeve	**33**	Trigger Spring		Buttplate
15	Safety Lock	**34**	Trigger Spring Adjusting Nuts		Buttplate Screws
16	Breechbolt Sleeve Lock	**35**	Sear		Buttstock
17	Breechbolt Sleeve Lock Spring	**36**	Sear Spring		
18	Breechbolt Sleeve Lock Pin	**37**	Sear Pin		
19	Firing Pin Stop Screw	**38**	Magazine		

Model 71 Lever-Action Rifle

Courtesy of James M. Triggs

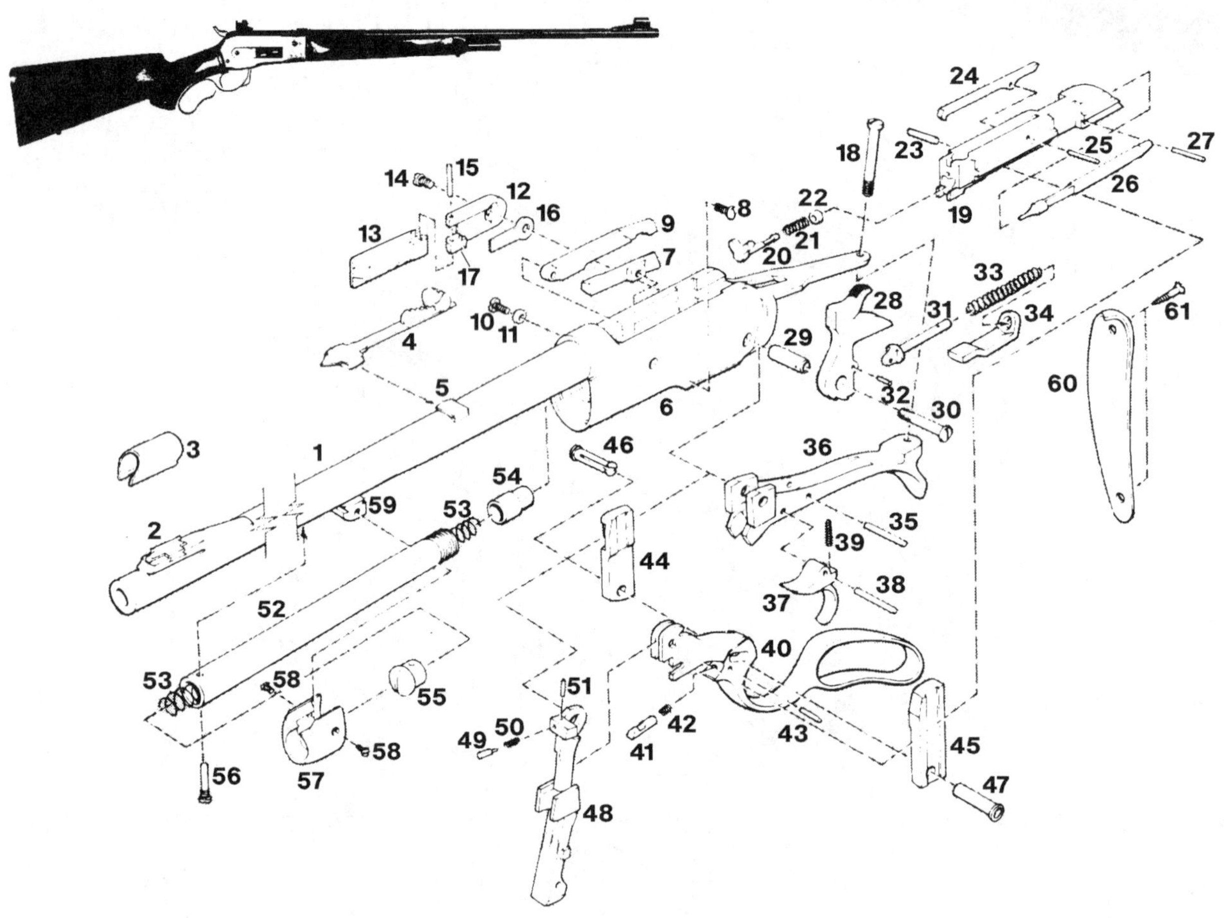

1	Barrel	**23**	Finger Lever Connecting Pin	**45**	Locking Bolt, Left
2	Front Sight	**24**	Extractor	**46**	Finger Lever Bushing Pin
3	Front Sight Cover	**25**	Extractor Pin	**47**	Finger Lever Bushing
4	Rear Sight	**26**	Firing Pin	**48**	Carrier
5	Rear Sight Blank	**27**	Firing Pin Stop Pin	**49**	Carrier Plunger
6	Receiver	**28**	Hammer	**50**	Carrier Plunger Spring
7	Cartridge Stop	**29**	Hammer Screw Bushing	**51**	Carrier Plunger Pin
8	Cartridge Stop Screw	**30**	Hammer Screw	**52**	Magazine Tube
9	Cartridge Guide	**31**	Hammer Spring Guide Rod	**53**	Magazine Spring
10	Cartridge Guide Screw	**32**	Hammer Spring Guide Rod Pin	**54**	Magazine Follower
11	Cartridge Guide Screw Bushing	**33**	Hammer Spring	**55**	Magazine Plug
12	Spring Cover Base	**34**	Hammer Spring Abutment	**56**	Magazine Plug Screw
13	Spring Cover Leaf	**35**	Hammer Spring Abutment Pin	**57**	Forearm Tip
14	Spring Cover Base Screw	**36**	Lower Tang	**58**	Forearm Tip Screws
15	Spring Cover Leaf Pin	**37**	Trigger	**59**	Forearm Tip Tenon
16	Spring Cover Spring	**38**	Trigger Pin	**60**	Buttplate
17	Spring Cover Stop Pin	**39**	Trigger Spring	**61**	Buttplate Screws
18	Upper Tang Screw	**40**	Finger Lever	**Parts Not Shown**	
19	Breechbolt	**41**	Friction Stud		Forearm
20	Ejector	**42**	Friction Stud Spring		Stock
21	Ejector Spring	**43**	Friction Stud Stop Pin		
22	Ejector Collar	**44**	Locking Bolt, Right		

Model 74 Autoloading Rifle

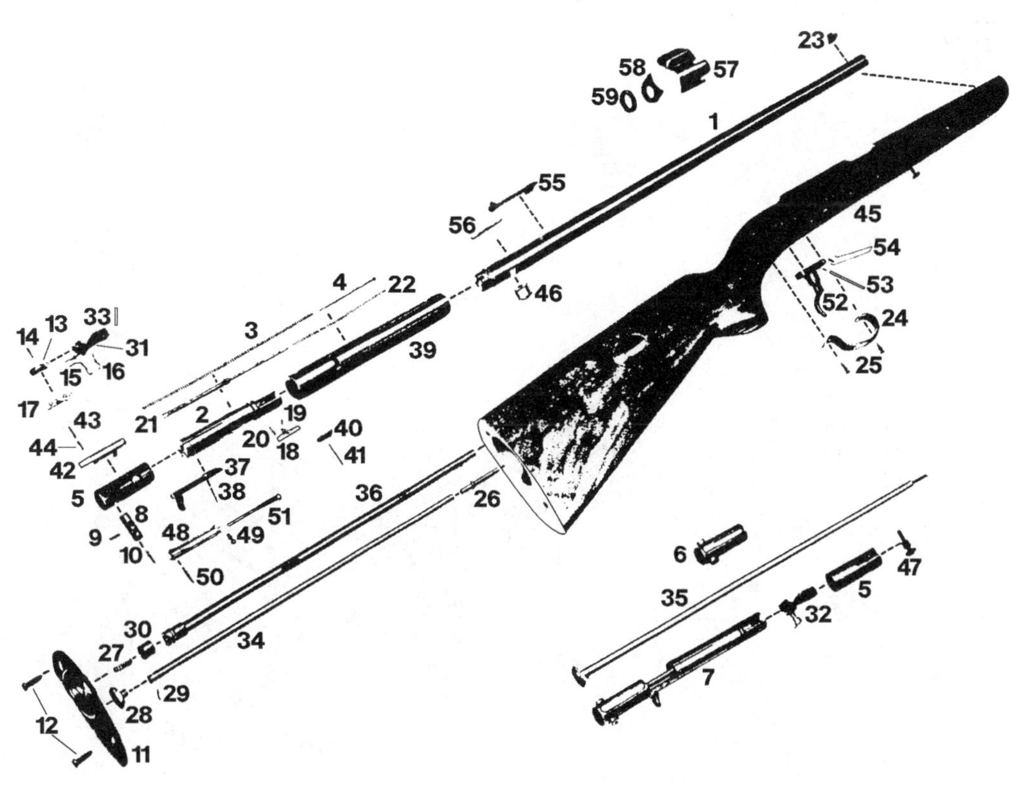

1	Barrel
2	Bolt
3	Bolt Spring
4	Bolt Spring Rod
5	Bolt Stop
6	Bolt Stop Complete
7	Bolt and Bolt Stop Complete
8	Bolt Stop Plunger
9	Bolt Stop Plunger Pin
10	Bolt Stop Plunger Spring
11	Buttplate
12	Buttplate Screws
13	Cartridge Guide
14	Cartridge Guide Pin
15	Cartridge Cutoff, Right
16	Cartridge Cutoff, Left
17	Ejector
18	Extractor
19	Extractor Pin
20	Extractor Spring
21	Firing Pin
22	Firing Pin Spring
23	Front Sight
24	Trigger Guard Bow
25	Trigger Guard Bow Screws
26	Magazine Follower
27	Magazine Lifting Spring
28	Magazine Plug
29	Magazine Plug Pin
30	Magazine Sleeve Nut
31	Magazine Throat
32	Magazine Throat, Complete
33	Magazine Throat Pin
34	Magazine Inside Tube
35	Magazine Inside Tube Complete
36	Magazine Outside Tube
37	Operating Slide
38	Operating Slide Pin
39	Receiver
40	Safety Lock
41	Safety Lock Spring
42	Sear
43	Sear Pin
44	Sear Spring
45	Stock
46	Stock Stud
47	Stock Stud Screw and Escutcheon
48	Timing Rocker
49	Timing Rocker Guide Screw
50	Timing Rocker Pin
51	Timing Rocker Spring
52	Trigger
53	Trigger Pin
54	Trigger Spring
55	Rear Sight
56	Rear Sight Elevator
57	Shell Reflector with Pin
58	Smoke Eliminator, Front
59	Smoke Eliminator, Rear
Parts Not Shown	
	Cartridge Cutoff Pins

Model 75 Bolt-Action Rifle

Courtesy of James M. Triggs

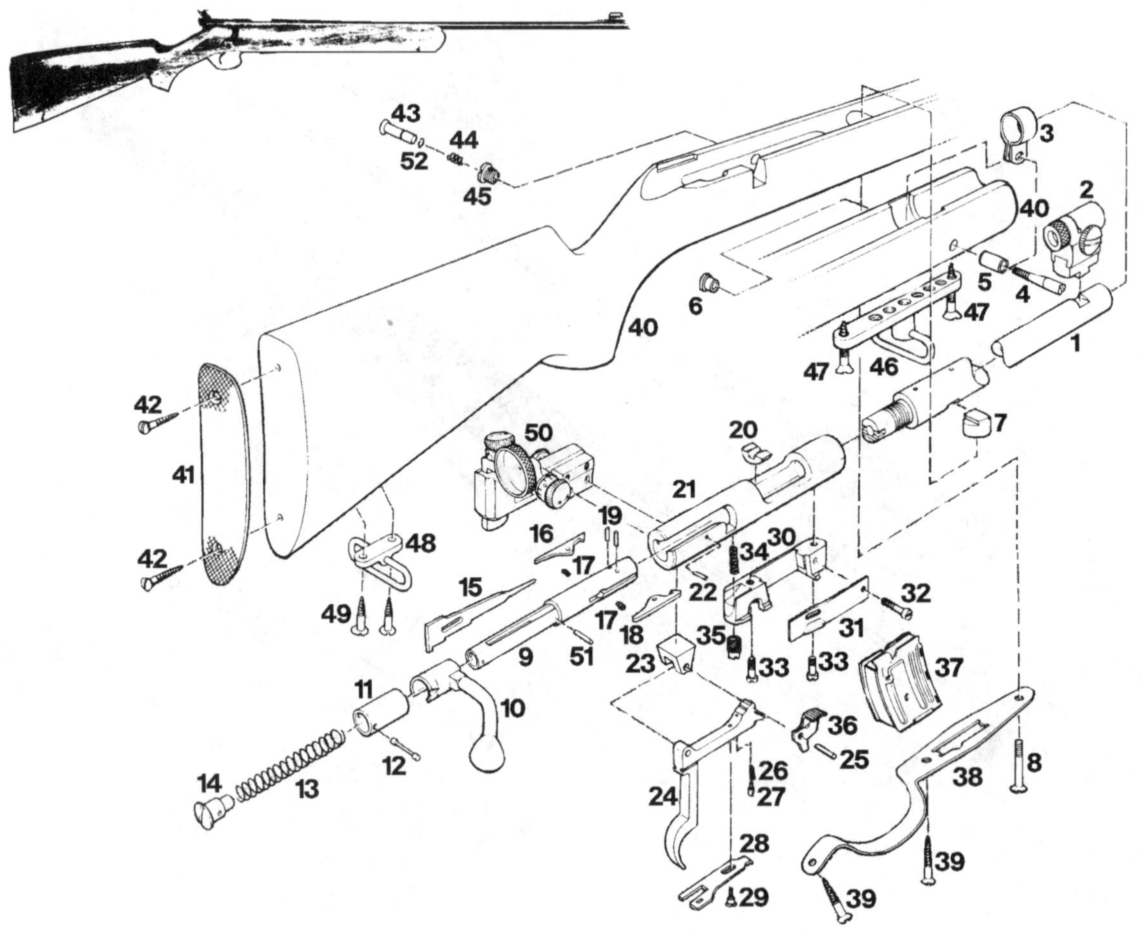

1	Barrel	**20**	Ejector	**40**	Buttstock
2	Front Sight Assembly	**21**	Receiver	**41**	Buttplate
3	Barrel Band	**22**	Safety-Lever Stop Pin	**42**	Buttplate Screws
4	Barrel Band Screw	**23**	Trigger Base	**43**	Magazine Release Plunger
5	Barrel Band Screw Bushing	**24**	Trigger	**44**	Magazine Release Plunger Spring
6	Barrel Band Screw Escutcheon	**25**	Trigger Pin	**45**	Magazine Release Plunger Escutcheon
7	Stock Stud	**26**	Safety Lock Plunger Spring	**46**	Forearm Adjustment Base Assembly
8	Stock Stud Screw	**27**	Safety Lock Plunger	**47**	Forearm Adjustment Base Screws
9	Breechbolt	**28**	Safety Lock	**48**	Stock Swivel Base Assembly
10	Breechbolt Handle and Cocking Sleeve	**29**	Safety Lock Screw	**49**	Stock Swivel Base Assembly Screws
11	Breechbolt Sleeve	**30**	Magazine Holder	**50**	Receiver Sight Assembly
12	Breechbolt Sleeve Pin	**31**	Magazine Catch	**51**	Firing Pin Stop Pin
13	Firing Pin Spring	**32**	Magazine Catch Screw	**52**	Magazine Release Plunger Stop
14	Breechbolt Plug	**33**	Magazine Holder Screws		
15	Firing Pin	**34**	Trigger Spring		
16	Left Extractor	**35**	Trigger Spring Adjusting Screw		
17	Extractor Springs	**36**	Safety-Lever		
18	Right Extractor	**37**	Magazine Assembly		
19	Extractor Pins	**38**	Guard Bow		
		39	Guard Bow Screws		

Model 77 Autoloading Rifle

Courtesy of James M. Triggs

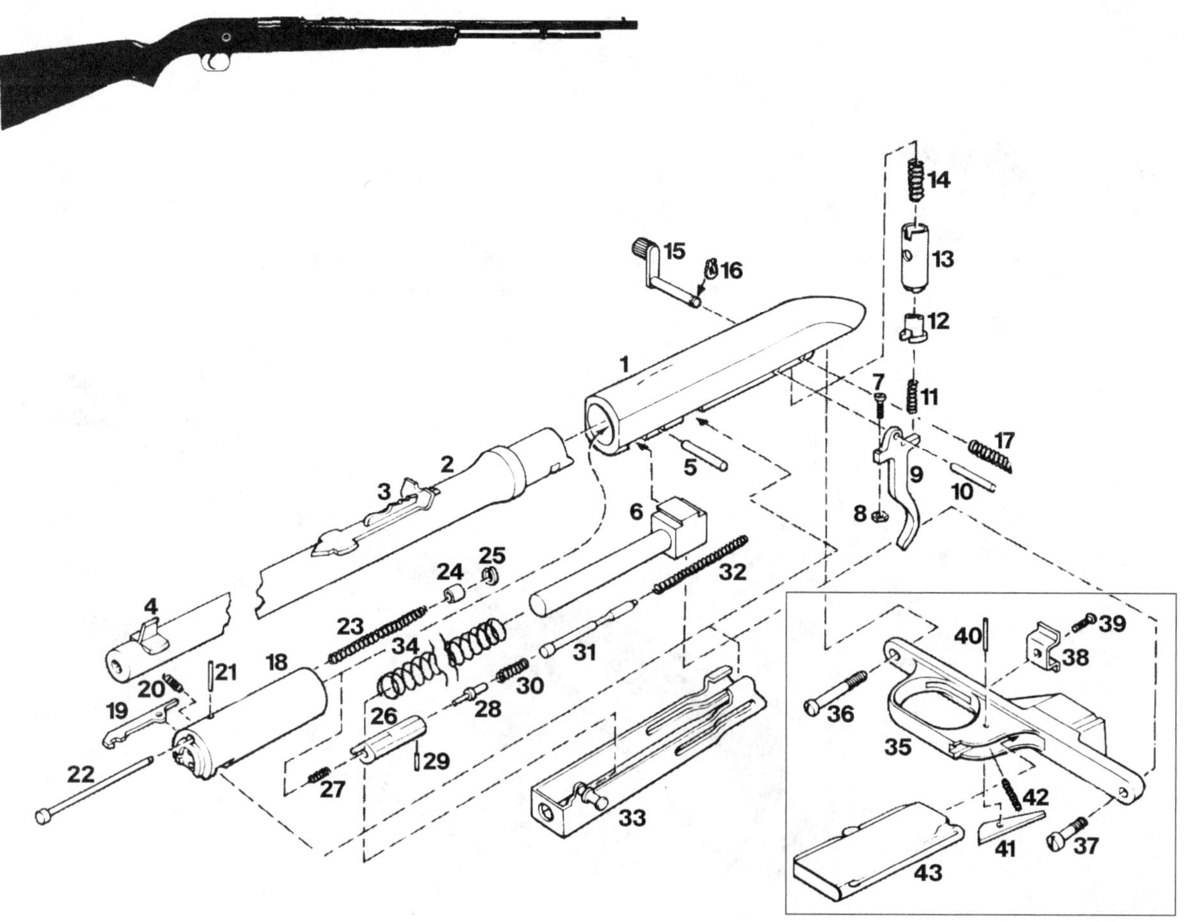

1	Receiver	**17**	Safety Spring	**33**	Operating Slide Assembly
2	Barrel	**18**	Bolt	**34**	Mainspring
3	Rear Sight	**19**	Extractor	**35**	Guard
4	Front Sight	**20**	Extractor Spring	**36**	Recoil Block Screw
5	Barrel Locating Pin	**21**	Extractor Pin	**37**	Stock Stud Screw
6	Operating Slide Guide Assembly	**22**	Timing Rod	**38**	Guard Screw Escutcheon
7	Trigger Stop Screw	**23**	Timing Rod Spring	**39**	Guard Screw
8	Trigger Stop Screw Nut	**24**	Timing Rod Collar	**40**	Magazine Lock Pin
9	Trigger	**25**	Timing Rod Retaining Ring	**41**	Magazine Lock
10	Trigger Pin	**26**	Firing Pin	**42**	Magazine Lock Spring
11	Disconnector Spring	**27**	Firing Pin Retracting Spring	**43**	Magazine
12	Disconnector	**28**	Ejector	**Parts Not Shown**	
13	Sear	**29**	Ejector Spring Pin		Buttplate
14	Sear Spring	**30**	Ejector Spring		Buttplate Screws
15	Safety-Lever	**31**	Firing Pin Striker		Buttstock
16	Safety-Lever Retaining Washer	**32**	Firing Pin Striker Spring		

WINCHESTER

Model 88 Lever-Action Rifle

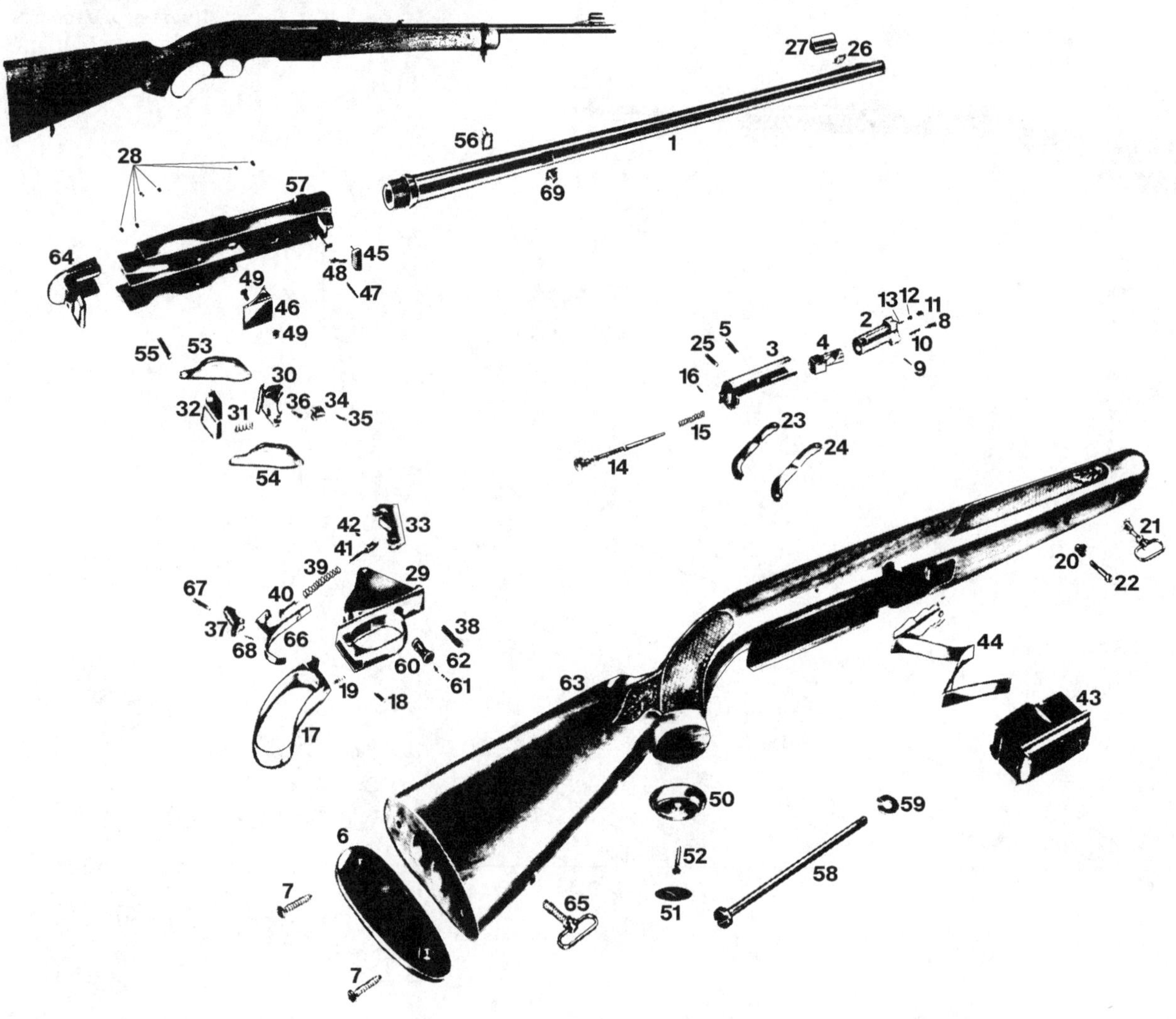

1	Barrel	**25**	Front Link Pin	**46**	Magazine Housing
2	Bolt	**26**	Front Sight	**47**	Magazine Lock Pin
3	Bolt Sleeve	**27**	Front Sight Cover	**48**	Magazine Lock Spring
4	Bolt Sleeve Lock	**28**	Front and Rear Base Plug Screws	**49**	Magazine Housing Screws
5	Bolt Sleeve Lock Pin	**29**	Trigger Guard	**50**	Pistol Grip Cap
6	Buttplate	**30**	Trigger Guard Latch	**51**	Pistol Grip Cap Insert
7	Buttplate Screws	**31**	Trigger Guard Latch Spring	**52**	Pistol Grip Cap Screw
8	Ejector	**32**	Trigger Guard Latch Spring Abutment	**53**	Rear Link, Left
9	Ejector Pin	**33**	Hammer	**54**	Rear Link, Right
10	Ejector Springs	**34**	Hammer Catch	**55**	Rear Link Pin
11	Extractor	**35**	Hammer Catch Pin	**56**	Rear Sight
12	Extractor Plunger	**36**	Hammer Catch Spring	**57**	Receiver
13	Extractor Spring	**37**	Hammer Lock	**58**	Recoil Block Screw
14	Firing Pin	**38**	Hammer Pin	**59**	Recoil Block Screw Washer
15	Firing Pin Spring	**39**	Hammer Spring	**60**	Safety
16	Firing Pin Retaining Pin	**40**	Hammer Spring Guide	**61**	Safety Spring
17	Finger Lever	**41**	Hammer Spring Guide Rod	**62**	Safety Spring Plunger
18	Finger Lever Pin	**42**	Hammer Spring Guide Rod Pin	**63**	Stock
19	Finger Lever Spring	**43**	Magazine Complete	**64**	Recoil Block
20	Forend Escutcheon	**44**	Magazine Follower Assembly	**65**	Stock Swivel Bow
21	Forend Swivel Complete	**45**	Magazine Lock	**66**	Trigger
22	Forend Screw			**67**	Trigger Pin
23	Front Link, Left			**68**	Trigger Spring
24	Front Link, Right			**69**	Forend Stud

Model 9422 Lever-Action Carbine

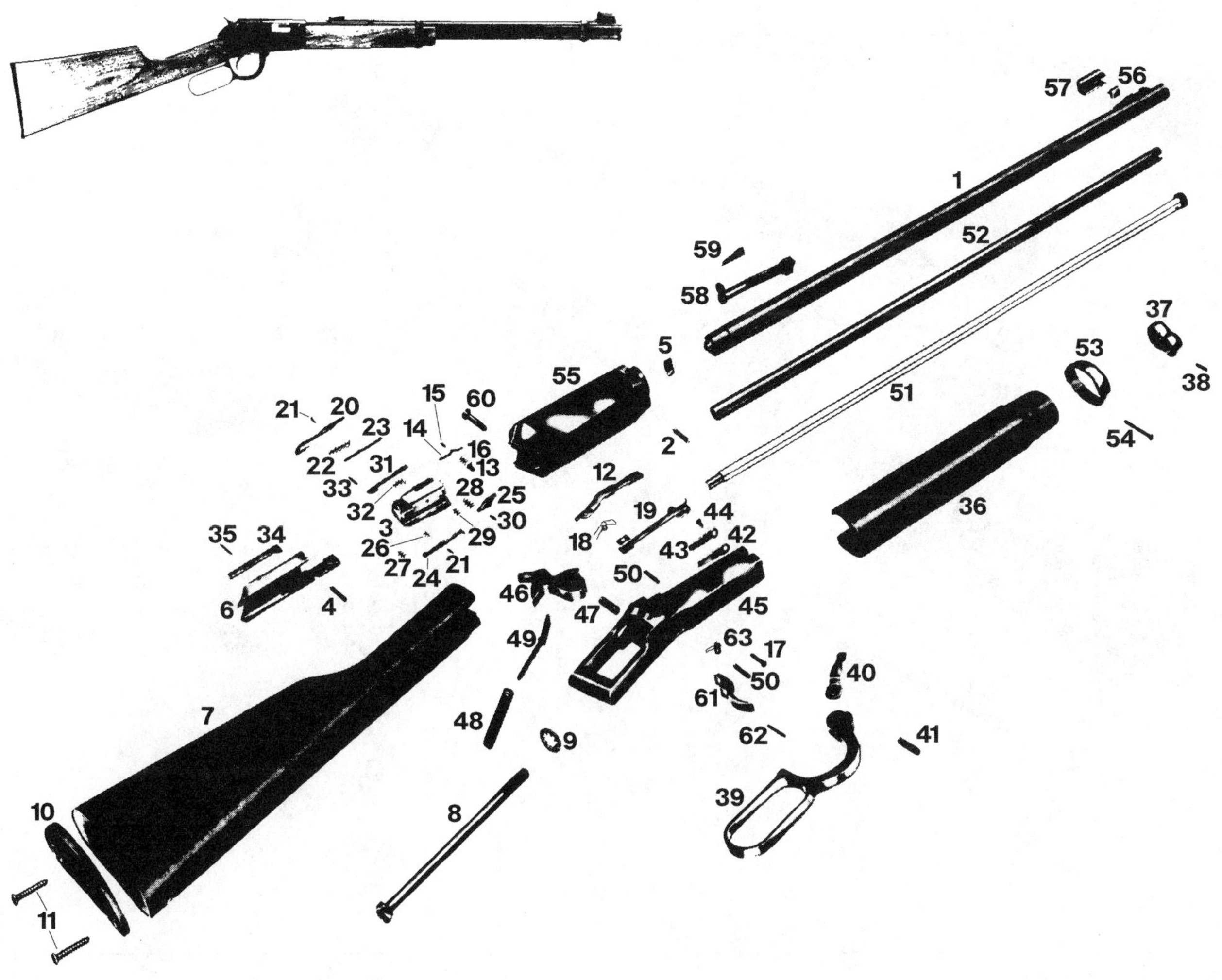

1	Barrel	**23**	Extractor, Left	**44**	Finger Lever Spring Screw
2	Barrel Retaining Pin	**24**	Extractor, Right	**45**	Frame
3	Breechbolt	**25**	Extractor, Upper Right	**46**	Hammer
4	Bolt Cam Pin	**26**	Extractor Spring, Right	**47**	Hammer Pivot Bushing
5	Bolt Guide with Pad	**27**	Extractor Helper Spring, Right	**48**	Hammer Spring
6	Bolt Slide	**28**	Extractor Spring, Upper Right	**49**	Hammer Spring Guide Rod
7	Buttstock	**29**	Extractor Helper Spring, Upper Right	**50**	Hammer Stop and Trigger Spring Pins
8	Buttstock Bolt	**30**	Extractor Pin, Upper Right	**51**	Magazine Tube Assembly, Inside
9	Buttstock Bolt Washer	**31**	Firing Pin	**52**	Magazine Tube, Outside
10	Buttplate	**32**	Firing Pin Spring	**53**	Rear Band
11	Buttplate Screws	**33**	Firing Pin Retainer Pin	**54**	Rear Band Screw
12	Carrier	**34**	Firing Pin Striker	**55**	Receiver
13	Carrier Pawl	**35**	Firing Pin Striker Retaining Pin	**56**	Front Sight
14	Carrier Pawl Retainer	**36**	Forend	**57**	Front Sight Cover
15	Carrier Pawl Retainer Pin	**37**	Front Band	**58**	Rear Sight
16	Carrier Pawl Spring	**38**	Front Band Screw	**59**	Rear Sight Elevator
17	Carrier Pin	**39**	Finger Lever	**60**	Takedown Screw
18	Carrier Spring	**40**	Finger Lever Arm	**61**	Trigger
19	Cartridge Cutoff	**41**	Finger Lever Pin	**62**	Trigger Pin
20	Ejector	**42**	Finger Lever Spring	**63**	Trigger Spring
21	Ejector and Extractor Pins	**43**	Finger Lever Spring Plate		
22	Ejector Spring				

Model 96 Over/Under Shotgun

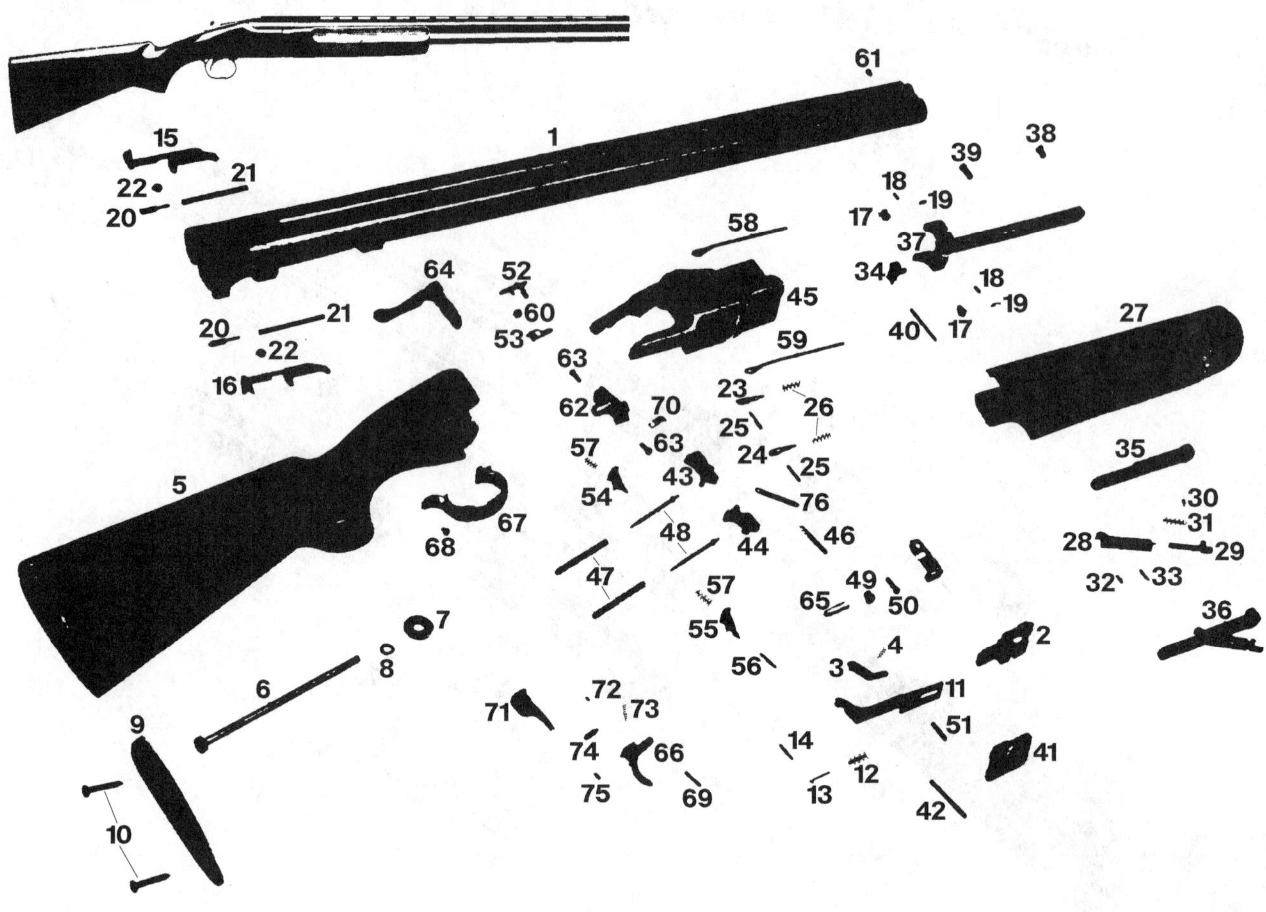

1	Barrels	25	Firing Pin Retaining Pins	50	Locking Pin Screw
2	Barrel Locking Plate	26	Firing Pin Springs	51	Pinion Screw
3	Barrel Locking Plate Latch	27	Forearm	52	Safety Button
4	Barrel Locking Plate Latch Spring	28	Forearm Catch	53	Safety Button Spring
5	Buttstock Assembly	29	Forearm Catch Release	54	Sear, Left
6	Buttstock Bolt	30	Forearm Catch Release Retaining Screw	55	Sear, Right
7	Buttstock Bolt Flat Washer	31	Forearm Catch Spring	56	Sear Pin
8	Buttstock Bolt Lock Washer	32	Forearm Catch Stop Pin	57	Sear Springs
9	Buttplate	33	Forearm Catch Retainer Pin	58	Selective Ejector Rod, Left
10	Buttplate Screws	34	Forearm Hinge Block	59	Selective Ejector Rod, Right
11	Cocking Plate	35	Forearm Plate, Lower	60	Selective Filler Block
12	Cocking Plate Spring	36	Forearm Plate Lower Complete	61	Sight
13	Cocking Plate Spring Guide Rod	37	Forearm Plate, Upper	62	Tang Spacer
14	Cocking Plate Spring Guide Rod Pin	38	Forearm Plate Screw, Front	63	Tang Spacer Screws
15	Ejector, Left	39	Forearm Plate Screw, Rear	64	Top-Lever Set
16	Ejector, Right	40	Forearm Hinge Block Pin	65	Top-Lever Spring
17	Ejector Hammer Catch	41	Frame Plate, Bottom	66	Trigger
18	Ejector Hammer Catch Pins	42	Frame Plate Pin, Bottom	67	Trigger Guard
19	Ejector Hammer Catch Springs	43	Hammer, Left	68	Trigger Guard Screw
20	Ejector Plungers	44	Hammer, Right	69	Trigger Pin
21	Ejector Springs	45	Frame	70	Trigger Recovery Spring
22	Ejector Retainers	46	Hammer Pin	71	Trigger Sear Catch
23	Firing Pin, Upper	47	Hammer Springs	72	Trigger Sear Catch Pin
24	Firing Pin, Lower	48	Hammer Spring Guide Rods	73	Trigger Spring
		49	Locking Pin Catch	74	Trigger Swivel Plunger
				75	Trigger Swivel Plunger Stop Pin
				76	Spacer

New Model 70 Lightweight Bolt-Action Rifle

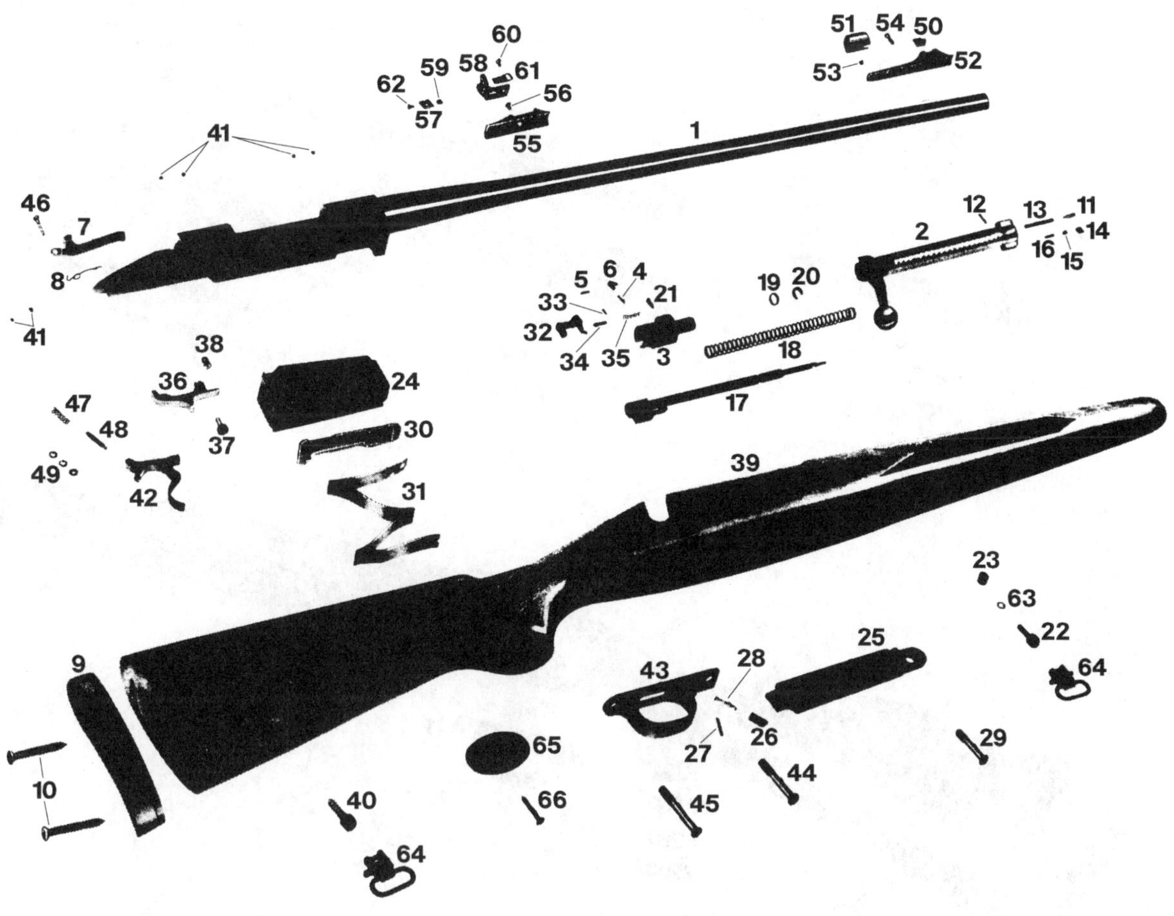

1	Barrel with Receiver Assembly	**24**	Magazine	**45**	Trigger Guard Screw, Rear
2	Breechbolt	**25**	Magazine Cover Complete	**46**	Trigger Pin
3	Breechbolt Sleeve	**26**	Magazine Cover Catch	**47**	Trigger Spring
4	Breechbolt Sleeve Lock	**27**	Magazine Cover Catch Pin	**48**	Trigger Stop Screw
5	Breechbolt Sleeve Lock Pin	**28**	Magazine Cover Catch Spring	**49**	Trigger Stop Screw Nuts
6	Breechbolt Sleeve Lock Spring	**29**	Magazine Cover Hinge Plate Screw	**50**	Front Sight
7	Breechbolt Stop	**30**	Magazine Follower	**51**	Front Sight Cover
8	Breechbolt Stop Spring	**31**	Magazine Spring	**52**	Front Sight Ramp
9	Buttpad	**32**	Safety	**53**	Front Sight Ramp Screw, Short
10	Buttpad Screws	**33**	Safety Pin	**54**	Front Sight Ramp Screw, Long
11	Ejector	**34**	Safety Plunger	**55**	Rear Sight Base
12	Ejector Pin	**35**	Safety Plunger Spring	**56**	Rear Sight Base Screw
13	Ejector Spring	**36**	Sear	**57**	Rear Sight Blade
14	Extractor	**37**	Sear Pin	**58**	Rear Sight Blade Holder Assembly
15	Extractor Plunger	**38**	Sear Spring	**59**	Rear Sight Blade Nut
16	Extractor Spring	**39**	Stock Complete	**60**	Rear Sight Blade Screw
17	Firing Pin	**40**	Stock Swivel Stud	**61**	Rear Sight Blade Spring
18	Firing Pin Spring	**41**	Telescope Sight Base Plug Screws	**62**	Rear Sight Windage Screw
19	Firing Pin Spring Retainer	**42**	Trigger	**63**	Washer
20	Firing Pin Spring Retainer Washer	**43**	Trigger Guard	**64**	Swivels
21	Firing Pin Stop Screw	**44**	Trigger Guard Screw, Front	**65**	Pistol Grip Cap
22	Forearm Screw Eye			**66**	Cap Screw
23	Forearm Screw Eye Escutcheon				

New Model 70A and 770 Bolt-Action Rifle

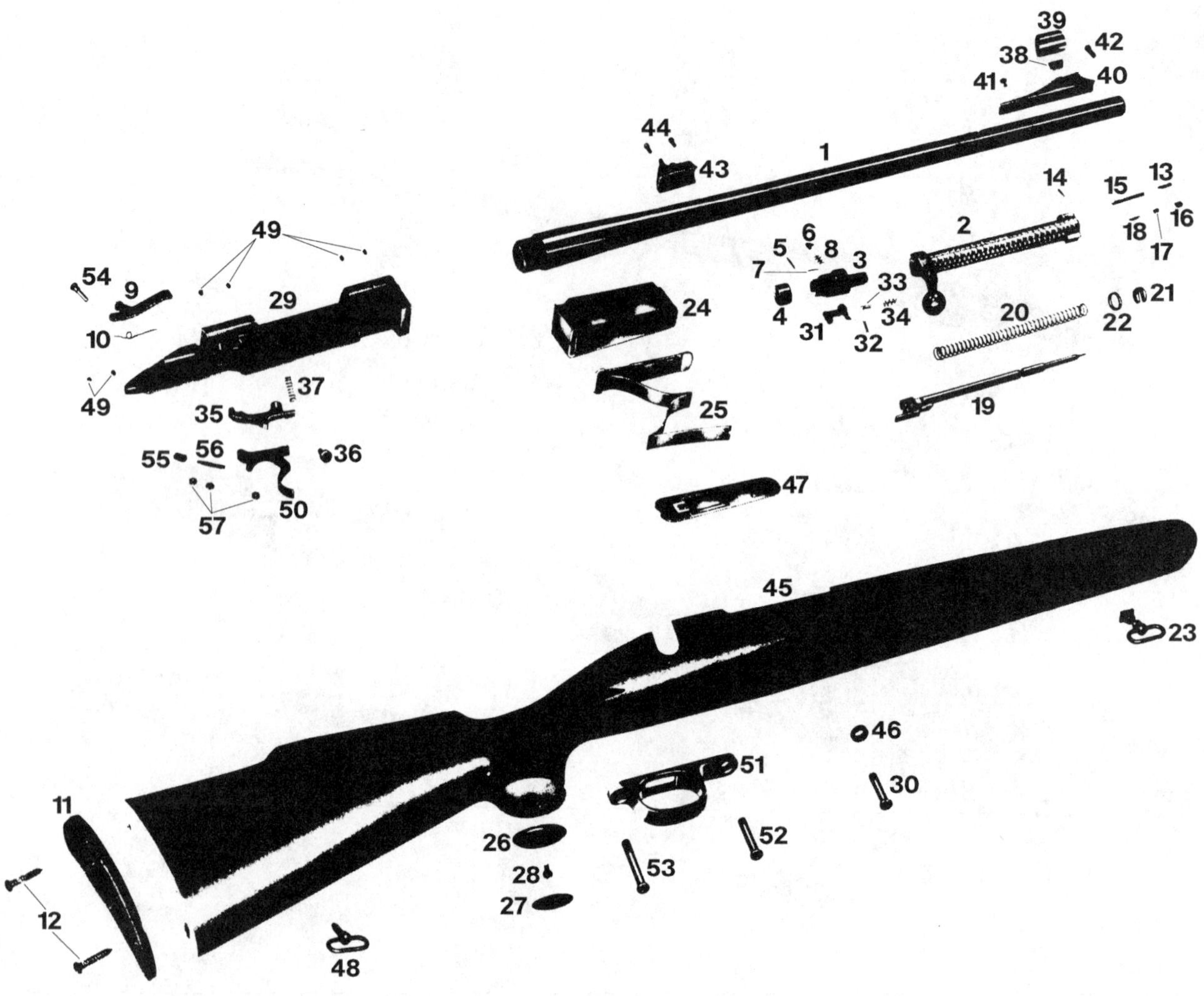

1	Barrel	21	Firing Pin Spring Retainer	39	Front Sight Cover
2	Breechbolt	22	Firing Pin Spring Washer	40	Front Sight Ramp
3	Breechbolt Sleeve	23	Forearm Screw Eye Swivel Complete	41	Front Sight Ramp Screw, Short
4	Breechbolt Sleeve Cap	24	Magazine	42	Front Sight Ramp Screw, Long
5	Breechbolt Sleeve Cap Pin	25	Magazine Follower and Spring Assembly	43	Rear Sight Assembly
6	Breechbolt Sleeve Lock	26	Pistol Grip Cap	44	Rear Sight Screws
7	Breechbolt Sleeve Lock Pin	27	Pistol Grip Cap Insert	45	Stock
8	Breechbolt Sleeve Lock Spring	28	Pistol Grip Cap Screw	46	Stock Escutcheon
9	Breechbolt Stop	29	Receiver	47	Stock Floorplate
10	Breechbolt Stop Spring	30	Receiver Screw, Front	48	Stock Swivel Bow
11	Buttplate	31	Safety	49	Telescope Sight Base Plug Screws
12	Buttplate Screws	32	Safety Pin	50	Trigger
13	Ejector	33	Safety Plunger	51	Trigger Guard
14	Ejector Pin	34	Safety Plunger Spring	52	Trigger Guard Screw, Front
15	Ejector Spring	35	Sear	53	Trigger Guard Screw, Rear
16	Extractor	36	Sear Pin	54	Trigger Pin
17	Extractor Plunger	37	Sear Spring	55	Trigger Spring
18	Extractor Spring	38	Front Sight	56	Trigger Stop Screw
19	Firing Pin			57	Trigger Stop Screw Nuts
20	Firing Pin Spring				

New Model 70 XTR Sporter Bolt-Action Rifle

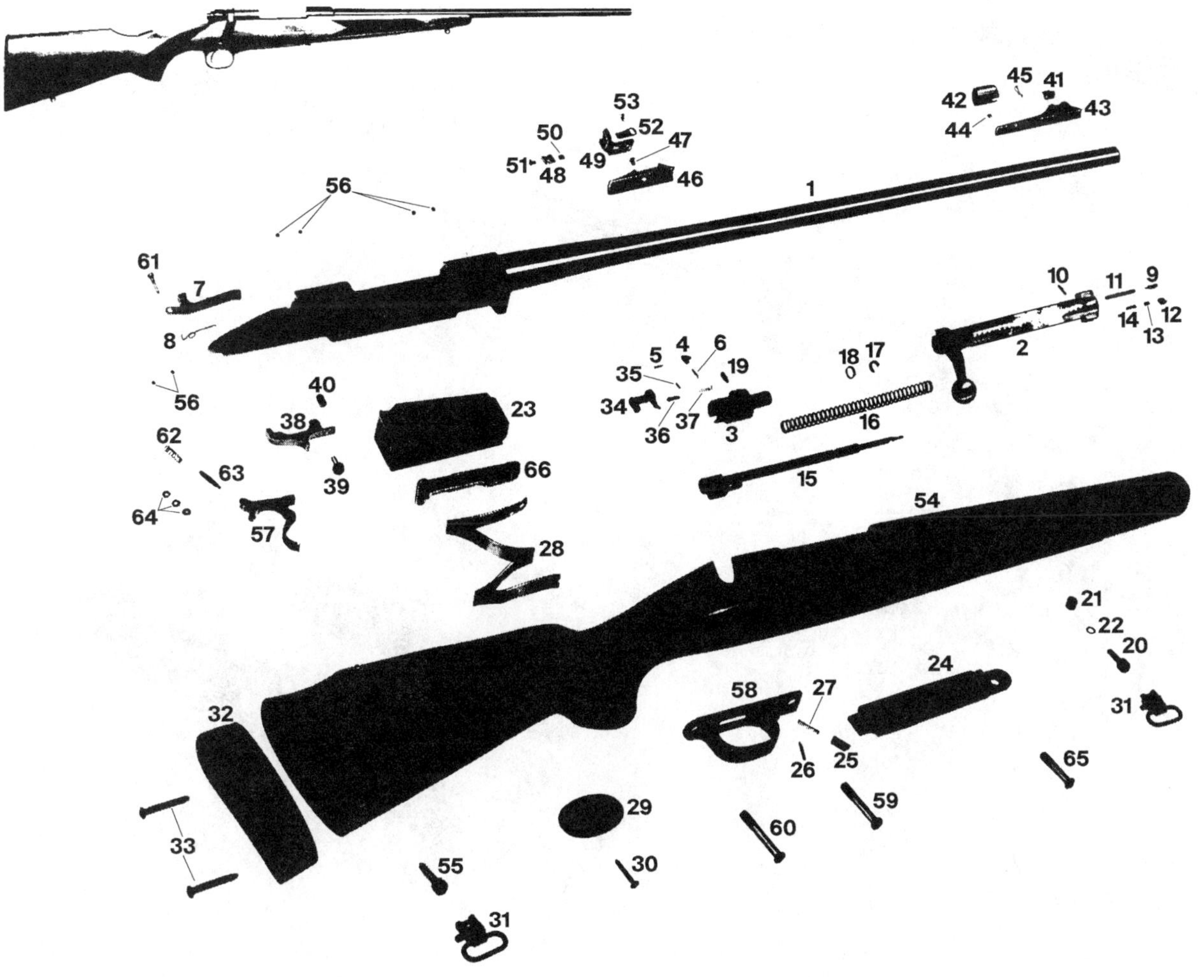

1	Barrel with Receiver Assembly	**24**	Magazine Cover Complete	**47**	Rear Sight Base Screw
2	Breechbolt	**25**	Magazine Cover Catch	**48**	Rear Sight Blade
3	Breechbolt Sleeve	**26**	Magazine Cover Catch Pin	**49**	Rear Sight Blade Holder Assembly
4	Breechbolt Sleeve Lock	**27**	Magazine Cover Catch Spring	**50**	Rear Sight Blade Nut
5	Breechbolt Sleeve Lock Pin	**28**	Magazine Spring	**51**	Rear Sight Blade Screw
6	Breechbolt Sleeve Lock Spring	**29**	Pistol Grip Cap	**52**	Rear Sight Blade Spring
7	Breechbolt Stop	**30**	Pistol Grip Cap Screw	**53**	Rear Sight Windage Screw
8	Breechbolt Stop Spring	**31**	Quick Detachable Swivels	**54**	Stock Complete
9	Ejector	**32**	Recoil Pad	**55**	Stock Swivel Stud
10	Ejector Pin	**33**	Recoil Pad Screws	**56**	Telescope Sight Base Plug Screws
11	Ejector Spring	**34**	Safety	**57**	Trigger
12	Extractor	**35**	Safety Pin	**58**	Trigger Guard
13	Extractor Plunger	**36**	Safety Plunger	**59**	Trigger Guard Screw, Front
14	Extractor Spring	**37**	Safety Plunger Spring	**60**	Trigger Guard Screw, Rear
15	Firing Pin	**38**	Sear	**61**	Trigger Pin
16	Firing Pin Spring	**39**	Sear Pin	**62**	Trigger Spring
17	Firing Pin Spring Retainer	**40**	Sear Spring	**63**	Trigger Stop Screw
18	Firing Pin Spring Washer	**41**	Front Sight	**64**	Trigger Stop Screw Nuts
19	Firing Pin Stop Screw	**42**	Front Sight Cover	**65**	Cover Hinge Plate Screw
20	Forearm Screw Eye	**43**	Front Sight Ramp	**66**	Magazine Follower
21	Forearm Screw Eye Escutcheon	**44**	Front Sight Ramp Screw, Short		
22	Forearm Screw Eye Washer	**45**	Front Sight Ramp Screw, Long		
23	Magazine	**46**	Rear Sight Base		

New Model 94 Angle Eject Lever-Action Rifle

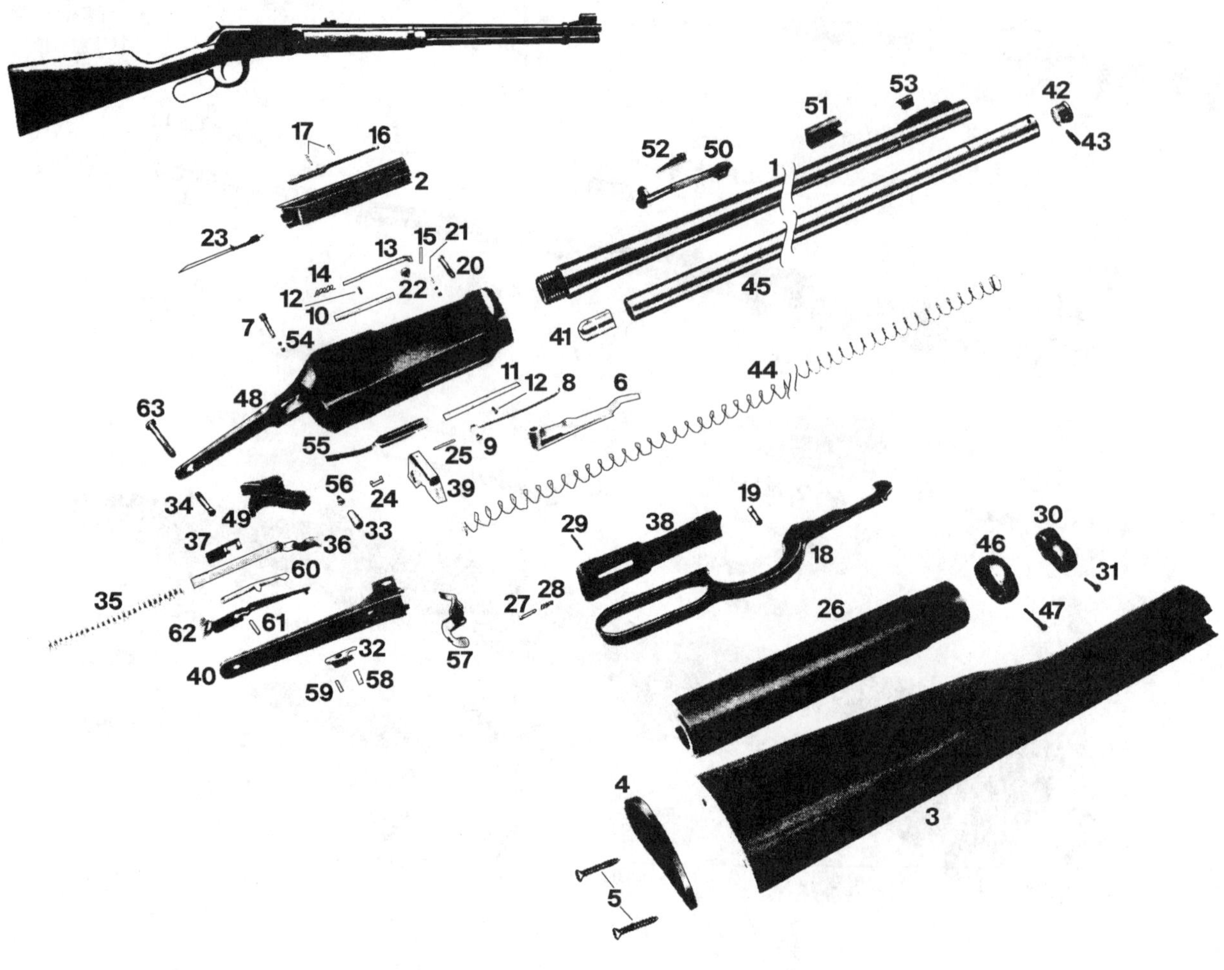

1	Barrel	23	Firing Pin	45	Magazine Tube
2	Breechbolt	24	Firing Pin Striker	46	Rear Band
3	Buttstock Complete	25	Firing Pin Striker Stop Pin	47	Rear Band Screw
4	Buttplate	26	Forearm	48	Receiver
5	Buttplate Screws	27	Friction Stud	49	Sear and Hammer
6	Carrier	28	Friction Stud Spring	50	Rear Sight Assembly
7	Carrier Screw	29	Friction Stud Stop Pin	51	Front Sight Cover
8	Carrier Spring	30	Front Band	52	Rear Sight Elevator
9	Carrier Spring Screw	31	Front Band Screw	53	Front Sight
10	Cartridge Guide, Left	32	Hammer and Sear	54	Telescope Front Sight Plug Screws
11	Cartridge Guide, Right	33	Hammer Bushing	55	Spring Cover
12	Cartridge Guide Screws	34	Hammer Screw	56	Spring Cover Screw
13	Ejector	35	Hammer Spring	57	Trigger with Hammer Block Assembly
14	Ejector Spring	36	Hammer Spring Guide Rod	58	Trigger/Sear Pin
15	Ejector Stop Pin	37	Hammer Spur Assembly	59	Trigger Spring
16	Extractor	38	Link Complete	60	Trigger Stop
17	Extractor Retaining Screws	39	Locking Bolt	61	Trigger Stop Pin
18	Finger Lever	40	Lower Tang	62	Trigger Stop Spring
19	Finger Lever Link Pin	41	Magazine Follower	63	Upper Tang Screw
20	Finger Lever Link Screw	42	Magazine Plug		
21	Finger Lever Pin	43	Magazine Plug Screw		
22	Finger Lever Pin Stop Screw	44	Magazine Spring		

New Model 94 Lever-Action Carbine

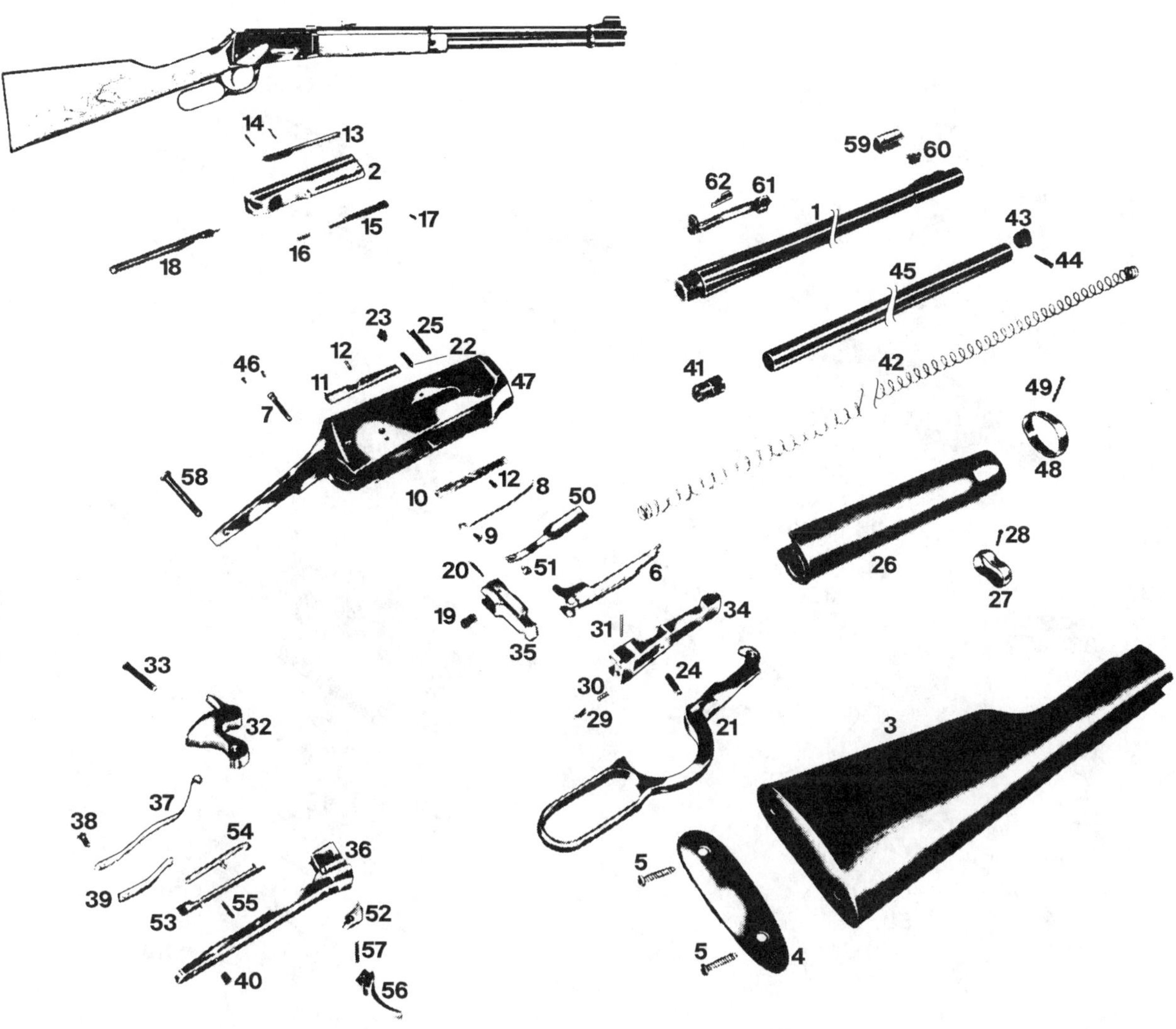

1	Barrel	**22**	Finger Lever Pin	**43**	Magazine Plug
2	Breechbolt	**23**	Finger Lever Pin Stop Screw	**44**	Magazine Plug Screw
3	Buttstock	**24**	Finger Lever Link Pin	**45**	Magazine Tube
4	Buttplate	**25**	Finger Lever Link Screw	**46**	Sight Plug Screws
5	Buttplate Screws	**26**	Forend	**47**	Receiver
6	Carrier	**27**	Front Band	**48**	Rear Band
7	Carrier Screw	**28**	Front Band Screw	**49**	Rear Band Screw
8	Carrier Spring	**29**	Friction Stud	**50**	Spring Cover
9	Carrier Spring Screw	**30**	Friction Stud Spring	**51**	Spring Cover Screw
10	Cartridge Guide, Right	**31**	Friction Stud Stop Pin	**52**	Sear
11	Cartridge Guide, Left	**32**	Hammer	**53**	Trigger Stop Spring
12	Cartridge Guide Screws	**33**	Hammer Link Screw	**54**	Trigger Stop
13	Extractor	**34**	Link	**55**	Trigger Stop Pin
14	Extractor Pins	**35**	Locking Bolt	**56**	Trigger
15	Ejector	**36**	Lower Tang	**57**	Trigger Pin
16	Ejector Spring	**37**	Mainspring	**58**	Upper Tang Screw
17	Ejector Stop Pin	**38**	Mainspring Screw	**59**	Front Sight Cover
18	Firing Pin	**39**	Mainspring Base	**60**	Front Sight
19	Firing Pin Striker	**40**	Mainspring Strain Screw	**61**	Rear Sight
20	Firing Pin Striker Pin	**41**	Magazine Follower	**62**	Rear Sight Elevator
21	Finger Lever	**42**	Magazine Spring		

New Model 94 Top-Eject Lever-Action Rifle

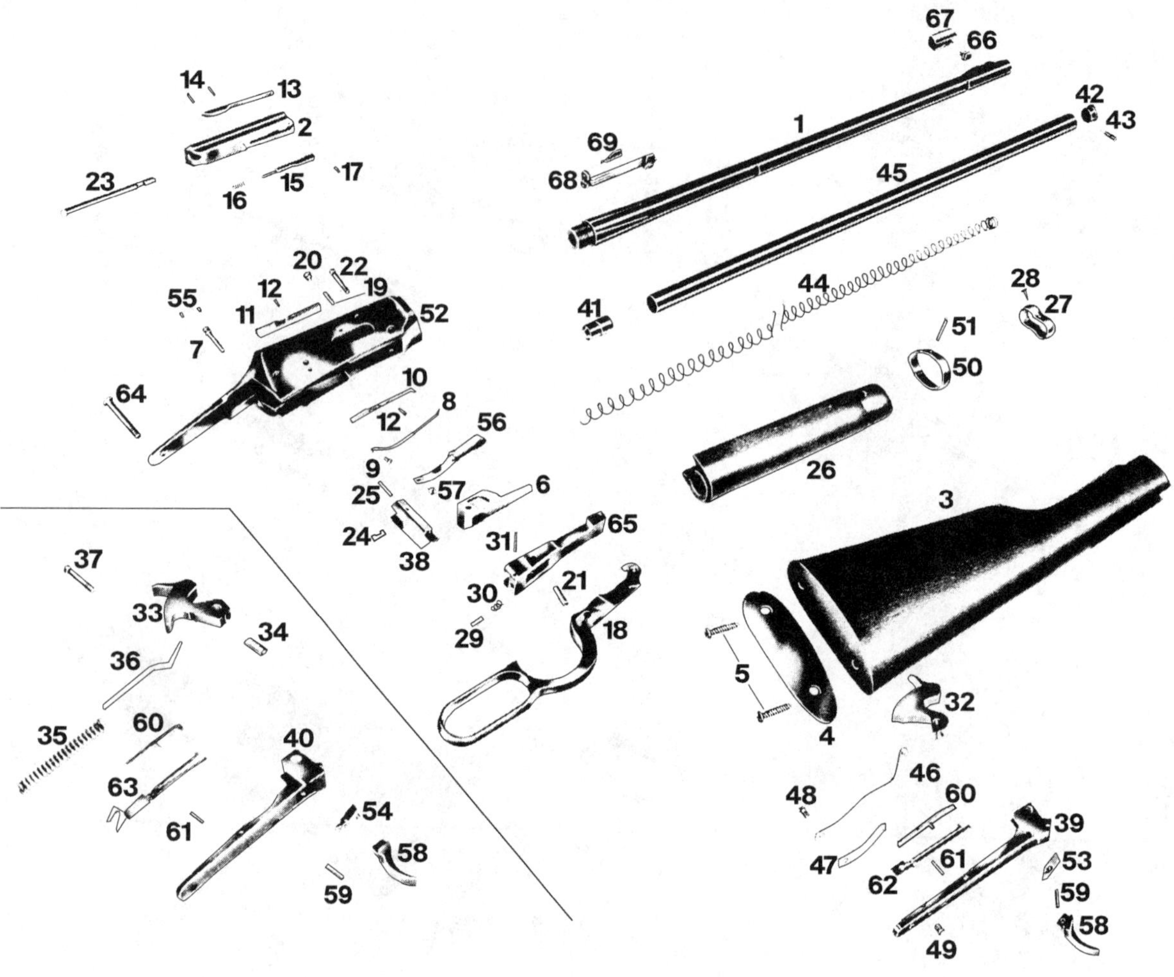

1	Barrel	24	Firing Pin Striker	47	Mainspring Base
2	Breechbolt	25	Firing Pin Striker Stop Pin	48	Mainspring Screw
3	Buttstock	26	Forearm	49	Mainspring Strain Screw
4	Buttplate	27	Front Band	50	Rear Band
5	Buttplate Screws	28	Front Band Screw	51	Rear Band Screw
6	Carrier	29	Friction Stud	52	Receiver
7	Carrier Screw	30	Friction Stud Spring	53	Sear
8	Carrier Spring	31	Friction Stud Stop Pin	54	Sear
9	Carrier Spring Screw	32	Hammer	55	Sight Plug Screws
10	Cartridge Guide, Right	33	Hammer	56	Spring Cover
11	Cartridge Guide, Left	34	Hammer Bushing	57	Spring Cover Screw
12	Cartridge Guide Screws	35	Hammer Spring	58	Trigger
13	Extractor	36	Hammer Spring Guide Rod	59	Trigger/Sear Pin
14	Extractor Pins	37	Hammer Screw	60	Trigger Stop
15	Ejector	38	Locking Bolt	61	Trigger Stop Pin
16	Ejector Spring	39	Lower Tang	62	Trigger Stop Spring
17	Ejector Stop Pin	40	Lower Tang	63	Trigger Stop Spring
18	Finger Lever	41	Magazine Follower	64	Upper Tang Screw
19	Finger Lever Pin	42	Magazine Plug	65	Link Complete
20	Finger Lever Pin Stop Screw	43	Magazine Plug Screw	66	Front Sight
21	Finger Lever Link Pin	44	Magazine Spring	67	Front Sight Cover
22	Finger Lever Link Screw	45	Magazine Tube	68	Rear Sight
23	Firing Pin	46	Mainspring	69	Rear Sight Elevator

Single Shot Rifle

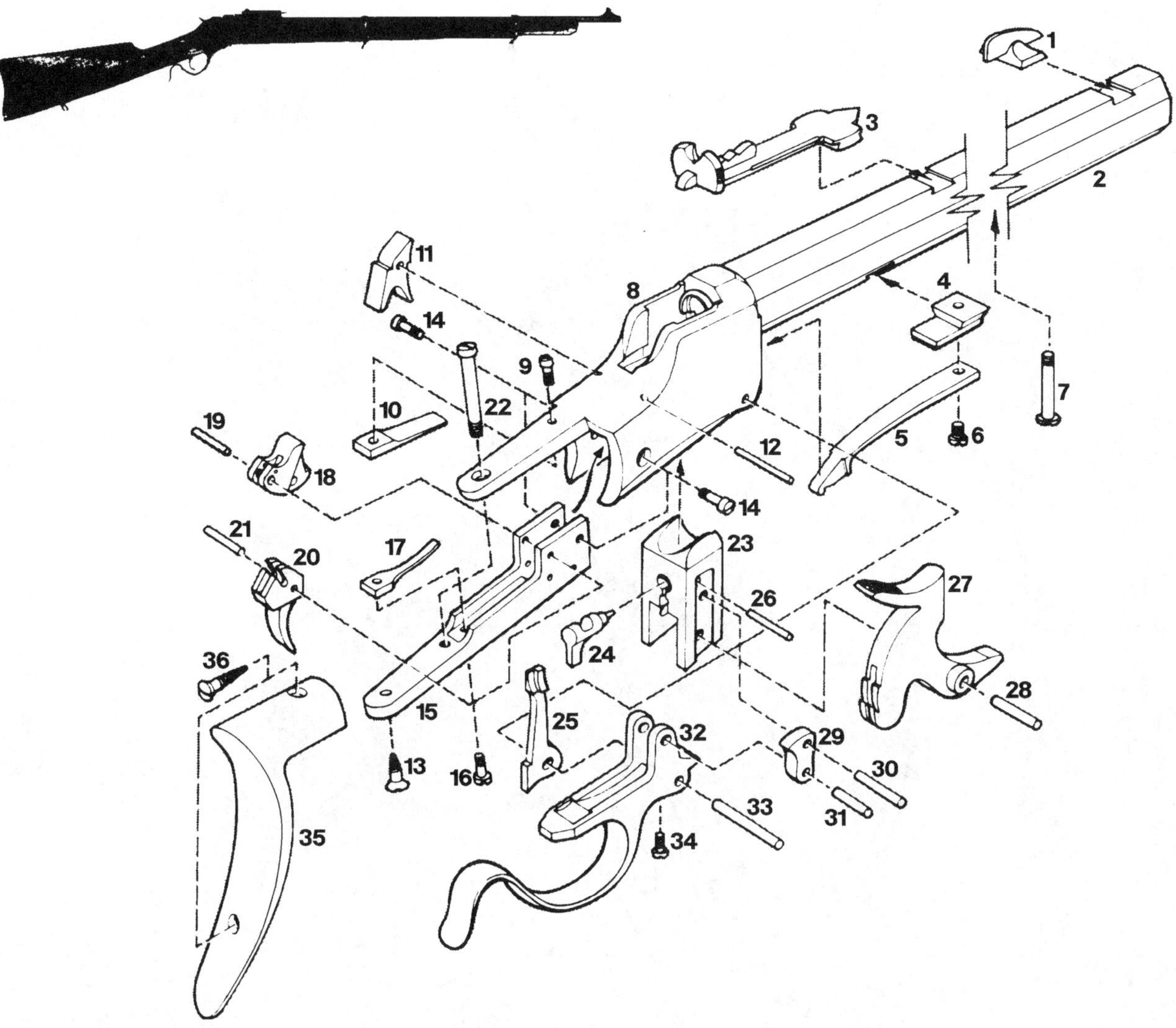

1	Front Sight	21	Trigger Pin
2	Barrel	22	Upper Tang Screw
3	Rear Sight	23	Breechblock
4	Mainspring Base	24	Firing Pin
5	Mainspring	25	Extractor
6	Mainspring Screw	26	Firing Pin Stop Pin
7	Forearm Screw	27	Hammer
8	Receiver	28	Hammer Pin
9	Sear Spring Screw	29	Link
10	Sear Spring	30	Link Pin, Long
11	Sear	31	Link Pin, Short
12	Sear Pin	32	Finger Lever
13	Lower Tang Screw	33	Finger Lever Pin
14	Side Tang Screws	34	Finger Lever Pin Stop Screw
15	Tang	35	Buttplate
16	Knock-Off Spring Screw	36	Buttplate Screws
17	Knock-Off Spring	**Parts Not Shown**	
18	Knock-Off		Buttstock
19	Knock-Off Pin		Forearm
20	Trigger		

Rifle

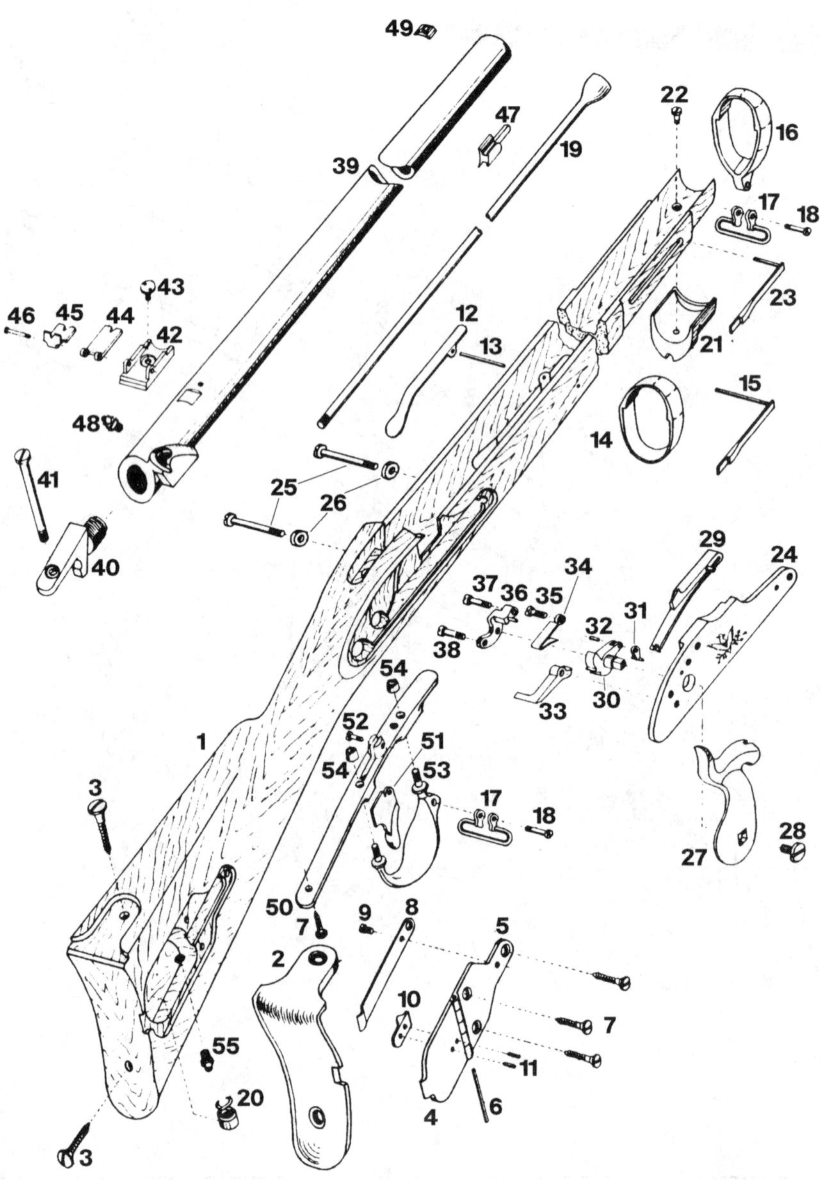

No.	Part	No.	Part	No.	Part
1	Stock	20	Worm	39	Barrel
2	Buttplate	21	Forend Tip	40	Breech Plug
3	Buttplate Screws	22	Forend Tip Screw	41	Breech Plug Screw
4	Patchbox Trap	23	Front Band Spring	42	Rear Sight Base
5	Patchbox Plate	24	Lockplate	43	Rear Sight Retainer Screw
6	Patchbox Hinge Pin	25	Lockplate Screws	44	Rear Sight Elevation Spring
7	Patchbox Cover Screws	26	Stock Bushings	45	Rear Sight Blade
8	Patchbox Spring	27	Hammer	46	Rear Sight Pin
9	Patchbox Spring Screw	28	Hammer Screw	47	Bayonet Stud
10	Patchbox Latch	29	Mainspring	48	Barrel Pin
11	Patchbox Retaining Pins	30	Tumbler	49	Front Sight
12	Ramrod Spoon	31	Bridle	50	Trigger Plate
13	Ramrod Spoon Pin	32	Bridle Pin	51	Trigger
14	Rear Band	33	Sear	52	Trigger Guard Screw
15	Rear Band Spring	34	Sear Spring	53	Trigger Guard
16	Front Band	35	Sear Spring Screw	54	Trigger Guard Nuts
17	Swivels	36	Tumbler Support Plate	55	Extra Nipple
18	Swivel Screws	37	Tumbler Plate Screw		
19	Ramrod	38	Sear Screw		

Ariete M1 Side-By-Side Shotgun

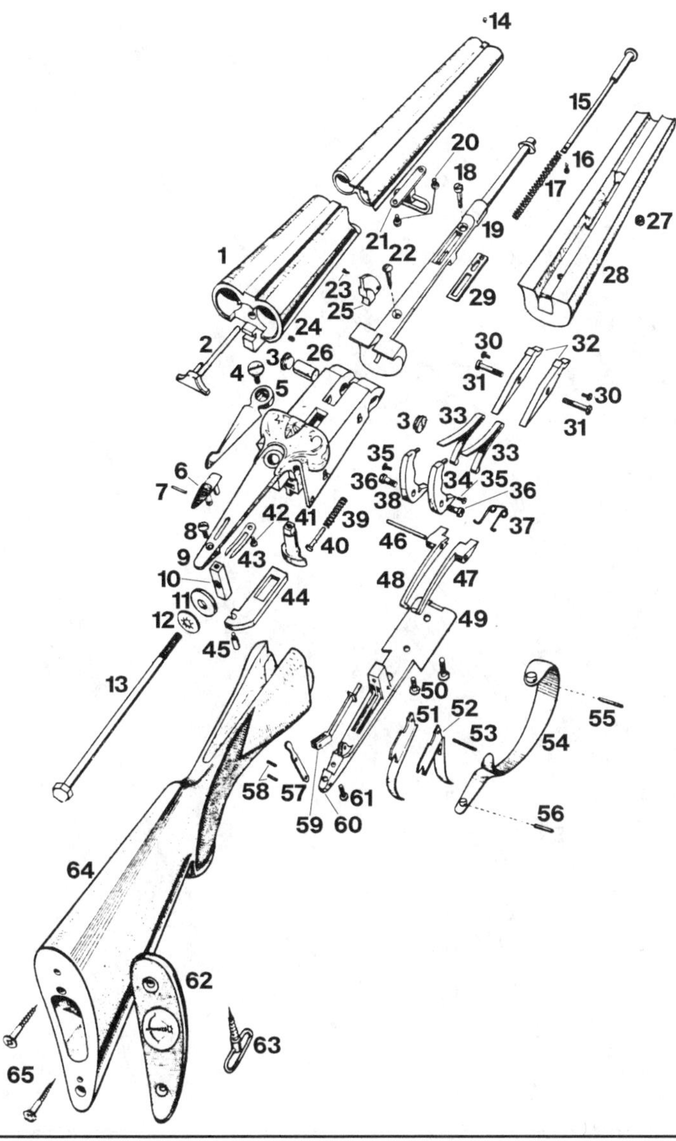

1	Barrels	**23**	Ejector Lever Screw	**45**	Locking Bolt Screw
2	Ejector	**24**	Ejector Retaining Screw	**46**	Sear Pin
3	Pivot Pin Retainers	**25**	Ejector Lever	**47**	Right Sear
4	Top Lever Screw	**26**	Barrel Pivot Pin	**48**	Left Sear
5	Top Lever	**27**	Forend Escutcheon	**49**	Trigger Plate
6	Safety Button	**28**	Forend Wood	**50**	Trigger Plate Screws
7	Safety Button Pin	**29**	Forend Latch	**51**	Rear Trigger
8	Top Tang Screw	**30**	Cocking Lever Pivot Retainer	**52**	Front Trigger
9	Frame	**31**	Cocking Lever Pivot	**53**	Trigger Pin
10	Tang Spacer Block	**32**	Cocking Levers	**54**	Trigger Guard
11	Stock Bolt Washer	**33**	Hammer Springs	**55**	Trigger Guard Pin, Front
12	Stock Bolt Lockwasher	**34**	Right Hammer	**56**	Trigger Guard Pin, Rear
13	Stock Bolt	**35**	Hammer Lock Screws	**57**	Safety Connector
14	Front Bead Sight	**36**	Hammer Screws	**58**	Safety Connector Pins
15	Forend Release	**37**	Sear Spring	**59**	Safety Block
16	Forend Release Spring	**38**	Left Hammer	**60**	Trigger Housing
17	Forend Release Spring Pin	**39**	Top Lever Dog Spring	**61**	Trigger Plate Screw
18	Forend Iron Screw, Front	**40**	Top Lever Dog Plunger	**62**	Buttplate
19	Forend Iron	**41**	Top Lever Dog	**63**	Sling Swivel, Rear
20	Sling Swivel Screws	**42**	Safety Spring Screw	**64**	Stock
21	Sling Swivel, Front	**43**	Safety Spring	**65**	Buttplate Screws
22	Forend Iron Screw, Rear	**44**	Locking Bolt		

Delfino Over/Under Shotgun

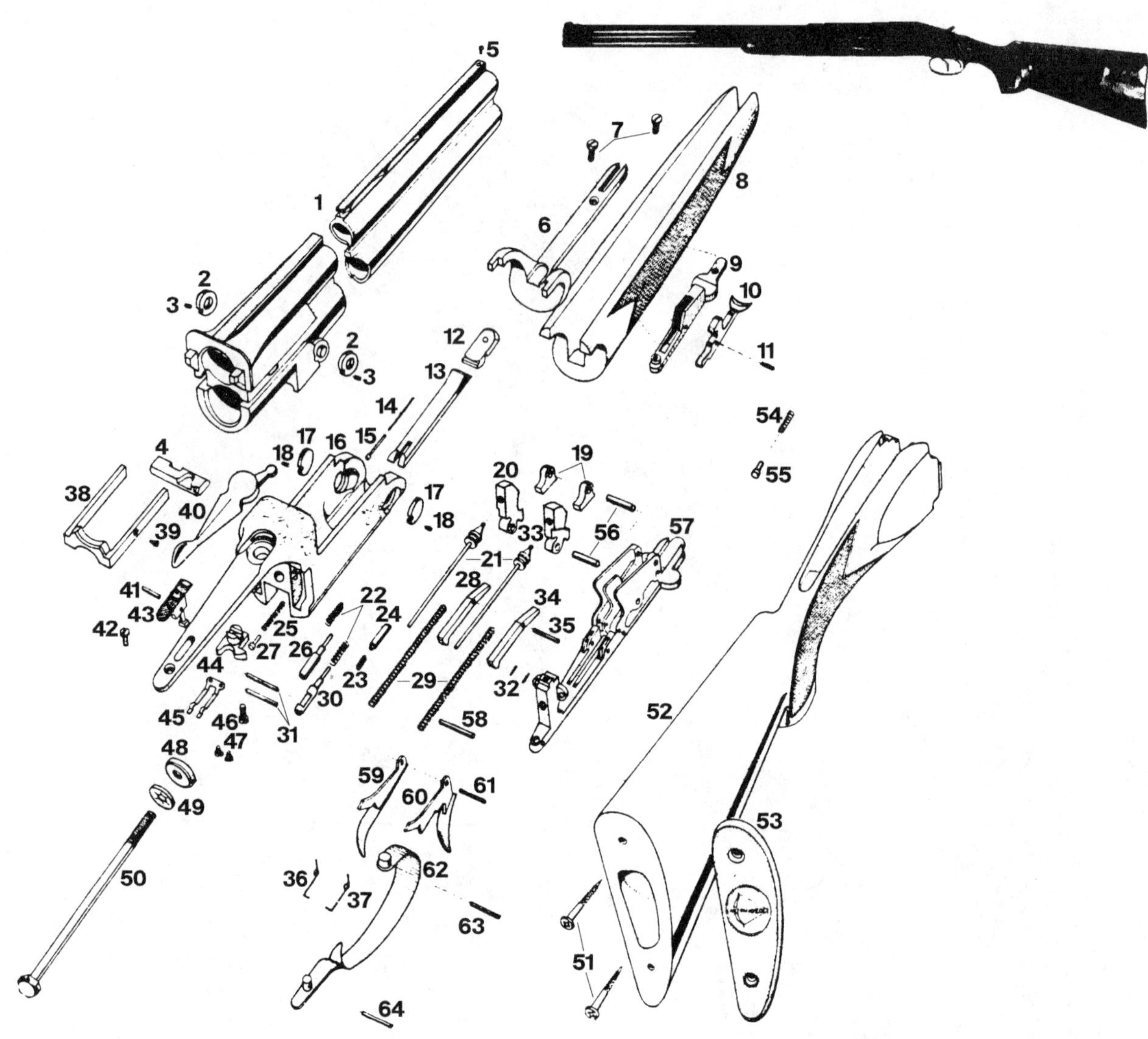

1	Barrels	23	Spring	45	Safety Button Spring
2	Barrel Pivot Rings	24	Plunger	46	Upper Tang Screw
3	Barrel Pivot Lock Screws	25	Top Lever Spring	47	Safety Button Spring Screws
4	Barrel Latch Bar	26	Firing Pin, Upper	48	Stock Bolt Washer
5	Front Bead Sight	27	Top Lever Spring Plunger	49	Stock Bolt Lockwasher
6	Forend Iron	28	Sear, Left	50	Stock Bolt
7	Forend Iron Screws	29	Hammer Springs	51	Buttplate Screws
8	Forend Wood	30	Firing Pin, Lower	52	Buttstock
9	Forend Release Housing	31	Firing Pin Retaining Pins	53	Buttplate
10	Forend Release Lever	32	Trigger Limit Pins	54	Forend Latch Spring
11	Forend Release Lever Pin	33	Hammer, Right	55	Forend Latch Spring Plunger
12	Cocking Slide Head	34	Sear, Right	56	Hammer and Cocking Lever Pivots
13	Cocking Slide	35	Sear Pivot Pin	57	Trigger Plate
14	Cocking Slide Spring	36	Sear Spring, Left	58	Cocking Slide Retaining Pin
15	Cocking Slide Spring Plunger	37	Sear Spring, Right	59	Bottom Trigger
16	Receiver	38	Ejector	60	Top Trigger
17	Pivot Cover Discs	39	Ejector Retaining Screw	61	Trigger Pivot
18	Pivot Cover Discs Screws	40	Top Lever	62	Trigger Guard
19	Cocking Levers	41	Safety Button Pin	63	Trigger Guard Pin, Front
20	Hammer, Left	42	Top Lever Base Screw	64	Trigger Guard Pin, Rear
21	Hammer Spring Guides	43	Safety Button		
22	Firing Pin Springs	44	Top Lever Base		

2005 GUN DIGEST DIRECTORY OF THE ARMS TRADE

The **Product Directory** contains 84 product categories. The **Manufacturer's Directory** alphabetically lists the manufacturers with their dresses, phone numbers, FAX numbers and Internet addresses, if available.

DIRECTORY OF THE ARMS TRADE INDEX

AMMUNITION COMPONENTS, SHOTSHELL

A.W. Peterson Gun Shop, Inc.
Ballistic Products, Inc.
Blount, Inc., Sporting Equipment Div.
CCI/Speer Div of ATK
Cheddite, France S.A.
Claybuster Wads & Harvester Bullets
Garcia National Gun Traders, Inc.
Guncrafter Industries
Peterson Gun Shop, Inc., A.W.
Precision Reloading, Inc.
Ravell Ltd.
Tar-Hunt Custom Rifles, Inc.
The A.W. Peterson Gun Shop, Inc.
Vitt/Boos

AMMUNITION COMPONENTS--BULLETS, POWDER, PRIMERS, CASES

A.W. Peterson Gun Shop, Inc.
Acadian Ballistic Specialties
Accuracy Unlimited
Accurate Arms Co., Inc.
Action Bullets & Alloy Inc.
ADCO Sales, Inc.
Alaska Bullet Works, Inc.
Alex, Inc.
Alliant Techsystems Smokeless Powder Group
Allred Bullet Co.
Alpha LaFranck Enterprises
American Products, Inc.
Arizona Ammunition, Inc.
Armfield Custom Bullets
A-Square Co.
Atlantic Rose, Inc.
Baer's Hollows
Ballard Rifle & Cartridge Co., LLC
Barnes
Barnes Bullets, Inc.
Beartooth Bullets
Bell Reloading, Inc.
Berger Bullets Ltd.
Berry's Mfg., Inc.
Big Bore Bullets of Alaska
Big Bore Express
Bitterroot Bullet Co.
Black Belt Bullets
(See Big Bore Express)
Black Hills Shooters Supply
Black Powder Products
Blount, Inc., Sporting Equipment Div.
Blue Mountain Bullets
Brenneke GmbH
Briese Bullet Co., Inc.
Brown Co., E. Arthur
Brown Dog Ent.
BRP, Inc. High Performance Cast Bullets
Buck Stix-SOS Products Co.
Buckeye Custom Bullets
Buckskin Bullet Co.
Buffalo Arms Co.
Buffalo Bullet Co., Inc.
Buffalo Rock Shooters Supply
Bull-X, Inc.
Butler Enterprises
Calhoon Mfg.
Cambos Outdoorsman
Canyon Cartridge Corp.
Cascade Bullet Co., Inc.
Cast Performance Bullet Company
Casull Arms Corp.
CCI/Speer Div of ATK
Champion's Choice, Inc.
Cheddite, France S.A.
CheVron Bullets
Chuck's Gun Shop
Clean Shot Technologies
Competitor Corp., Inc.
Cook Engineering Service
Corbin Mfg. & Supply, Inc.
Cummings Bullets
Curtis Cast Bullets
Curtis Gun Shop
(See Curtis Cast Bullets)
Custom Bullets by Hoffman
D.L. Unmussig Bullets
Dakota Arms, Inc.
Davide Pedersoli and Co.
DKT, Inc.
Dohring Bullets
Dutchman's Firearms, Inc.
Eichelberger Bullets, Wm.
Federal Cartridge Co.
Fiocchi of America, Inc.
Forkin Custom Classics
Fowler Bullets
Fowler, Bob
(See Black Powder Products)
Freedom Arms, Inc.
Garcia National Gun Traders, Inc.
Gehmann, Walter
(See Huntington Die Specialties)
GOEX, Inc.
Golden Bear Bullets
Gotz Bullets
Grayback Wildcats
Green Mountain Rifle Barrel Co., Inc.
Grier's Hard Cast Bullets
GTB-Custom Bullets
Gun City
Harris Enterprises
Harrison Bullets
Hart & Son, Inc.
Hawk Laboratories, Inc.
(See Hawk, Inc.)
Hawk, Inc.
Heidenstrom Bullets
Hercules, Inc. (See Alliant Techsystems, Smokeless)
Hi-Performance Ammunition Company
Hirtenberger AG
Hobson Precision Mfg. Co.
Hodgdon Powder Co.
Hornady Mfg. Co.
HT Bullets
Hunters Supply, Inc.
Huntington Die Specialties
Impact Case & Container, Inc.
Imperial Magnum Corp.
IMR Powder Co.
Intercontinental Distributors, Ltd.
J&D Components
J&L Superior Bullets
(See Huntington Die Special)
J.R. Williams Bullet Co.
Jamison International
Jensen Bullets
Jensen's Firearms Academy
Jericho Tool & Die Co., Inc.
Jester Bullets
JLK Bullets
JRP Custom Bullets
Ka Pu Kapili
Kaswer Custom, Inc.
Keith's Bullets
Keng's Firearms Specialty, Inc./US Tactical Systems
Ken's Kustom Kartridges
Knight Rifles
Knight Rifles
(See Modern Muzzle Loading, Inc.)
Lapua Ltd.
Lawrence Brand Shot
(See Precision Reloading)
Liberty Shooting Supplies
Lightning Performance Innovations, Inc.
Lindsley Arms Cartridge Co.
Littleton, J. F.
Lomont Precision Bullets
Lyman Products Corp.
Magnus Bullets
Maine Custom Bullets
Marchmon Bullets
Markesbery Muzzle Loaders, Inc.
MarMik, Inc.
Marshall Fish Mfg. Gunsmith Sptg. Co.
MAST Technology, Inc.
McMurdo, Lynn
(See Specialty Gunsmithing)
Meister Bullets (See Gander Mountain)
Men-Metallwerk Elisenhuette GmbH
Merkuria Ltd.
Midway Arms, Inc.
Mitchell Bullets, R.F.
MI-TE Bullets
Montana Precision Swaging
Mountain State Muzzleloading Supplies, Inc.
Mulhern, Rick
Murmur Corp.
Nagel's Custom Bullets
National Bullet Co.
Naval Ordnance Works
North American Shooting Systems
North Devon Firearms Services
Northern Precision
Nosler, Inc.
OK Weber, Inc.
Oklahoma Ammunition Co.
Old Wagon Bullets
Old Western Scrounger Ammunition Inc.
Oregon Trail Bullet Company
Pacific Rifle Co.
Page Custom Bullets
Pease Accuracy
Penn Bullets
Peterson Gun Shop, Inc., A.W.
Petro-Explo Inc.
Phillippi Custom Bullets, Justin
Pinetree Bullets
PMC/Eldorado Cartridge Corp.
Polywad, Inc.
Pony Express Reloaders
Power Plus Enterprises, Inc.
Precision Delta Corp.
Prescott Projectile Co.
Price Bullets, Patrick W.
PRL Bullets, c/o Blackburn Enterprises
Professional Hunter Supplies
(See Star Custom Bullets)
Proofmark Corp.
PWM Sales Ltd.
Quality Cartridge
Quarton Beamshot
R.I.S. Co., Inc.
Rainier Bmiscallistics
Ramon B. Gonzalez Guns
Ravell Ltd.
Redwood Bullet Works
Reloading Specialties, Inc.
Remington Arms Co., Inc.
Rhino
Robinson H.V. Bullets
Rubright Bullets
Russ Haydon's Shooters' Supply
SAECO (See Redding Reloading Equipment)
Scharch Mfg., Inc.-Top Brass
Schneider Bullets
Schroeder Bullets
Schumakers Gun Shop
Scot Powder
Seebeck Assoc., R.E.
Shappy Bullets
Sharps Arms Co., Inc., C.
Shilen, Inc.
Sierra Bullets
SOS Products Co.
(See Buck Stix-SOS Products Co.)
Southern Ammunition Co., Inc.
Specialty Gunsmithing
Speer Bullets
Spencer's Rifle Barrels, Inc.
SSK Industries
Stanley Bullets
Star Ammunition, Inc.
Star Custom Bullets
Starke Bullet Company
Starline, Inc.
Stewart's Gunsmithing
Swift Bullet Co.
T.F.C. S.p.A.
Taracorp Industries, Inc.
Tar-Hunt Custom Rifles, Inc.
TCCI
TCSR
The A.W. Peterson Gun Shop, Inc.
The Gun Works
The Ordnance Works
Thompson Bullet Lube Co.
Thompson Precision
TMI Products
(See Haselbauer Products, Jerry)
Traditions Performance Firearms
Trico Plastics
True Flight Bullet Co.
Tucson Mold, Inc.
USAC
Vann Custom Bullets
Vihtavuori Oy/Kaltron-Pettibone
Vincent's Shop
Viper Bullet and Brass Works
Walters Wads
Warren Muzzleloading Co., Inc.
Watson Bullets
Western Nevada West Coast Bullets
Widener's Reloading & Shooting Supply, Inc.
Winchester Div. Olin Corp.
Winkle Bullets
Woodleigh
(See Huntington Die Specialties)
Worthy Products, Inc.
Wyant Bullets
Wyoming Custom Bullets
Zero Ammunition Co., Inc.

AMMUNITION, COMMERCIAL

3-Ten Corp.
A.W. Peterson Gun Shop, Inc.
Ace Custom 45's, Inc.
Ad Hominem
Air Arms
American Ammunition
Arizona Ammunition, Inc.
Arms Corporation of the Philippines
Arundel Arms & Ammunition, Inc., A.
A-Square Co.
Atlantic Rose, Inc.
Badger Shooters Supply, Inc.
Ballistic Products, Inc.
Benjamin/Sheridan Co., Crosman
Big Bear Arms & Sporting Goods, Inc.
Black Hills Ammunition, Inc.
Blammo Ammo
Blount, Inc., Sporting Equipment Div.
Brenneke GmbH
Buffalo Arms Co.
Buffalo Bullet Co., Inc.
Bull-X, Inc.
Cabela's
Cambos Outdoorsman
Casull Arms Corp.
CBC
CCI/Speer Div of ATK
Champion's Choice, Inc.
Cor-Bon Inc./Glaser LLC
Crosman Airguns
Cubic Shot Shell Co., Inc.
Daisy Outdoor Products
Dead Eye's Sport Center
Delta Arms Ltd.
Delta Frangible Ammunition LLC
Dutchman's Firearms, Inc.
Dynamit Nobel-RWS, Inc.
Effebi SNC-Dr. Franco Beretta
Eley Ltd.
Elite Ammunition
Estate Cartridge, Inc.
Federal Cartridge Co.
Fiocchi of America, Inc.
Garcia National Gun Traders, Inc
Garrett Cartridges, Inc.
Garthwaite Pistolsmith, Inc., Jim
Gibbs Rifle Co., Inc.
Gil Hebard Guns, Inc.
Glaser LLC
Glaser Safety Slug, Inc.
GOEX, Inc.
Goodwin's Pawn Shop
Gun City
Guncrafter Industries
Hansen & Co.
Hart & Son, Inc.
Hi-Performance Ammunition Company
Hirtenberger AG
Hornady Mfg. Co.
Hunters Supply, Inc.
Intercontinental Distributors, Ltd.
Ion Industries, Inc.
Keng's Firearms Specialty, Inc./US Tactical Systems
Kent Cartridge America, Inc.
Knight Rifles
Lapua Ltd.
Lethal Force Institute
(See Police Bookshelf)
Lock's Philadelphia Gun Exchange
Lomont Precision Bullets
Magnum Research, Inc.
MagSafe Ammo Co.
Mandall Shooting Supplies Inc.
Markell, Inc.
Marshall Fish Mfg. Gunsmith Sptg.
McBros Rifle Co.
Men-Metallwerk Elisenhuette GmbH
Mullins Ammunition
New England Ammunition Co.
Oklahoma Ammunition Co.
Old Western Scrounger Ammunition Inc.
Outdoor Sports Headquarters, Inc.
P.S.M.G. Gun Co.
Paragon Sales & Services, Inc.
Parker & Sons Shooting Supply
Peterson Gun Shop, Inc., A.W.
PMC/Eldorado Cartridge Corp.
Police Bookshelf
Polywad, Inc.
Pony Express Reloaders
Precision Delta Corp.
Pro Load Ammunition, Inc.
Quality Cartridge
R.E.I.
Ravell Ltd.
Remington Arms Co., Inc.
Rucker Dist. Inc.
RWS (See U.S. Importer-Dynamit Nobel-RWS, Inc.)
Sellier & Bellot, USA, Inc.
Southern Ammunition Co., Inc.
Speer Bullets
TCCI
The A.W. Peterson Gun Shop, Inc.
The BulletMakers Workshop
The Gun Room Press
The Gun Works
Thompson Bullet Lube Co.
USAC
VAM Distribution Co. LLC

USA
ori Oy/Kaltron-Pettibone
Impact Targets
KGH GmbH
erby, Inc.
y Richards & Co. Ltd.
tone Lumber Corp.
er's Reloading & Shooting
ply, Inc.
n E. Phillips Firearms
ester Div. Olin Corp.
mmunition Co., Inc.

IUNITION, CUSTOM

Corp.
Peterson Gun Shop, Inc.
acy Unlimited
O Ammunition
Bullet Co.
can Derringer Corp.
can Products, Inc.
a Ammunition, Inc.
Corporation of the Philippines
tic Rose, Inc.
d Rifle & Cartridge Co., LLC
Arms
ng's Custom Gun Shop
er Bullets Ltd.
ore Bullets of Alaska
Hills Ammunition, Inc.
Mountain Bullets
n, Milton
skin Bullet Co.
alo Arms Co.

entures
nplin Firearms, Inc.
c Shot Shell Co., Inc.
om Tackle and Ammo
Unmussig Bullets
ota Arms, Inc.
d Eye's Sport Center
a Frangible Ammunition LLC
, Inc.
chman's Firearms, Inc.
Ammunition
ate Cartridge, Inc.
Enterprises
EX, Inc.
yback Wildcats
wk, Inc.
tenberger AG
oson Precision Mfg. Co.
izons Unlimited
rnady Mfg. Co.
nters Supply, Inc.
nsen Bullets
nsen's Custom Ammunition
nsen's Firearms Academy
swer Custom, Inc.
E. Jurras & Assoc.
A.R. Mfg., Inc.
thal Force Institute
(See Police Bookshelf)
ndsley Arms Cartridge Co.
nebaugh Custom Sixguns
ch Leven Industries/Convert-A-Pell
agSafe Ammo Co.
AST Technology, Inc.
cBros Rifle Co.
cMurdo, Lynn
(See Specialty Gunsmithing)
len-Metallwerk Elisenhuette GmbH
ilstor Corp.
ullins Ammunition
klahoma Ammunition Co.
.S.M.G. Gun Co.
eterson Gun Shop, Inc., A.W.
hillippi Custom Bullets, Justin
olice Bookshelf
ower Plus Enterprises, Inc.
recision Delta Corp.
Professional Hunter Supplies
(See Star Custom Bullets)
Quality Cartridge
R.E.I.
Ramon B. Gonzalez Guns
Sandia Die & Cartridge Co.
SOS Products Co.
(See Buck Stix-SOS Products Co.)
Specialty Gunsmithing
Spencer's Rifle Barrels, Inc.
SSK Industries
Star Custom Bullets
Stewart's Gunsmithing
TCCI
The A.W. Peterson Gun Shop, Inc.
The BulletMakers Workshop
The Country Armourer
Vitt/Boos
Vulpes Ventures, Inc., Fox Cartridge
Division
Warren Muzzleloading Co., Inc.
Watson Bullets
Worthy Products, Inc.
Zero Ammunition Co., Inc.

AMMUNITION, FOREIGN

A.W. Peterson Gun Shop, Inc.
Ad Hominem
AFSCO Ammunition
Armscorp USA, Inc.
Atlantic Rose, Inc.
B&P America
Cape Outfitters
CBC
Cheddite, France S.A.
Cubic Shot Shell Co., Inc.
Dead Eye's Sport Center
DKT, Inc.
Dynamit Nobel-RWS, Inc.
E. Arthur Brown Co.
Fiocchi of America, Inc.
Gamebore Division, Polywad, Inc.
Gibbs Rifle Co., Inc.
GOEX, Inc.
Goodwin's Pawn Shop
Gunsmithing, Inc.
Hansen & Co.
Heidenstrom Bullets
Hirtenberger AG
Hornady Mfg. Co.
I.S.S.
Intrac Arms International
Jack First, Inc.
K.B.I. Inc.
MagSafe Ammo Co.
Mandall Shooting Supplies Inc.
Marksman Products
MAST Technology, Inc.
Merkuria Ltd.
Mullins Ammunition
Navy Arms Company
Oklahoma Ammunition Co.
P.S.M.G. Gun Co.
Paragon Sales & Services, Inc.
Peterson Gun Shop, Inc., A.W.
Petro-Explo Inc.
Precision Delta Corp.
R.E.T. Enterprises
Ramon B. Gonzalez Guns
RWS (See U.S. Importer-Dynamit
Nobel-RWS, Inc.)
Samco Global Arms, Inc.
Sentinel Arms
Southern Ammunition Co., Inc.
Speer Bullets
Stratco, Inc.
T.F.C. S.p.A.
The A.W. Peterson Gun Shop, Inc.
The BulletMakers Workshop
The Paul Co.
Victory Ammunition
Vihtavuori Oy/Kaltron-Pettibone
Wolf Performance Ammunition

ANTIQUE ARMS DEALER

Ackerman & Co.
Ad Hominem
Antique American Firearms
Antique Arms Co.
Aplan Antiques & Art, James O.
Armoury, Inc., The
Arundel Arms & Ammunition, Inc., A.
Ballard Rifle & Cartridge Co., LLC
Bear Mountain Gun & Tool
Bob's Tactical Indoor Shooting Range
& Gun Shop
Buffalo Arms Co.
Cape Outfitters
Carlson, Douglas R, Antique American
Firearms
CBC-BRAZIL
Chadick's Ltd.
Chambers Flintlocks Ltd., Jim
Champlin Firearms, Inc.
Chuck's Gun Shop
Clements' Custom Leathercraft, Chas
Cole's Gun Works
D&D Gunsmiths, Ltd.
David R. Chicoine
Dixie Gun Works
Dixon Muzzleloading Shop, Inc.
Duffy, Charles E.
(See Guns Antique & Modern DBA)
Ed's Gun House
Enguix Import-Export
Fagan Arms
Flayderman & Co., Inc.
George Madis Winchester Consultants
Getz Barrel Company
Glass, Herb
Goergen's Gun Shop, Inc.
Golden Age Arms Co.
Goodwin's Pawn Shop
Gun Hunter Books
(See Gun Hunter Trading Co.)
Gun Hunter Trading Co.
Guns Antique & Modern DBA / Charles
E. Duffy
Hallowell & Co.
Hammans, Charles E.
HandCrafts Unltd.
(See Clements' Custom Leather)
Handgun Press
Hansen & Co.
Hunkeler, A.
(See Buckskin Machine Works)
Imperial Miniature Armory
James Wayne Firearms for Collectors
and Investors
Kelley's
Knight's Mfg. Co.
Ledbetter Airguns, Riley
LeFever Arms Co., Inc.
Lever Arms Service Ltd.
Lock's Philadelphia Gun Exchange
Log Cabin Sport Shop
Logdewood Mfg.
Mandall Shooting Supplies Inc.
Marshall Fish Mfg. Gunsmith Sptg. Co.
Martin's Gun Shop
Michael's Antiques
Mid-America Recreation, Inc.
Montana Outfitters, Lewis E. Yearout
Muzzleloaders Etcetera, Inc.
Navy Arms Company
New England Arms Co.
Olathe Gun Shop
P.S.M.G. Gun Co.
Peter Dyson & Son Ltd.
Pony Express Sport Shop
Powder Horn Ltd.
Ravell Ltd.
Reno, Wayne
Retting, Inc., Martin B.
Robert Valade Engraving
Rutgers Book Center
Samco Global Arms, Inc.
Sarco, Inc.
Scott Fine Guns Inc., Thad
Shootin' Shack
Sportsmen's Exchange & Western
Gun Traders, Inc.
Steves House of Guns
Stott's Creek Armory, Inc.
The Gun Room
The Gun Room Press
The Gun Works
Turnbull Restoration, Doug
Vic's Gun Refinishing
Wallace, Terry
Westley Richards & Co. Ltd.
Wild West Guns
Winchester Sutler, Inc., The
Wood, Frank (See Classic Guns, Inc.)
Yearout, Lewis E.
(See Montana Outfitters)

APPRAISER - GUNS, ETC.

A.W. Peterson Gun Shop, Inc.
Ackerman & Co.
Antique Arms Co.
Armoury, Inc., The
Arundel Arms & Ammunition, Inc., A.
Barta's Gunsmithing
Beitzinger, George
Blue Book Publications, Inc.
Bob's Tactical Indoor Shooting Range
& Gun Shop
Bonham's & Butterfields
Bullet N Press
Cape Outfitters
Chadick's Ltd.
Champlin Firearms, Inc.
Christie's East
Chuilli, Stephen
Clark Firearms Engraving
Clements' Custom Leathercraft, Chas
Cole's Gun Works
Colonial Arms, Inc.
Colonial Repair
Corry, John
Custom Tackle and Ammo
D&D Gunsmiths, Ltd.
David R. Chicoine
DGR Custom Rifles
Dietz Gun Shop & Range, Inc.
Dixie Gun Works
Dixon Muzzleloading Shop, Inc.
Duane's Gun Repair
(See DGR Custom Rifles)
Ed's Gun House
Eversull Co., Inc.
Fagan Arms
Ferris Firearms
Flayderman & Co., Inc.
Forty-Five Ranch Enterprises
Francotte & Cie S.A. Auguste
Frontier Arms Co., Inc.
Gene's Custom Guns
George Madis Winchester Consultants
Getz Barrel Company
Gillmann, Edwin
Goergen's Gun Shop, Inc.
Golden Age Arms Co.
Goodwin's Pawn Shop
Griffin & Howe, Inc.
Griffin & Howe, Inc.
Griffin & Howe, Inc.
Groenewold, John
Gun City
Gun Hunter Books
(See Gun Hunter Trading Co.)
Gun Hunter Trading Co.
Guncraft Books
(See Guncraft Sports, Inc.)
Guncraft Sports, Inc.
Guncraft Sports, Inc.
Gunsmithing, Inc.
Hallowell & Co.
Hammans, Charles E.
HandCrafts Unltd.
(See Clements' Custom Leather)
Handgun Press
Hank's Gun Shop
Hansen & Co.
Irwin, Campbell H.
Island Pond Gun Shop
Ithaca Classic Doubles
Jackalope Gun Shop
James Wayne Firearms for Collectors
and Investors
Jensen's Custom Ammunition
Kelley's
L.L. Bean, Inc.
Lampert, Ron
LaRocca Gun Works
Ledbetter Airguns, Riley
LeFever Arms Co., Inc.
Lock's Philadelphia Gun Exchange
Log Cabin Sport Shop
Logdewood Mfg.
Long, George F.
Mahony, Philip Bruce
Mandall Shooting Supplies Inc.
Marshall Fish Mfg. Gunsmith Sptg. Co.
Martin's Gun Shop
Mathews Gun Shop & Gunsmithing,
Inc.
McCann Industries
Mercer Custom Guns
Montana Outfitters, Lewis E. Yearout
Muzzleloaders Etcetera, Inc.
Navy Arms Company
New England Arms Co.
Nitex Gun Shop
Olathe Gun Shop
P&M Sales & Services, LLC
P.S.M.G. Gun Co.
Pasadena Gun Center
Pentheny de Pentheny
Perazone-Gunsmith, Brian
Peterson Gun Shop, Inc., A.W.
Pettinger Books, Gerald
Pony Express Sport Shop
Powder Horn Ltd.
R.A. Wells Custom Gunsmith
R.E.T. Enterprises
Ramon B. Gonzalez Guns
Retting, Inc., Martin B.
Robert Valade Engraving
Rutgers Book Center
Scott Fine Guns Inc., Thad
Shootin' Shack
Spencer Reblue Service
Sportsmen's Exchange & Western
Gun Traders, Inc.
Steven Dodd Hughes
Stott's Creek Armory, Inc.
Stratco, Inc.
Ten-Ring Precision, Inc.
The A.W. Peterson Gun Shop, Inc.
The Gun Room Press
The Gun Shop
The Gun Works
The Orvis Co.
The Swampfire Shop
(See Peterson Gun Shop, Inc.)
Thurston Sports, Inc.
Vic's Gun Refinishing
Walker Arms Co., Inc.
Wallace, Terry
Wasmundt, Jim
Weber & Markin Custom Gunsmiths
Werth, T. W.
Whildin & Sons Ltd, E.H.
Whitestone Lumber Corp.
Wild West Guns
Williams Shootin' Iron Service, The
Lynx-Line
Winchester Sutler, Inc., The

Wood, Frank (See Classic Guns, Inc.)
Yearout, Lewis E.
(See Montana Outfitters)

AUCTIONEER - GUNS, ETC.

"Little John's" Antique Arms
Bonham's & Butterfields
Buck Stix-SOS Products Co.
Christie's East
Fagan Arms
Pete de Coux Auction House
Sotheby's

BOOKS & MANUALS (PUBLISHERS & DEALERS)

"Su-Press-On", Inc.
Alpha 1 Drop Zone
American Handgunner Magazine
Armory Publications
Arms & Armour Press
Ballistic Products, Inc.
Ballistic Products, Inc.
Barnes Bullets, Inc.
Bauska Barrels
Beartooth Bullets
Beeman Precision Airguns
Blacksmith Corp.
Blacktail Mountain Books
Blue Book Publications, Inc.
Blue Ridge Machinery & Tools, Inc.
Boone's Custom Ivory Grips, Inc.
Brown Co., E. Arthur
Brownells, Inc.
Bullet N Press
C. Sharps Arms Co. Inc./Montana Armory
Cape Outfitters
Cheyenne Pioneer Products
Collector's Armoury, Ltd.
Colonial Repair
Corbin Mfg. & Supply, Inc.
DBI Books Division of Krause Publications
deHaas Barrels
Dixon Muzzleloading Shop, Inc.
Excalibur Publications
Executive Protection Institute
Fulton Armory
Galati International
GAR
Golden Age Arms Co.
Gun City
Gun Hunter Books
(See Gun Hunter Trading Co.)
Gun Hunter Trading Co.
Gun List (See Krause Publications)
Guncraft Books
(See Guncraft Sports, Inc.)
Guncraft Sports, Inc.
Gunnerman Books
GUNS Magazine
Gunsmithing, Inc.
H&P Publishing
Handgun Press
Harris Publications
Hawk Laboratories, Inc.
(See Hawk, Inc.)
Hawk, Inc.
Heritage/VSP Gun Books
Hodgdon Powder Co.
Home Shop Machinist, The Village Press Publications
Hornady Mfg. Co.
Huntington Die Specialties
I.D.S.A. Books
Info-Arm
Ironside International Publishers, Inc.
Jantz Supply
Kelley's
King & Co.
Koval Knives
Krause Publications, Inc.
L.B.T.
Lapua Ltd.
Lebeau-Courally
Lethal Force Institute
(See Police Bookshelf)
Lyman Products Corp.
Madis Books
Magma Engineering Co.
Mandall Shooting Supplies Inc.
MarMik, Inc.
Marshall Fish Mfg. Gunsmith Sptg. Co.
Montana Armory, Inc.
(See C. Sharps Arms Co. Inc.)
Montana Precision Swaging
Mountain State Muzzleloading Supplies, Inc.
Mulberry House Publishing
Navy Arms Company
Numrich Gun Parts Corporation
OK Weber, Inc.
Outdoor Sports Headquarters, Inc.
Paintball Games International Magazine Aceville
Pansch, Robert F
Pejsa Ballistics
Pettinger Books, Gerald
PFRB Co.
Police Bookshelf
Precision Reloading, Inc.
Precision Shooting, Inc.
Primedia Publishing Co.
Professional Hunter Supplies
(See Star Custom Bullets)
Ravell Ltd.
Ray Riling Arms Books Co.
Remington Double Shotguns
Russ Haydon's Shooters' Supply
Rutgers Book Center
S&S Firearms
Safari Press, Inc.
Saunders Gun & Machine Shop
Scharch Mfg., Inc.-Top Brass
Scharch Mfg., Inc.-Top Brass
Semmer, Charles
(See Remington Double Shotguns)
Sharps Arms Co., Inc., C.
Shotgun Sports Magazine, dba Shootin' Accessories Ltd.
Sierra Bullets
Speer Bullets
SPG LLC
Stackpole Books
Star Custom Bullets
Stewart Game Calls, Inc., Johnny
Stoeger Industries
Stoeger Publishing Co.
(See Stoeger Industries)
Swift Bullet Co.
The A.W. Peterson Gun Shop, Inc.
The Gun Room Press
The Gun Works
The NgraveR Co.
Thomas, Charles C.
Track of the Wolf, Inc.
Trafalgar Square
Trotman, Ken
Tru-Balance Knife Co.
Vega Tool Co.
Vintage Industries, Inc.
VSP Publishers
(See Heritage/VSP Gun Books)
W.E. Brownell Checkering Tools
WAMCO-New Mexico
Wells Creek Knife & Gun Works
Wilderness Sound Products Ltd.
Williams Gun Sight Co.
Wolfe Publishing Co.
Wolf's Western Traders

BULLET CASTING, ACCESSORIES

Ballisti-Cast, Inc.
Buffalo Arms Co.
Bullet Metals
Cast Performance Bullet Company
CFVentures
Cooper-Woodward Perfect Lube
Davide Pedersoli and Co.
Ferguson, Bill
Huntington Die Specialties
Lee Precision, Inc.
Lithi Bee Bullet Lube
Lyman Products Corp.
MA Systems, Inc.
Magma Engineering Co.
Ox-Yoke Originals, Inc.
Rapine Bullet Mould Mfg. Co.
SPG LLC
The A.W. Peterson Gun Shop, Inc.
The Hanned Line
United States Products Co.

BULLET CASTING, FURNACES & POTS

Ballisti-Cast, Inc.
Buffalo Arms Co.
Bullet Metals
Ferguson, Bill
GAR
Lee Precision, Inc.
Lyman Products Corp.
Magma Engineering Co.
Rapine Bullet Mould Mfg. Co.
RCBS/ATK
The A.W. Peterson Gun Shop, Inc.
The Gun Works
Thompson Bullet Lube Co.

BULLET CASTING, LEAD

Action Bullets & Alloy Inc.
Ames Metal Products
Buckskin Bullet Co.
Buffalo Arms Co.
Bullet Metals
Hunters Supply, Inc.
Jericho Tool & Die Co., Inc.
Lee Precision, Inc.
Lithi Bee Bullet Lube
Magma Engineering Co.
Montana Precision Swaging
Ox-Yoke Originals, Inc.
Penn Bullets
Proofmark Corp.
SPG LLC
Splitfire Sporting Goods, L.L.C.
The A.W. Peterson Gun Shop, Inc.
The Gun Works
Walters Wads

BULLET PULLERS

Battenfeld Technologies Inc.
Davide Pedersoli and Co.
Hollywood Engineering
Huntington Die Specialties
Royal Arms Gunstocks
The A.W. Peterson Gun Shop, Inc.
The Gun Works

BULLET TOOLS

Brynin, Milton
Camdex, Inc.
Corbin Mfg. & Supply, Inc.
Cumberland Arms
Eagan, Donald V.
Holland's Gunsmithing
Hollywood Engineering
Lee Precision, Inc.
Niemi Engineering, W. B.
North Devon Firearms Services
Rorschach Precision Products
Sport Flite Manufacturing Co.
The A.W. Peterson Gun Shop, Inc.
The Hanned Line
WTA Manufacturing

BULLET, CASE & DIE LUBRICANTS

Beartooth Bullets
Bonanza (See Forster Products)
Brown Co., E. Arthur
Buckskin Bullet Co.
Buffalo Arms Co.
Camp-Cap Products
CFVentures
Cooper-Woodward Perfect Lube
CVA
E-Z-Way Systems
Ferguson, Bill
Forster Products
GAR
Guardsman Products
Heidenstrom Bullets
Hollywood Engineering
Hornady Mfg. Co.
Imperial (See E-Z-Way Systems)
Knoell, Doug
L.B.T.
Le Clear Industries
(See E-Z-Way Systems)
Lee Precision, Inc.
Lithi Bee Bullet Lube
MI-TE Bullets
Paco's (See Small Custom Mould & Bullet Co.)
RCBS Operations/ATK
Reardon Products
Rooster Laboratories
Shay's Gunsmithing
Small Custom Mould & Bullet Co.
Tamarack Products, Inc.
The Hanned Line
Uncle Mike's
(See Michaels of Oregon Co.)
Warren Muzzleloading Co., Inc.
Widener's Reloading & Shooting Supply, Inc.
Young Country Arms

CARTRIDGES FOR COLLECTORS

Ackerman & Co.
Ad Hominem
Armory Publications
Cameron's
Campbell, Dick
Cherry Creek State Park Shooting Center
Cole's Gun Works
Colonial Repair
Cubic Shot Shell Co., Inc.
Duane's Gun Repair
(See DGR Custom Rifles)
Ed's Gun House
Ed's Gun House
Enguix Import-Export
Forty-Five Ranch Enterprises
George Madis Winchester Consultants
Goergen's Gun Shop, Inc.
Goodwin's Pawn Shop
Grayback Wildcats
Gun City
Gun Hunter Books
(See Gun Hunter Trading Co.)
Gun Hunter Trading Co.
Jack First, Inc.
Kelley's
Liberty Shooting Supplies
Mandall Shooting Supplies Inc.
MAST Technology, Inc.
Michael's Antiques
Montana Outfitters, Lewis E. Ye
Numrich Gun Parts Corporation
Pasadena Gun Center
Pete de Coux Auction House
Samco Global Arms, Inc.
SOS Products Co.
(See Buck Stix-SOS Products
Stone Enterprises Ltd.
The Country Armourer
The Gun Room Press
Ward & Van Valkenburg
Yearout, Lewis E.
(See Montana Outfitters)

CASE & AMMUNITION PROCESSORS, INSPECTORS, BOXER

Ammo Load, Inc.
Hafner World Wide, Inc.
Scharch Mfg., Inc.-Top Brass
The A.W. Peterson Gun Shop, Inc

CASE CLEANERS & POLISHING MEDIA

Battenfeld Technologies Inc.
Buffalo Arms Co.
G96 Products Co., Inc.
Huntington Die Specialties
Lee Precision, Inc.
Penn Bullets
The A.W. Peterson Gun Shop, Inc.
The Gun Works
Tru-Square Metal Products, Inc.
VibraShine, Inc.

CASE PREPARATION TOOLS

Battenfeld Technologies Inc.
High Precision
Hoehn Sales, Inc.
Huntington Die Specialties
J. Dewey Mfg. Co., Inc.
K&M Services
Lee Precision, Inc.
Match Prep-Doyle Gracey
Plum City Ballistic Range
PWM Sales Ltd.
RCBS Operations/ATK
Russ Haydon's Shooters' Supply
Sinclair International, Inc.
Stoney Point Products, Inc.
The A.W. Peterson Gun Shop, Inc.

CASE TRIMMERS, TRIM DIES & ACCESSORIES

Buffalo Arms Co.
Creedmoor Sports, Inc.
Fremont Tool Works
Goodwin's Pawn Shop
Hollywood Engineering
K&M Services
Lyman Products Corp.
Match Prep-Doyle Gracey
OK Weber, Inc.
Ozark Gun Works
PWM Sales Ltd.
RCBS/ATK
Redding Reloading Equipment
The A.W. Peterson Gun Shop, Inc.

E TUMBLERS, ATORS, MEDIA & ESSORIES

stom Die Co.
eld Technologies Inc.
Mfg., Inc.
Precision Products, Inc.
in's Pawn Shop
ullets
h Div. of Lyman Products Corp.
W. Peterson Gun Shop, Inc.
uare Metal Products, Inc.
hine, Inc.

ES, CABINETS, CKS & SAFES - GUN

e Products, Inc.
Co., Inc.
a Sport by Dee Zee
can Display Co.
can Security Products Co.
case
wel Enterprises Ltd.
aster Mfg., Inc.
mundi Corp.
's Mfg., Inc.
pring Enterprises "Bore Stores"
Studios
Sheep Brand
er Bros.
ning Arms Co.
master Hunting & Fishing
on Safe, Inc.
munk (See Oregon Arms, Inc.)
ecticut Shotgun Mfg. Co.
Industries (See D.J. Marketing)
Marketing
-Nes, Inc.
ee Nesci Enterprises, Inc.)
eeka Exports Pvt. Ltd.
ocil Mfg. Co., Inc.
International, Inc.
Co., Inc.
ish, Inc., A.G.
anced Presentations, Inc.
rsull Co., Inc.
nbeau, Inc.
Knox Security Products
edom Arms, Inc.
ntier Safe Co.
ati International
CO International Ltd.
n-Ho Sports Cases
Plastics, Inc., John
stings
mak
ppe's Div. Penguin Industries, Inc.
nter Co., Inc.
drosorbent Products
pact Case & Container, Inc.
nanssons Vapentillbehor, Bert
nnston Bros. (See C&T Corp. TA
Johnson Brothers)
lispel Case Line
Air International
(See Impact Case & Container Co.)
ock on Wood Antiques
lpin Outdoors, Inc.
kewood Products LLC
berty Safe
andall Shooting Supplies Inc.
arsh, Mike
cWelco Products
orton Booth Co.
PC
TM Molded Products Co., Inc.
alpak
ecessary Concepts, Inc.
esci Enterprises Inc.
regon Arms, Inc.
(See Rogue Rifle Co., Inc.)
Outa-Site Gun Carriers
Pflumm Mfg. Co.
Poburka, Philip (See Bison Studios)
Powell & Son (Gunmakers) Ltd., William
Prototech Industries, Inc.
Rogue Rifle Co., Inc.
Schulz Industries
Silhouette Leathers
Southern Security
Sportsman's Communicators
Sun Welding Safe Co.
Sweet Home, Inc.
The Outdoor Connection, Inc.
The Surecase Co.
Tinks & Ben Lee Hunting Products
(See Wellington)
Trulock Tool
Universal Sports
W. Waller & Son, Inc.
Whitestone Lumber Corp.
Wilson Case, Inc.
Woodstream
Zanotti Armor, Inc.
Ziegel Engineering

CHOKE DEVICES, RECOIL ABSORBERS & RECOIL PADS

3-Ten Corp.
Action Products, Inc.
Answer Products Co.
Arundel Arms & Ammunition, Inc., A.
Bansner's Ultimate Rifles, LLC
Bartlett Engineering
Battenfeld Technologies Inc.
Bob Allen Sportswear
Briley Mfg. Inc.
Brooks Tactical Systems-Agrip
Brownells, Inc.
B-Square Company, Inc.
Buffer Technologies
Bull Mountain Rifle Co.
C&H Research
Cation
Chicasaw Gun Works
Clearview Products
Colonial Arms, Inc.
Connecticut Shotgun Mfg. Co.
CRR, Inc./Marble's Inc.
Danuser Machine Co.
Dina Arms Corporation
Gentry Custom LLC
Goodwin's Pawn Shop
Graybill's Gun Shop
Gruning Precision, Inc.
Harry Lawson Co.
Hastings
Haydel's Game Calls, Inc.
Hogue Grips
Holland's Gunsmithing
I.N.C. Inc. (See Kickeez I.N.C., Inc.)
J.P. Enterprises Inc.
Jackalope Gun Shop
Jenkins Recoil Pads
KDF, Inc.
Kickeez I.N.C., Inc.
Lawson Co., Harry
London Guns Ltd.
Lyman Products Corp.
Mag-Na-Port International, Inc.
Mandall Shooting Supplies Inc.
Marble Arms
(See CRR, Inc./Marble's Inc.)
Menck, Gunsmith Inc., T.W.
Middlebrooks Custom Shop
Morrow, Bud
Nu-Line Guns,Inc.
One Of A Kind
Original Box, Inc.
P.S.M.G. Gun Co.
Palsa Outdoor Products
Parker & Sons Shooting Supply
Pro-Port Ltd.
Que Industries, Inc.
Shotguns Unlimited
Simmons Gun Repair, Inc.
Stan Baker Sports
Stone Enterprises Ltd.
The A.W. Peterson Gun Shop, Inc.
Time Precision
Truglo, Inc.
Trulock Tool
Uncle Mike's
(See Michaels of Oregon Co.)
Universal Sports
Virgin Valley Custom Guns
Williams Gun Sight Co.
Wilsom Combat
Wise Guns, Dale

CHRONOGRAPHS & PRESSURE TOOLS

Air Rifle Specialists
Brown Co., E. Arthur
C.W. Erickson's L.L.C.
Canons Delcour
Clearview Products
Competition Electronics, Inc.
Custom Chronograph, Inc.
D&H Precision Tooling
Hege Jagd-u. Sporthandels GmbH
Hutton Rifle Ranch
Mac-1 Airgun Distributors
Oehler Research, Inc.
P.A.C.T., Inc.
Romain's Custom Guns, Inc.
Savage Arms, Inc.
Stratco, Inc.
Tepeco

CLEANERS & DEGREASERS

Barnes Bullets, Inc.
Camp-Cap Products
Cubic Shot Shell Co., Inc.
G96 Products Co., Inc.
Goodwin's Pawn Shop
Hafner World Wide, Inc.
Half Moon Rifle Shop
Kleen-Bore, Inc.
LEM Gun Specialties, Inc. The Lewis Lead Remover
Modern Muzzleloading, Inc.
Northern Precision
Parker & Sons Shooting Supply
Parker Gun Finishes
PrOlixr Lubricants
R&S Industries Corp.
Ramon B. Gonzalez Guns
Rusteprufe Laboratories
Sheffield Knifemakers Supply, Inc.
Shooter's Choice Gun Care
Sierra Specialty Prod. Co.
Spencer's Rifle Barrels, Inc.
The A.W. Peterson Gun Shop, Inc.
The Gun Works
United States Products Co.

CLEANING & REFINISHING SUPPLIES

AC Dyna-tite Corp.
Alpha 1 Drop Zone
American Gas & Chemical Co., Ltd
Answer Products Co.
Armite Laboratories
Atlantic Mills, Inc.
Atsko/Sno-Seal, Inc.
Barnes Bullets, Inc.
Battenfeld Technologies Inc.
Beeman Precision Airguns
Bill's Gun Repair
Birchwood Casey
Blount, Inc., Sporting Equipment Div.
Blount/Outers ATK
Blue and Gray Products Inc.
(See Ox-Yoke Originals)
Break-Free, Inc.
Bridgers Best
Brown Co., E. Arthur
Brownells, Inc.
C.S. Van Gorden & Son, Inc.
Cambos Outdoorsman
Cambos Outdoorsman
Camp-Cap Products
CCI/Speer Div of ATK
Connecticut Shotgun Mfg. Co.
Creedmoor Sports, Inc.
CRR, Inc./Marble's Inc.
Custom Products
(See Jones Custom Products)
Cylinder & Slide, Inc., William R. Laughridge
Dara-Nes, Inc.
(See Nesci Enterprises, Inc.)
Deepeeka Exports Pvt. Ltd.
Desert Mountain Mfg.
Du-Lite Corp.
Dykstra, Doug
E&L Mfg., Inc.
Effebi SNC-Dr. Franco Beretta
Ekol Leather Care
Faith Associates
Flitz International Ltd.
Fluoramics, Inc.
Frontier Products Co.
G96 Products Co., Inc.
Golden Age Arms Co.
Guardsman Products
Gunsmithing, Inc.
Hafner World Wide, Inc.
Half Moon Rifle Shop
Hammans, Charles E.
Heatbath Corp.
Hoppe's Div. Penguin Industries, Inc.
Hornady Mfg. Co.
Hydrosorbent Products
Iosso Products
J. Dewey Mfg. Co., Inc.
Jantz Supply
Jantz Supply
Johnston Bros. (See C&T Corp. TA Johnson Brothers)
Jonad Corp.
K&M Industries, Inc.
Kellogg's Professional Products
Kesselring Gun Shop
Kleen-Bore, Inc.
Knight Rifles
Laurel Mountain Forge
Lee Supplies, Mark
LEM Gun Specialties, Inc. The Lewis Lead Remover
List Precision Engineering
LPS Laboratories, Inc.
Lyman Products Corp.
Mac-1 Airgun Distributors
Mandall Shooting Supplies Inc.
Marble Arms
(See CRR, Inc./Marble's Inc.)
Mark Lee Supplies
Micro Sight Co.
Minute Man High Tech Industries
Mountain State Muzzleloading Supplies, Inc.
MTM Molded Products Co., Inc.
Muscle Products Corp.
Nesci Enterprises Inc.
Northern Precision
October Country Muzzleloading
Old World Oil Products
Otis Technology, Inc.
Outers Laboratories Div. of ATK
Ox-Yoke Originals, Inc.
Parker & Sons Shooting Supply
Parker Gun Finishes
Pendleton Royal, c/o Swingler Buckland Ltd.
Pete Rickard, Inc.
Peter Dyson & Son Ltd.
Precision Airgun Sales, Inc.
Precision Reloading, Inc.
PrOlixr Lubricants
Pro-Shot Products, Inc.
R&S Industries Corp.
Radiator Specialty Co.
Rooster Laboratories
Russ Haydon's Shooters' Supply
Rusteprufe Laboratories
Rusty Duck Premium Gun Care Products
Saunders Gun & Machine Shop
Schumakers Gun Shop
Sheffield Knifemakers Supply, Inc.
Shooter's Choice Gun Care
Shotgun Sports Magazine, dba Shootin' Accessories Ltd.
Silencio/Safety Direct
Sinclair International, Inc.
Sno-Seal, Inc.
(See Atsko/Sno-Seal, Inc.)
Southern Bloomer Mfg. Co.
Splitfire Sporting Goods, L.L.C.
Starr Trading Co., Jedediah
Stoney Point Products, Inc.
Svon Corp.
T.F.C. S.p.A.
TDP Industries, Inc.
Tennessee Valley Mfg.
Tetra Gun Care
Texas Platers Supply Co.
The A.W. Peterson Gun Shop, Inc.
The Lewis Lead Remover
(See LEM Gun Specialties)
The Paul Co.
Track of the Wolf, Inc.
United States Products Co.
Van Gorden & Son Inc., C. S.
Venco Industries, Inc.
(See Shooter's Choice Gun Care)
VibraShine, Inc.
Volquartsen Custom Ltd.
Warren Muzzleloading Co., Inc.
Watson Bullets
WD-40 Co.
Wick, David E.
Willow Bend
Wolf's Western Traders
Young Country Arms

COMPUTER SOFTWARE - BALLISTICS

Action Target, Inc.
AmBr Software Group Ltd.
Arms Software
Arms, Programming Solutions
(See Arms Software)
Barnes Bullets, Inc.
Canons Delcour
Corbin Mfg. & Supply, Inc.
Data Tech Software Systems
Hodgdon Powder Co.
J.I.T. Ltd.
Jensen Bullets
Oehler Research, Inc.
Outdoor Sports Headquarters, Inc.
P.A.C.T., Inc.
Pejsa Ballistics
Powley Computer
(See Hutton Rifle Ranch)
RCBS Operations/ATK
Sierra Bullets
The Ballistic Program Co., Inc.
The Country Armourer
The Gun Works
Tioga Engineering Co., Inc.
W. Square Enterprises

Product & Service Directory

CUSTOM GUNSMITH

A&W Repair
A.A. Arms, Inc.
Acadian Ballistic Specialties
Accuracy Unlimited
Ace Custom 45's, Inc.
Acra-Bond Laminates
Adair Custom Shop, Bill
Ahlman Guns
Aldis Gunsmithing & Shooting Supply
Alpha Precision, Inc.
Alpine Indoor Shooting Range
Amrine's Gun Shop
Answer Products Co.
Antique Arms Co.
Armament Gunsmithing Co., Inc.
Arms Craft Gunsmithing
Armscorp USA, Inc.
Artistry in Wood
Art's Gun & Sport Shop, Inc.
Arundel Arms & Ammunition, Inc., A.
Autauga Arms, Inc.
Badger Creek Studio
Baelder, Harry
Bain & Davis, Inc.
Bansner's Ultimate Rifles, LLC
Barnes Bullets, Inc.
Baron Technology
Barrel & Gunworks
Barta's Gunsmithing
Bear Arms
Bear Mountain Gun & Tool
Behlert Precision, Inc.
Beitzinger, George
Belding's Custom Gun Shop
Bengtson Arms Co., L.
Bill Adair Custom Shop
Billings Gunsmiths
BlackStar AccuMax Barrels
BlackStar Barrel Accurizing
(See BlackStar AccuMax)
Bob Rogers Gunsmithing
Bond Custom Firearms
Borden Ridges Rimrock Stocks
Borovnik KG, Ludwig
Bowen Classic Arms Corp.
Brace, Larry D.
Briese Bullet Co., Inc.
Briganti, A.J.
Briley Mfg. Inc.
Broad Creek Rifle Works, Ltd.
Brockman's Custom Gunsmithing
Broken Gun Ranch
Brown Precision, Inc.
Brown Products, Inc., Ed
Buchsenmachermeister
Buckhorn Gun Works
Budin, Dave
Bull Mountain Rifle Co.
Bullberry Barrel Works, Ltd.
Burkhart Gunsmithing, Don
Cache La Poudre Rifleworks
Calhoon Mfg.
Cambos Outdoorsman
Cambos Outdoorsman
Campbell, Dick
Carolina Precision Rifles
Carter's Gun Shop
Caywood, Shane J.
CBC-BRAZIL
Chambers Flintlocks Ltd., Jim
Champlin Firearms, Inc.
Chicasaw Gun Works
Chuck's Gun Shop
Chuilli, Stephen
Clark Custom Guns, Inc.
Clark Firearms Engraving
Classic Arms Company
Classic Arms Corp.
Clearview Products
Cleland's Outdoor World, Inc
Coffin, Charles H.
Cogar's Gunsmithing
Cole's Gun Works
Colonial Arms, Inc.
Colonial Repair
Colorado Gunsmithing Academy
Colorado School of Trades
Colt's Mfg. Co., Inc.
Conrad, C. A.
Corkys Gun Clinic
Cullity Restoration
Custom Single Shot Rifles
D&D Gunsmiths, Ltd.
D.L. Unmussig Bullets
Dangler, Homer L.
D'Arcy Echols & Co.
Darlington Gun Works, Inc.
Dave's Gun Shop
David Miller Co.
David R. Chicoine
David W. Schwartz Custom Guns
Davis, Don
Delorge, Ed
Del-Sports, Inc.
DGR Custom Rifles
DGS, Inc., Dale A. Storey
Dietz Gun Shop & Range, Inc.
Dilliott Gunsmithing, Inc.
Don Klein Custom Guns
Donnelly, C. P.
Duane A. Hobbie Gunsmithing
Duane's Gun Repair
(See DGR Custom Rifles)
Duffy, Charles E.
(See Guns Antique & Modern DBA)
Duncan's Gun Works, Inc.
E. Arthur Brown Co.
Eckelman Gunsmithing
Ed Brown Products, Inc.
Eggleston, Jere D.
Entre`prise Arms, Inc.
Erhardt, Dennis
Eversull Co., Inc.
Evolution Gun Works, Inc.
FERLIB
Ferris Firearms
Fisher, Jerry A.
Fisher Custom Firearms
Fleming Firearms
Flynn's Custom Guns
Forkin Custom Classics
Forster, Kathy
(See Custom Checkering)
Forster, Larry L.
Forthofer's Gunsmithing & Knifemaking
Francotte & Cie S.A. Auguste
Fred F. Wells/Wells Sport Store
Frontier Arms Co., Inc.
Fullmer, Geo. M.
Fulton Armory
G.G. & G.
Galaxy Imports Ltd., Inc.
Garthwaite Pistolsmith, Inc., Jim
Gary Reeder Custom Guns
Gator Guns & Repair
Genecco Gun Works
Gene's Custom Guns
Gentry Custom LLC
George Hoenig, Inc.
Gillmann, Edwin
Gilmore Sports Concepts, Inc.
Giron, Robert E.
Goens, Dale W.
Gonic Arms/North American Arms, Inc.
Goodling's Gunsmithing
Goodwin's Pawn Shop
Grace, Charles E.
Grayback Wildcats
Graybill's Gun Shop
Green, Roger M.
Greg Gunsmithing Repair
Gre-Tan Rifles
Griffin & Howe, Inc.
Griffin & Howe, Inc.
Griffin & Howe, Inc.
Gruning Precision, Inc.
Guncraft Books
(See Guncraft Sports, Inc.)
Guncraft Sports, Inc.
Guncraft Sports, Inc.
Guns Antique & Modern DBA / Charles E. Duffy
Gunsite Training Center
Gunsmithing Ltd.
Hamilton, Alex B.
(See Ten-Ring Precision, Inc.)
Hammans, Charles E.
Hammerli Service-Precision Mac
Hammond Custom Guns Ltd.
Hank's Gun Shop
Hanson's Gun Center, Dick
Harry Lawson Co.
Hart & Son, Inc.
Hart Rifle Barrels, Inc.
Hartmann & Weiss GmbH
Harwood, Jack O.
Hawken Shop, The
(See Dayton Traister)
Hecht, Hubert J., Waffen-Hecht
Heilmann, Stephen
Heinie Specialty Products
Hensley, Gunmaker, Darwin
High Bridge Arms, Inc.
High Performance International
High Precision
High Standard Mfg. Co./F.I., Inc.
Highline Machine Co.
Hill, Loring F.
Hiptmayer, Armurier
Hiptmayer, Klaus
Hoag, James W.
Hodgson, Richard
Hoehn Sales, Inc.
Hofer Jagdwaffen, P.
Holland's Gunsmithing
Huebner, Corey O.
Hunkeler, A.
(See Buckskin Machine Works)
Imperial Magnum Corp.
Irwin, Campbell H.
Island Pond Gun Shop
Israel Arms Inc.
Ivanoff, Thomas G.
(See Tom's Gun Repair)
J&S Heat Treat
J.J. Roberts / Engraver
Jack Dever Co.
Jackalope Gun Shop
Jamison's Forge Works
Jarrett Rifles, Inc.
Jarvis, Inc.
Jay McCament Custom Gunmaker
Jeffredo Gunsight
Jensen's Custom Ammunition
Jim Norman Custom Gunstocks
Jim's Precision, Jim Ketchum
John Rigby & Co.
Jones Custom Products, Neil A.
Juenke, Vern
K. Eversull Co., Inc.
KDF, Inc.
Keith's Custom Gunstocks
Ken Eyster Heritage Gunsmiths, Inc.
Ken Starnes Gunmaker
Ketchum, Jim (See Jim's Precision)
Kilham & Co.
King's Gun Works
Kleinendorst, K. W.
KOGOT
Korzinek Riflesmith, J.
L. E. Jurras & Assoc.
LaFrance Specialties
Lampert, Ron
LaRocca Gun Works
Larry Lyons Gunworks
Lathrop's, Inc.
Laughridge, William R.
(See Cylinder & Slide Inc.)
Lawson Co., Harry
Lazzeroni Arms Co.
LeFever Arms Co., Inc.
Les Baer Custom, Inc.
Linebaugh Custom Sixguns
List Precision Engineering
Lock's Philadelphia Gun Exchange
Lone Star Rifle Company
Long, George F.
Mag-Na-Port International, Inc.
Mahony, Philip Bruce
Mahony, Philip Bruce
Mahovsky's Metalife
Makinson, Nicholas
Mandall Shooting Supplies Inc.
Marshall Fish Mfg. Gunsmith Sptg. Co.
Martin's Gun Shop
Martz, John V.
Mathews Gun Shop & Gunsmithing, Inc.
Mazur Restoration, Pete
McCann, Tom
McCluskey Precision Rifles
McGowen Rifle Barrels
McMillan Rifle Barrels
MCS, Inc.
Mercer Custom Guns
Michael's Antiques
Mid-America Recreation, Inc.
Middlebrooks Custom Shop
Miller Arms, Inc.
Miller Custom
Mills Jr., Hugh B.
Moeller, Steve
Monell Custom Guns
Morrison Custom Rifles, J. W.
Morrow, Bud
Mo's Competitor Supplies
(See MCS, Inc.)
Mowrey's Guns & Gunsmithing
Mullis Guncraft
Muzzleloaders Etcetera, Inc.
NCP Products, Inc.
Neil A. Jones Custom Products
Nelson's Custom Guns, Inc.
Nettestad Gun Works
New England Arms Co.
New England Custom Gun Service
Newman Gunshop
Nicholson Custom
Nickels, Paul R.
Nicklas, Ted
Nitex Gun Shop
North American Shooting Systems
Nu-Line Guns,Inc.
Old World Gunsmithing
Olson, Vic
Ottmar, Maurice
Ox-Yoke Originals, Inc.
Ozark Gun Works
P&M Sales & Services, LLC
P.S.M.G. Gun Co.
PAC-NOR Barreling
Pagel Gun Works, Inc.
Parker & Sons Shooting Supply
Parker Gun Finishes
Pasadena Gun Center
Paterson Gunsmithing
Paulsen Gunstocks
Peacemaker Specialists
PEM's Mfg. Co.
Pence Precision Barrels
Pennsylvania Gunsmith School
Penrod Precision
Pentheny de Pentheny
Perazone-Gunsmith, Brian
Performance Specialists
Pete Mazur Restoration
Peter Dyson & Son Ltd.
Peterson Gun Shop, Inc., A.W.
Piquette's Custom Engraving
Plum City Ballistic Range
Powell & Son (Gunmakers) Ltd. William
Power Custom, Inc.
Professional Hunter Supplies
(See Star Custom Bullets)
Quality Custom Firearms
R&J Gun Shop
R.A. Wells Custom Gunsmith
Ramon B. Gonzalez Guns
Ray's Gunsmith Shop
Renfrew Guns & Supplies
Ridgetop Sporting Goods
Ries, Chuck
RMS Custom Gunsmithing
Robert Valade Engraving
Robinson, Don
Rocky Mountain Arms, Inc.
Romain's Custom Guns, Inc.
Ron Frank Custom Classic Arms
Ruger's Custom Guns
Rupert's Gun Shop
Savage Arms, Inc.
Schiffman, Mike
Schumakers Gun Shop
Score High Gunsmithing
Sharp Shooter Supply
Shaw, Inc., E. R.
(See Small Arms Mfg. Co.)
Shay's Gunsmithing
Shockley, Harold H.
Shooters Supply
Shootin' Shack
Shooting Specialties
(See Titus, Daniel)
Shotguns Unlimited
Silver Ridge Gun Shop
(See Goodwin, Fred)
Simmons Gun Repair, Inc.
Singletary, Kent
Siskiyou Gun Works
(See Donnelly, C. P.)
Skeoch, Brian R.
Sklany's Machine Shop
Slezak, Jerome F.
Small Arms Mfg. Co.
Small Arms Specialists
Smith, Art
Snapp's Gunshop
Speiser, Fred D.
Spencer Reblue Service
Spencer's Rifle Barrels, Inc.
Splitfire Sporting Goods, L.L.C.
Sportsmen's Exchange & Western Gun Traders, Inc.
Springfield Armory
Springfield, Inc.
SSK Industries
Star Custom Bullets
Steelman's Gun Shop
Steffens, Ron
Steven Dodd Hughes
Stiles Custom Guns
Stott's Creek Armory, Inc.
Sturgeon Valley Sporters
Sullivan, David S.
(See Westwind Rifles, Inc.)
Swann, D. J.
Swenson's 45 Shop, A. D.
Swift River Gunworks
Szweda, Robert
(See RMS Custom Gunsmithing)
Taconic Firearms Ltd., Perry Lane
Tank's Rifle Shop
Tar-Hunt Custom Rifles, Inc.
Tarnhelm Supply Co., Inc.
Taylor & Robbins
Tennessee Valley Mfg.
Ten-Ring Precision, Inc.

PRODUCT & SERVICE DIRECTORY

. Kopp Professional
smithing
.W. Peterson Gun Shop, Inc.
mpetitive Pistol Shop
stom Shop
n Shop
ın Works
vis Co.
obar Co., Inc.
wampfire Shop
Peterson Gun Shop, Inc.)
Terry
ton Sports, Inc.
Precision
Gun Repair, Thomas G. Ivanoff
Gunshop
lion Gunstocks
ck Tool
r, James C.
ull Restoration, Doug
Missouri Trading Co.
lorn, Gil
atten, J. W.
Gunsmith Service
John
Gun Refinishing
Valley Custom Guns
ıartsen Custom Ltd.
er Arms Co., Inc.
ace, Terry
nundt, Jim
ne E. Schwartz Custom Guns
therby, Inc.
er & Markin Custom Gunsmiths
ms, Cecil
h, T. W.
singer Custom Guns & Engraving
tern Design
ee Alpha Gunsmith Division)
tley Richards & Co. Ltd.
twind Rifles, Inc., David S.
ullivan
te Barn Wor
te Rifles, Inc.
hita Arms, Inc.
be, Duane
d West Guns
iam E. Phillips Firearms
iams Gun Sight Co.
iams Shootin' Iron Service, The
ynx-Line
iamson Precision Gunsmithing
som Combat
nter, Robert M.
se Guns, Dale
seman and Co., Bill
od, Frank (See Classic Guns, Inc.)
orking Guns
ight's Gunstock Blanks
nkee Gunsmith "Just Glocks"
eryp, Russ

USTOM METALSMITH

&W Repair
ckerman & Co.
lman Guns
askan Silversmith, The
dis Gunsmithing & Shooting Supply
pha Precision, Inc.
nrine's Gun Shop
nswer Products Co.
ntique Arms Co.
tistry in Wood
aron Technology
arrel & Gunworks
ear Mountain Gun & Tool
ehlert Precision, Inc.
eitzinger, George
engtson Arms Co., L.
ill Adair Custom Shop
illings Gunsmiths
Billingsley & Brownell
Bob Rogers Gunsmithing
Bowen Classic Arms Corp.
Brace, Larry D.
Briganti, A.J.
Broad Creek Rifle Works, Ltd.
Brown Precision, Inc.
Buckhorn Gun Works
Bull Mountain Rifle Co.
Bullberry Barrel Works, Ltd.
Carter's Gun Shop
Caywood, Shane J.
Checkmate Refinishing
Cleland's Outdoor World, Inc
Colonial Repair
Colorado Gunsmithing Academy
Craftguard
Crandall Tool & Machine Co.
Cullity Restoration
Custom Single Shot Rifles
D&D Gunsmiths, Ltd.
D&H Precision Tooling
D'Arcy Echols & Co.
Dave's Gun Shop
Delorge, Ed
DGS, Inc., Dale A. Storey
Dietz Gun Shop & Range, Inc.
Dilliott Gunsmithing, Inc.
Don Klein Custom Guns
Duane's Gun Repair
(See DGR Custom Rifles)
Duncan's Gun Works, Inc.
Erhardt, Dennis
Eversull Co., Inc.
Ferris Firearms
Fisher, Jerry A.
Forster, Larry L.
Forthofer's Gunsmithing & Knifemaking
Fred F. Wells/Wells Sport Store
Fullmer, Geo. M.
Genecco Gun Works
Gentry Custom LLC
Grace, Charles E.
Grayback Wildcats
Graybill's Gun Shop
Green, Roger M.
Gunsmithing Ltd.
Hamilton, Alex B.
(See Ten-Ring Precision, Inc.)
Harry Lawson Co.
Hartmann & Weiss GmbH
Harwood, Jack O.
Hecht, Hubert J., Waffen-Hecht
Heilmann, Stephen
High Precision
Highline Machine Co.
Hiptmayer, Armurier
Hiptmayer, Klaus
Hoag, James W.
Holland's Gunsmithing
Island Pond Gun Shop
Ivanoff, Thomas G.
(See Tom's Gun Repair)
J J Roberts Firearm Engraver
J&S Heat Treat
J.J. Roberts / Engraver
Jamison's Forge Works
Jay McCament Custom Gunmaker
Jeffredo Gunsight
KDF, Inc.
Ken Eyster Heritage Gunsmiths, Inc.
Ken Starnes Gunmaker
Kilham & Co.
Kleinendorst, K. W.
Lampert, Ron
LaRocca Gun Works
Larry Lyons Gunworks
Lawson Co., Harry
Les Baer Custom, Inc.
List Precision Engineering
Lock's Philadelphia Gun Exchange
Mahovsky's Metalife
Makinson, Nicholas
Mandall Shooting Supplies Inc.
Mazur Restoration, Pete
McCann Industries
Mid-America Recreation, Inc.
Miller Arms, Inc.
Morrison Custom Rifles, J. W.
Morrow, Bud
Mullis Guncraft
Nelson's Custom Guns, Inc.
Nettestad Gun Works
New England Custom Gun Service
Nicholson Custom
Nitex Gun Shop
Noreen, Peter H.
Nu-Line Guns,Inc.
Olson, Vic
Ozark Gun Works
P.S.M.G. Gun Co.
Pagel Gun Works, Inc.
Parker & Sons Shooting Supply
Parker Gun Finishes
Pasadena Gun Center
Penrod Precision
Pete Mazur Restoration
Precision Specialties
Quality Custom Firearms
R.A. Wells Custom Gunsmith
Rice, Keith
(See White Rock Tool & Die)
Robert Valade Engraving
Robinson, Don
Rocky Mountain Arms, Inc.
Romain's Custom Guns, Inc.
Ron Frank Custom Classic Arms
Score High Gunsmithing
Simmons Gun Repair, Inc.
Singletary, Kent
Skeoch, Brian R.
Sklany's Machine Shop
Small Arms Specialists
Smith, Art
Smith, Sharmon
Snapp's Gunshop
Spencer Reblue Service
Spencer's Rifle Barrels, Inc.
Sportsmen's Exchange & Western Gun Traders, Inc.
SSK Industries
Steffens, Ron
Stiles Custom Guns
Taylor & Robbins
Ten-Ring Precision, Inc.
The A.W. Peterson Gun Shop, Inc.
The Custom Shop
The Gun Shop
The Robar Co., Inc.
Tom's Gun Repair, Thomas G. Ivanoff
Turnbull Restoration, Doug
Van Horn, Gil
Van Patten, J. W.
Vic's Gun Refinishing
Waldron, Herman
Wallace, Terry
Weber & Markin Custom Gunsmiths
Werth, T. W.
Wessinger Custom Guns & Engraving
White Rock Tool & Die
Wiebe, Duane
Wild West Guns
Williams Shootin' Iron Service, The Lynx-Line
Williamson Precision Gunsmithing
Winter, Robert M.
Wise Guns, Dale
Wood, Frank (See Classic Guns, Inc.)
Wright's Gunstock Blanks
Zufall, Joseph F.

DECOYS

Ad Hominem
Baekgaard Ltd.
Belding's Custom Gun Shop
Bill Russ Trading Post
Boyds' Gunstock Industries, Inc.
Carry-Lite, Inc.
Farm Form Decoys, Inc.
Feather, Flex Decoys
Flambeau, Inc.
G&H Decoys, Inc.
Grand Slam Hunting Products
Herter's Manufacturing Inc.
Klingler Woodcarving
Kolpin Outdoors, Inc.
L.L. Bean, Inc.
Molin Industries, Tru-Nord Division
Murphy, R.R. Co., Inc.
Original Deer Formula Co., The
Quack Decoy & Sporting Clays
Sports Innovations, Inc.
Tanglefree Industries
The A.W. Peterson Gun Shop, Inc.
Woods Wise Products

DIE ACCESSORIES, METALLIC

High Precision
King & Co.
MarMik, Inc.
Rapine Bullet Mould Mfg. Co.
Redding Reloading Equipment
Royal Arms Gunstocks
Sport Flite Manufacturing Co.
The A.W. Peterson Gun Shop, Inc.
Wolf's Western Traders

DIES, METALLIC

4-D Custom Die Co.
Badger Creek Studio
Buffalo Arms Co.
Competitor Corp., Inc.
Dakota Arms, Inc.
Dillon Precision Products, Inc.
Dixie Gun Works
Fremont Tool Works
Goodwin's Pawn Shop
Gruning Precision, Inc.
Jones Custom Products, Neil A.
King & Co.
Lee Precision, Inc.
Montana Precision Swaging
Neil A. Jones Custom Products
Ozark Gun Works
PWM Sales Ltd.
Rapine Bullet Mould Mfg. Co.
RCBS Operations/ATK
RCBS/ATK
Redding Reloading Equipment
Romain's Custom Guns, Inc.
Spencer's Rifle Barrels, Inc.
Sport Flite Manufacturing Co.
SSK Industries
The A.W. Peterson Gun Shop, Inc.
Vega Tool Co.
Wolf's Western Traders

DIES, SHOTSHELL

Goodwin's Pawn Shop
Hollywood Engineering
Lee Precision, Inc.
MEC, Inc.
The A.W. Peterson Gun Shop, Inc.

DIES, SWAGE

4-D Custom Die Co.
Bullet Swaging Supply, Inc.
Competitor Corp., Inc.
Corbin Mfg. & Supply, Inc.
D.L. Unmussig Bullets
Goodwin's Pawn Shop
Montana Precision Swaging
Sport Flite Manufacturing Co.
The A.W. Peterson Gun Shop, Inc.

ENGRAVER, ENGRAVING TOOLS

Ackerman & Co.
Adair Custom Shop, Bill
Ahlman Guns
Alaskan Silversmith, The
Alfano, Sam
Allard, Gary/Creek Side Metal & Woodcrafters
Allen Firearm Engraving
Altamont Co.
American Pioneer Video
Baron Technology
Barraclough, John K.
Bates Engraving, Billy
Bill Adair Custom Shop
Billy Bates Engraving
Boessler, Erich
Brooker, Dennis
Buchsenmachermeister
Churchill, Winston G.
Clark Firearms Engraving
Collings, Ronald
Creek Side Metal & Woodcrafters
Cullity Restoration
Cupp, Alana, Custom Engraver
Dayton Traister
Delorge, Ed
Dolbare, Elizabeth
Drain, Mark
Dremel Mfg. Co.
Dubber, Michael W.
Engraving Artistry
Engraving Only
Eversull Co., Inc.
Firearms Engraver's Guild of America
Forty-Five Ranch Enterprises
Fountain Products
Francotte & Cie S.A. Auguste
Frank Knives
Fred F. Wells/Wells Sport Store
Gary Reeder Custom Guns
Gene's Custom Guns
George Madis Winchester Consultants
Glimm's Custom Gun Engraving
Golden Age Arms Co.
Gournet Artistic Engraving
Grant, Howard V.
GRS / Glendo Corp.
Gurney, F. R.
Half Moon Rifle Shop
Harris Hand Engraving, Paul A.
Harwood, Jack O.
Hawken Shop, The
(See Dayton Traister)
Hiptmayer, Armurier
Hiptmayer, Heidemarie
Hofer Jagdwaffen, P.
Ingle, Ralph W.
J J Roberts Firearm Engraver
J.J. Roberts / Engraver
Jantz Supply
Jeff Flannery Engraving
Jim Blair Engraving
John J. Adams & Son Engravers
Kane, Edward
Kehr, Roger
Kelly, Lance
Ken Eyster Heritage Gunsmiths, Inc.
Kenneth W. Warren Engraver
Klingler Woodcarving
Larry Lyons Gunworks
LeFever Arms Co., Inc.
Leibowitz, Leonard
Lindsay Engraving & Tools
Little Trees Ramble
(See Scott Pilkington)
McCombs, Leo

PRODUCT & SERVICE DIRECTORY

McDonald, Dennis
McKenzie, Lynton
Mele, Frank
Mid-America Recreation, Inc.
Nelson, Gary K.
New Orleans Jewelers Supply Co.
Pedersen, C. R.
Pedersen, Rex C.
Peter Hale/Engraver
Pilgrim Pewter, Inc.
(See Bell Originals Inc. Sid)
Pilkington, Scott
(See Little Trees Ramble)
Piquette's Custom Engraving
Potts, Wayne E.
Quality Custom Firearms
Rabeno, Martin
Ralph Bone Engraving
Reed, Dave
Reno, Wayne
Riggs, Jim
Robert Evans Engraving
Robert Valade Engraving
Robinson, Don
Rohner, Hans
Rohner, John
Rosser, Bob
Rundell's Gun Shop
Sam Welch Gun Engraving
Sampson, Roger
Schiffman, Mike
Sheffield Knifemakers Supply, Inc.
Sherwood, George
Singletary, Kent
Smith, Mark A.
Smith, Ron
Smokey Valley Rifles
SSK Industries
Steve Kamyk Engraver
Swanson, Mark
The Gun Room
The NgraveR Co.
Theis, Terry
Thiewes, George W.
Thirion Gun Engraving, Denise
Viramontez Engraving
Vorhes, David
W.E. Brownell Checkering Tools
Wagoner, Vernon G.
Wallace, Terry
Warenski Engraving
Weber & Markin Custom Gunsmiths
Wells, Rachel
Wessinger Custom Guns & Engraving
Ziegel Engineering

GAME CALLS

African Import Co.
Bill Russ Trading Post
Bostick Wildlife Calls, Inc.
Cedar Hill Game Calls, Inc.
Crit'R Call (See Rocky Mountain Wildlife Products)
Custom Calls
D-Boone Ent., Inc.
Deepeeka Exports Pvt. Ltd.
Dr. O's Products Ltd.
Duck Call Specialists
Faulhaber Wildlocker
Faulk's Game Call Co., Inc.
Fibron Products, Inc.
Flambeau, Inc.
Glynn Scobey Duck & Goose Calls
Goodwin's Pawn Shop
Grand Slam Hunting Products
Green Head Game Call Co.
Hally Caller
Haydel's Game Calls, Inc.
Herter's Manufacturing Inc.
Hunter's Specialties Inc.
Keowee Game Calls
Kolpin Outdoors, Inc.
Lohman Mfg. Co., Inc.
Mallardtone Game Calls
Moss Double Tone, Inc.
Oakman Turkey Calls
Original Deer Formula Co., The
Outdoor Sports Headquarters, Inc.
Pete Rickard, Inc.
Philip S. Olt Co.
Primos Hunting Calls
Protektor Model
Quaker Boy, Inc.
Rocky Mountain Wildlife Products
Sceery Game Calls
Sports Innovations, Inc.
Stewart Game Calls, Inc., Johnny
Sure-Shot Game Calls, Inc.
Tanglefree Industries
The A.W. Peterson Gun Shop, Inc.
Tinks & Ben Lee Hunting Products
(See Wellington)
Tink's Safariland Hunting Corp.
Wellington Outdoors
Wilderness Sound Products Ltd.
Woods Wise Products
Wyant's Outdoor Products, Inc.

GAUGES, CALIPERS & MICROMETERS

Blue Ridge Machinery & Tools, Inc.
Goodwin's Pawn Shop
Gruning Precision, Inc.
Huntington Die Specialties
K&M Services
King & Co.
Peter Dyson & Son Ltd.
Spencer's Rifle Barrels, Inc.
Starrett Co., L. S.
Stoney Point Products, Inc.

GUN PARTS, U.S. & FOREIGN

"Su-Press-On", Inc.
A.A. Arms, Inc.
Ahlman Guns
Amherst Arms
Antique Arms Co.
Armscorp USA, Inc.
Auto-Ordnance Corp.
B.A.C.
Badger Shooters Supply, Inc.
Ballard Rifle & Cartridge Co., LLC
Bar-Sto Precision Machine
Bear Mountain Gun & Tool
Billings Gunsmiths
Bill's Gun Repair
Bob's Gun Shop
Briese Bullet Co., Inc.
Brown Products, Inc., Ed
Brownells, Inc.
Bryan & Assoc.
Buffer Technologies
Cambos Outdoorsman
Cambos Outdoorsman
Cape Outfitters
Caspian Arms, Ltd.
CBC-BRAZIL
Century International Arms, Inc.
Chicasaw Gun Works
Chip McCormick Corp.
Cole's Gun Works
Colonial Arms, Inc.
Colonial Repair
Colt's Mfg. Co., Inc.
Custom Riflestocks, Inc., Michael M. Kokolus
Cylinder & Slide, Inc., William R. Laughridge
Dan Wesson Firearms
David R. Chicoine
Delta Arms Ltd.
DGR Custom Rifles
Dibble, Derek A.
Dixie Gun Works
Duane's Gun Repair
(See DGR Custom Rifles)
Duffy, Charles E.
(See Guns Antique & Modern DBA)
E.A.A. Corp.
Elliott, Inc., G. W.
EMF Co., Inc.
Enguix Import-Export
Entre`prise Arms, Inc.
European American Armory Corp.
(See E.A.A. Corp.)
Evolution Gun Works, Inc.
Falcon Industries, Inc.
Federal Arms Corp. of America
Felk Pistols, Inc.
Fleming Firearms
Fulton Armory
Gentry Custom LLC
Glimm's Custom Gun Engraving
Goodwin's Pawn Shop
Granite Mountain Arms, Inc.
Greider Precision
Gre-Tan Rifles
Groenewold, John
Gun Hunter Books
(See Gun Hunter Trading Co.)
Gun Hunter Trading Co.
Guns Antique & Modern DBA / Charles E. Duffy
Gunsmithing, Inc.
Hastings
Hawken Shop, The
(See Dayton Traister)
High Performance International
High Standard Mfg. Co./F.I., Inc.
I.S.S.
Irwin, Campbell H.
Jack First, Inc.
Jamison's Forge Works
Jonathan Arthur Ciener, Inc.
Kimber of America, Inc.
Knight's Mfg. Co.
Krico Deutschland GmbH
LaFrance Specialties
Lampert, Ron
LaPrade
Laughridge, William R.
(See Cylinder & Slide Inc.)
Leapers, Inc.
List Precision Engineering
Lodewick, Walter H.
Logdewood Mfg.
Lomont Precision Bullets
Long, George F.
Mandall Shooting Supplies Inc.
Markell, Inc.
Martin's Gun Shop
MCS, Inc.
Merkuria Ltd.
Mid-America Recreation, Inc.
Morrow, Bud
Mo's Competitor Supplies
(See MCS, Inc.)
North Star West
Northwest Arms
Nu-Line Guns,Inc.
Numrich Gun Parts Corporation
Nygord Precision Products, Inc.
Olathe Gun Shop
Olympic Arms Inc.
P.S.M.G. Gun Co.
Pacific Armament Corp
Perazone-Gunsmith, Brian
Performance Specialists
Peter Dyson & Son Ltd.
Peterson Gun Shop, Inc., A.W.
Ranch Products
Randco UK
Ravell Ltd.
Retting, Inc., Martin B.
Romain's Custom Guns, Inc.
Ruger (See Sturm, Ruger & Co., Inc.)
Rutgers Book Center
S&S Firearms
Sabatti SPA
Samco Global Arms, Inc.
Sarco, Inc.
Scherer Supplies
Shockley, Harold H.
Shootin' Shack
Silver Ridge Gun Shop
(See Goodwin, Fred)
Simmons Gun Repair, Inc.
Smires, C. L.
Smith & Wesson
Southern Ammunition Co., Inc.
Sportsmen's Exchange & Western Gun Traders, Inc.
Springfield Sporters, Inc.
Springfield, Inc.
Steyr Mannlicher GmbH & Co KG
STI International
Strayer-Voigt, Inc.
Sturm Ruger & Co. Inc.
Sunny Hill Enterprises, Inc.
T&S Industries, Inc.
Tank's Rifle Shop
Tarnhelm Supply Co., Inc.
Terry K. Kopp Professional Gunsmithing
The A.W. Peterson Gun Shop, Inc.
The Gun Room Press
The Gun Shop
The Gun Works
The Southern Armory
The Swampfire Shop
(See Peterson Gun Shop, Inc.)
Tom Forrest, Inc.
VAM Distribution Co. LLC
Vektor USA
W. Waller & Son, Inc.
W.C. Wolff Co.
Walker Arms Co., Inc.
Wescombe, Bill (See North Star West)
Wild West Guns
Williams Mfg. of Oregon
Winchester Sutler, Inc., The
Wise Guns, Dale
Wisners, Inc.

GUNS & GUN PARTS, REPLICA & ANTIQUE

Ackerman & Co.
Ahlman Guns
Armi San Paolo
Auto-Ordnance Corp.
Ballard Rifle & Cartridge Co., LLC
Bear Mountain Gun & Tool
Billings Gunsmiths
Bob's Gun Shop
Buffalo Arms Co.
Cache La Poudre Rifleworks
Campbell, Dick
Cash Mfg. Co., Inc.
CBC-BRAZIL
CCL Security Products
Chambers Flintlocks Ltd., Jim
Chicasaw Gun Works
Cimarron F.A. Co.
Cogar's Gunsmithing
Cole's Gun Works
Colonial Repair
Colt Blackpowder Arms Co.
Colt's Mfg. Co., Inc.
Custom Riflestocks, Inc., Michael M. Kokolus
Custom Single Shot Rifles
David R. Chicoine
Delhi Gun House
Delta Arms Ltd.
Dilliott Gunsmithing, Inc.
Dixie Gun Works
Dixon Muzzleloading Shop, Inc.
Ed's Gun House
Euroarms of America, Inc.
Flintlocks, Etc.
Getz Barrel Company
Golden Age Arms Co.
Goodwin's Pawn Shop
Groenewold, John
Gun Hunter Books
(See Gun Hunter Trading Co.)
Gun Hunter Trading Co.
Hastings
Heidenstrom Bullets
Hunkeler, A.
(See Buckskin Machine Works)
IAR Inc.
Imperial Miniature Armory
Ithaca Classic Doubles
Jack First, Inc.
Ken Starnes Gunmaker
L&R Lock Co.
Leonard Day
List Precision Engineering
Lock's Philadelphia Gun Exchange
Logdewood Mfg.
Lone Star Rifle Company
Lucas, Edward E
Mandall Shooting Supplies Inc.
Martin's Gun Shop
Mathews Gun Shop & Gunsmithing, Inc.
Mid-America Recreation, Inc.
Mountain State Muzzleloading Supplies, Inc.
Mowrey Gun Works
Navy Arms Company
Neumann GmbH
North Star West
Nu-Line Guns,Inc.
Numrich Gun Parts Corporation
Olathe Gun Shop
Parker & Sons Shooting Supply
Pasadena Gun Center
Pecatonica River Longrifle
PEM's Mfg. Co.
Peter Dyson & Son Ltd.
Pony Express Sport Shop
R.A. Wells Custom Gunsmith
Randco UK
Ravell Ltd.
Retting, Inc., Martin B.
Rutgers Book Center
S&S Firearms
Samco Global Arms, Inc.
Sarco, Inc.
Shootin' Shack
Silver Ridge Gun Shop
(See Goodwin, Fred)
Simmons Gun Repair, Inc.
Sklany's Machine Shop
Southern Ammunition Co., Inc.
Starr Trading Co., Jedediah
Stott's Creek Armory, Inc.
Taylor's & Co., Inc.
Tennessee Valley Mfg.
The A.W. Peterson Gun Shop, Inc.
The Gun Room Press
The Gun Works
Tiger-Hunt Gunstocks
Turnbull Restoration, Doug
Upper Missouri Trading Co.
Vintage Industries, Inc.
VTI Gun Parts
Weber & Markin Custom Gunsmiths
Wescombe, Bill (See North Star West)
Whitestone Lumber Corp.
Winchester Sutler, Inc., The

GUNS, AIR

Air Arms
Air Rifle Specialists
Air Venture Airguns

PRODUCT & SERVICE DIRECTORY

e Airguns
Bullet Co.
orporation of the Philippines
c.
n Precision Airguns
in/Sheridan Co., Crosman
Eagle, Inc.
k Ltd.
& Assoc.
uns Ltd.
asseco, Ltd.
onent Concepts, Inc.
ol Scope Mounts
an Airguns
Outdoor Products
te Ltd.
o
it Nobel-RWS, Inc.
SNC-Dr. Franco Beretta
ean American Armory Corp.
E.A.A. Corp.)
erkbau Westinger & Altenburger
USA, Inc.
er Armes, S.A.
Lakes Airguns
ewold, John
erli Service-Precision Mac
c.
Anschutz GmbH & Co. KG
u, Inc.
ers, Inc.
Precision Engineering
1 Airgun Distributors
sman Products
land Paintball Supply
uria Ltd.
nwide Airgun Repair
rd Precision Products, Inc.
pic Arms Inc.
ini Armi Srl
sion Airgun Sales, Inc.
ision Sales International, Inc.
ey Rifles
nson, Don
S (See U.S. Importer-Dynamit
obel-RWS, Inc.)
ri Arms/Schuetzen Pistol Works
age Arms, Inc.
rt Parts
th & Wesson
r Mannlicher GmbH & Co KG
ne Enterprises Ltd.
A.W. Peterson Gun Shop, Inc.
Gun Room Press
Park Rifle Co., Ltd.
oman Pneumatics, Inc.
tar Sporting Arms, Ltd.
oper Walsh
raSport Arms, Inc.
ible Impact Targets
lther GmbH, Carl
bley and Scott Ltd.
ihrauch KG, Hermann
iscombe (See U.S. Importer-
Pelaire Products)

UNS, FOREIGN ANUFACTURER U.S. IPORTER

curacy Internationl Precision Rifles
(See U.S.)
curacy Int'l. North America, Inc.
Hominem
Arms
mas Garbi, S.A.
mas Kemen S. A.
(See U.S. Importers)
mi Perazzi S.P.A.
mi San Marco (See U.S. Importers-
Taylor's & Co.)
Armi Sport (See U.S. Importers-Cape
Outfitters)
Arms Corporation of the Philippines
Armscorp USA, Inc.
Arrieta S.L.
Astra Sport, S.A.
Atamec-Bretton
AYA (See U.S. Importer-New England
Custom Gun Serv)
B.A.C.
B.C. Outdoors
BEC, Inc.
Benelli Armi S.P.A.
Benelli USA Corp
Beretta S.P.A., Pietro
Beretta U.S.A. Corp.
Bernardelli, Vincenzo
Bersa S.A.
Bertuzzi (See U.S. Importer-New
England Arms Co)
Bill Hanus Birdguns
Blaser Jagdwaffen GmbH
Borovnik KG, Ludwig
Bosis (See U.S. Importer-New England
Arms Co.)
Brenneke GmbH
Browning Arms Co.
Bryan & Assoc.
BSA Guns Ltd.
Cabanas (See U.S. Importer-Mandall
Shooting Supply)
Cabela's
Cape Outfitters
CBC
Champlin Firearms, Inc.
Chapuis Armes
Churchill
(See U.S. Importer-Ellett Bros.)
Collector's Armoury, Ltd.
Conetrol Scope Mounts
Cosmi Americo & Figlio S.N.C.
Crucelegui, Hermanos (See U.S.
Importer-Mandall)
Cubic Shot Shell Co., Inc.
Dakota
(See U.S. Importer-EMF Co., Inc.)
Dakota Arms, Inc.
Daly, Charles/KBI
Davide Pedersoli and Co.
Domino
Dumoulin, Ernest
Eagle Imports, Inc.
EAW (See U.S. Importer-New England
Custom Gun Serv)
Ed's Gun House
Effebi SNC-Dr. Franco Beretta
EMF Co., Inc.
Eversull Co., Inc.
F.A.I.R.
Fabarm S.p.A.
FEG
Feinwerkbau Westinger & Altenburger
Felk Pistols, Inc.
FERLIB
Fiocchi Munizioni S.P.A.
(See U.S. Importer-Fiocch)
Firearms Co. Ltd. / Alpine
(See U.S. Importer-Mandall
Firearms International
Flintlocks, Etc.
Galaxy Imports Ltd., Inc.
Gamba S.p.A. Societa Armi Bresciane
Srl
Gamo (See U.S. Importers-Arms
United Corp, Daisy M)
Gaucher Armes, S.A.
Gibbs Rifle Co., Inc.
Glock GmbH
Goergen's Gun Shop, Inc.
Griffin & Howe, Inc.
Griffin & Howe, Inc.
Griffin & Howe, Inc.
Grulla Armes
Hammerli Ltd.
Hammerli USA
Hartford
(See U.S. Importer-EMF Co. Inc.)
Hartmann & Weiss GmbH
Heckler & Koch, Inc.
Hege Jagd-u. Sporthandels GmbH
Helwan (See U.S. Importer-Interarms)
Holland & Holland Ltd.
Howa Machinery, Ltd.
I.A.B. (See U.S. Importer-Taylor's &
Co. Inc.)
IAR Inc.
IGA (See U.S. Importer-Stoeger
Industries)
Imperial Magnum Corp.
Imperial Miniature Armory
Import Sports Inc.
Inter Ordnance of America LP
Intrac Arms International
J.G. Anschutz GmbH & Co. KG
JSL Ltd. (See U.S. Importer-Specialty
Shooters)
K. Eversull Co., Inc.
Kimar (See U.S. Importer-IAR,Inc)
Korth Germany GmbH
Krico Deutschland GmbH
Krieghoff Gun Co., H.
Lakefield Arms Ltd.
(See Savage Arms, Inc.)
Lapua Ltd.
Laurona Armas Eibar, S.A.L.
Lebeau-Courally
Lever Arms Service Ltd.
Llama Gabilondo Y Cia
Lomont Precision Bullets
London Guns Ltd.
Mandall Shooting Supplies Inc.
Marocchi F.lli S.p.A
Mauser Werke Oberndorf
Waffensysteme GmbH
McCann Industries
MEC-Gar S.R.L.
Merkel
Mitchell's Mauser
Morini (See U.S. Importers-Mandall
Shooting Supply)
New England Custom Gun Service
New SKB Arms Co.
Norica, Avnda Otaola
Norinco
Norma Precision AB
(See U.S. Importers-Dynamit)
Northwest Arms
Nygord Precision Products, Inc.
OK Weber, Inc.
Para-Ordnance Mfg., Inc.
Pardini Armi Srl
Perugini Visini & Co. S.r.l.
Peters Stahl GmbH
Pietta (See U.S. Importers-Navy Arms
Co, Taylor's)
Piotti (See U.S. Importer-Moore & Co.,
Wm. Larkin)
PMC/Eldorado Cartridge Corp.
Powell & Son (Gunmakers) Ltd.,
William
Prairie Gun Works
Ramon B. Gonzalez Guns
Rizzini F.lli (See U.S. Importers-Moore
& C England)
Rizzini SNC
Robinson Armament Co.
Rossi Firearms
Rottweil Compe
Rutten (See U.S. Importer-Labanu Inc)
RWS (See U.S. Importer-Dynamit
Nobel-RWS, Inc.)
S.A.R.L. G. Granger
S.I.A.C.E. (See U.S. Importer-IAR Inc)
Sabatti SPA
Sako Ltd (See U.S. Importer-Stoeger
Industries)
San Marco (See U.S. Importers-Cape
Outfitters-EMF)
Sarsilmaz Shotguns - Turkey
(See B.C. Outdoors)
Sauer (See U.S. Importers-Paul Co.,
The, Sigarms I)
Savage Arms (Canada), Inc.
SIG
Sigarms, Inc.
SIG-Sauer
(See U.S. Importer-Sigarms Inc.)
SKB Shotguns
Small Arms Specialists
Societa Armi Bresciane Srl (See U.S.
Importer-Cape)
Sphinx Systems Ltd.
Springfield Armory
Springfield, Inc.
Starr Trading Co., Jedediah
Steyr Mannlicher GmbH & Co KG
T.F.C. S.p.A.
Tanfoglio Fratelli S.r.l.
Tanner (See U.S. Importer-Mandall
Shooting Supply)
Taurus International Firearms
(See U.S. Importer)
Taurus S.A. Forjas
Taylor's & Co., Inc.
Techno Arms (See U.S. Importer-
Auto-Ordnance Corp
The A.W. Peterson Gun Shop, Inc.
Tikka (See U.S. Importer-Stoeger
Industries)
TOZ (See U.S. Importer-Nygord
Precision Products)
Ugartechea S. A., Ignacio
Ultralux (See U.S. Importer-Keng's
Firearms)
Unique/M.A.P.F.
Valtro USA, Inc.
Verney-Carron
Voere-KGH GmbH
Walther GmbH, Carl
Webley and Scott Ltd.
Weihrauch KG, Hermann
Westley Richards & Co. Ltd.
Whiscombe (See U.S. Importer-
Pelaire Products)
Wolf (See J.R. Distributing)
Yankee Gunsmith "Just Glocks"
Zabala Hermanos S.A.

GUNS, FOREIGN-IMPORTER

Accuracy International
AcuSport Corporation
Air Rifle Specialists
Auto-Ordnance Corp.
B.A.C.
B.C. Outdoors
Bell's Legendary Country Wear
Benelli USA Corp
Big Bear Arms & Sporting Goods, Inc.
Bill Hanus Birdguns
Bridgeman Products
British Sporting Arms
Browning Arms Co.
Cape Outfitters
Century International Arms, Inc.
Champion Shooters' Supply
Champion's Choice, Inc.
Chapuis USA
Cimarron F.A. Co.
CVA
CZ USA
Dixie Gun Works
Dynamit Nobel-RWS, Inc.
E&L Mfg., Inc.
E.A.A. Corp.
Eagle Imports, Inc.
Ellett Bros.
EMF Co., Inc.
Euroarms of America, Inc.
Eversull Co., Inc.
Fiocchi of America, Inc.
Flintlocks, Etc.
Franzen International, Inc.
(See U.S. Importer)
G.U., Inc. (See U.S. Importer for New
SKB Arms Co.)
Galaxy Imports Ltd., Inc.
Gamba, USA
Gamo USA, Inc.
Giacomo Sporting USA
Glock, Inc.
GSI, Inc.
Guncraft Books
(See Guncraft Sports, Inc.)
Guncraft Sports, Inc.
Gunsite Training Center
Hammerli USA
I.S.S.
IAR Inc.
Imperial Magnum Corp.
Imperial Miniature Armory
Import Sports Inc.
Intrac Arms International
K. Eversull Co., Inc.
K.B.I. Inc.
Kemen America
Keng's Firearms Specialty, Inc./US
Tactical Systems
Krieghoff International,Inc.
Labanu, Inc.
Legacy Sports International
Lion Country Supply
London Guns Ltd.
Magnum Research, Inc.
Marx, Harry
(See U.S. Importer for FERLIB)
MCS, Inc.
MEC-Gar U.S.A., Inc.
Mitchell Mfg. Corp.
Navy Arms Company
New England Arms Co.
Nu-Line Guns,Inc.
Nygord Precision Products, Inc.
OK Weber, Inc.
P.S.M.G. Gun Co.
Para-Ordnance, Inc.
Pelaire Products
Perazone-Gunsmith, Brian
Perazzi U.S.A. Inc.
Powell Agency, William
Precision Sales International, Inc.
Rocky Mountain Armoury
S.D. Meacham
Safari Arms/Schuetzen Pistol Works
Samco Global Arms, Inc.
Savage Arms, Inc.
Scott Fine Guns Inc., Thad
Sigarms, Inc.
SKB Shotguns
Small Arms Specialists
Southern Ammunition Co., Inc.
Specialty Shooters Supply, Inc.
Springfield, Inc.
Stoeger Industries
Stone Enterprises Ltd.
Swarovski Optik North America Ltd.
Taurus Firearms, Inc.
Taylor's & Co., Inc.
The A.W. Peterson Gun Shop, Inc.
The Gun Shop
The Orvis Co.
The Paul Co.
Track of the Wolf, Inc.
Traditions Performance Firearms
Tristar Sporting Arms, Ltd.
Trooper Walsh
U.S. Importer-Wm. Larkin Moore
VAM Distribution Co. LLC
Vektor USA
VTI Gun Parts

PRODUCT & SERVICE DIRECTORY

Westley Richards Agency USA
(See U.S. Importer)
Wingshooting Adventures

GUNS, SURPLUS, PARTS & AMMUNITION

Ahlman Guns
Alpha 1 Drop Zone
Armscorp USA, Inc.
Arundel Arms & Ammunition, Inc., A.
B.A.C.
Bob's Gun Shop
Cambos Outdoorsman
Century International Arms, Inc.
Cole's Gun Works
Conetrol Scope Mounts
Delta Arms Ltd.
Ed's Gun House
Fleming Firearms
Fulton Armory
Garcia National Gun Traders, Inc.
Goodwin's Pawn Shop
Gun City
Gun Hunter Books
(See Gun Hunter Trading Co.)
Gun Hunter Trading Co.
Hank's Gun Shop
Hege Jagd-u. Sporthandels GmbH
Jackalope Gun Shop
Ken Starnes Gunmaker
LaRocca Gun Works
Lever Arms Service Ltd.
Log Cabin Sport Shop
Martin's Gun Shop
Navy Arms Company
Nevada Pistol Academy, Inc.
Northwest Arms
Numrich Gun Parts Corporation
Oil Rod and Gun Shop
Olathe Gun Shop
Paragon Sales & Services, Inc.
Pasadena Gun Center
Power Plus Enterprises, Inc.
Ravell Ltd.
Retting, Inc., Martin B.
Rutgers Book Center
Samco Global Arms, Inc.
Sarco, Inc.
Shootin' Shack
Silver Ridge Gun Shop
(See Goodwin, Fred)
Simmons Gun Repair, Inc.
Sportsmen's Exchange & Western
Gun Traders, Inc.
Springfield Sporters, Inc.
T.F.C. S.p.A.
Tarnhelm Supply Co., Inc.
The A.W. Peterson Gun Shop, Inc.
The Gun Room Press
Thurston Sports, Inc.
Whitestone Lumber Corp.
Williams Shootin' Iron Service, The
Lynx-Line

GUNS, U.S. MADE

3-Ten Corp.
A.A. Arms, Inc.
Accu-Tek
Ace Custom 45's, Inc.
Acra-Bond Laminates
Ad Hominem
Airrow
Allred Bullet Co.
American Derringer Corp.
AR-7 Industries, LLC
ArmaLite, Inc.
Armscorp USA, Inc.
Arundel Arms & Ammunition, Inc., A.
A-Square Co.
Austin & Halleck, Inc.
Autauga Arms, Inc.
Auto-Ordnance Corp.
Ballard Rifle & Cartridge Co., LLC
Barrett Firearms Manufacturer, Inc.
Bar-Sto Precision Machine
Benjamin/Sheridan Co., Crosman
Beretta S.P.A., Pietro
Beretta U.S.A. Corp.
Big Bear Arms & Sporting Goods, Inc.
Bill Russ Trading Post
Bond Arms, Inc.
Borden Ridges Rimrock Stocks
Borden Rifles Inc.
Brockman's Custom Gunsmithing
Brown Co., E. Arthur
Brown Products, Inc., Ed
Browning Arms Co.
Bryan & Assoc.
Bushmaster Firearms, Inc.
C. Sharps Arms Co. Inc./Montana
Armory
Cabela's
Calico Light Weapon Systems
Cambos Outdoorsman
Cape Outfitters
Casull Arms Corp.
CCL Security Products
Century Gun Dist. Inc.
Champlin Firearms, Inc.
Charter 2000
Cobra Enterprises, Inc.
Colt's Mfg. Co., Inc.
Competitor Corp., Inc.
Competitor Corp., Inc.
Conetrol Scope Mounts
Connecticut Shotgun Mfg. Co.
Connecticut Valley Classics
(See CVC, BPI)
Cooper Arms
Crosman Airguns
Cumberland Arms
Cumberland Mountain Arms
CVA
Daisy Outdoor Products
Dakota Arms, Inc.
Dan Wesson Firearms
Dayton Traister
Detonics USA
Dixie Gun Works
Downsizer Corp.
DS Arms, Inc.
DunLyon R&D, Inc.
Dutchman's Firearms, Inc.
E&L Mfg., Inc.
E. Arthur Brown Co.
Eagle Arms, Inc. (See ArmaLite, Inc.)
Ed Brown Products, Inc.
Emerging Technologies, Inc.
(See Laseraim Technologies, Inc.)
Entre`prise Arms, Inc.
Essex Arms
Excel Industries, Inc.
Fletcher-Bidwell, LLC.
FN Manufacturing
Freedom Arms, Inc.
Fulton Armory
Galena Industries AMT
Garcia National Gun Traders, Inc.
Gary Reeder Custom Guns
Genecco Gun Works
Gentry Custom LLC
George Hoenig, Inc.
George Madis Winchester Consultants
Gibbs Rifle Co., Inc.
Gil Hebard Guns, Inc.
Gilbert Equipment Co., Inc.
Goergen's Gun Shop, Inc.
Goodwin's Pawn Shop
Granite Mountain Arms, Inc.
Grayback Wildcats
Guncrafter Industries
H&R 1871.LLC
Hammans, Charles E.
Hammerli USA
Harrington & Richardson
(See H&R 1871, Inc.)
Hart & Son, Inc.
Hatfield Gun
Hawken Shop, The
(See Dayton Traister)
Heritage Firearms
(See Heritage Mfg., Inc.)
Heritage Manufacturing, Inc.
Hesco-Meprolight
High Precision
High Standard Mfg. Co./F.I., Inc.
Hi-Point Firearms/MKS Supply
HJS Arms, Inc.
H-S Precision, Inc.
Hutton Rifle Ranch
IAR Inc.
Imperial Miniature Armory
Israel Arms Inc.
Ithaca Classic Doubles
Ithaca Gun Company LLC
J.P. Enterprises Inc.
Jim Norman Custom Gunstocks
John Rigby & Co.
John's Custom Leather
K.B.I. Inc.
Kahr Arms
Kehr, Roger
Kelbly, Inc.
Kel-Tec CNC Industries, Inc.
Keystone Sporting Arms, Inc.
(Crickett Rifles)
Kimber of America, Inc.
Knight Rifles
Knight's Mfg. Co.
Kolar
L.A.R. Mfg., Inc.
L.W. Seecamp Co., Inc.
LaFrance Specialties
Lakefield Arms Ltd.
(See Savage Arms, Inc.)
Laseraim Technologies, Inc.
Les Baer Custom, Inc.
Lever Arms Service Ltd.
Ljutic Industries, Inc.
Lock's Philadelphia Gun Exchange
Lomont Precision Bullets
Lone Star Rifle Company
Mag-Na-Port International, Inc.
Magnum Research, Inc.
Mandall Shooting Supplies Inc.
Marlin Firearms Co.
Marshall Fish Mfg. Gunsmith Sptg. Co.
Mathews Gun Shop & Gunsmithing,
Inc.
Maverick Arms, Inc.
McBros Rifle Co.
McCann Industries
Mid-America Recreation, Inc.
Miller Arms, Inc.
MKS Supply, Inc.
(See Hi-Point Firearms)
MOA Corporation
Montana Armory, Inc.
(See C. Sharps Arms Co. Inc.)
MPI Stocks
Navy Arms Company
NCP Products, Inc.
New Ultra Light Arms, LLC
Noreen, Peter H.
North American Arms, Inc.
North Star West
Northwest Arms
Nowlin Mfg. Co.
Olympic Arms Inc.
Oregon Arms, Inc.
(See Rogue Rifle Co., Inc.)
P&M Sales & Services, LLC
Parker & Sons Shooting Supply
Parker Gun Finishes
Phillips & Rogers, Inc.
Phoenix Arms
Precision Small Arms Inc.
ProWare, Inc.
Ramon B. Gonzalez Guns
Rapine Bullet Mould Mfg. Co.
Remington Arms Co., Inc.
Rifles, Inc.
Robinson Armament Co.
Rock River Arms
Rocky Mountain Arms, Inc.
Rogue Rifle Co., Inc.
Rogue River Rifleworks
Rohrbaugh
Romain's Custom Guns, Inc.
RPM
Ruger (See Sturm, Ruger & Co., Inc.)
Safari Arms/Schuetzen Pistol Works
Savage Arms (Canada), Inc.
Schumakers Gun Shop
Searcy Enterprises
Sharps Arms Co., Inc., C.
Sigarms, Inc.
Sklany's Machine Shop
Small Arms Specialists
Smith & Wesson
Sound Tech Silencers
Spencer's Rifle Barrels, Inc.
Springfield Armory
Springfield, Inc.
SSK Industries
STI International
Stoeger Industries
Strayer-Voigt, Inc.
Sturm Ruger & Co. Inc.
Sunny Hill Enterprises, Inc.
T&S Industries, Inc.
Taconic Firearms Ltd., Perry Lane
Tank's Rifle Shop
Tar-Hunt Custom Rifles, Inc.
Taurus Firearms, Inc.
Texas Armory (See Bond Arms, Inc.)
The A.W. Peterson Gun Shop, Inc.
The Gun Room Press
The Gun Works
Thompson/Center Arms
Time Precision
Tristar Sporting Arms, Ltd.
U.S. Fire Arms Mfg. Co., Inc.
U.S. Repeating Arms Co., Inc.
Uselton/Arms, Inc.
Visible Impact Targets
Volquartsen Custom Ltd.
Wallace, Terry
Weatherby, Inc.
Wescombe, Bill (See North Star West)
Wessinger Custom Guns & Engraving
Whildin & Sons Ltd, E.H.
Whitestone Lumber Corp.
Wichita Arms, Inc.
Wildey, Inc.
Wilsom Combat
Z-M Weapons

GUNSMITH SCHOOL

American Gunsmithing Institute
Bull Mountain Rifle Co.
Colorado Gunsmithing Academy
Colorado School of Trades
Cylinder & Slide, Inc., William R.
Laughridge
Lassen Community College,
Gunsmithing Dept.
Laughridge, William R.
(See Cylinder & Slide Inc.)
Log Cabin Sport Shop
Modern Gun Repair School
Murray State College
North American Correspondence
Schools The Gun Pro
Nowlin Mfg. Co.
NRI Gunsmith School
Pennsylvania Gunsmith School
Piedmont Community College
Pine Technical College
Professional Gunsmiths of Ame
Smith & Wesson
Southeastern Community Colle
Spencer's Rifle Barrels, Inc.
Trinidad St. Jr. Col. Gunsmith D
Wright's Gunstock Blanks
Yavapai College

GUNSMITH SUPPLIES TOOLS & SERVICES

Ace Custom 45's, Inc.
Actions by "T" Teddy Jacobson
Alaskan Silversmith, The
Aldis Gunsmithing & Shooting S
Alley Supply Co.
Allred Bullet Co.
Alpec Team, Inc.
American Gunsmithing Institute
Ballard Rifle & Cartridge Co., LLC
Bar-Sto Precision Machine
Battenfeld Technologies Inc.
Bauska Barrels
Bear Mountain Gun & Tool
Bengtson Arms Co., L.
Bill's Gun Repair
Blue Ridge Machinery & Tools, In
Boyds' Gunstock Industries, Inc.
Briley Mfg. Inc.
Brockman's Custom Gunsmithing
Brown Products, Inc., Ed
Brownells, Inc.
Bryan & Assoc.
B-Square Company, Inc.
Buffer Technologies
Bull Mountain Rifle Co.
Bushmaster Firearms, Inc.
C.S. Van Gorden & Son, Inc.
Carbide Checkering Tools
(See J&R Engineering)
Caywood, Shane J.
CBC-BRAZIL
Chapman Manufacturing Co.
Chicasaw Gun Works
Chip McCormick Corp.
Choate Machine & Tool Co., Inc.
Colonial Arms, Inc.
Colorado School of Trades
Colt's Mfg. Co., Inc.
Conetrol Scope Mounts
Corbin Mfg. & Supply, Inc.
CRR, Inc./Marble's Inc.
Cumberland Arms
Cumberland Mountain Arms
Custom Checkering Service, Kathy
Forster
Dan's Whetstone Co., Inc.
D'Arcy Echols & Co.
Dem-Bart Checkering Tools, Inc.
Dixie Gun Works
Dixie Gun Works
Dremel Mfg. Co.
Du-Lite Corp.
Entre`prise Arms, Inc.
Erhardt, Dennis
Evolution Gun Works, Inc.
Faith Associates
Falcon Industries, Inc.
FERLIB
Fisher, Jerry A.
Forgreens Tool & Mfg., Inc.
Forster, Kathy
(See Custom Checkering)
Gentry Custom LLC
Gilmore Sports Concepts, Inc.
Goodwin's Pawn Shop
Grace Metal Products
Gre-Tan Rifles
Gruning Precision, Inc.
Gunline Tools
Half Moon Rifle Shop
Hammond Custom Guns Ltd.

s
en Tool Co., Inc.
rformance International
ecision
's Gunsmithing
Sports Inc.
nter Co.
rms Inc.
Thomas G.
Tom's Gun Repair)
gineering
eat Treat
ey Mfg. Co., Inc.
upply
s Recoil Pads
ecision Tool Mfg., LLC
an Arthur Ciener, Inc.
Custom Products, Neil A.
Custom Guns Inc.
t Co., Inc.
ndorst, K. W.
ek Riflesmith, J.
nty Precision Reboring, Inc
ce Specialties
Mountain Forge
upplies, Mark
ecision Engineering
s Philadelphia Gun Exchange
n Guns Ltd.
vsky's Metalife
e Arms
e CRR, Inc./Marble's Inc.)
Lee Supplies
n, Mike
n's Gun Shop
land, Stan
k, Gunsmith Inc., T.W.
ife Industries
e Mahovsky's Metalife)
ael's Antiques
Sight Co.
ay Arms, Inc.

Competitor Supplies
e MCS, Inc.)
rey's Guns & Gunsmithing
A. Jones Custom Products
England Custom Gun Service
rontier Gunsmith Shop
mpic Arms Inc.
er & Sons Shooting Supply
er Gun Finishes
er Gun Finishes
sen Gunstocks
's Mfg. Co.
zone-Gunsmith, Brian
r Dyson & Son Ltd.
ver Custom, Inc.
ctical Tools, Inc.
cision Specialties
Wells Custom Gunsmith
ch Products
som International Corp.
rdon Products
e, Keith
See White Rock Tool & Die)
bert Valade Engraving
cky Mountain Arms, Inc.
main's Custom Guns, Inc.
yal Arms Gunstocks
steprufe Laboratories
arp Shooter Supply
ooter's Choice Gun Care
mmons Gun Repair, Inc.
nith Abrasives, Inc.
uthern Bloomer Mfg. Co.
encer Reblue Service
encer's Rifle Barrels, Inc.
radlin's
arr Trading Co., Jedediah
arrett Co., L. S.
les Custom Guns
oney Point Products, Inc.
Sullivan, David S.
(See Westwind Rifles, Inc.)
Sunny Hill Enterprises, Inc.
T&S Industries, Inc.
T.W. Menck Gunsmith, Inc.
Tank's Rifle Shop
Tar-Hunt Custom Rifles, Inc.
Texas Platers Supply Co.
The A.W. Peterson Gun Shop, Inc.
The Gun Works
The NgraveR Co.
The Robar Co., Inc.
Theis, Terry
Tom's Gun Repair, Thomas G. Ivanoff
Track of the Wolf, Inc.
Trinidad St. Jr. Col. Gunsmith Dept.
Trulock Tool
Turnbull Restoration, Doug
United States Products Co.
Van Gorden & Son Inc., C. S.
Venco Industries, Inc.
(See Shooter's Choice Gun Care)
W.C. Wolff Co.
Warne Manufacturing Co.
Washita Mountain Whetstone Co.
Weigand Combat Handguns, Inc.
Wessinger Custom Guns & Engraving
White Rock Tool & Die
Wilcox All-Pro Tools & Supply
Wild West Guns
Will-Burt Co.
Williams Gun Sight Co.
Williams Shootin' Iron Service, The Lynx-Line
Willow Bend
Windish, Jim
Wise Guns, Dale
Wright's Gunstock Blanks
Yavapai College
Ziegel Engineering

HANDGUN ACCESSORIES

"Su-Press-On", Inc.
A.A. Arms, Inc.
Ace Custom 45's, Inc.
Action Direct, Inc.
ADCO Sales, Inc.
Advantage Arms, Inc.
Aimtech Mount Systems
Ajax Custom Grips, Inc.
Alpha 1 Drop Zone
American Derringer Corp.
Arms Corporation of the Philippines
Astra Sport, S.A.
Autauga Arms, Inc.
Badger Creek Studio
Bagmaster Mfg., Inc.
Bar-Sto Precision Machine
Behlert Precision, Inc.
Berry's Mfg., Inc.
Blue and Gray Products Inc.
(See Ox-Yoke Originals)
Bond Custom Firearms
Bowen Classic Arms Corp.
Bridgeman Products
Broken Gun Ranch
Brooks Tactical Systems-Agrip
Brown Products, Inc., Ed
Bushmaster Hunting & Fishing
Butler Creek Corp.
Cannon Safe, Inc.
Centaur Systems, Inc.
Central Specialties Ltd
(See Trigger Lock Division
Charter 2000
Cheyenne Pioneer Products
Chicasaw Gun Works
Clark Custom Guns, Inc.
Classic Arms Company
Conetrol Scope Mounts
Crimson Trace Lasers
CRR, Inc./Marble's Inc.
Cylinder & Slide, Inc., William R. Laughridge
D&L Industries (See D.J. Marketing)
D.J. Marketing
Dade Screw Machine Products
Dan Wesson Firearms
Delhi Gun House
DeSantis Holster & Leather Goods, Inc.
Dixie Gun Works
Doskocil Mfg. Co., Inc.
E&L Mfg., Inc.
E. Arthur Brown Co.
E.A.A. Corp.
Eagle Imports, Inc.
Ed Brown Products, Inc.
Essex Arms
European American Armory Corp.
(See E.A.A. Corp.)
Evolution Gun Works, Inc.
Falcon Industries, Inc.
Federal Arms Corp. of America
Feinwerkbau Westinger & Altenburger
Fisher Custom Firearms
Fleming Firearms
Freedom Arms, Inc.
G.G. & G.
Galati International
GALCO International Ltd.
Garcia National Gun Traders, Inc.
Garthwaite Pistolsmith, Inc., Jim
Gil Hebard Guns, Inc.
Gilmore Sports Concepts, Inc.
Glock, Inc.
Goodwin's Pawn Shop
Gould & Goodrich
Gun-Alert
Gun-Ho Sports Cases
H.K.S. Products
Hafner World Wide, Inc.
Hammerli USA
Heinie Specialty Products
Henigson & Associates, Steve
High Standard Mfg. Co./F.I., Inc.
Hill Speed Leather, Ernie
HIP-GRIP Barami Corp.
Hi-Point Firearms/MKS Supply
Hobson Precision Mfg. Co.
Hoppe's Div. Penguin Industries, Inc.
H-S Precision, Inc.
Hume, Don
Hunter Co., Inc.
Impact Case & Container, Inc.
Import Sports Inc.
J.P. Enterprises Inc.
Jarvis, Inc.
JB Custom
Jeffredo Gunsight
Jim Noble Co.
John's Custom Leather
Jonathan Arthur Ciener, Inc.
Kalispel Case Line
KeeCo Impressions, Inc.
King's Gun Works
KK Air International
(See Impact Case & Container Co.)
Kolpin Outdoors, Inc.
L&S Technologies Inc.
(See Aimtech Mount Systems)
Lakewood Products LLC
LaserMax, Inc.
Les Baer Custom, Inc.
Loch Leven Industries/Convert-A-Pell
Lock's Philadelphia Gun Exchange
Lohman Mfg. Co., Inc.
Mag-Na-Port International, Inc.
Magnolia Sports, Inc.
Mag-Pack Corp.
Mahony, Philip Bruce
Mandall Shooting Supplies Inc.
Marble Arms
(See CRR, Inc./Marble's Inc.)
Markell, Inc.
MEC-Gar S.R.L.
Menck, Gunsmith Inc., T.W.
Merkuria Ltd.
Middlebrooks Custom Shop
Millett Sights
Mogul Co./Life Jacket
MTM Molded Products Co., Inc.
No-Sho Mfg. Co.
Numrich Gun Parts Corporation
Omega Sales
Outdoor Sports Headquarters, Inc.
Ox-Yoke Originals, Inc.
Pachmayr Div. Lyman Products
Pager Pal
Parker & Sons Shooting Supply
Pearce Grip, Inc.
Phoenix Arms
Practical Tools, Inc.
Precision Small Arms Inc.
Ram-Line ATK
Ranch Products
Ransom International Corp.
Ringler Custom Leather Co.
RPM
Seecamp Co. Inc., L. W.
Simmons Gun Repair, Inc.
Southern Bloomer Mfg. Co.
Springfield Armory
Springfield, Inc.
SSK Industries
Sturm Ruger & Co. Inc.
T.F.C. S.p.A.
Tactical Defense Institute
Tanfoglio Fratelli S.r.l.
The A.W. Peterson Gun Shop, Inc.
The Concealment Shop, Inc.
The Gun Works
The Keller Co.
The Protector Mfg. Co., Inc.
Thompson/Center Arms
Trigger Lock Division / Central Specialties Ltd.
Trijicon, Inc.
Triple-K Mfg. Co., Inc.
Truglo, Inc.
Tyler Manufacturing & Distributing
United States Products Co.
Universal Sports
Volquartsen Custom Ltd.
W. Waller & Son, Inc.
W.C. Wolff Co.
Warne Manufacturing Co.
Weigand Combat Handguns, Inc.
Wessinger Custom Guns & Engraving
Western Design
(See Alpha Gunsmith Division)
Whitestone Lumber Corp.
Wichita Arms, Inc.
Wild West Guns
Williams Gun Sight Co.
Wilsom Combat
Yankee Gunsmith "Just Glocks"
Ziegel Engineering

HANDGUN GRIPS

A.A. Arms, Inc.
African Import Co.
Ahrends, Kim
(See Custom Firearms, Inc)
Ajax Custom Grips, Inc.
Altamont Co.
American Derringer Corp.
American Gripcraft
Arms Corporation of the Philippines
Art Jewel Enterprises Ltd.
Baelder, Harry
Big Bear Arms & Sporting Goods, Inc.
Bob's Gun Shop
Boone Trading Co., Inc.
Boone's Custom Ivory Grips, Inc.
Boyds' Gunstock Industries, Inc.
Brooks Tactical Systems-Agrip
Brown Products, Inc., Ed
Clark Custom Guns, Inc.
Claro Walnut Gunstock Co.
Cole-Grip
Colonial Repair
Crimson Trace Lasers
Custom Firearms (See Ahrends, Kim)
Cylinder & Slide, Inc., William R. Laughridge
Dixie Gun Works
Dolbare, Elizabeth
E.A.A. Corp.
Eagle Imports, Inc.
EMF Co., Inc.
Essex Arms
European American Armory Corp.
(See E.A.A. Corp.)
Falcon Industries, Inc.
Feinwerkbau Westinger & Altenburger
Fibron Products, Inc.
Fisher Custom Firearms
Garthwaite Pistolsmith, Inc., Jim
Goodwin's Pawn Shop
Herrett's Stocks, Inc.
High Standard Mfg. Co./F.I., Inc.
HIP-GRIP Barami Corp.
Hogue Grips
H-S Precision, Inc.
Huebner, Corey O.
I.S.S.
Israel Arms Inc.
John Masen Co. Inc.
KeeCo Impressions, Inc.
Kim Ahrends Custom Firearms, Inc.
Korth Germany GmbH
Les Baer Custom, Inc.
Lett Custom Grips
Linebaugh Custom Sixguns
Lyman Products Corp.
Mandall Shooting Supplies Inc.
Michaels Of Oregon, Co.
Millett Sights
N.C. Ordnance Co.
Newell, Robert H.
Northern Precision
Pachmayr Div. Lyman Products
Pardini Armi Srl
Parker & Sons Shooting Supply
Pearce Grip, Inc.
Pilgrim Pewter, Inc.
(See Bell Originals Inc. Sid)
Precision Small Arms Inc.
Radical Concepts
Robinson, Don
Rosenberg & Son, Jack A.
Roy's Custom Grips
Spegel, Craig
Stoeger Industries
Sturm Ruger & Co. Inc.
Sunny Hill Enterprises, Inc.
Tactical Defense Institute
Taurus Firearms, Inc.
The A.W. Peterson Gun Shop, Inc.
Tirelli
Tom Forrest, Inc.
Triple-K Mfg. Co., Inc.
Tyler Manufacturing & Distributing
U.S. Fire Arms Mfg. Co., Inc.
Uncle Mike's
(See Michaels of Oregon Co.)
Vintage Industries, Inc.
Volquartsen Custom Ltd.
Western Mfg. Co.
Whitestone Lumber Corp.
Wright's Gunstock Blanks

HEARING PROTECTORS

Aero Peltor
Ajax Custom Grips, Inc.
Brown Co., E. Arthur
Browning Arms Co.

Creedmoor Sports, Inc.
David Clark Co., Inc.
Dillon Precision Products, Inc.
Dixie Gun Works
E-A-R, Inc.
Electronic Shooters Protection, Inc.
Gentex Corp.
Goodwin's Pawn Shop
Gunsmithing, Inc.
Hoppe's Div. Penguin Industries, Inc.
Kesselring Gun Shop
Mandall Shooting Supplies Inc.
Parker & Sons Shooting Supply
Paterson Gunsmithing
Peltor, Inc. (See Aero Peltor)
R.E.T. Enterprises
Ridgeline, Inc.
Rucker Dist. Inc.
Silencio/Safety Direct
Tactical Defense Institute
The A.W. Peterson Gun Shop, Inc.
The Gun Room Press
Triple-K Mfg. Co., Inc.
Watson Bullets
Whitestone Lumber Corp.

HOLSTERS & LEATHER GOODS

A&B Industries, Inc
(See Top-Line USA Inc.)
A.A. Arms, Inc.
Action Direct, Inc.
Action Products, Inc.
Aker International, Inc.
AKJ Concealco
Alessi Holsters, Inc.
Arratoonian, Andy
(See Horseshoe Leather Products)
Autauga Arms, Inc.
Bagmaster Mfg., Inc.
Baker's Leather Goods, Roy
Bandcor Industries, Div. of Man-Sew Corp.
Bang-Bang Boutique
(See Holster Shop, The)
Beretta S.P.A., Pietro
Bianchi International, Inc.
Bond Arms, Inc.
Brocock Ltd.
Brooks Tactical Systems-Agrip
Browning Arms Co.
Bull-X, Inc.
Cape Outfitters
Cathey Enterprises, Inc.
Chace Leather Products
Churchill Glove Co., James
Cimarron F.A. Co.
Classic Old West Styles
Clements' Custom Leathercraft, Chas
Cobra Sport S.R.I.
Collector's Armoury, Ltd.
Colonial Repair
Counter Assault
Delhi Gun House
DeSantis Holster & Leather Goods, Inc.
Dillon Precision Products, Inc.
Dixie Gun Works
Eagle Imports, Inc.
Ekol Leather Care
El Paso Saddlery Co.
EMF Co., Inc.
Faust Inc., T. G.
Freedom Arms, Inc.
Gage Manufacturing
GALCO International Ltd.
Garcia National Gun Traders, Inc.
Gil Hebard Guns, Inc.
Gilmore Sports Concepts, Inc.
GML Products, Inc.
Goodwin's Pawn Shop
Gould & Goodrich
Gun Leather Limited
Hafner World Wide, Inc.
HandCrafts Unltd.
(See Clements' Custom Leather)
Hank's Gun Shop
Heinie Specialty Products
Henigson & Associates, Steve
Hill Speed Leather, Ernie
HIP-GRIP Barami Corp.
Hobson Precision Mfg. Co.
Hogue Grips
Horseshoe Leather Products
Hume, Don
Hunter Co., Inc.
Import Sports Inc.
Jim Noble Co.
John's Custom Leather
K.L. Null Holsters Ltd.
Kirkpatrick Leather Co.
Kolpin Outdoors, Inc.
Korth Germany GmbH
Kramer Handgun Leather
L.A.R. Mfg., Inc.
Lawrence Leather Co.
Lock's Philadelphia Gun Exchange
Lone Star Gunleather
Magnolia Sports, Inc.
Mandall Shooting Supplies Inc.
Markell, Inc.
Marksman Products
Michaels Of Oregon, Co.
Minute Man High Tech Industries
Navy Arms Company
No-Sho Mfg. Co.
Null Holsters Ltd. K.L.
October Country Muzzleloading
Oklahoma Leather Products, Inc.
Old West Reproductions, Inc. R.M. Bachman
Pager Pal
Parker & Sons Shooting Supply
Pathfinder Sports Leather
Protektor Model
PWL Gunleather
Ramon B. Gonzalez Guns
Renegade
Ringler Custom Leather Co.
Rogue Rifle Co., Inc.
S&S Firearms
Safariland Ltd., Inc.
Safety Speed Holster, Inc.
Scharch Mfg., Inc.-Top Brass
Schulz Industries
Second Chance Body Armor
Silhouette Leathers
Smith Saddlery, Jesse W.
Sparks, Milt
Stalker, Inc.
Starr Trading Co., Jedediah
Strong Holster Co.
Stuart, V. Pat
Tabler Marketing
Tactical Defense Institute
Ted Blocker Holsters, Inc.
Tex Shoemaker & Sons, Inc.
Thad Rybka Custom Leather Equipment
The A.W. Peterson Gun Shop, Inc.
The Concealment Shop, Inc.
The Gun Works
The Keller Co.
The Outdoor Connection, Inc.
Torel, Inc.
Triple-K Mfg. Co., Inc.
Tristar Sporting Arms, Ltd.
Tyler Manufacturing & Distributing
Uncle Mike's
(See Michaels of Oregon Co.)
Venus Industries
W. Waller & Son, Inc.
Walt's Custom Leather, Walt Whinnery
Watson Bullets
Westley Richards & Co. Ltd.
Whinnery, Walt
(See Walt's Custom Leather)
Wild Bill's Originals
Wilsom Combat

HUNTING & CAMP GEAR, CLOTHING, ETC.

Action Direct, Inc.
Action Products, Inc.
Adventure 16, Inc.
All Rite Products, Inc.
Alpha 1 Drop Zone
Armor (See Buck Stop Lure Co., Inc.)
Atlanta Cutlery Corp.
Atsko/Sno-Seal, Inc.
B.B. Walker Co.
Baekgaard Ltd.
Bagmaster Mfg., Inc.
Barbour, Inc.
Bauer, Eddie
Bear Archery
Beaver Park Product, Inc.
Beretta S.P.A., Pietro
Better Concepts Co.
Bill Russ Trading Post
Bob Allen Sportswear
Boonie Packer Products
Boss Manufacturing Co.
Browning Arms Co.
Buck Stop Lure Co., Inc.
Bushmaster Hunting & Fishing
Cambos Outdoorsman
Cambos Outdoorsman
Camp-Cap Products
Carhartt, Inc.
Churchill Glove Co., James
Clarkfield Enterprises, Inc.
Classic Old West Styles
Clements' Custom Leathercraft, Chas
Coghlan's Ltd.
Cold Steel Inc.
Coleman Co., Inc.
Coulston Products, Inc.
Counter Assault
Dakota Corp.
Danner Shoe Mfg. Co.
Deepeeka Exports Pvt. Ltd.
Dr. O's Products Ltd.
Duofold, Inc.
Dynalite Products, Inc.
E-A-R, Inc.
Ekol Leather Care
Flambeau, Inc.
Forrest Tool Co.
Fox River Mills, Inc.
Frontier
G&H Decoys, Inc.
Gerber Legendary Blades
Glacier Glove
Grand Slam Hunting Products
HandCrafts Unltd.
(See Clements' Custom Leather)
High North Products, Inc.
Hinman Outfitters, Bob
Hodgman, Inc.
Houtz & Barwick
Hunter's Specialties Inc.
James Churchill Glove Co.
John's Custom Leather
K&M Industries, Inc.
Kamik Outdoor Footwear
Kolpin Outdoors, Inc.
L.L. Bean, Inc.
LaCrosse Footwear, Inc.
Leapers, Inc.
MAG Instrument, Inc.
Mag-Na-Port International, Inc.
McCann Industries
Molin Industries, Tru-Nord Division
Murphy, R.R. Co., Inc.
Northlake Outdoor Footwear
Original Deer Formula Co., The
Palsa Outdoor Products
Partridge Sales Ltd., John
Pointing Dog Journal, Village Press Publications
Powell & Son (Gunmakers) Ltd., William
Pro-Mark Div. of Wells Lamont
Ringler Custom Leather Co.
Robert Valade Engraving
Rocky Shoes & Boots
Scansport, Inc.
Sceery Game Calls
Schaefer Shooting Sports
Servus Footwear Co.
Simmons Outdoor Corp.
Sno-Seal, Inc.
(See Atsko/Sno-Seal, Inc.)
Swanndri New Zealand
TEN-X Products Group
The A.W. Peterson Gun Shop, Inc.
The Orvis Co.
The Outdoor Connection, Inc.
Tink's Safariland Hunting Corp.
Torel, Inc.
Triple-K Mfg. Co., Inc.
United Cutlery Corp.
Venus Industries
Wakina by Pic
Walls Industries, Inc.
Wideview Scope Mount Corp.
Wilderness Sound Products Ltd.
Winchester Sutler, Inc., The
Wolverine Footwear Group
Woolrich, Inc.
Wyoming Knife Corp.
Yellowstone Wilderness Supply

KNIVES & KNIFEMAKER'S SUPPLIES

A.G. Russell Knives, Inc.
Action Direct, Inc.
Adventure 16, Inc.
African Import Co.
Aitor-Cuchilleria Del Norte S.A.
American Target Knives
Art Jewel Enterprises Ltd.
Atlanta Cutlery Corp.
B&D Trading Co., Inc.
Barteaux Machete
Benchmark Knives
(See Gerber Legendary Blades)
Beretta S.P.A., Pietro
Beretta U.S.A. Corp.
Big Bear Arms & Sporting Goods, Inc.
Bill Russ Trading Post
Boker USA, Inc.
Boone Trading Co., Inc.
Boone's Custom Ivory Grips, Inc.
Bowen Knife Co., Inc.
Brooks Tactical Systems-Agrip
Browning Arms Co.
Buck Knives, Inc.
Buster's Custom Knives
Camillus Cutlery Co.
Campbell, Dick
Case & Sons Cutlery Co., W R
Chicago Cutlery Co.
Claro Walnut Gunstock Co.
Clements' Custom Leathercraft, Chas
Cold Steel Inc.
Coleman Co., Inc.
Collector's Armoury, Ltd.
Compass Industries, Inc.
Crosman Blades
(See Coleman Co., Inc.)
CRR, Inc./Marble's Inc.
Cutco Cutlery
damascususa@inteliport.com
Dan's Whetstone Co., Inc.
Deepeeka Exports Pvt. Ltd.
Degen Inc. (See Aristocrat Knives)
Delhi Gun House
DeSantis Holster & Leather Go
Inc.
Diamond Machining Technolog
(See DMT)
Dixie Gun Works
Dolbare, Elizabeth
EdgeCraft Corp., S. Weiner
Empire Cutlery Corp.
Eze-Lap Diamond Prods.
Flitz International Ltd.
Forrest Tool Co.
Forthofer's Gunsmithing & Knifemaking
Fortune Products, Inc.
Frank Knives
Frost Cutlery Co.
Galati International
George Ibberson (Sheffield) Ltd
Gerber Legendary Blades
Glock, Inc.
Golden Age Arms Co.
H&B Forge Co.
Hafner World Wide, Inc.
Hammans, Charles E.
HandCrafts Unltd.
(See Clements' Custom Leathe
Harris Publications
High North Products, Inc.
Hoppe's Div. Penguin Industries,
Hunter Co., Inc.
Imperial Schrade Corp.
J.A. Blades, Inc.
(See Christopher Firearms Co.)
J.A. Henckels Zwillingswerk Inc.
Jackalope Gun Shop
Jantz Supply
Jenco Sales, Inc.
Jim Blair Engraving
Johnson Wood Products
KA-BAR Knives
Kasenit Co., Inc.
Kershaw Knives
Knifeware, Inc.
Koval Knives
Lamson & Goodnow Mfg. Co.
Lansky Sharpeners
Leapers, Inc.
Leatherman Tool Group, Inc.
Lethal Force Institute
(See Police Bookshelf)
Linder Solingen Knives
Mandall Shooting Supplies Inc.
Marble Arms
(See CRR, Inc./Marble's Inc.)
Marshall Fish Mfg. Gunsmith Sptg.
Matthews Cutlery
McCann Industries
Molin Industries, Tru-Nord Divisio
Mountain State Muzzleloading Supplies, Inc.
Normark Corp.
October Country Muzzleloading
Outdoor Edge Cutlery Corp.
Pilgrim Pewter, Inc.
(See Bell Originals Inc. Sid)
Plaza Cutlery, Inc.
Police Bookshelf
Queen Cutlery Co.
R&C Knives & Such
R. Murphy Co., Inc.
Randall-Made Knives
Ringler Custom Leather Co.
Robert Valade Engraving
Scansport, Inc.
Schiffman, Mike
Sheffield Knifemakers Supply, Inc.
Smith Saddlery, Jesse W.
Springfield Armory
Spyderco, Inc.
T.F.C. S.p.A.
The A.W. Peterson Gun Shop, Inc.
The Creative Craftsman, Inc.

Room
Works
erry
ns Performance Firearms
ns Performance Firearms
ance Knife Co.
Cutlery Corp.
itlery Co.
ndustries
ase & Sons Cutlery Co.
a Mountain Whetstone Co.
reek Knife & Gun Works
North America/Precise Int'l.
n Cutlery
Camillus Cutlery Co.)
ry, Walt
Walt's Custom Leather)
ew Scope Mount Corp.
holm (See Ibberson [Sheffield]
George)
ng Knife Corp.

ELS, BOXES & TRIDGE HOLDERS

c Products, Inc.
s Mfg., Inc.
ck Ltd.
Co., E. Arthur
t Mtn. Outfitters Scents & Lures
nne Pioneer Products
y Products
tis Holster & Leather Goods,

eau, Inc.
vin's Pawn Shop
r World Wide, Inc.
roducts, Inc.
n Outdoors, Inc.
y Shooting Supplies
ay Arms, Inc.
Molded Products Co., Inc.
eton Royal, c/o Swingler
ckland Ltd.
s Custom Leather, Walt Whinnery
l Engineering

AD WIRES & WIRE TTERS

s Metal Products
Bore Express
t Swaging Supply, Inc.
Unmussig Bullets
dwin's Pawn Shop
rty Metals
tning Performance Innovations,
c.
tana Precision Swaging
hern Precision
rt Flite Manufacturing Co.
Ammunition, Inc.

AD TESTING & ODUCT TESTING

istic Research
lgeman Products
se Bullet Co., Inc.
kskin Bullet Co.
l Mountain Rifle Co.
/entures
ybuster Wads & Harvester Bullets
arview Products
H Precision Tooling
ad Eye's Sport Center
fense Training International, Inc.
ane's Gun Repair
See DGR Custom Rifles)
uning Precision, Inc.
P. White Laboratory, Inc.
nk's Gun Shop

Henigson & Associates, Steve
Hutton Rifle Ranch
J&J Sales
Jackalope Gun Shop
Jensen Bullets
Jonathan Arthur Ciener, Inc.
L. E. Jurras & Assoc.
Liberty Shooting Supplies
Linebaugh Custom Sixguns
Lomont Precision Bullets
MAST Technology, Inc.
McMurdo, Lynn
(See Specialty Gunsmithing)
Middlebrooks Custom Shop
Modern Gun Repair School
Multiplex International
Northwest Arms
Oil Rod and Gun Shop
Plum City Ballistic Range
R.A. Wells Custom Gunsmith
Ramon B. Gonzalez Guns
Rupert's Gun Shop
Small Custom Mould & Bullet Co.
SOS Products Co.
(See Buck Stix-SOS Products Co.)
Spencer's Rifle Barrels, Inc.
Tar-Hunt Custom Rifles, Inc.
Trinidad St. Jr. Col. Gunsmith Dept.
Vulpes Ventures, Inc., Fox Cartridge Division
W. Square Enterprises
X-Spand Target Systems

LOADING BLOCKS, METALLIC & SHOTSHELL

Battenfeld Technologies Inc.
Buffalo Arms Co.
Huntington Die Specialties
Jericho Tool & Die Co., Inc.
Sinclair International, Inc.
The A.W. Peterson Gun Shop, Inc.

LUBRISIZERS, DIES & ACCESSORIES

Ballisti-Cast, Inc.
Buffalo Arms Co.
Cast Performance Bullet Company
Cooper-Woodward Perfect Lube
Corbin Mfg. & Supply, Inc.
GAR
Hart & Son, Inc.
Javelina Lube Products
Lee Precision, Inc.
Lithi Bee Bullet Lube
Lyman Products Corp.
Magma Engineering Co.
PWM Sales Ltd.
RCBS Operations/ATK
Redding Reloading Equipment
S&S Firearms
SPG LLC
The A.W. Peterson Gun Shop, Inc.
Thompson Bullet Lube Co.
United States Products Co.
WTA Manufacturing

MOULDS & MOULD ACCESSORIES

Ad Hominem
American Products, Inc.
Ballisti-Cast, Inc.
Buffalo Arms Co.
Bullet Swaging Supply, Inc.
Cast Performance Bullet Company
Corbin Mfg. & Supply, Inc.
Davide Pedersoli and Co.
GAR
Huntington Die Specialties
Lee Precision, Inc.
Lyman Products Corp.
Magma Engineering Co.
Old West Bullet Moulds
Pacific Rifle Co.
Penn Bullets
Rapine Bullet Mould Mfg. Co.
RCBS Operations/ATK
Redding Reloading Equipment
S&S Firearms
Small Custom Mould & Bullet Co.
The A.W. Peterson Gun Shop, Inc.
The Gun Works
Wolf's Western Traders

MUZZLE-LOADING GUNS, BARRELS & EQUIPMENT

Accuracy Unlimited
Ackerman & Co.
Adkins, Luther
Allen Mfg.
Armi San Paolo
Armoury, Inc., The
Austin & Halleck, Inc.
Bauska Barrels
Bentley, John
Big Bore Express
Birdsong & Assoc., W. E.
Black Powder Products
Blount/Outers ATK
Blue and Gray Products Inc.
(See Ox-Yoke Originals)
Bridgers Best
Buckskin Bullet Co.
Bullberry Barrel Works, Ltd.
Butler Creek Corp.
Cabela's
Cache La Poudre Rifleworks
California Sights
(See Fautheree, Andy)
Cash Mfg. Co., Inc.
Caywood Gunmakers
CBC-BRAZIL
Chambers Flintlocks Ltd., Jim
Chicasaw Gun Works
Cimarron F.A. Co.
Claybuster Wads & Harvester Bullets
Cogar's Gunsmithing
Colonial Repair
Colt Blackpowder Arms Co.
Conetrol Scope Mounts
Cousin Bob's Mountain Products
Cumberland Arms
Cumberland Mountain Arms
Curly Maple Stock Blanks
(See Tiger-Hunt)
CVA
Dangler, Homer L.
Davide Pedersoli and Co.
Dayton Traister
deHaas Barrels
Delhi Gun House
Dixie Gun Works
Dixie Gun Works
Dixon Muzzleloading Shop, Inc.
Dolbare, Elizabeth
EMF Co., Inc.
Euroarms of America, Inc.
Feken, Dennis
Flintlocks, Etc.
Fort Hill Gunstocks
Fowler, Bob
(See Black Powder Products)
Frontier
Getz Barrel Company
Goergen's Gun Shop, Inc.
Golden Age Arms Co.
Gonic Arms/North American Arms, Inc.
Goodwin's Pawn Shop
Green Mountain Rifle Barrel Co., Inc.
H&R 1871.LLC
Hastings
Hawken Shop, The
(See Dayton Traister)
Hege Jagd-u. Sporthandels GmbH
Hodgdon Powder Co.
Hoppe's Div. Penguin Industries, Inc.
Hornady Mfg. Co.
House of Muskets, Inc., The
Hunkeler, A.
(See Buckskin Machine Works)
IAR Inc.
Impact Case & Container, Inc.
Ironsighter Co.
J. Dewey Mfg. Co., Inc.
Jamison's Forge Works
Jones Co., Dale
K&M Industries, Inc.
Kalispel Case Line
Kennedy Firearms
Knight Rifles
Knight Rifles
(See Modern Muzzle Loading, Inc.)
Kolar
L&R Lock Co.
L&S Technologies Inc.
(See Aimtech Mount Systems)
Lakewood Products LLC
Lodgewood Mfg.
Log Cabin Sport Shop
Lothar Walther Precision Tool Inc.
Lyman Products Corp.
Markesbery Muzzle Loaders, Inc.
Mathews Gun Shop & Gunsmithing, Inc.
McCann, Tom
Michaels Of Oregon, Co.
Millennium Designed Muzzleloaders
Modern Muzzleloading, Inc.
Mountain State Muzzleloading Supplies, Inc.
Mowrey Gun Works
Navy Arms Company
Newman Gunshop
North Star West
October Country Muzzleloading
Oklahoma Leather Products, Inc.
Olson, Myron
Orion Rifle Barrel Co.
Ox-Yoke Originals, Inc.
Pacific Rifle Co.
Parker & Sons Shooting Supply
Parker Gun Finishes
Pecatonica River Longrifle
Peter Dyson & Son Ltd.
Pioneer Arms Co.
Prairie River Arms
Rossi Firearms
Rusty Duck Premium Gun Care Products
S&S Firearms
Selsi Co., Inc.
Simmons Gun Repair, Inc.
Sklany's Machine Shop
Smokey Valley Rifles
South Bend Replicas, Inc.
Southern Bloomer Mfg. Co.
Splitfire Sporting Goods, L.L.C.
Starr Trading Co., Jedediah
Stone Mountain Arms
Sturm Ruger & Co. Inc.
Taylor's & Co., Inc.
Tennessee Valley Mfg.
The A.W. Peterson Gun Shop, Inc.
The Gun Works
The Hawken Shop
Thompson Bullet Lube Co.
Thompson/Center Arms
Tiger-Hunt Gunstocks
Track of the Wolf, Inc.
Traditions Performance Firearms
Truglo, Inc.
Uncle Mike's
(See Michaels of Oregon Co.)
Universal Sports
Upper Missouri Trading Co.
Venco Industries, Inc.
(See Shooter's Choice Gun Care)
Village Restorations & Consulting, Inc.
Virgin Valley Custom Guns
Voere-KGH GmbH
W.E. Birdsong & Assoc.
Warne Manufacturing Co.
Warren Muzzleloading Co., Inc.
Wescombe, Bill (See North Star West)
White Rifles, Inc.
William E. Phillips Firearms
Woodworker's Supply
Wright's Gunstock Blanks
Young Country Arms
Ziegel Engineering

PISTOLSMITH

A.W. Peterson Gun Shop, Inc.
Acadian Ballistic Specialties
Accuracy Unlimited
Ace Custom 45's, Inc.
Actions by "T" Teddy Jacobson
Adair Custom Shop, Bill
Ahlman Guns
Ahrends, Kim
(See Custom Firearms, Inc)
Aldis Gunsmithing & Shooting Supply
Alpha Precision, Inc.
Alpine Indoor Shooting Range
Armament Gunsmithing Co., Inc.
Arundel Arms & Ammunition, Inc., A.
Badger Creek Studio
Bain & Davis, Inc.
Bar-Sto Precision Machine
Behlert Precision, Inc.
Bengtson Arms Co., L.
Bill Adair Custom Shop
Billings Gunsmiths
Bob Rogers Gunsmithing
Bowen Classic Arms Corp.
Broken Gun Ranch
Caraville Manufacturing
Chicasaw Gun Works
Chip McCormick Corp.
Clark Custom Guns, Inc.
Cleland's Outdoor World, Inc
Colonial Repair
Colorado School of Trades
Colt's Mfg. Co., Inc.
Corkys Gun Clinic
Custom Firearms (See Ahrends, Kim)
Cylinder & Slide, Inc., William R. Laughridge
D&D Gunsmiths, Ltd.
D&L Sports
David R. Chicoine
Dayton Traister
Dilliott Gunsmithing, Inc.
Ellicott Arms, Inc. / Woods Pistolsmithing
Evolution Gun Works, Inc.
Ferris Firearms
Fisher Custom Firearms
Forkin Custom Classics
G.G. & G.
Garthwaite Pistolsmith, Inc., Jim
Gary Reeder Custom Guns
Genecco Gun Works
Gentry Custom LLC
Greider Precision
Guncraft Sports, Inc.
Guncraft Sports, Inc.
Gunsite Training Center
Hamilton, Alex B.
(See Ten-Ring Precision, Inc.)
Hammerli Service-Precision Mac
Hammond Custom Guns Ltd.
Hank's Gun Shop

Hanson's Gun Center, Dick
Harwood, Jack O.
Hawken Shop, The
(See Dayton Traister)
Heinie Specialty Products
High Bridge Arms, Inc.
High Standard Mfg. Co./F.I., Inc.
Highline Machine Co.
Hoag, James W.
Irwin, Campbell H.
Island Pond Gun Shop
Ivanoff, Thomas G.
(See Tom's Gun Repair)
J&S Heat Treat
Jarvis, Inc.
Jeffredo Gunsight
Jensen's Custom Ammunition
Jungkind, Reeves C.
Kaswer Custom, Inc.
Ken Starnes Gunmaker
Kilham & Co.
Kim Ahrends Custom Firearms, Inc.
King's Gun Works
La Clinique du .45
LaFrance Specialties
LaRocca Gun Works
Lathrop's, Inc.
Lawson, John G.
(See Sight Shop, The)
Leckie Professional Gunsmithing
Les Baer Custom, Inc.
Linebaugh Custom Sixguns
List Precision Engineering
Long, George F.
Mag-Na-Port International, Inc.
Mahony, Philip Bruce
Mahovsky's Metalife
Mandall Shooting Supplies Inc.
Marvel, Alan
Mathews Gun Shop & Gunsmithing, Inc.
MCS, Inc.
Middlebrooks Custom Shop
Miller Custom
Mitchell's Accuracy Shop
MJK Gunsmithing, Inc.
Modern Gun Repair School
Mo's Competitor Supplies
(See MCS, Inc.)
Mowrey's Guns & Gunsmithing
Mullis Guncraft
NCP Products, Inc.
Novak's, Inc.
Nowlin Mfg. Co.
Olathe Gun Shop
Paris, Frank J.
Pasadena Gun Center
Peacemaker Specialists
PEM's Mfg. Co.
Performance Specialists
Peterson Gun Shop, Inc., A.W.
Pierce Pistols
Piquette's Custom Engraving
Power Custom, Inc.
Precision Specialties
Ramon B. Gonzalez Guns
Randco UK
Ries, Chuck
Rim Pac Sports, Inc.
Rocky Mountain Arms, Inc.
RPM
Ruger's Custom Guns
Score High Gunsmithing
Shooters Supply
Shootin' Shack
Singletary, Kent
Springfield, Inc.
SSK Industries
Swenson's 45 Shop, A. D.
Swift River Gunworks
Ten-Ring Precision, Inc.
Terry K. Kopp Professional Gunsmithing
The A.W. Peterson Gun Shop, Inc.
The Gun Works
The Robar Co., Inc.
The Sight Shop
Thurston Sports, Inc.
Time Precision
Tom's Gun Repair, Thomas G. Ivanoff
Turnbull Restoration, Doug
Vic's Gun Refinishing
Volquartsen Custom Ltd.
Walker Arms Co., Inc.
Walters Industries
Wardell Precision Handguns Ltd.
Wessinger Custom Guns & Engraving
White Barn Wor
Wichita Arms, Inc.
Wild West Guns
Williams Gun Sight Co.
Williamson Precision Gunsmithing
Wilson Combat
Wright's Gunstock Blanks

POWDER MEASURES, SCALES, FUNNELS & ACCESSORIES

4-D Custom Die Co.
Battenfeld Technologies Inc.
Buffalo Arms Co.
Davide Pedersoli and Co.
Dillon Precision Products, Inc.
Fremont Tool Works
Frontier
GAR
High Precision
Hoehn Sales, Inc.
Jones Custom Products, Neil A.
Modern Muzzleloading, Inc.
Neil A. Jones Custom Products
Pacific Rifle Co.
Peter Dyson & Son Ltd.
Precision Reloading, Inc.
Ramon B. Gonzalez Guns
RCBS Operations/ATK
RCBS/ATK
Redding Reloading Equipment
Saunders Gun & Machine Shop
Schumakers Gun Shop
Spencer's Rifle Barrels, Inc.
The A.W. Peterson Gun Shop, Inc.
Vega Tool Co.
VibraShine, Inc.
VTI Gun Parts

PRESS ACCESSORIES, METALLIC

Buffalo Arms Co.
Corbin Mfg. & Supply, Inc.
Hollywood Engineering
Huntington Die Specialties
MA Systems, Inc.
R.E.I.
Redding Reloading Equipment
Royal Arms Gunstocks
The A.W. Peterson Gun Shop, Inc.
Thompson Tool Mount
Vega Tool Co.

PRESS ACCESSORIES, SHOTSHELL

Hollywood Engineering
Lee Precision, Inc.
MEC, Inc.
Precision Reloading, Inc.
R.E.I.
The A.W. Peterson Gun Shop, Inc.

PRESSES, ARBOR

Blue Ridge Machinery & Tools, Inc.
Goodwin's Pawn Shop
Hoehn Sales, Inc.
K&M Services
RCBS Operations/ATK
Spencer's Rifle Barrels, Inc.
The A.W. Peterson Gun Shop, Inc.

PRESSES, METALLIC

4-D Custom Die Co.
Battenfeld Technologies Inc.
Dillon Precision Products, Inc.
Fremont Tool Works
Goodwin's Pawn Shop
Hornady Mfg. Co.
Huntington Die Specialties
Lee Precision, Inc.
Midway Arms, Inc.
R.E.I.
Ramon B. Gonzalez Guns
RCBS Operations/ATK
RCBS/ATK
Redding Reloading Equipment
Spencer's Rifle Barrels, Inc.
The A.W. Peterson Gun Shop, Inc.

PRESSES, SHOTSHELL

Ballistic Products, Inc.
Dillon Precision Products, Inc.
Goodwin's Pawn Shop
Hornady Mfg. Co.
MEC, Inc.
Precision Reloading, Inc.
Spolar Power Load, Inc.
The A.W. Peterson Gun Shop, Inc.

PRESSES, SWAGE

Bullet Swaging Supply, Inc.
The A.W. Peterson Gun Shop, Inc.

PRIMING TOOLS & ACCESSORIES

GAR
Goodwin's Pawn Shop
Hart & Son, Inc.
Huntington Die Specialties
K&M Services
RCBS Operations/ATK
Simmons, Jerry
Sinclair International, Inc.
The A.W. Peterson Gun Shop, Inc.

REBORING & RERIFLING

Ahlman Guns
Barrel & Gunworks
Bauska Barrels
BlackStar AccuMax Barrels
BlackStar Barrel Accurizing
(See BlackStar AccuMax)
Buffalo Arms Co.
Champlin Firearms, Inc.
Ed's Gun House
Fred F. Wells/Wells Sport Store
Ivanoff, Thomas G.
(See Tom's Gun Repair)
Jackalope Gun Shop
Jonathan Arthur Ciener, Inc.
LaBounty Precision Reboring, Inc
NCP Products, Inc.
Pence Precision Barrels
Redman's Rifling & Reboring
Rice, Keith
(See White Rock Tool & Die)
Ridgetop Sporting Goods
Savage Arms, Inc.
Shaw, Inc., E. R.
(See Small Arms Mfg. Co.)
Siegrist Gun Shop
Simmons Gun Repair, Inc.
Stratco, Inc.
Terry K. Kopp Professional Gunsmithing
The Gun Works
Time Precision
Tom's Gun Repair, Thomas G. Ivanoff
Turnbull Restoration, Doug
Van Patten, J. W.
White Rock Tool & Die
Zufall, Joseph F.

RELOADING TOOLS AND ACCESSORIES

4-D Custom Die Co.
Advance Car Mover Co., Rowell Div.
American Products, Inc.
Ammo Load, Inc.
Armfield Custom Bullets
Armite Laboratories
Arms Corporation of the Philippines
Atlantic Rose, Inc.
Atsko/Sno-Seal, Inc.
Bald Eagle Precision Machine Co.
Ballistic Products, Inc.
Berger Bullets Ltd.
Berry's Mfg., Inc.
Blount, Inc., Sporting Equipment Div.
Blue Mountain Bullets
Blue Ridge Machinery & Tools, Inc.
Bonanza (See Forster Products)
Brown Co., E. Arthur
BRP, Inc. High Performance Cast Bullets
Brynin, Milton
B-Square Company, Inc.
Buck Stix-SOS Products Co.
Buffalo Arms Co.
Bull Mountain Rifle Co.
C&D Special Products (See Claybuster Wads & Harvester Bullets)
Camdex, Inc.
Camp-Cap Products
Canyon Cartridge Corp.
Case Sorting System
CCI/Speer Div of ATK
CH Tool & Die Co.
(See 4-D Custom Die Co.)
CheVron Bullets
Claybuster Wads & Harvester Bullets
Cook Engineering Service
Crouse's Country Cover
Cumberland Arms
Curtis Cast Bullets
Custom Products
(See Jones Custom Products)
CVA
D.C.C. Enterprises
Davide Pedersoli and Co.
Davis, Don
Davis Products, Mike
Denver Instrument Co.
Dillon Precision Products, Inc.
Dropkick
E&L Mfg., Inc.
Eagan, Donald V.
Eichelberger Bullets, Wm.
Enguix Import-Export
Euroarms of America, Inc.
E-Z-Way Systems
Federated-Fry (See Fry Metals)
Feken, Dennis
Ferguson, Bill
Fisher Custom Firearms
Flambeau, Inc.
Flitz International Ltd.
Forster Products
Fremont Tool Works
Fry Metals
Gehmann, Walter
(See Huntington Die Special
Graf & Sons
Graphics Direct
Graves Co.
Green, Arthur S.
Greenwood Precision
GTB-Custom Bullets
Gun City
Hanned Precision
(See The Hanned Line)
Harrell's Precision
Harris Enterprises
Harrison Bullets
Heidenstrom Bullets
High Precision
Hirtenberger AG
Hodgdon Powder Co.
Hoehn Sales, Inc.
Holland's Gunsmithing
Hondo Ind.
Hornady Mfg. Co.
Howell Machine
Hunters Supply, Inc.
Hutton Rifle Ranch
Image Ind. Inc.
Imperial Magnum Corp.
INTEC International, Inc.
Iosso Products
J&L Superior Bullets
(See Huntington Die Special)
Jack First, Inc.
Javelina Lube Products
JGS Precision Tool Mfg., LLC
JLK Bullets
Jonad Corp.
Jones Custom Products, Neil A.
Jones Moulds, Paul
K&M Services
Kapro Mfg. Co. Inc. (See R.E.I.)
Knoell, Doug
Korzinek Riflesmith, J.
L.A.R. Mfg., Inc.
L.E. Wilson, Inc.
Lapua Ltd.
Le Clear Industries
(See E-Z-Way Systems)
Lee Precision, Inc.
Liberty Metals
Liberty Shooting Supplies
Lightning Performance Innovatior Inc.
Lithi Bee Bullet Lube
Littleton, J. F.
Lock's Philadelphia Gun Exchange
Lortone Inc.
Lyman Instant Targets, Inc.
(See Lyman Products)
Lyman Products Corp.
MA Systems, Inc.
Magma Engineering Co.
MarMik, Inc.
Marquart Precision Co.
Match Prep-Doyle Gracey
Mayville Engineering Co.
(See MEC, Inc.)
MCS, Inc.
MEC, Inc.
Midway Arms, Inc.
MI-TE Bullets
Montana Armory, Inc.
(See C. Sharps Arms Co. Inc.)
Mo's Competitor Supplies
(See MCS, Inc.)
Mountain State Muzzleloading Supplies, Inc.
MTM Molded Products Co., Inc.
MWG Co.
Navy Arms Company
Newman Gunshop
North Devon Firearms Services
Old West Bullet Moulds

Box, Inc.
Sports Headquarters, Inc.
'See Small Custom Mould & Co.)
Sales & Services, Inc.
ccuracy
e Bullets
ss/Warren
River Arms
Reloading
ional Hunter Supplies
Star Custom Bullets)
ot Products, Inc.
ells Custom Gunsmith

o., Inc.
Bullet Mould Mfg. Co.
ing Specialties, Inc.
eith
White Rock Tool & Die)
ster Lead Works
r Laboratories
ach Precision Products
)
Redding Reloading Equipment)
Die & Cartridge Co.
ers Gun & Machine Shop
Iron Co.
e Greenwood Precision)
ck Assoc., R.E.
Shooter Supply
s Arms Co., Inc., C.
Specialty Prod. Co.
Eagle Machining
Machine
Custom Mould & Bullet Co.
Seal, Inc.
e Atsko/Sno-Seal, Inc.)
Products Co.
e Buck Stix-SOS Products Co.)
cer's Rifle Barrels, Inc.
LLC
Industries
art Corporation
Custom Bullets
Trading Co., Jedediah
vell, Robert
ey Point Products, Inc.
co, Inc.
arack Products, Inc.
corp Industries, Inc.

R
Industries, Inc.
a Gun Care
Hanned Line
Protector Mfg. Co., Inc.
mpson/Center Arms
Products
See Haselbauer Products, Jerry)
a Tool Co.
co Industries, Inc.
See Shooter's Choice Gun Care)
aShine, Inc.
a-Tek Co.
tavuori Oy/Kaltron-Pettibone
/Boos
B. Niemi Engineering
J. Riebe Co.
)-40 Co.
bster Scale Mfg. Co.
ite Rock Tool & Die
dener's Reloading & Shooting Supply, Inc.
se Custom Guns
odleigh
(See Huntington Die Specialties)
steryear Armory & Supply
ung Country Arms

RESTS BENCH, PORTABLE AND ACCESSORIES

Adventure 16, Inc.
Armor Metal Products
Bald Eagle Precision Machine Co.
Bartlett Engineering
Battenfeld Technologies Inc.
Blount/Outers ATK
Browning Arms Co.
B-Square Company, Inc.
Bull Mountain Rifle Co.
Canons Delcour
Clift Mfg., L. R.
Desert Mountain Mfg.
Greenwood Precision
Harris Engineering Inc.
Hart & Son, Inc.
Hidalgo, Tony
Hoehn Sales, Inc.
Hoppe's Div. Penguin Industries, Inc.
J&J Sales
Keng's Firearms Specialty, Inc./US Tactical Systems
Kolpin Outdoors, Inc.
Kramer Designs
Midway Arms, Inc.
Millett Sights
Protektor Model
Ransom International Corp.
Russ Haydon's Shooters' Supply
Saville Iron Co.
(See Greenwood Precision)
Sinclair International, Inc.
Stoney Point Products, Inc.
The A.W. Peterson Gun Shop, Inc.
The Outdoor Connection, Inc.
Thompson Target Technology
Tonoloway Tack Drives
Varmint Masters, LLC
Wichita Arms, Inc.
Zanotti Armor, Inc.
Ziegel Engineering

RIFLE BARREL MAKER

Airrow
American Safe Arms, Inc.
Barrel & Gunworks
Bauska Barrels
BlackStar AccuMax Barrels
BlackStar Barrel Accurizing
(See BlackStar AccuMax)
Border Barrels Ltd.
Brown Co., E. Arthur
Buchsenmachermeister
Bullberry Barrel Works, Ltd.
Bushmaster Firearms, Inc.
Canons Delcour
Carter's Gun Shop
Christensen Arms
Cincinnati Swaging
D.L. Unmussig Bullets
deHaas Barrels
Dilliott Gunsmithing, Inc.
DKT, Inc.
Donnelly, C. P.
Douglas Barrels, Inc.
Fred F. Wells/Wells Sport Store
Gaillard Barrels
Getz Barrel Company
Getz Barrel Company
Granite Mountain Arms, Inc.
Green Mountain Rifle Barrel Co., Inc.
Gruning Precision, Inc.
Half Moon Rifle Shop
Hart Rifle Barrels, Inc.
Hastings
Hofer Jagdwaffen, P.
H-S Precision, Inc.
Jackalope Gun Shop
Krieger Barrels, Inc.
Les Baer Custom, Inc.
Lilja Precision Rifle Barrels
Lothar Walther Precision Tool Inc.
McGowen Rifle Barrels
McMillan Rifle Barrels
Mid-America Recreation, Inc.
Modern Gun Repair School
Morrison Precision
N.C. Ordnance Co.
Obermeyer Rifled Barrels
Olympic Arms Inc.
Orion Rifle Barrel Co.
PAC-NOR Barreling
Pence Precision Barrels
Perazone-Gunsmith, Brian
Rogue Rifle Co., Inc.
Sabatti SPA
Savage Arms, Inc.
Schneider Rifle Barrels, Inc.
Shaw, Inc., E. R.
(See Small Arms Mfg. Co.)
Shilen, Inc.
Siskiyou Gun Works
(See Donnelly, C. P.)
Small Arms Mfg. Co.
Specialty Shooters Supply, Inc.
Spencer's Rifle Barrels, Inc.
Steyr Mannlicher GmbH & Co KG
Strutz Rifle Barrels, Inc., W. C.
Swift River Gunworks
Terry K. Kopp Professional Gunsmithing
The Gun Works
The Wilson Arms Co.
Turnbull Restoration, Doug
Verney-Carron
Virgin Valley Custom Guns
William E. Phillips Firearms
Wiseman and Co., Bill

SCOPES, MOUNTS, ACCESSORIES, OPTICAL EQUIPMENT

A.R.M.S., Inc.
Accu-Tek
Ackerman, Bill
(See Optical Services Co.)
Action Direct, Inc.
ADCO Sales, Inc.
Aimtech Mount Systems
Air Rifle Specialists
Air Venture Airguns
All Rite Products, Inc.
Alley Supply Co.
Alpec Team, Inc.
Apel GmbH, Ernst
ArmaLite, Inc.
Arundel Arms & Ammunition, Inc., A.
B.A.C.
Badger Creek Studio
Bansner's Ultimate Rifles, LLC
Barrett Firearms Manufacturer, Inc.
Beaver Park Product, Inc.
BEC, Inc.
Beeman Precision Airguns
Benjamin/Sheridan Co., Crosman
Bill Russ Trading Post
BKL Technologies
Blount, Inc., Sporting Equipment Div.
Blount/Outers ATK
Borden Rifles Inc.
Broad Creek Rifle Works, Ltd.
Brockman's Custom Gunsmithing
Brocock Ltd.
Brown Co., E. Arthur
Brownells, Inc.
Brunton U.S.A.
BSA Optics
B-Square Company, Inc.
Bull Mountain Rifle Co.
Burris Co., Inc.
Bushmaster Firearms, Inc.
Bushnell Sports Optics Worldwide
Butler Creek Corp.
Cabela's
Carl Zeiss Inc.
Center Lock Scope Rings
Chuck's Gun Shop
Clark Custom Guns, Inc.
Clearview Mfg. Co., Inc.
Compass Industries, Inc.
Compasseco, Ltd.
Concept Development Corp.
Conetrol Scope Mounts
Creedmoor Sports, Inc.
Crimson Trace Lasers
Crosman Airguns
Custom Quality Products, Inc.
D.C.C. Enterprises
D.L. Unmussig Bullets
Daisy Outdoor Products
Del-Sports, Inc.
DHB Products
Dolbare, Elizabeth
E. Arthur Brown Co.
Eagle Imports, Inc.
Eclectic Technologies, Inc.
Edmund Scientific Co.
Ednar, Inc.
Eggleston, Jere D.
Emerging Technologies, Inc.
(See Laseraim Technologies, Inc.)
Entre`prise Arms, Inc.
Euro-Imports
Evolution Gun Works, Inc.
Excalibur Electro Optics, Inc.
Excel Industries, Inc.
Falcon Industries, Inc.
Farr Studio, Inc.
Federal Arms Corp. of America
Freedom Arms, Inc.
Fujinon, Inc.
G.G. & G.
Galati International
Gentry Custom LLC
Gil Hebard Guns, Inc.
Gilmore Sports Concepts, Inc.
Goodwin's Pawn Shop
GSI, Inc.
Gun South, Inc. (See GSI, Inc.)
Guns Div. of D.C. Engineering, Inc.
Gunsmithing, Inc.
Hakko Co. Ltd.
Hammerli USA
Hart & Son, Inc.
Harvey, Frank
Highwood Special Products
Hiptmayer, Armurier
Hiptmayer, Klaus
Holland's Gunsmithing
Hunter Co., Inc.
Impact Case & Container, Inc.
Ironsighter Co.
Jeffredo Gunsight
Jena Eur
Jerry Phillips Optics
Jewell Triggers, Inc.
John Masen Co. Inc.
John's Custom Leather
Kahles A. Swarovski Company
Kalispel Case Line
KDF, Inc.
Keng's Firearms Specialty, Inc./US Tactical Systems
Kesselring Gun Shop
Kimber of America, Inc.
Knight's Mfg. Co.
Kowa Optimed, Inc.
KVH Industries, Inc.
Kwik-Site Co.
L&S Technologies Inc.
(See Aimtech Mount Systems)
L.A.R. Mfg., Inc.
Laser Devices, Inc.
Laseraim Technologies, Inc.
LaserMax, Inc.
Leapers, Inc.
Leica USA, Inc.
Les Baer Custom, Inc.
Leupold & Stevens, Inc.
List Precision Engineering
Lohman Mfg. Co., Inc.
Lomont Precision Bullets
London Guns Ltd.
Mac-1 Airgun Distributors
Mag-Na-Port International, Inc.
Mandall Shooting Supplies Inc.
Marksman Products
Maxi-Mount Inc.
McBros Rifle Co.
McMillan Optical Gunsight Co.
MCS, Inc.
MDS
Merit Corp.
Military Armament Corp.
Millett Sights
Mirador Optical Corp.
Mitchell Optics, Inc.
MMC
Mo's Competitor Supplies
(See MCS, Inc.)
MWG Co.
Navy Arms Company
New England Custom Gun Service
Nikon, Inc.
Norincoptics (See BEC, Inc.)
Olympic Optical Co.
Op-Tec
Optical Services Co.
Orchard Park Enterprise
Oregon Arms, Inc.
(See Rogue Rifle Co., Inc.)
Ozark Gun Works
Parker & Sons Shooting Supply
Parsons Optical Mfg. Co.
PECAR Herbert Schwarz GmbH
PEM's Mfg. Co.
Pentax Corp.
PMC/Eldorado Cartridge Corp.
Precision Sport Optics
Premier Reticles
Quarton Beamshot
R.A. Wells Custom Gunsmith
Ram-Line ATK
Ramon B. Gonzalez Guns
Ranch Products
Randolph Engineering, Inc.
Rice, Keith
(See White Rock Tool & Die)
Robinson Armament Co.
Rogue Rifle Co., Inc.
Romain's Custom Guns, Inc.
S&K Scope Mounts
Saunders Gun & Machine Shop
Schmidt & Bender, Inc.
Schumakers Gun Shop
Scope Control, Inc.
Score High Gunsmithing
Seecamp Co. Inc., L. W.
Segway Industries
Selsi Co., Inc.
Sharp Shooter Supply
Shepherd Enterprises, Inc.
Sightron, Inc.
Simmons Outdoor Corp.
Six Enterprises
Southern Bloomer Mfg. Co.
Spencer's Rifle Barrels, Inc.
Splitfire Sporting Goods, L.L.C.
Sportsmatch U.K. Ltd.
Springfield Armory
Springfield, Inc.
SSK Industries
Stiles Custom Guns
Stoeger Industries
Stoney Point Products, Inc.
Sturm Ruger & Co. Inc.
Sunny Hill Enterprises, Inc.

PRODUCT & SERVICE DIRECTORY

Swarovski Optik North America Ltd.
Swift Instruments, Inc.
T.K. Lee Co.
Talley, Dave
Tasco Sales, Inc.
Tele-Optics
The A.W. Peterson Gun Shop, Inc.
The Outdoor Connection, Inc.
Thompson/Center Arms
Traditions Performance Firearms
Trijicon, Inc.
Truglo, Inc.
U.S. Optics, A Division of Zeitz Optics U.S.A.
Ultra Dot Distribution
Uncle Mike's (See Michaels of Oregon Co.)
Unertl Optical Co., Inc.
United Binocular Co.
Virgin Valley Custom Guns
Visible Impact Targets
Voere-KGH GmbH
Warne Manufacturing Co.
Warren Muzzleloading Co., Inc.
Watson Bullets
Weaver Products ATK
Weaver Scope Repair Service
Webley and Scott Ltd.
Weigand Combat Handguns, Inc.
Wessinger Custom Guns & Engraving
Westley Richards & Co. Ltd.
White Rifles, Inc.
White Rock Tool & Die
Whitestone Lumber Corp.
Wideview Scope Mount Corp.
Wilcox Industries Corp.
Wild West Guns
Williams Gun Sight Co.
York M-1 Conversion
Zanotti Armor, Inc.

SHELLHOLDERS

Corbin Mfg. & Supply, Inc.
Fremont Tool Works
GAR
Goodwin's Pawn Shop
Hart & Son, Inc.
Hollywood Engineering
Huntington Die Specialties
K&M Services
King & Co.
Protektor Model
PWM Sales Ltd.
RCBS Operations/ATK
Redding Reloading Equipment
The A.W. Peterson Gun Shop, Inc.
Vega Tool Co.

SHOOTING/TRAINING SCHOOL

Alpine Indoor Shooting Range
American Gunsmithing Institute
American Small Arms Academy
Auto Arms
Beretta U.S.A. Corp.
Bob's Tactical Indoor Shooting Range & Gun Shop
Bridgeman Products
Chapman Academy of Practical Shooting
Chelsea Gun Club of New York City Inc.
Cherry Creek State Park Shooting Center
Cleland's Outdoor World, Inc
CQB Training
Defense Training International, Inc.
Executive Protection Institute
Ferris Firearms
Front Sight Firearms Training Institute
G.H. Enterprises Ltd.
Gene's Custom Guns
Gilmore Sports Concepts, Inc.
Griffin & Howe, Inc.
Griffin & Howe, Inc.
Griffin & Howe, Inc.
Guncraft Books (See Guncraft Sports, Inc.)
Guncraft Sports, Inc.
Guncraft Sports, Inc.
Gunsite Training Center
Henigson & Associates, Steve
Jensen's Custom Ammunition
Jensen's Firearms Academy
Kemen America
L.L. Bean, Inc.
Lethal Force Institute (See Police Bookshelf)
Loch Leven Industries/Convert-A-Pell
Long, George F.
McMurdo, Lynn (See Specialty Gunsmithing)
Mendez, John A.
NCP Products, Inc.
Nevada Pistol Academy, Inc.
North American Shooting Systems
North Mountain Pine Training Center
Nowlin Mfg. Co.
Paxton Quigley's Personal Protection Strategies
Pentheny de Pentheny
Performance Specialists
Police Bookshelf
Protektor Model
SAFE
Shoot Where You Look
Shooter's World
Shooters, Inc.
Sigarms, Inc.
Smith & Wesson
Specialty Gunsmithing
Starlight Training Center, Inc.
Tactical Defense Institute
The Firearm Training Center
The Midwest Shooting School
The Shooting Gallery
Thunden Ranch
Western Missouri Shooters Alliance
Yankee Gunsmith "Just Glocks"
Yavapai Firearms Academy Ltd.

SHOTSHELL MISCELLANY

American Products, Inc.
Ballistic Products, Inc.
Bridgeman Products
Goodwin's Pawn Shop
Lee Precision, Inc.
MEC, Inc.
Precision Reloading, Inc.
R.E.I.
RCBS Operations/ATK
T&S Industries, Inc.
The A.W. Peterson Gun Shop, Inc.
The Gun Works
Vitt/Boos
Ziegel Engineering

SIGHTS, METALLIC

100 Straight Products, Inc.
Accura-Site (See All's, The Jim Tembelis Co., Inc.)
Ad Hominem
Alley Supply Co.
All's, The Jim J. Tembelis Co., Inc.
Alpec Team, Inc.
Andela Tool & Machine, Inc.
AO Sight Systems
ArmaLite, Inc.
Ashley Outdoors, Inc.
Aspen Outfitting Co.
Axtell Rifle Co.
B.A.C.
Ballard Rifle & Cartridge Co., LLC
BEC, Inc.
Bob's Gun Shop
Bo-Mar Tool & Mfg. Co.
Bond Custom Firearms
Bowen Classic Arms Corp.
Brockman's Custom Gunsmithing
Brooks Tactical Systems-Agrip
Brown Co., E. Arthur
Brown Dog Ent.
Brownells, Inc.
Buffalo Arms Co.
Bushmaster Firearms, Inc.
C. Sharps Arms Co. Inc./Montana Armory
California Sights (See Fautheree, Andy)
Campbell, Dick
Cape Outfitters
Cape Outfitters
Cash Mfg. Co., Inc.
Center Lock Scope Rings
Champion's Choice, Inc.
Chip McCormick Corp.
C-More Systems
Colonial Repair
CRR, Inc./Marble's Inc.
Davide Pedersoli and Co.
DHB Products
Dixie Gun Works
DPMS (Defense Procurement Manufacturing Services, Inc.)
E. Arthur Brown Co.
Effebi SNC-Dr. Franco Beretta
Evolution Gun Works, Inc.
Falcon Industries, Inc.
Farr Studio, Inc.
G.G. & G.
Garthwaite Pistolsmith, Inc., Jim
Goergen's Gun Shop, Inc.
Goodwin's Pawn Shop
Guns Div. of D.C. Engineering, Inc.
Gunsmithing, Inc.
Hank's Gun Shop
Heidenstrom Bullets
Heinie Specialty Products
Hesco-Meprolight
Hiptmayer, Armurier
Hiptmayer, Klaus
I.S.S.
Innovative Weaponry Inc.
J.G. Anschutz GmbH & Co. KG
J.P. Enterprises Inc.
Keng's Firearms Specialty, Inc./US Tactical Systems
Knight Rifles
Knight's Mfg. Co.
L.P.A. Inc.
Leapers, Inc.
Les Baer Custom, Inc.
List Precision Engineering
London Guns Ltd.
Lyman Instant Targets, Inc. (See Lyman Products)
Mandall Shooting Supplies Inc.
Marble Arms (See CRR, Inc./Marble's Inc.)
MCS, Inc.
MEC-Gar S.R.L.
Meprolight (See Hesco-Meprolight)
Merit Corp.
Mid-America Recreation, Inc.
Middlebrooks Custom Shop
Millett Sights
MMC
Modern Muzzleloading, Inc.
Montana Armory, Inc. (See C. Sharps Arms Co. Inc.)
Montana Vintage Arms
Mo's Competitor Supplies (See MCS, Inc.)
Navy Arms Company
New England Custom Gun Service
Newman Gunshop
Novak's, Inc.
OK Weber, Inc.
One Ragged Hole
Parker & Sons Shooting Supply
PEM's Mfg. Co.
Perazone-Gunsmith, Brian
RPM
Sharps Arms Co., Inc., C.
Slug Site
STI International
T.F.C. S.p.A.
Talley, Dave
Tank's Rifle Shop
The A.W. Peterson Gun Shop, Inc.
The Gun Doctor
Trijicon, Inc.
Truglo, Inc.
U.S. Optics, A Division of Zeitz Optics U.S.A.
Warne Manufacturing Co.
Weigand Combat Handguns, Inc.
Wichita Arms, Inc.
Wild West Guns
Williams Gun Sight Co.
Wilsom Combat
Wilsom Combat

STOCK MAKER

Acra-Bond Laminates
Amrine's Gun Shop
Antique Arms Co.
Artistry in Wood
Aspen Outfitting Co.
Bain & Davis, Inc.
Bansner's Ultimate Rifles, LLC
Baron Technology
Belding's Custom Gun Shop
Billings Gunsmiths
Bob Rogers Gunsmithing
Boltin, John M.
Borden Ridges Rimrock Stocks
Bowerly, Kent
Boyds' Gunstock Industries, Inc.
Brace, Larry D.
Briganti, A.J.
Broad Creek Rifle Works, Ltd.
Brown Precision, Inc.
Buchsenmachermeister
Bull Mountain Rifle Co.
Bullberry Barrel Works, Ltd.
Burkhart Gunsmithing, Don
Cambos Outdoorsman
Cambos Outdoorsman
Caywood, Shane J.
Chicasaw Gun Works
Chuck's Gun Shop
Claro Walnut Gunstock Co.
Coffin, Charles H.
Colorado Gunsmithing Academy
Custom Riflestocks, Inc., Michael M. Kokolus
Custom Single Shot Rifles
D&D Gunsmiths, Ltd.
Dangler, Homer L.
D'Arcy Echols & Co.
DGR Custom Rifles
DGR Custom Rifles
DGS, Inc., Dale A. Storey
Don Klein Custom Guns
Erhardt, Dennis
Eversull Co., Inc.
Fieldsport Ltd.
Fisher, Jerry A.
Forster, Larry L.
Fred F. Wells/Wells Sport Store
Gary Goudy Classic Stocks
Genecco Gun Works
Gene's Custom Guns
Gillmann, Edwin
Grace, Charles E.
Great American Gunstock Co.
Gruning Precision, Inc.
Gunsmithing Ltd.
Hank's Gun Shop
Harper's Custom Stocks
Harry Lawson Co.
Heilmann, Stephen
Hensley, Gunmaker, Darwin
Heydenberk, Warren R.
High Tech Specialties, Inc.
Hofer Jagdwaffen, P.
Huebner, Corey O.
Island Pond Gun Shop
Jack Dever Co.
Jamison's Forge Works
Jay McCament Custom Gunmak
Jim Norman Custom Gunstocks
John Rigby & Co.
K. Eversull Co., Inc.
Keith's Custom Gunstocks
Ken Eyster Heritage Gunsmiths,
Larry Lyons Gunworks
Marshall Fish Mfg. Gunsmith Spt
Mathews Gun Shop & Gunsmith Inc.
McGowen Rifle Barrels
Mercer Custom Guns
Mid-America Recreation, Inc.
Mike Yee Custom Stocking
Mitchell, Jack
Modern Gun Repair School
Morrow, Bud
Nelson's Custom Guns, Inc.
Nettestad Gun Works
Nickels, Paul R.
Paul and Sharon Dressel
Paul D. Hillmer Custom Gunstock
Paulsen Gunstocks
Pawling Mountain Club
Pecatonica River Longrifle
Pentheny de Pentheny
Quality Custom Firearms
R&J Gun Shop
R.A. Wells Custom Gunsmith
Ralph Bone Engraving
RMS Custom Gunsmithing
Robinson, Don
Ron Frank Custom Classic Arms
Royal Arms Gunstocks
Royal Arms Gunstocks
Ruger's Custom Guns
Six Enterprises
Skeoch, Brian R.
Smith, Art
Smith, Sharmon
Speiser, Fred D.
Steven Dodd Hughes
Stott's Creek Armory, Inc.
Sturgeon Valley Sporters
Taylor & Robbins
Tennessee Valley Mfg.
The Custom Shop
Tiger-Hunt Gunstocks
Trico Plastics
Tucker, James C.
Turnbull Restoration, Doug
Vest, John
Walker Arms Co., Inc.
Wayne E. Schwartz Custom Guns
Weber & Markin Custom Gunsmiths
Wenig Custom Gunstocks
Wiebe, Duane
Wild West Guns
Williamson Precision Gunsmithing
Winter, Robert M.
Working Guns

:KS (COMMERCIAL)

:y Unlimited
nd Laminates
Import Co.
Guns
Outfitting Co.

, Harry
, Joe
r's Ultimate Rifles, LLC
Bullets, Inc.
eld Technologies Inc.
ger, George
's Custom Gun Shop
Carlson, Inc.
, Inc., Sporting Equipment Div.
/Outers ATK
Gun Shop
Ridges Rimrock Stocks
Rifles Inc.
ly, Kent
' Gunstock Industries, Inc.
nan's Custom Gunsmithing
Co., E. Arthur
orn Gun Works
ountain Rifle Co.
Creek Corp.
Hardwoods, Inc.
Outfitters
ood, Shane J.
bers Flintlocks Ltd., Jim
saw Gun Works
i, Stephen
Walnut Gunstock Co.
, Charles H.
, Jim (See Working Guns)
ial Repair
ado Gunsmithing Academy
ado School of Trades
ad, C. A.
Maple Stock Blanks
ee Tiger-Hunt)
om Checkering Service, Kathy
ster
om Riflestocks, Inc., Michael M.
kolus
Gunsmiths, Ltd.
Precision Duplicators
ee Greene Precision)
d W. Schwartz Custom Guns
de Pedersoli and Co.
Custom Rifles
ne's Gun Repair
ee DGR Custom Rifles)
can's Gun Works, Inc.
oi SNC-Dr. Franco Beretta
eston, Jere D.
ardt, Dennis
rsull Co., Inc.
on Industries, Inc.
on Industries, Inc.
on Products, Inc.
dsport Ltd.
er, Jerry A.
ks, Donald E.
ster, Kathy
See Custom Checkering)
hofer's Gunsmithing &
Knifemaking
ncotte & Cie S.A. Auguste
me Haven Gunstocks
orge Hoenig, Inc.
rvais, Mike
mann, Edwin
on, Robert E.
ens, Dale W.
lden Age Arms Co.
odwin's Pawn Shop
eat American Gunstock Co.
een, Roger M.
Greenwood Precision
Guns Div. of D.C. Engineering, Inc.
Hammerli USA
Hanson's Gun Center, Dick
Harper's Custom Stocks
Harry Lawson Co.
Harwood, Jack O.
Hecht, Hubert J., Waffen-Hecht
Hensley, Gunmaker, Darwin
High Tech Specialties, Inc.
Hiptmayer, Armurier
Hiptmayer, Klaus
Hogue Grips
H-S Precision, Inc.
Huebner, Corey O.
Island Pond Gun Shop
Israel Arms Inc.
Ivanoff, Thomas G.
(See Tom's Gun Repair)
Jackalope Gun Shop
Jarrett Rifles, Inc.
Jim Norman Custom Gunstocks
John Masen Co. Inc.
Johnson Wood Products
KDF, Inc.
Keith's Custom Gunstocks
Kelbly, Inc.
Kilham & Co.
Klingler Woodcarving
Lawson Co., Harry
Mandall Shooting Supplies Inc.
McBros Rifle Co.
McDonald, Dennis
McMillan Fiberglass Stocks, Inc.
Michaels Of Oregon, Co.
Mid-America Recreation, Inc.
Miller Arms, Inc.
Mitchell, Jack
Morrison Custom Rifles, J. W.
MPI Stocks
MWG Co.
NCP Products, Inc.
Nelson's Custom Guns, Inc.
New England Arms Co.
New England Custom Gun Service
Newman Gunshop
Nickels, Paul R.
Oil Rod and Gun Shop
Old World Gunsmithing
One Of A Kind
Ottmar, Maurice
Pagel Gun Works, Inc.
Paragon Sales & Services, Inc.
Parker & Sons Shooting Supply
Paul and Sharon Dressel
Paul D. Hillmer Custom Gunstocks
Paulsen Gunstocks
Pawling Mountain Club
Pecatonica River Longrifle
PEM's Mfg. Co.
Perazone-Gunsmith, Brian
Powell & Son (Gunmakers) Ltd., William
Precision Gun Works
R&J Gun Shop
R.A. Wells Custom Gunsmith
Ram-Line ATK
Ramon B. Gonzalez Guns
Rampart International
Richards Micro-Fit Stocks
RMS Custom Gunsmithing
Robinson, Don
Robinson Armament Co.
Robinson Firearms Mfg. Ltd.
Romain's Custom Guns, Inc.
Ron Frank Custom Classic Arms
Royal Arms Gunstocks
Saville Iron Co.
(See Greenwood Precision)
Schiffman, Mike
Score High Gunsmithing
Simmons Gun Repair, Inc.
Six Enterprises
Speiser, Fred D.
Stan De Treville & Co.
Stiles Custom Guns
Swann, D. J.
Swift River Gunworks
Szweda, Robert
(See RMS Custom Gunsmithing)
T.F.C. S.p.A.
Tecnolegno S.p.A.
The A.W. Peterson Gun Shop, Inc.
The Gun Shop
The Orvis Co.
Tiger-Hunt Gunstocks
Tirelli
Tom's Gun Repair, Thomas G. Ivanoff
Track of the Wolf, Inc.
Trevallion Gunstocks
Tuttle, Dale
Vic's Gun Refinishing
Vintage Industries, Inc.
Virgin Valley Custom Guns
Volquartsen Custom Ltd.
Walker Arms Co., Inc.
Weber & Markin Custom Gunsmiths
Weems, Cecil
Wenig Custom Gunstocks
Werth, T. W.
Western Mfg. Co.
Wild West Guns
Williams Gun Sight Co.
Windish, Jim
Working Guns
Wright's Gunstock Blanks
Zeeryp, Russ

STUCK CASE REMOVERS

GAR
Goodwin's Pawn Shop
Huntington Die Specialties
MarMik, Inc.
The A.W. Peterson Gun Shop, Inc.
Tom's Gun Repair, Thomas G. Ivanoff

TARGETS, BULLET & CLAYBIRD TRAPS

Action Target, Inc.
Air Arms
American Target
Autauga Arms, Inc.
Beeman Precision Airguns
Benjamin/Sheridan Co., Crosman
Birchwood Casey
Blount, Inc., Sporting Equipment Div.
Blount/Outers ATK
Blue and Gray Products Inc.
(See Ox-Yoke Originals)
Brown Precision, Inc.
Bull-X, Inc.
Caswell International
Champion Target Co.
Creedmoor Sports, Inc.
Crosman Airguns
D.C.C. Enterprises
Daisy Outdoor Products
Diamond Mfg. Co.
Federal Champion Target Co.
G.H. Enterprises Ltd.
H-S Precision, Inc.
Hunterjohn
J.G. Dapkus Co., Inc.
Kennebec Journal
Kleen-Bore, Inc.
Lakefield Arms Ltd.
(See Savage Arms, Inc.)
Leapers, Inc.
Littler Sales Co.
Lyman Instant Targets, Inc.
(See Lyman Products)
Marksman Products
Mendez, John A.
Mountain Plains Industries
MSR Targets
N.B.B., Inc.
National Target Co.
North American Shooting Systems
Outers Laboratories Div. of ATK
Ox-Yoke Originals, Inc.
Palsa Outdoor Products
Passive Bullet Traps, Inc.
(See Savage Range Systems, Inc.)
PlumFire Press, Inc.
Precision Airgun Sales, Inc.
Protektor Model
Quack Decoy & Sporting Clays
Remington Arms Co., Inc.
Rockwood Corp.
Rocky Mountain Target Co.
Savage Range Systems, Inc.
Schaefer Shooting Sports
Seligman Shooting Products
Shooters Supply
Shoot-N-C Targets
(See Birchwood Casey)
Target Shooting, Inc.
The A.W. Peterson Gun Shop, Inc.
Thompson Target Technology
Trius Traps, Inc.
Universal Sports
Visible Impact Targets
Watson Bullets
Woods Wise Products
World of Targets
(See Birchwood Casey)
X-Spand Target Systems

TAXIDERMY

African Import Co.
Bill Russ Trading Post
Kulis Freeze Dry Taxidermy
World Trek, Inc.

TRAP & SKEET SHOOTER'S EQUIPMENT

American Products, Inc.
Bagmaster Mfg., Inc.
Ballistic Products, Inc.
Beretta S.P.A., Pietro
Blount/Outers ATK
Bob Allen Sportswear
Bridgeman Products
C&H Research
Cape Outfitters
Claybuster Wads & Harvester Bullets
Fiocchi of America, Inc.
G.H. Enterprises Ltd.
Hoppe's Div. Penguin Industries, Inc.
Jamison's Forge Works
Jenkins Recoil Pads
Jim Noble Co.
Kalispel Case Line
Kolar
Lakewood Products LLC
Ljutic Industries, Inc.
Mag-Na-Port International, Inc.
MEC, Inc.
Moneymaker Guncraft Corp.
MTM Molded Products Co., Inc.
NCP Products, Inc.
Pachmayr Div. Lyman Products
Palsa Outdoor Products
Pro-Port Ltd.
Protektor Model
Quack Decoy & Sporting Clays
Remington Arms Co., Inc.
Rhodeside, Inc.
Shooting Specialties
(See Titus, Daniel)
Shotgun Sports Magazine, dba Shootin' Accessories Ltd.
Stan Baker Sports
T&S Industries, Inc.
TEN-X Products Group
The Gun Works
Trius Traps, Inc.
Truglo, Inc.
Universal Sports
Warne Manufacturing Co.
Weber & Markin Custom Gunsmiths
X-Spand Target Systems
Ziegel Engineering

TRIGGERS, RELATED EQUIPMENT

Actions by "T" Teddy Jacobson
B&D Trading Co., Inc.
Behlert Precision, Inc.
Bond Custom Firearms
Boyds' Gunstock Industries, Inc.
Broad Creek Rifle Works, Ltd.
Bull Mountain Rifle Co.
Chicasaw Gun Works
Dayton Traister
Dolbare, Elizabeth
Electronic Trigger Systems, Inc.
Eversull Co., Inc.
Feinwerkbau Westinger & Altenburger
Gentry Custom LLC
Goodwin's Pawn Shop
Hart & Son, Inc.
Hawken Shop, The
(See Dayton Traister)
Hoehn Sales, Inc.
Holland's Gunsmithing
Impact Case & Container, Inc.
J.P. Enterprises Inc.
Jewell Triggers, Inc.
John Masen Co. Inc.
Jones Custom Products, Neil A.
K. Eversull Co., Inc.
KK Air International
(See Impact Case & Container Co.)
Knight's Mfg. Co.
L&R Lock Co.
Les Baer Custom, Inc.
List Precision Engineering
London Guns Ltd.
M.H. Canjar Co.
Mahony, Philip Bruce
Master Lock Co.
Miller Single Trigger Mfg. Co.
NCP Products, Inc.
Neil A. Jones Custom Products
Nowlin Mfg. Co.
PEM's Mfg. Co.
Penrod Precision
Perazone-Gunsmith, Brian
Ramon B. Gonzalez Guns
Robinson Armament Co.
Sharp Shooter Supply
Shilen, Inc.
Simmons Gun Repair, Inc.
Spencer's Rifle Barrels, Inc.
Tank's Rifle Shop
Target Shooting, Inc.
The A.W. Peterson Gun Shop, Inc.
The Gun Works
Watson Bullets

MANUFACTURER'S DIRECTORY

A

A Zone Bullets, 2039 Walter Rd., Billings, MT 59105 / 800-252-3111; FAX: 406-248-1961

A&B Industries, Inc (See Top-Line USA Inc.)

A&W Repair, 2930 Schneider Dr., Arnold, MO 63010 / 617-287-3725

A.A. Arms, Inc., 4811 Persimmont Ct., Monroe, NC 28110 / 704-289-5356; or 800-935-1119; FAX: 704-289-5859

A.B.S. III, 9238 St. Morritz Dr., Fern Creek, KY 40291

A.G. Russell Knives, Inc., 1920 North 26th Street, Springdale, AR 72764 / 479-751-7341; FAX: 479-751-4520 ag@agrussell.com agrussell.com

A.R.M.S., Inc., 230 W. Center St., West Bridgewater, MA 02379-1620 / 508-584-7816; FAX: 508-588-8045

A.W. Peterson Gun Shop, Inc., 4255 W. Old U.S. 441, Mt. Dora, FL 32757-3299 / 352-383-4258; FAX: 352-735-1001

AC Dyna-tite Corp., 155 Kelly St., P.O. Box 0984, Elk Grove Village, IL 60007 / 847-593-5566; FAX: 847-593-1304

Acadian Ballistic Specialties, P.O. Box 787, Folsom, LA 70437 / 504-796-0078 gunsmith@neasolft.com

Accuracy International, Foster, PO Box 111, Wilsall, MT 59086 / 406-587-7922; FAX: 406-585-9434

Accuracy Internationl Precision Rifles (See U.S.)

Accuracy Int'l. North America, Inc., PO Box 5267, Oak Ridge, TN 37831 / 423-482-0330; FAX: 423-482-0336

Accuracy Unlimited, 16036 N. 49 Ave., Glendale, AZ 85306 / 602-978-9089; FAX: 602-978-9089 fglenn@cox.net www.glenncustom.com

Accuracy Unlimited, 7479 S. DePew St., Littleton, CO 80123

Accura-Site (See All's, The Jim Tembelis Co., Inc.)

Accurate Arms Co., Inc., 5891 Hwy. 230 West, McEwen, TN 37101 / 931-729-4207; FAX: 931-729-4211 burrensburg@aac-ca.com www.accuratepowder.com

Accu-Tek, 4510 Carter Ct., Chino, CA 91710

Ace Custom 45's, Inc., 1880 1/2 Upper Turtle Creek Rd., Kerrville, TX 78028 / 830-257-4290; FAX: 830-257-5724 www.acecustom45.com

Ackerman & Co., Box 133 US Highway Rt. 7, Pownal, VT 05261 / 802-823-9874 muskets@togsther.net

Ackerman, Bill (See Optical Services Co.)

Acra-Bond Laminates, 134 Zimmerman Rd., Kalispell, MT 59901 / 406-257-9003; FAX: 406-257-9003 merlins@digisys.net www.acrabondlaminates.com

Action Bullets & Alloy Inc., RR 1, P.O. Box 189, Quinter, KS 67752 / 785-754-3609; FAX: 785-754-3629 bullets@ruraltel.net

Action Direct, Inc., P.O. Box 770400, Miami, FL 33177 / 305-969-0056; FAX: 305-256-3541 www.action-direct.com

Action Products, Inc., 22 N. Mulberry St., Hagerstown, MD 21740 / 301-797-1414; FAX: 301-733-2073

Action Target, Inc., PO Box 636, Provo, UT 84603 / 801-377-8033; FAX: 801-377-8096

Actions by "T" Teddy Jacobson, 16315 Redwood Forest Ct., Sugar Land, TX 77478 / 281-277-4008; FAX: 281-277-9112 tjacobson@houston.rr.com www.actionsbyt.us

AcuSport Corporation, 1 Hunter Place, Bellefontaine, OH 43311-3001 / 513-593-7010; FAX: 513-592-5625

Ad Hominem, 3130 Gun Club Lane, RR #3, Orillia, ON L3V 6H3 CANADA / 705-689-5303; FAX: 705-689-5303

Adair Custom Shop, Bill, 2886 Westridge, Carrollton, TX 75006

ADCO Sales, Inc., 4 Draper St. #A, Woburn, MA 01801 / 781-935-1799; FAX: 781-935-1011

Adkins, Luther, 1292 E. McKay Rd., Shelbyville, IN 46176-8706 / 317-392-3795

Advance Car Mover Co., Rowell Div., P.O. Box 1, 240 N. Depot St., Juneau, WI 53039 / 414-386-4464; FAX: 414-386-4416

Advantage Arms, Inc., 25163 W. Ave. Stanford, Valencia, CA 91355 / 661-257-2290

Adventure 16, Inc., 4620 Alvarado Canyon Rd., San Diego, CA 92120 / 619-283-6314

Aero Peltor, 90 Mechanic St., Southbridge, MA 01550 / 508-764-5500; FAX: 508-764-0188

African Import Co., 22 Goodwin Rd, Plymouth, MA 02360 / 508-746-8552; FAX: 508-746-0404 africanimport@aol.com

AFSCO Ammunition, 731 W. Third St., P.O. Box L, Owen, WI 54460 / 715-229-2516 sailers@webtv.net

Ahlman Guns, 9525 W. 230th St., Morristown, MN 55052 / 507-685-4243; FAX: 507-685-4280 www.ahlmans.com

Ahrends, Kim (See Custom Firearms, Inc), Box 203, Clarion, IA 50525 / 515-532-3449; FAX: 515-532-3926

Aimtech Mount Systems, P.O. Box 223, Thomasville, GA 31799 / 229-226-4313; FAX: 229-227-0222 mail@aimtech-mounts.com www.aimtech-mounts.com

Air Arms, Hailsham Industrial Park, Diplocks Way, Hailsham, E. Sussex, BN27 3JF ENGLAND / 011-0323-845853

Air Rifle Specialists, P.O. Box 138, 130 Holden Rd., Pine City, NY 14871-0138 / 607-734-7340; FAX: 607-733-3261 ars@stny.rr.com www.air-rifles.com

Air Venture Airguns, 9752 E. Flower St., Bellflower, CA 90706 / 562-867-6355

AirForce Airguns, P.O. Box 2478, Fort Worth, TX 76113 / 817-451-8966; FAX: 817-451-1613 www.airforceairguns.com

Airrow, 11 Monitor Hill Rd., Newtown, CT 06470 / 203-270-6343

Aitor-Cuchilleria Del Norte S.A., Izelaieta, 17, 48260, Ermua, S SPAIN / 43-17-08-50 info@aitor.com www.ailor.com

Ajax Custom Grips, Inc., 9130 Viscount Row, Dallas, TX 75247 / 214-630-8893; FAX: 214-630-4942

Aker International, Inc., 2248 Main St., Suite 6, Chula Vista, CA 91911 / 619-423-5182; FAX: 619-423-1363 aker@akerleather.com www.akerleather.com

AKJ Concealco, P.O. Box 871596, Vancouver, WA 98687-1596 / 360-891-8222; FAX: 360-891-8221 Concealco@aol.com www.greatholsters.com

Alana Cupp Custom Engraver, P.O. Box 207, Annabella, UT 84711 / 801-896-4834

Alaska Bullet Works, Inc., 9978 Crazy Horse Drive, Juneau, AK 99801 / 907-789-3834; FAX: 907-789-3433

Alaskan Silversmith, The, 2145 Wagner Hollow Rd., Fort Plain, NY 13339 / 518-993-3983 sidbell@capital.net www.sidbell.cizland.com

Aldis Gunsmithing & Shooting Supply, 502 S. Montezuma St., Prescott, AZ 86303 / 602-445-6723; FAX: 602-445-6763

Alessi Holsters, Inc., 2465 Niagara Falls Blvd., Amherst, NY 14228-3527 / 716-691-5615

Alex, Inc., 3420 Cameron Bridge Rd., Manhattan, MT 59741-8523 / 406-282-7396; FAX: 406-282-7396

Alfano, Sam, 36180 Henry Gaines Rd., Pearl River, LA 70452 / 504-863-3364; FAX: 504-863-7715

All American Lead Shot Corp., P.O. Box 224566, Dallas, TX 75062

All Rite Products, Inc., 9554 Wells Circle, Suite D, West Jordan, UT 84088-6226 / 800-771-8471; FAX: 801-280-8302 info@allriteproducts.com www.allriteproducts.com

Allard, Gary/Creek Side Metal & Woodcrafters, Fishers Hill, VA 22626 / 703-465-3903

Allen Co., Inc., 525 Burbank St., Broomfield, CO 80020 / 303-469-1857; or 800-876-8600; FAX: 303-466-7437

Allen Firearm Engraving, P.O. Box 155, Camp Verde, AZ 86322 / 928-567-6711 rosebudmukco@netzero.com

Allen Mfg., 6449 Hodgson Rd., Circle Pines, MN 55014 / 612-429-8231

Alley Supply Co., PO Box 848, Gardnerville, NV 89410 / 775-782-3800; FAX: 775-782-3827 jetalley@aol.com www.alleysupplyco.com

Alliant Techsystems Smokeless Powder Group, P.O. Box 6, Rt. 114, Bldg. 229, Radford, VA 24141-0096 www.alliantpowder.com

Allred Bullet Co., 932 Evergreen Drive, Logan, UT 84321 / 435-752-6983; FAX: 435-752-6983

All's, The Jim J. Tembelis Co., Inc., 216 Loper Ct., Neenah, WI 54956 / 920-725-5251; FAX: 920-725-5251

Alpec Team, Inc., 201 Ricken Backer Cir., Livermore, CA 94550 / 510-606-8245; FAX: 510-606-4279

Alpha 1 Drop Zone, 2121 N. Tyler, Wichita, KS 67212 / 316-729-0800; FAX: 316-729-4262 www.alpha1dropzone.com

Alpha LaFranck Enterprises, P.O. Box 81072, Lincoln, NE 68501 / 402-466-3193

Alpha Precision, Inc., 3238 Della Slaton Rd., Comer, GA 30629-2212 / 706-783-2131 jim@alphaprecisioninc.com www.alphaprecisioninc.com

Alpine Indoor Shooting Range, 2401 Government Way, Coeur d'Alene, ID 83814 / 208-676-8824; FAX: 208-676-8824

Altamont Co., 901 N. Church St., P.O. Box 309, Thomasboro, IL 61878 / 217-643-3125; or 800-626-5774; FAX: 217-643-7973

Alumna Sport by Dee Zee, 1572 NE 58th Ave., P.O. Box 3090, Des Moines, IA 50316 / 800-798-9899

Amadeo Rossi S.A., Rua: Amadeo Rossi, 143, Sao Leopoldo, RS 93030-220 BRAZIL / 051-592-5566

AmBr Software Group Ltd., P.O. Box 301, Reistertown, MD 21136-0301 / 800-888-1917; FAX: 410-526-7212

American Ammunition, 3545 NW 71st St., Miami, FL 33147 / 305-835-7400; FAX: 305-694-0037

American Derringer Corp., 127 N. Lacy Dr., Waco, TX 7 / 800-642-7817; or 254-799-9111; FAX: 254-799-

American Display Co., 55 Cromwell St., Providence, RI / 401-331-2464; FAX: 401-421-1264

American Gas & Chemical Co., Ltd, 220 Pegasus Ave, Northvale, NJ 07647 / 201-767-7300

American Gripcraft, 3230 S Dodge 2, Tucson, AZ 857 602-790-1222

American Gunsmithing Institute, 1325 Imola Ave #504, CA 94559 / 707-253-0462; FAX: 707-253-7149

American Handgunner Magazine, 591 Camino de la Re Ste. 200, San Diego, CA 92108 / 619-297-5350; F 619-297-5353

American Pioneer Video, PO Box 50049, Bowling Gree 42102-2649 / 800-743-4675

American Products, Inc., 14729 Spring Valley Road, Morrison, IL 61270 / 815-772-3336; FAX: 815-772

American Safe Arms, Inc., 1240 Riverview Dr., Garland 84312 / 801-257-7472; FAX: 801-785-8156

American Security Products Co., 11925 Pacific Ave., Fo CA 92337 / 909-685-9680; or 800-421-6142; FAX 909-685-9685

American Small Arms Academy, P.O. Box 12111, Pres AZ 86304 / 602-778-5623

American Target, 1328 S. Jason St., Denver, CO 80223 303-733-0433; FAX: 303-777-0311

American Target Knives, 1030 Brownwood NW, Grand Rapids, MI 49504 / 616-453-1998

Americase, P.O. Box 271, 1610 E. Main, Waxahachie, T 75165 / 800-880-3629; FAX: 214-937-8373

Ames Metal Products, 4323 S. Western Blvd., Chicago, 60609 / 773-523-3230; or 800-255-6937; FAX: 773-523-3854

Amherst Arms, P.O. Box 1457, Englewood, FL 34295 / 941-475-2020; FAX: 941-473-1212

Ammo Load, Inc., 1560 E. Edinger, Suite G, Santa Ana, 92705 / 714-558-8858; FAX: 714-569-0319

Amrine's Gun Shop, 937 La Luna, Ojai, CA 93023 / 805-646-2376

Amsec, 11925 Pacific Ave., Fontana, CA 92337

Analog Devices, Box 9106, Norwood, MA 02062

Andela Tool & Machine, Inc., RD3, Box 246, Richfield Springs, NY 13439

Anderson Manufacturing Co., Inc., 22602 53rd Ave. SE, Bothell, WA 98021 / 206-481-1858; FAX: 206-481-

Andres & Dworsky KG, Bergstrasse 18, A-3822 Karlsteir Thaya, AUSTRIA / 0 28 44-285; FAX: 02844 28619 andres.dnorsky@wvnet.as

Angelo & Little Custom Gun Stock Blanks, P.O. Box 240 Dell, MT 59724-0046

Answer Products Co., 1519 Westbury Drive, Davison, M 48423 / 810-653-2911

Antique American Firearms, P.O. Box 71035, Dept. GD, D Moines, IA 50325 / 515-224-6552

Antique Arms Co., 1110 Cleveland Ave., Monett, MO 6570 417-235-6501

AO Sight Systems, 2401 Ludelle St., Fort Worth, TX 7610 888-744-4880; or 817-536-0136; FAX: 817-536-351

Apel GmbH, Ernst, Am Kirschberg 3, D-97218, Gerbrunn GERMANY / 0 (931) 707192 info@eaw.de www.eaw

Aplan Antiques & Art, James O., James O., HC 80, Box 793-25, Piedmont, SD 57769 / 605-347-5016

AR-7 Industries, LLC, 998 N. Colony Rd., Meriden, CT 064 / 203-630-3536; FAX: 203-630-3637

Arizona Ammunition, Inc., 21421 No. 14th Ave., Suite E, Phoenix, AZ 85027 / 623-516-9004; FAX: 623-516-90 www.azammo.com

ArmaLite, Inc., P.O. Box 299, Geneseo, IL 61254 / 800-336-0184; or 309-944-6939; FAX: 309-944-6949

Armament Gunsmithing Co., Inc., 525 Rt. 22, Hillside, NJ 07205 / 908-686-0960; FAX: 718-738-5019 armamentgunsmithing@worldnet.att.net

Armas Garbi, S.A., 12-14 20.600 Urki, 12, Eibar (Guipuzco SPAIN / 943203873; FAX: 943203873 armosgarbi@euskalnet.n

Armas Kemen S. A. (See U.S. Importers)

Armfield Custom Bullets, 10584 County Road 100, Carthag MO 64836 / 417-359-8480; FAX: 417-359-8497

Armi Perazzi S.P.A., Via Fontanelle 1/3, 1-25080, Botticino Mattina, ITALY / 030-2692591; FAX: 030 2692594

Armi San Marco (See U.S. Importers-Taylor's & Co.)

Armi San Paolo, 172-A, I-25062, via Europa, ITALY / 030-2751725

Armi Sport (See U.S. Importers-Cape Outfitters)

Armite Laboratories, 1560 Superior Ave., Costa Mesa, CA 92627 / 213-587-7768; FAX: 213-587-5075

Armoloy Co. of Ft. Worth, 204 E. Daggett St., Fort Worth, T 76104 / 817-332-5604; FAX: 817-335-6517

Armor (See Buck Stop Lure Co., Inc.)

MANUFACTURER'S DIRECTORY

Metal Products, P.O. Box 4609, Helena, MT 59604 / -442-5560; FAX: 406-442-5650
Publications, 2120 S. Reserve St., PMB 253, ssoula, MT 59801 / 406-549-7670; FAX: -728-0597 armorypub@aol.com w.armorypub.com
y, Inc., The, Rt. 202, Box 2340, New Preston, CT 777 / 860-868-0001; FAX: 860-868-2919
Armour Press, Wellington House, 125 Strand, ndon, WC2R 0BB ENGLAND / 0171-420-5555; FAX: 71-240-7265
Corporation of the Philippines, Bo. Parang Marikina, etro Manila, PHILIPPINES / 632-941-6243; or 2-941-6244; FAX: 632-942-0682
Craft Gunsmithing, 1106 Linda Dr., Arroyo Grande, CA 420 / 805-481-2830
Software, 4851 SW Madrona St., Lake Oswego, OR 035 / 800-366-5559; or 503-697-0533; FAX: 3-697-3337
Programming Solutions (See Arms Software)
cor Precision, 5740 S. Arville St. #219, Las Vegas, NV 118 / 702-362-7750
corp USA, Inc., 4424 John Ave., Baltimore, MD 21227 / 0-247-6200; FAX: 410-247-6205 fo@armscorpusa.com www.armscorpusa.com
onian, Andy (See Horseshoe Leather Products)
a S.L., Morkaiko 5, 20870, Elgoibar, SPAIN / 4-43-743150; FAX: 34-43-743154
wel Enterprises Ltd., Eagle Business Ctr., 460 Randy d., Carol Stream, IL 60188 / 708-260-0400
y in Wood, 134 Zimmerman Rd., Kalispell, MT 59901 / 06-257-9003; FAX: 406-257-9167 merlins@digisys.net ww.acrabondlaminates.com
Gun & Sport Shop, Inc., 6008 Hwy. Y, Hillsboro, MO 3050
del Arms & Ammunition, Inc., A., 24A Defense St., nnapolis, MD 21401 / 410-224-8683
y Outdoors, Inc., 2401 Ludelle St., Fort Worth, TX 6105 / 888-744-4880; FAX: 800-734-7939
n Outfitting Co., Jon Hollinger, 9 Dean St., Aspen, CO 1611 / 970-925-3406
uare Co., 205 Fairfield Ave., Jeffersonville, IN 47130 / 12-283-0577; FAX: 812-283-0375
Sport, S.A., Apartado 3, 48300 Guernica, Espagne, SPAIN / 34-4-6250100; FAX: 34-4-6255186
ec-Bretton, 19 rue Victor Grignard, F-42026, St.-Etienne Cedex 1, FRANCE / 77-93-54-69; FAX: 33-77-93-57-98
ta Cutlery Corp., 2143 Gees Mill Rd., Box 839 CIS, Conyers, GA 30207 / 800-883-0300; FAX: 404-388-0246
tic Mills, Inc., 1295 Towbin Ave., Lakewood, NJ 08701-5934 / 800-242-7374
tic Rose, Inc., P.O. Box 10717, Bradenton, FL 34282-0717
o/Sno-Seal, Inc., 2664 Russell St., Orangeburg, SC 29115 / 803-531-1820; FAX: 803-531-2139 info@atsko.com www.atsko.com
ste Francotte & Cie S.A., rue du Trois Juin 109, 4400 Herstal-Liege, BELGIUM / 32-4-248-13-18; FAX: 32-4-948-11-79
tin & Halleck, Inc., 2150 South 950 East, Provo, UT 84606-6285 / 877-543-3256; or 801-374-9990; FAX: 801-374-9998 www.austinhallek.com
tin Sheridan USA, Inc., P.O. Box 577, 36 Haddam Quarter Rd., Durham, CT 06422 / 860-349-1772; FAX: 860-349-1771 swalzer@palm.net
auga Arms, Inc., Pratt Plaza Mall No. 13, Prattville, AL 36067 / 800-262-9563; FAX: 334-361-2961
o Arms, 738 Clearview, San Antonio, TX 78228 / 512-434-5450
o-Ordnance Corp., PO Box 220, Blauvelt, NY 10913 / 914-353-7770
umn Sales, Inc. (Blaser), 1320 Lake St., Fort Worth, TX 76102 / 817-335-1634; FAX: 817-338-0119
nda Otaola Norica, 16 Apartado 68, 20600, Eibar, SPAIN
C Systems Technology, P.O. Box 41938, Phoenix, AZ 85080-1938 / 623-780-1050; FAX: 623-780-2967 awc@awcsystech.com www.awcsystech.com
tell Rifle Co., 353 Mill Creek Road, Sheridan, MT 59749 / 406-842-5814
A (See U.S. Importer-New England Custom Gun Serv

B

&D Trading Co., Inc., 3935 Fair Hill Rd., Fair Oaks, CA 95628 / 800-334-3790; or 916-967-9366; FAX: 916-967-4873
&P America, 12321 Brittany Cir., Dallas, TX 75230 / 972-726-9069
B.A.C., 17101 Los Modelos St., Fountain Valley, CA 92708 / 435-586-3286
B.B. Walker Co., PO Box 1167, 414 E Dixie Dr, Asheboro, NC 27204 / 910-625-1380; FAX: 910-625-8125
B.C. Outdoors, Larry McGhee, PO Box 61497, Boulder City, NV 89006 / 702-294-3056; FAX: 702-294-0413 jdalton@pmcammo.com www.pmcammo.com
B.M.F. Activator, Inc., 12145 Mill Creek Run, Plantersville, TX 77363 / 936-894-2397; FAX: 936-894-2397 bmf25years@aol.com
Badger Creek Studio, 1629 Via Monserate, Fallbrook, CA 92028 / 760-723-9279; or 619-728-2663
Badger Shooters Supply, Inc., P.O. Box 397, Owen, WI 54460 / 800-424-9069; FAX: 715-229-2332
Baekgaard Ltd., 1855 Janke Dr., Northbrook, IL 60062 / 708-498-3040; FAX: 708-493-3106
Baelder, Harry, Alte Goennebeker Strasse 5, 24635, Rickling, GERMANY / 04328-722732; FAX: 04328-722733
Baer's Hollows, P.O. Box 284, Eads, CO 81036 / 719-438-5718
Bagmaster Mfg., Inc., 2731 Sutton Ave., St. Louis, MO 63143 / 314-781-8002; FAX: 314-781-3363 sales@bagmaster.com www.bagmaster.com
Bain & Davis, Inc., 307 E. Valley Blvd., San Gabriel, CA 91776-3522 / 626-573-4241 baindavis@aol.com
Baker, Stan. See: STAN BAKER SPORTS
Baker's Leather Goods, Roy, PO Box 893, Magnolia, AR 71754 / 870-234-0344 pholsters@ipa.net
Bald Eagle Precision Machine Co., 101-A Allison St., Lock Haven, PA 17745 / 570-748-6772; FAX: 570-748-4443
Balickie, Joe, 408 Trelawney Lane, Apex, NC 27502 / 919-362-5185
Ballard, Donald. See: BALLARD INDUSTRIES
Ballard Industries, Donald Ballard Sr., PO Box 2035, Arnold, CA 95223 / 408-996-0957; FAX: 408-257-6828
Ballard Rifle & Cartridge Co., LLC, 113 W. Yellowstone Ave., Cody, WY 82414 / 307-587-4914; FAX: 307-527-6097 ballard@wyoming.com www.ballardrifles.com
Ballistic Products, Inc., 20015 75th Ave. North, Corcoran, MN 55340-9456 / 763-494-9237; FAX: 763-494-9236 info@ballisticproducts.com www.ballisticproducts.com
Ballistic Research, 1108 W. May Ave., McHenry, IL 60050 / 815-385-0037
Ballisti-Cast, Inc., P.O. Box 1057, Minot, ND 58702-1057 / 701-497-3333; FAX: 701-497-3335
Bandcor Industries, Div. of Man-Sew Corp., 6108 Sherwin Dr., Port Richey, FL 34668 / 813-848-0432
Bang-Bang Boutique (See Holster Shop, The)
Bansner's Ultimate Rifles, LLC, P.O. Box 839, 261 E. Main St., Adamstown, PA 19501 / 717-484-2370; FAX: 717-484-0523 bansner@aol.com www.bansnersrifle.com
Barbour, Inc., 55 Meadowbrook Dr., Milford, NH 03055 / 603-673-1313; FAX: 603-673-6510
Barnes, 4347 Tweed Dr., Eau Claire, WI 54703-6302
Barnes Bullets, Inc., P.O. Box 215, American Fork, UT 84003 / 801-756-4222; or 800-574-9200; FAX: 801-756-2465 email@barnesbullets.com www.barnesbullets.com
Baron Technology, 62 Spring Hill Rd., Trumbull, CT 06611 / 203-452-0515; FAX: 203-452-0663 dbaron@baronengraving.com www.baronengraving.com
Barraclough, John K., 55 Merit Park Dr., Gardena, CA 90247 / 310-324-2574 johnbar120@aol.com
Barramundi Corp., P.O. Drawer 4259, Homosassa Springs, FL 32687 / 904-628-0200
Barrel & Gunworks, 2601 Lake Valley Rd., Prescott Valley, AZ 86314 / 928-772-4060 www.cutrifle.com
Barrett Firearms Manufacturer, Inc., P.O. Box 1077, Murfreesboro, TN 37133 / 615-896-2938; FAX: 615-896-7313
Bar-Sto Precision Machine, 73377 Sullivan Rd., PO Box 1838, Twentynine Palms, CA 92277 / 760-367-2747; FAX: 760-367-2407 barsto@eee.org www.barsto.com
Barta's Gunsmithing, 10231 US Hwy. 10, Cato, WI 54230 / 920-732-4472
Barteaux Machete, 1916 SE 50th Ave., Portland, OR 97215-3238 / 503-233-5880
Bartlett Engineering, 40 South 200 East, Smithfield, UT 84335-1645 / 801-563-5910
Bates Engraving, Billy, 2302 Winthrop Dr. SW, Decatur, Al 35603 / 256-355-3690 bbrn@aol.com
Battenfeld Technologies Inc., 5885 W. Van Horn Tavern Rd., Columbia, MO 65203 / 573-445-9200; FAX: 573-447-4158 battenfeldtechnologies.com
Bauer, Eddie, 15010 NE 36th St., Redmond, WA 98052
Baumgartner Bullets, 3011 S. Alane St., W. Valley City, UT 84120
Bauska Barrels, 105 9th Ave. W., Kalispell, MT 59901 / 406-752-7706
Bear Archery, RR 4, 4600 Southwest 41st Blvd., Gainesville, FL 32601 / 904-376-2327
Bear Arms, 374-A Carson Road, St. Mathews, SC 29135
Bear Mountain Gun & Tool, 120 N. Plymouth, New Plymouth, ID 83655 / 208-278-5221; FAX: 208-278-5221
Beartooth Bullets, PO Box 491, Dept. HLD, Dover, ID 83825-0491 / 208-448-1865 bullets@beartoothbullets.com beartoothbullets.com
Beaver Park Product, Inc., 840 J St., Penrose, CO 81240 / 719-372-6744
BEC, Inc., 1227 W. Valley Blvd., Suite 204, Alhambra, CA 91803 / 626-281-5751; FAX: 626-293-7073
Beeks, Mike. See: GRAYBACK WILDCATS
Beeman Precision Airguns, 5454 Argosy Dr., Huntington Beach, CA 92649 / 714-890-4808; FAX: 714-890-4808
Behlert Precision, Inc., P.O. Box 288, 7067 Easton Rd., Pipersville, PA 18947 / 215-766-8681; or 215-766-7301; FAX: 215-766-8681
Beitzinger, George, 116-20 Atlantic Ave., Richmond Hill, NY 11419 / 718-847-7661
Belding's Custom Gun Shop, 10691 Sayers Rd., Munith, MI 49259 / 517-596-2388
Bell & Carlson, Inc., Dodge City Industrial Park, 101 Allen Rd., Dodge City, KS 67801 / 800-634-8586; or 620-225-6688; FAX: 620-225-6688 email@bellandcarlson.com www.bellandcarlson.com
Bell Reloading, Inc., 1725 Harlin Lane Rd., Villa Rica, GA 30180
Bell's Gun & Sport Shop, 3309-19 Mannheim Rd, Franklin Park, IL 60131
Bell's Legendary Country Wear, 22 Circle Dr., Bellmore, NY 11710 / 516-679-1158
Benchmark Knives (See Gerber Legendary Blades)
Benelli Armi S.P.A., Via della Stazione, 61029, Urbino, ITALY / 39-722-307-1; FAX: 39-722-327427
Benelli USA Corp, 17603 Indian Head Hwy, Accokeek, MD 20607 / 301-283-6981; FAX: 301-283-6988 benelliusa.com
Bengtson Arms Co., L., 6345-B E. Akron St., Mesa, AZ 85205 / 602-981-6375
Benjamin/Sheridan Co., Crosman, Rts. 5 and 20, E. Bloomfield, NY 14443 / 716-657-6161; FAX: 716-657-5405 www.crosman.com
Bentley, John, 128-D Watson Dr., Turtle Creek, PA 15145
Beretta S.P.A., Pietro, Via Beretta, 18, 25063, Gardone Vae Trompia, ITALY / 39-30-8341-1 info@benetta.com www.benetta.com
Beretta U.S.A. Corp., 17601 Beretta Drive, Accokeek, MD 20607 / 301-283-2191; FAX: 301-283-0435
Berger Bullets Ltd., 5443 W. Westwind Dr., Glendale, AZ 85310 / 602-842-4001; FAX: 602-934-9083
Bernardelli, Vincenzo, P.O. Box 460243, Houston, TX 77056-8243 www.bernardelli.com
Bernardelli, Vincenzo, Via Grande, 10, Sede Legale Torbole Casaglia, Brescia, ITALY / 39-30-8912851-2-3; FAX: 39-030-2150963 bernardelli@bernardelli.com www.bernardelli.com
Berry's Mfg., Inc., 401 North 3050 East St., St. George, UT 84770 / 435-634-1682; FAX: 435-634-1683 sales@berrysmfg.com www.berrysmfg.com
Bersa S.A., Benso Bonadimani, Magallanes 775 B1704 FLC, Ramos Mejia, ARGENTINA / 011-4656-2377; FAX: 011-4656-2093+ info@bersa-sa.com.dr www.bersa-sa.com.ar
Bert Johanssons Vapentillbehor, S-430 20 Veddige, SWEDEN,
Bertuzzi (See U.S. Importer-New England Arms Co)
Better Concepts Co., 663 New Castle Rd., Butler, PA 16001 / 412-285-9000
Beverly, Mary, 3201 Horseshoe Trail, Tallahassee, FL 32312
Bianchi International, Inc., 100 Calle Cortez, Temecula, CA 92590 / 909-676-5621; FAX: 909-676-6777
Big Bear Arms & Sporting Goods, Inc., 1112 Milam Way, Carrollton, TX 75006 / 972-416-8051; or 800-400-BEAR; FAX: 972-416-0771
Big Bore Bullets of Alaska, PO Box 521455, Big Lake, AK 99652 / 907-373-2673; FAX: 907-373-2673 doug@mtaonline.net ww.awloo.com/bbb/index.
Big Bore Express, 16345 Midway Rd., Nampa, ID 83651 / 208-466-9975; FAX: 208-466-6927 bigbore.com
Big Spring Enterprises "Bore Stores", P.O. Box 1115, Big Spring Rd., Yellville, AR 72687 / 870-449-5297; FAX: 870-449-4446
Bilal, Mustafa. See: TURK'S HEAD PRODUCTIONS
Bilinski, Bryan. See: FIELDSPORT LTD.
Bill Adair Custom Shop, 2886 Westridge, Carrollton, TX 75006 / 972-418-0950

Manufacturer's Directory

Bill Austin's Calls, Box 284, Kaycee, WY 82639 / 307-738-2552

Bill Hanus Birdguns, P.O. Box 533, Newport, OR 97365 / 541-265-7433; FAX: 541-265-7400 www.billhanusbirdguns.com

Bill Russ Trading Post, William A. Russ, 25 William St., Addison, NY 14801-1326 / 607-359-3896

Bill Wiseman and Co., P.O. Box 3427, Bryan, TX 77805 / 409-690-3456; FAX: 409-690-0156

Billeb, Stepehn. See: QUALITY CUSTOM FIREARMS

Billings Gunsmiths, 1841 Grand Ave., Billings, MT 59102 / 406-256-8390; FAX: 406-256-6530 blgsgunsmiths@msn.com www.billingsgunsmiths.net

Billingsley & Brownell, P.O. Box 25, Dayton, WY 82836 / 307-655-9344

Bill's Gun Repair, 1007 Burlington St., Mendota, IL 61342 / 815-539-5786

Billy Bates Engraving, 2302 Winthrop Dr. SW, Decatur, AL 35603 / 256-355-3690 bbrn@aol.com

Birchwood Casey, 7900 Fuller Rd., Eden Prairie, MN 55344 / 800-328-6156; or 612-937-7933; FAX: 612-937-7979

Birdsong & Assoc., W. E., 1435 Monterey Rd, Florence, MS 39073-9748 / 601-366-8270

Bismuth Cartridge Co., 3500 Maple Ave., Suite 1650, Dallas, TX 75219 / 214-521-5880; FAX: 214-521-9035

Bison Studios, 1409 South Commerce St., Las Vegas, NV 89102 / 702-388-2891; FAX: 702-383-9967

Bitterroot Bullet Co., 2001 Cedar Ave., Lewiston, ID 83501-0412 / 208-743-5635 brootbil@lewiston.com

BKL Technologies, PO Box 5237, Brownsville, TX 78523

Black Belt Bullets (See Big Bore Express)

Black Hills Ammunition, Inc., P.O. Box 3090, Rapid City, SD 57709-3090 / 605-348-5150; FAX: 605-348-9827

Black Hills Shooters Supply, P.O. Box 4220, Rapid City, SD 57709 / 800-289-2506

Black Powder Products, 67 Township Rd. 1411, Chesapeake, OH 45619 / 614-867-8047

Black Sheep Brand, 3220 W. Gentry Parkway, Tyler, TX 75702 / 903-592-3853; FAX: 903-592-0527

Blacksmith Corp., P.O. Box 280, North Hampton, OH 45349 / 937-969-8389; FAX: 937-969-8399 sales@blacksmithcorp.com www.blacksmithcorp.com

BlackStar AccuMax Barrels, 11501 Brittmoore Park Drive, Houston, TX 77041 / 281-721-6040; FAX: 281-721-6041

BlackStar Barrel Accurizing (See BlackStar AccuMax)

Blacktail Mountain Books, 42 First Ave. W., Kalispell, MT 59901 / 406-257-5573

Blammo Ammo, P.O. Box 1677, Seneca, SC 29679 / 803-882-1768

Blaser Jagdwaffen GmbH, D-88316, Isny Im Allgau, GERMANY

Blount, Inc., Sporting Equipment Div., 2299 Snake River Ave., P.O. Box 856, Lewiston, ID 83501 / 800-627-3640; or 208-746-2351; FAX: 208-799-3904

Blount/Outers ATK, P.O. Box 39, Onalaska, WI 54650 / 608-781-5800; FAX: 608-781-0368

Blue and Gray Products Inc. (See Ox-Yoke Originals)

Blue Book Publications, Inc., 8009 34th Ave. S., Ste. 175, Minneapolis, MN 55425 / 952-854-5229; FAX: 952-853-1486 bluebook@bluebookinc.com www.bluebookinc.com

Blue Mountain Bullets, 64146 Quail Ln., Box 231, John Day, OR 97845 / 541-820-4594; FAX: 541-820-4594

Blue Ridge Machinery & Tools, Inc., P.O. Box 536-GD, Hurricane, WV 25526 / 800-872-6500; FAX: 304-562-5311 blueridgemachine@worldnet.att.net www.blueridgemachinery.com

BMC Supply, Inc., 26051 - 179th Ave. S.E., Kent, WA 98042

Bob Allen Co., P.O. Box 477, 214 SW Jackson, Des Moines, IA 50315 / 800-685-7020; FAX: 515-283-0779

Bob Allen Sportswear, 220 S. Main St., Osceola, IA 50213 / 210-344-8531; FAX: 210-342-2703 sales@bob-allen.com www.bob-allen.com

Bob Rogers Gunsmithing, P.O. Box 305, 344 S. Walnut St., Franklin Grove, IL 61031 / 815-456-2685; FAX: 815-456-2685

Bob's Gun Shop, P.O. Box 200, Royal, AR 71968 / 501-767-1970; FAX: 501-767-1970 gunparts@hsnp.com www.gun-parts.com

Bob's Tactical Indoor Shooting Range & Gun Shop, 90 Lafayette Rd., Salisbury, MA 01952 / 508-465-5561

Boessler, Erich, Am Vogeltal 3, 97702, Munnerstadt, GERMANY

Boker USA, Inc., 1550 Balsam Street, Lakewood, CO 80214 / 303-462-0662; FAX: 303-462-0668 sales@bokerusa.com bokerusa.com

Boltin, John M., P.O. Box 644, Estill, SC 29918 / 803-625-2185

Bo-Mar Tool & Mfg. Co., 6136 State Hwy. 300, Longview, TX 75604 / 903-759-4784; FAX: 903-759-9141 marykor@earthlink.net bo-mar.com

Bonadimani, Benso. See: BERSA S.A.

Bonanza (See Forster Products), 310 E. Lanark Ave., Lanark, IL 61046 / 815-493-6360; FAX: 815-493-2371

Bond Arms, Inc., P.O. Box 1296, Granbury, TX 76048 / 817-573-4445; FAX: 817-573-5636

Bond Custom Firearms, 8954 N. Lewis Ln., Bloomington, IN 47408 / 812-332-4519

Bonham's & Butterfields, 220 San Bruno Ave., San Francisco, CA 94103 / 415-861-7500; FAX: 415-861-0183 arms@butterfields.com www.butterfields.com

Boone Trading Co., Inc., PO Box 669, Brinnon, WA 98320 / 800-423-1945; or 360-796-4330; FAX: 360-796-4511 sales@boonetrading.com boonetrading.com

Boone's Custom Ivory Grips, Inc., 562 Coyote Rd., Brinnon, WA 98320 / 206-796-4330

Boonie Packer Products, P.O. Box 12517, Salem, OR 97309-0517 / 800-477-3244; or 503-581-3244; FAX: 503-581-3191 booniepacker@aol.com www.booniepacker.com

Borden Ridges Rimrock Stocks, RR 1 Box 250 BC, Springville, PA 18844 / 570-965-2505; FAX: 570-965-2328

Borden Rifles Inc., RD 1, Box 250BC, Springville, PA 18844 / 717-965-2505; FAX: 717-965-2328

Border Barrels Ltd., Riccarton Farm, Newcastleton, SCOTLAND UK

Borovnik KG, Ludwig, 9170 Ferlach, Bahnhofstrasse 7, AUSTRIA / 042 27 24 42; FAX: 042 26 43 49

Bosis (See U.S. Importer-New England Arms Co.)

Boss Manufacturing Co., 221 W. First St., Kewanee, IL 61443 / 309-852-2131; or 800-447-4581; FAX: 309-852-0848

Bostick Wildlife Calls, Inc., P.O. Box 728, Estill, SC 29918 / 803-625-2210; or 803-625-4512

Bowen Classic Arms Corp., P.O. Box 67, Louisville, TN 37777 / 865-984-3583 www.bowenclassicarms.com

Bowen Knife Co., Inc., P.O. Box 590, Blackshear, GA 31516 / 912-449-4794

Bowerly, Kent, 710 Golden Pheasant Dr., Redmond, OR 97756 / 541-923-3501 jkbowerly@aol.com

Boyds' Gunstock Industries, Inc., 25376 403 Rd. Ave., Mitchell, SD 57301 / 605-996-5011; FAX: 605-996-9878

Brace, Larry D., 771 Blackfoot Ave., Eugene, OR 97404 / 541-688-1278; FAX: 541-607-5833

Brass Eagle, Inc., 7050A Bramalea Rd., Unit 19, Mississauga,, ON L4Z 1C7 CANADA / 416-848-4844

Brauer Bros., 1520 Washington Avenue., St. Louis, MO 63103 / 314-231-2864; FAX: 314-249-4952 www.brauerbros.com

Break-Free, Inc., 13386 International Parkway, Jacksonville, FL 32218 / 800-428-0588; FAX: 904-741-5407 contactus@armorholdings.com www.break-free.com

Brenneke GmbH, P.O. Box 1646, 30837 Langenhagen, Langenhagen, GERMANY / +49-511-97262-0; FAX: +49-511-97262-62 info@brenneke.de brenneke.com

Bridgeman Products, Harry Jaffin, 153 B Cross Slope Court, Englishtown, NJ 07726 / 732-536-3604; FAX: 732-972-1004

Bridgers Best, P.O. Box 1410, Berthoud, CO 80513

Briese Bullet Co., Inc., 3442 42nd Ave. SE, Tappen, ND 58487 / 701-327-4578; FAX: 701-327-4579

Brigade Quartermasters, 1025 Cobb International Blvd., Dept. VH, Kennesaw, GA 30144-4300 / 404-428-1248; or 800-241-3125; FAX: 404-426-7726

Briganti, A.J., 512 Rt. 32, Highland Mills, NY 10930 / 914-928-9573

Briley Mfg. Inc., 1230 Lumpkin, Houston, TX 77043 / 800-331-5718; or 713-932-6995; FAX: 713-932-1043

Brill, R. See: ROYAL ARMS INTERNATIONAL

British Sporting Arms, RR1, Box 130, Millbrook, NY 12545 / 914-677-8303

Broad Creek Rifle Works, Ltd., 120 Horsey Ave., Laurel, DE 19956 / 302-875-5446; FAX: 302-875-1448 bcrw4guns@aol.com

Brockman's Custom Gunsmithing, P.O. Box 357, Gooding, ID 83330 / 208-934-5050

Brocock Ltd., 43 River Street, Digbeth, Birmingham, B5 5SA ENGLAND / 011-021-773-1200; FAX: 011-021-773-1211 sales@brocock.co.un www.brocock.co.uk

Broken Gun Ranch, 10739 126 Rd., Spearville, KS 67876 / 316-385-2587; FAX: 316-385-2597 nbowlin@ucom.net www.brokengunranch

Brooker, Dennis, Rt. 1, Box 12A, Derby, IA 50068 / 515-533-2103

Brooks Tactical Systems-Agrip, 279-C Shorewood Ct., Island, WA 98333 / 253-549-2866 FAX: 253-549- brooks@brookstactical.com www.brookstactical.c

Brown Co., E. Arthur, 3404 Pawnee Dr., Alexandria, M 56308 / 320-762-8847

Brown Dog Ent., 2200 Calle Camelia, 1000 Oaks, CA 91 805-497-2318; FAX: 805-497-1618

Brown Precision, Inc., 7786 Molinos Ave., Los Molinos 96055 / 530-384-2506; FAX: 916-384-1638 www.brownprecision.com

Brown Products, Inc., Ed, 43825 Muldrow Trail, Perry, 63462 / 573-565-3261; FAX: 573-565-2791 edbrown@edbrown.com www.edbrown.com

Brownells, Inc., 200 S. Front St., Montezuma, IA 5017 800-741-0015; FAX: 800-264-3068 orderdesk@brownells.com www.brownells.com

Browning Arms Co., One Browning Place, Morgan, UT 8 / 801-876-2711; FAX: 801-876-3331 www.browning.com

Browning Arms Co. (Parts & Service), 3005 Arnold Tent Rd., Arnold, MO 63010 / 617-287-6800; FAX: 617-287-9751

BRP, Inc. High Performance Cast Bullets, 1210 Alexand Rd., Colorado Springs, CO 80909 / 719-633-0658

Brunton U.S.A., 620 E. Monroe Ave., Riverton, WY 825 307-856-6559; FAX: 307-857-4702 info@brunton.c www.brunton.com

Bryan & Assoc., R D Sauls, PO Box 5772, Anderson, SC 29623-5772 / 864-261-6810 bryanandac@aol.com www.huntersweb.com/bryanandac

Brynin, Milton, P.O. Box 383, Yonkers, NY 10710 / 914-779-4333

BSA Guns Ltd., Armoury Rd. Small Heath, Birmingham 2PP, ENGLAND / 011-021-772-8543; FAX: 011-021-773-0845 sales@bsagun.com www.bsagun.com

BSA Optics, 3911 SW 47th Ave., Ste. 914, Ft. Lauderdale 33314 / 954-581-2144; FAX: 954-581-3165 4info@basaoptics.com www.bsaoptics.com

B-Square Company, Inc., P.O. Box 11281, 2708 St. Loui Ave., Ft. Worth, TX 76110 / 817-923-0964 or 800-433-2909; FAX: 817-926-7012

Buchsenmachermeister, Peter Hofer Jagdwaffen, Buchsenmachermeister, Kirchgasse 24 A-9170, Ferl AUSTRIA / 43 4227 3683; FAX: 43 4227 368330 peterhofer@hoferwaffen.com www.hoferwaffen.com

Buck Knives, Inc., 1900 Weld Blvd., P.O. Box 1267, El Ca CA 92020 / 619-449-1100; or 800-326-2825; FAX: 619-562-5774

Buck Stix-SOS Products Co., Box 3, Neenah, WI 54956

Buck Stop Lure Co., Inc., 3600 Grow Rd. NW, P.O. Box 6 Stanton, MI 48888 / 989-762-5091; FAX: 989-762-5 buckstop@nethawk.com www.buckstopscents.com

Buckeye Custom Bullets, 6490 Stewart Rd., Elida, OH 458 / 419-641-4463

Buckhorn Gun Works, 8109 Woodland Dr., Black Hawk, S 57718 / 605-787-6472

Buckskin Bullet Co., P.O. Box 1893, Cedar City, UT 84721 435-586-3286

Budin, Dave, 817 Main St., P.O. Box 685, Margaretville, N 12455 / 914-568-4103; FAX: 914-586-4105

Budin, Dave. See: DEL-SPORTS, INC.

Buenger Enterprises/Goldenrod Dehumidifier, 3600 S. Harbor Blvd., Oxnard, CA 93035 / 800-451-6797; or 805-985-5828; FAX: 805-985-1534

Buffalo Arms Co., 660 Vermeer Ct., Ponderay, ID 83852 / 208-263-6953; FAX: 208-265-2096 www.buffaloarms.com

Buffalo Bullet Co., Inc., 12637 Los Nietos Rd., Unit A, San Fe Springs, CA 90670 / 800-423-8069; FAX: 562-944-5054

Buffalo Gun Center, 3385 Harlem Rd., Buffalo, NY 14225 716-833-2581; FAX: 716-833-2265 www.buffaloguncenter.com

Buffalo Rock Shooters Supply, R.R. 1, Ottawa, IL 61350 / 815-433-2471

Buffer Technologies, P.O. Box 104930, Jefferson City, MO 65110 / 573-634-8529; FAX: 573-634-8522

Bull Mountain Rifle Co., 6327 Golden West Terrace, Billings MT 59106 / 406-656-0778

Bullberry Barrel Works, Ltd., 2430 W. Bullberry Ln., Hurricane, UT 84737 / 435-635-9866; FAX: 435-635-0348 fred@bullberry.com www.bullberry.com

Bullet Metals, Bill Ferguson, P.O. Box 1238, Sierra Vista, AZ 85636 / 520-458-5321; FAX: 520-458-1421 info@theantimonyman.com www.bullet-metals.com

Bullet N Press, 1210 Jones St., Gastonia, NC 28052 / 704-853-0265 bnpress@quik.com www.clt.quik.com/bnpress

MANUFACTURER'S DIRECTORY

Swaging Supply, Inc., P.O. Box 1056, 303 McMillan
d., West Monroe, LA 71291 / 318-387-3266; FAX:
18-387-7779 leblackmon@colla.com
, Inc., 411 E. Water St., Farmer City, IL 61842-1556 /
09-928-2574 or 800-248-3845; FAX: 309-928-2130
art Gunsmithing, Don, P.O. Box 852, Rawlins, WY
2301 / 307-324-6007
am Bros., P.O. Box 1148, Menard, TX 78659 /
15-396-4572; FAX: 915-396-4574
s Co., Inc., PO Box 1747, 331 E. 8th St., Greeley, CO
0631 / 970-356-1670; FAX: 970-356-8702
master Firearms, Inc., 999 Roosevelt Trail, Windham,
ME 04062 / 800-998-7928; FAX: 207-892-8068
nfo@bushmaster.com www.bushmaster.com
master Hunting & Fishing, 451 Alliance Ave., Toronto,
ON M6N 2J1 CANADA / 416-763-4040; FAX:
416-763-0623
nell Sports Optics Worldwide, 9200 Cody, Overland
Park, KS 66214 / 913-752-3400 or 800-423-3537; FAX:
913-752-3550
er's Custom Knives, P.O. Box 214, Richfield, UT 84701 /
435-896-5319; FAX: 435-896-8333
www.warenskiknives.com
er Creek Corp., 2100 S. Silverstone Way, Meridian, ID
83642-8151 / 800-423-8327 or 406-388-1356; FAX:
406-388-7204
er Enterprises, 834 Oberting Rd., Lawrenceburg, IN
47025 / 812-537-3584
Fletcher Custom Stockmaker, 117 Silver Road, P.O. Box
189, Taos, NM 87571 / 505-758-3486

C

Special Products (See Claybuster Wads & Harvester
Bullets)
Research, 115 Sunnyside Dr., Box 351, Lewis, KS
67552 / 316-324-5445; or 888-324-5445; FAX:
620-324-5984 info@mercuryrecoil.com
www.mercuryrecoil.com
Palmer Manufacturing Co., Inc., P.O. Box 220, West
Newton, PA 15089 / 412-872-8200; FAX: 412-872-8302
Sharps Arms Co. Inc./Montana Armory, 100 Centennial
Dr., PO Box 885, Big Timber, MT 59011 / 406-932-4353;
FAX: 406-932-4443
. Van Gorden & Son, Inc., 1815 Main St., Bloomer, WI
54724 / 715-568-2612 vangorden@bloomer.net
V. Erickson's L.L.C., 530 Garrison Ave. NE, PO Box 522,
Buffalo, MN 55313 / 763-682-3665; FAX: 763-682-4328
www.archerhunter.com
banas (See U.S. Importer-Mandall Shooting Supply
bela's, One Cabela Drive, Sidney, NE 69160 /
308-254-5505; FAX: 308-254-8420
binet Mtn. Outfitters Scents & Lures, P.O. Box 766, Plains,
MT 59859 / 406-826-3970
che La Poudre Rifleworks, 140 N. College, Ft. Collins, CO
80524 / 920-482-6913
lhoon Mfg., 4343 U.S. Highway 87, Havre, MT 59501 /
406-395-4079 www.jamescalhoon.com
li'co Hardwoods, Inc., 3580 Westwind Blvd., Santa Rosa,
CA 95403 / 707-546-4045; FAX: 707-546-4027
calicohardwoods@msn.com
lico Light Weapon Systems, 1489 Greg St., Sparks, NV
89431
alifornia Sights (See Fautheree, Andy)
ambos Outdoorsman, 532 E. Idaho Ave., Ontario, OR 97914
/ 541-889-3135; FAX: 541-889-2633
ambos Outdoorsman, Fritz Hallberg, 532 E. Idaho Ave,
Ontario, OR 97914 / 541-889-3135; FAX: 541-889-2633
amdex, Inc., 2330 Alger, Troy, MI 48083 / 810-528-2300;
FAX: 810-528-0989
ameron's, 16690 W. 11th Ave., Golden, CO 80401 /
303-279-7365; FAX: 303-628-5413
ncnoremac@aol.com
amillus Cutlery Co., 54 Main St., Camillus, NY 13031 /
315-672-8111; FAX: 315-672-8832
ampbell, Dick, 20000 Silver Ranch Rd., Conifer, CO 80433
/ 303-697-0150; FAX: 303-697-0150
dicksknives@aol.com
amp-Cap Products, P.O. Box 3805, Chesterfield, MO 63006
/ 314-532-4340; FAX: 314-532-4340
annon Safe, Inc., 216 S. 2nd Ave. #BLD-932, San
Bernardino, CA 92400 / 310-692-0636; or
800-242-1055; FAX: 310-692-7252
anons Delcour, Rue J.B. Cools, B-4040, Herstal, BELGIUM
/ 32.(0)42.40.61.40; FAX: 32(0)42.40.22.88
anyon Cartridge Corp., P.O. Box 152, Albertson, NY 11507
FAX: 516-294-8946

Cape Outfitters, 599 County Rd. 206, Cape Girardeau, MO
63701 / 573-335-4103; FAX: 573-335-1555
Caraville Manufacturing, P.O. Box 4545, Thousand Oaks, CA
91359 / 805-499-1234
Carbide Checkering Tools (See J&R Engineering)
Carhartt, Inc., P.O. Box 600, 3 Parklane Blvd., Dearborn, MI
48121 / 800-358-3825; or 313-271-8460; FAX:
313-271-3455
Carl Walther GmbH, B.P. 4325, D-89033, Ulm, GERMANY
Carl Zeiss Inc., 13005 N. Kingston Ave., Chester, VA 23836 /
800-441-3005; FAX: 804-530-8481
Carlson, Douglas R, Antique American Firearms, P.O. Box
71035, Dept GD, Des Moines, IA 50325 / 515-224-6552
Carolina Precision Rifles, 1200 Old Jackson Hwy., Jackson,
SC 29831 / 803-827-2069
Carrell, William. See: CARRELL'S PRECISION FIREARMS
Carrell's Precision Firearms, William Carrell, 1952 W.Silver
Falls Ct., Meridian, ID 83642-3837
Carry-Lite, Inc., P.O. Box 1587, Fort Smith, AR 72902 /
479-782-8971; FAX: 479-783-0234
Carter's Gun Shop, 225 G St., Penrose, CO 81240 /
719-372-6240
Cascade Bullet Co., Inc., 2355 South 6th St., Klamath Falls,
OR 97601 / 503-884-9316
Cascade Shooters, 2155 N.W. 12th St., Redwood, OR 97756
Case & Sons Cutlery Co., W R, Owens Way, Bradford, PA
16701 / 814-368-4123; or 800-523-6350; FAX:
814-768-5369
Case Sorting System, 12695 Cobblestone Creek Rd., Poway,
CA 92064 / 619-486-9340
Cash Mfg. Co., Inc., P.O. Box 130, 201 S. Klein Dr.,
Waunakee, WI 53597-0130 / 608-849-5664; FAX:
608-849-5664
Caspian Arms, Ltd., 14 North Main St., Hardwick, VT 05843
/ 802-472-6454; FAX: 802-472-6709
Cast Performance Bullet Company, P.O. Box 153, Riverton,
WY 82501 / 307-857-2940; FAX: 307-857-3132
castperform@wyoming.com castperformance.com
Casull Arms Corp., P.O. Box 1629, Afton, WY 83110 /
307-886-0200
Caswell International, 720 Industrial Dr. No. 112, Cary, IL
60013 / 847-639-7666; FAX: 847-639-7694
www.caswellintl.com
Cathey Enterprises, Inc., P.O. Box 2202, Brownwood, TX
76804 / 915-643-2553; FAX: 915-643-3653
Cation, 2341 Alger St., Troy, MI 48083 / 810-689-0658; FAX:
810-689-7558
Caywood, Shane J., P.O. Box 321, Minocqua, WI 54548 /
715-277-3866
Caywood Gunmakers, 18 Kings Hill Estates, Berryville, AR
72616 / 870-423-4741 www.caywoodguns.com
CBC, Avenida Humberto de Campos 3220, 09400-000,
Ribeirao Pires, SP, BRAZIL / 55 11 4822 8378; FAX: 55
11 4822 8323 export@cbc.com.bc www.cbc.com.bc
CBC-BRAZIL, 3 Cuckoo Lane, Honley, Yorkshire HD7 2BR,
ENGLAND / 44-1484-661062; FAX: 44-1484-663709
CCG Enterprises, 5217 E. Belknap St., Halton City, TX 76117
/ 800-819-7464
CCI/Speer Div of ATK, P.O. Box 856, 2299 Snake River Ave.,
Lewiston, ID 83501 / 800-627-3640 or 208-746-2351
CCL Security Products, 199 Whiting St, New Britain, CT
06051 / 800-733-8588
Cedar Hill Game Calls, Inc., 238 Vic Allen Rd, Downsville, LA
71234 / 318-982-5632; FAX: 318-368-2245
Centaur Systems, Inc., 1602 Foothill Rd., Kalispell, MT 59901
/ 406-755-8609; FAX: 406-755-8609
Center Lock Scope Rings, 9901 France Ct., Lakeville, MN
55044 / 952-461-2114; FAX: 952-461-2194
marklee55044@usfamily.net
Central Specialties Ltd (See Trigger Lock Division
Century Gun Dist. Inc., 1467 Jason Rd., Greenfield, IN 46140
/ 317-462-4524
Century International Arms, Inc., 1161 Holland Dr, Boca
Raton, FL 33487 / 800-527-1252; FAX: 561-998-1993
support@centuryarms.com www.centuryarms.com
CFVentures, 509 Harvey Dr., Bloomington, IN 47403-1715
paladinwilltravel@yahoo.com
www.caversam16.freeserve.co.uk
CH Tool & Die Co. (See 4-D Custom Die Co.), 711 N Sandusky
St., P.O. Box 889, Mt. Vernon, OH 43050-0889 /
740-397-7214; FAX: 740-397-6600
Chace Leather Products, 507 Alden St., Fall River, MA 02722
/ 508-678-7556; FAX: 508-675-9666 chacelea@aol.com
www.chaceleather.com
Chadick's Ltd., P.O. Box 100, Terrell, TX 75160 /
214-563-7577
Chambers Flintlocks Ltd., Jim, 116 Sams Branch Rd.,
Candler, NC 28715 / 828-667-8361; FAX: 828-665-0852
www.flintlocks.com

Champion Shooters' Supply, P.O. Box 303, New Albany, OH
43054 / 614-855-1603; FAX: 614-855-1209
Champion Target Co., 232 Industrial Parkway, Richmond, IN
47374 / 800-441-4971
Champion's Choice, Inc., 201 International Blvd., LaVergne,
TN 37086 / 615-793-4066; FAX: 615-793-4070
champ.choice@earthlink.net www.champchoice.com
Champlin Firearms, Inc., P.O. Box 3191, Woodring Airport,
Enid, OK 73701 / 580-237-7388; FAX: 580-242-6922
info@champlinarms.com www.champlinarms.com
Chapman Academy of Practical Shooting, 4350 Academy Rd.,
Hallsville, MO 65255 / 573-696-5544; FAX:
573-696-2266 ha@chapmanacademy.com
Chapman, J Ken. See: OLD WEST BULLET MOULDS
Chapman Manufacturing Co., 471 New Haven Rd., P.O. Box
250, Durham, CT 06422 / 860-349-9228; FAX:
860-349-0084 sales@chapmanmfg.com
www.chapmanmfg.com
Chapuis Armes, 21 La Gravoux, BP15, 42380, St.
Bonnet-le-Chatea, FRANCE / (33)77.50.06.96
Chapuis USA, 416 Business Park, Bedford, KY 40006
Charter 2000, 273 Canal St, Shelton, CT 06484 /
203-922-1652
Checkmate Refinishing, 370 Champion Dr., Brooksville, FL
34601 / 352-799-5774; FAX: 352-799-2986
checkmatecustom.com
Cheddite, France S.A., 99 Route de Lyon, F-26501,
Bourg-les-Valence, FRANCE / 33-75-56-4545; FAX:
33-75-56-3587 export@cheddite.com
Chelsea Gun Club of New York City Inc., 237 Ovington Ave.,
Apt. D53, Brooklyn, NY 11209 / 718-836-9422; or
718-833-2704
Cherry Creek State Park Shooting Center, 12500 E. Belleview
Ave., Englewood, CO 80111 / 303-693-1765
CheVron Bullets, RR1, Ottawa, IL 61350 / 815-433-2471
Cheyenne Pioneer Products, PO Box 28425, Kansas City, MO
64188 / 816-413-9196; FAX: 816-455-2859
cheyennepp@aol.com www.cartridgeboxes.com
Chicago Cutlery Co., 1536 Beech St., Terre Haute, IN 47804 /
800-457-2665
Chicasaw Gun Works, 4 Mi. Mkr., Pluto Rd., Box 868, Shady
Spring, WV 25918-0868 / 304-763-2848; FAX:
304-763-3725
Chip McCormick Corp., P.O. Box 1560, Manchaca, TX 78652
/ 800-328-2447; FAX: 512-280-4282
www.chipmccormick.com
Chipmunk (See Oregon Arms, Inc.)
Choate Machine & Tool Co., Inc., P.O. Box 218, 116 Lovers
Ln., Bald Knob, AR 72010 / 501-724-6193; or
800-972-6390; FAX: 501-724-5873
Christensen Arms, 192 East 100 North, Fayette, UT 84630 /
435-528-7999; FAX: 435-528-7494
www.christensenarms.com
Christie's East, 20 Rockefeller Plz., New York, NY
10020-1902 / 212-606-0406 christics.com
Chu Tani Ind., Inc., P.O. Box 2064, Cody, WY 82414-2064
Chuck's Gun Shop, P.O. Box 597, Waldo, FL 32694 /
904-468-2264
Chuilli, Stephen, 8895 N. Military Trl. Ste., Ste. 201E, Palm
Beach Gardens, FL 33410
Churchill (See U.S. Importer-Ellett Bros.)
Churchill, Winston G., 2838 20 Mile Stream Rd., Proctorville,
VT 05153 / 802-226-7772
Churchill Glove Co., James, PO Box 298, Centralia, WA 98531
/ 360-736-2816; FAX: 360-330-0151
CIDCO, 21480 Pacific Blvd., Sterling, VA 22170 /
703-444-5353
Cimarron F.A. Co., P.O. Box 906, Fredericksburg, TX
78624-0906 / 830-997-9090; FAX: 830-997-0802
cimgraph@koc.com www.cimarron-firearms.com
Cincinnati Swaging, 2605 Marlington Ave., Cincinnati, OH
45208
Clark Custom Guns, Inc., 336 Shootout Lane, Princeton, LA
71067 / 318-949-9884; FAX: 318-949-9829
Clark Firearms Engraving, P.O. Box 80746, San Marino, CA
91118 / 818-287-1652
Clarkfield Enterprises, Inc., 1032 10th Ave., Clarkfield, MN
56223 / 612-669-7140
Claro Walnut Gunstock Co., 1235 Stanley Ave., Chico, CA
95928 / 530-342-5188; FAX: 530-342-5199
wally@clarowalnutgunstocks.com
www.clarowalnutgunstocks.com
Classic Arms Company, Rt 1 Box 120F, Burnet, TX 78611 /
512-756-4001
Classic Arms Corp., P.O. Box 106, Dunsmuir, CA 96025-0106
/ 530-235-2000
Classic Old West Styles, 1060 Doniphan Park Circle C, El
Paso, TX 79936 / 915-587-0684

MANUFACTURER'S DIRECTORY

Claybuster Wads & Harvester Bullets, 309 Sequoya Dr., Hopkinsville, KY 42240 / 800-922-6287; or 800-284-1746; FAX: 502-885-8088
Clean Shot Technologies, 21218 St. Andrews Blvd. Ste 504, Boca Raton, FL 33433 / 888-866-2532
Clearview Mfg. Co., Inc., 413 S. Oakley St., Fordyce, AR 71742 / 501-352-8557; FAX: 501-352-7120
Clearview Products, 3021 N. Portland, Oklahoma City, OK 73107
Cleland's Outdoor World, Inc, 10306 Airport Hwy., Swanton, OH 43558 / 419-865-4713; FAX: 419-865-5865
Clements' Custom Leathercraft, Chas, 1741 Dallas St., Aurora, CO 80010-2018 / 303-364-0403; FAX: 303-739-9824 gryphons@home.com kuntaoslcat.com
Clenzoil Worldwide Corp, Jack Fitzgerald, 25670 1st St., Westlake, OH 44145-1430 / 440-899-0482; FAX: 440-899-0483
Clift Mfg., L. R., 3821 Hammonton Rd., Marysville, CA 95901 / 916-755-3390; FAX: 916-755-3393
Clymer Mfg. Co., 1645 W. Hamlin Rd., Rochester Hills, MI 48309-3312 / 248-853-5555; FAX: 248-853-1530
C-More Systems, P.O. Box 1750, 7553 Gary Rd., Manassas, VA 20108 / 703-361-2663; FAX: 703-361-5881
Cobra Enterprises, Inc., 1960 S. Milestone Drive, Suite F, Salt Lake City, UT 84104 FAX: 801-908-8301 www.cobrapistols@networld.com
Cobra Sport S.R.I., Via Caduti Nei Lager No. 1, 56020 San Romano, Montopoli v/Arno (Pi, ITALY / 0039-571-450490; FAX: 0039-571-450492
Coffin, Charles H., 3719 Scarlet Ave., Odessa, TX 79762 / 915-366-4729; FAX: 915-366-4729
Coffin, Jim (See Working Guns)
Coffin, Jim. See: WORKING GUNS
Cogar's Gunsmithing, 206 Redwine Dr., Houghton Lake, MI 48629 / 517-422-4591
Coghlan's Ltd., 121 Irene St., Winnipeg, MB R3T 4C7 CANADA / 204-284-9550; FAX: 204-475-4127
Cold Steel Inc., 3036 Seaborg Ave. Ste. A, Ventura, CA 93003 / 800-255-4716; or 800-624-2363; FAX: 805-642-9727
Cole-Grip, 16135 Cohasset St., Van Nuys, CA 91406 / 818-782-4424
Coleman Co., Inc., 3600 N. Hydraulic, Wichita, KS 67219 / 1-800-835-3278; www.coleman.com
Cole's Gun Works, Old Bank Building, Rt. 4 Box 250, Moyock, NC 27958 / 919-435-2345
Collector's Armoury, Ltd., Tom Nelson, 9404 Gunston Cove Rd., Lorton, VA 22079 / 703-493-9120; FAX: 703-493-9424 www.collectorsarmoury.com
Collings, Ronald, 1006 Cielta Linda, Vista, CA 92083
Colonial Arms, Inc., P.O. Box 636, Selma, AL 36702-0636 / 334-872-9455; FAX: 334-872-9540 colonialarms@mindspring.com www.colonialarms.com
Colonial Repair, 47 Navarre St., Roslindale, MA 02131-4725 / 617-469-4951
Colorado Gunsmithing Academy, RR 3 Box 79B, El Campo, TX 77437 / 719-336-4099; or 800-754-2046; FAX: 719-336-9642
Colorado School of Trades, 1575 Hoyt St., Lakewood, CO 80215 / 800-234-4594; FAX: 303-233-4723
Colt Blackpowder Arms Co., 110 8th Street, Brooklyn, NY 11215 / 718-499-4678; FAX: 718-768-8056
Colt's Mfg. Co., Inc., PO Box 1868, Hartford, CT 06144-1868 / 800-962-COLT; or 860-236-6311; FAX: 860-244-1449
Compass Industries, Inc., 104 East 25th St., New York, NY 10010 / 212-473-2614 or 800-221-9904; FAX: 212-353-0826
Compasseco, Ltd., 151 Atkinson Hill Ave., Bardtown, KY 40004 / 502-349-0910
Competition Electronics, Inc., 3469 Precision Dr., Rockford, IL 61109 / 815-874-8001; FAX: 815-874-8181
Competitor Corp., Inc., 26 Knight St. Unit 3, Jaffrey, NH 03452 / 603-532-9483; FAX: 603-532-8209 competitorcorp@aol.com competitor-pistol.com
Component Concepts, Inc., 530 S. Springbrook Road, Newberg, OR 97132 / 503-554-8095; FAX: 503-554-9370 cci@cybcon.com www.phantomonline.com
Concept Development Corp., 16610 E. Laser Drive, Suite 5, Fountain Hills, AZ 85268-6644
Conetrol Scope Mounts, 10225 Hwy. 123 S., Seguin, TX 78155 / 830-379-3030; or 800-CONETROL; FAX: 830-379-3030 email@conetrol.com www.conetrol.com
Connecticut Shotgun Mfg. Co., P.O. Box 1692, 35 Woodland St., New Britain, CT 06051 / 860-225-6581; FAX: 860-832-8707
Connecticut Valley Classics (See CVC, BPI)
Conrad, C. A., 3964 Ebert St., Winston-Salem, NC 27127 / 919-788-5469
Cook Engineering Service, 891 Highbury Rd., Vict, 3133 AUSTRALIA
Cooper Arms, P.O. Box 114, Stevensville, MT 59870 / 406-777-0373; FAX: 406-777-5228
Cooper-Woodward Perfect Lube, 4120 Oesterle Rd., Helena, MT 59602 / 406-459-2287 cwperfectlube@mt.net cwperfectlube.com
Corbin Mfg. & Supply, Inc., 600 Industrial Circle, P.O. Box 2659, White City, OR 97503 / 541-826-5211; FAX: 541-826-8669 sales@corbins.com www.corbins.com
Cor-Bon Inc./Glaser LLC, P.O. Box 173, 1311 Industry Rd., Sturgis, SD 57785 / 605-347-4544; or 800-221-3489; FAX: 605-347-5055 email@corbon.com www.corbon.com
Corkys Gun Clinic, 4401 Hot Springs Dr., Greeley, CO 80634-9226 / 970-330-0516
Corry, John, 861 Princeton Ct., Neshanic Station, NJ 08853 / 908-369-8019
Cosmi Americo & Figlio S.N.C., Via Flaminia 307, Ancona, ITALY / 071-888208; FAX: 39-071-887008
Coulston Products, Inc., P.O. Box 30, 201 Ferry St. Suite 212, Easton, PA 18044-0030 / 215-253-0167; or 800-445-9927; FAX: 215-252-1511
Counter Assault, 120 Industrial Court, Kalispell, MT 59901 / 406-257-4740; FAX: 406-257-6674
Cousin Bob's Mountain Products, 7119 Ohio River Blvd., Ben Avon, PA 15202 / 412-766-5114; FAX: 412-766-5114
CP Bullets, 1310 Industrial Hwy #5-6, South Hampton, PA 18966 / 215-953-7264; FAX: 215-953-7275
CQB Training, P.O. Box 1739, Manchester, MO 63011
Craftguard, 3624 Logan Ave., Waterloo, IA 50703 / 319-232-2959; FAX: 319-234-0804
Crandall Tool & Machine Co., 19163 21 Mile Rd., Tustin, MI 49688 / 616-829-4430
Creedmoor Sports, Inc., P.O. Box 1040, Oceanside, CA 92051 / 767-757-5529; FAX: 760-757-5558 shoot@creedmoorsports.com www.creedmoorsports.com
Creek Side Metal & Woodcrafters, Fishers Hill, VA 22626 / 703-465-3903
Creighton Audette, 19 Highland Circle, Springfield, VT 05156 / 802-885-2331
Crimson Trace Lasers, 8090 SW Cirrus Dr., Beverton, OR 97008 / 800-442-2406; FAX: 503-627-0166 www.crimsontrace.com
Crit'R Call (See Rocky Mountain Wildlife Products)
Crosman Airguns, Rts. 5 and 20, E. Bloomfield, NY 14443 / 716-657-6161; FAX: 716-657-5405
Crosman Blades (See Coleman Co., Inc.)
Crouse's Country Cover, P.O. Box 160, Storrs, CT 06268 / 860-423-8736
CRR, Inc./Marble's Inc., 420 Industrial Park, P.O. Box 111, Gladstone, MI 49837 / 906-428-3710; FAX: 906-428-3711
Crucelegui, Hermanos (See U.S. Importer-Mandall)
Cubic Shot Shell Co., Inc., 98 Fatima Dr., Campbell, OH 44405 / 330-755-0349
Cullity Restoration, 209 Old Country Rd., East Sandwich, MA 02537 / 508-888-1147
Cumberland Arms, 514 Shafer Road, Manchester, TN 37355 / 800-797-8414
Cumberland Mountain Arms, P.O. Box 710, Winchester, TN 37398 / 615-967-8414; FAX: 615-967-9199
Cummings Bullets, 1417 Esperanza Way, Escondido, CA 92027
Cupp, Alana, Custom Engraver, P.O. Box 207, Annabella, UT 84711 / 801-896-4834
Curly Maple Stock Blanks (See Tiger-Hunt)
Curtis Cast Bullets, 527 W. Babcock St., Bozeman, MT 59715 / 406-587-8117; FAX: 406-587-8117
Curtis Gun Shop (See Curtis Cast Bullets)
Custom Bullets by Hoffman, 2604 Peconic Ave., Seaford, NY 11783
Custom Calls, 607 N. 5th St., Burlington, IA 52601 / 319-752-4465
Custom Checkering Service, Kathy Forster, 2124 S.E. Yamhill St., Portland, OR 97214 / 503-236-5874
Custom Chronograph, Inc., 5305 Reese Hill Rd., Sumas, WA 98295 / 360-988-7801
Custom Firearms (See Ahrends, Kim)
Custom Products (See Jones Custom Products)
Custom Quality Products, Inc., 345 W. Girard Ave., P.O. Box 71129, Madison Heights, MI 48071 / 810-585-1616; FAX: 810-585-0644
Custom Riflestocks, Inc., Michael M. Kokolus, 7005 Herber Rd., New Tripoli, PA 18066 / 610-298-3013; FAX: 610-298-2431 mkokolus@prodigy.net
Custom Single Shot Rifles, 9651 Meadows Lane, Guthrie, OK 73044 / 405-282-3634
Custom Tackle and Ammo, P.O. Box 1886, Farmington, 87499 / 505-632-3539
Cutco Cutlery, P.O. Box 810, Olean, NY 14760 / 716-372-3111
CVA, 5988 Peachtree Corners East, Norcross, GA 3007[illegible] 770-449-4687; FAX: 770-242-8546 info@cva.com www.cva.com
Cylinder & Slide, Inc., William R. Laughridge, 245 E. 4th Fremont, NE 68025 / 402-721-4277; FAX: 402-721-[illegible] bill@cylinder-slide.com www.clinder-slide.com
CZ USA, PO Box 171073, Kansas City, KS 66117 / 913-321-1811; FAX: 913-321-4901

D

D&D Gunsmiths, Ltd., 363 E. Elmwood, Troy, MI 48083 810-583-1512; FAX: 810-583-1524
D&G Precision Duplicators (See Greene Precision)
D&H Precision Tooling, 7522 Barnard Mill Rd., Ringwoo[illegible] 60072 / 815-653-4011
D&L Industries (See D.J. Marketing)
D&L Sports, P.O. Box 651, Gillette, WY 82717 / 307-686-4008
D.C.C. Enterprises, 259 Wynburn Ave., Athens, GA 3060[illegible]
D.J. Marketing, 10602 Horton Ave., Downey, CA 90241 / 310-806-0891; FAX: 310-806-6231
D.L. Unmussig Bullets, 7862 Brentford Dr., Richmond, V[illegible] 23225 / 804-320-1165; FAX: 804-320-4587
Dade Screw Machine Products, 2319 NW 7th Ave., Miami, 33127 / 305-573-5050
Daisy Outdoor Products, P.O. Box 220, Rogers, AR 7275[illegible] 479-636-1200; FAX: 479-636-0573 www.daisy.com
Dakota (See U.S. Importer-EMF Co., Inc.)
Dakota Arms, Inc., 130 Industry Road, Sturgis, SD 57785 605-347-4686; FAX: 605-347-4459 info@dakotaarms.com www.dakotaarms.com
Dakota Corp., 77 Wales St., P.O. Box 543, Rutland, VT 057[illegible] / 802-775-6062; or 800-451-4167; FAX: 802-773-391[illegible]
Daly, Charles/KBI, P.O. Box 6625, Harrisburg, PA 17112 866-DALY GUN
Da-Mar Gunsmith's, Inc., 102 1st St., Solvay, NY 13209
damascususa@inteliport.com, 149 Deans Farm Rd., Tyne[illegible] NC 27980 / 252-221-2010; FAX: 252-221-2010 damascususa@inteliport.com
Dan Wesson Firearms, 5169 Rt. 12 South, Norwich, NY 13815 / 607-336-1174; FAX: 607-336-2730 danwessonfirearms@citlink.net danwessonfirearms.c[illegible]
Danforth, Mikael. See: VEKTOR USA
Dangler, Homer L., 2870 Lee Marie Dr., Adrian, MI 49221 517-266-1997
Danner Shoe Mfg. Co., 12722 NE Airport Way, Portland, O 97230 / 503-251-1100; or 800-345-0430; FAX: 503-251-1119
Dan's Whetstone Co., Inc., 130 Timbs Place, Hot Springs, A 71913 / 501-767-1616; FAX: 501-767-9598 questions@danswhetstone.com www.danswhetstone.com
Danuser Machine Co., 550 E. Third St., P.O. Box 368, Fultor MO 65251 / 573-642-2246; FAX: 573-642-2240 sales@danuser.com www.danuser.com
Dara-Nes, Inc. (See Nesci Enterprises, Inc.)
D'Arcy Echols & Co., P.O. Box 421, Millville, UT 84326 / 435-755-6842
Darlington Gun Works, Inc., P.O. Box 698, 516 S. 52 Bypass Darlington, SC 29532 / 803-393-3931
Dart Bell/Brass (See MAST Technology)
Darwin Hensley Gunmaker, P.O. Box 329, Brightwood, OR 97011 / 503-622-5411
Data Tech Software Systems, 19312 East Eldorado Drive, Aurora, CO 80013
Dave Norin Schrank's Smoke & Gun, 2010 Washington St., Waukegan, IL 60085 / 708-662-4034
Dave's Gun Shop, P.O. Box 2824, Casper, WY 82602-2824 / 307-754-9724
David Clark Co., Inc., P.O. Box 15054, Worcester, MA 01615 / 508-756-6216; FAX: 508-753-5827 sales@davidclark.com www.davidclark.com
David Condon, Inc., 109 E. Washington St., Middleburg, VA 22117 / 703-687-5642
David Miller Co., 3131 E. Greenlee Rd., Tucson, AZ 85716 / 520-326-3117
David R. Chicoine, 1210 Jones Street, Gastonia, NC 28052 / 704-853-0265 bnpress@quik.com www.icxquik.com/bnpress
David W. Schwartz Custom Guns, 2505 Waller St., Eau Claire, WI 54703 / 715-832-1735
Davide Pedersoli and Co., Via Artigiani 57, Gardone VT, Brescia 25063, ITALY / 030-8915000; FAX:

MANUFACTURER'S DIRECTORY

30-8911019 info@davidepedersoli.com www.davide_pedersoli.com
Don, 1619 Heights, Katy, TX 77493 / 713-391-3090
Industries (See Cobra Enterprises, Inc.)
Products, Mike, 643 Loop Dr., Moses Lake, WA 98837 / 509-765-6178; or 509-766-7281
ate Ltd., Birch House Lanee, Cotes Heath Staffs, T15.022, ENGLAND / 01782-791755; FAX: 1782-791617
n Traister, 4778 N. Monkey Hill Rd., P.O. Box 593, Oak Harbor, WA 98277 / 360-679-4657; FAX: 360-675-1114
Books Division of Krause Publications, 700 E. State St., ola, WI 54990-0001 / 715-445-2214
one Ent., Inc., 5900 Colwyn Dr., Harrisburg, PA 17109
Eye's Sport Center, 76 Baer Rd., Shickshinny, PA 18655 570-256-7432 deadeyeprizz@aol.com
eeka Exports Pvt. Ltd., D-78, Saket, Meerut-250-006, INDIA / 011-91-121-640363 or ; FAX: 11-91-121-640988 deepeeka@poboxes.com www.deepeeka.com
nse Training International, Inc., 749 S. Lemay, Ste. A3-337, Ft. Collins, CO 80524 / 303-482-2520; FAX: 303-482-0548
n Inc. (See Aristocrat Knives)
as Barrels, 20049 W. State Hwy. Z, Ridgeway, MO 64481 / 660-872-6308
Rey Products, P.O. Box 5134, Playa Del Rey, CA 90296-5134 / 213-823-0494
i Gun House, 1374 Kashmere Gate, New Delhi 110 006, INDIA / 2940974; or 394-0974; FAX: 2917344 dgh@vsnl.com
rge, Ed, 6734 W. Main, Houma, LA 70360 / 985-223-0206 delorge@triparish.net www.eddelorge.com
Sports, Inc., Dave Budin, Box 685, 817 Main St., Margaretville, NY 12455 / 845-586-4103; FAX: 845-586-4105
a Arms Ltd., P.O. Box 1000, Delta, VT 84624-1000
a Enterprises, 284 Hagemann Drive, Livermore, CA 94550
a Frangible Ammunition LLC, P.O. Box 2350, Stafford, VA 22555-2350 / 540-720-5778; or 800-339-1933; FAX: 540-720-5667 dfa@dfanet.com www.dfanet.com
n-Bart Checkering Tools, Inc., 1825 Bickford Ave., Snohomish, WA 98290 / 360-568-7356 walt@dembartco.com www.dembartco.com
nver Instrument Co., 6542 Fig St., Arvada, CO 80004 / 800-321-1135; or 303-431-7255; FAX: 303-423-4831
Santis Holster & Leather Goods, Inc., P.O. Box 2039, 149 Denton Ave., New Hyde Park, NY 11040-0701 / 516-354-8000; FAX: 516-354-7501
sert Mountain Mfg., P.O. Box 130184, Coram, MT 59913 / 800-477-0762; or 406-387-5361; FAX: 406-387-5361
tonics USA, 53 Perimeter Center East #200, Atlanta, GA 30346 / 866-759-1169
R Custom Rifles, 4191 37th Ave. SE, Tappen, ND 58487 / 701-327-8135
S, Inc., Dale A. Storey, 1117 E. 12th, Casper, WY 82601 / 307-237-2414; FAX: 307-237-2414 dalest@trib.com www.dgsrifle.com
B Products, 336 River View Dr., Verona, VA 24482-2547 / 703-836-2648
amond Machining Technology, Inc. (See DMT)
amond Mfg. Co., P.O. Box 174, Wyoming, PA 18644 / 800-233-9601
bble, Derek A., 555 John Downey Dr., New Britain, CT 06051 / 203-224-2630
etz Gun Shop & Range, Inc., 421 Range Rd., New Braunfels, TX 78132 / 210-885-4662
illiott Gunsmithing, Inc., 657 Scarlett Rd., Dandridge, TN 37725 / 865-397-9204 gunsmithd@aol.com dilliottgunsmithing.com
illon Precision Products, Inc., 8009 East Dillon's Way, Scottsdale, AZ 85260 / 480-948-8009; or 800-762-3845; FAX: 480-998-2786 sales@dillonprecision.com www.dillonprecision.com
ina Arms Corporation, P.O. Box 46, Royersford, PA 19468 / 610-287-0266; FAX: 610-287-0266
Dixie Gun Works, P.O. Box 130, Union City, TN 38281 / 731-885-0700; FAX: 731-885-0440 info@dixiegunworks.com www.dixiegunworks.com
Dixon Muzzleloading Shop, Inc., 9952 Kunkels Mill Rd., Kempton, PA 19529 / 610-756-6271 dixonmuzzleloading.com
DKT, Inc., 14623 Vera Drive, Union, MI 49130-9744 / 800-741-7083 orders; FAX: 616-641-2015
DLO Mfg., 10807 SE Foster Ave., Arcadia, FL 33821-7304
DMT--Diamond Machining Technology Inc., 85 Hayes Memorial Dr., Marlborough, MA 01752 FAX: 508-485-3924
Dohring Bullets, 100 W. 8 Mile Rd., Ferndale, MI 48220
Dolbare, Elizabeth, P.O. Box 502, Dubois, WY 82513-0502 / 307-450-7500 edolbare@hotmail.com www.scrimshaw-engraving.com
Domino, P.O. Box 108, 20019 Settimo Milanese, Milano, ITALY / 1-39-2-33512040; FAX: 1-39-2-33511587
Don Klein Custom Guns, 433 Murray Park Dr., Ripon, WI 54971 / 920-748-2931 daklein@charter.net www.donkleincustomguns.com
Donnelly, C. P., 405 Kubli Rd., Grants Pass, OR 97527 / 541-846-6604
Doskocil Mfg. Co., Inc., P.O. Box 1246, 4209 Barnett, Arlington, TX 76017 / 817-467-5116; FAX: 817-472-9810
Douglas Barrels, Inc., 5504 Big Tyler Rd., Charleston, WV 25313-1398 / 304-776-1341; FAX: 304-776-8560 www.benchrest.com/douglas
Downsizer Corp., P.O. Box 710316, Santee, CA 92072-0316 / 619-448-5510 www.downsizer.com
DPMS (Defense Procurement Manufacturing Services, Inc.), 13983 Industry Avenue, Becker, MN 55308 / 800-578-DPMS; or 763-261-5600; FAX: 763-261-5599
Dr. O's Products Ltd., P.O. Box 111, Niverville, NY 12130 / 518-784-3333; FAX: 518-784-2800
Drain, Mark, SE 3211 Kamilche Point Rd., Shelton, WA 98584 / 206-426-5452
Dremel Mfg. Co., 4915-21st St., Racine, WI 53406
Dri-Slide, Inc., 411 N. Darling, Fremont, MI 49412 / 616-924-3950
Dropkick, 1460 Washington Blvd., Williamsport, PA 17701 / 717-326-6561; FAX: 717-326-4950
DS Arms, Inc., P.O. Box 370, 27 West 990 Industrial Ave., Barrington, IL 60010 / 847-277-7258; FAX: 847-277-7259 www.dsarms.com
DTM International, Inc., 40 Joslyn Rd., P.O. Box 5, Lake Orion, MI 48362 / 313-693-6670
Duane A. Hobbie Gunsmithing, 2412 Pattie Ave., Wichita, KS 67216 / 316-264-8266
Duane's Gun Repair (See DGR Custom Rifles)
Dubber, Michael W., P.O. Box 312, Evansville, IN 47702 / 812-424-9000; FAX: 812-424-6551
Duck Call Specialists, P.O. Box 124, Jerseyville, IL 62052 / 618-498-9855
Duffy, Charles E. (See Guns Antique & Modern DBA), Williams Lane, P.O. Box 2, West Hurley, NY 12491 / 914-679-2997
Du-Lite Corp., 171 River Rd., Middletown, CT 06457 / 203-347-2505; FAX: 203-347-9404
Dumoulin, Ernest, Rue Florent Boclinville 8-10, 13-4041, Votten, BELGIUM / 41 27 78 92
Duncan's Gun Works, Inc., 1619 Grand Ave., San Marcos, CA 92069 / 760-727-0515
DunLyon R&D, Inc., 52151 E. US Hwy. 60, Miami, AZ 85539 / 928-473-9027
Duofold, Inc., RD 3 Rt. 309, Valley Square Mall, Tamaqua, PA 18252 / 717-386-2666; FAX: 717-386-3652
Dutchman's Firearms, Inc., 4143 Taylor Blvd., Louisville, KY 40215 / 502-366-0555
Dybala Gun Shop, P.O. Box 1024, FM 3156, Bay City, TX 77414 / 409-245-0866
Dykstra, Doug, 411 N. Darling, Fremont, MI 49412 / 616-924-3950
Dynalite Products, Inc., 215 S. Washington St., Greenfield, OH 45123 / 513-981-2124
Dynamit Nobel-RWS, Inc., 81 Ruckman Rd., Closter, NJ 07624 / 201-767-7971; FAX: 201-767-1589

E

E&L Mfg., Inc., 4177 Riddle Bypass Rd., Riddle, OR 97469 / 541-874-2137; FAX: 541-874-3107
E. Arthur Brown Co., 3404 Pawnee Dr., Alexandria, MN 56308 / 320-762-8847
E.A.A. Corp., P.O. Box 1299, Sharpes, FL 32959 / 407-639-4842; or 800-536-4442; FAX: 407-639-7006
Eagan, Donald V., P.O. Box 196, Benton, PA 17814 / 717-925-6134
Eagle Arms, Inc. (See ArmaLite, Inc.)
Eagle Grips, Eagle Business Center, 460 Randy Rd., Carol Stream, IL 60188 / 800-323-6144; or 708-260-0400; FAX: 708-260-0486
Eagle Imports, Inc., 1750 Brielle Ave., Unit B1, Wanamassa, NJ 07712 / 732-493-0333; FAX: 732-493-0301 gsodini@aol.com www.bersa-11ama.com
E-A-R, Inc., Div. of Cabot Safety Corp., 5457 W. 79th St., Indianapolis, IN 46268 / 800-327-3431; FAX: 800-488-8007
EAW (See U.S. Importer-New England Custom Gun Serv
Eckelman Gunsmithing, 3125 133rd St. SW, Fort Ripley, MN 56449 / 218-829-3176
Eclectic Technologies, Inc., 45 Grandview Dr., Suite A, Farmington, CT 06034
Ed Brown Products, Inc., P.O. Box 492, Perry, MO 63462 / 573-565-3261; FAX: 573-565-2791 edbrown@edbrown.com www.edbrown.com
Edenpine, Inc. c/o Six Enterprises, Inc., 320 D Turtle Creek Ct., San Jose, CA 95125 / 408-999-0201; FAX: 408-999-0216
EdgeCraft Corp., S. Weiner, 825 Southwood Road, Avondale, PA 19311 / 610-268-0500; or 800-342-3255; FAX: 610-268-3545 www.edgecraft.com
Edmisten Co., P.O. Box 1293, Boone, NC 28607
Edmund Scientific Co., 101 E. Gloucester Pike, Barrington, NJ 08033 / 609-543-6250
Ednar, Inc., 2-4-8 Kayabacho, Nihonbashi Chuo-ku, Tokyo, JAPAN / 81-3-3667-1651; FAX: 81-3-3661-8113
Ed's Gun House, Ed Kukowski, P.O. Box 62, Minnesota City, MN 55959 / 507-689-2925
Effebi SNC-Dr. Franco Beretta, via Rossa, 4, 25062, ITALY / 030-2751955; FAX: 030-2180414
Eggleston, Jere D., 400 Saluda Ave., Columbia, SC 29205 / 803-799-3402
Eichelberger Bullets, Wm., 158 Crossfield Rd., King Of Prussia, PA 19406
Ekol Leather Care, P.O. Box 2652, West Lafayette, IN 47906 / 317-463-2250; FAX: 317-463-7004
El Paso Saddlery Co., P.O. Box 27194, El Paso, TX 79926 / 915-544-2233; FAX: 915-544-2535 epsaddlery.com www.epsaddlery.com
Electro Prismatic Collimators, Inc., 1441 Manatt St., Lincoln, NE 68521
Electronic Shooters Protection, Inc., 15290 Gadsden Ct., Brighton, CO 80603 / 800-797-7791; FAX: 303-659-8668 esp@usa.net espamerican.com
Electronic Trigger Systems, Inc., P.O. Box 645, Park Rapids, MN 56470 / 218-732-5333
Eley Ltd., P.O. Box 705, Witton, Birmingham, B6 7UT ENGLAND / 021-356-8899; FAX: 021-331-4173
Elite Ammunition, P.O. Box 3251, Oakbrook, IL 60522 / 708-366-9006
Ellett Bros., 267 Columbia Ave., P.O. Box 128, Chapin, SC 29036 / 803-345-3751; or 800-845-3711; FAX: 803-345-1820
Ellicott Arms, Inc. / Woods Pistolsmithing, 8390 Sunset Dr., Ellicott City, MD 21043 / 410-465-7979
Elliott, Inc., G. W., 514 Burnside Ave, East Hartford, CT 06108 / 203-289-5741; FAX: 203-289-3137
EMAP USA, 6420 Wilshire Blvd., Los Angeles, CA 90048 / 213-782-2000; FAX: 213-782-2867
Emerging Technologies, Inc. (See Laseraim Technologies, Inc.)
EMF Co., Inc., 1900 E. Warner Ave., Suite 1-D, Santa Ana, CA 92705 / 949-261-6611; FAX: 949-756-0133
Empire Cutlery Corp., 12 Kruger Ct., Clifton, NJ 07013 / 201-472-5155; FAX: 201-779-0759
English, Inc., A.G., 708 S. 12th St., Broken Arrow, OK 74012 / 918-251-3399 agenglish@wedzone.net www.agenglish.com
Engraving Artistry, 36 Alto Rd., Burlington, CT 06013 / 860-673-6837 bobburt44@hotmail.com
Engraving Only, Box 55 Rabbit Gulch, Hill City, SD 57745 / 605-574-2239
Enguix Import-Export, Alpujarras 58, Alzira, Valencia, SPAIN / (96) 241 43 95; FAX: (96) 241 43 95
Enhanced Presentations, Inc., 5929 Market St., Wilmington, NC 28405 / 910-799-1622; FAX: 910-799-5004
Enlow, Charles, 895 Box, Beaver, OK 73932 / 405-625-4487
Entre`prise Arms, Inc., 15861 Business Center Dr., Irwindale, CA 91706
EPC, 1441 Manatt St., Lincoln, NE 68521 / 402-476-3946
Erhardt, Dennis, 4508 N. Montana Ave., Helena, MT 59602 / 406-442-4533
Essex Arms, P.O. Box 363, Island Pond, VT 05846 / 802-723-6203; FAX: 802-723-6203
Estate Cartridge, Inc., 900 Bob Ehlen Dr., Anoka, MN 55303-7502 / 409-856-7277; FAX: 409-856-5486
Euber Bullets, No. Orwell Rd., Orwell, VT 05760 / 802-948-2621
Euroarms of America, Inc., P.O. Box 3277, Winchester, VA 22604 / 540-662-1863; FAX: 540-662-4464 www.euroarms.net
Euro-Imports, 2221 Upland Ave. S., Pahrump, NV 89048 / 775-751-6671; FAX: 775-751-6671

MANUFACTURER'S DIRECTORY

European American Armory Corp. (See E.A.A. Corp.)
Eversull Co., Inc., 1 Tracemont, Boyce, LA 71409 / 318-793-8728; FAX: 318-793-5483 bestguns@aol.com
Evolution Gun Works, Inc., 4050 B-8 Skyron Dr., Doylestown, PA 18901 / 215-348-9892; FAX: 215-348-1056 egw@pil.net www.egw-guns.com
Excalibur Electro Optics, Inc., P.O. Box 400, Fogelsville, PA 18051-0400 / 610-391-9105; FAX: 610-391-9220
Excalibur Publications, P.O. Box 89667, Tucson, AZ 85752 / 520-575-9057 excalibureditor@earthlink.net
Excel Industries, Inc., 4510 Carter Ct., Chino, CA 91710 / 909-627-2404; FAX: 909-627-7817
Executive Protection Institute, P.O. Box 802, Berryville, VA 22611 / 540-554-2540; FAX: 540-554-2558 ruk@crosslink.net www.personalprotecion.com
Eze-Lap Diamond Prods., P.O. Box 2229, 15164 West State St., Westminster, CA 92683 / 714-847-1555; FAX: 714-897-0280
E-Z-Way Systems, P.O. Box 4310, Newark, OH 43058-4310 / 614-345-6645; or 800-848-2072; FAX: 614-345-6600

F

F.A.I.R., Via Gitti, 41, 25060 Marcheno Bresc, ITALY / 030/861162-8610344; FAX: 030/8610179 info@fair.it www.fair.it
Fabarm S.p.A., Via Averolda 31, 25039 Travagliato, Brescia, ITALY / 030-6863629; FAX: 030-6863684 info@fabarm.com www.fabarm.com
Fagan Arms, 22952 15 Mile Rd, Clinton Township, MI 48035 / 810-465-4637; FAX: 810-792-6996
Faith Associates, P.O. Box 549, Flat Rock, NC 28731-0549 FAX: 828-697-6827
Falcon Industries, Inc., P.O. Box 1060, Tijeras, NM 87059 / 505-281-3783; FAX: 505-281-3991 shines@ergogrips.net www.ergogrips.net
Far North Outfitters, Box 1252, Bethel, AK 99559
Farm Form Decoys, Inc., 1602 Biovu, P.O. Box 748, Galveston, TX 77553 / 409-744-0762; or 409-765-6361; FAX: 409-765-8513
Farr Studio, Inc., 183 Hunters Rd., Washington, VA 22747-2001 / 615-638-8825
Farrar Tool Co., Inc., 11855 Cog Hill Dr., Whittier, CA 90601-1902 / 310-863-4367; FAX: 310-863-5123
Faulhaber Wildlocker, Dipl.-Ing. Norbert Wittasek, Seilergasse 2, A-1010 Wien, AUSTRIA / 43-1-5137001; FAX: 43-1-5137001 faulhaber1@utanet.at
Faulk's Game Call Co., Inc., 616 18th St., Lake Charles, LA 70601 / 337-436-9726; FAX: 337-494-7205
Faust Inc., T. G., 544 Minor St, Reading, PA 19602 / 610-375-8549; FAX: 610-375-4488
Fautheree, Andy, P.O. Box 4607, Pagosa Springs, CO 81157 / 970-731-5003; FAX: 970-731-5009
Feather, Flex Decoys, 4500 Doniphan Dr., Neosho, MO 64850 / 318-746-8596; FAX: 318-742-4815
Federal Arms Corp. of America, 7928 University Ave., Fridley, MN 55432 / 612-780-8780; FAX: 612-780-8780
Federal Cartridge Co., 900 Ehlen Dr., Anoka, MN 55303 / 612-323-2300; FAX: 612-323-2506
Federal Champion Target Co., 232 Industrial Parkway, Richmond, IN 47374 / 800-441-4971; FAX: 317-966-7747
Federated-Fry (See Fry Metals)
FEG, Budapest, Soroksariut 158, H-1095, HUNGARY
Feinwerkbau Westinger & Altenburger, Neckarstrasse 43, 78727, Oberndorf a. N., GERMANY / 07423-814-00; FAX: 07423-814-200 info@feinwerkbau.de www.feinwerkbau.de
Feken, Dennis, Rt. 2, Box 124, Perry, OK 73077 / 405-336-5611
Felk Pistols, Inc., 2121 Castlebridge Rd., Midlothian, VA 23113 / 804-794-3744; FAX: 208-988-4834
Ferguson, Bill, P.O. Box 1238, Sierra Vista, AZ 85636 / 520-458-5321; FAX: 520-458-9125
Ferguson, Bill. See: BULLET METALS
FERLIB, Via Parte 33 Marcheno/BS, Marcheno/BS, ITALY / 00390308610191; FAX: 00390308966882 info@ferlib.com www.ferlib.com
Ferris Firearms, 7110 F.M. 1863, Bulverde, TX 78163 / 210-980-4424
Fibron Products, Inc., P.O. Box 430, Buffalo, NY 14209-0430 / 716-886-2378; FAX: 716-886-2394
Fieldsport Ltd., Bryan Bilinski, 3313 W. South Airport Rd., Traverse City, MI 49684 / 616-933-0767
Fiocchi Munizioni S.P.A. (See U.S. Importer-Fiocch
Fiocchi of America, Inc., 5030 Fremont Rd., Ozark, MO 65721 / 417-725-4118; or 800-721-2666; FAX: 417-725-1039
Firearms Co. Ltd. / Alpine (See U.S. Importer-Mandall
Firearms Engraver's Guild of America, 332 Vine St., Oregon City, OR 97045 / 503-656-5693
Firearms International, 5709 Hartsdale, Houston, TX 77036 / 713-460-2447
Fisher, Jerry A., 631 Crane Mt. Rd., Big Fork, MT 59911 / 406-837-2722
Fisher Custom Firearms, 2199 S. Kittredge Way, Aurora, CO 80013 / 303-755-3710
Fitzgerald, Jack. See: CLENZOIL WORLDWIDE CORP
Flambeau, Inc., 15981 Valplast Rd., Middlefield, OH 44062 / 216-632-1631; FAX: 216-632-1581 www.flambeau.com
Flayderman & Co., Inc., P.O. Box 2446, Ft. Lauderdale, FL 33303 / 954-761-8855
Fleming Firearms, 7720 E. 126th St. N., Collinsville, OK 74021-7016 / 918-665-3624
Fletcher-Bidwell, LLC., 305 E. Terhune St., Viroqua, WI 54665-1631 / 866-637-1860 fbguns@netscape.net
Flintlocks, Etc., 160 Rossiter Rd., P.O. Box 181, Richmond, MA 01254 / 413-698-3822; FAX: 413-698-3866 flintetc@berkshire.rr.com
Flitz International Ltd., 821 Mohr Ave., Waterford, WI 53185 / 414-534-5898; FAX: 414-534-2991
Fluoramics, Inc., 18 Industrial Ave., Mahwah, NJ 07430 / 800-922-0075; FAX: 201-825-7035
Flynn's Custom Guns, P.O. Box 7461, Alexandria, LA 71306 / 318-455-7130
FN Manufacturing, P.O. Box 24257, Columbia, SC 29224 / 803-736-0522
Folks, Donald E., 205 W. Lincoln St., Pontiac, IL 61764 / 815-844-7901
Foothills Video Productions, Inc., P.O. Box 651, Spartanburg, SC 29304 / 803-573-7023; or 800-782-5358
Foredom Electric Co., Rt. 6, 16 Stony Hill Rd., Bethel, CT 06801 / 203-792-8622
Forgett, Valmore. See: NAVY ARMS COMPANY
Forgreens Tool & Mfg., Inc., P.O. Box 955, Robert Lee, TX 76945 / 915-453-2800; FAX: 915-453-2460
Forkin Custom Classics, 205 10th Avenue S.W., White Sulphur Spring, MT 59645 / 406-547-2344
Forrest Tool Co., P.O. Box 768, 44380 Gordon Lane, Mendocino, CA 95460 / 707-937-2141; FAX: 717-937-1817
Forster, Kathy (See Custom Checkering)
Forster, Larry L., Box 212, 216 Highway 13 E., Gwinner, ND 58040-0212 / 701-678-2475
Forster Products, 310 E. Lanark Ave., Lanark, IL 61046 / 815-493-6360; FAX: 815-493-2371
Fort Hill Gunstocks, 12807 Fort Hill Rd., Hillsboro, OH 45133 / 513-466-2763
Fort Knox Security Products, 1051 N. Industrial Park Rd., Orem, UT 84057 / 801-224-7233; or 800-821-5216; FAX: 801-226-5493
Forthofer's Gunsmithing & Knifemaking, 5535 U.S. Hwy. 93S, Whitefish, MT 59937-8411 / 406-862-2674
Fortune Products, Inc., 205 Hickory Creek Rd., Marble Falls, TX 78654 / 210-693-6111; FAX: 210-693-6394 randy@accusharp.com
Forty-Five Ranch Enterprises, Box 1080, Miami, OK 74355-1080 / 918-542-5875
Foster, See: ACCURACY INTERNATIONAL
Fountain Products, 492 Prospect Ave., West Springfield, MA 01089 / 413-781-4651; FAX: 413-733-8217
4-D Custom Die Co., 711 N. Sandusky St., PO Box 889, Mt. Vernon, OH 43050-0889 / 740-397-7214; FAX: 740-397-6600 info@ch4d.com ch4d.com
Fowler Bullets, 806 Dogwood Dr., Gastonia, NC 28054 / 704-867-3259
Fowler, Bob (See Black Powder Products)
Fox River Mills, Inc., P.O. Box 298, 227 Poplar St., Osage, IA 50461 / 515-732-3798; FAX: 515-732-5128
Francotte & Cie S.A. Auguste, rue de Trois Juin 109, 4400 Herstal-Liege, BELGIUM / 32-4-248-13-18; FAX: 32-4-248-11-79
Frank Knives, 13868 NW Keleka Pl., Seal Rock, OR 97376 / 541-563-3041; FAX: 541-563-3041
Frank Mittermeier, Inc., P.O. Box 1, Bronx, NY 10465
Franzen International, Inc. (See U.S. Importer for)
Fred F. Wells/Wells Sport Store, 110 N Summit St., Prescott, AZ 86301 / 928-445-3655 www.wellssportstore@cableone-net
Freedom Arms, Inc., P.O. Box 150, Freedom, WY 83120 / 307-883-2468; FAX: 307-883-2005
Fremont Tool Works, 1214 Prairie, Ford, KS 67842 / 316-369-2327
Front Sight Firearms Training Institute, P.O. Box 2619, Aptos, CA 95001 / 800-987-7719; FAX: 408-684-2137
Frontier, 2910 San Bernardo, Laredo, TX 78040 / 956-723-5409; FAX: 956-723-1774
Frontier Arms Co., Inc., 401 W. Rio Santa Cruz, Green V AZ 85614-3932
Frontier Products Co., 2401 Walker Rd., Roswell, NM 88201-8950 / 614-262-9357
Frontier Safe Co., 3201 S. Clinton St., Fort Wayne, IN 4 / 219-744-7233; FAX: 219-744-6678
Frost Cutlery Co., P.O. Box 22636, Chattanooga, TN 37 615-894-6079; FAX: 615-894-9576
Fry Metals, 4100 6th Ave., Altoona, PA 16602 / 814-946-1611
Fujinon, Inc., 10 High Point Dr., Wayne, NJ 07470 / 201-633-5600; FAX: 201-633-5216
Fullmer, Geo. M., 2499 Mavis St., Oakland, CA 94601 / 510-533-4193
Fulton Armory, 8725 Bollman Place No. 1, Savage, MD 2 / 301-490-9485; FAX: 301-490-9547 www.fulton.armory.com
Furr Arms, 91 N. 970 W., Orem, UT 84057 / 801-226-3 FAX: 801-226-3877

G

G&H Decoys, Inc., P.O. Box 1208, Hwy. 75 North, Henry OK 74437 / 918-652-3314; FAX: 918-652-3400
G.C. Bullet Co., Inc., 40 Mokelumne River Dr., Lodi, CA 9
G.G. & G., 3602 E. 42nd Stravenue, Tucson, AZ 85713 / 520-748-7167; FAX: 520-748-7583 ggg&3@aol.com www.ggg&3.com
G.H. Enterprises Ltd., Bag 10, Okotoks, AB T0L 1T0 CANA / 403-938-6070
G.U., Inc. (See U.S. Importer for New SKB Arms Co.)
G.W. Elliott, Inc., 514 Burnside Ave., East Hartford, CT 06 / 203-289-5741; FAX: 203-289-3137
G96 Products Co., Inc., 85 5th Ave., Bldg. #6, Paterson, 07544 / 973-684-4050; FAX: 973-684-3848 g96prod@aol
Gage Manufacturing, 663 W. 7th St., A, San Pedro, CA 907 / 310-832-3546
Gaillard Barrels, P.O. Box 21, Pathlow, SK S0K 3B0 CANA / 306-752-3769; FAX: 306-752-5969
Gain Twist Barrel Co., Rifle Works and Armory, 707 12th Cody, WY 82414 / 307-587-4919; FAX: 307-527-60
Galati International, P.O. Box 10, 616 Burley Ridge Rd., Wesco, MO 65586 / 636-584-0785; FAX: 573-775-43 support@galatiinternational.com www.galatiinternational.com
Galaxy Imports Ltd., Inc., P.O. Box 3361, Victoria, TX 779 / 361-573-4867; FAX: 361-576-9622 galaxy@cox-internet.com
GALCO International Ltd., 2019 W. Quail Ave., Phoenix, A 85027 / 623-474-7070; FAX: 623-582-6854 customerservice@usgalco.com www.usgalco.com
Galena Industries AMT, 5463 Diaz St., Irwindale, CA 91706 626-856-8883; FAX: 626-856-8878
Gamba S.p.A. Societa Armi Bresciane Srl, Renato, Via Artigiani 93, ITALY / 30-8911640; FAX: 30-8911648
Gamba, USA, P.O. Box 60452, Colorado Springs, CO 80960 719-578-1145; FAX: 719-444-0731
Game Haven Gunstocks, 13750 Shire Rd., Wolverine, MI 49799 / 616-525-8257
Gamebore Division, Polywad, Inc., P.O. Box 7916, Macon, G 31209 / 478-477-0669; or 800-998-0669
Gamo (See U.S. Importers-Arms United Corp, Daisy M
Gamo USA, Inc., 3911 SW 47th Ave., Suite 914, Ft. Lauderdale, FL 33314 / 954-581-5822; FAX: 954-581-3165 gamousa@gate.net www.gamo.com
Gander Mountain, Inc., 12400 Fox River Rd., Wilmont, WI 53192 / 414-862-6848
GAR, 590 McBride Ave., West Paterson, NJ 07424 / 973-754-1114; FAX: 973-754-1114 garreloading@aol.com www.garreloading.com
Garcia National Gun Traders, Inc., 225 SW 22nd Ave., Miami FL 33135 / 305-642-2355
Garrett Cartridges, Inc., P.O. Box 178, Chehalis, WA 98532 360-736-0702 www.garrettcartridges.com
Garthwaite Pistolsmith, Inc., Jim, 12130 State Route 405, Watsontown, PA 17777 / 570-538-1566; FAX: 570-538-2965 www.garthwaite.com
Gary Goudy Classic Stocks, 1512 S. 5th St., Dayton, WA 99328 / 509-382-2726 goudy@innw.net
Gary Reeder Custom Guns, 2601 7th Avenue East, Flagstaff, AZ 86004 / 928-526-3313; FAX: 928-527-0840 gary@reedercustomguns.com www.reedercustomguns.com
Gator Guns & Repair, 7952 Kenai Spur Hwy., Kenai, AK 99611-8311

MANUFACTURER'S DIRECTORY

er Armes, S.A., 46 rue Desjoyaux, 42000, aint-Etienne, FRANCE / 04-77-33-38-92; FAX: 4-77-61-95-72
Enterprises, 409 Le Gardeur, Slidell, LA 70460 / 04-649-0693
ann, Walter (See Huntington Die Specialties)
, P.O. Box 5704, Asheville, NC 28803
cco Gun Works, 10512 Lower Sacramento Rd., tockton, CA 95210 / 209-951-0706; FAX: 09-931-3872
s Custom Guns, P.O. Box 10534, White Bear Lake, MN 5110 / 651-429-5105; FAX: 651-429-7365
x Corp., 5 Tinkham Ave., Derry, NH 03038 / 03-434-0311; FAX: 603-434-3002 ales@derry.gentexcorp.com www.derry.gentexcorp.com
er Bullets, 109 Woodlawn Ave., Upper Darby, PA 19082 610-352-9396
y Custom LLC, 314 N. Hoffman, Belgrade, MT 59714 / 406-388-GUNS davidgent@mcn.net www.gentrycustom.com
ge & Roy's, P.O. Box 2125, Sisters, OR 97759-2125 / 503-228-5424; or 800-553-3022; FAX: 503-225-9409
ge Hoenig, Inc., 6521 Morton Dr., Boise, ID 83704 / 208-375-1116; FAX: 208-375-1116
ge Ibberson (Sheffield) Ltd., 25-31 Allen St., Sheffield, S3 7AW ENGLAND / 0114-2766123; FAX: 0114-2738465 sales@eggintongroupco.uk www.eggintongroup.co.uk
ge Madis Winchester Consultants, George Madis, P.O. Box 545, Brownsboro, TX 75756 / 903-852-6480; FAX: 903-852-3045 gmadis@earthlink.com www.georgemadis.com
ber Legendary Blades, 14200 SW 72nd Ave., Portland, OR 97223 / 503-639-6161; or 800-950-6161; FAX: 503-684-7008
vais, Mike, 3804 S. Cruise Dr., Salt Lake City, UT 84109 / 801-277-7729
Barrel Company, P.O. Box 88, 426 E. Market St., Beavertown, PA 17813 / 570-658-7263; FAX: 570-658-4110 www.getzbrl.com
como Sporting USA, 6234 Stokes Lee Center Rd., Lee Center, NY 13363
bs Rifle Co., Inc., 219 Lawn St., Martinsburg, WV 25401 / 304-262-1651; FAX: 304-262-1658 support@gibbsrifle.com www.gibbsrifle.com
Hebard Guns, Inc., 125 Public Square, Knoxville, IL 61448 / 309-289-2700; FAX: 309-289-2233
bert Equipment Co., Inc., 960 Downtowner Rd., Mobile, AL 36609 / 205-344-3322
mann, Edwin, 33 Valley View Dr., Hanover, PA 17331 / 717-632-1662 gillmaned@super-pa.net
more Sports Concepts, Inc., 5949 S. Garnett Rd., Tulsa, OK 74146 / 918-250-3810; FAX: 918-250-3845 info@gilmoresports.com www.gilmoresports.com
ron, Robert E., 12671 Cousins Rd.., Peosta, IA 52068 / 412-731-6041
acier Glove, 4890 Aircenter Circle, Suite 210, Reno, NV 89502 / 702-825-8225; FAX: 702-825-6544
aser LLC, P.O. Box 173, Sturgis, SD 57785 / 605-347-4544; or 800-221-3489; FAX: 605-347-5055 email@corbon.com www.safetyslug.com
aser Safety Slug, Inc., P.O. Box 8223, Foster City, CA 94404 / 800-221-3489; FAX: 510-785-6685 safetyslug.com
ass, Herb, P.O. Box 25, Bullville, NY 10915 / 914-361-3021
imm, Jerome. See: GLIMM'S CUSTOM GUN ENGRAVING
imm's Custom Gun Engraving, Jerome C. Glimm, 19 S. Maryland, Conrad, MT 59425 / 406-278-3574 jandlglimm@mcn.net
lock GmbH, P.O. Box 50, A-2232, Deutsch Wagram, AUSTRIA
lock, Inc., P.O. Box 369, Smyrna, GA 30081 / 770-432-1202; FAX: 770-433-8719
lynn Scobey Duck & Goose Calls, Rt. 3, Box 37, Newbern, TN 38059 / 731-643-6128
ML Products, Inc., 394 Laredo Dr., Birmingham, AL 35226 / 205-979-4867
ner's Hard Cast Bullets, 1107 11th St., LaGrande, OR 97850 / 503-963-8796
oens, Dale W., P.O. Box 224, Cedar Crest, NM 87008 / 505-281-5419
oergen's Gun Shop, Inc., 17985 538th Ave., Austin, MN 55912 / 507-433-9280
GOEX, Inc., P.O. Box 659, Doyline, LA 71023-0659 / 318-382-9300; FAX: 318-382-9303 mfahringer@goexpowder.com www.goexpowder.com
Golden Age Arms Co., 115 E. High St., Ashley, OH 43003 / 614-747-2488
Golden Bear Bullets, 3065 Fairfax Ave., San Jose, CA 95148 / 408-238-9515
Gonic Arms/North American Arms, Inc., 134 Flagg Rd., Gonic, NH 03839 / 603-332-8456; or 603-332-8457
Goodling's Gunsmithing, 1950 Stoverstown Rd., Spring Grove, PA 17362 / 717-225-3350
Goodwin, Fred. See: GOODWIN'S PAWN SHOP
Goodwin's Pawn Shop, Fred Goodwin, Silver Ridge, ME 04776 / 207-365-4451
Gotz Bullets, 11426 Edgemere Ter., Roscoe, IL 61073-8232
Gould & Goodrich, 709 E. McNeil, Lillington, NC 27546 / 910-893-2071; FAX: 910-893-4742
Gournet Artistic Engraving, Geoffroy Gournet, 820 Paxinosa Ave., Easton, PA 18042 / 610-559-0710 www.geoffroygournet.com
Gournet, Geoffroy. See: GOURNET ARTISTIC ENGRAVING
Grace, Charles E., 718 E. 2nd, Trinidad, CO 81082 / 719-846-9435 chuckgrace@sensonics.org
Grace Metal Products, P.O. Box 67, Elk Rapids, MI 49629 / 616-264-8133
Graf & Sons, 4050 S. Clark St., Mexico, MO 65265 / 573-581-2266; FAX: 573-581-2875 customerservice@grafs.com www.grafs.com
Grand Slam Hunting Products, Box 121, 25454 Military Rd., Cascade, MD 21719 / 301-241-4900; FAX: 301-241-4900 rlj6call@aol.com
Granite Mountain Arms, Inc., 3145 W. Hidden Acres Trail, Prescott, AZ 86305 / 520-541-9758; FAX: 520-445-6826
Grant, Howard V., Hiawatha 15, Woodruff, WI 54568 / 715-356-7146
Graphics Direct, P.O. Box 372421, Reseda, CA 91337-2421 / 818-344-9002
Graves Co., 1800 Andrews Ave., Pompano Beach, FL 33069 / 800-327-9103; FAX: 305-960-0301
Grayback Wildcats, Mike Beeks, 5306 Bryant Ave., Klamath Falls, OR 97603 / 541-884-1072; FAX: 541-884-1072 graybackwildcats@aol.com
Graybill's Gun Shop, 1035 Ironville Pike, Columbia, PA 17512 / 717-684-2739
Great American Gunstock Co., 3420 Industrial Drive, Yuba City, CA 95993 / 800-784-4867; FAX: 530-671-3906 gunstox@hotmail.com www.gunstocks.com
Great Lakes Airguns, 6175 S. Park Ave., Hamburg, NY 14075 / 716-648-6666; FAX: 716-648-6666 www.greatlakesairguns.com
Green, Arthur S., 485 S. Robertson Blvd., Beverly Hills, CA 90211 / 310-274-1283
Green, Roger M., P.O. Box 984, 435 E. Birch, Glenrock, WY 82637 / 307-436-9804
Green Head Game Call Co., RR 1, Box 33, Lacon, IL 61540 / 309-246-2155
Green Mountain Rifle Barrel Co., Inc., P.O. Box 2670, 153 West Main St., Conway, NH 03818 / 603-447-1095; FAX: 603-447-1099 www.gmriflebarrel.com
Greenwood Precision, P.O. Box 407, Rogersville, MO 65742 / 417-725-2330
Greg Gunsmithing Repair, 3732 26th Ave. North, Robbinsdale, MN 55422 / 612-529-8103
Greg's Superior Products, P.O. Box 46219, Seattle, WA 98146
Greider Precision, 431 Santa Marina Ct., Escondido, CA 92029 / 760-480-8892; FAX: 760-480-9800 greider@msn.com
Gre-Tan Rifles, 29742 W.C.R. 50, Kersey, CO 80644 / 970-353-6176; FAX: 970-356-5940 www.gtrtooling.com
Grier's Hard Cast Bullets, 1107 11th St., LaGrande, OR 97850 / 503-963-8796
Griffin & Howe, Inc., 36 W. 44th St., Suite 1011, New York, NY 10036 / 212-921-0980 info@griffinhowe.com www.griffinhowe.com
Griffin & Howe, Inc., 340 W. Putnam Ave., Greenwich, CT 06830 / 203-618-0270 info@griffinhowe.com www.griffinhowe.com
Griffin & Howe, Inc., 33 Claremont Rd., Bernardsville, NJ 07924 / 908-766-2287; FAX: 908-766-1068 info@griffinhowe.com www.griffinhowe.com
Grifon, Inc., 58 Guinam St., Waltham, MS 02154
Groenewold, John, P.O. Box 830, Mundelein, IL 60060 / 847-566-2365; FAX: 847-566-4065 jgairguns@direcway.com http://jgairguns.tripod.com/airgun
GRS / Glendo Corp., P.O. Box 1153, 900 Overlander St., Emporia, KS 66801 / 620-343-1084; or 800-836-3519; FAX: 620-343-9640 glendo@glendo.com www.glendo.com
Grulla Armes, Apartado 453, Avda Otaloa 12, Eiber, SPAIN
Gruning Precision, Inc., 7101 Jurupa Ave., No. 12, Riverside, CA 92504 / 909-289-4371; FAX: 909-689-7791 gruningprecision@earthlink.net www.gruningprecision.com
GSI, Inc., 7661 Commerce Ln., Trussville, AL 35173 / 205-655-8299
GTB-Custom Bullets, 482 Comerwood Court, S. San Francisco, CA 94080 / 650-583-1550
Guarasi, Robert. See: WILCOX INDUSTRIES CORP.
Guardsman Products, 411 N. Darling, Fremont, MI 49412 / 616-924-3950
Gun City, 212 W. Main Ave., Bismarck, ND 58501 / 701-223-2304
Gun Hunter Books (See Gun Hunter Trading Co.), 5075 Heisig St., Beaumont, TX 77705 / 409-835-3006; FAX: 409-838-2266 gunhuntertrading@hotmail.com
Gun Hunter Trading Co., 5075 Heisig St., Beaumont, TX 77705 / 409-835-3006; FAX: 409-838-2266 gunhuntertrading@hotmail.com
Gun Leather Limited, 116 Lipscomb, Ft. Worth, TX 76104 / 817-334-0225; FAX: 800-247-0609
Gun List (See Krause Publications), 700 E State St., Iola, WI 54990 / 715-445-2214; FAX: 715-445-4087
Gun South, Inc. (See GSI, Inc.)
Gun Vault, 7339 E. Acoma Dr., Ste. 7, Scottsdale, AZ 85260 / 602-951-6855
Gun-Alert, 1010 N. Maclay Ave., San Fernando, CA 91340 / 818-365-0864; FAX: 818-365-1308
Guncraft Books (See Guncraft Sports, Inc.), 10737 Dutchtown Rd., Knoxville, TN 37932 / 865-966-4545; FAX: 865-966-4500 findit@guncraft.com www.guncraft.com
Guncraft Sports, Inc., 10737 Dutchtown Rd., Knoxville, TN 37932 / 865-966-4545; FAX: 865-966-4500 findit@guncraft.com www.usit.net/guncraft
Guncraft Sports, Inc., Marie C. Wiest, 10737 Dutchtown Rd., Knoxville, TN 37932 / 865-966-4545; FAX: 865-966-4500 findit@guncraft.com www.guncraft.com
Guncrafter Industries, 171 Madison 1510, Huntsville, AR 72740 / 479-665-2466 www.guncrafterindustries.com
Gun-Ho Sports Cases, 110 E. 10th St., St. Paul, MN 55101 / 612-224-9491
Gunline Tools, 2950 Saturn St., "O", Brea, CA 92821 / 714-993-5100; FAX: 714-572-4128
Gunnerman Books, P.O. Box 81697, Rochester Hills, MI 48308 / 248-608-2856
Guns Antique & Modern DBA / Charles E. Duffy, Williams Lane, West Hurley, NY 12491 / 914-679-2997
Guns Div. of D.C. Engineering, Inc., 8633 Southfield Fwy., Detroit, MI 48228 / 313-271-7111; or 800-886-7623; FAX: 313-271-7112 guns@rifletech.com www.rifletech.com
GUNS Magazine, 591 Camino de la Reina, Suite 200, San Diego, CA 92108 / 619-297-5350; FAX: 619-297-5353
Gunsite Training Center, P.O. Box 700, Paulden, AZ 86334 / 520-636-4565; FAX: 520-636-1236
Gunsmithing Ltd., 57 Unquowa Rd., Fairfield, CT 06824 / 203-254-0436; FAX: 203-254-1535
Gunsmithing, Inc., 30 West Buchanan St., Colorado Springs, CO 80907 / 719-632-3795; FAX: 719-632-3493
Gurney, F. R., Box 13, Sooke, BC V0S 1N0 CANADA / 604-642-5282; FAX: 604-642-7859

H

H&B Forge Co., Rt. 2, Geisinger Rd., Shiloh, OH 44878 / 419-895-1856
H&P Publishing, 7174 Hoffman Rd., San Angelo, TX 76905 / 915-655-5953
H&R 1871.LLC, 60 Industrial Rowe, Gardner, MA 01440 / 508-632-9393; FAX: 508-632-2300 hr1871@hr1871.com www.hr1871.com
H. Krieghoff Gun Co., Boschstrasse 22, D-89079, Ulm, GERMANY / 731-401820; FAX: 731-4018270
H.K.S. Products, 7841 Founion Dr., Florence, KY 41042 / 606-342-7841; or 800-354-9814; FAX: 606-342-5865
H.P. White Laboratory, Inc., 3114 Scarboro Rd., Street, MD 21154 / 410-838-6550; FAX: 410-838-2802
Hafner World Wide, Inc., P.O. Box 1987, Lake City, FL 32055 / 904-755-6481; FAX: 904-755-6595 hafner@isgroupe.net
Hakko Co. Ltd., 1-13-12, Narimasu, Itabashiku Tokyo, JAPAN / 03-5997-7870/2; FAX: 81-3-5997-7840
Half Moon Rifle Shop, 490 Halfmoon Rd., Columbia Falls, MT 59912 / 406-892-4409 halfmoonrs@centurytel.net
Hall Manufacturing, 142 CR 406, Clanton, AL 35045 / 205-755-4094
Hall Plastics, Inc., John, P.O. Box 1526, Alvin, TX 77512 / 713-489-8709
Hallberg, Fritz. See: CAMBOS OUTDOORSMAN

MANUFACTURER'S DIRECTORY

Hallowell & Co., P.O. Box 1445, Livingston, MT 59047 / 406-222-4770; FAX: 406-222-4792 morris@hallowellco.com www.hallowellco.com
Hally Caller, 443 Wells Rd., Doylestown, PA 18901 / 215-345-6354; FAX: 215-345-8892 info@hallycaller.com www.hallycaller.com
Hamilton, Alex B. (See Ten-Ring Precision, Inc.)
Hammans, Charles E., P.O. Box 788, 2022 McCracken, Stuttgart, AR 72160-0788 / 870-673-1388
Hammerli Ltd., Seonerstrasse 37, CH-5600, SWITZERLAND / 064-50 11 44; FAX: 064-51 38 27
Hammerli Service-Precision Mac, Rudolf Marent, 9711 Tiltree St., Houston, TX 77075 / 713-946-7028 rmarent@webtv.net
Hammerli USA, 19296 Oak Grove Circle, Groveland, CA 95321 FAX: 209-962-5311
Hammond Custom Guns Ltd., 619 S. Pandora, Gilbert, AZ 85234 / 602-892-3437
HandCrafts Unltd. (See Clements' Custom Leather), 1741 Dallas St., Aurora, CO 80010-2018 / 303-364-0403; FAX: 303-739-9824 gryphons@home.com kuntaoslcat.com
Handgun Press, P.O. Box 406, Glenview, IL 60025 / 847-657-6500; FAX: 847-724-8831 handgunpress@earthlink.net
Hank's Gun Shop, Box 370, 50 West 100 South, Monroe, UT 84754 / 801-527-4456
Hanned Precision (See The Hanned Line)
Hansen & Co., 244-246 Old Post Rd., Southport, CT 06490 / 203-259-6222; FAX: 203-254-3832
Hanson's Gun Center, Dick, 233 Everett Dr., Colorado Springs, CO 80911
Harford (See U.S. Importer-EMF Co. Inc.)
Harper's Custom Stocks, 928 Lombrano St., San Antonio, TX 78207 / 210-732-7174
Harrell's Precision, 5756 Hickory Dr., Salem, VA 24153 / 540-380-2683
Harrington & Richardson (See H&R 1871, Inc.)
Harris Engineering Inc., Dept GD54, Barlow, KY 42024 / 502-334-3633; FAX: 502-334-3000
Harris Enterprises, P.O. Box 105, Bly, OR 97622 / 503-353-2625
Harris Hand Engraving, Paul A., 113 Rusty Ln., Boerne, TX 78006-5746 / 512-391-5121
Harris Publications, 1115 Broadway, New York, NY 10010 / 212-807-7100; FAX: 212-627-4678
Harrison Bullets, 6437 E. Hobart St., Mesa, AZ 85205
Harry Lawson Co., 3328 N. Richey Blvd., Tucson, AZ 85716 / 520-326-1117; FAX: 520-326-1117
Hart & Son, Inc., Robert W., 401 Montgomery St., Nescopeck, PA 18635 / 717-752-3655; FAX: 717-752-1088
Hart Rifle Barrels, Inc., P.O. Box 182, 1690 Apulia Rd., Lafayette, NY 13084 / 315-677-9841; FAX: 315-677-9610 hartrb@aol.com hartbarrels.com
Hartford (See U.S. Importer-EMF Co. Inc.)
Hartmann & Weiss GmbH, Rahlstedter Bahnhofstr. 47, 22143, Hamburg, GERMANY / (40) 677 55 85; FAX: (40) 677 55 92 hartmannundweisst-online.de
Harvey, Frank, 218 Nightfall, Terrace, NV 89015 / 702-558-6998
Harwood, Jack O., 1191 S. Pendlebury Lane, Blackfoot, ID 83221 / 208-785-5368
Hastings, P.O. Box 224, Clay Center, KS 67432 / 785-632-3169; FAX: 785-632-6554
Hatfield Gun, 224 N. 4th St., St. Joseph, MO 64501
Hawk Laboratories, Inc. (See Hawk, Inc.), 849 Hawks Bridge Rd., Salem, NJ 08079 / 609-299-2700; FAX: 609-299-2800
Hawk, Inc., 849 Hawks Bridge Rd., Salem, NJ 08079 / 609-299-2700; FAX: 609-299-2800 info@hawkbullets.com www.hawkbullets.com
Hawken Shop, The (See Dayton Traister)
Haydel's Game Calls, Inc., 5018 Hazel Jones Rd., Bossier City, LA 71111 / 318-746-3586; FAX: 318-746-3711
Heatbath Corp., P.O. Box 2978, Springfield, MA 01101 / 413-543-3381
Hecht, Hubert J., Waffen-Hecht, P.O. Box 2635, Fair Oaks, CA 95628 / 916-966-1020
Heckler & Koch GmbH, PO Box 1329, 78722 Oberndorf, Neckar, GERMANY / 49-7423179-0; FAX: 49-7423179-2406
Heckler & Koch, Inc., 21480 Pacific Blvd., Sterling, VA 20166-8900 / 703-450-1900; FAX: 703-450-8160 www.hecklerkoch-usa.com
Hege Jagd-u. Sporthandels GmbH, P.O. Box 101461, W-7770, Ueberlingen a. Boden, GERMANY
Heidenstrom Bullets, Dalghte 86-3660 Rjukan, 35091818, NORWAY, olau.joh@online.tuo
Heilmann, Stephen, P.O. Box 657, Grass Valley, CA 95945 / 530-272-8758; FAX: 530-274-0285 sheilmann@jps.net www.metalwood.com
Heinie Specialty Products, 301 Oak St., Quincy, IL 62301-2500 / 217-228-9500; FAX: 217-228-9502 rheinie@heinie.com www.heinie.com
Helwan (See U.S. Importer-Interarms)
Henigson & Associates, Steve, PO Box 2726, Culver City, CA 90231 / 310-305-8288; FAX: 310-305-1905
Henriksen Tool Co., Inc., 8515 Wagner Creek Rd., Talent, OR 97540 / 541-535-2309; FAX: 541-535-2309
Henry Repeating Arms Co., 110 8th St., Brooklyn, NY 11215 / 718-499-5600; FAX: 718-768-8056 info@henryrepeating.com www.henryrepeating.com
Hensley, Gunmaker, Darwin, PO Box 329, Brightwood, OR 97011 / 503-622-5411
Heppler, Keith. See: KEITH'S CUSTOM GUNSTOCKS
Hercules, Inc. (See Alliant Techsystems, Smokeless)
Heritage Firearms (See Heritage Mfg., Inc.)
Heritage Manufacturing, Inc., 4600 NW 135th St., Opa Locka, FL 33054 / 305-685-5966; FAX: 305-687-6721 infohmi@heritagemfg.com www.heritagemfg.com
Heritage/VSP Gun Books, P.O. Box 887, McCall, ID 83638 / 208-634-4104; FAX: 208-634-3101 heritage@gunbooks.com www.gunbooks.com
Herrett's Stocks, Inc., P.O. Box 741, Twin Falls, ID 83303 / 208-733-1498
Herter's Manufacturing Inc., 111 E. Burnett St., P.O. Box 518, Beaver Dam, WI 53916-1811 / 414-887-1765; FAX: 414-887-8444
Hesco-Meprolight, 2139 Greenville Rd., LaGrange, GA 30241 / 706-884-7967; FAX: 706-882-4683
Hesse Arms, Robert Hesse, 1126 70th Street E., Inver Grove Heights, MN 55077-2416 / 651-455-5760; FAX: 612-455-5760
Hesse, Robert. See: HESSE ARMS
Heydenberk, Warren R., 1059 W. Sawmill Rd., Quakertown, PA 18951 / 215-538-2682
Hickman, Jaclyn, Box 1900, Glenrock, WY 82637
Hidalgo, Tony, 12701 SW 9th Pl., Davie, FL 33325 / 954-476-7645
High Bridge Arms, Inc., 3185 Mission St., San Francisco, CA 94110 / 415-282-8358
High North Products, Inc., P.O. Box 2, Antigo, WI 54409 / 715-627-2331; FAX: 715-623-5451
High Performance International, 5734 W. Florist Ave., Milwaukee, WI 53218 / 414-466-9040
High Precision, Bud Welsh, 80 New Road, E. Amherst, NY 14051 / 716-688-6344; FAX: 716-688-0425 welsh5168@aol.com www.high-precision.com
High Standard Mfg. Co./F.I., Inc., 5200 Mitchelldale St., Ste. E17, Houston, TX 77092-7222 / 713-462-4200; or 800-272-7816; FAX: 713-681-5665 info@highstandard.com www.highstandard.com
High Tech Specialties, Inc., P.O. Box 839, 293 E Main St., Rear, Adamstown, PA 19501 / 717-484-0405; FAX: 717-484-0523 bansner@aol.com www.bansmersrifle.com/hightech
Highline Machine Co., Randall Thompson, Randall Thompson, 654 Lela Place, Grand Junction, CO 81504 / 970-434-4971
Highwood Special Products, 1531 E. Highwood, Pontiac, MI 48340
Hi-Grade Imports, 8655 Monterey Rd., Gilroy, CA 95021 / 408-842-9301; FAX: 408-842-2374
Hill, Loring F., 304 Cedar Rd., Elkins Park, PA 19027
Hill Speed Leather, Ernie, 4507 N 195th Ave., Litchfield Park, AZ 85340 / 602-853-9222; FAX: 602-853-9235
Hinman Outfitters, Bob, 107 N Sanderson Ave., Bartonville, IL 61607-1839 / 309-691-8132
Hi-Performance Ammunition Company, 484 State Route 366, Apollo, PA 15613 / 412-327-8100
HIP-GRIP Barami Corp., P.O. Box 252224, West Bloomfield, MI 48325-2224 / 248-738-0462; FAX: 248-738-2542 hipgripja@aol.com www.hipgrip.com
Hi-Point Firearms/MKS Supply, 8611-A North Dixie Dr., Dayton, OH 45414 / 877-425-4867; FAX: 937-454-0503 www.hi-pointfirearms.com
Hiptmayer, Armurier, RR 112 750, P.O. Box 136, Eastman, PQ J0E 1P0 CANADA / 514-297-2492
Hiptmayer, Heidemarie, RR 112 750, P.O. Box 136, Eastman, PQ J0E 1P0 CANADA / 514-297-2492
Hiptmayer, Klaus, RR 112 750, P.O. Box 136, Eastman, PQ J0E 1P0 CANADA / 514-297-2492
Hirtenberger AG, Leobersdorferstrasse 31, A-2552, Hirtenberg, AUSTRIA / 43(0)2256 81184; FAX: 43(0)2256 81808 www.hirtenberger.ot
HJS Arms, Inc., P.O. Box 3711, Brownsville, TX 78523-3711 / 956-542-2767; FAX: 956-542-2767
Hoag, James W., 8523 Canoga Ave., Suite C, Canoga P... CA 91304 / 818-998-1510
Hobson Precision Mfg. Co., 210 Big Oak Ln., Brent, AL 3... / 205-926-4662; FAX: 205-926-3193 cahobbob@dbtech.net
Hodgdon Powder Co., 6231 Robinson, Shawnee Missio... 66202 / 913-362-9455; FAX: 913-362-1307
Hodgman, Inc., 1750 Orchard Rd., Montgomery, IL 605... 708-897-7555; FAX: 708-897-7558
Hodgson, Richard, 9081 Tahoe Lane, Boulder, CO 8030...
Hoehn Sales, Inc., 2045 Kohn Road, Wright City, MO 63... / 636-745-8144; FAX: 636-745-7868 hoehnsal@usmo.com
Hofer Jagdwaffen, P., Buchsenmachermeister, Kirchgas... 24, A-9170 Ferlach, AUSTRIA / 43 4227 3683; FAX:... 4227 368330 peterhofer@hoferwaffen.com www.hoferwaffen.com
Hoffman New Ideas, 821 Northmoor Rd., Lake Forest, IL 60045 / 312-234-4075
Hogue Grips, P.O. Box 1138, Paso Robles, CA 93447 / 800-438-4747 or 805-239-1440; FAX: 805-239-255...
Holland & Holland Ltd., 33 Bruton St., London, ENGLAN... 44-171-499-4411; FAX: 44-171-408-7962
Holland's Gunsmithing, P.O. Box 69, Powers, OR 97466 541-439-5155; FAX: 541-439-5155
Hollinger, Jon. See: ASPEN OUTFITTING CO.
Hollywood Engineering, 10642 Arminta St., Sun Valley, C... 91352 / 818-842-8376; FAX: 818-504-4168 cadqueenel1@aol.com
Homak, 5151 W. 73rd St., Chicago, IL 60638-6613 / 312-523-3100; FAX: 312-523-9455
Home Shop Machinist, The Village Press Publications, P.... Box 1810, Traverse City, MI 49685 / 800-447-7367; F... 616-946-3289
Hondo Ind., 510 S. 52nd St., I04, Tempe, AZ 85281
Hoppe's Div. Penguin Industries, Inc., P.O. Box 1690, Oreg... City, OR 97045-0690 / 610-384-6000
Horizons Unlimited, P.O. Box 426, Warm Springs, GA 318... / 706-655-3603; FAX: 706-655-3603
Hornady Mfg. Co., P.O. Box 1848, Grand Island, NE 6880... 800-338-3220 or 308-382-1390; FAX: 308-382-5761
Horseshoe Leather Products, Andy Arratoonian, The Cotta... Sharow, Ripon U.K., ENGLAND U.K. / 44-1765-6058... andy@horseshoe.co.uk www.holsters.org
House of Muskets, Inc., The, PO Box 4640, Pagosa Spring... CO 81157 / 970-731-2295
Houtz & Barwick, P.O. Box 435, W. Church St., Elizabeth Ci... NC 27909 / 800-775-0337; or 919-335-4191; FAX: 919-335-1152
Howa Machinery, Ltd., Sukaguchi, Shinkawa-cho Nishikasugai-gun, Aichi 452-8601, JAPAN / 81-52-408-1231; FAX: 81-52-401-4999 howa@howa.co.jp http://www.howa.cojpl
Howell Machine, 815 1/2 D St., Lewiston, ID 83501 / 208-743-7418
H-S Precision, Inc., 1301 Turbine Dr., Rapid City, SD 5770... / 605-341-3006; FAX: 605-342-8964
HT Bullets, 244 Belleville Rd., New Bedford, MA 02745 / 508-999-3338
Hubert J. Hecht Waffen-Hecht, P.O. Box 2635, Fair Oaks, C... 95628 / 916-966-1020
Huebner, Corey O., P.O. Box 564, Frenchtown, MT 59834 / 406-721-7168 bugsboys@hotmail.com
Huey Gun Cases, 820 Indiana St., Lawrence, KS 66044-2645 / 816-444-1637; FAX: 816-444-1637 hueycases@aol.com www.hueycases.com
Hume, Don, P.O. Box 351, Miami, OK 74355 / 800-331-2686 FAX: 918-542-4340 info@donhume.com www.donhume.com
Hunkeler, A. (See Buckskin Machine Works), 3235 S 358th St., Auburn, WA 98001 / 206-927-5412
Hunter Co., Inc., 3300 W. 71st Ave., Westminster, CO 80030 / 303-427-4626; FAX: 303-428-3980 debbiet@huntercompany.com www.huntercompany.com
Hunterjohn, PO Box 771457, St. Louis, MO 63177 / 314-531-7250 www.hunterjohn.com
Hunter's Specialties Inc., 6000 Huntington Ct. NE, Cedar Rapids, IA 52402-1268 / 319-395-0321; FAX: 319-395-0326
Hunters Supply, Inc., P.O. Box 313, Tioga, TX 76271 / 940-437-2458; FAX: 940-437-2228 hunterssupply@hotmail.com www.hunterssupply.net
Huntington Die Specialties, 601 Oro Dam Blvd., Oroville, CA 95965 / 530-534-1210; FAX: 530-534-1212 buy@huntingtons.com www.huntingtons.com
Hutton Rifle Ranch, P.O. Box 170317, Boise, ID 83717 / 208-345-8781 www.martinbrevik@aol.com

MANUFACTURER'S DIRECTORY

)sorbent Products, PO Box 437, Ashley Falls, MA 01222 800-448-7903; FAX: 413-229-8743 rders@dehumidify.com www.dehumidify.com

I

. (See U.S. Importer-Taylor's & Co. Inc.)
.A. Books, 1324 Stratford Drive, Piqua, OH 45356 / 937-773-4203; FAX: 937-778-1922
. Inc. (See Kickeez I.N.C., Inc.)
., P.O. Box 185234, Ft. Worth, TX 76181 / 817-595-2090; FAX: 817-595-2090 iss@concentric.net
V., 106 E. Cairo Dr., Tempe, AZ 85282
Inc., 33171 Camino Capistrano, San Juan Capistrano, CA 92675 / 949-443-3642; FAX: 949-443-3647 sales@iar-arms.com iar-arms.com
Ken. See: STURGEON VALLEY SPORTERS
(See U.S. Importer-Stoeger Industries)
ge Ind. Inc., 382 Balm Court, Wood Dale, IL 60191 / 630-766-2402; FAX: 630-766-7373
act Case & Container, Inc., P.O. Box 1129, Rathdrum, ID 83858 / 877-687-2452; FAX: 208-687-0632 bradk@icc-case.com www.icc-case.com
erial (See E-Z-Way Systems), P.O. Box 4310, Newark, OH 43058-4310 / 614-345-6645; FAX: 614-345-6600 ezway@infinet.com www.jcunald.com
erial Magnum Corp., P.O. Box 249, Oroville, WA 98844 / 604-495-3131; FAX: 604-495-2816
erial Miniature Armory, 10547 S. Post Oak Road, Houston, TX 77035-3305 / 713-729-8428; FAX: 713-729-2274 miniguns@aol.com www.1800miniature.com
oerial Schrade Corp., 7 Schrade Ct., Box 7000, Ellenville, NY 12428 / 914-647-7601; FAX: 914-647-8701 csc@schradeknives.com www.schradeknives.com
oort Sports Inc., 1750 Brielle Ave., Unit B1, Wanamassa, NJ 07712 / 732-493-0302; FAX: 732-493-0301 gsodini@aol.com www.bersa-11ama.com
R Powder Co., 1080 Military Turnpike, Suite 2, Plattsburgh, NY 12901 / 518-563-2253; FAX: 518-563-6916
o-Arm, P.O. Box 1262, Champlain, NY 12919 / 514-955-0355; FAX: 514-955-0357 infoarm@qc.aira.com
gle, Ralph W., Engraver, 112 Manchester Ct., Centerville, GA 31028 / 478-953-5824 riengraver@aol.com www.fega.com
novative Weaponry Inc., 2513 E. Loop 820 N., Fort Worth, TX 76118 / 817-284-0099 or 800-334-3573
TEC International, Inc., P.O. Box 5708, Scottsdale, AZ 85261 / 602-483-1708
ter Ordnance of America LP, 3305 Westwood Industrial Dr., Monroe, NC 28110-5204 / 704-821-8337; FAX: 704-821-8523
tercontinental Distributors, Ltd., PO Box 815, Beulah, ND 58523
trac Arms International, 5005 Chapman Hwy., Knoxville, TN 37920
on Industries, Inc., 3508 E Allerton Ave., Cudahy, WI 53110 / 414-486-2007; FAX: 414-486-2017
osso Products, 1485 Lively Blvd., Elk Grove Village, IL 60007 / 847-437-8400; FAX: 847-437-8478
ron Bench, 12619 Bailey Rd., Redding, CA 96003 / 916-241-4623
ronside International Publishers, Inc., P.O. Box 1050, Lorton, VA 22199
ronsighter Co., P.O. Box 85070, Westland, MI 48185 / 734-326-8731; FAX: 734-326-3378 www.ironsighter.com
rwin, Campbell H., 140 Hartland Blvd., East Hartland, CT 06027 / 203-653-3901
sland Pond Gun Shop, Cross St., Island Pond, VT 05846 / 802-723-4546
srael Arms Inc., 5625 Star Ln. #B, Houston, TX 77057 / 713-789-0745; FAX: 713-914-9515 www.israelarms.com
Ithaca Classic Doubles, Stephen Lamboy, No. 5 Railroad St., Victor, NY 14564 / 716-924-2710; FAX: 716-924-2737 ithacadoubles.com
Ithaca Gun Company LLC, 901 Rt. 34 B, King Ferry, NY 13081 / 315-364-7171; FAX: 315-364-5134 info@ithacagun.com
Ivanoff, Thomas G. (See Tom's Gun Repair)

J

J J Roberts Firearm Engraver, 7808 Lake Dr, Manassas, VA 20111 / 703-330-0448; FAX: 703-264-8600 james..roberts@angelfire.com www.angelfire.com/va2/engraver
J&D Components, 75 East 350 North, Orem, UT 84057-4719 / 801-225-7007 www.jdcomponents.com
J&J Products, Inc., 9240 Whitmore, El Monte, CA 91731 / 818-571-5228; FAX: 800-927-8361
J&J Sales, 1501 21st Ave. S., Great Falls, MT 59405 / 406-727-9789 mtshootingbench@yahoo.com www.j&jsales.us
J&L Superior Bullets (See Huntington Die Special)
J&R Engineering, P.O. Box 77, 200 Lyons Hill Rd., Athol, MA 01331 / 508-249-9241
J&R Enterprises, 4550 Scotts Valley Rd., Lakeport, CA 95453
J&S Heat Treat, 803 S. 16th St., Blue Springs, MO 64015 / 816-229-2149; FAX: 816-228-1135
J. Dewey Mfg. Co., Inc., P.O. Box 2014, Southbury, CT 06488 / 203-264-3064; FAX: 203-262-6907 deweyrods@worldnet.att.net www.deweyrods.com
J. Korzinek Riflesmith, RD 2, Box 73D, Canton, PA 17724 / 717-673-8512
J.A. Blades, Inc. (See Christopher Firearms Co.)
J.A. Henckels Zwillingswerk Inc., 9 Skyline Dr., Hawthorne, NY 10532 / 914-592-7370
J.G. Anschutz GmbH & Co. KG, Daimlerstr. 12, D-89079 Ulm, Ulm, GERMANY / 49 731 40120; FAX: 49 731 4012700 JGA-info@anschuetz-sport.com www.anschuetz-sport.com
J.G. Dapkus Co., Inc., Commerce Circle, P.O. Box 293, Durham, CT 06422 www.explodingtargets.com
J.I.T. Ltd., P.O. Box 230, Freedom, WY 83120 / 708-494-0937
J.J. Roberts / Engraver, 7808 Lake Dr., Manassas, VA 20111 / 703-330-0448 jjrengraver@aol.com www.angelfire.com/va2/engraver
J.P. Enterprises Inc., P.O. Box 378, Hugo, MN 55110 / 612-486-9064; FAX: 612-482-0970
J.R. Williams Bullet Co., 2008 Tucker Rd., Perry, GA 31069 / 912-987-0274
J.W. Morrison Custom Rifles, 4015 W. Sharon, Phoenix, AZ 85029 / 602-978-3754
J/B Adventures & Safaris Inc., 2275 E. Arapahoe Rd., Ste. 109, Littleton, CO 80122-1521 / 303-771-0977
Jack A. Rosenberg & Sons, 12229 Cox Ln., Dallas, TX 75234 / 214-241-6302
Jack Dever Co., 8520 NW 90th St., Oklahoma City, OK 73132 / 405-721-6393 jbdever1@home.com
Jack First, Inc., 1201 Turbine Dr., Rapid City, SD 57703 / 605-343-8481; FAX: 605-343-9420
Jack Jonas Appraisals & Taki, 13952 E. Marina Dr., #604, Aurora, CO 80014
Jackalope Gun Shop, 1048 S. 5th St., Douglas, WY 82633 / 307-358-3441
Jaffin, Harry. See: BRIDGEMAN PRODUCTS
Jagdwaffen, Peter. See: BUCHSENMACHERMEISTER
James Churchill Glove Co., PO Box 298, Centralia, WA 98531 / 360-736-2816; FAX: 360-330-0151 churchillglove@localaccess.com
James Wayne Firearms for Collectors and Investors, 2608 N. Laurent, Victoria, TX 77901 / 361-578-1258; FAX: 361-578-3559
Jamison International, Marc Jamison, 3551 Mayer Ave., Sturgis, SD 57785 / 605-347-5090; FAX: 605-347-4704 jbell2@masttechnology.com
Jamison, Marc. See: JAMISON INTERNATIONAL
Jamison's Forge Works, 4527 Rd. 6.5 NE, Moses Lake, WA 98837 / 509-762-2659
Jantz Supply, 309 West Main Dept HD, Davis, OK 73030-0584 / 580-369-2316; FAX: 580-369-3082 jantz@brightok.net www.knifemaking.com
Jarrett Rifles, Inc., 383 Brown Rd., Jackson, SC 29831 / 803-471-3616 www.jarrettrifles.com
Jarvis, Inc., 1123 Cherry Orchard Lane, Hamilton, MT 59840 / 406-961-4392
Javelina Lube Products, P.O. Box 337, San Bernardino, CA 92402 / 909-350-9556; FAX: 909-429-1211
Jay McCament Custom Gunmaker, Jay McCament, 1730-134th St. Ct. S., Tacoma, WA 98444 / 253-531-8832
JB Custom, P.O. Box 6912, Leawood, KS 66206 / 913-381-2329
Jeff Flannery Engraving, 11034 Riddles Run Rd., Union, KY 41091 / 859-384-3127; FAX: 859-384-2222 engraving@fuse.net http://home.fuse.net/engraving/
Jeffredo Gunsight, P.O. Box 669, San Marcos, CA 92079 / 760-728-2695
Jena Eur, PO Box 319, Dunmore, PA 18512
Jenco Sales, Inc., P.O. Box 1000, Manchaca, TX 78652 / 800-531-5301; FAX: 800-266-2373 jencosales@sbcglobal.net
Jenkins Recoil Pads, 5438 E. Frontage Ln., Olney, IL 62450 / 618-395-3416
Jensen Bullets, RR 1 Box 187, Arco, ID 83213 / 208-785-5590
Jensen's Custom Ammunition, 5146 E. Pima, Tucson, AZ 85712 / 602-325-3346; FAX: 602-322-5704
Jensen's Firearms Academy, 1280 W. Prince, Tucson, AZ 85705 / 602-293-8516
Jericho Tool & Die Co., Inc., 2917 St. Hwy. 7, Bainbridge, NY 13733 / 607-563-8222; FAX: 607-563-8560 jerichotool.com www.jerichotool.com
Jerry Phillips Optics, P.O. Box L632, Langhorne, PA 19047 / 215-757-5037; FAX: 215-757-7097.
Jesse W. Smith Saddlery, 0499 County Road J, Pritchett, CO 81064 / 509-325-0622
Jester Bullets, Rt. 1 Box 27, Orienta, OK 73737
Jewell Triggers, Inc., 3620 Hwy. 123, San Marcos, TX 78666 / 512-353-2999; FAX: 512-392-0543
JGS Precision Tool Mfg., LLC, 60819 Selander Rd., Coos Bay, OR 97420 / 541-267-4331; FAX: 541-267-5996 jgstools@harborside.com www.jgstools.com
Jim Blair Engraving, P.O. Box 64, Glenrock, WY 82637 / 307-436-8115 jblairengrav@msn.com
Jim Noble Co., 1305 Columbia St., Vancouver, WA 98660 / 360-695-1309; FAX: 360-695-6835 jnobleco@aol.com
Jim Norman Custom Gunstocks, 14281 Cane Rd., Valley Center, CA 92082 / 619-749-6252
Jim's Precision, Jim Ketchum, 1725 Moclips Dr., Petaluma, CA 94952 / 707-762-3014
JLK Bullets, 414 Turner Rd., Dover, AR 72837 / 501-331-4194
Johanssons Vapentillbehor, Bert, S-430 20, Veddige, SWEDEN
John Hall Plastics, Inc., P.O. Box 1526, Alvin, TX 77512 / 713-489-8709
John J. Adams & Son Engravers, 7040 VT Rt 113, Vershire, VT 05079 / 802-685-0019
John Masen Co. Inc., 1305 Jelmak, Grand Prairie, TX 75050 / 817-430-8732; FAX: 817-430-1715
John Partridge Sales Ltd., Trent Meadows Rugeley, Staffordshire, WS15 2HS ENGLAND
John Rigby & Co., 500 Linne Rd. Ste. D, Paso Robles, CA 93446 / 805-227-4236; FAX: 805-227-4723 jribgy@calinet www.johnrigbyandco.com
John's Custom Leather, 523 S. Liberty St., Blairsville, PA 15717 / 724-459-6802; FAX: 724-459-5996
Johnson Wood Products, 34897 Crystal Road, Strawberry Point, IA 52076 / 563-933-6504 johnsonwoodproducts@yahoo.com
Johnston Bros. (See C&T Corp. TA Johnson Brothers)
Jonad Corp., 2091 Lakeland Ave., Lakewood, OH 44107 / 216-226-3161
Jonathan Arthur Ciener, Inc., 8700 Commerce St., Cape Canaveral, FL 32920 / 321-868-2200; FAX: 321-868-2201 www.22lrconversions.com
Jones Co., Dale, 680 Hoffman Draw, Kila, MT 59920 / 406-755-4684
Jones Custom Products, Neil A., 17217 Brookhouser Rd., Saegertown, PA 16433 / 814-763-2769; FAX: 814-763-4228
Jones, J. See: SSK INDUSTRIES
Jones Moulds, Paul, 4901 Telegraph Rd., Los Angeles, CA 90022 / 213-262-1510
JP Sales, Box 307, Anderson, TX 77830
JRP Custom Bullets, RR2 2233 Carlton Rd., Whitehall, NY 12887 / 518-282-0084 or 802-438-5548
JSL Ltd. (See U.S. Importer-Specialty Shooters)
Juenke, Vern, 25 Bitterbush Rd., Reno, NV 89523 / 702-345-0225
Jungkind, Reeves C., 509 E. Granite St., Llano, TX 78643-3055 / 325-247-1151
Jurras, L. See: L. E. JURRAS & ASSOC.
Justin Phillippi Custom Bullets, P.O. Box 773, Ligonier, PA 15658 / 412-238-9671

K

K&M Industries, Inc., Box 66, 510 S. Main, Troy, ID 83871 / 208-835-2281; FAX: 208-835-5211
K&M Services, 5430 Salmon Run Rd., Dover, PA 17315 / 717-292-3175; FAX: 717-292-3175
K. Eversull Co., Inc., 1 Tracemont, Boyce, LA 71409 / 318-793-8728; FAX: 318-793-5483 bestguns@aol.com

K.B.I. Inc., P.O. Box 6625, Harrisburg, PA 17112 / 717-540-8518; FAX: 717-540-8567
K.L. Null Holsters Ltd., 161 School St. NW, Hill City Station, Resaca, GA 30735 / 706-625-5643; FAX: 706-625-9392 ken@klnullholsters.com www.klnullholsters.com
Ka Pu Kapili, P.O. Box 745, Honokaa, HI 96727 / 808-776-1644; FAX: 808-776-1731
KA-BAR Knives, 200 Homer St., Olean, NY 14760 / 800-282-0130; FAX: 716-790-7188 info@ka-bar.com www.ka-bar.com
Kahles A. Swarovski Company, 2 Slater Rd., Cranston, RI 02920 / 401-946-2220; FAX: 401-946-2587
Kahr Arms, PO Box 220, 630 Route 303, Blauvelt, NY 10913 / 845-353-7770; FAX: 845-353-7833 www.kahr.com
Kailua Custom Guns Inc., 51 N. Dean Street, Coquille, OR 97423 / 541-396-5413 kailuacustom@aol.com www.kailuacustom.com
Kalispel Case Line, P.O. Box 267, Cusick, WA 99119 / 509-445-1121
Kamik Outdoor Footwear, 554 Montee de Liesse, Montreal, PQ H4T 1P1 CANADA / 514-341-3950; FAX: 514-341-1861
Kane, Edward, P.O. Box 385, Ukiah, CA 95482 / 707-462-2937
Kapro Mfg. Co. Inc. (See R.E.I.)
Kasenit Co., Inc., 39 Park Ave., Highland Mills, NY 10930 / 845-928-9595; FAX: 845-986-8038
Kaswer Custom, Inc., 13 Surrey Drive, Brookfield, CT 06804 / 203-775-0564; FAX: 203-775-6872
KDF, Inc., 2485 Hwy. 46 N., Seguin, TX 78155 / 830-379-8141; FAX: 830-379-5420
KeeCo Impressions, Inc., 346 Wood Ave., North Brunswick, NJ 08902 / 800-468-0546
Kehr, Roger, 2131 Agate Ct. SE, Lacy, WA 98503 / 360-491-0691
Keith's Bullets, 942 Twisted Oak, Algonquin, IL 60102 / 708-658-3520
Keith's Custom Gunstocks, Keith M. Heppler, 540 Banyan Circle, Walnut Creek, CA 94598 / 925-934-3509; FAX: 925-934-3143 kmheppler@hotmail.com
Kelbly, Inc., 7222 Dalton Fox Lake Rd., North Lawrence, OH 44666 / 216-683-4674; FAX: 216-683-7349
Kelley's, P.O. Box 125, Woburn, MA 01801-0125 / 800-879-7273; FAX: 781-272-7077 kels@star.net www.kelsmilitary.com
Kellogg's Professional Products, 325 Pearl St., Sandusky, OH 44870 / 419-625-6551; FAX: 419-625-6167 skwigton@aol.com
Kelly, Lance, 1723 Willow Oak Dr., Edgewater, FL 32132 / 904-423-4933
Kel-Tec CNC Industries, Inc., PO Box 236009, Cocoa, FL 32923 / 407-631-0068; FAX: 407-631-1169
Kemen America, 2550 Hwy. 23, Wrenshall, MN 55797 / 218-384-3670 patrickl@midwestshootingschool.com midwestshootingschool.com
Ken Eyster Heritage Gunsmiths, Inc., 6441 Bisop Rd., Centerburg, OH 43011 / 740-625-6131; FAX: 740-625-7811
Ken Starnes Gunmaker, 15940 SW Holly Hill Rd., Hillsboro, OR 97123-9033 / 503-628-0705; FAX: 503-443-2096 kstarnes@kdsa.com
Keng's Firearms Specialty, Inc./US Tactical Systems, 875 Wharton Dr., P.O. Box 44405, Atlanta, GA 30336-1405 / 404-691-7611; FAX: 404-505-8445
Kennebec Journal, 274 Western Ave., Augusta, ME 04330 / 207-622-6288
Kennedy Firearms, 10 N. Market St., Muncy, PA 17756 / 717-546-6695
Kenneth W. Warren Engraver, P.O. Box 2842, Wenatchee, WA 98807 / 509-663-6123; FAX: 509-665-6123
Ken's Kustom Kartridges, 331 Jacobs Rd., Hubbard, OH 44425 / 216-534-4595
Kent Cartridge America, Inc., PO Box 849, 1000 Zigor Rd., Kearneysville, WV 25430
Keowee Game Calls, 608 Hwy. 25 North, Travelers Rest, SC 29690 / 864-834-7204; FAX: 864-834-7831
Kershaw Knives, 25300 SW Parkway Ave., Wilsonville, OR 97070 / 503-682-1966; or 800-325-2891; FAX: 503-682-7168
Kesselring Gun Shop, 4024 Old Hwy. 99N, Burlington, WA 98233 / 360-724-3113; FAX: 360-724-7003 info@kesselrings.com www.kesselrings.com
Ketchum, Jim (See Jim's Precision)
Keystone Sporting Arms, Inc. (Crickett Rifles), 8920 State Route 405, Milton, PA 17847 / 800-742-2777; FAX: 570-742-1455
Kickeez I.N.C., Inc., 301 Industrial Dr., Carl Junction, MO 64834-8806 / 419-649-2100; FAX: 417-649-2200 kickey@ipa.net
Kilham & Co., Main St., P.O. Box 37, Lyme, NH 03768 / 603-795-4112
Kim Ahrends Custom Firearms, Inc., Box 203, Clarion, IA 50525 / 515-532-3449; FAX: 515-532-3926
Kimar (See U.S. Importer-IAR,Inc)
Kimber of America, Inc., 1 Lawton St., Yonkers, NY 10705 / 800-880-2418; FAX: 914-964-9340
King & Co., P.O. Box 1242, Bloomington, IL 61702 / 309-473-3964; FAX: 309-473-2161
King's Gun Works, 1837 W. Glenoaks Blvd., Glendale, CA 91201 / 818-956-6010; FAX: 818-548-8606
Kirkpatrick Leather Co., PO Box 677, Laredo, TX 78040 / 956-723-6631; FAX: 956-725-0672 mike@kirkpatrickleather.com www.kirkpatrickleather.com
KK Air International (See Impact Case & Container Co.)
Kleen-Bore, Inc., 16 Industrial Pkwy., Easthampton, MA 01027 / 413-527-0300; FAX: 413-527-2522 info@kleen-bore.com www.kleen-bore.com
Kleinendorst, K. W., RR 1, Box 1500, Hop Bottom, PA 18824 / 717-289-4687
Klingler Woodcarving, P.O. Box 141, Thistle Hill, Cabot, VT 05647 / 802-426-3811
Knifeware, Inc., P.O. Box 3, Greenville, WV 24945 / 304-832-6878
Knight Rifles, 21852 Hwy. J46, P.O. Box 130, Centerville, IA 52544 / 515-856-2626; FAX: 515-856-2628 www.knightrifles.com
Knight Rifles (See Modern Muzzle Loading, Inc.)
Knight's Mfg. Co., 7750 Ninth St. SW, Vero Beach, FL 32968 / 561-562-5697; FAX: 561-569-2955 civiliansales@knightarmco.com
Knock on Wood Antiques, 355 Post Rd., Darien, CT 06820 / 203-655-9031
Knoell, Doug, 9737 McCardle Way, Santee, CA 92071 / 619-449-5189
Knopp, Gary. See: SUPER 6 LLC
KOGOT, 410 College, Trinidad, CO 81082 / 719-846-9406; FAX: 719-846-9406
Kolar, 1925 Roosevelt Ave., Racine, WI 53406 / 414-554-0800; FAX: 414-554-9093
Kolpin Outdoors, Inc., P.O. Box 107, 205 Depot St., Fox Lake, WI 53933 / 414-928-3118; FAX: 414-928-3687 cdutton@kolpin.com www.kolpin.com
Korth Germany GmbH, Robert Bosch Strasse, 11, D-23909, 23909 Ratzeburg, GERMANY / 4541-840363; FAX: 4541-84 05 35 info@korthwaffen.de www.korthwaffen.com
Korth USA, 437R Chandler St., Tewksbury, MA 01876 / 978-851-8656; FAX: 978-851-9462 info@kortusa.com www.korthusa.com
Korzinek Riflesmith, J., RD 2 Box 73D, Canton, PA 17724 / 717-673-8512
Koval Knives, 5819 Zarley St., Suite A, New Albany, OH 43054 / 614-855-0777; FAX: 614-855-0945 koval@kovalknives.com www.kovalknives.com
Kowa Optimed, Inc., 20001 S. Vermont Ave., Torrance, CA 90502 / 310-327-1913; FAX: 310-327-4177 scopekowa@kowa.com www.kowascope.com
Kramer Designs, P.O. Box 129, Clancy, MT 59634 / 406-933-8658; FAX: 406-933-8658
Kramer Handgun Leather, P.O. Box 112154, Tacoma, WA 98411 / 800-510-2666; FAX: 253-564-1214 www.kramerleather.com
Krause Publications, Inc., 700 E. State St., Iola, WI 54990 / 715-445-2214; FAX: 715-445-4087
Krico Deutschland GmbH, Nurnbergerstrasse 6, D-90602, Pyrbaum, GERMANY / 09180-2780; FAX: 09180-2661
Krieger Barrels, Inc., 2024 Mayfield Rd, Richfield, WI 53076 / 262-628-8558; FAX: 262-628-8748
Krieghoff Gun Co., H., Boschstrasse 22, D-89079 Elm, GERMANY / 731-4018270
Krieghoff International,Inc., 7528 Easton Rd., Ottsville, PA 18942 / 610-847-5173; FAX: 610-847-8691
Kukowski, Ed. See: ED'S GUN HOUSE
Kulis Freeze Dry Taxidermy, 725 Broadway Ave., Bedford, OH 44146 / 216-232-8352; FAX: 216-232-7305 jkulis@kastaway.com kastaway.com
KVH Industries, Inc., 110 Enterprise Center, Middletown, RI 02842 / 401-847-3327; FAX: 401-849-0045
Kwik-Site Co., 5555 Treadwell St., Wayne, MI 48184 / 734-326-1500; FAX: 734-326-4120 kwiksiteco@aol.com

L

L&R Lock Co., 1137 Pocalla Rd., Sumter, SC 29150 / 803-775-6127; FAX: 803-775-5171
L&S Technologies Inc. (See Aimtech Mount Systems)
L. Bengtson Arms Co., 6345-B E. Akron St., Mesa, AZ 85 / 602-981-6375
L. E. Jurras & Assoc., L. E. Jurras, P.O. Box 680, Washing IN 47501 / 812-254-6170; FAX: 812-254-6170 jurasgun@rtcc.net
L.A.R. Mfg., Inc., 4133 W. Farm Rd., West Jordan, UT 84 / 801-280-3505; FAX: 801-280-1972
L.B.T., Judy Smith, HCR 62, Box 145, Moyie Springs, ID 83845 / 208-267-3588
L.E. Wilson, Inc., Box 324, 404 Pioneer Ave., Cashmere, 98815 / 509-782-1328; FAX: 509-782-7200
L.L. Bean, Inc., Freeport, ME 04032 / 207-865-4761; FA 207-552-2802
L.P.A. Inc., Via Alfieri 26, Gardone V.T., Brescia, ITALY / 30-891-14-81; FAX: 30-891-09-51
L.R. Clift Mfg., 3821 Hammonton Rd., Marysville, CA 95 / 916-755-3390; FAX: 916-755-3393
L.W. Seecamp Co., Inc., PO Box 255, New Haven, CT 065 / 203-877-3429; FAX: 203-877-3429 seecamp@optonline.net
La Clinique du .45, 1432 Rougemont, Chambly, PQ J3L 2 CANADA / 514-658-1144
Labanu, Inc., 2201-F Fifth Ave., Ronkonkoma, NY 11779 516-467-6197; FAX: 516-981-4112
LaBoone, Pat. See: THE MIDWEST SHOOTING SCHOOL
LaBounty Precision Reboring, Inc, 7968 Silver Lake Rd., Box 186, Maple Falls, WA 98266 / 360-599-2047; FA 360-599-3018
LaCrosse Footwear, Inc., 18550 NE Riverside Parkway, Portland, OR 97230 / 503-766-1010; or 800-323-266 FAX: 503-766-1015
LaFrance Specialties, P.O. Box 87933, San Diego, CA 921 / 619-293-3373; FAX: 619-293-0819 timlafrance@att. lafrancespecialties.com
Lake Center Marina, PO Box 670, St. Charles, MO 63302 314-946-7500
Lakefield Arms Ltd. (See Savage Arms, Inc.)
Lakewood Products LLC, 275 June St., Berlin, WI 54923 800-872-8458; FAX: 920-361-7719 lakewood@centurytel.net www.lakewoodproducts.co
Lamboy, Stephen. See: ITHACA CLASSIC DOUBLES
Lampert, Ron, Rt. 1, 44857 Schoolcraft Trl., Guthrie, MN 56461 / 218-854-7345
Lamson & Goodnow Mfg. Co., 45 Conway St., Shelburne Falls, MA 03170 / 413-625-6564; or 800-872-6564; FA 413-625-9816 www.lamsonsharp.com
Lansky Levine, Arthur. See: LANSKY SHARPENERS
Lansky Sharpeners, Arthur Lansky Levine, PO Box 50830, Las Vegas, NV 89016 / 702-361-7511; FAX: 702-896-9511
LaPrade, PO Box 250, Ewing, VA 24248 / 423-733-2615
Lapua Ltd., P.O. Box 5, Lapua, FINLAND / 6-310111; FAX: 6-4388991
LaRocca Gun Works, 51 Union Place, Worcester, MA 0160 / 508-754-2887; FAX: 508-754-2887 www.laroccagunworks.com
Larry Lyons Gunworks, 110 Hamilton St., Dowagiac, MI 49047 / 616-782-9478
Laser Devices, Inc., 2 Harris Ct. A-4, Monterey, CA 93940 / 831-373-0701; FAX: 831-373-0903 sales@laserdevices.com www.laserdevices.com
Laseraim Technologies, Inc., P.O. Box 3548, Little Rock, AR 72203 / 501-375-2227
Laserlyte, 2201 Amapola Ct., Torrance, CA 90501
LaserMax, Inc., 3495 Winton Place, Bldg. B, Rochester, NY 14623-2807 / 800-527-3703; FAX: 716-272-5427 customerservice@lasermax-inc.com www.lasermax-inc.com
Lassen Community College, Gunsmithing Dept., P.O. Box 3000, Hwy. 139, Susanville, CA 96130 / 916-251-8800; FAX: 916-251-8838
Lathrop's, Inc., 5146 E. Pima, Tucson, AZ 85712 / 520-881-0266; or 800-875-4867; FAX: 520-322-5704
Laughridge, William R. (See Cylinder & Slide Inc.)
Laurel Mountain Forge, P.O. Box 52, Crown Point, IN 46308 / 219-548-2950; FAX: 219-548-2950
Laurona Armas Eibar, S.A.L., Avenida de Otaola 25, P.O. Box 260, Eibar 20600, SPAIN / 34-43-700600; FAX: 34-43-700616
Lawrence Brand Shot (See Precision Reloading)
Lawrence Leather Co., P.O. Box 1479, Lillington, NC 27546 / 910-893-2071; FAX: 910-893-4742
Lawson Co., Harry, 3328 N Richey Blvd., Tucson, AZ 85716 / 520-326-1117; FAX: 520-326-1117
Lawson, John. See: THE SIGHT SHOP
Lawson, John G. (See Sight Shop, The)
Lazzeroni Arms Co., PO Box 26696, Tucson, AZ 85726 / 888-492-7247; FAX: 520-624-4250

ar Industries (See E-Z-Way Systems), P.O. Box 4310, ›wark, OH 43058-4310 / 614-345-6645; FAX: 4-345-6600

's, Inc., 7675 Five Mile Rd., Northville, MI 48167 / 8-486-1231; FAX: 248-486-1430

rman Tool Group, Inc., 12106 NE Ainsworth Cir., P.O. ›x 20595, Portland, OR 97294 / 503-253-7826; FAX: 3-253-7830

u-Courally, Rue St. Gilles, 386 4000, Liege, BELGIUM)42-52-48-43; FAX: 32-4-252-2008 fo@lebeau-courally.com www.lebeau-courally.com

Professional Gunsmithing, 546 Quarry Rd., Ottsville, \ 18942 / 215-847-8594

tter Airguns, Riley, 1804 E Sprague St, Winston Salem, C 27107-3521 / 919-784-0676

recision, Inc., 4275 Hwy. U, Hartford, WI 53027 / 62-673-3075; FAX: 262-673-9273 fo@leeprecision.com www.leeprecision.com

upplies, Mark, 9901 France Ct., Lakeville, MN 55044 / 12-461-2114

er Arms Co., Inc., 6234 Stokes, Lee Center Rd., Lee enter, NY 13363 / 315-337-6722; FAX: 315-337-1543

cy Sports International, 206 S. Union St., Alexandria, VA 2314 / 703-548-4837 www.legacysports.com

witz, Leonard, 1205 Murrayhill Ave., Pittsburgh, PA 5217 / 412-361-5455

USA, Inc., 156 Ludlow Ave., Northvale, NJ 07647 / 201-767-7500; FAX: 201-767-8666

Gun Specialties, Inc. The Lewis Lead Remover, P.O. Box 2855, Peachtree City, GA 30269-2024 / 770-487-0556

ard Day, 6 Linseed Rd Box 1, West Hatfield, MA 01088-7505 / 413-337-8369

Baer Custom, Inc., 29601 34th Ave., Hillsdale, IL 61257 / 309-658-2716; FAX: 309-658-2610 www.lesbaer.com

Merises, Felix. See: ROCKY MOUNTAIN ARMOURY

al Force Institute (See Police Bookshelf), PO Box 122, Concord, NH 03301 / 603-224-6814; FAX: 603-226-3554

Custom Grips, 672 Currier Rd., Hopkinton, NH 03229-2652 / 800-421-5388; FAX: 603-226-4580 info@lettgrips.com www.lettgrips.com

pold & Stevens, Inc., 14400 NW Greenbrier Pky., Beaverton, OR 97006 / 503-646-9171; FAX: 503-526-1455

er Arms Service Ltd., 2131 Burrard St., Vancouver, BC V6J 3H7 CANADA / 604-736-2711; FAX: 604-738-3503 leverarms@leverarms.com www.leverarms.com

Horton Dist. Co., Inc., 15 Walkup Dr., Westboro, MA 01581 / 508-366-7400; FAX: 508-366-5332

erty Metals, 2233 East 16th St., Los Angeles, CA 90021 / 213-581-9171; FAX: 213-581-9351 libertymfgsolder@hotmail.com

erty Safe, 999 W. Utah Ave., Payson, UT 84651-1744 / 800-247-5625; FAX: 801-489-6409

erty Shooting Supplies, P.O. Box 357, Hillsboro, OR 97123 / 503-640-5518; FAX: 503-640-5518 info@libertyshootingsupplies.com www.libertyshootingsupplies.com

htning Performance Innovations, Inc., RD1 Box 555, Mohawk, NY 13407 / 315-866-8819; FAX: 315-867-5701

a Precision Rifle Barrels, P.O. Box 372, Plains, MT 59859 / 406-826-3084; FAX: 406-826-3083 lilja@riflebarrels.com www.riflebarrels.com

ncoln, Dean, Box 1886, Farmington, NM 87401

nder Solingen Knives, 4401 Sentry Dr. #B, Tucker, GA 30084 / 770-939-6915; FAX: 770-939-6738

ndsay Engraving & Tools, Steve Lindsay, 3714 W. Cedar Hills, Kearney, NE 68845 / 308-236-7885 steve@lindsayengraving.com www.handgravers.com

ndsay, Steve. See: LINDSAY ENGRAVING & TOOLS

ndsley Arms Cartridge Co., P.O. Box 757, 20 College Hill Rd., Henniker, NH 03242 / 603-428-3127

nebaugh Custom Sixguns, P.O. Box 455, Cody, WY 82414 / 307-645-3332 www.sixgunner.com

on Country Supply, P.O. Box 480, Port Matilda, PA 16870

st Precision Engineering, Unit 1 Ingley Works, 13 River Road, Barking, ENGLAND / 011-081-594-1686

ithi Bee Bullet Lube, 1728 Carr Rd., Muskegon, MI 49442 / 616-788-4479 lithibee@att.net

Little John's" Antique Arms, 1740 W. Laveta, Orange, CA 92668

Little Trees Ramble (See Scott Pilkington)

Littler Sales Co., 20815 W. Chicago, Detroit, MI 48228 / 313-273-6888; FAX: 313-273-1099 littlerptg@aol.com

Littleton, J. F., 275 Pinedale Ave., Oroville, CA 95966 / 916-533-6084

Ljutic Industries, Inc., 732 N. 16th Ave., Suite 22, Yakima, WA 98902 / 509-248-0476; FAX: 509-576-8233 ljuticgun@earthlink.net www.ljuticgun.com

Llama Gabilondo Y Cia, Apartado 290, E-01080, Victoria, SPAIN

Loch Leven Industries/Convert-A-Pell, P.O. Box 2751, Santa Rosa, CA 95405 / 707-573-8735; FAX: 707-573-0369

Lock's Philadelphia Gun Exchange, 6700 Rowland Ave., Philadelphia, PA 19149 / 215-332-6225; FAX: 215-332-4800 locks.gunshop@verizon.net

Lodewick, Walter H., 2816 NE Halsey St., Portland, OR 97232 / 503-284-2554 wlodewick@aol.com

Lodgewood Mfg., P.O. Box 611, Whitewater, WI 53190 / 262-473-5444; FAX: 262-473-6448 lodgewd@idcnet.com lodgewood.com

Log Cabin Sport Shop, 8010 Lafayette Rd., Lodi, OH 44254 / 330-948-1082; FAX: 330-948-4307 logcabin@logcabinshop.com www.logcabinshop.com

Logan, Harry M., Box 745, Honokaa, HI 96727 / 808-776-1644

Logdewood Mfg., P.O. Box 611, Whitewater, WI 53190 / 262-473-5444; FAX: 262-473-6448 lodgewd@idcnet.com www.lodgewood.com

Lohman Mfg. Co., Inc., 4500 Doniphan Dr., P.O. Box 220, Neosho, MO 64850 / 417-451-4438; FAX: 417-451-2576

Lomont Precision Bullets, 278 Sandy Creek Rd., Salmon, ID 83467 / 208-756-6819; FAX: 208-756-6824 www.klomont.com

London Guns Ltd., Box 3750, Santa Barbara, CA 93130 / 805-683-4141; FAX: 805-683-1712

Lone Star Gunleather, 1301 Brushy Bend Dr., Round Rock, TX 78681 / 512-255-1805

Lone Star Rifle Company, 11231 Rose Road, Conroe, TX 77303 / 936-856-3363; FAX: 936-856-3363 dave@lonestar.com

Long, George F., 1500 Rogue River Hwy., Ste. F, Grants Pass, OR 97527 / 541-476-7552

Lortone Inc., 2856 NW Market St., Seattle, WA 98107

Lothar Walther Precision Tool Inc., 3425 Hutchinson Rd., Cumming, GA 30040 / 770-889-9998; FAX: 770-889-4919 lotharwalther@mindspring.com www.lothar-walther.com

LPS Laboratories, Inc., 4647 Hugh Howell Rd., P.O. Box 3050, Tucker, GA 30084 / 404-934-7800

Lucas, Edward E, 32 Garfield Ave., East Brunswick, NJ 08816 / 201-251-5526

Lupton, Keith. See: PAWLING MOUNTAIN CLUB

Lyman Instant Targets, Inc. (See Lyman Products)

Lyman Products Corp., 475 Smith Street, Middletown, CT 06457-1541 / 800-423-9704; FAX: 860-632-1699 lymansales@cshore.com www.lymanproducts.com

M

M.H. Canjar Co., 6510 Raleigh St., Arvada, CO 80003 / 303-295-2638; FAX: 303-295-2638

MA Systems, Inc., P.O. Box 894, Pryor, OK 74362-0894 / 918-824-3705; FAX: 918-824-3710

Mac-1 Airgun Distributors, 13974 Van Ness Ave., Gardena, CA 90249-2900 / 310-327-3581; FAX: 310-327-0238 mac1@maclairgun.com www.mac1airgun.com

Madis Books, 2453 West Five Mile Pkwy., Dallas, TX 75233 / 214-330-7168

Madis, George. See: GEORGE MADIS WINCHESTER CONSULTANTS

MAG Instrument, Inc., 1635 S. Sacramento Ave., Ontario, CA 91761 / 909-947-1006; FAX: 909-947-3116

Magma Engineering Co., P.O. Box 161, 20955 E. Ocotillo Rd., Queen Creek, AZ 85242 / 602-987-9008; FAX: 602-987-0148

Mag-Na-Port International, Inc., 41302 Executive Dr., Harrison Twp., MI 48045-1306 / 586-469-6727; FAX: 586-469-0425 email@magnaport.com www.magnaport.com

Magnolia Sports, Inc., 211 W. Main, Magnolia, AR 71753 / 501-234-8410; or 800-530-7816; FAX: 501-234-8117

Magnum Power Products, Inc., P.O. Box 17768, Fountain Hills, AZ 85268

Magnum Research, Inc., 7110 University Ave. NE, Minneapolis, MN 55432 / 800-772-6168 or 763-574-1868; FAX: 763-574-0109 info@magnumresearch.com

Magnus Bullets, P.O. Box 239, Toney, AL 35773 / 256-420-8359; FAX: 256-420-8360

Mag-Pack Corp., P.O. Box 846, Chesterland, OH 44026 / 440-285-9480 magpack@hotmail.com

MagSafe Ammo Co., 4700 S US Highway 17/92, Casselberry, FL 32707-3814 / 407-834-9966; FAX: 407-834-8185 www.magsafeonline.com

Magtech Ammunition Co. Inc., 6845 20th Ave. S., Ste. 120, Centerville, MN 55038

Mahony, Philip Bruce, 67 White Hollow Rd., Lime Rock, CT 06039-2418 / 203-435-9341 filbalony-redbeard@snet.net

Mahovsky's Metalife, R.D. 1, Box 149a Eureka Road, Grand Valley, PA 16420 / 814-436-7747

Maine Custom Bullets, RFD 1, Box 1755, Brooks, ME 04921

Makinson, Nicholas, RR 3, Komoka, ON N0L 1R0 CANADA / 519-471-5462

Mallardtone Game Calls, 10406 96th St., Court West, Taylor Ridge, IL 61284 / 309-798-2481; FAX: 309-798-2501

Mandall Shooting Supplies Inc., 3616 N. Scottsdale Rd., Scottsdale, AZ 85251 / 480-945-2553; FAX: 480-949-0734

Marble Arms (See CRR, Inc./Marble's Inc.)

Marchmon Bullets, 6502 Riverdale Rd., Whitmore Lake, MI 48189

Marent, Rudolf. See: HAMMERLI SERVICE-PRECISION MAC

Mark Lee Supplies, 9901 France Ct., Lakeville, MN 55044 / 952-461-2114; FAX: 952-461-2194 marklee55044@usfamily.net

Markell, Inc., 422 Larkfield Center 235, Santa Rosa, CA 95403 / 707-573-0792; FAX: 707-573-9867

Markesbery Muzzle Loaders, Inc., 7785 Foundation Dr., Ste. 6, Florence, KY 41042 / 606-342-5553 or 606-342-2380

Marksman Products, 5482 Argosy Dr., Huntington Beach, CA 92649 / 714-898-7535; or 800-822-8005; FAX: 714-891-0782

Marlin Firearms Co., 100 Kenna Dr., North Haven, CT 06473 / 203-239-5621; FAX: 203-234-7991 www.marlinfirearms.com

MarMik, Inc., 2116 S. Woodland Ave., Michigan City, IN 46360 / 219-872-7231; FAX: 219-872-7231

Marocchi F.lli S.p.A, Via Galileo Galilei 8, I-25068 Zanano, ITALY

Marquart Precision Co., P.O. Box 1740, Prescott, AZ 86302 / 520-445-5646

Marsh, Mike, Croft Cottage, Main St., Derbyshire, DE4 2BY ENGLAND / 01629 650 669

Marshall Enterprises, 792 Canyon Rd., Redwood City, CA 94062

Marshall Fish Mfg. Gunsmith Sptg. Co., Rd. Box 2439, Westport, NY 12993 / 518-962-4897; FAX: 518-962-4897

Martin B. Retting Inc., 11029 Washington, Culver City, CA 90232 / 213-837-2412

Martini & Hagn, 1264 Jimsmith Lake Rd, Cranbrook, BC V1C 6V6 CANADA / 250-417-2926; FAX: 250-417-2928

Martin's Gun Shop, 937 S. Sheridan Blvd., Lakewood, CO 80226 / 303-922-2184

Martz, John V., 8060 Lakeview Lane, Lincoln, CA 95648 FAX: 916-645-3815

Marvel, Alan, 3922 Madonna Rd., Jarretsville, MD 21084 / 301-557-6545

Marx, Harry (See U.S. Importer for FERLIB)

Maryland Paintball Supply, 8507 Harford Rd., Parkville, MD 21234 / 410-882-5607

MAST Technology, Inc., 14555 US Hwy. 95 S., P.O. Box 60969, Boulder City, NV 89006 / 702-293-6969; FAX: 702-293-7255 info@masttechnology.com www.bellammo.com

Master Lock Co., 2600 N. 32nd St., Milwaukee, WI 53245 / 414-444-2800

Match Prep-Doyle Gracey, P.O. Box 155, Tehachapi, CA 93581 / 661-822-5383; FAX: 661-823-8680

Mathews Gun Shop & Gunsmithing, Inc., 10224 S. Paramount Blvd., Downey, CA 90241 / 562-928-2129; FAX: 562-928-8629

Matthews Cutlery, 4401 Sentry Dr. #B, Tucker, GA 30084 / 770-939-6915

Mauser Werke Oberndorf Waffensysteme GmbH, Postfach 1349, 78722, Oberndorf/N., GERMANY

Maverick Arms, Inc., 7 Grasso Ave., P.O. Box 497, North Haven, CT 06473 / 203-230-5300; FAX: 203-230-5420

Maxi-Mount Inc., P.O. Box 291, Willoughby Hills, OH 44096-0291 / 440-944-9456; FAX: 440-944-9456 maximount454@yahoo.com

Mayville Engineering Co. (See MEC, Inc.)

Mazur Restoration, Pete, 13083 Drummer Way, Grass Valley, CA 95949 / 530-268-2412

McBros Rifle Co., P.O. Box 86549, Phoenix, AZ 85080 / 602-582-3713; FAX: 602-581-3825

McCament, Jay. See: JAY MCCAMENT CUSTOM GUNMAKER

McCann, Tom, 14 Walton Dr., New Hope, PA 18938 / 215-862-2728

MANUFACTURER'S DIRECTORY

McCann Industries, P.O. Box 641, Spanaway, WA 98387 / 253-537-6919; FAX: 253-537-6919 mccann.machine@worldnet.att.net www.mccannindustries.com
McCluskey Precision Rifles, 10502 14th Ave. NW, Seattle, WA 98177 / 206-781-2776
McCombs, Leo, 1862 White Cemetery Rd., Patriot, OH 45658 / 740-256-1714
McDonald, Dennis, 8359 Brady St., Peosta, IA 52068 / 319-556-7940
McFarland, Stan, 2221 Idella Ct., Grand Junction, CO 81505 / 970-243-4704
McGhee, Larry. See: B.C. OUTDOORS
McGowen Rifle Barrels, 5961 Spruce Lane, St. Anne, IL 60964 / 815-937-9816; FAX: 815-937-4024
Mchalik, Gary. See: ROSSI FIREARMS
McKenzie, Lynton, 6940 N. Alvernon Way, Tucson, AZ 85718 / 520-299-5090
McMillan Fiberglass Stocks, Inc., 1638 W. Knudsen Dr. #102, Phoenix, AZ 85027 / 623-582-9635; FAX: 623-581-3825 mfsinc@mcmfamily.com www.mcmfamily.com
McMillan Optical Gunsight Co., 28638 N. 42nd St., Cave Creek, AZ 85331 / 602-585-7868; FAX: 602-585-7872
McMillan Rifle Barrels, P.O. Box 3427, Bryan, TX 77805 / 409-690-3456; FAX: 409-690-0156
McMurdo, Lynn (See Specialty Gunsmithing), PO Box 404, Afton, WY 83110 / 307-886-5535
MCS, Inc., 166 Pocono Rd., Brookfield, CT 06804-2023 / 203-775-1013; FAX: 203-775-9462
McWelco Products, 6730 Santa Fe Ave., Hesperia, CA 92345 / 619-244-8876; FAX: 619-244-9398 products@mcwelco.com www.mawelco.com
MDS, P.O. Box 1441, Brandon, FL 33509-1441 / 813-653-1180; FAX: 813-684-5953
Measurement Group Inc., Box 27777, Raleigh, NC 27611
Measures, Leon. See: SHOOT WHERE YOU LOOK
MEC, Inc., 715 South St., Mayville, WI 53050 / 414-387-4500; FAX: 414-387-5802 reloaders@mayul.com www.mayvl.com
MEC-Gar S.R.L., Via Madonnina 64, Gardone V.T. Brescia, ITALY / 39-30-8912687; FAX: 39-30-8910065
MEC-Gar U.S.A., Inc., Hurley Farms Industr. Park, 115, Hurley Road 6G, Oxford, CT 06478 / 203-262-1525; FAX: 203-262-1719 mecgar@aol.com www.mec-gar.com
Mech-Tech Systems, Inc., 1602 Foothill Rd., Kalispell, MT 59901 / 406-755-8055
Meister Bullets (See Gander Mountain)
Mele, Frank, 201 S. Wellow Ave., Cookeville, TN 38501 / 615-526-4860
Menck, Gunsmith Inc., T.W., 5703 S 77th St., Ralston, NE 68127
Mendez, John A., P.O. Box 620984, Orlando, FL 32862 / 407-344-2791
Men-Metallwerk Elisenhuette GmbH, P.O. Box 1263, Nassau/Lahn, D-56372 GERMANY / 2604-7819
Meprolight (See Hesco-Meprolight)
Mercer Custom Guns, 216 S. Whitewater Ave., Jefferson, WI 53549 / 920-674-3839
Merit Corp., PO Box 9044, Schenectady, NY 12309 / 518-346-1420 sales@meritcorporation.com www.meritcorporation.com
Merkel, Schutzenstrasse 26, D-98527 Suhl, Suhl, GERMANY FAX: 011-49-3681-854-203 www.merkel-waffen.de
Merkuria Ltd., Argentinska 38, 17005, Praha 7, CZECH REPUBLIC / 422-875117; FAX: 422-809152
Metal Merchants, PO Box 186, Walled Lake, MI 48390-0186
Metalife Industries (See Mahovsky's Metalife)
Michael's Antiques, Box 591, Waldoboro, ME 04572
Michaels Of Oregon, Co., P.O. Box 1690, Oregon City, OR 97045 www.michaels-oregon.com
Micro Sight Co., 242 Harbor Blvd., Belmont, CA 94002 / 415-591-0769; FAX: 415-591-7531
Microfusion Alfa S.A., Paseo San Andres N8, P.O. Box 271, Eibar, 20600 SPAIN / 34-43-11-89-16; FAX: 34-43-11-40-38
Mid-America Recreation, Inc., 1328 5th Ave., Moline, IL 61265 / 309-764-5089; FAX: 309-764-5089 fmilcusguns@aol.com www.midamericarecreation.com
Middlebrooks Custom Shop, 7366 Colonial Trail East, Surry, VA 23883 / 757-357-0881; FAX: 757-365-0442
Midway Arms, Inc., 5875 W. Van Horn Tavern Rd., Columbia, MO 65203 / 800-243-3220; or 573-445-6363; FAX: 573-446-1018
Midwest Gun Sport, 1108 Herbert Dr., Zebulon, NC 27597 / 919-269-5570
Midwest Sport Distributors, Box 129, Fayette, MO 65248
Mike Davis Products, 643 Loop Dr., Moses Lake, WA 98837 / 509-765-6178; or 509-766-7281
Mike Yee Custom Stocking, 29927 56 Pl. S., Auburn, WA 98001 / 253-839-3991
Military Armament Corp., P.O. Box 120, Mt. Zion Rd., Lingleville, TX 76461 / 817-965-3253
Millennium Designed Muzzleloaders, PO Box 536, Routes 11 & 25, Limington, ME 04049 / 207-637-2316
Miller Arms, Inc., P.O. Box 260 Purl St., St. Onge, SD 57779 / 605-642-5160; FAX: 605-642-5160
Miller Custom, 210 E. Julia, Clinton, IL 61727 / 217-935-9362
Miller Single Trigger Mfg. Co., 6680 Rt. 5-20, P.O. Box 471, Bloomfield, NY 14469 / 585-657-6338
Millett Sights, 7275 Murdy Circle, Adm. Office, Huntington Beach, CA 92647 / 714-842-5575 or 800-645-5388; FAX: 714-843-5707
Mills Jr., Hugh B., 3615 Canterbury Rd., New Bern, NC 28560 / 919-637-4631
Milstor Corp., 80-975 Indio Blvd. C-7, Indio, CA 92201 / 760-775-9998; FAX: 760-775-5229 milstor@webtv.net
Minute Man High Tech Industries, 10611 Canyon Rd. E., Suite 151, Puyallup, WA 98373 / 800-233-2734
Mirador Optical Corp., P.O. Box 11614, Marina Del Rey, CA 90295-7614 / 310-821-5587; FAX: 310-305-0386
Mitchell, Jack, c/o Geoff Gaebe, Addieville East Farm, 200 Pheasant Dr., Mapleville, RI 02839 / 401-568-3185
Mitchell Bullets, R.F., 430 Walnut St., Westernport, MD 21562
Mitchell Mfg. Corp., P.O. Box 9295, Fountain Valley, CA 92728 / 714-444-2220
Mitchell Optics, Inc., 2072 CR 1100 N, Sidney, IL 61877 / 217-688-2219; or 217-621-3018; FAX: 217-688-2505 mitche1@attglobal.net
Mitchell's Accuracy Shop, 68 Greenridge Dr., Stafford, VA 22554 / 703-659-0165
Mitchell's Mauser, P.O. Box 9295, Fountain Valley, CA 92728 / 714-979-7663; FAX: 714-899-3660
MI-TE Bullets, 1396 Ave. K, Ellsworth, KS 67439 / 785-472-4575; FAX: 785-472-5579
Mittleman, William, P.O. Box 65, Etna, CA 96027
Mixson Corp., 7635 W. 28th Ave., Hialeah, FL 33016 / 305-821-5190; or 800-327-0078; FAX: 305-558-9318
MJK Gunsmithing, Inc., 417 N. Huber Ct., E. Wenatchee, WA 98802 / 509-884-7683
MKS Supply, Inc. (See Hi-Point Firearms)
MMC, 5050 E. Belknap St., Haltom City, TX 76117 / 817-831-9557; FAX: 817-834-5508
MOA Corporation, 2451 Old Camden Pike, Eaton, OH 45320 / 937-456-3669 www.moaguns
Modern Gun Repair School, PO Box 846, Saint Albans, VT 05478 / 802-524-2223; FAX: 802-524-2053 jfwp@dlilearn.com www.mgsinfoadlifearn.com
Modern Muzzleloading, Inc., P.O. Box 130, Centerville, IA 52544 / 515-856-2626
Moeller, Steve, 1213 4th St., Fulton, IL 61252 / 815-589-2300
Mogul Co./Life Jacket, 500 N. Kimball Rd., Ste. 109, South Lake, TX 76092
Molin Industries, Tru-Nord Division, P.O. Box 365, 204 North 9th St., Brainerd, MN 56401 / 218-829-2870
Monell Custom Guns, 228 Red Mills Rd., Pine Bush, NY 12566 / 914-744-3021
Moneymaker Guncraft Corp., 1420 Military Ave., Omaha, NE 68131 / 402-556-0226
Montana Armory, Inc. (See C. Sharps Arms Co. Inc.), 100 Centennial Dr., P.O. Box 885, Big Timber, MT 59011 / 406-932-4353; FAX: 406-932-4443
Montana Outfitters, Lewis E. Yearout, 308 Riverview Dr. E., Great Falls, MT 59404 / 406-761-0859; or 406-727-4560
Montana Precision Swaging, P.O. Box 4746, Butte, MT 59702 / 406-494-0600; FAX: 406-494-0600
Montana Rifleman, Inc., 2593A Hwy. 2 East, Kalispell, MT 59901 / 406-755-4867
Montana Vintage Arms, 2354 Bear Canyon Rd., Bozeman, MT 59715
Morini (See U.S. Importers-Mandall Shooting Supply)
Morrison Custom Rifles, J. W., 4015 W Sharon, Phoenix, AZ 85029 / 602-978-3754
Morrison Precision, 6719 Calle Mango, Hereford, AZ 85615 / 520-378-6207 morprec@c2i2.com
Morrow, Bud, 11 Hillside Lane, Sheridan, WY 82801-9729 / 307-674-8360
Morton Booth Co., P.O. Box 123, Joplin, MO 64802 / 417-673-1962; FAX: 417-673-3642
Mo's Competitor Supplies (See MCS, Inc.)
Moss Double Tone, Inc., P.O. Box 1112, 2101 S. Kentucky, Sedalia, MO 65301 / 816-827-0827
Mountain Plains Industries, 3720 Otter Place, Lynchburg, VA 24503 / 800-687-3000; FAX: 434-845-6594 mpitargets@cstone.net
Mountain State Muzzleloading Supplies, Inc., Box 154-2, Williamstown, WV 26187 / 304-375-7842; FAX 304-375-3737
Mowrey Gun Works, P.O. Box 246, Waldron, IN 46182 317-525-6181; FAX: 317-525-9595
Mowrey's Guns & Gunsmithing, 119 Fredericks St., Canajoharie, NY 13317 / 518-673-3483
MPC, P.O. Box 450, McMinnville, TN 37110-0450 / 615-473-5513; FAX: 615-473-5516 thebox@blomand.net www.mpc-thebox.com
MPI Stocks, PO Box 83266, Portland, OR 97283 / 503-226-1215; FAX: 503-226-2661
MSR Targets, P.O. Box 1042, West Covina, CA 91793 / 818-331-7840
MTM Molded Products Co., Inc., 3370 Obco Ct., Daytor 45414 / 937-890-7461; FAX: 937-890-1747
Mulberry House Publishing, P.O. Box 2180, Apache Junc AZ 85217 / 888-738-1567; FAX: 480-671-1015
Mulhern, Rick, Rt. 5, Box 152, Rayville, LA 71269 / 318-728-2688
Mullins Ammunition, Rt. 2 Box 304N, Clintwood, VA 242 276-926-6772; FAX: 276-926-6092 mammo@extremeshockusa.com www.extremeshockusa
Mullis Guncraft, 3523 Lawyers Road E., Monroe, NC 281 704-283-6683
Multiplex International, 26 S. Main St., Concord, NH 03 FAX: 603-796-2223
Multipropulseurs, La Bertrandiere, 42580, FRANCE / 77 01 30; FAX: 77 93 19 34
Mundy, Thomas A., 69 Robbins Road, Somerville, NJ 08 / 201-722-2199
Murmur Corp., 2823 N. Westmoreland Ave., Dallas, TX 75 / 214-630-5400
Murphy, R.R. Murphy Co., Inc. See: MURPHY, R.R. CO.,
Murphy, R.R. Co., Inc., R.R. Murphy Co., Inc. Murphy, P Box 102, Ripley, TN 38063 / 901-635-4003; FAX: 901-635-2320
Murray State College, 1 Murray Campus St., Tishomingo, 73460 / 508-371-2371 darnold@mscok.edu
Muscle Products Corp., 112 Fennell Dr., Butler, PA 1600 800-227-7049; or 724-283-0567; FAX: 724-283-831 mpc@mpc_home.com www.mpc_home.com
Muzzleloaders Etcetera, Inc., 9901 Lyndale Ave. S., Bloomington, MN 55420 / 952-884-1161 www.muzzleloaders-etcetera.com
MWG Co., P.O. Box 971202, Miami, FL 33197 / 800-428-9394; or 305-253-8393; FAX: 305-232-124

N

N.B.B., Inc., 24 Elliot Rd., Sterling, MA 01564 / 508-422-7538; or 800-942-9444
N.C. Ordnance Co., P.O. Box 3254, Wilson, NC 27895 / 919-237-2440; FAX: 919-243-9845
Nagel's Custom Bullets, 100 Scott St., Baytown, TX 77520-2849
Nalpak, 1937-C Friendship Drive, El Cajon, CA 92020 / 619-258-1200
Nastoff, Steve. See: NASTOFFS 45 SHOP, INC.
Nastoffs 45 Shop, Inc., Steve Nastoff, 1057 Laverne Dr., Youngstown, OH 44511
National Bullet Co., 1585 E. 361 St., Eastlake, OH 44095 / 216-951-1854; FAX: 216-951-7761
National Target Co., 4690 Wyaconda Rd., Rockville, MD 20852 / 800-827-7060 or 301-770-7060; FAX: 301-770-7892
Nationwide Airgun Repair, 2310 Windsor Forest Dr., Louisville, KY 40272 / 502-937-2614; FAX: 812-637-1463 shortshoestring@insightbb.com
Naval Ordnance Works, Rt. 2, Box 919, Sheperdstown, WV 25443 / 304-876-0998
Navy Arms Co., 219 Lawn St., Martinsburg, WV 25401 / 304-262-9870; FAX: 304-262-1658
Navy Arms Company, Valmore J. Forgett Jr., 815 22nd Street Union City, NJ 07087 / 201-863-7100; FAX: 201-863-8770 info@navyarms.com www.navyarms.cor
NCP Products, Inc., 3500 12th St. N.W., Canton, OH 44708 / 330-456-5130; FAX: 330-456-5234
Necessary Concepts, Inc., P.O. Box 571, Deer Park, NY 11729 / 516-667-8509; FAX: 516-667-8588
NEI Handtools, Inc., 10960 Gary Player Dr., El Paso, TX 79935
Neil A. Jones Custom Products, 17217 Brookhouser Road, Saegertown, PA 16433 / 814-763-2769; FAX: 814-763-4228
Nelson, Gary K., 975 Terrace Dr., Oakdale, CA 95361 / 209-847-4590

MANUFACTURER'S DIRECTORY

, Stephen. See: NELSON'S CUSTOM GUNS, INC.
's Custom Guns, Inc., Stephen Nelson, 7430 Valley ew Dr. N.W., Corvallis, OR 97330 / 541-745-5232 lsons-custom@attbi.com
Enterprises Inc., P.O. Box 119, Summit St., East ampton, CT 06424 / 203-267-2588
Bay Precision, 22239 Big Valley Rd., Poulsbo, WA 370 / 206-697-3830
stad Gun Works, 38962 160th Avenue, Pelican Rapids, N 56572 / 218-863-4301
ann GmbH, Am Galgenberg 6, 90575, GERMANY / 9101/8258; FAX: 09101/6356
a Pistol Academy, Inc., 4610 Blue Diamond Rd., Las egas, NV 89139 / 702-897-1100
ngland Ammunition Co., 1771 Post Rd. East, Suite 223, Vestport, CT 06880 / 203-254-8048
England Arms Co., Box 278, Lawrence Lane, Kittery oint, ME 03905 / 207-439-0593; FAX: 207-439-0525 nfo@newenglandarms.com www.newenglandarms.com
England Custom Gun Service, 438 Willow Brook Rd., lainfield, NH 03781 / 603-469-3450; FAX: 03-469-3471 bestguns@cyborportal.net www.newenglandcustom.com
Orleans Jewelers Supply Co., 206 Charters St., New Orleans, LA 70130 / 504-523-3839; FAX: 504-523-3836
SKB Arms Co., C.P.O. Box 1401, Tokyo, JAPAN / 1-3-3943-9550; FAX: 81-3-3943-0695
Ultra Light Arms, LLC, P.O. Box 340, Granville, WV 26534
rk Electronics, 4801 N. Ravenswood Ave., Chicago, IL 60640
ell, Robert H., 55 Coyote, Los Alamos, NM 87544 / 505-662-7135
man Gunshop, 2035 Chester Ave. #411, Ottumwa, IA 52501-3715 / 515-937-5775
olson Custom, 17285 Thornlay Road, Hughesville, MO 65334 / 816-826-8746
els, Paul R., 4328 Seville St., Las Vegas, NV 89121 / 702-435-5318
las, Ted, 5504 Hegel Rd., Goodrich, MI 48438 / 810-797-4493
ni Engineering, W. B., Box 126 Center Rd., Greensboro, VT 05841 / 802-533-7180; FAX: 802-533-7141
n, Inc., 1300 Walt Whitman Rd., Melville, NY 11747 / 516-547-8623; FAX: 516-547-0309
x Gun Shop, P.O. Box 1706, Uvalde, TX 78801 / 830-278-8843
een, Peter H., 5075 Buena Vista Dr., Belgrade, MT 59714 / 406-586-7383
ica, Avnda Otaola, 16 Apartado 68, Eibar, SPAIN
inco, 7A Yun Tan N, Beijing, CHINA
incoptics (See BEC, Inc.)
rma Precision AB (See U.S. Importers-Dynamit)
rmark Corp., 10395 Yellow Circle Dr., Minnetonka, MN 55343-9101 / 612-933-7060; FAX: 612-933-0046
rth American Arms, Inc., 2150 South 950 East, Provo, UT 84606-6285 / 800-821-5783; or 801-374-9990; FAX: 801-374-9998
rth American Correspondence Schools The Gun Pro, Oak & Pawney St., Scranton, PA 18515 / 717-342-7701
rth American Shooting Systems, P.O. Box 306, Osoyoos, BC V0H 1V0 CANADA / 250-495-3131; FAX: 250-495-3131 rifle@cablerocket.com
rth Devon Firearms Services, 3 North St., Braunton, EX33 1AJ ENGLAND / 01271 813624; FAX: 01271 813624
rth Mountain Pine Training Center (See Executive
orth Star West, P.O. Box 488, Glencoe, CA 95232 / 209-293-7010 northstarwest.com
orthern Precision, 329 S. James St., Carthage, NY 13619 / 315-493-1711
orthlake Outdoor Footwear, P.O. Box 10, Franklin, TN 37065-0010 / 615-794-1556; FAX: 615-790-8005
orthside Gun Shop, 2725 NW 109th, Oklahoma City, OK 73120 / 405-840-2353
orthwest Arms, 26884 Pearl Rd., Parma, ID 83660 / 208-722-6771; FAX: 208-722-1062
o-Sho Mfg. Co., 10727 Glenfield Ct., Houston, TX 77096 / 713-723-5332
osler, Inc., P.O. Box 671, Bend, OR 97709 / 800-285-3701; or 541-382-3921; FAX: 541-388-4667 www.nosler.com
ovak's, Inc., 1206 1/2 30th St., P.O. Box 4045, Parkersburg, WV 26101 / 304-485-9295; FAX: 304-428-6722
owlin Mfg. Co., 20622 S 4092 Rd., Claremore, OK 74017 / 918-342-0689; FAX: 918-342-0624 nowlinguns@msn.com nowlinguns.com
RI Gunsmith School, P.O. Box 182968, Columbus, OH 43218-2968
Nu-Line Guns,Inc., 1053 Caulks Hill Rd., Harvester, MO 63304 / 314-441-4500; or 314-447-4501; FAX: 314-447-5018
Null Holsters Ltd. K.L., 161 School St NW, Resaca, GA 30735 / 706-625-5643; FAX: 706-625-9392
Numrich Gun Parts Corporation, 226 Williams Lane, P.O. Box 299, West Hurley, NY 12491 / 866-686-7424; FAX: 877-GUNPART info@gunpartscorp.com www.@-gunparts.com
Nygord Precision Products, Inc., P.O. Box 12578, Prescott, AZ 86304 / 928-717-2315; FAX: 928-717-2198 nygords@northlink.com www.nygordprecision.com

O

O.F. Mossberg & Sons, Inc., 7 Grasso Ave., North Haven, CT 06473 / 203-230-5300; FAX: 203-230-5420
Oakman Turkey Calls, RD 1, Box 825, Harrisonville, PA 17228 / 717-485-4620
Obermeyer Rifled Barrels, 23122 60th St., Bristol, WI 53104 / 262-843-3537; FAX: 262-843-2129
October Country Muzzleloading, P.O. Box 969, Dept. GD, Hayden, ID 83835 / 208-772-2068; FAX: 208-772-9230 ocinfo@octobercountry.com www.octobercountry.com
Oehler Research, Inc., P.O. Box 9135, Austin, TX 78766 / 512-327-6900; or 800-531-5125; FAX: 512-327-6903 www.oehler-research.com
Oil Rod and Gun Shop, 69 Oak St., East Douglas, MA 01516 / 508-476-3687
OK Weber, Inc., P.O. Box 7485, Eugene, OR 97401 / 541-747-0458; FAX: 541-747-5927 okweber@pacinfo www.okweber.com
Oker's Engraving, P.O. Box 126, Shawnee, CO 80475 / 303-838-6042
Oklahoma Ammunition Co., 3701A S. Harvard Ave., No. 367, Tulsa, OK 74135-2265 / 918-396-3187; FAX: 918-396-4270
Oklahoma Leather Products, Inc., 500 26th NW, Miami, OK 74354 / 918-542-6651; FAX: 918-542-6653
Olathe Gun Shop, 716-A South Rogers Road, Olathe, KS 66062 / 913-782-6900; FAX: 913-782-6902 info@olathegunshop.com www.olathegunshop.com
Old Wagon Bullets, 32 Old Wagon Rd., Wilton, CT 06897
Old West Bullet Moulds, J Ken Chapman, P.O. Box 519, Flora Vista, NM 87415 / 505-334-6970
Old West Reproductions, Inc. R.M. Bachman, 446 Florence S. Loop, Florence, MT 59833 / 406-273-2615; FAX: 406-273-2615 rick@oldwestreproductions.com www.oldwestreproductions.com
Old Western Scrounger Ammunition Inc., 50 Industrial Parkway, Carson City, NV 89706 / 775-246-2091; FAX: 775-246-2095 www.ows-ammunition.com
Old World Gunsmithing, 2901 SE 122nd St., Portland, OR 97236 / 503-760-7681
Old World Oil Products, 3827 Queen Ave. N., Minneapolis, MN 55412 / 612-522-5037
Ole Frontier Gunsmith Shop, 2617 Hwy. 29 S., Cantonment, FL 32533 / 904-477-8074
Olson, Myron, 989 W. Kemp, Watertown, SD 57201 / 605-886-9787
Olson, Vic, 5002 Countryside Dr., Imperial, MO 63052 / 314-296-8086
Olympic Arms Inc., 620-626 Old Pacific Hwy. SE, Olympia, WA 98513 / 360-456-3471; FAX: 360-491-3447 info@olyarms.com www.olyarms.com
Olympic Optical Co., P.O. Box 752377, Memphis, TN 38175-2377 / 901-794-3890; or 800-238-7120; FAX: 901-794-0676 80
Omega Sales, P.O. Box 1066, Mt. Clemens, MI 48043 / 810-469-7323; FAX: 810-469-0425
100 Straight Products, Inc., P.O. Box 6148, Omaha, NE 68106 / 402-556-1055; FAX: 402-556-1055
One Of A Kind, 15610 Purple Sage, San Antonio, TX 78255 / 512-695-3364
One Ragged Hole, P.O. Box 13624, Tallahassee, FL 32317-3624
Op-Tec, P.O. Box L632, Langhorn, PA 19047 / 215-757-5037; FAX: 215-757-7097
Optical Services Co., P.O. Box 1174, Santa Teresa, NM 88008-1174 / 505-589-3833
Orchard Park Enterprise, P.O. Box 563, Orchard Park, NY 14127 / 616-656-0356
Oregon Arms, Inc. (See Rogue Rifle Co., Inc.)
Oregon Trail Bullet Company, PO Box 529, Dept. P, Baker City, OR 97814 / 800-811-0548; FAX: 514-523-1803
Original Box, Inc., 700 Linden Ave., York, PA 17404 / 717-854-2897; FAX: 717-845-4276
Original Deer Formula Co., The, P.O. Box 1705, Dickson, TN 37056 / 800-874-6965; FAX: 615-446-0646 deerformula1@aol.com www.deerformula
Orion Rifle Barrel Co., RR2, 137 Cobler Village, Kalispell, MT 59901 / 406-257-5649
Otis Technology, Inc., RR 1 Box 84, Boonville, NY 13309 / 315-942-3320
Ottmar, Maurice, Box 657, 113 E. Fir, Coulee City, WA 99115 / 509-632-5717
Outa-Site Gun Carriers, 219 Market St., Laredo, TX 78040 / 210-722-4678; or 800-880-9715; FAX: 210-726-4858
Outdoor Edge Cutlery Corp., 4699 Nautilus Ct. S. Ste. 503, Boulder, CO 80301-5310 / 303-652-8212; FAX: 303-652-8238
Outdoor Enthusiast, 3784 W. Woodland, Springfield, MO 65807 / 417-883-9841
Outdoor Sports Headquarters, Inc., 967 Watertower Ln., West Carrollton, OH 45449 / 513-865-5855; FAX: 513-865-5962
Outers Laboratories Div. of ATK, Route 2, P.O. Box 39, Onalaska, WI 54650 / 608-781-5800; FAX: 608-781-0368
Ox-Yoke Originals, Inc., 34 Main St., Milo, ME 04463 / 800-231-8313; or 207-943-7351; FAX: 207-943-2416
Ozark Gun Works, 11830 Cemetery Rd., Rogers, AR 72756 / 479-631-1024; FAX: 479-631-1024 ogw@hotmail.com www.eocities.com/ocarkgunworks

P

P&M Sales & Services, LLC, 4697 Tote Rd. Bldg. H-B, Comins, MI 48619 / 989-848-8364; FAX: 989-848-8364 info@pmsales-online.com
P.A.C.T., Inc., P.O. Box 531525, Grand Prairie, TX 75053 / 214-641-0049
P.S.M.G. Gun Co., 10 Park Ave., Arlington, MA 02174 / 781-646-1699; FAX: 781-643-7212 psmg2@aol.com
Pachmayr Div. Lyman Products, 475 Smith St., Middletown, CT 06457 / 860-632-2020; or 800-225-9626; FAX: 860-632-1699 lymansales@cshore.com www.pachmayr.com
Pacific Armament Corp, 4813 Enterprise Way, Unit K, Modesto, CA 95356 / 209-545-2800 gunsparts@att.net
Pacific Rifle Co., P.O. Box 841, Carlton, OR 97111 / 503-852-6276 pacificrifle@aol.com
PAC-NOR Barreling, 99299 Overlook Rd., P.O. Box 6188, Brookings, OR 97415 / 503-469-7330; FAX: 503-469-7331 info@pac-nor.com www.pac-nor.com
Paco's (See Small Custom Mould & Bullet Co.)
Page Custom Bullets, P.O. Box 25, Port Moresby, NEW GUINEA
Pagel Gun Works, Inc., 2 SE 1st St., Grand Rapids, MN 55744
Pager Pal, 200 W Pleasantview, Hurst, TX 76054 / 800-561-1603; FAX: 817-285-8769 www.pagerpal.com
Paintball Games International Magazine Aceville, Castle House 97 High St., Essex, ENGLAND / 011-44-206-564840
Palsa Outdoor Products, P.O. Box 81336, Lincoln, NE 68501 / 402-488-5288; FAX: 402-488-2321
Pansch, Robert F, 1004 Main St. #10, Neenah, WI 54956 / 920-725-8175
Paragon Sales & Services, Inc., 2501 Theodore St., Crest Hill, IL 60435-1613 / 815-725-9212; FAX: 815-725-8974
Para-Ordnance Mfg., Inc., 980 Tapscott Rd., Scarborough, ON M1X 1E7 CANADA / 416-297-7855; FAX: 416-297-1289
Para-Ordnance, Inc., 1919 NE 45th St., Ste 215, Ft. Lauderdale, FL 33308 info@paraord.com www.paraord.com
Pardini Armi Srl, Via Italica 154, 55043, Lido Di Camaiore Lu, ITALY / 584-90121; FAX: 584-90122
Paris, Frank J., 17417 Pershing St., Livonia, MI 48152-3822
Parker & Sons Shooting Supply, 9337 Smoky Row Road, Strawberry Plains, TN 37871 / 865-933-3286; FAX: 865-932-8586
Parker Gun Finishes, 9337 Smokey Row Rd., Strawberry Plains, TN 37871 / 865-933-3286; FAX: 865-932-8586
Parsons Optical Mfg. Co., PO Box 192, Ross, OH 45061 / 513-867-0820; FAX: 513-867-8380 psscopes@concentric.net
Partridge Sales Ltd., John, Trent Meadows, Rugeley, ENGLAND
Pasadena Gun Center, 206 E. Shaw, Pasadena, TX 77506 / 713-472-0417; FAX: 713-472-1322
Passive Bullet Traps, Inc. (See Savage Range Systems, Inc.)
Paterson Gunsmithing, 438 Main St., Paterson, NJ 07502 / 201-345-4100

MANUFACTURER'S DIRECTORY

Pathfinder Sports Leather, 2920 E. Chambers St., Phoenix, AZ 85040 / 602-276-0016

Patrick W. Price Bullets, 16520 Worthley Drive, San Lorenzo, CA 94580 / 510-278-1547

Pattern Control, 114 N. Third St., P.O. Box 462105, Garland, TX 75046 / 214-494-3551; FAX: 214-272-8447

Paul A. Harris Hand Engraving, 113 Rusty Lane, Boerne, TX 78006-5746 / 512-391-5121

Paul and Sharon Dressel, 209 N. 92nd Ave., Yakima, WA 98908 / 509-966-9233; FAX: 509-966-3365 dressels@nwinfo.net www.dressels.com

Paul D. Hillmer Custom Gunstocks, 7251 Hudson Heights, Hudson, IA 50643 / 319-988-3941

Paul Jones Moulds, 4901 Telegraph Rd., Los Angeles, CA 90022 / 213-262-1510

Paulsen Gunstocks, Rt. 71, Box 11, Chinook, MT 59523 / 406-357-3403

Pawling Mountain Club, Keith Lupton, PO Box 573, Pawling, NY 12564 / 914-855-3825

Paxton Quigley's Personal Protection Strategies, 9903 Santa Monica Blvd., 300, Beverly Hills, CA 90212 / 310-281-1762 www.defend-net.com/paxton

Payne Photography, Robert, Robert, P.O. Box 141471, Austin, TX 78714 / 512-272-4554

Peacemaker Specialists, P.O. Box 157, Whitmore, CA 96096 / 530-472-3438 www.peacemakerspecialists.com

Pearce Grip, Inc., P.O. Box 40367, Fort Worth, TX 76140 / 817-568-9704; FAX: 817-568-9707 info@pearcegrip.com www.pearcegrip.com

Pease Accuracy, Bob, P.O. Box 310787, New Braunfels, TX 78131 / 210-625-1342

PECAR Herbert Schwarz GmbH, Kreuzbergstrasse 6, 10965, Berlin, GERMANY / 004930-785-7383; FAX: 004930-785-1934 michael.schwart@pecar-berlin.de www.pecar-berlin.de

Pecatonica River Longrifle, 5205 Nottingham Dr., Rockford, IL 61111 / 815-968-1995; FAX: 815-968-1996

Pedersen, C. R., 2717 S. Pere Marquette Hwy., Ludington, MI 49431 / 231-843-2061; FAX: 231-845-7695 fega@fega.com

Pedersen, Rex C., 2717 S. Pere Marquette Hwy., Ludington, MI 49431 / 231-843-2061; FAX: 231-845-7695 fega@fega.com

Peifer Rifle Co., P.O. Box 220, Nokomis, IL 62075

Pejsa Ballistics, 1314 Marquette Ave., Apt 906, Minneapolis, MN 55403 / 612-332-5073; FAX: 612-332-5204 pejsa@sprintmail.com pejsa.com

Pelaire Products, 5346 Bonky Ct., W. Palm Beach, FL 33415 / 561-439-0691; FAX: 561-967-0052

Peltor, Inc. (See Aero Peltor)

PEM's Mfg. Co., 5063 Waterloo Rd., Atwater, OH 44201 / 216-947-3721

Pence Precision Barrels, 7567 E. 900 S., S. Whitley, IN 46787 / 219-839-4745

Pendleton Royal, c/o Swingler Buckland Ltd., 4/7 Highgate St., Birmingham, ENGLAND / 44 121 440 3060; or 44 121 446 5898; FAX: 44 121 446 4165

Pendleton Woolen Mills, P.O. Box 3030, 220 N.W. Broadway, Portland, OR 97208 / 503-226-4801

Penn Bullets, P.O. Box 756, Indianola, PA 15051

Pennsylvania Gun Parts Inc., RR 7 Box 150, Mount Pleasant, PA 15666

Pennsylvania Gunsmith School, 812 Ohio River Blvd., Avalon, Pittsburgh, PA 15202 / 412-766-1812; FAX: 412-766-0855 pgs@pagunsmith.com www.pagunsmith.com

Penrod Precision, 312 College Ave., P.O. Box 307, N. Manchester, IN 46962 / 260-982-8385; FAX: 260-982-1819

Pentax Corp., 35 Inverness Dr. E., Englewood, CO 80112 / 303-799-8000; FAX: 303-790-1131

Pentheny de Pentheny, c/o H.P. Okelly, 321 S. Main St., Sebastopol, CA 95472 / 707-824-1637; FAX: 707-824-1637

Perazone-Gunsmith, Brian, Cold Spring Rd., Roxbury, NY 12474 / 607-326-4088; FAX: 607-326-3140 bpgunsmith@catskill.net www.bpgunsmith@catskill.net

Perazzi U.S.A. Inc., 1010 West Tenth, Azusa, CA 91702 / 626-334-1234; FAX: 626-334-0344 perazziusa@aol.com

Performance Specialists, 308 Eanes School Rd., Austin, TX 78746 / 512-327-0119

Perugini Visini & Co. S.r.l., Via Camprelle, 126, 25080 Nuvolera, ITALY / 30-6897535; FAX: 30-6897821 peruvisi@virgilia.it

Pete de Coux Auction House, HC 30 Box 932 G, Prescott, AZ 86305-7447 / 928-776-8285; FAX: 928-776-8276 pdbullets@commspeed.net

Pete Mazur Restoration, 13083 Drummer Way, Grass Valley, CA 95949 / 530-268-2412; FAX: 530-268-2412

Pete Rickard, Inc., 115 Roy Walsh Rd, Cobleskill, NY 12043 / 518-234-2731: FAX: 518-234-2454 rickard@telenet.net www.peterickard.com

Peter Dyson & Son Ltd., 3 Cuckoo Lane, Honley, Holmfirth, Yorkshire, HD9 6AS ENGLAND / 44-1484-661062; FAX: 44-1484-663709 peter@peterdyson.co.uk www.peterdyson.co.uk

Peter Hale/Engraver, 800 E. Canyon Rd., Spanish Fork, UT 84660 / 801-798-8215

Peters Stahl GmbH, Stettiner Strasse 42, D-33106, Paderborn, GERMANY / 05251-750025; FAX: 05251-75611

Peterson Gun Shop, Inc., A.W., 4255 W. Old U.S. 441, Mt. Dora, FL 32757-3299 / 352-383-4258; FAX: 352-735-1001

Petro-Explo Inc., 7650 U.S. Hwy. 287, Suite 100, Arlington, TX 76017 / 817-478-8888

Pettinger Books, Gerald, 47827 300th Ave., Russell, IA 50238 / 641-535-2239 gpettinger@lisco.com

Pflumm Mfg. Co., 10662 Widmer Rd., Lenexa, KS 66215 / 800-888-4867; FAX: 913-451-7857

PFRB Co., P.O. Box 1242, Bloomington, IL 61702 / 309-473-3964; or 800-914-5464; FAX: 309-473-2161

Philip S. Olt Co., P.O. Box 550, 12662 Fifth St., Pekin, IL 61554 / 309-348-3633; FAX: 309-348-3300

Phillippi Custom Bullets, Justin, P.O. Box 773, Ligonier, PA 15658 / 724-238-2962; FAX: 724-238-9671 jrp@wpa.net http://www.wpa.net~jrphil

Phillips & Rogers, Inc., 100 Hilbig #C, Conroe, TX 77301 / 409-435-0011

Phoenix Arms, 4231 Brickell St., Ontario, CA 91761 / 909-937-6900; FAX: 909-937-0060

Photronic Systems Engineering Company, 6731 Via De La Reina, Bonsall, CA 92003 / 619-758-8000

Piedmont Community College, P.O. Box 1197, Roxboro, NC 27573 / 336-599-1181; FAX: 336-597-3817 www.piedmont.cc.nc.us

Pierce Pistols, 55 Sorrellwood Lane, Sharpsburg, GA 30277-9523 / 404-253-8192

Pietta (See U.S. Importers-Navy Arms Co, Taylor's

Pilgrim Pewter, Inc. (See Bell Originals Inc. Sid)

Pilkington, Scott (See Little Trees Ramble)

Pine Technical College, 1100 4th St., Pine City, MN 55063 / 800-521-7463; FAX: 612-629-6766

Pinetree Bullets, 133 Skeena St., Kitimat, BC V8C 1Z1 CANADA / 604-632-3768; FAX: 604-632-3768

Pioneer Arms Co., 355 Lawrence Rd., Broomall, PA 19008 / 215-356-5203

Piotti (See U.S. Importer-Moore & Co., Wm. Larkin)

Piquette, Paul. See: PIQUETTE'S CUSTOM ENGRAVING

Piquette's Custom Engraving, Paul R. Piquette, 80 Bradford Dr., Feeding Hills, MA 01030 / 413-789-4582; FAX: 413-786-8118 ppiquette@aol.com www.pistoldynamics.com

Plaza Cutlery, Inc., 3333 Bristol, 161 South Coast Plaza, Costa Mesa, CA 92626 / 714-549-3932

Plum City Ballistic Range, N2162 80th St., Plum City, WI 54761 / 715-647-2539

PlumFire Press, Inc., 30-A Grove Ave., Patchogue, NY 11772-4112 / 800-695-7246; FAX: 516-758-4071

PMC/Eldorado Cartridge Corp., P.O. Box 62508, 12801 U.S. Hwy. 95 S., Boulder City, NV 89005 / 702-294-0025; FAX: 702-294-0121 kbauer@pmcammo.com www.pmcammo.com

Poburka, Philip (See Bison Studios)

Pointing Dog Journal, Village Press Publications, P.O. Box 968, Dept. PGD, Traverse City, MI 49685 / 800-272-3246; FAX: 616-946-3289

Police Bookshelf, PO Box 122, Concord, NH 03301 / 603-224-6814; FAX: 603-226-3554

Polywad, Inc., P.O. Box 7916, Macon, GA 31209 / 478-477-0669; or 800-998-0669 FAX: 478-477-0666 polywadmpb@aol.com www.polywad.com

Ponsness/Warren, 768 Ohio St., Rathdrum, ID 83858 / 800-732-0706; FAX: 208-687-2233

Pony Express Reloaders, 608 E. Co. Rd. D, Suite 3, St. Paul, MN 55117 / 612-483-9406; FAX: 612-483-9884

Pony Express Sport Shop, 23404 Lyons Ave., PMB 448, Newhall, CA 91321-2511 / 818-895-1231

Potts, Wayne E., 912 Poplar St., Denver, CO 80220 / 303-355-5462

Powder Horn Ltd., PO Box 565, Glenview, IL 60025 / 305-565-6060

Powell & Son (Gunmakers) Ltd., William, 35-37 Carrs Lane, Birmingham, B4 7SX ENGLAND / 121-643-0689; FAX: 121-631-3504 sales@william-powell.co.uk www.william-powell.co.uk

Powell Agency, William, 22 Circle Dr., Bellmore, NY 11710 / 516-679-1158

Power Custom, Inc., 29739 Hwy. J, Gravois Mills, MO 6 / 573-372-5684; FAX: 573-372-5799 rwpowers@laurie.net www.powercustom.com

Power Plus Enterprises, Inc., PO Box 38, Warm Spring 31830 / 706-655-2132

Powley Computer (See Hutton Rifle Ranch)

Practical Tools, Inc., 7067 Easton Rd., P.O. Box 133, Pipersville, PA 18947 / 215-766-7301; FAX: 215-766-8681

Prairie Gun Works, 1-761 Marion St., Winnipeg, MB R2 CANADA / 204-231-2976; FAX: 204-231-8566

Prairie River Arms, 1220 N. Sixth St., Princeton, IL 613 815-875-1616; or 800-445-1541; FAX: 815-875-14

Pranger, Ed G., 1414 7th St., Anacortes, WA 98221 / 206-293-3488

Precision Airgun Sales, Inc., 5247 Warrensville Ctr Rd., Maple Hts., OH 44137 / 216-587-5005; FAX: 216-587-5005

Precision Cast Bullets, 101 Mud Creek Lane, Ronan, MT 59864 / 406-676-5135

Precision Delta Corp., PO Box 128, Ruleville, MS 38771 662-756-2810; FAX: 662-756-2590

Precision Firearm Finishing, 25 N.W. 44th Avenue, Des Moines, IA 50313 / 515-288-8680; FAX: 515-244-3

Precision Gun Works, 104 Sierra Rd., Dept. GD, Kerrville 78028 / 830-367-4587

Precision Reloading, Inc., P.O. Box 122, Stafford Springs 06076 / 860-684-7979; FAX: 860-684-6788 info@precisionreloading.com www.precisionreloading.com

Precision Sales International, Inc., PO Box 1776, Westfie MA 01086 / 413-562-5055; FAX: 413-562-5056 precision-sales.com

Precision Shooting, Inc., 222 McKee St., Manchester, CT 06040 / 860-645-8776; FAX: 860-643-8215 www.theaccuraterifle.com

Precision Small Arms Inc., 9272 Jeronimo Rd, Ste 121, Irvine, CA 92618 / 800-554-5515; or 949-768-3530; FAX: 949-768-4808 www.tcbebe.com

Precision Specialties, 131 Hendom Dr., Feeding Hills, MA 01030 / 413-786-3365; FAX: 413-786-3365

Precision Sport Optics, 15571 Producer Lane, Unit G, Huntington Beach, CA 92649 / 714-891-1309; FAX: 714-892-6920

Premier Reticles, 920 Breckinridge Lane, Winchester, VA 22601-6707 / 540-722-0601; FAX: 540-722-3522

Prescott Projectile Co., 1808 Meadowbrook Road, Presco AZ 86303

Preslik's Gunstocks, 4245 Keith Ln., Chico, CA 95926 / 916-891-8236

Price Bullets, Patrick W., 16520 Worthley Dr., San Lorenz CA 94580 / 510-278-1547

Prime Reloading, 30 Chiswick End, Meldreth, ROYSTON U / 0763-260636

Primedia Publishing Co., 6420 Wilshire Blvd., Los Angeles CA 90048 / 213-782-2000; FAX: 213-782-2867

Primos Hunting Calls, 4436 North State St., Ste. A-7, Jackson, MS 39206 / 601-366-1288; FAX: 601-362-3274 www.primos.com

PRL Bullets, c/o Blackburn Enterprises, 114 Stuart Rd., Ste 110, Cleveland, TN 37312 / 423-559-0340

Pro Load Ammunition, Inc., 5180 E. Seltice Way, Post Falls ID 83854 / 208-773-9444; FAX: 208-773-9441

Professional Gunsmiths of America, Rt 1 Box 224, Lexingto MO 64067 / 660-259-2636

Professional Hunter Supplies (See Star Custom Bullets), P.O Box 608, 468 Main St., Ferndale, CA 95536 / 707-786-9140; FAX: 707-786-9117 wmebride@humboldt.com

PrOlixr Lubricants, P.O. Box 1348, Victorville, CA 92393 / 760-243-3129; FAX: 760-241-0148 prolix@accex.net www.prolixlubricant.com

Pro-Mark Div. of Wells Lamont, 6640 W. Touhy, Chicago, IL 60648 / 312-647-8200

Proofmark Corp., P.O. Box 357, Burgess, VA 22432 / 804-453-4337; FAX: 804-453-4337 proofmark@rivnet.net www.proofmarkbullets.com

Pro-Port Ltd., 41302 Executive Dr., Harrison Twp., MI 48045-1306 / 586-469-6727; FAX: 586-469-0425 e-mail@magnaport.com www.magnaport.com

Pro-Shot Products, Inc., P.O. Box 763, Taylorville, IL 62568 / 217-824-9133; FAX: 217-824-8861 www.proshotproducts.com

Protektor Model, 1-11 Bridge St., Galeton, PA 16922 / 814-435-2442 mail@protektormodel.com www.protektormodel.com

Prototech Industries, Inc., 10532 E Road, Delia, KS 66418 / 785-771-3571 prototec@grapevine.net

are, Inc., 15847 NE Hancock St., Portland, OR 97230 /)3-239-0159
Gunleather, P.O. Box 450432, Atlanta, GA 31145 /)0-960-4072; FAX: 770-822-1704 covert@pwlusa.com ww.pwlusa.com
Sales Ltd., N.D.F.S., Gowdall Lane, Pollington DN14 AU, ENGLAND / 01405862688; FAX: 01405862622 aulwelburn9@aol.com
nyd Stone Inter. Corp., 2447 Suffolk Lane, Pepper Pike, H 44124-4540

Q

k Decoy & Sporting Clays, 4 Ann & Hope Way, P.O. Box 8, Cumberland, RI 02864 / 401-723-8202; FAX: 01-722-5910
er Boy, Inc., 5455 Webster Rd., Orchard Parks, NY 4127 / 716-662-3979; FAX: 716-662-9426
ity Arms, Inc., Box 19477, Dept. GD, Houston, TX 77224 281-870-8377 arrieta2@excite.com www.gunshop.com
ity Cartridge, P.O. Box 445, Hollywood, MD 20636 / 301-373-3719 www.qual-cart.com
ity Custom Firearms, Stepehn Billeb, 22 Vista View Drive, Cody, WY 82414 / 307-587-4278; FAX: 307-587-4297 stevebilleb@wyoming.com
rton Beamshot, 4538 Centerview Dr., Ste. 149, San Antonio, TX 78228 / 800-520-8435; FAX: 210-735-1326 www.beamshot.com
Industries, Inc., PO Box 2471, Everett, WA 98203 / 425-303-9088; FAX: 206-514-3266 queinfo@queindustries.com
en Cutlery Co., PO Box 500, Franklinville, NY 14737 / 800-222-5233; FAX: 800-299-2618

R

C Knives & Such, 2136 CANDY CANE WALK, Manteca, CA 95336-9501 / 209-239-3722; FAX: 209-825-6947
D Gun Repair, Kenny Howell, RR1 Box 283, Beloit, WI 53511
J Gun Shop, 337 S. Humbolt St., Canyon City, OR 97820 / 541-575-2130 rjgunshop@highdestertnet.com
S Industries Corp., 8255 Brentwood Industrial Dr., St. Louis, MO 63144 / 314-781-5169 ron@miraclepolishingcloth.com www.miraclepolishingcloth.com
Murphy Co., Inc., 13 Groton-Harvard Rd., P.O. Box 376, Ayer, MA 01432 / 617-772-3481 www.r.murphyknives.com
A. Wells Custom Gunsmith, 3452 1st Ave., Racine, WI 53402 / 414-639-5223
E. Seebeck Assoc., P.O. Box 59752, Dallas, TX 75229
E.I., P.O. Box 88, Tallevast, FL 34270 / 813-755-0085
E.T. Enterprises, 2608 S. Chestnut, Broken Arrow, OK 74012 / 918-251-GUNS; FAX: 918-251-0587
F. Mitchell Bullets, 430 Walnut St., Westernport, MD 21562
I.S. Co., Inc., 718 Timberlake Circle, Richardson, TX 75080 / 214-235-0933
T. Eastman Products, P.O. Box 1531, Jackson, WY 83001 / 307-733-3217; or 800-624-4311
abeno, Martin, 530 The Eagle Pass, Durango, CO 81301 / 970-382-0353 fancygun@aol.com
adack Photography, Lauren, 21140 Jib Court L-12, Aventura, FL 33180 / 305-931-3110
adiator Specialty Co., 1900 Wilkinson Blvd., P.O. Box 34689, Charlotte, NC 28234 / 800-438-6947; FAX: 800-421-9525
adical Concepts, P.O. Box 1473, Lake Grove, OR 97035 / 503-538-7437
Rainier Ballistics, 4500 15th St. East, Tacoma, WA 98424 / 800-638-8722; FAX: 253-922-7854 sales@rainierballistics.com www.rainierballistics.com
Ralph Bone Engraving, 718 N. Atlanta St., Owasso, OK 74055 / 918-272-9745
Ram-Line ATK, P.O. Box 39, Onalaska, WI 54650
Ramon B. Gonzalez Guns, P.O. Box 370, Monticello, NY 12701 / 914-794-4515; FAX: 914-794-4515
Rampart International, 2781 W. MacArthur Blvd., B-283, Santa Ana, CA 92704 / 800-976-7240 or 714-557-6405
Ranch Products, P.O. Box 145, Malinta, OH 43535 / 313-277-3118; FAX: 313-565-8536
Randall-Made Knives, P.O. Box 1988, Orlando, FL 32802 / 407-855-8075
Randco UK, 286 Gipsy Rd., Welling, DA16 1JJ ENGLAND / 44 81 303 4118
Randolph Engineering, Inc., Ranger Shooting Glasses, 26 Thomas Patten Dr., Randolph, MA 02368 / 800-541-1405; FAX: 781-986-0337 sales@randolphusa.com www.randolphusa.com
Randy Duane Custom Stocks, 7822 Church St., Middletown, VA 22645-9521
Range Brass Products Company, P.O. Box 218, Rockport, TX 78381
Ransom International Corp., 1027 Spire Dr, Prescott, AZ 86302 / 520-778-7899; FAX: 520-778-7993 ransom@primenet.com www.ransom-intl.com
Rapine Bullet Mould Mfg. Co., 9503 Landis Lane, East Greenville, PA 18041 / 215-679-5413; FAX: 215-679-9795
Ravell Ltd., 289 Diputacion St., 08009, Barcelona, SPAIN / 34(3) 4874486; FAX: 34(3) 4881394
Ray Riling Arms Books Co., 6844 Gorsten St., Philadelphia, PA 19119 / 215-438-2456; FAX: 215-438-5395 sales@rayrilingarmsbooks.com www.rayrilingarmsbooks.com
Ray's Gunsmith Shop, 3199 Elm Ave., Grand Junction, CO 81504 / 970-434-6162; FAX: 970-434-6162
Raytech Div. of Lyman Products Corp., 475 Smith Street, Middletown, CT 06457-1541 / 860-632-2020 or 800-225-9626; FAX: 860-632-1699 raysales@cshore.com www.raytech-ind.com
RCBS Operations/ATK, 605 Oro Dam Blvd., Oroville, CA 95965 / 530-533-5191 or 800-533-5000; FAX: 530-533-1647 www.rcbs.com
Reardon Products, P.O. Box 126, Morrison, IL 61270 / 815-772-3155
Red Diamond Dist. Co., 1304 Snowdon Dr., Knoxville, TN 37912
Redding Reloading Equipment, 1089 Starr Rd., Cortland, NY 13045 / 607-753-3331; FAX: 607-756-8445 techline@redding-reloading.com www.redding-reloading.com
Redfield Media Resource Center, 4607 N.E. Cedar Creek Rd., Woodland, WA 98674 / 360-225-5000; FAX: 360-225-7616
Redman's Rifling & Reboring, 189 Nichols Rd., Omak, WA 98841 / 509-826-5512
Redwood Bullet Works, 3559 Bay Rd., Redwood City, CA 94063 / 415-367-6741
Reed, Dave, Rt. 1, Box 374, Minnesota City, MN 55959 / 507-689-2944
Reimer Johannsen, Inc., 438 Willow Brook Rd., Plainfield, NH 03781 / 603-469-3450; FAX: 603-469-3471
Reloaders Equipment Co., 4680 High St., Ecorse, MI 48229
Reloading Specialties, Inc., Box 1130, Pine Island, MN 55463 / 507-356-8500; FAX: 507-356-8800
Remington Arms Co., Inc., 870 Remington Drive, P.O. Box 700, Madison, NC 27025-0700 / 800-243-9700; FAX: 910-548-8700
Remington Double Shotguns, 7885 Cyd Dr., Denver, CO 80221 / 303-429-6947
Renato Gamba S.p.A.-Societa Armi Bresciane Srl., Via Artigiani 93, 25063 Gardone, Val Trompia (BS), ITALY / 30-8911640; FAX: 30-8911648
Renegade, P.O. Box 31546, Phoenix, AZ 85046 / 602-482-6777; FAX: 602-482-1952
Renfrew Guns & Supplies, R.R. 4, Renfrew, ON K7V 3Z7 CANADA / 613-432-7080
Reno, Wayne, 2808 Stagestop Road, Jefferson, CO 80456
Republic Arms, Inc. (See Cobra Enterprises, Inc.)
Retting, Inc., Martin B., 11029 Washington, Culver City, CA 90232 / 213-837-2412
RG-G, Inc., P.O. Box 935, Trinidad, CO 81082 / 719-845-1436
RH Machine & Consulting Inc., P.O. Box 394, Pacific, MO 63069 / 314-271-8465
Rhino, P.O. Box 787, Locust, NC 28097 / 704-753-2198
Rhodeside, Inc., 1704 Commerce Dr., Piqua, OH 45356 / 513-773-5781
Rice, Keith (See White Rock Tool & Die)
Richards Micro-Fit Stocks, 8331 N. San Fernando Ave., Sun Valley, CA 91352 / 818-767-6097; FAX: 818-767-7121
Ridgeline, Inc., Bruce Sheldon, P.O. Box 930, Dewey, AZ 86327-0930 / 800-632-5900; FAX: 520-632-5900
Ridgetop Sporting Goods, P.O. Box 306, 42907 Hilligoss Ln. East, Eatonville, WA 98328 / 360-832-6422; FAX: 360 832 6422
Ries, Chuck, 415 Ridgecrest Dr., Grants Pass, OR 97527 / 503-476-5623
Rifles, Inc., 3580 Leal Rd., Pleasanton, TX 78064 / 830-569-2055; FAX: 830-569-2297
Riggs, Jim, 206 Azalea, Boerne, TX 78006 / 210-249-8567
Riley Ledbetter Airguns, 1804 E. Sprague St., Winston Salem, NC 27107-3521 / 919-784-0676
Rim Pac Sports, Inc., 1034 N. Soldano Ave., Azusa, CA 91702-2135
Ringler Custom Leather Co., 31 Shining Mtn. Rd., Powell, WY 82435 / 307-645-3255
Ripley Rifles, 42 Fletcher Street, Ripley, Derbyshire, DE5 3LP ENGLAND / 011-0773-748353
Rizzini F.lli (See U.S. Importers-Moore & C England)
Rizzini SNC, Via 2 Giugno, 7/7Bis-25060, Marcheno (Brescia), ITALY
RLCM Enterprises, 110 Hill Crest Drive, Burleson, TX 76028
RMS Custom Gunsmithing, 4120 N. Bitterwell, Prescott Valley, AZ 86314 / 520-772-7626
Robert Evans Engraving, 332 Vine St., Oregon City, OR 97045 / 503-656-5693
Robert Valade Engraving, 931 3rd Ave., Seaside, OR 97138 / 503-738-7672
Robinett, R. G., P.O. Box 72, Madrid, IA 50156 / 515-795-2906
Robinson, Don, Pennsylvania Hse, 36 Fairfax Crescent, W Yorkshire, ENGLAND / 0422-364458 donrobinsonuk@yahoo.co.uk www.guns4u2.co.uk
Robinson Armament Co., PO Box 16776, Salt Lake City, UT 84116 / 801-355-0401; FAX: 801-355-0402 zdf@robarm.com www.robarm.com
Robinson Firearms Mfg. Ltd., 1699 Blondeaux Crescent, Kelowna, BC V1Y 4J8 CANADA / 604-868-9596
Robinson H.V. Bullets, 3145 Church St., Zachary, LA 70791 / 504-654-4029
Rochester Lead Works, 76 Anderson Ave., Rochester, NY 14607 / 716-442-8500; FAX: 716-442-4712
Rock River Arms, 101 Noble St., Cleveland, IL 61241
Rockwood Corp., Speedwell Division, 136 Lincoln Blvd., Middlesex, NJ 08846 / 800-243-8274; FAX: 980-560-7475
Rocky Mountain Armoury, Mr. Felix LesMerises, 610 Main Street, P.O. Box 691, Frisco, CO 80443-0691 / 970-668-0136; FAX: 970-668-4484 felix@rockymountainarmoury.com
Rocky Mountain Arms, Inc., 1813 Sunset Pl, Unit D, Longmont, CO 80501 / 800-375-0846; FAX: 303-678-8766
Rocky Mountain Target Co., 3 Aloe Way, Leesburg, FL 34788 / 352-365-9598
Rocky Mountain Wildlife Products, P.O. Box 999, La Porte, CO 80535 / 970-484-2768; FAX: 970-484-0807 critrcall@earthlink.net www.critrcall.com
Rocky Shoes & Boots, 294 Harper St., Nelsonville, OH 45764 / 800-848-9452; or 614-753-1951; FAX: 614-753-4024
Rogue Rifle Co., Inc., 1140 36th St. N., Ste. B, Lewiston, ID 83501 / 208-743-4355; FAX: 208-743-4163
Rogue River Rifleworks, 500 Linne Road #D, Paso Robles, CA 93446 / 805-227-4706; FAX: 805-227-4723 rrrifles@calinet.com
Rohner, Hans, 1148 Twin Sisters Ranch Rd., Nederland, CO 80466-9600
Rohner, John, 186 Virginia Ave, Asheville, NC 28806 / 303-444-3841
Rohrbaugh, P.O. Box 785, Bayport, NY 11705 / 631-363-2843; FAX: 631-363-2681 API380@aol.com
Romain's Custom Guns, Inc., RD 1, Whetstone Rd., Brockport, PA 15823 / 814-265-1948 romwhetstone@penn.com
Ron Frank Custom Classic Arms, 7131 Richland Rd., Ft. Worth, TX 76118 / 817-284-9300; FAX: 817-284-9300 rfrank3974@aol.com
Rooster Laboratories, P.O. Box 414605, Kansas City, MO 64141 / 816-474-1622; FAX: 816-474-7622
Rorschach Precision Products, 417 Keats Cir., Irving, TX 75061 / 214-790-3487
Rosenberg & Son, Jack A., 12229 Cox Ln., Dallas, TX 75234 / 214-241-6302
Ross, Don, 12813 West 83 Terrace, Lenexa, KS 66215 / 913-492-6982
Rosser, Bob, 2809 Crescent Ave., Suite 20, Homewood, AL 35209 / 205-870-4422; FAX: 205-870-4421 www.hand-engravers.com
Rossi Firearms, Gary Mchalik, 16175 NW 49th Ave., Miami, FL 33014-6314 / 305-474-0401; FAX: 305-623-7506
Rottweil Compe, 1330 Glassell, Orange, CA 92667
Roy Baker's Leather Goods, PO Box 893, Magnolia, AR 71754 / 870-234-0344
Royal Arms Gunstocks, 919 8th Ave. NW, Great Falls, MT 59404 / 406-453-1149 royalarms@lmt.net www.lmt.net/~royalarms
Royal Arms International, R J Brill, P.O. Box 6083, Woodland Hills, CA 91365 / 818-704-5110; FAX: 818-887-2059 royalarms.com

Roy's Custom Grips, 793 Mt. Olivet Church Rd., Lynchburg, VA 24504 / 434-993-3470
RPM, 15481 N. Twin Lakes Dr., Tucson, AZ 85739 / 520-825-1233; FAX: 520-825-3333
Rubright Bullets, 1008 S. Quince Rd., Walnutport, PA 18088 / 215-767-1339
Rucker Dist. Inc., P.O. Box 479, Terrell, TX 75160 / 214-563-2094
Ruger (See Sturm, Ruger & Co., Inc.)
Ruger, Chris. See: RUGER'S CUSTOM GUNS
Ruger's Custom Guns, Chris Ruger, 1050 Morton Blvd., Kingston, NY 12401 / 845-336-7106; FAX: 845-336-7106 rugerscustom@outdrs.net rugergunsmith.com
Rundell's Gun Shop, 6198 Frances Rd., Clio, MI 48420 / 313-687-0559
Rupert's Gun Shop, 2202 Dick Rd., Suite B, Fenwick, MI 48834 / 517-248-3252 17rupert@pathwaynet.com
Russ Haydon's Shooters' Supply, 15018 Goodrich Dr. NW, Gig Harbor, WA 98329 / 877-663-6249; FAX: 253-857-7884 www.shooters-supply.com
Russ, William. See: BILL RUSS TRADING POST
Rusteprufe Laboratories, 1319 Jefferson Ave., Sparta, WI 54656 / 608-269-4144; FAX: 608-366-1972 rusteprufe@centurytel.net www.rusteprufe.com
Rusty Duck Premium Gun Care Products, 7785 Foundation Dr., Suite 6, Florence, KY 41042 / 606-342-5553; FAX: 606-342-5556
Rutgers Book Center, 127 Raritan Ave., Highland Park, NJ 08904 / 732-545-4344; FAX: 732-545-6686 gunbooks@rutgersgunbooks.com www.rutgersgunbooks.com
Rutten (See U.S. Importer-Labanu Inc)
RWS (See U.S. Importer-Dynamit Nobel-RWS, Inc.), 81 Ruckman Rd., Closter, NJ 07624 / 201-767-7971; FAX: 201-767-1589

S

S&K Scope Mounts, RD 2 Box 72E, Sugar Grove, PA 16350 / 814-489-3091; or 800-578-9862; FAX: 814-489-5466 comments@scopemounts.com www.scopemounts.com
S&S Firearms, 74-11 Myrtle Ave., Glendale, NY 11385 / 718-497-1100; FAX: 718-497-1105 info@ssfirearms.com ssfirearms.com
S.A.R.L. G. Granger, 66 cours Fauriel, 42100, Saint Etienne, FRANCE / 04 77 25 14 73; FAX: 04 77 38 66 99
S.C.R.C., P.O. Box 660, Katy, TX 77492-0660 FAX: 281-492-6332
S.D. Meacham, 1070 Angel Ridge, Peck, ID 83545
S.I.A.C.E. (See U.S. Importer-IAR Inc)
Sabatti SPA, Via A Volta 90, 25063 Gandome V.T.(BS), Brescia, ITALY / 030-8912207-831312; FAX: 030-8912059 info@sabatti.it www.sabatti.com
SAECO (See Redding Reloading Equipment)
Safari Arms/Schuetzen Pistol Works, 620-626 Old Pacific Hwy. SE, Olympia, WA 98513 / 360-459-3471; FAX: 360-491-3447 info@yarms.com www.olyarms.com
Safari Press, Inc., 15621 Chemical Lane B, Huntington Beach, CA 92649 / 714-894-9080; FAX: 714-894-4949 info@safaripress.com www.safaripress.com
Safariland Ltd., Inc., 3120 E. Mission Blvd., P.O. Box 51478, Ontario, CA 91761 / 909-923-7300; FAX: 909-923-7400
SAFE, PO Box 864, Post Falls, ID 83877 / 208-773-3624; FAX: 208-773-6819 staysafe@safe-llc.com www.safe-llc.com
Safety Speed Holster, Inc., 910 S. Vail Ave., Montebello, CA 90640 / 323-723-4140; FAX: 323-726-6973 e-mail@safetyspeedholster.com www.safetyspeedholster.com
Sako Ltd (See U.S. Importer-Stoeger Industries)
Sam Welch Gun Engraving, Sam Welch, HC 64 Box 2110, Moab, UT 84532 / 435-259-8131
Samco Global Arms, Inc., 6995 NW 43rd St., Miami, FL 33166 / 305-593-9782; FAX: 305-593-1014 samco@samcoglobal.com www.samcoglobal.com
Sampson, Roger, 2316 Mahogany St., Mora, MN 55051 / 612-679-4868
San Marco (See U.S. Importers-Cape Outfitters-EMF
Sandia Die & Cartridge Co., 37 Atancacio Rd. NE, Albuquerque, NM 87123 / 505-298-5729
Sarco, Inc., 323 Union St., Stirling, NJ 07980 / 908-647-3800; FAX: 908-647-9413
Sarsilmaz Shotguns - Turkey (see B.C. Outdoors)
Sauer (See U.S. Importers-Paul Co., The, Sigarms I
Sauls, R. See: BRYAN & ASSOC.
Saunders Gun & Machine Shop, 145 Delhi Rd, Manchester, IA 52057 / 563-927-4026
Savage Arms (Canada), Inc., 248 Water St., P.O. Box 1240, Lakefield, ON K0L 2H0 CANADA / 705-652-8000; FAX: 705-652-8431 www.savagearms.com
Savage Arms, Inc., 100 Springdale Rd., Westfield, MA 01085 / 413-568-7001; FAX: 413-562-7764
Savage Range Systems, Inc., 100 Springdale Rd., Westfield, MA 01085 / 413-568-7001; FAX: 413-562-1152 snailtraps@savagearms.com www.snailtraps.com
Saville Iron Co. (See Greenwood Precision)
Savino, Barbara J., P.O. Box 51, West Burke, VT 05871-0051
Scansport, Inc., P.O. Box 700, Enfield, NH 03748 / 603-632-7654
Sceery Game Calls, P.O. Box 6520, Sante Fe, NM 87502 / 505-471-9110; FAX: 505-471-3476
Schaefer Shooting Sports, P.O. Box 1515, Melville, NY 11747-0515 / 516-643-5466; FAX: 516-643-2426 robert@robertschaefer.com www.schaefershooting.com
Scharch Mfg., Inc.-Top Brass, 10325 Co. Rd. 120, Salida, CO 81201 / 719-539-7242; or 800-836-4683; FAX: 719-539-3021 scharch@chaffee.net www.topbraass.tv
Scherer, Liz. See: SCHERER SUPPLIES
Scherer Supplies, Liz Scherer, Box 250, Ewing, VA 24248 FAX: 423-733-2073
Schiffman, Curt, 2938 S. Greenwood, Mesa, AZ 85212
Schiffman, Mike, 8233 S. Crystal Springs, McCammon, ID 83250 / 208-254-9114
Schmidt & Bender, Inc., P.O. Box 134, Meriden, NH 03770 / 603-469-3565; FAX: 603-469-3471 scopes@cyberportal.net www.schmidtbender.com
Schmidtke Group, 17050 W. Salentine Dr., New Berlin, WI 53151-7349
Schneider Bullets, 3655 West 214th St., Fairview Park, OH 44126
Schneider Rifle Barrels, Inc., 1403 W Red Baron Rd., Payson, AZ 85541 / 602-948-2525
Schroeder Bullets, 1421 Thermal Ave., San Diego, CA 92154 / 619-423-3523; FAX: 619-423-8124
Schulz Industries, 16247 Minnesota Ave., Paramount, CA 90723 / 213-439-5903
Schumakers Gun Shop, 512 Prouty Corner Lp. A, Colville, WA 99114 / 509-684-4848
Scope Control, Inc., 5775 Co. Rd. 23 SE, Alexandria, MN 56308 / 612-762-7295
Score High Gunsmithing, 9812-A, Cochiti SE, Albuquerque, NM 087123 / 800-326-5632 or 505-292-5532; FAX: 505-292-2592
Scot Powder, Rt.1 Box 167, McEwen, TN 37101 / 800-416-3006; FAX: 615-729-4211
Scott Fine Guns Inc., Thad, P.O. Box 412, Indianola, MS 38751 / 601-887-5929
Searcy Enterprises, P.O. Box 584, Boron, CA 93596 / 760-762-6771; FAX: 760-762-0191
Second Chance Body Armor, P.O. Box 578, Central Lake, MI 49622 / 616-544-5721; FAX: 616-544-9824
Seebeck Assoc., R.E., P. O. Box 59752, Dallas, TX 75229
Seecamp Co. Inc., L. W., PO Box 255, New Haven, CT 06502 / 203-877-3429; FAX: 203-877-3429
Segway Industries, P.O. Box 783, Suffern, NY 10901-0783 / 914-357-5510
Seligman Shooting Products, Box 133, Seligman, AZ 86337 / 602-422-3607 shootssp@yahoo.com
Sellier & Bellot, USA, Inc., P.O. Box 27006, Shawnee Mission, KS 66225 / 913-685-0916; FAX: 913-685-0917
Selsi Co., Inc., P.O. Box 10, Midland Park, NJ 07432-0010 / 201-935-0388; FAX: 201-935-5851
Semmer, Charles (See Remington Double Shotguns), 7885 Cyd Dr, Denver, CO 80221 / 303-429-6947
Sentinel Arms, P.O. Box 57, Detroit, MI 48231 / 313-331-1951; FAX: 313-331-1456
Servus Footwear Co., 1136 2nd St., Rock Island, IL 61204 / 309-786-7741; FAX: 309-786-9808
Shappy Bullets, 76 Milldale Ave., Plantsville, CT 06479 / 203-621-3704
Sharp Shooter Supply, 4970 Lehman Road, Delphos, OH 45833 / 419-695-3179
Sharps Arms Co., Inc., C., 100 Centennial, Box 885, Big Timber, MT 59011 / 406-932-4353
Shaw, Inc., E. R. (See Small Arms Mfg. Co.)
Shay's Gunsmithing, 931 Marvin Ave., Lebanon, PA 17042
Sheffield Knifemakers Supply, Inc., P.O. Box 741107, Orange City, FL 32774-1107 / 386-775-6453; FAX: 386-774-5754
Sheldon, Bruce. See: RIDGELINE, INC.
Shepherd Enterprises, Inc., Box 189, Waterloo, NE 68069 / 402-779-2424; FAX: 402-779-4010 sshepherd@shepherdscopes.com www.shepherdscopes.com
Sherwood, George, 46 N. River Dr., Roseburg, OR 97470 / 541-672-3159
Shilen, Inc., 205 Metro Park Blvd., Ennis, TX 75119 / 972-875-5318; FAX: 972-875-5402
Shiloh Rifle Mfg., P.O. Box 279, Big Timber, MT 59011
Shockley, Harold H., 204 E. Farmington Rd., Hanna City 61536 / 309-565-4524
Shoot Where You Look, Leon Measures, Dept GD, 408 Livingston, TX 77351
Shooters Arms Manufacturing, Inc., Rivergate Mall, Ger Maxilom Ave., Cebu City 6000, PHILIPPINES / 6332-254-8478 www.shootersarms.com.ph
Shooter's Choice Gun Care, 15050 Berkshire Ind. Pky., Middlefield, OH 44062 / 440-834-8888; FAX: 440-834-3388 www.shooterschoice.com
Shooter's Edge Inc., 3313 Creekstone Dr., Fort Collins, C 80525
Shooters Supply, 1120 Tieton Dr., Yakima, WA 98902 / 509-452-1181
Shooter's World, 3828 N. 28th Ave., Phoenix, AZ 85017 602-266-0170
Shooters, Inc., 5139 Stanart St., Norfolk, VA 23502 / 757-461-9152; FAX: 757-461-9155 gflocker@aol.co
Shootin' Shack, 357 Cypress Drive, No. 10, Tequesta, FL 33469 / 561-842-0990; FAX: 561-545-4861
Shooting Specialties (See Titus, Daniel)
Shooting Star, 1715 FM 1626 Ste 105, Manchaca, TX 786 / 512-462-0009
Shoot-N-C Targets (See Birchwood Casey)
Shotgun Sports, P.O. Box 6810, Auburn, CA 95604 / 530-889-2220; FAX: 530-889-9106 custsrv@shotgunsportsmagazine.com shotgunsportsmagazine.com
Shotgun Sports Magazine, dba Shootin' Accessories Ltd., P.O. Box 6810, Auburn, CA 95604 / 916-889-2220 custsrv@shotgunsportsmagazine.com shotgunspotsmagazine.com
Shotguns Unlimited, 2307 Fon Du Lac Rd., Richmond, VA 23229 / 804-752-7115
Siegrist Gun Shop, 8752 Turtle Road, Whittemore, MI 487 / 989-873-3929
Sierra Bullets, 1400 W. Henry St., Sedalia, MO 65301 / 816-827-6300; FAX: 816-827-6300
Sierra Specialty Prod. Co., 1344 Oakhurst Ave., Los Altos, C 94024 FAX: 415-965-1536
SIG, CH-8212 Neuhausen, SWITZERLAND
Sigarms, Inc., 18 Industrial Dr., Exeter, NH 03833 / 603-772-2302; FAX: 603-772-9082 www.sigarms.con
Sightron, Inc., 1672B Hwy. 96, Franklinton, NC 27525 / 919-528-8783; FAX: 919-528-0995 info@sightron.con www.sightron.com
SIG-Sauer (See U.S. Importer-Sigarms Inc.)
Silencio/Safety Direct, 56 Coney Island Dr., Sparks, NV 8943 / 800-648-1812 or 702-354-4451; FAX: 702-359-1074
Silent Hunter, 1100 Newton Ave., W. Collingswood, NJ 0810 / 609-854-3276
Silhouette Leathers, P.O. Box 1161, Gunnison, CO 81230 / 970-641-6630 oldshooter@yahoo.com
Silver Eagle Machining, 18007 N. 69th Ave., Glendale, AZ 85308
Silver Ridge Gun Shop (See Goodwin, Fred)
Simmons, Jerry, 715 Middlebury St., Goshen, IN 46528-271 / 574-533-8546
Simmons Gun Repair, Inc., 700 S. Rogers Rd., Olathe, KS 66062 / 913-782-3131; FAX: 913-782-4189
Simmons Outdoor Corp., 6001 Oak Canyon, Irvine, CA 92618 / 949-451-1450; FAX: 949-451-1460 www.meade.com
Sinclair International, Inc., 2330 Wayne Haven St., Fort Wayne, IN 46803 / 260-493-1858; FAX: 260-493-2530 sales@sinclairintl.com www.sinclairintl.com
Singletary, Kent, 4538 W Carol Ave., Glendale, AZ 85302 / 602-526-6836 kent@kscustom www.kscustom.com
Siskiyou Gun Works (See Donnelly, C. P.)
Six Enterprises, 320-D Turtle Creek Ct., San Jose, CA 95125 / 408-999-0201; FAX: 408-999-0216
SKB Shotguns, 4325 S. 120th St., Omaha, NE 68137 / 800-752-2767; FAX: 402-330-8040 skb@skbshotguns.com www.skbshotguns.com
Skeoch, Brian R., P.O. Box 279, Glenrock, WY 82637 / 307-436-9655 brianskeoch@aol.com
Skip's Machine, 364 29 Road, Grand Junction, CO 81501 / 303-245-5417
Sklany's Machine Shop, 566 Birch Grove Dr., Kalispell, MT 59901 / 406-755-4257
Slezak, Jerome F., 1290 Marlowe, Lakewood (Cleveland), OH 44107 / 216-221-1668
Slug Site, Ozark Wilds, 21300 Hwy. 5, Versailles, MO 65084 / 573-378-6430 john@ebeling.com john.ebeling.com
Small Arms Mfg. Co., 5312 Thoms Run Rd., Bridgeville, PA 15017 / 412-221-4343; FAX: 412-221-4303

MANUFACTURER'S DIRECTORY

Arms Specialists, 443 Firchburg Rd., Mason, NH 03048 603-878-0427; FAX: 603-878-3905 iniguns@empire.net miniguns.com
Custom Mould & Bullet Co., Box 17211, Tucson, AZ 5731
t Parts, 1203 Spring St., Latrobe, PA 15650 / 12-539-2660; FAX: 412-539-2298
s, C. L., 5222 Windmill Lane, Columbia, MD 1044-1328
& Wesson, 2100 Roosevelt Ave., Springfield, MA 1104 / 413-781-8300; FAX: 413-731-8980
, Art, P.O. Box 645, Park Rapids, MN 56470 / 18-732-5333;
, Mark A., P.O. Box 182, Sinclair, WY 82334 / 07-324-7929
, Michael, 2612 Ashmore Ave., Red Bank, TN 37415 / 15-267-8341
, Ron, 5869 Straley, Ft. Worth, TX 76114 / 17-732-6768
, Sharmon, 4545 Speas Rd., Fruitland, ID 83619 / 08-452-6329 sharmon@fmtc.com
Abrasives, Inc., 1700 Sleepy Valley Rd., P.O. Box 5095, Hot Springs, AR 71902-5095 / 501-321-2244; FAX: 501-321-9232
h, Judy. See: L.B.T.
h Saddlery, Jesse W., 0499 County Road J, Pritchett, CO 81064 / 509-325-0622
key Valley Rifles, E1976 Smokey Valley Rd., Scandinavia, WI 54977 / 715-467-2674
p's Gunshop, 6911 E. Washington Rd., Clare, MI 48617 / 989-386-9226 snapp@glccomputers.com
-Seal, Inc. (See Atsko/Sno-Seal, Inc.)
eta Armi Bresciane Srl (See U.S. Importer-Cape
Products Co. (See Buck Stix-SOS Products Co.), Box 3, Neenah, WI 54956
neby's, 1334 York Ave. at 72nd St., New York, NY 10021 / 212-606-7260
nd Tech Silencers, Box 391, Pelham, AL 35124 / 205-664-5860 silenceio@wmconnect.com www.soundtechsilencers.com
th Bend Replicas, Inc., 61650 Oak Rd., South Bend, IN 46614 / 219-289-4500
theastern Community College, 1015 S. Gear Ave., West Burlington, IA 52655 / 319-752-2731
thern Ammunition Co., Inc., 4232 Meadow St., Loris, SC 29569-3124 / 803-756-3262; FAX: 803-756-3583
thern Bloomer Mfg. Co., P.O. Box 1621, Bristol, TN 37620 / 615-878-6660; FAX: 615-878-8761
thern Security, 1700 Oak Hills Dr., Kingston, TN 37763 / 423-376-6297; FAX: 800-251-9992
arks, Milt, 605 E. 44th St. No. 2, Boise, ID 83714-4800
artan-Realtree Products, Inc., 1390 Box Circle, Columbus, GA 31907 / 706-569-9101; FAX: 706-569-0042
ecialty Gunsmithing, Lynn McMurdo, P.O. Box 404, Afton, WY 83110 / 307-886-5535
ecialty Shooters Supply, Inc., 3325 Griffin Rd., Suite 9mm, Fort Lauderdale, FL 33317
eer Bullets, P.O. Box 856, Lewiston, ID 83501 / 208-746-2351; www.speer-bullets.com
egel, Craig, P.O. Box 387, Nehalem, OR 97131 / 503-368-5653
eiser, Fred D., 2229 Dearborn, Missoula, MT 59801 / 406-549-8133
encer Reblue Service, 1820 Tupelo Trail, Holt, MI 48842 / 517-694-7474
encer's Rifle Barrels, Inc., 4107 Jacobs Creek Dr., Scottsville, VA 24590 / 804-293-6836; FAX: 804-293-6836 www.spencerriflebarrels.com
PG LLC, P.O. Box 1625, Cody, WY 82414 / 307-587-7621; FAX: 307-587-7695 spg@cody.wtp.net www.blackpowderspg.com
phinx Systems Ltd., Gesteigtstrasse 12, CH-3800, Matten, BRNE, SWITZERLAND
plitfire Sporting Goods, L.L.C., P.O. Box 1044, Orem, UT 84059-1044 / 801-932-7950; FAX: 801-932-7959 www.splitfireguns.com
polar Power Load, Inc., 17376 Filbert, Fontana, CA 92335 / 800-227-9667
port Flite Manufacturing Co., P.O. Box 1082, Bloomfield Hills, MI 48303 / 248-647-3747
Sporting Clays Of America, 9257 Bluckeye Rd, Sugar Grove, OH 43155-9632 / 740-746-8334; FAX: 740-746-8605
Sports Afield Magazine, 15621 Chemical Lane B, Huntington Beach, CA 92649 / 714-894-9080; FAX: 714-894-4949 info@sportsafield.com www.sportsafield.com
Sports Innovations, Inc., P.O. Box 5181, 8505 Jacksboro Hwy., Wichita Falls, TX 76307 / 817-723-6015
Sportsman Safe Mfg. Co., 6309-6311 Paramount Blvd., Long Beach, CA 90805 / 800-266-7150; or 310-984-5445
Sportsman's Communicators, 588 Radcliffe Ave., Pacific Palisades, CA 90272 / 800-538-3752
Sportsmatch U.K. Ltd., 16 Summer St. Leighton,, Buzzard Beds, Bedfordshire, LU7 8HT ENGLAND / 4401525-381638; FAX: 4401525-851236 info@sportsmatch-uk.com www.sportsmatch-uk.com
Sportsmen's Exchange & Western Gun Traders, Inc., 560 S. C St., Oxnard, CA 93030 / 805-483-1917
Spradlin's, 457 Shannon Rd., Texas CreekCotopaxi, CO 81223 / 719-275-7105; FAX: 719-275-3852 spradlins@prodigy.net www.spradlins.net
Springfield Armory, 420 W. Main St, Geneseo, IL 61254 / 309-944-5631; FAX: 309-944-3676 sales@springfield-armory.com www.springfieldarmory.com
Springfield Sporters, Inc., RD 1, Penn Run, PA 15765 / 412-254-2626; FAX: 412-254-9173
Springfield, Inc., 420 W. Main St., Geneseo, IL 61254 / 309-944-5631; FAX: 309-944-3676
Spyderco, Inc., 820 Spyderco Way, Golden, CO 80403 / 800-525-7770; or 800-525-7770; FAX: 303-278-2229 sales@spyderco.com www.spyderco.com
SSK Industries, J. D. Jones, 590 Woodvue Lane, Wintersville, OH 43953 / 740-264-0176; FAX: 740-264-2257 www.sskindustries.com
Stackpole Books, 5067 Ritter Rd., Mechanicsburg, PA 17055-6921 / 717-796-0411; or 800-732-3669; FAX: 717-796-0412 tmanney@stackpolebooks.com www.stackpolebooks.com
Stalker, Inc., P.O. Box 21, Fishermans Wharf Rd., Malakoff, TX 75148 / 903-489-1010
Stalwart Corporation, P.O. Box 46, Evanston, WY 82931 / 307-789-7687; FAX: 307-789-7688
Stan Baker Sports, Stan Baker, 10000 Lake City Way, Seattle, WA 98125 / 206-522-4575
Stan De Treville & Co., 4129 Normal St., San Diego, CA 92103 / 619-298-3393
Stanley Bullets, 2085 Heatheridge Ln., Reno, NV 89509
Star Ammunition, Inc., 5520 Rock Hampton Ct., Indianapolis, IN 46268 / 800-221-5927; FAX: 317-872-5847
Star Custom Bullets, P.O. Box 608, 468 Main St., Ferndale, CA 95536 / 707-786-9140; FAX: 707-786-9117 wmebridge@humboldt.com
Star Machine Works, P.O. Box 1872, Pioneer, CA 95666 / 209-295-5000
Starke Bullet Company, P.O. Box 400, 605 6th St. NW, Cooperstown, ND 58425 / 888-797-3431
Starkey Labs, 6700 Washington Ave. S., Eden Prairie, MN 55344
Starkey's Gun Shop, 9430 McCombs, El Paso, TX 79924 / 915-751-3030
Starlight Training Center, Inc., Rt. 1, P.O. Box 88, Bronaugh, MO 64728 / 417-843-3555
Starline, Inc., 1300 W. Henry St., Sedalia, MO 65301 / 660-827-6640; FAX: 660-827-6650 info@starlinebrass.com http://www.starlinebrass.com
Starr Trading Co., Jedediah, P.O. Box 2007, Farmington Hills, MI 48333 / 810-683-4343; FAX: 810-683-3282
Starrett Co., L. S., 121 Crescent St., Athol, MA 01331 / 978-249-3551; FAX: 978-249-8495
Steelman's Gun Shop, 10465 Beers Rd., Swartz Creek, MI 48473 / 810-735-4884
Steffens, Ron, 18396 Mariposa Creek Rd., Willits, CA 95490 / 707-485-0873
Stegall, James B., 26 Forest Rd., Wallkill, NY 12589
Steve Henigson & Associates, P.O. Box 2726, Culver City, CA 90231 / 310-305-8288; FAX: 310-305-1905
Steve Kamyk Engraver, 9 Grandview Dr., Westfield, MA 01085-1810 / 413-568-0457 stevek201@attbi
Steven Dodd Hughes, P.O. Box 545, Livingston, MT 59047 / 406-222-9377; FAX: 406-222-9377
Steves House of Guns, Rt. 1, Minnesota City, MN 55959 / 507-689-2573
Stewart Game Calls, Inc., Johnny, P.O. Box 7954, 5100 Fort Ave., Waco, TX 76714 / 817-772-3261; FAX: 817-772-3670
Stewart's Gunsmithing, P.O. Box 5854, Pietersburg North 0750, Transvaal, SOUTH AFRICA / 01521-89401
Steyr Mannlicher GmbH & Co KG, Mannlicherstrasse 1, 4400 Steyr, Steyr, AUSTRIA / 0043-7252-896-0; FAX: 0043-7252-78620 office@steyr-mannlicher.com www.steyr-mannlicher.com
STI International, 114 Halmar Cove, Georgetown, TX 78628 / 800-959-8201; FAX: 512-819-0465 www.stiguns.com
Stiles Custom Guns, 76 Cherry Run Rd., Box 1605, Homer City, PA 15748 / 712-479-9945
Stillwell, Robert, 421 Judith Ann Dr., Schertz, TX 78154
Stoeger Industries, 17603 Indian Head Hwy., Suite 200, Accokeek, MD 20607-2501 / 301-283-6300; FAX: 301-283-6986 www.stoegerindustries.com
Stoeger Publishing Co. (See Stoeger Industries)
Stone Enterprises Ltd., 426 Harveys Neck Rd., P.O. Box 335, Wicomico Church, VA 22579 / 804-580-5114; FAX: 804-580-8421
Stone Mountain Arms, 5988 Peachtree Corners E., Norcross, GA 30071 / 800-251-9412
Stoney Point Products, Inc., P.O. Box 234, 1822 N Minnesota St., New Ulm, MN 56073-0234 / 507-354-3360; FAX: 507-354-7236 stoney@newulmtel.net www.stoneypoint.com
Storm, Gary, P.O. Box 5211, Richardson, TX 75083 / 214-385-0862
Stott's Creek Armory, Inc., 2526 S. 475W, Morgantown, IN 46160 / 317-878-5489; FAX: 317-878-9489 sccalendar@aol.com www.Sccalendar.aol.com
Stratco, Inc., P.O. Box 2270, Kalispell, MT 59901 / 406-755-1221; FAX: 406-755-1226
Strayer, Sandy. See: STRAYER-VOIGT, INC.
Strayer-Voigt, Inc., Sandy Strayer, 3435 Ray Orr Blvd, Grand Prairie, TX 75050 / 972-513-0575
Strong Holster Co., 39 Grove St., Gloucester, MA 01930 / 508-281-3300; FAX: 508-281-6321
Strutz Rifle Barrels, Inc., W. C., P.O. Box 611, Eagle River, WI 54521 / 715-479-4766
Stuart, V. Pat, Rt.1, Box 447-S, Greenville, VA 24440 / 804-556-3845
Sturgeon Valley Sporters, Ken Ide, P.O. Box 283, Vanderbilt, MI 49795 / 517-983-4338 k.ide@mail.com
Sturm Ruger & Co. Inc., 200 Ruger Rd., Prescott, AZ 86301 / 928-541-8820; FAX: 520-541-8850 www.ruger.com
"Su-Press-On", Inc., P.O. Box 09161, Detroit, MI 48209 / 313-842-4222
Sullivan, David S. (See Westwind Rifles, Inc.)
Sun Welding Safe Co., 290 Easy St. No.3, Simi Valley, CA 93065 / 805-584-6678; or 800-729-SAFE; FAX: 805-584-6169 sunwelding.com
Sunny Hill Enterprises, Inc., W1790 Cty. HHH, Malone, WI 53049 / 920-795-4722; FAX: 920-795-4822
Super 6 LLC, Gary Knopp, 3806 W. Lisbon Ave., Milwaukee, WI 53208 / 414-344-3343; FAX: 414-344-0304
Sure-Shot Game Calls, Inc., P.O. Box 816, 6835 Capitol, Groves, TX 77619 / 409-962-1636; FAX: 409-962-5465
Svon Corp., 2107 W. Blue Heron Blvd., Riviera Beach, FL 33404 / 508-881-8852
Swann, D. J., 5 Orsova Close, Eltham North Vic., 3095 AUSTRALIA / 03-431-0323
Swanndri New Zealand, 152 Elm Ave., Burlingame, CA 94010 / 415-347-6158
Swanson, Mark, 975 Heap Avenue, Prescott, AZ 86301 / 928-778-4423
Swarovski Optik North America Ltd., 2 Slater Rd., Cranston, RI 02920 / 401-946-2220; or 800-426-3089; FAX: 401-946-2587
Sweet Home, Inc., P.O. Box 900, Orrville, OH 44667-0900
Swenson's 45 Shop, A. D., 3839 Ladera Vista Rd, Fallbrook, CA 92028-9431
Swift Bullet Co., P.O. Box 27, 201 Main St., Quinter, KS 67752 / 913-754-3959; FAX: 913-754-2359
Swift Instruments, Inc., 952 Dorchester Ave., Boston, MA 02125 / 617-436-2960; FAX: 617-436-3232
Swift River Gunworks, 450 State St., Belchertown, MA 01007 / 413-323-4052
Szweda, Robert (See RMS Custom Gunsmithing)

T

T&S Industries, Inc., 1027 Skyview Dr., W. Carrollton, OH 45449 / 513-859-8414
T.F.C. S.p.A., Via G. Marconi 118, B, Villa Carcina 25069, ITALY / 030-881271; FAX: 030-881826
T.G. Faust, Inc., 544 Minor St., Reading, PA 19602 / 610-375-8549; FAX: 610-375-4488
T.K. Lee Co., 1282 Branchwater Ln., Birmingham, AL 35216 / 205-913-5222 odonmich@aol.com www.scopedot.com
T.W. Menck Gunsmith, Inc., 5703 S. 77th St., Ralston, NE 68127 guntools@cox.net http://llwww.members.cox.net/guntools
Tabler Marketing, 2554 Lincoln Blvd., Suite 555, Marina Del Rey, CA 90291 / 818-755-4565; FAX: 818-755-0972
Taconic Firearms Ltd., Perry Lane, P.O. Box 553, Cambridge, NY 12816 / 518-677-2704; FAX: 518-677-5974
Tactical Defense Institute, 2174 Bethany Ridges, West Union, OH 45693 / 937-544-7228; FAX: 937-544-2887 tdiohio@dragonbbs.com www.tdiohio.com

Manufacturer's Directory

Talley, Dave, P.O. Box 821, Glenrock, WY 82637 / 307-436-8724; or 307-436-9315
Talon Industries Inc. (See Cobra Enterprises, Inc.)
Tamarack Products, Inc., P.O. Box 625, Wauconda, IL 60084 / 708-526-9333; FAX: 708-526-9353
Tanfoglio Fratelli S.r.l., via Valtrompia 39, 41, Brescia, ITALY / 30-8910361; FAX: 30-8910183
Tanglefree Industries, 1261 Heavenly Dr., Martinez, CA 94553 / 800-982-4868; FAX: 510-825-3874
Tank's Rifle Shop, P.O. Box 474, Fremont, NE 68026-0474 / 402-727-1317 jtank@tanksrifleshop.com www.tanksrifleshop.com
Tanner (See U.S. Importer-Mandall Shooting Supply)
Taracorp Industries, Inc., 1200 Sixteenth St., Granite City, IL 62040 / 618-451-4400
Target Shooting, Inc., P.O. Box 773, Watertown, SD 57201 / 605-882-6955; FAX: 605-882-8840
Tar-Hunt Custom Rifles, Inc., 101 Dogtown Rd., Bloomsburg, PA 17815 / 570-784-6368; FAX: 570-389-9150 www.tar-hunt.com
Tarnhelm Supply Co., Inc., 431 High St., Boscawen, NH 03303 / 603-796-2551; FAX: 603-796-2918 info@tarnhelm.com www.tarnhelm.com
Tasco Sales, Inc., 2889 Commerce Pky., Miramar, FL 33025
Taurus Firearms, Inc., 16175 NW 49th Ave., Miami, FL 33014 / 305-624-1115; FAX: 305-623-7506
Taurus International Firearms (See U.S. Importer)
Taurus S.A. Forjas, Avenida Do Forte 511, Porto Alegre, RS BRAZIL 91360 / 55-51-347-4050; FAX: 55-51-347-3065
Taylor & Robbins, P.O. Box 164, Rixford, PA 16745 / 814-966-3233
Taylor's & Co., Inc., 304 Lenoir Dr., Winchester, VA 22603 / 540-722-2017; FAX: 540-722-2018
TCCI, P.O. Box 302, Phoenix, AZ 85001 / 602-237-3823; FAX: 602-237-3858
TCSR, 3998 Hoffman Rd., White Bear Lake, MN 55110-4626 / 800-328-5323; FAX: 612-429-0526
TDP Industries, Inc., P.O. Box 249, Ottsville, PA 18942-0249 / 215-345-8687; FAX: 215-345-6057
Techno Arms (See U.S. Importer- Auto-Ordnance Corp
Tecnolegno S.p.A., Via A. Locatelli, 6 10, 24019 Zogno, I ITALY / 0345-55111; FAX: 0345-55155
Ted Blocker Holsters, Inc., 9396 S.W. Tigard St., Tigard, OR 97223 / 800-650-9742; FAX: 503-670-9692 www.tedblocker.com
Tele-Optics, 630 E. Rockland Rd., P.O. Box 6313, Libertyville, IL 60048 / 847-362-7757; FAX: 847-362-7757
Tennessee Valley Mfg., 14 County Road 521, Corinth, MS 38834 / 601-286-5014 tvm@avsia.com www.avsia.com/tvm
Ten-Ring Precision, Inc., Alex B. Hamilton, 1449 Blue Crest Lane, San Antonio, TX 78232 / 210-494-3063; FAX: 210-494-3066
TEN-X Products Group, 1905 N Main St, Suite 133, Cleburne, TX 76031-1305 / 972-243-4016; or 800-433-2225; FAX: 972-243-4112
Tepeco, P.O. Box 342, Friendswood, TX 77546 / 713-482-2702
Terry K. Kopp Professional Gunsmithing, Rt 1 Box 224, Lexington, MO 64067 / 816-259-2636
Testing Systems, Inc., 220 Pegasus Ave., Northvale, NJ 07647
Tetra Gun Care, 8 Vreeland Rd., Florham Park, NJ 07932 / 973-443-0004; FAX: 973-443-0263
Tex Shoemaker & Sons, Inc., 714 W. Cienega Ave., San Dimas, CA 91773 / 909-592-2071; FAX: 909-592-2378 texshoemaker@texshoemaker.com www.texshoemaker.com
Texas Armory (See Bond Arms, Inc.)
Texas Platers Supply Co., 2453 W. Five Mile Parkway, Dallas, TX 75233 / 214-330-7168
Thad Rybka Custom Leather Equipment, 2050 Canoe Creek Rd., Springvale, AL 35146-6709
Thad Scott Fine Guns, Inc., P.O. Box 412, Indianola, MS 38751 / 601-887-5929
The A.W. Peterson Gun Shop, Inc., 4255 West Old U.S. 441, Mount Dora, FL 32757-3299 / 352-383-4258
The Accuracy Den, 25 Bitterbrush Rd., Reno, NV 89523 / 702-345-0225
The Ballistic Program Co., Inc., 2417 N. Patterson St., Thomasville, GA 31792 / 912-228-5739 or 800-368-0835
The BulletMakers Workshop, RFD 1 Box 1755, Brooks, ME 04921
The Competitive Pistol Shop, 5233 Palmer Dr., Ft. Worth, TX 76117-2433 / 817-834-8479
The Concealment Shop, Inc., 3550 E. Hwy. 80, Mesquite, TX 75149 / 972-289-8997; or 800-444-7090; FAX: 972-289-4410 info@theconcealmentshop.com www.theconcealmentshop.com
The Country Armourer, P.O. Box 308, Ashby, MA 01431-0308 / 508-827-6797; FAX: 508-827-4845
The Creative Craftsman, Inc., 95 Highway 29 North, P.O. Box 331, Lawrenceville, GA 30246 / 404-963-2112; FAX: 404-513-9488
The Custom Shop, 890 Cochrane Crescent, Peterborough, ON K9H 5N3 CANADA / 705-742-6693
The Ensign-Bickford Co., 660 Hopmeadow St., Simsbury, CT 06070
The Firearm Training Center, 9555 Blandville Rd., West Paducah, KY 42086 / 502-554-5886
The Fouling Shot, 6465 Parfet St., Arvada, CO 80004
The Gun Doctor, 435 East Maple, Roselle, IL 60172 / 708-894-0668
The Gun Room, 1121 Burlington, Muncie, IN 47302 / 765-282-9073; FAX: 765-282-5270 bshstleguns@aol.com
The Gun Room Press, 127 Raritan Ave., Highland Park, NJ 08904 / 732-545-4344; FAX: 732-545-6686 gunbooks@rutgersgunbooks.com www.rutgersgunbooks.com
The Gun Shop, 62778 Spring Creek Rd., Montrose, CO 81401
The Gun Shop, 5550 S. 900 East, Salt Lake City, UT 84117 / 801-263-3633
The Gun Works, 247 S. 2nd St., Springfield, OR 97477 / 541-741-4118; FAX: 541-988-1097 gunworks@worldnet.att.net www.thegunworks.com
The Gunsight, 1712 North Placentia Ave., Fullerton, CA 92631
The Hanned Line, 4463 Madoc Way, San Jose, CA 95130 smith@hanned.com www.hanned.com
The Hawken Shop, P.O. Box 593, Oak Harbor, WA 98277 / 206-679-4657; FAX: 206-675-1114
The Keller Co., P.O. Box 4057, Port Angeles, WA 98363-0997 / 214-770-8585
The Lewis Lead Remover (See LEM Gun Specialties)
The Midwest Shooting School, Pat LaBoone, 2550 Hwy. 23, Wrenshall, MN 55797 / 218-384-3670 shootingschool@starband.net
The NgraveR Co., 67 Wawecus Hill Rd., Bozrah, CT 06334 / 860-823-1533; FAX: 860-887-6252 ngraver98@aol.com www.ngraver.com
The Ordnance Works, 2969 Pidgeon Point Road, Eureka, CA 95501 / 707-443-3252
The Orvis Co., Rt. 7, Manchester, VT 05254 / 802-362-3622; FAX: 802-362-3525
The Outdoor Connection, Inc., 7901 Panther Way, Waco, TX 76712-6556 / 800-533-6076 or 254-772-5575; FAX: 254-776-3553 floyd@outdoorconnection.com www.outdoorconnection.com
The Park Rifle Co., Ltd., Unit 6a Dartford Trade Park, Power Mill Lane, Dartford DA7 7NX, ENGLAND / 011-0322-222512
The Paul Co., 27385 Pressonville Rd., Wellsville, KS 66092 / 785-883-4444; FAX: 785-883-2525
The Protector Mfg. Co., Inc., 443 Ashwood Place, Boca Raton, FL 33431 / 407-394-6011
The Robar Co., Inc., 21438 N. 7th Ave., Suite B, Phoenix, AZ 85027 / 623-581-2648; FAX: 623-582-0059 info@robarguns.com www.robarguns.com
The School of Gunsmithing, 6065 Roswell Rd., Atlanta, GA 30328 / 800-223-4542
The Shooting Gallery, 8070 Southern Blvd., Boardman, OH 44512 / 216-726-7788
The Sight Shop, John G. Lawson, 1802 E. Columbia Ave., Tacoma, WA 98404 / 253-474-5465 parahellum9@aol.com www.thesightshop.org
The Southern Armory, 25 Millstone Road, Woodlawn, VA 24381 / 703-238-1343; FAX: 703-238-1453
The Surecase Co., 233 Wilshire Blvd., Ste. 900, Santa Monica, CA 90401 / 800-92ARMLOC
The Swampfire Shop (See Peterson Gun Shop, Inc.)
The Wilson Arms Co., 63 Leetes Island Rd., Branford, CT 06405 / 203-488-7297; FAX: 203-488-0135
Theis, Terry, 21452 FM 2093, Harper, TX 78631 / 830-864-4438
Thiewes, George W., 14329 W. Parada Dr., Sun City West, AZ 85375
Things Unlimited, 235 N. Kimbau, Casper, WY 82601 / 307-234-5277
Thirion Gun Engraving, Denise, PO Box 408, Graton, CA 95444 / 707-829-1876
Thomas, Charles C., 2600 S. First St., Springfield, IL 62704 / 217-789-8980; FAX: 217-789-9130 books@ccthomas.com ccthomas.com
Thompson Bullet Lube Co., P.O. Box 409, Wills Point, T 75169 / 866-476-1500; FAX: 866-476-1500 thompsonbulletlube.com www.thompsonbulletlube
Thompson Precision, 110 Mary St., P.O. Box 251, Warre 61087 / 815-745-3625
Thompson, Randall. See: HIGHLINE MACHINE CO.
Thompson Target Technology, 4804 Sherman Church A S.W., Canton, OH 44710 / 330-484-6480; FAX: 330-491-1087 www.thompsontarget.com
Thompson Tool Mount, 1550 Solomon Rd., Santa Maria 93455 / 805-934-1281 ttm@pronet.net www.thompsontoolmount.com
Thompson/Center Arms, P.O. Box 5002, Rochester, NH 03866 / 603-332-2394; FAX: 603-332-5133 tech@tcarms.com www.tcarms.com
3-Ten Corp., P.O. Box 269, Feeding Hills, MA 01030 / 413-789-2086; FAX: 413-789-1549
Thunden Ranch, HCR 1, Box 53, Mt. Home, TX 78058 / 830-640-3138
Thurston Sports, Inc., RD 3 Donovan Rd., Auburn, NY 13 / 315-253-0966
Tiger-Hunt Gunstocks, Box 379, Beaverdale, PA 15921 / 814-472-5161 tigerhunt4@aol.com www.gunstockwood.com
Tikka (See U.S. Importer-Stoeger Industries)
Time Precision, 4 Nicholas Sq., New Milford, CT 06776-3 / 203-775-8343
Tinks & Ben Lee Hunting Products (See Wellington)
Tink's Safariland Hunting Corp., P.O. Box 244, 1140 Monticello Rd., Madison, GA 30650 / 706-342-4915 FAX: 706-342-7568
Tioga Engineering Co., Inc., P.O. Box 913, 13 Cone St., Wellsboro, PA 16901 / 570-724-3533; FAX: 570-724-3895 tiogaeng@epix.net
Tippman Pneumatics, Inc., 2955 Adams Center Rd., Fort Wayne, IN 46803
Tirelli, Snc Di Tirelli Primo E.C., Via Matteotti No. 359, Gardone V.T. Brescia, I ITALY / 030-8912819; FAX: 030-832240
TM Stockworks, 6355 Maplecrest Rd., Fort Wayne, IN 468 / 219-485-5389
TMI Products (See Haselbauer Products, Jerry)
Tom Forrest, Inc., P.O. Box 326, Lakeside, CA 92040 / 619-561-5800; FAX: 888-GUN-CLIP info@gunmag.co www.gunmags.com
Tombstone Smoke`n' Deals, PO Box 31298, Phoenix, AZ 85046 / 602-905-7013; FAX: 602-443-1998
Tom's Gun Repair, Thomas G. Ivanoff, 76-6 Rt. Southfork Rd., Cody, WY 82414 / 307-587-6949
Tom's Gunshop, 3601 Central Ave., Hot Springs, AR 71913 501-624-3856
Tonoloway Tack Drives, HCR 81, Box 100, Needmore, PA 17238
Torel, Inc., 1708 N. South St., P.O. Box 592, Yoakum, TX 77995 / 512-293-2341; FAX: 512-293-3413
TOZ (See U.S. Importer-Nygord Precision Products)
Track of the Wolf, Inc., 18308 Joplin St. NW, Elk River, MN 55330-1773 / 763-633-2500; FAX: 763-633-2550
Traditions Performance Firearms, P.O. Box 776, 1375 Bosto Post Rd., Old Saybrook, CT 06475 / 860-388-4656; FA 860-388-4657 info@traditionsfirearms.com www.traditionsfirearms.com
Trafalgar Square, P.O. Box 257, N. Pomfret, VT 05053 / 802-457-1911
Trail Visions, 5800 N. Ames Terrace, Glendale, WI 53209 / 414-228-1328
Trax America, Inc., PO Box 898, 1150 Eldridge, Forrest City AR 72335 / 870-633-0410; or 800-232-2327; FAX: 870-633-4788 trax@ipa.net www.traxamerica.com
Treadlok Gun Safe, Inc., 1764 Granby St. NE, Roanoke, VA 24012 / 800-729-8732; or 703-982-6881; FAX: 703-982-1059
Treemaster, P.O. Box 247, Guntersville, AL 35976 / 205-878-3597
Trevallion Gunstocks, 9 Old Mountain Rd., Cape Neddick, ME 03902 / 207-361-1130
Trico Plastics, 28061 Diaz Rd., Temecula, CA 92590 / 909-676-7714; FAX: 909-676-0267 ustinfo@ustplastics.com www.tricoplastics.com
Trigger Lock Division / Central Specialties Ltd., 220-D Exchange Dr., Crystal Lake, IL 60014 / 847-639-3900; FAX: 847-639-3972
Trijicon, Inc., 49385 Shafer Ave., P.O. Box 930059, Wixom, MI 48393-0059 / 248-960-7700 or 800-338-0563
Trilby Sport Shop, 1623 Hagley Rd., Toledo, OH 43612-2024 / 419-472-6222
Trilux, Inc., P.O. Box 24608, Winston-Salem, NC 27114 / 910-659-9438; FAX: 910-768-7720

d St. Jr. Col. Gunsmith Dept., 600 Prospect St., nidad, CO 81082 / 719-846-5631; FAX: 719-846-5667
K Mfg. Co., Inc., 2222 Commercial St., San Diego, CA 113 / 619-232-2066; FAX: 619-232-7675 es@triplek.com www.triplek.com
Sporting Arms, Ltd., 1814 Linn St. #16, N. Kansas y, MO 64116-3627 / 816-421-1400; FAX: 6-421-4182 tristar@blitz-it.net ww.tristarsportingarms
raps, Inc., P.O. Box 25, 221 S. Miami Ave., Cleves, OH 002 / 513-941-5682; FAX: 513-941-7970 ustraps@fuse.net www.triustraps.com
r Walsh, 2393 N. Edgewood St., Arlington, VA 22207
an, Ken, 135 Ditton Walk, Unit 11, Cambridge, CB5 8PY GLAND / 01223-211030; FAX: 01223-212317 ww.kentrolman.com
lance Knife Co., P.O. Box 140555, Grand Rapids, MI 514 / 616-647-1215
light Bullet Co., 5581 Roosevelt St., Whitehall, PA 052 / 610-262-7630; FAX: 610-262-7806
, Inc., P.O. Box 1612, McKinna, TX 75070 / 2-774-0300; FAX: 972-774-0323 ww.truglosights.com
k Tool, P.O. Box 530, Whigham, GA 31797 / 29-762-4678; FAX: 229-762-4050 ulockchokes@hotmail.com trulockchokes.com
quare Metal Products, Inc., 640 First St. SW, P.O. Box 35, Auburn, WA 98071 / 253-833-2310; or 00-225-1017; FAX: 253-833-2349 tumbler@qwest.net
r, James C., P.O. Box 366, Medford, OR 97501 / 41-245-3887 jctstocker@yahoo.com
on Mold, Inc., 930 S. Plumer Ave., Tucson, AZ 85719 / 20-792-1075; FAX: 520-792-1075
s Head Productions, Mustafa Bilal, 908 NW 50th St., eattle, WA 98107-3634 / 206-782-4164; FAX: 06-783-5677 info@turkshead.com www.turkshead.com
bull Restoration, Doug, 6680 Rt. 5 & 20, P.O. Box 471, Bloomfield, NY 14469 / 585-657-6338; FAX: 85-657-6338 turnbullrest@mindspring.com www.turnbullrestoration.com
e, Dale, 4046 Russell Rd., Muskegon, MI 49445 / 16-766-2250
Manufacturing & Distributing, 3804 S. Eastern, Oklahoma City, OK 73129 / 405-677-1487; or 800-654-8415

U

Fire Arms Mfg. Co., Inc., 55 Van Dyke Ave., Hartford, CT 06106 / 877-227-6901; FAX: 800-644-7265 usfirearms.com
. Importer-Wm. Larkin Moore, 8430 E. Raintree Ste. B-7, Scottsdale, AZ 85260
. Optics, A Division of Zeitz Optics U.S.A., 5900 Dale St., Buena Park, CA 90621 / 714-994-4901; FAX: 714-994-4904 www.usoptics.com
. Repeating Arms Co., Inc., 275 Winchester Ave., Morgan, UT 84050-9333 / 801-876-3440; FAX: 801-876-3737 www.winchester-guns.com
. Tactical Systems (See Keng's Firearms Specialty)
artechea S. A., Ignacio, Chonta 26, Eibar, SPAIN / 43-121257; FAX: 43-121669
ra Dot Distribution, P.O. Box 362, 6304 Riverside Dr., Yankeetown, FL 34498 / 352-447-2255; FAX: 352-447-2266
ralux (See U.S. Importer-Keng's Firearms)
raSport Arms, Inc., 1955 Norwood Ct., Racine, WI 53403 / 414-554-3237; FAX: 414-554-9731
cle Bud's, HCR 81, Box 100, Needmore, PA 17238 / 717-294-6000; FAX: 717-294-6005
cle Mike's (See Michaels of Oregon Co.)
ertl Optical Co., Inc., 103 Grand Avenue, P.O. Box 895, Mars, PA 16046-0895 / 724-625-3810; FAX: 724-625-3819 unertl@nauticom.net www.unertloptics.net
nique/M.A.P.F., 10 Les Allees, 64700, Hendaye, FRANCE / 33-59 20 71 93
niTec, 1250 Bedford SW, Canton, OH 44710 / 216-452-4017
nited Binocular Co., 9043 S. Western Ave., Chicago, IL 60620
nited Cutlery Corp., 1425 United Blvd., Sevierville, TN 37876 / 865-428-2532; or 800-548-0835; FAX: 865-428-2267
United States Products Co., 518 Melwood Ave., Pittsburgh, PA 15213-1136 / 412-621-2130; FAX: 412-621-8740 sales@us-products.com www.us-products.com
Universal Sports, P.O. Box 532, Vincennes, IN 47591 / 812-882-8680; FAX: 812-882-8680
Upper Missouri Trading Co., P.O. Box 100, 304 Harold St., Crofton, NE 68730-0100 / 402-388-4844
USAC, 4500-15th St. East, Tacoma, WA 98424 / 206-922-7589
Uselton/Arms, Inc., 842 Conference Dr., Goodlettsville, TN 37072 / 615-851-4919
Utica Cutlery Co., 820 Noyes St., Utica, NY 13503 / 315-733-4663; FAX: 315-733-6602

V

V.H. Blackinton & Co., Inc., 221 John L. Dietsch, Attleboro Falls, MA 02763-0300 / 508-699-4436; FAX: 508-695-5349
Valdada Enterprises, P.O. Box 773122, 31733 County Road 35, Steamboat Springs, CO 80477 / 970-879-2983; FAX: 970-879-0851 www.valdada.com
Valtro USA, Inc., 1281 Andersen Dr., San Rafael, CA 94901 / 415-256-2575; FAX: 415-256-2576
VAM Distribution Co. LLC, 1141-B Mechanicsburg Rd., Wooster, OH 44691 www.rex10.com
Van Gorden & Son Inc., C. S., 1815 Main St., Bloomer, WI 54724 / 715-568-2612
Van Horn, Gil, P.O. Box 207, Llano, CA 93544
Van Patten, J. W., P.O. Box 145, Foster Hill, Milford, PA 18337 / 717-296-7069
Vann Custom Bullets, 2766 N. Willowside Way, Meridian, ID 83642
Van's Gunsmith Service, 224 Route 69-A, Parish, NY 13131 / 315-625-7251
Varmint Masters, LLC, Rick Vecqueray, P.O. Box 6724, Bend, OR 97708 / 541-318-7306; FAX: 541-318-7306 varmintmasters@bendcable.com www.varmintmasters.net
Vecqueray, Rick. See: VARMINT MASTERS, LLC
Vega Tool Co., c/o T.R. Ross, 4865 Tanglewood Ct., Boulder, CO 80301 / 303-530-0174 clanlaird@aol.com www.vegatool.com
Vektor USA, Mikael Danforth, 5139 Stanart St, Norfolk, VA 23502 / 888-740-0837; or 757-455-8895; FAX: 757-461-9155
Venco Industries, Inc. (See Shooter's Choice Gun Care)
Venus Industries, P.O. Box 246, Sialkot-1, PAKISTAN FAX: 92 432 85579
Verney-Carron, BP 72-54 Boulevard Thiers, 42002 St Etienne Cedex 1, St Etienne Cedex 1, FRANCE / 33-477791500; FAX: 33-477790702 email@verney-carron.com www.verney-carron.com
Vest, John, 1923 NE 7th St., Redmond, OR 97756 / 541-923-8898
VibraShine, Inc., P.O. Box 577, Taylorsville, MS 39168 / 601-785-9854; FAX: 601-785-9874 rdbekevibrashine.com www.vibrashine.com
Vibra-Tek Co., 1844 Arroya Rd., Colorado Springs, CO 80906 / 719-634-8611; FAX: 719-634-6886
Vic's Gun Refinishing, 6 Pineview Dr., Dover, NH 03820-6422 / 603-742-0013
Victory Ammunition, P.O. Box 1022, Milford, PA 18337 / 717-296-5768; FAX: 717-296-9298
Victory USA, P.O. Box 1021, Pine Bush, NY 12566 / 914-744-2060; FAX: 914-744-5181
Vihtavuori Oy, FIN-41330 Vihtavuori, FINLAND, / 358-41-3779211; FAX: 358-41-3771643
Vihtavuori Oy/Kaltron-Pettibone, 1241 Ellis St., Bensenville, IL 60106 / 708-350-1116; FAX: 708-350-1606
Viking Video Productions, P.O. Box 251, Roseburg, OR 97470
Village Restorations & Consulting, Inc., P.O. Box 569, Claysburg, PA 16625 / 814-239-8200; FAX: 814-239-2165 www.villagerestoration@yahoo.com
Vincent's Shop, 210 Antoinette, Fairbanks, AK 99701
Vintage Industries, Inc., 2772 Depot St., Sanford, FL 32773
Viper Bullet and Brass Works, 11 Brock St., Box 582, Norwich, ON N0J 1P0 CANADA
Viramontez Engraving, Ray Viramontez, 601 Springfield Dr., Albany, GA 31721 / 229-432-9683 sgtvira@aol.com
Viramontez, Ray. See: VIRAMONTEZ ENGRAVING
Virgin Valley Custom Guns, 450 E 800 N #20, Hurricane, UT 84737 / 435-635-8941; FAX: 435-635-8943 vvcguns@infowest.com www.virginvalleyguns.com
Visible Impact Targets, Rts. 5 & 20, E. Bloomfield, NY 14443 / 716-657-6161; FAX: 716-657-5405
Vitt/Boos, 1195 Buck Hill Rd., Townshend, VT 05353 / 802-365-9232
Voere-KGH GmbH, Untere Sparchen 56, A-6330 Kufstein, Tirol, AUSTRIA / 0043-5372-62547; FAX: 0043-5372-65752 voere@aon.com www.voere.com
Volquartsen Custom Ltd., 24276 240th Street, PO Box 397, Carroll, IA 51401 / 712-792-4238; FAX: 712-792-2542 vcl@netins.net www.volquartsen.com
Vorhes, David, 3042 Beecham St., Napa, CA 94558 / 707-226-9116; FAX: 707-253-7334
VSP Publishers (See Heritage/VSP Gun Books), P.O. Box 887, McCall, ID 83638 / 208-634-4104; FAX: 208-634-3101 heritage@gunbooks.com www.gunbooks.com
VTI Gun Parts, P.O. Box 509, Lakeville, CT 06039 / 860-435-8068; FAX: 860-435-8146 mail@vtigunparts.com www.vtigunparts.com
Vulpes Ventures, Inc., Fox Cartridge Division, P.O. Box 1363, Bolingbrook, IL 60440-7363 / 630-759-1229

W

W. Square Enterprises, 9826 Sagedale Dr., Houston, TX 77089 / 281-484-0935; FAX: 281-464-9940 lfdw@pdq.net www.loadammo.com
W. Waller & Son, Inc., 2221 Stoney Brook Rd., Grantham, NH 03753-7706 / 603-863-4177 www.wallerandson.com
W.B. Niemi Engineering, Box 126 Center Road, Greensboro, VT 05841 / 802-533-7180 or 802-533-7141
W.C. Wolff Co., P.O. Box 458, Newtown Square, PA 19073 / 610-359-9600; or 800-545-0077; mail@gunsprings.com www.gunsprings.com
W.E. Birdsong & Assoc., 1435 Monterey Rd., Florence, MS 39073-9748 / 601-366-8270
W.E. Brownell Checkering Tools, 9390 Twin Mountain Cir., San Diego, CA 92126 / 858-695-2479; FAX: 858-695-2479
W.J. Riebe Co., 3434 Tucker Rd., Boise, ID 83703
W.R. Case & Sons Cutlery Co., Owens Way, Bradford, PA 16701 / 814-368-4123; or 800-523-6350; FAX: 814-368-1736 jsullivan@wrcase.com www.wrcase.com
Wagoner, Vernon G., 2325 E. Encanto St., Mesa, AZ 85213-5917 / 480-835-1307
Wakina by Pic, 24813 Alderbrook Dr., Santa Clarita, CA 91321 / 800-295-8194
Waldron, Herman, Box 475, 80 N. 17th St., Pomeroy, WA 99347 / 509-843-1404
Walker Arms Co., Inc., 499 County Rd. 820, Selma, AL 36701 / 334-872-6231; FAX: 334-872-6262
Wallace, Terry, 385 San Marino, Vallejo, CA 94589 / 707-642-7041
Walls Industries, Inc., P.O. Box 98, 1905 N. Main, Cleburne, TX 76033 / 817-645-4366; FAX: 817-645-7946 www.wallsoutdoors.com
Walters Industries, 6226 Park Lane, Dallas, TX 75225 / 214-691-6973
Walters, John. See: WALTERS WADS
Walters Wads, John Walters, 500 N. Avery Dr., Moore, OK 73160 / 405-799-0376; FAX: 405-799-7727 www.tinwadman@cs.com
Walther America, P.O. Box 22, Springfield, MA 01102 / 413-747-3443 www.walther-usa.com
Walther GmbH, Carl, B.P. 4325, D-89033 Ulm, GERMANY
Walt's Custom Leather, Walt Whinnery, 1947 Meadow Creek Dr., Louisville, KY 40218 / 502-458-4361
WAMCO-New Mexico, P.O. Box 205, Peralta, NM 87042-0205 / 505-869-0826
Ward & Van Valkenburg, 114 32nd Ave. N., Fargo, ND 58102 / 701-232-2351
Ward Machine, 5620 Lexington Rd., Corpus Christi, TX 78412 / 512-992-1221
Wardell Precision Handguns Ltd., 48851 N. Fig Springs Rd., New River, AZ 85027-8513 / 602-465-7995
Warenski Engraving, Julie Warenski, 590 E. 500 N., Richfield, UT 84701 / 435-896-5319; FAX: 435-896-8333 julie@warenskiknives.com
Warenski, Julie. See: WARENSKI ENGRAVING
Warne Manufacturing Co., 9057 SE Jannsen Rd., Clackamas, OR 97015 / 503-657-5590 or 800-683-5590; FAX: 503-657-5695 info@warnescopemounts.com www.warnescopemounts.com
Warren Muzzleloading Co., Inc., Hwy. 21 North, P.O. Box 100, Ozone, AR 72854 / 501-292-3268
Washita Mountain Whetstone Co., P.O. Box 378, Lake Hamilton, AR 71951 / 501-525-3914
Wasmundt, Jim, P.O. Box 511, Fossil, OR 97830
Watson Bros., 39 Redcross Way, SE1 1H6, London, ENGLAND FAX: 44-171-403-336

MANUFACTURER'S DIRECTORY

Watson Bullets, 231 Allies Pass, Frostproof, FL 33843 / 863-635-7948 cbestbullet@aol.com
Wayne E. Schwartz Custom Guns, 970 E. Britton Rd., Morrice, MI 48857 / 517-625-4079
Wayne Firearms For Collectors & Investors
Wayne Specialty Services, 260 Waterford Drive, Florissant, MO 63033 / 413-831-7083
WD-40 Co., 1061 Cudahy Pl., San Diego, CA 92110 / 619-275-1400; FAX: 619-275-5823
Weatherby, Inc., 3100 El Camino Real, Atascadero, CA 93422 / 805-466-1767; FAX: 805-466-2527 www.weatherby.com
Weaver Products ATK, P.O. Box 39, Onalaska, WI 54650 / 800-648-9624 or 608-781-5800; FAX: 608-781-0368
Weaver Scope Repair Service, 1121 Larry Mahan Dr., Suite B, El Paso, TX 79925 / 915-593-1005
Webb, Bill, 6504 North Bellefontaine, Kansas City, MO 64119 / 816-453-7431
Weber & Markin Custom Gunsmiths, 4-1691 Powick Rd., Kelowna, BC V1X 4L1 CANADA / 250-762-7575; FAX: 250-861-3655 www.weberandmarkinguns.com
Webley and Scott Ltd., Frankley Industrial Park, Tay Rd., Birmingham, B45 0PA ENGLAND / 011-021-453-1864; FAX: 0121-457-7846 guns@webley.co.uk www.webley.co.uk
Webster Scale Mfg. Co., P.O. Box 188, Sebring, FL 33870 / 813-385-6362
Weems, Cecil, 510 W Hubbard St., Mineral Wells, TX 76067-4847 / 817-325-1462
Weigand Combat Handguns, Inc., 1057 South Main Rd., Mountain Top, PA 18707 / 570-868-8358; FAX: 570-868-5218 sales@jackweigand.com www.jackweigand.com
Weihrauch KG, Hermann, Industriestrasse 11, 8744 Mellrichstadt, Mellrichstadt, GERMANY
Welch, Sam. See: SAM WELCH GUN ENGRAVING
Wellington Outdoors, P.O. Box 244, 1140 Monticello Rd., Madison, GA 30650 / 706-342-4915; FAX: 706-342-7568
Wells, Rachel, 110 N. Summit St., Prescott, AZ 86301 / 928-445-3655 wellssportstore@cableone.net wellssportstore@cableone-net
Wells Creek Knife & Gun Works, 32956 State Hwy. 38, Scottsburg, OR 97473 / 541-587-4202; FAX: 541-587-4223
Welsh, Bud. See: HIGH PRECISION
Wenger North America/Precise Int'l., 15 Corporate Dr., Orangeburg, NY 10962 / 800-431-2996; FAX: 914-425-4700
Wenig Custom Gunstocks, 103 N. Market St., P.O. Box 249, Lincoln, MO 65338 / 660-547-3334; FAX: 660-547-2881 gustock@wenig.com www.wenig.com
Werth, T. W., 1203 Woodlawn Rd., Lincoln, IL 62656 / 217-732-1300
Wescombe, Bill (See North Star West)
Wessinger Custom Guns & Engraving, 268 Limestone Rd., Chapin, SC 29036 / 803-345-5677
West, Jack L., 1220 W. Fifth, P.O. Box 427, Arlington, OR 97812
Western Cutlery (See Camillus Cutlery Co.)
Western Design (See Alpha Gunsmith Division)
Western Mfg. Co., 550 Valencia School Rd., Aptos, CA 95003 / 831-688-5884 lotsabears@eathlink.net
Western Missouri Shooters Alliance, P.O. Box 11144, Kansas City, MO 64119 / 816-597-3950; FAX: 816-229-7350
Western Nevada West Coast Bullets, P.O. BOX 2270, DAYTON, NV 89403-2270 / 702-246-3941; FAX: 702-246-0836
Westley Richards & Co. Ltd., 40 Grange Rd., Birmingham, ENGLAND / 010-214722953; FAX: 010-214141138 sales@westleyrichards.com www.westleyrichards.com
Westley Richards Agency USA (See U.S. Importer for
Westwind Rifles, Inc., David S. Sullivan, P.O. Box 261, 640 Briggs St., Erie, CO 80516 / 303-828-3823
Weyer International, 2740 Nebraska Ave., Toledo, OH 43607 / 419-534-2020; FAX: 419-534-2697
Whildin & Sons Ltd, E.H., RR 2 Box 119, Tamaqua, PA 18252 / 717-668-6743; FAX: 717-668-6745
Whinnery, Walt (See Walt's Custom Leather)
Whiscombe (See U.S. Importer-Pelaire Products)
White Barn Wor, 431 County Road, Broadlands, IL 61816
White Pine Photographic Services, Hwy. 60, General Delivery, Wilno, ON K0J 2N0 CANADA / 613-756-3452
White Rifles, Inc., 234 S.1250 W., Linden, UT 84042 / 801-932-7950 www.whiterifles.com
White Rock Tool & Die, 6400 N. Brighton Ave., Kansas City, MO 64119 / 816-454-0478
Whitestone Lumber Corp., 148-02 14th Ave., Whitestone, NY 11357 / 718-746-4400; FAX: 718-767-1748 whstco@aol.com
Wichita Arms, Inc., 923 E. Gilbert, P.O. Box 11371, Wichita, KS 67211 / 316-265-0661; FAX: 316-265-0760 sales@wichitaarms.com www.wichitaarms.com
Wick, David E., 1504 Michigan Ave., Columbus, IN 47201 / 812-376-6960
Widener's Reloading & Shooting Supply, Inc., P.O. Box 3009 CRS, Johnson City, TN 37602 / 615-282-6786; FAX: 615-282-6651
Wideview Scope Mount Corp., 13535 S. Hwy. 16, Rapid City, SD 57702 / 605-341-3220; FAX: 605-341-9142 wvdon@rapidnet.com www.jii.to
Wiebe, Duane, 5300 Merchant Cir. #2, Placerville, CA 95667 / 530-344-1357; FAX: 530-344-1357 wiebe@d-wdb.com
Wiest, Marie. See: GUNCRAFT SPORTS, INC.
Wilcox All-Pro Tools & Supply, 4880 147th St., Montezuma, IA 50171 / 515-623-3138; FAX: 515-623-3104
Wilcox Industries Corp., Robert F Guarasi, 53 Durham St., Portsmouth, NH 03801 / 603-431-1331; FAX: 603-431-1221
Wild Bill's Originals, P.O. Box 13037, Burton, WA 98013 / 206-463-5738; FAX: 206-465-5925 wildbill@halcyon.com
Wild West Guns, 7521 Old Seward Hwy., Unit A, Anchorage, AK 99518 / 800-992-4570 or 907-344-4500; FAX: 907-344-4005 wwguns@ak.net www.wildwestguns.com
Wilderness Sound Products Ltd., 4015 Main St. A, Springfield, OR 97478 / 800-47-0006; FAX: 541-741-0263
Wildey, Inc., 45 Angevine Rd, Warren, CT 06754-1818 / 203-355-9000; FAX: 203-354-7759
Wildlife Research Center, Inc., 1050 McKinley St., Anoka, MN 55303 / 763-427-3350; or 800-USE-LURE; FAX: 763-427-8354
Will-Burt Co., 169 S. Main, Orrville, OH 44667
William E. Phillips Firearms, 38 Avondale Rd., Wigston, Leicester, ENGLAND / 0116 2886334; FAX: 0116 2810644 wephillips@aol.com
William Powell Agency, 22 Circle Dr., Bellmore, NY 11710 / 516-679-1158
Williams Gun Sight Co., 7389 Lapeer Rd., Box 329, Davison, MI 48423 / 810-653-2131 or 800-530-9028; FAX: 810-658-2140 williamsgunsight.com
Williams Mfg. of Oregon, 110 East B St., Drain, OR 97435 / 503-836-7461; FAX: 503-836-7245
Williams Shootin' Iron Service, The Lynx-Line, Rt. 2 Box 223A, Mountain Grove, MO 65711 / 417-948-0902; FAX: 417-948-0902
Williamson Precision Gunsmithing, 117 W. Pipeline, Hurst, TX 76053 / 817-285-0064; FAX: 817-280-0044
Willow Bend, P.O. Box 203, Chelmsford, MA 01824 / 978-256-8508; FAX: 978-256-8508
Wilsom Combat, 2234 CR 719, Berryville, AR 72616-4573 / 800-955-4856; FAX: 870-545-3310
Wilson Case, Inc., P.O. Box 1106, Hastings, NE 68902-1106 / 800-322-5493; FAX: 402-463-5276 sales@wilsoncase.com www.wilsoncase.com
Wilson Combat, 2234 CR 719, Berryville, AR 72616-4573 / 800-955-4856
Winchester Div. Olin Corp., 427 N. Shamrock, E. Alton, IL 62024 / 618-258-3566; FAX: 618-258-3599
Winchester Sutler, Inc., The, 270 Shadow Brook Lane, Winchester, VA 22603 / 540-888-3595; FAX: 540-888-4632
Windish, Jim, 2510 Dawn Dr., Alexandria, VA 22306 / 703-765-1994
Wingshooting Adventures, 0-1845 W. Leonard, Grand Rapids, MI 49544 / 616-677-1980; FAX: 616-677-1986
Winkle Bullets, R.R. 1, Box 316, Heyworth, IL 61745
Winter, Robert M., P.O. Box 484, 42975-287th St., Menno, SD 57045 / 605-387-5322
Wise Custom Guns, 1402 Blanco Rd., San Antonio, TX 78212-2716 / 210-828-3388
Wise Guns, Dale, 1402 Blanco Rd., San Antonio, TX 78212 / 210-734-9999
Wiseman and Co., Bill, P.O. Box 3427, Bryan, TX 77805 / 409-690-3456; FAX: 409-690-0156
Wisners, Inc., P.O. Box 58, Adna, WA 98522 / 360-748-4590; FAX: 360-748-6028 parts@gunpartsspecialist.com www.wisnersinc.com
Wolf (See J.R. Distributing)
Wolf Performance Ammunition, 2201 E. Winston Rd., Ste. K, Anaheim, CA 92806-5537 / 702-837-8506; FAX: 702-837-9250
Wolfe Publishing Co., 2625 Stearman Rd., Ste. A, Prescott, AZ 86301 / 928-445-7810; or 800-899-7810; FAX: 928-778-5124
Wolf's Western Traders, 1250 Santa Cora Ave. #613, Vista, CA 91913 / 619-482-1701 patwolf4570book@aol.com
Wolverine Footwear Group, 9341 Courtland Dr. NE, Rc MI 49351 / 616-866-5500; FAX: 616-866-5658
Wood, Frank (See Classic Guns, Inc.), 5305 Peachtre Blvd., Norcross, GA 30092 / 404-242-7944
Woodleigh (See Huntington Die Specialties)
Woods Wise Products, P.O. Box 681552, Franklin, TN / 800-735-8182; FAX: 615-726-2637
Woodstream, P.O. Box 327, Lititz, PA 17543 / 717-626-2125; FAX: 717-626-1912
Woodworker's Supply, 1108 North Glenn Rd., Caspe 82601 / 307-237-5354
Woolrich, Inc., Mill St., Woolrich, PA 17701 / 800-99 FAX: 717-769-6234/6259
Working Guns, Jim Coffin, 1224 NW Fernwood Cir., C OR 97330-2909 / 541-928-4391
World of Targets (See Birchwood Casey)
World Trek, Inc., 7170 Turkey Creek Rd., Pueblo, CO 81007-1046 / 719-546-2121; FAX: 719-543-688
Worthy Products, Inc., RR 1, P.O. Box 213, Martville 13111 / 315-324-5298
Wostenholm (See Ibberson [Sheffield] Ltd., George)
Wright's Gunstock Blanks, 8540 SE Kane Rd., Gresh 97080 / 503-666-1705 doyal@wrightsguns.com www.wrightsguns.com
WTA Manufacturing, P.O. Box 164, Kit Carson, CO 8 800-700-3054; FAX: 719-962-3570 wta@rebelte http://www.members.aol.com/ductman249/wta.
Wyant Bullets, Gen. Del., Swan Lake, MT 59911
Wyant's Outdoor Products, Inc., P.O. Box 9, Broadw 22815
Wyoming Custom Bullets, 1626 21st St., Cody, WY
Wyoming Knife Corp., 101 Commerce Dr., Ft. Collins 80524 / 303-224-3454

X

X-Spand Target Systems, 26-10th St. SE, Medicine H T1A 1P7 CANADA / 403-526-7997; FAX: 403-52

Y

Yankee Gunsmith "Just Glocks", 2901 Deer Flat Dr., Co Cove, TX 76522 / 817-547-8433; FAX: 254-547- ed@justglocks.com www.justglocks.com
Yavapai College, 1100 E. Sheldon St., Prescott, AZ 8 520-776-2353; FAX: 520-776-2355
Yavapai Firearms Academy Ltd., P.O. Box 27290, Pre Valley, AZ 86312 / 928-772-8262; FAX: 928-772 info@yfainc.corn www.yfainc.com
Yearout, Lewis E. (See Montana Outfitters), 308 River E., Great Falls, MT 59404 / 406-761-0859; or 406-727-4569
Yellowstone Wilderness Supply, P.O. Box 129, W. Yellowstone, MT 59758 / 406-646-7613
Yesteryear Armory & Supply, P.O. Box 408, Carthage 37030
York M-1 Conversion, 12145 Mill Creek Run, Planters 77363 / 936-894-2397; FAX: 936-894-2397 bmf25years@aol.com
Young Country Arms, William, 1409 Kuehner Dr. #13 Valley, CA 93063-4478

Z

Zabala Hermanos S.A., P.O. Box 97, 20600 Elbar, Elg Guipuzcoa, 20600 SPAIN / 943-768076; FAX: 943-768201 imanol@zabalahermanos.com www.zabalabermanos.com
Zander's Sporting Goods, 7525 Hwy 154 West, Baldw 62217-9706 / 800-851-4373; FAX: 618-785-232
Zanotti Armor, Inc., 123 W. Lone Tree Rd., Cedar Fal 50613 / 319-232-9650 www.zanottiarmor.com
Zeeryp, Russ, 1601 Foard Dr., Lynn Ross Manor, Morristown, TN 37814 / 615-586-2357
Zero Ammunition Co., Inc., 1601 22nd St. SE, P.O. Bo Cullman, AL 35056-1188 / 800-545-9376; FAX: 205-739-4683
Ziegel Engineering, 1390 E. Bunnett St. "F", Signal Hi 90755 / 562-596-9481; FAX: 562-598-4734 ziegel@aol.com www.ziegeleng.com
Zim's, Inc., 4370 S. 3rd West, Salt Lake City, UT 841 801-268-2505
Z-M Weapons, 203 South St., Bernardston, MA 0133 413-648-9501; FAX: 413-648-0219
Zufall, Joseph F., P.O. Box 304, Golden, CO 80402-0

PERIODICAL PUBLICATIONS

. News (M)
Cherokee Ave., Tampa, FL 33604. Official newsletter of merican Airgun Field Target Assn.

ccurate Rifle
sions Shooting, Inc., 222 Mckee Street, Manchester CT 0. $37 yr. Dedicated to the rifle accuracy enthusiast.

Pursuit Games Magazine (M)
Enterprises, Inc., 4201 W. Vanowen Pl., Burbank, CA 5 818-845-2656. $4.99 single copy U.S., $5.50 Canada. r: Dan Reeves. World's leading magazine of paintball s.

nner Magazine
e Courtyard, Denmark St., Wokingham, Berkshire RG11 England/011-44-734-771677. $U.S. $44 for 1 yr. Leading thly airgun magazine in U.K.

n Ads
33, Hamilton, MT 59840/406-363-3805; Fax: 363-4117. $35 1 yr. (for first mailing; $20 for second mailing; for Canada and foreign orders.) Monthly tabloid with nsive For Sale and Wanted airgun listings.

irgun Letter
p, Inc., 4614 Woodland Rd., Ellicott City, MD 42-6329/410-730-5496; Fax: 410-730-9544; e-mail: @airgnltr.net; http://www.airgunletter.com. $21 U.S., $24 ada, $27 Mexico and $33 other foreign orders, 1 yr. Monthly sletter for airgun users and collectors.

n World
e Courtyard, Denmark St., Wokingham, Berkshire RG40 , England/011-44-734-771677. Call for subscription rates. est monthly airgun magazine in the U.K., now a sister lication to *Air Gunner.*

ka Magazine
ris Communications, 735 Broad Street, Augusta, GA 01/706-722-6060. Hunting, Fishing and Life on the Last ntier articles of Alaska and western Canada.

rican Firearms Industry
'l. Assn. of Federally Licensed Firearms Dealers, 2455 E. rise Blvd., Suite 916, Ft. Lauderdale, FL 33304. $35.00 yr. firearms retailers, distributors and manufacturers.

rican Guardian
A, 11250 Waples Mill Rd., Fairfax, VA 22030. Publications sion. $15.00 1 yr. Magazine features personal protection; me-self-defense; family recreation shooting; women's issues;

rican Gunsmith
lvoir Publications, Inc., 75 Holly Hill Lane, Greenwich, CT 836-2626/203-661-6111. $49.00 (12 issues). Technical rnal of firearms repair and maintenance.

rican Handgunner*
blisher's Development Corp., 591 Camino de la Reina, Suite 0, San Diego, CA 92108/800-537-3006 $16.95 yr. Articles for ndgun enthusiasts, competitors, police and hunters.

rican Hunter (M)
ational Rifle Assn., 11250 Waples Mill Rd., Fairfax, VA 22030 ame address for both.) Publications Div. $35.00 yr. Wide ope of hunting articles.

rican Rifleman (M)
ational Rifle Assn., 11250 Waples Mill Rd., Fairfax, VA 22030 ame address for both). Publications Div. $35.00 yr. Firearms ticles of all kinds.

erican Survival Guide
cMullen Angus Publishing, Inc., 774 S. Placentia Ave., acentia, CA 92670-6846. 12 issues $19.95/714-572-2255; AX: 714-572-1864.

nes & Tir*
o FABECO, 38, rue de Trévise 75009 Paris, France. Articles r hunters, collectors, and shooters. French text.

ns Collecting (Q)
useum Restoration Service, P.O. Box 70, Alexandria Bay, NY 3607-0070. $22.00 yr.; $62.00 3 yrs.; $112.00 5 yrs.
ustralian Shooter *(formerly Australian Shooters Journal)*
porting Shooters' Assn. of Australia, Inc., P.O. Box 2066, ent Town SA 5071, Australia. $60.00 yr. locally; $65.00 yr. verseas surface mail. Hunting and shooting articles.

e Backwoodsman Magazine
.O. Box 627, Westcliffe, CO 81252. $16.00 for 6 issues per yr.; 30.00 for 2 yrs.; sample copy $2.75. Subjects include nuzzle-loading, woodslore, primitive survival, trapping, omesteading, blackpowder cartridge guns, 19th century ow-to.

ack Powder Cartridge News (Q)
SPG, Inc., P.O. Box 761, Livingston, MT 59047/Phone/Fax: 406-222-8416. $17 yr. (4 issues) ($6 extra 1st class mailing). For he blackpowder cartridge enthusiast.

ackpowder Hunting (M)
ntl. Blackpowder Hunting Assn., P.O. Box 1180Z, Glenrock, WY 82637/307-436-9817. $20.00 1 yr., $36.00 2 yrs. How-to and where-to features by experts on hunting; shooting; ballistics; traditional and modern blackpowder rifles, shotguns, pistols and cartridges.

lack Powder Times
P.O. Box 234, Lake Stevens, WA 98258. $20.00 yr.; add $5 per year for Canada, $10 per year other foreign. Tabloid newspaper for blackpowder activities; test reports.

lade Magazine
Krause Publications, 700 East State St., Iola, WI 54990-0001. $25.98 for 12 issues. Foreign price (including Canada-Mexico) $50.00. A magazine for all enthusiasts of handmade, factory and antique knives.

Caliber
GFI-Verlag, Theodor-Heuss Ring 62, 50668 Koln, Germany. For hunters, target shooters and reloaders.

The Caller (Q) (M)
National Wild Turkey Federation, P.O. Box 530, Edgefield, SC 29824. Tabloid newspaper for members; 4 issues per yr. (membership fee $25.00)

Cartridge Journal (M)
Robert Mellichamp, 907 Shirkmere, Houston, TX 77008/713-869-0558. Dues $12 for U.S. and Canadian members (includes the newsletter); 6 issues.

The Cast Bullet*(M)
Official journal of The Cast Bullet Assn. Director of Membership, 203 E. 2nd St., Muscatine, IA 52761. Annual membership dues $14, includes 6 issues.

Cibles
14, rue du Patronage-Laique, BP 2057, 52902 Chaumont, cedex 9, France. French-language arms magazine also carries a small amount of arms-related and historical content. 12 issues per year. Tel/03-25-03-87-47/Email cibeles@graphycom.com; Website: www.graphycom.com

COLTELLI, che Passione (Q)
Casella postale N.519, 20101 Milano, Italy/Fax:02-48402857. $15 1 yr., $27 2 yrs. Covers all types of knives—collecting, combat, historical. Italian text.

Combat Handguns*
Harris Publications, Inc., 1115 Broadway, New York, NY 10010.

Deer & Deer Hunting Magazine
Krause Publications, 700 E. State St., Iola, WI 54990-0001. $19.95 yr. (9 issues). For the serious deer hunter. Website: www.krause.com

The Derringer Peanut (M)
The National Association of Derringer Collectors, P.O. Box 20572, San Jose, CA 95160. A newsletter dedicated to developing the best derringer information. Write for details.

Deutsches Waffen Journal
Journal-Verlag Schwend GmbH, Postfach 100340, D-74503 Schwäbisch Hall, Germany/0791-404-500; FAX:0791-404-505 and 404-424. DM102 p. yr. (interior); DM125.30 (abroad), postage included. Antique and modern arms and equipment. German text.

Double Gun Journal
P.O. Box 550, East Jordan, MI 49727/800-447-1658. $35 for 4 issues.

Ducks Unlimited, Inc. (M)
1 Waterfowl Way, Memphis, TN 38120

The Engraver (M) (Q)
P.O. Box 4365, Estes Park, CO 80517/970-586-2388; Fax: 970-586-0394. Mike Dubber, editor. The journal of firearms engraving.

The Field
King's Reach Tower, Stamford St., London SE1 9LS England. £36.40 U.K. 1 yr.; 49.90 (overseas, surface mail) yr.; £82.00 (overseas, air mail) yr. Hunting and shooting articles, and all country sports.

Field & Stream
Time4 Media, Two Park Ave., New York, NY 10016/212-779-5000. 12 issues/$19.97. Monthly shooting column. Articles on hunting and fishing.

Field Tests
Belvoir Publications, Inc., 75 Holly Hill Lane; P.O. Box 2626, Greenwich, CT 06836-2626/203-661-6111; 800-829-3361 (subscription line). U.S. & Canada $29 1 yr., $58 2 yrs.; all other countries $45 1 yr., $90 2 yrs. (air).

Fur-Fish-Game
A.R. Harding Pub. Co., 2878 E. Main St., Columbus, OH 43209. $15.95 yr. Practical guidance regarding trapping, fishing and hunting.

The Gottlieb-Tartaro Report
Second Amendment Foundation, James Madison Bldg., 12500 NE 10th Pl., Bellevue, WA 98005/206-454-7012;Fax:206-451-3959. $30 for 12 issues. An insiders guide for gun owners.

Gray's Sporting Journal
Gray's Sporting Journal, P.O. Box 1207, Augusta, GA 30903. $36.95 per yr. for 6 issues. Hunting and fishing journals. Expeditions and Guides Book (Annual Travel Guide).

Gun List†
700 E. State St., Iola, WI 54990. $37.98 yr. (26 issues); $66.98 2 yrs. (52 issues). Indexed market publication for firearms collectors and active shooters; guns, supplies and services. Website: www.krause.com

Gun News Digest (Q)
Second Amendment Fdn., P.O. Box 488, Station C, Buffalo, NY 14209/716-885-6408; Fax:716-884-4471. $10 U.S.; $20 foreign.

The Gun Report
World Wide Gun Report, Inc., Box 38, Aledo, IL 61231-0038. $33.00 yr. For the antique and collectable gun dealer and collector.

Gunmaker (M) (Q)
ACGG, P.O. Box 812, Burlington, IA 52601-0812. The journal of custom gunmaking.

The Gunrunner
Div. of Kexco Publ. Co. Ltd., Box 565G, Lethbridge, Alb., Canada T1J 3Z4. $23.00 yr., sample $2.00. Monthly newspaper, listing everything from antiques to artillery.

Gun Show Calendar (Q)
700 E. State St., Iola, WI 54990. $14.95 yr. (4 issues). Gun shows listed; chronologically and by state. Website: www.krause.com

Gun Tests
11 Commerce Blvd., Palm Coast, FL 32142. The consumer resource for the serious shooter. Write for information.

Gun Trade News
Bruce Publishing Ltd., P.O. Box 82, Wantage, Ozon OX12 7A8, England/44-1-235-771770; Fax: 44-1-235-771848. Britain's only "trade only" magazine exclusive to the gun trade.

Gun Week†
Second Amendment Foundation, P.O. Box 488, Station C, Buffalo, NY 14209. $35.00 yr. U.S. and possessions; $45.00 yr. other countries. Tabloid paper on guns, hunting, shooting and collecting (36 issues).

Gun World
Y-Visionary Publishing, LP 265 South Anita Drive, Ste. 120, Orange, CA 92868. $21.97 yr.; $34.97 2 yrs. For the hunting, reloading and shooting enthusiast.

Guns & Ammo
Primedia, 6420 Wilshire Blvd., Los Angeles, CA 90048/213-782-2780. $23.94 yr. Guns, shooting, and technical articles.

Guns
Publishers Development Corporation, P.O. Box 85201, San Diego, CA 92138/800-537-3006. $19.95 yr. In-depth articles on a wide range of guns, shooting equipment and related accessories for gun collectors, hunters and shooters.

Guns Review
Ravenhill Publishing Co. Ltd., Box 35, Standard House, Bonhill St., London EC 2A 4DA, England. £20.00 sterling (approx. U.S. $38 USA & Canada) yr. For collectors and shooters.

H.A.C.S. Newsletter (M)
Harry Moon, Pres., P.O. Box 50117, South Slope RPO, Burnaby BC, V5J 5G3, Canada/604-438-0950; Fax:604-277-3646. $25 p. yr. U.S. and Canada. Official newsletter of The Historical Arms Collectors of B.C. (Canada).

Handgunner*
Richard A.J. Munday, Seychelles house, Brightlingsen, Essex CO7 ONN, England/012063-305201. £18.00 (sterling).

Handguns*
Primedia, 6420 Wilshire Blvd., Los Angeles, CA 90048/323-782-2868. For the handgunning and shooting enthusiast.

Handloader*
Wolfe Publishing Co., 2626 Stearman Road, Ste. A, Prescott, AZ 86301/520-445-7810;Fax:520-778-5124. $22.00 yr. The journal of ammunition reloading.

INSIGHTS*
NRA, 11250 Waples Mill Rd., Fairfax, VA 22030. Editor, John E. Robbins. $15.00 yr., which includes NRA junior membership; $10.00 for adult subscriptions (12 issues). Plenty of details for the young hunter and target shooter; emphasizes gun safety, marksmanship training, hunting skills.

International Arms & Militaria Collector (Q)
Arms & Militaria Press, P.O. Box 80, Labrador, Qld. 4215, Australia. A$39.50 yr. (U.S. & Canada), 2 yrs. A$77.50; A$37.50 (others), 1 yr., 2 yrs. $73.50 all air express mail; surface mail is less. Editor: Ian D. Skennerton.

International Shooting Sport*/UIT Journal
International Shooting Union (UIT), Bavariaring 21, D-80336 Munich, Germany. Europe: (Deutsche Mark) DM44.00 yr., 2 yrs. DM83.00; outside Europe: DM50.00 yr., 2 yrs. DM95.00 (air mail postage included.) For international sport shooting.

Internationales Waffen-Magazin
Habegger-Verlag Zürich, Postfach 9230, CH-8036 Zürich, Switzerland. SF 105.00 (approx. U.S. $73.00) surface mail for 10 issues. Modern and antique arms, self-defense. German text; English summary of contents.

The Journal of the Arms & Armour Society (M)
A. Dove, P.O. Box 10232, London, SW19 2ZD England. £15.00 surface mail; £20.00 airmail sterling only yr. Articles for the historian and collector.

Journal of the Historical Breechloading Smallarms Assn.
Published annually. P.O. Box 12778, London, SE1 6XB, England. $21.00 yr. Articles for the collector plus mailings of short articles on specific arms, reprints, newsletters, etc.

Knife World
Knife World Publications, P.O. Box 3395, Knoxville, TN 37927. $15.00 yr.; $25.00 2 yrs. Published monthly for knife enthusiasts and collectors. Articles on custom and factory knives; other knife-related interests, monthly column on knife identification, military knives.

Man At Arms*
P.O. Box 460, Lincoln, RI 02865. $27.00 yr., $52.00 2 yrs. plus $8.00 for foreign subscribers. The N.R.A. magazine of arms collecting-investing, with excellent articles for the collector of antique arms and militaria.

The Mannlicher Collector (Q)(M)
Mannlicher Collectors Assn., Inc., P.O. Box 7144, Salem Oregon 97303. $20/ yr. subscription included in membership.

MAGNUM
Rua Madre Rita Amada de Jesus, 182 , Granja Julieta, Sao Paulo – SP – 04721-050 Brazil. No details.

---

*Published bi-monthly
† Published weekly
‡Published three times per month. All others are published monthly.

M=Membership requirements; write for details.
Q=Published Quarterly.

PERIODICAL PUBLICATIONS

MAN/MAGNUM
S.A. Man (Pty) Ltd., P.O. Box 35204, Northway, Durban 4065, Republic of South Africa. SA Rand 200.00 for 12 issues. Africa's only publication on hunting, shooting, firearms, bushcraft, knives, etc.

The Marlin Collector (M)
R.W. Paterson, 407 Lincoln Bldg., 44 Main St., Champaign, IL 61820.

Muzzle Blasts (M)
National Muzzle Loading Rifle Assn., P.O. Box 67, Friendship, IN 47021/812-667-5131. $35.00 yr. annual membership. For the blackpowder shooter.

Muzzleloader Magazine*
Scurlock Publishing Co., Inc., Dept. Gun, Route 5, Box 347-M, Texarkana, TX 75501. $18.00 U.S.; $22.50 U.S./yr. for foreign subscribers. The publication for blackpowder shooters.

National Defense (M)*
American Defense Preparedness Assn., Two Colonial Place, Suite 400, 2101 Wilson Blvd., Arlington, VA 22201-3061/703-522-1820; FAX: 703-522-1885. $35.00 yr. Articles on both military and civil defense field, including weapons, materials technology, management.

National Knife Magazine (M)
Natl. Knife Coll. Assn., 7201 Shallowford Rd., P.O. Box 21070, Chattanooga, TN 37424-0070. Membership $35 yr.; $65.00 International yr.

National Rifle Assn. Journal (British) (Q)
Natl. Rifle Assn. (BR.), Bisley Camp, Brookwood, Woking, Surrey, England. GU24, OPB. £24.00 Sterling including postage.

National Wildlife*
Natl. Wildlife Fed., 1400 16th St. NW, Washington, DC 20036, $16.00 yr. (6 issues); *International Wildlife*, 6 issues, $16.00 yr. Both, $22.00 yr., includes all membership benefits. Write attn.: Membership Services Dept., for more information.

New Zealand GUNS*
Waitekauri Publishing, P.O. 45, Waikino 3060, New Zealand. $NZ90.00 (6 issues) yr. Covers the hunting and firearms scene in New Zealand.

New Zealand Wildlife (Q)
New Zealand Deerstalkers Assoc., Inc., P.O. Box 6514, Wellington, N.Z. $30.00 (N.Z.). Hunting, shooting and firearms/game research articles.

North American Hunter* (M)
P.O. Box 3401, Minnetonka, MN 55343/612-936-9333; e-mail: huntingclub@pclink.com. $18.00 yr. (7 issues). Articles on all types of North American hunting.

Outdoor Life
Time4 Media, Two Park Ave., New York, NY 10016. $14.97/10 issues. Extensive coverage of hunting and shooting. Shooting column by Jim Carmichel.

La Passion des Courteaux (Q)
Phenix Editions, 25 rue Mademoiselle, 75015 Paris, France. French text.

Paintball Games International Magazine
Aceville Publications, Castle House, 97 High St., Colchester, Essex, England CO1 1TH/011-44-206-564840. Write for subscription rates. Leading magazine in the U.K. covering competitive paintball activities.

Paintball News
PBN Publishing, P.O. Box 1608, 24 Henniker St., Hillsboro, NH 03244/603-464-6080. $35 U.S. 1 yr. Bi-weekly. Newspaper covering the sport of paintball, new product reviews and industry features.

Paintball Sports (Q)
Paintball Publications, Inc., 540 Main St., Mount Kisco, NY 10549/941-241-7400. $24.75 U.S. 1 yr., $32.75 foreign. Covering the competitive paintball scene.

Performance Shooter
Belvoir Publications, Inc., 75 Holly Hill Lane, Greenwich, CT 06836-2626/203-661-6111. $45.00 yr. (12 issues). Techniques and technology for improved rifle and pistol accuracy.

Petersen's HUNTING Magazine
Primedia, 6420 Wilshire Blvd., Los Angeles, CA 90048. $19.94 yr.; Canada $29.34 yr.; foreign countries $29.94 yr. Hunting articles for all game; test reports.

P.I. Magazine
America's Private Investigation Journal, 755 Bronx Dr., Toledo, OH 43609. Chuck Klein, firearms editor with column about handguns.

Pirsch
BLV Verlagsgesellschaft GmbH, Postfach 400320, 80703 Munich, Germany/089-12704-0;Fax:089-12705-354. German text.

Point Blank
Citizens Committee for the Right to Keep and Bear Arms (sent to contributors), Liberty Park, 12500 NE 10th Pl., Bellevue, WA 98005

POINTBLANK (M)
Natl. Firearms Assn., Box 4384 Stn. C, Calgary, AB T2T 5N2, Canada. Official publication of the NFA.

The Police Marksman*
6000 E. Shirley Lane, Montgomery, AL 36117. $17.95 yr. For law enforcement personnel.

Police Times (M)
3801 Biscayne Blvd., Miami, FL 33137/305-573-0070.

Popular Mechanics
Hearst Corp., 224 W. 57th St., New York, NY 10019. Firearms, camping, outdoor oriented articles.

Precision Shooting
Precision Shooting, Inc., 222 McKee St., Manchester, CT 06040. $37.00 yr. U.S. Journal of the International Benchrest Shooters, and target shooting in general. Also considerable coverage of varmint shooting, as well as big bore, small bore, schuetzen, lead bullet, wildcats and precision reloading.

Rifle*
Wolfe Publishing Co., 2626 Stearman Road, Ste. A, Prescott, AZ 86301/520-445-7810; Fax: 520-778-5124. $19.00 yr. The sporting firearms journal.

Rifle's Hunting Annual
Wolfe Publishing Co., 2626 Stearman Road, Ste. A, Prescott, AZ 86301/520-445-7810; Fax: 520-778-5124. $4.99 Annual. Dedicated to the finest pursuit of the hunt.

Rod & Rifle Magazine
Lithographic Serv. Ltd., P.O. Box 38-138, Wellington, New Zealand. $50.00 yr. (6 issues). Hunting, shooting and fishing articles.

Safari* (M)
Safari Magazine, 4800 W. Gates Pass Rd., Tucson, AZ 85745/602-620-1220. $55.00 (6 times). The journal of big game hunting, published by Safari Club International. Also publish *Safari Times*, a monthly newspaper, included in price of $55.00 national membership.

Second Amendment Reporter
Second Amendment Foundation, James Madison Bldg., 12500 NE 10th Pl., Bellevue, WA 98005. $15.00 yr. (non-contributors).

Shoot! Magazine*
Shoot! Magazine Corp., 1770 West State Stret PMB 340, Boise ID 83702/208-368-9920; Fax: 208-338-8428. Website: www.shootmagazine.com; $32.95 (6 times/yr.). Articles of interest to the cowboy action shooter, or others interested the Western-era firearms and ammunition.

Shooter's News
23146 Lorain Rd., Box 349, North Olmsted, OH 44070/216-979-5258;Fax:216-979-5259. $29 U.S. 1 yr., $54 2 yrs.; $52 foreign surface. A journal dedicated to precision riflery.

Shooting Industry
Publisher's Dev. Corp., 591 Camino de la Reina, Suite 200, San Diego, CA 92108. $50.00 yr. To the trade. $25.00.

Shooting Sports USA
National Rifle Assn. of America, 11250 Waples Mill Road, Fairfax, VA 22030. Annual subscriptions for NRA members are $5 for classified shooters and $10 for non-classified shooters. Non-NRA member subscriptions are $15. Covering events, techniques and personalities in competitive shooting.

Shooting Sportsman*
P.O. Box 11282, Des Moines, IA 50340/800-666-4955 (for subscriptions). Editorial: P.O. Box 1357, Camden, ME 04843. $19.95 for six issues. The magazine of wingshooting and fine guns.

The Shooting Times & Country Magazine (England)†
IPC Magazines Ltd., King's Reach Tower, Stamford St, 1 London SE1 9LS, England/0171-261-6180;Fax:0171-261-7179. £65 (approx. $98.00) yr.; £79 yr. overseas (52 issues). Game shooting, wild fowling, hunting, game fishing and firearms articles. Britain's best selling field sports magazine.

Shooting Times
Primedia, 2 News Plaza, P.O. Box 1790, Peoria, IL 61656/309-682-6626. $16.97 yr. Guns, shooting, reloading; articles on every gun activity.

The Shotgun News‡
Primedia, 2 News Plaza, P.O. Box 1790, Peoria, IL 61656/800-495-8362. 36 issues/ yr. @ $28.95; 12 issues/yr. @ $19.95. foreign subscription call for rates. Sample copy $4.00. Gun ads of all kinds.

SHOT Business
National Shooting Sports Foundation, Flintlock Ridge Office Center, 11 Mile Hill Rd., Newtown, CT 06470-2359/203-426-1320; FAX: 203-426-1087. For the shooting, hunting and outdoor trade retailer.

Shotgun Sports
P.O. Box 6810, Auburn, CA 95604/916-889-2220; FAX:916-889-9106. $31.00 yr. Trapshooting how-to's, shotshell reloading, shotgun patterning, shotgun tests and evaluations, Sporting Clays action, waterfowl/upland hunting. Call 1-800-676-8920 for a free sample copy.

The Single Shot Exhange Magazine
PO box 1055, York SC 29745/803-628-5326 phone/fax. $31.50/yr., monthly. Articles of interest to the blackpowder cartridge shooter and antique arms collector.

Single Shot Rifle Journal* (M)
Editor John Campbell, PO Box 595, Bloomfield Hills, MI 48303/248-458-8415. Email: jcampbel@dmbb.com Annual dues $35 for 6 issues. Journal of the American Single Shot Rifle Assn.

The Sixgunner (M)
Handgun Hunters International, P.O. Box 357, MAG, Bloomingdale, OH 43910

The Skeet Shooting Review
National Skeet Shooting Assn., 5931 Roft Rd., San Antonio, TX 78253. $20.00 yr. (Assn. membership includes mag.) Competition results, personality profiles of top Skeet shooters, how-to articles, technical, reloading information.

Soldier of Fortune
Subscription Dept., P.O. Box 348, Mt. Morris, IL 61054. $29.95 yr.; $39.95 Canada; $50.95 foreign.
Sporting Classics

Sporting Classics, Inc.
PO Box 23707, Columbia, SC 29223/1-800-849-1004. 1 yr/6 issues/$23.95; 2 yrs./12 issues/$38.95; 3 yrs./18 issues/$ Firearms & outdoor articles and columns.

Sporting Clays Magazine
Patch Communications, 5211 South Washington Ave., Titusville, FL 32780/407-268-5010; FAX: 407-267-7216. $ yr. (12 issues). Official publication of the National Sporti Clays Association.

Sporting Goods Business
Miller Freeman, Inc., One Penn Plaza, 10th Fl., New Yor 10119-0004. Trade journal.

Sporting Goods Dealer
Two Park Ave., New York, NY 10016. $100.00 yr. Sportir goods trade journal.

Sporting Gun
Bretton Court, Bretton, Peterborough PE3 8DZ, England. £27.00 (approx. U.S. $36.00), airmail £35.50 yr. For the g and clay enthusiasts.

Sports Afield
15621 Chemical Lane, Huntington Beach CA 92648. U.S./800-234-3537. International/714-894-9080. Nine iss for $29.97. Website: www.sportsafield.com. America's o outdoor publication is now devoted to high-end sporting pursuits, especially in North America and Africa.

The Squirrel Hunter
P.O. Box 368, Chireno, TX 75937. $14.00 yr. Articles abo squirrel hunting.

Stott's Creek Calendar
Stott's Creek Printers, 2526 S 475 W, Morgantown, IN 46160/317-878-5489. 1 yr (3 issues) $11.50; 2 yrs. (6 issu $20.00. Lists all gun shows everywhere in convenient cale form; call for information.

Super Outdoors
2695 Aiken Road, Shelbyville, KY 40065/502-722-9463; 800-404-6064; Fax: 502-722-8093. Mark Edwards, publish Contact for details.

TACARMI
Via E. De Amicis, 25; 20123 Milano, Italy. $100.00 yr. appr Antique and modern guns. (Italian text.)

Territorial Dispatch—1800s Historical Publication (M
National Assn. of Buckskinners, 4701 Marion St., Suite 324 Livestock Exchange Bldg., Denver, CO 80216. Michael A. Nester & Barbara Wyckoff, editors. 303-297-9671.

Trap & Field
1000 Waterway Blvd., Indianapolis, IN 46202. $25.00 yr. Off publ. Amateur Trapshooting Assn. Scores, averages, trapshooting articles.

Turkey Call* (M)
Natl. Wild Turkey Federation, Inc., P.O. Box 530, Edgefield, 29824. $25.00 with membership (6 issues per yr.)

Turkey & Turkey Hunting*
Krause Publications, 700 E. State St., Iola, WI 54990-0001. $13.95 (6 issue p. yr.). Magazine with leading-edge articles all aspects of wild turkey behavior, biology and the success ways to hunt better with that info. Learn the proper technique calling, the right equipment, and more.

The U.S. Handgunner* (M)
U.S. Revolver Assn., 40 Larchmont Ave., Taunton, MA 027 $10.00 yr. General handgun and competition articles. Bi-monthly sent to members.

U.S. Airgun Magazine
P.O. Box 2021, Benton, AR 72018/800-247-4867; Fax: 501-316-8549. 10 issues a yr. Cover the sport from hunting, 10-meter, field target and collecting. Write for details.

The Varmint Hunter Magazine (Q)
The Varmint Hunters Assn., Box 759, Pierre, SD 57501/800-528-4868. $24.00 yr.

Waffenmarkt-Intern
GFI-Verlag, Theodor-Heuss Ring 62, 50668 K"ln, Germany. Only for gunsmiths, licensed firearms dealers and their supplie in Germany, Austria and Switzerland.

Wild Sheep (M) (Q)
Foundation for North American Wild Sheep, 720 Allen Ave., Cody, WY 82414. Website: http://iigi.com/os/non/fnaws/fnaws.htm; e-mail: fnaws@wyoming.com. Official journal of the foundation.

Wisconsin Outdoor Journal
Krause Publications, 700 E. State St., Iola, WI 54990-0001. $17.97 yr. (8 issues). For Wisconsin's avid hunters and fishermen, with features from all over that state with regional reports, legislative updates, etc. Website: www.krause.com

Women & Guns
P.O. Box 488, Sta. C, Buffalo, NY 14209. $24.00 yr. U.S.; $72.00 foreign (12 issues). Only magazine edited by and for women gun owners.

World War II*
Cowles History Group, 741 Miller Dr. SE, Suite D-2, Leesburg VA 20175-8920. Annual subscriptions $19.95 U.S.; $25.95 Canada; 43.95 foreign. The title says it—WWII; good articles, ads, etc.

*Published bi-monthly
† Published weekly
‡Published three times per month. All others are published monthly.

M=Membership requirements; write for details.
Q=Published Quarterly.

ARMS ASSOCIATIONS

NITED STATES

ALABAMA

na Gun Collectors Assn.
ary, P.O. Box 70965,
oosa, AL 35407

ALASKA

Gun Collectors Assn., Inc.
oyd, Pres., 5240 Little Tree,
rage, AK 99507

ARIZONA

a Arms Assn.
eBusk, President, 4837
Ave., Glendale, AZ 85301

CALIFORNIA

rnia Cartridge Collectors
Montgomery, 1729 Christina,
ton, CA
/209-463-7216 evs.

rnia Waterfowl Assn.
Northgate Blvd., #150,
mento, CA 95834

er Calif. Arms & Collectors
d L. Bullock, 8291 Carburton
ong Beach, CA 90808-3302

ngeles Gun Ctg. Collectors
Ruffra, 20810 Amie Ave., Apt.
orrance, CA 90503

Gun Players Assn.
Appian Way, Long Beach,
0803

COLORADO

rado Gun Collectors Assn.
Bud) Greenwald, 2553 S.
man St., Denver, CO
9/303-935-3850

**y Mountain Cartridge
ectors Assn.**
Roth, P.O. Box 757, Conifer,
0433

CONNECTICUT

onnecticut Gun Guild, Inc.
Fraser, P.O. Box 425,
dsor, CT 06095

FLORIDA

ied Sportsmen of Florida
Box 6565, Tallahassee, FL
14

GEORGIA

rgia Arms Collectors Assn.,
hael Kindberg, President, P.O.
277, Alpharetta, GA
39-0277

ILLINOIS

nois State Rifle Assn.
Box 637, Chatsworth, IL
921

**ssissippi Valley Gun &
rtridge Coll. Assn.**
Filbert, P.O. Box 61, Port
ron, IL 61275/309-523-2593

k Trail Gun Collectors
rdell M. Matson, P.O. Box 1113,
an, IL 61264

**abash Valley Gun Collectors
sn., Inc.**
ger L. Dorsett, 2601 Willow Rd.,
bana, IL 61801/217-384-7302

INDIANA

diana State Rifle & Pistol Assn.
os. Glancy, P.O. Box 552,
esterton, IN 46304

**uthern Indiana Gun Collectors
sn., Inc.**
eila McClary, 309 W. Monroe
., Boonville, IN
601/812-897-3742

IOWA

eaver Creek Plainsmen Inc.
teve Murphy, Secy., P.O. Box 298,
Bondurant, IA 50035

Central States Gun Collectors Assn.
Dennis Greischar, Box 841, Mason City, IA 50402-0841

KANSAS

Kansas Cartridge Collectors Assn.
Bob Linder, Box 84, Plainville, KS 67663

KENTUCKY

Kentuckiana Arms Collectors Assn.
Charles Billips, President, Box 1776, Louisville, KY 40201

Kentucky Gun Collectors Assn., Inc.
Ruth Johnson, Box 64, Owensboro, KY 42302/502-729-4197

LOUISIANA

Washitaw River Renegades
Sandra Rushing, P.O. Box 256, Main St., Grayson, LA 71435

MARYLAND

Baltimore Antique Arms Assn.
Mr. Cillo, 1034 Main St., Darlington, MD 21304

MASSACHUSETTS

Bay Colony Weapons Collectors, Inc.
John Brandt, Box 111, Hingham, MA 02043

Massachusetts Arms Collectors
Bruce E. Skinner, P.O. Box 31, No. Carver, MA 02355/508-866-5259

MICHIGAN

Association for the Study and Research of .22 Caliber Rimfire Cartridges
George Kass, 4512 Nakoma Dr., Okemos, MI 48864

MINNESOTA

Sioux Empire Cartridge Collectors Assn.
Bob Cameron, 14597 Glendale Ave. SE, Prior Lake, MN 55372

MISSISSIPPI

Mississippi Gun Collectors Assn.
Jack E. Swinney, P.O. Box 16323, Hattiesburg, MS 39402

MISSOURI

Greater St. Louis Cartridge Collectors Assn.
Don MacChesney, 634 Scottsdale Rd., Kirkwood, MO 63122-1109

Mineral Belt Gun Collectors Assn.
D.F. Saunders, 1110 Cleveland Ave., Monett, MO 65708

Missouri Valley Arms Collectors Assn., Inc.
L.P Brammer II, Membership Secy., P.O. Box 33033, Kansas City, MO 64114

MONTANA

Montana Arms Collectors Assn.
Dean E. Yearout, Sr., Exec. Secy., 1516 21st Ave. S., Great Falls, MT 59405

Weapons Collectors Society of Montana
R.G. Schipf, Ex. Secy., 3100 Bancroft St., Missoula, MT 59801/406-728-2995

NEBRASKA

Nebraska Cartridge Collectors Club
Gary Muckel, P.O. Box 84442, Lincoln, NE 68501

NEW HAMPSHIRE

New Hampshire Arms Collectors, Inc.
James Stamatelos, Secy., P.O. Box 5, Cambridge, MA 02139

NEW JERSEY

Englishtown Benchrest Shooters Assn.
Michael Toth, 64 Cooke Ave., Carteret, NJ 07008

Jersey Shore Antique Arms Collectors
Joe Sisia, P.O. Box 100, Bayville, NJ 08721-0100

New Jersey Arms Collectors Club, Inc.
Angus Laidlaw, Vice President, 230 Valley Rd., Montclair, NJ 07042/201-746-0939; e-mail: acclaidlaw@juno.com

NEW YORK

Iroquois Arms Collectors Assn.
Bonnie Robinson, Show Secy., P.O. Box 142, Ransomville, NY 14131/716-791-4096

Mid-State Arms Coll. & Shooters Club
Jack Ackerman, 24 S. Mountain Terr., Binghamton, NY 13903

NORTH CAROLINA

North Carolina Gun Collectors Assn.
Jerry Ledford, 3231-7th St. Dr. NE, Hickory, NC 28601

OHIO

Ohio Gun Collectors Assn.
P.O. Box 9007, Maumee, OH 43537-9007/419-897-0861; Fax:419-897-0860

Shotshell Historical and Collectors Society
Madeline Bruemmer, 3886 Dawley Rd., Ravenna, OH 44266

The Stark Gun Collectors, Inc.
William I. Gann, 5666 Waynesburg Dr., Waynesburg, OH 44688

OREGON

Oregon Arms Collectors Assn., Inc.
Phil Bailey, P.O. Box 13000-A, Portland, OR 97213-0017/503-281-6864; off.:503-281-0918

Oregon Cartridge Collectors Assn.
Boyd Northrup, P.O. Box 285, Rhododendron, OR 97049

PENNSYLVANIA

Presque Isle Gun Collectors Assn.
James Welch, 156 E. 37 St., Erie, PA 16504

SOUTH CAROLINA

Belton Gun Club, Inc.
Attn. Secretary, P.O. Box 126, Belton, SC 29627/864-369-6767

Gun Owners of South Carolina
Membership Div.: William Strozier, Secretary, P.O. Box 70, Johns Island, SC 29457-0070/803-762-3240; Fax:803-795-0711; e-mail:76053.222@compuserve.com

SOUTH DAKOTA

Dakota Territory Gun Coll. Assn., Inc.
Curt Carter, Castlewood, SD 57223

TENNESSEE

Smoky Mountain Gun Coll. Assn., Inc.
Hugh W. Yabro, President, P.O. Box 23225, Knoxville, TN 37933

Tennessee Gun Collectors Assn., Inc.
M.H. Parks, 3556 Pleasant Valley Rd., Nashville, TN 37204-3419

TEXAS

Houston Gun Collectors Assn., Inc.
P.O. Box 741429, Houston, TX 77274-1429

Texas Gun Collectors Assn.
Bob Eder, Pres., P.O. Box 12067, El Paso, TX 79913/915-584-8183

Texas State Rifle Assn.
1131 Rockingham Dr., Suite 101, Richardson, TX 75080-4326

VIRGINIA

Virginia Gun Collectors Assn., Inc.
Addison Hurst, Secy., 38802 Charlestown Height, Waterford, VA 20197/540-882-3543

WASHINGTON

Association of Cartridge Collectors on the Pacific Northwest
Robert Jardin, 14214 Meadowlark Drive KPN, Gig Harbor, WA 98329

Washington Arms Collectors, Inc.
Joyce Boss, P.O. Box 389, Renton, WA, 98057-0389/206-255-8410

WISCONSIN

Great Lakes Arms Collectors Assn., Inc.
Edward C. Warnke, 2913 Woodridge Lane, Waukesha, WI 53188

Wisconsin Gun Collectors Assn., Inc.
Lulita Zellmer, P.O. Box 181, Sussex, WI 53089

WYOMING

Wyoming Weapons Collectors
P.O. Box 284, Laramie, WY 82073/307-745-4652 or 745-9530

NATIONAL ORGANIZATIONS

Amateur Trapshooting Assn.
David D. Bopp, Exec. Director, 601 W. National Rd., Vandalia, OH 45377/937-898-4638; Fax:937-898-5472

American Airgun Field Target Assn.
5911 Cherokee Ave., Tampa, FL 33604

American Coon Hunters Assn.
Opal Johnston, P.O. Cadet, Route 1, Box 492, Old Mines, MO 63630

American Custom Gunmakers Guild
Jan Billeb, Exec. Director, 22 Vista View Drive, Cody, WY 82414-9606 (307) 587-4297 (phone/fax). Email: acgg@acgg.org Website: www.acgg.org

American Defense Preparedness Assn.
Two Colonial Place, 2101 Wilson Blvd., Suite 400, Arlington, VA 22201-3061

American Paintball League
P.O. Box 3561, Johnson City, TN 37602/800-541-9169

American Pistolsmiths Guild
Alex B. Hamilton, Pres., 1449 Blue Crest Lane, San Antonio, TX 78232/210-494-3063

American Police Pistol & Rifle Assn.
3801 Biscayne Blvd., Miami, FL 33137

American Single Shot Rifle Assn.
Gary Staup, Secy., 709 Carolyn Dr., Delphos, OH 45833/419-692-3866. Website: www.assra.com

American Society of Arms Collectors
George E. Weatherly, P.O. Box 2567, Waxahachie, TX 75165

American Tactical Shooting Assn.(A.T.S.A.)
c/o Skip Gochenour, 2600 N. Third St., Harrisburg, PA 17110/717-233-0402; Fax:717-233-5340

Association of Firearm and Tool Mark Examiners
Lannie G. Emanuel, Secy., Southwest Institute of Forensic Sciences, P.O. Box 35728, Dallas, TX 75235/214-920-5979; Fax:214-920-5928; Membership Secy., Ann D. Jones, VA Div. of Forensic Science, P.O. Box 999, Richmond, VA 23208/804-786-4706; Fax:804-371-8328

Boone & Crockett Club
250 Station Dr., Missoula, MT 59801-2753

Browning Collectors Assn.
Secretary:Scherrie L. Brennac, 2749 Keith Dr., Villa Ridge, MO 63089/314-742-0571

The Cast Bullet Assn., Inc.
Ralland J. Fortier, Editor, 4103 Foxcraft Dr., Traverse City, MI 49684

Citizens Committee for the Right to Keep and Bear Arms
Natl. Hq., Liberty Park, 12500 NE Tenth Pl., Bellevue, WA 98005

Colt Collectors Assn.
25000 Highland Way, Los Gatos, CA 95030/408-353-2658.

Contemporary Longrifle Association
P.O. Box 2097, Staunton, VA 24402/540-886-6189. Website: www.CLA@longrifle.ws

Ducks Unlimited, Inc.
Natl. Headquarters, One Waterfowl Way, Memphis, TN 38120/901-758-3937

Fifty Caliber Shooters Assn.
PO Box 111, Monroe UT 84754-0111

Firearms Coalition/Neal Knox Associates
Box 6537, Silver Spring, MD 20906/301-871-3006

Firearms Engravers Guild of America
Rex C. Pedersen, Secy., 511 N. Rath Ave., Lundington, MI 49431/616-845-7695(Phone and Fax)

Foundation for North American Wild Sheep
720 Allen Ave., Cody, WY 82414-3402/web site: http://iigi.com/os/non/fnaws/fnaws.htm; e-mail: fnaws@wyoming.com

Freedom Arms Collectors Assn.
P.O. Box 160302, Miami, FL 33116-0302

Garand Collectors Assn.
P.O. Box 181, Richmond, KY 40475

Glock Collectors Association
P.O. Box 1063, Maryland Heights, MO 63043/314-878-2061 phone/FAX.

Glock Shooting Sports Foundation
BO Box 309, Smyrna GA 30081 770-432-1202 Website: www.gssfonline.com

Golden Eagle Collectors Assn. (G.E.C.A.)
Chris Showler, 11144 Slate Creek Rd., Grass Valley, CA 95945

Gun Owners of America
8001 Forbes Place, Suite 102, Springfield, VA 22151/703-321-8585

Handgun Hunters International
J.D. Jones, Director, P.O. Box 357

ARMS ASSOCIATIONS

MAG, Bloomingdale, OH 43910

Harrington & Richardson Gun Coll. Assn.
George L. Cardet, 330 S.W. 27th Ave., Suite 603, Miami, FL 33135

High Standard Collectors' Assn.
John J. Stimson, Jr., Pres., 540 W. 92nd St., Indianapolis, IN 46260 Website: www.highstandard.org

Hopkins & Allen Arms & Memorabilia Society (HAAMS)
P.O. Box 187, 1309 Pamela Circle, Delphos, OH 45833

International Ammunition Association, Inc.
C.R. Punnett, Secy., 8 Hillock Lane, Chadds Ford, PA 19317/610-358-1285;Fax:610-3 58-1560

International Benchrest Shooters
Joan Borden, RR1, Box 250BB, Springville, PA 18844/717-965-2366

International Blackpowder Hunting Assn.
P.O. Box 1180, Glenrock, WY 82637/307-436-9817

IHMSA (Intl. Handgun Metallic Silhouette Assn.)
PO Box 368, Burlington, IA 52601 Website: www.ihmsa.org

International Society of Mauser Arms Collectors
Michael Kindberg, Pres., P.O. Box 277, Alpharetta, GA 30239-0277

Jews for the Preservation of Firearms Ownership (JPFO) 501(c)(3)
2872 S. Wentworth Ave., Milwaukee, WI 53207/414-769-0760; Fax:414-483-8435

The Mannlicher Collectors Assn.
Membership Office: P.O. Box1249, The Dalles, Oregon 97058

Marlin Firearms Collectors Assn., Ltd.
Dick Paterson, Secy., 407 Lincoln Bldg., 44 Main St., Champaign, IL 61820

Merwin Hulbert Association,
2503 Kentwood Ct., High Point, NC 27265

Miniature Arms Collectors/Makers Society, Ltd.
Ralph Koebbeman, Pres., 4910 Kilburn Ave., Rockford, IL 61101/815-964-2569

M1 Carbine Collectors Assn. (M1-CCA)
623 Apaloosa Ln., Gardnerville, NV 89410-7840

National Association of Buckskinners (NAB)
Territorial Dispatch—1800s Historical Publication, 4701 Marion St., Suite 324, Livestock Exchange Bldg., Denver, CO 80216/303-297-9671

The National Association of Derringer Collectors
P.O. Box 20572, San Jose, CA 95160

National Assn. of Federally Licensed Firearms Dealers
Andrew Molchan, 2455 E. Sunrise, Ft. Lauderdale, FL 33304

National Association to Keep and Bear Arms
P.O. Box 78336, Seattle, WA 98178

National Automatic Pistol Collectors Assn.
Tom Knox, P.O. Box 15738, Tower Grove Station, St. Louis, MO 63163

National Bench Rest Shooters Assn., Inc.
Pat Ferrell, 2835 Guilford Lane, Oklahoma City, OK 73120-4404/405-842-9585; Fax: 405-842-9575

National Muzzle Loading Rifle Assn.
Box 67, Friendship, IN 47021 / 812-667-5131. Website: www.nmlra@nmlra.org

National Professional Paintball League (NPPL)
540 Main St., Mount Kisco, NY 10549/914-241-7400

National Reloading Manufacturers Assn.
One Centerpointe Dr., Suite 300, Lake Oswego, OR 97035

National Rifle Assn. of America
11250 Waples Mill Rd., Fairfax, VA 22030 / 703-267-1000. Website: www.nra.org

National Shooting Sports Foundation, Inc.
Doug Painter, President, Flintlock Ridge Office Center, 11 Mile Hill Rd., Newtown, CT 06470-2359/203-426-1320; FAX: 203-426-1087

National Skeet Shooting Assn.
Dan Snyuder, Director, 5931 Roft Road, San Antonio, TX 78253-9261/800-877-5338. Website: nssa-nsca.com

National Sporting Clays Association
Ann Myers, Director, 5931 Roft Road, San Antonio, TX 78253-9261/800-877-5338. Website: nssa-nsca.com

National Wild Turkey Federation, Inc.
P.O. Box 530, 770 Augusta Rd., Edgefield, SC 29824

North American Hunting Club
P.O. Box 3401, Minnetonka, MN 55343/612-936-9333; Fax: 612-936-9755

North American Paintball Referees Association (NAPRA)
584 Cestaric Dr., Milpitas, CA 95035

North-South Skirmish Assn., Inc.
Stevan F. Meserve, Exec. Secretary, 507 N. Brighton Court, Sterling, VA 20164-3919
Old West Shooter's Association 712 James Street, Hazel TX 76020 817-444-2049

Remington Society of America
Gordon Fosburg, Secretary, 11900 North Brinton Road, Lake, MI 48623

Rocky Mountain Elk Foundation
P.O. Box 8249, Missoula, MT 59807-8249/406-523-4500;Fax: 406-523-4581 Website: www.rmef.org

Ruger Collector's Assn., Inc.
P.O. Box 240, Greens Farms, CT 06436

Safari Club International
4800 W. Gates Pass Rd., Tucson, AZ 85745/520-620-1220

Sako Collectors Assn., Inc.
Jim Lutes, 202 N. Locust, Whitewater, KS 67154

Second Amendment Foundation
James Madison Building, 12500 NE 10th Pl., Bellevue, WA 98005

Single Action Shooting Society (SASS)
23255-A La Palma Avenue, Yorba Linda, CA 92887/714-694-1800; FAX: 714-694-1815/email: sasseot@aol.com Website: www.sassnet.com

Smith & Wesson Collectors Assn.
Cally Pletl, Admin. Asst.,PO Box 444, Afton, NY 13730

The Society of American Bayonet Collectors
P.O. Box 234, East Islip, NY 11730-0234

Southern California Schuetzen Society
Dean Lillard, 34657 Ave. E., Yucaipa, CA 92399

Sporting Arms and Ammunition Manufacturers' Institute (SAAMI)
Flintlock Ridge Office Center, 11 Mile Hill Rd., Newtown, CT 06470-2359/203-426-4358; FAX: 203-426-1087

Sporting Clays of America (SCA)
Ron L. Blosser, Pres., 9257 Buckeye Rd., Sugar Grove, OH 43155-9632/614-746-8334; Fax: 614-746-8605
Steel Challenge 23234 Via Barra, Valencia CA 91355 Website: www.steelchallenge.com

The Thompson/Center Assn.
Joe Wright, President, Box 792, Northboro, MA 01532/508-845-6960

U.S. Practical Shooting Assn./IPSC
Dave Thomas, P.O. Box 811, Sedro Woolley, WA 98284/360-855-2245 Website: www.uspsa.org

U.S. Revolver Assn.
Brian J. Barer, 40 Larchmont Ave., Taunton, MA 02780/508-824-4836

U.S.A. Shooting
U.S. Olympic Shooting Center, One Olympic Plaza, Colorado Springs, CO 80909/719-578-4670. Website: wwwusashooting.org

The Varmint Hunters Assn., Inc.
Box 759, Pierre, SD 57501/Member Services 800-528-4868

Weatherby Collectors Assn., Inc.
P.O. Box 478, Pacific, MO 63069 Website: www.weatherbycollectors.com Email: WCAsecretary@aol.com

The Wildcatters
P.O. Box 170, Greenville, WI 54942

Winchester Arms Collectors Assn.
P.O. Box 230, Brownsboro, TX 75756/903-852-4027

The Women's Shooting Sports Foundation (WSSF)
4620 Edison Avenue, Ste. C, Colorado Springs, CO 80915/719-638-1299; FAX: 719-638-1271/email: wssf@worldnet.att.net

ARGENTINA

Asociacion Argentina de Coleccionistas de Armes y Municiones
Castilla de Correos No. 28, Succursal I B, 1401 Buenos Aires, Republica Argentina

AUSTRALIA

Antique & Historical Arms Collectors of Australia
P.O. Box 5654, GCMC Queensland 9726, Australia

The Arms Collector's Guild of Queensland, Inc.
Ian Skennerton, P.O. Box 433, Ashmore City 4214, Queensland, Australia

Australian Cartridge Collectors Assn., Inc.
Bob Bennett, 126 Landscape Dr., E. Doncaster 3109, Victoria, Australia

Sporting Shooters Assn. of Australia, Inc.
P.O. Box 2066, Kent Town, SA 5071, Australia

BRAZIL

Associaçao de Armaria Coleçao e Tiro (ACOLTI) Rua do Senado, 258 - 2 andar, Centro, Rio de Janeiro - RJ - 20231-002 Brazil / tel: 0055-21-31817989

CANADA

ALBERTA

Canadian Historical Arms Society
P.O. Box 901, Edmonton, Alb., Canada T5J 2L8

National Firearms Assn.
Natl. Hq: P.O. Box 1779, Edmonton, Alb., Canada T5J 2P1

BRITISH COLUMBIA

The Historical Arms Collectors of B.C. (Canada)
Harry Moon, Pres., P.O. Box 50117, South Slope RPO, Burnaby, BC V5J 5G3, Canada/604-438-0950; Fax:604-277-3646

ONTARIO

Association of Canadian Cartridge Collectors
Monica Wright, RR 1, Millgrove, ON, LOR IVO, Canada

Tri-County Antique Arms Fair
P.O. Box 122, RR #1, North Lancaster, Ont., Canada K0C 1Z0

EUROPE

BELGIUM

European Cartridge Research Assn.
Graham Irving, 21 Rue Schaltin, 4900 Spa, Belgium/32.87.77.43.40; Fax:32.87.77.27.51

CZECHOSLOVAKIA

Spolecnost Pro Studium Naboju (Czech Cartridge Research Assn.)
JUDr. Jaroslav Bubak, Pod Homolko 1439, 26601 Beroun 2, Czech Republic

DENMARK

Aquila Dansk Jagtpatron Historic Forening (Danish Historical Cartridge Collectors Club)
Steen Elgaard Møller, Ulriksdalsvej 7, 4840 Nr. Alslev, Denmark 10045-53846218;Fax:00455384 6209

ENGLAND

Arms and Armour Society
Hon. Secretary A. Dove, P.O. Box 10232, London, 5W19 2ZD, England

Dutch Paintball Federation
Aceville Publ., Castle House 97 High Street, Colchester, Essex C01 1TH, England/011-44-206-564840

European Paintball Sports Foundation
c/o Aceville Publ., Castle House 97 High St., Colchester, Essex, C01 1TH, England

Historical Breechloading Smallarms Assn.
D.J. Penn M.A., Secy., P.O. Box 12778, London SE1 6BX, England. Journal and newsletter are $23 a yr., including airmail.

National Rifle Assn.
(Great Britain) Bisley Camp, Brookwood, Woking Surrey OPB, England/01483.79777 014730686275

United Kingdom Cartridge C
Ian Southgate, 20 Millfield, E Castle, Nr. Pershore, Worcestershire, WR10 3HR, England

FRANCE

STAC-Western Co.
3 Ave. Paul Doumer (N.311), 78360 Montesson, France/01.30.53-43-65; Fax: 01.30.53.19.10

GERMANY

Bund Deutscher Sportschütz e.v. (BDS)
Borsigallee 10, 53125 Bonn Germany

Deutscher Schützenbund
Lahnstrasse 120, 65195 Wiesbaden, Germany

NORWAY

Scandinavian Ammunition Research Assn.
c/o Morten Stoen, Annerudstubben 3, N-1383 A Norway

NEW ZEALAND

New Zealand Cartridge Collec Club
Terry Castle, 70 Tiraumea Dr., Pakuranga, Auckland, New Zealand

New Zealand Deerstalkers As
P.O. Box 6514 TE ARO, Wellington, New Zealand

SOUTH AFRICA

Historical Firearms Soc. of So Africa
P.O. Box 145, 7725 Newlands, Republic of South Africa

Republic of South Africa Cartridge Collectors Assn.
Arno Klee, 20 Eugene St., Malanshof Randburg, Gauteng 2194, Republic of South Africa

S.A.A.C.A. (Southern Africa Arms and Ammunition Assn.)
Gauteng office: P.O. Box 7597, Weltevreden Pa 1715, Republic of South Africa/011-679-1151; Fax: 011-679-1131; e-mail: saaaca@iafrica.com.
Kwa-Zulu Natal office: P.O. Box 4065, Northway, Kwazulu-Natal 4065, Republic o South Africa

SAGA (S.A. Gunowners' Assn.)
P.O. Box 35203, Northway, Kwazulu-Natal 4065, Republic o South Africa

SPAIN

Asociacion Espanola de Colleccionistas de Cartuchos (A.E.C.C.)
Secretary: Apdo. Correos No. 1086, 2880-Alcala de Henares (Madrid), Spain. President: Apdo Correos No. 682, 50080 Zaragoza Spain

SELECTED BIBLIOGRAPHY: GENERAL

STANDARD CATALOG OF FIREARM S, 14TH EDITION, THE ...CTOR'S PRICE & REFERENCE GUIDE, BY NED SCHWING, ... WI: KRAUSE PUBLISHING, 2003. 14TH EDITION. 1,384 ...S, ILLUSTRATED. 6,000+ B&W PHOTOS PLUS A 16-PAGE COLOR ...ON. SOFTCOVER. $34.95

...is the largest, most comprehensive and best-selling firearm ... of all time! And this year's edition is a blockbuster for both ...ters and firearm collectors. More than 25,000 firearms are listed ...priced in up to six grades of condition. That's almost 110,000 ...s! Gun enthusiasts will love the new full-color section of ...os highlighting the finest firearms sold at auction this past year.

...on Shooting: Cowboy Style, by John Taffin, Krause ...lications, Iola, WI, 1999. 320 pp., illustrated. $39.95

...ils on the guns and ammunition. Explanations of the rules used ...many events. The essential cowboy wardrobe.

...anced Muzzleloader's Guide, by Toby Bridges, Stoeger ...lishing Co., So. Hackensack, NJ, 1985. 256 pp., illus. ...er covers. $14.95

...complete guide to muzzle-loading rifles, pistols and shotguns—...ock and percussion.

...s to Musketry for Officers & NCOs, by Capt. B.J. Friend, ...alibur Publications, Latham, NY, 1996. 40 pp., illus. ...er covers. $7.95

...csimile edition of a pre-WWI British manual filled with useful ...rmation for training the common soldier.

...gun Odyssey, by Steve Hanson. Manchester, CT: ...cision Shooting, Inc., 2004. 1st edition. 175 pages. ...torial softcover. $28.95

... evolution of today's precision air rifle is traced from the early ...d recent) lever action B-B guns to the cost-in-four-figures ...et and hunting guns now available. The pros and cons of the ...un calibers are discussed in depth for both hunting and target ...plications. Airguns from foreign manufacturers are given in-depth ...iew as are the popular airgun-specializing gunsmiths operating ...ay. The book's chapter titles give a capsule of the book's ...ntents: Airgun Evolution & Trends... Airgun Propulsion Systems... ...gun Varmint Hunting & Pest Control... American Field Target... ...roduction to BR 4000 ... Airgun Tests/Current Production Guns... ...gun Tests/Classic & Discontinued Guns ... Spring-Piston Airgun ...ning... Building A New PCP Airgun for the Sport of American ...ld Target... Supplier's Index (Airgun Periodicals, Suppliers, ...vices, Parts & Accessories.

...merican Air Rifles, by James E. House. Krause ...blications, Iola, WI. 2002. 1st edition. 208 pages, with ...8 b&w photos. Softcover. $22.95

... rifle ballistics, sights, pellets, games, and hunting caliber ...commendations are thoroughly explained to help shooters get ...e most out of their American air rifles. Evaluation of more than a ...ozen American-made and American-imported air rifle models.

...e American B.B. Gun: A Collector's Guide, by Arni T. ...unathan. A.S. Barnes and Co., Inc., South Brunswick. ...001. 154 pages, illustrated with nearly 200 photographs, ...rawings and detailed diagrams. Hardcove. $35.00

...merican and Imported Arms, Ammunition and Shooting ...ccessories, Catalog No. 18 of the Shooter's Bible, Stoeger, Inc., ...printed by Fayette Arsenal, Fayetteville, NC, 1988. 142 pp., illus. ...aper covers. $10.95

... facsimile reprint of the 1932 Stoeger's Shooter's Bible.

America's Great Gunmakers, by Wayne van Zwoll, Stoeger Publishing Co., So. Hackensack, NJ, 1992. 288 pp., illus. Paper covers. $16.95

This book traces in great detail the evolution of guns and ammunition in America and the men who formed the companies that produced them.

Annie Oakley of the Wild West, by Walter Havighurst. New York: Castle Books, 2000. 246 pages. Hardcover. $10.00

This book brings to life the complete story of "Little Sureshot"—not only her phenomenal sharp-shooting techniques and career in the Wild West Show, but also her fifty-year marriage to Frank Butler, himself a professional marksman.

Armed and Female, by Paxton Quigley, E.P. Dutton, New York, NY, 2001. 237 pp., illus. Softcover $9.95

The first complete book on one of the hottest subjects in the media today, the arming of the American woman.

Arming the Glorious Cause: Weapons of the Second War for Independence, by James B. Whisker, Daniel D. Hartzler and Larry W. Yantz, R & R Books, Livonia, NY, 1998. 175 pp., illustrated. $45.00

A photographic study of Confederate weapons.

Arms & Armor in the Art Institute of Chicago, by Walter J. Karcheski, Jr., Bulfinch Press, Boston, MA, 1995. 128 pp., illus. $35.00

Now, for the first time, the Art Institute of Chicago's arms and armor collection is presented in the visual delight of 103 color illustrations.

Arms for the Nation: Springfield Longarms, edited by David C. Clark, Scott A. Duff, Export, PA, 1994. 73 pp., illus. Paper covers. $9.95

A brief history of the Springfield Armory and the arms made there.

Arsenal of Freedom, The Springfield Armory, 1890-1948: A Year-by-Year Account Drawn from Official Records, compiled and edited by Lt. Col. William S. Brophy, USAR Ret., Andrew Mowbray, Inc., Lincoln, RI, 1991. 400 pp., illus. Soft covers. $29.95

A "must buy" for all students of American military weapons, equipment and accoutrements.

Assault Pistols, Rifles and Submachine Guns, by Duncan Long, Paladin Press, Boulder, CO, 1997, 8 1/2 x 11, soft cover, photos, illus. 152 pp. $21.95

This book offers up-to-date, practical information on how to operate and field-strip modern military, police and civilian combat weapons. Covers new developments and trends such as the use of fiber optics, liquid-recoil systems and lessening of barrel length are covered. Troubleshooting procedures, ballistic tables and a list of manufacturers and distributors are also included.

Assault Weapons, 5th Edition, The Gun Digest Book of, edited by Jack Lewis and David E. Steele, DBI Books, a division of Krause Publications, Iola, WI, 2000. 256 pp., illustrated. Paper covers. $21.95

This is the latest word on true assault weaponry in use today by international military and law enforcement organizations.

The Belgian Rattlesnake: The Lewis Automatic Machine Gun, by William M. Easterly, Collector Grade Publications, Inc., Cobourg, Ont. Canada, 1998. 542 pp., illus. $79.95

A social and technical biography of the Lewis automatic machine gun and its inventors.

The Benchrest Shooting Primer, by Brennan, Dave

(Editor). Precision Shooting, Inc., Manchester, CT 2000. 2nd edition. 420 pages, illustrated with b&w photographs, drawings and detailed diagrams. Pictorial softcover. $24.95

The very best articles on shooting and reloading for the most challenging of all the rifle accuracy disciplines...benchrest shooting.

The Big Guns: Civil War Siege, Seacoast, and Naval Cannon, by Edwin Olmstead, Wayne E. Stark and Spencer C. Tucker, Museum Restoration Service, Bloomfield, Ontario, Canada, 1997. 360 pp., illus. $80.00

This book is designed to identify and record the heavy guns available to both sides during the Civil War.

Blackpowder Loading Manual, 3rd Edition, by Sam Fadala, DBI Books, a division of Krause Publications, Iola, WI, 1995. 368 pp., illus. Paper covers. $20.95

Revised and expanded edition of this landmark blackpowder loading book. Covers hundreds of loads for most of the popular blackpowder rifles, handguns and shotguns.

Black Powder, Pig Lead And Steel Silhouettes, by Paul A. Matthews. Wolfe Publishing, Prescott, AZ, 2002. 132 pages, illustrated with b&w photographs and detailed drawings and diagrams. Softcover. $16.95

Bolt Action Rifles, 4th Edition, by Frank de Haas, DBI Books, a division of Krause Publications, Iola, WI, 2004. 628 pp., illus. Paper covers. $27.95

A revised edition of the most definitive work on all major bolt-action rifle designs.

British Small Arms of World War 2, by Ian D. Skennerton, Arms & Militaria Press, Australia 1988. 110 pp., 37 illus. $25.00.

Co2 Pistols and Rifles, by James E. House. Iola, WI: Krause Publications, 2004. 1st edition. 240 pages, with 198 b&w photos. Softcover. $24.95

In this new guide to CO2-powered pistols and rifles, James E. House offers a comprehensive history of CO2 guns, dating back to the 1930s, and a discussion of propulsion, pellets, and sights. Beginning shooters are introduced to the market with a complete analysis on performance and accuracy of currently available products. Airgun enthusiasts are reunited with CO2 classics no longer being manufactured. This book also offers additional sections on target shooting, games, and varmints. Offers a comprehensive history of CO2 pistols and rifles dating back to the 1930s. Includes a categorical review of BB pistols, .177 caliber pistols, .20 and .22 caliber pistols, and rifles. Discover products currently available only on the secondary market.

Combat Handgunnery, 5th Edition, The Gun Digest Book of, by Chuck Taylor, DBI Books, a division of Krause Publications, Iola, WI, 2002. 256 pp., illus. Paper covers. $21.95

This edition looks at real world combat handgunnery from three different perspectives—military, police and civilian.

The Complete Blackpowder Handbook, 4th Edition, by Sam Fadala, DBI Books, a division of Krause Publications, Iola, WI, 2002. 400 pp., illus. Paper covers. $21.95.

Expanded and completely rewritten edition of the definitive book on the subject of blackpowder.

Custom Firearms Engraving, by Tom Turpin, Krause Publications, Iola, WI, 1999. 208 pp., illustrated. $49.95

Provides a broad and comprehensive look at the world of firearms engraving. The exquisite styles of more than 75 master engravers are shown on beautiful examples of handguns, rifles, shotguns, and other firearms, as well as knives.

Dead On, by Tony Noblitt and Warren Gabrilska, Pala Press, Boulder, CO, 1998. 176 pp., illustrated. Paper covers. $22.00

The long-range marksman's guide to extreme accuracy.

Early American Flintlocks, by Daniel D. Hartzler and James B. Whisker, Bedford Valley Press, Bedford, PA 2 192 pp., Illustrated. $45.00

Covers early Colonial Guns, New England Guns, Pennsylvania Guns and Souther Guns.

The Exercise of Armes, by Jacob de Gheyn, Dover Publications, Inc., Mineola, NY, 1999. 144 pp., illustrat Paper covers. $14.95

Republications of all 117 engravings from the 1607 classic milit manual. A meticulously accurate portrait of uniforms and weap of the 17th century Netherlands.

Fighting Iron; A Metals Handbook for Arms Collectors, Art Gogan, Mowbray Publishers, Inc., Lincoln, RI, 2002 176 pp., illustrated. $28.00

A guide that is easy to use, explains things in simple English and covers all of the different historical periods that we are interested in.

The Fighting Submachine Gun, Machine Pistol, and Shotgun, by Timothy J. Mullin, Paladin Press, Boulder, 1999. 224 pp., illustrated. Paper covers. $35.00

An invaluable reference for military, police and civilian shooters who may someday need to know how a specific weapon actual performs when the targets are shooting back and the margin of errors is measured in lives lost.

Firearms Assembly Disassembly; Part 4 : Centerfire Rifl (2nd Edition), by J. B. Wood, Iola, WI: Krause Publicatio 2004. 2nd edition. 576 pages, 1,750 b&w photos. Softcover. $24.95

The increasing cost of gunsmithing services has caused enthusia to perform minor repairs, refinishing, and deep cleaning on their own firearms. This updated edition shows how to easily disassemble and reassemble centerfire rifles and the correct tool needed. Sixty-six popular guns are taken apart and individually photographed. The cross-reference index identifies more than 40 similar or identical rifle patterns that also follow these disassemb and reassembly directions. Covers the Argentine Mauser to Marli Model 9 to Russian AK-47 to U.S. M-1 Garand to Winchester Model 1894.

From a Stranger's Doorstep to the Kremlin Gate, by Mikhail Kalashnikov, Ironside International Publishers, Inc., Alexandria, VA, 1999. 460 pp., illustrated. $34.95

A biography of the most influential rifle designer of the 20th century. His AK-47 assault rifle has become the most widely usec (and copied) assault rifle of this century.

The Frontier Rifleman, by H.B. LaCrosse Jr., Pioneer Pre Union City, TN, 1989. 183 pp., illus. Soft covers. $17.50

The Frontier rifleman's clothing and equipment during the era of the American Revolution, 1760-1800.

The Gatling Gun: 19th Century Machine Gun to 21st Century Vulcan, by Joseph Berk, Paladin Press, Boulder, CO, 1991. 136 pp., illus. $34.95

Here is the fascinating on-going story of a truly timeless weapon, from its beginnings during the Civil War to its current role as a state-of-the-art modern combat system.

German Artillery of World War Two, by Ian V. Hogg, Stackpole Books, Mechanicsburg, PA, 1997. 304 pp., illus. $44.95

plete details of German artillery use in WWII.

e Diggin: Memoirs Of A Civil War Relic Hunter, by y Law. Orange, VA: Publisher's Press, 2002. 1st edition ed. 151 pages, illustrated with b&w photos. $24.95

true story of one relic hunter's life - The author kept exacting rds of every relic hunt and every relic hunter he was with king with.

nd Old Lady of No Man's Land: The Vickers Machine , by Dolf L. Goldsmith, Collector Grade Publications, ourg, Canada, 1994. 600 pp., illus. $79.95.

lsmith brings his years of experience as a U.S. Army armourer, hine gun collector and shooter to bear on the Vickers, in a k sure to become a classic in its field.

enhill Military Manuals; Small Arms: Pistols and Rifles, an Hogg; London: Greenhill Press, 2003. Revised. 160 es, illustrated. Hardcover. $24.00

handy reference guide, by the leading small arms author, vides descriptions, technical specifications and illustrations of of the most important pistols and rifles, including the Heckler och USP/SOCOM pistols, the FN Five-seveN 5.7mm pistol, the kler & Koch G36 rifle and much more.

n Digest 2005, 59th Edition, edited by Ken Ramage, DBI oks a division of Krause Publications, Iola, WI, 2002. 544 ., illustrated. Paper covers. $27.95

s all new 58th edition continues the editorial excellence, quality, tent and comprehensive cataloguing that firearms enthusiasts e come to know and expect. The most read gun book in the rld for the last half century.

n Engraving, by C. Austyn, Safari Press Publication, ntington Beach, CA, 1998. 128 pp., plus 24 pages of lor photos. $50.00

vell-illustrated book on fine English and European gun gravers. Includes a fantastic pictorial section that lists types of gravings and prices.

n Talk, edited by Dave Moreton, Winchester Press, scataway, NJ, 1973. 256 pp., illus. $9.95

treasury of original writing by the top gun writers and editors in nerica. Practical advice about every aspect of the shooting sports.

ne Gun That Made the Twenties Roar, by Wm. J. Helmer, ne Gun Room Press, Highland Park, NJ, 1977. Over 300 p., illus. $24.95

storical account of John T. Thompson and his invention, the famous "Tommy Gun."

un Trader's Guide (2005 - 26th Edition), by Jarrett (ed.). ocomoke, MD: Stoeger Publishing, 2004. 26th edition. oftcover. $21.99

ne Gun Trader's Guide has been the standard reference for ollectors, dealers, shooters and gun enthusiasts since 1953. his 592 page edition provides complete updated specifications, ates of manufacture and current market average values for over ,000 handguns, rifles and shotguns, both foreign and domestic. complete index is provided for easy reference to all guns plus andy thumb tabs help readers find, identify and price firearms ith ease.

uns Illustrated 2004, 24th Edition, edited by Ken Ramage, BI Books a division of Krause Publications, Iola, WI, 003. 388 pp., illustrated. Softcovers. $24.95

ighly informative, technical articles on a wide range of shooting opics by some of the top writers in the industry. A catalog ection lists more than 3,000 firearms currently manufactured in or mported to the U.S.

uns & Shooting: A Selected Bibliography, by Ray Riling, Ray Riling Arms Books Co., Phila., PA, 1982. 434 pp., illus. Limited, numbered edition. $75.00

A limited edition of this superb bibliographical work, the only modern listing of books devoted to guns and shooting.

Guns, Bullets, and Gunfighters, by Jim Cirillo, Paladin Press, Boulder, CO, 1996. 119 pp., illus. Paper covers. $16.00

Lessons and tales from a modern-day gunfighter.

Hidden in Plain Sight, "A Practical Guide to Concealed Handgun Carry" (Revised 2nd Edition), by Trey Bloodworth and Mike Raley, Paladin Press, Boulder, CO, 1997, softcover, photos, 176 pp. $20.00

Concerned with how to comfortably, discreetly and safely exercise the privileges granted by a CCW permit? This invaluable guide offers the latest advice on what to look for when choosing a CCW, how to dress for comfortable, effective concealed carry, traditional and more unconventional carry modes, accessory holsters, customized clothing and accessories, accessibility data based on draw-time comparisons and new holsters on the market. Includes 40 new manufacturer listings.

HK Assault Rifle Systems, by Duncan Long, Paladin Press, Boulder, CO, 1995. 110 pp., illus. Paper covers. $27.95

The little known history behind this fascinating family of weapons tracing its beginnings from the ashes of World War Two to the present time.

The Hunter's Guide to Accurate Shooting, by Wayne Van Zwoll, Guilford, CT: Lyons Press, 2002. 1st edition. 288 pp. Hardcover. $29.95

Firearms expert Van Zwoll explains exactly how to shoot the big-game rifle accurately. Taking into consideration every pertinent factor, he shows a step-by-step analysis of shooting and hunting with the big-game rifle.

Jack O'Connor Catalogue of Letters, by Enzler-Herring, E. Cataloguer. Agoura CA: Trophy Room Books, 2002. 262 pages, 18 illustrations. Hardcover. $55.00

During a sixteen-year period beginning in 1960, O'Connor exchanged many letters with his pal, John Jobson. Material from nearly three hundred of these has been assembled and edited by Ellen Enzler Herring and published in chronological order. A number of the letters have been reproduced in full or part. They offer considerable insight into the beloved gun editor and "Dean of Outdoor Writers"over and beyond what we know about him from his books.

Jack O'Connor - The Legendary Life Of America's Greatest Gunwriter, by R. Anderson. Long Beach, CA: Safari Press, 2002. 1st edition. 240pp, profuse photos. Hardcover. $29.95

This is the book all hunters in North America have been waiting for--the long-awaited biography on Jack O'Connor! Jack O'Connor was the preeminent North American big-game hunter and gunwriter of the twentieth century, and Robert Anderson's masterfully written new work is a blockbuster filled with fascinating facts and stories about this controversial character. With the full cooperation of the O'Connor children, Anderson spent three years interviewing O'Connor's family and friends as well as delving into JOC's papers, photos, and letters, including the extensive correspondence between O'Connor and Bob Householder, and the O'Connor papers from Washington State University. O'Connor's lifelong friend Buck Buckner has contributed two chapters on his experiences with the master of North American hunting.

Joe Rychertinik Reflects on Guns, Hunting, and Days Gone by, by Joe Rychertinik, Precision Shooting, Inc., Manchester, CT, 1999. 281 pp., illustrated. Thirty articles

by a master story-teller. Paper covers. $16.95.

Kill or Get Killed, by Col. Rex Applegate, Paladin Press, Boulder, CO, 1996. 400 pp., illus. $49.95

The best and longest-selling book on close combat in history.

Manual for H&R Reising Submachine Gun and Semi-Auto Rifle, edited by George P. Dillman, Desert Publications, El Dorado, AZ, 1994. 81 pp., illus. Paper covers. $14.95

A reprint of the Harrington & Richardson 1943 factory manual and the rare military manual on the H&R submachine gun and semi-auto rifle.

Military Rifle & Machine Gun Cartridges, by Jean Huon, Paladin Press, Boulder, CO, 1990. 392 pp., illus. $34.95

Describes the primary types of military cartridges and their principal loadings, as well as their characteristics, origin and use.

Military Small Arms of the 20th Century, 7th Edition, by Ian V. Hogg and John Weeks, DBI Books, a division of Krause Publications, Iola, WI, 2000. 416 pp., illustrated. Paper covers. Over 800 photographs and illustrations. $24.95

Cover small arms of 46 countries.

Modern Custom Guns, Walnut, Steel, and Uncommon Artistry, by Tom Turpin, Krause Publications, Iola, WI, 1997. 206 pp., illus. $49.95

From exquisite engraving to breathtaking exotic woods, the mystique of today's custom guns is expertly detailed in word and awe-inspiring color photos of rifles, shotguns and handguns.

Modern Gun Values: 12th Edition, edited by Ken Ramage, Krause Publications, Iola, WI 2003. 608 Pages, 3,000+ b&w photos. Softcover. $21.95

Back by popular demand, this all-new expanded edition helps collectors identify the firearm, evaluate condition and determine value. Detailed specifications—and current values from specialized experts—are provided for domestic and imported handguns, rifles, shotguns and commemorative firearms. Heavily illustrated. Over 7,500 arms described and valued, in three grades of condition, according to the NRA's Modern standards.

Modern Machine Guns, by John Walter, Stackpole Books, Inc. Mechanicsburg, PA, 2000. 144 pp., with 146 illustrations. $22.95

A compact and authoritative guide to post-war machine-guns. A gun-by-gun directory identifying individual variants and types including detailed evaluations and technical data.

Modern Sporting Guns, by Christopher Austyn, Safari Press, Huntington Beach, CA, 1994. 128 pp., illus. $40.00

A discussion of the "best" English guns; round action, over-and-under, boxlocks, hammer guns, bolt action and double rifles as well as accessories.

The MP-40 Machine Gun, Desert Publications, El Dorado, AZ, 1995. 32 pp., illus. Paper covers. $11.95

A reprint of the hard-to-find operating and maintenance manual for one of the most famous machine guns of World War II.

Naval Percussion Locks and Primers, by Lt. J. A. Dahlgren, Museum Restoration Service, Bloomfield, Canada, 1996. 140 pp., illus. $35.00

First published as an Ordnance Memoranda in 1853, this is the finest existing study of percussion locks and primers origin and development.

The Official Soviet AKM Manual, translated by Maj. James F. Gebhardt (Ret.), Paladin Press, Boulder, CO, 1999. 120 pp., illustrated. Paper covers. $18.00

This official military manual, available in English for the first time, was originally published by the Soviet Ministry of Defence. Covers the history, function, maintenance, assembly and disassembly, etc. of the 7.62mm AKM assault rifle.

Practically Speaking: An Illustrated Guide - The Game, Guns and Gear of the International Defensive Pistol Association, by Walt Rauch. Lafayette Hills, PA: Privately Printed, 2002. 1st edition. 79 pages, illustated with drawings and color photos. Softcover. $24.95

The game, guns and gear of the International Defensive Pistol Association with real-world applications.

The Shooter's Bible 2004, No. 95, edited by William S. Jarrett, Stoeger Publishing Co., Wayne, NJ, 2003. 576 pp. illustrated. Paper covers. $23.95

Over 3,000 firearms currently offered by major American and foreign gunmakers. Represented are handguns, rifles, shotguns and black powder arms with complete specifications and retail prices.

Shooting Buffalo Rifles Of The Old West, by Mike Venturino, MLV Enterprises, Livingston, MT, 2002. 278 pages, illustrated with b&w photos. Softcover. $30.00

This tome will take you through the history, the usage, the many models, and the actual shooting (and how to's) of the many guns that saw service on the Frontier and are lovingly called "Buffalo Rifles" today. If you love to shoot your Sharps, Ballards, Remingtons, or Springfield "Trapdoors" for hunting or competition or simply love Old West history, your library WILL NOT be complete without this latest book from Mike Venturino!

Shooting Colt Single Actions, by Mike Venturino, MLV Enterprises, Livingston, MT 1997. 205 pp., illus. Softcover. $25.00

A complete examination of the Colt Single Action including styles calibers and generations. Black & white photos throughout.

Shooting Lever Guns Of The Old West, by Mike Venturino, MLV Enterprises, Livingston, MT, 1999. 300 pp., illustrated. Softcover. $27.95

Shooting the lever action type repeating rifles of our American West.

Shooting Sixguns of the Old West, by Mike Venturino, MLV Enterprises, Livingston, MT, 1997. 221 pp., illus. Paper covers. $26.50.

A comprehensive look at the guns of the early West: Colts, Smith & Wesson and Remingtons, plus blackpowder and reloading specs.

Shooters Bible 2005 No. 96, by Jarrett (editor). The World's Standard Firearms Reference Book. Pocomoke, MD: Stoeger Publishing Company, 2003. 2004 edition. 576 pages. Pictorial softcover. $23.95

The new edition of the Shooter's Bible offers gun enthusi asts everything they need to know about some 3,000 firearms and related equipment produced by U.S. and foreign gunmakers. It includes complete specifications and updated retail prices for handguns, rifles, shotguns, black powder arms and scopes and sights, all heavily illustrated throughout. Comprehensive ballistics tables for all major rifle cartridges simplify the reader's search for the latest information in one 20-page section. In addition, the 2004 edition contains an array of original articles by noted outdoor writers. New for this edition is a special Web Directory designed to complement the regular Reference section, including the popular Gunfinder index.

Small Arms of World War II, by Chris Chant. St. Paul, MN: MBI Publishing Company, 2001. 1st edition. 96 pages, single page on each weapon with photograph, description and a specifications table. Hardcover. New. $13.95

Detailing the design and development of each weapon, this book covers the most important infantry weapons used by both Allied

Axis soldiers between 1939 and 1945. These include both ...dard infantry bolt-action rifles, such as the German Kar 98 and ...British Lee-Enfield, plus the automatic rifles that entered service ...rd the end of the war, such as the Stg 43. As well as rifles, this ... also features submachine guns, machine guns and handguns ...a specifications table for each weapon.

...dard Catalog of Military Firearms 2nd Edition: The ...lector's Price & Reference Guide, by Ned Schwing. ..., WI: Krause Publishing, 2003. 2nd edition. 448 pages. ...cover. $22.99

...mpanion volume to Standard Catalog of Firearms, this revised ... expanded second edition comes complete with all the detailed ...rmation readers found useful and more. Listings beginning with ...early cartridge models of the 1870s to the latest high-tech sniper ...s have been expanded to include more models, variations, ...orical information, and data, offering more detail for the military ...rms collector, shooter, and history buff. Identification of specific ...rms is easier with nearly 250 additional photographs. Plus, ...ders will enjoy "snap shots," small personal articles from experts ...ting real-life experiences with exclusive models. Revised to ...ude every known military firearm available to the U.S. collector ...ore than 100 pages of expanded coverage * Special feature ...cles on focused aspects of collecting and shooting.

...vival Guns, by Mel Tappan, Desert Publications, El ...rado, AZ, 1993. 456 pp., illus. Paper covers. $25.00

...cusses in a frank and forthright manner which handguns, rifles ...l shotguns to buy for personal defense and securing food, and ... ones to avoid.

...e Ultimate Sniper, by Major John L. Plaster, ...ladin Press, Boulder, CO, 1994. 464 pp., illus. Paper ...vers. $49.95

... advanced training manual for military and police snipers.

...eapons of Delta Force, by Fred Pushies. St. Paul, MN: MBI ...blishing Company, 2002. 1st edition. 128 pgs., 100 b&w ...d 100 color illustrated. Hardcover. $24.95

...nerica's elite counter-terrorist organization, Delta Force, is a ...ndpicked group of the U.S. Army's finest soldiers. The group ...ecializes in hostage rescues and other difficult procedures to ...otect the lives of Americans throughout the world. Delta uses ...me of the most sophisticated weapons in the field today, and ... are detailed in this book. Pistols, sniper rifles, special mission ...rcraft, fast attack vehicles, SCUBA and paratrooper gear, and more ...e presented in this fully illustrated account of our country's heroes ...d their tools of the trade.

...eapons of the Waffen-SS, by Bruce Quarrie, Sterling Publishing ...., Inc., 1991. 168 pp., illus. $24.95

...n in-depth look at the weapons that made Hitler's Waffen-SS the ...arsome fighting machine it was.

...eatherby: The Man, The Gun, The Legend, by Grits and ...om Gresham, Cane River Publishing Co., Natchitoches, ...A, 1992. 290 pp., illus. $24.95

... fascinating look at the life of the man who changed the course of ...rearms development in America.

...he Winchester Era, by David Madis, Art & Reference ...Iouse, Brownsville, TX, 1984. 100 pp., illus. $19.95

...tory of the Winchester company, management, employees, etc.

...he World's Machine Pistols and Submachine Guns ...Vol. 2a 1964 to 1980, by Nelson & Musgrave, Ironside ...nternational, Alexandria, VA, 2000. 673 pages. $59.95

...ontaining data, history and photographs of over 200 weapons. ...With a special section covering shoulder stocked automatic pistols, ...100 additional photos.

The World's Sniping Rifles, by Ian V. Hogg, Stackpole Books, Mechanicsburg, 1998. 144 pp., illustrated. $24.00

A detailed manual with descriptions and illustrations of more than 50 high-precision rifles from 14 countries and a complete analysis of sights and systems.

SELECTED BIBLIOGRAPHY: GUNSMITHING

ACCURIZING THE FACTORY RIFLE, BY M.L. MCPHERESON, PRECISION SHOOTING, INC., MANCHESTER, CT, 1999. 335 PP., ILLUSTRATED. PAPER COVERS. $44.95

A long-awaiting book, which bridges the gap between the rudimentary (mounting sling swivels, scope blocks and that general level of accomplishment) and the advanced (precision chambering, barrel fluting, and that general level of accomplishment) books that are currently available today.

The Art of Engraving, by James B. Meek, F. Brownell & Son, Montezuma, IA, 1973. 196 pp., illus. $42.95

A complete, authoritative, imaginative and detailed study in training for gun engraving. The first book of its kind—and a great one.

Checkering and Carving of Gun Stocks, by Monte Kennedy, Stackpole Books, Harrisburg, PA, 1962. 175 pp., illus. $39.95

Revised, enlarged cloth-bound edition of a much sought-after, dependable work.

Firearms Assembly/Disassembly, Part I: Automatic Pistols, 2nd Revised Edition, The Gun Digest Book of, by J.B. Wood, DBI Books, a division of Krause Publications, Iola, WI, 1999. 480 pp., illus. Paper covers. $24.95

Covers 58 popular autoloading pistols plus nearly 200 variants of those models integrated into the text and completely cross-referenced in the index.

Firearms Assembly/Disassembly Part II: Revolvers, Revised Edition, The Gun Digest Book of, by J.B. Wood, DBI Books, a division of Krause Publications, Iola, WI, 1997. 480 pp., illus. Paper covers. $27.95

Covers 49 popular revolvers plus 130 variants. The most comprehensive and professional presentation available to either hobbyist or gunsmith.

Firearms Assembly/Disassembly Part III: Rimfire Rifles, Revised Edition, The Gun Digest Book of, by J. B. Wood, DBI Books, a division of Krause Publications, Iola, WI., 1994. 480 pp., illus. Paper covers. $19.95

Greatly expanded edition covering 65 popular rimfire rifles plus over 100 variants all completely cross-referenced in the index.

Firearms Assembly/Disassembly Part IV: Centerfire Rifles, 3rd Revised Edition, The Gun Digest Book of, by J.B. Wood, Krause Publications, Iola, WI, 2004. 480 pp., illus. Paper covers. $24.95

Covers 54 popular centerfire rifles plus 300 variants. The most comprehensive and professional presentation available to either hobbyist or gunsmith.

Firearms Assembly/Disassembly, Part V: Shotguns, Revised Edition, The Gun Digest Book of, by J.B. Wood, Krause Publications, Iola, WI, 2002. 480 pp., illus. Paper covers. $24.95

Covers 46 popular shotguns plus over 250 variants with step-by-step instructions on how to dismantle and reassemble each. The most comprehensive and professional presentation available to either hobbyist or gunsmith.

Firearms Assembly 3: The NRA Guide to Rifle and Shotguns, NRA Books, Wash., DC, 1980. 264 pp., illus.

Paper covers. $14.95

Text and illustrations explaining the takedown of 125 rifles and shotguns, domestic and foreign.

Firearms Assembly 4: The NRA Guide to Pistols and Revolvers, NRA Books, Wash., DC, 1980. 253 pp., illus. Paper covers. $13.95

Text and illustrations explaining the takedown of 124 pistol and revolver models, domestic and foreign.

Firearms Bluing and Browning, by R.H. Angier, Stackpole Books, Harrisburg, PA. 151 pp., illus. $19.95

A world master gunsmith reveals his secrets of building, repairing and renewing a gun, quite literally, lock, stock and barrel. A useful, concise text on chemical coloring methods for the gunsmith and mechanic.

Guns and Gunmaking Tools of Southern Appalachia, by John Rice Irwin, Schiffer Publishing Ltd., 1983. 118 pp., illus. Paper covers. $9.95

The story of the Kentucky rifle.

The Gunsmith Of Grenville County: Building The American Longrifle, by Peter Alexander, Texarkana, TX: Scurlock Publishing Co., 2002. 400 pages, with hundreds of illustrations, and six color photos of original rifles. Wire O Bind spine will lay flat on the workbench. Stiff paper covers. $45.00

The most extensive how to book on building longrifles ever published. Takes you through every step of building your own longrifle, from shop set up and tools to engraving, carving and finishing.

Gunsmithing: Pistols & Revolvers, by Patrick Sweeney, DBI Books, a division of Krause Publications, Iola, WI, 1998. 352 pp., illus. Paper covers. $24.95

Do-it-Yourself projects, diagnosis and repair for pistols and revolvers.

Gunsmithing: Rifles, by Patrick Sweeney, Krause Publications, Iola, WI, 1999. 352 pp., illustrated. Paper covers. $24.95

Tips for lever-action rifles. Building a custom Ruger 10/22. Building a better hunting rifle.

Gunsmithing Tips and Projects, a collection of the best articles from the Handloader and Rifle magazines, by various authors, Wolfe Publishing Co., Prescott, AZ, 1992. 443 pp., illus. Paper covers. $25.00

Includes such subjects as shop, stocks, actions, tuning, triggers, barrels, customizing, etc.

Gunsmith Kinks, by F.R. (Bob) Brownell, F. Brownell & Son, Montezuma, IA, 1st ed., 1969. 496 pp., well illus. $22.98

A widely useful accumulation of shop kinks, short cuts, techniques and pertinent comments by practicing gunsmiths from all over the world.

Gunsmith Kinks 2, by Bob Brownell, F. Brownell & Son, Publishers, Montezuma, IA, 1983. 496 pp., illus. $22.95

A collection of gunsmithing knowledge, shop kinks, new and old techniques, shortcuts and general know-how straight from those who do them best—the gunsmiths.

Gunsmith Kinks 3, edited by Frank Brownell, Brownells Inc., Montezuma, IA, 1993. 504 pp., illus. $24.95

Tricks, knacks and "kinks" by professional gunsmiths and gun tinkerers. Hundreds of valuable ideas are given in this volume.

Gunsmith Kinks 4, edited by Frank Brownell, Brownells Inc., Montezuma, IA, 2001. 564 pp., illus. $27.75

332 detailed illustrations. 560+ pages with 706 separate subject headings and over 5000 cross-indexed entries. An incredible gol mine of information.

Gunsmithing, by Roy F. Dunlap, Stackpole Books, Harrisburg, PA, 1990. 742 pp., illus. $34.95

A manual of firearm design, construction, alteration and remodeling. For amateur and professional gunsmiths and users c modern firearms.

Gunsmithing at Home: Lock, Stock and Barrel, by John Traister, Stoeger Publishing Co., Wayne, NJ, 1997. 320 p illus. Paper covers. $19.95

A complete step-by-step fully illustrated guide to the art of gunsmithing.

Home Gunsmithing the Colt Single Action Revolvers, by Loren W. Smith, Ray Riling Arms Books, Co., Phila., PA, 2001. 119 pp., illus. $29.95

Affords the Colt Single Action owner detailed, pertinent informati on the operating and servicing of this famous and historic handgu

How to Convert Military Rifles, Williams Gun Sight Co., Davision, MI, new and enlarged seventh edition, 1997. 7 pp., illus. Paper covers. $13.95

This latest edition updated the changes that have occured over the past thirty years. Tips, instructions and illustratons on how to convert popular military rifles as the Enfield, Mauser 96 nad SKS just to name a few are presented.

Mauser M98 & M96, by R.A. Walsh, Wolfe Publishing Co., Prescott, AR, 1998. 123 pp., illustrated. Paper covers. $32.50

How to build your own favorite custom Mauser rifle from two of the best bolt action rifle designs ever produced—the military Mauser Model 1898 and Model 1896 bolt rifles.

Mr. Single Shot's Gunsmithing-Idea-Book, by Frank de Haas, Mark de Haas, Orange City, IA, 1996. 168 pp., illus. Paper covers. $22.50

Offers easy to follow, step-by-step instructions for a wide variety o gunsmithing procedures all reinforced by plenty of photos.

Pistolsmithing, by George C. Nonte, Jr., Stackpole Books, Harrisburg, PA, 1974. 560 pp., illus. $34.95

A single source reference to handgun maintenance, repair, and modification at home, unequaled in value.

Professional Stockmaking, by D. Wesbrook, Wolfe Publishing Co., Prescott AZ, 1995. 308 pp., illus. $54.00

A step-by-step how-to with complete photographic support for every detail of the art of working wood into riflestocks.

Recreating the American Longrifle, by William Buchele, et al, George Shumway Publisher, York, Pa, 5th edition, 1999 175 pp., illustrated. $40.00

Includes full size plans for building a Kentucky rifle.

The Story of Pope's Barrels, by Ray M. Smith, R&R Books, Livonia, NY, 1993. 203 pp., illus. $39.00

A reissue of a 1960 book whose author knew Pope personally. It will be of special interest to Schuetzen rifle fans, since Pope's greatest days were at the height of the Schuetzen-era before WWI.

Survival Gunsmithing, by J.B. Wood, Desert Publications, Cornville, AZ, 1986. 92 pp., illus. Paper covers. $11.95

A guide to repair and maintenance of the most popular rifles, shotguns and handguns.

The Tactical 1911, by Dave Lauck, Paladin Press, Boulder, CO, 1998. 137 pp., illus. Paper covers. $20.00

Here is the only book you will ever need to teach you how to select, modify, employ and maintain your Colt.